MW01234605

Annotated Federal Acquisition Regulation Desk Reference

Volume 1

Steven N. Tomanelli

THOMSON REUTERS®

For Customer Assistance Call 1-800-328-4880

Mat #41884258

ISBN 978-0-314-98805-8

Significant Changes Included in This Edition

Starting with this 2017-1 Edition of the Annotated FAR, decisions of the Small Business Administration's Office of Hearings and Appeals (OHA) will be included where relevant to a FAR section.

- *Innovative Procurement Upheld Under Authority of the "Guiding Principles" (FAR 1.102, Note 1).* GSA awarded 60 IDIQ contracts to offerors that were the "highest technically rated with a fair and reasonable price" without conducting a tradeoff of price and non-price factors. The protester alleged that this evaluation method violated the requirement to evaluate price, since the proposed prices of offerors not technically rated in the top 60 were not considered. GAO denied the protest and noted that the "Guiding Principles" in FAR 1.102 authorize agencies to use any acquisition procedure unless prohibited by law or regulation. Although FAR Part 15 describes only two procedures (the tradeoff process and the low price/technically acceptable process), it does not prohibit the approach used by the GSA. Sevatec, Inc., et al., B-413559.3, et al., 2017 CPD ¶3 (Comp. Gen. 2017)

- *General FAR Paragraphs in Parts 1-51 Are Not Contractually Binding Unless Included in Contract (1.104, Note 1).* The ASBCA dismissed a Government claim alleging that the contractor breached its contract by not auditing its subcontractors or obtaining incurred cost data. The Government asserted that FAR 42.202 imposed these contractual duties because it states: "The prime contractor is responsible for managing its subcontractors." However, since FAR 42.202 is not a contract clause and was not included in the contract, the ASBCA held that the prime contractor is not subject to it and the alleged violation of this FAR paragraph could not form the basis for a breach of contract claim. Lockheed Martin Integrated Sys., Inc. ASBCA 59508, 59509, 17-1 BCA ¶36597 (Armed Serv. B.C.A. 2016)

- *Agencies Must Use Part 12 Commercial Item Procedures if Commercial Item Can Meet Government's Requirements (12.102, Note 2). Army* violated a procurement statute requiring that offerors of commercial items have an opportunity to compete in any procurement by issuing a solicitation for a contract to develop an intelligence software system, where Army was on notice that contractor offered a realistic, commercially available alternative product, but it failed in its market research report to fully consider its potential commercial options before pursuing a developmental only procurement. Palantir USG, Inc. v. U.S., 129 Fed.Cl. 218 (2016)

- Protest challenging the agency's past performance evaluation is sustained where the agency mechanically determined that, because the awardee and the protester both received "Satisfactory" past performance ratings, that past performance could be eliminated as a basis for award. The GAO held that this approach failed to "fulfill the requirement for a documented decision based on a comparative assessment of proposals against all source selection criteria in the solicitation. " EFW Inc., B-412608, et al., 2016 CPD ¶304 (Comp. Gen. 2016)

• Agency's past performance evaluation did not violate requirement that contractors receive impartial, fair, and equitable treatment, by evaluating ten task orders as one contract rather than as separate contracts, because the agency reasonably explained that " [h]earing from one COR on ten different task orders does not provide the same insight into a contractor's past performance as hearing from ten CORs on ten different contracts." Great S. Eng?g, Inc. v. U.S., 128 Fed. Cl. 739 (2016)

• Protest alleging that agency engaged in misleading discussions was sustained because the agency's discussion questions addressed the level effort proposed for only one aspect of performance even though the agency had concerns with the level of effort proposed on the entire line item. EFW Inc., B-412608, et al., 2016 CPD ¶304 (Comp. Gen. 2016)

• Price reasonableness and price realism are distinct concepts. The purpose of a price reasonableness review is to determine whether the prices offered are too high, as opposed to too low. Conversely, a price realism review is to determine whether prices are too low, such that there may be a risk of poor performance. EFW Inc., B-412608, et al., 2016 CPD ¶304 (Comp. Gen. 2016)

• Agency's cost realism analysis was flawed because the agency limited its analysis to internal cost data provided by the offerors and did not assess the realism of the proposed rates through such methods as comparison of the rates to the prevailing market rates, the rates paid to incumbent employees, or the rates proposed by other offerors. GAO considered the cost realism evaluation to be unreasonable and sustained the protest. Target Media Mid Atlantic, Inc., B-412468.6, 2016 CPD ¶358 (Comp. Gen. 2017)

• There is a rebuttable presumption that close family members have identical interests and must be treated as one person for purposes of determining if two firms are affiliated. A challenged firm may rebut the presumption of identity of interest if it is able to show "a clear line of fracture among the family members." Relevant factors include whether the firms share officers, employees, facilities, or equipment; whether the firms have different customers and lines of business; whether there is financial assistance, loans, or significant subcontracting between the firms; and whether the family members participate in multiple businesses together. Gregory Landscape Servs., SBA No. SIZ-5817, 2017 (S.B.A.), 2017 WL 1049487

• A concern that represents itself and qualifies as an SDVO SBC at the time of initial offer (or other formal response to a solicitation), which includes price, including a Multiple Award Contract, is considered an

SDVO SBC throughout the life of that contract. This means that if an SDVO SBC is qualified at the time of initial offer for a Multiple Award Contract, then it will be considered an SDVO SBC for each order issued against the contract, unless a contracting officer requests a new SDVO SBC certification in connection with a specific order. Redhorse Corp., SBA No. VET-261, 2017 (S.B.A.), 2017 WL 1104611

About the Author

Steven N. Tomanelli is an attorney specializing in government contract law in the Washington DC area. Mr. Tomanelli provides legal services, training and consulting services in all aspects of government procurement and federal appropriations law. He owns an acquisition consulting and training company, Steven N. Tomanelli & Associates, and teaches a broad variety of courses to government and contractor personnel, including contracting officers and technical staff, attorneys, financial managers, contractor proposal teams, support staff and program office personnel. Courses include: Performance-Based Contracting, Task Order Contracting, Source Selection, Advanced Source Selection, Federal Acquisition Regulation Workshop, Contract Disputes and Terminations, Introduction to Government Contracting, Procurement Ethics, Past Performance Evaluation, Oral Presentations for Best Value Source Selections, Federal Appropriations Law, Commercial Item Acquisition, as well as courses tailored for the specific customer.

Mr. Tomanelli is a retired Air Force Judge Advocate and has held numerous high-level procurement law positions, including Chief of Acquisition and Fiscal Law for the Air Force's Air Mobility Command and Senior DoD Counsel for the National Reconnaissance Office (NRO) in Chantilly, Virginia. He has provided consulting services and legal advice in support of highly classified major system acquisitions and has been a member of many source selection boards, advisory councils and "red teams." Mr. Tomanelli has a current TS/SCI security clearance. He provided legal support on numerous classified aerospace systems acquisitions for the NRO for five years and was a Professor of Contract and Fiscal Law at the Army Judge Advocate General's School in Charlottesville, Virginia, for three years where he provided instruction in a wide variety of procurement and fiscal law topics. In 2001, he was selected as "The Outstanding Career Judge Advocate of the Air Force."

Mr. Tomanelli received his B.A. and J.D. at Hofstra University, and his Master of Laws in Federal Procurement Law at George Washington University. While earning his Master of Laws degree in Procurement, Mr. Tomanelli worked as an Intern at the Armed Services Board of Contract Appeals.

Since 1995, Mr. Tomanelli has consistently been one of the highest rated acquisition trainers in the country according to student evaluations. He has authored over thirty-five course books and written numerous articles for national publications in federal procurement and fiscal law. Mr. Tomanelli has authored a comprehensive textbook titled, *A Practical Guide to Federal Appropriations Law* (MCI, 2003). He is a member of the Virginia, New York, and Florida Bars and serves on the Advisory Board of the *Government Contractor* (West Publishing).

For information on available training programs and consulting services, please visit the AcqTrainer website at: www.AcqTrainer.com.

GSA Contracts:
GS-02F-0080P (Schedule 69 – Acquisition Training and Consulting)

Foreword

The Federal Acquisition Regulation (FAR) directly affects the purchase and sale of over $600 billion worth of supplies, services and construction each year by federal and state procurement offices. This critically important document is comprehensive, complex, and evolving. All contract professionals involved in a FAR-based procurement must have a detailed working knowledge of the FAR to ensure that they are getting the best possible contract and that they are in full compliance with all applicable laws.

This edition of the FAR incorporates recent changes and facilitates easy access to all FAR Parts with a clear and comprehensive Table of Contents. Although comprehensive, this manual is readily transportable and will prove to be an invaluable desk reference.

Steven N. Tomanelli, J.D., LL.M.
STEVEN N. TOMANELLI & ASSOCIATES

THOMSON REUTERS PROVIEW™

This title is one of many now available on your tablet as an eBook.

Take your research mobile. Powered by the Thomson Reuters ProView™ app, our eBooks deliver the same trusted content as your print resources, but in a compact, on-the-go format.

ProView eBooks are designed for the way you work. You can add your own notes and highlights to the text, and all of your annotations will transfer electronically to every new edition of your eBook.

You can also instantly verify primary authority with built-in links to WestlawNext® and KeyCite®, so you can be confident that you're accessing the most current and accurate information.

To find out more about ProView eBooks and available discounts, call 1-800-344-5009.

Overview of the FAR

This overview is intended to give the relative newcomer to federal acquisitions a general understanding of the origin and evolution of the FAR so the reader has a contextual reference when consulting the actual document. The overview will discuss the historical background of the FAR, describe when the FAR applies and when it does not apply, explain the structure of the FAR and how it corresponds to agency FAR supplements, and, lastly, how the FAR is changed and how you can keep up with the changes.

Historical Background

The FAR became effective on 1 April 1984, replacing the Defense Acquisition Regulation (DAR), the Federal Procurement Regulation (FPR), and the NASA Procurement Regulation (NASAPR). The FAR was established to provide uniform policies for executive agency acquisitions.[1] The FAR is issued and maintained jointly, pursuant to the Office of Federal Procurement Policy Act of 1974 (Pub. L. 93-400), as amended by Pub. L. 96-83, through the coordinated action of two councils, the Defense Acquisition Regulations Council (DAR Council) and the Civilian Agency Acquisition Council (CAA Council). The Chairperson of the DAR Council is the Secretary of Defense; the Chairperson of the CAA is the Administrator of General Services. Statutory authorities to issue and revise the FAR have been delegated to the Procurement Executives in DOD, GSA and NASA. The General Services Administration is responsible for establishing and operating the FAR Secretariat to print, publish, and distribute the FAR through the Code of Federal Regulations system (including a loose-leaf edition with periodic updates). The FAR Secretariat also provides administrative support to the DAR and CAA Councils.

The FAR is Chapter 1 of the FAR system, which consists of the FAR and all of the FAR Supplements issued by executive agencies subject to the FAR.[2] The regulations comprising the FAR system are codified at Title 48 of the Code of Federal Regulations. Each agency FAR supplement is assigned a chapter number, e.g., DoD is Chapter 2, HHS is Chapter 3, etc. and, by inserting the agency Chapter number to a FAR citation (e.g., FAR 15.306), one can locate the corresponding FAR supplement paragraph. For example, because the Defense Federal Acquisition Supplement (DFARS) is Chapter 2 in the FAR System, one would insert a "2" in front of the FAR paragraph of interest. Therefore, DFARS 215.306 would correspond to FAR 15.306.

---

[1] Despite the overarching goal of uniformity, certain agencies are not required to use the FAR (e.g., the FAA) and not all procurements are subject to the FAR (e.g., procurements conducted under "Other Transaction" authority and procurements using non-appropriated funds.

[2] http://www.access.gpo.gov/nara/cfr/cfr-table-search.html#page1.

Agency FAR Supplements are generally intended to provide direction and guidance as to how statutory and regulatory requirements contained in the FAR are implemented within the particular agency. The FAR Supplements must not unnecessarily repeat, paraphrase, or otherwise restate material contained in the FAR or higher-level agency acquisition regulations and cannot conflict or be inconsistent with the FAR (except as required by law or as provided in an authorized FAR deviation under FAR Subpart 1.4).

Agency policy memoranda are not part of the FAR System. Although these references could significantly impact agency acquisitions, they are not subject to the statutory requirement for public notice and comment. However, many agencies (e.g., DoD and HHS) do post their policy memos on their websites and these references may be consulted to augment one's knowledge of the agency's acquisition practices.

Applicability of the FAR

The FAR applies to all "acquisitions," except where expressly excluded. FAR 2.101 defines an "acquisition" as follows:

"Acquisition" means the *acquiring by contract* with appropriated funds of supplies or services (including construction) by and for the use of the Federal Government through purchase or lease, whether the supplies or services are already in existence or must be created, developed, demonstrated, and evaluated [emphasis added].

FAR 2.101 defines a "contract" as follows:

"Contract" means a mutually binding legal relationship obligating the seller to furnish the supplies or services (including construction) and the buyer to pay for them. It includes all types of commitments that obligate the Government to an expenditure of appropriated funds and that, except as otherwise authorized, are in writing. In addition to bilateral instruments, contracts include (but are not limited to) awards and notices of awards; job orders or task letters issued under basic ordering agreements; letter contracts; orders, such as purchase orders, under which the contract becomes effective by written acceptance or performance; and bilateral contract modifications. Contracts do not include grants and cooperative agreements covered by 31 U.S.C. 6301, *et seq.*

Thus, the FAR and its supplements apply to contracts funded with appropriated funds. The parties may apply the FAR to grants and cooperative agreements, though they are not required to do so because grants and cooperative agreements are not "contracts."

Structure of the FAR

The FAR is subdivided into eight subchapters (A-H) and 53 Parts. Parts 1 to 51 provide guidance to agencies and contractors; Part 52 contains the provisions and clauses that are applicable to solicitations and contracts, respectively; and Part 53 contains the Standard Forms applicable to federal acquisitions.

To determine which provision or clause should be included in a solicitation or contract, the FAR includes a comprehensive matrix at Subpart 52.3. The matrix also indicates whether the clause may be incorporated by reference or must be included in full text and specifies in which section of the solicitation or contract the provision or clause should be located.

Some clauses state that they must be flowed down to subcontractors and if there are any preconditions to flowdown (e.g., dollar value), those preconditions will be identified in the clause. These clauses are referred to as "mandatory flowdown clauses," and are primarily intended to protect the Government's interests. There are many additional clauses that prudent prime contractors and higher tier subcontractors should flow down, even though not required to do so by the Government or by the clause itself. For example, the Termination for Convenience clause applicable to fixed price contracts (FAR 52.249-1) is not a mandatory flow down clause. Nevertheless, prime contractors will always want to flow it down to their subcontractors so they can terminate the subcontracts if the Government terminates the prime contract. Failure to flow down this clause would probably cause the prime contractor to owe more to its subcontractors than it could recover from the Government. Consequently, prime contractors and higher tier subcontractors should develop their own set of required flow down clauses, based on the specific circumstances of each procurement.

Changes to the FAR

Changes to the FAR are accomplished by issuance of either a proposed rule or an interim rule and allowing for public comment from interested parties. Notices of proposed and interim rules are published in the Federal Register in both paper form and electronically.[3] Interim rules are effective upon publication in the Federal Register unless otherwise specified. FAR changes are published as interim rules when they address matters that must be implemented immediately. In recent years several interim rules were issued to address post-9-11 security measures and, more recently, recordkeeping requirements under the American Recovery and Reinvestment Act (ARRA). Proposed rules are issued in all other cases.

After the notice and comment period, the FAR Councils will review the comments and can: 1) release the final rule without change; 2) release the final rule with changes; 3) withdraw the proposed or interim rule and start the process over; 4) withdraw the proposed or interim rule and take no further action. When a final rule is issued, it is released as part of a Federal Acquisition Circular (FAC) that contains the background for the change, the comments received and changes made or not made in response and a description of the changes made. To keep up with the FAR changes as they are made, one may subscribe to the FAR news at: http://www.acqnet.gov/FAR/loadmainre.html.

Steven N. Tomanelli, J.D., LL.M.

---

[3] http://www.gpoaccess.gov/fr.

STEVEN N. TOMANELLI & ASSOCIATES
October 2011

General Structure of the FAR

Subchapter A—General

Part 1—Federal Acquisition Regulations System

Part 2—Definitions of Words and Terms

Part 3—Improper Business Practices and Personal Conflicts of Interest

Part 4—Administrative Matters

Subchapter B—Competition and Acquisition Planning

Part 5—Publicizing Contract Actions

Part 6—Competition Requirements

Part 7—Acquisition Planning

Part 8—Required Sources of Supplies and Services

Part 9—Contractor Qualifications

Part 10—Market Research

Part 11—Describing Agency Needs

Part 12—Acquisition of Commercial Items

Subchapter C—Contracting Methods and Contract Types

Part 13—Simplified Acquisition Procedures

Part 14—Sealed Bidding

Part 15—Contracting by Negotiation

Part 16—Types of Contracts

Part 17—Special Contracting Methods

Part 18—Emergency Acquisitions

Subchapter D—Socioeconomic Programs

Part 19—Small Business Programs

Part 20—Reserved

Part 21—Reserved

Part 22—Application of Labor Laws to Government Acquisitions

Part 23—Environment, Energy and Water Efficiency, Renewable Energy

Part 24—Protection of Privacy and Freedom of Information

Part 25—Foreign Acquisition

Part 26—Other Socioeconomic Programs

Subchapter E—General Contracting Requirements

Summary of Contents

Volume 1

TITLE 48 FEDERAL ACQUISITION REGULATIONS SYSTEM

CHAPTER 1 FEDERAL ACQUISITION REGULATION

SUBCHAPTER A GENERAL

Volume 2

SUBCHAPTER G CONTRACT MANAGEMENT

Title 48 Federal Acquisition Regulations System

Chapter 1 Federal Acquisition Regulation

Subchapter A General

PART 1 FEDERAL ACQUISITION REGULATIONS SYSTEM

§ 1.000 Scope of part.

Subpart 1.1 Purpose, Authority, Issuance

§ 1.101 Purpose.
§ 1.102 Statement of guiding principles for the Federal Acquisition System.
§ 1.102-1 Discussion.
§ 1.102-2 Performance standards.
§ 1.102-3 Acquisition Team.
§ 1.102-4 Role of the Acquisition Team.
§ 1.103 Authority.
§ 1.104 Applicability.
§ 1.105 Issuance.
§ 1.105-1 Publication and code arrangement.
§ 1.105-2 Arrangement of regulations.
§ 1.105-3 Copies.
§ 1.106 OMB approval under the Paperwork Reduction Act.
§ 1.107 Certifications.
§ 1.108 FAR conventions.
§ 1.109 Statutory acquisition—related dollar thresholds—adjustment for inflation.
§ 1.110 Positive law codification.

Subpart 1.2 Administration

§ 1.201 Maintenance of the FAR.
§ 1.201-1 The two councils.
§ 1.201-2 FAR Secretariat.
§ 1.202 Agency compliance with the FAR.

Subpart 1.3 Agency Acquisition Regulations

§ 1.301 Policy.
§ 1.302 Limitations.
§ 1.303 Publication and codification.
§ 1.304 Agency control and compliance procedures.

Subpart 1.4 Deviations from the FAR

§ 1.400 Scope of subpart.
§ 1.401 Definition.
§ 1.402 Policy.
§ 1.403 Individual deviations.
§ 1.404 Class deviations.
§ 1.405 Deviations pertaining to treaties and executive agreements.

§ 1.000 Scope of part.

This part sets forth basic policies and general information about the Federal Acquisition Regulations System including purpose, authority, applicability, issuance, arrangement, numbering, dissemination, implementation, supplementation, maintenance, administration, and deviation. Subparts 1.2, 1.3, and 1.4 prescribe administrative procedures for maintaining the FAR System.

United States Code Annotated

Authority and functions of the Administrator, see 41 U.S.C.A. § 405.

Definitions, see 41 U.S.C.A. § 403.

Establishment of Office of Federal Procurement Policy, appointment of Administrator, see 41 U.S.C.A. § 404.

Federal Acquisition Regulatory Council, see 41 U.S.C.A. § 421.

Uniform Federal procurement regulations and procedures, see 41 U.S.C.A. § 405a.

Notes of Decisions

In general 1

1 In general

Federal Acquisition Regulations System (FAR) and the Department of Defense FAR

3

Supplement (DFARS) have force and effect of law. 48 C.F.R. § 1.301(b). Davies Precision Machining, Inc. v. U.S., 35 Fed. Cl. 651, 40 Cont. Cas. Fed. (CCH) P 76936 (1996). United States ⊙─65

Subpart 1.1 Purpose, Authority, Issuance

§ 1.101 Purpose.

The Federal Acquisition Regulations System is established for the codification and publication of uniform policies and procedures for acquisition by all executive agencies. The Federal Acquisition Regulations System consists of the Federal Acquisition Regulation (FAR), which is the primary document, and agency acquisition regulations that implement or supplement the FAR. The FAR System does not include internal agency guidance of the type described in 1.301(a)(2).

United States Code Annotated

Authority and functions of the Administrator, see 41 U.S.C.A. § 405.

Definitions, see 41 U.S.C.A. § 403.

Establishment of Office of Federal Procurement Policy, appointment of Administrator, see 41 U.S.C.A. § 404.

Federal Acquisition Regulatory Council, see 41 U.S.C.A. § 421.

Uniform Federal procurement regulations and procedures, see 41 U.S.C.A. § 405a.

Notes of Decisions

In general 1
Executive agency 2
Railroads 3

1 In general

The FAR provides general rules for use by agencies in all applicable acquisitions, including those of information resources such as ADPE and telecommunications resources. Protest of Julie Research Laboratories, Inc., G.S.B.C.A. No. 9474-P-R, 88-3 B.C.A. (CCH) ¶ 21079, 1988 WL 89497 (Gen. Services Admin. B.C.A. 1988).

Federal Acquisition Regulations System (FAR) and the Department of Defense FAR Supplement (DFARS) have force and effect of law. 48 C.F.R. § 1.301(b). Davies Precision Machining, Inc. v. U.S., 35 Fed. Cl. 651, 40 Cont. Cas. Fed. (CCH) P 76936 (1996). United States ⊙─65

The FAR is established for the codification and publication of uniform policies and procedures for acquisition by all executive agencies. The FAR is published in 48 C.F.R., Chapters 1–29 The federal acquisition system primarily consists of the regulations published in FAR and agency acquisition regulations that implement or supplement the FAR. The FAR does not include internal agency guidance of the type described in FAR § 1.301(a)(2)48 C.F.R. § 1.101. Davies Precision Machining, Inc. v. U.S., 35 Fed. Cl. 651, 40 Cont. Cas. Fed. (CCH) P 76936 (1996).

2 Executive agency

Federal Acquisition Regulation (FAR) does not apply to the Administrative Office of the United States Courts (AOUSC), as the AOUSC is not an "executive agency" within meaning of the FAR. 48 C.F.R. §§ 1.101, 2.101. Novell, Inc. v. U.S., 46 Fed. Cl. 601 (2000). United States ⊙─64.5

3 Railroads

Federal procurement regulations applicable to "executive agencies," defined to include any wholly owned government corporation, do not apply to National Railroad Passenger Corporation (Amtrak) which is mixed-ownership government corporation. 31 U.S.C.A. § 9101(2)(A), (3); 48 C.F.R. §§ 1.101, 2.101. Hill Intern., Inc. v. National R.R. Passenger Corp., 957 F. Supp. 548, 41 Cont. Cas. Fed. (CCH) P 77108 (D.N.J. 1996). Railroads ⊙─5.51; United States ⊙─64.5

§ 1.102 Statement of guiding principles for the Federal Acquisition System.

(a) The vision for the Federal Acquisition System is to deliver on a timely basis the best value product or service to the customer, while maintaining the public's trust and fulfilling public policy objectives. Participants in the acquisition process should work together as a team and should be empowered to make decisions within their area of responsibility.

(b) The Federal Acquisition System will—

(1) Satisfy the customer in terms of cost, quality, and timeliness of the delivered product or service by, for example—

(i) Maximizing the use of commercial products and services;

(ii) Using contractors who have a track record of successful past performance or who demonstrate a current superior ability to perform; and

(iii) Promoting competition;

(2) Minimize administrative operating costs;

(3) Conduct business with integrity, fairness, and openness; and

(4) Fulfill public policy objectives.

(c) The Acquisition Team consists of all participants in Government acquisition including not only representatives of the technical, supply, and procurement communities but also the customers they serve, and the contractors who provide the products and services.

(d) The role of each member of the Acquisition Team is to exercise personal initiative and sound business judgment in providing the best value product or service to meet the customer's needs. In exercising initiative, Government members of the Acquisition Team may assume if a specific strategy, practice, policy or procedure is in the best interests of the Government and is not addressed in the FAR, nor prohibited by law (statute or case law), Executive order or other regulation, that the strategy, practice, policy or procedure is a permissible exercise of authority.

United States Code Annotated

Authority and functions of the Administrator, see 41 U.S.C.A. § 405.

Definitions, see 41 U.S.C.A. § 403.

Establishment of Office of Federal Procurement Policy, appointment of Administrator, see 41 U.S.C.A. § 404.

Federal Acquisition Regulatory Council, see 41 U.S.C.A. § 421.

Uniform Federal procurement regulations and procedures, see 41 U.S.C.A. § 405a.

Notes of Decisions

In general 1
Duty of good faith and fair dealing 2

1 In general

To determine whether construction may be procured under an Indefinite Delivery/ Indefinite Quantity (ID/IQ) contract, the Federal Circuit stated that the proper inquiry is not whether the FAR authorizes IDIQ contracts for construction procurements, but whether any statutory or regulatory provisions preclude such use. The Federal Circuit found none. Under FAR 1.102(d), Government officers have authority to use any "strategy, practice, policy or procedure" that is not prohibited and "is in the best interests of the Government." The Federal Circuit agreed with the COFC that the Corps' use of IDIQ contracts for this procurement represents the type of innovation envisioned by FAR 1.102(d). Tyler Const. Group v. U.S., 570 F.3d 1329 (Fed. Cir. 2009)

Although the "Guiding Principles" permit a broad range of contracting officer discretion, the contracting officer's decision is subject to judicial oversight to ensure that this discretion is exercised consistent with law. Blackhawk Industries Products Group Unlimited, LLC. v. U.S. General Services Admin., 348 F. Supp. 2d 662 (E.D. Va. 2004). MTB Group, Inc., B-295463, 2005 CPD ¶ 40 (Comp. Gen. 2005).

While reverse auctions are not expressly recognized in the FAR as a permissible procurement vehicle for goods and services, neither does the FAR expressly prohibit the government from using reverse auctions. Under these circumstances, the "Guiding Principles" of FAR 1.102 would permit the use of reverse auctions. MTB Group, Inc., v. United States, 65

Fed.Cl. 516 (2005)

GSA awarded 60 IDIQ contracts to offerors that were the "highest technically rated with a fair and reasonable price" without conducting a tradeoff of price and non-price factors. The protester alleged that this evaluation method violated the requirement to evaluate price, since the proposed prices of offerors not technically rated in the top 60 were not considered. GAO denied the protest and noted that the "Guiding Principles" in FAR 1.102 authorize agencies to use any acquisition procedure unless prohibited by law or regulation. Although FAR Part 15 describes only two procedures (the tradeoff process and the low price/technically acceptable process), it does not prohibit the approach used by the GSA. Sevatec, Inc., et al., B-413559.3, et al., 2017 CPD ¶ 3 (Comp. Gen. 2017)

2 Duty of good faith and fair dealing

Every contract imposes upon each party a duty of good faith and fair dealing in its performance and its enforcement, but that duty does not deal with good faith in the *formation* of a contract. Agency did not breach its implied duty of good faith and fair dealing by failing to notify timber contractor that timber-sale contracts on which it was bidding were at risk of being suspended due to litigation brought by environmental groups; government's pre-award conduct could not have breached implied duty of good faith and fair dealing because duty does arise until a contract is signed between the parties. Scott Timber Co. v. U.S., 692 F.3d 1365 (Fed. Cir. 2012)

Government breached implied covenant of good faith and fair dealing by failing to communicate with licensee of trademark for HooAH! nutritional energy bars for eight months and by abandoning HooAH! name during period of cooperative research and development agreement (CRADA), granting licensee exclusive license to HooAH! trademark in order to commercialize nutritional bars in exchange for payment of royalties, since government's lack of cooperation and forthrightness in intentionally refusing to communicate with licensee was unreasonable, and government's evasive behavior leading to abandonment of HooAH! name without consulting licensee destroyed licensee's reasonable expectations regarding fruits of contract, as name was bargained for by licensee and was critical component of commercialization efforts. D'Andrea Bros. LLC v. U.S., 109 Fed.Cl. 243 (2013)

§ 1.102-1 Discussion.

(a) *Introduction.* The statement of Guiding Principles for the Federal Acquisition System (System) represents a concise statement designed to be user-friendly for all participants in Government acquisition. The following discussion of the principles is provided in order to illuminate the meaning of the terms and phrases used. The framework for the System includes the Guiding Principles for the System and the supporting policies and procedures in the FAR.

(b) *Vision.* All participants in the System are responsible for making acquisition decisions that deliver the best value product or service to the customer. Best value must be viewed from a broad perspective and is achieved by balancing the many competing interests in the System. The result is a system which works better and costs less.

United States Code Annotated

Authority and functions of the Administrator, see 41 U.S.C.A. § 405.

Definitions, see 41 U.S.C.A. § 403.

Establishment of Office of Federal Procurement Policy, appointment of Administrator, see 41 U.S.C.A. § 404.

Federal Acquisition Regulatory Council, see 41 U.S.C.A. § 421.

Uniform Federal procurement regulations and procedures, see 41 U.S.C.A. § 405a.

§ 1.102-2 Performance standards.

(a) Satisfy the customer in terms of cost, quality, and timeliness of the delivered product or service.

(1) The principal customers for the product or service provided by the System are the users and line managers, acting on behalf of the American taxpayer.

(2) The System must be responsive and adaptive to customer needs, concerns, and feedback. Implementation of acquisition policies and procedures, as well as consideration

of timeliness, quality, and cost throughout the process, must take into account the perspective of the user of the product or service.

(3) When selecting contractors to provide products or perform services, the Government will use contractors who have a track record of successful past performance or who demonstrate a current superior ability to perform.

(4) The Government must not hesitate to communicate with the commercial sector as early as possible in the acquisition cycle to help the Government determine the capabilities available in the commercial marketplace. The Government will maximize its use of commercial products and services in meeting Government requirements.

(5) It is the policy of the System to promote competition in the acquisition process.

(6) The System must perform in a timely, high quality, and cost-effective manner.

(7) All members of the Team are required to employ planning as an integral part of the overall process of acquiring products or services. Although advance planning is required, each member of the Team must be flexible in order to accommodate changing or unforeseen mission needs. Planning is a tool for the accomplishment of tasks, and application of its discipline should be commensurate with the size and nature of a given task.

(b) Minimize administrative operating costs.

(1) In order to ensure that maximum efficiency is obtained, rules, regulations, and policies should be promulgated only when their benefits clearly exceed the costs of their development, implementation, administration, and enforcement. This applies to internal administrative processes, including reviews, and to rules and procedures applied to the contractor community.

(2) The System must provide uniformity where it contributes to efficiency or where fairness or predictability is essential. The System should also, however, encourage innovation, and local adaptation where uniformity is not essential.

(c) Conduct business with integrity, fairness, and openness.

(1) An essential consideration in every aspect of the System is maintaining the public's trust. Not only must the System have integrity, but the actions of each member of the Team must reflect integrity, fairness, and openness. The foundation of integrity within the System is a competent, experienced, and well-trained, professional workforce. Accordingly, each member of the Team is responsible and accountable for the wise use of public resources as well as acting in a manner which maintains the public's trust. Fairness and openness require open communication among team members, internal and external customers, and the public.

(2) To achieve efficient operations, the System must shift its focus from "risk avoidance" to one of "risk management." The cost to the taxpayer of attempting to eliminate all risk is prohibitive. The Executive Branch will accept and manage the risk associated with empowering local procurement officials to take independent action based on their professional judgment.

(3) The Government shall exercise discretion, use sound business judgment, and comply with applicable laws and regulations in dealing with contractors and prospective contractors. All contractors and prospective contractors shall be treated fairly and impartially but need not be treated the same.

(d) *Fulfill public policy objectives.* The System must support the attainment of public policy goals adopted by the Congress and the President. In attaining these goals, and in its overall operations, the process shall ensure the efficient use of public resources.

United States Code Annotated

Authority and functions of the Administrator, see 41 U.S.C.A. § 405.

Definitions, see 41 U.S.C.A. § 403.

Establishment of Office of Federal Procurement Policy, appointment of Administrator, see 41 U.S.C.A. § 404.

Federal Acquisition Regulatory Council, see 41 U.S.C.A. § 421.

Uniform Federal procurement regulations and procedures, see 41 U.S.C.A. § 405a.

Notes of Decisions

In general 1

1 In general

To achieve efficient operations, the FAR shifts its focus from risk avoidance to one of risk management. FAR 1.102-2(c)(2). The FAR views the cost to the taxpayer of attempting to eliminate all risk as prohibitive. To avoid these costs, the FAR encourages the broad use of discretion. Wood v. U.S., 290 F.3d 29, 19 O.S.H. Cas. (BNA) 1905 (1st Cir. 2002).

Discretionary function exception to waiver of sovereign immunity under Federal Tort Claims Act (FTCA) applied to government's obligation to ensure that painting contractor was in compliance with contract, including safety requirements, precluding landowner liability claims asserted by injured employee of contractor; under Federal Acquisition Regulations (FAR) and mandated contract provisions, Navy had limited supervisory duties, its performance of safety oversight was discretionary, and decisions regarding safety oversight involved permissible exercise of policy judgment. 28 U.S.C.A. § 2680; 48 C.F.R. § 1.102-2(a, c), 1.602-2; Restatement (Second) of Torts §§ 343, 343A, 413, 414; Wood v. U.S., 290 F.3d 29, 19 O.S.H. Cas. (BNA) 1905 (1st Cir. 2002). United States ☞78(12)

Discretionary function exception to waiver of sovereign immunity under Federal Tort Claims Act (FTCA) applied to government's obligation to ensure that painting contractor was in compliance with contract, including safety requirements, precluding landowner liability claims asserted by injured employee of contractor; under Federal Acquisition Regulations (FAR) and mandated contract provisions, Navy had limited supervisory duties, its performance of safety oversight was discretionary, and decisions regarding safety oversight involved permissible exercise of policy judgment. 28 U.S.C.A. § 2680; 48 C.F.R. § 1.102-2(a, c), 1.602-2; Restatement (Second) of Torts §§ 343, 343A, 413, 414; Wood v. U.S., 290 F.3d 29, 19 O.S.H. Cas. (BNA) 1905 (1st Cir. 2002). United States ☞78(12)

Bid protester did not establish that contracting officer (CO) failed to evaluate all offers fairly, based on allegation that despite the fact that it and contract awardee were given the same scores for two subfactors within the overall performance risk category, when the subfactor scores were combined, awardee was unfairly given a more favorable score; CO permissibly chose to afford more weight to the financial risk and overall performance risk components of her analysis, and she identified specific "disadvantages" in protester's risk assessment not present in awardee's assessment. 48 C.F.R. § 1.102-2(c)(3). Ryder Move Management, Inc. v. U.S., 48 Fed. Cl. 380 (2001). United States ☞64.40(2)

Agency may request clarification from one offeror but not from another. The mere fact that an agency requests clarification from one offeror and not another, does not constitute unfair treatment under FAR 1.102-2(c)(3), which states that all contractors and prospective contractors must be treated fairly and impartially but need not be treated the same. Matter of Indus Technology, Inc., B-297800.13, 2007 CPD ¶ 116 (Comp. Gen. 2007).

Under the FSS, agencies are not required to conduct a competition before using their business judgment in determining whether ordering supplies or services from an FSS vendor represents the best value and meets the agency's needs at the lowest overall cost. However, selecting a vendor on an award basis different than that announced in the solicitation is not consistent with the agency's obligation to treat vendors fairly. Computer Products, Inc., B-284702, 2000 CPD ¶ 95 (Comp. Gen. 2000).

§ 1.102-3 Acquisition Team.

The purpose of defining the Federal Acquisition Team (Team) in the Guiding Principles is to ensure that participants in the System are identified beginning with the customer and ending with the contractor of the product or service. By identifying the team members in this manner, teamwork, unity of purpose, and open communication among the members of the Team in sharing the vision and achieving the goal of the System are encouraged. Individual team members will participate in the acquisition process at the appropriate time.

United States Code Annotated

Authority and functions of the Administrator, see 41 U.S.C.A. § 405.

Chief acquisition officers and senior procurement executives, see 41 U.S.C.A. § 414.

Definitions, see 41 U.S.C.A. § 403.

Establishment of Office of Federal Procurement Policy, appointment of Administrator, see 41 U.S.C.A. § 404.

Federal Acquisition Regulatory Council, see 41 U.S.C.A. § 421.

8

Uniform Federal procurement regulations and procedures, see 41 U.S.C.A. § 405a.

§ 1.102-4 Role of the Acquisition Team.

(a) Government members of the Team must be empowered to make acquisition decisions within their areas of responsibility, including selection, negotiation, and administration of contracts consistent with the Guiding Principles. In particular, the contracting officer must have the authority to the maximum extent practicable and consistent with law, to determine the application of rules, regulations, and policies, on a specific contract.

(b) The authority to make decisions and the accountability for the decisions made will be delegated to the lowest level within the System, consistent with law.

(c) The Team must be prepared to perform the functions and duties assigned. The Government is committed to provide training, professional development, and other resources necessary for maintaining and improving the knowledge, skills, and abilities for all Government participants on the Team, both with regard to their particular area of responsibility within the System, and their respective role as a team member. The contractor community is encouraged to do likewise.

(d) The System will foster cooperative relationships between the Government and its contractors consistent with its overriding responsibility to the taxpayers.

(e) The FAR outlines procurement policies and procedures that are used by members of the Acquisition Team. If a policy or procedure, or a particular strategy or practice, is in the best interest of the Government and is not specifically addressed in the FAR, nor prohibited by law (statute or case law), Executive order or other regulation, Government members of the Team should not assume it is prohibited. Rather, absence of direction should be interpreted as permitting the Team to innovate and use sound business judgment that is otherwise consistent with law and within the limits of their authority. Contracting officers should take the lead in encouraging business process innovations and ensuring that business decisions are sound.

United States Code Annotated

Authority and functions of the Administrator, see 41 U.S.C.A. § 405.

Chief acquisition officers and senior procurement executives, see 41 U.S.C.A. § 414.

Definitions, see 41 U.S.C.A. § 403.

Establishment of Office of Federal Procurement Policy, appointment of Administrator, see 41 U.S.C.A. § 404.

Federal Acquisition Regulatory Council, see 41 U.S.C.A. § 421.

Uniform Federal procurement regulations and procedures, see 41 U.S.C.A. § 405a.

Notes of Decisions

In general 1

1 In general

Although FAR 1.102-4 states that the absence of direction should be interpreted as permitting the Acquisition Team to innovate and use sound business judgment, this broad discretion does not permit the Acquisition Team or the Contracting Officer to disregard the terms of the contract. However, FAR 1.102-4 applies only when the "procedure . . . is in the best interest of the Government _and_ is not specifically addressed in the FAR." Because the procedure to issuing a notice to proceed is specifically addressed in FAR 11.404(b) (referencing FAR 52.211-10, the discretion permitted by FAR 1.102-4 does not apply in this situation. Tidewater Contractors, Inc. v. Dept. of Transportation, CBCA 50, 07-1 B.C.A. (CCH) ¶ 33525, 2007 WL 994555 (U.S. Civilian BCA 2007), modified on reconsideration, CBCA 50-R, 07-2 B.C.A. (CCH) ¶ 33618, 2007 WL 2045470 (U.S. Civilian BCA 2007).

§ 1.103 Authority.

(a) The development of the FAR System is in accordance with the requirements of 41 U.S.C. chapter 13, Acquisition Councils.

(b) The FAR is prepared, issued, and maintained, and the FAR System is prescribed jointly by the Secretary of Defense, the Administrator of General Services, and the

Administrator, National Aeronautics and Space Administration, under their several statutory authorities.

United States Code Annotated

Authority and functions of the Administrator, see 41 U.S.C.A. § 405.

Definitions, see 41 U.S.C.A. § 403.

Establishment of Office of Federal Procurement Policy, appointment of Administrator, see 41 U.S.C.A. § 404.

Federal Acquisition Regulatory Council, see 41 U.S.C.A. § 421.

Uniform Federal procurement regulations and procedures, see 41 U.S.C.A. § 405a.

Notes of Decisions

In general 2
Regulation vs. statute 1

1 Regulation vs. statute

Editor's Note: The court's conclusion that the FAR is not a statute, while obviously correct, does not necessarily mean that violation of a FAR section would *never* trigger the protections of the Whistleblower Protection Act. Because many FAR sections implement statutes verbatim (or nearly so), refusal to comply with an order to violate one of those sections would, presumably, preclude adverse personnel actions. Examples of such FAR sections include: FAR 3.104-3 (Procurement Integrity Act), FAR Part 6.1 (Competition in Contracting Act) and FAR 22.10 (Service Contract Act).

The Federal Circuit has held that the FAR is a regulation rather than a statute. The significance of this distinction is that a federal employee who refuses to comply with a supervisor's order to violate the FAR is subject to disciplinary action because the Whistleblower Protection Act of 1989 prohibits adverse personnel actions when an employee refuses "to obey an order that would require the individual to violate a *law*." 5 USC § 2302(b)(9)(D). Based on this distinction, the termination of a Contracting Officer's Representative for refusing to obey an order to violate the FAR, was upheld. Rainey v. MSPB, 824 F.3d 1359 (Fed. Cir. 2016).

2 In general

The FAR is prepared, issued, and maintained jointly by the Secretary of Defense, the Administrator of General Services, and the Administrator of the National Aeronautics and Space Administration. The Civilian Agency Acquisition Council, chaired by GSA, and the Defense Acquisition Regulations Council are charged with revising the FAR. Knowledge Connections, Inc. v. U.S., 76 Fed. Cl. 6 (2007)

The FAR were developed in accordance with the Office of Federal Procurement Policy Act of 1974, as amended by Pub.L. No. 96-83, and are the primary regulation for use by all federal agencies in their acquisition of supplies and services with appropriated funds. The FAR are promulgated by the Civilian Agency Council and Defense Acquisition Regulations Council. The FAR codified and published uniform policies and procedures for acquisition by all executive agencies. ATK Thiokol, Inc. v. U.S., 68 Fed. Cl. 612 (2005), aff'd, 598 F.3d 1329 (Fed. Cir. 2010).

Federal Acquisition Regulations System (FAR) and the Department of Defense FAR Supplement (DFARS) have force and effect of law. 48 C.F.R. § 1.301(b). Davies Precision Machining, Inc. v. U.S., 35 Fed. Cl. 651, 40 Cont. Cas. Fed. (CCH) P 76936 (1996). United States ⊸65

§ 1.104 Applicability.

The FAR applies to all acquisitions as defined in Part 2 of the FAR, except where expressly excluded.

United States Code Annotated

Authority and functions of the Administrator, see 41 U.S.C.A. § 405.

Definitions, see 41 U.S.C.A. § 403.

Establishment of Office of Federal Procurement Policy, appointment of Administrator, see

41 U.S.C.A. § 404.

Federal Acquisition Regulatory Council, see 41 U.S.C.A. § 421.

Uniform Federal procurement regulations and procedures, see 41 U.S.C.A. § 405a.

Notes of Decisions

In general 1
Executive Agency Procurements 2
Types of Transactions 3
Use of Appropriated Funds 4

1 In general

Where there is a question over the applicability of the procurement statutes, a contract is unenforceable only when the contractor caused the illegal award, or the illegality was so obvious that the contractor should have recognized it; when an illegality is not obvious, a contractor should be accorded the benefit of all reasonable doubts and the award upheld. The government may cancel a contract as illegal that violates procurement statutes or regulations. Rockies Express Pipeline LLC v. Salazar, 730 F.3d 1330 (Fed. Cir. 2013)

The FAR was established in 1983 for the purpose of codifying and publishing uniform practices and procedures for federal executive agencies to follow in making acquisitions. The FAR apply to all acquisitions, as defined in part 2 of the FAR, except where expressly excluded. Bear Medicine v. U.S., 47 F. Supp. 2d 1172 (D. Mont. 1999), judgment rev'd, 241 F.3d 1208, 31 Envtl. L. Rep. 20501 (9th Cir. 2001).

The ASBCA dismissed a Government claim alleging that the contractor breached its contract by not auditing its subcontractors or obtaining incurred cost data. The Government asserted that FAR 42.202 imposed these contractual duties because it states: "The prime contractor is responsible for managing its subcontractors." However, since FAR 42.202 is not a contract clause and was not included in the contract, the ASBCA held that the prime contractor is not subject to it and the alleged violation of this FAR paragraph could not form the basis for a breach of contract claim. Lockheed Martin Integrated Sys., Inc. ASBCA 59508, 59509, 17-1 BCA ¶ 36597 (Armed Serv. B.C.A. 2016)

2 Executive Agency Procurements

The Federal Acquisition Regulation is not applicable to United States Postal Service (USPS) contracts. Overflo Public Warehouse, Inc., PSBCA No. 4649, 04-1 BCA ¶ 32488 (Post. Serv. B.C.A. 2004)

Federal procurement regulations applicable to "executive agencies," defined to include any wholly owned government corporation, do not apply to National Railroad Passenger Corporation (Amtrak) which is mixed-ownership government corporation. 31 U.S.C.A. § 9101(2)(A), (3); 48 C.F.R. §§ 1.101, 2.101. Hill Intern., Inc. v. National R.R. Passenger Corp., 957 F. Supp. 548, 41 Cont. Cas. Fed. (CCH) P 77108 (D.N.J. 1996). Railroads ☞5.51; United States ☞64.5

The majority of government procurement actions are governed by title 48 of the Code of Federal Regulations, the FAR. However, as a legislative branch agency, the Architect of the Capital (AOC) is not subject to these rules. Architect of the Capitol Contract Ratification, B-306353, 2005 WL 2810714 (Comp. Gen. 2005).

While the FAR governs only executive agency procurements, and therefore is not controlling as to the procurements of legislative agencies such as the Library of Congress, it nevertheless is instructive as to the different definitions of nonprofit organization that are used in government. American Multi Media, Inc. - Reconsideration, B-293782.2, 2004 CPD ¶ 158 (Comp. Gen. 2004).

The FAR applies to Federal Executive agencies and does not in any way govern the filing of a protest involving a District government procurement. The timeliness provisions of the D.C. Procurement Practices Act of 1985 (PPA) applied to determine the timeliness of a protest. Protest of Smith & Wesson, 1989 WL 508649 (D.C. C.A.B. 1989).

3 Types of Transactions

The FAR governs the acquisition of supplies or services by all executive agencies. The

FAR covers procurement contracts, but does not cover grants or cooperative agreements as defined by 31 U.S.C. § 6301, et seq.48 C.F.R. § 2.101. Chem Service, Inc. v. Environmental Monitoring Systems Laboratory-Cincinnati of U.S. E.P.A., 12 F.3d 1256, 39 Cont. Cas. Fed. (CCH) P 76617 (3d Cir. 1993).

The FAR is applicable to federal agency "acquisitions," not sales and was not applicable to a Department of Agriculture contract for the sale of timber. Thus, the express provisions of those regulations dealing with allowable and unallowable costs are not of relevance. Therefore, much of the case law that addresses the allowability of attorney fees, is not directly relevant, because the rationale is grounded on cost principles that do not apply here. In re Reidhead Bros. Lumber Mill, A.G.B.C.A. No. 2000-126-1, 01-2 B.C.A. (CCH) ¶ 31486, 2001 WL 744077 (Dep't Agric. B.C.A. 2001).

Federal Acquisition Regulation (FAR) did not apply to sales contract whereby agency would release product movement sales data from military commissaries to contractor in exchange for a share in the revenue generated by sale of that information and for analytical support services for category management, since contract which did not utilize appropriated funds was not an "acquisition" within ambit of the FAR. 48 C.F.R. § 2.101. Marketing and Management Information, Inc. v. U.S., 57 Fed. Cl. 665 (2003). United States ⊙═62

Agreements entered into under an agency's "Other Transactions" authority, e.g., 10 U.S.C. sect. 2371(a), are not tantamount to the award of contracts for the procurement of goods and services and are, therefore, not subject to the FAR. Exploration Partners, LLC, B-298804, 2006 CPD ¶ 201 (Comp. Gen. 2006).

4 Use of Appropriated Funds

Revolving funds are considered to be appropriated funds and the FAR is, therefore, applicable to contracts funded with revolving funds. An agency funded a contract from the "Defense Business Operating Fund" (DBOF), a revolving fund. The DBOF fund was authorized by Public Law 102-172, § 8121 and 10 U.S.C. § 2208, which permit DoD to establish working-capital funds for industrial and commercial type activities; require reimbursement to such funds for the cost of services or work performed from available appropriations; provide for capital for such funds by appropriated amounts authorized by law; and provide that an agency may not incur a cost for services or work performed by industrial or commercial-type activities for which working capital funds are established, exceeding the amount of appropriations or other funds available for those purposes. An industrial or commercial type activity reimburses the DBOF from the activity's appropriations after award of contracts and the activity has been billed for the supplies or services. Most importantly, general appropriations principles and legislation apply to revolving funds. In re EROS Div. of Resource Recycling Intern., Inc., A.S.B.C.A. No. 48355, A.S.B.C.A. No. 48773, 99-1 B.C.A. (CCH) ¶ 30207, 1998 WL 919558 (Armed Serv. B.C.A. 1998), aff'd, 232 F.3d 912 (Fed. Cir. 2000)

Because contracts of the Army, Air Force Exchange Service (AAFES) do not obligate appropriated funds of the United States, such contracts are not subject to the FAR. Any agreements reached between AAFES and the Air Force with regard to reimbursement of AAFES funds expended on the project after the contract was awarded have no bearing upon the terms of the contractor's contract with AAFES. Therefore, even if appropriated funds were used by the Air Force to reimburse AAFES, the contract itself did not obligate appropriated funds. Accordingly, the FAR cost principles relied upon by appellant which permit supervisory costs to be charged as direct costs are not applicable to this AAFES contract. Appeal of Hermanson, A.S.B.C.A. No. 38384, 93-1 B.C.A. (CCH) ¶ 25403, 1992 WL 231899 (Armed Serv. B.C.A. 1992).

This concessionaire contract was not an "acquisition" that was funded by Congressional appropriation, and hence the FAR does not govern the procurement. However, the Contract Disputes Act does apply, 41 U.S.C. sec. 602(a). Appeal of Lumanlan Portrait & Painting Service, A.S.B.C.A. No. 35709, 91-2 B.C.A. (CCH) ¶ 23988, 1991 WL 121273 (Armed Serv. B.C.A. 1991).

The FAR applies only to acquisitions by the government of supplies or services with appropriated funds. Where an agency contracts for the operation of a government-owned facility, but does not pay the contractor for its services, the provisions of the FAR do not apply since no funds-and thus no appropriated funds-are being expended. Matter of: Good Food

Service, Inc.—Reconsideration, B-256526, B-256526.3, 94-2 CPD ¶ 16 (Comp. Gen. 1994).

Since the procurement of goods and services for publishing civilian enterprise newspapers does not involve the payment of appropriated funds to the contractor, the basic acquisition statutes and regulations, specifically, the Armed Services Procurement Act, 10 U.S.C. § 2301 et seq., and the FAR, do not apply. Gino Morena Enterprises, B-224235, 87-1 CPD ¶ 121 (Comp. Gen. 1987), on reconsideration, B-224235, B-224235.2, 87-1 CPD ¶ 501 (Comp. Gen. 1987).

§ 1.105 Issuance.

§ 1.105-1 Publication and code arrangement.
(a) The FAR is published in—
(1) The daily issue of the *Federal Register*;
(2) Cumulated form in the *Code of Federal Regulations* (CFR); and
(3) A separate loose-leaf edition.

(b) The FAR is issued as Chapter 1 of Title 48, CFR. Subsequent chapters are reserved for agency acquisition regulations that implement or supplement the FAR (see Subpart 1.3). The CFR Staff will assign chapter numbers to requesting agencies.

(c) Each numbered unit or segment (*e.g.*, part, subpart, section, etc.) of an agency acquisition regulation that is codified in the CFR shall begin with the chapter number. However, the chapter number assigned to the FAR will not be included in the numbered units or segments of the FAR.

United States Code Annotated
Authority and functions of the Administrator, see 41 U.S.C.A. § 405.

Definitions, see 41 U.S.C.A. § 403.

Establishment of Office of Federal Procurement Policy, appointment of Administrator, see 41 U.S.C.A. § 404.

Federal Acquisition Regulatory Council, see 41 U.S.C.A. § 421.

Uniform Federal procurement regulations and procedures, see 41 U.S.C.A. § 405a.

§ 1.105-2 Arrangement of regulations.
(a) *General.* The FAR is divided into subchapters, parts (each of which covers a separate aspect of acquisition), subparts, sections, and subsections.
(b) Numbering.
(1) The numbering system permits the discrete identification of every FAR paragraph. The digits to the left of the decimal point represent the part number. The numbers to the right of the decimal point and to the left of the dash represent, in order, the subpart (one or two digits), and the section (two digits). The number to the right of the dash represents the subsection. Subdivisions may be used at the section and subsection level to identify individual paragraphs. The following example illustrates the make-up of a FAR number citation (note that subchapters are not used with citations):

25.108-2

Part ◄
Subpart ◄
Section ◄
Subsection ◄

(2) Subdivisions below the section or subsection level consist of parenthetical alpha numerics using the following sequence:

$$(a)(1)(i)(A)(1)(i)$$

(c) References and citations.

(1) Unless otherwise stated, cross-references indicate parts, subparts, sections, subsections, paragraphs, subparagraphs, or subdivisions of this regulation.

(2) This regulation may be referred to as the Federal Acquisition Regulation or the FAR.

(3) Using the FAR coverage at 9.106-4(d) as a typical illustration, reference to the—

(i) Part would be "FAR part 9" outside the FAR and "part 9" within the FAR.

(ii) Subpart would be "FAR subpart 9.1" outside the FAR and "subpart 9.1" within the FAR.

(iii) Section would be "FAR 9.106" outside the FAR and "9.106" within the FAR.

(iv) Subsection would be "FAR 9.106-4" outside the FAR and "9.106-4" within the FAR.

(v) Paragraph would be "FAR 9.106-4(d)" outside the FAR and "9.106-4(d)" within the FAR.

(4) Citations of authority (e.g., statutes or Executive orders) in the FAR shall follow the *Federal Register* form guides.

United States Code Annotated

Authority and functions of the Administrator, see 41 U.S.C.A. § 405.

Definitions, see 41 U.S.C.A. § 403.

Establishment of Office of Federal Procurement Policy, appointment of Administrator, see 41 U.S.C.A. § 404.

Federal Acquisition Regulatory Council, see 41 U.S.C.A. § 421.

Uniform Federal procurement regulations and procedures, see 41 U.S.C.A. § 405a.

§ 1.105-3 Copies.

Copies of the FAR in *Federal Register*, loose-leaf, CD-ROM, and CFR form may be purchased from the—

Superintendent of Documents
Government Printing Office (GPO)
Washington, DC 20402.

United States Code Annotated

Authority and functions of the Administrator, see 41 U.S.C.A. § 405.

Definitions, see 41 U.S.C.A. § 403.

Establishment of Office of Federal Procurement Policy, appointment of Administrator, see 41 U.S.C.A. § 404.

Federal Acquisition Regulatory Council, see 41 U.S.C.A. § 421.

Uniform Federal procurement regulations and procedures, see 41 U.S.C.A. § 405a.

§ 1.106 OMB approval under the Paperwork Reduction Act.

The Paperwork Reduction Act of 1980 (44 U.S.C. chapter 35) imposes a requirement on Federal agencies to obtain approval from the Office of Management and Budget (OMB) before collecting information from 10 or more members of the public. The information collection and recordkeeping requirements contained in this regulation have been approved by the OMB. The following OMB control numbers apply:

FAR segment	OMB Control Number
3.103	9000-0018
3.11	9000-0183
4.102	9000-0033
4.5	9000-0137
4.605	9000-0145
4.607	9000-0145
4.7	9000-0034
4.9	9000-0097
4.14	9000-0177
4.17	9000-0179
5.405	9000-0036
7.2	9000-0082
8.5	9000-0113
9.1	9000-0011
9.2	9000-0083
14.201	9000-0034
14.202-4	9000-0040
14.202-5	9000-0039
14.205	9000-0037
14.407	9000-0038
14.5	9000-0041
15.2	9000-0037
15.209	9000-0034
15.4	9000-0013
15.404-1(f)	9000-0080
15.407-2	9000-0078
15.408	9000-0115
19.7	9000-0006 and 9000-0007
22.103	9000-0065
22.5	9000-0175
22.8	1250-0003
22.11	9000-0066
22.12	1235-0007 and 1235-0025
22.14	1250-0005
22.16	1215-0004
22.17	9000-0188
23.602	9000-0107
25.302	9000-0184
27.2	9000-0096
27.3	9000-0095
27.4	9000-0090
28.1	9000-0045
28.2	9000-0045
29.304	9000-0059
30.6	9000-0129
31.205-46	9000-0079

FAR segment	OMB Control Number
31.205-46(a)(3)	9000-0088
32.000	9000-0138
32.1	9000-0070 and 9000-0138
32.2	9000-0138
32.4	9000-0073
32.5	9000-0010 and 9000-0138
32.7	9000-0074
32.9	9000-0102
32.10	9000-0138
33	9000-0035
36.213-2	9000-0037
36.603	9000-0157
41.202(c)	9000-0125
42.7	9000-0013
42.12	9000-0076
42.13	9000-0076
42.15	9000-0142
44.305	9000-0132
45	9000-0075
46	9000-0077
47	9000-0061
47.208	9000-0056
48	9000-0027
49	9000-0028
50	9000-0029
51.1	9000-0031
51.2	9000-0032
52.203-2	9000-0018
52.203-7	9000-0091
52.203-13	9000-0164
52.203-16	9000-0183
52.204-3	9000-0097
52.204-6	9000-0145
52.204-7	9000-0159
52.204-10	9000-0177
52.204-12	9000-0145
52.204-13	9000-0159
52.204-14	9000-0179
52.204-15	9000-0179
52.204-16	9000-0185
52.204-17	9000-0185
52.204-18	9000-0185
52.204-20	9000-0189
52.207-3	9000-0114
52.207-4	9000-0082
52.208-8	9000-0113

FAR segment	OMB Control Number
52.208-9	9000-0113
52.209-1	9000-0083
52.209-1(b)	9000-0020
52.209-1(c)	9000-0083
52.207-2	9000-0190
52.209-5	9000-0094
52.209-6	9000-0094
52.209-7	9000-0174
52.209-9	9000-0174
52.209-10	9000-0190
52.209-11	9000-0193
52.209-12	9000-0193
52.211-7	9000-0153
52.211-8	9000-0043
52.211-9	9000-0043
52.212-1(k)	9000-0159
52.212-3	9000-0136
52.212-3(h)	9000-0094
52.212-4(t)	9000-0159
52.212-5	9000-0034
52.214-14	9000-0047
52.214-15	9000-0044
52.214-16	9000-0044
52.214-21	9000-0039
52.214-26	9000-0034
52.214-28	9000-0013
52.212-5	9000-0034
52.215-1(c)(2)(iv)	9000-0048
52.215-1(d)	9000-0044
52.215-2	9000-0034
52.215-6	9000-0047
52.215-9	9000-0078
52.215-12	9000-0013
52.215-13	9000-0013
52.215-14	9000-0080
52.215-19	9000-0115
52.215-20	9000-0013
52.215-21	9000-0013
	9000-0173
	9000-0173
52.216-2	9000-0068
52.216-3	9000-0068
52.216-4	9000-0068
52.216-5	9000-0071
52.216-6	9000-0071
52.216-7	9000-0069
52.216-10	9000-0067

FAR segment	OMB Control Number
52.216-15	9000-0069
52.216-16	9000-0067
52.216-17	9000-0067
52.219-9	9000-0006 and 9000-0007
52.219-10	9000-0006
52.219-28	9000-0163
52.219-29	3245-0374
52.219-30	3245-0374
52.222-2	9000-0065
52.222-4	1215-0023
52.222-6	1215-0023
52.222-8	1235-0008 and 1235-0018
52.222-11	9000-0014
52.222-17	1235-0007 and 1235-0025
52.222-18	9000-0155
52.222-21	1250-0003
52.222-22	1250-0003
52.222-23	1250-0003
52.222-25	1250-0003
52.222-26	1250-0003
52.222-27	1250-0003
52.222-32	9000-0154
52.222-35	1250-0004
52.222-36	1250-0005
52.222-37	1293-0004 and 1293-0005
52.222-38	1250-0004 and 1293-0005
52.222-40	1245-0004
52.222-41	1235-0018 and 1235-0007
52.222-46	9000-0066
52.222-50	9000-0188
52.222-54	1615-0092
52.222-55	1235-0018
52.222-56	9000-0188
52.223-2	9000-0180
52.223-4	9000-0134
52.223-5	9000-0147
52.223-6(b)(5)	9000-0101
52.223-7	9000-0107
52.223-9	9000-0134
52.223-11	9000-0191
52.223-12	9000-0191
52.225-2	9000-0024
52.225-4	9000-0024

FAR segment	OMB Control Number
52.225-6	9000-0024
52.225-8	9000-0022
52.225-9	9000-0024
52.225-10	9000-0024
52.225-11	9000-0024
52.225-12	9000-0024
52.225-18	9000-0161
52.225-21	9000-0024
52.225-23	9000-0024
52.225-26	9000-0184
52.227-2	9000-0096
52.227-6	9000-0096
52.227-9	9000-0096
52.227-11	9000-0095
52.227-13	9000-0095
52.227-14	9000-0090
52.227-15	9000-0090
52.227-16	9000-0090
52.227-17	9000-0090
52.227-18	9000-0090
52.227-19	9000-0090
52.227-20	9000-0090
52.227-21	9000-0090
52.227-22	9000-0090
52.227-23	9000-0090
52.228-1	9000-0045
52.228-2	9000-0045
52.228-12	9000-0135
52.228-13	9000-0045
52.228-14	9000-0045
52.228-15	9000-0045
52.228-16	9000-0045
52.229-2	9000-0059
52.230-6	9000-0129
52.232-1	9000-0070
52.232-2	9000-0070
52.232-3	9000-0070
52.232-4	9000-0070
52.232-5	9000-0102
52.232-6	9000-0070
52.232-7	9000-0070
52.232-8	9000-0070
52.232-9	9000-0070
52.232-10	9000-0070
52.232-11	9000-0070
52.232-12	9000-0073
52.232-13	9000-0010

FAR segment	OMB Control Number
52.232-14	9000-0010
52.232-15	9000-0010
52.232-16	9000-0010
52.232-20	9000-0074
52.232-22	9000-0074
52.232-27	9000-0102
52.232-29	9000-0138
52.232-30	9000-0138
52.232-31	9000-0138
52.232-32	9000-0138
52.232-33	9000-0144
52.232-34	9000-0144
52.233-1	9000-0035
52.236-5	9000-0062
52.236-13	9000-0060
52.236-15	9000-0058
52.236-19	9000-0064
52.237-10	9000-0152
52.241-1	9000-0126
52.241-3	9000-0122
52.241-7	9000-0123
52.241-13	9000-0124
52.242-13	9000-0108
52.243-1	9000-0026
52.243-2	9000-0026
52.243-3	9000-0026
52.243-4	9000-0026
52.243-6	9000-0026
52.243-7	9000-0026
52.244-2	9000-0149
52.244-2 (i)	9000-0132
52.245-1	9000-0075
52.245-9	9000-0075
52.246-2	9000-0077
52.246-3	9000-0077
52.246-4	9000-0077
52.246-5	9000-0077
52.246-6	9000-0077
52.246-7	9000-0077
52.246-8	9000-0077
52.246-12	9000-0077
52.246-15	9000-0077
52.247-2	9000-0053
52.247-6	9000-0061
52.247-29	9000-0061
52.247-30	9000-0061
52.247-31	9000-0061

§ 1.106

ANNOTATED FEDERAL ACQUISITION REGULATION

FAR segment	OMB Control Number
52.247-32	9000-0061
52.247-33	9000-0061
52.247-34	9000-0061
52.247-35	9000-0061
52.247-36	9000-0061
52.247-37	9000-0061
52.247-38	9000-0061
52.247-39	9000-0061
52.247-40	9000-0061
52.247-41	9000-0061
52.247-42	9000-0061
52.247-43	9000-0061
52.247-44	9000-0061
52.247-48	9000-0061
52.247-51	9000-0057
52.247-52	9000-0061
52.247-53	9000-0055
52.247-57	9000-0061
52.247-63	9000-0054
52.247-64	9000-0061
52.247-68	9000-0056
52.248-1	9000-0027
52.248-2	9000-0027
52.248-3	9000-0027
52.249-2	9000-0028
52.249-3	9000-0028
52.249-5	9000-0028
52.249-6	9000-0028
52.250-1	9000-0029
52.251-2	9000-0032
SF 24	9000-0045
SF 25	9000-0045
SF 25A	9000-0045
SF 28	9000-0001
SF 34	9000-0045
SF 35	9000-0045
SF 273	9000-0045
SF 274	9000-0045
SF 275	9000-0045
SF 294	9000-0006
SF 295	9000-0007
SF 330	9000-0157
SF 1403	9000-0011
SF 1404	9000-0011
SF 1405	9000-0011
SF 1406	9000-0011
SF 1407	9000-0011

22

FAR segment	OMB Control Number
SF 1408	9000-0011
SF 1413	9000-0014
SF 1416	9000-0045
SF 1418	9000-0045
SF 1428	9000-0075
SF 1429	9000-0075
SF 1435	9000-0012
SF 1436	9000-0012
SF 1437	9000-0012
SF 1438	9000-0012
SF 1439	9000-0012
SF 1440	9000-0012
SF 1443	9000-0010
SF 1444	9000-0089
SF 1445	9000-0089
SF 1446	9000-0089

§ 1.107 Certifications.

In accordance with 41 U.S.C. 1304, a new requirement for a certification by a contractor or offeror may not be included in this chapter unless—

(a) The certification requirement is specifically imposed by statute; or

(b) Written justification for such certification is provided to the Administrator for Federal Procurement Policy by the Federal Acquisition Regulatory Council, and the Administrator approves in writing the inclusion of such certification requirement.

United States Code Annotated

Authority and functions of the Administrator, see 41 U.S.C.A. § 405.

Definitions, see 41 U.S.C.A. § 403.

Establishment of Office of Federal Procurement Policy, appointment of Administrator, see 41 U.S.C.A. § 404.

Federal Acquisition Regulatory Council, see 41 U.S.C.A. § 421.

Uniform Federal procurement regulations and procedures, see 41 U.S.C.A. § 405a.

§ 1.108 FAR conventions.

The following conventions provide guidance for interpreting the FAR:

(a) *Words and terms.* Definitions in Part 2 apply to the entire regulation unless specifically defined in another part, subpart, section, provision, or clause. Words or terms defined in a specific part, subpart, section, provision, or clause have that meaning when used in that part, subpart, section, provision, or clause. Undefined words retain their common dictionary meaning.

(b) *Delegation of authority.* Each authority is delegable unless specifically stated otherwise (see 1.102-4(b)).

(c) *Dollar thresholds.* Unless otherwise specified, a specific dollar threshold for the purpose of applicability is the final anticipated dollar value of the action, including the dollar value of all options. If the action establishes a maximum quantity of supplies or services to be acquired or establishes a ceiling price or establishes the final price to be based on future events, the final anticipated dollar value must be the highest final priced alternative to the Government, including the dollar value of all options.

(d) *Application of FAR changes to solicitations and contracts.* Unless otherwise specified—

(1) FAR changes apply to solicitations issued on or after the effective date of the

change;

(2) Contracting officers may, at their discretion, include the FAR changes in solicitations issued before the effective date, provided award of the resulting contract(s) occurs on or after the effective date; and

(3) Contracting officers may, at their discretion, include the changes in any existing contract with appropriate consideration.

(e) *Citations.* When the FAR cites a statute, Executive order, Office of Management and Budget circular, Office of Federal Procurement Policy policy letter, or relevant portion of the *Code of Federal Regulations*, the citation includes all applicable amendments, unless otherwise stated.

(f) *Imperative sentences.* When an imperative sentence directs action, the contracting officer is responsible for the action, unless another party is expressly cited.

United States Code Annotated

Authority and functions of the Administrator, see 41 U.S.C.A. § 405.

Definitions, see 41 U.S.C.A. § 403.

Establishment of Office of Federal Procurement Policy, appointment of Administrator, see 41 U.S.C.A. § 404.

Federal Acquisition Regulatory Council, see 41 U.S.C.A. § 421.

Uniform Federal procurement regulations and procedures, see 41 U.S.C.A. § 405a.

Notes on Decisions
Applicability of FAR Changes 1

1 Applicability of FAR Changes

FAR changes apply to solicitations issued on or after the effective date of the change. FAR 1.108(d)(1). However, the FAR provides limited exceptions to this general rule when contracting officers wish to apply FAR amendments retroactively to pre-existing agreements. Specifically, contracting officers are permitted to include the FAR changes in solicitations issued before the effective date, provided that award of the resulting contract(s) occurs on or after the effective date. FAR 1.108(d)(2). Another option is for contracting officers to "include the changes in any existing contract with appropriate consideration." *Id.* at (d)(3). BearingPoint, Inc. v. U.S., 77 Fed. Cl. 189 (2007).

A new FAR section, which became effective after bid opening is not applicable and could not be used to assess the responsibility or responsiveness of the bidders. FAR changes apply to solicitations issued on or after the effective date of the change. FAR 1.108(d)(1). Matter of: Johnson Machine Works, Inc., B-297115, 2005 CPD ¶ 188 (Comp. Gen. 2005).

§ 1.109 Statutory acquisition—related dollar thresholds—adjustment for inflation.

(a) 41 U.S.C. 1908 requires that the FAR Council periodically adjust all statutory acquisition-related dollar thresholds in the FAR for inflation, except as provided in paragraph (c) of this section. This adjustment is calculated every 5 years, starting in October 2005, using the Consumer Price Index (CPI) for all-urban consumers, and supersedes the applicability of any other provision of law that provides for the adjustment of such acquisition-related dollar thresholds.

(b) The statute defines an acquisition-related dollar threshold as a dollar threshold that is specified in law as a factor in defining the scope of the applicability of a policy, procedure, requirement, or restriction provided in that law to the procurement of supplies or services by an executive agency, as determined by the FAR Council.

(c) The statute does not permit escalation of acquisition-related dollar thresholds established by:

(1) 40 U.S.C. chapter 31, subchapter IV, Wage Rate Requirements (Construction);

(2) 41 U.S.C. chapter 67, Service Contract Labor Standards; or

(3) The United States Trade Representative pursuant to the authority of the Trade Agreements Act of 1979 (19 U.S.C. 2511 et seq.).

(d) A matrix showing calculation of the most recent escalation adjustments of statutory acquisition-related dollar thresholds is available via the Internet at http://www.regulation s.gov (search FAR Case 2008-024).

§ 1.110 Positive law codification.

(a) Public Law 107-217 revised, codified, and enacted as title 40, United States Code, Public Buildings, Property, and Works, certain general and permanent laws of the United States.

(b) Public Law 111-350 revised, codified, and enacted as title 41, United States Code, Public Contracts, certain general and permanent laws of the United States.

(c) The following table provides cross references between the historical titles of the acts, and the current reference in title 40 or title 41.

Historical Title of Act	Division/ Chapter/ Subchapter	Title
Anti-Kickback Act	41 U.S.C. chapter 87	Kickbacks
Brooks Architect Engineer Act	40 U.S.C. chapter 11	Selection of Architects and Engineers
Buy American Act	41 U.S.C. chapter 83	Buy American
Contract Disputes Act of 1978	41 U.S.C. chapter 71	Contract Disputes
Contract Work Hours and Safety Standards Act	40 U.S.C. chapter 37	Contract Work Hours and Safety Standards
Davis-Bacon Act	40 U.S.C. chapter 31, Subchapter IV	Wage Rate Requirements (Construction)
Drug-Free Workplace Act	41 U.S.C. chapter 81	Drug-Free Workplace
Federal Property and Administrative Services Act of 1949, Title III.	41 U.S.C. Div. C of subtitle I*	Procurement
Javits-Wagner-O'Day Act	41 U.S.C. chapter 85	Committee for Purchase from People Who Are Blind or Severely Disabled
Miller Act	40 U.S.C. chapter 31, subchapter III	Bonds
Office of Federal Procurement Policy Act	41 U.S.C. Div. B of subtitle I**	Office of Federal Procurement Policy
Procurement Integrity Act	41 U.S.C. chapter 21	Restrictions on Obtaining and Disclosing Certain Information
Service Contract Act of 1965	41 U.S.C. chapter 67	Service Contract Labor Standards
Truth in Negotiations Act	41 U.S.C. chapter 35	Truthful Cost or Pricing Data
Walsh-Healey Public Contracts Act	41 U.S.C. chapter 65	Contracts for Materials, Supplies, Articles, and Equipment Exceeding $15,000.

* Except sections 3302, 3501(b), 3509, 3906, 4710, and 4711.

** Except sections 1704 and 2303.

Subpart 1.2 Administration

§ 1.201 Maintenance of the FAR.

§ 1.201-1 The two councils.

(a) Subject to the authorities discussed in 1.103, revisions to the FAR will be prepared and issued through the coordinated action of two councils, the Defense Acquisition Regulations Council (DAR Council) and the Civilian Agency Acquisition Council (CAA Council). Members of these councils shall—

(1) Represent their agencies on a full-time basis;

(2) Be selected for their superior qualifications in terms of acquisition experience and demonstrated professional expertise; and

(3) Be funded by their respective agencies.

(b) The chairperson of the CAA Council shall be the representative of the Administrator of General Services. The other members of this council shall be one each representative from the—

(1) Departments of Agriculture, Commerce, Energy, Health and Human Services, Homeland Security, Interior, Labor, State, Transportation, and Treasury; and

(2) Environmental Protection Agency, Social Security Administration, Small Business Administration, and Department of Veterans Affairs.

(c) The Director of the DAR Council shall be the representative of the Secretary of Defense. The operation of the DAR Council will be as prescribed by the Secretary of Defense. Membership shall include representatives of the military departments, the Defense Logistics Agency, the Defense Contract Management Agency, and the National Aeronautics and Space Administration.

(d) Responsibility for processing revisions to the FAR is apportioned by the two councils so that each council has cognizance over specified parts or subparts.

(e) Each council shall be responsible for—

(1) Agreeing on all revisions with the other council;

(2) Submitting to the FAR Secretariat (see 1.201-2) the information required under paragraphs 1.501-2(b) and (e) for publication in the *Federal Register* of a notice soliciting comments on a proposed revision to the FAR;

(3) Considering all comments received in response to notice of proposed revisions;

(4) Arranging for public meetings;

(5) Preparing any final revision in the appropriate FAR format and language; and

(6) Submitting any final revision to the FAR Secretariat for publication in the *Federal Register* and printing for distribution.

United States Code Annotated

Authority and functions of the Administrator, see 41 U.S.C.A. § 405.

Definitions, see 41 U.S.C.A. § 403.

Establishment of Office of Federal Procurement Policy, appointment of Administrator, see 41 U.S.C.A. § 404.

Federal Acquisition Regulatory Council, see 41 U.S.C.A. § 421.

Uniform Federal procurement regulations and procedures, see 41 U.S.C.A. § 405a.

Notes on Decisions

In general 1

1 In general

FAR 1.201 provides that the Defense Acquisition Regulations Council and the Civilian Agency Acquisition Council shall be responsible for preparation and issuance of revisions to the FAR. This includes the submittal of information necessary for publication of a notice soliciting comments on a proposed revision to the FAR. In re Johnson Controls World Services, Inc., A.S.B.C.A. No. 51640, A.S.B.C.A. No. 51766, A.S.B.C.A. No. 52127, A.S.B.C.A. No. 52262, 01-2, 01-2 B.C.A. (CCH) ¶ 31531, 2001 WL 865383 (Armed Serv. B.C.A.

2001).

The FAR is prepared, issued, and maintained jointly by the Secretary of Defense, the Administrator of General Services, and the Administrator of the National Aeronautics and Space Administration. The Civilian Agency Acquisition Council, chaired by GSA, and the Defense Acquisition Regulations Council are charged with revising the FAR. Knowledge Connections, Inc. v. U.S., 76 Fed. Cl. 6 (2007).

§ 1.201-2 FAR Secretariat.

(a) The General Services Administration is responsible for establishing and operating the FAR Secretariat to print, publish, and distribute the FAR through the *Code of Federal Regulations* system (including a loose-leaf edition with periodic updates).

(b) Additionally, the FAR Secretariat shall provide the two councils with centralized services for—

(1) Keeping a synopsis of current FAR cases and their status;

(2) Maintaining official files;

(3) Assisting parties interested in reviewing the files on completed cases; and

(4) Performing miscellaneous administrative tasks pertaining to the maintenance of the FAR.

United States Code Annotated

Authority and functions of the Administrator, see 41 U.S.C.A. § 405.

Definitions, see 41 U.S.C.A. § 403.

Establishment of Office of Federal Procurement Policy, appointment of Administrator, see 41 U.S.C.A. § 404.

Federal Acquisition Regulatory Council, see 41 U.S.C.A. § 421.

Uniform Federal procurement regulations and procedures, see 41 U.S.C.A. § 405a.

§ 1.202 Agency compliance with the FAR.

Agency compliance with the FAR (see 1.304) is the responsibility of the Secretary of Defense (for the military departments and defense agencies), the Administrator of General Services (for civilian agencies other than NASA), and the Administrator of NASA (for NASA activities).

United States Code Annotated

Authority and functions of the Administrator, see 41 U.S.C.A. § 405.

Definitions, see 41 U.S.C.A. § 403.

Establishment of Office of Federal Procurement Policy, appointment of Administrator, see 41 U.S.C.A. § 404.

Federal Acquisition Regulatory Council, see 41 U.S.C.A. § 421.

Uniform Federal procurement regulations and procedures, see 41 U.S.C.A. § 405a.

Subpart 1.3 Agency Acquisition Regulations

§ 1.301 Policy.

(a) (1) Subject to the authorities in paragraph (c) of this section and other statutory authority, an agency head may issue or authorize the issuance of agency acquisition regulations that implement or supplement the FAR and incorporate, together with the FAR, agency policies, procedures, contract clauses, solicitation provisions, and forms that govern the contracting process or otherwise control the relationship between the agency, including any of its suborganizations, and contractors or prospective contractors.

(2) Subject to the authorities in paragraph (c) of this section and other statutory authority, an agency head may issue or authorize the issuance of internal agency guidance at any organizational level (*e.g.*, designations and delegations of authority, assignments of responsibilities, work-flow procedures, and internal reporting requirements).

(b) Agency heads shall establish procedures to ensure that agency acquisition regulations are published for comment in the *Federal Register* in conformance with the procedures in Subpart 1.5 and as required by 41 U.S.C. 1707, and other applicable statutes, when they have a significant effect beyond the internal operating procedures of the agency or have a significant cost or administrative impact on contractors or offerors. However, publication is not required for issuances that merely implement or supplement higher level issuances that have previously undergone the public comment process, unless such implementation or supplementation results in an additional significant cost or administrative impact on contractors or offerors or effect beyond the internal operating procedures of the issuing organization. Issuances under 1.301(a)(2) need not be publicized for public comment.

(c) When adopting acquisition regulations, agencies shall ensure that they comply with the Paperwork Reduction Act (44 U.S.C. 3501, *et seq.*) as implemented in 5 CFR 1320 (see 1.106) and the Regulatory Flexibility Act (5 U.S.C. 601, *et seq.*). Normally, when a law requires publication of a proposed regulation, the Regulatory Flexibility Act applies and agencies must prepare written analyses, or certifications as provided in the law.

(d) Agency acquisition regulations implementing or supplementing the FAR are, for—

(1) The military departments and defense agencies, issued subject to the authority of the Secretary of Defense;

(2) NASA activities, issued subject to the authorities of the Administrator of NASA; and

(3) The civilian agencies other than NASA, issued by the heads of those agencies subject to the overall authority of the Administrator of General Services or independent authority the agency may have.

Notes of Decisions

In general 1

1 In general

While the FAR replaced the DAR, FPR, and procurement regulations of other agencies having statutory authority to issue such regulations, it allowed agencies to issue their own "FAR Supplement" for unique or special circumstances peculiar to a particular agency. DoD promptly established a Defense FAR Supplement (DFARS) and other agencies (including NASA) followed suit, setting up their own supplemental regulations. Space Gateway Support, LLC, ASBCA No. 55608, 2013 WL 518974 (Armed Serv. B.C.A. 2013)

Federal Acquisition Regulations System (FAR) and the Department of Defense FAR Supplement (DFARS) have force and effect of law. 48 C.F.R. § 1.301(b). Davies Precision Machining, Inc. v. U.S., 35 Fed. Cl. 651, 40 Cont. Cas. Fed. (CCH) P 76936 (1996). United States ☞65

Agencies must publish agency acquisition regulations in the Federal Register, 5 U.S.C. § 552(a)(1) (1988); FAR 1.301(b), although agencies are not generally required to publish issuances that merely implement or supplement higher level issuances that have previously undergone the public comment process. FAR 1.301(b). Petro Star, Inc., B-248019, 92-2 CPD ¶ 34 (Comp. Gen. 1992).

§ 1.302 Limitations.

Agency acquisition regulations shall be limited to—

(a) Those necessary to implement FAR policies and procedures within the agency; and

(b) Additional policies, procedures, solicitation provisions, or contract clauses that supplement the FAR to satisfy the specific needs of the agency.

Notes on Decisions

In general 1

1 In general

General Services Administration (GSA) regulation, providing that contractors must retroactively reimburse GSA for any wage or fringe benefit increases paid by GSA which are later determined by Secretary of Labor to be at substantial variance with prevailing wage and fringe benefits in the area, was not designed to satisfy specific need of the agency and thus, GSA regulation was not proper under Service Contract Act and Federal Acquisition Regulations (FAR); although rationale behind GSA regulation was cost savings, GSA had not explained how this need for cost savings was specific or unique to it. Service Contract Act of 1965, § 2 et seq., 41 U.S.C.A. § 351 et seq.Service Employees Intern. Union, AFL-CIO v. General Services Admin., 830 F. Supp. 5, 1 Wage & Hour Cas. 2d (BNA) 974 (D.D.C. 1993). Labor And Employment ☞2338

§ 1.303 Publication and codification.

(a) Agency-wide acquisition regulations shall be published in the *Federal Register* as required by law, shall be codified under an assigned chapter in Title 48, Code of Federal Regulations, and shall parallel the FAR in format, arrangement, and numbering system (but see 1.105-1(c)). Coverage in an agency acquisition regulation that implements a specific part, subpart, section, or subsection of the FAR shall be numbered and titled to correspond to the appropriate FAR number and title. Supplementary material for which there is no counterpart in the FAR shall be codified using chapter, part, subpart, section, or subsection numbers of 70 and up (*e.g.*, for the Department of Interior, whose assigned chapter number in Title 48 is 14, Part 1470, Subpart 1401.70, section 1401.370, or subsection 1401.301-70).

(b) Issuances under 1.301(a)(2) need not be published in the *Federal Register*.

Notes on Decisions
In general 1

1 In general

Clause in government contracts permitting either party to cancel contract upon 30 days' written notice did not conflict with second provision permitting "termination for convenience," and thus, even though 30-day provision had not been published in Federal Register, General Services Administration (GSA) could invoke that provision to cancel contracts upon suspending contractor due to its indictment for defrauding government; 30-day provision permitted either party to cancel entire multiple award schedule contract with requisite notice, while "termination for convenience" provision, which was included in most federal contracts, permitted either party to cancel individual orders. 48 C.F.R. § 1.401. Commercial Drapery Contractors, Inc. v. U.S., 133 F.3d 1, 328, 39 Fed. R. Serv. 3d 825 (D.C. Cir. 1998). United States ☞72.1(1)

Agencies must publish agency acquisition regulations in the Federal Register, 5 U.S.C. § 552(a)(1) (1988); FAR 1.301(b), although agencies are not generally required to publish issuances that merely implement or supplement higher level issuances that have previously undergone the public comment process. FAR 1.301(b). Petro Star, Inc., B-248019, 92-2 CPD ¶ 34 (Comp. Gen. 1992).

§ 1.304 Agency control and compliance procedures.

(a) Under the authorities of 1.301(d), agencies shall control and limit issuance of agency acquisition regulations and, in particular, local agency directives that restrain the flexibilities found in the FAR, and shall establish formal procedures for the review of these documents to assure compliance with this Part 1.

(b) Agency acquisition regulations shall not—

(1) Unnecessarily repeat, paraphrase, or otherwise restate material contained in the FAR or higher-level agency acquisition regulations; or

(2) Except as required by law or as provided in Subpart 1.4, conflict or be inconsistent with FAR content.

(c) Agencies shall evaluate all regulatory coverage in agency acquisition regulations to determine if it could apply to other agencies. Coverage that is not peculiar to one agency shall be recommended for inclusion in the FAR.

Notes on Decisions
In general 1

1 In general

Although the FAR forbids agency acquisition regulations from conflicting with FAR content, it also permits each agency head or his designee to authorize both individual deviations and class deviations from the body of Government-wide regulations. FAR 1.304(b) (2). A "class deviation" affects more than one contracting action, and may be made on a permanent basis. FAR 1.404. Ace Services, Inc. v. General Services Admin., G.S.B.C.A. No. 11331, 92-2 B.C.A. (CCH) ¶ 24943, 1992 WL 59426 (Gen. Services Admin. B.C.A. 1992).

An agency's supplement to the FAR is not permitted to conflict with the FAR, except when authorized. 48 C.F.R. § 1.304(b)(2). The Air Force's regulations, which did not preclude the consideration of key personnel, are not inconsistent with the FAR. SDS Intern. v. U.S., 48 Fed. Cl. 759 (2001)

Subpart 1.4 Deviations from the FAR

§ 1.400 Scope of subpart.

This subpart prescribes the policies and procedures for authorizing deviations from the FAR. Exceptions pertaining to the use of forms prescribed by the FAR are covered in Part 53 rather than in this subpart.

United States Code Annotated

Administrative determinations, see 41 U.S.C.A. § 257.

Chief acquisition officers and senior procurement executives, see 41 U.S.C.A. § 414.

Definitions, see 10 U.S.C.A. § 2302, 41 U.S.C.A. §§ 259, 403.

Determinations and decisions, see 10 U.S.C.A. § 2310, 41 U.S.C.A. § 262.

§ 1.401 Definition.

"Deviation" means any one or combination of the following:

(a) The issuance or use of a policy, procedure, solicitation provision (see definition in 2.101), contract clause (see definition in 2.101), method, or practice of conducting acquisition actions of any kind at any stage of the acquisition process that is inconsistent with the FAR.

(b) The omission of any solicitation provision or contract clause when its prescription requires its use.

(c) The use of any solicitation provision or contract clause with modified or alternate language that is not authorized by the FAR (see definition of " modification" in 52.101(a) and definition of "alternate" in 2.101(a)).

(d) The use of a solicitation provision or contract clause prescribed by the FAR on a "substantially as follows" or "substantially the same as" basis (see definitions in 2.101 and 52.101(a)), if such use is inconsistent with the intent, principle, or substance of the prescription or related coverage on the subject matter in the FAR.

(e) The authorization of lesser or greater limitations on the use of any solicitation provision, contract clause, policy, or procedure prescribed by the FAR.

(f) The issuance of policies or procedures that govern the contracting process or otherwise control contracting relationships that are not incorporated into agency acquisition regulations in accordance with 1.301(a).

United States Code Annotated

Administrative determinations, see 41 U.S.C.A. § 257.

Chief acquisition officers and senior procurement executives, see 41 U.S.C.A. § 414.

Definitions, see 10 U.S.C.A. § 2302, 41 U.S.C.A. §§ 259, 403.

Determinations and decisions, see 10 U.S.C.A. § 2310, 41 U.S.C.A. § 262.

Notes of Decisions

In general 1

1 In general

Any agreement to allow the Government to terminate the contract for convenience only in the event of a base closure would amount to a modification of the standard FAR convenience termination clauses. As there is no provision in the FAR authorizing the contracting officer to enter into that modification, it would constitute a deviation under FAR 1.401(c), requiring prior authorization by the agency head or his designee. Therefore, such a modification would be beyond the contracting officer's authority and, invalid. In re Empresa de Viacao Terceirense, A.S.B.C.A. No. 49827, 00-1 B.C.A. (CCH) ¶ 30796, 2000 WL 223808 (Armed Serv. B.C.A. 2000).

In order for there to be a deviation from the prescribed FAR Limitations of Funds clause, there must be action "inconsistent with the FAR." FAR 1.401. As described in DFARS 1.402(a)(1), there must be a contract clause covering the same subject matter which varies from the FAR or DoD FAR supplement coverage, or use of a collateral provision which modifies either the clause or its prescribed application. Appeal of COLSA, Inc., A.S.B.C.A. No. 45505, 94-1 B.C.A. (CCH) ¶ 26534, 1993 WL 502266 (Armed Serv. B.C.A. 1993).

Although the FAR forbids agency acquisition regulations from conflicting with FAR content, it also permits each agency head or his designee to authorize both individual deviations and class deviations from the body of Government-wide regulations. FAR 1.304(b) (2). A "class deviation" affects more than one contracting action, and may be made on a permanent basis. FAR 1.404. Ace Services, Inc. v. General Services Admin., G.S.B.C.A. No. 11331, 92-2 B.C.A. (CCH) ¶ 24943, 1992 WL 59426 (Gen. Services Admin. B.C.A. 1992).

§ 1.402 Policy.

Unless precluded by law, executive order, or regulation, deviations from the FAR may be granted as specified in this subpart when necessary to meet the specific needs and requirements of each agency. The development and testing of new techniques and methods of acquisition should not be stifled simply because such action would require a FAR deviation. The fact that deviation authority is required should not, of itself, deter agencies in their development and testing of new techniques and acquisition methods. Refer to 31.101 for instructions concerning deviations pertaining to the subject matter of Part 31, Contract Cost Principles and Procedures. Deviations are not authorized with respect to 30.201-3 and 30.201-4, or the requirements of the Cost Accounting Standards Board (CASB) rules and regulations (48 CFR Chapter 99 (FAR Appendix)). Refer to 30.201-5 for instructions concerning waivers pertaining to Cost Accounting Standards.

United States Code Annotated

Administrative determinations, see 41 U.S.C.A. § 257.

Chief acquisition officers and senior procurement executives, see 41 U.S.C.A. § 414.

Definitions, see 10 U.S.C.A. § 2302, 41 U.S.C.A. §§ 259, 403.

Determinations and decisions, see 10 U.S.C.A. § 2310, 41 U.S.C.A. § 262.

Notes on Decisions
In general 1

1 In general

FAR 52.211-10, expressly states that the project completion date will be extended by the number of calendar days after the seventieth day following bid opening. An internal Federal Highway Administration specification (FP-96, *Standard Specifications for Construction of Roads and Bridges on Federal Highway Projects*, 1996, § 108.03), which limits the extension of the completion date to those delays or modifications that affect critical activities, cannot modify a FAR clause unless a deviation is granted in accordance with FAR Subpart 1.4, which governs individual or class deviations to the FAR. Tidewater Contractors, Inc. v. Dept. of Transportation, CBCA 50-R, 07-2 B.C.A. (CCH) ¶ 33618, 2007 WL 2045470 (U.S. Civilian BCA 2007).

§ 1.403 Individual deviations.

Individual deviations affect only one contract action, and, unless 1.405(e) is applicable, may be authorized by the agency head. The contracting officer must document the justification and agency approval in the contract file.

United States Code Annotated

Administrative determinations, see 41 U.S.C.A. § 257.

Chief acquisition officers and senior procurement executives, see 41 U.S.C.A. § 414.

Definitions, see 10 U.S.C.A. § 2302, 41 U.S.C.A. §§ 259, 403.

Determinations and decisions, see 10 U.S.C.A. § 2310, 41 U.S.C.A. § 262.

Notes of Decisions

In general 1

1 In general

A contract modification of FAR's Advance Payment clause was found to be void and unenforceable where the CO has not obtained an individual deviation to do so. Johnson Management Group CFC, Inc. v. Martinez, 308 F.3d 1245 (Fed. Cir. 2002)

By varying from and modifying the prescribed application of the mandatory FAR 52.232-1 Payments clause, a special "PAYMENTS" provision at in Section H of the contract constitutes a deviation. DFARS 201.402. Unless such deviation has been authorized in accordance with the procedures prescribed by FAR 1.403 or 1.404 and DFARS 201.402 to.404, the deviation is unauthorized and unenforceable. Appeal of Revere Elec. Supply Co., A.S.B. C.A. No. 46413, 95-1 B.C.A. (CCH) ¶ 27385, 1994 WL 144265 (Armed Serv. B.C.A. 1994).

Three individual deviations obtained by the government for illegal economic price adjustment (EPA) clauses in five contracts were unauthorized and invalid, as governing sections of the Federal Acquisition Regulation (FAR) and the Defense Logistics Acquisition Regulation (DLAR) required that government obtain an individual deviation for each contract. 48 C.F.R. § 1.403. Sunoco, Inc. v. U.S., 59 Fed. Cl. 390 (2004) (abrogated by, Tesoro Hawaii Corp. v. U.S., 405 F.3d 1339, 15 A.L.R. Fed. 2d 755 (Fed. Cir. 2005)) (the court said on abrogation that "[t]he issue regarding the legality of the procedures used to obtain the individual and class deviations is moot in light of our determination that the clause that DESC sought permission to use was authorized by the FAR"). United States ⟶70(18)

Individual deviation or exemption from section of the Federal Acquisition Regulation (FAR) governing economic price adjustment clauses was invalid and illegal under the FAR, where deviation was applied not to a single contract but to multiple contracts issued under single solicitation, and was used to accommodate the government as a temporary measure until a permanent class deviation was obtained. 48 C.F.R. §§ 1.403, 1.404, 16.203-1. Calcasieu Refining Co. v. U.S., 2003 WL 22049528 (Ct. Fed. Cl. 2003). United States ⟶70(18)

Individual deviations from the Federal Acquisition Regulation (FAR) for economic price adjustment (EPA) clauses in contracts for supply of military jet fuel were obtained in violation of the FAR, where deviations were not sought for individual contracts, but for multiple-award solicitations under which suppliers received their particular contract awards. 48 C.F.R. § 1.403. Navajo Refining Co., L.P. v. U.S., 58 Fed. Cl. 200 (2003). United States ⟶70(18)

Individual deviations from the Federal Acquisition Regulation (FAR) for economic price adjustment (EPA) clause which the government obtained to cover all domestic fuel supply contracts for a period of one year were invalid under section of the Federal Acquisition Regulation (FAR) limiting individual deviations to single contracts. 48 C.F.R. § 1.401(a). Tesoro Hawaii Corp. v. U.S., 58 Fed. Cl. 65 (2003), rev'd, 405 F.3d 1339, 15 A.L.R. Fed. 2d 755 (Fed. Cir. 2005)(the court said on reversal that "[t]he issue regarding the legality of the procedures used to obtain the individual and class deviations is moot in light of our determination that the clause that DESC sought permission to use was authorized by the FAR").

Under reasonable reading of the Defense Logistics Acquisition Regulations (DLAR), agency's individual deviation from the Federal Acquisition Regulation (FAR) permitting use of economic price adjustment (EPA) clause that adopted market-based price index clearly extended to solicitations that encompassed the award of multiple contracts, and not just individual contracts. 48 C.F.R. § 1.403. Williams Alaska Petroleum, Inc. v. U.S., 57 Fed. Cl. 789 (2003). United States ⟶70(18)

Individual deviations from the Federal Acquisition Regulation (FAR) for economic price adjustment clause which the government obtained for two years of fuel supply procurements violated the FAR, as government's fuel procurements, which occurred in the fall and again in the spring, involved multiple contracts and required a class deviation rather than individual deviations. 48 C.F.R. §§ 1.403, 1.404. La Gloria Oil and Gas Co. v. U.S., 56 Fed. Cl. 211 (2003) (abrogated by, Tesoro Hawaii Corp. v. U.S., 405 F.3d 1339, 15 A.L.R. Fed. 2d 755 (Fed. Cir. 2005))(the court said on abrogation that "[t]he issue regarding the legality of the procedures used to obtain the individual and class deviations is moot in light of our determination that the clause that DESC sought permission to use was authorized by the FAR"). United States ☞70(18)

Phrase "one contract action" in section of the Federal Acquisition Regulation (FAR) defining individual deviation from the FAR affecting "only one contract action" means, unambiguously, an action related to one contract award. 48 C.F.R. § 1.403. La Gloria Oil and Gas Co. v. U.S., 56 Fed. Cl. 211 (2003) (abrogated by, Tesoro Hawaii Corp. v. U.S., 405 F.3d 1339, 15 A.L.R. Fed. 2d 755 (Fed. Cir. 2005)) (the court said on abrogation that "[t]he issue regarding the legality of the procedures used to obtain the individual and class deviations is moot in light of our determination that the clause that DESC sought permission to use was authorized by the FAR"). United States ☞70(25.1)

§ 1.404 Class deviations.

Class deviations affect more than one contract action. When an agency knows that it will require a class deviation on a permanent basis, it should propose a FAR revision, if appropriate. Civilian agencies, other than NASA, must furnish a copy of each approved class deviation to the FAR Secretariat.

(a) For civilian agencies except NASA, class deviations may be authorized by agency heads or their designees, unless 1.405(e) is applicable. Delegation of this authority shall not be made below the head of a contracting activity. Authorization of class deviations by agency officials is subject to the following limitations:

(1) An agency official who may authorize a class deviation, before doing so, shall consult with the chairperson of the Civilian Agency Acquisition Council (CAA Council), unless that agency official determines that urgency precludes such consultation.

(2) Recommended revisions to the FAR shall be transmitted to the FAR Secretariat by agency heads or their designees for authorizing class deviations.

(b) For DoD, class deviations shall be controlled, processed, and approved in accordance with the Defense FAR Supplement.

(c) For NASA, class deviations shall be controlled and approved by the Assistant Administrator for Procurement. Deviations shall be processed in accordance with agency regulations.

United States Code Annotated

Administrative determinations, see 41 U.S.C.A. § 257.

Chief acquisition officers and senior procurement executives, see 41 U.S.C.A. § 414.

Definitions, see 10 U.S.C.A. § 2302, 41 U.S.C.A. §§ 259, 403.

Determinations and decisions, see 10 U.S.C.A. § 2310, 41 U.S.C.A. § 262.

Notes of Decisions

In general 1

1 In general

Although the FAR forbids agency acquisition regulations from conflicting with FAR content, it also permits each agency head or his designee to authorize both individual deviations and class deviations from the body of Government-wide regulations. FAR 1.304(b)(2). A "class deviation" affects more than one contracting action, and may be made on a permanent basis. FAR 1.404. Ace Services, Inc. v. General Services Admin., G.S.B.C.A. No. 11331, 92-2 B.C.A. (CCH) ¶ 24943, 1992 WL 59426 (Gen. Services Admin. B.C.A. 1992).

The FAR does not specifically address publication requirements for class deviations. However, the FAR does require that for "significant revisions" to FAR provisions, "[t]he opportunity to submit written comments on proposed significant revisions shall be provided by placing a notice in the Federal Register." FAR 1.501-2(b). A significant revision "alter[s] the substantive meaning of any coverage in the FAR System having a significant cost or administrative impact on contractors or having a significant effect beyond the internal operating procedures of the issuing agency." Class deviation from the FAR for economic price adjustment (EPA) clause employing price indexes in military jet fuel supply contracts was not valid, where contracting agency did not comply with publication requirements. Navajo Refining Co., L.P. v. U.S., 58 Fed. Cl. 200 (2003)

Class deviation from the Federal Acquisition Regulation which permitted use of economic price adjustment (EPA) clause in military fuel supply contracts was unauthorized, where contracting agency implemented the class deviation without fulfilling publication requirements provided in the Defense Logistics Accusation Regulation (DLAR) and the Office of Federal Procurement Policy Act (OFPPA). Office of Federal Procurement Policy Act, § 22, as amended, 41 U.S.C.A. § 418b. Tesoro Hawaii Corp. v. U.S., 58 Fed. Cl. 65 (2003), rev'd, 405 F.3d 1339, 15 A.L.R. Fed. 2d 755 (Fed. Cir. 2005) (the court said on reversal that "[t]he issue regarding the legality of the procedures used to obtain the individual and class deviations is moot in light of our determination that the clause that DESC sought permission to use was authorized by the FAR").

Suppliers of military fuel were precluded from challenging agency's class deviation from the Federal Acquisition Regulation (FAR) on ground that agency failed to prepare a regulatory flexibility analysis describing the impact of the proposed deviation on small businesses, in compliance with the Regulatory Flexibility Act (RFA), as suppliers were not small businesses and their grievance did not concern a final agency action. 5 U.S.C.A. §§ 603(a), 611(a)(1). Williams Alaska Petroleum, Inc. v. U.S., 57 Fed. Cl. 789 (2003). United States ☞64.25

Class deviation from the Federal Acquisition Regulation (FAR) for economic price adjustment clause based on price index was not authorized and was not valid for 1997, 1998, and 1999 contracts for the procurement of military jet and diesel fuel, where the government obtained the class deviation in contravention of the publication requirements established by section of the Defense Logistics Acquisition Regulation, and section of the Office of Federal Procurement Policy (OFPP) Act; government did not publish notice of the proposed class deviation and published notice of a proposed permanent revision did not provide notice of the class deviation. Office of Federal Procurement Policy Act, § 22, as amended, 41 U.S.C.A. § 418b; 48 C.F.R. § 1.404. La Gloria Oil and Gas Co. v. U.S., 56 Fed. Cl. 211 (2003) (abrogated by, Tesoro Hawaii Corp. v. U.S., 405 F.3d 1339, 15 A.L.R. Fed. 2d 755 (Fed. Cir. 2005)) (the court said on abrogation that "[t]he issue regarding the legality of the procedures used to obtain the individual and class deviations is moot in light of our determination that the clause that DESC sought permission to use was authorized by the FAR"). United States ☞70(18)

§ 1.405 Deviations pertaining to treaties and executive agreements.

(a) "Executive agreements," as used in this section, means Government-to-Government agreements, including agreements with international organizations, to which the United States is a party.

(b) Any deviation from the FAR required to comply with a treaty to which the United States is a party is authorized, unless the deviation would be inconsistent with FAR coverage based on a law enacted after the execution of the treaty.

(c) Any deviation from the FAR required to comply with an executive agreement is authorized unless the deviation would be inconsistent with FAR coverage based on law.

(d) For civilian agencies other than NASA, a copy of the text deviation authorized under paragraph (b) or (c) of this section shall be transmitted to the FAR Secretariat through a central agency control point.

(e) For civilian agencies other than NASA, if a deviation required to comply with a treaty or an executive agreement is not authorized by paragraph (b) or (c) of this section, then the request for deviation shall be processed through the FAR Secretariat to the Civilian Agency Acquisition Council.

United States Code Annotated

Administrative determinations, see 41 U.S.C.A. § 257.

Chief acquisition officers and senior procurement executives, see 41 U.S.C.A. § 414.

Definitions, see 10 U.S.C.A. § 2302, 41 U.S.C.A. §§ 259, 403.

Determinations and decisions, see 10 U.S.C.A. § 2310, 41 U.S.C.A. § 262.

Subpart 1.5 Agency and Public Participation

§ 1.501 Solicitation of agency and public views.

§ 1.501-1 Definition.

"Significant revisions," as used in this subpart, means revisions that alter the substantive meaning of any coverage in the FAR System and which have a significant cost or administrative impact on contractors or offerors, or significant effect beyond the internal operating procedures of the issuing agency. This expression, for example, does not include editorial, stylistic, or other revisions that have no impact on the basic meaning of the coverage being revised.

§ 1.501-2 Opportunity for public comments.

(a) Views of agencies and nongovernmental parties or organizations will be considered in formulating acquisition policies and procedures.

(b) The opportunity to submit written comments on proposed significant revisions shall be provided by placing a notice in the *Federal Register*. Each of these notices shall include—

(1) The text of the revision or, if it is impracticable to publish the full text, a summary of the proposal;

(2) The address and telephone number of the individual from whom copies of the revision, in full text, can be requested and to whom comments thereon should be addressed; and

(3) When 1.501-3(b) is applicable, a statement that the revision is effective on a temporary basis pending completion of the public comment period.

(c) A minimum of 30 days and, normally, at least 60 days will be given for the receipt of comments.

Notes of Decisions

In general 1

1 In general

Defense Federal Acquisition Regulation Supplement (DFARS) rule prohibiting contractors and subcontractors under contract with Defense Department from delivering munitions that were acquired from a Communist Chinese military company was properly promulgated in accordance with notice and comment requirements of Office of Federal Procurement Policy Act and Federal Acquisition Regulation, not Administrative Procedure Act (APA), and thus criminal enforcement of prohibition to contract under which contractor was alleged to have delivered prohibited ammunition to Army did not violate ex post facto clause for prohibition's failure to have been promulgated under APA. United States v. AEY, INC., Efraim Diveroli, David Packouz, Alexander Podrizki, and Ralph Merrill, 603 F.Supp.2d 1363 (S.D. Fla. 2009)

The FAR does not specifically address publication requirements for class deviations. However, the FAR does require that for "significant revisions" to FAR provisions, "[t]he opportunity to submit written comments on proposed significant revisions shall be provided by placing a notice in the Federal Register." FAR 1.501-2(b). A significant revision "alter[s] the substantive meaning of any coverage in the FAR System having a significant cost or administrative impact on contractors or having a significant effect beyond the internal operating procedures of the issuing agency." Class deviation from the FAR for economic price adjustment (EPA) clause employing price indexes in military jet fuel supply contracts was not valid, where contracting agency did not comply with publication requirements. Navajo Refining Co., L.P. v. U.S., 58 Fed. Cl. 200 (2003)

By its terms, 41 U.S.C. § 418b(b) requires publication of proposed regulations which will have a significant effect on the procurement system. The FAR implements this law and requires that proposed significant revisions to the FAR system are to be published in the Federal Register with a minimum of 30 days for receipt of comments. FAR 1.501-2. Any change which alters the substantive meaning of any rule in the FAR system or has a significant cost or administrative impact on contractors is considered significant. Grimes Oil Company, Inc., General Oil Company, Phoenix Petroleum Co., and Las Energy Corp., B-239334, 69 Comp. Gen. 676, 90-2 CPD ¶ 141 (Comp. Gen. 1990)

The purpose of the notice and comment requirement is both to allow the agency to benefit from the experience and input of the parties who file comments and to see to it that the agency maintains a flexible and open-minded attitude towards its own rule. The notice and comment procedure encourages public participation in the administrative process and educates the agency, thereby helping to ensure informed agency decision-making. Grimes Oil Company, Inc., General Oil Company, Phoenix Petroleum Co., and Las Energy Corp., B-239334, 69 Comp. Gen. 676, 90-2 CPD ¶ 141 (Comp. Gen. 1990)

§ 1.501-3 Exceptions.

(a) Comments need not be solicited when the proposed coverage does not constitute a significant revision.

(b) Advance comments need not be solicited when urgent and compelling circumstances make solicitation of comments impracticable prior to the effective date of the coverage, such as when a new statute must be implemented in a relatively short period of time. In such case, the coverage shall be issued on a temporary basis and shall provide for at least a 30 day public comment period.

§ 1.502 Unsolicited proposed revisions.

Consideration shall also be given to unsolicited recommendations for revisions that have been submitted in writing with sufficient data and rationale to permit their evaluation.

§ 1.503 Public meetings.

Public meetings may be appropriate when a decision to adopt, amend, or delete FAR coverage is likely to benefit from significant additional views and discussion.

Subpart 1.6 Career Development, Contracting Authority, and Responsibilities

§ 1.601 General.

(a) Unless specifically prohibited by another provision of law, authority and responsibility to contract for authorized supplies and services are vested in the agency head. The agency head may establish contracting activities and delegate broad authority to manage the agency's contracting functions to heads of such contracting activities. Contracts may be entered into and signed on behalf of the Government only by contracting officers. In some agencies, a relatively small number of high level officials are designated contracting officers solely by virtue of their positions. Contracting officers below the level of a head of a contracting activity shall be selected and appointed under 1.603.

(b) Agency heads may mutually agree to—

(1) Assign contracting functions and responsibilities from one agency to another; and

(2) Create joint or combined offices to exercise acquisition functions and responsibilities.

United States Code Annotated

Administrative determinations, see 41 U.S.C.A. § 257.

Chief acquisition officers and senior procurement executives, see 41 U.S.C.A. § 414.

Definitions, see 10 U.S.C.A. § 2302, 41 U.S.C.A. §§ 259, 403.

Determinations and decisions, see 10 U.S.C.A. § 2310, 41 U.S.C.A. § 262.

Notes of Decisions

In general 1
Contract 4
Federal preemption 2
Modification of contract 5
Third party claims 3

1 In general

Contracting officer is competent to testify in Board of Contract Appeals hearing or in trial in Court of Federal Claims, subject to compliance with Federal Rules of Evidence. Contract

Disputes Act of 1978, § 6(a, c), 41 U.S.C.A. § 605(a, c). Wilner v. U.S., 24 F.3d 1397, 39 Cont. Cas. Fed. (CCH) P 76665 (Fed. Cir. 1994). Federal Courts ☞1113; United States ☞73(15)

Court of Federal Claims did not rely on contracting officer's testimony at trial, for purposes of determining whether court conducted de novo review as required under Contract Disputes Act (CDA), where contracting officer's testimony did not independently establish cause or number of days of delay for which court awarded compensation to contractor. Contract Disputes Act of 1978, §§ 2–15, 41 U.S.C.A. §§ 601–613. Wilner v. U.S., 24 F.3d 1397, 39 Cont. Cas. Fed. (CCH) P 76665 (Fed. Cir. 1994). Federal Courts ☞1115

Court of Federal Claims could not rely on contracting officer's decision, in contractor's action for compensation for delay, in determining any issues; rather, contractor had burden to prove de novo extent of delay, proximate cause of delay, and harm from delay. Contract Disputes Act of 1978, §§ 6(a), 10(a)(3), 41 U.S.C.A. §§ 605(a), 609(a)(3). Wilner v. U.S., 24 F.3d 1397, 39 Cont. Cas. Fed. (CCH) P 76665 (Fed. Cir. 1994). Federal Courts ☞1115; Federal Courts ☞1118

Under Contract Disputes Act (CDA), contracting officer's decision is not entitled to any presumption of correctness. Contract Disputes Act of 1978, §§ 6(a), 10(a)(3), 41 U.S.C.A. §§ 605(a), 609(a)(3). Wilner v. U.S., 24 F.3d 1397, 39 Cont. Cas. Fed. (CCH) P 76665 (Fed. Cir. 1994). United States ☞73(15)

In action for review of contracting officer's decision, contracting officer's findings of fact are not binding upon the parties and are not entitled to any deference; rather, contractor has burden to prove fundamental facts of liability and damages de novo. Contract Disputes Act of 1978, §§ 6(a), 10(a)(3), 41 U.S.C.A. §§ 605(a), 609(a)(3). Wilner v. U.S., 24 F.3d 1397, 39 Cont. Cas. Fed. (CCH) P 76665 (Fed. Cir. 1994). United States ☞73(15)

Constructive waiver of provision of government contract occurs where contracting officer possessed knowledge of work outside scope of contract, action or inaction by contracting officer indicated acceptance of nonspecification performance, reliance ensued by contractor on action or inactions of contracting officer, and inequity would result from retraction of acceptance by contracting officer. Miller Elevator Co., Inc. v. U.S., 30 Fed. Cl. 662, 39 Cont. Cas. Fed. (CCH) P 76635 (1994), dismissed, 36 F.3d 1111 (Fed. Cir. 1994). United States ☞70(36)

2 Federal preemption

Virginia could not require that contractors working solely for background investigation contract services program (BICS) of Federal Bureau of Investigation (FBI) comply with Virginia's licensing and registration requirements concerning private security services, inasmuch as, by adding to qualifications necessary for BICS contractors to work for FBI, Virginia's regulatory scheme impermissibly frustrated objectives of federal procurement laws. Federal Property and Administrative Services Act of 1949, § 303B(d)(3), as amended, 41 U.S.C.A. § 253b(d)(3); Office of Federal Procurement Policy Act, § 16(1), as amended, 41 U.S.C.A. § 414(1); Va.Code 1950, §§ 9-182, subd. B, 9-183.9; 48 C.F.R. §§ 1.601, 9.103(b), 9.104-1(a, c, d, e, g). U.S. v. Com. of Va., 139 F.3d 984, 42 Cont. Cas. Fed. (CCH) P 77271 (4th Cir. 1998). Detectives ☞1; Detectives ☞3; States ☞18.15

3 Third party claims

Incorporation of remittance address to subcontractor's escrow account into contract between contractor and government did not make subcontractor third-party beneficiary to contract, since contracting officers did not know purpose of that address and thus officers, and therefore government, did not have intent to benefit subcontractor directly. Flexfab, L.L.C. v. U.S., 424 F.3d 1254 (Fed. Cir. 2005). United States ☞70(5)

When a government agent with authority to contract on the government's behalf knows of a condition precedent to a third party's performance as a subcontractor, such as receipt of payment directly from the government, and specifically modifies the prime contract so as to ensure the third party's continued performance, the agent, and by implication the government itself, necessarily intends to benefit the third party, and that intent gives rise to standing as a third-party beneficiary to enforce the prime contract. Flexfab, L.L.C. v. U.S., 424 F.3d 1254 (Fed. Cir. 2005). United States ☞70(5)

For third-party beneficiary status to lie with regard to a contract with the government, the contracting officer must be put on notice, by either the contract language or the attendant circumstances, of the relationship between the prime contractor and the third-party subcontractor so that an intent to benefit the third party is fairly attributable to the contracting officer. Flexfab, L.L.C. v. U.S., 424 F.3d 1254 (Fed. Cir. 2005). United States ☞70(5)

Though a third-party beneficiary of a contract to which the government is a direct party may assert a claim against the government in accordance with the rules applicable to thirdparty claims, the law governing third-party beneficiaries is subject to the principle that the government can only be bound by those with authorization to do so. Flexfab, L.L.C. v. U.S., 424 F.3d 1254 (Fed. Cir. 2005). United States ☞70(5)

4 Contract

Implied in fact contract did not exist between subcontractor and government, whereby subcontractor was to be paid directly by government for supplying air-duct hose to contractor, where subcontractor could not show that there was mutual intent to contract, and actual authority to contract, on part of contracting officers. Flexfab, L.L.C. v. U.S., 424 F.3d 1254 (Fed. Cir. 2005). United States ☞69(4)

5 Modification of contract

A contracting officer for the United States has the authority to modify contracts. Flexfab, L.L.C. v. U.S., 424 F.3d 1254 (Fed. Cir. 2005). United States ☞72(3)

§ 1.602 Contracting officers.

§ 1.602-1 Authority.

(a) Contracting officers have authority to enter into, administer, or terminate contracts and make related determinations and findings. Contracting officers may bind the Government only to the extent of the authority delegated to them. Contracting officers shall receive from the appointing authority (see 1.603-1) clear instructions in writing regarding the limits of their authority. Information on the limits of the contracting officers' authority shall be readily available to the public and agency personnel.

(b) No contract shall be entered into unless the contracting officer ensures that all requirements of law, executive orders, regulations, and all other applicable procedures, including clearances and approvals, have been met.

United States Code Annotated

Administrative determinations, see 41 U.S.C.A. § 257.

Chief acquisition officers and senior procurement executives, see 41 U.S.C.A. § 414.

Definitions, see 10 U.S.C.A. § 2302, 41 U.S.C.A. §§ 259, 403.

Determinations and decisions, see 10 U.S.C.A. § 2310, 41 U.S.C.A. § 262.

Notes of Decisions

In general 1
Apparent authority 9
Bids and proposals 2
Certification of claim 4
Delegation of authority 5
Estoppel 6
Implied Authority 7
Implied Ratification 10
Ratification 8
Termination of contract 3

1 In general

Virgin Islands Water and Power Authority (WAPA), rather than United States, had contract with security services provider for protection of equipment used in providing emergency water supply after hurricane, and thus, WAPA was liable for paying for those services; although federal officials played major role in negotiating and overseeing contract, there was no evidence that any official involved with procuring those services had authority to bind United States, or that contract was ratified by someone in federal government who had authority to do so, which showing was necessary even if contract were implied-in-fact by emergency situation. 48 C.F.R. §§ 1.601(a), 1.602-1(a), 2.101, 4401.603-2(a), 4401.603-3. Gardiner v. Virgin Islands Water & Power Authority, 145 F.3d 635, 40 Fed. R. Serv. 3d 1440 (3d Cir. 1998). Territories ☞25; United States ☞60

A party who seeks to contract with the government bears the burden of making sure that the person who purportedly represents the government actually has that authority. 48 C.F.R. §§ 1.601(a), 1.602-1(a), 2.101, 4401.000. Gardiner v. Virgin Islands Water & Power Authority, 145 F.3d 635, 40 Fed. R. Serv. 3d 1440 (3d Cir. 1998). United States ☞59

Only those with specific authority can bind the government contractually, and even those persons may do so only to the extent that their authority permits. 48 C.F.R. §§ 1.601(a), 1.602-1(a), 2.101, 4401.000. Gardiner v. Virgin Islands Water & Power Authority, 145 F.3d 635, 40 Fed. R. Serv. 3d 1440 (3d Cir. 1998). United States ☞59

Property maintenance contractor's detrimental reliance on provision of its contract with Department of Housing and Urban Development (HUD), permitting it to satisfy its advance payments indebtedness by purchasing equipment for contract performance, did not estop government from asserting that contracting officer's actions in agreeing to the provision were unauthorized because it directly conflicted with the requirements of the Federal Acquisition Regulations (FAR). Federal Property and Administrative Services Act of 1949, § 305(a), 41 U.S.C.A. § 255(a); 48 C.F.R. § 52.232-12. Johnson Management Group CFC, Inc. v. Martinez, 308 F.3d 1245 (Fed. Cir. 2002). Estoppel ☞62.6

Contracting officer is competent to testify in Board of Contract Appeals hearing or in trial in Court of Federal Claims, subject to compliance with Federal Rules of Evidence. Contract Disputes Act of 1978, § 6(a, c), 41 U.S.C.A. § 605(a, c). Wilner v. U.S., 24 F.3d 1397, 39 Cont. Cas. Fed. (CCH) P 76665 (Fed. Cir. 1994). Federal Courts ☞1113; United States ☞73(15)

The ASBCA dismissed a contractor's claims because the contracting officer's representative lacked authority to order the work and the unauthorized orders were not ratified. Government contracts require that the official purporting to modify a contract have actual authority to bind the Government, and a contractor bears the risk of ascertaining the agent's authority. Appeals of Sinil Co., Ltd., A.S.B.C.A. No. 55819, 09-2 B.C.A. (CCH) ¶ 34213, 2009 WL 2359862 (Armed Serv. B.C.A. 2009)

Any agreement to allow the Government to terminate the contract for convenience only in the event of a base closure would amount to a modification of the standard FAR convenience termination clauses. As there is no provision in the FAR authorizing the contracting officer to enter into that modification, it would constitute a deviation under FAR 1.401(c), requiring prior authorization by the agency head or his designee. Therefore, such a modification would be beyond the contracting officer's authority and, invalid. In re Empresa de Viacao Terceirense, A.S.B.C.A. No. 49827, 00-1 B.C.A. (CCH) ¶ 30796, 2000 WL 223808 (Armed Serv. B.C.A. 2000).

A contractor was not entitled to compensation for work on a pilot program under a side agreement with a Postal Service official who lacked sufficient contracting authority to bind the Government, the COFC has held. Although the official was a district manager and had limited authority to make small online purchases of supplies, she did not have express authority to contract for a pilot program. Moreover, because that authority was not necessary for performance of her duties, she did not have implied authority to contract for the pilot program. The Government did not ratify the unauthorized agreement, and the contractor could not recover under a quantum meruit theory. BioFunction, LLC v. U.S., 92 Fed. Cl. 167 (2010)

Member of United States Foreign Service did not have the authority to enter a purported lease contract to provide housing for employees of government contractors simply by virtue of his position as charge d'affaires of embassy. Foreign Service Buildings Act 1926, §§ 1, 10, as amended, 502(c), 22 U.S.C.A. §§ 291, 301, 3982(c); 48 C.F.R. § 1.601. Sam Gray Enterprises, Inc. v. U.S., 43 Fed. Cl. 596 (1999), decision aff'd, 250 F.3d 755 (Fed. Cir. 2000). United States ☞60

Contracting officer's technical representative (COTR) did not have implied actual authority to modify contract; contract itself specified that COTR lacked authority. Aero-Abre, Inc. v. U.S., 39 Fed. Cl. 654, 442 Cont. Cas. Fed. (CCH) P 77226 (1997). United States ☞72(3)

Even if government representative compels additional work, government escapes contractual liability absent adherence to terms of contract, such as written authorization of contracting officer. Miller Elevator Co., Inc. v. U.S., 30 Fed. Cl. 662, 39 Cont. Cas. Fed. (CCH) P 76635 (1994), dismissed, 36 F.3d 1111 (Fed. Cir. 1994). United States ☞70(25.1)

An agency's decision to exclude an offeror from a competition because the offeror obtained a copy of the Government's internal cost estimate requires a balancing of competing interests set forth in the FAR. On the one hand, contracting officers are granted wide latitude in their business judgments to safeguard the interests of the United States in its contractual relationships. FAR 1.602-2. On the other hand, the same section of the FAR requires contracting officers to ensure impartial, fair, and equitable treatment of all contractors. A contracting officer may protect the integrity of the competitive procurement system by disqualifying an offeror from a competition where the firm may have obtained an unfair competitive advantage, even if no actual impropriety can be shown, so long as the determination is based on facts and not mere innuendo or suspicion. Protest sustained because the Government could have shared the estimate with all the vendors to neutralize competitive advantage. IGIT, Inc., B-271823, 96-2 CPD ¶ 51 (Comp. Gen. 1996).

A handwritten note from a contract specialist, written on personal stationery, requesting that the bidder confirm its bid, acknowledge some corrections, acknowledge the amendments and stating, "we are awarding only price schedule A, B & C," was insufficient to form a contract. The note was signed by the contracting specialist. The handwritten note lacked any indicia of a binding agreement between the parties since it specifically requested information preparatory to any award and provided information about the award terms. In any event, the government is not bound beyond the actual authority conferred upon its agents. FAR 4.101 provides that only contracting officers shall sign contracts on behalf of the United States. The note was not executed by a contracting officer and thus could not bind the agency contractually. Environmental Safety Consultants, Inc., B-241714, 91-1 CPD ¶ 213 (Comp. Gen. 1991).

2 Bids and proposals

Contracting officer's decision to disqualify government contractor based on appearance of impropriety stemming from contractor's substantial downward revision of its bid after hiring former technical representative of contracting officer was not unreasonable or irrational. NKF Engineering, Inc. v. U.S., 805 F.2d 372, 33 Cont. Cas. Fed. (CCH) P 74691 (Fed. Cir. 1986). United States ☞64.20

Contracting officer has authority to disqualify bidder on government contract to protect integrity of procurement process from potential for unfair competitive advantage. NKF Engineering, Inc. v. U.S., 805 F.2d 372, 33 Cont. Cas. Fed. (CCH) P 74691 (Fed. Cir. 1986). United States ☞64.20

Contracting officer may disqualify bidder on government contract on belief that actual impropriety has occurred in regard to its bid, provided that officer bases his decision on hard facts and that his conclusion is rational. NKF Engineering, Inc. v. U.S., 805 F.2d 372, 33 Cont. Cas. Fed. (CCH) P 74691 (Fed. Cir. 1986). United States ☞64.20

Decision of contracting officer for government lease to allow late submission of proposal after deadline for initial proposals was contrary to Competition in Contracting Act of 1984 (CICA) requirement for provision of notice of due date for initial proposals in solicitation for offers (SFO) and Federal Acquisition Regulation (FAR) requiring that bidders submit initial offers by deadline for initial proposals as established in SFO, and thus Court of Federal Claims would enjoin award of instant contract to late bidder. Federal Property and Administrative Services Act of 1949, § 303A(b), (b)(2)(B)(ii), as amended, 41 U.S.C.A. § 253a(b), (b)(2)(B)(ii). Aerolease Long Beach v. U.S., 31 Fed. Cl. 342, 39 Cont. Cas. Fed. (CCH) P 76654, 39 Cont. Cas. Fed. (CCH) P 76655, 39 Cont. Cas. Fed. (CCH) P 76656 (1994), aff'd, 39 F.3d 1198 (Fed. Cir. 1994). Injunction ☞86; United States ☞64.40(1)

3 Termination of contract

Contracting officer may not terminate government contract for convenience in bad faith, for example, simply to acquire better bargain from another source. Krygoski Const. Co., Inc. v. U.S., 94 F.3d 1537, 41 Cont. Cas. Fed. (CCH) P 76985 (Fed. Cir. 1996). United States ☞72.1(2)

Government contractor failed to establish that contracting officer's motivations and actions in terminating contract for default constituted bad faith, based on performance disputes; contractor failed to identify the necessary specific instances of ill will on the part of the government. Green Management Corp. v. U.S., 42 Fed. Cl. 411 (1998). United States ⊕74(11)

It was within the discretion of the contracting officer to terminate for default a contract to provide management services for properties owned by the Department of Housing and Urban Development (HUD), where contractor specifically admitted to failing to comply with the contractual requirement that inspection reports be submitted within 10 days. 48 C.F.R. § 52.249-8. Green Management Corp. v. U.S., 42 Fed. Cl. 411 (1998). United States ⊕72.1(2)

4 Certification of claim

Federal Acquisition Regulation (FAR) on who may certify claim to contracting officer is not interpretative and, therefore, could not be waived by contracting officer. Contract Disputes Act of 1978, § 6(c)(1), as amended, 41 U.S.C.A. § 605(c)(1). Newport News Shipbuilding and Dry Dock Co. v. Garrett, 6 F.3d 1547, 39 Cont. Cas. Fed. (CCH) P 76577 (Fed. Cir. 1993)

5 Delegation of authority

Where a delegation of contracting authority possessed by agency head has not been made, high-ranking officials of agencies—even those that supervise contracting officials—do not themselves possess contracting authority. 48 C.F.R. § 1.601. Sam Gray Enterprises, Inc. v. U.S., 43 Fed. Cl. 596 (1999), decision aff'd, 250 F.3d 755 (Fed. Cir. 2000). United States ⊕60

Failure of Department of the Army to follow statutory procedures in awarding contract for computer driven battle simulation exercises did not mean that contracting officer lost her delegation of authority, and thus nullification of award was not warranted on ground of lack of contracting authority. 48 C.F.R. §§ 1.601, 1.602-1(a). Cubic Applications, Inc. v. U.S., 37 Fed. Cl. 345, 41 Cont. Cas. Fed. (CCH) P 77075 (1997). United States ⊕60

6 Estoppel

Government waived requirements of elevator maintenance contract that contractor obtain written authorization of contracting officer for additional work considered outside scope of contract and written invoicing for overtime callback services when government representatives repeatedly granted oral authorization for extra work under contract as well as prior maintenance contracts, estopping government from escaping liability for constructive changes to contract based on contractor's failure to obtain written authorization. Miller Elevator Co., Inc. v. U.S., 30 Fed. Cl. 662, 39 Cont. Cas. Fed. (CCH) P 76635 (1994), dismissed, 36 F.3d 1111 (Fed. Cir. 1994). United States ⊕70(36)

7 Implied Authority

A contractor was not entitled to compensation for work on a pilot program under a side agreement with a Postal Service official who lacked sufficient contracting authority to bind the Government, the COFC has held. Although the official was a district manager and had limited authority to make small online purchases of supplies, she did not have express authority to contract for a pilot program. Moreover, because that authority was not necessary for performance of her duties, she did not have implied authority to contract for the pilot program. The Government did not ratify the unauthorized agreement, and the contractor could not recover under a quantum meruit theory. BioFunction, LLC v. U.S., 92 Fed. Cl. 167 (2010)

Although apparent authority is insufficient to bind the Government, express actual authority and implied actual authority suffice. An official has implied authority to contract on behalf of the Government if contracting authority is an integral part of the duties assigned to the employee. Because contracting on behalf of the Government was appropriate and essential to the duties of Department of Defense officials, they had implied authority to contract on behalf of the Government, the Court of Federal Claims has held. Correspondence between the officials and plaintiffs showed that they had agreed that DOD would reimburse certain costs and, therefore, had a valid implied-in-fact contract entitling plaintiffs to reimbursement. Stevens Van Lines, Inc. v. U.S., 80 Fed. Cl. 276 (2008)

Government employee who performed functions of informally designated contracting officer by repeatedly approving additional repair and maintenance work in seeming conformity with explicit provision of contract which allowed only contracting officer to authorize such work had implied authority to accept work outside scope of elevator maintenance contract. Miller Elevator Co., Inc. v. U.S., 30 Fed. Cl. 662, 39 Cont. Cas. Fed. (CCH) P 76635 (1994), dismissed, 36 F.3d 1111 (Fed. Cir. 1994). United States ☞70(28)

8 Ratification

Even assuming that government employee did not have implied authority to authorize additional repairs and maintenance under elevator maintenance contract, government could be held liable for equitable adjustment by ratification; contracting officer had frequently approved repairs and other maintenance work outside scope of contract without requiring adherence to contract provision requiring contracting officer approval. Miller Elevator Co., Inc. v. U.S., 30 Fed. Cl. 662, 39 Cont. Cas. Fed. (CCH) P 76635 (1994), dismissed, 36 F.3d 1111 (Fed. Cir. 1994). United States ☞70(28)

9 Apparent authority

The United States Postal Service (ISPS) had no duty to verify the authority of an individual to agree to the termination of a contractor's USPS contract, because the contractor created the appearance of authority in the individual by allowing the individual to sign a contract as "vice president", even though the individual was not even an employee of the contractor. Near the time the contract was signed, the contractor told the USPS that the person worked with the contractor. It did not disclose any restriction on the person's authority until long after the contract was terminated, the COFC said. Distribution Postal Consultants, Inc. v. U.S., 90 Fed. Cl. 569 (2009)

10 Implied Ratification

Although air base engineer lacked contracting authority to direct road repair work, agency was liable for performance costs on the basis of implied ratification. The roads that were repaired were wholly within the base where the contracting officer was located. The court stated, "[i]t seems incredible that he did not know all about the agreement and by his inaction ratify it. Certainly he did not repudiate the agreement." Since the government received a benefit from the work and because the contracting was aware that the work was being performed, the agency was directed to pay for the value of the services rendered by the plaintiffs. Williams v. United States, 130 Ct. Cl. 435 (1955).

§ 1.602-2 Responsibilities.

Contracting officers are responsible for ensuring performance of all necessary actions for effective contracting, ensuring compliance with the terms of the contract, and safeguarding the interests of the United States in its contractual relationships. In order to perform these responsibilities, contracting officers should be allowed wide latitude to exercise business judgment. Contracting officers shall—

(a) Ensure that the requirements of 1.602-1(b) have been met, and that sufficient funds are available for obligation;

(b) Ensure that contractors receive impartial, fair, and equitable treatment;

(c) Request and consider the advice of specialists in audit, law, engineering, information security, transportation, and other fields, as appropriate; and

(d) Designate and authorize, in writing and in accordance with agency procedures, a contracting officer's representative (COR) on all contracts and orders other than those that are firm-fixed price, and for firm-fixed-price contracts and orders as appropriate, unless the contracting officer retains and executes the COR duties. See 7.104(e). COR—

(1) Shall be a Government employee, unless otherwise authorized in agency regulations;

(2) Shall be certified and maintain certification in accordance with the current Office of Management and Budget memorandum on the Federal Acquisition Certification for Contracting Officer Representatives (FAC-COR) guidance, or for DoD, in accordance with the current applicable DoD policy guidance;

(3) Shall be qualified by training and experience commensurate with the responsibilities to be delegated in accordance with agency procedures;

(4) May not be delegated responsibility to perform functions that have been delegated

under 42.202 to a contract administration office, but may be assigned some duties at 42.302 by the contracting officer;

(5) Has no authority to make any commitments or changes that affect price, quality, quantity, delivery, or other terms and conditions of the contract nor in any way direct the contractor or its subcontractors to operate in conflict with the contract terms and conditions;

(6) Shall be nominated either by the requiring activity or in accordance with agency procedures; and

(7) Shall be designated in writing, with copies furnished to the contractor and the contract administration office—

(i) Specifying the extent of the COR's authority to act on behalf of the contracting officer;

(ii) Identifying the limitations on the COR's authority;

(iii) Specifying the period covered by the designation;

(iv) Stating the authority is not redelegable; and

(v) Stating that the COR may be personally liable for unauthorized acts.

§ 1.602-3 Ratification of unauthorized commitments.

(a) *Definitions.*

"Ratification," as used in this subsection, means the act of approving an unauthorized commitment by an official who has the authority to do so.

"Unauthorized commitment," as used in this subsection, means an agreement that is not binding solely because the Government representative who made it lacked the authority to enter into that agreement on behalf of the Government.

(b) Policy.

(1) Agencies should take positive action to preclude, to the maximum extent possible, the need for ratification actions. Although procedures are provided in this section for use in those cases where the ratification of an unauthorized commitment is necessary, these procedures may not be used in a manner that encourages such commitments being made by Government personnel.

(2) Subject to the limitations in paragraph (c) of this subsection, the head of the contracting activity, unless a higher level official is designated by the agency, may ratify an unauthorized commitment.

(3) The ratification authority in paragraph (b)(2) of this subsection may be delegated in accordance with agency procedures, but in no case shall the authority be delegated below the level of chief of the contracting office.

(4) Agencies should process unauthorized commitments using the ratification authority of this subsection instead of referring such actions to the Government Accountability Office for resolution. (See 1.602-3(d).)

(5) Unauthorized commitments that would involve claims subject to resolution under 41 U.S.C. chapter 71, Contract Disputes, should be processed in accordance with Subpart 33.2, Disputes and Appeals.

(c) *Limitations.* The authority in paragraph (b)(2) of this subsection may be exercised only when—

(1) Supplies or services have been provided to and accepted by the Government, or the Government otherwise has obtained or will obtain a benefit resulting from performance of the unauthorized commitment;

(2) The ratifying official has the authority to enter into a contractual commitment;

(3) The resulting contract would otherwise have been proper if made by an appropriate contracting officer;

(4) The contracting officer reviewing the unauthorized commitment determines the price to be fair and reasonable;

(5) The contracting officer recommends payment and legal counsel concurs in the recommendation, unless agency procedures expressly do not require such concurrence;

(6) Funds are available and were available at the time the unauthorized commitment was made; and

(7) The ratification is in accordance with any other limitations prescribed under agency

procedures.

(d) *Nonratifiable commitments.* Cases that are not ratifiable under this subsection may be subject to resolution as recommended by the Government Accountability Office under its claim procedure (GAO Policy and Procedures Manual for Guidance of Federal Agencies, Title 4, Chapter 2), or as authorized by FAR Subpart 50.1. Legal advice should be obtained in these cases.

United States Code Annotated

Administrative determinations, see 41 U.S.C.A. § 257.

Chief acquisition officers and senior procurement executives, see 41 U.S.C.A. § 414.

Definitions, see 10 U.S.C.A. § 2302, 41 U.S.C.A. §§ 259, 403.

Determinations and decisions, see 10 U.S.C.A. § 2310, 41 U.S.C.A. § 262.

Notes of Decisions

In general 1
Performance or breach of contracts 4
Rights and remedies of contractors 5
Termination or rescission 3

1 In general

With respect to contracts for supplies and services, the federal government has given the authority to enter into and modify contracts to only a limited class of government employees: contracting officers. Where a government agent without contracting authority acts to bind the government, the government will be bound only if the action is subsequently ratified by those with authority if the ratifying officials have actual or constructive knowledge of the unauthorized acts. Winter v. Cath-dr/Balti Joint Venture, 497 F.3d 1339, 1344 (Fed.Cir.2007)

Institutional ratification may occur giving rise to a contract where a government agency accepts benefits followed by a promise of payment by the agency or approval of payment by a senior agency official with authority to obtain reimbursement for the one providing those benefits. Institutional ratification occurred where the government received benefits and senior agency officials were aware of the unauthorized agreement by a government representative and allowed performance to continue Janowsky v. U.S., 133 F.3d 888, 891 (Fed. Cir. 1998).

A government representative with contract authority, who has actual or constructive knowledge of the material facts with respect to an unauthorized contract action by a government representative, may ratify the action so as to bind the government provided the authorized representative expressly or by implication adopts the unauthorized contract action. Constructive knowledge may be imputed to the government representative with contracting authority, if the government representative knew or should have known of the unauthorized action. Appeals of Real Estate Technical Advisors, Inc., A.S.B.C.A. No. 53427, A.S.B.C.A. No. 53501, 03-1 B.C.A. (CCH) ¶ 32074, 2002 WL 31648261 (Armed Serv. B.C.A. 2002).

Even assuming that government employee did not have implied authority to authorize additional repairs and maintenance under elevator maintenance contract, government could be held liable for equitable adjustment by ratification; contracting officer had frequently approved repairs and other maintenance work outside scope of contract without requiring adherence to contract provision requiring contracting officer approval. Miller Elevator Co., Inc. v. U.S., 30 Fed. Cl. 662, 39 Cont. Cas. Fed. (CCH) P 76635 (1994), dismissed, 36 F.3d 1111 (Fed. Cir. 1994). United States ⚖70(28)

The Director of Procurement of the Architect of the Capital (AOC) executed a modification that served as a ratification of an unauthorized commitment, because an authorized agent, knowing of the facts surrounding the unauthorized act, may ratify the unauthorized transaction and because all of the conditions set forth in FAR 1.602-3 were met. AOC may use appropriated funds to pay the costs incurred under the directive letters, because Contract Modification 36 represents a valid ratification of the unauthorized commitments. Architect of the Capitol Contract Ratification, B-306353, 2005 WL 2810714 (Comp. Gen. 2005).

Contract improperly made in Fiscal Year 1981 and ratified by authorized official in Fiscal Year 1982 should be charged to Fiscal Year 1981 appropriation. Ratification relates back to the time of the initial agreement, which is when the services were needed and the work was performed. Fish and Wildlife Service-Fiscal Year Chargeable on Ratification of Contract, B-208730, 83-1 CPD ¶ 75 (Comp. Gen. 1983).

3 Termination or rescission

It was within the discretion of the contracting officer to terminate for default a contract to provide management services for properties owned by the Department of Housing and Urban Development (HUD), where contractor specifically admitted to failing to comply with the contractual requirement that inspection reports be submitted within 10 days. 48 C.F.R. § 52.249-8. Green Management Corp. v. U.S., 42 Fed. Cl. 411 (1998). United States ☞72.1(2)

4 Performance or breach of contracts

Reply letters from Immigration and Naturalization Service denying city's claims for payment for emergency medical services rendered to illegal aliens constituted final decisions of contracting officer for purposes of Contract Disputes Act, as required for Claims Court to exercise jurisdiction over claims. Contract Disputes Act of 1978, § 6, 41 U.S.C.A. § 605. City of El Centro v. U.S., 922 F.2d 816, 37 Cont. Cas. Fed. (CCH) P 76044 (Fed. Cir. 1990). United States ☞73(9)

City submitted claims for payment for emergency medical services rendered to illegal aliens "to the contracting officer," as required by Contract Disputes Act, by submitting claims to official Immigration and Naturalization Service identified as "the one to determine payment." Contract Disputes Act of 1978, § 6(a), 41 U.S.C.A. § 605(a). City of El Centro v. U.S., 922 F.2d 816, 37 Cont. Cas. Fed. (CCH) P 76044 (Fed. Cir. 1990). United States ☞73(9)

5 Rights and remedies of contractors

Government contractor failed to establish that contracting officer's motivations and actions in terminating contract for default constituted bad faith, based on performance disputes; contractor failed to identify the necessary specific instances of ill will on the part of the government. Green Management Corp. v. U.S., 42 Fed. Cl. 411 (1998). United States ☞74(11)

§ 1.603 Selection, appointment, and termination of appointment for contracting officers.

§ 1.603-1 General.

41 U.S.C. 1702(b)(3)(F) requires agency heads to establish and maintain a procurement career management program and a system for the selection, appointment, and termination of appointment of contracting officers. Agency heads or their designees may select and appoint contracting officers and terminate their appointments. These selections and appointments shall be consistent with Office of Federal Procurement Policy's (OFPP) standards for skill-based training in performing contracting and purchasing duties as published in OFPP Policy Letter No. 05-01, Developing and Managing the Acquisition Workforce, April 15, 2005.

United States Code Annotated

Chief acquisition officers and senior procurement executives, see 41 U.S.C.A. § 414.

Definitions, see 41 U.S.C.A. § 403.

§ 1.603-2 Selection.

In selecting contracting officers, the appointing official shall consider the complexity and dollar value of the acquisitions to be assigned and the candidate's experience, training, education, business acumen, judgment, character, and reputation. Examples of selection criteria include—

(a) Experience in Government contracting and administration, commercial purchasing, or related fields;

(b) Education or special training in business administration, law, accounting, engineering, or related fields;

(c) Knowledge of acquisition policies and procedures, including this and other applicable regulations;

(d) Specialized knowledge in the particular assigned field of contracting; and

(e) Satisfactory completion of acquisition training courses.

United States Code Annotated

Chief acquisition officers and senior procurement executives, see 41 U.S.C.A. § 414.

Definitions, see 41 U.S.C.A. § 403.

§ 1.603-3 Appointment.

(a) Contracting officers shall be appointed in writing on an SF 1402, Certificate of Appointment, which shall state any limitations on the scope of authority to be exercised, other than limitations contained in applicable law or regulation. Appointing officials shall maintain files containing copies of all appointments that have not been terminated.

(b) Agency heads are encouraged to delegate micro-purchase authority to individuals who are employees of an executive agency or members of the Armed Forces of the United States who will be using the supplies or services being purchased. Individuals delegated this authority are not required to be appointed on an SF 1402, but shall be appointed in writing in accordance with agency procedures.

United States Code Annotated

Chief acquisition officers and senior procurement executives, see 41 U.S.C.A. § 414.

Definitions, see 41 U.S.C.A. § 403.

§ 1.603-4 Termination.

Termination of a contracting officer appointment will be by letter, unless the Certificate of Appointment contains other provisions for automatic termination. Terminations may be for reasons such as reassignment, termination of employment, or unsatisfactory performance. No termination shall operate retroactively.

United States Code Annotated

Chief acquisition officers and senior procurement executives, see 41 U.S.C.A. § 414.

Definitions, see 41 U.S.C.A. § 403.

§ 1.604 Contracting Officer's Representative (COR).

A contracting officer's representative (COR) assists in the technical monitoring or administration of a contract (see 1.602-2(d)). The COR shall maintain a file for each assigned contract. The file must include, at a minimum—

(a) A copy of the contracting officer's letter of designation and other documents describing the COR's duties and responsibilities;

(b) A copy of the contract administration functions delegated to a contract administration office which may not be delegated to the COR (see 1.602-2(d)(4)); and

(c) Documentation of COR actions taken in accordance with the delegation of authority.

Subpart 1.7 Determinations and Findings

§ 1.700 Scope of subpart.

This subpart prescribes general policies and procedures for the use of determinations and findings (D&F's). Requirements for specific types of D&F's can be found with the appropriate subject matter.

United States Code Annotated

Administrative determinations, see 41 U.S.C.A. § 257.

Chief acquisition officers and senior procurement executives, see 41 U.S.C.A. § 414.

Definitions, see 10 U.S.C.A. § 2302, 41 U.S.C.A. §§ 259, 403.
Determinations and decisions, see 10 U.S.C.A. § 2310, 41 U.S.C.A. § 262.

§ 1.701 Definition.

"Determination and Findings" means a special form of written approval by an authorized official that is required by statute or regulation as a prerequisite to taking certain contract actions. The "determination" is a conclusion or decision supported by the "findings." The findings are statements of fact or rationale essential to support the determination and must cover each requirement of the statute or regulation.

United States Code Annotated

Administrative determinations, see 41 U.S.C.A. § 257.

Chief acquisition officers and senior procurement executives, see 41 U.S.C.A. § 414.

Definitions, see 10 U.S.C.A. § 2302, 41 U.S.C.A. §§ 259, 403.

Determinations and decisions, see 10 U.S.C.A. § 2310, 41 U.S.C.A. § 262.

§ 1.702 General.

(a) A D&F shall ordinarily be for an individual contract action. Unless otherwise prohibited, class D&F's may be executed for classes of contract actions (see 1.703). The approval granted by a D&F is restricted to the proposed contract action(s) reasonably described in that D&F. D&F's may provide for a reasonable degree of flexibility. Furthermore, in their application, reasonable variations in estimated quantities or prices are permitted, unless the D&F specifies otherwise.

(b) When an option is anticipated, the D&F shall state the approximate quantity to be awarded initially and the extent of the increase to be permitted by the option.

United States Code Annotated

Administrative determinations, see 41 U.S.C.A. § 257.

Chief acquisition officers and senior procurement executives, see 41 U.S.C.A. § 414.

Definitions, see 10 U.S.C.A. § 2302, 41 U.S.C.A. §§ 259, 403.

Determinations and decisions, see 10 U.S.C.A. § 2310, 41 U.S.C.A. § 262.

§ 1.703 Class determinations and findings.

(a) A class D&F provides authority for a class of contract actions. A class may consist of contract actions for the same or related supplies or services or other contract actions that require essentially identical justification.

(b) The findings in a class D&F shall fully support the proposed action either for the class as a whole or for each action. A class D&F shall be for a specified period, with the expiration date stated in the document.

(c) The contracting officer shall ensure that individual actions taken pursuant to the authority of a class D&F are within the scope of the D&F.

United States Code Annotated

Administrative determinations, see 41 U.S.C.A. § 257.

Chief acquisition officers and senior procurement executives, see 41 U.S.C.A. § 414.

Definitions, see 10 U.S.C.A. § 2302, 41 U.S.C.A. §§ 259, 403.

Determinations and decisions, see 10 U.S.C.A. § 2310, 41 U.S.C.A. § 262.

§ 1.704 Content.

Each D&F shall set forth enough facts and circumstances to clearly and convincingly justify the specific determination made. As a minimum, each D&F shall include, in the prescribed agency format, the following information:

(a) Identification of the agency and of the contracting activity and specific identification of the document as a "Determination and Findings."

(b) Nature and/or description of the action being approved.

(c) Citation of the appropriate statute and/or regulation upon which the D&F is based.

(d) Findings that detail the particular circumstances, facts, or reasoning essential to support the determination. Necessary supporting documentation shall be obtained from appropriate requirements and technical personnel.

(e) A determination, based on the findings, that the proposed action is justified under the applicable statute or regulation.

(f) Expiration date of the D&F, if required (see 1.706).

(g) The signature of the official authorized to sign the D&F (see 1.707) and the date signed.

United States Code Annotated

Administrative determinations, see 41 U.S.C.A. § 257.

Chief acquisition officers and senior procurement executives, see 41 U.S.C.A. § 414.

Definitions, see 10 U.S.C.A. § 2302, 41 U.S.C.A. §§ 259, 403.

Determinations and decisions, see 10 U.S.C.A. § 2310, 41 U.S.C.A. § 262.

§ 1.705 Supersession and modification.

(a) If a D&F is superseded by another D&F, that action shall not render invalid any action taken under the original D&F prior to the date of its supersession.

(b) The contracting officer need not cancel the solicitation if the D&F, as modified, supports the contract action.

United States Code Annotated

Administrative determinations, see 41 U.S.C.A. § 257.

Chief acquisition officers and senior procurement executives, see 41 U.S.C.A. § 414.

Definitions, see 10 U.S.C.A. § 2302, 41 U.S.C.A. §§ 259, 403.

Determinations and decisions, see 10 U.S.C.A. § 2310, 41 U.S.C.A. § 262.

§ 1.706 Expiration.

Expiration dates are required for class D&F's and are optional for individual D&F's. Authority to act under an individual D&F expires when it is exercised or on an expiration date specified in the document, whichever occurs first. Authority to act under a class D&F expires on the expiration date specified in the document. When a solicitation has been furnished to prospective offerors before the expiration date, the authority under the D&F will continue until award of the contract(s) resulting from the solicitation.

United States Code Annotated

Administrative determinations, see 41 U.S.C.A. § 257.

Chief acquisition officers and senior procurement executives, see 41 U.S.C.A. § 414.

Definitions, see 10 U.S.C.A. § 2302, 41 U.S.C.A. §§ 259, 403.

Determinations and decisions, see 10 U.S.C.A. § 2310, 41 U.S.C.A. § 262.

§ 1.707 Signatory authority.

When a D&F is required, it shall be signed by the appropriate official in accordance with agency regulations. Authority to sign or delegate signature authority for the various D&F's is as shown in the applicable FAR part.

United States Code Annotated

Administrative determinations, see 41 U.S.C.A. § 257.

Chief acquisition officers and senior procurement executives, see 41 U.S.C.A. § 414.

Definitions, see 10 U.S.C.A. § 2302, 41 U.S.C.A. §§ 259, 403.

Determinations and decisions, see 10 U.S.C.A. § 2310.

PART 2 DEFINITIONS OF WORDS AND TERMS

§ 2.000 Scope of part.

Subpart 2.1 Definitions

§ 2.101 Definitions.

Subpart 2.2 Definitions Clause

§ 2.201 Contract clause.

§ 2.000 Scope of part.

(a) This part—

(1) Defines words and terms that are frequently used in the FAR;

(2) Provides cross-references to other definitions in the FAR of the same word or term; and

(3) Provides for the incorporation of these definitions in solicitations and contracts by reference.

(b) Other parts, subparts, and sections of this regulation (48 CFR Chapter 1) may define other words or terms and those definitions only apply to the part, subpart, or section where the word or term is defined.

United States Code Annotated

Definitions, see 10 USCA § 2302, 41 USCA §§ 259, 403.

Subpart 2.1 Definitions

§ 2.101 Definitions.

(a) A word or a term, defined in this section, has the same meaning throughout this regulation (48 CFR Chapter 1), unless—

(1) The context in which the word or term is used clearly requires a different meaning; or

(2) Another FAR part, subpart, or section provides a different definition for the particular part or portion of the part.

(b) If a word or term that is defined in this section is defined differently in another part, subpart, or section of this regulation (48 CFR Chapter 1), the definition in—

(1) This section includes a cross-reference to the other definitions; and

(2) That part, subpart, or section applies to the word or term when used in that part, subpart, or section.

"Acquisition" means the acquiring by contract with appropriated funds of supplies or services (including construction) by and for the use of the Federal Government through purchase or lease, whether the supplies or services are already in existence or must be created, developed, demonstrated, and evaluated. Acquisition begins at the point when agency needs are established and includes the description of requirements to satisfy agency needs, solicitation and selection of sources, award of contracts, contract financing, contract performance, contract administration, and those technical and management functions directly related to the process of fulfilling agency needs by contract.

"Acquisition planning" means the process by which the efforts of all personnel responsible for an acquisition are coordinated and integrated through a comprehensive plan for fulfilling the agency need in a timely manner and at a reasonable cost. It includes developing the overall strategy for managing the acquisition.

"Activity Address Code (AAC)" means a distinct six-position code consisting of a combination of alpha and/or numeric characters assigned to identify specific agency offices, units, activities, or organizations by the General Services Administration for civilian agencies and by the Department of Defense for defense agencies.

"Adequate evidence" means information sufficient to support the reasonable belief that a particular act or omission has occurred.

"Advisory and assistance services" means those services provided under contract by non-governmental sources to support or improve: organizational policy development; decision-making; management and administration; program and/or project management and administration; or R&D activities. It can also mean the furnishing of professional advice or assistance rendered to improve the effectiveness of Federal management processes or procedures (including those of an engineering and technical nature). In rendering the foregoing services, outputs may take the form of information, advice, opinions, alternatives, analyses, evaluations, recommendations, training and the day-to-day aid of support personnel needed for the successful performance of ongoing Federal operations. All advisory and assistance services are classified in one of the following definitional subdivisions:

(1) Management and professional support services, i.e., contractual services that provide assistance, advice or training for the efficient and effective management and operation of organizations, activities (including management and support services for R&D activities), or systems. These services are normally closely related to the basic responsibilities and mission of the agency originating the requirement for the acquisition of services by contract. Included are efforts that support or contribute to improved organization of program management, logistics management, project monitoring and reporting, data collection, budgeting, accounting, performance auditing, and administrative technical support for conferences and training programs.

(2) Studies, analyses and evaluations, i.e., contracted services that provide organized, analytical assessments/evaluations in support of policy development, decision-making, management, or administration. Included are studies in support of R&D activities. Also included are acquisitions of models, methodologies, and related software supporting studies, analyses or evaluations.

(3) Engineering and technical services, i.e., contractual services used to support the program office during the acquisition cycle by providing such services as systems engineering and technical direction (see 9.505-1(b)) to ensure the effective operation and maintenance of a weapon system or major system as defined in OMB Circular No. A-109 or to provide direct support of a weapon system that is essential to research, development, production, operation or maintenance of the system.

"Affiliates" means associated business concerns or individuals if, directly or indirectly—

(1) Either one controls or can control the other; or

(2) A third party controls or can control both.

"Agency head" or "head of the agency" means the Secretary, Attorney General, Administrator, Governor, Chairperson, or other chief official of an executive agency, unless otherwise indicated, including any deputy or assistant chief official of an executive agency.

"Alternate" means a substantive variation of a basic provision or clause prescribed for use in a defined circumstance. It adds wording to, deletes wording from, or substitutes specified wording for a portion of the basic provision or clause. The alternate version of a provision or clause is the basic provision or clause as changed by the addition, deletion, or substitution (see 52.105(a)).

"Architect-engineer services," as defined in 40 U.S.C. 1102, means—

(1) Professional services of an architectural or engineering nature, as defined by State law, if applicable, that are required to be performed or approved by a person licensed, registered, or certified to provide those services;

(2) Professional services of an architectural or engineering nature performed by contract that are associated with research, planning, development, design, construction, alteration, or repair of real property; and

(3) Those other professional services of an architectural or engineering nature, or incidental services, that members of the architectural and engineering professions (and individuals in their employ) may logically or justifiably perform, including studies, investigations, surveying and mapping, tests, evaluations, consultations, comprehensive planning, program management, conceptual designs, plans and specifications, value engineering, construction phase services, soils engineering, drawing reviews, preparation of operating and maintenance manuals, and other related services.

"Assignment of claims" means the transfer or making over by the contractor to a bank, trust company, or other financing institution, as security for a loan to the contractor, of its right to be paid by the Government for contract performance.

"Assisted acquisition" means a type of interagency acquisition where a servicing agency performs acquisition activities on a requesting agency's behalf, such as awarding and administering a contract, task order, or delivery order.

"Basic research" means that research directed toward increasing knowledge in science. The primary aim of basic research is a fuller knowledge or understanding of the subject under study, rather than any practical application of that knowledge.

"Best value" means the expected outcome of an acquisition that, in the Government's estimation, provides the greatest overall benefit in response to the requirement.

"Bid sample" means a product sample required to be submitted by an offeror to show characteristics of the offered products that cannot adequately be described by specifications, purchase descriptions, or the solicitation (e.g., balance, facility of use, or pattern).

"Biobased product" means a product determined by the U.S. Department of Agriculture to be a commercial or industrial product (other than food or feed) that is composed, in whole or in significant part, of biological products, including renewable domestic agricultural materials and forestry materials.

"Broad agency announcement" means a general announcement of an agency's research interest including criteria for selecting proposals and soliciting the participation of all offerors capable of satisfying the Government's needs (see 6.102(d)(2)).

"Building or work" means construction activity as distinguished from manufacturing, furnishing of materials, or servicing and maintenance work. The terms include, without limitation, buildings, structures, and improvements of all types, such as bridges, dams, plants, highways, parkways, streets, subways, tunnels, sewers, mains, power lines, pumping stations, heavy generators, railways, airports, terminals, docks, piers, wharves, ways, lighthouses, buoys, jetties, breakwaters, levees, canals, dredging, shoring, rehabilitation and reactivation of plants, scaffolding, drilling, blasting, excavating, clearing, and landscaping. The manufacture or furnishing of materials, articles, supplies, or equipment (whether or not a Federal or State agency acquires title to such materials, articles, supplies, or equipment during the course of the manufacture or furnishing, or owns the materials from which they are manufactured or furnished) is not "building" or "work" within the meaning of this definition unless conducted in connection with and at the site of such building or work as is described in the foregoing sentence, or under the United States Housing Act of 1937 and the Housing Act of 1949 in the construction or development of the project.

"Bundled contract" means a contract where the requirements have been consolidated by bundling. (See the definition of bundling.)

"Bundling" means—

(1) Consolidating two or more requirements for supplies or services, previously provided or performed under separate smaller contracts, into a solicitation for a single contract that is likely to be unsuitable for award to a small business concern due to—

(i) The diversity, size, or specialized nature of the elements of the performance specified;

(ii) The aggregate dollar value of the anticipated award;

(iii) The geographical dispersion of the contract performance sites; or

(iv) Any combination of the factors described in paragraphs (1)(i), (ii), and (iii) of this definition.

(2) "Separate smaller contract" as used in this definition, means a contract that has been performed by one or more small business concerns or that was suitable for award to one or more small business concerns.

(3) "Single contract" as used in this definition, includes—

(i) Multiple awards of indefinite-quantity contracts under a single solicitation for the same or similar supplies or services to two or more sources (see FAR 16.504(c)); and

(ii) An order placed against an indefinite quantity contract under a—

(A) Federal Supply Schedule contract; or

(B) Task-order contract or delivery-order contract awarded by another agency (i.e., Governmentwide acquisition contract or multi-agency contract).

(4) This definition does not apply to a contract that will be awarded and performed

entirely outside of the United States.

"Business unit" means any segment of an organization, or an entire business organization that is not divided into segments.

"Certified cost or pricing data" means "cost or pricing data" that were required to be submitted in accordance with FAR 15.403-4 and 15.403-5 and have been certified, or is required to be certified, in accordance with 15.406-2. This certification states that, to the best of the person's knowledge and belief, the cost or pricing data are accurate, complete, and current as of a date certain before contract award. Cost or pricing data are required to be certified in certain procurements (10 U.S.C. 2306a and 41 U.S.C. chapter 35).

"Change-of-name agreement" means a legal instrument executed by the contractor and the Government that recognizes the legal change of name of the contractor without disturbing the original contractual rights and obligations of the parties.

"Change order" means a written order, signed by the contracting officer, directing the contractor to make a change that the Changes clause authorizes the contracting officer to order without the contractor's consent.

"Chief Acquisition Officer" means an executive level acquisition official responsible for agency performance of acquisition activities and acquisition programs created pursuant to 41 U.S.C. 1702.

"Chief of mission" means the principal officer in charge of a diplomatic mission of the United States or of a United States office abroad which is designated by the Secretary of State as diplomatic in nature, including any individual assigned under section 502(c) of the Foreign Service Act of 1980 (Public Law 96-465) to be temporarily in charge of such a mission or office.

"Claim" means a written demand or written assertion by one of the contracting parties seeking, as a matter of right, the payment of money in a sum certain, the adjustment or interpretation of contract terms, or other relief arising under or relating to the contract. However, a written demand or written assertion by the contractor seeking the payment of money exceeding $100,000 is not a claim under 41 U.S.C. chapter 71, Contract Disputes, until certified as required by the statute. A voucher, invoice, or other routine request for payment that is not in dispute when submitted is not a claim. The submission may be converted to a claim, by written notice to the contracting officer as provided in 33.206(a), if it is disputed either as to liability or amount or is not acted upon in a reasonable time.

"Classified acquisition" means an acquisition in which offerors must have access to classified information to properly submit an offer or quotation, to understand the performance requirements, or to perform the contract.

"Classified contract" means any contract in which the contractor or its employees must have access to classified information during contract performance. A contract may be a classified contract even though the contract document itself is unclassified.

"Classified information" means any knowledge that can be communicated or any documentary material, regardless of its physical form or characteristics, that—

(1) (i) Is owned by, is produced by or for, or is under the control of the United States Government; or

(ii) Has been classified by the Department of Energy as privately generated restricted data following the procedures in 10 CFR 1045.21; and

(2) Must be protected against unauthorized disclosure according to Executive Order 12958, Classified National Security Information, April 17, 1995, or classified in accordance with the Atomic Energy Act of 1954.

"Cognizant Federal agency" means the Federal agency that, on behalf of all Federal agencies, is responsible for establishing final indirect cost rates and forward pricing rates, if applicable, and administering cost accounting standards for all contracts in a business unit.

"Combatant commander" means the commander of a unified or specified combatant command established in accordance with 10 U.S.C. 161.

"Commercial component" means any component that is a commercial item.

"Commercial computer software" means any computer software that is a commercial item.

"Commercial item" means—

(1) Any item, other than real property, that is of a type customarily used by the general

public or by non-governmental entities for purposes other than governmental purposes, and—

    (i) Has been sold, leased, or licensed to the general public; or

    (ii) Has been offered for sale, lease, or license to the general public;

  (2) Any item that evolved from an item described in paragraph (1) of this definition through advances in technology or performance and that is not yet available in the commercial marketplace, but will be available in the commercial marketplace in time to satisfy the delivery requirements under a Government solicitation;

  (3) Any item that would satisfy a criterion expressed in paragraphs (1) or (2) of this definition, but for—

    (i) Modifications of a type customarily available in the commercial marketplace; or

    (ii) Minor modifications of a type not customarily available in the commercial marketplace made to meet Federal Government requirements. Minor modifications means modifications that do not significantly alter the nongovernmental function or essential physical characteristics of an item or component, or change the purpose of a process. Factors to be considered in determining whether a modification is minor include the value and size of the modification and the comparative value and size of the final product. Dollar values and percentages may be used as guideposts, but are not conclusive evidence that a modification is minor;

  (4) Any combination of items meeting the requirements of paragraphs (1), (2), (3), or (5) of this definition that are of a type customarily combined and sold in combination to the general public;

  (5) Installation services, maintenance services, repair services, training services, and other services if—

    (i) Such services are procured for support of an item referred to in paragraph (1), (2), (3), or (4) of this definition, regardless of whether such services are provided by the same source or at the same time as the item; and

    (ii) The source of such services provides similar services contemporaneously to the general public under terms and conditions similar to those offered to the Federal Government;

  (6) Services of a type offered and sold competitively in substantial quantities in the commercial marketplace based on established catalog or market prices for specific tasks performed or specific outcomes to be achieved and under standard commercial terms and conditions. For purposes of these services—

    (i) "Catalog price" means a price included in a catalog, price list, schedule, or other form that is regularly maintained by the manufacturer or vendor, is either published or otherwise available for inspection by customers, and states prices at which sales are currently, or were last, made to a significant number of buyers constituting the general public; and

    (ii) "Market prices" means current prices that are established in the course of ordinary trade between buyers and sellers free to bargain and that can be substantiated through competition or from sources independent of the offerors.

  (7) Any item, combination of items, or service referred to in paragraphs (1) through (6) of this definition, notwithstanding the fact that the item, combination of items, or service is transferred between or among separate divisions, subsidiaries, or affiliates of a contractor; or

  (8) A nondevelopmental item, if the procuring agency determines the item was developed exclusively at private expense and sold in substantial quantities, on a competitive basis, to multiple State and local governments.

"Commercially available off-the-shelf (COTS) item—"

  (1) Means any item of supply (including construction material) that is—

    (i) A commercial item (as defined in paragraph (1) of the definition in this section);

    (ii) Sold in substantial quantities in the commercial marketplace; and

    (iii) Offered to the Government, under a contract or subcontract at any tier, without modification, in the same form in which it is sold in the commercial marketplace; and

  (2) Does not include bulk cargo, as defined in 46 U.S.C. 40102(4), such as agricultural products and petroleum products.

"Common item" means material that is common to the applicable Government contract and the contractor's other work.

"Component" means any item supplied to the Government as part of an end item or of another component, except that for use in—

    (1) part 25, see the definition in 25.003;

    (2) 52.225-1 and 52.225-3, see the definition in 52.225-1(a) and 52.225-3(a);

    (3) 52.225-9 and 52.225-11, see the definition in 52.225-9(a) and 52.225-11(a); and

    (4) 52.225-21 and 52.225-23, see the definition in 52.225-21(a) and 52.225-23(a).

"Computer database" or "database" means a collection of recorded information in a form capable of, and for the purpose of, being stored in, processed, and operated on by a computer. The term does not include computer software.

"Computer software" —

    (1) Means

        (i) Computer programs that comprise a series of instructions, rules, routines, or statements, regardless of the media in which recorded, that allow or cause a computer to perform a specific operation or series of operations; and

        (ii) Recorded information comprising source code listings, design details, algorithms, processes, flow charts, formulas, and related material that would enable the computer program to be produced, created, or compiled.

    (2) Does not include computer databases or computer software documentation.

"Computer software documentation" means owner's manuals, user's manuals, installation instructions, operating instructions, and other similar items, regardless of storage medium, that explain the capabilities of the computer software or provide instructions for using the software.

"Consent to subcontract" means the contracting officer's written consent for the prime contractor to enter into a particular subcontract.

"Construction" means construction, alteration, or repair (including dredging, excavating, and painting) of buildings, structures, or other real property. For purposes of this definition, the terms "buildings, structures, or other real property" include, but are not limited to, improvements of all types, such as bridges, dams, plants, highways, parkways, streets, subways, tunnels, sewers, mains, power lines, cemeteries, pumping stations, railways, airport facilities, terminals, docks, piers, wharves, ways, lighthouses, buoys, jetties, breakwaters, levees, canals, and channels. Construction does not include the manufacture, production, furnishing, construction, alteration, repair, processing, or assembling of vessels, aircraft, or other kinds of personal property (except that for use in subpart 22.5, see the definition at 22.502).

"Contiguous United States (CONUS)" means the 48 contiguous States and the District of Columbia.

"Contingency operation" (10 U.S.C. 101(a)(13)) means a military operation that—

    (1) Is designated by the Secretary of Defense as an operation in which members of the armed forces are or may become involved in military actions, operations, or hostilities against an enemy of the United States or against an opposing military force; or

    (2) Results in the call or order to, or retention on, active duty of members of the uniformed services under sections 688, 12301(a), 12302, 12304, 12304(a), 12305, or 12406 of title 10 of the United States Code, Chapter 15 of title 10 of the United States Code, or any other provision of law during a war or during a national emergency declared by the President or Congress.

"Continued portion of the contract" means the portion of a contract that the contractor must continue to perform following a partial termination.

"Contract" means a mutually binding legal relationship obligating the seller to furnish the supplies or services (including construction) and the buyer to pay for them. It includes all types of commitments that obligate the Government to an expenditure of appropriated funds and that, except as otherwise authorized, are in writing. In addition to bilateral instruments, contracts include (but are not limited to) awards and notices of awards; job orders or task letters issued under basic ordering agreements; letter contracts; orders, such as purchase orders, under which the contract becomes effective by written acceptance or performance; and bilateral contract modifications. Contracts do not include grants and cooperative agreements covered by 31 U.S.C. 6301, et seq. For discussion of various types of contracts, see part 16.

"Contract administration office" means an office that performs—

(1) Assigned postaward functions related to the administration of contracts; and

(2) Assigned preaward functions.

"Contract clause" or "clause" means a term or condition used in contracts or in both solicitations and contracts, and applying after contract award or both before and after award.

"Contract modification" means any written change in the terms of a contract (see 43.103).

"Contracting" means purchasing, renting, leasing, or otherwise obtaining supplies or services from nonfederal sources. Contracting includes description (but not determination) of supplies and services required, selection and solicitation of sources, preparation and award of contracts, and all phases of contract administration. It does not include making grants or cooperative agreements.

"Contracting activity" means an element of an agency designated by the agency head and delegated broad authority regarding acquisition functions.

"Contracting office" means an office that awards or executes a contract for supplies or services and performs postaward functions not assigned to a contract administration office (except for use in part 48, see also 48.001).

"Contracting officer" means a person with the authority to enter into, administer, and/or terminate contracts and make related determinations and findings. The term includes certain authorized representatives of the contracting officer acting within the limits of their authority as delegated by the contracting officer. "Administrative contracting officer (ACO)" refers to a contracting officer who is administering contracts. "Termination contracting officer (TCO)" refers to a contracting officer who is settling terminated contracts. A single contracting officer may be responsible for duties in any or all of these areas. Reference in this regulation (48 CFR Chapter 1) to administrative contracting officer or termination contracting officer does not—

(1) Require that a duty be performed at a particular office or activity; or

(2) Restrict in any way a contracting officer in the performance of any duty properly assigned.

"Contracting officer's representative (COR)" means an individual, including a contracting officer's technical representative (COTR), designated and authorized in writing by the contracting officer to perform specific technical or administrative functions.

"Conviction" means a judgment or conviction of a criminal offense by any court of competent jurisdiction, whether entered upon a verdict or a plea, and includes a conviction entered upon a plea of nolo contendere. For use in subpart 23.5, see the definition at 23.503.

"Cost or pricing data" (10 U.S.C. 2306a(h)(1) and 41 U.S.C. chapter 35) means all facts that, as of the date of price agreement, or, if applicable, an earlier date agreed upon between the parties that is as close as practicable to the date of agreement on price, prudent buyers and sellers would reasonably expect to affect price negotiations significantly. Cost or pricing data are factual, not judgmental; and are verifiable. While they do not indicate the accuracy of the prospective contractor's judgment about estimated future costs or projections, they do include the data forming the basis for that judgment. Cost or pricing data are more than historical accounting data; they are all the facts that can be reasonably expected to contribute to the soundness of estimates of future costs and to the validity of determinations of costs already incurred. They also include, but are not limited to, such factors as—

(1) Vendor quotations;

(2) Nonrecurring costs;

(3) Information on changes in production methods and in production or purchasing volume;

(4) Data supporting projections of business prospects and objectives and related operations costs;

(5) Unit-cost trends such as those associated with labor efficiency;

(6) Make-or-buy decisions;

(7) Estimated resources to attain business goals; and

(8) Information on management decisions that could have a significant bearing on costs.

"Cost realism" means that the costs in an offeror's proposal—

(1) Are realistic for the work to be performed;

(2) Reflect a clear understanding of the requirements; and

(3) Are consistent with the various elements of the offeror's technical proposal.

"Cost sharing" means an explicit arrangement under which the contractor bears some of the burden of reasonable, allocable, and allowable contract cost.

"Customs territory of the United States" means the 50 States, the District of Columbia, and Puerto Rico.

"Data other than certified cost or pricing data" means pricing data, cost data, and judgmental information necessary for the contracting officer to determine a fair and reasonable price or to determine cost realism. Such data may include the identical types of data as certified cost or pricing data, consistent with Table 15-2 of 15.408, but without the certification. The data may also include, for example, sales data and any information reasonably required to explain the offeror's estimating process, including, but not limited to—

(1) The judgmental factors applied and the mathematical or other methods used in the estimate, including those used in projecting from known data; and

(2) The nature and amount of any contingencies included in the proposed price.

"Data Universal Numbering System (DUNS) number" means the 9-digit number assigned by Dun and Bradstreet, Inc. (D&B), to identify unique business entities, which is used as the identification number for Federal contractors.

"Data Universal Numbering System +4 (DUNS+4) number" means the DUNS number assigned by D&B plus a 4-character suffix that may be assigned by a business concern. (D&B has no affiliation with this 4-character suffix.) This 4-character suffix may be assigned at the discretion of the business concern to establish additional System for Award Management records for identifying alternative Electronic Funds Transfer (EFT) accounts (see subpart 32.11) for the same concern.

"Day" means, unless otherwise specified, a calendar day.

"Debarment" means action taken by a debarring official under 9.406 to exclude a contractor from Government contracting and Government-approved subcontracting for a reasonable, specified period; a contractor that is excluded is "debarred."

"Delivery order" means an order for supplies placed against an established contract or with Government sources.

"Depreciation" means a charge to current operations that distributes the cost of a tangible capital asset, less estimated residual value, over the estimated useful life of the asset in a systematic and logical manner. It does not involve a process of valuation. Useful life refers to the prospective period of economic usefulness in a particular contractor's operations as distinguished from physical life; it is evidenced by the actual or estimated retirement and replacement practice of the contractor.

"Descriptive literature" means information provided by an offeror, such as cuts, illustrations, drawings, and brochures, that shows a product's characteristics or construction of a product or explains its operation. The term includes only that information needed to evaluate the acceptability of the product and excludes other information for operating or maintaining the product.

"Design-to-cost" means a concept that establishes cost elements as management goals to achieve the best balance between life-cycle cost, acceptable performance, and schedule. Under this concept, cost is a design constraint during the design and development phases and a management discipline throughout the acquisition and operation of the system or equipment.

"Designated operational area" means a geographic area designated by the combatant commander or subordinate joint force commander for the conduct or support of specified military operations.

"Direct cost" means any cost that is identified specifically with a particular final cost objective. Direct costs are not limited to items that are incorporated in the end product as material or labor. Costs identified specifically with a contract are direct costs of that contract. All costs identified specifically with other final cost objectives of the contractor are direct costs of those cost objectives.

"Direct acquisition" means a type of interagency acquisition where a requesting agency places an order directly against a servicing agency's indefinite-delivery contract. The servicing agency manages the indefinite-delivery contract but does not participate in the placement or administration of an order.

"Disaster Response Registry" means a voluntary registry of contractors who are willing to perform debris removal, distribution of supplies, reconstruction, and other disaster or emergency relief activities established in accordance with 6 U.S.C. 796, Registry of Disaster Response Contractors. The Registry contains information on contractors who are willing to perform disaster or emergency relief activities within the United States and its outlying areas. The Registry is accessed via https://www.acquisition.gov and alternately through the FEMA website at http://www.fema.gov/business/index.shtm. (See 26.205.)

"Drug-free workplace" means the site(s) for the performance of work done by the contractor in connection with a specific contract where employees of the contractor are prohibited from engaging in the unlawful manufacture, distribution, dispensing, possession, or use of a controlled substance.

"Earned value management system" means a project management tool that effectively integrates the project scope of work with cost, schedule and performance elements for optimum project planning and control. The qualities and operating characteristics of an earned value management system are described in American National Standards Institute /Electronics Industries Alliance (ANSI/EIA) Standard-748, Earned Value Management Systems. (See OMB Circular A-11, Part 7.)

"Economically disadvantaged women-owned small business (EDWOSB) concern"—(see definition of "Women-Owned Small Business (WOSB) Program" in this section).

"Effective date of termination" means the date on which the notice of termination requires the contractor to stop performance under the contract. If the contractor receives the termination notice after the date fixed for termination, then the effective date of termination means the date the contractor receives the notice.

"Electronic and information technology (EIT)" has the same meaning as "information technology" except EIT also includes any equipment or interconnected system or subsystem of equipment that is used in the creation, conversion, or duplication of data or information. The term EIT, includes, but is not limited to, telecommunication products (such as telephones), information kiosks and transaction machines, worldwide websites, multimedia, and office equipment (such as copiers and fax machines).

"Electronic commerce" means electronic techniques for accomplishing business transactions including electronic mail or messaging, World Wide Web technology, electronic bulletin boards, purchase cards, electronic funds transfer, and electronic data interchange.

"Electronic data interchange (EDI)" means a technique for electronically transferring and storing formatted information between computers utilizing established and published formats and codes, as authorized by the applicable Federal Information Processing Standards.

"Electronic Funds Transfer (EFT)" means any transfer of funds, other than a transaction originated by cash, check, or similar paper instrument, that is initiated through an electronic terminal, telephone, computer, or magnetic tape, for the purpose of ordering, instructing, or authorizing a financial institution to debit or credit an account. The term includes Automated Clearing House transfers, Fedwire transfers, and transfers made at automatic teller machines and point-of-sale terminals. For purposes of compliance with 31 U.S.C. 3332 and implementing regulations at 31 CFR Part 208, the term "electronic funds transfer" includes a Governmentwide commercial purchase card transaction.

"End product" means supplies delivered under a line item of a Government contract, except for use in part 25 and the associated clauses at 52.225-1, 52.225-3, and 52.225-5, see the definitions in 25.003, 52.225-1(a), 52.225-3(a), and 52.225-5(a).

"Energy-efficient product"—

(1) Means a product that—

(i) Meets Department of Energy and Environmental Protection Agency criteria for use of the Energy Star trademark label; or

(ii) Is in the upper 25 percent of efficiency for all similar products as designated by the Department of Energy's Federal Energy Management Program.

(2) As used in this definition, the term "product" does not include any energy-consuming

product or system designed or procured for combat or combat-related missions (42 U.S.C. 8259b).

"Energy-efficient standby power devices" means products that use—

(1) External standby power devices, or that contain an internal standby power function; and

(2) No more than one watt of electricity in their standby power consuming mode or meet recommended low standby levels as designated by the Department of Energy Federal Energy Management Program.

"Energy-savings performance contract" means a contract that requires the contractor to—

(1) Perform services for the design, acquisition, financing, installation, testing, operation, and where appropriate, maintenance and repair, of an identified energy conservation measure or series of measures at one or more locations;

(2) Incur the costs of implementing the energy savings measures, including at least the cost (if any) incurred in making energy audits, acquiring and installing equipment, and training personnel in exchange for a predetermined share of the value of the energy savings directly resulting from implementation of such measures during the term of the contract; and

(3) Guarantee future energy and cost savings to the Government.

"Environmentally preferable" means products or services that have a lesser or reduced effect on human health and the environment when compared with competing products or services that serve the same purpose. This comparison may consider raw materials acquisition, production, manufacturing, packaging, distribution, reuse, operation, maintenance, or disposal of the product or service.

"Excess personal property" means any personal property under the control of a Federal agency that the agency head determines is not required for its needs or for the discharge of its responsibilities.

"Executive agency" means an executive department, a military department, or any independent establishment within the meaning of 5 U.S.C. 101, 102, and 104(1), respectively, and any wholly owned Government corporation within the meaning of 31 U.S.C. 9101.

"Facilities capital cost of money" means "cost of money as an element of the cost of facilities capital" as used at 48 CFR 9904.414—Cost Accounting Standard—Cost of Money as an Element of the Cost of Facilities Capital.

"Federal agency" means any executive agency or any independent establishment in the legislative or judicial branch of the Government (except the Senate, the House of Representatives, the Architect of the Capitol, and any activities under the Architect's direction).

"Federally-controlled facilities" means—

(1) Federally-owned buildings or leased space, whether for single or multi-tenant occupancy, and its grounds and approaches, all or any portion of which is under the jurisdiction, custody or control of a department or agency;

(2) Federally-controlled commercial space shared with non-government tenants. For example, if a department or agency leased the 10th floor of a commercial building, the Directive applies to the 10th floor only;

(3) Government-owned, contractor-operated facilities, including laboratories engaged in national defense research and production activities; and

(4) Facilities under a management and operating contract, such as for the operation, maintenance, or support of a Government-owned or Government-controlled research, development, special production, or testing establishment.

"Federally-controlled information system" means an information system (44 U.S.C. 3502(8) used or operated by a Federal agency, or a contractor or other organization on behalf of the agency (44 U.S.C. 3544(a)(1)(A)).

"Federally Funded Research and Development Centers (FFRDC's)" means activities that are sponsored under a broad charter by a Government agency (or agencies) for the purpose of performing, analyzing, integrating, supporting, and/or managing basic or applied research and/or development, and that receive 70 percent or more of their financial support from the Government; and—

(1) A long-term relationship is contemplated;

(2) Most or all of the facilities are owned or funded by the Government; and

(3) The FFRDC has access to Government and supplier data, employees, and facilities beyond that common in a normal contractual relationship.

"Final indirect cost rate" means the indirect cost rate established and agreed upon by the Government and the contractor as not subject to change. It is usually established after the close of the contractor's fiscal year (unless the parties decide upon a different period) to which it applies. For cost-reimbursement research and development contracts with educational institutions, it may be predetermined; that is, established for a future period on the basis of cost experience with similar contracts, together with supporting data.

"First article" means a preproduction model, initial production sample, test sample, first lot, pilot lot, or pilot models.

"First article testing" means testing and evaluating the first article for conformance with specified contract requirements before or in the initial stage of production.

"F.o.b." means free on board. This term is used in conjunction with a physical point to determine—

(1) The responsibility and basis for payment of freight charges; and

(2) Unless otherwise agreed, the point where title for goods passes to the buyer or consignee.

"F.o.b. destination" means free on board at destination; i.e., the seller or consignor delivers the goods on seller's or consignor's conveyance at destination. Unless the contract provides otherwise, the seller or consignor is responsible for the cost of shipping and risk of loss. For use in the clause at 52.247-34, see the definition at 52.247-34(a).

"F.o.b. origin" means free on board at origin; i.e., the seller or consignor places the goods on the conveyance. Unless the contract provides otherwise, the buyer or consignee is responsible for the cost of shipping and risk of loss. For use in the clause at 52.247-29, see the definition at 52.247-29(a).

"F.o.b.". . .(For other types of F.o.b., see 47.303).

"Forward pricing rate agreement" means a written agreement negotiated between a contractor and the Government to make certain rates available during a specified period for use in pricing contracts or modifications. These rates represent reasonable projections of specific costs that are not easily estimated for, identified with, or generated by a specific contract, contract end item, or task. These projections may include rates for such things as labor, indirect costs, material obsolescence and usage, spare parts provisioning, and material handling.

"Forward pricing rate recommendation" means a rate set unilaterally by the administrative contracting officer for use by the Government in negotiations or other contract actions when forward pricing rate agreement negotiations have not been completed or when the contractor will not agree to a forward pricing rate agreement.

"Freight" means supplies, goods, and transportable property.

"Full and open competition," when used with respect to a contract action, means that all responsible sources are permitted to compete.

"General and administrative (G&A) expense" means any management, financial, and other expense which is incurred by or allocated to a business unit and which is for the general management and administration of the business unit as a whole. G&A expense does not include those management expenses whose beneficial or causal relationship to cost objectives can be more directly measured by a base other than a cost input base representing the total activity of a business unit during a cost accounting period.

"Global warming potential" means how much a given mass of a chemical contributes to global warming over a given time period compared to the same mass of carbon dioxide. Carbon dioxide's global warming potential is defined as 1.0.

"Governmentwide acquisition contract (GWAC)" means a task-order or delivery-order contract for information technology established by one agency for Governmentwide use that is operated—

(1) By an executive agent designated by the Office of Management and Budget pursuant to 40 U.S.C. 11302(e); or

(2) Under a delegation of procurement authority issued by the General Services Administration (GSA) prior to August 7, 1996, under authority granted GSA by former section 40 U.S.C. 759, repealed by Pub. L. 104-106. The Economy Act does not apply to

orders under a Governmentwide acquisition contract.

"Governmentwide point of entry (GPE)" means the single point where Government business opportunities greater than $25,000, including synopses of proposed contract actions, solicitations, and associated information, can be accessed electronically by the public. The GPE is located at http://www.fedbizopps.gov.

"Head of the agency" (see "agency head").

"Head of the contracting activity" means the official who has overall responsibility for managing the contracting activity.

"High global warming potential hydrofluorocarbons" means any hydrofluorocarbons in a particular end use for which EPA's Significant New Alternatives Policy (SNAP) program has identified other acceptable alternatives that have lower global warming potential. The SNAP list of alternatives is found at 40 CFR part 82 subpart G with supplemental tables of alternatives available at http://www.epa.gov/snap/).

"Historically black college or university" means an institution determined by the Secretary of Education to meet the requirements of 34 CFR 608.2.

"HUBZone" means a historically underutilized business zone that is an area located within one or more qualified census tracts, qualified nonmetropolitan counties, lands within the external boundaries of an Indian reservation, qualified base closure areas, or redesignated areas, as defined in 13 CFR 126.103.

"HUBZone contract" means a contract awarded to a "HUBZone small business" concern through any of the following procurement methods:

(1) A sole source award to a HUBZone small business concern.

(2) Set-aside awards based on competition restricted to HUBZone small business concerns.

(3) Awards to HUBZone small business concerns through full and open competition after a price evaluation preference in favor of HUBZone small business concerns.

"HUBZone small business concern" means a small business concern that appears on the List of Qualified HUBZone Small Business Concerns maintained by the Small Business Administration (13 CFR 126.103).

"Humanitarian or peacekeeping operation" means a military operation in support of the provision of humanitarian or foreign disaster assistance or in support of a peacekeeping operation under Chapter VI or VII of the Charter of the United Nations. The term does not include routine training, force rotation, or stationing (10 U.S.C. 2302(8) and 41 U.S.C. 153(2)).

"Hydrofluorocarbons" means compounds that contain only hydrogen, fluorine, and carbon.

"In writing," "writing," or "written" means any worded or numbered expression that can be read, reproduced, and later communicated, and includes electronically transmitted and stored information.

"Indirect cost" means any cost not directly identified with a single final cost objective, but identified with two or more final cost objectives or with at least one intermediate cost objective.

"Indirect cost rate" means the percentage or dollar factor that expresses the ratio of indirect expense incurred in a given period to direct labor cost, manufacturing cost, or another appropriate base for the same period (see also "final indirect cost rate").

"Ineligible" means excluded from Government contracting (and subcontracting, if appropriate) pursuant to statutory, Executive order, or regulatory authority other than this regulation (48 CFR chapter 1) and its implementing and supplementing regulations; for example, pursuant to—

(1) 40 U.S.C. chapter 31, subchapter IV, Wage Rate Requirements (Construction), and its related statutes and implementing regulations;

(2) 41 U.S.C. chapter 67, Service Contract Labor Standards;

(3) The Equal Employment Opportunity Acts and Executive orders;

(4) 41 U.S.C. chapter 65, Contracts for Material, Supplies, Articles, and Equipment Exceeding $15,000;

(5) 41 U.S.C. chapter 83, Buy American; or

(6) The Environmental Protection Acts and Executive orders.

"Information security" means protecting information and information systems from unauthorized access, use, disclosure, disruption, modification, or destruction in order to provide—

(1) Integrity, which means guarding against improper information modification or destruction, and includes ensuring information nonrepudiation and authenticity;

(2) Confidentiality, which means preserving authorized restrictions on access and disclosure, including means for protecting personal privacy and proprietary information; and

(3) Availability, which means ensuring timely and reliable access to, and use of, information.

"Information technology" means any equipment, or interconnected system(s) or subsystem(s) of equipment, that is used in the automatic acquisition, storage, analysis, evaluation, manipulation, management, movement, control, display, switching, interchange, transmission, or reception of data or information by the agency.

(1) For purposes of this definition, equipment is used by an agency if the equipment is used by the agency directly or is used by a contractor under a contract with the agency that requires—

(i) Its use; or

(ii) To a significant extent, its use in the performance of a service or the furnishing of a product.

(2) The term "information technology" includes computers, ancillary equipment (including imaging peripherals, input, output, and storage devices necessary for security and surveillance), peripheral equipment designed to be controlled by the central processing unit of a computer, software, firmware and similar procedures, services (including support services), and related resources.

(3) The term "information technology" does not include any equipment that—

(i) Is acquired by a contractor incidental to a contract; or

(ii) Contains imbedded information technology that is used as an integral part of the product, but the principal function of which is not the acquisition, storage, analysis, evaluation, manipulation, management, movement, control, display, switching, interchange, transmission, or reception of data or information. For example, HVAC (heating, ventilation, and air conditioning) equipment, such as thermostats or temperature control devices, and medical equipment where information technology is integral to its operation, are not information technology.

"Inherently governmental function" means, as a matter of policy, a function that is so intimately related to the public interest as to mandate performance by Government employees. This definition is a policy determination, not a legal determination. An inherently governmental function includes activities that require either the exercise of discretion in applying Government authority, or the making of value judgments in making decisions for the Government. Governmental functions normally fall into two categories: the act of governing, i.e., the discretionary exercise of Government authority, and monetary transactions and entitlements.

(1) An inherently governmental function involves, among other things, the interpretation and execution of the laws of the United States so as to—

(i) Bind the United States to take or not to take some action by contract, policy, regulation, authorization, order, or otherwise;

(ii) Determine, protect, and advance United States economic, political, territorial, property, or other interests by military or diplomatic action, civil or criminal judicial proceedings, contract management, or otherwise;

(iii) Significantly affect the life, liberty, or property of private persons;

(iv) Commission, appoint, direct, or control officers or employees of the United States; or

(v) Exert ultimate control over the acquisition, use, or disposition of the property, real or personal, tangible or intangible, of the United States, including the collection, control, or disbursement of Federal funds.

(2) Inherently governmental functions do not normally include gathering information for or providing advice, opinions, recommendations, or ideas to Government officials. They also do not include functions that are primarily ministerial and internal in nature, such as building security, mail operations, operation of cafeterias, housekeeping, facilities

operations and maintenance, warehouse operations, motor vehicle fleet management operations, or other routine electrical or mechanical services.

"Inspection" means examining and testing supplies or services (including, when appropriate, raw materials, components, and intermediate assemblies) to determine whether they conform to contract requirements.

"Insurance" means a contract that provides that for a stipulated consideration, one party undertakes to indemnify another against loss, damage, or liability arising from an unknown or contingent event.

"Interagency acquisition" means a procedure by which an agency needing supplies or services (the requesting agency) obtains them from another agency (the servicing agency), by an assisted acquisition or a direct acquisition. The term includes—

(1) Acquisitions under the Economy Act (31 U.S.C. 1535); and

(2) Non-Economy Act acquisitions completed under other statutory authorities, (e.g., General Services Administration Federal Supply Schedules in subpart 8.4 and Governmentwide acquisition contracts (GWACs)).

"Invoice" means a contractor's bill or written request for payment under the contract for supplies delivered or services performed (see also "proper invoice").

"Irrevocable letter of credit" means a written commitment by a federally insured financial institution to pay all or part of a stated amount of money, until the expiration date of the letter, upon the Government's (the beneficiary) presentation of a written demand for payment. Neither the financial institution nor the offeror/contractor can revoke or condition the letter of credit.

"Labor surplus area" means a geographical area identified by the Department of Labor in accordance with 20 CFR Part 654, Subpart A, as an area of concentrated unemployment or underemployment or an area of labor surplus.

"Labor surplus area concern" means a concern that together with its first-tier subcontractors will perform substantially in labor surplus areas. Performance is substantially in labor surplus areas if the costs incurred under the contract on account of manufacturing, production, or performance of appropriate services in labor surplus areas exceed 50 percent of the contract price.

"Latent defect" means a defect that exists at the time of acceptance but cannot be discovered by a reasonable inspection.

"Major system" means that combination of elements that will function together to produce the capabilities required to fulfill a mission need. The elements may include hardware, equipment, software, or any combination thereof, but exclude construction or other improvements to real property. A system is a major system if—

(1) The Department of Defense is responsible for the system and the total expenditures for research, development, test, and evaluation for the system are estimated to be more than $185 million based on Fiscal Year 2014 constant dollars or the eventual total expenditure for the acquisition exceeds $835 million based on Fiscal Year 2014 constant dollars (or any update of these thresholds based on a more recent fiscal year, as specified in the DoD Instruction 5000.02, "Operation of the Defense Acquisition System");

(2) A civilian agency is responsible for the system and total expenditures for the system are estimated to exceed $2 million or the dollar threshold for a "major system" established by the agency pursuant to Office of Management and Budget Circular A-109, entitled "Major System Acquisitions," whichever is greater; or

(3) The system is designated a "major system" by the head of the agency responsible for the system (10 U.S.C. 2302 and 41 U.S.C. 109).

"Make-or-buy program" means that part of a contractor's written plan for a contract identifying those major items to be produced or work efforts to be performed in the prime contractor's facilities and those to be subcontracted.

Manufactured end product means any end product in product and service codes (PSC) 1000-9999, except—

(1) PSC 5510, Lumber and Related Basic Wood Materials;

(2) Product or service group (PSG) 87, Agricultural Supplies;

(3) PSG 88, Live Animals;

(4) PSG 89, Subsistence;

(5) PSC 9410, Crude Grades of Plant Materials;

(6) PSC 9430, Miscellaneous Crude Animal Products, Inedible;

(7) PSC 9440, Miscellaneous Crude Agricultural and Forestry Products;

(8) PSC 9610, Ores;

(9) PSC 9620, Minerals, Natural and Synthetic; and

(10) PSC 9630, Additive Metal Materials.

"Market research" means collecting and analyzing information about capabilities within the market to satisfy agency needs.

"Master solicitation" means a document containing special clauses and provisions that have been identified as essential for the acquisition of a specific type of supply or service that is acquired repetitively.

"May" denotes the permissive. However, the words "no person may . . ." mean that no person is required, authorized, or permitted to do the act described.

"Micro-purchase" means an acquisition of supplies or services using simplified acquisition procedures, the aggregate amount of which does not exceed the micro-purchase threshold.

"Micro-purchase threshold" means $3,500, except it means—

(1) For acquisitions of construction subject to 40 U.S.C. chapter 31, subchapter IV, Wage Rate Requirements (Construction), $2,000;

(2) For acquisitions of services subject to 41 U.S.C. chapter 67, Service Contract Labor Standards, $2,500; and

(3) For acquisitions of supplies or services that, as determined by the head of the agency, are to be used to support a contingency operation or to facilitate defense against or recovery from nuclear, biological, chemical or radiological attack as described in 13.201(g)(1), except for construction subject to 40 U.S.C. chapter 31, subchapter IV, Wage Rate Requirements (Construction) (41 U.S.C. 1903)—

(i) $20,000 in the case of any contract to be awarded and performed, or purchase to be made, inside the United States; and

(ii) $30,000 in the case of any contract to be awarded and performed, or purchase to be made, outside the United States.

"Minority Institution" means an institution of higher education meeting the requirements of Section 365(3) of the Higher Education Act of 1965 (20 U.S.C. 1067k), including a Hispanic-serving institution of higher education, as defined in Section 502(a) of the Act (20 U.S.C. 1101a).

"Multi-agency contract (MAC)" means a task-order or delivery-order contract established by one agency for use by Government agencies to obtain supplies and services, consistent with the Economy Act (see 17.502-2). Multi-agency contracts include contracts for information technology established pursuant to 40 U.S.C. 11314(a)(2).

"Multiple-award contract" means a contract that is—

(1) A Multiple Award Schedule contract issued by GSA (e.g., GSA Schedule Contract) or agencies granted Multiple Award Schedule contract authority by GSA (e.g., Department of Veterans Affairs) as described in FAR part 38;

(2) A multiple-award task-order or delivery-order contract issued in accordance with FAR subpart 16.5, including Governmentwide acquisition contracts; or

(3) Any other indefinite-delivery, indefinite-quantity contract entered into with two or more sources pursuant to the same solicitation.

"Must" (see "shall").

"National defense" means any activity related to programs for military or atomic energy production or construction, military assistance to any foreign nation, stockpiling, or space, except that for use in subpart 11.6, see the definition in 11.601.

"Neutral person" means an impartial third party, who serves as a mediator, fact finder, or arbitrator, or otherwise functions to assist the parties to resolve the issues in controversy. A neutral person may be a permanent or temporary officer or employee of the Federal Government or any other individual who is acceptable to the parties. A neutral person must have no official, financial, or personal conflict of interest with respect to the issues in controversy, unless the interest is fully disclosed in writing to all parties and all parties agree that the neutral person may serve (5 U.S.C. 583).

"Nondevelopmental item" means—

(1) Any previously developed item of supply used exclusively for governmental purposes by a Federal agency, a State or local government, or a foreign government with which the United States has a mutual defense cooperation agreement;

(2) Any item described in paragraph (1) of this definition that requires only minor modification or modifications of a type customarily available in the commercial marketplace in order to meet the requirements of the procuring department or agency; or

(3) Any item of supply being produced that does not meet the requirements of paragraphs (1) or (2) solely because the item is not yet in use.

"Novation agreement" means a legal instrument—

(1) Executed by the—

   (i) Contractor (transferor);

   (ii) Successor in interest (transferee); and

   (iii) Government; and

(2) By which, among other things, the transferor guarantees performance of the contract, the transferee assumes all obligations under the contract, and the Government recognizes the transfer of the contract and related assets.

"Offer" means a response to a solicitation that, if accepted, would bind the offeror to perform the resultant contract. Responses to invitations for bids (sealed bidding) are offers called "bids" or "sealed bids"; responses to requests for proposals (negotiation) are offers called "proposals"; however, responses to requests for quotations (simplified acquisition) are "quotations," not offers. For unsolicited proposals, see subpart 15.6.

"Offeror" means offeror or bidder.

"Office of Small and Disadvantaged Business Utilization" means the Office of Small Business Programs when referring to the Department of Defense.

"OMB Uniform Guidance at 2 CFR part 200" is the abbreviated title for Uniform Administrative Requirements, Cost Principles, and Audit Requirements for Federal Awards (2 CFR part 200), which supersedes OMB Circulars A-21, A-87, A-89, A-102, A-110, A-122, and A-133, and the guidance in Circular A-50 on Audit Followup.

"Option" means a unilateral right in a contract by which, for a specified time, the Government may elect to purchase additional supplies or services called for by the contract, or may elect to extend the term of the contract.

"Organizational conflict of interest" means that because of other activities or relationships with other persons, a person is unable or potentially unable to render impartial assistance or advice to the Government, or the person's objectivity in performing the contract work is or might be otherwise impaired, or a person has an unfair competitive advantage.

"Outlying areas" means—

(1) Commonwealths.

   (i) Puerto Rico.

   (ii) The Northern Mariana Islands;

(2) Territories.

   (i) American Samoa.

   (ii) Guam.

   (iii) U.S. Virgin Islands; and

(3) Minor outlying islands.

   (i) Baker Island.

   (ii) Howland Island.

   (iii) Jarvis Island.

   (iv) Johnston Atoll.

   (v) Kingman Reef.

   (vi) Midway Islands.

   (vii) Navassa Island.

   (viii) Palmyra Atoll.

   (ix) Wake Atoll.

"Overtime" means time worked by a contractor's employee in excess of the employee's normal workweek.

"Overtime premium" means the difference between the contractor's regular rate of pay to an employee for the shift involved and the higher rate paid for overtime. It does not include shift premium, i.e., the difference between the contractor's regular rate of pay to an employee and the higher rate paid for extra-pay-shift work.

"Ozone-depleting substance" means any substance the Environmental Protection Agency designates in 40 CFR part 82 as—

(1) Class I, including, but not limited to, chlorofluorocarbons, halons, carbon tetrachloride, and methyl chloroform; or

(2) Class II, including, but not limited to, hydrochlorofluorocarbons.

"Partial termination" means the termination of a part, but not all, of the work that has not been completed and accepted under a contract.

"Past performance" means an offeror's or contractor's performance on active and physically completed contracts (see 4.804-4).

"Performance-based acquisition (PBA)" means an acquisition structured around the results to be achieved as opposed to the manner by which the work is to be performed.

"Performance Work Statement (PWS)" means a statement of work for performance-based acquisitions that describes the required results in clear, specific and objective terms with measurable outcomes.

"Personal property" means property of any kind or interest in it except real property, records of the Federal Government, and naval vessels of the following categories:

(1) Battleships;

(2) Cruisers;

(3) Aircraft carriers;

(4) Destroyers; and

(5) Submarines.

"Personal services contract" means a contract that, by its express terms or as administered, makes the contractor personnel appear to be, in effect, Government employees (see 37.104).

"Plant clearance officer" means an authorized representative of the contracting officer, appointed in accordance with agency procedures, responsible for screening, redistributing, and disposing of contractor inventory from a contractor's plant or work site. The term "Contractor's plant" includes, but is not limited to, Government-owned contractor-operated plants, Federal installations, and Federal and non-Federal industrial operations, as may be required under the scope of the contract.

"Pollution prevention" means any practice that—

(1) (i) Reduces the amount of any hazardous substance, pollutant, or contaminant entering any waste stream or otherwise released into the environment (including fugitive emissions) prior to recycling, treatment, or disposal; and

(ii) Reduces the hazards to public health and the environment associated with the release of such substances, pollutants, and contaminants;

(2) Reduces or eliminates the creation of pollutants through increased efficiency in the use of raw materials, energy, water, or other resources; or

(3) Protects natural resources by conservation.

"Power of attorney" means the authority given one person or corporation to act for and obligate another, as specified in the instrument creating the power; in corporate suretyship, an instrument under seal that appoints an attorney-in-fact to act in behalf of a surety company in signing bonds (see also "attorney-in-fact" at 28.001).

"Preaward survey" means an evaluation of a prospective contractor's capability to perform a proposed contract.

"Preponderance of the evidence" means proof by information that, compared with that opposing it, leads to the conclusion that the fact at issue is more probably true than not.

"Pricing" means the process of establishing a reasonable amount or amounts to be paid for supplies or services.

"Principal" means an officer, director, owner, partner, or a person having primary management or supervisory responsibilities within a business entity (e.g., general manager; plant manager; head of a division or business segment; and similar positions).

"Procurement" (see "acquisition").

"Procuring activity" means a component of an executive agency having a significant acquisition function and designated as such by the head of the agency. Unless agency regulations specify otherwise, the term "procuring activity" is synonymous with "contracting activity."

"Products" has the same meaning as "supplies."

"Projected average loss" means the estimated long-term average loss per period for periods of comparable exposure to risk of loss.

"Proper invoice" means an invoice that meets the minimum standards specified in 32.905(b).

"Purchase order," when issued by the Government, means an offer by the Government to buy supplies or services, including construction and research and development, upon specified terms and conditions, using simplified acquisition procedures.

"Qualification requirement" means a Government requirement for testing or other quality assurance demonstration that must be completed before award of a contract.

"Qualified products list (QPL)" means a list of products that have been examined, tested, and have satisfied all applicable qualification requirements.

"Receiving report" means written evidence that indicates Government acceptance of supplies delivered or services performed (see subpart 46.6). Receiving reports must meet the requirements of 32.905(c).

"Recovered material" means waste materials and by-products recovered or diverted from solid waste, but the term does not include those materials and by-products generated from, and commonly reused within, an original manufacturing process. For use in subpart 11.3 for paper and paper products, see the definition at 11.301.

"Registered in the System for Award Management (SAM) database" means that—

(1) The Contractor has entered all mandatory information, including the DUNS number or the DUNS+4 number, the Contractor and Government Entity (CAGE) code, as well as data required by the Federal Funding Accountability and Transparency Act of 2006 (see subpart 4.14), into the SAM database;

(2) The Contractor has completed the Core, Assertions, Representations and Certifications, and Points of Contact sections of the registration in the SAM database;

(3) The Government has validated all mandatory data fields, to include validation of the Taxpayer Identification Number (TIN) with the Internal Revenue Service (IRS). The contractor will be required to provide consent for TIN validation to the Government as a part of the SAM registration process; and

(4) The Government has marked the record Active.

"Renewable energy" means energy produced by solar, wind, geothermal, biomass, landfill gas, ocean (including tidal, wave, current, and thermal), municipal solid waste, or new hydroelectric generation capacity achieved from increased efficiency or additions of new capacity at an existing hydroelectric project (Energy Policy Act of 2005, 42 U.S.C. 15852).

"Renewable energy technology" means—

(1) Technologies that use renewable energy to provide light, heat, cooling, or mechanical or electrical energy for use in facilities or other activities; or

(2) The use of integrated whole-building designs that rely upon renewable energy resources, including passive solar design.

"Requesting agency" means the agency that has the requirement for an interagency acquisition.

"Residual value" means the proceeds, less removal and disposal costs, if any, realized upon disposition of a tangible capital asset. It usually is measured by the net proceeds from the sale or other disposition of the asset, or its fair value if the asset is traded in on another asset. The estimated residual value is a current forecast of the residual value.

"Responsible audit agency" means the agency that is responsible for performing all required contract audit services at a business unit.

"Responsible prospective contractor" means a contractor that meets the standards in 9.104.

"Scrap" means personal property that has no value except its basic metallic, mineral, or organic content.

"Segment" means one of two or more divisions, product departments, plants, or other subdivisions of an organization reporting directly to a home office, usually identified with responsibility for profit and/or producing a product or service. The term includes—

(1) Government-owned contractor-operated (GOCO) facilities; and

(2) Joint ventures and subsidiaries (domestic and foreign) in which the organization has—

(i) A majority ownership; or

(ii) Less than a majority ownership, but over which it exercises control.

"Self-insurance" means the assumption or retention of the risk of loss by the contractor, whether voluntarily or involuntarily. Self-insurance includes the deductible portion of purchased insurance.

"Senior procurement executive" means the individual appointed pursuant to 41 U.S.C. 1702(c) who is responsible for management direction of the acquisition system of the executive agency, including implementation of the unique acquisition policies, regulations, and standards of the executive agency.

"Service-disabled veteran-owned small business concern"—

(1) Means a small business concern—

(i) Not less than 51 percent of which is owned by one or more service-disabled veterans or, in the case of any publicly owned business, not less than 51 percent of the stock of which is owned by one or more service-disabled veterans; and

(ii) The management and daily business operations of which are controlled by one or more service-disabled veterans or, in the case of a service-disabled veteran with permanent and severe disability, the spouse or permanent caregiver of such veteran.

(2) Service-disabled veteran means a veteran, as defined in 38 U.S.C. 101(2), with a disability that is service-connected, as defined in 38 U.S.C. 101(16).

"Servicing agency" means the agency that will conduct an assisted acquisition on behalf of the requesting agency.

"Shall" means the imperative.

"Shipment" means freight transported or to be transported.

"Shop drawings" means drawings submitted by the construction contractor or a subcontractor at any tier or required under a construction contract, showing in detail either or both of the following:

(1) The proposed fabrication and assembly of structural elements.

(2) The installation (i.e., form, fit, and attachment details) of materials or equipment.

"Should" means an expected course of action or policy that is to be followed unless inappropriate for a particular circumstance.

"Signature" or "signed" means the discrete, verifiable symbol of an individual that, when affixed to a writing with the knowledge and consent of the individual, indicates a present intention to authenticate the writing. This includes electronic symbols.

"Simplified acquisition procedures" means the methods prescribed in part 13 for making purchases of supplies or services.

"Simplified acquisition threshold" means $150,000 (41 U.S.C. 134), except for—

(1) Acquisitions of supplies or services that, as determined by the head of the agency, are to be used to support a contingency operation or to facilitate defense against or recovery from nuclear, biological, chemical, or radiological attack (41 U.S.C. 1903), the term means—

(i) $300,000 for any contract to be awarded and performed, or purchase to be made, inside the United States; and

(ii) $1 million for any contract to be awarded and performed, or purchase to be made, outside the United States; and

(2) Acquisitions of supplies or services that, as determined by the head of the agency, are to be used to support a humanitarian or peacekeeping operation (10 U.S.C. 2302), the term means $300,000 for any contract to be awarded and performed, or purchase to be made, outside the United States.

"Single, Governmentwide point of entry," means the one point of entry to be designated by the Administrator of OFPP that will allow the private sector to electronically access procurement opportunities Governmentwide.

"Small business concern" means a concern, including its affiliates, that is independently owned and operated, not dominant in the field of operation in which it is bidding on Government contracts, and qualified as a small business under the criteria and size standards in 13 CFR part 121 (see 19.102). Such a concern is "not dominant in its field of operation" when it does not exercise a controlling or major influence on a national basis in a kind of business activity in which a number of business concerns are primarily engaged. In determining whether dominance exists, consideration must be given to all appropriate factors, including volume of business, number of employees, financial resources, competitive status or position, ownership or control of materials, processes, patents, license agreements, facilities, sales territory, and nature of business activity. (See 15 U.S.C. 632.)

"Small business subcontractor" means a concern, including affiliates, that for subcontracts valued at—

(1) $15,000 or less, does not have more than 500 employees; and

(2) More than $15,000, does not have employees or average annual receipts exceeding the size standard in 13 CFR Part 121 (see 19.102) for the product or service it is providing on the subcontract.

"Small disadvantaged business concern" consistent with 13 CFR 124.1002, means a small business concern under the size standard applicable to the acquisition, that:

(1) Is at least 51 percent unconditionally and directly owned (as defined at 13 CFR 124.105) by—

(i) One or more socially disadvantaged (as defined at 13 CFR 124.103) and economically disadvantaged (as defined at 13 CFR 124.104) individuals who are citizens of the United States; and

(ii) Each individual claiming economic disadvantage has a net worth not exceeding $750,000 after taking into account the applicable exclusions set forth at 13 CFR 124.104(c)(2); and

(2) The management and daily business operations of which are controlled (as defined at 13 CFR 124.106) by individuals who meet the criteria in paragraphs (1)(i) and (ii) of this definition.

"Sole source acquisition" means a contract for the purchase of supplies or services that is entered into or proposed to be entered into by an agency after soliciting and negotiating with only one source.

"Solicitation" means any request to submit offers or quotations to the Government. Solicitations under sealed bid procedures are called "invitations for bids." Solicitations under negotiated procedures are called "requests for proposals." Solicitations under simplified acquisition procedures may require submission of either a quotation or an offer.

"Solicitation provision or provision" means a term or condition used only in solicitations and applying only before contract award.

"Source selection information" means any of the following information that is prepared for use by an agency for the purpose of evaluating a bid or proposal to enter into an agency procurement contract, if that information has not been previously made available to the public or disclosed publicly:

(1) Bid prices submitted in response to an agency invitation for bids, or lists of those bid prices before bid opening.

(2) Proposed costs or prices submitted in response to an agency solicitation, or lists of those proposed costs or prices.

(3) Source selection plans.

(4) Technical evaluation plans.

(5) Technical evaluations of proposals.

(6) Cost or price evaluations of proposals.

(7) Competitive range determinations that identify proposals that have a reasonable chance of being selected for award of a contract.

(8) Rankings of bids, proposals, or competitors.

(9) Reports and evaluations of source selection panels, boards, or advisory councils.

(10) Other information marked as "Source Selection Information—See FAR 2.101 and 3.104" based on a case-by-case determination by the head of the agency or the contract-

ing officer, that its disclosure would jeopardize the integrity or successful completion of the Federal agency procurement to which the information relates.

"Special competency" means a special or unique capability, including qualitative aspects, developed incidental to the primary functions of the Federally Funded Research and Development Centers to meet some special need.

"Special test equipment" means either single or multipurpose integrated test units engineered, designed, fabricated, or modified to accomplish special purpose testing in performing a contract. It consists of items or assemblies of equipment including foundations and similar improvements necessary for installing special test equipment, and standard or general purpose items or components that are interconnected and interdependent so as to become a new functional entity for special testing purposes. Special test equipment does not include material, special tooling, real property, and equipment items used for general testing purposes or property that with relatively minor expense can be made suitable for general purpose use.

"Special tooling" means jigs, dies, fixtures, molds, patterns, taps, gauges, and all components of these items including foundations and similar improvements necessary for installing special tooling, and which are of such a specialized nature that without substantial modification or alteration their use is limited to the development or production of particular supplies or parts thereof or to the performance of particular services. Special tooling does not include material, special test equipment, real property, equipment, machine tools, or similar capital items.

"State and local taxes" means taxes levied by the States, the District of Columbia, outlying areas of the United States, or their political subdivisions.

"Statement of Objectives (SOO)" means a Government-prepared document incorporated into the solicitation that states the overall performance objectives. It is used in solicitations when the Government intends to provide the maximum flexibility to each offeror to propose an innovative approach.

"Substantial evidence" means information sufficient to support the reasonable belief that a particular act or omission has occurred.

"Substantially as follows" or "substantially the same as," when used in the prescription and introductory text of a provision or clause, means that authorization is granted to prepare and utilize a variation of that provision or clause to accommodate requirements that are peculiar to an individual acquisition; provided that the variation includes the salient features of the FAR provision or clause, and is not inconsistent with the intent, principle, and substance of the FAR provision or clause or related coverage of the subject matter.

"Supplemental agreement" means a contract modification that is accomplished by the mutual action of the parties.

"Supplies" means all property except land or interest in land. It includes (but is not limited to) public works, buildings, and facilities; ships, floating equipment, and vessels of every character, type, and description, together with parts and accessories; aircraft and aircraft parts, accessories, and equipment; machine tools; and the alteration or installation of any of the foregoing.

"Supporting a diplomatic or consular mission" means performing outside the United States under a contract administered by Federal agency personnel who are subject to the direction of a Chief of Mission.

"Surety" means an individual or corporation legally liable for the debt, default, or failure of a principal to satisfy a contractual obligation. The types of sureties referred to are as follows:

(1) An individual surety is one person, as distinguished from a business entity, who is liable for the entire penal amount of the bond.

(2) A corporate surety is licensed under various insurance laws and, under its charter, has legal power to act as surety for others.

(3) A cosurety is one of two or more sureties that are jointly liable for the penal sum of the bond. A limit of liability for each surety may be stated.

"Surplus property" means excess personal property not required by any Federal agency as determined by the Administrator of the General Services Administration (GSA). (See 41 CFR 102-36.40).

"Suspension" means action taken by a suspending official under 9.407 to disqualify a contractor temporarily from Government contracting and Government-approved subcontracting; a contractor that is disqualified is "suspended."

"Sustainable acquisition" means acquiring goods and services in order to create and maintain conditions—

(1) Under which humans and nature can exist in productive harmony; and

(2) That permit fulfilling the social, economic, and other requirements of present and future generations.

"System for Award Management (SAM)" means the primary Government repository for prospective Federal awardee and Federal awardee information and the centralized Government system for certain contracting, grants, and other assistance-related processes. It includes—

(1) Data collected from prospective Federal awardees required for the conduct of business with the Government;

(2) Prospective contractor-submitted annual representations and certifications in accordance with FAR subpart 4.12; and

(3) Identification of those parties excluded from receiving Federal contracts, certain subcontracts, and certain types of Federal financial and non-financial assistance and benefits.

"Task order" means an order for services placed against an established contract or with Government sources.

"Taxpayer Identification Number (TIN)" means the number required by the IRS to be used by the offeror in reporting income tax and other returns. The TIN may be either a Social Security Number or an Employer Identification Number.

"Technical data" means recorded information (regardless of the form or method of the recording) of a scientific or technical nature (including computer databases and computer software documentation). This term does not include computer software or financial, administrative, cost or pricing, or management data or other information incidental to contract administration. The term includes recorded information of a scientific or technical nature that is included in computer databases (See 41 U.S.C. 116).

"Termination for convenience" means the exercise of the Government's right to completely or partially terminate performance of work under a contract when it is in the Government's interest.

"Termination for default" means the exercise of the Government's right to completely or partially terminate a contract because of the contractor's actual or anticipated failure to perform its contractual obligations.

"Termination inventory" means any property purchased, supplied, manufactured, furnished, or otherwise acquired for the performance of a contract subsequently terminated and properly allocable to the terminated portion of the contract. It includes Government-furnished property. It does not include any facilities, material, special test equipment, or special tooling that are subject to a separate contract or to a special contract requirement governing their use or disposition.

"Terminated portion of the contract" means the portion of a contract that the contractor is not to perform following a partial termination. For construction contracts that have been completely terminated for convenience, it means the entire contract, notwithstanding the completion of, and payment for, individual items of work before termination.

"Unallowable cost" means any cost that, under the provisions of any pertinent law, regulation, or contract, cannot be included in prices, cost-reimbursements, or settlements under a Government contract to which it is allocable.

"Unique and innovative concept," when used relative to an unsolicited research proposal, means that—

(1) In the opinion and to the knowledge of the Government evaluator, the meritorious proposal—

(i) Is the product of original thinking submitted confidentially by one source;

(ii) Contains new, novel, or changed concepts, approaches, or methods;

(iii) Was not submitted previously by another; and

(iv) Is not otherwise available within the Federal Government.

(2) In this context, the term does not mean that the source has the sole capability of performing the research.

"United States," when used in a geographic sense, means the 50 States and the District of Columbia, except as follows:

(1) For use in subpart 3.10, see the definition at 3.1001.

(2) For use in subpart 22.8, see the definition at 22.801.

(3) For use in subpart 22.10, see the definition at 22.1001.

(4) For use in subpart 22.12, see the definition at 22.1201.

(5) For use in subpart 22.13, see the definition at 22.1301.

(6) For use in subpart 22.16, see the definition at 22.1601.

(7) For use in subpart 22.17, see the definition at 22.1702.

(8) For use in subpart 22.18, see the definition at 22.1801.

(9) For use in part 23, see definition at 23.001.

(10) For use in part 25, see the definition at 25.003.

(11) For use in part 27, see the definition at 27.001.

(12) For use in subpart 47.4, see the definition at 47.401.

"Unsolicited proposal" means a written proposal for a new or innovative idea that is submitted to an agency on the initiative of the offeror for the purpose of obtaining a contract with the Government, and that is not in response to a request for proposals, Broad Agency Announcement, Small Business Innovation Research topic, Small Business Technology Transfer Research topic, Program Research and Development Announcement, or any other Government-initiated solicitation or program.

"Value engineering" means an analysis of the functions of a program, project, system, product, item of equipment, building, facility, service, or supply of an executive agency, performed by qualified agency or contractor personnel, directed at improving performance, reliability, quality, safety, and life-cycle costs (41 U.S.C. 1711). For use in the clause at 52.248-2, see the definition at 52.248-2(b).

"Value engineering change proposal (VECP)"—

(1) Means a proposal that—

(i) Requires a change to the instant contract to implement; and

(ii) Results in reducing the overall projected cost to the agency without impairing essential functions or characteristics, provided, that it does not involve a change—

(A) In deliverable end item quantities only;

(B) In research and development (R&D) items or R&D test quantities that are due solely to results of previous testing under the instant contract; or

(C) To the contract type only.

(2) For use in the clauses at—

(i) 52.248-2, see the definition at 52.248-2(b); and

(ii) 52.248-3, see the definition at 52.248-3(b).

"Veteran-owned small business concern" means a small business concern—

(1) Not less than 51 percent of which is owned by one or more veterans (as defined at 38 U.S.C. 101(2)) or, in the case of any publicly owned business, not less than 51 percent of the stock of which is owned by one or more veterans; and

(2) The management and daily business operations of which are controlled by one or more veterans.

"Virgin material" means—

(1) Previously unused raw material, including previously unused copper, aluminum, lead, zinc, iron, other metal or metal ore; or

(2) Any undeveloped resource that is, or with new technology will become, a source of raw materials.

"Voluntary consensus standards" means common and repeated use of rules, conditions, guidelines or characteristics for products, or related processes and production methods and related management systems. Voluntary Consensus Standards are developed or adopted by domestic and international voluntary consensus standard making bodies (e.g., International Organization for Standardization (ISO) and ASTM-International). See OMB Circular A-119.

"Warranty" means a promise or affirmation given by a contractor to the Government regarding the nature, usefulness, or condition of the supplies or performance of services furnished under the contract.

"Waste reduction" means preventing or decreasing the amount of waste being generated through waste prevention, recycling, or purchasing recycled and environmentally preferable products.

"Water consumption intensity" means water consumption per square foot of building space.

"Women-owned small business concern" means—

(1) A small business concern—

(i) That is at least 51 percent owned by one or more women; or, in the case of any publicly owned business, at least 51 percent of the stock of which is owned by one or more women; and

(ii) Whose management and daily business operations are controlled by one or more women; or

(2) A small business concern eligible under the Women-Owned Small Business Program in accordance with 13 CFR part 127 (see subpart 19.15).

"Women-Owned Small Business (WOSB) Program."

(1) "Women-Owned Small Business (WOSB) Program" means a program that authorizes contracting officers to limit competition, including award on a sole source basis, to—

(i) Economically disadvantaged women-owned small business (EDWOSB) concerns eligible under the WOSB Program for Federal contracts assigned a North American Industry Classification Systems (NAICS) code in an industry in which the Small Business Administration (SBA) has determined that WOSB concerns are underrepresented in Federal procurement; and

(ii) WOSB concerns eligible under the WOSB Program for Federal contracts assigned a NAICS code in an industry in which SBA has determined that WOSB concerns are substantially underrepresented in Federal procurement.

(2) "Economically disadvantaged women-owned small business (EDWOSB) concern" means a small business concern that is at least 51 percent directly and unconditionally owned by, and the management and daily business operations of which are controlled by, one or more women who are citizens of the United States and who are economically disadvantaged in accordance with 13 CFR part 127. It automatically qualifies as a women-owned small business (WOSB) concern eligible under the WOSB Program.

(3) "Women-owned small business (WOSB)" concern eligible under the WOSB Program means a small business concern that is at least 51 percent directly and unconditionally owned by, and the management and daily business operations of which are controlled by, one or more women who are citizens of the United States (13 CFR part 127).

"Writing or written" (see "in writing").

Notes of Decisions

Acquisition 1
Affidavits 33
Affiliates 36
Best value 2
Cardinal change 3
Claim 4
Commercial item 6
Connection with 7
Constructive change 8
Constructive suspension 9
Contract 10
Contracting officer 11
Cost or Pricing Data 37
Direct Cost 38
Divisions, subsidiaries, or affiliates 12
Economic price adjustment 13

1 Acquisition

That Pennsylvania Avenue Development Corporation (PADC) followed Federal Acquisition Regulation (FAR) system when it arranged for outside contractor to help it evaluate developer's applications to develop Federal Triangle Development Project did not establish that PADC thought it was bound by FAR in selecting developer; even when PADC conducted its customary development competitions, i.e., competitions for right to develop private projects, its contracts for professional services were "acquisitions" subject to FAR and Competitions in Contracts Act (CICA). Federal Triangle Development Act, §§ 2-10, 40 U.S.C.A. §§ 1101–1109; 31 U.S.C.A. § 9101(3)(H); Federal Property and Administrative Services Act of 1949, § 303 et seq., as amended, 41 U.S.C.A. § 253 et seq. Saratoga Development Corp. v. U.S., 21 F.3d 445, 305, 39 Cont. Cas. Fed. (CCH) P 76649 (D.C. Cir. 1994). United States ☞64.5; United States ☞64.40(1)

Federal Acquisition Regulation (FAR) did not apply to sales contract whereby agency would release product movement sales data from military commissaries to contractor in exchange for a share in the revenue generated by sale of that information and for analytical support services for category management, since contract which did not utilize appropriated funds was not an "acquisition" within ambit of the FAR. 48 C.F.R. § 2.101. Marketing and Management Information, Inc. v. U.S., 57 Fed. Cl. 665 (2003). United States ☞62

Federal Acquisition Regulation (FAR) did not apply to sales contract whereby agency would release product movement sales data from military commissaries to contractor in exchange for a share in the revenue generated by sale of that information and for analytical support services for category management, since contract which did not utilize appropriated funds was not an "acquisition" within ambit of the FAR. 48 C.F.R. § 2.101. Marketing and Management Information, Inc. v. U.S., 57 Fed. Cl. 665 (2003). United States ☞62

2 Best value

Bid protestor's burden is particularly great in negotiated procurements because the contracting officer is entrusted with a relatively high degree of discretion, and greater still, where the procurement is a "best-value" procurement. 48 C.F.R. § 15.605(c). JWK Intern. Corp. v. U.S., 52 Fed. Cl. 650 (2002), aff'd, 56 Fed. Appx. 474 (Fed. Cir. 2003). United States

👉64.60(3.1)

A bid protestor's burden is particularly great in negotiated procurements because the contracting officer is entrusted with a relatively high degree of discretion, and greater still, where the procurement is a "best-value" procurement. 48 C.F.R. § 15.605(c). ManTech Telecommunications and Information Systems Corp. v. U.S., 49 Fed. Cl. 57 (2001), decision aff'd, 30 Fed. Appx. 995 (Fed. Cir. 2002). United States 👉64.60(3.1)

Solicitation which indicated that the greater the equality of the proposals, the more important price would become in selecting "best value," provided a measure of latitude in the best value determination, permitting some price consideration with technically unequal proposals. ITT Federal Services Corp. v. U.S., 45 Fed. Cl. 174 (1999). United States 👉64.40(1)

Solicitation which indicated that the greater the equality of the proposals, the more important price would become in selecting "best value," provided a measure of latitude in the best value determination, permitting some price consideration with technically unequal proposals. ITT Federal Services Corp. v. U.S., 45 Fed. Cl. 174 (1999). United States 👉64.40(1)

3 Cardinal change

"Cardinal change" describes change outside scope of government contract and thus is not governed by changes clause. Miller Elevator Co., Inc. v. U.S., 30 Fed. Cl. 662, 39 Cont. Cas. Fed. (CCH) P 76635 (1994), dismissed, 36 F.3d 1111 (Fed. Cir. 1994). United States 👉73(17)

4 Claim

A claim is a written demand by a party "seeking, as a matter of right, the payment of money in a sum certain, the adjustment or interpretation of contract terms, or other relief arising under or relating to the contract." 48 CFR 2.101 (2006). Appellant's first request for relief, seeking, "costs incurred, fines, and penalties," does not meet the definition of a claim since it requests money, but not in an amount that is a sum certain. Accordingly, this Board has no jurisdiction over the first alternative request for relief. Winslow v. General Services Administration, CBCA 560, 07-2 B.C.A. (CCH) ¶ 33589, 2007 WL 1760947 (U.S. Civilian BCA 2007).

Armed Services Board of Contract Appeals did not have jurisdiction under Contract Disputes Act (CDA) over contractor's appeal from contracting officer's award of termination settlement costs following termination of its contract with Navy to provide guard services at shipyard, where contractor did not submit either a claim or termination settlement proposal that could have ripened into a claim prior to the contracting officer's settlement proposal. Contract Disputes Act of 1978, § 6(a), 41 U.S.C.A. § 605(a); 48 C.F.R. § 2.201. England v. The Swanson Group, Inc., 353 F.3d 1375 (Fed. Cir. 2004). United States 👉73(15)

Under governing version of federal acquisition regulation, request for equitable adjustment (REA) was not "claim" under Contract Disputes Act (CDA) when submitted by government contractor to contracting officer, inasmuch as regulation excluded from definition of "claim" a written demand or assertion seeking payment of more than $100,000 that had not been certified under CDA, and REA, while certified pursuant to defense acquisition regulations, was not certified in accordance with regulation applicable to contractor claims submitted under CDA. 10 U.S.C.A. § 2410(a); Contract Disputes Act of 1978, § 2 et seq., 41 U.S.C.A. § 601 et seq.; 48 C.F.R. §§ 2.101, 33.201, 33.207(c), 243.204-70. Johnson v. Advanced Engineering & Planning Corp., Inc., 292 F. Supp. 2d 846 (E.D. Va. 2003). United States 👉73(9)

Letter from timber purchaser to contracting officer (CO) asserting that timber sale contract was modified pursuant to prior letters from CO proposing modification and its acceptance by down payment, and requesting CO to respond within ten days, constituted a "claim" within meaning of the Contract Disputes Act (CDA). Mills v. U.S., 69 Fed. Cl. 358 (2006). United States 👉73(9)

Letter from contracting officer (CO) responding to letter of timber purchaser in which CO denied there had been any modification to the contract arising from prior letters, and explaining that the parties failed to execute a written agreement to modify the contract constituted a "final decision" for purposes of the Contract Disputes Act (CDA) with respect to purchaser claim that contract had been modified. Mills v. U.S., 69 Fed. Cl. 358 (2006).

United States ☞73(15)

Letter from timber purchaser to contracting officer (CO) asserting that timber sale contract was modified pursuant to prior letters from CO proposing modification and its acceptance by down payment, and requesting CO to respond within ten days, constituted a "claim" within meaning of the Contract Disputes Act (CDA). Mills v. U.S., 69 Fed. Cl. 358 (2006). United States ☞73(9)

Contractor's letters to contracting officer (CO) in which it asked CO to "confirm" its interpretation of exclusivity provision of contract constituted a valid "claim" within meaning of the Contract Disputes Act (CDA), since they sought "interpretation of contract terms" by the CO, in light of impending solicitation which contractor believed violated exclusivity provision. CW Government Travel, Inc. v. U.S., 63 Fed. Cl. 369 (2004). United States ☞73(9)

Contractor's letters to contracting officer (CO) in which it asked CO to "confirm" its interpretation of exclusivity provision of contract constituted a valid "claim" within meaning of the Contract Disputes Act (CDA), since they sought "interpretation of contract terms" by the CO, in light of impending solicitation which contractor believed violated exclusivity provision. CW Government Travel, Inc. v. U.S., 63 Fed. Cl. 369 (2004). United States ☞73(9)

Contractor did not make written demand seeking payment of money in sum certain that would qualify as claim within meaning of Contract Disputes Act (CDA) when it sent letter itemizing amount sought to government employee who was not contracting officer and who was not primary contact on underlying contract, and did not allege that contracting officer timely received its letter, and therefore contractor failed to invoke jurisdiction of Court of Federal Claims with respect to claimed amount. Danka de Puerto Rico, Inc. v. U.S., 63 Fed. Cl. 20 (2004). Federal Courts ☞1076

Contractor did not make written demand seeking payment of money in sum certain that would qualify as claim within meaning of Contract Disputes Act (CDA) when it sent letter itemizing amount sought to government employee who was not contracting officer and who was not primary contact on underlying contract, and did not allege that contracting officer timely received its letter, and therefore contractor failed to invoke jurisdiction of Court of Federal Claims with respect to claimed amount. Danka de Puerto Rico, Inc. v. U.S., 63 Fed. Cl. 20 (2004). Federal Courts ☞1076

Under the Contract Disputes Act (CDA), government contractor filed valid termination for convenience claim with contracting officer (CO) when it submitted second filing to the CO, which was specifically labeled a "claim," updating with increased costs the claims asserted in termination settlement proposal (TSP), and explicitly requesting a final decision from the CO. Contract Disputes Act of 1978, § 6(a), 41 U.S.C.A. § 605(a). Advanced Materials, Inc. v. U.S., 46 Fed. Cl. 697 (2000). United States ☞73(9)

Under the Contract Disputes Act (CDA), government contractor filed valid termination for convenience claim with contracting officer (CO) when it submitted second filing to the CO, which was specifically labeled a "claim," updating with increased costs the claims asserted in termination settlement proposal (TSP), and explicitly requesting a final decision from the CO. Contract Disputes Act of 1978, § 6(a), 41 U.S.C.A. § 605(a). Advanced Materials, Inc. v. U.S., 46 Fed. Cl. 697 (2000). United States ☞73(9)

Under Contract Disputes Act, term "claim" generally refers to each claim for money that is part of divisible case. Contract Disputes Act of 1978, § 6, 41 U.S.C.A. § 605. Alaska Pulp Corp. v. U.S., 34 Fed. Cl. 100, 40 Cont. Cas. Fed. (CCH) P 76841 (1995). United States ☞73(9)

Government contracting officer's notice, to company operating pulp mill under agreement with Forest Service, that it was terminating contract, was "government claim," for purposes of Contract Disputes Act; claim placed in litigation when operator appealed contracting officer's decision. Contract Disputes Act of 1978, § 6, 41 U.S.C.A. § 605. Alaska Pulp Corp. v. U.S., 34 Fed. Cl. 100, 40 Cont. Cas. Fed. (CCH) P 76841 (1995). United States ☞73(9)

Under Contract Disputes Act, term "claim" generally refers to each claim for money that is part of divisible case. Contract Disputes Act of 1978, § 6, 41 U.S.C.A. § 605. Alaska Pulp Corp. v. U.S., 34 Fed. Cl. 100, 40 Cont. Cas. Fed. (CCH) P 76841 (1995). United States ☞73(9)

Government contracting officer's notice, to company operating pulp mill under agreement with Forest Service, that it was terminating contract, was "government claim," for purposes of Contract Disputes Act; claim placed in litigation when operator appealed contracting officer's decision. Contract Disputes Act of 1978, § 6, 41 U.S.C.A. § 605. Alaska Pulp Corp. v. U.S., 34 Fed. Cl. 100, 40 Cont. Cas. Fed. (CCH) P 76841 (1995). United States ☞73(9)

To determine whether claim meets all Contract Disputes Act requirements, entire submission is examined. Contract Disputes Act of 1978, § 6(c)(1), 41 U.S.C.A. § 605(c)(1). McDonnell Douglas Corp. v. U.S., 25 Cl. Ct. 342, 37 Cont. Cas. Fed. (CCH) P 76273, 1992 WL 30189 (1992). United States ☞73(9)

To determine whether claim meets all Contract Disputes Act requirements, entire submission is examined. Contract Disputes Act of 1978, § 6(c)(1), 41 U.S.C.A. § 605(c)(1). McDonnell Douglas Corp. v. U.S., 25 Cl. Ct. 342, 37 Cont. Cas. Fed. (CCH) P 76273, 1992 WL 30189 (1992). United States ☞73(9)

5 Third party claims

Though a third-party beneficiary of a contract to which the government is a direct party may assert a claim against the government in accordance with the rules applicable to third party claims, the law governing third-party beneficiaries is subject to the principle that the government can only be bound by those with authorization to do so. Flexfab, L.L.C. v. U.S., 424 F.3d 1254 (Fed. Cir. 2005). United States ☞70(5)

6 Commercial item

—Commercial Services

Protester challenged the award of a contract for stacking, banding, and weighing zinc lead by alleging that the awardee was not proposing commercial services, as required by the solicitation. The argument is based on paragraph (5) of the commercial item definition at FAR 2.101, which states that services are commercial when they are in support of a commercial item and are obtained from sources that offer them to the general public and the federal government contemporaneously and under similar terms and conditions. GAO found that the lead handling services here do not fall within the scope of this definition because the services here (stacking, banding, weighing, and moving lead and zinc ingots) are not support-type services in the same sense as the categories listed in paragraph (5). Lynwood Machine & Engineering, Inc., B-287652, 2001 CPD ¶ 138 (Comp. Gen. 2001).

Forest Service concluded, based upon an informal market survey, that tree thinning services qualify as a commercial item because the services are not unique, are not used exclusively by the government, and are offered and sold competitively by forestry and nursery firms. There were more than 150 potential offerors on the mailing list for the services, that the local telephone book contained numerous sources for tree thinning services, and that the agency has personal knowledge of several commercial companies engaged in various types of tree services. SHABA does not dispute any of these findings. Thus, these services constituted a commercial item and were required to be solicited under FAR Part 12. SHABA Contracting, B-287430, 2001 CPD ¶ 105 (Comp. Gen. 2001).

The protester, CW Government Travel, Inc. protested the terms of an RFP issued by the Navy for travel management services. The protester alleged that, since the requirement qualified as "commercial services," the Navy could not impose pricing terms that are inconsistent with commercial practices unless it obtained a waiver. The GAO noted, "[b]ased on the research conducted, the contracting officer determined that the services required by the Navy under this procurement fall outside the FAR definition of commercial services; that is, that portions of the travel service requirements were not sold in substantial quantities in the commercial marketplace based on established catalog or market prices performed under standard terms and conditions. . . . Specifically, the contracting officer identified several mandatory tasking requirements that she believed precluded the procurement from being considered an acquisition of commercial services, including: required contractor response to mobilization, contingency operations, and evaluations; mandatory booking of lodging in government bachelor quarters; and required contractor reconciliation of the centrally billed accounts of the Navy's charge card contractor." The GAO stated the general rule that "determining whether a product or service is a commercial item is largely within the discretion of the contracting agency." GAO held that the pricing term being challenged by the protester was consistent with industry practice so that even if the services qualified as "commercial" (as alleged by the protester), the Navy would still be authorized to use the pricing term. Accordingly, GAO denied the protest. CW Government Travel, Inc. d/b/a Carlson Wagonlit Travel; AmericanExpress Travel Related Services Company, Inc., B-283408, B-283408.2, 99-2 CPD ¶ 89 (Comp. Gen. 1999).

DoD issued a commercial item RFP for the movement of household goods of military personnel worldwide. Almost 120 companies that had previously provided this service to the DoD under non-commercial contracts protested, alleging that moving services for DoD are not commercial services because: 1) movements of the household goods of military personnel from one base to another are not like movements of the household goods of non-military personnel; 2) international shipments of household goods are not commercial services because such international shipments are not based on established catalog or market prices; and 3) many of the RFPs requirements are inconsistent with customary commercial practice and depart from standard commercial terms and conditions in the moving industry. GAO denied the protest, and responded to the protester's first argument by finding that moving the household goods of military personnel was not materially different from moving the household goods of non-military personnel (e.g. both involve packing, loading, transport, storing, and delivering). GAO responded to the second allegation by noting that is an established market rate for moving household goods (based on weight of goods moved and distance). Finally, GAO did not find that differences in terms and conditions changed the commercial nature of the services, holding that "there is no requirement that all specifications reflect commercial practice." Aalco Forwarding, Inc., et al., B-277241, B-277241.8, B-277241.9, 97-2 CPD ¶ 110 (Comp. Gen. 1997)

—Sold, leased or licensed or offered for sale lease or license

Protester was not eligible for award of a commercial item contract based on finding by agency that protester failed to propose off-the-shelf commercial items and that the protester was offering test systems that have not been designed yet. Based on this finding alone, the protester was not responsive to the requirements of the solicitation, did not have a substantial chance, or any chance, of winning the award and, therefore, was not prejudiced by selection of another vendor for award. Chant Engineering Co., Inc. v. U.S., 75 Fed. Cl. 62 (2007)

Commerciality was established where the offerors proposed pedestrian monitor had been regularly sold to laboratories, nuclear plants, and scrap metal dealers. Information furnished by the offeror to the agency, identifying commercial sales to power plants in Argentina, Germany, and Switzerland, confirms the commercial nature of the item. Canberra Industries, Inc., B-271016, 96-1 CPD ¶ 269 (Comp. Gen. 1996)

Actual sale or license to the general public is not required for an item to be considered a commercial product. The determination of whether a product is a commercial item is largely within the discretion of the contracting agency, and will not be disturbed by our Office unless it is shown to be unreasonable. Coherent, Inc., B-270998, 96-1 CPD ¶ 214 (Comp. Gen. 1996).

—Minor Modifications

Awardee's proposed explosive ordinance disposal total containment vessel (TCV) is a commercial item, even though it is a modified version of an existing commercially available TCV, where the modification is minor and customarily available in the commercial marketplace. NABCO, Inc., B-293027, B-293027.2, 2004 CPD ¶ 15 (Comp. Gen. 2004) There is no prohibition against making a modification to a commercial item. Under the FAR, commercial item modifications of a type customarily available in the commercial marketplace, or commercial item of a type not customarily available in the commercial marketplace, made to meet government requirements, are permitted. While the RFQ did not incorporate the FAR's commercial item definition, it did not provide for anything different concerning modifications. Rather, the only restriction was that the unit could not be a "prototype unit, pre-production model, or experimental unit." The protester has not shown that the alleged change in the waste disposal system was so significant a modification that it violated this restriction, and the mere fact that Flow may have quoted a TomCat modified in this way does not establish that the unit was not a current production model. NLB Corporation, B-286846, 2001 CPD ¶ 67 (Comp. Gen. 2001)

Agency reasonably determined that awardee's offered product was a commercial item, where the awardee proposed a modified version of its standard commercial product and the modifications were of a type customarily offered in the commercial marketplace and were also minor. Premier Engineering & Manufacturing, Inc., B-283028, B-283028.2, 99-2 CPD ¶ 65 (Comp. Gen. 1999)

Procuring agency reasonably determined that protester's proposal was unacceptable and excluded it from the competitive range in a solicitation for a commercial item where the protester was not offering "commercial off the shelf equipment," as required, but was merely offering to fabricate, for the first time after award, equipment that met the specification. Chant Engineering Company, Inc., B-281521, 99-1 CPD ¶ 45 (Comp. Gen. 1999)

In a procurement for an aircraft test stand, the RFP required that "the test stand shall be an already developed, state-of-the-art, market proven, commercial test stand with a proven reliability track record. Minor modifications are allowed to the existing test stand. . . . The proposed test stand shall be a commercial NDI test stand." Avtron protested, alleging that the awardee's test stand was not an NDI because it had not previously developed the identical test stand that it was proposing to provide to the agency. The GAO denied the protest because it found that the awardee had submitted lists of commercial customers for its commercial test stand, and the stand needed only minor modifications to meet the agency's requirements. The GAO noted that, prior to award, a team of government personnel visited the eventual awardee's production facility and determined that its commercial test stand was very similar to that which it was proposing. This additional effort by the agency enabled the GAO to conclude that "[w]e therefore have no basis to disagree with the agency's conclusion that [the awardee's] proposed test stand met the requirements of the solicitation." Avtron Manufacturing, INc., B-280758, 98-2 CPD ¶ 148 (Comp. Gen. 1998).

The GSA issued a solicitation for the lease of exhibit booths and related services in which it provided 15 days from the RFP release date and the proposal due date. Although an agency must generally allow at lease 30 days for the submission of proposals, FAR 5.203(c), it may allow fewer days when it is acquiring commercial items. FAR 12.205(c). In an effort to support its protest allegation that the agency was required to allow more time for proposal submission, the protester contended that the exhibition booths were not commercial items because "they will have to be extensively modified to meet GSA's specific requirements." In denying the protest, the GAO noted that the FAR definition authorizes minor modifications of commercial items and concluded that "[o]ur review of the record indicates that the modifications at issue here are not so extensive as to fall outside this definition." American Artisan Productions, Inc., B-281409, 98-2 CPD ¶ 155 (Comp. Gen. 1998).

The Coast Guard issued a commercial item solicitation for an emergency exit lighting system to be used in its helicopters. At the debriefing for the protester, the agency inaccurately stated that the awardee lighting system would be custom made for the Coast Guard. The protester alleged that the awardee was ineligible for award because its "custom made" lighting system could not qualify as a commercial item. In the Agency Report, the Coast Guard clarified its debriefing statement, explaining that only certain parts (e.g., brackets and mounting hardware) were being custom made and that the system was "an adaptation of a system commercially available to the general public." The protester did not challenge the Coast Guard's explanation and the GAO considered the issue abandoned. Stratus Systems, Inc., B-281645, 99-1 CPD ¶ 67 (Comp. Gen. 1999).

Agency properly accepted awardee's certification that its proposed pedestrian radiation detector complied with the solicitation's commercial item requirement where the product has been sold to the general public and the modified product offered, based on newer software, is the result of a minor modification which does not change the product's physical characteristics or function. Canberra Industries, Inc., B-271016, 96-1 CPD ¶ 269 (Comp. Gen. 1996).

—General

Radioactive waste disposal service called for in solicitation was not a "commercial item" subject to mandatory procedures of the Federal Acquisition Regulation (FAR), where there were no market prices for the service, and no competitive market for the service. 48 C.F.R. § 2.101, 12.102(a). Envirocare of Utah, Inc. v. U.S., 44 Fed. Cl. 474 (1999), dismissed, 217 F.3d 852 (Fed. Cir. 1999). United States ☞64.10

Regarding the commercial item status of Rados's monitor, the determination of whether a product is a commercial item is largely within the discretion of the contracting agency, and will not be disturbed by our Office unless it is shown to be unreasonable. Canberra Industries, Inc., B-271016, 96-1 CPD ¶ 269 (Comp. Gen. 1996)

Commerciality was established where the offerors proposed pedestrian monitor had been regularly sold to laboratories, nuclear plants, and scrap metal dealers. Information furnished by the offeror to the agency, identifying commercial sales to power plants in Argentina, Germany, and Switzerland, confirms the commercial nature of the item. Canberra Industries, Inc., B-271016, 96-1 CPD ¶ 269 (Comp. Gen. 1996).

—Non-Developmental Items

Incorporation of remittance address to subcontractor's escrow account into contract between contractor and government did not make subcontractor third-party beneficiary to contract, since contracting officers did not know purpose of that address and thus officers, and therefore government, did not have intent to benefit subcontractor directly. Flexfab, L.L.C. v. U.S., 424 F.3d 1254 (Fed. Cir. 2005). United States ☞70(5)

When a government agent with authority to contract on the government's behalf knows of a condition precedent to a third party's performance as a subcontractor, such as receipt of payment directly from the government, and specifically modifies the prime contract so as to ensure the third party's continued performance, the agent, and by implication the government itself, necessarily intends to benefit the third party, and that intent gives rise to standing as a third-party beneficiary to enforce the prime contract. Flexfab, L.L.C. v. U.S., 424 F.3d 1254 (Fed. Cir. 2005). United States ☞70(5)

For third-party beneficiary status to lie with regard to a contract with the government, the contracting officer must be put on notice, by either the contract language or the attendant circumstances, of the relationship between the prime contractor and the third-party subcontractor so that an intent to benefit the third party is fairly attributable to the contracting officer. Flexfab, L.L.C. v. U.S., 424 F.3d 1254 (Fed. Cir. 2005). United States ☞70(5)

Radioactive waste disposal service called for in solicitation was not a "commercial item" subject to mandatory procedures of the Federal Acquisition Regulation (FAR), where there were no market prices for the service, and no competitive market for the service. 48 C.F.R. § 2.101, 12.102(a). Envirocare of Utah, Inc. v. U.S., 44 Fed. Cl. 474 (1999), dismissed, 217 F.3d 852 (Fed. Cir. 1999). United States ☞64.10

In a negotiated procurement for a hand-held global positioning system receiver, award could not properly be made to an offeror whose proposal did not demonstrate that it satisfied the solicitation's requirement for a nondevelopmental item. The RFP included the standard "Definition" clause, FAR § 52.202-1, that defined NDI as including any previously developed item that does not require more than minor modification to satisfy the agency's needs. GAO held: "This definition is in accord with the statutory definition. Thus, to the extent that the agency believes that the term "NDI" is not clearly defined and allows the agency to buy, as NDI, items that require more than minor modification to meet its needs, the agency is simply mistaken." Trimble Navigation, Ltd., B-271882, B-271882.2, 96-2 CPD ¶ 102 (Comp. Gen. 1996).

7 Connection with

Contract awarded by the Bureau of Reclamation to construct a visitors center and parking structure at the Hoover Dam was "in connection with" the Boulder Canyon Project, and thus could be incrementally funded under the authority of section of the Reclamation Project Act authorizing the Secretary of Interior to enter into construction contracts "in which the liability of the United States shall be contingent upon appropriations being made therefor." 43 U.S.C.A. § 388. PCL Const. Services, Inc. v. U.S., 41 Fed. Cl. 242, 42 Cont. Cas. Fed. (CCH) P 77325 (1998), aff'd, 96 Fed. Appx. 672 (Fed. Cir. 2004). United States ☞70(15.1)

8 Constructive change

Constructive change to government contract entails two basic components, the change component and the order or fault component; "change" component describes work outside scope of contract, while "order/fault" component describes reason that contractor performed work. Miller Elevator Co., Inc. v. U.S., 30 Fed. Cl. 662, 39 Cont. Cas. Fed. (CCH) P 76635

(1994), dismissed, 36 F.3d 1111 (Fed. Cir. 1994). United States ☞70(25.1); United States ☞73(17)

To demonstrate constructive change for disputes over contract requirements, contractor must show performance of work in addition to or different from that required under contract, the "change" component, either by express or implied direction of government or by government fault, the "order/fault" component. Miller Elevator Co., Inc. v. U.S., 30 Fed. Cl. 662, 39 Cont. Cas. Fed. (CCH) P 76635 (1994), dismissed, 36 F.3d 1111 (Fed. Cir. 1994). United States ☞73(17)

"Constructive change" occurs where contractor performs work beyond contract requirements, without formal order under changes clause, either by informal order of government or by fault of government. Miller Elevator Co., Inc. v. U.S., 30 Fed. Cl. 662, 39 Cont. Cas. Fed. (CCH) P 76635 (1994), dismissed, 36 F.3d 1111 (Fed. Cir. 1994). United States ☞73(17)

9 Constructive suspension

"Constructive suspension" occurs when work is stopped absent an express order by the contracting officer and the government is found to be responsible for the work stoppage. P.R. Burke Corp. v. U.S., 277 F.3d 1346 (Fed. Cir. 2002). United States ☞73(20)

Government contract was not under "constructive suspension" after government acknowledged that change order should issue and therefore delay in completion of contract was not chargeable to government; government was not obligated under contract to issue change order, even though it agreed to do so, because contract was performable as written, nothing government did or said prevented contractor from submitting contract-compliant plan at any time, and any delay attributable to government was reasonable following its agreement to issue change order. P.R. Burke Corp. v. U.S., 277 F.3d 1346 (Fed. Cir. 2002). United States ☞73(20)

10 Contract

United States' alleged agreement to guaranty payment of monies owed by contractor to subcontractor was governed by Federal Acquisition Regulation (FAR); alleged contract was means chosen by United States to secure subcontractor's services, and those services were intended to benefit United States. 48 C.F.R. §§ 1.000 et seq., 1.104, 2.101. Pacord, Inc. v. U.S., 139 F.3d 1320, 42 Cont. Cas. Fed. (CCH) P 77272, 1999 A.M.C. 909 (9th Cir. 1998). United States ☞70(1)

United States' alleged agreement to guaranty payment of monies owed by contractor to subcontractor was governed by Federal Acquisition Regulation (FAR); alleged contract was means chosen by United States to secure subcontractor's services, and those services were intended to benefit United States. 48 C.F.R. §§ 1.000 et seq., 1.104, 2.101. Pacord, Inc. v. U.S., 139 F.3d 1320, 42 Cont. Cas. Fed. (CCH) P 77272, 1999 A.M.C. 909 (9th Cir. 1998). United States ☞70(1).

The Federal Circuit determined that a Request for Quotations (RFQ) is a "solicitation" and the resulting order is a "contract" as those terms are defined by FAR 2.101. The FAR states: "Solicitation means any request to submit offers or quotations to the Government." Similarly, the FAR defines a "contract" as including "orders, such as purchase orders." CGI Federal Inc. v. U.S., 779 F.3d 1346 (Fed. Cir. 2015).

Implied in fact contract did not exist between subcontractor and government, whereby subcontractor was to be paid directly by government for supplying air-duct hose to contractor, where subcontractor could not show that there was mutual intent to contract, and actual authority to contract, on part of contracting officers. Flexfab, L.L.C. v. U.S., 424 F.3d 1254 (Fed. Cir. 2005). United States ☞69(4)

An Indefinite Delivery/Indefinite Quantity (ID/IQ) contract for services contemplates the issuance of orders for the performance of tasks during the period of the contract. Such orders are contracts within the overall ID/IQ contract. FAR § 2.101. Sea-Land Service, Inc., B-278404, B-278404.2, 98-1 CPD ¶ 47 (Comp. Gen. 1998).

11 Contracting officer

Only those with specific authority can bind the government contractually, and even those persons may do so only to the extent that their authority permits. 48 C.F.R. §§ 1.601(a), 1.602-1(a), 2.101, 4401.000. Gardiner v. Virgin Islands Water & Power Authority, 145 F.3d

635, 40 Fed. R. Serv. 3d 1440 (3d Cir. 1998). United States ☞59

Only those with specific authority can bind the government contractually, and even those persons may do so only to the extent that their authority permits. 48 C.F.R. §§ 1.601(a), 1.602-1(a), 2.101, 4401.000. Gardiner v. Virgin Islands Water & Power Authority, 145 F.3d 635, 40 Fed. R. Serv. 3d 1440 (3d Cir. 1998). United States ☞59

A party who seeks to contract with the government bears the burden of making sure that the person who purportedly represents the government actually has that authority. 48 C.F.R. §§ 1.601(a), 1.602-1(a), 2.101, 4401.000. Gardiner v. Virgin Islands Water & Power Authority, 145 F.3d 635, 40 Fed. R. Serv. 3d 1440 (3d Cir. 1998). United States ☞59

A contracting officer for the United States has the authority to modify contracts. Flexfab, L.L.C. v. U.S., 424 F.3d 1254 (Fed. Cir. 2005). United States ☞72(3)

A contracting officer for the United States has the authority to modify contracts. Flexfab, L.L.C. v. U.S., 424 F.3d 1254 (Fed. Cir. 2005). United States ☞72(3)

Contracting officer, as official representative of government in doing business with public, has authority to modify public contracts. 48 C.F.R. § 2.101. LDG Timber Enterprises, Inc. v. Glickman, 114 F.3d 1140, 41 Cont. Cas. Fed. (CCH) P 77109 (Fed. Cir. 1997). United States ☞72(3)

12 Divisions, subsidiaries, or affiliates

Common control did not exist between defense contractor and temporary staffing company for purposes of regulation limiting profits on sales between "divisions, subdivisions, subsidiaries or affiliates" under contractor's common control, given that company's sole shareholders held no direct shareholder interest in contractor and did not hold any positions of management, employment, or influence with contractor, shareholders ceded management and daily operational decision- making for company to its president-chief executive officer (CEO), president-CEO did not hold ownership interest in, or occupy any official or management position with, contractor, two businesses did not share common space or engage in business in same industry, and relationship between two businesses was fully disclosed to government entity that was responsible for ensuring that contractor's contract billings complied with federal regulations in all respects, which did not object in any of its audit reports. 48 C.F.R. §§ 2.101, 19.101, 31.205-26(e). U.S. ex rel. Kholi v. General Atomics, 2003 WL 21536816 (S.D. Cal. 2003). United States ☞70(12.1)

13 Economic price adjustment

Section of the Federal Acquisition Regulation (FAR) which authorizes the government's use of "[f]ixed-price contracts with economic price adjustment" authorized the use of economic price adjustment (EPA) clauses that adopt marketbased price indexes to provide adjustments in a contractor's established prices. 48 C.F.R. § 16.203-1. Williams Alaska Petroleum, Inc. v. U.S., 57 Fed. Cl. 789 (2003). United States ☞70(18)

14 Effective date

Determination of Defense Logistics Agency (DLA) that it did not have jurisdiction over whistleblower claim by employee of defense contractor, under statute prohibiting discrimination against defense contractor whistleblowers, because contract was entered into with contractor prior to effective date of statute, and none of the modifications of contract were "contracts entered into" after statute's effective date, in that modifications were contemplated in original contract, was reasonable interpretation of statute, which had to be deferred to under Chevron. 10 U.S.C.(1994 Ed.) § 2409a. Micalizzi Micalizzi v. Rumsfeld, 247 F. Supp. 2d 556 (D. Vt. 2003). West's Key Number Digest, United States ☞72(1.1)

Phrase "in effect on the date of this contract" in pricing of adjustments clause of letter contract was unambiguous and meant the designated effective date of the contract rather than the date the contract was executed, for purposes of applicable cost accounting standards (CAS); thus, cost accounting standard preventing contractor from recovering costs on stepped-up assets was not applicable because contract's designated effective date preceded the effective date of the standard. 48 C.F.R. § 31.205-52. DynCorp Information Systems, LLC v. U.S., 58 Fed. Cl. 446 (2003). West's Key Number Digest, United States ☞70(18)

15 Equitable adjustment

In determining whether costs incurred by Navy contractor in preparing request for equitable adjustment (REA) which did not qualify as claim under Contract Disputes Act (CDA) were recoverable contract administration costs, rather than costs incurred in connection with prosecution of CDA claim against government, Armed Services Board of Contract Appeals could consider the course of negotiations between the parties to determine the objective purpose behind contractor's submission of REA. Contract Disputes Act of 1978, § 2 et seq., 41 U.S.C.A. § 601 et seq.; 48 C.F.R. §§ 2.101, 31.205-33(d), 33.201. Johnson v. Advanced Engineering & Planning Corp., Inc., 292 F. Supp. 2d 846 (E.D. Va. 2003). United States ⊙74(12.1)

"Equitable adjustment" encompasses quantitative difference between reasonable cost of performance of government contract without added, deleted, or substituted work and reasonable costs or performance with addition, deletion, or substitution. Miller Elevator Co., Inc. v. U.S., 30 Fed. Cl. 662, 39 Cont. Cas. Fed. (CCH) P 76635 (1994), dismissed, 36 F.3d 1111 (Fed. Cir. 1994). United States ⊙70(22.1)

16 Established prices

Economic price adjustment (EPA) clause in contracts for supply of jet fuel was not valid under the Federal Acquisition Regulation (FAR) as an "adjustment based on established prices," where clause used as escalator the PPI Index derived from the Petroleum Marketing Monthly (PPM), a monthly government publication of petroleum sales data setting forth average prices for petroleum products, as term "established prices" refers to established market prices. 48 C.F.R. § 16.203-1(a). Calcasieu Refining Co. v. U.S., 2003 WL 22049528 (Ct. Fed. Cl. 2003), Unreported. United States ⊙70(18)

17 Estoppel

In government contracts, "estoppel" proscribes government from escaping liability for statements, actions, or inactions relied upon by another contracting party; "estoppel" thus prevents undue hardship to contractor who has detrimentally relied upon earlier inconsistent position of government. Miller Elevator Co., Inc. v. U.S., 30 Fed. Cl. 662, 39 Cont. Cas. Fed. (CCH) P 76635 (1994), dismissed, 36 F.3d 1111 (Fed. Cir. 1994). United States ⊙70(36)

18 Executive agencies

Federal procurement regulations applicable to "executive agencies," defined to include any wholly owned government corporation, do not apply to National Railroad Passenger Corporation (Amtrak) which is mixed-ownership government corporation. 31 U.S.C.A. § 9101(2)(A), (3); 48 C.F.R. §§ 1.101, 2.101. Hill Intern., Inc. v. National R.R. Passenger Corp., 957 F. Supp. 548, 41 Cont. Cas. Fed. (CCH) P 77108 (D.N.J. 1996). Railroads ⊙5.51; United States ⊙64.5

Federal Acquisition Regulation (FAR) does not apply to the Administrative Office of the United States Courts (AOUSC), as the AOUSC is not an "executive agency" within meaning of the FAR. 48 C.F.R. §§ 1.101, 2.101. Novell, Inc. v. U.S., 46 Fed. Cl. 601 (2000). United States ⊙64.5

19 Interested party

Manufacturer of office automation systems was "interested party," for purposes of Tucker Act, and thus had standing to challenge Department of Labor's (DOL) decision to standardize its software applications exclusively to software manufactured by competitor as violative of Competition in Contracting Act (CICA), where DOL refused to engage in competitive procurement for its office automation systems, and manufacturer submitted bid nonetheless. 10 U.S.C.A. § 2304; 28 U.S.C.A. § 1491(b)(1); Federal Property and Administrative Services Act of 1949, § 303, as amended, 41 U.S.C.A. § 253; 48 C.F.R. §§ 16.501-1, 16.501-2. Corel Corp. v. U.S., 165 F. Supp. 2d 12 (D.D.C. 2001). United States ⊙64.60(2)

20 Meaningful

Discussions with offerors whose proposals are found to be in the competitive range must be "meaningful," and requirement is not met if an offeror is not advised, in some way, of defects in its proposal that do not meet the requirements of the solicitation. 48 C.F.R. § 15.306(d). ManTech Telecommunications and Information Systems Corp. v. U.S., 49 Fed. Cl. 57 (2001), decision aff'd, 30 Fed. Appx. 995 (Fed. Cir. 2002). United States ⊙64.40(1)

21 Open period

Provision in Pennsylvania Avenue Development Corporation (PADC) procedures authorizing modifications of or additions to timely submissions in developer competition under Federal Triangle Development Act in cases where PADC sets "open period" during which all developers are allowed to submit modifications did not oblige PADC to hold "open period." Federal Triangle Development Act, §§ 2-10, 40 U.S.C.A. §§ 1101–1109. Saratoga Development Corp. v. U.S., 21 F.3d 445, 305, 39 Cont. Cas. Fed. (CCH) P 76649 (D.C. Cir. 1994). United States ☞64.40(4)

Pennsylvania Avenue Development Corporation's (PADC's) failure to hold "open period" during which offerors could modify their proposals to develop federal office complex under Federal Triangle Development Act in response to PADC's adoption of affirmative action resolution was not abuse of discretion. Federal Triangle Development Act, §§ 2-10, 40 U.S.C.A. §§ 1101–1109. Saratoga Development Corp. v. U.S., 21 F.3d 445, 305, 39 Cont. Cas. Fed. (CCH) P 76649 (D.C. Cir. 1994). United States ☞64.40(4)

Pennsylvania Avenue Development Corporation's (PADC's) failure to hold "open period" during which offerors could modify their proposals to develop Federal Triangle Development Project in response to PADC's deletion of financing criteria was not abuse of discretion, where PADC specifically asked each developer, both by letter and in oral presentation, whether deletion of financial criterion would have any impact on its proposal and neither protesting developer nor any other development team identified any such impact, and protesting developer offered, even on appeal, only contradictory and ill supported claims of how it would have changed its application in response to deletion of financing criterion. Federal Triangle Development Act, §§ 2-10, 40 U.S.C.A. §§ 1101–1109. Saratoga Development Corp. v. U.S., 21 F.3d 445, 305, 39 Cont. Cas. Fed. (CCH) P 76649 (D.C. Cir. 1994). United States ☞64.40(4)

22 Performance contract

Government contract for demolition and construction of sewage treatment plant was "performance contract," performable as written; although contractor asserted that contract was design contract and that government's poor design entitled contractor to time extension and associated costs to remedy alleged design deficiencies, nothing in description of contract dictated manner in which contractor was to perform, contract merely identified what contractor was required to have completed by end of performance. P.R. Burke Corp. v. U.S., 277 F.3d 1346 (Fed. Cir. 2002). United States ☞70(8)

23 Procurement

Arrangement whereby private hospital agreed to pay one half of the cost of acquisition by Veterans Affairs Medical Center of a piece of medical equipment, with the equipment to be placed in the private hospital and used by both the VA and the hospital, was not a "procurement" for purposes of the Competition in Contracting Act (CICA). Federal Property and Administrative Services Act of 1949, § 303(a), as amended, 41 U.S.C.A. § 253(a). Rapides Regional Medical Center v. Secretary, Dept. of Veterans' Affairs, 974 F.2d 565, 38 Cont. Cas. Fed. (CCH) P 76445 (5th Cir. 1992). United States ☞64.10

Definition of "procurement" in the Federal Procurement Policy Act which establishes the Office of Federal Procurement Policy within the Office of Management and Budget does not apply to the Competition in Contracting Act (CICA). Office of Federal Procurement Policy Act, § 4, 41 U.S.C.A. § 403; Federal Property and Administrative Services Act of 1949, § 303(a), as amended, 41 U.S.C.A. § 253(a). Rapides Regional Medical Center v. Secretary, Dept. of Veterans' Affairs, 974 F.2d 565, 38 Cont. Cas. Fed. (CCH) P 76445 (5th Cir. 1992). United States ☞64.10

Even if agreement between hospital and Veterans Affairs Medical Center for acquisition and use of piece of medical equipment was a "procurement" for purposes of the Competition in Contracting Act (CICA), statute authorizing the Veterans Administration to enter into such arrangements was a procurement procedure "expressly authorized by statute" and thus not subject to the full and open competition requirements of CICA. 38 U.S.C.A. §§ 8153, 8153(b); Federal Property and Administrative Services Act of 1949, § 303(a)(1), as amended, 41 U.S.C.A. § 253(a)(1). Rapides Regional Medical Center v. Secretary, Dept. of Veterans' Affairs, 974 F.2d 565, 38 Cont. Cas. Fed. (CCH) P 76445 (5th Cir. 1992). United States ☞64.10

Existing procedures of Pennsylvania Avenue Development Corporation (PADC) for development competition for construction of federal office complex, pursuant to Federal Triangle Development Act, did not have to include compliance with Federal Acquisition Regulations (FAR) system or Competition in Contracting Act (CICA); although PADC, as wholly owned government corporation, was subject to those authorities, FAR applied only to acquisitions and CICA applied only to government procurements, and choosing developer for project did not constitute "acquiring" or "procuring" within meaning of FAR and CICA. Federal Triangle Development Act, §§ 2-10, 40 U.S.C.A. §§ 1101–1109; 31 U.S.C.A. § 9101(3)(H); Federal Property and Administrative Services Act of 1949, § 303 et seq., as amended, 41 U.S.C.A. § 253 et seq. Saratoga Development Corp. v. U.S., 21 F.3d 445, 305, 39 Cont. Cas. Fed. (CCH) P 76649 (D.C. Cir. 1994). United States ☞64.5; United States ☞64.40(1)

United States Department of Labor's (DOL) decision to standardize its office software applications to those manufactured by single software manufacturer was not "procurement" decision to which Competition in Contracting Act's (CICA) sole source or name-brand only rules applied; decision did not involve actual purchase of software, and DOL subsequently elected to utilize procurement procedures expressly authorized by Federal Acquisition Streamlining Act (FASA) rather than engage in full and open competition under CICA. Federal Property and Administrative Services Act of 1949, §§ 303(a)(1), 303J(a)(2), as amended, 41 U.S.C.A. §§ 253(a)(1), 253j(a)(2); 48 C.F.R. § 6.001(f). Corel Corp. v. U.S., 165 F. Supp. 2d 12 (D.D.C. 2001). United States ☞64.10

United States Department of Labor's (DOL) decision to standardize its office software applications to those manufactured by single software manufacturer was not "procurement" decision to which Competition in Contracting Act's (CICA) sole source or name-brand only rules applied; decision did not involve actual purchase of software, and DOL subsequently elected to utilize procurement procedures expressly authorized by Federal Acquisition Streamlining Act (FASA) rather than engage in full and open competition under CICA. Federal Property and Administrative Services Act of 1949, §§ 303(a)(1), 303J(a)(2), as amended, 41 U.S.C.A. §§ 253(a)(1), 253j(a)(2); 48 C.F.R. § 6.001(f). Corel Corp. v. U.S., 165 F. Supp. 2d 12 (D.D.C. 2001). United States ☞64.10

Term "procurement," as used in competition in Contracting Act (CICA), means payment of money or conferral of other benefits to obtain goods or services. Federal Property and Administrative Services Act of 1949, § 302(a), 41 U.S.C.A. § 252(a). Health Systems Architects, Inc. v. Shalala, 992 F. Supp. 804 (D. Md. 1998). United States ☞64.10

Term "procurement," as used in competition in Contracting Act (CICA), means payment of money or conferral of other benefits to obtain goods or services. Federal Property and Administrative Services Act of 1949, § 302(a), 41 U.S.C.A. § 252(a). Health Systems Architects, Inc. v. Shalala, 992 F. Supp. 804 (D. Md. 1998). United States ☞64.10

Pursuant to the Competition in Contracting Act, government is required to specify its needs and solicit proposals "in a manner designed to achieve full and open competition for the procurement," and fact that the procurement is a commercial item acquisition does not relieve government of such obligation. 10 U.S.C.A. § 2305(a)(1)(A)(i). Candle Corp. v. U.S., 40 Fed. Cl. 658, 42 Cont. Cas. Fed. (CCH) P 77276 (1998). United States ☞64.10

Pursuant to the Competition in Contracting Act, government is required to specify its needs and solicit proposals "in a manner designed to achieve full and open competition for the procurement," and fact that the procurement is a commercial item acquisition does not relieve government of such obligation. 10 U.S.C.A. § 2305(a)(1)(A)(i). Candle Corp. v. U.S., 40 Fed. Cl. 658, 42 Cont. Cas. Fed. (CCH) P 77276 (1998). United States ☞6410.

24 Remain in operation

Contractor's interpretation of phrase, "remain in operation," in government contract, to mean that component of sewage treatment process could be shut down during construction, was unreasonable; although contractor asserted that latent ambiguity existed in contract, on basis that it was impossible to perform contract while component was in operation, and therefore contract was required to be interpreted in its favor, part of plant that contractor sought to shut down was key component of sewage treatment system and therefore could not be shut down if plant was to "remain in operation." P.R. Burke Corp. v. U.S., 277 F.3d 1346 (Fed. Cir. 2002). United States ☞70(8)

25 Responsible bidder

The federal government decides who is a "responsible bidder," for purposes of an award of a procurement contract, using applicable federal laws and regulations. 48 C.F.R. § 9.104-1. LeBoeuf, Lamb, Greene & MacRae, LLP v. Abraham, 215 F. Supp. 2d 73 (D.D.C. 2002), opinion vacated, 347 F.3d 315 (D.C. Cir. 2003) (vacated and remanded to district court for determination of the adequacy of the Department of Energy's evaluation of an apparent conflict of interest, and, if plaintiff prevails, the nature of appropriate relief in light of the DOE's need for expert legal services). United States ⊶64.45(2)

26 Specifications

"Performance specifications" set forth an objective or standard to be achieved, and the successful bidder is expected to exercise his ingenuity in achieving that objective or standard of performance, selecting the means and assuming a corresponding responsibility for that selection; "design specifications," on the other hand, describe in precise detail the materials to be employed and the manner in which the work is to be performed and the contractor has no discretion to deviate from the specifications, but is required to follow them as a road map. P.R. Burke Corp. v. U.S., 277 F.3d 1346 (Fed. Cir. 2002). United States ⊶73(1)

27 Subject to availability of funds

Government contractor waived any objection to "subject to the availability of funds" clause in contract, which purported to make government's obligation contingent upon the availability of appropriated funds, where use of clause was apparent on face of solicitation, but contractor raised no objection prior to submission of bids, rather than subsequent to contract completion. PCL Const. Services, Inc. v. U.S., 41 Fed. Cl. 242, 42 Cont. Cas. Fed. (CCH) P 77325 (1998), aff'd, 96 Fed. Appx. 672 (Fed. Cir. 2004). United States ⊶74(6)

"Subject to the availability of funds" clause, which the Federal Acquisition Regulation requires for the use of indefinite- quantity or requirements contracts for services, may be used beyond those specialized contracting situations. 48 C.F.R. § 52.232-19. PCL Const. Services, Inc. v. U.S., 41 Fed. Cl. 242, 42 Cont. Cas. Fed. (CCH) P 77325 (1998), aff'd, 96 Fed. Appx. 672 (Fed. Cir. 2004). United States ⊶70(15.1)

28 Supplies

The term "supplies" as used in a contract provision incorporating the Cargo Preference Act requirement to use United States flag vessels to transport military cargo was not ambiguous and included both components and end items. 10 U.S.C.A. § 2631. Craft Mach. Works, Inc. v. U.S., 926 F.2d 1110, 36 Cont. Cas. Fed. (CCH) P 76020 (Fed. Cir. 1991). United States ⊶70(12.1)

29 Termination

Determination by Court of Appeals that Armed Services Board of Contract Appeals lacked jurisdiction over contractor's appeal from contracting officer's award of termination settlement costs following termination of its contract with Navy did not bar contractor from submitting a termination settlement proposal to the contracting officer; such a proposal would put contracting officer in a position either to reject it on the ground that it was untimely or to consider it on the merits. Contract Disputes Act of 1978, § 6(a), 41 U.S.C.A. § 605(a); 48 C.F.R. § 2.201. England v. The Swanson Group, Inc., 353 F.3d 1375 (Fed. Cir. 2004). United States ⊶74(6)

30 Total cost

"Total cost" method of calculating damages under government contract calculates monetary difference between amount of costs anticipated in bid price from actual cost of performance plus profit. Miller Elevator Co., Inc. v. U.S., 30 Fed. Cl. 662, 39 Cont. Cas. Fed. (CCH) P 76635 (1994), dismissed, 36 F.3d 1111 (Fed. Cir. 1994). United States ⊶74(13)

31 Waiver

"Express waiver" involves exchange of relinquishment of contract right for defined consideration; however, waiver may also occur by implication. Miller Elevator Co., Inc. v. U.S., 30 Fed. Cl. 662, 39 Cont. Cas. Fed. (CCH) P 76635 (1994), dismissed, 36 F.3d 1111 (Fed. Cir. 1994). United States ⊶73(3)

"Waiver" describes abdication of right under government contract. Miller Elevator Co., Inc. v. U.S., 30 Fed. Cl. 662, 39 Cont. Cas. Fed. (CCH) P 76635 (1994), dismissed, 36 F.3d 1111 (Fed. Cir. 1994). United States ☞70(36); United States ☞74(6)

32 Writing

United States' alleged oral agreement to guaranty payment of monies owed by government contractor to subcontractor was not necessarily invalid, even though it was governed by Federal Acquisition Regulation (FAR), which required that commitments obligating United States to expenditure of appropriated funds be in writing. 48 C.F.R. § 2.101. Pacord, Inc. v. U.S., 139 F.3d 1320, 42 Cont. Cas. Fed. (CCH) P 77272, 1999 A.M.C. 909 (9th Cir. 1998). United States ☞65; United States ☞69(1)

Where the regulations require that a contract modification be written, an "oral" modification not reduced to writing and signed by both parties simply is not effective. In re Kato Corp., A.S.B.C.A. No. 51462, 6-2 B.C.A. (CCH) ¶ 33,293, 2006 WL 1461129 (Armed Serv. B.C.A. 2006).

33 Affidavits

Bid protestor would not be permitted to supplement the record with affidavits of its employees and purported statements of government officials; statements in employees' affidavits were irrelevant in that they did not purport to contain statements by contracting (CO) officer or his authorized representative, and purported statements by government employees were inadmissible hearsay. Cardinal Maintenance Service, Inc. v. U.S., 63 Fed. Cl. 98 (2004). West's Key Number Digest, United States ☞64.60(3.1)

34 Jurisdiction

Even if government contractor's claim for amounts allegedly due on copy machines purportedly covered under leaseto- own plan qualified as non-routine request for compensation, such that there did not have to be pre-existing dispute between parties, lack of written demand to contracting officer for payment of sum certain required under Contract Disputes Act (CDA) precluded contractor's invocation of jurisdiction of Court of Federal Claims. Danka de Puerto Rico, Inc. v. U.S., 63 Fed. Cl. 20 (2004). Federal Courts ☞1076

Pursuant to Contract Disputes Act (CDA), government contractor failed to invoke jurisdiction of Court of Federal Claims with respect to its claim for $109,040.91 allegedly due on copy machines purportedly covered under lease-to-own plan when contractor did not make written demand upon contracting officer for such amount, and did not certify that claim was made in good faith, that supporting data was accurate and complete to the best of contractor's knowledge and belief, and that amount accurately reflected contract adjustment for which contractor believed government was liable. Danka de Puerto Rico, Inc. v. U.S., 63 Fed. Cl. 20 (2004). Federal Courts ☞1076

35 Final decision

Letter from contracting officer (CO) responding to letter of timber purchaser in which CO denied there had been any modification to the contract arising from prior letters, and explaining that the parties failed to execute a written agreement to modify the contract constituted a "final decision" for purposes of the Contract Disputes Act (CDA) with respect to purchaser claim that contract had been modified. Mills v. U.S., 69 Fed. Cl. 358 (2006). United States ☞73(15)

36 Affiliates

Common control did not exist between defense contractor and temporary staffing company for purposes of regulation limiting profits on sales between "divisions, subdivisions, subsidiaries or affiliates" under contractor's common control, given that company's sole shareholders held no direct shareholder interest in contractor and did not hold any positions of management, employment, or influence with contractor, shareholders ceded management and daily operational decision- making for company to its president-chief executive officer (CEO), president-CEO did not hold ownership interest in, or occupy any official or management position with, contractor, two businesses did not share common space or engage in business in same industry, and relationship between two businesses was fully disclosed to government entity that was responsible for ensuring that contractor's contract billings complied with federal regulations in all respects, which did not object in any of its audit reports. 48 C.F.R. §§ 2.101, 19.101, 31.205-26(e). U.S. ex rel. Kholi v. General Atomics, 2003 WL 21536816 (S.D. Cal. 2003), Unreported. United States ☞70(12.1)

37 Cost or Pricing Data

A proposal does not fall under the definition of cost or pricing data as prescribed by the regulations. Cost or pricing data consist of all facts which reasonably can be expected to contribute to sound estimates of future costs as well as to the validity of costs already incurred. A contractor's proposal is not a set of facts consistent with this definition. Rather, a contractor's offer is a mix of judgments as to how best to accomplish contract work at a price that is developed to cover anticipated cost and a satisfactory profit. That a verifiable "fact" may be included in such a document does not detract from its overall judgmental nature. The government's for contract price reduction based upon proposal misstatements or inaccuracies are not cognizable under TINA since a proposal is not cost or pricing data. United Technologies Corp., Appeals of, A.S.B.C.A. No. 51410, 04-1 B.C.A. (CCH) ¶ 32556, 2004 WL 483216 (Armed Serv. B.C.A. 2004), on reconsideration, A.S.B.C.A. No. 51410, A.S.B.C.A. No. 53089, A.S.B.C.A. No. 53349, 05-1 B.C.A. (CCH) ¶ 32860, 2005 WL 147601 (Armed Serv. B.C.A. 2005), decision aff'd, 463 F.3d 1261 (Fed. Cir. 2006).

A purchase history, including vendor quotes and price/cost analysis, for recent purchase of the same parts as those at issue falls within the definition of cost or pricing data at FAR 15.801 [presently at FAR 2.101]. The fact that the purchase history pertained to a contract other than the one being negotiated was not persuasive to the board. In re McDonnell Douglas Helicopter Systems, A.S.B.C.A. No. 50447, A.S.B.C.A. No. 50448, A.S.B.C.A. No. 50449, 2000 WL 1286267 (Armed Serv. B.C.A. 2000).

If price agreement occurred on 22 May 1986, a 4 June 1986 vendor quote was not "cost or pricing data" for purposes of the Truth in Negotiations Act. Under the definition of cost or pricing data applicable here, cost or pricing data consists of "all facts as of the time of price agreement . . . ." Consequently, the quote would not be cost or pricing data since it would have been received after the date of agreement on price. Appeals of Arral Industries, Inc., A.S.B.C.A. No. 41493, A.S.B.C.A. No. 41494, 96-1 B.C.A. (CCH) ¶ 28030, 1995 WL 645737 (Armed Serv. B.C.A. 1995).

Direct labor hours available prior to execution of the certificate of current cost or pricing data constitute cost or pricing data that the contractor must update prior to execution of the certification. Appeal of Lambert Engineering Co., A.S.B.C.A. No. 13338, 69-1 B.C.A. (CCH) ¶ 7663, 1969 WL 934 (Armed Serv. B.C.A. 1969).

38 Direct Cost

A direct cost is any cost that can be identified specifically with a particular final cost objective. Costs identified specifically with the contract are direct costs of the contract and are to be charged directly to the contract. Bid and proposal costs incurred pursuant to the terms of a Memorandum of Agreement (MOA) do not support multiple cost objectives and cannot be allocated as indirect costs. Such costs must be allocated directly to the MOA. U.S. v. TRW, Inc., 2000 WL 33400196 (C.D. Cal. 2000).

39 Latent Defect

Discovery of a deficiency after acceptance, which is unknown at the time of acceptance, does not automatically equate to a latent defect. Generally, a latent defect is defined as one which existed at the time of acceptance, but which could not have been discovered by reasonable care or inspection. In proving the existence of a latent defect, therefore, the Government must demonstrate that a defect existed at the time of acceptance and that this defect could not have been discovered by reasonable care or inspection. Appeal of Ahern Painting Contractors, Inc., G.S.B.C.A. No. 7912, G.S.B.C.A. No. 8368, G.S.B.C.A. No. 8697, 90-1 B.C.A. (CCH) ¶ 22291, 1989 WL 112842 (Gen. Services Admin. B.C.A. 1989).

Government's contention that the defective pointing and caulking are latent defects fails for the reason that the agency chose not to undertake a very simple series of tests which, under the circumstances, were the only reasonable form of inspection to insure compliance with contract requirements. With the exercise of reasonable and due care, the defects in pointing and caulking complained of by the agency could have been readily discovered prior to acceptance. Appeal of Ahern Painting Contractors, Inc., G.S.B.C.A. No. 7912, G.S.B.C.A.

No. 8368, G.S.B.C.A. No. 8697, 90-1 B.C.A. (CCH) ¶ 22291, 1989 WL 112842 (Gen. Services Admin. B.C.A. 1989).

40 Source selection information

Disclosure to one vendor, prior to release of the information to other competitors, that the scope of work under the solicitation would consolidate two existing contracts, and that the procurement would be conducted as an 8(a) set-aside did not violate the Procurement Integrity Act's prohibition of non-disclosure of source selection information. Neither the Act nor the implementing regulations confer source selection information status on every piece of information relevant to a given procurement. The information said to have been improperly disclosed generally relates to matters that are administrative in nature and does not fall into any of the categories of information expressly identified in the regulation. Cexec, Inc. v. Department of Energy, G.S.B.C.A. No. 12909-P, 95-1 B.C.A. (CCH) ¶ 27380, 1994 WL 706767 (Gen. Services Admin. B.C.A. 1994).

41 Signature or signed

Signature or signed means "the discrete, verifiable symbol of an individual which, when affixed to a writing with the knowledge and consent of the individual, indicates a present intention to authenticate the writing. This includes electronic symbols." A stamp bearing the company's name ("Tokyo Company - For General Contracting & Services, Baghdad-Iraq Build 23 St Al-Karadaa") and the typed but unsigned name "Beniamen Monadhil" as "General Manager of Company" are not particularized and do not specifically identify the person purporting to sign the certification. Therefore, the stamp does not satisfy the definition of "signature" of "signed." Tokyo Co., ASBCA No. 59059, 14-1 BCA ¶ 35590 (Armed Serv.B.C.A. 2014)

Subpart 2.2 Definitions Clause

§ 2.201 Contract clause.

Insert the clause at 52.202-1, Definitions, in solicitations and contracts that exceed the simplified acquisition threshold.

PART 3 IMPROPER BUSINESS PRACTICES AND PERSONAL CONFLICTS OF INTEREST

§ 3.000 Scope of part.

Subpart 3.1 Safeguards

Subpart 3.2 Contractor Gratuities to Government Personnel

Subpart 3.3 Reports of Suspected Antitrust Violations

Subpart 3.4 Contingent Fees

Subpart 3.10 Contractor Code of Business Ethics and Conduct

Subpart 3.11 Preventing Personal Conflicts of Interest for Contractor Employees Performing Acquisition Functions

§ 3.000 Scope of part.

This part prescribes policies and procedures for avoiding improper business practices and personal conflicts of interest and for dealing with their apparent or actual occurrence.

Notes of Decisions
Standards of conduct, generally 1

1 Standards of conduct, generally

Purpose of regulation regarding government-contractor relationships is to set a general standard of conduct for agency procurement practices. 48 C.F.R. § 3.101-1. INSLAW, Inc. v. U.S., 40 Fed. Cl. 843, 42 Cont. Cas. Fed. (CCH) P 77302 (1998). United States ☞64.5

Prospective Veterans Administration contractor, whose bid on contract for construction of VA facility was not accepted due to appearance of conflict of interest in negotiating process, was not entitled to timely notice and hearing before VA refused to award contract and formally advertised procurement, as contractor had no property interest in award of public contract which would entitle it to due process hearing. U.S.C.A. Const.Amends. 5, 14. Refine Const. Co., Inc. v. U.S., 12 Cl. Ct. 56, 34 Cont. Cas. Fed. (CCH) P 75242 (1987). Constitutional Law ☞277(1)

Subpart 3.1 Safeguards

§ 3.101 Standards of conduct.

§ 3.101-1 General.

Government business shall be conducted in a manner above reproach and, except as authorized by statute or regulation, with complete impartiality and with preferential treatment for none. Transactions relating to the expenditure of public funds require the highest degree of public trust and an impeccable standard of conduct. The general rule is to avoid strictly any conflict of interest or even the appearance of a conflict of interest in Government-contractor relationships. While many Federal laws and regulations place restrictions on the actions of Government personnel, their official conduct must, in addition, be such that they would have no reluctance to make a full public disclosure of their actions.

United States Code Annotated

Definitions, see 41 U.S.C.A. § 403.

Restrictions on disclosing and obtaining contractor bid or proposal information or source selection information, see 41 U.S.C.A. § 423.

Notes of Decisions

In general 1
Conflict of interest 2
Private right of action 3

1 In general

Participation of four local managers on evaluation boards did not constitute prejudicial conflict of interest in A-76 cost comparison study of whether maintenance and motor transport services at naval air station should be contracted out to private contractor, where only one of the managers was directly associated with a function under study, and he was a military officer not concerned with loss of employment. 48 C.F.R. § 3.101-1. JWK Intern. Corp. v. U.S., 52 Fed. Cl. 650 (2002), aff'd, 56 Fed. Appx. 474 (Fed. Cir. 2003). United States ☞64.40(1)

Purpose of regulation regarding government-contractor relationships is to set a general standard of conduct for agency procurement practices. 48 C.F.R. § 3.101-1. INSLAW, Inc. v. U.S., 40 Fed. Cl. 843, 42 Cont. Cas. Fed. (CCH) P 77302 (1998). United States ☞64.5

Impeccable-conduct standard set forth in regulation concerning government-contractor relationships was not appropriate standard of care to apply to contractor's equitable claim in congressional reference case; type of harm alleged, misuse of the contractor's data rights, was not contemplated by regulation on its face, and although the hazard of unfair treatment of contractors is arguably addressed by the regulation, its primary purpose is clearly to protect the integrity of the government procurement system. 48 C.F.R. § 3.101-1. INSLAW, Inc. v. U.S., 40 Fed. Cl. 843, 42 Cont. Cas. Fed. (CCH) P 77302 (1998). United States ☞74(7)

In participating on behalf of contractor in contractor's negotiations with Veterans Administration for construction of VA facility, VA employee violated executive order and VA regulations forbidding any activity adversely affecting confidence of public and integrity of Government; although contractor was preselected by Small Business Administration, resulting in contractor having no competition for contract, VA employee's actions in appearing on behalf of contractor and in misrepresenting to contractor that he had received permission from his VA supervisor to participate in negotiations created appearance of conflict of interest. Executive Order No. 11222, § 201(c)(6), 18 U.S.C.A. § 201 note. Refine Const. Co., Inc. v. U.S., 12 Cl. Ct. 56, 34 Cont. Cas. Fed. (CCH) P 75242 (1987). United States ☞41

Agency failed to determine whether the evaluators of the protester's proposal under a Small Business Innovation Research program solicitation had a conflict of interest, where the evaluators were employed by firms that promote a type of technology that assertedly is directly challenged by the type of technology offered in the protester's proposal. Celadon

Laboratories, Inc., B-298533, 2006 CPD ¶ 158 (Comp. Gen. 2006).

In addressing organizational conflicts of interest, where the record establishes that a conflict exists, GAO will presume that the protester was prejudiced, unless the record establishes the absence of prejudice. Similarly, where the record establishes that a procurement official was biased in favor of one offeror, and was a significant participant in agency activities that culminated in the decisions forming the basis for protest, the need to maintain the integrity of the procurement process requires that a protest challenged be sustained, unless there is compelling evidence that the protester was not prejudiced. Lockheed Martin Corporation, B-295402, 2005 CPD ¶ 24 (Comp. Gen. 2005).

Where a senior procurement official who functioned as the source selection authority has acknowledged bias in favor of the awardee, and was materially involved in the evaluation of proposals, indicating during the evaluation process that she believed the awardee's technical ratings should be raised in various areas and that the protesters' technical ratings should be lowered in various areas, the protests are sustained based on the agency's failure to demonstrate that the senior official's acknowledged bias did not prejudice the protesters and that the integrity of the procurement process was not compromised. Lockheed Martin Aeronautics Company; L-3 Communications Integrated Systems L.P.; BAE Systems Integrated Defense Solutions, Inc., B-295401, B-295401.2, B-295401.3, B-295401.4, B-295401.5, B-295401.6, B-295401.7, 2005 WL 502840 (Comp. Gen. 2005).

A conflict of interest was created when 14 of the 16 evaluators who were responsible for evaluating private-sector proposals in an A-76 study also held positions that were subject to the study. The fact that the employees with the conflict of interest were most familiar with the subject matter did not affect the conclusion. DZS/Baker LLC; Morrison Knudsen Corporation, B-281224, B-281224.2, B-281224.3, B-281224.4, B-281224.5, B-281224.6, 99-1 CPD ¶ 19 (Comp. Gen. 1999).

A protester challenged the propriety of an award because the director of the contracting activity, who appointed the Source Selection Official, had a close personal relationship with the president of the awardee and failed to obtain a formal recusal from the procurement. Although FAR 3.104-5 requires procurement officials who wish to discuss future employment or business opportunities with a competing contractor during the conduct of a procurement to provide a written proposal of disqualification from further participation in the procurement which relates to that competing contractor, there is no similar requirement for a written recusal based on a close personal relationship with personnel employed by a competing vendor. Since the director, in fact, did not participate in the procurement, the absence of a written recusal would constitute a mere formality that would not affect the propriety of the award. Centra Technology, Inc., B-274744, 97-1 CPD ¶ 35 (Comp. Gen. 1996).

Protest that personal conflict of interest of government employee initially designated as source selection official impermissibly tainted evaluation and award process is denied where government employee recused himself from the selection decision, and record contains no evidence that employee with conflict influenced agency's technical evaluators or replacement source selection official, or that awardee gained access to any competitor's proposal or other sensitive information. FAR 1.602 requires procurement officials to safeguard the government's interests in its contractual relationships. Consequently, contracting agencies are to avoid any conflict of interest or even the appearance of a conflict of interest in government procurements. Matter of: Lancaster & Company, B-254418, 93-2 CPD ¶ 319 (Comp. Gen. 1993).

2 Conflict of interest

Contracting agency's failure to answer bidder's e-mail questions in amendment to solicitation did not constitute a violation of section of the Federal Acquisition Regulation (FAR) directing government officials to conduct their business in a manner above reproach and to avoid any conflict of interest between government officials and potential bidders. KSEND v. U.S., 69 Fed. Cl. 103 (2005), aff'd, 184 Fed. Appx. 956 (Fed. Cir. 2006). United States ☞64.40(2) Even assuming that conflict-of-interest provision of the Federal Acquisition Regulation (FAR) was violated when supervisor of motor transport department was placed on evaluation board involved in A-76 cost comparison to determine if function of department should be contracted out, contractor was not prejudiced by supervisor's participation, considering that supervisor was only one of six individuals on the board, and there was no dissent on board's "poor" rating of contractor. 48 C.F.R. § 3.101-1. JWK Intern. Corp. v. U.S., 52 Fed. Cl. 650 (2002), aff'd, 56 Fed. Appx. 474 (Fed. Cir. 2003). United States ☞64.55(1)

Prospective Veterans Administration contractor, whose bid on contract for construction of VA facility was not accepted due to appearance of conflict of interest in negotiating process, was not entitled to timely notice and hearing before VA refused to award contract and formally advertised procurement, as contractor had no property interest in award of public contract which would entitle it to due process hearing. U.S.C.A. Const.Amends. 5, 14. Refine Const. Co., Inc. v. U.S., 12 Cl. Ct. 56, 34 Cont. Cas. Fed. (CCH) P 75242 (1987). Constitutional Law ☞277(1)

3 Private right of action

Federal acquisition regulation requiring government business to be conducted in a manner above reproach does not create a private right of action. 48 C.F.R. § 3.101-1. INSLAW, Inc. v. U.S., 39 Fed. Cl. 307, Fed. Sec. L. Rep. (CCH) P 77317 (1997), report and recommendation adopted, 40 Fed. Cl. 843, 42 Cont. Cas. Fed. (CCH) P 77302 (1998). United States ☞74(1)

§ 3.101-2 Solicitation and acceptance of gratuities by Government personnel.

As a rule, no Government employee may solicit or accept, directly or indirectly, any gratuity, gift, favor, entertainment, loan, or anything of monetary value from anyone who (a) has or is seeking to obtain Government business with the employee's agency, (b) conducts activities that are regulated by the employee's agency, or (c) has interests that may be substantially affected by the performance or nonperformance of the employee's official duties. Certain limited exceptions are authorized in agency regulations.

United States Code Annotated

Definitions, see 41 U.S.C.A. § 403.

Restrictions on disclosing and obtaining contractor bid or proposal information or source selection information, see 41 U.S.C.A. § 423.

§ 3.101-3 Agency regulations.

(a) Agencies are required by Executive Order 11222 of May 8, 1965, and 5 CFR 735 to prescribe "Standards of Conduct." These agency standards contain—

(1) Agency-authorized exceptions to 3.101-2; and

(2) Disciplinary measures for persons violating the standards of conduct.

(b) Requirements for employee financial disclosure and restrictions on private employment for former Government employees are in Office of Personnel Management and agency regulations implementing Public Law 95-521, which amended 18 U.S.C. 207.

United States Code Annotated

Definitions, see 41 U.S.C.A. § 403.

Restrictions on disclosing and obtaining contractor bid or proposal information or source selection information, see 41 U.S.C.A. § 423.

§ 3.102 [Reserved]

§ 3.103 Independent pricing.

§ 3.103-1 Solicitation provision.

The contracting officer shall insert the provision at 52.203-2, Certificate of Independent Price Determination, in solicitations when a firm-fixed-price contract or fixed-price contract with economic price adjustment is contemplated, unless—

(a) The acquisition is to be made under the simplified acquisition procedures in Part 13;

(b) [Reserved]

(c) The solicitation is a request for technical proposals under two-step sealed bidding procedures; or

(d) The solicitation is for utility services for which rates are set by law or regulation.

United States Code Annotated

Administrative determinations, see 41 U.S.C.A. § 257.

Contract requirements, see 41 U.S.C.A. § 254.

Contracts, planning, solicitation, evaluation, and award procedures, see 10 U.S.C.A. § 2305.

Definitions, see 10 U.S.C.A. § 2302, 41 U.S.C.A. §§ 259, 403.

Determinations and decisions, see 10 U.S.C.A. § 2310, 41 U.S.C.A. § 262.

Kinds of contracts, see 10 U.S.C.A. § 2306.

Planning and solicitation requirements, see 41 U.S.C.A. § 253a.

Restrictions on disclosing and obtaining contractor bid or proposal information or source selection information, see 41 U.S.C.A. § 423.

Notes of Decisions

In general 1

1 In general

The certificate of independent price determination is generally required to be included in all solicitations. FAR § 3.103-1. The purpose of the certification is to aid in enforcement of the antitrust laws and to assure that offerors do not collude among themselves to set prices or to restrict competition by inducing others not to bid. Topgallant Group, Inc., B-227865, B-227865.4, 88-2 CPD ¶ 594 (Comp. Gen. 1988).

§ 3.103-2 Evaluating the certification.

(a) Evaluation guidelines.

(1) None of the following, in and of itself, constitutes "disclosure" as it is used in paragraph (a)(2) of the Certificate of Independent Price Determination (hereafter, the certificate):

(i) The fact that a firm has published price lists, rates, or tariffs covering items being acquired by the Government.

(ii) The fact that a firm has informed prospective customers of proposed or pending publication of new or revised price lists for items being acquired by the Government.

(iii) The fact that a firm has sold the same items to commercial customers at the same prices being offered to the Government.

(2) For the purpose of paragraph (b)(2) of the certificate, an individual may use a blanket authorization to act as an agent for the person(s) responsible for determining the offered prices if—

(i) The proposed contract to which the certificate applies is clearly within the scope of the authorization; and

(ii) The person giving the authorization is the person within the offeror's organization who is responsible for determining the prices being offered at the time the certification is made in the particular offer.

(3) If an offer is submitted jointly by two or more concerns, the certification provided by the representative of each concern applies only to the activities of that concern.

(b) Rejection of offers suspected of being collusive.

(1) If the offeror deleted or modified paragraph (a)(1) or (a)(3) or paragraph (b) of the certificate, the contracting officer shall reject the offeror's bid or proposal.

(2) If the offeror deleted or modified paragraph (a)(2) of the certificate, the offeror must have furnished with its offer a signed statement of the circumstances of the disclosure of prices contained in the bid or proposal. The chief of the contracting office shall review the altered certificate and the statement and shall determine, in writing, whether the disclosure was made for the purpose or had the effect of restricting competition. If the determination is positive, the bid or proposal shall be rejected; if it is negative, the bid or proposal shall be considered for award.

(3) Whenever an offer is rejected under paragraph (b)(1) or (b)(2) of this section, or the certificate is suspected of being false, the contracting officer shall report the situation to

the Attorney General in accordance with 3.303.

(4) The determination made under paragraph (b)(2) of this section shall not prevent or inhibit the prosecution of any criminal or civil actions involving the occurrences or transactions to which the certificate relates.

United States Code Annotated

Administrative determinations, see 41 U.S.C.A. § 257.

Contract requirements, see 41 U.S.C.A. § 254.

Contracts, planning, solicitation, evaluation, and award procedures, see 10 U.S.C.A. § 2305.

Definitions, see 10 U.S.C.A. § 2302, 41 U.S.C.A. §§ 259, 403.

Determinations and decisions, see 10 U.S.C.A. § 2310, 41 U.S.C.A. § 262.

Kinds of contracts, see 10 U.S.C.A. § 2306.

Planning and solicitation requirements, see 41 U.S.C.A. § 253a.

Restrictions on disclosing and obtaining contractor bid or proposal information or source selection information, see 41 U.S.C.A. § 423.

Notes of Decisions
In general 1

1 In general

Prior to submission of final revised proposals, Delco advised the contracting officer that another offeror, J. Morris, had contacted Delco and disclosed its price after advising that it was the low bidder and would receive the award. Based upon this disclosure the agency rejected the proposals of both companies pursuant to FAR 3.103-2(b)(2), which provides that the agency must determine whether the disclosure was made for the purpose or had the effect of restricting competition and that if the determination is positive, the bid or proposal shall be rejected. The Air Force found that Delco's and J. Morris's exchange of pricing information restricted competition. The agency's decision to eliminate both firms from the competition was upheld. Delco Construction, Inc., B-237116, 90-1 CPD ¶ 157 (Comp. Gen. 1990).

Agency's rejection of proposal was reasonable where contracting officer specifically found that competitors' exchange of pricing information had the effect of restricting competition. The agency noted that both offerors changed their proposed prices, after these discussions, before BAFOs were submitted. One of the offerors lowered its price to displace another offeror. GAO determined that rejection of the proposal was reasonable under FAR 3.103-2(b)(2). Delco Construction, Inc., B-237116, 90-1 CPD ¶ 157 (Comp. Gen. 1990).

If a contracting officer suspects a certificate of independent price determination to be false, he is required to report the situation to the Department of Justice for prosecution under the antitrust laws. Topgallant Group, Inc., B-227865, B-227865.4, 88-2 CPD ¶ 594 (Comp. Gen. 1988).

§ 3.103-3 The need for further certifications.

A contractor that properly executed the certificate before award does not have to submit a separate certificate with each proposal to perform a work order or similar ordering instrument issued pursuant to the terms of the contract, where the Government's requirements cannot be met from another source.

United States Code Annotated

Administrative determinations, see 41 U.S.C.A. § 257.

Contract requirements, see 41 U.S.C.A. § 254.

Contracts, planning, solicitation, evaluation, and award procedures, see 10 U.S.C.A. § 2305.

Definitions, see 10 U.S.C.A. § 2302, 41 U.S.C.A. §§ 259, 403.

Determinations and decisions, see 10 U.S.C.A. § 2310, 41 U.S.C.A. § 262.

Kinds of contracts, see 10 U.S.C.A. § 2306.

Planning and solicitation requirements, see 41 U.S.C.A. § 253a.

Restrictions on disclosing and obtaining contractor bid or proposal information or source selection information, see 41 U.S.C.A. § 423.

§ 3.104 Procurement integrity.

§ 3.104-1 Definitions.

As used in this section—

"Agency ethics official" means the designated agency ethics official described in 5 CFR 2638.201 or other designated person, including—

(1) Deputy ethics officials described in 5 CFR 2638.204, to whom authority under 3.104-6 has been delegated by the designated agency ethics official; and

(2) Alternate designated agency ethics officials described in 5 CFR 2638.202(b).

"Compensation" means wages, salaries, honoraria, commissions, professional fees, and any other form of compensation, provided directly or indirectly for services rendered. Compensation is indirectly provided if it is paid to an entity other than the individual, specifically in exchange for services provided by the individual.

"Contractor bid or proposal information" means any of the following information submitted to a Federal agency as part of or in connection with a bid or proposal to enter into a Federal agency procurement contract, if that information has not been previously made available to the public or disclosed publicly:

(1) Cost or pricing data (as defined by 10 U.S.C. 2306a(h)) with respect to procurements subject to that section, and 41 U.S.C. 3501(a)(2), with respect to procurements subject to that section.

(2) Indirect costs and direct labor rates.

(3) Proprietary information about manufacturing processes, operations, or techniques marked by the contractor in accordance with applicable law or regulation.

(4) Information marked by the contractor as "contractor bid or proposal information" in accordance with applicable law or regulation.

(5) Information marked in accordance with 52.215-1(e).

"Decision to award a subcontract or modification of subcontract" means a decision to designate award to a particular source.

"Federal agency procurement" means the acquisition (by using competitive procedures and awarding a contract) of goods or services (including construction) from non-Federal sources by a Federal agency using appropriated funds. For broad agency announcements and small business innovation research programs, each proposal received by an agency constitutes a separate procurement for purposes of 41 U.S.C. chapter 21.

"In excess of $10,000,000" means—

(1) The value, or estimated value, at the time of award, of the contract, including all options;

(2) The total estimated value at the time of award of all orders under an indefinite-delivery, indefinite-quantity, or requirements contract;

(3) Any multiple award schedule contract, unless the contracting officer documents a lower estimate;

(4) The value of a delivery order, task order, or an order under a Basic Ordering Agreement;

(5) The amount paid or to be paid in settlement of a claim; or

(6) The estimated monetary value of negotiated overhead or other rates when applied to the Government portion of the applicable allocation base.

"Official" means—

(1) An officer, as defined in 5 U.S.C. 2104;

(2) An employee, as defined in 5 U.S.C. 2105;

(3) A member of the uniformed services, as defined in 5 U.S.C. 2101(3); or

(4) A special Government employee, as defined in 18 U.S.C. 202.

"Participating personally and substantially in a Federal agency procurement" means—

(1) Active and significant involvement of an official in any of the following activities

directly related to that procurement:

(i) Drafting, reviewing, or approving the specification or statement of work for the procurement.

(ii) Preparing or developing the solicitation.

(iii) Evaluating bids or proposals, or selecting a source.

(iv) Negotiating price or terms and conditions of the contract.

(v) Reviewing and approving the award of the contract.

(2) "Participating personally" means participating directly, and includes the direct and active supervision of a subordinate's participation in the matter.

(3) "Participating substantially" means that the official's involvement is of significance to the matter. Substantial participation requires more than official responsibility, knowledge, perfunctory involvement, or involvement on an administrative or peripheral issue. Participation may be substantial even though it is not determinative of the outcome of a particular matter. A finding of substantiality should be based not only on the effort devoted to a matter, but on the importance of the effort. While a series of peripheral involvements may be insubstantial, the single act of approving or participating in a critical step may be substantial. However, the review of procurement documents solely to determine compliance with regulatory, administrative, or budgetary procedures, does not constitute substantial participation in a procurement.

(4) Generally, an official will not be considered to have participated personally and substantially in a procurement solely by participating in the following activities:

(i) Agency-level boards, panels, or other advisory committees that review program milestones or evaluate and make recommendations regarding alternative technologies or approaches for satisfying broad agency-level missions or objectives.

(ii) The performance of general, technical, engineering, or scientific effort having broad application not directly associated with a particular procurement, notwithstanding that such general, technical, engineering, or scientific effort subsequently may be incorporated into a particular procurement.

(iii) Clerical functions supporting the conduct of a particular procurement.

(iv) For procurements to be conducted under the procedures of OMB Circular A-76, participation in management studies, preparation of in-house cost estimates, preparation of "most efficient organization" analyses, and furnishing of data or technical support to be used by others in the development of performance standards, statements of work, or specifications.

"Source selection evaluation board" means any board, team, council, or other group that evaluates bids or proposals.

United States Code Annotated

Administrative determinations, see 41 U.S.C.A. § 257.

Contract requirements, see 41 U.S.C.A. § 254.

Contracts, planning, solicitation, evaluation, and award procedures, see 10 U.S.C.A. § 2305.

Definitions, see 10 U.S.C.A. § 2302, 41 U.S.C.A. §§ 259, 403.

Determinations and decisions, see 10 U.S.C.A. § 2310, 41 U.S.C.A. § 262.

Kinds of contracts, see 10 U.S.C.A. § 2306.

Planning and solicitation requirements, see 41 U.S.C.A. § 253a.

Restrictions on disclosing and obtaining contractor bid or proposal information or source selection information, see 41 U.S.C.A. § 423.

Notes of Decisions
Contractor bid or proposal information 1

1 Contractor bid or proposal information

Transcripts of offerors' oral presentations of their technical proposals constituted contractor proposal information, defined to include proprietary information about operations or techniques. The oral presentation encompassed details of the offerors' team composition and structure; management approach; personnel and transition plans; its approach to performing each of the task orders; and the processes that would be used to perform the tasks. The transcripts also constituted source selection information, defined to include any information prepared for the purpose of evaluating a proposal which has not previously been made publicly available. Computer Technology Associates, Inc., B-288622, 2001 CPD ¶ 187 (Comp. Gen. 2001).

§ 3.104-2 General.

(a) This section implements 41 U.S.C. chapter 21, Restrictions on Obtaining and Disclosing Certain Information. Agency supplementation of 3.104, including specific definitions to identify individuals who occupy positions specified in 3.104-3(d)(1)(ii), and any clauses required by 3.104 must be approved by the senior procurement executive of the agency, unless a law establishes a higher level of approval for that agency.

(b) Agency officials are reminded that there are other statutes and regulations that deal with the same or related prohibited conduct, for example—

(1) The offer or acceptance of a bribe or gratuity is prohibited by 18 U.S.C. 201 and 10 U.S.C. 2207. The acceptance of a gift, under certain circumstances, is prohibited by 5 U.S.C. 7353 and 5 CFR Part 2635;

(2) Contacts with an offeror during the conduct of an acquisition may constitute "seeking employment," (see Subpart F of 5 CFR Part 2636 and 3.104-3(c)(2)). Government officers and employees (employees) are prohibited by 18 U.S.C. 208 and 5 CFR Part 2635 from participating personally and substantially in any particular matter that would affect the financial interests of any person with whom the employee is seeking employment. An employee who engages in negotiations or is otherwise seeking employment with an offeror or who has an arrangement concerning future employment with an offeror must comply with the applicable disqualification requirements of 5 CFR 2635.604 and 2635. 606. The statutory prohibition in 18 U.S.C. 208 also may require an employee's disqualification from participation in the acquisition even if the employee's duties may not be considered "participating personally and substantially," as this term is defined in 3.104-1;

(3) Post-employment restrictions are covered by 18 U.S.C. 207 and 5 CFR parts 2637 and 2641, that prohibit certain activities by former Government employees, including representation of a contractor before the Government in relation to any contract or other particular matter involving specific parties on which the former employee participated personally and substantially while employed by the Government. Additional restrictions apply to certain senior Government employees and for particular matters under an employee's official responsibility;

(4) Parts 14 and 15 place restrictions on the release of information related to procurements and other contractor information that must be protected under 18 U.S.C. 1905;

(5) Release of information both before and after award (see 3.104-4) may be prohibited by the Privacy Act (5 U.S.C. 552a), the Trade Secrets Act (18 U.S.C. 1905), and other laws; and

(6) Using nonpublic information to further an employee's private interest or that of another and engaging in a financial transaction using nonpublic information are prohibited by 5 CFR 2635.703.

United States Code Annotated

Administrative determinations, see 41 U.S.C.A. § 257.

Contract requirements, see 41 U.S.C.A. § 254.

Contracts, planning, solicitation, evaluation, and award procedures, see 10 U.S.C.A. § 2305.

Definitions, see 10 U.S.C.A. § 2302, 41 U.S.C.A. §§ 259, 403.

Determinations and decisions, see 10 U.S.C.A. § 2310, 41 U.S.C.A. § 262.

Kinds of contracts, see 10 U.S.C.A. § 2306.

Planning and solicitation requirements, see 41 U.S.C.A. § 253a.

Restrictions on disclosing and obtaining contractor bid or proposal information or source selection information, see 41 U.S.C.A. § 423.

Notes of Decisions

In general 1

1 In general

Recognizing the disadvantage to a contractor whose protected information is exploited by its competitors, Congress did not limit remedies to Procurement Integrity Act violations only to overturning procurement decisions or excluding particular contractors. The act enforces the prohibition of releasing protected information by placing criminal sanctions on potential violators, including up to five years in prison, thereby emphasizing the importance of maintaining the integrity in government contracting. Avtel Services, Inc. v. U.S., 70 Fed. Cl. 173 (2006).

In participating on behalf of contractor in contractor's negotiations with Veterans Administration for construction of VA facility, VA employee violated executive order and VA regulations forbidding any activity adversely affecting confidence of public and integrity of Government; although contractor was preselected by Small Business Administration, resulting in contractor having no competition for contract, VA employee's actions in appearing on behalf of contractor and in misrepresenting to contractor that he had received permission from his VA supervisor to participate in negotiations created appearance of conflict of interest. Executive Order No. 11222, § 201(c)(6), 18 U.S.C.A. § 201 note. Refine Const. Co., Inc. v. U.S., 12 Cl. Ct. 56, 34 Cont. Cas. Fed. (CCH) P 75242 (1987). United States ☞41

§ 3.104-3 Statutory and related prohibitions, restrictions, and requirements.

(a) Prohibition on disclosing procurement information (41 U.S.C. 2102).

(1) A person described in paragraph (a)(2) of this subsection must not, other than as provided by law, knowingly disclose contractor bid or proposal information or source selection information before the award of a Federal agency procurement contract to which the information relates. (See 3.104-4(a).)

(2) Paragraph (a)(1) of this subsection applies to any person who—

(i) Is a present or former official of the United States, or a person who is acting or has acted for or on behalf of, or who is advising or has advised the United States with respect to, a Federal agency procurement; and

(ii) By virtue of that office, employment, or relationship, has or had access to contractor bid or proposal information or source selection information.

(b) *Prohibition on obtaining procurement information* (41 U.S.C. 2102). A person must not, other than as provided by law, knowingly obtain contractor bid or proposal information or source selection information before the award of a Federal agency procurement contract to which the information relates.

(c) Actions required when an agency official contacts or is contacted by an offeror regarding non-Federal employment (41 U.S.C. 2103).

(1) If an agency official, participating personally and substantially in a Federal agency procurement for a contract in excess of the simplified acquisition threshold, contacts or is contacted by a person who is an offeror in that Federal agency procurement regarding possible non-Federal employment for that official, the official must—

(i) Promptly report the contact in writing to the official's supervisor and to the agency ethics official; and

(ii) Either reject the possibility of non-Federal employment or disqualify himself or herself from further personal and substantial participation in that Federal agency procurement (see 3.104-5) until such time as the agency authorizes the official to resume participation in that procurement, in accordance with the requirements of 18 U.S.C. 208 and applicable agency regulations, because—

(A) The person is no longer an offeror in that Federal agency procurement; or

(B) All discussions with the offeror regarding possible non-Federal employment have terminated without an agreement or arrangement for employment.

(2) A contact is any of the actions included as "seeking employment" in 5 CFR 2635.603(b). In addition, unsolicited communications from offerors regarding possible employment are considered contacts.

(3) Agencies must retain reports of employment contacts for 2 years from the date the report was submitted.

(4) Conduct that complies with *41 U.S.C. 2104* may be prohibited by other criminal statutes and the Standards of Ethical Conduct for Employees of the Executive Branch.

See 3.104-2(b)(2).

(d) Prohibition on former official's acceptance of compensation from a contractor (41 U.S.C. 2104).

(1) A former official of a Federal agency may not accept compensation from a contractor that has been awarded a competitive or sole source contract, as an employee, officer, director, or consultant of the contractor within a period of 1 year after such former official—

(i) Served, at the time of selection of the contractor or the award of a contract to that contractor, as the procuring contracting officer, the source selection authority, a member of a source selection evaluation board, or the chief of a financial or technical evaluation team in a procurement in which that contractor was selected for award of a contract in excess of $10,000,000;

(ii) Served as the program manager, deputy program manager, or administrative contracting officer for a contract in excess of $10,000,000 awarded to that contractor; or

(iii) Personally made for the Federal agency a decision to—

(A) Award a contract, subcontract, modification of a contract or subcontract, or a task order or delivery order in excess of $10,000,000 to that contractor;

(B) Establish overhead or other rates applicable to a contract or contracts for that contractor that are valued in excess of $10,000,000;

(C) Approve issuance of a contract payment or payments in excess of $10,000,000 to that contractor; or

(D) Pay or settle a claim in excess of $10,000,000 with that contractor.

(2) The 1-year prohibition begins on the date—

(i) Of contract award for positions described in paragraph (d)(1)(i) of this subsection, or the date of contractor selection if the official was not serving in the position on the date of award;

(ii) The official last served in one of the positions described in paragraph (d)(1)(ii) of this subsection; or

(iii) The official made one of the decisions described in paragraph (d)(1)(iii) of this subsection.

(3) Nothing in paragraph (d)(1) of this subsection may be construed to prohibit a former official of a Federal agency from accepting compensation from any division or affiliate of a contractor that does not produce the same or similar products or services as the entity of the contractor that is responsible for the contract referred to in paragraph (d)(1) of this subsection.

United States Code Annotated

Administrative determinations, see 41 U.S.C.A. § 257.

Contract requirements, see 41 U.S.C.A. § 254.

Contracts, planning, solicitation, evaluation, and award procedures, see 10 U.S.C.A. § 2305.

Definitions, see 10 U.S.C.A. § 2302, 41 U.S.C.A. §§ 259, 403.

Determinations and decisions, see 10 U.S.C.A. § 2310, 41 U.S.C.A. § 262.

Kinds of contracts, see 10 U.S.C.A. § 2306.

Planning and solicitation requirements, see 41 U.S.C.A. § 253a.

Restrictions on disclosing and obtaining contractor bid or proposal information or source selection information, see 41 U.S.C.A. § 423.

Notes of Decisions

In general 1
Disclosure of information 2
Injunctions 5
Obtaining information 3
Source selection information 4

1 In general

A former agency official's work for a contractor was permissible "behind-the-scenes" consulting and did not create an appearance of impropriety. The record does not support the contracting officer's determination that an appearance of impropriety had been created by the protester's hiring of a former government employee as a consultant, because the record shows that the determination was based on assumptions, rather than hard facts, and relied on an incorrect understanding of the statutes and regulations that apply to post-government employment activities. VSE Corp., B-404833.4, 2011 CPD ¶ 268 (Comp. Gen. 2011)

GAO Bid Protest Regulations and the Procurement Integrity Act (PIA) require, as a condition precedent to GAO's consideration of a matter, that a protester first report the alleged violation of the PIA to the contracting agency within 14 days after becoming aware of the facts giving rise to the alleged violation. 41 U.S.C. § 423(g); 4 C.F.R. § 21.5(d) (2008). At a minimum, a protester must diligently pursue the information necessary to establish its basis for protest. A protester does not meet its obligation of diligently pursuing the information on which it bases its protest where it allows more than 5 months to elapse after learning of a possible basis for protest. Matter of: Orbital Sciences Corporation, B-400589, B-400589.2, 2008 WL 5790105 (Comp. Gen. 2008).

2 Disclosure of information

Government procurement to provide building for Veterans Administration (VA) was flawed, and procurement was improperly awarded, where General Services Administration (GSA) improperly disclosed to successful bidder that its first best and final offers (BAFO) was not lowest bid, successful bidder prevented GSA from making thorough evaluation of its financial capability by failing to disclose material information and misrepresenting material information, GSA erroneously resolved flood plain issue relating to unsuccessful bid without affording unsuccessful bidder opportunity to respond, successful bidder made number of attempts to sell award before it even built building, and it did not appear that selected site was in fact even minimally acceptable. 48 C.F.R. § 3.104-4(b), (b)(3), (k)(2)(viii). Ralvin Pacific Properties, Inc. v. U.S., 871 F. Supp. 468 (D.D.C. 1994). United States ⬤64.40(1)

3 Obtaining information

Unsuccessful bidder on government procurement contract failed to demonstrate that successful bidders improperly used confidential and proprietary information of competitors in computing successful bid, for purposes of showing that successful bidders were unjustly enriched. Connelly Containers, Inc. v. Bernard, 717 F. Supp. 202 (S.D. N.Y. 1989). United States ⬤64.60(5.1)

A "Reverse Auction," in which other bidders and their subcontractors will be able to obtain or derive the bid prices and pricing strategy that could be used to the bidders' disadvantage in an ongoing auction and in procurements, did not violate the Procurement Integrity Act. In a reverse auction, the bidder's are releasing their prices and 41 U.S.C. § 423(h)(2) allows a contractor to disclose its own bid or proposal information. As such, the reverse auction's price disclosure falls within the exceptions of 41 U.S.C. § 423(h)(1) and (2). MTB Group, Inc. v. U.S., 65 Fed. Cl. 516 (2005)

Contracting agency and successful bidder did not violate the Procurement Integrity Act when they received personnel and compensation information concerning employees of another bidder, where the information did not constitute "contractor bid or proposal information" as defined by the Federal Acquisition Regulation. Office of Federal Procurement Policy Act, § 27, as amended, 41 U.S.C.A. § 423; 48 C.F.R. § 3.104-3. Synetics, Inc. v. U.S., 45 Fed. Cl. 1 (1999). United States ⬤64.45(1)

In pre-award bid protest action, under discovery order allowing disappointed bidder access to information relating to its own proposal, and denying access to any information relating to proposals of other bidders, discovery could not be used as vehicle for acquisition of proprietary information and trade secrets of other bidders. 48 C.F.R. §§ 15.005(e), 15.006(e) (1997); 48 C.F.R. § 15.1004(d, e) (1996). Pikes Peak Family Housing, LLC v. U.S., 40 Fed. Cl. 673, 42 Cont. Cas. Fed. (CCH) P 77280 (1998). Federal Courts ⬤1112

4 Source selection information

Federal Acquisition Regulations forbid procurement officials from revealing source selection information during course of procurement proceedings, including disclosure of ranking of bids, proposals, or competitors. 48 C.F.R. § 3.104-4(b), (b)(3), (k)(2)(viii). Ralvin Pacific Properties, Inc. v. U.S., 871 F. Supp. 468 (D.D.C. 1994). United States ⊕64.40(1)

5 Injunctions

Contractor who filed pre-award bid protest was not entitled to permanent injunction preventing the Department of Housing and Urban Development (HUD) from employing online reverse auction procedure to procure housing inspection services, as contractor failed to show any likelihood of success on the merits of its claim that procedure violated procurement statute and regulation prohibiting disclosure or obtaining of contractor bid or source selection information. MTB Group, Inc. v. U.S., 65 Fed. Cl. 516 (2005). Injunction ⊕86

§ 3.104-4 Disclosure, protection, and marking of contractor bid or proposal information and source selection information.

(a) Except as specifically provided for in this subsection, no person or other entity may disclose contractor bid or proposal information or source selection information to any person other than a person authorized, in accordance with applicable agency regulations or procedures, by the agency head or the contracting officer to receive such information.

(b) Contractor bid or proposal information and source selection information must be protected from unauthorized disclosure in accordance with 14.401, 15.207, applicable law, and agency regulations.

(c) Individuals unsure if particular information is source selection information, as defined in 2.101, should consult with agency officials as necessary. Individuals responsible for preparing material that may be source selection information as described at paragraph (10) of the "source selection information" definition in 2.101 must mark the cover page and each page that the individual believes contains source selection information with the legend "*Source Selection Information—See FAR 2.101 and 3.104.*" Although the information in paragraphs (1) through (9) of the definition in 2.101 is considered to be source selection information whether or not marked, all reasonable efforts must be made to mark such material with the same legend.

(d) Except as provided in paragraph (d)(3) of this subsection, the contracting officer must notify the contractor in writing if the contracting officer believes that proprietary information, contractor bid or proposal information, or information marked in accordance with 52.215-1(e) has been inappropriately marked. The contractor that has affixed the marking must be given an opportunity to justify the marking.

(1) If the contractor agrees that the marking is not justified, or does not respond within the time specified in the notice, the contracting officer may remove the marking and release the information.

(2) If, after reviewing the contractor's justification, the contracting officer determines that the marking is not justified, the contracting officer must notify the contractor in writing before releasing the information.

(3) For technical data marked as proprietary by a contractor, the contracting officer must follow the procedures in 27.404-5.

(e) This section does not restrict or prohibit—

(1) A contractor from disclosing its own bid or proposal information or the recipient from receiving that information;

(2) The disclosure or receipt of information, not otherwise protected, relating to a Federal agency procurement after it has been canceled by the Federal agency, before contract award, unless the Federal agency plans to resume the procurement;

(3) Individual meetings between a Federal agency official and an offeror or potential offeror for, or a recipient of, a contract or subcontract under a Federal agency procurement, provided that unauthorized disclosure or receipt of contractor bid or proposal information or source selection information does not occur; or

(4) The Government's use of technical data in a manner consistent with the Government's rights in the data.

(f) This section does not authorize—

(1) The withholding of any information pursuant to a proper request from the Congress, any committee or subcommittee thereof, a Federal agency, the Comptroller General, or

an Inspector General of a Federal agency, except as otherwise authorized by law or regulation. Any release containing contractor bid or proposal information or source selection information must clearly identify the information as contractor bid or proposal information or source selection information related to the conduct of a Federal agency procurement and notify the recipient that the disclosure of the information is restricted by 41 U.S.C. chapter 21;

(2) The withholding of information from, or restricting its receipt by, the Comptroller General in the course of a protest against the award or proposed award of a Federal agency procurement contract;

(3) The release of information after award of a contract or cancellation of a procurement if such information is contractor bid or proposal information or source selection information that pertains to another procurement; or

(4) The disclosure, solicitation, or receipt of bid or proposal information or source selection information after award if disclosure, solicitation, or receipt is prohibited by law. (See 3.104-2(b)(5) and Subpart 24.2.)

United States Code Annotated

Administrative determinations, see 41 U.S.C.A. § 257.

Contract requirements, see 41 U.S.C.A. § 254.

Contracts, planning, solicitation, evaluation, and award procedures, see 10 U.S.C.A. § 2305.

Definitions, see 10 U.S.C.A. § 2302, 41 U.S.C.A. §§ 259, 403.

Determinations and decisions, see 10 U.S.C.A. § 2310, 41 U.S.C.A. § 262.

Kinds of contracts, see 10 U.S.C.A. § 2306.

Planning and solicitation requirements, see 41 U.S.C.A. § 253a.

Restrictions on disclosing and obtaining contractor bid or proposal information or source selection information, see 41 U.S.C.A. § 423.

Notes of Decisions

In general 1
Contractor bid or proposal information 2
Injunctions 4
Source selection information 3

1 In general

FAR 3.104-4(a) prohibits disclosure of contractor bid or proposal or source selection information unless one of the listed exceptions applies. Under the Freedom of Information Act (FOIA), government agencies are obligated to make information available to the public, unless one of the listed exceptions applies. Once information enters the public domain, however, it is no longer confidential and parties may not make claims of confidentiality regarding such information. Avtel Services, Inc. v. U.S., 70 Fed. Cl. 173 (2006).

Contracting agency and successful bidder did not violate the Procurement Integrity Act when they received personnel and compensation information concerning employees of another bidder, where the information did not constitute "contractor bid or proposal information" as defined by the Federal Acquisition Regulation. Office of Federal Procurement Policy Act, § 27, as amended, 41 U.S.C.A. § 423; 48 C.F.R. § 3.104-3. Synetics, Inc. v. U.S., 45 Fed. Cl. 1 (1999). United States ☞64.45(1)

In pre-award bid protest action, under discovery order allowing disappointed bidder access to information relating to its own proposal, and denying access to any information relating to proposals of other bidders, discovery could not be used as vehicle for acquisition of proprietary information and trade secrets of other bidders. 48 C.F.R. §§ 15.005(e), 15.006(e) (1997); 48 C.F.R. § 15.1004(d, e) (1996). Pikes Peak Family Housing, LLC v. U.S., 40 Fed. Cl. 673, 42 Cont. Cas. Fed. (CCH) P 77280 (1998). Federal Courts ☞1112

2 Contractor bid or proposal information

A "Reverse Auction," in which other bidders and their subcontractors will be able to obtain or derive the bid prices and pricing strategy that could be used to the bidders' disadvantage in an ongoing auction and in procurements, did not violate the Procurement Integrity Act. In a reverse auction, the bidder's are releasing their prices and 41 U.S.C. § 423(h)(2) allows a contractor to disclose its own bid or proposal information. As such, the reverse auction's price disclosure falls within the exceptions of 41 U.S.C. § 423(h)(1) and (2). MTB Group, Inc. v. U.S., 65 Fed. Cl. 516 (2005).

Contracting agency acted arbitrarily, capriciously, or otherwise not in accordance with law when it released incumbent contractor's current and future unit prices to a competitor under the Freedom of Information Act (FOIA) and the Trade Secrets Act, where prices were released in face of an imminent re-solicitation of a substantially similar contract covering largely the same period as contractor's prices released on unperformed option years, thereby creating appearance of impropriety, i.e., that the sole purpose of the resolicitation was the underbidding of the current contract unit prices. 5 U.S.C.A. § 552(b)(4); 18 U.S.C.A. § 1905; 48 C.F.R. § 1.602-2. R & W Flammann GmbH v. U.S., 53 Fed. Cl. 647 (2002), judgment rev'd, 339 F.3d 1320 (Fed. Cir. 2003).

Contracting agency and successful bidder did not violate the Procurement Integrity Act when they received personnel and compensation information concerning employees of another bidder, where the information did not constitute "contractor bid or proposal information" as defined by the Federal Acquisition Regulation. Office of Federal Procurement Policy Act, § 27, as amended, 41 U.S.C.A. § 423; 48 C.F.R. § 3.104-3. Synetics, Inc. v. U.S., 45 Fed. Cl. 1 (1999). United States ☞64.45(1)

Neither the Procurement Integrity Act nor the FAR contemplates the absolute prohibition of the release of an offeror's pricing information, but rather make clear that the contracting officer is authorized to disclose pricing information under certain circumstances. The Procurement Integrity Act provides in relevant part that "[t]his section does not . . . restrict the disclosure of information to, or its receipt by, any person or class of persons authorized, in accordance with applicable agency regulations or procedures, to receive that information." Where an unsuccessful offeror lawfully obtains proprietary information, such as a competitor's prices and technical scores, and the agency subsequently properly reopens negotiations, the agency may disclose similar information to all competitors to eliminate any competitive advantage obtained. DGS Contract Service, Inc. v. U.S., 43 Fed. Cl. 227 (1999).

In pre-award bid protest action, under discovery order allowing disappointed bidder access to information relating to its own proposal, and denying access to any information relating to proposals of other bidders, discovery could not be used as vehicle for acquisition of proprietary information and trade secrets of other bidders. 48 C.F.R. §§ 15.005(e), 15.006(e) (1997); 48 C.F.R. § 15.1004(d, e) (1996). Pikes Peak Family Housing, LLC v. U.S., 40 Fed. Cl. 673, 42 Cont. Cas. Fed. (CCH) P 77280 (1998). Federal Courts ☞1112

Providing an on-site tour to potential competitor did not disclose protected contractor bid or proposal information pertaining to on-site incumbent's staffing and management approach. The GAO determined that staffing and management information was neither contractor bid or proposal information nor source selection information, as those terms are defined in the applicable statutory provisions and implementing regulations, because much of the information was available in the public domain or could be derived though visits to the government facility. Matter of: Accent Service Company, Inc., B-299888, 2007 CPD ¶ 169 (Comp. Gen. 2007).

Transcripts of oral presentations of offerors' technical proposals constituted contractor proposal information, defined to include proprietary information about operations or techniques. The transcripts contained details of team composition and structure; management approach; personnel and transition plans and task order performance approach. Computer Technology Associates, Inc., B-288622, 2001 CPD ¶ 187 (Comp. Gen. 2001).

3 Source selection information

Government procurement to provide building for Veterans Administration (VA) was flawed, and procurement was improperly awarded, where General Services Administration (GSA) improperly disclosed to successful bidder that its first best and final offers (BAFO) was not lowest bid. 48 C.F.R. § 3.104-4(b), (b)(3), (k)(2)(viii). Ralvin Pacific Properties, Inc. v. U.S., 871 F. Supp. 468 (D.D.C. 1994). United States ☞64.40(1)

Disclosure to one vendor, prior to release of the information to other competitors, that the scope of work under the solicitation would consolidate two existing contracts, and that the procurement would be conducted as an 8(a) set-aside did not violate the Procurement Integrity Act's prohibition of non-disclosure of source selection information. Neither the Act nor the implementing regulations confer source selection information status on every piece of information relevant to a given procurement. The information said to have been improperly disclosed generally relates to matters that are administrative in nature and does not fall into any of the categories of information expressly identified in the regulation. Cexec, Inc. v. Department of Energy, G.S.B.C.A. No. 12909-P, 95-1 B.C.A. (CCH) ¶ 27380, 1994 WL 706767 (Gen. Services Admin. B.C.A. 1994).

Awardees possession of a list of employees and bonus compensation paid by another offeror did not violate the Procurement Integrity Act because such information did not meet the definition of "contractor bid and proposal information." The protester's personnel and bonus information was not any of the following: cost or pricing data; indirect costs and direct labor rates; proprietary information about manufacturing; information marked by the contractor as "contractor bid or proposal information"; or information marked in accordance with 52.215-1(e). Synetics, Inc. v. U.S., 45 Fed. Cl. 1 (1999).

Protest alleging procurement integrity violation is denied where the only source selection information disclosed by the agency to the awardee was the advance notification that the awardee was in line for award, and protester has not demonstrated that it suffered prejudice as a result of the advance notification. Matter of: East West, Inc., B-400325.7, B-400325.8, 2010 CPD ¶ 187 (Comp. Gen. 2010)

The Procurement Integrity Act, as implemented by the FAR, prohibits anyone from "knowingly obtain[ing] contractor bid or proposal information or source selection information before the award" of a "contract to which the information relates." 41 U.S.C. § 423(b); FAR 3.104-4(b). Where there is a violation or possible violation of the Act, the contracting officer must determine whether the violation or possible violation has any impact on the pending award or source selection and, if an impact is found, must refer the matter to the Head of the Contracting Activity or designee. FAR 3.104-10(a). Computer Technology Associates, Inc., B-288622, 2001 CPD ¶ 187 (Comp. Gen. 2001).

The Procurement Integrity Act was violated when an offeror obtained copies of oral presentation transcripts pertaining to two other offerors. The Act is violated where a person "knowingly obtain[s] contractor bid or proposal information" prior to award. 41 U.S.C. § 423(b); FAR § 3.104-4(b). Prior to the award of blanket purchase agreements (BPAs) an employee of one of the offerors obtained the oral presentation transcripts pertaining to two other offerors. The employee produced copies, and then disseminated them to the Project Manager, who in turn provided them to the Deputy Project Manager. Computer Technology Associates, Inc., B-288622, 2001 CPD ¶ 187 (Comp. Gen. 2001).

An agency's decision to exclude an offeror from a competition because the offeror obtained a copy of the Government's internal cost estimate requires a balancing of competing interests set forth in the FAR. On the one hand, contracting officers are granted wide latitude in their business judgments to safeguard the interests of the United States in its contractual relationships. FAR 1.602-2. On the other hand, the same section of the FAR requires contracting officers to ensure impartial, fair, and equitable treatment of all contractors. A contracting officer may protect the integrity of the competitive procurement system by disqualifying an offeror from a competition where the firm may have obtained an unfair competitive advantage, even if no actual impropriety can be shown, so long as the determination is based on facts and not mere innuendo or suspicion. Protest sustained because the Government could have shared the estimate with all the vendors to neutralize competitive advantage. IGIT, Inc., B-271823, 96-2 CPD ¶ 51 (Comp. Gen. 1996).

4 Injunctions

Contractor who filed pre-award bid protest was not entitled to permanent injunction preventing the Department of Housing and Urban Development (HUD) from employing online reverse auction procedure to procure housing inspection services, as contractor failed to show any likelihood of success on the merits of its claim that procedure violated procurement statute and regulation prohibiting disclosure or obtaining of contractor bid or source selection information. MTB Group, Inc. v. U.S., 65 Fed. Cl. 516 (2005). Injunction ☞86

§ 3.104-5 Disqualification.

(a) *Contacts through agents or other intermediaries.* Employment contacts between the employee and the offeror, that are conducted through agents, or other intermediaries, may require disqualification under 3.104-3(c)(1). These contacts may also require disqualification under other statutes and regulations. (See 3.104-2(b)(2).)

(b) *Disqualification notice.* In addition to submitting the contact report required by 3.104-3(c)(1), an agency official who must disqualify himself or herself pursuant to 3.104-3(c)(1)(ii) must promptly submit written notice of disqualification from further participation in the procurement to the contracting officer, the source selection authority if other than the contracting officer, and the agency official's immediate supervisor. As a minimum, the notice must—

(1) Identify the procurement;

(2) Describe the nature of the agency official's participation in the procurement and specify the approximate dates or time period of participation; and

(3) Identify the offeror and describe its interest in the procurement.

(c) Resumption of participation in a procurement.

(1) The official must remain disqualified until such time as the agency, at its sole and exclusive discretion, authorizes the official to resume participation in the procurement in accordance with 3.104-3(c)(1)(ii).

(2) After the conditions of 3.104-3(c)(1)(ii)(A) or (B) have been met, the head of the contracting activity (HCA), after consultation with the agency ethics official, may authorize the disqualified official to resume participation in the procurement, or may determine that an additional disqualification period is necessary to protect the integrity of the procurement process. In determining the disqualification period, the HCA must consider any factors that create an appearance that the disqualified official acted without complete impartiality in the procurement. The HCA's reinstatement decision should be in writing.

(3) Government officer or employee must also comply with the provisions of 18 U.S.C. 208 and 5 CFR Part 2635 regarding any resumed participation in a procurement matter. Government officer or employee may not be reinstated to participate in a procurement matter affecting the financial interest of someone with whom the individual is seeking employment, unless the individual receives—

(i) A waiver pursuant to 18 U.S.C. 208(b)(1) or (b)(3); or

(ii) An authorization in accordance with the requirements of Subpart F of 5 CFR Part 2635.

United States Code Annotated

Administrative determinations, see 41 U.S.C.A. § 257.

Contract requirements, see 41 U.S.C.A. § 254.

Contracts, planning, solicitation, evaluation, and award procedures, see 10 U.S.C.A. § 2305.

Definitions, see 10 U.S.C.A. § 2302, 41 U.S.C.A. §§ 259, 403.

Determinations and decisions, see 10 U.S.C.A. § 2310, 41 U.S.C.A. § 262.

Kinds of contracts, see 10 U.S.C.A. § 2306.

Planning and solicitation requirements, see 41 U.S.C.A. § 253a.

Restrictions on disclosing and obtaining contractor bid or proposal information or source selection information, see 41 U.S.C.A. § 423.

Notes of Decisions

In general 1

1 In general

Agency's disqualification of the protester from further participation in two task order competitions for combat support services issued under an indefinite-delivery/ indefinite-quantity contract was reasonable, where an employee of the protester improperly accessed source selection sensitive and proprietary information, and the protester, in response to a request from the agency that the employee be isolated from the two open task order competitions for which the improperly accessed proprietary information would be competitively useful, refused to do so. Matter of: Kellogg Brown & Root Services, Inc., B-400787.2, B-400861, 2009 CPD ¶ 54 (Comp. Gen. 2009)

A contracting officer may protect the integrity of the procurement system by disqualifying an offeror from the competition where the firm may have obtained an unfair competitive advantage, even if no actual impropriety can be shown, so long as the determination is based on facts and not mere innuendo or suspicion. Matter of: Kellogg Brown & Root Services, Inc., B-400787.2, B-400861, 2009 CPD ¶ 54 (Comp. Gen. 2009).

Wherever an offeror has improperly obtained proprietary proposal information during the course of a procurement, the integrity of the procurement is at risk, and an agency's decision to disqualify the firm is generally reasonable, absent unusual circumstances. Computer Technology Associates, Inc., B-288622, 2001 CPD ¶ 187 (Comp. Gen. 2001).

A protester challenged the propriety of an award because the director of the contracting activity, who appointed the Source Selection Official, had a close personal relationship with the president of the awardee and failed to obtain a formal recusal from the procurement. Although FAR 3.104-5 requires procurement officials who wish to discuss future employment or business opportunities with a competing contractor during the conduct of a procurement to provide a written proposal of disqualification from further participation in the procurement which relates to that competing contractor, there is no similar requirement for a written recusal based on a close personal relationship with personnel employed by a competing vendor. Since the director, in fact, did not participate in the procurement, the absence of a written recusal would constitute a mere formality that would not affect the propriety of the award. Centra Technology, Inc., B-274744, 97-1 CPD ¶ 35 (Comp. Gen. 1996).

§ 3.104-6 Ethics advisory opinions regarding prohibitions on a former official's acceptance of compensation from a contractor.

(a) An official or former official of a Federal agency who does not know whether he or she is or would be precluded by 41 U.S.C. 2104 (see 3.104-3(d)) from accepting compensation from a particular contractor may request advice from the appropriate agency ethics official before accepting such compensation.

(b) The request for an advisory opinion must be in writing, include all relevant information reasonably available to the official or former official, and be dated and signed. The request must include information about the—

(1) Procurement(s), or decision(s) on matters under 3.104-3(d)(1)(iii), involving the particular contractor, in which the individual was or is involved, including contract or solicitation numbers, dates of solicitation or award, a description of the supplies or services procured or to be procured, and contract amount;

(2) Individual's participation in the procurement or decision, including the dates or time periods of that participation, and the nature of the individual's duties, responsibilities, or actions; and

(3) Contractor, including a description of the products or services produced by the division or affiliate of the contractor from whom the individual proposes to accept compensation.

(c) Within 30 days after receipt of a request containing complete information, or as soon thereafter as practicable, the agency ethics official should issue an opinion on whether the proposed conduct would violate 41 U.S.C. 2104.

(d) (1) If complete information is not included in the request, the agency ethics official may ask the requester to provide more information or request information from other persons, including the source selection authority, the contracting officer, or the requester's immediate supervisor.

(2) In issuing an opinion, the agency ethics official may rely upon the accuracy of information furnished by the requester or other agency sources, unless he or she has reason to believe that the information is fraudulent, misleading, or otherwise incorrect.

(3) If the requester is advised in a written opinion by the agency ethics official that the requester may accept compensation from a particular contractor, and accepts such compensation in good faith reliance on that advisory opinion, then neither the requester nor the contractor will be found to have knowingly violated 41 U.S.C. 2104. If the requester or the contractor has actual knowledge or reason to believe that the opinion is based upon fraudulent, misleading, or otherwise incorrect information, their reliance upon the opinion will not be deemed to be in good faith.

United States Code Annotated

Administrative determinations, see 41 U.S.C.A. § 257.

Contract requirements, see 41 U.S.C.A. § 254.

Contracts, planning, solicitation, evaluation, and award procedures, see 10 U.S.C.A. § 2305.

Definitions, see 10 U.S.C.A. § 2302, 41 U.S.C.A. §§ 259, 403.

Determinations and decisions, see 10 U.S.C.A. § 2310, 41 U.S.C.A. § 262.

Kinds of contracts, see 10 U.S.C.A. § 2306.

Planning and solicitation requirements, see 41 U.S.C.A. § 253a.

Restrictions on disclosing and obtaining contractor bid or proposal information or source selection information, see 41 U.S.C.A. § 423.

§ 3.104-7 Violations or possible violations.

(a) A contracting officer who receives or obtains information of a violation or possible violation of 41 U.S.C. 2102, 2103, or 2104 (see 3.104-3) must determine if the reported violation or possible violation has any impact on the pending award or selection of the contractor.

(1) If the contracting officer concludes that there is no impact on the procurement, the contracting officer must forward the information concerning the violation or possible violation and documentation supporting a determination that there is no impact on the procurement to an individual designated in accordance with agency procedures.

(i) If that individual concurs, the contracting officer may proceed with the procurement.

(ii) If that individual does not concur, the individual must promptly forward the information and documentation to the HCA and advise the contracting officer to withhold award.

(2) If the contracting officer concludes that the violation or possible violation impacts the procurement, the contracting officer must promptly forward the information to the HCA.

(b) The HCA must review all information available and, in accordance with agency procedures, take appropriate action, such as—

(1) Advise the contracting officer to continue with the procurement;

(2) Begin an investigation;

(3) Refer the information disclosed to appropriate criminal investigative agencies;

(4) Conclude that a violation occurred; or

(5) Recommend that the agency head determine that the contractor, or someone acting for the contractor, has engaged in conduct constituting an offense punishable under 41 U.S.C. 2105, for the purpose of voiding or rescinding the contract.

(c) Before concluding that an offeror, contractor, or person has violated 41 U.S.C. Chapter 21, the HCA may consider that the interests of the Government are best served by requesting information from appropriate parties regarding the violation or possible violation.

(d) If the HCA concludes that 41 U.S.C. Chapter 21 has been violated, the HCA may direct the contracting officer to—

(1) If a contract has not been awarded—

(i) Cancel the procurement;

(ii) Disqualify an offeror; or

(iii) Take any other appropriate actions in the interests of the Government.

(2) If a contract has been awarded—

(i) Effect appropriate contractual remedies, including profit recapture under the clause at 52.203-10, Price or Fee Adjustment for Illegal or Improper Activity, or, if the contract has been rescinded under paragraph (d)(2)(ii) of this subsection, recovery of the amount expended under the contract;

(ii) Void or rescind the contract with respect to which—

(A) The contractor or someone acting for the contractor has been convicted for an offense where the conduct constitutes a violation of 41 U.S.C. 2102 for the purpose of either—

(1) Exchanging the information covered by the subsections for anything of

value; or

(2) Obtaining or giving anyone a competitive advantage in the award of a Federal agency procurement contract; or

(B) The agency head has determined, based upon a preponderance of the evidence, that the contractor or someone acting for the contractor has engaged in conduct constituting an offense punishable under 41 U.S.C. 2105(a) or

(iii) Take any other appropriate actions in the best interests of the Government.

(3) Refer the matter to the agency suspending or debarring official.

(e) The HCA should recommend or direct an administrative or contractual remedy commensurate with the severity and effect of the violation.

(f) If the HCA determines that urgent and compelling circumstances justify an award, or award is otherwise in the interests of the Government, the HCA, in accordance with agency procedures, may authorize the contracting officer to award the contract or execute the contract modification after notifying the agency head.

(g) The HCA may delegate his or her authority under this subsection to an individual at least one organizational level above the contracting officer and of General Officer, Flag, Senior Executive Service, or equivalent rank.

United States Code Annotated

Administrative determinations, see 41 U.S.C.A. § 257.

Contract requirements, see 41 U.S.C.A. § 254.

Contracts, planning, solicitation, evaluation, and award procedures, see 10 U.S.C.A. § 2305.

Definitions, see 10 U.S.C.A. § 2302, 41 U.S.C.A. §§ 259, 403.

Determinations and decisions, see 10 U.S.C.A. § 2310, 41 U.S.C.A. § 262.

Kinds of contracts, see 10 U.S.C.A. § 2306.

Planning and solicitation requirements, see 41 U.S.C.A. § 253a.

Restrictions on disclosing and obtaining contractor bid or proposal information or source selection information, see 41 U.S.C.A. § 423.

Notes of Decisions

In general 1

1 In general

Contracting officer's decision to disqualify government contractor based on appearance of impropriety stemming from contractor's substantial downward revision of its bid after hiring former technical representative of contracting officer was not unreasonable or irrational. NKF Engineering, Inc. v. U.S., 805 F.2d 372, 33 Cont. Cas. Fed. (CCH) P 74691 (Fed. Cir. 1986). United States ⊕64.20

A contracting officer who receives or obtains information of a violation or possible violation of the Procurement Integrity Act must determine if the reported violation or possible violation has any impact on the pending award or selection of the contractor. Kola Nut Travel, Inc. v. U.S., 68 Fed. Cl. 195 (2005).

Protest that awardee gained an unfair competitive advantage by employing a former high-level agency official was sustained where the record demonstrated that the agency failed to meaningfully consider whether the official had access to non-public, competitively useful information. Int'l Res. Group, B-409346.2, 2014 CPD ¶ 365 (Comp. Gen. 2014)

In meeting their responsibility to safeguard the interests of the government in its contractual relationships, contracting officers are granted wide latitude to exercise business judgment and may impose a variety of restrictions, not explicitly provided for in the regulations, where the needs of the agency or the nature of the procurement dictates the use of those restrictions. Matter of: Kellogg Brown & Root Services, Inc., B-400787.2, B-400861, 2009 CPD ¶ 54 (Comp. Gen. 2009).

Wherever an offeror has improperly obtained proprietary proposal information during the course of a procurement, the integrity of the procurement is at risk, and an agency's decision to disqualify the firm is generally reasonable, absent unusual circumstances. Computer

Technology Associates, Inc., B-288622, 2001 CPD ¶ 187 (Comp. Gen. 2001).

GAO Bid Protest Regulations and the Procurement Integrity Act require, as a condition precedent to GAO considering the matter, that a protester have reported the alleged violation of the Act to the contracting agency within 14 days after becoming aware of the information or facts giving rise to the alleged violation. 41 U.S.C.A. § 423(g); 4 C.F.R. § 21.5(d) (1997). The 14-day reporting requirement affords the agency an opportunity to investigate alleged improper action during the conduct of an acquisition and, in appropriate circumstances, to take remedial action before completing the tainted procurement. SRS Technlogies, B-277366, 97-2 CPD ¶ 42 (Comp. Gen. 1997).

§ 3.104-8 Criminal and civil penalties, and further administrative remedies.

Criminal and civil penalties, and administrative remedies, may apply to conduct that violates 41 U.S.C. Chapter 21 (see 3.104-3). See 33.102(f) for special rules regarding bid protests. See 3.104-7 for administrative remedies relating to contracts.

(a) An official who knowingly fails to comply with the requirements of 3.104-3 is subject to the penalties and administrative action set forth in 41 U.S.C. 2105.

(b) An offeror who engages in employment discussion with an official subject to the restrictions of 3.104-3, knowing that the official has not complied with 3.104-3(c)(1), is subject to the criminal, civil, or administrative penalties set forth in subsection 27(e) of the Act.

(c) An official who refuses to terminate employment discussions (see 3.104-5) may be subject to agency administrative actions under 5 CFR 2635.604(d) if the official's disqualification from participation in a particular procurement interferes substantially with the individual's ability to perform assigned duties.

United States Code Annotated

Administrative determinations, see 41 U.S.C.A. § 257.

Contract requirements, see 41 U.S.C.A. § 254.

Contracts, planning, solicitation, evaluation, and award procedures, see 10 U.S.C.A. § 2305.

Definitions, see 10 U.S.C.A. § 2302, 41 U.S.C.A. §§ 259, 403.

Determinations and decisions, see 10 U.S.C.A. § 2310, 41 U.S.C.A. § 262.

Kinds of contracts, see 10 U.S.C.A. § 2306.

Planning and solicitation requirements, see 41 U.S.C.A. § 253a.

Restrictions on disclosing and obtaining contractor bid or proposal information or source selection information, see 41 U.S.C.A. § 423.

§ 3.104-9 Contract clauses.

In solicitations and contracts for other than commercial items that exceed the simplified acquisition threshold, insert the clauses at—

(a) 52.203-8, Cancellation, Rescission, and Recovery of Funds for Illegal or Improper Activity; and

(b) 52.203-10, Price or Fee Adjustment for Illegal or Improper Activity.

United States Code Annotated

Administrative determinations, see 41 U.S.C.A. § 257.

Contract requirements, see 41 U.S.C.A. § 254.

Contracts, planning, solicitation, evaluation, and award procedures, see 10 U.S.C.A. § 2305.

Definitions, see 10 U.S.C.A. § 2302, 41 U.S.C.A. §§ 259, 403.

Determinations and decisions, see 10 U.S.C.A. § 2310, 41 U.S.C.A. § 262.

Kinds of contracts, see 10 U.S.C.A. § 2306.

Planning and solicitation requirements, see 41 U.S.C.A. § 253a.

Restrictions on disclosing and obtaining contractor bid or proposal information or source selection information, see 41 U.S.C.A. § 423.

Subpart 3.2 Contractor Gratuities to Government Personnel

§ 3.201 Applicability.

This subpart applies to all executive agencies, except that coverage concerning exemplary damages applies only to the Department of Defense (10 U.S.C. 2207).

United States Code Annotated

Contract requirements, see 41 U.S.C.A. § 254.

Contracts, planning, solicitation, evaluation, and award procedures, see 10 U.S.C.A. § 2305.

Definitions, see 10 U.S.C.A. § 2302, 41 U.S.C.A. §§ 259, 403.

Kinds of contracts, see 10 U.S.C.A. § 2306.

Planning and solicitation requirements, see 41 U.S.C.A. § 253a.

§ 3.202 Contract clause.

The contracting officer shall insert the clause at 52.203-3, Gratuities, in solicitations and contracts with a value exceeding the simplified acquisition threshold, except those for personal services and those between military departments or defense agencies and foreign governments that do not obligate any funds appropriated to the Department of Defense.

United States Code Annotated

Contract requirements, see 41 U.S.C.A. § 254.

Contracts, planning, solicitation, evaluation, and award procedures, see 10 U.S.C.A. § 2305.

Definitions, see 10 U.S.C.A. § 2302, 41 U.S.C.A. §§ 259, 403.

Kinds of contracts, see 10 U.S.C.A. § 2306.

Planning and solicitation requirements, see 41 U.S.C.A. § 253a.

§ 3.203 Reporting suspected violations of the Gratuities clause.

Agency personnel shall report suspected violations of the Gratuities clause to the contracting officer or other designated official in accordance with agency procedures. The agency reporting procedures shall be published as an implementation of this section 3.203 and shall clearly specify—

(a) What to report and how to report it; and

(b) The channels through which reports must pass, including the function and authority of each official designated to review them.

United States Code Annotated

Contract requirements, see 41 U.S.C.A. § 254.

Contracts, planning, solicitation, evaluation, and award procedures, see 10 U.S.C.A. § 2305.

Definitions, see 10 U.S.C.A. § 2302, 41 U.S.C.A. §§ 259, 403.

Kinds of contracts, see 10 U.S.C.A. § 2306.

Planning and solicitation requirements, see 41 U.S.C.A. § 253a.

§ 3.204 Treatment of violations.

(a) Before taking any action against a contractor, the agency head or a designee shall determine, after notice and hearing under agency procedures, whether the contractor, its agent, or another representative, under a contract containing the Gratuities clause—

(1) Offered or gave a gratuity (e.g., an entertainment or gift) to an officer, official, or employee of the Government; and

(2) Intended by the gratuity to obtain a contract or favorable treatment under a contract (intent generally must be inferred).

(b) Agency procedures shall afford the contractor an opportunity to appear with counsel, submit documentary evidence, present witnesses, and confront any person the agency presents. The procedures should be as informal as practicable, consistent with principles of fundamental fairness.

(c) When the agency head or designee determines that a violation has occurred, the Government may—

(1) Terminate the contractor's right to proceed;

(2) Initiate debarment or suspension measures as set forth in Subpart 9.4; and

(3) Assess exemplary damages, if the contract uses money appropriated to the Department of Defense.

United States Code Annotated

Contract requirements, see 41 U.S.C.A. § 254.

Contracts, planning, solicitation, evaluation, and award procedures, see 10 U.S.C.A. § 2305.

Definitions, see 10 U.S.C.A. § 2302, 41 U.S.C.A. §§ 259, 403.

Expenditure of appropriations: limitation, see 10 U.S.C.A. § 2207.

Kinds of contracts, see 10 U.S.C.A. § 2306.

Planning and solicitation requirements, see 41 U.S.C.A. § 253a.

Notes of Decisions

In general 2
Employee disciplinary proceedings 1

1 Employee disciplinary proceedings

Discharge of Social Security Administration employee for accepting gratuity and divulging confidential information to potential subcontractor did not constitute disparate treatment, absent allegation that agency knowingly treated employee differently. Baker v. Department of Health and Human Services, 912 F.2d 1448 (Fed. Cir. 1990). Officers And Public Employees ☞69.7

Finding that Social Security Administration employee accepted gratuitous lunch from potential subcontractor was based on substantial evidence, despite employee's contention that lunch was a social engagement between friends. Baker v. Department of Health and Human Services, 912 F.2d 1448 (Fed. Cir. 1990). Officers And Public Employees ☞72.63

Discharge of Social Security Administration employee for accepting gratuity and divulging confidential information to potential subcontractor was not a grossly disproportionate penalty. Baker v. Department of Health and Human Services, 912 F.2d 1448 (Fed. Cir. 1990). Officers And Public Employees ☞69.7

2 In general

E-mails from a contractor's employee requesting favorable ratings and his gifts to the Government employee responsible for the ratings were sufficient evidence of guilt of violating an illegal gratuity statute, even though a favorable rating was never given, the U.S. Court of Appeals for the Eighth Circuit has held, affirming a district court decision. U.S. v. Hoffmann, 556 F.3d 871 (8th Cir. 2009)

Subpart 3.3 Reports of Suspected Antitrust Violations

§ 3.301 General.

(a) Practices that eliminate competition or restrain trade usually lead to excessive prices and may warrant criminal, civil, or administrative action against the participants. Examples of anticompetitive practices are collusive bidding, follow-the-leader pricing, rotated low bids, collusive price estimating systems, and sharing of the business.

(b) Contracting personnel are an important potential source of investigative leads for antitrust enforcement and should therefore be sensitive to indications of unlawful behavior by offerors and contractors. Agency personnel shall report, in accordance with agency regulations, evidence of suspected antitrust violations in acquisitions for possible referral to—

(1) The Attorney General under 3.303 and

(2) The agency office responsible for contractor debarment and suspension under Subpart 9.4.

United States Code Annotated

Contract requirements, see 41 U.S.C.A. § 254.

Contracts, planning, solicitation, evaluation, and award procedures, see 10 U.S.C.A. § 2305.

Definitions, see 10 U.S.C.A. § 2302, 41 U.S.C.A. §§ 259, 403.

Evaluation and award, see 41 U.S.C.A. § 253b.

Expenditure of appropriations: limitation, see 10 U.S.C.A. § 2207.

Kinds of contracts, see 10 U.S.C.A. § 2306.

Planning and solicitation requirements, see 41 U.S.C.A. § 253a.

§ 3.302 Definitions.

As used in this subpart—

"Identical bids" means bids for the same line item that are determined to be identical as to unit price or total line item amount, with or without the application of evaluation factors (*e.g.,* discount or transportation cost).

"Line item" means an item of supply or service, specified in a solicitation, that the offeror must separately price.

United States Code Annotated

Contract requirements, see 41 U.S.C.A. § 254.

Contracts, planning, solicitation, evaluation, and award procedures, see 10 U.S.C.A. § 2305.

Definitions, see 10 U.S.C.A. § 2302, 41 U.S.C.A. §§ 259, 403.

Evaluation and award, see 41 U.S.C.A. § 253b.

Expenditure of appropriations: limitation, see 10 U.S.C.A. § 2207.

Kinds of contracts, see 10 U.S.C.A. § 2306.

Planning and solicitation requirements, see 41 U.S.C.A. § 253a.

§ 3.303 Reporting suspected antitrust violations.

(a) Agencies are required by 41 U.S.C. 3707 and 10 U.S.C. 2305(b)(9) to report to the Attorney General any bids or proposals that evidence a violation of the antitrust laws. These reports are in addition to those required by Subpart 9.4.

(b) The antitrust laws are intended to ensure that markets operate competitively. Any agreement or mutual understanding among competing firms that restrains the natural operation of market forces is suspect. Paragraph (c) of this section identifies behavior patterns that are often associated with antitrust violations. Activities meeting the descriptions in paragraph (c) are not necessarily improper, but they are sufficiently questionable to warrant notifying the appropriate authorities, in accordance with agency procedures.

(c) Practices or events that may evidence violations of the antitrust laws include—

(1) The existence of an "industry price list" or "price agreement" to which contractors refer in formulating their offers;

(2) A sudden change from competitive bidding to identical bidding;

(3) Simultaneous price increases or follow-the-leader pricing;

(4) Rotation of bids or proposals, so that each competitor takes a turn in sequence as low bidder, or so that certain competitors bid low only on some sizes of contracts and high on other sizes;

(5) Division of the market, so that certain competitors bid low only for contracts awarded by certain agencies, or for contracts in certain geographical areas, or on certain products, and bid high on all other jobs;

(6) Establishment by competitors of a collusive price estimating system;

(7) The filing of a joint bid by two or more competitors when at least one of the competitors has sufficient technical capability and productive capacity for contract performance;

(8) Any incidents suggesting direct collusion among competitors, such as the appearance of identical calculation or spelling errors in two or more competitive offers or the submission by one firm of offers for other firms; and

(9) Assertions by the employees, former employees, or competitors of offerors, that an agreement to restrain trade exists.

(d) Identical bids shall be reported under this section if the agency has some reason to believe that the bids resulted from collusion.

(e) For offers from foreign contractors for contracts to be performed outside the United States and its outlying areas, contracting officers may refer suspected collusive offers to the authorities of the foreign government concerned for appropriate action.

(f) Agency reports shall be addressed to the—

Attorney General
U.S. Department of Justice
Washington DC 20530
Attention: Assistant Attorney General
Antitrust Division

and shall include—

(1) A brief statement describing the suspected practice and the reason for the suspicion; and

(2) The name, address, and telephone number of an individual in the agency who can be contacted for further information.

(g) Questions concerning this reporting requirement may be communicated by telephone directly to the Office of the Assistant Attorney General, Antitrust Division.

United States Code Annotated

Contract requirements, see 41 U.S.C.A. § 254.

Contracts, planning, solicitation, evaluation, and award procedures, see 10 U.S.C.A. § 2305.

Definitions, see 10 U.S.C.A. § 2302, 41 U.S.C.A. §§ 259, 403.

Evaluation and award, see 41 U.S.C.A. § 253b.

Expenditure of appropriations: limitation, see 10 U.S.C.A. § 2207.

Kinds of contracts, see 10 U.S.C.A. § 2306.

Planning and solicitation requirements, see 41 U.S.C.A. § 253a.

Notes of Decisions

In general 1

1 In general

FAR 3.303(a) states that the antitrust laws are intended to ensure that markets operate competitively. Any agreement or mutual understanding among competing firms that restrains the natural operation of market forces is suspect. Practices or events that may evidence violations of the antitrust laws include: "Assertions by the employees, former employees, or competitors of offerors, that an agreement to restrain trade exists." 48 C.F.R. 3.303(c)(9). Inducing a prospective subcontractor to quote higher prices to other prospective prime contractors to ensure award of the contract is a per se violation of the Sherman Act. 15 U.S.C. § 3 (2005). Suspected antitrust violations are to be reported to the Attorney General, who enforces the Sherman Act, as well as to the debarring and suspending official of the appropriate agency. 48 CFR 3.301, 3.303. Turner Construction Co. v. General Services Administration, G.S.B.C.A. No. 15502, 05-2 B.C.A. (CCH) ¶ 33118, 2005 WL 2789442 (Gen. Services Admin. B.C.A. 2005).

Subpart 3.4 Contingent Fees

§ 3.400 Scope of subpart.

This subpart prescribes policies and procedures that restrict contingent fee arrangements for soliciting or obtaining Government contracts to those permitted by 10 U.S.C. 2306(b) and 41 U.S.C. 3901.

United States Code Annotated

Contract requirements, see 41 U.S.C.A. § 254.

Definitions, see 10 U.S.C.A. § 2302, 41 U.S.C.A. §§ 259, 403.

Kinds of contracts, see 10 U.S.C.A. § 2306.

Notes of Decisions

In general 1

1 In general

By their terms, 10 U.S.C. § 2306(b) and 41 U.S.C. § 254(a) (1988), the statutory basis for the contingent fee prohibition, only apply to negotiated contracts. As a matter of policy the statutory prohibition for negotiated contracts has been extended to sealed bids. FAR 3.403. Accordingly, the contingent fee prohibition applies to all federal procurements. General Sales Agency, B-247529, B-247529.2, 92-2 CPD ¶ 80 (Comp. Gen. 1992).

§ 3.401 Definitions.

As used in this subpart—

"Bona fide agency" means an established commercial or selling agency, maintained by a contractor for the purpose of securing business, that neither exerts nor proposes to exert improper influence to solicit or obtain Government contracts nor holds itself out as being able to obtain any Government contract or contracts through improper influence.

"Bona fide employee" means a person, employed by a contractor and subject to the contractor's supervision and control as to time, place, and manner of performance, who neither exerts nor proposes to exert improper influence to solicit or obtain Government contracts nor holds out as being able to obtain any Government contract or contracts through improper influence.

"Contingent fee" means any commission, percentage, brokerage, or other fee that is contingent upon the success that a person or concern has in securing a Government contract.

"Improper influence" means any influence that induces or tends to induce a Government employee or officer to give consideration or to act regarding a Government contract on any basis other than the merits of the matter.

United States Code Annotated

Contract requirements, see 41 U.S.C.A. § 254.

Definitions, see 10 U.S.C.A. § 2302, 41 U.S.C.A. §§ 259, 403.

Kinds of contracts, see 10 U.S.C.A. § 2306.

Notes of Decisions

In general 1

1 In general

A contingent fee agreement is only enforceable if it exists between a contractor and its bona fide employee or agency. FAR 3.402(b). Although a selling agent agreed to assist the awardee in securing business from the government, there is no indication that the agent exerted or proposed to exert influence upon government contracting personnel in its efforts on behalf of the awardee. An established selling agency that obtains necessary solicitation documents and provides other administrative services-arranging for a client to be placed on an agency's list of prospective bidders, reviewing a procurement's requirements, and assisting a client with the preparation and submission of its bid-falls within the definition of a bona fide selling agency under 10 U.S.C. § 2306(b) and FAR § 3.402(b). Howard Johnson Lodge-Reconsideration, B-244302, B-244302.2, 1992 WL 62441 (Comp. Gen. 1992).

§ 3.402 Statutory requirements.

Contractors' arrangements to pay contingent fees for soliciting or obtaining Government contracts have long been considered contrary to public policy because such arrangements may lead to attempted or actual exercise of improper influence. In 10 U.S.C. 2306(b) and 41 U.S.C. 3901, Congress affirmed this public policy but permitted certain exceptions. These statutes—

(a) Require in every negotiated contract a warranty by the contractor against contingent fees;

(b) Permit, as an exception to the warranty, contingent fee arrangements between contractors and bona fide employees or bona fide agencies; and

(c) Provide that, for breach or violation of the warranty by the contractor, the Government may annul the contract without liability or deduct from the contract price or consideration, or otherwise recover, the full amount of the contingent fee.

United States Code Annotated

Contract requirements, see 41 U.S.C.A. § 254.

Definitions, see 10 U.S.C.A. § 2302, 41 U.S.C.A. §§ 259, 403.

Kinds of contracts, see 10 U.S.C.A. § 2306.

Notes of Decisions

In general 1

1 In general

The fact that an agent's fee is contingent upon the contractor's successful performance of the contract, or even upon receiving the contract award, is not sufficient, by itself, to bring a fee agreement under the contingent fee prohibition; rather, the regulation contemplates a specific demonstration that an agent is retained for the express purpose of contacting government officials, where such contact poses a threat of the exertion of improper influence to obtain government contracts. Matter of: Kola Nut Travel, Inc., B-296090.4, 2005 CPD ¶ 184 (Comp. Gen. 2005).

No violation of the contingent fee prohibition was found where awardees' consultant will earn a fee based on profits earned during the awardees' performance of the contract, and there is no evidence of improper influence on government officials regarding the contract award decisions. The record reflects that award was made on the basis of the awardees' significantly lower prices and higher rated technical proposals. Therefore, the agreement between the awardees and the consultant does not violate the statutory and regulatory limitations on contingent fees. Matter of: Kola Nut Travel, Inc., B-296090.4, 2005 CPD ¶ 184 (Comp. Gen. 2005).

A contingent fee agreement is only enforceable if it exists between a contractor and its bona fide employee or selling agent. FAR3.402(b). Although a selling agent agreed to assist the awardee in securing business from the government, there is no indication that the agent exerted or proposed to exert influence upon government contracting personnel in its efforts on behalf of the awardee. An established selling agency that obtains necessary solicitation documents and provides other administrative services-arranging for a client to be placed on an agency's list of prospective bidders, reviewing a procurement's requirements, and assisting a client with the preparation and submission of its bid-falls within the definition of a bona fide selling agency under 10 U.S.C. § 2306(b) and FAR § 3.402(b). Howard Johnson Lodge-Reconsideration, B-244302, B-244302.2, 1992 WL 62441 (Comp. Gen. 1992).

§ 3.403 Applicability.

This subpart applies to all contracts. Statutory requirements for negotiated contracts are, as a matter of policy, extended to sealed bid contracts.

United States Code Annotated

Contract requirements, see 41 U.S.C.A. § 254.

Definitions, see 10 U.S.C.A. § 2302, 41 U.S.C.A. §§ 259, 403.

Kinds of contracts, see 10 U.S.C.A. § 2306.

Notes of Decisions

In general 1

1 In general

FAR section prohibiting enforcement of contracts entered into by a government agency with a contractor that has employed or retained a third-party to secure the government contract, in exchange for a fee that is contingent upon the third-party's success in securing the government contract, did not apply to a federal housing authority's contract with a provider of utility cost-savings consulting services; the percentage-based fee at issue was not to be paid to the provider by a third-party wishing to secure a contract with the government, but rather, was to be paid to the provider by the housing authority itself, as a percentage of the cost savings realized. Lowell Housing Authority v. PSC Intern., Inc., 692 F.Supp.2d 180 (D. Mass. 2010)

By their terms, 10 U.S.C. § 2306(b) and 41 U.S.C. § 254(a) (1988), the statutory bases for the contingent fee prohibition, only apply to negotiated contracts. However, as a matter of policy, the statutory prohibition for negotiated contracts has been extended to sealed bids. FAR 3.403. Accordingly, the contingent fee prohibition applies to all federal procurements. General Sales Agency, B-247529, B-247529.2, 92-2 CPD ¶ 80 (Comp. Gen. 1992); Convention Marketing Services, B-245660, B-245660.3, B-246175, 92-1 CPD ¶ 144 (Comp. Gen. 1992).

§ 3.404 Contract clause.

The contracting officer shall insert the clause at 52.203-5, Covenant Against Contingent Fees, in all solicitations and contracts exceeding the simplified acquisition threshold, other than those for commercial items (see Parts 2 and 12).

United States Code Annotated

Contract requirements, see 41 U.S.C.A. § 254.

Definitions, see 10 U.S.C.A. § 2302, 41 U.S.C.A. §§ 259, 403.

Kinds of contracts, see 10 U.S.C.A. § 2306.

§ 3.405 Misrepresentations or violations of the Covenant Against Contingent Fees.

(a) Government personnel who suspect or have evidence of attempted or actual exercise of improper influence, misrepresentation of a contingent fee arrangement, or other violation of the Covenant Against Contingent Fees shall report the matter promptly to the contracting officer or appropriate higher authority in accordance with agency procedures.

(b) When there is specific evidence or other reasonable basis to suspect one or more of the violations in paragraph (a) of this section, the chief of the contracting office shall review the facts and, if appropriate, take or direct one or more of the following, or other, actions:

(1) If before award, reject the bid or proposal.

(2) If after award, enforce the Government's right to annul the contract or to recover the fee.

(3) Initiate suspension or debarment action under Subpart 9.4.

(4) Refer suspected fraudulent or criminal matters to the Department of Justice, as prescribed in agency regulations.

United States Code Annotated

Contract requirements, see 41 U.S.C.A. § 254.

Definitions, see 10 U.S.C.A. § 2302, 41 U.S.C.A. §§ 259, 403.

Kinds of contracts, see 10 U.S.C.A. § 2306.

Notes of Decisions

Improper influence 1

1 Improper influence

Issues of material fact existed as to whether governmental relations firm proposed to exert improper influence to assist cable television facilities operator to obtain government contract, such that firm would not be bona fide established commercial or selling agency and operator would not be exempted from statute prohibiting contingent fee arrangements for procurement of government services, precluding summary judgment. Federal Property and Administrative Services Act of 1949, § 304(a), 41 U.S.C.A. § 254(a); Fed. Rules Civ.Proc. Rule 56(c), 28 U.S.C.A.; 48 C.F.R. § 3.401. Keefe Co. v. Americable Intern., Inc., 169 F.3d 34, 335 (D.C. Cir. 1999), certified question answered, 755 A.2d 469 (D.C. 2000), answer to certified question conformed to Keefe Co. v. Americable Intern., Inc., 219 F.3d 669, 343 (D.C. Cir. 2000). Federal Civil Procedure ⚖2492

§ 3.406 Records.

For enforcement purposes, agencies shall preserve any specific evidence of one or more of the violations in 3.405(a), together with all other pertinent data, including a record of actions taken. Contracting offices shall not retire or destroy these records until it is certain that they are no longer needed for enforcement purposes. If the original record is maintained in a central file, a copy must be retained in the contract file.

United States Code Annotated
Contract requirements, see 41 U.S.C.A. § 254.

Definitions, see 10 U.S.C.A. § 2302, 41 U.S.C.A. §§ 259, 403.

Kinds of contracts, see 10 U.S.C.A. § 2306.

Subpart 3.5 Other Improper Business Practices

§ 3.501 Buying-in.

§ 3.501-1 Definition.
"Buying-in," as used in this section, means submitting an offer below anticipated costs, expecting to—

(1) Increase the contract amount after award (e.g., through unnecessary or excessively priced change orders); or

(2) Receive follow-on contracts at artificially high prices to recover losses incurred on the buy-in contract.

United States Code Annotated
Contract requirements, see 41 U.S.C.A. § 254.

Contracts, planning, solicitation, evaluation, and award procedures, see 10 U.S.C.A. § 2305.

Definitions, see 10 U.S.C.A. § 2302, 41 U.S.C.A. §§ 259, 403.

Kinds of contracts, see 10 U.S.C.A. § 2306.

Planning and solicitation requirements, see 41 U.S.C.A. § 253a.

Notes of Decisions
In general 1

1 In general
Protester challenged the agency's decision to accept the awardee's proposed cost recovery cap, alleging that the cap violates the prohibition against "buying-in." FAR 3.501. The effect of a cap is to convert a portion of this cost-type contract to a fixed-price contract, which is analogous to a below-cost bid or offer in a fixed-price environment. However, the FAR does not bar submission or acceptance of below cost offers. Rather, the FAR states that contracting officers faced with the possibility of a buy-in must take steps to ensure that an offeror's buying-in losses are not recovered from the government through change orders or follow-on efforts. FAR 3.501-2(a). In fact, the FAR suggests that one way to minimize such an offeror's likelihood of recovering such losses through other means is to seek a price commitment covering as much of the program as possible-something the contracting officer has done here. Matter of: Halifax Technical Services, Inc., B-246236, B-246236.6, B-246236.7, B-246236.9, 94-1 CPD ¶ 30 (Comp. Gen. 1994).

§ 3.501-2 General.
(a) Buying-in may decrease competition or result in poor contract performance. The

contracting officer must take appropriate action to ensure buying-in losses are not recovered by the contractor through the pricing of—

(1) Change orders; or

(2) Follow-on contracts subject to cost analysis.

(b) The Government should minimize the opportunity for buying-in by seeking a price commitment covering as much of the entire program concerned as is practical by using—

(1) Multiyear contracting, with a requirement in the solicitation that a price be submitted only for the total multiyear quantity; or

(2) Priced options for additional quantities that, together with the firm contract quantity, equal the program requirements (see Subpart 17.2).

(c) Other safeguards are available to the contracting officer to preclude recovery of buying-in losses (*e.g.*, amortization of nonrecurring costs (see 15.408, Table 15-2, paragraph A, column (2) under "Formats for Submission of Line Item Summaries") and treatment of unreasonable price quotations (see 15.405).

United States Code Annotated

Contract requirements, see 41 U.S.C.A. § 254.

Contracts, planning, solicitation, evaluation, and award procedures, see 10 U.S.C.A. § 2305.

Definitions, see 10 U.S.C.A. § 2302, 41 U.S.C.A. §§ 259, 403.

Kinds of contracts, see 10 U.S.C.A. § 2306.

Planning and solicitation requirements, see 41 U.S.C.A. § 253a.

Notes of Decisions

In general 1

1 In general

"Buying-in' is the prohibited practice of intentionally underpricing a contract. It triggers no Government duty to verify the bid, but only the duty to ensure that the contractor does not recover its buying-in losses improperly. FAR 3.501-2. Appeal of Triax Pacific, Inc., A.S.B.C.A. No. 41891, 94-1 B.C.A. (CCH) ¶ 26529, 1993 WL 492228 (Armed Serv. B.C.A. 1993).

An offeror, for various reasons, in its business judgment, may decide to submit a below-cost offer, and such an offer is not inherently invalid. Whether an awardee can perform the contract at the price offered is a matter of responsibility which we will not review absent a showing of possible fraud or bad faith or that definitive responsibility criteria have not been met. However, contracting agencies are encouraged to minimize the opportunity for buying-in by seeking a price commitment covering as much of the entire program concerned as is practical and contracting officers must take appropriate action to ensure buying-in losses are not recovered by the contractor. Femme Comp Inc. v. U.S., 83 Fed.Cl. 704 (Fed.Cl. ,2008)

Contracting officers faced with the possibility of a buy-in must take steps to ensure that an offeror's buying-in losses are not recovered from the government through change orders or follow-on efforts. FAR 3.501-2(a). One way to minimize such an offeror's likelihood of recovering such losses through other means is to seek a price commitment covering as much of the program as possible, as the contracting officer has done here. See FAR 3.501-2(b)(1). Halifax Technical Services, Inc., B-246236, B-246236.6, B-246236.7, B-246236.9, 94-1 CPD ¶ 30 (Comp. Gen. 1994).

§ 3.502 Subcontractor kickbacks.

§ 3.502-1 Definitions.

As used in this section—

"Kickback" means any money, fee, commission, credit, gift, gratuity, thing of value, or compensation of any kind which is provided to any prime contractor, prime contractor employee, subcontractor, or subcontractor employee for the purpose of improperly obtaining or rewarding favorable treatment in connection with a prime contract or in connection with a subcontract relating to a prime contract.

"Person" means a corporation, partnership, business association of any kind, trust, joint-stock company, or individual.

"Prime contract" means a contract or contractual action entered into by the United States for the purpose of obtaining supplies, materials, equipment, or services of any kind.

"Prime Contractor" means a person who has entered into a prime contr the United States.

"Prime Contractor employee" means any officer, partner, employee, or agent of a prime contractor.

"Subcontract" means a contract or contractual action entered into by a prime contractor or subcontractor for the purpose of obtaining supplies, materials, equipment, or services of any kind under a prime contract.

"Subcontractor" (1) means any person, other than the prime contractor, who offers to furnish or furnishes any supplies, materials, equipment, or services of any kind under a prime contract or a subcontract entered into in connection with such prime contract; and (2) includes any person who offers to furnish or furnishes general supplies to the prime contractor or a higher tier subcontractor.

United States Code Annotated

Administrative offsets, see 41 U.S.C.A. § 56.

Civil actions, see 41 U.S.C.A. § 55.

Contract requirements, see 41 U.S.C.A. § 254.

Contractor responsibilities, see 41 U.S.C.A. § 57.

Contracts, planning, solicitation, evaluation, and award procedures, see 10 U.S.C.A. § 2305.

Criminal penalties, see 41 U.S.C.A. § 54.

Definitions, see 10 U.S.C.A. § 2302, 41 U.S.C.A. §§ 259, 403.

Inspection authority, see 41 U.S.C.A. § 58.

Kinds of contracts, see 10 U.S.C.A. § 2306.

Planning and solicitation requirements, see 41 U.S.C.A. § 253a.

Prohibited conduct, see 41 U.S.C.A. § 53.

§ 3.502-2 Subcontractor kickbacks.

The Anti-Kickback Act of 1986 (now codified at 41 U.S.C. chapter 87, Kickbacks,) was passed to deter subcontractors from making payments and contractors from accepting payments for the purpose of improperly obtaining or rewarding favorable treatment in connection with a prime contract or a subcontract relating to a prime contract. The Kickbacks statute—

(a) Prohibits any person from—

(1) Providing, attempting to provide, or offering to provide any kickback;

(2) Soliciting, accepting, or attempting to accept any kickback; or

(3) Including, directly or indirectly, the amount of any kickback in the contract price charged by a subcontractor to a prime contractor or a higher tier subcontractor or in the contract price charged by a prime contractor to the United States.

(b) Imposes criminal penalties on any person who knowingly and willfully engages in the prohibited conduct addressed in paragraph (a) of this subsection.

(c) Provides for the recovery of civil penalties by the United States from any person who knowingly engages in such prohibited conduct and from any person whose employee, subcontractor, or subcontractor employee provides, accepts, or charges a kickback.

(d) Provides that—

(1) The contracting officer may offset the amount of a kickback against monies owed by the United States to the prime contractor under the prime contract to which such kickback relates;

(2) The contracting officer may direct a prime contractor to withhold from any sums

owed to a subcontractor under a subcontract of the prime contract the amount of any kickback which was or may be offset against the prime contractor under paragraph (d)(1) of this subsection; and

(3) An offset under paragraph (d)(1) or a direction under paragraph (d)(2) of this subsection is a claim by the Government for the purposes of 41 U.S.C. chapter 71, Contract Disputes.

(e) Authorizes contracting officers to order that sums withheld under paragraph (d)(2) of this subsection be paid to the contracting agency, or if the sum has already been offset against the prime contractor, that it be retained by the prime contractor.

(f) Requires the prime contractor to notify the contracting officer when the withholding under paragraph (d)(2) of this subsection has been accomplished unless the amount withheld has been paid to the Government.

(g) Requires a prime contractor or subcontractor to report in writing to the inspector general of the contracting agency, the head of the contracting agency if the agency does not have an inspector general, or the Attorney General any possible violation of the Kickbacks statute when the prime contractor or subcontractor has reasonable grounds to believe such violation may have occurred.

(h) Provides that, for the purpose of ascertaining whether there has been a violation of the Kickbacks statute with respect to any prime contract, the Government Accountability Office and the inspector general of the contracting agency, or a representative of such contracting agency designated by the head of the agency if the agency does not have an inspector general, shall have access to and may inspect the facilities and audit the books and records, including any electronic data or records, of any prime contractor or subcontractor under a prime contract awarded by such agency.

(i) Requires each contracting agency to include in each prime contract exceeding $150,000 for other than commercial items (see Part 12), a requirement that the prime contractor shall—

(1) Have in place and follow reasonable procedures designed to prevent and detect violations of the Kickbacks statute in its own operations and direct business relationships (e.g., company ethics rules prohibiting kickbacks by employees, agents, or subcontractors; education programs for new employees and subcontractors, explaining policies about kickbacks, related company procedures and the consequences of detection; procurement procedures to minimize the opportunity for kickbacks; audit procedures designed to detect kickbacks; periodic surveys of subcontractors to elicit information about kickbacks; procedures to report kickbacks to law enforcement officials; annual declarations by employees of gifts or gratuities received from subcontractors; annual employee declarations that they have violated no company ethics rules; personnel practices that document unethical or illegal behavior and make such information available to prospective employers); and

(2) Cooperate fully with any Federal agency investigating a possible violation of the Kickbacks statute.

(j) Notwithstanding paragraph (i) of this section, a prime contractor shall cooperate fully with any Federal Government agency investigating a violation of 41 U.S.C. 8702 (see 41 U.S.C. 8703(b)).

United States Code Annotated

Administrative offsets, see 41 U.S.C.A. § 56.

Civil actions, see 41 U.S.C.A. § 55.

Contract requirements, see 41 U.S.C.A. § 254.

Contractor responsibilities, see 41 U.S.C.A. § 57.

Contracts, planning, solicitation, evaluation, and award procedures, see 10 U.S.C.A. § 2305.

Criminal penalties, see 41 U.S.C.A. § 54.

Definitions, see 10 U.S.C.A. § 2302, 41 U.S.C.A. §§ 259, 403.

Inspection authority, see 41 U.S.C.A. § 58.

Kinds of contracts, see 10 U.S.C.A. § 2306.

Planning and solicitation requirements, see 41 U.S.C.A. § 253a.

Prohibited conduct, see 41 U.S.C.A. § 53.

Notes of Decisions

In general 1

1 In general

Express provision for government's recovery of kickbacks in connection with government contracts did not preclude government from cancellation of prime contract where three of prime contractor's principal employees had accepted kickbacks from subcontractors. U.S. v. Acme Process Equipment Co., 385 U.S. 138, 87 S.Ct. 350 (1966)

Cancellation by government of prime contract because three of principal employees of prime contractor had been paid kickbacks by subcontractors was consistent with effectuating public policy embodied in Anti-Kickback Act. U.S. v. Acme Process Equipment Co., 385 U.S. 138, 87 S. Ct. 350, 17 L.Ed. 2d 249 (1966).

That none of officers of prime contractor were aware of kickbacks by subcontractors did not preclude government from cancelling prime contract on basis of the kickbacks, where those of prime contractor's employees and agents who did know were in the upper echelon of its managers, one of guilty employees was general manager of one of company's chief plants and son of president of prime contractor, and the other two kickback receivers were in charge of operations, sales and government contracts. U.S. v. Acme Process Equipment Co., 385 U.S. 138, 87 S.Ct. 350, 17 L. Ed. 2d 249 (1966).

Although kickbacks from subcontractors to three principal employees of prime contractor took place after prime contract had been awarded, where kickback arrangements existed either at time prime contract was awarded or shortly thereafter, one of kickbacking subcontractors actually participated in negotiation of prime contract, and prime contract contained price redetermination feature, there was great likelihood that cost of prime contract to government and reliability of prime contractor's performance under it would be directly affected by fact that prime contract was to be performed largely through subcontracts obtained by kickbacks and government was entitled to cancel prime contract. Lowell Housing Authority v. PSC Intern., Inc., 692 F.Supp.2d 180 (D. Mass. 2010)

The relevant portion of the Anti-Kickback Act, 41 U.S.C. § 56(c) states that the contracting officer's offset "is a claim of the Government for the purposes of the [CDA]." The House Report pertaining to the statute states: [T]he Committee intends that the contracting officer's actions and decisions under section 6(b) be governed by the Contract Disputes Act of 1978, in cases of offsets against the contract connected with the kickback. A prime contractor may seek review under the Contract Disputes Act when it disagrees with a contracting officer's decision or actions under Section 6(b). H.R. Rep. No. 99-964, at 17 (1986). Therefore, a government claim under 41 U.S.C. § 56 is subject to the full set of procedures available under the CDA, including the choice of appellate forum. In short, boards of contract appeals and the United States Court of Federal Claims possess concurrent jurisdiction over appeals of contracting officer's decisions made under the Turner Construction Co. v. General Services Administration, G.S.B.C.A. No. 16840, 06-2 B.C.A. (CCH) ¶ 33391, 2006 WL 2506768 (Gen. Services Admin. B.C.A. 2006).

Under the Anti-Kickback Act, the authority of the contracting officer is limited to determining the amount of the kickback. Criminal or civil liability and the resulting penalties must be determined in either a criminal or civil action brought in the name of the United States by the Department of Justice in a court of competent jurisdiction. 41 U.S.C. §§ 54, 55; 28 U.S.C. § 516. Consequently, the existence of an Anti-Kickback Act violation is outside the purview of both the contracting officer's authority and the CDA jurisdiction of a Board of Contract Appeals. Turner Construction Co. v. GSA, 06-2 BCA ¶ 33391 (G.S.B.C.A. 2006)

Acceptance by support services contractor's food service manager of $20,000 from subcontractor while performing his obligations under an umbrella contract to provide dining facility services to United States Army in Kuwait and Iraq was a kickback for which contractor was strictly liable under Anti-Kickback Act; although manager characterized money as a serious investment by subcontractor in exploring potential of acquiring a restaurant franchise, it was provided to manager while he was still employed by contractor, and no more money was forthcoming following his departure. Kellogg Brown & Root Services, Inc. v. U.S., 103 Fed. Cl. 714 (2012)

When government contractor's employees received kickbacks about which contractor had no knowledge, contractor did not violate, as distinguished from wrongdoers, obvious ethical or moral standards, and contract with government could not be cancelled on that ground. Acme Process Equipment Co. v. U. S., 171 Ct. Cl. 324, 347 F.2d 509 (1965), judgment rev'd, 385 U.S. 138, 87 S. Ct. 350, 17 L. Ed.2d 249 (1966) and (rejected by, R.P. Wallace, Inc. v. U.S., 63 Fed. Cl. 402 (2004)).

In a contract for household goods moving services, relocation brokers who receive commissions and tariff rebates from moving companies receiving subcontracts do not necessarily violate the Anti-Kickback Act. Both the express language of the Anti-Kickback statute and the Act's legislative history specify that the prohibition applies to payments or solicitations for payment that are made for an "improper" purpose (for example, payments made to a prime contractor to induce the award of a subcontract). No evidence was presented that the commissions or tariff rebates received by brokers were for an improper purpose such as to violate the Anti-Kickback Act. Aalco Forwarding, Inc., et al., B-277241, B-277241.8, B-277241.9, 97-2 CPD ¶ 110 (Comp. Gen. 1997)

§ 3.502-3 Contract clause.

The contracting officer shall insert the clause at 52.203-7, Anti-Kickback Procedures, in solicitations and contracts exceeding the simplified acquisition threshold, other than those for commercial items (see Part 12).

United States Code Annotated

Administrative offsets, see 41 U.S.C.A. § 56.

Civil actions, see 41 U.S.C.A. § 55.

Contract requirements, see 41 U.S.C.A. § 254.

Contractor responsibilities, see 41 U.S.C.A. § 57.

Contracts, planning, solicitation, evaluation, and award procedures, see 10 U.S.C.A. § 2305.

Criminal penalties, see 41 U.S.C.A. § 54.

Definitions, see 10 U.S.C.A. § 2302, 41 U.S.C.A. §§ 259, 403.

Inspection authority, see 41 U.S.C.A. § 58.

Kinds of contracts, see 10 U.S.C.A. § 2306.

Planning and solicitation requirements, see 41 U.S.C.A. § 253a.

Prohibited conduct, see 41 U.S.C.A. § 53.

§ 3.503 Unreasonable restrictions on subcontractor sales.

§ 3.503-1 Policy.

10 U.S.C. 2402 and 41 U.S.C. 4704 require that subcontractors not be unreasonably precluded from making direct sales to the Government of any supplies or services made or furnished under a contract. However, this does not preclude contractors from asserting rights that are otherwise authorized by law or regulation.

United States Code Annotated

Contract requirements, see 41 U.S.C.A. § 254.

Contracts, planning, solicitation, evaluation, and award procedures, see 10 U.S.C.A. § 2305.

Definitions, see 10 U.S.C.A. § 2302, 41 U.S.C.A. §§ 259, 403.

Kinds of contracts, see 10 U.S.C.A. § 2306.

Planning and solicitation requirements, see 41 U.S.C.A. § 253a.

Prohibition of contractors limiting subcontractor sales directly to the United States, see 10 U.S.C.A. § 2402, 41 U.S.C.A. § 253g.

§ 3.503-2 Contract clause.

The contracting officer shall insert the clause at 52.203-6, Restrictions on Subcontractor Sales to the Government, in solicitations and contracts exceeding the simplified acquisition threshold. For the acquisition of commercial items, the contracting officer shall use the clause with its Alternate I.

United States Code Annotated

Contract requirements, see 41 U.S.C.A. § 254.

Contracts, planning, solicitation, evaluation, and award procedures, see 10 U.S.C.A. § 2305.

Definitions, see 10 U.S.C.A. § 2302, 41 U.S.C.A. §§ 259, 403.

Kinds of contracts, see 10 U.S.C.A. § 2306.

Planning and solicitation requirements, see 41 U.S.C.A. § 253a.

Prohibition of contractors limiting subcontractor sales directly to the United States, see 10 U.S.C.A. § 2402, 41 U.S.C.A. § 253g.

Subpart 3.6 Contracts with Government Employees or Organizations Owned or Controlled by Them

§ 3.601 Policy.

(a) Except as specified in 3.602, a contracting officer shall not knowingly award a contract to a Government employee or to a business concern or other organization owned or substantially owned or controlled by one or more Government employees. This policy is intended to avoid any conflict of interest that might arise between the employees' interests and their Government duties, and to avoid the appearance of favoritism or preferential treatment by the Government toward its employees.

(b) For purposes of this subpart, special Government employees (as defined in 18 U.S.C. 202) performing services as experts, advisors, or consultants, or as members of advisory committees, are not considered Government employees unless—

(1) The contract arises directly out of the individual's activity as a special Government employee;

(2) In the individual's capacity as a special Government employee, the individual is in a position to influence the award of the contract; or

(3) Another conflict of interest is determined to exist.

United States Code Annotated

Contracting functions performed by Federal personnel, see 41 U.S.C.A. § 419.

Contracts, planning, solicitation, evaluation, and award procedures, see 10 U.S.C.A. § 2305.

Definitions, see 10 U.S.C.A. § 2302, 41 U.S.C.A. §§ 259, 403.

Evaluation and award, see 41 U.S.C.A. § 253b.

Planning and solicitation requirements, see 41 U.S.C.A. § 253a.

Notes of Decisions

In general 1
Conflict of interest 2

1 In general

At the time of the bidding, the president of the eventual awardee was employed by the federal government as a project engineer. At the time of award, the president was no longer employed by the government. FAR 3.601 prohibits *awarding* a contract to a company owned or controlled by a federal employee, but does not prohibit submission of a bid or proposal by a federal employee. Where the language of the regulation is unambiguous, the court will apply it as written. Accordingly, there was no violation of FAR 3.401. Speakman Co. v. Weinberger, 837 F.2d 1171, 267, 34 Cont. Cas. Fed. (CCH) P 75431 (D.C. Cir. 1988).

Protest alleging that the agency knowingly awarded a contract to a company substantially owned or controlled by a government employee in violation of FAR 3.601 was denied where the record shows that the contracting officer did not know of the facts alleged by the protester until after award. Metro Offices, Inc., B-408477, 2013 CPD ¶ 239 (Comp. Gen.

2013)

This prohibition in FAR 3.601 is intended to avoid any conflict of interest that might arise between an employee's interests and government duties, and to avoid the appearance, much less the fact, of favoritism or preferential treatment. A bidder's designation of a government employee as president of the closely-held corporation, the preparation of the bid by the government employee, as president, and the fact that all of the agency's dealings with the bidder were with the government employee provided the reasonable factual basis for the contracting officer to conclude that the government employee had a substantially controlling interest. Matter of: KSR, Inc., B-250160, 93-1 CPD ¶ 37 (Comp. Gen. 1993).

Procuring agency properly rejected the bid of a firm listing government employees as its president and vice president since the agency had reason to believe that these government employees substantially controlled the firm's business. Matter of: Gurley's Inc., B-253852, 1993 WL 335056 (Comp. Gen. 1993).

An agency is not required to establish with certainty that a government employee has a substantially controlling interest; the agency need only have "reason to believe" that a government employee has such control. The protester's listing government employees as the firm's president and vice president and their daughter as secretary provided a reasonable factual basis for the contracting officer's determination that government employees had a substantially controlling interest in the bidding entity. Matter of: Gurley's Inc., B-253852, 1993 WL 335056 (Comp. Gen. 1993).

This regulation is intended to avoid any conflict of interest that might arise between the employees' interests and their government duties, and to avoid the appearance of favoritism or preferential treatment by the government toward its employees. FAR 3.601. HH & K Builders, Inc., B-238095, 90-1 CPD ¶ 219 (Comp. Gen. 1990).

The government is generally precluded from contracting with a business controlled or owned by an employee of a government agency, whether or not it is the contracting agency. Tamara L. Wolf, B-233317, 89-1 CPD ¶ 99 (Comp. Gen. 1989).

2 Conflict of interest

Even assuming that conflict-of-interest provision of the Federal Acquisition Regulation (FAR) was violated when supervisor of motor transport department was placed on evaluation board involved in A-76 cost comparison to determine if function of department should be contracted out, contractor was not prejudiced by supervisor's participation, considering that supervisor was only one of six individuals on the board, and there was no dissent on board's "poor" rating of contractor. 48 C.F.R. § 3.101-1. JWK Intern. Corp. v. U.S., 52 Fed. Cl. 650 (2002), aff'd, 56 Fed. Appx. 474 (Fed. Cir. 2003). United States ☞64.55(1)

Prospective Veterans Administration contractor, whose bid on contract for construction of VA facility was not accepted due to appearance of conflict of interest in negotiating process, was not entitled to timely notice and hearing before VA refused to award contract and formally advertised procurement, as contractor had no property interest in award of public contract which would entitle it to due process hearing. U.S.C.A. Const.Amends. 5, 14. Refine Const. Co., Inc. v. U.S., 12 Cl. Ct. 56, 34 Cont. Cas. Fed. (CCH) P 75242 (1987). Constitutional Law ☞277(1)

Veterans Administration's decision not to accept bid of contractor which had been preselected by Small Business Administration and which was only company negotiating with VA for construction of VA facility was not arbitrary or capricious, and contractor was not entitled to recover its bid preparation and negotiating costs; decision not to award contract was based on appearance of conflict of interest caused by contractor's representation during negotiation process by VA employee, in violation of executive order, VA regulations, and statute prohibiting government employee from acting as agent for anyone in connection with matter in which Government is party or has direct and substantial interest. 18 U.S.C.A. § 205; Executive Order No. 11222, § 201(c)(6), 18 U.S.C.A. § 201 note. Refine Const. Co., Inc. v. U.S., 12 Cl. Ct. 56, 34 Cont. Cas. Fed. (CCH) P 75242 (1987). United States ☞64.60(6)

Pursuant to federal acquisition regulation (FAR), bidder on government contract may be disqualified based on appearance of impropriety when bidder may have gained unfair competitive advantage through actual or potential conflict of interest in procurement process. 48 C.F.R. § 1.000 et seq. Medco Behavioral Care Corp. of Iowa v. State, Dept. of Human

Services, 553 N.W.2d 556 (Iowa 1996). Public Contracts ⚖11

Mere conjecture, innuendo, or speculation of actual or potential conflict of interest, without factual support, provide no basis for disqualification of government contract bidder under federal acquisition regulation (FAR). 48 C.F.R. § 1.000 et seq. Medco Behavioral Care Corp. of Iowa v. State, Dept. of Human Services, 553 N.W.2d 556 (Iowa 1996). Public Contracts ⚖11

§ 3.602 Exceptions.

The agency head, or a designee not below the level of the head of the contracting activity, may authorize an exception to the policy in 3.601 only if there is a most compelling reason to do so, such as when the Government's needs cannot reasonably be otherwise met.

United States Code Annotated

Contracting functions performed by Federal personnel, see 41 U.S.C.A. § 419.

Contracts, planning, solicitation, evaluation, and award procedures, see 10 U.S.C.A. § 2305.

Definitions, see 10 U.S.C.A. § 2302, 41 U.S.C.A. §§ 259, 403.

Evaluation and award, see 41 U.S.C.A. § 253b.

Planning and solicitation requirements, see 41 U.S.C.A. § 253a.

Notes of Decisions

In general 1

1 In general

Regulation prohibiting award of government contract to business substantially owned or controlled by government employees did not bar award of such contract to business whose owner had left federal employment between bid opening and award. Speakman Co. v. Weinberger, 837 F.2d 1171, 267, 34 Cont. Cas. Fed. (CCH) P 75431 (D.C. Cir. 1988). United States ⚖64.20

§ 3.603 Responsibilities of the contracting officer.

a) Before awarding a contract, the contracting officer shall obtain an authorization under 3.602 if—

(1) The contracting officer knows, or has reason to believe, that a prospective contractor is one to which award is otherwise prohibited under 3.601; and

(2) There is a most compelling reason to make an award to that prospective contractor.

(b) The contracting officer shall comply with the requirements and guidance in Subpart 9.5 before awarding a contract to an organization owned or substantially owned or controlled by Government employees.

United States Code Annotated

Contracting functions performed by Federal personnel, see 41 U.S.C.A. § 419.

Contracts, planning, solicitation, evaluation, and award procedures, see 10 U.S.C.A. § 2305.

Definitions, see 10 U.S.C.A. § 2302, 41 U.S.C.A. §§ 259, 403.

Evaluation and award, see 41 U.S.C.A. § 253b.

Planning and solicitation requirements, see 41 U.S.C.A. § 253a.

Notes of Decisions

In general 1

1 In general

Regulation prohibiting award of government contract to business substantially owned or controlled by government employees did not bar award of such contract to business whose owner had left federal employment between bid opening and award. Speakman Co. v. Weinberger, 837 F.2d 1171, 267, 34 Cont. Cas. Fed. (CCH) P 75431 (D.C. Cir. 1988). United States ⚖64.20

Subpart 3.7 Voiding and Rescinding Contracts

§ 3.700 Scope of subpart.

(a) This subpart prescribes Governmentwide policies and procedures for exercising discretionary authority to declare void and rescind contracts in relation to which—

(1) There has been a final conviction for bribery, conflict of interest, disclosure or receipt of contractor bid or proposal information or source selection information in exchange for a thing of value or to give anyone a competitive advantage in the award of a Federal agency procurement contract, or similar misconduct; or

(2) There has been an agency head determination that contractor bid or proposal information or source selection information has been disclosed or received in exchange for a thing of value, or for the purpose of obtaining or giving anyone a competitive advantage in the award of a Federal agency procurement contract.

(b) This subpart does not prescribe policies or procedures for, or govern the exercise of, any other remedy available to the Government with respect to such contracts, including but not limited to, the common law right of avoidance, rescission, or cancellation.

§ 3.701 Purpose.

This subpart provides—

(a) An administrative remedy with respect to contracts in relation to which there has been—

(1) A final conviction for bribery, conflict of interest, disclosure or receipt of contractor bid or proposal information or source selection information in exchange for a thing of value or to give anyone a competitive advantage in the award of a Federal agency procurement contract, or similar misconduct; or

(2) An agency head determination that contractor bid or proposal information or source selection information has been disclosed or received in exchange for a thing of value, or for the purpose of obtaining or giving anyone a competitive advantage in the award of a Federal agency procurement contract; and

(b) A means to deter similar misconduct in the future by those who are involved in the award, performance, and administration of Government contracts.

United States Code Annotated

Definitions, see 18 U.S.C.A. § 202, 41 U.S.C.A. § 403.

Restrictions on disclosing and obtaining contractor bid or proposal information or source selection information, see 41 U.S.C.A. § 423.

Voiding transactions in violation of chapter, recovery by the United States, see 18 U.S.C.A. § 218.

§ 3.702 Definition.

"Final conviction" means a conviction, whether entered on a verdict or plea, including a plea of nolo contendere, for which a sentence has been imposed.

United States Code Annotated

Definitions, see 18 U.S.C.A. § 202, 41 U.S.C.A. § 403.

Restrictions on disclosing and obtaining contractor bid or proposal information or source selection information, see 41 U.S.C.A. § 423.

Voiding transactions in violation of chapter, recovery by the United States, see 18 U.S.C.A. § 218.

§ 3.703 Authority.

(a) Section 1(e) of Public Law 87-849, 18 U.S.C. 218 ("the Act"), empowers the President or the heads of executive agencies acting under regulations prescribed by the President, to declare void and rescind contracts and other transactions enumerated in the Act, in relation to which there has been a final conviction for bribery, conflict of interest, or any other violation of Chapter 11 of Title 18 of the United States Code (18 U.S.C. 201–224). Executive Order 12448, November 4, 1983, delegates the President's authority under the Act to the heads of the executive agencies and military departments.

(b) 41 U.S.C. 2105(c) requires a Federal agency, upon receiving information that a contractor or a person has violated 41 U.S.C. 2102, to consider rescission of a contract with respect to which—

(1) The contractor or someone acting for the contractor has been convicted for an offense punishable under 41 U.S.C. 2105(a); or

(2) The head of the agency, or designee, has determined, based upon a preponderance of the evidence, that the contractor or someone acting for the contractor has engaged in conduct constituting such an offense.

United States Code Annotated

Definitions, see 18 U.S.C.A. § 202, 41 U.S.C.A. § 403.

Restrictions on disclosing and obtaining contractor bid or proposal information or source selection information, see 41 U.S.C.A. § 423.

Voiding transactions in violation of chapter, recovery by the United States, see 18 U.S.C.A. § 218.

§ 3.704 Policy.

(a) In cases in which there is a final conviction for any violation of 18 U.S.C. 201–224 involving or relating to contracts awarded by an agency, the agency head or designee, shall consider the facts available and, if appropriate, may declare void and rescind contracts, and recover the amounts expended and property transferred by the agency in accordance with the policies and procedures of this subpart.

(b) Since a final conviction under 18 U.S.C. 201–224 relating to a contract also may justify the conclusion that the party involved is not presently responsible, the agency should consider initiating debarment proceedings in accordance with Subpart 9.4, Debarment, Suspension, and Ineligibility, if debarment has not been initiated, or is not in effect at the time the final conviction is entered.

(c) If there is a final conviction for an offense punishable under 41 U.S.C. 2105, or if the head of the agency, or designee, has determined, based upon a preponderance of the evidence, that the contractor or someone acting for the contractor has engaged in conduct constituting such an offense, then the head of the contracting activity shall consider, in addition to any other penalty prescribed by law or regulation—

(1) Declaring void and rescinding contracts, as appropriate, and recovering the amounts expended under the contracts by using the procedures at 3.705 (see 3.104-7); and

(2) Recommending the initiation of suspension or debarment proceedings in accordance with Subpart 9.4.

United States Code Annotated

Definitions, see 18 U.S.C.A. § 202, 41 U.S.C.A. § 403.

Restrictions on disclosing and obtaining contractor bid or proposal information or source selection information, see 41 U.S.C.A. § 423.

Voiding transactions in violation of chapter, recovery by the United States, see 18 U.S.C.A. § 218.

§ 3.705 Procedures.

(a) *Reporting.* The facts concerning any final conviction for any violation of 18 U.S.C. 201–224 involving or relating to agency contracts shall be reported promptly to the agency head or designee for that official's consideration. The agency head or designee shall promptly notify the Civil Division, Department of Justice, that the action is being considered under this subpart.

(b) *Decision.* Following an assessment of the facts, the agency head or designee may declare void and rescind contracts with respect to which a final conviction has been entered, and recover the amounts expended and the property transferred by the agency under the terms of the contracts involved.

(c) *Decision-making process.* Agency procedures governing the voiding and rescinding decision-making process shall be as informal as practicable, consistent with the principles of fundamental fairness. As a minimum, however, agencies shall provide the following:

(1) A notice of proposed action to declare void and rescind the contract shall be made in writing and sent by certified mail, return receipt requested.

(2) A thirty calendar day period after receipt of the notice, for the contractor to submit pertinent information before any final decision is made.

(3) Upon request made within the period for submission of pertinent information, an opportunity shall be afforded for a hearing at which witnesses may be presented, and any witness the agency presents may be confronted. However, no inquiry shall be made regarding the validity of a conviction.

(4) If the agency head or designee decides to declare void and rescind the contracts involved, that official shall issue a written decision which—

(i) States that determination;

(ii) Reflects consideration of the fair value of any tangible benefits received and retained by the agency; and

(iii) States the amount due and the property to be returned to the agency.

(d) *Notice of proposed action.* The notice of proposed action, as a minimum shall—

(1) Advise that consideration is being given to declaring void and rescinding contracts awarded by the agency, and recovering the amounts expended and property transferred therefor, under the provisions of 18 U.S.C. 218;

(2) Specifically identify the contracts affected by the action;

(3) Specifically identify the offense or final conviction on which the action is based;

(4) State the amounts expended and property transferred under each of the contracts involved, and the money and the property demanded to be returned;

(5) Identify any tangible benefits received and retained by the agency under the contract, and the value of those benefits, as calculated by the agency;

(6) Advise that pertinent information may be submitted within 30 calendar days after receipt of the notice, and that, if requested within that time, a hearing shall be held at which witnesses may be presented and any witness the agency presents may be confronted; and

(7) Advise that action shall be taken only after the agency head or designee issues a final written decision on the proposed action.

(e) *Final agency decision.* The final agency decision shall be based on the information available to the agency head or designee, including any pertinent information submitted or, if a hearing was held, presented at the hearing. If the agency decision declares void and rescinds the contract, the final decision shall specify the amounts due and property to be returned to the agency, and reflect consideration of the fair value of any tangible benefits received and retained by the agency. Notice of the decision shall be sent promptly by certified mail, return receipt requested. Rescission of contracts under the authority of the Act and demand for recovery of the amounts expended and property transferred therefor, is not a claim within the meaning of 41 U.S.C. chapter 71, Contract Disputes, or Part 32. Therefore, the procedures required by the statute and the FAR for the issuance of a final contracting officer decision are not applicable to final agency decisions under this subpart, and shall not be followed.

United States Code Annotated

Definitions, see 18 U.S.C.A. § 202, 41 U.S.C.A. § 403.

Restrictions on disclosing and obtaining contractor bid or proposal information or source selection information, see 41 U.S.C.A. § 423.

Voiding transactions in violation of chapter, recovery by the United States, see 18 U.S.C.A. § 218.

Notes of Decisions

In general 1

1 In general

Where plaintiff entered into an agreement with the Government to sell to the Government the S.S. Medric at an agreed price; and where, upon delivery of the vessel, defendant refused to accept and pay for the vessel on the ground that there had been misrepresentations of material facts as to the condition of the vessel amounting to fraud; and where it is shown by the evidence that plaintiff did make fraudulent representations concerning the vessel which were properly relied upon by defendant's representative; it is held that the defendant was justified in rescinding the agreement as to the price and in refusing to accept the vessel and to execute the written contract, and plaintiff is not entitled to recover. Taylor v. Burr Printing Co., 26 F.2d 331 (C.C.A. 2d Cir. 1928). Shipping Key Number ☞27; United States Key Number ☞72.1(2)

Government may avoid contract that is tainted by fraud, kickbacks, conflicts of interest, or bribery, regardless of whether there is criminal conviction, whether wrongdoing adversely affected contract, or whether prime contractor is innocent. Godley v. U.S., 5 F.3d 1473, 39 Cont. Cas. Fed. (CCH) ¶ 76581 (Fed. Cir. 1993). United States Key Number ☞72.1(2)

Subpart 3.8 Limitations on the Payment of Funds to Influence Federal Transactions

§ 3.800 Scope of subpart.

This subpart prescribes policies and procedures implementing 31 U.S.C. 1352, "Limitation on use of appropriated funds to influence certain Federal contracting and financial transactions."

United States Code Annotated

Contract requirements, see 41 U.S.C.A. § 254.

Contracts, planning, solicitation, evaluation, and award procedures, see 10 U.S.C.A. § 2305.

Definitions, see 10 U.S.C.A. § 2302, 41 U.S.C.A. §§ 259, 403.

Kinds of contracts, see 10 U.S.C.A. § 2306.

Limitation on use of appropriated funds to influence certain Federal contracting and financial transactions, see 31 U.S.C.A. § 1352.

Planning and solicitation requirements, see 41 U.S.C.A. § 253a.

§ 3.801 Definitions.

As used in this subpart—

"Agency" means "executive agency" as defined in 2.101.

"Covered Federal action" means any of the following actions:

(1) Awarding any Federal contract.

(2) Making any Federal grant.

(3) Making any Federal loan.

(4) Entering into any cooperative agreement.

(5) Extending, continuing, renewing, amending, or modifying any Federal contract, grant, loan, or cooperative agreement.

"Indian tribe" and "tribal organization" have the meaning provided in section 4 of the Indian Self-Determination and Education Assistance Act (25 U.S.C. 450B) and include Alaskan Natives.

"Influencing or attempting to influence" means making, with the intent to influence, any communication to or appearance before an officer or employee of any agency, a Member of Congress, an officer or employee of Congress, or an employee of a Member of Congress in connection with any covered Federal action.

"Local government" means a unit of government in a State and, if chartered, established, or otherwise recognized by a State for the performance of a governmental duty, including a local public authority, a special district, an intrastate district, a council of governments, a sponsor group representative organization, and any other instrumentality of a local government.

"Officer or employee of an agency" includes the following individuals who are employed by an agency:

(1) An individual who is appointed to a position in the Government under Title 5,

United States Code, including a position under a temporary appointment.

(2) A member of the uniformed services, as defined in subsection 101(3), Title 37, United States Code.

(3) A special Government employee, as defined in section 202, Title 18, United States Code.

(4) An individual who is a member of a Federal advisory committee, as defined by the Federal Advisory Committee Act, Title 5, United States Code, appendix 2.

"Person" means an individual, corporation, company, association, authority, firm, partnership, society, State, and local government, regardless of whether such entity is operated for profit or not for profit. This term excludes an Indian tribe, tribal organization, or any other Indian organization eligible to receive Federal contracts, grants, cooperative agreements, or loans from an agency, but only with respect to expenditures by such tribe or organization that are made for purposes specified in paragraph 3.802(a) and are permitted by other Federal law.

"Reasonable compensation" means, with respect to a regularly employed officer or employee of any person, compensation that is consistent with the normal compensation for such officer or employee for work that is not furnished to, not funded by, or not furnished in cooperation with the Federal Government.

"Reasonable payment" means, with respect to professional and other technical services, a payment in an amount that is consistent with the amount normally paid for such services in the private sector.

"Recipient" includes the contractor and all subcontractors. This term excludes an Indian tribe, tribal organization, or any other Indian organization eligible to receive Federal contracts, grants, cooperative agreements, or loans from an agency, but only with respect to expenditures by such tribe or organization that are made for purposes specified in paragraph 3.802(a) and are permitted by other Federal law.

"Regularly employed" means, with respect to an officer or employee of a person requesting or receiving a Federal contract, an officer or employee who is employed by such person for at least 130 working days within 1 year immediately preceding the date of the submission that initiates agency consideration of such person for receipt of such contract. An officer or employee who is employed by such person for less than 130 working days within 1 year immediately preceding the date of the submission that initiates agency consideration of such person shall be considered to be regularly employed as soon as he or she is employed by such person for 130 working days.

"State" means a State of the United States, the District of Columbia, an outlying area of the United States, an agency or instrumentality of a State, and multi-State, regional, or interstate entity having governmental duties and powers.

United States Code Annotated

Contract requirements, see 41 U.S.C.A. § 254.

Contracts, planning, solicitation, evaluation, and award procedures, see 10 U.S.C.A. § 2305.

Definitions, see 10 U.S.C.A. § 2302, 41 U.S.C.A. §§ 259, 403.

Kinds of contracts, see 10 U.S.C.A. § 2306.

Limitation on use of appropriated funds to influence certain Federal contracting and financial transactions, see 31 U.S.C.A. § 1352.

Planning and solicitation requirements, see 41 U.S.C.A. § 253a.

§ 3.802 Statutory prohibition and requirement.

(a) 31 U.S.C. 1352 prohibits a recipient of a Federal contract, grant, loan, or cooperative agreement from using appropriated funds to pay any person for influencing or attempting to influence an officer or employee of any agency, a Member of Congress, an officer or employee of Congress, or an employee of a Member of Congress in connection with any covered Federal actions.

(1) For purposes of this subpart the term "appropriated funds" does not include profit or fee from a covered Federal action.

(2) To the extent a person can demonstrate that the person has sufficient monies, other

than Federal appropriated funds, the Government shall assume that these other monies were spent for any influencing activities that would be unallowable if paid for with Federal appropriated funds.

(b) 31 U.S.C. 1352 also requires offerors to furnish a declaration consisting of both a certification and a disclosure, with periodic updates of the disclosure after contract award. These requirements are contained in the provision at 52.203-11, Certification and Disclosure Regarding Payments to Influence Certain Federal Transactions, and the clause at 52.203-12, Limitation on Payments to Influence Certain Federal Transactions.

United States Code Annotated

Contract requirements, see 41 U.S.C.A. § 254.

Contracts, planning, solicitation, evaluation, and award procedures, see 10 U.S.C.A. § 2305.

Definitions, see 10 U.S.C.A. § 2302, 41 U.S.C.A. §§ 259, 403.

Kinds of contracts, see 10 U.S.C.A. § 2306.

Limitation on use of appropriated funds to influence certain Federal contracting and financial transactions, see 31 U.S.C.A. § 1352.

Planning and solicitation requirements, see 41 U.S.C.A. § 253a.

§ 3.803 Exceptions.

(a) The prohibition of paragraph 3.802(a) does not apply under the following conditions:

(1) *Agency and legislative liaison by own employees.*

(i) Payment of reasonable compensation made to an officer or employee of a person requesting or receiving a covered Federal action if the payment is for agency and legislative liaison activities not directly related to a covered Federal action. For purposes of this paragraph, providing any information specifically requested by an agency or Congress is permitted at any time.

(ii) Participating with an agency in discussions that are not related to a specific solicitation for any covered Federal action, but that concern—

(A) The qualities and characteristics (including individual demonstrations) of the person's products or services, conditions or terms of sale, and service capabilities; or

(B) The application or adaptation of the person's products or services for an agency's use.

(iii) Providing prior to formal solicitation of any covered Federal action any information not specifically requested but necessary for an agency to make an informed decision about initiation of a covered Federal action.

(iv) Participating in technical discussions regarding the preparation of an unsolicited proposal prior to its official submission.

(v) Making capability presentations prior to formal solicitation of any covered Federal action when seeking an award from an agency pursuant to the provision of the Small Business Act, as amended by Pub L. 95-507, and subsequent amendments.

(2) *Professional and technical services.*

(i) Payment of reasonable compensation made to an officer or employee of a person requesting or receiving a covered Federal action, if payment is for professional or technical services rendered directly in the preparation, submission, or negotiation of any bid, proposal, or application for that Federal action or for meeting requirements imposed by or pursuant to law as a condition of receiving that Federal action;

(ii) Any reasonable payment to a person, other than an officer or employee of a person requesting or receiving a covered Federal action, if the payment is for professional or technical services rendered directly in the preparation, submission, or negotiation of any bid, proposal, or application for that Federal action, or for meeting requirements imposed by or pursuant to law as a condition for receiving that Federal action. Persons other than officers or employees of a person requesting or receiving a covered Federal action include consultant and trade associations.

(iii) As used in this paragraph (a)(2) of this section "professional and technical services" are limited to advice and analysis directly applying any professional or technical discipline. For example, drafting of a legal document accompanying a bid or proposal by a lawyer is allowable. Similarly, technical advice provided by an engineer on the performance or operational capability of a piece of equipment rendered directly in the negotiation of a contract is allowable. However, communications tithe the intent to influence made by a professional or a technical person are not allowable under this section unless they provide advice and analysis directly applying their professional or technical expertise and unless the advice or analysis is rendered directly and solely in the preparation, submission or negotiation of a covered Federal action. Thus, for example, communications with the intent to influence made by a lawyer that do not provide legal advice or analysis directly and solely related to the legal aspects of his or her client's proposal, but generally advocate one proposal over another, are not allowable under this section because the lawyer is not providing professional legal services. Similarly, communications with the intent to influence made by an engineer providing an engineering analysis prior to the preparation or submission of a bid or proposal are not allowable under his section since the engineer is providing technical services but not directly in the preparation, submission or negotiation of a covered Federal action.

(iv) Requirements imposed by or pursuant to law as a condition for receiving a covered Federal award include those required by law or regulation and any other requirements in the actual award documents.

(b) Only those communications and services expressly authorized by paragraph (a) of this section are permitted.

(c) The disclosure requirements of paragraph 3.802(b) do not apply with respect to payments of reasonable compensation made to regularly employed officers or employees of a person.

United States Code Annotated

Contract requirements, see 41 U.S.C.A. § 254.

Contracts, planning, solicitation, evaluation, and award procedures, see 10 U.S.C.A. § 2305.

Definitions, see 10 U.S.C.A. § 2302, 41 U.S.C.A. §§ 259, 403.

Kinds of contracts, see 10 U.S.C.A. § 2306.

Limitation on use of appropriated funds to influence certain Federal contracting and financial transactions, see 31 U.S.C.A. § 1352.

Planning and solicitation requirements, see 41 U.S.C.A. § 253a.

§ 3.804 Policy.

The contracting officer shall obtain certifications and disclosures as required by the provision at 52.203-11, Certification and Disclosure Regarding Payments to Influence Certain Federal Transactions, prior to the award of any contract exceeding $150,000.

United States Code Annotated

Contract requirements, see 41 U.S.C.A. § 254.

Contracts, planning, solicitation, evaluation, and award procedures, see 10 U.S.C.A. § 2305.

Definitions, see 10 U.S.C.A. § 2302, 41 U.S.C.A. §§ 259, 403.

Kinds of contracts, see 10 U.S.C.A. § 2306.

Limitation on use of appropriated funds to influence certain Federal contracting and financial transactions, see 31 U.S.C.A. § 1352.

Planning and solicitation requirements, see 41 U.S.C.A. § 253a.

§ 3.805 Exemption.

The Secretary of Defense may exempt, on a case-by-case basis, a covered Federal action from the prohibitions of this subpart whenever the Secretary determines, in writing, that such an exemption is in the national interest. The Secretary shall transmit a copy of the exemption to Congress immediately after making the determination.

United States Code Annotated

Contract requirements, see 41 U.S.C.A. § 254.

Contracts, planning, solicitation, evaluation, and award procedures, see 10 U.S.C.A. § 2305.

Definitions, see 10 U.S.C.A. § 2302, 41 U.S.C.A. §§ 259, 403.

Kinds of contracts, see 10 U.S.C.A. § 2306.

Limitation on use of appropriated funds to influence certain Federal contracting and financial transactions, see 31 U.S.C.A. § 1352.

Planning and solicitation requirements, see 41 U.S.C.A. § 253a.

§ 3.806 Processing suspected violations.

The contracting officer shall report suspected violations of the requirements of 31 U.S.C. 1352 in accordance with agency procedures.

United States Code Annotated

Contract requirements, see 41 U.S.C.A. § 254.

Contracts, planning, solicitation, evaluation, and award procedures, see 10 U.S.C.A. § 2305.

Definitions, see 10 U.S.C.A. § 2302, 41 U.S.C.A. §§ 259, 403.

Kinds of contracts, see 10 U.S.C.A. § 2306.

Limitation on use of appropriated funds to influence certain Federal contracting and financial transactions, see 31 U.S.C.A. § 1352.

Planning and solicitation requirements, see 41 U.S.C.A. § 253a.

§ 3.807 Civil penalties.

Agencies shall impose and collect civil penalties pursuant to the provisions of the Program Fraud and Civil Remedies Act, 31 U.S.C. 3803 (except subsection (c)), 3804–3808, and 3812, insofar as the provisions therein are not inconsistent with the requirements of this subpart.

United States Code Annotated

Contract requirements, see 41 U.S.C.A. § 254.

Contracts, planning, solicitation, evaluation, and award procedures, see 10 U.S.C.A. § 2305.

Definitions, see 10 U.S.C.A. § 2302, 41 U.S.C.A. §§ 259, 403.

Kinds of contracts, see 10 U.S.C.A. § 2306.

Limitation on use of appropriated funds to influence certain Federal contracting and financial transactions, see 31 U.S.C.A. § 1352.

Planning and solicitation requirements, see 41 U.S.C.A. § 253a.

§ 3.808 Solicitation provision and contract clause.

(a) Insert the provision at 52.203-11, Certification and Disclosure Regarding Payments to Influence Certain Federal Transactions, in solicitations expected to exceed $150,000.

(b) Insert the clause at 52.203-12, Limitation on Payments to Influence Certain Federal Transactions, in solicitations and contracts expected to exceed $150,000.

United States Code Annotated

Contract requirements, see 41 U.S.C.A. § 254.

Contracts, planning, solicitation, evaluation, and award procedures, see 10 U.S.C.A. § 2305.

Definitions, see 10 U.S.C.A. § 2302, 41 U.S.C.A. §§ 259, 403.

Kinds of contracts, see 10 U.S.C.A. § 2306.

Limitation on use of appropriated funds to influence certain Federal contracting and financial transactions, see 31 U.S.C.A. § 1352.

Planning and solicitation requirements, see 41 U.S.C.A. § 253a.

Subpart 3.9 Whistleblower Protections for Contractor Employees

§ 3.900 Scope of subpart.

This subpart implements three different statutory whistleblower programs. This subpart does not implement 10 U.S.C. 2409, which is applicable only to DoD, NASA, and the Coast Guard.

(a) 41 U.S.C. 4705 (in effect before July 1, 2013 and on or after January 2, 2017). Sections 3.901 through 3.906 of this subpart implement 41 U.S.C. 4705, applicable to civilian agencies other than NASA and the Coast Guard, except as provided in paragraph (c) of this section. These sections are not in effect for the duration of the pilot program described in paragraph (b) of this section.

(b) 41 U.S.C. 4712 (in effect on July 1, 2013 through January 1, 2017). Section 3.908 of this subpart implements the pilot program, applicable to civilian agencies other than NASA and the Coast Guard, except as provided in paragraph (c) of this section.

(c) Contracts funded by the American Recovery and Reinvestment Act. Section 3.907 of this subpart implements section 1553 of the American Recovery and Reinvestment Act of 2009 (Pub. L. 111-5), and applies to all contracts funded in whole or in part by that Act.

§ 3.901 Definitions.

As used in this subpart—

"Authorized official of an agency" means an officer or employee responsible for contracting, program management, audit, inspection, investigation, or enforcement of any law or regulation relating to Government procurement or the subject matter of the contract.

"Authorized official of the Department of Justice" means any person responsible for the investigation, enforcement, or prosecution of any law or regulation.

"Inspector General" means an Inspector General appointed under the Inspector General Act of 1978, as amended. In the Department of Defense that is the DoD Inspector General. In the case of an executive agency that does not have an Inspector General, the duties shall be performed by an official designated by the head of the executive agency.

United States Code Annotated

Contractor employees: protection from reprisal for disclosure of certain information, see 10 U.S.C.A. § 2409, 41 U.S.C.A. 265.

Definitions, see 10 U.S.C.A. § 2302, 41 U.S.C.A. §§ 259, 403.

§ 3.902 [Reserved]

§ 3.903 Policy.

Government contractors shall not discharge, demote or otherwise discriminate against an employee as a reprisal for disclosing information to a Member of Congress, or an authorized official of an agency or of the Department of Justice, relating to a substantial violation of law related to a contract (including the competition for or negotiation of a contract).

United States Code Annotated

Contractor employees: protection from reprisal for disclosure of certain information, see 10 U.S.C.A. § 2409, 41 U.S.C.A. 265.

Definitions, see 10 U.S.C.A. § 2302, 41 U.S.C.A. §§ 259, 403.

§ 3.904 Procedures for filing complaints.

(a) Any employee of a contractor who believes that he or she has been discharged, demoted, or otherwise discriminated against contrary to the policy in 3.903 may file a complaint with the Inspector General of the agency that awarded the contract.

(b) The complaint shall be signed and shall contain—

(1) The name of the contractor;

(2) The contract number, if known; if not, a description reasonably sufficient to identify

the contract(s) involved;

(3) The substantial violation of law giving rise to the disclosure;

(4) The nature of the disclosure giving rise to the discriminatory act; and

(5) The specific nature and date of the reprisal.

United States Code Annotated

Contractor employees: protection from reprisal for disclosure of certain information, see 10 U.S.C.A. § 2409, 41 U.S.C.A. 265.

Definitions, see 10 U.S.C.A. § 2302, 41 U.S.C.A. §§ 259, 403.

§ 3.905 Procedures for investigating complaints.

(a) Upon receipt of a complaint, the Inspector General shall conduct an initial inquiry. If the Inspector General determines that the complaint is frivolous or for other reasons does not merit further investigation, the Inspector General shall advise the complainant that no further action on the complaint will be taken.

(b) If the Inspector General determines that the complaint merits further investigation, the Inspector General shall notify the complainant, contractor, and head of the contracting activity. The Inspector General shall conduct an investigation and provide a written report of findings to the head of the agency or designee.

(c) Upon completion of the investigation, the head of the agency or designee shall ensure that the Inspector General provides the report of findings to—

(1) The complainant and any person acting on the complainant's behalf;

(2) The contractor alleged to have committed the violation; and

(3) The head of the contracting activity.

(d) The complainant and contractor shall be afforded the opportunity to submit a written response to the report of findings within 30 days to the head of the agency or designee. Extensions of time to file a written response may be granted by the head of the agency or designee.

(e) At any time, the head of the agency or designee may request additional investigative work be done on the complaint.

United States Code Annotated

Contractor employees: protection from reprisal for disclosure of certain information, see 10 U.S.C.A. § 2409, 41 U.S.C.A. 265.

Definitions, see 10 U.S.C.A. § 2302, 41 U.S.C.A. §§ 259, 403.

§ 3.906 Remedies.

(a) If the head of the agency or designee determines that a contractor has subjected one of its employees to a reprisal for providing information to a Member of Congress, or an authorized official of an agency or of the Department of Justice, the head of the agency or designee may take one or more of the following actions:

(1) Order the contractor to take affirmative action to abate the reprisal.

(2) Order the contractor to reinstate the person to the position that the person held before the reprisal, together with the compensation (including back pay), employment benefits, and other terms and conditions of employment that would apply to the person in that position if the reprisal had not been taken.

(3) Order the contractor to pay the complainant an amount equal to the aggregate amount of all costs and expenses (including attorneys' fees and expert witnesses' fees) that were reasonably incurred by the complainant for, or in connection with, bringing the complaint regarding the reprisal.

(b) Whenever a contractor fails to comply with an order, the head of the agency or designee shall request the Department of Justice to file an action for enforcement of such order in the United States district court for a district in which the reprisal was found to have occurred. In any action brought under this section, the court may grant appropriate relief, including injunctive relief and compensatory and exemplary damages.

(c) Any person adversely affected or aggrieved by an order issued under this section may obtain review of the order's conformance with the law, and this subpart, in the United States Court of Appeals for a circuit in which the reprisal is alleged in the order to have occurred. No petition seeking such review may be filed more than 60 days after issuance of the order by the head of the agency or designee. Review shall conform to Chapter 7 of Title 5, United States Code.

United States Code Annotated

Contractor employees: protection from reprisal for disclosure of certain information, see 10 U.S.C.A. § 2409, 41 U.S.C.A. 265.

Definitions, see 10 U.S.C.A. § 2302, 41 U.S.C.A. §§ 259, 403.

Notes of Decisions
In general 1

1 In general

Subsection (c) of 10 U.S.C. § 2409 authorizes "heads of agencies" to take action against a contractor who is found to have engaged in reprisals against a whistleblower. This subsection allows the head of an agency to intervene in these situations and order the contactor to abate the reprisal including reinstating the whistleblower with back pay and any other benefit denied to the whistleblower. Neither subsection (b) nor subsection (c) of 10 U.S.C. § 2409 provides an aggrieved employee the right to bring a private cause of action as an alternative to the remedial scheme established by the statute. Rogers v. U.S. Army, 13 Wage & Hour Cas. 2d (BNA) 119, 2007 WL 1217964 (S.D. Tex. 2007).

§ 3.907 Whistleblower Protections Under the American Recovery and Reinvestment Act of 2009 (the Recovery Act).

§ 3.907-1 Definitions.

As used in this section—

"Board" means the Recovery Accountability and Transparency Board established by Section 1521 of the Recovery Act.

"Covered funds" means any contract payment, grant payment, or other payment received by a contractor if—

(1) The Federal Government provides any portion of the money or property that is provided, requested, or demanded; and

(2) At least some of the funds are appropriated or otherwise made available by the Recovery Act.

"Covered information" means information that the employee reasonably believes is evidence of gross mismanagement of the contract or subcontract related to covered funds, gross waste of covered funds, a substantial and specific danger to public health or safety related to the implementation or use of covered funds, an abuse of authority related to the implementation or use of covered funds, or a violation of law, rule, or regulation related to an agency contract (including the competition for or negotiation of a contract) awarded or issued relating to covered funds.

"Inspector General" means an Inspector General appointed under the Inspector General Act of 1978. In the Department of Defense that is the DoD Inspector General. In the case of an executive agency that does not have an Inspector General, the duties shall be performed by an official designated by the head of the executive agency.

"Non-Federal employer," as used in this section, means any employer that receives Recovery Act funds, including a contractor, subcontractor, or other recipient of funds pursuant to a contract or other agreement awarded and administered in accordance with the Federal Acquisition Regulation.

§ 3.907-2 Policy.

Non-Federal employers are prohibited from discharging, demoting, or otherwise discriminating against an employee as a reprisal for disclosing covered information to any of the following entities or their representatives:

(1) The Board.

(2) An Inspector General.

(3) The Comptroller General.

(4) A member of Congress.

(5) A State or Federal regulatory or law enforcement agency.

(6) A person with supervisory authority over the employee or such other person working for the employer who has the authority to investigate, discover, or terminate misconduct.

(7) A court or grand jury.

(8) The head of a Federal agency.

§ 3.907-3 Procedures for filing complaints.

(a) An employee who believes that he or she has been subjected to reprisal prohibited by the Recovery Act, Section 1553 as set forth in 3.907-2, may submit a complaint regarding the reprisal to the Inspector General of the agency that awarded the contract.

(b) The complaint shall be signed and shall contain—

(1) The name of the contractor;

(2) The contract number, if known; if not, a description reasonably sufficient to identify the contract(s) involved;

(3) The covered information giving rise to the disclosure;

(4) The nature of the disclosure giving rise to the discriminatory act; and

(5) The specific nature and date of the reprisal.

(c) A contracting officer who receives a complaint of reprisal of the type described in 3.907-2 shall forward it to the Office of Inspector General and to other designated officials in accordance with agency procedures (*e.g.*, agency legal counsel).

§ 3.907-4 Procedures for investigating complaints.

Investigation of complaints will be in accordance with section 1553 of the Recovery Act.

§ 3.907-5 Access to investigative file of Inspector General.

(a) The employee alleging reprisal under this section shall have access to the investigation file of the Inspector General, in accordance with the Privacy Act, 5 U.S.C. 552a. The investigation of the Inspector General shall be deemed closed for the purposes of disclosure under such section when an employee files an appeal to the agency head or a court of competent jurisdiction.

(b) In the event the employee alleging reprisal brings a civil action under section 1553(c)(3) of the Recovery Act, the employee alleging the reprisal and the non-Federal employer shall have access to the investigative file of the Inspector General in accordance with the Privacy Act.

(c) The Inspector General may exclude from disclosures made under 3.907-5(a) or (b)—

(1) Information protected from disclosure by a provision of law; and

(2) Any additional information the Inspector General determines disclosure of which would impede a continuing investigation, provided that such information is disclosed once such disclosure would no longer impede such investigation, unless the Inspector General determines that the disclosure of law enforcement techniques, procedures, or information could reasonably be expected to risk circumvention of the law or disclose the identity of a confidential source.

(d) An Inspector General investigating an alleged reprisal under this section may not respond to any inquiry or disclose any information from or about any person alleging such reprisal, except in accordance with 5 U.S.C. 552a or as required by any other applicable Federal law.

§ 3.907-6 Remedies and enforcement authority.

(a) *Burden of Proof.*

(1) Disclosure as contributing factor in reprisal.

(i) An employee alleging a reprisal under this section shall be deemed to have affirmatively established the occurrence of the reprisal if the employee demonstrates that a disclosure described in section 3.907-2 was a contributing factor in the reprisal.

(ii) A disclosure may be demonstrated as a contributing factor in a reprisal for purposes of this paragraph by circumstantial evidence, including—

(A) Evidence that the official undertaking the reprisal knew of the disclosure; or

(B) Evidence that the reprisal occurred within a period of time after the disclosure such that a reasonable person could conclude that the disclosure was a contributing factor in the reprisal.

(2) *Opportunity for rebuttal.* The head of an agency may not find the occurrence of a reprisal with respect to a reprisal that is affirmatively established under section 3.907-6(a) (1) if the non-Federal employer demonstrates by clear and convincing evidence that the non-Federal employer would have taken the action constituting the reprisal in the absence of the disclosure.

(b) No later than 30 days after receiving an Inspector General report in accordance with section 1553 of the Recovery Act, the head of the agency concerned shall determine whether there is sufficient basis to conclude that the non-Federal employer has subjected the complainant to a reprisal prohibited by subsection 3.907-2 and shall either issue an order denying relief in whole or in part or shall take one or more of the following actions:

(1) Order the employer to take affirmative action to abate the reprisal.

(2) Order the employer to reinstate the person to the position that the person held before the reprisal, together with the compensation (including back pay), compensatory damages, employment benefits, and other terms and conditions of employment that would apply to the person in that position if the reprisal had not been taken.

(3) Order the employer to pay the complainant an amount equal to the aggregate amount of all costs and expenses (including attorneys' fees and expert witnesses' fees) that were reasonably incurred by the complainant for, or in connection with, bringing the complaint regarding the reprisal.

(c)

(1) The complainant shall be deemed to have exhausted all administrative remedies with respect to the complaint, and the complainant may bring a de novo action at law or equity against the employer to seek compensatory damages and other relief available under this section in the appropriate district court of United States, which shall have jurisdiction over such an action without regard to the amount in controversy if

(i) The head of an agency—

(A) Issues an order denying relief in whole or in part under paragraph (a) of this section;

(B) Has not issued an order within 210 days after the submission of a complaint in accordance with section 1553 of the Recovery Act, or in the case of an extension of time in accordance with section 1553 of the Recovery Act, within 30 days after the expiration of the extension of time; or

(C) Decides in accordance with section 1553 of the Recovery Act not to investigate or to discontinue an investigation; and

(ii) There is no showing that such delay or decision is due to the bad faith of the complainant.

(2) Such an action shall, at the request of either party to the action, be tried by the court with a jury.

(d) Whenever an employer fails to comply with an order issued under this section, the head of the agency shall request the Department of Justice to file an action for enforcement of such order in the United States district court for a district in which the reprisal was found to have occurred. In any action brought under this section, the court may grant appropriate relief, including injunctive relief, compensatory and exemplary damages, and attorneys fees and costs.

(e) Any person adversely affected or aggrieved by an order issued under paragraph (b) of this subsection may obtain review of the order's conformance with the law, and this section, in the United States Court of Appeals for a circuit in which the reprisal is alleged in the order to have occurred. No petition seeking such review may be filed more than 60 days after issuance of the order by the head of the agency.

§ 3.907-7 Contract clause.

Use the clause at 52.203-15, Whistleblower Protections Under the American Recovery and Reinvestment Act of 2009 in all solicitations and contracts funded in whole or in part with Recovery Act funds.

§ 3.908 Pilot program for enhancement of contractor employee whistleblower protections.

§ 3.908-1 Scope of section.

(a) This section implements 41 U.S.C. 4712.

(b) This section does not apply to—

(1) DoD, NASA, and the Coast Guard; or

(2) Any element of the intelligence community, as defined in section 3(4) of the National Security Act of 1947 (50 U.S.C. 3003(4)). This section does not apply to any disclosure made by an employee of a contractor or subcontractor of an element of the intelligence community if such disclosure-

(i) Relates to an activity of an element of the intelligence community; or

(ii) Was discovered during contract or subcontract services provided to an element of the intelligence community.

§ 3.908-2 Definitions.

As used in this section—

"Abuse of authority" means an arbitrary and capricious exercise of authority that is inconsistent with the mission of the executive agency concerned or the successful performance of a contract of such agency.

"Inspector General" means an Inspector General appointed under the Inspector General Act of 1978 and any Inspector General that receives funding from, or has oversight over contracts awarded for, or on behalf of, the executive agency concerned.

§ 3.908-3 Policy.

(a) Contractors and subcontractors are prohibited from discharging, demoting, or otherwise discriminating against an employee as a reprisal for disclosing, to any of the entities listed at paragraph (b) of this subsection, information that the employee reasonably believes is evidence of gross mismanagement of a Federal contract, a gross waste of Federal funds, an abuse of authority relating to a Federal contract, a substantial and specific danger to public health or safety, or a violation of law, rule, or regulation related to a Federal contract (including the competition for or negotiation of a contract). A reprisal is prohibited even if it is undertaken at the request of an executive branch official, unless the request takes the form of a non-discretionary directive and is within the authority of the executive branch official making the request.

(b) Entities to whom disclosure may be made.

(1) A Member of Congress or a representative of a committee of Congress.

(2) An Inspector General.

(3) The Government Accountability Office.

(4) A Federal employee responsible for contract oversight or management at the relevant agency.

(5) An authorized official of the Department of Justice or other law enforcement agency.

(6) A court or grand jury.

(7) A management official or other employee of the contractor or subcontractor who has the responsibility to investigate, discover, or address misconduct.

(c) An employee who initiates or provides evidence of contractor or subcontractor misconduct in any judicial or administrative proceeding relating to waste, fraud, or abuse on a Federal contract shall be deemed to have made a disclosure.

§ 3.908-4 Filing complaints.

A contractor or subcontractor employee who believes that he or she has been discharged, demoted, or otherwise discriminated against contrary to the policy in 3.908-3 of this section may submit a complaint with the Inspector General of the agency concerned. Procedures for submitting fraud, waste, abuse, and whistleblower complaints are generally accessible on agency Office of Inspector General Hotline or Whistleblower Internet sites. A complaint by the employee may not be brought under 41 U.S.C. 4712 more than three years after the date on which the alleged reprisal took place.

§ 3.908-5 Procedures for investigating complaints.

(a) Investigation of complaints will be in accordance with 41 U.S.C. 4712(b).

(b) Upon completion of the investigation, the head of the agency or designee shall ensure that the Inspector General provides the report of findings to—

(1) The complainant and any person acting on the complainant's behalf;

(2) The contractor alleged to have committed the violation; and

(3) The head of the contracting activity.

(c) The complainant and contractor shall be afforded the opportunity to submit a written response to the report of findings within 30 days to the head of the agency or designee. Extensions of time to file a written response may be granted by the head of the agency or designee.

(d) At any time, the head of the agency or designee may request additional investigative work be done on the complaint.

§ 3.908-6 Remedies.

(a) Agency response to Inspector General report. Not later than 30 days after receiving an Inspector General report in accordance with 41 U.S.C. 4712, the head of the agency shall—

(1) Determine whether sufficient basis exists to conclude that the contractor or subcontractor has subjected the employee who submitted the complaint to a reprisal as prohibited by 3.908-3; and

(2) Issue an order denying relief or take one or more of the following actions:

(i) Order the contractor to take affirmative action to abate the reprisal.

(ii) Order the contractor or subcontractor to reinstate the complainant-employee to the position that the person held before the reprisal, together with compensatory damages (including back pay), employment benefits, and other terms and conditions of employment that would apply to the person in that position if the reprisal had not been taken.

(iii) Order the contractor or subcontractor to pay the complainant-employee an amount equal to the aggregate amount of all costs and expenses (including attorneys' fees and expert witnesses' fees) that were reasonably incurred by the complainant for, or in connection with, bringing the complaint regarding the reprisal, as determined by the head of the agency.

(b) Complainant's right to go to court. If the head of the agency issues an order denying relief or has not issued an order within 210 days after the submission of the complaint or within 30 days after the expiration of an extension of time granted in accordance with 41 U.S.C. 4712(b)(2)(B) for the submission of the Inspector General's report on the investigative findings of the complaint to the head of the agency, the contractor or subcontractor, and the complainant, and there is no showing that such delay is due to the bad faith of the complainant—

(1) The complainant shall be deemed to have exhausted all administrative remedies with respect to the complaint; and

(2) The complainant may bring a de novo action at law or equity against the contractor or subcontractor to seek compensatory damages and other relief available under 41 U.S.C. 4712 in the appropriate district court of the United States, which shall have jurisdiction over such an action without regard to the amount in controversy. Such an action shall, at the request of either party to the action, be tried by the court with a jury. An action under this authority may not be brought more than two years after the date on which remedies are deemed to have been exhausted.

(c) Admissibility in evidence. An Inspector General determination and an agency head order denying relief under this section shall be admissible in evidence in any de novo action at law or equity brought pursuant to 41 U.S.C. 4712.

(d) No waiver. The rights and remedies provided for in 41 U.S.C. 4712 may not be waived by any agreement, policy, form, or condition of employment.

§ 3.908-7 Enforcement of orders.

(a) Whenever a contractor or subcontractor fails to comply with an order issued under 3.908-6(a)(2) of this section, the head of the agency concerned shall file an action for enforcement of the order in the U.S. district court for a district in which the reprisal was found to have occurred. In any action brought pursuant to this authority, the court may grant appropriate relief, including injunctive relief, compensatory and exemplary damages, and attorney fees and costs. The complainant-employee upon whose behalf an order was issued may also file such an action or join in an action filed by the head of the agency.

(b) Any person adversely affected or aggrieved by an order issued under 3.908-6(a)(2) may obtain review of the order's conformance with 41 U.S.C. 4712 and its implementing regulations, in the U.S. court of appeals for a circuit in which the reprisal is alleged in the order to have occurred. No petition seeking such review may be filed more than 60 days after issuance of the order by the head of the agency. Filing such an appeal shall not act to stay the enforcement of the order of the head of an agency, unless a stay is specifically entered by the court.

§ 3.908-8 Classified information.

41 U.S.C. 4712 does not provide any right to disclose classified information not otherwise provided by law.

§ 3.908-9 Contract clause.

The contracting officer shall insert the clause at 52.203-17, Contractor Employee Whistleblower Rights and Requirement to Inform Employees of Whistleblower Rights, in all solicitations and contracts that exceed the simplified acquisition threshold.

Subpart 3.10 Contractor Code of Business Ethics and Conduct

§ 3.1000 Scope of subpart.

This subpart—

(a) Implements 41 U.S.C. 3509, Notification of Violations of Federal Criminal Law or Overpayments; and

(b) Prescribes policies and procedures for the establishment of contractor codes of business ethics and conduct, and display of agency Office of Inspector General (OIG) fraud hotline posters.

§ 3.1001 Definitions.

As used in this subpart—

"Subcontract" means any contract entered into by a subcontractor to furnish supplies or services for performance of a prime contract or a subcontract.

"Subcontractor" means any supplier, distributor, vendor, or firm that furnished supplies or services to or for a prime contractor or another subcontractor.

"United States" means the 50 States, the District of Columbia, and outlying areas.

§ 3.1002 Policy.

(a) Government contractors must conduct themselves with the highest degree of integrity and honesty.

(b) Contractors should have a written code of business ethics and conduct. To promote compliance with such code of business ethics and conduct, contractors should have an employee business ethics and compliance training program and an internal control system that—

(1) Are suitable to the size of the company and extent of its involvement in Government contracting;

(2) Facilitate timely discovery and disclosure of improper conduct in connection with Government contracts; and

(3) Ensure corrective measures are promptly instituted and carried out.

§ 3.1003 Requirements.

a) *Contractor Requirements.*

(1) Although the policy in section 3.1002 applies as guidance to all Government contractors, the contractual requirements set forth in the clauses at 52.203-13, Contractor Code of Business Ethics and Conduct, and 52.203-14, Display of Hotline Poster(s), are mandatory if the contracts meet the conditions specified in the clause prescriptions at 3.1004.

(2) Whether or not the clause at 52.203-13 is applicable, a contractor may be suspended and/or debarred for knowing failure by a principal to timely disclose to the Government, in connection with the award, performance, or closeout of a Government contract performed by the contractor or a subcontract awarded thereunder, credible evidence of a violation of Federal criminal law involving fraud, conflict of interest, bribery, or gratuity violations found in Title 18 of the United States Code or a violation of the civil False Claims Act. Knowing failure to timely disclose credible evidence of any of the above violations remains a cause for suspension and/or debarment until 3 years after final payment on a contract (see 9.406-2(b)(1)(vi) and 9.407-2(a)(8)).

(3) The Payment clauses at FAR 52.212-4(i)(5), 52.232-25(d), 52.232-26(c), and 52.232-27(l) require that, if the contractor becomes aware that the Government has overpaid on a contract financing or invoice payment, the contractor shall remit the overpayment amount to the Government. A contractor may be suspended and/or debarred for knowing failure by a principal to timely disclose credible evidence of a significant overpayment, other than overpayments resulting from contract financing payments as defined in 32.001 (see 9.406-2(b)(1)(vi) and 9.407-2(a)(8)).

(b) *Notification of possible contractor violation.* If the contracting officer is notified of possible contractor violation of Federal criminal law involving fraud, conflict of interest, bribery, or gratuity violations found in Title 18 U.S.C.; or a violation of the civil False Claims Act, the contracting officer shall—

(1) Coordinate the matter with the agency Office of the Inspector General; or

(2) Take action in accordance with agency procedures.

(c) *Fraud Hotline Poster.*

(1) Agency OIGs are responsible for determining the need for, and content of, their respective agency OIG fraud hotline poster(s).

(2) When requested by the Department of Homeland Security, agencies shall ensure that contracts funded with disaster assistance funds require display of any fraud hotline poster applicable to the specific contract. As established by the agency OIG, such posters may be displayed in lieu of, or in addition to, the agency's standard poster.

§ 3.1004 Contract clauses.

(a) Insert the clause at FAR 52.203-13, Contractor Code of Business Ethics and Conduct, in solicitations and contracts if the value of the contract is expected to exceed $5.5 million and the performance period is 120 days or more.

(b) (1) Unless the contract is for the acquisition of a commercial item or will be performed entirely outside the United States, insert the clause at FAR 52.203-14, Display of Hotline Poster(s), if—

(i) The contract exceeds $5.5 million or a lesser amount established by the agency; and

(ii) (A) The agency has a fraud hotline poster; or

(B) The contract is funded with disaster assistance funds.

(2) In paragraph (b)(3) of the clause, the contracting officer shall—

(i) Identify the applicable posters; and

(ii) Insert the website link(s) or other contact information for obtaining the agency and/or Department of Homeland Security poster.

(3) In paragraph (d) of the clause, if the agency has established policies and procedures for display of the OIG fraud hotline poster at a lesser amount, the contracting officer shall replace "$5.5 million" with the lesser amount that the agency has established.

Subpart 3.11 Preventing Personal Conflicts of Interest for Contractor Employees Performing Acquisition Functions

§ 3.1100 Scope of subpart.

This subpart implements policy on personal conflicts of interest by employees of Government contractors as required by 41 U.S.C. 2303.

§ 3.1101 Definitions.

As used in this subpart—

"Acquisition function closely associated with inherently governmental functions" means supporting or providing advice or recommendations with regard to the following activities of a Federal agency:

(1) Planning acquisitions.

(2) Determining what supplies or services are to be acquired by the Government, including developing statements of work.

(3) Developing or approving any contractual documents, to include documents defining requirements, incentive plans, and evaluation criteria.

(4) Evaluating contract proposals.

(5) Awarding Government contracts.

(6) Administering contracts (including ordering changes or giving technical direction in contract performance or contract quantities, evaluating contractor performance, and accepting or rejecting contractor products or services).

(7) Terminating contracts.

(8) Determining whether contract costs are reasonable, allocable, and allowable.

"Covered employee" means an individual who performs an acquisition function closely associated with inherently governmental functions and is—

(1) An employee of the contractor; or

(2) A subcontractor that is a self-employed individual treated as a covered employee of the contractor because there is no employer to whom such an individual could submit the required disclosures.

"Personal conflict of interest" means a situation in which a covered employee has a financial interest, personal activity, or relationship that could impair the employee's ability to act impartially and in the best interest of the Government when performing under the contract. (A de minimis interest that would not "impair the employee's ability to act impartially and in the best interest of the Government" is not covered under this definition.)

(1) Among the sources of personal conflicts of interest are—

(i) Financial interests of the covered employee, of close family members, or of other members of the covered employee's household;

(ii) Other employment or financial relationships (including seeking or negotiating for prospective employment or business); and

(iii) Gifts, including travel.

(2) For example, financial interests referred to in paragraph (1) of this definition may arise from—

(i) Compensation, including wages, salaries, commissions, professional fees, or fees for business referrals;

(ii) Consulting relationships (including commercial and professional consulting and service arrangements, scientific and technical advisory board memberships, or serving as an expert witness in litigation);

(iii) Services provided in exchange for honorariums or travel expense reimbursements;

(iv) Research funding or other forms of research support;

(v) Investment in the form of stock or bond ownership or partnership interest (excluding diversified mutual fund investments);

(vi) Real estate investments;

(vii) Patents, copyrights, and other intellectual property interests; or

(viii) Business ownership and investment interests.

§ 3.1102 Policy.

The Government's policy is to require contractors to—

(a) Identify and prevent personal conflicts of interest of their covered employees; and

(b) Prohibit covered employees who have access to non-public information by reason of performance on a Government contract from using such information for personal gain.

§ 3.1103 Procedures.

(a) By use of the contract clause at 52.203-16, as prescribed at 3.1106, the contracting officer shall require each contractor whose employees perform acquisition functions closely associated with inherently Government functions to—

(1) Have procedures in place to screen covered employees for potential personal conflicts of interest by—

(i) Obtaining and maintaining from each covered employee, when the employee is initially assigned to the task under the contract, a disclosure of interests that might be affected by the task to which the employee has been assigned, as follows:

(A) Financial interests of the covered employee, of close family members, or of other members of the covered employee's household.

(B) Other employment or financial relationships of the covered employee (including seeking or negotiating for prospective employment or business).

(C) Gifts, including travel; and

(ii) Requiring each covered employee to update the disclosure statement whenever the employee's personal or financial circumstances change in such a way that a new personal conflict of interest might occur because of the task the covered employee is performing.

(2) For each covered employee—

(i) Prevent personal conflicts of interest, including not assigning or allowing a covered employee to perform any task under the contract for which the Contractor has identified a personal conflict of interest for the employee that the Contractor or employee cannot satisfactorily prevent or mitigate in consultation with the contracting agency;

(ii) Prohibit use of non-public information accessed through performance of a Government contract for personal gain; and

(iii) Obtain a signed non-disclosure agreement to prohibit disclosure of non-public information accessed through performance of a Government contract.

(3) Inform covered employees of their obligation—

(i) To disclose and prevent personal conflicts of interest;

(ii) Not to use non-public information accessed through performance of a Government contract for personal gain; and

(iii) To avoid even the appearance of personal conflicts of interest;

(4) Maintain effective oversight to verify compliance with personal conflict-of-interest safeguards;

(5) Take appropriate disciplinary action in the case of covered employees who fail to comply with policies established pursuant to this section; and

(6) Report to the contracting officer any personal conflict-of-interest violation by a covered employee as soon as identified. This report shall include a description of the violation and the proposed actions to be taken by the contractor in response to the violation, with follow-up reports of corrective actions taken, as necessary.

(b) If a contractor reports a personal conflict-of-interest violation by a covered employee to the contracting officer in accordance with paragraph (b)(6) of the clause at 52.203-16, Preventing Personal Conflicts of Interest, the contracting officer shall—

(1) Review the actions taken by the contractor;

(2) Determine whether any action taken by the contractor has resolved the violation satisfactorily; and

(3) If the contracting officer determines that the contractor has not resolved the violation satisfactorily, take any appropriate action in consultation with agency legal counsel.

§ 3.1104 Mitigation or waiver.

(a) In exceptional circumstances, if the contractor cannot satisfactorily prevent a personal conflict of interest as required by paragraph (b)(2)(i) of the clause at 52.203-16, Preventing Personal Conflicts of Interest, the contractor may submit a request, through the contracting officer, for the head of the contracting activity to—

(1) Agree to a plan to mitigate the personal conflict of interest; or

(2) Waive the requirement to prevent personal conflicts of interest.

(b) If the head of the contracting activity determines in writing that such action is in the best interest of the Government, the head of the contracting activity may impose conditions that provide mitigation of a personal conflict of interest or grant a waiver.

(c) This authority shall not be redelegated.

§ 3.1105 Violations.

If the contracting officer suspects violation by the contractor of a requirement of paragraph (b), (c)(3), or (d) of the clause at 52.203-16, Preventing Personal Conflicts of Interest, the contracting officer shall contact the agency legal counsel for advice and/or recommendations on a course of action.

§ 3.1106 Contract clause.

(a) Insert the clause at 52.203-16, Preventing Personal Conflicts of Interest, in solicitations and contracts that—

(1) Exceed the simplified acquisition threshold; and

(2) Include a requirement for services by contractor employee(s) that involve performance of acquisition functions closely associated with inherently governmental functions for, or on behalf of, a Federal agency or department.

(b) If only a portion of a contract is for the performance of acquisition functions closely associated with inherently governmental functions, then the contracting officer shall still insert the clause, but shall limit applicability of the clause to that portion of the contract that is for the performance of such services.

(c) Do not insert the clause in solicitations or contracts with a self-employed individual if the acquisition functions closely associated with inherently governmental functions are to be performed entirely by the self-employed individual, rather than an employee of the contractor.

PART 4 ADMINISTRATIVE MATTERS

§ 4.000 Scope of part.
§ 4.001 Definitions.

Subpart 4.1 Contract Execution

§ 4.101 Contracting officer's signature.
§ 4.102 Contractor's signature.
§ 4.103 Contract clause.

Subpart 4.2 Contract Distribution

§ 4.201 Procedures.
§ 4.202 Agency distribution requirements.
§ 4.203 Taxpayer identification information.

Subpart 4.3 Paper Documents

§ 4.300 Scope of subpart.
§ 4.301 Definition.
§ 4.302 Policy.
§ 4.303 Contract clause.

Subpart 4.4 Safeguarding Classified Information Within Industry

§ 4.401 [Reserved]
§ 4.402 General.
§ 4.403 Responsibilities of contracting officers.
§ 4.404 Contract clause.

Subpart 4.5 Electronic Commerce in Contracting

§ 4.500 Scope of subpart.
§ 4.501 [Reserved]
§ 4.502 Policy.

Subpart 4.6 —Contract Reporting

§ 4.600 Scope of subpart.
§ 4.601 Definitions.
§ 4.602 General.
§ 4.603 Policy.
§ 4.604 Responsibilities.
§ 4.605 Procedures.
§ 4.606 Reporting Data.
§ 4.607 Solicitation provisions and contract clause.

Subpart 4.7 Contractor Records Retention

§ 4.700 Scope of subpart.
§ 4.701 Purpose.
§ 4.702 Applicability.
§ 4.703 Policy.
§ 4.704 Calculation of retention periods.

Subpart 4.14 Reporting Executive Compensation and First-Tier Subcontract Awards

§ 4.1400 Scope of subpart
§ 4.1401 Applicability
§ 4.1402 Procedures
§ 4.1403 Contract clause

Subpart 4.15 [Reserved]

§ 4.1500 [Reserved]
§ 4.1501 [Reserved]
§ 4.1502 [Reserved]

Subpart 4.16 —Unique Procurement Instrument Identifiers

§ 4.1600 Scope of subpart.
§ 4.1601 Policy.
§ 4.1602 Identifying the PIID and supplementary PIID.
§ 4.1603 Procedures.

Subpart 4.17 Service Contracts Inventory

§ 4.1700 Scope of subpart.
§ 4.1701 Definitions.
§ 4.1702 Applicability.
§ 4.1703 Reporting requirements.
§ 4.1704 Contracting officer responsibilities.
§ 4.1705 Contract clauses.

Subpart 4.18 —Commercial and Government Entity Code

§ 4.1800 Scope of subpart.
§ 4.1801 Definitions.
§ 4.1802 Policy.
§ 4.1803 Verifying CAGE codes prior to award.
§ 4.1804 Solicitation provisions and contract clause.

Subpart 4.19 Basic Safeguarding of Covered Contractor Information Systems

§ 4.1901 Definitions.
§ 4.1902 Applicability.
§ 4.1903 Contract clause.

§ 4.000 Scope of part.

This part prescribes policies and procedures relating to the administrative aspects of contract execution, contractor-submitted paper documents, distribution, reporting, retention, and files.

§ 4.001 Definitions.

As used in this part—

"Procurement Instrument Identifier (PIID)" means the Government-unique identifier for each solicitation, contract, agreement, or order. For example, an agency may use as its PIID for procurement actions, such as delivery and task orders or basic ordering agreements, the order or agreement number in conjunction with the contract number (see 4.1602).

"Supplementary procurement instrument identifier" means the non-unique identifier for a procurement action that is used in conjunction with the Government-unique identifier. For example, an agency may use as its PIID for an amended solicitation, the Government-unique identifier for a solicitation number (*e.g.*, N0002309R0009) in conjunction with a non-unique amendment number (*e.g.*, 0001). The non-unique amendment number represents the supplementary PIID.

Subpart 4.1 Contract Execution

§ 4.101 Contracting officer's signature.

Only contracting officers shall sign contracts on behalf of the United States. The contracting officer's name and official title shall be typed, stamped, or printed on the contract. The contracting officer normally signs the contract after it has been signed by the contractor. The contracting officer shall ensure that the signer(s) have authority to bind the contractor (see specific requirements in 4.102 of this subpart).

United States Code Annotated

Contract requirements, see 41 U.S.C.A. § 254.

Contracts, planning, solicitation, evaluation, and award procedures, see 10 U.S.C.A. § 2305.

Definitions, see 10 U.S.C.A. § 2302, 41 U.S.C.A. §§ 259, 403.

Kinds of contracts, see 10 U.S.C.A. § 2306.

Planning and solicitation requirements, see 41 U.S.C.A. § 253a.

Notes of Decisions

In general 1

1 In general

A handwritten note from a contract specialist, written on personal stationery, requesting that the bidder confirm its bid, acknowledge some corrections, acknowledge the amendments and stating, "we are awarding only price schedule A, B & C," was insufficient to form a contract. The note was signed by the contracting specialist. The handwritten note lacked any indicia of a binding agreement between the parties since it specifically requested information preparatory to any award and provided information about the award terms. In any event, the government is not bound beyond the actual authority conferred upon its agents. FAR 4.101 provides that only contracting officers shall sign contracts on behalf of the United States. The note was not executed by a contracting officer and thus could not bind the agency contractually. Environmental Safety Consultants, Inc., B-241714, 91-1 CPD ¶ 213 (Comp. Gen. 1991).

§ 4.102 Contractor's signature.

(a) *Individuals.* A contract with an individual shall be signed by that individual. A contract with an individual doing business as a firm shall be signed by that individual, and the signature shall be followed by the individual's typed, stamped, or printed name and the words, "an individual doing business as _____" [*insert name of firm*].

(b) *Partnerships.* A contract with a partnership shall be signed in the partnership name. Before signing for the Government, the contracting officer shall obtain a list of all partners and ensure that the individual(s) signing for the partnership have authority to bind the partnership.

(c) *Corporations.* A contract with a corporation shall be signed in the corporate name, followed by the word "by" and the signature and title of the person authorized to sign. The contracting officer shall ensure that the person signing for the corporation has authority to bind the corporation.

(d) *Joint venturers.* A contract with joint venturers may involve any combination of individuals, partnerships, or corporations. The contract shall be signed by each participant in the joint venture in the manner prescribed in paragraphs (a) through (c) of this section for each type of participant. When a corporation is participating, the contracting officer shall verify that the corporation is authorized to participate in the joint venture.

(e) *Agents.* When an agent is to sign the contract, other than as stated in paragraphs (a) through (d) of this section, the agent's authorization to bind the principal must be established by evidence satisfactory to the contracting officer.

United States Code Annotated

Contract requirements, see 41 U.S.C.A. § 254.

Contracts, planning, solicitation, evaluation, and award procedures, see 10 U.S.C.A. § 2305.

Definitions, see 10 U.S.C.A. § 2302, 41 U.S.C.A. §§ 259, 403.

Kinds of contracts, see 10 U.S.C.A. § 2306.

Planning and solicitation requirements, see 41 U.S.C.A. § 253a.

Notes of Decisions

In general 1

1 In general

FAR 4.102(d) states that, in the case of a joint venture, "[t]he contract shall be signed by each participant in the joint venture in the manner prescribed in paragraphs (a) through (c) of this section for each type of participant." When one of the joint venture members is a partnership, the signature of only one partner is sufficient to bind the partnership. FAR 4.102(b). The contracting officer misconstrued the FAR by requiring each partner in the joint venture to sign the bid. In rejecting a bid because only one partner signed the bid, the contracting officer was unaware of the general principle of joint venture law providing that the signature of one partner is sufficient to bind the joint venture. PCI/RCI v. U.S., 37 Fed. Cl. 785 (1997)

Regulation requiring that contract with joint venture be signed by each participant in joint venture did not become part of bid by implication under regulation requiring bid to be considered only if award on bid would result in binding contract with terms and conditions that did not vary from terms and conditions of invitation; bidders could not be held subject to unpublicized requirement. 48 C.F.R. §§ 4.102(d), 14.301(d). PCI/RCI v. U. S., 36 Fed. Cl. 761, 41 Cont. Cas. Fed. (CCH) P 77015 (1996). United States ☞64.30

Regulation requiring contract with joint venture to be signed by each participant in joint venture did not require bids submitted by joint venture to be signed by each partner of joint venture. 48 C.F.R. § 4.102(d). PCI/RCI v. U. S., 36 Fed. Cl. 761, 41 Cont. Cas. Fed. (CCH) P 77015 (1996). United States ☞64.30

Protest that contracting agency improperly awarded contract is sustained where the record reflects that the legal entity awarded the contract did not participate in the procurement and appears to be a different legal entity from the offering entity. The awardee had changed its organizational structure from a corporation to a limited liability corporation (LLC) and proposed as an LLC even though the DUNS Number pertained to the prior corporate entity and award was made to the corporation. W.B. Constr. & Sons, Inc., B-405874, 2011 CPD ¶ 282 (Comp. Gen 2011)

The low bidder, a corporate entity, submitted a signed bid but did not place the word 'by' before the signature, as required by FAR 4.102. The protester, while not challenging the authority of the person who signed for the low bidder, contended that the bid should have been rejected as non-responsive because the low bidder did not comply with the literal wording of FAR 4.102. The GAO denied the protest because FAR 4.102 deals with a contractor's signature on a *contract*, rather than on a bid, and there is no indication that FAR 4.102 was intended to apply to offers in response to a solicitation. Further, FAR 14.405 permits waiver of minor informalities or irregularities when their effect on price, quantity, quality, or delivery is negligible. As an example of a minor informality or irregularity, FAR, § 14.405(c)(1), lists an unsigned bid which is accompanied by other material indicating the bidder's intention to be bound by the unsigned bid. IBI Security Service, Inc., B-215732, 84-2 CPD ¶ 118 (Comp. Gen. 1984).

§ 4.103 Contract clause.

The contracting officer shall insert the clause at 52.204-1, Approval of Contract, in solicitations and contracts if required by agency procedures.

United States Code Annotated

Contract requirements, see 41 U.S.C.A. § 254.

Contracts, planning, solicitation, evaluation, and award procedures, see 10 U.S.C.A. § 2305.

Definitions, see 10 U.S.C.A. § 2302, 41 U.S.C.A. §§ 259, 403.

Kinds of contracts, see 10 U.S.C.A. § 2306.

Planning and solicitation requirements, see 41 U.S.C.A. § 253a.

Subpart 4.2 Contract Distribution

§ 4.201 Procedures.

Contracting officers shall distribute copies of contracts or modifications within 10 working days after execution by all parties. As a minimum, the contracting officer shall—

(a) Distribute simultaneously one signed copy or reproduction of the signed contract to the contractor and the paying office;

(b) When a contract is assigned to another office for contract administration (see Subpart 42.2), provide to that office—

(1) One copy or reproduction of the signed contract and of each modification; and

(2) A copy of the contract distribution list, showing those offices that should receive copies of modifications, and any changes to the list as they occur;

(c) Distribute one copy to each accounting and finance office (funding office) whose funds are cited in the contract;

(d) When the contract is not assigned for administration but contains a Cost Accounting Standards clause, provide one copy of the contract to the cognizant administrative contracting officer and mark the copy *"For Cost Accounting Standards Administration Only"* (see 30.601(b));

(e) Provide one copy of each contract or modification that requires audit service to the appropriate field audit office listed in the "Directory of Federal Contract Audit Offices" (copies of this directory can be ordered from the—

U.S. Government Printing Office
Superintendent of Document
Washington, DC 20402

referencing stock numbers 008-007-03189-9 and 008-007-03190-2 for Volumes I and II, respectively); and

(f) Provide copies of contracts and modifications to those organizations required to perform contract administration support functions (*e.g.,* when manufacturing is performed at multiple sites, the contract administration office cognizant of each location).

United States Code Annotated

Contract requirements, see 41 U.S.C.A. § 254.

Contracts, planning, solicitation, evaluation, and award procedures, see 10 U.S.C.A. § 2305.

Definitions, see 10 U.S.C.A. § 2302, 41 U.S.C.A. §§ 259, 403.

Kinds of contracts, see 10 U.S.C.A. § 2306.

Planning and solicitation requirements, see 41 U.S.C.A. § 253a.

§ 4.202 Agency distribution requirements.

Agencies shall limit additional distribution requirements to the minimum necessary for proper performance of essential functions. When contracts are assigned for administration to a contract administration office located in an agency different from that of the contracting office (see Part 42), the two agencies shall agree on any necessary distribution in addition to that prescribed in 4.201.

United States Code Annotated

Contract requirements, see 41 U.S.C.A. § 254.

Contracts, planning, solicitation, evaluation, and award procedures, see 10 U.S.C.A.

§ 2305.

Definitions, see 10 U.S.C.A. § 2302, 41 U.S.C.A. §§ 259, 403.

Kinds of contracts, see 10 U.S.C.A. § 2306.

Planning and solicitation requirements, see 41 U.S.C.A. § 253a.

§ 4.203 Taxpayer identification information.

(a) If the contractor has furnished a Taxpayer Identification Number (TIN) when completing the solicitation provision at 52.204-3, Taxpayer Identification, or paragraph (l) of the solicitation provision at 52.212-3, Offeror Representations and Certifications—Commercial Items, the contracting officer shall, unless otherwise provided in agency procedures, attach a copy of the completed solicitation provision as the last page of the copy of the contract sent to the payment office.

(b) If the TIN or type of organization is derived from a source other than the provision at 52.204-3 or 52.212-3(l), the contracting officer shall annotate the last page of the contract or order forwarded to the payment office to state the contractor's TIN and type of organization, unless this information is otherwise provided to the payment office in accordance with agency procedures.

(c) If the contractor provides its TIN or type of organization to the contracting officer after award, the contracting officer shall forward the information to the payment office within 7 days of its receipt.

(d) *Federal Supply Schedule contracts.* Each contracting officer that places an order under a Federal Supply Schedule contract (see Subpart 8.4) shall provide the TIN and type of organization information to the payment office in accordance with paragraph (b) of this section.

(e) Basic ordering agreements and indefinite-delivery contracts (other than Federal Supply Schedule contracts).

(1) Each contracting officer that issues a basic ordering agreement or indefinite-delivery contract (other than a Federal Supply Schedule contract) shall provide to contracting officers placing orders under the agreement or contract (if the contractor is not required to provide this information to the System for Award Management)—

(i) A copy of the agreement or contract with a copy of the completed solicitation provision at 52.204-3 or 52.212-3(l) as the last page of the agreement or contract; or

(ii) The contractor's TIN and type of organization information.

(2) Each contracting officer that places an order under a basic ordering agreement or indefinite-delivery contract (other than a Federal Supply Schedule contract) shall provide the TIN and type of organization information to the payment office in accordance with paragraph (a) or (b) of this section.

Subpart 4.3 Paper Documents

§ 4.300 Scope of subpart.

This subpart provides policies and procedures on contractor-submitted paper documents.

United States Code Annotated

Contract requirements, see 41 U.S.C.A. § 254.

Contracts, planning, solicitation, evaluation, and award procedures, see 10 U.S.C.A. § 2305.

Definitions, see 10 U.S.C.A. § 2302, 41 U.S.C.A. §§ 259, 403.

Kinds of contracts, see 10 U.S.C.A. § 2306.

Planning and solicitation requirements, see 41 U.S.C.A. § 253a.

§ 4.301 Definition.

"Printed or copied double-sided," as used in this subpart, means printing or reproducing a document so that information is on both sides of a sheet of paper.

United States Code Annotated

Contract requirements, see 41 U.S.C.A. § 254.

Contracts, planning, solicitation, evaluation, and award procedures, see 10 U.S.C.A. § 2305.

Definitions, see 10 U.S.C.A. § 2302, 41 U.S.C.A. §§ 259, 403.

Kinds of contracts, see 10 U.S.C.A. § 2306.

Planning and solicitation requirements, see 41 U.S.C.A. § 253a.

§ 4.302 Policy.

(a) Section 3(a) of E.O. 13423, Strengthening Federal Environmental, Energy, and Transportation Management, directs agencies to implement waste prevention. In addition, section 2(e) of E.O. 13514, Federal Leadership in Environmental, Energy, and Economic Performance, directs agencies to eliminate waste. Electronic commerce methods (see 4.502) and double-sided printing and copying are best practices for waste prevention.

(b) When electronic commerce methods (see 4.502) are not used, agencies shall require contractors to submit paper documents to the Government relating to an acquisition printed or copied double-sided on at least 30 percent postconsumer fiber paper whenever practicable. If the contractor cannot print or copy double-sided, it shall print or copy single-sided on at least 30 percent postconsumer fiber paper.

United States Code Annotated

Contract requirements, see 41 U.S.C.A. § 254.

Contracts, planning, solicitation, evaluation, and award procedures, see 10 U.S.C.A. § 2305.

Definitions, see 10 U.S.C.A. § 2302, 41 U.S.C.A. §§ 259, 403.

Kinds of contracts, see 10 U.S.C.A. § 2306.

Planning and solicitation requirements, see 41 U.S.C.A. § 253a.

§ 4.303 Contract clause.

Insert the clause at 52.204-4, Printed or Copied Double-Sided on Recycled Paper, in solicitations and contracts that exceed the simplified acquisition threshold.

United States Code Annotated

Contract requirements, see 41 U.S.C.A. § 254.

Contracts, planning, solicitation, evaluation, and award procedures, see 10 U.S.C.A. § 2305.

Definitions, see 10 U.S.C.A. § 2302, 41 U.S.C.A. §§ 259, 403.

Kinds of contracts, see 10 U.S.C.A. § 2306.

Planning and solicitation requirements, see 41 U.S.C.A. § 253a.

Subpart 4.4 Safeguarding Classified Information Within Industry

§ 4.401 [Reserved]

§ 4.402 General.

(a) Executive Order 12829, January 6, 1993 (58 FR 3479, January 8, 1993), entitled "National Industrial Security Program" (NISP), establishes a program to safeguard Federal Government classified information that is released to contractors, licensees, and grantees of the United States Government. Executive Order 12829 amends Executive Order 10865, February 20, 1960 (25 FR 1583, February 25, 1960), entitled "Safeguarding Classified Information Within Industry," as amended by Executive Order 10909, January 17, 1961 (26 FR 508, January 20, 1961).

(b) The National Industrial Security Program Operating Manual (NISPOM) incorporates the requirements of these Executive orders. The Secretary of Defense, in consultation with all affected agencies and with the concurrence of the Secretary of Energy, the Chairman of the Nuclear Regulatory Commission, and the Director of Central Intelligence, is responsible for issuance and maintenance of this Manual. The following DoD publications implement the program:

(1) National Industrial Security Program Operating Manual (NISPOM) (DoD 5220.22-M).

(2) Industrial Security Regulation (DoD 5220.22-R).

(c) Procedures for the protection of information relating to foreign classified contracts awarded to U.S. industry, and instructions for the protection of U.S. information relating to classified contracts awarded to foreign firms, are prescribed in Chapter 10 of the NISPOM.

(d) Part 27—Patents, Data, and Copyrights, contains policy and procedures for safeguarding classified information in patent applications and patents.

United States Code Annotated

Contract requirements, see 41 U.S.C.A. § 254.

Contracts, planning, solicitation, evaluation, and award procedures, see 10 U.S.C.A. § 2305.

Definitions, see 10 U.S.C.A. § 2302, 41 U.S.C.A. §§ 259, 403.

Kinds of contracts, see 10 U.S.C.A. § 2306.

Planning and solicitation requirements, see 41 U.S.C.A. § 253a.

§ 4.403 Responsibilities of contracting officers.

(a) *Presolicitation phase.* Contracting officers shall review all proposed solicitations to determine whether access to classified information may be required by offerors, or by a contractor during contract performance.

(1) If access to classified information of another agency may be required, the contracting officer shall—

(i) Determine if the agency is covered by the NISP; and

(ii) Follow that agency's procedures for determining the security clearances of firms to be solicited.

(2) If the classified information required is from the contracting officer's agency, the contracting officer shall follow agency procedures.

(b) *Solicitation phase.* Contracting officers shall—

(1) Ensure that the classified acquisition is conducted as required by the NISP or agency procedures, as appropriate; and

(2) Include—

(i) An appropriate Security Requirements clause in the solicitation (see 4.404); and

(ii) As appropriate, in solicitations and contracts when the contract may require access to classified information, a requirement for security safeguards in addition to those provided in the clause (52.204-2, Security Requirements).

(c) *Award phase.* Contracting officers shall inform contractors and subcontractors of the security classifications and requirements assigned to the various documents, materials, tasks, subcontracts, and components of the classified contract as follows:

(1) Agencies covered by the NISP shall use the Contract Security Classification Specification, DD Form 254. The contracting officer, or authorized representative, is the approving official for the form and shall ensure that it is prepared and distributed in accordance with the Industrial Security Regulation.

(2) Contracting officers in agencies not covered by the NISP shall follow agency procedures.

United States Code Annotated

Contract requirements, see 41 U.S.C.A. § 254.

Contracts, planning, solicitation, evaluation, and award procedures, see 10 U.S.C.A. § 2305.

Definitions, see 10 U.S.C.A. § 2302, 41 U.S.C.A. §§ 259, 403.

Kinds of contracts, see 10 U.S.C.A. § 2306.

Planning and solicitation requirements, see 41 U.S.C.A. § 253a.

Notes of Decisions

In general 1

1 In general

Court of Federal Claims dismissed protest on grounds that agency's efforts to process a security clearance were adequate and therefore did not cause the protester's failure to comply with the request for quotations requirement to hold a security clearance prior to award. MVS USA, Inc. v. U.S., 111 Fed.Cl. 639 (Fed. Cl. June 27, 2013)

Solicitation requirement that an offeror possess a Top Secret facility clearance at the time final proposal revisions are submitted does not unduly restrict competition where the record shows that the requirement is reasonably related to the agency's needs. CompTech–CDO, LLC, B-409949.2, 2015 CPD ¶ 62 (Comp.Gen. 2015)

§ 4.404 Contract clause.

(a) The contracting officer shall insert the clause at 52.204-2, Security Requirements, in solicitations and contracts when the contract may require access to classified information, unless the conditions specified in paragraph (d) of this section apply.

(b) If a cost contract (see 16.302) for research and development with an educational institution is contemplated, the contracting officer shall use the clause with its Alternate I.

(c) If a construction or architect-engineer contract where employee identification is required for security reasons is contemplated, the contracting officer shall use the clause with its Alternate II.

(d) If the contracting agency is not covered by the NISP and has prescribed a clause and alternates that are substantially the same as those at 52.204-2, the contracting officer shall use the agency-prescribed clause as required by agency procedures.

United States Code Annotated

Contract requirements, see 41 U.S.C.A. § 254.

Contracts, planning, solicitation, evaluation, and award procedures, see 10 U.S.C.A. § 2305.

Definitions, see 10 U.S.C.A. § 2302, 41 U.S.C.A. §§ 259, 403.

Kinds of contracts, see 10 U.S.C.A. § 2306.

Planning and solicitation requirements, see 41 U.S.C.A. § 253a.

Subpart 4.5 Electronic Commerce in Contracting

§ 4.500 Scope of subpart.

This subpart provides policy and procedures for the establishment and use of electronic commerce in Federal acquisition as required by 41 U.S.C. 2301.

United States Code Annotated

Definitions, see 41 U.S.C.A. § 403.

Implementation of electronic commerce capability, see 10 U.S.C.A. § 2302c.

Use of electronic commerce in Federal procurement, see 41 U.S.C.A. § 426.

§ 4.501 [Reserved]

§ 4.502 Policy.

(a) The Federal Government shall use electronic commerce whenever practicable or cost-effective. The use of terms commonly associated with paper transactions (*e.g.,* "copy," "document," "page," "printed," "sealed envelope," and "stamped") shall not be interpreted to restrict the use of electronic commerce. Contracting officers may supplement electronic transactions by using other media to meet the requirements of any contract action governed by the FAR (*e.g.,* transmit hard copy of drawings).

(b) Agencies may exercise broad discretion in selecting the hardware and software that will be used in conducting electronic commerce. However, as required by 41 U.S.C. 2301, the head of each agency, after consulting with the Administrator of OFPP, shall ensure that systems, technologies, procedures, and processes used by the agency to conduct electronic commerce—

(1) Are implemented uniformly throughout the agency, to the maximum extent practicable;

(2) Are implemented only after considering the full or partial use of existing infrastructures;

(3) Facilitate access to Government acquisition opportunities by small business concerns, small disadvantaged business concerns, women-owned, veteran-owned, HUBZone, and service-disabled veteran-owned small business concerns;

(4) Include a single means of providing widespread public notice of acquisition opportunities through the Governmentwide point of entry and a means of responding to notices or solicitations electronically; and

(5) Comply with nationally and internationally recognized standards that broaden interoperability and ease the electronic interchange of information, such as standards established by the National Institute of Standards and Technology.

(c) Before using electronic commerce, the agency head shall ensure that the agency systems are capable of ensuring authentication and confidentiality commensurate with the risk and magnitude of the harm from loss, misuse, or unauthorized access to or modification of the information.

(d) Agencies may accept electronic signatures and records in connection with Government contracts.

United States Code Annotated

Definitions, see 41 U.S.C.A. § 403.

Implementation of electronic commerce capability, see 10 U.S.C.A. § 2302c.

Use of electronic commerce in Federal procurement, see 41 U.S.C.A. § 426.

Notes of Decisions

In general 1

1 In general

Electronic proposal transmitted 11 minutes before the 1:00 deadline and received at the agency's initial point of entry (a Unix mail relay host server) between 8 and 10 minutes before the deadline, was late because it took approximately 17 to 33 minutes for the proposal to complete the agency's virus scanning process and did not arrive at the e-mail address designated in the RFP until over 7 minutes after the deadline. Sea Box, Inc., B-291056, 2002 CPD ¶ 181 (Comp. Gen. 2002).

In a procurement conducted by electronic commerce, where the solicitation materials were available only on the Internet, protest that it was improper for the agency to post an amendment with a short response time without specifically advising the protester was denied where the record shows that the protester failed to avail itself of every reasonable opportunity to obtain the amendment by either registering for e-mail notification or checking the Internet site, and that this failure was the reason the protester allegedly had insufficient time to protest the solicitation's terms. USA Information Systems, Inc., B-291488, 2002 CPD ¶ 205 (Comp. Gen. 2002).

Subpart 4.6 —Contract Reporting

§ 4.600 Scope of subpart.

This subpart prescribes uniform reporting requirements for the Federal Procurement Data System (FPDS).

United States Code Annotated

Contract requirements, see 41 U.S.C.A. § 254.

Contracts, planning, solicitation, evaluation, and award procedures, see 10 U.S.C.A. § 2305.

Definitions, see 10 U.S.C.A. § 2302, 41 U.S.C.A. §§ 259, 403.

Kinds of contracts, see 10 U.S.C.A. § 2306.

Planning and solicitation requirements, see 41 U.S.C.A. § 253a.

Record requirements, see 41 U.S.C.A. § 417.

§ 4.601 Definitions.

As used in this subpart—

"Contract action" means any oral or written action that results in the purchase, rent, or lease of supplies or equipment, services, or construction using appropriated dollars over the micro-purchase threshold, or modifications to these actions regardless of dollar value. Contract action does not include grants, cooperative agreements, other transactions, real property leases, requisitions from Federal stock, training authorizations, or other non-FAR based transactions.

"Contract action report (CAR)" means contract action data required to be entered into the Federal Procurement Data System (FPDS).

"Definitive contract" means any contract that must be reported to FPDS other than an indefinite delivery vehicle. This definition is only for FPDS, and is not intended to apply to Part 16.

"Entitlement program" means a Federal program that guarantees a certain level of benefits to persons or other entities who meet requirements set by law, such as Social Security, farm price supports, or unemployment benefits.

"Generic DUNS number" means a DUNS number assigned to a category of vendors not specific to any individual or entity.

"Indefinite delivery vehicle (IDV)" means an indefinite delivery contract or agreement that has one or more of the following clauses:

(1) 52.216-18, Ordering.

(2) 52.216-19, Order Limitations.

(3) 52.216-20, Definite Quantity.

(4) 52.216-21, Requirements.

(5) 52.216-22, Indefinite Quantity.

(6) Any other clause allowing ordering.

United States Code Annotated

Contract requirements, see 41 U.S.C.A. § 254.

Contracts, planning, solicitation, evaluation, and award procedures, see 10 U.S.C.A. § 2305.

Definitions, see 10 U.S.C.A. § 2302, 41 U.S.C.A. §§ 259, 403.

Kinds of contracts, see 10 U.S.C.A. § 2306.

Planning and solicitation requirements, see 41 U.S.C.A. § 253a.

Record requirements, see 41 U.S.C.A. § 417.

§ 4.602 General.

(a) The FPDS provides a comprehensive web-based tool for agencies to report contract actions. The resulting data provides—

(1) A basis for recurring and special reports to the President, the Congress, the Government Accountability Office, Federal executive agencies, and the general public;

(2) A means of measuring and assessing the effect of Federal contracting on the Nation's economy and the extent to which small, veteran-owned small, service-disabled veteran-owned small, HUBZone small, small disadvantaged, women-owned small business concerns, and AbilityOne nonprofit agencies operating under 41 U.S.C. chapter 85, Committee for Purchase from People Who Are Blind or Severely Disabled, are sharing in Federal contracts;

(3) A means of measuring and assessing the effect of Federal contracting for promoting sustainable technologies, materials, products, and high-performance sustainable buildings. This is accomplished by collecting and reporting agency data on sustainable acquisition, including types of products purchased, the purchase costs, and the exceptions

used for other than sustainable acquisition; and

(4) A means of measuring and assessing the effect of other policy and management initiatives (e.g., performance based acquisitions and competition).

(b) FPDS does not provide reports for certain acquisition information used in the award of a contract action (e.g., subcontracting data, funding data, or accounting data).

(c) The FPDS Web site, https://www.fpds.gov, provides instructions for submitting data. It also provides—

(1) A complete list of departments, agencies, and other entities that submit data to the FPDS;

(2) Technical and end-user guidance;

(3) A computer-based tutorial; and

(4) Information concerning reports not generated in FPDS.

United States Code Annotated

Contract requirements, see 41 U.S.C.A. § 254.

Contracts, planning, solicitation, evaluation, and award procedures, see 10 U.S.C.A. § 2305.

Definitions, see 10 U.S.C.A. § 2302, 41 U.S.C.A. §§ 259, 403.

Kinds of contracts, see 10 U.S.C.A. § 2306.

Planning and solicitation requirements, see 41 U.S.C.A. § 253a.

Record requirements, see 41 U.S.C.A. § 417.

§ 4.603 Policy.

(a) In accordance with the Federal Funding Accountability and Transparency Act of 2006 (Pub. L. 109-282), all unclassified Federal award data must be publicly accessible.

(b) Executive agencies shall use FPDS to maintain publicly available information about all unclassified contract actions exceeding the micro-purchase threshold, and any modifications to those actions that change previously reported contract action report data, regardless of dollar value.

(c) Agencies awarding assisted acquisitions or direct acquisitions must report these actions and identify the Program/Funding Agency and Office Codes from the applicable agency codes maintained by each agency at FPDS. These codes represent the agency and office that has provided the predominant amount of funding for the contract action. For assisted acquisitions, the requesting agency will receive socioeconomic credit for meeting agency small business goals, where applicable. Requesting agencies shall provide the appropriate agency/bureau component code as part of the written interagency agreement between the requesting and servicing agencies (see 17.502-1(b)(1)).

(d) Agencies awarding contract actions with a mix of appropriated and non-appropriated funding shall only report the full appropriated portion of the contract action in FPDS.

United States Code Annotated

Contract requirements, see 41 U.S.C.A. § 254.

Contracts, planning, solicitation, evaluation, and award procedures, see 10 U.S.C.A. § 2305.

Definitions, see 10 U.S.C.A. § 2302, 41 U.S.C.A. §§ 259, 403.

Kinds of contracts, see 10 U.S.C.A. § 2306.

Planning and solicitation requirements, see 41 U.S.C.A. § 253a.

Record requirements, see 41 U.S.C.A. § 417.

§ 4.604 Responsibilities.

(a) The Senior Procurement Executive in coordination with the head of the contracting activity is responsible for developing and monitoring a process to ensure timely and accurate reporting of contractual actions to FPDS.

(b) (1) The responsibility for the completion and accuracy of the individual contract action report (CAR) resides with the contracting officer who awarded the contract action. CARs in a draft or error status in FPDS are not considered complete.

(2) The CAR must be confirmed for accuracy by the contracting officer prior to release of the contract award. The CAR must then be completed in FPDS within three business days after contract award.

(3) For any action awarded in accordance with FAR 6.302-2 or pursuant to any of the authorities listed at FAR subpart 18.2, the CAR must be completed in FPDS within 30 days after contract award.

(4) When the contracting office receives written notification that a contractor has changed its size status in accordance with the clause at 52.219-28, Post-Award Small Business Program Rerepresentation, the contracting officer shall update the size status in FPDS within 30 days after receipt of contractor's notification of rerepresentation.

(5) If after award of a contract, the contracting officer receives written notification of SBA's final decision on a protest concerning a size determination, the contracting officer shall update FPDS to reflect the final decision.

(c) The chief acquisition officer of each agency required to report its contract actions must submit to the General Services Administration (GSA), in accordance with FPDS guidance, within 120 days after the end of each fiscal year, an annual certification of whether, and to what degree, agency CAR data for the preceding fiscal year is complete and accurate.

§ 4.605 Procedures.

(a) *Procurement Instrument Identifier (PIID).* Agencies shall have in place a process that ensures that each PIID reported to FPDS is unique Governmentwide, for all solicitations, contracts, blanket purchase agreements, basic agreements, basic ordering agreements, or orders in accordance with 4.1601 to 4.1603, and will remain so for at least 20 years from the date of contract award. Other pertinent PIID instructions for FPDS reporting can be found at https://www.fpds.gov.

(b) Data Universal Numbering System. The contracting officer must identify and report a Data Universal Numbering System (DUNS) number (Contractor Identification Number) for the successful offeror on a contract action. The DUNS number reported must identify the successful offeror's name and address as stated in the offer and resultant contract, and as registered in the System for Award Management database in accordance with the provision at 52.204-7, System for Award Management. The contracting officer must ask the offeror to provide its DUNS number by using either the provision at 52.204-6, Data Universal Numbering System Number, the provision at 52.204-7, System for Award Management, or the provision at 52.212-1, Instructions to Offerors-Commercial Items. (For a discussion of the Commercial and Government Entity (CAGE) Code, which is a different identification number, see subpart 4.18.)

(c) Generic DUNS number.

(1) The use of a generic DUNS number should be limited, and only used in the situations described in paragraph (c)(2) of this section. Use of a generic DUNS number does not supersede the requirements of either provisions 52.204-6 or 52.204-7 (if present in the solicitation) for the contractor to have a DUNS number assigned.

(2) Authorized generic DUNS numbers, maintained by the Integrated Award Environment (IAE) program office (https://www.acquisition.gov), may be used to report contracts in lieu of the contractor's actual DUNS number only for—

(i) Contract actions valued at or below $30,000 that are awarded to a contractor that is—

(A) A student;

(B) A dependent of either a veteran, foreign service officer, or military member assigned outside the United States and its outlying areas (as defined in 2.101); or

(C) Located outside the United States and its outlying areas for work to be performed outside the United States and its outlying areas and the contractor does not otherwise have a DUNS number;

(ii) Contracts valued above $30,000 awarded to individuals located outside the United States and its outlying areas for work to be performed outside the United States and its outlying areas; or

(iii) Contracts when specific public identification of the contracted party could endanger the mission, contractor, or recipients of the acquired goods or services. The contracting officer must include a written determination in the contract file of a decision applicable to authority under this paragraph (c)(2)(iii).

(d) American Recovery and Reinvestment Act actions. The contracting officer, when entering data in FPDS, shall use the instructions at https://www.fpds.gov to identify any action funded in whole or in part by the American Recovery and Reinvestment Act of 2009 (Pub. L. 111-5).

(e) Office Codes. Agencies shall by March 1, 2016–

(1) Use the Activity Address Code (AAC), as defined in 2.101, assigned to the issuing contracting office as the contracting office code, and

(2) Use the AAC assigned to the program/funding office providing the predominance of funding for the contract action as the program/funding office code.

§ 4.606 Reporting Data.

(a) *Actions required to be reported to FPDS*.

(1) As a minimum, agencies must report the following contract actions over the micro-purchase threshold, regardless of solicitation process used, and agencies must report any modification to these contract actions that change previously reported contract action data, regardless of dollar value:

(i) Definitive contracts, including purchase orders and imprest fund buys over the micro-purchase threshold awarded by a contracting officer.

(ii) Indefinite delivery vehicle (identified as an "IDV" in FPDS). Examples of IDVs include the following:

(A) Task and Delivery Order Contracts (see Subpart 16.5), including—

(1) Government-wide acquisition contracts.

(2) Multi-agency contracts.

(B) GSA Federal supply schedules.

(C) Blanket Purchase Agreements (see 13.303).

(D) Basic Ordering Agreements (see 16.703).

(E) Any other agreement or contract against which individual orders or purchases may be placed.

(iii) All calls and orders awarded under the indefinite delivery vehicles identified in paragraph (a)(1)(ii) of this section.

(2) The GSA Office of Charge Card Management will provide the Government purchase card data, at a minimum annually, and GSA will incorporate that data into FPDS for reports.

(3) Agencies may use the FPDS Express Reporting capability for consolidated multiple action reports for a vendor when it would be overly burdensome to report each action individually. When used, Express Reporting should be done at least monthly.

(b) *Reporting Other Actions*. Agencies may submit actions other than those listed at paragraph (a)(1) of this section only if they are able to be segregated from FAR-based actions and this is approved in writing by the FPDS Program Office. Prior to the commencement of reporting, agencies must contact the FPDS Program Office if they desire to submit any of the following types of activity:

(1) Transactions at or below the micro-purchase threshold, except as provided in paragraph (a)(2) of this section.

(2) Any non-appropriated fund (NAF) or NAF portion of a contract action using a mix of appropriated and nonappropriated funding.

(3) Lease and supplemental lease agreements for real property.

(4) Grants and entitlement actions.

(c) *Actions not reported*. The following types of contract actions are not to be reported to FPDS:

(1) Imprest fund transactions below the micro-purchase threshold, including those made via the Government purchase card (unless specific agency procedures prescribe reporting these actions).

(2) Orders from GSA stock and the GSA Global Supply Program.

(3) Purchases made at GSA or AbilityOne service stores, as these items stocked for

resale have already been reported by GSA.

(4) Purchases made using non-appropriated fund activity cards, chaplain fund cards, individual Government personnel training orders, and Defense Printing orders.

(5) Actions that, pursuant to other authority, will not be entered in FPDS (*e.g.*, reporting of the information would compromise national security).

(6) Contract actions in which the required data would constitute classified information.

(7) Resale activity (*i.e.*, commissary or exchange activity).

(8) Revenue generating arrangements (*i.e.*, concessions).

(9) Training expenditures not issued as orders or contracts.

(10) Interagency agreements other than inter-agency acquisitions required to be reported at 4.606(a)(1).

(11) Letters of obligation used in the A-76 process.

(d) Agencies not subject to the FAR. Agencies not subject to the FAR may be required by other authority (*e.g.*, statute, OMB, or internal agency policy) to report certain information to FPDS. Those agencies not subject to the FAR must first receive approval from the FPDS Program Office prior to reporting to FPDS.

§ 4.607 Solicitation provisions and contract clause.

(a) Insert the provision at 52.204-5, Women-Owned Business (Other Then Small Business), in all solicitations that—

(1) Are not set aside for small business concerns;

(2) Exceed the simplified acquisition threshold; and

(3) Are for contracts that will be performed in the United States or its outlying areas.

(b) Insert the provision at 52.204-6, Data Universal Numbering System Number, in solicitations that do not contain the provision at 52.204-7, System for Award Management, or meet a condition at 4.605(c)(2).

(c) Insert the clause at 52.204-12, Data Universal Numbering System Number Maintenance, in solicitations and resulting contracts that contain the provision at 52.204-6, Data Universal Numbering System.

Subpart 4.7 Contractor Records Retention

§ 4.700 Scope of subpart.

This subpart provides policies and procedures for retention of records by contractors to meet the records review requirements of the Government. In this subpart, the terms "contracts" and "contractors" include "subcontracts" and "subcontractors."

United States Code Annotated

Definitions, see 10 U.S.C.A. § 2302, 41 U.S.C.A. §§ 259, 403.

Examination of records of contractor, see 10 U.S.C.A. § 2313, 41 U.S.C.A. § 254d.

§ 4.701 Purpose.

The purpose of this subpart is to generally describe records retention requirements and to allow reductions in the retention period for specific classes of records under prescribed circumstances.

United States Code Annotated

Definitions, see 10 U.S.C.A. § 2302, 41 U.S.C.A. §§ 259, 403.

Examination of records of contractor, see 10 U.S.C.A. § 2313, 41 U.S.C.A. § 254d.

§ 4.702 Applicability.

(a) This subpart applies to records generated under contracts that contain one of the following clauses:

(1) Audit and Records—Sealed Bidding (52.214-26).

(2) Audit and Records—Negotiation (52.215-2).

(b) This subpart is not mandatory on Department of Energy contracts for which the Comptroller General allows alternative records retention periods. Apart from this exception, this subpart applies to record retention periods under contracts that are subject to Chapter 137, Title 10, U.S.C., or 40 U.S.C. 101, et seq.

United States Code Annotated

Definitions, see 10 U.S.C.A. § 2302, 41 U.S.C.A. §§ 259, 403.

Examination of records of contractor, see 10 U.S.C.A. § 2313, 41 U.S.C.A. § 254d.

§ 4.703 Policy.

(a) Except as stated in 4.703(b), contractors shall make available records, which includes books, documents, accounting procedures and practices, and other data, regardless of type and regardless of whether such items are in written form, in the form of computer data, or in any other form, and other supporting evidence to satisfy contract negotiation, administration, and audit requirements of the contracting agencies and the Comptroller General for—

(1) 3 years after final payment or, for certain records;

(2) The period specified in 4.705 through 4.705-3, whichever of these periods expires first.

(b) Contractors shall make available the foregoing records and supporting evidence for a longer period of time than is required in 4.703(a) if—

(1) A retention period longer than that cited in 4.703(a) is specified in any contract clause; or

(2) The contractor, for its own purposes, retains the foregoing records and supporting evidence for a longer period. Under this circumstance, the retention period shall be the period of the contractor's retention or 3 years after final payment, whichever period expires first.

(3) The contractor does not meet the original due date for submission of final indirect cost rate proposals specified in paragraph (d)(2) of the clause at 52.216-7, Allowable Cost and Payment. Under these circumstances, the retention periods in 4.705 shall be automatically extended one day for each day the proposal is not submitted after the original due date.

(c) Nothing in this section shall be construed to preclude a contractor from duplicating or storing original records in electronic form unless they contain significant information not shown on the record copy. Original records need not be maintained or produced in an audit if the contractor or subcontractor provides photographic or electronic images of the original records and meets the following requirements:

(1) The contractor or subcontractor has established procedures to ensure that the imaging process preserves accurate images of the original records, including signatures and other written or graphic images, and that the imaging process is reliable and secure so as to maintain the integrity of the records.

(2) The contractor or subcontractor maintains an effective indexing system to permit timely and convenient access to the imaged records.

(3) The contractor or subcontractor retains the original records for a minimum of one year after imaging to permit periodic validation of the imaging systems.

(d) If the information described in paragraph (a) of this section is maintained on a computer, contractors shall retain the computer data on a reliable medium for the time periods prescribed. Contractors may transfer computer data in machine readable form from one reliable computer medium to another. Contractors' computer data retention and transfer procedures shall maintain the integrity, reliability, and security of the original computer data. Contractors shall also retain an audit trail describing the data transfer. For the record retention time periods prescribed, contractors shall not destroy, discard, delete, or write over such computer data.

United States Code Annotated

Definitions, see 10 U.S.C.A. § 2302, 41 U.S.C.A. §§ 259, 403.

Examination of records of contractor, see 10 U.S.C.A. § 2313, 41 U.S.C.A. § 254d.

§ 4.704 Calculation of retention periods.

(a) The retention periods in 4.705 are calculated from the end of the contractor's fiscal year in which an entry is made charging or allocating a cost to a Government contract or subcontract. If a specific record contains a series of entries, the retention period is calculated from the end of the contractor's fiscal year in which the final entry is made. The contractor should cut off the records in annual blocks and retain them for block disposal under the prescribed retention periods.

(b) When records generated during a prior contract are relied upon by a contractor for certified cost or pricing data in negotiating a succeeding contract, the prescribed periods shall run from the date of the succeeding contract.

(c) If two or more of the record categories described in 4.705 are interfiled and screening for disposal is not practical, the contractor shall retain the entire record series for the longest period prescribed for any category of records.

United States Code Annotated

Definitions, see 10 U.S.C.A. § 2302, 41 U.S.C.A. §§ 259, 403.

Examination of records of contractor, see 10 U.S.C.A. § 2313, 41 U.S.C.A. § 254d.

§ 4.705 Specific retention periods.

The contractor shall retain the records identified in 4.705-1 through 4.705-3 for the periods designated, provided retention is required under 4.702. Records are identified in this subpart in terms of their purpose or use and not by specific name or form number. Although the descriptive identifications may not conform to normal contractor usage or filing practices, these identifications apply to all contractor records that come within the description.

United States Code Annotated

Definitions, see 10 U.S.C.A. § 2302, 41 U.S.C.A. §§ 259, 403.

Examination of records of contractor, see 10 U.S.C.A. § 2313, 41 U.S.C.A. § 254d.

§ 4.705-1 Financial and cost accounting records.

(a) Accounts receivable invoices, adjustments to the accounts, invoice registers, carrier freight bills, shipping orders, and other documents which detail the material or services billed on the related invoices: Retain 4 years.

(b) Material, work order, or service order files, consisting of purchase requisitions or purchase orders for material or services, or orders for transfer of material or supplies: Retain 4 years. *

(c) Cash advance recapitulations, prepared as posting entries to accounts receivable ledgers for amounts of expense vouchers prepared for employees' travel and related expenses: Retain 4 years.

(d) Paid, canceled, and voided checks, other than those issued for the payment of salary and wages: Retain 4 years.

(e) Accounts payable records to support disbursements of funds for materials, equipment, supplies, and services, containing originals or copies of the following and related documents: remittance advices and statements, vendors' invoices, invoice audits and distribution slips, receiving and inspection reports or comparable certifications of receipt and inspection of material or services, and debit and credit memoranda: Retain 4 years.

(f) Labor cost distribution cards or equivalent documents: Retain 2 years.

(g) Petty cash records showing description of expenditures, to whom paid, name of person authorizing payment, and date, including copies of vouchers and other supporting documents: Retain 2 years.

United States Code Annotated

Definitions, see 10 U.S.C.A. § 2302, 41 U.S.C.A. §§ 259, 403.

Examination of records of contractor, see 10 U.S.C.A. § 2313, 41 U.S.C.A. § 254d.

Notes of Decisions

In general 1
Laches and stale demands 2

1 In general

Contractor's labor recap sheets showing time each employee worked on specific government contract during given month were required to be retained by contractor for three years from date of final payment; labor recap sheets were more properly classified as documents which detailed material or services billed on related invoices rather than labor cost distribution cards or equivalent documentation, retention period for which was only two years. JANA, Inc. v. U.S., 936 F.2d 1265, 37 Cont. Cas. Fed. (CCH) P 76116 (Fed. Cir. 1991). United States ⊕88

2 Laches and stale demands

Government's delay in conducting audit of contractor and resulting delay in issuance of contracting officer's decision assessing overcharges were not unreasonable and inexcusable so as to invoke defense of laches, where Government began audit within period which contractor was required to maintain records and Government had no knowledge of any overcharges by contractor until audit was concluded. JANA, Inc. v. U.S., 936 F.2d 1265, 37 Cont. Cas. Fed. (CCH) P 76116 (Fed. Cir. 1991). United States ⊕88

Defense of laches requires showing of two things: unreasonable and unexcused delay by claimant, and prejudice to other party, either economic prejudice or defense prejudice, i.e., impairment of abilities to mount defense due to circumstances such as loss of records, destruction of evidence, or witness unavailability. JANA, Inc. v. U.S., 936 F.2d 1265, 37 Cont. Cas. Fed. (CCH) P 76116 (Fed. Cir. 1991). Equity ⊕72(1); Equity ⊕73

§ 4.705-2 Pay administration records.

(a) Payroll sheets, registers, or their equivalent, of salaries and wages paid to individual employees for each payroll period; change slips; and tax withholding statements: Retain 4 years.

(b) Clock cards or other time and attendance cards: Retain 2 years.

(c) Paid checks, receipts for wages paid in cash, or other evidence of payments for services rendered by employees: Retain 2 years.

United States Code Annotated

Definitions, see 10 U.S.C.A. § 2302, 41 U.S.C.A. §§ 259, 403.

Examination of records of contractor, see 10 U.S.C.A. § 2313, 41 U.S.C.A. § 254d.

§ 4.705-3 Acquisition and supply records.

(a) Store requisitions for materials, supplies, equipment, and services: Retain 2 years.

(b) Work orders for maintenance and other services: Retain 4 years.

(c) Equipment records, consisting of equipment usage and status reports and equipment repair orders: Retain 4 years.

(d) Expendable property records, reflecting accountability for the receipt and use of material in the performance of a contract: Retain 4 years.

(e) Receiving and inspection report records, consisting of reports reflecting receipt and inspection of supplies, equipment, and materials: Retain 4 years.

(f) Purchase order files for supplies, equipment, material, or services used in the performance of a contract; supporting documentation and backup files including, but not limited to, invoices, and memoranda; e.g., memoranda of negotiations showing the principal elements of subcontract price negotiations (see 52.244-2): Retain 4 years.

(g) Production records of quality control, reliability, and inspection: Retain 4 years.

(h) Property records (see FAR 45.101 and 52.245-1): Retain 4 years.

United States Code Annotated

Definitions, see 10 U.S.C.A. § 2302, 41 U.S.C.A. §§ 259, 403.

Examination of records of contractor, see 10 U.S.C.A. § 2313, 41 U.S.C.A. § 254d.

Subpart 4.8 Government Contract Files

§ 4.800 Scope of subpart.

This subpart prescribes requirements for establishing, maintaining, and disposing of contract files.

United States Code Annotated

Definitions, see 41 U.S.C.A. § 403.

Record requirements, see 41 U.S.C.A. § 417.

§ 4.801 General.

(a) The head of each office performing contracting, contract administration, or paying functions shall establish files containing the records of all contractual actions.

(b) The documentation in the files (see 4.803) shall be sufficient to constitute a complete history of the transaction for the purpose of—

(1) Providing a complete background as a basis for informed decisions at each step in the acquisition process;

(2) Supporting actions taken;

(3) Providing information for reviews and investigations; and

(4) Furnishing essential facts in the event of litigation or congressional inquiries.

(c) The files to be established include—

(1) A file for cancelled solicitations;

(2) A file for each contract; and

(3) A file such as a contractor general file, containing documents relating—for example—to—

(i) No specific contract;

(ii) More than one contract; or

(iii) The contractor in a general way (e.g., contractor's management systems, past performance, or capabilities).

United States Code Annotated

Definitions, see 41 U.S.C.A. § 403.

Record requirements, see 41 U.S.C.A. § 417.

Notes of Decisions

In general 1

1 In general

A failure to maintain required contract file documentation in accordance with FAR 4.801 may be considered as evidence that an agency procurement decision was arbitrary. Matter of: Southwest Marine, Inc.; American Systems Engineering Corporation, B-265865, B-265865.3, B-265865.4, 96-1 CPD ¶ 56 (Comp. Gen. 1996).

§ 4.802 Contract files.

(a) A contract file should generally consist of—

(1) The contracting office contract file that documents the basis for the acquisition and the award, the assignment of contract administration (including payment responsibilities), and any subsequent actions taken by the contracting office;

(2) The contract administration office contract file that documents actions reflecting the basis for and the performance of contract administration responsibilities; and

(3) The paying office contract file that documents actions prerequisite to, substantiating, and reflecting contract payments.

(b) Normally, each file should be kept separately; however, if appropriate, any or all of the files may be combined; e.g., if all functions or any combination of the functions are performed by the same office.

(c) Files must be maintained at organizational levels that ensure—

(1) Effective documentation of contract actions;

(2) Ready accessibility to principal users;

(3) Minimal establishment of duplicate and working files;

(4) The safeguarding of classified documents; and

(5) Conformance with agency regulations for file location and maintenance.

(d) If the contract files or file segments are decentralized (*e.g.*, by type or function) to various organizational elements or to other outside offices, responsibility for their maintenance must be assigned. A central control and, if needed, a locator system should be established to ensure the ability to locate promptly any contract files.

(e) Contents of contract files that are contractor bid or proposal information or source selection information as defined in 2.101 must be protected from disclosure to unauthorized persons (see 3.104-4).

(f) Agencies may retain contract files in any medium (paper, electronic, microfilm, etc.) or any combination of media, as long as the requirements of this subpart are satisfied.

United States Code Annotated

Definitions, see 41 U.S.C.A. § 403.

Record requirements, see 41 U.S.C.A. § 417.

§ 4.803 Contents of contract files.

The following are examples of the records normally contained, if applicable, in contract files:

(a) Contracting office contract file.

(1) Purchase request, acquisition planning information, and other presolicitation documents.

(2) Justifications and approvals, determinations and findings, and associated documents.

(3) Evidence of availability of funds.

(4) Synopsis of proposed acquisition as required by Part 5 or a reference to the synopsis.

(5) The list of sources solicited, and a list of any firms or persons whose requests for copies of the solicitation were denied, together with the reasons for denial.

(6) Set-aside decision including the type and extent of market research conducted.

(7) Government estimate of contract price.

(8) A copy of the solicitation and all amendments thereto.

(9) Security requirements and evidence of required clearances.

(10) A copy of each offer or quotation, the related abstract, and records of determinations concerning late offers or quotations. Unsuccessful offers or quotations may be maintained separately, if cross-referenced to the contract file. The only portions of the unsuccessful offer or quotation that need be retained are—

(i) Completed solicitation sections A, B, and K;

(ii) Technical and management proposals;

(iii) Cost/price proposals; and

(iv) Any other pages of the solicitation that the offeror or quoter has altered or annotated.

(11) Contractor's representations and certifications (see 4.1201(c)).

(12) Preaward survey reports or reference to previous preaward survey reports relied upon.

(13) Source selection documentation.

(14) Contracting officer's determination of the contractor's responsibility.

(15) Small Business Administration Certificate of Competency.

(16) Records of contractor's compliance with labor policies including equal employment opportunity policies.

(17) Data and information related to the contracting officer's determination of a fair

and reasonable price. This may include—

    (i) Certified cost or pricing data;

    (ii) Data other than certified cost or pricing data;

    (iii) Justification for waiver from the requirement to submit certified cost or pricing data; or

    (iv) Certificates of Current Cost or Pricing Data.

(18) Packaging and transportation data.

(19) Cost or price analysis.

(20) Audit reports or reasons for waiver.

(21) Record of negotiation.

(22) Justification for type of contract.

(23) Authority for deviations from this regulation, statutory requirements, or other restrictions.

(24) Required approvals of award and evidence of legal review.

(25) Notice of award.

(26) The original of—

    (i) The signed contract or award;

    (ii) All contract modifications; and

    (iii) Documents supporting modifications executed by the contracting office.

(27) Synopsis of award or reference thereto.

(28) Notice to unsuccessful quoters or offerors and record of any debriefing.

(29) Acquisition management reports (see subpart 4.6).

(30) Bid, performance, payment, or other bond documents, or a reference thereto, and notices to sureties.

(31) Report of postaward conference.

(32) Notice to proceed, stop orders, and any overtime premium approvals granted at the time of award.

(33) Documents requesting and authorizing modification in the normal assignment of contract administration functions and responsibility.

(34) Approvals or disapprovals of requests for waivers or deviations from contract requirements.

(35) Rejected engineering change proposals.

(36) Royalty, invention, and copyright reports (including invention disclosures) or reference thereto.

(37) Contract completion documents.

(38) Documentation regarding termination actions for which the contracting office is responsible.

(39) Cross-references to pertinent documents that are filed elsewhere.

(40) Any additional documents on which action was taken or that reflect actions by the contracting office pertinent to the contract.

(41) A current chronological list identifying the awarding and successor contracting officers, with inclusive dates of responsibility.

(42) When limiting competition, or awarding on a sole source basis, to economically disadvantaged women-owned small business (EDWOSB) concerns or women-owned small business (WOSB) concerns eligible under the WOSB Program in accordance with subpart 19.15, include documentation—

    (i) Of the type and extent of market research; and

    (ii) That the NAICS code assigned to the acquisition is for an industry that SBA has designated as—

        (A) Underrepresented for EDWOSB concerns; or

        (B) Substantially underrepresented for WOSB concerns.

(b) Contract administration office contract file.

(1) Copy of the contract and all modifications, together with official record copies of supporting documents executed by the contract administration office.

(2) Any document modifying the normal assignment of contract administration functions and responsibility.

(3) Security requirements.

(4) Certified cost or pricing data, Certificates of Current Cost or Pricing Data, or data other than certified cost or pricing data; cost or price analysis; and other documentation supporting contractual actions executed by the contract administration office.

(5) Preaward survey information.

(6) Purchasing system information.

(7) Consent to subcontract or purchase.

(8) Performance and payment bonds and surety information.

(9) Postaward conference records.

(10) Orders issued under the contract.

(11) Notice to proceed and stop orders.

(12) Insurance policies or certificates of insurance or references to them.

(13) Documents supporting advance or progress payments.

(14) Progressing, expediting, and production surveillance records.

(15) Quality assurance records.

(16) Property administration records.

(17) Documentation regarding termination actions for which the contract administration office is responsible.

(18) Cross reference to other pertinent documents that are filed elsewhere.

(19) Any additional documents on which action was taken or that reflect actions by the contract administration office pertinent to the contract.

(20) Contract completion documents.

(c) Paying office contract file.

(1) Copy of the contract and any modifications.

(2) Bills, invoices, vouchers, and supporting documents.

(3) Record of payments or receipts.

(4) Other pertinent documents.

United States Code Annotated

Definitions, see 41 U.S.C.A. § 403.

Record requirements, see 41 U.S.C.A. § 417.

§ 4.804 Closeout of contract files.

§ 4.804-1 Closeout by the office administering the contract.

(a) Except as provided in paragraph (c) of this section, time standards for closing out contract files are as follows:

(1) Files for contracts using simplified acquisition procedures should be considered closed when the contracting officer receives evidence of receipt of property and final payment, unless otherwise specified by agency regulations.

(2) Files for firm-fixed-price contracts, other than those using simplified acquisition procedures, should be closed within 6 months after the date on which the contracting officer receives evidence of physical completion.

(3) Files for contracts requiring settlement of indirect cost rates should be closed within 36 months of the month in which the contracting officer receives evidence of physical completion.

(4) Files for all other contracts should be closed within 20 months of the month in which the contracting officer receives evidence of physical completion.

(b) When closing out the contract files at 4.804-1(a)(2), (3), and (4), the contracting officer shall use the closeout procedures at 4.804-5. However, these closeout actions may be modified to reflect the extent of administration that has been performed. Quick closeout procedures (see 42.708) should be used, when appropriate, to reduce administrative costs and to enable deobligation of excess funds.

(c) A contract file shall not be closed if—

(1) The contract is in litigation or under appeal; or

(2) In the case of a termination, all termination actions have not been completed.

United States Code Annotated

Definitions, see 41 U.S.C.A. § 403.

Record requirements, see 41 U.S.C.A. § 417.

§ 4.804-2 Closeout of the contracting office files if another office administers the contract.

(a) Contract files for contracts using simplified acquisition procedures should be considered closed when the contracting officer receives evidence of receipt of property and final payment, unless otherwise specified by agency regulation.

(b) All other contract files shall be closed as soon as practicable after the contracting officer receives a contract completion statement from the contract administration office. The contracting officer shall ensure that all contractual actions required have been completed and shall prepare a statement to that effect. This statement is authority to close the contract file and shall be made a part of the official contract file.

United States Code Annotated

Definitions, see 41 U.S.C.A. § 403.

Record requirements, see 41 U.S.C.A. § 417.

§ 4.804-3 Closeout of paying office contract files.

The paying office shall close the contract file upon issuance of the final payment voucher.

United States Code Annotated

Definitions, see 41 U.S.C.A. § 403.

Record requirements, see 41 U.S.C.A. § 417.

§ 4.804-4 Physically completed contracts.

(a) Except as provided in paragraph (b) of this section, a contract is considered to be physically completed when—

(1) (i) The contractor has completed the required deliveries and the Government has inspected and accepted the supplies;

(ii) The contractor has performed all services and the Government has accepted these services; and

(iii) All option provisions, if any, have expired; or

(2) The Government has given the contractor a notice of complete contract termination.

(b) Rental, use, and storage agreements are considered to be physically completed when—

(1) The Government has given the contractor a notice of complete contract termination; or

(2) The contract period has expired.

United States Code Annotated

Definitions, see 41 U.S.C.A. § 403.

Record requirements, see 41 U.S.C.A. § 417.

Notes of Decisions

Physically completed 1

1 Physically completed

Under regulations in effect when Navy contract for underwater marking devices was closed, contract was not "physically completed" before contractor submitted its value engineering change proposal (VECP), inasmuch as contractor had not completed all deliveries required under contract, given one $5 spare part that remained to be delivered, and contracting officer had not given contractor notice of government's intent to declare contract complete. 48 C.F.R. §§ 4.804-4(a)(1-2), 4.804.5(a), (b)(8), 52.248-1. Vantage Associates, Inc. v. England, 25 Fed. Appx. 859 (Fed. Cir. 2001). United States ☞70(15.1)

§ 4.804-5 Procedures for closing out contract files.

(a) The contract administration office is responsible for initiating (automated or manual) administrative closeout of the contract after receiving evidence of its physical completion. At the outset of this process, the contract administration office must review the contract funds status and notify the contracting office of any excess funds the contract administration office might deobligate. When complete, the administrative closeout procedures must ensure that—

(1) Disposition of classified material is completed;

(2) *Final patent report is cleared*. If a final patent report is required, the contracting officer may proceed with contract closeout in accordance with the following procedures, or as otherwise prescribed by agency procedures:

(i) Final patent reports should be cleared within 60 days of receipt.

(ii) If the final patent report is not received, the contracting officer shall notify the contractor of the contractor's obligations and the Government's rights under the applicable patent rights clause, in accordance with 27.303. If the contractor fails to respond to this notification, the contracting officer may proceed with contract closeout upon consultation with the agency legal counsel responsible for patent matters regarding the contractor's failure to respond.

(3) Final royalty report is cleared;

(4) There is no outstanding value engineering change proposal;

(5) Plant clearance report is received;

(6) Property clearance is received;

(7) All interim or disallowed costs are settled;

(8) Price revision is completed;

(9) Subcontracts are settled by the prime contractor;

(10) Prior year indirect cost rates are settled;

(11) Termination docket is completed;

(12) Contract audit is completed;

(13) Contractor's closing statement is completed;

(14) Contractor's final invoice has been submitted; and

(15) Contract funds review is completed and excess funds deobligated.

(b) When the actions in paragraph (a) of this subsection have been verified, the contracting officer administering the contract must ensure that a contract completion statement, containing the following information, is prepared:

(1) Contract administration office name and address (if different from the contracting office).

(2) Contracting office name and address.

(3) Contract number.

(4) Last modification number.

(5) Last call or order number.

(6) Contractor name and address.

(7) Dollar amount of excess funds, if any.

(8) Voucher number and date, if final payment has been made.

(9) Invoice number and date, if the final approved invoice has been forwarded to a disbursing office of another agency or activity and the status of the payment is unknown.

(10) A statement that all required contract administration actions have been fully and satisfactorily accomplished.

(11) Name and signature of the contracting officer.

(12) Date.

(c) When the statement is completed, the contracting officer must ensure that—

(1) The signed original is placed in the contracting office contract file (or forwarded to the contracting office for placement in the files if the contract administration office is different from the contracting office); and

(2) A signed copy is placed in the appropriate contract administration file if administration is performed by a contract administration office.

United States Code Annotated

Definitions, see 41 U.S.C.A. § 403.

Record requirements, see 41 U.S.C.A. § 417.

Notes of Decisions

Physically completed 1

1 Physically completed

Under regulations in effect when Navy contract for underwater marking devices was closed, contract was not "physically completed" before contractor submitted its value engineering change proposal (VECP), inasmuch as contractor had not completed all deliveries required under contract, given one $5 spare part that remained to be delivered, and contracting officer had not given contractor notice of government's intent to declare contract complete. 48 C.F.R. §§ 4.804-4(a)(1-2), 4.804.5(a), (b)(8), 52.248-1. Vantage Associates, Inc. v. England, 25 Fed. Appx. 859 (Fed. Cir. 2001). United States ☞70(15.1)

When all costs are settled, the affected contracts then will be "closed out," pursuant to FAR 4.804-5, providing that, in order to close out a contract, the contracting officer and the contractor must: settle prior year indirect cost rates; complete a contract audit; review the contractor's final invoice; and, if necessary, de-obligate any excess funds over the course of the contract). ATK Thiokol, Inc. v. U.S., 76 Fed. Cl. 654 (2007).

§ 4.805 Storage, handling, and contract files.

(a) Agencies must prescribe procedures for the handling, storing, and disposing of contract files, in accordance with the National Archives and Records Administration (NARA) General Records Schedule 1.1, Financial Management and Reporting Records. The Financial Management and Reporting Records can be found at http://www.archives.gov/records-mgm t/grs.html. These procedures must take into account documents held in all types of media, including microfilm and various electronic media. Agencies may change the original medium to facilitate storage as long as the requirements of Part 4, law, and other regulations are satisfied. The process used to create and store records must record and reproduce the original document, including signatures and other written and graphic images completely, accurately, and clearly. Data transfer, storage, and retrieval procedures must protect the original data from alteration. Unless law or other regulations require signed originals to be kept, they may be destroyed after the responsible agency official verifies that record copies on alternate media and copies reproduced from the record copy are accurate, complete, and clear representations of the originals. When original documents have been converted to alternate media for storage, the requirements in Table 4-1 of this section also apply to the record copies in the alternate media.

(b) If administrative records are mixed with program records and cannot be economically segregated, the entire file should be kept for the period of time approved for the program records. Similarly, if documents described in the following table are part of a subject or case file that documents activities that are not described in the table, they should be treated in the same manner as the files of which they are a part.

(c) An agency that requires a shorter retention period than those identified in Table 4-1 shall request approval from NARA through the agency's records officer.

TABLE 4-1—RETENTION PERIODS

Record	Retention Period
(1) Contracts (and related records or documents, including successful and unsuccessful proposals, except see paragraph (c)(2) of this section regarding contractor payrolls submitted under construction contracts).	6 years after final payment.

Record	Retention Period
(2) Contractor's payrolls submitted under construction contracts in accordance with Department of Labor regulations (29 CFR 5.5(a)(3)), with related certifications, anti-kickback affidavits, and other related records.	3 years after contract completion unless contract performance is the subject of an enforcement action on that date (see paragraph (c)(8) of this section).
(3) Unsolicited proposals not accepted by a department or agency.	Retain in accordance with agency procedures.
(4) Files for canceled solicitations.	6 years after cancellation.
(5) Other copies of procurement file records used for administrative purposes.	When business use ceases.
(6) Documents pertaining generally to the contractor as described at 4.801(c)(3).	Until superseded or obsolete.
(7) Data submitted to the Federal Procurement Data System (FPDS). Electronic data file maintained by fiscal year, containing unclassified records of all procurements exceeding the micropurchase threshold, and information required under 4.603.	6 years after submittal to FPDS.
(8) Investigations, cases pending or in litigation (including protests), or similar matters (including enforcement actions).	Until final clearance or settlement, or, if related to a document identified in paragraphs (c)(1) through (7) of this section, for the retention period specified for the related document, whichever is later.

United States Code Annotated

Definitions, see 41 U.S.C.A. § 403.

Record requirements, see 41 U.S.C.A. § 417.

Subpart 4.9 Taxpayer Identification Number Information

§ 4.900 Scope of subpart.

This subpart provides policies and procedures for obtaining—

(a) Taxpayer Identification Number (TIN) information that may be used for debt collection purposes; and

(b) Contract information and payment information for submittal to the payment office for Internal Revenue Service (IRS) reporting purposes.

United States Code Annotated

Contracts, planning, solicitation, evaluation, and award procedures, see 10 U.S.C.A. § 2305.

Definitions, see 41 U.S.C.A. § 403.

Planning and solicitation requirements, see 41 U.S.C.A. § 253a.

§ 4.901 Definition.

"Common parent," as used in this subpart, means that corporate entity that owns or controls an affiliated group of corporations that files its Federal income tax returns on a consolidated basis, and of which the offeror is a member.

United States Code Annotated

Contracts, planning, solicitation, evaluation, and award procedures, see 10 U.S.C.A. § 2305.

Definitions, see 41 U.S.C.A. § 403.

Planning and solicitation requirements, see 41 U.S.C.A. § 253a.

§ 4.902 General.

(a) *Debt collection.* 31 U.S.C. 7701(c) requires each contractor doing business with a Government agency to furnish its TIN to that agency. 31 U.S.C. 3325(d) requires the Government to include, with each certified voucher prepared by the Government payment office and submitted to a disbursing official, the TIN of the contractor receiving payment under the voucher. The TIN may be used by the Government to collect and report on any delinquent amounts arising out of the contractor's relationship with the Government.

(b) *Information reporting to the IRS.* The TIN is also required for Government reporting of certain contract information (see 4.903) and payment information (see 4.904) to the IRS.

United States Code Annotated

Contracts, planning, solicitation, evaluation, and award procedures, see 10 U.S.C.A. § 2305.

Definitions, see 41 U.S.C.A. § 403.

Planning and solicitation requirements, see 41 U.S.C.A. § 253a.

§ 4.903 Reporting contract information to the IRS.

(a) 26 U.S.C. 6050M, as implemented in 26 CFR, requires heads of Federal executive agencies to report certain information to the IRS.

(b) (1) The required information applies to contract modifications—

(i) Increasing the amount of a contract awarded before January 1, 1989, by $50,000 or more; and

(ii) Entered into on or after April 1, 1990.

(2) The reporting requirement also applies to certain contracts and modifications thereto in excess of $25,000 entered into on or after January 1, 1989.

(c) The information to report is—

(1) Name, address, and TIN of the contractor;

(2) Name and TIN of the common parent (if any);

(3) Date of the contract action;

(4) Amount obligated on the contract action; and

(5) Estimated contract completion date.

(d) Transmit the information to the IRS through the Federal Procurement Data System (see Subpart 4.6 and implementing instructions).

United States Code Annotated

Contracts, planning, solicitation, evaluation, and award procedures, see 10 U.S.C.A. § 2305.

Definitions, see 41 U.S.C.A. § 403.

Planning and solicitation requirements, see 41 U.S.C.A. § 253a.

§ 4.904 Reporting payment information to the IRS.

26 U.S.C. 6041 and 6041A, as implemented in 26 CFR, in part, require payors, including Government agencies, to report to the IRS, on Form 1099, payments made to certain contractors. 26 U.S.C. 6109 requires a contractor to provide its TIN if a Form 1099 is required. The payment office is responsible for submitting reports to the IRS.

United States Code Annotated

Contracts, planning, solicitation, evaluation, and award procedures, see 10 U.S.C.A. § 2305.

Definitions, see 41 U.S.C.A. § 403.

Planning and solicitation requirements, see 41 U.S.C.A. § 253a.

§ 4.905 Solicitation provision.

The contracting officer shall insert the provision at 52.204-3, Taxpayer Identification, in solicitations that—

(a) Do not include the provision at 52.204-7, System for Award Management; and

(b) Are not conducted under the procedures of Part 12.

Subpart 4.10 Contract Line Items

§ 4.1001 Policy.

Contracts may identify the items or services to be acquired as separately identified line items. Contract line items should provide unit prices or lump sum prices for separately identifiable contract deliverables, and associated delivery schedules or performance periods. Line items may be further subdivided or stratified for administrative purposes (*e.g.*, to provide for traceable accounting classification citations).

United States Code Annotated

Contract requirements, see 41 U.S.C.A. § 254.

Definitions, see 10 U.S.C.A. § 2302, 41 U.S.C.A. §§ 259, 403.

Kinds of contracts, see 10 U.S.C.A. § 2306.

Subpart 4.11 System for Award Management

§ 4.1100 Scope.

This subpart prescribes policies and procedures for requiring contractor registration in the System for Award Management (SAM) database to—

(a) Increase visibility of vendor sources (including their geographical locations) for specific supplies and services; and

(b) Establish a common source of vendor data for the Government.

§ 4.1101 Definition.

As used in this subpart—

"Agreement" means basic agreement, basic ordering agreement, or blanket purchase agreement.

§ 4.1102 Policy.

(a) Prospective contractors shall be registered in the SAM database prior to award of a contract or agreement, except for—

(1) Purchases under the micro-purchase threshold that use a Governmentwide commercial purchase card as both the purchasing and payment mechanism, as opposed to using the purchase card for payment only;

(2) Classified contracts (see 2.101) when registration in the SAM database, or use of SAM data, could compromise the safeguarding of classified information or national security;

(3) Contracts awarded by—

(i) Deployed contracting officers in the course of military operations, including, but not limited to, contingency operations as defined in 10 U.S.C. 101(a)(13) or humanitarian or peacekeeping operations as defined in 10 U.S.C. 2302(8);

(ii) Contracting officers located outside the United States and its outlying areas, as defined in 2.101, for work to be performed in support of diplomatic or developmental operations, including those performed in support of foreign assistance programs overseas, in an area that has been designated by the Department of State as a danger pay post (see http://aoprals.state.gov/Web920/danger_pay_all.asp); or

(iii) Contracting officers in the conduct of emergency operations, such as responses to natural or environmental disasters or national or civil emergencies, e.g., Robert T. Stafford Disaster Relief and Emergency Assistance Act (42 U.S.C. 5121);

(4) Contracts with individuals for performance outside the United States and its outlying areas;

(5) Contracts to support unusual or compelling needs (see 6.302-2);

(6) Contract actions at or below $30,000 awarded to foreign vendors for work performed

outside the United States, if it is impractical to obtain System for Award Management registration; and

(7) Micro-purchases that do not use the electronic funds transfer (EFT) method for payment and are not required to be reported (see Subpart 4.6).

(b) If practical, the contracting officer shall modify the contract or agreement awarded under paragraph (a)(3) of this section to require SAM registration.

(c) (1) (i) If a contractor has legally changed its business name, "doing business as" name, or division name (whichever is shown on the contract), or has transferred the assets used in performing the contract, but has not completed the necessary requirements regarding novation and change-of-name agreements in Subpart 42.12, the contractor shall provide the responsible contracting officer a minimum of one business day's written notification of its intention to change the name in the SAM database; comply with the requirements of Subpart 42.12; and agree in writing to the timeline and procedures specified by the responsible contracting officer. The contractor must provide with the notification sufficient documentation to support the legally changed name.

(ii) If the contractor fails to comply with the requirements of paragraph (c)(1)(i) of the clause at 52.204-13, System for Award Management Maintenance, or fails to perform the agreement at 52.204-13, paragraph (c)(1)(i)(C), and, in the absence of a properly executed novation or change-of-name agreement, the SAM information that shows the contractor to be other than the contractor indicated in the contract will be considered to be incorrect information within the meaning of the "Suspension of Payment" paragraph of the EFT clause of the contract.

(2) The contractor shall not change the name or address for electronic funds transfer payments (EFT) or manual payments, as appropriate, in the SAM record to reflect an assignee for the purpose of assignment of claims (see Subpart 32.8, Assignment of Claims).

(3) Assignees shall be separately registered in the SAM database. Information provided to the contractor's SAM record that indicates payments, including those made by EFT, to an ultimate recipient other than that contractor will be considered to be incorrect information within the meaning of the "Suspension of payment" paragraph of the EFT clause of the contract.

Notes of Decisions

In general 1

1 In general

Protest that the awardee's proposal was unacceptable because the awardee was not registered in the System for Award Management at the time proposals were due, as required by the solicitation, is denied where the awardee was registered at the time of award, as provided for by the Federal Acquisition Regulation, and there is no basis to conclude that the protester was prejudiced by the agency's apparent waiver of the registration provision. C.L.R. Development Group, B-409398, 2014 CPD ¶ 141 (Comp.Gen. 2014)

§ 4.1103 Procedures.

(a) Unless the acquisition is exempt under 4.1102, the contracting officer—

(1) Shall verify that the prospective contractor is registered in the SAM database (see paragraph (b) of this section) before awarding a contract or agreement. Contracting officers are encouraged to check the SAM early in the acquisition process, after the competitive range has been established, and then communicate to the unregistered offerors that they must register;

(2) Should use the DUNS number or, if applicable, the DUNS+4 number, to verify registration—

(i) Via the Internet via https://www.acquisition.gov;

(ii) As otherwise provided by agency procedures; and

(3) Need not verify registration before placing an order or call if the contract or agreement includes the provision at 52.204-7, or the clause at 52.212-4, or a similar agency clause, except when use of the Governmentwide commercial purchase card is contemplated as a method of payment. (See 32.1108(b)(2)).

(b) If the contracting officer, when awarding a contract or agreement, determines that a prospective contractor is not registered in the SAM database and an exception to the registration requirements for the award does not apply (see 4.1102), the contracting officer shall—

(1) If the needs of the requiring activity allow for a delay, make award after the apparently successful offeror has registered in the SAM database. The contracting officer shall advise the offeror of the number of days it will be allowed to become registered. If the offeror does not become registered by the required date, the contracting officer shall award to the next otherwise successful registered offeror following the same procedures (*i.e.*, if the next apparently successful offeror is not registered, the contracting officer shall advise the offeror of the number of days it will be allowed to become registered, etc.); or

(2) If the needs of the requiring activity do not allow for a delay, proceed to award to the next otherwise successful registered offeror, provided that written approval is obtained at one level above the contracting officer; or

(3) If the contract action is being awarded pursuant to 6.302-2, the contractor must be registered in the System for Award Management within 30 days after contract award, or at least three days prior to submission of the first invoice, whichever occurs first.

(c) Agencies shall protect against improper disclosure of contractor SAM information.

(d) The contracting officer shall, on contractual documents transmitted to the payment office, provide the DUNS number, or, if applicable, the DUNS+4, in accordance with agency procedures.

§ 4.1104 Disaster Response Registry.

Contracting officers shall consult the Disaster Response Registry via https://www.acquisition.gov when contracting for debris removal, distribution of supplies, reconstruction, and other disaster or emergency relief activities inside the United States and outlying areas. (See 26.205).

§ 4.1105 Solicitation provision and contract clauses.

(a) (1) Except as provided in 4.1102(a), use the provisions at 52.204-7, System for Award Management, in solicitations.

(2) If the solicitation is anticipated to be awarded in accordance with 4.1102(a)(5), the contracting officer shall use the provision at 52.204-7, System for Award Management, with its Alternate I.

(b) Insert the clause at 52.204-13, System for Award Management Maintenance, in solicitations that contain the provision at 52.204-7, and resulting contracts.

Subpart 4.12 —Representations and Certifications

§ 4.1200 Scope.

This subpart prescribes policies and procedures for requiring submission and maintenance of representations and certifications via the System for Award Management (SAM) to—

(a) Eliminate the administrative burden for contractors of submitting the same information to various contracting offices;

(b) Establish a common source for this information to procurement offices across the Government; and

(c) Incorporate by reference the contractor's representations and certifications in the awarded contract.

§ 4.1201 Policy.

(a) Prospective contractors shall complete electronic annual representations and certifications at SAM accessed via https://www.acquisition.gov as a part of required registration (see FAR 4.1102).

(b) (1) Prospective contractors shall update the representations and certifications submitted to SAM as necessary, but at least annually, to ensure they are kept current, accurate, and complete. The representations and certifications are effective until one year from date of submission or update to SAM.

(2) When any of the conditions in paragraph (b) of the clause at 52.219-28, Post-Award Small Business Program Rerepresentation, apply, contractors that represented they were

small businesses prior to award of a contract must update the representations and certifications in SAM as directed by the clause. Contractors that represented they were other than small businesses prior to award of a contract may update the representations and certifications in SAM as directed by the clause, if their size status has changed since contract award.

(c) Data in SAM is archived and is electronically retrievable. Therefore, when a prospective contractor has completed representations and certifications electronically via SAM, the contracting officer must reference the date of SAM verification in the contract file, or include a paper copy of the electronically-submitted representations and certifications in the file. Either of these actions satisfies contract file documentation requirements of 4.803(a)(11). However, if an offeror identifies changes to SAM data pursuant to the FAR provisions at 52.204-8(d) or 52.212-3(b), the contracting officer must include a copy of the changes in the contract file.

(d) The contracting officer shall incorporate the representations and certifications by reference in the contract (see 52.204-19, or for acquisitions of commercial items see 52.212-4(v)).

Notes of Decisions
In general 1

1 In general

Agency improperly awarded contract based upon a proposal where the offeror expressly declined to certify that the product to be provided would comply with the Trade Agreements Act as was required by the terms of the solicitation. Wyse Technology, Inc., B- 297454, 2006 CPD ¶ 23 (Comp.Gen. 2006)

§ 4.1202 Solicitation provision and contract clause.

(a) Except for commercial item solicitations issued under FAR part 12, insert in solicitations the provision at 52.204-8, Annual Representations and Certifications. The contracting officer shall check the applicable provisions at 52.204-8(c)(2). When the provision at 52.204-7, System for Award Management, is included in the solicitation, do not include the following representations and certifications:

(1) 52.203-2, Certificate of Independent Price Determination.

(2) 52.203-11, Certification and Disclosure Regarding Payments to Influence Certain Federal Transactions.

(3) 52.204-3, Taxpayer Identification.

(4) 52.204-5, Women-Owned Business (Other Than Small Business).

(5) 52.204-17, Ownership or Control of Offeror.

(6) 52.204-20, Predecessor of Offeror.

(7) 52.209-2, Prohibition on Contracting with Inverted Domestic Corporations—Representation.

(8) 52.209-5, Certification Regarding Responsibility Matters.

(9) 52.209-11, Representation by Corporations Regarding Delinquent Tax Liability or a Felony Conviction under any Federal Law.

(10) 52.214-14, Place of Performance—Sealed Bidding.

(11) 52.215-6, Place of Performance.

(12) 52.219-1, Small Business Program Representations (Basic & Alternate I).

(13) 52.219-2, Equal Low Bids.

(14) [Reserved]

(15) 52.222-18, Certification Regarding Knowledge of Child Labor for Listed End Products.

(16) 52.222-22, Previous Contracts and Compliance Reports.

(17) 52.222-25, Affirmative Action Compliance.

(18) 52.222-38, Compliance with Veterans' Employment Reporting Requirements.

(19) 52.222-48, Exemption from Application of the Service Contract Labor Standards to Contracts for Maintenance, Calibration, or Repair of Certain Equipment–Certification.

(20) 52.222-52, Exemption from Application of the Service Contract Labor Standards to

Contracts for Certain Services—Certification.

(21) 52.223-1, Biobased Product Certification.

(22) 52.223-4, Recovered Material Certification.

(23) 52.223-9, Estimate of Percentage of Recovered Material Content for EPA-Designated Items (Alternate I only).

(24) 52.225-2, Buy American Certificate.

(25) 52.225-4, Buy American—Free Trade Agreements—Israeli Trade Act Certificate (Basic, Alternates I, II, and III).

(26) 52.225-6, Trade Agreements Certificate.

(27) 52.225-20, Prohibition on Conducting Restricted Business Operations in Sudan—Certification.

(28) 52.225-25, Prohibition on Contracting with Entities Engaging in Certain Activities or Transactions Relating to Iran-Representation and Certifications.

(29) 52.226-2, Historically Black College or University and Minority Institution Representation.

(30) 52.227-6, Royalty Information (Basic & Alternate I).

(31) 52.227-15, Representation of Limited Rights Data and Restricted Computer Software.

(b) The contracting officer shall insert the clause at 52.204-19, Incorporation by Reference of Representations and Certifications, in solicitations and contracts.

Subpart 4.13 Personal Identity Verification

§ 4.1300 Scope of subpart.

This subpart provides policy and procedures associated with Personal Identity Verification as required by—

(a) Federal Information Processing Standards Publication (FIPS PUB) Number 201, "Personal Identity Verification of Federal Employees and Contractors"; and

(b) Office of Management and Budget (OMB) Guidance M-05-24, dated August 5, 2005, "Implementation of Homeland Security Presidential Directive (HSPD) 12-Policy for a Common Identification Standard for Federal Employees and Contractors."

§ 4.1301 Policy.

(a) Agencies must follow FIPS PUB Number 201 and the associated OMB implementation guidance for personal identity verification for all affected contractor and subcontractor personnel when contract performance requires contractors to have routine physical access to a Federally-controlled facility and/or routine access to a Federally-controlled information system.

(b) Agencies must include their implementation of FIPS PUB 201 and OMB Guidance M-05-24 in solicitations and contracts that require the contractor to have routine physical access to a Federally-controlled facility and/or routine access to a Federally-controlled information system.

(c) Agencies must designate an official responsible for verifying contractor employee personal identity.

(d) (1) Agency procedures for the return of Personal Identity Verification (PIV) products shall ensure that Government contractors account for all forms of Government-provided identification issued to Government contractor employees under a contract, *i.e.*, the PIV cards or other similar badges, and shall ensure that contractors return such identification to the issuing agency as soon as any of the following occurs, unless otherwise determined by the agency:

(i) When no longer needed for contract performance.

(ii) Upon completion of a contractor employee's employment.

(iii) Upon contract completion or termination.

(2) The contracting officer may delay final payment under a contract if the contractor fails to comply with these requirements.

§ 4.1302 Acquisition of approved products and services for personal identity verification.

(a) In order to comply with FIPS PUB 201, agencies must purchase only approved personal identity verification products and services.

(b) Agencies may acquire the approved products and services from the GSA, Federal Supply Schedule 70, Special Item Number (SIN) 132-62, HSPD-12 Product and Service Components, in accordance with ordering procedures outlined in FAR Subpart 8.4.

(c) When acquiring personal identity verification products and services not using the process in paragraph (b) of this section, agencies must ensure that the applicable products and services are approved as compliant with FIPS PUB 201 including—

(1) Certifying the products and services procured meet all applicable Federal standards and requirements;

(2) Ensuring interoperability and conformance to applicable Federal standards for the lifecycle of the components; and

(3) Maintaining a written plan for ensuring ongoing conformance to applicable Federal standards for the lifecycle of the components.

(d) For more information on personal identity verification products and services see htt p://www.idmanagement.gov.

§ 4.1303 Contract clause.

The contracting officer shall insert the clause at 52.204-9, Personal Identity Verification of Contractor Personnel, in solicitations and contracts when contract performance requires contractors to have routine physical access to a Federally-controlled facility and/or routine access to a Federally-controlled information system. The clause shall not be used when contractors require only intermittent access to Federally-controlled facilities.

Subpart 4.14 Reporting Executive Compensation and First-Tier Subcontract Awards

§ 4.1400 Scope of subpart

This subpart implements section 2 of the Federal Funding Accountability and Transparency Act of 2006 (Pub. L. 109-282), as amended by section 6202 of the Government Funding Transparency Act of 2008 (Pub. L. 110-252), which requires contractors to report subcontract award data and the total compensation of the five most highly compensated executives of the contractor and subcontractor. The public may view first-tier subcontract award data at http://usaspending.gov.

§ 4.1401 Applicability

(a) This subpart applies to all contracts with a value of $30,000 or more. Nothing in this subpart requires the disclosure of classified information.

(b) Reporting of subcontract information will be limited to the first-tier subcontractor.

§ 4.1402 Procedures

(a) Agencies shall ensure that contractors comply with the reporting requirements of 52.204-10, Reporting Executive Compensation and First-Tier Subcontract Awards. Agencies shall review contractor reports on a quarterly basis to ensure the information is consistent with contract information. The agency is not required to address data for which the agency would not normally have supporting information, such as the compensation information required of contractors and first-tier subcontractors. However, the agency shall inform the contractor of any inconsistencies with the contract information and require that the contractor correct the report, or provide a reasonable explanation as to why it believes the information is correct. Agencies may review the reports at http://www.fsrs.gov.

(b) When contracting officers report the contract action to the Federal Procurement Data System (FPDS) in accordance with FAR Subpart 4.6, certain data will then pre-populate from FPDS, to assist contractors in completing and submitting their reports. If data originating from FPDS is found by the contractor to be in error when the contractor completes the subcontract report, the contractor should notify the Government contracting officer, who is responsible for correcting the data in FPDS. Contracts reported using the generic DUNS number allowed at FAR 4.605(c)(2) will interfere with the contractor's ability to comply with this reporting requirement, because the data will not pre-populate from FPDS.

(c) If the contractor fails to comply with the reporting requirements, the contracting officer shall exercise appropriate contractual remedies. In addition, the contracting officer shall make the contractor's failure to comply with the reporting requirements a part of the contractor's performance information under Subpart 42.15.

(d) There is a reporting exception in 52.204-10(g) for contractors and subcontractors who had gross income in the previous tax year under $300,000.

§ 4.1403 Contract clause

(a) Except as provided in paragraph (b) of this section, the contracting officer shall insert the clause at 52.204-10, Reporting Executive Compensation and First-Tier Subcontract Awards, in all solicitations and contracts of $30,000 or more.

(b) The clause is not prescribed for contracts that are not required to be reported in the Federal Procurement Data System (FPDS) (see Subpart 4.6).

Subpart 4.15 [Reserved]

§ 4.1500 [Reserved]

§ 4.1501 [Reserved]

§ 4.1502 [Reserved]

Subpart 4.16 —Unique Procurement Instrument Identifiers

§ 4.1600 Scope of subpart.

This subpart prescribes policies and procedures for assigning unique Procurement Instrument Identifiers (PIID) for each solicitation, contract, agreement, or order and related procurement instrument.

§ 4.1601 Policy.

(a) *Establishment of a Procurement Instrument Identifier (PIID)*. Agencies shall have in place a process that ensures that each PIID used to identify a solicitation or contract action is unique Governmentwide, and will remain so for at least 20 years from the date of contract award. The PIID shall be used to identify all solicitation and contract actions. The PIID shall also be used to identify solicitation and contract actions in designated support and reporting systems (*e.g.*, Federal Procurement Data System, System for Award Management), in accordance with regulations, applicable authorities, and agency policies and procedures.)

(b) *Transition of PIID numbering*. No later than October 1, 2017, agencies shall comply with paragraph (a) of this section and use the requirements in 4.1602 and 4.1603 for all new solicitations and contract awards. Until an agency's transition is complete, it shall maintain its 2013 PIID format that is on record with the General Services Administration's Integrated Award Environment Program Office (which maintains a registry of the agency unique identifier scheme). The 2013 PIID format consisted of alpha characters in the first positions to indicate the agency, followed by alpha-numeric characters; the 2017 format instead has the AAC in the beginning 6 positions.

(c) Change in the Procurement Instrument Identifier after its assignment.

(1) Agencies shall not change the PIID unless one of the following two circumstances apply:

(i) The PIID serial numbering system is exhausted. In this instance, the contracting officer may assign a new PIID by issuing a contract modification.

(ii) Continued use of a PIID is administratively burdensome (*e.g.*, for implementations of new agency contract writing systems). In this instance, the contracting officer may assign a new PIID by issuing a contract modification.

(2) The modification shall clearly identify both the original and the newly assigned

PIID. Issuance of a new PIID is an administrative change (see 43.101).

§ 4.1602 Identifying the PIID and supplementary PIID.

(a) *Identifying the PIID in solicitation and contract award documentation (including forms and electronic generated formats).* Agencies shall include all PIIDs for all related procurement actions as identified in paragraphs (a)(1) through (a)(5) of this section.

(1) *Solicitation.* Identify the PIID for all solicitations. For amendments to solicitations, identify a supplementary PIID, in conjunction with the PIID for the solicitation.

(2) *Contracts and purchase orders.* Identify the PIID for contracts and purchase orders.

(3) *Delivery and task orders.* For delivery and task orders placed by an agency under a contract (*e.g.*, indefinite delivery indefinite quantity (IDIQ) contracts, multi-agency contracts (MAC), Governmentwide acquisition contracts (GWACs), or Multiple Award Schedule (MAS) contracts), identify the PIID for the delivery and task order and the PIID for the contract.

(4) *Blanket purchase agreements and basic ordering agreements.* Identify the PIID for blanket purchase agreements issued in accordance with 13.303, and for basic agreements and basic ordering agreements issued in accordance with subpart 16.7. For blanket purchase agreements issued in accordance with subpart 8.4 under a MAS contract, identify the PIID for the blanket purchase agreement and the PIID for the MAS contract.

(i) *Orders.* For orders against basic ordering agreements or blanket purchase agreements issued in accordance with 13.303, identify the PIID for the order and the PIID for the blanket purchase agreement or basic ordering agreement.

(ii) *Orders under subpart* 8.4. For orders against a blanket purchase agreement established under a MAS contract, identify the PIID for the order, the PIID for the blanket purchase agreement, and the PIID for the MAS contract.

(5) *Modifications.* For modifications to actions described in paragraphs (a)(2) through (a)(4) of this section, and in accordance with agency procedures, identify a supplementary PIID for the modification in conjunction with the PIID for the contract, order, or agreement being modified.

(b) *Placement of the PIID on forms.* When the form (including electronic generated format) does not provide spaces or fields for the PIID or supplementary PIID required in paragraph (a) of this section, identify the PIID in accordance with agency procedures.

(c) *Additional agency specific identification information.* If agency procedures require additional identification information in solicitations, contracts, or other related procurement instruments for administrative purposes, separate and clearly identify the additional information from the PIID.

§ 4.1603 Procedures.

(a) *Elements of a PIID.* The PIID consists of a combination of thirteen to seventeen alpha and/or numeric characters sequenced to convey certain information. Do not use special characters (such as hyphens, dashes, or spaces).

(1) *Positions 1 through 6.* The first six positions identify the department/agency and office issuing the instrument. Use the AAC assigned to the issuing office for positions 1 through 6. Civilian agency points of contact for obtaining an AAC are on the AAC Contact list maintained by the General Services Administration and can be found at http://www.gsa.gov/graphics/fas/Civilian_contacts.pdf. For Department of Defense (DoD) inquiries, contact the service/agency Central Service Point or DoDAAC Monitor, or if unknown, email mailto:DODAADHQ@DLA.MIL for assistance.

(2) *Positions 7 through 8.* The seventh and eighth positions are the last two digits of the fiscal year in which the procurement instrument is issued or awarded. This is the date the action is signed, not the effective date if the effective date is different.

(3) *Position 9.* Indicate the type of instrument by entering one of the following upper case letters in position nine. Departments and independent agencies may assign those letters identified for department use below in accordance with their agency policy; however, any use must be applied to the entire department or agency.

Instrument	Letter Designation
(i) Blanket purchase agreements.	A
(ii) Invitations for bids.	B
(iii) Contracts of all types except indefinite-delivery contracts (see subpart 16.5).	C
(iv) Indefinite-delivery contracts (including Federal Supply Schedules, Governmentwide acquisition contracts (GWACs), and multi-agency contracts).	D
(v) Reserved for future Federal Governmentwide use.	E
(vi) Task orders, delivery orders or calls under– • Indefinite-delivery contracts (including Federal Supply Schedules, Governmentwide acquisition contracts (GWACs), and multi-agency contracts); • Blanket purchase agreements; or • Basic ordering agreements.	F
(vii) Basic ordering agreements.	G
(viii) Agreements, including basic agreements and loan agreements, but excluding blanket purchase agreements, basic ordering agreements, and leases. Do not use this code for contracts or agreements with provisions for orders or calls.	H
(ix) Do not use this letter.	I
(x) Reserved for future Federal Governmentwide use.	J
(xi) Reserved for departmental or agency use.	K
(xii) Lease agreements.	L
(xiii) Reserved for departmental or agency use.	M
(xiv) Reserved for departmental or agency use.	N
(xv) Do not use this letter.	O
(xvi) Purchase orders (assign V if numbering capacity of P is exhausted during a fiscal year).	P
(xvii) Requests for quotations (assign U if numbering capacity of Q is exhausted during a fiscal year).	Q
(xviii) Requests for proposals.	R
(xix) Reserved for departmental or agency use.	S
(xx) Reserved for departmental or agency use	T
(xxi) See Q, requests for quotations.	U
(xxii) See P, purchase orders.	V
(xxiii) Reserved for future Federal Governmentwide use.	W
(xxiv) Reserved for future Federal Governmentwide use.	X
(xxv) Imprest fund.	Y
(xxvi) Reserved for future Federal Governmentwide use.	Z

(4) *Positions 10 through 17.* Enter the number assigned by the issuing agency in these positions. Agencies may choose a minimum of four characters up to a maximum of eight characters to be used, but the same number of characters must be used agency-wide. If a number less than the maximum is used, do not use leading or trailing zeroes to make it equal the maximum in any system or data transmission. A separate series of numbers may be used for any type of instrument listed in paragraph (a)(3) of this section. An agency may reserve blocks of numbers or alpha-numeric numbers for use by its various components.

(5) *Illustration of PIID.* The following illustrates a properly configured PIID using four characters in the final positions:

Position	Contents				
		N00062	17	C	0001
1-6	Identification of department/agency office (AAC)				
7-8	Last two digits of the fiscal year in which the procurment instrument is issued or				
9	Type of instrument				
10-13	Four position agency assigned number				

(b) *Elements of a supplementary PIID.* Use the supplementary PIID to identify amendments to solicitations and modifications to contracts, orders, and agreements.

(1) *Amendments to solicitations.* Number amendments to solicitations sequentially using a four position numeric serial number added to the 13-17 character PIID beginning with 0001.

(2) *Modifications to contracts, orders, and agreements.* Number modifications to contracts, orders, and agreements using a six position alpha or numeric, or a combination thereof, added to the 13-17 character PIID. For example, a modification could be numbered P00001. This would be added to the end of the 13-17 character PIID illustrated in (a)(5) of this section.

(i) *Position 1.* Identify the office issuing the modification. The letter P shall be designated for modifications issued by the procuring contracting office. The letter A shall be used for modifications issued by the contract administration office (if other than the procuring contracting office).

(ii) *Positions 2 through 6.* These positions may be alpha, numeric, or a combination thereof, in accordance with agency procedures.

Each office authorized to issue modifications shall assign the supplementary identification numbers in sequence (unless provided otherwise in agency procedures). Do not assign the numbers until it has been determined that a modification is to be issued.

Subpart 4.17 Service Contracts Inventory

§ 4.1700 Scope of subpart.

This subpart implements section 743(a) of Division C of the Consolidated Appropriations Act, 2010 (Pub. L. 111-117), which requires agencies to report annually to the Office of Management and Budget (OMB) on activities performed by service contractors. Section 743(a) applies to executive agencies, other than the Department of Defense (DoD), covered by the Federal Activities Inventory Reform Act (Pub. L. 105-270) (FAIR Act). The information reported in the inventory will be publicly accessible.

§ 4.1701 Definitions.

As used in this subpart–

"FAIR Act agencies" means the agencies required under the FAIR Act to submit inventories annually of the activities performed by Government personnel.

"First-tier subcontract" means a subcontract awarded directly by the contractor for the purpose of acquiring supplies or services (including construction) for performance of a prime contract. It does not include the contractor's supplier agreements with vendors, such as long-term arrangements for materials or supplies that benefit multiple contracts and/or the costs of which are normally applied to a contractor's general and administrative expenses or indirect costs.

§ 4.1702 Applicability.

(a) This subpart applies to–

(1) All FAIR Act agencies, except DoD as specified in 4.1705;

(2) Solicitations, contracts, and orders for services (including construction) that meet or exceed the thresholds at 4.1703; and

(3) Contractors and first-tier subcontractors.

(b) Procedures for compiling and submitting agency service contract inventories are governed by section 743(a)(3) of Division C of Pub. L. 111-117 and Office of Federal Procurement Policy (OFPP) guidance. The guidance is available at the following Web site: *http://www.whitehouse.gov/omb/procurement-service-contract-inventories*.

(c) This subpart addresses requirements for obtaining information from, and reporting by, agency service contractors.

§ 4.1703 Reporting requirements.

(a) Thresholds.

(1) Except as exempted by OFPP guidance, service contractor reporting shall be

required for contracts and first-tier subcontracts for services based on type of contract and estimated total value. For indefinite-delivery contracts, reporting shall be determined based on the type and estimated total value of each order under the contract. Indefinite-delivery contracts include, but are not limited to, contracts such as indefinite-delivery indefinite-quantity (IDIQ) contracts, Federal Supply Schedule contracts (FSSs), Governmentwide acquisition contracts (GWACs), and multi-agency contracts.

(2) Reporting is required according to the following thresholds:

(i) All cost-reimbursement, time-and-materials, and labor-hour service contracts and orders with an estimated total value above the simplified acquisition threshold.

(ii) All fixed-price service contracts awarded and orders issued according to the following thresholds:

(A) Awarded or issued in Fiscal Year 2014, with an estimated total value of $2.5 million or greater.

(B) Awarded or issued in Fiscal Year 2015, with an estimated total value of $1 million or greater.

(C) Awarded or issued in Fiscal Year 2016, and subsequent years, with an estimated total value of $500,000 or greater.

(3) Reporting is required for all first-tier subcontracts for services as prescribed in paragraphs (a)(2)(i) and (ii) of this section.

(b) Agency reporting responsibilities.

(1) Agencies shall ensure that contractors comply with the reporting requirements of 52.204-14, Service Contract Reporting Requirements and 52.204-15, Service Contract Reporting Requirements for Indefinite-Delivery Contracts. Agencies shall review contractor reported information for reasonableness and consistency with available contract information. The agency is not required to address data for which the agency would not normally have supporting information. In the event the agency believes that revisions to the contractor reported information are warranted, the agency shall notify the contractor no later than November 15. By November 30, the contractor shall revise the report, or document its rationale for the agency. Authorized agency officials may review the reports at www.sam.gov.

(2) Agencies are required to compile annually an inventory of service contracts performed for, or on behalf of, the agency during the prior fiscal year in order to determine the extent of the agency's reliance on service contractors. Agencies shall submit a service contract inventory to OMB by January 15 annually. Then, each agency must post the inventory on its Web site and publish a Federal Register Notice of Availability by February 15 annually.

(3) Most of the required information is already collected in the Federal Procurement Data System (FPDS). Information not collected in FPDS will be provided by the contractor, as specified in 52.204-14, Service Contract Reporting Requirements and 52.204-15, Service Contract.

§ 4.1704 Contracting officer responsibilities.

(a) For other than indefinite-delivery contracts, the contracting officer shall ensure that 52.204-14, Service Reporting Requirement, is included in solicitations, contracts, and orders as prescribed at 4.1705. For indefinite-delivery contracts, the contracting officer who awarded the contract shall ensure that 52.204-15 Service Contract Reporting Requirements for Indefinite-Delivery Contracts, is included in solicitations and contracts as prescribed at 4.1705. The contracting officer at the order level shall verify the clause's inclusion in the contract.

(b) If the contractor fails to submit a report in a timely manner, the contracting officer shall exercise appropriate contractual remedies. In addition, the contracting officer shall make the contractor's failure to comply with the reporting requirements a part of the contractor's performance information under Subpart 42.15.

§ 4.1705 Contract clauses.

(a) The contracting officer shall insert the clause at 52.204-14, Service Contract Reporting Requirements, in solicitations and contracts for services (including construction) that meet or exceed the thresholds at 4.1703, except for indefinite-delivery contracts. This clause is not required for actions entirely funded by DoD, contracts awarded with a generic

DUNS number, or in classified solicitations, contracts, or orders.

(b) The contracting officer shall insert the clause at 52.204-15, Service Contract Reporting Requirements for Indefinite-Delivery Contracts, in solicitations and indefinite-delivery contracts for services (including construction) where one or more orders issued thereunder are expected to each meet or exceed the thresholds at 4.1703. This clause is not required for actions entirely funded by DoD, contracts awarded with a generic DUNS number, or in classified solicitations, contracts, or orders.

Subpart 4.18 —Commercial and Government Entity Code

§ 4.1800 Scope of subpart.

(a) This subpart prescribes policies and procedures for identification of commercial and government entities. The Commercial and Government Entity (CAGE) code system may be used, among other things, to–

(1) Exchange data with another contracting activity, including contract administration activities and contract payment activities.

(2) Exchange data with another system that requires the unique identification of a contractor entity; or

(3) Identify when offerors are owned or controlled by another entity.

(b) For information on the Data Universal Numbering System (DUNS) number, which is a different identification number, see 4.605 and the provisions at 52.204-6 and 52.204-7.

§ 4.1801 Definitions.

As used in this part–

"Commercial and Government Entity (CAGE) code" means–

(1) An identifier assigned to entities located in the United States or its outlying areas by the Defense Logistics Agency (DLA) Commercial and Government Entity (CAGE) Branch to identify a commercial or government entity; or

(2) An identifier assigned by a member of the North Atlantic Treaty Organization (NATO) or by the NATO Support and Procurement Agency (NSPA) to entities located outside the United States and its outlying areas that the DLA Commercial and Government Entity (CAGE) Branch records and maintains in the CAGE master file. This type of code is known as a NATO CAGE (NCAGE) code.

"Highest-level owner" means the entity that owns or controls an immediate owner of the offeror, or that owns or controls one or more entities that control an immediate owner of the offeror. No entity owns or exercises control of the highest level owner.

"Immediate owner" means an entity, other than the offeror, that has direct control of the offeror. Indicators of control include, but are not limited to, one or more of the following: ownership or interlocking management, identity of interests among family members, shared facilities and equipment, and the common use of employees.

§ 4.1802 Policy.

(a) Commercial and Government Entity code.

(1) Offerors shall provide the contracting officer the Commercial and Government Entity (CAGE) code assigned to that offeror's location prior to the award of a contract action above the micro-purchase threshold, when there is a requirement to be registered in SAM or a requirement to have a DUNS Number in the solicitation.

(2) The contracting officer shall include the contractor's CAGE code in the contract and in any electronic transmissions of the contract data to other systems when it is provided in accordance with paragraph (a)(1) of this section.

(b) Ownership or control of offeror. Offerors, if owned or controlled by another entity, shall provide the contracting officer with the CAGE code and legal name of that entity prior to the award of a contract action above the micro-purchase threshold, when there is a requirement to be registered in SAM or a requirement to have a DUNS Number in the solicitation.

§ 4.1803 Verifying CAGE codes prior to award.

(a) Contracting officers shall verify the offeror's CAGE code by reviewing the entity's registration in the System for Award Management (SAM). Active registrations in SAM have had the associated CAGE codes verified.

(b) For entities not required to be registered in SAM, the contracting officer shall validate the CAGE code using the CAGE code search feature at https://cage.dla.mil.

§ 4.1804 Solicitation provisions and contract clause.

(a) Insert the provision at 52.204-16, Commercial and Government Entity Code Reporting, in all solicitations that include–

(1) 52.204-6, Data Universal Numbering System Number; or

(2) 52.204-7, System for Award Management.

(b) Insert the provision at 52.204-17, Ownership or Control of Offeror, in all solicitations that include the provision at 52.204-16, Commercial and Government Entity Code Reporting.

(c) Insert the clause at 52.204-18, Commercial and Government Entity Code Maintenance, in all solicitations and contracts when the solicitation contains the provision at 52.204-16, Commercial and Government Entity Code Reporting.

(d) Insert the provision at 52.204-20, Predecessor of Offeror, in all solicitations that include the provision at 52.204-16, Commercial and Government Entity Code Reporting.

Subpart 4.19 Basic Safeguarding of Covered Contractor Information Systems

§ 4.1901 Definitions.

As used in this subpart–

"Covered contractor information system" means an information system that is owned or operated by a contractor that processes, stores, or transmits Federal contract information.

"Federal contract information" means information, not intended for public release, that is provided by or generated for the Government under a contract to develop or deliver a product or service to the Government, but not including information provided by the Government to the public (such as that on public websites) or simple transactional information, such as that necessary to process payments.

"Information" means any communication or representation of knowledge such as facts, data, or opinions in any medium or form, including textual, numerical, graphic, cartographic, narrative, or audiovisual (Committee on National Security Systems Instruction (CNSSI) 4009).

"Information system" means a discrete set of information resources organized for the collection, processing, maintenance, use, sharing, dissemination, or disposition of information (44 U.S.C. 3502).

"Safeguarding" means measures or controls that are prescribed to protect information systems.

§ 4.1902 Applicability.

This subpart applies to all acquisitions, including acquisitions of commercial items other than commercially available off-the-shelf items, when a contractor's information system may contain Federal contract information.

§ 4.1903 Contract clause.

The contracting officer shall insert the clause at 52.204-21, Basic Safeguarding of Covered Contractor Information Systems, in solicitations and contracts when the contractor or a subcontractor at any tier may have Federal contract information residing in or transiting through its information system.

Subchapter B Competition and Acquisition Planning

PART 5 PUBLICIZING CONTRACT ACTIONS

§ 5.000 Scope of part.
§ 5.001 Definition.
§ 5.002 Policy.
§ 5.003 Governmentwide point of entry.

Subpart 5.1 Dissemination of Information

§ 5.101 Methods of disseminating information.
§ 5.102 Availability of solicitations.

Subpart 5.2 Synopses of Proposed Contract Actions

§ 5.201 General.
§ 5.202 Exceptions.
§ 5.203 Publicizing and response time.
§ 5.204 Presolicitation notices.
§ 5.205 Special situations.
§ 5.206 Notices of subcontracting opportunities.
§ 5.207 Preparation and transmittal of synopses.

Subpart 5.3 Synopses of Contract Awards

§ 5.301 General.
§ 5.302 Preparation and transmittal of synopses of awards.
§ 5.303 Announcement of contract awards.

Subpart 5.4 Release of Information

§ 5.401 General.
§ 5.402 General public.
§ 5.403 Requests from Members of Congress.
§ 5.404 Release of long-range acquisition estimates.
§ 5.404-1 Release procedures.
§ 5.404-2 Announcements of long-range acquisition estimates.
§ 5.405 Exchange of acquisition information.
§ 5.406 Public disclosure of justification documents for certain contract actions.

Subpart 5.5 Paid Advertisements

§ 5.501 Definitions.
§ 5.502 Authority.
§ 5.503 Procedures.
§ 5.504 Use of advertising agencies.

Subpart 5.6 Publicizing Multi-Agency Use Contracts

§ 5.601 Governmentwide database of contracts.

Subpart 5.7 Publicizing Requirements Under the American Recovery and Reinvestment Act of 2009

§ 5.701 Scope.

§ 5.702 Applicability.

§ 5.703 Definition.

§ 5.704 Publicizing preaward.

§ 5.705 Publicizing postaward.

§ 5.000 Scope of part.

This part prescribes policies and procedures for publicizing contract opportunities and award information.

United States Code Annotated

Competition requirements, see 41 U.S.C.A. § 253.

Contracts, competition requirements, see 10 U.S.C.A. § 2304.

Contracts, planning, solicitation, evaluation, and award procedures, see 10 U.S.C.A. § 2305.

Contracts, prohibition on competition between Department of Defense and small businesses and certain other entities, see 10 U.S.C.A. § 2304e.

Definitions, see 10 U.S.C.A. § 2302, 41 U.S.C.A. §§ 259, 403.

Encouragement of new competition, see 41 U.S.C.A. § 253c.

Encouragement of new competitors, see 10 U.S.C.A. § 2319.

Planning and solicitation requirements, see 41 U.S.C.A. § 253a.

Procurement notice, see 41 U.S.C.A. § 416.

§ 5.001 Definition.

"Contract action," as used in this part, means an action resulting in a contract, as defined in Subpart 2.1, including actions for additional supplies or services outside the existing contract scope, but not including actions that are within the scope and under the terms of the existing contract, such as contract modifications issued pursuant to the Changes clause, or funding and other administrative changes.

§ 5.002 Policy.

Contracting officers must publicize contract actions in order to—

(a) Increase competition;

(b) Broaden industry participation in meeting Government requirements; and

(c) Assist small business concerns, veteran-owned small business concerns, service-disabled veteran-owned small business concerns, HUBZone small business concerns, small disadvantaged business concerns, and women-owned small business concerns in obtaining contracts and subcontracts.

United States Code Annotated

Competition requirements, see 41 U.S.C.A. § 253.

Contracts, competition requirements, see 10 U.S.C.A. § 2304.

Contracts, planning, solicitation, evaluation, and award procedures, see 10 U.S.C.A. § 2305.

Contracts, prohibition on competition between Department of Defense and small businesses and certain other entities, see 10 U.S.C.A. § 2304e.

Definitions, see 10 U.S.C.A. § 2302; 41 U.S.C.A. §§ 259, 403.

Encouragement of new competition, see 41 U.S.C.A. § 253c.

Encouragement of new competitors, see 10 U.S.C.A. § 2319.

Planning and solicitation requirements, see 41 U.S.C.A. § 253a.

Procurement notice, see 41 U.S.C.A. § 416.

Notes of Decisions

1 Contract Action

NASA did not synopsize and publicize a modification in the Commerce Business Daily (CBD) as either a proposed contract action or actual contract award. Protester contends that NASA violated FAR 5.201, which requires publication of proposed contract actions. FAR 5.001 defines contract action as "an action resulting in a contract, but not including contract modifications that are within the scope and under the terms of the contract." Since contracting action as defined in FAR 5.001 does not include modifications within the scope of the contract, there was no requirement for a published notice and therefore no violation of FAR 5.301. Pacific Bell v. National Aeronautics and Space Admin., G.S.B.C.A. No. 12814-P, 94-3 B.C.A. (CCH) ¶ 27067, 1994 WL 323408 (Gen. Services Admin. B.C.A. 1994).

Phrase "one contract action" in section of the Federal Acquisition Regulation (FAR) defining individual deviation from the FAR affecting "only one contract action" means, unambiguously, an action related to one contract award. 48 C.F.R. § 1.403. La Gloria Oil and Gas Co. v. U.S., 56 Fed. Cl. 211 (2003) (abrogated on other grounds by, Tesoro Hawaii Corp. v. U.S., 405 F.3d 1339, 15 A.L.R. Fed. 2d 755 (Fed. Cir. 2005)). United States ☞70(25.1)

Under FAR part 5, only "contract actions" are required to be synopsized. Contract actions are defined as actions "resulting in a contract." FAR 5.001. The placement of an order consistent with the terms of an IDIQ contract does not result in a new contract, that is, in a new contractual relationship, and therefore the order is not required to be published in the CBD. The Honorable John Conyers, Jr. Chairman, Committee on Government Operations House of Representatives, B-158766, B-158766.16, 1989 WL 251138 (Comp. Gen. 1989).

§ 5.003 Governmentwide point of entry.

For any requirement in the FAR to publish a notice, the contracting officer must transmit the notices to the GPE.

United States Code Annotated

Competition requirements, see 41 U.S.C.A. § 253.

Contracts, competition requirements, see 10 U.S.C.A. § 2304.

Contracts, planning, solicitation, evaluation, and award procedures, see 10 U.S.C.A. § 2305.

Contracts, prohibition on competition between Department of Defense and small businesses and certain other entities, see 10 U.S.C.A. § 2304e.

Definitions, see 10 U.S.C.A. § 2302; 41 U.S.C.A. §§ 259, 403.

Encouragement of new competition, see 41 U.S.C.A. § 253c.

Encouragement of new competitors, see 10 U.S.C.A. § 2319.

Planning and solicitation requirements, see 41 U.S.C.A. § 253a.

Procurement notice, see 41 U.S.C.A. § 416.

Subpart 5.1 Dissemination of Information

§ 5.101 Methods of disseminating information.

(a) As required by the Small Business Act (15 U.S.C. 637(e)) and the Office of Federal Procurement Policy Act (41 U.S.C. 1708), contracting officers must disseminate information on proposed contract actions as follows:

(1) For proposed contract actions expected to exceed $25,000, by synopsizing in the GPE (see 5.201).

(2) For proposed contract actions expected to exceed $15,000, but not expected to exceed $25,000, by displaying in a public place, or by any appropriate electronic means, an unclassified notice of the solicitation or a copy of the solicitation satisfying the requirements of 5.207(c). The notice must include a statement that all responsible sources may submit a response which, if timely received, must be considered by the agency. The information must be posted not later than the date the solicitation is issued, and must remain posted for at least 10 days or until after quotations have been opened, whichever is later.

(i) If solicitations are posted instead of a notice, the contracting officer may employ various methods of satisfying the requirements of 5.207(c). For example, the contracting officer may meet the requirements of 5.207(c) by stamping the solicitation, by a cover sheet to the solicitation, or by placing a general statement in the display room.

(ii) The contracting officer need not comply with the display requirements of this section when the exemptions at 5.202(a)(1), (a)(4) through (a)(9), or (a)(11) apply, when oral solicitations are used, or when providing access to a notice of proposed contract action and solicitation through the GPE and the notice permits the public to respond to the solicitation electronically.

(iii) Contracting officers may use electronic posting of requirements in a place accessible by the general public at the Government installation to satisfy the public display requirement. Contracting offices using electronic systems for public posting that are not accessible outside the installation must periodically publicize the methods for accessing the information.

(b) In addition, one or more of the following methods may be used:

(1) Preparing periodic handouts listing proposed contracts, and displaying them as in 5.101(a)(2).

(2) Assisting local trade associations in disseminating information to their members.

(3) Making brief announcements of proposed contracts to newspapers, trade journals, magazines, or other mass communication media for publication without cost to the Government.

(4) Placing paid advertisements in newspapers or other communications media, subject to the following limitations:

(i) Contracting officers shall place paid advertisements of proposed contracts only when it is anticipated that effective competition cannot be obtained otherwise (see 5.205(d)).

(ii) Contracting officers shall not place advertisements of proposed contracts in a newspaper published and printed in the District of Columbia unless the supplies or services will be furnished, or the labor performed, in the District of Columbia or adjoining counties in Maryland or Virginia (44 U.S.C. 3701).

(iii) Advertisements published in newspapers must be under proper written authority in accordance with 44 U.S.C. 3702 (see 5.502(a)).

§ 5.102 Availability of solicitations.

(a) (1) Except as provided in paragraph (a)(5) of this section, the contracting officer must make available through the GPE solicitations synopsized through the GPE, including specifications, technical data, and other pertinent information determined necessary by the contracting officer. Transmissions to the GPE must be in accordance with the interface description available via the Internet at http://www.fedbizopps.gov.

(2) The contracting officer is encouraged, when practicable and cost-effective, to make accessible through the GPE additional information related to a solicitation.

(3) The contracting officer must ensure that solicitations transmitted using electronic commerce are forwarded to the GPE to satisfy the requirements of paragraph (a)(1) of this section.

(4) When an agency determines that a solicitation contains information that requires additional controls to monitor access and distribution (e.g., technical data, specifications, maps, building designs, schedules, etc.), the information shall be made available through the enhanced controls of the GPE, unless an exception in paragraph (a)(5) of this section applies. The GPE meets the synopsis and advertising requirements of this part.

(5) The contracting officer need not make a solicitation available through the GPE as required in paragraph (a)(4) of this section, when—

(i) Disclosure would compromise the national security (e.g., would result in disclosure of classified information, or information subject to export controls) or create other security risks. The fact that access to classified matter may be necessary to submit a proposal or perform the contract does not, in itself, justify use of this exception;

(ii) The nature of the file (e.g., size, format) does not make it cost-effective or practicable for contracting officers to provide access to the solicitation through the GPE; or

(iii) The agency's senior procurement executive makes a written determination that access through the GPE is not in the Government's interest.

(6) When an acquisition contains brand name specifications, the contracting officer shall include with the solicitation the justification or documentation required by 6.302-1(c), 13.106-1(b), or 13.501, redacted as necessary (see 6.305).

(b) When the contracting officer does not make a solicitation available through the GPE pursuant to paragraph (a)(5) of this section, the contracting officer—

(1) Should employ other electronic means (e.g., CD-ROM or electronic mail) whenever practicable and cost- effective. When solicitations are provided electronically on physical media (e.g., disks) or in paper form, the contracting officer must—

(i) Maintain a reasonable number of copies of solicitations, including specifications and other pertinent information determined necessary by the contracting officer (upon request, potential sources not initially solicited should be mailed or provided copies of solicitations, if available);

(ii) Provide copies on a "first-come-first-served" basis, for pickup at the contracting office, to publishers, trade associations, information services, and other members of the public having a legitimate interest (for construction, see 36.211); and

(iii) Retain a copy of the solicitation and other documents for review by and duplication for those requesting copies after the initial number of copies is exhausted; and

(2) May require payment of a fee, not exceeding the actual cost of duplication, for a copy of the solicitation document.

(c) In addition to the methods of disseminating proposed contract information in 5.101(a) and (b), provide, upon request to small business concerns, as required by 15 U.S.C. 637(b)—

(1) A copy of the solicitation and specifications. In the case of solicitations disseminated by electronic data interchange, solicitations may be furnished directly to the electronic address of the small business concern;

(2) The name and telephone number of an employee of the contracting office who will answer questions on the solicitation; and

(3) Adequate citations to each applicable major Federal law or agency rule with which small business concerns must comply in performing the contract.

(d) When electronic commerce (see Subpart 4.5) is used in the solicitation process, availability of the solicitation may be limited to the electronic medium.

(e) Provide copies of a solicitation issued under other than full and open competition to firms requesting copies that were not initially solicited, but only after advising the requester of the determination to limit the solicitation to a specified firm or firms as authorized under Part 6.

(f) This section 5.102 applies to classified contracts to the extent consistent with agency security requirements (see 5.202(a)(1)).

United States Code Annotated

Competition requirements, see 41 U.S.C.A. § 253.

Contracts, competition requirements, see 10 U.S.C.A. § 2304.

Contracts, planning, solicitation, evaluation, and award procedures, see 10 U.S.C.A. § 2305.

Contracts, prohibition on competition between Department of Defense and small businesses and certain other entities, see 10 U.S.C.A. § 2304e.

Definitions, see 10 U.S.C.A. § 2302; 41 U.S.C.A. §§ 259, 403.

Encouragement of new competition, see 41 U.S.C.A. § 253c.

Encouragement of new competitors, see 10 U.S.C.A. § 2319.

Planning and solicitation requirements, see 41 U.S.C.A. § 253a.

Procurement notice, see 41 U.S.C.A. § 416.

Notes of Decisions

In general 1

1 In general

Though the government failed to attach a copy of a specification as to peanut content to a request for proposals (RFP) to supply mixed nuts, as appeared to have been its customary practice, contractor's decision to bid on the contract without having looked up the maximum allowable peanut content could not be construed to be a "misreading" of the specification, supporting rescission of contract, where contractor identified no regulation requiring that the specification be attached to the solicitation, though the government is required to send contractors copies of the specifications upon request, it appeared that contractor never requested one, and contractor's president testified that he knew the importance of the Commercial Item Description (CID) reference in the RFP, and that he knew how to go to the library and look it up, but that he left this work to a broker. 48 C.F.R. § 5.102. Giesler v. U.S., 232 F.3d 864 (Fed. Cir. 2000). United States ☞74(4)

FedBizOpps is the currently designated Governmentwide Point of Entry (GPE) and is the single point where Government business opportunities greater than $25,000, including synopses of proposed contract actions, solicitations, and associated information, can be accessed electronically by the public. Beyond this requirement, there are no further requirements to individually notify potential offerors, or to post notice of a contract action on an agency's own website. Bestcare, Inc., B-403585, 2010 CPD ¶ 278 (Comp. Gen. 2010)

Protest of agency's failure to post solicitation on FedBizOpps Internet website, as required by regulation, was denied because protester did not avail itself of every reasonable opportunity to obtain the solicitation. The presolicitation notice indicated an anticipated August 20, 2003 closing time, as that time approached and passed, protester did not contact agency to determine status of solicitation, and finally inquired as to status approximately 7 weeks after closing time. Notwithstanding the agency's error in failing to post the RFP to FedBizOpps, the protester's inability to compete was primarily the result of its failure to fulfill its obligation to avail itself of every reasonable opportunity to obtain the RFP. Allied Materials & Equipment Company, Inc., B-293231, 2004 CPD ¶ 27 (Comp. Gen. 2004).

Subpart 5.2 Synopses of Proposed Contract Actions

§ 5.201 General.

(a) As required by the Small Business Act (15 U.S.C. 637(e)) and the Office of Federal Procurement Policy Act (41 U.S.C. 1708), agencies must make notices of proposed contract actions available as specified in paragraph (b) of this section.

(b) (1) For acquisitions of supplies and services, other than those covered by the exceptions in 5.202 and the special situations in 5.205, the contracting officer must transmit a notice to the GPE, for each proposed—

(i) Contract action meeting the threshold in 5.101(a)(1);

(ii) Modification to an existing contract for additional supplies or services that meets the threshold in 5.101(a)(1); or

(iii) Contract action in any amount when advantageous to the Government.

(2) When transmitting notices using electronic commerce, contracting officers must ensure the notice is forwarded to the GPE.

(c) The primary purposes of the notice are to improve small business access to acquisition information and enhance competition by identifying contracting and subcontracting opportunities.

(d) The GPE may be accessed via the Internet at http://www.fedbizopps.gov.

United States Code Annotated

Competition requirements, see 41 U.S.C.A. § 253.

Contracts, competition requirements, see 10 U.S.C.A. § 2304.

Contracts, planning, solicitation, evaluation, and award procedures, see 10 U.S.C.A. § 2305.

Contracts, prohibition on competition between Department of Defense and small businesses and certain other entities, see 10 U.S.C.A. § 2304e.

Definitions, see 10 U.S.C.A. § 2302; 41 U.S.C.A. §§ 259, 403.

Encouragement of new competition, see 41 U.S.C.A. § 253c.

Encouragement of new competitors, see 10 U.S.C.A. § 2319.

Planning and solicitation requirements, see 41 U.S.C.A. § 253a.

Procurement notice, see 41 U.S.C.A. § 416.

Notes of Decisions

In general 1
Applicability to simplified acquisitions 3
Prejudice required 2

1 In general

If a modification to the contract is for "additional supplies or services," i.e., it was outside the scope of the Changes clause, it must be synopsized in the CBD. If the procurement action here involved, i.e., the contract modification, was within the ambit of the Changes clause, the modification was not required to be synopsized. Wiltel, Inc. v. General Services Admin., G.S.B.C.A. No. 11857-P, 1992 WL 145738 (Gen. Services Admin. B.C.A. 1992)

An agency's notice must provide an accurate description of the property or services to be purchased so prospective contractors can make an informed business judgment as to whether to request a copy of the solicitation. In this regard, the FAR requires agencies to use one of the procurement classification codes identified at the FedBizOpps website to identify services or supplies in its notices on FedBizOpps and contracting officers must use the most appropriate classification category. Protest was sustained because the agency failed to effectively notify potential offerors of the nature of the procurement by misclassifying an acquisition for support services under a miscellaneous code for products. TMI Management Systems, Inc., B-401530, 2009 CPD ¶ 191 (Comp. Gen. 2009)

Protester was not placed on notice of proposed contract action because agency did not publish its intent to enter into a sole-source contract with awardee, nor provide notice of the award on FedBizOpps. Agency's posting on DefenseLink does not substitute for FedBizOpps because DefenseLink has not been designated by statute or regulation as an official public medium for providing notice of contracting actions, as FedBizOpps has. GAO refused to dismiss protest as untimely because it determined that posting on DefenseLink did not provide actual or constructive notice. WorldWide Language Resources, Inc.; SOS International Ltd., B-296984, B-296984.2, B-296984.3, B-296984.4, B-296993, B-296993.2, B-296993.3, 2005 CPD ¶ 206 (Comp. Gen. 2005).

Protest challenging as unclear the terms of a CBD notice seeking expressions of interest (EOI) for a decontamination, decommissioning, and recycling project for the Department of Energy (DOE) is denied where on its face, the announcement reasonably described the work to be performed and provided sufficient information, considering the nature of the procurement, to enable all interested parties, including the protester, to prepare EOIs in response, particularly given that prior to publishing the announcement DOE held a workshop to discuss the agency's goals with respect to the project with private industry, and protester attended that workshop, presented its proposed approach to DOE officials, and was a team member of a consortium that subsequently submitted a proposal to DOE to complete the project. SouthEastern Technologies, Inc., B-275636, 97-1 CPD ¶ 96 (Comp. Gen. 1997).

Protest that the agency deprived a potential offeror of an opportunity to compete because the firm allegedly did not receive a mailed copy of the solicitation and amendment is denied where the record shows that the agency followed established procedures for disseminating solicitation documents, and there is no evidence in the record of any deficiencies in the agency's solicitation process or of a deliberate attempt by the agency to exclude the protester. Chem-Fab Corporation, B-277795, 97-2 CPD ¶ 120 (Comp. Gen. 1997).

The fundamental purpose of the presolicitation notice requirement is to improve small business access to acquisition information and thereby enhance competition by identifying contracting and subcontracting opportunities. FAR 5.201(c). Pacific Sky Supply, Inc., B-225420, 87-1 CPD ¶ 206 (Comp. Gen. 1987), modified, B-225420, B-225420.2, 87-2 CPD ¶ 162 (Comp. Gen. 1987).

2 Prejudice required

Protest denied where protester asserted that agency failed to synopsize the current RFQ in the Commerce Business Daily because protester was well aware of the solicitation and apparently intended to submit a quote. GAO determined that there was no harm to protester and held that, absent prejudice, there is no basis to sustain the protest. Borders Consulting, Inc., B-281606, 99-1 CPD ¶ 56 (Comp. Gen. 1999).

3 Applicability to simplified acquisitions

Regardless of whether a simplified acquisition is competed or reserved for only one source, the simplified acquisition procedures require synopsis of procurements in excess of $25,000 in accordance with the Small Business Act, 15 U.S.C. § 637(e), and the Office of Federal Procurement Policy Act, 41 U.S.C. § 416 (2000). Information Ventures, Inc., B-293541, 2004 CPD ¶ 81 (Comp. Gen. 2004).

If an exception to the synopsis requirement applies, it applies regardless of whether the procurement is conducted under Part 13, Simplified Acquisitions, or any other FAR Part. RFQs were exempted under the exception at FAR 5.202(a)(12) for defense agency contract actions made and performed outside of the United States when only local sources are solicited. Protester argued that the introductory clause of FAR 5.202 specifically limits the exceptions to the synopsis notification requirements of FAR 5.201, which leaves unaffected the allegedly separate displaying requirements of FAR 5.101. GAO disagreed, holding that FAR 13.105, which governs both the synopsis and displaying requirements applicable to simplified acquisition procedures, states that the public display requirements of FAR §§ 5.101 and 5.203 are not applicable if an exception in FAR 5.202 applies. Thus, the FAR 5.101, 5.201 and 5.203 requirements are not applicable to these RFQs. Military Agency Services Pty., Ltd., B-290414, B-290441, B-290468, B-290496, 2002 CPD ¶ 130 (Comp. Gen. 2002).

To determine whether public display and synopsis requirements apply to a proposed purchase under simplified procedures, FAR 13.104(b) refers to FAR 5.101 and 5.202. Under FAR 5.101(2), agencies must publicly display a solicitation where the proposed contract action is expected to exceed $10,000 but not expected to exceed $25,000. Here, the agency states that it did not expect the procurement to exceed the $10,000 threshold and thus determined that the display requirement did not apply. In fact, the purchase order was placed at a price below the $10,000 threshold. Under the circumstances presented, the agency was not required to post a notice of the solicitation, and it satisfied the requirement for competition by requesting estimates from three firms. Continental Transport & Moving, Inc., B-280612, 1998 WL 746134 (Comp. Gen. 1998).

§ 5.202 Exceptions.

The contracting officer need not submit the notice required by 5.201 when—

(a) The contracting officer determines that—

(1) The synopsis cannot be worded to preclude disclosure of an agency's needs and such disclosure would compromise the national security (*e.g.*, would result in disclosure of classified information). The fact that a proposed solicitation or contract action contains classified information, or that access to classified matter may be necessary to submit a proposal or perform the contract does not, in itself, justify use of this exception to synopsis;

(2) The proposed contract action is made under the conditions described in 6.302-2 (or, for purchases conducted using simplified acquisition procedures, if unusual and compelling urgency precludes competition to the maximum extent practicable) and the Government would be seriously injured if the agency complies with the time periods specified in 5.203;

(3) The proposed contract action is one for which either the written direction of a foreign government reimbursing the agency for the cost of the acquisition of the supplies or services for such government, or the terms of an international agreement or treaty between the United States and a foreign government, or international organizations, has the effect of requiring that the acquisition shall be from specified sources;

(4) The proposed contract action is expressly authorized or required by a statute to be made through another Government agency, including acquisitions from the Small Business Administration (SBA) using the authority of section 8(a) of the Small Business Act (but see 5.205(f)), or from a specific source such as a workshop for the blind under the rules of the Committee for Purchase from People Who Are Blind or Severely Disabled;

(5) The proposed contract action is for utility services other than telecommunications services and only one source is available;

(6) The proposed contract action is an order placed under subpart 16.5. When the order contains brand-name specifications, see especially 16.505(a)(4);

(7) The proposed contract action results from acceptance of a proposal under the Small Business Innovation Development Act of 1982 (Pub. L. 97-219);

(8) The proposed contract action results from the acceptance of an unsolicited research proposal that demonstrates a unique and innovative concept (see 2.101) and publication of any notice complying with 5.207 would improperly disclose the originality of thought or innovativeness of the proposed research, or would disclose proprietary information associated with the proposal. This exception does not apply if the proposed contract action results from an unsolicited research proposal and acceptance is based solely upon the unique capability of the source to perform the particular research services proposed (see 6.302-1(a)(2)(i));

(9) The proposed contract action is made for perishable subsistence supplies, and advance notice is not appropriate or reasonable;

(10) The proposed contract action is made under conditions described in 6.302-3, or 6.302-5 with regard to brand name commercial items for authorized resale, or 6.302-7, and advance notice is not appropriate or reasonable;

(11) The proposed contract action is made under the terms of an existing contract that was previously synopsized in sufficient detail to comply with the requirements of 5.207 with respect to the current proposed contract action;

(12) The proposed contract action is by a Defense agency and the proposed contract action will be made and performed outside the United States and its outlying areas, and only local sources will be solicited. This exception does not apply to proposed contract actions covered by the World Trade Organization Government Procurement Agreement or a Free Trade Agreement (see Subpart 25.4);

(13) The proposed contract action—

(i) Is for an amount not expected to exceed the simplified acquisition threshold;

(ii) Will be made through a means that provides access to the notice of proposed contract action through the GPE; and

(iii) Permits the public to respond to the solicitation electronically; or

(14) The proposed contract action is made under conditions described in 6.302-3 with respect to the services of an expert to support the Federal Government in any current or anticipated litigation or dispute.

(b) The head of the agency determines in writing, after consultation with the Administrator for Federal Procurement Policy and the Administrator of the Small Business Administration, that advance notice is not appropriate or reasonable.

United States Code Annotated

Competition requirements, see 41 U.S.C.A. § 253.

Contracts, competition requirements, see 10 U.S.C.A. § 2304.

Contracts, planning, solicitation, evaluation, and award procedures, see 10 U.S.C.A. § 2305.

Contracts, prohibition on competition between Department of Defense and small businesses and certain other entities, see 10 U.S.C.A. § 2304e.

Definitions, see 10 U.S.C.A. § 2302; 41 U.S.C.A. §§ 259, 403.

Encouragement of new competition, see 41 U.S.C.A. § 253c.

Encouragement of new competitors, see 10 U.S.C.A. § 2319.

Planning and solicitation requirements, see 41 U.S.C.A. § 253a.

Procurement notice, see 41 U.S.C.A. § 416.

Notes of Decisions

In general 1
Contract performed outside the United States 4
Public interest exception 5
Restriction by foreign buyer 3
Unusual and compelling circumstances 2

1 In general

There is no requirement to synopsize in the Commerce Business Daily delivery orders placed against mandatory FSS contracts. Information Marketing International, B-216945, 85-1 CPD ¶ 740 (Comp. Gen. 1985).

2 Unusual and compelling circumstances

Protest that an agency did not synopsize its simplified acquisition requirement is denied, where the agency reasonably found that the requirement was too urgent to allow public posting of the solicitation. Coast Guard's determination of urgency was reasonable given the short time (six days) between its request for quotations and the need to provide housing for incoming Coast Guard personnel. U.S. Hotel Sourcing, LLC, B-406726, 2012 CPD ¶ 232 (Comp. Gen. 2012)

An agency is not required to synopsize such urgent contract actions where the government would be seriously injured if the agency were to comply with the time periods required for publication of the synopsis. The contract was for deployable circuit analyzers that will allow for badly needed field checks on the MH-60G helicopters used by the Special Operations Forces. The helicopters are used primarily in the rescue of downed pilots in hostile areas. Eclypse Int'l Corp., B-274507, 96-2 CPD ¶ 179 (Comp. Gen. 1996).

Protest that agency violated applicable synopsis and time period requirements in the FAR was denied where procurement is being conducted on an urgent and compelling basis and thus is exempt from these requirements, and, in any event, the protester has not shown how these alleged solicitation improprieties resulted in any competitive prejudice to the protester. Agency determined that it's need for the shuttle bus services was urgent, and, consequently, the resolicitation was conducted on an urgent and compelling basis under FAR 6.302-2. As such, the resolicitation is exempt from the FAR's general synopsis and time period requirements. FAR 5.202(a)(2). Matter of: JRW Management Company, Inc., B-260396, B-260396.2, 95-1 CPD ¶ 276 (Comp. Gen. 1995).

3 Restriction by foreign buyer

In a foreign military sales (FMS) procurement conducted under the Arms Export Control Act, the agency is not required to publish notice in the CBD before making a sole source award on behalf of FMS customers, because the law provides an exemption from the requirement where written directions of the foreign customers have the effect of requiring sole-source procurements. 41 U.S.C. § 416(c)(2). Kahn Industries, Inc., B-225491, B-225533, 87-1 CPD ¶ 343 (Comp. Gen. 1987).

4 Contract performed outside the United States

FAR 5.303(a)(12) provides that a proposed contract action need not be advertised in the CBD where "[t]he contract action is by a Defense agency and the contract action will be made and performed outside the United States, its possessions, or Puerto Rico, and only local sources will be solicited." At the time the Army initiated the procurement in the war zone in Saudi Arabia, the contracting officer expected the competition to be limited to firms in that region and planned to solicit only local sources. Although delivery of the washers under the contract ultimately took place at Dover AFB (Deleware), there is no indication that at the time the RFP was issued in Saudi Arabia the agency expected contract award and performance to take place anywhere other than in Saudi Arabia or that offers from other than local sources would be received. Thus, pursuant to the publication exception at FAR 5.303(a)(12), there is no basis to challenge the agency's determination not to advertise the proposed contract action in the CBD. American Kleaner Mfg. Co., Inc., B-243901, B-243901.2, B-243901.3, 91-2 CPD ¶ 235 (Comp. Gen. 1991).

5 Public interest exception

FAR 5.201 generally requires that agencies provide advance notice in the CBD prior to awarding a contract. However, FAR 5.202(a)(10) states that "the contracting officer need not submit the notice required by 5.201 when the contract is made under conditions described in 6.302.7 (exception to competition based on the public interest), and advance notice is not reasonable." Because the agency determined that sole source award was in the public interest and the contracting determined that advance notice was not reasonable, the agency was not required to publish notice in the Varicon Intern. v. Office of Personnel

Management, 934 F. Supp. 440, 41 Cont. Cas. Fed. (CCH) P 77011 (D.D.C. 1996).

§ 5.203 Publicizing and response time.

Whenever agencies are required to publicize notice of proposed contract actions under 5.201, they must proceed as follows:

(a) An agency must transmit a notice of proposed contract action to the GPE (see 5.201). All publicizing and response times are calculated based on the date of publication. The publication date is the date the notice appears on the GPE. The notice must be published at least 15 days before issuance of a solicitation, or a proposed contract action the Government intends to solicit and negotiate with only one source under the authority of 6.302, except that, for acquisitions of commercial items, the contracting officer may—

(1) Establish a shorter period for issuance of the solicitation; or

(2) Use the combined synopsis and solicitation procedure (see 12.603).

(b) The contracting officer must establish a solicitation response time that will afford potential offerors a reasonable opportunity to respond to each proposed contract action, (including actions where the notice of proposed contract action and solicitation information is accessible through the GPE), in an amount estimated to be greater than $25,000, but not greater than the simplified acquisition threshold; or each contract action for the acquisition of commercial items in an amount estimated to be greater than $25,000. The contracting officer should consider the circumstances of the individual acquisition, such as the complexity, commerciality, availability, and urgency, when establishing the solicitation response time.

(c) Except for the acquisition of commercial items (see 5.203(b)), agencies shall allow at least a 30-day response time for receipt of bids or proposals from the date of issuance of a solicitation, if the proposed contract action is expected to exceed the simplified acquisition threshold.

(d) Agencies shall allow at least a 30 day response time from the date of publication of a proper notice of intent to contract for architect-engineer services or before issuance of an order under a basic ordering agreement or similar arrangement if the proposed contract action is expected to exceed the simplified acquisition threshold.

(e) Agencies must allow at least a 45-day response time for receipt of bids or proposals from the date of publication of the notice required in 5.201 for proposed contract actions categorized as research and development if the proposed contract action is expected to exceed the simplified acquisition threshold.

(f) Nothing in this subpart prohibits officers or employees of agencies from responding to requests for information.

(g) Contracting officers may, unless they have evidence to the contrary, presume the notice was published one day after transmission to the GPE. This presumption does not negate the mandatory waiting or response times specified in paragraphs (a) through (d) of this section. Upon learning that a particular notice has not in fact been published within the presumed timeframes, contracting officers should consider whether the date for receipt of offers can be extended or whether circumstances have become sufficiently compelling to justify proceeding with the proposed contract action under the authority of 5.202(a)(2).

(h) In addition to other requirements set forth in this section, for acquisitions covered by the World Trade Organization Government Procurement Agreement or a Free Trade Agreement (see Subpart 25.4), the period of time between publication of the synopsis notice and receipt of offers must be no less than 40 days. However, if the acquisition falls within a general category identified in an annual forecast, the availability of which is published, the contracting officer may reduce this time period to as few as 10 days.

United States Code Annotated

Competition requirements, see 41 U.S.C.A. § 253.

Contracts, competition requirements, see 10 U.S.C.A. § 2304.

Contracts, planning, solicitation, evaluation, and award procedures, see 10 U.S.C.A. § 2305.

Contracts, prohibition on competition between Department of Defense and small businesses and certain other entities, see 10 U.S.C.A. § 2304e.

Definitions, see 10 U.S.C.A. § 2302; 41 U.S.C.A. §§ 259, 403.

Encouragement of new competition, see 41 U.S.C.A. § 253c.

Encouragement of new competitors, see 10 U.S.C.A. § 2319.

Planning and solicitation requirements, see 41 U.S.C.A. § 253a.

Procurement notice, see 41 U.S.C.A. § 416.

Notes of Decisions

Reasonable time 1

1 Reasonable time

Commercial items

Because the items and services acquired by the VA were commercial items, the thirty day response time to prepare bids or proposals was not applicable. Instead, the VA was only required to allow "offerors a reasonable opportunity to respond." Software Testing Solutions, Inc. v. U.S., 58 Fed. Cl. 533 (2003).

After synopsizing a procurement, agencies must provide potential offerors a reasonable opportunity to respond. 41 U.S.C. § 426(c); FAR 5.203(b), 13.003(h)(2). What constitutes a reasonable opportunity to respond will depend on "the circumstances of the particular acquisition, such as complexity, commerciality, availability, and urgency." FAR 5.203(b). The fundamental purpose of these notices, including the circumstance where an agency contemplates a sole-source award, is to enhance the possibility of competition. The time provided by an agency was determined unreasonable because, other than the New Year's Day holiday and the weekend following it, the agency allowed a total response time of 1 1/2 business days and there was no evidence supporting the agency's contention that the services had to be completed as quickly as the agency alleged. Under these circumstances, a response time of 1 1/2 business days was not a reasonable amount of time to require IVI to prepare a submission to demonstrate its capabilities. Information Ventures, Inc., B-293541, 2004 CPD ¶ 81 (Comp. Gen. 2004).

The decision as to the appropriate proposal preparation time lies within the discretion of the contracting officer. Three-day period to respond to solicitation amendment was reasonable because the changes were relatively minor, and the protester had advance notice of the agency's intent to issue the purchase order by the end of the fiscal year. Under the circumstances, protester did not demonstrate that the contracting officer abused her discretion. USA Information Systems, Inc., B-291488, 2002 CPD ¶ 205 (Comp. Gen. 2002).

Protest that agency established unreasonably short deadline to respond to Request for Quotations (RFQ) issued under the Federal Supply Schedule (FSS) program is denied, where protester admits it could have timely responded but chose not to because it objected to the mode of transmission specified by the agency. The agency faxed an RFQ to FSS vendors at 9:15 pm on a Friday evening, seeking a "technical and price proposal in accordance with your GSA schedule contract" for A-76 consulting services. The agency had to make award on Monday, the last day of the fiscal year. FAR Subpart 8.4 does not require that vendors be permitted a specific minimum amount of time to respond to an RFQ; what is reasonable and sufficient depends on the facts and circumstances of the case. In this case, protester could have prepared the proposal in the time allotted by refused to transmit the proposal by any means other than e-mail, which was not permitted by the agency. GAO treated protester's decision not to respond as a business judgment and denied the protest. Warden Associates, Inc., B-291440, B-291440.2, 2002 CPD ¶ 223 (Comp. Gen. 2002).

Agency may allow fewer than 30 days to respond to an RFP when it is acquiring commercial items. FAR 12.205(c). When acquiring commercial items, the contracting officer should afford potential offerors a reasonable opportunity to respond; when establishing the solicitation response time, the contracting officer should consider the complexity, commerciality, availability, and urgency of the acquisition. Contracting officer's decision to specify a 15-day response period was reasonable because it was based on prior year's procurement for a more complex requirement, which resulted in adequate competition and no complaints from offerors. American Artisan Productions, Inc., B-281409, 98-2 CPD ¶ 155 (Comp. Gen. 1998).

§ 5.204 Presolicitation notices.

Contracting officers must provide access to presolicitation notices through the GPE (see

15.201 and 36.213-2). The contracting officer must synopsize a proposed contract action before issuing any resulting solicitation (see 5.201 and 5.203).

United States Code Annotated

Competition requirements, see 41 U.S.C.A. § 253.

Contracts, competition requirements, see 10 U.S.C.A. § 2304.

Contracts, planning, solicitation, evaluation, and award procedures, see 10 U.S.C.A. § 2305.

Contracts, prohibition on competition between Department of Defense and small businesses and certain other entities, see 10 U.S.C.A. § 2304e.

Definitions, see 10 U.S.C.A. § 2302; 41 U.S.C.A. §§ 259, 403.

Encouragement of new competition, see 41 U.S.C.A. § 253c.

Encouragement of new competitors, see 10 U.S.C.A. § 2319.

Planning and solicitation requirements, see 41 U.S.C.A. § 253a.

Procurement notice, see 41 U.S.C.A. § 416.

§ 5.205 Special situations.

(a) *Research and development (R&D) advance notices.* Contracting officers may transmit to the GPE advance notices of their interest in potential R&D programs whenever market research does not produce a sufficient number of concerns to obtain adequate competition. Advance notices must not be used where security considerations prohibit such publication. Advance notices will enable potential sources to learn of R&D programs and provide these sources with an opportunity to submit information which will permit evaluation of their capabilities. Contracting officers must consider potential sources which respond to advance notices for a subsequent solicitation. Advanced notices must be entitled "Research and Development Sources Sought" and include the name and telephone number of the contracting officer or other contracting activity official from whom technical details of the project can be obtained. This will enable sources to submit information for evaluation of their R&D capabilities. Contracting officers must synopsize (see 5.201) all subsequent solicitations for R&D contracts, including those resulting from a previously synopsized advance notice, unless one of the exceptions in 5.202 applies.

(b) *Federally Funded Research and Development Centers.* Before establishing a Federally Funded Research and Development Center (FFRDC) (see Part 35) or before changing its basic purpose and mission, the sponsor must transmit at least three notices over a 90-day period to the GPE and the *Federal Register*, indicating the agency's intention to sponsor an FFRDC or change the basic purpose and mission of an FFRDC. The notice must indicate the scope and nature of the effort to be performed and request comments. Notice is not required where the action is required by law.

(c) *Special notices.* Contracting officers may transmit to the GPE special notices of procurement matters such as business fairs, long-range procurement estimates, prebid or preproposal conferences, meetings, and the availability of draft solicitations or draft specifications for review.

(d) *Architect-engineering services.* Contracting officers must publish notices of intent to contract for architect-engineering services as follows:

(1) Except when exempted by 5.202, contracting officers must transmit to the GPE a synopsis of each proposed contract action for which the total fee (including phases and options) is expected to exceed $25,000.

(2) When the total fee is expected to exceed $15,000 but not exceed $25,000, the contracting officer must comply with 5.101(a)(2). When the proposed contract action is not required to be synopsized under paragraph (d)(1) of this section, the contracting officer must display a notice of the solicitation or a copy of the solicitation in a public place at the contracting office. Other optional publicizing methods are authorized in accordance with 5.101(b).

(e) Public-private competitions under OMB Circular A-76.

(1) The contracting officer shall make a formal public announcement for each streamlined or standard competition. The public announcement shall include, at a minimum, the agency, agency component, location, type of competition (streamlined or stan-

dard), activity being competed, incumbent service providers, number of Government personnel performing the activity, name of the Competitive Sourcing Official, name of the contracting officer, name of the Agency Tender Official, and projected end date of the competition.

(2) The contracting officer shall announce the end of the streamlined or standard competition by making a formal public announcement of the performance decision. (See OMB Circular A-76.)

(f) *Section 8(a) competitive acquisition.* When a national buy requirement is being considered for competitive acquisition limited to eligible 8(a) concerns under Subpart 19.8, the contracting officer must transmit a synopsis of the proposed contract action to the GPE. The synopsis may be transmitted to the GPE concurrent with submission of the agency offering (see 19.804-2) to the Small Business Administration (SBA). The synopsis should also include information—

(1) Advising that the acquisition is being offered for competition limited to eligible 8(a) concerns;

(2) Specifying the North American Industry Classification System (NAICS) code;

(3) Advising that eligibility to participate may be restricted to firms in either the developmental stage or the developmental and transitional stages; and

(4) Encouraging interested 8(a) firms to request a copy of the solicitation as expeditiously as possible since the solicitation will be issued without further notice upon SBA acceptance of the requirement for the section 8(a) program.

United States Code Annotated

Competition requirements, see 41 U.S.C.A. § 253.

Contracts, competition requirements, see 10 U.S.C.A. § 2304.

Contracts, planning, solicitation, evaluation, and award procedures, see 10 U.S.C.A. § 2305.

Contracts, prohibition on competition between Department of Defense and small businesses and certain other entities, see 10 U.S.C.A. § 2304e.

Definitions, see 10 U.S.C.A. § 2302; 41 U.S.C.A. §§ 259, 403.

Encouragement of new competition, see 41 U.S.C.A. § 253c.

Encouragement of new competitors, see 10 U.S.C.A. § 2319.

Planning and solicitation requirements, see 41 U.S.C.A. § 253a.

Procurement notice, see 41 U.S.C.A. § 416.

§ 5.206 Notices of subcontracting opportunities.

(a) The following entities may transmit a notice to the GPE to seek competition for subcontracts, to increase participation by qualified HUBZone small business, small, small disadvantaged, women-owned small business, veteran-owned small business and service-disabled veteran-owned small business concerns, and to meet established subcontracting plan goals:

(1) A contractor awarded a contract exceeding $150,000 that is likely to result in the award of any subcontracts.

(2) A subcontractor or supplier, at any tier, under a contract exceeding $150,000, that has a subcontracting opportunity exceeding $15,000.

(b) The notices must describe—

(1) The business opportunity;

(2) Any prequalification requirements; and

(3) Where to obtain technical data needed to respond to the requirement.

United States Code Annotated

Competition requirements, see 41 U.S.C.A. § 253.

Contracts, competition requirements, see 10 U.S.C.A. § 2304.

Contracts, planning, solicitation, evaluation, and award procedures, see 10 U.S.C.A. § 2305.

Contracts, prohibition on competition between Department of Defense and small businesses and certain other entities, see 10 U.S.C.A. § 2304e.

Definitions, see 10 U.S.C.A. § 2302; 41 U.S.C.A. §§ 259, 403.

Encouragement of new competition, see 41 U.S.C.A. § 253c.

Encouragement of new competitors, see 10 U.S.C.A. § 2319.

Planning and solicitation requirements, see 41 U.S.C.A. § 253a.

Procurement notice, see 41 U.S.C.A. § 416.

§ 5.207 Preparation and transmittal of synopses.

(a) *Content.* Each synopsis transmitted to the GPE must address the following data elements, as applicable:

(1) Action Code.

(2) Date.

(3) Year.

(4) Contracting Office ZIP Code.

(5) Classification Code.

(6) Contracting Office Address.

(7) Subject.

(8) Proposed Solicitation Number.

(9) Closing Response Date.

(10) Contact Point or Contracting Officer.

(11) Contract Award and Solicitation Number.

(12) Contract Award Dollar Amount.

(13) Contract Line Item Number.

(14) Contract Award Date.

(15) Contractor.

(16) Description.

(17) Place of Contract Performance.

(18) Set-aside Status.

(b) *Transmittal.* Transmissions to the GPE must be in accordance with the interface description available via the Internet at http://www.fedbizopps.gov.

(c) *General format for "Description."* Prepare a clear and concise description of the supplies or services that is not unnecessarily restrictive of competition and will allow a prospective offeror to make an informed business judgment as to whether a copy of the solicitation should be requested including the following, as appropriate:

(1) National Stock Number (NSN) if assigned.

(2) Specification and whether an offeror, its product, or service must meet a qualification requirement in order to be eligible for award, and identification of the office from which additional information about the qualification requirement may be obtained (see Subpart 9.2).

(3) Manufacturer, including part number, drawing number, etc.

(4) Size, dimensions, or other form, fit or functional description.

(5) Predominant material of manufacture.

(6) Quantity, including any options for additional quantities.

(7) Unit of issue.

(8) Destination information.

(9) Delivery schedule.

(10) Duration of the contract period.

(11) Sustainable acquisition requirements (or a description of high-performance sustainable building practices required, if for design, construction, renovation, repair, or deconstruction) (see parts 23 or 36).

(12) For a proposed contract action in an amount estimated to be greater than $25,000 but not greater than the simplified acquisition threshold, enter—

(i) A description of the procedures to be used in awarding the contract (*e.g.,* request for oral or written quotation or solicitation); and

(ii) The anticipated award date.

(13) For Architect-Engineer projects and other projects for which the supply or service codes are insufficient, provide brief details with respect to: location, scope of services required, cost range and limitations, type of contract, estimated starting and completion dates, and any significant evaluation factors.

(14) (i) If the solicitation will include the FAR clause at 52.225-3, Buy American—Free Trade Agreements—Israeli Trade Act, or an equivalent agency clause, insert the following notice in the synopsis: "One or more of the items under this acquisition is subject to Free Trade Agreements."

(ii) If the solicitation will include the FAR clause at 52.225-5, Trade Agreements, or an equivalent agency clause, insert the following notice in the synopsis: "One or more of the items under this acquisition is subject to the World Trade Organization Government Procurement Agreement and Free Trade Agreements."

(iii) If the solicitation will include the FAR clause at 52.225-11, Buy American-Construction Materials under Trade Agreements, 52.225-23, Required Use of American Iron, Steel, and Manufactured Goods-Buy American Statute-Construction Materials under Trade Agreements, or an equivalent agency clause, insert the following notice in the synopsis: "One or more of the items under this acquisition is subject to the World Trade Organization Government Procurement Agreement and Free Trade Agreements."

(15) In the case of noncompetitive contract actions (including those that do not exceed the simplified acquisition threshold), identify the intended source and insert a statement of the reason justifying the lack of competition.

(16) (i) Except when using the sole source authority at 6.302-1, insert a statement that all responsible sources may submit a bid, proposal, or quotation which shall be considered by the agency.

(ii) When using the sole source authority at 6.302-1, insert a statement that all responsible sources may submit a capability statement, proposal, or quotation, which shall be considered by the agency.

(17) If solicitations synopsized through the GPE will not be made available through the GPE, provide information on how to obtain the solicitation.

(18) If the solicitation will be made available to interested parties through electronic data interchange, provide any information necessary to obtain and respond to the solicitation electronically.

(19) If the technical data required to respond to the solicitation will not be furnished as part of such solicitation, identify the source in the Government, such as http://www.fedbizopps.gov/, from which the technical data may be obtained.

(d) *Set-asides.* When the proposed acquisition provides for a total or partial small business program set-aside, or when the proposed acquisition provides for a local area set-aside (see Subpart 26.2), the contracting officer shall identify the type of set-aside in the synopsis and in the solicitation.

(e) *Codes to be used in Synopses to identify services or supplies.* Contracting officers must use one of the classification codes identified at http://www.fedbizopps.gov/ to identify services or supplies in synopses.

(f) *Notice of solicitation cancellation.* Contracting officers may publish notices of solicitation cancellations (or indefinite suspensions) of proposed contract actions in the GPE.

United States Code Annotated

Competition requirements, see 41 U.S.C.A. § 253.

Contracts, competition requirements, see 10 U.S.C.A. § 2304.

Contracts, planning, solicitation, evaluation, and award procedures, see 10 U.S.C.A. § 2305.

Contracts, prohibition on competition between Department of Defense and small businesses and certain other entities, see 10 U.S.C.A. § 2304e.

Definitions, see 10 U.S.C.A. § 2302; 41 U.S.C.A. §§ 259, 403.

Encouragement of new competition, see 41 U.S.C.A. § 253c.

Encouragement of new competitors, see 10 U.S.C.A. § 2319.

Planning and solicitation requirements, see 41 U.S.C.A. § 253a.

Procurement notice, see 41 U.S.C.A. § 416.

Notes of Decisions

In general 1
Judicial review 3
Numbered notes 2

1 In general

By providing an inadequate description of its sole-source procurement in the synopsis, DOE restricted competition in violation of statute and regulation. Moreover, DOE compounded the shortcomings of the notice by providing no information on the availability of a statement of work and by stating in the synopsis that the notice "is for informational purposes only and is not a request for proposals or other information." GAO sustained the protest, finding that the language of the synopsis discouraged, and may have been intended to discourage, responses. Matter of: M.D. Thompson Consulting, LLC; PMTech, Inc., B-297616, B-297616.2, 2006 CPD ¶ 41 (Comp. Gen. 2006).

2 Numbered notes

Inclusion in published solicitation of Note 22, requiring government consideration of any proposal submitted within a 45-day period despite the sole-source nature of the procurement, necessarily precludes the imposition of a protest-filing deadline that falls before any such proposal has been considered. 48 C.F.R. § 5.207(e)(3). FN Mfg., Inc. v. U.S., 41 Fed. Cl. 186, 42 Cont. Cas. Fed. (CCH) P 77329 (1998). United States ☞64.55(1)

3 Judicial review

Contractor's response to sole source procurement notice did not amount to a waiver of its right to protest the procurement; contractor expressed sufficient interest in the procurement in telephonic communication with contracting agency, and although contractor did not articulate its capability to perform the work, its inability to do so resulted from the agency's failure to obtain certain data from the awardee. 10 U.S.C.A. § 2304(f)(1)(C); 48 C.F.R. § 5.207(e)(3). Cubic Defense Systems, Inc. v. U.S., 45 Fed. Cl. 239 (1999), dismissed, 230 F.3d 1375 (Fed. Cir. 1999). United States ☞64.60(2)

Subpart 5.3 Synopses of Contract Awards

§ 5.301 General.

(a) Except for contract actions described in paragraph (b) of this section and as provided in 5.003, contracting officers must synopsize through the GPE the following:

 (1) Contract awards exceeding $25,000 that are—

  (i) Covered by the World Trade Organization Government Procurement Agreement or a Free Trade Agreement (see subpart 25.4); or

  (ii) Likely to result in the award of any subcontracts. However, the dollar threshold is not a prohibition against publicizing an award of a smaller amount when publicizing would be advantageous to industry or to the Government.

 (2) Certain contract actions greater than the simplified acquisition threshold as follows—

  (i) Federal Supply Schedule (FSS) orders or Blanket Purchase Agreements supported by a limited-source justification (excluding brand name) in accordance with 8.405-6; or

  (ii) Task or delivery orders awarded without providing fair opportunity in accordance with 16.505(b)(2).

 (3) A notice is not required under this section if the notice would disclose the executive agency's needs and the disclosure of such needs would compromise the national security.

(b) A notice is not required under paragraph (a)(1) of this section if—

 (1) The award results from acceptance of an unsolicited research proposal that demonstrates a unique and innovative research concept and publication of any notice would disclose the originality of thought or innovativeness of the proposed research or would disclose proprietary information associated with the proposal;

(2) The award results from a proposal submitted under the Small Business Innovation Development Act of 1982 (Pub. L. 97-219);

(3) The contract action is an order placed under subpart 16.5 or 8.4, except see paragraph (a)(2) of this section;

(4) The award is made for perishable subsistence supplies;

(5) The award is for utility services, other than telecommunications services, and only one source is available;

(6) The contract action—

(i) Is for an amount not greater than the simplified acquisition threshold;

(ii) Was made through a means where access to the notice of proposed contract action was provided through the GPE; and

(iii) Permitted the public to respond to the solicitation electronically; or

(7) The award is for the services of an expert to support the Federal Government in any current or anticipated litigation or dispute pursuant to the exception to full and open competition authorized at 6.302-3.

(c) With respect to acquisitions covered by the World Trade Organization Government Procurement Agreement or a Free Trade Agreement, contracting officers must submit synopses in sufficient time to permit their publication in the GPE not later than 60 days after award.

(d) Posting is required of the justifications for—

(1) Contracts awarded using other than full and open competition in accordance with 6.305;

(2) FSS orders or Blanket Purchase Agreements with an estimated value greater than the simplified acquisition threshold and supported by a limited-sources justification (see 8.405-6(a)); or

(3) Task or delivery orders greater than the simplified acquisition threshold and awarded without providing for fair opportunity in accordance with 16.505(b)(2)(ii)(B) and (D).

United States Code Annotated

Competition requirements, see 41 U.S.C.A. § 253.

Contracts, competition requirements, see 10 U.S.C.A. § 2304.

Contracts, planning, solicitation, evaluation, and award procedures, see 10 U.S.C.A. § 2305.

Contracts, prohibition on competition between Department of Defense and small businesses and certain other entities, see 10 U.S.C.A. § 2304e.

Definitions, see 10 U.S.C.A. § 2302; 41 U.S.C.A. §§ 259, 403.

Planning and solicitation requirements, see 41 U.S.C.A. § 253a.

Procurement notice, see 41 U.S.C.A. § 416.

Notes of Decisions

In general 1

1 In general

For publication purposes, since contracting action as defined in FAR 5.001 does not include modifications within the scope of the contract, there was no requirement for a published notice of the in-scope modification and therefore no violation of FAR 5.301. Pacific Bell v. National Aeronautics and Space Admin., G.S.B.C.A. No. 12814-P, 94-3 B.C.A. (CCH) ¶ 27067, 1994 WL 323408 (Gen. Services Admin. B.C.A. 1994).

Agency was required to provide notice of award on FedBizOpps, pursuant to FAR 5.301(a), for contract awards exceeding $25,000 that are either: (1) covered by the World Trade Organization Government Procurement Agreement or a Free Trade Agreement; or (2) "likely to result in the award of any subcontracts." Since the agency expected that the award would result in the award of subcontracts, it failed to comply with FAR 5.301, which requires publication of awards when it is "likely" to result in "any" subcontracts. WorldWide Language Resources, Inc.; SOS International Ltd., B-296984, B-296984.2, B-296984.3, B-296984.4,

B-296993, B-296993.2, B-296993.3, 2005 CPD ¶ 206 (Comp. Gen. 2005).

§ 5.302 Preparation and transmittal of synopses of awards.

Contracting officers shall transmit synopses of contract awards in the same manner as prescribed in 5.207.

United States Code Annotated

Competition requirements, see 41 U.S.C.A. § 253.

Contracts, competition requirements, see 10 U.S.C.A. § 2304.

Contracts, planning, solicitation, evaluation, and award procedures, see 10 U.S.C.A. § 2305.

Contracts, prohibition on competition between Department of Defense and small businesses and certain other entities, see 10 U.S.C.A. § 2304e.

Definitions, see 10 U.S.C.A. § 2302; 41 U.S.C.A. §§ 259, 403.

Planning and solicitation requirements, see 41 U.S.C.A. § 253a.

Procurement notice, see 41 U.S.C.A. § 416.

§ 5.303 Announcement of contract awards.

(a) *Public announcement.* Contracting officers shall make information available on awards over $4 million (unless another dollar amount is specified in agency acquisition regulations) in sufficient time for the agency concerned to announce it by 5 p.m. Washington, DC, time on the day of award. Agencies shall not release information on awards before the public release time of 5 p.m. Washington, DC time. Contracts excluded from this reporting requirement include—

(1) Those placed with the Small Business Administration under Section 8(a) of the Small Business Act;

(2) Those placed with foreign firms when the place of delivery or performance is outside the United States and its outlying areas; and

(3) Those for which synopsis was exempted under 5.202(a)(1).

(b) *Local announcement.* Agencies may also release information on contract awards to the local press or other media. When local announcements are made for contract awards in excess of the simplified acquisition threshold, they shall include—

(1) For awards after sealed bidding, a statement that the contract was awarded after competition by sealed bidding, the number of offers solicited and received, and the basis for selection (*e.g.,* the lowest responsible bidder); or

(2) For awards after negotiation, the information prescribed by 15.503(b), and after competitive negotiation (either price or design competition), a statement to this effect, and in general terms the basis for selection.

United States Code Annotated

Competition requirements, see 41 U.S.C.A. § 253.

Contracts, competition requirements, see 10 U.S.C.A. § 2304.

Contracts, planning, solicitation, evaluation, and award procedures, see 10 U.S.C.A. § 2305.

Contracts, prohibition on competition between Department of Defense and small businesses and certain other entities, see 10 U.S.C.A. § 2304e.

Definitions, see 10 U.S.C.A. § 2302; 41 U.S.C.A. §§ 259, 403.

Planning and solicitation requirements, see 41 U.S.C.A. § 253a.

Procurement notice, see 41 U.S.C.A. § 416.

Subpart 5.4 Release of Information

§ 5.401 General.

(a) A high level of business security must be maintained in order to preserve the integrity of the acquisition process. When it is necessary to obtain information from potential contractors and others outside the Government for use in preparing Government estimates, contracting officers shall ensure that the information is not publicized or discussed with potential contractors.

(b) Contracting officers may make available maximum information to the public, except information—

(1) On plans that would provide undue or discriminatory advantage to private or personal interests;

(2) Received in confidence from an offeror;

(3) Otherwise requiring protection under Freedom of Information Act (see Subpart 24.2) or Privacy Act (see Subpart 24.1); or

(4) Pertaining to internal agency communications (*e.g.*, technical reviews, contracting authority or other reasons, or recommendations referring thereto).

(c) This policy applies to all Government personnel who participate directly or indirectly in any stage of the acquisition cycle.

United States Code Annotated

Competition requirements, see 41 U.S.C.A. § 253.

Contracts, competition requirements, see 10 U.S.C.A. § 2304.

Contracts, planning, solicitation, evaluation, and award procedures, see 10 U.S.C.A. § 2305.

Contracts, prohibition on competition between Department of Defense and small businesses and certain other entities, see 10 U.S.C.A. § 2304e.

Definitions, see 10 U.S.C.A. § 2302; 41 U.S.C.A. §§ 259, 403.

Encouragement of new competition, see 41 U.S.C.A. § 253c.

Encouragement of new competitors, see 10 U.S.C.A. § 2319.

Planning and solicitation requirements, see 41 U.S.C.A. § 253a.

Procurement notice, see 41 U.S.C.A. § 416.

§ 5.402 General public.

Contracting officers shall process requests for specific information from the general public, including suppliers, in accordance with Subpart 24.1 or 24.2, as appropriate.

United States Code Annotated

Competition requirements, see 41 U.S.C.A. § 253.

Contracts, competition requirements, see 10 U.S.C.A. § 2304.

Contracts, planning, solicitation, evaluation, and award procedures, see 10 U.S.C.A. § 2305.

Contracts, prohibition on competition between Department of Defense and small businesses and certain other entities, see 10 U.S.C.A. § 2304e.

Definitions, see 10 U.S.C.A. § 2302; 41 U.S.C.A. §§ 259, 403.

Encouragement of new competition, see 41 U.S.C.A. § 253c.

Encouragement of new competitors, see 10 U.S.C.A. § 2319.

Planning and solicitation requirements, see 41 U.S.C.A. § 253a.

Procurement notice, see 41 U.S.C.A. § 416.

§ 5.403 Requests from Members of Congress.

Contracting officers shall give Members of Congress, upon their request, detailed information regarding any particular contract. When responsiveness would result in disclosure of classified matter, business confidential information, or information prejudicial to competitive acquisition, the contracting officer shall refer the proposed reply, with full documentation, to the agency head and inform the legislative liaison office of the action.

United States Code Annotated

Competition requirements, see 41 U.S.C.A. § 253.

Contracts, competition requirements, see 10 U.S.C.A. § 2304.

Contracts, planning, solicitation, evaluation, and award procedures, see 10 U.S.C.A. § 2305.

Contracts, prohibition on competition between Department of Defense and small businesses and certain other entities, see 10 U.S.C.A. § 2304e.

Definitions, see 10 U.S.C.A. § 2302; 41 U.S.C.A. §§ 259, 403.

Encouragement of new competition, see 41 U.S.C.A. § 253c.

Encouragement of new competitors, see 10 U.S.C.A. § 2319.

Planning and solicitation requirements, see 41 U.S.C.A. § 253a.

Procurement notice, see 41 U.S.C.A. § 416.

§ 5.404 Release of long-range acquisition estimates.

To assist industry planning and to locate additional sources of supply, it may be desirable to publicize estimates of unclassified long-range acquisition requirements. Estimates may be publicized as far in advance as possible.

United States Code Annotated

Competition requirements, see 41 U.S.C.A. § 253.

Contracts, competition requirements, see 10 U.S.C.A. § 2304.

Contracts, planning, solicitation, evaluation, and award procedures, see 10 U.S.C.A. § 2305.

Contracts, prohibition on competition between Department of Defense and small businesses and certain other entities, see 10 U.S.C.A. § 2304e.

Definitions, see 10 U.S.C.A. § 2302; 41 U.S.C.A. §§ 259, 403.

Encouragement of new competition, see 41 U.S.C.A. § 253c.

Encouragement of new competitors, see 10 U.S.C.A. § 2319.

Planning and solicitation requirements, see 41 U.S.C.A. § 253a.

Procurement notice, see 41 U.S.C.A. § 416.

§ 5.404-1 Release procedures.

(a) *Application*. The agency head, or a designee, may release long-range acquisition estimates if the information will—

(1) Assist industry in its planning and facilitate meeting the acquisition requirements;

(2) Not encourage undesirable practices (*e.g.*, attempts to corner the market or hoard industrial materials); and

(3) Not indicate the existing or potential mobilization of the industry as a whole.

(b) *Conditions*. The agency head shall ensure that—

(1) Classified information is released through existing security channels in accordance with agency security regulations;

(2) The information is publicized as widely as practicable to all parties simultaneously by any of the means described in this part;

(3) Each release states that—

(i) The estimate is based on the best information available,

(ii) The information is subject to modification and is in no way binding on the Government, and

(iii) More specific information relating to any individual item or class of items will not be furnished until the proposed action is synopsized through the GPE or the solicitation is issued;

(4) Each release contains the name and address of the contracting officer that will process the acquisition;

(5) Modifications to the original release are publicized as soon as possible, in the same manner as the original; and

(6) Each release—

(i) Is coordinated in advance with small business, public information, and public relations personnel, as appropriate;

(ii) Contains, if applicable, a statement that small business set-asides may be involved, but that a determination can be made only when acquisition action is initiated; and

(iii) Contains the name or description of the item, and the estimated quantity to be acquired by calendar quarter, fiscal year, or other period. It may also contain such additional information as the number of units last acquired, the unit price, and the name of the last supplier.

United States Code Annotated

Competition requirements, see 41 U.S.C.A. § 253.

Contracts, competition requirements, see 10 U.S.C.A. § 2304.

Contracts, planning, solicitation, evaluation, and award procedures, see 10 U.S.C.A. § 2305.

Contracts, prohibition on competition between Department of Defense and small businesses and certain other entities, see 10 U.S.C.A. § 2304e.

Definitions, see 10 U.S.C.A. § 2302; 41 U.S.C.A. §§ 259, 403.

Encouragement of new competition, see 41 U.S.C.A. § 253c.

Encouragement of new competitors, see 10 U.S.C.A. § 2319.

Planning and solicitation requirements, see 41 U.S.C.A. § 253a.

Procurement notice, see 41 U.S.C.A. § 416.

§ 5.404-2 Announcements of long-range acquisition estimates.

Further publicizing, consistent with the needs of the individual case, may be accomplished by announcing through the GPE that long-range acquisition estimates have been published and are obtainable, upon request, from the contracting officer.

United States Code Annotated

Competition requirements, see 41 U.S.C.A. § 253.

Contracts, competition requirements, see 10 U.S.C.A. § 2304.

Contracts, planning, solicitation, evaluation, and award procedures, see 10 U.S.C.A. § 2305.

Contracts, prohibition on competition between Department of Defense and small businesses and certain other entities, see 10 U.S.C.A. § 2304e.

Definitions, see 10 U.S.C.A. § 2302; 41 U.S.C.A. §§ 259, 403.

Encouragement of new competition, see 41 U.S.C.A. § 253c.

Encouragement of new competitors, see 10 U.S.C.A. § 2319.

Planning and solicitation requirements, see 41 U.S.C.A. § 253a.

Procurement notice, see 41 U.S.C.A. § 416.

§ 5.405 Exchange of acquisition information.

(a) When the same item or class of items is being acquired by more than one agency, or by more than one contracting activity within an agency, the exchange and coordination of pertinent information, particularly cost and pricing data, between these agencies or contracting activities is necessary to promote uniformity of treatment of major issues and the resolution of particularly difficult or controversial issues. The exchange and coordination of information is particularly beneficial during the period of acquisition planning, presolicitation, evaluation, and pre-award survey.

(b) When substantial acquisitions of major items are involved or when the contracting activity deems it desirable, the contracting activity shall request appropriate information (on both the end item and on major subcontracted components) from other agencies or contracting activities responsible for acquiring similar items. Each agency or contracting activity receiving such a request shall furnish the information requested. The contracting officer, early in a negotiation of a contract, or in connection with the review of a subcontract, shall request the contractor to furnish information as to the contractor's or subcontractor's previous Government contracts and subcontracts for the same or similar end items and major subcontractor components.

United States Code Annotated

Competition requirements, see 41 U.S.C.A. § 253.

Contracts, competition requirements, see 10 U.S.C.A. § 2304.

Contracts, planning, solicitation, evaluation, and award procedures, see 10 U.S.C.A. § 2305.

Contracts, prohibition on competition between Department of Defense and small businesses and certain other entities, see 10 U.S.C.A. § 2304e.

Definitions, see 10 U.S.C.A. § 2302; 41 U.S.C.A. §§ 259, 403.

Encouragement of new competition, see 41 U.S.C.A. § 253c.

Encouragement of new competitors, see 10 U.S.C.A. § 2319.

Planning and solicitation requirements, see 41 U.S.C.A. § 253a.

Procurement notice, see 41 U.S.C.A. § 416.

§ 5.406 Public disclosure of justification documents for certain contract actions.

(a) Justifications and approvals for other than full and open competition must be posted in accordance with 6.305.

(b) Limited-source justifications (excluding brand name) for FSS orders or blanket purchase agreements with an estimated value greater than the simplified acquisition threshold must be posted in accordance with 8.405-6(a)(2).

(c) Justifications for task or delivery orders greater than the simplified acquisition threshold and awarded without providing for fair opportunity must be posted in accordance with 16.505(b)(2)(ii)(D).

Subpart 5.5 Paid Advertisements

§ 5.501 Definitions.

As used in this subpart—

"Advertisement" means any single message prepared for placement in communication media, regardless of the number of placements.

"Publication" means—

(1) The placement of an advertisement in a newspaper, magazine, trade or professional journal, or any other printed medium; or

(2) The broadcasting of an advertisement over radio or television.

United States Code Annotated

Advertisements not to be published without written authority, see 44 U.S.C.A. § 3702.

Competition requirements, see 41 U.S.C.A. § 253.

Contracts, competition requirements, see 10 U.S.C.A. § 2304.

Contracts, planning, solicitation, evaluation, and award procedures, see 10 U.S.C.A. § 2305.

Contracts, prohibition on competition between Department of Defense and small businesses and certain other entities, see 10 U.S.C.A. § 2304e.

Definitions, see 10 U.S.C.A. § 2302; 41 U.S.C.A. §§ 259, 403.

Encouragement of new competition, see 41 U.S.C.A. § 253c.

Encouragement of new competitors, see 10 U.S.C.A. § 2319.

Planning and solicitation requirements, see 41 U.S.C.A. § 253a.

Procurement notice, see 41 U.S.C.A. § 416.

Rate of payment for advertisements, notices, and proposals, see 44 U.S.C.A. § 3703.

§ 5.502 Authority.

(a) *Newspapers.* Authority to approve the publication of paid advertisements in newspapers is vested in the head of each agency (44 U.S.C. 3702). This approval authority may be delegated (5 U.S.C. 302(b)). Contracting officers shall obtain written authorization in accordance with policy procedures before advertising in newspapers.

(b) *Other media.* Unless the agency head determines otherwise, advance written authorization is not required to place advertisements in media other than newspapers.

United States Code Annotated

Advertisements not to be published without written authority, see 44 U.S.C.A. § 3702.

Competition requirements, see 41 U.S.C.A. § 253.

Contracts, competition requirements, see 10 U.S.C.A. § 2304.

Contracts, planning, solicitation, evaluation, and award procedures, see 10 U.S.C.A. § 2305.

Contracts, prohibition on competition between Department of Defense and small businesses and certain other entities, see 10 U.S.C.A. § 2304e.

Definitions, see 10 U.S.C.A. § 2302; 41 U.S.C.A. §§ 259, 403.

Encouragement of new competition, see 41 U.S.C.A. § 253c.

Encouragement of new competitors, see 10 U.S.C.A. § 2319.

Planning and solicitation requirements, see 41 U.S.C.A. § 253a.

Procurement notice, see 41 U.S.C.A. § 416.

Rate of payment for advertisements, notices, and proposals, see 44 U.S.C.A. § 3703.

§ 5.503 Procedures.

(a) *General.* (1) Orders for paid advertisements may be placed directly with the media or through an advertising agency. Contracting officers shall give small, small disadvantaged, women-owned, veteran-owned, HUBZone, and service-disabled veteran-owned small business concerns maximum opportunity to participate in these acquisitions.

(2) The contracting officer shall use the SF 1449 for paper solicitations. The SF 1449 shall be used to make awards or place orders unless the award/order is made by using electronic commerce or by using the Governmentwide commercial purchase card for micropurchases.

(b) *Rates.* Advertisements may be paid for at rates not over the commercial rates charged private individuals, with the usual discounts (44 U.S.C. 3703).

(c) *Proof of advertising.* Every invoice for advertising shall be accompanied by a copy of the advertisement or an affidavit of publication furnished by the publisher, radio or television station, or advertising agency concerned (44 U.S.C. 3703). Paying offices shall retain the proof of advertising until the Government Accountability Office settles the paying office's account.

(d) *Payment.* Upon receipt of an invoice supported by proof of advertising, the contracting officer shall attach a copy of the written authority (see 5.502(a)) and submit the invoice for payment under agency procedures.

United States Code Annotated

Advertisements not to be published without written authority, see 44 U.S.C.A. § 3702.

Competition requirements, see 41 U.S.C.A. § 253.

Contracts, competition requirements, see 10 U.S.C.A. § 2304.

Contracts, planning, solicitation, evaluation, and award procedures, see 10 U.S.C.A. § 2305.

Contracts, prohibition on competition between Department of Defense and small businesses and certain other entities, see 10 U.S.C.A. § 2304e.

Definitions, see 10 U.S.C.A. § 2302; 41 U.S.C.A. §§ 259, 403.

Encouragement of new competition, see 41 U.S.C.A. § 253c.

Encouragement of new competitors, see 10 U.S.C.A. § 2319.

Planning and solicitation requirements, see 41 U.S.C.A. § 253a.

Procurement notice, see 41 U.S.C.A. § 416.

Rate of payment for advertisements, notices, and proposals, see 44 U.S.C.A. § 3703.

§ 5.504 Use of advertising agencies.

(a) *General.* Basic ordering agreements may be placed with advertising agencies for assistance in producing and placing advertisements when a significant number will be placed in several publications and in national media. Services of advertising agencies include, but are not limited to, counseling as to selection of the media for placement of the advertisement, contacting the media in the interest of the Government, placing orders, selecting and ordering typography, copywriting, and preparing rough layouts.

(b) *Use of commission-paying media.* The services of advertising agencies in placing advertising with media often can be obtained at no cost to the Government, over and above the space cost, as many media give advertising agencies a commission or discount on the space cost that is not given to the Government.

(c) *Use of noncommission-paying media.* Some media do not grant advertising agencies a commission or discount, meaning the Government can obtain the same rate as the advertising agency. If the advertising agency agrees to place advertisements in noncommission-paying media as a no-cost service, the basic ordering agreement shall so provide. If the advertising agency will not agree to place advertisements at no cost, the agreement shall—

(1) Provide that the Government may place orders directly with the media; or

(2) Specify an amount that the Government will pay if the agency places the orders.

(d) *Art work, supplies, and incidentals.* The basic ordering agreement also may provide for the furnishing by the advertising agency of art work, supplies, and incidentals, including brochures and pamphlets, but not their printing. "Incidentals" may include telephone calls, telegrams, and postage incurred by the advertising agency on behalf of the Government.

United States Code Annotated

Advertisements not to be published without written authority, see 44 U.S.C.A. § 3702.

Competition requirements, see 41 U.S.C.A. § 253.

Contracts, competition requirements, see 10 U.S.C.A. § 2304.

Contracts, planning, solicitation, evaluation, and award procedures, see 10 U.S.C.A. § 2305.

Contracts, prohibition on competition between Department of Defense and small businesses and certain other entities, see 10 U.S.C.A. § 2304e.

Definitions, see 10 U.S.C.A. § 2302; 41 U.S.C.A. §§ 259, 403.

Encouragement of new competition, see 41 U.S.C.A. § 253c.

Encouragement of new competitors, see 10 U.S.C.A. § 2319.

Planning and solicitation requirements, see 41 U.S.C.A. § 253a.

Procurement notice, see 41 U.S.C.A. § 416.

Rate of payment for advertisements, notices, and proposals, see 44 U.S.C.A. § 3703.

Subpart 5.6 Publicizing Multi-Agency Use Contracts

§ 5.601 Governmentwide database of contracts.

(a) A Governmentwide database of contracts and other procurement instruments intended for use by multiple agencies is available via the Internet at https://www.contractdirectory.g ov/contractdirectory/. This searchable database is a tool that may be used to identify existing contracts and other procurement instruments that may be used to fulfill Government needs.

(b) The contracting activity shall—

(1) Enter the information specified at https://www.contractdirectory.gov/contractdirecto ry/, in accordance with the instructions on that web site, within ten days of award of a Governmentwide acquisition contract (GWAC), multi-agency contract, Federal Supply Schedule contract, or any other procurement instrument intended for use by multiple agencies, including blanket purchase agreements (BPAs) under Federal Supply Schedule contracts.

(2) Enter the information specified at https://www.contractdirectory.gov/contractdirect ory/ in accordance with the instructions on that web site by October 31, 2003, for all

contracts and other procurement instruments intended for use by multiple agencies that were awarded before July 24, 2003.

United States Code Annotated

Competition requirements, see 41 U.S.C.A. § 253.

Contracts, competition requirements, see 10 U.S.C.A. § 2304.

Contracts, planning, solicitation, evaluation, and award procedures, see 10 U.S.C.A. § 2305.

Contracts, prohibition on competition between Department of Defense and small businesses and certain other entities, see 10 U.S.C.A. § 2304e.

Definitions, see 10 U.S.C.A. § 2302; 41 U.S.C.A. §§ 259, 403.

Encouragement of new competition, see 41 U.S.C.A. § 253c.

Encouragement of new competitors, see 10 U.S.C.A. § 2319.

Planning and solicitation requirements, see 41 U.S.C.A. § 253a.

Procurement notice, see 41 U.S.C.A. § 416.

Subpart 5.7 Publicizing Requirements Under the American Recovery and Reinvestment Act of 2009

§ 5.701 Scope.

This subpart prescribes posting requirements for presolicitation and award notices for actions funded in whole or in part by the American Recovery and Reinvestment Act of 2009 (Pub. L. 111-5) (Recovery Act). The requirements of this subpart enhance transparency to the public.

§ 5.702 Applicability.

This subpart applies to all actions expected to exceed $25,000 funded in whole or in part by the Recovery Act. Unlike subparts 5.2 and 5.3, this subpart includes additional requirements for orders and for actions that are not both fixedprice and competitive.

§ 5.703 Definition.

As used in this subpart—

"Task or delivery order contract" means a "delivery order contract," and a "task order contract," as defined in 16.501-1. For example, it includes Governmentwide Acquisition Contracts (GWACs), multi-agency contracts (MACs), and other indefinite-delivery/indefinite-quantity contracts, whether single award or multiple award. It also includes Federal Supply Schedule contracts (including Blanket Purchase Agreements under Subpart 8.4).

§ 5.704 Publicizing preaward.

(a) (1) Follow the publication procedures at 5.201.

(2) In addition, notices of proposed contract actions are required for orders exceeding $25,000, funded in whole or in part by the Recovery Act, which are issued under task or delivery order contracts. This does not include modifications to existing orders, but these modifications are covered postaward, see 5.705. These notices are for "informational purposes only," therefore, 5.203 does not apply. Contracting officers should concurrently use their usual solicitation practice (*e.g.*, e-Buy).

(b) Contracting officers shall identify proposed contract actions, funded in whole or in part by the Recovery Act, by using the following instructions which are also available in the Recovery FAQs under "Buyers/Engineers" at the Governmentwide Point of Entry (GPE) (https://www.fedbizopps.gov):

(1) If submitting notices electronically via ftp or email, enter the word "Recovery" as the first word in the title field.

(2) If using the GPE directly, select the "yes" radio button for the "Is this a Recovery and Reinvestment Act action" field on the "Notice Details" form (Step 2) located below the "NAICS Code" field. In addition, enter the word "Recovery" as the first word in the title

field.

(c) In preparing the description required by 5.207(a)(16), use clear and concise language to describe the planned procurement. Use descriptions of the goods and services (including construction), that can be understood by the general public. Avoid the use of acronyms or terminology that is not widely understood by the general public.

§ 5.705 Publicizing postaward.

Follow usual publication procedures at 5.301, except that the following supersede the exceptions at 5.301(b)(2) through (7):

(a) (1) Publicize the award notice for any action exceeding $500,000, funded in whole or in part by the Recovery Act, including—

    (i) Contracts;

    (ii) Modifications to existing contracts;

    (iii) Orders which are issued under task or delivery order contracts; and

    (iv) Modifications to orders under task or delivery order contracts.

(2) Contracting officers shall identify contract actions, funded in whole or in part by the Recovery Act, by using the following instructions which are also available in the Recovery FAQS under "Buyers/Engineers" at the Governmentwide Point of Entry (GPE) (https://www.fedbizopps.gov):

    (i) If submitting notices electronically via ftp or email, enter the word "Recovery" as the first word in the title field.

    (ii) If using the GPE directly, select the "yes" radio button for the "Is this a Recovery and Reinvestment Act action" field on the "Notice Details" form (Step 2) located below the "NAICS Code" field. In addition, enter the word "Recovery" as the first word in the title field.

(3) In preparing the description required by 5.207(a)(16), use clear and concise language to describe the planned procurement. Use descriptions of the goods and services (including construction), that can be understood by the general public. Avoid the use of acronyms or terminology that is not widely understood by the general public.

(b) Regardless of dollar value, if the contract action, including all modifications and orders under task or delivery order contracts, is not both fixed-price and competitively awarded, publicize the award notice and include in the description the rationale for using other than a fixed-priced and/or competitive approach. Include in the description a statement specifically noting if the contract action was not awarded competitively, or was not fixed-price, or was neither competitive nor fixed-price. These notices and the rationale will be available to the public at the GPE, so do not include any proprietary information or information that would compromise national security. The following table provides examples for when a rationale is required.

Posting of Rationale—Examples

	DESCRIPTION OF CONTRACT ACTION	RATIONALE REQUIRED
(1)	A contract is competitively awarded and is fixed-price.	Not Required.
(2)	A contract is awarded that is not fixed-price.	Required.
(3)	A contract is awarded without competition.	Required.
(4)	An order is issued under a new or existing single award IDIQ contract.	Required if order is made under a contract described in (2) or (3).
(5)	An order is issued under a new or existing multiple award IDIQ contract.	Required if one or both of the following conditions exist: (i) The order is not fixed-price. (ii) The order is awarded pursuant to an exception to the competition requirements applicable to the underlying vehicle (e.g., award is made pursuant to an exception to the fair opportunity process).

	DESCRIPTION OF CONTRACT ACTION	RATIONALE REQUIRED
(6)	A modification is issued.	Required if modification is made— (i) To a contract described in (2) or (3) above; or (ii) To an order requiring posting as described in (4) or (5) above.
(7)	A contract or order is awarded pursuant to a small business contracting authority (*e.g.*, SBA's section 8(a) program).	Required if one or both of the following conditions exist: (i) the contract or order is not fixed-price; (ii) the contract or order was not awarded using competition (*e.g.*, a non-competitive 8(a) award).

(c) Contracting officers shall use the instructions available in the Recovery FAQs under "Buyers/Engineers" at the GPE (https://www.fedbizopps.gov) to identify actions funded in whole or in part by the Recovery Act.

PART 6 COMPETITION REQUIREMENTS

§ 6.000 Scope of part.
§ 6.001 Applicability.
§ 6.002 Limitations.
§ 6.003 [Reserved]

Subpart 6.1 Full and Open Competition

§ 6.100 Scope of subpart.
§ 6.101 Policy.
§ 6.102 Use of competitive procedures.

Subpart 6.2 Full and Open Competition After Exclusion of Sources

§ 6.200 Scope of subpart.
§ 6.201 Policy.
§ 6.202 Establishing or maintaining alternative sources.
§ 6.203 Set-asides for small business concerns.
§ 6.204 Section 8(a) competition.
§ 6.205 Set-asides for HUBZone small business concerns.
§ 6.206 Set-asides for service-disabled veteran-owned small business concerns.
§ 6.207 Set-asides for economically disadvantaged women-owned small business (EDWOSB) concerns or women-owned small business (WOSB) concerns eligible under the WOSB Program.
§ 6.208 Set-asides for local firms during a major disaster or emergency.

Subpart 6.3 Other Than Full and Open Competition

§ 6.300 Scope of subpart.
§ 6.301 Policy.
§ 6.302 Circumstances permitting other than full and open competition.
§ 6.302-1 Only one responsible source and no other supplies or services will satisfy agency requirements.
§ 6.302-2 Unusual and compelling urgency.
§ 6.302-3 Industrial mobilization; engineering, developmental, or research capability; or expert services.
§ 6.302-4 International agreement.
§ 6.302-5 Authorized or required by statute.
§ 6.302-6 National security.
§ 6.302-7 Public interest.
§ 6.303 Justifications.
§ 6.303-1 Requirements.
§ 6.303-2 Content.
§ 6.304 Approval of the justification.
§ 6.305 Availability of the justification.

Subpart 6.4 Sealed Bidding and Competitive Proposals

§ 6.401 Sealed bidding and competitive proposals.

Subpart 6.5 Competition Advocates
§ 6.501 Requirement.
§ 6.502 Duties and responsibilities.

§ 6.000 Scope of part.
This part prescribes policies and procedures to promote full and open competition in the acquisition process and to provide for full and open competition, full and open competition after exclusion of sources, other than full and open competition, and advocates for competition. This part does not deal with the results of competition (*e.g.*, adequate price competition), that are addressed in other parts (*e.g.*, Part 15).

United States Code Annotated
Advocates for competition, see 41 U.S.C.A. § 418.

Competition requirements, see 41 U.S.C.A. § 253.

Contract goal for small disadvantaged businesses and certain institutions of higher education, see 10 U.S.C.A. § 2323.

Contracts, competition requirements, see 10 U.S.C.A. § 2304.

Contracts, planning, solicitation, evaluation, and award procedures, see 10 U.S.C.A. § 2305.

Contracts, prohibition on competition between Department of Defense and small businesses and certain other entities, see 10 U.S.C.A. § 2304e.

Credit for Indian contracting in meeting certain subcontracting goals for small disadvantaged businesses and certain institutions of higher education, see 10 U.S.C.A. § 2323a.

Definitions, see 10 U.S.C.A. § 2302; 41 U.S.C.A. §§ 259, 403.

Design-build selection procedures, see 10 U.S.C.A. § 2305a; 41 U.S.C.A. § 253m.

Encouragement of new competition, see 41 U.S.C.A. § 253c.

Encouragement of new competitors, see 10 U.S.C.A. § 2319.

Planning and solicitation requirements, see 41 U.S.C.A. § 253a.

Procurement notice, see 41 U.S.C.A. § 416.

§ 6.001 Applicability.
This part applies to all acquisitions except—

(a) Contracts awarded using the simplified acquisition procedures of Part 13 (but see 13.501 for requirements pertaining to sole source acquisitions of commercial items under Subpart 13.5);

(b) Contracts awarded using contracting procedures (other than those addressed in this part) that are expressly authorized by statute;

(c) Contract modifications, including the exercise of priced options that were evaluated as part of the initial competition (see 17.207(f)), that are within the scope and under the terms of an existing contract;

(d) Orders placed under requirements contracts or definite-quantity contracts;

(e) Orders placed under indefinite-quantity contracts that were entered into pursuant to this part when—

(1) The contract was awarded under Subpart 6.1 or 6.2 and all responsible sources were realistically permitted to compete for the requirements contained in the order; or

(2) The contract was awarded under Subpart 6.3 and the required justification and approval adequately covers the requirements contained in the order; or

(f) Orders placed against task order and delivery order contracts entered into pursuant to Subpart 16.5.

United States Code Annotated
Advocates for competition, see 41 U.S.C.A. § 418.

Competition requirements, see 41 U.S.C.A. § 253.

Contract goal for small disadvantaged businesses and certain institutions of higher

education, see 10 U.S.C.A. § 2323.

Contracts, competition requirements, see 10 U.S.C.A. § 2304.

Contracts, planning, solicitation, evaluation, and award procedures, see 10 U.S.C.A. § 2305.

Contracts, prohibition on competition between Department of Defense and small businesses and certain other entities, see 10 U.S.C.A. § 2304e.

Credit for Indian contracting in meeting certain subcontracting goals for small disadvantaged businesses and certain institutions of higher education, see 10 U.S.C.A. § 2323a.

Definitions, see 10 U.S.C.A. § 2302; 41 U.S.C.A. §§ 259, 403.

Design-build selection procedures, see 10 U.S.C.A. § 2305a; 41 U.S.C.A. § 253m.

Encouragement of new competition, see 41 U.S.C.A. § 253c.

Encouragement of new competitors, see 10 U.S.C.A. § 2319.

Planning and solicitation requirements, see 41 U.S.C.A. § 253a.

Procurement notice, see 41 U.S.C.A. § 416.

Notes of Decisions

In general 1
Commercial items 6
Construction and application 2
Federal preemption 3
Grants and cooperative agreements 9
Indefinite delivery/indefinite quantity (ID/IQ) contracts 7
In-scope modifications 5
Out-of-scope modifications 4
Statutory exemptions 8

1 In general

Even if agreement between hospital and Veterans Affairs Medical Center for acquisition and use of piece of medical equipment was a "procurement" for purposes of the Competition in Contracting Act (CICA), statute authorizing the Veterans Administration to enter into such arrangements was a procurement procedure "expressly authorized by statute" and thus not subject to the full and open competition requirements of CICA. 38 U.S.C.A. §§ 8153, 8153(b); Federal Property and Administrative Services Act of 1949, § 303(a)(1), as amended, Rapides Regional Medical Center v. Secretary, Dept. of Veterans' Affairs, 974 F.2d 565, 38 Cont. Cas. Fed. (CCH) P 76445 (5th Cir. 1992). United States ☞64.10

Arrangement whereby private hospital agreed to pay one half of the cost of acquisition by Veterans Affairs Medical Center of a piece of medical equipment, with the equipment to be placed in the private hospital and used by both the VA and the hospital, was not a "procurement" for purposes of the Competition in Contracting Act (CICA). Federal Property and Administrative Services Act of 1949, § 303(a), as amended, Rapides Regional Medical Center v. Secretary, Dept. of Veterans' Affairs, 974 F.2d 565, 38 Cont. Cas. Fed. (CCH) P 76445 (5th Cir. 1992). United States ☞64.10

Existing procedures of Pennsylvania Avenue Development Corporation (PADC) for development competition for construction of federal office complex, pursuant to Federal Triangle Development Act, did not have to include compliance with Federal Acquisition Regulations (FAR) system or Competition in Contracting Act (CICA); although PADC, as wholly owned government corporation, was subject to those authorities, FAR applied only to acquisitions and CICA applied only to government procurements, and choosing developer for project did not constitute "acquiring" or "procuring" within meaning of FAR and CICA. Federal Triangle Development Act, §§ 2-10, 40 U.S.C.A. §§ 1101–1109; 31 U.S.C.A. § 9101(3) (H); Federal Property and Administrative Services Act of 1949, § 303 et seq., as amended, 41 U.S.C.A. § 253 et seq.Saratoga Development Corp. v. U.S., 21 F.3d 445, 305, 39 Cont. Cas. Fed. (CCH) P 76649 (D.C. Cir. 1994). United States ☞64.5; United States ☞64.40(1)

Term "procurement," as used in competition in Contracting Act (CICA), means payment of money or conferral of other benefits to obtain goods or services. Federal Property and

Administrative Services Act of 1949, § 302(a), 41 U.S.C.A. § 252(a). Health Systems Architects, Inc. v. Shalala, 992 F. Supp. 804 (D. Md. 1998). United States ☞64.10

Health Care Financing Administration (HCFA) did not procure any goods or services, so as to become subject to competition in Contracting Act (CICA), when it directed subcontractors providing accounting services for Medicare to standardize on single software system; HCFA was using previously granted license rights to use software, rather than seeking to acquire anything new. Federal Property and Administrative Services Act of 1949, § 302(a), 41 U.S.C.A. § 252(a). Health Systems Architects, Inc. v. Shalala, 992 F. Supp. 804 (D. Md. 1998). United States ☞64.10

Air Force's Electronics Security Command was not prohibited by Competition in Contracting Act, in procuring automated data processing equipment, from changing from full and open competition procurement under that Act to procurement from another agency through existing contract under the Economy Act. 10 U.S.C.A. § 2304(a)(1), (c); National Gateway Telecom, Inc. v. Aldridge, 701 F. Supp. 1104 (D.N.J. 1988), judgment aff'd, 879 F.2d 858 (3d Cir. 1989). United States ☞64.10

Government was under no obligation to solicit incumbent contractor on a delivery order from a Federal Supply Services (FSS) schedule contract, as sealed bidding regulation is not applicable to placement of a delivery order from an FSS schedule. 48 C.F.R. §§ 8.401(a, b), 14.205-4(b). Cybertech Group, Inc. v. U.S., 48 Fed. Cl. 638 (2001). United States ☞64.10

2 Construction and application

Procurement regulations providing authority for award of contracts where there is other than full and open competition do not affect determination of whether CDA is applicable to particular contract. Contract Disputes Act of 1978, § 2 et seq., 41 U.S.C.A. § 601 et seq.; 48 C.F.R. § 6.300. Oroville-Tonasket Irr. Dist. v. U.S., 33 Fed. Cl. 14, 40 Cont. Cas. Fed. (CCH) P 76746 (1995). United States ☞73(9)

3 Federal preemption

References to rates or prices "fixed by law or regulations" in 1962 procurement statute are merely minor collateral accommodations to those situations where, within limits of federal procurement regulations and the statute, the federal procurement official decides that the practical way to obtain the supplies needed is by following state price-fixing or ratefixing system, and statute does not show a congressional purpose to abandon competitive bidding or show a desire to make the federal procurement policy bow to state pricefixing in the face of contrary policy expressed in the Procurement Regulation. 10 U.S.C.A. §§ 2304(g), 2305(a, c), 2306(f). Paul v. U.S., 371 U.S. 245, 83 S. Ct. 426, 9 L. Ed. 2d 292 (1963). States ☞18.89; United States ☞64.10

Government procurement statutes and regulations designed to ensure active competition so that the United States receives the most advantageous contract did not defer to South Dakota Utilities Franchise Law and did not prevent federal enclave from procuring electric services by means of competitive bidding. Competition in Contracting Act of 1984, § 2701 et seq., 98 Stat. 1175; SDCL 49-34A-44. Black Hills Power and Light Co. v. Weinberger, 808 F.2d 665, 33 Cont. Cas. Fed. (CCH) P 74929 (8th Cir. 1987). United States ☞3

Federal statute requiring United States Army to privatize gas and electric utility systems at its military installations through competitive bidding process preempted any contrary state public utility laws precluding competition. 10 U.S.C.A. § 2688. Baltimore Gas and Elec. Co. v. U.S., 133 F. Supp. 2d 721 (D. Md. 2001). States ☞18.93; United States ☞64.10

4 Out-of-scope modifications

Addition of traditional travel services to contract to provide military travel services using a paperless automated travel management system to be known as the common user interface (CUI) was a cardinal change, and failure of contracting agency to issue a competitive solicitation for traditional travel services added by the modification violated the Competition in Contracting Act (CICA); potential contractor bidding on the original contract would not have anticipated that it could also be called upon under the changes clause to provide traditional travel services, as reflected in fact that no provider of traditional travel services bid on the original contract. Federal Property and Administrative Services Act of 1949, § 303(a), 41 U.S.C.A. § 253(a). CW Government Travel, Inc. v. U.S., 61 Fed. Cl. 559

(2004), opinion corrected, 2004 WL 2358246 (Ct. Fed. Cl. 2004) and opinion clarified on denial of reconsideration, 63 Fed. Cl. 459 (2005), aff'd, 163 Fed. Appx. 853 (Fed. Cir. 2005) and aff'd, 163 Fed. Appx. 853 (Fed. Cir. 2005). United States ☞64.10; United States ☞73(17)

Modifying a government contract after its award so that it materially departs from the scope of the original procurement violates the Competition in Contracting Act (CICA) by preventing potential bidders from participating or competing for what should be a new procurement. Federal Property and Administrative Services Act of 1949, § 303(a)(1)(A), 41 U.S.C.A. § 253(a)(1)(A). CESC Plaza Ltd. Partnership v. U.S., 52 Fed. Cl. 91 (2002). United States ☞64.10; United States ☞72(1.1)

If the government procures services through competition, but then changes the contract work being performed by the contract awardee, such changes may effectively circumvent the competition requirements of the Competition in Contracting Act (CICA). 10 U.S.C.A. § 2304(a)(1)(A). Northrop Grumman Corp. v. U.S., 50 Fed. Cl. 443 (2001). United States ☞64.10

In determining whether a contract modification represents a new procurement requiring use of competitive procedures under the Competition in Contracting Act (CICA), it is relevant to inquire into whether potential bidders at the time of the original contract would have been on notice that the later modification was within the reasonable scope of the solicited material or services. Federal Property and Administrative Services Act of 1949, § 303(a)(1)(A), 41 U.S.C.A. § 253(a)(1)(A). VMC Behavioral Healthcare Services, Div. of Vasquez Group, Inc. v. U.S., 50 Fed. Cl. 328 (2001). United States ☞64.10

Modification of government contract for employee assistance program (EAP) services to include EAP services for approximately 850,000 Postal Service employees was not beyond scope of original contract, so as to constitute a new procurement without competition in violation of the Competition in Contracting Act (CICA), where original solicitation contained statement that services to Postal Service might be added to the contract in the future. Federal Property and Administrative Services Act of 1949, § 303(a)(1)(A), 41 U.S.C.A. § 253(a)(1)(A). VMC Behavioral Healthcare Services, Div. of Vasquez Group, Inc. v. U.S., 50 Fed. Cl. 328 (2001). United States ☞64.10

Statutory requirement for full and open competition in the Competition in Contracting Act (CICA) cannot be circumvented through the use of contract modifications. Federal Property and Administrative Services Act of 1949, § 303(a)(1)(A), 41 U.S.C.A. § 253(a)(1)(A). VMC Behavioral Healthcare Services, Div. of Vasquez Group, Inc. v. U.S., 50 Fed. Cl. 328 (2001). United States ☞64.10

Armed Services Procurement Act (ASPA) does not require a new bid procedure for every change made to an existing contract; rather, only modifications outside the scope of the original competed contract fall under the statutory competition requirement. 10 U.S.C.A. § 2304. Phoenix Air Group, Inc. v. U.S., 46 Fed. Cl. 90 (2000), dismissed, 243 F.3d 555 (Fed. Cir. 2000). United States ☞64.10

Competition in Contracting Act (CICA) competitive procedures requirement cannot be avoided by using device of contract modification. 10 U.S.C.A. § 2304(a)(1)(A). CCL, Inc. v. U.S., 39 Fed. Cl. 780, 42 Cont. Cas. Fed. (CCH) P 77237 (1997). United States ☞64.10

Under Competition in Contracting Act (CICA), contract modifications may not materially depart from scope of original procurement; otherwise, modification prevents complaining party, and other potential bidders, from competing for what is, in reality, a new and different contract. 10 U.S.C.A. § 2304(a)(1)(A). CCL, Inc. v. U.S., 39 Fed. Cl. 780, 42 Cont. Cas. Fed. (CCH) P 77237 (1997). United States ☞64.10; United States ☞72(1.1)

Whether given modification is within scope of original government contract is determined by comparing modified contract with scope of competition conducted to achieve original contract, with overall inquiry being whether modification is of nature which potential offerors would reasonably have anticipated; inquiry is primarily objective one viewed from perspective of potential bidders for first procurement. 10 U.S.C.A. § 2304(a)(1)(A). CCL, Inc. v. U.S., 39 Fed. Cl. 780, 42 Cont. Cas. Fed. (CCH) P 77237 (1997). United States ☞64.10

Contract modification exceeded scope of government's original contract with contractor for installation and maintenance of computers, and thus government violated Competition in Contracting Act (CICA) by procuring goods and services without competition or findings excusing competition, where number of sites at which work could be performed was increased from six to sixteen, and number of "client" entities was increased from single agency within Air Force to several agencies within Department of Defense across all service boundaries. 10 U.S.C.A. § 2304(a)(1)(A). CCL, Inc. v. U.S., 39 Fed. Cl. 780, 42 Cont. Cas. Fed. (CCH) P 77237 (1997). United States ⊕64.10

Protest alleging that agency issued an improper, out-of-scope, sole-source modification to a previously-awarded Federal Supply Schedule delivery order was sustained where the original contract was for basic IT technical support and various Microsoft™ products and the modification added cloud-based support and another software product that was not included in the original acquisition. GAO recommended that the agency either fulfill its requirement through full and open competition or justify use of an exception to competition. Onix Networking Corp., B-411841, 2015 CPD ¶ 330 (Comp. Gen. 2015)

5 In-scope modifications

Government did not violate the Armed Services Procurement Act (ASPA) by its sole-source acquisition of training flight services in Hawaii and the Far East pursuant to existing contract without any competition, as the procurements were within scope of the contract, which covered training flight services for the Navy across the globe. 10 U.S.C.A. § 2304. Phoenix Air Group, Inc. v. U.S., 46 Fed. Cl. 90 (2000), dismissed, 243 F.3d 555 (Fed. Cir. 2000). United States ⊕64.10

6 Commercial items

Pursuant to the Competition in Contracting Act, government is required to specify its needs and solicit proposals "in a manner designed to achieve full and open competition for the procurement," and fact that the procurement is a commercial item acquisition does not relieve government of such obligation. 10 U.S.C.A. § 2305(a)(1)(A)(i). Candle Corp. v. U.S., 40 Fed. Cl. 658, 42 Cont. Cas. Fed. (CCH) P 77276 (1998). United States ⊕64.10

7 Indefinite delivery/indefinite quantity (ID/IQ) contracts

Bid protestor did not establish that agency's focus on experience with dredge disposal area maintenance in the context of an indefinite delivery/indefinite quantity (ID/IQ) contract effectively converted the contract into an illegal sole source contract because incumbent contractor was the only qualified small-business contractor in the Small Business Administration geographic region that had experience with dredge disposal area maintenance; actual results of competition in which five eligible offerors submitted proposals that were found to be within the competitive range belied any notion that the solicitation was a disguised sole source procurement. Gulf Group, Inc. v. U.S., 56 Fed. Cl. 391 (2003). United States ⊕64.10

8 Statutory exemptions

Randolph-Sheppard Act, which authorized Secretary of Department of Education to secure operation of cafeterias on federal property by blind licensees, by contract or otherwise, was procurement statute under Competition in Contracting Act (CICA), and thus came within exception from CICA's open competition requirements for federal procurements. 10 U.S.C.A. § 2302(3)(A); Randolph-Sheppard Vending Stand Act, § 7(d), as amended, 20 U.S.C.A. § 107d-3(d); 48 C.F.R. § 6.302-5(b). NISH v. Cohen, 247 F.3d 197 (4th Cir. 2001). United States ⊕57

Subcontracts under Small Business Administration's program for awarding government procurement contracts to small business concerns owned by "socially or economically disadvantaged persons" may be awarded on a noncompetitive basis. Small Business Act, § 2[8](a), 15 U.S.C.A. § 637(a). Ray Baillie Trash Hauling, Inc. v. Kleppe, 477 F.2d 696 (5th Cir. 1973). United States ⊕64.10

While CICA governs the manner in which most procurements are conducted, it exempts those covered by "procurement procedures that are otherwise expressly authorized by statute." 41 U.S.C. § 253(a)(1). The National Park Service (NPS) Concessions Management Improvement Act of 1998, 16 U.S.C. § 5951 et seq. (2000) establishes such procedures for the award of NPS concession contracts. Where CICA and the implementing FAR do not apply, GAO will review the record to determine if the agency's actions were reasonable and consistent with any statutes and regulations that do apply. Great South Bay Marina, Inc.,

B-293649, 2004 CPD ¶ 108 (Comp. Gen. 2004).

Under the Federal Acquisition Streamlining Act of 1994 (FASA), procurements conducted using simplified acquisition procedures-used to purchase supplies and services, including construction, research and development, and commercial items, the aggregate amount of which does not exceed $100,000—are excepted from the general requirement that agencies obtain full and open competition through the use of competitive procedures when conducting procurements. 10 U.S.C. §§ 2304(a)(1)(A), (g)(1), (g)(3) (1994 & Supp. IV 1998). FASA requires only that agencies obtain competition to the maximum extent practicable when they utilize simplified acquisition procedures. 10 U.S.C. § 2304(g)(3); FAR § 13.104. This standard is usually met if an agency solicits at least three sources. GMA Cover Corporation, B-288018, 2001 CPD ¶ 144 (Comp. Gen. 2001)

9 Grants and cooperative agreements

Competitive bidding requirements of CICA did not apply to Fish and Wildlife Service's cooperative agreements that were authorized by regulation Service enacted pursuant to statute authorizing Service to provide assistance to, and cooperate with, Federal, State, and public or private agencies and organizations, in fulfilling its goals; no provision in CICA's text indicated that Congress meant to replace the cooperative agreement provisions of the earlier legislations. Hymas v. U.S., 2016 WL 158470 (Fed. Cir. 2016)

Cooperative agreements under the Federal Grant And Cooperative Agreement Act, 31 USCA §§ 6301–6308 (FGCAA) are not procurement contracts and are not, therefore, subject to the Competition In Contracting Act. CMS Contract Management Services v. United States, 110 Fed.Cl. 537 (Fed.Cl., 2013)

§ 6.002 Limitations.

No agency shall contract for supplies or services from another agency for the purpose of avoiding the requirements of this part.

United States Code Annotated

Advocates for competition, see 41 U.S.C.A. § 418.

Competition requirements, see 41 U.S.C.A. § 253.

Contract goal for small disadvantaged businesses and certain institutions of higher education, see 10 U.S.C.A. § 2323.

Contracts, competition requirements, see 10 U.S.C.A. § 2304.

Contracts, planning, solicitation, evaluation, and award procedures, see 10 U.S.C.A. § 2305.

Contracts, prohibition on competition between Department of Defense and small businesses and certain other entities, see 10 U.S.C.A. § 2304e.

Credit for Indian contracting in meeting certain subcontracting goals for small disadvantaged businesses and certain institutions of higher education, see 10 U.S.C.A. § 2323a.

Definitions, see 10 U.S.C.A. § 2302; 41 U.S.C.A. §§ 259, 403.

Design-build selection procedures, see 10 U.S.C.A. § 2305a; 41 U.S.C.A. § 253m.

Encouragement of new competition, see 41 U.S.C.A. § 253c.

Encouragement of new competitors, see 10 U.S.C.A. § 2319.

Planning and solicitation requirements, see 41 U.S.C.A. § 253a.

Procurement notice, see 41 U.S.C.A. § 416.

§ 6.003 [Reserved]

Subpart 6.1 Full and Open Competition

§ 6.100 Scope of subpart.

This subpart prescribes the policy and procedures that are to be used to promote and provide for full and open competition.

United States Code Annotated

Advocates for competition, see 41 U.S.C.A. § 418.

Competition requirements, see 41 U.S.C.A. § 253.

Contract goal for small disadvantaged businesses and certain institutions of higher education, see 10 U.S.C.A. § 2323.

Contracts, competition requirements, see 10 U.S.C.A. § 2304.

Contracts, planning, solicitation, evaluation, and award procedures, see 10 U.S.C.A. § 2305.

Contracts, prohibition on competition between Department of Defense and small businesses and certain other entities, see 10 U.S.C.A. § 2304e.

Credit for Indian contracting in meeting certain subcontracting goals for small disadvantaged businesses and certain institutions of higher education, see 10 U.S.C.A. § 2323a.

Definitions, see 10 U.S.C.A. § 2302; 41 U.S.C.A. §§ 259, 403.

Design-build selection procedures, see 10 U.S.C.A. § 2305a; 41 U.S.C.A. § 253m.

Encouragement of new competition, see 41 U.S.C.A. § 253c.

Encouragement of new competitors, see 10 U.S.C.A. § 2319.

Planning and solicitation requirements, see 41 U.S.C.A. § 253a.

Procurement notice, see 41 U.S.C.A. § 416.

§ 6.101 Policy.

(a) 10 U.S.C. 2304 and 41 U.S.C. 3301 require, with certain limited exceptions (see Subpart 6.2 and 6.3), that contracting officers shall promote and provide for full and open competition in soliciting offers and awarding Government contracts.

(b) Contracting officers shall provide for full and open competition through use of the competitive procedure(s) contained in this subpart that are best suited to the circumstances of the contract action and consistent with the need to fulfill the Government's requirements efficiently (10 U.S.C. 2304 and 41 U.S.C. 3301).

United States Code Annotated

Advocates for competition, see 41 U.S.C.A. § 418.

Competition requirements, see 41 U.S.C.A. § 253.

Contract goal for small disadvantaged businesses and certain institutions of higher education, see 10 U.S.C.A. § 2323.

Contracts, competition requirements, see 10 U.S.C.A. § 2304.

Contracts, planning, solicitation, evaluation, and award procedures, see 10 U.S.C.A. § 2305.

Contracts, prohibition on competition between Department of Defense and small businesses and certain other entities, see 10 U.S.C.A. § 2304e.

Credit for Indian contracting in meeting certain subcontracting goals for small disadvantaged businesses and certain institutions of higher education, see 10 U.S.C.A. § 2323a.

Definitions, see 10 U.S.C.A. § 2302; 41 U.S.C.A. §§ 259, 403.

Design-build selection procedures, see 10 U.S.C.A. § 2305a; 41 U.S.C.A. § 253m.

Encouragement of new competition, see 41 U.S.C.A. § 253c.

Encouragement of new competitors, see 10 U.S.C.A. § 2319.

Planning and solicitation requirements, see 41 U.S.C.A. § 253a.

Procurement notice, see 41 U.S.C.A. § 416.

Notes of Decisions

Discretion of administrative agency 2
Full and open competition 3
Judicial review 5
Purpose 1
Solicitation 4

1 Purpose

Purpose of the Competition in Contracting Act (CICA) is to save money, curb cost growth, promote innovation and the development of high quality technology, and maintain the integrity of the expenditure of public funds. American Federation of Government Employees v. Rumsfeld, 262 F.3d 649 (7th Cir. 2001). United States ☞64.10

In enacting Competition in Contracting Act (CICA), Congress intended to promote competition in government's procurement of goods and services. 31 U.S.C.A. §§ 3551–3556, 3554(c). U.S. v. Instruments, S.A., Inc., 807 F. Supp. 811, 38 Cont. Cas. Fed. (CCH) P 76466 (D.D.C. 1992). United States ☞64.10

2 Discretion of administrative agency

Whether a federal procurement officer negotiates contracts for milk at military installations or uses competitive bidding is dependent on his informed discretion and not on state price-fixing policy and if he negotiates, federal Procurement Regulation requires price quotations from all such qualified sources of supplies as are deemed necessary to assure full and free competition. 10 U.S.C.A. §§ 2304(a, f, g), 2305(a, c), 2306(f). Paul v. U.S., 371 U.S. 245, 83 S. Ct. 426, 9 L. Ed. 2d 292 (1963). United States ☞64.10

Failure of agency to make determination that government contract should be negotiated, rather than made the subject of two-step formal advertising, constitutes an action committed to agency discretion by law, within the Administrative Procedure Act. 5 U.S.C.A. § 701(a) (2); 10 U.S.C.A. § 2304(a) (14). Wheelabrator Corp. v. Chafee, 455 F.2d 1306, 147 (D.C. Cir. 1971). Administrative Law And Procedure ☞756; United States ☞64.10

No abuse of discretion was shown in initiating two-step formal advertising procedure with respect to procurement of portable ship hull cleaning device for Navy, rather than negotiating contract with company which had allegedly developed new and unique device and acquired body of technology, special equipment and tooling, in absence of showing that formal advertising would be likely to result either in additional cost to the government by reason of duplication of investment or in duplication of necessary preparation which would unduly delay the procurement. Wheelabrator Corp. v. Chafee, 455 F.2d 1306, 147 (D.C. Cir. 1971). United States ☞64.10

Pursuant to section of Armed Services Procurement Act which requires Department of the Navy to solicit proposals from the maximum number of qualified sources, matters of technical expertise and certain evaluative judgments may lie within Navy's discretion, and the duty to pursue competition is not absolute; however, the obligation to consider and pursue competition in good faith is mandatory and cannot be avoided as a matter of discretion. 10 U.S.C.A. § 2304(g). Aero Corp. v. Department of the Navy, 558 F. Supp. 404 (D.D.C. 1983). United States ☞64.10

Secretary of Navy's decision to use competitive procedure for awarding procurement contract, in accordance with statute requiring use of competitive bid process to award contracts, despite alleged presence of three of seven exceptions prescribed in statute that allow use of noncompetitive procedure, was not abuse of discretion, in light of determination by Navy that circumstances had changed since original award of contract, subsequent variants in system ordered, determination that awarding contract on competitive basis would lead to financial savings, and fact that original contractor was given opportunity to present its views. 10 U.S.C.A. § 2304. Westinghouse Elec. Corp. v. U.S. Dept. of Navy, 894 F. Supp. 204, 40 Cont. Cas. Fed. (CCH) P 76848 (W.D. Pa. 1995). United States ☞64.10

Statute allowing agency to withdraw procurement contract from competitive bid process, and instead use noncompetitive procedure, when one of prescribed exceptions applied was discretionary, and did not require agency to forego competitive bid process when exception was present. 10 U.S.C.A. § 2304(c). Westinghouse Elec. Corp. v. U.S. Dept. of Navy, 894 F. Supp. 204, 40 Cont. Cas. Fed. (CCH) P 76848 (W.D. Pa. 1995). United States ☞64.10

In determining whether there are genuine issues of fact regarding allegation that government has violated legal duty to provide full and open competition while soliciting bids and awarding contracts, court should not substitute its judgment for that of procuring agency and should intervene only when it is clear that agency's determinations were irrational or unreasonable. 10 U.S.C.A. § 2304(a)(1)(A); 41 U.S.C.A. § 253(a)(1)(A); 48 C.F.R. § 6.101(b). Mike Hooks, Inc. v. U.S., 39 Fed. Cl. 147, 42 Cont. Cas. Fed. (CCH) P 77191 (1997). United States ☞64.60(4)

Procurement by negotiation contemplates the exercise of greater discretion overall by a contracting officer than does procurement by formal advertising. DeMat Air, Inc. v. U.S., 2 Cl. Ct. 197, 30 Cont. Cas. Fed. (CCH) P 70980 (1983). United States ☞64.10

3 Full and open competition

In enacting section of the Continuing Appropriations Act prohibiting use of appropriated funds to procure electricity in a manner inconsistent with state law, Congress did not intend to amend extensive body of federal procurement law which establishes that federal agencies must use full and open competitive procedures in procurement of their property and services. Act Dec. 22, 1987, § 8093, 101 Stat. 1329; West River Elec. Ass'n, Inc. v. Black Hills Power and Light Co., 918 F.2d 713, 118 Pub. Util. Rep. 4th (PUR) 510 (8th Cir. 1990). United States ☞64.10

Federal Acquisition Streamlining Act (FASA) permitted Department of Labor (DOL) to enter into indefinite delivery contract with retailer for purchase of single manufacturer's software products without conducting full and open competition among manufacturers pursuant to Competition in Contracting Act (CICA), as long as DOL previously conducted full and open competition among retailers. Federal Property and Administrative Services Act of 1949, §§ 303, 303J, as amended, Corel Corp. v. U.S., 165 F. Supp. 2d 12 (D.D.C. 2001). United States ☞64.10

Air Force's Electronics Security Command was not prohibited by Competition in Contracting Act, in procuring automated data processing equipment, from changing from full and open competition procurement under that Act to procurement from another agency through existing contract under the Economy Act. 10 U.S.C.A. § 2304(a)(1), (c); 31 U.S.C.A. § 1535. National Gateway Telecom, Inc. v. Aldridge, 701 F. Supp. 1104 (D.N.J. 1988), judgment aff'd, 879 F.2d 858 (3d Cir. 1989). United States ☞64.10

Statutory exception from competitive bidding procedures for personal service contracts confers no right upon those seeking government contracts to demand that competitive bidding not be used. 41 U.S.C.A. § 5(4). Goldhaber v. Foley, 519 F. Supp. 466 (E.D. Pa. 1981). United States ☞64.10

Pursuant to the Competition in Contracting Act, government is required to specify its needs and solicit proposals "in a manner designed to achieve full and open competition for the procurement," and fact that the procurement is a commercial item acquisition does not relieve government of such obligation. 10 U.S.C.A. § 2305(a)(1)(A)(i). Candle Corp. v. U.S., 40 Fed. Cl. 658, 42 Cont. Cas. Fed. (CCH) P 77276 (1998). United States ☞64.10

4 Solicitation

Statute providing that in all negotiated procurements in excess of $2,500 in which rates or prices are not fixed by law or regulation proposals shall be solicited from maximum number of qualified sources and discussions shall be conducted with responsible offerors who submitted proposals does not require federal procurement to follow state rate-fixing and state price-fixing contrary to federal regulation providing for competitive bidding. 10 U.S.C.A. § 2304(g). Paul v. U.S., 371 U.S. 245, 83 S. Ct. 426, 9 L. Ed. 2d 292 (1963). United States ☞64.10

Absence of incumbent contractor from bidding process for paper towels significantly diminished level of competition for paper towel contract and no level of competition could cure such clearly prejudicial violation of General Services Administration's procurement regulations, so that General Services Administration's initial decision to resolicit only 14 of 33 items was not in accordance with Competition in Contracting Act. Federal Property and Administrative Services Act of 1949, § 301 et seq., as amended, 41 U.S.C.A. § 251 et seq.Abel Converting, Inc. v. U.S., 679 F. Supp. 1133, 34 Cont. Cas. Fed. (CCH) P 75449 (D.D.C. 1988). United States ☞64.10

In reviewing Army's solicitation, court is limited to determining whether agency acted in accord with applicable statutes and regulations and had rational basis for its decisions. New York Telephone Co. v. Secretary of Army, 657 F. Supp. 18 (D.D.C. 1986). United States ☞64.60(4)

Plaintiff has standing to challenge army's allegedly anticompetitive solicitation plan if it establishes that it has suffered injury in fact; that injury is one arguably within zone of interests protected by applicable statutes and regulations; and that statutes in question do not reflect clear and convincing intent to preclude review. New York Telephone Co. v. Secretary of Army, 657 F. Supp. 18 (D.D.C. 1986). United States ☞64.60(2)

Even a determination that a firm is possessed of superior performance potential and is likely to perform procurement contract at lowest cost to government does not spare procurement officer from presumption favoring solicitation and evaluation of proposals from other competent firms. Aero Corp. v. Department of the Navy, 540 F. Supp. 180, 29 Cont. Cas. Fed. (CCH) P 82290 (D.D.C. 1982). United States ☞64.10

Section of the Resource Conservation and Recovery Act (RCRA) requiring that all federal agencies engaged in disposal of solid waste comply with state requirements and Washington statute requiring that a solid waste collection company obtain a certificate of public convenience and necessity from the Washington Utilities and Transportation Commission (WUTC) do not mandate that a federal agency must solicit bids only from or award a contract exclusively to a solid waste disposal contractor with a WUTC certification; moreover, such a requirement would violate the Competition in Contracting Act (CICA). 10 U.S.C.A. § 2305(b)(3); Solid Waste Disposal Act, § 6001(a), as amended, 42 U.S.C.A. § 6961(a); Blue Dot Energy Co., Inc. v. U.S., 61 Fed. Cl. 548 (2004). United States ☞64.10

Government was under no obligation to solicit incumbent contractor on a delivery order from a Federal Supply Services (FSS) schedule contract, as sealed bidding regulation is not applicable to placement of a delivery order from an FSS schedule. 48 C.F.R. §§ 8.401(a, b), 14.205-4(b). Cybertech Group, Inc. v. U.S., 48 Fed. Cl. 638 (2001). United States ☞64.10

5 Judicial review

In determining whether there are genuine issues of fact regarding allegation that government has violated legal duty to provide full and open competition while soliciting bids and awarding contracts, court should not substitute its judgment for that of procuring agency and should intervene only when it is clear that agency's determinations were irrational or unreasonable. 10 U.S.C.A. § 2304(a)(1)(A); 41 U.S.C.A. § 253(a)(1)(A); 48 C.F.R. § 6.101(b). Mike Hooks, Inc. v. U.S., 39 Fed. Cl. 147, 42 Cont. Cas. Fed. (CCH) P 77191 (1997). United States ☞64.60(4)

§ 6.102 Use of competitive procedures.

The competitive procedures available for use in fulfilling the requirement for full and open competition are as follows:

(a) *Sealed bids*. (See 6.401(a).)

(b) *Competitive proposals*. (See 6.401(b).) If sealed bids are not appropriate under paragraph (a) of this section, contracting officers shall request competitive proposals or use the other competitive procedures under paragraph (c) or (d) of this section.

(c) *Combination of competitive procedures*. If sealed bids are not appropriate, contracting officers may use any combination of competitive procedures (*e.g.*, two-step sealed bidding).

(d) Other competitive procedures.

(1) Selection of sources for architect-engineer contracts in accordance with the provisions of 40 U.S.C. 1102 *et seq.* is a competitive procedure (see Subpart 36.6 for procedures).

(2) Competitive selection of basic and applied research and that part of development not related to the development of a specific system or hardware procurement is a competitive procedure if award results from—

(i) A broad agency announcement that is general in nature identifying areas of research interest, including criteria for selecting proposals, and soliciting the participation of all offerors capable of satisfying the Government's needs; and

(ii) A peer or scientific review.

(3) Use of multiple award schedules issued under the procedures established by the Administrator of General Services consistent with the requirement of 41 U.S.C. 152(3)(A) for the multiple award schedule program of the General Services Administration is a competitive procedure.

United States Code Annotated

Advocates for competition, see 41 U.S.C.A. § 418.

Competition requirements, see 41 U.S.C.A. § 253.

Contract goal for small disadvantaged businesses and certain institutions of higher

education, see 10 U.S.C.A. § 2323.

Contracts, competition requirements, see 10 U.S.C.A. § 2304.

Contracts, planning, solicitation, evaluation, and award procedures, see 10 U.S.C.A. § 2305.

Contracts, prohibition on competition between Department of Defense and small businesses and certain other entities, see 10 U.S.C.A. § 2304e.

Credit for Indian contracting in meeting certain subcontracting goals for small disadvantaged businesses and certain institutions of higher education, see 10 U.S.C.A. § 2323a.

Definitions, see 10 U.S.C.A. § 2302; 41 U.S.C.A. §§ 259, 403.

Design-build selection procedures, see 10 U.S.C.A. § 2305a; 41 U.S.C.A. § 253m.

Encouragement of new competition, see 41 U.S.C.A. § 253c.

Encouragement of new competitors, see 10 U.S.C.A. § 2319.

Planning and solicitation requirements, see 41 U.S.C.A. § 253a.

Procurement notice, see 41 U.S.C.A. § 416.

Notes of Decisions

In general 1
Armed forces contracts 15
Basic and applied research 12
Broad agency announcements 21
Capability of performing work 13
Choosing sealed bidding or negotiated procedures 11
Commercial items 8
Construction and application 3
Construction with other laws 4
Cost or pricing data 14
Discretion of administrative agency 5
Federal preemption 6
Full and open competition 9
GSA Federal Supply Schedule 22
Judiciary contracts 17
Parties 20
Procurement or acquisitions, generally 7
Purpose 2
Security clearances 23
Small business contracts 18
Solicitation, generally 10
Telecommunications 19
Veterans Administration contracts 16

1 In general

Competitive bidding is the cornerstone of federal procurement policy. 10 U.S.C.A. § 2304(a) (9, 10). U.S. v. Warne, 190 F. Supp. 645 (N.D. Cal. 1960), judgment aff'd in part, vacated in part, 371 U.S. 245, 83 S. Ct. 426, 9 L. Ed. 2d 292 (1963). United States ☞64.10

There is no constitutional or statutory requirement that the federal government offer all of its business through competitive bidding. Jets Services, Inc. v. Hoffman, 420 F. Supp. 1300 (M.D. Fla. 1976). United States ☞64.10

2 Purpose

Under statutes governing procurement and providing for competitive bidding, purpose of section providing that head of agency may negotiate such purchase or contract if it is for property or services for which it is impracticable to obtain competition was to place the maximum responsibility for decisions as to when it is impracticable to secure competition in hands of the agency concerned. 10 U.S.C.A. §§ 2301–2314, 2304(a) (10, 12). Public Utilities Commission of State of Cal. v. U.S., 355 U.S. 534, 78 S. Ct. 446, 2 L. Ed. 2d 470, 23 Pub. Util. Rep. 3d (PUR) 55 (1958). United States ⊕64.10

Purpose of the Competition in Contracting Act (CICA) is to save money, curb cost growth, promote innovation and the development of high quality technology, and maintain the integrity of the expenditure of public funds. 10 U.S.C.A. § 2304. American Federation of Government Employees v. Rumsfeld, 262 F.3d 649 (7th Cir. 2001). United States ⊕64.10

In enacting Competition in Contracting Act (CICA), Congress intended to promote competition in government's procurement of goods and services. 31 U.S.C.A. §§ 3551–3556, 3554(c). U.S. v. Instruments, S.A., Inc., 807 F. Supp. 811, 38 Cont. Cas. Fed. (CCH) P 76466 (D.D.C. 1992). United States ⊕64.10

3 Construction and application

Pennsylvania Avenue Development Corporation (PADC) did not follow Competition in Contracts Act (CICA) and Federal Acquisition Regulations (FAR) voluntarily in conducting its development competitions for building of federal office complex under Federal Triangle Development Act, and thus, PADC's process for selecting developer was not governed by FAR and CICA. Federal Triangle Development Act, §§ 2–10, 40 U.S.C.A. §§ 1101–1109; 31 U.S.C.A. § 9101(3)(H); Federal Property and Administrative Services Act of 1949, § 303 et seq., as amended, 41 U.S.C.A. § 253 et seq.Saratoga Development Corp. v. U.S., 21 F.3d 445, 305, 39 Cont. Cas. Fed. (CCH) P 76649 (D.C. Cir. 1994). United States ⊕64.5; United States ⊕64.40(1)

Procurement regulations providing authority for award of contracts where there is other than full and open competition do not affect determination of whether CDA is applicable to particular contract. Contract Disputes Act of 1978, § 2 et seq., 41 U.S.C.A. § 601 et seq.; 48 C.F.R. § 6.300. Oroville-Tonasket Irr. Dist. v. U.S., 33 Fed. Cl. 14, 40 Cont. Cas. Fed. (CCH) P 76746 (1995). United States ⊕73(9)

4 Construction with other laws

Randolph-Sheppard Act, which authorized Secretary of Department of Education to secure operation of cafeterias on federal property by blind licensees, by contract or otherwise, was procurement statute under Competition in Contracting Act (CICA), and thus came within exception from CICA's open competition requirements for federal procurements. 10 U.S.C.A. § 2302(3)(A); Randolph-Sheppard Vending Stand Act, § 7(d), as amended, 20 U.S.C.A. § 107d-3(d); 48 C.F.R. § 6.302-5(b). NISH v. Cohen, 247 F.3d 197 (4th Cir. 2001). United States ⊕57

General Services Administration's (GSA) execution of lease with winning developer to develop federal office complex under Federal Triangle Development Act did not violate federal statute providing that GSA may acquire leasehold interest in any building which is constructed for lease to, and for predominant use by, United States only by use of competitive procedures required by Competition in Contracts Act (CICA); just as Congress overrode Federal Acquisition Regulation (FAR) system and CICA when it enacted legislation entrusting Federal Triangle Development Project to Pennsylvania Avenue Development Corporation (PADC), it obviously overrode aforementioned statute when it directed GSA to enter into lease with whichever developer won PADC's development competition. Public Buildings Act of 1959, § 18(b) as amended, 40 U.S.C.A. § 618(b); Federal Triangle Development Act, §§ 5(a)(3), 6, 40 U.S.C.A. §§ 1104(a)(3), 1105; 31 U.S.C.A. § 9101(3)(H); Federal Property and Administrative Services Act of 1949, § 303 et seq., as amended, 41 U.S.C.A. § 253 et seq.Saratoga Development Corp. v. U.S., 21 F.3d 445, 305, 39 Cont. Cas. Fed. (CCH) P 76649 (D.C. Cir. 1994). United States ⊕64.10

Under Federal Triangle Development Act, Pennsylvania Avenue Development Corporation (PADC), which was in charge of selecting developer for federal office complex, was not governed by Federal Acquisition Regulations (FAR) system nor Competition in Contracting Act (CICA), where Congress stipulated that competition for project must be conducted in accordance with existing policies and procedures of PADC for development competition which referred to only procedures PADC ever characterized as procedures for development competition, i.e., those used for private development initiated by PADC. Federal Triangle Development Act, §§ 2–10, 40 U.S.C.A. §§ 1101–1109; 31 U.S.C.A. § 9101(3)(H); Federal Property and Administrative Services Act of 1949, § 303 et seq., as amended, 41 U.S.C.A. § 253 et seq.Saratoga Development Corp. v. U.S., 21 F.3d 445, 305, 39 Cont. Cas. Fed.

(CCH) P 76649 (D.C. Cir. 1994). United States ☞64.10; United States ☞64.40(1)

5 Discretion of administrative agency

Whether a federal procurement officer negotiates contracts for milk at military installations or uses competitive bidding is dependent on his informed discretion and not on state price-fixing policy and if he negotiates, federal Procurement Regulation requires price quotations from all such qualified sources of supplies as are deemed necessary to assure full and free competition. 10 U.S.C.A. §§ 2304(a, f, g), 2305(a, c), 2306(f). Paul v. U.S., 371 U.S. 245, 83 S. Ct. 426, 9 L. Ed. 2d 292 (1963). United States ☞64.10

Failure of agency to make determination that government contract should be negotiated, rather than made the subject of two-step formal advertising, constitutes an action committed to agency discretion by law, within the Administrative Procedure Act. 5 U.S.C.A. § 701(a) (2); 10 U.S.C.A. § 2304(a) (14). Wheelabrator Corp. v. Chafee, 455 F.2d 1306, 147 (D.C. Cir. 1971). Administrative Law And Procedure ☞756; United States ☞64.10

No abuse of discretion was shown in initiating two-step formal advertising procedure with respect to procurement of portable ship hull cleaning device for Navy, rather than negotiating contract with company which had allegedly developed new and unique device and acquired body of technology, special equipment and tooling, in absence of showing that formal advertising would be likely to result either in additional cost to the government by reason of duplication of investment or in duplication of necessary preparation which would unduly delay the procurement. Wheelabrator Corp. v. Chafee, 455 F.2d 1306, 147 (D.C. Cir. 1971). United States ☞64.10

Pursuant to section of Armed Services Procurement Act which requires Department of the Navy to solicit proposals from the maximum number of qualified sources, matters of technical expertise and certain evaluative judgments may lie within Navy's discretion, and the duty to pursue competition is not absolute; however, the obligation to consider and pursue competition in good faith is mandatory and cannot be avoided as a matter of discretion. 10 U.S.C.A. § 2304(g). Aero Corp. v. Department of the Navy, 558 F. Supp. 404 (D.D.C. 1983). United States ☞64.10

Secretary of Navy's decision to use competitive procedure for awarding procurement contract, in accordance with statute requiring use of competitive bid process to award contracts, despite alleged presence of three of seven exceptions prescribed in statute that allow use of noncompetitive procedure, was not abuse of discretion, in light of determination by Navy that circumstances had changed since original award of contract, subsequent variants in system ordered, determination that awarding contract on competitive basis would lead to financial savings, and fact that original contractor was given opportunity to present its views. 10 U.S.C.A. § 2304. Westinghouse Elec. Corp. v. U.S. Dept. of Navy, 894 F. Supp. 204, 40 Cont. Cas. Fed. (CCH) P 76848 (W.D. Pa. 1995). United States ☞64.10

Statute allowing agency to withdraw procurement contract from competitive bid process, and instead use noncompetitive procedure, when one of prescribed exceptions applied was discretionary, and did not require agency to forego competitive bid process when exception was present. 10 U.S.C.A. § 2304(c). Westinghouse Elec. Corp. v. U.S. Dept. of Navy, 894 F. Supp. 204, 40 Cont. Cas. Fed. (CCH) P 76848 (W.D. Pa. 1995). United States ☞64.10

6 Federal preemption

References to rates or prices "fixed by law or regulations" in 1962 procurement statute are merely minor collateral accommodations to those situations where, within limits of federal procurement regulations and the statute, the federal procurement official decides that the practical way to obtain the supplies needed is by following state price-fixing or ratefixing system, and statute does not show a congressional purpose to abandon competitive bidding or show a desire to make the federal procurement policy bow to state pricefixing in the face of contrary policy expressed in the Procurement Regulation. 10 U.S.C.A. §§ 2304(g), 2305(a, c), 2306(f). Paul v. U.S., 371 U.S. 245, 83 S. Ct. 426, 9 L. Ed. 2d 292 (1963). States ☞18.89; United States ☞64.10

Government procurement statutes and regulations designed to ensure active competition so that the United States receives the most advantageous contract did not defer to South Dakota Utilities Franchise Law and did not prevent federal enclave from procuring electric services by means of competitive bidding. Competition in Contracting Act of 1984, § 2701 et seq., 98 Stat. 1175; SDCL 49-34A-44. Black Hills Power and Light Co. v. Weinberger, 808 F.2d 665, 33 Cont. Cas. Fed. (CCH) P 74929 (8th Cir. 1987). United States ☞3

Federal statute requiring United States Army to privatize gas and electric utility systems at its military installations through competitive bidding process preempted any contrary state public utility laws precluding competition. 10 U.S.C.A. § 2688. Baltimore Gas and Elec. Co. v. U.S., 133 F. Supp. 2d 721 (D. Md. 2001). States ☞18.93; United States ☞64.10

7 Procurement or acquisitions, generally

Even if agreement between hospital and Veterans Affairs Medical Center for acquisition and use of piece of medical equipment was a "procurement" for purposes of the Competition in Contracting Act (CICA), statute authorizing the Veterans Administration to enter into such arrangements was a procurement procedure "expressly authorized by statute" and thus not subject to the full and open competition requirements of CICA. 38 U.S.C.A. §§ 8153, 8153(b); Federal Property and Administrative Services Act of 1949, § 303(a)(1), as amended, 41 U.S.C.A. § 253(a)(1). Rapides Regional Medical Center v. Secretary, Dept. of Veterans' Affairs, 974 F.2d 565, 38 Cont. Cas. Fed. (CCH) P 76445 (5th Cir. 1992). United States ☞64.10

Arrangement whereby private hospital agreed to pay one half of the cost of acquisition by Veterans Affairs Medical Center of a piece of medical equipment, with the equipment to be placed in the private hospital and used by both the VA and the hospital, was not a "procurement" for purposes of the Competition in Contracting Act (CICA). Federal Property and Administrative Services Act of 1949, § 303(a), as amended, 41 U.S.C.A. § 253(a). Rapides Regional Medical Center v. Secretary, Dept. of Veterans' Affairs, 974 F.2d 565, 38 Cont. Cas. Fed. (CCH) P 76445 (5th Cir. 1992). United States ☞64.10

Definition of "procurement" in the Federal Procurement Policy Act which establishes the Office of Federal Procurement Policy within the Office of Management and Budget does not apply to the Competition in Contracting Act (CICA). Office of Federal Procurement Policy Act, § 4, 41 U.S.C.A. § 403; Federal Property and Administrative Services Act of 1949, § 303(a), as amended, 41 U.S.C.A. § 253(a). Rapides Regional Medical Center v. Secretary, Dept. of Veterans' Affairs, 974 F.2d 565, 38 Cont. Cas. Fed. (CCH) P 76445 (5th Cir. 1992). United States ☞64.10

Term "procurement," as used in competition in Contracting Act (CICA), means payment of money or conferral of other benefits to obtain goods or services. Federal Property and Administrative Services Act of 1949, § 302(a), 41 U.S.C.A. § 252(a). Health Systems Architects, Inc. v. Shalala, 992 F. Supp. 804 (D. Md. 1998). United States ☞64.10

Health Care Financing Administration (HCFA) did not procure any goods or services, so as to become subject to competition in Contracting Act (CICA), when it directed subcontractors providing accounting services for Medicare to standardize on single software system; HCFA was using previously granted license rights to use software, rather than seeking to acquire anything new. Federal Property and Administrative Services Act of 1949, § 302(a), 41 U.S.C.A. § 252(a). Health Systems Architects, Inc. v. Shalala, 992 F. Supp. 804 (D. Md. 1998). United States ☞64.10

8 Commercial items

Pursuant to the Competition in Contracting Act, government is required to specify its needs and solicit proposals "in a manner designed to achieve full and open competition for the procurement," and fact that the procurement is a commercial item acquisition does not relieve government of such obligation. 10 U.S.C.A. § 2305(a)(1)(A)(i). Candle Corp. v. U.S., 40 Fed. Cl. 658, 42 Cont. Cas. Fed. (CCH) P 77276 (1998). United States ☞64.10

9 Full and open competition

Federal Acquisition Streamlining Act (FASA) permitted Department of Labor (DOL) to enter into indefinite delivery contract with retailer for purchase of single manufacturer's software products without conducting full and open competition among manufacturers pursuant to Competition in Contracting Act (CICA), as long as DOL previously conducted full and open competition among retailers. Federal Property and Administrative Services Act of 1949, §§ 303, 303J, as amended, 41 U.S.C.A. §§ 253, 253j. Corel Corp. v. U.S., 165 F. Supp. 2d 12 (D.D.C. 2001). United States ☞64.10

Air Force's Electronics Security Command was not prohibited by Competition in Contracting Act, in procuring automated data processing equipment, from changing from full and open competition procurement under that Act to procurement from another agency through existing contract under the Economy Act. 10 U.S.C.A. § 2304(a)(1), (c); 31 U.S.C.A. § 1535. National Gateway Telecom, Inc. v. Aldridge, 701 F. Supp. 1104 (D.N.J. 1988), judgment aff'd, 879 F.2d 858 (3d Cir. 1989). United States ☞64.10

Statutory exception from competitive bidding procedures for personal service contracts confers no right upon those seeking government contracts to demand that competitive bidding not be used. 41 U.S.C.A. § 5(4). Goldhaber v. Foley, 519 F. Supp. 466 (E.D. Pa. 1981). United States ☞64.10

Pursuant to the Competition in Contracting Act, government is required to specify its needs and solicit proposals "in a manner designed to achieve full and open competition for the procurement," and fact that the procurement is a commercial item acquisition does not relieve government of such obligation. 10 U.S.C.A. § 2305(a)(1)(A)(i). Candle Corp. v. U.S., 40 Fed. Cl. 658, 42 Cont. Cas. Fed. (CCH) P 77276 (1998). United States ☞64.10

10 Solicitation, generally

Competition in Contracting Act and procurement regulations imposed upon General Services Administration general obligation to solicit bids for paper towels through most effectively competitive mechanism possible and to take affirmative steps to ensure that potentially responsible bidders, including incumbent, as previously successful bidder, be permitted to submit bids and be on bidder's mailing list. Office of Federal Procurement Policy Act, § 4(7), 41 U.S.C.A. § 403(7). Abel Converting, Inc. v. U.S., 679 F. Supp. 1133, 34 Cont. Cas. Fed. (CCH) P 75449 (D.D.C. 1988). United States ☞64.10

Unless and until a procurement officer makes a rational determination that a single firm is only possible source for every phase of a procurement, section of Armed Services Procurement Act providing for solicitation of proposals from maximum number of qualified sources requires the procurement officer to position himself to compete all feasible contracts within the overall procurement. 10 U.S.C.A. § 2304(g). Aero Corp. v. Department of the Navy, 540 F. Supp. 180, 29 Cont. Cas. Fed. (CCH) P 82290 (D.D.C. 1982). United States ☞64.10

Even a determination that a firm is possessed of superior performance potential and is likely to perform procurement contract at lowest cost to government does not spare procurement officer from presumption favoring solicitation and evaluation of proposals from other competent firms. Aero Corp. v. Department of the Navy, 540 F. Supp. 180, 29 Cont. Cas. Fed. (CCH) P 82290 (D.D.C. 1982). United States ☞64.10

11 Choosing sealed bidding or negotiated procedures

Armed Services Procurement Regulation requires that negotiations or, wherever possible, advertising for bids, shall reflect active competition so that the United States may receive the most advantageous contracts and the Regulation does more than merely authorize procurement officers to negotiate for lower rates. 10 U.S.C.A. §§ 2304(a) (8, 9, 10, 15), 2305(a, c). Paul v. U.S., 371 U.S. 245, 83 S. Ct. 426, 9 L. Ed. 2d 292 (1963). United States ☞64.10

Federal statute providing that commodities purchased for resale may be procured by negotiations rather than by formal advertising was intended to cover purchases for commissaries which are generally not made by specifications but by brand names, and purchases of milk for resale at commissaries did not fit the category of commodities for which the statute was designed, but in any event the exception to formal advertising was permissive and a procurement officer may negotiate for articles to be resold but he is not required to do so and he is free to purchase by formal advertising from responsible bidder whose bid is the most advantageous to the United States. 10 U.S.C.A. §§ 2304(a) (8), 2305(c). Paul v. U.S., 371 U.S. 245, 83 S. Ct. 426, 9 L. Ed. 2d 292 (1963). United States ☞64.10

Bidder on contract for navy portable ship hull cleaner, contending that the contract should have been negotiated with such bidder rather than made subject of two-step formal advertising, failed to establish, by reliance on affidavits based in great part on conjecture or belief, that any of the criteria set forth in the procurement regulations as compelling twostep formal advertising were absent. 10 U.S.C.A. § 2301 et seq.Wheelabrator Corp. v. Chafee, 455 F.2d 1306, 147 (D.C. Cir. 1971). United States ☞64.10

Statute and armed forces procurement regulation authorizing negotiation of contracts rather than formal advertising when the latter would be likely to result in additional cost to the government or would unduly delay the procurement are permissive only. 10 U.S.C.A. § 2304(a) (14). Wheelabrator Corp. v. Chafee, 455 F.2d 1306, 147 (D.C. Cir. 1971). United States ☞64.10

Authorization for Air Force to negotiate individual contract for design and development of transmitter and its "integration into the total [radar] system" permitted Air Force to negotiate individual contract for new, integrated system without engaging in usual process of competitive, advertised process with award to lowest responsible bidder. 10 U.S.C.A. § 2304(a). Whittaker Electronic Systems v. Dalton, 124 F.3d 1443, 41 Cont. Cas. Fed. (CCH) P 77168 (Fed. Cir. 1997). United States ☞64.10

Determination by responsible Navy officials that they should buy and use aircraft of type already in use by Army and Air Force and that formal advertising was impracticable was grounded upon legally sufficient consideration that Navy would be able to have planes serviced at existing worldwide Army and Air Force bases, and thus Navy's failure to advertise formally or otherwise permit competition for contract for purchase of turboprop light utility transport aircraft did not violate Armed Services Procurement Act. 28 U.S.C.A. § 1331; 10 U.S.C.A. §§ 2301 et seq., 2310(b). Cessna Aircraft Co. v. Brown, 452 F. Supp. 1245, 25 Cont. Cas. Fed. (CCH) P 82437 (D.D.C. 1978). United States ☞64.10

It is the general policy of Congress that government contracts, unless specifically excepted, shall be awarded by means of maximum competitive bidding, whether formal advertising or negotiation is used; such policy is binding on the Small Business Administration in making of contract awards to small businesses. Small Business Act, § 2 [8] (a), 15 U.S.C.A. § 637(a). Ray Baillie Trash Hauling, Inc. v. Kleppe, 334 F. Supp. 194 (S.D. Fla. 1971), decision rev'd on other grounds, 477 F.2d 696 (5th Cir. 1973). United States ☞64.10

Circumstances held to show emergency authorizing War Department to purchase, without readvertising for proposals after rejecting unsatisfactory proposals, caskets for reburial of soldiers who died in World War service in France. 41 U.S.C.A. § 5. U.S. v. Heller, 1 F. Supp. 1 (D. Md. 1932). United States ☞64.10

That a public exigency may not be administratively created and used as basis for making awards of government contracts for supplies without advertising for competition, as required by law, does not mean that a public exigency existing may not be recognized and dealt with administratively. 41 U.S.C.A. § 5. Good Roads Machinery Co. of New England v. U.S., 19 F. Supp. 652 (D. Mass. 1937). United States ☞64.10

A "public exigency" demanding immediate delivery of government supplies and obviating statutory necessity of advertising for competitive bids is a sudden and unexpected happening, an unforeseen occurrence or condition, a perplexing contingency or complication of circumstances, or a sudden or unexpected occasion for action. 41 U.S.C.A. § 5. Good Roads Machinery Co. of New England v. U.S., 19 F. Supp. 652 (D. Mass. 1937). United States ☞64.10

Purchases of material and equipment for civil works project by administrator who had authority to make purchases were made under "public exigency" requiring immediate delivery, and hence seller's right to recover purchase price was not barred because of failure to advertise for competitive bids, especially where government had paid for other purchases from same seller. 41 U.S.C.A. § 5. Good Roads Machinery Co. of New England v. U.S., 19 F. Supp. 652 (D. Mass. 1937). United States ☞64.10

Statute requiring that purchases and contracts for supplies in any department of federal government shall be made by due advertising for proposals requires that proposal most advantageous to government be accepted, provided that it is made by responsible person, 41 U.S.C.A. § 5. O'Brien v. Carney, 6 F. Supp. 761 (D. Mass. 1934). United States ☞64.10

Determination by Army to conduct negotiated procurement of rifle sight-post assembly rather than procurement through formal advertising had rational basis, and thus such determination could not be overturned on judicial review, where there was ample reason for procurement officer to believe that at most only a few companies would bid on contract, and it was shown that public interest was likely to best be served through negotiated bidding. Self-Powered Lighting, Ltd. v. U.S., 492 F. Supp. 1267, 27 Cont. Cas. Fed. (CCH) P 80472 (S.D. N.Y. 1980). United States ☞64.10

The procedure of advertising for bids on construction of apartment and of invitation to submit further sealed bid specifying amount each bidder would be willing to deduct by reason of alternate proposal after all original bids had been found to exceed funds available did not substantially depart from the "competitive bidding plan". Contel Const. Corp. v. Parker, 261 F. Supp. 428 (E.D. Pa. 1966). United States ☞64.10

The procurement system is based on premise that the government's needs are best served when "full and free competition" exists among prospective government contractors, and to ensure competition, Congress has provided that property and services should be procured by formal advertising whenever possible. 10 U.S.C.A. §§ 2304(a, g), 2305. Continental Business Enterprises, Inc. v. U. S., 196 Ct. Cl. 627, 452 F.2d 1016 (1971). United States ☞64.10

Statutory provisions requiring the advertising for competitive bids in connection with Government contracts are for the protection of the Government and not those dealing with it. In reletting a contract which had been terminated for default, the Government need not advertise for competitive bids. H & H Mfg. Co. Inc. v. U.S., 168 Ct. Cl. 873, 1964 WL 8568 (1964). United States ☞64.10; United States ☞72.1(6)

Public policy requires governmental needs to be supplied pursuant to contracts with low bidders ascertained by public advertisement. 10 U.S.C.A. § 2301 et seq.; G.S. § 143-129. Douglas Aircraft Co. v. Local Union 379 of Intern. Broth. of Elec. Workers (A. F. of L.), 247 N.C. 620, 101 S.E.2d 800, 41 L.R.R.M. (BNA) 2594, 34 Lab. Cas. (CCH) P 71352 (1958). United States ☞64.10

Public contract with the United States for construction of a dam could only be let to the lowest responsible bidder after advertisement for proposals. Constructors Ass'n of Western Pennsylvania v. Seeds, 142 Pa. Super. 59, 15 A.2d 467 (1940). United States ☞64.10

12 Basic and applied research

Custom Services' use of Broad Agency Announcement (BAA) to secure from one supplier mobile x-ray device for detection of contraband was utilization of noncompetitive method of procurement in violation of Competition in Contracting Act (CICA); specific device was called for, by specifications, rather than basic or applied research covered by BAA. Federal Property and Administrative Services Act of 1949, § 303(a)(1), 41 U.S.C.A. § 253(a)(1); 48 C.F.R. § 6.102(d)(2). American Science and Engineering, Inc. v. Kelly, 69 F. Supp. 2d 227 (D. Mass. 1999). United States ☞64.10

Only when what is procured through a Broad Agency Announcement (BAA) is either basic research, applied research, or development not related to the development of a specific system or hardware procurement will the process be considered competitive. Federal Property and Administrative Services Act of 1949, § 303(a)(1), 41 U.S.C.A. § 253(a)(1); 48 C.F.R. § 6.102(d)(2). American Science and Engineering, Inc. v. Kelly, 69 F. Supp. 2d 227 (D. Mass. 1999). United States ☞64.10

13 Capability of performing work

Public interest in competition is not vindicated until a procurement officer invites and evaluates proposals from firms that are capable of performing the work; if in that process market forces lead a technically-competent firm to make an offer ultimately unfavorable to itself, procurement officer may decide with competing offers before him whether bargain will be so difficult for offeror to keep that government's interest will be jeopardized. Aero Corp. v. Department of the Navy, 540 F. Supp. 180, 29 Cont. Cas. Fed. (CCH) P 82290 (D.D.C. 1982). United States ☞64.10

14 Cost or pricing data

Statute requiring contractors to submit cost or pricing data for any negotiated contract but providing for waiver of such data if prices of some commodities included in contract have been set by law or regulation does not require federal procurement officers to abandon competitive bidding where prices are set by law or regulation. 10 U.S.C.A. § 2306(f). Paul v. U.S., 371 U.S. 245, 83 S. Ct. 426, 9 L. Ed. 2d 292 (1963). United States ☞64.10

15 Armed forces contracts

Award of contract for construction of nuclear-powered submarine to particular shipyard on basis of price alone did not violate competitive acquisition strategy and Appropriations

Act; nothing in language of statutory requirement that Navy consider desirability of competitive acquisition strategy for the entire submarine program required Navy to award contract in such a way that would insure future existence of competing shipyards. Department of Defense Appropriations Act, 1991, 104 Stat. 1856; 10 U.S.C.A. § 2438. Newport News Shipbuilding and Dry Dock Co. v. General Dynamics Corp., 960 F.2d 386, 37 Cont. Cas. Fed. (CCH) P 76285 (4th Cir. 1992). United States ☞64.10

In making its decision whether to provide its own commercial supplies and services or whether to contract with private sector, Army must compare costs and choose the least costly alternative. Diebold v. U.S., 947 F.2d 787, 37 Cont. Cas. Fed. (CCH) P 76208 (6th Cir. 1991), rehearing denied, rehearing denied Diebold v. U.S., 961 F.2d 97 (6th Cir. 1992). United States ☞64.10

Competition in Contracting Act (CICA) lists a number of situations in which the armed forces are not required to follow the procedures for competition set forth in the Act. 10 U.S.C.A. § 2304(c)(1). American Federation of Government Employees v. Rumsfeld, 262 F.3d 649 (7th Cir. 2001). United States ☞64.10

General Services Administration (GSA) was not required to competitively bid drapery order for Army, where order was awarded to contractor pursuant to multiple award schedule for amount no greater than maximum order limitation. 48 C.F.R. § 8.404-1. Commercial Drapery Contractors, Inc. v. U.S., 967 F. Supp. 1, 41 Cont. Cas. Fed. (CCH) P 77172 (D.D.C. 1997), judgment aff'd, 133 F.3d 1, 39 Fed. R. Serv. 3d 825 (D.C. Cir. 1998). United States ☞64.10

Navy correctly refused to provide information to competitor of contractor that provided prototype of cylindrical orthogonal cylindrical arrangement air compressor that was new technology; if Government were forced to divulge every detail of new idea to competitor, then no company would be willing to go to government with novel or innovative concept. 10 U.S.C.A. § 2304(c)(1). Single Screw Compressor, Inc. v. U.S. Dept. of Navy, 791 F. Supp. 7, 38 Cont. Cas. Fed. (CCH) P 76403 (D.D.C. 1992). United States ☞64.10

Business which manufactured and dealt military and commercial spare parts but do not have capability to build entire MK-46 torpedo was not an alternative responsible source entitled to receive technical data on procurement under the Competition in Colonial Trading Corp. v. Department of Navy, 735 F. Supp. 429, 36 Cont. Cas. Fed. (CCH) P 75985 (D.D.C. 1990). United States ☞64.10

Statement in Air Force's undefinitized contract award for electronic monitors, that failure to meet delivery schedule would result in work stoppage by aircraft manufacturer and additional charges, complied with statute which permits use of undefinitized contracts only when request for authorization includes description of "anticipated effect on requirements of the military department concerned if a delay is incurred." Mil-Com Electronics Corp. v. Aldridge, 712 F. Supp. 232, 35 Cont. Cas. Fed. (CCH) P 75658 (D.D.C. 1989). United States ☞64.10

Contracting officer's statements showed that definitized contract for electronic monitors could not have been completed in time to meet required delivery schedule to avoid costly delays, and thus Air Force, in issuing undefinitized contract award, complied with regulation providing that such contracts may be issued only when negotiation of definitive contract action is not possible in sufficient time to meet government's requirements, and government's interests demand that contractor be given "binding commitment" so that contract performance can begin immediately. Mil-Com Electronics Corp. v. Aldridge, 712 F. Supp. 232, 35 Cont. Cas. Fed. (CCH) P 75658 (D.D.C. 1989). United States ☞64.10

Evidence that Air Force allowed use of its spare component parts by manufacturer of electronic monitors did not prove that there was no emergency and that Air Force inappropriately awarded undefinitized contract; rather, fact that Air Force was willing to allow its usual quantity of spare parts to be used to meet deadline showed that Air Force approached procurement as an urgent one. Mil-Com Electronics Corp. v. Aldridge, 712 F. Supp. 232, 35 Cont. Cas. Fed. (CCH) P 75658 (D.D.C. 1989). United States ☞64.10

Air Force could make undefinitized contract award even while request for proposals was outstanding. Mil-Com Electronics Corp. v. Aldridge, 712 F. Supp. 232, 35 Cont. Cas. Fed. (CCH) P 75658 (D.D.C. 1989). United States ☞64.10

Contracting officer's decision that manufacturer was not qualified to produce electronic monitors for Air Force had rational basis and was final, thereby allowing Air Force to make undefinitized contract award to the only remaining offeror which was qualified. Mil-Com Electronics Corp. v. Aldridge, 712 F. Supp. 232, 35 Cont. Cas. Fed. (CCH) P 75658 (D.D.C. 1989). United States ⊸64.10

Although there is an overriding public interest, expressed by statute, to foster competition in procurement to the maximum practical extent, the public is also concerned with expeditious and undisrupted procurement and this is especially true when military procurements are involved. Aero Corp. v. Department of the Navy, 493 F. Supp. 558, 27 Cont. Cas. Fed. (CCH) P 80203 (D.D.C. 1980). United States ⊸64.10

Private award of subcontracts for collection on removal of refuse from air force base by administrator of Small Business Administration, with active assistance of Secretary of the Department of the Air Force, violated statutory requirements obligating them to secure maximum competitive bidding practicable and arbitrarily and capriciously deprived other small businesses, which sought to bid, of benefits extended to them by means of Small Business Act; such contracts were unauthorized by law and illegal. Small Business Act, § 2 [8] (a), 15 U.S.C.A. § 637(a). Ray Baillie Trash Hauling, Inc. v. Kleppe, 334 F. Supp. 194 (S.D. Fla. 1971), decision rev'd, 477 F.2d 696 (5th Cir. 1973). United States ⊸64.10

Although Air Force's sole source procurement to standardize its network security systems violated the Competition in Contracting Act, protester's request for injunctive relief was denied because the Air Force's security needs outweighed the potential harm to protester in that any delay in obtaining and installing firewalls on that network would render network susceptible to complete shutdown or infiltration by hostile forces. McAfee, Inc. v. U.S., 111 Fed.Cl. 696 (Fed. Cl. 2013)

Authority of an agency to purchase products against the Federal Supply Schedule (FSS) does not extend to incidentals and does not exempt use of competitive procedures in procuring incidentals. 10 U.S.C.A. § 2302(2). ATA Defense Industries, Inc. v. U.S., 38 Fed. Cl. 489, 41 Cont. Cas. Fed. (CCH) P 77147 (1997). United States ⊸64.10

16 Veterans Administration contracts

Veterans Administration regulation did not circumvent requirements of Competition in Contracting Act, inasmuch as regulation antedated provision of Act allowing exceptions to Act that are "expressly authorized by statute." Federal Property and Administrative Services Act of 1949, § 303(a), as amended, 41 U.S.C.A. § 253(a). Rapides Regional Medical Center v. Derwinski, 783 F. Supp. 1006 (W.D. La. 1991), decision rev'd on other grounds, 974 F.2d 565, 38 Cont. Cas. Fed. (CCH) P 76445 (5th Cir. 1992). United States ⊸64.10

Veterans Administration's involvement in 1990 Advanced Technology Medical Equipment Shared Acquisition Program was subject to Competition in Contracting Act. 38 U.S.C.A. § 8153; Federal Property and Administrative Services Act of 1949, §§ 301 et seq., 302, as amended, 41 U.S.C.A. §§ 251 et seq., 252. Rapides Regional Medical Center v. Derwinski, 783 F. Supp. 1006 (W.D. La. 1991), decision rev'd on other grounds, 974 F.2d 565, 38 Cont. Cas. Fed. (CCH) P 76445 (5th Cir. 1992). United States ⊸64.10

17 Judiciary contracts

Competition in Contracting Act (CICA) does not apply to the Administrative Office of the United States Courts (AOUSC), as the AOUSC is not an "executive agency" within meaning of the CICA. Federal Property and Administrative Services Act of 1949, § 302(a), 41 U.S.C.A. § 252(a). Novell, Inc. v. U.S., 46 Fed. Cl. 601 (2000). United States ⊸64.10

Procurement chapter of the Guide to Judiciary Policies and Procedures which establishes the procedure for the Administrative Office of the United States Courts (AOUSC) to conduct competitive acquisitions does not have the effect of a regulation binding the AOUSC, as the Guide has not been published for the public and is not available to the general public. Novell, Inc. v. U.S., 46 Fed. Cl. 601 (2000). United States ⊸64.10

18 Small business contracts

There is no constitutional duty to offer government procurement contracts for competitive bidding. Small Business Act, § 2[8](a), 15 U.S.C.A. § 637(a). Ray Baillie Trash Hauling, Inc. v. Kleppe, 477 F.2d 696 (5th Cir. 1973). United States ⊸64.10

Subcontracts under Small Business Administration's program for awarding government procurement contracts to small business concerns owned by "socially or economically disadvantaged persons" may be awarded on a noncompetitive basis. Small Business Act, § 2[8](a), 15 U.S.C.A. § 637(a). Ray Baillie Trash Hauling, Inc. v. Kleppe, 477 F.2d 696 (5th Cir. 1973). United States ☞64.10

General policy of competitive bidding in federal procurement is wholly inapplicable to a contract which the Small Business Administration has specific statutory authority to enter. Small Business Act, § 2 [8] (a), (a)(2), 15 U.S.C.A. § 637(a), (a)(2); 41 U.S.C.A. § 252(c)(10). Fortec Constructors v. Kleppe, 350 F. Supp. 171 (D.D.C. 1972). United States ☞64.10

19 Telecommunications

United States Information Agency (USIA) could produce television news broadcasts for transmission to Cuba in-house, rather than through use of independent contractors procured by contract, without comparing costs of each alternative as required by Economy Act and Office of Management and Budget Circular; TV Marti Act called for "maximum utilization" of agency resources, and its specific requirements controlled over those of Economy Act, a statute having general applicability. Television Broadcasting to Cuba Act, § 244(b), 22 U.S.C.A. § 1465cc(b); 31 U.S.C.A. § 1535(a). Techniarts Engineering v. U.S., 51 F.3d 301, 311, 40 Cont. Cas. Fed. (CCH) P 76774 (D.C. Cir. 1995), rehearing and suggestion for rehearing in banc denied. United States ☞64.10

Postal Service's management instruction for "acquiring pay telephones" addressed leasing of phones per se, and thus did not preempt general competitive bidding requirements of Service's procurement manual when Service sought to contract out management of public pay telephones on its property. AT&T Corp. v. U.S. Postal Service, 57 F. Supp. 2d 522 (N.D. Ill. 1998). United States ☞64.10

Geographic scope of contract for local telecommunications services for federal agencies in an area consisting of the five boroughs of New York City and suburban locations in New York and New Jersey did not violate the Competition in Contracting Act (CICA) on theory that it gave unfair advantage to the incumbent, as the only company with sufficient facilities to service the entire area directly; boundary of the contract area was reasonably drawn, and size of the area did not preclude anyone from competing. Federal Property and Administrative Services Act of 1949, § 303(a)(2), as amended, WinStar Communications, Inc. v. U.S., 41 Fed. Cl. 748, 42 Cont. Cas. Fed. (CCH) P 77371 (1998). United States ☞64.10

20 Parties

Manufacturer of office automation systems was "interested party," for purposes of Tucker Act, and thus had standing to challenge Department of Labor's (DOL) decision to standardize its software applications exclusively to software manufactured by competitor as violative of Competition in Contracting Act (CICA), where DOL refused to engage in competitive procurement for its office automation systems, and manufacturer submitted bid nonetheless. 10 U.S.C.A. § 2304; 28 U.S.C.A. § 1491(b)(1); Federal Property and Administrative Services Act of 1949, § 303, as amended, 41 U.S.C.A. § 253; 48 C.F.R. §§ 16.501-1, 16. 501-2. Corel Corp. v. U.S., 165 F. Supp. 2d 12 (D.D.C. 2001). United States ☞64.60(2)

Contractor established that it was an "interested party" within meaning of provision of the Tucker Act conferring jurisdiction on the Court of Federal Claims over actions claiming violation of a procurement statute or regulation; contractor demonstrated its connection to the procurement it challenged because of its communications with contracting agency, and it had an economic interest based on its allegation that it would have competed for the contract if the agency had not decided to award the contract without competition. 28 U.S.C.A. § 1491(b)(1). Cubic Defense Systems, Inc. v. U.S., 45 Fed. Cl. 239 (1999), dismissed, 230 F.3d 1375 (Fed. Cir. 1999). Federal Courts ☞1110; United States ☞64.60(2)

21 Broad agency announcements

Custom Services' use of Broad Agency Announcement (BAA) to secure from one supplier mobile x-ray device for detection of contraband was utilization of noncompetitive method of procurement in violation of Competition in Contracting Act (CICA); specific device was called for, by specifications, rather than basic or applied research covered by BAA. Federal Property and Administrative Services Act of 1949, § 303(a)(1), 41 U.S.C.A. § 253(a)(1); 48 C.F.R. § 6.102(d)(2). American Science and Engineering, Inc. v. Kelly, 69 F. Supp. 2d 227 (D.

Mass. 1999). United States ☞64.10

22 GSA Federal Supply Schedule

General Services Administration (GSA) was not required to competitively bid drapery order for Army, where order was awarded to contractor pursuant to multiple award schedule for amount no greater than maximum order limitation. 48 C.F.R. § 8.404-1. Commercial Drapery Contractors, Inc. v. U.S., 967 F. Supp. 1, 41 Cont. Cas. Fed. (CCH) P 77172 (D.D.C. 1997), judgment aff'd, 133 F.3d 1, 39 Fed. R. Serv. 3d 825 (D.C. Cir. 1998). United States ☞64.10

Contracting agencies must obtain full and open competition in the procurement of supplies and services. The Federal Supply Schedule provides agencies with a simplified process for obtaining commonly used commercial supplies and services. FAR 8.401(a). The procedures established for the FSS program satisfy the requirement for full and open competition. 41 U.S.C. sect. 259(b)(3); FAR 6.102(d)(3). However, supplies and services not on the FSS may not be purchased using FSS procedures; instead, their purchase requires compliance with the applicable procurement laws and regulations, including those requiring full and open competition, unless some other exception applies. Information Ventures, Inc., B-299422, B-299422.2, 2007 CPD ¶ 88 (Comp. Gen. 2007)

Protest that contracting agency's issuance of a delivery order to a firm pursuant to its General Services Administration (GSA), Federal Supply Schedule contract was improper is sustained where the product to be furnished is outside of the scope of the firm's GSA schedule contract and the agency unreasonably determined that the selected product met the solicitation specifications. Armed Forces Merchandise Outlet, Inc., B-294281, 2004 CPD ¶ 218 (Comp. Gen. 2004)

23 Security clearances

Solicitation requirement that an offeror possess a Top Secret facility clearance at the time final proposal revisions are submitted does not unduly restrict competition where the record shows that the requirement is reasonably related to the agency's needs. CompTech–CDO, LLC, B-409949.2, 2015 CPD ¶ 62 (Comp.Gen. 2015)

Subpart 6.2 Full and Open Competition After Exclusion of Sources

§ 6.200 Scope of subpart.

This subpart prescribes policy and procedures for providing for full and open competition after excluding one or more sources.

United States Code Annotated

Advocates for competition, see 41 U.S.C.A. § 418.

Competition requirements, see 41 U.S.C.A. § 253.

Contract goal for small disadvantaged businesses and certain institutions of higher education, see 10 U.S.C.A. § 2323.

Contracts, competition requirements, see 10 U.S.C.A. § 2304.

Contracts, planning, solicitation, evaluation, and award procedures, see 10 U.S.C.A. § 2305.

Contracts, prohibition on competition between Department of Defense and small businesses and certain other entities, see 10 U.S.C.A. § 2304e.

Credit for Indian contracting in meeting certain subcontracting goals for small disadvantaged businesses and certain institutions of higher education, see 10 U.S.C.A. § 2323a.

Definitions, see 10 U.S.C.A. § 2302; 41 U.S.C.A. §§ 259, 403.

Design-build selection procedures, see 10 U.S.C.A. § 2305a; 41 U.S.C.A. § 253m.

Encouragement of new competition, see 41 U.S.C.A. § 253c.

Encouragement of new competitors, see 10 U.S.C.A. § 2319.

Planning and solicitation requirements, see 41 U.S.C.A. § 253a.

Procurement notice, see 41 U.S.C.A. § 416.

§ 6.201 Policy.

Acquisitions made under this subpart require use of the competitive procedures prescribed in 6.102.

United States Code Annotated

Advocates for competition, see 41 U.S.C.A. § 418.

Contract goal for small disadvantaged businesses and certain institutions of higher education, see 10 U.S.C.A. § 2323.

Contracts, competition requirements, see 10 U.S.C.A. § 2304.

Contracts, planning, solicitation, evaluation, and award procedures, see 10 U.S.C.A. § 2305.

Contracts, prohibition on competition between Department of Defense and small businesses and certain other entities, see 10 U.S.C.A. § 2304e.

Credit for Indian contracting in meeting certain subcontracting goals for small disadvantaged businesses and certain institutions of higher education, see 10 U.S.C.A. § 2323a.

Definitions, see 10 U.S.C.A. § 2302; 41 U.S.C.A. §§ 259, 403.

Design-build selection procedures, see 10 U.S.C.A. § 2305a; 41 U.S.C.A. § 253m.

Encouragement of new competition, see 41 U.S.C.A. § 253c.

Encouragement of new competitors, see 10 U.S.C.A. § 2319.

Planning and solicitation requirements, see 41 U.S.C.A. § 253a.

Procurement notice, see 41 U.S.C.A. § 416.

Notes of Decisions

In general 1
Full and open competition 3
Purpose 2

1 In general

There is no constitutional or statutory requirement that the federal government offer all of its business through competitive bidding. Jets Services, Inc. v. Hoffman, 420 F. Supp. 1300 (M.D. Fla. 1976). United States ☞64.10

2 Purpose

Under statutes governing procurement and providing for competitive bidding, purpose of section providing that head of agency may negotiate such purchase or contract if it is for property or services for which it is impracticable to obtain competition was to place the maximum responsibility for decisions as to when it is impracticable to secure competition in hands of the agency concerned. 10 U.S.C.A. §§ 2301–2314, 2304(a) (10, 12). Public Utilities Commission of State of Cal. v. U.S., 355 U.S. 534, 78 S. Ct. 446, 2 L. Ed. 2d 470, 23 Pub. Util. Rep. 3d (PUR) 55 (1958). United States ☞64.10

Purpose of the Competition in Contracting Act (CICA) is to save money, curb cost growth, promote innovation and the development of high quality technology, and maintain the integrity of the expenditure of public funds. American Federation of Government Employees v. Rumsfeld, 262 F.3d 649 (7th Cir. 2001). United States ☞64.10

Competitive bidding is the cornerstone of federal procurement policy. U.S. v. Warne, 190 F. Supp. 645 (N.D. Cal. 1960), judgment aff'd in part, vacated in part, 371 U.S. 245, 83 S. Ct. 426, 9 L. Ed. 2d 292 (1963). United States ☞64.10

In enacting Competition in Contracting Act (CICA), Congress intended to promote competition in government's procurement of goods and services. U.S. v. Instruments, S.A., Inc., 807 F. Supp. 811, 38 Cont. Cas. Fed. (CCH) P 76466 (D.D.C. 1992). United States ☞64.10

3 Full and open competition

Under congressional comprehensive policy governing procurement, while competitive bidding is a general policy, negotiation was contemplated where rates, fixed by a government agency, are involved. 10 U.S.C.A. §§ 2301–2314, 2304(a) (2, 10). Public Utilities Commission of State of Cal. v. U.S., 355 U.S. 534, 78 S. Ct. 446, 2 L. Ed. 2d 470, 23 Pub. Util. Rep. 3d (PUR) 55 (1958). United States ☞64.10

In enacting section of the Continuing Appropriations Act prohibiting use of appropriated funds to procure electricity in a manner inconsistent with state law, Congress did not intend to amend extensive body of federal procurement law which establishes that federal agencies must use full and open competitive procedures in procurement of their property and services. Act Dec. 22, 1987, § 8093, 101 Stat. 1329; 10 U.S.C.A. §§ 2301–2316. West River Elec. Ass'n, Inc. v. Black Hills Power and Light Co., 918 F.2d 713, 118 Pub. Util. Rep. 4th (PUR) 510 (8th Cir. 1990). United States ☞64.10

Winning bidder's postaward substitution of personnel to perform computer facility operation contract was properly reviewable in bid protest action; allegations that winning bidder had misrepresented personnel to be used on contract raised issue of whether full and open competition in bidding and award of contract had been achieved. Planning Research Corp. v. U.S., 971 F.2d 736, 38 Cont. Cas. Fed. (CCH) P 76383 (Fed. Cir. 1992). United States ☞64.60(3.1)

Federal Acquisition Streamlining Act (FASA) permitted Department of Labor (DOL) to enter into indefinite delivery contract with retailer for purchase of single manufacturer's software products without conducting full and open competition among manufacturers pursuant to Competition in Contracting Act (CICA), as long as DOL previously conducted full and open competition among retailers. Federal Property and Administrative Services Act of 1949, §§ 303, 303J, as amended, Corel Corp. v. U.S., 165 F. Supp. 2d 12 (D.D.C. 2001). United States ☞64.10

Trial court would not bar performance of contract to provide Customs Service with mobile x-ray for detection of contraband, even though Customs Service erroneously used Broad Agency Announcement (BAA) single source procurement procedure to avoid competitive bidding when BAA was available only for research or applied research contracts; Customs Service had good faith belief that BAA procedure could be used, and protestor requesting relief was not prejudiced, as it was previous sole source for x-ray equipment, and Customs Service wanted second source and could have legitimately requested bids from potential suppliers excluding protestor. Federal Property and Administrative Services Act of 1949, § 303(a)(1), (b)(1), 41 U.S.C.A. § 253(a)(1), (b)(1); 48 C.F.R. §§ 6.102(d)(2), 6.201, 6.202(b)(1). American Science and Engineering, Inc. v. Kelly, 69 F. Supp. 2d 227 (D. Mass. 1999). United States ☞64.60(5.1)

Air Force's Electronics Security Command was not prohibited by Competition in Contracting Act, in procuring automated data processing equipment, from changing from full and open competition procurement under that Act to procurement from another agency through existing contract under the Economy Act. 10 U.S.C.A. § 2304(a)(1), (c); National Gateway Telecom, Inc. v. Aldridge, 701 F. Supp. 1104 (D.N.J. 1988), judgment aff'd, 879 F.2d 858 (3d Cir. 1989). United States ☞64.10

Statutory exception from competitive bidding procedures for personal service contracts confers no right upon those seeking government contracts to demand that competitive bidding not be used. 41 U.S.C.A. § 5(4). Goldhaber v. Foley, 519 F. Supp. 466 (E.D. Pa. 1981). United States ☞64.10

Pursuant to the Competition in Contracting Act, government is required to specify its needs and solicit proposals "in a manner designed to achieve full and open competition for the procurement," and fact that the procurement is a commercial item acquisition does not relieve government of such obligation. 10 U.S.C.A. § 2305(a)(1)(A)(i). Candle Corp. v. U.S., 40 Fed. Cl. 658, 42 Cont. Cas. Fed. (CCH) P 77276 (1998). United States ☞64.10

Requirement in solicitation for bids to dredge river bottom did not violate requirement that Army Corps of Engineers obtain full and open competition, by applying estimate of production rate using water injection wedge (WID) that was same as that for alternate metal cutterhead technology using 24 inch head, which according to complaining bidder caused a disadvantage to bidders using cutterheads; estimate was based on results of three WID demonstrations, in conditions either similar to or easier than those to be encountered under proposed contract, and estimate was reasonable in light of results from demonstrations. 41 U.S.C.A. § 253(a)(1)(A); 48 C.F.R. § 6.101(b). Mike Hooks, Inc. v. U.S., 39 Fed. Cl. 147, 42 Cont. Cas. Fed. (CCH) P 77191 (1997). United States ☞64.25

Agency must evaluate its options and make any determination prior to entering the contract to use other than full and open competition in procurement and to award contract using other than competitive procedures; agency may not award a contract without justifying in writing the use of noncompetitive procedures and must specify in the contract the statutory basis for the exception. 10 U.S.C.A. § 2304(f)(1); 48 C.F.R. § 6.301(b). ATA Defense Industries, Inc. v. U.S., 38 Fed. Cl. 489, 41 Cont. Cas. Fed. (CCH) P 77147 (1997). United States ☞64.10

§ 6.202 Establishing or maintaining alternative sources.

(a) Agencies may exclude a particular source from a contract action in order to establish or maintain an alternative source or sources for the supplies or services being acquired if the agency head determines that to do so would—

(1) Increase or maintain competition and likely result in reduced overall costs for the acquisition, or for any anticipated acquisition;

(2) Be in the interest of national defense in having a facility (or a producer, manufacturer, or other supplier) available for furnishing the supplies or services in case of a national emergency or industrial mobilization;

(3) Be in the interest of national defense in establishing or maintaining an essential engineering, research, or development capability to be provided by an educational or other nonprofit institution or a federally funded research and development center;

(4) Ensure the continuous availability of a reliable source of supplies or services;

(5) Satisfy projected needs based on a history of high demand; or

(6) Satisfy a critical need for medical, safety, or emergency supplies.

(b) (1) Every proposed contract action under the authority of paragraph (a) of this section shall be supported by a determination and findings (D&F) (see Subpart 1.7) signed by the head of the agency or designee. This D&F shall not be made on a class basis.

(2) Technical and requirements personnel are responsible for providing all necessary data to support their recommendation to exclude a particular source.

(3) When the authority in paragraph (a)(1) of this section is cited, the findings shall include a description of the estimated reduction in overall costs and how the estimate was derived.

United States Code Annotated

Advocates for competition, see 41 U.S.C.A. § 418.

Competition requirements, see 41 U.S.C.A. § 253.

Contract goal for small disadvantaged businesses and certain institutions of higher education, see 10 U.S.C.A. § 2323.

Contracts, competition requirements, see 10 U.S.C.A. § 2304.

Contracts, planning, solicitation, evaluation, and award procedures, see 10 U.S.C.A. § 2305.

Contracts, prohibition on competition between Department of Defense and small businesses and certain other entities, see 10 U.S.C.A. § 2304e.

Credit for Indian contracting in meeting certain subcontracting goals for small disadvantaged businesses and certain institutions of higher education, see 10 U.S.C.A. § 2323a.

Definitions, see 10 U.S.C.A. § 2302; 41 U.S.C.A. §§ 259, 403.

Design-build selection procedures, see 10 U.S.C.A. § 2305a; 41 U.S.C.A. § 253m.

Encouragement of new competition, see 41 U.S.C.A. § 253c.

Encouragement of new competitors, see 10 U.S.C.A. § 2319.

Planning and solicitation requirements, see 41 U.S.C.A. § 253a.

Procurement notice, see 41 U.S.C.A. § 416.

Notes of Decisions

In general 1

1 In general

Trial court would not bar performance of contract to provide Customs Service with mobile x-ray for detection of contraband, even though Customs Service erroneously used Broad Agency Announcement (BAA) single source procurement procedure to avoid competitive bidding when BAA was available only for research or applied research contracts; Customs Service had good faith belief that BAA procedure could be used, and protestor requesting relief was not prejudiced, as it was previous sole source for x-ray equipment, and Customs Service wanted second source and could have legitimately requested bids from potential suppliers excluding protestor. Federal Property and Administrative Services Act of 1949, § 303(a)(1), (b)(1), 41 U.S.C.A. § 253(a)(1), (b)(1); 48 C.F.R. §§ 6.102(d)(2), 6.201, 6.202(b)(1). American Science and Engineering, Inc. v. Kelly, 69 F. Supp. 2d 227 (D. Mass. 1999). United States ☞64.60(5.1)

Agency properly determined to exclude protester from the competition for award of batteries, where the protester currently held a contract for the same batteries and the agency reasonably found that another source was necessary to ensure the batteries' continuous availability, to satisfy projected needs, to provide for future competition, and to satisfy national defense interests. Hawker Eternacell, Inc., B-283586, 99-2 CPD ¶ 96 (Comp. Gen. 1999)

§ 6.203 Set-asides for small business concerns.

(a) To fulfill the statutory requirements relating to small business concerns, contracting officers may set aside solicitations to allow only such business concerns to compete. This includes contract actions conducted under the Small Business Innovation Research Program established under Pub. L. 97-219.

(b) No separate justification or determination and findings is required under this part to set aside a contract action for small business concerns.

(c) Subpart 19.5 prescribes policies and procedures that shall be followed with respect to set-asides.

United States Code Annotated

Notes of Decisions
In general 1

1 In general

There is no constitutional duty to offer government procurement contracts for competitive bidding. Small Business Act, § 2[8](a), 15 U.S.C.A. § 637(a). Ray Baillie Trash Hauling, Inc. v. Kleppe, 477 F.2d 696 (5th Cir. 1973). United States ☞64.10

With respect to small business set-asides, CICA defines "competitive procedures" as including set-aside procurements conducted in furtherance of section 15 of the Small Business Act (15 U.S.C. § 644) as long as all responsible small business concerns are permitted to compete. The FAR implements these CICA requirements by providing for full and open competition after the exclusion of one or more sources, such as, for example, business concerns that do not satisfy the size standards in a small business set-aside. FAR 6.203. Where a small business set-aside procurement is used, the law generally provides for full and open competition among eligible small business concerns. Department of the Army—Request for Modification of Recommendation, B-290682.2, 2003 CPD ¶ 23 (Comp. Gen. 2003)

§ 6.204 Section 8(a) competition.

(a) To fulfill statutory requirements relating to section 8(a) of the Small Business Act, as amended by Pub. L. 100-656, contracting officers may limit competition to eligible 8(a) contractors (see Subpart 19.8).

(b) No separate justification or determination and findings is required under this part to limit competition to eligible 8(a) contractors. (But see 6.302-5 and 6.303-1 for sole source 8(a) awards over $22 million.)

United States Code Annotated

Advocates for competition, see 41 U.S.C.A. § 418.

Competition requirements, see 41 U.S.C.A. § 253.

Contract goal for small disadvantaged businesses and certain institutions of higher education, see 10 U.S.C.A. § 2323.

Contracts, competition requirements, see 10 U.S.C.A. § 2304.

Contracts, planning, solicitation, evaluation, and award procedures, see 10 U.S.C.A. § 2305.

Contracts, prohibition on competition between Department of Defense and small businesses and certain other entities, see 10 U.S.C.A. § 2304e.

Credit for Indian contracting in meeting certain subcontracting goals for small disadvantaged businesses and certain institutions of higher education, see 10 U.S.C.A. § 2323a.

Definitions, see 10 U.S.C.A. § 2302; 41 U.S.C.A. §§ 259, 403.

Design-build selection procedures, see 10 U.S.C.A. § 2305a; 41 U.S.C.A. § 253m.

Encouragement of new competition, see 41 U.S.C.A. § 253c.

Encouragement of new competitors, see 10 U.S.C.A. § 2319.

Planning and solicitation requirements, see 41 U.S.C.A. § 253a.

Procurement notice, see 41 U.S.C.A. § 416.

Notes of Decisions
Small business contracts 1

1 Small business contracts

Generally, before a procuring agency may award an 8(a) sole-source contract, it must submit an offer letter for the procurement to the SBA, and the SBA must accept it. 13 C.F.R. § 124.502(a). However, section 8(a) regulations provide that when the value of a proposed contract falls below the simplified acquisition threshold, an agency that has sent an offer letter for the contract to the SBA "may assume the offer is accepted and proceed with award" of the contract if the agency "does not receive a reply [from the SBA] within two days" of sending the offer letter. 13 C.F.R. § 124.503(a)(4)(i). Eagle Collaborative Computing Services, Inc., B-401043.3 (Comp. Gen. 2011)

There is no constitutional duty to offer government procurement contracts for competitive bidding. Small Business Act, § 2[8](a), 15 U.S.C.A. § 637(a). Ray Baillie Trash Hauling, Inc. v. Kleppe, 477 F.2d 696 (5th Cir. 1973). United States ⚖64.10

Subcontracts under Small Business Administration's program for awarding government procurement contracts to small business concerns owned by "socially or economically disadvantaged persons" may be awarded on a noncompetitive basis. Small Business Act, § 2[8](a), 15 U.S.C.A. § 637(a). Ray Baillie Trash Hauling, Inc. v. Kleppe, 477 F.2d 696 (5th Cir. 1973). United States ⚖64.10

General policy of competitive bidding in federal procurement is wholly inapplicable to a contract which the Small Business Administration has specific statutory authority to enter. Small Business Act, § 2 [8] (a), (a)(2), 15 U.S.C.A. § 637(a), (a)(2); Fortec Constructors v. Kleppe, 350 F. Supp. 171 (D.D.C. 1972). United States ⊕64.10

§ 6.205 Set-asides for HUBZone small business concerns.

(a) To fulfill the statutory requirements relating to the HUBZone Act of 1997 (15 U.S.C. 631 note), contracting officers in participating agencies (see 19.1302) may set aside solicitations to allow only qualified HUBZone small business concerns to compete (see 19.1305).

(b) No separate justification or determination and findings is required under this part to set aside a contract action for qualified HUBZone small business concerns.

United States Code Annotated

Advocates for competition, see 41 U.S.C.A. § 418.

Competition requirements, see 41 U.S.C.A. § 253.

Contract goal for small disadvantaged businesses and certain institutions of higher education, see 10 U.S.C.A. § 2323.

Contracts, competition requirements, see 10 U.S.C.A. § 2304.

Contracts, planning, solicitation, evaluation, and award procedures, see 10 U.S.C.A. § 2305.

Contracts, prohibition on competition between Department of Defense and small businesses and certain other entities, see 10 U.S.C.A. § 2304e.

Credit for Indian contracting in meeting certain subcontracting goals for small disadvantaged businesses and certain institutions of higher education, see 10 U.S.C.A. § 2323a.

Definitions, see 10 U.S.C.A. § 2302; 41 U.S.C.A. §§ 259, 403.

Design-build selection procedures, see 10 U.S.C.A. § 2305a; 41 U.S.C.A. § 253m.

Encouragement of new competition, see 41 U.S.C.A. § 253c.

Encouragement of new competitors, see 10 U.S.C.A. § 2319.

Planning and solicitation requirements, see 41 U.S.C.A. § 253a.

Procurement notice, see 41 U.S.C.A. § 416.

§ 6.206 Set-asides for service-disabled veteran-owned small business concerns.

(a) To fulfill the statutory requirements relating to the Veterans Benefits Act of 2003 (15 U.S.C. 657f), contracting officers may set-aside solicitations to allow only service-disabled veteran-owned small business concerns to compete (see 19.1405).

(b) No separate justification or determination and findings are required under this part to set aside a contract action for service-disabled veteran-owned small business concerns.

United States Code Annotated

Advocates for competition, see 41 U.S.C.A. § 418.

Competition requirements, see 41 U.S.C.A. § 253.

Contract goal for small disadvantaged businesses and certain institutions of higher education, see 10 U.S.C.A. § 2323.

Contracts, competition requirements, see 10 U.S.C.A. § 2304.

Contracts, planning, solicitation, evaluation, and award procedures, see 10 U.S.C.A. § 2305.

Contracts, prohibition on competition between Department of Defense and small businesses and certain other entities, see 10 U.S.C.A. § 2304e.

Credit for Indian contracting in meeting certain subcontracting goals for small disadvantaged businesses and certain institutions of higher education, see 10 U.S.C.A. § 2323a.

Definitions, see 10 U.S.C.A. § 2302; 41 U.S.C.A. §§ 259, 403.

Design-build selection procedures, see 10 U.S.C.A. § 2305a; 41 U.S.C.A. § 253m.

Encouragement of new competition, see 41 U.S.C.A. § 253c.

Encouragement of new competitors, see 10 U.S.C.A. § 2319.

Planning and solicitation requirements, see 41 U.S.C.A. § 253a.

Procurement notice, see 41 U.S.C.A. § 416.

§ 6.207 Set-asides for economically disadvantaged women-owned small business (EDWOSB) concerns or women-owned small business (WOSB) concerns eligible under the WOSB Program.

(a) To fulfill the statutory requirements relating to 15 U.S.C. 637(m), contracting officers may set aside solicitations for only EDWOSB concerns or WOSB concerns eligible under the WOSB Program (see 19.1505).

(b) No separate justification or determination and findings is required under this part to set aside a contract action for EDWOSB concerns or WOSB concerns eligible under the WOSB Program.

§ 6.208 Set-asides for local firms during a major disaster or emergency.

(a) To fulfill the statutory requirements relating to 42 U.S.C. 5150, contracting officers may set aside solicitations to allow only offerors residing or doing business primarily in the area affected by such major disaster or emergency to compete (see Subpart 26.2).

(b) No separate justification or determination and findings is required under this part to set aside a contract action. The set-aside area specified by the contracting officer shall be a geographic area within the area identified in a Presidential declaration(s) of major disaster or emergency and any additional geographic areas identified by the Department of Homeland Security.

Subpart 6.3 Other Than Full and Open Competition

§ 6.300 Scope of subpart.

This subpart prescribes policies and procedures, and identifies the statutory authorities, for contracting without providing for full and open competition.

United States Code Annotated

Administrative determinations, see 41 U.S.C.A. § 257.

Advocates for competition, see 41 U.S.C.A. § 418.

Competition requirements, see 41 U.S.C.A. § 253.

Contract goal for small disadvantaged businesses and certain institutions of higher education, see 10 U.S.C.A. § 2323.

Contracts, competition requirements, see 10 U.S.C.A. § 2304.

Contracts, planning, solicitation, evaluation, and award procedures, see 10 U.S.C.A. § 2305.

Contracts, prohibition on competition between Department of Defense and small businesses and certain other entities, see 10 U.S.C.A. § 2304e.

Credit for Indian contracting in meeting certain subcontracting goals for small disadvantaged businesses and certain institutions of higher education, see 10 U.S.C.A. § 2323a.

Definitions, see 10 U.S.C.A. § 2302; 41 U.S.C.A. §§ 259, 403.

Design-build selection procedures, see 10 U.S.C.A. § 2305a; 41 U.S.C.A. § 253m.

Determinations and decisions, see 10 U.S.C.A. § 2310; 41 U.S.C.A. § 262.

Encouragement of new competition, see 41 U.S.C.A. § 253c.

Encouragement of new competitors, see 10 U.S.C.A. § 2319.

Planning and solicitation requirements, see 41 U.S.C.A. § 253a.

Procurement notice, see 41 U.S.C.A. § 416.

§ 6.301 Policy.

(a) 41 U.S.C. 3304 and 10 U.S.C. 2304(c) each authorize, under certain conditions, contracting without providing for full and open competition. The Department of Defense, Coast Guard, and National Aeronautics and Space Administration are subject to 10 U.S.C. 2304(c). Other executive agencies are subject to 41 U.S.C. 3304. Contracting without providing for full and open competition or full and open competition after exclusion of sources is a violation of statute, unless permitted by one of the exceptions in 6.302.

(b) Each contract awarded without providing for full and open competition shall contain a reference to the specific authority under which it was so awarded. Contracting officers shall use the U.S. Code citation applicable to their agency (see 6.302).

(c) Contracting without providing for full and open competition shall not be justified on the basis of—

(1) A lack of advance planning by the requiring activity; or

(2) Concerns related to the amount of funds available (e.g., funds will expire) to the agency or activity for the acquisition of supplies or services.

(d) When not providing for full and open competition, the contracting officer shall solicit offers from as many potential sources as is practicable under the circumstances.

(e) For contracts under this subpart, the contracting officer shall use the contracting procedures prescribed in 6.102(a) or (b), if appropriate, or any other procedures authorized by this regulation.

United States Code Annotated

Administrative determinations, see 41 U.S.C.A. § 257.

Advocates for competition, see 41 U.S.C.A. § 418.

Competition requirements, see 41 U.S.C.A. § 253.

Contract goal for small disadvantaged businesses and certain institutions of higher education, see 10 U.S.C.A. § 2323.

Contracts, competition requirements, see 10 U.S.C.A. § 2304.

Contracts, planning, solicitation, evaluation, and award procedures, see 10 U.S.C.A. § 2305.

Contracts, prohibition on competition between Department of Defense and small businesses and certain other entities, see 10 U.S.C.A. § 2304e.

Credit for Indian contracting in meeting certain subcontracting goals for small disadvantaged businesses and certain institutions of higher education, see 10 U.S.C.A. § 2323a.

Definitions, see 10 U.S.C.A. § 2302; 41 U.S.C.A. §§ 259, 403.

Design-build selection procedures, see 10 U.S.C.A. § 2305a; 41 U.S.C.A. § 253m.

Determinations and decisions, see 10 U.S.C.A. § 2310; 41 U.S.C.A. § 262.

Encouragement of new competition, see 41 U.S.C.A. § 253c.

Encouragement of new competitors, see 10 U.S.C.A. § 2319.

Planning and solicitation requirements, see 41 U.S.C.A. § 253a.

Procurement notice, see 41 U.S.C.A. § 416.

Notes of Decisions

In general 1
Full and open competition 3
Lack of advance planning 5
Purpose 2
Solicitation, generally 4

1 In general

There is no constitutional or statutory requirement that the federal government offer all of its business through competitive bidding. Jets Services, Inc. v. Hoffman, 420 F. Supp. 1300 (M.D. Fla. 1976). United States ☞64.10

A lack of advance planning may not justify a noncompetitive procurement. 10 U.S.C.A. § 2304(f)(5); Federal Property and Administrative Services Act of 1949, § 303(f)(5), 41 U.S.C.A. § 253(f)(5). Cubic Defense Systems, Inc. v. U.S., 45 Fed. Cl. 239 (1999), dismissed, 230 F.3d 1375 (Fed. Cir. 1999). United States ☞64.10

2 Purpose

Under statutes governing procurement and providing for competitive bidding, purpose of section providing that head of agency may negotiate such purchase or contract if it is for property or services for which it is impracticable to obtain competition was to place the maximum responsibility for decisions as to when it is impracticable to secure competition in hands of the agency concerned. 10 U.S.C.A. §§ 2301–2314, 2304(a) (10, 12). Public Utilities Commission of State of Cal. v. U.S., 355 U.S. 534, 78 S. Ct. 446, 2 L. Ed. 2d 470, 23 Pub. Util. Rep. 3d (PUR) 55 (1958). United States ⚏64.10

Purpose of the Competition in Contracting Act (CICA) is to save money, curb cost growth, promote innovation and the development of high quality technology, and maintain the integrity of the expenditure of public funds. 10 U.S.C.A. § 2304. American Federation of Government Employees v. Rumsfeld, 262 F.3d 649 (7th Cir. 2001). United States ⚏64.10

Competitive bidding is the cornerstone of federal procurement policy. 10 U.S.C.A. § 2304(a) (9, 10). U.S. v. Warne, 190 F. Supp. 645 (N.D. Cal. 1960), judgment aff'd in part, vacated in part, 371 U.S. 245, 83 S. Ct. 426, 9 L. Ed. 2d 292 (1963). United States ⚏64.10

In enacting Competition in Contracting Act (CICA), Congress intended to promote competition in government's procurement of goods and services. 31 U.S.C.A. §§ 3551–3556, 3554(c). U.S. v. Instruments, S.A., Inc., 807 F. Supp. 811, 38 Cont. Cas. Fed. (CCH) P 76466 (D.D.C. 1992). United States ⚏64.10

3 Full and open competition

In enacting section of the Continuing Appropriations Act prohibiting use of appropriated funds to procure electricity in a manner inconsistent with state law, Congress did not intend to amend extensive body of federal procurement law which establishes that federal agencies must use full and open competitive procedures in procurement of their property and services. Act Dec. 22, 1987, § 8093, 101 Stat. 1329; 10 U.S.C.A. §§ 2301–2316. West River Elec. Ass'n, Inc. v. Black Hills Power and Light Co., 918 F.2d 713, 118 Pub. Util. Rep. 4th (PUR) 510 (8th Cir. 1990). United States ⚏64.10

Winning bidder's postaward substitution of personnel to perform computer facility operation contract was properly reviewable in bid protest action; allegations that winning bidder had misrepresented personnel to be used on contract raised issue of whether full and open competition in bidding and award of contract had been achieved. Planning Research Corp. v. U.S., 971 F.2d 736, 38 Cont. Cas. Fed. (CCH) P 76383 (Fed. Cir. 1992). United States ⚏64.60(3.1)

Federal Acquisition Streamlining Act (FASA) permitted Department of Labor (DOL) to enter into indefinite delivery contract with retailer for purchase of single manufacturer's software products without conducting full and open competition among manufacturers pursuant to Competition in Contracting Act (CICA), as long as DOL previously conducted full and open competition among retailers. Federal Property and Administrative Services Act of 1949, §§ 303, 303J, as amended, 41 U.S.C.A. §§ 253, 253j. Corel Corp. v. U.S., 165 F. Supp. 2d 12 (D.D.C. 2001). United States ⚏64.10

Air Force's Electronics Security Command was not prohibited by Competition in Contracting Act, in procuring automated data processing equipment, from changing from full and open competition procurement under that Act to procurement from another agency through existing contract under the Economy Act. 10 U.S.C.A. § 2304(a)(1), (c); 31 U.S.C.A. § 1535. National Gateway Telecom, Inc. v. Aldridge, 701 F. Supp. 1104 (D.N.J. 1988), judgment aff'd, 879 F.2d 858 (3d Cir. 1989). United States ⚏64.10

Statutory exception from competitive bidding procedures for personal service contracts confers no right upon those seeking government contracts to demand that competitive bidding not be used. 41 U.S.C.A. § 5(4). Goldhaber v. Foley, 519 F. Supp. 466 (E.D. Pa. 1981). United States ⚏64.10

Pursuant to the Competition in Contracting Act, government is required to specify its needs and solicit proposals "in a manner designed to achieve full and open competition for the procurement," and fact that the procurement is a commercial item acquisition does not relieve government of such obligation. 10 U.S.C.A. § 2305(a)(1)(A)(i). Candle Corp. v. U.S., 40 Fed. Cl. 658, 42 Cont. Cas. Fed. (CCH) P 77276 (1998). United States ⚏64.10

Requirement in solicitation for bids to dredge river bottom did not violate requirement that Army Corps of Engineers obtain full and open competition, by applying estimate of production rate using water injection wedge (WID) that was same as that for alternate metal cutterhead technology using 24 inch head, which according to complaining bidder caused a disadvantage to bidders using cutterheads; estimate was based on results of three WID demonstrations, in conditions either similar to or easier than those to be encountered under proposed contract, and estimate was reasonable in light of results from demonstrations. 41 U.S.C.A. § 253(a)(1)(A); 48 C.F.R. § 6.101(b). Mike Hooks, Inc. v. U.S., 39 Fed. Cl. 147, 42 Cont. Cas. Fed. (CCH) P 77191 (1997). United States ⊕64.25

Requirement that agency determine prior to contract award the precise exception upon which it will rely to justify use of noncompetitive procedures is part of comprehensive plan to improve efficiency with which federal agencies procure products and services. 10 U.S.C.A. § 2304; 48 C.F.R. § 6.301(b). ATA Defense Industries, Inc. v. U.S., 38 Fed. Cl. 489, 41 Cont. Cas. Fed. (CCH) P 77147 (1997). United States ⊕64.10

Agency must evaluate its options and make any determination prior to entering the contract to use other than full and open competition in procurement and to award contract using other than competitive procedures; agency may not award a contract without justifying in writing the use of noncompetitive procedures and must specify in the contract the statutory basis for the exception. 10 U.S.C.A. § 2304(f)(1); 48 C.F.R. § 6.301(b). ATA Defense Industries, Inc. v. U.S., 38 Fed. Cl. 489, 41 Cont. Cas. Fed. (CCH) P 77147 (1997). United States ⊕64.10

4 Solicitation, generally

Statute providing that in all negotiated procurements in excess of $2,500 in which rates or prices are not fixed by law or regulation proposals shall be solicited from maximum number of qualified sources and discussions shall be conducted with responsible offerors who submitted proposals does not require federal procurement to follow state rate-fixing and state price-fixing contrary to federal regulation providing for competitive bidding. 10 U.S.C.A. § 2304(g). Paul v. U.S., 371 U.S. 245, 83 S. Ct. 426, 9 L. Ed. 2d 292 (1963). United States ⊕64.10

Competition in Contracting Act and procurement regulations imposed upon General Services Administration general obligation to solicit bids for paper towels through most effectively competitive mechanism possible and to take affirmative steps to ensure that potentially responsible bidders, including incumbent, as previously successful bidder, be permitted to submit bids and be on bidder's mailing list. Office of Federal Procurement Policy Act, § 4(7), 41 U.S.C.A. § 403(7). Abel Converting, Inc. v. U.S., 679 F. Supp. 1133, 34 Cont. Cas. Fed. (CCH) P 75449 (D.D.C. 1988). United States ⊕64.10

Absence of incumbent contractor from bidding process for paper towels significantly diminished level of competition for paper towel contract and no level of competition could cure such clearly prejudicial violation of General Services Administration's procurement regulations, so that General Services Administration's initial decision to resolicit only 14 of 33 items was not in accordance with Competition in Contracting Act. Federal Property and Administrative Services Act of 1949, § 301 et seq., as amended, 41 U.S.C.A. § 251 et seq.Abel Converting, Inc. v. U.S., 679 F. Supp. 1133, 34 Cont. Cas. Fed. (CCH) P 75449 (D.D.C. 1988). United States ⊕64.10

Absence of incumbent contractor from bidding process for paper towel contract, which resulted in only two bids on 17 of line items, one bid on 14 line item and three or more on two line items, impaired competitiveness of process to prejudice of incumbent contractor in violation of Competition in Contracting Act and procurement regulations, so that resolicitation of all 33 line items was appropriate remedy for failure to mail incumbent contractor copy of solicitation. Federal Property and Administrative Services Act of 1949, § 301 et seq., as amended, 41 U.S.C.A. § 251 et seq.Abel Converting, Inc. v. U.S., 679 F. Supp. 1133, 34 Cont. Cas. Fed. (CCH) P 75449 (D.D.C. 1988). United States ⊕64.10; United States ⊕64.60(5.1)

In reviewing Army's solicitation, court is limited to determining whether agency acted in accord with applicable statutes and regulations and had rational basis for its decisions. New York Telephone Co. v. Secretary of Army, 657 F. Supp. 18 (D.D.C. 1986). United States ⊕64.60(4)

Plaintiff has standing to challenge army's allegedly anticompetitive solicitation plan if it establishes that it has suffered injury in fact; that injury is one arguably within zone of interests protected by applicable statutes and regulations; and that statutes in question do not reflect clear and convincing intent to preclude review. New York Telephone Co. v. Secretary of Army, 657 F. Supp. 18 (D.D.C. 1986). United States ⏚64.60(2)

Unless and until a procurement officer makes a rational determination that a single firm is only possible source for every phase of a procurement, section of Armed Services Procurement Act providing for solicitation of proposals from maximum number of qualified sources requires the procurement officer to position himself to compete all feasible contracts within the overall procurement. 10 U.S.C.A. § 2304(g). Aero Corp. v. Department of the Navy, 540 F. Supp. 180, 29 Cont. Cas. Fed. (CCH) P 82290 (D.D.C. 1982). United States ⏚64.10

Even a determination that a firm is possessed of superior performance potential and is likely to perform procurement contract at lowest cost to government does not spare procurement officer from presumption favoring solicitation and evaluation of proposals from other competent firms. Aero Corp. v. Department of the Navy, 540 F. Supp. 180, 29 Cont. Cas. Fed. (CCH) P 82290 (D.D.C. 1982). United States ⏚64.10

Where decision by Army to conduct negotiated procurement for rifle sight-post assembly, rather than one by formal advertising, was apparent on face of solicitation, unsuccessful bidder failed timely to object to it as required by applicable regulations, and the unsuccessful bidder subsequently participated in procurement procedures, the unsuccessful bidder waived any objection to any impropriety in decision to conduct negotiated procurement. Self-Powered Lighting, Ltd. v. U.S., 492 F. Supp. 1267, 27 Cont. Cas. Fed. (CCH) P 80472 (S.D. N.Y. 1980). United States ⏚64.10

Section of the Resource Conservation and Recovery Act (RCRA) requiring that all federal agencies engaged in disposal of solid waste comply with state requirements and Washington statute requiring that a solid waste collection company obtain a certificate of public convenience and necessity from the Washington Utilities and Transportation Commission (WUTC) do not mandate that a federal agency must solicit bids only from or award a contract exclusively to a solid waste disposal contractor with a WUTC certification; moreover, such a requirement would violate the Competition in Contracting Act (CICA). 10 U.S.C.A. § 2305(b)(3); Solid Waste Disposal Act, § 6001(a), as amended, 42 U.S.C.A. § 6961(a); Blue Dot Energy Co., Inc. v. U.S., 61 Fed. Cl. 548 (2004). United States ⏚64.10

Government was under no obligation to solicit incumbent contractor on a delivery order from a Federal Supply Services (FSS) schedule contract, as sealed bidding regulation is not applicable to placement of a delivery order from an FSS schedule. 48 C.F.R. §§ 8.401(a, b), 14.205-4(b). Cybertech Group, Inc. v. U.S., 48 Fed. Cl. 638 (2001). United States ⏚64.10

In determining whether there are genuine issues of fact regarding allegation that government has violated legal duty to provide full and open competition while soliciting bids and awarding contracts, court should not substitute its judgment for that of procuring agency and should intervene only when it is clear that agency's determinations were irrational or unreasonable. 10 U.S.C.A. § 2304(a)(1)(A); 41 U.S.C.A. § 253(a)(1)(A); 48 C.F.R. § 6.101(b). Mike Hooks, Inc. v. U.S., 39 Fed. Cl. 147, 42 Cont. Cas. Fed. (CCH) P 77191 (1997). United States ⏚64.60(4)

5 Lack of advance planning

Protest of sole source extension of contract was sustained because of the agency's lack of adequate and reasonable advance planning where, despite knowing of and documenting the need for detailed solicitation requirements nearly 4 years prior to the end of the current contract, the agency issued the solicitation containing only "high level" requirements and then cancelled the solicitation because it failed to include sufficiently detailed requirements. XTec, Inc., B-410778.3, 2015 CPD ¶ 292 (Comp.Gen. 2015)

§ 6.302 Circumstances permitting other than full and open competition.

The following statutory authorities (including applications and limitations) permit contracting without providing for full and open competition. Requirements for justifications to support the use of these authorities are in 6.303.

United States Code Annotated

Administrative determinations, see 41 U.S.C.A. § 257.

Advocates for competition, see 41 U.S.C.A. § 418.

Competition requirements, see 41 U.S.C.A. § 253.

Contract goal for small disadvantaged businesses and certain institutions of higher education, see 10 U.S.C.A. § 2323.

Contracts, competition requirements, see 10 U.S.C.A. § 2304.

Contracts, planning, solicitation, evaluation, and award procedures, see 10 U.S.C.A. § 2305.

Contracts, prohibition on competition between Department of Defense and small businesses and certain other entities, see 10 U.S.C.A. § 2304e.

Credit for Indian contracting in meeting certain subcontracting goals for small disadvantaged businesses and certain institutions of higher education, see 10 U.S.C.A. § 2323a.

Definitions, see 10 U.S.C.A. § 2302; 41 U.S.C.A. §§ 259, 403.

Design-build selection procedures, see 10 U.S.C.A. § 2305a; 41 U.S.C.A. § 253m.

Determinations and decisions, see 10 U.S.C.A. § 2310; 41 U.S.C.A. § 262.

Encouragement of new competition, see 41 U.S.C.A. § 253c.

Encouragement of new competitors, see 10 U.S.C.A. § 2319.

Planning and solicitation requirements, see 41 U.S.C.A. § 253a.

Procurement notice, see 41 U.S.C.A. § 416.

Notes of Decisions
In general 1

1 In general

Exceptions to the Competition in Contracting Act's (CICA's) competitive bidding practices, including the sole source exception, reference situations in which either a national emergency or a narrow set of compelling circumstances requires that a branch of the armed services must contract with a particular private entity. 10 U.S.C.A. § 2304(c). American Federation of Government Employees v. Rumsfeld, 262 F.3d 649 (7th Cir. 2001). United States ☞64.10

§ 6.302-1 Only one responsible source and no other supplies or services will satisfy agency requirements.

(a) Authority.

(1) Citations: 10 U.S.C. 2304(c)(1) or 41 U.S.C. 3304(a)(1).

(2) When the supplies or services required by the agency are available from only one responsible source, or, for DoD, NASA, and the Coast Guard, from only one or a limited number of responsible sources, and no other type of supplies or services will satisfy agency requirements, full and open competition need not be provided for.

(i) Supplies or services may be considered to be available from only one source if the source has submitted an unsolicited research proposal that—

(A) Demonstrates a unique and innovative concept (see definition at 2.101), or, demonstrates a unique capability of the source to provide the particular research services proposed;

(B) Offers a concept or services not otherwise available to the Government; and

(C) Does not resemble the substance of a pending competitive acquisition. (See 10 U.S.C. 2304(d)(1)(A) and 41 U.S.C. 3304(b)(1).)

(ii) Supplies may be deemed to be available only from the original source in the case of a follow-on contract for the continued development or production of a major system or highly specialized equipment, including major components thereof, when it is likely that award to any other source would result in—

(A) Substantial duplication of cost to the Government that is not expected to be recovered through competition; or

(B) Unacceptable delays in fulfilling the agency's requirements. (See 10 U.S.C. 2304(d)(1)(B) or 41 U.S.C. 3304(b)(2).)

(iii) For DoD, NASA, and the Coast Guard, services may be deemed to be available only from the original source in the case of follow-on contracts for the continued provision of highly specialized services when it is likely that award to any other source would result in—

(A) Substantial duplication of cost to the Government that is not expected to be recovered through competition; or

(B) Unacceptable delays in fulfilling the agency's requirements. (See 10 U.S.C. 2304(d)(1)(B).)

(b) *Application.* This authority shall be used, if appropriate, in preference to the authority in 6.302-7; it shall not be used when any of the other circumstances is applicable. Use of this authority may be appropriate in situations such as the following (these examples are not intended to be all inclusive and do not constitute authority in and of themselves):

(1) When there is a reasonable basis to conclude that the agency's minimum needs can only be satisfied by—

(i) Unique supplies or services available from only one source or only one supplier with unique capabilities; or

(ii) For DoD, NASA, and the Coast Guard, unique supplies or services available from only one or a limited number of sources or from only one or a limited number of suppliers with unique capabilities.

(2) The existence of limited rights in data, patent rights, copyrights, or secret processes; the control of basic raw material; or similar circumstances, make the supplies and services available from only one source (however, the mere existence of such rights or circumstances does not in and of itself justify the use of these authorities) (see Part 27).

(3) When acquiring utility services (see 41.101), circumstances may dictate that only one supplier can furnish the service (see 41.202); or when the contemplated contract is for construction of a part of a utility system and the utility company itself is the only source available to work on the system.

(4) When the agency head has determined in accordance with the agency's standardization program that only specified makes and models of technical equipment and parts will satisfy the agency's needs for additional units or replacement items, and only one source is available.

(c) Application for brand-name descriptions.

(1) An acquisition or portion of an acquisition that uses a brand-name description or other purchase description to specify a particular brand-name, product, or feature of a product, peculiar to one manufacturer—

(i) Does not provide for full and open competition, regardless of the number of sources solicited; and

(ii) Shall be justified and approved in accordance with 6.303 and 6.304.

(A) If only a portion of the acquisition is for a brand-name product or item peculiar to one manufacturer, the justification and approval is to cover only the portion of the acquisition which is brand-name or peculiar to one manufacturer. The justification should state it is covering only the portion of the acquisition which is brand-name or peculiar to one manufacturer, and the approval level requirements will then only apply to that portion;

(B) The justification should indicate that the use of such descriptions in the acquisition or portion of an acquisition is essential to the Government's requirements, thereby precluding consideration of a product manufactured by another company; and

(C) The justification shall be posted with the solicitation (see 5.102(a)(6)).

(2) Brand-name or equal descriptions, and other purchase descriptions that permit prospective contractors to offer products other than those specifically referenced by brand-name, provide for full and open competition and do not require justifications and approvals to support their use.

(d) Limitations.

(1) Contracts awarded using this authority shall be supported by the written justifications and approvals described in 6.303 and 6.304.

(2) For contracts awarded using this authority, the notices required by 5.201 shall have been published and any bids, proposals, quotations, or capability statements must have been considered.

United States Code Annotated

Administrative determinations, see 41 U.S.C.A. § 257.

Advocates for competition, see 41 U.S.C.A. § 418.

Competition requirements, see 41 U.S.C.A. § 253.

Contract goal for small disadvantaged businesses and certain institutions of higher education, see 10 U.S.C.A. § 2323.

Contracts, competition requirements, see 10 U.S.C.A. § 2304.

Contracts, planning, solicitation, evaluation, and award procedures, see 10 U.S.C.A. § 2305.

Contracts, prohibition on competition between Department of Defense and small businesses and certain other entities, see 10 U.S.C.A. § 2304e.

Credit for Indian contracting in meeting certain subcontracting goals for small disadvantaged businesses and certain institutions of higher education, see 10 U.S.C.A. § 2323a.

Definitions, see 10 U.S.C.A. § 2302; 41 U.S.C.A. §§ 259, 403.

Design-build selection procedures, see 10 U.S.C.A. § 2305a; 41 U.S.C.A. § 253m.

Determinations and decisions, see 10 U.S.C.A. § 2310; 41 U.S.C.A. § 262.

Encouragement of new competition, see 41 U.S.C.A. § 253c.

Encouragement of new competitors, see 10 U.S.C.A. § 2319.

Planning and solicitation requirements, see 41 U.S.C.A. § 253a.

Procurement notice, see 41 U.S.C.A. § 416.

Notes of Decisions

Adequate justification 7
Brand Name Specification 6
Expert services 9
Inadequate justification 8
Injunctions—Sole source acquisitions, injunctions 10
Justifications-generally 4
Publication Requirement 5
Sole source acquisitions—In general 2
Sole source acquisitions—Armed forces contracts, sole source acquisitions 3
Solicitation 1

1 Solicitation

Statute providing that in all negotiated procurements in excess of $2,500 in which rates or prices are not fixed by law or regulation proposals shall be solicited from maximum number of qualified sources and discussions shall be conducted with responsible offerors who submitted proposals does not require federal procurement to follow state rate-fixing and state price-fixing contrary to federal regulation providing for competitive bidding. 10 U.S.C.A. § 2304(g). Paul v. U.S., 371 U.S. 245, 83 S. Ct. 426, 9 L. Ed. 2d 292 (1963). United States ⊄64.10

Competition in Contracting Act and procurement regulations imposed upon General Services Administration general obligation to solicit bids for paper towels through most effectively competitive mechanism possible and to take affirmative steps to ensure that potentially responsible bidders, including incumbent, as previously successful bidder, be permitted to submit bids and be on bidder's mailing list. Office of Federal Procurement Policy Act, § 4(7), 41 U.S.C.A. § 403(7). Abel Converting, Inc. v. U.S., 679 F. Supp. 1133, 34 Cont. Cas. Fed. (CCH) P 75449 (D.D.C. 1988). United States ⊄64.10

Absence of incumbent contractor from bidding process for paper towels significantly diminished level of competition for paper towel contract and no level of competition could cure such clearly prejudicial violation of General Services Administration's procurement regulations, so that General Services Administration's initial decision to resolicit only 14 of 33 items was not in accordance with Competition in Contracting Act. Federal Property and Administrative Services Act of 1949, § 301 et seq., as amended, 41 U.S.C.A. § 251 et seq. Abel Converting, Inc. v. U.S., 679 F. Supp. 1133, 34 Cont. Cas. Fed. (CCH) P 75449 (D.D.C. 1988). United States ⊄64.10

Absence of incumbent contractor from bidding process for paper towel contract, which resulted in only two bids on 17 of line items, one bid on 14 line item and three or more on two line items, impaired competitiveness of process to prejudice of incumbent contractor in violation of Competition in Contracting Act and procurement regulations, so that resolicitation of all 33 line items was appropriate remedy for failure to mail incumbent contractor copy of solicitation. Federal Property and Administrative Services Act of 1949, § 301 et seq., as amended, 41 U.S.C.A. § 251 et seq.Abel Converting, Inc. v. U.S., 679 F. Supp. 1133, 34 Cont. Cas. Fed. (CCH) P 75449 (D.D.C. 1988). United States ☜64.10; United States ☜64.60(5.1)

In reviewing Army's solicitation, court is limited to determining whether agency acted in accord with applicable statutes and regulations and had rational basis for its decisions. New York Telephone Co. v. Secretary of Army, 657 F. Supp. 18 (D.D.C. 1986). United States ☜64.60(4)

Plaintiff has standing to challenge army's allegedly anticompetitive solicitation plan if it establishes that it has suffered injury in fact; that injury is one arguably within zone of interests protected by applicable statutes and regulations; and that statutes in question do not reflect clear and convincing intent to preclude review. New York Telephone Co. v. Secretary of Army, 657 F. Supp. 18 (D.D.C. 1986). United States ☜64.60(2)

Unless and until a procurement officer makes a rational determination that a single firm is only possible source for every phase of a procurement, section of Armed Services Procurement Act providing for solicitation of proposals from maximum number of qualified sources requires the procurement officer to position himself to compete all feasible contracts within the overall procurement. 10 U.S.C.A. § 2304(g). Aero Corp. v. Department of the Navy, 540 F. Supp. 180, 29 Cont. Cas. Fed. (CCH) P 82290 (D.D.C. 1982). United States ☜64.10

Even a determination that a firm is possessed of superior performance potential and is likely to perform procurement contract at lowest cost to government does not spare procurement officer from presumption favoring solicitation and evaluation of proposals from other competent firms. Aero Corp. v. Department of the Navy, 540 F. Supp. 180, 29 Cont. Cas. Fed. (CCH) P 82290 (D.D.C. 1982). United States ☜64.10

Where decision by Army to conduct negotiated procurement for rifle sight-post assembly, rather than one by formal advertising, was apparent on face of solicitation, unsuccessful bidder failed timely to object to it as required by applicable regulations, and the unsuccessful bidder subsequently participated in procurement procedures, the unsuccessful bidder waived any objection to any impropriety in decision to conduct negotiated procurement. National Military Establishment Appropriation Act, § 633, 41 U.S.C.A. § 10d. Self-Powered Lighting, Ltd. v. U.S., 492 F. Supp. 1267, 27 Cont. Cas. Fed. (CCH) P 80472 (S.D. N.Y. 1980). United States ☜64.10

Section of the Resource Conservation and Recovery Act (RCRA) requiring that all federal agencies engaged in disposal of solid waste comply with state requirements and Washington statute requiring that a solid waste collection company obtain a certificate of public convenience and necessity from the Washington Utilities and Transportation Commission (WUTC) do not mandate that a federal agency must solicit bids only from or award a contract exclusively to a solid waste disposal contractor with a WUTC certification; moreover, such a requirement would violate the Competition in Contracting Act (CICA). 10 U.S.C.A. § 2305(b)(3); Solid Waste Disposal Act, § 6001(a), as amended, 42 U.S.C.A. § 6961(a); Blue Dot Energy Co., Inc. v. U.S., 61 Fed. Cl. 548 (2004). United States ☜64.10

Government was under no obligation to solicit incumbent contractor on a delivery order from a Federal Supply Services (FSS) schedule contract, as sealed bidding regulation is not applicable to placement of a delivery order from an FSS schedule. 48 C.F.R. §§ 8.401(a, b), 14.205-4(b). Cybertech Group, Inc. v. U.S., 48 Fed. Cl. 638 (2001). United States ☜64.10

In determining whether there are genuine issues of fact regarding allegation that government has violated legal duty to provide full and open competition while soliciting bids and awarding contracts, court should not substitute its judgment for that of procuring agency and should intervene only when it is clear that agency's determinations were irrational or unreasonable. 10 U.S.C.A. § 2304(a)(1)(A); 41 U.S.C.A. § 253(a)(1)(A); 48 C.F.R. § 6.101(b). Mike Hooks, Inc. v. U.S., 39 Fed. Cl. 147, 42 Cont. Cas. Fed. (CCH) P 77191 (1997). United States ☜64.60(4)

2 Sole source acquisitions—In general

Exceptions to the Competition in Contracting Act's (CICA's) competitive bidding practices, including the sole source exception, reference situations in which either a national emergency or a narrow set of compelling circumstances requires that a branch of the armed services must contract with a particular private entity. American Federation of Government Employees v. Rumsfeld, 262 F.3d 649 (7th Cir. 2001). United States ☞64.10

Party challenging award of sole-source government contract may meet its heavy burden of showing that award decision had no rational basis by showing: (1) agency's decision to conduct sole-source procurement process lacked rational basis; (2) agency's sole-source requirements lacked rational basis; or (3) based on sole-source requirements, selection of sole-source awardee lacked rational basis. 5 U.S.C.A. § 706(2). Emery Worldwide Airlines, Inc. v. U.S., 264 F.3d 1071 (Fed. Cir. 2001). United States ☞64.10

Statutory provision requiring United States Postal Service (USPS) to make "fair and equitable distribution of mail business to carriers providing similar modes of transportation services to the Postal Service" did not preclude USPS from awarding non-competitive single-source contract for its air transportation network services to deliver certain classes of mail, where contract award was based on rational requirements in light of relevant data from several potential carriers. 39 U.S.C.A. § 101(f). Emery Worldwide Airlines, Inc. v. U.S., 264 F.3d 1071 (Fed. Cir. 2001). United States ☞64.10

United States Department of Labor's (DOL) decision to standardize its office software applications to those manufactured by single software manufacturer was not "procurement" decision to which Competition in Contracting Act's (CICA) sole source or name-brand only rules applied; decision did not involve actual purchase of software, and DOL subsequently elected to utilize procurement procedures expressly authorized by Federal Acquisition Streamlining Act (FASA) rather than engage in full and open competition under CICA. Federal Property and Administrative Services Act of 1949, §§ 303(a)(1), 303J(a)(2), as amended, 41 U.S.C.A. §§ 253(a)(1), 253j(a)(2); 48 C.F.R. § 6.001(f). Corel Corp. v. U.S., 165 F. Supp. 2d 12 (D.D.C. 2001). United States ☞64.10

Department of Labor (DOL) was not bound by senior DOL officials' mistaken belief that Competition in Contracting Act's (CICA) sole source and brand-name only requirements applied to its decision to standardize its office software applications, where officers' correspondence occurred before DOL made its ultimate decision to procure software from single manufacturer under Federal Acquisition Streamlining Act (FASA). Federal Property and Administrative Services Act of 1949, §§ 303, 303J, as amended, 41 U.S.C.A. §§ 253, 253j. Corel Corp. v. U.S., 165 F. Supp. 2d 12 (D.D.C. 2001). United States ☞64.10

Under the contracting scheme established by Javits-Wagner- O'Day (JWOD) Act, until a service is placed on the procurement list for qualified nonprofit agencies which employ blind or severely disabled persons, a federal agency may, under various contracting authorities, contract with any provider, including a qualified nonprofit agency for the severely disabled, even before the qualified nonprofit agency becomes a mandatory sole-source for those services; once a service is added to the procurement list, however, an agency must contract with one of the qualified providers. Wagner- O'Day Act, § 2, 41 U.S.C.A. § 47. Brothers Cleaning Service, Inc. v. Chair, Committee for Purchase from People Who are Blind or Severely Disabled, 26 F. Supp. 2d 1 (D.D.C. 1998). United States ☞64.10

United States Postal Service's award of sole-source contract to manage public pay telephones on Postal Service property was "purchase," within meaning of procurement manual's competitive bidding requirements, even though contractor was to be paid by retention of commissions from money generated from calls. AT&T Corp. v. U.S. Postal Service, 57 F. Supp. 2d 518 (N.D. Ill. 1997). United States ☞64.10

Trial court would not bar performance of contract to provide Customs Service with mobile x-ray for detection of contraband, even though Customs Service erroneously used Broad Agency Announcement (BAA) single source procurement procedure to avoid competitive bidding when BAA was available only for research or applied research contracts; Customs Service had good faith belief that BAA procedure could be used, and protestor requesting relief was not prejudiced, as it was previous sole source for x-ray equipment, and Customs Service wanted second source and could have legitimately requested bids from potential suppliers excluding protestor. Federal Property and Administrative Services Act of 1949, § 303(a)(1), (b)(1), 41 U.S.C.A. § 253(a)(1), (b)(1); 48 C.F.R. §§ 6.102(d)(2), 6.201, 6.202(b)(1). American Science and Engineering, Inc. v. Kelly, 69 F. Supp. 2d 227 (D. Mass. 1999). United States ☞64.60(5.1)

Bid protestor did not establish that agency's focus on experience with dredge disposal area maintenance in the context of an indefinite delivery/indefinite quantity (ID/IQ) contract effectively converted the contract into an illegal sole source contract because incumbent contractor was the only qualified small-business contractor in the Small Business Administration geographic region that had experience with dredge disposal area maintenance; actual results of competition in which five eligible offerors submitted proposals that were found to be within the competitive range belied any notion that the solicitation was a disguised sole source procurement. Gulf Group, Inc. v. U.S., 56 Fed. Cl. 391 (2003). United States ☞64.10

When deciding whether to award a contract to a potential sole-source supplier, procurement officials are not required to speculate as to every possible scenario that might enable other industry players to qualify. Emery Worldwide Airlines, Inc. v. U.S., 49 Fed. Cl. 211 (2001), aff'd, 264 F.3d 1071 (Fed. Cir. 2001). United States ☞64.10

Postal Service's decision to award sole-source contract for air transportation of mail was not arbitrary or capricious; decision was soundly grounded in adequate market research, as well as a reasonable operational and financial analysis, and its decision to rely on publicly available data was reasonable, based on its conclusion that the process of obtaining carriersupplied information would be tantamount to conducting a solicitation. Emery Worldwide Airlines, Inc. v. U.S., 49 Fed. Cl. 211 (2001), aff'd, 264 F.3d 1071 (Fed. Cir. 2001). United States ☞64.10

Statute providing that the Postal Service "make a fair and equitable distribution of mail business to carriers providing similar modes of transportation services to the Postal Service" does not preclude a non-competitive sole-source award. 39 U.S.C.A. §§ 101(f), 5402(d). Emery Worldwide Airlines, Inc. v. U.S., 49 Fed. Cl. 211 (2001), aff'd, 264 F.3d 1071 (Fed. Cir. 2001). United States ☞64.10

Delivery order placed against a General Services Administration (GSA) supply schedule was not an unlawful sole source award, notwithstanding that the order was placed with the one contractor who responded to the request for quotes. 48 C.F.R. § 8.404. Cybertech Group, Inc. v. U.S., 48 Fed. Cl. 638 (2001). United States ☞64.10

Contractor's history as a supplier and its prior participation in a related procurement did not satisfy requirements of notice of planned sole-source procurement that interested parties identify their interest and capability to respond to the requirement or submit proposals, as notice required affirmative action. 10 U.S.C.A. § 2304(f)(1)(C); 48 C.F.R. § 5.207(e)(3). Cubic Defense Systems, Inc. v. U.S., 45 Fed. Cl. 239 (1999), dismissed, 230 F.3d 1375 (Fed. Cir. 1999). United States ☞64.30

Contractor's response to sole source procurement notice did not amount to a waiver of its right to protest the procurement; contractor expressed sufficient interest in the procurement in telephonic communication with contracting agency, and although contractor did not articulate its capability to perform the work, its inability to do so resulted from the agency's failure to obtain certain data from the awardee. 10 U.S.C.A. § 2304(f)(1)(C); 48 C.F.R. § 5.207(e)(3). Cubic Defense Systems, Inc. v. U.S., 45 Fed. Cl. 239 (1999), dismissed, 230 F.3d 1375 (Fed. Cir. 1999). United States ☞64.60(2)

Sole-source contract for supply of M461M4A1 carbines represented a lawful exercise of procurement authority under the Competition in Contracting Act, where the government's acknowledgment in settlement of supplier's proprietary data rights precluded procurement of the weapon on a competitive basis. 10 U.S.C.A. § 2304. FN Manufacturing, Inc. v. U.S., 44 Fed. Cl. 449 (1999). United States ☞64.10

Government adequately explained its justification for awarding sole-source contract for modification of radar simulator which emits electronic warfare threats for training purposes, as required by the Competition in Contracting Act (CICA); contract was awarded to current manufacturer of simulator, and agency explained that the current manufacturer was the only source capable of performing as the total system integrator. 10 U.S.C.A. § 2304(c), (f)(1)(A); 48 C.F.R. § 6.303-2(a)(5). Metric Systems Corp. v. U.S., 42 Fed. Cl. 306 (1998). United States ☞64.45(1)

Clause in contracts for development of anti-submarine warfare system did not grant contractor sole-source status for life of the program; while clause did state that successful offeror would become the sole producer for the program, it did not state that offeror would become the sole producer, let alone sole-source, for the life of the program; moreover, contracts were for specific duration of four years, and clause had to be viewed as component of four-year contract. Westinghouse Elec. Corp. v. U.S., 41 Fed. Cl. 229, 42 Cont. Cas. Fed. (CCH) P 77332 (1998). United States ⚭64.10

Sole source concept relating to government contracts relate mainly to procurement, not to sales. 10 U.S.C.A. § 2304; Federal Property and Administrative Services Act of 1949, § 302(c), 41 U.S.C.A. § 252(c). Siller Bros., Inc. v. U. S., 228 Ct. Cl. 76, 655 F.2d 1039, 28 Cont. Cas. Fed. (CCH) P 81482 (1981). United States ⚭64.10

3 Sole source acquisitions—Armed forces contracts, sole source acquisitions

Sole source procurement by Navy was permissible for prototype of cylindrical orthogonal cylindrical arrangement air compressor that was unique concept available only from one contractor. 10 U.S.C.A. § 2304(c)(1). Single Screw Compressor, Inc. v. U.S. Dept. of Navy, 791 F. Supp. 7, 38 Cont. Cas. Fed. (CCH) P 76403 (D.D.C. 1992). United States ⚭64.10

Fact that under a court's direction Navy commissioned review team to investigate possibility of limited competition with respect to awarding of contracts to overhaul certain navy planes did not excuse navy's failure, during long pendency of review team's investigation, to take steps necessary for competition until it received final report, and therefore Navy was not entitled during that time to pursue a solesource program merely because firm the contracts were awarded to was only firm it was certain could perform the work. 10 U.S.C.A. § 2304(g). Aero Corp. v. Department of the Navy, 540 F. Supp. 180, 29 Cont. Cas. Fed. (CCH) P 82290 (D.D.C. 1982). United States ⚭64.10

Post-award bid protest challenging Army's sole-source procurement of helicopter engine filters raised justiciable claims, notwithstanding government's contention that the Court of Federal Claims could not supply relief because it could not determine the number of engine filters necessary to fulfill the operational needs of the armed forces in Iraq; test for "unusual and compelling urgency" invocation of exception to the full and open competition requirement of the Competition in Contracting Act (CICA) provided a manageable standard by which Court could judge the procurement. 10 U.S.C.A. § 2304(c)(2). Filtration Development Co., LLC v. U.S., 59 Fed. Cl. 658 (2004). United States ⚭64.60(1)

Government did not violate the Armed Services Procurement Act (ASPA) by its sole-source acquisition of training flight services in Hawaii and the Far East pursuant to existing contract without any competition, as the procurements were within scope of the contract, which covered training flight services for the Navy across the globe. 10 U.S.C.A. § 2304. Phoenix Air Group, Inc. v. U.S., 46 Fed. Cl. 90 (2000), dismissed, 243 F.3d 555 (Fed. Cir. 2000). United States ⚭64.10

Decision of the Air Force to issue a sole-source contract to contractor for contractor logistics support services at air base for pilot training system was not arbitrary, capricious or otherwise in violation of law or regulation. Cubic Defense Systems, Inc. v. U.S., 45 Fed. Cl. 239 (1999), dismissed, 230 F.3d 1375 (Fed. Cir. 1999). United States ⚭64.45(1)

The Air Force inappropriately used a non-appropriated fund instrumentality (NAFI) to provide mission essential food services on a non-competitive basis because it failed to comply with the requirement for a Justification and Approval of sole source award. GAO rejected the Air Force's contention that the NAFI statute (10 USC § 2492) authorized the transaction because the GAO found that the statute does not extend to contracts for mission essential food services, but instead applies to contracts in support of morale, welfare, and recreation (MWR). Asiel Enters., B-406780, 2012 CPD ¶ 242 (Comp. Gen. 2012)

4 Justifications-generally

Contracting officer's decision to award portion of contract for products and services without subjecting it to full and open competition, that was based on sole source justification and was abuse of discretion, could not be upheld on theory that goods and services were incidental to goods in rest of contract that were purchased against Federal Supply Schedule (FSS) contract, as officer's decision was not based on incidentals rationale but instead rationale was post hoc rationalization by government counsel; furthermore, congressional mandate requiring use of competitive procedures in conducting procurement does not include incidentals exception. 10 U.S.C.A. § 2304(a)(1)(A); 48 C.F.R. § 6.302-1. ATA Defense Industries, Inc. v. U.S., 38 Fed. Cl. 489, 41 Cont. Cas. Fed. (CCH) P 77147 (1997). United States ⚭64.10

Contracting officer's justification for not subjecting portion of contract to full and open competition, that goods and services could not have been purchased on the open market, was not legally sufficient to support award of contract, was abuse of discretion, and was not in accordance with law, where contracting officer was reasonably on notice that products and services purchased under contract on sole source basis were available competitively, and that successful bidder intended to purchase those products and services on the open market. 10 U.S.C.A. § 2304; 48 C.F.R. § 6.302-1. ATA Defense Industries, Inc. v. U.S., 38 Fed. Cl. 489, 41 Cont. Cas. Fed. (CCH) P 77147 (1997). United States ⊙64.10

Justification and approval prepared in support of a sole-source award expanding the scope of the contract was unreasonable where justification was premised on the conclusion that the awardee was the only responsible source, yet the capabilities of firms other than the awardee were not in fact considered. WorldWide Language Resources, Inc.; SOS International Ltd., B-296984, B-296984.2, B-296984.3, B-296984.4, B-296993, B-296993.2, B-296993.3, 2005 CPD ¶ 206 (Comp. Gen. 2005).

5 Publication Requirement

The FAR requires publication of a synopsis of a sole-source procurement in accordance with the Small Business Act, 15 U.S.C. § 637(e), and the Office of Federal Procurement Policy Act, 41 U.S.C. § 416, unless the procurement fits one of the exceptions to the synopsis requirement set forth in the regulations. FAR 5.101(a)(1), 6.302-1(d)(2). Matter of: M.D. Thompson Consulting, LLC; PMTech, Inc., B-297616, B-297616.2, 2006 CPD ¶ 41 (Comp. Gen. 2006).

6 Brand Name Specification

The U.S. Court of Appeals for the Federal Circuit (CAFC) found that a specification for "an integrated financial, acquisition and asset management system that is currently fully operational" within the Government did not unduly restrict competition, even though the protester contended that only an Oracle system could satisfy such a specification. The CAFC found that the specification addressed the agency's legitimate need for a fully integrated system because of difficulties experienced in past procurements in which the contractors could not provide functional integration among components of the system. Savantage Financial Services, Inc. v. U.S., 595 F.3d 1282 (Fed. Cir. 2010)

Solicitation for an emergency mass notification system, telephony and training that was limited on a brand name basis is overly restrictive because the agency failed to demonstrate a reasonable basis for the brand name restriction. The agency's justification was deficient because it failed to adequately define the supplies or services required to meet its needs, or any essential feature of the supplies or services that is unique to the brand name product. Further, the justification was deficient because the agency failed to document adequately its market research of other vendors' similar products. Desktop Alert, Inc., B-408196, 2013 CPD ¶ 179 (Comp.Gen. 2013)

Protest that solicitation is unduly restrictive because it requires firms to submit proposals based solely on a brand name list of particular products is sustained where the solicitation does not include salient characteristics for the brand name products, and the agency has not taken the steps necessary to procure its requirements using other than full and open competition. Matter of: California Industrial Facilities Resources, Inc., d/b/a CAMSS Shelters, B-403397.3, 2011 CPD ¶ 71 (Comp. Gen. 2011)

Where the solicitation given to protester only solicited offers for a designated model manufactured by the protester and did not indicate that equal products would be acceptable, but award was made to another offeror for its model, the specifications misled and prejudiced the protester, who assertedly could have proposed less expensive models conforming to the agency's needs. Deknatel Division, Pfizer Hospital Products Group, Inc., B-243408, 91-2 CPD ¶ 97 (Comp. Gen. 1991).

7 Adequate justification

Sole source procurement by Navy was permissible for prototype of cylindrical orthogonal cylindrical arrangement air compressor that was unique concept available only from one contractor. 10 U.S.C.A. § 2304(c)(1). Single Screw Compressor, Inc. v. U.S. Dept. of Navy, 791 F. Supp. 7, 38 Cont. Cas. Fed. (CCH) P 76403 (D.D.C. 1992). United States ⊙64.10

An agency's desire to avoid administrative inconvenience and rely upon an incumbent contractor's experience with its needs is no justification for sole-source procurement. Aero Corp. v. Department of the Navy, 540 F. Supp. 180, 29 Cont. Cas. Fed. (CCH) P 82290 (D.D.C. 1982). United States ☞64.10

Sole-source contract for supply of M461M4A1 carbines represented a lawful exercise of procurement authority under the Competition in Contracting Act, where the government's acknowledgment in settlement of supplier's proprietary data rights precluded procurement of the weapon on a competitive basis. 10 U.S.C.A. § 2304. FN Manufacturing, Inc. v. U.S., 44 Fed. Cl. 449 (1999). United States ☞64.10

Government adequately explained its justification for awarding sole-source contract for modification of radar simulator which emits electronic warfare threats for training purposes, as required by the Competition in Contracting Act (CICA); contract was awarded to current manufacturer of simulator, and agency explained that the current manufacturer was the only source capable of performing as the total system integrator. 10 U.S.C.A. § 2304(c), (f)(1)(A); 48 C.F.R. § 6.303-2(a)(5). Metric Systems Corp. v. U.S., 42 Fed. Cl. 306 (1998). United States ☞64.45(1)

Protest that agency improperly awarded interim "bridge" contract on sole-source basis is denied where award of long-term contract for same services was delayed by litigation and agency reasonably determined that only the incumbent contractor was in a position to perform urgently required services. J & J Colombia Services MV LTDA, B-299595.3, 2007 CPD ¶ 126 (Comp. Gen. 2007)

Agency's proposed award of a sole-source contract for autotitrators to be used in nuclear submarines is unobjectionable where the agency reasonably determined that it needed to acquire the same autotitrator previously fielded on other nuclear submarines for purposes of standardization and safety across the nuclear submarine fleet. The Navy determined that the sole source award was necessary because no other autotitrator is directly interchangeable in form fit and function with the currently fielded unit so that introducing a different unit would undermine the advantage of having Navy personnel operate a single standard unit, thereby increasing the risk of incorrect chemical analyses and, in turn, increasing the risk to the safety of Navy personnel and equipment. Matter of: Brinkmann Instruments, Inc., B-309946, B-309946.2, 2007 CPD ¶ 188 (Comp. Gen. 2007)

An agency may restrict a procurement to a single contractor to ensure that one firm is responsible for a technical system so that the government is relieved of the need to analyze the source of technical problems and to avoid "finger pointing" between contractors or to ensure the technical integrity and performance of a computer system. Under the protester's alternative proposal, two firms who have an admittedly contentious relationship would share responsibility for the successful functioning of mission-critical software. Under these circumstances, the agency properly considered the potential pitfalls in the protester's alternative proposal and reasonably decided that this approach would not meet its needs. eFedBudget Corporation, B-298627, 2006 CPD ¶ 159 (Comp. Gen. 2006)

Protester did not meet its burden of demonstrating that the contract could be performed without access to the awardee's source code and without violating the license agreement. In fact, the record demonstrates the need for any contractor other than the awardee to have access to the proprietary software, by means of a license from the awardee, to adequately perform the full scope of work. An agency may properly take into account the existence of software licenses when determining whether only one responsible source exists. eFedBudget Corporation, B-298627, 2006 CPD ¶ 159 (Comp. Gen. 2006)

8 Inadequate justification

Fact that under a court's direction Navy commissioned review team to investigate possibility of limited competition with respect to awarding of contracts to overhaul certain navy planes did not excuse navy's failure, during long pendency of review team's investigation, to take steps necessary for competition until it received final report, and therefore Navy was not entitled during that time to pursue a solesource program merely because firm the contracts were awarded to was only firm it was certain could perform the work. 10 U.S.C.A. § 2304(g). Aero Corp. v. Department of the Navy, 540 F. Supp. 180, 29 Cont. Cas. Fed. (CCH) P 82290 (D.D.C. 1982). United States ☞64.10

An agency's desire to avoid administrative inconvenience and rely upon an incumbent contractor's experience with its needs is no justification for sole-source procurement. Aero

Corp. v. Department of the Navy, 540 F. Supp. 180, 29 Cont. Cas. Fed. (CCH) P 82290 (D.D.C. 1982). United States ☞64.10

Contracting officer's justification for not subjecting portion of contract to full and open competition, that goods and services could not have been purchased on the open market, was not legally sufficient to support award of contract, was abuse of discretion, and was not in accordance with law, where contracting officer was reasonably on notice that products and services purchased under contract on sole source basis were available competitively, and that successful bidder intended to purchase those products and services on the open market. 10 U.S.C.A. § 2304; 48 C.F.R. § 6.302-1. ATA Defense Industries, Inc. v. U.S., 38 Fed. Cl. 489, 41 Cont. Cas. Fed. (CCH) P 77147 (1997). United States ☞64.10

Protest challenging sole-source procurement justified on the ground that only one source is available is sustained where the record shows that the presolicitation notice generated an expression of interest from a second source that has made significant progress towards becoming an approved source under the agency's source approval rules, and the remaining time required for approval is not long; as a result, a sole-source award, without considering the viability of the second source as part of the justification and approval process, is improper. Barnes Aerospace Group, B-298864, B-298864.2, 2006 CPD ¶ 204 (Comp. Gen. 2006)

Protest that agency improperly awarded requirement on a sole-source basis because it determined that only one firm could meet its requirements is sustained where record shows that another potential vendor was given an incorrect understanding of the agency's requirements; agencies are required to provide potential sources an opportunity to demonstrate their ability to meet the agency's requirements based on an accurate portrayal of the agency's needs. Lockheed Martin Systems Integration -- Owego, B-287190.2, B-287190.3, 2001 CPD ¶ 110 (Comp. Gen. 2001)

Agency's justification for sole-source procurement is inadequate where the documentation does not reasonably show that only one vendor's product will satisfy the agency's needs, and does not show that the agency's need for the item is of unusual and compelling urgency that was not created by a lack of advance planning. National Aerospace Group, Inc., B-282843, 99-2 CPD ¶ 43 (Comp. Gen. 1999)

Protest is sustained where agency did not provide protester with a reasonable opportunity to demonstrate the acceptability of its alternate product prior to, or in conjunction with, procurement restricted to a sole source, and where rejection of alternate item is based entirely on agency's unsupported assertion that it cannot evaluate alternate without the original equipment manufacturer's technical data. National Aerospace Group, Inc., B-282843, 99-2 CPD ¶ 43 (Comp. Gen. 1999)

9 Expert services

While contracting agency improperly relied upon the "expert" exception to full and open competition to justify the award of a sole-source contract to an incumbent contractor for litigation support services, protests that the agency's sole-source award based upon that exception are denied where the record reasonably supports the conclusion that the agency's action more properly should be viewed as a procurement under the exception to full and open competition where there is only one source capable of meeting the agency's needs. SEMCOR, Inc.; HJ Ford Associates, Inc., B-279794, B-279794.2, B-279794.3, 98-2 CPD ¶ 43 (Comp. Gen. 1998)

10 Injunctions—Sole source acquisitions, injunctions

Although Air Force's sole source procurement to standardize its network security systems violated the Competition in Contracting Act, protester's request for injunctive relief was denied because the Air Force's security needs outweighed the potential harm to protester in that any delay in obtaining and installing firewalls on that network would render network susceptible to complete shutdown or infiltration by hostile forces. McAfee, Inc. v. U.S., 111 Fed.Cl. 696 (Fed. Cl. 2013)

Contractor who protested award of sole source contract modification to incumbent contractor was not entitled to preliminary injunction enjoining performance of the modification; determination of head of contracting agency that sole source modification advanced the underlying public interest was clearly and convincingly justified, and thus protestor could not prevail on the merits. Federal Property and Administrative Services Act of 1949, § 303(c)(7), 41 U.S.C. § 253(c)(7); 48 C.F.R. § 6.302-7. Spherix, Inc. v. U.S., 58 Fed. Cl. 514 (2003)

If Claims Court finds, for purposes of imposing preliminary injunction against government award of contract to competitor, that prospective bidder casts strong doubt on government's justifications for sole-source award, then prospective bidder has strong likelihood of success on merits. Magnavox Electronic Systems Co. v. U.S., 26 Cl. Ct. 1373, 38 Cont. Cas. Fed. (CCH) P 76414, 1992 WL 277980 (1992)

Government's decision to proceed on sole-source procurement for fuses without further investigating prospective bidder's capabilities by conducting preaward survey was unreasonable and violation of regulations and thus, for purposes of preliminarily enjoining contract award, prospective bidder had likely success on merits. Magnavox Electronic Systems Co. v. U.S., 26 Cl. Ct. 1373, 38 Cont. Cas. Fed. (CCH) P 76414, 1992 WL 277980 (1992).

§ 6.302-2 Unusual and compelling urgency.

(a) Authority.

(1) Citations: 10 U.S.C. 2304(c)(2) or 41 U.S.C. 3304(a)(2).

(2) When the agency's need for the supplies or services is of such an unusual and compelling urgency that the Government would be seriously injured unless the agency is permitted to limit the number of sources from which it solicits bids or proposals, full and open competition need not be provided for.

(b) *Application.* This authority applies in those situations where—

(1) An unusual and compelling urgency precludes full and open competition; and

(2) Delay in award of a contract would result in serious injury, financial or other, to the Government.

(c) Limitations.

(1) Contracts awarded using this authority shall be supported by the written justifications and approvals described in 6.303 and 6.304. These justifications may be made and approved after contract award when preparation and approval prior to award would unreasonably delay the acquisition.

(2) This statutory authority requires that agencies shall request offers from as many potential sources as is practicable under the circumstances.

(d) Period of Performance.

(1) The total period of performance of a contract awarded using this authority—

(i) May not exceed the time necessary—

(A) To meet the unusual and compelling requirements of the work to be performed under the contract; and

(B) For the agency to enter into another contract for the required goods and services through the use of competitive procedures; and

(ii) May not exceed one year unless the head of the agency entering into the contract determines that exceptional circumstances apply.

(2) The requirements in paragraph (d)(1) of this section shall apply to any contract in an amount greater than the simplified acquisition threshold.

(3) The determination of exceptional circumstances is in addition to the approval of the justification in 6.304.

(4) The determination may be made after contract award when making the determination prior to award would unreasonably delay the acquisition.

United States Code Annotated

Administrative determinations, see 41 U.S.C.A. § 257.

Advocates for competition, see 41 U.S.C.A. § 418.

Competition requirements, see 41 U.S.C.A. § 253.

Contract goal for small disadvantaged businesses and certain institutions of higher education, see 10 U.S.C.A. § 2323.

Contracts, competition requirements, see 10 U.S.C.A. § 2304.

Contracts, planning, solicitation, evaluation, and award procedures, see 10 U.S.C.A.

§ 2305.

Contracts, prohibition on competition between Department of Defense and small businesses and certain other entities, see 10 U.S.C.A. § 2304e.

Credit for Indian contracting in meeting certain subcontracting goals for small disadvantaged businesses and certain institutions of higher education, see 10 U.S.C.A. § 2323a.

Definitions, see 10 U.S.C.A. § 2302; 41 U.S.C.A. §§ 259, 403.

Design-build selection procedures, see 10 U.S.C.A. § 2305a; 41 U.S.C.A. § 253m.

Determinations and decisions, see 10 U.S.C.A. § 2310; 41 U.S.C.A. § 262.

Encouragement of new competition, see 41 U.S.C.A. § 253c.

Encouragement of new competitors, see 10 U.S.C.A. § 2319.

Planning and solicitation requirements, see 41 U.S.C.A. § 253a.

Procurement notice, see 41 U.S.C.A. § 416.

Notes of Decisions

In general 1
Adequate justification 5
Armed forces contracts 2
Inadequate justification 6
Lack of advance planning 3
Limitations 4

1 In general

A "public exigency" demanding immediate delivery of government supplies and obviating statutory necessity of advertising for competitive bids is a sudden and unexpected happening, an unforeseen occurrence or condition, a perplexing contingency or complication of circumstances, or a sudden or unexpected occasion for action. Good Roads Machinery Co. of New England v. U.S., 19 F. Supp. 652 (D. Mass. 1937). United States ☞64.10

For purposes of award of attorney fees under the Equal Access to Justice Act (EAJA) to bid protestor, government's conduct at the agency level and during litigation was not substantially justified with regard to unusual and compelling urgency exception to the Competition in Contracting Act (CICA) which it invoked for procurement of engine filters for military helicopters; although initial invocation of exception was substantially justified, government did not attempt to scope and duration of exception to quantity of filters needed satisfy urgent requirements. Filtration Development Co., LLC v. U.S., 63 Fed. Cl. 612 (2005). United States ☞147(12)

Contracting agency's invocation of the "unusual and compelling urgency" exception to the full and open competition requirement of the Competition in Contracting Act (CICA), and its inherent limitations, is subject to judicial review. 10 U.S.C.A. § 2304(c)(2). Filtration Development Co., LLC v. U.S., 59 Fed. Cl. 658 (2004). United States ☞64.10

"Unusual and compelling urgency" exception to the full and open competition requirement of the Competition in Contracting Act (CICA) contains an implicit limitation that the agency take reasonable steps to accurately determine its needs and describe them; the agency head's discretion is subject to such limitation because the urgency justification cannot support the procurement of more than a minimum quantity needed to satisfy the immediate urgent requirement. 10 U.S.C.A. § 2304(c)(2). Filtration Development Co., LLC v. U.S., 59 Fed. Cl. 658 (2004). United States ☞64.10

Contracting agency's invocation of the "unusual and compelling urgency" exception to the full and open competition requirement of the Competition in Contracting Act (CICA) did not preclude challenge to procurement based on allegation that agency violated organizational conflict of interest (OCI) regulations. 10 U.S.C.A. § 2304(c)(2); 48 C.F.R. § 9. 505-1. Filtration Development Co., LLC v. U.S., 59 Fed. Cl. 658 (2004). United States ☞64.15

The exception for unusual and compelling urgency permits executive agencies to limit the number of sources from which it solicits bids or proposals. However, an agency must obtain the maximum level of competition that circumstances allow and may not simply ignore the potential for competition. 41 U.S.C. sect. 253(e); FAR 6.302-2(c)(2). Bausch & Lomb, Inc., B-298444, 2006 CPD ¶ 135 (Comp. Gen. 2006)

2 Armed forces contracts

Bid protestor who prevailed on merits of claim that Army procurement of helicopter engine filters did not adhere to organizational conflict of interest (OCI) requirements and exceeded permissible bounds of the unusual and compelling urgency exception of the Competition in Contracting Act (CICA) was not entitled to injunctive relief with respect to 183 "A kits" and 150 "B kits" for which funding had been allocated and delivery schedule had been set, as that order was justified by needs of Operation Iraqi Freedom; however, Army would be enjoined to conduct any procurement in excess of those amounts on a competitive basis unless an independent justification for invoking an exception to full and open competition was provided. 10 U.S.C.A. § 2304(c)(2). Filtration Development Co., LLC v. U.S., 60 Fed. Cl. 371 (2004). Injunction ☞86

Army properly invoked the "unusual and compelling urgency" exception to the full and open competition requirement of the Competition in Contracting Act (CICA) to make sole-source procurement of helicopter engine filter kits based on urgent need to acquire filters for helicopters deployed to Iraq during Operation Iraqi Freedom; however, Army through its actions revealed that emergency situation encompassed only 183 "A kits" and 150 "B kits." Filtration Development Co., LLC v. U.S., 60 Fed. Cl. 371 (2004). United States ☞64.10

Post-award bid protest challenging Army's sole-source procurement of helicopter engine filters raised justiciable claims, notwithstanding government's contention that the Court of Federal Claims could not supply relief because it could not determine the number of engine filters necessary to fulfill the operational needs of the armed forces in Iraq; test for "unusual and compelling urgency" invocation of exception to the full and open competition requirement of the Competition in Contracting Act (CICA) provided a manageable standard by which Court could judge the procurement. 10 U.S.C.A. § 2304(c)(2). Filtration Development Co., LLC v. U.S., 59 Fed. Cl. 658 (2004). United States ☞64.60(1)

Military agency reasonably awarded a contract on a sole source basis for urgently required deployable circuit analyzers for use in helicopter maintenance and repair to the only approved source of the items, where the record evidences that no other source is or will become an approved source of the circuit analyzers in time to meet the urgent requirement. Eclypse Int'l Corp., B-274507, 96-2 CPD ¶ 179 (Comp. Gen. 1996).

3 Lack of advance planning

Agency improperly extended a contract on a sole-source basis because it did not consider other contractors and created the urgency that led to the sole-source award through a lack of advance procurement planning. The GAO rejected the agency's contention that the extension was justified because market research for the new procurement took longer than expected. Decision Matter of: Major Contracting Services, Inc., B-401472, 2009 CPD ¶ 170 (Comp. Gen. 2009)

Protest to a sole source award based on unusual and compelling circumstances was sustained because the agency failed to adequately plan. When an agency restricts competition to pre-approved sources, it must give other potential sources a reasonable opportunity to qualify. Agency's failure to act upon a vendor's request for approval within a reasonable period of time deprived the vendor of an opportunity to compete. Decision Matter of: RBC Bearings Incorporated, B-401661, B-401661.2, 2009 CPD ¶ 207 (Comp. Gen. 2009)

Protests challenging agency's award of sole-source contract for bilingual-bicultural advisors utilizing other than competitive procedures based on unusual and compelling urgency are sustained where the agency initially attempted to place the requirement under an environmental services contract, which, on its face, did not include within its scope the bilingual-bicultural advisor requirement. This obvious error constituted lack of advance planning, which compromised the agency's ability to obtain any meaningful competition and directly resulted in the sole-source award. WorldWide Language Resources, Inc.; SOS International Ltd., B-296984, B-296984.2, B-296984.3, B-296984.4, B-296993, B-296993.2, B-296993.3, 2005 CPD ¶ 206 (Comp. Gen. 2005).

4 Limitations

The invocation of the unusual and compelling urgency exception is constrained by several inherent limitations as to scope and duration. The agency must take reasonable steps to accurately determine its needs and describe them. The urgency justification cannot support the procurement of more than a minimum quantity needed to satisfy the immediate urgent requirement. In addition, the invocation of the exception should not continue for more than a minimum time. Filtration Development Co., LLC v. U.S., 63 Fed. Cl. 612 (2005).

Contracting officer's after-the-fact reliance upon Federal Acquisition Regulation that allows use of other than competitive procedures when there is an unusual and compelling urgency was too late to justify issuance of purchase order contract without the benefit of full and open competition. 10 U.S.C.A. § 2304; 48 C.F.R. § 6.302-2. ATA Defense Industries, Inc. v. U.S., 38 Fed. Cl. 489, 41 Cont. Cas. Fed. (CCH) P 77147 (1997). United States ⬤═64.10

5 Adequate justification

Army properly invoked the "unusual and compelling urgency" exception to the full and open competition requirement of the Competition in Contracting Act (CICA) to make sole-source procurement of helicopter engine filter kits based on urgent need to acquire filters for helicopters deployed to Iraq during Operation Iraqi Freedom; however, Army through its actions revealed that emergency situation encompassed only 183 "A kits" and 150 "B kits." 10 U.S.C.A. § 2304(c)(2). Filtration Development Co., LLC v. U.S., 60 Fed. Cl. 371 (2004). United States ⬤═64.10

Protest against sole-source award of contract for maintenance and operation of foreign threat systems is denied where agency reasonably determined that protester's performance under its current contract was unacceptable, and that protester had not adequately addressed the unacceptable performance, casting protester's ability to satisfactorily perform new contract into doubt. Although the agency must request offers from as many sources as practicable under the circumstances, 10 U.S.C. § 2304(e), FAR 6.302-2(c)(2), it nevertheless may limit the procurement to the only firm it reasonably believes can properly perform the work in the available time. Research Analysis & Maintenance, Inc., B-296206, B-296206.2, 2005 CPD ¶ 182 (Comp. Gen. 2005)

6 Inadequate justification

Navy's conclusory justification and approval, which contained no operative facts to support award of contract for mobile facility units, minimally complied with statute, that permits less than full and open competition in case of unusual and compelling urgency to prevent serious injury to United States, where justification and approval stated that inability to obtain units in shortest possible time would injuriously delay weapon system operational requirements and influence readiness of fleet. 10 U.S.C.A. § 2304(c), (c)(2), (f), (f)(1)(B)(ii). McDonald Welding & Mach. Co., Inc. v. Lehman, 648 F. Supp. 1338 (N.D. Ohio 1986), judgment rev'd on other grounds, 829 F.2d 593, 34 Cont. Cas. Fed. (CCH) P 75362 (6th Cir. 1987). United States ⬤═64.10

Agency failed to demonstrate that it had a reasonable basis to make sole-source orders under the unusual and compelling urgency exception. The agency did not reasonably demonstrate why it could not have opened the requirement up to an expedited limited competition among those firms that had expressed interest in the acquisition. There is no evidence in the record that the agency ever considered whether the protester's equipment proposed, or the equipment of any other firm, would meet its urgent requirements. Bausch & Lomb, Inc., B-298444, 2006 CPD ¶ 135 (Comp. Gen. 2006)

§ 6.302-3 Industrial mobilization; engineering, developmental, or research capability; or expert services.

    (a) Authority.

        (1) Citations: 10 U.S.C. 2304(c)(3) or 41 U.S.C. 3304(a)(3).

        (2) Full and open competition need not be provided for when it is necessary to award the contract to a particular source or sources in order—

            (i) To maintain a facility, producer, manufacturer, or other supplier available for furnishing supplies or services in case of a national emergency or to achieve industrial mobilization;

            (ii) To establish or maintain an essential engineering, research, or development capability to be provided by an educational or other nonprofit institution or a federally funded research and development center; or

(iii) To acquire the services of an expert or neutral person for any current or anticipated litigation or dispute.

(b) Application.

(1) Use of the authority in paragraph (a)(2)(i) of this subsection may be appropriate when it is necessary to—

(i) Keep vital facilities or suppliers in business or make them available in the event of a national emergency;

(ii) Train a selected supplier in the furnishing of critical supplies or services; prevent the loss of a supplier's ability and employees' skills; or maintain active engineering, research, or development work;

(iii) Maintain properly balanced sources of supply for meeting the requirements of acquisition programs in the interest of industrial mobilization (when the quantity required is substantially larger than the quantity that must be awarded in order to meet the objectives of this authority, that portion not required to meet such objectives will be acquired by providing for full and open competition, as appropriate, under this part);

(iv) Create or maintain the required domestic capability for production of critical supplies by limiting competition to items manufactured in—

(A) The United States or its outlying areas; or

(B) The United States, its outlying areas, or Canada.

(v) Continue in production, contractors that are manufacturing critical items, when there would otherwise be a break in production; or

(vi) Divide current production requirements among two or more contractors to provide for an adequate industrial mobilization base.

(2) Use of the authority in paragraph (a)(2)(ii) of this subsection may be appropriate when it is necessary to—

(i) Establish or maintain an essential capability for theoretical analyses, exploratory studies, or experiments in any field of science or technology;

(ii) Establish or maintain an essential capability for engineering or developmental work calling for the practical application of investigative findings and theories of a scientific or technical nature; or

(iii) Contract for supplies or services as are necessary incident to paragraphs (b)(2)(i) or (ii) of this subsection.

(3) Use of the authority in paragraph (a)(2)(iii) of this subsection may be appropriate when it is necessary to acquire the services of either—

(i) An expert to use, in any litigation or dispute (including any reasonably foreseeable litigation or dispute) involving the Government in any trial, hearing, or proceeding before any court, administrative tribunal, or agency, whether or not the expert is expected to testify. Examples of such services include, but are not limited to:

(A) Assisting the Government in the analysis, presentation, or defense of any claim or request for adjustment to contract terms and conditions, whether asserted by a contractor or the Government, which is in litigation or dispute, or is anticipated to result in dispute or litigation before any court, administrative tribunal, or agency; or

(B) Participating in any part of an alternative dispute resolution process, including but not limited to evaluators, fact finders, or witnesses, regardless of whether the expert is expected to testify; or

(ii) A neutral person, *e.g.,* mediators or arbitrators, to facilitate the resolution of issues in an alternative dispute resolution process.

(c) *Limitations.* Contracts awarded using this authority shall be supported by the written justifications and approvals described in 6.303 and 6.304.

United States Code Annotated

Administrative determinations, see 41 U.S.C.A. § 257.

Advocates for competition, see 41 U.S.C.A. § 418.

Competition requirements, see 41 U.S.C.A. § 253.

Contract goal for small disadvantaged businesses and certain institutions of higher education, see 10 U.S.C.A. § 2323.

Contracts, competition requirements, see 10 U.S.C.A. § 2304.

Contracts, planning, solicitation, evaluation, and award procedures, see 10 U.S.C.A. § 2305.

Contracts, prohibition on competition between Department of Defense and small businesses and certain other entities, see 10 U.S.C.A. § 2304e.

Credit for Indian contracting in meeting certain subcontracting goals for small disadvantaged businesses and certain institutions of higher education, see 10 U.S.C.A. § 2323a.

Definitions, see 10 U.S.C.A. § 2302; 41 U.S.C.A. §§ 259, 403.

Design-build selection procedures, see 10 U.S.C.A. § 2305a; 41 U.S.C.A. § 253m.

Determinations and decisions, see 10 U.S.C.A. § 2310; 41 U.S.C.A. § 262.

Encouragement of new competition, see 41 U.S.C.A. § 253c.

Encouragement of new competitors, see 10 U.S.C.A. § 2319.

Planning and solicitation requirements, see 41 U.S.C.A. § 253a.

Procurement notice, see 41 U.S.C.A. § 416.

Notes of Decisions

Expert services 2
Industrial mobilization 1

1 Industrial mobilization

Award of contract to construct nuclear-powered submarine for Navy on basis of price alone violated Appropriations Act provision requiring contract be awarded pursuant to acquisition strategy for submarine program, where strategy required industrial mobilization award to provide for competition between two competing shipyards throughout life of submarine program. 10 U.S.C. § 2305a. Newport News Shipbuilding and Dry Dock Co. v. U.S. Dept. of Navy, 771 F. Supp. 739, 37 Cont. Cas. Fed. (CCH) P 76230 (E.D. Va. 1991), judgment rev'd, 960 F.2d 386, 37 Cont. Cas. Fed. (CCH) P 76285 (4th Cir. 1992)

For purposes of particular procurement decision, "industrial mobilization" refers to exception to general requirement that government contracts be awarded on basis of price competition. 10 U.S.C. §§ 2304(c)(3), 4501. Newport News Shipbuilding and Dry Dock Co. v. U.S. Dept. of Navy, 771 F. Supp. 739, 37 Cont. Cas. Fed. (CCH) P 76230 (E.D. Va. 1991), judgment rev'd, 960 F.2d 386, 37 Cont. Cas. Fed. (CCH) P 76285 (4th Cir. 1992)

The Competition in Contracting Act, 10 U.S.C. § 2304, permits restriction of competition to insure suppliers of critical items constantly maintain the production capacity that would be needed in the event of a national emergency. GAO's standard of review recognizes substantial agency discretion in the establishment and composition of a mobilization base. The Honorable Dan Burton House of Representatives, B-265884, 1995 WL 684894 (Comp. Gen. 1995)

2 Expert services

While contracting agency improperly relied upon the "expert" exception to full and open competition to justify the award of a sole-source contract to an incumbent contractor for litigation support services, protests that the agency's sole-source award based upon that exception are denied where the record reasonably supports the conclusion that the agency's action more properly should be viewed as a procurement under the exception to full and open competition where there is only one source capable of meeting the agency's needs. SEMCOR, Inc.; HJ Ford Associates, Inc., B-279794, B-279794.2, B-279794.3, 98-2 CPD ¶ 43 (Comp. Gen. 1998)

§ 6.302-4 International agreement.

(a) Authority.

(1) Citations: 10 U.S.C. 2304(c)(4) or 41 U.S.C. 3304(a)(4).

(2) Full and open competition need not be provided for when precluded by the terms of an international agreement or a treaty between the United States and a foreign government or international organization, or the written directions of a foreign government reimbursing the agency for the cost of the acquisition of the supplies or services for such government.

(b) *Application.* This authority may be used in circumstances such as—

(1) When a contemplated acquisition is to be reimbursed by a foreign country that requires that the product be obtained from a particular firm as specified in official written direction such as a Letter of Offer and Acceptance; or

(2) When a contemplated acquisition is for services to be performed, or supplies to be used, in the sovereign territory of another country and the terms of a treaty or agreement specify or limit the sources to be solicited.

(c) *Limitations.* Except for DoD, NASA, and the Coast Guard, contracts awarded using this authority shall be supported by written justifications and approvals described in 6.303 and 6.304.

United States Code Annotated

Administrative determinations, see 41 U.S.C.A. § 257.

Advocates for competition, see 41 U.S.C.A. § 418.

Competition requirements, see 41 U.S.C.A. § 253.

Contract goal for small disadvantaged businesses and certain institutions of higher education, see 10 U.S.C.A. § 2323.

Contracts, competition requirements, see 10 U.S.C.A. § 2304.

Contracts, planning, solicitation, evaluation, and award procedures, see 10 U.S.C.A. § 2305.

Contracts, prohibition on competition between Department of Defense and small businesses and certain other entities, see 10 U.S.C.A. § 2304e.

Credit for Indian contracting in meeting certain subcontracting goals for small disadvantaged businesses and certain institutions of higher education, see 10 U.S.C.A. § 2323a.

Definitions, see 10 U.S.C.A. § 2302; 41 U.S.C.A. §§ 259, 403.

Design-build selection procedures, see 10 U.S.C.A. § 2305a; 41 U.S.C.A. § 253m.

Determinations and decisions, see 10 U.S.C.A. § 2310; 41 U.S.C.A. § 262.

Encouragement of new competition, see 41 U.S.C.A. § 253c.

Encouragement of new competitors, see 10 U.S.C.A. § 2319.

Planning and solicitation requirements, see 41 U.S.C.A. § 253a.

Procurement notice, see 41 U.S.C.A. § 416.

Notes of Decisions

In general 1
Directions of foreign government 3
Treaties 2

1 In general

Authority to enter foreign military sale (FMS) sole source contracts required conformance to written justifications and approvals requirement, and contracting officer did not have authority to enter into sole source contract upon receipt of sole source procurement request from FMS customer. 10 U.S.C.A. § 2304(c)(4). Kollsman, a Div. of Sequa Corp. v. U.S., 25 Cl. Ct. 500, 37 Cont. Cas. Fed. (CCH) P 76283, 1992 WL 48773 (1992). United States ⊙═64.10

2 Treaties

Affiliated status of Icelandic company and United States flag carrier that submitted bids for separate portions of military contract for shipping between United States and Iceland did not transform bidding process into something other than a "competition," as required by treaty and memorandum of understanding (MOU), since company and carrier were separate corporate entities despite their common ownership. Iceland S.S. Co., Ltd.-Eimskip v. U.S. Dept. of Army, 201 F.3d 451, 458, 2000 A.M.C. 1487 (D.C. Cir. 2000). Treaties ⊙⇒8; United States ⊙⇒64.10

3 Directions of foreign government

Under DFARS 225.7304(a) the contracting officer "shall honor" a foreign customer's request for a directed subcontract when the "written direction sufficiently fulfills the requirements of FAR 6.3." Insofar as pertinent, FAR 6.302-4(a) allows for other than full and open competition pursuant to the "written directions of a foreign government reimbursing the agency for the cost of the acquisition . . .." We find that the foreign government's written direction as to a directed subcontract materially complied with FAR 6.302-4(a). Appeals of Lockheed Martin Tactical Aircraft Systems, A.S.B.C.A. No. 49530, A.S.B.C.A. No. 50057, 00-1 B.C.A. (CCH) ¶ 30852, 2000 WL 307741 (Armed Serv. B.C.A. 2000), adhered to on denial of reconsideration, A.S.B.C.A. No. 49530, 00-2 B.C.A. (CCH) ¶ 30930, 2000 WL 655947 (Armed Serv. B.C.A. 2000)

The Foreign Assistance Act, 22 U.S.C. §§ 2311(a)(3) (1994), permits transfer of military assistance funds to a country's Foreign Military Sales (FMS) trust account for use in meeting the obligations of that FMS customer arising from purchases made under the Arms Export Control Act. Once funds are deposited in a foreign country's account to be used to meet the obligations of the FMS customer, FMS rules and procedures apply, including the honoring of a customer's designation of a sole source supplier as provided for in FAR 6.302-4. Accordingly, there is no basis to object to the agency's actions here. Goddard Industries, Inc., B-275643, 97-1 CPD ¶ 104 (Comp. Gen. 1997)

§ 6.302-5 Authorized or required by statute.

(a) Authority.

(1) Citations: 10 U.S.C. 2304(c)(5) or 41 U.S.C. 3304(a)(5).

(2) Full and open competition need not be provided for when—

(i) A statute expressly authorizes or requires that the acquisition be made through another agency or from a specified source; or

(ii) The agency's need is for a brand name commercial item for authorized resale.

(b) Application. This authority may be used when statutes, such as the following, expressly authorize or require that acquisition be made from a specified source or through another agency:

(1) Federal Prison Industries (UNICOR)—18 U.S.C. 4124 (see subpart 8.6).

(2) Qualified nonprofit agencies for the blind or other severely disabled—41 U.S.C. chapter 85, Committee for Purchase From People Who Are Blind or Severely Disabled (see subpart 8.7).

(3) Government Printing and Binding—44 U.S.C. 501–504, 1121 (see subpart 8.8).

(4) Sole source awards under the 8(a) Program (15 U.S.C. 637), but see 6.303 for requirements for justification and approval of sole-source 8(a) awards over $22 million. (See subpart 19.8).

(5) Sole source awards under the HUBZone Act of 1997—15 U.S.C. 657a (see 19.1306).

(6) Sole source awards under the Veterans Benefits Act of 2003 (15 U.S.C. 657f).

(7) Sole source awards under the WOSB Program–15 U.S.C. 637(m) (see 19.1506).

(c) Limitations.

(1) This authority shall not be used when a provision of law requires an agency to award a new contract to a specified non-Federal Government entity unless the provision of law specifically—

(i) Identifies the entity involved;

(ii) Refers to 10 U.S.C. 2304(k) for armed services acquisitions or 41 U.S.C. 3105 for civilian agency acquisitions; and

(iii) States that award to that entity shall be made in contravention of the merit-based selection procedures in 10 U.S.C. 2304(k) or 41 U.S.C. 3105, as appropriate. However, this limitation does not apply—

(A) When the work provided for in the contract is a continuation of the work performed by the specified entity under a preceding contract; or

(B) To any contract requiring the National Academy of Sciences to investigate, examine, or experiment upon any subject of science or art of significance to an executive agency and to report on those matters to the Congress or any agency of the Federal Government.

(2) Contracts awarded using this authority shall be supported by the written justifications and approvals described in 6.303 and 6.304, except for—

(i) Contracts awarded under (a)(2)(ii) or (b)(2) of this subsection;

(ii) Contracts awarded under (a)(2)(i) of this subsection when the statute expressly requires that the procurement be made from a specified source. (Justification and approval requirements apply when the statute authorizes, but does not require, that the procurement be made from a specified source); or

(iii) Contracts less than or equal to $22 million awarded under (b)(4) of this subsection.

(3) The authority in (a)(2)(ii) of this subsection may be used only for purchases of brand-name commercial items for resale through commissaries or other similar facilities. Ordinarily, these purchases will involve articles desired or preferred by customers of the selling activities (but see 6.301(d)).

United States Code Annotated

Administrative determinations, see 41 U.S.C.A. § 257.

Advocates for competition, see 41 U.S.C.A. § 418.

Competition requirements, see 41 U.S.C.A. § 253.

Contract goal for small disadvantaged businesses and certain institutions of higher education, see 10 U.S.C.A. § 2323.

Contracts, competition requirements, see 10 U.S.C.A. § 2304.

Contracts, planning, solicitation, evaluation, and award procedures, see 10 U.S.C.A. § 2305.

Contracts, prohibition on competition between Department of Defense and small businesses and certain other entities, see 10 U.S.C.A. § 2304e.

Credit for Indian contracting in meeting certain subcontracting goals for small disadvantaged businesses and certain institutions of higher education, see 10 U.S.C.A. § 2323a.

Definitions, see 10 U.S.C.A. § 2302; 41 U.S.C.A. §§ 259, 403.

Design-build selection procedures, see 10 U.S.C.A. § 2305a; 41 U.S.C.A. § 253m.

Determinations and decisions, see 10 U.S.C.A. § 2310; 41 U.S.C.A. § 262.

Encouragement of new competition, see 41 U.S.C.A. § 253c.

Encouragement of new competitors, see 10 U.S.C.A. § 2319.

Planning and solicitation requirements, see 41 U.S.C.A. § 253a.

Procurement notice, see 41 U.S.C.A. § 416.

Notes of Decisions

Commercial items 2
Construction with other laws 1
Purchases from disabled individuals 3

1 Construction with other laws

General Services Administration's (GSA) execution of lease with winning developer to develop federal office complex under Federal Triangle Development Act did not violate federal statute providing that GSA may acquire leasehold interest in any building which is constructed for lease to, and for predominant use by, United States only by use of competitive procedures required by Competition in Contracts Act (CICA); just as Congress overrode Federal Acquisition Regulation (FAR) system and CICA when it enacted legislation entrusting Federal Triangle Development Project to Pennsylvania Avenue Development Corporation (PADC), it obviously overrode aforementioned statute when it directed GSA to enter into lease with whichever developer won PADC's development competition. Public Buildings Act of 1959, § 18(b) as amended, 40 U.S.C.A. § 618(b); Federal Triangle Development Act, §§ 5(a)(3), 6, 40 U.S.C.A. §§ 1104(a)(3), 1105; 31 U.S.C.A. § 9101(3)(H); Federal Property and Administrative Services Act of 1949, § 303 et seq., as amended, 41 U.S.C.A. § 253 et seq.Saratoga Development Corp. v. U.S., 21 F.3d 445, 305, 39 Cont. Cas. Fed. (CCH) P 76649 (D.C. Cir. 1994). United States ☞64.10

When Congress directed Pennsylvania Avenue Development Corporation (PADC) to use its existing procedures for competition to select developer for federal office complex under Federal Triangle Development Act, it intended to supplant Competition in Contracts Act (CICA) and Federal Acquisition Regulation (FAR) system, rather than impose requirement that PADC follow not only CICA and FAR but also its own procedures, where Congress not only authorized, but directed PADC to follow its own policy and procedures regarding development competitions, Federal Triangle Project was hybrid project since it was publicly funded in sense that government would eventually pay all development costs in form of rent, but title to building would actually be in private hands for first 35 years, and Congress entrusted construction of building to corporation whose primary success had come in superintending private projects. Federal Triangle Development Act, §§ 2–10, 40 U.S.C.A. §§ 1101–1109; 31 U.S.C.A. § 9101(3)(H); Federal Property and Administrative Services Act of 1949, § 303 et seq., as amended, 41 U.S.C.A. § 253 et seq.Saratoga Development Corp. v. U.S., 21 F.3d 445, 305, 39 Cont. Cas. Fed. (CCH) P 76649 (D.C. Cir. 1994). United States ☞64.5; United States ☞64.40(1)

Under Federal Triangle Development Act, Pennsylvania Avenue Development Corporation (PADC), which was in charge of selecting developer for federal office complex, was not governed by Federal Acquisition Regulations (FAR) system nor Competition in Contracting Act (CICA), where Congress stipulated that competition for project must be conducted in accordance with existing policies and procedures of PADC for development competition which referred to only procedures PADC ever characterized as procedures for development competition, i.e., those used for private development initiated by PADC. Federal Triangle Development Act, §§ 2–10, 40 U.S.C.A. §§ 1101–1109; 31 U.S.C.A. § 9101(3)(H); Federal Property and Administrative Services Act of 1949, § 303 et seq., as amended, 41 U.S.C.A. § 253 et seq.Saratoga Development Corp. v. U.S., 21 F.3d 445, 305, 39 Cont. Cas. Fed. (CCH) P 76649 (D.C. Cir. 1994). United States ☞64.10; United States ☞64.40(1)

Concessions contract issued pursuant to the Concessions Policy Act (CPA) was not subject to Federal Acquisition Regulations (FAR). National Park System Concessions Policy Act, §§ 2, 3, 16 U.S.C.A. §§ 20a, 20b; Federal Property and Administrative Services Act of 1949, § 303(a)(1), 41 U.S.C.A. § 253(a)(1). YRT Services Corp. v. U.S., 28 Fed. Cl. 366, 38 Cont. Cas. Fed. (CCH) P 76512 (1993). United States ☞57; United States ☞64.10

Contention that a Justification and Approval (J & A) does not properly support an agency's decision to limit a competition for debris cleanup under the Stafford Act to firms residing, or primarily doing business, in Mississippi is denied where the agency's J & A reasonably explains and justifies the actions taken, and where the record shows that those actions are within the discretion provided by the Stafford Act. The FAR provision implementing the statutory authority at 10 U.S.C. sect. 2304(c)(5) expressly identifies the Stafford Act as one of the statutes that may be used to support a decision to use other than full and open competition in a federal procurement. FAR sect. 6.302-5(b)(5). AshBritt Inc., B-297889, B-297889.2, 2006 CPD ¶ 48 (Comp. Gen. 2006)

2 Commercial items

Radioactive waste disposal service called for in solicitation was not a "commercial item" subject to mandatory procedures of the Federal Acquisition Regulation (FAR), where there were no market prices for the service, and no competitive market for the service. 48 C.F.R. § 2.101, 12.102(a). Envirocare of Utah, Inc. v. U.S., 44 Fed. Cl. 474 (1999), dismissed, 217 F.3d 852 (Fed. Cir. 1999). United States ☞64.10

3 Purchases from disabled individuals

Randolph-Sheppard Act, which authorized Secretary of Department of Education to secure operation of cafeterias on federal property by blind licensees, by contract or otherwise, was procurement statute under Competition in Contracting Act (CICA), and thus came within exception from CICA's open competition requirements for federal procurements. 10 U.S.C.A. § 2302(3)(A); Randolph-Sheppard Vending Stand Act, § 7(d), as amended, 20 U.S.C.A. § 107d-3(d); 48 C.F.R. § 6.302-5(b). NISH v. Cohen, 247 F.3d 197 (4th Cir. 2001). United States ☞57

Evidence did not support factual conclusions of committee for purchase from the blind and other severely handicapped that workshops for the blind would be able to produce requisite quantities of computer tabulating machine paper at fair market price, for purposes of adding paper to list of commodities to be purchased by federal government from workshops for the blind and handicapped. Wagner-O'Day Act, §§ 2(a–c), 3, 5(3, 5), as amended, 41 U.S.C.A. §§ 47(a–c), 48, 48b(3, 5). McGregor Printing Corp. v. Kemp, 20 F.3d 1188, 1194 (D.C. Cir. 1994). United States ☞64.10

Record was insufficient to support conclusion, if any, of committee for purchase from the blind and other severely handicapped that it could add computer tabulating machine paper to list of commodities to be procured from workshop for the blind even if workshop could not produce paper at fair market price; former supplier presented evidence that workshop could produce paper only at a loss even if it sold paper at calculated fair market price. Wagner-O'Day Act, § 2(b), as amended, 41 U.S.C.A. § 47(b). McGregor Printing Corp. v. Kemp, 20 F.3d 1188, 1196 (D.C. Cir. 1994). United States ☞64.10

For commodity to be added to list of commodities and services which federal government procures solely from workshops for the blind, 75% of man-hours of direct labor required for production or provision of commodity must be performed by blind persons; commodity may not be added if less work is performed by the blind, even if 75% of workshop's total work is performed by the blind. Wagner-O'Day Act, § 5(3)(C), as amended, 41 U.S.C.A. § § 47(a-c). McGregor Printing Corp. v. Kemp, 20 F.3d 1188, 305 (D.C. Cir. 1994). United States ☞64.10

The Committee for Purchase from the Blind and other Severely Handicapped, acting pursuant to the Wagner-O'Day Act, did not act arbitrarily or capriciously in determining that involved floor wax product was "suitable," that the blind workshop was capable of producing acceptable floor wax, and that the adverse impact on competitive bidder was not so serious as to preclude the Committee's action of adding floor wax to procurement list for mandatory government purchase from qualified blind workshops. Wagner-O'Day Act, §§ 1–3, 41 U.S.C.A. §§ 46 to 48. Barrier Industries, Inc. v. Eckard, 584 F.2d 1074, 1083, 25 Cont. Cas. Fed. (CCH) P 82589 (D.C. Cir. 1978). United States ☞64.10

Notice required by the Wagner-O'Day Act, which authorizes government purchase from qualified blind and handicapped workshops, is publication in the Federal Register and direct notice to other competitive bidders seeking to supply product purchased is not required. Wagner-O'Day Act, § 2(a)(2), 41 U.S.C.A. § 47(a)(2). Barrier Industries, Inc. v. Eckard, 584 F.2d 1074, 190, 25 Cont. Cas. Fed. (CCH) P 82589 (D.C. Cir. 1978). United States ☞64.10

Central nonprofit agency acted consistently with its responsibilities under Javits-Wagner-O'Day (JWOD) Act when it recommended certain nonprofit agency which employed blind or severely disabled persons to the Committee for Purchase from People Who Are Blind or Severely Disabled as a provider of custodial services for federal agency, even if central nonprofit agency acted to facilitate such employment before Committee added the custodial services to procurement list. Wagner-O'Day Act, § 2, 41 U.S.C.A. § 47. Brothers Cleaning Service, Inc. v. Chair, Committee for Purchase from People Who are Blind or Severely Disabled, 26 F. Supp. 2d 1 (D.D.C. 1998). United States ☞64.10

Committee for Purchase from People Who Are Blind or Severely Disabled did not act arbitrarily or capriciously in refusing to reconsider its original placement, under Javits-Wagner-O'Day (JWOD) Act, of custodial services contract on procurement list which was open only to nonprofit agencies which employed blind or severely disabled persons. Wagner-O'Day Act, § 2, 41 U.S.C.A. § 47; 41 C.F.R. § 51-2.6. Brothers Cleaning Service, Inc. v. Chair, Committee for Purchase from People Who are Blind or Severely Disabled, 26 F. Supp. 2d 1 (D.D.C. 1998). United States ☞64.10

Committee for Purchase from People Who Are Blind or Severely Disabled reasonably concluded, when it added custodial services contract to procurement list which was open only to nonprofit agencies which employed blind or severely disabled persons, that contractor which previously provided such custodial services was not the "current contractor" or "most recent contractor" with regard to the project, and therefore Committee was not required under Javits-Wagner- O'Day (JWOD) Act to conduct impact study on the contractor. Wagner-O'Day Act, § 2, 41 U.S.C.A. § 47; 41 C.F.R. §§ 51-2.4(a)(4)(ii), 51-2.6. Brothers Cleaning Service, Inc. v. Chair, Committee for Purchase from People Who are Blind or Severely Disabled, 26 F. Supp. 2d 1 (D.D.C. 1998). United States ☞64.10

Committee for Purchase from People Who Are Blind or Severely Disabled complied with

30-day notice requirement, under Javits-Wagner-O'Day (JWOD) Act, before adding custodial services contract to procurement list which listed those services for which federal agencies could only contract with qualified nonprofit agencies which employed blind or severely disabled persons. Wagner-O'Day Act, § 2(a)(2), 41 U.S.C.A. § 47(a)(2); 41 C.F.R. § 51-2.3. Brothers Cleaning Service, Inc. v. Chair, Committee for Purchase from People Who are Blind or Severely Disabled, 26 F. Supp. 2d 1 (D.D.C. 1998). United States ☞64.10

Committee for Purchase from People Who Are Blind or Severely Disabled had no authority under Javits-Wagner- O'Day (JWOD) Act to prevent federal agency from contracting with provider for custodial services before such services were added, pursuant to JWOD Act, to procurement list which listed those services for which federal agencies could only contract with qualified nonprofit agencies which employed blind or severely disabled persons. Wagner-O'Day Act, § 2, 41 U.S.C.A. § 47. Brothers Cleaning Service, Inc. v. Chair, Committee for Purchase from People Who are Blind or Severely Disabled, 26 F. Supp. 2d 1 (D.D.C. 1998). United States ☞64.10

Committee for Purchase from the Blind and Other Severely Handicapped did not exceed its statutory authority under JWOD (Javits-Wagner-O'Day) Act in deciding to add computer tabulating paper to list of commodities and services which federal government procured solely from blind and handicapped workshops; although NIB (National Industries for the Blind) played central role in providing initial information, Committee did not yield its authority to NIB, and nothing in Act or in its legislative history or any regulation limited set-asides to workshops already manufacturing the commodity involved. Wagner-O'Day Act, §§ 1–6, as amended, McGregor Printing Corp. v. Kemp, 802 F. Supp. 519 (D.D.C. 1992), rev'd on other grounds, 20 F.3d 1188 (D.C. Cir. 1994). United States ☞64.10

Committee for Purchase from the Blind and Other Severely Handicapped acted within scope of APA (Administrative Procedure Act) and relevant regulations in process of making informal rule-making decision to add computer tabulating paper to list of commodities and services which federal government procured solely from blind and handicapped workshops; Committee issued its notice for proposed rule making 30 days in advance of rule's effective date and prior government contractor's shortened response time was due to its own failure to see that notice until ten days before deadline, terms of notice adequately identified issue, contractor's extensive comments on economic repercussions of decision also indicated that it was sufficiently apprised and given adequate opportunity to comment, and final rule sufficiently addressed critical issues raised by contractor's comments. 5 U.S.C.A. § 553(b–d). McGregor Printing Corp. v. Kemp, 802 F. Supp. 519 (D.D.C. 1992), rev'd on other grounds, 20 F.3d 1188 (D.C. Cir. 1994). United States ☞64.10

Committee for Purchase from the Blind and Other Severely Handicapped did not act arbitrarily and capriciously in determining that blind and handicapped workshops were "capable" of producing computer tabulating paper using 75% blind labor, for purposes of contractor's challenge to its informal rule-making decision to add that paper to list of commodities and services purchased by federal government solely from such workshops; Committee's initial finding of capability was reasonable given the information which it received, and regulation required that percentage of blind labor for production of all commodities, not per product. 5 U.S.C.A. § 706(2); Wagner-O'Day Act, §§ 1–6, as amended, McGregor Printing Corp. v. Kemp, 802 F. Supp. 519 (D.D.C. 1992), rev'd on other grounds, 20 F.3d 1188 (D.C. Cir. 1994). United States ☞64.10

Committee for Purchase from the Blind and Other Severely Handicapped conducted adequate fair market price analysis before deciding to add computer tabulating paper to list of commodities and services which federal government procured solely from blind and handicapped workshops; Committee was not under any obligation to explain basis of its fair price determination, price arrived at through use of publicly available mathematical averaging formula based on average price of previous bids was not arbitrary, and Committee reasonably interpreted regulation as not requiring it to independently investigate whether workshops were actually able to produce commodity at fair market price, rather than relying on NIB (National Industries for the Blind) findings on that matter. Wagner-O'Day Act, §§ 1–6, as amended, McGregor Printing Corp. v. Kemp, 802 F. Supp. 519 (D.D.C. 1992), rev'd on other grounds, 20 F.3d 1188 (D.C. Cir. 1994). United States ☞64.10

Committee for Purchase from the Blind and Other Severely Handicapped adequately investigated and analyzed the adverse impact on past or current contractors of decision to add computer tabulating paper to list of commodities and services which federal government procured solely from blind and handicapped workshops, and its conclusion that a 2.7% loss of sales was not serious enough to exclude that commodity from procurement list was reasonable. 5 U.S.C.A. § 706(2); Wagner-O'Day Act, §§ 1–6, as amended, McGregor Printing Corp. v. Kemp, 802 F. Supp. 519 (D.D.C. 1992), rev'd on other grounds, 20 F.3d 1188 (D.C. Cir. 1994). United States ⊗⊸64.10

Committee for Purchase from Blind and Other Severely Handicapped properly rejected so called alternative proposal by former supplier of medals and competitor of sheltered workshop in its determination whether to add procurement of certain medals to Committee's list, where "proposal" was no more than bargaining with Committee which would tie Committee's hands and result in abdication of Committee's responsibility to add suitable commodities and services to procurement list. HLI Lordship Industries, Inc. v. Committee for Purchase From Blind and Other Severely Handicapped, 663 F. Supp. 246 (E.D. Va. 1987). United States ⊗⊸64.10

Harm asserted by former supplier of medals to government was insufficient to negate curative effect of republished notice which added medal and six medal sets to procurement list of Committee for Purchase from the Blind and Other Severely Handicapped, where allegation merely speculated that Department of Defense withdrew invitation for bids on two of seven medals upon which former supplier had intended to submit bids, in response to defective first publication. 5 U.S.C.A. § 553(d). HLI Lordship Industries, Inc. v. Committee for Purchase From Blind and Other Severely Handicapped, 663 F. Supp. 246 (E.D. Va. 1987). United States ⊗⊸64.10

Given fact that members of Committee for Purchase From the Blind and Other Severely Handicapped did not wish to have circulated their objections to take particular medals and medal sets out of competitive bidding and placed on list as commodities suitable for procurement by government from qualified nonprofit agencies for the blind or other severely handicapped, it was reasonable for the executive director of the Committee to not circulate the objections. HLI Lordship Industries, Inc. v. Committee for Purchase from the Blind & Other Severely Handicapped, 615 F. Supp. 970 (E.D. Va. 1985), decision rev'd on other grounds, 791 F.2d 1136 (4th Cir. 1986). United States ⊗⊸64.10

Committee for Purchase From the Blind and Other Severely Handicapped did not abuse its discretion in considering impact on competitive bidder of its decision that medals and medal sets were commodities suitable for procurement by government from qualified nonprofit agencies for the blind or other severely handicapped, and thus, items would not be subject to competitive bidding and in concluding that the impact of its decision was not serious enough to warrant voting against the proposal. 41 U.S.C.A. § 46 et seq. HLI Lordship Industries, Inc. v. Committee for Purchase from the Blind & Other Severely Handicapped, 615 F. Supp. 970 (E.D. Va. 1985), decision rev'd on other grounds, 791 F.2d 1136 (4th Cir. 1986). United States ⊗⊸64.10

Committee for Purchase From the Blind and Other Severely Handicapped had necessary information for its decision that medals and medal sets were commodities suitable for procurement by government from qualified nonprofit agencies for the blind or other severely handicapped, and thus, would not be subjected to competitive bidding, and any error that may have occurred with respect to consideration of the evidence was harmless. 5 U.S.C.A. § 553. HLI Lordship Industries, Inc. v. Committee for Purchase from the Blind & Other Severely Handicapped, 615 F. Supp. 970 (E.D. Va. 1985), decision rev'd on other grounds, 791 F.2d 1136 (4th Cir. 1986). United States ⊗⊸64.10

Because over 75% of man-hours of direct labor needed to assemble medals and medal sets was done by severely handicapped employees, employer was a qualified nonprofit agency under the Javits-Wagner-O'Day Act [41 U.S.C.A. § 46 et seq.] and thus public contract for medals could be withdrawn from competitive bidding. HLI Lordship Industries, Inc. v. Committee for Purchase from the Blind & Other Severely Handicapped, 615 F. Supp. 970 (E.D. Va. 1985), decision rev'd on other grounds, 791 F.2d 1136 (4th Cir. 1986). United States ⊗⊸64.10

Committee for Purchase From the Blind and Other Severely Handicapped did not violate the Administrative Procedure Act [5 U.S.C.A. § 553(c)] when it published statement explaining basis of decision to take particular medals and medal sets out of competitive bidding and to place them on list for commodities suitable for procurement by government from qualified nonprofit agencies for the blind or other severely handicapped where Committee published concise general statement of basis and purpose of decision to place commodities on procurement list; Committee was not required to disclose every fact or opinion contained in public comments. HLI Lordship Industries, Inc. v. Committee for Purchase from the Blind & Other Severely Handicapped, 615 F. Supp. 970 (E.D. Va. 1985), decision rev'd on other grounds, 791 F.2d 1136 (4th Cir. 1986). United States ☞64.10

An agency's decision to issue orders on a sole source basis under Javits-Wagner-O'Day (JWOD) Act authority was improper because the procured items were not on the Procurement List maintained by the Committee for Purchase From People Who Are Blind or Severely Disabled. Matter of: OSC Solutions, Inc., B-401498, 2009 CPD ¶ 185 (Comp. Gen. 2009)

§ 6.302-6 National security.

(a) Authority.

(1) Citations: 10 U.S.C. 2304(c)(6) or 41 U.S.C. 3304(a)(6).

(2) Full and open competition need not be provided for when the disclosure of the agency's needs would compromise the national security unless the agency is permitted to limit the number of sources from which it solicits bids or proposals.

(b) *Application.* This authority may be used for any acquisition when disclosure of the Government's needs would compromise the national security (*e.g.,* would violate security requirements); it shall not be used merely because the acquisition is classified, or merely because access to classified matter will be necessary to submit a proposal or to perform the contract.

(c) Limitations.

(1) Contracts awarded using this authority shall be supported by the written justifications and approvals described in 6.303 and 6.304.

(2) See 5.202(a)(1) for synopsis requirements.

(3) This statutory authority requires that agencies shall request offers from as many potential sources as is practicable under the circumstances.

United States Code Annotated

Administrative determinations, see 41 U.S.C.A. § 257.

Advocates for competition, see 41 U.S.C.A. § 418.

Competition requirements, see 41 U.S.C.A. § 253.

Contract goal for small disadvantaged businesses and certain institutions of higher education, see 10 U.S.C.A. § 2323.

Contracts, competition requirements, see 10 U.S.C.A. § 2304.

Contracts, planning, solicitation, evaluation, and award procedures, see 10 U.S.C.A. § 2305.

Contracts, prohibition on competition between Department of Defense and small businesses and certain other entities, see 10 U.S.C.A. § 2304e.

Credit for Indian contracting in meeting certain subcontracting goals for small disadvantaged businesses and certain institutions of higher education, see 10 U.S.C.A. § 2323a.

Definitions, see 10 U.S.C.A. § 2302; 41 U.S.C.A. §§ 259, 403.

Design-build selection procedures, see 10 U.S.C.A. § 2305a; 41 U.S.C.A. § 253m.

Determinations and decisions, see 10 U.S.C.A. § 2310; 41 U.S.C.A. § 262.

Encouragement of new competition, see 41 U.S.C.A. § 253c.

Encouragement of new competitors, see 10 U.S.C.A. § 2319.

Planning and solicitation requirements, see 41 U.S.C.A. § 253a.

Procurement notice, see 41 U.S.C.A. § 416.

§ 6.302-7 Public interest.

(a) Authority.

(1) Citations: 10 U.S.C. 2304(c)(7) or 41 U.S.C. 3304(a)(7).

(2) Full and open competition need not be provided for when the agency head determines that it is not in the public interest in the particular acquisition concerned.

(b) *Application.* This authority may be used when none of the other authorities in 6.302 apply.

(c) Limitations.

(1) A written determination to use this authority shall be made in accordance with Subpart 1.7, by—

(i) The Secretary of Defense, the Secretary of the Army, the Secretary of the Navy, the Secretary of the Air Force, the Secretary of Homeland Security for the Coast Guard, or the Administrator of the National Aeronautics and Space Administration; or

(ii) The head of any other executive agency. This authority may not be delegated.

(2) The Congress shall be notified in writing of such determination not less than 30 days before award of the contract.

(3) If required by the head of the agency, the contracting officer shall prepare a justification to support the determination under paragraph (c)(1) of this subsection.

(4) This Determination and Finding (D&F) shall not be made on a class basis.

United States Code Annotated

Administrative determinations, see 41 U.S.C.A. § 257.

Advocates for competition, see 41 U.S.C.A. § 418.

Competition requirements, see 41 U.S.C.A. § 253.

Contract goal for small disadvantaged businesses and certain institutions of higher education, see 10 U.S.C.A. § 2323.

Contracts, competition requirements, see 10 U.S.C.A. § 2304.

Contracts, planning, solicitation, evaluation, and award procedures, see 10 U.S.C.A. § 2305.

Contracts, prohibition on competition between Department of Defense and small businesses and certain other entities, see 10 U.S.C.A. § 2304e.

Credit for Indian contracting in meeting certain subcontracting goals for small disadvantaged businesses and certain institutions of higher education, see 10 U.S.C.A. § 2323a.

Definitions, see 10 U.S.C.A. § 2302; 41 U.S.C.A. §§ 259, 403.

Design-build selection procedures, see 10 U.S.C.A. § 2305a; 41 U.S.C.A. § 253m.

Determinations and decisions, see 10 U.S.C.A. § 2310; 41 U.S.C.A. § 262.

Encouragement of new competition, see 41 U.S.C.A. § 253c.

Encouragement of new competitors, see 10 U.S.C.A. § 2319.

Planning and solicitation requirements, see 41 U.S.C.A. § 253a.

Procurement notice, see 41 U.S.C.A. § 416.

Notes of Decisions

In general 1

1 In general

Contractor who protested award of sole source contract modification to incumbent contractor was not entitled to preliminary injunction enjoining performance of the modification; determination of head of contracting agency that sole source modification advanced the underlying public interest was clearly and convincingly justified, and thus protestor could not prevail on the merits. Federal Property and Administrative Services Act of 1949, § 303(c)(7), 41 U.S.C.A. § 253(c)(7); 48 C.F.R. § 6.302-7. Spherix, Inc. v. U.S., 58 Fed. Cl. 514 (2003). Injunction ⋘138.63

With regard to statute establishing procedures for the use of noncompetitive contract awards, including when head of agency determines that noncompetitive procedures are in the public interest, agency head's public interest determination is not committed to agency discretion by law, so as to preclude judicial review; section of the Federal Acquisition Regulation (FAR) requiring agency head to adopt a written finding setting out facts and circumstances that clearly and convincingly justify such determination provides a meaningful standard of review. Federal Property and Administrative Services Act of 1949, § 303(c)(7), 41 U.S.C.A. § 253(c)(7); 48 C.F.R. § 6.302-7(c). Spherix, Inc. v. U.S., 58 Fed. Cl. 351 (2003).

United States ☞64.10

Protest of agency's use of public interest exception under 10 U.S.C. § 2304(c)(7) to justify transferring an appropriated fund, mission essential requirement to a nonappropriated fund instrumentality using a Memorandum of Agreement was sustained because the public interest exception is applicable only to procurements, and a Memorandum of Agreement is not a procurement. Asiel Enterprises, Inc., B-408315.2, 2013 CPD ¶ 205 (Comp. Gen. 2013)

§ 6.303 Justifications.

§ 6.303-1 Requirements.

(a) A contracting officer shall not commence negotiations for a sole source contract, commence negotiations for a contract resulting from an unsolicited proposal, or award any other contract without providing for full and open competition unless the contracting officer—

(1) Justifies, if required in 6.302, the use of such actions in writing;

(2) Certifies the accuracy and completeness of the justification; and

(3) Obtains the approval required by 6.304.

(b) The contracting officer shall not award a sole-source contract under the 8(a) authority (15 U.S.C. 637(a)) for an amount exceeding $22 million unless —

(1) The contracting officer justifies the use of a sole-source contract in writing in accordance with 6.303-2;

(2) The justification is approved by the appropriate official designated at 6.304; and

(3) The justification and related information are made public after award in accordance with 6.305.

(c) Technical and requirements personnel are responsible for providing and certifying as accurate and complete necessary data to support their recommendation for other than full and open competition.

(d) Justifications required by paragraph (a) of this section may be made on an individual or class basis. Any justification for contracts awarded under the authority of 6.302-7 shall only be made on an individual basis. Whenever a justification is made and approved on a class basis, the contracting officer must ensure that each contract action taken pursuant to the authority of the class justification and approval is within the scope of the class justification and approval and shall document the contract file for each contract action accordingly.

(e) The justifications for contracts awarded under the authority cited in 6.302-2 may be prepared and approved within a reasonable time after contract award when preparation and approval prior to award would unreasonably delay the acquisitions.

United States Code Annotated

Administrative determinations, see 41 U.S.C.A. § 257.

Advocates for competition, see 41 U.S.C.A. § 418.

Competition requirements, see 41 U.S.C.A. § 253.

Contract goal for small disadvantaged businesses and certain institutions of higher education, see 10 U.S.C.A. § 2323.

Contracts, competition requirements, see 10 U.S.C.A. § 2304.

Contracts, planning, solicitation, evaluation, and award procedures, see 10 U.S.C.A. § 2305.

Contracts, prohibition on competition between Department of Defense and small businesses and certain other entities, see 10 U.S.C.A. § 2304e.

Credit for Indian contracting in meeting certain subcontracting goals for small disadvantaged businesses and certain institutions of higher education, see 10 U.S.C.A. § 2323a.

Definitions, see 10 U.S.C.A. § 2302; 41 U.S.C.A. §§ 259, 403.

Design-build selection procedures, see 10 U.S.C.A. § 2305a; 41 U.S.C.A. § 253m.

Determinations and decisions, see 10 U.S.C.A. § 2310; 41 U.S.C.A. § 262.

Encouragement of new competition, see 41 U.S.C.A. § 253c.

Encouragement of new competitors, see 10 U.S.C.A. § 2319.

Planning and solicitation requirements, see 41 U.S.C.A. § 253a.

Procurement notice, see 41 U.S.C.A. § 416.

Notes of Decisions

In general 1
Requirements 3
Sole source acquisitions 2

1 In general

United States Department of Labor's (DOL) decision to standardize its software applications exclusively to software manufactured by one company was not arbitrary and capricious, even if DOL misstated number of competitor's office suites that had already been installed and consequently miscalculated relative cost savings in converting to company's product, some of DOL's constituent departments leveled harsh criticism at justification's cost-benefit analysis, and recommendation to standardize to company's product was formulated before competitor was given opportunity to make its presentation, where there was evidence that DOL had experienced problems with competitor's software applications operating on company's operating systems, private company's conversion to single office suite had permitted it to achieve increased efficiency, some product reviews chose company's product over that of competitor, company had largest market share, and DOL officials considered information provided by competitor in formulating their ultimate recommendation. Corel Corp. v. U.S., 165 F. Supp. 2d 12 (D.D.C. 2001). United States ☞64.45(1)

With regard to statute establishing procedures for the use of noncompetitive contract awards, including when head of agency determines that noncompetitive procedures are in the public interest, agency head's public interest determination is not committed to agency discretion by law, so as to preclude judicial review; section of the Federal Acquisition Regulation (FAR) requiring agency head to adopt a written finding setting out facts and circumstances that clearly and convincingly justify such determination provides a meaningful standard of review. Federal Property and Administrative Services Act of 1949, § 303(c)(7), 41 U.S.C.A. § 253(c)(7); 48 C.F.R. § 6.302-7(c). Spherix, Inc. v. U.S., 58 Fed. Cl. 351 (2003). United States ☞64.10

To justify a noncompetitive procurement, advance planning need not be entirely error-free or even actually successful; all that is required is that the planning actions be reasonable. 10 U.S.C.A. § 2304(f)(5); Federal Property and Administrative Services Act of 1949, § 303(f)(5), 41 U.S.C.A. § 253(f)(5). Cubic Defense Systems, Inc. v. U.S., 45 Fed. Cl. 239 (1999), dismissed, 230 F.3d 1375 (Fed. Cir. 1999). United States ☞64.10

A lack of advance planning may not justify a noncompetitive procurement. 10 U.S.C.A. § 2304(f)(5); Federal Property and Administrative Services Act of 1949, § 303(f)(5), 41 U.S.C.A. § 253(f)(5). Cubic Defense Systems, Inc. v. U.S., 45 Fed. Cl. 239 (1999), dismissed, 230 F.3d 1375 (Fed. Cir. 1999). United States ☞64.10

Requirement that agency determine prior to contract award the precise exception upon which it will rely to justify use of noncompetitive procedures is part of comprehensive plan to improve efficiency with which federal agencies procure products and services. 10 U.S.C.A. § 2304; 48 C.F.R. § 6.301(b). ATA Defense Industries, Inc. v. U.S., 38 Fed. Cl. 489, 41 Cont. Cas. Fed. (CCH) P 77147 (1997). United States ☞64.10

Exceptions applicable to negotiated procurements and requirement for a determination and finding justifying a negotiated rather than a competitive procurement were inapplicable to two-step, formally advertised procurement. Eagle Const. Corp. v. U.S., 4 Cl. Ct. 470, 31 Cont. Cas. Fed. (CCH) P 72046 (1984). United States ☞64.10

2 Sole source acquisitions

United States Postal Service (USPS) had rational basis for contracting out its air transportation network services to deliver certain classes of mail on sole-source basis; competitive bidding process would have taken much longer to perform than negotiating sole-source award and would have required USPS to expend great amount of resources to design appropriate potential networks with each viable competitor, existing piecemeal system resulted in cost inefficiencies, commercial airlines that currently transported some mail were unreliable. Emery Worldwide Airlines, Inc. v. U.S., 264 F.3d 1071 (Fed. Cir.

2001). United States ☞64.10

Party challenging award of sole-source government contract may meet its heavy burden of showing that award decision had no rational basis by showing: (1) agency's decision to conduct sole-source procurement process lacked rational basis; (2) agency's sole-source requirements lacked rational basis; or (3) based on sole-source requirements, selection of sole-source awardee lacked rational basis. Emery Worldwide Airlines, Inc. v. U.S., 264 F.3d 1071 (Fed. Cir. 2001)United States ☞64.10

United States Postal Service (USPS) had rational basis for awarding on non-competitive basis sole-source contract for its air transportation network services to deliver certain classes of mail; publicly available information indicated that it was unlikely that unsuccessful provider could have met USPS's national network requirements at cost effective price without relying on postal payments for significant portion of its overall revenue. Emery Worldwide Airlines, Inc. v. U.S., 264 F.3d 1071 (Fed. Cir. 2001). United States ☞64.10

An agency's desire to avoid administrative inconvenience and rely upon an incumbent contractor's experience with its needs is no justification for sole-source procurement. Aero Corp. v. Department of the Navy, 540 F. Supp. 180, 29 Cont. Cas. Fed. (CCH) P 82290 (D.D.C. 1982). United States ☞64.10

A sole-source procurement award is justified by urgency only if awardee is only firm that can supply the item by required delivery date. Aero Corp. v. Department of the Navy, 540 F. Supp. 180, 29 Cont. Cas. Fed. (CCH) P 82290 (D.D.C. 1982). United States ☞64.10

Technical and administrative superiority of one firm over all other possible sources is not a justification for sole-source procurement from that firm. Aero Corp. v. Department of the Navy, 540 F. Supp. 180, 29 Cont. Cas. Fed. (CCH) P 82290 (D.D.C. 1982). United States ☞64.10

Air Force did not violate restrictions against unjustified sole source contracts in procuring automated data processing equipment from another agency through existing contract, in that 40% increase in purchase price did not represent acquisition outside scope of contract. 10 U.S.C.A. § 2304(f)(1). National Gateway Telecom, Inc. v. Aldridge, 701 F. Supp. 1104 (D.N.J. 1988), judgment aff'd, 879 F.2d 858 (3d Cir. 1989). United States ☞64.10

Contracting officer's justification for not subjecting portion of contract to full and open competition, that goods and services could not have been purchased on the open market, was not legally sufficient to support award of contract, was abuse of discretion, and was not in accordance with law, where contracting officer was reasonably on notice that products and services purchased under contract on sole source basis were available competitively, and that successful bidder intended to purchase those products and services on the open market. 10 U.S.C.A. § 2304; 48 C.F.R. § 6.302-1. ATA Defense Industries, Inc. v. U.S., 38 Fed. Cl. 489, 41 Cont. Cas. Fed. (CCH) P 77147 (1997). United States ☞64.10

Contracting officer's decision to award portion of contract for products and services without subjecting it to full and open competition, that was based on sole source justification and was abuse of discretion, could not be upheld on theory that goods and services were incidental to goods in rest of contract that were purchased against Federal Supply Schedule (FSS) contract, as officer's decision was not based on incidentals rationale but instead rationale was post hoc rationalization by government counsel; furthermore, congressional mandate requiring use of competitive procedures in conducting procurement does not include incidentals exception. 10 U.S.C.A. § 2304(a)(1)(A); 48 C.F.R. § 6.302-1. ATA Defense Industries, Inc. v. U.S., 38 Fed. Cl. 489, 41 Cont. Cas. Fed. (CCH) P 77147 (1997). United States ☞64.10

Authority to enter foreign military sale (FMS) sole source contracts required conformance to written justifications and approvals requirement, and contracting officer did not have authority to enter into sole source contract upon receipt of sole source procurement request from FMS customer. 10 U.S.C.A. § 2304(c)(4). Kollsman, a Div. of Sequa Corp. v. U.S., 25 Cl. Ct. 500, 37 Cont. Cas. Fed. (CCH) P 76283, 1992 WL 48773 (1992). United States ☞64.10

Lack of written justification and approval for foreign military sale (FMS) sole source contract did not defeat contractor's claim based on implied-in-fact contract to produce military hardware for precontract costs incurred to meet FMS customer's schedule. 10

U.S.C.A. § 2304(c)(4). Kollsman, a Div. of Sequa Corp. v. U.S., 25 Cl. Ct. 500, 37 Cont. Cas. Fed. (CCH) P 76283, 1992 WL 48773 (1992). United States ☞69(6)

3 Requirements

To justify a noncompetitive procurement, advance planning need not be entirely error-free or even actually successful; all that is required is that the planning actions be reasonable. 10 U.S.C.A. § 2304(f)(5); Federal Property and Administrative Services Act of 1949, § 303(f)(5), 41 U.S.C.A. § 253(f)(5). Cubic Defense Systems, Inc. v. U.S., 45 Fed. Cl. 239 (1999), dismissed, 230 F.3d 1375 (Fed. Cir. 1999). United States ☞64.10

Agency must evaluate its options and make any determination prior to entering the contract to use other than full and open competition in procurement and to award contract using other than competitive procedures; agency may not award a contract without justifying in writing the use of noncompetitive procedures and must specify in the contract the statutory basis for the exception. 10 U.S.C.A. § 2304(f)(1); 48 C.F.R. § 6.301(b). ATA Defense Industries, Inc. v. U.S., 38 Fed. Cl. 489, 41 Cont. Cas. Fed. (CCH) P 77147 (1997). United States ☞64.10

Contracting officer's after-the-fact reliance upon Federal Acquisition Regulation that allows use of other than competitive procedures when there is an unusual and compelling urgency was too late to justify issuance of purchase order contract without the benefit of full and open competition. 10 U.S.C.A. § 2304; 48 C.F.R. § 6.302-2. ATA Defense Industries, Inc. v. U.S., 38 Fed. Cl. 489, 41 Cont. Cas. Fed. (CCH) P 77147 (1997). United States ☞64.10

Authority to enter foreign military sale (FMS) sole source contracts required conformance to written justifications and approvals requirement, and contracting officer did not have authority to enter into sole source contract upon receipt of sole source procurement request from FMS customer. 10 U.S.C.A. § 2304(c)(4). Kollsman, a Div. of Sequa Corp. v. U.S., 25 Cl. Ct. 500, 37 Cont. Cas. Fed. (CCH) P 76283, 1992 WL 48773 (1992). United States ☞64.10

The FAR regulations that implement CICA expressly anticipate limiting full and open competition to accommodate the Stafford Act's preference for using local businesses to clean up debris resulting from a major disaster. FAR 6.302-5(b)(5). The FAR does not require the generation of a J&A when a statute expressly requires that a procurement be made from a specified source; rather, the FAR advises that "when the statute authorizes, but does not require, that the procurement be made from a specified source" the agency must prepare a J&A. FAR 6.302-5(c)(2)(ii). As we hold in this decision, the Stafford Act authorizes, but does not require, that a procurement be made from specified sources (*i.e.*, firms within the area affected by a major disaster). Accordingly, a J&A was required in this case. AshBritt Inc., B-297889, B-297889.2, 2006 CPD ¶ 48 (Comp. Gen. 2006).

When an agency uses noncompetitive procedures under section 2304(c)(1), it must execute a written J&A with sufficient facts and rationale to support the use of the specific authority, FAR 6.302-1(c), 6.303, 6.304, and publish a notice in the CBD to permit potential competitors to challenge the agency's intent to procure without full and open competition. 10 U.S.C. § 2304(f). GAO's review of an agency's decision to conduct a sole-source procurement focuses on the adequacy of the rationale and conclusions set forth in the J&A. When the J&A sets forth reasonable justifications for the agency's actions, GAO will not object to the award. On the other hand, where the record shows that the agency has failed to adequately justify its sole-source award decision, GAO will sustain the protest. Lockheed Martin Systems Integration -- Owego, B-287190.2, B-287190.3, 2001 CPD ¶ 110 (Comp. Gen. 2001)

§ 6.303-2 Content.

(a) Each justification shall contain sufficient facts and rationale to justify the use of the specific authority cited.

(b) As a minimum, each justification, except those for sole-source 8(a) contracts over $22 million (see paragraph (d) of this section), shall include the following information:

(1) Identification of the agency and the contracting activity, and specific identification of the document as a "Justification for other than full and open competition."

(2) Nature and/or description of the action being approved.

(3) A description of the supplies or services required to meet the agency's needs (including the estimated value).

(4) An identification of the statutory authority permitting other than full and open competition.

(5) A demonstration that the proposed contractor's unique qualifications or the nature of the acquisition requires use of the authority cited.

(6) A description of efforts made to ensure that offers are solicited from as many potential sources as is practicable, including whether a notice was or will be publicized as required by subpart 5.2 and, if not, which exception under 5.202 applies.

(7) A determination by the contracting officer that the anticipated cost to the Government will be fair and reasonable.

(8) A description of the market research conducted (see Part 10) and the results or a statement of the reason market research was not conducted.

(9) Any other facts supporting the use of other than full and open competition, such as:

(i) Explanation of why technical data packages, specifications, engineering descriptions, statements of work, or purchase descriptions suitable for full and open competition have not been developed or are not available.

(ii) When 6.302-1 is cited for follow-on acquisitions as described in 6.302-1(a)(2)(ii), an estimate of the cost to the Government that would be duplicated and how the estimate was derived.

(iii) When 6.302-2 is cited, data, estimated cost, or other rationale as to the extent and nature of the harm to the Government.

(10) A listing of the sources, if any, that expressed, in writing, an interest in the acquisition.

(11) A statement of the actions, if any, the agency may take to remove or overcome any barriers to competition before any subsequent acquisition for the supplies or services required.

(12) Contracting officer certification that the justification is accurate and complete to the best of the contracting officer's knowledge and belief.

(c) Each justification shall include evidence that any supporting data that is the responsibility of technical or requirements personnel (e.g., verifying the Government's minimum needs or schedule requirements or other rationale for other than full and open competition) and which form a basis for the justification have been certified as complete and accurate by the technical or requirements personnel.

(d) As a minimum, each justification for a sole-source 8(a) contract over $22 million shall include the following information:

(1) A description of the needs of the agency concerned for the matters covered by the contract.

(2) A specification of the statutory provision providing the exception from the requirement to use competitive procedures in entering into the contract (see 19.805-1).

(3) A determination that the use of a sole-source contract is in the best interest of the agency concerned.

(4) A determination that the anticipated cost of the contract will be fair and reasonable.

(5) Such other matters as the head of the agency concerned shall specify for purposes of this section.

United States Code Annotated

Administrative determinations, see 41 U.S.C.A. § 257.

Advocates for competition, see 41 U.S.C.A. § 418.

Competition requirements, see 41 U.S.C.A. § 253.

Contract goal for small disadvantaged businesses and certain institutions of higher education, see 10 U.S.C.A. § 2323.

Contracts, competition requirements, see 10 U.S.C.A. § 2304.

Contracts, planning, solicitation, evaluation, and award procedures, see 10 U.S.C.A. § 2305.

Contracts, prohibition on competition between Department of Defense and small businesses and certain other entities, see 10 U.S.C.A. § 2304e.

Credit for Indian contracting in meeting certain subcontracting goals for small disadvantaged businesses and certain institutions of higher education, see 10 U.S.C.A. § 2323a.

Definitions, see 10 U.S.C.A. § 2302; 41 U.S.C.A. §§ 259, 403.

Design-build selection procedures, see 10 U.S.C.A. § 2305a; 41 U.S.C.A. § 253m.

Determinations and decisions, see 10 U.S.C.A. § 2310; 41 U.S.C.A. § 262.

Encouragement of new competition, see 41 U.S.C.A. § 253c.

Encouragement of new competitors, see 10 U.S.C.A. § 2319.

Planning and solicitation requirements, see 41 U.S.C.A. § 253a.

Procurement notice, see 41 U.S.C.A. § 416.

Notes of Decisions

In general 1
Substantiation required 2

1 In general

Government adequately explained its justification for awarding sole-source contract for modification of radar simulator which emits electronic warfare threats for training purposes, as required by the Competition in Contracting Act (CICA); contract was awarded to current manufacturer of simulator, and agency explained that the current manufacturer was the only source capable of performing as the total system integrator. 10 U.S.C.A. § 2304(c), (f)(1)(A); 48 C.F.R. § 6.303-2(a)(5). Metric Systems Corp. v. U.S., 42 Fed. Cl. 306 (1998). United States ☞64.45(1)

2 Substantiation required

Justification and approval prepared in support of a sole-source award expanding the scope of the contract was unreasonable where justification was premised on the conclusion that the awardee was the only responsible source, yet the capabilities of firms other than the awardee were not in fact considered. WorldWide Language Resources, Inc.; SOS International Ltd., B-296984, B-296984.2, B-296984.3, B-296984.4, B-296993, B-296993.2, B-296993.3, 2005 CPD ¶ 206 (Comp. Gen. 2005).

§ 6.304 Approval of the justification.

(a) Except for paragraph (b) of this section, the justification for other than full and open competition shall be approved in writing—

(1) For a proposed contract not exceeding $700,000, the contracting officer's certification required by 6.303-2(b)(12) will serve as approval unless a higher approving level is established in agency procedures.

(2) For a proposed contract over $700,000 but not exceeding $13.5 million, by the advocate for competition for the procuring activity designated pursuant to 6.501 or an official described in paragraph (a)(3) or (a)(4) of this section. This authority is not delegable.

(3) For a proposed contract over $13.5 million, but not exceeding $68 million, or, for DoD, NASA, and the Coast Guard, not exceeding $93 million, by the head of the procuring activity, or a designee who—

(i) If a member of the armed forces, is a general or flag officer; or

(ii) If a civilian, is serving in a position in a grade above GS-15 under the General Schedule (or in a comparable or higher position under another schedule).

(4) For a proposed contract over $68 million or, for DoD, NASA, and the Coast Guard, over $93 million, by the senior procurement executive of the agency designated pursuant to 41 U.S.C. 1702(c) in accordance with agency procedures.This authority is not delegable except in the case of the Under Secretary of Defense for Acquisition, Technology, and Logistics, acting as the senior procurement executive for the Department of Defense.

(b) Any justification for a contract awarded under the authority of 6.302-7, regardless of dollar amount, shall be considered approved when the determination required by 6.302-7(c)(1) is made.

(c) A class justification for other than full and open competition shall be approved in writing in accordance with agency procedures. The approval level shall be determined by the estimated total value of the class.

(d) The estimated dollar value of all options shall be included in determining the approval level of a justification

United States Code Annotated

Administrative determinations, see 41 U.S.C.A. § 257.

Advocates for competition, see 41 U.S.C.A. § 418.

Competition requirements, see 41 U.S.C.A. § 253.

Contract goal for small disadvantaged businesses and certain institutions of higher education, see 10 U.S.C.A. § 2323.

Contracts, competition requirements, see 10 U.S.C.A. § 2304.

Contracts, planning, solicitation, evaluation, and award procedures, see 10 U.S.C.A. § 2305.

Contracts, prohibition on competition between Department of Defense and small businesses and certain other entities, see 10 U.S.C.A. § 2304e.

Credit for Indian contracting in meeting certain subcontracting goals for small disadvantaged businesses and certain institutions of higher education, see 10 U.S.C.A. § 2323a.

Definitions, see 10 U.S.C.A. § 2302; 41 U.S.C.A. §§ 259, 403.

Design-build selection procedures, see 10 U.S.C.A. § 2305a; 41 U.S.C.A. § 253m.

Determinations and decisions, see 10 U.S.C.A. § 2310; 41 U.S.C.A. § 262.

Encouragement of new competition, see 41 U.S.C.A. § 253c.

Encouragement of new competitors, see 10 U.S.C.A. § 2319.

Planning and solicitation requirements, see 41 U.S.C.A. § 253a.

Procurement notice, see 41 U.S.C.A. § 416.

§ 6.305 Availability of the justification.

(a) The agency shall make publicly available the justification required by 6.303-1 as required by 10 U.S.C. 2304(l) and 41 U.S.C. 3304(f). Except for the circumstances in paragraphs (b) and (c) of this section, the justification shall be made publicly available within 14 days after contract award.

(b) In the case of a contract award permitted under 6.302-2, the justification shall be posted within 30 days after contract award.

(c) In the case of a brand name justification under 6.302-1(c), the justification shall be posted with the solicitation (see 5.102(a)(6)).

(d) The justifications shall be made publicly available—

(1) At the Government Point of Entry (GPE) www.fedbizopps.gov;

(2) On the website of the agency, which may provide access to the justifications by linking to the GPE; and

(3) Must remain posted for a minimum of 30 days.

(e) Contracting officers shall carefully screen all justifications for contractor proprietary data and remove all such data, and such references and citations as are necessary to protect the proprietary data, before making the justifications available for public inspection. Contracting officers shall also be guided by the exemptions to disclosure of information contained in the Freedom of Information Act (5 U.S.C. 552) and the prohibitions against disclosure in 24.202 in determining whether the justification, or portions of it, are exempt from posting. Although the submitter notice process set out in EO 12600, entitled "Predisclosure Notification Procedures for Confidential Commercial Information," does not apply, if the justification appears to contain proprietary data, the contracting officer should provide the contractor that submitted the information an opportunity to review the justification for proprietary data, before making the justification available for public inspection, redacted as necessary. This process must not prevent or delay the posting of the justification in accordance with the timeframes required in paragraphs (a) through (c).

(f) The requirements of paragraphs (a) through (d) do not apply if posting the justification would disclose the executive agency's needs and disclosure of such needs would compromise national security or create other security risks.

United States Code Annotated

Administrative determinations, see 41 U.S.C.A. § 257.

Advocates for competition, see 41 U.S.C.A. § 418.

Competition requirements, see 41 U.S.C.A. § 253.

Contract goal for small disadvantaged businesses and certain institutions of higher education, see 10 U.S.C.A. § 2323.

Contracts, competition requirements, see 10 U.S.C.A. § 2304.

Contracts, planning, solicitation, evaluation, and award procedures, see 10 U.S.C.A. § 2305.

Contracts, prohibition on competition between Department of Defense and small businesses and certain other entities, see 10 U.S.C.A. § 2304e.

Credit for Indian contracting in meeting certain subcontracting goals for small disadvantaged businesses and certain institutions of higher education, see 10 U.S.C.A. § 2323a.

Definitions, see 10 U.S.C.A. § 2302; 41 U.S.C.A. §§ 259, 403.

Design-build selection procedures, see 10 U.S.C.A. § 2305a; 41 U.S.C.A. § 253m.

Determinations and decisions, see 10 U.S.C.A. § 2310; 41 U.S.C.A. § 262.

Encouragement of new competition, see 41 U.S.C.A. § 253c.

Encouragement of new competitors, see 10 U.S.C.A. § 2319.

Planning and solicitation requirements, see 41 U.S.C.A. § 253a.

Procurement notice, see 41 U.S.C.A. § 416.

Notes of Decisions

In general 1

1 In general

In a sole-source procurement, the Notice of Intent issued by the government may invite potential vendors to submit statements of capability to convince the government that it should hold a full competition instead of awarding on a sole-source basis. Where a protester failed to submit a statement of capability within the required time, the Federal Circuit held that the protest must be dismissed because the protester is not an "actual or prospective bidder" and is not, therefore, an "interested party" with standing to file a protest. Digitalis Educ. Solutions, Inc. v. U.S., 664 F.3d 1380 (Fed. Cir. 2012).

Subpart 6.4 Sealed Bidding and Competitive Proposals

§ 6.401 Sealed bidding and competitive proposals.

Sealed bidding and competitive proposals, as described in Parts 14 and 15, are both acceptable procedures for use under Subparts 6.1, 6.2; and, when appropriate, under Subpart 6.3.

(a) *Sealed bids.* (See Part 14 for procedures.) Contracting officers shall solicit sealed bids if—

(1) Time permits the solicitation, submission, and evaluation of sealed bids;

(2) The award will be made on the basis of price and other price-related factors;

(3) It is not necessary to conduct discussions with the responding offerors about their bids; and

(4) There is a reasonable expectation of receiving more than one sealed bid.

(b) *Competitive proposals. (See Part 15 for procedures.)*(1) Contracting officers may request competitive proposals if sealed bids are not appropriate under paragraph (a) of this section.

(2) Because of differences in areas such as law, regulations, and business practices, it is generally necessary to conduct discussions with offerors relative to proposed contracts to be made and performed outside the United States and its outlying areas. Competitive proposals will therefore be used for these contracts unless discussions are not required and the use of sealed bids is otherwise appropriate.

United States Code Annotated

Advocates for competition, see 41 U.S.C.A. § 418.

Competition requirements, see 41 U.S.C.A. § 253.

Contract goal for small disadvantaged businesses and certain institutions of higher education, see 10 U.S.C.A. § 2323.

Contracts, competition requirements, see 10 U.S.C.A. § 2304.

Contracts, planning, solicitation, evaluation, and award procedures, see 10 U.S.C.A. § 2305.

Contracts, prohibition on competition between Department of Defense and small businesses and certain other entities, see 10 U.S.C.A. § 2304e.

Credit for Indian contracting in meeting certain subcontracting goals for small disadvantaged businesses and certain institutions of higher education, see 10 U.S.C.A. § 2323a.

Definitions, see 10 U.S.C.A. § 2302; 41 U.S.C.A. §§ 259, 403.

Design-build selection procedures, see 10 U.S.C.A. § 2305a; 41 U.S.C.A. § 253m.

Determinations and decisions, see 10 U.S.C.A. § 2310; 41 U.S.C.A. § 262.

Encouragement of new competition, see 41 U.S.C.A. § 253c.

Encouragement of new competitors, see 10 U.S.C.A. § 2319.

Planning and solicitation requirements, see 41 U.S.C.A. § 253a.

Procurement notice, see 41 U.S.C.A. § 416.

Notes of Decisions

In general 1
Substantiation required 2

1 In general

No abuse of discretion was shown in initiating two-step formal advertising procedure with respect to procurement of portable ship hull cleaning device for Navy, rather than negotiating contract with company which had allegedly developed new and unique device and acquired body of technology, special equipment and tooling, in absence of showing that formal advertising would be likely to result either in additional cost to the government by reason of duplication of investment or in duplication of necessary preparation which would unduly delay the procurement. Wheelabrator Corp. v. Chafee, 455 F.2d 1306, 147 (D.C. Cir. 1971). United States ☞64.10

Procurement by negotiation contemplates the exercise of greater discretion overall by a contracting officer than does procurement by formal advertising. DeMat Air, Inc. v. U.S., 2 Cl. Ct. 197, 30 Cont. Cas. Fed. (CCH) P 70980 (1983). United States ☞64.10

The procurement system is based on premise that the government's needs are best served when "full and free competition" exists among prospective government contractors, and to ensure competition, Congress has provided that property and services should be procured by formal advertising whenever possible. 10 U.S.C.A. §§ 2304(a, g), 2305. Continental Business Enterprises, Inc. v. U. S., 196 Ct. Cl. 627, 452 F.2d 1016 (1971). United States ☞64.10

If a construction project requires complex coordination and a compressed time frame, it is reasonable for an agency to consider non-price evaluation factors and award the project using negotiated procedures. Although several similar projects may have been awarded using sealed bidding procedures, that alone is not dispositive on whether the agency is prohibited from using negotiated procedures. Matter of: Ceres Environmental Services, Inc., B-310902, 2008 CPD ¶ 48 (Comp. Gen. 2008)

2 Substantiation required

Protest challenging use of negotiated procedures rather than sealed bidding to acquire waste management services is denied where the record shows that the agency reasonably concluded that discussions might be required before award. The agency reasonably anticipated that discussions may be necessary in view of the substantial discretion vested in offerors to structure programs to meet the agency's needs. Also, the agency points out that numerous disputes arose during the last contract regarding the recycling requirement and it believed that discussions prior to award could minimize post-award disputes. Enviro-clean Systems, Inc., B-278261, 97-2 CPD ¶ 172 (Comp. Gen. 1997)

Where record supports agency determination that the need for providing a smooth transition between civilian and military life mandated consideration of offeror's past performance in solicitation for lodging and transportation of applicants for military service, use of negotiated procedures was justified, since award would not be based on price alone. Comfort Inn South, B-270819, B-270819.2, 96-1 CPD ¶ 225 (Comp. Gen. 1996).

Agency decision to use sealed bidding procedures instead of competitive negotiation to acquire fire prevention system inspection and maintenance services is justified where the agency reasonably concludes that technical proposals and/or discussions with offerors are unnecessary to ensure understanding of requirements. Matter of: Eagle Fire Inc, B-257951, 94-2 CPD ¶ 214 (Comp. Gen. 1994)

Subpart 6.5 Competition Advocates

§ 6.501 Requirement.

As required by 41 U.S.C. 1705, the head of each executive agency shall designate an advocate for competition for the agency and for each procuring activity of the agency. The advocates for competition shall—

(a) Be in positions other than that of the agency senior procurement executive;

(b) Not be assigned any duties or responsibilities that are inconsistent with 6.502; and

(c) Be provided with staff or assistance (*e.g.*, specialists in engineering, technical operations, contract administration, financial management, supply management, and utilization of small business concerns), as may be necessary to carry out the advocate's duties and responsibilities.

United States Code Annotated

Advocates for competition, see 10 U.S.C.A. § 2318; 41 U.S.C.A. § 418.

Competition requirements, see 41 U.S.C.A. § 253.

Contract goal for small disadvantaged businesses and certain institutions of higher education, see 10 U.S.C.A. § 2323.

Contracts, competition requirements, see 10 U.S.C.A. § 2304.

Contracts, planning, solicitation, evaluation, and award procedures, see 10 U.S.C.A. § 2305.

Contracts, prohibition on competition between Department of Defense and small businesses and certain other entities, see 10 U.S.C.A. § 2304e.

Credit for Indian contracting in meeting certain subcontracting goals for small disadvantaged businesses and certain institutions of higher education, see 10 U.S.C.A. § 2323a.

Definitions, see 10 U.S.C.A. § 2302; 41 U.S.C.A. §§ 259, 403.

Design-build selection procedures, see 10 U.S.C.A. § 2305a; 41 U.S.C.A. § 253m.

Determinations and decisions, see 10 U.S.C.A. § 2310; 41 U.S.C.A. § 262.

Encouragement of new competition, see 41 U.S.C.A. § 253c.

Encouragement of new competitors, see 10 U.S.C.A. § 2319.

Planning and solicitation requirements, see 41 U.S.C.A. § 253a.

Procurement notice, see 41 U.S.C.A. § 416.

Notes of Decisions

Small business contracts 1

1 Small business contracts

There is no constitutional duty to offer government procurement contracts for competitive bidding. Small Business Act, § 2[8](a), 15 U.S.C.A. § 637(a). Ray Baillie Trash Hauling, Inc. v. Kleppe, 477 F.2d 696 (5th Cir. 1973). United States ⊛64.10

Subcontracts under Small Business Administration's program for awarding government procurement contracts to small business concerns owned by "socially or economically disadvantaged persons" may be awarded on a noncompetitive basis. Small Business Act, § 2[8](a), 15 U.S.C.A. § 637(a). Ray Baillie Trash Hauling, Inc. v. Kleppe, 477 F.2d 696 (5th Cir. 1973). United States ☞64.10

General policy of competitive bidding in federal procurement is wholly inapplicable to a contract which the Small Business Administration has specific statutory authority to enter. Small Business Act, § 2 [8] (a), (a)(2), 15 U.S.C.A. § 637(a), (a)(2); Fortec Constructors v. Kleppe, 350 F. Supp. 171 (D.D.C. 1972). United States ☞64.10

§ 6.502 Duties and responsibilities.

(a) Agency and procuring activity advocates for competition are responsible for promoting the acquisition of commercial items, promoting full and open competition, challenging requirements that are not stated in terms of functions to be performed, performance required or essential physical characteristics, and challenging barriers to the acquisition of commercial items and full and open competition such as unnecessarily restrictive statements of work, unnecessarily detailed specifications, and unnecessarily burdensome contract clauses.

(b) Agency advocates for competition shall—

(1) Review the contracting operations of the agency and identify and report to the agency senior procurement executive and the chief acquisition officer—

(i) Opportunities and actions taken to acquire commercial items to meet the needs of the agency;

(ii) Opportunities and actions taken to achieve full and open competition in the contracting operations of the agency;

(iii) Actions taken to challenge requirements that are not stated in terms of functions to be performed, performance required or essential physical characteristics;

(iv) Any condition or action that has the effect of unnecessarily restricting the acquisition of commercial items or competition in the contract actions of the agency;

(2) Prepare and submit an annual report to the agency senior procurement executive and the chief acquisition officer in accordance with agency procedures, describing—

(i) Such advocate's activities under this subpart;

(ii) New initiatives required to increase the acquisition of commercial items;

(iii) New initiatives required to increase competition;

(iv) New initiatives to ensure requirements are stated in terms of functions to be performed, performance required or essential physical characteristics;

(v) Any barriers to the acquisition of commercial items or competition that remain;

(vi) Other ways in which the agency has emphasized the acquisition of commercial items and competition in areas such as acquisition training and research; and

(vii) Initiatives that ensure task and delivery orders over $1,000,000 issued under multiple award contracts are properly planned, issued, and comply with 8.405 and 16.505.

(3) Recommend goals and plans for increasing competition on a fiscal year basis to the agency senior procurement executive and the chief acquisition officer; and

(4) Recommend to the agency senior procurement executive and the chief acquisition officer a system of personal and organizational accountability for competition, which may include the use of recognition and awards to motivate program managers, contracting officers, and others in authority to promote competition in acquisition.

United States Code Annotated

Advocates for competition, see 10 U.S.C.A. § 2318; 41 U.S.C.A. § 418.

Competition requirements, see 41 U.S.C.A. § 253.

Contract goal for small disadvantaged businesses and certain institutions of higher education, see 10 U.S.C.A. § 2323.

Contracts, competition requirements, see 10 U.S.C.A. § 2304.

Contracts, planning, solicitation, evaluation, and award procedures, see 10 U.S.C.A. § 2305.

Contracts, prohibition on competition between Department of Defense and small businesses and certain other entities, see 10 U.S.C.A. § 2304e.

Credit for Indian contracting in meeting certain subcontracting goals for small disadvantaged businesses and certain institutions of higher education, see 10 U.S.C.A. § 2323a.

Definitions, see 10 U.S.C.A. § 2302; 41 U.S.C.A. §§ 259, 403.

Design-build selection procedures, see 10 U.S.C.A. § 2305a; 41 U.S.C.A. § 253m.

Determinations and decisions, see 10 U.S.C.A. § 2310; 41 U.S.C.A. § 262.

Encouragement of new competition, see 41 U.S.C.A. § 253c.

Encouragement of new competitors, see 10 U.S.C.A. § 2319.

Planning and solicitation requirements, see 41 U.S.C.A. § 253a.

Procurement notice, see 41 U.S.C.A. § 416.

Notes of Decisions

Commercial items 1

1 Commercial items

Radioactive waste disposal service called for in solicitation was not a "commercial item" subject to mandatory procedures of the Federal Acquisition Regulation (FAR), where there were no market prices for the service, and no competitive market for the service. 48 C.F.R. § 2.101, 12.102(a). Envirocare of Utah, Inc. v. U.S., 44 Fed. Cl. 474 (1999), dismissed, 217 F.3d 852 (Fed. Cir. 1999). United States ⊛64.10

PART 7 ACQUISITION PLANNING

§ 7.000 Scope of part.

Subpart 7.1 Acquisition Plans

Subpart 7.2 Planning for the Purchase of Supplies in Economic Quantities

Subpart 7.3 Contractor Versus Government Performance

Subpart 7.4 Equipment Lease or Purchase

Subpart 7.5 Inherently Governmental Functions

§ 7.000 Scope of part.

This part prescribes policies and procedures for—

(a) Developing acquisition plans;

(b) Determining whether to use commercial or Government resources for acquisition of supplies or services;

(c) Deciding whether it is more economical to lease equipment rather than purchase it;

and

(d) Determining whether functions are inherently governmental.

United States Code Annotated

Commercially available off-the-shelf item acquisitions, lists of inapplicable laws in Federal Acquisition Regulation, see 41 U.S.C.A. § 431.

Competition requirements, see 41 U.S.C.A. § 253.

Contracts, competition requirements, see 10 U.S.C.A. § 2304.

Contracts, planning, solicitation, evaluation, and award procedures, see 10 U.S.C.A. § 2305.

Contracts, prohibition on competition between Department of Defense and small businesses and certain other entities, see 10 U.S.C.A. § 2304e.

Definitions, see 10 U.S.C.A. § 2302; 41 U.S.C.A. §§ 259, 403.

Encouragement of new competition, see 41 U.S.C.A. § 253c.

Encouragement of new competitors, see 10 U.S.C.A. § 2319.

Planning and solicitation requirements, see 41 U.S.C.A. § 253a.

Preference for acquisition of commercial items, see 10 U.S.C.A. § 2377; 41 U.S.C.A. § 264b.

Procurement notice, see 41 U.S.C.A. § 416.

Subpart 7.1 Acquisition Plans

§ 7.101 Definitions.

As used in this subpart—

"Acquisition streamlining" means any effort that results in more efficient and effective use of resources to design and develop, or produce quality systems. This includes ensuring that only necessary and cost-effective requirements are included, at the most appropriate time in the acquisition cycle, in solicitations and resulting contracts for the design, development, and production of new systems, or for modifications to existing systems that involve redesign of systems or subsystems.

"Life-cycle cost" means the total cost to the Government of acquiring, operating, supporting, and (if applicable) disposing of the items being acquired.

"Order" means an order placed under a—

(1) Federal Supply Schedule contract; or

(2) Task-order contract or delivery-order contract awarded by another agency, (i.e., Governmentwide acquisition contract or multi-agency contract).

"Planner" means the designated person or office responsible for developing and maintaining a written plan, or for the planning function in those acquisitions not requiring a written plan.

United States Code Annotated

Commercially available off-the-shelf item acquisitions, lists of inapplicable laws in Federal Acquisition Regulation, see 41 U.S.C.A. § 431.

Competition requirements, see 41 U.S.C.A. § 253.

Contracts, competition requirements, see 10 U.S.C.A. § 2304.

Contracts, planning, solicitation, evaluation, and award procedures, see 10 U.S.C.A. § 2305.

Contracts, prohibition on competition between Department of Defense and small businesses and certain other entities, see 10 U.S.C.A. § 2304e.

Definitions, see 10 U.S.C.A. § 2302; 41 U.S.C.A. §§ 259, 403.

Encouragement of new competition, see 41 U.S.C.A. § 253c.

Encouragement of new competitors, see 10 U.S.C.A. § 2319.

Planning and solicitation requirements, see 41 U.S.C.A. § 253a.

Preference for acquisition of commercial items, see 10 U.S.C.A. § 2377; 41 U.S.C.A. § 264b.

Procurement notice, see 41 U.S.C.A. § 416.

Notes of Decisions

In general 1

1 In general

Acquisition planning and market research are required to ensure that agencies, among other things, develop a plan to suitably satisfy their needs in a timely manner and at a reasonable cost. See FAR 7.101, 10.000. The Federal Supply Schedule (FSS) program specifically satisfies these goals by allowing the government to acquire a wide range of commercial products and services in a timely fashion and at fair and reasonable prices. Thus, we think that, as a general rule, obtaining information from the FSS program and FSS vendors satisfies the agency's obligations to conduct procurement planning and market research. Sales Resources Consultants, Inc., B-284943, B-284943.2, 2000 CPD ¶ 102 (Comp. Gen. 2000)

CICA requires that agencies use market research during the planning stage for the procurement of property or services. 41 U.S.C. § 253a(a)(1)(B). A market survey is an acceptable method of market research to ascertain whether other qualified sources capable of satisfying the government's requirements exist and may be informal, i.e., phone calls to federal or non-federal experts, or formal, i.e., sources-sought announcements in the CBD or solicitations for information or planning purposes. FAR 7.101. Matter of: Coulter Corporation; Nova Biomedical; Ciba Corning Diagnostics Corp, B-258713, B-258714, 1995 WL 64156 (Comp. Gen. 1995)

§ 7.102 Policy.

(a) Agencies shall perform acquisition planning and conduct market research (see Part 10) for all acquisitions in order to promote and provide for—

(1) Acquisition of commercial items or, to the extent that commercial items suitable to meet the agency's needs are not available, nondevelopmental items, to the maximum extent practicable (10 U.S.C. 2377 and 41 U.S.C. 3307); and

(2) Full and open competition (see Part 6) or, when full and open competition is not required in accordance with Part 6, to obtain competition to the maximum extent practicable, with due regard to the nature of the supplies or services to be acquired (10 U.S.C. 2305(a)(1)(A) and 41 U.S.C. 3306a(1)).

(3) Selection of appropriate contract type in accordance with Part 16; and

(4) Appropriate consideration of the use of pre-existing contracts, including interagency and intra-agency contracts, to fulfill the requirement, before awarding new contracts. (See 8.002 through 8.004 and Subpart 17.5).

(b) This planning shall integrate the efforts of all personnel responsible for significant aspects of the acquisition. The purpose of this planning is to ensure that the Government meets its needs in the most effective, economical, and timely manner. Agencies that have a detailed acquisition planning system in place that generally meets the requirements of 7.104 and 7.105 need not revise their system to specifically meet all of these requirements.

§ 7.103 Agency-head responsibilities.

The agency head or a designee shall prescribe procedures for—

(a) Promoting and providing for full and open competition (see part 6) or, when full and open competition is not required in accordance with part 6, for obtaining competition to the maximum extent practicable, with due regard to the nature of the supplies and services to be acquired (10 U.S.C. 2305(a)(1)(A) and 41 U.S.C. 3306(a)(1)).

(b) Encouraging offerors to supply commercial items, or to the extent that commercial items suitable to meet the agency needs are not available, nondevelopmental items in response to agency solicitations (10 U.S.C. 2377 and 41 U.S.C. 3307); and

(c) Ensuring that acquisition planners address the requirement to specify needs, develop specifications, and to solicit offers in such a manner to promote and provide for full and open competition with due regard to the nature of the supplies and services to be acquired (10 U.S.C. 2305(a)(1)(A) and 41 U.S.C. 3306(a)(1)). (See part 6 and 10.002.)

(d) Ensuring that acquisition planners document the file to support the selection of the contract type in accordance with subpart 16.1.

(e) Establishing criteria and thresholds at which increasingly greater detail and formality in the planning process is required as the acquisition becomes more complex and costly, including for cost-reimbursement and other high-risk contracts (e.g., other than firm-fixed-price contracts) requiring a written acquisition plan. A written plan shall be prepared for cost reimbursement and other high-risk contracts other than firm-fixed-price contracts, although written plans may be required for firm-fixed-price contracts as appropriate.

(f) Ensuring that the statement of work is closely aligned with performance outcomes and cost estimates.

(g) Writing plans either on a systems basis, on an individual contract basis, or on an individual order basis, depending upon the acquisition.

(h) Ensuring that the principles of this subpart are used, as appropriate, for those acquisitions that do not require a written plan as well as for those that do.

(i) Designating planners for acquisitions.

(j) Reviewing and approving acquisition plans and revisions to these plans to ensure compliance with FAR requirements including 7.104 and part 16. For other than firm-fixed-price contracts, ensuring that the plan is approved and signed at least one level above the contracting officer.

(k) Establishing criteria and thresholds at which design-to-cost and life-cycle-cost techniques will be used.

(l) Establishing standard acquisition plan formats, if desired, suitable to agency needs; and

(m) Waiving requirements of detail and formality, as necessary, in planning for acquisitions having compressed delivery or performance schedules because of the urgency of the need.

(n) Assuring that the contracting officer, prior to contracting, reviews:

(1) The acquisition history of the supplies and services; and

(2) A description of the supplies, including, when necessary for adequate description, a picture, drawing, diagram, or other graphic representation.

(o) Ensuring that agency planners include use of the metric system of measurement in proposed acquisitions in accordance with 15 U.S.C. 205b (see 11.002(b)) and agency metric plans and guidelines.

(p) Ensuring that agency planners—

(1) Specify needs for printing and writing paper consistent with the 30 percent postconsumer fiber minimum content standards specified in section 2(d)(ii) of Executive Order 13423 of January 24, 2007, Strengthening Federal Environmental, Energy, and Transportation Management, and section 2(e)(iv) of Executive Order 13514 of October 5, 2009 (see 11.303)

(2) Comply with the policy in 11.002(d) regarding procurement of biobased products, products containing recovered materials, environmentally preferable products and services (including Electronic Product Environmental Assessment Tool (EPEAT®)-registered electronic products, nontoxic or low-toxic alternatives), ENERGY STAR® and Federal Energy Management Program-designated products, renewable energy, water-efficient products, non-ozone-depleting products, and products and services that minimize or eliminate, when feasible, the use, release, or emission of high global warming potential hydrofluorocarbons, such as by using reclaimed instead of virgin hydrofluorocarbons;

(3) Comply with the Guiding Principles for Federal Leadership in High-Performance and Sustainable Buildings (Guiding Principles), for the design, construction, renovation, repair, or deconstruction of Federal buildings. The Guiding Principles can be accessed at http://www.wbdg.org/pdfs/hpsb_guidance.pdf; and

(4) Require contractor compliance with Federal environmental requirements, when the contractor is operating Government-owned facilities or vehicles, to the same extent as the agency would be required to comply if the agency operated the facilities or vehicles.

(q) Ensuring that acquisition planners specify needs and develop plans, drawings, work statements, specifications, or other product descriptions that address Electronic and Information Technology Accessibility Standards (see 36 CFR Part 1194) in proposed acquisitions (see 11.002(e)) and that these standards are included in requirements planning, as appropriate (see subpart 39.2).

(r) Making a determination, prior to issuance of a solicitation for advisory and assistance services involving the analysis and evaluation of proposals submitted in response to a solicitation, that a sufficient number of covered personnel with the training and capability to perform an evaluation and analysis of proposals submitted in response to a solicitation are not readily available within the agency or from another Federal agency in accordance with the guidelines at 37.204.

(s) Ensuring that no purchase request is initiated or contract entered into that would result in the performance of an inherently governmental function by a contractor and that all contracts or orders are adequately managed so as to ensure effective official control over contract or order performance.

(t) Ensuring that knowledge gained from prior acquisitions is used to further refine requirements and acquisition strategies. For services, greater use of performance-based acquisition methods should occur for follow-on acquisitions.

(u) Ensuring that acquisition planners, to the maximum extent practicable—

(1) Structure contract requirements to facilitate competition by and among small business concerns; and

(2) Avoid unnecessary and unjustified bundling that precludes small business participation as contractors (see 7.107) (15 U.S.C. 631(j)).

(v) Ensuring that agency planners on information technology acquisitions comply with the capital planning and investment control requirements in 40 U.S.C. 11312 and OMB Circular A-130.

(w) Ensuring that agency planners on information technology acquisitions comply with the information technology security requirements in the Federal Information Security Management Act (44 U.S.C. 3544), OMB's implementing policies including Appendix III of OMB Circular A-130, and guidance and standards from the Department of Commerce's National Institute of Standards and Technology.

(x) Encouraging agency planners to consider the use of a project labor agreement (see subpart 22.5).

(y) Ensuring that contracting officers consult the Disaster Response Registry via https://www.acquisition.gov as a part of acquisition planning for debris removal, distribution of supplies, reconstruction, and other disaster or emergency relief activities inside the United States and outlying areas. (See 26.205).

United States Code Annotated

Commercially available off-the-shelf item acquisitions, lists of inapplicable laws in Federal Acquisition Regulation, see 41 U.S.C.A. § 431.

Competition requirements, see 41 U.S.C.A. § 253.

Contracts, competition requirements, see 10 U.S.C.A. § 2304.

Contracts, planning, solicitation, evaluation, and award procedures, see 10 U.S.C.A. § 2305.

Contracts, prohibition on competition between Department of Defense and small businesses and certain other entities, see 10 U.S.C.A. § 2304e.

Definitions, see 10 U.S.C.A. § 2302; 41 U.S.C.A. §§ 259, 403.

Encouragement of new competition, see 41 U.S.C.A. § 253c.

Encouragement of new competitors, see 10 U.S.C.A. § 2319.

Planning and solicitation requirements, see 41 U.S.C.A. § 253a.

Preference for acquisition of commercial items, see 10 U.S.C.A. § 2377; 41 U.S.C.A. § 264b.

Procurement notice, see 41 U.S.C.A. § 416.

§ 7.104 General procedures.

(a) Acquisition planning should begin as soon as the agency need is identified, preferably well in advance of the fiscal year in which contract award or order placement is necessary. In developing the plan, the planner shall form a team consisting of all those who will be responsible for significant aspects of the acquisition, such as contracting, fiscal, legal, and technical personnel. If contract performance is to be in a designated operational area or supporting a diplomatic or consular mission, the planner shall also consider inclusion of the combatant commander or chief of mission, as appropriate. The planner should review previous plans for similar acquisitions and discuss them with the key personnel involved in those acquisitions. At key dates specified in the plan or whenever significant changes occur, and no less often than annually, the planner shall review the plan and, if appropriate, revise it.

(b) Requirements and logistics personnel should avoid issuing requirements on an urgent basis or with unrealistic delivery or performance schedules, since it generally restricts competition and increases prices. Early in the planning process, the planner should consult with requirements and logistics personnel who determine type, quality, quantity, and delivery requirements.

(c) The planner shall coordinate with and secure the concurrence of the contracting officer in all acquisition planning. If the plan proposes using other than full and open competition when awarding a contract, the plan shall also be coordinated with the cognizant advocate for competition.

(d) (1) The planner shall coordinate the acquisition plan or strategy with the cognizant small business specialist when the strategy contemplates an acquisition meeting the dollar amounts in paragraph (d)(2) of this section unless the contract or order is entirely reserved or set-aside for small business under part 19. The small business specialist shall notify the agency Office of Small and Disadvantaged Business Utilization if the strategy involves contract bundling that is unnecessary, unjustified, or not identified as bundled by the agency. If the strategy involves substantial bundling, the small business specialist shall assist in identifying alternative strategies that would reduce or minimize the scope of the bundling.

(2) (i) The strategy shall be coordinated with the cognizant small business specialist in accordance with paragraph (d)(1) of this section if the estimated contract or order value is—

(A) $9 million or more for the Department of Defense;

(B) $6.5 million or more for the National Aeronautics and Space Administration, the General Services Administration, and the Department of Energy; and

(C) $2.5 million or more for all other agencies.

(ii) If the strategy contemplates the award of multiple contracts or orders, the thresholds in paragraph (d)(2)(i) of this section apply to the cumulative maximum potential value, including options, of the contracts and orders.

(e) The planner shall ensure that a COR is nominated as early as practicable in the acquisition process by the requirements official or in accordance with agency procedures. The contracting officer shall designate and authorize a COR as early as practicable after the nomination. See 1.602-2(d).

§ 7.105 Contents of written acquisition plans.

In order to facilitate attainment of the acquisition objectives, the plan must identify those milestones at which decisions should be made (see paragraph (b)(21) of this section). The plan must address all the technical, business, management, and other significant considerations that will control the acquisition. The specific content of plans will vary, depending on the nature, circumstances, and stage of the acquisition. In preparing the plan, the planner must follow the applicable instructions in paragraphs (a) and (b) of this section, together with the agency's implementing procedures. Acquisition plans for service contracts or orders must describe the strategies for implementing performance-based acquisition methods or must provide rationale for not using those methods (see subpart 37.6).

(a) Acquisition background and objectives—

(1) Statement of need. Introduce the plan by a brief statement of need. Summarize the technical and contractual history of the acquisition. Discuss feasible acquisition alternatives, the impact of prior acquisitions on those alternatives, and any related in-house effort.

(2) Applicable conditions. State all significant conditions affecting the acquisition, such as—

(i) Requirements for compatibility with existing or future systems or programs; and

(ii) Any known cost, schedule, and capability or performance constraints.

(3) Cost. Set forth the established cost goals for the acquisition and the rationale supporting them, and discuss related cost concepts to be employed, including, as appropriate, the following items:

(i) Life-cycle cost. Discuss how life-cycle cost will be considered. If it is not used, explain why. If appropriate, discuss the cost model used to develop life-cycle-cost estimates.

(ii) Design-to-cost. Describe the design-to-cost objective(s) and underlying assumptions, including the rationale for quantity, learning-curve, and economic adjustment factors. Describe how objectives are to be applied, tracked, and enforced. Indicate specific related solicitation and contractual requirements to be imposed.

(iii) Application of should-cost. Describe the application of should-cost analysis to the acquisition (see 15.407-4).

(4) Capability or performance. Specify the required capabilities or performance characteristics of the supplies or the performance standards of the services being acquired and state how they are related to the need.

(5) Delivery or performance-period requirements. Describe the basis for establishing delivery or performance-period requirements (see subpart 11.4). Explain and provide reasons for any urgency if it results in concurrency of development and production or constitutes justification for not providing for full and open competition.

(6) Trade-offs. Discuss the expected consequences of trade-offs among the various cost, capability or performance, and schedule goals.

(7) Risks. Discuss technical, cost, and schedule risks and describe what efforts are planned or underway to reduce risk and the consequences of failure to achieve goals. If concurrency of development and production is planned, discuss its effects on cost and schedule risks.

(8) Acquisition streamlining. If specifically designated by the requiring agency as a program subject to acquisition streamlining, discuss plans and procedures to—

(i) Encourage industry participation by using draft solicitations, presolicitation conferences, and other means of stimulating industry involvement during design and development in recommending the most appropriate application and tailoring of contract requirements;

(ii) Select and tailor only the necessary and cost-effective requirements; and

(iii) State the timeframe for identifying which of those specifications and standards, originally provided for guidance only, shall become mandatory.

(b) Plan of action—

(1) Sources. Indicate the prospective sources of supplies or services that can meet the need. Consider required sources of supplies or services (see part 8) and sources identifiable through databases including the Governmentwide database of contracts and other procurement instruments intended for use by multiple agencies available at https://www.contractdirectory.gov/contractdirectory/. Include consideration of small business, veteran-owned small business, service-disabled veteran-owned small business, HUBZone small business, small disadvantaged business, and women-owned small business concerns (see part 19), and the impact of any bundling that might affect their participation in the acquisition (see 7.107) (15 U.S.C. 644(e)). When the proposed acquisition strategy involves bundling, identify the incumbent contractors and contracts affected by the bundling. Address the extent and results of the market research and indicate their impact on the various elements of the plan (see part 10).

(2) Competition.

(i) Describe how competition will be sought, promoted, and sustained throughout the course of the acquisition. If full and open competition is not contemplated, cite the authority in 6.302, discuss the basis for the application of that authority, identify the source(s), and discuss why full and open competition cannot be obtained.

(ii) Identify the major components or subsystems. Discuss component breakout plans relative to these major components or subsystems. Describe how competition will be sought, promoted, and sustained for these components or subsystems.

(iii) Describe how competition will be sought, promoted, and sustained for spares and repair parts. Identify the key logistic milestones, such as technical data delivery schedules and acquisition method coding conferences, that affect competition.

(iv) When effective subcontract competition is both feasible and desirable, describe how such subcontract competition will be sought, promoted, and sustained throughout the course of the acquisition. Identify any known barriers to increasing subcontract competition and address how to overcome them.

(3) Contract type selection. Discuss the rationale for the selection of contract type. For other than firm-fixed-price contracts, see 16.103(d) for additional documentation guidance. Acquisition personnel shall document the acquisition plan with findings that detail the particular facts and circumstances, (e.g., complexity of the requirements, uncertain duration of the work, contractor's technical capability and financial responsibility, or adequacy of the contractor's accounting system), and associated reasoning essential to support the contract type selection. The contracting officer shall ensure that requirements and technical personnel provide the necessary documentation to support the contract type selection.

(4) Source-selection procedures. Discuss the source-selection procedures for the acquisition, including the timing for submission and evaluation of proposals, and the relationship of evaluation factors to the attainment of the acquisition objectives (see subpart 15.3). When an EVMS is required (see FAR 34.202(a)) and a pre-award IBR is contemplated, the acquisition plan must discuss—

(i) How the pre-award IBR will be considered in the source selection decision;

(ii) How it will be conducted in the source selection process (see FAR 15.306); and

(iii) Whether offerors will be directly compensated for the costs of participating in a pre-award IBR.

(5) Acquisition considerations.

(i) For each contract contemplated, discuss use of multiyear contracting, options, or other special contracting methods (see part 17); any special clauses, special solicitation provisions, or FAR deviations required (see subpart 1.4); whether sealed bidding or negotiation will be used and why; whether equipment will be acquired by lease or purchase (see subpart 7.4) and why; and any other contracting considerations. Provide rationale if a performance-based acquisition will not be used or if a performance-based acquisition for services is contemplated on other than a firm-fixed-price basis (see 37.102(a), 16.103(d), and 16.505(a)(3)).

(ii) For each order contemplated, discuss—

(A) For information technology acquisitions, how the capital planning and investment control requirements of 40 U.S.C. 11312 and OMB Circular A-130 will be met (see 7.103(v) and part 39); and

(B) Why this action benefits the Government, such as when—

(1) The agency can accomplish its mission more efficiently and effectively (e.g., take advantage of the servicing agency's specialized expertise; or gain access to contractors with needed expertise); or

(2) Ordering through an indefinite delivery contract facilitates access to small business concerns, including small disadvantaged business concerns, 8(a) contractors, women-owned small business concerns, HUBZone small business concerns, veteran-owned small business concerns, or service-disabled veteran-owned small business concerns.

(iii) For information technology acquisitions using Internet Protocol, discuss whether the requirements documents include the Internet Protocol compliance requirements specified in 11.002(g) or a waiver of these requirements has been granted by the agency's Chief Information Officer.

(iv) For each contract (and order) contemplated, discuss the strategy to transition to firm-fixed-price contracts to the maximum extent practicable. During the requirements development stage, consider structuring the contract requirements, e.g., contract line items (CLINS), in a manner that will permit some, if not all, of the requirements to be awarded on a firm-fixed-price basis, either in the current contract, future option years, or follow-on contracts. This will facilitate an easier transition to a firm-fixed-price contact because a cost history will be developed for a recurring definitive requirement.

(6) Budgeting and funding. Include budget estimates, explain how they were derived, and discuss the schedule for obtaining adequate funds at the time they are required (see subpart 32.7).

(7) *Product or service descriptions.* Explain the choice of product or service description types (including performance-based acquisition descriptions) to be used in the acquisition.

(8) *Priorities, allocations, and allotments.* When urgency of the requirement dictates a particularly short delivery or performance schedule, certain priorities may apply. If so, specify the method for obtaining and using priorities, allocations, and allotments, and the reasons for them (see subpart 11.6).

(9) *Contractor versus Government performance.* Address the consideration given to OMB Circular No. A-76 (see subpart 7.3).

(10) *Inherently governmental functions.* Address the consideration given to subpart 7.5.

(11) *Management information requirements.* Discuss, as appropriate, what management system will be used by the Government to monitor the contractor's effort. If an Earned Value Management System is to be used, discuss the methodology the Government will employ to analyze and use the earned value data to assess and monitor contract performance. In addition, discuss how the offeror's/contractor's EVMS will be verified for compliance with the American National Standards Institute/Electronics Industries Alliance (ANSI/EIA) Standard-748, Earned Value Management Systems, and the timing and conduct of integrated baseline reviews (whether prior to or post award). (See 34.202.)

(12) *Make or buy.* Discuss any consideration given to make-or-buy programs (see 15.407-2).

(13) *Test and evaluation.* To the extent applicable, describe the test program of the contractor and the Government. Describe the test program for each major phase of a major system acquisition. If concurrency is planned, discuss the extent of testing to be accomplished before production release.

(14) *Logistics considerations.* Describe—

(i) The assumptions determining contractor or agency support, both initially and over the life of the acquisition, including consideration of contractor or agency maintenance and servicing (see subpart 7.3), support for contracts to be performed in a designated operational area or supporting a diplomatic or consular mission (see 25.301-3); and distribution of commercial items;

(ii) The reliability, maintainability, and quality assurance requirements, including any planned use of warranties (see part 46);

(iii) The requirements for contractor data (including repurchase data) and data rights, their estimated cost, and the use to be made of the data (see part 27); and

(iv) Standardization concepts, including the necessity to designate, in accordance with agency procedures, technical equipment as "standard" so that future purchases of the equipment can be made from the same manufacturing source.

(15) *Government-furnished property.* Indicate any Government property to be furnished to contractors, and discuss any associated considerations, such as its availability or the schedule for its acquisition (see 45.102).

(16) *Government-furnished information.* Discuss any Government information, such as manuals, drawings, and test data, to be provided to prospective offerors and contractors. Indicate which information that requires additional controls to monitor access and distribution (e.g., technical specifications, maps, building designs, schedules, etc.), as determined by the agency, is to be posted via the enhanced controls of the GPE at http://www.fedbizopps.gov (see 5.102(a)).

(17) *Environmental and energy conservation objectives.* Discuss all applicable environmental and energy conservation objectives associated with the acquisition (see part 23), the applicability of an environmental assessment or environmental impact statement (see 40 CFR 1502), the proposed resolution of environmental issues, and any environmentally-related requirements to be included in solicitations and contracts (see 11.002 and 11.303).

(18) *Security considerations.*

(i) For acquisitions dealing with classified matters, discuss how adequate security will be established, maintained, and monitored (see subpart 4.4).

(ii) For information technology acquisitions, discuss how agency information security requirements will be met.

(iii) For acquisitions requiring routine contractor physical access to a Federally-controlled facility and/or routine access to a Federally-controlled information system, discuss how agency requirements for personal identity verification of contractors will be met (see subpart 4.13).

(iv) or acquisitions that may require Federal contract information to reside in or transit through contractor information systems, discuss compliance with subpart 4.19.

(19) Contract administration. Describe how the contract will be administered. In contracts for services, include how inspection and acceptance corresponding to the work statement's performance criteria will be enforced.

(20) Other considerations. Discuss, as applicable:

(i) Standardization concepts;

(ii) The industrial readiness program;

(iii) The Defense Production Act;

(iv) The Occupational Safety and Health Act;

(v) Support Anti-terrorism by Fostering Effective Technologies Act of 2002 (SAFETY Act) (see subpart 50.2);

(vi) Foreign sales implications;

(vii) Special requirements for contracts to be performed in a designated operational area or supporting a diplomatic or consular mission; and

(viii) Any other matters germane to the plan not covered elsewhere.

(21) Milestones for the acquisition cycle. Address the following steps and any others appropriate:

Acquisition plan approval.

Statement of work.

Specifications.

Data requirements.

Completion of acquisition-package preparation.

Purchase request.

Justification and approval for other than full and open competition where applicable and/or any required D&F approval.

Issuance of synopsis.

Issuance of solicitation.

Evaluation of proposals, audits, and field reports.

Beginning and completion of negotiations.

Contract preparation, review, and clearance.

Contract award.

(22) Identification of participants in acquisition plan preparation. List the individuals who participated in preparing the acquisition plan, giving contact information for each.

United States Code Annotated

Commercially available off-the-shelf item acquisitions, lists of inapplicable laws in Federal Acquisition Regulation, see 41 U.S.C.A. § 431.

Competition requirements, see 41 U.S.C.A. § 253.

Contracts, competition requirements, see 10 U.S.C.A. § 2304.

Contracts, planning, solicitation, evaluation, and award procedures, see 10 U.S.C.A. § 2305.

Contracts, prohibition on competition between Department of Defense and small businesses and certain other entities, see 10 U.S.C.A. § 2304e.

Definitions, see 10 U.S.C.A. § 2302; 41 U.S.C.A. §§ 259, 403.

Encouragement of new competition, see 41 U.S.C.A. § 253c.

Encouragement of new competitors, see 10 U.S.C.A. § 2319.

Planning and solicitation requirements, see 41 U.S.C.A. § 253a.

Preference for acquisition of commercial items, see 10 U.S.C.A. § 2377; 41 U.S.C.A. § 264b.

Procurement notice, see 41 U.S.C.A. § 416.

1 In general

An agency decision to procure photocopier machines and related services on a total package basis was legally unobjectionable where the agency's acquisition planning documents demonstrated that the agency reasonably believed that this contracting method would reduce administrative costs attributable to duplicate efforts; allow greater flexibility in redistributing copiers to meet changing needs; and increase competition for certain categories of copiers. Canon U.S.A., Inc., B-232262, 88-2 CPD ¶ 538 (Comp. Gen. 1988)

§ 7.106 Additional requirements for major systems.

(a) In planning for the solicitation of a major system (see Part 34) development contract, planners shall consider requiring offerors to include, in their offers, proposals to incorporate in the design of a major system—

(1) Items which are currently available within the supply system of the agency responsible for the major system, available elsewhere in the national supply system, or commercially available from more than one source; and

(2) Items which the Government will be able to acquire competitively in the future if they are likely to be needed in substantial quantities during the system's service life.

(b) In planning for the solicitation of a major system (see Part 34) production contract, planners shall consider requiring offerors to include, in their offers, proposals identifying opportunities to assure that the Government will be able to obtain, on a competitive basis, items acquired in connection with the system that are likely to be acquired in substantial quantities during the service life of the system. Proposals submitted in response to such requirements may include the following:

(1) Proposals to provide the Government the right to use technical data to be provided under the contract for competitive future acquisitions, together with the cost to the Government, if any, of acquiring such technical data and the right to use such data.

(2) Proposals for the qualification or development of multiple sources of supply for competitive future acquisitions.

(c) In determining whether to apply paragraphs (a) and (b) of this section, planners shall consider the purposes for which the system is being acquired and the technology necessary to meet the system's required capabilities. If such proposals are required, the contracting officer shall consider them in evaluating competing offers. In noncompetitive awards, the factors in paragraphs (a) and (b) of this section, may be considered by the contracting officer as objectives in negotiating the contract.

United States Code Annotated

Commercially available off-the-shelf item acquisitions, lists of inapplicable laws in Federal Acquisition Regulation, see 41 U.S.C.A. § 431.

Competition requirements, see 41 U.S.C.A. § 253.

Contracts, competition requirements, see 10 U.S.C.A. § 2304.

Contracts, planning, solicitation, evaluation, and award procedures, see 10 U.S.C.A. § 2305.

Contracts, prohibition on competition between Department of Defense and small businesses and certain other entities, see 10 U.S.C.A. § 2304e.

Definitions, see 10 U.S.C.A. § 2302; 41 U.S.C.A. §§ 259, 403.

Encouragement of new competition, see 41 U.S.C.A. § 253c.

Encouragement of new competitors, see 10 U.S.C.A. § 2319.

Planning and solicitation requirements, see 41 U.S.C.A. § 253a.

Preference for acquisition of commercial items, see 10 U.S.C.A. § 2377; 41 U.S.C.A. § 264b.

Procurement notice, see 41 U.S.C.A. § 416.

§ 7.107 Additional requirements for acquisitions involving bundling.

(a) Bundling may provide substantial benefits to the Government. However, because of the potential impact on small business participation, the head of the agency must conduct market research to determine whether bundling is necessary and justified (15 U.S.C. 644(e) (2)). Market research may indicate that bundling is necessary and justified if an agency or the Government would derive measurably substantial benefits (see 10.001(a)(2)(iv) and (a)(3)(vi)).

(b) Measurably substantial benefits may include, individually or in any combination or aggregate, cost savings or price reduction, quality improvements that will save time or improve or enhance performance or efficiency, reduction in acquisition cycle times, better terms and conditions, and any other benefits. The agency must quantify the identified benefits and explain how their impact would be measurably substantial. Except as provided in paragraph (d) of this section, the agency may determine bundling to be necessary and justified if, as compared to the benefits that it would derive from contracting to meet those requirements if not bundled, it would derive measurably substantial benefits equivalent to—

(1) Ten percent of the estimated contract or order value (including options) if the value is $102 million or less; or

(2) Five percent of the estimated contract or order value (including options) or $10.2 million, whichever is greater, if the value exceeds $102 million.

(c) Without power of delegation, the service acquisition executive for the military departments, the Under Secretary of Defense for Acquisition, Technology and Logistics for the defense agencies, or the Deputy Secretary or equivalent for the civilian agencies may determine that bundling is necessary and justified when—

(1) The expected benefits do not meet the thresholds in paragraphs (b)(1) and (b)(2) of this section but are critical to the agency's mission success; and

(2) The acquisition strategy provides for maximum practicable participation by small business concerns.

(d) Reduction of administrative or personnel costs alone is not sufficient justification for bundling unless the cost savings are expected to be at least 10 percent of the estimated contract or order value (including options) of the bundled requirements.

(e) Substantial bundling is any bundling that results in a contract or order that meets the dollar amounts specified in 7.104(d)(2). When the proposed acquisition strategy involves substantial bundling, the acquisition strategy must additionally—

(1) Identify the specific benefits anticipated to be derived from bundling;

(2) Include an assessment of the specific impediments to participation by small business concerns as contractors that result from bundling;

(3) Specify actions designed to maximize small business participation as contractors, including provisions that encourage small business teaming;

(4) Specify actions designed to maximize small business participation as subcontractors (including suppliers) at any tier under the contract, or order, that may be awarded to meet the requirements;

(5) Include a specific determination that the anticipated benefits of the proposed bundled contract or order justify its use; and

(6) Identify alternative strategies that would reduce or minimize the scope of the bundling, and the rationale for not choosing those alternatives.

(f) The contracting officer must justify bundling in acquisition strategy documentation.

(g) In assessing whether cost savings would be achieved through bundling, the contracting officer must consider the cost that has been charged or, where data is available, could be charged by small business concerns for the same or similar work.

(h) The requirements of this section, except for paragraph (e), do not apply if a cost comparison analysis will be performed in accordance with OMB Circular A-76.

United States Code Annotated

Commercially available off-the-shelf item acquisitions, lists of inapplicable laws in Federal Acquisition Regulation, see 41 U.S.C.A. § 431.

Competition requirements, see 41 U.S.C.A. § 253.

Contracts, competition requirements, see 10 U.S.C.A. § 2304.

Contracts, planning, solicitation, evaluation, and award procedures, see 10 U.S.C.A. § 2305.

Contracts, prohibition on competition between Department of Defense and small businesses and certain other entities, see 10 U.S.C.A. § 2304e.

Definitions, see 10 U.S.C.A. § 2302; 41 U.S.C.A. §§ 259, 403.

Encouragement of new competition, see 41 U.S.C.A. § 253c.

Encouragement of new competitors, see 10 U.S.C.A. § 2319.

Planning and solicitation requirements, see 41 U.S.C.A. § 253a.

Preference for acquisition of commercial items, see 10 U.S.C.A. § 2377; 41 U.S.C.A. § 264b.

Procurement notice, see 41 U.S.C.A. § 416.

Notes of Decisions

In general 1

1 In general

The agency articulated a rational basis for soliciting a single provider for computer hardware and software maintenance, the U.S. Court of Appeals for the Federal Circuit held, rejecting an assertion that the bundled procurement violated the Competition in Contracting Act requirement for full and open competition. The agency justified bundling hardware and software maintenance because, although separate contracts might be feasible, such an approach would increase the risk to the agency's complex computing environment, which might jeopardize national security. CHE Consulting, Inc. v. U.S., 552 F.3d 1351 (Fed. Cir. 2008)

§ 7.108 Additional requirements for telecommuting.

In accordance with 41 U.S.C. 3306(f), an agency shall generally not discourage a contractor from allowing its employees to telecommute in the performance of Government contracts. Therefore, agencies shall not—

(a) Include in a solicitation a requirement that prohibits an offeror from permitting its employees to telecommute unless the contracting officer first determines that the requirements of the agency, including security requirements, cannot be met if telecommuting is permitted. The contracting officer shall document the basis for the determination in writing and specify the prohibition in the solicitation; or

(b) When telecommuting is not prohibited, unfavorably evaluate an offer because it includes telecommuting, unless the contracting officer first determines that the requirements of the agency, including security requirements, would be adversely impacted if telecommuting is permitted. The contracting officer shall document the basis for the determination in writing and address the evaluation procedures in the solicitation.

Subpart 7.2 Planning for the Purchase of Supplies in Economic Quantities

§ 7.200 Scope of subpart.

This subpart prescribes policies and procedures for gathering information from offerors to assist the Government in planning the most advantageous quantities in which supplies should be purchased.

United States Code Annotated

Commercially available off-the-shelf item acquisitions, lists of inapplicable laws in Federal Acquisition Regulation, see 41 U.S.C.A. § 431.

Competition requirements, see 41 U.S.C.A. § 253.

Contracts, competition requirements, see 10 U.S.C.A. § 2304.

Contracts, planning, solicitation, evaluation, and award procedures, see 10 U.S.C.A. § 2305.

Contracts, prohibition on competition between Department of Defense and small businesses and certain other entities, see 10 U.S.C.A. § 2304e.

Definitions, see 10 U.S.C.A. § 2302; 41 U.S.C.A. §§ 259, 403.

Economic order quantities, see 41 U.S.C.A. § 253f.

Encouragement of new competition, see 41 U.S.C.A. § 253c.

Encouragement of new competitors, see 10 U.S.C.A. § 2319.

Planning and solicitation requirements, see 41 U.S.C.A. § 253a.

Preference for acquisition of commercial items, see 10 U.S.C.A. § 2377; 41 U.S.C.A. § 264b.

Procurement notice, see 41 U.S.C.A. § 416.

Supplies, economic order quantities, see 10 U.S.C.A. § 2384a.

§ 7.201 [Reserved]

§ 7.202 Policy.

(a) Agencies are required by 10 U.S.C. 2384a and 41 U.S.C. 3310 to procure supplies in such quantity as—

(1) Will result in the total cost and unit cost most advantageous to the Government, where practicable; and

(2) Does not exceed the quantity reasonably expected to be required by the agency.

(b) Each solicitation for a contract for supplies is required, if practicable, to include a provision inviting each offeror responding to the solicitation—

(1) To state an opinion on whether the quantity of the supplies proposed to be acquired is economically advantageous to the Government; and

(2) If applicable, to recommend a quantity or quantities which would be more economically advantageous to the Government. Each such recommendation is required to include a quotation of the total price and the unit price for supplies procured in each recommended quantity.

United States Code Annotated

Commercially available off-the-shelf item acquisitions, lists of inapplicable laws in Federal Acquisition Regulation, see 41 U.S.C.A. § 431.

Competition requirements, see 41 U.S.C.A. § 253.

Contracts, competition requirements, see 10 U.S.C.A. § 2304.

Contracts, planning, solicitation, evaluation, and award procedures, see 10 U.S.C.A. § 2305.

Contracts, prohibition on competition between Department of Defense and small businesses and certain other entities, see 10 U.S.C.A. § 2304e.

Definitions, see 10 U.S.C.A. § 2302; 41 U.S.C.A. §§ 259, 403.

Economic order quantities, see 41 U.S.C.A. § 253f.

Encouragement of new competition, see 41 U.S.C.A. § 253c.

Encouragement of new competitors, see 10 U.S.C.A. § 2319.

Planning and solicitation requirements, see 41 U.S.C.A. § 253a.

Preference for acquisition of commercial items, see 10 U.S.C.A. § 2377; 41 U.S.C.A. § 264b.

Procurement notice, see 41 U.S.C.A. § 416.

Supplies, economic order quantities, see 10 U.S.C.A. § 2384a.

Notes of Decisions

In general 1

1 In general

The requirement that agencies purchase economic order quantities, when practicable, FAR 7.202(a)(1), does not apply when the procuring agency does not have sufficient funding available and it is not possible to procure the entire system under one procurement. Matter of: AAI ACL Technologies, Inc., B-258679, B-258679.4, 95-2 CPD ¶ 243 (Comp. Gen. 1995).

§ 7.203 Solicitation provision.

Contracting officers shall insert the provision at 52.207-4, Economic Purchase Quantity—

Supplies, in solicitations for supplies. The provision need not be inserted if the solicitation is for a contract under the General Services Administration's multiple award schedule contract program, or if the contracting officer determines that—

(a) The Government already has the data;

(b) The data is otherwise readily available; or

(c) It is impracticable for the Government to vary its future requirements.

United States Code Annotated

Commercially available off-the-shelf item acquisitions, lists of inapplicable laws in Federal Acquisition Regulation, see 41 U.S.C.A. § 431.

Competition requirements, see 41 U.S.C.A. § 253.

Contracts, competition requirements, see 10 U.S.C.A. § 2304.

Contracts, planning, solicitation, evaluation, and award procedures, see 10 U.S.C.A. § 2305.

Contracts, prohibition on competition between Department of Defense and small businesses and certain other entities, see 10 U.S.C.A. § 2304e.

Definitions, see 10 U.S.C.A. § 2302; 41 U.S.C.A. §§ 259, 403.

Economic order quantities, see 41 U.S.C.A. § 253f.

Encouragement of new competition, see 41 U.S.C.A. § 253c.

Encouragement of new competitors, see 10 U.S.C.A. § 2319.

Planning and solicitation requirements, see 41 U.S.C.A. § 253a.

Preference for acquisition of commercial items, see 10 U.S.C.A. § 2377; 41 U.S.C.A. § 264b.

Procurement notice, see 41 U.S.C.A. § 416.

Supplies, economic order quantities, see 10 U.S.C.A. § 2384a.

§ 7.204 Responsibilities of contracting officers.

(a) Contracting officers are responsible for transmitting offeror responses to the solicitation provision at 52.207-4 to appropriate inventory management/requirements development activities in accordance with agency procedures. The economic purchase quantity data so obtained are intended to assist inventory managers in establishing and evaluating economic order quantities for supplies under their cognizance.

(b) In recognition of the fact that economic purchase quantity data furnished by offerors are only one of many data inputs required for determining the most economical order quantities, contracting officers should generally take no action to revise quantities to be acquired in connection with the instant procurement. However, if a significant price variation is evident from offeror responses, and the potential for significant savings is apparent, the contracting officer shall consult with the cognizant inventory manager or requirements development activity before proceeding with an award or negotiations. If this consultation discloses that the Government should be ordering an item of supply in different quantities and the inventory manager/requirements development activity concurs, the solicitation for the item should be amended or canceled and a new requisition should be obtained.

United States Code Annotated

Commercially available off-the-shelf item acquisitions, lists of inapplicable laws in Federal Acquisition Regulation, see 41 U.S.C.A. § 431.

Competition requirements, see 41 U.S.C.A. § 253.

Contracts, competition requirements, see 10 U.S.C.A. § 2304.

Contracts, planning, solicitation, evaluation, and award procedures, see 10 U.S.C.A. § 2305.

Contracts, prohibition on competition between Department of Defense and small businesses and certain other entities, see 10 U.S.C.A. § 2304e.

Definitions, see 10 U.S.C.A. § 2302; 41 U.S.C.A. §§ 259, 403.

Economic order quantities, see 41 U.S.C.A. § 253f.

Encouragement of new competition, see 41 U.S.C.A. § 253c.

Encouragement of new competitors, see 10 U.S.C.A. § 2319.

Planning and solicitation requirements, see 41 U.S.C.A. § 253a.

Preference for acquisition of commercial items, see 10 U.S.C.A. § 2377; 41 U.S.C.A. § 264b.

Procurement notice, see 41 U.S.C.A. § 416.

Supplies, economic order quantities, see 10 U.S.C.A. § 2384a.

Subpart 7.3 Contractor Versus Government Performance

§ 7.300 [Reserved]

§ 7.301 Definitions.

Definitions of "inherently governmental activity" and other terms applicable to this subpart are set forth at Attachment D of the Office of Management and Budget Circular No. A-76 (Revised), Performance of Commercial Activities, dated May 29, 2003 (the Circular).

United States Code Annotated

Administrative determinations, see 41 U.S.C.A. § 257.

Commercially available off-the-shelf item acquisitions, lists of inapplicable laws in Federal Acquisition Regulation, see 41 U.S.C.A. § 431.

Competition requirements, see 41 U.S.C.A. § 253.

Contracts, competition requirements, see 10 U.S.C.A. § 2304.

Contracts, planning, solicitation, evaluation, and award procedures, see 10 U.S.C.A. § 2305.

Contracts, prohibition on competition between Department of Defense and small businesses and certain other entities, see 10 U.S.C.A. § 2304e.

Definitions, see 10 U.S.C.A. § 2302; 41 U.S.C.A. §§ 259, 403.

Determinations and decisions, see 10 U.S.C.A. § 2310; 41 U.S.C.A. § 262.

Encouragement of new competition, see 41 U.S.C.A. § 253c.

Encouragement of new competitors, see 10 U.S.C.A. § 2319.

Evaluation and award, see 41 U.S.C.A. § 253b.

Planning and solicitation requirements, see 41 U.S.C.A. § 253a.

Preference for acquisition of commercial items, see 10 U.S.C.A. § 2377; 41 U.S.C.A. § 264b.

Procurement notice, see 41 U.S.C.A. § 416.

§ 7.302 Policy.

(a) The Circular provides that it is the policy of the Government to—

   (1) Perform inherently governmental activities with Government personnel; and

   (2) Subject commercial activities to the forces of competition.

(b) As provided in the Circular, agencies shall—

   (1) Not use contractors to perform inherently governmental activities;

   (2) Conduct public-private competitions in accordance with the provisions of the Circular and, as applicable, these regulations;

   (3) Give appropriate consideration relative to cost when making performance decisions between agency and contractor performance in public-private competitions;

   (4) Consider the Agency Tender Official an interested party in accordance with 31 U.S.C. 3551 to 3553 for purposes of filing a protest at the Government Accountability Office; and

   (5) Hear contests in accordance with OMB Circular A-76, Attachment B, Paragraph F.

(c) When using sealed bidding in public-private competitions under OMB Circular A-76, contracting officers shall not hold discussions to correct deficiencies.

United States Code Annotated

Administrative determinations, see 41 U.S.C.A. § 257.

Commercially available off-the-shelf item acquisitions, lists of inapplicable laws in Federal Acquisition Regulation, see 41 U.S.C.A. § 431.

Competition requirements, see 41 U.S.C.A. § 253.

Contracts, competition requirements, see 10 U.S.C.A. § 2304.

Contracts, planning, solicitation, evaluation, and award procedures, see 10 U.S.C.A. § 2305.

Contracts, prohibition on competition between Department of Defense and small businesses and certain other entities, see 10 U.S.C.A. § 2304e.

Definitions, see 10 U.S.C.A. § 2302; 41 U.S.C.A. §§ 259, 403.

Determinations and decisions, see 10 U.S.C.A. § 2310; 41 U.S.C.A. § 262.

Encouragement of new competition, see 41 U.S.C.A. § 253c.

Encouragement of new competitors, see 10 U.S.C.A. § 2319.

Evaluation and award, see 41 U.S.C.A. § 253b.

Planning and solicitation requirements, see 41 U.S.C.A. § 253a.

Preference for acquisition of commercial items, see 10 U.S.C.A. § 2377; 41 U.S.C.A. § 264b.

Procurement notice, see 41 U.S.C.A. § 416.

Notes of Decisions

In general 1
Conflict of Interest 2

1 In general

Secretary of Defense may not contract out services to private company as a matter of discretion, nor may that decision rest on whether the Secretary deems the contract or the in house service to cost less; governing statute requires a measurable, objective comparison of costs. 10 U.S.C.A. § 2462. Diebold v. U.S., 947 F.2d 787, 37 Cont. Cas. Fed. (CCH) P 76208 (6th Cir. 1991). United States ⊕64.10

Air Force's decision to in-source the work which contractor had been performing at four Air Force bases and continued to perform at five other locations was a decision that was made "in connection with a procurement" within meaning of Tucker Act provision enabling contractor to challenge decision in Court of Federal Claims (28 USCA § 1491(b)(1)). Additionally, contractor was an "interested party" with standing to challenge the in-sourcing decision. Santa Barbara Applied Research, Inc. v. U.S., 98 Fed. Cl. 536 (2011)

The Navy's evaluation and documentation under an Office of Management and Budget Circular A-76 competition was inadequate because the Navy classified the agency tender as "acceptable" despite identified weaknesses, and then conducted further discussions. In a lowest-priced, technically acceptable OMB A-76 competition, an agency may not conduct discussions after a tender is rated acceptable. Matter of: Rosemary Livingston-Agency Tender Official, B-401102.2, 2009 CPD ¶ 135 (Comp. Gen. 2009)

An agency's cost-realism evaluation was found unreasonable because the agency failed to consider whether the agency tender's material and supply costs were realistic under an Office of Management and Budget Circular A-76 competition. Although the agency also prepared an analysis report on cost realism and reasonableness, it did not address the elements of the awardee's material and supply costs, or their reduction in the final revised proposal. Matter of: New Dynamics Corporation, B-401272, 2009 CPD ¶ 150 (Comp. Gen. 2009)

If no acceptable private-sector offers are received in response to a solicitation issued for a public-private competition under Office of Management and Budget Circular A-76, the agency must revise and reissue the solicitation, or implement the agency tender. Under these alternatives, there is no prejudice to the agency tender official, the U.S. Comptroller General stated in dismissing the ATO's protest. Decision Matter of: Clark E. Myatt, Agency Tender Official, B-311234.2, 2008 CPD ¶ 74 (Comp. Gen. 2008)

2 Conflict of Interest

Participation of four local managers on evaluation boards did not constitute prejudicial conflict of interest in A-76 cost comparison study of whether maintenance and motor transport services at naval air station should be contracted out to private contractor, where only one of the managers was directly associated with a function under study, and he was a military officer not concerned with loss of employment. 48 C.F.R. § 3.101-1. JWK Intern. Corp. v. U.S., 52 Fed. Cl. 650 (2002), aff'd, 56 Fed. Appx. 474 (Fed. Cir. 2003). United States ☜64.40(1)

The organizational conflict of interest rules in Subpart 9.5 may be applied to Government personnel involved in cost comparison studies conducted under OMB Circular A-76. The rationale for applying Subpart 9.5 to the "Most Efficient Organization" (MEO) is the reality that MEO teams are, in fact, competing to perform the Performance Work Statement. Department of the Navy—Reconsideration, B-286194.7, 2002 CPD ¶ 76 (Comp. Gen. 2002).

§ 7.303 [Reserved]

§ 7.304 [Reserved]

§ 7.305 Solicitation provisions and contract clause.

(a) The contracting officer shall, when soliciting offers and tenders, insert in solicitations issued for standard competitions the provision at 52.207-1, Notice of Standard Competition.

(b) The contracting officer shall, when soliciting offers, insert in solicitations issued for streamlined competitions the provision at 52.207-2, Notice of Streamlined Competition.

(c) The contracting officer shall insert the clause at 52.207-3, Right of First Refusal of Employment, in all solicitations which may result in a conversion from in-house performance to contract performance of work currently being performed by the Government and in contracts that result from the solicitations, whether or not a public-private competition is conducted. The 10-day period in the clause may be varied by the contracting officer up to a period of 90 days.

United States Code Annotated

Administrative determinations, see 41 U.S.C.A. § 257.

Commercially available off-the-shelf item acquisitions, lists of inapplicable laws in Federal Acquisition Regulation, see 41 U.S.C.A. § 431.

Competition requirements, see 41 U.S.C.A. § 253.

Contracts, competition requirements, see 10 U.S.C.A. § 2304.

Contracts, planning, solicitation, evaluation, and award procedures, see 10 U.S.C.A. § 2305.

Contracts, prohibition on competition between Department of Defense and small businesses and certain other entities, see 10 U.S.C.A. § 2304e.

Definitions, see 10 U.S.C.A. § 2302; 41 U.S.C.A. §§ 259, 403.

Determinations and decisions, see 10 U.S.C.A. § 2310; 41 U.S.C.A. § 262.

Encouragement of new competition, see 41 U.S.C.A. § 253c.

Encouragement of new competitors, see 10 U.S.C.A. § 2319.

Evaluation and award, see 41 U.S.C.A. § 253b.

Planning and solicitation requirements, see 41 U.S.C.A. § 253a.

Preference for acquisition of commercial items, see 10 U.S.C.A. § 2377; 41 U.S.C.A. § 264b.

Procurement notice, see 41 U.S.C.A. § 416.

Notes of Decisions

Protest Jurisdiction 1

1 Protest Jurisdiction

Air Force's decision to in-source performance of base supply services, rather than exercising option to renew contract with incumbent contractor, was "in connection with a procurement or proposed procurement," within meaning of bid protest jurisdictional statute 28 USC § 1491), since in-sourcing decision necessarily included process for determining need for services that incumbent contractor provided, and statutorily-required cost comparison was beginning of contracting process. Also, incumbent contractor challenging Air Force's decision to in-source performance of base supply services, rather than exercising option to renew contract, had financial interest in maintaining incumbency, as required to qualify as "interested party" with standing to pursue bid protest, since contractor desired renewal of contract, was rated excellent on contract performance, and had substantial chance of continued performance but for in-sourcing decision. Elmendorf Support Services Joint Venture v. U.S., 105 Fed. Cl. 203 (2012)

Subpart 7.4 Equipment Lease or Purchase

§ 7.400 Scope of subpart.

This subpart provides guidance pertaining to the decision to acquire equipment by lease or purchase. It applies to both the initial acquisition of equipment and the renewal or extension of existing equipment leases.

United States Code Annotated

Commercially available off-the-shelf item acquisitions, lists of inapplicable laws in Federal Acquisition Regulation, see 41 U.S.C.A. § 431.

Competition requirements, see 41 U.S.C.A. § 253.

Contracts, competition requirements, see 10 U.S.C.A. § 2304.

Contracts, planning, solicitation, evaluation, and award procedures, see 10 U.S.C.A. § 2305.

Contracts, prohibition on competition between Department of Defense and small businesses and certain other entities, see 10 U.S.C.A. § 2304e.

Definitions, see 10 U.S.C.A. § 2302, 41 U.S.C.A. §§ 259, 403.

Encouragement of new competition, see 41 U.S.C.A. § 253c.

Encouragement of new competitors, see 10 U.S.C.A. § 2319.

Lease of vehicles, equipment, vessels, and aircraft, see 10 U.S.C.A. § 2401a.

Planning and solicitation requirements, see 41 U.S.C.A. § 253a.

Preference for acquisition of commercial items, see 10 U.S.C.A. § 2377, 41 U.S.C.A. § 264b.

Procurement notice, see 41 U.S.C.A. § 416.

§ 7.401 Acquisition considerations.

(a) Agencies should consider whether to lease or purchase equipment based on a case-by-case evaluation of comparative costs and other factors. The following factors are the minimum that should be considered:

(1) Estimated length of the period the equipment is to be used and the extent of use within that period.

(2) Financial and operating advantages of alternative types and makes of equipment.

(3) Cumulative rental payments for the estimated period of use.

(4) Net purchase price.

(5) Transportation and installation costs.

(6) Maintenance and other service costs.

(7) Potential obsolescence of the equipment because of imminent technological improvements.

(b) The following additional factors should be considered, as appropriate, depending on the type, cost, complexity, and estimated period of use of the equipment:

(1) Availability of purchase options.

(2) Potential for use of the equipment by other agencies after its use by the acquiring agency is ended.

(3) Trade-in or salvage value.

(4) Imputed interest.

(5) Availability of a servicing capability, especially for highly complex equipment; e.g., can the equipment be serviced by the Government or other sources if it is purchased?

United States Code Annotated

Commercially available off-the-shelf item acquisitions, lists of inapplicable laws in Federal Acquisition Regulation, see 41 U.S.C.A. § 431.

Competition requirements, see 41 U.S.C.A. § 253.

Contracts, competition requirements, see 10 U.S.C.A. § 2304.

Contracts, planning, solicitation, evaluation, and award procedures, see 10 U.S.C.A. § 2305.

Contracts, prohibition on competition between Department of Defense and small businesses and certain other entities, see 10 U.S.C.A. § 2304e.

Definitions, see 10 U.S.C.A. § 2302, 41 U.S.C.A. §§ 259, 403.

Encouragement of new competition, see 41 U.S.C.A. § 253c.

Encouragement of new competitors, see 10 U.S.C.A. § 2319.

Lease of vehicles, equipment, vessels, and aircraft, see 10 U.S.C.A. § 2401a.

Planning and solicitation requirements, see 41 U.S.C.A. § 253a.

Preference for acquisition of commercial items, see 10 U.S.C.A. § 2377, 41 U.S.C.A. § 264b.

Procurement notice, see 41 U.S.C.A. § 416.

Notes of Decisions

In general 1

1 In general

Army's exclusion of telephone company from participation in solicitation of bids for telecommunications equipment, on ground that company's tariffs required it to lease and maintain its equipment, did not violate Army Services Procurement Act or federal acquisition regulation, and its decision that proposed lease arrangement would directly conflict with objective of combining operation and maintenance responsibilities under single central management was rational. 10 U.S.C.A. § 2301 et seq.; 28 U.S.C.A. § 1491(a)(3). New York Telephone Co. v. Secretary of Army, 657 F. Supp. 18 (D.D.C. 1986). United States ☞64.15

§ 7.402 Acquisition methods.

(a) *Purchase method.* (1) Generally, the purchase method is appropriate if the equipment will be used beyond the point in time when cumulative leasing costs exceed the purchase costs.

(2) Agencies should not rule out the purchase method of equipment acquisition in favor of leasing merely because of the possibility that future technological advances might make the selected equipment less desirable.

(b) *Lease method.* (1) The lease method is appropriate if it is to the Government's advantage under the circumstances. The lease method may also serve as an interim measure when the circumstances—

(i) Require immediate use of equipment to meet program or system goals; but

(ii) Do not currently support acquisition by purchase.

(2) If a lease is justified, a lease with option to purchase is preferable.

(3) Generally, a long term lease should be avoided, but may be appropriate if an option to purchase or other favorable terms are included.

(4) If a lease with option to purchase is used, the contract shall state the purchase price or provide a formula which shows how the purchase price will be established at the time of purchase.

United States Code Annotated

Commercially available off-the-shelf item acquisitions, lists of inapplicable laws in Federal Acquisition Regulation, see 41 U.S.C.A. § 431.

Competition requirements, see 41 U.S.C.A. § 253.

Contracts, competition requirements, see 10 U.S.C.A. § 2304.

Contracts, planning, solicitation, evaluation, and award procedures, see 10 U.S.C.A. § 2305.

Contracts, prohibition on competition between Department of Defense and small businesses and certain other entities, see 10 U.S.C.A. § 2304e.

Definitions, see 10 U.S.C.A. § 2302, 41 U.S.C.A. §§ 259, 403.

Encouragement of new competition, see 41 U.S.C.A. § 253c.

Encouragement of new competitors, see 10 U.S.C.A. § 2319.

Lease of vehicles, equipment, vessels, and aircraft, see 10 U.S.C.A. § 2401a.

Planning and solicitation requirements, see 41 U.S.C.A. § 253a.

Preference for acquisition of commercial items, see 10 U.S.C.A. § 2377, 41 U.S.C.A. § 264b.

Procurement notice, see 41 U.S.C.A. § 416.

Notes of Decisions

In general 1

1 In general

Army's solicitation plan for bidding on telecommunications equipment, excluding telephone company from participation on ground that its tariffs required it to lease and maintain its equipment, did not violate Department of Defense policy and Department of Defense findings recommending consideration of all procurement options, where army was receptive to bids from any source that could provide needed equipment without impairing its objective of combining operation and maintenance responsibilities under single central management. New York Telephone Co. v. Secretary of Army, 657 F. Supp. 18 (D.D.C. 1986). United States ☞64.15

Army's exclusion of telephone company from participation in solicitation of bids for telecommunications equipment, on ground that company's tariffs required it to lease and maintain its equipment, did not violate Army Services Procurement Act or federal acquisition regulation, and its decision that proposed lease arrangement would directly conflict with objective of combining operation and maintenance responsibilities under single central management was rational. 10 U.S.C.A. § 2301 et seq.; 28 U.S.C.A. § 1491(a)(3). New York Telephone Co. v. Secretary of Army, 657 F. Supp. 18 (D.D.C. 1986). United States ☞64.15

§ 7.403 General Services Administration assistance.

(a) When requested by an agency, the General Services Administration (GSA) will assist in lease or purchase decisions by providing information such as—

    (1) Pending price adjustments to Federal Supply Schedule contracts;

    (2) Recent or imminent technological developments;

    (3) New techniques; and

    (4) Industry or market trends.

(b) Agencies may request information from the following GSA office: U.S. General Services Administration, Federal Acquisition Service, Office of Acquisition Management, 2200 Crystal Drive, Room 806, Arlington, VA. 22202. Email: mailto:fasam@gsa.gov.

United States Code Annotated

Commercially available off-the-shelf item acquisitions, lists of inapplicable laws in Federal Acquisition Regulation, see 41 U.S.C.A. § 431.

Competition requirements, see 41 U.S.C.A. § 253.

Contracts, competition requirements, see 10 U.S.C.A. § 2304.

Contracts, planning, solicitation, evaluation, and award procedures, see 10 U.S.C.A. § 2305.

Contracts, prohibition on competition between Department of Defense and small businesses and certain other entities, see 10 U.S.C.A. § 2304e.

Definitions, see 10 U.S.C.A. § 2302, 41 U.S.C.A. §§ 259, 403.

Encouragement of new competition, see 41 U.S.C.A. § 253c.

Encouragement of new competitors, see 10 U.S.C.A. § 2319.

Lease of vehicles, equipment, vessels, and aircraft, see 10 U.S.C.A. § 2401a.

Planning and solicitation requirements, see 41 U.S.C.A. § 253a.

Preference for acquisition of commercial items, see 10 U.S.C.A. § 2377, 41 U.S.C.A. § 264b.

Procurement notice, see 41 U.S.C.A. § 416.

§ 7.404 Contract clause.

The contracting officer shall insert a clause substantially the same as the clause in 52. 207-5, Option to Purchase Equipment, in solicitations and contracts involving a lease with option to purchase. 7.4-2

United States Code Annotated

Commercially available off-the-shelf item acquisitions, lists of inapplicable laws in Federal Acquisition Regulation, see 41 U.S.C.A. § 431.

Competition requirements, see 41 U.S.C.A. § 253.

Contracts, competition requirements, see 10 U.S.C.A. § 2304.

Contracts, planning, solicitation, evaluation, and award procedures, see 10 U.S.C.A. § 2305.

Contracts, prohibition on competition between Department of Defense and small businesses and certain other entities, see 10 U.S.C.A. § 2304e.

Definitions, see 10 U.S.C.A. § 2302, 41 U.S.C.A. §§ 259, 403.

Encouragement of new competition, see 41 U.S.C.A. § 253c.

Encouragement of new competitors, see 10 U.S.C.A. § 2319.

Lease of vehicles, equipment, vessels, and aircraft, see 10 U.S.C.A. § 2401a.

Planning and solicitation requirements, see 41 U.S.C.A. § 253a.

Preference for acquisition of commercial items, see 10 U.S.C.A. § 2377, 41 U.S.C.A. § 264b.

Procurement notice, see 41 U.S.C.A. § 416.

Subpart 7.5 Inherently Governmental Functions

§ 7.500 Scope of subpart.

The purpose of this subpart is to prescribe policies and procedures to ensure that inherently governmental functions are not performed by contractors.

United States Code Annotated

Commercially available off-the-shelf item acquisitions, lists of inapplicable laws in Federal Acquisition Regulation, see 41 U.S.C.A. § 431.

Competition requirements, see 41 U.S.C.A. § 253.

Contracts, competition requirements, see 10 U.S.C.A. § 2304.

Contracts, planning, solicitation, evaluation, and award procedures, see 10 U.S.C.A. § 2305.

Contracts, prohibition on competition between Department of Defense and small businesses and certain other entities, see 10 U.S.C.A. § 2304e.

Definitions, see 10 U.S.C.A. § 2302, 41 U.S.C.A. §§ 259, 403.

Encouragement of new competition, see 41 U.S.C.A. § 253c.

Encouragement of new competitors, see 10 U.S.C.A. § 2319.

Planning and solicitation requirements, see 41 U.S.C.A. § 253a.

Preference for acquisition of commercial items, see 10 U.S.C.A. § 2377, 41 U.S.C.A. § 264b.

Procurement notice, see 41 U.S.C.A. § 416.

§ 7.501 [Reserved]

§ 7.502 Applicability.

The requirements of this subpart apply to all contracts for services. This subpart does not apply to services obtained through either personnel appointments, advisory committees, or personal services contracts issued under statutory authority.

United States Code Annotated

Commercially available off-the-shelf item acquisitions, lists of inapplicable laws in Federal Acquisition Regulation, see 41 U.S.C.A. § 431.

Competition requirements, see 41 U.S.C.A. § 253.

Contracts, competition requirements, see 10 U.S.C.A. § 2304.

Contracts, planning, solicitation, evaluation, and award procedures, see 10 U.S.C.A. § 2305.

Contracts, prohibition on competition between Department of Defense and small businesses and certain other entities, see 10 U.S.C.A. § 2304e.

Definitions, see 10 U.S.C.A. § 2302, 41 U.S.C.A. §§ 259, 403.

Encouragement of new competition, see 41 U.S.C.A. § 253c.

Encouragement of new competitors, see 10 U.S.C.A. § 2319.

Planning and solicitation requirements, see 41 U.S.C.A. § 253a.

Preference for acquisition of commercial items, see 10 U.S.C.A. § 2377, 41 U.S.C.A. § 264b.

Procurement notice, see 41 U.S.C.A. § 416.

§ 7.503 Policy.

(a) Contracts shall not be used for the performance of inherently governmental functions.

(b) Agency decisions which determine whether a function is or is not an inherently governmental function may be reviewed and modified by appropriate Office of Management and Budget officials.

(c) The following is a list of examples of functions considered to be inherently governmental functions or which shall be treated as such. This list is not all inclusive:

(1) The direct conduct of criminal investigations.

(2) The control of prosecutions and performance of adjudicatory functions other than those relating to arbitration or other methods of alternative dispute resolution.

(3) The command of military forces, especially the leadership of military personnel who are members of the combat, combat support, or combat service support role.

(4) The conduct of foreign relations and the determination of foreign policy.

(5) The determination of agency policy, such as determining the content and application of regulations, among other things.

(6) The determination of Federal program priorities for budget requests.

(7) The direction and control of Federal employees.

(8) The direction and control of intelligence and counter-intelligence operations.

(9) The selection or non-selection of individuals for Federal Government employment, including the interviewing of individuals for employment.

(10) The approval of position descriptions and performance standards for Federal employees.

(11) The determination of what Government property is to be disposed of and on what terms (although an agency may give contractors authority to dispose of property at prices within specified ranges and subject to other reasonable conditions deemed appropriate by the agency).

(12) In Federal procurement activities with respect to prime contracts—

(i) Determining what supplies or services are to be acquired by the Government (although an agency may give contractors authority to acquire supplies at prices within specified ranges and subject to other reasonable conditions deemed appropriate by the agency);

(ii) Participating as a voting member on any source selection boards;

(iii) Approving any contractual documents, to include documents defining requirements, incentive plans, and evaluation criteria;

(iv) Awarding contracts;

(v) Administering contracts (including ordering changes in contract performance or contract quantities, taking action based on evaluations of contractor performance, and accepting or rejecting contractor products or services);

(vi) Terminating contracts;

(vii) Determining whether contract costs are reasonable, allocable, and allowable; and

(viii) Participating as a voting member on performance evaluation boards.

(13) The approval of agency responses to Freedom of Information Act requests (other than routine responses that, because of statute, regulation, or agency policy, do not require the exercise of judgment in determining whether documents are to be released or withheld), and the approval of agency responses to the administrative appeals of denials of Freedom of Information Act requests.

(14) The conduct of administrative hearings to determine the eligibility of any person for a security clearance, or involving actions that affect matters of personal reputation or eligibility to participate in Government programs.

(15) The approval of Federal licensing actions and inspections.

(16) The determination of budget policy, guidance, and strategy.

(17) The collection, control, and disbursement of fees, royalties, duties, fines, taxes, and other public funds, unless authorized by statute, such as 31 U.S.C. 952 (relating to private collection contractors) and 31 U.S.C. 3718 (relating to private attorney collection services), but not including—

(i) Collection of fees, fines, penalties, costs, or other charges from visitors to or patrons of mess halls, post or base exchange concessions, national parks, and similar entities or activities, or from other persons, where the amount to be collected is easily calculated or predetermined and the funds collected can be easily controlled using standard case management techniques; and

(ii) Routine voucher and invoice examination.

(18) The control of the treasury accounts.

(19) The administration of public trusts.

(20) The drafting of Congressional testimony, responses to Congressional correspondence, or agency responses to audit reports from the Inspector General, the Government Accountability Office, or other Federal audit entity.

(d) The following is a list of examples of functions generally not considered to be inherently governmental functions. However, certain services and actions that are not considered to be inherently governmental functions may approach being in that category because of the nature of the function, the manner in which the contractor performs the contract, or the manner in which the Government administers contractor performance. This list is not all inclusive:

(1) Services that involve or relate to budget preparation, including workload modeling, fact finding, efficiency studies, and should-cost analyses, etc.

(2) Services that involve or relate to reorganization and planning activities.

(3) Services that involve or relate to analyses, feasibility studies, and strategy options to be used by agency personnel in developing policy.

(4) Services that involve or relate to the development of regulations.

(5) Services that involve or relate to the evaluation of another contractor's performance.

(6) Services in support of acquisition planning.

(7) Contractors providing assistance in contract management (such as where the contractor might influence official evaluations of other contractors).

(8) Contractors providing technical evaluation of contract proposals.

(9) Contractors providing assistance in the development of statements of work.

(10) Contractors providing support in preparing responses to Freedom of Information Act requests.

(11) Contractors working in any situation that permits or might permit them to gain access to confidential business information and/or any other sensitive information (other than situations covered by the National Industrial Security Program described in 4.402(b)).

(12) Contractors providing information regarding agency policies or regulations, such as attending conferences on behalf of an agency, conducting community relations campaigns, or conducting agency training courses.

(13) Contractors participating in any situation where it might be assumed that they are agency employees or representatives.

(14) Contractors participating as technical advisors to a source selection board or participating as voting or nonvoting members of a source evaluation board.

(15) Contractors serving as arbitrators or providing alternative methods of dispute resolution.

(16) Contractors constructing buildings or structures intended to be secure from electronic eavesdropping or other penetration by foreign governments.

(17) Contractors providing inspection services.

(18) Contractors providing legal advice and interpretations of regulations and statutes to Government officials.

(19) Contractors providing special non-law enforcement, security activities that do not directly involve criminal investigations, such as prisoner detention or transport and non-military national security details.

(e) Agency implementation shall include procedures requiring the agency head or designated requirements official to provide the contracting officer, concurrent with transmittal of the statement of work (or any modification thereof), a written determination that none of the functions to be performed are inherently governmental. This assessment should place emphasis on the degree to which conditions and facts restrict the discretionary authority, decision-making responsibility, or accountability of Government officials using contractor services or work products. Disagreements regarding the determination will be resolved in accordance with agency procedures before issuance of a solicitation.

Notes of Decisions

In general 1

1 In general

Protester objected to participation as a technical advisor of a non-governmental employee of the contractor performing privatized management functions at MacDill AFB under the "A-76 initiative" and requested that this individual not be allowed to participate in the selection process. However, the FAR specifically provides that government contractors may participate as "technical advisors to a source selection board or . . . as voting or nonvoting members of a source evaluation board," as such functions are "generally not considered to be inherently governmental." FAR 7.503(d)(14). Gulf Group Inc. v. U.S., 61 Fed. Cl. 338 (2004)

Contractor authorized to select carriers; negotiate, execute, and manage subcontracts; ensure subcontractor compliance with federal regulations regarding public liability and cargo liability insurance; facilitate the resolution of government claims for loss or damage to cargo; and interpret and enforce cargo liability terms was held not to be performing inherently governmental functions. 2B Brokers et al., B-298651, 2006 CPD ¶ 178 (Comp. Gen. 2006)

PART 8 REQUIRED SOURCES OF SUPPLIES AND SERVICES

§ 8.000 Scope of part.

This part deals with prioritizing sources of supplies and services for use by the Government.

§ 8.001 General.

Regardless of the source of supplies or services to be acquired, information technology acquisitions shall comply with capital planning and investment control requirements in 40 U.S.C. 11312 and OMB Circular A-130.

§ 8.002 Priorities for use of mandatory Government sources.

(a) Except as required by 8.003, or as otherwise provided by law, agencies shall satisfy requirements for supplies and services from or through the sources and publications listed below in descending order of priority:

(1) *Supplies.*

(i) Inventories of the requiring.

(ii) Excess from other agencies (see Subpart 8.1).

(iii) Federal Prison Industries, Inc. (see Subpart 8.6).

(iv) Supplies which are on the Procurement List maintained by the Committee for Purchase From People Who Are Blind or Severely Disabled (see Subpart 8.7).

(v) Wholesale supply sources, such as stock programs of the General Services Administration (GSA) (see 41 CFR 101-26.3), the Defense Logistics Agency (see 41 CFR 101-26.6), the Department of Veterans Affairs (see 41 CFR 101-26.704), and military inventory control points.

(2) *Services.* Services that are on the Procurement List maintained by the Committee for Purchase From People Who Are Blind or Severely Disabled (see Subpart 8.7).

(b) Sources other than those listed in paragraph (a) of this section may be used as prescribed in 41 CFR 101-26.301 and in an unusual and compelling urgency as prescribed in 6.302-2 and in 41 CFR 101-25.101-5.

(c) The statutory obligation for Government agencies to satisfy their requirements for supplies or services available from the Committee for Purchase From People Who Are Blind or Severely Disabled also applies when contractors purchase the supplies or services for Government use.

§ 8.003 Use of other mandatory sources.

Agencies shall satisfy requirements for the following supplies or services from or through specified sources, as applicable:

(a) Public utility services (see Part 41).

(b) Printing and related supplies (see Subpart 8.8).

(c) Leased motor vehicles (see Subpart 8.11).

(d) Strategic and critical materials (*e.g.,* metals and ores) from inventories exceeding Defense National Stockpile requirements (detailed information is available from the DLA Strategic Materials, 8725 John J. Kingman Rd., Suite 3229, Fort Belvoir, VA 22060-6223).

(e) Helium (see Subpart 8.5—Acquisition of Helium).

§ 8.004 Use of other sources.

If an agency is unable to satisfy requirements for supplies and services from the mandatory sources listed in 8.002 and 8.003, agencies are encouraged to consider satisfying requirements from or through the non-mandatory sources listed in paragraph (a) of this section (not listed in any order of priority) before considering the non-mandatory source listed in paragraph (b) of this section. When satisfying requirements from non-mandatory sources, see 7.105(b) and Part 19 regarding consideration of small business, veteran-owned small business, service-disabled veteran-owned small business, HUBZone small business, small disadvantaged business (including 8(a) participants), and women-owned small business concerns.

(a) (1) *Supplies.* Federal Supply Schedules, Governmentwide acquisition contracts, multi-agency contracts, and any other procurement instruments intended for use by multiple agencies, including blanket purchase agreements (BPAs) under Federal Supply Schedule contracts (*e.g.*, Federal Strategic Sourcing Initiative (FSSI) agreements accessible at *http://www.gsa.gov/fssi* (see also 5.601)).

(2) *Services.* Agencies are encouraged to consider Federal Prison Industries, Inc., as well as the sources listed in paragraph (a)(1) of this section (see Subpart 8.6).

(b) Commercial sources (including educational and non-profit institutions) in the open market.

§ 8.005 Contract clause.

Insert the clause at 52.208-9, Contractor Use of Mandatory Sources of Supply and Services, in solicitations and contracts that require a contractor to provide supplies or services for Government use that are on the Procurement List maintained by the Committee for Purchase From People Who Are Blind or Severely Disabled. The contracting officer shall identify in the contract schedule the supplies or services that shall be purchased from a mandatory source and the specific source.

Subpart 8.1 Excess Personal Property

§ 8.101 [Reserved]

§ 8.102 Policy.

When practicable, agencies must use excess personal property as the first source of supply for agency and cost-reimbursement contractor requirements. Agency personnel must make positive efforts to satisfy agency requirements by obtaining and using excess personal property (including that suitable for adaptation or substitution) before initiating a contract action.

United States Code Annotated

Commercially available off-the-shelf item acquisitions, lists of inapplicable laws in Federal Acquisition Regulation, see 41 USCA § 431.

Contracts, planning, solicitation, evaluation, and award procedures, see 10 USCA § 2305.

Definitions, see 10 USCA § 2302, 41 USCA §§ 259, 403.

Planning and solicitation requirements, see 41 USCA § 253a.

Preference for acquisition of commercial items, see 10 USCA § 2377, 41 USCA § 264b.

§ 8.103 Information on available excess personal property.

Information regarding the availability of excess personal property can be obtained through—

(a) Review of excess personal property catalogs and bulletins issued by the General Services Administration (GSA);

(b) Personal contact with GSA or the activity holding the property;

(c) Submission of supply requirements to the regional offices of GSA (GSA Form 1539, Request for Excess Personal Property, is available for this purpose); and

(d) Examination and inspection of reports and samples of excess personal property in GSA regional offices.

United States Code Annotated

Commercially available off-the-shelf item acquisitions, lists of inapplicable laws in Federal Acquisition Regulation, see 41 USCA § 431.

Contracts, planning, solicitation, evaluation, and award procedures, see 10 USCA § 2305.

Definitions, see 10 USCA § 2302, 41 USCA §§ 259, 403.

Planning and solicitation requirements, see 41 USCA § 253a.

Preference for acquisition of commercial items, see 10 USCA § 2377, 41 USCA § 264b.

§ 8.104 Obtaining nonreportable property.

GSA will assist agencies in meeting their requirements for supplies of the types excepted from reporting as excess by the Federal Management Regulations (41 CFR 102-36.90). Federal agencies requiring such supplies should contact the appropriate GSA regional office.

United States Code Annotated

Commercially available off-the-shelf item acquisitions, lists of inapplicable laws in Federal Acquisition Regulation, see 41 USCA § 431.

Contracts, planning, solicitation, evaluation, and award procedures, see 10 USCA § 2305.

Definitions, see 10 USCA § 2302, 41 USCA §§ 259, 403.

Planning and solicitation requirements, see 41 USCA § 253a.

Preference for acquisition of commercial items, see 10 USCA § 2377, 41 USCA § 264b.

Subpart 8.2 [Reserved]

Subpart 8.3 [Reserved]

Subpart 8.4 Federal Supply Schedules

§ 8.401 Definitions.

As used in this subpart—

"Ordering activity" means an activity that is authorized to place orders, or establish blanket purchase agreements (BPA), against the General Services Administration's (GSA) Multiple Award Schedule contracts. A list of eligible ordering activities is available at http://www.gsa.gov/schedules (click "For Customers Ordering from Schedules" and then "Eligibility to Use GSA Sources").

"Multiple Award Schedule (MAS)" means contracts awarded by GSA or the Department of Veterans Affairs (VA) for similar or comparable supplies, or services, established with more than one supplier, at varying prices. The primary statutory authorities for the MAS program are 41 U.S.C. 152(3), *Competitive Procedures,* and 40 U.S.C. 501, Services for Executive Agencies.

"Requiring agency" means the agency needing the supplies or services.

"Schedules e-Library" means the on-line source for GSA and VA Federal Supply Schedule contract award information. Schedules e-Library may be accessed at http://www.gsa.gov/elibrary.

"Special Item Number (SIN)" means a group of generically similar (but not identical) supplies or services that are intended to serve the same general purpose or function.

United States Code Annotated

Commercially available off-the-shelf item acquisitions, lists of inapplicable laws in Federal Acquisition Regulation, see 41 USCA § 431.

Contracts, planning, solicitation, evaluation, and award procedures, see 10 USCA § 2305.

Definitions, see 10 USCA § 2302, 41 USCA §§ 259, 403.

Planning and solicitati on requirements, see 41 USCA § 253a.

Preference for acquisition of commercial items, see 10 USCA § 2377, 41 USCA § 264b.

§ 8.402 General.

(a) The Federal Supply Schedule program is also known as the GSA Schedules Program or the Multiple Award Schedule Program. The Federal Supply Schedule program is directed and managed by GSA and provides Federal agencies (see 8.004) with a simplified process for obtaining commercial supplies and services at prices associated with volume buying. Indefinite delivery contracts are awarded to provide supplies and services at stated prices for given periods of time. GSA may delegate certain responsibilities to other agencies (*e.g.,* GSA has delegated authority to the VA to procure medical supplies under the VA Federal Supply Schedules program). Orders issued under the VA Federal Supply Schedule program are covered by this subpart. Additionally, the Department of Defense (DoD) manages similar systems of schedule-type contracting for military items; however, DoD systems are not covered by this subpart.

(b) GSA schedule contracts require all schedule contractors to publish an "Authorized Federal Supply Schedule Pricelist" (pricelist). The pricelist contains all supplies and services offered by a schedule contractor. In addition, each pricelist contains the pricing and the terms and conditions pertaining to each Special Item Number that is on schedule. The schedule contractor is required to provide one copy of its pricelist to any ordering activity upon request. Also, a copy of the pricelist may be obtained from the Federal Supply Service by submitting a written e-mail request to mailto:schedules.infocenter@gsa.gov or by telephone at 1-800-488-3111. This subpart, together with the pricelists, contain necessary information for placing delivery or task orders with schedule contractors. In addition, the GSA schedule contracting office issues Federal Supply Schedules publications that contain a general overview of the Federal Supply Schedule (FSS) program and address pertinent topics. Ordering activities may request copies of schedules publications by contacting the Centralized Mailing List Service through the Internet at http://www.gsa.gov/cmls, submitting written e-mail requests to mailto:CMLS@gsa.gov; or by completing GSA Form 457, FSS Publications Mailing List Application, and mailing it to the GSA Centralized Mailing List Service (7SM), P.O. Box 6477, Fort Worth, TX 76115. Copies of GSA Form 457 may also be obtained from the above-referenced points of contact.

(c) (1) GSA offers an on-line shopping service called "GSA Advantage!" through which ordering activities may place orders against Schedules. (Ordering activities may also use GSA Advantage! to place orders through GSA's Global Supply System, a GSA wholesale supply source, formerly known as "GSA Stock" or the "Customer Supply Center." FAR Subpart 8.4 is not applicable to orders placed through the GSA Global Supply System.) Ordering activities may access GSA Advantage! through the GSA Federal Supply Service Home Page (http://www.gsa.gov/fas) or the GSA Federal Supply Schedule Home Page at http://www.gsa.gov/schedules.

(2) GSA Advantage! enables ordering activities to search specific information (*i.e.,* national stock number, part number, common name), review delivery options, place orders directly with Schedule contractors (except see 8.405-6) and pay for orders using the Governmentwide commercial purchase card.

(d) (1) *e-Buy,* GSA's electronic Request for Quotation (RFQ) system, is a part of a suite of on-line tools which complement GSA Advantage!. E-Buy allows ordering activities to post requirements, obtain quotes, and issue orders electronically. Posting an RFQ on e-Buy—

(i) Is one medium for providing fair notice to all schedule contractors offering such supplies and services as required by 8.405-1, 8.405-2, and 8.405-3; and

(ii) Is required when an order contains brand-name specifications (see 8.405-6).

(2) Ordering activities may access e-Buy at http://www.ebuy.gsa.gov. For more information or assistance on either GSA Advantage! or e-Buy, contact GSA at Internet e-mail address mailto:gsa.advantage@gsa.gov.

(e) For more information or assistance regarding the Federal Supply Schedule Program, review the following website: http://www.gsa.gov/schedules. Additionally, for on-line training courses regarding the Schedules Program, review the following website: http://www.gsa.gov/training.

(f) For administrative convenience, an ordering activity contracting officer may add items not on the Federal Supply Schedule (also referred to as open market items) to a Federal Supply Schedule blanket purchase agreement (BPA) or an individual task or delivery order only if—

(1) All applicable acquisition regulations pertaining to the purchase of the items not on the Federal Supply Schedule have been followed (*e.g.,* publicizing (Part 5), competition requirements (Part 6), acquisition of commercial items (Part 12), contracting methods (Parts 13, 14, and 15), and small business programs (Part 19));

(2) The ordering activity contracting officer has determined the price for the items not on the Federal Supply Schedule is fair and reasonable;

(3) The items are clearly labeled on the order as items not on the Federal Supply Schedule; and

(4) All clauses applicable to items not on the Federal Supply Schedule are included in the order.

(g) When using the Governmentwide commercial purchase card as a method of payment, orders at or below the micro-purchase threshold are exempt from verification in the System for Award Management database as to whether the contractor has a delinquent debt subject to collection under the Treasury Offset Program (TOP).

United States Code Annotated

Commercially available off-the-shelf item acquisitions, lists of inapplicable laws in Federal Acquisition Regulation, see 41 USCA § 431.

Contracts, planning, solicitation, evaluation, and award procedures, see 10 USCA § 2305.

Definitions, see 10 USCA § 2302, 41 USCA §§ 259, 403.

Planning and solicitation requirements, see 41 USCA § 253a.

Preference for acquisition of commercial items, see 10 USCA § 2377, 41 USCA § 264b.

Notes of Decisions
In general 1

1 In general

Because a procuring agency did not preserve information on the e-Buy website related to the protested procurement, the Court of Federal Claims barred the Government from offering secondary evidence of the website's contents. Considering the merits of the protest, the Court held that the information on e-Buy did not change the submission due date set out in the solicitation. As a result, the Court found that the agency improperly rejected the protester's submission as untimely. Lab. Corp. of Am. v. U.S., 108 Fed. Cl. 549 (2012)

The FSS program provides federal agencies with a "simplified process for obtaining commercial supplies and services at prices associated with volume buying." FAR 8.402(a). Orders placed against FSS contracts are not subject to FAR Part 15, which prescribes procedures for most negotiated contracts. See FAR 8.404(a). As long as orders are placed against schedule contracts using the procedures in FAR Subpart 8.4, however, those orders are "considered to be issued using full and open competition." Data Management Services Joint Venture v. U.S., 78 Fed. Cl. 366 (2007)

The FSS program "provides Federal agencies with a simplified process for obtaining commonly used commercial supplies and services at prices associated with volume buying." FAR 8.401(a). Under the program, an agency may select products and services from a list of eligible contractors whose pricing schemes have been pre-approved by GSA. An agency procuring goods or services pursuant to an FSS contract need not comply with the more formal and rigorous procedures for negotiated procurements set forth in FAR Part 15. Labat-Anderson Inc. v. U.S., 50 Fed. Cl. 99 (2001).

§ 8.403 Applicability.

(a) Procedures in this subpart apply to—

(1) Individual orders for supplies or services placed against Federal Supply Schedules contracts; and

(2) BPAs established against Federal Supply Schedule contracts.

(b) GSA may establish special ordering procedures for a particular schedule. In this case, that schedule will specify those special ordering procedures. Unless otherwise noted, special ordering procedures established for a Federal Supply Schedule take precedence over the procedures in 8.405.

(c) In accordance with section 1427(b) of Public Law 108-136 (40 U.S.C. 1103 note), for requirements that substantially or to a dominant extent specify performance of architect-engineer services (as defined in 2.101), agencies—

(1) Shall use the procedures at Subpart 36.6; and

(2) Shall not place orders for such requirements under a Federal Supply Schedule.

United States Code Annotated

Commercially available off-the-shelf item acquisitions, lists of inapplicable laws in Federal Acquisition Regulation, see 41 USCA § 431.

Contracts, planning, solicitation, evaluation, and award procedures, see 10 USCA § 2305.

Definitions, see 10 USCA § 2302, 41 USCA §§ 259, 403.

Planning and solicitation requirements, see 41 USCA § 253a.

Preference for acquisition of commercial items, see 10 USCA § 2377, 41 USCA § 264b.

§ 8.404 Use of Federal Supply Schedules.

(a) General. Parts 13 (except 13.303-2(c)(3)), 14, 15, and 19 (except for the requirement at 19.202-1(e)(1)(iii)) do not apply to BPAs or orders placed against Federal Supply Schedules contracts (but see 8.405-5). BPAs and orders placed against a MAS, using the procedures in this subpart, are considered to be issued using full and open competition (see 6.102(d)(3)). Therefore, when establishing a BPA (as authorized by 13.303-2(c)(3)), or placing orders under Federal Supply Schedule contracts using the procedures of 8.405, ordering activities shall not seek competition outside of the Federal Supply Schedules or synopsize the requirement; but see paragraph (g) of this section.

(b) (1) The contracting officer, when placing an order or establishing a BPA, is responsible for applying the regulatory and statutory requirements applicable to the agency for which the order is placed or the BPA is established. The requiring agency shall provide the information on the applicable regulatory and statutory requirements to the contracting officer responsible for placing the order.

(2) For orders over $550,000, see subpart 17.5 for additional requirements for interagency acquisitions. For example, the requiring agency shall make a determination that use of the Federal Supply Schedule is the best procurement approach, in accordance with 17.502-1(a).

(c) Acquisition planning. Orders placed under a Federal Supply Schedule contract—

(1) Are not exempt from the development of acquisition plans (see subpart 7.1), and an information technology acquisition strategy (see Part 39);

(2) Must comply with all FAR requirements for a bundled contract when the order meets the definition of "bundled contract" (see 2.101(b)); and

(3) Must, whether placed by the requiring agency, or on behalf of the requiring agency, be consistent with the requiring agency's statutory and regulatory requirements applicable to the acquisition of the supply or service.

(d) Pricing. Supplies offered on the schedule are listed at fixed prices. Services offered on the schedule are priced either at hourly rates, or at a fixed price for performance of a specific task (e.g., installation, maintenance, and repair). GSA has already determined the prices of supplies and fixed-price services, and rates for services offered at hourly rates, under schedule contracts to be fair and reasonable. Therefore, ordering activities are not required to make a separate determination of fair and reasonable pricing, except for a price evaluation as required by 8.405-2(d). By placing an order against a schedule contract using the procedures in 8.405, the ordering activity has concluded that the order represents the best value (as defined in FAR 2.101) and results in the lowest overall cost alternative (considering price, special features, administrative costs, etc.) to meet the Government's needs. Although GSA has already negotiated fair and reasonable pricing, ordering activities may seek additional discounts before placing an order (see 8.405-4).

(e) The procedures under subpart 33.1 are applicable to the issuance of an order or the establishment of a BPA against a schedule contract.

(f) If the ordering activity issues an RFQ, the ordering activity shall provide the RFQ to any schedule contractor that requests a copy of it.

(g) (1) Ordering activities shall publicize contract actions funded in whole or in part by the American Recovery and Reinvestment Act of 2009 (Pub. L. 111-5):

(i) Notices of proposed MAS orders (including orders issued under BPAs) that are for "informational purposes only" exceeding $25,000 shall follow the procedures in 5.704 for posting orders.

(ii) Award notices for MAS orders (including orders issued under BPAs) shall follow the procedures in 5.705.

(2) When an order is awarded or a Blanket Purchase Agreement is established with an estimated value greater than the simplified acquisition threshold and supported by a limited-source justification at 8.405-6(a), the ordering activity contracting officer must—

(i) Publicize the action (see 5.301); and

(ii) Post the justification in accordance with 8.405-6(a)(2).

(h) Type-of-order preference for services.

(1) The ordering activity shall specify the order type (i.e., firm-fixed price, time-and-materials, or labor-hour) for the services offered on the schedule priced at hourly rates.

(2) Agencies shall use fixed-price orders for the acquisition of commercial services to the maximum extent practicable.

(3) (i) A time-and-materials or labor-hour order may be used for the acquisition of commercial services only when it is not possible at the time of placing the order to estimate accurately the extent or duration of the work or to anticipate costs with any reasonable degree of confidence.

(ii) Prior to the issuance of a time-and-materials or labor-hour order, the contracting officer shall—

(A) Execute a determination and findings (D&F) for the order, in accordance with paragraph (h)(3)(iii) of this section that a fixed-price order is not suitable;

(B) Include a ceiling price in the order that the contractor exceeds at its own risk; and

(C) When the total performance period, including options, is more than three years, the D&F prepared in accordance with this paragraph shall be signed by the contracting officer and approved by the head of the contracting activity prior to the execution of the base period.

(iii) The D&F required by paragraph (h)(3)(ii)(A) of this section shall contain sufficient facts and rationale to justify that a fixed-price order is not suitable. At a minimum, the D&F shall—

(A) Include a description of the market research conducted (see 8.404(c) and 10.002(e));

(B) Establish that it is not possible at the time of placing the order to accurately estimate the extent or duration of the work or anticipate costs with any reasonable degree of confidence;

(C) Establish that the current requirement has been structured to maximize the use of fixed-price orders (e.g., by limiting the value or length of the time-and-materials/labor-hour order; or, establishing fixed prices for portions of the requirement) on future acquisitions for the same or similar requirements; and

(D) Describe actions to maximize the use of fixed-price orders on future acquisitions for the same requirements.

(iv) Prior to an increase in the ceiling price of a time-and-materials or labor-hour order, the ordering activity shall—

(A) Conduct an analysis of pricing and other relevant factors to determine if the action is in the best interest of the Government and document the order file;

(B) Follow the procedures at 8.405-6 for a change that modifies the general scope of the order; and

(C) Comply with the requirements at 8.402(f) when modifying an order to add open market items.

(i) Ensure that service contractor reporting requirements are met in accordance with subpart 4.17, Service Contracts Inventory.

United States Code Annotated

Commercially available off-the-shelf item acquisitions, lists of inapplicable laws in Federal Acquisition Regulation, see 41 USCA § 431.

Contracts, planning, solicitation, evaluation, and award procedures, see 10 USCA § 2305.

Definitions, see 10 USCA § 2302, 41 USCA §§ 259, 403.

Planning and solicitation requirements, see 41 USCA § 253a.

Preference for acquisition of commercial items, see 10 USCA § 2377, 41 USCA § 264b.

Notes of Decisions

In general 1
Cancellation of solicitation 3
Protest of FSS orders 2

1 In general

Agency has discretion to procure via GSA's Federal Supply Schedules (FSS), rather than set-aside the procurement for small businesses, even though requirement had been previously performed by an 8(a) small business. Neither the Small Business Act, 15 USCA §§ 631–657, nor applicable regulations require the Government to obtain a service from a small business, including 8(a) firms, if it can meet its needs through the FSS. K-Lak Corp. v. U.S., 98 Fed. Cl. 1 (2011)

Agency is not required to order supplies under non-mandatory Federal Supply Schedule (FSS) contract, and where it is in agency's best interests-including need to establish "best value" among potential offerors-agency may compete its requirements among commercial sources of supply instead of under non-mandatory FSS. Murray×Benjamin Electric Company, LP, B-298481, 2006 CPD ¶ 129 (Comp. Gen. 2006)

Agency decision not to provide the protester with a solicitation for an acquisition of a unified financial management system under the Federal Supply Schedule program was reasonable, where the agency reasonably determined that the protester did not appear to offer best value (price and other factors considered) when compared to schedule vendors that were provided with the solicitation. Savantage Financial Services, Inc., B-292046, B-292046.2, 2003 CPD ¶ 113 (Comp. Gen. 2003)

2 Protest of FSS orders

Provision of the Federal Acquisition Streamlining Act (FASA) prohibiting bid protests in connection with issuance of a task order or delivery order does not apply to protests relating to the placement of orders under GSA Federal Supply Schedule (FSS) contracts. 10 U.S.C.A. §§ 2304a, 2304b, 2304c(d). Idea Intern., Inc. v. U.S., 74 Fed. Cl. 129 (2006)

Federal Acquisition Streamlining Act (FASA) which prohibits protests "in connection with the issuance or proposed issuance of a task or delivery order" except under certain circumstances did not bar protest of award of blanket purchase agreement (BPA), as task order restriction does not apply to Federal Supply Schedule (FSS) procurements. Federal Property and Administrative Services Act of 1949, § 303j(d), as amended, 41 U.S.C.A. § 253j(d); FAR 8.404(b)(4). Labat-Anderson Inc. v. U.S., 50 Fed. Cl. 99 (2001).

3 Cancellation of solicitation

Under FAR subpart 8.4 procedures, an agency need only advance a reasonable basis to cancel a solicitation. Where an agency concludes that cancellation is warranted because of ambiguous or inadequate specifications, GAO will not disturb that determination unless it is shown to be arbitrary, capricious, or not supported by substantial evidence. Strategic Technology Institute, Inc., B-408005.2, 2013 CPD ¶ 229 (Comp. Gen. 2013)

§ 8.405 Ordering procedures for Federal Supply Schedules.

Ordering activities shall use the ordering procedures of this section when placing an order or establishing a BPA for supplies or services. The procedures in this section apply to all schedules. For establishing BPAs and for orders under BPAs see 8.405-3.

United States Code Annotated

Commercially available off-the-shelf item acquisitions, lists of inapplicable laws in Federal Acquisition Regulation, see 41 USCA § 431.

Contracts, planning, solicitation, evaluation, and award procedures, see 10 USCA § 2305.

Definitions, see 10 USCA § 2302, 41 USCA §§ 259, 403.

Planning and solicitation requirements, see 41 USCA § 253a.

Preference for acquisition of commercial items, see 10 USCA § 2377, 41 USCA § 264b.

Notes of Decisions

Cancellation of solicitation 11
Commercial terms 8
Competition requirements 1
Compliance requirements 10
Meaningful discussions 7
Non-compliant quotations 9

Open market items 6
Procurement methods 4
Responsibility determination 5
Solicitation of incumbent 3
Time to submit proposal 2

1 Competition requirements

When conducting a procurement under the Federal Supply Schedule (FSS) program, contracting agency satisfies applicable statutory and regulatory competition requirements when it solicits quotations from at least three FSS contractors able to meet the agency's needs; the agency is not required to solicit the incumbent FSS contractor to participate in the competition. Allmond & Company, B-298946, 2007 CPD ¶ 8 (Comp. Gen. 2007)

Award of purchase order for printers to Federal Supply Service (FSS) vendor without providing protester an opportunity to compete was proper where agency determined that only one printer was compatible with the system with which it was to operate, and protester does not submit any evidence showing that it offers a compatible printer listed on the FSS. Card Technology Corporation, B-275385, B-275385.2, 97-1 CPD ¶ 76 (Comp. Gen. 1997)

2 Time to submit proposal

Agency properly rejected quotation that was not received by the agency by the time specified in the Request for Quotations (RFQ) due to the agency's network security firewall. Although the protester timely uploaded its quotation onto GSA's "E-Buy" system, the RFQ required submission directly to the agency Contract Specialist and GAO held that the agency was not required to check E-Buy. Advanced Decisions Vectors, Inc., B-412307, 2016 CPD ¶ 18 (Comp. Gen. 2016)

Protest that agency established unreasonably short deadline to respond to Request for Quotations (RFQ) issued under the Federal Supply Schedule (FSS) program is denied, where protester admits it could have timely responded but chose not to because it objected to the mode of transmission specified by the agency. The agency faxed an RFQ to FSS vendors at 9:15 pm on a Friday evening, seeking a "technical and price proposal in accordance with your GSA schedule contract" for A-76 consulting services. The agency had to make award on Monday, the last day of the fiscal year. FAR Subpart 8.4 does not require that vendors be permitted a specific minimum amount of time to respond to an RFQ; what is reasonable and sufficient depends on the facts and circumstances of the case. In this case, protester could have prepared the proposal in the time allotted but refused to transmit the proposal by any means other than e-mail, which was not permitted by the agency. GAO treated protester's decision not to respond as a business judgment and denied the protest. Warden Associates, Inc., B-291440, B-291440.2, 2002 CPD ¶ 223 (Comp. Gen. 2002)

3 Solicitation of incumbent

Government was under no obligation to solicit incumbent contractor on a delivery order from a Federal Supply Services (FSS) schedule contract, as sealed bidding regulation is not applicable to placement of a delivery order from an FSS schedule. 48 C.F.R. §§ 8.401(a, b), 14.205-4(b). Cybertech Group, Inc. v. U.S., 48 Fed. Cl. 638 (2001). United States ☞64.10

4 Procurement methods

When agency conducting a Federal Supply Schedule (FSS) procurement chooses to engage in a more comprehensive selection process than contemplated by the FSS scheme, bid protester cannot prevail on the theory that the procurement procedure involved a clear and prejudicial violation of applicable statutes and regulations, because no applicable procedural regulations are contained in the FSS regulation; rather, protester must rely on establishing that the government officials involved in the procurement process were without a rational and reasonable basis for their decision. FAR 8.401. Ellsworth Associates, Inc. v. U.S., 45 Fed. Cl. 388 (1999), dismissed, 6 Fed. Appx. 867 (Fed. Cir. 2001)

When ordering services priced at hourly rates from vendors holding FSS contracts, and when a statement of work is required, an agency is required under FAR 8.405-2(d) to consider a vendor's proposed level of effort and labor mix in its selection decision. Advanced Technology Systems, Inc., B-296493.6, 2006 CPD ¶ 151 (Comp. Gen. 2006)

Where agency initially set Federal Supply Schedule (FSS) procurement aside for small businesses, but subsequently decided to conduct purchase on non-set-aside basis, agency's elimination of set-aside was unobjectionable; small business set-aside requirements do not apply to FSS purchases. Global Analytic Information Technology Services, Inc., B-297200.3, 2006 CPD ¶ 53 (Comp. Gen. 2006)

Protest that procurement should have been set aside for small businesses is denied, where the agency reasonably determined that the items to be procured were available under the Federal Supply Schedule (FSS); agencies need not consider small business programs when purchasing from the FSS. Future Solutions, Inc., B-293194, 2004 CPD ¶ 39 (Comp. Gen. 2004)

Agency's conduct of discussions with two other FSS vendors without affording protester an opportunity to address technical deficiencies in its proposal is unobjectionable where agency reasonably concluded that protester's proposal should be excluded from further consideration because of reasonable concerns about its technical compliance and its higher price. Venturi Technology Partners, B-292060, 2003 CPD ¶ 114 (Comp. Gen. 2003)

The procedures of FAR Part 15, governing contracting by negotiation, do not govern competitive procurements under the Federal Supply Schedule (FSS). This does not mean, however, that the agency can announce one basis for award and then make award on another basis. Under the FSS, agencies are not required to conduct a competition before using their business judgment in determining whether ordering supplies or services from an FSS vendor represents the best value and meets the agency's needs at the lowest overall cost. However, where an agency conducts a competition, GAO will review the agency's actions to ensure that the evaluation was reasonable and consistent with the terms of the solicitation. Selecting a vendor on an award basis different than that announced in the solicitation is not consistent with the agency's obligation to treat vendors fairly. Computer Products, Inc., B-284702, 2000 CPD ¶ 95 (Comp. Gen. 2000).

5 Responsibility determination

An ordering agency is not required to perform a responsibility determination when placing a task or delivery order under a Federal Supply Schedule (FSS) contract, since the General Services Administration performed a responsibility determination at the time of award of the underlying contract. Advanced Technology Systems, Inc., B-296493.6, 2006 CPD ¶ 151 (Comp. Gen. 2006)

6 Open market items

✻ GSA inappropriately awarded a Federal Supply Schedule (FSS) task order to a vendor whose FSS contract scope did not include all of the required services. The GAO held, that "the relevant inquiry as to whether a vendor's services are outside its FSS contract's scope is "not whether the vendor is willing to provide the services that the agency is seeking, but whether the services or positions offered are actually included in the vendor's FSS contract. Matter of: American Security Programs, Inc., B-402069, B-402069.2, 2010 CPD ¶ 2 (Comp. Gen. 2010)

7 Meaningful discussions

The procedures of FAR Part 15 concerning exchanges with offerors after receipt of proposals do not apply to competitive procurements under GSA's Federal Supply Schedule (FSS) program. There is no requirement in FAR Subpart 8.4 that an agency conduct discussions with vendors when conducting a best value procurement under the FSS. However, if exchanges are conducted with vendors in such a procurement, the exchanges must be fair and equitable. GAO looks to the standards in FAR Part 15 as guidance to make this determination. Protest was sustained because the agency's discussions did not address the aspect of the protester's proposal that rendered it unacceptable. Kardex Remstar, LLC, B-409030, 2014 CPD ¶ 1 (Comp. Gen. 2014)

8 Commercial terms

The FAR requirement (12.302) that commercial item contracts include only those clauses determined to be consistent with "customary commercial practice" applied to a Request for Quotations (RFQ) posted on GSA's E-Buy portal. Although the FAR does not explicitly state that the "customary commercial practice" provision applied to orders placed under GSA Schedule contracts, the provision does apply to "acquisitions" and purchases through the use of RFQs meet the broad definition of an "acquisition" under FAR 2.101. CGI Federal Inc. v. U.S., 779 F.3d 1346 (Fed. Cir. 2015)

9 Non-compliant quotations

GAO sustained a protest to the award of orders under GSA's Federal Supply Schedule 70 because the awardees quotation violated the solicitation requirement to use a 12-point font (the awardee used a 10 point font in several tables included in the quotation) and the requirement to use "single spacing" (the awardee used a line spacing of less than 1.0). DKW Commc'ns, Inc., B-412652.3,et al., 2016 CPD ¶ 143 (Comp. Gen. 2016)

10 Compliance requirements

A solicitation issued under Federal Supply Schedule 70 requiring the "contractor" to comply with FISMA IT security standards did not require offerors to demonstrate compliance before the source selection decision. Such compliance is a performance requirement to be satisfied after award during contract performance. Discover Techs. LLC, B-412773, 2016 CPD ¶ 142 (Comp. Gen. 2016)

11 Cancellation of solicitation

An agency reasonably decided to cancel a solicitationin light of the agency's determination that doing the work with agency employees would savecosts. In the absence of convincing evidence of badfaith, the protester's argument that the cancellationwas a pretext to avoid scrutiny of organizationalconflicts of interests (OCIs) was not enough to overcomethe presumption that Government officials actin good faith. Inalab Consulting, Inc., B-413044 et al., 2016 CPD ¶ 195 (Comp. Gen.2016)

§ 8.405-1 Ordering procedures for supplies, and services not requiring a statement of work.

(a) Ordering activities shall use the procedures of this subsection when ordering supplies and services that are listed in the schedules contracts at a fixed price for the performance of a specific task, where a statement of work is not required (*e.g.,* installation, maintenance, and repair). For establishing BPAs and for orders under BPAs see 8.405-3.

(b) *Orders at or below the micro-purchase threshold.* Ordering activities may place orders at, or below, the micro-purchase threshold with any Federal Supply Schedule contractor that can meet the agency's needs. Although not required to solicit from a specific number of schedule contractors, ordering activities should attempt to distribute orders among contractors.

(c) *Orders exceeding the micro-purchase threshold but not exceeding the simplified acquisition threshold.* Ordering activities shall place orders with the schedule contractor that can provide the supply or service that represents the best value. Before placing an order, an ordering activity shall:

(1) Consider reasonably available information about the supply or service offered under MAS contracts by surveying at least three schedule contractors through the GSA Advantage! on-line shopping service, by reviewing the catalogs or pricelists of at least three schedule contractors, or by requesting quotations from at least three schedule contractors (see 8.405-5); or

(2) Document the circumstances for restricting consideration to fewer than three schedule contractors based on one of the reasons at 8.405-6(a);

(d) For proposed orders exceeding the simplified acquisition threshold.

(1) Each order shall be placed on a competitive basis in accordance with (d)(2) and (3) of this section, unless this requirement is waived on the basis of a justification that is prepared and approved in accordance with 8.405-6.

(2) The ordering activity contracting officer shall provide an RFQ that includes a description of the supplies to be delivered or the services to be performed and the basis upon which the selection will be made (see 8.405-1(f)).

(3) The ordering activity contracting officer shall—

(i) Post the RFQ on e-Buy to afford all schedule contractors offering the required supplies or services under the appropriate multiple award schedule(s) an opportunity to submit a quote; or

(ii) Provide the RFQ to as many schedule contractors as practicable, consistent with market research appropriate to the circumstances, to reasonably ensure that quotes will be received from at least three contractors that can fulfill the requirements. When fewer than three quotes are received from schedule contractors that can fulfill the requirement, the contracting officer shall prepare a written determination explaining that no additional contractors capable of fulfilling the requirement could be identified despite reasonable efforts to do so. The determination must clearly explain efforts made to obtain quotes from at least three schedule contractors.

(4) The ordering activity contracting officer shall ensure that all quotes received are fairly considered and award is made in accordance with the basis for selection in the RFQ.

(e) When an order contains brand-name specifications, the contracting officer shall post the RFQ on e-Buy along with the justification or documentation, as required by 8.405-6. An RFQ is required when a purchase description specifies a brand-name.

(f) In addition to price (see 8.404(d) and 8.405-4), when determining best value, the ordering activity may consider, among other factors, the following:

(1) Past performance.

(2) Special features of the supply or service required for effective program performance.

(3) Trade-in considerations.

(4) Probable life of the item selected as compared with that of a comparable item.

(5) Warranty considerations.

(6) Maintenance availability.

(7) Environmental and energy efficiency considerations.

(8) Delivery terms.

(g) *Minimum documentation.* The ordering activity shall document—

(1) The schedule contracts considered, noting the contractor from which the supply or service was purchased;

(2) A description of the supply or service purchased;

(3) The amount paid;

(4) When an order exceeds the simplified acquisition threshold, evidence of compliance with the ordering procedures at 8.405-1(d); and

(5) The basis for the award decision.

United States Code Annotated

Commercially available off-the-shelf item acquisitions, lists of inapplicable laws in Federal Acquisition Regulation, see 41 USCA § 431.

Contracts, planning, solicitation, evaluation, and award procedures, see 10 USCA § 2305.

Definitions, see 10 USCA § 2302, 41 USCA §§ 259, 403.

Planning and solicitation requirements, see 41 USCA § 253a.

Preference for acquisition of commercial items, see 10 USCA § 2377, 41 USCA § 264b.

Notes of Decisions

Competition requirements 1
Improper orders 3
Procurement methods 2
Responsibility determination 4

1 Competition requirements

General Services Administration (GSA) was not required to competitively bid drapery order for Army, where order was awarded to contractor pursuant to multiple award schedule for amount no greater than maximum order limitation. 48 C.F.R. § 8.404-1. Commercial Drapery Contractors, Inc. v. U.S., 967 F. Supp. 1, 41 Cont. Cas. Fed. (CCH) P 77172 (D.D.C. 1997), judgment aff'd, 133 F.3d 1, 39 Fed. R. Serv. 3d 825 (D.C. Cir. 1998). United States ☞64.10

Contracting agencies must obtain full and open competition in the procurement of supplies and services. The Federal Supply Schedule provides agencies with a simplified process for obtaining commonly used commercial supplies and services. FAR 8.401(a). The procedures established for the FSS program satisfy the requirement for full and open competition. 41 U.S.C. sect. 259(b)(3); FAR 6.102(d)(3). However, supplies and services not on the FSS may not be purchased using FSS procedures; instead, their purchase requires compliance with the applicable procurement laws and regulations, including those requiring full and open competition, unless some other exception applies. Information Ventures, Inc., B-299422, B-299422.2, 2007 CPD ¶ 88 (Comp. Gen. 2007)

Protest is sustained where contracting office furnished request for quotations (RFQ) for furniture system to only 2 of the 13 Federal Supply Schedule (FSS) contractors for which it had brochures on hand, since the applicable FSS calls for the purchasing office to furnish copies of the RFQ to all contractors for whom brochures are on hand, and FAR 8.405-1(a), in effect at the time the procurement was conducted, directed agencies ordering from FSS contracts to review the schedule price lists that were reasonably available at the ordering office. Matter of: Knoll North America, Inc, B-259112, B-259113, 95-1 CPD ¶ 141 (Comp. Gen. 1995)

2 Procurement methods

The whole of Part 15 is not applied to a solicitation under the Federal Supply Schedule (FSS) merely because it employs some Part 15 procedures. Rather, only those portions that are particularly implicated by the procedures used will be applied to the solicitation. Where the solicitation did not specifically provide for a post-award debriefing, the post-award debriefing requirements found in subpart 15.506 are not applicable. Systems Plus, Inc. v. U.S., 68 Fed. Cl. 206 (2005)

3 Improper orders

The GAO determined that an agency improperly issued a Federal Supply Schedule (FSS) purchase order to a vendor for open market items because the vendor's FSS contract did not include all the items identified in the order. GAO rejected the agency's argument that a $0 item fell within the micropurchase exception because the item's cost was shifted to other items included in the order. Matter of: Rapiscan Systems, Inc., B-401773.2, B-401773.3, 2010 CPD ¶ 60 (Comp. Gen. 2010).

Protest was sustained where a solicitation limited competition to vendors holding a GSA contracts for the specified items but the agency's purchase order included two items that were not on the awardee's GSA contract. The agency contended that the purchase was proper because, although the two items were not listed on the awardee's GSA contract at the time the agency issued the purchase order, the agency believed that the items would be added to the GSA contract by the delivery date specified in the purchase order. GAO rejected this argument because subsequent inclusion of the items on the awardee's GSA contract was uncertain. Decision Matter of: Science Applications International Corporation, B-401773, 2009 CPD ¶ 229 (Comp. Gen. 2009)

Protest that contracting agency's issuance of a delivery order to a firm pursuant to its General Services Administration (GSA), Federal Supply Schedule contract was improper is sustained where the product to be furnished is outside of the scope of the firm's GSA schedule contract and the agency unreasonably determined that the selected product met the solicitation specifications. Armed Forces Merchandise Outlet, Inc., B-294281, 2004 CPD ¶ 218 (Comp. Gen. 2004)

An agency may no longer rely on the "incidentals" test to justify the purchase of non-FSS items in connection with an FSS buy; where an agency buys non-FSS items for an amount above the micro-purchase threshold, it must follow applicable acquisition regulations. Pyxis Corporation, B-282469, B-282469.2, 99-2 CPD ¶ 18 (Comp. Gen. 1999)

4 Responsibility determination

An ordering agency is not required to perform a responsibility determination when placing a task or delivery order under a Federal Supply Schedule (FSS) contract, since the General Services Administration performed a responsibility determination at the time of award of the underlying contract. Advanced Technology Systems, Inc., B-296493.6, 2006 CPD ¶ 151 (Comp. Gen. 2006)

§ 8.405-2 Ordering procedures for services requiring a statement of work.

(a) *General.* Ordering activities shall use the procedures in this subsection when ordering services priced at hourly rates as established by the schedule contracts. The applicable services will be identified in the Federal Supply Schedule publications and the contractor's pricelists. For establishing BPAs and for orders under BPAs see 8.405-3.

(b) *Statements of Work (SOWs)*. All Statements of Work shall include a description of work to be performed; location of work; period of performance; deliverable schedule; applicable performance standards; and any special requirements (*e.g.*, security clearances, travel, special knowledge). To the maximum extent practicable, agency requirements shall be performance-based statements (see Subpart 37.6).

(c) *Request for Quotation procedures*. The ordering activity must provide the Request for Quotation (RFQ), which includes the statement of work and evaluation criteria (*e.g.*, experience and past performance), to schedule contractors that offer services that will meet the agency's needs. The RFQ may be posted to GSA's electronic RFQ system, e-Buy (see 8.402(d)).

(1) *Orders at, or below, the micro-purchase threshold*. Ordering activities may place orders at, or below, the micro-purchase threshold with any Federal Supply Schedule contractor that can meet the agency's needs. The ordering activity should attempt to distribute orders among contractors.

(2) *For orders exceeding the micro-purchase threshold, but not exceeding the simplified acquisition threshold.*

(i) The ordering activity shall develop a statement of work, in accordance with 8.405-2(b).

(ii) The ordering activity shall provide the RFQ (including the statement of work and evaluation criteria) to at least three schedule contractors that offer services that will meet the agency's needs or document the circumstances for restricting consideration to fewer than three schedule contractors based on one of the reasons at 8.405-6(a).

(iii) The ordering activity shall specify the type of order (*i.e.*, firm-fixed-price, labor-hour) for the services identified in the statement of work. The contracting officer should establish firm-fixed-prices, as appropriate.

(3) For proposed orders exceeding the simplified acquisition threshold. In addition to meeting the requirements of 8.405-2(c)(2)(i) and (iii), the following procedures apply:

(i) Each order shall be placed on a competitive basis in accordance with (c)(3)(ii) and (iii) of this section, unless this requirement is waived on the basis of a justification that is prepared and approved in accordance with 8.405-6.

(ii) The ordering activity contracting officer shall provide an RFQ that includes a statement of work and the evaluation criteria.

(iii) The ordering activity contracting officer shall—

(A) Post the RFQ on e-Buy to afford all schedule contractors offering the required services under the appropriate multiple-award schedule(s) an opportunity to submit a quote; or

(B) Provide the RFQ to as many schedule contractors as practicable, consistent with market research appropriate to the circumstances, to reasonably ensure that quotes will be received from at least three contractors that can fulfill the requirements. When fewer than three quotes are received from schedule contractors that can fulfill the requirements, the contracting officer shall prepare a written determination to explain that no additional contractors capable of fulfilling the requirements could be identified despite reasonable efforts to do so. The determination must clearly explain efforts made to obtain quotes from at least three schedule contractors.

(C) Ensure all quotes received are fairly considered and award is made in accordance with the evaluation criteria in the RFQ.

(4) The ordering activity shall provide the RFQ (including the statement of work and the evaluation criteria) to any schedule contractor who requests a copy of it.

(d) *Evaluation*. The ordering activity shall evaluate all responses received using the evaluation criteria provided to the schedule contractors. The ordering activity is responsible for considering the level of effort and the mix of labor proposed to perform a specific task being ordered, and for determining that the total price is reasonable. Place the order with the schedule contractor that represents the best value (see 8.404(d) and 8.405-4). After award, ordering activities should provide timely notification to unsuccessful offerors. If an unsuccessful offeror requests information on an award that was based on factors other than price alone, a brief explanation of the basis for the award decision shall be provided.

(e) *Use of time-and-materials and labor-hour orders for services.* When placing a time-and-materials or labor-hour order for services, see 8.404(h).

(f) *Minimum documentation.* The ordering activity shall document—

(1) The schedule contracts considered, noting the contractor from which the service was purchased;

(2) A description of the service purchased;

(3) The amount paid;

(4) The evaluation methodology used in selecting the contractor to receive the order;

(5) The rationale for any tradeoffs in making the selection;

(6) The price reasonableness determination required by paragraph (d) of this subsection;

(7) The rationale for using other than—

(i) A firm-fixed price order; or

(ii) A performance-based order; and

(8) When an order exceeds the simplified acquisition threshold, evidence of compliance with the ordering procedures at 8.405-2(c).

United States Code Annotated

Commercially available off-the-shelf item acquisitions, lists of inapplicable laws in Federal Acquisition Regulation, see 41 USCA § 431.

Contracts, planning, solicitation, evaluation, and award procedures, see 10 USCA § 2305.

Definitions, see 10 USCA § 2302, 41 USCA §§ 259, 403.

Planning and solicitation requirements, see 41 USCA § 253a.

Preference for acquisition of commercial items, see 10 USCA § 2377, 41 USCA § 264b.

Notes of Decisions

In general 1
Documentation requirements 2
Failure to acknowledge amendment to statement of work 3
Failure to satisfy solicitation requirements 5
Price reasonableness 4

1 In general

The whole of Part 15 is not applied to a solicitation under the Federal Supply Schedule (FSS) merely because it employs some Part 15 procedures. Rather, only those portions that are particularly implicated by the procedures used will be applied to the solicitation. Where the solicitation did not specifically provide for a post-award debriefing, the post-award debriefing requirements found in subpart 15.506 are not applicable. Systems Plus, Inc. v. U.S., 68 Fed. Cl. 206 (2005)

In a procurement conducted pursuant to Federal Supply Schedule procedures, an agency, when ordering services priced at hourly rates and when a statement of work is included, must consider the level of effort and the mix of labor offered to perform a specific task being ordered and determine that the total price is reasonable. Matter of: U S Information Technologies Corporation, B-404357, B-404357.2, 2011 CPD ¶ 74 (Comp. Gen. 2011)

An agency improperly awarded a task order to a GSA vendor whose proposal took exception to a solicitation requirement to propose a fixed price by conditioning its offered price on a greater use of government facilities than contemplated or authorized by the solicitation, such that its offered price was conditional not firm. Matter of: Solers, Inc., B-404032.3, B-404032.4, 2011 CPD ¶ 83 (Comp. Gen. 2011)

Where an agency announces its intention to order from an existing GSA FSS contractor, it means that the agency intends to order all items using GSA FSS procedures and that all items are required to be within the scope of the vendor's FSS contract. Non-FSS products and services may not be purchased using FSS procedures; instead, their purchase requires compliance with the applicable procurement laws and regulations, including those requiring the use of competitive procedures. Tarheel Specialties, Inc., B-298197, B-298197.2, 2006 CPD ¶ 140 (Comp. Gen. 2006)

The FSS program, directed and managed by the General Services Administration (GSA), gives federal agencies a simplified process for obtaining commonly used commercial supplies and services. FAR 8.401(a). Where an agency issues an RFQ under FAR Subpart 8.4, conducts a competition, and uses vendors' responses as the basis for a detailed technical evaluation and price/technical tradeoff, which is more like a competition in a negotiated procurement than a simple FSS buy, GAO will review the record to ensure that the agency's evaluation is reasonable and consistent with the terms of the solicitation. CourtSmart Digital Systems, Inc., B-292995.2, B-292995.3, 2004 CPD ¶ 79 (Comp. Gen. 2004)

2 Documentation requirements

Protest challenging source selection decision in a best-value procurement conducted under a Blanket Purchase Agreement (BPA) under GSA's Federal Supply Schedule was sustained where the agency selected awardee's higher-rated quotation without meaningfully considering the protester's lower price. The agency's selection decision stated: "Given [awardee's] rating of 'exceptional,' with no other bidders having received an equivalent or higher rating, thereby rendering further analysis under the trade-off approach unnecessary, [awardee] was selected for award." The protest was sustained because the agency did not consider price or conduct a tradeoff analysis as required by the solicitation. NikSoft Sys. Corp., B-406179, 2012 CPD ¶ 104 (Comp. Gen. 2012)

3 Failure to acknowledge amendment to statement of work

Protest was sustained where agency rejected awardee's quote for failure to acknowledge an amendment posted on GSA's E-Buy website that was immaterial and did not impose any legal obligations on the contractor in addition to those to which it had already agreed. Infoshred LLC, B-407086, 2012 CPD ¶ 298 (Comp. Gen. 2012)

4 Price reasonableness

While the GSA has already determined that the rates for services offered at hourly rates under FSS contracts are fair and reasonable (and, thus, ordering activities are generally not required to make a separate determination of fair and reasonable pricing), when a statement of work is required, the ordering agency must still perform a price evaluation to determine that the offeror's total price is reasonable. Beltway Transportation Service, B-411458, 2015 CPD ¶ 225 (Comp.Gen. 2015)

In a procurement conducted pursuant to Federal Supply Schedule procedures, an agency, when ordering services priced at hourly rates and when a statement of work is included, is required to consider the level of effort and the mix of labor offered to perform a specific task being ordered and determine that the total price is reasonable. U.S. Information Technologies Corp., B-404357, 2011 CPD ¶ 74 (Comp.Gen. 2011)

5 Failure to satisfy solicitation requirements

Protest of a task order issued under GSA's Federal Supply Schedule (FSS) was sustained because the task order was based on a labor category that did not meet solicitation requirements. If a quoted labor category description under a firm's FSS contract does not satisfy solicitation requirements, the firm cannot alter the labor category description via its quotation to satisfy the requirement. Rather, the failure to satisfy solicitation requirements precludes the agency from issuing a task order to the firm. AllWorld Language Consultants, Inc., B-411481.3, 2016 CPD ¶ 12 (Comp. Gen. 2016)

§ 8.405-3 Blanket purchase agreements (BPAs).

(a) Establishment.

(1) Ordering activities may establish BPAs under any schedule contract to fill repetitive needs for supplies or services. Ordering activities shall establish the BPA with the schedule contractor(s) that can provide the supply or service that represents the best value.

(2) In addition to price (see 8.404(d) and 8.405-4), when determining best value, the ordering activity may consider, among other factors, the following:

(i) Past performance.

(ii) Special features of the supply or service required for effective program performance.

(iii) Trade-in considerations.

(iv) Probable life of the item selected as compared with that of a comparable item.

(v) Warranty considerations.

(vi) Maintenance availability.

(vii) Environmental and energy efficiency considerations.

(viii) Delivery terms.

(3) (i) The ordering activity contracting officer shall, to the maximum extent practicable, give preference to establishing multiple-award BPAs, rather than establishing a single-award BPA.

(ii) No single-award BPA with an estimated value exceeding $112 million (including any options), may be awarded unless the head of the agency determines in writing that—

(A) The orders expected under the BPA are so integrally related that only a single source can reasonably perform the work;

(B) The BPA provides only for firm-fixed priced orders for—

(1) Products with unit prices established in the BPA; or

(2) Services with prices established in the BPA for specific tasks to be performed;

(C) Only one source is qualified and capable of performing the work at a reasonable price to the Government; or

(D) It is necessary in the public interest to award the BPA to a single source for exceptional circumstances.

(iii) The requirement for a determination for a single-award BPA greater than $112 million is in addition to any applicable requirement for a limited-source justification at 8.405-6. However, the two documents may be combined into one document.

(iv) In determining how many multiple-award BPAs to establish or that a single-award BPA is appropriate, the contracting officer should consider the following factors and document the decision in the acquisition plan or BPA file:

(A) The scope and complexity of the requirement(s);

(B) The benefits of on-going competition and the need to periodically compare multiple technical approaches or prices;

(C) The administrative costs of BPAs; and

(D) The technical qualifications of the schedule contractor(s).

(4) BPAs shall address the frequency of ordering, invoicing, discounts, requirements (e.g., estimated quantities, work to be performed), delivery locations, and time.

(5) When establishing multiple-award BPAs, the ordering activity shall specify the procedures for placing orders under the BPAs in accordance with 8.405-3(c)(2).

(6) Establishment of a multi-agency BPA against a Federal Supply Schedule contract is permitted if the multi-agency BPA identifies the participating agencies and their estimated requirements at the time the BPA is established.

(7) Minimum documentation. The ordering activity contracting officer shall include in the BPA file documentation the—

(i) Schedule contracts considered, noting the contractor to which the BPA was awarded;

(ii) Description of the supply or service purchased;

(iii) Price;

(iv) Required justification for a limited-source BPA (see 8.405-6), if applicable;

(v) Determination for a single-award BPA exceeding $112 million, if applicable (see (a)(3)(ii)) of this section);

(vi) Documentation supporting the decision to establish multiple-award BPAs or a single-award BPA (see (a)(3)(iv));

(vii) Evidence of compliance with paragraph (b) of this section, for competitively awarded BPAs, if applicable; and

(viii) Basis for the award decision. This should include the evaluation methodology used in selecting the contractor, the rationale for any tradeoffs in making the selection, and a price reasonableness determination for services requiring a statement of work.

(b) Competitive procedures for establishing a BPA. This paragraph applies to the establishment of a BPA, in addition to applicable instructions in paragraph (a).

(1) For supplies, and for services not requiring a statement of work. The procedures of this paragraph apply when establishing a BPA for supplies and services that are listed in the schedule contract at a fixed price for the performance of a specific task, where a statement of work is not required (e.g., installation, maintenance, and repair).

(i) If the estimated value of the BPA does not exceed the simplified acquisition threshold.

(A) The ordering activity shall:

(1) Consider reasonably available information about the supply or service offered under MAS contracts by surveying at least three schedule contractors through the GSA Advantage! on-line shopping service, by reviewing the catalogs or pricelists of at least three schedule contractors, or by requesting quotations from at least three schedule contractors (see 8.405-5); or

(2) Document the circumstances for restricting consideration to fewer than three schedule contractors based on one of the reasons at 8.405-6(a).

(B) The ordering activity shall establish the BPA with the schedule contractor(s) that can provide the best value.

(ii) If the estimated value of the BPA exceeds the simplified acquisition threshold. The ordering activity contracting officer:

(A) Shall provide an RFQ that includes a description of the supplies to be delivered or the services to be performed and the basis upon which the selection will be made.

(B) (1) Shall post the RFQ on e-Buy to afford all schedule contractors offering the required supplies or services under the appropriate multiple award schedule(s) an opportunity to submit a quote; or

(2) Shall provide the RFQ to as many schedule contractors as practicable, consistent with market research appropriate to the circumstances, to reasonably ensure that quotes will be received from at least three contractors that can fulfill the requirements. When fewer than three quotes are received from schedule contractors that can fulfill the requirements, the contracting officer shall prepare a written determination explaining that no additional contractors capable of fulfilling the requirements could be identified despite reasonable efforts to do so. The determination must clearly explain efforts made to obtain quotes from at least three schedule contractors.

(C) Shall ensure all quotes received are fairly considered and award is made in accordance with the basis for selection in the RFQ. After seeking price reductions (see 8.405-4), establish the BPA with the schedule contractor(s) that provides the best value.

(D) The BPA must be established in accordance with paragraphs (b)(1)(ii)(B) and (C) of this section, unless the requirement is waived on the basis of a justification that is prepared and approved in accordance with 8.405-6.

(2) For services requiring a statement of work. This applies when establishing a BPA that requires services priced at hourly rates, as provided by the schedule contract. The applicable services will be identified in the Federal Supply Schedule publications and the contractor's pricelists.

(i) Statements of Work (SOWs). The ordering activity shall develop a statement of work. All Statements of Work shall include a description of work to be performed; location of work; period of performance; deliverable schedule; applicable performance standards; and any special requirements (e.g., security clearances, travel, and special knowledge). To the maximum extent practicable, agency requirements shall be performance-based statements (see subpart 37.6).

(ii) Type-of-order preference. The ordering activity shall specify the order type (i.e., firm-fixed price, time-and-materials, or labor-hour) for the services identified in the statement of work. The contracting officer should establish firm-fixed priced orders to the maximum extent practicable. For time-and-materials and labor-hour orders, the contracting officer shall follow the procedures at 8.404(h).

(iii) Request for Quotation procedures. The ordering activity must provide a RFQ, which includes the statement of work and evaluation criteria (e.g., experience and past performance), to schedule contractors that offer services that will meet the agency's needs. The RFQ may be posted to GSA's electronic RFQ system, e-Buy (see 8.402(d)).

(iv) If the estimated value of the BPA does not exceed the simplified acquisition threshold. The ordering activity shall provide the RFQ (including the statement of work and evaluation criteria) to at least three schedule contractors that offer services that will meet the agency's needs.

(v) If estimated value of the BPA exceeds the simplified acquisition threshold. The ordering activity contracting officer-

(A) Shall post the RFQ on e-Buy to afford all schedule contractors offering the required supplies or services under the appropriate multiple-award schedule an opportunity to submit a quote; or

(B) Shall provide the RFQ, which includes the statement of work and evaluation criteria, to as many schedule contractors as practicable, consistent with market research appropriate to the circumstances, to reasonably ensure that quotes will be received from at least three contractors that can fulfill the requirements. When fewer than three quotes are received from schedule contractors that can fulfill the requirements, the contracting officer shall document the file. The contracting officer shall prepare a written determination explaining that no additional contractors capable of fulfilling the requirements could be identified despite reasonable efforts to do so. The determination must clearly explain efforts made to obtain quotes from at least three schedule contractors.

(vi) The ordering activity contracting officer shall ensure all quotes received are fairly considered and award is made in accordance with the basis for selection in the RFQ. The ordering activity is responsible for considering the level of effort and the mix of labor proposed to perform, and for determining that the proposed price is reasonable.

(vii) The BPA must be established in accordance with paragraph (b)(2)(iv) or (v), and with paragraph (b)(2)(vi) of this section, unless the requirement is waived on the basis of a justification that is prepared and approved in accordance with 8.405-6.

(viii) The ordering activity contracting officer shall establish the BPA with the schedule contractor(s) that represents the best value (see 8.404(d) and 8.405-4).

(3) After award, ordering activities should provide timely notification to unsuccessful offerors. If an unsuccessful offeror requests information on an award that was based on factors other than price alone, a brief explanation of the basis for the award decision shall be provided.

(c) Ordering from BPAs. The procedures in this paragraph (c) are not required for BPAs established on or before May 16, 2011. However, ordering activities are encouraged to use the procedures for such BPAs.

(1) Single-award BPA. If the ordering activity establishes a single-award BPA, authorized users may place the order directly under the established BPA when the need for the supply or service arises.

(2) Multiple-award BPAs.

(i) Orders at or below the micro-purchase threshold. The ordering activity may place orders at or below the micro-purchase threshold with any BPA holder that can meet the agency needs. The ordering activity should attempt to distribute any such orders among the BPA holders.

(ii) Orders exceeding the micro-purchase threshold but not exceeding the simplified acquisition threshold.

(A) The ordering activity must provide each multiple-award BPA holder a fair opportunity to be considered for each order exceeding the micro-purchase threshold, but not exceeding the simplified acquisition threshold unless one of the exceptions at 8.405-6(a)(1)(i) applies.

(B) The ordering activity need not contact each of the multiple-award BPA holders before placing an order if information is available to ensure that each BPA holder is provided a fair opportunity to be considered for each order.

(C) The ordering activity contracting officer shall document the circumstances when restricting consideration to less than all multiple-award BPA holders offering the required supplies and services.

(iii) Orders exceeding the simplified acquisition threshold.

(A) The ordering activity shall place an order in accordance with paragraphs (c)(2)(iii)(A)(1), (2) and (3) of this paragraph, unless the requirement is waived on the basis of a justification that is prepared and approved in accordance with 8.405-6. The ordering activity shall—

(1) Provide an RFQ to all BPA holders offering the required supplies or services under the multiple-award BPAs, to include a description of the supplies to be delivered or the services to be performed and the basis upon which the selection will be made;

(2) Afford all BPA holders responding to the RFQ an opportunity to submit a quote; and

(3) Fairly consider all responses received and make award in accordance with the selection procedures.

(B) The ordering activity shall document evidence of compliance with these procedures and the basis for the award decision.

(3) BPAs for hourly-rate services. If the BPA is for hourly-rate services, the ordering activity shall develop a statement of work for each order covered by the BPA. Ordering activities should place these orders on a firm-fixed price basis to the maximum extent practicable. For time-and-materials and labor-hour orders, the contracting officer shall follow the procedures at 8.404(h). All orders under the BPA shall specify a price for the performance of the tasks identified in the statement of work. The ordering activity is responsible for considering the level of effort and the mix of labor proposed to perform a specific task being ordered, and for determining that the total price is reasonable through appropriate analysis techniques, and documenting the file accordingly.

(d) Duration of BPAs.

(1) Multiple-award BPAs generally should not exceed five years in length, but may do so to meet program requirements.

(2) A single-award BPA shall not exceed one year. It may have up to four one-year options. See paragraph (e) of this section for requirements associated with option exercise.

(3) Contractors may be awarded BPAs that extend beyond the current term of their GSA Schedule contract, so long as there are option periods in their GSA Schedule contract that, if exercised, will cover the BPA's period of performance.

(e) Review of BPAs.

(1) The ordering activity contracting officer shall review the BPA and determine in writing, at least once a year (e.g., at option exercise), whether—

(i) The schedule contract, upon which the BPA was established, is still in effect;

(ii) The BPA still represents the best value (see 8.404(d)); and

(iii) Estimated quantities/amounts have been exceeded and additional price reductions can be obtained.

(2) The determination shall be included in the BPA file documentation.

United States Code Annotated

Commercially available off-the-shelf item acquisitions, lists of inapplicable laws in Federal Acquisition Regulation, see 41 USCA § 431.

Contracts, planning, solicitation, evaluation, and award procedures, see 10 USCA § 2305.

Definitions, see 10 USCA § 2302, 41 USCA §§ 259, 403.

Planning and solicitation requirements, see 41 USCA § 253a.

Preference for acquisition of commercial items, see 10 USCA § 2377, 41 USCA § 264b.

Notes of Decisions

In general 1

1 In general

GAO sustained a protest alleging that agency failed to meaningfully consider price in issuing blanket purchase agreements(BPAs) under GSA's Federal Supply Schedule because the agency selected vendors only on the basis of their technical evaluation scores and did not consider price. The GAO rejected the agency's contention that it was not feasible to conduct a price evaluation at the time the BPAs were established because the agency was not procuring specific services at that time, which precluded a price comparison. Glotech, Inc., B-406761, 2012 CPD ¶ 248

Contracting agency was not required to suspend performance of blanket purchase agreement (BPA) awarded under Federal Supply Schedule (FSS) of the General Services Administration (GSA) pending review of post-award bid protest by the Government Accountability Office (GAO), under statute requiring such suspension if agency receives notice of protest within 5 days after debriefing offered to unsuccessful offeror if debriefing is required, as such debriefing was not required for an award under a multiple award schedule of the GSA, which is not awarded on the basis of a "competitive proposal." 31 U.S.C.A. § 3553(d)(4)(B). Systems Plus, Inc. v. U.S., 68 Fed. Cl. 206 (2005)

GAO sustained a protest alleging that agency issued an improper, out-of-scope, sole-source delivery order for cloud-based software licensesunder a vendor's GSA Federal Supply Schedule BPA where the vendor's BPA catalog did not include cloud based IT services, but instead included only site-based licenses. Tempus Nova, Inc., B-412821, 2016 CPD ¶ 161 (Comp. Gen. 2016)

Protest challenging source selection decision in a best-value procurement conducted under a Blanket Purchase Agreement (BPA) under GSA's Federal Supply Schedule was sustained where the agency selected awardee's higher-rated quotation without meaningfully considering the protester's lower price. The agency's selection decision stated: "Given [awardee's] rating of 'exceptional,' with no other bidders having received an equivalent or higher rating, thereby rendering further analysis under the trade-off approach unnecessary, [awardee] was selected for award." The protest was sustained because the agency did not consider price or conduct a tradeoff analysis as required by the solicitation. NikSoft Sys. Corp., B-406179, 2012 CPD ¶ 104 (Comp. Gen. 2012)

Protest challenging the terms of a commercial item solicitation contemplating the establishment of a BPA with GSA contractors was sustained because the agency failed to perform adequate market research to demonstrate that the "Price Maintenance", "Sales Leakage" and "International Roaming" clauses were consistent with customary commercial practice, as required by FAR 12.301. Verizon Wireless, B-406854, 2012 CPD ¶ 260 (Comp. Gen. 2012)

§ 8.405-4 Price reductions.

Ordering activities may request a price reduction at any time before placing an order, establishing a BPA, or in conjunction with the annual BPA review. However, the ordering activity shall seek a price reduction when the order or BPA exceeds the simplified acquisition threshold. Schedule contractors are not required to pass on to all schedule users a price reduction extended only to an individual ordering activity for a specific order or BPA.

United States Code Annotated

Commercially available off-the-shelf item acquisitions, lists of inapplicable laws in Federal Acquisition Regulation, see 41 USCA § 431.

Contracts, planning, solicitation, evaluation, and award procedures, see 10 USCA § 2305.

Definitions, see 10 USCA § 2302, 41 USCA §§ 259, 403.

Planning and solicitation requirements, see 41 USCA § 253a.

Preference for acquisition of commercial items, see 10 USCA § 2377, 41 USCA § 264b.

§ 8.405-5 Small business.

(a) Although the preference programs of part 19 are not mandatory in this subpart, in accordance with section 1331 of Public Law 111-240 (15 U.S.C. 644(r))—

    (1) Ordering activity contracting officers may, at their discretion—

        (i) Set aside orders for any of the small business concerns identified in 19.000(a)(3); and

        (ii) Set aside BPAs for any of the small business concerns identified in 19.000(a)(3).

(2) When setting aside orders and BPAs—

(i) Follow the ordering procedures for Federal Supply Schedules at 8.405-1, 8.405-2, and 8.405-3; and

(ii) The specific small business program eligibility requirements identified in part 19 apply.

(b) Orders placed against schedule contracts may be credited toward the ordering activity's small business goals. For purposes of reporting an order placed with a small business schedule contractor, an ordering agency may only take credit if the awardee meets a size standard that corresponds to the work performed. Ordering activities should rely on the small business representations made by schedule contractors at the contract level.

(c) Ordering activities may consider socio-economic status when identifying contractor(s) for consideration or competition for award of an order or BPA. At a minimum, ordering activities should consider, if available, at least one small business, veteran-owned small business, service disabled veteran-owned small business, HUBZone small business, women-owned small business, or small disadvantaged business schedule contractor(s). GSA Advantage! and Schedules e-Library at http://www.gsa.gov/fas contain information on the small business representations of Schedule contractors.

(d) For orders exceeding the micro-purchase threshold, ordering activities should give preference to the items of small business concerns when two or more items at the same delivered price will satisfy the requirement.

United States Code Annotated

Commercially available off-the-shelf item acquisitions, lists of inapplicable laws in Federal Acquisition Regulation, see 41 USCA § 431.

Contracts, planning, solicitation, evaluation, and award procedures, see 10 USCA § 2305.

Definitions, see 10 USCA § 2302, 41 USCA §§ 259, 403.

Planning and solicitation requirements, see 41 USCA § 253a.

Preference for acquisition of commercial items, see 10 USCA § 2377, 41 USCA § 264b.

Notes of Decisions

Contracting officer authority 1

1 Contracting officer authority

Air Force's contracting officer's demand that contractor pay reprocurement costs was invalid, and Court of Federal Claims accordingly lacked jurisdiction over demand, where General Services Administration's (GSA's) contracting officer, rather than Air Force's officer, was the appropriate officer to resolve whether contractor's alleged default was excusable and contract termination accordingly should be considered one for convenience of Government, thus affecting liability for reprocurement costs, and GSA's officer had not made a determination. 48 C.F.R. §§ 8.405-5, 32.610(a), 49.401(b), 49.402-6, 52.249-10(b)(1). United Partition Systems, Inc. v. U.S., 59 Fed. Cl. 627, 12 A.L.R. Fed. 2d 867 (2004). United States ⚬═73(4)

Air Force's contracting officer lacked authority to issue "final decision" on contractor's claim for work completed on prefabricated modular building in light of excusability defense raised by contractor; contractor had Multiple Award Schedule (MAS) contract as part of Federal Supply Schedule (FSS) program with General Services Administration (GSA) to provide prefabricated buildings to federal agencies for five years, Air Force chose to purchase from contractor after solicitation to FSS-MAS contract holders, and contractual default clause and regulation applicable to FSS schedule contracts provided that determination of whether failure was excusable was to be made by GSA's contracting officer. Contract Disputes Act of 1978, § 6, 41 U.S.C.A. § 605; 48 C.F.R. §§ 8.402, 8.405-5. United Partition Systems, Inc. v. U.S., 59 Fed. Cl. 627, 12 A.L.R. Fed. 2d 867 (2004). United States ⚬═73(9)

Air Force's contracting officer retained some authority to resolve contractual disputes on contractor's claim for work completed on prefabricated modular building, although final decision regarding excusability defense raised by contractor with Multiple Award Schedule (MAS) contract as part of Federal Supply Schedule (FSS) program was to be resolved by General Services Administration's (GSA's) contracting officer, and thus, Air Force's officer could have issued change order in response to contractor's previous request for equitable adjustment, decided whether to accept and pay for materials delivered by contractor, required contractor to dispose of materials that had been delivered, or issued counterclaim against contractor if excusability defense were rejected by GSA's officer. 48 C.F.R. §§ 8.402, 8.405-5, 8.405-7, 52.246-12, 52.233-1, 52.243-4. United Partition Systems, Inc. v. U.S., 59 Fed. Cl. 627, 12 A.L.R. Fed. 2d 867 (2004). United States ☜73(9)

Contractor's submission of claim seeking written decision to Air Force's contracting officer triggered time for governmental action or having claim deemed denied, for purposes of further judicial review, where two agencies' contracting officers had concurrent, partial authority over claim; upon receipt of claim, Air Force's contracting officer had responsibility for evaluating claim, determining appropriate official to address aspects of claim, forwarding claim as necessary, and either issuing final decision or notifying contractor of date by which valid final decision would be issued, and officer's erroneous decision that he was authorized to issue decision on excusability defense and his failure to forward claim to General Services Administration's (GSA's) contracting officer could not be held against contractor. Contract Disputes Act of 1978, § 6(c)(2, 5), 41 U.S.C.A. § 605(c)(2, 5); 48 C.F.R. §§ 8.402, 8.405-5. United Partition Systems, Inc. v. U.S., 59 Fed. Cl. 627, 12 A.L.R. Fed. 2d 867 (2004). United States ☜73(13)

General Services Administration's (GSA's) contracting officer went beyond scope of her authority by issuing demand for reprocurement costs against claimant, even though Court of Federal Claims had revested officer with authority to issue final decision on claim which was subject of litigation; officer was expressly charged with responsibility and authority to consider claimant's excusability defense, but contract and applicable regulations vested authority in Air Force's contracting officer to issue demand for reprocurement costs. Contract Disputes Act of 1978, § 6(c)(5), 41 U.S.C.A. § 605(c)(5); 48 C.F.R. §§ 8.402, 8.405-5, 8.405-7, 49.402-6, 52.246-12, 52.233-1, 52.243-4. United Partition Systems, Inc. v. U.S., 59 Fed. Cl. 627, 12 A.L.R. Fed. 2d 867 (2004). United States ☜73(9)

§ **8.405-6 Limiting sources.**

Orders placed or BPAs established under Federal Supply Schedules are exempt from the requirements in part 6. However, an ordering activity must justify its action when restricting consideration in accordance with paragraphs (a) or (b) of this section—

(a) Orders or BPAs exceeding the micro-purchase threshold based on a limited sources justification.

(1) Circumstances justifying limiting the source.

(i) For a proposed order or BPA with an estimated value exceeding the micro-purchase threshold not placed or established in accordance with the procedures in 8.405-1, 8.405-2, or 8.405-3, the only circumstances that may justify the action are—

(A) An urgent and compelling need exists, and following the procedures would result in unacceptable delays;

(B) Only one source is capable of providing the supplies or services required at the level of quality required because the supplies or services are unique or highly specialized; or

(C) In the interest of economy and efficiency, the new work is a logical follow-on to an original Federal Supply Schedule order provided that the original order was placed in accordance with the applicable Federal Supply Schedule ordering procedures. The original order or BPA must not have been previously issued under sole-source or limited-sources procedures.

(ii) See 8.405-6(c) for the content of the justification for an order or BPA exceeding the simplified acquisition threshold.

(2) Posting.

(i) Within 14 days after placing an order or establishing a BPA exceeding the simplified acquisition threshold that is supported by a limited-sources justification permitted under any of the circumstances under paragraph (a)(1) of this section, the ordering activity shall—

(A) Publish a notice in accordance with 5.301; and

(B) Post the justification—

(1) At the GPE www.fedbizopps.gov;

(2) On the Web site of the ordering activity agency, which may provide access to the justification by linking to the GPE; and

(3) For a minimum of 30 days.

(ii) In the case of an order or BPA permitted under paragraph (a)(1)(i)(A) of this section, the justification shall be posted within 30 days after award.

(iii) Contracting officers shall carefully screen all justifications for contractor proprietary data and remove all such data, and such references and citations as are necessary to protect the proprietary data, before making the justifications available for public inspection. Contracting officers shall also be guided by the exemptions to disclosure of information contained in the Freedom of Information Act (5 U.S.C. 552) and the prohibitions against disclosure in 24.202 in determining whether other data should be removed. Although the submitter notice process set out in Executive Order 12600 "Predisclosure Notification Procedures for Confidential Commercial Information" does not apply, if the justification appears to contain proprietary data, the contracting officer should provide the contractor that submitted the information an opportunity to review the justification for proprietary data before making the justification available for public inspection, redacted as necessary. This process must not prevent or delay the posting of the justification in accordance with the timeframes required in paragraphs (a)(2)(i) and (ii) of this section.

(iv) This posting requirement does not apply when disclosure would compromise the national security (e.g., would result in disclosure of classified information) or create other security risks.

(b) Items peculiar to one manufacturer. An item peculiar to one manufacturer can be a particular brand name, product, or a feature of a product, peculiar to one manufacturer). A brand name item, whether available on one or more schedule contracts, is an item peculiar to one manufacturer.

(1) Brand name specifications shall not be used unless the particular brand name, product, or feature is essential to the Government's requirements, and market research indicates other companies' similar products, or products lacking the particular feature, do not meet, or cannot be modified to meet, the agency's needs.

(2) Documentation.

(i) For proposed orders or BPAs with an estimated value exceeding the micro-purchase threshold, but not exceeding the simplified acquisition threshold, the ordering activity contracting officer shall document the basis for restricting consideration to an item peculiar to one manufacturer.

(ii) For proposed orders or BPAs with an estimated value exceeding the simplified acquisition threshold, see paragraph (c) of this section.

(iii) The documentation or justification must be completed and approved at the time the requirement for a brand-name item is determined. In addition, the justification for a brand-name item is required at the order level when a justification for the brand-name item was not completed for the BPA or does not adequately cover the requirements in the order.

(3) Posting.

(i) The ordering activity shall post the following information along with the Request for Quotation (RFQ) to e-Buy (http://www.ebuy.gsa.gov):

(A) For proposed orders or BPAs with an estimated value exceeding $25,000, but not exceeding the simplified acquisition threshold, the documentation required by paragraph (b)(2)(i) of this section.

(B) For proposed orders or BPAs with an estimated value exceeding the simplified acquisition threshold, the justification required by paragraph (c) of this section.

(C) The documentation in paragraph (b)(2)(i) and the justification in paragraph (c) of this subsection is subject to the screening requirement in paragraph (a)(2)(iii) of this section.

(ii) The posting requirement of paragraph (b)(3)(i) of this section does not apply when—

(A) Disclosure would compromise the national security (e.g., would result in disclosure of classified information) or create other security risks. The fact that access to classified matter may be necessary to submit a proposal or perform the contract does not, in itself, justify use of this exception;

(B) The nature of the file (e.g., size, format) does not make it cost-effective or practicable for contracting officers to provide access through e-Buy; or

(C) The agency's senior procurement executive makes a written determination that access through e-Buy is not in the Government's interest.

(4) When applicable, the documentation and posting requirements in paragraphs (b)(2) and (3) of this subsection apply only to the portion of the order or BPA that requires a brand-name item. If the justification and approval is to cover only the portion of the acquisition which is brand-name, then it should so state; the approval level requirements will then only apply to that portion.

(c) An order or BPA with an estimated value exceeding the simplified acquisition threshold.

(1) For a proposed order or BPA exceeding the simplified acquisition threshold, the requiring activity shall assist the ordering activity contracting officer in the preparation of the justification. The justification shall cite that the acquisition is conducted under the authority of the Multiple-Award Schedule Program (see 8.401).

(2) At a minimum, each justification shall include the following information:

(i) Identification of the agency and the contracting activity, and specific identification of the document as a "Limited-Sources Justification."

(ii) Nature and/or description of the action being approved.

(iii) A description of the supplies or services required to meet the agency's needs (including the estimated value).

(iv) The authority and supporting rationale (see 8.405-6(a)(1)(i) and (b)(1)) and, if applicable, a demonstration of the proposed contractor's unique qualifications to provide the required supply or service.

(v) A determination by the ordering activity contracting officer that the order represents the best value consistent with 8.404(d).

(vi) A description of the market research conducted among schedule holders and the results or a statement of the reason market research was not conducted.

(vii) Any other facts supporting the justification.

(viii) A statement of the actions, if any, the agency may take to remove or overcome any barriers that led to the restricted consideration before any subsequent acquisition for the supplies or services is made.

(ix) The ordering activity contracting officer's certification that the justification is accurate and complete to the best of the contracting officer's knowledge and belief.

(x) Evidence that any supporting data that is the responsibility of technical or requirements personnel (e.g., verifying the Government's minimum needs or requirements or other rationale for limited sources) and which form a basis for the justification have been certified as complete and accurate by the technical or requirements personnel.

(xi) For justifications under 8.405-6(a)(1), a written determination by the approving official identifying the circumstance that applies.

(d) Justification approvals.

(1) For a proposed order or BPA with an estimated value exceeding the simplified acquisition threshold, but not exceeding $700,000, the ordering activity contracting officer's certification that the justification is accurate and complete to the best of the ordering activity contracting officer's knowledge and belief will serve as approval, unless a higher approval level is established in accordance with agency procedures.

(2) For a proposed order or BPA with an estimated value exceeding $700,000, but not exceeding $13.5 million, the justification must be approved by the advocate for competition of the activity placing the order, or by an official named in paragraph (d)(3) or (d)(4) of this section. This authority is not delegable.

(3) For a proposed order or BPA with an estimated value exceeding $13.5 million, but not exceeding $68 million (or, for DoD, NASA, and the Coast Guard, not exceeding $93 million), the justification must be approved by—

(i) The head of the procuring activity placing the order;

(ii) A designee who—

(A) If a member of the armed forces, is a general or flag officer;

(B) If a civilian, is serving in a position in a grade above GS-15 under the General Schedule (or in a comparable or higher position under another schedule); or

(iii) An official named in paragraph (d)(4) of this section.

(4) For a proposed order or BPA with an estimated value exceeding $68 million (or, for DoD, NASA, and the Coast Guard, over $93 million), the justification must be approved by the senior procurement executive of the agency placing the order. This authority is not delegable, except in the case of the Under Secretary of Defense for Acquisition, Technology, and Logistics, acting as the senior procurement executive for the Department of Defense.

United States Code Annotated

Commercially available off-the-shelf item acquisitions, lists of inapplicable laws in Federal Acquisition Regulation, see 41 USCA § 431.

Contracts, planning, solicitation, evaluation, and award procedures, see 10 USCA § 2305.

Definitions, see 10 USCA § 2302, 41 USCA §§ 259, 403.

Planning and solicitation requirements, see 41 USCA § 253a.

Preference for acquisition of commercial items, see 10 USCA § 2377, 41 USCA § 264b.

Notes of Decisions

In general 1

1 In general

After 19 July 2004, FAR 8.406-4, Termination for cause, not only authorized the ordering activity CO to terminate a Delivery Order for default, but also authorized the CO to determine whether the default was excusable. If the FSS contractor asserts that the failure was excusable, the ordering activity CO must follow the disputes procedures at FAR 8.406-6, which authorize an ordering activity CO to issue a final decision on disputes arising from performance of an order under a FSS contract. In re Spectrum Healthcare Resources, Inc., A.S.B.C.A. No. 55120, 06-2 B.C.A. (CCH) ¶ 33377, 2006 WL 2349230 (Armed Serv. B.C.A. 2006).

§ 8.405-7 Payment.

Agencies may make payments for oral or written orders by any authorized means, including the Governmentwide commercial purchase card (but see 32.1108(b)(2)).

United States Code Annotated

Commercially available off-the-shelf item acquisitions, lists of inapplicable laws in Federal Acquisition Regulation, see 41 USCA § 431.

Contracts, planning, solicitation, evaluation, and award procedures, see 10 USCA § 2305.

Definitions, see 10 USCA § 2302, 41 USCA §§ 259, 403.

Planning and solicitation requirements, see 41 USCA § 253a.

Preference for acquisition of commercial items, see 10 USCA § 2377, 41 USCA § 264b.

§ 8.406 Ordering activity responsibilities.

§ 8.406-1 Order placement.

(a) Ordering activities may place orders orally, except for—

(1) Supplies and services not requiring a statement of work exceeding the simplified acquisition threshold;

(2) Services requiring a statement of work (SOW); and

(3) Orders containing brand-name specifications that exceed $25,000.

(b) Ordering activities may use Optional Form 347, an agency-prescribed form, or an established electronic communications format to order supplies or services from schedule contracts.

(c) The ordering activity shall place an order directly with the contractor in accordance with the terms and conditions of the pricelists (see 8.402(b)). Prior to placement of the order, the ordering activity shall ensure that the regulatory and statutory requirements of the requiring agency have been applied.

(d) Orders shall include the following information in addition to any information required by the schedule contract:

(1) Complete shipping and billing addresses.

(2) Contract number and date.

(3) Agency order number.

(4) F.o.b. delivery point; *i.e.*, origin or destination.

(5) Discount terms.

(6) Delivery time or period of performance.

(7) Special item number or national stock number.

(8) A statement of work for services, when required, or a brief, complete description of each item (when ordering by model number, features and options such as color, finish, and electrical characteristics, if available, must be specified).

(9) Quantity and any variation in quantity.

(10) Number of units.

(11) Unit price.

(12) Total price of order.

(13) Points of inspection and acceptance.

(14) Other pertinent data; *e.g.*, delivery instructions or receiving hours and size-of-truck limitation.

(15) Marking requirements.

(16) Level of preservation, packaging, and packing.

United States Code Annotated

Commercially available off-the-shelf item acquisitions, lists of inapplicable laws in Federal Acquisition Regulation, see 41 USCA § 431.

Contracts, planning, solicitation, evaluation, and award procedures, see 10 USCA § 2305.

Definitions, see 10 USCA § 2302, 41 USCA §§ 259, 403.

Planning and solicitation requirements, see 41 USCA § 253a.

Preference for acquisition of commercial items, see 10 USCA § 2377, 41 USCA § 264b.

Notes of Decisions

In general 1

1 In general

GAO rejected the agency's argument that, because quotations are not "offers" that the agency can accept to form a binding contract, the agency may select a quotation that does not comply with the RFQ's requirements, if the agency finds that the quotation will otherwise satisfy its needs. The legal nature of a quotation vis-à-vis "offer" and "acceptance" in the context of a RFQ issued to Federal Supply Schedule (FSS) vendors does not alter the fundamental requirement that the FSS competition be conducted fairly and in a manner that affords vendors an opportunity to compete on an equal basis. Hanel Storage Sys., L.P., B-409030.2, 2015 CPD ¶ 87 (Comp. Gen. 2015)

Agency's acceptance of a quotation that failed to conform to a material solicitation requirement is unreasonable; a technically unacceptable quotation may not form the basis for award. J. Squared Inc., dba University Loft Co., B-407302, 2013 CPD ¶ 9 (Comp. Gen. 2013)

§ 8.406-2 Inspection and acceptance.

(a) *Supplies.* (1) Consignees shall inspect supplies at destination except when—

(i) The schedule contract indicates that mandatory source inspection is required by the schedule contracting agency; or

(ii) A schedule item is covered by a product description, and the ordering activity determines that the schedule contracting agency's inspection assistance is needed (based on the ordering volume, the complexity of the supplies, or the past performance of the supplier).

(2) When the schedule contracting agency performs the inspection, the ordering activity will provide two copies of the order specifying source inspection to the schedule contracting agency. The schedule contracting agency will notify the ordering activity of acceptance or rejection of the supplies.

(3) Material inspected at source by the schedule contracting agency, and determined to conform with the product description of the schedule, shall not be reinspected for the same purpose. The consignee shall limit inspection to kind, count, and condition on receipt.

(4) Unless otherwise provided in the schedule contract, acceptance is conclusive, except as regards latent defects, fraud, or such gross mistakes as amount to fraud.

(b) *Services.* The ordering activity has the right to inspect all services in accordance with the contract requirements and as called for by the order. The ordering activity shall perform inspections and tests as specified in the order's quality assurance surveillance plan in a manner that will not unduly delay the work.

United States Code Annotated

Commercially available off-the-shelf item acquisitions, lists of inapplicable laws in Federal Acquisition Regulation, see 41 USCA § 431.

Contracts, planning, solicitation, evaluation, and award procedures, see 10 USCA § 2305.

Definitions, see 10 USCA § 2302, 41 USCA §§ 259, 403.

Planning and solicitation requirements, see 41 USCA § 253a.

Preference for acquisition of commercial items, see 10 USCA § 2377, 41 USCA § 264b.

§ 8.406-3 Remedies for nonconformance.

(a) If a contractor delivers a supply or service, but it does not conform to the order requirements, the ordering activity shall take appropriate action in accordance with the inspection and acceptance clause of the contract, as supplemented by the order.

(b) If the contractor fails to perform an order, or take appropriate corrective action, the ordering activity may terminate the order for cause or modify the order to establish a new delivery date (after obtaining consideration, as appropriate). Ordering activities shall follow the procedures at 8.406-4 when terminating an order for cause.

United States Code Annotated

Commercially available off-the-shelf item acquisitions, lists of inapplicable laws in Federal Acquisition Regulation, see 41 USCA § 431.

Contracts, planning, solicitation, evaluation, and award procedures, see 10 USCA § 2305.

Definitions, see 10 USCA § 2302, 41 USCA §§ 259, 403.

Planning and solicitation requirements, see 41 USCA § 253a.

Preference for acquisition of commercial items, see 10 USCA § 2377, 41 USCA § 264b.

§ 8.406-4 Termination for cause.

(a) (1) An ordering activity contracting officer may terminate individual orders for cause. Termination for cause shall comply with FAR 12.403, and may include charging the contractor with excess costs resulting from repurchase.

(2) The schedule contracting office shall be notified of all instances where an ordering activity contracting officer has terminated for cause an individual order to a Federal Supply Schedule contractor, or if fraud is suspected.

(b) If the contractor asserts that the failure was excusable, the ordering activity contracting officer shall follow the procedures at 8.406-6, as appropriate.

(c) If the contractor is charged excess costs, the following apply:

(1) Any repurchase shall be made at as low a price as reasonable, considering the quality required by the Government, delivery requirement, and administrative expenses. Copies of all repurchase orders, except the copy furnished to the contractor or any other

commercial concern, shall include the notation:

Repurchase against the account of _____ [*insert contractor's name*] under Order _____ [*insert number*] under Contract _____ [*insert number*].

(2) When excess costs are anticipated, the ordering activity may withhold funds due the contractor as offset security. Ordering activities shall minimize excess costs to be charged against the contractor and collect or set-off any excess costs owed.

(3) If an ordering activity is unable to collect excess repurchase costs, it shall notify the schedule contracting office after final payment to the contractor.

(i) The notice shall include the following information about the terminated order:

(A) Name and address of the contractor.

(B) Schedule, contract, and order number.

(C) National stock or special item number(s), and a brief description of the item(s).

(D) Cost of schedule items involved.

(E) Excess costs to be collected.

(F) Other pertinent data.

(ii) The notice shall also include the following information about the purchase contract:

(A) Name and address of the contractor.

(B) Item repurchase cost.

(C) Repurchase order number and date of payment.

(D) Contract number, if any.

(E) Other pertinent data.

(d) Only the schedule contracting officer may modify the contract to terminate for cause any, or all, supplies or services covered by the schedule contract. If the schedule contracting officer has terminated any supplies or services covered by the schedule contract, no further orders may be placed for those items. Orders placed prior to termination for cause shall be fulfilled by the contractor, unless terminated for the convenience of the Government by the ordering activity contracting officer.

(e) *Reporting.* An ordering activity contracting officer, in accordance with agency procedures, shall ensure that information related to termination for cause notices and any amendments are reported. In the event the termination for cause is subsequently converted to a termination for convenience, or is otherwise withdrawn, the contracting officer shall ensure that a notice of the conversion or withdrawal is reported. All reporting shall be in accordance with 42.1503(h).

§ 8.406-5 Termination for the Government's convenience.

(a) An ordering activity contracting officer may terminate individual orders for the Government's convenience. Terminations for the Government's convenience shall comply with FAR 12.403.

(b) Before terminating orders for the Government's convenience, the ordering activity contracting officer shall endeavor to enter into a "no cost" settlement agreement with the contractor.

(c) Only the schedule contracting officer may modify the schedule contract to terminate any, or all, supplies or services covered by the schedule contract for the Government's convenience.

United States Code Annotated

Commercially available off-the-shelf item acquisitions, lists of inapplicable laws in Federal Acquisition Regulation, see 41 USCA § 431.

Contracts, planning, solicitation, evaluation, and award procedures, see 10 USCA § 2305.

Definitions, see 10 USCA § 2302, 41 USCA §§ 259, 403.

Planning and solicitation requirements, see 41 USCA § 253a.

Preference for acquisition of commercial items, see 10 USCA § 2377, 41 USCA § 264b.

§ 8.406-6 Disputes.

(a) *Disputes pertaining to the performance of orders under a schedule contract.* (1) Under the Disputes clause of the schedule contract, the ordering activity contracting officer may—

(i) Issue final decisions on disputes arising from performance of the order (but see paragraph (b) of this section); or

(ii) Refer the dispute to the schedule contracting officer.

(2) The ordering activity contracting officer shall notify the schedule contracting officer promptly of any final decision.

(b) *Disputes pertaining to the terms and conditions of schedule contracts.* The ordering activity contracting officer shall refer all disputes that relate to the contract terms and conditions to the schedule contracting officer for resolution under the Disputes clause of the contract and notify the schedule contractor of the referral.

(c) *Appeals.* Contractors may appeal final decisions to either the Board of Contract Appeals servicing the agency that issued the final decision or the U.S. Court of Federal Claims.

(d) *Alternative dispute resolution.* The contracting officer should use the alternative dispute resolution (ADR) procedures, to the maximum extent practicable (see 33.204 and 33.214).

United States Code Annotated

Commercially available off-the-shelf item acquisitions, lists of inapplicable laws in Federal Acquisition Regulation, see 41 USCA § 431.

Contracts, planning, solicitation, evaluation, and award procedures, see 10 USCA § 2305.

Definitions, see 10 USCA § 2302, 41 USCA §§ 259, 403.

Planning and solicitation requirements, see 41 USCA § 253a.

Preference for acquisition of commercial items, see 10 USCA § 2377, 41 USCA § 264b.

Notes of Decisions

In general 1

1 In general

An ordering contracting officer lacks authority to decide a dispute requiring interpretation of a Federal Supply Schedule contract clause, in whole or in part, regardless of whether the parties frame the dispute as pertaining to the performance of the order. The ordering CO does have authority to construe the terms of the order under an FSS contract, if the dispute does not involve interpretation of the schedule contract. A decision by the proper CO is a prerequisite to BCA jurisdiction. Sharp Elecs. Corp. v. McHugh, 707 F.3d 1367 (Fed. Cir. 2013)

Ordering agency contracting officer may decide a claim arising under an order placed against a Blanket Purchase Agreement (BPA) established under a GSA Federal Supply Schedule (FSS), because the claim did not require interpretation of the FSS contract and was properly submitted to the ordering agency contracting officer. The ASBCA also determined that claims arising from orders under a BPA are properly decided by the ordering agency (Army) instead of the agency that issued the BPA (Navy). A BPA is not a contract, and a contract is formed only when an order is issued. Therefore, it was proper for the Army CO to address claims arising from the Navy BPA orders. Hewlett-Packard Co., ASBCA 57940 (Armed Serv. B.C.A. 2013)

A contractor's claim for fees due for early termination of a delivery order for the lease of equipment pertained to the terms of a GSA Multiple Award Schedule contract, and therefore the ordering activity contracting officer did not have authority to resolve the dispute. Therefore, the deemed denial of the contractor's claim could not serve as the basis for the ASBCA's jurisdiction. Sharp Elecs. Corp., ASBCA 57583, 12-1 B.C.A. (CCH) ¶ 34903, 2011 WL 6337659 (Armed Serv. B.C.A. 2011)

Board of Contract Appeals lacked jurisdiction because contracting officer did not have authority to issue final decision on claim arising under FSS order. Under the FAR, all disputes relating to the contract terms and conditions must be referred to GSA's schedule contracting officer. FAR 8.406-6. The contracting officer had no authority to issue a final decision on the contractor's claim and the "final decision" is, therefore, a nullity. The contracting officer is obligated under the FAR to refer the matter to the GSA. Under the Contract Disputes Act without a proper final decision, the Board has no jurisdiction over the appeal. Appeal of CritiCom, Inc., V.A.B.C.A. No. 7538, 06-2 B.C.A. (CCH) ¶ 33369, 2006 WL 2328778 (Veterans Admin. B.C.A. 2006)

After 19 July 2004, FAR 8.406-4, Termination for cause, not only authorized the ordering activity CO to terminate a Delivery Order for default, but also authorized the CO to determine whether the default was excusable. If the FSS contractor asserts that the failure was excusable, the ordering activity CO must follow the disputes procedures at FAR 8.406-6, which authorize an ordering activity CO to issue a final decision on disputes arising from performance of an order under a FSS contract, provided that the dispute does not pertain to the terms or conditions of the FSS contract itself. In re Spectrum Healthcare Resources, Inc., A.S.B.C.A. No. 55120, 06-2 B.C.A. (CCH) ¶ 33377, 2006 WL 2349230 (Armed Serv. B.C.A. 2006).

Air Force's contracting officer lacked authority to issue "final decision" on contractor's claim for work completed on prefabricated modular building in light of excusability defense raised by contractor; contractor had Multiple Award Schedule (MAS) contract as part of Federal Supply Schedule (FSS) program with General Services Administration (GSA) to provide prefabricated buildings to federal agencies for five years, Air Force chose to purchase from contractor after solicitation to FSS-MAS contract holders, and contractual default clause and regulation applicable to FSS schedule contracts provided that determination of whether failure was excusable was to be made by GSA's contracting officer. Contract Disputes Act of 1978, § 6, 41 U.S.C.A. § 605; FAR 8.402, 8.405-5. United Partition Systems, Inc. v. U.S., 59 Fed. Cl. 627, 12 A.L.R. Fed. 2d 867 (2004)

§ 8.406-7 Contractor Performance Evaluation.

Ordering activities must prepare at least annually and at the time the work under the order is completed, an evaluation of contractor performance for each order that exceeds the simplified acquisition threshold in accordance with 42.1502(c).

Subpart 8.5 Acquisition of Helium

§ 8.500 Scope of subpart.

This subpart implements the requirements of the Helium Act (50 U.S.C. 167, *et seq.*) concerning the acquisition of liquid or gaseous helium by Federal agencies or by Government contractors or subcontractors for use in the performance of a Government contract (also see 43 CFR Part 3195).

United States Code Annotated

Commercially available off-the-shelf item acquisitions, lists of inapplicable laws in Federal Acquisition Regulation, see 41 USCA § 431.

Contracts, planning, solicitation, evaluation, and award procedures, see 10 USCA § 2305.

Definitions, see 10 USCA § 2302, 41 USCA §§ 259, 403.

Planning and solicitation requirements, see 41 USCA § 253a.

Preference for acquisition of commercial items, see 10 USCA § 2377, 41 USCA § 264b.

§ 8.501 Definitions.

As used in this subpart—

"Bureau of Land Management" means the—

Department of the Interior
Bureau of Land Management
Amarillo Field Office
Helium Operations
801 South Fillmore Street
Suite 500
Amarillo, TX 79101-3545.

"Federal helium supplier" means a private helium vendor that has an in-kind crude helium sales contract with the Bureau of Land Management (BLM) and that is on the BLM Amarillo Field Office's Authorized List of Federal Helium Suppliers available via the Internet at http://blm.gov/8pjd.

"Major helium requirement" means an estimated refined helium requirement greater than 200,000 standard cubic feet (scf) (measured at 14.7 pounds per square inch absolute pressure and 70 degrees Fahrenheit temperature) of gaseous helium or 7510 liters of liquid helium delivered to a helium use location per year.

United States Code Annotated

Commercially available off-the-shelf item acquisitions, lists of inapplicable laws in Federal Acquisition Regulation, see 41 USCA § 431.

Contracts, planning, solicitation, evaluation, and award procedures, see 10 USCA § 2305.

Definitions, see 10 USCA § 2302, 41 USCA §§ 259, 403.

Planning and solicitation requirements, see 41 USCA § 253a.

Preference for acquisition of commercial items, see 10 USCA § 2377, 41 USCA § 264b.

§ 8.502 Policy.

Agencies and their contractors and subcontractors must purchase major helium requirements from Federal helium suppliers, to the extent that supplies are available.

United States Code Annotated

Commercially available off-the-shelf item acquisitions, lists of inapplicable laws in Federal Acquisition Regulation, see 41 USCA § 431.

Contracts, planning, solicitation, evaluation, and award procedures, see 10 USCA § 2305.

Definitions, see 10 USCA § 2302, 41 USCA §§ 259, 403.

Planning and solicitation requirements, see 41 USCA § 253a.

Preference for acquisition of commercial items, see 10 USCA § 2377, 41 USCA § 264b.

§ 8.503 Exception.

The requirements of this subpart do not apply to contracts or subcontracts in which the helium was acquired by the contractor prior to award of the contract or subcontract.

United States Code Annotated

Commercially available off-the-shelf item acquisitions, lists of inapplicable laws in Federal Acquisition Regulation, see 41 USCA § 431.

Contracts, planning, solicitation, evaluation, and award procedures, see 10 USCA § 2305.

Definitions, see 10 USCA § 2302, 41 USCA §§ 259, 403.

Planning and solicitation requirements, see 41 USCA § 253a.

Preference for acquisition of commercial items, see 10 USCA § 2377, 41 USCA § 264b.

§ 8.504 Procedures.

The contracting officer must forward the following information to the Bureau of Land Management within 45 days of the close of each fiscal quarter:

(a) The name of any company that supplied a major helium requirement.

(b) The amount of helium purchased.

(c) The delivery date(s).

(d) The location where the helium was used.

United States Code Annotated

Commercially available off-the-shelf item acquisitions, lists of inapplicable laws in Federal Acquisition Regulation, see 41 USCA § 431.

Contracts, planning, solicitation, evaluation, and award procedures, see 10 USCA § 2305.

Definitions, see 10 USCA § 2302, 41 USCA §§ 259, 403.

Planning and solicitation requirements, see 41 USCA § 253a.

Preference for acquisition of commercial items, see 10 USCA § 2377, 41 USCA § 264b.

§ 8.505 Contract clause.

Insert the clause at 52.208-8, Required Sources for Helium and Helium Usage Data, in solicitations and contracts if it is anticipated that performance of the contract involves a major helium requirement.

United States Code Annotated

Commercially available off-the-shelf item acquisitions, lists of inapplicable laws in Federal Acquisition Regulation, see 41 USCA § 431.

Contracts, planning, solicitation, evaluation, and award procedures, see 10 USCA § 2305.

Definitions, see 10 USCA § 2302, 41 USCA §§ 259, 403.

Planning and solicitation requirements, see 41 USCA § 253a.

Preference for acquisition of commercial items, see 10 USCA § 2377, 41 USCA § 264b.

Subpart 8.6 Acquisition from Federal Prison Industries, Inc.

§ 8.601 General.

(a) Federal Prison Industries, Inc. (FPI), also referred to as UNICOR, is a self-supporting, wholly owned Government corporation of the District of Columbia.

(b) FPI provides training and employment for prisoners confined in Federal penal and correctional institutions through the sale of its supplies and services to Government agencies (18 U.S.C. 4121–4128).

(c) FPI diversifies its supplies and services to minimize adverse impact on private industry.

(d) Supplies manufactured and services performed by FPI are listed in the FPI Schedule, which can be accessed at http://www.unicor.gov or by submitting a written request to Federal Prison Industries, Inc., Department of Justice, Washington, DC 20534.

(e) Agencies are encouraged to purchase FPI supplies and services to the maximum extent practicable.

United States Code Annotated

Commercially available off-the-shelf item acquisitions, lists of inapplicable laws in Federal Acquisition Regulation, see 41 USCA § 431.

Contracts, planning, solicitation, evaluation, and award procedures, see 10 USCA § 2305.

Definitions, see 10 USCA § 2302, 41 USCA §§ 259, 403.

Planning and solicitation requirements, see 41 USCA § 253a.

Preference for acquisition of commercial items, see 10 USCA § 2377, 41 USCA § 264b.

§ 8.602 Policy.

(a) In accordance with 10 U.S.C. 2410n and Section 637 of Division H of the Consolidated Appropriations Act, 2005 (Pub. L. 108-447) (18 U.S.C. 4124 note), and except as provided in paragraph (b) of this section, agencies shall—

(1) Before purchasing an item of supply listed in the FPI Schedule, conduct market research to determine whether the FPI item is comparable to supplies available from the private sector that best meet the Government's needs in terms of price, quality, and time of delivery. This is a unilateral determination made at the discretion of the contracting officer. The arbitration provisions of 18 U.S.C. 4124(b) do not apply.

(2) Prepare a written determination that includes supporting rationale explaining the assessment of price, quality, and time of delivery, based on the results of market research comparing the FPI item to supplies available from the private sector.

(3) If the FPI item is comparable, purchase the item from FPI following the ordering procedures at http://www.unicor.gov, unless a waiver is obtained in accordance with 8.604.

(4) If the FPI item is not comparable in one or more of the areas of price, quality, and time of delivery—

(i) Acquire the item using—

(A) Competitive procedures (e.g., the procedures in 6.102, the set-aside procedures in Subpart 19.5, or competition conducted in accordance with Part 13); or

(B) The fair opportunity procedures in 16.505, if placing an order under a multiple award delivery-order contract;

(ii) Include FPI in the solicitation process and consider a timely offer from FPI for award in accordance with the item description or specifications, and evaluation factors in the solicitation—

(A) If the solicitation is available through the Governmentwide point of entry (FedBizOpps), it is not necessary to provide a separate copy of the solicitation to FPI;

(B) If the solicitation is not available through FedBizOpps, provide a copy of the solicitation to FPI;

(iii) When using a multiple award schedule issued under the procedures in Subpart 8.4 or when using the fair opportunity procedures in 16.505—

(A) Establish and communicate to FPI the item description or specifications, and evaluation factors that will be used as the basis for selecting a source, so that an offer from FPI can be evaluated on the same basis as the contract or schedule holder; and

(B) Consider a timely offer from FPI;

(iv) Award to the source offering the item determined by the agency to provide the best value to the Government; and

(v) When the FPI item is determined to provide the best value to the Government as a result of FPI's response to a competitive solicitation, follow the ordering procedures at http://www.unicor.gov.

(b) The procedures in paragraph (a) of this section do not apply if an exception in 8.605(b) through (g) applies.

(c) In some cases where FPI and an AbilityOne participating nonprofit agency produce identical items (see 8.603), FPI grants a waiver to permit the Government to purchase a portion of its requirement from the AbilityOne participating nonprofit agency. When this occurs, the portion of the requirement for which FPI has granted a waiver—

(1) Shall be purchased from the AbilityOne participating nonprofit agency using the procedures in Subpart 8.7; and

(2) Shall not be subject to the procedures in paragraph (a) of this section.

(d) Disputes regarding price, quality, character, or suitability of supplies produced by FPI, except for determinations under paragraph (a)(1) of this section, are subject to arbitration as specified in 18 U.S.C. 4124. The statute provides that the arbitration shall be conducted by a board consisting of the Comptroller General of the United States, the Administrator of General Services, and the President, or their representatives. The decisions of the board are final and binding on all parties.

United States Code Annotated

Commercially available off-the-shelf item acquisitions, lists of inapplicable laws in Federal Acquisition Regulation, see 41 USCA § 431.

Contracts, planning, solicitation, evaluation, and award procedures, see 10 USCA § 2305.

Definitions, see 10 USCA § 2302, 41 USCA §§ 259, 403.

Planning and solicitation requirements, see 41 USCA § 253a.

Preference for acquisition of commercial items, see 10 USCA § 2377, 41 USCA § 264b.

Notes of Decisions

In general 1
Administrative hearings and adjudications 7
Discretion of agency 6
Eminent domain and just compensation 2
Judicial review 11
Jurisdiction 9
Laches and stale demands 8

Market share analysis 4
Protests and disputes 3
Standing 10
Waiver of objections 5

1 In general

Agencies must purchase supplies manufactured by FPI where, after conducting market research, the agency determines that supplies produced by FPI are comparable to those of the private sector in terms of price, quality, and time of delivery. FAR 8.602(a)(1), (3). Management Solutions, L.C. d/b/a EssTech Engineering, B-298883, B-298883.2, 2006 CPD ¶ 197 (Comp. Gen. 2006)

2 Eminent domain and just compensation

The increases in federal office furniture production by Federal Prison Industries (FPI) did not result in onerous and unreasonable restrictions on the use of private manufacturers, property as to constitute a Fifth Amendment taking, where manufacturers merely lost market share, rather than suffered direct appropriation of property. U.S.C.A. Const. Amend. 5; 18 U.S.C.A. § 4122. Coalition for Government Procurement v. Federal Prison Industries, 154 F. Supp. 2d 1140 (W.D. Mich. 2001), aff'd in part, remanded in part, 365 F.3d 435, 2004 FED App. 0101P (6th Cir. 2004). Eminent Domain ⟜2.39

Where there has been no direct appropriation of property by governmental agencies, consequential damages resulting from the exercise of lawful regulations are not compensable takings within the purview of the Fifth Amendment. U.S.C.A. Const.Amend. 5. Coalition for Government Procurement v. Federal Prison Industries, 154 F. Supp. 2d 1140 (W.D. Mich. 2001), aff'd in part, remanded in part, 365 F.3d 435, 2004 FED App. 0101P (6th Cir. 2004). Eminent Domain ⟜2.1

3 Protests and disputes

General Accounting Office will not review protest of agency's determination that Federal Prison Industry's (UNICOR) product was not comparable to private sector products, since UNICOR's enabling statute provides for binding resolution of such disputes by an arbitration board. 18 U.S.C. § 4124(b). Federal Prison Industries, Inc., B-290546, 2002 CPD ¶ 112 (Comp. Gen. 2002)

4 Market share analysis

Non-profit trade association representing manufacturers of office furniture suffered no discernible prejudice as result of error by agency charged with managing federal-inmate labor in authorizing start-up of new systems furniture factory at federal prison without performing requisite market share analysis, since subsequent review of market share revealed allowable increase. 5 U.S.C.A. § 706. Coalition for Government Procurement v. Federal Prison Industries, Inc., 365 F.3d 435, 2004 FED App. 0101P (6th Cir. 2004). Convicts' ⟜10(5)

Agency charged with managing federal-inmate labor was not required to perform Comprehensive Advanced Review Process (CARP) or market share analysis before authorizing new systems furniture factory at federal prison, since, by the time factory opened, agency's production of systems furniture was within approved levels. 18 U.S.C.A. § 4122. Coalition for Government Procurement v. Federal Prison Industries, Inc., 365 F.3d 435, 2004 FED App. 0101P (6th Cir. 2004). Convicts ⟜10(5)

Agency charged with managing federal-inmate labor was not required to perform market share analysis when dorm and quarters (D&Q) furniture factory manufactured special order of office seating furniture, since agency offset $44,545 in office-seating sales at D&Q factory with corresponding decrease of $1.8 million in sales at four office seating factories. 18 U.S.C.A. § 4122. Coalition for Government Procurement v. Federal Prison Industries, Inc., 365 F.3d 435, 2004 FED App. 0101P (6th Cir. 2004). Convicts ⟜10(5)

Agency charged with managing federal-inmate labor was not required to perform Comprehensive Advanced Review Process (CARP) before increasing inmate employment at office seating furniture factories by more than 10%, since agency estimated that its market share would decrease, and, even though market share actually increased, increase was within agency's allowable market share. 18 U.S.C.A. § 4122. Coalition for Government Procurement v. Federal Prison Industries, Inc., 365 F.3d 435, 2004 FED App. 0101P (6th Cir. 2004). Convicts ☞10(5)

Agency charged with managing federal-inmate labor was not required to perform market share analysis before increasing employment levels at office seating furniture factories, or authorizing activation of new factories, since agency's operating plan for year estimated decrease in sales from previous year. 18 U.S.C.A. § 4122. Coalition for Government Procurement v. Federal Prison Industries, Inc., 365 F.3d 435, 2004 FED App. 0101P (6th Cir. 2004). Convicts ☞10(5)

5 Waiver of objections

Coalition of manufacturers, distributors, and businesses waived its objections to Federal Prison Industries' (FPI) expansion of its furniture production, where coalition members did not raise objections during three separate meetings of the FPI Board, and coalition members were aware of meetings, aware that procedural violations were to be raised at the meeting, and had fully participated at the meetings. Coalition for Government Procurement v. Federal Prison Industries, 154 F. Supp. 2d 1140 (W.D. Mich. 2001), aff'd in part, remanded in part, 365 F.3d 435, 2004 FED App. 0101P (6th Cir. 2004). Convicts ☞10(5)

6 Discretion of agency

Coalition of manufacturers, distributors, and businesses were unable to show injury in fact resulting from Federal Prison Industries' (FPI) practice of exercising its discretion as to whether it would require private contractors of federal agency to purchase furniture from FPI or whether FPI would waive its right to supply the agency with furniture, and thus did not have standing to challenge the practice. 18 U.S.C.A. § 4122. Coalition for Government Procurement v. Federal Prison Industries, 154 F. Supp. 2d 1140 (W.D. Mich. 2001), aff'd in part, remanded in part, 365 F.3d 435, 2004 FED App. 0101P (6th Cir. 2004). Convicts ☞10(5)

"Pass-through" sales of Federal Prison Industries (FPI), which occurred when FPI was unable to meet a production deadline and would purchase the product from a private manufacturer and resell it to the purchasing federal agency, were within the scope of the discretion granted to the FPI and its Board under its governing statute. 18 U.S.C.A. § 4122. Coalition for Government Procurement v. Federal Prison Industries, 154 F. Supp. 2d 1140 (W.D. Mich. 2001), aff'd in part, remanded in part, 365 F.3d 435, 2004 FED App. 0101P (6th Cir. 2004). Convicts ☞10(5)

7 Administrative hearings and adjudications

Requirement of issue exhaustion, precluding court reviewing agency decision from considering arguments not raised before administrative agency, did not apply to challenge by non-profit trade association representing manufacturers of office furniture to decision by agency charged with managing federal-inmate labor to significantly expand production of office furniture as violation of agency's organic statute, since agency's board's significant expansion hearings were not adversarial; rules governing hearings vested full fact-finding authority with board and limited record to be considered by board, and hearings bore hallmarks of inquisitorial proceedings. 18 U.S.C.A. § 4122. Coalition for Government Procurement v. Federal Prison Industries, Inc., 365 F.3d 435, 2004 FED App. 0101P (6th Cir. 2004). Administrative Law And Procedure ☞501; Convicts ☞10(5)

8 Laches and stale demands

Claims by non-profit trade association representing manufacturers of office furniture that expansion by agency charged with managing federal-inmate labor of production of office furniture violated agency's organic statute were not barred by laches; association filed its complaint well within analogous limitations period, and association could not be said to have unreasonably delayed in filing suit. 18 U.S.C.A. § 4122; 28 U.S.C.A. § 2401(a). Coalition for Government Procurement v. Federal Prison Industries, Inc., 365 F.3d 435, 2004 FED App. 0101P (6th Cir. 2004). Equity ☞87(1)

9 Jurisdiction

Tucker Act did not require non-profit trade association representing manufacturers of office furniture to bring Fifth Amendment just compensation claim against agency charged with managing federal-inmate labor in Federal Court of Claims, since agency was self-sufficient corporation that did not operate with appropriated funds. U.S.C.A. Const. Amend. 5; 28 U.S.C.A. § 1491(a)(1). Coalition for Government Procurement v. Federal Prison Industries, Inc., 365 F.3d 435, 2004 FED App. 0101P (6th Cir. 2004). Federal Courts ⬥1139

Claim for just compensation asserted against United States under Fifth Amendment must be brought to Federal Court of Claims in first instance, unless Congress has otherwise withdrawn Tucker Act grant of jurisdiction. U.S.C.A. Const.Amend. 5; 28 U.S.C.A. § 1491(a)(1). Coalition for Government Procurement v. Federal Prison Industries, Inc., 365 F.3d 435, 2004 FED App. 0101P (6th Cir. 2004). Federal Courts ⬥1139

Claims by non-profit trade association representing manufacturers of office furniture that unauthorized significant expansions by agency charged with managing federal-inmate labor of production of office furniture violated Administrative Procedure Act (APA) presented actual cases or controversies under Article III, since court had broad discretionary authority to award relief in manner akin to "equitable volume sales replacement remedy" proposed by association. U.S.C.A. Const. Art. 3, § 2, cl. 1; 5 U.S.C.A. § 551 et seq. Coalition for Government Procurement v. Federal Prison Industries, Inc., 365 F.3d 435, 2004 FED App. 0101P (6th Cir. 2004). Federal Courts ⬥13

Statute permitting, but not requiring, private sector contractors employed on projects for Department of Defense (DOD) to purchase office furniture from agency charged with managing federal-inmate labor did not moot claim by nonprofit trade association representing manufacturers of office furniture that agency's practice of enforcing its mandatorysource preference by selling office furniture directly to private sector contractors for installation in federal facility violated statutory prohibition on agency's sale of goods to public in competition with private enterprise, since agency's practice extended beyond DOD projects. 18 U.S.C.A. § 4122. Coalition for Government Procurement v. Federal Prison Industries, Inc., 365 F.3d 435, 2004 FED App. 0101P (6th Cir. 2004). Federal Courts ⬥13

Claim by non-profit trade association representing manufacturers of office furniture that unauthorized significant expansion by agency charged with managing federal-inmate labor of production of office furniture violated agency's organic statute and Administrative Procedure Act (APA) presented justiciable case or controversy under Article III, since association's proposed equitable remedies ordering "rollback" or "capping" of agency's production would have impacted agency's current production levels. U.S.C.A. Const. Art. 3, § 2, cl. 1; 5 U.S.C.A. § 551 et seq.; 18 U.S.C.A. § 4122 et seq. Coalition for Government Procurement v. Federal Prison Industries, Inc., 365 F.3d 435, 2004 FED App. 0101P (6th Cir. 2004). Federal Courts ⬥13

10 Standing

Non-profit trade association representing manufacturers of office furniture had standing to challenge practice of agency charged with managing federal-inmate labor of enforcing its mandatory-source preference by selling office furniture directly to private sector contractor for installation in federal facility, as violation of statutory prohibition on agency's sale of goods to public in competition with private enterprise, since association member identified alleged injury resulting from practice; member identified instance when general contractor ultimately purchased office furniture from agency, rather than member. 18 U.S.C.A. § 4122. Coalition for Government Procurement v. Federal Prison Industries, Inc., 365 F.3d 435, 2004 FED App. 0101P (6th Cir. 2004). Convicts ⬥10(5)

Coalition of manufacturers, distributors, and businesses lacked standing to raise challenge that Federal Prison Industries (FPI) would purchase a product directly from a private manufacturer and resell it to a federal agency as a "passthrough," in violation of FPI's governing statute, where coalition members could not show an injury in fact. 18 U.S.C.A. § 4122. Coalition for Government Procurement v. Federal Prison Industries, 154 F. Supp. 2d 1140 (W.D. Mich. 2001), aff'd in part, remanded in part, 365 F.3d 435, 2004 FED App. 0101P (6th Cir. 2004). Convicts ⬥10(5)

11 Judicial review

Remand to agency charged with managing federal-inmate labor for further action consistent with correct legal standards was unnecessary after Court of Appeals determined that agency lacked authority to retroactively authorize prior significant expansion of production of office seating furniture, since agency had already complied with only instructions Court of Appeals could have given it; agency had already elicited public comments on expansion, and made specific findings as to whether it had obtained more than reasonable share of market. 18 U.S.C.A. § 4122. Coalition for Government Procurement v. Federal Prison Industries, Inc., 365 F.3d 435, 2004 FED App. 0101P (6th Cir. 2004). Convicts ⊂⊃10(5)

On review, decisions of Federal Prison Industries (FPI) Board are entitled to a presumption of regularity. 5 U.S.C.A. § 706(2)(A–D); 18 U.S.C.A. § 4122. Coalition for Government Procurement v. Federal Prison Industries, 154 F. Supp. 2d 1140 (W.D. Mich. 2001), aff'd in part, remanded in part, 365 F.3d 435, 2004 FED App. 0101P (6th Cir. 2004). Convicts ⊂⊃10(5)

§ 8.603 Purchase priorities.

FPI and nonprofit agencies participating in the AbilityOne Program under 41 U.S.C. chapter 85, Committee for Purchase from People Who Are Blind or Severely Disabled (see Subpart 8.7) may produce identical supplies or services. When this occurs, ordering offices shall purchase supplies and services in the following priorities:

(a) Supplies.

(1) Federal Prison Industries, Inc. (41 U.S.C. 8504).

(2) AbilityOne participating nonprofit agencies.

(3) Commercial sources.

(b) Services.

(1) AbilityOne participating nonprofit agencies.

(2) Federal Prison Industries, Inc., or commercial sources.

United States Code Annotated

Commercially available off-the-shelf item acquisitions, lists of inapplicable laws in Federal Acquisition Regulation, see 41 USCA § 431.

Contracts, planning, solicitation, evaluation, and award procedures, see 10 USCA § 2305.

Definitions, see 10 USCA § 2302, 41 USCA §§ 259, 403.

Planning and solicitation requirements, see 41 USCA § 253a.

Preference for acquisition of commercial items, see 10 USCA § 2377, 41 USCA § 264b.

§ 8.604 Waivers.

FPI may grant a waiver for purchase of supplies in the FPI Schedule from another source. FPI waivers ordinarily are of the following types:

(a) General or blanket waivers issued when classes of supplies are not available from FPI.

(b) Formal waivers issued in response to requests from offices desiring to acquire, from other sources, supplies listed in the FPI Schedule and not covered by a general waiver. Agencies shall process waiver requests in accordance with the procedures at http://www.un icor.gov.

United States Code Annotated

Commercially available off-the-shelf item acquisitions, lists of inapplicable laws in Federal Acquisition Regulation, see 41 USCA § 431.

Contracts, planning, solicitation, evaluation, and award procedures, see 10 USCA § 2305.

Definitions, see 10 USCA § 2302, 41 USCA §§ 259, 403.

Planning and solicitation requirements, see 41 USCA § 253a.

Preference for acquisition of commercial items, see 10 USCA § 2377, 41 USCA § 264b.

§ 8.605 Exceptions.

Purchase from FPI is not mandatory and a waiver is not required if—

(a) (1) The contracting officer makes a determination that the FPI item of supply is not comparable to supplies available from the private sector that best meet the Government's needs in terms of price, quality, and time of delivery; and

(2) The item is acquired in accordance with 8.602(a)(4);

(b) Public exigency requires immediate delivery or performance;

(c) Suitable used or excess supplies are available;

(d) The supplies are acquired and used outside the United States;

(e) Acquiring listed items totaling $3,500 or less;

(f) Acquiring items that FPI offers exclusively on a competitive (non-mandatory) basis, as identified in the FPI Schedule; or

(g) Acquiring services.

United States Code Annotated

Commercially available off-the-shelf item acquisitions, lists of inapplicable laws in Federal Acquisition Regulation, see 41 USCA § 431.

Contracts, planning, solicitation, evaluation, and award procedures, see 10 USCA § 2305.

Definitions, see 10 USCA § 2302, 41 USCA §§ 259, 403.

Planning and solicitation requirements, see 41 USCA § 253a.

Preference for acquisition of commercial items, see 10 USCA § 2377, 41 USCA § 264b.

§ 8.606 Evaluating FPI performance.

Agencies shall evaluate FPI contract performance in accordance with Subpart 42.15. Performance evaluations do not negate the requirements of 8.602 and 8.604, but they may be used to support a waiver request in accordance with 8.604.

United States Code Annotated

Commercially available off-the-shelf item acquisitions, lists of inapplicable laws in Federal Acquisition Regulation, see 41 USCA § 431.

Contracts, planning, solicitation, evaluation, and award procedures, see 10 USCA § 2305.

Definitions, see 10 USCA § 2302, 41 USCA §§ 259, 403.

Planning and solicitation requirements, see 41 USCA § 253a.

Preference for acquisition of commercial items, see 10 USCA § 2377, 41 USCA § 264b.

§ 8.607 Performance as a subcontractor.

Agencies shall not require a contractor, or subcontractor at any tier, to use FPI as a subcontractor for performance of a contract by any means, including means such as—

(a) A solicitation provision requiring a potential contractor to offer to make use of FPI supplies or services;

(b) A contract specification requiring the contractor to use specific supplies or services (or classes of supplies or services) offered by FPI; or

(c) Any contract modification directing the use of FPI supplies or services.

United States Code Annotated

Commercially available off-the-shelf item acquisitions, lists of inapplicable laws in Federal Acquisition Regulation, see 41 USCA § 431.

Contracts, planning, solicitation, evaluation, and award procedures, see 10 USCA § 2305.

Definitions, see 10 USCA § 2302, 41 USCA §§ 259, 403.

Planning and solicitation requirements, see 41 USCA § 253a.

Preference for acquisition of commercial items, see 10 USCA § 2377, 41 USCA § 264b.

§ 8.608 Protection of classified and sensitive information.

Agencies shall not enter into any contract with FPI that allows an inmate worker access to any—

(a) Classified data;

(b) Geographic data regarding the location of—

(1) Surface and subsurface infrastructure providing communications or water or electrical power distribution;

(2) Pipelines for the distribution of natural gas, bulk petroleum products, or other commodities; or

(3) Other utilities; or

(c) Personal or financial information about any individual private citizen, including information relating to such person's real property however described, without the prior consent of the individual.

United States Code Annotated

Commercially available off-the-shelf item acquisitions, lists of inapplicable laws in Federal Acquisition Regulation, see 41 USCA § 431.

Contracts, planning, solicitation, evaluation, and award procedures, see 10 USCA § 2305.

Definitions, see 10 USCA § 2302, 41 USCA §§ 259, 403.

Planning and solicitation requirements, see 41 USCA § 253a.

Preference for acquisition of commercial items, see 10 USCA § 2377, 41 USCA § 264b.

Subpart 8.7 Acquisition from Nonprofit Agencies Employing People Who Are Blind or Severely Disabled

§ 8.700 Scope of subpart.

This subpart prescribes the policies and procedures for implementing the Javits-Wagner-O'Day Act (41 U.S.C. 46–48c) and the rules of the Committee for Purchase from People Who Are Blind or Severely Disabled (41 CFR Chapter 51) which implements the AbilityOne Program.

United States Code Annotated

Commercially available off-the-shelf item acquisitions, lists of inapplicable laws in Federal Acquisition Regulation, see 41 USCA § 431.

Committee for Purchase From People Who Are Blind or Severely Disabled, see 41 USCA § 46.

Contracts, planning, solicitation, evaluation, and award procedures, see 10 USCA § 2305.

Definitions, see 10 USCA § 2302, 41 USCA §§ 259, 403.

Duties and powers of the Committee, see 41 USCA § 47.

Planning and solicitation requirements, see 41 USCA § 253a.

Preference for acquisition of commercial items, see 10 USCA § 2377, 41 USCA § 264b.

Procurement requirements for the Government, nonapplication to prison-made products, see 41 USCA § 48.

§ 8.701 Definitions.

As used in this subpart—

"Allocation" means an action taken by a central nonprofit agency to designate the AbilityOne participating nonprofit agencies that will furnish definite quantities of supplies or perform specific services upon receipt of orders from ordering offices.

"Central nonprofit agency" means National Industries for the Blind (NIB), which has been designated to represent people who are blind; or NISH, which has been designated to represent AbilityOne participating nonprofit agencies serving people with severe disabilities other than blindness.

"Committee" means the Committee for Purchase from People Who Are Blind or Severely Disabled.

"Government" or "entity of the Government" means any entity of the legislative or judicial branch, any executive agency, military department, Government corporation, or independent establishment, the U.S. Postal Service, or any nonappropriated-fund instrumentality of the Armed Forces.

"Ordering office" means any activity in an entity of the Government that places orders for the purchase of supplies or services under the AbilityOne Program.

"Procurement List" means a list of supplies (including military resale commodities) and services that the Committee has determined are suitable for purchase by the Government under the 41 U.S.C. chapter 85.

"Nonprofit agency serving people who are blind" or "nonprofit agency serving people with other severe disabilities" (referred to jointly as AbilityOne participating nonprofit agencies) means a qualified nonprofit agency employing people who are blind or have other severe disabilities approved by the Committee to furnish a commodity or a service to the Government under the 41 U.S.C. chapter 85.

United States Code Annotated

Commercially available off-the-shelf item acquisitions, lists of inapplicable laws in Federal Acquisition Regulation, see 41 USCA § 431.

Committee for Purchase From People Who Are Blind or Severely Disabled, see 41 USCA § 46.

Contracts, planning, solicitation, evaluation, and award procedures, see 10 USCA § 2305.

Definitions, see 10 USCA § 2302, 41 USCA §§ 259, 403.

Duties and powers of the Committee, see 41 USCA § 47.

Planning and solicitation requirements, see 41 USCA § 253a.

Preference for acquisition of commercial items, see 10 USCA § 2377, 41 USCA § 264b.

Procurement requirements for the Government, nonapplication to prison-made products, see 41 USCA § 48.

§ 8.702 General.

The Committee is an independent Government activity with members appointed by the President of the United States. It is responsible for—

(a) Determining those supplies and services to be purchased by all entities of the Government from AbilityOne participating nonprofit agencies;

(b) Establishing prices for the supplies and services; and

(c) Establishing rules and regulations to implement the 41 U.S.C. chapter 85.

United States Code Annotated

Commercially available off-the-shelf item acquisitions, lists of inapplicable laws in Federal Acquisition Regulation, see 41 USCA § 431.

Committee for Purchase From People Who Are Blind or Severely Disabled, see 41 USCA § 46.

Contracts, planning, solicitation, evaluation, and award procedures, see 10 USCA § 2305.

Definitions, see 10 USCA § 2302, 41 USCA §§ 259, 403.

Duties and powers of the Committee, see 41 USCA § 47.

Planning and solicitation requirements, see 41 USCA § 253a.

Preference for acquisition of commercial items, see 10 USCA § 2377, 41 USCA § 264b.

Procurement requirements for the Government, nonapplication to prison-made products, see 41 USCA § 48.

§ 8.703 Procurement List.

The Committee maintains a Procurement List of all supplies and services required to be purchased from AbilityOne participating nonprofit agencies. The Procurement List may be accessed at: http://www.abilityone.gov. Questions concerning whether a supply item or service is on the Procurement List may be submitted at Internet e-mail address mailto:info@a bilityone.gov or referred to the Committee offices at the following address and telephone number:

Committee for Purchase From People
Who Are Blind or Severely Disabled,
1401 S. Clark Street, Suite 10800,
Arlington, VA 22202-3259,
(703) 603-7740.

Many items on the Procurement List are identified in the General Services Administration (GSA) Supply Catalog and GSA's Customer Service Center Catalogs with a black square and the words "NIB/NISH Mandatory Source," and in similar catalogs issued by the Defense Logistics Agency (DLA) and the Department of Veterans Affairs (VA). GSA, DLA, and VA are central supply agencies from which other Federal agencies are required to purchase certain supply items on the Procurement List.

§ 8.704 Purchase priorities.

(a) The 41 U.S.C. chapter 85 requires the Government to purchase supplies or services on the Procurement List, at prices established by the Committee, from AbilityOne participating nonprofit agencies if they are available within the period required. When identical supplies or services are on the Procurement List and the Schedule of Products issued by Federal Prison Industries, Inc., ordering offices shall purchase supplies and services in the following priorities:

(1) Supplies:

(i) Federal Prison Industries, Inc. (41 U.S.C. chapter 8504).

(ii) AbilityOne participating nonprofit agencies.

(iii) Commercial sources.

(2) Services:

(i) AbilityOne participating nonprofit agencies.

(ii) Federal Prison Industries, Inc., or commercial sources.

(b) No other provision of the FAR shall be construed as permitting an exception to the mandatory purchase of items on the Procurement List.

(c) The Procurement List identifies those supplies for which the ordering office must obtain a formal waiver (8.604) from Federal Prison Industries, Inc., before making any purchases from AbilityOne participating nonprofit agencies.

United States Code Annotated

Commercially available off-the-shelf item acquisitions, lists of inapplicable laws in Federal Acquisition Regulation, see 41 USCA § 431.

Committee for Purchase From People Who Are Blind or Severely Disabled, see 41 USCA § 46.

Contracts, planning, solicitation, evaluation, and award procedures, see 10 USCA § 2305.

Definitions, see 10 USCA § 2302, 41 USCA §§ 259, 403.

Duties and powers of the Committee, see 41 USCA § 47.

Planning and solicitation requirements, see 41 USCA § 253a.

Preference for acquisition of commercial items, see 10 USCA § 2377, 41 USCA § 264b.

Procurement requirements for the Government, nonapplication to prison-made products, see 41 USCA § 48.

Notes of Decisions

In general 1

1 In general

Contracting officer lacked rational basis for failing to comply with Department of Veterans Affairs' (DVA) guidelines (which give first priority to service-disabled veteran-owned (SDVO) and veteran-owned (VO) small businesses) by awarding laundry services contract on a sole-source basis to JWOD contractor under AbilityOne program, since agency guidelines did not exempt placements on AbilityOne procurement list. Angelica Textile Services, Inc. v. U.S., 95 Fed. Cl. 208 (2010)

An agency's decision to issue orders on a sole source basis under Javits-Wagner-O'Day (JWOD) Act authority was improper because the procured items were not on the Procurement List maintained by the Committee for Purchase From People Who Are Blind or Severely Disabled. Matter of: OSC Solutions, Inc., B-401498, 2009 CPD ¶ 185 (Comp. Gen. 2009)

The JWOD Act provides authority for noncompetitive acquisitions for specified supplies or services. The Act establishes the Committee for Purchase from People Who Are Blind or Severely Disabled (the Committee), and grants it exclusive authority to establish and maintain a procurement list of supplies and services provided by qualified nonprofit agencies for the blind or disabled. 41 U.S.C. §§ 46(a), 47(a); see FAR Subpart 8.7. Once a service has been added to the procurement list, contracting agencies are required to acquire that service directly from a qualified workshop, if the service is available within the period required. 41 U.S.C. § 48; FAR 8.704. Aleman & Associates, Inc., B-287275.2, B-287356.2, 2001 CPD ¶ 120 (Comp. Gen. 2001)

§ 8.705 Procedures.

§ 8.705-1 General.

(a) Ordering offices shall obtain supplies and services on the Procurement List from the central nonprofit agency or its designated AbilityOne participating nonprofit agencies, except that supplies identified on the Procurement List as available from DLA, GSA, or VA supply distribution facilities shall be obtained through DLA, GSA, or VA procedures. If a distribution facility cannot provide the supplies, it shall inform the ordering office, which shall then order from the AbilityOne participating nonprofit agency designated by the Committee.

(b) Supply distribution facilities in DLA and GSA shall obtain supplies on the Procurement List from the central nonprofit agency identified or its designated AbilityOne participating nonprofit agency.

United States Code Annotated

Commercially available off-the-shelf item acquisitions, lists of inapplicable laws in Federal Acquisition Regulation, see 41 USCA § 431.

Committee for Purchase From People Who Are Blind or Severely Disabled, see 41 USCA § 46.

Contracts, planning, solicitation, evaluation, and award procedures, see 10 USCA § 2305.

Definitions, see 10 USCA § 2302, 41 USCA §§ 259, 403.

Duties and powers of the Committee, see 41 USCA § 47.

Planning and solicitation requirements, see 41 USCA § 253a.

Preference for acquisition of commercial items, see 10 USCA § 2377, 41 USCA § 264b.

Procurement requirements for the Government, nonapplication to prison-made products, see 41 USCA § 48.

§ 8.705-2 Direct-order process.

Central nonprofit agencies may authorize ordering offices to transmit orders for specific supplies or services directly to an AbilityOne participating nonprofit agency. The written authorization remains valid until it is revoked by the central nonprofit agency or the Committee. The central nonprofit agency shall specify the normal delivery or performance lead time required by the nonprofit agency. The ordering office shall reflect this lead time in its orders.

United States Code Annotated

Commercially available off-the-shelf item acquisitions, lists of inapplicable laws in Federal Acquisition Regulation, see 41 USCA § 431.

Committee for Purchase From People Who Are Blind or Severely Disabled, see 41 USCA § 46.

Contracts, planning, solicitation, evaluation, and award procedures, see 10 USCA § 2305.

Definitions, see 10 USCA § 2302, 41 USCA §§ 259, 403.

Duties and powers of the Committee, see 41 USCA § 47.

Planning and solicitation requirements, see 41 USCA § 253a.

Preference for acquisition of commercial items, see 10 USCA § 2377, 41 USCA § 264b.

Procurement requirements for the Government, nonapplication to prison-made products, see 41 USCA § 48.

Notes of Decisions

In general 1

1 In general

Notice required by the Wagner-O'Day Act, which authorizes government purchase from qualified blind and handicapped workshops, is publication in the Federal Register and direct notice to other competitive bidders seeking to supply product purchased is not required. Wagner-O'Day Act, § 2(a)(2), 41 U.S.C.A. § 47(a)(2). Barrier Industries, Inc. v. Eckard, 584 F.2d 1074, 1082, 25 Cont. Cas. Fed. (CCH) P 82589 (D.C. Cir. 1978)

§ 8.705-3 Allocation process.

(a) When the direct order process has not been authorized, the ordering office shall submit a letter request for allocation (requesting the designation of the AbilityOne participating nonprofit agency to produce the supplies or perform the service) to the central nonprofit agency designated in the Procurement List. Ordering offices shall request allocations in sufficient time for a reply, for orders to be placed, and for the nonprofit agency to produce the supplies or provide the service within the required delivery or performance schedule.

(b) The ordering office's request to the central nonprofit agency for allocation shall include the following information:

(1) For supplies—Item name, stock number, latest specification, quantity, unit price, date delivery is required, and destination to which delivery is to be made.

(2) For services—Type and location of service required, latest specification, work to be performed, estimated volume, and required date or dates for completion.

(3) Other requirements; *e.g.*, packing, marking, as necessary.

(c) When an allocation is received, the ordering office shall promptly issue an order to the specified AbilityOne participating nonprofit agency or to the central nonprofit agency, as instructed by the allocation. If the issuance of an order is to be delayed for more than 15 days beyond receipt of the allocation, or canceled, the ordering office shall advise the central nonprofit agency immediately.

(d) Ordering offices may issue orders without limitation as to dollar amount and shall record them upon issuance as obligations. Each order shall include, as a minimum, the information contained in the request for allocation. Ordering offices shall also include additional instructions necessary for performance under the order; *e.g.*, on the handling of Governmentfurnished property, reports required, and notification of shipment.

United States Code Annotated

Commercially available off-the-shelf item acquisitions, lists of inapplicable laws in Federal Acquisition Regulation, see 41 USCA § 431.

Committee for Purchase From People Who Are Blind or Severely Disabled, see 41 USCA § 46.

Contracts, planning, solicitation, evaluation, and award procedures, see 10 USCA § 2305.

Definitions, see 10 USCA § 2302, 41 USCA §§ 259, 403.

Duties and powers of the Committee, see 41 USCA § 47.

Planning and solicitation requirements, see 41 USCA § 253a.

Preference for acquisition of commercial items, see 10 USCA § 2377, 41 USCA § 264b.

Procurement requirements for the Government, nonapplication to prison-made products, see 41 USCA § 48.

§ 8.705-4 Compliance with orders.

(a) The central nonprofit agency shall inform the ordering office of changes in lead time experienced by its AbilityOne participating nonprofit agencies to minimize requests for extension once the ordering office places an order.

(b) The ordering office shall grant a request by a central nonprofit agency or AbilityOne participating nonprofit agency for revision in the delivery or completion schedule, if feasible. If extension of the delivery or completion date is not feasible, the ordering office shall notify the appropriate central nonprofit agency and request that it reallocate the order, or grant a purchase exception authorizing acquisition from commercial sources.

(c) When an AbilityOne participating nonprofit agency fails to perform under the terms of an order, the ordering office shall make every effort to resolve the noncompliance with the nonprofit agency involved and to negotiate an adjustment before taking action to cancel the order. If the problem cannot be resolved with the nonprofit agency, the ordering office shall refer the matter for resolution first to the central nonprofit agency and then, if necessary, to the Committee.

(d) When, after complying with 8.705-4(c), the ordering office determines that it must cancel an order, it shall notify the central nonprofit agency and, if practical, request a reallocation of the order. When the central nonprofit agency cannot reallocate the order, it shall grant a purchase exception permitting use of commercial sources, subject to approval by the Committee when the value of the purchase exception is $25,000 or more.

United States Code Annotated

Commercially available off-the-shelf item acquisitions, lists of inapplicable laws in Federal Acquisition Regulation, see 41 USCA § 431.

Committee for Purchase From People Who Are Blind or Severely Disabled, see 41 USCA § 46.

Contracts, planning, solicitation, evaluation, and award procedures, see 10 USCA § 2305.

Definitions, see 10 USCA § 2302, 41 USCA §§ 259, 403.

Duties and powers of the Committee, see 41 USCA § 47.

Planning and solicitation requirements, see 41 USCA § 253a.

Preference for acquisition of commercial items, see 10 USCA § 2377, 41 USCA § 264b.

Procurement requirements for the Government, nonapplication to prison-made products, see 41 USCA § 48.

§ 8.706 Purchase exceptions.

(a) Ordering offices may acquire supplies or services on the Procurement List from commercial sources only if the acquisition is specifically authorized in a purchase exception granted by the designated central nonprofit agency.

(b) The central nonprofit agency shall promptly grant purchase exceptions when—

(1) The AbilityOne participating nonprofit agencies cannot provide the supplies or services within the time required, and commercial sources can provide them significantly sooner in the quantities required; or

(2) The quantity required cannot be produced or provided economically by the AbilityOne participating nonprofit agencies.

(c) The central nonprofit agency granting the exception shall specify the quantity and delivery or performance period covered by the exception.

(d) When a purchase exception is granted, the contracting officer shall—

(1) Initiate purchase action within 15 days following the date of the exception or any extension granted by the central nonprofit agency; and

(2) Provide a copy of the solicitation to the central nonprofit agency when it is issued.

(e) The Committee may also grant a purchase exception, under any circumstances it considers appropriate.

United States Code Annotated

Commercially available off-the-shelf item acquisitions, lists of inapplicable laws in Federal Acquisition Regulation, see 41 USCA § 431.

Committee for Purchase From People Who Are Blind or Severely Disabled, see 41 USCA § 46.

Contracts, planning, solicitation, evaluation, and award procedures, see 10 USCA § 2305.

Definitions, see 10 USCA § 2302, 41 USCA §§ 259, 403.

Duties and powers of the Committee, see 41 USCA § 47.

Planning and solicitation requirements, see 41 USCA § 253a.

Preference for acquisition of commercial items, see 10 USCA § 2377, 41 USCA § 264b.

Procurement requirements for the Government, nonapplication to prison-made products, see 41 USCA § 48.

Notes of Decisions

In general 1

1 In general

Evidence did not support factual conclusions of committee for purchase from the blind and other severely handicapped that workshops for the blind would be able to produce requisite quantities of computer tabulating machine paper at fair market price, for purposes of adding paper to list of commodities to be purchased by federal government from workshops for the blind and handicapped. Wagner-O'Day Act, §§ 2(a–c), 3, 5(3, 5), as amended, 41 U.S.C.A. §§ 47(a–c), 48, 48b(3, 5). McGregor Printing Corp. v. Kemp, 20 F.3d 1188, 1194 (D.C. Cir. 1994)

The Committee for Purchase from the Blind and other Severely Handicapped, acting pursuant to the Wagner-O'Day Act, did not act arbitrarily or capriciously in determining that involved floor wax product was "suitable," that the blind workshop was capable of producing acceptable floor wax, and that the adverse impact on competitive bidder was not so serious as to preclude the Committee's action of adding floor wax to procurement list for mandatory government purchase from qualified blind workshops. Wagner-O'Day Act, §§ 1–3, 41 U.S.C.A. §§ 46–48. Barrier Industries, Inc. v. Eckard, 584 F.2d 1074, 1083, 25 Cont. Cas. Fed. (CCH) P 82589 (D.C. Cir. 1978)

Central nonprofit agency acted consistently with its responsibilities under Javits-Wagner-O'Day (JWOD) Act when it recommended certain nonprofit agency which employed blind or severely disabled persons to the Committee for Purchase from People Who Are Blind or Severely Disabled as a provider of custodial services for federal agency, even if central nonprofit agency acted to facilitate such employment before Committee added the custodial services to procurement list. Wagner-O'Day Act, § 2, 41 U.S.C.A. § 47. Brothers Cleaning Service, Inc. v. Chair, Committee for Purchase from People Who are Blind or Severely Disabled, 26 F. Supp. 2d 1 (D.D.C. 1998)

Committee for Purchase from People Who Are Blind or Severely Disabled did not act arbitrarily or capriciously in refusing to reconsider its original placement, under Javits-Wagner-O'Day (JWOD) Act, of custodial services contract on procurement list which was open only to nonprofit agencies which employed blind or severely disabled persons. Wagner-O'Day Act, § 2, 41 U.S.C.A. § 47; 41 C.F.R. § 51-2.6. Brothers Cleaning Service, Inc. v. Chair, Committee for Purchase from People Who are Blind or Severely Disabled, 26 F. Supp. 2d 1 (D.D.C. 1998)

Committee for Purchase from People Who Are Blind or Severely Disabled reasonably concluded, when it added custodial services contract to procurement list which was open only to nonprofit agencies which employed blind or severely disabled persons, that contractor which previously provided such custodial services was not the "current contractor" or "most recent contractor" with regard to the project, and therefore Committee was not required under Javits-Wagner- O'Day (JWOD) Act to conduct impact study on the contractor. Wagner-O'Day Act, § 2, 41 U.S.C.A. § 47; 41 C.F.R. §§ 51-2.4(a)(4)(ii), 51-2.6. Brothers Cleaning Service, Inc. v. Chair, Committee for Purchase from People Who are Blind or Severely Disabled, 26 F. Supp. 2d 1 (D.D.C. 1998)

Committee for Purchase from the Blind and Other Severely Handicapped did not exceed its statutory authority under JWOD (Javits-Wagner-O'Day) Act in deciding to add computer tabulating paper to list of commodities and services which federal government procured solely from blind and handicapped workshops; although NIB (National Industries for the Blind) played central role in providing initial information, Committee did not yield its authority to NIB, and nothing in Act or in its legislative history or any regulation limited set-asides to workshops already manufacturing the commodity involved. Wagner-O'Day Act, §§ 1–6, as amended, 41 U.S.C.A. §§ 46–48c. McGregor Printing Corp. v. Kemp, 802 F. Supp. 519 (D.D.C. 1992), rev'd on other grounds, 20 F.3d 1188 (D.C. Cir. 1994)

Because over 75% of man-hours of direct labor needed to assemble medals and medal sets was done by severely handicapped employees, employer was a qualified nonprofit agency under the Javits-Wagner-O'Day Act [41 U.S.C.A. § 46 et seq.] and thus public contract for medals could be withdrawn from competitive bidding. HLI Lordship Industries,

Inc. v. Committee for Purchase from the Blind & Other Severely Handicapped, 615 F. Supp. 970 (E.D. Va. 1985), decision rev'd on other grounds, 791 F.2d 1136 (4th Cir. 1986)

The granting of an exception does not have the effect of removing the contract from the JWOD procurement list-such a "deletion" is accomplished under an entirely different regulation, 41 C.F.R. § 51-6.8. Magic Brite Janitorial v. U.S., 69 Fed. Cl. 319 (2006)

§ 8.707 Prices.

(a) The prices of items on the Procurement List are fair market prices established by the Committee. All prices for supplies ordered under this subpart are f.o.b. origin.

(b) Prices for supplies are normally adjusted semiannually. Prices for services are normally adjusted annually.

(c) The Committee may request the agency responsible for acquiring the supplies or service to assist it in establishing or revising the fair market price. The Committee has the authority to establish prices without prior coordination with the responsible contracting office.

(d) Price changes shall normally apply to all orders received by the AbilityOne participating nonprofit agency on or after the effective date of the change. In special cases, after considering the views of the ordering office, the Committee may make price changes applicable to orders received by the AbilityOne participating nonprofit agency prior to the effective date of the change.

(e) If an ordering office desires packing, packaging, or marking of supplies other than the standard pack as provided on the Procurement List, any difference in costs shall be included as a separate item on the nonprofit agency's invoice. The ordering office shall reimburse the nonprofit agency for these costs.

(f) Ordering offices may make recommendations to the Committee at any time for price revisions for supplies and services on the Procurement List.

United States Code Annotated

Commercially available off-the-shelf item acquisitions, lists of inapplicable laws in Federal Acquisition Regulation, see 41 USCA § 431.

Committee for Purchase From People Who Are Blind or Severely Disabled, see 41 USCA § 46.

Contracts, planning, solicitation, evaluation, and award procedures, see 10 USCA § 2305.

Definitions, see 10 USCA § 2302, 41 USCA §§ 259, 403.

Duties and powers of the Committee, see 41 USCA § 47.

Planning and solicitation requirements, see 41 USCA § 253a.

Preference for acquisition of commercial items, see 10 USCA § 2377, 41 USCA § 264b.

Procurement requirements for the Government, nonapplication to prison-made products, see 41 USCA § 48.

§ 8.708 Shipping.

(a) Delivery is accomplished when a shipment is placed aboard the vehicle of the initial carrier. The time of delivery is the date shipment is released to and accepted by the initial carrier.

(b) Shipment is normally under Government bills of lading. However, for small orders, ordering offices may specify other shipment methods.

(c) When shipments are under Government bills of lading, the bills of lading may accompany orders or be otherwise furnished promptly. Failure of an ordering office to furnish bills of lading or to designate a method of transportation may result in an excusable delay in delivery.

(d) AbilityOne participating nonprofit agencies shall include transportation costs for small shipments paid by the nonprofit agencies as an item on the invoice. The ordering office shall reimburse the nonprofit agencies for these costs.

United States Code Annotated

Commercially available off-the-shelf item acquisitions, lists of inapplicable laws in Federal Acquisition Regulation, see 41 USCA § 431.

Committee for Purchase From People Who Are Blind or Severely Disabled, see 41 USCA § 46.

Contracts, planning, solicitation, evaluation, and award procedures, see 10 USCA § 2305.

Definitions, see 10 USCA § 2302, 41 USCA §§ 259, 403.

Duties and powers of the Committee, see 41 USCA § 47.

Planning and solicitation requirements, see 41 USCA § 253a.

Preference for acquisition of commercial items, see 10 USCA § 2377, 41 USCA § 264b.

Procurement requirements for the Government, nonapplication to prison-made products, see 41 USCA § 48.

§ 8.709 Payments.

The ordering office shall make payments for supplies or services on the Procurement List within 30 days after shipment or after receipt of a proper invoice or voucher.

United States Code Annotated

Commercially available off-the-shelf item acquisitions, lists of inapplicable laws in Federal Acquisition Regulation, see 41 USCA § 431.

Committee for Purchase From People Who Are Blind or Severely Disabled, see 41 USCA § 46.

Contracts, planning, solicitation, evaluation, and award procedures, see 10 USCA § 2305.

Definitions, see 10 USCA § 2302, 41 USCA §§ 259, 403.

Duties and powers of the Committee, see 41 USCA § 47.

Planning and solicitation requirements, see 41 USCA § 253a.

Preference for acquisition of commercial items, see 10 USCA § 2377, 41 USCA § 264b.

Procurement requirements for the Government, nonapplication to prison-made products, see 41 USCA § 48.

§ 8.710 Quality of merchandise.

Supplies and services provided by AbilityOne participating nonprofit agencies shall comply with the applicable Government specifications and standards cited in the order. When no specifications or standards exist—

(a) Supplies shall be of the highest quality and equal to similar items available on the commercial market; and

(b) Services shall conform to good commercial practices.

United States Code Annotated

Commercially available off-the-shelf item acquisitions, lists of inapplicable laws in Federal Acquisition Regulation, see 41 USCA § 431.

Committee for Purchase From People Who Are Blind or Severely Disabled, see 41 USCA § 46.

Contracts, planning, solicitation, evaluation, and award procedures, see 10 USCA § 2305.

Definitions, see 10 USCA § 2302, 41 USCA §§ 259, 403.

Duties and powers of the Committee, see 41 USCA § 47.

Planning and solicitation requirements, see 41 USCA § 253a.

Preference for acquisition of commercial items, see 10 USCA § 2377, 41 USCA § 264b.

Procurement requirements for the Government, nonapplication to prison-made products, see 41 USCA § 48.

§ 8.711 Quality complaints.

(a) When the quality of supplies or services received is unsatisfactory, the using activity shall take the following actions:

(1) For supplies received from DLA supply centers, GSA supply distribution facilities, or Department of Veterans Affairs distribution division, notify the supplying agency.

(2) For supplies or services received from AbilityOne participating nonprofit agencies, address complaints to the individual nonprofit agency involved, with a copy to the appropriate central nonprofit agency.

(b) When quality problems cannot be resolved by the AbilityOne participating nonprofit agency and the ordering office, the ordering office shall first contact the central nonprofit agency and then, if necessary, the Committee for resolution.

United States Code Annotated

Commercially available off-the-shelf item acquisitions, lists of inapplicable laws in Federal Acquisition Regulation, see 41 USCA § 431.

Committee for Purchase From People Who Are Blind or Severely Disabled, see 41 USCA § 46.

Contracts, planning, solicitation, evaluation, and award procedures, see 10 USCA § 2305.

Definitions, see 10 USCA § 2302, 41 USCA §§ 259, 403.

Duties and powers of the Committee, see 41 USCA § 47.

Planning and solicitation requirements, see 41 USCA § 253a.

Preference for acquisition of commercial items, see 10 USCA § 2377, 41 USCA § 264b.

Procurement requirements for the Government, nonapplication to prison-made products, see 41 USCA § 48.

§ 8.712 Specification changes.

(a) The contracting activity shall notify the AbilityOne participating nonprofit agency and appropriate central nonprofit agency of any change in specifications or descriptions. In the absence of such written notification, the AbilityOne participating nonprofit agency shall furnish the supplies or services under the specification or description cited in the order.

(b) The contracting activity shall provide 90-days advance notification to the Committee and the central nonprofit agency on actions that affect supplies on the Procurement List and shall permit them to comment before action is taken, particularly when it involves—

(1) Changes that require new national stock numbers or item designations;

(2) Deleting items from the supply system;

(3) Standardization; or

(4) Developing new items to replace items on the Procurement List.

(c) For services, the contracting activity shall notify the AbilityOne participating nonprofit agency and central nonprofit agency concerned at least 90 days prior to the date that any changes in the scope of work or other conditions will be required.

(d) When, in order to meet its emergency needs, a contracting activity is unable to give the 90-day notification required in paragraphs (b) and (c) of this section, the contracting activity shall, at the time it places the order or change notice, inform the AbilityOne participating nonprofit agency and the central nonprofit agency in writing of the reasons that it cannot meet the 90-day notification requirement.

United States Code Annotated

Commercially available off-the-shelf item acquisitions, lists of inapplicable laws in Federal Acquisition Regulation, see 41 USCA § 431.

Committee for Purchase From People Who Are Blind or Severely Disabled, see 41 USCA § 46.

Contracts, planning, solicitation, evaluation, and award procedures, see 10 USCA § 2305.

Definitions, see 10 USCA § 2302, 41 USCA §§ 259, 403.

Duties and powers of the Committee, see 41 USCA § 47.

Planning and solicitation requirements, see 41 USCA § 253a.

Preference for acquisition of commercial items, see 10 USCA § 2377, 41 USCA § 264b.

Procurement requirements for the Government, nonapplication to prison-made products, see 41 USCA § 48.

§ 8.713 Optional acquisition of supplies and services.

(a) Ordering offices may acquire supplies and services not included on the Procurement

List from an AbilityOne participating nonprofit agency that is the low responsive, responsible offeror under a solicitation issued by other authorized acquisition methods.

(b) Ordering offices should forward solicitations to AbilityOne participating nonprofit agencies that may be qualified to provide the supplies or services required.

United States Code Annotated

Commercially available off-the-shelf item acquisitions, lists of inapplicable laws in Federal Acquisition Regulation, see 41 USCA § 431.

Committee for Purchase From People Who Are Blind or Severely Disabled, see 41 USCA § 46.

Contracts, planning, solicitation, evaluation, and award procedures, see 10 USCA § 2305.

Definitions, see 10 USCA § 2302, 41 USCA §§ 259, 403.

Duties and powers of the Committee, see 41 USCA § 47.

Planning and solicitation requirements, see 41 USCA § 253a.

Preference for acquisition of commercial items, see 10 USCA § 2377, 41 USCA § 264b.

Procurement requirements for the Government, nonapplication to prison-made products, see 41 USCA § 48.

§ 8.714 Communications with the central nonprofit agencies and the Committee.

(a) The addresses of the central nonprofit agencies are:

(1) National Industries for the Blind

1310 Braddock Place
Alexandria, VA 22314-1691
(703) 310-0500; and

(2) NISH

8401 Old Courthouse Road
Vienna, VA 22182
(571) 226-4660.

(b) Any matter requiring referral to the Committee shall be addressed to:

Executive Director of the Committee,
1401 S. Clark Street, Suite 10800,
Arlington, VA 22202-3259.

§ 8.715 Replacement commodities.

When a commodity on the Procurement List is replaced by another commodity which has not been previously acquired, and a qualified AbilityOne participating nonprofit agency can furnish the replacement commodity in accordance with the Government's quality standards and delivery schedules and at a fair market price, the replacement commodity is automatically on the Procurement List and shall be acquired from the AbilityOne participating nonprofit agency designated by the Committee. The commodity being replaced shall continue to be included on the Procurement List until there is no longer a requirement for that commodity.

United States Code Annotated

Commercially available off-the-shelf item acquisitions, lists of inapplicable laws in Federal Acquisition Regulation, see 41 USCA § 431.

Committee for Purchase From People Who Are Blind or Severely Disabled, see 41 USCA § 46.

Contracts, planning, solicitation, evaluation, and award procedures, see 10 USCA § 2305.

Definitions, see 10 USCA § 2302, 41 USCA §§ 259, 403.

Duties and powers of the Committee, see 41 USCA § 47.

Planning and solicitation requirements, see 41 USCA § 253a. Preference for acquisition of commercial items, see 10 USCA § 2377, 41 USCA § 264b.

Procurement requirements for the Government, nonapplication to prison-made products, see 41 USCA § 48.

§ 8.716 Change-of-name and successor in interest procedures.

When the Committee recognizes a name change or a successor in interest for an AbilityOne participating nonprofit agency providing supplies or services on the Procurement List—

(a) The Committee will provide a notice of a change to the Procurement List to the cognizant contracting officers; and

(b) Upon receipt of a notice of a change to the Procurement List from the Committee, the contracting officer must—

(1) Prepare a Standard Form (SF) 30, Amendment of Solicitation/Modification of Contract, incorporating a summary of the notice and attaching a list of contracts affected; and

(2) Distribute the SF 30, including a copy to the Committee.

United States Code Annotated

Commercially available off-the-shelf item acquisitions, lists of inapplicable laws in Federal Acquisition Regulation, see 41 USCA § 431.

Committee for Purchase From People Who Are Blind or Severely Disabled, see 41 USCA § 46.

Contracts, planning, solicitation, evaluation, and award procedures, see 10 USCA § 2305.

Definitions, see 10 USCA § 2302, 41 USCA §§ 259, 403.

Duties and powers of the Committee, see 41 USCA § 47.

Planning and solicitation requirements, see 41 USCA § 253a.

Preference for acquisition of commercial items, see 10 USCA § 2377, 41 USCA § 264b.

Procurement requirements for the Government, nonapplication to prison-made products, see 41 USCA § 48.

Subpart 8.8 Acquisition of Printing and Related Supplies

§ 8.800 Scope of subpart.

This subpart provides policy for the acquisition of Government printing and related supplies.

United States Code Annotated

Commercially available off-the-shelf item acquisitions, lists of inapplicable laws in Federal Acquisition Regulation, see 41 USCA § 431.

Contracts, planning, solicitation, evaluation, and award procedures, see 10 USCA § 2305.

Definitions, see 10 USCA § 2302, 41 USCA §§ 259, 403.

Direct purchase of printing, binding, and blank-book work by Government agencies, see 44 USCA § 504.

Government printing, binding, and blank-book work to be done at Government Printing Office, see 44 USCA § 501.

Planning and solicitation requirements, see 41 USCA § 253a.

Preference for acquisition of commercial items, see 10 USCA § 2377, 41 USCA § 264b.

§ 8.801 Definitions.

As used in this subpart—

"Government printing" means printing, binding, and blankbook work for the use of an executive department, independent agency, or establishment of the Government.

"Related supplies" means supplies that are used and equipment that is usable in printing and binding operations.

United States Code Annotated

Commercially available off-the-shelf item acquisitions, lists of inapplicable laws in Federal Acquisition Regulation, see 41 USCA § 431.

Contracts, planning, solicitation, evaluation, and award procedures, see 10 USCA § 2305.

Definitions, see 10 USCA § 2302, 41 USCA §§ 259, 403.

Direct purchase of printing, binding, and blank-book work by Government agencies, see 44 USCA § 504.

Government printing, binding, and blank-book work to be done at Government Printing Office, see 44 USCA § 501.

Planning and solicitation requirements, see 41 USCA § 253a.

Preference for acquisition of commercial items, see 10 USCA § 2377, 41 USCA § 264b.

§ 8.802 Policy.

(a) Government printing must be done by or through the Government Printing Office (GPO) (44 U.S.C. 501), unless—

(1) The GPO cannot provide the printing service (44 U.S.C. 504);

(2) The printing is done in field printing plants operated by an executive agency (44 U.S.C. 501(2));

(3) The printing is acquired by an executive agency from allotments for contract field printing (44 U.S.C. 501(2)); or

(4) The printing is specifically authorized by statute to be done other than by the GPO.

(b) The head of each agency shall designate a central printing authority; that central printing authority may serve as the liaison with the Congressional Joint Committee on Printing (JCP) and the Public Printer on matters related to printing. Contracting officers shall obtain approval from their designated central printing authority before contracting in any manner, whether directly or through contracts for supplies or services, for the items defined in 8.801 and for composition, platemaking, presswork, binding, and micrographics (when used as a substitute for printing).

(c) (1) Further, 44 U.S.C. 1121 provides that the Public Printer may acquire and furnish paper and envelopes (excluding envelopes printed in the course of manufacture) in common use by two or more Government departments, establishments, or services within the District of Columbia, and provides for reimbursement of the Public Printer from available appropriations or funds. Paper and envelopes that are furnished by the Public Printer may not be acquired in any other manner.

(2) Paper and envelopes for use by Executive agencies outside the District of Columbia and stocked by GSA shall be requisitioned from GSA in accordance with the procedures listed in Federal Property Management Regulations (FPMR) Subpart 101-26.3.

United States Code Annotated

Commercially available off-the-shelf item acquisitions, lists of inapplicable laws in Federal Acquisition Regulation, see 41 USCA § 431.

Contracts, planning, solicitation, evaluation, and award procedures, see 10 USCA § 2305.

Definitions, see 10 USCA § 2302, 41 USCA §§ 259, 403.

Direct purchase of printing, binding, and blank-book work by Government agencies, see 44 USCA § 504.

Government printing, binding, and blank-book work to be done at Government Printing Office, see 44 USCA § 501.

Planning and solicitation requirements, see 41 USCA § 253a.

Preference for acquisition of commercial items, see 10 USCA § 2377, 41 USCA § 264b.

Subpart 8.9 [Reserved]

Subpart 8.10 [Reserved]

Subpart 8.11 Leasing of Motor Vehicles

§ 8.1100 Scope of subpart.

This subpart covers the procedures for the leasing, from commercial concerns, of motor vehicles that comply with Federal Motor Vehicle Safety Standards and applicable State motor vehicle safety regulations. It does not apply to motor vehicles leased outside the United States and its outlying areas.

United States Code Annotated

Commercially available off-the-shelf item acquisitions, lists of inapplicable laws in Federal Acquisition Regulation, see 41 USCA § 431.

Contracts, planning, solicitation, evaluation, and award procedures, see 10 USCA § 2305.

Definitions, see 10 USCA § 2302, 41 USCA §§ 259, 403.

Planning and solicitation requirements, see 41 USCA § 253a.

Preference for acquisition of commercial items, see 10 USCA § 2377, 41 USCA § 264b.

§ 8.1101 Definitions.

As used in this subpart—

"Leasing" means the acquisition of motor vehicles, other than by purchase from private or commercial sources, and includes the synonyms "hire" and "rent."

"Motor vehicle" means an item of equipment, mounted on wheels and designed for highway and/or land use, that—

(1) Derives power from a self-contained power unit; or

(2) Is designed to be towed by and used in conjunction with self-propelled equipment.

United States Code Annotated

Commercially available off-the-shelf item acquisitions, lists of inapplicable laws in Federal Acquisition Regulation, see 41 USCA § 431.

Contracts, planning, solicitation, evaluation, and award procedures, see 10 USCA § 2305.

Definitions, see 10 USCA § 2302, 41 USCA §§ 259, 403.

Planning and solicitation requirements, see 41 USCA § 253a.

Preference for acquisition of commercial items, see 10 USCA § 2377, 41 USCA § 264b.

Notes of Decisions

Implied lease 2
Leasing, generally 1

1 Leasing, generally

Federal employee's use of credit card issued to him by his employing agency as government traveler did not convert employee's car rental agreement with private car rental company into government lease for purposes of statute imposing one-month suspension on federal employee who misuses vehicle owned or leased by the government; under credit card agreement, government employees would pay credit card bills themselves and then would submit reimbursement requests to government, government assumed no liability for charges incurred on credit cards, and employee was solely responsible to rental company to pay car rental fees; moreover, fact that government employees may obtain government rates for official travel expenses did not convert employee's individual contract with car rental company into lease between government and rental company; lease agreement was solely between employee and rental company at preset government rate. 31 U.S.C.A. § 1349(b); 41 C.F.R. § 301-15.44(c, h). Chufo v. Department of Interior, 45 F.3d 419 (Fed. Cir. 1995). Officers And Public Employees ⚯69.12

Rented vehicle which was basis for misuse charge against federal employee was not "leased by the United States government" within meaning of misuse statute; lease which employee entered into with private car rental company did not comply with regulatory requirements for a government lease as no contracting officer procured lease of car and government did not assume any responsibility to make lease payments under the rental agreement; moreover, rental agreement was only between employee and car rental company as contract was standard form-contract that listed employee alone as customer and bore only his signature, contract did not list employee's employer, even though space was provided for this information, and no language in contract indicated that vehicle was leased by government. 48 C.F.R. § 52.208-4. Chufo v. Department of Interior, 45 F.3d 419 (Fed. Cir. 1995). Officers And Public Employees ⊸69.7

2 Implied lease

Mere fact that federal employee rented vehicle for government use did not create an implied lease between government and private car rental company for purposes of statute imposing one-month suspension on federal employee who misuses vehicle owned or leased by government; government did not contract with rental company for the car, name of employing agency did not appear on rental agreement, employee alone signed contract, employee never sought to bind government through his car rental agreement, employee himself paid rental company and then sought reimbursement for the expense, and government was never bound to pay rental company. 31 U.S.C.A. § 1349(b). Chufo v. Department of Interior, 45 F.3d 419 (Fed. Cir. 1995). Officers And Public Employees ⊸69.12

An implied lease between government and private company requires demonstration of mutual intent to contract, offer and acceptance, and contractual authority vested in individual seeking to bind government. Chufo v. Department of Interior, 45 F.3d 419 (Fed. Cir. 1995). Municipal Corporations ⊸249

§ 8.1102 Presolicitation requirements.

(a) Except as specified in 8.1102(b), before preparing solicitations for leasing of motor vehicles, contracting officers shall obtain from the requiring activity a written certification that—

(1) The vehicles requested are of maximum fuel efficiency and minimum body size, engine size, and equipment (if any) necessary to fulfill operational needs, and meet prescribed fuel economy standards;

(2) The head of the requiring agency, or a designee, has certified that the requested passenger automobiles (sedans and station wagons) larger than Type IA, IB, or II (small, subcompact, or compact) are essential to the agency's mission;

(3) Internal approvals have been received; and

(4) The General Services Administration has advised that it cannot furnish the vehicles.

(b) With respect to requirements for leasing motor vehicles for a period of less than 60 days, the contracting officer need not obtain the certification specified in 8.1102(a)—

(1) If the requirement is for type 1A, 1B, or II vehicles, which are by definition fuel efficient; or

(2) If the requirement is for passenger vehicles larger than 1A, 1B, or II, and the agency has established procedures for advance approval, on a case-by-case basis, of such requirements.

(c) Generally, solicitations shall not be limited to current year production models. However, with the prior approval of the head of the contracting office, solicitations may be limited to current models on the basis of overall economy.

United States Code Annotated

Commercially available off-the-shelf item acquisitions, lists of inapplicable laws in Federal Acquisition Regulation, see 41 USCA § 431.

Contracts, planning, solicitation, evaluation, and award procedures, see 10 USCA § 2305.

Definitions, see 10 USCA § 2302, 41 USCA §§ 259, 403.

Planning and solicitation requirements, see 41 USCA § 253a.

Preference for acquisition of commercial items, see 10 USCA § 2377, 41 USCA § 264b.

§ 8.1103 Contract requirements.

Contracting officers shall include the following items in each contract for leasing motor vehicles:

(a) Scope of contract.

(b) Method of computing payments.

(c) A listing of the number and type of vehicles required, and the equipment and accessories to be provided with each vehicle.

(d) Responsibilities of the contractor or the Government for furnishing gasoline, motor oil, antifreeze, and similar items.

(e) Unless it is determined that it will be more economical for the Government to perform the work, a statement that the contractor shall perform all maintenance on the vehicles.

(f) A statement as to the applicability of pertinent State and local laws and regulations, and the responsibility of each party for compliance with them.

(g) Responsibilities of the contractor or the Government for emergency repairs and services.

United States Code Annotated

Acquisition procedures, see 10 USCA 2302b, 41 USCA § 252b.

Commercially available off-the-shelf item acquisitions, lists of inapplicable laws in Federal Acquisition Regulation, see 41 USCA § 431.

Contracts, planning, solicitation, evaluation, and award procedures, see 10 USCA § 2305.

Definitions, see 10 USCA § 2302, 41 USCA §§ 259, 403.

Planning and solicitation requirements, see 41 USCA § 253a.

Preference for acquisition of commercial items, see 10 USCA § 2377, 41 USCA § 264b.

§ 8.1104 Contract clauses.

Insert the following clauses in solicitations and contracts for leasing of motor vehicles, unless the motor vehicles are leased in foreign countries:

(a) The clause at 52.208-4, Vehicle Lease Payments.

(b) The clause at 52.208-5, Condition of Leased Vehicles.

(c) The clause at 52.208-6, Marking of Leased Vehicles.

(d) A clause substantially the same as the clause at 52.208-7, Tagging of Leased Vehicles, for vehicles leased over 60 days (see Subpart B of 41 CFR Part 102-34).

(e) The provisions and clauses prescribed elsewhere in the FAR for solicitations and contracts for supplies when a fixed-price contract is contemplated, but excluding—

(1) The clause at 52.211-16, Variation in Quantity;

(2) The clause at 52.232-1, Payments;

(3) The clause at 52.222-20, Contracts for Materials, Supplies, Articles, and Equipment Exceeding $15,000; and

(4) The clause at 52.246-16, Responsibility for Supplies.

United States Code Annotated

Commercially available off-the-shelf item acquisitions, lists of inapplicable laws in Federal Acquisition Regulation, see 41 USCA § 431.

Contracts, planning, solicitation, evaluation, and award procedures, see 10 USCA § 2305.

Definitions, see 10 USCA § 2302, 41 USCA §§ 259, 403.

Planning and solicitation requirements, see 41 USCA § 253a.

Preference for acquisition of commercial items, see 10 USCA § 2377, 41 USCA § 264b.

PART 9 CONTRACTOR QUALIFICATIONS

§ 9.000 Scope of part.

Subpart 9.1 —Responsible Prospective Contractors

Subpart 9.2 Qualifications Requirements

§ 9.507-2 Contract clause.
§ 9.508 Examples.

Subpart 9.6 Contractor Team Arrangements
§ 9.601 Definition.
§ 9.602 General.
§ 9.603 Policy.
§ 9.604 Limitations.

Subpart 9.7 Defense Production Pools and Research and Development Pools
§ 9.701 Definition.
§ 9.702 Contracting with pools.
§ 9.703 Contracting with individual pool members.

§ 9.000 Scope of part.
This part prescribes policies, standards, and procedures pertaining to prospective contractors' responsibility; debarment, suspension, and ineligibility; qualified products; first article testing and approval; contractor team arrangements; defense production pools and research and development pools; and organizational conflicts of interest.

United States Code Annotated
Administrative determinations, see 41 USCA § 257.

Contracts, planning, solicitation, evaluation, and award procedures, see 10 USCA § 2305.

Definitions, see 10 USCA § 2302, 41 USCA §§ 259, 403.

Determinations and decisions, see 10 USCA § 2310, 41 USCA § 262.

Planning and solicitation requirements, see 41 USCA § 253a.

Subpart 9.1 —Responsible Prospective Contractors

§ 9.100 Scope of subpart.
This subpart prescribes policies, standards, and procedures for determining whether prospective contractors and subcontractors are responsible.

§ 9.101 Definitions.
"Administrative proceeding" means a non-judicial process that is adjudicatory in nature in order to make a determination of fault or liability (e.g., Securities and Exchange Commission Administrative Proceedings, Civilian Board of Contract Appeals Proceedings, and Armed Services Board of Contract Appeals Proceedings). This includes administrative proceedings at the Federal and state level but only in connections with performance of a Federal contract or grant. It does not include agency actions such as contract audits, site visits, corrective plans, or inspection of deliverables.

"Surveying activity," as used in this subpart, means the cognizant contract administration office or, if there is no such office, another organization designated by the agency to conduct preaward surveys.

United States Code Annotated
Administrative determinations, see 41 USCA § 257.

Contracts, planning, solicitation, evaluation, and award procedures, see 10 USCA § 2305.

Definitions, see 10 USCA § 2302, 41 USCA §§ 259, 403.

Determinations and decisions, see 10 USCA § 2310, 41 USCA § 262.

Planning and solicitation requirements, see 41 USCA § 253a.

Notes of Decisions

In general 1

1 In general

Unlike determining "responsiveness" of bid, in assessing contractor's "responsibility," contracting officer is not limited to information contained in bid when opened; rather, contracting officer may solicit and contractor may supply additional information to demonstrate that contractor is capable of performing contract work. VMS Hotel Partners v. U.S., 30 Fed. Cl. 512, 39 Cont. Cas. Fed. (CCH) P 76631 (1994). United States ⚷64.45(2)

"Responsibility" for purposes of public contract addresses performance capability of bidder including financial resources, experience, management, past performance, place of performance, and integrity, and evidence may be presented after bid opening until time of award. Bean Dredging Corp. v. U.S., 22 Cl. Ct. 519, 36 Cont. Cas. Fed. (CCH) P 76017, 1991 WL 15601 (1991). Public Contracts ⚷11

In identifying whether particular requirement is related to responsiveness or to responsibility, responsibility concerns question of bidder's performance capability and responsiveness concerns promise to perform contract. Bean Dredging Corp. v. U.S., 22 Cl. Ct. 519, 36 Cont. Cas. Fed. (CCH) P 76017, 1991 WL 15601 (1991). Public Contracts ⚷8; Public Contracts ⚷11

When examining whether clause in bid related to bidder "responsiveness" or "responsibility," "responsiveness" refers to question whether bidder has promised to perform in precise manner requested by Government, whereas "responsibility" involves inquiry into bidder's ability and will to perform subject contract as promised. Blount, Inc. v. U.S., 22 Cl. Ct. 221, 36 Cont. Cas. Fed. (CCH) P 75981, 1990 WL 210734 (1990). United States ⚷64.30

Fact that contracting officer requested clarification of bidder's response to business management questionnaire question in which bidder indicated that it intended to self-perform only 10% of contract work, while invitation for bid required self-performance of 20%, could not convert issue of nonresponsiveness of bid into issue of responsibility; procuring agency's authority to permit correction of bid mistakes is limited to bids that are responsive to solicitation. Blount, Inc. v. U.S., 22 Cl. Ct. 221, 36 Cont. Cas. Fed. (CCH) P 75981, 1990 WL 210734 (1990). United States ⚷64.30

Term "responsibility" concerns how bidder will accomplish conformance with material provisions of contract; "responsibility" addresses performance capability of bidder, and normally involves inquiry into potential contractor's financial resources, experience, management, past performance, place of performance, and integrity. Blount, Inc. v. U.S., 22 Cl. Ct. 221, 36 Cont. Cas. Fed. (CCH) P 75981, 1990 WL 210734 (1990). United States ⚷64.45(2)

Bidder is not "responsible bidder," entitled to award of contract, if it fails to meet certain standards indicating that it does not have necessary manpower, financing, ability, desire, perseverance, equipment, and experience, which cumulatively would indicate that bidder lacked ability successfully to complete contract. International Verbatim Reporters, Inc. v. U.S., 9 Cl. Ct. 710, 33 Cont. Cas. Fed. (CCH) P 74323 (1986). United States ⚷64.45(2)

§ 9.102 Applicability.

(a) This subpart applies to all proposed contracts with any prospective contractor that is located—

(1) In the United States or its outlying areas; or

(2) Elsewhere, unless application of the subpart would be inconsistent with the laws or customs where the contractor is located.

(b) This subpart does not apply to proposed contracts with—

(1) Foreign, State, or local governments;

(2) Other U.S. Government agencies or their instrumentalities; or

(3) Agencies for people who are blind or severely disabled (see subpart 8.7).

United States Code Annotated

Administrative determinations, see 41 USCA § 257.

Contracts, planning, solicitation, evaluation, and award procedures, see 10 USCA § 2305.

Definitions, see 10 USCA § 2302, 41 USCA §§ 259, 403.

Determinations and decisions, see 10 USCA § 2310, 41 USCA § 262.

Notes of Decisions

In general 1

1 In general

An ordering agency is not required to perform a responsibility determination when placing a task or delivery order under a Federal Supply Schedule (FSS) contract, since the General Services Administration performed a responsibility determination at the time of award of the underlying contract. Advanced Technology Systems, Inc., B-296493.6, 2006 CPD ¶ 151 (Comp. Gen. 2006)

§ 9.103 Policy.

(a) Purchases shall be made from, and contracts shall be awarded to, responsible prospective contractors only.

(b) No purchase or award shall be made unless the contracting officer makes an affirmative determination of responsibility. In the absence of information clearly indicating that the prospective contractor is responsible, the contracting officer shall make a determination of nonresponsibility. If the prospective contractor is a small business concern, the contracting officer shall comply with subpart 19.6, Certificates of Competency and Determinations of Responsibility. (If Section 8(a) of the Small Business Act (15 U.S.C. 637) applies, see subpart 19.8.)

(c) The award of a contract to a supplier based on lowest evaluated price alone can be false economy if there is subsequent default, late deliveries, or other unsatisfactory performance resulting in additional contractual or administrative costs. While it is important that Government purchases be made at the lowest price, this does not require an award to a supplier solely because that supplier submits the lowest offer. A prospective contractor must affirmatively demonstrate its responsibility, including, when necessary, the responsibility of its proposed subcontractors.

United States Code Annotated

Administrative determinations, see 41 USCA § 257.

Contracts, planning, solicitation, evaluation, and award procedures, see 10 USCA § 2305.

Definitions, see 10 USCA § 2302, 41 USCA §§ 259, 403.

Determinations and decisions, see 10 USCA § 2310, 41 USCA § 262.

Planning and solicitation requirements, see 41 USCA § 253a.

Notes of Decisions

Discretion of contracting officers 4
Due process of law 3
Federal preemption 1
Hearing 6
Judicial review 7
Responsibility, generally 2
Timeliness 5

1 Federal preemption

Virginia could not require that contractors working solely for background investigation contract services program (BICS) of Federal Bureau of Investigation (FBI) comply with Virginia's licensing and registration requirements concerning private security services, inasmuch as, by adding to qualifications necessary for BICS contractors to work for FBI, Virginia's regulatory scheme impermissibly frustrated objectives of federal procurement laws. Federal Property and Administrative Services Act of 1949, § 303B(d)(3), as amended, 41 U.S.C.A. § 253b(d)(3); Office of Federal Procurement Policy Act, § 16(1), as amended, 41 U.S.C.A. § 414(1); Va.Code 1950, §§ 9-182, subd. B, 9-183.9; 48 C.F.R. §§ 1.601, 9.103(b), 9.104-1(a, c, d, e, g). U.S. v. Com. of Va., 139 F.3d 984, 42 Cont. Cas. Fed. (CCH) P 77271 (4th Cir. 1998). Detectives ⚖1; Detectives ⚖3; States ⚖18.15

2 Responsibility, generally

The federal government decides who is a "responsible bidder," for purposes of an award of a procurement contract, using applicable federal laws and regulations. 48 C.F.R. § 9.104-1. LeBoeuf, Lamb, Greene & MacRae, LLP v. Abraham, 215 F. Supp. 2d 73 (D.D.C. 2002), opinion vacated, 347 F.3d 315, 358 (D.C. Cir. 2003) (The court vacated the judgment and remanded the case for a determination as to an apparent conflict of interest was considered as required by regulations, and whether the Department's need for expert legal services on the project supported a direct award of the contract to LeBoeuf or an award of other relief.) United States ☞64.45(2)

Air Force properly conducted responsibility determination as required by statute regulating government procurement contracts, though disappointed bidder claimed that Air Force released no rationale for its finding that successful bidder was "responsible"; statute explicitly states that contracting officer's signature on contract constitutes determination of responsibility, and no other rationale is required. Marwais Steel Co. v. Department of Air Force, 871 F. Supp. 1448, 40 Cont. Cas. Fed. (CCH) P 76781 (D.D.C. 1994). United States ☞64.45(2)

"Responsibility" in context of public contracts refers to bidder's apparent ability and capacity to perform contract's requirements. Applications Research Corp. v. Naval Air Development Center, 752 F. Supp. 660, 37 Cont. Cas. Fed. (CCH) P 76045 (E.D. Pa. 1990). Public Contracts ☞11

Under the Federal Acquisition Regulation (FAR), a contracting officer (CO) is required to make a responsibility determination only for the one bidder selected for award; FAR does not require procuring agencies to evaluate conclusively the responsibility of other bidders. Greenleaf Const. Co., Inc. v. U.S., 67 Fed. Cl. 350 (2005). United States ☞64.45(2)

FAR 9.104-1 requires a CO to assess the responsibility of a putative awardee prior to award. The determination is independent of the award decision itself, although it may well be related to both technical and pricing aspects of the proposal. The responsibility assessment entails such matters as whether an offeror has "adequate financial resources," can comply with the proposed performance schedule, has a satisfactory performance record, has the necessary "organization, experience, and technical skills" to perform the contract, and has the facilities necessary to perform. Orca Northwest Real Estate Services v. U.S., 65 Fed. Cl. 1 (2005), on reconsideration, 65 Fed. Cl. 419 (2005)

"Definitive responsibility criteria" are specific and objective standards established by an agency for use in a particular procurement for the measurement of a bidder's ability to perform the contract; they limit the class of bidders to those meeting specified qualitative and quantitative qualifications necessary for contract performance. News Printing Co., Inc. v. U.S., 46 Fed. Cl. 740 (2000). United States ☞64.45(2)

Two characteristics mark definitive responsibility criteria in a government contract solicitation: they must be specific and objective, and the bidders have to be warned of them. News Printing Co., Inc. v. U.S., 46 Fed. Cl. 740 (2000). United States ☞64.45(2)

Contracting officer's responsibility determination focuses on the bidder's ability to satisfy its contractual commitments encompassed within its responsive bid. 48 C.F.R. § 9.103. Ryan Co. v. U.S., 43 Fed. Cl. 646 (1999). United States ☞64.40(1)

Prospective government contractor is not entitled to contract award merely because it is the low bidder; prospective contractor must also prove that it is capable of performing the contract. 27 C.F.R. § 9.103(c). CRC Marine Services, Inc. v. U.S., 41 Fed. Cl. 66, 42 Cont. Cas. Fed. (CCH) P 77310 (1998). United States ☞64.55(1)

In typical government contract case, solicitation and related regulations require contracting officer to make separate determinations on issue of bid's "responsiveness" to terms of solicitation and "responsibility" of bidder to perform contract work covered in solicitation prior to awarding contract to apparent low bidder. VMS Hotel Partners v. U.S., 30 Fed. Cl. 512, 39 Cont. Cas. Fed. (CCH) P 76631 (1994). United States ☞64.30; United States ☞64.45(2)

Unlike determining "responsiveness" of bid, in assessing contractor's "responsibility," contracting officer is not limited to information contained in bid when opened; rather, contracting officer may solicit and contractor may supply additional information to demonstrate that contractor is capable of performing contract work. VMS Hotel Partners v. U.S., 30 Fed. Cl. 512, 39 Cont. Cas. Fed. (CCH) P 76631 (1994). United States ☞64.45(2)

"Responsibility" for purposes of public contract addresses performance capability of bidder including financial resources, experience, management, past performance, place of performance, and integrity, and evidence may be presented after bid opening until time of award. Bean Dredging Corp. v. U.S., 22 Cl. Ct. 519, 36 Cont. Cas. Fed. (CCH) P 76017, 1991 WL 15601 (1991). Public Contracts ☞11

In identifying whether particular requirement is related to responsiveness or to responsibility, responsibility concerns question of bidder's performance capability and responsiveness concerns promise to perform contract. Bean Dredging Corp. v. U.S., 22 Cl. Ct. 519, 36 Cont. Cas. Fed. (CCH) P 76017, 1991 WL 15601 (1991). Public Contracts ☞8; Public Contracts ☞11

When examining whether clause in bid related to bidder "responsiveness" or "responsibility," "responsiveness" refers to question whether bidder has promised to perform in precise manner requested by Government, whereas "responsibility" involves inquiry into bidder's ability and will to perform subject contract as promised. Blount, Inc. v. U.S., 22 Cl. Ct. 221, 36 Cont. Cas. Fed. (CCH) P 75981, 1990 WL 210734 (1990). United States ☞64.30

Fact that contracting officer requested clarification of bidder's response to business management questionnaire question in which bidder indicated that it intended to self-perform only 10% of contract work, while invitation for bid required self-performance of 20%, could not convert issue of nonresponsiveness of bid into issue of responsibility; procuring agency's authority to permit correction of bid mistakes is limited to bids that are responsive to solicitation. Blount, Inc. v. U.S., 22 Cl. Ct. 221, 36 Cont. Cas. Fed. (CCH) P 75981, 1990 WL 210734 (1990). United States ☞64.30

Term "responsibility" concerns how bidder will accomplish conformance with material provisions of contract; "responsibility" addresses performance capability of bidder, and normally involves inquiry into potential contractor's financial resources, experience, management, past performance, place of performance, and integrity. Blount, Inc. v. U.S., 22 Cl. Ct. 221, 36 Cont. Cas. Fed. (CCH) P 75981, 1990 WL 210734 (1990). United States ☞64.45(2)

Bidder is not "responsible bidder," entitled to award of contract, if it fails to meet certain standards indicating that it does not have necessary manpower, financing, ability, desire, perseverance, equipment, and experience, which cumulatively would indicate that bidder lacked ability successfully to complete contract. International Verbatim Reporters, Inc. v. U.S., 9 Cl. Ct. 710, 33 Cont. Cas. Fed. (CCH) P 74323 (1986). United States ☞64.45(2)

Under 32 C.F.R. § 1-904.1 (1970), the award of a procurement contract to a prospective contractor by the contracting officer constitutes an affirmative determination that the contractor is "responsible" within the meaning of 32 C.F.R. § 1-902. Transcountry Packing Co. v. U. S., 215 Ct. Cl. 390, 568 F.2d 1333, 24 Cont. Cas. Fed. (CCH) P 82055 (1978). United States ☞64.45(2)

A contractor is presumed nonresponsible until the contracting officer affirmatively finds that there is information clearly indicating that the offeror is responsible. Protest was sustained because the contracting officer shifted the presumption to one of responsibility until "proven" nonresponsible. FCi Fed., Inc., B-408558.4, 2014 CPD ¶ 308 (Comp. Gen. 2014)

Protest that awardee in fixed-price sealed bid acquisition submitted unrealistically low prices is dismissed, since question of whether a firm's pricing is too low does not involve the responsiveness of the firm's bid, but rather the firm's responsibility; agency, in making award, made an affirmative determination of responsibility, which is not for consideration under our Bid Protest Regulations except in circumstances not alleged by protester. AllWorld Language Consultants, Inc., B-298831, 2006 CPD ¶ 198 (Comp. Gen. 2006)

Responsibility is a term used to describe the offeror's ability to meet its contract obligations. See generally Federal Acquisition Regulation (FAR) subpart 9.1. In most cases, responsibility is determined on the basis of what the FAR refers to as general standards of responsibility, such as adequacy of financial resources, ability to meet delivery schedules, and a satisfactory record of past performance and of business integrity and ethics. FAR 9.104-1. In some cases, however, an agency will include in a solicitation a special standard of responsibility, FAR 9.104-2, which is often referred to as a definitive criterion of responsibility. Definitive responsibility criteria are specific and objective standards established by an agency as a precondition to award which are designed to measure a prospective contractor's ability to perform the contract. Vador Ventures, Inc., B-296394, 2005

CPD ¶ 155 (Comp. Gen. 2005)

3 Due process of law

Small Business Administration (SBA) is responsible for determining the responsibility of small businesses. SBA's investigation of government contract bidder, resulting in denial of certificate of competency, was thorough and unbiased, and did not violate bidder's due process rights, absent any evidence that SBA deviated from its standard operating procedure or in any manner deprived bidder of its right to submit pertinent information and to explain its case for a certificate of competency. U.S.C.A. Const.Amend. 5. PNM Const., Inc. v. U.S., 13 Cl. Ct. 745, 34 Cont. Cas. Fed. (CCH) P 75409, 1987 WL 20987 (1987). Constitutional Law ☞276(2); United States ☞64.20

4 Discretion of contracting officers

Protest challenging an agency's negative responsibility determination was sustained because the agency's determination was based on incomplete information and unsubstantiated conclusions and the contracting officer failed to consider readily available evidence demonstrating responsibility. Engility Corp., B-413202, 2016 WL 5047471 (Comp.Gen. 2016)

Determination of government contracting officer that Icelandic company was a responsible contractor, in awarding company portion of military contract for shipping between United States and Iceland, had a rational basis, even if company's proffered letter of credit was tentative and was addressed to an affiliated company, in view of discretionary nature of responsibility determination and agency's self interest in making proper responsibility determinations. Iceland S.S. Co., Ltd.-Eimskip v. U.S. Dept. of Army, 201 F.3d 451, 462, 2000 A.M.C. 1487 (D.C. Cir. 2000). United States ☞64.45(2)

Contracting officers are generally given wide discretion in making responsibility determinations with respect to prospective government contractors and in determining the amount of information that is required to make a responsibility determination. 48 C.F.R. § 9.103(a). Bender Shipbuilding & Repair Co., Inc. v. U.S., 297 F.3d 1358 (Fed. Cir. 2002). United States ☞64.45(2)

Contracting officers are generally given wide discretion in making responsibility determinations and in determining the amount of information that is required to make a responsibility determination. Impresa Construzioni Geom. Domenico Garufi v. U.S., 238 F.3d 1324 (Fed. Cir. 2001). United States ☞64.45(2)

Although contracting officer is given discretion to seek additional or clarifying responsibility information from contractor, he is not obligated to do so. 48 C.F.R. § 9.105-1(a). John C. Grimberg Co., Inc. v. U.S., 185 F.3d 1297 (Fed. Cir. 1999). United States ☞64.45(2)

Although finding of responsibility by bidder is discretionary finding involving balancing of many factors, discretion is necessary only for factors as to which federal contracting officer is exercising business judgment. Action Service Corp. v. Garrett, 797 F. Supp. 82 (D.P.R. 1992). United States ☞64.45(2)

In making a determination of responsibility, a contracting officer in general has wide discretion both in making a determination of responsibility and in determining the amount of information required to make the determination. While a contracting officer is required to explain a determination of nonresponsibility, the FAR does not require an explanation that the offeror is responsible. The burden is on the disappointed offeror to establish that the contracting officer acted arbitrarily and capriciously. Responsibility determination based only on review of the Excluded Parties List and Dun & Bradstreet reports was adequate. Southern Foods, Inc. v. U.S., 76 Fed. Cl. 769 (2007)

Agency has great discretion in determining the scope of an evaluation factor in a procurement, and can give more weight to one past contract over another if it is more relevant to an offeror's future performance on the solicited contract. Gulf Group, Inc. v. U.S., 56 Fed. Cl. 391 (2003). United States ☞64.45(2)

Agency representative has broad discretion to decide whether to communicate with a contractor concerning its performance history, under section of the Federal Acquisition Regulation (FAR) providing that offerors "may" be given the opportunity to clarify certain aspects of proposals, including past performance information, where award will be made without conducting discussions. 48 C.F.R. § 15.306(a)(2). JWK Intern. Corp. v. U.S., 52 Fed.

Cl. 650 (2002), aff'd, 56 Fed. Appx. 474 (Fed. Cir. 2003). United States ⊸64.45(2)

An agency has broad discretion in making past performance evaluations for purpose of procurement. SDS Intern. v. U.S., 48 Fed. Cl. 759 (2001). United States ⊸64.45(2) It is within the discretion of the procuring agency to find that some of an offeror's past contracts are not relevant to the procurement at hand. SDS Intern. v. U.S., 48 Fed. Cl. 742 (2001). United States ⊸64.45(2)

Contracting agency has broad discretion in making responsibility determinations since it must bear the brunt of difficulties experienced in obtaining the required performance. News Printing Co., Inc. v. U.S., 46 Fed. Cl. 740 (2000). United States ⊸64.45(2)

Responsibility determinations by contracting agency are of necessity a matter of business judgment and such judgments must be based on fact and reached in good faith. News Printing Co., Inc. v. U.S., 46 Fed. Cl. 740 (2000). United States ⊸64.45(2)

Agency personnel engaged in procurement are generally given great discretion in determining what references to review in evaluating past performance of bidders; thus, there is no requirement that all references listed in a proposal be checked. Seattle Sec. Services, Inc. v. U.S., 45 Fed. Cl. 560 (2000). United States ⊸64.45(2)

Defaulted contractor may be considered for award of reprocurement contract; however, whether it receives the award lies within contracting officer's discretionary authority. Venice Maid Co., Inc. v. U. S., 225 Ct. Cl. 418, 639 F.2d 690, 28 Cont. Cas. Fed. (CCH) P 80851 (1980). United States ⊸64.45(2)

Protest challenging rejection of small business protester's offer on the ground that the agency's decision constituted a nonresponsibility determination that should have been referred to the Small Business Administration is sustained where the basis of the agency's determination-that protester would be unable to obtain the required parts-relates directly to the firm's capability to perform the contract. Fabritech, Inc., B-298247, B-298247.2, 2006 CPD ¶ 112 (Comp. Gen. 2006)

5 Timeliness

Responsibility determinations in relation to bids are made at time of award; bidder may present evidence subsequent to bid opening but prior to award to demonstrate bidder's responsibility. Blount, Inc. v. U.S., 22 Cl. Ct. 221, 36 Cont. Cas. Fed. (CCH) P 75981, 1990 WL 210734 (1990). United States ⊸64.30

6 Hearing

Acquisition regulations did not mandate any right of hearing to bidder prior to determination by contracting officer that bidder was a "nonresponsible contractor," and, absent clear and convincing evidence that officer's decision was irrational or that bidder was de facto debarred, bidder's due process rights were not violated by the "nonresponsibility" determination. U.S.C.A. Const.Amend. 5. PNM Const., Inc. v. U.S., 13 Cl. Ct. 745, 34 Cont. Cas. Fed. (CCH) P 75409, 1987 WL 20987 (1987). Administrative Law And Procedure ⊸470; Constitutional Law ⊸276(2); United States ⊸64.45(2)

7 Judicial review

Agency's determination of government contractor's responsibility is only reviewable upon showing of agency fraud, bad faith or misapplication of responsibility criteria. 48 C.F.R. § 9.104-1 (1996). City & County of San Francisco v. U.S., 130 F.3d 873, 42 Cont. Cas. Fed. (CCH) P 77215 (9th Cir. 1997). United States ⊸64.60(3.1)

Because of the special nature of government contracting determinations, review of such determinations by the Court of Appeals is an especially deferential application of the arbitrary and capricious standard. Iceland S.S. Co., Ltd.-Eimskip v. U.S. Dept. of Army, 201 F.3d 451, 461, 2000 A.M.C. 1487 (D.C. Cir. 2000). United States ⊸64.60(4)

Bidder responsibility is ultimately question of fact. 41 U.S.C.A. § 253(b). Northeast Const. Co. v. Romney, 485 F.2d 752, 759, 5 Fair Empl. Prac. Cas. (BNA) 746, 6 Fair Empl. Prac. Cas. (BNA) 119, 5 Empl. Prac. Dec. (CCH) P 8495, 6 Empl. Prac. Dec. (CCH) P 8784 (D.C. Cir. 1973). United States ⊸64.45(2)

Reviewing court cannot substitute its judgment for that of contracting officer in making responsibility determinations with respect to prospective government contractors. 48 C.F.R.

§ 9.103(a). Bender Shipbuilding & Repair Co., Inc. v. U.S., 297 F.3d 1358 (Fed. Cir. 2002). United States ☞64.60(3.1)

In reviewing, under Administrative Procedure Act (APA), bid protest challenging contracting officer's failure to find successful bidder non-responsible due to alleged misrepresentation in its certification, Court of Appeals would require explanation by deposition of contracting officer's reasons for accepting certification, given absence of articulation in the record of what contracting officer concluded when reviewing certification and given evidence raising serious questions as to accuracy of certification. 5 U.S.C.A. § 551 et seq.; 48 C.F.R. §§ 9.104-1(g), 52.209-5. Impresa Construzioni Geom. Domenico Garufi v. U.S., 238 F.3d 1324 (Fed. Cir. 2001). United States ☞64.60(1)

On judicial review under Administrative Procedure Act (APA) of bid protest challenging contracting officer's failure to find bidder non-responsible due to alleged misrepresentation in its certification, court was required to assume that contracting officer considered certification and concluded that it was not misleading, then ask whether this conclusion was arbitrary. 5 U.S.C.A. § 551 et seq.; 48 C.F.R. §§ 9.104-1(g), 52.209-5. Impresa Construzioni Geom. Domenico Garufi v. U.S., 238 F.3d 1324 (Fed. Cir. 2001). United States ☞64.60(4)

Appropriate course for obtaining reasons for contracting officer's responsibility determination for joint venture awarded government contract, so as to permit reviewing court to address whether determination was arbitrary and capricious under Administrative Procedure Act (APA), was to order contracting officer's deposition, confined strictly to placing on the record the basis for conclusion that joint venture had satisfactory record of performance, integrity, and business ethics. 5 U.S.C.A. § 551 et seq.; 48 C.F.R. § 9.105-1(a). Impresa Construzioni Geom. Domenico Garufi v. U.S., 238 F.3d 1324 (Fed. Cir. 2001). United States ☞64.60(1)

Absence of allegations of fraud or bad faith by contracting officer did not shield officer's responsibility determination in contract procurement process from judicial review; Administrative Procedure Act (APA) allowed for review of responsibility determination if there was violation of statute or regulation, or, alternatively, if determination lacked rational basis. 5 U.S.C.A. § 706; 28 U.S.C.A. § 1491(b). Impresa Construzioni Geom. Domenico Garufi v. U.S., 238 F.3d 1324 (Fed. Cir. 2001). United States ☞64.45(2); United States ☞64.60(1)

Past criminal activities by a corporate officer do not automatically establish that bidder for federal contract fails responsibility requirement. Impresa Construzioni Geom. Domenico Garufi v. U.S., 238 F.3d 1324 (Fed. Cir. 2001). United States ☞64.45(2); United States ☞64.60(1)

Decision by contracting officer whether to allow contractor to cure problems related to its responsibility or to make nonresponsibility determination based on existing record, without giving contractor opportunity to explain or defend against adverse evidence, is reviewed for abuse of discretion. John C. Grimberg Co., Inc. v. U.S., 185 F.3d 1297 (Fed. Cir. 1999). United States ☞64.45(2)

Particular deference is due a contracting officer's determination involving the responsibility of a bidder for government contract to perform under the contract. ANADAC, Inc. v. U.S. Dept. of Justice, I.N.S., 44 F. Supp. 2d 306 (D.D.C. 1999). United States ☞64.45(2)

Certificate of competency issued by Small Business Administration to successful low bidder on Navy contract for procurement of six marine thruster units would be set aside for failure to review compliance with "standard commercial product" clause in invitation for bids; Navy made no assessment of compliance despite fact that clause was part of product specification; SBA made only an after-the-fact, offhanded assessment of whether bidder met the specifications, accepting without question as evidence of "current offering for sale" a one-page flyer which described bidder's ability to produce all manner of thrust or propulsion systems. Small Business Act, § 2[8](b)(7), 15 U.S.C.A. § 637(b)(7). Ulstein Maritime, Ltd. v. U.S., 646 F. Supp. 720, 27 Wage & Hour Cas. (BNA) 1641 (D.R.I. 1986), judgment aff'd, 833 F.2d 1052, 34 Cont. Cas. Fed. (CCH) P 75405 (1st Cir. 1987). United States ☞64.60(5.1)

Record supported the Coast Guard's conclusion that plaintiff, low bidder on contract to construct medium endurance cutters and to provide spare parts, was a responsible bidder, that the determination to award contract to plaintiff was neither arbitrary nor capricious, that it was made in good faith, that determination did not lack reasonable or rational basis, and that there was no clear and prejudicial violation of any procurement regulation. Robert E. Derecktor of Rhode Island, Inc. v. Goldschmidt, 516 F. Supp. 1085, 29 Cont. Cas. Fed. (CCH) P 81853 (D.R.I. 1981). United States ☞64.45(2)

A responsibility determination by a contracting officer (CO) is not immune from judicial review simply because allegations of fraud or bad faith are absent; rather, traditional standard of review based on the Administrative Procedure Act (APA) allows for review of an agency's responsibility determination if there has been a violation of a statute or regulation, or alternatively, if the agency determination lacked a rational basis. 5 U.S.C.A. § 551 et seq.; 48 C.F.R. § 9.103(b). Impresa Construzioni Geom. Domenico Garufi v. U.S., 52 Fed. Cl. 421 (2002). United States ☞64.60(1)

General responsibility determinations of contracting agency will not be overturned on judicial review, absent allegations of fraud or bad faith. News Printing Co., Inc. v. U.S., 46 Fed. Cl. 740 (2000). United States ☞64.45(2)

Judicial review of agency's preaward procurement decision is limited in scope, with such decision being accorded great deference; it is through narrow lens that reviewing court is charged with determining whether government has satisfied implied contractual condition that each bid, received by government in response to request for proposals, will be fairly and honestly evaluated. YRT Services Corp. v. U.S., 28 Fed. Cl. 366, 38 Cont. Cas. Fed. (CCH) P 76512 (1993). United States ☞64.60(3.1)

Government is entitled to some deference in its decision making regarding responsibility determination under Federal Acquisition Regulations (FAR) and standard of review of regarding actions of government official who has made responsibility determination under FAR is difficult one for plaintiff to meet. YRT Services Corp. v. U.S., 28 Fed. Cl. 366, 38 Cont. Cas. Fed. (CCH) P 76512 (1993). United States ☞64.60(3.1)

Aggrieved bidder has burden to show that there was no rational basis for determination made by Army Corps of Engineers in preaward procurement action; court should not substitute its judgment for that of agency but should intervene only if agency acted irrationally or unreasonably. Bean Dredging Corp. v. U.S., 22 Cl. Ct. 519, 36 Cont. Cas. Fed. (CCH) P 76017, 1991 WL 15601 (1991). United States ☞64.60(4)

§ 9.104 Standards.

§ 9.104-1 General standards.

To be determined responsible, a prospective contractor must—

(a) Have adequate financial resources to perform the contract, or the ability to obtain them (see 9.104-3(a));

(b) Be able to comply with the required or proposed delivery or performance schedule, taking into consideration all existing commercial and governmental business commitments;

(c) Have a satisfactory performance record (see 9.104-3(b) and subpart 42.15). A prospective contractor shall not be determined responsible or nonresponsible solely on the basis of a lack of relevant performance history, except as provided in 9.104-2;

(d) Have a satisfactory record of integrity and business ethics (for example, see subpart 42.15).

(e) Have the necessary organization, experience, accounting and operational controls, and technical skills, or the ability to obtain them (including, as appropriate, such elements as production control procedures, property control systems, quality assurance measures, and safety programs applicable to materials to be produced or services to be performed by the prospective contractor and subcontractors). (See 9.104-3(a).)

(f) Have the necessary production, construction, and technical equipment and facilities, or the ability to obtain them (see 9.104-3(a)); and

(g) Be otherwise qualified and eligible to receive an award under applicable laws and regulations (see also inverted domestic corporation prohibition at 9.108).

United States Code Annotated

Administrative determinations, see 41 USCA § 257.

Contracts, planning, solicitation, evaluation, and award procedures, see 10 USCA § 2305.

Definitions, see 10 USCA § 2302, 41 USCA §§ 259, 403.

Determinations and decisions, see 10 USCA § 2310, 41 USCA § 262.

Planning and solicitation requirements, see 41 USCA § 253a.

Notes of Decisions

In general 1
Business integrity 2
Financial responsibility 3
Licensing 4
Number of employees 5
Poor performance 6
Schedule compliance 7
Understanding and capability 8

1 In general

"Responsibility" in context of public contracts refers to bidder's apparent ability and capacity to perform contract's requirements. Applications Research Corp. v. Naval Air Development Center, 752 F. Supp. 660, 37 Cont. Cas. Fed. (CCH) P 76045 (E.D. Pa. 1990). Public Contracts ☞11

"Definitive responsibility criteria" are specific and objective standards established by an agency for use in a particular procurement for the measurement of a bidder's ability to perform the contract; they limit the class of bidders to those meeting specified qualitative and quantitative qualifications necessary for contract performance. News Printing Co., Inc. v. U.S., 46 Fed. Cl. 740 (2000). United States ☞64.45(2)

Two characteristics mark definitive responsibility criteria in a government contract solicitation: they must be specific and objective, and the bidders have to be warned of them. News Printing Co., Inc. v. U.S., 46 Fed. Cl. 740 (2000). United States ☞64.45(2)

Contracting officer's responsibility determination focuses on the bidder's ability to satisfy its contractual commitments encompassed within its responsive bid. 48 C.F.R. § 9.103. Ryan Co. v. U.S., 43 Fed. Cl. 646 (1999). United States ☞64.40(1)

Prospective government contractor is not entitled to contract award merely because it is the low bidder; prospective contractor must also prove that it is capable of performing the contract. 27 C.F.R. § 9.103(c). CRC Marine Services, Inc. v. U.S., 41 Fed. Cl. 66, 42 Cont. Cas. Fed. (CCH) P 77310 (1998). United States ☞64.55(1)

In typical government contract case, solicitation and related regulations require contracting officer to make separate determinations on issue of bid's "responsiveness" to terms of solicitation and "responsibility" of bidder to perform contract work covered in solicitation prior to awarding contract to apparent low bidder. VMS Hotel Partners v. U.S., 30 Fed. Cl. 512, 39 Cont. Cas. Fed. (CCH) P 76631 (1994). United States ☞64.30; United States ☞64.45(2)

Unlike determining "responsiveness" of bid, in assessing contractor's "responsibility," contracting officer is not limited to information contained in bid when opened; rather, contracting officer may solicit and contractor may supply additional information to demonstrate that contractor is capable of performing contract work. VMS Hotel Partners v. U.S., 30 Fed. Cl. 512, 39 Cont. Cas. Fed. (CCH) P 76631 (1994). United States ☞64.45(2)

"Responsibility" for purposes of public contract addresses performance capability of bidder including financial resources, experience, management, past performance, place of performance, and integrity, and evidence may be presented after bid opening until time of award. Bean Dredging Corp. v. U.S., 22 Cl. Ct. 519, 36 Cont. Cas. Fed. (CCH) P 76017, 1991 WL 15601 (1991). Public Contracts ☞11

Bidder is not "responsible bidder," entitled to award of contract, if it fails to meet certain standards indicating that it does not have necessary manpower, financing, ability, desire, perseverance, equipment, and experience, which cumulatively would indicate that bidder lacked ability successfully to complete contract. International Verbatim Reporters, Inc. v. U.S., 9 Cl. Ct. 710, 33 Cont. Cas. Fed. (CCH) P 74323 (1986). United States ☞64.45(2)

Responsibility is a term used to describe the offeror's ability to meet its contract obligations. See generally Federal Acquisition Regulation (FAR) subpart 9.1. In most cases, responsibility is determined on the basis of what the FAR refers to as general standards of responsibility, such as adequacy of financial resources, ability to meet delivery schedules, and a satisfactory record of past performance and of business integrity and ethics. FAR 9.104-1. In some cases, however, an agency will include in a solicitation a special standard of responsibility, FAR 9.104-2, which is often referred to as a definitive criterion of responsibility. Definitive responsibility criteria are specific and objective standards established by an agency as a precondition to award which are designed to measure a prospective contractor's ability to perform the contract. Vador Ventures, Inc., B-296394, 2005 CPD ¶ 155 (Comp. Gen. 2005)

2 Business integrity

Protest challenging an agency's affirmative determination of the awardee's responsibility on the ground that there is evidence raising serious concerns that the contracting officer (CO) unreasonably failed to consider available relevant information suggesting that the awardee does not have a satisfactory record of integrity and business ethics is denied where the record shows that: (1) while the awardee was investigated for possible fraud, it was neither indicted nor proposed for debarment; (2) the CO was aware of the information that led to the questions about the awardee's activities under certain previous contracts and did not ignore the matter; and (3) the CO's more recent dealings with the company provided a rational basis for her conclusion that the awardee is a responsible contractor. Matter of: FN Manufacturing, Inc., B-297172, B-297172.2, 2005 CPD ¶ 212 (Comp. Gen. 2005)

Contracting officer's affirmative determination of the awardee's responsibility is not reasonably based where, despite having general awareness of misconduct by some of awardee's principals and parent company, the contracting officer did not obtain sufficient information about or consider the awardee's record of integrity and business ethics in making his responsibility determination. Southwestern Bell Telephone Company, B-292476, 2003 CPD ¶ 177 (Comp. Gen. 2003)

Determination by contracting officer that offeror, should it be in line for award, would be nonresponsible for lack of integrity because of criminal conviction in connection with obtaining, attempting to obtain, or performing a public contract is reasonable and therefore offeror is not an interested party to protest evaluation of proposals since it would not receive award in any event. Service Deli, Inc., B-276251, 97-1 CPD ¶ 110 (Comp. Gen. 1997)

3 Financial responsibility

Contracting officer's determination that bidder for Army ship-building contract was financially responsible was not arbitrary or capricious, or without adequate factual basis, notwithstanding contentions that decision overlooked fact that money which bidder would receive and have available as working capital was subject to creditors' liens and that contracting officer failed to check with creditors or bankruptcy court in which bidder's Chapter 11 case was pending to determine whether they would permit bidder to use such funds to perform contract; contracting officer examined all relevant financial data before him and carefully articulated detailed explanation for his decision, which was amply supported by the record, including indications that it was likely that creditors and bankruptcy court would authorize bidder to use funds it received to perform contract. Bender Shipbuilding & Repair Co., Inc. v. U.S., 297 F.3d 1358 (Fed. Cir. 2002)

Affirmative determination of awardee's financial responsibility was not reasonable where, despite knowing awardee had sold an affiliated company, contracting officer nevertheless based responsibility determination on financial capability assessment by Defense Contract Audit Agency that was based in significant measure on financial resources of company that had been sold. Matter of: Greenleaf Construction Company, Inc., B-293105.18, B-293105.19, 2006 CPD ¶ 19 (Comp. Gen. 2006)

Agency reasonably determined that protester was nonresponsible where, in making the nonresponsibility determination immediately prior to the protester's bankruptcy filing, the contracting officer performed a detailed financial review which established that the firm's unsatisfactory and deteriorating financial condition made it an unacceptable financial risk; the contracting officer had recognized the implications of an anticipated bankruptcy filing and reasonably concluded that it was unlikely that the bankruptcy reorganization plan would significantly reduce the financial risk, and that, even if successful, the bankruptcy reorganization was itself likely to create contract performance risk. XO Communications, Inc., B-290981, 2002 CPD ¶ 179 (Comp. Gen. 2002)

Agency reasonably determined that protester was nonresponsible to perform construction/ lease contract based on lack of financial capability, where protester's financial information contained significant discrepancies and indicated that protester had proposed a rental rate insufficient to cover the cost of construction. Acquest Development LLC, B-287439, 2001 CPD ¶ 101 (Comp. Gen. 2001)

Contracting officer's rejection of proposal based on concerns regarding offeror's financial responsibility was reasonable even thought the RFP did not specifically require vendors to demonstrate financial responsibility. Before awarding a contract, a contracting officer must make an affirmative determination that the prospective contractor is responsible. FAR 9.103(b). The RFP included GSAR clause 552.212-73, "Evaluation- Commercial Items (Multiple Award Schedule)," which provides that award would be made to "those responsible offerors that offer reasonable pricing . . ." Moreover, FAR Part 9, "Contractor Qualifications," provides that "[n]o purchase or award shall be made unless the contracting officer makes an affirmative determination of responsibility." FAR § 9.103(b). Although Part 9 was not included in the solicitation, FAR 9.100 states that subpart 9.1 prescribes policies, standards, and procedures for determining whether prospective contractors are responsible, and FAR 9.102 provides that subpart 9.1 "applies to all proposed contracts with any prospective contractor . . . in the United States . . ." Concepts Building Systems, Inc., B-281995, 99-1 CPD ¶ 95 (Comp. Gen. 1999)

Protest challenging nonresponsibility determination on ground that agency's alleged failure to consider protester's financial information resulted in Small Business Administration's failure to receive vital information bearing on protester's financial capability is denied where: (1) small business protester failed to respond to three separate requests by contracting agency for financial information; and (2) Small Business Administration conducted its own investigation before affirming agency's determination that protester was nonresponsible. Matter of: International Shipbuilding, Inc., B-257071, B-257071.2, 94-2 CPD ¶ 245 (Comp. Gen. 1994)

Contracting officer reasonably determined that protester lacked the financial resources for performance and was therefore nonresponsible where protester's financial statements reflected a lack of available working capital, deficit retained earnings, negative net worth, and a large volume of past due payments, and where protester failed to furnish references from a financial institution confirming the availability of a line of credit. Matter of: Bernard Johnson Incorporated, B-252481, 93-1 CPD ¶ 476 (Comp. Gen. 1993)

4 Licensing

Protest challenging an agency's affirmative determination of the awardees responsibility on the ground that the contracting officer failed to consider the fact that the awardee did not possess a North Carolina unlimited general contractors license at the time of award, and could not likely obtain the required license in a timely manner, if at all, is dismissed where the record shows that the license was not required to perform most of the work called for under the solicitation, if any work at all; thus, information regarding the awardees ability to obtain the license is not the type of information that would be expected to have a strong bearing on the awardees responsibility, and, as a result, an allegation that the agency failed to consider such information is not sufficient to trigger review by GAO of the agency's affirmative responsibility determination. Transcontinental Enterprises, Inc., B-294765, 2004 CPD ¶ 240 (Comp. Gen. 2004)

5 Number of employees

Term "number of employees" in regulation permitting contracting officer to waive or permit correction of minor informality or irregularity relates to a firm's capacity and capabilities, a matter of "responsibility." Northeast Const. Co. v. Romney, 485 F.2d 752, 795, 5 Fair Empl. Prac. Cas. (BNA) 746, 6 Fair Empl. Prac. Cas. (BNA) 119, 5 Empl. Prac. Dec. (CCH) P 8495, 6 Empl. Prac. Dec. (CCH) P 8784 (D.C. Cir. 1973). United States ☞64.45(2)

6 Poor performance

Protest against nonresponsibility determination is denied where the determination was reasonably based upon the contracting officer's conclusion that the protester's recent contract performance on similar work was inadequate because of consistently high volume of unresolved customer complaints, notwithstanding protester's disagreement with the agency's interpretation of the underlying facts. Pacific Photocopy and Research Services, B-281127, 98-2 CPD ¶ 164 (Comp. Gen. 1998)

7 Schedule compliance

Contention that agency wrongly rejected protester's offer after determining that the protester was nonresponsible is denied where the record shows that the agency reasonably concluded that protester had not clearly established that it could meet the solicitation's delivery schedule. The CO looked at protester's previous delinquencies for delivery of the same items under the current contract, at the company's proposed schedule for addressing its previously delinquent contracts, and at the delivery schedule under the follow-on contract, and concluded it did not appear that the protester would be able to make the deliveries required under the solicitation. Kilgore Flares Company, B-292944, B-292944.2, B-292944.3, 2004 CPD ¶ 8 (Comp. Gen. 2003)

Contracting officer reasonably found protester nonresponsible where the protester failed to promptly provide the necessary proof that it would be able to comply with the required performance schedule. 50 State Security Service, Inc., B-272114, 96-2 CPD ¶ 123 (Comp. Gen. 1996)

8 Understanding and capability

Agency's determination, based on information acquired during preaward survey, that offeror lacked the understanding and capability to implement its proposed approach to meeting the specification requirements, constituted a nonresponsibility determination, not a revised technical evaluation. Agency therefore was not required to reopen discussions and request revised proposals. Matter of: TAAS-Israel Industries, Inc., B-251789, B-251789.3, 94-1 CPD ¶ 197 (Comp. Gen. 1994)

§ 9.104-2 Special standards.

(a) When it is necessary for a particular acquisition or class of acquisitions, the contracting officer shall develop, with the assistance of appropriate specialists, special standards of responsibility. Special standards may be particularly desirable when experience has demonstrated that unusual expertise or specialized facilities are needed for adequate contract performance. The special standards shall be set forth in the solicitation (and so identified) and shall apply to all offerors.

(b) Contracting officers shall award contracts for subsistence only to those prospective contractors that meet the general standards in 9.104-1 and are approved in accordance with agency sanitation standards and procedures.

United States Code Annotated

Administrative determinations, see 41 USCA § 257.

Contracts, planning, solicitation, evaluation, and award procedures, see 10 USCA § 2305.

Definitions, see 10 USCA § 2302, 41 USCA §§ 259, 403.

Determinations and decisions, see 10 USCA § 2310, 41 USCA § 262.

Planning and solicitation requirements, see 41 USCA § 253a.

Notes of Decisions

In general 1
Examples 2
Judicial review 3
Small business subcontracting plans 4

1 In general

Valid special standard of responsibility in bid solicitation must be specific, objective, and mandatory. 48 C.F.R. § 9.104-2(a). John C. Grimberg Co., Inc. v. U.S., 185 F.3d 1297 (Fed. Cir. 1999). Public Contracts ⊙7

Contracting officer (CO) can only impose special standards of responsibility if they are set forth in the solicitation and so identified. News Printing Co., Inc. v. U.S., 46 Fed. Cl.

740 (2000). United States ☞64.45(2)

Responsibility is a term used to describe the offeror's ability to meet its contract obligations. See generally Federal Acquisition Regulation (FAR) subpart 9.1. In most cases, responsibility is determined on the basis of what the FAR refers to as general standards of responsibility, such as adequacy of financial resources, ability to meet delivery schedules, and a satisfactory record of past performance and of business integrity and ethics. FAR 9.104-1. In some cases, however, an agency will include in a solicitation a special standard of responsibility, FAR 9.104-2, which is often referred to as a definitive criterion of responsibility. Definitive responsibility criteria are specific and objective standards established by an agency as a precondition to award which are designed to measure a prospective contractor's ability to perform the contract. Vador Ventures, Inc., B-296394, 2005 CPD ¶ 155 (Comp. Gen. 2005)

Definitive responsibility criteria are specific and objective standards established by an agency for use in a particular procurement to measure a bidder's ability to perform the contract. FAR 9.104-2. These special standards of responsibility limit the class of bidders to those meeting specified qualitative and quantitative qualifications necessary for adequate contract performance. HK Systems, Inc.—Protest and Reconsideration, B-291647.6, B-291647.7, 2003 CPD ¶ 159 (Comp. Gen. 2003)

2 Examples

Factors contained in Building Comparison Chart, which agency used to evaluate whether bidder on renovation project satisfied special standard of responsibility that bidder have completed three projects within past six years involving restoration or renovation of building interiors and exteriors of historic properties that were "of the size and complexity of the proposed project" were not themselves special standards required to be provided to bidders in the solicitation; no quantitative requirement had to be met under any of the criteria, and solicitation was sufficiently specific and provided bidders with reasonable notice of what would satisfy special "size and complexity" standard. 48 C.F.R. § 9.104-2(a). John C. Grimberg Co., Inc. v. U.S., 185 F.3d 1297 (Fed. Cir. 1999). United States ☞64.25

Requirement of invitation for bids on patent printing contract that low bidder pass a pre-award test which called for it to print 100 patents from a data tape in accordance with specifications was not a definitive or special responsibility criterion, and contracting agency's finding that bidder successfully completed the pre-award test was not reviewable absent fraud or bad faith. News Printing Co., Inc. v. U.S., 46 Fed. Cl. 740 (2000). United States ☞64.45(2)

Plain language of section of the bid solicitation set forth definitive responsibility criteria which included the submission of a listing which had to specify at least five contracts similar to the scope, size, and dollar value of the present project, performed within the last three years. 48 C.F.R. 9.104-2. Charles H. Tompkins Co. v. U.S., 43 Fed. Cl. 716 (1999). United States ☞64.25

Protest that awardee's proposed key personnel do not meet solicitation's definitive responsibility criteria requiring experience managing or supervising the operation of an 800,000 square foot building is denied where the agency has reasonably determined that experience of awardee's personnel with two buildings (totaling 971,425 square feet), operated in major respects as one building, and having integrated systems with equipment sized to operate the two buildings together, satisfied the requirements. Vador Ventures, Inc., B-296394, 2005 CPD ¶ 155 (Comp. Gen. 2005)

3 Judicial review

Only if bidder responsibility standards are "special" or "definitive responsibility criteria," is the Court of Federal Claims able to do a typical bid protest review of contracting agency's responsibility determinations for abuse of discretion. News Printing Co., Inc. v. U.S., 46 Fed. Cl. 740 (2000). United States ☞64.45(2)

4 Small business subcontracting plans

In a negotiated procurement that provided for the evaluation of small business subcontracting plans on a pass/fail basis, the rejection of the protester's proposal as technically unacceptable on the basis of the acceptability of its small business subcontracting plan was unreasonable. Because the plans were evaluated on a pass/fail basis, the agency's evaluation of those plans concern an offeror's responsibility and not the technical merit of the offeror's proposal. Since there was no indication that the offeror would not be able to comply with the terms of the subcontracting plan, rejection of the proposal was unreasonable. MANCON, B-405663, 2012 CPD ¶ 68 (Comp. Gen 2012)

§ 9.104-3 Application of standards.

(a) Ability to obtain resources. Except to the extent that a prospective contractor has sufficient resources or proposes to perform the contract by subcontracting, the contracting officer shall require acceptable evidence of the prospective contractor's ability to obtain required resources (see 9.104-1(a), (e), and (f)). Acceptable evidence normally consists of a commitment or explicit arrangement, that will be in existence at the time of contract award, to rent, purchase, or otherwise acquire the needed facilities, equipment, other resources, or personnel. Consideration of a prime contractor's compliance with limitations on subcontracting shall take into account the time period covered by the contract base period or quantities plus option periods or quantities, if such options are considered when evaluating offers for award.

(b) Satisfactory performance record. A prospective contractor that is or recently has been seriously deficient in contract performance shall be presumed to be nonresponsible, unless the contracting officer determines that the circumstances were properly beyond the contractor's control, or that the contractor has taken appropriate corrective action. Past failure to apply sufficient tenacity and perseverance to perform acceptably is strong evidence of nonresponsibility. Failure to meet the quality requirements of the contract is a significant factor to consider in determining satisfactory performance. The contracting officer shall consider the number of contracts involved and the extent of deficient performance in each contract when making this determination. If the pending contract requires a subcontracting plan pursuant to subpart 19.7, The Small Business Subcontracting Program, the contracting officer shall also consider the prospective contractor's compliance with subcontracting plans under recent contracts.

(c) Affiliated concerns. Affiliated concerns (see "Concern" in 19.001 and "Affiliates" in 19.101) are normally considered separate entities in determining whether the concern that is to perform the contract meets the applicable standards for responsibility. However, the contracting officer shall consider the affiliate's past performance and integrity when they may adversely affect the prospective contractor's responsibility.

(d) (1) Small business concerns. Upon making a determination of nonresponsibility with regard to a small business concern, the contracting officer shall refer the matter to the Small Business Administration, which will decide whether to issue a Certificate of Competency (see subpart 19.6).

(2) A small business that is unable to comply with the limitations on subcontracting at 52.219-14 may be considered nonresponsible.

United States Code Annotated

Administrative determinations, see 41 USCA § 257.

Contracts, planning, solicitation, evaluation, and award procedures, see 10 USCA § 2305.

Definitions, see 10 USCA § 2302, 41 USCA §§ 259, 403.

Determinations and decisions, see 10 USCA § 2310, 41 USCA § 262.

Planning and solicitation requirements, see 41 USCA § 253a.

Notes of Decisions

Equipment and facilities 1
Performance record—In general 2
Small business concerns 3

1 Equipment and facilities

Responsibility determination of government contracting officer that United States flag carrier had shown sufficient evidence of right to control a vessel to perform military contract for shipping between United States and Iceland had a rational basis, in view of carrier's submission of four letters from marine companies pledging the availability of vessels. Iceland S.S. Co., Ltd.-Eimskip v. U.S. Dept. of Army, 201 F.3d 451, 462, 2000 A.M.C. 1487

(D.C. Cir. 2000). United States ☞64.45(2)

Requirement of invitation for bids that low bidder submit evidence of its ability to bill electronically during a pre-award survey was not a definitive responsibility requirement, and thus agency's determination that bidder met requirement was not subject to judicial scrutiny. 48 C.F.R. § 9.104-1(f). News Printing Co., Inc. v. U.S., 46 Fed. Cl. 740 (2000). United States ☞64.45(2)

Requirement of invitation for bids that low bidder submit for government approval a written quality control program addressing seven specific factors was not a definitive or special responsibility standard, and contracting agency's determination that bidder met requirement was not subject to judicial review for abuse of discretion. 48 C.F.R. § 9.104-1(f). News Printing Co., Inc. v. U.S., 46 Fed. Cl. 740 (2000). United States ☞64.45(2)

2 Performance record—In general

Federal Aviation Administration (FAA) determination that bidder on contract to provide operations and maintenance services satisfied the solicitation's past performance provision, which required experience managing a facility with over 60 employees, based in part on its experience managing a correctional facility with 60 workers, including 44 inmates, was not arbitrary or capricious, where the FAA found the inmates were employees because they were both paid and supervised by the bidder. J.A. Jones Management Services v. F.A.A., 225 F.3d 761, 765 (D.C. Cir. 2000). United States ☞64.45(2)

However, government violated dairy products supplier's due process liberty right, where it rejected the supplier's bids to supply dairy products to the government based on contracting officers' determinations that supplier lacked integrity and responsibility without giving the supplier any notice that its integrity was in issue. Old Dominion Dairy Products, Inc. v. Secretary of Defense, 631 F.2d 953, 27 Cont. Cas. Fed. (CCH) P 80584 (D.C. Cir. 1980) United States ☞64.45(2)

Determination of contracting officer that bidder on lease for office space was nonresponsible offeror was not abuse of discretion, where decision was based on bidder's failure to pay property taxes for four years and report revealing that business ventures which bidder had funded had history of going bankrupt, ceasing operations, or experiencing financial difficulties. Community Economic Development Corp., Inc. v. U.S., 577 F. Supp. 425 (D.D.C. 1983). United States ☞64.45(2)

Audit reports indicating that bidder had not complied with terms of prior contracts in several substantial respects provided ample basis for rejections of bids on basis that bidder was not responsible, and thus determinations by contracting officers as to nonresponsibility of bidder were reasonable. Old Dominion Dairy Products, Inc. v. Brown, 471 F. Supp. 300, 26 Cont. Cas. Fed. (CCH) P 83300 (D.D.C. 1979), judgment rev'd, 631 F.2d 953, 27 Cont. Cas. Fed. (CCH) P 80584 (D.C. Cir. 1980).

Contracting officer's ultimate decision to disqualify lowest bidder on government procurement contract for chairs as financially nonresponsible was not arbitrary and capricious since contracting officer considered planned facilities report, bidder's past performance under government contracts, and adverse financial analysis of bidder. 5 U.S.C.A. § 706(2) (A, D). Harvard Interiors Mfg. Co. v. U.S., 798 F. Supp. 565 (E.D. Mo. 1992). United States ☞64.45(2)

Contracting officer did not abuse his discretion in failing to award reprocurement contract to plaintiff, which willfully defaulted on first contract for manufacture and delivery of over 40,000 cans of chili con carne by failing to procure appropriate meat or request a waiver, which had no previous contract experience with government and which was low bidder on reprocurement contract as to east coast delivery items. Venice Maid Co., Inc. v. U. S., 225 Ct. Cl. 418, 639 F.2d 690, 28 Cont. Cas. Fed. (CCH) P 80851 (1980). United States ☞64.45(2)

GAO generally will not disturb a nonresponsibility determination absent a showing either that the agency had no reasonable basis for the determination, or acted in bad faith. Id. In our review of nonresponsibility determinations, we consider only whether the negative determination was reasonably based on the information available to the contracting officer at the time it was made. Acquest Development LLC, B-287439, 2001 CPD ¶ 101 (Comp. Gen. 2001)

3 Small business concerns

United States ☞64.45(2)

Responsibility factors may be considered in the course of proposal evaluation without referral to the Small Business Administration. Delta Data Systems Corp. v. Webster, 744 F.2d 197, 240, 32 Cont. Cas. Fed. (CCH) P 73066 (D.C. Cir. 1984).

While Small Business Administration's issuance of certificate of competency is binding on contracting officer, refusal to issue that certificate does not prevent contracting officer from later reversing denial of contract for nonresponsibility on basis of new evidence. Small Business Act, § 2[8], as amended, 15 U.S.C.A. § 637. Cavalier Clothes, Inc. v. U.S., 810 F.2d 1108, 33 Cont. Cas. Fed. (CCH) P 74983 (Fed. Cir. 1987). United States ☞64.45(2)

Statute governing government procurement contracts specifies seven factors which prospective contractor must satisfy in order to be deemed "responsible," including qualification under all relevant statutes and regulations, including Small Business Act (SBA) and Walsh-Healey Act. Walsh-Healey Act, § 1 et seq., 41 U.S.C.A § 35 et seq.Marwais Steel Co. v. Department of Air Force, 871 F. Supp. 1448, 40 Cont. Cas. Fed. (CCH) P 76781 (D.D.C. 1994). United States ☞64.45(2)

Military agency's decision to award public contract for supply of water storage systems to low bidder was rational and reasonable, as bidder was low by 25% margin, agency had prior successful contracting experience with bidder, and both preaward survey and investigation by Small Business Administration (SBA) confirmed bidder's ability to perform contract, notwithstanding bidder's alleged loss in fulfilling contract obligations or alleged factual disputes. J.G.B. Enterprises, Inc. v. U.S., 921 F. Supp. 91, 40 Cont. Cas. Fed. (CCH) P 76941 (N.D. N.Y. 1996). United States ☞64.45(2)

Navy as contracting agency, rather than Small Business Administration (SBA), had duty to make responsibility determination with respect to best bidder and competitive bid. Small Business Act, § 2[8](a), as amended, 15 U.S.C.A. § 637(a). Action Service Corp. v. Garrett, 797 F. Supp. 82 (D.P.R. 1992). United States ☞64.45(2)

Government agency's failure to conduct responsibility determination prior to awarding procurement contract was material and not subject to correction by another agency's review; procurement regulations specifically require two separate evaluations of contracting firm's responsibility, one by contracting agency and one by Small Business Administration, and contracting agency can neither abdicate nor delegate its obligation to conduct responsibility determination. Small Business Act, § 2[8](a), 15 U.S.C.A. § 637(a). Action Service Corp. v. Garrett, 790 F. Supp. 1188, 38 Cont. Cas. Fed. (CCH) P 76347 (D.P.R. 1992). United States ☞64.45(2)

Agency's failure to perform responsibility analysis of awardee prior to award of government contract constituted clear error prejudicial to disappointed bidder; contracting agency was required under applicable regulations to independently evaluate awardee's responsibility, and had awardee been found nonresponsible by agency and failed to receive certificate of competency from Small Business Administration, disappointed bidder would have had chance to win contract. Small Business Act, § 2[8](a), 15 U.S.C.A. § 637(a). Action Service Corp. v. Garrett, 790 F. Supp. 1188, 38 Cont. Cas. Fed. (CCH) P 76347 (D.P.R. 1992). United States ☞64.45(2); United States ☞64.60(5.1)

Government agency is not required to give contract to contractor certified with respect to capacity and credit, and it was not improper for government agency to reject defaulting contractor's bid on replacement contract, even though his bid was lowest received and he had received Small Defense Plants Administration certification. Defense Production Act of 1950, § 714(f) (1), as added in 1951, 50 U.S.C.A.Appendix, § 2163a(f) (1). U.S. v. Thompson, 168 F. Supp. 281 (N.D. W. Va. 1958), judgment aff'd, 268 F.2d 426 (4th Cir. 1959). United States ☞64.45(2)

In reviewing contractor's application for certificate of competency (COC), the Small Business Administration (SBA) violated section of the Federal Acquisition Regulation (FAR) charging agency evaluators to "consider the number of contracts involved and the extent of deficient performance in each contract" when making responsibility determinations, where SBA contacted only 3 of 35 project references submitted by contractor for the period since 2000 to the present. 48 C.F.R. § 9.104-3(b). CSE Const. Co., Inc. v. U.S., 58 Fed. Cl. 230 (2003). United States ☞64.45(2)

Failure of the Small Business Administration (SBA), on review of bidder's application for certificate of competency (COC), to consider whether bidder's past performance problems arose from circumstances beyond its control and whether bidder took appropriate corrective action to remedy the problems constituted a violation of SBA's obligations under both the solicitation and section of the Federal Acquisition Regulation (FAR). 48 C.F.R. § 9.104-3(b). CSE Const. Co., Inc. v. U.S., 58 Fed. Cl. 230 (2003). United States ☞64.45(2)

In reviewing a contractor's certificate of competency (COC) application, the Small Business Administration (SBA) is bound by the responsibility criteria set forth in the Federal Acquisition Regulation (FAR), and the criteria set out in the solicitation itself. Small Business Act, § 2[8](b)(7)(A), as amended, 15 U.S.C.A. § 637(b)(7)(A). CSE Const. Co., Inc. v. U.S., 58 Fed. Cl. 230 (2003). United States ☞64.45(2)

Upon bidder's application for certificate of competency (COC) from the Small Business Administration (SBA), contracting agency was required by regulation to supply the SBA with the results of its investigation into bidder's past performance, and the SBA was required to give consideration to the information collected by the agency concerning bidder's past performance. 13 C.F.R. § 125.5(c)(1); 48 C.F.R. § 19.602-1(c). CSE Const. Co., Inc. v. U.S., 58 Fed. Cl. 230 (2003). United States ☞64.45(2)

On review of bidder's application for a certificate of competency, the Small Business Administration (SBA) was not required to give bidder the opportunity to clarify unfavorable past performance references the SBA had collected. CSE Const. Co., Inc. v. U.S., 58 Fed. Cl. 230 (2003). United States ☞64.45(2)

Decision of the Small Business Administration (SBA) to deny bidder a certificate of competency (COC) on the basis of poor past performance lacked a rational basis, where the SBA checked only three past references from extensive list of 105 submitted by bidder, and ignored contracting agency's conclusion that bidder's past performance was "very good"; moreover, SBA did not consider whether negative comments concerning past performance stemmed from circumstances beyond bidder's control, or even whether bidder had taken appropriate corrective action in the three instances. CSE Const. Co., Inc. v. U.S., 58 Fed. Cl. 230 (2003). United States ☞64.45(2)

Government contractor failed to establish that Small Business Administration (SBA) was arbitrary or capricious in denying its application for a certificate of competency (COC) with respect to its bid on solicitation for transportation by barge of reactor vessels and steam generators. CRC Marine Services, Inc. v. U.S., 41 Fed. Cl. 66, 42 Cont. Cas. Fed. (CCH) P 77310 (1998). United States ☞64.45(2)

Government contractor did not establish that its prior debarment was a significant factor in determination of the Small Business Administration (SBA) to deny contractor a certificate of competency (COC); although report of SBA official referred to history of debarment, official was not a member of committee who made decision, and committee's minutes did not mention debarment. CRC Marine Services, Inc. v. U.S., 41 Fed. Cl. 66, 42 Cont. Cas. Fed. (CCH) P 77310 (1998). United States ☞64.45(2)

When Small Business Administration (SBA) makes responsibility determination, for purposes of deciding whether to issue Certificate of Competency (COC) to government contractor, it is not limited to deficiencies cited in referring agency's non-responsibility decision, but may consider all aspects of responsibility it considers germane. 13 C.F.R. § 125. 5(a)(1). Stapp Towing Inc. v. U.S., 34 Fed. Cl. 300, 40 Cont. Cas. Fed. (CCH) P 76839 (1995). United States ☞64.45(2)

Decision by Small Business Administration's certificate of competency (COC) review committee, that contractor seeking to haul government fuel was nonresponsible, and thus not entitled to COC, was not arbitrary and capricious; committee noted its concern that contractor had not completed installation of fuel gauges and alarms on equipment it proposed to use, that contractor had not fully implemented safety program, and that contractor had unacceptable number of oil spills. Stapp Towing Inc. v. U.S., 34 Fed. Cl. 300, 40 Cont. Cas. Fed. (CCH) P 76839 (1995). United States ☞64.45(2)

Small Business Administration (SBA) may perform financial analysis in Miller Act cases, which require posting of performance and payment bonds for public contract award, but SBA must consider bonding requirement in assessing responsibility. Miller Act, § 1 et seq., 40 U.S.C.A. § 270a et seq.C & G Excavating, Inc. v. U.S., 32 Fed. Cl. 231, 39 Cont. Cas. Fed. (CCH) P 76715 (1994). United States ☞64.15; United States ☞64.45(2)

Evidence that contractor had outstanding Internal Revenue Service (IRS) deficiency and that it omitted 1993 financial statement demonstrated that Small Business Administration (SBA) did not act arbitrarily and capriciously in failing to pursue additional information or seek clarification before making finding of nonresponsibility in certification of competency review. C & G Excavating, Inc. v. U.S., 32 Fed. Cl. 231, 39 Cont. Cas. Fed. (CCH) P 76715 (1994). United States ☞64.40(3); United States ☞64.45(2)

Small Business Administration (SBA) properly considered contractor's financial status in making responsibility determination, though contracting officer cited capacity as only basis for her nonresponsibility decision; SBA may consider all aspects of responsibility in making certificate of competency determination. Small Business Act, § 2[8](a)(16)(A), (b)(7), 15 U.S.C.A. § 637(a)(16)(A), (b)(7); 13 C.F.R. § 125.5(e). C & G Excavating, Inc. v. U.S., 32 Fed. Cl. 231, 39 Cont. Cas. Fed. (CCH) P 76715 (1994). United States ☞64.45(2)

Small Business Administration (SBA) was under no obligation to perform site visit to evaluate contractor's financial condition, given that subject of referral was another aspect of contractor responsibility. Small Business Act, § 2[8](b)(7), 15 U.S.C.A. § 637(b)(7). C & G Excavating, Inc. v. U.S., 32 Fed. Cl. 231, 39 Cont. Cas. Fed. (CCH) P 76715 (1994). United States ☞64.45(2)

Exception to mandatory requirement that if small business concern's offer is to be rejected because of determination of nonresponsibility, contracting officers shall refer the matter to the Small Business Administration (SBA), which will decide whether to issue certificate of competency, did not apply to Department of State's rejection of disadvantaged small business for contract based on accounting system deficiencies identified in audit; exception applies if contracting officer determines business is unqualified because it does not meet standard of being "otherwise qualified and eligible to receive award," but different subsection lists as specific responsibility requirement that prospective contractor have necessary accounting and operational controls, so exception did not apply. Celtech, Inc. v. U.S., 24 Cl. Ct. 269, 37 Cont. Cas. Fed. (CCH) P 76181, 1991 WL 193295 (1991), vacated pursuant to settlement, 25 Cl. Ct. 368, 1992 WL 46122 (1992). United States ☞64.15

Despite language in first paragraph of letter from contracting officer to authorized representative of bidder, that "your firm has been determined non-responsible," suggesting letter was finding that bidder was non-responsible in Small Business Act sense of that term, as would allegedly have required referral of finding to Small Business Administration, evidence established that letter was finding that bidder's proposal bond, rather than bidder, was nonresponsible; letter explained "[t]he basis of this determination is your inability to submit acceptable proposal bond within the allotted time frame." Small Business Act, § 2[8](b)(7)(A), as amended, 15 U.S.C.A. § 637(b)(7)(A). RADVA Corp. v. U.S., 17 Cl. Ct. 812, 35 Cont. Cas. Fed. (CCH) P 75706, 1989 WL 91318 (1989), judgment aff'd, 914 F.2d 271 (Fed. Cir. 1990). United States ☞64.45(2)

Small Business Administration did not exceed its statutory authority, in ruling on bidder's certificate of competence application, by considering the contract specifications and conformity of the bid thereto; that aspect of review was a proper exercise of SBA's investigative responsibilities, particularly in view of bidder's track record of marginal and unsatisfactory performance on other government contracts. PNM Const., Inc. v. U.S., 13 Cl. Ct. 745, 34 Cont. Cas. Fed. (CCH) P 75409, 1987 WL 20987 (1987). United States ☞64.45(2)

In participating on behalf of contractor in contractor's negotiations with Veterans Administration or for construction of VA facility, VA employee did not violate executive order or VA standards of ethical conduct prohibiting giving of preferential treatment to any organization or person; contractor had been preselected by Small Business Administration, resulting in procurement being sole source procurement for which contractor had no competition. Order No. 11222, § 201(c)(2), 18 U.S.C.A. § 201 note. Refine Const. Co., Inc. v. U.S., 12 Cl. Ct. 56, 34 Cont. Cas. Fed. (CCH) P 75242 (1987). United States ☞41

§ 9.104-4 Subcontractor responsibility.

(a) Generally, prospective prime contractors are responsible for determining the responsibility of their prospective subcontractors (but see 9.405 and 9.405-2 regarding debarred, ineligible, or suspended firms). Determinations of prospective subcontractor responsibility may affect the Government's determination of the prospective prime contractor's responsibility. A prospective contractor may be required to provide written evidence of a proposed subcontractor's responsibility.

(b) When it is in the Government's interest to do so, the contracting officer may directly determine a prospective subcontractor's responsibility (e.g., when the prospective contract involves medical supplies, urgent requirements, or substantial subcontracting). In this case, the same standards used to determine a prime contractor's responsibility shall be used by the Government to determine subcontractor responsibility.

United States Code Annotated

Administrative determinations, see 41 USCA § 257.

Contracts, planning, solicitation, evaluation, and award procedures, see 10 USCA § 2305.

Definitions, see 10 USCA § 2302, 41 USCA §§ 259, 403.

Determinations and decisions, see 10 USCA § 2310, 41 USCA § 262.

Planning and solicitation requirements, see 41 USCA § 253a.

Notes of Decisions

In general 1

1 In general

The contracting officer properly considered the performance record of a proposed subcontractor in making a determination that an offeror was nonresponsible. A contracting officer must make an affirmative determination that a prospective prime contractor is responsible before awarding a contract. FAR 9.104(b). The quality of the subcontractors that a prospective prime contractor designates may influence the contracting officer's determination. FAR 9.104-4(a). While a prospective prime contractor generally determines the responsibility of its subcontractors, federal regulations authorize a contracting officer directly to determine a subcontractor's responsibility when a contract involves substantial subcontracting. Matter of: L & M Mercadeo Internacional, S.A., B-250637, 93-1 CPD ¶ 124 (Comp. Gen. 1993)

§ 9.104-5 Representation and certifications regarding responsibility matters.

(a) When an offeror provides an affirmative response in paragraph (a)(1) of the provision at 52.209-5, Certification Regarding Responsibility Matters, or paragraph (h) of provision 52.212-3, the contracting officer shall—

(1) Promptly, upon receipt of offers, request such additional information from the offeror as the offeror deems necessary in order to demonstrate the offeror's responsibility to the contracting officer (but see 9.405); and

(2) Notify, prior to proceeding with award, in accordance with agency procedures (see 9.406-3(a) and 9.407-3(a)), the agency official responsible for initiating debarment or suspension action, where an offeror indicates the existence of an indictment, charge, conviction, or civil judgment, or Federal tax delinquency in an amount that exceeds $3,500.

(b) The provision at 52.209-11, Representation by Corporations Regarding Delinquent Tax Liability or a Felony Conviction under any Federal Law, implements sections 744 and 745 of Division E of the Consolidated and Further Continuing Appropriations Act, 2015 (Pub. L. 113-235) (and similar provisions in subsequent appropriations acts). When an offeror provides an affirmative response in paragraph (b)(1) or (2) of the provision at 52.209-11 or paragraph (q)(2)(i) or (ii) of provision 52.212-3, the contracting officer shall—

(1) Promptly, upon receipt of offers, request such additional information from the offeror as the offeror deems necessary in order to demonstrate the offeror's responsibility to the contracting officer (but see 9.405);

(2) Notify, in accordance with agency procedures (see 9.406-3(a) and 9.407-3(a)), the agency official responsible for initiating debarment or suspension action; and

(3) Not award to the corporation unless an agency suspending or debarring official has considered suspension or debarment of the corporation and made a determination that suspension or debarment is not necessary to protect the interests of the Government.

(c) If the provision at 52.209-12, Certification Regarding Tax Matters, is applicable (see 9.104-7(e)), then the contracting officer shall not award any contract in an amount greater than $5,000,000, unless the offeror affirmatively certified in its offer, as required by paragraph (b)(1), (2), and (3) of the provision.

(d) Offerors who do not furnish the representation or certifications or such information as may be requested by the contracting officer shall be given an opportunity to remedy the deficiency. Failure to furnish the representation or certifications or such information may render the offeror nonresponsible.

§ 9.104-6 Federal Awardee Performance and Integrity Information System.

(a) (1) Before awarding a contract in excess of the simplified acquisition threshold, the contracting officer shall review the performance and integrity information available in the Federal Awardee Performance and Integrity Information System (FAPIIS), (available at www.ppirs.gov, then select FAPIIS), including FAPIIS information from the System for Award Management (SAM) Exclusions and the Past Performance Information Retrieval System (PPIRS).

(2) In accordance with 41 U.S.C. 2313(d)(3), FAPIIS also identifies—

(i) An affiliate that is an immediate owner or subsidiary of the offeror, if any (see 52.204-17, Ownership or Control of Offeror); and

(ii) All predecessors of the offeror that held a Federal contract or grant within the last three years (see 52.204-20, Predecessor of Offeror).

(b) (1) When making a responsibility determination, the contracting officer shall consider all the information available through FAPIIS with regard to the offeror and any immediate owner, predecessor, or subsidiary identified for that offeror in FAPIIS, as well as other past performance information on the offeror (see subpart 42.15).

(2) For evaluation of information available through FAPIIS relating to an affiliate of the offeror, see 9.104-3(c).

(3) For source selection evaluations of past performance, see 15.305(a)(2). Contracting officers shall use sound judgment in determining the weight and relevance of the information contained in FAPIIS and how it relates to the present acquisition.

(4) Since FAPIIS may contain information on any of the offeror's previous contracts and information covering a five-year period, some of that information may not be relevant to a determination of present responsibility, e.g., a prior administrative action such as debarment or suspension that has expired or otherwise been resolved, or information relating to contracts for completely different products or services.

(5) Because FAPIIS is a database that provides information about prime contractors, the contracting officer posts information required to be posted about a subcontractor, such as trafficking in persons violations, to the record of the prime contractor (see 42.1503(h)(1)(v)). The prime contractor has the opportunity to post in FAPIIS any mitigating factors. The contracting officer shall consider any mitigating factors posted in FAPIIS by the prime contractor, such as degree of compliance by the prime contractor with the terms of FAR clause 52.222-50.

(c) If the contracting officer obtains relevant information from FAPIIS regarding criminal, civil, or administrative proceedings in connection with the award or performance of a Government contract; terminations for default or cause; determinations of nonresponsibility because the contractor does not have a satisfactory performance record or a satisfactory record of integrity and business ethics; or comparable information relating to a grant, the contracting officer shall, unless the contractor has already been debarred or suspended—

(1) Promptly request such additional information from the offeror as the offeror deems necessary in order to demonstrate the offeror's responsibility to the contracting officer (but see 9.405); and

(2) Notify, prior to proceeding with award, in accordance with agency procedures (see 9.406-3(a) and 9.407-3(a)), the agency official responsible for initiating debarment or suspension action, if the information appears appropriate for the official's consideration.

(d) The contracting officer shall document the contract file for each contract in excess of the simplified acquisition threshold to indicate how the information in FAPIIS was considered in any responsibility determination, as well as the action that was taken as a result of the information. A contracting officer who makes a nonresponsibility determination is required to document that information in FAPIIS in accordance with 9.105-2 (b)(2).

§ 9.104-7 Solicitation provisions and contract clauses.

(a) The contracting officer shall insert the provision at 52.209-5, Certification Regarding Responsibility Matters, in solicitations where the contract value is expected to exceed the simplified acquisition threshold.

(b) The contracting officer shall insert the provision at 52.209-7, Information Regarding Responsibility Matters, in solicitations where the resultant contract value is expected to exceed $550,000.

(c) The contracting officer shall insert the clause at 52.209-9, Updates of Publicly Available Information Regarding Responsibility Matters—

(1) In solicitations where the resultant contract value is expected to exceed $550,000; and

(2) In contracts in which the offeror checked "has" in paragraph (b) of the provision at 52.209-7.

(d) The contracting officer shall insert the provision 52.209-11, Representation by Corporations Regarding Delinquent Tax Liability or a Felony Conviction under any Federal Law, in all solicitations.

(e) For agencies receiving funds subject to section 523 of Division B of the Consolidated and Further Continuing Appropriations Act, 2015 (Pub. L. 113-235) and similar provisions in subsequent appropriations acts, the contracting officer shall insert the provision 52.209-12, Certification Regarding Tax Matters, in solicitations for which the resultant contract (including options) may have a value greater than $5,000,000. Division B of the Consolidated and Continuing Further Appropriations Act, 2015 appropriates funds for the following agencies: the Department of Commerce, the Department of Justice, the National Aeronautics and Space Administration, the Office of Science and Technology Policy, the National Science Foundation, the Commission on Civil Rights, the Equal Employment Opportunity Commission, the U.S. International Trade Commission, the Legal Services Corporation, the Marine Mammal Commission, the Office of the United States Trade Representative, and the State Justice Institute.

§ 9.105 Procedures.

§ 9.105-1 Obtaining information.

(a) Before making a determination of responsibility, the contracting officer shall possess or obtain information sufficient to be satisfied that a prospective contractor currently meets the applicable standards in 9.104.

(b) (1) Generally, the contracting officer shall obtain information regarding the responsibility of prospective contractors, including requesting preaward surveys when necessary (see 9.106), promptly after a bid opening or receipt of offers. However, in negotiated contracting, especially when research and development is involved, the contracting officer may obtain this information before issuing the request for proposals. Requests for information shall ordinarily be limited to information concerning—

(i) The low bidder; or

(ii) Those offerors in range for award.

(2) Preaward surveys shall be managed and conducted by the surveying activity.

(i) If the surveying activity is a contract administration office—

(A) That office shall advise the contracting officer on prospective contractors' financial competence and credit needs; and

(B) The administrative contracting officer shall obtain from the auditor any information required concerning the adequacy of prospective contractors' accounting systems and these systems' suitability for use in administering the proposed type of contract.

(ii) If the surveying activity is not a contract administration office, the contracting officer shall obtain from the auditor any information required concerning prospective contractors' financial competence and credit needs, the adequacy of their accounting systems, and these systems' suitability for use in administering the proposed type of contract.

(3) Information on financial resources and performance capability shall be obtained or updated on as current a basis as is feasible up to the date of award.

(c) In making the determination of responsibility, the contracting officer shall consider information available through FAPIIS (see 9.104-6), with regard to the offeror and any immediate owner, predecessor, or subsidiary identified for that offeror in FAPIIS, including information that is linked to FAPIIS such as from SAM, and PPIRS, as well as any other relevant past performance information on the offeror (see 9.104-1(c) and subpart 42.15). In addition, the contracting officer should use the following sources of information to support such determinations:

(1) Records and experience data, including verifiable knowledge of personnel within the contracting office, audit offices, contract administration offices, and other contracting offices.

(2) The prospective contractor-including bid or proposal information (including the certification at 52.209-5 or 52.212-3(h) (see 9.104-5)), questionnaire replies, financial data, information on production equipment, and personnel information.

(3) Commercial sources of supplier information of a type offered to buyers in the private sector.

(4) Preaward survey reports (see 9.106).

(5) Other sources such as publications; suppliers, subcontractors, and customers of the prospective contractor; financial institutions; Government agencies; and business and trade associations.

(d) Contracting offices and cognizant contract administration offices that become aware of circumstances casting doubt on a contractor's ability to perform contracts successfully shall promptly exchange relevant information.

§ 9.105-2 Determinations and documentation.

(a) Determinations.

(1) The contracting officer's signing of a contract constitutes a determination that the prospective contractor is responsible with respect to that contract. When an offer on which an award would otherwise be made is rejected because the prospective contractor is found to be nonresponsible, the contracting officer shall make, sign, and place in the contract file a determination of nonresponsibility, which shall state the basis for the determination.

(2) If the contracting officer determines that a responsive small business lacks certain elements of responsibility, the contracting officer shall comply with the procedures in subpart 19.6. When a Certificate of Competency is issued for a small business concern (see subpart 19.6), the contracting officer shall accept the Small Business Administration's decision to issue a Certificate of Competency and award the contract to the concern.

(b) Support documentation.

(1) Documents and reports supporting a determination of responsibility or nonresponsibility, including any preaward survey reports, the use of FAPIIS information (see 9.104-6), and any applicable Certificate of Competency, must be included in the contract file.

(2) (i) The contracting officer shall document the determination of nonresponsibility in FAPIIS (available at www.cpars.gov, then select FAPIIS) if—

(A) The contract is valued at more than the simplified acquisition threshold;

(B) The determination of nonresponsibility is based on lack of satisfactory performance record or satisfactory record of integrity and business ethics; and

(C) The Small Business Administration does not issue a Certificate of Competency.

(ii) The contracting officer is responsible for the timely submission, within 3 working days, and sufficiency, and accuracy of the documentation regarding the nonresponsibility determination.

(iii) As required by section 3010 of the Supplemental Appropriations Act, 2010 (Pub. L. 111-212), all information posted in FAPIIS on or after April 15, 2011, except past performance reviews, will be publicly available. FAPIIS consists of two segments—

(A) The non-public segment, into which Government officials and contractors post information, which can only be viewed by—

(1) Government personnel and authorized users performing business on behalf of the Government; or

(2) An offeror or contractor, when viewing data on itself; and

(B) The publicly-available segment, to which all data in the non-public segment of FAPIIS is automatically transferred after a waiting period of 14 calendar days, except for—

(1) Past performance reviews required by subpart 42.15;

(2) Information that was entered prior to April 15, 2011; or

(3) Information that is withdrawn during the 14-calendar-day waiting period by the Government official who posted it in accordance with paragraph (b)(2)(iv) of this section.

(iv) The contracting officer, or any other Government official, shall not post any information in the non-public segment of FAPIIS that is covered by a disclosure exemption under the Freedom of Information Act. If the contractor asserts within 7 calendar days, to the Government official who posted the information, that some of the information posted to the non-public segment of FAPIIS is covered by a disclosure exemption under the Freedom of Information Act, the Government official who posted the information must within 7 calendar days remove the posting from FAPIIS and resolve the issue in accordance with agency Freedom of Information Act procedures, prior to reposting the releasable information.

United States Code Annotated

Administrative determinations, see 41 USCA § 257.

Contracts, planning, solicitation, evaluation, and award procedures, see 10 USCA § 2305.

Definitions, see 10 USCA § 2302, 41 USCA §§ 259, 403.

Determinations and decisions, see 10 USCA § 2310, 41 USCA § 262.

Planning and solicitation requirements, see 41 USCA § 253a.

Notes of Decisions

In general 1
Signing of contract 2
Support documentation 3

1 In general

The federal government decides who is a "responsible bidder," for purposes of an award of a procurement contract, using applicable federal laws and regulations. 48 C.F.R. § 9.104-1. LeBoeuf, Lamb, Greene & MacRae, LLP v. Abraham, 215 F. Supp. 2d 73 (D.D.C. 2002), opinion vacated, 347 F.3d 315, 358 (D.C. Cir. 2003) (The court vacated the judgment and remanded the case for a determination as to an apparent conflict of interest was considered as required by regulations, and whether the Department's need for expert legal services on the project supported a direct award of the contract to LeBoeuf or an award of other relief.) United States ☞64.45(2)

Air Force properly conducted responsibility determination as required by statute regulating government procurement contracts, though disappointed bidder claimed that Air Force released no rationale for its finding that successful bidder was "responsible"; statute explicitly states that contracting officer's signature on contract constitutes determination of responsibility, and no other rationale is required. Marwais Steel Co. v. Department of Air Force, 871 F. Supp. 1448, 40 Cont. Cas. Fed. (CCH) P 76781 (D.D.C. 1994). United States ☞64.45(2)

Under 32 C.F.R. § 1-904.1 (1970), the award of a procurement contract to a prospective contractor by the contracting officer constitutes an affirmative determination that the contractor is "responsible" within the meaning of 32 C.F.R. § 1-902. Transcountry Packing Co. v. U. S., 215 Ct. Cl. 390, 568 F.2d 1333, 24 Cont. Cas. Fed. (CCH) P 82055 (1978). United States ☞64.45(2)

2 Signing of contract

When contracting officer makes determination of responsibility, as opposed to situation in which he makes determination of non-responsibility, regulations do not require contracting officer to "make, sign and place in the contract file a determination of" responsibility which states the basis for the determination. 48 C.F.R. § 9.105-2(a). Impresa Construzioni Geom. Domenico Garufi v. U.S., 238 F.3d 1324 (Fed. Cir. 2001). United States ☞64.45(2)

Air Force properly conducted responsibility determination as required by statute regulating government procurement contracts, though disappointed bidder claimed that Air Force released no rationale for its finding that successful bidder was "responsible"; statute explicitly states that contracting officer's signature on contract constitutes determination of responsibility, and no other rationale is required. Marwais Steel Co. v. Department of Air Force, 871 F. Supp. 1448, 40 Cont. Cas. Fed. (CCH) P 76781 (D.D.C. 1994). United States ☞64.45(2)

3 Support documentation

Where contracting officer had all the documents supporting his nonresponsibility decision with respect to contractor in a file in his office area at time he entered the determination, he substantially complied with regulation even though he did not make separate copies of such documents for each of the "contract files." Shermco Industries, Inc. v. Secretary of the Air Force, 584 F. Supp. 76, 32 Cont. Cas. Fed. (CCH) P 72713 (N.D. Tex. 1984). United States ☞64.45(2)

Contracting officer who made nonresponsibility determination with regard to contractor did not violate regulations because he did not include copy of report of FBI investigation of colonel's dealings with contractor in his files and never took it into his possession but merely reviewed it at security police office, since officer did not base his determination on the report. Shermco Industries, Inc. v. Secretary of the Air Force, 584 F. Supp. 76, 32 Cont. Cas. Fed. (CCH) P 72713 (N.D. Tex. 1984). United States ☞64.45(2)

§ 9.105-3 Disclosure of preaward information.

(a) Except as provided in subpart 24.2, Freedom of Information Act, information (including the preaward survey report) accumulated for purposes of determining the responsibility of a prospective contractor shall not be released or disclosed outside the Government.

(b) The contracting officer may discuss preaward survey information with the prospective contractor before determining responsibility. After award, the contracting officer or, if it is appropriate, the head of the surveying activity or a designee may discuss the findings of the preaward survey with the company surveyed.

(c) Preaward survey information may contain proprietary or source selection information and should be marked with the appropriate legend and protected accordingly (see 3.104-4).

United States Code Annotated

Administrative determinations, see 41 USCA § 257.

Contracts, planning, solicitation, evaluation, and award procedures, see 10 USCA § 2305.

Definitions, see 10 USCA § 2302, 41 USCA §§ 259, 403.

Determinations and decisions, see 10 USCA § 2310, 41 USCA § 262.

Planning and solicitation requirements, see 41 USCA § 253a.

Notes of Decisions

In general 1

1 In general

Agency was not obligated to discuss the findings and recommendation of the pre-award survey team with the protester. While the FAR allows the contracting officer to discuss pre-award survey information with the prospective contractor, such discussions are not required. FAR 9.105-3(b). Matter of: Bernard Johnson Incorporated, B-252481, 93-1 CPD ¶ 476 (Comp. Gen. 1993)

§ 9.106 Preaward surveys.

§ 9.106-1 Conditions for preaward surveys.

(a) A preaward survey is normally required only when the information on hand or readily available to the contracting officer, including information from commercial sources, is not sufficient to make a determination regarding responsibility. In addition, if the contemplated contract will have a fixed price at or below the simplified acquisition threshold or will involve the acquisition of commercial items (see Part 12), the contracting officer should not request a preaward survey unless circumstances justify its cost.

(b) When a cognizant contract administration office becomes aware of a prospective award to a contractor about which unfavorable information exists and no preaward survey has been requested, it shall promptly obtain and transmit details to the contracting officer.

(c) Before beginning a preaward survey, the surveying activity shall ascertain whether the prospective contractor is debarred, suspended, or ineligible (see subpart 9.4). If the prospective contractor is debarred, suspended, or ineligible, the surveying activity shall advise the contracting officer promptly and not proceed with the preaward survey unless specifically requested to do so by the contracting officer.

United States Code Annotated

Administrative determinations, see 41 USCA § 257.

Contracts, planning, solicitation, evaluation, and award procedures, see 10 USCA § 2305.

Definitions, see 10 USCA § 2302, 41 USCA §§ 259, 403.

Determinations and decisions, see 10 USCA § 2310, 41 USCA § 262.

Planning and solicitation requirements, see 41 USCA § 253a.

Notes of Decisions

In general 1

1 In general

The government, through its pre-award survey of the subcontractor, did not become aware of contractor's intention to supply a nonconforming mix on contract to supply mixed nuts, so as to allow contractor equitable relief of rescission; inspector apparently asked subcontractor's officer for a written verification of the content of the nut mix, but officer did not have one prepared, and though the inspector's questioning did not uncover the discrepancy between the nut mix sought by the government and the nut mix that subcontractor intended to produce, and though inspector filled out the pre-award survey form prior to receiving the written verification of the content of the nut mix, it was clear that inspector carried out his responsibility in giving subcontractor an opportunity to raise any issues it might have had regarding the nut mix. 48 C.F.R. § 9.106-1. Giesler v. U.S., 232 F.3d 864 (Fed. Cir. 2000). United States ⊕74(4)

Failure to complete preaward survey of prospective contractor's financial capability in connection with government procurement contract was not clear violation of applicable procedures warranting overturning of administrative decision disqualifying lowest bidder on grounds of financial nonresponsibility since form recording general analysis was submitted by contracting officer in accordance with usual procedure and lack of survey did not substantially prejudice bidder in that it would have been deemed financially nonresponsible even if survey had been used. 5 U.S.C.A. § 706(2)(A). Harvard Interiors Mfg. Co. v. U.S., 798 F. Supp. 565 (E.D. Mo. 1992). United States ⊕64.45(2)

Survey of prospective contractor financial capability is not required in government procurement contract process unless form is submitted by requesting contracting officer based on officer's evaluation of prospective contractor. 5 U.S.C.A. § 706(2)(A). Harvard Interiors Mfg. Co. v. U.S., 798 F. Supp. 565 (E.D. Mo. 1992). United States ⊕64.45(2)

Unsuccessful offeror on Navy contract to supply auto parts failed to establish Navy's bias in favor of successful offeror and, thus, failed to establish that contract award was infected with bad faith; there was no proof that Navy improperly advanced information to successful offeror before release of request for proposals, and although successful offeror received negative preaward survey, preaward survey was merely a recommendation that contracting officer, exercising his independent judgment, could follow or not, depending upon other relevant circumstances. Howard Cooper Corp. v. U.S., 763 F. Supp. 829, 37 Cont. Cas. Fed. (CCH) P 76169 (E.D. Va. 1991). United States ⊕64.40(2)

Preaward survey determination of contractor's responsibility did not amount to a tacit approval of contractor's accounting system, rendering it eligible for progress payments "as a matter of course"; responsibility determination addresses in a general way the financial wherewithal and general business competence of a bidder, while progress payment survey focuses on specific factors seen as preconditions to receiving progress payments. 48 C.F.R. §§ 9.105-1, 32.503-3. Florida Engineered Const. Products Corp. v. U.S., 41 Fed. Cl. 534, 42 Cont. Cas. Fed. (CCH) P 77355 (1998). United States ⊕70(15.1)

Government's decision to proceed on sole-source procurement for fuses without further investigating prospective bidder's capabilities by conducting preaward survey was unreasonable and violation of regulations and thus, for purposes of preliminarily enjoining contract award, prospective bidder had likely success on merits. Magnavox Electronic Systems Co. v. U.S., 26 Cl. Ct. 1373, 38 Cont. Cas. Fed. (CCH) P 76414, 1992 WL 277980 (1992). Injunction ☞138.63

A pre-award survey involves an evaluation of a prospective contractor's capability to perform the proposed contract—that is, the contractor's responsibility. As a matter pertaining to contractor responsibility, the contracting official has broad discretion as to whether a pre-award survey should be conducted; although a contracting official may request such a survey to help determine whether the proposed awardee is responsible, a pre-award survey is not a prerequisite to an affirmative determination of responsibility. In this regard, an agency is not required to conduct such a survey if the information on hand or readily available is sufficient to allow the contracting officer to make a determination of responsibility. FAR 9.106-1(a). Oliver Products Company, B-245762, B-245762.2, 92-1 CPD ¶ 501 (Comp. Gen. 1992)

§ 9.106-2 Requests for preaward surveys.

The contracting officer's request to the surveying activity (Preaward Survey of Prospective Contractor (General), SF 1403) shall—

(a) Identify additional factors about which information is needed;

(b) Include the complete solicitation package (unless it has previously been furnished), and any information indicating prior unsatisfactory performance by the prospective contractor;

(c) State whether the contracting office will participate in the survey;

(d) Specify the date by which the report is required. This date should be consistent with the scope of the survey requested and normally shall allow at least 7 working days to conduct the survey; and

(e) When appropriate, limit the scope of the survey.

United States Code Annotated

Administrative determinations, see 41 USCA § 257.

Contracts, planning, solicitation, evaluation, and award procedures, see 10 USCA § 2305.

Definitions, see 10 USCA § 2302, 41 USCA §§ 259, 403.

Determinations and decisions, see 10 USCA § 2310, 41 USCA § 262.

Planning and solicitation requirements, see 41 USCA § 253a.

§ 9.106-3 Interagency preaward surveys.

When the contracting office and the surveying activity are in different agencies, the procedures of this section 9.106 and subpart 42.1 shall be followed along with the regulations of the agency in which the surveying activity is located, except that reasonable special requests by the contracting office shall be accommodated (also see subpart 17.5).

United States Code Annotated

Administrative determinations, see 41 USCA § 257.

Contracts, planning, solicitation, evaluation, and award procedures, see 10 USCA § 2305.

Definitions, see 10 USCA § 2302, 41 USCA §§ 259, 403.

Determinations and decisions, see 10 USCA § 2310, 41 USCA § 262.

Planning and solicitation requirements, see 41 USCA § 253a.

§ 9.106-4 Reports.

(a) The surveying activity shall complete the applicable parts of SF 1403, Preaward Survey of Prospective Contractor (General); SF 1404, Preaward Survey of Prospective Contractor—Technical; SF 1405, Preaward Survey of Prospective Contractor—Production; SF 1406, Preaward Survey of Prospective Contractor—Quality Assurance; SF 1407, Preaward Survey of Prospective Contractor—Financial Capability; and SF 1408, Preaward Survey of Prospective Contractor—Accounting System; and provide a narrative discussion sufficient to support both the evaluation ratings and the recommendations.

(b) When the contractor surveyed is a small business that has received preferential treatment on an ongoing contract under Section 8(a) of the Small Business Act (15 U.S.C. 637) or has received a Certificate of Competency during the last 12 months, the surveying activity shall consult the appropriate Small Business Administration field office before making an affirmative recommendation regarding the contractor's responsibility or nonresponsibility.

(c) When a preaward survey discloses previous unsatisfactory performance, the surveying activity shall specify the extent to which the prospective contractor plans, or has taken, corrective action. Lack of evidence that past failure to meet contractual requirements was the prospective contractor's fault does not necessarily indicate satisfactory performance. The narrative shall report any persistent pattern of need for costly and burdensome Government assistance (e.g., engineering, inspection, or testing) provided in the Government's interest but not contractually required.

(d) When the surveying activity possesses information that supports a recommendation of complete award without an on-site survey and no special areas for investigation have been requested, the surveying activity may provide a short-form preaward survey report. The short-form report shall consist solely of the Preaward Survey of Prospective Contractor (General), SF 1403. Sections III and IV of this form shall be completed and block 21 shall be checked to show that the report is a short-form preaward report.

United States Code Annotated

Administrative determinations, see 41 USCA § 257.

Contracts, planning, solicitation, evaluation, and award procedures, see 10 USCA § 2305.

Definitions, see 10 USCA § 2302, 41 USCA §§ 259, 403.

Determinations and decisions, see 10 USCA § 2310, 41 USCA § 262.

Planning and solicitation requirements, see 41 USCA § 253a.

§ 9.107 Surveys of nonprofit agencies participating in the AbilityOne Program.

(a) The Committee for Purchase From People Who Are Blind or Severely Disabled (Committee), as authorized by 41 U.S.C. chapter 85, determines what supplies and services Federal agencies are required to purchase from AbilityOne participating nonprofit agencies serving people who are blind or have other severe disabilities (see subpart 8.7). The Committee is required to find an AbilityOne participating nonprofit agency capable of furnishing the supplies or services before the nonprofit agency can be designated as a mandatory source under the AbilityOne Program. The Committee may request a contracting office to assist in assessing the capabilities of a nonprofit agency.

(b) The contracting office, upon request from the Committee, shall request a capability survey from the activity responsible for performing preaward surveys, or notify the Committee that the AbilityOne participating nonprofit agency is capable, with supporting rationale, and that the survey is waived. The capability survey will focus on the technical and production capabilities and applicable preaward survey elements to furnish specific supplies or services being considered for addition to the Procurement List.

(c) The contracting office shall use the Standard Form 1403 to request a capability survey of organizations employing people who are blind or have other severe disabilities.

(d) The contracting office shall furnish a copy of the completed survey, or notice that the AbilityOne participating nonprofit agency is capable and the survey is waived, to the Executive Director, Committee for Purchase From People Who Are Blind or Severely Disabled.

United States Code Annotated

Administrative determinations, see 41 USCA § 257.

Contracts, planning, solicitation, evaluation, and award procedures, see 10 USCA § 2305.

Definitions, see 10 USCA § 2302, 41 USCA §§ 259, 403.

Determinations and decisions, see 10 USCA § 2310, 41 USCA § 262.

Planning and solicitation requirements, see 41 USCA § 253a.

§ 9.108 Prohibition on contracting with inverted domestic corporations.

§ 9.108-1 Definitions.

As used in this section—

"Inverted domestic corporation" means a foreign incorporated entity that meets the definition of an inverted domestic corporation under 6 U.S.C. 395(b), applied in accordance with the rules and definitions of 6 U.S.C. 395(c).

"Subsidiary" means an entity in which more than 50 percent of the entity is owned—

(1) Directly by a parent corporation; or

(2) Through another subsidiary of a parent corporation.

§ 9.108-2 Prohibition.

(a) Section 745 of Division D of the Consolidated Appropriations Act, 2008 (Pub. L. 110-161) and its successor provisions in subsequent appropriations acts (and as extended in continuing resolutions) prohibit, on a Governmentwide basis, the use of appropriated (or otherwise made available) funds for contracts with either an inverted domestic corporation, or a subsidiary of such a corporation, except as provided in paragraph (b) of this section and in 9.108-4 Waiver.

(b)(1) Section 745 and its successor provisions include the following exception: This section shall not apply to any Federal Government contract entered into before the date of the enactment of this Act, or to any task order issued pursuant to such contract.

(2) To ensure appropriate application of the prohibition and this exception, contracting officers should consult with legal counsel if, during the performance of a contract, a contractor becomes an inverted domestic corporation or a subsidiary of one.

Notes of Decisions

In general 1

1 In general

Protest alleging awardee is inverted domestic corporation and therefore award violated restriction in FAR 9.108-2 against award to such corporations is denied where contracting officer knew agency legal counsel previously investigated matter in response to prior allegations by protester and determined awardee not to be inverted domestic corporation. Inchcape Shipping Services (Dubai) LLC, B-409465, B-409465.2, 2014 CPD ¶ 152 (Comp.Gen. 2014)

§ 9.108-3 Representation by the offeror.

(a) In order to be eligible for contract award, an offeror must represent that it is neither an inverted domestic corporation, nor a subsidiary of an inverted domestic corporation. Any offeror that cannot so represent is ineligible for award of a contract, unless waived in accordance with the procedures at 9.108-4.

(b) The contracting officer may rely on an offeror's representation that it is not an inverted domestic corporation unless the contracting officer has reason to question the representation.

§ 9.108-4 Waiver.

Any agency head may waive the prohibition in subsection 9.108-2 and the requirement of subsection 9.108-3 for a specific contract if the agency head determines in writing that the waiver is required in the interest of national security, documents the determination, and reports it to the Congress.

§ 9.108-5 Solicitation provision and contract clause.

The contracting officer shall—

(a) Include the provision at 52.209-2, Prohibition on Contracting with Inverted Domestic Corporations—Representation, in each solicitation for the acquisition of products or services (including construction); and

(b) Include the clause at 52.209-10, Prohibition on Contracting with Inverted Domestic Corporations, in each solicitation and contract for the acquisition of products or services (including construction).

Subpart 9.2 Qualifications Requirements

§ 9.200 Scope of subpart.

This subpart implements 10 U.S.C. 2319 and 41 U.S.C. 3311 and prescribes policies and procedures regarding qualification requirements and the acquisitions that are subject to such requirements.

United States Code Annotated

Administrative determinations, see 41 USCA § 257.

Contracts, planning, solicitation, evaluation, and award procedures, see 10 USCA § 2305.

Definitions, see 10 USCA § 2302, 41 USCA §§ 259, 403.

Determinations and decisions, see 10 USCA § 2310, 41 USCA § 262.

Encouragement of new competition, see 41 USCA § 253c.

Encouragement of new competitors, see 10 USCA § 2319.

Planning and solicitation requirements, see 41 USCA § 253a.

§ 9.201 Definitions.

As used in this subpart—

"Qualified bidders list (QBL)" means a list of bidders who have had their products examined and tested and who have satisfied all applicable qualification requirements for that product or have otherwise satisfied all applicable qualification requirements.

"Qualified manufacturers list (QML)" means a list of manufacturers who have had their products examined and tested and who have satisfied all applicable qualification requirements for that product.

United States Code Annotated

Administrative determinations, see 41 USCA § 257.

Contracts, planning, solicitation, evaluation, and award procedures, see 10 USCA § 2305.

Definitions, see 10 USCA § 2302, 41 USCA §§ 259, 403.

Determinations and decisions, see 10 USCA § 2310, 41 USCA § 262.

Encouragement of new competition, see 41 USCA § 253c.

Encouragement of new competitors, see 10 USCA § 2319.

Planning and solicitation requirements, see 41 USCA § 253a.

§ 9.202 Policy.

(a) (1) The head of the agency or designee shall, before establishing a qualification requirement, prepare a written justification—

(i) Stating the necessity for establishing the qualification requirement and specifying why the qualification requirement must be demonstrated before contract award;

(ii) Estimating the likely costs for testing and evaluation which will be incurred by the potential offeror to become qualified; and

(iii) Specifying all requirements that a potential offeror (or its product) must satisfy in order to become qualified. Only those requirements which are the least restrictive to meet the purposes necessitating the establishment of the qualification requirements shall be specified.

(2) Upon request to the contracting activity, potential offerors shall be provided—

(i) All requirements that they or their products must satisfy to become qualified; and

(ii) At their expense (but see 9.204(a)(2) with regard to small businesses), a prompt opportunity to demonstrate their abilities to meet the standards specified for qualification using qualified personnel and facilities of the agency concerned, or of another agency obtained through interagency agreements or under contract, or other methods approved by the agency (including use of approved testing and evaluation services not provided under contract to the agency).

(3) If the services in (a)(2)(ii) of this section are provided by contract, the contractors

401

selected to provide testing and evaluation services shall be—

(i) Those that are not expected to benefit from an absence of additional qualified sources; and

(ii) Required by their contracts to adhere to any restriction on technical data asserted by the potential offeror seeking qualification.

(4) A potential offeror seeking qualification shall be promptly informed as to whether qualification is attained and, in the event it is not, promptly furnished specific reasons why qualification was not attained.

(b) When justified under the circumstances, the agency activity responsible for establishing a qualification requirement shall submit to the advocate for competition for the procuring activity responsible for purchasing the item subject to the qualification requirement, a determination that it is unreasonable to specify the standards for qualification which a prospective offeror (or its product) must satisfy. After considering any comments of the advocate for competition reviewing the determination, the head of the procuring activity may waive the requirements of 9.202(a)(1)(ii) through (4) for up to 2 years with respect to the item subject to the qualification requirement. A copy of the waiver shall be furnished to the head of the agency or other official responsible for actions under 9.202(a)(1). The waiver authority provided in this paragraph does not apply with respect to qualification requirements contained in a QPL, QML, or QBL.

(c) If a potential offeror can demonstrate to the satisfaction of the contracting officer that the potential offeror (or its product) meets the standards established for qualification or can meet them before the date specified for award of the contract, a potential offeror may not be denied the opportunity to submit and have considered an offer for a contract solely because the potential offeror—

(1) Is not on a QPL, QML, or QBL maintained by the Department of Defense (DoD) or the National Aeronautics and Space Administration (NASA); or

(2) Has not been identified as meeting a qualification requirement established after October 19, 1984, by DoD or NASA; or

(3) Has not been identified as meeting a qualification requirement established by a civilian agency (not including NASA).

(d) The procedures in Subpart 19.6 for referring matters to the Small Business Administration are not mandatory on the contracting officer when the basis for a referral would involve a challenge by the offeror to either the validity of the qualification requirement or the offeror's compliance with such requirement.

(e) The contracting officer need not delay a proposed award in order to provide a potential offeror with an opportunity to demonstrate its ability to meet the standards specified for qualification. In addition, when approved by the head of an agency or designee, a procurement need not be delayed in order to comply with 9.202(a).

(f) Within 7 years following enforcement of a QPL, QML, or QBL by DoD or NASA, or within 7 years after any qualification requirement was originally established by a civilian agency other than NASA, the qualification requirement shall be examined and revalidated in accordance with the requirements of 9.202(a). For DoD and NASA, qualification requirements other than QPL's, QML's and QBL's shall be examined and revalidated within 7 years after establishment of the requirement under 9.202(a). Any periods for which a waiver under 9.202(b) is in effect shall be excluded in computing the 7 years within which review and revalidation must occur.

United States Code Annotated

Administrative determinations, see 41 USCA § 257.

Contracts, planning, solicitation, evaluation, and award procedures, see 10 USCA § 2305.

Definitions, see 10 USCA § 2302, 41 USCA §§ 259, 403.

Determinations and decisions, see 10 USCA § 2310, 41 USCA § 262.

Encouragement of new competition, see 41 USCA § 253c.

Encouragement of new competitors, see 10 USCA § 2319.

Planning and solicitation requirements, see 41 USCA § 253a.

Notes of Decisions

Purpose 1

Qualification for award under other laws and regulations 3
Qualification requirement, generally 2

1 Purpose

The purpose of the procedural safeguards in statute governing qualification requirements when soliciting bids for a contract is to ensure that qualification requirements are used only when and to the extent necessary to ensure product quality, reliability, and maintainability, rather than to inappropriately restrict competition, and qualification requirements imposed without following the procedures set out by Congress must be struck down. 10 U.S.C.A. §§ 2319, 2319(b); 48 C.F.R. § 9.206-1(a). W.G. Yates & Sons Const. Co., Inc. v. Caldera, 192 F.3d 987 (Fed. Cir. 1999). United States ☞64.15

Qualification requirements are government requirements for testing or other quality assurance demonstrations that must be completed before the award of a contract. Matter of: Warren Pumps, Inc, B-258710, 1995 WL 64154 (Comp. Gen. 1995), on reconsideration, B-258710, B-258710.2, 95-2 CPD ¶ 20 (Comp. Gen. 1995)

2 Qualification requirement, generally

Statute addressing bid specifications did not govern subcontractor qualification requirements to be completed after award of the prime contract; "specifications" are the requirements of the particular project for which the bids are sought, such as design requirements, functional requirements, or performance requirements, while "qualification requirements" are activities which establish the experience and abilities of the bidder to assure the government that the bidder has the ability to carry out and complete the contract. 10 U.S.C.A. §§ 2305(a)(1)(B)(ii), (a)(1)(C), 2319. W.G. Yates & Sons Const. Co., Inc. v. Caldera, 192 F.3d 987 (Fed. Cir. 1999). United States ☞64.25

Fact that contracting officer (CO) informed prospective subcontractor during a telephone conversation 17 days prior to contract award that the three week pre-bid qualification requirement would be waived did not remove remaining bid solicitation requirements from the statutory definition of "qualification requirement," and thus when the Army did not follow the statutory and regulatory requirements, the qualification requirement was rendered invalid and unenforceable, as subcontractor still had to satisfy the explicit "before award" requirement as determined by the CO, which required submission of evidence of having manufactured similar systems which were operating satisfactorily for at least five years prior to the date of the award. 10 U.S.C.A. §§ 2305(a)(1)(B)(ii), 2319, 2319(b); 48 C.F.R. § 9. 206-1(a). W.G. Yates & Sons Const. Co., Inc. v. Caldera, 192 F.3d 987 (Fed. Cir. 1999). United States ☞64.15

Protest that award was improper because contracting activity that approved awardee's part for addition to qualified products list did not have approval authority is denied, where contracting officer found part approval valid based on consideration of information from cognizant activities, consistent with his authority under 10 U.S.C. § 2319. Phaostron Instrument & Electronic Company, B-284456, 2000 CPD ¶ 65 (Comp. Gen. 2000)

The purpose of the QPL system is to allow the efficient procurement of items which require substantial testing to demonstrate compliance with specification requirements. The procurement of qualified products is a two-step process in which (1) products are tested for compliance with specifications and, if found in compliance, listed on the appropriate QPL, and (2) products on the QPL may be then procured. While the QPL system is intended to be used prior to, and independent of, any specific procurement action, it nevertheless is one facet of the integral system of procuring qualified products. Matter of, B-247363, B-247363.6, 92-2 CPD ¶ 315 (Comp. Gen. 1992)

The use of a QPL in the procurement of qualified products is inherently restrictive of competition. Nonetheless, where, as here, the government's minimum needs require the qualification of products for inclusion on an applicable QPL (and statutory and regulatory requirements have been satisfied), the restriction of a procurement to a product on the QPL is not improper. Matter of, B-247363, B-247363.6, 92-2 CPD ¶ 315 (Comp. Gen. 1992)

3 Qualification for award under other laws and regulations

Aircraft refueling business was not responsible entity, in context of county code, and thus did not meet minimum standards county required of entities doing business on airport property, as would support business's claim that county and airport officials engaged in anti-competitive practices by preventing government from awarding refueling contracts to business; business owners had repeatedly engaged in fraudulent transfers to funnel business assets for personal uses, business had failed to pay income tax for over 15 years, business had filed for bankruptcy, and fuel contamination issues existed. 48 C.F.R. § 9.104-1. Top Flight Aviation, Inc. v. Washington County Regional Airport Com'n, 224 F. Supp. 2d 966 (D. Md. 2002). Monopolies ⊸28(1.6)

The government need not delay the award of a contract in order to provide a potential offeror with an opportunity to qualify. FAR 9.202(e). SAI Industries Corp. v. U.S., 60 Fed. Cl. 731 (2004)

Where, pursuant to 10 U.S.C. § 2865 (authorizing simplified method of awarding energy savings performance contracts (ESPC), including use of a list of prequalified firms), agency initiated process of selecting firms for award of ESPCs in 1997, agency reasonably limited consideration of firms to those on the 1997 prequalified list, the only list available at the time. Even though the actual selection will not be made until 1998, agency is not required to consider firms which subsequently were included on the 1998 list; the resulting delay and cost would be inconsistent with the simplified and cost-conscious selection process authorized by the statute and the statutory goal of accelerating the use of ESPCs. Strategic Resource Solutions Corporation, B-278732, 98-1 CPD ¶ 74 (Comp. Gen. 1998)

§ 9.203 QPL's, QML's, and QBL's.

(a) Qualification and listing in a QPL, QML, or QBL is the process by which products are obtained from manufacturers or distributors, examined and tested for compliance with specification requirements, or manufacturers or potential offerors, are provided an opportunity to demonstrate their abilities to meet the standards specified for qualification. The names of successful products, manufacturers, or potential offerors are included on lists evidencing their status. Generally, qualification is performed in advance and independently of any specific acquisition action. After qualification, the products, manufacturers, or potential offerors are included in a Federal or Military QPL, QML, or QBL. (See 9.202(a)(2) with regard to any product, manufacturer, or potential offeror not yet included on an applicable list.)

(b) Specifications requiring a qualified product are included in the following publications:

(1) GSA Index of Federal Specifications, Standards and Commercial Item Descriptions, FPMR 101-29.1.

(2) Department of Defense Acquisition Streamlining and Standardization Information System (ASSIST) at (*https://assist.dla.mil/online/start/*).

(c) Instructions concerning qualification procedures are included in the following publications:

(1) Federal Standardization Manual, FSPM-0001.

(2) Defense Standardization Manual 4120.24-M, Appendix 2, as amended by Military Standards 961 and 962.

(d) The publications listed in paragraphs (b) and (c) of this section are sold to the public. The publications in paragraphs (b)(1) and (c)(1) of this section may be obtained from the addressee in 11.201(d)(1). The publications in paragraphs (b)(2) and (c)(2) of this section may be obtained from the addressee in 11.201(d)(2).

United States Code Annotated

Administrative determinations, see 41 USCA § 257.

Contracts, planning, solicitation, evaluation, and award procedures, see 10 USCA § 2305.

Definitions, see 10 USCA § 2302, 41 USCA §§ 259, 403.

Determinations and decisions, see 10 USCA § 2310, 41 USCA § 262.

Encouragement of new competition, see 41 USCA § 253c.

Encouragement of new competitors, see 10 USCA § 2319.

Planning and solicitation requirements, see 41 USCA § 253a.

Notes of Decisions

In general 1

1 In general

Where, pursuant to 10 U.S.C. § 2865 (authorizing simplified method of awarding energy savings performance contracts (ESPC), including use of a list of prequalified firms), agency initiated process of selecting firms for award of ESPCs in 1997, agency reasonably limited consideration of firms to those on the 1997 prequalified list, the only list available at the time. Even though the actual selection will not be made until 1998, agency is not required to consider firms which subsequently were included on the 1998 list; the resulting delay and cost would be inconsistent with the simplified and cost-conscious selection process authorized by the statute and the statutory goal of accelerating the use of ESPCs. Strategic Resource Solutions Corporation, B-278732, 98-1 CPD ¶ 74 (Comp. Gen. 1998)

§ **9.204 Responsibilities for establishment of a qualification requirement.**

The responsibilities of agency activities that establish qualification requirements include the following:

(a) Arranging publicity for the qualification requirements. If active competition on anticipated future qualification requirements is likely to be fewer than two manufacturers or the products of two manufacturers, the activity responsible for establishment of the qualification requirements must—

(1) Periodically furnish through the Governmentwide point of entry (GPE) a notice seeking additional sources or products for qualification unless the contracting officer determines that such publication would compromise the national security.

(2) Bear the cost of conducting the specified testing and evaluation (excluding the costs associated with producing the item or establishing the production, quality control, or other system to be tested and evaluated) for a small business concern or a product manufactured by a small business concern which has met the standards specified for qualification and which could reasonably be expected to compete for a contract for that requirement. However, such costs may be borne only if it is determined in accordance with agency procedures that such additional qualified sources or products are likely to result in cost savings from increased competition for future requirements sufficient to amortize the costs incurred by the agency within a reasonable period of time, considering the duration and dollar value of anticipated future requirements. A prospective contractor requesting the United States to bear testing and evaluation costs must certify as to its status as a small business concern under Section 3 of the Small Business Act in order to receive further consideration.

(b) Qualifying products that meet specification requirements.

(c) Listing manufacturers and suppliers whose products are qualified in accordance with agency procedures.

(d) Furnishing QPL's, QML's, or QBL's or the qualification requirements themselves to prospective offerors and the public upon request (see 9.202(a)(2)(i)).

(e) Clarifying, as necessary, qualification requirements.

(f) In appropriate cases, when requested by the contracting officer, providing concurrence in a decision not to enforce a qualification requirement for a solicitation.

(g) Withdrawing or omitting qualification of a listed product, manufacturer or offeror, as necessary.

(h) Advising persons furnished any list of products, manufacturers or offerors meeting a qualification requirement and suppliers whose products are on any such list that—

(1) The list does not constitute endorsement of the product, manufacturer, or other source by the Government;

(2) The products or sources listed have been qualified under the latest applicable specification;

(3) The list may be amended without notice;

(4) The listing of a product or source does not release the supplier from compliance with the specification; and

(5) Use of the list for advertising or publicity is permitted. However, it must not be stated or implied that a particular product or source is the only product or source of that type qualified, or that the Government in any way recommends or endorses the products or the sources listed.

(i) Reexamining a qualified product or manufacturer when—

(1) The manufacturer has modified its product, or changed the material or the processing sufficiently so that the validity of previous qualification is questionable;

(2) The requirements in the specification have been amended or revised sufficiently to affect the character of the product; or

(3) It is otherwise necessary to determine that the quality of the product is maintained in conformance with the specification.

United States Code Annotated

Administrative determinations, see 41 USCA § 257.

Contracts, planning, solicitation, evaluation, and award procedures, see 10 USCA § 2305.

Definitions, see 10 USCA § 2302, 41 USCA §§ 259, 403.

Determinations and decisions, see 10 USCA § 2310, 41 USCA § 262.

Encouragement of new competition, see 41 USCA § 253c.

Encouragement of new competitors, see 10 USCA § 2319.

Planning and solicitation requirements, see 41 USCA § 253a.

Notes of Decisions

Amendment of specifications 2
Qualification requirement, generally 1

1 Qualification requirement, generally

Statute addressing bid specifications did not govern subcontractor qualification requirements to be completed postaward of the prime contract; "specifications" are the requirements of the particular project for which the bids are sought, such as design requirements, functional requirements, or performance requirements, while "qualification requirements" are activities which establish the experience and abilities of the bidder to assure the government that the bidder has the ability to carry out and complete the contract. 10 U.S.C.A. §§ 2305(a)(1)(B)(ii), (a)(1)(C), 2319. W.G. Yates & Sons Const. Co., Inc. v. Caldera, 192 F.3d 987 (Fed. Cir. 1999). United States ☞64.25

Fact that contracting officer (CO) informed prospective subcontractor during a telephone conversation 17 days prior to contract award that the three week pre-bid qualification requirement would be waived did not remove remaining bid solicitation requirements from the statutory definition of "qualification requirement," and thus when the Army did not follow the statutory and regulatory requirements, the qualification requirement was rendered invalid and unenforceable, as subcontractor still had to satisfy the explicit "before award" requirement as determined by the CO, which required submission of evidence of having manufactured similar systems which were operating satisfactorily for at least five years prior to the date of the award. 10 U.S.C.A. §§ 2305(a)(1)(B)(ii), 2319, 2319(b); 48 C.F.R. § 9. 206-1(a). W.G. Yates & Sons Const. Co., Inc. v. Caldera, 192 F.3d 987 (Fed. Cir. 1999). United States ☞64.15

2 Amendment of specifications

Justification and approval procedures in Federal Acquisition Regulations (FAR) applicable to acquisitions involving qualification requirements did not apply to amendment made by Forest Service to its specification for fire retardant; altering the fire-retardant ingredients for enhanced efficiency and safety did not substantially effect the character of the product. Fire-Trol Holdings, LLC v. U.S., 66 Fed. Cl. 36 (2005). United States ☞64.25

§ 9.205 Opportunity for qualification before award.

(a) If an agency determines that a qualification requirement is necessary, the agency activity responsible for establishing the requirement must urge manufacturers and other potential sources to demonstrate their ability to meet the standards specified for qualification and, when possible, give sufficient time to arrange for qualification before award. The responsible agency activity must, before establishing any qualification requirement, furnish notice through the GPE. The notice must include—

(1) Intent to establish a qualification requirement;

(2) The specification number and name of the product;

(3) The name and address of the activity to which a request for the information and op-

portunity described in 9.202(a)(2) should be submitted;

(4) The anticipated date that the agency will begin awarding contracts subject to the qualification requirement;

(5) A precautionary notice that when a product is submitted for qualification testing, the applicant must furnish any specific information that may be requested of the manufacturer before testing will begin; and

(6) The approximate time period following submission of a product for qualification testing within which the applicant will be notified whether the product passed or failed the qualification testing (see 9.202(a)(4)).

(b) The activity responsible for establishing a qualification requirement must keep any list maintained of those already qualified open for inclusion of additional products, manufacturers, or other potential sources.

United States Code Annotated

Administrative determinations, see 41 USCA § 257.

Contracts, planning, solicitation, evaluation, and award procedures, see 10 USCA § 2305.

Definitions, see 10 USCA § 2302, 41 USCA §§ 259, 403.

Determinations and decisions, see 10 USCA § 2310, 41 USCA § 262.

Encouragement of new competition, see 41 USCA § 253c.

Encouragement of new competitors, see 10 USCA § 2319.

Planning and solicitation requirements, see 41 USCA § 253a.

Notes of Decisions

In general 1

1 In general

Contracting officers are authorized to find that a product meets (or will meet) a qualification requirement by the time of contract award, regardless of whether the item is listed on the QPL. 10 U.S.C. § 2319(c)(3); FAR 9.206-1(c).

Government violated requirement of procurement regulation by failing to urge potential offeror to demonstrate its ability to meet qualification requirements. 48 C.F.R. § 9.205. SAI Industries Corp. v. U.S., 60 Fed. Cl. 731 (2004). United States ☞64.5

Section of the FAR regarding opportunity for qualification before a contract award requires the government to make a meaningful and bona fide effort to urge potential offerors to pre-qualify before an award. 48 C.F.R. § 9.205. SAI Industries Corp. v. U.S., 60 Fed. Cl. 731 (2004). United States ☞64.5

Bid protestor proved that it was prejudiced by government's failure to properly and promptly notify it of its removal as an approved source, and its failure to urge it to requalify at any point after its removal; but for the failures, protestor would have had more than 7-1/2 months to requalify as a pre-approved supplier, and if it had requalified, there was a substantial chance it would have received the contractor, as it was the incumbent contractor who was awarded three of the last four contracts. 48 C.F.R. §§ 9.205, 9.207(b). SAI Industries Corp. v. U.S., 60 Fed. Cl. 731 (2004). United States ☞64.55(1)

When an incumbent offeror loses its pre-qualification status, and said offeror is never informed of such change, in violation of procurement regulation requiring prompt notification of de-listing, the government also violates regulation requiring the government to make a meaningful and bona fide effort to urge potential offerors to pre-qualify before an award; incumbent offeror is a readily identifiable "potential offeror" that the government should "urge" to qualify, an incumbent offeror unaware that it is no longer pre-qualified to bid on future contracts is least likely to seek re-qualification without government urging, and an incumbent offeror may be more likely than a non-incumbent offeror to attempt to re-qualify upon learning that it is no longer qualified. 48 C.F.R. §§ 9.205, 9.207(b). SAI Industries Corp. v. U.S., 60 Fed. Cl. 731 (2004). United States ☞64.5

Nothing in the statute limits the contracting officer's authority to approve a product for a procurement based on whether the product has been tested or approved by a particular entity. Indeed, consistent with the statutory objective of enhancing competition for products subject to a qualification requirement, we have approved an agency's use of an alternate method of source approval—a licensing agreement with the original equipment manufacturer—in lieu of approval by an authorized agency activity. Phaostron Instrument & Electronic Company, B-284456, 2000 CPD ¶ 65 (Comp. Gen. 2000)

§ 9.206 Acquisitions subject to qualification requirements.

§ 9.206-1 General.

(a) Agencies may not enforce any QPL, QML, or QBL without first complying with the requirements of 9.202(a). However, qualification requirements themselves, whether or not previously embodied in a in a QPL, QML, or QBL, may be enforced without regard to 9.202(a) if they are in either of the following categories:

(1) Any qualification requirement established by statute prior to October 30, 1984, for civilian agencies (not including NASA); or

(2) Any qualification requirement established by statute or administrative action prior to October 19, 1984, for DoD or NASA. Qualification requirements established after the above dates must comply with 9.202(a) to be enforceable.

(b) Except when the agency head or designee determines that an emergency exists, whenever an agency elects, whether before or after award, not to enforce a qualification requirement which it established, the requirement may not thereafter be enforced unless the agency complies with 9.202(a).

(c) If a qualification requirement applies, the contracting officer need consider only those offers identified as meeting the requirement or included on the applicable QPL, QML, or QBL, unless an offeror can satisfactorily demonstrate to the contracting officer that it or its product or its subcontractor or its product can meet the standards established for qualification before the date specified for award.

(d) If a product subject to a qualification requirement is to be acquired as a component of an end item, the contracting officer must ensure that all such components and their qualification requirements are properly identified in the solicitation since the product or source must meet the standards specified for qualification before award.

(e) In acquisitions subject to qualification requirements, the contracting officer shall take the following steps:

(1) Use presolicitation notices in appropriate cases to advise potential suppliers before issuing solicitations involving qualification requirements. The notices shall identify the specification containing the qualification requirement and establish an allowable time period, consistent with delivery requirements, for prospective offerors to demonstrate their abilities to meet the standards specified for qualification. The notice shall be publicized in accordance with 5.204. Whether or not a presolicitation notice is used, the general synopsizing requirements of Subpart 5.2 apply.

(2) Distribute solicitations to prospective contractors whether or not they have been identified as meeting applicable qualification requirements.

(3) When appropriate, request in accordance with agency procedures that a qualification requirement not be enforced in a particular acquisition and, if granted, so specify in the solicitation (see 9.206-1(b)).

(4) Forward requests from potential suppliers for information on a qualification requirement to the agency activity responsible for establishing the requirement.

(5) Allow the maximum time, consistent with delivery requirements, between issuing the solicitation and the contract award. As a minimum, contracting officers shall comply with the time frames specified in 5.203 when applicable.

United States Code Annotated

Administrative determinations, see 41 USCA § 257.

Contracts, planning, solicitation, evaluation, and award procedures, see 10 USCA § 2305.

Definitions, see 10 USCA § 2302, 41 USCA §§ 259, 403.

Determinations and decisions, see 10 USCA § 2310, 41 USCA § 262.

Encouragement of new competition, see 41 USCA § 253c.

Encouragement of new competitors, see 10 USCA § 2319.

Planning and solicitation requirements, see 41 USCA § 253a.

Notes of Decisions

In general 2
Purpose 1

1 Purpose

The purpose of the procedural safeguards in statute governing qualification requirements when soliciting bids for a contract is to ensure that qualification requirements are used only when and to the extent necessary to ensure product quality, reliability, and maintainability, rather than to inappropriately restrict competition, and qualification requirements imposed without following the procedures set out by Congress must be struck down. 10 U.S.C.A. §§ 2319, 2319(b); 48 C.F.R. § 9.206-1(a). W.G. Yates & Sons Const. Co., Inc. v. Caldera, 192 F.3d 987 (Fed. Cir. 1999). United States ☞64.15

2 In general

Fact that contracting officer (CO) informed prospective subcontractor during a telephone conversation 17 days prior to contract award that the three week pre-bid qualification requirement would be waived did not remove remaining bid solicitation requirements from the statutory definition of "qualification requirement," and thus when the Army did not follow the statutory and regulatory requirements, the qualification requirement was rendered invalid and unenforceable, as subcontractor still had to satisfy the explicit "before award" requirement as determined by the CO, which required submission of evidence of having manufactured similar systems which were operating satisfactorily for at least five years prior to the date of the award. 10 U.S.C.A. §§ 2305(a)(1)(B)(ii), 2319, 2319(b); 48 C.F.R. § 9. 206-1(a). W.G. Yates & Sons Const. Co., Inc. v. Caldera, 192 F.3d 987 (Fed. Cir. 1999). United States ☞64.15

§ 9.206-2 Contract clause.

The contracting officer shall insert the clause at 52.209-1, Qualification Requirements, in solicitations and contracts when the acquisition is subject to a qualification requirement.

United States Code Annotated

Administrative determinations, see 41 USCA § 257.

Contracts, planning, solicitation, evaluation, and award procedures, see 10 USCA § 2305.

Definitions, see 10 USCA § 2302, 41 USCA §§ 259, 403.

Determinations and decisions, see 10 USCA § 2310, 41 USCA § 262.

Encouragement of new competition, see 41 USCA § 253c.

Encouragement of new competitors, see 10 USCA § 2319.

Planning and solicitation requirements, see 41 USCA § 253a.

§ 9.206-3 Competition.

(a) *Presolicitation.* If a qualification requirement applies to an acquisition, the contracting officer shall review the applicable QPL, QML, or QBL or other identification of those sources which have met the requirement before issuing a solicitation to ascertain whether the number of sources is adequate for competition. (See 9.204(a) for duties of the agency activity responsible for establishment of the qualification requirement.) If the number of sources is inadequate, the contracting officer shall request the agency activity which established the requirement to—

(1) Indicate the anticipated date on which any sources presently undergoing evaluation will have demonstrated their abilities to meet the qualification requirement so that the solicitation could be rescheduled to allow as many additional sources as possible to qualify; or

(2) Indicate whether a means other than the qualification requirement is feasible for testing or demonstrating quality assurance.

(b) *Post solicitation.* The contracting officer shall submit to the agency activity which established the qualification requirement the names and addresses of concerns which expressed interest in the acquisition but are not included on the applicable QPL, QML, or QBL or identified as meeting the qualification requirement. The activity will then assist interested concerns in meeting the standards specified for qualification (see 9.202(a)(2) and

(4)).

United States Code Annotated

Administrative determinations, see 41 USCA § 257.

Contracts, planning, solicitation, evaluation, and award procedures, see 10 USCA § 2305.

Definitions, see 10 USCA § 2302, 41 USCA §§ 259, 403.

Determinations and decisions, see 10 USCA § 2310, 41 USCA § 262.

Encouragement of new competition, see 41 USCA § 253c.

Encouragement of new competitors, see 10 USCA § 2319.

Planning and solicitation requirements, see 41 USCA § 253a.

§ 9.207 Changes in status regarding qualification requirements.

(a) The contracting officer shall promptly report to the agency activity which established the qualification requirement any conditions which may merit removal or omission from a QPL, QML, or QBL or affect whether a source should continue to be otherwise identified as meeting the requirement. These conditions exist when—

(1) Products or services are submitted for inspection or acceptance that do not meet the qualification requirement;

(2) Products or services were previously rejected and the defects were not corrected when submitted for inspection or acceptance;

(3) A supplier fails to request reevaluation following change of location or ownership of the plant where the product which met the qualification requirement was manufactured (see the clause at 52.209-1, Qualification Requirements);

(4) A manufacturer of a product which met the qualification requirement has discontinued manufacture of the product;

(5) A source requests removal from a QPL, QML, or QBL;

(6) A condition of meeting the qualification requirement was violated; *e.g.*, advertising or publicity contrary to 9.204(h)(5);

(7) A revised specification imposes a new qualification requirement;

(8) Manufacturing or design changes have been incorporated in the qualification requirement;

(9) The source is listed in the System for Award Management Exclusions (see Subpart 9.4); or

(10) Performance of a contract subject to a qualification requirement is otherwise unsatisfactory.

(b) After considering any of the above or other conditions reasonably related to whether a product or source continues to meet the standards specified for qualification, an agency may take appropriate action without advance notification. The agency shall, however, promptly notify the affected parties if a product or source is removed from a QPL, QML, or QBL, or will no longer be identified as meeting the standards specified for qualification. This notice shall contain specific information why the product or source no longer meets the qualification requirement.

Subpart 9.3 First Article Testing and Approval

§ 9.301 Definition.

"Approval," as used in this subpart, means the contracting officer's written notification to the contractor accepting the test results of the first article.

United States Code Annotated

Contract requirements, see 41 USCA § 254.

Contracts, planning, solicitation, evaluation, and award procedures, see 10 USCA § 2305.

Definitions, see 10 USCA § 2302, 41 USCA §§ 259, 403.

Kinds of contracts, see 10 USCA § 2306.

Planning and solicitation requirements, see 41 USCA § 253a.

§ 9.302 General.

First article testing and approval (hereafter referred to as testing and approval) ensures that the contractor can furnish a product that conforms to all contract requirements for acceptance. Before requiring testing and approval, the contracting officer shall consider the—

(a) Impact on cost or time of delivery;

(b) Risk to the Government of foregoing such test; and

(c) Availability of other, less costly, methods of ensuring the desired quality.

United States Code Annotated

Contract requirements, see 41 USCA § 254.

Contracts, planning, solicitation, evaluation, and award procedures, see 10 USCA § 2305.

Definitions, see 10 USCA § 2302, 41 USCA §§ 259, 403.

Kinds of contracts, see 10 USCA § 2306.

Planning and solicitation requirements, see 41 USCA § 253a.

Notes of Decisions

In general 1

1 In general

Appellant's failure to timely deliver its First Article submission and its refusal to proceed with contract performance unless the Government agreed to appellant's demands for an increase in the contract price establish a *prima facie* case of default. Appeal of Dae Shin Enterprises, Inc., A.S.B.C.A. No. 50533, 03-1 B.C.A. (CCH) ¶ 32096, 2002 WL 31741516 (Armed Serv. B.C.A. 2002)

The standard FAR 52.209-3, first article testing clause, which permits contractors to request a waiver, does not introduce legally objectionable competitive risk into the procurement. The purpose of the testing requirement is to ensure that the contractor can furnish a product that conforms to all contract requirements for acceptance. FAR 9.302. The standard first article testing clause is required by FAR § 9.3081(a) to ensure that this purpose is met. The clause does not confer any right to a waiver upon any bidder, nor is the inherent advantage gained by a bidder, which properly receives a waiver for the first article testing requirement, objectionable. Matter of Automated Power Systems, Inc, B-257178, B-257178.2, 1994 WL 480181 (Comp. Gen. 1994)

First article testing and approval ensures that the contractor can furnish a product that conforms to all contract requirements. FAR 9.302. An agency decision to waive or not to waive first article testing for a particular contractor is subject to question only where found to be unreasonable. Aerospace Design, Inc., B-247938, 92-2 CPD ¶ 33 (Comp. Gen. 1992)

Agency reasonably waived first article testing requirement for firm which successfully produced items under previous contracts with the agency, and whose specifications for the items were used by the agency as the basis for the solicitation specifications. Marine Instrument Company, B-241292, B-241292.3, 91-1 CPD ¶ 317 (Comp. Gen. 1991)

§ 9.303 Use.

Testing and approval may be appropriate when—

(a) The contractor has not previously furnished the product to the Government;

(b) The contractor previously furnished the product to the Government, but—

(1) There have been subsequent changes in processes or specifications;

(2) Production has been discontinued for an extended period of time; or

(3) The product acquired under a previous contract developed a problem during its life;

(c) The product is described by a performance specification; or

(d) It is essential to have an approved first article to serve as a manufacturing standard.

United States Code Annotated

Contract requirements, see 41 USCA § 254.

Contracts, planning, solicitation, evaluation, and award procedures, see 10 USCA § 2305.

Definitions, see 10 USCA § 2302, 41 USCA §§ 259, 403.

Kinds of contracts, see 10 USCA § 2306.

Planning and solicitation requirements, see 41 USCA § 253a.

Notes of Decisions
In general 1

1 In general

The Federal Acquisition Regulation (FAR) states that first article testing may be appropriate in a number of situations including where a contractor has not previously furnished a product to the government and where the product acquired under a previous contract developed a problem during its life. Whittaker Technical Products, Inc., B-239428, 90-2 CPD ¶ 174 (Comp. Gen. 1990)

Agency decision not to waive first article testing requirement for protester, a current producer of certain batteries and cells being procured for use on deep submergence rescue vehicles, was reasonable where the protester's products have never successfully completed first article testing and problems have arisen during performance by the protester's products which raise doubt as to whether they can perform in accordance with the specifications. Whittaker Technical Products, Inc., B-239428, 90-2 CPD ¶ 174 (Comp. Gen. 1990)

§ 9.304 Exceptions.

Normally, testing and approval is not required in contracts for—

(a) Research or development;

(b) Products requiring qualification before award (e.g., when an applicable qualified products list exists (see Subpart 9.2));

(c) Products normally sold in the commercial market; or

(d) Products covered by complete and detailed technical specifications, unless the requirements are so novel or exacting that it is questionable whether the products would meet the requirements without testing and approval.

United States Code Annotated

Contract requirements, see 41 USCA § 254.

Contracts, planning, solicitation, evaluation, and award procedures, see 10 USCA § 2305.

Definitions, see 10 USCA § 2302, 41 USCA §§ 259, 403.

Kinds of contracts, see 10 USCA § 2306.

Planning and solicitation requirements, see 41 USCA § 253a.

Notes of Decisions
In general 1

1 In general

Normally, first article testing and approval are not required in contracts for products requiring qualification before award. FAR 9.304. Where a solicitation contains a First Article Test (FAT) requirement, it must provide the performance or other characteristics that the first article must meet for approval. FAR § 9.306(a),(b). Further, either the government must provide detailed technical requirements for the approval tests (in the case of testing to be performed by the offeror, § 9.306(a)) or the government must provide the tests to which the first article will be subjected (in the case of government testing, § 9.306(b)). The FAR does not express a preference for FAT procedures or preaward qualification testing. Matter of: Advanced Seal Technology, Inc., B-250106, 93-1 CPD ¶ 23 (Comp. Gen. 1993)

§ 9.305 Risk.

Before first article approval, the acquisition of materials or components, or commencement of production, is normally at the sole risk of the contractor. To minimize this risk, the contracting officer shall provide sufficient time in the delivery schedule for acquisition of materials and components, and for production after receipt of first article approval. When Government requirements preclude this action, the contracting officer may, before approval of the first article, authorize the contractor to acquire specific materials or components or commence production to the extent essential to meet the delivery schedule (see Alternate II of the clause at 52.209-3, First Article Approval—Contractor Testing, and Alternate II of the clause at 52.209-4, First Article Approval—Government Testing). Costs incurred based on this authorization are allocable to the contract for—

(1) Progress payments; and

(2) Termination settlements if the contract is terminated for the convenience of the Government.

United States Code Annotated

Contract requirements, see 41 USCA § 254.

Contracts, planning, solicitation, evaluation, and award procedures, see 10 USCA § 2305.

Definitions, see 10 USCA § 2302, 41 USCA §§ 259, 403.

Kinds of contracts, see 10 USCA § 2306.

Planning and solicitation requirements, see 41 USCA § 253a.

Notes of Decisions

In general 1

1 In general

Where first article approval is required, it is the contractor, not the government, that must normally bear the risk until first article approval is obtained. Nebraska Aluminum Castings, Inc.-Reconsideration, B-222476, B-222476.2, 86-2 CPD ¶ 335 (Comp. Gen. 1986), on reconsideration, B-222476, B-222476.3, 86-2 CPD ¶ 515 (Comp. Gen. 1986)

§ 9.306 Solicitation requirements.

Solicitations containing a testing and approval requirement shall—

(a) Provide, in the circumstance where the contractor is to be responsible for the first article approval testing—

(1) The performance or other characteristics that the first article must meet for approval;

(2) The detailed technical requirements for the tests that must be performed for approval; and

(3) The necessary data that must be submitted to the Government in the first article approval test report;

(b) Provide, in the circumstance where the Government is to be responsible for the first article approval testing—

(1) The performance or other characteristics that the first article must meet for approval; and

(2) The tests to which the first article will be subjected for approval;

(c) Inform offerors that the requirement may be waived when supplies identical or similar to those called for have previously been delivered by the offeror and accepted by the Government (see 52.209-3(h) and 52.209-4(i));

(d) Permit the submission of alternative offers, one including testing and approval and the other excluding testing and approval (if eligible under 9.306(c));

(e) State clearly the first article's relationship to the contract quantity (see paragraph (e) of the clause at 52.209-3, First Article Approval—Contractor Testing, or 52.209-4, First Article Approval—Government Testing);

(f) Contain a delivery schedule for the production quantity (see 12.104). The delivery schedule may—

(1) Be the same whether or not testing and approval is waived; or

(2) Provide for earlier delivery when testing and approval is waived and the Government desires earlier delivery. In the latter case, any resulting difference in delivery schedules shall not be a factor in evaluation for award. The clause at 52.209-4, First Article Approval—Government Testing, shall contain the delivery schedule for the first

article;

(g) Provide for the submission of contract numbers, if any, to document the offeror's eligibility under 9.306(c);

(h) State whether the approved first article will serve as a manufacturing standard; and

(i) Include, when the Government is responsible for first article testing, the Government's estimated testing costs as a factor for use in evaluating offers (when appropriate).

(j) Inform offerors that the prices for first articles and first article tests in relation to production quantities shall not be materially unbalanced (see 15.404-1(g)) if first article test items or tests are to be separately priced.

United States Code Annotated

Contract requirements, see 41 USCA § 254.

Contracts, planning, solicitation, evaluation, and award procedures, see 10 USCA § 2305.

Definitions, see 10 USCA § 2302, 41 USCA §§ 259, 403.

Kinds of contracts, see 10 USCA § 2306.

Planning and solicitation requirements, see 41 USCA § 253a.

Notes of Decisions

In general 1

1 In general

Normally, first article testing and approval are not required in contracts for products requiring qualification before award. FAR 9.304. Where a solicitation contains a First Article Test (FAT) requirement, it must provide the performance or other characteristics that the first article must meet for approval. FAR 9.306(a),(b). Further, either the government must provide detailed technical requirements for the approval tests (in the case of testing to be performed by the offeror, § 9.306(a)) or the government must provide the tests to which the first article will be subjected (in the case of government testing, § 9.306(b)). The FAR does not express a preference for FAT procedures or preaward qualification testing. Matter of: Advanced Seal Technology, Inc., B-250106, 93-1 CPD ¶ 23 (Comp. Gen. 1993)

§ 9.307 Government administration procedures.

(a) Before the contractor ships the first article, or the first article test report, to the Government laboratory or other activity responsible for approval at the address specified in the contract, the contract administration office shall provide that activity with as much advance notification as is feasible of the forthcoming shipment, and—

(1) Advise that activity of the contractual requirements for testing and approval, or evaluation, as appropriate;

(2) Call attention to the notice requirement in paragraph (b) of the clause at 52.209-3, First Article Approval—Contractor Testing, or 52.209-4, First Article Approval—Government Testing; and

(3) Request that the activity inform the contract administration office of the date when testing or evaluation will be completed.

(b) The Government laboratory or other activity responsible for first article testing or evaluation shall inform the contracting office whether to approve, conditionally approve, or disapprove the first article. The contracting officer shall then notify the contractor of the action taken and furnish a copy of the notice to the contract administration office. The notice shall include the first article shipment number, when available, and the applicable contract line item number. Any changes in the drawings, designs, or specifications determined by the contracting officer to be necessary shall be made under the Changes clause, and not by the notice of approval, conditional approval, or disapproval furnished the contractor.

United States Code Annotated

Contract requirements, see 41 USCA § 254.

Contracts, planning, solicitation, evaluation, and award procedures, see 10 USCA § 2305.

Definitions, see 10 USCA § 2302, 41 USCA §§ 259, 403.

Kinds of contracts, see 10 USCA § 2306.

Planning and solicitation requirements, see 41 USCA § 253a.

§ 9.308 Contract clauses.

§ 9.308-1 Testing performed by the contractor.

(a) (1) The contracting officer shall insert the clause at 52.209-3, First Article Approval—Contractor Testing, in solicitations and contracts when a fixed-price contract is contemplated and it is intended that the contract require—

(i) First article approval; and

(ii) That the contractor be required to conduct the first article testing.

(2) If it is intended that the contractor be required to produce the first article and the production quantity at the same facility, the contracting officer shall use the clause with its Alternate I.

(3) If it is necessary to authorize the contractor to purchase material or to commence production before first article approval, the contracting officer shall use the clause with its Alternate II.

(b) (1) The contracting officer shall insert a clause substantially the same as the clause at 52.209-3, First Article Approval—Contractor Testing, in solicitations and contracts when a cost-reimbursement contract is contemplated and it is intended that the contract require—

(i) First article approval; and

(ii) That the contractor be required to conduct the first article test.

(2) If it is intended that the contractor be required to produce the first article and the production quantity at the same facility, the contracting officer shall use a clause substantially the same as the clause at 52.209-3, First Article Approval— Contractor Testing, with its Alternate I.

(3) If it is necessary to authorize the contractor to purchase material or to commence production before first article approval, the contracting officer shall use a clause substantially the same as the clause at 52.209-3, First Article Approval—Contractor Testing, with its Alternate II.

United States Code Annotated

Contract requirements, see 41 USCA § 254.

Contracts, planning, solicitation, evaluation, and award procedures, see 10 USCA § 2305.

Definitions, see 10 USCA § 2302, 41 USCA §§ 259, 403.

Kinds of contracts, see 10 USCA § 2306.

Planning and solicitation requirements, see 41 USCA § 253a.

§ 9.308-2 Testing performed by the Government.

(a) (1) The contracting officer shall insert the clause at 52.209-4, First Article Approval—Government Testing, in solicitations and contracts when a fixed-price contract is contemplated and it is intended that the contract require first article approval and that the Government will be responsible for conducting the first article test.

(2) If it is intended that the contractor be required to produce the first article and the production quantity at the same facility, the contracting officer shall use the basic clause with its Alternate I.

(3) If it is necessary to authorize the contractor to purchase material or to commence production before first article approval, the contracting officer shall use the basic clause with its Alternate II.

(b) (1) The contracting officer shall insert a clause substantially the same as the clause at 52.209-4, First Article Approval—Government Testing, in solicitations and contracts when a cost-reimbursement contract is contemplated and it is intended that the contract require first article approval and that the Government be responsible for conducting the first article test.

(2) If it is intended that the contractor be required to produce the first article and the production quantity at the same facility, the contracting officer shall use a clause

substantially the same as the clause at 52.209-4, First Article Approval— Government Testing, with its Alternate I.

(3) If it is necessary to authorize the contractor to purchase material or to commence production before first article approval, the contracting officer shall use a clause substantially the same as the clause at 52.209-4, First Article Approval—Government Testing, with its Alternate II.

United States Code Annotated

Contract requirements, see 41 USCA § 254.

Contracts, planning, solicitation, evaluation, and award procedures, see 10 USCA § 2305.

Definitions, see 10 USCA § 2302, 41 USCA §§ 259, 403.

Kinds of contracts, see 10 USCA § 2306.

Planning and solicitation requirements, see 41 USCA § 253a.

Subpart 9.4 Debarment, Suspension, and Ineligibility

§ 9.400 Scope of subpart.

(a) This subpart—

(1) Prescribes policies and procedures governing the debarment and suspension of contractors by agencies for the causes given in 9.406-2 and 9.407-2;

(2) Provides for the listing of contractors debarred, suspended, proposed for debarment, and declared ineligible (see the definition of "ineligible" in 2.101); and

(3) Sets forth the consequences of this listing.

(b) Although this subpart does cover the listing of ineligible contractors (9.404) and the effect of this listing (9.405(b)), it does not prescribe policies and procedures governing declarations of ineligibility.

United States Code Annotated

Administrative determinations, see 41 USCA § 257.

Contract requirements, see 41 USCA § 254.

Contractor responsibilities, see 41 USCA § 57.

Contracts, planning, solicitation, evaluation, and award procedures, see 10 USCA § 2305.

Definitions, see 10 USCA § 2302, 41 USCA §§ 259, 403.

Determinations and decisions, see 10 USCA § 2310, 41 USCA § 262.

Kinds of contracts, see 10 USCA § 2306.

Planning and solicitation requirements, see 41 USCA § 253a.

Notes of Decisions

In general 1
Ineligibility distinguished 5
Purpose 2
Retroactive or prospective application 3
Validity 4

1 In general

Suspension and debarment of bidder for government contract occur when Government formally or constructively precludes contractor from participating in future, government contracts or when contracting official's decisions effectively prevent contractor from participating in that and future procurements. BMY, A Div. of HARSCO Corp. v. U.S., 693 F. Supp. 1232, 35 Cont. Cas. Fed. (CCH) P 75552 (D.D.C. 1988). United States ⊜64.20

2 Purpose

Executive order providing for government-wide debarment and suspension of contractors who are debarred or suspended by particular agency was a managerial tool and not shown to be for the benefit of contractors, and thus did not provide basis for challenging government-wide debarment order on ground that, under the executive order, a prior agency debarment arising from the same circumstances should have been government-wide, precluding later imposition of the same penalty. Executive Order No. 12549, §§ 1 et seq., 1(a), 31 U.S.C.A. § 6101 note. Facchiano Const. Co., Inc. v. U.S. Dept. of Labor, 987 F.2d 206, 1 Wage & Hour Cas. 2d (BNA) 468, 39 Cont. Cas. Fed. (CCH) P 76542, 124 Lab. Cas. (CCH) P 35782 (3d Cir. 1993). United States ☞64.20

3 Retroactive or prospective application

Executive order providing for government-wide debarment and suspension of government contractors debarred or suspended by particular agency did not become effective until issuance of guidelines by Office of Management and Budget (OMB) and subsequent implementing regulations and, in the interim, Department of Labor (DOL) properly continued operating according to its existing regulations. Executive Order No. 12549, § 6, 31 U.S.C.A. § 6101 note. Facchiano Const. Co., Inc. v. U.S. Dept. of Labor, 987 F.2d 206, 1 Wage & Hour Cas. 2d (BNA) 468, 39 Cont. Cas. Fed. (CCH) P 76542, 124 Lab. Cas. (CCH) P 35782 (3d Cir. 1993). United States ☞64.20

4 Validity

Federal acquisitions regulations governing debarment of government contractors are not unreasonable or unconstitutional. Joseph Const. Co. v. Veterans Admin. of U.S., 595 F. Supp. 448, 32 Cont. Cas. Fed. (CCH) P 73082 (N.D. Ill. 1984). United States ☞64.20

5 Ineligibility distinguished

FAR subpart 9.4, Debarment, Suspension, and Ineligibility, distinguishes between debarment and ineligibility. "Debarment" refers to actions taken by debarring officials under FAR 9.406. "Ineligible" refers to exclusion from contracts pursuant to statutes such as the Service Contract Act. For purposes of determining whether an offeror falsely certified its debarment status, the ASBCA will construe the terminology in the Debarment clause in accordance with these definitions. Offeror was not proposed for debarment; rather, the Department of Labor was seeking to have it declared ineligible. Further, offeror was not ineligible at the time of certification. Accordingly, its certification was not false. In re Plum Run, Inc., A.S.B.C.A. No. 46091, A.S.B.C.A. No. 49203, 05-1 B.C.A. (CCH) ¶ 32977, 2005 WL 1271527 (Armed Serv. B.C.A. 2005)

§ 9.401 Applicability.

In accordance with Public Law 103-355, Section 2455 (31 U.S.C. 6101, note), and Executive Order 12689, any debarment, suspension or other Governmentwide exclusion initiated under the Nonprocurement Common Rule implementing Executive Order 12549 on or after August 25, 1995, shall be recognized by and effective for Executive Branch agencies as a debarment or suspension under this subpart. Similarly, any debarment, suspension, proposed debarment or other Governmentwide exclusion initiated on or after August 25, 1995, under this subpart shall also be recognized by and effective for those agencies and participants as an exclusion under the Nonprocurement Common Rule.

United States Code Annotated

Administrative determinations, see 41 USCA § 257.

Contract requirements, see 41 USCA § 254.

Contractor responsibilities, see 41 USCA § 57.

Contracts, planning, solicitation, evaluation, and award procedures, see 10 USCA § 2305.

Definitions, see 10 USCA § 2302, 41 USCA §§ 259, 403.

Determinations and decisions, see 10 USCA § 2310, 41 USCA § 262.

Kinds of contracts, see 10 USCA § 2306.

Planning and solicitation requirements, see 41 USCA § 253a.

Notes of Decisions

Construction and application 2
Construction with other laws 3
Deference to agency interpretation 5

Due process of law 6
Injunctions 7
Purpose 1
Retroactive or prospective application 4

1 Purpose

Executive order providing for government-wide debarment and suspension of contractors who are debarred or suspended by particular agency was a managerial tool and not shown to be for the benefit of contractors, and thus did not provide basis for challenging government-wide debarment order on ground that, under the executive order, a prior agency debarment arising from the same circumstances should have been government-wide, precluding later imposition of the same penalty. Executive Order No. 12549, §§ 1 et seq., 1(a), 31 U.S.C.A. § 6101 note. Facchiano Const. Co., Inc. v. U.S. Dept. of Labor, 987 F.2d 206, 1 Wage & Hour Cas. 2d (BNA) 468, 39 Cont. Cas. Fed. (CCH) P 76542, 124 Lab. Cas. (CCH) P 35782 (3d Cir. 1993). United States ☞64.20

2 Construction and application

Once navy officials determined to suspend bidder rather than to reject its bids for nonresponsibility, the navy officials likewise determined to subject themselves to their own regulations and body of case law prescribing fair method for executing such a suspension. ATL, Inc. v. U.S., 736 F.2d 677, 32 Cont. Cas. Fed. (CCH) P 72528 (Fed. Cir. 1984). United States ☞64.20

3 Construction with other laws

National Labor Relations Act (NLRA) provision guaranteeing management's right to hire permanent replacements during labor strikes preempted Executive Order made under authority of Procurement Act, barring federal government from contracting with employers who hire permanent replacements during lawful strike. National Labor Relations Act, § 1 et seq., as amended, 29 U.S.C.A. § 151 et seq.; Federal Property and Administrative Services Act of 1949, § 2, 40 U.S.C.A. § 471. Chamber of Commerce of U.S. v. Reich, 74 F.3d 1322, 316, 151 L.R.R.M. (BNA) 2353, 40 Cont. Cas. Fed. (CCH) P 76878, 131 Lab. Cas. (CCH) P 11496 (D.C. Cir. 1996). Labor And Employment ☞1434; United States ☞64.20

4 Retroactive or prospective application

Executive order providing for government-wide debarment and suspension of government contractors debarred or suspended by particular agency did not become effective until issuance of guidelines by Office of Management and Budget (OMB) and subsequent implementing regulations and, in the interim, Department of Labor (DOL) properly continued operating according to its existing regulations. Executive Order No. 12549, § 6, 31 U.S.C.A. § 6101 note. Facchiano Const. Co., Inc. v. U.S. Dept. of Labor, 987 F.2d 206, 1 Wage & Hour Cas. 2d (BNA) 468, 39 Cont. Cas. Fed. (CCH) P 76542, 124 Lab. Cas. (CCH) P 35782 (3d Cir. 1993). United States ☞64.20

5 Deference to agency interpretation

Although agency's interpretation of its own regulations is entitled to considerable deference, court construed regulations dealing with debarment of government contractors with minimal deference; regulations were written and promulgated not only by Department of Defense, but also by General Services Administration and National Aeronautics and Space Administration, and interpretation of regulations was given by debarring official not by head of agency. Caiola v. Carroll, 851 F.2d 395, 399, 34 Cont. Cas. Fed. (CCH) P 75514 (D.C. Cir. 1988). Administrative Law And Procedure ☞413; United States ☞64.20

6 Due process of law

Suspension of contractor from eligibility for government contracts pursuant to Federal Acquisition Regulations System (FAR), following contractor's indictment on charges involving fraud or dishonesty, satisfied requirements of procedural due process; although private interest at stake was important, initial reliability of indictment coupled with contractor's opportunity to rebut its conclusions greatly minimized risk of erroneous or irrational deprivation of its interest, and government interests in having responsible contractors perform its contracts and avoiding impairment of conduct of its business which would result if every governmental decision required full hearing involving all parties affected were significant. U.S.C.A. Const.Amend. 14; 48 C.F.R. §§ 9.401–9.407. Rutigliano Paper Stock, Inc. v. U.S. General Services Admin., 967 F. Supp. 757, 41 Cont. Cas. Fed. (CCH) P 77156 (E.D. N.Y. 1997). Constitutional Law ⬥276(2); United States ⬥64.20

For purpose of determining extent of process due contractor upon suspension of its eligibility for government contracts pursuant to Federal Acquisition Regulations System (FAR), such suspension, if based upon contractor's indictment, is considered to be based upon independent fact finding process that produced indictment, which process is considered sufficiently reliable to effect temporary but total deprivation of liberty. 48 C.F.R. §§ 9.401–9.407. Rutigliano Paper Stock, Inc. v. U.S. General Services Admin., 967 F. Supp. 757, 41 Cont. Cas. Fed. (CCH) P 77156 (E.D. N.Y. 1997). Constitutional Law ⬥276(2); United States ⬥64.20

Due process is satisfied with respect to suspension of contractor from eligibility for government contracts under Federal Acquisition Regulations System (FAR) if meaningful opportunity to be heard on issue of appropriateness of suspension is granted within reasonable time and contractor is afforded opportunity to demonstrate that imposition of suspension would be irrational or contrary to government's interests. U.S.C.A. Const.Amend. 14; 48 C.F.R. §§ 9.401–9.407. Rutigliano Paper Stock, Inc. v. U.S. General Services Admin., 967 F. Supp. 757, 41 Cont. Cas. Fed. (CCH) P 77156 (E.D. N.Y. 1997). Constitutional Law ⬥276(2); United States ⬥64.20

Requirements of due process did not dictate that Federal Acquisition Regulations System (FAR) require justification for contractor's suspension from eligibility for government contracts beyond fact of contractor's indictment on charges involving fraud or dishonesty; indictment merely gave rise to rebuttable presumption that suspension was justified, contractor was entitled to provide contradictory evidence, indictment gave rise to presumption of probable cause and was sufficiently reliable to provide adequate basis for suspension, and judicial review of any improper suspension was available pursuant to Administrative Procedures Act. U.S.C.A. Const. Amend. 14; 5 U.S.C.A. § 551 et seq.; 48 C.F.R. §§ 9.401–9.407. Rutigliano Paper Stock, Inc. v. U.S. General Services Admin., 967 F. Supp. 757, 41 Cont. Cas. Fed. (CCH) P 77156 (E.D. N.Y. 1997). Constitutional Law ⬥276(2); United States ⬥64.20

Contractor's indictment gives rise to presumption of probable cause, such that grounding of rebuttable presumption that suspension from eligibility for government contracts pursuant to Federal Acquisition Regulations System (FAR) is warranted upon such indictment does not violate contractor's due process rights. U.S.C.A. Const.Amend. 14; 48 C.F.R. §§ 9.401–9.407. Rutigliano Paper Stock, Inc. v. U.S. General Services Admin., 967 F. Supp. 757, 41 Cont. Cas. Fed. (CCH) P 77156 (E.D. N.Y. 1997). Constitutional Law ⬥276(2); United States ⬥64.20

Requirements of due process did not dictate that Federal Acquisition Regulations System (FAR) provide additional fact finding hearing upon suspension of contractor from eligibility for government contracts, where basis for suspension was contractor's indictment on charges involving fraud or dishonesty, although government was obligated to inform contractor clearly of its opportunity to present evidence which might rebut indictment; General Services Administration (GSA) lacked power to find facts related to indictment, and purpose of contractor's opportunity to be heard was not to contest indictment. U.S.C.A. Const.Amend. 14; 48 C.F.R. §§ 9.401–9.407. Rutigliano Paper Stock, Inc. v. U.S. General Services Admin., 967 F. Supp. 757, 41 Cont. Cas. Fed. (CCH) P 77156 (E.D. N.Y. 1997). Constitutional Law ⬥276(2); United States ⬥64.20

In context of contractor's suspension from eligibility for government contracts under Federal Acquisition Regulations System (FAR) following contractor's indictment, due process does not require full adversarial hearing and fact finding; purpose of contractor's opportunity to be heard is not to contest indictment, but rather to demonstrate that suspension should not be imposed, either because it is not in government's interest to do so, or because in light of compelling evidence presented by contractor, governmental decision to rely only on indictment would be arbitrary, capricious, or abuse of discretion. U.S.C.A. Const.Amend. 14; 48 C.F.R. §§ 9.401–9.407. Rutigliano Paper Stock, Inc. v. U.S. General Services Admin., 967 F. Supp. 757, 41 Cont. Cas. Fed. (CCH) P 77156 (E.D. N.Y. 1997). Constitutional Law ⬥276(2); United States ⬥64.20

Requirements of due process did not dictate that General Services Administration (GSA) provide suspended contractor with independent review by individual not directly involved with its decision to suspend contractor's eligibility for government contracts; applicable regulations did not call for such review, no process provided for therein could be construed as independent review, and district court review was available under Administrative Procedures Act. U.S.C.A. Const.Amend. 14; 5 U.S.C.A. § 551 et seq.; 48 C.F.R. §§ 9.401–9. 407. Rutigliano Paper Stock, Inc. v. U.S. General Services Admin., 967 F. Supp. 757, 41 Cont. Cas. Fed. (CCH) P 77156 (E.D. N.Y. 1997). Constitutional Law ⟐276(2); United States ⟐64.20

Contractor suspended from eligibility for government contracts by General Services Administration (GSA) pursuant to Federal Acquisition Regulations System (FAR) had protected liberty interest in its eligibility to bid for federal contracts, where suspension was based upon contractor's indictment on charges involving fraud and dishonesty. 48 C.F.R. §§ 9.401–9.407. Rutigliano Paper Stock, Inc. v. U.S. General Services Admin., 967 F. Supp. 757, 41 Cont. Cas. Fed. (CCH) P 77156 (E.D. N.Y. 1997). Constitutional Law ⟐276(2)

Provision of Federal Acquisition Regulations System (FAR) continuing contractors' suspension from eligibility for government contracts until conclusion of significant activity in criminal action did not violate due process as applied, despite delay in trial on charges in indictment; contractors had been permitted to present evidence indicating that suspension was not in government's interest despite existence of indictment, and no significant activity in state criminal case was pending that would prolong suspension. U.S.C.A. Const. Amend. 14; 48 C.F.R. §§ 9.401–9.407. Rutigliano Paper Stock, Inc. v. U.S. General Services Admin., 967 F. Supp. 757, 41 Cont. Cas. Fed. (CCH) P 77156 (E.D. N.Y. 1997). Constitutional Law ⟐276(2); United States ⟐64.20

7 Injunctions

Air Force debarment of company CEO was enjoined because the Air Force debarring official did not adequately consider the CEO's submissions challenging agency assertions about late deliveries of freight. In addition, the agency appeared to have improperly relied on the CEO's position in the company to impute misconduct to the Alf v. Donley, 666 F. Supp. 2d 60 (D.D.C. 2009)

For purpose of determining contractor's entitlement to injunction against enforcement of Federal Acquisition Regulations System (FAR), contractor's almost total loss of business and inability to bid on new contracts as result of suspension from eligibility for government contracts constituted "irreparable harm" incapable of being remedied by monetary damages alone. 48 C.F.R. §§ 9.401–9.407. Rutigliano Paper Stock, Inc. v. U.S. General Services Admin., 967 F. Supp. 757, 41 Cont. Cas. Fed. (CCH) P 77156 (E.D. N.Y. 1997). Injunction ⟐86

§ 9.402 Policy.

(a) Agencies shall solicit offers from, award contracts to, and consent to subcontracts with responsible contractors only. Debarment and suspension are discretionary actions that, taken in accordance with this subpart, are appropriate means to effectuate this policy.

(b) The serious nature of debarment and suspension requires that these sanctions be imposed only in the public interest for the Government's protection and not for purposes of punishment. Agencies shall impose debarment or suspension to protect the Government's interest and only for the causes and in accordance with the procedures set forth in this subpart.

(c) Agencies are encouraged to establish methods and procedures for coordinating their debarment or suspension actions.

(d) When more than one agency has an interest in the debarment or suspension of a contractor, the Interagency Committee on Debarment and Suspension, established under Executive Order 12549, and authorized by Section 873 of the National Defense Authorization Act for Fiscal Year 2009 (Pub. L. 110-417) (31 U.S.C. 6101, note), shall resolve the lead agency issue and coordinate such resolution among all interested agencies prior to the initiation of any suspension, debarment, or related administrative action by any agency.

(e) Agencies shall establish appropriate procedures to implement the policies and procedures of this subpart.

United States Code Annotated

Administrative determinations, see 41 USCA § 257.

Contract requirements, see 41 USCA § 254.

Contractor responsibilities, see 41 USCA § 57.

Contracts, planning, solicitation, evaluation, and award procedures, see 10 USCA § 2305.

Definitions, see 10 USCA § 2302, 41 USCA §§ 259, 403.

Determinations and decisions, see 10 USCA § 2310, 41 USCA § 262.

Kinds of contracts, see 10 USCA § 2306.

Planning and solicitation requirements, see 41 USCA § 253a.

Notes of Decisions

Double jeopardy 2
Injunctions 3
Purpose 1

1 Purpose

Executive order providing for government-wide debarment and suspension of contractors who are debarred or suspended by particular agency was a managerial tool and not shown to be for the benefit of contractors, and thus did not provide basis for challenging government-wide debarment order on ground that, under the executive order, a prior agency debarment arising from the same circumstances should have been government-wide, precluding later imposition of the same penalty. Executive Order No. 12549, §§ 1 et seq., 1(a), 31 U.S.C.A. § 6101 note. Facchiano Const. Co., Inc. v. U.S. Dept. of Labor, 987 F.2d 206, 1 Wage & Hour Cas. 2d (BNA) 468, 39 Cont. Cas. Fed. (CCH) P 76542, 124 Lab. Cas. (CCH) P 35782 (3d Cir. 1993). United States ☞64.20

Debarment, so as to preclude contractor from being awarded federal government contracts, is designed to insure integrity of government contracts. 48 C.F.R. § 9.402(a). Ali v. U.S., 932 F. Supp. 1206 (N.D. Cal. 1996). United States ☞64.20

2 Double jeopardy

Debarment of government contractor for 26 months was not sufficiently punitive to implicate double jeopardy clause and require the dismissal of criminal prosecution against him, as contractor failed to show disbarment was disproportionate to benefits received by government in protecting it against effects of willful failures to perform in accordance with terms of government contracts, effects of history of failures to perform, and adverse effect of having government contract with irresponsible contractor. U.S.C.A. Const. Amend. 5; 48 C.F.R. §§ 9.402(b), 9.403, 9.406-2, 9.406-3(b)(1), (d)(3). U.S. v. Hatfield, 108 F.3d 67 (4th Cir. 1997). Double Jeopardy ☞24

Debarment of government contractor did not have to be subjected to a "particularized assessment" to determine whether it was punitive for double jeopardy purposes, where government did not seek the return of particular quantity of funds but instead sought to protect the quality of its acquisition programs. 48 C.F.R. §§ 9.402(b), 9.406-2(b)(1), 48 C.F.R. §§ 9.402(b), (c), 9.406-4. U.S. v. Hatfield, 108 F.3d 67 (4th Cir. 1997). Double Jeopardy ☞24

Four-year debarment of defense contractor from government contracting was not so overwhelmingly disproportionate to harm caused by defendant's conduct, in knowingly supplying nonconforming parts to Department of Defense (DOD), as to constitute punishment for double jeopardy purposes, even though regulations generally provided for three-year maximum debarment, as debarment served important nonpunitive goals of preventing further dissipation of public funds and protecting DOD programs by preventing supply of substandard or defective parts, and extra year could be viewed as evidence of intent to protect government from particularly egregious conduct, where government paid company more than $40,000 for nonconforming parts. U.S.C.A. Const.Amend. 5; 18 U.S.C.A. § 287; 48 C.F.R. §§ 9.402, 9.406-2(b), 9.406-4. U.S. v. Glymph, 96 F.3d 722 (4th Cir. 1996). Double Jeopardy ☞24

3 Injunctions

Contractor's officer was not entitled to temporary restraining order against his expired debarment by Department of Health and Human Services (DHHS), which had precluded officer from being awarded government contracts; officer was not likely to succeed on the merits of his challenge to debarment, as administrative record revealed substantial evidence upon which debarring official could have concluded that contractor committed forgery and that officer knew or should have known of it, officer apparently received all due process guarantees required by debarment regulations, and government agencies had not waived all fraud claims against officer, and balance of hardships did not tip in officer's favor, as officer had delayed two years in filing action and seeking injunction, any harm to officer was economic, speculative, or both, and government had strong interest in maintaining integrity of its contractors. 48 C.F.R. §§ 9.402(a), 9.406-2(c), 9.406-3(b)(1), (d)(1), (d)(2)(i), 9.406-5(b). Ali v. U.S., 932 F. Supp. 1206 (N.D. Cal. 1996). Injunction ⊕⃬150

§ 9.403 Definitions.

As used in this subpart—

"Affiliates." Business concerns, organizations, or individuals are affiliates of each other if, directly or indirectly, (1) either one controls or has the power to control the other, or (2) a third party controls or has the power to control both. Indicia of control include, but are not limited to, interlocking management or ownership, identity of interests among family members, shared facilities and equipment, common use of employees, or a business entity organized following the debarment, suspension, or proposed debarment of a contractor which has the same or similar management, ownership, or principal employees as the contractor that was debarred, suspended, or proposed for debarment.

"Agency" means any executive department, military department or defense agency, or other agency or independent establishment of the executive branch.

"Civil judgment" means a judgment or finding of a civil offense by any court of competent jurisdiction.

"Contractor" means any individual or other legal entity that—

(1) Directly or indirectly (*e.g.*, through an affiliate), submits offers for or is awarded, or reasonably may be expected to submit offers for or be awarded, a Government contract, including a contract for carriage under Government or commercial bills of lading, or a subcontract under a Government contract; or

(2) Conducts business, or reasonably may be expected to conduct business, with the Government as an agent or representative of another contractor.

"Debarring official" means—

(1) An agency head; or

(2) A designee authorized by the agency head to impose debarment.

"Indictment" means indictment for a criminal offense. An information or other filing by competent authority charging a criminal offense is given the same effect as an indictment.

"Legal proceedings" means any civil judicial proceeding to which the Government is a party or any criminal proceeding. The term includes appeals from such proceedings.

"Nonprocurement Common Rule" means the procedures used by Federal Executive Agencies to suspend, debar, or exclude individuals or entities from participation in nonprocurement transactions under Executive Order 12549. Examples of nonprocurement transactions are grants, cooperative agreements, scholarships, fellowships, contracts of assistance, loans, loan guarantees, subsidies, insurance, payments for specified use, and donation agreements.

"Suspending official" means—

(1) An agency head; or

(2) A designee authorized by the agency head to impose suspension.

"Unfair trade practices" means the commission of any or the following acts by a contractor:

(1) A violation of Section 337 of the Tariff Act of 1930 (19 U.S.C. 1337) as determined by the International Trade Commission.

(2) A violation, as determined by the Secretary of Commerce, of any agreement of the group known as the "Coordination Committee" for purposes of the Export Administration Act of 1979 (50 U.S.C. App. 2401, et seq.) or any similar bilateral or multilateral export control agreement.

(3) A knowingly false statement regarding a material element of a certification concerning the foreign content of an item of supply, as determined by the Secretary of the

Department or the head of the agency to which such certificate was furnished.

United States Code Annotated

Administrative determinations, see 41 USCA § 257.

Contract requirements, see 41 USCA § 254.

Contractor responsibilities, see 41 USCA § 57.

Contracts, planning, solicitation, evaluation, and award procedures, see 10 USCA § 2305.

Definitions, see 10 USCA § 2302, 41 USCA §§ 259, 403.

Determinations and decisions, see 10 USCA § 2310, 41 USCA § 262.

Kinds of contracts, see 10 USCA § 2306.

Planning and solicitation requirements, see 41 USCA § 253a.

Notes of Decisions

In general 1
Double jeopardy 2
Falsification of records 4
Indictment 3

1 In general

The purpose of the affiliate rule is evident: to prevent a debarred contractor from reorganizing or changing the name of a corporation and continuing to do business with the Government. The regulations can also prevent a corporation, which is controlled by a debarred corporation or individual, from doing business with the Government. The regulations equate affiliation to control. An organization is the affiliate of an individual if the organization "is controlled by" the individual. This is a broad standard and there are no guidelines on how to treat affiliates. It is the mere status of being an affiliate being controlled by a debarred contractor or individual, rather than any wrongful act on the part of the affiliate, that can give rise to a debarment action under the regulation. Balboa Ambulance, Inc., VABCA No. D&S-93-001, 1993 WL 428087 (V.A.B.C.A.), September 15, 1993

Contracting officer reasonably determined that the protester was ineligible for award because of its affiliation with a debarred contractor where the record shows, among other things, that: (1) the protester is a newly activated company, purchased by a key employee of the debarred company and reorganized shortly after its affiliate was debarred; (2) the protester and the debarred contractor share several key management employees; (3) the protester and the debarred firm share a common street address and the protester will lease the debarred contractor's manufacturing equipment and other facilities; and (4) the protester planned to subcontract with the debarred firm. Matter of: Detek, Inc., B-261678, 95-2 CPD ¶ 177 (Comp. Gen. 1995)

2 Double jeopardy

Debarment of government contractor for 26 months was not sufficiently punitive to implicate double jeopardy clause and require the dismissal of criminal prosecution against him, as contractor failed to show disbarment was disproportionate to benefits received by government in protecting it against effects of willful failures to perform in accordance with terms of government contracts, effects of history of failures to perform, and adverse effect of having government contract with irresponsible contractor. U.S.C.A. Const. Amend. 5; 48 C.F.R. §§ 9.402(b), 9.403, 9.406-2, 9.406-3(b)(1), (d)(3). U.S. v. Hatfield, 108 F.3d 67 (4th Cir. 1997). Double Jeopardy ⊸24

Halper balancing test for determining whether debarment of government contractor is punitive for double jeopardy purposes—weighing government's harm against penalty's size—is inapplicable, where sanction and purposes it seeks to achieve are qualitative rather than merely quantitative, and question becomes whether debarment is in effect so punitive, that court must conclude that the proceeding is not civil but criminal in nature. U.S.C.A. Const.Amend. 5; 48 C.F.R. § 9.403. U.S. v. Hatfield, 108 F.3d 67 (4th Cir. 1997). Double Jeopardy ⊸24

To determine whether debarment of government contractor is civil or criminal, for purposes of claim that debarment precluded criminal prosecution of double jeopardy grounds, court examines whether procedure was designed to be remedial, and whether remedy provided, even if designated as civil, is so unreasonable or excessive that it transforms what was clearly intended as civil remedy into a criminal penalty. U.S.C.A. Const.Amend. 5; 48 C.F.R. § 9.403. U.S. v. Hatfield, 108 F.3d 67 (4th Cir. 1997). Double Jeopardy ⊸24

3 Indictment

Moving and storage company that was not indicted for antitrust violations was nonetheless properly placed on Department of Army's list of disqualified bidders, when company was an affiliate of company named in indictment. Coleman American Moving Services, Inc. v. Weinberger, 716 F. Supp. 1405, 36 Cont. Cas. Fed. (CCH) P 75786 (M.D. Ala. 1989). United States ⊸64.20

Suspension of contractor was based on adequate evidence, where suspension board gave careful consideration to criminal indictment against contractor and additional information supporting indictment before it recommended suspension. Shermco Industries, Inc. v. Secretary of the Air Force, 584 F. Supp. 76, 32 Cont. Cas. Fed. (CCH) P 72713 (N.D. Tex. 1984). United States ⊸64.20

Where there was no showing that new suspension of contractor from contracting for federal contracts as a result of indictment charging false statements and fraud in connection with performance of prior government contracts was not in accordance with applicable regulations, and where there was no contention that the regulations were invalid, the Navy could not presently award four contracts on which contractor was low bidder to contractor and there was no basis for enjoining awards to others or preventing them from proceeding on awards already made. ATL, Inc. v. U.S., 6 Cl. Ct. 539, 32 Cont. Cas. Fed. (CCH) P 73067 (1984). United States ⊸64.20

4 Falsification of records

Although government contractor was properly debarred from doing business with government for three-year term for falsification of laboratory test results, debarment of president and secretary of contractor on ground that they had reason to know of contractor's criminal conduct, although they did not have actual knowledge of conduct, was not supported by preponderance of evidence and, therefore, their debarment was unreasonable. Caiola v. Carroll, 851 F.2d 395, 399, 34 Cont. Cas. Fed. (CCH) P 75514 (D.C. Cir. 1988). United States ⊸64.20

§ 9.404 System for Award Management Exclusions.

(a) The General Services Administration (GSA)—

　(1) Operates the web-based System for Award Management (SAM) Exclusions; and

　(2) Provides technical assistance to Federal agencies in the use of SAM.

(b) The SAM Exclusions contains the—

　(1) Names and addresses of all contractors debarred, suspended, proposed for debarment, declared ineligible, or excluded or disqualified under the nonprocurement common rule, with cross-references when more than one name is involved in a single action;

　(2) Name of the agency or other authority taking the action;

　(3) Cause for the action (see 9.406-2 and 9.407-2 for causes authorized under this subpart) or other statutory or regulatory authority;

　(4) Effect of the action;

　(5) Termination date for each listing;

　(6) Data Universal Numbering System number;

　(7) Social Security Number (SSN), Employer Identification Number (EIN), or other Taxpayer Identification Number (TIN), if available; and

　(8) Name and telephone number of the agency point of contact for the action.

(c) Each agency must—

　(1) Obtain password(s) from GSA to access SAM for data entry;

　(2) Notify GSA in the event a password needs to be rescinded (e.g., when an agency employee leaves or changes function);

(3) Enter the information required by paragraph (b) of this section within 3 working days after the action becomes effective;

(4) Determine whether it is legally permitted to enter the SSN, EIN, or other TIN, under agency authority to suspend or debar;

(5) Update SAM Exclusions, generally within 5 working days after modifying or rescinding an action;

(6) In accordance with internal retention procedures, maintain records relating to each debarment, suspension, or proposed debarment taken by the agency;

(7) Establish procedures to ensure that the agency does not solicit offers from, award contracts to, or consent to subcontracts with contractors whose names are in SAM Exclusions, except as otherwise provided in this subpart;

(8) Direct inquiries concerning listed contractors to the agency or other authority that took the action; and

(9) Contact GSA for technical assistance with SAM, via the support e-mail address or on the technical support phone line available at the SAM web site provided in paragraph (d) of this section.

(d) SAM is available via https://www.acquisition.gov.

§ 9.405 Effect of listing.

(a) Contractors debarred, suspended, or proposed for debarment are excluded from receiving contracts, and agencies shall not solicit offers from, award contracts to, or consent to subcontracts with these contractors, unless the agency head determines that there is a compelling reason for such action (see 9.405-1(b), 9.405-2, 9.406-1(c), 9.407-1(d), and 23.506(e)). Contractors debarred, suspended, or proposed for debarment are also excluded from conducting business with the Government as agents or representatives of other contractors.

(b) Contractors included in SAM Exclusions as having been declared ineligible on the basis of statutory or other regulatory procedures are excluded from receiving contracts, and if applicable, subcontracts, under the conditions and for the period set forth in the statute or regulation. Agencies shall not solicit offers from, award contracts to, or consent to subcontracts with these contractors under those conditions and for that period.

(c) Contractors debarred, suspended, or proposed for debarment are excluded from acting as individual sureties (see Part 28).

(d) (1) After the opening of bids or receipt of proposals, the contracting officer shall review SAM Exclusions.

(2) Bids received from any listed contractor in response to an invitation for bids shall be entered on the abstract of bids, and rejected unless the agency head determines in writing that there is a compelling reason to consider the bid.

(3) Proposals, quotations, or offers received from any listed contractor shall not be evaluated for award or included in the competitive range, nor shall discussions be conducted with a listed offeror during a period of ineligibility, unless the agency head determines, in writing, that there is a compelling reason to do so. If the period of ineligibility expires or is terminated prior to award, the contracting officer may, but is not required to, consider such proposals, quotations, or offers.

(4) Immediately prior to award, the contracting officer shall again review SAM Exclusions to ensure that no award is made to a listed contractor.

§ 9.405-1 Continuation of current contracts.

(a) Notwithstanding the debarment, suspension, or proposed debarment of a contractor, agencies may continue contracts or subcontracts in existence at the time the contractor was debarred, suspended, or proposed for debarment unless the agency head directs otherwise. A decision as to the type of termination action, if any, to be taken should be made only after review by agency contracting and technical personnel and by counsel to ensure the propriety of the proposed action.

(b) For contractors debarred, suspended, or proposed for debarment, unless the agency head makes a written determination of the compelling reasons for doing so, ordering activities shall not—

(1) Place orders exceeding the guaranteed minimum under indefinite quantity

contracts;

(2) Place orders under Federal Supply Schedule contracts, blanket purchase agreements, or basic ordering agreements; or

(3) Add new work, exercise options, or otherwise extend the duration of current contracts or orders.

§ 9.405-2 Restrictions on subcontracting.

(a) When a contractor debarred, suspended, or proposed for debarment is proposed as a subcontractor for any subcontract subject to Government consent (see Subpart 44.2), contracting officers shall not consent to subcontracts with such contractors unless the agency head states in writing the compelling reasons for this approval action. (See 9.405(b) concerning declarations of ineligibility affecting sub-contracting.)

(b) The Government suspends or debars contractors to protect the Government's interests. By operation of the clause at 52.209-6, Protecting the Government's Interests When Subcontracting with Contractors Debarred, Suspended or Proposed for Debarment, contractors shall not enter into any subcontract in excess of $35,000, other than a subcontract for a commercially available off-the-shelf item, with a contractor that has been debarred, suspended, or proposed for debarment unless there is a compelling reason to do so. If a contractor intends to enter into a subcontract in excess of $35,000, other than a subcontract for a commercially available off-the-shelf item, with a party that is debarred, suspended, or proposed for debarment as evidenced by the parties' listing in SAM Exclusions (see 9.404), a corporate officer or designee of the contractor is required by operation of the clause at 52.209-6, Protecting the Government's Interests when Subcontracting with Contractors Debarred, Suspended, or Proposed for Debarment, to notify the contracting officer, in writing, before entering into such subcontract. For contracts for the acquisition of commercial items, the notification requirement applies only for first-tier subcontracts. For all other contracts, the notification requirement applies to subcontracts at any tier. The notice must provide the following:

(1) The name of the subcontractor;

(2) The contractor's knowledge of the reasons for the subcontractor being listed in SAM Exclusions;

(3) The compelling reason(s) for doing business with the subcontractor notwithstanding its listed in SAM Exclusions; and

(4) The systems and procedures the contractor has established to ensure that it is fully protecting the Government's interests when dealing with such subcontractor in view of the specific basis for the party's debarment, suspension, or proposed debarment.

(c) The contractor's compliance with the requirements of 52.209-6 will be reviewed during Contractor Purchasing System Reviews (see Subpart 44.3).

§ 9.406 Debarment.

§ 9.406-1 General.

(a) It is the debarring official's responsibility to determine whether debarment is in the Government's interest. The debarring official may, in the public interest, debar a contractor for any of the causes in 9.406-2, using the procedures in 9.406-3. The existence of a cause for debarment, however, does not necessarily require that the contractor be debarred; the seriousness of the contractor's acts or omissions and any remedial measures or mitigating factors should be considered in making any debarment decision. Before arriving at any debarment decision, the debarring official should consider factors such as the following:

(1) Whether the contractor had effective standards of conduct and internal control systems in place at the time of the activity which constitutes cause for debarment or had adopted such procedures prior to any Government investigation of the activity cited as a cause for debarment.

(2) Whether the contractor brought the activity cited as a cause for debarment to the attention of the appropriate Government agency in a timely manner.

(3) Whether the contractor has fully investigated the circumstances surrounding the cause for debarment and, if so, made the result of the investigation available to the debarring official.

(4) Whether the contractor cooperated fully with Government agencies during the

investigation and any court or administrative action.

(5) Whether the contractor has paid or has agreed to pay all criminal, civil, and administrative liability for the improper activity, including any investigative or administrative costs incurred by the Government, and has made or agreed to make full restitution.

(6) Whether the contractor has taken appropriate disciplinary action against the individuals responsible for the activity which constitutes cause for debarment.

(7) Whether the contractor has implemented or agreed to implement remedial measures, including any identified by the Government.

(8) Whether the contractor has instituted or agreed to institute new or revised review and control procedures and ethics training programs.

(9) Whether the contractor has had adequate time to eliminate the circumstances within the contractor's organization that led to the cause for debarment.

(10) Whether the contractor's management recognizes and understands the seriousness of the misconduct giving rise to the cause for debarment and has implemented programs to prevent recurrence.

The existence or nonexistence of any mitigating factors or remedial measures such as set forth in this paragraph (a) is not necessarily determinative of a contractor's present responsibility. Accordingly, if a cause for debarment exists, the contractor has the burden of demonstrating, to the satisfaction of the debarring official, its present responsibility and that debarment is not necessary.

(b) Debarment constitutes debarment of all divisions or other organizational elements of the contractor, unless the debarment decision is limited by its terms to specific divisions, organizational elements, or commodities. The debarring official may extend the debarment decision to include any affiliates of the contractor if they are—

(1) Specifically named; and

(2) Given written notice of the proposed debarment and an opportunity to respond (see 9.406-3(c)).

(c) A contractor's debarment, or proposed debarment, shall be effective throughout the executive branch of the Government, unless the agency head or a designee (except see 23. 506(e)) states in writing the compelling reasons justifying continued business dealings between that agency and the contractor.

(d) (1) When the debarring official has authority to debar contractors from both acquisition contracts pursuant to this regulation and contracts for the purchase of Federal personal property pursuant to the Federal Property Management Regulations (FPMR) 101-45.6, that official shall consider simultaneously debarring the contractor from the award of acquisition contracts and from the purchase of Federal personal property.

(2) When debarring a contractor from the award of acquisition contracts and from the purchase of Federal personal property, the debarment notice shall so indicate and the appropriate FAR and FPMR citations shall be included.

United States Code Annotated

Administrative determinations, see 41 USCA § 257.

Contract requirements, see 41 USCA § 254.

Contractor responsibilities, see 41 USCA § 57.

Contracts, planning, solicitation, evaluation, and award procedures, see 10 USCA § 2305.

Definitions, see 10 USCA § 2302, 41 USCA §§ 259, 403.

Determinations and decisions, see 10 USCA § 2310, 41 USCA § 262.

Kinds of contracts, see 10 USCA § 2306.

Planning and solicitation requirements, see 41 USCA § 253a.

Notes of Decisions

In general 2
Agriculture Department 23
Antitrust violations and anticompetitive activities 14
Armed services and defense 24
Cause of serious and compelling nature 17

1 Validity

Federal acquisitions regulations governing debarment of government contractors are not unreasonable or unconstitutional. Joseph Const. Co. v. Veterans Admin. of U.S., 595 F. Supp. 448, 32 Cont. Cas. Fed. (CCH) P 73082 (N.D. Ill. 1984). United States ⊸64.20

2 In general

Suspension and debarment of bidder for government contract occur when Government formally or constructively precludes contractor from participating in future, government contracts or when contracting official's decisions effectively prevent contractor from participating in that and future procurements. BMY, A Div. of HARSCO Corp. v. U.S., 693 F. Supp. 1232, 35 Cont. Cas. Fed. (CCH) P 75552 (D.D.C. 1988). United States ⊸64.20

3 Purpose

Executive order providing for government-wide debarment and suspension of contractors who are debarred or suspended by particular agency was a managerial tool and not shown to be for the benefit of contractors, and thus did not provide basis for challenging government-wide debarment order on ground that, under the executive order, a prior agency debarment arising from the same circumstances should have been government-wide, precluding later imposition of the same penalty. Executive Order No. 12549, §§ 1 et seq., 1(a), 31 U.S.C.A. § 6101 note. Facchiano Const. Co., Inc. v. U.S. Dept. of Labor, 987 F.2d 206, 1 Wage & Hour Cas. 2d (BNA) 468, 39 Cont. Cas. Fed. (CCH) P 76542, 124 Lab. Cas. (CCH) P 35782 (3d Cir. 1993). United States ⊸64.20

4 Deference to agency interpretation

Although agency's interpretation of its own regulations is entitled to considerable deference, court construed regulations dealing with debarment of government contractors with minimal deference; regulations were written and promulgated not only by Department of Defense, but also by General Services Administration and National Aeronautics and Space Administration, and interpretation of regulations was given by debarring official not by head of agency. Caiola v. Carroll, 851 F.2d 395, 399, 34 Cont. Cas. Fed. (CCH) P 75514 (D.C. Cir. 1988). Administrative Law And Procedure ☞413; United States ☞64.20

5 Retroactive or prospective application

Executive order providing for government-wide debarment and suspension of government contractors debarred or suspended by particular agency did not become effective until issuance of guidelines by Office of Management and Budget (OMB) and subsequent implementing regulations and, in the interim, Department of Labor (DOL) properly continued operating according to its existing regulations. Executive Order No. 12549, § 6, 31 U.S.C.A. § 6101 note. Facchiano Const. Co., Inc. v. U.S. Dept. of Labor, 987 F.2d 206, 1 Wage & Hour Cas. 2d (BNA) 468, 39 Cont. Cas. Fed. (CCH) P 76542, 124 Lab. Cas. (CCH) P 35782 (3d Cir. 1993). United States ☞64.20

6 Due process of law

Allowing Department of Housing and Urban Development (HUD) employee to act as an advisor to the hearing official, even though he had previously participated in the investigation and prosecution of matter involving another property owned by contractor, did not violate contractor's due process rights, absent showing advisor exerted any improper influence upon the hearing official, that hearing official was otherwise biased as a result of any HUD participant, that other matter entered into debarring official's determination, or that decision was tainted or otherwise rendered unsupportable by roles of any other HUD employees participating in debarment proceeding. U.S.C.A. Const.Amend. 14. Marshall v. Cuomo, 192 F.3d 473 (4th Cir. 1999). Constitutional Law ☞276(2); United States ☞64.20

In recognition of the serious nature of debarment, the FAR sets out detailed procedures to ensure that this sanction, which is intended to safeguard the integrity of the acquisitions process, itself is applied in conformity with principles of fundamental fairness. Accordingly, the debarment procedures specified in the FAR provide for an opportunity to appear with counsel, submit documentary evidence, and confront any person the agency presents, if it is found that the contractor's submission in opposition raises a genuine dispute over facts material to the proposed debarment. Sameena Inc. v. U.S. Air Force, 147 F.3d 1148, 42 Cont. Cas. Fed. (CCH) P 77335 (9th Cir. 1998)

Agricultural Stabilization and Conservation Service (ASCS) debarment procedures comported with fundamental fairness requirements of due process even though they were not conducted by administrative law judge; under regulations, debarring officer was not member of investigative branch of agency and regulations did not facially merge functions of prosecutor and decision maker. U.S.C.A. Const. Amend. 14. Girard v. Klopfenstein, 930 F.2d 738 (9th Cir. 1991). Constitutional Law ☞291.6; United States ☞64.20

To sustain a denial of contractor's liberty interest by debarment, it must be established that contract awards to contractor involve a threat to interests of Government. Peter Kiewit Sons' Co. v. U. S. Army Corps of Engineers, 534 F. Supp. 1139, 29 Cont. Cas. Fed. (CCH) P 82291 (D.D.C. 1982), judgment rev'd, 714 F.2d 163, 31 Cont. Cas. Fed. (CCH) P 71395, 1983-2 Trade Cas. (CCH) ¶ 65528 (D.C. Cir. 1983). United States ☞64.20

Debarment proceedings did not violate procedural due process rights of defense contractor where proceedings were conducted in compliance with Department of Defense procedural requirements, contractor was given opportunity to submit information and argument in opposition to proposed debarment and chose to do so in writing, and no genuine dispute of material fact was created by contractor's opposition to debarment as would require fact-finding hearing, even though contractor contended that lack of opportunity to cross-examine government witnesses violated its due process rights. U.S.C.A. Const.Amend. 5. IMCO, Inc. v. U.S., 33 Fed. Cl. 312 (1995), judgment aff'd, 97 F.3d 1422 (Fed. Cir. 1996). Constitutional Law ☞276(2); United States ☞64.20

7 Double jeopardy

Debarment of government contractor for 26 months was not sufficiently punitive to implicate double jeopardy clause and require the dismissal of criminal prosecution against him, as contractor failed to show disbarment was disproportionate to benefits received by government in protecting it against effects of willful failures to perform in accordance with terms of government contracts, effects of history of failures to perform, and adverse effect of having government contract with irresponsible contractor. U.S.C.A. Const. Amend. 5; 48 C.F.R. §§ 9.402(b), 9.403, 9.406-2, 9.406-3(b)(1), (d)(3). U.S. v. Hatfield, 108 F.3d 67 (4th Cir. 1997). Double Jeopardy ☞24

Debarment of government contractor did not have to be subjected to a "particularized assessment" to determine whether it was punitive for double jeopardy purposes, where government did not seek the return of particular quantity of funds but instead sought to protect the quality of its acquisition programs. 48 C.F.R. §§ 9.402(b), 9.406-2(b)(1), (c), 9.406-4. U.S. v. Hatfield, 108 F.3d 67 (4th Cir. 1997). Double Jeopardy ☞24

To determine whether debarment of government contractor is civil or criminal, for purposes of claim that debarment precluded criminal prosecution of double jeopardy grounds, court examines whether procedure was designed to be remedial, and whether remedy provided, even if designated as civil, is so unreasonable or excessive that it transforms what was clearly intended as civil remedy into a criminal penalty. U.S.C.A. Const.Amend. 5; 48 C.F.R. § 9.403. U.S. v. Hatfield, 108 F.3d 67 (4th Cir. 1997). Double Jeopardy ☞24

Halper balancing test for determining whether debarment of government contractor is punitive for double jeopardy purposes—weighing government's harm against penalty's size—is inapplicable, where sanction and purposes it seeks to achieve are qualitative rather than merely quantitative, and question becomes whether debarment is in effect so punitive, that court must conclude that the proceeding is not civil but criminal in nature. U.S.C.A. Const.Amend. 5; 48 C.F.R. § 9.403. U.S. v. Hatfield, 108 F.3d 67 (4th Cir. 1997). Double Jeopardy ☞24

Four-year debarment of defense contractor from government contracting was not so overwhelmingly disproportionate to harm caused by defendant's conduct, in knowingly supplying nonconforming parts to Department of Defense (DOD), as to constitute punishment for double jeopardy purposes, even though regulations generally provided for three-year maximum debarment, as debarment served important nonpunitive goals of preventing further dissipation of public funds and protecting DOD programs by preventing supply of substandard or defective parts, and extra year could be viewed as evidence of intent to protect government from particularly egregious conduct, where government paid company more than $40,000 for nonconforming parts. U.S.C.A. Const.Amend. 5; 18 U.S.C.A. § 287; 48 C.F.R. §§ 9.402, 9.406-2(b), 9.406-4. U.S. v. Glymph, 96 F.3d 722 (4th Cir. 1996). Double Jeopardy ☞24

Intent of provision for administrative debarment from government contracting is to purge government programs of corrupt influences and prevent improper dissipation of public funds, and debarment is thus not punitive, for double jeopardy purposes, but constitutes "rough remedial justice" permissible as prophylactic governmental action. U.S.C.A. Const. Amend. 5; 48 C.F.R. § 9.406-2(b). U.S. v. Glymph, 96 F.3d 722 (4th Cir. 1996). Double Jeopardy ☞24

8 Searches and seizures

Requiring a federal contractor to submit to an enforcement proceeding by Office of Federal Contract Compliance Programs (OFCCP) based on evidence illegally obtained in violation of the Fourth Amendment would not itself be an actionable constitutional wrong. U.S.C.A. Const.Amend. 4. Nationsbank Corp. v. Herman, 174 F.3d 424, 79 Fair Empl. Prac. Cas. (BNA) 1113, 75 Empl. Prac. Dec. (CCH) P 45814 (4th Cir. 1999). United States ☞64.20

Government contractor could not show irreparable injury arising from seizure and retention of its business records pursuant to search warrant, and thus was not entitled to return of the records, where it had been allowed to copy all the records and real motive in bringing motion was to have search declared illegal; claimed business losses as to result of alleged illegal conduct and reliance on search warrant affidavit to determine that contractor was not a responsible contractor and was ineligible to be awarded contracts were result of investigation of suspected wrongdoing and not the consequence of the search and seizure. Fed.Rules Cr.Proc. Rule 41(e), 18 U.S.C.A.U.S. v. A Bldg. Housing a Business Known as Mach. Products Co., Inc., 139 F.R.D. 111 (W.D. Wis. 1990). Searches And Seizures ☞84

9 Debarment—In general

"Debarment" is administrative action which excludes nonresponsible contractors from government contracting. Caiola v. Carroll, 851 F.2d 395, 398, 34 Cont. Cas. Fed. (CCH) P 75514 (D.C. Cir. 1988). United States ☞64.20

Debarment, so as to preclude contractor from being awarded federal government contracts, is designed to insure integrity of government contracts. 48 C.F.R. § 9.402(a). Ali v. U.S., 932 F. Supp. 1206 (N.D. Cal. 1996). United States ☞64.20

"Debarment" of government contractor is discretionary measure taken to protect public interest and to promote agency's policy of conducting business only with responsible persons. 40 C.F.R. § 32.115(a). Burke v. U.S. E.P.A., 127 F. Supp. 2d 235, 51 Env't. Rep. Cas. (BNA) 2210 (D.D.C. 2001). United States ☞64.20

Federal Acquisition Regulations (FARs) provide for automatic debarment in the case of conviction or civil judgment against contractor; because another fact finder has already found one of the bases for debarment beyond a reasonable doubt or by a preponderance of the evidence, there is no statutory, regulatory, or due process requirement of additional hearing to determine the underlying facts. U.S.C.A. Const.Amend. 14; 48 C.F.R. §§ 9.406-2(a), 9.406-3(d). Waterhouse v. U.S., 874 F. Supp. 5 (D.D.C. 1994). United States ☞64.20

To sustain a debarment from bidding on Government contracts, there must be found some threat to Government interests arising from contracting with debarred contractor. Peter Kiewit Sons' Co. v. U. S. Army Corps of Engineers, 534 F. Supp. 1139, 29 Cont. Cas. Fed. (CCH) P 82291 (D.D.C. 1982), judgment rev'd, 714 F.2d 163, 31 Cont. Cas. Fed. (CCH) P 71395, 1983-2 Trade Cas. (CCH) ¶ 65528 (D.C. Cir. 1983). United States ☞64.20

Congressional interference in contractor debarment proceeding rendered debarment proceedings null and void. Peter Kiewit Sons' Co. v. U. S. Army Corps of Engineers, 534 F. Supp. 1139, 29 Cont. Cas. Fed. (CCH) P 82291 (D.D.C. 1982), judgment rev'd, 714 F.2d 163, 31 Cont. Cas. Fed. (CCH) P 71395, 1983-2 Trade Cas. (CCH) ¶ 65528 (D.C. Cir. 1983). United States ☞64.20

10 Debarment—Officers of corporation, debarment

Individual could not be debarred from government contracts for willful and aggravated violations of Davis-Bacon Act and related Acts solely on the basis of his status as president of offending contractor. Davis-Bacon Act, §§ 1-6, as amended, 40 U.S.C.A. §§ 276a to 276a-5; 40 U.S.C.A. § 276c; Contract Work Hours and Safety Standards Act, §§ 101-107, as amended, 40 U.S.C.A. §§ 327–333; Portal-to-Portal Act of 1947, § 6(a), as amended, 29 U.S.C.A. § 255(a). Facchiano Const. Co., Inc. v. U.S. Dept. of Labor, 987 F.2d 206, 1 Wage & Hour Cas. 2d (BNA) 468, 39 Cont. Cas. Fed. (CCH) P 76542, 124 Lab. Cas. (CCH) P 35782 (3d Cir. 1993). United States ☞64.20

Government contractor's president and chief executive officer did not have "reason to know" of contractor's misconduct, so as to justify his debarment from government contracting; although president admitted that he became "generally aware" of some customer complaints after four years of alleged misconduct, there was no evidence that he was informed of their continuing nature, and president also claimed that he was told that complaints concerned problems that contractor had no obligation to report to the government. Novicki v. Cook, 946 F.2d 938, 942–943, 37 Cont. Cas. Fed. (CCH) P 76198 (D.C. Cir. 1991). United States ☞64.20

In deciding to debar two officers but not a third on basis that the two officers had reason to know of the corporation's criminal conduct while third officer did not, the debarring official did not treat the officers equally and the debarments would be set aside; debarring official's determination did not explain why third officer, the treasurer of the corporation, escaped the treatment meted out to the other officers. Caiola v. Carroll, 851 F.2d 395, 401, 34 Cont. Cas. Fed. (CCH) P 75514 (D.C. Cir. 1988). United States ☞64.20

Probable cause to believe that president of government contractor had reason to know that his company was defrauding Department of Defense was not prerequisite to Department's initiation of debarment proceeding against president. Novicki v. Cook, 743 F. Supp. 11, 36 Cont. Cas. Fed. (CCH) P 76009 (D.D.C. 1990), judgment rev'd, 946 F.2d 938, 37 Cont. Cas. Fed. (CCH) P 76198 (D.C. Cir. 1991). United States ☞64.20

Defense Logistics Agency's decision to debar president of government contractor upon Agency's conclusion that president had reason to know that his company was defrauding

Department of Defense was neither arbitrary nor capricious, even though the contracting company itself was not debarred; company was acquired by different company, and drastic changes in management and operation were made. Novicki v. Cook, 743 F. Supp. 11, 36 Cont. Cas. Fed. (CCH) P 76009 (D.D.C. 1990), judgment rev'd, 946 F.2d 938, 37 Cont. Cas. Fed. (CCH) P 76198 (D.C. Cir. 1991) (On reversing judgment and remanding, the circuit court said "[a]ssuming... that the agency official did apply the definition of "reason to know" that... was appropriate... we do not think the record reasonably supports the agency's decision, because there is not substantial evidence to establish that Novicki had 'reason to know.' ") United States ☞64.20

Department of Defense was not precluded from debarring executive of government contractor, who knew or had reason to know, that his company was defrauding Department after fraud had occurred, but before it was uncovered by government, and who failed to take remedial action of any sort. Novicki v. Cook, 743 F. Supp. 11, 36 Cont. Cas. Fed. (CCH) P 76009 (D.D.C. 1990), judgment rev'd, 946 F.2d 938, 37 Cont. Cas. Fed. (CCH) P 76198 (D.C. Cir. 1991) (On reversing judgment and remanding, the circuit court said "[a]ssuming... that the agency official did apply the definition of "reason to know" that... was appropriate... we do not think the record reasonably supports the agency's decision, because there is not substantial evidence to establish that Novicki had 'reason to know.' ") United States ☞64.20

11 De facto suspension or debarment

De facto debarment of contractor from bidding on government contracts, although final action, was illegal and could not form the basis for dissolution of interim action, the ongoing debarment proceeding. Peter Kiewit Sons' Co. v. U.S. Army Corps of Engineers, 714 F.2d 163, 230, 31 Cont. Cas. Fed. (CCH) P 71395, 1983-2 Trade Cas. (CCH) ¶ 65528 (D.C. Cir. 1983). United States ☞64.20

"De facto suspension" of a contractor may be shown by successive denial of a number of contracts on which the contractor is low bidder, though contractor's other actions and statements may also support its existence. Shermco Industries, Inc. v. Secretary of the Air Force, 584 F. Supp. 76, 32 Cont. Cas. Fed. (CCH) P 72713 (N.D. Tex. 1984). United States ☞64.20

Air Force's de facto suspension of contractor, as evidenced by fact that suspension of contractor was not ordered until seven and one-half months after contractor submitted low bid on contract which was rejected and almost five months after nonresponsibility determination, injured contractor, entitling it to relief. Shermco Industries, Inc. v. Secretary of the Air Force, 584 F. Supp. 76, 32 Cont. Cas. Fed. (CCH) P 72713 (N.D. Tex. 1984). United States ☞64.20

A finding of de facto suspension of a contractor is not justified at time of a first determination of nonresponsibility unless there is evidence that the procuring body has decided that from that point forward it will award no further contracts. Shermco Industries, Inc. v. Secretary of the Air Force, 584 F. Supp. 76, 32 Cont. Cas. Fed. (CCH) P 72713 (N.D. Tex. 1984). United States ☞64.20

"De facto debarment" occurs when an agency bars a contractor from competing for government contracts for a certain period of time without following the applicable debarment procedures found in the Federal Acquisition Regulations (FAR). 48 C.F.R. § 9.406-3. TLT Const. Corp. v. U.S., 50 Fed. Cl. 212 (2001). United States ☞64.20

To succeed on a claim of de facto debarment, bidder must demonstrate a systematic effort by the procuring agency to reject all of the bidder's contract bids. TLT Const. Corp. v. U.S., 50 Fed. Cl. 212 (2001). United States ☞64.20

Two options exist to establish a de facto debarment claim: (1) by an agency's statement that it will not award the contractor future contracts; or (2) by an agency's conduct demonstrating that it will not award the contractor future contracts. TLT Const. Corp. v. U.S., 50 Fed. Cl. 212 (2001). United States ☞64.20

Government's failure to pursue discussions with disappointed bidder over its past performance did not amount to a de facto debarment, absent evidence that bidder was being disqualified from government contracts on a systematic basis. TLT Const. Corp. v. U.S., 50 Fed. Cl. 212 (2001). United States ☞64.20

To establish a de facto debarment claim, a disappointed bidder must show evidence of a systematic effort by the procuring agency to reject all of the bidder's contract bids; showing may be accomplished by evidence of an agency's statement that it will not award any contracts to the bidder in the future as well as by an agency's conduct to that effect. CRC Marine Services, Inc. v. U.S., 41 Fed. Cl. 66, 42 Cont. Cas. Fed. (CCH) P 77310 (1998). United States ☞64.20

Low bidder on solicitation for transportation by barge of reactor vessels and steam generators did not establish that agency's decision to award contract to other bidder constituted unlawful de facto debarment, based on allegation that contracting officer's finding of low bidder's nonresponsibility was based on its prior debarment. CRC Marine Services, Inc. v. U.S., 41 Fed. Cl. 66, 42 Cont. Cas. Fed. (CCH) P 77310 (1998). United States ☞64.20

Bidder on spot bid solicitation for shipment by barge of nuclear reactor vessels and steam generators failed to establish that rejection of its bid as "disqualified" constituted unlawful de facto debarment; rather, evidence established that bidder failed to meet solicitation's requirements. CRC Marine Services, Inc. v. U.S., 41 Fed. Cl. 66, 42 Cont. Cas. Fed. (CCH) P 77310 (1998). United States ☞64.20

Unsuccessful bidder failed to show systematic effort by procuring government agency to reject all of bidder's contract bids, as required to show de facto debarment. Stapp Towing Inc. v. U.S., 34 Fed. Cl. 300, 40 Cont. Cas. Fed. (CCH) P 76839 (1995). United States ☞64.20

A de facto suspension or debarment from participation in government business arises when procuring body refuses, for indefinite period of time, to grant awards to particular contractor, but successive determinations of nonresponsibility on same grounds are improper, and procuring agency must initiate suspension or debarment procedures at earliest practical date following first determination of nonresponsibility. 18 U.S.C.A. § 287; Small Business Act, § 2 [2–18], 15 U.S.C.A. §§ 631–647. Shermco Industries, Inc. v. U.S., 6 Cl. Ct. 588, 32 Cont. Cas. Fed. (CCH) P 73068 (1984). United States ☞64.20

12 Conviction of crime, generally

A debarment from contracting with executive branch of government need not be proportional to severity of a prior criminal sentence, for a criminal sentence is a statutory sanction quite distinct from a debarment. Shane Meat Co., Inc. v. U.S. Dept. of Defense, 800 F.2d 334, 91 A.L.R. Fed. 857 (3d Cir. 1986). United States ☞64.20

Agency's decision to debar government contractor was arbitrary, capricious and abuse of discretion, though contractor pled guilty to misdemeanor for conversion of government property, where government continued to enter into contracts with contractor for six years after misrepresentations that served as basis for misdemeanor conviction. Silverman v. U.S. Dept. of Defense, 817 F. Supp. 846, 39 Cont. Cas. Fed. (CCH) P 76540 (S.D. Cal. 1993). United States ☞64.20

Debarment of government contractors from all government procurement and sales contracting for three years was not arbitrary or capricious; contractors were convicted of crime in connection with performance of government contract. Delta Rocky Mountain Petroleum, Inc. v. U.S. Dept. of Defense, 726 F. Supp. 278, 36 Cont. Cas. Fed. (CCH) P 75888 (D. Colo. 1989). United States ☞64.15

Contractor's guilty plea to charge of making a false statement for purpose of influencing action of a bank and the legitimate inferences to be drawn therefrom constituted substantial evidence in support of administrative decision to debar him from further participation in HUD programs. Agan v. Pierce, 576 F. Supp. 257 (N.D. Ga. 1983). United States ☞64.20

Where agency considered not only criminal conviction of president of government contractor, but also mitigating factors submitted by contractor in debarment proceedings, decision to debar contractor for period of one year was not arbitrary, capricious or abuse of discretion. Federal Property and Administrative Services Act of 1949, § 303(b), 41 U.S.C.A. § 253(b). Joseph Const. Co. v. Veterans Admin. of U.S., 595 F. Supp. 448, 32 Cont. Cas. Fed. (CCH) P 73082 (N.D. Ill. 1984). United States ☞64.20

13 Nolo contendere pleas

Under regulations, conviction of contractor based upon plea of nolo contendere or otherwise, does not, ipso facto, support a debarment from bidding in Government contracts. Peter Kiewit Sons' Co. v. U. S. Army Corps of Engineers, 534 F. Supp. 1139, 29 Cont. Cas. Fed. (CCH) P 82291 (D.D.C. 1982), judgment rev'd, 714 F.2d 163, 31 Cont. Cas. Fed. (CCH)

P 71395, 1983-2 Trade Cas. (CCH) ¶ 65528 (D.C. Cir. 1983). United States ☞64.20

Debarment of contractor from bidding on Government contracts may not be imposed for further punishment after plea of nolo contendere. Peter Kiewit Sons' Co. v. U. S. Army Corps of Engineers, 534 F. Supp. 1139, 29 Cont. Cas. Fed. (CCH) P 82291 (D.D.C. 1982), judgment rev'd, 714 F.2d 163, 31 Cont. Cas. Fed. (CCH) P 71395, 1983-2 Trade Cas. (CCH) ¶ 65528 (D.C. Cir. 1983). United States ☞64.20

14 Antitrust violations and anticompetitive activities

Department of Army followed appropriate procedures in placing moving and storage companies who were under antitrust indictment on restricted contractor list, companies received adequate notice of suspension and were fully informed of their appeals rights. Coleman American Moving Services, Inc. v. Weinberger, 716 F. Supp. 1405, 36 Cont. Cas. Fed. (CCH) P 75786 (M.D. Ala. 1989). United States ☞64.20

Suspension of companies furnishing moving and storage service to Department of Army, based on indictment charging them with antitrust violations, was not invalid due to failure of Department to make specific determination that immediate action was necessary to protect government's interest, as evidence of bid rigging as claimed in antitrust complaint was implicitly contrary to government's interest. Coleman American Moving Services, Inc. v. Weinberger, 716 F. Supp. 1405, 36 Cont. Cas. Fed. (CCH) P 75786 (M.D. Ala. 1989). United States ☞64.20

Moving and storage companies who were indicted and suspended from contracting with Department of Army were not entitled to make-up tonnage following their acquittal in antitrust action, as make-up tonnage was available only to contractors who were wrongfully suspended and suspension during pendency of antitrust action had been valid. Coleman American Moving Services, Inc. v. Weinberger, 716 F. Supp. 1405, 36 Cont. Cas. Fed. (CCH) P 75786 (M.D. Ala. 1989). United States ☞64.20

Moving and storage companies were not entitled to makeup tonnage under contract with Department of Army, as they had not established bad faith on part of Department in suspending them during pendency of antitrust litigation against them. Coleman American Moving Services, Inc. v. Weinberger, 716 F. Supp. 1405, 36 Cont. Cas. Fed. (CCH) P 75786 (M.D. Ala. 1989). United States ☞64.20

Moving and storage companies who were suspended from contracting with Department of Army because of indictment under antitrust charges were not prevented from adequately exercising their right to contest suspension by fact that it would have required person capable of refuting charges to waive his Fifth Amendment right against self-incrimination, as only relevance of his testimony would be denying existence of indictment or denying that defendants were named in indictment and testimony on these subjects would have posed no hazard of self-incrimination for individual. U.S.C.A. Const.Amend. 5. Coleman American Moving Services, Inc. v. Weinberger, 716 F. Supp. 1405, 36 Cont. Cas. Fed. (CCH) P 75786 (M.D. Ala. 1989). United States ☞64.20; Witnesses ☞297(8.1)

Suspension proceedings brought against moving and storage companies by Department of Army following filing of antitrust indictment against them did not impermissibly extend right of government to discovery in case involving companies' claim for back-up tonnage after companies were acquitted and restored to bidders list, as there was little opportunity for abuse of discovery in postsuspension hearing which covered only evidence refuting existence of indictment or refuting that companies were named in indictment. Coleman American Moving Services, Inc. v. Weinberger, 716 F. Supp. 1405, 36 Cont. Cas. Fed. (CCH) P 75786 (M.D. Ala. 1989). United States ☞64.20

Substantial evidence supported finding, in support of three-year debarment of bidder from government surplus auctions, that bidder had engaged in anticompetitive activity; arrangements described by bidder did not appear to be joint ventures and presented situation more akin to bid rigging. Textor v. Cheney, 757 F. Supp. 51, 37 Cont. Cas. Fed. (CCH) P 76028 (D.D.C. 1991). United States ☞64.20

15 Falsification of records

Although government contractor was properly debarred from doing business with government for three-year term for falsification of laboratory test results, debarment of president and secretary of contractor on ground that they had reason to know of contractor's criminal conduct, although they did not have actual knowledge of conduct, was not supported by preponderance of evidence and, therefore, their debarment was unreasonable. Caiola v. Carroll, 851 F.2d 395, 399, 34 Cont. Cas. Fed. (CCH) P 75514 (D.C. Cir. 1988). United States ☞64.20

16 Made in America labels

Under the Buy America Act (BAA), whenever agency head determines that violation has taken place, imposition of three-year period of debarment from receiving government contract is mandatory. Buy American Act, § 3(b), 41 U.S.C.A. § 10b(b). Glazer Const. Co., Inc. v. U.S., 50 F. Supp. 2d 85, 185 A.L.R. Fed. 717 (D. Mass. 1999). United States ☞64.20

Contractor would be deemed in violation of Buy American Act (BAA), and would be barred from receiving contract for three years, even though value of materials found to violate BAA was only 0.01% of materials used in project. Buy American Act, § 3, 41 U.S.C.A. § 10b. Glazer Const. Co., Inc. v. U.S., 50 F. Supp. 2d 85, 185 A.L.R. Fed. 717 (D. Mass. 1999). United States ☞64.20

Violations of Buy America Act by contractors do not have to be intentional in order for liability to attach. Buy American Act, § 3, 41 U.S.C.A. § 10b. Glazer Const. Co., Inc. v. U.S., 50 F. Supp. 2d 85, 185 A.L.R. Fed. 717 (D. Mass. 1999). United States ☞64.20

17 Cause of serious and compelling nature

Even in the absence of conviction or civil judgment against government contractor, contractor may be debarred, based on preponderance of the evidence, for cause of serious and compelling nature, but debarring official must give notice to contractor or proposal to debar and must invite the contractor to submit information or argument in opposition to the proposed debarment. 48 C.F.R. §§ 9.406-2(c), 9.406-3(c)(4). Waterhouse v. U.S., 874 F. Supp. 5 (D.D.C. 1994). United States ☞64.20

Hearing officer's finding that government contractor violated terms of purchase orders with Department of Housing and Urban Development constituting "causes of such serious and compelling nature, affecting responsibility," and demonstrating at least implicitly that suspension under the facts was in the best interest of HUD, which determination was sustained by assistant secretary of HUD, was adequate finding on which to base suspension of government contractor. Adamo Wrecking Co. v. Department of Housing and Urban Development, 414 F. Supp. 877 (D.D.C. 1976). United States ☞64.20

18 Collusive bidding

Bidder for purchase of surplus property from federal government could properly be found to have engaged in collusive bidding agreements warranting debarment even if he committed no overt acts in furtherance of such agreements. Leitman v. McAusland, 934 F.2d 46, 37 Cont. Cas. Fed. (CCH) P 76107 (4th Cir. 1991). United States ☞64.20

Bidder could be debarred from purchasing surplus property from federal government based on collusive bidding agreements upon determination at administrative hearing that bidder had entered into such agreements, even though he had suffered no conviction or civil judgment on such agreements. Leitman v. McAusland, 934 F.2d 46, 37 Cont. Cas. Fed. (CCH) P 76107 (4th Cir. 1991). United States ☞64.20

Finding that bidder for purchase of surplus property from federal government had entered into collusive bidding agreements warranting debarment was sufficiently supported by testimony of informant and investigator, along with transcript of telephone conversation in which agreement was made. Leitman v. McAusland, 934 F.2d 46, 37 Cont. Cas. Fed. (CCH) P 76107 (4th Cir. 1991). United States ☞64.20

19 Failure to perform contract

Evidence supported finding cause for debarring certified public accounting firm from doing work for federal government for violation of regulation through willful failure to perform in accordance with terms of public agreements or transactions; contract stipulated that audit report had to be executed according to generally accepted accounting principles and Department of Housing and Urban Development (HUD) requirements, but audit report for city public housing authority which did business with HUD did not contain qualifying opinion or finding regarding unusual manner in which city authority reported cash in its financial statements, and firm made no attempt to issue revised report. Sellers v. Kemp, 749 F. Supp. 1001, 36 Cont. Cas. Fed. (CCH) P 75996 (W.D. Mo. 1990). United States ☞64.20

Government's decision to remove incumbent contractor from approved source list for the production of T-37 aircraft tailpipes was not arbitrary or capricious; four separate metallurgical reports concluded that manufacturing defects caused tailpipe failures during contractor's performance of its last two contracts, and contractor did not prove that the defects were due to design defects. SAI Industries Corp. v. U.S., 60 Fed. Cl. 731 (2004). United States ☞64.20

Debarment of defense contractor was supported by evidence that contractor had defaulted on two contracts and not performed on total of nine contracts, contractor had positive balance sheet at time of nonperformance, and contracts which contractor failed to perform were relatively small and would have required little capital, even though contractor contended that its difficulties in performing contracts were due to delays in obtaining settlement funds from government in connection with earlier disputed contracts and that it was financially unable to perform. IMCO, Inc. v. U.S., 33 Fed. Cl. 312 (1995), judgment aff'd, 97 F.3d 1422 (Fed. Cir. 1996). United States ☞64.20

Material issue of fact as to whether government contractor's failure to perform was willful precluded summary disbarment of contractor, where there was circumstantial evidence that Government requested acceleration of deliveries, government representative knew or should have known of prefirst article approved cutting of government furnished material, contractor did not have physical means of reworking incorrectly cut coats, and subsequent defaults on government contracts were due to Government's threat of offsetting losses on contract against progress payments on other defaulted contracts. Sterlingwear of Boston, Inc. v. U.S., 11 Cl. Ct. 879, 34 Cont. Cas. Fed. (CCH) P 75210 (1987). United States ☞64.20

20 Present responsibility test

Trust agreement leaving ultimate decision-making authority for government contractor to someone other than individual accused of bid rigging, and sworn affidavits that accused bid rigger had little or no present contact with company, did not establish contractor's present responsibility to do business with government, for purpose of debarment proceeding; although agreement gave trustee direct authority over all company operations it contained no specific term barring alleged bid rigger from either acting on behalf of company or participating in its management, and, more importantly, nothing in trust agreement or any other company submission gave government any assurance that alleged bid rigger would not conduct illicit dealings on behalf of company entirely outside company channels. Robinson v. Cheney, 876 F.2d 152, 277, 35 Cont. Cas. Fed. (CCH) P 75666 (D.C. Cir. 1989). United States ☞64.20

Federal acquisition regulation permitting agency to debar contractor for lack of "present responsibility" was not unconstitutionally vague as applied or on its face. U.S.C.A. Const. Amend. 5. Robinson v. Cheney, 876 F.2d 152, 277, 35 Cont. Cas. Fed. (CCH) P 75666 (D.C. Cir. 1989). United States ☞64.20

Analysis of present responsibility of contractor in review of debarment action focuses on seriousness of offense, length of time elapsed since offense, and contractor's conduct in interim period. Silverman v. U.S. Dept. of Defense, 817 F. Supp. 846, 39 Cont. Cas. Fed. (CCH) P 76540 (S.D. Cal. 1993). Public Contracts ☞11; United States ☞64.20

Ultimate inquiry in debarment of contractor to insure that government contracts are awarded only to responsible bidders must be directed to present responsibility of contractor; agency is required to carefully consider any favorable evidence of responsibility to insure that all findings are based on realistic and articulable threat of harm to government's propriety interest. Silverman v. U.S. Dept. of Defense, 817 F. Supp. 846, 39 Cont. Cas. Fed. (CCH) P 76540 (S.D. Cal. 1993). United States ☞64.20

Test for whether "debarment," an administrative action which excludes nonresponsible contractors from government contracting, is warranted is present responsibility of contractor; contractor can meet test of present responsibility by demonstrating that it has taken steps to ensure that wrongful acts will not recur. Delta Rocky Mountain Petroleum, Inc. v. U.S. Dept. of Defense, 726 F. Supp. 278, 36 Cont. Cas. Fed. (CCH) P 75888 (D. Colo. 1989). United States ☞64.15

Air Force's decision to debar contractor from having contract for three years, due to violation of Buy America Act (BAA), on factually undisputed ground that contractor lacked present responsibility to hold contract, allowed for affirmance of Air Force's debarment decision without holding of hearing required on other ground, that contractor's conduct was wilful. Buy American Act, § 3, 41 U.S.C.A. § 10b. Glazer Const. Co., Inc. v. U.S., 50 F. Supp. 2d 85, 185 A.L.R. Fed. 717 (D. Mass. 1999). United States ☞64.20

Air Force official issuing order debarring contractor from receiving contract for three years, due to violation of Buy American Act (BAA), did not act arbitrarily and capriciously in determining that contractor did not show degree of present responsibility to be government contractor, when contractor claimed without research that Canadian wall base found in construction project was unavailable in United States, did not dispute official's conclusion that statement was false, and presented program to prevent recurrence of violations that was unacceptable to official. Buy American Act, § 3(b), 41 U.S.C.A. § 10b(b); 48 C.F.R. § 9.406-2(c). Glazer Const. Co., Inc. v. U.S., 50 F. Supp. 2d 85, 185 A.L.R. Fed. 717 (D. Mass. 1999). United States ☞64.20

Concept of "present responsibility," as will potentially prevent debarment of government contractor, encompasses contractor's ability to successfully perform government contract. IMCO, Inc. v. U.S., 33 Fed. Cl. 312 (1995), judgment aff'd, 97 F.3d 1422 (Fed. Cir. 1996). United States ☞64.20

21 New facts and circumstances

Contractor's conviction for making false statements in connection with defense contracts was a "new fact or circumstance" for purpose of regulation precluding further debarment solely on basis of facts and circumstances upon which an initial debarment action was based. Wellham v. Cheney, 934 F.2d 305 (11th Cir. 1991). United States ☞64.20

22 Solicitation

Cancellation of government contract did not constitute breach of government's implied contractually duty to fairly and honestly consider bid of defense contractor where contractor was eliminated from consideration for bid after being proposed for debarment, subsequent debarment of contractor was not arbitrary and capricious, next lowest bidder had gone out of business, and remaining bids were determined to be either outdated or unreasonably high. IMCO, Inc, v. U.S., 33 Fed. Cl. 312 (1995), judgment aff'd, 97 F.3d 1422 (Fed. Cir. 1996). United States ☞64.50

23 Agriculture Department

Procurement process for panel support services contract with United States Department of Agriculture was not arbitrary or capricious based on exclusion of company whose president had sought appointment to panel from consideration for that contract on conflict of interest grounds; by the time it was learned that president had not been selected for panel, contractor selection was sufficiently complete from Department's perspective that evaluation process could not reasonably begin anew. Information Resources Inc. v. U.S., 676 F. Supp. 293, 34 Cont. Cas. Fed. (CCH) P 75357 (D.D.C. 1987). United States ☞64.20

Department of Agriculture's order barring meat supplier from bidding on or being awarded contracts to supply meat for USDA programs was supported by substantial evidence as to the supplier's affiliation with another suspended supplier and as to illegal activities involving movement of unwholesome meat in Department of Agriculture programs. Rules and Regulations, §§ 1-1.601-1(e), 1-1.605-2(b), 1-1.605-3, 41 U.S.C.A.App. Stanko Packing Co., Inc. v. Bergland, 489 F. Supp. 947, 27 Cont. Cas. Fed. (CCH) P 80419 (D.D.C. 1980). Food ☞12; United States ☞64.20

24 Armed services and defense

Administrative proceedings in which Air Force had threatened to suspend or disbar contractor from entering into contracts with Department of Defense constituted "alternate remedy" to qui tam action under False Claims Act (FCA), and thus contractor's former employee who commenced qui tam action based on contractor's use of defective damping fluid and falsification of test results was entitled under FCA to relator's share of proceeds from settlement agreement arising from proceedings which required contractor to repair and replace defective flight data transmitters and to replace defective damping fluid, even though suspension or debarment proceeding was significantly different from FCA action, where government declined to intervene in qui tam action arising from defective fluid, choosing instead to go forward with suspension or debarment proceeding based on conduct that formed basis of action, and then settled relator's action for false testing, with result that relator was later found barred by claim preclusion from pursuing action for defective damping fluid. 31 U.S.C.A. § 3730(c)(5). U.S. ex rel. Barajas v. U.S., 258 F.3d 1004 (9th Cir. 2001). United States ☞122

The Air Force should have followed its own regulation, calling for notice and a hearing before debarring a supplier from bidding for contracts for a period of years, when the supplier raised a genuine issue of fact challenging the debarment; the supplier presented evidence that a debarred person was mistakenly listed as an officer of the supplier, and that if the debarred person was not considered an officer the supplier's answer to questions regarding its prior procurement record would be correct and the basis for its debarment would be removed. 48 C.F.R. § 9.406-3(b). Sameena Inc. v. U.S. Air Force, 147 F.3d 1148, 42 Cont. Cas. Fed. (CCH) P 77335 (9th Cir. 1998). United States ☞64.20

The Defense Logistics Agency (DLA) did not act arbitrarily or capriciously in determining that contractor's false statements about two pre-1984 defense contracts were new facts and circumstances for purposes of regulation providing that debarment may not be extended on basis of facts and circumstances upon which initial debarment action was based, where memorandum accompanying initial 1985 debarment explained that contractor was being debarred for submitting "fraudulent test reports or certificates of conformance" in enumerated contracts, and memorandum accompanying subsequent 1989 debarment explained that contractor was being debarred for submitting false statements in connection with other contracts not mentioned in original debarment memorandum. Wellham v. Cheney, 934 F.2d 305 (11th Cir. 1991). United States ☞64.20

Army lacked authority to bind Government to a contract with low bidder as long as bidder was suspended from receiving any government contracts and therefore low bidder's suit to enjoin temporarily the award of two Army Corps of Engineers contracts to any other bidders did not constitute a "bid protest" case over which Claims Court had jurisdiction. ATL, Inc. v. U.S., 735 F.2d 1343 (Fed. Cir. 1984). Federal Courts ☞1074; United States ☞64.20; United States ☞64.60(1)

Claims Court lacked jurisdiction to consider claim that Department of Army failed to apply procedures governing suspension of government contractors and allotment of make-up tonnage, as its jurisdiction was limited to "contractual undertaking" where remedy was money damages. 28 U.S.C.A. § 1491(a)(1). Coleman American Moving Services, Inc. v. Weinberger, 716 F. Supp. 1405, 36 Cont. Cas. Fed. (CCH) P 75786 (M.D. Ala. 1989). Federal Courts ☞1074

In Air Force suspension or debarment proceeding against defense contractor, government lacks any power to compel production of evidence or attendance of witnesses. 48 C.F.R. §§ 9.406-1 et seq., 9.407-1 et seq.U.S. ex rel. Barajas v. Northrop Corp., 65 F. Supp. 2d 1097 (C.D. Cal. 1999), rev'd and remanded on other grounds, 258 F.3d 1004 (9th Cir. 2001). United States ☞64.20

A procuring agency cannot make successive determinations of nonresponsibility with regard to a contractor on the same basis; rather, it must initiate suspension or debarment procedures at the earliest practicable date following the first determination of nonresponsibility. Shermco Industries, Inc. v. Secretary of the Air Force, 584 F. Supp. 76, 32 Cont. Cas. Fed. (CCH) P 72713 (N.D. Tex. 1984). United States ☞64.20

25 Labor Department

Government contractor's violation of unambiguous regulation promulgated under McNamara-O'Hara Service Contract Act, without more, cannot justify debarment. Service Contract Act of 1965, § 2 et seq., 41 U.S.C.A. § 351 et seq.Dantran, Inc. v. U.S. Dept. of Labor, 171 F.3d 58, 5 Wage & Hour Cas. 2d (BNA) 334, 137 Lab. Cas. (CCH) P 33837 (1st Cir. 1999). United States ☞64.20

Structure and legislative history of Contract Work Hours and Safety Standards Act supported Secretary of Labor's authority to debar contractor for violating overtime hours and pay provisions of Act. Davis-Bacon Act, §§ 1-6, as amended, 40 U.S.C.A. §§ 276a to 276a-5; Housing and Community Development Act of 1974, §§ 110, 802(g), 42 U.S.C.A. §§ 5310,

1440(g); Contract Work Hours and Safety Standards Act, §§ 102, 103, 104(a), 106, as amended, 40 U.S.C.A. §§ 328, 329, 330(a), 332; Department of Defense Authorization Act, 1986, § 1 et seq., 99 Stat. 583; 23 U.S.C.A. § 113(a). Janik Paving & Const., Inc. v. Brock, 828 F.2d 84, 28 Wage & Hour Cas. (BNA) 417, 34 Cont. Cas. Fed. (CCH) P 75363, 107 Lab. Cas. (CCH) P 34958 (2d Cir. 1987). Labor And Employment ⚖2345; United States ⚖64.20

Fact that Contract Work Hours and Safety Standards Act did not expressly authorize Secretary of Labor to debar contractors for violating Act did not require invalidation of Secretary's debarment regulations even though, in later statutes, Congress expressly granted debarment authority. Davis-Bacon Act, §§ 1-6, as amended, 40 U.S.C.A. §§ 276a to 276a-5; Housing and Community Development Act of 1974, §§ 110, 802(g), 42 U.S.C.A. §§ 5310, 1440(g); Contract Work Hours and Safety Standards Act, §§ 102, 103, 104(a), 106, as amended, 40 U.S.C.A. §§ 328, 329, 330(a), 332; Department of Defense Authorization Act, 1986, § 1 et seq., 99 Stat. 583; 23 U.S.C.A. § 113(a). Janik Paving & Const., Inc. v. Brock, 828 F.2d 84, 28 Wage & Hour Cas. (BNA) 417, 34 Cont. Cas. Fed. (CCH) P 75363, 107 Lab. Cas. (CCH) P 34958 (2d Cir. 1987). Labor And Employment ⚖2338; United States ⚖64.20

Department of Labor's prima facie case for debarment of contractor, based on violation of overtime hours and pay provisions of Contract Work Hours and Safety Standards Act, was not weakened by fact that testimony of former employees or other evidence offered by Department may have been too vague to demonstrate with some precision the amount and extent of undercompensated overtime work for each affected employee; amount allegedly underpaid was merely incidental. Davis-Bacon Act, §§ 1-6, as amended, 40 U.S.C.A. §§ 276a to 276a-5; Housing and Community Development Act of 1974, §§ 110, 802(g), 42 U.S.C.A. §§ 5310, 1440(g); Contract Work Hours and Safety Standards Act, §§ 102, 103, 104(a), 106, as amended, 40 U.S.C.A. §§ 328, 329, 330(a), 332; Department of Defense Authorization Act, 1986, § 1 et seq., 99 Stat. 583; 23 U.S.C.A. § 113(a). Janik Paving & Const., Inc. v. Brock, 828 F.2d 84, 28 Wage & Hour Cas. (BNA) 417, 34 Cont. Cas. Fed. (CCH) P 75363, 107 Lab. Cas. (CCH) P 34958 (2d Cir. 1987). Labor And Employment ⚖2347; United States ⚖64.20

Debarment of contractor for violating overtime hours and pay provisions of Contract Work Hours and Safety Standards Act was intended to compel compliance with Act, and was not penalty, and, therefore, Secretary of Labor had authority to adopt regulations for debarment, even though Act did not specifically authorize debarment as sanction. Davis-Bacon Act, §§ 1-6, as amended, 40 U.S.C.A. §§ 276a to 276a-5; Housing and Community Development Act of 1974, §§ 110, 802(g), 42 U.S.C.A. §§ 5310, 1440(g); Contract Work Hours and Safety Standards Act, §§ 102, 103, 104(a), 106, as amended, 40 U.S.C.A. §§ 328, 329, 330(a), 332; Department of Defense Authorization Act, 1986, § 1 et seq., 99 Stat. 583; 23 U.S.C.A. § 113(a). Janik Paving & Const., Inc. v. Brock, 828 F.2d 84, 28 Wage & Hour Cas. (BNA) 417, 34 Cont. Cas. Fed. (CCH) P 75363, 107 Lab. Cas. (CCH) P 34958 (2d Cir. 1987). Labor And Employment ⚖2338; United States ⚖64.20

Substantial evidence supported Secretary of Labor's order debarring contractor for violating overtime hours and pay provisions of Contract Work Hours and Safety Standards Act, even though there was five-year hiatus between alleged wage violations and administrative hearing at which employees testified that overtime hours for which they were paid were consistently lower than those actually reported to contractor. Davis-Bacon Act, §§ 1-6, as amended, 40 U.S.C.A. §§ 276a to 276a-5; Housing and Community Development Act of 1974, §§ 110, 802(g), 42 U.S.C.A. §§ 5310, 1440(g); Contract Work Hours and Safety Standards Act, §§ 102, 103, 104(a), 106, as amended, 40 U.S.C.A. §§ 328, 329, 330(a), 332; Department of Defense Authorization Act, 1986, § 1 et seq., 99 Stat. 583; 23 U.S.C.A. § 113(a). Janik Paving & Const., Inc. v. Brock, 828 F.2d 84, 28 Wage & Hour Cas. (BNA) 417, 34 Cont. Cas. Fed. (CCH) P 75363, 107 Lab. Cas. (CCH) P 34958 (2d Cir. 1987). Labor And Employment ⚖2347; United States ⚖64.20

Regulation authorized debarment of individual corporate officers and not merely corporate contractor for willful violation of labor standards. Facchiano Const. Co., Inc. v. U.S. Dept. of Labor, 987 F.2d 206, 1 Wage & Hour Cas. 2d (BNA) 468, 39 Cont. Cas. Fed. (CCH) P 76542, 124 Lab. Cas. (CCH) P 35782 (3d Cir. 1993). United States ⚖64.20

Federal contractor failed to show that Department of Labor's Office of Federal Contract Compliance Programs (OFCCP) lacked jurisdiction over it; exemption from OFCCP's review authority cited by contractor was limited to state and local governments, and contractor failed to identify any regulations providing it with exemption and failed to argue that it reached those regulations' exemption requirements. Trinity Industries, Inc. v. Reich, 33 F.3d 942 (8th Cir. 1994). United States ☞64.15; United States ☞64.20

26 Environmental Protection Agency

Exceptional circumstances did not justify district court's intervention in ongoing debarment process initiated by Environmental Protection Agency against superfund contractor; process was initiated by proper agency official, contractor received proper notice of proceeding, and EPA procedures satisfied requirements of both its own regulations and due process. U.S.C.A. Const.Amends. 5, 14. Baranowski v. E.P.A., 699 F. Supp. 1119, 29 Env't. Rep. Cas. (BNA) 1213 (E.D. Pa. 1988), judgment aff'd, 902 F.2d 1558 (3d Cir. 1990). United States ☞64.20

Director of Grants Administration Division is only Environmental Protection Agency official who has authority to debar or suspend contractor or to issue notice proposing debarment or suspension. Baranowski v. E.P.A., 699 F. Supp. 1119, 29 Env't. Rep. Cas. (BNA) 1213 (E.D. Pa. 1988), judgment aff'd, 902 F.2d 1558 (3d Cir. 1990). Environmental Law ☞15

27 Housing and Urban Development

Department of Housing and Urban Development's (HUD) initiating debarment proceedings did not violate settlement agreement, under which HUD received title to other subsidized housing property which contractor also allegedly failed to maintain in a decent, safe, and sanitary condition; settlement agreement did not prohibit HUD from pursuing future administrative action against contractor arising out of substandard conditions existing at other subsidized properties owned by contractor or his affiliated companies, and debarment was fully supported by evidence of conditions at subject property. Marshall v. Cuomo, 192 F.3d 473 (4th Cir. 1999). United States ☞64.20

Department of Housing and Urban Development (HUD) neither conducted debarment proceeding improperly nor violated provision of Administrative Procedure Act (APA) prohibiting an employee or agent engaged in the performance of investigative or prosecuting functions for an agency from participating or advising in the decision, even though HUD advisor to debarring official had previously participated in the investigation and prosecution of matter involving another property owned by contractor. 5 U.S.C.A. § 554(d). Marshall v. Cuomo, 192 F.3d 473 (4th Cir. 1999). United States ☞64.20

Provision of Administrative Procedure Act (APA) prohibiting an employee or agent engaged in the performance of investigative or prosecuting functions for an agency from participating or advising in the decision did not apply to Department of Housing and Urban Development's (HUD) debarment proceeding, which was not statutorily required. 5 U.S.C.A. § 554(d). Marshall v. Cuomo, 192 F.3d 473 (4th Cir. 1999). United States ☞64.20

Department of Housing and Urban Development (HUD) did not have to show that officer of suspended HUD coinsured lender was final decision maker in lender's passthrough procedures in violation of requirements of Government National Mortgage Assistance (GNMA) to sustain officer's debarment from participating in primary and lower tier covered transactions throughout executive branch of federal government for three years, and HUD was justified in debarring officer based upon substantial evidence that officer not only had reason to know of lender's misconduct, but also participated in it; fact that officer was participant, and not ultimate decision maker and that decisions were made on advice of counsel did not insulate him from sanction of debarment. Kisser v. Cisneros, 14 F.3d 615, 622 (D.C. Cir. 1994). United States ☞53(9)

Decision of Department of Housing and Urban Development (HUD) not to initiate debarment proceedings against certain officers of suspended HUD coinsured lender was unreviewable, and thus, district court's requirement that HUD give reasoned explanation for its decision to take debarment action against one former officer, but not other similarly situated officers was improper; no statute expressly provided for debarment actions or contained guidelines that informed HUD's decision to bring such actions, HUD's own regulations did not provide sufficient standards circumscribing HUD's enforcement discretion over debarment actions to rebut presumption of unreviewability, and there was no procedural step at initiation of debarment process which would provide focus for judicial review of HUD's nonenforcement decisions. 5 U.S.C.A. § 706(2); Executive Order No. 12549, § 1 et seq., 31 U.S.C.A. § 6101 note. Kisser v. Cisneros, 14 F.3d 615, 619 (D.C. Cir. 1994).

United States ☞53(9)

28 Forest Service

Government's refusal to permit rebidding by contractor who had not cut any timber pursuant to prior contract was proper. Siller Bros., Inc. v. U. S., 228 Ct. Cl. 76, 655 F.2d 1039, 28 Cont. Cas. Fed. (CCH) P 81482 (1981). United States ☞58(3); United States ☞64.20

Refusal of forest supervisor to permit contractor which had defaulted on prior timber cutting contract to rebid was an implicit determination that awarding contract to such contractor would not be in the public interest. Siller Bros., Inc. v. U. S., 228 Ct. Cl. 76, 655 F.2d 1039, 28 Cont. Cas. Fed. (CCH) P 81482 (1981). United States ☞58(3); United States ☞64.20

29 Exhaustion of administrative remedies

Exhaustion of administrative remedies is not required when constitutionality or statutory validity of Agricultural Stabilization and Conservation Service (ASCS) debarment hearing regulations are challenged. Girard v. Klopfenstein, 930 F.2d 738 (9th Cir. 1991). Administrative Law And Procedure ☞229; United States ☞64.20

President and sales manager of farmers cooperative were not required to exhaust their administrative remedies before challenging constitutional validity of debarment hearing by Agricultural Stabilization and Conservation Service (ASCS); exhaustion of remedies would not have assisted court in determining validity of allowing hearing before allegedly biased administrative officer rather than administrative law judge. Girard v. Klopfenstein, 930 F.2d 738 (9th Cir. 1991). Administrative Law And Procedure ☞229; United States ☞64.20

Congressional interference with proceedings to debar contractor from bidding on government contracts did not so taint the administrative process that said contractor's rights were clearly and significantly violated; accordingly, the finality and exhaustion requirements, in regard to review of an agency action, were not dispensed with. Peter Kiewit Sons' Co. v. U.S. Army Corps of Engineers, 714 F.2d 163, 230, 31 Cont. Cas. Fed. (CCH) P 71395, 1983-2 Trade Cas. (CCH) ¶ 65528 (D.C. Cir. 1983). United States ☞64.20

District court, in voiding ongoing administrative proceeding pertaining to debarment of contractor from bidding on government contracts, interrupted a process in which neither exhaustion nor finality requirements had been met, and there was no such congressional interference as to create an exceptional situation which would compel circumvention of the twin requirements of exhaustion and finality. Peter Kiewit Sons' Co. v. U.S. Army Corps of Engineers, 714 F.2d 163, 230, 31 Cont. Cas. Fed. (CCH) P 71395, 1983-2 Trade Cas. (CCH) ¶ 65528 (D.C. Cir. 1983). United States ☞64.20

30 Res judicata and collateral estoppel

Causes of action by the Department of Housing and Urban Development (HUD) debarring contractor from HUD programs and by the Department of Labor (DOL) debarring contractor government-wide for labor standards violations were not the same for res judicata purposes, nor were issues identical for collateral estoppel effect, where HUD debarment was based solely on criminal conviction of officer of contractor for mail fraud in violation of HUD regulations, while DOL was seeking to debar contractor and three officers based on willful and aggravated violations of Davis Bacon Act or related Acts. Davis-Bacon Act, §§ 1–6, as amended, 40 U.S.C.A. §§ 276a to 276a-5; 40 U.S.C.A. § 276c; Contract Work Hours and Safety Standards Act, §§ 101-107, as amended, 40 U.S.C.A. §§ 327–333; Portal-to-Portal Act of 1947, § 6(a), as amended, 29 U.S.C.A. § 255(a). Facchiano Const. Co., Inc. v. U.S. Dept. of Labor, 987 F.2d 206, 1 Wage & Hour Cas. 2d (BNA) 468, 39 Cont. Cas. Fed. (CCH) P 76542, 124 Lab. Cas. (CCH) P 35782 (3d Cir. 1993). United States ☞64.20

The Department of Labor (DOL) and the Department of Housing and Urban Development (HUD) were not in "privity" for purposes of giving res judicata effect to HUD order debarring contractor from HUD contracts, so as to preclude later government-wide debarment order by DOL; since scope of HUD's enforcement authority was limited to HUD programs, while DOL had broad delegated authority to debar contractors from all federal contracts for labor standards violations, HUD did not have authority to represent United States in final adjudication of the issue in controversy. Reorganization Plan No. 14 of 1950, 5 U.S.C.A.App. § 1; Department of Housing and Urban Development Act, § 7(d), 42 U.S.C.A.

§ 3535(d); Davis-Bacon Act, §§ 1-6, as amended, 40 U.S.C.A. §§ 276a to 276a-5; 40 U.S.C.A. § 276c; Contract Work Hours and Safety Standards Act, §§ 101-107, as amended, 40 U.S.C.A. §§ 327–333; Portal-to-Portal Act of 1947, § 6(a), as amended, 29 U.S.C.A. § 255(a). Facchiano Const. Co., Inc. v. U.S. Dept. of Labor, 987 F.2d 206, 1 Wage & Hour Cas. 2d (BNA) 468, 39 Cont. Cas. Fed. (CCH) P 76542, 124 Lab. Cas. (CCH) P 35782 (3d Cir. 1993). United States ☞64.20

31 Injunctions—In general

Superfund contractor was not entitled to preliminary injunction against Environmental Protection Agency debarment proceeding because it failed to establish likelihood of success on merits of claim that EPA had denied due process and had initiated debarment proceeding for improper purpose after contractor had been acquitted on criminal charges in connection with clean-up contract. U.S.C.A. Const. Amends. 5, 14. Baranowski v. E.P.A., 699 F. Supp. 1119, 29 Env't. Rep. Cas. (BNA) 1213 (E.D. Pa. 1988), judgment aff'd, 902 F.2d 1558 (3d Cir. 1990). Environmental Law ☞701

Statute providing that no injunction or other similar process shall be issued against administrator of small business administration or his property did not deprive Claims Court of jurisdiction to enjoin, on preliminary basis, Department of Defense from awarding procurement contract to anyone other than apparent low bidder, even though proposed debarment of contractor resulted in SBA decision to discontinue its efforts to award bidder certificate of competency; declining to follow Speco Corp. v. U.S., 2 Cl. Ct. 335, 31 Cont. Cas. Fed. (CCH) P 71137 (1983) (rejected by, Cavalier Clothes, Inc. v. U.S., 810 F.2d 1108, 33 Cont. Cas. Fed. (CCH) P 74983 (Fed. Cir. 1987)). Small Business Act, § 2[5](b), as amended, 15 U.S.C.A. § 634(b). Sterlingwear of Boston, Inc. v. U.S., 10 Cl. Ct. 644, 33 Cont. Cas. Fed. (CCH) P 74560 (1986). Federal Courts ☞1080

32 Injunctions—Preliminary injunctions and restraining orders

For purposes of determining whether to grant temporary restraining order, debarment from being awarded federal government contracts is not sufficient to establish "irreparable harm." Ali v. U.S., 932 F. Supp. 1206 (N.D. Cal. 1996). Injunction ☞150

Contractor's officer was not entitled to temporary restraining order against his expired debarment by Department of Health and Human Services (DHHS), which had precluded officer from being awarded government contracts; officer was not likely to succeed on the merits of his challenge to debarment, as administrative record revealed substantial evidence upon which debarring official could have concluded that contractor committed forgery and that officer knew or should have known of it, officer apparently received all due process guarantees required by debarment regulations, and government agencies had not waived all fraud claims against officer, and balance of hardships did not tip in officer's favor, as officer had delayed two years in filing action and seeking injunction, any harm to officer was economic, speculative, or both, and government had strong interest in maintaining integrity of its contractors. 48 C.F.R. §§ 9.402(a), 9.406-2(c), 9.406-3(b)(1), (d)(1), (d)(2)(i), 9.406-5(b). Ali v. U.S., 932 F. Supp. 1206 (N.D. Cal. 1996). Injunction ☞150

Notwithstanding debarment of apparent low bidder for Government contract, bidder was entitled to preliminary injunction to enjoin Government from awarding procurement contract to anyone other than bidder where denial of relief would visit immediate and irreparable harm on bidder, challenge of debarment proceeding in United States district court was not adequate "remedy at law," as remedy in district court would be equitable, bidder was likely to succeed on merits, and grant of preliminary injunction was in public interest. Sterlingwear of Boston, Inc. v. U.S., 11 Cl. Ct. 517, 33 Cont. Cas. Fed. (CCH) P 74956 (1987). Injunction ☞138.63

Public interest favored grant of preliminary injunction to prevent Department of Defense from awarding government contract to anyone other than apparent low bidder based on alleged lack of rationality in decision to seek debarment of bidder. Sterlingwear of Boston, Inc. v. U.S., 10 Cl. Ct. 644, 33 Cont. Cas. Fed. (CCH) P 74560 (1986). Injunction ☞138.63

Apparent low bidder on defense procurement contract had no adequate remedy at law for proposed debarment based on commonality of management with another corporation which had defaulted on its government contracts and, therefore, bidder was entitled to preliminary injunction to prevent Department of Defense from awarding contract to anyone other than bidder. Sterlingwear of Boston, Inc. v. U.S., 10 Cl. Ct. 644, 33 Cont. Cas. Fed. (CCH) P

74560 (1986). Injunction ☞138.63

Denial of preliminary injunction to prevent Department of Defense from awarding procurement contract to anyone other than apparent low bidder would visit immediate and irreparable harm on bidder where bidder would need to engage in extensive postaward activities to restore status quo, particularly in light of Department's failure to demonstrate any injury to itself if preliminary injunction were granted pending definitive determination on proposed debarment of bidder based on alleged "commonality with management" with another corporation which had defaulted on its contracts. Sterlingwear of Boston, Inc. v. U.S., 10 Cl. Ct. 644, 33 Cont. Cas. Fed. (CCH) P 74560 (1986). Injunction ☞138.63

Apparent low bidder on defense procurement contract presented evidence reflecting substantial likelihood of success on merits of its claim that there was no rational basis for decision to reject bid for lack of tenacity, perseverance and capacity based on alleged "commonality" between bidder and another corporation which had defaulted on two government contracts and decision to recommend debarment on identical grounds and, therefore, bidder was entitled to preliminary injunction to prevent Department of Defense from awarding contract to anyone other than low bidder. Sterlingwear of Boston, Inc. v. U.S., 10 Cl. Ct. 644, 33 Cont. Cas. Fed. (CCH) P 74560 (1986). Injunction ☞147

33 Jurisdiction

Any issue regarding ability of deputy administrator of Agricultural Stabilization and Conservation Service (ASCS) to serve as impartial debarring officer became moot upon his resignation. Girard v. Klopfenstein, 930 F.2d 738 (9th Cir. 1991). Federal Courts ☞13

Contractor's claim that wrongful debarment by General Services Administration (GSA) unfairly excluded him from possibility of entering future government procurement contracts established only tangential connection between alleged wrongful act by government and procurement contract, and, thus, Board of Contract Appeals did not have jurisdiction over claim under Contract Disputes Act. Contract Disputes Act, § 402(a), as amended, 41 U.S.C.A. § 602(a). Schickler v. Davis, 10 Fed. Appx. 944 (Fed. Cir. 2001). United States ☞64.20; United States ☞73(15)

Court of Federal Claims does not have jurisdiction to review propriety of agency's decision to debar contractor; such challenge must be brought in district court under Administrative Procedure Act. 5 U.S.C.A. §§ 701–706; 28 U.S.C.A. § 1491(a)(1). IMCO, Inc. v. U.S., 97 F.3d 1422 (Fed. Cir. 1996). United States ☞64.60(1)

Court of Federal Claims exceeded its jurisdiction in reviewing propriety of actual debarment from government contracting, when only proposed debarment rendered contractor ineligible for contract award. IMCO, Inc. v. U.S., 97 F.3d 1422 (Fed. Cir. 1996). United States ☞64.60(3.1)

Contractor who brought suit for contract damages against the United States could not raise debarment issue in the Court of Federal Claims, where debarment did not interfere with the contract at issue, but only served to preclude future contracts Medina Const., Ltd. v. U.S., 43 Fed. Cl. 537 (1999). Federal Courts ☞1073.1

Jurisdiction in the Court of Federal Claims to consider an agency decision to debar a contractor is appropriate, within carefully defined limits, only in the context of affording complete relief in bid protest claims. Medina Const., Ltd. v. U.S., 43 Fed. Cl. 537 (1999). Federal Courts ☞1073.1

The Tucker Act does not give the Court of Federal Claims jurisdiction to review the propriety of an agency's decision to debar a contractor; such a challenge must be brought in district court under the Administrative Procedures Act (APA). 5 U.S.C.A. § 551 et seq.; 28 U.S.C.A. §§ 1346, 1491. Medina Const., Ltd. v. U.S., 43 Fed. Cl. 537 (1999). Federal Courts ☞1141

Claims Court did not have bid protest jurisdiction over complaint alleging that action of contracting officer in requesting that debarment proceedings be instituted effectively prohibited apparent low bidder from being awarded contract and any other contract without due process of law, as any hearing provided by Department of Defense Regulations would not stay any action of contracting officer or small business administration. 28 U.S.C.A. §§ 1491, 1491(a)(3); U.S.C.A. Const.Amends. 5, 14. Sterlingwear of Boston, Inc. v. U.S., 10 Cl. Ct. 644, 33 Cont. Cas. Fed. (CCH) P 74560 (1986). Federal Courts ☞1076

34 Parties

Only proper defendant, in helicopter owner's action alleging wrongful debarment of Department of Interior contract work, was Secretary of Interior. 5 U.S.C.A. § 702. Dynamic Aviation v. Department of Interior, 898 F. Supp. 11 (D.D.C. 1995), aff'd, 132 F.3d 1481 (D.C. Cir. 1997). United States ☞64.20

35 Presumptions and burden of proof

Proposed debarment of government contractor, which rendered its bid ineligible for award of federal contract, was not arbitrary and capricious, and, thus, government did not breach its implied contractual duty to consider bid fairly and honestly, where there was no evidence of bad faith by procurement fraud division officer making recommendation. IMCO, Inc. v. U.S., 97 F.3d 1422 (Fed. Cir. 1996)

Government contractor has burden of demonstrating, to satisfaction of debarring official, that sufficient mitigating factors make debarment unnecessary. 48 C.F.R. § 9.406-1(a)(1) (10). Burke v. U.S. E.P.A., 127 F. Supp. 2d 235, 51 Env't. Rep. Cas. (BNA) 2210 (D.D.C. 2001). United States ☞64.20

Government contractor has burden of demonstrating, to satisfaction of debarring official, that sufficient mitigating factors make debarment unnecessary. 48 C.F.R. § 9.406-1(a)(1) (10). Burke v. U.S. E.P.A., 127 F. Supp. 2d 235, 51 Env't. Rep. Cas. (BNA) 2210 (D.D.C. 2001). United States ☞64.20

§ 9.406-2 Causes for debarment.

The debarring official may debar—

(a) A contractor for a conviction of or civil judgment for—

(1) Commission of fraud or a criminal offense in connection with—

(i) Obtaining;

(ii) Attempting to obtain; or

(iii) Performing a public contract or subcontract.

(2) Violation of Federal or State antitrust statutes relating to the submission of offers;

(3) Commission of embezzlement, theft, forgery, bribery, falsification or destruction of records, making false statements, tax evasion, violating Federal criminal tax laws, or receiving stolen property;

(4) Intentionally affixing a label bearing a "Made in America" inscription (or any inscription having the same meaning) to a product sold in or shipped to the United States or its outlying areas, when the product was not made in the United States or its outlying areas (see Section 202 of the Defense Production Act (Public Law 102-558)); or

(5) Commission of any other offense indicating a lack of business integrity or business honesty that seriously and directly affects the present responsibility of a Government contractor or subcontractor.

(b) (1) A contractor, based upon a preponderance of the evidence, for any of the following—

(i) Violation of the terms of a Government contract or subcontract so serious as to justify debarment, such as—

(A) Willful failure to perform in accordance with the terms of one or more contracts; or

(B) A history of failure to perform, or of unsatisfactory performance of, one or more contracts.

(ii) Violations of 41 U.S.C. chapter 81, Drug-Free Workplace, as indicated by—

(A) Failure to comply with the requirements of the clause at 52.223-6, Drug-Free Workplace; or

(B) Such a number of contractor employees convicted of violations of criminal drug statutes occurring in the workplace as to indicate that the contractor has failed to make a good faith effort to provide a drug-free workplace (see 23.504).

(iii) Intentionally affixing a label bearing a "Made in America" inscription (or any inscription having the same meaning) to a product sold in or shipped to the United States or its outlying areas, when the product was not made in the United States or its outlying areas (see Section 202 of the Defense Production Act (Public Law 102-558)).

(iv) Commission of an unfair trade practice as defined in 9.403 (see Section 201 of the Defense Production Act (Pub. L. 102-558)).

(v) Delinquent Federal taxes in an amount that exceeds $3,500.

(A) Federal taxes are considered delinquent for purposes of this provision if both of the following criteria apply:

(1) The tax liability is finally determined. The liability is finally determined if it has been assessed. A liability is not finally determined if there is a pending administrative or judicial challenge. In the case of a judicial challenge to the liability, the liability is not finally determined until all judicial appeal rights have been exhausted.

(2) The taxpayer is delinquent in making payment. A taxpayer is delinquent if the taxpayer has failed to pay the tax liability when full payment was due and required. A taxpayer is not delinquent in cases where enforced collection action is precluded.

(B) Examples.

(1) The taxpayer has received a statutory notice of deficiency, under I.R.C. § 6212, which entitles the taxpayer to seek Tax Court review of a proposed tax deficiency. This is not a delinquent tax because it is not a final tax liability. Should the taxpayer seek Tax Court review, this will not be a final tax liability until the taxpayer has exercised all judicial appeal rights.

(2) The IRS has filed a notice of Federal tax lien with respect to an assessed tax liability, and the taxpayer has been issued a notice under I.R.C. § 6320 entitling the taxpayer to request a hearing with the IRS Office of Appeals contesting the lien filing, and to further appeal to the Tax Court if the IRS determines to sustain the lien filing. In the course of the hearing, the taxpayer is entitled to contest the underlying tax liability because the taxpayer has had no prior opportunity to contest the liability. This is not a delinquent tax because it is not a final tax liability. Should the taxpayer seek tax court review, this will not be a final tax liability until the taxpayer has exercised all judicial appeal rights.

(3) The taxpayer has entered into an installment agreement pursuant to I.R.C. § 6159. The taxpayer is making timely payments and is in full compliance with the agreement terms. The taxpayer is not delinquent because the taxpayer is not currently required to make full payment.

(4) The taxpayer has filed for bankruptcy protection. The taxpayer is not delinquent because enforced collection action is stayed under 11 U.S.C. 362 (the Bankruptcy Code).

(vi) Knowing failure by a principal, until 3 years after final payment on any Government contract awarded to the contractor, to timely disclose to the Government, in connection with the award, performance, or closeout of the contract or a subcontract thereunder, credible evidence of—

(A) Violation of Federal criminal law involving fraud, conflict of interest, bribery, or gratuity violations found in Title 18 of the United States Code;

(B) Violation of the civil False Claims Act (31 U.S.C. 3729–3733); or

(C) Significant overpayment(s) on the contract, other than overpayments resulting from contract financing payments as defined in 32.001.

(2) A contractor, based on a determination by the Secretary of Homeland Security or the Attorney General of the United States, that the contractor is not in compliance with Immigration and Nationality Act employment provisions (see Executive Order 12989, as amended by Executive Order 13286). Such determination is not reviewable in the debarment proceedings.

(c) A contractor or subcontractor based on any other cause of so serious or compelling a nature that it affects the present responsibility of the contractor or subcontractor.

United States Code Annotated

Administrative determinations, see 41 USCA § 257.

Contract requirements, see 41 USCA § 254.

Contractor responsibilities, see 41 USCA § 57.

Contracts, planning, solicitation, evaluation, and award procedures, see 10 USCA § 2305.

Definitions, see 10 USCA § 2302, 41 USCA §§ 259, 403.

Determinations and decisions, see 10 USCA § 2310, 41 USCA § 262.

Kinds of contracts, see 10 USCA § 2306.

Planning and solicitation requirements, see 41 USCA § 253a.

Notes of Decisions

Agriculture Department 13
Antitrust violations and anticompetitive activities 5
Armed services and defense 14
Cause of serious and compelling nature 8
Collusive bidding 9
Conviction of crime, generally 3
Double jeopardy 2
Environmental Protection Agency 16
Failure to perform contract 10
Falsification of records 6
Forest Service 18
Hearing 21
Housing and Urban Development 17
Injunctions 19
Labor Department 15
Made in America labels 7
New facts and circumstances 11
Nolo contendere pleas 4
Present responsibility test 12
Presumptions and burden of proof 20
Validity 1

1 Validity

Federal acquisitions regulations governing debarment of government contractors are not unreasonable or unconstitutional. Joseph Const. Co. v. Veterans Admin. of U.S., 595 F. Supp. 448, 32 Cont. Cas. Fed. (CCH) P 73082 (N.D. Ill. 1984). United States ☞64.20

2 Double jeopardy

Debarment of government contractor for 26 months was not sufficiently punitive to implicate double jeopardy clause and require the dismissal of criminal prosecution against him, as contractor failed to show disbarment was disproportionate to benefits received by government in protecting it against effects of willful failures to perform in accordance with terms of government contracts, effects of history of failures to perform, and adverse effect of having government contract with irresponsible contractor. U.S.C.A. Const. Amend. 5; 48 C.F.R. §§ 9.402(b), 9.403, 9.406-2, 9.406-3(b)(1), (d)(3). U.S. v. Hatfield, 108 F.3d 67 (4th Cir. 1997). Double Jeopardy ☞24

Debarment of government contractor did not have to be subjected to a "particularized assessment" to determine whether it was punitive for double jeopardy purposes, where government did not seek the return of particular quantity of funds but instead sought to protect the quality of its acquisition programs. 48 C.F.R. §§ 9.402(b), 9.406-2(b)(1), (c), 9.406-4. U.S. v. Hatfield, 108 F.3d 67 (4th Cir. 1997). Double Jeopardy ☞24

Four-year debarment of defense contractor from government contracting was not so overwhelmingly disproportionate to harm caused by defendant's conduct, in knowingly supplying nonconforming parts to Department of Defense (DOD), as to constitute punishment for double jeopardy purposes, even though regulations generally provided for three-year maximum debarment, as debarment served important nonpunitive goals of preventing further dissipation of public funds and protecting DOD programs by preventing supply of substandard or defective parts, and extra year could be viewed as evidence of intent to protect government from particularly egregious conduct, where government paid company more than $40,000 for nonconforming parts. U.S.C.A. Const.Amend. 5; 18 U.S.C.A. § 287; 48 C.F.R. §§ 9.402, 9.406-2(b), 9.406-4. U.S. v. Glymph, 96 F.3d 722 (4th Cir. 1996). Double Jeopardy ☜24

Intent of provision for administrative debarment from government contracting is to purge government programs of corrupt influences and prevent improper dissipation of public funds, and debarment is thus not punitive, for double jeopardy purposes, but constitutes "rough remedial justice" permissible as prophylactic governmental action. U.S.C.A. Const. Amend. 5; 48 C.F.R. § 9.406-2(b). U.S. v. Glymph, 96 F.3d 722 (4th Cir. 1996). Double Jeopardy ☜24

3 Conviction of crime, generally

A debarment from contracting with executive branch of government need not be proportional to severity of a prior criminal sentence, for a criminal sentence is a statutory sanction quite distinct from a debarment. Shane Meat Co., Inc. v. U.S. Dept. of Defense, 800 F.2d 334, 91 A.L.R. Fed. 857 (3d Cir. 1986). United States ☜64.20

Agency's decision to debar government contractor was arbitrary, capricious and abuse of discretion, though contractor pled guilty to misdemeanor for conversion of government property, where government continued to enter into contracts with contractor for six years after misrepresentations that served as basis for misdemeanor conviction. Silverman v. U.S. Dept. of Defense, 817 F. Supp. 846, 39 Cont. Cas. Fed. (CCH) P 76540 (S.D. Cal. 1993). United States ☜64.20

Debarment of government contractors from all government procurement and sales contracting for three years was not arbitrary or capricious; contractors were convicted of crime in connection with performance of government contract. Delta Rocky Mountain Petroleum, Inc. v. U.S. Dept. of Defense, 726 F. Supp. 278, 36 Cont. Cas. Fed. (CCH) P 75888 (D. Colo. 1989). United States ☜64.15

Contractor's guilty plea to charge of making a false statement for purpose of influencing action of a bank and the legitimate inferences to be drawn therefrom constituted substantial evidence in support of administrative decision to debar him from further participation in HUD programs. Agan v. Pierce, 576 F. Supp. 257 (N.D. Ga. 1983). United States ☜64.20

Where agency considered not only criminal conviction of president of government contractor, but also mitigating factors submitted by contractor in debarment proceedings, decision to debar contractor for period of one year was not arbitrary, capricious or abuse of discretion. Federal Property and Administrative Services Act of 1949, § 303(b), 41 U.S.C.A. § 253(b). Joseph Const. Co. v. Veterans Admin. of U.S., 595 F. Supp. 448, 32 Cont. Cas. Fed. (CCH) P 73082 (N.D. Ill. 1984). United States ☜64.20

4 Nolo contendere pleas

Under regulations, conviction of contractor based upon plea of nolo contendere or otherwise, does not, ipso facto, support a debarment from bidding in Government contracts. Peter Kiewit Sons' Co. v. U. S. Army Corps of Engineers, 534 F. Supp. 1139, 29 Cont. Cas. Fed. (CCH) P 82291 (D.D.C. 1982), judgment rev'd, 714 F.2d 163, 31 Cont. Cas. Fed. (CCH) P 71395, 1983-2 Trade Cas. (CCH) ¶ 65528 (D.C. Cir. 1983). United States ☜64.20

Debarment of contractor from bidding on Government contracts may not be imposed for further punishment after plea of nolo contendere. Peter Kiewit Sons' Co. v. U. S. Army Corps of Engineers, 534 F. Supp. 1139, 29 Cont. Cas. Fed. (CCH) P 82291 (D.D.C. 1982), judgment rev'd, 714 F.2d 163, 31 Cont. Cas. Fed. (CCH) P 71395, 1983-2 Trade Cas. (CCH) ¶ 65528 (D.C. Cir. 1983). United States ☜64.20

5 Antitrust violations and anticompetitive activities

Department of Army followed appropriate procedures in placing moving and storage companies who were under antitrust indictment on restricted contractor list, companies received adequate notice of suspension and were fully informed of their appeals rights. Coleman American Moving Services, Inc. v. Weinberger, 716 F. Supp. 1405, 36 Cont. Cas. Fed. (CCH) P 75786 (M.D. Ala. 1989). United States ☜64.20

Suspension of companies furnishing moving and storage service to Department of Army, based on indictment charging them with antitrust violations, was not invalid due to failure of Department to make specific determination that immediate action was necessary to protect government's interest, as evidence of bid rigging as claimed in antitrust complaint was implicitly contrary to government's interest. Coleman American Moving Services, Inc. v. Weinberger, 716 F. Supp. 1405, 36 Cont. Cas. Fed. (CCH) P 75786 (M.D. Ala. 1989). United States ☞64.20

Moving and storage companies who were indicted and suspended from contracting with Department of Army were not entitled to make-up tonnage following their acquittal in antitrust action, as make-up tonnage was available only to contractors who were wrongfully suspended and suspension during pendency of antitrust action had been valid. Coleman American Moving Services, Inc. v. Weinberger, 716 F. Supp. 1405, 36 Cont. Cas. Fed. (CCH) P 75786 (M.D. Ala. 1989). United States ☞64.20

Moving and storage companies were not entitled to makeup tonnage under contract with Department of Army, as they had not established bad faith on part of Department in suspending them during pendency of antitrust litigation against them. Coleman American Moving Services, Inc. v. Weinberger, 716 F. Supp. 1405, 36 Cont. Cas. Fed. (CCH) P 75786 (M.D. Ala. 1989). United States ☞64.20

Moving and storage companies who were suspended from contracting with Department of Army because of indictment under antitrust charges were not prevented from adequately exercising their right to contest suspension by fact that it would have required person capable of refuting charges to waive his Fifth Amendment right against self-incrimination, as only relevance of his testimony would be denying existence of indictment or denying that defendants were named in indictment and testimony on these subjects would have posed no hazard of self-incrimination for individual. U.S.C.A. Const.Amend. 5. Coleman American Moving Services, Inc. v. Weinberger, 716 F. Supp. 1405, 36 Cont. Cas. Fed. (CCH) P 75786 (M.D. Ala. 1989). United States ☞64.20; Witnesses ☞297(8.1)

Suspension proceedings brought against moving and storage companies by Department of Army following filing of antitrust indictment against them did not impermissibly extend right of government to discovery in case involving companies' claim for back-up tonnage after companies were acquitted and restored to bidders list, as there was little opportunity for abuse of discovery in postsuspension hearing which covered only evidence refuting existence of indictment or refuting that companies were named in indictment. Coleman American Moving Services, Inc. v. Weinberger, 716 F. Supp. 1405, 36 Cont. Cas. Fed. (CCH) P 75786 (M.D. Ala. 1989). United States ☞64.20

Substantial evidence supported finding, in support of three-year debarment of bidder from government surplus auctions, that bidder had engaged in anticompetitive activity; arrangements described by bidder did not appear to be joint ventures and presented situation more akin to bid rigging. Textor v. Cheney, 757 F. Supp. 51, 37 Cont. Cas. Fed. (CCH) P 76028 (D.D.C. 1991). United States ☞64.20

6 Falsification of records

Although government contractor was properly debarred from doing business with government for three-year term for falsification of laboratory test results, debarment of president and secretary of contractor on ground that they had reason to know of contractor's criminal conduct, although they did not have actual knowledge of conduct, was not supported by preponderance of evidence and, therefore, their debarment was unreasonable. Caiola v. Carroll, 851 F.2d 395, 399, 34 Cont. Cas. Fed. (CCH) P 75514 (D.C. Cir. 1988). United States ☞64.20

7 Made in America labels

Under the Buy America Act (BAA), whenever agency head determines that violation has taken place, imposition of three-year period of debarment from receiving government contract is mandatory. Buy American Act, § 3(b), 41 U.S.C.A. § 10b(b). Glazer Const. Co., Inc. v. U.S., 50 F. Supp. 2d 85, 185 A.L.R. Fed. 717 (D. Mass. 1999). United States ☞64.20

Contractor would be deemed in violation of Buy American Act (BAA), and would be barred from receiving contract for three years, even though value of materials found to violate BAA was only 0.01% of materials used in project. Buy American Act, § 3, 41 U.S.C.A. § 10b. Glazer Const. Co., Inc. v. U.S., 50 F. Supp. 2d 85, 185 A.L.R. Fed. 717 (D. Mass. 1999). United States ☞64.20

Violations of Buy America Act by contractors do not have to be intentional in order for liability to attach. Buy American Act, § 3, 41 U.S.C.A. § 10b. Glazer Const. Co., Inc. v. U.S., 50 F. Supp. 2d 85, 185 A.L.R. Fed. 717 (D. Mass. 1999). United States ⚷64.20

8 Cause of serious and compelling nature

Even in the absence of conviction or civil judgment against government contractor, contractor may be debarred, based on preponderance of the evidence, for cause of serious and compelling nature, but debarring official must give notice to contractor or proposal to debar and must invite the contractor to submit information or argument in opposition to the proposed debarment. 48 C.F.R. §§ 9.406-2(c), 9.406-3(c)(4). Waterhouse v. U.S., 874 F. Supp. 5 (D.D.C. 1994). United States ⚷64.20

Hearing officer's finding that government contractor violated terms of purchase orders with Department of Housing and Urban Development constituting "causes of such serious and compelling nature, affecting responsibility," and demonstrating at least implicitly that suspension under the facts was in the best interest of HUD, which determination was sustained by assistant secretary of HUD, was adequate finding on which to base suspension of government contractor. Adamo Wrecking Co. v. Department of Housing and Urban Development, 414 F. Supp. 877 (D.D.C. 1976). United States ⚷64.20

9 Collusive bidding

Bidder for purchase of surplus property from federal government could properly be found to have engaged in collusive bidding agreements warranting debarment even if he committed no overt acts in furtherance of such agreements. Leitman v. McAusland, 934 F.2d 46, 37 Cont. Cas. Fed. (CCH) P 76107 (4th Cir. 1991). United States ⚷64.20

Bidder could be debarred from purchasing surplus property from federal government based on collusive bidding agreements upon determination at administrative hearing that bidder had entered into such agreements, even though he had suffered no conviction or civil judgment on such agreements. Leitman v. McAusland, 934 F.2d 46, 37 Cont. Cas. Fed. (CCH) P 76107 (4th Cir. 1991). United States ⚷64.20

Finding that bidder for purchase of surplus property from federal government had entered into collusive bidding agreements warranting debarment was sufficiently supported by testimony of informant and investigator, along with transcript of telephone conversation in which agreement was made. Leitman v. McAusland, 934 F.2d 46, 37 Cont. Cas. Fed. (CCH) P 76107 (4th Cir. 1991). United States ⚷64.20

10 Failure to perform contract

Evidence supported finding cause for debarring certified public accounting firm from doing work for federal government for violation of regulation through willful failure to perform in accordance with terms of public agreements or transactions; contract stipulated that audit report had to be executed according to generally accepted accounting principles and Department of Housing and Urban Development (HUD) requirements, but audit report for city public housing authority which did business with HUD did not contain qualifying opinion or finding regarding unusual manner in which city authority reported cash in its financial statements, and firm made no attempt to issue revised report. Sellers v. Kemp, 749 F. Supp. 1001, 36 Cont. Cas. Fed. (CCH) P 75996 (W.D. Mo. 1990). United States ⚷64.20

Government's decision to remove incumbent contractor from approved source list for the production of T-37 aircraft tailpipes was not arbitrary or capricious; four separate metallurgical reports concluded that manufacturing defects caused tailpipe failures during contractor's performance of its last two contracts, and contractor did not prove that the defects were due to design defects. SAI Industries Corp. v. U.S., 60 Fed. Cl. 731 (2004). United States ⚷64.20

Debarment of defense contractor was supported by evidence that contractor had defaulted on two contracts and not performed on total of nine contracts, contractor had positive balance sheet at time of nonperformance, and contracts which contractor failed to perform were relatively small and would have required little capital, even though contractor contended that its difficulties in performing contracts were due to delays in obtaining settlement funds from government in connection with earlier disputed contracts and that it was financially unable to perform. IMCO, Inc. v. U.S., 33 Fed. Cl. 312 (1995), judgment aff'd, 97 F.3d 1422 (Fed. Cir. 1996). United States ☞64.20

Material issue of fact as to whether government contractor's failure to perform was willful precluded summary disbarment of contractor, where there was circumstantial evidence that Government requested acceleration of deliveries, government representative knew or should have known of prefirst article approved cutting of government furnished material, contractor did not have physical means of reworking incorrectly cut coats, and subsequent defaults on government contracts were due to Government's threat of offsetting losses on contract against progress payments on other defaulted contracts. Sterlingwear of Boston, Inc. v. U.S., 11 Cl. Ct. 879, 34 Cont. Cas. Fed. (CCH) P 75210 (1987). United States ☞64.20

11 New facts and circumstances

Contractor's conviction for making false statements in connection with defense contracts was a "new fact or circumstance" for purpose of regulation precluding further debarment solely on basis of facts and circumstances upon which an initial debarment action was based. Wellham v. Cheney, 934 F.2d 305 (11th Cir. 1991). United States ☞64.20

12 Present responsibility test

Trust agreement leaving ultimate decision-making authority for government contractor to someone other than individual accused of bid rigging, and sworn affidavits that accused bid rigger had little or no present contact with company, did not establish contractor's present responsibility to do business with government, for purpose of debarment proceeding; although agreement gave trustee direct authority over all company operations it contained no specific term barring alleged bid rigger from either acting on behalf of company or participating in its management, and, more importantly, nothing in trust agreement or any other company submission gave government any assurance that alleged bid rigger would not conduct illicit dealings on behalf of company entirely outside company channels. Robinson v. Cheney, 876 F.2d 152, 277, 35 Cont. Cas. Fed. (CCH) P 75666 (D.C. Cir. 1989). United States ☞64.20

Federal acquisition regulation permitting agency to debar contractor for lack of "present responsibility" was not unconstitutionally vague as applied or on its face. U.S.C.A. Const. Amend. 5. Robinson v. Cheney, 876 F.2d 152, 277, 35 Cont. Cas. Fed. (CCH) P 75666 (D.C. Cir. 1989). United States ☞64.20

Analysis of present responsibility of contractor in review of debarment action focuses on seriousness of offense, length of time elapsed since offense, and contractor's conduct in interim period. Silverman v. U.S. Dept. of Defense, 817 F. Supp. 846, 39 Cont. Cas. Fed. (CCH) P 76540 (S.D. Cal. 1993). Public Contracts ☞11; United States ☞64.20

Ultimate inquiry in debarment of contractor to insure that government contracts are awarded only to responsible bidders must be directed to present responsibility of contractor; agency is required to carefully consider any favorable evidence of responsibility to insure that all findings are based on realistic and articulable threat of harm to government's propriety interest. Silverman v. U.S. Dept. of Defense, 817 F. Supp. 846, 39 Cont. Cas. Fed. (CCH) P 76540 (S.D. Cal. 1993). United States ☞64.20

Test for whether "debarment," an administrative action which excludes nonresponsible contractors from government contracting, is warranted is present responsibility of contractor; contractor can meet test of present responsibility by demonstrating that it has taken steps to ensure that wrongful acts will not recur. Delta Rocky Mountain Petroleum, Inc. v. U.S. Dept. of Defense, 726 F. Supp. 278, 36 Cont. Cas. Fed. (CCH) P 75888 (D. Colo. 1989). United States ☞64.15

Air Force's decision to debar contractor from having contract for three years, due to violation of Buy America Act (BAA), on factually undisputed ground that contractor lacked present responsibility to hold contract, allowed for affirmance of Air Force's debarment decision without holding of hearing required on other ground, that contractor's conduct was wilful. Buy American Act, § 3, 41 U.S.C.A. § 10b. Glazer Const. Co., Inc. v. U.S., 50 F. Supp. 2d 85, 185 A.L.R. Fed. 717 (D. Mass. 1999). United States ☞64.20

Air Force official issuing order debarring contractor from receiving contract for three years, due to violation of Buy American Act (BAA), did not act arbitrarily and capriciously in determining that contractor did not show degree of present responsibility to be government contractor, when contractor claimed without research that Canadian wall base found in construction project was unavailable in United States, did not dispute official's conclusion that statement was false, and presented program to prevent recurrence of violations that was unacceptable to official. Buy American Act, § 3(b), 41 U.S.C.A. § 10b(b); 48 C.F.R. § 9.406-2(c). Glazer Const. Co., Inc. v. U.S., 50 F. Supp. 2d 85, 185 A.L.R. Fed. 717 (D. Mass. 1999). United States ☞64.20

Concept of "present responsibility," as will potentially prevent debarment of government contractor, encompasses contractor's ability to successfully perform government contract. IMCO, Inc. v. U.S., 33 Fed. Cl. 312 (1995), judgment aff'd, 97 F.3d 1422 (Fed. Cir. 1996). United States ☞64.20

13 Agriculture Department

Procurement process for panel support services contract with United States Department of Agriculture was not arbitrary or capricious based on exclusion of company whose president had sought appointment to panel from consideration for that contract on conflict of interest grounds; by the time it was learned that president had not been selected for panel, contractor selection was sufficiently complete from Department's perspective that evaluation process could not reasonably begin anew. Information Resources Inc. v. U.S., 676 F. Supp. 293, 34 Cont. Cas. Fed. (CCH) P 75357 (D.D.C. 1987). United States ☞64.20

Department of Agriculture's order barring meat supplier from bidding on or being awarded contracts to supply meat for USDA programs was supported by substantial evidence as to the supplier's affiliation with another suspended supplier and as to illegal activities involving movement of unwholesome meat in Department of Agriculture programs. Rules and Regulations, §§ 1-1.601-1(e), 1-1.605-2(b), 1-1.605-3, 41 U.S.C.A.App. Stanko Packing Co., Inc. v. Bergland, 489 F. Supp. 947, 27 Cont. Cas. Fed. (CCH) P 80419 (D.D.C. 1980). Food ☞12; United States ☞64.20

14 Armed services and defense

Administrative proceedings in which Air Force had threatened to suspend or disbar contractor from entering into contracts with Department of Defense constituted "alternate remedy" to qui tam action under False Claims Act (FCA), and thus contractor's former employee who commenced qui tam action based on contractor's use of defective damping fluid and falsification of test results was entitled under FCA to relator's share of proceeds from settlement agreement arising from proceedings which required contractor to repair and replace defective flight data transmitters and to replace defective damping fluid, even though suspension or debarment proceeding was significantly different from FCA action, where government declined to intervene in qui tam action arising from defective fluid, choosing instead to go forward with suspension or debarment proceeding based on conduct that formed basis of action, and then settled relator's action for false testing, with result that relator was later found barred by claim preclusion from pursuing action for defective damping fluid. 31 U.S.C.A. § 3730(c)(5). U.S. ex rel. Barajas v. U.S., 258 F.3d 1004 (9th Cir. 2001). United States ☞122

The Air Force should have followed its own regulation, calling for notice and a hearing before debarring a supplier from bidding for contracts for a period of years, when the supplier raised a genuine issue of fact challenging the debarment; the supplier presented evidence that a debarred person was mistakenly listed as an officer of the supplier, and that if the debarred person was not considered an officer the supplier's answer to questions regarding its prior procurement record would be correct and the basis for its debarment would be removed. 48 C.F.R. § 9.406-3(b). Sameena Inc. v. U.S. Air Force, 147 F.3d 1148, 42 Cont. Cas. Fed. (CCH) P 77335 (9th Cir. 1998). United States ☞64.20

The Defense Logistics Agency (DLA) did not act arbitrarily or capriciously in determining that contractor's false statements about two pre-1984 defense contracts were new facts and circumstances for purposes of regulation providing that debarment may not be extended on basis of facts and circumstances upon which initial debarment action was based, where memorandum accompanying initial 1985 debarment explained that contractor was being debarred for submitting "fraudulent test reports or certificates of conformance" in enumerated contracts, and memorandum accompanying subsequent 1989 debarment explained that contractor was being debarred for submitting false statements in connection with other contracts not mentioned in original debarment memorandum. Wellham v. Cheney, 934 F.2d 305 (11th Cir. 1991). United States ☞64.20

Army lacked authority to bind Government to a contract with low bidder as long as bidder was suspended from receiving any government contracts and therefore low bidder's suit to enjoin temporarily the award of two Army Corps of Engineers contracts to any other bidders did not constitute a "bid protest" case over which Claims Court had jurisdiction. ATL, Inc. v. U.S., 735 F.2d 1343 (Fed. Cir. 1984). Federal Courts ⚷1074; United States ⚷64.20; United States ⚷64.60(1)

Claims Court lacked jurisdiction to consider claim that Department of Army failed to apply procedures governing suspension of government contractors and allotment of make-up tonnage, as its jurisdiction was limited to "contractual undertaking" where remedy was money damages. 28 U.S.C.A. § 1491(a)(1). Coleman American Moving Services, Inc. v. Weinberger, 716 F. Supp. 1405, 36 Cont. Cas. Fed. (CCH) P 75786 (M.D. Ala. 1989). Federal Courts ⚷1074

In Air Force suspension or debarment proceeding against defense contractor, government lacks any power to compel production of evidence or attendance of witnesses. 48 C.F.R. §§ 9.406-1 et seq., 9.407-1 et seq.U.S. ex rel. Barajas v. Northrop Corp., 65 F. Supp. 2d 1097 (C.D. Cal. 1999), rev'd and remanded on other grounds, 258 F.3d 1004 (9th Cir. 2001). United States ⚷64.20

A procuring agency cannot make successive determinations of nonresponsibility with regard to a contractor on the same basis; rather, it must initiate suspension or debarment procedures at the earliest practicable date following the first determination of nonresponsibility. Shermco Industries, Inc. v. Secretary of the Air Force, 584 F. Supp. 76, 32 Cont. Cas. Fed. (CCH) P 72713 (N.D. Tex. 1984). United States ⚷64.20

15 Labor Department

Government contractor's violation of unambiguous regulation promulgated under McNamara-O'Hara Service Contract Act, without more, cannot justify debarment. Service Contract Act of 1965, § 2 et seq., 41 U.S.C.A. § 351 et seq.Dantran, Inc. v. U.S. Dept. of Labor, 171 F.3d 58, 5 Wage & Hour Cas. 2d (BNA) 334, 137 Lab. Cas. (CCH) P 33837 (1st Cir. 1999). United States ⚷64.20

Structure and legislative history of Contract Work Hours and Safety Standards Act supported Secretary of Labor's authority to debar contractor for violating overtime hours and pay provisions of Act. Davis-Bacon Act, §§ 1-6, as amended, 40 U.S.C.A. §§ 276a to 276a-5; Housing and Community Development Act of 1974, §§ 110, 802(g), 42 U.S.C.A. §§ 5310, 1440(g); Contract Work Hours and Safety Standards Act, §§ 102, 103, 104(a), 106, as amended, 40 U.S.C.A. §§ 328, 329, 330(a), 332; Department of Defense Authorization Act, 1986, § 1 et seq., 99 Stat. 583; 23 U.S.C.A. § 113(a). Janik Paving & Const., Inc. v. Brock, 828 F.2d 84, 28 Wage & Hour Cas. (BNA) 417, 34 Cont. Cas. Fed. (CCH) P 75363, 107 Lab. Cas. (CCH) P 34958 (2d Cir. 1987). Labor And Employment ⚷2345; United States ⚷64.20

Fact that Contract Work Hours and Safety Standards Act did not expressly authorize Secretary of Labor to debar contractors for violating Act did not require invalidation of Secretary's debarment regulations even though, in later statutes, Congress expressly granted debarment authority. Davis-Bacon Act, §§ 1-6, as amended, 40 U.S.C.A. §§ 276a to 276a-5; Housing and Community Development Act of 1974, §§ 110, 802(g), 42 U.S.C.A. §§ 5310, 1440(g); Contract Work Hours and Safety Standards Act, §§ 102, 103, 104(a), 106, as amended, 40 U.S.C.A. §§ 328, 329, 330(a), 332; Department of Defense Authorization Act, 1986, § 1 et seq., 99 Stat. 583; 23 U.S.C.A. § 113(a). Janik Paving & Const., Inc. v. Brock, 828 F.2d 84, 28 Wage & Hour Cas. (BNA) 417, 34 Cont. Cas. Fed. (CCH) P 75363, 107 Lab. Cas. (CCH) P 34958 (2d Cir. 1987). Labor And Employment ⚷2338; United States ⚷64.20

Department of Labor's prima facie case for debarment of contractor, based on violation of overtime hours and pay provisions of Contract Work Hours and Safety Standards Act, was not weakened by fact that testimony of former employees or other evidence offered by Department may have been too vague to demonstrate with some precision the amount and extent of undercompensated overtime work for each affected employee; amount allegedly underpaid was merely incidental. Davis-Bacon Act, §§ 1-6, as amended, 40 U.S.C.A. §§ 276a to 276a-5; Housing and Community Development Act of 1974, §§ 110, 802(g), 42 U.S.C.A. §§ 5310, 1440(g); Contract Work Hours and Safety Standards Act, §§ 102, 103, 104(a), 106, as amended, 40 U.S.C.A. §§ 328, 329, 330(a), 332; Department of Defense Authorization Act, 1986, § 1 et seq., 99 Stat. 583; 23 U.S.C.A. § 113(a). Janik Paving & Const., Inc. v. Brock, 828 F.2d 84, 28 Wage & Hour Cas. (BNA) 417, 34 Cont. Cas. Fed. (CCH) P 75363,

107 Lab. Cas. (CCH) P 34958 (2d Cir. 1987). Labor And Employment ⟋2347; United States ⟋64.20

Debarment of contractor for violating overtime hours and pay provisions of Contract Work Hours and Safety Standards Act was intended to compel compliance with Act, and was not penalty, and, therefore, Secretary of Labor had authority to adopt regulations for debarment, even though Act did not specifically authorize debarment as sanction. Davis-Bacon Act, §§ 1-6, as amended, 40 U.S.C.A. §§ 276a to 276a-5; Housing and Community Development Act of 1974, §§ 110, 802(g), 42 U.S.C.A. §§ 5310, 1440(g); Contract Work Hours and Safety Standards Act, §§ 102, 103, 104(a), 106, as amended, 40 U.S.C.A. §§ 328, 329, 330(a), 332; Department of Defense Authorization Act, 1986, § 1 et seq., 99 Stat. 583; 23 U.S.C.A. § 113(a). Janik Paving & Const., Inc. v. Brock, 828 F.2d 84, 28 Wage & Hour Cas. (BNA) 417, 34 Cont. Cas. Fed. (CCH) P 75363, 107 Lab. Cas. (CCH) P 34958 (2d Cir. 1987). Labor And Employment ⟋2338; United States ⟋64.20

Substantial evidence supported Secretary of Labor's order debarring contractor for violating overtime hours and pay provisions of Contract Work Hours and Safety Standards Act, even though there was five-year hiatus between alleged wage violations and administrative hearing at which employees testified that overtime hours for which they were paid were consistently lower than those actually reported to contractor. Davis-Bacon Act, §§ 1-6, as amended, 40 U.S.C.A. §§ 276a to 276a-5; Housing and Community Development Act of 1974, §§ 110, 802(g), 42 U.S.C.A. §§ 5310, 1440(g); Contract Work Hours and Safety Standards Act, §§ 102, 103, 104(a), 106, as amended, 40 U.S.C.A. §§ 328, 329, 330(a), 332; Department of Defense Authorization Act, 1986, § 1 et seq., 99 Stat. 583; 23 U.S.C.A. § 113(a). Janik Paving & Const., Inc. v. Brock, 828 F.2d 84, 28 Wage & Hour Cas. (BNA) 417, 34 Cont. Cas. Fed. (CCH) P 75363, 107 Lab. Cas. (CCH) P 34958 (2d Cir. 1987). Labor And Employment ⟋2347; United States ⟋64.20

Regulation authorized debarment of individual corporate officers and not merely corporate contractor for willful violation of labor standards. Facchiano Const. Co., Inc. v. U.S. Dept. of Labor, 987 F.2d 206, 1 Wage & Hour Cas. 2d (BNA) 468, 39 Cont. Cas. Fed. (CCH) P 76542, 124 Lab. Cas. (CCH) P 35782 (3d Cir. 1993). United States ⟋64.20

Federal contractor failed to show that Department of Labor's Office of Federal Contract Compliance Programs (OFCCP) lacked jurisdiction over it; exemption from OFCCP's review authority cited by contractor was limited to state and local governments, and contractor failed to identify any regulations providing it with exemption and failed to argue that it reached those regulations' exemption requirements. Trinity Industries, Inc. v. Reich, 33 F.3d 942 (8th Cir. 1994). United States ⟋64.15; United States ⟋64.20

16 Environmental Protection Agency

Exceptional circumstances did not justify district court's intervention in ongoing debarment process initiated by Environmental Protection Agency against superfund contractor; process was initiated by proper agency official, contractor received proper notice of proceeding, and EPA procedures satisfied requirements of both its own regulations and due process. U.S.C.A. Const.Amends. 5, 14. Baranowski v. E.P.A., 699 F. Supp. 1119, 29 Env't. Rep. Cas. (BNA) 1213 (E.D. Pa. 1988), judgment aff'd, 902 F.2d 1558 (3d Cir. 1990). United States ⟋64.20

Director of Grants Administration Division is only Environmental Protection Agency official who has authority to debar or suspend contractor or to issue notice proposing debarment or suspension. Baranowski v. E.P.A., 699 F. Supp. 1119, 29 Env't. Rep. Cas. (BNA) 1213 (E.D. Pa. 1988), judgment aff'd, 902 F.2d 1558 (3d Cir. 1990). Environmental Law ⟋15

17 Housing and Urban Development

Department of Housing and Urban Development's (HUD) initiating debarment proceedings did not violate settlement agreement, under which HUD received title to other subsidized housing property which contractor also allegedly failed to maintain in a decent, safe, and sanitary condition; settlement agreement did not prohibit HUD from pursuing future administrative action against contractor arising out of substandard conditions existing at other subsidized properties owned by contractor or his affiliated companies, and debarment was fully supported by evidence of conditions at subject property. Marshall v. Cuomo, 192 F.3d 473 (4th Cir. 1999). United States ⟋64.20

Department of Housing and Urban Development (HUD) neither conducted debarment proceeding improperly nor violated provision of Administrative Procedure Act (APA) prohibiting an employee or agent engaged in the performance of investigative or prosecuting functions for an agency from participating or advising in the decision, even though HUD advisor to debarring official had previously participated in the investigation and prosecution of matter involving another property owned by contractor. 5 U.S.C.A. § 554(d). Marshall v. Cuomo, 192 F.3d 473 (4th Cir. 1999). United States ☞64.20

Provision of Administrative Procedure Act (APA) prohibiting an employee or agent engaged in the performance of investigative or prosecuting functions for an agency from participating or advising in the decision did not apply to Department of Housing and Urban Development's (HUD) debarment proceeding, which was not statutorily required. 5 U.S.C.A. § 554(d). Marshall v. Cuomo, 192 F.3d 473 (4th Cir. 1999). United States ☞64.20

Department of Housing and Urban Development (HUD) did not have to show that officer of suspended HUD coinsured lender was final decision maker in lender's passthrough procedures in violation of requirements of Government National Mortgage Assistance (GNMA) to sustain officer's debarment from participating in primary and lower tier covered transactions throughout executive branch of federal government for three years, and HUD was justified in debarring officer based upon substantial evidence that officer not only had reason to know of lender's misconduct, but also participated in it; fact that officer was participant, and not ultimate decision maker and that decisions were made on advice of counsel did not insulate him from sanction of debarment. Kisser v. Cisneros, 14 F.3d 615, 622 (D.C. Cir. 1994). United States ☞53(9)

Decision of Department of Housing and Urban Development (HUD) not to initiate debarment proceedings against certain officers of suspended HUD coinsured lender was unreviewable, and thus, district court's requirement that HUD give reasoned explanation for its decision to take debarment action against one former officer, but not other similarly situated officers was improper; no statute expressly provided for debarment actions or contained guidelines that informed HUD's decision to bring such actions, HUD's own regulations did not provide sufficient standards circumscribing HUD's enforcement discretion over debarment actions to rebut presumption of unreviewability, and there was no procedural step at initiation of debarment process which would provide focus for judicial review of HUD's nonenforcement decisions. 5 U.S.C.A. § 706(2); Executive Order No. 12549, § 1 et seq., 31 U.S.C.A. § 6101 note. Kisser v. Cisneros, 14 F.3d 615, 620 (D.C. Cir. 1994). United States ☞53(9)

18 Forest Service

Government's refusal to permit rebidding by contractor who had not cut any timber pursuant to prior contract was proper. Siller Bros., Inc. v. U. S., 228 Ct. Cl. 76, 655 F.2d 1039, 28 Cont. Cas. Fed. (CCH) P 81482 (1981). United States ☞58(3); United States ☞64.20

Refusal of forest supervisor to permit contractor which had defaulted on prior timber cutting contract to rebid was an implicit determination that awarding contract to such contractor would not be in the public interest. Siller Bros., Inc. v. U. S., 228 Ct. Cl. 76, 655 F.2d 1039, 28 Cont. Cas. Fed. (CCH) P 81482 (1981). United States ☞58(3); United States ☞64.20

19 Injunctions

Contractor's officer was not entitled to temporary restraining order against his expired debarment by Department of Health and Human Services (DHHS), which had precluded officer from being awarded government contracts; officer was not likely to succeed on the merits of his challenge to debarment, as administrative record revealed substantial evidence upon which debarring official could have concluded that contractor committed forgery and that officer knew or should have known of it, officer apparently received all due process guarantees required by debarment regulations, and government agencies had not waived all fraud claims against officer, and balance of hardships did not tip in officer's favor, as officer had delayed two years in filing action and seeking injunction, any harm to officer was economic, speculative, or both, and government had strong interest in maintaining integrity of its contractors. 48 C.F.R. §§ 9.402(a), 9.406-2(c), 9.406-3(b)(1), (d)(1), (d)(2)(i), 9.406-5(b). Ali v. U.S., 932 F. Supp. 1206 (N.D. Cal. 1996). Injunction ☞150

20 Presumptions and burden of proof

Government contractor has burden of demonstrating, to satisfaction of debarring official, that sufficient mitigating factors make debarment unnecessary. 48 C.F.R. § 9.406-1(a)(1) (10). Burke v. U.S. E.P.A., 127 F. Supp. 2d 235, 51 Env't. Rep. Cas. (BNA) 2210 (D.D.C. 2001). United States ⚷64.20

Charges against bidder need only be supported by preponderance of evidence in order to support debarment from participation in government surplus auctions. Textor v. Cheney, 757 F. Supp. 51, 37 Cont. Cas. Fed. (CCH) P 76028 (D.D.C. 1991). United States ⚷64.20

21 Hearing

Evidence that contracting officer received goods and services from supplier and never paid for them by cash or currency and that he gave an automobile to the supplier's church, taking a tax deduction, established basis for debarment and did not raise any genuine issues requiring debarring official to hold evidentiary hearing. 48 C.F.R. §§ 9.406-2(c), 9.406-3(b)(2). Waterhouse v. U.S., 874 F. Supp. 5 (D.D.C. 1994). United States ⚷64.20

Federal Acquisition Regulations (FARs) provide for automatic debarment in the case of conviction or civil judgment against contractor; because another fact finder has already found one of the bases for debarment beyond a reasonable doubt or by a preponderance of the evidence, there is no statutory, regulatory, or due process requirement of additional hearing to determine the underlying facts. U.S.C.A. Const.Amend. 14; 48 C.F.R. §§ 9.406-2(a), 9.406-3(d). Waterhouse v. U.S., 874 F. Supp. 5 (D.D.C. 1994). United States ⚷64.20

§ 9.406-3 Procedures.

(a) *Investigation and referral.* Agencies shall establish procedures for the prompt reporting, investigation, and referral to the debarring official of matters appropriate for that official's consideration.

(b) Decisionmaking process.

(1) Agencies shall establish procedures governing the debarment decisionmaking process that are as informal as is practicable, consistent with principles of fundamental fairness. These procedures shall afford the contractor (and any specifically named affiliates) an opportunity to submit, in person, in writing, or through a representative, information and argument in opposition to the proposed debarment.

(2) In actions not based upon a conviction or civil judgment, if it is found that the contractor's submission in opposition raises a genuine dispute over facts material to the proposed debarment, agencies shall also—

(i) Afford the contractor an opportunity to appear with counsel, submit documentary evidence, present witnesses, and confront any person the agency presents; and

(ii) Make a transcribed record of the proceedings and make it available at cost to the contractor upon request, unless the contractor and the agency, by mutual agreement, waive the requirement for a transcript.

(c) *Notice of proposal to debar.* A notice of proposed debarment shall be issued by the debarring official advising the contractor and any specifically named affiliates, by certified mail, return receipt requested—

(1) That debarment is being considered;

(2) Of the reasons for the proposed debarment in terms sufficient to put the contractor on notice of the conduct or transaction(s) upon which it is based;

(3) Of the cause(s) relied upon under 9.406-2 for proposing debarment;

(4) That, within 30 days after receipt of the notice, the contractor may submit, in person, in writing, or through a representative, information and argument in opposition to the proposed debarment, including any additional specific information that raises a genuine dispute over the material facts;

(5) Of the agency's procedures governing debarment decisionmaking;

(6) Of the effect of the issuance of the notice of proposed debarment; and

(7) Of the potential effect of an actual debarment.

(d) Debarring official's decision.

(1) In actions based upon a conviction or civil judgment, or in which there is no genuine dispute over material facts, the debarring official shall make a decision on the basis of all the information in the administrative record, including any submission made by the

contractor. If no suspension is in effect, the decision shall be made within 30 working days after receipt of any information and argument submitted by the contractor, unless the debarring official extends this period for good cause.

(2) (i) In actions in which additional proceedings are necessary as to disputed material facts, written findings of fact shall be prepared. The debarring official shall base the decision on the facts as found, together with any information and argument submitted by the contractor and any other information in the administrative record.

(ii) The debarring official may refer matters involving disputed material facts to another official for findings of fact. The debarring official may reject any such findings, in whole or in part, only after specifically determining them to be arbitrary and capricious or clearly erroneous.

(iii) The debarring official's decision shall be made after the conclusion of the proceedings with respect to disputed facts.

(3) In any action in which the proposed debarment is not based upon a conviction or civil judgment, the cause for debarment must be established by a preponderance of the evidence.

(e) Notice of debarring official's decision.

(1) If the debarring official decides to impose debarment, the contractor and any affiliates involved shall be given prompt notice by certified mail, return receipt requested—

(i) Referring to the notice of proposed debarment;

(ii) Specifying the reasons for debarment;

(iii) Stating the period of debarment, including effective dates; and

(iv) Advising that the debarment is effective throughout the executive branch of the Government unless the head of an agency or a designee makes the statement called for by 9.406-1(c).

(2) If debarment is not imposed, the debarring official shall promptly notify the contractor and any affiliates involved, by certified mail, return receipt requested.

(f) (1) If the contractor enters into an administrative agreement with the Government in order to resolve a debarment proceeding, the debarring official shall access the website (available at www.cpars.csd.disa.mil, then select FAPIIS) and enter the requested information.

(2) The debarring official is responsible for the timely submission, within 3 working days, and accuracy of the documentation regarding the administrative agreement.

(3) With regard to information that may be covered by a disclosure exemption under the Freedom of Information Act, the debarring official shall follow the procedures at 9.105-2(b)(2)(iv).

United States Code Annotated

Administrative determinations, see 41 USCA § 257.

Contract requirements, see 41 USCA § 254.

Contractor responsibilities, see 41 USCA § 57.

Contracts, planning, solicitation, evaluation, and award procedures, see 10 USCA § 2305.

Definitions, see 10 USCA § 2302, 41 USCA §§ 259, 403.

Determinations and decisions, see 10 USCA § 2310, 41 USCA § 262.

Kinds of contracts, see 10 USCA § 2306.

Planning and solicitation requirements, see 41 USCA § 253a.

Notes of Decisions

In general 2
Debarring official's decision 19
De facto debarment 7
Deference to agency interpretation 4
Double jeopardy 23
Due process of law 6
Equal protection of laws 21
Evidence 18

1 Validity

Federal acquisitions regulations governing debarment of government contractors are not unreasonable or unconstitutional. Joseph Const. Co. v. Veterans Admin. of U.S., 595 F. Supp. 448, 32 Cont. Cas. Fed. (CCH) P 73082 (N.D. Ill. 1984). United States ⊕→64.20

2 In general

Competition in Contracting Act (CICA) and the Federal Acquisition Regulations (FAR) implementing it do not allow contracting officer to eliminate competitors from initial competitive range if there is any reasonable chance that they will be selected. Federal Property and Administrative Services Act of 1949, § 301 et seq., as amended, 41 U.S.C.A. § 251 et seq.Birch & Davis Intern., Inc. v. Christopher, 4 F.3d 970, 39 Cont. Cas. Fed. (CCH) P 76561 (Fed. Cir. 1993). United States ⊕→64.20

Suspension and debarment of bidder for government contract occur when Government formally or constructively precludes contractor from participating in future, government contracts or when contracting official's decisions effectively prevent contractor from participating in that and future procurements. BMY, A Div. of HARSCO Corp. v. U.S., 693 F. Supp. 1232, 35 Cont. Cas. Fed. (CCH) P 75552 (D.D.C. 1988). United States ⊕→64.20

3 Purpose

Executive order providing for government-wide debarment and suspension of contractors who are debarred or suspended by particular agency was a managerial tool and not shown to be for the benefit of contractors, and thus did not provide basis for challenging government-wide debarment order on ground that, under the executive order, a prior agency debarment arising from the same circumstances should have been government-wide, precluding later imposition of the same penalty. Executive Order No. 12549, §§ 1 et seq., 1(a), 31 U.S.C.A. § 6101 note. Facchiano Const. Co., Inc. v. U.S. Dept. of Labor, 987 F.2d 206, 1 Wage & Hour Cas. 2d (BNA) 468, 39 Cont. Cas. Fed. (CCH) P 76542, 124 Lab. Cas. (CCH) P 35782 (3d Cir. 1993). United States ⊕→64.20

4 Deference to agency interpretation

Although agency's interpretation of its own regulations is entitled to considerable deference, court construed regulations dealing with debarment of government contractors with minimal deference; regulations were written and promulgated not only by Department of Defense, but also by General Services Administration and National Aeronautics and Space Administration, and interpretation of regulations was given by debarring official not by head of agency. Caiola v. Carroll, 851 F.2d 395, 399, 34 Cont. Cas. Fed. (CCH) P 75514 (D.C. Cir. 1988). Administrative Law And Procedure ⊕→413; United States ⊕→64.20

5 Retroactive or prospective application

Executive order providing for government-wide debarment and suspension of government contractors debarred or suspended by particular agency did not become effective until issuance of guidelines by Office of Management and Budget (OMB) and subsequent implementing regulations and, in the interim, Department of Labor (DOL) properly continued operating according to its existing regulations. Executive Order No. 12549, § 6, 31 U.S.C.A. § 6101 note. Facchiano Const. Co., Inc. v. U.S. Dept. of Labor, 987 F.2d 206, 1 Wage & Hour Cas. 2d (BNA) 468, 39 Cont. Cas. Fed. (CCH) P 76542, 124 Lab. Cas. (CCH) P 35782 (3d Cir. 1993). United States ☞64.20

6 Due process of law

Allowing Department of Housing and Urban Development (HUD) employee to act as an advisor to the hearing official, even though he had previously participated in the investigation and prosecution of matter involving another property owned by contractor, did not violate contractor's due process rights, absent showing advisor exerted any improper influence upon the hearing official, that hearing official was otherwise biased as a result of any HUD participant, that other matter entered into debarring official's determination, or that decision was tainted or otherwise rendered unsupportable by roles of any other HUD employees participating in debarment proceeding. U.S.C.A. Const.Amend. 14. Marshall v. Cuomo, 192 F.3d 473 (4th Cir. 1999). Constitutional Law ☞276(2); United States ☞64.20

In recognition of the serious nature of debarment, the FAR sets out detailed procedures to ensure that this sanction, which is intended to safeguard the integrity of the acquisitions process, itself is applied in conformity with principles of fundamental fairness. Accordingly, the debarment procedures specified in the FAR provide for an opportunity to appear with counsel, submit documentary evidence, and confront any person the agency presents, if it is found that the contractor's submission in opposition raises a genuine dispute over facts material to the proposed debarment. Sameena Inc. v. U.S. Air Force, 147 F.3d 1148, 42 Cont. Cas. Fed. (CCH) P 77335 (9th Cir. 1998)

Agricultural Stabilization and Conservation Service (ASCS) debarment procedures comported with fundamental fairness requirements of due process even though they were not conducted by administrative law judge; under regulations, debarring officer was not member of investigative branch of agency and regulations did not facially merge functions of prosecutor and decision maker. U.S.C.A. Const. Amend. 14. Girard v. Klopfenstein, 930 F.2d 738 (9th Cir. 1991). Constitutional Law ☞291.6; United States ☞64.20

Bidder for Navy contract was not deprived of due process, though it was not given opportunity to respond to charges before contracting officer disqualified it for appearance of impropriety, where bidder participated in protest hearing conducted by General Accounting Office. U.S.C.A. Const. Amend. 5. Compliance Corp. v. U.S., 960 F.2d 157, 37 Cont. Cas. Fed. (CCH) P 76296 (Fed. Cir. 1992). Constitutional Law ☞276(2); United States ☞64.20

To sustain a denial of contractor's liberty interest by debarment, it must be established that contract awards to contractor involve a threat to interests of Government. Peter Kiewit Sons' Co. v. U. S. Army Corps of Engineers, 534 F. Supp. 1139, 29 Cont. Cas. Fed. (CCH) P 82291 (D.D.C. 1982), judgment rev'd, 714 F.2d 163, 31 Cont. Cas. Fed. (CCH) P 71395, 1983-2 Trade Cas. (CCH) ¶ 65528 (D.C. Cir. 1983). United States ☞64.20

Debarment proceedings did not violate procedural due process rights of defense contractor where proceedings were conducted in compliance with Department of Defense procedural requirements, contractor was given opportunity to submit information and argument in opposition to proposed debarment and chose to do so in writing, and no genuine dispute of material fact was created by contractor's opposition to debarment as would require fact-finding hearing, even though contractor contended that lack of opportunity to cross-examine government witnesses violated its due process rights. U.S.C.A. Const.Amend. 5. IMCO, Inc. v. U.S., 33 Fed. Cl. 312 (1995), judgment aff'd, 97 F.3d 1422 (Fed. Cir. 1996). Constitutional Law ☞276(2); United States ☞64.20

7 De facto debarment

De facto debarment of contractor from bidding on government contracts, although final action, was illegal and could not form the basis for dissolution of interim action, the ongoing debarment proceeding. Peter Kiewit Sons' Co. v. U.S. Army Corps of Engineers, 714 F.2d 163, 230, 31 Cont. Cas. Fed. (CCH) P 71395, 1983-2 Trade Cas. (CCH) ¶ 65528 (D.C. Cir. 1983). United States ☞64.20

"De facto debarment" occurs when an agency bars a contractor from competing for government contracts for a certain period of time without following the applicable debarment procedures found in the Federal Acquisition Regulations (FAR). 48 C.F.R. § 9.406-3. TLT Const. Corp. v. U.S., 50 Fed. Cl. 212 (2001). United States ☞64.20

To succeed on a claim of de facto debarment, bidder must demonstrate a systematic effort by the procuring agency to reject all of the bidder's contract bids. TLT Const. Corp. v. U.S., 50 Fed. Cl. 212 (2001). United States ☞64.20

Government's failure to pursue discussions with disappointed bidder over its past performance did not amount to a de facto debarment, absent evidence that bidder was being disqualified from government contracts on a systematic basis. TLT Const. Corp. v. U.S., 50 Fed. Cl. 212 (2001). United States ☞64.20

Two options exist to establish a de facto debarment claim: (1) by an agency's statement that it will not award the contractor future contracts; or (2) by an agency's conduct demonstrating that it will not award the contractor future contracts. TLT Const. Corp. v. U.S., 50 Fed. Cl. 212 (2001). United States ☞64.20

To establish a de facto debarment claim, a disappointed bidder must show evidence of a systematic effort by the procuring agency to reject all of the bidder's contract bids; showing may be accomplished by evidence of an agency's statement that it will not award any contracts to the bidder in the future as well as by an agency's conduct to that effect. CRC Marine Services, Inc. v. U.S., 41 Fed. Cl. 66, 42 Cont. Cas. Fed. (CCH) P 77310 (1998). United States ☞64.20

Low bidder on solicitation for transportation by barge of reactor vessels and steam generators did not establish that agency's decision to award contract to other bidder constituted unlawful de facto debarment, based on allegation that contracting officer's finding of low bidder's nonresponsibility was based on its prior debarment. CRC Marine Services, Inc. v. U.S., 41 Fed. Cl. 66, 42 Cont. Cas. Fed. (CCH) P 77310 (1998). United States ☞64.20

Bidder on spot bid solicitation for shipment by barge of nuclear reactor vessels and steam generators failed to establish that rejection of its bid as "disqualified" constituted unlawful de facto debarment; rather, evidence established that bidder failed to meet solicitation's requirements. CRC Marine Services, Inc. v. U.S., 41 Fed. Cl. 66, 42 Cont. Cas. Fed. (CCH) P 77310 (1998). United States ☞64.20

Unsuccessful bidder failed to show systematic effort by procuring government agency to reject all of bidder's contract bids, as required to show de facto debarment. Stapp Towing Inc. v. U.S., 34 Fed. Cl. 300, 40 Cont. Cas. Fed. (CCH) P 76839 (1995). United States ☞64.20

A de facto suspension or debarment from participation in government business arises when procuring body refuses, for indefinite period of time, to grant awards to particular contractor, but successive determinations of nonresponsibility on same grounds are improper, and procuring agency must initiate suspension or debarment procedures at earliest practical date following first determination of nonresponsibility. 18 U.S.C.A. § 287; Small Business Act, § 2 [2–18], 15 U.S.C.A. §§ 631–647. Shermco Industries, Inc. v. U.S., 6 Cl. Ct. 588, 32 Cont. Cas. Fed. (CCH) P 73068 (1984). United States ☞64.20

8 Exhaustion of administrative remedies

District court, in voiding ongoing administrative proceeding pertaining to debarment of contractor from bidding on

Even if Office of Federal Contract Compliance Programs (OFCCP) admitted that it had blanket policy of denying all waiver requests, federal contractor which sought waiver from OFCCP would be required to exhaust administrative remedies before bringing suit, since contractor's administrative remedies did not end with OFCCP. Trinity Industries, Inc. v. Reich, 33 F.3d 942 (8th Cir. 1994). United States ☞64.15; United States ☞64.20

Exhaustion of administrative remedies is not required when constitutionality or statutory validity of Agricultural Stabilization and Conservation Service (ASCS) debarment hearing regulations are challenged. Girard v. Klopfenstein, 930 F.2d 738 (9th Cir. 1991). Administrative Law And Procedure ☞229; United States ☞64.20

President and sales manager of farmers cooperative were not required to exhaust their administrative remedies before challenging constitutional validity of debarment hearing by Agricultural Stabilization and Conservation Service (ASCS); exhaustion of remedies would not have assisted court in determining validity of allowing hearing before allegedly biased administrative officer rather than administrative law judge. Girard v. Klopfenstein, 930 F.2d 738 (9th Cir. 1991). Administrative Law And Procedure ⟨key⟩229; United States ⟨key⟩64.20

Congressional interference with proceedings to debar contractor from bidding on government contracts did not so taint the administrative process that said contractor's rights were clearly and significantly violated; accordingly, the finality and exhaustion requirements, in regard to review of an agency action, were not dispensed with. Peter Kiewit Sons' Co. v. U.S. Army Corps of Engineers, 714 F.2d 163, 230, 31 Cont. Cas. Fed. (CCH) P 71395, 1983-2 Trade Cas. (CCH) ¶ 65528 (D.C. Cir. 1983). United States ⟨key⟩64.20

9 Res judicata and collateral estoppel

Causes of action by the Department of Housing and Urban Development (HUD) debarring contractor from HUD programs and by the Department of Labor (DOL) debarring contractor government-wide for labor standards violations were not the same for res judicata purposes, nor were issues identical for collateral estoppel effect, where HUD debarment was based solely on criminal conviction of officer of contractor for mail fraud in violation of HUD regulations, while DOL was seeking to debar contractor and three officers based on willful and aggravated violations of Davis Bacon Act or related Acts. Davis-Bacon Act, §§ 1-6, as amended; 40 U.S.C.A. §§ 276a to 276a-5; 40 U.S.C.A. § 276c; Contract Work Hours and Safety Standards Act, §§ 101-107, as amended, 40 U.S.C.A. §§ 327–333; Portal-to-Portal Act of 1947, § 6(a), as amended, 29 U.S.C.A. § 255(a). Facchiano Const. Co., Inc. v. U.S. Dept. of Labor, 987 F.2d 206, 1 Wage & Hour Cas. 2d (BNA) 468, 39 Cont. Cas. Fed. (CCH) P 76542, 124 Lab. Cas. (CCH) P 35782 (3d Cir. 1993). United States ⟨key⟩64.20

The Department of Labor (DOL) and the Department of Housing and Urban Development (HUD) were not in "privity" for purposes of giving res judicata effect to HUD order debarring contractor from HUD contracts, so as to preclude later government-wide debarment order by DOL; since scope of HUD's enforcement authority was limited to HUD programs, while DOL had broad delegated authority to debar contractors from all federal contracts for labor standards violations, HUD did not have authority to represent United States in final adjudication of the issue in controversy. Reorganization Plan No. 14 of 1950, 5 U.S.C.A.App. § 1; Department of Housing and Urban Development Act, § 7(d), 42 U.S.C.A. § 3535(d); Davis-Bacon Act, §§ 1-6, as amended, 40 U.S.C.A. §§ 276a to 276a-5; 40 U.S.C.A. § 276c; Contract Work Hours and Safety Standards Act, §§ 101-107, as amended, 40 U.S.C.A. §§ 327–333; Portal-to-Portal Act of 1947, § 6(a), as amended, 29 U.S.C.A. § 255(a). Facchiano Const. Co., Inc. v. U.S. Dept. of Labor, 987 F.2d 206, 1 Wage & Hour Cas. 2d (BNA) 468, 39 Cont. Cas. Fed. (CCH) P 76542, 124 Lab. Cas. (CCH) P 35782 (3d Cir. 1993). United States ⟨key⟩64.20

10 Injunctions—In general

Superfund contractor was not entitled to preliminary injunction against Environmental Protection Agency debarment proceeding because it failed to establish likelihood of success on merits of claim that EPA had denied due process and had initiated debarment proceeding for improper purpose after contractor had been acquitted on criminal charges in connection with clean-up contract. U.S.C.A. Const. Amends. 5, 14. Baranowski v. E.P.A., 699 F. Supp. 1119, 29 Env't. Rep. Cas. (BNA) 1213 (E.D. Pa. 1988), judgment aff'd, 902 F.2d 1558 (3d Cir. 1990). Environmental Law ⟨key⟩701

Statute providing that no injunction or other similar process shall be issued against administrator of small business administration or his property did not deprive Claims Court of jurisdiction to enjoin, on preliminary basis, Department of Defense from awarding procurement contract to anyone other than apparent low bidder, even though proposed debarment of contractor resulted in SBA decision to discontinue its efforts to award bidder certificate of competency; declining to follow Speco Corp. v. U.S., 2 Cl. Ct. 335, 31 Cont. Cas. Fed. (CCH) P 71137 (1983) (rejected by, Cavalier Clothes, Inc. v. U.S., 810 F.2d 1108, 33 Cont. Cas. Fed. (CCH) P 74983 (Fed. Cir. 1987)). Small Business Act, § 2[5](b), as amended, 15 U.S.C.A. § 634(b). Sterlingwear of Boston, Inc. v. U.S., 10 Cl. Ct. 644, 33 Cont. Cas. Fed. (CCH) P 74560 (1986). Federal Courts ⟨key⟩1080

11 Injunctions—Preliminary injunctions and restraining orders

For purposes of determining whether to grant temporary restraining order, debarment from being awarded federal government contracts is not sufficient to establish "irreparable harm." Ali v. U.S., 932 F. Supp. 1206 (N.D. Cal. 1996). Injunction ☞150

Contractor's officer was not entitled to temporary restraining order against his expired debarment by Department of Health and Human Services (DHHS), which had precluded officer from being awarded government contracts; officer was not likely to succeed on the merits of his challenge to debarment, as administrative record revealed substantial evidence upon which debarring official could have concluded that contractor committed forgery and that officer knew or should have known of it, officer apparently received all due process guarantees required by debarment regulations, and government agencies had not waived all fraud claims against officer, and balance of hardships did not tip in officer's favor, as officer had delayed two years in filing action and seeking injunction, any harm to officer was economic, speculative, or both, and government had strong interest in maintaining integrity of its contractors. 48 C.F.R. §§ 9.402(a), 9.406-2(c), 9.406-3(b)(1), (d)(1), (d)(2)(i), 9.406-5(b). Ali v. U.S., 932 F. Supp. 1206 (N.D. Cal. 1996). Injunction ☞150

Notwithstanding debarment of apparent low bidder for Government contract, bidder was entitled to preliminary injunction to enjoin Government from awarding procurement contract to anyone other than bidder where denial of relief would visit immediate and irreparable harm on bidder, challenge of debarment proceeding in United States district court was not adequate "remedy at law," as remedy in district court would be equitable, bidder was likely to succeed on merits, and grant of preliminary injunction was in public interest. Sterlingwear of Boston, Inc. v. U.S., 11 Cl. Ct. 517, 33 Cont. Cas. Fed. (CCH) P 74956 (1987). Injunction ☞138.63

Public interest favored grant of preliminary injunction to prevent Department of Defense from awarding government contract to anyone other than apparent low bidder based on alleged lack of rationality in decision to seek debarment of bidder. Sterlingwear of Boston, Inc. v. U.S., 10 Cl. Ct. 644, 33 Cont. Cas. Fed. (CCH) P 74560 (1986). Injunction ☞138.63

Apparent low bidder on defense procurement contract had no adequate remedy at law for proposed debarment based on commonality of management with another corporation which had defaulted on its government contracts and, therefore, bidder was entitled to preliminary injunction to prevent Department of Defense from awarding contract to anyone other than bidder. Sterlingwear of Boston, Inc. v. U.S., 10 Cl. Ct. 644, 33 Cont. Cas. Fed. (CCH) P 74560 (1986). Injunction ☞138.63

Denial of preliminary injunction to prevent Department of Defense from awarding procurement contract to anyone other than apparent low bidder would visit immediate and irreparable harm on bidder where bidder would need to engage in extensive postaward activities to restore status quo, particularly in light of Department's failure to demonstrate any injury to itself if preliminary injunction were granted pending definitive determination on proposed debarment of bidder based on alleged "commonality with management" with another corporation which had defaulted on its contracts. Sterlingwear of Boston, Inc. v. U.S., 10 Cl. Ct. 644, 33 Cont. Cas. Fed. (CCH) P 74560 (1986). Injunction ☞138.63

Apparent low bidder on defense procurement contract presented evidence reflecting substantial likelihood of success on merits of its claim that there was no rational basis for decision to reject bid for lack of tenacity, perseverance and capacity based on alleged "commonality" between bidder and another corporation which had defaulted on two government contracts and decision to recommend debarment on identical grounds and, therefore, bidder was entitled to preliminary injunction to prevent Department of Defense from awarding contract to anyone other than low bidder. Sterlingwear of Boston, Inc. v. U.S., 10 Cl. Ct. 644, 33 Cont. Cas. Fed. (CCH) P 74560 (1986). Injunction ☞147

12 Jurisdiction

Any issue regarding ability of deputy administrator of Agricultural Stabilization and Conservation Service (ASCS) to serve as impartial debarring officer became moot upon his resignation. Girard v. Klopfenstein, 930 F.2d 738 (9th Cir. 1991). Federal Courts ☞13

Contractor's claim that wrongful debarment by General Services Administration (GSA) unfairly excluded him from possibility of entering future government procurement contracts established only tangential connection between alleged wrongful act by government and procurement contract, and, thus, Board of Contract Appeals did not have jurisdiction over claim under Contract Disputes Act. Contract Disputes Act, § 402(a), as amended, 41

U.S.C.A. § 602(a). Schickler v. Davis, 10 Fed. Appx. 944 (Fed. Cir. 2001). United States ⊂64.20; United States ⊂73(15).

Court of Federal Claims does not have jurisdiction to review propriety of agency's decision to debar contractor; such challenge must be brought in district court under Administrative Procedure Act. 5 U.S.C.A. §§ 701–706; 28 U.S.C.A. § 1491(a)(1). IMCO, Inc. v. U.S., 97 F.3d 1422 (Fed. Cir. 1996). United States ⊂64.60(1)

Court of Federal Claims exceeded its jurisdiction in reviewing propriety of actual debarment from government contracting, when only proposed debarment rendered contractor ineligible for contract award. IMCO, Inc. v. U.S., 97 F.3d 1422 (Fed. Cir. 1996). United States ⊂64.60(3.1)

Contractor who brought suit for contract damages against the United States could not raise debarment issue in the Court of Federal Claims, where debarment did not interfere with the contract at issue, but only served to preclude future contracts Medina Const., Ltd. v. U.S., 43 Fed. Cl. 537 (1999). Federal Courts ⊂1073.1

Jurisdiction in the Court of Federal Claims to consider an agency decision to debar a contractor is appropriate, within carefully defined limits, only in the context of affording complete relief in bid protest claims. Medina Const., Ltd. v. U.S., 43 Fed. Cl. 537 (1999). Federal Courts ⊂1073.1

The Tucker Act does not give the Court of Federal Claims jurisdiction to review the propriety of an agency's decision to debar a contractor; such a challenge must be brought in district court under the Administrative Procedures Act (APA). 5 U.S.C.A. § 551 et seq.; 28 U.S.C.A. §§ 1346, 1491. Medina Const., Ltd. v. U.S., 43 Fed. Cl. 537 (1999). Federal Courts ⊂1141

Claims Court did not have bid protest jurisdiction over complaint alleging that action of contracting officer in requesting that debarment proceedings be instituted effectively prohibited apparent low bidder from being awarded contract and any other contract without due process of law, as any hearing provided by Department of Defense Regulations would not stay any action of contracting officer or small business administration. 28 U.S.C.A. §§ 1491, 1491(a)(3); U.S.C.A. Const.Amends. 5, 14. Sterlingwear of Boston, Inc. v. U.S., 10 Cl. Ct. 644, 33 Cont. Cas. Fed. (CCH) P 74560 (1986). Federal Courts ⊂1076

13 Parties

Only proper defendant, in helicopter owner's action alleging wrongful debarment of Department of Interior contract work, was Secretary of Interior. 5 U.S.C.A. § 702. Dynamic Aviation v. Department of Interior, 898 F. Supp. 11 (D.D.C. 1995), aff'd, 132 F.3d 1481 (D.C. Cir. 1997). United States ⊂64.20

14 Procedures, generally

The Air Force should have followed its own regulation, calling for notice and a hearing before debarring a supplier from bidding for contracts for a period of years, when the supplier raised a genuine issue of fact challenging the debarment; the supplier presented evidence that a debarred person was mistakenly listed as an officer of the supplier, and that if the debarred person was not considered an officer the supplier's answer to questions regarding its prior procurement record would be correct and the basis for its debarment would be removed. 48 C.F.R. § 9.406-3(b). Sameena Inc. v. U.S. Air Force, 147 F.3d 1148, 42 Cont. Cas. Fed. (CCH) P 77335 (9th Cir. 1998). United States ⊂64.20

Concept of "fundamental fairness," within meaning of Federal Acquisition Regulations providing that debarment procedures established by government agencies must be consistent with principles of fundamental fairness, includes right to impartial decision maker. Girard v. Klopfenstein, 930 F.2d 738 (9th Cir. 1991). United States ⊂64.20

Risk of error in government contract bidder suspension or debarment proceeding based on charges of false statements and fraudulent acts or conduct in nature of fraud in performance of contracts is great and calls for pinpointing of specific acts, right of confrontation and cross-examination of witnesses. U.S.C.A. Const.Amends. 5, 14. ATL, Inc. v. U.S., 736 F.2d 677, 32 Cont. Cas. Fed. (CCH) P 72528 (Fed. Cir. 1984). United States ⊂64.20

15 Notice of charges

Impropriety of Government's failure to provide contractor with requisite notice and opportunity to be heard on alleged debarment for more than four months was not cured by after-the-fact issuance of notice of proposed debarment or by another debarment hearing. Peter Kiewit Sons' Co. v. U. S. Army Corps of Engineers, 534 F. Supp. 1139, 29 Cont. Cas. Fed. (CCH) P 82291 (D.D.C. 1982), judgment rev'd, 714 F.2d 163, 31 Cont. Cas. Fed. (CCH) P 71395, 1983-2 Trade Cas. (CCH) ¶ 65528 (D.C. Cir. 1983). United States ☞64.20

Notice of proposed debarment precludes issuing agency from awarding contracts to contractor pending resolution of debarment proceeding. Baranowski v. E.P.A., 699 F. Supp. 1119, 29 Env't. Rep. Cas. (BNA) 1213 (E.D. Pa. 1988), judgment aff'd, 902 F.2d 1558 (3d Cir. 1990). United States ☞64.20

16 Hearings

HUD debarment from participation in HUD-sponsored contracts was sufficiently adjudicatory and final to enable debarred construction companies to raise preclusion defense in later Department of Labor debarment proceedings seeking to disqualify construction companies from all government contracts, where companies had had opportunity to present their case to administrative law judge in HUD proceedings and a judge filed detailed opinion containing factual findings and rulings. Facchiano v. U.S. Dept. of Labor, 859 F.2d 1163, 28 Wage & Hour Cas. (BNA) 1529, 35 Cont. Cas. Fed. (CCH) P 75572, 110 Lab. Cas. (CCH) P 35140 (3d Cir. 1988). Administrative Law And Procedure ☞501; United States ☞64.20

Hearing officer, in action to debar bidder from purchasing surplus property from federal government, did not violate statute prohibiting him from acting as prosecuting officer, even if statute was applicable to proceeding; though officer participated in questioning of witnesses, questioning was similar to that generally permitted trial judge, with questions asked for clarification or to move proceedings along. 5 U.S.C.A. § 554. Leitman v. McAusland, 934 F.2d 46, 37 Cont. Cas. Fed. (CCH) P 76107 (4th Cir. 1991). Administrative Law And Procedure ☞445; United States ☞64.20

Agricultural Stabilization and Conservation Service (ASCS) debarment hearing is not statutorily required and, thus, Administrative Procedure Act does not apply to such hearings so as to require that administrative law judge preside, even if hearing is "on the record." 5 U.S.C.A. § 554(a). Girard v. Klopfenstein, 930 F.2d 738 (9th Cir. 1991). Administrative Law And Procedure ☞470; United States ☞64.20

Person subject to debarment for improper conduct in performing government contract has no statutory right to evidentiary hearing; debarment is within inherent authority of contracting agencies and, as such, it is informal procedure for which hearing is not required. 5 U.S.C.A. § 554(a). Girard v. Klopfenstein, 930 F.2d 738 (9th Cir. 1991). United States ☞64.20

Defense logistics agency was not required to hold hearing in debarment proceeding on issues of whether alleged bid rigging actually occurred and whether contractor was presently responsible by virtue of irrevocable trust agreement transferring all of alleged bid rigger's right, title, and interest in company to trustee. Robinson v. Cheney, 876 F.2d 152, 277, 35 Cont. Cas. Fed. (CCH) P 75666 (D.C. Cir. 1989). Administrative Law And Procedure ☞470; United States ☞64.20

Government contractor may not, without hearing, be debarred or suspended from qualification for government work on grounds of lack of integrity or fraud. ATL, Inc. v. U.S., 736 F.2d 677, 32 Cont. Cas. Fed. (CCH) P 72528 (Fed. Cir. 1984). United States ☞64.20

Federal Acquisition Regulations (FARs) provide for automatic debarment in the case of conviction or civil judgment against contractor; because another fact finder has already found one of the bases for debarment beyond a reasonable doubt or by a preponderance of the evidence, there is no statutory, regulatory, or due process requirement of additional hearing to determine the underlying facts. U.S.C.A. Const.Amend. 14; 48 C.F.R. §§ 9.406-2(a), 9.406-3(d). Waterhouse v. U.S., 874 F. Supp. 5 (D.D.C. 1994). United States ☞64.20

Evidence that contracting officer received goods and services from supplier and never paid for them by cash or currency and that he gave an automobile to the supplier's church, taking a tax deduction, established basis for debarment and did not raise any genuine issues requiring debarring official to hold evidentiary hearing. 48 C.F.R. §§ 9.406-2(c), 9.406-3(b)(2). Waterhouse v. U.S., 874 F. Supp. 5 (D.D.C. 1994). United States ☞64.20

Principles of fundamental fairness were not violated in debarment proceedings against bidder for alleged anticompetitive activities in connection with government surplus auctions, even though financial constraints prevented bidder from appearing in person at hearing held in another city; defendant was afforded opportunity to appear via telephone, was represented by two attorneys and had unlimited opportunity to testify and to introduce evidence on his own behalf; situs chosen was not arbitrary, and bidder was not entitled to have hearing officer and witnesses come to him. U.S.C.A. Const.Amend. 5. Textor v. Cheney, 757 F. Supp. 51, 37 Cont. Cas. Fed. (CCH) P 76028 (D.D.C. 1991). United States ☞64.20

Combined with proper notice of pending debarment proceeding, hearing requirement can be met by providing federal government contractor with opportunity to present information or argument, in person, in writing or through representation. U.S.C.A. Const.Amend. 5. Joseph Const. Co. v. Veterans Admin. of U.S., 595 F. Supp. 448, 32 Cont. Cas. Fed. (CCH) P 73082 (N.D. Ill. 1984). United States ☞64.20

Contractor was not entitled to appear with counsel, submit documentary evidence, present witnesses, and confront agency witnesses in debarment hearing, absent determination by agency that contractor's submission in opposition raised a genuine dispute over facts material to the suspension. 48 C.F.R. § 9.407-3(b)(2). Lion Raisins, Inc. v. U.S., 51 Fed. Cl. 238 (2001). United States ☞64.20

Fact that different government agency concludes that contractor is responsible does not itself create genuine dispute of fact as will warrant fact finding proceeding to be held in connection with debarment proceedings instituted against contractor; whether nor not contractor is responsible is determination which debarment official is empowered to make. IMCO, Inc. v. U.S., 33 Fed. Cl. 312 (1995), judgment aff'd, 97 F.3d 1422 (Fed. Cir. 1996). Administrative Law And Procedure ☞489.1; United States ☞64.20

Debarment official did not err in concluding that material facts were not in dispute and proceeding with disbarment of defense contractor without holding fact finding proceeding where contractor's arguments against validity of default terminations were primarily of two kinds, based on financial inability and onerous quality verification requirements, and it was not unreasonable for debarment official to conclude that relevant evidence was primarily in written form and that contractor's cross-examination of government witnesses was pointless. IMCO, Inc. v. U.S., 33 Fed. Cl. 312 (1995), judgment aff'd, 97 F.3d 1422 (Fed. Cir. 1996). Administrative Law And Procedure ☞489.1; United States ☞64.20

Supplementation of administrative record was not warranted in action challenging debarment of defense contractor where no relevant information was ignored in making determinations, reasons for debarment were clearly expressed in debarment decision memorandum and could be traced to existing administrative record, and proffered documents sought to be added to record would not have affected result. IMCO, Inc. v. U.S., 33 Fed. Cl. 312 (1995), judgment aff'd, 97 F.3d 1422 (Fed. Cir. 1996). Administrative Law And Procedure ☞506; United States ☞64.20

Presentation by defense contractor of matters in opposition to proposed debarment of contractor did not require hearing where with respect to contractor's delinquency rate and total number of contracts debarment official had contractor's figures before him and figures were not seriously contested by procuring department or Procurement Fraud Division (PFD). IMCO, Inc. v. U.S., 33 Fed. Cl. 312 (1995), judgment aff'd, 97 F.3d 1422 (Fed. Cir. 1996). United States ☞64.20

Debarring official's decision not to hold full fact-finding proceeding was improper where it was made prior to time contractor submitted written opposition to proposed debarment. Sterlingwear of Boston, Inc. v. U.S., 11 Cl. Ct. 879, 34 Cont. Cas. Fed. (CCH) P 75210 (1987). United States ☞64.20

17 Presumptions and burden of proof

Government contractor has burden of demonstrating, to satisfaction of debarring official, that sufficient mitigating factors make debarment unnecessary. 48 C.F.R. § 9.406-1(a)(1) (10). Burke v. U.S. E.P.A., 127 F. Supp. 2d 235, 51 Env't. Rep. Cas. (BNA) 2210 (D.D.C. 2001). United States ☞64.20

Even in the absence of conviction or civil judgment against government contractor, contractor may be debarred, based on preponderance of the evidence, for cause of serious and compelling nature, but debarring official must give notice to contractor or proposal to debar and must invite the contractor to submit information or argument in opposition to the proposed debarment. 48 C.F.R. §§ 9.406-2(c), 9.406-3(c)(4). Waterhouse v. U.S., 874 F. Supp. 5 (D.D.C. 1994). United States ☜64.20

Charges against bidder need only be supported by preponderance of evidence in order to support debarment from participation in government surplus auctions. Textor v. Cheney, 757 F. Supp. 51, 37 Cont. Cas. Fed. (CCH) P 76028 (D.D.C. 1991). United States ☜64.20

18 Evidence

Affidavit submitted by the contract specialist assigned to an Air Force procurement of laptop computers was admissible in an administrative hearing to determine if a bidder should be debarred for providing a false statement regarding prior debarments; the affidavit set forth facts linked to the present case and established the status of the specialist to manage the procurement in question. Sameena Inc. v. U.S. Air Force, 147 F.3d 1148, 42 Cont. Cas. Fed. (CCH) P 77335 (9th Cir. 1998). United States ☜64.20

Government met its burden of showing by preponderance of evidence in debarment proceeding that contractor participated in bid rigging scheme, through unsworn statement of indicted government contract official that contractor's sole shareholder orchestrated bids by suppliers, three of which he controlled, on contract for camouflage pants and paid official $10,000, in two $5,000 installments, for his help in directing contract, notwithstanding statements by contractor's employees denying any personal knowledge of either bid rigging or improper payments; official's statement, standing alone, provided sufficient proof even though official was seeking leniency or immunity, and while shareholder had probably acted alone and made illegal payments off company's books, that misconduct could be imputed to company pursuant to unchallenged regulation. Robinson v. Cheney, 876 F.2d 152, 277, 35 Cont. Cas. Fed. (CCH) P 75666 (D.C. Cir. 1989). United States ☜64.20

Testimony of witnesses in superfund contractor's criminal trial, as well as exhibits introduced in that trial, could have probative value in subsequent debarment proceeding even though criminal prosecution failed to prove contractor guilty beyond reasonable doubt. Baranowski v. E.P.A., 699 F. Supp. 1119, 29 Env't. Rep. Cas. (BNA) 1213 (E.D. Pa. 1988), judgment aff'd, 902 F.2d 1558 (3d Cir. 1990). United States ☜64.20

19 Debarring official's decision

Proposed debarment of government contractor, which rendered its bid ineligible for award of federal contract, was not arbitrary and capricious, and, thus, government did not breach its implied contractual duty to consider bid fairly and honestly, where there was no evidence of bad faith by procurement fraud division officer making recommendation. IMCO, Inc. v. U.S., 97 F.3d 1422 (Fed. Cir. 1996). United States ☜64.20; United States ☜64.40(2)

If, after receiving information from contractor, debarring official concludes that there is no genuine dispute over the material facts, he make a decision to debar based on all the information of the record. 48 C.F.R. §§ 9.406-3(d). Waterhouse v. U.S., 874 F. Supp. 5 (D.D.C. 1994). United States ☜64.20

20 Judicial review

Defense Logistics Agency's determination that meat company and owner of company should be debarred from contracting with government for period of three years, based on special assistant's consideration of relevant factors established by administrative regulation, required district court to uphold agency action on review and district court's disagreement with determination of weight of mitigating factors and its construction of evidence exceeded its limited scope of review and was substitution of its own judgment for that of agency. Shane Meat Co., Inc. v. U.S. Dept. of Defense, 800 F.2d 334, 91 A.L.R. Fed. 857 (3d Cir. 1986). Administrative Law And Procedure ☜758; United States ☜64.60(3.1)

District judge reviewing decision of Defense Logistics Agency debarring meat company from contracting with executive branch of government does not sit as agency official responsible for weighing evidence and making initial debarment decision; rather, trial judge is limited in his authority to finding whether agency action was rational, based on relevant factors, and within agency's statutory authority. Shane Meat Co., Inc. v. U.S. Dept. of Defense, 800 F.2d 334, 91 A.L.R. Fed. 857 (3d Cir. 1986)

Court of Appeals' review of decision of Department of Housing and Urban Development (HUD) to debar former officer of suspended HUD coinsured lender from participating in primary and lower tier covered transactions throughout executive branch of federal government for three years was governed by traditional arbitrary and capricious standard as set forth in Administrative Procedures Act (APA); review was highly deferential, and Court of Appeals had to assume validity of agency action. 5 U.S.C.A. § 706(2)(A). Kisser v. Cisneros, 14 F.3d 615, 619 (D.C. Cir. 1994). United States ⬤53(9)

General Accounting Office, under its bid protest function, does not review protests that an agency improperly proposed a contractor for debarment, as the contracting agency is the appropriate forum for suspension and debarment disputes. Triton Electronic Enterprises, Inc., B-294221, B-294248, B-294249, 2004 CPD ¶ 139 (Comp. Gen. 2004)

21 Equal protection of laws

Mere allegation that moving and storage companies were denied make-up tonnage following their removal from Department of Army suspended contractor list when acquitted of antitrust violations did not establish protectible Fifth Amendment equal protection right, as no fundamental interest or suspect classifications were involved and discretionary element of regulations was rationally related to Department's legitimate interest in ensuring efficient storage and carrier service. U.S.C.A. Const.Amend. 5. Coleman American Moving Services, Inc. v. Weinberger, 716 F. Supp. 1405, 36 Cont. Cas. Fed. (CCH) P 75786 (M.D. Ala. 1989). Constitutional Law ⬤225.4; United States ⬤64.20

Procedure affording companies who have not been indicted for antitrust violations a hearing prior to their placement on list of suspended government contractors, while denying hearing to companies who have been indicted, did not violate equal protection rights of indicted companies as reason for hearing was to determine if suspension would be rationally related to government objectives and fact of indictment provided sufficient reason to proceed with suspension. U.S.C.A. Const.Amend. 5. Coleman American Moving Services, Inc. v. Weinberger, 716 F. Supp. 1405, 36 Cont. Cas. Fed. (CCH) P 75786 (M.D. Ala. 1989). Constitutional Law ⬤225.4; United States ⬤64.20

22 Right to counsel

In recognition of the serious nature of debarment, the FAR sets out detailed procedures to ensure that this sanction, which is intended to safeguard the integrity of the acquisitions process, itself is applied in conformity with principles of fundamental fairness. Accordingly, the debarment procedures specified in the FAR provide for an opportunity to appear with counsel, submit documentary evidence, and confront any person the agency presents, if it is found that the contractor's submission in opposition raises a genuine dispute over facts material to the proposed debarment. Sameena Inc. v. U.S. Air Force, 147 F.3d 1148, 42 Cont. Cas. Fed. (CCH) P 77335 (9th Cir. 1998)

Moving and storage companies which were placed on Department of Army's suspended bidders list following filing of antitrust indictments against them were not deprived of their right to counsel, as such right extends only to cases where deprivation of personal liberty may result from proceeding and companies' antitrust exposure was limited to property loss. U.S.C.A. Const.Amend. 6. Coleman American Moving Services, Inc. v. Weinberger, 716 F. Supp. 1405, 36 Cont. Cas. Fed. (CCH) P 75786 (M.D. Ala. 1989). Criminal Law ⬤641.2(4)

23 Double jeopardy

Debarment of government contractor for 26 months was not sufficiently punitive to implicate double jeopardy clause and require the dismissal of criminal prosecution against him, as contractor failed to show disbarment was disproportionate to benefits received by government in protecting it against effects of willful failures to perform in accordance with terms of government contracts, effects of history of failures to perform, and adverse effect of having government contract with irresponsible contractor. U.S.C.A. Const. Amend. 5; 48 C.F.R. §§ 9.402(b), 9.403, 9.406-2, 9.406-3(b)(1), (d)(3). U.S. v. Hatfield, 108 F.3d 67 (4th Cir. 1997). Double Jeopardy ⬤24

Debarment of government contractor did not have to be subjected to a "particularized assessment" to determine whether it was punitive for double jeopardy purposes, where government did not seek the return of particular quantity of funds but instead sought to protect the quality of its acquisition programs. 48 C.F.R. §§ 9.402(b), 9.406-2(b)(1), (c), 9.406-4. U.S. v. Hatfield, 108 F.3d 67 (4th Cir. 1997). Double Jeopardy ⬤24

To determine whether debarment of government contractor is civil or criminal, for purposes of claim that debarment precluded criminal prosecution of double jeopardy grounds, court examines whether procedure was designed to be remedial, and whether remedy provided, even if designated as civil, is so unreasonable or excessive that it transforms what was clearly intended as civil remedy into a criminal penalty. U.S.C.A. Const.Amend. 5; 48 C.F.R. § 9.403. U.S. v. Hatfield, 108 F.3d 67 (4th Cir. 1997). Double Jeopardy ☞24

Halper balancing test for determining whether debarment of government contractor is punitive for double jeopardy purposes—weighing government's harm against penalty's size—is inapplicable, where sanction and purposes it seeks to achieve are qualitative rather than merely quantitative, and question becomes whether debarment is in effect so punitive, that court must conclude that the proceeding is not civil but criminal in nature. U.S.C.A. Const.Amend. 5; 48 C.F.R. § 9.403. U.S. v. Hatfield, 108 F.3d 67 (4th Cir. 1997). Double Jeopardy ☞24

Four-year debarment of defense contractor from government contracting was not so overwhelmingly disproportionate to harm caused by defendant's conduct, in knowingly supplying nonconforming parts to Department of Defense (DOD), as to constitute punishment for double jeopardy purposes, even though regulations generally provided for three-year maximum debarment, as debarment served important nonpunitive goals of preventing further dissipation of public funds and protecting DOD programs by preventing supply of substandard or defective parts, and extra year could be viewed as evidence of intent to protect government from particularly egregious conduct, where government paid company more than $40,000 for nonconforming parts. U.S.C.A. Const.Amend. 5; 18 U.S.C.A. § 287; 48 C.F.R. §§ 9.402, 9.406-2(b), 9.406-4. U.S. v. Glymph, 96 F.3d 722 (4th Cir. 1996). Double Jeopardy ☞24

Intent of provision for administrative debarment from government contracting is to purge government programs of corrupt influences and prevent improper dissipation of public funds, and debarment is thus not punitive, for double jeopardy purposes, but constitutes "rough remedial justice" permissible as prophylactic governmental action. U.S.C.A. Const. Amend. 5; 48 C.F.R. § 9.406-2(b). U.S. v. Glymph, 96 F.3d 722 (4th Cir. 1996). Double Jeopardy ☞24

24 Searches and seizures

Requiring a federal contractor to submit to an enforcement proceeding by Office of Federal Contract Compliance Programs (OFCCP) based on evidence illegally obtained in violation of the Fourth Amendment would not itself be an actionable constitutional wrong. U.S.C.A. Const.Amend. 4. Nationsbank Corp. v. Herman, 174 F.3d 424, 79 Fair Empl. Prac. Cas. (BNA) 1113, 75 Empl. Prac. Dec. (CCH) P 45814 (4th Cir. 1999). United States ☞64.20

Government contractor could not show irreparable injury arising from seizure and retention of its business records pursuant to search warrant, and thus was not entitled to return of the records, where it had been allowed to copy all the records and real motive in bringing motion was to have search declared illegal; claimed business losses as to result of alleged illegal conduct and reliance on search warrant affidavit to determine that contractor was not a responsible contractor and was ineligible to be awarded contracts were result of investigation of suspected wrongdoing and not the consequence of the search and seizure. Fed.Rules Cr.Proc. Rule 41(e), 18 U.S.C.A.U.S. v. A Bldg. Housing a Business Known as Mach. Products Co., Inc., 139 F.R.D. 111 (W.D. Wis. 1990). Searches And Seizures ☞84

§ 9.406-4 Period of debarment.

(a) (1) Debarment shall be for a period commensurate with the seriousness of the cause(s). Generally, debarment should not exceed 3 years, except that—

(i) Debarment for violation of the provisions of the Drug-Free Workplace Act of 1988 (see 23.506) may be for a period not to exceed 5 years; and

(ii) Debarments under 9.406-2(b)(2) shall be for one year unless extended pursuant to paragraph (b) of this subsection.

(2) If suspension precedes a debarment, the suspension period shall be considered in determining the debarment period.

(b) The debarring official may extend the debarment for an additional period, if that official determines that an extension is necessary to protect the Government's interest.

However, a debarment may not be extended solely on the basis of the facts and circumstances upon which the initial debarment action was based. Debarments under 9.406-2(b)(2) may be extended for additional periods of one year if the Secretary of Homeland Security or the Attorney General determines that the contractor continues to be in violation of the employment provisions of the Immigration and Nationality Act. If debarment for an additional period is determined to be necessary, the procedures of 9.406-3 shall be followed to extend the debarment.

(c) The debarring official may reduce the period or extent of debarment, upon the contractor's request, supported by documentation, for reasons such as—

(1) Newly discovered material evidence;

(2) Reversal of the conviction or civil judgment upon which the debarment was based;

(3) Bona fide change in ownership or management;

(4) Elimination of other causes for which the debarment was imposed; or

(5) Other reasons the debarring official deems appropriate.

United States Code Annotated

Administrative determinations, see 41 USCA § 257.

Contract requirements, see 41 USCA § 254.

Contractor responsibilities, see 41 USCA § 57.

Contracts, planning, solicitation, evaluation, and award procedures, see 10 USCA § 2305.

Definitions, see 10 USCA § 2302, 41 USCA §§ 259, 403.

Determinations and decisions, see 10 USCA § 2310, 41 USCA § 262.

Kinds of contracts, see 10 USCA § 2306.

Planning and solicitation requirements, see 41 USCA § 253a.

Notes of Decisions

Double jeopardy 1
Period of debarment 2

1 Double jeopardy

Debarment of government contractor did not have to be subjected to a "particularized assessment" to determine whether it was punitive for double jeopardy purposes, where government did not seek the return of particular quantity of funds but instead sought to protect the quality of its acquisition programs. 48 C.F.R. §§ 9.402(b), 9.406-2(b)(1), (c), 9.406-4. U.S. v. Hatfield, 108 F.3d 67 (4th Cir. 1997). Double Jeopardy ⬯24

Four-year debarment of defense contractor from government contracting was not so overwhelmingly disproportionate to harm caused by defendant's conduct, in knowingly supplying nonconforming parts to Department of Defense (DOD), as to constitute punishment for double jeopardy purposes, even though regulations generally provided for three-year maximum debarment, as debarment served important nonpunitive goals of preventing further dissipation of public funds and protecting DOD programs by preventing supply of substandard or defective parts, and extra year could be viewed as evidence of intent to protect government from particularly egregious conduct, where government paid company more than $40,000 for nonconforming parts. U.S.C.A. Const.Amend. 5; 18 U.S.C.A. § 287; 48 C.F.R. §§ 9.402, 9.406-2(b), 9.406-4. U.S. v. Glymph, 96 F.3d 722 (4th Cir. 1996). Double Jeopardy ⬯24

2 Period of debarment

While there are no bright lines delineating arbitrariness, district court's conclusory declaration that a one year debarment of meat company and sole owner of company from contracting with executive branch of government was justified, but that a longer debarment would be arbitrary or capricious could not be sustained absent a carefully reasoned analysis explaining the demarcation at one year, despite explicit administrative regulatory authorization of debarment for up to three years. Shane Meat Co., Inc. v. U.S. Dept. of Defense, 800 F.2d 334, 91 A.L.R. Fed. 857 (3d Cir. 1986). United States ⬯64.60(4)

Bidder failed to prove that his three-year debarment from participation in government surplus auctions was excessive and therefore retaliatory, even though second bidder, who was involved in some of same activities, received only sixmonth debarment, where bidders were not in identical positions with respect to conduct and second bidder cooperated, admitted her wrongdoing and acceded to government's conditions. Textor v. Cheney, 757 F. Supp. 51, 37 Cont. Cas. Fed. (CCH) P 76028 (D.D.C. 1991). United States ☞64.20

The 90-day period for forwarding the name of a wage and fringe benefit violator to the Comptroller General for placement on list of debarred contractors ran from date order of administrative law judge became final, after expiration of time for appeal, not from date of initial order and, in any event, period of debarment ran from date of publication of violator's name on debarment list, not from date on which name was forwarded to the Comptroller. Service Contract Act of 1965, § 5(a), as amended, 41 U.S.C.A. § 354(a). Cimpi v. Dole, 739 F. Supp. 25, 29 Wage & Hour Cas. (BNA) 1436, 36 Cont. Cas. Fed. (CCH) P 75987, 117 Lab. Cas. (CCH) P 35412 (D.D.C. 1990). United States ☞64.20

Mitigating circumstances warranted reduction in length of debarment of public accounting firm from contracting with federal government, where accounting firm could not be found to have been uncooperative after its proprietor was made aware of problem with original audit report provided to federal agency, but sincerely tried to remedy problems raised by federal agency, and federal agency was aware of unusual accounting procedures followed by audited city authority that were not noted in audit report. Sellers v. Kemp, 749 F. Supp. 1001, 36 Cont. Cas. Fed. (CCH) P 75996 (W.D. Mo. 1990). United States ☞64.20

§ 9.406-5 Scope of debarment.

(a) The fraudulent, criminal, or other seriously improper conduct of any officer, director, shareholder, partner, employee, or other individual associated with a contractor may be imputed to the contractor when the conduct occurred in connection with the individual's performance of duties for or on behalf of the contractor, or with the contractor's knowledge, approval, or acquiescence. The contractor's acceptance of the benefits derived from the conduct shall be evidence of such knowledge, approval, or acquiescence.

(b) The fraudulent, criminal, or other seriously improper conduct of a contractor may be imputed to any officer, director, shareholder, partner, employee, or other individual associated with the contractor who participated in, knew of, or had reason to know of the contractor's conduct.

(c) The fraudulent, criminal, or other seriously improper conduct of one contractor participating in a joint venture or similar arrangement may be imputed to other participating contractors if the conduct occurred for or on behalf of the joint venture or similar arrangement, or with the knowledge, approval, or acquiescence of these contractors. Acceptance of the benefits derived from the conduct shall be evidence of such knowledge, approval, or acquiescence.

United States Code Annotated

Administrative determinations, see 41 USCA § 257.

Contract requirements, see 41 USCA § 254.

Contractor responsibilities, see 41 USCA § 57.

Contracts, planning, solicitation, evaluation, and award procedures, see 10 USCA § 2305.

Definitions, see 10 USCA § 2302, 41 USCA §§ 259, 403.

Determinations and decisions, see 10 USCA § 2310, 41 USCA § 262.

Kinds of contracts, see 10 USCA § 2306.

Planning and solicitation requirements, see 41 USCA § 253a.

Notes of Decisions

Cause of serious and compelling nature 3
Conviction of crime, generally 2
Debarment of officers of corporation 1
Injunctions 4

1 Debarment of officers of corporation

Individual could not be debarred from government contracts for willful and aggravated violations of Davis-Bacon Act and related Acts solely on the basis of his status as president of offending contractor. Davis-Bacon Act, §§ 1-6, as amended, 40 U.S.C.A. §§ 276a to 276a-5; 40 U.S.C.A. § 276c; Contract Work Hours and Safety Standards Act, §§ 101-107, as amended, 40 U.S.C.A. §§ 327–333; Portal-to-Portal Act of 1947, § 6(a), as amended, 29 U.S.C.A. § 255(a). Facchiano Const. Co., Inc. v. U.S. Dept. of Labor, 987 F.2d 206, 1 Wage & Hour Cas. 2d (BNA) 468, 39 Cont. Cas. Fed. (CCH) P 76542, 124 Lab. Cas. (CCH) P 35782 (3d Cir. 1993). United States ⚬—64.20

Government contractor's president and chief executive officer did not have "reason to know" of contractor's misconduct, so as to justify his debarment from government contracting; although president admitted that he became "generally aware" of some customer complaints after four years of alleged misconduct, there was no evidence that he was informed of their continuing nature, and president also claimed that he was told that complaints concerned problems that contractor had no obligation to report to the government. Novicki v. Cook, 946 F.2d 938, 942, 37 Cont. Cas. Fed. (CCH) P 76198 (D.C. Cir. 1991). United States ⚬—64.20

In deciding to debar two officers but not a third on basis that the two officers had reason to know of the corporation's criminal conduct while third officer did not, the debarring official did not treat the officers equally and the debarments would be set aside; debarring official's determination did not explain why third officer, the treasurer of the corporation, escaped the treatment meted out to the other officers. Caiola v. Carroll, 851 F.2d 395, 400, 34 Cont. Cas. Fed. (CCH) P 75514 (D.C. Cir. 1988). United States ⚬—64.20

In regard to debarment from government contracting of former president and chief executive officer of government contractor, preponderance of evidence showed that president had reason to know that his company was defrauding Department of Defense by, among other things, submitting fabricated test results and false quality control reports; problem with faulty resistors and complaints from dissatisfied customers extended over number of years, and president's explanation—that he asked his subordinates about problem and that they informed him that failures resulted from customer's improper soldering techniques—was improbable, in view of number of customers involved, all of which were large manufacturers skilled in assembling hightech components, and in view of assumption underlying alleged explanation that all of those customers made virtually identical mistakes on numerous occasions. Novicki v. Cook, 743 F. Supp. 11, 36 Cont. Cas. Fed. (CCH) P 76009 (D.D.C. 1990), judgment rev'd, 946 F.2d 938, 37 Cont. Cas. Fed. (CCH) P 76198 (D.C. Cir. 1991)(On reversing judgment and remanding, the circuit court said "[a]ssuming... that the agency official did apply the definition of "reason to know" that... was appropriate... we do not think the record reasonably supports the agency's decision, because there is not substantial evidence to establish that Novicki had 'reason to know.' ") United States ⚬—64.20

Probable cause to believe that president of government contractor had reason to know that his company was defrauding Department of Defense was not prerequisite to Department's initiation of debarment proceeding against president. Novicki v. Cook, 743 F. Supp. 11, 36 Cont. Cas. Fed. (CCH) P 76009 (D.D.C. 1990), judgment rev'd, 946 F.2d 938, 37 Cont. Cas. Fed. (CCH) P 76198 (D.C. Cir. 1991)(On reversing judgment and remanding, the circuit court said "[a]ssuming... that the agency official did apply the definition of 'reason to know' that... was appropriate... we do not think the record reasonably supports the agency's decision, because there is not substantial evidence to establish that Novicki had 'reason to know.' ") United States ⚬—64.20

Defense Logistics Agency's decision to debar president of government contractor upon Agency's conclusion that president had reason to know that his company was defrauding Department of Defense was neither arbitrary nor capricious, even though the contracting company itself was not debarred; company was acquired by different company, and drastic changes in management and operation were made. Novicki v. Cook, 743 F. Supp. 11, 36 Cont. Cas. Fed. (CCH) P 76009 (D.D.C. 1990), judgment rev'd, 946 F.2d 938, 37 Cont. Cas. Fed. (CCH) P 76198 (D.C. Cir. 1991)(On reversing judgment and remanding, the circuit court said "[a]ssuming... that the agency official did apply the definition of reason to know' that... was appropriate... we do not think the record reasonably supports the agency's decision, because there is not substantial evidence to establish that Novicki had 'reason to know.' ") United States ⚬—64.20

Department of Defense was not precluded from debarring executive of government contractor, who knew or had reason to know, that his company was defrauding Department after fraud had occurred, but before it was uncovered by government, and who failed to take remedial action of any sort. Novicki v. Cook, 743 F. Supp. 11, 36 Cont. Cas. Fed. (CCH) P 76009 (D.D.C. 1990), judgment rev'd, 946 F.2d 938, 37 Cont. Cas. Fed. (CCH) P 76198 (D.C. Cir. 1991)(On reversing judgment and remanding, the circuit court said "[a]ssuming... that the agency official did apply the definition of 'reason to know' that... was appropriate... we do not think the record reasonably supports the agency's decision, because there is not substantial evidence to establish that Novicki had 'reason to know.' ") United States ⊶64.20

2 Conviction of crime, generally

A debarment from contracting with executive branch of government need not be proportional to severity of a prior criminal sentence, for a criminal sentence is a statutory sanction quite distinct from a debarment. Shane Meat Co., Inc. v. U.S. Dept. of Defense, 800 F.2d 334, 91 A.L.R. Fed. 857 (3d Cir. 1986). United States ⊶64.20

Agency's decision to debar government contractor was arbitrary, capricious and abuse of discretion, though contractor pled guilty to misdemeanor for conversion of government property, where government continued to enter into contracts with contractor for six years after misrepresentations that served as basis for misdemeanor conviction. Silverman v. U.S. Dept. of Defense, 817 F. Supp. 846, 39 Cont. Cas. Fed. (CCH) P 76540 (S.D. Cal. 1993). United States ⊶64.20

Debarment of government contractors from all government procurement and sales contracting for three years was not arbitrary or capricious; contractors were convicted of crime in connection with performance of government contract. Delta Rocky Mountain Petroleum, Inc. v. U.S. Dept. of Defense, 726 F. Supp. 278, 36 Cont. Cas. Fed. (CCH) P 75888 (D. Colo. 1989). United States ⊶64.15

Contractor's guilty plea to charge of making a false statement for purpose of influencing action of a bank and the legitimate inferences to be drawn therefrom constituted substantial evidence in support of administrative decision to debar him from further participation in HUD programs. Agan v. Pierce, 576 F. Supp. 257 (N.D. Ga. 1983). United States ⊶64.20

Where agency considered not only criminal conviction of president of government contractor, but also mitigating factors submitted by contractor in debarment proceedings, decision to debar contractor for period of one year was not arbitrary, capricious or abuse of discretion. Federal Property and Administrative Services Act of 1949, § 303(b), 41 U.S.C.A. § 253(b). Joseph Const. Co. v. Veterans Admin. of U.S., 595 F. Supp. 448, 32 Cont. Cas. Fed. (CCH) P 73082 (N.D. Ill. 1984). United States ⊶64.20

3 Cause of serious and compelling nature

Even in the absence of conviction or civil judgment against government contractor, contractor may be debarred, based on preponderance of the evidence, for cause of serious and compelling nature, but debarring official must give notice to contractor or proposal to debar and must invite the contractor to submit information or argument in opposition to the proposed debarment. 48 C.F.R. §§ 9.406-2(c), 9.406-3(c)(4). Waterhouse v. U.S., 874 F. Supp. 5 (D.D.C. 1994). United States ⊶64.20

4 Injunctions

Contractor's officer was not entitled to temporary restraining order against his expired debarment by Department of Health and Human Services (DHHS), which had precluded officer from being awarded government contracts; officer was not likely to succeed on the merits of his challenge to debarment, as administrative record revealed substantial evidence upon which debarring official could have concluded that contractor committed forgery and that officer knew or should have known of it, officer apparently received all due process guarantees required by debarment regulations, and government agencies had not waived all fraud claims against officer, and balance of hardships did not tip in officer's favor, as officer had delayed two years in filing action and seeking injunction, any harm to officer was economic, speculative, or both, and government had strong interest in maintaining integrity of its contractors. 48 C.F.R. §§ 9.402(a), 9.406-2(c), 9.406-3(b)(1), (d)(1), (d)(2)(i), 9.406-5(b). Ali v. U.S., 932 F. Supp. 1206 (N.D. Cal. 1996). Injunction ⊶150

§ 9.407 Suspension.

§ 9.407-1 General.

(a) The suspending official may, in the public interest, suspend a contractor for any of the causes in 9.407-2, using the procedures in 9.407-3.

(b) (1) Suspension is a serious action to be imposed on the basis of adequate evidence, pending the completion of investigation or legal proceedings, when it has been determined that immediate action is necessary to protect the Government's interest. In assessing the adequacy of the evidence, agencies should consider how much information is available, how credible it is given the circumstances, whether or not important allegations are corroborated, and what inferences can reasonably be drawn as a result. This assessment should include an examination of basic documents such as contracts, inspection reports, and correspondence.

(2) The existence of a cause for suspension does not necessarily require that the contractor be suspended. The suspending official should consider the seriousness of the contractor's acts or omissions and may, but is not required to, consider remedial measures or mitigating factors, such as those set forth in 9.406-1(a). A contractor has the burden of promptly presenting to the suspending official evidence of remedial measures or mitigating factors when it has reason to know that a cause for suspension exists. The existence or nonexistence of any remedial measures or mitigating factors is not necessarily determinative of a contractor's present responsibility.

(c) Suspension constitutes suspension of all divisions or other organizational elements of the contractor, unless the suspension decision is limited by its terms to specific divisions, organizational elements, or commodities. The suspending official may extend the suspension decision to include any affiliates of the contractor if they are—

(1) Specifically named; and

(2) Given written notice of the suspension and an opportunity to respond (see 9.407-3(c)).

(d) A contractor's suspension shall be effective throughout the executive branch of the Government, unless the agency head or a designee (except see 23.506(e)) states in writing the compelling reasons justifying continued business dealings between that agency and the contractor.

(e) (1) When the suspending official has authority to suspend contractors from both acquisition contracts pursuant to this regulation and contracts for the purchase of Federal personal property pursuant to FPMR 101-45.6, that official shall consider simultaneously suspending the contractor from the award of acquisition contracts and from the purchase of Federal personal property.

(2) When suspending a contractor from the award of acquisition contracts and from the purchase of Federal personal property, the suspension notice shall so indicate and the appropriate FAR and FPMR citations shall be included.

United States Code Annotated

Administrative determinations, see 41 USCA § 257.

Contract requirements, see 41 USCA § 254.

Contractor responsibilities, see 41 USCA § 57.

Contracts, planning, solicitation, evaluation, and award procedures, see 10 USCA § 2305.

Definitions, see 10 USCA § 2302, 41 USCA §§ 259, 403.

Determinations and decisions, see 10 USCA § 2310, 41 USCA § 262.

Kinds of contracts, see 10 USCA § 2306.

Planning and solicitation requirements, see 41 USCA § 253a.

Notes of Decisions

In general 2
Agriculture Department 16
Antitrust violations and anticompetitive activities 10
Armed services and defense 17
Cause of serious and compelling nature 11
Construction and application 4
De facto suspension 9
Due process of law 6
Environmental Protection Agency 18

1 Validity

Federal acquisitions regulations governing debarment of government contractors are not unreasonable or unconstitutional. Joseph Const. Co. v. Veterans Admin. of U.S., 595 F. Supp. 448, 32 Cont. Cas. Fed. (CCH) P 73082 (N.D. Ill. 1984). United States ☞64.20

2 In general

Suspension and debarment of bidder for government contract occur when Government formally or constructively precludes contractor from participating in future, government contracts or when contracting official's decisions effectively prevent contractor from participating in that and future procurements. BMY, A Div. of HARSCO Corp. v. U.S., 693 F. Supp. 1232, 35 Cont. Cas. Fed. (CCH) P 75552 (D.D.C. 1988). United States ☞64.20

3 Purpose

Executive order providing for government-wide debarment and suspension of contractors who are debarred or suspended by particular agency was a managerial tool and not shown to be for the benefit of contractors, and thus did not provide basis for challenging government-wide debarment order on ground that, under the executive order, a prior agency debarment arising from the same circumstances should have been government-wide, precluding later imposition of the same penalty. Executive Order No. 12549, §§ 1 et seq., 1(a), 31 U.S.C.A. § 6101 note. Facchiano Const. Co., Inc. v. U.S. Dept. of Labor, 987 F.2d 206, 1 Wage & Hour Cas. 2d (BNA) 468, 39 Cont. Cas. Fed. (CCH) P 76542, 124 Lab. Cas. (CCH) P 35782 (3d Cir. 1993). United States ☞64.20

4 Construction and application

Once navy officials determined to suspend bidder rather than to reject its bids for nonresponsibility, the navy officials likewise determined to subject themselves to their own regulations and body of case law prescribing fair method for executing such a suspension. ATL, Inc. v. U.S., 736 F.2d 677, 32 Cont. Cas. Fed. (CCH) P 72528 (Fed. Cir. 1984). United States ☞64.20

5 Retroactive or prospective application

Executive order providing for government-wide debarment and suspension of government contractors debarred or suspended by particular agency did not become effective until issuance of guidelines by Office of Management and Budget (OMB) and subsequent implementing regulations and, in the interim, Department of Labor (DOL) properly continued operating according to its existing regulations. Executive Order No. 12549, § 6, 31 U.S.C.A. § 6101 note. Facchiano Const. Co., Inc. v. U.S. Dept. of Labor, 987 F.2d 206, 1 Wage & Hour Cas. 2d (BNA) 468, 39 Cont. Cas. Fed. (CCH) P 76542, 124 Lab. Cas. (CCH) P 35782 (3d Cir. 1993). United States ☞64.20

6 Due process of law

General Services Administration (GSA) did not violate contractor's due process rights by denying contractor's request for formal hearing upon suspension of contractor and cancellation of its existing contracts due to contractor's indictment for defrauding government; contractor received both notice and informal hearing, and GSA official in charge of making suspension decision conferred with prosecutor and concluded that formal hearing could compromise ongoing criminal investigation. U.S.C.A. Const.Amend. 5. Commercial Drapery Contractors, Inc. v. U.S., 133 F.3d 1, 6, 39 Fed. R. Serv. 3d 825 (D.C. Cir. 1998). Constitutional Law ⚮276(2); United States ⚮64.20; United States ⚮72.1(1)

Agency may not impose even temporary suspension on government contractor without providing core requirements of due process, i.e., adequate notice and meaningful hearing. U.S.C.A. Const.Amend. 5. Commercial Drapery Contractors, Inc. v. U.S., 133 F.3d 1, 7, 39 Fed. R. Serv. 3d 825 (D.C. Cir. 1998). Constitutional Law ⚮276(2)

Airline's due process interest in having fuller notice and hearing before Commercial Airline Review Board (CARB) suspended airline from military airlift transportation program did not outweigh government interest in avoiding administrative and financial burdens. U.S.C.A. Const.Amend. 5; 10 U.S.C.A. § 2640(c, d). Reeve Aleutian Airways, Inc. v. U.S., 982 F.2d 594, 602 (D.C. Cir. 1993), as amended on denial of reh'g, (Mar. 26, 1993). Constitutional Law ⚮276(2); United States ⚮64.20

Procedures that Commercial Airline Review Board (CARB) employed in suspending airline from military airlift transportation program did not violate due process, even though airline had significant interest in avoiding deprivation of reputational and economic interests caused by even temporary suspension; CARB provided specific notice, detailed statement of evidence, and opportunity to seek clarification of any confusion caused by notice. U.S.C.A. Const.Amend. 5; 10 U.S.C.A. § 2640(c, d). Reeve Aleutian Airways, Inc. v. U.S., 982 F.2d 594, 602 (D.C. Cir. 1993), as amended on denial of reh'g, (Mar. 26, 1993). Constitutional Law ⚮276(2); United States ⚮64.20

Airline had liberty interest in avoiding damage to its reputation and business caused by stigmatizing suspension by Commercial Airline Review Board (CARB), for purposes of due process challenge to procedures employed by CARB in suspending airline. U.S.C.A. Const. Amend. 5; 10 U.S.C.A. § 2640(c, d). Reeve Aleutian Airways, Inc. v. U.S., 982 F.2d 594, 602 (D.C. Cir. 1993), as amended on denial of reh'g, (Mar. 26, 1993). Constitutional Law ⚮276(2); United States ⚮64.20

Due process rights of airline were not violated by notice airline received from Commercial Airline Review Board (CARB) prior to hearing at which CARB suspended airline from military airlift transportation program on basis that airline did not receive adequate notice; CARB's notification letter was not inadequate for not saying which portions of report formed basis for CARB's actions, in that the whole report was of interest to CARB and airline was told explicitly what dispute was about and airline could be expected to have sufficient know-how to separate important from unimportant in report, moreover, notification letter offered follow-up contact during which airline could request additional information. U.S.C.A. Const.Amend. 5; 10 U.S.C.A. § 2640(c, d). Reeve Aleutian Airways, Inc. v. U.S., 982 F.2d 594, 599 (D.C. Cir. 1993), as amended on denial of reh'g, (Mar. 26, 1993). Constitutional Law ⚮276(2); United States ⚮64.20

Hearing before Commercial Airline Review Board (CARB) did not deprive airline, which was suspended from military airlift transportation program, of its right to due process, even though CARB was not required to present any witnesses thus allegedly depriving airline of opportunity to confront its accusers; airline had detailed specific statement of evidence against it in its possession months before hearing took place and airline apparently had chance to counter that evidence through oral or written presentation of whatever type or length it thought best, and had chance to engage in direct discussion of disputed topics with ultimate decision makers. U.S.C.A. Const.Amend. 5; 10 U.S.C.A. § 2640(c, d). Reeve Aleutian Airways, Inc. v. U.S., 982 F.2d 594, 601 (D.C. Cir. 1993), as amended on denial of reh'g, (Mar. 26, 1993). Constitutional Law ⚮276(2); United States ⚮64.20

Moving and storage companies were not entitled to increased tonnage under contracts with Department of Army to compensate them for period of time they were on suspended list of bidders for contracts, as they had no constitutionally protected due process right to receive make-up tonnage. U.S.C.A. Const.Amend. 5. Coleman American Moving Services, Inc. v. Weinberger, 716 F. Supp. 1405, 36 Cont. Cas. Fed. (CCH) P 75786 (M.D. Ala. 1989). Constitutional Law ⚮276(2); United States ⚮64.20

Moving and storage companies placed on Department of Army's suspended contractor list following filing of criminal antitrust indictments against them were not denied due process by suffering loss of corporate liberty interest to be free from stigmatizing government defamation, as whatever stigma was involved flowed not from Department's action but from indictment. U.S.C.A. Const.Amend. 5. Coleman American Moving Services, Inc. v. Weinberger, 716 F. Supp. 1405, 36 Cont. Cas. Fed. (CCH) P 75786 (M.D. Ala. 1989). Constitutional Law ☞276(2); United States ☞64.20

Due process clause was not violated when moving and storage companies were placed on Department of Army's suspended contractors list following filing of antitrust indictments against them, as companies were merely bidders and as such had no constitutionally protectable property interest. U.S.C.A. Const.Amend. 5. Coleman American Moving Services, Inc. v. Weinberger, 716 F. Supp. 1405, 36 Cont. Cas. Fed. (CCH) P 75786 (M.D. Ala. 1989). Constitutional Law ☞277(1); United States ☞64.20

Government drapery contractor's late receipt of documents relating to subsequent cancellation action did not violate due process in proceeding to suspend contracts based on indictment of contractor and its owner, where contractor had full opportunity to rebut information on which General Services Administration's (GSA) decision to suspend was based, and was not prejudiced by late receipt of documents unrelated to grounds for suspension. U.S.C.A. Const.Amend. 14; 48 C.F.R. §§ 509.406-3(b)(6), 509.407-3(b)(5). Commercial Drapery Contractors, Inc. v. U.S., 967 F. Supp. 1, 41 Cont. Cas. Fed. (CCH) P 77172 (D.D.C. 1997), judgment aff'd, 133 F.3d 1, 39 Fed. R. Serv. 3d 825 (D.C. Cir. 1998). Constitutional Law ☞276(2); United States ☞75(3)

Procedures that preceded suspension of government drapery contractor and its affiliate based on indictment of contractor and its president satisfied requirements of due process, although formal evidentiary hearing was not conducted; procedures included contractor's meeting with suspending official and opportunity to submit additional evidence. U.S.C.A. Const.Amend. 14; 48 C.F.R. § 509.407-3(b)(6). Commercial Drapery Contractors, Inc. v. U.S., 967 F. Supp. 1, 41 Cont. Cas. Fed. (CCH) P 77172 (D.D.C. 1997), judgment aff'd, 133 F.3d 1, 39 Fed. R. Serv. 3d 825 (D.C. Cir. 1998). Constitutional Law ☞276(2); United States ☞75(3)

Formal or constructive suspension or debarment of government contractor is legal only if contractor has been afforded full due process protections. U.S.C.A. Const. Amends. 5, 14. BMY, A Div. of HARSCO Corp. v. U.S., 693 F. Supp. 1232, 35 Cont. Cas. Fed. (CCH) P 75552 (D.D.C. 1988). Constitutional Law ☞276(2); United States ☞64.20

Suspension of contractor from eligibility for government contracts pursuant to Federal Acquisition Regulations System (FAR), following contractor's indictment on charges involving fraud or dishonesty, satisfied requirements of procedural due process; although private interest at stake was important, initial reliability of indictment coupled with contractor's opportunity to rebut its conclusions greatly minimized risk of erroneous or irrational deprivation of its interest, and government interests in having responsible contractors perform its contracts and avoiding impairment of conduct of its business which would result if every governmental decision required full hearing involving all parties affected were significant. U.S.C.A. Const.Amend. 14; 48 C.F.R. §§ 9.401–9.407. Rutigliano Paper Stock, Inc. v. U.S. General Services Admin., 967 F. Supp. 757, 41 Cont. Cas. Fed. (CCH) P 77156 (E.D. N.Y. 1997). Constitutional Law ☞276(2); United States ☞64.20

For purpose of determining extent of process due contractor upon suspension of its eligibility for government contracts pursuant to Federal Acquisition Regulations System (FAR), such suspension, if based upon contractor's indictment, is considered to be based upon independent fact finding process that produced indictment, which process is considered sufficiently reliable to effect temporary but total deprivation of liberty. 48 C.F.R. §§ 9.401–9.407. Rutigliano Paper Stock, Inc. v. U.S. General Services Admin., 967 F. Supp. 757, 41 Cont. Cas. Fed. (CCH) P 77156 (E.D. N.Y. 1997). Constitutional Law ☞276(2); United States ☞64.20

Provision of Federal Acquisition Regulations System (FAR) continuing contractors' suspension from eligibility for government contracts until conclusion of significant activity in criminal action did not violate due process as applied, despite delay in trial on charges in indictment; contractors had been permitted to present evidence indicating that suspension was not in government's interest despite existence of indictment, and no significant activity in state criminal case was pending that would prolong suspension. U.S.C.A. Const. Amend. 14; 48 C.F.R. §§ 9.401–9.407. Rutigliano Paper Stock, Inc. v. U.S. General Services Admin.,

967 F. Supp. 757, 41 Cont. Cas. Fed. (CCH) P 77156 (E.D. N.Y. 1997). Constitutional Law ☞276(2); United States ☞64.20

Due process is satisfied with respect to suspension of contractor from eligibility for government contracts under Federal Acquisition Regulations System (FAR) if meaningful opportunity to be heard on issue of appropriateness of suspension is granted within reasonable time and contractor is afforded opportunity to demonstrate that imposition of suspension would be irrational or contrary to government's interests. U.S.C.A. Const.Amend. 14; 48 C.F.R. §§ 9.401–9.407. Rutigliano Paper Stock, Inc. v. U.S. General Services Admin., 967 F. Supp. 757, 41 Cont. Cas. Fed. (CCH) P 77156 (E.D. N.Y. 1997). Constitutional Law ☞276(2); United States ☞64.20

Requirements of due process did not dictate that Federal Acquisition Regulations System (FAR) require justification for contractor's suspension from eligibility for government contracts beyond fact of contractor's indictment on charges involving fraud or dishonesty; indictment merely gave rise to rebuttable presumption that suspension was justified, contractor was entitled to provide contradictory evidence, indictment gave rise to presumption of probable cause and was sufficiently reliable to provide adequate basis for suspension, and judicial review of any improper suspension was available pursuant to Administrative Procedures Act. U.S.C.A. Const. Amend. 14; 5 U.S.C.A. § 551 et seq.; 48 C.F.R. §§ 9.401–9.407. Rutigliano Paper Stock, Inc. v. U.S. General Services Admin., 967 F. Supp. 757, 41 Cont. Cas. Fed. (CCH) P 77156 (E.D. N.Y. 1997). Constitutional Law ☞276(2); United States ☞64.20

Contractor's indictment gives rise to presumption of probable cause, such that grounding of rebuttable presumption that suspension from eligibility for government contracts pursuant to Federal Acquisition Regulations System (FAR) is warranted upon such indictment does not violate contractor's due process rights. U.S.C.A. Const.Amend. 14; 48 C.F.R. §§ 9.401–9.407. Rutigliano Paper Stock, Inc. v. U.S. General Services Admin., 967 F. Supp. 757, 41 Cont. Cas. Fed. (CCH) P 77156 (E.D. N.Y. 1997). Constitutional Law ☞276(2); United States ☞64.20

Requirements of due process did not dictate that Federal Acquisition Regulations System (FAR) provide additional fact finding hearing upon suspension of contractor from eligibility for government contracts, where basis for suspension was contractor's indictment on charges involving fraud or dishonesty, although government was obligated to inform contractor clearly of its opportunity to present evidence which might rebut indictment; General Services Administration (GSA) lacked power to find facts related to indictment, and purpose of contractor's opportunity to be heard was not to contest indictment. U.S.C.A. Const.Amend. 14; 48 C.F.R. §§ 9.401–9.407. Rutigliano Paper Stock, Inc. v. U.S. General Services Admin., 967 F. Supp. 757, 41 Cont. Cas. Fed. (CCH) P 77156 (E.D. N.Y. 1997). Constitutional Law ☞276(2); United States ☞64.20

In context of contractor's suspension from eligibility for government contracts under Federal Acquisition Regulations System (FAR) following contractor's indictment, due process does not require full adversarial hearing and fact finding; purpose of contractor's opportunity to be heard is not to contest indictment, but rather to demonstrate that suspension should not be imposed, either because it is not in government's interest to do so, or because in light of compelling evidence presented by contractor, governmental decision to rely only on indictment would be arbitrary, capricious, or abuse of discretion. U.S.C.A. Const.Amend. 14; 48 C.F.R. §§ 9.401–9.407. Rutigliano Paper Stock, Inc. v. U.S. General Services Admin., 967 F. Supp. 757, 41 Cont. Cas. Fed. (CCH) P 77156 (E.D. N.Y. 1997). Constitutional Law ☞276(2); United States ☞64.20

Requirements of due process did not dictate that General Services Administration (GSA) provide suspended contractor with independent review by individual not directly involved with its decision to suspend contractor's eligibility for government contracts; applicable regulations did not call for such review, no process provided for therein could be construed as independent review, and district court review was available under Administrative Procedures Act. U.S.C.A. Const.Amend. 14; 5 U.S.C.A. § 551 et seq.; 48 C.F.R. §§ 9.401–9.407. Rutigliano Paper Stock, Inc. v. U.S. General Services Admin., 967 F. Supp. 757, 41 Cont. Cas. Fed. (CCH) P 77156 (E.D. N.Y. 1997). Constitutional Law ☞276(2); United States ☞64.20

Contractor suspended from eligibility for government contracts by General Services Administration (GSA) pursuant to Federal Acquisition Regulations System (FAR) had protected liberty interest in its eligibility to bid for federal contracts, where suspension was based upon contractor's indictment on charges involving fraud and dishonesty. 48 C.F.R. §§ 9.401–9.407. Rutigliano Paper Stock, Inc. v. U.S. General Services Admin., 967 F. Supp. 757, 41 Cont. Cas. Fed. (CCH) P 77156 (E.D. N.Y. 1997). Constitutional Law ☞276(2)

Contractors established protected liberty interest, where suspension of their participation in Department of Transportation financial assistance programs was based upon indictment charging contractors with creating false and fraudulent joint minority business enterprise in connection with construction project, and with falsifying records as part of that fraud. U.S.C.A. Const.Amend. 5. Mainelli v. U.S., 611 F. Supp. 606 (D.R.I. 1985). Constitutional Law ☞291.6

With regard to a contractor's suspension from bidding, due process requirements of the Federal Acquisition Regulation (FAR) are satisfied when the contractor has been provided all of the information relied on by the suspending official. U.S.C.A. Const.Amend. 5; 48 C.F.R. § 9.407-3(b)(1). Lion Raisins, Inc. v. U.S., 51 Fed. Cl. 238 (2001). United States ☞64.20

Individual has a right to notice and opportunity to be heard before he is debarred, suspended, or denied license to practice profession by government agency. U.S.C.A. Const. Amend. 14. ATL, Inc. v. U.S., 3 Cl. Ct. 259, 31 Cont. Cas. Fed. (CCH) P 71393 (1983). Constitutional Law ☞276(2); United States ☞64.20

Agency's failure to give proper written notice to an affiliate of a suspended contractor pursuant to FAR 9.407-1(c) is a procedural defect that does not deprive the affiliate of due process or affect the validity of the rejection of the affiliate's bid based on the suspended contractor's ineligibility, where the suspended contractor had actual notice of the intended suspension and the ownership and control of the suspended contractor is the same as for the affiliate. TS Generalbau GmbH; Thomas Stadlbauer, B-246034, B-246036, B-246037, B-246037.2, B-246038, B-246039, B-246040, B-246040.2, B-246042, B-246042.2, B-246043, B-246043.2, 92-1 CPD ¶ 189 (Comp. Gen. 1992)

7 Equal protection of laws

Mere allegation that moving and storage companies were denied make-up tonnage following their removal from Department of Army suspended contractor list when acquitted of antitrust violations did not establish protectible Fifth Amendment equal protection right, as no fundamental interest or suspect classifications were involved and discretionary element of regulations was rationally related to Department's legitimate interest in ensuring efficient storage and carrier service. U.S.C.A. Const.Amend. 5. Coleman American Moving Services, Inc. v. Weinberger, 716 F. Supp. 1405, 36 Cont. Cas. Fed. (CCH) P 75786 (M.D. Ala. 1989). Constitutional Law ☞225.4; United States ☞64.20

Procedure affording companies who have not been indicted for antitrust violations a hearing prior to their placement on list of suspended government contractors, while denying hearing to companies who have been indicted, did not violate equal protection rights of indicted companies as reason for hearing was to determine if suspension would be rationally related to government objectives and fact of indictment provided sufficient reason to proceed with suspension. U.S.C.A. Const.Amend. 5. Coleman American Moving Services, Inc. v. Weinberger, 716 F. Supp. 1405, 36 Cont. Cas. Fed. (CCH) P 75786 (M.D. Ala. 1989). Constitutional Law ☞225.4; United States ☞64.20

8 Right to counsel

Moving and storage companies which were placed on Department of Army's suspended bidders list following filing of antitrust indictments against them were not deprived of their right to counsel, as such right extends only to cases where deprivation of personal liberty may result from proceeding and companies' antitrust exposure was limited to property loss. U.S.C.A. Const.Amend. 6. Coleman American Moving Services, Inc. v. Weinberger, 716 F. Supp. 1405, 36 Cont. Cas. Fed. (CCH) P 75786 (M.D. Ala. 1989). Criminal Law ☞641.2(4)

9 De facto suspension

"De facto suspension" of a contractor may be shown by successive denial of a number of contracts on which the contractor is low bidder, though contractor's other actions and statements may also support its existence. Shermco Industries, Inc. v. Secretary of the Air Force,

584 F. Supp. 76, 32 Cont. Cas. Fed. (CCH) P 72713 (N.D. Tex. 1984). United States ⚖64.20

Air Force's de facto suspension of contractor, as evidenced by fact that suspension of contractor was not ordered until seven and one-half months after contractor submitted low bid on contract which was rejected and almost five months after nonresponsibility determination, injured contractor, entitling it to relief. Shermco Industries, Inc. v. Secretary of the Air Force, 584 F. Supp. 76, 32 Cont. Cas. Fed. (CCH) P 72713 (N.D. Tex. 1984). United States ⚖64.20

A finding of de facto suspension of a contractor is not justified at time of a first determination of nonresponsibility unless there is evidence that the procuring body has decided that from that point forward it will award no further contracts. Shermco Industries, Inc. v. Secretary of the Air Force, 584 F. Supp. 76, 32 Cont. Cas. Fed. (CCH) P 72713 (N.D. Tex. 1984). United States ⚖64.20

A de facto suspension or debarment from participation in government business arises when procuring body refuses, for indefinite period of time, to grant awards to particular contractor, but successive determinations of nonresponsibility on same grounds are improper, and procuring agency must initiate suspension or debarment procedures at earliest practical date following first determination of nonresponsibility. 18 U.S.C.A. § 287; Small Business Act, § 2 [2–18], 15 U.S.C.A. §§ 631–647. Shermco Industries, Inc. v. U.S., 6 Cl. Ct. 588, 32 Cont. Cas. Fed. (CCH) P 73068 (1984). United States ⚖64.20

10 Antitrust violations and anticompetitive activities

Department of Army followed appropriate procedures in placing moving and storage companies who were under antitrust indictment on restricted contractor list, companies received adequate notice of suspension and were fully informed of their appeals rights. Coleman American Moving Services, Inc. v. Weinberger, 716 F. Supp. 1405, 36 Cont. Cas. Fed. (CCH) P 75786 (M.D. Ala. 1989). United States ⚖64.20

Suspension of companies furnishing moving and storage service to Department of Army, based on indictment charging them with antitrust violations, was not invalid due to failure of Department to make specific determination that immediate action was necessary to protect government's interest, as evidence of bid rigging as claimed in antitrust complaint was implicitly contrary to government's interest. Coleman American Moving Services, Inc. v. Weinberger, 716 F. Supp. 1405, 36 Cont. Cas. Fed. (CCH) P 75786 (M.D. Ala. 1989). United States ⚖64.20

Moving and storage companies who were indicted and suspended from contracting with Department of Army were not entitled to make-up tonnage following their acquittal in antitrust action, as make-up tonnage was available only to contractors who were wrongfully suspended and suspension during pendency of antitrust action had been valid. Coleman American Moving Services, Inc. v. Weinberger, 716 F. Supp. 1405, 36 Cont. Cas. Fed. (CCH) P 75786 (M.D. Ala. 1989). United States ⚖64.20

Moving and storage companies were not entitled to makeup tonnage under contract with Department of Army, as they had not established bad faith on part of Department in suspending them during pendency of antitrust litigation against them. Coleman American Moving Services, Inc. v. Weinberger, 716 F. Supp. 1405, 36 Cont. Cas. Fed. (CCH) P 75786 (M.D. Ala. 1989). United States ⚖64.20

Moving and storage companies who were suspended from contracting with Department of Army because of indictment under antitrust charges were not prevented from adequately exercising their right to contest suspension by fact that it would have required person capable of refuting charges to waive his Fifth Amendment right against self-incrimination, as only relevance of his testimony would be denying existence of indictment or denying that defendants were named in indictment and testimony on these subjects would have posed no hazard of self-incrimination for individual. U.S.C.A. Const.Amend. 5. Coleman American Moving Services, Inc. v. Weinberger, 716 F. Supp. 1405, 36 Cont. Cas. Fed. (CCH) P 75786 (M.D. Ala. 1989). United States ⚖64.20; Witnesses ⚖297(8.1)

Suspension proceedings brought against moving and storage companies by Department of Army following filing of antitrust indictment against them did not impermissibly extend right of government to discovery in case involving companies' claim for back-up tonnage after companies were acquitted and restored to bidders list, as there was little opportunity for abuse of discovery in postsuspension hearing which covered only evidence refuting existence of indictment or refuting that companies were named in indictment. Coleman American Moving Services, Inc. v. Weinberger, 716 F. Supp. 1405, 36 Cont. Cas. Fed. (CCH) P 75786 (M.D. Ala. 1989). United States ⊶64.20

11 Cause of serious and compelling nature

Hearing officer's finding that government contractor violated terms of purchase orders with Department of Housing and Urban Development constituting "causes of such serious and compelling nature, affecting responsibility," and demonstrating at least implicitly that suspension under the facts was in the best interest of HUD, which determination was sustained by assistant secretary of HUD, was adequate finding on which to base suspension of government contractor. Adamo Wrecking Co. v. Department of Housing and Urban Development, 414 F. Supp. 877 (D.D.C. 1976). United States ⊶64.20

12 Present responsibility test

General Services Administration's (GSA) suspension of contractor and its affiliate upon indictment of contractor and its president for defrauding government was proper, despite contractor's claim that it had ensured its "present responsibility" by incorporating safeguards into its corporate structure, such as president's resignation and transfer of control to management committee; president remained employed by contractor, thereby casting doubt on independence of new management committee, which was composed of several longtime friends and associates of president. 48 C.F.R. §§ 9.407-1(a), (b)(2). Commercial Drapery Contractors, Inc. v. U.S., 133 F.3d 1, 6, 39 Fed. R. Serv. 3d 825 (D.C. Cir. 1998). United States ⊶64.20

Evidence supported suspending official's decision not to make finding of "present responsibility" following indictment of government drapery contractor and contractor's owner for misconduct relating to prior contracts; evidence indicated that owner maintained close associations with contractor, that friends and relatives of owner continued to manage company and that contractor failed to investigate allegations in indictment. 48 C.F.R. § 9.407-1(b)(2). Commercial Drapery Contractors, Inc. v. U.S., 967 F. Supp. 1, 41 Cont. Cas. Fed. (CCH) P 77172 (D.D.C. 1997), judgment aff'd, 133 F.3d 1, 39 Fed. R. Serv. 3d 825 (D.C. Cir. 1998). United States ⊶75(4)

13 Suspension, generally

Notifying potential contractor of suspension of processing of particular potential contract, without purporting to restrict contractor's participation in agency programs for a specified period of time, was not a "Limited Denial of Participation" under regulation so as to entitle contractor to notice and hearing. Pro-Mark, Inc. v. Kemp, 781 F. Supp. 1172, 38 Cont. Cas. Fed. (CCH) P 76368 (S.D. Miss. 1991), aff'd, 952 F.2d 401 (5th Cir. 1992). United States ⊶64.20

Federal Acquisition Regulations System (FAR) provided constitutionally adequate direction to agency officials seeking to determine whether suspension of contractor from eligibility for government contracts upon contractor's indictment was appropriate; regulations specified that suspension was to further policy that agencies contract only with responsible contractors and was to be imposed only upon determination that doing so was in government's interest, set forth specific qualifying causes for suspension, and directed suspending official to consider evidence against contractor, its reliability, and gravity of alleged offense, and permitted contractor to present for consideration any form of credible exculpatory evidence showing that suspension would not be in government's interest. U.S.C.A. Const.Amend. 14; 48 C.F.R. §§ 9.401–9.407. Rutigliano Paper Stock, Inc. v. U.S. General Services Admin., 967 F. Supp. 757, 41 Cont. Cas. Fed. (CCH) P 77156 (E.D. N.Y. 1997). United States ⊶64.20

A procuring body cannot hold a contractor in "suspended animation" for an indefinite period of time without affording it procedural protections associated with a formal suspension or debarment; contractor is entitled to receive such protection even though procuring body did not label its action a "suspension." Shermco Industries, Inc. v. Secretary of the Air Force, 584 F. Supp. 76, 32 Cont. Cas. Fed. (CCH) P 72713 (N.D. Tex. 1984). United States ⊶64.20

Agency acted arbitrarily and capriciously in suspending contractor from bidding on government contracts for one year, where it deemed contractor both responsible and nonresponsible for the same time period and based on the same evidence, as demonstrated by grant of five interim contracts to contractor, and thus suspension appeared to be in the nature of punishment rather than a response to a real need for immediate action. 48 C.F.R. § 9.407-2(a)(7), (b). Lion Raisins, Inc. v. U.S., 51 Fed. Cl. 238 (2001). United States ☞64.20

14 Indictment for crime

Moving and storage company that was not indicted for antitrust violations was nonetheless properly placed on Department of Army's list of disqualified bidders, when company was an affiliate of company named in indictment. Coleman American Moving Services, Inc. v. Weinberger, 716 F. Supp. 1405, 36 Cont. Cas. Fed. (CCH) P 75786 (M.D. Ala. 1989). United States ☞64.20

Suspension of contractor was based on adequate evidence, where suspension board gave careful consideration to criminal indictment against contractor and additional information supporting indictment before it recommended suspension. Shermco Industries, Inc. v. Secretary of the Air Force, 584 F. Supp. 76, 32 Cont. Cas. Fed. (CCH) P 72713 (N.D. Tex. 1984). United States ☞64.20

Where there was no showing that new suspension of contractor from contracting for federal contracts as a result of indictment charging false statements and fraud in connection with performance of prior government contracts was not in accordance with applicable regulations, and where there was no contention that the regulations were invalid, the Navy could not presently award four contracts on which contractor was low bidder to contractor and there was no basis for enjoining awards to others or preventing them from proceeding on awards already made. ATL, Inc. v. U.S., 6 Cl. Ct. 539, 32 Cont. Cas. Fed. (CCH) P 73067 (1984). United States ☞64.20

15 Rescission or termination

Clause in government contracts permitting either party to cancel contract upon 30 days' written notice did not conflict with second provision permitting "termination for convenience," and thus, even though 30-day provision had not been published in Federal Register, General Services Administration (GSA) could invoke that provision to cancel contracts upon suspending contractor due to its indictment for defrauding government; 30-day provision permitted either party to cancel entire multiple award schedule contract with requisite notice, while "termination for convenience" provision, which was included in most federal contracts, permitted either party to cancel individual orders. 48 C.F.R. § 1.401. Commercial Drapery Contractors, Inc. v. U.S., 133 F.3d 1, 6, 39 Fed. R. Serv. 3d 825 (D.C. Cir. 1998). United States ☞72.1(1)

Federal Acquisition Regulation (FAR) permitting continuation of contracts despite contractor's suspension, rather than General Services Administration's (GSA) implementing regulations, applied to GSA's cancellation of government drapery contracts following contractor's suspension; GSA regulation only provided implementing rules to deal with situations involving default or significant risk to government. 48 C.F.R. §§ 9.405-1, 509.405-1. Commercial Drapery Contractors, Inc. v. U.S., 967 F. Supp. 1, 41 Cont. Cas. Fed. (CCH) P 77172 (D.D.C. 1997), judgment aff'd, 133 F.3d 1, 39 Fed. R. Serv. 3d 825 (D.C. Cir. 1998). United States ☞72.1(1)

Small Business Act and Competition in Contracting Act provisions applicable when company is being considered for contract award are inapplicable to General Services Administration (GSA) action suspending or terminating government contract. Small Business Act, § 2[8](b)(7), as amended, 15 U.S.C.A. § 637(b)(7); Federal Property and Administrative Services Act of 1949, § 303B(c), (d)(2), as amended, 41 U.S.C.A. § 253b(c), (d)(2); 48 C.F.R. § 19.602-1(a)(2)(ii). Commercial Drapery Contractors, Inc. v. U.S., 967 F. Supp. 1, 41 Cont. Cas. Fed. (CCH) P 77172 (D.D.C. 1997), judgment aff'd, 133 F.3d 1, 39 Fed. R. Serv. 3d 825 (D.C. Cir. 1998). United States ☞72.1(1)

16 Agriculture Department

Department of Agriculture's order barring meat supplier from bidding on or being awarded contracts to supply meat for USDA programs was supported by substantial evidence as to the supplier's affiliation with another suspended supplier and as to illegal activities involving movement of unwholesome meat in Department of Agriculture programs. Rules and Regulations, §§ 1-1.601-1(e), 1-1.605-2(b), 1-1.605-3, 41 U.S.C.A.App.

Stanko Packing Co., Inc. v. Bergland, 489 F. Supp. 947, 27 Cont. Cas. Fed. (CCH) P 80419 (D.D.C. 1980). Food ⏄12; United States ⏄64.20

17 Armed services and defense

Administrative proceedings in which Air Force had threatened to suspend or disbar contractor from entering into contracts with Department of Defense constituted "alternate remedy" to qui tam action under False Claims Act (FCA), and thus contractor's former employee who commenced qui tam action based on contractor's use of defective damping fluid and falsification of test results was entitled under FCA to relator's share of proceeds from settlement agreement arising from proceedings which required contractor to repair and replace defective flight data transmitters and to replace defective damping fluid, even though suspension or debarment proceeding was significantly different from FCA action, where government declined to intervene in qui tam action arising from defective fluid, choosing instead to go forward with suspension or debarment proceeding based on conduct that formed basis of action, and then settled relator's action for false testing, with result that relator was later found barred by claim preclusion from pursuing action for defective damping fluid. 31 U.S.C.A. § 3730(c)(5). U.S. ex rel. Barajas v. U.S., 258 F.3d 1004 (9th Cir. 2001). United States ⏄122

Army lacked authority to bind Government to a contract with low bidder as long as bidder was suspended from receiving any government contracts and therefore low bidder's suit to enjoin temporarily the award of two Army Corps of Engineers contracts to any other bidders did not constitute a "bid protest" case over which Claims Court had jurisdiction. ATL, Inc. v. U.S., 735 F.2d 1343 (Fed. Cir. 1984). Federal Courts ⏄1074; United States ⏄64.20; United States ⏄64.60(1)

Claims Court lacked jurisdiction to consider claim that Department of Army failed to apply procedures governing suspension of government contractors and allotment of make-up tonnage, as its jurisdiction was limited to "contractual undertaking" where remedy was money damages. 28 U.S.C.A. § 1491(a)(1). Coleman American Moving Services, Inc. v. Weinberger, 716 F. Supp. 1405, 36 Cont. Cas. Fed. (CCH) P 75786 (M.D. Ala. 1989). Federal Courts ⏄1074

In Air Force suspension or debarment proceeding against defense contractor, government lacks any power to compel production of evidence or attendance of witnesses. 48 C.F.R. §§ 9.406-1 et seq., 9.407-1 et seq.U.S. ex rel. Barajas v. Northrop Corp., 65 F. Supp. 2d 1097 (C.D. Cal. 1999), rev'd and remanded on other grounds, 258 F.3d 1004 (9th Cir. 2001). United States ⏄64.20

A procuring agency cannot make successive determinations of nonresponsibility with regard to a contractor on the same basis; rather, it must initiate suspension or debarment procedures at the earliest practicable date following the first determination of nonresponsibility. Shermco Industries, Inc. v. Secretary of the Air Force, 584 F. Supp. 76, 32 Cont. Cas. Fed. (CCH) P 72713 (N.D. Tex. 1984). United States ⏄64.20

18 Environmental Protection Agency

Director of Grants Administration Division is only Environmental Protection Agency official who has authority to debar or suspend contractor or to issue notice proposing debarment or suspension. Baranowski v. E.P.A., 699 F. Supp. 1119, 29 Env't. Rep. Cas. (BNA) 1213 (E.D. Pa. 1988), judgment aff'd, 902 F.2d 1558 (3d Cir. 1990). Environmental Law ⏄15

19 Housing and Urban Development

Decision of Department of Housing and Urban Development (HUD) not to initiate debarment proceedings against certain officers of suspended HUD coinsured lender was unreviewable, and thus, district court's requirement that HUD give reasoned explanation for its decision to take debarment action against one former officer, but not other similarly situated officers was improper; no statute expressly provided for debarment actions or contained guidelines that informed HUD's decision to bring such actions, HUD's own regulations did not provide sufficient standards circumscribing HUD's enforcement discretion over debarment actions to rebut presumption of unreviewability, and there was no procedural step at initiation of debarment process which would provide focus for judicial review of HUD's nonenforcement decisions. 5 U.S.C.A. § 706(2); Executive Order No. 12549,

§ 1 et seq., 31 U.S.C.A. § 6101 note. Kisser v. Cisneros, 14 F.3d 615, 619 (D.C. Cir. 1994). United States ⇒53(9)

Department of Housing and Urban Development (HUD) did not have to show that officer of suspended HUD coinsured lender was final decision maker in lender's passthrough procedures in violation of requirements of Government National Mortgage Assistance (GNMA) to sustain officer's debarment from participating in primary and lower tier covered transactions throughout executive branch of federal government for three years, and HUD was justified in debarring officer based upon substantial evidence that officer not only had reason to know of lender's misconduct, but also participated in it; fact that officer was participant, and not ultimate decision maker and that decisions were made on advice of counsel did not insulate him from sanction of debarment. Kisser v. Cisneros, 14 F.3d 615, 622 (D.C. Cir. 1994). United States ⇒53(9)

20 Exhaustion of administrative remedies

Exhaustion of administrative remedies rule barred judicial review of res judicata-collateral estoppel defense to suspension by United States Department of Transportation of contractors from participation in Department financial assistance programs. Mainelli v. U.S., 611 F. Supp. 606 (D.R.I. 1985). United States ⇒82(7)

21 Res judicata and collateral estoppel

Intervening indictment against contractors was changed circumstance rendering collateral estoppel inapplicable in action brought by contractors seeking preliminary injunction prohibiting Department of Transportation from suspending them from participation in Department sponsored financial assistance programs. Mainelli v. U.S., 611 F. Supp. 606 (D.R.I. 1985). Judgment ⇒739

22 Injunctions—In general

For purpose of determining contractor's entitlement to injunction against enforcement of Federal Acquisition Regulations System (FAR), contractor's almost total loss of business and inability to bid on new contracts as result of suspension from eligibility for government contracts constituted "irreparable harm" incapable of being remedied by monetary damages alone. 48 C.F.R. §§ 9.401–9.407. Rutigliano Paper Stock, Inc. v. U.S. General Services Admin., 967 F. Supp. 757, 41 Cont. Cas. Fed. (CCH) P 77156 (E.D. N.Y. 1997). Injunction ⇒86

Bidder failed to establish substantial likelihood that it would prevail on merits of its claim that its suspension from further contracting with any agency in executive branch of government violated federal acquisition regulations or that it was denied due process and, therefore, bidder was not entitled to preliminary injunction to prevent Air Force from awarding contract to install new windows at Air Force bases; bidder had been suspended from competition after it was indicted for making false claims and false statements. U.S.C.A. Const.Amends. 5, 14. JDL Const., Inc. v. U.S., 14 Cl. Ct. 825, 34 Cont. Cas. Fed. (CCH) P 75502, 1988 WL 58047 (1988). Civil Rights ⇒1457(7); Injunction ⇒138.63

23 Injunctions—Preliminary injunctions and restraining orders

Contractor who had been indicted for filing false claims in connection with navy contracts was not entitled to preliminary injunction prohibiting Secretaries of Army, Navy and Air Force from suspending him and his company for competing for government contracts, where contractor was not likely to prevail on his constitutional challenge to acquisition regulations, public interest favored allowing suspension of contractors indicted for fraud against government and loss of opportunity to bid on undetermined number of military contracts during suspension period did not constitute irreparable harm. James A. Merritt and Sons v. Marsh, 791 F.2d 328, 33 Cont. Cas. Fed. (CCH) P 74391 (4th Cir. 1986). Injunction ⇒138.63

Contractors were not entitled to preliminary injunction prohibiting Department of Transportation from suspending them from participation in Department financial assistance programs, where contractors were not likely to succeed on their claims that Department was barred from suspending them by doctrines of res judicata and collateral estoppel based upon determination by Rhode Island Department of Transportation that they had committed no substantive violations of minority business enterprise regulation through its subcontracting, that suspension regulations were procedurally defective in that they failed to give contractors hearing before suspension, that regulations were unconstitutional because Government was free to base suspension on indictment alone, irrespective of showing made by contractor at hearing, and that regulation under which they were suspended violated, on its face, Fifth Amendment privilege against selfincrimination. U.S.C.A. Const. Amend. 5. Mainelli v. U.S., 611 F. Supp. 606 (D.R.I. 1985). Injunction ☞138.63

Government contractors accused of intentionally defrauding Government by selling substandard neoprene tubing to Defense Department were not entitled to preliminary injunction prohibiting Government from placing their names on suspended contractors list; Defense Logistics Agency (DLA) acted in accordance with applicable statutes and regulations and had rational basis for its decision, and contractors made no attempt at redressing their suspension with DLA official. RSI, Inc. v. U.S., 772 F. Supp. 956 (W.D. Tex. 1991). Injunction ☞138.63

Possible harm to Government if preliminary injunction were granted, preventing Air Force from awarding window installation contract, outweighed threatened harm to bidder and, therefore, bidder was not entitled to injunctive relief based on its challenge to suspension from competition after it had been indicted for making false claims and false statements. JDL Const., Inc. v. U.S., 14 Cl. Ct. 825, 34 Cont. Cas. Fed. (CCH) P 75502, 1988 WL 58047 (1988). Injunction ☞138.63

Bidder failed to show that it would be irreparably harmed, absent preliminary injunction to prevent Air Force from awarding window installation contract to anyone else; bidder's suspension from competition after it had been indicted for making false claims and false statements was not permanent and, even if contract could have been completed before contractor opposed suspension, Claims Court retained full, equitable jurisdiction to fashion any appropriate relief if bidder prevailed in its suit. JDL Const., Inc. v. U.S., 14 Cl. Ct. 825, 34 Cont. Cas. Fed. (CCH) P 75502, 1988 WL 58047 (1988). Injunction ☞138.63

24 Jurisdiction

Contractors' action against United States, challenging General Services Administration's (GSA) termination of two current contracts and suspension of further contracting pending completion of criminal proceedings, was not at its essence a contract action, and thus, Court of Appeals had jurisdiction over appeal from district court's decision; even though contractors complained about termination clause in their contracts, basis of their claim was that GSA's repeated attempts to extricate government from financial dealings with them constituted unlawful "blacklisting," and dispute over termination clause in their contracts was embedded within that broader claim, and was not independent cause of action. 28 U.S.C.A. § 1346(a)(2); Contract Disputes Act of 1978, §§ 8(g), 10(a)(1), 41 U.S.C.A. §§ 607(g), 609(a)(1). Commercial Drapery Contractors, Inc. v. U.S., 133 F.3d 1, 4, 39 Fed. R. Serv. 3d 825 (D.C. Cir. 1998). Federal Courts ☞1139

§ 9.407-2 Causes for suspension.

(a) The suspending official may suspend a contractor suspected, upon adequate evidence, of—

(1) Commission of fraud or a criminal offense in connection with—

(i) Obtaining;

(ii) Attempting to obtain; or

(iii) Performing a public contract or subcontract.

(2) Violation of Federal or State antitrust statutes relating to the submission of offers;

(3) Commission of embezzlement, theft, forgery, bribery, falsification or destruction of records, making false statements, tax evasion, violating Federal criminal tax laws, or receiving stolen property;

(4) Violations of 41 U.S.C. chapter 81, Drug-Free Workplace, as indicated by—

(i) Failure to comply with the requirements of the clause at 52.223-6, Drug-Free Workplace; or

(ii) Such a number of contractor employees convicted of violations of criminal drug statutes occurring in the workplace as to indicate that the contractor has failed to make a good faith effort to provide a drug-free workplace (see 23.504);

(5) Intentionally affixing a label bearing a "Made in America" inscription (or any

inscription having the same meaning) to a product sold in or shipped to the United States or its outlying areas, when the product was not made in the United States or its outlying areas (see Section 202 of the Defense Production Act (Public Law 102-558));

(6) Commission of an unfair trade practice as defined in 9.403 (see section 201 of the Defense Production Act (Pub. L. 102-558));

(7) Delinquent Federal taxes in an amount that exceeds $3,500. See the criteria at 9.406-2(b)(1)(v) for determination of when taxes are delinquent;

(8) Knowing failure by a principal, until 3 years after final payment on any Government contract awarded to the contractor, to timely disclose to the Government, in connection with the award, performance, or closeout of the contract or a subcontract thereunder, credible evidence of—

(i) Violation of Federal criminal law involving fraud, conflict of interest, bribery, or gratuity violations found in Title 18 of the United States Code;

(ii) Violation of the civil False Claims Act (31 U.S.C. 3729–3733); or

(iii) Significant overpayment(s) on the contract, other than overpayments resulting from contract financing payments as defined in 32.001; or

(9) Commission of any other offense indicating a lack of business integrity or business honesty that seriously and directly affects the present responsibility of a Government contractor or subcontractor.

(b) Indictment for any of the causes in paragraph (a) of this section constitutes adequate evidence for suspension.

(c) The suspending official may upon adequate evidence also suspend a contractor for any other cause of so serious or compelling a nature that it affects the present responsibility of a Government contractor or subcontractor.

United States Code Annotated

Administrative determinations, see 41 USCA § 257.

Contract requirements, see 41 USCA § 254.

Contractor responsibilities, see 41 USCA § 57.

Contracts, planning, solicitation, evaluation, and award procedures, see 10 USCA § 2305.

Definitions, see 10 USCA § 2302, 41 USCA §§ 259, 403.

Determinations and decisions, see 10 USCA § 2310, 41 USCA § 262.

Kinds of contracts, see 10 USCA § 2306.

Planning and solicitation requirements, see 41 USCA § 253a.

Notes of Decisions

Armed services and defense 4
Environmental Protection Agency 5
Housing and Urban Development 6
Indictment for crime 3
Rescission or termination 1
Suspension, generally 2

1 Rescission or termination

Substantial evidence supported General Services Administration's (GSA) cancellation of drapery contracts with contractor and its affiliate based on the indictment of contractor and its owner for misconduct related to prior contracts. 48 C.F.R. §§ 9.407-1, 9.407-2(a, b). Commercial Drapery Contractors, Inc. v. U.S., 967 F. Supp. 1, 41 Cont. Cas. Fed. (CCH) P 77172 (D.D.C. 1997), judgment aff'd, 133 F.3d 1, 39 Fed. R. Serv. 3d 825 (D.C. Cir. 1998). United States ⊙⊸72.1(2); United States ⊙⊸75(4)

2 Suspension, generally

Notifying potential contractor of suspension of processing of particular potential contract, without purporting to restrict contractor's participation in agency programs for a specified period of time, was not a "Limited Denial of Participation" under regulation so as to entitle contractor to notice and hearing. Pro-Mark, Inc. v. Kemp, 781 F. Supp. 1172, 38 Cont. Cas. Fed. (CCH) P 76368 (S.D. Miss. 1991), aff'd, 952 F.2d 401 (5th Cir. 1992). United States

☞64.20

Federal Acquisition Regulations System (FAR) provided constitutionally adequate direction to agency officials seeking to determine whether suspension of contractor from eligibility for government contracts upon contractor's indictment was appropriate; regulations specified that suspension was to further policy that agencies contract only with responsible contractors and was to be imposed only upon determination that doing so was in government's interest, set forth specific qualifying causes for suspension, and directed suspending official to consider evidence against contractor, its reliability, and gravity of alleged offense, and permitted contractor to present for consideration any form of credible exculpatory evidence showing that suspension would not be in government's interest. U.S.C.A. Const.Amend. 14; 48 C.F.R. §§ 9.401–9.407. Rutigliano Paper Stock, Inc. v. U.S. General Services Admin., 967 F. Supp. 757, 41 Cont. Cas. Fed. (CCH) P 77156 (E.D. N.Y. 1997). United States ☞64.20

A procuring body cannot hold a contractor in "suspended animation" for an indefinite period of time without affording it procedural protections associated with a formal suspension or debarment; contractor is entitled to receive such protection even though procuring body did not label its action a "suspension." Shermco Industries, Inc. v. Secretary of the Air Force, 584 F. Supp. 76, 32 Cont. Cas. Fed. (CCH) P 72713 (N.D. Tex. 1984). United States ☞64.20

Agency acted arbitrarily and capriciously in suspending contractor from bidding on government contracts for one year, where it deemed contractor both responsible and nonresponsible for the same time period and based on the same evidence, as demonstrated by grant of five interim contracts to contractor, and thus suspension appeared to be in the nature of punishment rather than a response to a real need for immediate action. 48 C.F.R. § 9.407-2(a)(7), (b). Lion Raisins, Inc. v. U.S., 51 Fed. Cl. 238 (2001). United States ☞64.20

Protester was properly excluded from competition where it had been suspended on the basis of detailed, unrebutted allegations of misconduct which were contained in a civil complaint filed by a federal government entity in Matter of: SDA Inc., B-253322, B-253355, B-253577, B-253577.2, 93-2 CPD ¶ 132 (Comp. Gen. 1993) Suspensions are imposed for a temporary period before suspected misconduct is proven and while an investigation of the contractor is taking place. FAR 9.407-4.

An agency may suspend a contractor suspected, upon "adequate evidence," of misconduct indicating a lack of business integrity. FAR § 9.407-2. "Adequate evidence" is more than uncorroborated suspicion or accusation. The FAR provides that, in assessing the adequacy of the evidence, agencies should consider, among other factors, "how much information is available, how credible it is given the circumstances, [and] whether or not important allegations are corroborated." Matter of: SDA Inc., B-253322, B-253355, B-253577, B-253577.2, 93-2 CPD ¶ 132 (Comp. Gen. 1993)

When a protester alleges that it has been improperly suspended or debarred during the pendency of a procurement in which it was competing, the General Accounting Office will review the matter to ensure that the agency has not acted arbitrarily to avoid making an award to the bidder otherwise entitled to the award and also to ensure that minimum standards of due process have been met. Agency had a reasonable basis to suspend an individual, who was authorized to sign contracts for a suspended contractor, since the agency had adequate evidence to impute the suspended contractor's misconduct (involving bribery to obtain government contracts) to the individual. TS Generalbau GmbH; Thomas Stadlbauer, B-246034, B-246036, B-246037, B-246037.2, B-246038, B-246039, B-246040, B-246040.2, B-246042, B-246042.2, B-246043, B-246043.2, 92-1 CPD ¶ 189 (Comp. Gen. 1992)

3 Indictment for crime

Moving and storage company that was not indicted for antitrust violations was nonetheless properly placed on Department of Army's list of disqualified bidders, when company was an affiliate of company named in indictment. Coleman American Moving Services, Inc. v. Weinberger, 716 F. Supp. 1405, 36 Cont. Cas. Fed. (CCH) P 75786 (M.D. Ala. 1989). United States ☞64.20

Suspension of contractor was based on adequate evidence, where suspension board gave careful consideration to criminal indictment against contractor and additional information supporting indictment before it recommended suspension. Shermco Industries, Inc. v.

Secretary of the Air Force, 584 F. Supp. 76, 32 Cont. Cas. Fed. (CCH) P 72713 (N.D. Tex. 1984). United States ☞64.20

Where there was no showing that new suspension of contractor from contracting for federal contracts as a result of indictment charging false statements and fraud in connection with performance of prior government contracts was not in accordance with applicable regulations, and where there was no contention that the regulations were invalid, the Navy could not presently award four contracts on which contractor was low bidder to contractor and there was no basis for enjoining awards to others or preventing them from proceeding on awards already made. ATL, Inc. v. U.S., 6 Cl. Ct. 539, 32 Cont. Cas. Fed. (CCH) P 73067 (1984). United States ☞64.20

4 Armed services and defense

Administrative proceedings in which Air Force had threatened to suspend or disbar contractor from entering into contracts with Department of Defense constituted "alternate remedy" to qui tam action under False Claims Act (FCA), and thus contractor's former employee who commenced qui tam action based on contractor's use of defective damping fluid and falsification of test results was entitled under FCA to relator's share of proceeds from settlement agreement arising from proceedings which required contractor to repair and replace defective flight data transmitters and to replace defective damping fluid, even though suspension or debarment proceeding was significantly different from FCA action, where government declined to intervene in qui tam action arising from defective fluid, choosing instead to go forward with suspension or debarment proceeding based on conduct that formed basis of action, and then settled relator's action for false testing, with result that relator was later found barred by claim preclusion from pursuing action for defective damping fluid. 31 U.S.C.A. § 3730(c)(5). U.S. ex rel. Barajas v. U.S., 258 F.3d 1004 (9th Cir. 2001). United States ☞122

Army lacked authority to bind Government to a contract with low bidder as long as bidder was suspended from receiving any government contracts and therefore low bidder's suit to enjoin temporarily the award of two Army Corps of Engineers contracts to any other bidders did not constitute a "bid protest" case over which Claims Court had jurisdiction. ATL, Inc. v. U.S., 735 F.2d 1343 (Fed. Cir. 1984). Federal Courts ☞1074; United States ☞64.20; United States ☞64.60(1)

Claims Court lacked jurisdiction to consider claim that Department of Army failed to apply procedures governing suspension of government contractors and allotment of make-up tonnage, as its jurisdiction was limited to "contractual undertaking" where remedy was money damages. 28 U.S.C.A. § 1491(a)(1). Coleman American Moving Services, Inc. v. Weinberger, 716 F. Supp. 1405, 36 Cont. Cas. Fed. (CCH) P 75786 (M.D. Ala. 1989). Federal Courts ☞1074

In Air Force suspension or debarment proceeding against defense contractor, government lacks any power to compel production of evidence or attendance of witnesses. 48 C.F.R. §§ 9.406-1 et seq., 9.407-1 et seq.U.S. ex rel. Barajas v. Northrop Corp., 65 F. Supp. 2d 1097 (C.D. Cal. 1999), rev'd and remanded on other grounds, 258 F.3d 1004 (9th Cir. 2001). United States ☞64.20

A procuring agency cannot make successive determinations of nonresponsibility with regard to a contractor on the same basis; rather, it must initiate suspension or debarment procedures at the earliest practicable date following the first determination of nonresponsibility. Shermco Industries, Inc. v. Secretary of the Air Force, 584 F. Supp. 76, 32 Cont. Cas. Fed. (CCH) P 72713 (N.D. Tex. 1984). United States ☞64.20

5 Environmental Protection Agency

Director of Grants Administration Division is only Environmental Protection Agency official who has authority to debar or suspend contractor or to issue notice proposing debarment or suspension. Baranowski v. E.P.A., 699 F. Supp. 1119, 29 Env't. Rep. Cas. (BNA) 1213 (E.D. Pa. 1988), judgment aff'd, 902 F.2d 1558 (3d Cir. 1990). Environmental Law ☞15

6 Housing and Urban Development

Decision of Department of Housing and Urban Development (HUD) not to initiate debarment proceedings against certain officers of suspended HUD coinsured lender was unreviewable, and thus, district court's requirement that HUD give reasoned explanation for its decision to take debarment action against one former officer, but not other similarly situated officers was improper; no statute expressly provided for debarment actions or contained guidelines that informed HUD's decision to bring such actions, HUD's own regulations did not provide sufficient standards circumscribing HUD's enforcement discretion over debarment actions to rebut presumption of unreviewability, and there was no procedural step at initiation of debarment process which would provide focus for judicial review of HUD's nonenforcement decisions. 5 U.S.C.A. § 706(2); Executive Order No. 12549, § 1 et seq., 31 U.S.C.A. § 6101 note. Kisser v. Cisneros, 14 F.3d 615, 619 (D.C. Cir. 1994). United States ☞53(9)

Department of Housing and Urban Development (HUD) did not have to show that officer of suspended HUD coinsured lender was final decision maker in lender's passthrough procedures in violation of requirements of Government National Mortgage Assistance (GNMA) to sustain officer's debarment from participating in primary and lower tier covered transactions throughout executive branch of federal government for three years, and HUD was justified in debarring officer based upon substantial evidence that officer not only had reason to know of lender's misconduct, but also participated in it; fact that officer was participant, and not ultimate decision maker and that decisions were made on advice of counsel did not insulate him from sanction of debarment. Kisser v. Cisneros, 14 F.3d 615, 622 (D.C. Cir. 1994). United States ☞53(9)

§ 9.407-3 Procedures.

(a) *Investigation and referral*. Agencies shall establish procedures for the prompt reporting, investigation, and referral to the suspending official of matters appropriate for that official's consideration.

(b) Decisionmaking process.

(1) Agencies shall establish procedures governing the suspension decisionmaking process that are as informal as is practicable, consistent with principles of fundamental fairness. These procedures shall afford the contractor (and any specifically named affiliates) an opportunity, following the imposition of suspension, to submit, in person, in writing, or through a representative, information and argument in opposition to the suspension.

(2) In actions not based on an indictment, if it is found that the contractor's submission in opposition raises a genuine dispute over facts material to the suspension and if no determination has been made, on the basis of Department of Justice advice, that substantial interests of the Government in pending or contemplated legal proceedings based on the same facts as the suspension would be prejudiced, agencies shall also—

(i) Afford the contractor an opportunity to appear with counsel, submit documentary evidence, present witnesses, and confront any person the agency presents; and

(ii) Make a transcribed record of the proceedings and make it available at cost to the contractor upon request, unless the contractor and the agency, by mutual agreement, waive the requirement for a transcript.

(c) *Notice of suspension*. When a contractor and any specifically named affiliates are suspended, they shall be immediately advised by certified mail, return receipt requested—

(1) That they have been suspended and that the suspension is based on an indictment or other adequate evidence that the contractor has committed irregularities—

(i) Of a serious nature in business dealings with the Government or

(ii) Seriously reflecting on the propriety of further Government dealings with the contractor—any such irregularities shall be described in terms sufficient to place the contractor on notice without disclosing the Government's evidence;

(2) That the suspension is for a temporary period pending the completion of an investigation and such legal proceedings as may ensue;

(3) Of the cause(s) relied upon under 9.407-2 for imposing suspension;

(4) Of the effect of the suspension;

(5) That, within 30 days after receipt of the notice, the contractor may submit, in person, in writing, or through a representative, information and argument in opposition to the suspension, including any additional specific information that raises a genuine

dispute over the material facts; and

(6) That additional proceedings to determine disputed material facts will be conducted unless—

(i) The action is based on an indictment; or

(ii) A determination is made, on the basis of Department of Justice advice, that the substantial interests of the Government in pending or contemplated legal proceedings based on the same facts as the suspension would be prejudiced.

(d) Suspending official's decision.

(1) In actions—

(i) Based on an indictment;

(ii) In which the contractor's submission does not raise a genuine dispute over material facts; or

(iii) In which additional proceedings to determine disputed material facts have been denied on the basis of Department of Justice advice, the suspending official's decision shall be based on all the information in the administrative record, including any submission made by the contractor.

(2) (i) In actions in which additional proceedings are necessary as to disputed material facts, written findings of fact shall be prepared. The suspending official shall base the decision on the facts as found, together with any information and argument submitted by the contractor and any other information in the administrative record.

(ii) The suspending official may refer matters involving disputed material facts to another official for findings of fact. The suspending official may reject any such findings, in whole or in part, only after specifically determining them to be arbitrary and capricious or clearly erroneous.

(iii) The suspending official's decision shall be made after the conclusion of the proceedings with respect to disputed facts.

(3) The suspending official may modify or terminate the suspension or leave it in force (for example, see 9.406-4(c) for the reasons for reducing the period or extent of debarment). However, a decision to modify or terminate the suspension shall be without prejudice to the subsequent imposition of—

(i) Suspension by any other agency; or

(ii) Debarment by any agency.

(4) Prompt written notice of the suspending official's decision shall be sent to the contractor and any affiliates involved, by certified mail, return receipt requested.

(e) (1) If the contractor enters into an administrative agreement with the Government in order to resolve a suspension proceeding, the suspending official shall access the website (available at www.cpars.csd.disa.mil, then select FAPIIS) and enter the requested information.

(2) The suspending official is responsible for the timely submission, within 3 working days, and accuracy of the documentation regarding the administrative agreement.

(3) With regard to information that may be covered by a disclosure exemption under the Freedom of Information Act, the suspending official shall follow the procedures at 9.105-2(b)(2)(iv).

United States Code Annotated

Administrative determinations, see 41 USCA § 257.

Contract requirements, see 41 USCA § 254.

Contractor responsibilities, see 41 USCA § 57.

Contracts, planning, solicitation, evaluation, and award procedures, see 10 USCA § 2305.

Definitions, see 10 USCA § 2302, 41 USCA §§ 259, 403.

Determinations and decisions, see 10 USCA § 2310, 41 USCA § 262.

Kinds of contracts, see 10 USCA § 2306.

Planning and solicitation requirements, see 41 USCA § 253a.

Notes of Decisions
In general 2

1 Validity

Federal acquisitions regulations governing debarment of government contractors are not unreasonable or unconstitutional. Joseph Const. Co. v. Veterans Admin. of U.S., 595 F. Supp. 448, 32 Cont. Cas. Fed. (CCH) P 73082 (N.D. Ill. 1984). United States ☞64.20

2 In general

Suspension and debarment of bidder for government contract occur when Government formally or constructively precludes contractor from participating in future, government contracts or when contracting official's decisions effectively prevent contractor from participating in that and future procurements. BMY, A Div. of HARSCO Corp. v. U.S., 693 F. Supp. 1232, 35 Cont. Cas. Fed. (CCH) P 75552 (D.D.C. 1988). United States ☞64.20

3 Purpose

Executive order providing for government-wide debarment and suspension of contractors who are debarred or suspended by particular agency was a managerial tool and not shown to be for the benefit of contractors, and thus did not provide basis for challenging government-wide debarment order on ground that, under the executive order, a prior agency debarment arising from the same circumstances should have been government-wide, precluding later imposition of the same penalty. Executive Order No. 12549, §§ 1 et seq., 1(a), 31 U.S.C.A. § 6101 note. Facchiano Const. Co., Inc. v. U.S. Dept. of Labor, 987 F.2d 206, 1 Wage & Hour Cas. 2d (BNA) 468, 39 Cont. Cas. Fed. (CCH) P 76542, 124 Lab. Cas. (CCH) P 35782 (3d Cir. 1993). United States ☞64.20

4 Retroactive or prospective application

Executive order providing for government-wide debarment and suspension of government contractors debarred or suspended by particular agency did not become effective until issuance of guidelines by Office of Management and Budget (OMB) and subsequent implementing regulations and, in the interim, Department of Labor (DOL) properly continued operating according to its existing regulations. Executive Order No. 12549, § 6, 31 U.S.C.A. § 6101 note. Facchiano Const. Co., Inc. v. U.S. Dept. of Labor, 987 F.2d 206, 1 Wage & Hour Cas. 2d (BNA) 468, 39 Cont. Cas. Fed. (CCH) P 76542, 124 Lab. Cas. (CCH) P 35782 (3d Cir. 1993). United States ☞64.20

5 Due process of law

General Services Administration (GSA) did not violate contractor's due process rights by denying contractor's request for formal hearing upon suspension of contractor and cancellation of its existing contracts due to contractor's indictment for defrauding government; contractor received both notice and informal hearing, and GSA official in charge of making suspension decision conferred with prosecutor and concluded that formal hearing could compromise ongoing criminal investigation. U.S.C.A. Const.Amend. 5. Commercial Drapery Contractors, Inc. v. U.S., 133 F.3d 1, 6, 39 Fed. R. Serv. 3d 825 (D.C. Cir. 1998).

Constitutional Law ☞276(2); United States ☞64.20; United States ☞72.1(1)

Agency may not impose even temporary suspension on government contractor without providing core requirements of due process, i.e., adequate notice and meaningful hearing. U.S.C.A. Const.Amend. 5. Commercial Drapery Contractors, Inc. v. U.S., 133 F.3d 1, 6, 39 Fed. R. Serv. 3d 825 (D.C. Cir. 1998). Constitutional Law ☞276(2)

Airline's due process interest in having fuller notice and hearing before Commercial Airline Review Board (CARB) suspended airline from military airlift transportation program did not outweigh government interest in avoiding administrative and financial burdens. U.S.C.A. Const.Amend. 5; 10 U.S.C.A. § 2640(c, d). Reeve Aleutian Airways, Inc. v. U.S., 982 F.2d 594, 602 (D.C. Cir. 1993), as amended on denial of reh'g, (Mar. 26, 1993). Constitutional Law ☞276(2); United States ☞64.20

Procedures that Commercial Airline Review Board (CARB) employed in suspending airline from military airlift transportation program did not violate due process, even though airline had significant interest in avoiding deprivation of reputational and economic interests caused by even temporary suspension; CARB provided specific notice, detailed statement of evidence, and opportunity to seek clarification of any confusion caused by notice. U.S.C.A. Const.Amend. 5; 10 U.S.C.A. § 2640(c, d). Reeve Aleutian Airways, Inc. v. U.S., 982 F.2d 594, 602 (D.C. Cir. 1993), as amended on denial of reh'g, (Mar. 26, 1993). Constitutional Law ☞276(2); United States ☞64.20

Airline had liberty interest in avoiding damage to its reputation and business caused by stigmatizing suspension by Commercial Airline Review Board (CARB), for purposes of due process challenge to procedures employed by CARB in suspending airline. U.S.C.A. Const. Amend. 5; 10 U.S.C.A. § 2640(c, d). Reeve Aleutian Airways, Inc. v. U.S., 982 F.2d 594, 599 (D.C. Cir. 1993), as amended on denial of reh'g, (Mar. 26, 1993). Constitutional Law ☞276(2); United States ☞64.20

Due process rights of airline were not violated by notice airline received from Commercial Airline Review Board (CARB) prior to hearing at which CARB suspended airline from military airlift transportation program on basis that airline did not receive adequate notice; CARB's notification letter was not inadequate for not saying which portions of report formed basis for CARB's actions, in that the whole report was of interest to CARB and airline was told explicitly what dispute was about and airline could be expected to have sufficient know-how to separate important from unimportant in report, moreover, notification letter offered follow-up contact during which airline could request additional information. U.S.C.A. Const.Amend. 5; 10 U.S.C.A. § 2640(c, d). Reeve Aleutian Airways, Inc. v. U.S., 982 F.2d 594, 599 (D.C. Cir. 1993), as amended on denial of reh'g, (Mar. 26, 1993). Constitutional Law ☞276(2); United States ☞64.20

Hearing before Commercial Airline Review Board (CARB) did not deprive airline, which was suspended from military airlift transportation program, of its right to due process, even though CARB was not required to present any witnesses thus allegedly depriving airline of opportunity to confront its accusers; airline had detailed specific statement of evidence against it in its possession months before hearing took place and airline apparently had chance to counter that evidence through oral or written presentation of whatever type or length it thought best, and had chance to engage in direct discussion of disputed topics with ultimate decision makers. U.S.C.A. Const.Amend. 5; 10 U.S.C.A. § 2640(c, d). Reeve Aleutian Airways, Inc. v. U.S., 982 F.2d 594, 601 (D.C. Cir. 1993), as amended on denial of reh'g, (Mar. 26, 1993). Constitutional Law ☞276(2); United States ☞64.20

Moving and storage companies were not entitled to increased tonnage under contracts with Department of Army to compensate them for period of time they were on suspended list of bidders for contracts, as they had no constitutionally protected due process right to receive make-up tonnage. U.S.C.A. Const.Amend. 5. Coleman American Moving Services, Inc. v. Weinberger, 716 F. Supp. 1405, 36 Cont. Cas. Fed. (CCH) P 75786 (M.D. Ala. 1989). Constitutional Law ☞276(2); United States ☞64.20

Moving and storage companies placed on Department of Army's suspended contractor list following filing of criminal antitrust indictments against them were not denied due process by suffering loss of corporate liberty interest to be free from stigmatizing government defamation, as whatever stigma was involved flowed not from Department's action but from indictment. U.S.C.A. Const.Amend. 5. Coleman American Moving Services, Inc. v. Weinberger, 716 F. Supp. 1405, 36 Cont. Cas. Fed. (CCH) P 75786 (M.D. Ala. 1989).

Constitutional Law ☜276(2); United States ☜64.20

Due process clause was not violated when moving and storage companies were placed on Department of Army's suspended contractors list following filing of antitrust indictments against them, as companies were merely bidders and as such had no constitutionally protectable property interest. U.S.C.A. Const.Amend. 5. Coleman American Moving Services, Inc. v. Weinberger, 716 F. Supp. 1405, 36 Cont. Cas. Fed. (CCH) P 75786 (M.D. Ala. 1989). Constitutional Law ☜277(1); United States ☜64.20

Government drapery contractor's late receipt of documents relating to subsequent cancellation action did not violate due process in proceeding to suspend contracts based on indictment of contractor and its owner, where contractor had full opportunity to rebut information on which General Services Administration's (GSA) decision to suspend was based, and was not prejudiced by late receipt of documents unrelated to grounds for suspension. U.S.C.A. Const.Amend. 14; 48 C.F.R. §§ 509.406-3(b)(6), 509.407-3(b)(5). Commercial Drapery Contractors, Inc. v. U.S., 967 F. Supp. 1, 41 Cont. Cas. Fed. (CCH) P 77172 (D.D.C. 1997), judgment aff'd, 133 F.3d 1, 39 Fed. R. Serv. 3d 825 (D.C. Cir. 1998). Constitutional Law ☜276(2); United States ☜75(3)

Procedures that preceded suspension of government drapery contractor and its affiliate based on indictment of contractor and its president satisfied requirements of due process, although formal evidentiary hearing was not conducted; procedures included contractor's meeting with suspending official and opportunity to submit additional evidence. U.S.C.A. Const.Amend. 14; 48 C.F.R. § 509.407-3(b)(6). Commercial Drapery Contractors, Inc. v. U.S., 967 F. Supp. 1, 41 Cont. Cas. Fed. (CCH) P 77172 (D.D.C. 1997), judgment aff'd, 133 F.3d 1, 39 Fed. R. Serv. 3d 825 (D.C. Cir. 1998). Constitutional Law ☜276(2); United States ☜75(3)

Formal or constructive suspension or debarment of government contractor is legal only if contractor has been afforded full due process protections. U.S.C.A. Const. Amends. 5, 14. BMY, A Div. of HARSCO Corp. v. U.S., 693 F. Supp. 1232, 35 Cont. Cas. Fed. (CCH) P 75552 (D.D.C. 1988). Constitutional Law ☜276(2); United States ☜64.20

Suspension of contractor from eligibility for government contracts pursuant to Federal Acquisition Regulations System (FAR), following contractor's indictment on charges involving fraud or dishonesty, satisfied requirements of procedural due process; although private interest at stake was important, initial reliability of indictment coupled with contractor's opportunity to rebut its conclusions greatly minimized risk of erroneous or irrational deprivation of its interest, and government interests in having responsible contractors perform its contracts and avoiding impairment of conduct of its business which would result if every governmental decision required full hearing involving all parties affected were significant. U.S.C.A. Const.Amend. 14; 48 C.F.R. §§ 9.401–9.407. Rutigliano Paper Stock, Inc. v. U.S. General Services Admin., 967 F. Supp. 757, 41 Cont. Cas. Fed. (CCH) P 77156 (E.D. N.Y. 1997). Constitutional Law ☜276(2); United States ☜64.20

For purpose of determining extent of process due contractor upon suspension of its eligibility for government contracts pursuant to Federal Acquisition Regulations System (FAR), such suspension, if based upon contractor's indictment, is considered to be based upon independent fact finding process that produced indictment, which process is considered sufficiently reliable to effect temporary but total deprivation of liberty. 48 C.F.R. §§ 9.401–9.407. Rutigliano Paper Stock, Inc. v. U.S. General Services Admin., 967 F. Supp. 757, 41 Cont. Cas. Fed. (CCH) P 77156 (E.D. N.Y. 1997). Constitutional Law ☜276(2); United States ☜64.20

Provision of Federal Acquisition Regulations System (FAR) continuing contractors' suspension from eligibility for government contracts until conclusion of significant activity in criminal action did not violate due process as applied, despite delay in trial on charges in indictment; contractors had been permitted to present evidence indicating that suspension was not in government's interest despite existence of indictment, and no significant activity in state criminal case was pending that would prolong suspension. U.S.C.A. Const. Amend. 14; 48 C.F.R. §§ 9.401–9.407. Rutigliano Paper Stock, Inc. v. U.S. General Services Admin., 967 F. Supp. 757, 41 Cont. Cas. Fed. (CCH) P 77156 (E.D. N.Y. 1997). Constitutional Law ☜276(2); United States ☜64.20

Due process is satisfied with respect to suspension of contractor from eligibility for government contracts under Federal Acquisition Regulations System (FAR) if meaningful opportunity to be heard on issue of appropriateness of suspension is granted within reasonable time and contractor is afforded opportunity to demonstrate that imposition of suspension would be irrational or contrary to government's interests. U.S.C.A. Const.Amend. 14; 48 C.F.R. §§ 9.401–9.407. Rutigliano Paper Stock, Inc. v. U.S. General Services Admin., 967 F. Supp. 757, 41 Cont. Cas. Fed. (CCH) P 77156 (E.D. N.Y. 1997). Constitutional Law ☞276(2); United States ☞64.20

Requirements of due process did not dictate that Federal Acquisition Regulations System (FAR) require justification for contractor's suspension from eligibility for government contracts beyond fact of contractor's indictment on charges involving fraud or dishonesty; indictment merely gave rise to rebuttable presumption that suspension was justified, contractor was entitled to provide contradictory evidence, indictment gave rise to presumption of probable cause and was sufficiently reliable to provide adequate basis for suspension, and judicial review of any improper suspension was available pursuant to Administrative Procedures Act. U.S.C.A. Const. Amend. 14; 5 U.S.C.A. § 551 et seq.; 48 C.F.R. §§ 9.401–9.407. Rutigliano Paper Stock, Inc. v. U.S. General Services Admin., 967 F. Supp. 757, 41 Cont. Cas. Fed. (CCH) P 77156 (E.D. N.Y. 1997). Constitutional Law ☞276(2); United States ☞64.20

Contractor's indictment gives rise to presumption of probable cause, such that grounding of rebuttable presumption that suspension from eligibility for government contracts pursuant to Federal Acquisition Regulations System (FAR) is warranted upon such indictment does not violate contractor's due process rights. U.S.C.A. Const.Amend. 14; 48 C.F.R. §§ 9.401–9.407. Rutigliano Paper Stock, Inc. v. U.S. General Services Admin., 967 F. Supp. 757, 41 Cont. Cas. Fed. (CCH) P 77156 (E.D. N.Y. 1997). Constitutional Law ☞276(2); United States ☞64.20

Requirements of due process did not dictate that Federal Acquisition Regulations System (FAR) provide additional fact finding hearing upon suspension of contractor from eligibility for government contracts, where basis for suspension was contractor's indictment on charges involving fraud or dishonesty, although government was obligated to inform contractor clearly of its opportunity to present evidence which might rebut indictment; General Services Administration (GSA) lacked power to find facts related to indictment, and purpose of contractor's opportunity to be heard was not to contest indictment. U.S.C.A. Const.Amend. 14; 48 C.F.R. §§ 9.401–9.407. Rutigliano Paper Stock, Inc. v. U.S. General Services Admin., 967 F. Supp. 757, 41 Cont. Cas. Fed. (CCH) P 77156 (E.D. N.Y. 1997). Constitutional Law ☞276(2); United States ☞64.20

In context of contractor's suspension from eligibility for government contracts under Federal Acquisition Regulations System (FAR) following contractor's indictment, due process does not require full adversarial hearing and fact finding; purpose of contractor's opportunity to be heard is not to contest indictment, but rather to demonstrate that suspension should not be imposed, either because it is not in government's interest to do so, or because in light of compelling evidence presented by contractor, governmental decision to rely only on indictment would be arbitrary, capricious, or abuse of discretion. U.S.C.A. Const.Amend. 14; 48 C.F.R. §§ 9.401–9.407. Rutigliano Paper Stock, Inc. v. U.S. General Services Admin., 967 F. Supp. 757, 41 Cont. Cas. Fed. (CCH) P 77156 (E.D. N.Y. 1997). Constitutional Law ☞276(2); United States ☞64.20

Requirements of due process did not dictate that General Services Administration (GSA) provide suspended contractor with independent review by individual not directly involved with its decision to suspend contractor's eligibility for government contracts; applicable regulations did not call for such review, no process provided for therein could be construed as independent review, and district court review was available under Administrative Procedures Act. U.S.C.A. Const.Amend. 14; 5 U.S.C.A. § 551 et seq.; 48 C.F.R. §§ 9.401–9.407. Rutigliano Paper Stock, Inc. v. U.S. General Services Admin., 967 F. Supp. 757, 41 Cont. Cas. Fed. (CCH) P 77156 (E.D. N.Y. 1997). Constitutional Law ☞276(2); United States ☞64.20

Contractor suspended from eligibility for government contracts by General Services Administration (GSA) pursuant to Federal Acquisition Regulations System (FAR) had protected liberty interest in its eligibility to bid for federal contracts, where suspension was based upon contractor's indictment on charges involving fraud and dishonesty. 48 C.F.R. §§ 9.401–9.407. Rutigliano Paper Stock, Inc. v. U.S. General Services Admin., 967 F. Supp. 757, 41 Cont. Cas. Fed. (CCH) P 77156 (E.D. N.Y. 1997). Constitutional Law ☞276(2)

Contractors established protected liberty interest, where suspension of their participation in Department of Transportation financial assistance programs was based upon indictment charging contractors with creating false and fraudulent joint minority business enterprise in connection with construction project, and with falsifying records as part of that fraud. U.S.C.A. Const.Amend. 5. Mainelli v. U.S., 611 F. Supp. 606 (D.R.I. 1985). Constitutional Law ⚖291.6

With regard to a contractor's suspension from bidding, due process requirements of the Federal Acquisition Regulation (FAR) are satisfied when the contractor has been provided all of the information relied on by the suspending official. U.S.C.A. Const.Amend. 5; 48 C.F.R. § 9.407-3(b)(1). Lion Raisins, Inc. v. U.S., 51 Fed. Cl. 238 (2001). United States ⚖64.20

In light of renewed suspension on other grounds of contractor's eligibility to receive government contracts, contractor, which alleged that prior proceedings did not measure up to standards for procedural due process, had no present right to be awarded a government contract and no right to enjoin anyone else from receiving or performing it. U.S.C.A. Const. Amend. 5. ATL, Inc. v. U.S., 6 Cl. Ct. 539, 32 Cont. Cas. Fed. (CCH) P 73067 (1984). Injunction ⚖114(2); United States ⚖64.20

Individual has a right to notice and opportunity to be heard before he is debarred, suspended, or denied license to practice profession by government agency. U.S.C.A. Const. Amend. 14. ATL, Inc. v. U.S., 3 Cl. Ct. 259, 31 Cont. Cas. Fed. (CCH) P 71393 (1983). Constitutional Law ⚖276(2); United States ⚖64.20

Due process for a suspension requires notice sufficiently specific to enable the suspended party to marshal evidence on its behalf so as to make the subsequent opportunity for response meaningful. Agency is not required to inform persons of proposed suspensions to allow them an opportunity to submit evidence; such evidence is properly presented in the person's post-suspension response to the action. TS Generalbau GmbH; Thomas Stadlbauer, B-246034, B-246036, B-246037, B-246037.2, B-246038, B-246039, B-246040, B-246040.2, B-246042, B-246042.2, B-246043, B-246043.2, 92-1 CPD ¶ 189 (Comp. Gen. 1992)

6 Equal protection of laws

Mere allegation that moving and storage companies were denied make-up tonnage following their removal from Department of Army suspended contractor list when acquitted of antitrust violations did not establish protectible Fifth Amendment equal protection right, as no fundamental interest or suspect classifications were involved and discretionary element of regulations was rationally related to Department's legitimate interest in ensuring efficient storage and carrier service. U.S.C.A. Const.Amend. 5. Coleman American Moving Services, Inc. v. Weinberger, 716 F. Supp. 1405, 36 Cont. Cas. Fed. (CCH) P 75786 (M.D. Ala. 1989). Constitutional Law ⚖225.4; United States ⚖64.20

Procedure affording companies who have not been indicted for antitrust violations a hearing prior to their placement on list of suspended government contractors, while denying hearing to companies who have been indicted, did not violate equal protection rights of indicted companies as reason for hearing was to determine if suspension would be rationally related to government objectives and fact of indictment provided sufficient reason to proceed with suspension. U.S.C.A. Const.Amend. 5. Coleman American Moving Services, Inc. v. Weinberger, 716 F. Supp. 1405, 36 Cont. Cas. Fed. (CCH) P 75786 (M.D. Ala. 1989). Constitutional Law ⚖225.4; United States ⚖64.20

7 Right to counsel

Moving and storage companies which were placed on Department of Army's suspended bidders list following filing of antitrust indictments against them were not deprived of their right to counsel, as such right extends only to cases where deprivation of personal liberty may result from proceeding and companies' antitrust exposure was limited to property loss. U.S.C.A. Const.Amend. 6. Coleman American Moving Services, Inc. v. Weinberger, 716 F. Supp. 1405, 36 Cont. Cas. Fed. (CCH) P 75786 (M.D. Ala. 1989). Criminal Law ⚖641.2(4)

8 Exhaustion of administrative remedies

Exhaustion of administrative remedies rule barred judicial review of res judicata-collateral estoppel defense to suspension by United States Department of Transportation of contractors from participation in Department financial assistance programs. Mainelli v. U.S., 611 F. Supp. 606 (D.R.I. 1985). United States ☞82(7)

9 Res judicata and collateral estoppel

Intervening indictment against contractors was changed circumstance rendering collateral estoppel inapplicable in action brought by contractors seeking preliminary injunction prohibiting Department of Transportation from suspending them from participation in Department sponsored financial assistance programs. Mainelli v. U.S., 611 F. Supp. 606 (D.R.I. 1985). Judgment ☞739

10 Injunctions—In general

For purpose of determining contractor's entitlement to injunction against enforcement of Federal Acquisition Regulations System (FAR), contractor's almost total loss of business and inability to bid on new contracts as result of suspension from eligibility for government contracts constituted "irreparable harm" incapable of being remedied by monetary damages alone. 48 C.F.R. §§ 9.401–9.407. Rutigliano Paper Stock, Inc. v. U.S. General Services Admin., 967 F. Supp. 757, 41 Cont. Cas. Fed. (CCH) P 77156 (E.D. N.Y. 1997). Injunction ☞86

Bidder failed to establish substantial likelihood that it would prevail on merits of its claim that its suspension from further contracting with any agency in executive branch of government violated federal acquisition regulations or that it was denied due process and, therefore, bidder was not entitled to preliminary injunction to prevent Air Force from awarding contract to install new windows at Air Force bases; bidder had been suspended from competition after it was indicted for making false claims and false statements. U.S.C.A. Const.Amends. 5, 14. JDL Const., Inc. v. U.S., 14 Cl. Ct. 825, 34 Cont. Cas. Fed. (CCH) P 75502, 1988 WL 58047 (1988). Civil Rights ☞1457(7); Injunction ☞138.63

11 Injunctions—Preliminary injunctions and restraining orders

Contractor who had been indicted for filing false claims in connection with navy contracts was not entitled to preliminary injunction prohibiting Secretaries of Army, Navy and Air Force from suspending him and his company for competing for government contracts, where contractor was not likely to prevail on his constitutional challenge to acquisition regulations, public interest favored allowing suspension of contractors indicted for fraud against government and loss of opportunity to bid on undetermined number of military contracts during suspension period did not constitute irreparable harm. James A. James A. Merritt and Sons v. Marsh, 791 F.2d 328, 33 Cont. Cas. Fed. (CCH) P 74391 (4th Cir. 1986). Injunction ☞138.63

Contractors were not entitled to preliminary injunction prohibiting Department of Transportation from suspending them from participation in Department financial assistance programs, where contractors were not likely to succeed on their claims that Department was barred from suspending them by doctrines of res judicata and collateral estoppel based upon determination by Rhode Island Department of Transportation that they had committed no substantive violations of minority business enterprise regulation through its subcontracting, that suspension regulations were procedurally defective in that they failed to give contractors hearing before suspension, that regulations were unconstitutional because Government was free to base suspension on indictment alone, irrespective of showing made by contractor at hearing, and that regulation under which they were suspended violated, on its face, Fifth Amendment privilege against selfincrimination. U.S.C.A. Const. Amend. 5. Mainelli v. U.S., 611 F. Supp. 606 (D.R.I. 1985). Injunction ☞138.63

Government contractors accused of intentionally defrauding Government by selling substandard neoprene tubing to Defense Department were not entitled to preliminary injunction prohibiting Government from placing their names on suspended contractors list; Defense Logistics Agency (DLA) acted in accordance with applicable statutes and regulations and had rational basis for its decision, and contractors made no attempt at redressing their suspension with DLA official. RSI, Inc. v. U.S., 772 F. Supp. 956 (W.D. Tex. 1991). Injunction ☞138.63

Possible harm to Government if preliminary injunction were granted, preventing Air Force from awarding window installation contract, outweighed threatened harm to bidder and, therefore, bidder was not entitled to injunctive relief based on its challenge to suspension from competition after it had been indicted for making false claims and false statements. JDL Const., Inc. v. U.S., 14 Cl. Ct. 825, 34 Cont. Cas. Fed. (CCH) P 75502, 1988 WL 58047 (1988). Injunction ⊕138.63

Bidder failed to show that it would be irreparably harmed, absent preliminary injunction to prevent Air Force from awarding window installation contract to anyone else; bidder's suspension from competition after it had been indicted for making false claims and false statements was not permanent and, even if contract could have been completed before contractor opposed suspension, Claims Court retained full, equitable jurisdiction to fashion any appropriate relief if bidder prevailed in its suit. JDL Const., Inc. v. U.S., 14 Cl. Ct. 825, 34 Cont. Cas. Fed. (CCH) P 75502, 1988 WL 58047 (1988). Injunction ⊕138.63

12 Jurisdiction

Contractors' action against United States, challenging General Services Administration's (GSA) termination of two current contracts and suspension of further contracting pending completion of criminal proceedings, was not at its essence a contract action, and thus, Court of Appeals had jurisdiction over appeal from district court's decision; even though contractors complained about termination clause in their contracts, basis of their claim was that GSA's repeated attempts to extricate government from financial dealings with them constituted unlawful "blacklisting," and dispute over termination clause in their contracts was embedded within that broader claim, and was not independent cause of action. 28 U.S.C.A. § 1346(a)(2); Contract Disputes Act of 1978, §§ 8(g), 10(a)(1), 41 U.S.C.A. §§ 607(g), 609(a)(1). Commercial Drapery Contractors, Inc. v. U.S., 133 F.3d 1, 4, 39 Fed. R. Serv. 3d 825 (D.C. Cir. 1998). Federal Courts ⊕1139

13 Discovery

Contractor that sued General Services Administration (GSA) after GSA suspended contractor and terminated its existing contracts failed to sufficiently assert Bivens claim against GSA officials, and thus, contractor was not entitled to discovery on that claim; complaint contained no such claim, damages were not mentioned, there was no indication that officials were being sued in their individual capacities, and, while counsel for contractor alluded to Bivens claim at hearing on temporary injunction, he never amended complaint or even moved to do so. Commercial Drapery Contractors, Inc. v. U.S., 133 F.3d 1, 7–8, 39 Fed. R. Serv. 3d 825 (D.C. Cir. 1998). Federal Civil Procedure ⊕1264; United States ⊕50.20

Contractor who sued United States, challenging General Services Administration's (GSA) suspension of contractor and cancellation of its existing contracts, was not entitled to discovery of GSA's decisionmaking process, as contractor failed to show that GSA acted in bad faith; basis for "bad faith" claim was affidavit by contractor's president stating that employee told him that GSA had barred contractor from participating in trade show and said bad things about contractor to its business partners and potential customers, such hearsay was inadmissible to oppose GSA's summary judgment motion, and, in any event, affidavit was not produced to support specific discovery request before district court. 5 U.S.C.A. § 706(2)(A, B); Fed.Rules Civ.Proc.Rule 56(e), 28 U.S.C.A.Commercial Drapery Contractors, Inc. v. U.S., 133 F.3d 1, 7, 39 Fed. R. Serv. 3d 825 (D.C. Cir. 1998). Federal Civil Procedure ⊕1272.1

14 Procedures, generally

Since suspended contractor's bid was turned down by the Navy within a month of the suspension, and since the government must be permitted a reasonable time, after notifying a contractor of his suspension status, before it must provide the contractor an opportunity to offer evidence to rebut the charges the action of the Navy in turning down the bid was not improper, even though no opportunity had at the time been accorded the contractor to rebut the "adequate evidence" against it. Horne Bros., Inc. v. Laird, 463 F.2d 1268, 1272 (D.C. Cir. 1972). United States ⊕64.20

Under any proper procedural scheme, the government should be permitted a reasonable time, after it has notified a suspended bidder of his suspension status, before it must conduct a proceeding attended by the subcontractor and his representatives, to provide an opportunity to offer evidence to rebut the charges and confront his accusers, in short, to demonstrate the lack of "adequate evidence" to warrant the suspension. Horne Bros., Inc. v.

Laird, 463 F.2d 1268, 1272 (D.C. Cir. 1972). United States ☞64.20

Risk of error in government contract bidder suspension or debarment proceeding based on charges of false statements and fraudulent acts or conduct in nature of fraud in performance of contracts is great and calls for pinpointing of specific acts, right of confrontation and cross-examination of witnesses. U.S.C.A. Const.Amends. 5, 14. ATL, Inc. v. U.S., 736 F.2d 677, 32 Cont. Cas. Fed. (CCH) P 72528 (Fed. Cir. 1984). United States ☞64.20

In light of severe economic consequences of suspension of a contractor, whether exercise of suspension is proper depends on procedural protections afforded the contractor. Shermco Industries, Inc. v. Secretary of the Air Force, 584 F. Supp. 76, 32 Cont. Cas. Fed. (CCH) P 72713 (N.D. Tex. 1984). United States ☞64.20

15 Hearings

A government action that "suspends" a contractor and contemplates that he may dangle in suspension for a period of one year or more is such as to require the government to insure fundamental fairness to the contractor whose economic life may depend on his ability to bid on government contracts; such fairness requires that the bidder be given specific notice as to at least some charges alleged against him and be given, in the usual case, an opportunity to rebut those charges. Horne Bros., Inc. v. Laird, 463 F.2d 1268, 1271 (D.C. Cir. 1972). Administrative Law And Procedure ☞454; United States ☞64.20

Although there may be circumstances where substantial government interests in national security and maintenance of a criminal prosecution would be prejudiced even by a disclosure of enough facts to show "adequate evidence" for the suspension of a bidder from participating in government contract awards, the government may not, in that event, simply ignore the interests of the contractor; rather, an appropriate government official, one vested with sufficient discretionary power, must make a formal determination that significant injury would result if a hearing were to be held; and a real abuse of such discretionary authority would be subject to judicial review. Horne Bros., Inc. v. Laird, 463 F.2d 1268, 1272 (D.C. Cir. 1972). United States ☞64.20

Where period between official notice of suspension of government contractor and original date for hearing on suspension was filled with numerous discussions and negotiations between contractor and government and contractor apparently sought to resolve matter by means other than adjudicatory process, contractor had waived right to prompt hearing. Adamo Wrecking Co. v. Department of Housing and Urban Development, 414 F. Supp. 877 (D.D.C. 1976). United States ☞64.20

Where suspension from receiving government contracts was used impermissibly as device to preclude disclosing to contractor and to Small Business Administration factual basis for Navy's determination that contractor lacked integrity, contractor was entitled to prerejection hearing, and, by same count, contractor remained entitled to SBA review of decision not to award contracts to contractor upon "lack of integrity" finding. Small Business Act, § 2[8](b)(7)(A), as amended, 15 U.S.C.A. § 637(b)(7)(A). ATL, Inc. v. U.S., 3 Cl. Ct. 259, 31 Cont. Cas. Fed. (CCH) P 71393 (1983). United States ☞64.20

16 Presumptions and burden of proof

Contractor suspended from eligibility for government contracts pursuant to Federal Acquisition Regulations System (FAR) failed to present facts to support inference of some form of impermissible bias or prejudice on part of suspending official, as required to overcome presumption of regularity of suspension decision by official of General Services Administration (GSA). 48 C.F.R. §§ 9.401–9.407. Rutigliano Paper Stock, Inc. v. U.S. General Services Admin., 967 F. Supp. 757, 41 Cont. Cas. Fed. (CCH) P 77156 (E.D. N.Y. 1997). United States ☞64.20

17 Judicial review

Court of Appeals' review of decision of Department of Housing and Urban Development (HUD) to debar former officer of suspended HUD coinsured lender from participating in primary and lower tier covered transactions throughout executive branch of federal government for three years was governed by traditional arbitrary and capricious standard as set forth in Administrative Procedures Act (APA); review was highly deferential, and Court of Appeals had to assume validity of agency action. 5 U.S.C.A. § 706(2)(A). Kisser v. Cisneros,

14 F.3d 615, 619 (D.C. Cir. 1994). United States ☞53(9)

Administrative record could be supplemented by declaration of agency official to extent that it assisted court in understanding the sequence of events that preceded agency decision to suspend contractor from bidding on contracts for one year, but declaration could not be considered insofar as it provided a new and alternative rationale for agency's decision. Lion Raisins, Inc. v. U.S., 51 Fed. Cl. 238 (2001). United States ☞64.60(1)

§ 9.407-4 Period of suspension.

(a) Suspension shall be for a temporary period pending the completion of investigation and any ensuing legal proceedings, unless sooner terminated by the suspending official or as provided in this subsection.

(b) If legal proceedings are not initiated within 12 months after the date of the suspension notice, the suspension shall be terminated unless an Assistant Attorney General requests its extension, in which case it may be extended for an additional 6 months. In no event may a suspension extend beyond 18 months, unless legal proceedings have been initiated within that period.

(c) The suspending official shall notify the Department of Justice of the proposed termination of the suspension, at least 30 days before the 12-month period expires, to give that Department an opportunity to request an extension.

United States Code Annotated

Administrative determinations, see 41 USCA § 257.

Contract requirements, see 41 USCA § 254.

Contractor responsibilities, see 41 USCA § 57.

Contracts, planning, solicitation, evaluation, and award procedures, see 10 USCA § 2305.

Definitions, see 10 USCA § 2302, 41 USCA §§ 259, 403.

Determinations and decisions, see 10 USCA § 2310, 41 USCA § 262.

Kinds of contracts, see 10 USCA § 2306.

Planning and solicitation requirements, see 41 USCA § 253a.

Notes of Decisions

In general 1

1 In general

While the government may temporarily suspend a contractor for a short period, not to exceed one month, without any provision for according him an opportunity to confront his accusers and rebut the "adequate evidence" against him, a protracted suspension requires that the government adopt and utilize procedures to assure fundamental fairness to contractor. Horne Bros., Inc. v. Laird, 463 F.2d 1268, 1270 (D.C. Cir. 1972). United States ☞64.20

While the initial thrust of a suspension of a bidder from participating in government contract awards may be likened to an ex parte temporary restraining order, the continuance of the suspension beyond a 30-day period is more fairly likened to a preliminary injunction after notice, maintainable only on a showing of adequate evidence that is not selfdetermined. Horne Bros., Inc. v. Laird, 463 F.2d 1268, 1272 (D.C. Cir. 1972). United States ☞64.20

Although it may be lawful in exceptional circumstances for Government to suspend contractor temporarily pending investigation without providing requisite notice and hearing, period of temporary suspension should not exceed 30 days and should be countenanced only in extreme situations such as those involving national security. Peter Kiewit Sons' Co. v. U. S. Army Corps of Engineers, 534 F. Supp. 1139, 29 Cont. Cas. Fed. (CCH) P 82291 (D.D.C. 1982), judgment rev'd, 714 F.2d 163, 31 Cont. Cas. Fed. (CCH) P 71395, 1983-2 Trade Cas. (CCH) ¶ 65528 (D.C. Cir. 1983). United States ☞64.20

Under regulation providing that suspension of government contractor is for temporary period pending completion of investigation and such legal proceedings as may ensue, investigation may include consideration of suspended party's arguments and contentions. Adamo Wrecking Co. v. Department of Housing and Urban Development, 414 F. Supp. 877

(D.D.C. 1976). United States ⊝64.20

Department of Housing and Urban Development was entitled to five weeks after completing preliminary decision process on suspending government contractor in which to complete its investigation and initiate such legal proceedings as might ensue to continue suspension. Adamo Wrecking Co. v. Department of Housing and Urban Development, 414 F. Supp. 877 (D.D.C. 1976). United States ⊝64.20

§ 9.407-5 Scope of suspension.

The scope of suspension shall be the same as that for debarment (see 9.406-5), except that the procedures of 9.407-3 shall be used in imposing suspension.

United States Code Annotated

Administrative determinations, see 41 USCA § 257.

Contract requirements, see 41 USCA § 254.

Contractor responsibilities, see 41 USCA § 57.

Contracts, planning, solicitation, evaluation, and award procedures, see 10 USCA § 2305.

Definitions, see 10 USCA § 2302, 41 USCA §§ 259, 403.

Determinations and decisions, see 10 USCA § 2310, 41 USCA § 262.

Kinds of contracts, see 10 USCA § 2306.

Planning and solicitation requirements, see 41 USCA § 253a.

§ 9.408 [Reserved]

§ 9.409 Contract clause.

The contracting officer shall insert the clause at 52.209-6, Protecting the Government's Interests when Subcontracting with Contractors Debarred, Suspended, or Proposed for Debarment, in solicitations and contracts where the contract value exceeds $35,000.

United States Code Annotated

Administrative determinations, see 41 USCA § 257.

Contract requirements, see 41 USCA § 254.

Contractor responsibilities, see 41 USCA § 57.

Contracts, planning, solicitation, evaluation, and award procedures, see 10 USCA § 2305.

Definitions, see 10 USCA § 2302, 41 USCA §§ 259, 403.

Determinations and decisions, see 10 USCA § 2310, 41 USCA § 262.

Kinds of contracts, see 10 USCA § 2306.

Planning and solicitation requirements, see 41 USCA § 253a.

Notes of Decisions

In general 1

1 In general

Vagueness challenge to federal acquisition regulations was inappropriate where regulations proscribed no conduct and were not enforced against defendants. 18 U.S.C.A. § 1001; 48 C.F.R. §§ 9.409(a), 52.209-5(a)(2). U.S. v. Ali, 27 Fed. Appx. 728 (9th Cir. 2001). Constitutional Law ⊝46(1)

Cancellation of government contract did not constitute breach of government's implied contractually duty to fairly and honestly consider bid of defense contractor where contractor was eliminated from consideration for bid after being proposed for debarment, subsequent debarment of contractor was not arbitrary and capricious, next lowest bidder had gone out of business, and remaining bids were determined to be either outdated or unreasonably high. IMCO, Inc. v. U.S., 33 Fed. Cl. 312 (1995), judgment aff'd, 97 F.3d 1422 (Fed. Cir. 1996). United States ⊝64.50

Subpart 9.5 Organizational and Consultant Conflicts of Interest

§ 9.500 Scope of subpart.

This subpart—

(a) Prescribes responsibilities, general rules, and procedures for identifying, evaluating, and resolving organizational conflicts of interest;

(b) Provides examples to assist contracting officers in applying these rules and procedures to individual contracting situations; and

(c) Implements section 8141 of the 1989 Department of Defense Appropriation Act, Pub. L. 100-463, 102 Stat. 2270-47 (1988).

United States Code Annotated

Administrative determinations, see 41 USCA § 257.

Conflict of interest standards for individuals providing consulting services, see 41 USCA § 405b.

Contract requirements, see 41 USCA § 254.

Contracting functions performed by Federal personnel, see 41 USCA § 419.

Contracts, planning, solicitation, evaluation, and award procedures, see 10 USCA § 2305.

Definitions, see 10 USCA § 2302, 41 USCA §§ 259, 403.

Determinations and decisions, see 10 USCA § 2310, 41 USCA § 262.

Kinds of contracts, see 10 USCA § 2306.

Planning and solicitation requirements, see 41 USCA § 253a.

§ 9.501 Definition.

"Marketing consultant," as used in this subpart, means any independent contractor who furnishes advice, information, direction, or assistance to an offeror or any other contractor in support of the preparation or submission of an offer for a Government contract by that offeror. An independent contractor is not a marketing consultant when rendering—

(1) Services excluded in Subpart 37.2;

(2) Routine engineering and technical services (such as installation, operation, or maintenance of systems, equipment, software, components, or facilities);

(3) Routine legal, actuarial, auditing, and accounting services; and

(4) Training services.

United States Code Annotated

Administrative determinations, see 41 USCA § 257.

Conflict of interest standards for individuals providing consulting services, see 41 USCA § 405b.

Contract requirements, see 41 USCA § 254.

Contracting functions performed by Federal personnel, see 41 USCA § 419.

Contracts, planning, solicitation, evaluation, and award procedures, see 10 USCA § 2305.

Definitions, see 10 USCA § 2302, 41 USCA §§ 259, 403.

Determinations and decisions, see 10 USCA § 2310, 41 USCA § 262.

Kinds of contracts, see 10 USCA § 2306.

Planning and solicitation requirements, see 41 USCA § 253a.

§ 9.502 Applicability.

(a) This subpart applies to contracts with either profit or nonprofit organizations, including nonprofit organizations created largely or wholly with Government funds.

(b) The applicability of this subpart is not limited to any particular kind of acquisition. However, organizational conflicts of interest are more likely to occur in contracts involving—

(1) Management support services;

(2) Consultant or other professional services;

(3) Contractor performance of or assistance in technical evaluations; or

(4) Systems engineering and technical direction work performed by a contractor that does not have overall contractual responsibility for development or production.

(c) An organizational conflict of interest may result when factors create an actual or potential conflict of interest on an instant contract, or when the nature of the work to be performed on the instant contract creates an actual or potential conflict of interest on a future acquisition. In the latter case, some restrictions on future activities of the contractor may be required.

(d) Acquisitions subject to unique agency organizational conflict of interest statutes are excluded from the requirements of this subpart.

United States Code Annotated

Administrative determinations, see 41 USCA § 257.

Conflict of interest standards for individuals providing consulting services, see 41 USCA § 405b.

Contract requirements, see 41 USCA § 254.

Contracting functions performed by Federal personnel, see 41 USCA § 419.

Contracts, planning, solicitation, evaluation, and award procedures, see 10 USCA § 2305.

Definitions, see 10 USCA § 2302, 41 USCA §§ 259, 403.

Determinations and decisions, see 10 USCA § 2310, 41 USCA § 262.

Kinds of contracts, see 10 USCA § 2306.

Planning and solicitation requirements, see 41 USCA § 253a.

Notes of Decisions

Access to information 3
Appearance of impropriety 2
Applicability to educational institutions 10
Applicability to government agencies and personnel 9
Avoidance or mitigation of conflict 4
Conjecture or speculation 8
Consultants, generally 1
Evaluation services 7
Preparing specifications or work statements 6
Providing systems engineering and technical direction 5

1 Consultants, generally

Federal acquisitions regulations do not mandate adoption of principle that vendors can never serve as contract consultants to government agencies even when they are prohibited from competing for contract on which they consult and subject to other appropriate restrictions. Informatics General Corp. v. Weinberger, 617 F. Supp. 331 (D.D.C. 1985). United States ☞64.5

2 Appearance of impropriety

Disqualification of successful bidder for state Medicaid managed mental health care contract, based on organizational conflicts of interest, was warranted by appearance of impropriety that tainted procurement process resulting from bidder's direct connection, as subsidiaries of same company, with contractor that assisted state in policy analysis that served as springboard for state's request for proposals (RFP), and indirect connection through undisclosed business relationship between bidder's cosubsidiary and company that actually prepared RFP. Medco Behavioral Care Corp. of Iowa v. State, Dept. of Human Services, 553 N.W.2d 556 (Iowa 1996). Health ☞486; Health ☞503(3); States ☞98

Pursuant to federal acquisition regulation (FAR), bidder on government contract may be disqualified based on appearance of impropriety when bidder may have gained unfair competitive advantage through actual or potential conflict of interest in procurement process. 48 C.F.R. § 1.000 et seq.Medco Behavioral Care Corp. of Iowa v. State, Dept. of Human Services, 553 N.W.2d 556 (Iowa 1996). Public Contracts ☞11

District court properly held as a matter of law that successful bidder for state Medicaid managed mental health care contract was disqualified due to organizational conflicts of interest, inasmuch as appearance of impropriety arising from bidder's connections with insiders that helped superintend process for receiving and evaluating bids could not be mitigated, despite self-structured embargoes on communications between bidder and insiders. Medco Behavioral Care Corp. of Iowa v. State, Dept. of Human Services, 553 N.W.2d 556 (Iowa 1996). States ☞98

District court applied correct legal standard in testing for existence of organizational conflict of interest requiring disqualification of successful bidder for Medicaid managed mental health care contract when it determined that mere appearance of impropriety was sufficient to support disqualification, and that actual conflict of interest did not have to be shown. I.C.A. § 249A.4; 45 C.F.R. Part 74, App. G, § 10 (1995); 48 C.F.R. §§ 1.101, 9.51, 9.502(b, c), 9.504(a)(1, 2), (e), 9.505. Medco Behavioral Care Corp. of Iowa v. State, Dept. of Human Services, 553 N.W.2d 556 (Iowa 1996). States ☞98

3 Access to information

Protest was sustained because the awardee had organizational conflicts of interest (OCIs) based on "biased ground rules" and "unequal access to information." The awardee's subcontractor provided procurement-development services to the agency and had access to competitively useful, nonpublic information. Matter of: L-3 Services, Inc., B-400134.11, B-400134.12, 2009 CPD ¶ 171 (Comp. Gen. 2009)

Successful bidder for state Medicaid managed mental health care contract could be disqualified based on organizational conflicts of interest, even though actual improper sharing of information between bidder and its contacts was not established. Medco Behavioral Care Corp. of Iowa v. State, Dept. of Human Services, 553 N.W.2d 556 (Iowa 1996). States ☞98

4 Avoidance or mitigation of conflict

Federal Acquisition Regulation (FAR) under which contracting officers are required to avoid, neutralize, or mitigate conflicts of interest and to notify bidding contractor of any basis for withholding of contract applies only to conflicts that are recognized before contract is awarded, and does not apply to contract termination situation or to agency's decision to follow General Accounting Office (GAO) decision recommending award of contract to entity other than one whose contract was terminated due to unmitigatable organizational conflict of interest (OCI). 48 C.F.R. § 9.504(e). QualMed, Inc. v. Office of Civilian Health and Medical Program of Uniformed Services, 934 F. Supp. 1227 (D. Colo. 1996). United States ☞64.40(1); United States ☞64.55(2)

Finding by General Accounting Office (GAO) that organizational conflict of interest (OCI) involving successful bidder on government contract was unmitigatable, which provided basis for GAO's recommendation that contract be terminated, was not irrational or unlawful; Federal Acquisition Regulation (FAR) requiring contracting officer to assist in mitigating conflicts was not applicable, as conflict appeared after contract was awarded, and GAO in any event considered contract and determined that appearance of impropriety rendered conflict unmitigatable. 48 C.F.R. § 9.504(e). QualMed, Inc. v. Office of Civilian Health and Medical Program of Uniformed Services, 934 F. Supp. 1227 (D. Colo. 1996). United States ☞64.40(1)

Speculative conflicts of interest in connection with awards of government contracts do not amount to violations of federal acquisitions regulations, which require only that agencies avoid or mitigate "significant potential conflicts," and not that all conceivable conflicts be avoided. Informatics General Corp. v. Weinberger, 617 F. Supp. 331 (D.D.C. 1985). United States ☞64.45(1)

Under acquisition regulation governing organizational conflicts of interest (OCI), contracting officer had to consider whether any potential OCIs could be avoided or mitigated and explain reasons for her conclusion before denying contract award to an otherwise qualified bidder. 48 C.F.R. § 9.504(e). Informatics Corp. v. U.S., 40 Fed. Cl. 508, 42 Cont. Cas. Fed. (CCH) P 77311 (1998). United States ☞64.15

5 Providing systems engineering and technical direction

Actual organizational conflict of interest (OCI) existed where contractor performed systems engineering and technical direction (SETA) tasks for procurement in which one of its divisions received sole source contract award for supply of helicopter engine filter kits, and presumption of harm to the procurement process and prejudice arose from contractor's dual role which was not rebutted by existence of unsigned and unapproved mitigation plans contractor submitted to contracting officer (CO). 48 C.F.R. §§ 9.505-1(a), 9.508(a). Filtration Development Co., LLC v. U.S., 60 Fed. Cl. 371 (2004). United States ☞64.15

6 Preparing specifications or work statements

Under developmental contractor exception to organizational conflict of interest (OCI) rules, contractor which had overall contractual responsibility for weapons system program was not precluded from bidding on production contract even after providing the specifications for the procurement; moreover, fact that contractor was successor to original developmental contractor by virtue of its purchase of related assets did not remove it from exception. 48 C.F.R. §§ 9.505-1(a), 9.508(e). Vantage Associates, Inc. v. U.S., 59 Fed. Cl. 1 (2003). United States ☞64.15

Industry representative exception to organizational conflict of interest (OCI) rules applied to development and design contractor which prepared new specifications for Navy weapons system procurement, and thus it could compete in the procurement, where contractor was acting as industry representative and under Navy auspices in preparing the specifications. 48 C.F.R. § 9.505-2(a)(1)(ii). Vantage Associates, Inc. v. U.S., 59 Fed. Cl. 1 (2003). United States ☞64.15

Contracting officer acted reasonably when she concluded that subcontractor which developed the plan for a new scheduling organization for the Air Force was precluded by an organizational conflict of interest (OCI) from competing in solicitation to provide contract support for the new scheduling organization, stemming from the input it had provided and continued to provide in developing the organization. 48 C.F.R. § 9.505-2(b)(2). DSD Laboratories, Inc. v. U.S., 46 Fed. Cl. 467 (2000). United States ☞64.15

7 Evaluation services

Even assuming that conflict-of-interest provision of the Federal Acquisition Regulation (FAR) was violated when supervisor of motor transport department was placed on evaluation board involved in A-76 cost comparison to determine if function of department should be contracted out, contractor was not prejudiced by supervisor's participation, considering that supervisor was only one of six individuals on the board, and there was no dissent on board's "poor" rating of contractor. 48 C.F.R. § 3.101-1. JWK Intern. Corp. v. U.S., 52 Fed. Cl. 650 (2002), aff'd, 56 Fed. Appx. 474 (Fed. Cir. 2003). United States ☞64.55(1)

Participation of four local managers on evaluation boards did not constitute prejudicial conflict of interest in A-76 cost comparison study of whether maintenance and motor transport services at naval air station should be contracted out to private contractor, where only one of the managers was directly associated with a function under study, and he was a military officer not concerned with loss of employment. 48 C.F.R. § 3.101-1. JWK Intern. Corp. v. U.S., 52 Fed. Cl. 650 (2002), aff'd, 56 Fed. Appx. 474 (Fed. Cir. 2003). United States ☞64.40(1)

An agency unreasonably failed to consider a potential organizational conflict of interest (OCI) because the contract would have required the offeror to review its own information technology designs proposed under a separate contract, and the offeror's mitigation plan did not adequately address the dual roles, GAO found. GAO determined that this OCI would not be cured by the fact that the agency would not rely solely on the offeror's input, nor by the fact that the agency retained the ultimate decision-making authority. Nortel Government Solutions, Inc., B-299522.5, 2009 CPD ¶ 10 (Comp. Gen. 2008)

The organizational conflict of interest rules in Subpart 9.5 may be applied to Government personnel involved in cost comparison studies conducted under OMB Circular A-76. The rationale for applying Subpart 9.5 to the "Most Efficient Organization" (MEO) is the reality that MEO teams are, in fact, competing to perform the Performance Work Statement. Department of the Navy--Reconsideration, B-286194.7, 2002 CPD ¶ 76 (Comp. Gen. 2002).

A conflict of interest existed in an Office of Management and Budget Circular A-76 commercial activities study where a Navy employee and a private-sector consultant wrote and edited the performance work statement and then prepared the management plan for in-house performance. The IT Facility Services-Joint Venture, B-285841, 2000 CPD ¶ 177 (Comp. Gen. 2000).

Agency reasonably determined that employees within the function under study in a cost comparison under Office of Management and Budget Circular A-76 could be on the source selection evaluation board for the competition among private-sector offerors, where the agency determined that these employees would not be directly affected by the cost comparison because their positions were not in jeopardy. IT Facility Services-Joint Venture, B-285841, 2000 CPD ¶ 177 (Comp. Gen. 2000)

Protest challenging the agency's use of a contractor to assist the agency in the preparation of the most efficient organization (MEO) and the evaluation of private-sector offers, including the preparation of an independent government estimate, in connection with a solicitation issued under Office of Management and Budget Circular A-76, is denied, where the contractor used discrete sets of employees to perform the various tasks and used a "firewall" to keep confidential the preparation of the MEO and management study, as well as the evaluation of the offers. IT Facility Services-Joint Venture, B-285841, 2000 CPD ¶ 177 (Comp. Gen. 2000)

8 Conjecture or speculation

Mere conjecture, innuendo, or speculation of actual or potential conflict of interest, without factual support, provide no basis for disqualification of government contract bidder under federal acquisition regulation (FAR). 48 C.F.R. § 1.000 et seq.Medco Behavioral Care Corp. of Iowa v. State, Dept. of Human Services, 553 N.W.2d 556 (Iowa 1996). Public Contracts ⊙11

9 Applicability to government agencies and personnel

In a cost comparison study pursuant to Office of Management and Budget Circular No. A-76, where 14 of 16 agency evaluators held positions under the study and thus subject to being contracted out, a conflict of interest that could not be mitigated was created, and protests challenging the evaluators' conclusion that all private-sector offers were unacceptable are therefore sustained. DZS/Baker LLC; DZS/Baker LLC; Morrison Knudsen Corporation, B-281224, B-281224.2, B-281224.3, B-281224.4, B-281224.5, B-281224.6, 99-1 CPD ¶ 19 (Comp. Gen. 1999)

10 Applicability to educational institutions

Organizational conflicts of interest exist for educational institutions submitting offers under a solicitation for educational support services where, as a contractor, the institution could advise government personnel to enroll in courses offered by that institution or verify billing statements submitted by the institution. Under such circumstances, the solicitation is required to contain a provision addressing the conflicts in accordance with Federal Acquisition Regulation Subpart 9.5. J&E Associates, Inc., B-278771, 98-1 CPD ¶ 77 (Comp. Gen. 1998)

§ 9.503 Waiver.

The agency head or a designee may waive any general rule or procedure of this subpart by determining that its application in a particular situation would not be in the Government's interest. Any request for waiver must be in writing, shall set forth the extent of the conflict, and requires approval by the agency head or a designee. Agency heads shall not delegate waiver authority below the level of head of a contracting activity.

United States Code Annotated

Administrative determinations, see 41 USCA § 257.

Conflict of interest standards for individuals providing consulting services, see 41 USCA § 405b.

Contract requirements, see 41 USCA § 254.

Contracting functions performed by Federal personnel, see 41 USCA § 419.

Contracts, planning, solicitation, evaluation, and award procedures, see 10 USCA § 2305.

Definitions, see 10 USCA § 2302, 41 USCA §§ 259, 403.

Determinations and decisions, see 10 USCA § 2310, 41 USCA § 262.

Kinds of contracts, see 10 USCA § 2306.

Planning and solicitation requirements, see 41 USCA § 253a.

Notes of Decisions
In general 1

1 In general

Protest alleging that the awardee had an organizational conflict of interest was denied because the agency properly waived the OCI in accordance with the procedures of FAR 9.503, finding that, "the waiver request and approval described the OCIs being waived, and the waiver was approved by the Head of Contracting Activity (HCA). Concurrent Techs. Corp., B-412795.2 et al., 2017 CPD ¶ 25 (Comp. Gen. 2017)

The OCI regulations require that, where an actual or apparent conflict of interest arises, the agency is required to carefully analyze the situation and either take action to avoid, neutralize or mitigate any possible advantage that might accrue from the circumstances, or make a specific determination to waive the application of the OCI requirements where the head of the contracting agency determines that it is in the best interests of the government to do so. Ktech Corporation, B-285330, B-285330.2, 2002 CPD ¶ 77 (Comp. Gen. 2000)

§ 9.504 Contracting officer responsibilities.

(a) Using the general rules, procedures, and examples in this subpart, contracting officers shall analyze planned acquisitions in order to—

(1) Identify and evaluate potential organizational conflicts of interest as early in the acquisition process as possible; and

(2) Avoid, neutralize, or mitigate significant potential conflicts before contract award.

(b) Contracting officers should obtain the advice of counsel and the assistance of appropriate technical specialists in evaluating potential conflicts and in developing any necessary solicitation provisions and contract clauses (see 9.506).

(c) Before issuing a solicitation for a contract that may involve a significant potential conflict, the contracting officer shall recommend to the head of the contracting activity a course of action for resolving the conflict (see 9.506).

(d) In fulfilling their responsibilities for identifying and resolving potential conflicts, contracting officers should avoid creating unnecessary delays, burdensome information requirements, and excessive documentation. The contracting officer's judgment need be formally documented only when a substantive issue concerning potential organizational conflict of interest exists.

(e) The contracting officer shall award the contract to the apparent successful offeror unless a conflict of interest is determined to exist that cannot be avoided or mitigated. Before determining to withhold award based on conflict of interest considerations, the contracting officer shall notify the contractor, provide the reasons therefor, and allow the contractor a reasonable opportunity to respond. If the contracting officer finds that it is in the best interest of the United States to award the contract notwithstanding a conflict of interest, a request for waiver shall be submitted in accordance with 9.503. The waiver request and decision shall be included in the contract file.

United States Code Annotated

Administrative determinations, see 41 USCA § 257.

Conflict of interest standards for individuals providing consulting services, see 41 USCA § 405b.

Contract requirements, see 41 USCA § 254.

Contracting functions performed by Federal personnel, see 41 USCA § 419.

Contracts, planning, solicitation, evaluation, and award procedures, see 10 USCA § 2305.

Definitions, see 10 USCA § 2302, 41 USCA §§ 259, 403.

Determinations and decisions, see 10 USCA § 2310, 41 USCA § 262.

Kinds of contracts, see 10 USCA § 2306.

Planning and solicitation requirements, see 41 USCA § 253a.

Notes of Decisions

1 Due process of law

Successful bidder on government contract whose contract was terminated after contracting agency accepted recommendation of General Accounting Office (GAO) that contract be terminated due to unmitigatable organizational conflict of interest (OCI) was not entitled under Federal Acquisition Regulation (FAR) to statement of reasons why OCI existed or to opportunity to respond, and thus, failure to provide such opportunity did not violate bidder's due process rights; FAR provision requiring such notice applies only to conflicts recognized before contract is awarded. U.S.C.A. Const. Amend. 5; 48 C.F.R. § 9.504(e). QualMed, Inc. v. Office of Civilian Health and Medical Program of Uniformed Services, 934 F. Supp. 1227 (D. Colo. 1996). Constitutional Law ⬉276(2); United States ⬉64.55(2)

Contracting officer's decision to disqualify offeror based on alleged possession of competitor information was procedurally flawed and contrary to law in that it did not provide notice to the disqualified vendor or an opportunity to be heard. Consequently, the vendor was provided no opportunity to address or to contest the contracting officer's suspicions. This process violated Section 555(b) of the Administrative Procedures Act (APA), which provides, in pertinent part, that a party is entitled to be heard in an agency proceeding, absent exigent circumstances. In short, the contracting officer's action contravened "the minimal requirements" for informal adjudication set forth in Section 555 of the APA and is, therefore, invalid. Systems Plus, Inc. v. U.S., 69 Fed. Cl. 757 (2006)

2 Consultants, generally

Federal acquisitions regulations do not mandate adoption of principle that vendors can never serve as contract consul tract award to an otherwise qualified bidder. 48 C.F.R. § 9. 504(e). Informatics Corp. v. U.S., 40 Fed. Cl. 508, 42 Cont. Cas. Fed. (CCH) P 77311 (1998). United States ⬉64.15

3 Conjecture or speculation

Speculative conflicts of interest in connection with awards of government contracts do not amount to violations of federal acquisitions regulations, which require only that agencies avoid or mitigate "significant potential conflicts," and not that all conceivable conflicts be avoided. Informatics General Corp. v. Weinberger, 617 F. Supp. 331 (D.D.C. 1985). United States ⬉64.45(1)

Protest alleging that a firm should be excluded from competition under a solicitation for information technology services because it assisted in the preparation of the solicitation is denied, where the allegation is based on inference and suspicion rather than substantial facts or hard evidence, and the agency unequivocally and credibly asserts that the firm did not assist in the preparation of the solicitation. Snell Enterprises, Inc., B-290113, B-290113.2, 2002 CPD ¶ 115 (Comp. Gen. 2002)

Protester's speculation that a competing firm has an incentive to falsely conclude that certain items being acquired by agency are not compatible with firm's software used to process the items, thereby improving its chances for subsequent awards for the items, does not provide a basis to require that the firm be prohibited from competing. B3H Corporation, B-280374, 98-2 CPD ¶ 88 (Comp. Gen. 1998)

Mere conjecture, innuendo, or speculation of actual or potential conflict of interest, without factual support, provide no basis for disqualification of government contract bidder under federal acquisition regulation (FAR). 48 C.F.R. § 1.000 et seq.Medco Behavioral Care Corp. of Iowa v. State, Dept. of Human Services, 553 N.W.2d 556 (Iowa 1996). Public Contracts ⊙⇒11

4 Appearance of impropriety

Disqualification of successful bidder for state Medicaid managed mental health care contract, based on organizational conflicts of interest, was warranted by appearance of impropriety that tainted procurement process resulting from bidder's direct connection, as subsidiaries of same company, with contractor that assisted state in policy analysis that served as springboard for state's request for proposals (RFP), and indirect connection through undisclosed business relationship between bidder's co-subsidiary and company that actually prepared RFP. Medco Behavioral Care Corp. of Iowa v. State, Dept. of Human Services, 553 N.W.2d 556 (Iowa 1996). Health ⊙⇒486; Health ⊙⇒503(3); States ⊙⇒98

Pursuant to federal acquisition regulation (FAR), bidder on government contract may be disqualified based on appearance of impropriety when bidder may have gained unfair competitive advantage through actual or potential conflict of interest in procurement process. 48 C.F.R. § 1.000 et seq.Medco Behavioral Care Corp. of Iowa v. State, Dept. of Human Services, 553 N.W.2d 556 (Iowa 1996). Public Contracts ⊙⇒11

District court properly held as a matter of law that successful bidder for state Medicaid managed mental health care contract was disqualified due to organizational conflicts of interest, inasmuch as appearance of impropriety arising from bidder's connections with insiders that helped superintend process for receiving and evaluating bids could not be mitigated, despite self-structured embargoes on communications between bidder and insiders. Medco Behavioral Care Corp. of Iowa v. State, Dept. of Human Services, 553 N.W.2d 556 (Iowa 1996). States ⊙⇒98

District court applied correct legal standard in testing for existence of organizational conflict of interest requiring disqualification of successful bidder for Medicaid managed mental health care contract when it determined that mere appearance of impropriety was sufficient to support disqualification, and that actual conflict of interest did not have to be shown. I.C.A. § 249A.4; 45 C.F.R. Part 74, App. G, § 10 (1995); 48 C.F.R. §§ 1.101, 9.51, 9.502(b, c), 9.504(a)(1, 2), (e), 9.505. Medco Behavioral Care Corp. of Iowa v. State, Dept. of Human Services, 553 N.W.2d 556 (Iowa 1996). States ⊙⇒98

5 Access to information

The exercise of common sense, good judgement, and sound discretion is required in both the decision on whether a significant potential conflict exists and, if it does, the development of an appropriate means for resolving it' (FAR 9.504). One of the underlying principles is preventing an unfair competitive advantage. The fact that protester hired the Chairman of the agency's evaluation panel during the source selection process, and then dropped their cost so drastically, much more than they would have been expected to under normal circumstances, indicates a strong possibility that they were aware of information which gave them an unfair competitive advantage and therefore damages the integrity of the proposal system. NKF Engineering, Inc. v. U.S., 805 F.2d 372, 33 Cont. Cas. Fed. (CCH) ¶ 74691 (Fed. Cir. 1986)

The Court of Federal Claims (COFC) held that an agency's decision to implement a GAO recommendation to recompete a contract because the award was tainted with an Organizational Conflict of Interest (OCI) was arbitrary and capricious. GAO had sustained a protest based on an OCI because the awardee's design subcontractor had access to competitively useful information through the firm retained by the agency to provide technical support services for the same project. The parent company of the agency's technical support contractor was negotiating a merger with the awardee's design subcontractor. The COFC found that the GAO decision was irrational because it failed to cite any hard facts to support the conclusion that the awardee had unequal access to competitively useful information. Because the GAO decision was irrational, the agency was not justified in relying on it. The COFC ordered the agency to restore the contract to the original awardee. Turner Const. Co., Inc. v. U.S., 94 Fed. Cl. 561 (2010), motion for stay pending appeal denied, 94 Fed. Cl. 586 (2010) and motion for stay pending appeal denied, 410 Fed. Appx. 319 (Fed. Cir. 2010) and appeal dismissed in part, 407 Fed. Appx. 478 (Fed. Cir. 2011) and aff'd, 645 F.3d 1377 (Fed. Cir. 2011)

Bid protestor failed to establish that in awarding a contract for space and missile defense integration, the Department of the Army violated regulations governing organizational conflicts of interest by allowing the awardee to have unequal access to information; based upon its prior experience, protestor had as much information as awardee regarding the various systems that were related to the task order that was the subject of the solicitation, and the information that awardee had was not particularly competitively useful in responding to the task order. ARINC Engineering Services, LLC v. U.S., 77 Fed. Cl. 196 (2007)

With regard to mitigation of situations in which one offeror has unequal access to information, the disclosure of information to equalize competition is an appropriate alternative to eliminating an offeror from a competition due to prior disclosure of information that could result in an unfair competitive advantage. Systems Plus, Inc. v. U.S., 69 Fed. Cl. 757 (2006)

Protest that the awardee should not have been permitted to receive the award of a contract for certain services because the awardee, through its performance of a task order for the agency, was given access to information that the protester now claims as proprietary and was exposed to certain agency information that gave the awardee an unfair competitive advantage, was denied, where the agency reasonably concluded that the protester furnished its information voluntarily without restrictions on its use, and the record did not support the protester's contention that the awardee had an unfair competitive advantage by virtue of the experience it gained from performing the task order. Matter of: CACI, Inc.-Federal, B-403064.2, 2011 CPD ¶ 31 (Comp. Gen. 2011)

Successful bidder for state Medicaid managed mental health care contract could be disqualified based on organizational conflicts of interest, even though actual improper sharing of information between bidder and its contacts was not established. Medco Behavioral Care Corp. of Iowa v. State, Dept. of Human Services, 553 N.W.2d 556 (Iowa 1996). States ⊃98

6 Avoidance or mitigation of conflict

Contracting officer has authority to disqualify bidder on government contract to protect integrity of procurement process from potential for unfair competitive advantage. NKF Engineering, Inc. v. U.S., 805 F.2d 372, 33 Cont. Cas. Fed. (CCH) P 74691 (Fed. Cir. 1986). United States ⊃64.20

QualMed, Inc. v. Office of Civilian Health and Medical Program of Uniformed Services, 934 F. Supp. 1227 (D. Colo. 1996). United States ⊃64.40(1); United States ⊃64.55(2)

Finding by General Accounting Office (GAO) that organizational conflict of interest (OCI) involving successful bidder on government contract was unmitigatable, which provided basis for GAO's recommendation that contract be terminated, was not irrational or unlawful; Federal Acquisition Regulation (FAR) requiring contracting officer to assist in mitigating conflicts was not applicable, as conflict appeared after contract was awarded, and GAO in any event considered contract and determined that appearance of impropriety rendered conflict unmitigatable. 48 C.F.R. § 9.504(e). QualMed, Inc. v. Office of Civilian Health and Medical Program of Uniformed Services, 934 F. Supp. 1227 (D. Colo. 1996). United States ⊃64.40(1)

General Accounting Office (GAO) had authority to review determination by federal agency charged with providing health care to dependents of military personnel with respect to plan to mitigate organizational conflict of interest (OCI) which had arisen with respect to bidding on government contract to provide services for agency. 31 U.S.C.A. § 3554(b)(1); 48 C.F.R. §§ 9.501–9.504. QualMed, Inc. v. Office of Civilian Health and Medical Program of Uniformed Services, 934 F. Supp. 1227 (D. Colo. 1996). United States ⊃64.55(2)

Since General Accounting Office (GAO) has authority to determine whether findings of governmental agency regarding organizational conflict of interest (OCI) which arises in connection with bidding on government contract are reasonable, it follows that GAO also has authority to determine whether mitigation plans approved by agency are reasonable. 31 U.S.C.A. § 3554(b)(1); 48 C.F.R. §§ 9.501–9.504. QualMed, Inc. v. Office of Civilian

Health and Medical Program of Uniformed Services, 934 F. Supp. 1227 (D. Colo. 1996). United States ⊶64.55(2)

General Accounting Office (GAO) is required to determine whether government contracts are awarded in accordance with procurement statutes and regulations, including regulations regarding organizational conflicts of interest (OCI's), and in making determination may overturn agency's determination as to whether actual or apparent conflict of interest exists and whether it can be mitigated if agency's determination is unreasonable. 31 U.S.C.A. § 3554(b)(1); 48 C.F.R. §§ 9.501–9.504. QualMed, Inc. v. Office of Civilian Health and Medical Program of Uniformed Services, 934 F. Supp. 1227 (D. Colo. 1996). United States ⊶64.55(2)

Although RFQ categorized all its non-purchased care requirements into three broad categories for the purposes of identifying, avoiding or mitigating against OCIs in accordance with FAR Subpart 9.5, it did not prohibit award of the Task Order to an offeror with an actual or potential OCI. Instead, the RFQ required that a voluntary mitigation plan be implemented to identify and mitigate any such conflict. In this case, however, the CO failed to identify and evaluate *potential* organizational conflicts of interest nor did the CO do so "as early in the acquisition process as possible." FAR 9.504(a)(1). The FAR clearly places a duty on the CO to identify, analyze, and mitigate both potential and actual conflicts. Axiom Resource Management, Inc. v. U.S., 78 Fed. Cl. 576 (2007)

Contracting officer (CO) abused his discretion in violation of FAR Subpart 9.5 regarding organizational conflicts of interest (OCIs) by awarding task order to awardee with multiple OCIs without developing a mitigation plan that did not afford awardee any significant competitive advantages, was enforceable, *i.e.*, subject to court order, and otherwise did not impose any anticompetitive effects on future competition. Axiom Resource Management, Inc. v. U.S., 78 Fed. Cl. 576 (2007)

With regard to mitigation of situations in which one offeror has unequal access to information, the disclosure of information to equalize competition is an appropriate alternative to eliminating an offeror from a competition due to prior disclosure of information that could result in an unfair competitive advantage. Systems Plus, Inc. v. U.S., 69 Fed. Cl. 757 (2006)

Contracting officer acted reasonably when she concluded that subcontractor which developed the plan for a new scheduling organization for the Air Force was precluded by an organizational conflict of interest (OCI) from competing in solicitation to provide contract support for the new scheduling organization, stemming from the input it had provided and continued to provide in developing the organization. DSD Laboratories, Inc. v. U.S., 46 Fed. Cl. 467 (2000). United States ⊶64.15

Under acquisition regulation governing organizational conflicts of interest (OCI), contracting officer had to consider whether any potential OCIs could be avoided or mitigated and explain reasons for her conclusion before denying con tract award to an otherwise qualified bidder. 48 C.F.R. § 9.504(e). Informatics Corp. v. U.S., 40 Fed. Cl. 508, 42 Cont. Cas. Fed. (CCH) P 77311 (1998). United States ⊶64.15

An agency's disqualification of an offeror for a perceived organizational conflict of interest (OCI) was unreasonable because the agency did not explore ways to avoid the conflict as required by the request for proposals. The agency also did not give the protester an opportunity to address OCI concerns, the U.S. Comptroller General found in sustaining the protest. Matter of: Richard Bowers & Company, B-400276, 2008 CPD ¶ 171 (Comp. Gen. 2008)

The responsibility for determining whether a contractor has a conflict of interest and should be excluded from competition rests with the contracting officer, who must exercise 'common sense, good judgment and sound discretion' in assessing whether a significant potential conflict exists and in developing appropriate ways to resolve it. Greenleaf Construction Company, Inc., B-293105.21, B-293105.22, B-293105.23, 2007 CPD ¶ 84 (Comp. Gen. 2007)

The Federal Acquisition Regulation (FAR) instructs agencies to identify potential OCIs as early as possible in the procurement process, and to avoid, neutralize, or mitigate significant conflicts before contract award so as to prevent unfair competitive advantage or the existence of conflicting roles that might impair a contractor's objectivity. Greenleaf Construction Company, Inc., B-293105.21, B-293105.22, B-293105.23, 2007 CPD ¶ 84

(Comp. Gen. 2007)

Agency reasonably concluded that potential for conflict of interest stemming from awardee's proposed use of a subcontractor who had served as an evaluator for the agency in connection with a previous procurement was mitigated where the subcontractor had signed a non-disclosure agreement in connection with her performance as an evaluator and the agency reasonably found that the subcontractor did not aid the awardee in preparing its proposal other than to submit a subcontract proposal. Maden Technologies, B-298543.2, 2006 CPD ¶ 167 (Comp. Gen. 2006)

Protester's contention that the agency failed to adequately mitigate the risk of organizational conflicts of interest (OCI) associated with the selection of the awardee is denied where the record shows that: the contracting officer reasonably concluded that the risk of a conflict of interest in this procurement is not great; the agency requested a detailed OCI mitigation plan from the awardee and sought additional information about, and modifications to, the plan; and the contracting officer reasonably concluded, after performing a detailed analysis, that the modified plan-together with certain steps designed to increase agency oversight of the contractor-was sufficient to protect the government's interest. Overlook Systems Technologies, Inc., B-298099.4, B-298099.5, 2006 CPD ¶ 185 (Comp. Gen. 2006)

Protest challenging agency's exclusion of an offeror from participation in a procurement is denied where the agency reasonably determined that the protester has an organizational conflict of interest arising from its preparation of technical specifications used by the agency in the solicitation. Lucent Technologies World Services, Inc., B-295462, 2005 CPD ¶ 55 (Comp. Gen. 2005)

Agency properly concluded that there was no organizational conflict of interest on the part of the firm in line for award where the firm was not involved in creation of the solicitation's statement of work (SOW); SOW was not essentially derived from materials furnished by the firm; and the firm did not play a role in the source selection process. CDR Enterprises, Inc., B-293557, 2004 CPD ¶ 46 (Comp. Gen. 2004)

Contracting agency reasonably determined not to reject the quotation from the vendor selected to receive an order for augmentation of the agency's procurement staff on the basis of organizational conflicts of interest (OCI) where any potential OCI can be avoided by the careful assignment of work under the contract to ensure that the vendor's contracting specialists do not handle matters (procurements or contracts) in which the vendor has an interest. The The LEADS Corporation, B-292465, 2003 CPD ¶ 197 (Comp. Gen. 2003)

Protest alleging that, in connection with procurement for loan support services, the awardee had an organizational conflict of interest that was not properly mitigated, is denied where the record shows that the contracting agency reasonably determined that the awardee's proposal adequately mitigated any conflict of interest through the use of a subcontractor to perform loan servicing on those properties where the awardee had previously been involved in handling administrative matters for the agency related to the same properties. Deutsche Bank, B-289111, 2001 CPD ¶ 210 (Comp. Gen. 2001)

There is a presumption of prejudice to competing offerors where an organizational conflict of interest (other than a de minimis matter) is not resolved. Organizational conflicts of interest call into question the integrity of the competitive procurement process, and, as with other such circumstances, no specific prejudice need be shown to warrant corrective action. Aetna Government Health Plans, Inc., Matter of: Aetna Government Health Plans, Inc., Foundation Health Federal Services, Inc., B-254397, B-254397.15, B-254397.16, B-254397.17, B-254397.18, B-254397.19, 95-2 CPD ¶ 129 (Comp. Gen. 1995).

7 Unusual and compelling urgency

Contracting agency's invocation of the "unusual and compelling urgency" exception to the full and open competition requirement of the Competition in Contracting Act (CICA) did not preclude challenge to procurement based on allegation that agency violated organizational conflict of interest (OCI) regulations. 10 U.S.C.A. § 2304(c)(2); 48 C.F.R. § 9. 505-1. Filtration Development Co., LLC v. U.S., 59 Fed. Cl. 658 (2004). United States ☞64.15

8 Documentation

Since the contracting officer in a government procurement case need not document his or her considerations unless a substantive issue concerning a conflict of interest exists, the lack of documentation is not a violation or abuse of discretion. LeBoeuf, Lamb, Greene & MacRae, LLP v. Abraham, 215 F. Supp. 2d 73 (D.D.C. 2002), opinion vacated, 347 F.3d 315, 358 (D.C. Cir. 2003)(The court vacated the judgment and remanded the case for a determination as to an apparent conflict of interest was considered as required by regulations, and whether the Department's need for expert legal services on the project supported a direct award of the contract to LeBoeuf or an award of other relief.) United States ☞64.45(1)

9 Injunctions

Bid protestor who prevailed on merits of claim that Army procurement of helicopter engine filters did not adhere to organizational conflict of interest (OCI) requirements and exceeded permissible bounds of the unusual and compelling urgency exception of the Competition in Contracting Act (CICA) was not entitled to injunctive relief with respect to 183 "A kits" and 150 "B kits" for which funding had been allocated and delivery schedule had been set, as that order was justified by needs of Operation Iraqi Freedom; however, Army would be enjoined to conduct any procurement in excess of those amounts on a competitive basis unless an independent justification for invoking an exception to full and open competition was provided. 10 U.S.C.A. § 2304(c)(2). Filtration Development Co., LLC v. U.S., 60 Fed. Cl. 371 (2004). Injunction ☞86

Contractor was not entitled to preliminary injunctive relief to prevent award of contract for support of Air Force combat scheduling organization; contractor was not likely to succeed on the merits because of an organizational conflict of interest (OCI), and there was a strong public interest in avoiding OCIs, and in proceeding with a solicitation support of contingency operations crises management. DSD Laboratories, Inc. v. U.S., 46 Fed. Cl. 467 (2000). Injunction ☞138.63

10 Mootness

Fact that Department of Energy (DOE) cancelled legal services contract awarded to law firm's competitor after only two of the ten years contemplated by the request for proposal (RFP) did not render moot law firm's request for directed award of contract, based on claim alleging that award to competitor violated Department's own regulations. 48 C.F.R. § 9. 504(a)(1). LeBoeuf, Lamb, Greene & MacRae, L.L.P. v. Abraham, 347 F.3d 315, 358 (D.C. Cir. 2003). Federal Courts ☞13

11 Discovery

Bid protestor was not entitled to discovery into whether contracting agency properly conducted organizational conflict of interest review required by the Federal Acquisition Regulation (FAR), where protestor failed to present any evidence suggesting that agency's conflict of interest determination was arbitrary and capricious, but merely pointed to lack of any mention of an organizational conflict of interest in the procurement record. 48 C.F.R. § 9.504(d). Beta Analytics Intern., Inc. v. U.S., 61 Fed. Cl. 223 (2004). United States ☞64.60(3.1)

12 Summary judgment

Genuine issues of material fact regarding whether Department of Energy (DOE) conducted adequate evaluation of potential organizational conflict of interest before awarding contract for legal services in connection with nuclear waste depository site project to law firm's competitor, who had provided legal services to subcontractor conducting studies of site, precluded summary judgment on firm's claim challenging award of contract as arbitrary, capricious, and contrary to Department's own procurement regulations. 48 C.F.R. § 9.504(a)(1); Fed.Rules Civ.Proc.Rule 56(c), 28 U.S.C.A.LeBoeuf, Lamb, Greene & MacRae, L.L.P. v. Abraham, 347 F.3d 315, 358 (D.C. Cir. 2003). Federal Civil Procedure ☞2492

13 Judicial review

In conflict of interest cases involving government procurement contract awards, courts afford great deference to the contracting officer's and agency's determination that no conflict of interest exists, and the court should not disturb a contracting agency's determination unless plaintiff can show that the determination is unreasonable; mere disagreement with the contracting officer's evaluation does not itself render the evaluation unreasonable. LeBoeuf, Lamb, Greene & MacRae, LLP v. Abraham, 215 F. Supp. 2d 73 (D.D.C. 2002), opinion vacated, 347 F.3d 315, 358 (D.C. Cir. 2003)(The court vacated the judgment and remanded the case for a determination as to an apparent conflict of interest was considered as required by regulations, and whether the Department's need for expert legal services on the project supported a direct award of the contract to LeBoeuf or an award of other relief.) United States ☞64.60(4)

For purposes of law firm's request for bid-preparation costs, in its action alleging violations of Administrative Procedure Act (APA) in award by Department of Energy (DOE) of contract for legal services, contract award was not arbitrary, capricious, an abuse of discretion, or in violation of law; DOE did not violate procurement rules and regulations in determining that winning law firm had no conflict of interest, Nevada Code of Professional Responsibility did not apply in federal government procurement context, and DOE did not act in bad faith in awarding contract. 5 U.S.C.A. § 701 et seq.LeBoeuf, Lamb, Greene & MacRae, LLP v. Abraham, 215 F. Supp. 2d 73 (D.D.C. 2002), opinion vacated, 347 F.3d 315, 358 (D.C. Cir. 2003)(The court vacated the judgment and remanded the case for a determination as to an apparent conflict of interest was considered as required by regulations, and whether the Department's need for expert legal services on the project supported a direct award of the contract to LeBoeuf or an award of other relief.) United States ☞64.60(6)

Determination of contracting officer (CO) regarding whether an acquisition involves a significant organizational conflict of interest will be overturned only on a showing of unreasonableness. 48 C.F.R. § 9.504. Filtration Development Co., LLC v. U.S., 60 Fed. Cl. 371 (2004). United States ☞64.15

Contracting agency's determination regarding a conflict of interest that disqualifies bidder should not be disturbed, unless it is shown to be unreasonable. Informatics Corp. v. U.S., 40 Fed. Cl. 508, 42 Cont. Cas. Fed. (CCH) P 77311 (1998). United States ☞64.60(4)

14 Nature of the contracting officer's responsibility

Contracting officers must avoid and address not only actual, but apparent, conflicts of interest. Thus, a protestor need not show that the persons who drafted an offeror's proposal were actually in possession of proprietary information as a result of their employees' work for the agency, but merely must show that the information was accessible to those employees and that the potential OCI created by that access has not been avoided or adequately mitigated. NetStar-1 Gov't Consulting, Inc. v. U.S., 101 Fed. Cl. 511 (2011)

Agency's investigation of awardee's alleged unequal access to information organizational conflict of interest was unreasonable, where the agency concluded that the awardee's hiring of a high-level government employee from the office responsible for the project being procured created a potential conflict, but limited its review to what responsibility and role the government employee had in the procurement prior to his retirement without any consideration of the employee's access to non-public, source selection information, and where the record establishes the employee's continued daily contact with members of the source selection team and access to inside information concerning the agency's build-to-budget concept. PCCP Constructors, et al., B-405036, 2011 CPD ¶ 156 (Comp. Gen. 2011)

An agency unreasonably failed to consider a potential organizational conflict of interest (OCI) because the contract would have required the offeror to review its own information technology designs proposed under a separate contract, and the offeror's mitigation plan did not adequately address the dual roles. Matter of: Nortel Government Solutions, Inc., B-299522.5, B-299522.6, 2009 CPD ¶ 10 (Comp. Gen. 2008)

15 Impaired objectivity

GAO sustained a protest based on impaired objectivity of the awardee where the awardee could potentially be required to evaluate the performance of its parent organization. During the source selection, the eventual awardee submitted an OCI mitigation plan stating that, if it is required to evaluate the performance of its parent organization, the parent would either divest its interest in the awardee company or subcontract the work that the awardee company (its subsidiary) would have to evaluate. The GAO determined the agency's acceptance of this mitigation approach was unreasonable because the plan lacked the detail necessary to assess its viability. Matter of: Cahaba Safeguard Administrators, LLC, B-401842.2, 2010 CPD ¶ 39 (Comp. Gen. 2010)

16 Biased ground rules

A biased ground rules organizational conflict of interest (OCI) exists if a contractor sets the ground rules for a Government contract, potentially skewing the competition in its favor. The Court of Federal Claims (COFC) held that an agency's decision to implement a GAO recommendation to recompete a contract because the award was tainted with a "biased ground rules" OCI was arbitrary and capricious. The COFC determined that the GAO's finding of a "biased ground rules" OCI was irrational because it was not supported by the record and because it failed to consider the agency's findings that no OCI existed. The COFC ordered the agency to restore the contract to the original awardee. Turner Const. Co., Inc. v. U.S., 94 Fed. Cl. 561 (2010), motion for stay pending appeal denied, 94 Fed. Cl. 586 (2010) and motion for stay pending appeal denied, 410 Fed. Appx. 319 (Fed. Cir. 2010) and appeal dismissed in part, 407 Fed. Appx. 478 (Fed. Cir. 2011) and aff'd, 645 F.3d 1377 (Fed. Cir. 2011)

Agency reasonably concluded that the protester had an organizational conflict of interest (OCI) and properly eliminated the protester from the competition where the agency found that a member of the protester's team was involved in developing the statement of work, solicitation, and other key acquisition documents and strategies, resulting in a biased ground rules OCI. IBM Corp., B-410639, B- 410639.2, 2015 CPD ¶ 41 (Comp.Gen. 2015)

§ 9.505 General rules.

The general rules in 9.505-1 through 9.505-4 prescribe limitations on contracting as the means of avoiding, neutralizing, or mitigating organizational conflicts of interest that might otherwise exist in the stated situations. Some illustrative examples are provided in 9.508. Conflicts may arise in situations not expressly covered in this section 9.505 or in the examples in 9.508. Each individual contracting situation should be examined on the basis of its particular facts and the nature of the proposed contract. The exercise of common sense, good judgment, and sound discretion is required in both the decision on whether a significant potential conflict exists and, if it does, the development of an appropriate means for resolving it. The two underlying principles are—

(a) Preventing the existence of conflicting roles that might bias a contractor's judgment; and

(b) Preventing unfair competitive advantage. In addition to the other situations described in this subpart, an unfair competitive advantage exists where a contractor competing for award of any Federal contract possesses—

(1) Proprietary information that was obtained from a Government official without proper authorization; or

(2) Source selection information (as defined in 2.101) that is relevant to the contract but is not available to all competitors, and such information would assist that contractor in obtaining the contract.

United States Code Annotated

Administrative determinations, see 41 USCA § 257.

Conflict of interest standards for individuals providing consulting services, see 41 USCA § 405b.

Contract requirements, see 41 USCA § 254.

Contracting functions performed by Federal personnel, see 41 USCA § 419.

Contracts, planning, solicitation, evaluation, and award procedures, see 10 USCA § 2305.

Definitions, see 10 USCA § 2302, 41 USCA §§ 259, 403.

Determinations and decisions, see 10 USCA § 2310, 41 USCA § 262.

Kinds of contracts, see 10 USCA § 2306.

Planning and solicitation requirements, see 41 USCA § 253a.

Notes of Decisions

Appearance of impropriety 2
Conjecture or speculation 3
Consultants, generally 1
Unusual and compelling urgency 4

1 Consultants, generally

Federal acquisitions regulations do not mandate adoption of principle that vendors can never serve as contract consultants to government agencies even when they are prohibited from competing for contract on which they consult and subject to other appropriate restrictions. Informatics General Corp. v. Weinberger, 617 F. Supp. 331 (D.D.C. 1985). United States ☞64.5

2 Appearance of impropriety

Pursuant to Federal Acquisition Regulation (FAR), bidder on government contract may be disqualified based on appearance of impropriety when bidder may have gained unfair competitive advantage through actual or potential conflict of interest in procurement process. 48 C.F.R. § 1.000 et seq.Medco Behavioral Care Corp. of Iowa v. State, Dept. of Human Services, 553 N.W.2d 556 (Iowa 1996). Public Contracts ☞11

Disqualification of successful bidder for state Medicaid managed mental health care contract, based on organizational conflicts of interest, was warranted by appearance of impropriety that tainted procurement process resulting from bidder's direct connection, as subsidiaries of same company, with contractor that assisted state in policy analysis that served as springboard for state's request for proposals (RFP), and indirect connection through undisclosed business relationship between bidder's cosubsidiary and company that actually prepared RFP. Medco Behavioral Care Corp. of Iowa v. State, Dept. of Human Services, 553 N.W.2d 556 (Iowa 1996). Health ☞486; Health ☞503(3); States ☞98

Pursuant to federal acquisition regulation (FAR), bidder on government contract may be disqualified based on appearance of impropriety when bidder may have gained unfair competitive advantage through actual or potential conflict of interest in procurement process. 48 C.F.R. § 1.000 et seq.Medco Behavioral Care Corp. of Iowa v. State, Dept. of Human Services, 553 N.W.2d 556 (Iowa 1996). Public Contracts ☞11

District court properly held as a matter of law that successful bidder for state Medicaid managed mental health care contract was disqualified due to organizational conflicts of interest, inasmuch as appearance of impropriety arising from bidder's connections with insiders that helped superintend process for receiving and evaluating bids could not be mitigated, despite self-structured embargoes on communications between bidder and insiders. Medco Behavioral Care Corp. of Iowa v. State, Dept. of Human Services, 553 N.W.2d 556 (Iowa 1996). States ☞98

District court applied correct legal standard in testing for existence of organizational conflict of interest requiring disqualification of successful bidder for Medicaid managed mental health care contract when it determined that mere appearance of impropriety was sufficient to support disqualification, and that actual conflict of interest did not have to be shown. I.C.A. § 249A.4; 45 C.F.R. Part 74, App. G, § 10 (1995); 48 C.F.R. §§ 1.101, 9.51, 9.502(b, c), 9.504(a)(1, 2), (e), 9.505. Medco Behavioral Care Corp. of Iowa v. State, Dept. of Human Services, 553 N.W.2d 556 (Iowa 1996). States ☞98

3 Conjecture or speculation

Protest that agency's decisions to eliminate protester from the competition and award the contract to the awardee were tainted because an improper conflict of interest existed between a member of the technical evaluation panel and an individual proposed by the awardee due to their prior co-authorship of various publications is denied where there is no evidence of any current economic relationship between the two individuals, and no evidence that the evaluator exerted improper influence in the procurement on behalf of the awardee or against the protester. Matter of: DRI/McGraw-Hill, B-261181, B-261181.2, 95-2 CPD ¶ 76 (Comp. Gen. 1995)

Mere conjecture, innuendo, or speculation of actual or potential conflict of interest, without factual support, provide no basis for disqualification of government contract bidder under federal acquisition regulation (FAR). 48 C.F.R. § 1.000 et seq.Medco Behavioral Care Corp. of Iowa v. State, Dept. of Human Services, 553 N.W.2d 556 (Iowa 1996). Public Contracts ☞11

4 Unusual and compelling urgency

Contracting agency's invocation of the "unusual and compelling urgency" exception to the full and open competition requirement of the Competition in Contracting Act (CICA) did not preclude challenge to procurement based on allegation that agency violated organizational conflict of interest (OCI) regulations. 10 U.S.C.A. § 2304(c)(2); 48 C.F.R. § 9. 505-1. Filtration Development Co., LLC v. U.S., 59 Fed. Cl. 658 (2004). United States ☞64.15

§ 9.505-1 Providing systems engineering and technical direction.

(a) A contractor that provides systems engineering and technical direction for a system but does not have overall contractual responsibility for its development, its integration, assembly, and checkout, or its production shall not—

(1) Be awarded a contract to supply the system or any of its major components; or

(2) Be a subcontractor or consultant to a supplier of the system or any of its major components.

(b) Systems engineering includes a combination of substantially all of the following activities: determining specifications, identifying and resolving interface problems, developing test requirements, evaluating test data, and supervising design. Technical direction includes a combination of substantially all of the following activities: developing work statements, determining parameters, directing other contractors' operations, and resolving technical controversies. In performing these activities, a contractor occupies a highly influential and responsible position in determining a system's basic concepts and supervising their execution by other contractors. Therefore this contractor should not be in a position to make decisions favoring its own products or capabilities.

United States Code Annotated

Administrative determinations, see 41 USCA § 257.

Conflict of interest standards for individuals providing consulting services, see 41 USCA § 405b.

Contract requirements, see 41 USCA § 254.

Contracting functions performed by Federal personnel, see 41 USCA § 419.

Contracts, planning, solicitation, evaluation, and award procedures, see 10 USCA § 2305.

Definitions, see 10 USCA § 2302, 41 USCA §§ 259, 403.

Determinations and decisions, see 10 USCA § 2310, 41 USCA § 262.

Kinds of contracts, see 10 USCA § 2306.

Planning and solicitation requirements, see 41 USCA § 253a.

Notes of Decisions
In general 1
Biased ground rules 2

1 In general

Although the CO ultimately cured a prior failure to identify and analyze a potential "unequal access to information" conflict the CO did not identify the potential "impaired objectivity" conflict, as required by FAR § 9.504(a). Axiom Resource Management, Inc. v. U.S., 78 Fed. Cl. 576 (2007)

Actual organizational conflict of interest (OCI) existed where contractor performed systems engineering and technical direction (SETA) tasks for procurement in which one of its divisions received sole source contract award for supply of helicopter engine filter kits, and presumption of harm to the procurement process and prejudice arose from contractor's dual role which was not rebutted by existence of unsigned and unapproved mitigation plans contractor submitted to contracting officer (CO). 48 C.F.R. §§ 9.505-1(a), 9.508(a). Filtration Development Co., LLC v. U.S., 60 Fed. Cl. 371 (2004). United States ☞64.15

Protest is sustained where record does not support the agency's conclusion that awardee's conflicts of interest will be minimal, with limited impact on quality of contract performance, where awardee, a manufacturer of spectrum-dependent products, will perform analysis and evaluation and exercise subjective judgment regarding formulation of policies and regulations that may affect the sale or use of spectrum-dependent products manufactured by the awardee or the awardee's competitors, and those deployed by the awardee's customers. Matter of: Alion Science & Technology Corporation, B-297342, 2006 CPD ¶ 1 (Comp. Gen. 2006)

Protest is sustained where agency failed to reasonably consider or evaluate potential conflicts of interest that will be created by awardees involvement in evaluating the performance of undersea warfare systems that have been manufactured by the awardee or by the awardees competitors. PURVIS Systems, Inc., B-293807.3, B-293807.4, 2004 CPD ¶ 177 (Comp. Gen. 2004)

Contractor's development of a quality assurance program to track scheduled maintenance events does not create an organizational conflict of interest (OCI) because the contractor is not responsible for making judgments as to what maintenance is required or how well the maintenance is being performed. Monitoring, standing alone, does not necessarily create the potential for impaired objectivity. Rather, an impaired objectivity OCI typically arises where a firm is evaluating its own (or a related firm's) activities, because the objectivity necessary to impartially evaluate performance may be impaired by the firm's interest in the entity being evaluated. Where the contractor's responsibilities are not based on subjective judgments or evaluations, there is no basis for finding that the objectivity of the contractor will be impaired. Computers Universal, Inc., B-292794, 2003 CPD ¶ 201 (Comp. Gen. 2003)

Contracting agency reasonably determined that contractor's performance of both a contract for operation of the agency's highest echelon calibration laboratory and a contract for operation of lower echelon calibration laboratories did not pose an organizational conflict of interest where government personnel who are responsible for monitoring and measuring contractor performance under both contracts rely primarily on information other than feedback from other contractors in performing these functions. Wyle Laboratories, Inc., B-288892, B-288892.2, 2002 CPD ¶ 12 (Comp. Gen. 2001)

2 Biased ground rules

Bid protestor did not establish contract awardee's prior work with contracting agency providing information technology services created an organizational conflict of interest (OCI) by making it the beneficiary of "biased ground rules," absent evidence that awardee was involved in setting specifications for solicitation or writing the solicitation itself. Systems Plus, Inc. v. U.S., 69 Fed. Cl. 757 (2006). United States ⊛64.15

§ 9.505-2 Preparing specifications or work statements.

(a) (1) If a contractor prepares and furnishes complete specifications covering nondevelopmental items, to be used in a competitive acquisition, that contractor shall not be allowed to furnish these items, either as a prime contractor or as a subcontractor, for a reasonable period of time including, at least, the duration of the initial production contract. This rule shall not apply to—

(i) Contractors that furnish at Government request specifications or data regarding a product they provide, even though the specifications or data may have been paid for separately or in the price of the product; or

(ii) Situations in which contractors, acting as industry representatives, help Government agencies prepare, refine, or coordinate specifications, regardless of source, provided this assistance is supervised and controlled by Government representatives.

(2) If a single contractor drafts complete specifications for nondevelopmental equipment, it should be eliminated for a reasonable time from competition for production based on the specifications. This should be done in order to avoid a situation in which the contractor could draft specifications favoring its own products or capabilities. In this way the Government can be assured of getting unbiased advice as to the content of the specifications and can avoid allegations of favoritism in the award of production contracts.

(3) In development work, it is normal to select firms that have done the most advanced work in the field. These firms can be expected to design and develop around their own prior knowledge. Development contractors can frequently start production earlier and more knowledgeably than firms that did not participate in the development, and this can affect the time and quality of production, both of which are important to the Government. In many instances the Government may have financed the development. Thus, while the development contractor has a competitive advantage, it is an unavoidable one that is not considered unfair; hence no prohibition should be imposed.

(b) (1) If a contractor prepares, or assists in preparing, a work statement to be used in competitively acquiring a system or services—or provides material leading directly, predictably, and without delay to such a work statement—that contractor may not supply the system, major components of the system, or the services unless—

(i) It is the sole source;

(ii) It has participated in the development and design work; or

(iii) More than one contractor has been involved in preparing the work statement.

(2) Agencies should normally prepare their own work statements. When contractor assistance is necessary, the contractor might often be in a position to favor its own products or capabilities. To overcome the possibility of bias, contractors are prohibited from supplying a system or services acquired on the basis of work statements growing out of their services, unless excepted in paragraph (b)(1) of this section.

(3) For the reasons given in 9.505-2(a)(3), no prohibitions are imposed on development and design contractors.

United States Code Annotated

Administrative determinations, see 41 USCA § 257.

Conflict of interest standards for individuals providing consulting services, see 41 USCA § 405b.

Contract requirements, see 41 USCA § 254.

Contracting functions performed by Federal personnel, see 41 USCA § 419.

Contracts, planning, solicitation, evaluation, and award procedures, see 10 USCA § 2305.

Definitions, see 10 USCA § 2302, 41 USCA §§ 259, 403.

Determinations and decisions, see 10 USCA § 2310, 41 USCA § 262.

Kinds of contracts, see 10 USCA § 2306.

Planning and solicitation requirements, see 41 USCA § 253a.

Notes of Decisions

In general 1

1 In general

Contractor that served as Department of Housing and Urban Development's (HUD) financial advisor for HUD's mortgage loan sales program did not create conflict of interest in violation of the False Claims Act (FCA) when it advised HUD that it needed a crosscutting financial advisor who could look across HUD's different portfolios and help advise the agency on how to dispose of its loans, then competed for the resulting crosscutting financial advisor contract. U.S. ex rel. Ervin and Associates, Inc. v. Hamilton Securities Group, Inc., 370 F. Supp. 2d 18 (D.D.C. 2005). United States ⊸120.1

A biased ground rules organizational conflict of interest (OCI) exists if a contractor sets the ground rules for a Government contract, potentially skewing the competition in its favor. The Court of Federal Claims (COFC) held that an agency's decision to implement a GAO recommendation to recompete a contract because the award was tainted with a "biased ground rules" OCI was arbitrary and capricious. The COFC determined that the GAO's finding of a "biased ground rules" OCI was irrational because it was not supported by the record and because it failed to consider the agency's findings that no OCI existed. The COFC ordered the agency to restore the contract to the original awardee. Turner Const. Co., Inc. v. U.S., 94 Fed. Cl. 561 (2010), motion for stay pending appeal denied, 94 Fed. Cl. 586 (2010) and motion for stay pending appeal denied, 410 Fed. Appx. 319 (Fed. Cir. 2010) and appeal dismissed in part, 407 Fed. Appx. 478 (Fed. Cir. 2011) and aff'd, 645 F.3d 1377 (Fed. Cir. 2011)

Under developmental contractor exception to organizational conflict of interest (OCI) rules, contractor which had overall contractual responsibility for weapons system program was not precluded from bidding on production contract even after providing the specifications for the procurement; moreover, fact that contractor was successor to original developmental contractor by virtue of its purchase of related assets did not remove it from exception. 48 C.F.R. §§ 9.505-1(a), 9.508(e). Vantage Associates, Inc. v. U.S., 59 Fed. Cl. 1 (2003). United States ⊸64.15

Industry representative exception to organizational conflict of interest (OCI) rules applied to development and design contractor which prepared new specifications for Navy weapons system procurement, and thus it could compete in the procurement, where contractor was acting as industry representative and under Navy auspices in preparing the specifications. 48 C.F.R. § 9.505-2(a)(1)(ii). Vantage Associates, Inc. v. U.S., 59 Fed. Cl. 1 (2003). United States ⊕64.15

Contracting officer acted reasonably when she concluded that subcontractor which developed the plan for a new scheduling organization for the Air Force was precluded by an organizational conflict of interest (OCI) from competing in solicitation to provide contract support for the new scheduling organization, stemming from the input it had provided and continued to provide in developing the organization. 48 C.F.R. § 9.505-2(b)(2). DSD Laboratories, Inc. v. U.S., 46 Fed. Cl. 467 (2000). United States ⊕64.15

Protest that awardee has an organizational conflict of interest arising from performance of contracts for similar work is denied where there is no support in the record for allegation that the awardee participated in drafting the performance requirements for the current procurement. Philadelphia Produce Market Wholesalers, LLC, B-298751.5, 2007 CPD ¶ 87 (Comp. Gen. 2007)

Protest alleging that firm that developed technical data package (TDP) for item to be procured has an unfair informational advantage over other competitors is denied where record establishes that TDP contained sufficient information to permit prospective offerors to formulate proposals. A competitive advantage that derives from an offeror's previous performance under a government contract is not an unfair competitive advantage that agency is required to neutralize. Lakota Technical Solutions, Inc., B-298297, 2006 CPD ¶ 118 (Comp. Gen. 2006)

Contracting agency reasonably concluded that awardee's use of a subcontractor which had participated in the development of the solicitation's specifications did not present an organizational conflict of interest because the subcontractor had worked only on design aspects of the specifications, more than one contractor was involved in preparing the specifications, and the subcontractor was not in a position to draft specifications favoring its own products. American Artisan Productions, Inc., B-292559, B-292559.2, 2003 CPD ¶ 176 (Comp. Gen. 2003)

Incumbent contractor did not have organizational conflict of interest or unfair competitive advantage where, contrary to the protester's assertion, the agency, not the incumbent, drafted the statement of work used in the protested procurement. M&W Construction Corporation, B-288649.2, 2002 CPD ¶ 30 (Comp. Gen. 2001)

Agency reasonably excluded protester from participating in procurement where protester has an organizational conflict of interest arising from its preparation of the statement of work and cost estimates used by the agency in the procurement. SSR Engineers, Inc., B-282244, 99-2 CPD ¶ 27 (Comp. Gen. 1999)

Agency properly excluded a firm from competing under a solicitation where the firm has an organizational conflict of interest with respect to competing under that solicitation because it prepared the statement of work and cost estimate which the agency used for the solicitation. Basile, Baumann, Prost & Associates, Inc., B-274870, 97-1 CPD ¶ 15 (Comp. Gen. 1997)

Protest that firm should be excluded from the competition for an economic development contract in Uganda based upon its prior involvement in preparing a concept paper for the project is denied where the record shows that the concept paper did not lead directly, predictably, and without delay to the solicitation's work statement; that the concept paper is a publicly available document; and that any competitive advantage obtained by the firm by virtue of its preparation of the concept paper was not created by any improper preference or other unfair action by the agency. Daniel Eke and Associates, P.C., B-271962, 96-2 CPD ¶ 9 (Comp. Gen. 1996)

§ 9.505-3 Providing evaluation services.

Contracts for the evaluation of offers for products or services shall not be awarded to a contractor that will evaluate its own offers for products or services, or those of a competitor, without proper safeguards to ensure objectivity to protect the Government's interests.

United States Code Annotated

Administrative determinations, see 41 USCA § 257.

Conflict of interest standards for individuals providing consulting services, see 41 USCA § 405b.

Contract requirements, see 41 USCA § 254.

Contracting functions performed by Federal personnel, see 41 USCA § 419.

Contracts, planning, solicitation, evaluation, and award procedures, see 10 USCA § 2305.

Definitions, see 10 USCA § 2302, 41 USCA §§ 259, 403.

Determinations and decisions, see 10 USCA § 2310, 41 USCA § 262.

Kinds of contracts, see 10 USCA § 2306.

Planning and solicitation requirements, see 41 USCA § 253a.

Notes of Decisions

In general 1

1 In general

Even assuming that conflict-of-interest provision of the Federal Acquisition Regulation (FAR) was violated when supervisor of motor transport department was placed on evaluation board involved in A-76 cost comparison to determine if function of department should be contracted out, contractor was not prejudiced by supervisor's participation, considering that supervisor was only one of six individuals on the board, and there was no dissent on board's "poor" rating of contractor. 48 C.F.R. § 3.101-1. JWK Intern. Corp. v. U.S., 52 Fed. Cl. 650 (2002), aff'd, 56 Fed. Appx. 474 (Fed. Cir. 2003). United States ⊙64.55(1)

Participation of four local managers on evaluation boards did not constitute prejudicial conflict of interest in A-76 cost comparison study of whether maintenance and motor transport services at naval air station should be contracted out to private contractor, where only one of the managers was directly associated with a function under study, and he was a military officer not concerned with loss of employment. 48 C.F.R. § 3.101-1. JWK Intern. Corp. v. U.S., 52 Fed. Cl. 650 (2002), aff'd, 56 Fed. Appx. 474 (Fed. Cir. 2003). United States ⊙64.40(1)

Agency reasonably concluded that potential for conflict of interest stemming from awardee's proposed use of a subcontractor who had served as an evaluator for the agency in connection with a previous procurement was mitigated where the subcontractor had signed a non-disclosure agreement in connection with her performance as an evaluator and the agency reasonably found that the subcontractor did not aid the awardee in preparing its proposal other than to submit a subcontract proposal. Maden Technologies, B-298543.2, 2006 CPD ¶ 167 (Comp. Gen. 2006)

Protest that awardee has impaired objectivity type of organizational conflict of interest is sustained where record shows that, under the terms of another contract, proposed subcontractor will be making recommendations that could benefit the awardee, and the proposed subcontractor could be called upon to evaluate the performance of the awardee team. Johnson Controls World Services, Inc., B-286714.2, 2001 CPD ¶ 20 (Comp. Gen. 2001)

A conflict of interest existed in an Office of Management and Budget Circular A-76 commercial activities study where a Navy employee and a private-sector consultant wrote and edited the performance work statement and then prepared the management plan for in-house performance. IT Facility Services-Joint Venture, B-285841, 2000 CPD ¶ 177 (Comp. Gen. 2000)

Significant organizational conflict of interest exists where an affiliate of one offeror's major subcontractor evaluates proposals for the procuring agency. Such a conflict of interest could not be mitigated by an OCI Mitigation Plan. Matter of: Aetna Government Health Plans, Inc., Foundation Health Federal Services, Inc., B-254397, B-254397.15, B-254397.16, B-254397.17, B-254397.18, B-254397.19, 95-2 CPD ¶ 129 (Comp. Gen. 1995)

§ 9.505-4 Obtaining access to proprietary information.

(a) When a contractor requires proprietary information from others to perform a Government contract and can use the leverage of the contract to obtain it, the contractor may gain an unfair competitive advantage unless restrictions are imposed. These restrictions protect the information and encourage companies to provide it when necessary for contract performance. They are not intended to protect information—

(1) Furnished voluntarily without limitations on its use; or

(2) Available to the Government or contractor from other sources without restriction.

(b) A contractor that gains access to proprietary information of other companies in performing advisory and assistance services for the Government must agree with the other companies to protect their information from unauthorized use or disclosure for as long as it remains proprietary and refrain from using the information for any purpose other than that for which it was furnished. The contracting officer shall obtain copies of these agreements and ensure that they are properly executed.

(c) Contractors also obtain proprietary and source selection information by acquiring the services of marketing consultants which, if used in connection with an acquisition, may give the contractor an unfair competitive advantage. Contractors should make inquiries of marketing consultants to ensure that the marketing consultant has provided no unfair competitive advantage.

United States Code Annotated

Administrative determinations, see 41 USCA § 257.

Conflict of interest standards for individuals providing consulting services, see 41 USCA § 405b.

Contract requirements, see 41 USCA § 254.

Contracting functions performed by Federal personnel, see 41 USCA § 419.

Contracts, planning, solicitation, evaluation, and award procedures, see 10 USCA § 2305.

Definitions, see 10 USCA § 2302, 41 USCA §§ 259, 403.

Determinations and decisions, see 10 USCA § 2310, 41 USCA § 262.

Kinds of contracts, see 10 USCA § 2306.

Planning and solicitation requirements, see 41 USCA § 253a.

Notes of Decisions

In general 1
Access to information 2
Sufficiency of evidence 3

1 In general

Successful bidder for state Medicaid managed mental health care contract could be disqualified based on organizational conflicts of interest, even though actual improper sharing of information between bidder and its contacts was not established. Medco Behavioral Care Corp. of Iowa v. State, Dept. of Human Services, 553 N.W.2d 556 (Iowa 1996). States ⊜98

2 Access to information

Awardee of blanket purchase agreement (BPA) to provide program management support services for agency had significant potential organizational conflict of interest (OCI) from unequal access to information that was not available to other bidders and could have provided awardee with significant competitive advantage in preparing bid and obtaining BPA, where awardee's employees had access to bid protestor's trade secrets including labor rates, due to awardee's performance of other contracts for the procuring agency, and awardee's lower price was determining factor in awarding contract. NetStar-1 Gov't Consulting, Inc. v. U.S., 101 Fed. Cl. 511 (2011)

The Court of Federal Claims (COFC) held that an agency's decision to implement a GAO recommendation to recompete a contract because the award was tainted with an Organizational Conflict of Interest (OCI) was arbitrary and capricious. GAO had sustained a protest based on an OCI because the awardee's design subcontractor had access to competitively useful information through the firm retained by the agency to provide technical support services for the same project. The parent company of the agency's technical support contractor was negotiating a merger with the awardee's design subcontractor. The COFC found that the GAO decision was irrational because it failed to cite any hard facts to support the conclusion that the awardee had unequal access to competitively useful information. Because the GAO decision was irrational, the agency was not justified in relying on it. The COFC ordered the agency to restore the contract to the original awardee. Turner Const. Co., Inc. v. U.S., 94 Fed. Cl. 561 (2010), motion for stay pending appeal denied, 94 Fed. Cl. 586 (2010) and motion for stay pending appeal denied, 410 Fed. Appx. 319 (Fed. Cir. 2010) and appeal dismissed in part, 407 Fed. Appx. 478 (Fed. Cir. 2011) and aff'd, 645 F.3d 1377 (Fed. Cir. 2011)

For an organizational conflict of interest (OIE) to exist based upon unequal access to information, there must be something more than mere incumbency, that is, indication that: (1) the awardee was so embedded in the agency as to provide it with insight into the agency's operations beyond that which would be expected of a typical government contractor; (2) the awardee had obtained materials related to the specifications or statement of work for the instant procurement; or (3) some other preferred treatment or agency action has occurred. ARINC Engineering Services, LLC v. U.S., 77 Fed. Cl. 196 (2007)

The awardee's prior performance as a subcontractor to the incumbent contractor did not create an unfair competitive advantage based on "unequal access to information." The awardee gained knowledge about how to perform the work, and supported the agency's internal daily operations meetings, as well as the agency's project management and administrative meetings, the knowledge gained through these activities Although the awardee may have had an advantage over some other bidders in these areas, the knowledge gained is not the kind of specific, sensitive information that would create an OCI. Systems Plus, Inc. v. U.S., 69 Fed. Cl. 757 (2006). United States ☞64.15

Protest that awardee's subcontractor had an unmitigated unequal access to information organizational conflict of interest is denied where, although the contracting officer did not follow the requirements of the FAR to ensure that contractors enter into non-disclosure agreements with other contractors to prevent competitive harm arising from disclosures of information, there was no competitive prejudice to the protester because the contracting officer obtained different kinds of non-disclosure agreements from the awardee's subcontractor's personnel, which provided adequate protections of the protester's confidential and proprietary information. Enter. Info. Servs. Inc., et. al., 2011 CPD ¶ 174 (Comp. Gen. 2011)

Protest that the awardee should not have been permitted to receive the award of a contract for certain services because the awardee, through its performance of a task order for the agency, was given access to information that the protester now claims as proprietary and was exposed to certain agency information that gave the awardee an unfair competitive advantage, was denied, where the agency reasonably concluded that the protester furnished its information voluntarily without restrictions on its use, and the record did not support the protester's contention that the awardee had an unfair competitive advantage by virtue of the experience it gained from performing the task order. Matter of: CACI, Inc.-Federal, B-403064.2, 2011 CPD ¶ 31 (Comp. Gen. 2011)

3 Sufficiency of evidence

Bid protestor did not establish that contract awardee's prior work with agency providing information technology services created an organizational conflict of interest (OCI) by giving it access to specific nonpublic information concerning agency which gave it a competitive advantage, absent evidence that awardee was "embedded" within agency such that it had such information; even though awardee might have gained some insights by performing planning, architecture, and design work, knowledge gained provided no more advantage than that usually enjoyed by incumbent contractor in solicitation process. Systems Plus, Inc. v. U.S., 69 Fed. Cl. 757 (2006). United States ☞64.15

Agency's determination that awardee's major subcontractor did not have a significant organizational conflict of interest because of its work as a support services contractor for the agency has not been shown to be unreasonable, where there was no evidence in record showing that the subcontractor had an unfair competitive advantage resulting from access to the proprietary information of competitors, or to competitively useful or source selection sensitive information not available to the other offerors. Mechanical Equipment Company, Inc.; Highland Engineering, Inc.; Etnyre International, Ltd.; Mechanical Equipment Company, Inc.; Highland Engineering, Inc.; Etnyre International, Ltd.; Kara Aerospace, Inc., B-292789.2, B-292789.3, B-292789.4, B-292789.5, B-292789.6, B-292789.7, 2004 CPD ¶ 192 (Comp. Gen. 2003)

Protest that a firm should be excluded from competition under a solicitation for information technology services because the firm, through its performance of a delivery order for the agency, was given access to information that the protester now claims as proprietary, is denied, where the information was furnished voluntarily and without restrictions on its use. Snell Enterprises, Inc., B-290113, B-290113.2, 2002 CPD ¶ 115 (Comp. Gen. 2002)

Protest that awardee had unfair competitive advantage due to organizational conflict of interest is sustained where awardee's proposed subcontractor possessed information through its work as a government contractor, the information was not available to other offerors, the agency took no steps to identify or mitigate the conflict in advance, and there were no meaningful procedures in place to prevent interaction between the employees possessing the information and the employees preparing the proposal. Johnson Controls World Services, Inc., B-286714.2, 2001 CPD ¶ 20 (Comp. Gen. 2001)

Protest that awardee's subcontractor has impermissible conflict of interest is sustained where record shows that agency did not consider possibility that subcontractor may have improperly obtained, through performance of earlier government contract, information confidential to protester and used it to enhance capabilities made available to awardee, and agency did not analyze possible conflicting roles that subcontractor may be required to perform under protested contract and subcontractor's other government work. Ktech Corporation, B-285330, B-285330.2, 2002 CPD ¶ 77 (Comp. Gen. 2000)

§ 9.506 Procedures.

(a) If information concerning prospective contractors is necessary to identify and evaluate potential organizational conflicts of interest or to develop recommended actions, contracting officers first should seek the information from within the Government or from other readily available sources. Government sources include the files and the knowledge of personnel within the contracting office, other contracting offices, the cognizant contract administration and audit activities and offices concerned with contract financing. Non-Government sources include publications and commercial services, such as credit rating services, trade and financial journals, and business directories and registers.

(b) If the contracting officer decides that a particular acquisition involves a significant potential organizational conflict of interest, the contracting officer shall, before issuing the solicitation, submit for approval to the chief of the contracting office (unless a higher level official is designated by the agency)—

(1) A written analysis, including a recommended course of action for avoiding, neutralizing, or mitigating the conflict, based on the general rules in 9.505 or on another basis not expressly stated in that section;

(2) A draft solicitation provision (see 9.507-1); and

(3) If appropriate, a proposed contract clause (see 9.507-2).

(c) The approving official shall—

(1) Review the contracting officer's analysis and recommended course of action, including the draft provision and any proposed clause;

(2) Consider the benefits and detriments to the Government and prospective contractors; and

(3) Approve, modify, or reject the recommendations in writing.

(d) The contracting officer shall—

(1) Include the approved provision(s) and any approved clause(s) in the solicitation or the contract, or both;

(2) Consider additional information provided by prospective contractors in response to the solicitation or during negotiations; and

(3) Before awarding the contract, resolve the conflict or the potential conflict in a manner consistent with the approval or other direction by the head of the contracting activity.

(e) If, during the effective period of any restriction (see 9.507), a contracting office transfers acquisition responsibility for the item or system involved, it shall notify the successor contracting office of the restriction, and send a copy of the contract under which the restriction was imposed.

United States Code Annotated

Administrative determinations, see 41 USCA § 257.

Conflict of interest standards for individuals providing consulting services, see 41 USCA § 405b.

Contract requirements, see 41 USCA § 254.

Contracting functions performed by Federal personnel, see 41 USCA § 419.

Contracts, planning, solicitation, evaluation, and award procedures, see 10 USCA § 2305.

Definitions, see 10 USCA § 2302, 41 USCA §§ 259, 403.

Determinations and decisions, see 10 USCA § 2310, 41 USCA § 262.

Kinds of contracts, see 10 USCA § 2306.

Planning and solicitation requirements, see 41 USCA § 253a.

Notes of Decisions

In general 1
Agency investigation 8
Discovery 4
Documentation 2
Due process of law 7
Injunctions 3
Judicial review 6
Summary judgment 5

1 In general

Contracting officer's decision to disqualify offeror based on alleged possession of competitor information was procedurally flawed and contrary to law in that it did not provide notice to the disqualified vendor or an opportunity to be heard. Consequently, the vendor was provided no opportunity to address or to contest the contracting officer's suspicions. This process violated Section 555(b) of the Administrative Procedures Act (APA), which provides, in pertinent part, that a party is entitled to be heard in an agency proceeding, absent exigent circumstances. In short, the contracting officer's action contravened "the minimal requirements" for informal adjudication set forth in Section 555 of the APA and is, therefore, invalid. Systems Plus, Inc. v. U.S., 69 Fed. Cl. 757 (2006)

Contracting officer acted reasonably when she concluded that subcontractor which developed the plan for a new scheduling organization for the Air Force was precluded by an organizational conflict of interest (OCI) from competing in solicitation to provide contract support for the new scheduling organization, stemming from the input it had provided and continued to provide in developing the organization. DSD Laboratories, Inc. v. U.S., 46 Fed. Cl. 467 (2000). United States ⊗64.15

Protest is sustained where Department of Housing and Urban Development failed to reasonably consider or evaluate potential organizational conflict of interest arising due to the fact that the owner of the management and marketing (M & M) services contractor in Ohio will be receiving payments from the owner of the closing agent contractor for Ohio, the activities of which the M & M contractor will oversee. Matter of: Greenleaf Construction Company, Inc., B-293105.18, B-293105.19, 2006 CPD ¶ 19 (Comp. Gen. 2006)

Where agency acknowledges that awardee's substantial involvement in activities that are subject to environmental regulations could create a conflict of interest in performing certain tasks contemplated by the solicitation's scope of work, and agency gave no consideration to the impact of such potential conflicts in selecting awardee's proposal for contract award, agency failed to comply with Federal Acquisition Regulation requirement that it "identify and evaluate potential organizational conflicts of interest." Science Applications International Corporation, B-293601, B-293601.2, B-293601.3, 2004 CPD ¶ 96 (Comp. Gen. 2004)

Contracting agency reasonably concluded that awardee's use of a subcontractor which had participated in the development of the solicitation's specifications did not present an organizational conflict of interest because the subcontractor had worked only on design aspects of the specifications, more than one contractor was involved in preparing the specifications, and the subcontractor was not in a position to draft specifications favoring its own products. American Artisan Productions, Inc., B-292559, B-292559.2, 2003 CPD ¶ 176 (Comp. Gen. 2003)

Contracting agency reasonably determined not to reject the quotation from the vendor selected to receive an order for augmentation of the agency's procurement staff on the basis of organizational conflicts of interest (OCI) where any potential OCI can be avoided by the careful assignment of work under the contract to ensure that the vendor's contracting specialists do not handle matters (procurements or contracts) in which the vendor has an interest. The The LEADS Corporation, B-292465, 2003 CPD ¶ 197 (Comp. Gen. 2003)

Protest that awardee had unfair competitive advantage due to organizational conflict of interest is sustained where awardee's proposed subcontractor possessed information through its work as a government contractor, the information was not available to other offerors, the agency took no steps to identify or mitigate the conflict in advance, and there were no meaningful procedures in place to prevent interaction between the employees possessing the information and the employees preparing the proposal. Johnson Controls World Services, Inc., B-286714.2, 2001 CPD ¶ 20 (Comp. Gen. 2001)

There is a presumption of prejudice to competing offerors where an organizational conflict of interest (other than a de minimis matter) is not resolved. Organizational conflicts of interest call into question the integrity of the competitive procurement process, and, as with other such circumstances, no specific prejudice need be shown to warrant corrective action. Matter of: Aetna Government Health Plans, Inc., Foundation Health Federal Services, Inc., B-254397, B-254397.15, B-254397.16, B-254397.17, B-254397.18, B-254397.19, 95-2 CPD ¶ 129 (Comp. Gen. 1995).

2 Documentation

Since the contracting officer in a government procurement case need not document his or her considerations unless a substantive issue concerning a conflict of interest exists, the lack of documentation is not a violation or abuse of discretion. LeBoeuf, Lamb, Greene & MacRae, LLP v. Abraham, 215 F. Supp. 2d 73 (D.D.C. 2002), opinion vacated, 347 F.3d 315, 358 (D.C. Cir. 2003)(The court vacated the judgment and remanded the case for a determination as to an apparent conflict of interest was considered as required by regulations, and whether the Department's need for expert legal services on the project supported a direct award of the contract to LeBoeuf or an award of other relief.) United States ⚖64.45(1)

3 Injunctions

Bid protestor who prevailed on merits of claim that Army procurement of helicopter engine filters did not adhere to organizational conflict of interest (OCI) requirements and exceeded permissible bounds of the unusual and compelling urgency exception of the Competition in Contracting Act (CICA) was not entitled to injunctive relief with respect to 183 "A kits" and 150 "B kits" for which funding had been allocated and delivery schedule had been set, as that order was justified by needs of Operation Iraqi Freedom; however, Army would be enjoined to conduct any procurement in excess of those amounts on a competitive basis unless an independent justification for invoking an exception to full and open competition was provided. 10 U.S.C.A. § 2304(c)(2). Filtration Development Co., LLC v. U.S., 60 Fed. Cl. 371 (2004). Injunction ⚖86

Contractor was not entitled to preliminary injunctive relief to prevent award of contract for support of Air Force combat scheduling organization; contractor was not likely to succeed on the merits because of an organizational conflict of interest (OCI), and there was a strong public interest in avoiding OCIs, and in proceeding with a solicitation support of contingency operations crises management. DSD Laboratories, Inc. v. U.S., 46 Fed. Cl. 467 (2000). Injunction ⚖138.63

4 Discovery

Bid protestor was not entitled to discovery into whether contracting agency properly conducted organizational conflict of interest review required by the Federal Acquisition Regulation (FAR), where protestor failed to present any evidence suggesting that agency's conflict of interest determination was arbitrary and capricious, but merely pointed to lack of any mention of an organizational conflict of interest in the procurement record. 48 C.F.R. § 9.504(d). Beta Analytics Intern., Inc. v. U.S., 61 Fed. Cl. 223 (2004). United States ⚖64.60(3.1)

5 Summary judgment

Genuine issues of material fact regarding whether Department of Energy (DOE)

conducted adequate evaluation of potential organizational conflict of interest before awarding contract for legal services in connection with nuclear waste depository site project to
law firm's competitor, who had provided legal services to subcontractor conducting studies
of site, precluded summary judgment on firm's claim challenging award of contract as
arbitrary, capricious, and contrary to Department's own procurement regulations. 48 C.F.R.
§ 9.504(a)(1); Fed.Rules Civ.Proc.Rule 56(c), 28 U.S.C.A.LeBoeuf, Lamb, Greene & MacRae,
L.L.P. v. Abraham, 347 F.3d 315, 358 (D.C. Cir. 2003). Federal Civil Procedure ☞2492

6 Judicial review

In conflict of interest cases involving government procurement contract awards, courts
afford great deference to the contracting officer's and agency's determination that no
conflict of interest exists, and the court should not disturb a contracting agency's determination unless plaintiff can show that the determination is unreasonable; mere disagreement with the contracting officer's evaluation does not itself render the evaluation
unreasonable. (The court vacated the judgment and remanded the case for a determination
as to an apparent conflict of interest was considered as required by regulations, and whether
the Department's need for expert legal services on the project supported a direct award of
the contract to LeBoeuf or an award of other relief.) United States ☞64.60(4)

For purposes of law firm's request for bid-preparation costs, in its action alleging violations of Administrative Procedure Act (APA) in award by Department of Energy (DOE) of
contract for legal services, contract award was not arbitrary, capricious, an abuse of discretion, or in violation of law; DOE did not violate procurement rules and regulations in
determining that winning law firm had no conflict of interest, Nevada Code of Professional
Responsibility did not apply in federal government procurement context, and DOE did not
act in bad faith in awarding contract. 5 U.S.C.A. § 701 et seq.LeBoeuf, Lamb, Greene &
MacRae, LLP v. Abraham, 215 F. Supp. 2d 73 (D.D.C. 2002), opinion vacated, 347 F.3d 315,
358 (D.C. Cir. 2003)(The court vacated the judgment and remanded the case for a determination as to an apparent conflict of interest was considered as required by regulations, and
whether the Department's need for expert legal services on the project supported a direct
award of the contract to LeBoeuf or an award of other relief.) United States ☞64.60(6)

Because FAR 9.504(d) states that the contracting officer need not make an official notation if he does not believe that there is a conflict of interest, this Court must assume that
the contracting officer not only performed the conflict of interest review, but that he did not
discover any conflicts. Beta Analytics Intern., Inc. v. U.S., 61 Fed. Cl. 223 (2004)

Determination of contracting officer (CO) regarding whether an acquisition involves a
significant organizational conflict of interest will be overturned only on a showing of
unreasonableness. 48 C.F.R. § 9.504. Filtration Development Co., LLC v. U.S., 60 Fed. Cl.
371 (2004). United States ☞64.15

Contracting agency's determination regarding a conflict of interest that disqualifies bidder should not be disturbed, unless it is shown to be unreasonable. Informatics Corp. v.
U.S., 40 Fed. Cl. 508, 42 Cont. Cas. Fed. (CCH) P 77311 (1998). United States ☞64.60(4)

7 Due process of law

Successful bidder on government contract whose contract was terminated after contracting agency accepted recommendation of General Accounting Office (GAO) that contract be
terminated due to unmitigatable organizational conflict of interest (OCI) was not entitled
under Federal Acquisition Regulation (FAR) to statement of reasons why OCI existed or to
opportunity to respond, and thus, failure to provide such opportunity did not violate bidder's due process rights; FAR provision requiring such notice applies only to conflicts
recognized before contract is awarded. U.S.C.A. Const. Amend. 5; 48 C.F.R. § 9.504(e).
QualMed, Inc. v. Office of Civilian Health and Medical Program of Uniformed Services, 934
F. Supp. 1227 (D. Colo. 1996). Constitutional Law ☞276(2); United States ☞64.55(2)

8 Agency investigation

Contracting officers must avoid and address not only actual, but apparent, conflicts of
interest. Thus, a protestor need not show that the persons who drafted an offeror's proposal
were actually in possession of proprietary information as a result of their employees' work
for the agency, but merely must show that the information was accessible to those employees and that the potential OCI created by that access has not been avoided or adequately

mitigated. NetStar-1 Gov't Consulting, Inc. v. U.S., 101 Fed. Cl. 511 (2011)

Agency's investigation of awardee's alleged unequal access to information organizational conflict of interest was unreasonable, where the agency concluded that the awardee's hiring of a high-level government employee from the office responsible for the project being procured created a potential conflict, but limited its review to what responsibility and role the government employee had in the procurement prior to his retirement without any consideration of the employee's access to non-public, source selection information, and where the record establishes the employee's continued daily contact with members of the source selection team and access to inside information concerning the agency's build-to-budget concept. PCCP Constructors, et al., B-405036, 2011 CPD ¶ 156 (Comp.Gen. 2011)

§ 9.507 Solicitation provisions and contract clause.

§ 9.507-1 Solicitation provisions.

As indicated in the general rules in 9.505, significant potential organizational conflicts of interest are normally resolved by imposing some restraint, appropriate to the nature of the conflict, upon the contractor's eligibility for future contracts or subcontracts. Therefore, affected solicitations shall contain a provision that—

(a) Invites offerors' attention to this subpart;

(b) States the nature of the potential conflict as seen by the contracting officer;

(c) States the nature of the proposed restraint upon future contractor activities; and

(d) Depending on the nature of the acquisition, states whether or not the terms of any proposed clause and the application of this subpart to the contract are subject to negotiation.

United States Code Annotated

Administrative determinations, see 41 USCA § 257.

Conflict of interest standards for individuals providing consulting services, see 41 USCA § 405b.

Contract requirements, see 41 USCA § 254.

Contracting functions performed by Federal personnel, see 41 USCA § 419.

Contracts, planning, solicitation, evaluation, and award procedures, see 10 USCA § 2305.

Definitions, see 10 USCA § 2302, 41 USCA §§ 259, 403.

Determinations and decisions, see 10 USCA § 2310, 41 USCA § 262.

Kinds of contracts, see 10 USCA § 2306.

Planning and solicitation requirements, see 41 USCA § 253a.

Notes of Decisions

In general 1

1 In general

Consulting firm which was not vendor of computer systems and which challenged letting of government systems engineering and technical assistance contract to hospital automation systems vendor failed to carry its burden of demonstrating that award of contract lacked rational basis or clearly and prejudicially violated applicable conflict of interest statutes and regulations; contract solicitation explicitly included provisions designed to eliminate or minimize conflicts in interest that might arise if contract were awarded to contractor that was also hospital automation systems provider and Department of Defense had exercised its contractual right to modify terms of contract to avoid potential conflicts identified after contract was awarded. Informatics General Corp. v. Weinberger, 617 F. Supp. 331 (D.D.C. 1985). United States ☞64.60(4)

§ 9.507-2 Contract clause.

(a) If, as a condition of award, the contractor's eligibility for future prime contract or subcontract awards will be restricted or the contractor must agree to some other restraint, the solicitation shall contain a proposed clause that specifies both the nature and duration of the proposed restraint. The contracting officer shall include the clause in the contract, first negotiating the clause's final terms with the successful offeror, if it is appropriate to do so (see 9.506(d) of this subsection).

(b) The restraint imposed by a clause shall be limited to a fixed term of reasonable duration, sufficient to avoid the circumstance of unfair competitive advantage or potential bias. This period varies. It might end, for example, when the first production contract using the contractor's specifications or work statement is awarded, or it might extend through the entire life of a system for which the contractor has performed systems engineering and technical direction. In every case, the restriction shall specify termination by a specific date or upon the occurrence of an identifiable event.

United States Code Annotated

Administrative determinations, see 41 USCA § 257.

Conflict of interest standards for individuals providing consulting services, see 41 USCA § 405b.

Contract requirements, see 41 USCA § 254.

Contracting functions performed by Federal personnel, see 41 USCA § 419.

Contracts, planning, solicitation, evaluation, and award procedures, see 10 USCA § 2305.

Definitions, see 10 USCA § 2302, 41 USCA §§ 259, 403.

Determinations and decisions, see 10 USCA § 2310, 41 USCA § 262.

Kinds of contracts, see 10 USCA § 2306.

Planning and solicitation requirements, see 41 USCA § 253a.

§ 9.508 Examples.

The examples in paragraphs (a) through (i) following illustrate situations in which questions concerning organizational conflicts of interest may arise. They are not all inclusive, but are intended to help the contracting officer apply the general rules in 9.505 to individual contract situations.

(a) Company A agrees to provide systems engineering and technical direction for the Navy on the powerplant for a group of submarines (*i.e.*, turbines, drive shafts, propellers, etc.). Company A should not be allowed to supply any powerplant components. Company A can, however, supply components of the submarine unrelated to the powerplant (*e.g.*, fire control, navigation, etc.). In this example, the system is the powerplant, not the submarine, and the ban on supplying components is limited to those for the system only.

(b) Company A is the systems engineering and technical direction contractor for system X. After some progress, but before completion, the system is canceled. Later, system Y is developed to achieve the same purposes as system X, but in a fundamentally different fashion. Company B is the systems engineering and technical direction contractor for system Y. Company A may supply system Y or its components.

(c) Company A develops new electronic equipment and, as a result of this development, prepares specifications. Company A may supply the equipment.

(d) XYZ Tool Company and PQR Machinery Company, representing the American Tool Institute, work under Government supervision and control to refine specifications or to clarify the requirements of a specific acquisition. These companies may supply the item.

(e) Before an acquisition for information technology is conducted, Company A is awarded a contract to prepare data system specifications and equipment performance criteria to be used as the basis for the equipment competition. Since the specifications are the basis for selection of commercial hardware, a potential conflict of interest exists. Company A should be excluded from the initial follow-on information technology hardware acquisition.

(f) Company A receives a contract to define the detailed performance characteristics an agency will require for purchasing rocket fuels. Company A has not developed the particular fuels. When the definition contract is awarded, it is clear to both parties that the agency will use the performance characteristics arrived at to choose competitively a contractor to develop or produce the fuels. Company A may not be awarded this follow-on contract.

(g) Company A receives a contract to prepare a detailed plan for scientific and technical training of an agency's personnel. It suggests a curriculum that the agency endorses and incorporates in its request for proposals to institutions to establish and conduct the training. Company A may not be awarded a contract to conduct the training.

(h) Company A is selected to study the use of lasers in communications. The agency intends to ask that firms doing research in the field make proprietary information available to Company A. The contract must require Company A to—

(1) Enter into agreements with these firms to protect any proprietary information they provide; and

(2) Refrain from using the information in supplying lasers to the Government or for any purpose other than that for which it was intended.

(i) An agency that regulates an industry wishes to develop a system for evaluating and processing license applications. Contractor X helps develop the system and process the applications. Contractor X should be prohibited from acting as a consultant to any of the applicants during its period of performance and for a reasonable period thereafter.

United States Code Annotated

Administrative determinations, see 41 USCA § 257.

Conflict of interest standards for individuals providing consulting services, see 41 USCA § 405b.

Contract requirements, see 41 USCA § 254.

Contracting functions performed by Federal personnel, see 41 USCA § 419.

Contracts, planning, solicitation, evaluation, and award procedures, see 10 USCA § 2305.

Definitions, see 10 USCA § 2302, 41 USCA §§ 259, 403.

Determinations and decisions, see 10 USCA § 2310, 41 USCA § 262.

Kinds of contracts, see 10 USCA § 2306.

Planning and solicitation requirements, see 41 USCA § 253a.

Subpart 9.6 Contractor Team Arrangements

§ 9.601 Definition.

"Contractor team arrangement," as used in this subpart, means an arrangement in which—

(1) Two or more companies form a partnership or joint venture to act as a potential prime contractor; or

(2) A potential prime contractor agrees with one or more other companies to have them act as its subcontractors under a specified Government contract or acquisition program.

United States Code Annotated

Contracts, planning, solicitation, evaluation, and award procedures, see 10 USCA § 2305.

Definitions, see 10 USCA § 2302, 41 USCA §§ 259, 403.

Planning and solicitation requirements, see 41 USCA § 253a.

Notes of Decisions

Contract to act as team 1
Definition 2
Federal jurisdiction 3

1 Contract to act as team

Agency's consideration of an offeror's subcontractor's capabilities as well as the offeror's in determining offeror capability was proper where the amended solicitation allowed for the potential prime contractor in agreement with its identified subcontractors to perform the contract services as a team and for the offeror's capability to be determined on that basis. Matter of: The Analytic Sciences Corporation, B-259013, 95-1 CPD ¶ 122 (Comp. Gen. 1995)

Protest is sustained where awardee's use of a Federally Funded Research and Development Center (FFRDC) as a significant teaming partner was contrary to Federal Acquisition Regulation prohibition against FFRDCs competing with private firms under government solicitations. Energy Compression Research Corporation, B-243650, B-243650.2, 91-2 CPD ¶ 466 (Comp. Gen. 1991)

2 Definition

Agency properly rejected quotation of vendor under request for quotations (RFQ) for the award of basic ordering agreements with Federal Supply Schedule (FSS) contract holders, where the vendor did not propose a contract teaming agreement (CTA) in accordance with the conditions imposed by the RFQ and did not satisfy the RFQ requirement applicable where an offering vendor is not a CTA that a single offeror hold all of the FSS Schedule contracts required by the RFQ. Matter of: Computer Cite, B-299858, 2007 CPD ¶ 166 (Comp. Gen. 2007)

3 Federal jurisdiction

The federal government's authorization and recognition of the use of teaming agreements in government contracting, FAR 9.601–604, is not evidence of a unique federal interest in teaming agreements sufficient to support federal common law jurisdiction. The cited regulations do not confer jurisdiction on the federal courts to hear disputes arising from teaming agreements. Simply because teaming agreements are *permitted* by federal law does not automatically convert them into subjects of unique federal interest. Northrop Corp. v. AIL Systems, Inc., 959 F.2d 1424, 22 Fed. R. Serv. 3d 626 (7th Cir. 1992)

While a contracting agency is not precluded from inquiring into the details of a contractor teaming agreement, there is no requirement that a contracting agency resolve disputes arising from such these agreements; an allegation that a teaming agreement has been breached is a dispute between private parties. PRB Associates, Inc., B-277994, B-277994.2, 98-1 CPD ¶ 13 (Comp. Gen. 1997)

§ 9.602 General.

(a) Contractor team arrangements may be desirable from both a Government and industry standpoint in order to enable the companies involved to—

(1) Complement each other's unique capabilities; and

(2) Offer the Government the best combination of performance, cost, and delivery for the system or product being acquired.

(b) Contractor team arrangements may be particularly appropriate in complex research and development acquisitions, but may be used in other appropriate acquisitions, including production.

(c) The companies involved normally form a contractor team arrangement before submitting an offer. However, they may enter into an arrangement later in the acquisition process, including after contract award.

United States Code Annotated

Contracts, planning, solicitation, evaluation, and award procedures, see 10 USCA § 2305.

Definitions, see 10 USCA § 2302, 41 USCA §§ 259, 403.

Planning and solicitation requirements, see 41 USCA § 253a.

Notes of Decisions

Contract to act as team 1
Pleadings 2
Summary judgment 3

1 Contract to act as team

Plaintiff could use evidence of a course of conduct of the parties, both in earlier arrangements and in dealings in the instant matter, to support its evidence of an exchange of oral promises to be a team and, as a team, submit a subcontract bid to defense contractor. Cable & Computer Technology Inc. v. Lockheed Sanders, Inc., 214 F.3d 1030, 2000-2 Trade Cas. (CCH) ¶ 72991 (9th Cir. 2000). Contracts ⊱16

In certain contexts, contractors may reach an actionable agreement to be a team and to submit a bid together as a team. City Solutions, Inc. v. Clear Channel Communications, Inc., 201 F. Supp. 2d 1035 (N.D. Cal. 2001). Joint Adventures ⊱1

General rules governing contract formation apply to agreements between contractors to be a team and to submit bid together as team, inasmuch as there is no freestanding duty to negotiate in good faith absent an agreement to do so that meets the standards necessary for a legally binding obligation; under these general rules, the parties must intend to be bound by the agreement, and terms regarded as material to the teaming agreement cannot be left outstanding from that agreement. City Solutions, Inc. v. Clear Channel Communications, Inc., 201 F. Supp. 2d 1035 (N.D. Cal. 2001). Joint Adventures ⊕1.2(4); Joint Adventures ⊕1.10

2 Pleadings

Claim of fraud, in that defendant allegedly made promises of making a team effort to obtain a subcontract, when it had no intention of keeping the promises and with the purpose of ultimately disabling plaintiff as a competitor for the subcontract, was not insufficiently particular in failing to identify which of plaintiff's officials defendant's representative spoke to when he reconfirmed the agreement on behalf of defendant. Fed.Rules Civ.Proc.Rule 9(b), 28 U.S.C.A. Cable & Computer Technology Inc. v. Lockheed Sanders, Inc., 214 F.3d 1030, 2000-2 Trade Cas. (CCH) ¶ 72991 (9th Cir. 2000). Federal Civil Procedure ⊕636

3 Summary judgment

There was issue of fact, precluding summary judgment on breach of contract claim, as to whether plaintiff and defendant entered into an oral contract to be a team and, as a team, submit a subcontract bid to defense contractor, though contemplated written team agreement was never executed. Cable & Computer Technology Inc. v. Lockheed Sanders, Inc., 214 F.3d 1030, 2000-2 Trade Cas. (CCH) ¶ 72991 (9th Cir. 2000). Federal Civil Procedure ⊕2492

§ 9.603 Policy.

The Government will recognize the integrity and validity of contractor team arrangements; *provided*, the arrangements are identified and company relationships are fully disclosed in an offer or, for arrangements entered into after submission of an offer, before the arrangement becomes effective. The Government will not normally require or encourage the dissolution of contractor team arrangements.

United States Code Annotated

Contracts, planning, solicitation, evaluation, and award procedures, see 10 USCA § 2305.

Definitions, see 10 USCA § 2302, 41 USCA §§ 259, 403.

Planning and solicitation requirements, see 41 USCA § 253a.

Notes of Decisions

Contract to act as team 1

1 Contract to act as team

Plaintiff could use evidence of a course of conduct of the parties, both in earlier arrangements and in dealings in the instant matter, to support its evidence of an exchange of oral promises to be a team and, as a team, submit a subcontract bid to defense contractor. Cable & Computer Technology Inc. v. Lockheed Sanders, Inc., 214 F.3d 1030, 2000-2 Trade Cas. (CCH) ¶ 72991 (9th Cir. 2000). Contracts ⊕16

In certain contexts, contractors may reach an actionable agreement to be a team and to submit a bid together as a team. City Solutions, Inc. v. Clear Channel Communications, Inc., 201 F. Supp. 2d 1035 (N.D. Cal. 2001). Joint Adventures ⊕1

General rules governing contract formation apply to agreements between contractors to be a team and to submit bid together as team, inasmuch as there is no freestanding duty to negotiate in good faith absent an agreement to do so that meets the standards necessary for a legally binding obligation; under these general rules, the parties must intend to be bound by the agreement, and terms regarded as material to the teaming agreement cannot be left outstanding from that agreement. City Solutions, Inc. v. Clear Channel Communications, Inc., 201 F. Supp. 2d 1035 (N.D. Cal. 2001). Joint Adventures ⊕1.2(4); Joint Adventures ⊕1.10

§ 9.604 Limitations.

Nothing in this subpart authorizes contractor team arrangements in violation of antitrust statutes or limits the Government's rights to—

(a) Require consent to subcontracts (see Subpart 44.2);

(b) Determine, on the basis of the stated contractor team arrangement, the responsibility of the prime contractor (see Subpart 9.1);

(c) Provide to the prime contractor data rights owned or controlled by the Government;

(d) Pursue its policies on competitive contracting, subcontracting, and component breakout after initial production or at any other time; and

(e) Hold the prime contractor fully responsible for contract performance, regardless of any team arrangement between the prime contractor and its subcontractors.

United States Code Annotated

Contracts, planning, solicitation, evaluation, and award procedures, see 10 USCA § 2305.

Definitions, see 10 USCA § 2302, 41 USCA §§ 259, 403.

Planning and solicitation requirements, see 41 USCA § 253a.

Subpart 9.7 Defense Production Pools and Research and Development Pools

§ 9.701 Definition.

"Pool," as used in this subpart, means a group of concerns (see 19.001) that have—

(1) Associated together in order to obtain and perform, jointly or in conjunction with each other, defense production or research and development contracts;

(2) Entered into an agreement governing their organization, relationship, and procedures; and

(3) Obtained approval of the agreement by either—

(i) The Small Business Administration (SBA) under section 9 or 11 of the Small Business Act (15 U.S.C. 638 or 640) (see 13 CFR 125); or

(ii) A designated official under Part V of Executive Order 10480, August 14, 1953 (18 FR 4939, August 20, 1953) and section 708 of the Defense Production Act of 1950 (50 U.S.C. App. 2158).

United States Code Annotated

Contracts, planning, solicitation, evaluation, and award procedures, see 10 USCA § 2305.

Definitions, see 10 USCA § 2302, 41 USCA §§ 259, 403.

Planning and solicitation requirements, see 41 USCA § 253a.

§ 9.702 Contracting with pools.

(a) Except as specified in this subpart, a pool shall be treated the same as any other prospective or actual contractor.

(b) The contracting officer shall not award a contract to a pool unless the offer leading to the contract is submitted by the pool in its own name or by an individual pool member expressly stating that the offer is on behalf of the pool.

(c) Upon receipt of an offer submitted by a group representing that it is a pool, the contracting officer shall verify its approved status with the SBA District Office Director or other approving agency and document the contract file that the verification was made.

(d) Pools approved by the SBA under the Small Business Act are entitled to the preferences and privileges accorded to small business concerns. Approval under the Defense Production Act does not confer these preferences and privileges.

(e) Before awarding a contract to an unincorporated pool, the contracting officer shall require each pool member participating in the contract to furnish a certified copy of a power of attorney identifying the agent authorized to sign the offer or contract on that member's behalf. The contracting officer shall attach a copy of each power of attorney to each signed copy of the contract retained by the Government.

United States Code Annotated

Contracts, planning, solicitation, evaluation, and award procedures, see 10 USCA § 2305.

Definitions, see 10 USCA § 2302, 41 USCA §§ 259, 403.

Planning and solicitation requirements, see 41 USCA § 253a.

§ 9.703 Contracting with individual pool members.

(a) Pool members may submit individual offers, independent of the pool. However, the contracting officer shall not consider an independent offer by a pool member if that pool member participates in a competing offer submitted by the pool.

(b) If a pool member submits an individual offer, independent of the pool, the contracting officer shall consider the pool agreement, along with other factors, in determining whether that pool member is a responsible prospective contractor under Subpart 9.1.

United States Code Annotated

Contracts, planning, solicitation, evaluation, and award procedures, see 10 USCA § 2305.

Definitions, see 10 USCA § 2302, 41 USCA §§ 259, 403.

Planning and solicitation requirements, see 41 USCA § 253a.

PART 10 MARKET RESEARCH

§ 10.000 Scope of part.
§ 10.001 Policy.
§ 10.002 Procedures.
§ 10.003 Contract clause.

§ 10.000 Scope of part.

This part prescribes policies and procedures for conducting market research to arrive at the most suitable approach to acquiring, distributing, and supporting supplies and services. This part implements the requirements of 41 U.S.C. 3306(a)(1), 41 U.S.C. 3307, 10 U.S.C. 2377, and 6 U.S.C. 796.

United States Code Annotated

Contracts, planning, solicitation, evaluation, and award procedures, see 10 USCA § 2305.

Definitions, see 10 USCA § 2302, 41 USCA §§ 259, 403.

Planning and solicitation requirements, see 41 USCA § 253a.

Preference for acquisition of commercial items, see 10 USCA § 2377, 41 USCA § 264b.

Notes of Decisions

In general 1

1 In general

Acquisition planning and market research are required to ensure that agencies, among other things, develop a plan to suitably satisfy their needs in a timely manner and at a reasonable cost. FAR 7.101, 10.000. The Federal Supply Schedule (FSS) program specifically satisfies these goals by allowing the government to acquire a wide range of commercial products and services in a timely fashion and at fair and reasonable prices. Thus, we think that, as a general rule, obtaining information from the FSS program and FSS vendors satisfies the agency's obligations to conduct procurement planning and market research. Sales Resources Consultants, Inc., B-284943, B-284943.2, 2000 CPD ¶ 102 (Comp. Gen. 2000)

§ 10.001 Policy.

(a) Agencies must—

(1) Ensure that legitimate needs are identified and trade-offs evaluated to acquire items that meet those needs;

(2) Conduct market research appropriate to the circumstances—

(i) Before developing new requirements documents for an acquisition by that agency;

(ii) Before soliciting offers for acquisitions with an estimated value in excess of the simplified acquisition threshold;

(iii) Before soliciting offers for acquisitions with an estimated value less than the simplified acquisition threshold when adequate information is not available and the circumstances justify its cost;

(iv) Before soliciting offers for acquisitions that could lead to a bundled contract (15 U.S.C. 644(e)(2)(A));

(v) Before awarding a task or delivery order under an indefinite-delivery/indefinite-quantity (ID/IQ) contract (e.g., GWACs, MACs) for a noncommercial item in excess of the simplified acquisition threshold (10 U.S.C. 2377(c)); and

(vi) On an ongoing basis, take advantage (to the maximum extent practicable) of commercially available market research methods in order to effectively identify the capabilities of small businesses and new entrants into Federal contracting that are available in the marketplace for meeting the requirements of the agency in furtherance of—

(A) A contingency operation or defense against or recovery from nuclear, biological, chemical, or radiological attack; and

(B) Disaster relief to include debris removal, distribution of supplies, reconstruction, and other disaster or emergency relief activities. (See 26.205).

(3) Use the results of market research to—

(i) Determine if sources capable of satisfying the agency's requirements exist;

(ii) Determine if commercial items or, to the extent commercial items suitable to meet the agency's needs are not available, nondevelopmental items are available that—

(A) Meet the agency's requirements;

(B) Could be modified to meet the agency's requirements; or

(C) Could meet the agency's requirements if those requirements were modified to a reasonable extent;

(iii) Determine the extent to which commercial items or nondevelopmental items could be incorporated at the component level;

(iv) Determine the practices of firms engaged in producing, distributing, and supporting commercial items, such as type of contract, terms for warranties, buyer financing, maintenance and packaging, and marking;

(v) Ensure maximum practicable use of recovered materials (see Subpart 23.4) and promote energy conservation and efficiency; and

(vi) Determine whether bundling is necessary and justified (see 7.107) (15 U.S.C. 644(e)(2)(A)).

(vii) Assess the availability of electronic and information technology that meets all or part of the applicable accessibility standards issued by the Architectural and Transportation Barriers Compliance Board at 36 CFR Part 1194 (see Subpart 39.2).

(b) When conducting market research, agencies should not request potential sources to submit more than the minimum information necessary.

(c) If an agency contemplates awarding a bundled contract, the agency—

(1) When performing market research, should consult with the local Small Business Administration procurement center representative (PCR). If a PCR is not assigned, see 19.402(a); and

(2) At least 30 days before release of the solicitation or 30 days prior to placing an order without a solicitation—

(i) Must notify any affected incumbent small business concerns of the Government's intention to bundle the requirement; and

(ii) Should notify any affected incumbent small business concerns of how the concerns may contact the appropriate Small Business Administration representative.

(d) See 10.003 for the requirement for a prime contractor to perform market research in contracts in excess of $5.5 million for the procurement of items other than commercial items in accordance with section 826 of Public Law 110-181.

United States Code Annotated

Contracts, planning, solicitation, evaluation, and award procedures, see 10 USCA § 2305.

Definitions, see 10 USCA § 2302, 41 USCA §§ 259, 403.

Planning and solicitation requirements, see 41 USCA § 253a.

Preference for acquisition of commercial items, see 10 USCA § 2377, 41 USCA § 264b.

Simplified acquisition procedures, see 41 USCA § 427.

Notes of Decisions

In general 1

1 In general

Protest challenging bundling of system engineering and support services with other requirements under a single-award BPA issued under awardee's Federal Supply Schedule contract is sustained, where agency failed to perform bundling analysis or satisfy the requirements of FAR 10.001(c)(2) and 19.202-1. Sigmatech, Inc., B-296401, 2005 CPD ¶ 156 (Comp. Gen. 2005)

Agencies must conduct market research pursuant to FAR part 10 to determine whether commercial items are available that could meet the agency's requirements. FAR 12.101(a). If through market research the agency determines that the government's needs can be met by an item customarily available in the commercial marketplace that meets the FAR 2.101 definition of a commercial item, the agency is required to use the procedures in FAR part 12 to solicit and award any resultant contract. SHABA Contracting, B-287430, 2001 CPD ¶ 105 (Comp. Gen. 2001)

Agency properly determined, based on market research, that household goods moving services for military personnel could be acquired under Federal Acquisition Regulation part 12 commercial item procedures, notwithstanding the inclusion of government-unique requirements in the solicitation that are not present in commercial contracts for moving services. Aalco Forwarding, Inc., et al., B-277241, B-277241.8, B-277241.9, 97-2 CPD ¶ 110 (Comp. Gen. 1997)

§ 10.002 Procedures.

(a) Acquisitions begin with a description of the Government's needs stated in terms sufficient to allow conduct of market research.

(b) Market research is then conducted to determine if commercial items or nondevelopmental items are available to meet the Government's needs or could be modified to meet the Government's needs.

(1) The extent of market research will vary, depending on such factors as urgency, estimated dollar value, complexity, and past experience. The contracting officer may use market research conducted within 18 months before the award of any task or delivery order if the information is still current, accurate, and relevant. Market research involves obtaining information specific to the item being acquired and should include—

(i) Whether the Government's needs can be met by—

(A) Items of a type customarily available in the commercial marketplace;

(B) Items of a type customarily available in the commercial marketplace with modifications; or

(C) Items used exclusively for governmental purposes;

(ii) Customary practices regarding customizing, modifying or tailoring of items to meet customer needs and associated costs;

(iii) Customary practices, including warranty, buyer financing, discounts, contract type considering the nature and risk associated with the requirement, etc., under which commercial sales of the products or services are made;

(iv) The requirements of any laws and regulations unique to the item being acquired;

(v) The availability of items that contain recovered materials and items that are energy efficient;

(vi) The distribution and support capabilities of potential suppliers, including alternative arrangements and cost estimates; and

(vii) Size and status of potential sources (see Part 19).

(2) Techniques for conducting market research may include any or all of the following:

(i) Contacting knowledgeable individuals in Government and industry regarding market capabilities to meet requirements.

(ii) Reviewing the results of recent market research undertaken to meet similar or identical requirements.

(iii) Publishing formal requests for information in appropriate technical or scientific journals or business publications.

(iv) Querying the Governmentwide database of contracts and other procurement instruments intended for use by multiple agencies available at https://www.contractdir ectory.gov/contractdirectory/ and other Government and commercial databases that provide information relevant to agency acquisitions.

(v) Participating in interactive, on-line communication among industry, acquisition personnel, and customers.

(vi) Obtaining source lists of similar items from other contracting activities or agencies, trade associations or other sources.

(vii) Reviewing catalogs and other generally available product literature published by manufacturers, distributors, and dealers or available on-line.

(viii) Conducting interchange meetings or holding presolicitation conferences to involve potential offerors early in the acquisition process.

(c) If market research indicates commercial or nondevelopmental items might not be available to satisfy agency needs, agencies shall reevaluate the need in accordance with 10.001(a)(3)(ii) and determine whether the need can be restated to permit commercial or nondevelopmental items to satisfy the agency's needs.

(d) (1) If market research establishes that the Government's need may be met by a type of item or service customarily available in the commercial marketplace that would meet the definition of a commercial item at Subpart 2.1, the contracting officer shall solicit and award any resultant contract using the policies and procedures in Part 12.

(2) If market research establishes that the Government's need cannot be met by a type of item or service customarily available in the marketplace, Part 12 shall not be used. When publication of the notice at 5.201 is required, the contracting officer shall include a notice to prospective offerors that the Government does not intend to use Part 12 for the acquisition.

(e) Agencies should document the results of market research in a manner appropriate to the size and complexity of the acquisition.

United States Code Annotated

Contracts, planning, solicitation, evaluation, and award procedures, see 10 USCA § 2305.

Definitions, see 10 USCA § 2302, 41 USCA §§ 259, 403.

Planning and solicitation requirements, see 41 USCA § 253a.

Preference for acquisition of commercial items, see 10 USCA § 2377, 41 USCA § 264b.

Simplified acquisition procedures, see 41 USCA § 427.

Notes of Decisions

In general 1

1 In general

The amount of market research that is a matter of agency discretion. Protest that agency should have conducted additional market research to determine if there were other sources capable of producing the item acquired through a sole source award was denied. FAR 10.002 does not set forth any specific method required to be used to conduct market research and recognizes that the extent of market research will vary, depending on such factors as urgency, estimated dollar value, complexity, and past experience. KSD, Inc. v. U.S., 72 Fed. Cl. 236 (2006)

Protest challenging adequacy of agency's market research was denied where the agency's market research included review of an extensive independent report comparing various firms' approaches to automated and robotic pharmacy systems, numerous meetings with these firms to obtain additional information, site visits to inspect various systems, and comparisons of the various features of each firms' systems and such efforts were appropriate to the circumstances of the particular acquisition. McKesson Automation Systems, Inc., B-290969.2, B-290969.3, 2003 CPD ¶ 24 (Comp. Gen. 2003)

Army violated a procurement statute requiring that offerors of commercial items have an opportunity to compete in any procurement by issuing a solicitation for a contract to develop an intelligence software system, where Army was on notice that contractor offered a realistic, commercially available alternative product, but it failed in its market research report to fully consider its potential commercial options before pursuing a developmental only procurement. Palantir USG, Inc. v. U.S., 129 Fed.Cl. 218 (2016)

CICA requires that agencies use market research during the planning stage for the procurement of property or services. 41 U.S.C. § 253a(a)(1)(B). A market survey is an acceptable method of market research to ascertain whether other qualified sources capable of satisfying the government's requirements exist and may be informal, i.e., phone calls to federal or non-federal experts, or formal, i.e., sources-sought announcements in the CBD or solicitations for information or planning purposes. FAR 7.101. Matter of: Coulter Corporation; Nova Biomedical; Ciba Corning Diagnostics Corp, B-258713, B-258714, 1995 WL 64156 (Comp. Gen. 1995)

§ 10.003 Contract clause.

The contracting officer shall insert the clause at 52.210-1, Market Research, in solicitations and contracts over $5.5 million for the procurement of items other than commercial items.

PART 11 DESCRIBING AGENCY NEEDS

Subpart 11.7 Variation in Quantity
§ 11.701 Supply contracts.
§ 11.702 Construction contracts.
§ 11.703 Contract clauses.

Subpart 11.8 Testing
§ 11.801 Preaward in-use evaluation.

§ 11.000 Scope of part.
This part prescribes policies and procedures for describing agency needs.

United States Code Annotated
Contracts, planning, solicitation, evaluation, and award procedures, see 10 USCA § 2305.
Definitions, see 10 USCA § 2302, 41 USCA §§ 259, 403.
Planning and solicitation requirements, see 41 USCA § 253a.
Preference for acquisition of commercial items, see 10 USCA § 2377, 41 USCA § 264b.
Simplified acquisition procedures, see 41 USCA § 427.

§ 11.001 Definitions.
As used in this part—

"Reconditioned" means restored to the original normal operating condition by readjustments and material replacement.

"Remanufactured" means factory rebuilt to original specifications.

United States Code Annotated
Contracts, planning, solicitation, evaluation, and award procedures, see 10 USCA § 2305.
Definitions, see 10 USCA § 2302, 41 USCA §§ 259, 403.
Planning and solicitation requirements, see 41 USCA § 253a.
Preference for acquisition of commercial items, see 10 USCA § 2377, 41 USCA § 264b.
Simplified acquisition procedures, see 41 USCA § 427.

§ 11.002 Policy.
(a) In fulfilling requirements of 10 U.S.C. 2305(a)(1), 10 U.S.C. 2377, 41 U.S.C. 3306(a), and 41 U.S.C. 3307, agencies shall—

(1) Specify needs using market research in a manner designed to—

(i) Promote full and open competition (see Part 6), or maximum practicable competition when using simplified acquisition procedures, with due regard to the nature of the supplies or services to be acquired; and

(ii) Only include restrictive provisions or conditions to the extent necessary to satisfy the needs of the agency or as authorized by law.

(2) To the maximum extent practicable, ensure that acquisition officials—

(i) State requirements with respect to an acquisition of supplies or services in terms of—

(A) Functions to be performed;

(B) Performance required; or

(C) Essential physical characteristics;

(ii) Define requirements in terms that enable and encourage offerors to supply commercial items, or, to the extent that commercial items suitable to meet the agency's needs are not available, nondevelopmental items, in response to the agency solicitations;

(iii) Provide offerors of commercial items and nondevelopmental items an opportunity to compete in any acquisition to fill such requirements;

(iv) Require prime contractors and subcontractors at all tiers under the agency contracts to incorporate commercial items or nondevelopmental items as components of items supplied to the agency; and

(v) Modify requirements in appropriate cases to ensure that the requirements can be met by commercial items or, to the extent that commercial items suitable to meet the agency's needs are not available, nondevelopmental items.

(b) The Metric Conversion Act of 1975, as amended by the Omnibus Trade and Competitiveness Act of 1988 (15 U.S.C. 205a, et seq.), designates the metric system of measurement as the preferred system of weights and measures for United States trade and commerce, and it requires that each agency use the metric system of measurement in its acquisitions, except to the extent that such use is impracticable or is likely to cause significant inefficiencies or loss of markets to United States firms. Requiring activities are responsible for establishing guidance implementing this policy in formulating their requirements for acquisitions.

(c) To the extent practicable and consistent with Subpart 9.5, potential offerors should be given an opportunity to comment on agency requirements or to recommend application and tailoring of requirements documents and alternative approaches. Requiring agencies should apply specifications, standards, and related documents initially for guidance only, making final decisions on the application and tailoring of these documents as a product of the design and development process. Requiring agencies should not dictate detailed design solutions prematurely (see 7.101 and 7.105(a)(8)).

(d) (1) When agencies acquire products and services, various statutes and executive orders (identified in part 23) require consideration of sustainable acquisition (see subpart 23.1) including—

(i) Energy-efficient and water-efficient services and products (including products containing energy-efficient standby power devices) (subpart 23.2);

(ii) Products and services that utilize renewable energy technologies (subpart 23.2);

(iii) Products containing recovered materials (subpart 23.4);

(iv) Biobased products (subpart 23.4);

(v) Environmentally preferable products and services, including EPEAT®-registered electronic products and non-toxic or low-toxic alternatives (subpart 23.7); and

(vi) Non-ozone-depleting substances, and products and services that minimize or eliminate, when feasible, the use, release, or emission of high global warming potential hydrofluorocarbons, such as by using reclaimed instead of virgin hydrofluorocarbons (subpart 23.8).

(2) Unless an exception applies and is documented by the requiring activity, Executive agencies shall, to the maximum practicable, require the use of products and services listed in paragraph (d)(1) of this section when—

(i) Developing, reviewing, or revising Federal and military specifications, product descriptions (including commercial item descriptions) and standards;

(ii) Describing Government requirements for products and services; and

(iii) Developing source-selection factors.

(e) Some or all of the performance levels or performance specifications in a solicitation may be identified as targets rather than as fixed or minimum requirements.

(f) In accordance with Section 508 of the Rehabilitation Act of 1973 (29 U.S.C. 794d), requiring activities must prepare requirements documents for electronic and information technology that comply with the applicable accessibility standards issued by the Architectural and Transportation Barriers Compliance Board at 36 CFR Part 1194 (see Subpart 39.2).

(g) Unless the agency Chief Information Officer waives the requirement, when acquiring information technology using Internet Protocol, the requirements documents must include reference to the appropriate technical capabilities defined in the USGv6 Profile (NIST Special Publication 500-267) and the corresponding declarations of conformance defined in the USGv6 Test Program. The applicability of IPv6 to agency networks, infrastructure, and applications specific to individual acquisitions will be in accordance with the agency's Enterprise Architecture (see OMB Memorandum M-05-22 dated August 2, 2005).

(h) Agencies shall not include in a solicitation a requirement that prohibits an offeror from permitting its employees to telecommute unless the contracting officer executes a written determination in accordance with FAR 7.108(a).

United States Code Annotated

Contracts, planning, solicitation, evaluation, and award procedures, see 10 USCA § 2305.

Definitions, see 10 USCA § 2302, 41 USCA §§ 259, 403.

Planning and solicitation requirements, see 41 USCA § 253a.

Preference for acquisition of commercial items, see 10 USCA § 2377, 41 USCA § 264b.

Simplified acquisition procedures, see 41 USCA § 427.

Notes of Decisions

In general 1

1 In general

To be valid and enforceable, contract must have both consideration, to ensure mutuality of obligation, and sufficient definiteness, to provide basis for determining existence of breach and for giving appropriate remedy. Ace-Federal Reporters, Inc. v. Barram, 226 F.3d 1329 (Fed. Cir. 2000)

Although restrictive provisions in solicitations are allowed only to the extent necessary to satisfy the needs of the agency or as authorized by law, requirement for computer hardware maintenance that contractor be able to acquire original equipment manufacturer (OEM) support without government intervention was not unduly restrictive, given contracting agency's judgment that OEM support might be necessary to perform timely repair. CHE Consulting, Inc. v. U.S., 74 Fed. Cl. 742 (2006)

Pursuant to the Competition in Contracting Act (CICA), the government is required to specify its needs and solicit proposals in a manner designed to achieve full and open competition for the procurement. A consequence of this duty is the requirement that solicitation provisions which restrict competition be used only to the extent necessary to satisfy the needs of the agency or as authorized by law. Unnecessarily restrictive specifications or requirements that might unduly limit the number of bidders are prohibited. Charles H. Tompkins Co. v. U.S., 43 Fed. Cl. 716 (1999)

Solicitation concerning past performance evaluation was overstated and overly restrictive of competition to the prejudice of other potential offerors in violation of the Competition in Contracting Act (CICA), warranting cancellation of solicitation. 10 U.S.C.A. § 2305(a)(1)(B) (ii); Federal Property and Administrative Services Act of 1949, § 303(a)(2)(B), 41 U.S.C.A. § 253(a)(2)(B); 48 C.F.R. § 14.101(a). Charles H. Tompkins Co. v. U.S., 43 Fed. Cl. 716 (1999). United States ☞64.50

In preparing a solicitation for supplies or services, a contracting agency must specify its needs in a manner designed to achieve full and open competition and may include restrictive provisions only to the extent necessary to satisfy its needs. 41 U.S.C. § 253a(a)(1)(A), (a)(2)(B) (1994). However, an agency is not required to neutralize the competitive advantages some potential offerors enjoy simply because of their own particular circumstances rather than any government action. WinStar Communications, Inc. v. U.S., 41 Fed. Cl. 748, 42 Cont. Cas. Fed. (CCH) ¶ 77371 (1998)

Geographic scope of contract for local telecommunications services for federal agencies in an area consisting of the five boroughs of New York City and suburban locations in New York and New Jersey did not violate the Competition in Contracting Act (CICA) on theory that it gave unfair advantage to the incumbent, as the only company with sufficient facilities to service the entire area directly; boundary of the contract area was reasonably drawn, and size of the area did not preclude anyone from competing. Federal Property and Administrative Services Act of 1949, § 303(a)(2), as amended, 41 U.S.C.A. § 253(a)(2). WinStar Communications, Inc. v. U.S., 41 Fed. Cl. 748, 42 Cont. Cas. Fed. (CCH) P 77371 (1998). United States ☞64.10

Pursuant to the Competition in Contracting Act, government is required to specify its needs and solicit proposals "in a manner designed to achieve full and open competition for the procurement," and fact that the procurement is a commercial item acquisition does not relieve government of such obligation. 10 U.S.C.A. § 2305(a)(1)(A)(i). Candle Corp. v. U.S., 40 Fed. Cl. 658, 42 Cont. Cas. Fed. (CCH) P 77276 (1998). United States ☞64.10

Solicitation requirement that an offeror possess a Top Secret facility clearance at the time final proposal revisions are submitted does not unduly restrict competition where the record shows that the requirement is reasonably related to the agency's needs. CompTech–CDO, LLC, B-409949.2, 2015 CPD ¶ 62 (Comp.Gen. 2015)

Protest that agency improperly made award of a contract for its actual requirements that differed significantly from the requirements solicited is sustained, where record shows that agency's actual requirements are for less than 30% of the requirements solicited. Agencies must accurately specify their requirements in a manner that affords offerors an opportunity to compete for the agency's actual requirements. Sys. Studies & Simulation, Inc., B-409375.2 et al., 2014 CPD ¶ 153 (Comp. Gen. 2014)

A contracting agency must specify its needs in a manner designed to achieve full and open competition and may include restrictive requirements only to the extent they are necessary to satisfy the agency's legitimate needs. Agency regulations permitted limiting a competition to a specific U.S. citizen category and the agency reasonably limited the competition for ship management services to entities that are U.S.-owned at all tiers. Maersk Line, Ltd., B-406586, 2012 CPD ¶ 200 (Comp. Gen. 2012)

Protest of agency requirement that any non-U.S.-based cloud computing data centers be located in Trade Agreements Act Designated Countries is sustained where the agency failed to establish a connection to any legitimate government need. Technosource Info. Sys., LLC, B-405296, 2011 CPD ¶ 220 (Comp. Gen. 2011)

A solicitation requirement that offerors present evidence of certification under ISO standards at proposal submission, rather than at the time of award or performance, exceeded the agency's reasonable needs. Matter of: USA Jet Airlines, Inc.; Active Aero Group, Inc., B-404666, 2011 CPD ¶ 91 (Comp. Gen. 2011)

In a commercial item acquisition for the repair and overhaul of pumps, protest of agency solicitation requiring vendors to be an original equipment manufacturer's (OEM) authorized repair facility was sustained, because the agency did not show that the restriction on competition were necessary to meet its needs. Decision Matter of: Missouri Machinery & Engineering Company, B-403561, 2010 CPD ¶ 276 (Comp. Gen. 2010)

Agency's solicitation requirements that computers and monitors be from the same manufacturer and use Intel-based microprocessors were overly restrictive because the agency did not demonstrate a reasonable basis for the requirements. Matter of: NCS Technologies, Inc., B-403435, 2010 CPD ¶ 281 (Comp. Gen. 2010)

A certification requirement for equipment does not need to be met at the time of quotation submission if the agency's rationale for this requirement is unreasonable. Restrictive requirements may only be included to the extent necessary to satisfy legitimate needs. Matter of: SMARTnet, Inc., B-400651.2, 2009 CPD ¶ 34 (Comp. Gen. 2009)

Agency may properly include in a work statement for fuels management services a minimum staffing requirement that the agency has shown to be necessary, without violating FAR 11.002(a)(2)(i), 37.602-1(b), which generally require that, to the maximum extent practicable, the agency's needs be described in terms of performance-based standards. United Paradyne Corporation, B-296609, 2005 CPD ¶ 164 (Comp. Gen. 2005)

Although specifications for the lease of commercial washers and dryers are stated in broad functional terms and include only minimal physical characteristics, protest that the specifications should be more clearly defined is denied since the specifications are sufficiently detailed so as to provide all offerors with a common understanding of what is required under the contract in order that they can compete intelligently on a relatively equal basis. Wincor Management Group, Inc., B-278925, 98-1 CPD ¶ 106 (Comp. Gen. 1998)

The protester challenged the agency's method for describing its software needs because the agency listed the critical functional requirements for the software in the RFP and did not name the commercially available software which the agency learned as part of its market research efforts would satisfy the RFP requirements. GAO disagreed and held that "there is no requirement that the agency, in defining its needs for commercial items, do so by listing commercial brand names. Rather, FAR 11.002(a)(2)(i) authorizes an agency to describe its needs for commercial supplies or services in terms of functions to be performed, performance required, or essential physical characteristics. Omega World Travel, Inc., B-280456, B-280456.2, 98-2 CPD ¶ 73 (Comp. Gen. 1998).

Solicitation provision which requires offeror to have completed 5 asbestos abatement projects with the last 3 years but also to have 5 years of an established asbestos abatement business is unduly restrictive in the absence of any rational explanation as to why agency's needs require such a restrictive provision. Keeson, Inc.; Ingram Demolition, Inc., B-245625, B-245655, 92-1 CPD ¶ 108 (Comp. Gen. 1992)

Subpart 11.1 Selecting and Developing Requirements Documents

§ 11.101 Order of precedence for requirements documents.

(a) Agencies may select from existing requirements documents, modify or combine existing requirements documents, or create new requirements documents to meet agency needs, consistent with the following order of precedence:

(1) Documents mandated for use by law.

(2) Performance-oriented documents (*e.g.,* a PWS or SOO). (See 2.101.)

(3) Detailed design-oriented documents.

(4) Standards, specifications and related publications issued by the Government outside the Defense or Federal series for the non-repetitive acquisition of items.

(b) In accordance with OMB Circular A-119, "Federal Participation in the Development and Use of Voluntary Consensus Standards and in Conformity Assessment Activities," and Section 12(d) of the National Technology Transfer and Advancement Act of 1995, Pub. L. 104-113 (15 U.S.C. 272 note), agencies must use voluntary consensus standards, when they exist, in lieu of Government-unique standards, except where inconsistent with law or otherwise impractical. The private sector manages and administers voluntary consensus standards. Such standards are not mandated by law (*e.g.,* industry standards such as ISO 9000, and IEEE 1680).

United States Code Annotated

Contracts, planning, solicitation, evaluation, and award procedures, see 10 USCA § 2305.

Definitions, see 10 USCA § 2302, 41 USCA §§ 259, 403.

Planning and solicitation requirements, see 41 USCA § 253a.

Preference for acquisition of commercial items, see 10 USCA § 2377, 41 USCA § 264b.

Simplified acquisition procedures, see 41 USCA § 427.

Notes of Decisions

Performance specifications 1

1 Performance specifications

"Performance specifications" set forth an objective or standard to be achieved, and the successful bidder is expected to exercise his ingenuity in achieving that objective or standard of performance, selecting the means and assuming a corresponding responsibility for that selection; "design specifications," on the other hand, describe in precise detail the materials to be employed and the manner in which the work is to be performed and the contractor has no discretion to deviate from the specifications, but is required to follow them as a road map. P.R. Burke Corp. v. U.S., 277 F.3d 1346 (Fed. Cir. 2002). United States ☞73(1)

"Performance specifications" in government contracts set forth an objective or standard to be achieved, and the successful bidder is expected to exercise his ingenuity in achieving that objective or standard of performance; "design specifications" are explicit, unquestionable specifications which tell the contractor exactly how the contract is to be performed and no deviation therefrom is possible. Conner Brothers Const. Co., Inc. v. U.S., 65 Fed. Cl. 657 (2005)

§ 11.102 Standardization program.

Agencies shall select existing requirements documents or develop new requirements documents that meet the needs of the agency in accordance with the guidance contained in the Federal Standardization Manual, FSPM-0001; for DoD components, DoD 4120.24-M,

Defense Standardization Program Policies and Procedures; and for IT standards and guidance, the Federal Information Processing Standards Publications (FIPS PUBS). The Federal Standardization Manual may be obtained from the General Services Administration (see address in 11.201(d)(1)). DoD 4120.24-M may be obtained from DoD (see 11.201(d)(2) or 11.201(d)(3)). FIPS PUBS may be obtained from the Government Printing Office (GPO), or the Department of Commerce's National Technical Information Service (NTIS) (see address in 11.201(d)(4)).

United States Code Annotated

Contracts, planning, solicitation, evaluation, and award procedures, see 10 USCA § 2305.

Definitions, see 10 USCA § 2302, 41 USCA §§ 259, 403.

Planning and solicitation requirements, see 41 USCA § 253a.

Preference for acquisition of commercial items, see 10 USCA § 2377, 41 USCA § 264b.

Simplified acquisition procedures, see 41 USCA § 427.

§ 11.103 Market acceptance.

(a) 41 U.S.C. 3307(e) provides that, in accordance with agency procedures, the head of an agency may, under appropriate circumstances, require offerors to demonstrate that the items offered—

(1) Have either—

(i) Achieved commercial market acceptance; or

(ii) Been satisfactorily supplied to an agency under current or recent contracts for the same or similar requirements; and

(2) Otherwise meet the item description, specifications, or other criteria prescribed in the public notice and solicitation.

(b) Appropriate circumstances may, for example, include situations where the agency's minimum need is for an item that has a demonstrated reliability, performance or product support record in a specified environment. Use of market acceptance is inappropriate when new or evolving items may meet the agency's needs.

(c) In developing criteria for demonstrating that an item has achieved commercial market acceptance, the contracting officer shall ensure the criteria in the solicitation—

(1) Reflect the minimum need of the agency and are reasonably related to the demonstration of an item's acceptability to meet the agency's minimum need;

(2) Relate to an item's performance and intended use, not an offeror's capability;

(3) Are supported by market research;

(4) Include consideration of items supplied satisfactorily under recent or current Government contracts, for the same or similar items; and

(5) Consider the entire relevant commercial market, including small business concerns.

(d) Commercial market acceptance shall not be used as a sole criterion to evaluate whether an item meets the Government's requirements.

(e) When commercial market acceptance is used, the contracting officer shall document the file to—

(1) Describe the circumstances justifying the use of commercial market acceptance criteria; and

(2) Support the specific criteria being used.

United States Code Annotated

Contracts, planning, solicitation, evaluation, and award procedures, see 10 USCA § 2305.

Definitions, see 10 USCA § 2302, 41 USCA §§ 259, 403.

Planning and solicitation requirements, see 41 USCA § 253a.

Preference for acquisition of commercial items, see 10 USCA § 2377, 41 USCA § 264b.

Simplified acquisition procedures, see 41 USCA § 427.

§ 11.104 Use of brand name or equal purchase descriptions.

(a) While the use of performance specifications is preferred to encourage offerors to propose innovative solutions, the use of brand name or equal purchase descriptions may be advantageous under certain circumstances.

(b) Brand name or equal purchase descriptions must include, in addition to the brand name, a general description of those salient physical, functional, or performance characteristics of the brand name item that an "equal" item must meet to be acceptable for award. Use brand name or equal descriptions when the salient characteristics are firm requirements.

United States Code Annotated

Contracts, planning, solicitation, evaluation, and award procedures, see 10 USCA § 2305.

Definitions, see 10 USCA § 2302, 41 USCA §§ 259, 403.

Planning and solicitation requirements, see 41 USCA § 253a.

Preference for acquisition of commercial items, see 10 USCA § 2377, 41 USCA § 264b.

Simplified acquisition procedures, see 41 USCA § 427.

Notes of Decisions

In general 1

1 In general

Agency unreasonably evaluated the protester's bid of an equal product under a brand name or equal solicitation conducted under simplified acquisition procedures where the solicitation lacked salient characteristics and the equal product was not shown to be significantly different from the brand name product. Veterans Healthcare Supply Solutions, Inc., B-407223.2, 2013 CPD ¶ 3 (Comp. Gen. 2013)

Protest that solicitation is unduly restrictive because it requires firms to submit proposals based solely on a brand name list of particular products is sustained where the solicitation does not include salient characteristics for the brand name products, and the agency has not taken the steps necessary to procure its requirements using other than full and open competition. Matter of: California Industrial Facilities Resources, Inc., d/b/a CAMSS Shelters, B-403397.3, 2011 CPD ¶ 71 (Comp. Gen. 2011)

Acquisitions conducted under FAR Parts 12 and 13 are not exempt from the requirement for the agency to identify salient characteristics of an item described in a brand name or equal specification. A brand name or equal RFQ is defective because it did not list salient characteristics, so that quoters offering equal products were left to guess at the desired essential qualities of the brand-name item. Where an agency does not include a list of salient characteristics in the solicitation, it is precluded from rejecting a quote offering an equal product for noncompliance with some performance or design feature, unless the offered item is significantly different from the brand-name product. Elementar Americas, Inc., B-289115, 2002 CPD ¶ 20 (Comp. Gen. 2002)

FAR 11.104(a) expresses only a preference for performance specifications and recognizes that the use of brand name or equal purchase descriptions may be advantageous under certain circumstances. Moreover, there is no requirement that agencies use only performance specifications in a brand name or equal purchase description. USA Information Systems, Inc., B-291417, 2002 CPD ¶ 224 (Comp. Gen. 2002)

Where there is no requirement that an agency define its needs for commercial-off-the-shelf software by commercial brand name, the agency appropriately defined its needs for commercially available travel management software by using a broad commercial item description stated in terms of functional requirements. Omega World Travel, Inc., B-280456, B-280456.2, 98-2 CPD ¶ 73 (Comp. Gen. 1998).

§ 11.105 Items peculiar to one manufacturer.

Agency requirements shall not be written so as to require a particular brand name, product, or a feature of a product, peculiar to one manufacturer, thereby precluding consideration of a product manufactured by another company, unless—

(a) (1) The particular brand name, product, or feature is essential to the Government's requirements, and market research indicates other companies' similar products, or products lacking the particular feature, do not meet, or cannot be modified to meet, the agency's needs;

(2) (i) The authority to contract without providing for full and open competition is supported by the required justifications and approvals (see 6.302-1); or

(ii) The basis for not providing for maximum practicable competition is documented in the file (see 13.106-1(b)) or justified (see 13.501) when the acquisition is awarded using simplified acquisition procedures.

(3) The documentation or justification is posted for acquisitions over $25,000. (See 5.102(a)(6).)

(b) For multiple award schedule orders, see 8.405-6.

(c) For orders under indefinite-quantity contracts, see 16.505(a)(4).

United States Code Annotated

Contracts, planning, solicitation, evaluation, and award procedures, see 10 USCA § 2305.

Definitions, see 10 USCA § 2302, 41 USCA §§ 259, 403.

Planning and solicitation requirements, see 41 USCA § 253a.

Preference for acquisition of commercial items, see 10 USCA § 2377, 41 USCA § 264b.

Simplified acquisition procedures, see 41 USCA § 427.

§ 11.106 Purchase descriptions for service contracts.

In drafting purchase descriptions for service contracts, agency requiring activities shall ensure that inherently governmental functions (see Subpart 7.5) are not assigned to a contractor. These purchase descriptions shall—

(a) Reserve final determination for Government officials;

(b) Require proper identification of contractor personnel who attend meetings, answer Government telephones, or work in situations where their actions could be construed as acts of Government officials unless, in the judgment of the agency, no harm can come from failing to identify themselves; and

(c) Require suitable marking of all documents or reports produced by contractors.

United States Code Annotated

Contracts, planning, solicitation, evaluation, and award procedures, see 10 USCA § 2305.

Definitions, see 10 USCA § 2302, 41 USCA §§ 259, 403.

Planning and solicitation requirements, see 41 USCA § 253a.

Preference for acquisition of commercial items, see 10 USCA § 2377, 41 USCA § 264b.

Simplified acquisition procedures, see 41 USCA § 427.

§ 11.107 Solicitation provision.

(a) Insert the provision at 52.211-6, Brand Name or Equal, when brand name or equal purchase descriptions are included in a solicitation.

(b) Insert the provision at 52.211-7, Alternatives to Government-Unique Standards, in solicitations that use Government-unique standards when the agency uses the transaction-based reporting method to report its use of voluntary consensus standards to the National Institute of Standards and Technology (see OMB Circular A-119, "Federal Participation in the Development and Use of Voluntary Consensus Standards and in Conformity Assessment Activities"). Use of the provision is optional for agencies that report their use of voluntary consensus standards to the National Institute of Standards and Technology using the categorical reporting method. Agencies that manage their specifications on a contract-by-contract basis use the transaction-based method of reporting. Agencies that manage their specifications centrally use the categorical method of reporting. Agency regulations regarding specification management describe which method is used.

United States Code Annotated

Contracts, planning, solicitation, evaluation, and award procedures, see 10 USCA § 2305.

Definitions, see 10 USCA § 2302, 41 USCA §§ 259, 403.

Planning and solicitation requirements, see 41 USCA § 253a.

Preference for acquisition of commercial items, see 10 USCA § 2377, 41 USCA § 264b.

Simplified acquisition procedures, see 41 USCA § 427.

Subpart 11.2 Using and Maintaining Requirements Documents

§ 11.201 Identification and availability of specifications.

(a) Solicitations citing requirements documents listed in the General Services Administration (GSA) Index of Federal Specifications, Standards and Commercial Item Descriptions, the DoD Acquisition Streamlining and Standardization Information System (ASSIST), or other agency index shall identify each document's approval date and the dates of any applicable amendments and revisions. Do not use general identification references, such as "the issue in effect on the date of the solicitation." Contracting offices will not normally furnish these cited documents with the solicitation, except when—

(1) The requirements document must be furnished with the solicitation to enable prospective contractors to make a competent evaluation of the solicitation;

(2) In the judgment of the contracting officer, it would be impracticable for prospective contractors to obtain the documents in reasonable time to respond to the solicitation; or

(3) A prospective contractor requests a copy of a Government promulgated requirements document.

(b) Contracting offices shall clearly identify in the solicitation any pertinent documents not listed in the GSA Index of Federal Specifications, Standards and Commercial Item Descriptions or ASSIST. Such documents shall be furnished with the solicitation or specific instructions shall be furnished for obtaining or examining such documents.

(c) When documents refer to other documents, such references shall—

(1) Be restricted to documents, or appropriate portions of documents, that apply in the acquisition;

(2) Cite the extent of their applicability;

(3) Not conflict with other documents and provisions of the solicitation; and

(4) Identify all applicable first tier references.

(d) (1) The GSA Index of Federal Specifications, Standards and Commercial Item Descriptions, FPMR Part 101-29, may be purchased from the—

General Services Administration
Federal Supply Service
Specifications Section
Suite 8100
470 East L'Enfant Plaza, SW
Washington, DC 20407
Telephone (202) 619-8925.

(2) Most unclassified Defense specifications and standards may be downloaded from the following ASSIST website:

(i) ASSIST (https://assist.dla.mil/online/start/).

(ii) Quick Search (http://quicksearch.dla.mil/).

(iii) ASSISTdocs.com (http://assistdocs.com).

(3) Documents not available from ASSIST may be ordered from the Department of Defense Single Stock Point (DoDSSP) by—

(i) Using the ASSIST Shopping Wizard (https://assist.dla.mil/wizard/index.cfm);

(ii) Phoning the DoDSSP Customer Service Desk, (215) 697-2179, Mon-Fri, 0730 to 1600 EST; or

(iii) Ordering from DoDSSP, Building 4, Section D, 700 Robbins Avenue, Philadelphia, PA 19111-5094, Telephone (215) 697-2667/2179, Facsimile (215) 697-1462.

(4) The FIPS PUBS may be obtained from—http://www.itl.nist.gov/fipspubs/, or purchased from the—

Superintendent of Documents,
U.S. Government Printing Office,
Washington, DC 20402,
Telephone (202) 512-1800,

Facsimile (202) 512-2250; or

National Technical Information Service (NTIS),
5285 Port Royal Road,
Springfield, VA 22161,
Telephone (703) 605-6000,
Facsimile (703) 605-6900,
Email: mailto:orders@ntis.gov.

(e) Agencies may purchase some nongovernment standards, including voluntary consensus standards, from the National Technical Information Service's Fedworld Information Network. Agencies may also obtain nongovernment standards from the standards developing organization responsible for the preparation, publication, or maintenance of the standard, or from an authorized document reseller. The National Institute of Standards and Technology can assist agencies in identifying sources for, and content of, nongovernment standards. DoD activities may obtain from the DoDSSP those nongovernment standards, including voluntary consensus standards, adopted for use by defense activities.

United States Code Annotated

Contracts, planning, solicitation, evaluation, and award procedures, see 10 USCA § 2305.
Definitions, see 10 USCA § 2302, 41 USCA §§ 259, 403.
Planning and solicitation requirements, see 41 USCA § 253a.
Preference for acquisition of commercial items, see 10 USCA § 2377, 41 USCA § 264b.
Simplified acquisition procedures, see 41 USCA § 427.

§ 11.202 Maintenance of standardization documents.

(a) Recommendations for changes to standardization documents listed in the GSA Index of Federal Specifications, Standards and Commercial Item Descriptions should be submitted to the—

General Services Administration
Federal Supply Service
Office of Acquisition
Washington, DC 20406.

Agencies shall submit recommendations for changes to standardization documents listed in the DoDISS to the cognizant preparing activity.

(b) When an agency cites an existing standardization document but modifies it to meet its needs, the agency shall follow the guidance in Federal Standardization Manual and, for Defense components, DoD 4120.24-M, Defense Standardization Program Policies and Procedures.

United States Code Annotated

Contracts, planning, solicitation, evaluation, and award procedures, see 10 USCA § 2305.
Definitions, see 10 USCA § 2302, 41 USCA §§ 259, 403.
Planning and solicitation requirements, see 41 USCA § 253a.
Preference for acquisition of commercial items, see 10 USCA § 2377, 41 USCA § 264b.
Simplified acquisition procedures, see 41 USCA § 427.

§ 11.203 Customer satisfaction.

Acquisition organizations shall communicate with customers to determine how well the requirements document reflects the customer's needs and to obtain suggestions for corrective actions. Whenever practicable, the agency may provide affected industry an opportunity to comment on the requirements documents.

United States Code Annotated

Contracts, planning, solicitation, evaluation, and award procedures, see 10 USCA § 2305.

Definitions, see 10 USCA § 2302, 41 USCA §§ 259, 403.

Planning and solicitation requirements, see 41 USCA § 253a.

Preference for acquisition of commercial items, see 10 USCA § 2377, 41 USCA § 264b.

Simplified acquisition procedures, see 41 USCA § 427.

§ 11.204 Solicitation provisions and contract clauses.

(a) The contracting officer shall insert the provision at 52.211-1, Availability of Specifications Listed in the GSA Index of Federal Specifications, Standards and Commercial Item Descriptions, FPMR Part 101-29, in solicitations that cite specifications listed in the Index that are not furnished with the solicitation.

(b) The contracting officer shall insert the provision at 52.211-2, Availability of Specifications, Standards, and Data Item Descriptions Listed in the Acquisition Streamlining and Standardization Information System (ASSIST), in solicitations that cite specifications listed in the ASSIST that are not furnished with the solicitation.

(c) The contracting officer shall insert a provision substantially the same as the provision at 52.211-3, Availability of Specifications Not Listed in the GSA Index of Federal Specifications, Standards and Commercial Item Descriptions, in solicitations that cite specifications that are not listed in the Index and are not furnished with the solicitation, but may be obtained from a designated source.

(d) The contracting officer shall insert a provision substantially the same as the provision at 52.211-4, Availability for Examination of Specifications Not Listed in the GSA Index of Federal Specifications, Standards and Commercial Item Descriptions, in solicitations that cite specifications that are not listed in the Index and are available for examination at a specified location.

United States Code Annotated

Contracts, planning, solicitation, evaluation, and award procedures, see 10 USCA § 2305.

Definitions, see 10 USCA § 2302, 41 USCA §§ 259, 403.

Planning and solicitation requirements, see 41 USCA § 253a.

Preference for acquisition of commercial items, see 10 USCA § 2377, 41 USCA § 264b.

Simplified acquisition procedures, see 41 USCA § 427.

Subpart 11.3 Acceptable Material

§ 11.301 Definitions.

As used in this subpart—

"Postconsumer material" means a material or finished product that has served its intended use and has been discarded for disposal or recovery, having completed its life as a consumer item. Postconsumer material is a part of the broader category of "recovered material." For paper and paper products, postconsumer material means "postconsumer fiber" defined by the U.S. Environmental Protection Agency (EPA) as—

(1) Paper, paperboard, and fibrous materials from retail stores, office buildings, homes, and so forth, after they have passed through their end-usage as a consumer item, including: used corrugated boxes; old newspapers; old magazines; mixed waste paper; tabulating cards; and used cordage; or

(2) All paper, paperboard, and fibrous materials that enter and are collected from municipal solid waste; but not

(3) Fiber derived from printers' over-runs, converters' scrap, and over-issue publications.

"Recovered material" for paper and paper products, is defined by EPA in its Comprehensive Procurement Guideline as "recovered fiber" and means the following materials:

(1) Postconsumer fiber.

(2) Manufacturing wastes such as—

(i) Dry paper and paperboard waste generated after completion of the papermaking process (that is, those manufacturing operations up to and including the cutting and trimming of the paper machine reel into smaller rolls or rough sheets) including: envelope cuttings, bindery trimmings, and other paper and paperboard waste resulting from printing, cutting, forming, and other converting operations; bag, box, and carton manufacturing wastes; and butt rolls, mill wrappers, and rejected unused stock; and

(ii) Repulped finished paper and paperboard from obsolete inventories of paper and paperboard manufacturers, merchants, wholesalers, dealers, printers, converters, or others.

United States Code Annotated

Contract requirements, see 41 USCA § 254.

Contracts, planning, solicitation, evaluation, and award procedures, see 10 USCA § 2305.

Definitions, see 10 USCA § 2302, 41 USCA §§ 259, 403.

Kinds of contracts, see 10 USCA § 2306.

Planning and solicitation requirements, see 41 USCA § 253a.

Preference for acquisition of commercial items, see 10 USCA § 2377, 41 USCA § 264b.

Simplified acquisition procedures, see 41 USCA § 427.

§ 11.302 Policy.

(a) Agencies must not require virgin material or supplies composed of or manufactured using virgin material unless compelled by law or regulation or unless virgin material is vital for safety or meeting performance requirements of the contract.

(b) (1) When acquiring other than commercial items, agencies must require offerors to identify used, reconditioned, or remanufactured supplies; or unused former Government surplus property proposed for use under the contract. These supplies or property may not be used in contract performance unless authorized by the contracting officer.

(2) When acquiring commercial items, the contracting officer must consider the customary practices in the industry for the item being acquired. The contracting officer may require offerors to provide information on used, reconditioned, or remanufactured supplies, or unused former Government surplus property proposed for use under the contract. The request for the information must be included in the solicitation, and to the maximum extent practicable must be limited to information or standards consistent with normal commercial practices.

(c)

(1) When the contracting officer needs additional information to determine whether supplies meet minimum recovered material or biobased standards stated in the solicitation, the contracting officer may require offerors to submit additional information on the recycled or biobased content or related standards. The request for the information must be included in the solicitation. When acquiring commercial items, limit the information to the maximum extent practicable to that available under normal commercial practices.

(2) For biobased products, agencies may not require, as a condition of purchase of such products, the vendor or manufacturer to provide more data than would typically be provided by other business entities offering products for sale to the agency, other than data confirming the biobased content of a product (see 7 CFR 3201.8).

United States Code Annotated

Contract requirements, see 41 USCA § 254.

Contracts, planning, solicitation, evaluation, and award procedures, see 10 USCA § 2305.

Definitions, see 10 USCA § 2302, 41 USCA §§ 259, 403.

Kinds of contracts, see 10 USCA § 2306.

Planning and solicitation requirements, see 41 USCA § 253a.

Preference for acquisition of commercial items, see 10 USCA § 2377, 41 USCA § 264b.

Simplified acquisition procedures, see 41 USCA § 427.

§ 11.303 Special requirements for paper.

(a) The following applies when agencies acquire paper in the United States (as defined in 23.001):

(1) Section 2(d)(ii) of Executive Order 13423, Strengthening Federal Environmental, Energy, and Transportation Management, establishes a 30 percent postconsumer fiber content standards for agency paper use. Section 2(d)(ii) requires that an agency's paper products must meet or exceed the minimum content standard.

(2) Section 2(e)(iv) of Executive Order 13514 requires acquisition of uncoated printing and writing paper containing at least 30 percent postconsumer fiber.

(b) *Exceptions.* If paper under paragraphs (a)(1) or (a)(2) of this section containing at least 30 percent postconsumer fiber is not reasonably available, does not meet reasonable performance requirements, or is only available at an unreasonable price, then the agency must purchase—

(1) Printing and writing paper containing no less than 20 percent postconsumer fiber; or

(2) Paper, other than printing and writing paper, with the maximum practicable percentage of postconsumer fiber that is reasonably available at a reasonable price and that meets reasonable performance requirements.

United States Code Annotated

Contract requirements, see 41 USCA § 254.

Contracts, planning, solicitation, evaluation, and award procedures, see 10 USCA § 2305.

Definitions, see 10 USCA § 2302, 41 USCA §§ 259, 403.

Kinds of contracts, see 10 USCA § 2306.

Planning and solicitation requirements, see 41 USCA § 253a.

Preference for acquisition of commercial items, see 10 USCA § 2377, 41 USCA § 264b.

Simplified acquisition procedures, see 41 USCA § 427.

§ 11.304 Contract clause.

Insert the clause at 52.211-5, Material Requirements, in solicitations and contracts for supplies that are not commercial items.

United States Code Annotated

Contract requirements, see 41 USCA § 254.

Contracts, planning, solicitation, evaluation, and award procedures, see 10 USCA § 2305.

Definitions, see 10 USCA § 2302, 41 USCA §§ 259, 403.

Kinds of contracts, see 10 USCA § 2306.

Planning and solicitation requirements, see 41 USCA § 253a.

Preference for acquisition of commercial items, see 10 USCA § 2377, 41 USCA § 264b.

Simplified acquisition procedures, see 41 USCA § 427.

Subpart 11.4 Delivery or Performance Schedules

§ 11.401 General.

(a) The time of delivery or performance is an essential contract element and shall be clearly stated in solicitations. Contracting officers shall ensure that delivery or performance schedules are realistic and meet the requirements of the acquisition. Schedules that are unnecessarily short or difficult to attain—

(1) Tend to restrict competition,

(2) Are inconsistent with small business policies, and

(3) May result in higher contract prices.

(b) Solicitations shall, except when clearly unnecessary, inform bidders or offerors of the basis on which their bids or proposals will be evaluated with respect to time of delivery or performance.

(c) If timely delivery or performance is unusually important to the Government, liquidated damages clauses may be used (see Subpart 11.5).

United States Code Annotated

Contract requirements, see 41 USCA § 254.

Contracts, planning, solicitation, evaluation, and award procedures, see 10 USCA § 2305.

Definitions, see 10 USCA § 2302, 41 USCA §§ 259, 403.

Kinds of contracts, see 10 USCA § 2306.

Planning and solicitation requirements, see 41 USCA § 253a.

Preference for acquisition of commercial items, see 10 USCA § 2377, 41 USCA § 264b.

Simplified acquisition procedures, see 41 USCA § 427.

§ 11.402 Factors to consider in establishing schedules.

(a) *Supplies or services.* When establishing a contract delivery or performance schedule, consideration shall be given to applicable factors such as the—

(1) Urgency of need;

(2) Industry practices;

(3) Market conditions;

(4) Transportation time;

(5) Production time;

(6) Capabilities of small business concerns;

(7) Administrative time for obtaining and evaluating offers and for awarding contracts;

(8) Time for contractors to comply with any conditions precedent to contract performance; and

(9) Time for the Government to perform its obligations under the contract; *e.g.,* furnishing Government property.

(b) *Construction.* When scheduling the time for completion of a construction contract, the contracting officer shall consider applicable factors such as the—

(1) Nature and complexity of the project;

(2) Construction seasons involved;

(3) Required completion date;

(4) Availability of materials and equipment;

(5) Capacity of the contractor to perform; and

(6) Use of multiple completion dates. (In any given contract, separate completion dates may be established for separable items of work. When multiple completion dates are used, requests for extension of time must be evaluated with respect to each item, and the affected completion dates modified when appropriate.)

United States Code Annotated

Contract requirements, see 41 USCA § 254.

Contracts, planning, solicitation, evaluation, and award procedures, see 10 USCA § 2305.

Definitions, see 10 USCA § 2302, 41 USCA §§ 259, 403.

Kinds of contracts, see 10 USCA § 2306.

Planning and solicitation requirements, see 41 USCA § 253a.

Preference for acquisition of commercial items, see 10 USCA § 2377, 41 USCA § 264b.

Simplified acquisition procedures, see 41 USCA § 427.

§ 11.403 Supplies or services.

(a) The contracting officer may express contract delivery or performance schedules in terms of—

(1) Specific calendar dates;

(2) Specific periods from the date of the contract; *i.e.,* from the date of award or acceptance by the Government, or from the date shown as the effective date of the contract;

(3) Specific periods from the date of receipt by the contractor of the notice of award or acceptance by the Government (including notice by receipt of contract document executed by the Government); or

(4) Specific time for delivery after receipt by the contractor of each individual order issued under the contract, as in indefinite delivery type contracts and GSA schedules.

(b) The time specified for contract performance should not be curtailed to the prejudice of the contractor because of delay by the Government in giving notice of award.

(c) If the delivery schedule is based on the date of the contract, the contracting officer shall mail or otherwise furnish to the contractor the contract, notice of award, acceptance of proposal, or other contract document not later than the date of the contract.

(d) If the delivery schedule is based on the date the contractor receives the notice of award, or if the delivery schedule is expressed in terms of specific calendar dates on the assumption that the notice of award will be received by a specified date, the contracting officer shall send the contract, notice of award, acceptance of proposal, or other contract document by certified mail, return receipt requested, or by any other method that will provide evidence of the date of receipt.

(e) In invitations for bids, if the delivery schedule is based on the date of the contract, and a bid offers delivery based on the date the contractor receives the contract or notice of award, the contracting officer shall evaluate the bid by adding 5 calendar days (as representing the normal time for arrival through ordinary mail). If the contract or notice of award will be transmitted electronically, (1) the solicitation shall so state; and (2) the contracting officer shall evaluate delivery schedule based on the date of contract receipt or notice of award, by adding one working day. (The term "working day" excludes weekends and U.S. Federal holidays.) If the offered delivery date computed with mailing or transmittal time is later than the delivery date required by the invitation for bids, the bid shall be considered nonresponsive and rejected. If award is made, the delivery date will be the number of days offered in the bid after the contractor actually receives the notice of award.

United States Code Annotated

Contract requirements, see 41 USCA § 254.

Contracts, planning, solicitation, evaluation, and award procedures, see 10 USCA § 2305.

Definitions, see 10 USCA § 2302, 41 USCA §§ 259, 403.

Kinds of contracts, see 10 USCA § 2306.

Planning and solicitation requirements, see 41 USCA § 253a.

Preference for acquisition of commercial items, see 10 USCA § 2377, 41 USCA § 264b.

Simplified acquisition procedures, see 41 USCA § 427.

§ 11.404 Contract clauses.

(a) *Supplies or services.* (1) The contracting officer may use a time of delivery clause to set forth a required delivery schedule and to allow an offeror to propose an alternative delivery schedule. The clauses and their alternates may be used in solicitations and contracts for other than construction and architect-engineering substantially as shown, or they may be changed or new clauses written.

(2) The contracting officer may insert in solicitations and contracts other than those for construction and architectengineering, a clause substantially the same as the clause at 52.211-8, Time of Delivery, if the Government requires delivery by a particular time and the delivery schedule is to be based on the date of the contract. If the delivery schedule is expressed in terms of specific calendar dates or specific periods and is based on an assumed date of award, the contracting officer may use the clause with its Alternate I. If the delivery schedule is expressed in terms of specific calendar dates or specific periods and is based on an assumed date the contractor will receive notice of award, the contracting officer may use the clause with its Alternate II. If the delivery schedule is to be based on the actual date the contractor receives a written notice of award, the contracting officer may use the clause with its Alternate III.

(3) The contracting officer may insert in solicitations and contracts other than those for construction and architectengineering, a clause substantially the same as the clause at 52.211-9, Desired and Required Time of Delivery, if the Government desires delivery by a certain time but requires delivery by a specified later time, and the delivery schedule is to be based on the date of the contract. If the delivery schedule is expressed in terms of specific calendar dates or specific periods and is based on an assumed date of award, the contracting officer may use the clause with its Alternate I. If the delivery schedule is expressed in terms of specific calendar dates or specific periods and is based on an assumed date the contractor will receive notice of award, the contracting officer may use

the clause with its Alternate II. If the delivery schedule is to be based on the actual date the contractor receives a written notice of award, the contracting officer may use the clause with its Alternate III.

(b) *Construction*. The contracting officer shall insert the clause at 52.211-10, Commencement, Prosecution, and Completion of Work, in solicitations and contracts when a fixedprice construction contract is contemplated. The clause may be changed to accommodate the issuance of orders under indefinite-delivery contracts. If the completion date is expressed as a specific calendar date, computed on the basis of the contractor receiving the notice to proceed by a certain day, the contracting officer may use the clause with its Alternate I.

United States Code Annotated
Contract requirements, see 41 USCA § 254.

Contracts, planning, solicitation, evaluation, and award procedures, see 10 USCA § 2305.

Definitions, see 10 USCA § 2302, 41 USCA §§ 259, 403.

Kinds of contracts, see 10 USCA § 2306.

Planning and solicitation requirements, see 41 USCA § 253a.

Preference for acquisition of commercial items, see 10 USCA § 2377, 41 USCA § 264b.

Simplified acquisition procedures, see 41 USCA § 427.

Notes of Decisions
In general 1

1 In general
Although FAR 1.102-4 states that the absence of direction should be interpreted as permitting the Acquisition Team to innovate and use sound business judgment, this broad discretion does not permit the Acquisition Team or the Contracting Officer to disregard the terms of the contract. However, FAR 1.102-4 applies only when the "procedure . . . is in the best interest of the Government *and* is not specifically addressed in the FAR." Because the procedure to issuing a notice to proceed is specifically addressed in FAR 11.404(b) (referencing FAR 52.211-10), the discretion permitted by FAR 1.102-4 does not apply in this situation. Tidewater Contractors, Inc. v. Dept. of Transportation, CBCA 50, 07-1 B.C.A. (CCH) ¶ 33525, 2007 WL 994555 (U.S. Civilian BCA 2007), modified on reconsideration, CBCA 50-R, 07-2 B.C.A. (CCH) ¶ 33618, 2007 WL 2045470 (U.S. Civilian BCA 2007).

Subpart 11.5 Liquidated Damages

§ 11.500 Scope.
This subpart prescribes policies and procedures for using liquidated damages clauses in solicitations and contracts for supplies, services, research and development, and construction. This subpart does not apply to liquidated damages for subcontracting plans (see 19.705-7) or liquidated damages related to the Contract Work Hours and Safety Standards statute (see Subpart 22.3).

United States Code Annotated
Contract requirements, see 41 USCA § 254.

Contracts, planning, solicitation, evaluation, and award procedures, see 10 USCA § 2305.

Definitions, see 10 USCA § 2302, 41 USCA §§ 259, 403.

Kinds of contracts, see 10 USCA § 2306.

Planning and solicitation requirements, see 41 USCA § 253a.

Preference for acquisition of commercial items, see 10 USCA § 2377, 41 USCA § 264b.

Remission of liquidated damages, see 10 USCA § 2312.

Simplified acquisition procedures, see 41 USCA § 427.

Waiver of liquidated damages, see 41 USCA § 256a.

§ 11.501 Policy.
(a) The contracting officer must consider the potential impact on pricing, competition,

and contract administration before using a liquidated damages clause. Use liquidated damages clauses only when—

(1) The time of delivery or timely performance is so important that the Government may reasonably expect to suffer damage if the delivery or performance is delinquent; and

(2) The extent or amount of such damage would be difficult or impossible to estimate accurately or prove.

(b) Liquidated damages are not punitive and are not negative performance incentives (see 16.402-2). Liquidated damages are used to compensate the Government for probable damages. Therefore, the liquidated damages rate must be a reasonable forecast of just compensation for the harm that is caused by late delivery or untimely performance of the particular contract. Use a maximum amount or a maximum period for assessing liquidated damages if these limits reflect the maximum probable damage to the Government. Also, the contracting officer may use more than one liquidated damages rate when the contracting officer expects the probable damage to the Government to change over the contract period of performance.

(c) The contracting officer must take all reasonable steps to mitigate liquidated damages. If the contract contains a liquidated damages clause and the contracting officer is considering terminating the contract for default, the contracting officer should seek expeditiously to obtain performance by the contractor or terminate the contract and repurchase (see Subpart 49.4). Prompt contracting officer action will prevent excessive loss to defaulting contractors and protect the interests of the Government.

(d) The head of the agency may reduce or waive the amount of liquidated damages assessed under a contract, if the Commissioner, Financial Management Service, or designee approves (see Treasury Order 145-10).

United States Code Annotated

Contract requirements, see 41 USCA § 254.

Contracts, planning, solicitation, evaluation, and award procedures, see 10 USCA § 2305.

Definitions, see 10 USCA § 2302, 41 USCA §§ 259, 403.

Kinds of contracts, see 10 USCA § 2306.

Planning and solicitation requirements, see 41 USCA § 253a.

Preference for acquisition of commercial items, see 10 USCA § 2377, 41 USCA § 264b.

Remission of liquidated damages, see 10 USCA § 2312.

Simplified acquisition procedures, see 41 USCA § 427.

Waiver of liquidated damages, see 41 USCA § 256a.

Notes of Decisions

In general 1

1 In general

When damages are uncertain or difficult to measure, a liquidated damages liquidated damages clause will be enforced as long as the amount stipulated for is not so extravagant, or disproportionate to the amount of property loss, as to show that compensation was not the object aimed at or as to imply fraud, mistake, circumvention or oppression; the test is objective, and regardless of how the liquidated damages figure was arrived at, the liquidated damages clause will be enforced if the amount stipulated is reasonable for the particular agreement at the time it is made. K–CON Building Systems, Inc. v. United States, 778 F.3d 1000 (Fed.Cir. 2015)

Liquidated damages clause in government contract for construction of prefabricated metal building that set rate of $589 per day of delay for $582,641 contract did not impose impermissible penalty and thus was enforceable under Contract Disputes Act (CDA); even if government made certain errors in arriving at $589 figure for inclusion in contract, ultimate rate of $589 per day was reasonable, and it was foreseeable at time of contracting that delay would create number of costs for government, including costs for travel, inspection, and other work by government personnel that should have ended but continued beyond date for completion. K–CON Building Systems, Inc. v. United States, 778 F.3d 1000 (Fed.Cir. 2015)

§ 11.502 Procedures.

(a) Include the applicable liquidated damages clause and liquidated damages rates in solicitations when the contract will contain liquidated damages provisions.

(b) Construction contracts with liquidated damages provisions must describe the rate(s) of liquidated damages assessed per day of delay. The rate(s) should include the estimated daily cost of Government inspection and superintendence. The rate(s) should also include an amount for other expected expenses associated with delayed completion such as—

(1) Renting substitute property; or

(2) Paying additional allowance for living quarters.

United States Code Annotated

Contract requirements, see 41 USCA § 254.

Contracts, planning, solicitation, evaluation, and award procedures, see 10 USCA § 2305.

Definitions, see 10 USCA § 2302, 41 USCA §§ 259, 403.

Kinds of contracts, see 10 USCA § 2306.

Planning and solicitation requirements, see 41 USCA § 253a.

Preference for acquisition of commercial items, see 10 USCA § 2377, 41 USCA § 264b.

Remission of liquidated damages, see 10 USCA § 2312.

Simplified acquisition procedures, see 41 USCA § 427.

Waiver of liquidated damages, see 41 USCA § 256a.

Notes of Decisions

In general 1

1 In general

Although the contracting officer did not issue a final decision assessing liquidated damages, the contractor's claim for damages was untimely because it was not asserted within six years of the date that the claim for recovery of the liquidated damages accrued. R.R. Gregory Corp., ASBCA 58517, 14-1 BCA ¶ 35524 (Armed Serv. B.C.A. 2014)

Liquidated damages provisions are authorized where the government reasonably expects to suffer damages if the contract is improperly performed and the extent of such damages would be difficult to ascertain. FAR 11.502(a). Before we will rule that a liquidated damages provision imposes a penalty, the protester must show that there is no possible relationship between the amounts stipulated for liquidated damages and losses which are contemplated by the parties. Sea-Land Service, Inc., B-278404, B-278404.2, 98-1 CPD ¶ 47 (Comp. Gen. 1998)

§ 11.503 Contract clauses.

(a) Use the clause at 52.211-11, Liquidated Damages—Supplies, Services, or Research and Development, in fixed-price solicitations and contracts for supplies, services, or research and development when the contracting officer determines that liquidated damages are appropriate (see 11.501(a)).

(b) Use the clause at 52.211-12, Liquidated Damages—Construction, in solicitations and contracts for construction, other than cost-plus-fixed-fee, when the contracting officer determines that liquidated damages are appropriate (see 11.501(a)). If the contract specifies more than one completion date for separate parts or stages of the work, revise paragraph (a) of the clause to state the amount of liquidated damages for delay of each separate part or stage of the work.

(c) Use the clause at 52.211-13, Time Extensions, in solicitations and contracts for construction that use the clause at 52.211-12, Liquidated Damages—Construction, when that clause has been revised as provided in paragraph (b) of this section.

United States Code Annotated

Contract requirements, see 41 USCA § 254.

Contracts, planning, solicitation, evaluation, and award procedures, see 10 USCA § 2305.

Definitions, see 10 USCA § 2302, 41 USCA §§ 259, 403.

Kinds of contracts, see 10 USCA § 2306.

Planning and solicitation requirements, see 41 USCA § 253a.

Preference for acquisition of commercial items, see 10 USCA § 2377, 41 USCA § 264b.

Remission of liquidated damages, see 10 USCA § 2312.

Simplified acquisition procedures, see 41 USCA § 427.

Waiver of liquidated damages, see 41 USCA § 256a.

Subpart 11.6 Priorities and Allocations

§ 11.600 Scope of subpart.

This subpart implements the Defense Priorities and Allocations System (DPAS), a Department of Commerce regulation in support of approved national defense, emergency preparedness, and energy programs (see 15 CFR part 700).

United States Code Annotated

Contract requirements, see 41 USCA § 254.

Contracts, planning, solicitation, evaluation, and award procedures, see 10 USCA § 2305.

Definitions, see 10 USCA § 2302, 41 USCA §§ 259, 403.

Kinds of contracts, see 10 USCA § 2306.

Limitation on actions without Congressional authorization, see 50 App. USCA § 2074.

Penalties, see 50 App. USCA § 2073.

Planning and solicitation requirements, see 41 USCA § 253a.

Preference for acquisition of commercial items, see 10 USCA § 2377, 41 USCA § 264b.

Priority in contracts and orders, see 50 App. USCA § 2071.

Simplified acquisition procedures, see 41 USCA § 427.

§ 11.601 Definitions.

As used in this subpart—

"Approved program" means a program determined as necessary or appropriate for priorities and allocations support to promote the national defense by the Secretary of Defense, the Secretary of Energy, or the Secretary of Homeland Security, under the authority of the Defense Production Act, the Stafford Act, and Executive Order 12919, or the Selective Service Act and related statutes and Executive Order 12742.

"Delegate Agency" means a Government agency authorized by delegation from the Department of Commerce to place priority ratings on contracts or orders needed to support approved programs.

"National defense" means programs for military and energy production or construction, military assistance to any foreign nation, stockpiling, space, and any directly related activity. Such term includes emergency preparedness activities conducted pursuant to title VI of The Robert T. Stafford Disaster Relief and Emergency Assistance Act (42 U.S.C. 5195 et seq.) and critical infrastructure protection and restoration. (50 U.S.C. App. § 2152).

"Rated order" means a prime contract, a subcontract, or a purchase order in support of an approved program issued in accordance with the provisions of the DPAS regulation (15 CFR part 700).

United States Code Annotated

Contract requirements, see 41 USCA § 254.

Contracts, planning, solicitation, evaluation, and award procedures, see 10 USCA § 2305.

Definitions, see 10 USCA § 2302, 41 USCA §§ 259, 403.

Kinds of contracts, see 10 USCA § 2306.

Limitation on actions without Congressional authorization, see 50 App. USCA § 2074.

Penalties, see 50 App. USCA § 2073.

Planning and solicitation requirements, see 41 USCA § 253a.

Preference for acquisition of commercial items, see 10 USCA § 2377, 41 USCA § 264b.

Priority in contracts and orders, see 50 App. USCA § 2071.

Simplified acquisition procedures, see 41 USCA § 427.

§ **11.602 General.**

(a) Under Title I of the Defense Production Act of 1950 (50 U.S.C. App. 2061, *et seq.*), the President is authorized to require preferential acceptance and performance of contracts and orders supporting certain approved national defense and energy programs and to allocate materials, services, and facilities in such a manner as to promote these approved programs.

(b) The President delegated the priorities and allocations authorities of the Defense Production Act in Executive Order 12919. As part of that delegation, the President designated the Secretary of Commerce to administer the DPAS. For more information, check the DPAS website at: *www.bis.doc.gov/dpas*.

United States Code Annotated

Contract requirements, see 41 USCA § 254.

Contracts, planning, solicitation, evaluation, and award procedures, see 10 USCA § 2305.

Definitions, see 10 USCA § 2302, 41 USCA §§ 259, 403.

Kinds of contracts, see 10 USCA § 2306.

Limitation on actions without Congressional authorization, see 50 App. USCA § 2074.

Penalties, see 50 App. USCA § 2073.

Planning and solicitation requirements, see 41 USCA § 253a.

Preference for acquisition of commercial items, see 10 USCA § 2377, 41 USCA § 264b.

Priority in contracts and orders, see 50 App. USCA § 2071.

Simplified acquisition procedures, see 41 USCA § 427.

§ **11.603 Procedures.**

(a) There are two levels of priority for rated orders established by the DPAS, identified by the rating symbols "DO" and "DX". All DO rated orders have equal priority with each other and take preference over unrated orders. All DX rated orders have equal priority with each other and take preference over DO rated and unrated orders (see 15 CFR 700.11). The DPAS regulation contains provisions concerning the elements of a rated order (see 15 CFR 700.12); acceptance and rejection of rated orders (see 15 CFR 700.13); preferential scheduling (see 15 CFR 700.14); extension of priority ratings (flowdown) (see 15 CFR 700.15); changes or cancellations of priority ratings and rated orders (see 15 CFR 700.16); use of rated orders (see 15 CFR 700.17); and limitations on placing rated orders (see 15 CFR 700.18).

(b) The Delegate Agencies have been given authority by the Department of Commerce to place rated orders in support of approved programs (see Schedule I of the DPAS). Other U.S. Government agencies, Canada, and foreign nations may apply for priority rating authority.

(c) Rated orders shall be placed in accordance with the provisions of the DPAS.

(d) Agency heads shall ensure compliance with the DPAS by contracting activities within their agencies.

(e) Agency heads shall provide contracting activities with specific guidance on the issuance of rated orders in support of approved agency programs, including the general limitations and jurisdictional limitations on placing rated orders (see 15 CFR 700.18 and Executive Order 12919).

(f) Contracting officers shall follow agency procedural instructions concerning the use of rated orders in support of approved agency programs.

(g) Contracting officers, contractors, or subcontractors at any tier, that experience difficulty placing rated orders, obtaining timely delivery under rated orders, locating a contractor or supplier to fill a rated order, ensuring that rated orders receive preferential treatment by contractors or suppliers, or require rating authority for items not automatically ratable under the DPAS, should promptly seek special priorities assistance in accordance with agency procedures (see 15 CFR 700.50–700.55 and 700.80).

(h) The Department of Commerce may take specific official actions (Ratings Authorizations, Directives, Letters of Understanding, Administrative Subpoenas, Demands for Information, and Inspection Authorizations) to implement or enforce the provisions of the DPAS (see 15 CFR 700.60–700.71).

(i) Contracting officers shall report promptly any violations of the DPAS in accordance with agency procedures to the Office of Strategic Industries and Economic Security, U.S. Department of Commerce, Room 3876, Washington, DC 20230, Ref: DPAS; telephone: (202) 482-3634 or fax: (202) 482-5650.

United States Code Annotated

Contract requirements, see 41 USCA § 254.

Contracts, planning, solicitation, evaluation, and award procedures, see 10 USCA § 2305.

Definitions, see 10 USCA § 2302, 41 USCA §§ 259, 403.

Kinds of contracts, see 10 USCA § 2306.

Limitation on actions without Congressional authorization, see 50 App. USCA § 2074.

Penalties, see 50 App. USCA § 2073.

Planning and solicitation requirements, see 41 USCA § 253a.

Preference for acquisition of commercial items, see 10 USCA § 2377, 41 USCA § 264b.

Priority in contracts and orders, see 50 App. USCA § 2071.

Simplified acquisition procedures, see 41 USCA § 427.

Notes of Decisions

In general 1

1 In general

Contractor terminated for default failed to establish an excusable delay under a rated order issued under the Defense Priorities and Allocations System (DPAS) based on the unavailability of monoethanolamine (MEA) because the contractor failed to exercise due diligence in locating suppliers of MEA. The contractor's failure to attempt to obtain a mandatory allocation for MEA under the procedures of the DPAS at the outset of performance of the contract was held not to be excusable. Beeston, Inc., ASBCA No. 38969, 91-3 BCA ¶ 24241 (ASBCA 1991)

When work will be performed on the basis of the Defense Priorities and Allocations Systems rated orders are identified as DO and DX. All DO orders have equal priority and take precedence over unrated orders. All DX orders have equal priority and take precedence over DO and unrated orders. FAR 11.603(a). Thus, companies may be required to work on the basis of the ratings, not the amount of fee. Boeing Sikorsky Aircraft Support, B-277263, B-277263.2, B-277263.3, 97-2 CPD ¶ 91 (Comp. Gen. 1997)

§ 11.604 Solicitation provision and contract clause.

(a) Contracting officers shall insert the provision at 52.211-14, Notice of Priority Rating for National Defense, Emergency Preparedness, and Energy Program Use, in solicitations when the contract to be awarded will be a rated order.

(b) Contracting officers shall insert the clause at 52.211-15, Defense Priority and Allocation Requirements, in contracts that are rated orders.

United States Code Annotated

Contract requirements, see 41 USCA § 254.

Contracts, planning, solicitation, evaluation, and award procedures, see 10 USCA § 2305.

Definitions, see 10 USCA § 2302, 41 USCA §§ 259, 403.

Kinds of contracts, see 10 USCA § 2306.

Limitation on actions without Congressional authorization, see 50 App. USCA § 2074.

Penalties, see 50 App. USCA § 2073.

Planning and solicitation requirements, see 41 USCA § 253a.

Preference for acquisition of commercial items, see 10 USCA § 2377, 41 USCA § 264b.

Priority in contracts and orders, see 50 App. USCA § 2071.

Simplified acquisition procedures, see 41 USCA § 427.

Subpart 11.7 Variation in Quantity

§ 11.701 Supply contracts.

(a) A fixed-price supply contract may authorize Government acceptance of a variation in the quantity of items called for if the variation is caused by conditions of loading, shipping, or packing, or by allowances in manufacturing processes. Any permissible variation shall be stated as a percentage and it may be an increase, a decrease, or a combination of both; however, contracts for subsistence items may use other applicable terms of variation in quantity.

(b) There should be no standard or usual variation percentage. The overrun or underrun permitted in each contract should be based upon the normal commercial practices of a particular industry for a particular item, and the permitted percentage should be no larger than is necessary to afford a contractor reasonable protection. The permissible variation shall not exceed plus or minus 10 percent unless a different limitation is established in agency regulations. Consideration shall be given to the quantity to which the percentage variation applies. For example, when delivery will be made to multiple destinations and it is desired that the quantity variation apply to the item quantity for each destination, this requirement must be stated in the contract.

(c) Contractors are responsible for delivery of the specified quantity of items in a fixed-price contract, within allowable variations, if any. If a contractor delivers a quantity of items in excess of the contract requirements plus any allowable variation in quantity, particularly small dollar value overshipments, it results in unnecessary administrative costs to the Government in determining disposition of the excess quantity. Accordingly, the contract may include the clause at 52.211-17, Delivery of Excess Quantities, to provide that—

(1) Excess quantities of items totaling up to $250 in value may be retained without compensating the contractor; and

(2) Excess quantities of items totaling over $250 in value may, at the Government's option, be either returned at the contractor's expense or retained and paid for at the contract unit price.

United States Code Annotated

Contract requirements, see 41 USCA § 254.

Contracts, planning, solicitation, evaluation, and award procedures, see 10 USCA § 2305.

Definitions, see 10 USCA § 2302, 41 USCA §§ 259, 403.

Kinds of contracts, see 10 USCA § 2306.

Planning and solicitation requirements, see 41 USCA § 253a.

Preference for acquisition of commercial items, see 10 USCA § 2377, 41 USCA § 264b.

Simplified acquisition procedures, see 41 USCA § 427.

Notes of Decisions

In general 1

1 In general

Contractor was entitled to increased compensation for indirect costs because of the shortfall in the number of service hours ordered by the government in the base year of the contract. The contract's variation-in-quantity clause included the indirect and overhead costs sought by the contractor. Brink's/Hermes Joint Venture v. Dept. of State, CBCA 1188, 09-2 B.C.A. (CCH) ¶ 34209, 2009 WL 2351798 (U.S. Civilian BCA 2009)

§ 11.702 Construction contracts.

Construction contracts may authorize a variation in estimated quantities of unit-priced items. When the variation between the estimated quantity and the actual quantity of a unit-priced item is more than plus or minus 15 percent, an equitable adjustment in the contract price shall be made upon the demand of either the Government or the contractor. The contractor may request an extension of time if the quantity variation is such as to cause an increase in the time necessary for completion. The contracting officer must receive the request in writing within 10 days from the beginning of the period of delay. However, the contracting officer may extend this time limit before the date of final settlement of the contract. The contracting officer shall ascertain the facts and make any adjustment for extending the completion date that the findings justify.

United States Code Annotated

Contract requirements, see 41 USCA § 254.

Contracts, planning, solicitation, evaluation, and award procedures, see 10 USCA § 2305.

Definitions, see 10 USCA § 2302, 41 USCA §§ 259, 403.

Kinds of contracts, see 10 USCA § 2306.

Planning and solicitation requirements, see 41 USCA § 253a.

Preference for acquisition of commercial items, see 10 USCA § 2377, 41 USCA § 264b.

Simplified acquisition procedures, see 41 USCA § 427.

§ 11.703 Contract clauses.

(a) The contracting officer shall insert the clause at 52.211-16, Variation in Quantity, in solicitations and contracts, if authorizing a variation in quantity in fixed-price contracts for supplies or for services that involve the furnishing of supplies.

(b) The contracting officer may insert the clause at 52.211-17, Delivery of Excess Quantities, in solicitations and contracts when a fixed-price supply contract is contemplated.

(c) The contracting officer shall insert the clause at 52.211-18, Variation in Estimated Quantity, in solicitations and contracts when a fixed-price construction contract is contemplated that authorizes a variation in the estimated quantity of unit-priced items.

United States Code Annotated

Contract requirements, see 41 USCA § 254.

Contracts, planning, solicitation, evaluation, and award procedures, see 10 USCA § 2305.

Definitions, see 10 USCA § 2302, 41 USCA §§ 259, 403.

Kinds of contracts, see 10 USCA § 2306.

Planning and solicitation requirements, see 41 USCA § 253a.

Preference for acquisition of commercial items, see 10 USCA § 2377, 41 USCA § 264b.

Simplified acquisition procedures, see 41 USCA § 427.

Subpart 11.8 Testing

§ 11.801 Preaward in-use evaluation.

Supplies may be evaluated under comparable in-use conditions without a further test plan, provided offerors are so advised in the solicitation. The results of such tests or demonstrations may be used to rate the proposal, to determine technical acceptability, or otherwise to evaluate the proposal (see 15.305).

United States Code Annotated

Contracts, planning, solicitation, evaluation, and award procedures, see 10 USCA § 2305.

Definitions, see 10 USCA § 2302, 41 USCA §§ 259, 403.

Planning and solicitation requirements, see 41 USCA § 253a.

Preference for acquisition of commercial items, see 10 USCA § 2377, 41 USCA § 264b.

Simplified acquisition procedures, see 41 USCA § 427.

PART 12 ACQUISITION OF COMMERCIAL ITEMS

Subpart 12.5 Applicability of Certain Laws to the Acquisition of Commercial Items and Commercially Available Off-The-Shelf Items

§ 12.500 Scope of subpart.
§ 12.501 Applicability.
§ 12.502 Procedures.
§ 12.503 Applicability of certain laws to Executive agency contracts for the acquisition of commercial items.
§ 12.504 Applicability of certain laws to subcontracts for the acquisition of commercial items.
§ 12.505 Applicability of certain laws to contracts for the acquisition of COTS items.

Subpart 12.6 Streamlined Procedures for Evaluation and Solicitation for Commercial Items

§ 12.601 General.
§ 12.602 Streamlined evaluation of offers.
§ 12.603 Streamlined solicitation for commercial items.

§ 12.000 Scope of part.

This part prescribes policies and procedures unique to the acquisition of commercial items. It implements the Federal Government's preference for the acquisition of commercial items contained in 41 U.S.C. 1906, 1907, and 3307 and 10 U.S.C. 2375–2377 by establishing acquisition policies more closely resembling those of the commercial marketplace and encouraging the acquisition of commercial items and components.

United States Code Annotated

Administrative determinations, see 41 USCA § 257.

Commercially available off-the-shelf item acquisitions, lists of inapplicable laws in Federal Acquisition Regulation, see 41 USCA § 431.

Contract requirements, see 41 USCA § 254.

Contracts, planning, solicitation, evaluation, and award procedures, see 10 USCA § 2305.

Definitions, see 10 USCA § 2302, 41 USCA §§ 259, 403.

Definitions relating to procurement of commercial items, see 10 USCA § 2376, 41 USCA § 264a.

Determinations and decisions, see 10 USCA § 2310, 41 USCA § 262.

Evaluation and award, see 41 USCA § 253b.

Kinds of contracts, see 10 USCA § 2306.

List of laws inapplicable to procurements of commercial items in Federal Acquisition Regulation, see 41 USCA § 430.

Planning and solicitation requirements, see 41 USCA § 253a.

Preference for acquisition of commercial items, see 10 USCA § 2377, 41 USCA § 264b.

Relationship of commercial item provisions to other provisions of law, see 10 USCA § 2375, 41 USCA § 264.

Simplified acquisition procedures, see 41 USCA § 427.

§ 12.001 Definition.

"Subcontract," as used in this part, includes, but is not limited to, a transfer of commercial items between divisions, subsidiaries, or affiliates of a contractor or subcontractor.

United States Code Annotated

Administrative determinations, see 41 USCA § 257.

Commercially available off-the-shelf item acquisitions, lists of inapplicable laws in Federal Acquisition Regulation, see 41 USCA § 431.

Contract requirements, see 41 USCA § 254.

Contracts, planning, solicitation, evaluation, and award procedures, see 10 USCA § 2305.

Definitions, see 10 USCA § 2302, 41 USCA §§ 259, 403.

Definitions relating to procurement of commercial items, see 10 USCA § 2376, 41 USCA § 264a.

Determinations and decisions, see 10 USCA § 2310, 41 USCA § 262.

Evaluation and award, see 41 USCA § 253b.

Kinds of contracts, see 10 USCA § 2306.

List of laws inapplicable to procurements of commercial items in Federal Acquisition Regulation, see 41 USCA § 430.

Planning and solicitation requirements, see 41 USCA § 253a.

Preference for acquisition of commercial items, see 10 USCA § 2377, 41 USCA § 264b.

Relationship of commercial item provisions to other provisions of law, see 10 USCA § 2375, 41 USCA § 264.

Simplified acquisition procedures, see 41 USCA § 427.

Subpart 12.1 Acquisition of Commercial Items—General

§ 12.101 Policy.

Agencies shall—

(a) Conduct market research to determine whether commercial items or nondevelopmental items are available that could meet the agency's requirements;

(b) Acquire commercial items or nondevelopmental items when they are available to meet the needs of the agency; and

(c) Require prime contractors and subcontractors at all tiers to incorporate, to the maximum extent practicable, commercial items or nondevelopmental items as components of items supplied to the agency.

United States Code Annotated

Administrative determinations, see 41 USCA § 257.

Commercially available off-the-shelf item acquisitions, lists of inapplicable laws in Federal Acquisition Regulation, see 41 USCA § 431.

Contract requirements, see 41 USCA § 254.

Contracts, planning, solicitation, evaluation, and award procedures, see 10 USCA § 2305.

Definitions, see 10 USCA § 2302, 41 USCA §§ 259, 403.

Definitions relating to procurement of commercial items, see 10 USCA § 2376, 41 USCA § 264a.

Determinations and decisions, see 10 USCA § 2310, 41 USCA § 262.

Evaluation and award, see 41 USCA § 253b.

Kinds of contracts, see 10 USCA § 2306.

List of laws inapplicable to procurements of commercial items in Federal Acquisition Regulation, see 41 USCA § 430.

Planning and solicitation requirements, see 41 USCA § 253a.

Preference for acquisition of commercial items, see 10 USCA § 2377, 41 USCA § 264b.

Relationship of commercial item provisions to other provisions of law, see 10 USCA § 2375, 41 USCA § 264.

Simplified acquisition procedures, see 41 USCA § 427.

Notes of Decisions

In general 1

1 In general

Agencies are required to conduct market research pursuant to FAR part 10 to determine whether commercial items are available that could meet the agency's requirements. FAR 12.102(a). If through market research the agency determines that the government's needs can be met by an item customarily available in the commercial marketplace that meets the FAR § 2.101 definition of a commercial item, the agency is required to use the procedures in FAR part 12 to solicit and award any resultant contract. SHABA Contracting, B-287430, 2001 CPD ¶ 105, 2001 WL 695080 (Comp.Gen.), June 18, 2001.

Agency properly determined, based on market research, that helicopter services could be acquired under Federal Acquisition Regulation part 12 commercial item procedures because the services solicited are the type of services offered and sold competitively by the aviation industry in substantial quantities to commercial entities; none of the requirements pertaining to pilot and mechanic qualifications and invoicing, which were included in the solicitations, transformed the type of services sought here to something other than a commercial item. Crescent Helicopters, B-284734, 2000 CPD ¶ 90, 2000 WL 706977 (Comp.Gen.), May 30, 2000

§ 12.102 Applicability.

(a) This part shall be used for the acquisition of supplies or services that meet the definition of commercial items at 2.101.

(b) Contracting officers shall use the policies in this part in conjunction with the policies and procedures for solicitation, evaluation and award prescribed in Part 13, Simplified Acquisition Procedures; Part 14, Sealed Bidding; or Part 15, Contracting by Negotiation, as appropriate for the particular acquisition.

(c) Contracts for the acquisition of commercial items are subject to the policies in other parts of the FAR. When a policy in another part of the FAR is inconsistent with a policy in this part, this part 12 shall take precedence for the acquisition of commercial items.

(d) The definition of commercial item in section 2.101 uses the phrase "purposes other than governmental purposes." These purposes are those that are not unique to a government.

(e) This part shall not apply to the acquisition of commercial items—

(1) At or below the micro-purchase threshold;

(2) Using the Standard Form 44 (see 13.306);

(3) Using the imprest fund (see 13.305);

(4) Using the Governmentwide commercial purchase card as a method of purchase rather than only as a method of payment; or

(5) Directly from another Federal agency.

(f) (1) Contracting officers may treat any acquisition of supplies or services that, as determined by the head of the agency, are to be used to facilitate defense against or recovery from nuclear, biological, chemical, or radiological attack, as an acquisition of commercial items.

(2) A contract in an amount greater than $19 million that is awarded on a sole source basis for an item or service treated as a commercial item under paragraph (f)(1) of this section but does not meet the definition of a commercial item as defined at FAR 2.101 shall not be exempt from—

(i) Cost accounting standards (see subpart 30.2); or

(ii) Certified cost or pricing data requirements (see 15.403).

(g) (1) In accordance with 41 U.S.C. 2310, the contracting officer also may use Part 12 for any acquisition for services that does not meet the definition of commercial item in FAR 2.101, if the contract or task order—

(i) Is entered into on or before November 24, 2013;

(ii) Has a value of $29.5 million or less;

(iii) Meets the definition of performance-based acquisition at FAR 2.101;

(iv) Uses a quality assurance surveillance plan;

(v) Includes performance incentives where appropriate;

(vi) Specifies a firm-fixed price for specific tasks to be performed or outcomes to be achieved; and

(vii) Is awarded to an entity that provides similar services to the general public under terms and conditions similar to those in the contract or task order.

(2) In exercising the authority specified in paragraph (g)(1) of this section, the contracting officer may tailor paragraph (a) of the clause at FAR 52.212-4 as may be necessary to ensure the contract's remedies adequately protect the Government's interests.

Notes of Decisions

Commercial item 1
Mandatory use of Part 12 procedures 2

1 Commercial item

The FAR definition of commercial item speaks in terms of services of a 'type' offered and sold in the commercial marketplace under standard commercial terms and conditions; it does not require that the services be identical to what offerors provide their commercial customers." Cresent Helicopters, B-284706, 2000 CPD ¶ 90 (Comp. Gen. 2000).

2 Mandatory use of Part 12 procedures

Army violated a procurement statute requiring that offerors of commercial items have an opportunity to compete in any procurement by issuing a solicitation for a contract to develop an intelligence software system, where Army was on notice that contractor offered a realistic, commercially available alternative product, but it failed in its market research report to fully consider its potential commercial options before pursuing a developmental only procurement. Palantir USG, Inc. v. U.S., 129 Fed.Cl. 218 (2016)

§ 12.103 Commercially available off-the-shelf (COTS) items.

Commercially available off-the-shelf (COTS) items are defined in 2.101. Unless indicated otherwise, all of the policies that apply to commercial items also apply to COTS items. Section 12.505 lists the laws that are not applicable to COTS (in addition to 12.503 and 12.504).

Subpart 12.2 Special Requirements for the Acquisition of Commercial Items

§ 12.201 General.

This subpart identifies special requirements for the acquisition of commercial items intended to more closely resemble those customarily used in the commercial marketplace, as well as other considerations necessary for proper planning, solicitation, evaluation, and award of contracts for commercial items.

United States Code Annotated

Administrative determinations, see 41 USCA § 257.

Commercially available off-the-shelf item acquisitions, lists of inapplicable laws in Federal Acquisition Regulation, see 41 USCA § 431.

Contract requirements, see 41 USCA § 254.

Contracts, planning, solicitation, evaluation, and award procedures, see 10 USCA § 2305.

Definitions, see 10 USCA § 2302, 41 USCA §§ 259, 403.

Definitions relating to procurement of commercial items, see 10 USCA § 2376, 41 USCA § 264a.

Determinations and decisions, see 10 USCA § 2310, 41 USCA § 262.

Evaluation and award, see 41 USCA § 253b.

Kinds of contracts, see 10 USCA § 2306.

List of laws inapplicable to procurements of commercial items in Federal Acquisition Regulation, see 41 USCA § 430.

Planning and solicitation requirements, see 41 USCA § 253a.

Preference for acquisition of commercial items, see 10 USCA § 2377, 41 USCA § 264b.

Relationship of commercial item provisions to other provisions of law, see 10 USCA § 2375, 41 USCA § 264.

Simplified acquisition procedures, see 41 USCA § 427.

Notes of Decisions
Effect of regulations 1

1 Effect of regulations

Regulations governing acquisition of commercial items by federal agencies do not create rule of substantive law requiring liquidated damages clause to be struck down unless liquidated damages rate is specially tailored to particular contract in advance, but merely recognize that a court may refuse to enforce liquidated damages clause if liquidated damages amount or rate is shown not to be reasonably related to actual damages that promisee could suffer as result of breach and advise that care should be taken to ensure that rate or amount is not unreasonable in light of possible actual damages that could flow from breach. 48 C.F.R. § 12.202(b). DJ Mfg. Corp. v. U.S., 86 F.3d 1130, 40 Cont. Cas. Fed. (CCH) P 76963 (Fed. Cir. 1996). Damages ☞80(1)

§ 12.202 Market research and description of agency need.

(a) Market research (see 10.001) is an essential element of building an effective strategy for the acquisition of commercial items and establishes the foundation for the agency description of need (see Part 11), the solicitation, and resulting contract.

(b) The description of agency need must contain sufficient detail for potential offerors of commercial items to know which commercial products or services may be suitable. Generally, for acquisitions in excess of the simplified acquisition threshold, an agency's statement of need for a commercial item will describe the type of product or service to be acquired and explain how the agency intends to use the product or service in terms of function to be performed, performance requirement or essential physical characteristics. Describing the agency's needs in these terms allows offerors to propose methods that will best meet the needs of the Government.

(c) Follow the procedures in Subpart 11.2 regarding the identification and availability of specifications, standards and commercial item descriptions.

(d) Requirements documents for electronic and information technology must comply with the applicable accessibility standards issued by the Architectural and Transportation Barriers Compliance Board at 36 CFR Part 1194 (see Subpart 39.2).

(e) When acquiring information technology using Internet Protocol, agencies must include the appropriate Internet Protocol compliance requirements in accordance with 11.002(g).

United States Code Annotated

Administrative determinations, see 41 USCA § 257.

Commercially available off-the-shelf item acquisitions, lists of inapplicable laws in Federal Acquisition Regulation, see 41 USCA § 431.

Contract requirements, see 41 USCA § 254.

Contracts, planning, solicitation, evaluation, and award procedures, see 10 USCA § 2305.

Definitions, see 10 USCA § 2302, 41 USCA §§ 259, 403.

Definitions relating to procurement of commercial items, see 10 USCA § 2376, 41 USCA § 264a.

Determinations and decisions, see 10 USCA § 2310, 41 USCA § 262.

Evaluation and award, see 41 USCA § 253b.

Kinds of contracts, see 10 USCA § 2306.

List of laws inapplicable to procurements of commercial items in Federal Acquisition Regulation, see 41 USCA § 430.

Planning and solicitation requirements, see 41 USCA § 253a.

Preference for acquisition of commercial items, see 10 USCA § 2377, 41 USCA § 264b.

Relationship of commercial item provisions to other provisions of law, see 10 USCA § 2375, 41 USCA § 264.

Simplified acquisition procedures, see 41 USCA § 427.

Notes of Decisions
Commerciality determination 1
Description of requirement 2

1 Commerciality determination

Determining whether a particular service is a commercial item is a determination largely within the agency's discretion, which will not be disturbed by our Office, unless it is shown to be unreasonable. Agencies are required to conduct market research pursuant to FAR part 10 to determine whether commercial items are available that could meet the agency's requirements. FAR § 12.101(a). If through market research the agency determines that the government's needs can be met by an item customarily available in the commercial marketplace that meets the FAR § 2.101 definition of a commercial item, the agency is required to use the procedures in FAR part 12 to solicit and award any resultant contract. SHABA Contracting, B-287430, 2001 CPD ¶ 105 (Comp. Gen. 2001)

Agency properly determined, based on market research, that helicopter services could be acquired under Federal Acquisition Regulation part 12 commercial item procedures because the services solicited are the type of services offered and sold competitively by the aviation industry in substantial quantities to commercial entities; none of the requirements pertaining to pilot and mechanic qualifications and invoicing, which were included in the solicitations, transformed the type of services sought here to something other than a commercial item. Crescent Helicopters, B-284706, B-284707, B-284734, B-284735, 2000 CPD ¶ 90 (Comp. Gen. 2000)

Agency properly determined, based on market research, that household goods moving services for military personnel could be acquired under Federal Acquisition Regulation part 12 commercial item procedures, notwithstanding the inclusion of government-unique requirements in the solicitation that are not present in commercial contracts for moving services. Aalco Forwarding, Inc., et al., B-277241, B-277241.8, B-277241.9, 97-2 CPD ¶ 110 (Comp. Gen. 1997)

2 Description of requirement

The clear implication in the FAR is that the VA, by choosing to acquire an item by using commercial items acquisition procedures forgoes the option to include detailed design or performance specifications and, instead, is to rely on the marketplace to meet its needs. In re Fischer Imaging Corp., V.A.B.C.A. No. 6125, V.A.B.C.A. No. 6126, V.A.B.C.A. No. 6127, 02-2 B.C.A. (CCH) ¶ 32003, 2002 WL 31057467 (Veterans Admin. B.C.A. 2002),

Pursuant to the Competition in Contracting Act, government is required to specify its needs and solicit proposals "in a manner designed to achieve full and open competition for the procurement," and fact that the procurement is a commercial item acquisition does not relieve government of such obligation. 10 U.S.C.A. § 2305(a)(1)(A)(i). Candle Corp. v. U.S., 40 Fed. Cl. 658, 42 Cont. Cas. Fed. (CCH) P 77276 (1998). United States ⊗64.10

Acquisitions conducted under FAR Parts 12 and 13 are not exempt from the requirement for the agency to identify salient characteristics of an item described in a brand name or equal specification. A brand name or equal RFQ is defective because it did not list salient characteristics, so that quoters offering equal products were left to guess at the desired essential qualities of the brand-name item. Where an agency does not include a list of salient characteristics in the solicitation, it is precluded from rejecting a quote offering an equal product for noncompliance with some performance or design feature, unless the offered item is significantly different from the brand-name product. Elementar Americas, Inc., B-289115, 2002 CPD ¶ 20 (Comp. Gen. 2002)

The protester challenged the agency's method for describing its software needs because the agency listed the critical functional requirements for the software in the RFP and did not name the commercially available software which the agency learned as part of its market research efforts would satisfy the RFP requirements. GAO disagreed and held that "there is no requirement that the agency, in defining its needs for commercial items, do so by listing commercial brand names. Rather, FAR 11.002(a)(2)(i) authorizes an agency to describe its needs for commercial supplies or services in terms of functions to be performed, performance required, or essential physical characteristics. Omega World Travel, Inc., B-280456, B-280456.2, 98-2 CPD ¶ 73 (Comp. Gen. 1998).

Although Federal Acquisition Regulation (FAR) Part 12, dealing with purchases of commercial products, permits requirements to be stated in broad functional or performance terms instead of in detailed specifications, it requires a contracting agency to describe its need for commercial items in "sufficient detail for potential offerors of commercial items to know which commercial products or services to offer," such that a solicitation is flawed where it does not include sufficient information to allow commercial vendors to understand the agency's requirements. National Aeronautics and Space Administration— Reconsideration and Modification of Remedy, B-274748, B-274748.3, 97-1 CPD ¶ 159 (Comp. Gen. 1997)

Protest of rejection of equal products offered in response to a brand name or equal procurement for commercial items is sustained where rejection was based on failure of proposal to meet requirements that were not conveyed by the solicitation. Access Logic, Inc., B-274748, B-274748.2, 97-1 CPD ¶ 36 (Comp. Gen. 1997), on reconsideration, B-274748, B-274748.3, 97-1 CPD ¶ 159 (Comp. Gen. 1997)

§ 12.203 Procedures for solicitation, evaluation, and award.

Contracting officers shall use the policies unique to the acquisition of commercial items prescribed in this part in conjunction with the policies and procedures for solicitation, evaluation and award prescribed in Part 13, Simplified Acquisition Procedures; Part 14, Sealed Bidding; or Part 15, Contracting by Negotiation, as appropriate for the particular acquisition. The contracting officer may use the streamlined procedure for soliciting offers for commercial items prescribed in 12.603. For acquisitions of commercial items exceeding the simplified acquisition threshold but not exceeding $7 million ($13 million for acquisitions as described in 13.500(c)), including options, contracting activities may use any of the simplified procedures authorized by subpart 13.5.

United States Code Annotated

Administrative determinations, see 41 USCA § 257.

Commercially available off-the-shelf item acquisitions, lists of inapplicable laws in Federal Acquisition Regulation, see 41 USCA § 431.

Contract requirements, see 41 USCA § 254.

Contracts, planning, solicitation, evaluation, and award procedures, see 10 USCA § 2305.

Definitions, see 10 USCA § 2302, 41 USCA §§ 259, 403.

Definitions relating to procurement of commercial items, see 10 USCA § 2376, 41 USCA § 264a.

Determinations and decisions, see 10 USCA § 2310, 41 USCA § 262.

Evaluation and award, see 41 USCA § 253b.

Kinds of contracts, see 10 USCA § 2306.

List of laws inapplicable to procurements of commercial items in Federal Acquisition Regulation, see 41 USCA § 430.

Planning and solicitation requirements, see 41 USCA § 253a.

Preference for acquisition of commercial items, see 10 USCA § 2377, 41 USCA § 264b.

Relationship of commercial item provisions to other provisions of law, see 10 USCA § 2375, 41 USCA § 264.

Simplified acquisition procedures, see 41 USCA § 427.

Notes of Decisions

In general 1
Injunctions 2

1 In general

Bid on solicitation for radar test system for the Army was non-responsive, where solicitation required standard commercial warranty, but bid refused to warrant performance if the hardware, software, or firmware was modified by anyone but bidder without its concurrence. Tel-Instrument Electronics Corp. v. U.S., 56 Fed. Cl. 174 (2003), aff'd, 87 Fed. Appx. 752 (Fed. Cir. 2004). United States ☞64.30

Pursuant to the Competition in Contracting Act, government is required to specify its needs and solicit proposals "in a manner designed to achieve full and open competition for the procurement," and fact that the procurement is a commercial item acquisition does not relieve government of such obligation. 10 U.S.C.A. § 2305(a)(1)(A)(i). Candle Corp. v. U.S., 40 Fed. Cl. 658, 42 Cont. Cas. Fed. (CCH) P 77276 (1998). United States ☞64.10

2 Injunctions

Pre-award bid protestor was not entitled to preliminary injunction enjoining contracting agency from accepting final proposal revisions and directing it to re-evaluate all offers in competitive range; plaintiff did not demonstrate that it was likely to succeed on the merits of its claim that agency acted arbitrarily, capriciously, or contrary to law in conducting the solicitation, and did not allege extraordinary injury. Seaborn Health Care, Inc. v. U.S., 55 Fed. Cl. 520 (2003). Injunction ☞138.63

§ 12.204 Solicitation/contract form.

(a) The contracting officer shall use the Standard Form 1449, Solicitation/Contract/Order for Commercial Items, if (1) the acquisition is expected to exceed the simplified acquisition threshold; (2) a paper solicitation or contract is being issued; and (3) procedures at 12.603 are not being used. Use of the SF 1449 is nonmandatory but encouraged for commercial acquisitions not exceeding the simplified acquisition threshold.

(b) Consistent with the requirements at 5.203(a) and (h), the contracting officer may allow fewer than 15 days before issuance of the solicitation.

United States Code Annotated

Administrative determinations, see 41 USCA § 257.

Commercially available off-the-shelf item acquisitions, lists of inapplicable laws in Federal Acquisition Regulation, see 41 USCA § 431.

Contract requirements, see 41 USCA § 254.

Contracts, planning, solicitation, evaluation, and award procedures, see 10 USCA § 2305.

Definitions, see 10 USCA § 2302, 41 USCA §§ 259, 403.

Definitions relating to procurement of commercial items, see 10 USCA § 2376, 41 USCA § 264a.

Determinations and decisions, see 10 USCA § 2310, 41 USCA § 262.

Evaluation and award, see 41 USCA § 253b.

Kinds of contracts, see 10 USCA § 2306.

List of laws inapplicable to procurements of commercial items in Federal Acquisition Regulation, see 41 USCA § 430.

Planning and solicitation requirements, see 41 USCA § 253a.

Preference for acquisition of commercial items, see 10 USCA § 2377, 41 USCA § 264b.

Relationship of commercial item provisions to other provisions of law, see 10 USCA § 2375, 41 USCA § 264.

Simplified acquisition procedures, see 41 USCA § 427.

§ 12.205 Offers.

(a) Where technical information is necessary for evaluation of offers, agencies should, as part of market research, review existing product literature generally available in the industry to determine its adequacy for purposes of evaluation. If adequate, contracting officers shall request existing product literature from offerors of commercial items in lieu of unique technical proposals.

(b) Contracting officers should allow offerors to propose more than one product that will meet a Government need in response to solicitations for commercial items. The contracting officer shall evaluate each product as a separate offer.

(c) Consistent with the requirements at 5.203(b), the contracting officer may allow fewer than 30 days response time for receipt of offers for commercial items, unless the acquisition is covered by the World Trade Organization Government Procurement Agreement or a Free Trade Agreement (see 5.203(h)).

United States Code Annotated

Administrative determinations, see 41 USCA § 257.

Commercially available off-the-shelf item acquisitions, lists of inapplicable laws in Federal Acquisition Regulation, see 41 USCA § 431.

Contract requirements, see 41 USCA § 254.

Contracts, planning, solicitation, evaluation, and award procedures, see 10 USCA § 2305.

Definitions, see 10 USCA § 2302, 41 USCA §§ 259, 403.

Definitions relating to procurement of commercial items, see 10 USCA § 2376, 41 USCA § 264a.

Determinations and decisions, see 10 USCA § 2310, 41 USCA § 262.

Evaluation and award, see 41 USCA § 253b.

Kinds of contracts, see 10 USCA § 2306.

List of laws inapplicable to procurements of commercial items in Federal Acquisition Regulation, see 41 USCA § 430.

Planning and solicitation requirements, see 41 USCA § 253a.

Preference for acquisition of commercial items, see 10 USCA § 2377, 41 USCA § 264b.

Relationship of commercial item provisions to other provisions of law, see 10 USCA § 2375, 41 USCA § 264.

Simplified acquisition procedures, see 41 USCA § 427.

Notes of Decisions

Responsiveness 1
Time to respond 2

1 Responsiveness

Bid on solicitation for radar test system for the Army was non-responsive, where solicitation required standard commercial warranty, but bid refused to warrant performance if the hardware, software, or firmware was modified by anyone but bidder without its concurrence. Tel-Instrument Electronics Corp. v. U.S., 56 Fed. Cl. 174 (2003), aff'd, 87 Fed. Appx. 752 (Fed. Cir. 2004). United States ⚯64.30

2 Time to respond

Agency may allow fewer than 30 days to respond to an RFP when it is acquiring commercial items. FAR § 12.205(c). When acquiring commercial items, the contracting officer should afford potential offerors a reasonable opportunity to respond; when establishing the solicitation response time, the contracting officer should consider the complexity, commerciality, availability, and urgency of the acquisition. Contracting officer's decision to specify a 15-day response period was reasonable because it was based on prior year's procurement for a more complex requirement, which resulted in adequate competition and no complaints from offerors. American Artisan Productions, Inc., B-281409, 98-2 CPD ¶ 155 (Comp. Gen. 1998)

§ 12.206 Use of past performance.

Past performance should be an important element of every evaluation and contract award for commercial items. Contracting officers should consider past performance data from a wide variety of sources both inside and outside the Federal Government in accordance with the policies and procedures contained in Subpart 9.1, 13.106, or Subpart 15.3, as applicable.

United States Code Annotated

Administrative determinations, see 41 USCA § 257.

Commercially available off-the-shelf item acquisitions, lists of inapplicable laws in Federal Acquisition Regulation, see 41 USCA § 431.

Contract requirements, see 41 USCA § 254.

Contracts, planning, solicitation, evaluation, and award procedures, see 10 USCA § 2305.

Definitions, see 10 USCA § 2302, 41 USCA §§ 259, 403.

Definitions relating to procurement of commercial items, see 10 USCA § 2376, 41 USCA § 264a.

Determinations and decisions, see 10 USCA § 2310, 41 USCA § 262.

Evaluation and award, see 41 USCA § 253b.

Kinds of contracts, see 10 USCA § 2306.

List of laws inapplicable to procurements of commercial items in Federal Acquisition

Regulation, see 41 USCA § 430.

Planning and solicitation requirements, see 41 USCA § 253a.

Preference for acquisition of commercial items, see 10 USCA § 2377, 41 USCA § 264b.

Relationship of commercial item provisions to other provisions of law, see 10 USCA § 2375, 41 USCA § 264.

Simplified acquisition procedures, see 41 USCA § 427.

Notes of Decisions

In general 1

1 In general

Protester's contention that an agency's decision to assign a weight of 5 percent to a solicitation's past performance evaluation factor violates FAR § 12.206 (providing that past performance should be an important element of every evaluation) is denied as the FAR provision is discretionary, not mandatory. Finlen Complex, Inc., B-288280, 2001 CPD ¶ 167 (Comp. Gen. 2001).

§ 12.207 Contract type.

(a) Except as provided in paragraph (b) of this section, agencies shall use firm-fixed-price contracts or fixed-price contracts with economic price adjustment for the acquisition of commercial items.

(b)

(1) A time-and-materials contract or labor-hour contract (see Subpart 16.6) may be used for the acquisition of commercial services when—

(i) The service is acquired under a contract awarded using—

(A) Competitive procedures (e.g., the procedures in 6.102, the set-aside procedures in Subpart 19.5, or competition conducted in accordance with Part 13);

(B) The procedures for other than full and open competition in 6.3 provided the agency receives offers that satisfy the Government's expressed requirement from two or more responsible offerors; or

(C) The fair opportunity procedures in 16.505 (including discretionary small business set-asides under 16.505(b)(2)(i)(F)), if placing an order under a multiple-award delivery-order contract; and

(ii) The contracting officer—

(A) Executes a determination and findings (D&F) for the contract, in accordance with paragraph (b)(2) of this section (but see paragraph (c) of this section for indefinite-delivery contracts), that no other contract type authorized by this subpart is suitable;

(B) Includes a ceiling price in the contract or order that the contractor exceeds at its own risk; and

(C) Prior to increasing the ceiling price of a time-and-materials or labor-hour contract or order, shall—

(1) Conduct an analysis of pricing and other relevant factors to determine if the action is in the best interest of the Government;

(2) Document the decision in the contract or order file; and

(3) When making a change that modifies the general scope of—

(i) A contract, follow the procedures at 6.303;

(ii) An order issued under the Federal Supply Schedules, follow the procedures at 8.405-6; or

(iii) An order issued under multiple award task and delivery order contracts, follow the procedures at 16.505(b)(2).

(2) Each D&F required by paragraph (b)(1)(ii)(A) of this section shall contain sufficient facts and rationale to justify that no other contract type authorized by this subpart is suitable. At a minimum, the D&F shall—

(i) Include a description of the market research conducted (see 10.002(e));

(ii) Establish that it is not possible at the time of placing the contract or order to accurately estimate the extent or duration of the work or to anticipate costs with any reasonable degree of confidence;

(iii) Establish that the requirement has been structured to maximize the use of firm-fixed-price or fixed-price with economic price adjustment contracts (*e.g.*, by limiting the value or length of the time-and-material/labor-hour contract or order; establishing fixed prices for portions of the requirement) on future acquisitions for the same or similar requirements; and

(iv) Describe actions planned to maximize the use of firm-fixed-price or fixed-price with economic price adjustment contracts on future acquisitions for the same requirements.

(3) See 16.601(d)(1) for additional approval required for contracts expected to extend beyond three years.

(4) See 8.404(h) for the requirement for determination and findings when using Federal Supply Schedules.

(c) (1) Indefinite-delivery contracts (see Subpart 16.5) may be used when—

(i) The prices are established based on a firm-fixed-price or fixed-price with economic price adjustment; or

(ii) Rates are established for commercial services acquired on a time-and-materials or labor-hour basis.

(2) When an indefinite-delivery contract is awarded with services priced on a time-and-materials or labor-hour basis, contracting officers shall, to the maximum extent practicable, also structure the contract to allow issuance of orders on a firm-fixed-price or fixed-price with economic price adjustment basis. For such contracts, the contracting officer shall execute the D&F required by paragraph (b)(2) of this section, for each order placed on a time-and-materials or labor-hour basis. Placement of orders shall be in accordance with Subpart 8.4 or 16.5, as applicable.

(3) If an indefinite-delivery contract only allows for the issuance of orders on a time-and-materials or labor-hour basis, the D&F required by paragraph (b)(2) of this section shall be executed to support the basic contract and shall also explain why providing for an alternative firm-fixed-price or fixed-price with economic price adjustment pricing structure is not practicable. The D&F for this contract shall be approved one level above the contracting officer. Placement of orders shall be in accordance with Subpart 16.5.

(d) The contract types authorized by this subpart may be used in conjunction with an award fee and performance or delivery incentives when the award fee or incentive is based solely on factors other than cost (see 16.202-1 and 16.203-1).

(e) Use of any contract type other than those authorized by this subpart to acquire commercial items is prohibited.

United States Code Annotated

Administrative determinations, see 41 USCA § 257.

Commercially available off-the-shelf item acquisitions, lists of inapplicable laws in Federal Acquisition Regulation, see 41 USCA § 431.

Contract requirements, see 41 USCA § 254.

Contracts, planning, solicitation, evaluation, and award procedures, see 10 USCA § 2305.

Definitions, see 10 USCA § 2302, 41 USCA §§ 259, 403.

Definitions relating to procurement of commercial items, see 10 USCA § 2376, 41 USCA § 264a.

Determinations and decisions, see 10 USCA § 2310, 41 USCA § 262.

Evaluation and award, see 41 USCA § 253b.

Kinds of contracts, see 10 USCA § 2306.

List of laws inapplicable to procurements of commercial items in Federal Acquisition Regulation, see 41 USCA § 430.

Planning and solicitation requirements, see 41 USCA § 253a.

Preference for acquisition of commercial items, see 10 USCA § 2377, 41 USCA § 264b.

Relationship of commercial item provisions to other provisions of law, see 10 USCA § 2375, 41 USCA § 264.

Simplified acquisition procedures, see 41 USCA § 427.

§ 12.208 Contract quality assurance.

Contracts for commercial items shall rely on contractors' existing quality assurance systems as a substitute for Government inspection and testing before tender for acceptance unless customary market practices for the commercial item being acquired include in-process inspection. Any in-process inspection by the Government shall be conducted in a manner consistent with commercial practice.

United States Code Annotated

Administrative determinations, see 41 USCA § 257.

Commercially available off-the-shelf item acquisitions, lists of inapplicable laws in Federal Acquisition Regulation, see 41 USCA § 431.

Contract requirements, see 41 USCA § 254.

Contracts, planning, solicitation, evaluation, and award procedures, see 10 USCA § 2305.

Definitions, see 10 USCA § 2302, 41 USCA §§ 259, 403.

Definitions relating to procurement of commercial items, see 10 USCA § 2376, 41 USCA § 264a.

Determinations and decisions, see 10 USCA § 2310, 41 USCA § 262.

Evaluation and award, see 41 USCA § 253b.

Kinds of contracts, see 10 USCA § 2306.

List of laws inapplicable to procurements of commercial items in Federal Acquisition Regulation, see 41 USCA § 430.

Planning and solicitation requirements, see 41 USCA § 253a.

Preference for acquisition of commercial items, see 10 USCA § 2377, 41 USCA § 264b.

Relationship of commercial item provisions to other provisions of law, see 10 USCA § 2375, 41 USCA § 264.

Simplified acquisition procedures, see 41 USCA § 427.

§ 12.209 Determination of price reasonableness.

While the contracting officer must establish price reasonableness in accordance with 13. 106-3, 14.408-2, or Subpart 15.4, as applicable, the contracting officer should be aware of customary commercial terms and conditions when pricing commercial items. Commercial item prices are affected by factors that include, but are not limited to, speed of delivery, length and extent of warranty, limitations of seller's liability, quantities ordered, length of the performance period, and specific performance requirements. The contracting officer must ensure that contract terms, conditions, and prices are commensurate with the Government's need.

United States Code Annotated

Administrative determinations, see 41 USCA § 257.

Commercially available off-the-shelf item acquisitions, lists of inapplicable laws in Federal Acquisition Regulation, see 41 USCA § 431.

Contract requirements, see 41 USCA § 254.

Contracts, planning, solicitation, evaluation, and award procedures, see 10 USCA § 2305.

Definitions, see 10 USCA § 2302, 41 USCA §§ 259, 403.

Definitions relating to procurement of commercial items, see 10 USCA § 2376, 41 USCA § 264a.

Determinations and decisions, see 10 USCA § 2310, 41 USCA § 262.

Evaluation and award, see 41 USCA § 253b.

Kinds of contracts, see 10 USCA § 2306.

List of laws inapplicable to procurements of commercial items in Federal Acquisition Regulation, see 41 USCA § 430.

Planning and solicitation requirements, see 41 USCA § 253a.

Preference for acquisition of commercial items, see 10 USCA § 2377, 41 USCA § 264b.

Relationship of commercial item provisions to other provisions of law, see 10 USCA § 2375, 41 USCA § 264.

Simplified acquisition procedures, see 41 USCA § 427.

§ 12.210 Contract financing.

Customary market practice for some commercial items may include buyer contract financing. The contracting officer may offer Government financing in accordance with the policies and procedures in Part 32.

United States Code Annotated

Administrative determinations, see 41 USCA § 257.

Commercially available off-the-shelf item acquisitions, lists of inapplicable laws in Federal Acquisition Regulation, see 41 USCA § 431.

Contract requirements, see 41 USCA § 254.

Contracts, planning, solicitation, evaluation, and award procedures, see 10 USCA § 2305.

Definitions, see 10 USCA § 2302, 41 USCA §§ 259, 403.

Definitions relating to procurement of commercial items, see 10 USCA § 2376, 41 USCA § 264a.

Determinations and decisions, see 10 USCA § 2310, 41 USCA § 262.

Evaluation and award, see 41 USCA § 253b.

Kinds of contracts, see 10 USCA § 2306.

List of laws inapplicable to procurements of commercial items in Federal Acquisition Regulation, see 41 USCA § 430.

Planning and solicitation requirements, see 41 USCA § 253a.

Preference for acquisition of commercial items, see 10 USCA § 2377, 41 USCA § 264b.

Relationship of commercial item provisions to other provisions of law, see 10 USCA § 2375, 41 USCA § 264.

Simplified acquisition procedures, see 41 USCA § 427.

§ 12.211 Technical data.

Except as provided by agency-specific statutes, the Government shall acquire only the technical data and the rights in that data customarily provided to the public with a commercial item or process. The contracting officer shall presume that data delivered under a contract for commercial items was developed exclusively at private expense. When a contract for commercial items requires the delivery of technical data, the contracting officer shall include appropriate provisions and clauses delineating the rights in the technical data in addenda to the solicitation and contract (see Part 27 or agency FAR supplements).

United States Code Annotated

Administrative determinations, see 41 USCA § 257.

Commercially available off-the-shelf item acquisitions, lists of inapplicable laws in Federal Acquisition Regulation, see 41 USCA § 431.

Contract requirements, see 41 USCA § 254.

Contracts, planning, solicitation, evaluation, and award procedures, see 10 USCA § 2305.

Definitions, see 10 USCA § 2302, 41 USCA §§ 259, 403.

Definitions relating to procurement of commercial items, see 10 USCA § 2376, 41 USCA § 264a.

Determinations and decisions, see 10 USCA § 2310, 41 USCA § 262.

Evaluation and award, see 41 USCA § 253b.

Kinds of contracts, see 10 USCA § 2306.

List of laws inapplicable to procurements of commercial items in Federal Acquisition Regulation, see 41 USCA § 430.

Planning and solicitation requirements, see 41 USCA § 253a.

Preference for acquisition of commercial items, see 10 USCA § 2377, 41 USCA § 264b.

Relationship of commercial item provisions to other provisions of law, see 10 USCA § 2375, 41 USCA § 264.

Simplified acquisition procedures, see 41 USCA § 427.

§ 12.212 Computer software.

(a) Commercial computer software or commercial computer software documentation shall be acquired under licenses customarily provided to the public to the extent such licenses are consistent with Federal law and otherwise satisfy the Government's needs. Generally, offerors and contractors shall not be required to—

(1) Furnish technical information related to commercial computer software or commercial computer software documentation that is not customarily provided to the public; or

(2) Relinquish to, or otherwise provide, the Government rights to use, modify, reproduce, release, perform, display, or disclose commercial computer software or commercial computer software documentation except as mutually agreed to by the parties.

(b) With regard to commercial computer software and commercial computer software documentation, the Government shall have only those rights specified in the license contained in any addendum to the contract. For additional guidance regarding the use and negotiation of license agreements for commercial computer software, see 27.405-3.

United States Code Annotated

Administrative determinations, see 41 USCA § 257.

Commercially available off-the-shelf item acquisitions, lists of inapplicable laws in Federal Acquisition Regulation, see 41 USCA § 431.

Contract requirements, see 41 USCA § 254.

Contracts, planning, solicitation, evaluation, and award procedures, see 10 USCA § 2305.

Definitions, see 10 USCA § 2302, 41 USCA §§ 259, 403.

Definitions relating to procurement of commercial items, see 10 USCA § 2376, 41 USCA § 264a.

Determinations and decisions, see 10 USCA § 2310, 41 USCA § 262.

Evaluation and award, see 41 USCA § 253b.

Kinds of contracts, see 10 USCA § 2306.

List of laws inapplicable to procurements of commercial items in Federal Acquisition Regulation, see 41 USCA § 430.

Planning and solicitation requirements, see 41 USCA § 253a.

Preference for acquisition of commercial items, see 10 USCA § 2377, 41 USCA § 264b.

Relationship of commercial item provisions to other provisions of law, see 10 USCA § 2375, 41 USCA § 264.

Simplified acquisition procedures, see 41 USCA § 427.

§ 12.213 Other commercial practices.

It is a common practice in the commercial marketplace for both the buyer and seller to propose terms and conditions written from their particular perspectives. The terms and conditions prescribed in this part seek to balance the interests of both the buyer and seller. These terms and conditions are generally appropriate for use in a wide range of acquisitions. However, market research may indicate other commercial practices that are appropriate for the acquisition of the particular item. These practices should be considered for incorporation into the solicitation and contract if the contracting officer determines them appropriate in concluding a business arrangement satisfactory to both parties and not otherwise precluded by law or Executive order.

United States Code Annotated

Administrative determinations, see 41 USCA § 257.

Commercially available off-the-shelf item acquisitions, lists of inapplicable laws in Federal Acquisition Regulation, see 41 USCA § 431.

Contract requirements, see 41 USCA § 254.

Contracts, planning, solicitation, evaluation, and award procedures, see 10 USCA § 2305.

Definitions, see 10 USCA § 2302, 41 USCA §§ 259, 403.

Definitions relating to procurement of commercial items, see 10 USCA § 2376, 41 USCA § 264a.

Determinations and decisions, see 10 USCA § 2310, 41 USCA § 262.

Evaluation and award, see 41 USCA § 253b.

Kinds of contracts, see 10 USCA § 2306.

List of laws inapplicable to procurements of commercial items in Federal Acquisition Regulation, see 41 USCA § 430.

Planning and solicitation requirements, see 41 USCA § 253a.

Preference for acquisition of commercial items, see 10 USCA § 2377, 41 USCA § 264b.

Relationship of commercial item provisions to other provisions of law, see 10 USCA § 2375, 41 USCA § 264.

Simplified acquisition procedures, see 41 USCA § 427.

Notes of Decisions

In general 1

1 In general

FAR 12.213 provides that the contracting officer "should consider" commercial practices that might be suitable for incorporation into a solicitation. However, the regulation leaves it within the contracting officer's discretion to determine whether a commercial practice is "appropriate in concluding a business arrangement satisfactory to both parties . . . ." Although ownership costs may sometimes be evaluated in commercial buys, an agency may determine that evaluation of such costs is not appropriate due to the unavailability of reliable data for potential vendors' cost of equipment. NLB Corporation, B-286846, 2001 CPD ¶ 67 (Comp. Gen. 2001)

§ 12.214 Cost Accounting Standards.

Cost Accounting Standards (CAS) do not apply to contracts and subcontracts for the acquisition of commercial items when these contracts and subcontracts are firm-fixedprice or fixed-price with economic price adjustment (provided that the price adjustment is not based on actual costs incurred). See 30.201-1 for CAS applicability to fixed-price with economic price adjustment contracts and subcontracts for commercial items when the price adjustment is based on actual costs incurred. When CAS applies, the contracting officer shall insert the appropriate provisions and clauses as prescribed in 30.201.

United States Code Annotated

Administrative determinations, see 41 USCA § 257.

Commercially available off-the-shelf item acquisitions, lists of inapplicable laws in Federal Acquisition Regulation, see 41 USCA § 431.

Contract requirements, see 41 USCA § 254.

Contracts, planning, solicitation, evaluation, and award procedures, see 10 USCA § 2305.

Definitions, see 10 USCA § 2302, 41 USCA §§ 259, 403.

Definitions relating to procurement of commercial items, see 10 USCA § 2376, 41 USCA § 264a.

Determinations and decisions, see 10 USCA § 2310, 41 USCA § 262.

Evaluation and award, see 41 USCA § 253b.

Kinds of contracts, see 10 USCA § 2306.

List of laws inapplicable to procurements of commercial items in Federal Acquisition Regulation, see 41 USCA § 430.

Planning and solicitation requirements, see 41 USCA § 253a.

Preference for acquisition of commercial items, see 10 USCA § 2377, 41 USCA § 264b.

Relationship of commercial item provisions to other provisions of law, see 10 USCA § 2375, 41 USCA § 264.

Simplified acquisition procedures, see 41 USCA § 427.

§ 12.215 Notification of overpayment.

If the contractor notifies the contracting officer of a duplicate payment or that the Government has otherwise overpaid, the contracting officer shall follow the procedures at 32.604.

United States Code Annotated

Administrative determinations, see 41 USCA § 257.

Commercially available off-the-shelf item acquisitions, lists of inapplicable laws in Federal Acquisition Regulation, see 41 USCA § 431.

Contract requirements, see 41 USCA § 254.

Contracts, planning, solicitation, evaluation, and award procedures, see 10 USCA § 2305.

Definitions, see 10 USCA § 2302, 41 USCA §§ 259, 403.

Definitions relating to procurement of commercial items, see 10 USCA § 2376, 41 USCA § 264a.

Determinations and decisions, see 10 USCA § 2310, 41 USCA § 262.

Evaluation and award, see 41 USCA § 253b.

Kinds of contracts, see 10 USCA § 2306.

List of laws inapplicable to procurements of commercial items in Federal Acquisition Regulation, see 41 USCA § 430.

Planning and solicitation requirements, see 41 USCA § 253a.

Preference for acquisition of commercial items, see 10 USCA § 2377, 41 USCA § 264b.

Relationship of commercial item provisions to other provisions of law, see 10 USCA § 2375, 41 USCA § 264.

Simplified acquisition procedures, see 41 USCA § 427.

§ 12.216 Unenforceability of unauthorized obligations.

Many supplies or services are acquired subject to supplier license agreements. These are particularly common in information technology acquisitions, but they may apply to any supply or service. For example, computer software and services delivered through the internet (web services) are often subject to license agreements, referred to as End User License Agreements (EULA), Terms of Service (TOS), or other similar legal instruments or agreements. Many of these agreements contain indemnification clauses that are inconsistent with Federal law and unenforceable, but which could create a violation of the Anti-Deficiency Act (31 U.S.C. 1341) if agreed to by the Government. Paragraph (u) of the clause at 52.212-4 prevents any such violations.

Subpart 12.3 Solicitation Provisions and Contract Clauses for the Acquisition of Commercial Items

§ 12.300 Scope of subpart.

This subpart establishes provisions and clauses to be used when acquiring commercial items.

United States Code Annotated

Commercially available off-the-shelf item acquisitions, lists of inapplicable laws in Federal Acquisition Regulation, see 41 USCA § 431.

Contract requirements, see 41 USCA § 254.

Contracts, planning, solicitation, evaluation, and award procedures, see 10 USCA § 2305.

Definitions, see 10 USCA § 2302, 41 USCA §§ 259, 403.

Definitions relating to procurement of commercial items, see 10 USCA § 2376, 41 USCA § 264a.

Kinds of contracts, see 10 USCA § 2306.

List of laws inapplicable to procurements of commercial items in Federal Acquisition Regulation, see 41 USCA § 430.

Planning and solicitation requirements, see 41 USCA § 253a.

Preference for acquisition of commercial items, see 10 USCA § 2377, 41 USCA § 264b.

Relationship of commercial item provisions to other provisions of law, see 10 USCA § 2375, 41 USCA § 264.

Simplified acquisition procedures, see 41 USCA § 427.

§ 12.301 Solicitation provisions and contract clauses for the acquisition of commercial items.

(a) In accordance with 41 U.S.C. 3307, contracts for the acquisition of commercial items shall, to the maximum extent practicable, include only those clauses—

(1) Required to implement provisions of law or executive orders applicable to the acquisition of commercial items; or

(2) Determined to be consistent with customary commercial practice.

(b) Insert the following provisions in solicitations for the acquisition of commercial items, and clauses in solicitations and contracts for the acquisition of commercial items:

(1) The provision at, Instructions to Offerors—Commercial Items. This provision provides a single, streamlined set of instructions to be used when soliciting offers for commercial items and is incorporated in the solicitation by reference (see Block 27a, SF 1449). The contracting officer may tailor these instructions or provide additional instructions tailored to the specific acquisition in accordance with 12.302.

(2) The provision at 52.212-3, Offeror Representations and Certifications—Commercial Items. This provision provides a single, consolidated list of representations and certifications for the acquisition of commercial items and is attached to the solicitation for offerors to complete. This provision may not be tailored except in accordance with subpart 1.4. Use the provision with its Alternate I in solicitations issued by DoD, NASA, or the Coast Guard.

(3) The clause at 52.212-4, Contract Terms and Conditions—Commercial Items. This clause includes terms and conditions which are, to the maximum extent practicable, consistent with customary commercial practices and is incorporated in the solicitation and contract by reference (see Block 27, SF 1449). Use this clause with its Alternate I when a time-and-materials or labor-hour contract will be awarded. The contracting officer may tailor this clause in accordance with 12.302.

(4) The clause at 52.212-5, Contract Terms and Conditions Required to Implement Statutes or Executive Orders—Commercial Items. This clause incorporates by reference only those clauses required to implement provisions of law or Executive orders applicable to the acquisition of commercial items.The contracting officer shall attach this clause to the solicitation and contract and, using the appropriate clause prescriptions, indicate which, if any, of the additional clauses cited in 52.212-5(b) or (c) are applicable to the specific acquisition. Some of the clauses require fill-in; the fill-in language should be inserted as directed by 52.104(d). When cost information is obtained pursuant to Part 15 to establish the reasonableness of prices for commercial items, the contracting officer shall insert the clauses prescribed for this purpose in an addendum to the solicitation and contract. This clause may not be tailored.

(i) Use the clause with its Alternate I when the head of the agency has waived the examination of records by the Comptroller General in accordance with 25.1001.

(ii) (A) If the acquisition will use funds appropriated or otherwise made available by the American Recovery and Reinvestment Act of 2009 (Pub. L. 111-5), the contracting officer shall use the clause with its Alternate II.

(B)

(1) In the case of a bilateral contract modification that will use funds appropriated or otherwise made available by the American Recovery and Reinvestment Act of 2009, the contracting officer shall specify applicability of Alternate II to that modification.

(2) In the case of a task- or delivery-order contract in which not all orders will use funds appropriated or otherwise made available by the American Recovery and Reinvestment Act of 2009, the contracting officer shall specify the task or delivery orders to which Alternate II applies.

(C) The contracting officer may not use Alternate I when Alternate II applies.

(c) When the use of evaluation factors is appropriate, the contracting officer may—

(1) Insert the provision at 52.212-2, Evaluation—Commercial Items, in solicitations for commercial items (see 12.602); or

(2) Include a similar provision containing all evaluation factors required by 13.106, subpart 14.2 or subpart 15.3, as an addendum (see 12.302(d)).

(d) Other required provisions and clauses. Notwithstanding prescriptions contained elsewhere in the FAR, when acquiring commercial items, contracting officers shall be required to use only those provisions and clauses prescribed in this part. The provisions and clauses prescribed in this part shall be revised, as necessary, to reflect the applicability of statutes and executive orders to the acquisition of commercial items.

(1) Insert the provision at 52.204-16, Commercial and Government Entity Code Reporting, when there is a requirement to be registered in SAM or a requirement to have a DUNS Number in the solicitation.

(2) Insert the clause at 52.204-18, Commercial and Government Entity Code Maintenance, when there is a requirement to be registered in SAM or a requirement to have a DUNS Number in the solicitation.

(3) Insert the clause at 52.204-21, Basic Safeguarding of Covered Contractor Information Systems, in solicitations and contracts (except for acquisitions of COTS items), as prescribed in 4.1903.

(4) Insert the provision at 52.209-7, Information Regarding Responsibility Matters, as prescribed in 9.104-7(b).

(5) Insert the provision at 52.209-12, Certification Regarding Tax Matters, as prescribed at 9.104-7(e).

(6) Insert the provision at 52.222-56, Certification Regarding Trafficking in Persons Compliance Plan, in solicitations as prescribed at 22.1705(b).

(7) Insert the clause at 52.225-19, Contractor Personnel in a Designated Operational Area or Supporting a Diplomatic or Consular Mission outside the United States, as prescribed in 25.301-4.

(8) Insert the clause at 52.232-40, Providing Accelerated Payments to Small Business Subcontractors, as prescribed in 32.009-2.

(e) Discretionary use of FAR provisions and clauses. The contracting officer may include in solicitations and contracts by addendum other FAR provisions and clauses when their use is consistent with the limitations contained in 12.302. For example:

(1) The contracting officer may include appropriate clauses when an indefinite-delivery type of contract will be used. The clauses prescribed at 16.506 may be used for this purpose.

(2) The contracting officer may include appropriate provisions and clauses when the use of options is in the Government's interest. The provisions and clauses prescribed in 17.208 may be used for this purpose. If the provision at 52.212-2 is used, paragraph (b) provides for the evaluation of options.

(3) The contracting officer may use the provisions and clauses contained in Part 23 regarding the use of products containing recovered materials and biobased products when appropriate for the item being acquired.

(4) When setting aside under the Stafford Act (subpart 26.2), include the provision at 52.226-3, Disaster or Emergency Area Representation, in the solicitation. The representation in this provision is not in the System for Award Management database.

(f) Agencies may supplement the provisions and clauses prescribed in this part (to require use of additional provisions and clauses) only as necessary to reflect agency unique statutes applicable to the acquisition of commercial items or as may be approved by the agency senior procurement executive, or the individual responsible for representing the agency on the FAR Council, without power of delegation.

Notes of Decisions

Full and open competition 2
Transportation services 3
Use of terms inconsistent with commercial practice 1

1 Use of terms inconsistent with commercial practice

The agency's market research failed to show that solicitation terms requiring offerors to propose fixed prices for a three-year base period and three four-year option periods are consistent with commercial practice. FAR 12.301(a) requires that "contracts for the acquisition of commercial items shall, to the maximum extent practicable, include only those clauses . . . [d]etermined to be consistent with customary commercial practice." The COFC concluded that the 15-year fixed pricing schedule was inconsistent with the requirements of FAR 12.301(a)(2), were contrary to law and therefore invalid. CW Gov't Travel, Inc. v. U.S., 99 Fed. Cl. 666 (2011)

Although RFP requirement that vendors identify country of origin of product is inconsistent with customary commercial practice (and therefore, inconsistent with the general policy of FAR 12.302 that commercial item contracts adopt commercial terms), the provision was reasonably related to ensuring compliance with the Trade Agreements Act. FAR clause 52.212-4(q) requires a contractor under a commercial items contract to "comply with all applicable Federal, State and local laws, executive orders, rules and regulations applicable to its performance under [the] contract." Bridges System Integration, LLC, B-411020, 2015 CPD ¶ 144 (Comp.Gen. 2015).

Protest challenging the terms of a commercial item solicitation contemplating the establishment of a BPA with GSA contractors was sustained because the agency failed to perform adequate market research to demonstrate that the "Price Maintenance", Sales Leakage" and "International Roaming" clauses were consistent with customary commercial practice, as required by FAR 12.301. Verizon Wireless, B-406854, 2012 CPD ¶ 260 (Comp. Gen. 2012)

GAO found that this amount of market research was insufficient to support the agency's decision to tailor the standard commercial item clauses and stated: "The agency does not assert, however, nor does the record otherwise show, that the specific terms challenged by Smelkinson were ever researched or discussed by the agency with industry representatives at these conferences or elsewhere . . . Here, we think that the agency has failed to meet its obligation to conduct appropriate market research to show that the challenged terms are consistent with customary commercial practice." Smelkinson Sysco Food Services, B-281631, 99-1 CPD ¶ 57 (Comp. Gen. 1999).

2 Full and open competition

Pursuant to the Competition in Contracting Act, government is required to specify its needs and solicit proposals "in a manner designed to achieve full and open competition for the procurement," and fact that the procurement is a commercial item acquisition does not relieve government of such obligation. 10 U.S.C.A. § 2305(a)(1)(A)(i). Candle Corp. v. U.S., 40 Fed. Cl. 658, 42 Cont. Cas. Fed. (CCH) P 77276 (1998). United States ⊙64.10

In a commercial item acquisition for the repair and overhaul of pumps, protest of agency solicitation requiring vendors to be an original equipment manufacturer's (OEM) authorized repair facility was sustained, because the agency did not show that the restriction on competition were necessary to meet its needs. Decision Matter of: Missouri Machinery & Engineering Company, B-403561, 2010 CPD ¶ 276 (Comp. Gen. 2010)

Agency's solicitation requirements that computers and monitors be from the same manufacturer and use Intel-based microprocessors were overly restrictive because the agency did not demonstrate a reasonable basis for the requirements. Matter of: NCS Technologies, Inc., B-403435, 2010 CPD ¶ 281 (Comp. Gen. 2010)

3 Transportation services

Section of the Federal Acquisition Regulation (FAR) which requires a contracting agency to allow offerors on transportation contracts to offer rates for specific transportation services was not applicable to commercial items procurement conducted under FAR Part 12 and governed by the provisions therein. 48 C.F.R. §§ 12.301(d), 47.207-6(b). ABF Freight System, Inc. v. U.S., 55 Fed. Cl. 392 (2003). United States ⊙64.30

§ 12.302 Tailoring of provisions and clauses for the acquisition of commercial items.

(a) *General.* The provisions and clauses established in this subpart are intended to address, to the maximum extent practicable, commercial market practices for a wide range of potential Government acquisitions of commercial items. However, because of the broad range of commercial items acquired by the Government, variations in commercial practices, and the relative volume of the Government's acquisitions in the specific market, contracting officers may, within the limitations of this subpart, and after conducting appropriate market research, tailor the provision at 52.212-1, Instructions to Offerors—Commercial Items, and the clause at 52.212-4, Contract Terms and Conditions—Commercial Items, to adapt to the market conditions for each acquisition.

(b) *Tailoring 52.212-4, Contract Terms and Conditions—Commercial Items*. The following paragraphs of the clause at 52.212-4, Contract Terms and Conditions—Commercial Items, implement statutory requirements and shall not be tailored—

(1) Assignments;

(2) Disputes;

(3) Payment (except as provided in subpart 32.11);

(4) Invoice;

(5) Other compliances;

(6) Compliance with laws unique to Government contracts; and

(7) Unauthorized obligations.

(c) *Tailoring inconsistent with customary commercial practice*. The contracting officer shall not tailor any clause or otherwise include any additional terms or conditions in a solicitation or contract for commercial items in a manner that is inconsistent with customary commercial practice for the item being acquired unless a waiver is approved in accordance with agency procedures. The request for waiver must describe the customary commercial practice found in the marketplace, support the need to include a term or condition that is inconsistent with that practice and include a determination that use of the customary commercial practice is inconsistent with the needs of the Government. A waiver may be requested for an individual or class of contracts for that specific item.

(d) Tailoring shall be by addenda to the solicitation and contract. The contracting officer shall indicate in Block 27a of the SF 1449 if addenda are attached. These addenda may include, for example, a continuation of the schedule of supplies/services to be acquired from blocks 18 through 21 of the SF 1449; a continuation of the description of the supplies/services being acquired; further elaboration of any other item(s) on the SF 1449; any other terms or conditions necessary for the performance of the proposed contract (such as options, ordering procedures for indefinite-delivery type contracts, warranties, contract financing arrangements, etc.).

Notes of Decisions

In general 1
Applicability to Federal Supply Schedule acquisitions 3
Use of non-commercial terms 2

1 In general

FAR 12.302 does not prohibit approval of a waiver granting permission to use terms and conditions that are inconsistent with commercial practices after release of the solicitation. Crescent Helicopters, B-284706, B-284707, B-284734, B-284735, 2000 CPD ¶ 90 (Comp. Gen. 2000)

2 Use of non-commercial terms

An agency issued a solicitation containing a pricing term that it tailored based on its determination that the term was consistent with the commercial practice in the food services industry. A potential offeror protested the terms of the solicitation. The GAO sustained the protest because the agency failed to conduct adequate market research to support its determination that the challenged terms (requiring, among other things, that profit associated with interorganizational transfers of food items be disclosed) are consistent with customary commercial practice, or, alternatively, because the agency failed to obtain the waiver that is required to tailor standard commercial item provision in a manner inconsistent with customary commercial practice. Smelkinson Sysco Food Services, B-281631, Mar. 15, 1999, 99-1 CPD ¶ 57

GAO found that this amount of market research was insufficient to support the agency's decision to tailor the standard commercial item clauses and stated: "The agency does not assert, however, nor does the record otherwise show, that the specific terms challenged by

Smelkinson were ever researched or discussed by the agency with industry representatives at these conferences or elsewhere . . . Here, we think that the agency has failed to meet its obligation to conduct appropriate market research to show that the challenged terms are consistent with customary commercial practice." Smelkinson Sysco Food Services, B-281631, Mar. 15, 1999, 99-1 CPD ¶ 57

Although RFP requirement that vendors identify country of origin of product is inconsistent with customary commercial practice (and therefore, inconsistent with the general policy of FAR 12.302 that commercial item contracts adopt commercial terms), the provision was reasonably related to ensuring compliance with the Trade Agreements Act. FAR clause 52.212-4(q) requires a contractor under a commercial items contract to "comply with all applicable Federal, State and local laws, executive orders, rules and regulations applicable to its performance under [the] contract." Bridges System Integration, LLC, B-411020, 2015 CPD ¶ 144 (Comp.Gen. 2015).

In deciding whether the solicitation requirements asserted to be inconsistent with customary commercial practices require a waiver, the GAO will consider whether the challenged terms of a solicitation are individually or in total of such a nature as to transform the type of services sought [in the solicitation] to something other than a commercial item. Aalco Forwarding, Inc., et al., B-277241, 97-2 CPD ¶ 110, 1997 WL 649182 (Comp.Gen.), October 21, 1997

Agency properly issued waiver in accordance with FAR 12.302(c) for commercial item solicitation requirements that may be inconsistent with customary commercial practice where agency followed its procedures and reasonably found that the requirements subject to the waiver were legitimate agency needs. Aalco Forwarding, Inc., et al., B-277241, 97-2 CPD ¶ 110, 1997 WL 649182 (Comp.Gen.), October 21, 1997

Protest that agency improperly included in commercial item solicitation for helicopter services pilot and mechanic qualification requirements that were inconsistent with commercial practice is denied where the record showed that commercial contracts had similar requirements, and for those requirements that were not in commercial contracts, the agency properly issued waiver in accordance with FAR 2.302(c). Crescent Helicopters, B-284734, 2000 CPD ¶ 90, 2000 WL 706977 (Comp.Gen.), May 30, 2000

FAR 12.302 does not prohibit approval of a waiver granting permission to use terms and conditions that are inconsistent with commercial practices after release of the solicitation. Crescent Helicopters, B-284734, 2000 CPD ¶ 90, 2000 WL 706977 (Comp.Gen.), May 30, 2000

3 Applicability to Federal Supply Schedule acquisitions

The FAR requirement (12.302) that commercial item contracts include only those clauses determined to be consistent with "customary commercial practice" applied to a Request for Quotations (RFQ) posted on GSA's E-Buy portal. Although the FAR does not explicitly state that the "customary commercial practice" provision applied to orders placed under GSA Schedule contracts, the provision does apply to "acquisitions" and purchases through the use of RFQs meet the broad definition of an "acquisition" under FAR 2.101. CGI Federal Inc. v. U.S., 779 F.3d 1346 (Fed. Cir. 2015)

Protest challenging the terms of a commercial item solicitation contemplating the establishment of a BPA with GSA contractors was sustained because the agency failed to perform adequate market research to demonstrate that the "Price Maintenance", Sales Leakage" and "International Roaming" clauses were consistent with customary commercial practice, as required by FAR 12.301. Verizon Wireless, B-406854, 2012 CPD ¶ 260 (Comp. Gen. 2012)

§ 12.303 Contract format.

Solicitations and contracts for the acquisition of commercial items prepared using this Part 12 shall be assembled, to the maximum extent practicable, using the following format:

(a) Standard Form (SF) 1449;

(b) Continuation of any block from SF 1449, such as—

(1) Block 10 if an incentive subcontracting clause is used (the contracting officer shall indicate the applicable percentage);

(2) Block 18B for remittance address;

(3) Block 19 for contract line item numbers;

(4) Block 20 for schedule of supplies/services; or

(5) Block 25 for accounting data;

(c) Contract clauses—

(1) 52.212-4, Contract Terms and Conditions—Commercial Items, by reference (see SF 1449 block 27a);

(2) Any addendum to 52.212-4; and

(3) 52.212-5, Contract Terms and Conditions Required to Implement Statutes and Executive orders;

(d) Any contract documents, exhibits or attachments; and

(e) Solicitation provisions—

(1) 52.212-1, Instructions to Offerors—Commercial Items, by reference (see SF 1449, Block 27a);

(2) Any addendum to 52.212-1;

(3) 52.212-2, Evaluation—Commercial Items, or other description of evaluation factors for award, if used; and

(4) 52.212-3, Offeror Representations and Certifications—Commercial Items.

United States Code Annotated

Commercially available off-the-shelf item acquisitions, lists of inapplicable laws in Federal Acquisition Regulation, see 41 USCA § 431.

Contract requirements, see 41 USCA § 254.

Contracts, planning, solicitation, evaluation, and award procedures, see 10 USCA § 2305.

Definitions, see 10 USCA § 2302, 41 USCA §§ 259, 403.

Definitions relating to procurement of commercial items, see 10 USCA § 2376, 41 USCA § 264a.

Kinds of contracts, see 10 USCA § 2306.

List of laws inapplicable to procurements of commercial items in Federal Acquisition Regulation, see 41 USCA § 430.

Planning and solicitation requirements, see 41 USCA § 253a.

Preference for acquisition of commercial items, see 10 USCA § 2377, 41 USCA § 264b.

Relationship of commercial item provisions to other provisions of law, see 10 USCA § 2375, 41 USCA § 264.

Simplified acquisition procedures, see 41 USCA § 427.

Subpart 12.4 Unique Requirements Regarding Terms and Conditions for Commercial Items

§ 12.401 General.

This subpart provides—

(a) Guidance regarding tailoring of the paragraphs in the clause at 52.212-4, Contract Terms and Conditions—Commercial Items, when the paragraphs do not reflect the customary practice for a particular market; and

(b) Guidance on the administration of contracts for commercial items in those areas where the terms and conditions in 52.212-4 differ substantially from those contained elsewhere in the FAR.

United States Code Annotated

Administrative determinations, see 41 USCA § 257.

Commercially available off-the-shelf item acquisitions, lists of inapplicable laws in Federal Acquisition Regulation, see 41 USCA § 431.

Contract requirements, see 41 USCA § 254.

Contracts, planning, solicitation, evaluation, and award procedures, see 10 USCA § 2305.

Definitions, see 10 USCA § 2302, 41 USCA §§ 259, 403.

Definitions relating to procurement of commercial items, see 10 USCA § 2376, 41 USCA

§ 264a.

Determinations and decisions, see 10 USCA § 2310, 41 USCA § 262.

Evaluation and award, see 41 USCA § 253b.

Kinds of contracts, see 10 USCA § 2306.

List of laws inapplicable to procurements of commercial items in Federal Acquisition Regulation, see 41 USCA § 430.

Planning and solicitation requirements, see 41 USCA § 253a.

Preference for acquisition of commercial items, see 10 USCA § 2377, 41 USCA § 264b.

Relationship of commercial item provisions to other provisions of law, see 10 USCA § 2375, 41 USCA § 264.

Simplified acquisition procedures, see 41 USCA § 427.

Notes of Decisions

Changes 1

1 Changes

Although FAR 52.212-4(c) states that changes to a commercial items contract may "be made only by written agreement of the parties," this clause must be read in conjunction with FAR 52.212-4(s), the commercial item order of precedence clause. That paragraph states that the clauses at FAR 52.212-5 take precedence over the clauses at FAR 52.212-4 in the event of inconsistency. FAR 52.212-5 includes FAR 52.233-3, Protest After Award, which authorizes the contracting officer to unilaterally issue and lift stop work orders and reestablish a delivery date in conjunction with a bid protest. To the extent there is an inconsistency between FAR 52.212-4(c), which requires bilateral changes, and FAR 52.233-3, which permits unilateral changes, FAR 52.233-3 took precedence. Accordingly, a contracting officer may issue a contract modification unilaterally reestablishing a delivery date after lifting a stop work order issued in conjunction with a bid protest, notwithstanding FAR 52.212-4(c). In re Double B Enterprises, Inc., A.S.B.C.A. No. 52010, A.S.B.C.A. No. 52192, 01-1 B.C.A. (CCH) ¶ 31396, 2001 WL 520824 (Armed Serv. B.C.A. 2001),

§ 12.402 Acceptance.

(a) The acceptance paragraph in 52.212-4 is based upon the assumption that the Government will rely on the contractor's assurances that the commercial item tendered for acceptance conforms to the contract requirements. The Government inspection of commercial items will not prejudice its other rights under the acceptance paragraph. Additionally, although the paragraph does not address the issue of rejection, the Government always has the right to refuse acceptance of nonconforming items. This paragraph is generally appropriate when the Government is acquiring noncomplex commercial items.

(b) Other acceptance procedures may be more appropriate for the acquisition of complex commercial items or commercial items used in critical applications. In such cases, the contracting officer shall include alternative inspection procedure(s) in an addendum and ensure these procedures and the postaward remedies adequately protect the interests of the Government. The contracting officer must carefully examine the terms and conditions of any express warranty with regard to the effect it may have on the Government's available postaward remedies (see 12.404).

(c) The acquisition of commercial items under other circumstances such as on an "as is" basis may also require acceptance procedures different from those contained in 52.212-4. The contracting officer should consider the effect the specific circumstances will have on the acceptance paragraph as well as other paragraphs of the clause.

United States Code Annotated

Administrative determinations, see 41 USCA § 257.

Commercially available off-the-shelf item acquisitions, lists of inapplicable laws in Federal Acquisition Regulation, see 41 USCA § 431.

Contract requirements, see 41 USCA § 254.

Contracts, planning, solicitation, evaluation, and award procedures, see 10 USCA § 2305.

Definitions, see 10 USCA § 2302, 41 USCA §§ 259, 403.

Definitions relating to procurement of commercial items, see 10 USCA § 2376, 41 USCA

§ 264a.

Determinations and decisions, see 10 USCA § 2310, 41 USCA § 262.

Evaluation and award, see 41 USCA § 253b.

Kinds of contracts, see 10 USCA § 2306.

List of laws inapplicable to procurements of commercial items in Federal Acquisition Regulation, see 41 USCA § 430.

Planning and solicitation requirements, see 41 USCA § 253a.

Preference for acquisition of commercial items, see 10 USCA § 2377, 41 USCA § 264b.

Relationship of commercial item provisions to other provisions of law, see 10 USCA § 2375, 41 USCA § 264.

Simplified acquisition procedures, see 41 USCA § 427.

§ **12.403 Termination.**

(a) *General.* The clause at 52.212-4 permits the Government to terminate a contract for commercial items either for the convenience of the Government or for cause. However, the paragraphs in 52.212-4 entitled "Termination for the Government's Convenience" and "Termination for Cause" contain concepts which differ from those contained in the termination clauses prescribed in Part 49. Consequently, the requirements of Part 49 do not apply when terminating contracts for commercial items and contracting officers shall follow the procedures in this section. Contracting officers may continue to use Part 49 as guidance to the extent that Part 49 does not conflict with this section and the language of the termination paragraphs in 52.212-4.

(b) *Policy.* The contracting officer should exercise the Government's right to terminate a contract for commercial items either for convenience or for cause only when such a termination would be in the best interests of the Government. The contracting officer should consult with counsel prior to terminating for cause.

(c) Termination for cause.

(1) The paragraph in 52.212-4 entitled "Excusable Delay" requires contractors notify the contracting officer as soon as possible after commencement of any excusable delay. In most situations, this requirement should eliminate the need for a show cause notice prior to terminating a contract. The contracting officer shall send a cure notice prior to terminating a contract for a reason other than late delivery.

(2) The Government's rights after a termination for cause shall include all the remedies available to any buyer in the marketplace. The Government's preferred remedy will be to acquire similar items from another contractor and to charge the defaulted contractor with any excess reprocurement costs together with any incidental or consequential damages incurred because of the termination.

(3) When a termination for cause is appropriate, the contracting officer shall send the contractor a written notification regarding the termination. At a minimum, this notification shall—

(i) Indicate the contract is terminated for cause;

(ii) Specify the reasons for the termination;

(iii) Indicate which remedies the Government intends to seek or provide a date by which the Government will inform the contractor of the remedy; and

(iv) State that the notice constitutes a final decision of the contracting officer and that the contractor has the right to appeal under the Disputes clause (see 33.211).

(4) The contracting officer, in accordance with agency procedures, shall ensure that information related to termination for cause notices and any amendments are reported. In the event the termination for cause is subsequently converted to a termination for convenience, or is otherwise withdrawn, the contracting officer shall ensure that a notice of the conversion or withdrawal is reported. All reporting shall be in accordance with 42.1503(h).

(d) Termination for the Government's convenience.

(1) When the contracting officer terminates a contract for commercial items for the Government's convenience, the contractor shall be paid—

(i)

(A) The percentage of the contract price reflecting the percentage of the work performed prior to the notice of the termination for fixed-price or fixed-price with economic price adjustment contracts; or

(B) An amount for direct labor hours (as defined in the Schedule of the contract) determined by multiplying the number of direct labor hours expended before the effective date of termination by the hourly rate(s) in the Schedule; and

(ii) Any charges the contractor can demonstrate directly resulted from the termination. The contractor may demonstrate such charges using its standard record keeping system and is not required to comply with the cost accounting standards or the contract cost principles in Part 31. The Government does not have any right to audit the contractor's records solely because of the termination for convenience.

(2) Generally, the parties should mutually agree upon the requirements of the termination proposal. The parties must balance the Government's need to obtain sufficient documentation to support payment to the contractor against the goal of having a simple and expeditious settlement

Notes of Decisions

In general 1

1 In general

GSA properly terminated for cause a commercial item contract for acquisition training services awarded to BMRA for non-delivery of scheduled courses. The Board of Contract Appeals rejected BMRA's argument that the termination was defective because GSA did not issue a cure notice prior to terminating the contract The FAR sections governing commercial item contracts do not require an agency to send a cure notice before terminating a contract for late delivery or non-delivery. FAR 12.403(c). BMRA vs. GSA, CBCA 464, 07-1 BCA ¶ 33486 (Civilian B.C.A. 2007)

ASBCA sustained appeal seeking recovery of lease costs incurred to perform a commercial item contract that was terminated for convenience prior to issuance of any task orders. The Board held, "as a result of the 0013 Contract convenience termination, SWR has incurred an unavoidable reasonable charge for a deposit of $75,000 in preparing to perform the 0013 Contract which it is entitled to recover." SWR, Inc., ASBCA No. 56708, 15-1 BCA ¶ 35832 (Armed Serv. B.C.A. 2014)

Although the commercial item contract termination for cause clause does not mention sending a cure notice, the regulations which apply to commercial item contracts require the Government to send a cure notice before terminating for any reason other than late delivery. The regulations do not require a set number of days for the cure period. Geo-Marine, Inc., v. GSA, GSBCA No. 16247, 05-2 BCA ¶ 33048 (G.S.B.C.A. 2005)

Under the standard (non-commercial item) termination for convenience clause, when a contract is partially terminated the contractor may recover an equitable adjustment for increased costs on the continuing work caused by the termination for convenience. However, the termination for convenience clause under commercial contracts does not provide for recovery of such costs because the contractor is not required to adhere to contract cost principles and the government has no right to audit contractor's termination proposals. Individual Development Associates, Inc., ASBCA No. 53910, 04-2 BCA ¶ 32740 (Armed Serv. B.C.A. 2004)

Although the agency's termination notice under a commercial item contract erroneously stated that the termination was for default, when the termination was actually for cause, this error did not nullify the effect of the notification. The commercial item contract did not contain a termination for default clause. Instead, it contained FAR 52.212-4, which permitted the agency to terminate the contract for cause if the contractor defaulted by not performing. There is no evidence to show that the reference in the notice to a termination for default was anything more than an error on the part of the person who drafted the notice. Rowe Inc. v. General Services Admin., GSBCA No. 14136, 00-1 BCA ¶ 30668 (G.S.B. C.A. 1999)

Agency was not required to notify the SBA of its termination for cause of a commercial item contract awarded to a small business, as required by Part 49 of the FAR because the requirements of Part 49 do not apply to commercial item contracts. FAR 12.403 does not require an agency to follow any of the procedures set out in Part 49 of the FAR when it terminates a commercial item contract for cause. Rowe Inc. v. General Services Admin.,

GSBCA No. 14136, 00-1 BCA ¶ 30668 (G.S.B.C.A. 1999)

§ 12.404 Warranties.

(a) *Implied warranties.* The Government's post award rights contained in 52.212-4 are the implied warranty of merchantability, the implied warranty of fitness for particular purpose and the remedies contained in the acceptance paragraph.

(1) The implied warranty of merchantability provides that an item is reasonably fit for the ordinary purposes for which such items are used. The items must be of at least average, fair or medium-grade quality and must be comparable in quality to those that will pass without objection in the trade or market for items of the same description.

(2) The implied warranty of fitness for a particular purpose provides that an item is fit for use for the particular purpose for which the Government will use the items. The Government can rely upon an implied warranty of fitness for particular purpose when—

(i) The seller knows the particular purpose for which the Government intends to use the item; and

(ii) The Government relied upon the contractor's skill and judgment that the item would be appropriate for that particular purpose.

(3) Contracting officers should consult with legal counsel prior to asserting any claim for a breach of an implied warranty.

(b) *Express warranties.* 41 U.S.C. 3307(e)(5)(B) requires contracting officers to take advantage of commercial warranties. To the maximum extent practicable, solicitations for commercial items shall require offerors to offer the Government at least the same warranty terms, including offers of extended warranties, offered to the general public in customary commercial practice. Solicitations may specify minimum warranty terms, such as minimum duration, appropriate for the Government's intended use of the item.

(1) Any express warranty the Government intends to rely upon must meet the needs of the Government. The contracting officer should analyze any commercial warranty to determine if—

(i) The warranty is adequate to protect the needs of the Government, *e.g.,* items covered by the warranty and length of warranty;

(ii) The terms allow the Government effective postaward administration of the warranty to include the identification of warranted items, procedures for the return of warranted items to the contractor for repair or replacement, and collection of product performance information; and

(iii) The warranty is cost-effective.

(2) In some markets, it may be customary commercial practice for contractors to exclude or limit the implied warranties contained in 52.212-4 in the provisions of an express warranty. In such cases, the contracting officer shall ensure that the express warranty provides for the repair or replacement of defective items discovered within a reasonable period of time after acceptance.

(3) Express warranties shall be included in the contract by addendum (see 12.302).

United States Code Annotated

Administrative determinations, see 41 USCA § 257.

Commercially available off-the-shelf item acquisitions, lists of inapplicable laws in Federal Acquisition Regulation, see 41 USCA § 431.

Contract requirements, see 41 USCA § 254.

Contracts, planning, solicitation, evaluation, and award procedures, see 10 USCA § 2305.

Definitions, see 10 USCA § 2302, 41 USCA §§ 259, 403.

Definitions relating to procurement of commercial items, see 10 USCA § 2376, 41 USCA § 264a.

Determinations and decisions, see 10 USCA § 2310, 41 USCA § 262.

Evaluation and award, see 41 USCA § 253b.

Kinds of contracts, see 10 USCA § 2306.

List of laws inapplicable to procurements of commercial items in Federal Acquisition Regulation, see 41 USCA § 430.

Planning and solicitation requirements, see 41 USCA § 253a.

Preference for acquisition of commercial items, see 10 USCA § 2377, 41 USCA § 264b.

Relationship of commercial item provisions to other provisions of law, see 10 USCA § 2375, 41 USCA § 264.

Simplified acquisition procedures, see 41 USCA § 427.

Notes of Decisions

In general 1

1 In general

Even if diving suits had been delivered on time, they were not merchantable. The "Contract Terms and Conditions—Commercial Items" clause requires that contractors warrant that deliverables are "merchantable" and "fit for the particular purpose" described in the contract. The diving suits procured under a commercial item contract did not satisfy this warranty because they leaked. Additionally, the manner by which the suits were repaired made future leaking possible and made the suits awkward and uncomfortable. FAR 12.404 defines merchantability as goods that are of at least average, fair or medium-grade quality and must be comparable in quality to those that will pass without objection in the trade or market for items of the same description. The leaking diving suits did not meet this standard. Appeal of Falls Manufacturing, Inc., D.O.T.C.A.B. No. 4149, 04-2 B.C.A. (CCH) ¶ 32632, 2004 WL 1126270 (D.O.T. Cont. Adj. Bd. 2004), aff'd, 128 Fed. Appx. 153 (Fed. Cir. 2005)

Subpart 12.5 Applicability of Certain Laws to the Acquisition of Commercial Items and Commercially Available Off-The-Shelf Items

§ 12.500 Scope of subpart.

(a) As required by 41 U.S.C. 1906 and 1907, this subpart lists provisions of law that are not applicable to—

(1) Contracts for the acquisition of commercial items;

(2) Subcontracts, at any tier, for the acquisition of commercial items; and

(3) Contracts and subcontracts, at any tier, for the acquisition of COTS items.

(b) This subpart also lists provisions of law that have been amended to eliminate or modify their applicability to either contracts or subcontracts for the acquisition of commercial items.

United States Code Annotated

Commercially available off-the-shelf item acquisitions, lists of inapplicable laws in Federal Acquisition Regulation, see 41 USCA § 431.

Contract requirements, see 41 USCA § 254.

Contracts, planning, solicitation, evaluation, and award procedures, see 10 USCA § 2305.

Definitions, see 10 USCA § 2302, 41 USCA §§ 259, 403.

Definitions relating to procurement of commercial items, see 10 USCA § 2376, 41 USCA § 264a.

Kinds of contracts, see 10 USCA § 2306.

List of laws inapplicable to procurements of commercial items in Federal Acquisition Regulation, see 41 USCA § 430.

Planning and solicitation requirements, see 41 USCA § 253a.

Preference for acquisition of commercial items, see 10 USCA § 2377, 41 USCA § 264b.

Relationship of commercial item provisions to other provisions of law, see 10 USCA § 2375, 41 USCA § 264.

Simplified acquisition procedures, see 41 USCA § 427.

§ 12.501 Applicability.

(a) This subpart applies to any contract or subcontract at any tier for the acquisition of commercial items.

(b) Nothing in this subpart shall be construed to authorize the waiver of any provision of law with respect to any subcontract if the prime contractor is reselling or distributing commercial items of another contractor without adding value. This limitation is intended to preclude establishment of unusual contractual arrangements solely for the purpose of Government sales.

(c) For purposes of this subpart, contractors awarded subcontracts under subpart 19.8, Contracting with the Small Business Administration (the 8(a) Program), shall be considered prime contractors.

United States Code Annotated

Commercially available off-the-shelf item acquisitions, lists of inapplicable laws in Federal Acquisition Regulation, see 41 USCA § 431.

Contract requirements, see 41 USCA § 254.

Contracts, planning, solicitation, evaluation, and award procedures, see 10 USCA § 2305.

Definitions, see 10 USCA § 2302, 41 USCA §§ 259, 403.

Definitions relating to procurement of commercial items, see 10 USCA § 2376, 41 USCA § 264a.

Kinds of contracts, see 10 USCA § 2306.

List of laws inapplicable to procurements of commercial items in Federal Acquisition Regulation, see 41 USCA § 430.

Planning and solicitation requirements, see 41 USCA § 253a.

Preference for acquisition of commercial items, see 10 USCA § 2377, 41 USCA § 264b.

Relationship of commercial item provisions to other provisions of law, see 10 USCA § 2375, 41 USCA § 264.

Simplified acquisition procedures, see 41 USCA § 427.

§ 12.502 Procedures.

(a) The FAR prescription for the provision or clause for each of the laws listed in 12.503 has been revised in the appropriate part to reflect its proper application to prime contracts for the acquisition of commercial items.

(b) For subcontracts for the acquisition of commercial items or commercial components, the clauses at 52.212-5, Contract Terms and Conditions Required to Implement Statutes or Executive Orders—Commercial Items, and 52.244-6, Subcontracts for Commercial Items, reflect the applicability of the laws listed in 12.504 by identifying the only provisions and clauses that are required to be included in a subcontract at any tier for the acquisition of commercial items or commercial components.

(c) The FAR prescription for the provision or clause for each of the laws listed in 12.505 has been revised in the appropriate part to reflect its proper application to contracts and subcontracts for the acquisition of COTS items.

United States Code Annotated

Commercially available off-the-shelf item acquisitions, lists of inapplicable laws in Federal Acquisition Regulation, see 41 USCA § 431.

Contract requirements, see 41 USCA § 254.

Contracts, planning, solicitation, evaluation, and award procedures, see 10 USCA § 2305.

Definitions, see 10 USCA § 2302, 41 USCA §§ 259, 403.

Definitions relating to procurement of commercial items, see 10 USCA § 2376, 41 USCA § 264a.

Kinds of contracts, see 10 USCA § 2306.

List of laws inapplicable to procurements of commercial items in Federal Acquisition Regulation, see 41 USCA § 430.

Planning and solicitation requirements, see 41 USCA § 253a.

Preference for acquisition of commercial items, see 10 USCA § 2377, 41 USCA § 264b.

Relationship of commercial item provisions to other provisions of law, see 10 USCA § 2375, 41 USCA § 264.

Simplified acquisition procedures, see 41 USCA § 427.

§ 12.503 Applicability of certain laws to Executive agency contracts for the acquisition of commercial items.

(a) The following laws are not applicable to Executive agency contracts for the acquisition of commercial items:

(1) 41 U.S.C. chapter 65, Contracts for Materials, Supplies, Articles, and Equipment Exceeding $15,000 (see subpart 22.6).

(2) 41 U.S.C. 3901(b) and 10 U.S.C. 2306(b), Contingent Fees (see 3.404).

(3) 41 U.S.C. 1708(e)(3), Minimum Response Time for Offers (see 5.203).

(4) 41 U.S.C. chapter 81, Drug-Free Workplace (see 23.501).

(5) 31 U.S.C. 1354(a), Limitation on use of appropriated funds for contracts with entities not meeting veterans' employment reporting requirements (see 22.1302).

(6) [Reserved]

(7) Section 806(a)(3) of Pub. L. 102-190, as amended by Sections 2091 and 8105 of Pub. L. 103-355, (10 U.S.C. 2302 note), Payment Protections for Subcontractors and Suppliers (see 28.106-6).

(8) 41 U.S.C. 4706(d)(1) and 10 U.S.C. 2313(c)(1), GAO Access to Contractor Employees, Section 871 of Pub. L. 110-417 (see 52.214-26 and 52.215-2).

(9) 41 U.S.C. 2303, Policy on Personal Conflicts of Interest by Contractor Employees (see subpart 3.11).

(b) Certain requirements of the following laws are not applicable to executive agency contracts for the acquisition of commercial items:

(1) 40 U.S.C. chapter 37, Requirement for a certificate and clause under the Contract Work Hours and Safety Standards statute (see 22.305).

(2) 41 U.S.C. 8703 and 8703, Requirement for a clause and certain other requirements related to kickbacks (see 3.502).

(3) 49 U.S.C. 40118, Requirement for a clause under the Fly American provisions (see 47.405).

(c) The applicability of the following laws have been modified in regards to Executive agency contracts for the acquisition of commercial items:

(1) 41 U.S.C. 4704 and 10 U.S.C. 2402, Prohibition on Limiting Subcontractor Direct Sales to the United States (see 3.503).

(2) 41 U.S.C. chapter 35, Truthful Cost or Pricing Data, and 10 U.S.C. 2306a, Truth in Negotiations Act (see 15.403).

(3) 41 U.S.C. chapter 15, Cost Accounting Standards (48 CFR Chapter 99) (see 12.214).

United States Code Annotated

Commercially available off-the-shelf item acquisitions, lists of inapplicable laws in Federal Acquisition Regulation, see 41 USCA § 431.

Contract requirements, see 41 USCA § 254.

Contracts, planning, solicitation, evaluation, and award procedures, see 10 USCA § 2305.

Definitions, see 10 USCA § 2302, 41 USCA §§ 259, 403.

Definitions relating to procurement of commercial items, see 10 USCA § 2376, 41 USCA § 264a.

Kinds of contracts, see 10 USCA § 2306.

List of laws inapplicable to procurements of commercial items in Federal Acquisition Regulation, see 41 USCA § 430.

Planning and solicitation requirements, see 41 USCA § 253a.

Preference for acquisition of commercial items, see 10 USCA § 2377, 41 USCA § 264b.

Relationship of commercial item provisions to other provisions of law, see 10 USCA § 2375, 41 USCA § 264.

Simplified acquisition procedures, see 41 USCA § 427.

Notes of Decisions

In general 1

1 In general

Section of the FAR which requires a contracting agency to allow offerors on transportation contracts to offer rates for specific transportation services was not applicable to commercial items procurement conducted under FAR Part 12 and governed by the provisions therein. 48 C.F.R. §§ 12.301(d), 47.207-6(b). ABF Freight System, Inc. v. U.S., 55 Fed. Cl. 392 (2003). United States ☞64.30

§ 12.504 Applicability of certain laws to subcontracts for the acquisition of commercial items.

(a) The following laws are not applicable to subcontracts at any tier for the acquisition of commercial items or commercial components at any tier:

(1) 10 U.S.C. 2631, Transportation of Supplies by Sea (except for the types of subcontracts listed at 47.504(d)).

(2) 15 U.S.C. 644(d), Requirements relative to labor surplus areas under the Small Business Act (see subpart 19.2).

(3) [Reserved]

(4) 41 U.S.C. 6505, Contracts for Materials, Supplies, Articles, and Equipment Exceeding $15,000 (see subpart 22.6).

(5) 41 U.S.C. 4703, Validation of Proprietary Data restrictions (see subpart 27.4).

(6) 41 U.S.C. 3901(b) and 10 U.S.C. 2306(b), Contingent Fees (see subpart 3.4).

(7) 41 U.S.C. 4706(d) and 10 U.S.C. 2313(c), Examination of Records of Contractor, when a subcontractor is not required to provide certified cost or pricing data (see15.209(b)), unless using funds appropriated or otherwise made available by the American Recovery and Reinvestment Act of 2009 (Pub. L. 111-5).

(8) 41 U.S.C. 1708(e)(3), Minimum Response Time for Offers (see subpart 5.2).

(9) 41 U.S.C. 2302, Rights in Technical Data (see subpart 27.4).

(10) 41 U.S.C. chapter 81, Drug-Free Workplace Act (see subpart 23.5).

(11) 46 U.S.C. App. 1241(b), Transportation in American Vessels of Government Personnel and Certain Cargo (see subpart 47.5) (except for the types of subcontracts listed at 47.504(d)).

(12) 49 U.S.C. 40118, Fly American provisions (see subpart 47.4).

(13) Section 806(a)(3) of Pub. L. 102-190, as amended by Sections 2091 and 8105 of Pub. L. 103-355 (10 U.S.C. 2302 note), Payment Protections for Subcontractors and Suppliers (see 28.106-6).

(b) The requirements for a certificate and clause under the Contract Work Hours and Safety Standards statute, 40 U.S.C. 37, (see subpart 22.3) are not applicable to subcontracts at any tier for the acquisition of commercial items or commercial components.

(c) The applicability of the following laws has been modified in regards to subcontracts at any tier for the acquisition of commercial items or commercial components:

(1) 41 U.S.C. 4704 and 10 U.S.C. 2402, Prohibition on Limiting Subcontractor Direct Sales to the United States (see subpart 3.5).

(2) 41 U.S.C. chapter 35, Truthful Cost or Pricing Data, and 10 U.S.C. 2306a, Truth in Negotiations (see subpart 15.4).

(3) 41 U.S.C. chapter 15, Cost Accounting Standards (48 CFR Chapter 99) (see 12.214).

United States Code Annotated

Commercially available off-the-shelf item acquisitions, lists of inapplicable laws in Federal Acquisition Regulation, see 41 USCA § 431.

Contract requirements, see 41 USCA § 254.

Contracts, planning, solicitation, evaluation, and award procedures, see 10 USCA § 2305.

Definitions, see 10 USCA § 2302, 41 USCA §§ 259, 403.

Definitions relating to procurement of commercial items, see 10 USCA § 2376, 41 USCA § 264a.

Kinds of contracts, see 10 USCA § 2306.

List of laws inapplicable to procurements of commercial items in Federal Acquisition Regulation, see 41 USCA § 430.

Planning and solicitation requirements, see 41 USCA § 253a.

Preference for acquisition of commercial items, see 10 USCA § 2377, 41 USCA § 264b.

Relationship of commercial item provisions to other provisions of law, see 10 USCA § 2375, 41 USCA § 264.

Simplified acquisition procedures, see 41 USCA § 427.

§ 12.505 Applicability of certain laws to contracts for the acquisition of COTS items.

COTS items are a subset of commercial items. Therefore, any laws listed in sections 12.503 and 12.504 are also inapplicable or modified in their applicability to contracts or subcontracts for the acquisition of COTS items. In addition, the following laws are not applicable to contracts for the acquisition of COTS items:

(a) (1) The portion of 41 U.S.C. 8302(a)(1), that reads "substantially all from articles, materials, or supplies mined, produced, or manufactured, in the United States," Buy American- Supplies, component test (see 52.225-1 and 52.225-3).

(2) The portion of 41 U.S.C. 8303(a)(2), that reads "substantially all from articles, materials, or supplies mined, produced, or manufactured in the United States," Buy American- Construction Materials, component test (see 52.225-9 and 52.225-11).

(b) 42 U.S.C. 6962(c)(3)(A), Certification and Estimate of Percentage of Recovered Material.

(c) Compliance Plan and Certification Requirement, section 1703 of the National Defense Authorization Act for Fiscal Year 2013 (Pub. L. 112-239), Title XVII, Ending trafficking in Government Contracting (see 52.222-50(h) and 52.222-56).

Subpart 12.6 Streamlined Procedures for Evaluation and Solicitation for Commercial Items

§ 12.601 General.

This subpart provides optional procedures for (a) streamlined evaluation of offers for commercial items; and (b) streamlined solicitation of offers for commercial items for use where appropriate. These procedures are intended to simplify the process of preparing and issuing solicitations, and evaluating offers for commercial items consistent with customary commercial practices.

United States Code Annotated

Commercially available off-the-shelf item acquisitions, lists of inapplicable laws in Federal Acquisition Regulation, see 41 USCA § 431.

Contract requirements, see 41 USCA § 254.

Contracts, planning, solicitation, evaluation, and award procedures, see 10 USCA § 2305.

Definitions, see 10 USCA § 2302, 41 USCA §§ 259, 403.

Definitions relating to procurement of commercial items, see 10 USCA § 2376, 41 USCA § 264a.

Evaluation and award, see 41 USCA § 253b.

Kinds of contracts, see 10 USCA § 2306.

List of laws inapplicable to procurements of commercial items in Federal Acquisition Regulation, see 41 USCA § 430.

Planning and solicitation requirements, see 41 USCA § 253a.

Preference for acquisition of commercial items, see 10 USCA § 2377, 41 USCA § 264b.

Relationship of commercial item provisions to other provisions of law, see 10 USCA § 2375, 41 USCA § 264.

Simplified acquisition procedures, see 41 USCA § 427.

Notes of Decisions

In general 1

1 In general

Procuring agency properly determined tree thinning services were a commercial item and used Federal Acquisition Regulation subpart 12.6, Streamlined Procedures for Evaluation and Solicitation for Commercial Items, to acquire the services. SHABA Contracting, B-287430, 2001 CPD ¶ 105 (Comp. Gen. 2001).

§ 12.602 Streamlined evaluation of offers.

(a) When evaluation factors are used, the contracting officer may insert a provision substantially the same as the provision at 52.212-2, Evaluation—Commercial Items, in solicitations for commercial items or comply with the procedures in 13.106 if the acquisition is being made using simplified acquisition procedures. When the provision at 52.212-2 is used, paragraph (a) of the provision shall be tailored to the specific acquisition to describe the evaluation factors and relative importance of those factors. However, when using the simplified acquisition procedures in Part 13, contracting officers are not required to describe the relative importance of evaluation factors.

(b) Offers shall be evaluated in accordance with the criteria contained in the solicitation. For many commercial items, the criteria need not be more detailed than technical (capability of the item offered to meet the agency need), price and past performance. Technical capability may be evaluated by how well the proposed products meet the Government requirement instead of predetermined subfactors. Solicitations for commercial items do not have to contain subfactors for technical capability when the solicitation adequately describes the item's intended use. A technical evaluation would normally include examination of such things as product literature, product samples (if requested), technical features and warranty provisions. Past performance shall be evaluated in accordance with the procedures in 13.106 or Subpart 15.3, as applicable. The contracting officer shall ensure the instructions provided in the provision at 52.212-1, Instructions to Offerors—Commercial Items, and the evaluation criteria provided in the provision at 52.212-2, Evaluation—Commercial Items, are in agreement.

(c) Select the offer that is most advantageous to the Government based on the factors contained in the solicitation. Fully document the rationale for selection of the successful offeror including discussion of any trade-offs considered.

United States Code Annotated

Commercially available off-the-shelf item acquisitions, lists of inapplicable laws in Federal Acquisition Regulation, see 41 USCA § 431.

Contract requirements, see 41 USCA § 254.

Contracts, planning, solicitation, evaluation, and award procedures, see 10 USCA § 2305.

Definitions, see 10 USCA § 2302, 41 USCA §§ 259, 403.

Definitions relating to procurement of commercial items, see 10 USCA § 2376, 41 USCA § 264a.

Evaluation and award, see 41 USCA § 253b.

Kinds of contracts, see 10 USCA § 2306.

List of laws inapplicable to procurements of commercial items in Federal Acquisition Regulation, see 41 USCA § 430.

Planning and solicitation requirements, see 41 USCA § 253a.

Preference for acquisition of commercial items, see 10 USCA § 2377, 41 USCA § 264b.

Relationship of commercial item provisions to other provisions of law, see 10 USCA § 2375, 41 USCA § 264.

Simplified acquisition procedures, see 41 USCA § 427.

Notes of Decisions

In general 1

1 In general

Under FAR subpart 12.6, Streamlined Procedures for Evaluation and Solicitation for Commercial Items, the contracting officer is required to [s]elect the offer that is most advantageous to the Government based on the factors contained in the solicitation, and to [f]ully document the rationale for selection of the successful offeror including discussion of any trade-offs considered. FAR 12.602(c). Although the FAR does not specify what is required for compliance with the mandate that the contracting officer [f]ully document the rationale for the source selection, the fundamental principle of government accountability dictates that an agency maintain a record adequate to allow for meaningful review. Tiger Enterprises, Inc., B-293951, 2004 CPD ¶ 141 (Comp. Gen. 2004)

Consistent with FAR § 12.602(b), an RFP in a commercial item procurement does not have to specify predetermined evaluation subfactors. Thus, the agency has the discretion to specify the data that offerors must submit, in conjunction with technical descriptions, to enable the agency to perform a technical evaluation to determine whether the proposed product(s) meet or exceed the Government's requirements. InterOcean Systems, Inc., B-290916, 2002 CPD ¶ 178 (Comp. Gen. 2002)

Notwithstanding statement in solicitation that simplified acquisition procedures were being used and authority at FAR 12.602(a) not to disclose the relative weight of evaluation factors when using simplified procedures, an agency's failure to disclose the relative weight of evaluation factors was unreasonable because basic fairness dictated disclosure of the relative weights where the agency required offerors to prepare detailed written proposals addressing unique government requirements. Finlen Complex, Inc., B-288280, 2001 CPD ¶ 167 (Comp. Gen. 2001).

FAR 12.301(c) permits inclusion of FAR § 52.212-2 (Evaluation-Commercial Items) or a similar provision setting forth the evaluation factors when the use of evaluation factors is appropriate. If a solicitation does not incorporate FAR 52.212-2 or otherwise provide for a comparative evaluation of technical submissions, but instead provides only for the evaluation of past performance and price, the agency must select the vendor judged to be best in terms of past performance and price if the vendors technical submission is at least minimally acceptable. APTUS Company, B-281289, 99-1 CPD ¶ 40 (Comp. Gen. 1999)

Protest that agency failed to conduct discussions with protester consistent with the requirements of part 15 of the Federal Acquisition Regulation (FAR) is denied where the procurement is a commercial item acquisition being conducted under simplified acquisition procedures, which is not subject to the FAR part 15 requirements. United Marine International LLC, B-281512, 99-1 CPD ¶ 44 (Comp. Gen. 1999)

Although FAR 12.602(b) states that "[t]echnical capability may be evaluated by how well the proposed products meet the Government requirement instead of predetermined subfactors," it also states that such subfactors are not necessary "when the solicitation adequately describes the item's intended use." Thus, a prerequisite for an appropriate evaluation of commercial items, consistent with FAR Part 12, is an adequate description of the agency's needs. National Aeronautics and Space Administration-- Reconsideration and Modification of Remedy, B-274748, B-274748.3, 97-1 CPD ¶ 159 (Comp. Gen. 1997)

Protest that agency failed to evaluate and consider the alleged technical superiority of a proposal for a commercial item is denied where the solicitation did not include any technical evaluation factors and it is clear that award was to be made on the basis of low price. Vistron, Inc., B-277497, 97-2 CPD ¶ 107 (Comp. Gen. 1997)

§ 12.603 Streamlined solicitation for commercial items.

(a) When a written solicitation will be issued, the contracting officer may use the following procedure to reduce the time required to solicit and award contracts for the acquisition of commercial items. This procedure combines the synopsis required by 5.203 and the issuance of the solicitation into a single document.

(b) When using the combined synopsis/solicitation procedure, the SF 1449 is not used for issuing the solicitation.

(c) To use these procedures, the contracting officer shall—

(1) Prepare the synopsis as described at 5.207.

(2) In the Description, include the following additional information:

(i) The following statement:

This is a combined synopsis/solicitation for commercial items prepared in accordance with the format in Subpart 12.6, as supplemented with additional information included in this notice. This announcement constitutes the only solicitation; proposals are being requested and a written solicitation will not be issued.

(ii) The solicitation number and a statement that the solicitation is issued as an invitation to bid (IFB), request for quotation (RFQ) or request for proposal (RFP).

(iii) A statement that the solicitation document and incorporated provisions and clauses are those in effect through Federal Acquisition Circular ____.

(iv) A notice regarding any set-aside and the associated NAICS code and small business size standard.

(v) A list of contract line item number(s) and items, quantities and units of measure, (including option(s), if applicable).

(vi) Description of requirements for the items to be acquired.

(vii) Date(s) and place(s) of delivery and acceptance and FOB point.

(viii) A statement that the provision at 52.212-1, Instructions to Offerors—Commercial, applies to this acquisition and a statement regarding any addenda to the provision.

(ix) A statement regarding the applicability of the provision at 52.212-2, Evaluation—Commercial Items, if used, and the specific evaluation criteria to be included in paragraph (a) of that provision. If this provision is not used, describe the evaluation procedures to be used.

(x) A statement advising offerors to include a completed copy of the provision at 52.212-3, Offeror Representations and Certifications—Commercial Items, with its offer.

(xi) A statement that the clause at 52.212-4, Contract Terms and Conditions—Commercial Items, applies to this acquisition and a statement regarding any addenda to the clause.

(xii) A statement that the clause at 52.212-5, Contract Terms and Conditions Required To Implement Statutes or Executive Orders—Commercial Items, applies to this acquisition and a statement regarding which, if any, of the additional FAR clauses cited in the clause are applicable to the acquisition.

(xiii) A statement regarding any additional contract requirement(s) or terms and conditions (such as contract financing arrangements or warranty requirements) determined by the contracting officer to be necessary for this acquisition and consistent with customary commercial practices.

(xiv) A statement regarding the Defense Priorities and Allocations System (DPAS) and assigned rating, if applicable.

(xv) The date, time and place offers are due.

(xvi) The name and telephone number of the individual to contact for information regarding the solicitation.

(3) Allow response time for receipt of offers as follows:

(i) Because the synopsis and solicitation are contained in a single document, it is not necessary to publicize a separate synopsis 15 days before the issuance of the solicitation.

(ii) When using the combined synopsis and solicitation, contracting officers must establish a response time in accordance with 5.203(b) (but see 5.203(h)).

(4) Publicize amendments to solicitations in the same manner as the initial synopsis and solicitation.

United States Code Annotated

Commercially available off-the-shelf item acquisitions, lists of inapplicable laws in Federal Acquisition Regulation, see 41 USCA § 431.

Contract requirements, see 41 USCA § 254.

Contracts, planning, solicitation, evaluation, and award procedures, see 10 USCA § 2305.

Definitions, see 10 USCA § 2302, 41 USCA §§ 259, 403.

Definitions relating to procurement of commercial items, see 10 USCA § 2376, 41 USCA § 264a.

Evaluation and award, see 41 USCA § 253b.

Kinds of contracts, see 10 USCA § 2306.

List of laws inapplicable to procurements of commercial items in Federal Acquisition Regulation, see 41 USCA § 430.

Planning and solicitation requirements, see 41 USCA § 253a.

Preference for acquisition of commercial items, see 10 USCA § 2377, 41 USCA § 264b.

Relationship of commercial item provisions to other provisions of law, see 10 USCA

§ 2375, 41 USCA § 264.

Simplified acquisition procedures, see 41 USCA § 427.

Notes of Decisions

In general 1

1 In general

Agency may allow fewer than 30 days to respond to an RFP when it is acquiring commercial items. FAR 12.205(c). When acquiring commercial items, the contracting officer should afford potential offerors a reasonable opportunity to respond; when establishing the solicitation response time, the contracting officer should consider the complexity, commerciality, availability, and urgency of the acquisition. Contracting officer's decision to specify a 15-day response period was reasonable because it was based on prior year's procurement for a more complex requirement, which resulted in adequate competition and no complaints from offerors. American Artisan Productions, Inc., B-281409, 98-2 CPD ¶ 155 (Comp. Gen. 1998)

Subchapter C Contracting Methods and Contract Types

PART 13 SIMPLIFIED ACQUISITION PROCEDURES

Subpart 13.1 Procedures

Subpart 13.2 Actions at or Below the Micro-Purchase Threshold

Subpart 13.3 Simplified Acquisition Methods

§ 13.303-8 Optional clause.
§ 13.304 [Reserved]
§ 13.305 Imprest funds and third party drafts.
§ 13.305-1 General.
§ 13.305-2 Agency responsibilities.
§ 13.305-3 Conditions for use.
§ 13.305-4 Procedures.
§ 13.306 SF 44, Purchase Order—Invoice—Voucher.
§ 13.307 Forms.

Subpart 13.4 Fast Payment Procedure

§ 13.401 General.
§ 13.402 Conditions for use.
§ 13.403 Preparation and execution of orders.
§ 13.404 Contract clause.

Subpart 13.5 Simplified Procedures for Certain Commercial Items

§ 13.500 General.
§ 13.501 Special documentation requirements.

§ 13.000 Scope of part.

This part prescribes policies and procedures for the acquisition of supplies and services, including construction, research and development, and commercial items, the aggregate amount of which does not exceed the simplified acquisition threshold (see 2.101). subpart 13.5 provides special authority for acquisitions of commercial items exceeding the simplified acquisition threshold but not exceeding $7 million ($13 million for acquisitions as described in 13.500(c)), including options. See Part 12 for policies applicable to the acquisition of commercial items exceeding the micro-purchase threshold. See 36.602-5 for simplified procedures to be used when acquiring architect-engineer services.

United States Code Annotated

Commercially available off-the-shelf item acquisitions, lists of inapplicable laws in Federal Acquisition Regulation, see 41 USCA § 431.

Competition requirements, see 41 USCA § 253.

Contract requirements, see 41 USCA § 254.

Contracts, competition requirements, see 10 USCA § 2304.

Contracts, planning, solicitation, evaluation, and award procedures, see 10 USCA § 2305.

Definitions, see 10 USCA § 2302, 41 USCA §§ 259, 403.

Definitions relating to procurement of commercial items, see 10 USCA § 2376, 41 USCA § 264a.

Implementation of simplified acquisition procedures, see 10 USCA § 2302b, 41 USCA § 252b.

Kinds of contracts, see 10 USCA § 2306.

List of laws inapplicable to contracts not greater than simplified acquisition threshold in Federal Acquisition Regulation, see 41 USCA § 429.

List of laws inapplicable to procurements of commercial items in Federal Acquisition Regulation, see 41 USCA § 430.

Planning and solicitation requirements, see 41 USCA § 253a.

Preference for acquisition of commercial items, see 10 USCA § 2377, 41 USCA § 264b.

Relationship of commercial item provisions to other provisions of law, see 10 USCA § 2375, 41 USCA § 264.

Simplified acquisition procedures, see 41 USCA § 427.

§ 13.001 Definitions.

As used in this part—

"Authorized individual" means a person who has been granted authority, in accordance with agency procedures, to acquire supplies and services in accordance with this part.

"Governmentwide commercial purchase card" means a purchase card, similar in nature to a commercial credit card, issued to authorized agency personnel to use to acquire and to pay for supplies and services.

"Imprest fund" means a cash fund of a fixed amount established by an advance of funds, without charge to an appropriation, from an agency finance or disbursing officer to a duly appointed cashier, for disbursement as needed from time to time in making payment in cash for relatively small amounts.

"Third party draft" means an agency bank draft, similar to a check, that is used to acquire and to pay for supplies and services. (See Treasury Financial Management Manual, Section 3040.70.)

United States Code Annotated

Commercially available off-the-shelf item acquisitions, lists of inapplicable laws in Federal Acquisition Regulation, see 41 USCA § 431.

Competition requirements, see 41 USCA § 253.

Contract requirements, see 41 USCA § 254.

Contracts, competition requirements, see 10 USCA § 2304.

Contracts, planning, solicitation, evaluation, and award procedures, see 10 USCA § 2305.

Definitions, see 10 USCA § 2302, 41 USCA §§ 259, 403.

Definitions relating to procurement of commercial items, see 10 USCA § 2376, 41 USCA § 264a.

Implementation of simplified acquisition procedures, see 10 USCA § 2302b, 41 USCA § 252b.

Kinds of contracts, see 10 USCA § 2306.

List of laws inapplicable to contracts not greater than simplified acquisition threshold in Federal Acquisition Regulation, see 41 USCA § 429.

List of laws inapplicable to procurements of commercial items in Federal Acquisition Regulation, see 41 USCA § 430.

Planning and solicitation requirements, see 41 USCA § 253a.

Preference for acquisition of commercial items, see 10 USCA § 2377, 41 USCA § 264b.

Relationship of commercial item provisions to other provisions of law, see 10 USCA § 2375, 41 USCA § 264.

Simplified acquisition procedures, see 41 USCA § 427.

§ 13.002 Purpose.

The purpose of this part is to prescribe simplified acquisition procedures in order to—

(a) Reduce administrative costs;

(b) Improve opportunities for small, small disadvantaged, women-owned, veteran-owned, HUBZone, and service-disabled veteran-owned small business concerns to obtain a fair proportion of Government contracts;

(c) Promote efficiency and economy in contracting; and

(d) Avoid unnecessary burdens for agencies and contractors.

United States Code Annotated

Commercially available off-the-shelf item acquisitions, lists of inapplicable laws in Federal Acquisition Regulation, see 41 USCA § 431.

Competition requirements, see 41 USCA § 253.

Contract requirements, see 41 USCA § 254.

Contracts, competition requirements, see 10 USCA § 2304.

Contracts, planning, solicitation, evaluation, and award procedures, see 10 USCA § 2305.

Definitions, see 10 USCA § 2302, 41 USCA §§ 259, 403.

Definitions relating to procurement of commercial items, see 10 USCA § 2376, 41 USCA § 264a.

Implementation of simplified acquisition procedures, see 10 USCA § 2302b, 41 USCA § 252b.

Kinds of contracts, see 10 USCA § 2306.

List of laws inapplicable to contracts not greater than simplified acquisition threshold in Federal Acquisition Regulation, see 41 USCA § 429.

List of laws inapplicable to procurements of commercial items in Federal Acquisition Regulation, see 41 USCA § 430.

Planning and solicitation requirements, see 41 USCA § 253a.

Preference for acquisition of commercial items, see 10 USCA § 2377, 41 USCA § 264b.

Relationship of commercial item provisions to other provisions of law, see 10 USCA § 2375, 41 USCA § 264.

Simplified acquisition procedures, see 41 USCA § 427.

Simplified acquisition procedures, see 41 USCA § 427.

Notes of Decisions

In general 1
Splitting orders 2

1 In general

Contracting officer did not abuse his discretion in failing to set aside spot tug boat work for small business, where only evidence was that there were less than two such businesses available in area. 48 C.F.R. § 13.003(b)(1). Petchem, Inc. v. U.S., 99 F. Supp. 2d 50 (D.D.C. 2000). United States ⊶64.15

Part 13 is aimed at streamlining the procurement process and advises agencies to use simplified acquisition procedures where the value of the acquisition is below the simplified acquisition threshold; to make simplified purchases in the most suitable, efficient, and economical manner based on the circumstances of the acquisition; and to use innovative procedures to the maximum extent practicable. Reverse auctions are consistent with these goals of FAR Part 13 and promote the underlying purpose of that regulation. MTB Group, Inc., B-295463, 2005 CPD ¶ 40 (Comp. Gen. 2005).

2 Splitting orders

Federal agency may not fragment procurement order that would otherwise fall above simplified acquisition threshold simply to take advantage of simplified procedures. 10 U.S.C.A. § 2304(g)(2); 48 C.F.R. § 13.003. Petchem, Inc. v. U.S., 99 F. Supp. 2d 50 (D.D.C. 2000). United States ⊶64.10

Navy did not improperly fragment contract for procurement of tug boat services when, after determining that solicited bids were too high, it canceled solicitation and began procuring tug services on piecemeal, spot-bid basis; spot-bid practice was not attempt to evade competitive bidding procedures, and contract requirements were not precisely known. 10 U.S.C.A. § 2304(g)(2); 48 C.F.R. § 13.003. Petchem, Inc. v. U.S., 99 F. Supp. 2d 50 (D.D.C. 2000). United States ⊶64.25

§ 13.003 Policy.

(a) Agencies shall use simplified acquisition procedures to the maximum extent practicable for all purchases of supplies or services not exceeding the simplified acquisition threshold (including purchases at or below the micro-purchase threshold). This policy does not apply if an agency can meet its requirement using—

(1) Required sources of supply under Part 8 (e.g., Federal Prison Industries, Committee for Purchase from People Who are Blind or Severely Disabled, and Federal Supply Schedule contracts);

(2) Existing indefinite delivery/indefinite quantity contracts; or

(3) Other established contracts.

(b) (1) Acquisitions of supplies or services that have an anticipated dollar value exceeding

$3,500 ($20,000 for acquisitions as described in 13.201(g)(1)) but not exceeding $150,000 ($300,000 for acquisitions described in paragraph (1)(i) of the simplified acquisition threshold definition at 2.101) are reserved exclusively for small business concerns and shall be set aside (see 19.000, 19.203, and subpart 19.5).

(2) The contracting officer may make an award to a small business concern under the—

(i) 8(a) Program (see subpart 19.8);

(ii) Historically Underutilized Business Zone (HUBZone) Program (but see 19.1305 and 19.1306(a)(4));

(iii) Service-Disabled Veteran-Owned Small Business (SDVOSB) Program (see subpart 19.14); or

(iv) Women-Owned Small Business (WOSB) Program (see subpart 19.15).

(3) The following contracting officer's decisions for acquisitions at or below the simplified acquisition threshold are not subject to review under subpart 19.4:

(i) A decision not to make an award under the 8(a) Program.

(ii) A decision not to set aside an acquisition for HUBZone small business concerns, service-disabled veteran-owned small business concerns, or EDWOSB concerns and WOSB concerns eligible under the WOSB Program.

(4) Each written solicitation under a set-aside shall contain the appropriate provisions prescribed by part 19. If the solicitation is oral, however, information substantially identical to that in the provision shall be given to potential quoters.

(c) (1) The contracting officer shall not use simplified acquisition procedures to acquire supplies and services if the anticipated award will exceed—

(i) The simplified acquisition threshold; or

(ii) $7 million ($13 million for acquisitions as described in 13.500(c)), including options, for acquisitions of commercial items using subpart 13.5.

(2) Do not break down requirements aggregating more than the simplified acquisition threshold (or for commercial items, the threshold in subpart 13.5) or the micro-purchase threshold into several purchases that are less than the applicable threshold merely to—

(i) Permit use of simplified acquisition procedures; or

(ii) Avoid any requirement that applies to purchases exceeding the micro-purchase threshold.

(d) An agency that has specific statutory authority to acquire personal services (see 37.104) may use simplified acquisition procedures to acquire those services.

(e) Agencies shall use the Governmentwide commercial purchase card and electronic purchasing techniques to the maximum extent practicable in conducting simplified acquisitions (but see 32.1108(b)(2)).

(f) Agencies shall maximize the use of electronic commerce when practicable and cost-effective (see subpart 4.5). Drawings and lengthy specifications can be provided off-line in hard copy or through other appropriate means.

(g) Authorized individuals shall make purchases in the simplified manner that is most suitable, efficient, and economical based on the circumstances of each acquisition. For acquisitions not expected to exceed—

(1) The simplified acquisition threshold for other than commercial items, use any appropriate combination of the procedures in Parts 13, 14, 15, 35, or 36, including the use of Standard Form 1442, Solicitation, Offer, and Award (Construction, Alteration, or Repair), for construction contracts (see 36.701(a)); or

(2) $7 million ($13 million for acquisitions as described in 13.500(c)), for commercial items, use any appropriate combination of the procedures in Parts 12, 13, 14, and 15 (see paragraph (d) of this section).

(h) In addition to other considerations, contracting officers shall—

(1) Promote competition to the maximum extent practicable (see 13.104);

(2) Establish deadlines for the submission of responses to solicitations that afford suppliers a reasonable opportunity to respond (see 5.203);

(3) Consider all quotations or offers that are timely received. For evaluation of quotations or offers received electronically, see 13.106-2(b)(3); and

(4) Use innovative approaches, to the maximum extent practicable, in awarding

contracts using simplified acquisition procedures.

United States Code Annotated

Commercially available off-the-shelf item acquisitions, lists of inapplicable laws in Federal Acquisition Regulation, see 41 USCA § 431.

Competition requirements, see 41 USCA § 253.

Contract requirements, see 41 USCA § 254.

Contracts, competition requirements, see 10 USCA § 2304.

Contracts, planning, solicitation, evaluation, and award procedures, see 10 USCA § 2305.

Definitions, see 10 USCA § 2302, 41 USCA §§ 259, 403.

Definitions relating to procurement of commercial items, see 10 USCA § 2376, 41 USCA § 264a.

Implementation of simplified acquisition procedures, see 10 USCA § 2302b, 41 USCA § 252b.

Kinds of contracts, see 10 USCA § 2306.

List of laws inapplicable to contracts not greater than simplified acquisition threshold in Federal Acquisition Regulation, see 41 USCA § 429.

List of laws inapplicable to procurements of commercial items in Federal Acquisition Regulation, see 41 USCA § 430.

Planning and solicitation requirements, see 41 USCA § 253a.

Preference for acquisition of commercial items, see 10 USCA § 2377, 41 USCA § 264b.

Relationship of commercial item provisions to other provisions of law, see 10 USCA § 2375, 41 USCA § 264.

Simplified acquisition procedures, see 41 USCA § 427.

Notes of Decisions

Fragmentation of order 2
Small businesses 1

1 Small businesses

Contracting officer did not abuse his discretion in failing to set aside spot tug boat work for small business, where only evidence was that there were less than two such businesses available in area. 48 C.F.R. § 13.003(b)(1). Petchem, Inc. v. U.S., 99 F. Supp. 2d 50 (D.D.C. 2000). United States ☞64.15

2 Fragmentation of order

Navy did not improperly fragment contract for procurement of tug boat services when, after determining that solicited bids were too high, it canceled solicitation and began procuring tug services on piecemeal, spot-bid basis; spot-bid practice was not attempt to evade competitive bidding procedures, and contract requirements were not precisely known. 10 U.S.C.A. § 2304(g)(2); 48 C.F.R. § 13.003. Petchem, Inc. v. U.S., 99 F. Supp. 2d 50 (D.D.C. 2000). United States ☞64.25

Federal agency may not fragment procurement order that would otherwise fall above simplified acquisition threshold simply to take advantage of simplified procedures. 10 U.S.C.A. § 2304(g)(2); 48 C.F.R. § 13.003. Petchem, Inc. v. U.S., 99 F. Supp. 2d 50 (D.D.C. 2000). United States ☞64.10

The procurement history showed that the value of a requirement was likely to exceed the $100,000 simplified acquisition threshold and thus precluded the use of simplified acquisition procedures. The GAO used the highest and lowest historical prices listed in the RFQ to estimate the potential value as between $205,881 and $343,977. Although DLA argued that it was not obligated to purchase the estimated quantity, the Comp. Gen. held that there was "no basis for DLA's approach of using simplified acquisition procedures where its estimated requirement for these filters cannot reasonably be expected to fall within the applicable threshold." Decision Matter of: Critical Process Filtration, Inc., B-400746, B-400747, B-400750, B-400751, B-400752, B-400785, 2009 CPD ¶ 25 (Comp. Gen. 2009)

§ 13.004 Legal effect of quotations.

(a) A quotation is not an offer and, consequently, cannot be accepted by the Government to form a binding contract. Therefore, issuance by the Government of an order in response to a supplier's quotation does not establish a contract. The order is an offer by the Government to the supplier to buy certain supplies or services upon specified terms and conditions. A contract is established when the supplier accepts the offer.

(b) When appropriate, the contracting officer may ask the supplier to indicate acceptance of an order by notification to the Government, preferably in writing, as defined at 2.101. In other circumstances, the supplier may indicate acceptance by furnishing the supplies or services ordered or by proceeding with the work to the point where substantial performance has occurred.

(c) If the Government issues an order resulting from a quotation, the Government may (by written notice to the supplier, at any time before acceptance occurs) withdraw, amend, or cancel its offer. (See 13.302-4 for procedures on termination or cancellation of purchase orders.)

United States Code Annotated

Commercially available off-the-shelf item acquisitions, lists of inapplicable laws in Federal Acquisition Regulation, see 41 USCA § 431.

Competition requirements, see 41 USCA § 253.

Contract requirements, see 41 USCA § 254.

Contracts, competition requirements, see 10 USCA § 2304.

Contracts, planning, solicitation, evaluation, and award procedures, see 10 USCA § 2305.

Definitions, see 10 USCA § 2302, 41 USCA §§ 259, 403.

Definitions relating to procurement of commercial items, see 10 USCA § 2376, 41 USCA § 264a.

Implementation of simplified acquisition procedures, see 10 USCA § 2302b, 41 USCA § 252b.

Kinds of contracts, see 10 USCA § 2306.

List of laws inapplicable to contracts not greater than simplified acquisition threshold in Federal Acquisition Regulation, see 41 USCA § 429.

List of laws inapplicable to procurements of commercial items in Federal Acquisition Regulation, see 41 USCA § 430.

Planning and solicitation requirements, see 41 USCA § 253a.

Preference for acquisition of commercial items, see 10 USCA § 2377, 41 USCA § 264b.

Relationship of commercial item provisions to other provisions of law, see 10 USCA § 2375, 41 USCA § 264.

Simplified acquisition procedures, see 41 USCA § 427.

Notes of Decisions

Acceptance 3
Late quotations 2
Non-conforming quotations 4
Purchase orders 1

1 Purchase orders

Purchase order cancellation and termination provisions of the Federal Acquisition Regulation (FAR) were not applicable to purchase order which lapsed when supplier failed to perform by the delivery date, as such provisions are only applicable where the government cancels or terminates a purchase order before the purchase order's delivery date. FAR 13.004(c), 13.302-4. Kaeper Machine, Inc. v. U.S., 74 Fed. Cl. 1 (2006)

Supplier's performance of government purchase order did not establish a contract with government under regulation providing that purchase orders may be accepted by "substantial performance," where government had received no benefit whatsoever when delivery date specified in purchase order passed. Smart Business Machines v. U.S., 72 Fed. Cl. 706 (2006). United States ☞66

2 Late quotations

Partial performance in response to agency purchase orders (POs) created an option allowing the company to accept the agency's offers by completing performance according to the offers' terms. Because the company did not complete performance by the date specified in the POs, the offers lapsed. In re Comptech Corp., A.S.B.C.A. No. 55526, 08-2, 08-2 B.C.A. (CCH) ¶ 33982, 2008 WL 4628786 (Armed Serv. B.C.A. 2008)

The Government, moreover, was under no obligation to issue a purchase order to the lowest priced quoter where the quote was submitted more than a week after the estimated performance start date. The quote was, at best, a counteroffer that the Government could reject. Appeal of Harney County Gypsum Co., A.G.B.C.A. No. 93-190-1, 94-1 B.C.A. (CCH) ¶ 26455, 1993 WL 439498 (Dep't Agric. B.C.A. 1993)

GAO sustained a protest of a purchase order issued by the Government Printing Office (GPO) because the awardee's quotation was received after the deadline and the solicitation terms specifically excluded untimely quotations. Because the contract was already performed, GAO recommended reimbursement of the protester's costs of preparing its quotation and pursuing the protest, including attorneys' fees and costs. Decision Matter of: Data Integrators, Inc., B-310928, 2008 CPD ¶ 27 (Comp. Gen. 2008)

The strict standard applicable to late bids and proposals does not generally apply to quotations submitted in response to a Request for Quotations (RFQ). An RFQ, unlike a request for proposals (or an invitation for bids), does not seek offers that can be accepted by the government to form a contract. Rather, the government's purchase order represents the offer that the vendor may accept through performance or by a formal acceptance document. Therefore, language in an RFQ requesting quotations by a certain date cannot be construed as establishing a firm closing date for receipt of quotations, absent a late quotation provision expressly providing that quotations must be received by that date to be considered. Armed Forces Merchandise Outlet, Inc., B-294281, 2004 CPD ¶ 218 (Comp. Gen. 2004)

Language in an RFQ requesting quotations by a certain date does not establish a firm closing date for receipt of quotations, absent a late submission provision expressly providing that quotations must be received by that date to be considered. Instruments & Controls Service Company, B-222122, 86-2 CPD ¶ 16 (Comp. Gen. 1986)

3 Acceptance

A purchase order such as this PO is an offer by the government to the supplier to buy certain supplies or services upon specified terms and conditions. A contract is established when the supplier accepts the order, by furnishing the supplies or services ordered or by proceeding with the work to the point of substantial performance prior to the due date. In re Friedman Enterprises, Inc., A.S.B.C.A. No. 54886, 05-2 B.C.A. (CCH) ¶ 32991, 2005 WL 1385135 (Armed Serv. B.C.A. 2005)

A quotation in response to an RFQ, which is provided for only by the simplified acquisition procedures in FAR Part 13, unlike a proposal in response to an RFP ("request for proposals") under FAR Part 15, does not give the government the power of acceptance, but only the power to make an offer that, in turn, may be accepted by the vendor, at its option. See FAR 13.004(a). Seaborn Health Care, Inc. v. U.S., 55 Fed. Cl. 520 (2003)

A quotation submitted in response to an agency's Request for Quotations (RFQ) is not a submission for acceptance by the government to form a binding contract. Rather, vendor quotations are purely informational. In the RFQ context, it is the government that makes the offer, albeit generally based on the information provided by the vendor in its quotation, and no binding agreement is created until the vendor accepts the offer. Sea Box, Inc., B-405711.2, 2012 CPD ¶ 116 (Comp. Gen. 2012)

Under a request for quotations issued in a competitive procurement under the Federal Supply Schedule, protest that the agency improperly made award based on a price discount that had expired by the terms of the vendor's quotation is denied as the vendor's submission was not an offer to which the standard for expired bids generally applies. Computer Associates International, Inc., B-292077.3, B-292077.4, B-292077.5, 2004 CPD ¶ 163 (Comp. Gen. 2004)

4 Non-conforming quotations

GAO rejected the agency's argument that, because quotations are not "offers" that the agency can accept to form a binding contract, the agency may select a quotation that does not comply with the RFQ's requirements, if the agency finds that the quotation will otherwise satisfy its needs. The legal nature of a quotation vis-à-vis "offer" and "acceptance" in the context of a RFQ issued to Federal Supply Schedule (FSS) vendors does not alter the fundamental requirement that the FSS competition be conducted fairly and in a manner that affords vendors an opportunity to compete on an equal basis. Hanel Storage Sys., L.P., B-409030.2, 2015 CPD ¶ 87 (Comp. Gen. 2015)

§ 13.005 List of laws inapplicable to contracts and subcontracts at or below the simplified acquisition threshold.

(a) The following laws are inapplicable to all contracts and subcontracts (if otherwise applicable to subcontracts) at or below the simplified acquisition threshold pursuant to 41 U.S.C. 1905:

(1) 41 U.S.C. 8703 and (Kickbacks statute). (Only the requirement for the incorporation of the contractor procedures for the prevention and detection of violations, and the contractual requirement for contractor cooperation in investigations are inapplicable.)

(2) 40 U.S.C. 3131 (Bonds statute). (Although the Bonds statute does not apply to contracts at or below the simplified acquisition threshold, alternative forms of payment protection for suppliers of labor and material (see 28.102) are still required if the contract exceeds $35,000 (40 U.S.C. 3132).)

(3) 40 U.S.C. chapter 37 et seq. (Contract Work Hours and Safety Standards-Overtime Compensation).

(4) 41 U.S.C. 8102(a)(1) (Drug-Free Workplace), except for individuals.

(5) 42 U.S.C. 6962 (Solid Waste Disposal Act). (The requirement to provide an estimate of recovered material utilized in contract performance does not apply unless the contract value exceeds $150,000.)

(6) 10 U.S.C. 2306(b) and 41 U.S.C. 3901(b) (Contract Clause Regarding Contingent Fees).

(7) 10 U.S.C. 2313 and 41 U.S.C. 7406 (Authority to Examine Books and Records of Contractors).

(8) 10 U.S.C. 2402 and 41 U.S.C. 4704 (Prohibition on Limiting Subcontractors Direct Sales to the United States).

(9) 15 U.S.C. 631 note (HUBZone Act of 1997), except for 15 U.S.C. 657a(b)(2)(B), which is optional for the agencies subject to the requirements of the Act.

(10) 31 U.S.C. 1354(a) (Limitation on use of appropriated funds for contracts with entities not meeting veterans' employment reporting requirements).

(b) The Federal Acquisition Regulatory (FAR) Council will include any law enacted after October 13, 1994, that sets forth policies, procedures, requirements, or restrictions for the acquisition of property or services, on the list set forth in paragraph (a) of this section. The FAR Council may make exceptions when it determines in writing that it is in the best interest of the Government that the enactment should apply to contracts or subcontracts not greater than the simplified acquisition threshold.

(c) The provisions of paragraph (b) of this section do not apply to laws that—

(1) Provide for criminal or civil penalties; or

(2) Specifically state that notwithstanding the language of 41 U.S.C. 1905, the enactment will be applicable to contracts or subcontracts in amounts not greater than the simplified acquisition threshold.

(d) Any individual may petition the Administrator, Office of Federal Procurement Policy (OFPP), to include any applicable provision of law not included on the list set forth in paragraph (a) of this section unless the FAR Council has already determined in writing that the law is applicable. The Administrator, OFPP, will include the law on the list in paragraph (a) of this section unless the FAR Council makes a determination that it is applicable within 60 days of receiving the petition.

United States Code Annotated

Commercially available off-the-shelf item acquisitions, lists of inapplicable laws in Federal Acquisition Regulation, see 41 USCA § 431.

Competition requirements, see 41 USCA § 253.

Contract requirements, see 41 USCA § 254.

Contracts, competition requirements, see 10 USCA § 2304.

Contracts, planning, solicitation, evaluation, and award procedures, see 10 USCA § 2305.

Definitions, see 10 USCA § 2302, 41 USCA §§ 259, 403.

Definitions relating to procurement of commercial items, see 10 USCA § 2376, 41 USCA § 264a.

Implementation of simplified acquisition procedures, see 10 USCA § 2302b, 41 USCA § 252b.

Kinds of contracts, see 10 USCA § 2306.

List of laws inapplicable to contracts not greater than simplified acquisition threshold in Federal Acquisition Regulation, see 41 USCA § 429.

List of laws inapplicable to procurements of commercial items in Federal Acquisition Regulation, see 41 USCA § 430.

Planning and solicitation requirements, see 41 USCA § 253a.

Preference for acquisition of commercial items, see 10 USCA § 2377, 41 USCA § 264b.

Relationship of commercial item provisions to other provisions of law, see 10 USCA § 2375, 41 USCA § 264.

Simplified acquisition procedures, see 41 USCA § 427.

§ 13.006 Inapplicable provisions and clauses.

While certain statutes still apply, pursuant to Public Law 103-355, the following provisions and clauses are inapplicable to contracts and subcontracts at or below the simplified acquisition threshold:

(a) 52.203-5, Covenant Against Contingent Fees.

(b) 52.203-6, Restrictions on Subcontractor Sales to the Government.

(c) 52.203-7, Anti-Kickback Procedures.

(d) 52.215-2, Audits and Records—Negotiation, except as used with its Alternate I, when using funds appropriated or otherwise made available by the American Recovery and Reinvestment Act of 2009 (Pub. L. 111-5).

(e) 52.222-4, Contract Work Hours and Safety Standards—Overtime Compensation.

(f) 52.223-6, Drug-Free Workplace, except for individuals.

(g) 52.223-9, Estimate of Percentage of Recovered Material Content for EPA-Designated Items.

United States Code Annotated

Commercially available off-the-shelf item acquisitions, lists of inapplicable laws in Federal Acquisition Regulation, see 41 USCA § 431.

Competition requirements, see 41 USCA § 253.

Contract requirements, see 41 USCA § 254.

Contracts, competition requirements, see 10 USCA § 2304.

Contracts, planning, solicitation, evaluation, and award procedures, see 10 USCA § 2305.

Definitions, see 10 USCA § 2302, 41 USCA §§ 259, 403.

Definitions relating to procurement of commercial items, see 10 USCA § 2376, 41 USCA § 264a.

Implementation of simplified acquisition procedures, see 10 USCA § 2302b, 41 USCA § 252b.

Kinds of contracts, see 10 USCA § 2306.

List of laws inapplicable to contracts not greater than simplified acquisition threshold in Federal Acquisition Regulation, see 41 USCA § 429.

List of laws inapplicable to procurements of commercial items in Federal Acquisition Regulation, see 41 USCA § 430.

Planning and solicitation requirements, see 41 USCA § 253a.

Preference for acquisition of commercial items, see 10 USCA § 2377, 41 USCA § 264b.

Relationship of commercial item provisions to other provisions of law, see 10 USCA § 2375, 41 USCA § 264.

Simplified acquisition procedures, see 41 USCA § 427.

Subpart 13.1 Procedures

§ 13.101 General.

(a) In making purchases, contracting officers shall—

(1) Comply with the policy in 7.202 relating to economic purchase quantities, when practicable;

(2) Satisfy the procedures described in Subpart 19.6 with respect to Certificates of Competency before rejecting a quotation, oral or written, from a small business concern determined to be nonresponsible (see Subpart 9.1); and

(3) Provide for the inspection of supplies or services as prescribed in 46.404.

(b) In making purchases, contracting officers should—

(1) Include related items (such as small hardware items or spare parts for vehicles) in one solicitation and make award on an "all-or-none" or "multiple award" basis provided suppliers are so advised when quotations or offers are requested;

(2) Incorporate provisions and clauses by reference in solicitations and in awards under requests for quotations, provided the requirements in 52.102 are satisfied;

(3) Make maximum effort to obtain trade and prompt payment discounts (see 14.408-3). Prompt payment discounts shall not be considered in the evaluation of quotations; and

(4) Use bulk funding to the maximum extent practicable. Bulk funding is a system whereby the contracting officer receives authorization from a fiscal and accounting officer to obligate funds on purchase documents against a specified lump sum of funds reserved for the purpose for a specified period of time rather than obtaining individual obligational authority on each purchase document. Bulk funding is particularly appropriate if numerous purchases using the same type of funds are to be made during a given period.

United States Code Annotated

Commercially available off-the-shelf item acquisitions, lists of inapplicable laws in Federal Acquisition Regulation, see 41 USCA § 431.

Competition requirements, see 41 USCA § 253.

Contract requirements, see 41 USCA § 254.

Contracts, competition requirements, see 10 USCA § 2304.

Contracts, planning, solicitation, evaluation, and award procedures, see 10 USCA § 2305.

Definitions, see 10 USCA § 2302, 41 USCA §§ 259, 403.

Definitions relating to procurement of commercial items, see 10 USCA § 2376, 41 USCA § 264a.

Implementation of simplified acquisition procedures, see 10 USCA § 2302b, 41 USCA § 252b.

Kinds of contracts, see 10 USCA § 2306.

List of laws inapplicable to contracts not greater than simplified acquisition threshold in Federal Acquisition Regulation, see 41 USCA § 429.

List of laws inapplicable to procurements of commercial items in Federal Acquisition Regulation, see 41 USCA § 430.

Planning and solicitation requirements, see 41 USCA § 253a.

Preference for acquisition of commercial items, see 10 USCA § 2377, 41 USCA § 264b.

Relationship of commercial item provisions to other provisions of law, see 10 USCA § 2375, 41 USCA § 264.

Simplified acquisition procedures, see 41 USCA § 427.

§ 13.102 Source list.

(a) Contracting officers should use the System for Award Management database (see subpart 4.11) via https://www.acquisition.gov as their primary sources of vendor information. Offices maintaining additional vendor source files or listings should identify the status of each source (when the status is made known to the contracting office) in the following categories:

(1) Small business.

(2) Small disadvantaged business.

(3) Women-owned small business concern, including economically disadvantaged women-owned small business concerns and women-owned small business concerns eligible under the Women-owned Small Business (WOSB) Program.

(4) HUBZone small business.

(5) Service-disabled veteran-owned small business.

(6) Veteran-owned small business.

(b) The status information may be used as the basis to ensure that small business concerns are provided the maximum practicable opportunities to respond to solicitations issued using simplified acquisition procedures.

§ 13.103 Use of standing price quotations.

Authorized individuals do not have to obtain individual quotations for each purchase. Standing price quotations may be used if—

(a) The pricing information is current; and

(b) The Government obtains the benefit of maximum discounts before award.

United States Code Annotated

Commercially available off-the-shelf item acquisitions, lists of inapplicable laws in Federal Acquisition Regulation, see 41 USCA § 431.

Competition requirements, see 41 USCA § 253.

Contract requirements, see 41 USCA § 254.

Contracts, competition requirements, see 10 USCA § 2304.

Contracts, planning, solicitation, evaluation, and award procedures, see 10 USCA § 2305.

Definitions, see 10 USCA § 2302, 41 USCA §§ 259, 403.

Definitions relating to procurement of commercial items, see 10 USCA § 2376, 41 USCA § 264a.

Implementation of simplified acquisition procedures, see 10 USCA § 2302b, 41 USCA § 252b.

Kinds of contracts, see 10 USCA § 2306.

List of laws inapplicable to contracts not greater than simplified acquisition threshold in Federal Acquisition Regulation, see 41 USCA § 429.

List of laws inapplicable to procurements of commercial items in Federal Acquisition Regulation, see 41 USCA § 430.

Planning and solicitation requirements, see 41 USCA § 253a.

Preference for acquisition of commercial items, see 10 USCA § 2377, 41 USCA § 264b.

Relationship of commercial item provisions to other provisions of law, see 10 USCA § 2375, 41 USCA § 264.

Simplified acquisition procedures, see 41 USCA § 427.

§ 13.104 Promoting competition.

The contracting officer must promote competition to the maximum extent practicable to obtain supplies and services from the source whose offer is the most advantageous to the Government, considering the administrative cost of the purchase.

(a) The contracting officer must not—

(1) Solicit quotations based on personal preference; or

(2) Restrict solicitation to suppliers of well-known and widely distributed makes or brands.

(b) If using simplified acquisition procedures and not providing access to the notice of proposed contract action and solicitation information through the Governmentwide point of entry (GPE), maximum practicable competition ordinarily can be obtained by soliciting quotations or offers from sources within the local trade area. Unless the contract action requires synopsis pursuant to 5.101 and an exception under 5.202 is not applicable, consider solicitation of at least three sources to promote competition to the maximum extent practicable. Whenever practicable, request quotations or offers from two sources not included in the previous solicitation.

United States Code Annotated

Commercially available off-the-shelf item acquisitions, lists of inapplicable laws in Federal Acquisition Regulation, see 41 USCA § 431.

Competition requirements, see 41 USCA § 253.

Contract requirements, see 41 USCA § 254.

Contracts, competition requirements, see 10 USCA § 2304.

Contracts, planning, solicitation, evaluation, and award procedures, see 10 USCA § 2305.

Definitions, see 10 USCA § 2302, 41 USCA §§ 259, 403.

Definitions relating to procurement of commercial items, see 10 USCA § 2376, 41 USCA § 264a.

Implementation of simplified acquisition procedures, see 10 USCA § 2302b, 41 USCA § 252b.

Kinds of contracts, see 10 USCA § 2306.

List of laws inapplicable to contracts not greater than simplified acquisition threshold in Federal Acquisition Regulation, see 41 USCA § 429.

List of laws inapplicable to procurements of commercial items in Federal Acquisition Regulation, see 41 USCA § 430.

Planning and solicitation requirements, see 41 USCA § 253a.

Preference for acquisition of commercial items, see 10 USCA § 2377, 41 USCA § 264b.

Relationship of commercial item provisions to other provisions of law, see 10 USCA § 2375, 41 USCA § 264.

Simplified acquisition procedures, see 41 USCA § 427.

Notes of Decisions

In general 1
Brand name solicitation 2

1 In general

Generally, before a procuring agency may award an 8(a) sole-source contract, it must submit an offer letter for the procurement to the SBA, and the SBA must accept it. 13 C.F.R. § 124.502(a). However, section 8(a) regulations provide that when the value of a proposed contract falls below the simplified acquisition threshold, an agency that has sent an offer letter for the contract to the SBA "may assume the offer is accepted and proceed with award" of the contract if the agency "does not receive a reply [from the SBA] within two days" of sending the offer letter. 13 C.F.R. § 124.503(a)(4)(i). Eagle Collaborative Computing Services, Inc., B-401043.3 (Comp. Gen. 2011)

Part 13 of the FAR establishes procedures for simplified acquisitions, which are designed to promote efficiency and economy in contracting and to avoid unnecessary burdens for agencies and contractors. To facilitate these objectives, the Federal Acquisition Streamlining Act (FASA) requires only that contracting agencies obtain competition to the "maximum extent practicable." Logan, LLC, B-294974.6, 2006 CPD ¶ 188 (Comp. Gen. 2006)

Agency unreasonably awarded a contract for the design and construction of an exhibition pavilion on a sole-source basis under simplified acquisition procedures to a firm that the agency believed the exhibit organizer required be used, where the agency's belief was erroneous and unreasonable. That the agency acted in good faith based on the best information available at the time is not a legitimate defense to a protest. GAO's review is based on whether the agency's sole-source decision was reasonable based on the information reasonably available to the agency at the time of the sole-source decision, not whether the agency acted in good faith. Matter of: Europe Displays, Inc., B-297099, 2005 CPD ¶ 214 (Comp. Gen. 2005)

Under the Federal Acquisition Streamlining Act of 1994 (FASA), procurements conducted using simplified acquisition procedures-used to purchase supplies and services, including construction, research and development, and commercial items, the aggregate amount of which does not exceed $100,000—are excepted from the general requirement that agencies obtain full and open competition through the use of competitive procedures when conducting procurements. 10 U.S.C. §§ 2304(a)(1)(A), (g)(1), (g)(3) (1994 & Supp. IV 1998). FASA requires only that agencies obtain competition to the maximum extent practicable when they utilize simplified acquisition procedures. 10 U.S.C. § 2304(g)(3); FAR § 13.104. This standard is usually met if an agency solicits at least three sources. GMA Cover Corporation, B-288018, 2001 CPD ¶ 144 (Comp. Gen. 2001)

Where agency determines that an item should be procured under small purchase procedures on a sole-source basis but provides for other offerors to supply pertinent information to demonstrate ability to provide required item, agency's failure to evaluate and determine the acceptability of protester's alternate item in a timely manner denies protester a reasonable opportunity to qualify as a source and to compete for award and violates the requirement under the small purchase procedures to obtain competition to the maximum extent practicable. Helitune, Inc., B-243617, B-243617.2, 1992 WL 59229 (Comp. Gen. 1992)

2 Brand name solicitation

Agency unreasonably evaluated the protester's bid of an equal product under a brand name or equal solicitation conducted under simplified acquisition procedures where the solicitation lacked salient characteristics and the equal product was not shown to be significantly different from the brand name product. Veterans Healthcare Supply Solutions, Inc., B-407223.2, 2013 CPD ¶ 3 (Comp. Gen. 2013)

Acquisitions conducted under FAR Parts 12 and 13 are not exempt from the requirement for the agency to identify salient characteristics of an item described in a brand name or equal specification. A brand name or equal RFQ is defective because it did not list salient characteristics, so that quoters offering equal products were left to guess at the desired essential qualities of the brand-name item. Where an agency does not include a list of salient characteristics in the solicitation, it is precluded from rejecting a quote offering an equal product for noncompliance with some performance or design feature, unless the offered item is significantly different from the brand-name product. Elementar Americas, Inc., B-289115, 2002 CPD ¶ 20 (Comp. Gen. 2002)

§ 13.105 Synopsis and posting requirements.

(a) The contracting officer must comply with the public display and synopsis requirements of 5.101 and 5.203 unless an exception in 5.202 applies.

(b) When acquiring commercial items or supplies or services procured in accordance with 12.102(f)(1), the contracting officer may use a combined synopsis and solicitation. In these cases, a separate solicitation is not required. The contracting officer must include enough information to permit suppliers to develop quotations or offers.

(c) See 5.102(a)(6) for the requirement to post a brand name justification or documentation required by 13.106-1(b) or 13.501.

(d) When publicizing contract actions funded in whole or in part by the American Recovery and Reinvestment Act of 2009 (Pub. L. 111-5):

(1) Notices of proposed contract actions shall follow the procedures in 5.704 for posting orders.

(2) Award notices shall follow the procedures in 5.705.

United States Code Annotated

Commercially available off-the-shelf item acquisitions, lists of inapplicable laws in Federal Acquisition Regulation, see 41 USCA § 431.

Competition requirements, see 41 USCA § 253.

Contract requirements, see 41 USCA § 254.

Contracts, competition requirements, see 10 USCA § 2304.

Contracts, planning, solicitation, evaluation, and award procedures, see 10 USCA § 2305.

Definitions, see 10 USCA § 2302, 41 USCA §§ 259, 403.

Definitions relating to procurement of commercial items, see 10 USCA § 2376, 41 USCA § 264a.

Implementation of simplified acquisition procedures, see 10 USCA § 2302b, 41 USCA § 252b.

Kinds of contracts, see 10 USCA § 2306.

List of laws inapplicable to contracts not greater than simplified acquisition threshold in Federal Acquisition Regulation, see 41 USCA § 429.

List of laws inapplicable to procurements of commercial items in Federal Acquisition Regulation, see 41 USCA § 430.

Planning and solicitation requirements, see 41 USCA § 253a.

Preference for acquisition of commercial items, see 10 USCA § 2377, 41 USCA § 264b.

Relationship of commercial item provisions to other provisions of law, see 10 USCA § 2375, 41 USCA § 264.

Simplified acquisition procedures, see 41 USCA § 427.

Notes of Decisions

In general 1

1 In general

Regardless of whether a simplified acquisition is competed or reserved for only one source, the simplified acquisition procedures require synopsis of procurements in excess of $25,000 in accordance with the Small Business Act, 15 U.S.C. § 637(e), and the Office of Federal Procurement Policy Act, 41 U.S.C. § 416 (2000). Information Ventures, Inc., B-293541, 2004 CPD ¶ 81 (Comp. Gen. 2004)

Where agency contemplated a sole source purchase under simplified acquisition procedures, and its December 31, 2003, announcement of the intended award established a response period for capability statements from potential sources of 1 1/2 business days (until January 5, 2004), the agency did not provide potential sources with a reasonable opportunity to respond, particularly where the record does not show a need for the short response period and the agency knew of the requirement well in advance of issuing the notice. Information Ventures, Inc., B-293541, 2004 CPD ¶ 81 (Comp. Gen. 2004)

Protest that published synopsis expressing an agency's intent to award a sole-source contract under simplified acquisition procedures was improper because the synopsis lacked necessary information is sustained where the synopsis did not accurately describe the agency's requirements in that the synopsis and work statement were materially inconsistent and misleading. Information Ventures, Inc., B-293518, B-293518.2, 2004 WL 626215 (Comp. Gen. 2004)

If an exception to the synopsis requirement applies, it applies regardless of whether the procurement is conducted under Part 13, Simplified Acquisitions, or any other FAR Part. RFQs were exempted under the exception at FAR 5.202(a)(12) for defense agency contract actions made and performed outside of the United States when only local sources are solicited. Protester argued that the introductory clause of FAR 5.202 specifically limits the exceptions to the synopsis notification requirements of FAR 5.201, which leaves unaffected the allegedly separate displaying requirements of FAR 5.101. GAO disagreed, holding that FAR 13.105, which governs both the synopsis and displaying requirements applicable to simplified acquisition procedures, states that the public display requirements of FAR §§ 5.101 and 5.203 are not applicable if an exception in FAR 5.202 applies. Thus, the FAR 5.101, 5.201 and 5.203 requirements are not applicable to these RFQs. Military Agency Services Pty., Ltd., B-290414, B-290441, B-290468, B-290496, 2002 CPD ¶ 130 (Comp. Gen. 2002)

GAO denied protest alleging that agency's issuance of purchase orders to maintain interim services while competitive procurement for the same services was ongoing violated FAR requirements because (1) they were not procured using full and open competition; (2) their requirements were not synopsized in the Commerce Business Daily (CBD); and (3) the protester was not sent a copy of the solicitations, is denied. The purchase orders were issued using the simplified acquisition procedures of FAR Part 13 which generally do not require full and open competition or CBD synopsis, and did not mandate distribution of the solicitations to the protester. Aleman & Associates, Inc., B-287275, 2001 CPD ¶ 93 (Comp. Gen. 2001)

To determine whether public display and synopsis requirements apply to a proposed purchase under simplified procedures, FAR 13.104(b) refers to FAR 5.101 and 5.202. Under

FAR 5.101(2), agencies must publicly display a solicitation where the proposed contract action is expected to exceed $10,000 but not expected to exceed $25,000. Here, the agency states that it did not expect the procurement to exceed the $10,000 threshold and thus determined that the display requirement did not apply. In fact, the purchase order was placed at a price below the $10,000 threshold. Under the circumstances presented, the agency was not required to post a notice of the solicitation, and it satisfied the requirement for competition by requesting estimates from three firms. Continental Transport & Moving, Inc., B-280612, 1998 WL 746134 (Comp. Gen. 1998)

§ 13.106 Soliciting competition, evaluation of quotations or offers, award and documentation.

§ 13.106-1 Soliciting competition.

(a) Considerations. In soliciting competition, the contracting officer shall consider the guidance in 13.104 and the following before requesting quotations or offers:

(1) (i) The nature of the article or service to be purchased and whether it is highly competitive and readily available in several makes or brands, or is relatively noncompetitive.

(ii) An electronic commerce method that employs widespread electronic public notice is not available; and

(iii) The urgency of the proposed purchase.

(iv) The dollar value of the proposed purchase.

(v) Past experience concerning specific dealers' prices.

(2) When soliciting quotations or offers, the contracting officer shall notify potential quoters or offerors of the basis on which award will be made (price alone or price and other factors, e.g., past performance and quality). Contracting officers are encouraged to use best value. Solicitations are not required to state the relative importance assigned to each evaluation factor and subfactor, nor are they required to include subfactors.

(b) Soliciting from a single source.

(1) For purchases not exceeding the simplified acquisition threshold.

(i) Contracting officers may solicit from one source if the contracting officer determines that the circumstances of the contract action deem only one source reasonably available (e.g., urgency, exclusive licensing agreements, brand-name or industrial mobilization).

(ii) Where a single source is identified to provide a portion of a purchase because that portion of the purchase specifies a particular brand-name item, the documentation in paragraph (b)(1)(i) of this section only applies to the portion of the purchase requiring the brand-name item. The documentation should state it is covering only the portion of the acquisition which is brand-name.

(2) For purchases exceeding the simplified acquisition threshold. The requirements at 13.501(a) apply to sole-source (including brand-name) acquisitions of commercial items conducted pursuant to subpart 13.5.

(3) See 5.102(a)(6) for the requirement to post the brand-name justification or documentation.

(c) Soliciting orally.

(1) The contracting officer shall solicit quotations orally to the maximum extent practicable, if—

(i) The acquisition does not exceed the simplified acquisition threshold;

(ii) Oral solicitation is more efficient than soliciting through available electronic commerce alternatives; and

(iii) Notice is not required under 5.101.

(2) However, an oral solicitation may not be practicable for contract actions exceeding $25,000 unless covered by an exception in 5.202.

(d) Written solicitations. If obtaining electronic or oral quotations is uneconomical or impracticable, the contracting officer should issue paper solicitations for contract actions likely to exceed $25,000. The contracting officer shall issue a written solicitation for construction requirements exceeding $2,000.

(e) Use of options. Options may be included in solicitations, provided the requirements of subpart 17.2 are met and the aggregate value of the acquisition and all options does not exceed the dollar threshold for use of simplified acquisition procedures.

(f) Inquiries. An agency should respond to inquiries received through any medium (including electronic commerce) if doing so would not interfere with the efficient conduct of the acquisition.

United States Code Annotated

Commercially available off-the-shelf item acquisitions, lists of inapplicable laws in Federal Acquisition Regulation, see 41 USCA § 431.

Competition requirements, see 41 USCA § 253.

Contract requirements, see 41 USCA § 254.

Contracts, competition requirements, see 10 USCA § 2304.

Contracts, planning, solicitation, evaluation, and award procedures, see 10 USCA § 2305.

Definitions, see 10 USCA § 2302, 41 USCA §§ 259, 403.

Definitions relating to procurement of commercial items, see 10 USCA § 2376, 41 USCA § 264a.

Implementation of simplified acquisition procedures, see 10 USCA § 2302b, 41 USCA § 252b.

Kinds of contracts, see 10 USCA § 2306.

List of laws inapplicable to contracts not greater than simplified acquisition threshold in Federal Acquisition Regulation, see 41 USCA § 429.

List of laws inapplicable to procurements of commercial items in Federal Acquisition Regulation, see 41 USCA § 430.

Planning and solicitation requirements, see 41 USCA § 253a.

Preference for acquisition of commercial items, see 10 USCA § 2377, 41 USCA § 264b.

Relationship of commercial item provisions to other provisions of law, see 10 USCA § 2375, 41 USCA § 264.

Simplified acquisition procedures, see 41 USCA § 427.

Notes of Decisions

In general 1
Adequacy of RFQ 8
Amendment of RFQ 7
Cancellation of RFQ 6
Oral Solicitation 5
Purchase descriptions. 4
Time to respond 2
Urgency Exception 3
Weight of factors and subfactors 9

1 In general

Where an agency solicits fixed-price quotations, it is not permitted to accept quotations that are not fixed-price. It is fundamental that an agency may not solicit quotes on one basis and then issue an order on a materially different basis when other vendors would be prejudiced by such an agency action. M. Braun, Inc., B-298935.2, 2007 CPD ¶ 96 (Comp. Gen. 2007)

Protest challenging contracting agency's failure to solicit incumbent contractor in a small purchase, small business set-aside procurement is sustained where contracting officer deliberately decided not to send copy of solicitation to incumbent based solely on remarks purportedly made by incumbent to another contracting official during conversation concerning incumbent's performance under then-current contract. J. Sledge Janitorial Service, B-241843, B-241845, 91-1 CPD ¶ 225 (Comp. Gen. 1991)

2 Time to respond

Agency properly rejected quotation that was not received by the agency by the time specified in the Request for Quotations (RFQ) due to the agency's network security firewall. Although the protester timely uploaded its quotation onto GSA's "E-Buy" system, the RFQ required submission directly to the agency Contract Specialist and GAO held that the agency was not required to check E-Buy. Advanced Decisions Vectors, Inc., B-412307, 2016 CPD ¶ 18 (Comp. Gen. 2016)

Where agency contemplated a sole source purchase under simplified acquisition procedures, and its December 31, 2003, announcement of the intended award established a response period for capability statements from potential sources of 1 1/2 business days (until January 5, 2004), the agency did not provide potential sources with a reasonable opportunity to respond, particularly where the record does not show a need for the short response period and the agency knew of the requirement well in advance of issuing the notice. Information Ventures, Inc., B-293541, 2004 CPD ¶ 81 (Comp. Gen. 2004)

Agency's request for responses to requests for quotations within 24 hours for picket boat services conducted under simplified acquisition procedures is unobjectionable, where the requirements were needed shortly after when responses were due, the contracting office was only requisitioned to obtain the requirements shortly before requesting quotes, only prices were solicited, and all requested sources timely submitted quotes. Military Agency Services Pty., Ltd., B-290414, B-290441, B-290468, B-290496, 2002 CPD ¶ 130 (Comp. Gen. 2002)

3 Urgency Exception

FAR 13.104 requires only that agencies obtain competition to the maximum extent practicable when they utilize simplified acquisition procedures. This standard is usually met if an agency solicits at least three sources. However, the competition may be limited to fewer than three, including limiting the competition to only one source reasonably capable of performing the work, and the solicitation conducted orally without public notice, if the agency's needs must be satisfied on an urgent basis. FAR 13.106-1(a)(1)(iii). GMA Cover Corporation, B-288018, 2001 CPD ¶ 144 (Comp. Gen. 2001).

4 Purchase descriptions.

Agency may use manufacturer part numbers as item descriptions in procurements conducted under Federal Acquisition Regulation (FAR) small purchase procedures so long as equal items can be offered, thus satisfying the FAR requirement that those procurements be competed to the maximum extent practicable. Helitune, Inc., B-243617, 91-2 CPD ¶ 77 (Comp. Gen. 1991)

A procuring agency is not required to use mandatory specifications and standards when procuring an item under the small purchase procedures of the FAR. Instead, it can use other adequate part identification (e.g., National Stock Number) to permit full and open competition. East West Research, Inc., B-238633, 90-1 CPD ¶ 555 (Comp. Gen. 1990)

5 Oral Solicitation

Agency's failure to solicit a quote from the protester for an urgently needed item under an oral solicitation conducted under simplified acquisition procedures is unobjectionable where the contracting officer solicited the sources that she was aware had supplied the item and she was unaware of the protester's interest in submitting a quote, notwithstanding that the protester had supplied the item for another agency and had submitted quotes on prior agency simplified procedure acquisitions of the item. GMA Cover Corporation, B-288018, 2001 CPD ¶ 144 (Comp. Gen. 2001).

6 Cancellation of RFQ

GAO sustained protest challenging cancellation of a Request for Quotations, stating that, "[i]n the absence of an adequate agency record to support its actions, and in the absence of any reasonable explanation for its actions, we are left with no option but to make an adverse inference in this matter. We therefore conclude that the record here does not establish that the agency had a reasonable basis for the cancellation of the solicitation and sustain the protest." Walker Dev. & Trading Group, Inc., B-413924, 2017 CPD ¶ 21 (Comp. Gen. 2017)

Cancellation of request for quotations issued under small purchase procedures is proper where agency determines that amount involved will exceed authorized ceiling for use of small purchase procedures. All Star Carpet and Bedding, Inc., B-242490, B-242490.3, 91-1 CPD ¶ 352 (Comp. Gen. 1991)

7 Amendment of RFQ

Protest that agency improperly selected vendor that did not quote system specified in synopsis/solicitation is denied where, although no written amendment was issued, agency advised protester that other systems would be considered for award; protester therefore was not prejudiced by absence of written amendment. Matter of: Aqua-Flo, Inc., B-283944, 1999 WL 1285479 (Comp. Gen. 1999)

8 Adequacy of RFQ

Agency did not have a reasonable basis to reject the protester's quotation under request for quotations (RFQ) for training services where the RFQ required submission of a technical proposal but gave no guidance as to its content or how it would be evaluated; the protester submitted a technical proposal; and the agency then rejected the proposal as "unresponsive" because it was too short and too general and failed to provide evidence that the firm understood how to perform the work or to include a plan showing how the firm would implement the substance of the work. SKJ & Associates, Inc., B-291533, 2003 CPD ¶ 3 (Comp. Gen. 2003)

9 Weight of factors and subfactors

Where a solicitation failed to disclose the relative weight of the listed subfactors of the primary technical factor, the subfactors should have been considered approximately equal in weight, even though the procurement was intended to be conducted using Federal Acquisition Regulation (FAR) Part 13 simplified acquisition procedures and FAR sect. 13.106-1(a)(2) states that the relative importance of evaluation factors and subfactors need not be disclosed in a solicitation, because the solicitation did not indicate that the acquisition was being conducted under FAR Part 13 and the acquisition was conducted in a manner that was not distinguishable from a negotiated acquisition conducted under FAR Part 15, which requires that the relative weights of the evaluation factors and subfactors be stated in the solicitation. Bio-Rad Laboratories, Inc., B-297553, 2007 CPD ¶ 58 (Comp. Gen. 2006)

Agency's selection of a proposal for award was unreasonable where the solicitation was silent as to the relative weights of the subfactors of the primary technical evaluation factor, and the agency, rather than treating the subfactors as equal in weight in evaluating the relative merits of the competing proposals, considered the subfactors as listed in descending order of importance. Bio-Rad Laboratories, Inc., B-297553, 2007 CPD ¶ 58 (Comp. Gen. 2006)

Notwithstanding statement in solicitation that simplified acquisition procedures were being used and authority at FAR 12.602(a) not to disclose the relative weight of evaluation factors when using simplified procedures, an agency's failure to disclose the relative weight of evaluation factors was unreasonable because basic fairness dictated disclosure of the relative weights where the agency required offerors to prepare detailed written proposals addressing unique government requirements. Finlen Complex, Inc., B-288280, 2001 CPD ¶ 167 (Comp. Gen. 2001).

§ 13.106-2 Evaluation of quotations or offers.

(a) *General.* (1) The contracting officer shall evaluate quotations or offers—

(i) In an impartial manner; and

(ii) Inclusive of transportation charges from the shipping point of the supplier to the delivery destination.

(2) Quotations or offers shall be evaluated on the basis established in the solicitation.

(3) All quotations or offers shall be considered (see paragraph (b) of this subsection).

(b) *Evaluation procedures.* (1) The contracting officer has broad discretion in fashioning suitable evaluation procedures. The procedures prescribed in Parts 14 and 15 are not mandatory. At the contracting officer's discretion, one or more, but not necessarily all, of the evaluation procedures in Part 14 or 15 may be used.

(2) If telecommuting is not prohibited, agencies shall not unfavorably evaluate an offer

because it includes telecommuting unless the contracting officer executes a written determination in accordance with FAR 7.108(b).

(3) If using price and other factors, ensure that quotations or offers can be evaluated in an efficient and minimally burdensome fashion. Formal evaluation plans and establishing a competitive range, conducting discussions, and scoring quotations or offers are not required. Contracting offices may conduct comparative evaluations of offers. Evaluation of other factors, such as past performance—

(i) Does not require the creation or existence of a formal data base; and

(ii) May be based on one or more of the following:

(A) The contracting officer's knowledge of and previous experience with the supply or service being acquired;

(B) Customer surveys, and past performance questionnaire replies;

(C) The Governmentwide Past Performance Information Retrieval System (PPIRS) at *www.ppirs.gov*; or

(D) Any other reasonable basis.

(4) For acquisitions conducted using a method that permits electronic response to the solicitation, the contracting officer may—

(i) After preliminary consideration of all quotations or offers, identify from all quotations or offers received one that is suitable to the user, such as the lowest priced brand name product, and quickly screen all lower priced quotations or offers based on readily discernible value indicators, such as past performance, warranty conditions, and maintenance availability; or

(ii) Where an evaluation is based only on price and past performance, make an award based on whether the lowest priced of the quotations or offers having the highest past performance rating possible represents the best value when compared to any lower priced quotation or offer.

United States Code Annotated

Commercially available off-the-shelf item acquisitions, lists of inapplicable laws in Federal Acquisition Regulation, see 41 USCA § 431.

Competition requirements, see 41 USCA § 253.

Contract requirements, see 41 USCA § 254.

Contracts, competition requirements, see 10 USCA § 2304.

Contracts, planning, solicitation, evaluation, and award procedures, see 10 USCA § 2305.

Definitions, see 10 USCA § 2302, 41 USCA §§ 259, 403.

Definitions relating to procurement of commercial items, see 10 USCA § 2376, 41 USCA § 264a.

Implementation of simplified acquisition procedures, see 10 USCA § 2302b, 41 USCA § 252b.

Kinds of contracts, see 10 USCA § 2306.

List of laws inapplicable to contracts not greater than simplified acquisition threshold in Federal Acquisition Regulation, see 41 USCA § 429.

List of laws inapplicable to procurements of commercial items in Federal Acquisition Regulation, see 41 USCA § 430.

Planning and solicitation requirements, see 41 USCA § 253a.

Preference for acquisition of commercial items, see 10 USCA § 2377, 41 USCA § 264b.

Relationship of commercial item provisions to other provisions of law, see 10 USCA § 2375, 41 USCA § 264.

Simplified acquisition procedures, see 41 USCA § 427.

Notes of Decisions

In general 1
Discretion of contracting officer 2

1 In general

Protest was sustained in a simplified acquisition procurement where agency engaged in discussions with the awardee and permitted the awardee to change the pricing terms in its quotation, but did not conduct discussions with the protester. Although an agency is not required to conduct discussions under simplified acquisition procedures, where an agency avails itself of negotiated procurement procedures, the agency should treat offerors fairly and reasonably in the conduct of those procedures. Int'l Waste Indus., B-411338, 2015 CPD ¶ 196 (Comp. Gen. 2015).

Where simplified acquisition procedures are used, the evaluation procedures provided for in FAR Parts 14 and 15, including the procedures for the correction of mistakes, are not mandatory. FAR 13.106-2(b). Paraclete Contracts, B-299883, 2007 CPD ¶ 153 (Comp. Gen. 2007).

Under procurement conducted under simplified acquisition procedures, there was nothing improper in obtaining clarifications from the awardee and not giving the protester an opportunity to correct a major deficiency under one of the evaluation factors that rendered its quotation unacceptable under that factor. The solicitation advised vendors that award may be made on initial quotations and discussions were not conducted with any of the quoters. Houston Air, Inc., B-292382, 2003 CPD ¶ 144 (Comp. Gen. 2003)

Under a request for quotations, issued under simplified acquisition procedures, under which oral presentations constituted the vendors' technical submissions and which provided for award based upon a price/technical tradeoff, protest challenging source selection decision is sustained, where the contracting officer's selection of the higher-priced, higher-rated quotation reflected a failure to meaningful consider price, given that the price/technical tradeoff was based primarily upon a technical consideration which the contracting officer testified he did not understand and for which he obtained no advice. e-LYNXX Corporation, B-292761, 2003 CPD ¶ 219 (Comp. Gen. 2003)

Agency did not have a reasonable basis to reject the protester's quotation under request for quotations (RFQ) for training services where the RFQ required submission of a technical proposal but gave no guidance as to its content or how it would be evaluated; the protester submitted a technical proposal; and the agency then rejected the proposal as "unresponsive" because it was too short and too general and failed to provide evidence that the firm understood how to perform the work or to include a plan showing how the firm would implement the substance of the work. SKJ & Associates, Inc., B-291533, 2003 CPD ¶ 3 (Comp. Gen. 2003)

In a procurement under simplified acquisition procedures where the agency elected to establish a competitive range and conduct discussions, the agency improperly excluded the protester's low-priced quote from the competitive range and conducted discussions with only the awardee, where the protester's and awardee's quotes failed to satisfy the same solicitation requirements and the record did not support the agency's determination that the protester would not have had a realistic chance of receiving award if it had been afforded discussions. Kathryn Huddleston and Associates, Ltd., B-289453, 2002 CPD ¶ 57 (Comp. Gen. 2002)

Agency properly considered as acceptable a quotation stating a delivery period longer than identified in the request for quotations (RFQ) conducted under simplified acquisition procedures, and reasonably evaluated delivery, where the RFQ permitted firms to quote delivery periods longer than that requested, and stated that delivery would be an evaluation factor. Multi-Spec Products Corporation, B-287135, 2001 CPD ¶ 72 (Comp. Gen. 2001)

Protest that agency failed to conduct discussions with protester consistent with the requirements of part 15 of the Federal Acquisition Regulation (FAR) is denied where the procurement is a commercial item acquisition being conducted under simplified acquisition procedures, which is not subject to the FAR part 15 requirements. United Marine International LLC, B-281512, 99-1 CPD ¶ 44 (Comp. Gen. 1999)

Agency reasonably eliminated quotation from consideration in a procurement conducted using simplified acquisition procedures where the solicitation required the submission of documentation describing similar contract experience for evaluation of past performance and the quotation did not include such documentation; there was no obligation for the agency to conduct discussions regarding the failure to provide the required documentation. CDS Network Systems, Inc., B-281200, 98-2 CPD ¶ 154 (Comp. Gen. 1998)

2 Discretion of contracting officer

Contracting officer (CO) did not abuse her discretion by failing to conduct a comprehensive individual comparison of offerors' unit prices for 1,500 individual commercial hardware items listed in solicitation; comparison of overall price was sufficient to satisfy price reasonableness determination under regulations governing simplified acquisition procedures. CC Distributors, Inc. v. U.S., 69 Fed. Cl. 277 (2006). United States ⚿64.40(1)

§ 13.106-3 Award and documentation.

(a) *Basis for award.* Before making award, the contracting officer must determine that the proposed price is fair and reasonable.

(1) Whenever possible, base price reasonableness on competitive quotations or offers.

(2) If only one response is received, include a statement of price reasonableness in the contract file. The contracting officer may base the statement on—

(i) Market research;

(ii) Comparison of the proposed price with prices found reasonable on previous purchases;

(iii) Current price lists, catalogs, or advertisements. However, inclusion of a price in a price list, catalog, or advertisement does not, in and of itself, establish fairness and reasonableness of the price;

(iv) A comparison with similar items in a related industry;

(v) The contracting officer's personal knowledge of the item being purchased;

(vi) Comparison to an independent Government estimate; or

(vii) Any other reasonable basis.

(3) Occasionally an item can be obtained only from a supplier that quotes a minimum order price or quantity that either unreasonably exceeds stated quantity requirements or results in an unreasonable price for the quantity required. In these instances, the contracting officer should inform the requiring activity of all facts regarding the quotation or offer and ask it to confirm or alter its requirement. The file shall be documented to support the final action taken.

(b) *File documentation and retention.* Keep documentation to a minimum. Purchasing offices shall retain data supporting purchases (paper or electronic) to the minimum extent and duration necessary for management review purposes (see Subpart 4.8). The following illustrate the extent to which quotation or offer information should be recorded:

(1) *Oral solicitations.* The contracting office should establish and maintain records of oral price quotations in order to reflect clearly the propriety of placing the order at the price paid with the supplier concerned. In most cases, this will consist merely of showing the names of the suppliers contacted and the prices and other terms and conditions quoted by each.

(2) *Written solicitations* (see 2.101). For acquisitions not exceeding the simplified acquisition threshold, limit written records of solicitations or offers to notes or abstracts to show prices, delivery, references to printed price lists used, the supplier or suppliers contacted, and other pertinent data.

(3) *Special situations.* Include additional statements—

(i) Explaining the absence of competition (see 13.106-1 for brand name purchases) if only one source is solicited and the acquisition does not exceed the simplified acquisition threshold (does not apply to an acquisition of utility services available from only one source); or

(ii) Supporting the award decision if other than pricerelated factors were considered in selecting the supplier.

(c) *Notification.* For acquisitions that do not exceed the simplified acquisition threshold and for which automatic notification is not provided through an electronic commerce method that employs widespread electronic public notice, notification to unsuccessful suppliers shall be given only if requested or required by 5.301.

(d) *Request for information.* If a supplier requests information on an award that was based on factors other than price alone, a brief explanation of the basis for the contract award decision shall be provided (see 15.503(b)(2)).

(e) *Taxpayer Identification Number.* If an oral solicitation is used, the contracting officer shall ensure that the copy of the award document sent to the payment office is annotated with the contractor's Taxpayer Identification Number (TIN) and type of organization (see 4.203), unless this information will be obtained from some other source (*e.g.*, centralized database). The contracting officer shall disclose to the contractor that the TIN may be used by the Government to collect and report on any delinquent amounts arising out of the contractor's relationship with the Government (31 U.S.C. 7701(c)(3)).

United States Code Annotated

Commercially available off-the-shelf item acquisitions, lists of inapplicable laws in Federal Acquisition Regulation, see 41 USCA § 431.

Competition requirements, see 41 USCA § 253.

Contract requirements, see 41 USCA § 254.

Contracts, competition requirements, see 10 USCA § 2304.

Contracts, planning, solicitation, evaluation, and award procedures, see 10 USCA § 2305.

Definitions, see 10 USCA § 2302, 41 USCA §§ 259, 403.

Definitions relating to procurement of commercial items, see 10 USCA § 2376, 41 USCA § 264a.

Implementation of simplified acquisition procedures, see 10 USCA § 2302b, 41 USCA § 252b.

Kinds of contracts, see 10 USCA § 2306.

List of laws inapplicable to contracts not greater than simplified acquisition threshold in Federal Acquisition Regulation, see 41 USCA § 429.

List of laws inapplicable to procurements of commercial items in Federal Acquisition Regulation, see 41 USCA § 430.

Planning and solicitation requirements, see 41 USCA § 253a.

Preference for acquisition of commercial items, see 10 USCA § 2377, 41 USCA § 264b.

Relationship of commercial item provisions to other provisions of law, see 10 USCA § 2375, 41 USCA § 264.

Simplified acquisition procedures, see 41 USCA § 427.

Notes of Decisions
In general 1
Discretion of contracting officer 2

1 In general

The Government, moreover, was under no obligation to issue a purchase order to the lowest priced quoter where the quote was submitted more than a week after the estimated performance start date. The quote was, at best, a counteroffer that the Government could reject. Appeal of Harney County Gypsum Co., A.G.B.C.A. No. 93-190-1, 94-1 B.C.A. (CCH) ¶ 26455, 1993 WL 439498 (Dep't Agric. B.C.A. 1993)

Even under simplified acquisition procedures, award decision is not reasonable where the record does not provide any documentation or explanation which supports the price/technical tradeoff, and the award determination appears to be based entirely on a comparison of total technical point scores without consideration of protester's lower technically scored, but low priced proposal. Universal Building Maintenance, Inc., B-282456, 99-2 CPD ¶ 32 (Comp. Gen. 1999)

2 Discretion of contracting officer

Contracting officer (CO) did not abuse her discretion by failing to conduct a comprehensive individual comparison of offerors' unit prices for 1,500 individual commercial hardware items listed in solicitation; comparison of overall price was sufficient to satisfy price reasonableness determination under regulations governing simplified acquisition procedures. CC Distributors, Inc. v. U.S., 69 Fed. Cl. 277 (2006). United States ⚘64.40(1)

Subpart 13.2 Actions at or Below the Micro-Purchase Threshold

§ 13.201 General.

(a) Agency heads are encouraged to delegate micro-purchase authority (see 1.603-3).

(b) The Governmentwide commercial purchase card shall be the preferred method to purchase and to pay for micro-purchases (see 2.101).

(c) Purchases at or below the micro-purchase threshold may be conducted using any of the methods described in Subpart 13.3, provided the purchaser is authorized and trained, pursuant to agency procedures, to use those methods.

(d) Micro-purchases do not require provisions or clauses, except as provided at 13.202 and 32.1110. This paragraph takes precedence over any other FAR requirement to the contrary, but does not prohibit the use of any clause.

(e) The requirements in Part 8 apply to purchases at or below the micro-purchase threshold.

(f) The procurement requirements in subparts 23.1, 23.2, 23.4, and 23.7 apply to purchases at or below the micro-purchase threshold.

(g) (1) For acquisitions of supplies or services that, as determined by the head of the agency, are to be used to support a contingency operation or to facilitate defense against or recovery from nuclear, biological, chemical, or radiological attack, the micro-purchase threshold is —

(i) $20,000 in the case of any contract to be awarded and performed, or purchase to be made, inside the United States; and

(ii) $30,000 in the case of any contract to be awarded and performed, or purchase to be made, outside the United States.

(2) Purchases using this authority must have a clear and direct relationship to the support of a contingency operation or the defense against or recovery from nuclear, biological, chemical, or radiological attack.

(h) When using the Governmentwide commercial purchase card as a method of payment, purchases at or below the micro-purchase threshold are exempt from verification in the System for Award Management database as to whether the contractor has a delinquent debt subject to collection under the Treasury Offset Program (TOP).

§ 13.202 Unenforceability of unauthorized obligations in micro-purchases.

Many supplies or services are acquired subject to supplier license agreements. These are particularly common in information technology acquisitions, but they may apply to any supply or service. For example, computer software and services delivered through the internet (web services) are often subject to license agreements, referred to as End User License Agreements (EULA), Terms of Service (TOS), or other similar legal instruments or agreements. Many of these agreements contain indemnification clauses that are inconsistent with Federal law and unenforceable, but which could create a violation of the Anti-Deficiency Act (31 U.S.C. 1341) if agreed to by the Government. The clause at 52.232-39, Unenforceability of Unauthorized Obligations, automatically applies to any micro-purchase, including those made with the Governmentwide purchase card. This clause prevents such violations of the Anti-Deficiency Act (31 U.S.C. 1341).

§ 13.203 Purchase guidelines.

(a) Solicitation, evaluation of quotations, and award.

(1) To the extent practicable, micro-purchases shall be distributed equitably among qualified suppliers.

(2) Micro-purchases may be awarded without soliciting competitive quotations if the contracting officer or individual appointed in accordance with 1.603-3(b) considers the price to be reasonable.

(3) The administrative cost of verifying the reasonableness of the price for purchases may more than offset potential savings from detecting instances of overpricing. Therefore, action to verify price reasonableness need only be taken if—

(i) The contracting officer or individual appointed in accordance with 1.603-3(b) suspects or has information to indicate that the price may not be reasonable (*e.g.,* comparison to the previous price paid or personal knowledge of the supply or service); or

(ii) Purchasing a supply or service for which no comparable pricing information is readily available (*e.g.,* a supply or service that is not the same as, or is not similar to, other supplies or services that have recently been purchased on a competitive basis).

(b) *Documentation.* If competitive quotations were solicited and award was made to other than the low quoter, documentation to support the purchase may be limited to identification of the solicited concerns and an explanation for the award decision.

Subpart 13.3 Simplified Acquisition Methods

§ 13.301 Governmentwide commercial purchase card.

(a) Except as provided in 32.1108(b)(2), the Governmentwide commercial purchase card is authorized for use in making and/or paying for purchases of supplies, services, or construction. The Governmentwide commercial purchase card may be used by contracting officers and other individuals designated in accordance with 1.603-3. The card may be used only for purchases that are otherwise authorized by law or regulation.

(b) Agencies using the Governmentwide commercial purchase card shall establish procedures for use and control of the card that comply with the Treasury Financial Manual for Guidance of Departments and Agencies (TFM 4-4500) and that are consistent with the terms and conditions of the current GSA credit card contract. Agency procedures should not limit the use of the Governmentwide commercial purchase card to micro-purchases. Agency procedures should encourage use of the card in greater dollar amounts by contracting officers to place orders and to pay for purchases against contracts established under Part 8 procedures, when authorized; and to place orders and/or make payment under other contractual instruments, when agreed to by the contractor. See 32.1110(d) for instructions for use of the appropriate clause when payment under a written contract will be made through use of the card.

(c) The Governmentwide commercial purchase card may be used to—

(1) Make micro-purchases;

(2) Place a task or delivery order (if authorized in the basic contract, basic ordering agreement, or blanket purchase agreement); or

(3) Make payments, when the contractor agrees to accept payment by the card (but see 32.1108(b)(2)).

United States Code Annotated

Commercially available off-the-shelf item acquisitions, lists of inapplicable laws in Federal Acquisition Regulation, see 41 USCA § 431.

Competition requirements, see 41 USCA § 253.

Contract requirements, see 41 USCA § 254.

Contracts, competition requirements, see 10 USCA § 2304.

Contracts, planning, solicitation, evaluation, and award procedures, see 10 USCA § 2305.

Definitions, see 10 USCA § 2302, 41 USCA §§ 259, 403.

Definitions relating to procurement of commercial items, see 10 USCA § 2376, 41 USCA § 264a.

Implementation of simplified acquisition procedures, see 10 USCA § 2302b, 41 USCA § 252b.

Kinds of contracts, see 10 USCA § 2306.

List of laws inapplicable to contracts not greater than simplified acquisition threshold in Federal Acquisition Regulation, see 41 USCA § 429.

List of laws inapplicable to procurements of commercial items in Federal Acquisition Regulation, see 41 USCA § 430.

Planning and solicitation requirements, see 41 USCA § 253a.

Preference for acquisition of commercial items, see 10 USCA § 2377, 41 USCA § 264b.

Relationship of commercial item provisions to other provisions of law, see 10 USCA § 2375, 41 USCA § 264.

Simplified acquisition procedures, see 41 USCA § 427.

§ 13.302 Purchase orders.

§ 13.302-1 General.

(a) Except as provided under the unpriced purchase order method (see 13.302-2), purchase orders generally are issued on a fixed-price basis. See 12.207 for acquisition of commercial items.

(b) Purchase orders shall—

(1) Specify the quantity of supplies or scope of services ordered;

(2) Contain a determinable date by which delivery of the supplies or performance of the services is required;

(3) Provide for inspection as prescribed in Part 46. Generally, inspection and acceptance should be at destination. Source inspection should be specified only if required by Part 46. When inspection and acceptance will be performed at destination, advance copies of the purchase order or equivalent notice shall be furnished to the consignee(s) for material receipt purposes. Receiving reports shall be accomplished immediately upon receipt and acceptance of supplies;

(4) Specify f.o.b. destination for supplies to be delivered within the United States, except Alaska or Hawaii, unless there are valid reasons to the contrary; and

(5) Include any trade and prompt payment discounts that are offered, consistent with the applicable principles at 14.408-3.

(c) The contracting officer's signature on purchase orders shall be in accordance with 4.101 and the definitions at 2.101. Facsimile and electronic signature may be used in the production of purchase orders by automated methods.

(d) Limit the distribution of copies of purchase orders and related forms to the minimum deemed essential for administration and transmission of contractual information.

(e) In accordance with 31 U.S.C. 3332, electronic funds transfer (EFT) is required for payments except as provided in 32.1110. See Subpart 32.11 for instructions for use of the appropriate clause in purchase orders. When obtaining oral quotes, the contracting officer shall inform the quoter of the EFT clause that will be in any resulting purchase order.

United States Code Annotated

Commercially available off-the-shelf item acquisitions, lists of inapplicable laws in Federal Acquisition Regulation, see 41 USCA § 431.

Competition requirements, see 41 USCA § 253.

Contract requirements, see 41 USCA § 254.

Contracts, competition requirements, see 10 USCA § 2304.

Contracts, planning, solicitation, evaluation, and award procedures, see 10 USCA § 2305.

Definitions, see 10 USCA § 2302, 41 USCA §§ 259, 403.

Definitions relating to procurement of commercial items, see 10 USCA § 2376, 41 USCA § 264a.

Implementation of simplified acquisition procedures, see 10 USCA § 2302b, 41 USCA § 252b.

Kinds of contracts, see 10 USCA § 2306.

List of laws inapplicable to contracts not greater than simplified acquisition threshold in Federal Acquisition Regulation, see 41 USCA § 429.

List of laws inapplicable to procurements of commercial items in Federal Acquisition Regulation, see 41 USCA § 430.

Planning and solicitation requirements, see 41 USCA § 253a.

Preference for acquisition of commercial items, see 10 USCA § 2377, 41 USCA § 264b.

Relationship of commercial item provisions to other provisions of law, see 10 USCA § 2375, 41 USCA § 264.

Simplified acquisition procedures, see 41 USCA § 427.

Notes of Decisions

In general 1
Fragmentation of order 2
Modification of contract 3

1 In general

Purchase order cancellation and termination provisions of the Federal Acquisition Regulation (FAR) were not applicable to purchase order which lapsed when supplier failed to perform by the delivery date, as such provisions are only applicable where the government cancels or terminates a purchase order before the purchase order's delivery date. FAR 13.004(c), 13.302-4. Kaeper Machine, Inc. v. U.S., 74 Fed. Cl. 1 (2006)

Once purchase orders lapse, they can be revived by words or conduct of the Government seeking or encouraging continued performance. Once the Government revives its offer, it remains open for the time specified, or if no time is specified, for a reasonable time. Davies Precision Machining, Inc. v. U.S., 35 Fed. Cl. 651, 40 Cont. Cas. Fed. (CCH) ¶ 76936 (1996)

2 Fragmentation of order

Navy did not improperly fragment contract for procurement of tug boat services when, after determining that solicited bids were too high, it canceled solicitation and began procuring tug services on piecemeal, spot-bid basis; spot-bid practice was not attempt to evade competitive bidding procedures, and contract requirements were not precisely known. 10 U.S.C.A. § 2304(g)(2); 48 C.F.R. § 13.003. Petchem, Inc. v. U.S., 99 F. Supp. 2d 50 (D.D.C. 2000). United States ☞64.25

Federal agency may not fragment procurement order that would otherwise fall above simplified acquisition threshold simply to take advantage of simplified procedures. 10 U.S.C.A. § 2304(g)(2); 48 C.F.R. § 13.003. Petchem, Inc. v. U.S., 99 F. Supp. 2d 50 (D.D.C. 2000). United States ☞64.10

3 Modification of contract

In unilateral procurements, provisions of schedule relative to delivery time and compliance with line item specifications determines supplier's obligations and cannot be changed absent action by contract officer. 48 C.F.R. § 13.000 (1993). Davies Precision Machining, Inc. v. U.S., 35 Fed. Cl. 651, 40 Cont. Cas. Fed. (CCH) P 76936 (1996). United States ☞72(1.1)

§ 13.302-2 Unpriced purchase orders.

(a) An unpriced purchase order is an order for supplies or services, the price of which is not established at the time of issuance of the order.

(b) An unpriced purchase order may be used only when—

(1) It is impractical to obtain pricing in advance of issuance of the purchase order; and

(2) The purchase is for—

(i) Repairs to equipment requiring disassembly to determine the nature and extent of repairs;

(ii) Material available from only one source and for which cost cannot readily be established; or

(iii) Supplies or services for which prices are known to be competitive, but exact prices are not known (*e.g.*, miscellaneous repair parts, maintenance agreements).

(c) Unpriced purchase orders may be issued on paper or electronically. A realistic monetary limitation, either for each line item or for the total order, shall be placed on each unpriced purchase order. The monetary limitation shall be an obligation subject to adjustment when the firm price is established. The contracting office shall follow up on each order to ensure timely pricing. The contracting officer or the contracting officer's designated representative shall review the invoice price and, if reasonable (see 13.106-3(a)), process the invoice for payment.

United States Code Annotated

Commercially available off-the-shelf item acquisitions, lists of inapplicable laws in Federal Acquisition Regulation, see 41 USCA § 431.

Competition requirements, see 41 USCA § 253.

Contract requirements, see 41 USCA § 254.

Contracts, competition requirements, see 10 USCA § 2304.

Contracts, planning, solicitation, evaluation, and award procedures, see 10 USCA § 2305.

Definitions, see 10 USCA § 2302, 41 USCA §§ 259, 403.

Definitions relating to procurement of commercial items, see 10 USCA § 2376, 41 USCA § 264a.

Implementation of simplified acquisition procedures, see 10 USCA § 2302b, 41 USCA § 252b.

Kinds of contracts, see 10 USCA § 2306.

List of laws inapplicable to contracts not greater than simplified acquisition threshold in Federal Acquisition Regulation, see 41 USCA § 429.

List of laws inapplicable to procurements of commercial items in Federal Acquisition Regulation, see 41 USCA § 430.

Planning and solicitation requirements, see 41 USCA § 253a.

Preference for acquisition of commercial items, see 10 USCA § 2377, 41 USCA § 264b.

Relationship of commercial item provisions to other provisions of law, see 10 USCA § 2375, 41 USCA § 264.

Simplified acquisition procedures, see 41 USCA § 427.

§ 13.302-3 Obtaining contractor acceptance and modifying purchase orders.

(a) When it is desired to consummate a binding contract between the parties before the contractor undertakes performance, the contracting officer shall require written (see 2.101) acceptance of the purchase order by the contractor.

(b) Each purchase order modification shall identify the order it modifies and shall contain an appropriate modification number.

(c) A contractor's written acceptance of a purchase order modification may be required only if—

(1) Determined by the contracting officer to be necessary to ensure the contractor's compliance with the purchase order as revised; or

(2) Required by agency regulations.

United States Code Annotated

Commercially available off-the-shelf item acquisitions, lists of inapplicable laws in Federal Acquisition Regulation, see 41 USCA § 431.

Competition requirements, see 41 USCA § 253.

Contract requirements, see 41 USCA § 254.

Contracts, competition requirements, see 10 USCA § 2304.

Contracts, planning, solicitation, evaluation, and award procedures, see 10 USCA § 2305.

Definitions, see 10 USCA § 2302, 41 USCA §§ 259, 403.

Definitions relating to procurement of commercial items, see 10 USCA § 2376, 41 USCA § 264a.

Implementation of simplified acquisition procedures, see 10 USCA § 2302b, 41 USCA § 252b.

Kinds of contracts, see 10 USCA § 2306.

List of laws inapplicable to contracts not greater than simplified acquisition threshold in Federal Acquisition Regulation, see 41 USCA § 429.

List of laws inapplicable to procurements of commercial items in Federal Acquisition Regulation, see 41 USCA § 430.

Planning and solicitation requirements, see 41 USCA § 253a.

Preference for acquisition of commercial items, see 10 USCA § 2377, 41 USCA § 264b.

Relationship of commercial item provisions to other provisions of law, see 10 USCA § 2375, 41 USCA § 264.

Simplified acquisition procedures, see 41 USCA § 427.

Notes of Decisions

In general 1

1 In general

When there is no written acceptance of the purchase order, suppliers may accept the Government's offers by delivering the requested supplies in accordance with the specified terms and conditions. A supplier may also indicate its mutual assent by beginning performance and, thus, "accept" an option contract, and the Government's offer becomes irrevocable. Davies Precision Machining, Inc. v. U.S., 35 Fed. Cl. 651, 40 Cont. Cas. Fed. (CCH) ¶ 76936 (1996)

§ 13.302-4 Termination or cancellation of purchase orders.

(a) If a purchase order that has been accepted in writing by the contractor is to be terminated, the contracting officer shall process the termination in accordance with—

(1) 12.403 and 52.212-4(l) or (m) for commercial items; or

(2) Part 49 or 52.213-4 for other than commercial items.

(b) If a purchase order that has not been accepted in writing by the contractor is to be canceled, the contracting officer shall notify the contractor in writing that the purchase order has been canceled, request the contractor's written acceptance of the cancellation, and proceed as follows:

(1) If the contractor accepts the cancellation and does not claim that costs were incurred as a result of beginning performance under the purchase order, no further action is required (*i.e.*, the purchase order shall be considered canceled).

(2) If the contractor does not accept the cancellation or claims that costs were incurred as a result of beginning performance under the purchase order, the contracting officer shall process the action as a termination prescribed in paragraph (a) of this subsection.

United States Code Annotated

Commercially available off-the-shelf item acquisitions, lists of inapplicable laws in Federal Acquisition Regulation, see 41 USCA § 431.

Competition requirements, see 41 USCA § 253.

Contract requirements, see 41 USCA § 254.

Contracts, competition requirements, see 10 USCA § 2304.

Contracts, planning, solicitation, evaluation, and award procedures, see 10 USCA § 2305.

Definitions, see 10 USCA § 2302, 41 USCA §§ 259, 403.

Definitions relating to procurement of commercial items, see 10 USCA § 2376, 41 USCA § 264a.

Implementation of simplified acquisition procedures, see 10 USCA § 2302b, 41 USCA § 252b.

Kinds of contracts, see 10 USCA § 2306.

List of laws inapplicable to contracts not greater than simplified acquisition threshold in Federal Acquisition Regulation, see 41 USCA § 429.

List of laws inapplicable to procurements of commercial items in Federal Acquisition Regulation, see 41 USCA § 430.

Planning and solicitation requirements, see 41 USCA § 253a.

Preference for acquisition of commercial items, see 10 USCA § 2377, 41 USCA § 264b.

Relationship of commercial item provisions to other provisions of law, see 10 USCA § 2375, 41 USCA § 264.

Simplified acquisition procedures, see 41 USCA § 427.

Notes of Decisions

In general 1
Lapsed purchase orders 2

1 In general

Once purchase orders lapse, they can be revived by words or conduct of the Government seeking or encouraging continued performance. Once the Government revives its offer, it remains open for the time specified, or if no time is specified, for a reasonable time. Davies Precision Machining, Inc. v. U.S., 35 Fed. Cl. 651, 40 Cont. Cas. Fed. (CCH) ¶ 76936 (1996)

2 Lapsed purchase orders

Purchase order cancellation and termination provisions of the Federal Acquisition Regulation (FAR) were not applicable to purchase order which lapsed when supplier failed to perform by the delivery date, as such provisions are only applicable where the government cancels or terminates a purchase order before the purchase order's delivery date. Kaeper Machine, Inc. v. U.S., 74 Fed. Cl. 1 (2006). United States ☞70(35)

§ 13.302-5 Clauses.

(a) Each purchase order (and each purchase order modification (see 13.302-3)) shall incorporate all clauses prescribed for the particular acquisition.

(b) The contracting officer shall insert the clause at 52.213-2, Invoices, in purchase orders that authorize advance payments (see 31 U.S.C. 3324(d)(2)) for subscriptions or other charges for newspapers, magazines, periodicals, or other publications (*i.e.,* any publication printed, microfilmed, photocopied, or magnetically or otherwise recorded for auditory or visual usage).

(c) The contracting officer shall insert the clause at 52.213-3, Notice to Supplier, in unpriced purchase orders.

(d) (1) The contracting officer may use the clause at 52.213-4, Terms and Conditions—Simplified Acquisitions (Other Than Commercial Items), in simplified acquisitions exceeding the micro-purchase threshold that are for other than commercial items (see 12.301).

(2) The clause—

(i) Is a compilation of the most commonly used clauses that apply to simplified acquisitions; and

(ii) May be modified to fit the individual acquisition to add other needed clauses, or those clauses may be added separately. Modifications (*i.e.,* additions, deletions, or substitutions) must not create a void or internal contradiction in the clause. For example, do not add an inspection and acceptance or termination for convenience requirement unless the existing requirement is deleted. Also, do not delete a paragraph without providing for an appropriate substitute.

(3) (i) When an acquisition for supplies for use within the United States cannot be set aside for small business concerns and trade agreements apply (see Subpart 25.4), substitute the clause at FAR 52.225-3, Buy American—Free Trade Agreements—Israeli Trade Act, used with Alternate I or Alternate II, if appropriate, instead of the clause at FAR 52.225-1, Buy American—Supplies.

(ii) When acquiring supplies for use outside the United States, delete clause 52.225-1 from the clause list at 52.213-4(b).

United States Code Annotated

Commercially available off-the-shelf item acquisitions, lists of inapplicable laws in Federal Acquisition Regulation, see 41 USCA § 431.

Competition requirements, see 41 USCA § 253.

Contract requirements, see 41 USCA § 254.

Contracts, competition requirements, see 10 USCA § 2304.

Contracts, planning, solicitation, evaluation, and award procedures, see 10 USCA § 2305.

Definitions, see 10 USCA § 2302, 41 USCA §§ 259, 403.

Definitions relating to procurement of commercial items, see 10 USCA § 2376, 41 USCA § 264a.

Implementation of simplified acquisition procedures, see 10 USCA § 2302b, 41 USCA § 252b.

Kinds of contracts, see 10 USCA § 2306.

List of laws inapplicable to contracts not greater than simplified acquisition threshold in Federal Acquisition Regulation, see 41 USCA § 429.

List of laws inapplicable to procurements of commercial items in Federal Acquisition Regulation, see 41 USCA § 430.

Planning and solicitation requirements, see 41 USCA § 253a.

Preference for acquisition of commercial items, see 10 USCA § 2377, 41 USCA § 264b.

Relationship of commercial item provisions to other provisions of law, see 10 USCA § 2375, 41 USCA § 264.

Simplified acquisition procedures, see 41 USCA § 427.

§ 13.303 Blanket purchase agreements (BPAs).

§ 13.303-1 General.

(a) A blanket purchase agreement (BPA) is a simplified method of filling anticipated repetitive needs for supplies or services by establishing "charge accounts" with qualified sources of supply (see Subpart 16.7 for additional coverage of agreements).

(b) BPAs should be established for use by an organization responsible for providing supplies for its own operations or for other offices, installations, projects, or functions. Such organizations, for example, may be organized supply points, separate independent or detached field parties, or one-person posts or activities.

(c) The use of BPAs does not exempt an agency from the responsibility for keeping obligations and expenditures within available funds.

United States Code Annotated

Commercially available off-the-shelf item acquisitions, lists of inapplicable laws in Federal Acquisition Regulation, see 41 USCA § 431.

Competition requirements, see 41 USCA § 253.

Contract requirements, see 41 USCA § 254.

Contracts, competition requirements, see 10 USCA § 2304.

Contracts, planning, solicitation, evaluation, and award procedures, see 10 USCA § 2305.

Definitions, see 10 USCA § 2302, 41 USCA §§ 259, 403.

Definitions relating to procurement of commercial items, see 10 USCA § 2376, 41 USCA § 264a.

Implementation of simplified acquisition procedures, see 10 USCA § 2302b, 41 USCA § 252b.

Kinds of contracts, see 10 USCA § 2306.

List of laws inapplicable to contracts not greater than simplified acquisition threshold in Federal Acquisition Regulation, see 41 USCA § 429.

List of laws inapplicable to procurements of commercial items in Federal Acquisition Regulation, see 41 USCA § 430.

Planning and solicitation requirements, see 41 USCA § 253a.

Preference for acquisition of commercial items, see 10 USCA § 2377, 41 USCA § 264b.

Relationship of commercial item provisions to other provisions of law, see 10 USCA § 2375, 41 USCA § 264.

Simplified acquisition procedures, see 41 USCA § 427.

Notes of Decisions

In general 1

1 In general

BPA between contractor and agency for providing various specified supplies as needed reflected illusory promises that did not impose obligations on either party, and therefore the BPAs did not constitute valid contracts with the United States sufficient to establish Tucker Act jurisdiction at the Court of Federal Claims The agency was not required to place any orders with contractor, and, likewise, contractor promised only to accept orders to the extent it was "willing and able" and was thus perfectly free not to accept any orders at all. Crewzers Fire Crew Transp., Inc. v. U.S., 2014 WL 463780 (Fed. Cir. 2014)

Immigration and Naturalization Service's (INS) establishment of 11-month delivery schedule for live-scan fingerprint systems by contract awardee did not constitute improper waiver under Federal Acquisition Regulations of 90- to 120-day terms of blanket purchase agreement, as alleged by unsuccessful bidder seeking to enjoin performance of contract; fact that purchase agreement required successful bidder to be able to deliver within shorter period did not require INS to schedule delivery within that period. 48 C.F.R. §§ 8.401(a), 13. 303-1(a). ANADAC, Inc. v. U.S. Dept. of Justice, I.N.S., 44 F. Supp. 2d 306 (D.D.C. 1999). United States ☞73(3)

§ 13.303-2 Establishment of BPAs.

(a) The following are circumstances under which contracting officers may establish BPAs:

(1) There is a wide variety of items in a broad class of supplies or services that are generally purchased, but the exact items, quantities, and delivery requirements are not known in advance and may vary considerably.

(2) There is a need to provide commercial sources of supply for one or more offices or projects in a given area that do not have or need authority to purchase otherwise.

(3) The use of this procedure would avoid the writing of numerous purchase orders.

(4) There is no existing requirements contract for the same supply or service that the contracting activity is required to use.

(b) After determining a BPA would be advantageous, contracting officers shall—

(1) Establish the parameters to limit purchases to individual items or commodity groups or classes, or permit the supplier to furnish unlimited supplies or services; and

(2) Consider suppliers whose past performance has shown them to be dependable, who offer quality supplies or services at consistently lower prices, and who have provided numerous purchases at or below the simplified acquisition threshold.

(c) BPAs may be established with—

(1) More than one supplier for supplies or services of the same type to provide maximum practicable competition;

(2) A single firm from which numerous individual purchases at or below the simplified acquisition threshold will likely be made in a given period; or

(3) Federal Supply Schedule contractors, if not inconsistent with the terms of the applicable schedule contract.

(d) BPAs should be prepared without a purchase requisition and only after contacting suppliers to make the necessary arrangements for—

(1) Securing maximum discounts;

(2) Documenting individual purchase transactions;

(3) Periodic billings; and

(4) Incorporating other necessary details.

United States Code Annotated

Commercially available off-the-shelf item acquisitions, lists of inapplicable laws in Federal Acquisition Regulation, see 41 USCA § 431.

Competition requirements, see 41 USCA § 253.

Contract requirements, see 41 USCA § 254.

Contracts, competition requirements, see 10 USCA § 2304.

Contracts, planning, solicitation, evaluation, and award procedures, see 10 USCA § 2305.

Definitions, see 10 USCA § 2302, 41 USCA §§ 259, 403.

Definitions relating to procurement of commercial items, see 10 USCA § 2376, 41 USCA § 264a.

Implementation of simplified acquisition procedures, see 10 USCA § 2302b, 41 USCA § 252b.

Kinds of contracts, see 10 USCA § 2306.

List of laws inapplicable to contracts not greater than simplified acquisition threshold in Federal Acquisition Regulation, see 41 USCA § 429.

List of laws inapplicable to procurements of commercial items in Federal Acquisition Regulation, see 41 USCA § 430.

Planning and solicitation requirements, see 41 USCA § 253a.

Preference for acquisition of commercial items, see 10 USCA § 2377, 41 USCA § 264b.

Relationship of commercial item provisions to other provisions of law, see 10 USCA § 2375, 41 USCA § 264.

Simplified acquisition procedures, see 41 USCA § 427.

Notes of Decisions

In general 1

1 In general

Statutory requirement to obtain maximum practicable competition in simplified acquisitions is met where agency uses competitive procedures in establishing blanket purchase agreements (BPA) with multiple vendors; under those circumstances, there is no requirement that the agency conduct a further competition among the BPA holders in connection with each individual purchase order subsequently issued under the BPAs. Logan, LLC, B-294974.6, 2006 CPD ¶ 188 (Comp. Gen. 2006)

§ **13.303-3 Preparation of BPAs.**

Prepare BPAs on the forms specified in 13.307. Do not cite accounting and appropriation data (see 13.303-5(e)(4)).

(a) The following terms and conditions are mandatory:

(1) *Description of agreement.* A statement that the supplier shall furnish supplies or services, described in general terms, if and when requested by the contracting officer (or the authorized representative of the contracting officer) during a specified period and within a stipulated aggregate amount, if any.

(2) *Extent of obligation.* A statement that the Government is obligated only to the extent of authorized purchases actually made under the BPA.

(3) *Purchase limitation.* A statement that specifies the dollar limitation for each individual purchase under the BPA (see 13.303-5(b)).

(4) *Individuals authorized to purchase under the BPA.* A statement that a list of individuals authorized to purchase under the BPA, identified either by title of position or by name of individual, organizational component, and the dollar limitation per purchase for each position title or individual shall be furnished to the supplier by the contracting officer.

(5) *Delivery tickets.* A requirement that all shipments under the agreement, except those for newspapers, magazines, or other periodicals, shall be accompanied by delivery tickets or sales slips that shall contain the following minimum information:

(i) Name of supplier.

(ii) BPA number.

(iii) Date of purchase.

(iv) Purchase number.

(v) Itemized list of supplies or services furnished.

(vi) Quantity, unit price, and extension of each item, less applicable discounts (unit prices and extensions need not be shown when incompatible with the use of automated systems, provided that the invoice is itemized to show this information).

(vii) Date of delivery or shipment.

(6) *Invoices.* One of the following statements shall be included (except that the statement in paragraph (a)(6)(iii) of this subsection should not be used if the accumulation of the individual invoices by the Government materially increases the administrative costs of this purchase method):

(i) A summary invoice shall be submitted at least monthly or upon expiration of this BPA, whichever occurs first, for all deliveries made during a billing period, identifying the delivery tickets covered therein, stating their total dollar value, and supported by receipt copies of the delivery tickets.

(ii) An itemized invoice shall be submitted at least monthly or upon expiration of this BPA, whichever occurs first, for all deliveries made during a billing period and for which payment has not been received. These invoices need not be supported by copies of delivery tickets.

(iii) When billing procedures provide for an individual invoice for each delivery, these invoices shall be accumulated, provided that—

(A) A consolidated payment will be made for each specified period; and

(B) The period of any discounts will commence on the final date of the billing period or on the date of receipt of invoices for all deliveries accepted during the billing period, whichever is later.

(iv) An invoice for subscriptions or other charges for newspapers, magazines, or other periodicals shall show the starting and ending dates and shall state either that ordered subscriptions have been placed in effect or will be placed in effect upon receipt of payment.

(b) If the fast payment procedure is used, include the requirements stated in 13.403.

United States Code Annotated

Commercially available off-the-shelf item acquisitions, lists of inapplicable laws in Federal Acquisition Regulation, see 41 USCA § 431.

Competition requirements, see 41 USCA § 253.

Contract requirements, see 41 USCA § 254.

Contracts, competition requirements, see 10 USCA § 2304.

Contracts, planning, solicitation, evaluation, and award procedures, see 10 USCA § 2305.

Definitions, see 10 USCA § 2302, 41 USCA §§ 259, 403.

Definitions relating to procurement of commercial items, see 10 USCA § 2376, 41 USCA § 264a.

Implementation of simplified acquisition procedures, see 10 USCA § 2302b, 41 USCA § 252b.

Kinds of contracts, see 10 USCA § 2306.

List of laws inapplicable to contracts not greater than simplified acquisition threshold in Federal Acquisition Regulation, see 41 USCA § 429.

List of laws inapplicable to procurements of commercial items in Federal Acquisition Regulation, see 41 USCA § 430.

Planning and solicitation requirements, see 41 USCA § 253a.

Preference for acquisition of commercial items, see 10 USCA § 2377, 41 USCA § 264b.

Relationship of commercial item provisions to other provisions of law, see 10 USCA § 2375, 41 USCA § 264.

Simplified acquisition procedures, see 41 USCA § 427.

§ 13.303-4 Clauses.

(a) The contracting officer shall insert in each BPA the clauses prescribed elsewhere in this part that are required for or applicable to the particular BPA.

(b) Unless a clause prescription specifies otherwise (e.g., see 22.305(a), 22.605(a)(5), or 22.1006), if the prescription includes a dollar threshold, the amount to be compared to that threshold is that of any particular order under the BPA.

United States Code Annotated

Commercially available off-the-shelf item acquisitions, lists of inapplicable laws in Federal Acquisition Regulation, see 41 USCA § 431.

Competition requirements, see 41 USCA § 253.

Contract requirements, see 41 USCA § 254.

Contracts, competition requirements, see 10 USCA § 2304.

Contracts, planning, solicitation, evaluation, and award procedures, see 10 USCA § 2305.

Definitions, see 10 USCA § 2302, 41 USCA §§ 259, 403.

Definitions relating to procurement of commercial items, see 10 USCA § 2376, 41 USCA § 264a.

Implementation of simplified acquisition procedures, see 10 USCA § 2302b, 41 USCA § 252b.

Kinds of contracts, see 10 USCA § 2306.

List of laws inapplicable to contracts not greater than simplified acquisition threshold in Federal Acquisition Regulation, see 41 USCA § 429.

List of laws inapplicable to procurements of commercial items in Federal Acquisition Regulation, see 41 USCA § 430.

Planning and solicitation requirements, see 41 USCA § 253a.

Preference for acquisition of commercial items, see 10 USCA § 2377, 41 USCA § 264b.

Relationship of commercial item provisions to other provisions of law, see 10 USCA § 2375, 41 USCA § 264.

Simplified acquisition procedures, see 41 USCA § 427.

§ 13.303-5 Purchases under BPAs.

(a) Use a BPA only for purchases that are otherwise authorized by law or regulation.

(b) Individual purchases shall not exceed the simplified acquisition threshold. However, agency regulations may establish a higher threshold consistent with the following:

(1) The simplified acquisition threshold and the $7 million limitation for individual purchases ($13 million for purchases entered into under the authority of 12.102(f)(1)) do not apply to BPAs established in accordance with 13.303-2(c)(3).

(2) The limitation for individual purchases for commercial item acquisitions conducted under subpart 13.5 is $7 million ($13 million for acquisitions as described in 13.500(c)).

(c) The existence of a BPA does not justify purchasing from only one source or avoiding small business set-asides. The requirements of 13.003(b) and subpart 19.5 also apply to each order.

(d) If, for a particular purchase greater than the micro-purchase threshold, there is an insufficient number of BPAs to ensure maximum practicable competition, the contracting officer shall—

(1) Solicit quotations from other sources (see 13.105) and make the purchase as appropriate; and

(2) Establish additional BPAs to facilitate future purchases if—

(i) Recurring requirements for the same or similar supplies or services seem likely;

(ii) Qualified sources are willing to accept BPAs; and

(iii) It is otherwise practical to do so.

(e) Limit documentation of purchases to essential information and forms as follows:

(1) Purchases generally should be made electronically, or orally when it is not considered economical or practical to use electronic methods.

(2) A paper purchase document may be issued if necessary to ensure that the supplier and the purchaser agree concerning the transaction.

(3) Unless a paper document is issued, record essential elements (e.g., date, supplier, supplies or services, price, delivery date) on the purchase requisition, in an informal memorandum, or on a form developed locally for the purpose.

(4) Cite the pertinent purchase requisitions and the accounting and appropriation data.

(5) When delivery is made or the services are performed, the supplier's sales document, delivery document, or invoice may (if it reflects the essential elements) be used for the purpose of recording receipt and acceptance of the supplies or services. However, if the purchase is assigned to another activity for administration, the authorized Government representative shall document receipt and acceptance of supplies or services by signing and dating the agency specified form after verification and after notation of any exceptions.

United States Code Annotated

Commercially available off-the-shelf item acquisitions, lists of inapplicable laws in Federal Acquisition Regulation, see 41 USCA § 431.

Competition requirements, see 41 USCA § 253.

Contract requirements, see 41 USCA § 254.

Contracts, competition requirements, see 10 USCA § 2304.

Contracts, planning, solicitation, evaluation, and award procedures, see 10 USCA § 2305.

Definitions, see 10 USCA § 2302, 41 USCA §§ 259, 403.

Definitions relating to procurement of commercial items, see 10 USCA § 2376, 41 USCA § 264a.

Implementation of simplified acquisition procedures, see 10 USCA § 2302b, 41 USCA § 252b.

Kinds of contracts, see 10 USCA § 2306.

List of laws inapplicable to contracts not greater than simplified acquisition threshold in Federal Acquisition Regulation, see 41 USCA § 429.

List of laws inapplicable to procurements of commercial items in Federal Acquisition Regulation, see 41 USCA § 430.

Planning and solicitation requirements, see 41 USCA § 253a.

Preference for acquisition of commercial items, see 10 USCA § 2377, 41 USCA § 264b.

Relationship of commercial item provisions to other provisions of law, see 10 USCA § 2375, 41 USCA § 264.

Simplified acquisition procedures, see 41 USCA § 427.

Notes of Decisions

In general 1

1 In general

Statutory requirement to obtain maximum practicable competition in simplified acquisitions is met where agency uses competitive procedures in establishing blanket purchase agreements (BPA) with multiple vendors; under those circumstances, there is no requirement that the agency conduct a further competition among the BPA holders in connection with each individual purchase order subsequently issued under the BPAs. Logan, LLC, B-294974.6, 2006 CPD ¶ 188 (Comp. Gen. 2006)

After a BPA is established otherwise applicable competition requirements still apply to all procurements under the BPA. FAR 13.303-5(a) The existence of a BPA does not justify purchasing from only one source. FAR 13.303-5(c). If, for a procurement in excess of the micropurchase threshold there is an insufficient number of established BPAs to ensure maximum practicable competition, the contracting officer must solicit quotations from other sources. FAR 13.303-5(d)(1). Envirosolve, LLC, B-294974.4, 2005 CPD ¶ 106 (Comp. Gen. 2005)

§ 13.303-6 Review procedures.

(a) The contracting officer placing orders under a BPA, or the designated representative of the contracting officer, shall review a sufficient random sample of the BPA files at least annually to ensure that authorized procedures are being followed.

(b) The contracting officer that entered into the BPA shall—

(1) Ensure that each BPA is reviewed at least annually and, if necessary, updated at that time; and

(2) Maintain awareness of changes in market conditions, sources of supply, and other pertinent factors that may warrant making new arrangements with different suppliers or modifying existing arrangements.

(c) If an office other than the purchasing office that established a BPA is authorized to make purchases under that BPA, the agency that has jurisdiction over the office authorized to make the purchases shall ensure that the procedures in paragraph (a) of this subsection are being followed.

United States Code Annotated

Commercially available off-the-shelf item acquisitions, lists of inapplicable laws in Federal Acquisition Regulation, see 41 USCA § 431.

Competition requirements, see 41 USCA § 253.

Contract requirements, see 41 USCA § 254.

Contracts, competition requirements, see 10 USCA § 2304.

Contracts, planning, solicitation, evaluation, and award procedures, see 10 USCA § 2305.

Definitions, see 10 USCA § 2302, 41 USCA §§ 259, 403.

Definitions relating to procurement of commercial items, see 10 USCA § 2376, 41 USCA § 264a.

Implementation of simplified acquisition procedures, see 10 USCA § 2302b, 41 USCA § 252b.

Kinds of contracts, see 10 USCA § 2306.

List of laws inapplicable to contracts not greater than simplified acquisition threshold in Federal Acquisition Regulation, see 41 USCA § 429.

List of laws inapplicable to procurements of commercial items in Federal Acquisition Regulation, see 41 USCA § 430.

Planning and solicitation requirements, see 41 USCA § 253a.

Preference for acquisition of commercial items, see 10 USCA § 2377, 41 USCA § 264b.

Relationship of commercial item provisions to other provisions of law, see 10 USCA § 2375, 41 USCA § 264.

Simplified acquisition procedures, see 41 USCA § 427.

§ 13.303-7 Completion of BPAs.

An individual BPA is considered complete when the purchases under it equal its total dollar limitation, if any, or when its stated time period expires.

United States Code Annotated

Commercially available off-the-shelf item acquisitions, lists of inapplicable laws in Federal Acquisition Regulation, see 41 USCA § 431.

Competition requirements, see 41 USCA § 253.

Contract requirements, see 41 USCA § 254.

Contracts, competition requirements, see 10 USCA § 2304.

Contracts, planning, solicitation, evaluation, and award procedures, see 10 USCA § 2305.

Definitions, see 10 USCA § 2302, 41 USCA §§ 259, 403.

Definitions relating to procurement of commercial items, see 10 USCA § 2376, 41 USCA § 264a.

Implementation of simplified acquisition procedures, see 10 USCA § 2302b, 41 USCA § 252b.

Kinds of contracts, see 10 USCA § 2306.

List of laws inapplicable to contracts not greater than simplified acquisition threshold in Federal Acquisition Regulation, see 41 USCA § 429.

List of laws inapplicable to procurements of commercial items in Federal Acquisition Regulation, see 41 USCA § 430.

Planning and solicitation requirements, see 41 USCA § 253a.

Preference for acquisition of commercial items, see 10 USCA § 2377, 41 USCA § 264b.

Relationship of commercial item provisions to other provisions of law, see 10 USCA § 2375, 41 USCA § 264.

Simplified acquisition procedures, see 41 USCA § 427.

§ 13.303-8 Optional clause.

The clause at 52.213-4, Terms and Conditions—Simplified Acquisitions (Other Than Commercial Items), may be used in BPAs established under this section.

United States Code Annotated

Commercially available off-the-shelf item acquisitions, lists of inapplicable laws in Federal Acquisition Regulation, see 41 USCA § 431.

Competition requirements, see 41 USCA § 253.

Contract requirements, see 41 USCA § 254.

Contracts, competition requirements, see 10 USCA § 2304.

Contracts, planning, solicitation, evaluation, and award procedures, see 10 USCA § 2305.

Definitions, see 10 USCA § 2302, 41 USCA §§ 259, 403.

Definitions relating to procurement of commercial items, see 10 USCA § 2376, 41 USCA § 264a.

Implementation of simplified acquisition procedures, see 10 USCA § 2302b, 41 USCA § 252b.

Kinds of contracts, see 10 USCA § 2306.

List of laws inapplicable to contracts not greater than simplified acquisition threshold in Federal Acquisition Regulation, see 41 USCA § 429.

List of laws inapplicable to procurements of commercial items in Federal Acquisition Regulation, see 41 USCA § 430.

Planning and solicitation requirements, see 41 USCA § 253a.

Preference for acquisition of commercial items, see 10 USCA § 2377, 41 USCA § 264b.

Relationship of commercial item provisions to other provisions of law, see 10 USCA § 2375, 41 USCA § 264.

Simplified acquisition procedures, see 41 USCA § 427.

§ 13.304 [Reserved]

§ 13.305 Imprest funds and third party drafts.

§ 13.305-1 General.

Imprest funds and third party drafts may be used to acquire and to pay for supplies or services. Policies and regulations concerning the establishment of and accounting for imprest funds and third party drafts, including the responsibilities of designated cashiers and alternates, are contained in Part IV of the Treasury Financial Manual for Guidance of Departments and Agencies, Title 7 of the GAO Policy and Procedures Manual for Guidance of Federal Agencies, and the agency implementing regulations. Agencies also shall be guided by the Manual of Procedures and Instructions for Cashiers, issued by the Financial Management Service, Department of the Treasury.

United States Code Annotated

Commercially available off-the-shelf item acquisitions, lists of inapplicable laws in Federal Acquisition Regulation, see 41 USCA § 431.

Competition requirements, see 41 USCA § 253.

Contract requirements, see 41 USCA § 254.

Contracts, competition requirements, see 10 USCA § 2304.

Contracts, planning, solicitation, evaluation, and award procedures, see 10 USCA § 2305.

Definitions, see 10 USCA § 2302, 41 USCA §§ 259, 403.

Definitions relating to procurement of commercial items, see 10 USCA § 2376, 41 USCA § 264a.

Implementation of simplified acquisition procedures, see 10 USCA § 2302b, 41 USCA § 252b.

Kinds of contracts, see 10 USCA § 2306.

List of laws inapplicable to contracts not greater than simplified acquisition threshold in Federal Acquisition Regulation, see 41 USCA § 429.

List of laws inapplicable to procurements of commercial items in Federal Acquisition Regulation, see 41 USCA § 430.

Planning and solicitation requirements, see 41 USCA § 253a.

Preference for acquisition of commercial items, see 10 USCA § 2377, 41 USCA § 264b.

Relationship of commercial item provisions to other provisions of law, see 10 USCA § 2375, 41 USCA § 264.

Simplified acquisition procedures, see 41 USCA § 427.

§ 13.305-2 Agency responsibilities.

Each agency using imprest funds and third party drafts shall—

(a) Periodically review and determine whether there is a continuing need for each fund or third party draft account established, and that amounts of those funds or accounts are not in excess of actual needs;

(b) Take prompt action to have imprest funds or third party draft accounts adjusted to a level commensurate with demonstrated needs whenever circumstances warrant such action; and

(c) Develop and issue appropriate implementing regulations. These regulations shall include (but are not limited to) procedures covering—

(1) Designation of personnel authorized to make purchases using imprest funds or third party drafts; and

(2) Documentation of purchases using imprest funds or third party drafts, including documentation of—

(i) Receipt and acceptance of supplies and services by the Government;

(ii) Receipt of cash or third party draft payments by the suppliers; and

(iii) Cash advances and reimbursements.

United States Code Annotated

Commercially available off-the-shelf item acquisitions, lists of inapplicable laws in Federal Acquisition Regulation, see 41 USCA § 431.

Competition requirements, see 41 USCA § 253.

Contract requirements, see 41 USCA § 254.

Contracts, competition requirements, see 10 USCA § 2304.

Contracts, planning, solicitation, evaluation, and award procedures, see 10 USCA § 2305.

Definitions, see 10 USCA § 2302, 41 USCA §§ 259, 403.

Definitions relating to procurement of commercial items, see 10 USCA § 2376, 41 USCA § 264a.

Implementation of simplified acquisition procedures, see 10 USCA § 2302b, 41 USCA § 252b.

Kinds of contracts, see 10 USCA § 2306.

List of laws inapplicable to contracts not greater than simplified acquisition threshold in Federal Acquisition Regulation, see 41 USCA § 429.

List of laws inapplicable to procurements of commercial items in Federal Acquisition Regulation, see 41 USCA § 430.

Planning and solicitation requirements, see 41 USCA § 253a.

Preference for acquisition of commercial items, see 10 USCA § 2377, 41 USCA § 264b.

Relationship of commercial item provisions to other provisions of law, see 10 USCA § 2375, 41 USCA § 264.

Simplified acquisition procedures, see 41 USCA § 427.

§ 13.305-3 Conditions for use.

Imprest funds or third party drafts may be used for purchases when—

(a) The imprest fund transaction does not exceed $500 or such other limits as have been approved by the agency head;

(b) The third party draft transaction does not exceed $2,500, unless authorized at a higher level in accordance with Treasury restrictions;

(c) The use of imprest funds or third party drafts is considered to be advantageous to the Government; and

(d) The use of imprest funds or third party drafts for the transaction otherwise complies with any additional conditions established by agencies and with the policies and regulations referenced in 13.305-1.

United States Code Annotated

Commercially available off-the-shelf item acquisitions, lists of inapplicable laws in Federal Acquisition Regulation, see 41 USCA § 431.

Competition requirements, see 41 USCA § 253.

Contract requirements, see 41 USCA § 254.

Contracts, competition requirements, see 10 USCA § 2304.

Contracts, planning, solicitation, evaluation, and award procedures, see 10 USCA § 2305.

Definitions, see 10 USCA § 2302, 41 USCA §§ 259, 403.

Definitions relating to procurement of commercial items, see 10 USCA § 2376, 41 USCA § 264a.

Implementation of simplified acquisition procedures, see 10 USCA § 2302b, 41 USCA § 252b.

Kinds of contracts, see 10 USCA § 2306.

List of laws inapplicable to contracts not greater than simplified acquisition threshold in Federal Acquisition Regulation, see 41 USCA § 429.

List of laws inapplicable to procurements of commercial items in Federal Acquisition

Regulation, see 41 USCA § 430.

Planning and solicitation requirements, see 41 USCA § 253a.

Preference for acquisition of commercial items, see 10 USCA § 2377, 41 USCA § 264b.

Relationship of commercial item provisions to other provisions of law, see 10 USCA § 2375, 41 USCA § 264.

Simplified acquisition procedures, see 41 USCA § 427.

§ 13.305-4 Procedures.

(a) Each purchase using imprest funds or third party drafts shall be based upon an authorized purchase requisition, contracting officer verification statement, or other agency approved method of ensuring that adequate funds are available for the purchase.

(b) Normally, purchases should be placed orally and without soliciting competition if prices are considered reasonable.

(c) Since there is, for all practical purposes, simultaneous placement of the order and delivery of the items, clauses are not required for purchases using imprest funds or third party drafts.

(d) Forms prescribed at 13.307(e) may be used if a written order is considered necessary (*e.g.*, if required by the supplier for discount, tax exemption, or other reasons). If a purchase order is used, endorse it "Payment to be made from Imprest Fund" (or "Payment to be made from Third Party Draft," as appropriate).

(e) The individual authorized to make purchases using imprest funds or third party drafts shall—

(1) Furnish to the imprest fund or third party draft cashier a copy of the document required under paragraph (a) of this subsection annotated to reflect—

(i) That an imprest fund or third party draft purchase has been made;

(ii) The unit prices and extensions; and

(iii) The supplier's name and address; and

(2) Require the supplier to include with delivery of the supplies an invoice, packing slip, or other sales instrument giving—

(i) The supplier's name and address;

(ii) List and quantity of items supplied;

(iii) Unit prices and extensions; and

(iv) Cash discount, if any.

United States Code Annotated

Commercially available off-the-shelf item acquisitions, lists of inapplicable laws in Federal Acquisition Regulation, see 41 USCA § 431.

Competition requirements, see 41 USCA § 253.

Contract requirements, see 41 USCA § 254.

Contracts, competition requirements, see 10 USCA § 2304.

Contracts, planning, solicitation, evaluation, and award procedures, see 10 USCA § 2305.

Definitions, see 10 USCA § 2302, 41 USCA §§ 259, 403.

Definitions relating to procurement of commercial items, see 10 USCA § 2376, 41 USCA § 264a.

Implementation of simplified acquisition procedures, see 10 USCA § 2302b, 41 USCA § 252b.

Kinds of contracts, see 10 USCA § 2306.

List of laws inapplicable to contracts not greater than simplified acquisition threshold in Federal Acquisition Regulation, see 41 USCA § 429.

List of laws inapplicable to procurements of commercial items in Federal Acquisition Regulation, see 41 USCA § 430.

Planning and solicitation requirements, see 41 USCA § 253a.

Preference for acquisition of commercial items, see 10 USCA § 2377, 41 USCA § 264b.

Relationship of commercial item provisions to other provisions of law, see 10 USCA

§ 2375, 41 USCA § 264.

Simplified acquisition procedures, see 41 USCA § 427.

§ 13.306 SF 44, Purchase Order—Invoice—Voucher.

The SF 44, Purchase Order—Invoice—Voucher, is a multipurpose pocket-size purchase order form designed primarily for on-the-spot, over-the-counter purchases of supplies and nonpersonal services while away from the purchasing office or at isolated activities. It also can be used as a receiving report, invoice, and public voucher.

(a) This form may be used if all of the following conditions are satisfied:

(1) The amount of the purchase is at or below the micropurchase threshold, except for purchases made under unusual and compelling urgency or in support of contingency operations. Agencies may establish higher dollar limitations for specific activities or items.

(2) The supplies or services are immediately available.

(3) One delivery and one payment will be made.

(4) Its use is determined to be more economical and efficient than use of other simplified acquisition procedures.

(b) General procedural instructions governing the form's use are printed on the form and on the inside front cover of each book of forms.

(c) Since there is, for all practical purposes, simultaneous placement of the order and delivery of the items, clauses are not required for purchases using this form.

(d) Agencies shall provide adequate safeguards regarding the control of forms and accounting for purchases.

United States Code Annotated

Commercially available off-the-shelf item acquisitions, lists of inapplicable laws in Federal Acquisition Regulation, see 41 USCA § 431.

Competition requirements, see 41 USCA § 253.

Contract requirements, see 41 USCA § 254.

Contracts, competition requirements, see 10 USCA § 2304.

Contracts, planning, solicitation, evaluation, and award procedures, see 10 USCA § 2305.

Definitions, see 10 USCA § 2302, 41 USCA §§ 259, 403.

Definitions relating to procurement of commercial items, see 10 USCA § 2376, 41 USCA § 264a.

Implementation of simplified acquisition procedures, see 10 USCA § 2302b, 41 USCA § 252b.

Kinds of contracts, see 10 USCA § 2306.

List of laws inapplicable to contracts not greater than simplified acquisition threshold in Federal Acquisition Regulation, see 41 USCA § 429.

List of laws inapplicable to procurements of commercial items in Federal Acquisition Regulation, see 41 USCA § 430.

Planning and solicitation requirements, see 41 USCA § 253a.

Preference for acquisition of commercial items, see 10 USCA § 2377, 41 USCA § 264b.

Relationship of commercial item provisions to other provisions of law, see 10 USCA § 2375, 41 USCA § 264.

Simplified acquisition procedures, see 41 USCA § 427.

§ 13.307 Forms.

(a) *Commercial items.* For use of the SF 1449, Solicitation/Contract/Order for Commercial Items, see 12.204.

(b) *Other than commercial items.* (1) Except when quotations are solicited electronically or orally, the SF 1449; SF 18, Request for Quotations; or an agency form/automated format may be used. Each agency request for quotations form/automated format should conform with the SF 18 or SF 1449 to the maximum extent practicable.

(2) Both SF 1449 and OF 347, Order for Supplies or Services, are multipurpose forms used for negotiated purchases of supplies or services, delivery or task orders, inspection and receiving reports, and invoices. An agency form/automated format also may be used.

(c) *Forms used for both commercial and other than commercial items.* (1) OF 336, Continuation Sheet, or an agency form/automated format may be used when additional space is needed.

(2) OF 348, Order for Supplies or Services Schedule— Continuation, or an agency form/automated format may be used for negotiated purchases when additional space is needed. Agencies may print on these forms the clauses considered to be generally suitable for purchases.

(3) SF 30, Amendment of Solicitation/Modification of Contract, or a purchase order form may be used to modify a purchase order, unless an agency form/automated format is prescribed in agency regulations.

(d) SF 44, Purchase Order—Invoice—Voucher, is a multipurpose pocket-size purchase order form that may be used as outlined in 13.306.

(e) SF 1165, Receipt for Cash—Subvoucher, or an agency purchase order form may be used for purchases using imprest funds or third party drafts.

United States Code Annotated

Commercially available off-the-shelf item acquisitions, lists of inapplicable laws in Federal Acquisition Regulation, see 41 USCA § 431.

Competition requirements, see 41 USCA § 253.

Contract requirements, see 41 USCA § 254.

Contracts, competition requirements, see 10 USCA § 2304.

Contracts, planning, solicitation, evaluation, and award procedures, see 10 USCA § 2305.

Definitions, see 10 USCA § 2302, 41 USCA §§ 259, 403.

Definitions relating to procurement of commercial items, see 10 USCA § 2376, 41 USCA § 264a.

Implementation of simplified acquisition procedures, see 10 USCA § 2302b, 41 USCA § 252b.

Kinds of contracts, see 10 USCA § 2306.

List of laws inapplicable to contracts not greater than simplified acquisition threshold in Federal Acquisition Regulation, see 41 USCA § 429.

List of laws inapplicable to procurements of commercial items in Federal Acquisition Regulation, see 41 USCA § 430.

Planning and solicitation requirements, see 41 USCA § 253a.

Preference for acquisition of commercial items, see 10 USCA § 2377, 41 USCA § 264b.

Relationship of commercial item provisions to other provisions of law, see 10 USCA § 2375, 41 USCA § 264.

Simplified acquisition procedures, see 41 USCA § 427.

Subpart 13.4 Fast Payment Procedure

§ 13.401 General.

(a) The fast payment procedure allows payment under limited conditions to a contractor prior to the Government's verification that supplies have been received and accepted. The procedure provides for payment for supplies based on the contractor's submission of an invoice that constitutes a certification that the contractor—

(1) Has delivered the supplies to a post office, common carrier, or point of first receipt by the Government; and

(2) Shall replace, repair, or correct supplies not received at destination, damaged in transit, or not conforming to purchase agreements.

(b) The contracting officer shall be primarily responsible for determining the amount of debts resulting from failure of contractors to properly replace, repair, or correct supplies lost, damaged, or not conforming to purchase requirements (see 32.602 and 32.603).

United States Code Annotated

Commercially available off-the-shelf item acquisitions, lists of inapplicable laws in

Federal Acquisition Regulation, see 41 USCA § 431.

Contract requirements, see 41 USCA § 254.

Contracts, planning, solicitation, evaluation, and award procedures, see 10 USCA § 2305.

Definitions, see 10 USCA § 2302, 41 USCA §§ 259, 403.

Definitions relating to procurement of commercial items, see 10 USCA § 2376, 41 USCA § 264a.

Implementation of simplified acquisition procedures, see 10 USCA § 2302b, 41 USCA § 252b.

Kinds of contracts, see 10 USCA § 2306.

List of laws inapplicable to contracts not greater than simplified acquisition threshold in Federal Acquisition Regulation, see 41 USCA § 429.

List of laws inapplicable to procurements of commercial items in Federal Acquisition Regulation, see 41 USCA § 430.

Planning and solicitation requirements, see 41 USCA § 253a.

Preference for acquisition of commercial items, see 10 USCA § 2377, 41 USCA § 264b.

Relationship of commercial item provisions to other provisions of law, see 10 USCA § 2375, 41 USCA § 264.

Simplified acquisition procedures, see 41 USCA § 427.

§ 13.402 Conditions for use.

If the conditions in paragraphs (a) through (f) of this section are present, the fast payment procedure may be used, provided that use of the procedure is consistent with the other conditions of the purchase. The conditions for use of the fast payment procedure are as follows:

(a) Individual purchasing instruments do not exceed $35,000, except that executive agencies may permit higher dollar limitations for specified activities or items on a case-by-case basis.

(b) Deliveries of supplies are to occur at locations where there is both a geographical separation and a lack of adequate communications facilities between Government receiving and disbursing activities that will make it impractical to make timely payment based on evidence of Government acceptance.

(c) Title to the supplies passes to the Government—

(1) Upon delivery to a post office or common carrier for mailing or shipment to destination; or

(2) Upon receipt by the Government if the shipment is by means other than Postal Service or common carrier.

(d) The supplier agrees to replace, repair, or correct supplies not received at destination, damaged in transit, or not conforming to purchase requirements.

(e) The purchasing instrument is a firm-fixed-price contract, a purchase order, or a delivery order for supplies.

(f) A system is in place to ensure—

(1) Documentation of evidence of contractor performance under fast payment purchases;

(2) Timely feedback to the contracting officer in case of contractor deficiencies; and

(3) Identification of suppliers that have a current history of abusing the fast payment procedure (also see Subpart 9.1).

United States Code Annotated

Commercially available off-the-shelf item acquisitions, lists of inapplicable laws in Federal Acquisition Regulation, see 41 USCA § 431.

Contract requirements, see 41 USCA § 254.

Contracts, planning, solicitation, evaluation, and award procedures, see 10 USCA § 2305.

Definitions, see 10 USCA § 2302, 41 USCA §§ 259, 403.

Definitions relating to procurement of commercial items, see 10 USCA § 2376, 41 USCA § 264a.

Implementation of simplified acquisition procedures, see 10 USCA § 2302b, 41 USCA

§ 252b.

Kinds of contracts, see 10 USCA § 2306.

List of laws inapplicable to contracts not greater than simplified acquisition threshold in Federal Acquisition Regulation, see 41 USCA § 429.

List of laws inapplicable to procurements of commercial items in Federal Acquisition Regulation, see 41 USCA § 430.

Planning and solicitation requirements, see 41 USCA § 253a.

Preference for acquisition of commercial items, see 10 USCA § 2377, 41 USCA § 264b.

Relationship of commercial item provisions to other provisions of law, see 10 USCA § 2375, 41 USCA § 264.

Simplified acquisition procedures, see 41 USCA § 427.

§ 13.403 Preparation and execution of orders.

Priced or unpriced contracts, purchase orders, or BPAs using the fast payment procedure shall include the following:

(a) A requirement that the supplies be shipped transportation or postage prepaid.

(b) A requirement that invoices be submitted directly to the finance or other office designated in the order, or in the case of unpriced purchase orders, to the contracting officer (see 13.302-2(c)).

(c) The following statement on the consignee's copy:

Consignee's Notification to Purchasing Activity of Nonreceipt, Damage, or Nonconformance

The consignee shall notify the purchasing office promptly after the specified date of delivery of supplies not received, damaged in transit, or not conforming to specifications of the purchase order. Unless extenuating circumstances exist, the notification should be made not later than 60 days after the specified date of delivery.

United States Code Annotated

Commercially available off-the-shelf item acquisitions, lists of inapplicable laws in Federal Acquisition Regulation, see 41 USCA § 431.

Contract requirements, see 41 USCA § 254.

Contracts, planning, solicitation, evaluation, and award procedures, see 10 USCA § 2305.

Definitions, see 10 USCA § 2302, 41 USCA §§ 259, 403.

Definitions relating to procurement of commercial items, see 10 USCA § 2376, 41 USCA § 264a.

Implementation of simplified acquisition procedures, see 10 USCA § 2302b, 41 USCA § 252b.

Kinds of contracts, see 10 USCA § 2306.

List of laws inapplicable to contracts not greater than simplified acquisition threshold in Federal Acquisition Regulation, see 41 USCA § 429.

List of laws inapplicable to procurements of commercial items in Federal Acquisition Regulation, see 41 USCA § 430.

Planning and solicitation requirements, see 41 USCA § 253a.

Preference for acquisition of commercial items, see 10 USCA § 2377, 41 USCA § 264b.

Relationship of commercial item provisions to other provisions of law, see 10 USCA § 2375, 41 USCA § 264.

Simplified acquisition procedures, see 41 USCA § 427.

§ 13.404 Contract clause.

The contracting officer shall insert the clause at 52.213-1, Fast Payment Procedure, in solicitations and contracts when the conditions in 13.402 are applicable and it is intended that the fast payment procedure be used in the contract (in the case of BPAs, the contracting officer may elect to insert the clause either in the BPA or in orders under the BPA).

United States Code Annotated

Commercially available off-the-shelf item acquisitions, lists of inapplicable laws in

Federal Acquisition Regulation, see 41 USCA § 431.

Contract requirements, see 41 USCA § 254.

Contracts, planning, solicitation, evaluation, and award procedures, see 10 USCA § 2305.

Definitions, see 10 USCA § 2302, 41 USCA §§ 259, 403.

Definitions relating to procurement of commercial items, see 10 USCA § 2376, 41 USCA § 264a.

Implementation of simplified acquisition procedures, see 10 USCA § 2302b, 41 USCA § 252b.

Kinds of contracts, see 10 USCA § 2306.

List of laws inapplicable to contracts not greater than simplified acquisition threshold in Federal Acquisition Regulation, see 41 USCA § 429.

List of laws inapplicable to procurements of commercial items in Federal Acquisition Regulation, see 41 USCA § 430.

Planning and solicitation requirements, see 41 USCA § 253a.

Preference for acquisition of commercial items, see 10 USCA § 2377, 41 USCA § 264b.

Relationship of commercial item provisions to other provisions of law, see 10 USCA § 2375, 41 USCA § 264.

Simplified acquisition procedures, see 41 USCA § 427.

Subpart 13.5 Simplified Procedures for Certain Commercial Items

§ 13.500 General.
(a) This subpart authorizes the use of simplified procedures for the acquisition of supplies and services in amounts greater than the simplified acquisition threshold but not exceeding $7 million ($13 million for acquisitions as described in 13.500(c)), including options, if the contracting officer reasonably expects, based on the nature of the supplies or services sought, and on market research, that offers will include only commercial items. Contracting officers may use any simplified acquisition procedure in this part, subject to any specific dollar limitation applicable to the particular procedure. The purpose of these simplified procedures is to vest contracting officers with additional procedural discretion and flexibility, so that commercial item acquisitions in this dollar range may be solicited, offered, evaluated, and awarded in a simplified manner that maximizes efficiency and economy and minimizes burden and administrative costs for both the Government and industry (10 U.S.C. 2304(g) and 2305 and 41 U.S.C. 3305, 3306, and chapter 37, Awarding of Contracts.

(b) When acquiring commercial items using the procedures in this part, the requirements of part 12 apply subject to the order of precedence provided at 12.102(c). This includes use of the provisions and clauses in subpart 12.3.

(c) Under 41 U.S.C. 1903, the simplified acquisition procedures authorized in this subpart may be used for acquisitions that do not exceed $13 million when—

(1) The acquisition is for commercial items that, as determined by the head of the agency, are to be used in support of a contingency operation or to facilitate the defense against or recovery from nuclear, biological, chemical, or radiological attack; or

(2) The acquisition will be treated as an acquisition of commercial items in accordance with 12.102(f)(1).

United States Code Annotated
Commercially available off-the-shelf item acquisitions, lists of inapplicable laws in Federal Acquisition Regulation, see 41 USCA § 431.

Competition requirements, see 41 USCA § 253.

Contract requirements, see 41 USCA § 254.

Contracts, competition requirements, see 10 USCA § 2304.

Contracts, planning, solicitation, evaluation, and award procedures, see 10 USCA § 2305.

Definitions, see 10 USCA § 2302, 41 USCA §§ 259, 403.

Definitions relating to procurement of commercial items, see 10 USCA § 2376, 41 USCA

§ 264a.

Implementation of simplified acquisition procedures, see 10 USCA § 2302b, 41 USCA § 252b.

Kinds of contracts, see 10 USCA § 2306.

List of laws inapplicable to contracts not greater than simplified acquisition threshold in Federal Acquisition Regulation, see 41 USCA § 429.

List of laws inapplicable to procurements of commercial items in Federal Acquisition Regulation, see 41 USCA § 430.

Planning and solicitation requirements, see 41 USCA § 253a.

Preference for acquisition of commercial items, see 10 USCA § 2377, 41 USCA § 264b.

Relationship of commercial item provisions to other provisions of law, see 10 USCA § 2375, 41 USCA § 264.

Simplified acquisition procedures, see 41 USCA § 427.

Notes of Decisions

In general 1

1 In general

Protest is sustained where agency had no authority to use small purchase procedures to acquire a commercial item because the anticipated contract value was in excess of $5 million, contrary to applicable regulation limiting use of these procedures to purchases at or below $5 million. Global Communications Solutions, Inc., B-299044, B-299044.2, 2007 CPD ¶ 30 (Comp. Gen. 2007)

§ 13.501 Special documentation requirements.

(a) Sole source (including brand name) acquisitions.

(1) Acquisitions conducted under simplified acquisition procedures are exempt from the requirements in part 6. However, contracting officers must—

(i) Conduct sole source acquisitions, as defined in 2.101, (including brand name) under this subpart only if the need to do so is justified in writing and approved at the levels specified in paragraph (a)(2) of this section;

(ii) Prepare sole source (including brand name) justifications using the format at 6.303-2, modified to reflect that the procedures in FAR subpart 13.5 were used in accordance with 41 U.S.C. 1901 or the authority of 41 U.S.C. 1903;

(iii) Make publicly available the justifications (excluding brand name) required by 6.305(a) within 14 days after contract award or in the case of unusual and compelling urgency within 30 days after contract award, in accordance with 6.305 procedures at paragraphs (b), (d), (e), and (f); and

(iv) Make publicly available brand name justifications with the solicitation, in accordance with 5.102(a)(6).

(2) Justifications and approvals are required under this subpart for sole-source (including brand-name) acquisitions or portions of an acquisition requiring a brand-name. If the justification is to cover only the portion of the acquisition which is brand-name, then it should so state; the approval level requirements will then only apply to that portion.

(i) For a proposed contract exceeding $150,000, but not exceeding $700,000, the contracting officer's certification that the justification is accurate and complete to the best of the contracting officer's knowledge and belief will serve as approval, unless a higher approval level is established in accordance with agency procedures.

(ii) For a proposed contract exceeding $700,000, but not exceeding $13.5 million, the advocate for competition for the procuring activity, designated pursuant to 6.501; or an official described in 6.304(a)(3) or (a)(4) must approve the justification and approval. This authority is not delegable.

(iii) For a proposed contract exceeding $13.5 million but not exceeding $68 million or, for DoD, NASA, and the Coast Guard, not exceeding $93 million, the head of the procuring activity or the official described in 6.304(a)(3) or (a)(4) must approve the justification and approval. This authority is not delegable.

(iv) For a proposed contract exceeding $68 million or, for DoD, NASA, and the Coast

Guard, $93 million, the official described in 6.304(a)(4) must approve the justification and approval. This authority is not delegable except as provided in 6.304(a)(4).

(b) Contract file documentation. The contract file must include—

(1) A brief written description of the procedures used in awarding the contract, including the fact that the procedures in FAR subpart 13.5 were used;

(2) The number of offers received;

(3) An explanation, tailored to the size and complexity of the acquisition, of the basis for the contract award decision; and

(4) Any justification approved under paragraph (a) of this section.

United States Code Annotated

Commercially available off-the-shelf item acquisitions, lists of inapplicable laws in Federal Acquisition Regulation, see 41 USCA § 431.

Competition requirements, see 41 USCA § 253.

Contract requirements, see 41 USCA § 254.

Contracts, competition requirements, see 10 USCA § 2304.

Contracts, planning, solicitation, evaluation, and award procedures, see 10 USCA § 2305.

Definitions, see 10 USCA § 2302, 41 USCA §§ 259, 403.

Definitions relating to procurement of commercial items, see 10 USCA § 2376, 41 USCA § 264a.

Implementation of simplified acquisition procedures, see 10 USCA § 2302b, 41 USCA § 252b.

Kinds of contracts, see 10 USCA § 2306.

List of laws inapplicable to contracts not greater than simplified acquisition threshold in Federal Acquisition Regulation, see 41 USCA § 429.

List of laws inapplicable to procurements of commercial items in Federal Acquisition Regulation, see 41 USCA § 430.

Planning and solicitation requirements, see 41 USCA § 253a.

Preference for acquisition of commercial items, see 10 USCA § 2377, 41 USCA § 264b.

Relationship of commercial item provisions to other provisions of law, see 10 USCA § 2375, 41 USCA § 264.

Simplified acquisition procedures, see 41 USCA § 427.

Notes of Decisions

In general 1

1 In general

When an agency plans to use simplified procedures in a procurement for commercial items that exceeds the simplified acquisition threshold under the Test Program, the agency must state that it is invoking the Subpart 13.5 test program and: (1) that the procurement is being conducted under the subpart 13.5 test program; (2) that simplified acquisition procedures apply; and (3) whether the agency will conduct the procurement according to parts 12, 14 or 15 of the FAR, or some combination thereof. In the event that an agency chooses to utilize a combination of these parts, it must provide notice of which procedural provisions it will apply. Failure to provide this information leaves the procurement subject to challenge on the ground that the lack of notice prejudicially affected the protestor's ability to compete for award. Dubinsky v. U.S., 43 Fed. Cl. 243 (1999).

Even in a commercial acquisition using simplified procedures, where an agency requests detailed written proposals, a selection decision is improper where it lacks a rationale which sets forth a basis for the tradeoffs made, including an explanation of any perceived benefits associated with additional costs. Finlen Complex, Inc., B-288280, 2001 CPD ¶ 167 (Comp. Gen. 2001).

Under the test program for commercial items, the agency must include in the contract file "[a]n explanation, tailored to the size and complexity of the acquisition, of the basis for the contract award decision." FAR 13.501(b)(3). A selection decision is flawed where the contracting officer makes no qualitative comparison of the technical differences between the proposals to determine whether the awardee's technical superiority justifies the price premium. Universal Building Maintenance, Inc., B-282456, 99-2 CPD ¶ 32 (Comp. Gen. 1999)

Subpart 14.3 Submission of Bids

Subpart 14.4 Opening of Bids and Award of Contract

Subpart 14.5 Two-Step Sealed Bidding

§ 14.000 Scope of part.

This part prescribes—

(a) The basic requirements of contracting for supplies and services (including construction) by sealed bidding;

(b) The information to be included in the solicitation (invitation for bids);

(c) Procedures concerning the submission of bids;

(d) Requirements for opening and evaluating bids and awarding contracts; and

(e) Procedures for two-step sealed bidding.

United States Code Annotated

Contract requirements, see 41 USCA § 254.

Contracts, planning, solicitation, evaluation, and award procedures, see 10 USCA § 2305.

Definitions, see 10 USCA § 2302, 41 USCA §§ 259, 403.

Evaluation and award, see 41 USCA § 253b.

Kinds of contracts, see 10 USCA § 2306.

Planning and solicitation requirements, see 41 USCA § 253a.

Subpart 14.1 Use of Sealed Bidding

§ 14.101 Elements of sealed bidding.

Sealed bidding is a method of contracting that employs competitive bids, public opening of bids, and awards. The following steps are involved:

(a) *Preparation of invitations for bids*. Invitations must describe the requirements of the Government clearly, accurately, and completely. Unnecessarily restrictive specifications or requirements that might unduly limit the number of bidders are prohibited. The invitation includes all documents (whether attached or incorporated by reference) furnished prospective bidders for the purpose of bidding.

(b) *Publicizing the invitation for bids*. Invitations must be publicized through distribution to prospective bidders, posting in public places, and such other means as may be appropriate. Publicizing must occur a sufficient time before public opening of bids to enable prospective bidders to prepare and submit bids.

(c) *Submission of bids*. Bidders must submit sealed bids to be opened at the time and place stated in the solicitation for the public opening of bids.

(d) *Evaluation of bids*. Bids shall be evaluated without discussions.

(e) *Contract award*. After bids are publicly opened, an award will be made with reasonable promptness to that responsible bidder whose bid, conforming to the invitation for bids, will be most advantageous to the Government, considering only price and the price-related factors included in the invitation.

United States Code Annotated

Contract requirements, see 41 USCA § 254.

Contracts, planning, solicitation, evaluation, and award procedures, see 10 USCA § 2305.

Definitions, see 10 USCA § 2302, 41 USCA §§ 259, 403.

Evaluation and award, see 41 USCA § 253b.

Kinds of contracts, see 10 USCA § 2306.

Planning and solicitation requirements, see 41 USCA § 253a.

Notes of Decisions

1 Construction and application of statutes and regulations

General Accounting Office (GAO) cannot rely on principles of procurement law, even well-established ones, when reliance is inconsistent with federal statutes and regulations. 48 C.F.R. § 14.101(a). Mark Dunning Industries, Inc. v. Perry, 890 F. Supp. 1504, 40 Cont. Cas. Fed. (CCH) P 76846 (M.D. Ala. 1995). United States ☜64.45(1)

2 Discretion and authority of agency—In general

Federal Acquisition Regulations confer discretionary authority upon contracting officers to permit correction of mistakes in bidding disclosed before government contract is awarded. 48 C.F.R. § 14.406-3. McKnight Const. Co., Inc. v. Perry, 888 F. Supp. 1178 (S.D. Ga. 1994). United States ☜64.5

If evidence available to government officer at time he made decision to award government contract did not clearly and convincingly establish bidder's intended bid, officer would lack authority to allow correction in bid. 48 C.F.R. § 14.406-3. McKnight Const. Co., Inc. v. Perry, 888 F. Supp. 1178 (S.D. Ga. 1994). United States ☜64.5

Generally, government has discretion to reject all bids for a variety of reasons; that is to say, sealed bid solicitation does not per se limit agency's discretion. Arrowhead Metals, Ltd. v. U.S., 8 Cl. Ct. 703, 33 Cont. Cas. Fed. (CCH) P 74026 (1985). United States ☜64.50

Procurement by negotiation contemplates the exercise of greater discretion overall by a contracting officer than does procurement by formal advertising. DeMat Air, Inc. v. U.S., 2 Cl. Ct. 197, 30 Cont. Cas. Fed. (CCH) P 70980 (1983). United States ☜64.10

3 Discretion and authority of agency—Cancellation of invitations, discretion of agency

The authority vested in a contracting officer (CO) to decide whether to cancel an invitation for bids (IFB) and readvertise is extremely broad; CO's determination concerning the unreasonableness of the prices bid is a matter of administrative discretion which should not be questioned unless the determination is shown to be unreasonable or that there is a showing of fraud or bad faith. 48 C.F.R. § 14.404-1(c)(6). First Enterprise v. U.S., 61 Fed. Cl. 109 (2004). United States ☜64.50

In the context of pre-award negotiations, a contracting officer is given latitude in deciding whether to cancel a solicitation and request new bids after price offers have been disclosed. Griffy's Landscape Maintenance LLC v. U.S., 51 Fed. Cl. 667 (2001). United States ☜64.50

Authority vested in the contracting officer to decide whether to cancel an invitation for bids (IFB) and readvertise is extremely broad. 48 C.F.R. § 14.404-1(a)(1). Overstreet Elec. Co., Inc. v. U.S., 47 Fed. Cl. 728 (2000). United States ☜64.50

Contracting officer's generally broad discretion to cancel a solicitation is substantially narrowed after bid opening to prevent harm to the integrity of the bidding system. 48 C.F.R. § 14.404-1. California Marine Cleaning, Inc. v. U.S., 42 Fed. Cl. 281, 42 Cont. Cas. Fed. (CCH) P 77398 (1998). United States ☜64.50

Procurement official's decision to cancel solicitation in negotiated procurement is inherently discretionary. Shields Enterprises, Inc. v. U.S., 28 Fed. Cl. 615, 38 Cont. Cas. Fed. (CCH) P 76526 (1993). United States ☜64.50

Contracting officer did not act arbitrarily or capriciously by cancelling solicitation because supplies being contracted for were no longer required; solicitation granted to officer gave substantial discretion to reject bid or to cancel or amend solicitation. Durable Metals Products, Inc. v. U.S., 27 Fed. Cl. 472, 38 Cont. Cas. Fed. (CCH) P 76471 (1993), judgment aff'd, 11 F.3d 1071 (Fed. Cir. 1993). United States ☜64.50

Government reasonably and within its discretion determined that specifications in solicitation for bids for providing armed-guard services were ambiguous or inadequate with respect to Government's need for two supervisors per eight hour shift, and thus Government properly cancelled solicitation. Vanguard Sec. Inc. v. U.S., 20 Cl. Ct. 90, 1990 WL 38036 (1990). United States ☜64.50

United States Mint did not abandon its discretion to Congress in determining whether to cancel solicitation for bids in connection with contract for production of coins, but rather considered, in exercise of its own discretion, that public and congressional outcry raised issues worthy of investigation. Arrowhead Metals, Ltd. v. U.S., 8 Cl. Ct. 703, 33 Cont. Cas. Fed. (CCH) P 74026 (1985). United States ☜64.50

4 Preparation of invitations for bids

Although communications between successful bidder and Alabama Department of Transportation (ADOT) officials, after ADOT realized that traffic control term had been omitted from plans, specifications, and estimates (PS & E) for highway construction project, during which bidder assured ADOT that omitted term would not affect its bid was certainly not advisable sort of communication, communication did not amount to kind of "reverse bid rigging" that required Federal Highway Administration (FHWA) to reject bidder as proposed awardee under FHWA policy memorandum, where ADOT clearly did not seek by its limited communication with bidder to gain reduction in price of construction contract and bidder did not attempt to thwart purposes of competitive bidding process by explaining that omitted note would have no effect on its bid and instead communications simply served as means for ADOT to evaluate materiality of omitted note. 23 U.S.C.A. § 112(c); 23 C.F.R. § 630.205(b, c); 48 C.F.R. § 14.101(a). Clark Const. Co., Inc. v. Pena, 895 F. Supp. 1483 (M.D. Ala. 1995). Highways ☜113(1)

Federal Highway Administration (FHWA) and Alabama Department of Transportation (ADOT), rather than prospective bidders on highway construction contract, were charged with duty to insure that plans, specifications and estimates (PS & E) contained all agreed-to terms no matter how trivial. 23 U.S.C.A. § 101 et seq.; 23 C.F.R. § 630.205(b, c); 48 C.F.R. § 14.101(a). Clark Const. Co., Inc. v. Pena, 895 F. Supp. 1483 (M.D. Ala. 1995). Highways ☜113(1)

5 Solicitation of bids—In general

Bid protestor did not establish that agency acted arbitrarily and capriciously when it issued solicitation, based on its assertions that agency was required to base its funding request on an independent government estimate of $3,596,111, not the agency's own construction estimate of $3,218,781, and that agency issued the solicitation without intent to award a contract because it should have known that using its own estimate would result in insufficient funding for the project. First Enterprise v. U.S., 61 Fed. Cl. 109 (2004). United States ☞64.25

Where air force official was merely expressing opinion when he stated that resolicitation for proposals for lease of aircraft by Air Force could occur in future, statement did not bind Air Force to future course of action. Aviation Enterprises, Inc. v. U.S., 8 Cl. Ct. 1, 32 Cont. Cas. Fed. (CCH) P 73403 (1985). United States ☞64.40(5)

6 Solicitation of bids—Incumbent contractor, solicitation of bids

Absence of incumbent contractor from bidding process for paper towel contract, which resulted in only two bids on 17 of line items, one bid on 14 line item and three or more on two line items, impaired competitiveness of process to prejudice of incumbent contractor in violation of Competition in Contracting Act and procurement regulations, so that resolicitation of all 33 line items was appropriate remedy for failure to mail incumbent contractor copy of solicitation. Federal Property and Administrative Services Act of 1949, § 301 et seq., as amended, 41 U.S.C.A. § 251 et seq.Abel Converting, Inc. v. U.S., 679 F. Supp. 1133, 34 Cont. Cas. Fed. (CCH) P 75449 (D.D.C. 1988). United States ☞64.10; United States ☞64.60(5.1)

Absence of incumbent contractor from bidding process for paper towels significantly diminished level of competition for paper towel contract and no level of competition could cure such clearly prejudicial violation of General Services Administration's procurement regulations, so that General Services Administration's initial decision to resolicit only 14 of 33 items was not in accordance with Competition in Contracting Act. Federal Property and Administrative Services Act of 1949, § 301 et seq., as amended, 41 U.S.C.A. § 251 et seq.Abel Converting, Inc. v. U.S., 679 F. Supp. 1133, 34 Cont. Cas. Fed. (CCH) P 75449 (D.D.C. 1988). United States ☞64.10

Competition in Contracting Act and procurement regulations imposed upon General Services Administration general obligation to solicit bids for paper towels through most effectively competitive mechanism possible and to take affirmative steps to ensure that potentially responsible bidders, including incumbent, as previously successful bidder, be permitted to submit bids and be on bidder's mailing list. Office of Federal Procurement Policy Act, § 4(7), 41 U.S.C.A. § 403(7). Abel Converting, Inc. v. U.S., 679 F. Supp. 1133, 34 Cont. Cas. Fed. (CCH) P 75449 (D.D.C. 1988). United States ☞64.10

General Services Administration's efforts to notify potential bidders, including publication in Commerce Business Daily, a compendium of all federal government contracting opportunities, mailing of several hundred preinvitation notice letters, and posting of solicitation of paper towel contract in General Services Administration's business centers was not sufficient to put incumbent contractor which did not receive copy of solicitation from General Services Administration on notice of solicitation, and because incumbent was not among small number of potential responsible bidders, General Service Administration's efforts were insufficient to satisfy competition requirements of Competition in Contracting Act. Federal Property and Administrative Services Act of 1949, § 301 et seq., as amended, 41 U.S.C.A. § 251 et seq.Abel Converting, Inc. v. U.S., 679 F. Supp. 1133, 34 Cont. Cas. Fed. (CCH) P 75449 (D.D.C. 1988). United States ☞64.25

Fact that incumbent contractor was nonbidder did not preclude incumbent contractor from challenging government procurement decision inasmuch as incumbent contractor was denied right to submit bid as a result of negligence of General Services Administration in failing to send solicitation notice. Abel Converting, Inc. v. U.S., 679 F. Supp. 1133, 34 Cont. Cas. Fed. (CCH) P 75449 (D.D.C. 1988). United States ☞64.60(2)

General Services Administration's failure to send solicitation to incumbent contractor in compliance with regulations injured incumbent by denying it opportunity to bid, failure to send solicitation was arguably within zone of interest intended to be protected by Competition in Contracting Act, and there was no clear and convincing congressional intent to withhold judicial review, so that prudential considerations permitted incumbent standing to challenge General Services Administration's failure to mail solicitation to incumbent. Federal Property and Administrative Services Act of 1949, § 301 et seq., as amended, 41 U.S.C.A. § 251 et seq.Abel Converting, Inc. v. U.S., 679 F. Supp. 1133, 34 Cont. Cas. Fed. (CCH) P 75449 (D.D.C. 1988). United States ☞64.60(2)

Incumbent contractor's burden was to demonstrate that General Services Administration's failure to follow its own regulations or its violation of Competition in Contracting Act, if any, by failing to mail incumbent copy of solicitation prejudiced incumbent's interest by excluding incumbent from bidding process and that General Services Administration's violations of its own regulation could not be excused or that violation diminished competition in order to obtain injunction requiring resolicitation of bid. Federal Property and Administrative Services Act of 1949, § 301 et seq., as amended, 41 U.S.C.A. § 251 et seq.Abel Converting, Inc. v. U.S., 679 F. Supp. 1133, 34 Cont. Cas. Fed. (CCH) P 75449 (D.D.C. 1988). United States ☞64.60(3.1)

Incumbent contractor was injured by General Services Administration's failure to follow its regulations requiring mailing of copy of solicitation to incumbent which resulted in denial to incumbent of opportunity to bid, and order by court directing resolicitation would redress injury, so that incumbent contractor had constitutional standing to seek relief from General Services Administration's failure to mail it a solicitation. U.S.C.A. Const. Art. 3, § 1 et seq.Abel Converting, Inc. v. U.S., 679 F. Supp. 1133, 34 Cont. Cas. Fed. (CCH) P 75449 (D.D.C. 1988). United States ☞64.60(2)

Incumbent government contractor failed to establish that agency official, acting in coordination with consultant, acted in bad faith by "steering" contract award to another contractor and requesting that contracting agency not solicit incumbent on the contract; there was testimony that agency officials were genuinely displeased with incumbent's performance, and it was another agency official who made the determination not to solicit a quote from incumbent for delivery order. Cybertech Group, Inc. v. U.S., 48 Fed. Cl. 638 (2001). United States ☞64.40(2)

Operator of civil engineering supply store at military base was not "incumbent operator" entitled under federal regulations to be solicited when government sought to procure new base operating support services, where there were major differences between prior and new procurements, including broad new requirements in many new functional area groupings, and operator's function was only small part of new procurement. 48 C.F.R. §§ 14.205, 15. 403. CC Distributors, Inc. v. U.S., 38 Fed. Cl. 771, 42 Cont. Cas. Fed. (CCH) P 77180 (1997). United States ☞64.25

7 Solicitation of bids—Amendment of solicitation of bids

Material change in terms of sealed bid solicitation, after bid is complete and contract awarded, cannot be imposed upon bidder with impunity. Lockheed Martin IR Imaging Systems, Inc. v. West, 108 F.3d 319, 41 Cont. Cas. Fed. (CCH) P 77052 (Fed. Cir. 1997). United States ☞72(1.1)

Prospective bidder failed to establish that contracting agency violated regulation by failing to notify it of amendment of solicitation on basis of evidence of non-receipt of email notification; although printouts of bulk mail screens related to the procurement were somewhat inconsistent, and reflect a shortened display name for prospective bidder, contracting officer (CO) presented affidavits in which she stated that she used a bulk mailing feature to send amendment, that plaintiff was on the list, that she routinely asked for return receipts when she sent out an e-mail, that, shortly after sending amendment 2, she began to receive receipt confirmations. 48 C.F.R. § 14.205-1(c). Razorcom Teleph & Net, LLC v. U.S., 56 Fed. Cl. 140 (2003). United States ☞64.25

Contracting agency's issuance of amendment to solicitation after bid submission did not violate the Federal Acquisition Regulation (FAR) on ground it altered a material term of the solicitation after the bid submission date; although amendment did affect technical and pricing aspects of bid proposals, and thus was material, there was no prejudice where final proposal revisions were not due until twenty-eight days after the issuance of amendment. 48 C.F.R. § 14.208. ABF Freight System, Inc. v. U.S., 55 Fed. Cl. 392 (2003). United States ☞64.25

8 Solicitation of bids—Construction of solicitation of bids

Contractor reasonably interpreted contract as not binding contractor to provide any option quantity United States Army might choose on same terms as were bid for 100% option, and Army's requirement that lesser amounts be provided was thus constructive change for which appropriate unit price adjustment was warranted; solicitation provided that government could "require" delivery of 100% option, and another section providing that bidder "may" offer additional option prices for varying option quantities and order dates did not require contractor to offer other than 100% option. Lockheed Martin IR Imaging Systems, Inc. v. West, 108 F.3d 319, 41 Cont. Cas. Fed. (CCH) P 77052 (Fed. Cir. 1997). United States ☞70(30)

Clause in solicitation which stated that contracting agency would "not accept any offers which are submitted only as an 'ALL OR NONE' offer" did not prohibit bidders from submitting any "all or none" offers; rather, clause unambiguously prohibited offerors from submitting only an "all or none" offer. 48 C.F.R. § 14.404-5. AmerisourceBergen Drug Corp. v. U.S., 60 Fed. Cl. 30 (2004). United States ☞64.30

An exception to a bidder's duty to inquire concerning a patent ambiguity in a government solicitation exists when the government has notice of the ambiguity or defect, and either fails to notify all bidders, or otherwise fails to clarify the flaw. Metcalf Const. Co., Inc. v. U.S., 53 Fed. Cl. 617 (2002). United States ☞70(30)

Under doctrine of patent ambiguity, when a solicitation presents conflicting signals, a contractor is under an affirmative duty to call the ambiguity to the attention of the contracting official; if it fails to do so, it may not argue before the Court of Federal Claims that its interpretation is proper. Ryan Co. v. U.S., 43 Fed. Cl. 646 (1999). United States ☞64.25

An invitation for bids (IFB) should be read as a whole in order to give effect to all of the provisions of the solicitation. Ryan Co. v. U.S., 43 Fed. Cl. 646 (1999). United States ☞64.25

9 Information given to prospective bidder

Government was not required to provide to all prospective bidders clarification which was given to one bidder that mistakenly construed unambiguous contract. Hunt Const. Group, Inc. v. U.S., 281 F.3d 1369 (Fed. Cir. 2002). United States ☞64.40(2)

Government's duty to notify other prospective bidders on contract of clarification given to one prospective bidder arises only if contract is ambiguous; if contract is unambiguous on its face, interpretations given to the contract by other bidders are not material, and are not required to be disclosed. 48 C.F.R. § 14.208(c). Hunt Const. Group, Inc. v. U.S., 281 F.3d 1369 (Fed. Cir. 2002). United States ☞64.25

10 Submission of bids—In general

Procurement officials' conduct in not ordering any contract line items from successful bidder's base year schedule, on ground that base year had already expired before contract was awarded, and in ordering items only from first option year schedule did not render procurement process irrational, and did not entitle unsuccessful bidder to recover its bid solicitation costs, on theory that, if unsuccessful bidder had known that procurement officials would bypass base year and order items only from first option year schedule, it would have offered lower option year prices; unsuccessful bidder was on notice of need to submit its best unit prices, and could not complain if it failed to do so. E.W. Bliss Co. v. U.S., 33 Fed. Cl. 123, 40 Cont. Cas. Fed. (CCH) P 76769 (1995), judgment aff'd, 77 F.3d 445, 40 Cont. Cas. Fed. (CCH) P 76893 (Fed. Cir. 1996). United States ☞64.30

11 Submission of bids—Timeliness, submission of bids

Air Force violated Federal Acquisition Regulation in soliciting business for contract to provide parachute releases by rejecting bids that did not comply with solicitation's technical requirements, then negotiating with bidder whose proposal did not meet deadline for critical design review or schedule for delivery. Irvin Industries Canada, Ltd. v. U.S. Air Force, 924 F.2d 1068, 1073, 36 Cont. Cas. Fed. (CCH) P 76008 (D.C. Cir. 1990). United States ☞64.40(1)

Government's determination as to whether a bid is responsive must be based solely upon the bid documents as they appear at the time of the opening. 48 C.F.R. § 14.301(a). Interstate Rock Products, Inc. v. U.S., 50 Fed. Cl. 349 (2001), aff'd, 48 Fed. Appx. 331 (Fed. Cir. 2002). United States ☞64.30

Generally, only bids that are timely received by the procuring agency may be considered for award; to be considered timely, a bid must be delivered to the place specified in an invitation for bids (IFB) on or before the time and date specified in the IFB. 48 C.F.R. §§ 14. 301(a), 14.302(a). California Marine Cleaning, Inc. v. U.S., 42 Fed. Cl. 281, 42 Cont. Cas.

Fed. (CCH) P 77398 (1998). United States ☞64.30

Bid protester bears the burden of proving by a preponderance of the evidence that its bid was timely submitted. California Marine Cleaning, Inc. v. U.S., 42 Fed. Cl. 281, 42 Cont. Cas. Fed. (CCH) P 77398 (1998). United States ☞64.55(2)

Fact that agency placed bid box in reception area and allowed bidders to date stamp their own bids did not afford a compelling reason for canceling and resoliciting the procurement; although agency's practice created difficulties in resolving timeliness of one bid, it did not call into question the entire solicitation or breach the integrity of the bidding system. 48 C.F.R. § 14.404-1(a)(1). California Marine Cleaning, Inc. v. U.S., 42 Fed. Cl. 281, 42 Cont. Cas. Fed. (CCH) P 77398 (1998). United States ☞64.50

Responsiveness, vel non, is determined at time of bid opening, and bid that is nonresponsive on opening may not be made responsive by subsequent submissions or communications. Firth Const. Co., Inc. v. U.S., 36 Fed. Cl. 268, 41 Cont. Cas. Fed. (CCH) P 76970 (1996). United States ☞64.30

Statement of requirements for second phase of concessions contract clearly required that applicants submit its best presentation of requested information at time application was sent to National Park Service (NPS) and, thus, applicant was not entitled to more time to submit information confirming commitments to satisfy $12 million capital equity requirement. YRT Services Corp. v. U.S., 28 Fed. Cl. 366, 38 Cont. Cas. Fed. (CCH) P 76512 (1993). United States ☞64.30

Matters of bid responsiveness must be discerned solely by reference to materials submitted with bid and facts available to Government at time of bid opening. Blount, Inc. v. U.S., 22 Cl. Ct. 221, 36 Cont. Cas. Fed. (CCH) P 75981, 1990 WL 210734 (1990). United States ☞64.30

General Accounting Office's (GAO's) determination in bid protest case, that contractor's bid was submitted simultaneously with bid opening officer's announcement that time for receipt of bids had passed, had rational basis, precluding unsuccessful bidder from enjoining award of Navy construction contract to successful bidder. 28 U.S.C.A. § 1491(a)(3); 31 U.S.C.A. §§ 3551–3556. Carothers Const. Inc. v. U.S., 18 Cl. Ct. 745, 35 Cont. Cas. Fed. (CCH) P 75758, 1989 WL 143515 (1989). United States ☞64.30

12 Responsiveness of bids—In general

Bidder's failure to complete Buy American Certificate or check foreign source certificate in connection with its bid for contract from Washington Metropolitan Area Transit Authority (WMATA) rendered bid unresponsive; had bidder checked second option of foreign source certificate, either before or after opening of bids, WMATA would have been required by regulations to increase plaintiff's bid price by 10%, and allowing contractor to make choice after bids were submitted would thus have permitted material alteration of bid by allowing postbidding manipulation based on bids of other competitors. Buy American Act, §§ 1–3, 41 U.S.C.A. §§ 10c, 10a, 10b. Seal and Co., Inc. v. Washington Metropolitan Area Transit Authority, 768 F. Supp. 1150 (E.D. Va. 1991). Urban Railroads ☞8

Offer in response to solicitation by the Department of Veterans Affairs (VA) for distribution of pharmaceutical products in 14 VA regions was an "all or none offer" within meaning of the Federal Acquisition Regulation (FAR), notwithstanding that offer recognized that the VA maintained the right to set aside three regions for small business concerns, where proposal limited acceptance to "all regions" contained in the offer. 48 C.F.R. § 14.404-5. AmerisourceBergen Drug Corp. v. U.S., 60 Fed. Cl. 30 (2004). United States ☞64.30

It was rational for contracting officer (CO) to reject bid bond as non-responsive because it was accompanied by a photocopied rather than original power of attorney, and absence of original power of attorney failed to provide sufficient authority to bind surety. 48 C.F.R. § 14.404-2(j). All Seasons Const., Inc. v. U.S., 55 Fed. Cl. 175 (2003). United States ☞64.35

Rationale for bid responsiveness requirement is to avoid unfairness to other contractors who submitted a sealed bid on the understanding that they must comply with all of the specifications and conditions in the invitation for bids, and who could have made a better proposal if they imposed conditions upon or variances from the contractual terms the government had specified. 10 U.S.C.A. § 2305(b)(3); Federal Property and Administrative Services Act of 1949, § 303B(c), 41 U.S.C.A. § 253b(c); 48 C.F.R. § 14.301. Ryan Co. v. U.S.,

43 Fed. Cl. 646 (1999). United States ☞64.30

In determining bid responsiveness, the contracting officer juxtaposes the bid against the invitation for bids to deter mine whether the former conforms in all material respects to the latter. 10 U.S.C.A. § 2305(b)(3); Federal Property and Administrative Services Act of 1949, § 303B(c), 41 U.S.C.A. § 253b(c); 48 C.F.R. § 14.301. Ryan Co. v. U.S., 43 Fed. Cl. 646 (1999). United States ☞64.30

Request in invitation for bids (IFB) for submission of "catalog cuts" on major equipment for high voltage electrical power system was a matter of bid responsiveness, rather than bid responsibility, and bidder's failure to submit such descriptive information rendered its bid nonresponsive, where IFB informed bidders that such information would be used for bid evaluation, and that failure to furnish it would require rejection of the bid. 48 C.F.R. § 52.214-21. Ryan Co. v. U.S., 43 Fed. Cl. 646 (1999). United States ☞64.30

Regulation requiring that contract with joint venture be signed by each participant in joint venture did not become part of bid by implication under regulation requiring bid to be considered only if award on bid would result in binding contract with terms and conditions that did not vary from terms and conditions of invitation; bidders could not be held subject to unpublicized requirement. 48 C.F.R. §§ 4.102(d), 14.301(d). PCI/RCI v. U. S., 36 Fed. Cl. 761, 41 Cont. Cas. Fed. (CCH) P 77015 (1996). United States ☞64.30

Bid package was nonresponsive to invitation for bids; bond commitment and period of bid validity were entirely omitted from package, and such missing terms could not be incorporated by reference through amendment to invitation since bidder submitted only first page of that amendment, which did not contain omitted material terms. Firth Const. Co., Inc. v. U.S., 36 Fed. Cl. 268, 41 Cont. Cas. Fed. (CCH) P 76970 (1996). United States ☞64.30

In typical government contract case, solicitation and related regulations require contracting officer to make separate determinations on issue of bid's "responsiveness" to terms of solicitation and "responsibility" of bidder to perform contract work covered in solicitation prior to awarding contract to apparent low bidder. VMS Hotel Partners v. U.S., 30 Fed. Cl. 512, 39 Cont. Cas. Fed. (CCH) P 76631 (1994). United States ☞64.30; United States ☞64.45(2)

Apparent low bidder's designation of place of performance in bid to provide meals, lodging, and transportation for members of armed services raised exclusively issue of whether bidder was responsible to perform contract work covered in solicitation, rather than responsiveness of bid, and therefore contracting officer properly allowed bidder to change its place of performance after opening bids but before awarding contract. VMS Hotel Partners v. U.S., 30 Fed. Cl. 512, 39 Cont. Cas. Fed. (CCH) P 76631 (1994). United States ☞64.40(4)

Unlike determining "responsiveness" of bid, in assessing contractor's "responsibility," contracting officer is not limited to information contained in bid when opened; rather, contracting officer may solicit and contractor may supply additional information to demonstrate that contractor is capable of performing contract work. VMS Hotel Partners v. U.S., 30 Fed. Cl. 512, 39 Cont. Cas. Fed. (CCH) P 76631 (1994). United States ☞64.45(2)

"Responsive bid" to solicitation issued by Government is one that, if accepted by Government as submitted, will obligate contractor to perform exact thing called for in solicitation. Bean Dredging Corp. v. U.S., 22 Cl. Ct. 519, 36 Cont. Cas. Fed. (CCH) P 76017, 1991 WL 15601 (1991). United States ☞64.30

Bidder's exception to bid in business questionnaire rendered bid nonresponsive to invitation for bid, notwithstanding claim that questionnaire was not contract document but merely informative in nature; material submitted with bid which takes exception to IFB requirement renders bid nonresponsive. Blount, Inc. v. U.S., 22 Cl. Ct. 221, 36 Cont. Cas. Fed. (CCH) P 75981, 1990 WL 210734 (1990). United States ☞64.30

Bidder's failure to submit properly and completely executed certification regarding debarment, suspension, proposed debarment and other responsibility matters with bid at bid opening does not affect firm's material obligations under solicitation and therefore does not render bid nonresponsive. Intermountain Electric, Inc., B-236953, B-236953.2, 90-1 CPD ¶ 143 (Comp. Gen. 1990)

13 Responsiveness of bids—Amendment of bid

Contracting officer's interpretation of solicitation to enable apparent low bidder to change place of performance would not have enabled apparent low bidder to terminate its bid, penalty free, by not finding suitable facility for performance and, therefore, did not impermissibly give apparent low bidder "two bites at the apple," whereby it could have waited to determine whether it would affirm or withdraw its bid after it became award of its competitor's bids. VMS Hotel Partners v. U.S., 30 Fed. Cl. 512, 39 Cont. Cas. Fed. (CCH) P 76631 (1994). United States ☞64.40(4)

Were contracting officer to award contract to bidder who had submitted nonresponsive bid after permitting bidder to change its response, award would be void ab initio. Blount, Inc. v. U.S., 22 Cl. Ct. 221, 36 Cont. Cas. Fed. (CCH) P 75981, 1990 WL 210734 (1990). United States ☞64.30

Bidder's failure to submit properly and completely executed certification regarding debarment, suspension, proposed debarment and other responsibility matters with bid at bid opening does not affect firm's material obligations under solicitation and therefore does not render bid nonresponsive. Intermountain Electric, Inc., B-236953, B-236953.2, 90-1 CPD ¶ 143 (Comp. Gen. 1990)

14 Opening of bids

Officer in charge of bid opening violated federal acquisition regulation by giving apparently late bid back to bidder's bonding agent, but mistake was cured by testing envelope to determine if someone had opened and resealed it. Washington Mechanical Contractors, Inc. v. U.S. Dept. of Navy, 612 F. Supp. 1243 (N.D. Cal. 1984). United States ☞64.30

Process of sealed bidding does not afford the opportunity for each bidder that might submit a defective bid bond to manifest its intent post-bid opening. 48 C.F.R. §§ 14.101(d), 14.208. Interstate Rock Products, Inc. v. U.S., 50 Fed. Cl. 349 (2001), aff'd, 48 Fed. Appx. 331 (Fed. Cir. 2002). United States ☞64.30

Defense National Stockpile Center's (DNSC) domestic preference in solicitations for surplus material through formal advertising violated Federal Acquisition Regulations (FAR) to extent preference allowed bids to be modified after being opened. Federal Property and Administrative Services Act of 1949, § 303A(a)(2), as amended, 41 U.S.C.A. § 253a(a) (2); Strategic and Critical Materials Stock Piling Act, § 6(b), as amended, 50 U.S.C.A. § 98e(b); 48 C.F.R. § 14.408-6. Minor Metals, Inc. v. U.S., 38 Fed. Cl. 16, 41 Cont. Cas. Fed. (CCH) P 77145 (1997). United States ☞64.15

15 Rejection of bid—In general

Public housing authority's vote to award contract to bidder did not preclude authority from later rejecting bid, where authority indicated that, before executing contract, its legal counsel would review issues. Professional Bldg. Concepts, Inc. v. City of Cent. Falls, 974 F.2d 1, 38 Cont. Cas. Fed. (CCH) P 76395 (1st Cir. 1992). United States ☞82(3.3)

Bid for public contract is mathematically unbalanced, such that bid is nonresponsive and must be rejected, when each line item in the bid does not reflect actual costs to bidder. 48 C.F.R. §§ 14.404-2(g), 15.814. McKnight Const. Co., Inc. v. Department of Defense, 85 F.3d 565, 40 Cont. Cas. Fed. (CCH) P 76942 (11th Cir. 1996). Public Contracts ☞8

Government's obligation to treat fairly responsive bids it receives is independent of Government's good-faith obligation and limits contracting officer's discretion to the extent officer may not act arbitrarily and capriciously in rejecting responsive bids. Arthur Forman Enterprises, Inc. v. U.S., 960 F.2d 154 (Fed. Cir. 1991). United States ☞64.40(2)

Although Government has discretion to reject responsive bids as unreasonable, after bid opening, discretion is limited by requirement that contracting officer have cogent and compelling reasons to reject bids. Arthur Forman Enterprises, Inc. v. U.S., 960 F.2d 154 (Fed. Cir. 1991). United States ☞64.40(2)

Government's rejection of bid for purchase of textile fabrics and clothing articles was arbitrary and capricious; Government failed to establish that it based its rejection of bid on finding that it was unreasonable and there were no cogent and compelling reasons for its decision to reject bid. Arthur Forman Enterprises, Inc. v. U.S., 960 F.2d 154 (Fed. Cir. 1991). United States ☞64.40(2)

Decision to reject all bids on timber at oral auction is matter within discretion of United

States Forest Service; Forest Service is not required to offer a cogent or compelling reason. Prineville Sawmill Co., Inc. v. U.S., 859 F.2d 905, 35 Cont. Cas. Fed. (CCH) P 75569 (Fed. Cir. 1988). United States ⟠58(3)

The United States Forest Service acted within its discretion in rejecting all bids at oral auction of timber, after announcing high bidder, based on errors in estimating volume of timber being sold equalling almost ten percent of value of high bid, even though bidders had been warned in advance that estimates of volume were not guarantees and that they should make their own estimates, where bidders had been informed of Service's right to reject any and all bids by advertisement and short-form bid. National Forest Management Act of 1976, § 14(e)(1)(A), 16 U.S.C.A. § 472a(e)(1)(A). Prineville Sawmill Co., Inc. v. U.S., 859 F.2d 905, 35 Cont. Cas. Fed. (CCH) P 75569 (Fed. Cir. 1988). United States ⟠58(3)

Determination of what is "so far out of line" on particular contract as to allow contracting agency to reject bid is a matter particularly committed to agency and contracting officer's discretion. 48 C.F.R. § 14.406-3(g)(5)(i, ii). Orbas & Associates v. Secretary of Navy, 863 F. Supp. 1186, 40 Cont. Cas. Fed. (CCH) P 76740 (E.D. Cal. 1994). United States ⟠64.30

Contracting officer's decision to deny award of contract to low bidder was fully rational and reasonable; contracting officer was faced with very low bid, with significant disparities in two of three options, bidder's failure to respond to numerous requests for verification, nonresponsive representative at specially set bid verification meeting, unexplained discrepancies between portions of bid and subcontractor bids submitted to bidder, and lack of original bid worksheets. 48 C.F.R. § 14.406-3(g)(5)(i). Orbas & Associates v. Secretary of Navy, 863 F. Supp. 1186, 40 Cont. Cas. Fed. (CCH) P 76740 (E.D. Cal. 1994). United States ⟠64.40(1); United States ⟠64.40(3)

Sale of low bidder to another company did not provide grounds for Government Accounting Office's (GAO) recommendation of termination of contract between low bidder and Immigration and Naturalization Service (INS) to provide security guard services; bidder was an ongoing business with substantial tangible and intangible assets, bidder retained its pre-sale assets and employees after sale, and bidder continued to perform its contracts and to conduct business as it had for 14 years. Federal Property and Administrative Services Act of 1949, § 303B(c), as amended, 41 U.S.C.A. § 253B(c); 48 C.F.R. § 14.404-2. Lyons Sec. Services, Inc. v. U.S., 38 Fed. Cl. 783 (1997). United States ⟠72.1(2)

Bids that fail to conform to essential requirements of invitation for bids must be rejected. 48 C.F.R. § 14.404-2(a). Firth Const. Co., Inc. v. U.S., 36 Fed. Cl. 268, 41 Cont. Cas. Fed. (CCH) P 76970 (1996). United States ⟠64.40(1)

Where considerable authority is granted to contracting officer to reject bids, high degree of proof is needed to establish right to recover bid preparation costs. Durable Metals Products, Inc. v. U.S., 27 Fed. Cl. 472, 38 Cont. Cas. Fed. (CCH) P 76471 (1993), judgment aff'd, 11 F.3d 1071 (Fed. Cir. 1993). United States ⟠64.60(6)

Bid on public contract which contains material nonconformity must be rejected; material nonconformity goes to substance of bid which affects price, quality, quantity, or delivery of article or service offered. Bean Dredging Corp. v. U.S., 22 Cl. Ct. 519, 36 Cont. Cas. Fed. (CCH) P 76017, 1991 WL 15601 (1991). Public Contracts ⟠8

Rejection of a bid based on the determination of ineligibility should not be overturned unless no rational basis exists for the contracting officer's determination. Walsh-Healey Act, § 1 et seq., 41 U.S.C.A. § 35 et seq.Mil-Tech Systems, Inc. v. U.S., 6 Cl. Ct. 26, 32 Cont. Cas. Fed. (CCH) P 72719 (1984). United States ⟠64.60(4)

16 Rejection of bid—Reason for rejection of bid

Contracting officer has discretion to reject bid based upon unreasonable price alone. Arthur Forman Enterprises, Inc. v. U.S., 960 F.2d 154 (Fed. Cir. 1991). United States ⟠64.60(1)

If agency relies upon improper basis to cancel procurement, cancellation may be upheld if another proper basis for cancellation exists which is reasonable and not abuse of discretion. Shields Enterprises, Inc. v. U.S., 28 Fed. Cl. 615, 38 Cont. Cas. Fed. (CCH) P 76526 (1993). United States ⟠64.60(3.1)

17 Rejection of bid—Mistakes, rejection of bids

Not every error requires rejection of an agency's procurement action, and the court will not overturn a contract award based on de minimis errors made during the procurement process. Anderson Columbia Environmental, Inc. v. U.S., 43 Fed. Cl. 693 (1999). United States ☞64.55(1)

Absent other considerations, an obvious clerical error that deceives no one does not require rejection of bid. Sciaba Const. Corp. v. City of Boston, 35 Mass. App. Ct. 181, 617 N.E.2d 1023 (1993). Public Contracts ☞8

18 Cancellation of invitations—In general

Army was not required to cancel invitation for bids where invitation overstated Army's minimum needs. Delta Chemical Corp. v. West, 33 F.3d 380, 39 Cont. Cas. Fed. (CCH) P 76693 (4th Cir. 1994). United States ☞64.50

Army did not act arbitrarily and capriciously when it refused to cancel invitation for bids after determining that invitation overstated its minimum needs, where unsuccessful bidder was not prejudiced because its bid was nonresponsive for reason unrelated to overstatement. Delta Chemical Corp. v. West, 33 F.3d 380, 39 Cont. Cas. Fed. (CCH) P 76693 (4th Cir. 1994). United States ☞64.50; United States ☞64.60(4)

Omission, from invitation for bid for manufacture of propeller shaft assembly approximately 56 feet long, of Defense Department restriction mandating against procurement of certain foreign forging products, including ship propulsion shafts greater than 50 feet in length, rendered invitation for bid defective under Federal Acquisition Regulations System and, thus, supported cancellation of invitation for bid. 10 U.S.C.A. § 2304(a)(16); Executive Order No. 11490, Oct. 28, 1969. National Forge Co. v. U.S., 779 F.2d 665, 33 Cont. Cas. Fed. (CCH) P 74149 (Fed. Cir. 1985). United States ☞64.25

Contracting officer (CO) did not act arbitrarily or capriciously in canceling invitation for bids (IFB) after lowest bidder withdrew, where all remaining bids were in excess of amount available for construction, and all the remaining bids when added to design costs exceeded $4,000,000 cap for minor construction projects. 48 C.F.R. § 14.404-1(c)(6). First Enterprise v. U.S., 61 Fed. Cl. 109 (2004). United States ☞64.50

Solicitation concerning past performance evaluation was overstated and overly restrictive of competition to the prejudice of other potential offerors in violation of the Competition in Contracting Act (CICA), warranting cancellation of solicitation. 10 U.S.C.A. § 2305(a)(1)(B) (ii); Federal Property and Administrative Services Act of 1949, § 303(a)(2)(B), 41 U.S.C.A. § 253(a)(2)(B); 48 C.F.R. § 14.101(a). Charles H. Tompkins Co. v. U.S., 43 Fed. Cl. 716 (1999). United States ☞64.50

Agency's decision to cancel solicitation after bid opening could not be justified as an effort to avoid litigation in the Court of Federal Claims; agency's cancellation decision must be supported by evidence in the administrative record at the time of decision, not based upon post hoc rationalization, and the rationale could not be considering "compelling." 48 C.F.R. § 14.404-1(a)(1). California Marine Cleaning, Inc. v. U.S., 42 Fed. Cl. 281, 42 Cont. Cas. Fed. (CCH) P 77398 (1998). United States ☞64.50

Cancellation of an invitation for bids (IFB) is disfavored after bid opening and is generally inappropriate when other bidders would not be prejudiced by an award under an ostensibly deficient solicitation and when such an award would serve the actual needs of the government. 48 C.F.R. § 14.404-1. California Marine Cleaning, Inc. v. U.S., 42 Fed. Cl. 281, 42 Cont. Cas. Fed. (CCH) P 77398 (1998). United States ☞64.50

When it becomes evident that solicitation fails to adequately reflect government's needs, it is proper to cancel solicitation; rule applies to sealed bidding and other competitive negotiation procedures. Shields Enterprises, Inc. v. U.S., 28 Fed. Cl. 615, 38 Cont. Cas. Fed. (CCH) P 76526 (1993). United States ☞64.50

For purpose of determining whether Government reasonably cancelled solicitation for bids for providing unarmed guard services, Government's need for two supervisors per eight-hour shift could not be inferred from provision of solicitation requiring that Government and contractor immediately after contract award coordinate to review performance requirements for guard post assignments. Vanguard Sec. Inc. v. U.S., 20 Cl. Ct. 90, 1990 WL 38036 (1990). United States ☞64.50

Regulatory admonitions that agency should not cancel solicitations just because their needs are for greater quantities than those listed in solicitation are meaningful only in context of supply contracts, as opposed to service contracts. Vanguard Sec. Inc. v. U.S., 20 Cl. Ct. 90, 1990 WL 38036 (1990). United States ☞64.50

For purpose of determining whether Government reasonably cancelled solicitation for bids for providing unarmed guard services, Government's need for two supervisors per eight-hour shift could not be inferred from solicitation's requirement that contractor furnish supervision on 24-houra-day basis. Vanguard Sec. Inc. v. U.S., 20 Cl. Ct. 90, 1990 WL 38036 (1990). United States ☞64.50

There was no basis for measuring decision to cancel solicitation of bids relating to coin production against standards or procedures contained in Office of Management Budget circular A-76, which stated that it is government policy to use private sources for government commercial activities in appropriate circumstances, since cancellation decision was based upon issue that is "jurisdictional" prerequisites of circular, that is, nongovernmental functions. Arrowhead Metals, Ltd. v. U.S., 8 Cl. Ct. 703, 33 Cont. Cas. Fed. (CCH) P 74026 (1985). United States ☞64.50

Office of Management Budget Circular A-76, which stated that it was government policy to use private sources for government commercial activities in appropriate circumstances, did not support claim that Government, in its cost analysis regarding coin production, as it related to decision to cancel solicitation of bids for production of coinage blanks, had to utilize historical costs for "strip" and could not utilize latest "strip" cost data. Arrowhead Metals, Ltd. v. U.S., 8 Cl. Ct. 703, 33 Cont. Cas. Fed. (CCH) P 74026 (1985). United States ☞64.50

It was not improper for United States Mint to consider actions taken or concerns raised by members of Congress in determining whether or not to cancel solicitation for bids in connection with contract for coin production; rather, issue was whether those factors affected contractor's right to full and fair consideration of its proposal. Arrowhead Metals, Ltd. v. U.S., 8 Cl. Ct. 703, 33 Cont. Cas. Fed. (CCH) P 74026 (1985). United States ☞64.50

Cancellation of solicitation bids in connection with contract for production of coins served interest of Government by allowing for further study of important policy issue of whether contracting out such work involved inherently governmental functions. Arrowhead Metals, Ltd. v. U.S., 8 Cl. Ct. 703, 33 Cont. Cas. Fed. (CCH) P 74026 (1985). United States ☞64.50

Foreign contractor's claim that United States Mint officials were prejudiced against it, thus leading to cancellation of solicitation for bids in connection with production of coins, could not be premised on language of Trade Agreement Act [Trade Agreements Act of 1979, §§ 1(a)-1112, 19 U.S.C.A. §§ 2501–2582] inasmuch as Act expressly denies private remedies not specifically provided for therein. Trade Agreements Act of 1979, §§ 3(f), 421, 19 U.S.C.A. § 2504(d), 2551. Arrowhead Metals, Ltd. v. U.S., 8 Cl. Ct. 703, 33 Cont. Cas. Fed. (CCH) P 74026 (1985). United States ☞64.60(1)

Offeror failed to establish that United States Air Force cancelled solicitation for lease of four aircraft in order to avoid bidder's protest or that air force air staff orchestrated plan to cancel solicitation and then rewrite specification to allow for use of C-12 aircraft at air field, either of which may have rendered cancellation of solicitation unreasonable. Aviation Enterprises, Inc. v. U.S., 8 Cl. Ct. 1, 32 Cont. Cas. Fed. (CCH) P 73403 (1985). United States ☞64.50

19 Cancellation of invitations—Reason for cancellation of invitations

Government Printing Office can cancel bids only for compelling reasons once bids have been opened and made public. U.S. v. International Business Machines Corp., 892 F.2d 1006, 36 Cont. Cas. Fed. (CCH) P 75772 (Fed. Cir. 1989). United States ☞64.50

Federal Energy Regulatory Commission (FERC) contracting officer did not have compelling reason for cancelling bid solicitation for stenographic services contract, making cancellation of contract abuse of discretion; reasons given for cancelling solicitation, including omission of clause requiring bid and performance bond, omission of organizational conflict of interest clause and omission of clause referring to potential loss of exhibits by stenographer, were inconsistent with reasons stated by FERC when initially cancelling the solicitation. Ace-Federal Reporters, Inc. v. F.E.R.C., 734 F. Supp. 20, 36 Cont. Cas. Fed. (CCH) P 75868 (D.D.C. 1990). United States ☞64.50

Decision of contracting officer (CO) to cancel solicitation for harbor dredging because its specifications were inadequate was arbitrary and capricious; administrative record did not support government's contentions that solicitation was defective because it did not contain sufficient information regarding the hardness of the rock to be dredged, it prohibited blasting or other pre-treatment of the rock, and it did not provide for an open-water disposal site, resulting in decreased competition and inflated bids from those companies that did compete. 48 C.F.R. § 14.404-1(c)(1). Great Lakes Dredge & Dock Co. v. U.S., 60 Fed. Cl. 350 (2004). United States ☞64.50

Absent a compromise to the competitive bidding process, agency lacks a compelling reason for cancellation of a solicitation after bid opening. 48 C.F.R. § 14.404-1(a)(1). California Marine Cleaning, Inc. v. U.S., 42 Fed. Cl. 281, 42 Cont. Cas. Fed. (CCH) P 77398 (1998). United States ☞64.50

Social Security Administration's (SSA's) need to reassess whether some of work on computer contracts should be done in-house as well as its conclusion that it needed to revise scope of work, as articulated at time of cancellation, formed reasonable basis for cancelling request for proposals and was not arbitrary and capricious. Shields Enterprises, Inc. v. U.S., 28 Fed. Cl. 615, 38 Cont. Cas. Fed. (CCH) P 76526 (1993). United States ☞64.50

Government's principal motivation for cancellation of solicitation for bids for providing unarmed guard services, that solicitation did not allow Immigration and Naturalization Service to obtain additional services on immediate basis, lacked rational basis both in law and fact and could not be upheld as permissible exercise of agency's discretion. Vanguard Sec. Inc. v. U.S., 20 Cl. Ct. 90, 1990 WL 38036 (1990). United States ☞64.50

Government's decision to cancel solicitation for bids for providing unarmed guard services, based on perceived prejudice to bidders from ambiguity in contract as to whether bidders had to resubmit pricing information for additional hours, was without factual predicate, where no pricing sheet called for such information, and pricing sheet, which took precedence over instructions, specified that additional hours were to be compensated at unit price bid per hour. Vanguard Sec. Inc. v. U.S., 20 Cl. Ct. 90, 1990 WL 38036 (1990). United States ☞64.50

In determining whether Government reasonably cancelled solicitation for bids, Government would be allowed to advance post hoc justifications for cancellation. Vanguard Sec. Inc. v. U.S., 20 Cl. Ct. 90, 1990 WL 38036 (1990). United States ☞64.50

It is not the case that only decisions to cancel solicitation for bids based on changed requirements will be overridden due to agency's failure to make every effort timely to identify such changes. Vanguard Sec. Inc. v. U.S., 20 Cl. Ct. 90, 1990 WL 38036 (1990). United States ☞64.50

Procurement regulation, which required Government to make every effort to both anticipate changes in a requirement before bid opening and to notify bidders of resulting modification or cancellation so that bidders may change bids and so that Government may prevent unnecessary exposure of bid prices, was merely hortatory, and thus Government did not violate regulation when it cancelled solicitation for bids for providing unnamed guard services on basis that solicitation did not contain adequate personnel requirements, even though there was no evidence that procurement personnel made any effort to confirm that solicitation reflected actual, present, and prospective requirements for production guards. Vanguard Sec. Inc. v. U.S., 20 Cl. Ct. 90, 1990 WL 38036 (1990). United States ☞64.50

Government's failure to state needs adequately in solicitation for bids, such that significant modification to contract would be required if agency's needs were to be met during performance, is compelling reason to cancel solicitation. Vanguard Sec. Inc. v. U.S., 20 Cl. Ct. 90, 1990 WL 38036 (1990). United States ☞64.50

Government's understatement of guard post assignments in solicitation for bids for providing unarmed guard services was error which rendered solicitation defective, and thus Government reasonably and within its discretion deemed specifications inadequate and cancelled solicitation. Vanguard Sec. Inc. v. U.S., 20 Cl. Ct. 90, 1990 WL 38036 (1990). United States ☞64.50

Decision of Department of Treasury to cancel solicitation of bids for contract in connection with coin production was "compelling" as well as reasonable and rational, where critical reason was desire to review and weigh implications of contracting out coin blanking operations to private sector. Arrowhead Metals, Ltd. v. U.S., 8 Cl. Ct. 703, 33 Cont. Cas.

Fed. (CCH) P 74026 (1985). United States ⚏64.50

Decision of Department of Treasury to cancel solicitation of bids for contract relating to coin production was not without rational basis, given concern as to propriety and/or national interest factor of contracting out work that overseeing House subcommittee and others considered governmental function. Arrowhead Metals, Ltd. v. U.S., 8 Cl. Ct. 703, 33 Cont. Cas. Fed. (CCH) P 74026 (1985). United States ⚏64.50

If party challenging cancellation of solicitation is unable to show that government officials involved in procurement process lacked rational or reasonable basis for their cancellation decision, party must present evidence of clear and prejudicial violation of applicable statute or regulations. Aviation Enterprises, Inc. v. U.S., 8 Cl. Ct. 1, 32 Cont. Cas. Fed. (CCH) P 73403 (1985). Public Contracts ⚏5.1

Alleged violations of regulations requiring contracting officers to give reason for cancellation of solicitation and to assure prospective bidders of their opportunity to bid on any resolicitation of bids was insufficient to warrant any equitable or legal relief, where neither alleged violation denied dissatisfied bidder fair and full consideration of its proposal. Aviation Enterprises, Inc. v. U.S., 8 Cl. Ct. 1, 32 Cont. Cas. Fed. (CCH) P 73403 (1985). United States ⚏64.50

Violation of regulation requiring that bidders be given reason for cancellation of solicitation was at most harmless error, where bidders were informed of reason for cancellation within reasonable time after first notification of cancellation. Aviation Enterprises, Inc. v. U.S., 8 Cl. Ct. 1, 32 Cont. Cas. Fed. (CCH) P 73403 (1985). United States ⚏64.50

Contracting officer had both compelling reason to cancel solicitation, and cancellation was in public interest, thereby satisfying regulations governing cancellation of bids both before and after opening of bids, where it was necessary to rework specifications in order to include turbo-prop aircraft, and tenor and intent behind reasons justifying cancellation after opening encompassed overstated specifications in solicitation. Aviation Enterprises, Inc. v. U.S., 8 Cl. Ct. 1, 32 Cont. Cas. Fed. (CCH) P 73403 (1985). United States ⚏64.50

In procurement terms "requirement" was synonymous with request for proposal and did not indicate that using facility need no longer existed at air force base; thus, notification of cancellation of solicitation in which it was noted there was no longer any requirement for aircraft was not inconsistent with official reason for cancellation that specifications were overstated. Aviation Enterprises, Inc. v. U.S., 8 Cl. Ct. 1, 32 Cont. Cas. Fed. (CCH) P 73403 (1985). United States ⚏64.50

Defective specifications, mistaken contractual provisions and erroneous specifications, in appropriate cases, may be compelling reasons within discretion of contracting officer for rejection of all bids. Caddell Const. Co. v. U.S., 7 Cl. Ct. 236, 32 Cont. Cas. Fed. (CCH) P 73206 (1985). United States ⚏64.50

In the circumstances, conclusion that unacceptably high prices were present because plaintiff's bid was 13.87 percent and only other bid was 16.7 percent over Government's estimate for construction of a submarine headquarters administration building was not unreasonable, and cancellation of the invitation for bids was appropriate. Caddell Const. Co. v. U.S., 7 Cl. Ct. 236, 32 Cont. Cas. Fed. (CCH) P 73206 (1985). United States ⚏64.50

Protest challenging the agency's cancellation of an invitation for bids (IFB) is denied where the agency concerns regarding an ambiguity in the IFB regarding the price to be paid for mobilization and demobilization provided a compelling basis for cancellation. Great Lakes Dredge & Dock Co., LLC, B-407502.2, 2013 CPD ¶ 48 (Comp. Gen. 2013)

20 Cancellation of invitations—Bad faith, cancellation of invitations

Inference of bad faith of personnel of United States Mint in cancelling solicitation for bids to perform "blanking," annealing and upsetting processes could not be drawn from Mint's postbid opening cost analysis efforts. Arrowhead Metals, Ltd. v. U.S., 8 Cl. Ct. 703, 33 Cont. Cas. Fed. (CCH) P 74026 (1985). United States ⚏64.50

Speculation that if foreign contractor were not low bidder on United States Treasury Department contract and American firm was low bidder, solicitation would not have been cancelled, did not support assertion of bad faith on part of Mint personnel in cancelling solicitation of bids. Arrowhead Metals, Ltd. v. U.S., 8 Cl. Ct. 703, 33 Cont. Cas. Fed. (CCH) P 74026 (1985). United States ⚏64.50

Criteria for determining whether bid cancellation decisions lack rational basis include determination of existence of bad faith on part of defendant that deprive bidder of fair and honest consideration of its proposal; determination of whether reasonable basis for administrative decision exists; degree of proof needed for recovery is related to amount of discretion entrusted to procurement officials; and/or in some instances, proven violation of statute or regulation can be grounds for recovery. Arrowhead Metals, Ltd. v. U.S., 8 Cl. Ct. 703, 33 Cont. Cas. Fed. (CCH) P 74026 (1985). United States ☞64.50

Criteria used to evaluate whether Government lacked rational or reasonable basis for its decision or acted in arbitrary and capricious manner in cancelling solicitation of bids include: determination of existence of bad faith on part of Government which deprived bidder of fair and honest consideration of its proposal, and determination of whether reasonable basis for administrative decision exists; furthermore, degree of proof needed for recovery is related to amount of discretion entrusted to procurement officials, and in some instances, proven violation of statute or regulation can be grounds for recovery. Aviation Enterprises, Inc. v. U.S., 8 Cl. Ct. 1, 32 Cont. Cas. Fed. (CCH) P 73403 (1985). Public Contracts ☞5.1

21 Cancellation of invitations—Presumptions and burden of proof, cancellation of invitations

Foreign contractor failed to meet heavy burden required to overcome presumption of good faith on part of personnel of United States Mint in performing their official duties in cancelling bid solicitation; cancellation occurred due to concern over whether it was consistent with Mint's responsibilities for it to contract out "blanking" to private sector, director of Mint stated that Mint was fully prepared at time to award contract to lowest responsible bidder, whether foreign or domestic, and contractor remained eligible to bid on Mint procurements for "strip." Arrowhead Metals, Ltd. v. U.S., 8 Cl. Ct. 703, 33 Cont. Cas. Fed. (CCH) P 74026 (1985). United States ☞64.50

In establishing that cancellation of solicitation for bids was improper, party challenging cancellation has burden of showing that government officials involved in procurement process lacked rational or reasonable basis for their cancellation decision. Aviation Enterprises, Inc. v. U.S., 8 Cl. Ct. 1, 32 Cont. Cas. Fed. (CCH) P 73403 (1985). Public Contracts ☞5.1

To overcome presumption that government officials acted properly in procuring bids or cancelling solicitations law requires well-nigh irrefragable proof. Aviation Enterprises, Inc. v. U.S., 8 Cl. Ct. 1, 32 Cont. Cas. Fed. (CCH) P 73403 (1985). United States ☞64.25; United States ☞64.50

22 Cancellation of invitations—Attorneys fees, cancellation of invitations

Contracting agency was not substantially justified, so as to preclude an award of attorney fees to a bid protestor under the Equal Access to Justice Act (EAJA), when it attempted to convert solicitation from a sealed bid to negotiated procurement and when it failed to follow the procedures required by the Federal Acquisition Regulation for cancellation of an invitation for bids (IFB). 28 U.S.C.A. § 2412(d)(1)(A); 48 C.F.R. § 14.404-1. Brickwood Contractors, Inc. v. U.S., 49 Fed. Cl. 148 (2001). United States ☞147(12)

Agency's decision to cancel solicitation was not substantially justified, so as to preclude an award of attorney fees under the Equal Access to Justice Act (EAJA), where agency canceled solicitation in reliance on determination of the General Accounting Office (GAO) that one bid was untimely, as untimeliness of one bid did not provide a rational basis for canceling the solicitation. 28 U.S.C.A. § 2412(d). California Marine Cleaning, Inc. v. U.S., 43 Fed. Cl. 724 (1999). United States ☞147(12)

23 Minor informalities or irregularities—In general

Bidder's submission of noncertified corporate check, rather than certified check as required by invitation of bids on public housing project, constituted material noncompliance with bidding process that warranted bidder's rejection. Professional Bldg. Concepts, Inc. v. City of Cent. Falls, 974 F.2d 1, 38 Cont. Cas. Fed. (CCH) P 76395 (1st Cir. 1992). United States ☞64.30; United States ☞82(3.3)

Determination of whether a defect in a bid is material is committed to agency discretion. 48 C.F.R. §§ 14.301, 14.405. Tel-Instrument Electronics Corp. v. U.S., 56 Fed. Cl. 174

(2003), aff'd, 87 Fed. Appx. 752 (Fed. Cir. 2004). United States ☞64.30

While a contract is to be awarded only to a bidder who fully responds to the federal government invitation for bids, where defect or omission in nonresponsive bid is trivial or a matter of a mere formality, law does not require that entire bid be rejected; rather, bidder may be given an opportunity to cure defect or government may waive those terms to which bid does not respond. Grade-Way Const. v. U.S., 7 Cl. Ct. 263, 32 Cont. Cas. Fed. (CCH) P 73209 (1985). United States ☞64.30

24 Minor informalities or irregularities—Responsiveness of bids, minor informalities or irregularities

If a bidder on a government contract attempts to impose conditions that would modify material requirements of the solicitation, the bid is not responsive and must be rejected; "material requirements" include those affecting price, quantity, quality, or delivery of the solicited products, and thus are not minor informalities or irregularities. 48 C.F.R. § 14.405. Tel-Instrument Electronics Corp. v. U.S., 56 Fed. Cl. 174 (2003), aff'd, 87 Fed. Appx. 752 (Fed. Cir. 2004). United States ☞64.30

When a bid fails to conform with the invitation for bids, it will be rejected if it is nonconforming in a material respect; it follows that when a bid's only defect is an immaterial nonconformity, it is responsive. 48 C.F.R. § 14.301(a). Interstate Rock Products, Inc. v. U.S., 50 Fed. Cl. 349 (2001), aff'd, 48 Fed. Appx. 331 (Fed. Cir. 2002). United States ☞64.30

To be deemed responsive, bid as submitted must obligate bidder to perform exactly what is being called for in solicitation. 48 C.F.R. §§ 14.301(a), 14.404-2(a). ECDC Environmental, L.C. v. U.S., 40 Fed. Cl. 236, 42 Cont. Cas. Fed. (CCH) P 77250 (1998). United States ☞64.30

Bidder's failure to submit properly and completely executed certification regarding debarment, suspension, proposed debarment and other responsibility matters with bid at bid opening does not affect firm's material obligations under solicitation and therefore does not render bid nonresponsive. Intermountain Electric, Inc., B-236953, B-236953.2, 90-1 CPD ¶ 143 (Comp. Gen. 1990)

25 Minor informalities or irregularities—Rejection of bids, minor informalities or irregularities

"Substantial deviation" that will require rejection of bid due to failure to conform with essential requirements of invitation for bids is defined as one which affects either price, quantity, or quality of article offered. 48 C.F.R. § 14.404-2(a). Firth Const. Co., Inc. v. U.S., 36 Fed. Cl. 268, 41 Cont. Cas. Fed. (CCH) P 76970 (1996). United States ☞64.40(1)

26 Mistake—In general

When the government has notice of a mistake in a particular bid, the government may have a duty to verify that bid by calling attention to the specific error suspected; however, this duty arises only where the contractor's mistake is a clear-cut clerical or arithmetical error, or a misreading of the specifications. Hunt Const. Group, Inc. v. U.S., 281 F.3d 1369 (Fed. Cir. 2002). United States ☞64.40(3)

Though the government has a general duty to examine bids for mistakes, this duty does not extend to errors that may be contained in a contractor's subsequent filings. 48 C.F.R. §§ 14.407-1 to 14.407-3. Giesler v. U.S., 232 F.3d 864 (Fed. Cir. 2000). United States ☞64.40(1)

The government has no legal duty to examine for mistakes any paperwork submitted by contractors and subcontractors subsequent to the opening and acceptance of their bids, and after the completion of the pre-award survey report. 48 C.F.R. §§ 9.106, 14.407. Giesler v. U.S., 232 F.3d 864 (Fed. Cir. 2000). United States ☞64.40(1)

In limited circumstances, if the government has knowledge, or constructive knowledge, that a contractor's bid is based on a mistake, and the government accepts the bid and awards the contract despite knowledge of this mistake, then a trial court may reform or rescind the contract, but, generally, a contractor may obtain reformation or rescission of the contract only if the contractor establishes that its bid error resulted from a clear-cut clerical or arithmetical error, or a misreading of the specifications. Giesler v. U.S., 232 F.3d 864 (Fed. Cir. 2000). United States ☞72(1.1); United States ☞74(4)

In limited circumstances, if the government has breached its explicit regulatory duty to examine the contractor's bid for mistakes, then court may rescind a contract, despite an otherwise inexcusable error by the contractor. 48 C.F.R. § 14.407-1. Giesler v. U.S., 232 F.3d 864 (Fed. Cir. 2000). United States ☞74(4)

Rescission of contract to supply mixed nuts was not warranted due to the government's failure to examine subcontractor's facsimile which would have disclosed discrepancy between the requested nut mix and the nut mix subcontractor intended to produce; where the fax arrived after contractor's bid was opened and verified, and after the government had completed its pre-award survey of subcontractor, the government had no duty to examine the fax for errors. 48 C.F.R. §§ 14.407-1 to 14.407-3. Giesler v. U.S., 232 F.3d 864 (Fed. Cir. 2000). United States ☞74(4)

Contracting officer reasonably suspected mistake and took appropriate steps where low bidder's aggregate bid on government procurement contract was 11% lower than government's estimate and 17% lower than next qualified bidder, and low bidder's base bid was 16% lower than government's estimate, while its option three bid was 957% higher than government's estimate. 48 C.F.R. § 14.406-3(g)(1)(i). Orbas & Associates v. Secretary of Navy, 863 F. Supp. 1186, 40 Cont. Cas. Fed. (CCH) P 76740 (E.D. Cal. 1994). United States ☞64.40(3)

Contractor's mistake in bid was not so gross that enforcement of contract without allowing for reformation was unconscionable, where contractor alleged that its mistake had affected its total bid of $17.2 million by $438,000, or about 2.5 percent; moreover, without correction of its bid mistake, contractor, at the time of award, still anticipated a profit of approximately 1.6%. Will H. Hall and Son, Inc. v. U.S., 54 Fed. Cl. 436 (2002). Reformation Of Instruments ☞17(1); United States ☞74(4)

A government contract may be reformed or rescinded if the contracting officer accepts a bid with actual or constructive knowledge that the bid contains a compensable mistake. Will H. Hall and Son, Inc. v. U.S., 54 Fed. Cl. 436 (2002). Reformation Of Instruments ☞17(1); United States ☞72(1.1)

Contracting officer's alleged failure to advise bidder of its option to withdraw after bidder discovered mistake in bid did not constitute a violation of the Federal Acquisition Regulation (FAR), as bidder was deemed to have constructive knowledge of applicable regulations allowing withdrawal, and FAR places an affirmative obligation on the bidder to request withdrawal. 48 C.F.R. § 14.407-3(a, b). Will H. Hall and Son, Inc. v. U.S., 54 Fed. Cl. 436 (2002). United States ☞64.40(4)

Bidder's alleged mistake in relying on quote from subcontractor which did not include work on a specification section was not an error in business judgment for which equitable relief was not available; although bidder's handling of quote was careless, it did not rise to the level of gross negligence, and bidder discovered the error six days after submitting its bid, and immediately notified the contracting officer. Will H. Hall and Son, Inc. v. U.S., 54 Fed. Cl. 436 (2002). United States ☞64.40(4)

An error in business judgment by a bidder is not a mistake for which equitable relief is available; such an error occurs where the bidder has the facts necessary to make the proper conclusion but, because of improper assumptions or faulty assessments of those facts, makes a bad business decision. Will H. Hall and Son, Inc. v. U.S., 54 Fed. Cl. 436 (2002). United States ☞74(4)

Since bid was responsive, bidder should have been allowed to correct mistake in its bid, omission of front-side of standard step-two form through clerical error, pursuant to mistake-in-bid procedures set out in regulation. 48 C.F.R. § 14.407. ECDC Environmental, L.C. v. U.S., 40 Fed. Cl. 236, 42 Cont. Cas. Fed. (CCH) P 77250 (1998). United States ☞64.30

Contracting officer has duty to verify bid if all facts and circumstances suggest that it was reasonable to believe mistake had been made. 48 C.F.R. § 14.406-1. Dakota Tribal Industries v. U.S., 34 Fed. Cl. 593, 40 Cont. Cas. Fed. (CCH) P 76867 (1995). United States ☞64.40(3)

27 Mistake—Mutual mistake

Government contractor could not invoke doctrine of mutual mistake to reform contract to include state sales tax in contract price, although both parties were mistaken concerning treatment of states sales tax in the contract, where contractor's mistake concerned the tax exemption status of materials used in the project, and government's mistake concerned the inclusion of state sales tax in unit prices contained in agency's Unit Price Book (UPB), and thus errors were separate and not mutual. C.W. Over & Sons, Inc. v. U.S., 54 Fed. Cl. 514 (2002). Reformation Of Instruments ☞19(2)

28 Mistake—Unilateral mistake

Where reformation of contract is sought due to contractor's unilateral bid mistake, contractor must show by clear and convincing evidence that: (1) mistake in fact occurred prior to contract award; (2) mistake was clear-cut, clerical or mathematical error or misreading of specifications and not judgmental error; (3) prior to award Government knew, or should have known, that mistake had been made and, therefore, should have requested bid verification; (4) Government did not request bid verification or its request for bid verification was inadequate; and (5) proof of intended bid is established. 48 C.F.R. §§ 14.406-1, 14.406-3(g) (1992). McClure Elec. Constructors, Inc. v. Dalton, 132 F.3d 709, 42 Cont. Cas. Fed. (CCH) P 77246 (Fed. Cir. 1997). United States ☞72(1.1)

Bid verification request sent out by contracting officer was adequate to put contractor on notice of suspected bid mistake, and thus, contractor was not entitled to contract reformation to correct its unilateral bid mistake; although contracting officer did not expressly state that she suspected error, she did reveal amounts of all bids, and with this information in hand, contractor could see that next lowest bid was almost 20% higher than its bid, and that government estimate was almost twice contractor's bid. 48 C.F.R. §§ 14.406-1, 14.406-3(g) (1992). McClure Elec. Constructors, Inc. v. Dalton, 132 F.3d 709, 42 Cont. Cas. Fed. (CCH) P 77246 (Fed. Cir. 1997). United States ☞72(1.1)

To be entitled to reformation under unilateral mistake, government contractor must show that the contracting officer knew or should have known of the contractor's unilateral mistake at the time its bid was accepted; moreover, the mistaken proposal must contain a clear cut clerical or arithmetical error, or misreading of the specifications. C.W. Over & Sons, Inc. v. U.S., 54 Fed. Cl. 514 (2002). Reformation Of Instruments ☞17(1)

In order to attain rescission on ground of unilateral mistake, government contractor must show: (1) the mistake in fact occurred prior to contract award; (2) the mistake was clerical, mathematical, or misreading of specification, not an error in judgment; (3) prior to award the government knew, or should have known, that a mistake had been made; and (4) the government did not request bid verification or the request was inadequate. Giesler v. U.S., 44 Fed. Cl. 737 (1999), rev'd in part on other grounds, 232 F.3d 864 (Fed. Cir. 2000). United States ☞72(1.1); United States ☞74(4)

Policy underlying doctrine of unilateral mistake is designed to prevent the government from overreaching by awarding a contract where it knows the contractor has made a significant mistake. Giesler v. U.S., 44 Fed. Cl. 737 (1999), rev'd in part on other grounds, 232 F.3d 864 (Fed. Cir. 2000). United States ☞74(4)

Doctrine of "unilateral mistake" holds that a government contract may be reformed or rescinded if the contracting officer accepts a bid with actual or constructive knowledge that it contains an error. Giesler v. U.S., 44 Fed. Cl. 737 (1999), rev'd in part on other grounds, 232 F.3d 864 (Fed. Cir. 2000). United States ☞74(4)

With respect to doctrine of unilateral mistake, the reasonableness of contractor's mistake is not relevant to the creation or discharge of the government's verification duty. Giesler v. U.S., 44 Fed. Cl. 737 (1999), rev'd in part on other grounds, 232 F.3d 864 (Fed. Cir. 2000). United States ☞74(4)

29 Mistake—Clerical mistakes

Misunderstanding of the requirements of base bid and option three of government procurement contract did not fall within definition of "clerical mistake" for which bidder could be permitted to correct bid. 48 C.F.R. § 14.406-2. Orbas & Associates v. Secretary of Navy, 863 F. Supp. 1186, 40 Cont. Cas. Fed. (CCH) P 76740 (E.D. Cal. 1994). United States ☞64.40(3)

There was ample evidence before contracting officer that low bid on procurement contract could contain significant nonclerical errors; low bidder's aggregate bid was 11% lower than government's estimate and 17% lower than next lowest bidder, its base bid was 16% lower than government's estimate while its option three bid was 957% higher than government's estimate, bidder never verified original bid or error, and never specified in writing true amount of error, and there were other suspected errors in the bid. 48 C.F.R. § 14.406-3(g) (1). Orbas & Associates v. Secretary of Navy, 863 F. Supp. 1186, 40 Cont. Cas. Fed. (CCH) P 76740 (E.D. Cal. 1994). United States ☞64.40(3)

Contracting officer could not correct bidder's "clerical mistake" where bidder never verified original bid or error and never specified in writing true amount of the error. 48 C.F.R. § 14.406-2(a). Orbas & Associates v. Secretary of Navy, 863 F. Supp. 1186, 40 Cont. Cas. Fed. (CCH) P 76740 (E.D. Cal. 1994). United States ☞64.40(3)

Bidder's failure to submit a properly executed bid guarantee by omitting penal sum on bid bond rendered its bid nonresponsive, and contracting agency was not permitted to consider bidder's explanation that omission of penal sum was a clerical error; moreover, bidder was not entitled to alter its bid with additional documents to correct the error following bid opening. 48 C.F.R. §§ 14.301(a), 14.404-2. Interstate Rock Products, Inc. v. U.S., 50 Fed. Cl. 349 (2001), aff'd, 48 Fed. Appx. 331 (Fed. Cir. 2002). United States ☞64.30

Contracting agency's failure to inquire concerning absence of insurance information in bid was arbitrary and capricious, where absence of the information clearly indicated a clerical mistake, and bidder had performed two previous contracts for agency. 48 C.F.R. § 14.406-1 (1994). Griffy's Landscape Maintenance LLC v. U.S., 46 Fed. Cl. 257 (2000). United States ☞64.40(3)

30 Mistake—Evidence, mistake

Army Corps of Engineers' rule stating that uncorroborated statement is insufficient to satisfy the clear and convincing evidence standard required to show that the submitted bid was mistaken and what was the actual intended bid, such that bid is subject to correction, is not arbitrary and fact that some honest contractors may lose contracts because of minor errors on their part does not render Army's rule arbitrary. 48 C.F.R. § 14.406-3(a) (Repealed). McKnight Const. Co., Inc. v. Department of Defense, 85 F.3d 565, 40 Cont. Cas. Fed. (CCH) P 76942 (11th Cir. 1996). United States ☞64.30

Mistake, if any, in bidder's failure to include mark up in its bid price for beef patties to be supplied for federal child nutrition programs was noncompensable error in judgment; evidence showed that prevailing market prices for beef at time of bid solicitation were lower than those subsequently claimed by bidder, warranting inference that bidder knowingly decided to mark up its bids by lesser amount. Goldberger Foods, Inc. v. U.S., 960 F.2d 155 (Fed. Cir. 1992). United States ☞70(29)

Bidder on contract to furnish beef patties for federal child nutrition programs failed to establish that its omission of mark up from bid price was type of mistake that would have warranted allowing bidder to withdraw or correct its bid; bidder offered no evidence of raw beef prices quoted by its suppliers, prevailing market prices at time of solicitation were substantially lower than those claimed by bidder, and it was likely that bidder included substantial portion of mark up in preparing its bid. Goldberger Foods, Inc. v. U.S., 960 F.2d 155 (Fed. Cir. 1992). United States ☞70(29)

For purposes of correcting mistakes in government contract bids under Federal Acquisitions Regulations, there is no requirement that contractor's work papers be related in any way to specific line items of the bid. 48 C.F.R. § 14.406-3. McKnight Const. Co., Inc. v. Perry, 888 F. Supp. 1178 (S.D. Ga. 1994). United States ☞64.5

Under Federal Acquisition Regulations, bid work papers can be relied upon as best objective evidence of intended bid on government contract, but intended bid need not be established only from bid working papers in all cases of mistake. 48 C.F.R. § 14.406-3(g)(2). McKnight Const. Co., Inc. v. Perry, 888 F. Supp. 1178 (S.D. Ga. 1994). United States ☞64.60(1)

Bidder on federal government contract to renovate Army barracks presented sufficient evidence to clearly and convincingly establish its intended bid, even though bidder had made mistake in bid by transposing some of the line items in bid, where casual inspection of bid abstract revealed transpositional character of mistake, and bidder's company president submitted sworn affidavit in conjunction with bid itself that clarified the mistake. 48 C.F.R. § 14.406-3. McKnight Const. Co., Inc. v. Perry, 888 F. Supp. 1178 (S.D. Ga. 1994). United States ☞64.60(1)

Government contractor could not invoke doctrine of unilateral mistake to reform contract to include state sales tax in contract price, absent evidence that contracting officers knew of alleged mistake which was contractor's erroneous interpretation of contract clause as indicating that entire project was exempt from state tax; moreover, even if contracting officers should have known of contractor's mistake, it was a mistake in judgment and not a misreading of specifications, and thus was not compensable under the doctrine. C.W. Over & Sons, Inc. v. U.S., 54 Fed. Cl. 514 (2002). Reformation Of Instruments ☞17(1)

Under the Federal Acquisition Regulation (FAR), a bidder's request for an upward correction of its bid before award of the contract may be granted where the request is supported by clear and convincing evidence of both the existence of a mistake and the intended bid; the intended bid does not need to be an exact figure, as long as the bidder provides clear and convincing evidence to establish that the bid would fall within a narrow range of uncertainty and would remain the low bid if corrected. 48 C.F.R. § 14.407-3(a). Will H. Hall and Son, Inc. v. U.S., 54 Fed. Cl. 436 (2002). United States ☞64.40(4)

Bidder who alleged that its bid amount was based on mistake in subcontractor's quote failed to present clear and convincing evidence of its intended bid within a relatively narrow range, as required for correction of bid, where bidder would have had at least six options for its intended bid, and there was a range of 27 to 38.6 percent in possible intended bids. 48 C.F.R. § 14.407-3(a). Will H. Hall and Son, Inc. v. U.S., 54 Fed. Cl. 436 (2002). United States ☞64.40(4)

Pursuant to the Federal Acquisition Regulation (FAR), if the evidence is clear and convincing as to the existence of a bid mistake, but not the amount of the intended bid, or if the evidence only reasonably supports the existence of a mistake but is not clear and convincing, an agency official above the contracting officer may permit withdrawal of the bid. 48 C.F.R. § 14.407-3(c). Will H. Hall and Son, Inc. v. U.S., 54 Fed. Cl. 436 (2002). United States ☞64.40(4)

Affidavit of bidder's secretary and treasurer, who prepared and submitted its bid, which stated that he was unaware that subcontractor's quote was incomplete, did not rise to level of clear and convincing evidence of bid mistake, where bidder's worksheets did not corroborate that bidder was unaware that subcontractor's quote excluded certain work called for in contract. 48 C.F.R. § 14.407-3(a). Will H. Hall and Son, Inc. v. U.S., 54 Fed. Cl. 436 (2002). United States ☞74(11)

31 Evaluation of bids

Failure of contracting agency to perform a cost realism analysis on contract awardee's offer was not error, as there was no requirement for such an analysis, where solicitation contemplated award of firm fixed price contract and contracting officer (CO) deemed awardee responsible to perform the project at the offered price. 48 C.F.R. § 15.404-1(d)(1). First Enterprise v. U.S., 61 Fed. Cl. 109 (2004). United States ☞64.40(1)

After lowest bidder withdrew, contracting officer (CO) acted properly in not awarding contract to the next lowest bidder, and instead concluding that remaining bids were unreasonable, where all the remaining bids were over the maximum amount the agency could spend on the construction portion of the contract. First Enterprise v. U.S., 61 Fed. Cl. 109 (2004). United States ☞64.50

In assessing contractor's responsibility, the contracting officer is not limited to the information contained in the bid when opened, but instead is expected to solicit additional information demonstrating that the contractor is capable of performing the contract work. 48 C.F.R. § 9.105-1. Ryan Co. v. U.S., 43 Fed. Cl. 646 (1999). United States ☞64.40(1)

Contracting officer's duty to verify bid does not necessarily arise because of price disparity among bids; variance from government estimates, prior procurement, market value, or other bids should be considered, and other factors may negate inference of contractor error, especially where they offer reasonable explanations for disparity. Small Business Act, § 2[8](a), 15 U.S.C.A. § 637(a); 48 C.F.R. § 14.406-1. Dakota Tribal Industries v. U.S., 34 Fed. Cl. 593, 40 Cont. Cas. Fed. (CCH) P 76867 (1995). United States ☞64.40(3)

Cancellation of government contract did not constitute breach of government's implied contractually duty to fairly and honestly consider bid of defense contractor where contractor was eliminated from consideration for bid after being proposed for debarment, subsequent debarment of contractor was not arbitrary and capricious, next lowest bidder had gone out of business, and remaining bids were determined to be either outdated or unreasonably high. IMCO, Inc. v. U.S., 33 Fed. Cl. 312 (1995), judgment aff'd, 97 F.3d 1422 (Fed. Cir. 1996). United States ☞64.50

Unsuccessful bidder for government contract failed to demonstrate that agency did not exercise good faith in evaluating its proposal and in cancelling request for proposals (RFP); bidder did not show bad faith through evidence that government specifically intended to injure bidder or that government operated with prejudice towards bidder. Shields Enterprises, Inc. v. U.S., 28 Fed. Cl. 615, 38 Cont. Cas. Fed. (CCH) P 76526 (1993). United States ☞64.50; United States ☞64.60(6)

United States Army Corps of Engineers, in soliciting bids for performance of maintenance dredging on stream, breached its implied-in-fact contract obligation to treat every bid in full, fair and honest manner by failing to prepare fair and reasonable estimate of costs to be incurred on project, with result that agency rejected all bids as exceeding its estimate by more than 25%; agency's estimate was based, inter alia, on unrealistic assumption of 29 effective dredging days per month. 33 U.S.C.A. § 624. Bean Dredging Corp. v. U.S., 22 Cl. Ct. 519, 36 Cont. Cas. Fed. (CCH) P 76017, 1991 WL 15601 (1991). United States ☞64.40(2)

32 Award of contract—In general

Addendum attached by Army when awarding contract was not way to correct flawed solicitation, and could not change conditions of award in way materially benefitting one side and materially prejudicing another. Lockheed Martin IR Imaging Systems, Inc. v. West, 108 F.3d 319, 41 Cont. Cas. Fed. (CCH) P 77052 (Fed. Cir. 1997). United States ☞64.45(4)

Decision of contracting officer (CO) to select contract awardee's bid on alternate bid item 6, instead of bid protestor's offer on alternate bid item 5, was not arbitrary and capricious, where awardee's bid on alternate bid item 6 was lower than the independent government estimate for item 6, and awarding the contract to protestor for its bid on alternate bid item 5 would have exceeded the allocated funding. First Enterprise v. U.S., 61 Fed. Cl. 109 (2004). United States ☞64.45(1)

Under the arbitrary and capricious standard applicable to bid protests, a bid award may be set aside if either: (1) the procurement official's decision lacked a rational basis; or (2) the procurement procedure involved a violation of a regulation or procedure. 5 U.S.C.A. § 706(2)(A); 28 U.S.C.A. § 1491(b)(4). First Enterprise v. U.S., 61 Fed. Cl. 109 (2004). United States ☞64.60(3.1); United States ☞64.60(4)

33 Award of contract—Delay, award of contract

Regulation concerning governmental delay in awarding bid is aimed at administrative efficiency and no substantive right is created on which contractor can erect damage claim. 48 C.F.R. § 14.404-1(d). Smith v. U.S., 34 Fed. Cl. 313, 40 Cont. Cas. Fed. (CCH) P 76854 (1995). United States ☞73(20)

34 Powers of attorney

Contracting officer (CO) was not reasonable in rejecting computer-generated powers of attorney appointing officer to execute bid bonds and accompanying certificates on ground that mechanical signatures were applied after powers of attorney were generated. 48 C.F.R. § 52.228-1. Hawaiian Dredging Const. Co., Inc. v. U.S., 59 Fed. Cl. 305 (2004). United States ☞64.35

Powers of attorney appointing officer to execute bid bonds which contained mechanically applied signatures, as opposed to original, or wet, signatures, were adequate to establish unequivocally that surety intended to be bound, where powers of attorney were submitted with certificates restating board resolutions by which surety bound itself to facsimile signatures on a power of attorney or any certificate relating to the power of attorney, appointment was facially valid, and original corporate seal was affixed to the documents. 48 C.F.R. § 52.228-1. Hawaiian Dredging Const. Co., Inc. v. U.S., 59 Fed. Cl. 305 (2004). United States ☞64.35

35 Negotiation procedure

Duty of verification of bid exists regardless of whether a solicitation is characterized as negotiated or sealed. 48 C.F.R. § 14.406-1 (1994). Griffy's Landscape Maintenance LLC v. U.S., 46 Fed. Cl. 257 (2000). United States ☞64.40(3)

Determination of evaluation panel, during second phase of application process for awarding concessions contract, that applicant did not satisfy financing criteria did not preclude applicant from further consideration, in view of use of negotiation procedure rather than sealed bidding procedure in awarding contract; applicant was considered at each stage of review, but was not awarded contract when competitor was found to have submitted best overall offer. YRT Services Corp. v. U.S., 28 Fed. Cl. 366, 38 Cont. Cas. Fed. (CCH) P 76512 (1993). United States ☞64.15

36 Costs of bid preparation

Claim for bid preparation costs depended on propriety of government cancellation of solicitation. Durable Metals Products, Inc. v. U.S., 27 Fed. Cl. 472, 38 Cont. Cas. Fed. (CCH) P 76471 (1993), judgment aff'd, 11 F.3d 1071 (Fed. Cir. 1993). United States ☞64.60(6)

Government's conduct in cancelling solicitation for bids is pertinent to bidder's claim for bid preparation costs. Vanguard Sec. Inc. v. U.S., 20 Cl. Ct. 90, 1990 WL 38036 (1990). United States ☞64.60(6)

Foreign contractor was not entitled to bid preparation costs after United States Mint had cancelled solicitation of bids, where cancellation decision had rational basis and where, at time solicitation was made, Mint had no knowledge, or reason to anticipate, that there would be any problems with solicitation. Arrowhead Metals, Ltd. v. U.S., 8 Cl. Ct. 703, 33 Cont. Cas. Fed. (CCH) P 74026 (1985). United States ☞64.60(6)

37 Federal supply services schedule

Government was under no obligation to solicit incumbent contractor on a delivery order from a Federal Supply Services (FSS) schedule contract, as sealed bidding regulation is not applicable to placement of a delivery order from an FSS schedule. 48 C.F.R. §§ 8.401(a, b), 14.205-4(b). Cybertech Group, Inc. v. U.S., 48 Fed. Cl. 638 (2001). United States ☞64.10

38 Restrictive specifications

In a commercial item acquisition for the repair and overhaul of pumps, protest of agency solicitation requiring vendors to be an original equipment manufacturer's (OEM) authorized repair facility was sustained, because the agency did not show that the restriction on competition were necessary to meet its needs. Decision Matter of: Missouri Machinery & Engineering Company, B-403561, 2010 CPD ¶ 276 (Comp. Gen. 2010)

§ 14.102 [Reserved]

§ 14.103 Policy.

§ 14.103-1 General.
(a) Sealed bidding shall be used whenever the conditions in 6.401(a) are met. This requirement applies to any proposed contract action under Part 6.

(b) Sealed bidding may be used for classified acquisitions if its use does not violate agency security requirements.

(c) The policy for pricing modifications of sealed bid contract appears in 15.403-4(a)(1) (iii).

United States Code Annotated
Contract requirements, see 41 USCA § 254.

Contracts, planning, solicitation, evaluation, and award procedures, see 10 USCA § 2305.

Definitions, see 10 USCA § 2302, 41 USCA §§ 259, 403.

Evaluation and award, see 41 USCA § 253b.

Kinds of contracts, see 10 USCA § 2306.

Planning and solicitation requirements, see 41 USCA § 253a.

Notes of Decisions
In general 1

1 In general

When an agency decides not to use sealed bidding in basic construction work, such as dredging, the Court of Federal Claims expects to see some legal discussion of why sealed bidding is not appropriate. The agency's justification is lacking when it provides no mention in the administrative record of subjects or issues that should have been addressed, such as whether (i) time permits the solicitation, submission, and evaluation of sealed bids; (ii) the award will be made on the basis of price and other price-related factors; (iii) it is necessary to conduct discussions with the responding sources about their bids; and (iv) there is a reasonable expectation of receiving more than one sealed bid. Weeks Marine, Inc. v. U.S., 79 Fed. Cl. 22 (2007), aff'd in part, rev'd in part on other grounds, 575 F.3d 1352 (Fed. Cir. 2009)

If a construction project requires complex coordination and a compressed time frame, it is reasonable for an agency to consider non-price evaluation factors and award the project using negotiated procedures. Although several similar projects may have been awarded using sealed bidding procedures, that alone is not dispositive on whether the agency is prohibited from using negotiated procedures. Matter of: Ceres Environmental Services, Inc., B-310902, 2008 CPD ¶ 48 (Comp. Gen. 2008)

§ 14.103-2 Limitations.

No awards shall be made as a result of sealed bidding unless—

(a) Bids have been solicited as required by Subpart 14.2;

(b) Bids have been submitted as required by Subpart 14.3;

(c) The requirements of 1.602-1(b) and Part 6 have been met; and

(d) An award is made to the responsible bidder (see 9.1) whose bid is responsive to the terms of the invitation for bids and is most advantageous to the Government, considering only price and the price related factors included in the invitation, as provided in Subpart 14.4.

United States Code Annotated

Contract requirements, see 41 USCA § 254.

Contracts, planning, solicitation, evaluation, and award procedures, see 10 USCA § 2305.

Definitions, see 10 USCA § 2302, 41 USCA §§ 259, 403.

Evaluation and award, see 41 USCA § 253b.

Kinds of contracts, see 10 USCA § 2306.

Planning and solicitation requirements, see 41 USCA § 253a.

§ 14.104 Types of contracts.

Firm-fixed-price contracts shall be used when the method of contracting is sealed bidding, except that fixed-price contracts with economic price adjustment clauses may be used if authorized in accordance with 16.203 when some flexibility is necessary and feasible. Such clauses must afford all bidders an equal opportunity to bid.

United States Code Annotated

Contract requirements, see 41 USCA § 254.

Contracts, planning, solicitation, evaluation, and award procedures, see 10 USCA § 2305.

Definitions, see 10 USCA § 2302, 41 USCA §§ 259, 403.

Evaluation and award, see 41 USCA § 253b.

Kinds of contracts, see 10 USCA § 2306.

Planning and solicitation requirements, see 41 USCA § 253a.

§ 14.105 Solicitations for informational or planning purposes.

(See 15.201(e).)

United States Code Annotated

Contract requirements, see 41 USCA § 254.

Contracts, planning, solicitation, evaluation, and award procedures, see 10 USCA § 2305.

Definitions, see 10 USCA § 2302, 41 USCA §§ 259, 403.

Evaluation and award, see 41 USCA § 253b.

Kinds of contracts, see 10 USCA § 2306.

Planning and solicitation requirements, see 41 USCA § 253a.

Subpart 14.2 Solicitation of Bids

§ 14.201 Preparation of invitations for bids.

§ 14.201-1 Uniform contract format.

(a) Contracting officers shall prepare invitations for bids and contracts using the uniform contract format outlined in Table 14-1 to the maximum practicable extent. The use of the format facilitates preparation of the solicitation and contract as well as reference to, and use of, those documents by bidders and contractors. It need not be used for acquisition of the following:

(1) Construction (see Part 36).

(2) Shipbuilding (including design, construction, and conversion), ship overhaul, and ship repair.

(3) Subsistence items.

(4) Supplies or services requiring special contract forms prescribed elsewhere in this regulation that are inconsistent with the uniform contract format.

(5) Firm-fixed-price or fixed-price with economic price adjustment acquisitions that use the simplified contract format (see 14.201-9).

(b) Information suitable for inclusion in invitations for bids under the uniform contract format shall also be included in invitations for bids not subject to that format if applicable.

(c) Solicitations to which the uniform contract format applies shall include Parts I, II, III, and IV. If any section of the uniform contract format does not apply, the contracting officer should so mark that section in the solicitation. Upon award, the contracting officer shall not physically include Part IV in the resulting contract, but shall retain it in the contract file. (See 14.201(c).) Award by acceptance of a bid on the award portion of Standard Form 33, Solicitation, Offer and Award (SF 33), Standard Form 26, Award/Contract (SF 26), or Standard Form 1447, Solicitation/Contract (SF 1447), incorporates Section K, Representations, certifications, and other statements of bidders, in the resultant contract even though not physically attached. The representations and certifications shall be incorporated by reference in the contract by using 52.204-19 (see 4.1202(b)) or for acquisitions of commercial items see 52.212-4(v).

TABLE 14-1—UNIFORM CONTRACT FORMAT

SECTION	TITLE
Part I—The Schedule	
A	Solicitation/contract form
B	Supplies or services and prices
C	Description/specifications
D	Packaging and marking
E	Inspection and acceptance
F	Deliveries or performance
G	Contract administration data
H	Special contract requirements
Part II—Contract Clauses	
I	Contract clauses
Part III—List of Documents, Exhibits, and Other Attachments	
J	List of documents, exhibits, and other attachments
Part IV—Representations and Instructions	
K	Representations, certifications, and other statements of bidders

Section	Title
L	Instructions, conditions, and notices to bidders
M	Evaluation factors for award

United States Code Annotated

Contract requirements, see 41 USCA § 254.

Contracts, planning, solicitation, evaluation, and award procedures, see 10 USCA § 2305.

Definitions, see 10 USCA § 2302, 41 USCA §§ 259, 403.

Evaluation and award, see 41 USCA § 253b.

Kinds of contracts, see 10 USCA § 2306.

Planning and solicitation requirements, see 41 USCA § 253a.

§ 14.201-2 Part I—The Schedule.

The contracting officer shall prepare the Schedule as follows:

(a) *Section A, Solicitation/contract form.* (1) Prepare the invitation for bids on SF 33, unless otherwise permitted by this regulation. The SF 33 is the first page of the solicitation and includes Section A of the uniform contract format. When the SF 1447 is used as the solicitation document, the information in subdivisions (a)(2)(i) and (a)(2)(iv) of this subsection shall be inserted in block 9 of the SF 1447.

(2) When the SF 33 or SF 1447 is not used, include the following on the first page of the invitation for bids:

(i) Name, address, and location of issuing activity, including room and building where bids must be submitted.

(ii) Invitation for bids number.

(iii) Date of issuance.

(iv) Time specified for receipt of bids.

(v) Number of pages.

(vi) Requisition or other purchase authority.

(vii) Requirement for bidder to provide its name and complete address, including street, city, county, state, and ZIP code.

(viii) A statement that bidders should include in the bid the address to which payment should be mailed, if that address is different from that of the bidder.

(b) *Section B, Supplies or services and prices.* Include a brief description of the supplies or services; *e.g.,* item number, national stock number/part number if applicable, title or name identifying the supplies or services, and quantities (see Part 11). The SF 33 and the SF 1447 may be supplemented as necessary by the Optional Form 336 (OF 336), Continuation Sheet (53.302–336).

(c) *Section C, Description/specifications.* Include any description or specifications needed in addition to Section B to permit full and open competition (see Part 11).

(d) *Section D, Packaging and marking.* Provide packaging, packing, preservation, and marking requirements, if any.

(e) *Section E, Inspection and acceptance.* Include inspection, acceptance, quality assurance, and reliability requirements (see Part 46, Quality Assurance).

(f) *Section F, Deliveries or performance.* Specify the requirements for time, place, and method of delivery or performance (see Subpart 11.4, Delivery or Performance Schedules).

(g) *Section G, Contract administration data.* Include any required accounting and appropriation data and any required contract administration information or instructions other than those on the solicitation form.

(h) *Section H, Special contract requirements.* Include a clear statement of any special contract requirements that are not included in Section I, Contract clauses, or in other sections of the uniform contract format.

United States Code Annotated

Contract requirements, see 41 USCA § 254.

Contracts, planning, solicitation, evaluation, and award procedures, see 10 USCA § 2305.

Definitions, see 10 USCA § 2302, 41 USCA §§ 259, 403.

Evaluation and award, see 41 USCA § 253b.

Kinds of contracts, see 10 USCA § 2306.

Planning and solicitation requirements, see 41 USCA § 253a.

§ 14.201-3 Part II—Contract clauses.

Section I, Contract clauses. The contracting officer shall include in this section the clauses required by law or by this regulation and any additional clauses expected to apply to any resulting contract, if these clauses are not required to be included in any other section of the uniform contract format.

United States Code Annotated

Contract requirements, see 41 USCA § 254.

Contracts, planning, solicitation, evaluation, and award procedures, see 10 USCA § 2305.

Definitions, see 10 USCA § 2302, 41 USCA §§ 259, 403.

Evaluation and award, see 41 USCA § 253b.

Kinds of contracts, see 10 USCA § 2306.

Planning and solicitation requirements, see 41 USCA § 253a.

§ 14.201-4 Part III—Documents, exhibits, and other attachments.

Section J, List of documents, exhibits, and other attachments. The contracting officer shall list the title, date, and number of pages for each attached document.

United States Code Annotated

Contract requirements, see 41 USCA § 254.

Contracts, planning, solicitation, evaluation, and award procedures, see 10 USCA § 2305.

Definitions, see 10 USCA § 2302, 41 USCA §§ 259, 403.

Evaluation and award, see 41 USCA § 253b.

Kinds of contracts, see 10 USCA § 2306.

Planning and solicitation requirements, see 41 USCA § 253a.

§ 14.201-5 Part IV—Representations and instructions.

The contracting officer shall prepare the representations and instructions as follows:

(a) *Section K, Representations, certifications, and other statements of bidders.* Include in this section those solicitation provisions that require representations, certifications, or the submission of other information by bidders.

(b) *Section L, Instructions, conditions, and notices to bidders.* Insert in this section solicitation provisions and other information and instructions not required elsewhere to guide bidders. Invitations shall include the time and place for bid openings, and shall advise bidders that bids will be evaluated without discussions (see 52.214-10 and, for construction contracts, 52.214-19).

(c) *Section M, Evaluation factors for award.* Identify the price related factors other than the bid price that will be considered in evaluating bids and awarding the contract. See 14. 202-8.

United States Code Annotated

Contract requirements, see 41 USCA § 254.

Contracts, planning, solicitation, evaluation, and award procedures, see 10 USCA § 2305.

Definitions, see 10 USCA § 2302, 41 USCA §§ 259, 403.

Evaluation and award, see 41 USCA § 253b.

Kinds of contracts, see 10 USCA § 2306.

Planning and solicitation requirements, see 41 USCA § 253a.

Notes of Decisions

In general 1

1 In general

Bidder's failure to complete Buy American Certificate or check foreign source certificate in connection with its bid for contract from Washington Metropolitan Area Transit Authority (WMATA) rendered bid unresponsive; had bidder checked second option of foreign source certificate, either before or after opening of bids, WMATA would have been required by regulations to increase plaintiff's bid price by 10%, and allowing contractor to make choice after bids were submitted would thus have permitted material alteration of bid by allowing postbidding manipulation based on bids of other competitors. Buy American Act, §§ 1–3, 41 U.S.C.A. §§ 10c, 10a, 10b. Seal and Co., Inc. v. Washington Metropolitan Area Transit Authority, 768 F. Supp. 1150 (E.D. Va. 1991). Urban Railroads ☞8

§ 14.201-6 Solicitation provisions.

(a) the provisions prescribed in this subsection apply to preparation and submission of bids in general. see other far parts for provisions and clauses related to specific acquisition requirements.

(b) insert in all invitations for bids the provisions at—

(1) 52.214-3, amendments to invitations for bids; and

(2) 52.214-4, false statements in bids.

(c) insert the following provisions in invitations for bids:

(1) 52.214-5, submission of bids.

(2) 52.214-6, explanation to prospective bidders.

(3) 52.214-7, late submissions, modifications, and withdrawals of bids.

(d) [reserved]

(e) insert in all invitations for bids, except those for construction, the provisions at 52.214-10, contract award—sealed bidding.

(f) insert in invitations for bids to which the uniform contract format applies, the provision at 52.214-12, preparation of bids.

(g) (1) insert the provision at 52.214-13, telegraphic bids, in invitations for bids if the contracting officer decides to authorize telegraphic bids.

(2) use the provision with its alternate i in invitations for bids that are for perishable subsistence, and when the contracting officer considers that offerors will be unwilling to provide acceptance periods long enough to allow written confirmation.

(h) insert the provision at 52.214-14, place of performance— sealed bidding, in invitations for bids except those in which the place of performance is specified by the government.

(i) insert the provision at 52.214-15, period for acceptance of bids, in invitations for bids (ifb's) that are not issued on SF 33 or SF 1447 except ifb's—

(1) for construction work; or

(2) in which the government specifies a minimum acceptance period.

(j) insert the provision at 52.214-16, minimum bid acceptance period, in invitations for bids, except for construction, if the contracting officer determines that a minimum acceptance period must be specified.

(k) [reserved]

(l) insert the provision at 52.214-18, preparation of bids— construction, in invitations for bids for construction work.

(m) insert the provision at 52.214-19, contract award— sealed bidding—construction, in all invitations for bids for construction work.

(n) [reserved]

(o) (1) insert the provision at 52.214-20, bid samples, in invitations for bids if bid samples are required.

(2) if it appears that the conditions in 14.202-4(e)(1) will apply and the contracting officer anticipates granting waivers and—

(i) if the nature of the required product does not necessitate limiting the grant of a waiver to a product produced at the same plant in which the product previously acquired or tested was produced, use the provision with its alternate i; or

(ii) if the nature of the required product necessitates limiting the grant of a waiver to a product produced at the same plant in which the product previously acquired or tested was produced, use the provision with its alternate ii.

(3) see 14.202-4(e)(2) regarding waiving the requirement for all bidders.

(p) (1) insert the provision at 52.214-21, descriptive literature, in invitations for bids if—

(i) descriptive literature is required to evaluate the technical acceptability of an offered product; and

(ii) the required information will not be readily available unless it is submitted by bidders.

(2) use the basic clause with its alternate i if the possibility exists that the contracting officer may waive the requirement for furnishing descriptive literature for a bidder offering a previously supplied product that meets specification requirements of the current solicitation.

(3) see 14.202-5(d)(2) regarding waiving the requirement for all bidders.

(q) insert the provision at 52.214-22, evaluation of bids for multiple awards, in invitations for bids if the contracting officer determines that multiple awards might be made if doing so is economically advantageous to the government.

(r) insert the provision at 52.214-23, late submissions, modifications, revisions, and withdrawals of technical proposals under two-step sealed bidding, in solicitations for technical proposals in step one of two-step sealed bidding.

(s) insert the provision at 52.214-24, multiple technical proposals, in solicitations for technical proposals in step one of two-step sealed bidding if the contracting officer permits the submission of multiple technical proposals.

(t) insert the provision at 52.214-25, step two of two-step sealed bidding, in invitations for bids issued under step two of two-step sealed bidding.

(u) [reserved]

(v) insert the provision at 52.214-31, facsimile bids, in solicitations if facsimile bids are authorized (see 14.202-7).

(w) insert the provision at 52.214-34, submission of offers in the english language, in solicitations that include any of the clauses prescribed in 25.1101 or 25.1102. it may be included in other solicitations when the contracting officer decides that it is necessary.

(x) insert the provision at 52.214-35, submission of offers in u.s. currency, in solicitations that include any of the clauses prescribed in 25.1101 or 25.1102, unless the contracting officer includes the clause at 52.225-17, Evaluation of Foreign Currency Offers, as prescribed in 25.1103(d). It may be included in other solicitations when the contracting officer decides that it is necessary.

United States Code Annotated

Contract requirements, see 41 USCA § 254.

Contracts, planning, solicitation, evaluation, and award procedures, see 10 USCA § 2305.

Definitions, see 10 USCA § 2302, 41 USCA §§ 259, 403.

Evaluation and award, see 41 USCA § 253b.

Kinds of contracts, see 10 USCA § 2306.

Planning and solicitation requirements, see 41 USCA § 253a.

Notes of Decisions

In general 1
Amendment of solicitation of bids 2
Construction of solicitation of bids 3
Facsimile bids 5
Multiple awards 4

1 In general

Bid protestor did not establish that agency acted arbitrarily and capriciously when it issued solicitation, based on its assertions that agency was required to base its funding request on an independent government estimate of $3,596,111, not the agency's own construction estimate of $3,218,781, and that agency issued the solicitation without intent to award a contract because it should have known that using its own estimate would result in insufficient funding for the project. First Enterprise v. U.S., 61 Fed. Cl. 109 (2004). United States ☞64.25

Where air force official was merely expressing opinion when he stated that resolicitation for proposals for lease of aircraft by Air Force could occur in future, statement did not bind Air Force to future course of action. Aviation Enterprises, Inc. v. U.S., 8 Cl. Ct. 1, 32 Cont. Cas. Fed. (CCH) P 73403 (1985). United States ☞64.40(5)

2 Amendment of solicitation of bids

Material change in terms of sealed bid solicitation, after bid is complete and contract awarded, cannot be imposed upon bidder with impunity. Lockheed Martin IR Imaging Systems, Inc. v. West, 108 F.3d 319, 41 Cont. Cas. Fed. (CCH) P 77052 (Fed. Cir. 1997). United States ☞72(1.1)

Prospective bidder failed to establish that contracting agency violated regulation by failing to notify it of amendment of solicitation on basis of evidence of non-receipt of email notification; although printouts of bulk mail screens related to the procurement were somewhat inconsistent, and reflect a shortened display name for prospective bidder, contracting officer (CO) presented affidavits in which she stated that she used a bulk mailing feature to send amendment, that plaintiff was on the list, that she routinely asked for return receipts when she sent out an e-mail, that, shortly after sending amendment 2, she began to receive receipt confirmations. 48 C.F.R. § 14.205-1(c). Razorcom Teleph & Net, LLC v. U.S., 56 Fed. Cl. 140 (2003). United States ☞64.25

Contracting agency's issuance of amendment to solicitation after bid submission did not violate the Federal Acquisition Regulation (FAR) on ground it altered a material term of the solicitation after the bid submission date; although amendment did affect technical and pricing aspects of bid proposals, and thus was material, there was no prejudice where final proposal revisions were not due until twenty-eight days after the issuance of amendment. 48 C.F.R. § 14.208. ABF Freight System, Inc. v. U.S., 55 Fed. Cl. 392 (2003). United States ☞64.25

3 Construction of solicitation of bids

When a government solicitation contains a patent ambiguity, a government contractor has a duty to seek clarification from the government, and its failure to do so precludes acceptance of its interpretation in a subsequent action against the government.A defect in a government bid solicitation is "patent" if it is an obvious omission, inconsistency, or discrepancy of significance; by contrast, a "latent" ambiguity, which need not be raised pre-award, is a hidden or concealed defect which is not apparent on the face of the document, could not be discovered by reasonable and customary care, and is not so patent and glaring as to impose an affirmative duty on bidder to seek clarification. Per Aarsleff A/S v. U.S., 2016 WL 3869790 (Fed.Cir. 2016)

Contractor reasonably interpreted contract as not binding contractor to provide any option quantity United States Army might choose on same terms as were bid for 100% option, and Army's requirement that lesser amounts be provided was thus constructive change for which appropriate unit price adjustment was warranted; solicitation provided that government could "require" delivery of 100% option, and another section providing that bidder "may" offer additional option prices for varying option quantities and order dates did not require contractor to offer other than 100% option. Lockheed Martin IR Imaging Systems, Inc. v. West, 108 F.3d 319, 41 Cont. Cas. Fed. (CCH) P 77052 (Fed. Cir. 1997). United States ☞70(30)

Clause in solicitation which stated that contracting agency would "not accept any offers which are submitted only as an 'ALL OR NONE' offer" did not prohibit bidders from submitting any "all or none" offers; rather, clause unambiguously prohibited offerors from submitting only an "all or none" offer. 48 C.F.R. § 14.404-5. AmerisourceBergen Drug Corp. v. U.S., 60 Fed. Cl. 30 (2004). United States ☞64.30

An exception to a bidder's duty to inquire concerning a patent ambiguity in a government solicitation exists when the government has notice of the ambiguity or defect, and either fails to notify all bidders, or otherwise fails to clarify the flaw. Metcalf Const. Co., Inc. v. U.S., 53 Fed. Cl. 617 (2002). United States ☞70(30)

Under doctrine of patent ambiguity, when a solicitation presents conflicting signals, a contractor is under an affirmative duty to call the ambiguity to the attention of the contracting official; if it fails to do so, it may not argue before the Court of Federal Claims that its interpretation is proper. Ryan Co. v. U.S., 43 Fed. Cl. 646 (1999). United States ☞64.25

An invitation for bids (IFB) should be read as a whole in order to give effect to all of the provisions of the solicitation. Ryan Co. v. U.S., 43 Fed. Cl. 646 (1999). United States ☞64.25

4 Multiple awards

In the context of sealed bidding, the FAR advises that IFBs are to provide for multiple awards where the contracting officer determines that multiple awards "might be made if doing so is economically advantageous to the Government." FAR 14.201-6(q). After the receipt of bids, the contracting officer shall assume, for the purpose of making multiple awards, that $500 would be the administrative cost to the Government for issuing and administering each contract awarded under a solicitation. Para Scientific Company, B-299046.2, 2007 CPD ¶ 37 (Comp. Gen. 2007)

5 Facsimile bids

The rules regarding the acceptance of facsimile bid modifications are well settled: a facsimile bid modification must be rejected where the solicitation does not expressly authorize its submission. The government cannot orally modify an IFB to allow for receipt of facsimile bid modifications where the IFB prohibits their submission, because to do so may be prejudicial to the other bidders. PBM Construction, Inc., B-271344, 96-1 CPD ¶ 216 (Comp. Gen. 1996)

§ 14.201-7 Contract clauses.

(a) When contracting by sealed bidding, the contracting officer shall insert the clause at 52.214-26, Audit and Records—Sealed Bidding, in solicitations and contracts as follows:

(1) Use the basic clause if—

(i) The acquisition will not use funds appropriated or otherwise made available by the American Recovery and Reinvestment Act of 2009 (Pub. L. 111-5); and

(ii) The contract amount is expected to exceed the threshold at 15.403-4(a)(1) for submission of certified cost or pricing data.

(2) (i) If the acquisition will use funds appropriated or otherwise made available by the American Recovery and Reinvestment Act of 2009, use the clause with its Alternate I in all solicitations and contracts.

(ii) (A) In the case of a bilateral contract modification that will use funds appropriated or otherwise made available by the American Recovery and Reinvestment Act of 2009, the contracting officer shall specify applicability of Alternate I to that modification.

(B) In the case of a task- or delivery-order contract in which not all orders will use funds appropriated or otherwise made available by the American Recovery and Reinvestment Act of 2009, the contracting officer shall specify the task or delivery orders to which Alternate I applies.

(b) (1) When contracting by sealed bidding, the contracting officer shall insert the clause at 52.214-27, Price Reduction for Defective Certified Cost or Pricing Data—Modifications—Sealed Bidding, in solicitations and contracts if the contract amount is expected to exceed the threshold for submission of certified cost or pricing data at 15.403-4(a)(1).

(2) In exceptional cases, the head of the contracting activity may waive the requirement for inclusion of the clause in a contract with a foreign government or agency of that government. The authorizations for the waiver and the reasons for granting it shall be in writing.

(c) (1) When contracting by sealed bidding, the contracting officer shall insert the clause at 52.214-28, Subcontractor Certified Cost or Pricing Data—Modifications—Sealed Bidding, in solicitations and contracts if the contract amount is expected to exceed the threshold for submission of certified cost or pricing data at 15.403-4(a)(1).

(2) In exceptional cases, the head of the contracting activity may waive the requirement for inclusion of the clause in a contract with a foreign government or agency of that government. The authorizations for the waiver and the reasons for granting it shall be in

writing.

(d) When contracting by sealed bidding the contracting officer shall insert the clause at 52.214-29, Order of Precedence—Sealed Bidding, in solicitations and contracts to which the uniform contract format applies.

United States Code Annotated

Contract requirements, see 41 USCA § 254.

Contracts, planning, solicitation, evaluation, and award procedures, see 10 USCA § 2305.

Definitions, see 10 USCA § 2302, 41 USCA §§ 259, 403.

Evaluation and award, see 41 USCA § 253b.

Kinds of contracts, see 10 USCA § 2306.

Planning and solicitation requirements, see 41 USCA § 253a.

§ 14.201-8 Price related factors.

The factors set forth in paragraphs (a) through (e) of this subsection may be applicable in evaluation of bids for award and shall be included in the solicitation when applicable. (See 14.201-5(c).)

(a) Foreseeable costs or delays to the Government resulting from such factors as differences in inspection, locations of supplies, and transportation. If bids are on an f.o.b. origin basis (see 47.303 and 47.305), transportation costs to the designated points shall be considered in determining the lowest cost to the Government.

(b) Changes made, or requested by the bidder, in any of the provisions of the invitation for bids, if the change does not constitute a ground for rejection under 14.404.

(c) Advantages or disadvantages to the Government that might result from making more than one award (see 14.201-6(q)). The contracting officer shall assume, for the purpose of making multiple awards, that $500 would be the administrative cost to the Government for issuing and administering each contract awarded under a solicitation. Individual awards shall be for the items or combinations of items that result in the lowest aggregate cost to the Government, including the assumed administrative costs.

(d) Federal, state, and local taxes (see Part 29).

(e) Origin of supplies, and, if foreign, the application of the Buy American statute or any other prohibition on foreign purchases (see Part 25).

United States Code Annotated

Contract requirements, see 41 USCA § 254.

Contracts, planning, solicitation, evaluation, and award procedures, see 10 USCA § 2305.

Definitions, see 10 USCA § 2302, 41 USCA §§ 259, 403.

Evaluation and award, see 41 USCA § 253b.

Kinds of contracts, see 10 USCA § 2306.

Planning and solicitation requirements, see 41 USCA § 253a.

Notes of Decisions

In general 1

1 In general

Under FAR 14.201-8, the evaluation of price-related factors, including foreseeable costs "to the Government resulting from such factors as differences in inspection, locations of supplies, and transportation," is a proper basis for award in a sealed bidding procurement. However, solicitation for ship repair is improper where the record evidences that the stated foreseeable costs to be added to each bidder's bid price to determine the low bidder are grossly understated. Todd Pacific Shipyards Corporation, 99-1 CPD ¶ 28 (Comp. Gen. 1999)

Protest that solicitation's provisions for evaluation of foreseeable costs to the agency (based on bidder's place of performance) unduly restrict competition and are ambiguous is denied where they provide for the proper evaluation of actual cost to the agency and, as amended, provide sufficient information to allow bidders to intelligently prepare their bids.

Cascade General, Inc., B-272271, 96-2 CPD ¶ 52 (Comp. Gen. 1996)

Protest challenging award under invitation for bids (IFB) for home oxygen respiratory equipment and services is sustained where IFB failed (1) to identify oxygen cylinder rental charges as a price-related factor to be considered in the evaluation of bids, (2) to advise bidders how the charges would factor into the evaluation, and (3) to provide bidders with the agency's estimate of the number of cylinders to which rental charges would apply. Matter of: Respiratory & Convalescent Specialties Inc., B-255176, 94-1 CPD ¶ 101 (Comp. Gen. 1994)

Agency reasonably considered for bid evaluation purposes the actual cost to the government of delivering and returning a vessel, along with the bid price, where the agency was responsible for transporting the vessel to and from the contractor's facility. Matter of: Marlen C. Robb & Son, Boatyard & Marina, Inc., B-256516, 94-1 CPD ¶ 392 (Comp. Gen. 1994)

Provision in solicitation for construction contract requiring bidders to propose overhead rates to which they will be bound in negotiation of change orders does not subject contractors to unreasonable risk; formula for evaluating impact of each bidder's proposed delivery schedule and overhead on price is neither contrary to Competition in Contracting Act of 1984, which requires that award decision consider only price and price-related factors, nor unreasonable where agency bases estimate of increase in cost of performance due to change orders on best historical data available. Matter of: ACS Construction Company, Inc. of Mississippi; ECI Construction, Inc.; C Construction Co., Inc., B-250372, B-250372.2, B-250372.3, 93-1 CPD ¶ 106 (Comp. Gen. 1993)

Addition of royalty fee evaluation factor to bids is not improper merely because it is not included under FAR 14.201-8, which lists only certain price-related factors that may be applicable, since this listing is not by its terms exclusive of other price-related factors which may be reasonable to evaluate when in the best interest of the government. Tek-Lite, Inc., B-230298, 88-1 CPD ¶ 241 (Comp. Gen. 1988)

§ 14.201-9 Simplified contract format.

Policy. For firm-fixed-price or fixed-price with economic price adjustment acquisitions of supplies and services, the contracting officer may use the simplified contract format in lieu of the uniform contract format (see 14.201-1). The contracting officer has flexibility in preparation and organization of the simplified contract format. However, the following format should be used to the maximum practical extent:

(a) *Solicitation/contract form.* Standard Form (SF) 1447, Solicitation/Contract, shall be used as the first page of the solicitation.

(b) *Contract schedule.* Include the following for each contract line item:

(1) Contract line item number.

(2) Description of supplies or services, or data sufficient to identify the requirement.

(3) Quantity and unit of issue.

(4) Unit price and amount.

(5) Packaging and marking requirements.

(6) Inspection and acceptance, quality assurance, and reliability requirements.

(7) Place of delivery, performance and delivery dates, period of performance, and f.o.b. point.

(8) Other item-peculiar information as necessary (*e.g.,* individual fund citations).

(c) *Clauses.* Include the clauses required by this regulation. Additional clauses shall be incorporated only when considered absolutely necessary to the particular acquisition.

(d) *List of documents and attachments.* Include if necessary.

(e) *Representations and instructions—* (1) *Representations and certifications.* Insert those solicitation provisions that require representations, certifications, or the submission of other information by offerors.

(2) *Instructions, conditions, and notices.* Include the solicitation provisions required by 14.201-6. Include any other information/instructions necessary to guide offerors.

(3) *Evaluation factors for award.* Insert all evaluation factors and any significant subfactors for award.

(4) Upon award, the contracting officer need not physically include the provisions in

paragraphs (e)(1), (2), and (3) of this subsection in the resulting contract, but shall retain them in the contract file. Award by acceptance of a bid on the award portion of SF 1447 incorporates the representations, certifications, and other statements of bidders in the resultant contract even though not physically attached.

United States Code Annotated

Contract requirements, see 41 USCA § 254.

Contracts, planning, solicitation, evaluation, and award procedures, see 10 USCA § 2305.

Definitions, see 10 USCA § 2302, 41 USCA §§ 259, 403.

Evaluation and award, see 41 USCA § 253b.

Kinds of contracts, see 10 USCA § 2306.

Planning and solicitation requirements, see 41 USCA § 253a.

§ 14.202 General rules for solicitation of bids.

§ 14.202-1 Bidding time.

(a) *Policy.* A reasonable time for prospective bidders to prepare and submit bids shall be allowed in all invitations, consistent with the needs of the Government. (For construction contracts, see 36.213-3(a).) A bidding time (*i.e.,* the time between issuance of the solicitation and opening of bids) of at least 30 calendar days shall be provided, when synopsis is required by Subpart 5.2.

(b) *Factors to be considered.* Because of unduly limited bidding time, some potential sources may be precluded from bidding and others may be forced to include amounts for contingencies that, with additional time, could be eliminated. To avoid unduly restricting competition or paying higher-thannecessary prices, consideration shall be given to such factors as the following in establishing a reasonable bidding time:

(1) Degree of urgency;

(2) Complexity of requirement;

(3) Anticipated extent of subcontracting;

(4) Whether use was made of presolicitation notices;

(5) Geographic distribution of bidders; and

(6) Normal transmittal time for both invitations and bids.

United States Code Annotated

Contract requirements, see 41 USCA § 254.

Contracts, planning, solicitation, evaluation, and award procedures, see 10 USCA § 2305.

Definitions, see 10 USCA § 2302, 41 USCA §§ 259, 403.

Evaluation and award, see 41 USCA § 253b.

Kinds of contracts, see 10 USCA § 2306.

Planning and solicitation requirements, see 41 USCA § 253a.

§ 14.202-2 Telegraphic bids.

(a) Telegraphic bids and mailgrams shall be authorized only when—

(1) The date for the opening of bids will not allow bidders sufficient time to submit bids in the prescribed format; or

(2) Prices are subject to frequent changes.

(b) If telegraphic bids are to be authorized, see 14.201-6(g). Unauthorized telegraphic bids shall not be considered (see 14.301(b)).

United States Code Annotated

Contract requirements, see 41 USCA § 254.

Contracts, planning, solicitation, evaluation, and award procedures, see 10 USCA § 2305.

Definitions, see 10 USCA § 2302, 41 USCA §§ 259, 403.

Evaluation and award, see 41 USCA § 253b.

Kinds of contracts, see 10 USCA § 2306.

Planning and solicitation requirements, see 41 USCA § 253a.

§ 14.202-3 Bid envelopes.

(a) Postage or envelopes bearing "Postage and Fees Paid" indicia shall not be distributed with the invitation for bids or otherwise supplied to prospective bidders.

(b) To provide for ready identification and proper handling of bids, Optional Form 17, Offer Label, may be furnished with each bid set. The form may be obtained from the General Services Administration (see 53.107).

United States Code Annotated

Contract requirements, see 41 USCA § 254.

Contracts, planning, solicitation, evaluation, and award procedures, see 10 USCA § 2305.

Definitions, see 10 USCA § 2302, 41 USCA §§ 259, 403.

Evaluation and award, see 41 USCA § 253b.

Kinds of contracts, see 10 USCA § 2306.

Planning and solicitation requirements, see 41 USCA § 253a.

§ 14.202-4 Bid samples.

(a) *Policy.* (1) Bidders shall not be required to furnish bid samples unless there are characteristics of the product that cannot be described adequately in the specification or purchase description.

(2) Bid samples will be used only to determine the responsiveness of the bid and will not be used to determine a bidder's ability to produce the required items.

(3) Bid samples may be examined for any required characteristic, whether or not such characteristic is adequately described in the specification, if listed in accordance with subdivision (e)(1)(ii) of this section.

(4) Bids will be rejected as nonresponsive if the sample fails to conform to each of the characteristics listed in the invitation.

(b) *When to use.* The use of bid samples would be appropriate for products that must be suitable from the standpoint of balance, facility of use, general "feel," color, pattern, or other characteristics that cannot be described adequately in the specification. However, when more than a minor portion of the characteristics of the product cannot be adequately described in the specification, products should be acquired by two-step sealed bidding or negotiation, as appropriate.

(c) *Justification.* The reasons why acceptable products cannot be acquired without the submission of bid samples shall be set forth in the contract file, except where the submission is required by the formal specifications (Federal, Military, or other) applicable to the acquisition.

(d) *Requirements for samples in invitations for bids.* (1) Invitations for bids shall—

(i) State the number and, if appropriate, the size of the samples to be submitted and otherwise fully describe the samples required; and

(ii) List all the characteristics for which the samples will be examined.

(2) If bid samples are required, see 14.201-6(o).

(e) *Waiver of requirement for bid samples.* (1) The requirement for furnishing bid samples may be waived when a bidder offers a product previously or currently being contracted for or tested by the Government and found to comply with specification requirements conforming in every material respect with those in the current invitation for bids. When the requirement may be waived, see 14.201-6(o)(2).

(2) Where samples required by a Federal, Military, or other formal specification are not considered necessary and a waiver of the sample requirements of the specification has been authorized, a statement shall be included in the invitation that notwithstanding the requirements of the specification, samples will not be required.

(f) *Unsolicited samples.* Bid samples furnished with a bid that are not required by the invitation generally will not be considered as qualifying the bid and will be disregarded. However, the bid sample will not be disregarded if it is clear from the bid or accompanying papers that the bidder's intention was to qualify the bid. (See 14.404-2(d) if the qualification does not conform to the solicitation.)

(g) *Handling bid samples.* (1) Samples that are not destroyed in testing shall be returned to bidders at their request and expense, unless otherwise specified in the invitation.

(2) Disposition instructions shall be requested from bidders and samples disposed of accordingly.

(3) Samples ordinarily will be returned collect to the address from which received if disposition instructions are not received within 30 days. Small items may be returned by mail, postage prepaid.

(4) Samples that are to be retained for inspection purposes in connection with deliveries shall be transmitted to the inspecting activity concerned, with instructions to retain the sample until completion of the contract or until disposition instructions are furnished.

(5) Where samples are consumed or their usefulness is impaired by tests, they will be disposed of as scrap unless the bidder requests their return.

United States Code Annotated

Contract requirements, see 41 USCA § 254.

Contracts, planning, solicitation, evaluation, and award procedures, see 10 USCA § 2305.

Definitions, see 10 USCA § 2302, 41 USCA §§ 259, 403.

Evaluation and award, see 41 USCA § 253b.

Kinds of contracts, see 10 USCA § 2306.

Planning and solicitation requirements, see 41 USCA § 253a.

Notes of Decisions

In general 1

1 In general

Agency decision to require bid samples in lieu of technical proposals in procurement for test sets is reasonable where the agency did not have adequate specifications to describe the facility of use characteristics it required in the test sets. Matter of: Pynco, Inc, B-257853, 94-2 CPD ¶ 190 (Comp. Gen. 1994)

Agency decision to require bid samples in lieu of technical proposals and first article testing is reasonable where: (1) solicitation contained detailed drawings and technical specifications enabling bidders to manufacture noncomplex component parts; and (2) agency did not have adequate specifications to describe facility of use characteristics it required in the components. Matter of: Machinewerks, Inc., B-258123, 94-2 CPD ¶ 238 (Comp. Gen. 1994)

§ 14.202-5 Descriptive literature.

(a) *Policy.* Contracting officers must not require bidders to furnish descriptive literature unless it is needed before award to determine whether the products offered meet the specification and to establish exactly what the bidder proposes to furnish.

(b) *Justification.* The contracting officer must document in the contract file the reasons why product acceptability cannot be determined without the submission of descriptive literature, except when the contract specifications require submission.

(c) *Requirements of invitation for bids.* (1) The invitation must clearly state—

(i) What descriptive literature the bidders must furnish;

(ii) The purpose for requiring the literature;

(iii) The extent of its consideration in the evaluation of bids; and

(iv) The rules that will apply if a bidder fails to furnish the literature before bid opening or if the literature provided does not comply with the requirements of the invitation.

(2) If bidders must furnish descriptive literature, see 14.201-6(p).

(d) *Waiver of requirement for descriptive literature.* (1) The contracting officer may waive the requirement for descriptive literature if—

(i) The bidder states in the bid that the product being offered is the same as a product previously or currently being furnished to the contracting activity; and

(ii) The contracting officer determines that the product offered by the bidder complies with the specification requirements of the current invitation for bids. When the contracting officer waives the requirement, see 14.201-6(p)(2).

(2) When descriptive literature is not necessary and a waiver of literature requirements of a specification has been authorized, the contracting officer must include a statement in the invitation that, despite the requirements of the specifications, descriptive literature will not be required.

(3) If the solicitation provides for a waiver, a bidder may submit a bid on the basis of either the descriptive literature furnished with the bid or a previously furnished product. If the bid is submitted on one basis, the bidder may not have it considered on the other basis after bids are opened.

(e) *Unsolicited descriptive literature.* If descriptive literature is furnished when it is not required by the invitation for bids, the procedures set forth in 14.202-4(f) must be followed.

United States Code Annotated

Contract requirements, see 41 USCA § 254.

Contracts, planning, solicitation, evaluation, and award procedures, see 10 USCA § 2305.

Definitions, see 10 USCA § 2302, 41 USCA §§ 259, 403.

Evaluation and award, see 41 USCA § 253b.

Kinds of contracts, see 10 USCA § 2306.

Planning and solicitation requirements, see 41 USCA § 253a.

Notes of Decisions

In general 1

1 In general

Where invitation for bids contained the standard descriptive literature clause but did not specify what type of literature was required and for what purpose, the solicitation effectively did not require submission of descriptive literature; bid which did not include descriptive literature thus cannot be rejected as nonresponsive. Matter of: Allotech, B-259154, 1995 WL 64176 (Comp. Gen. 1995)

Where the invitation for bids (IFB) clearly required, for purposes of determining the responsiveness of a bid, as opposed to the responsibility of the bidder, the submission of descriptive literature and technical data sheets in order to establish that a bidder's specifically identified equipment would satisfy the IFB's listed salient characteristics, the contracting officer properly rejected the protester's bid as nonresponsive where the protester did not identify in its bid the specific equipment being offered and did not submit with its bid descriptive materials demonstrating that its unidentified equipment would satisfy the salient characteristics. Matter of: Alaska Unlimited, B-257156, 94-2 CPD ¶ 87 (Comp. Gen. 1994)

Agency could not properly disregard unsolicited descriptive literature in a sealed bid procurement where the cover letter included with the bid referenced the solicitation number and expressly included the literature as pertinent information; since the phase-in schedule contained in the unsolicited literature reasonably raised a question whether the bid complied with a material solicitation requirement, the bid was properly rejected as nonresponsive. Matter of: Balantine's South Bay Caterers, Inc., B-250223, 93-1 CPD ¶ 39 (Comp. Gen. 1993)

Agency properly rejected as nonresponsive a bid which contained unsolicited descriptive literature concerning the product offered, which established that the product did not comply with a material solicitation requirement. Matter of: Amjay Chemicals, B-252502, 93-1 CPD ¶ 426 (Comp. Gen. 1993)

Proposed awardee's bid was properly determined responsive where the firm did not take exception in its unsolicited descriptive literature submitted with its bid, or elsewhere in its bid, to the solicitation's technical requirements and where the firm's unsolicited descriptive literature shows that its offered equipment will perform in accordance with the solicitation's technical requirements. Matter of: Williams Environmental Services, Inc., B-250404, 93-1 CPD ¶ 80 (Comp. Gen. 1993)

Protest challenging the rejection of a bid as nonresponsive on the basis that descriptive literature submitted with the bid failed to establish that the offered equipment conformed to the specifications is sustained where the solicitation effectively did not require descriptive literature, and the bid did not take exception to any of the solicitation's requirements. Matter of: Aidco, Inc., B-249736, B-249736.2, 92-2 CPD ¶ 407 (Comp. Gen. 1992)

§ 14.202-6 Final review of invitations for bids.

Each invitation for bids shall be thoroughly reviewed before issuance to detect and correct discrepancies or ambiguities that could limit competition or result in the receipt of nonresponsive bids. Contracting officers are responsible for the reviews.

United States Code Annotated

Contract requirements, see 41 USCA § 254.

Contracts, planning, solicitation, evaluation, and award procedures, see 10 USCA § 2305.

Definitions, see 10 USCA § 2302, 41 USCA §§ 259, 403.

Evaluation and award, see 41 USCA § 253b.

Kinds of contracts, see 10 USCA § 2306.

Planning and solicitation requirements, see 41 USCA § 253a.

§ 14.202-7 Facsimile bids.

(a) Unless prohibited or otherwise restricted by agency procedures, contracting officers may authorize facsimile bids (see 14.201-6(v)). In determining whether or not to authorize facsimile bids, the contracting officer shall consider factors such as—

(1) Anticipated bid size and volume;

(2) Urgency of the requirement;

(3) Frequency of price changes;

(4) Availability, reliability, speed, and capacity of the receiving facsimile equipment; and

(5) Adequacy of administrative procedures and controls for receiving, identifying, recording, and safeguarding facsimile bids, and ensuring their timely delivery to the bids opening location.

(b) If facsimile bids are authorized, contracting officers may, after the date set for bid opening, request the apparently successful offeror to provide the complete, original signed bid.

United States Code Annotated

Contract requirements, see 41 USCA § 254.

Contracts, planning, solicitation, evaluation, and award procedures, see 10 USCA § 2305.

Definitions, see 10 USCA § 2302, 41 USCA §§ 259, 403.

Evaluation and award, see 41 USCA § 253b.

Kinds of contracts, see 10 USCA § 2306.

Planning and solicitation requirements, see 41 USCA § 253a.

Notes of Decisions

In general 1

1 In general

Bidder that allegedly submitted its bid extension by facsimile transmission assumed the risk of nonreceipt by the agency, and the bidder's evidence of its facsimile transmission does not establish receipt where, as here, the agency denies receipt and there is no other evidence of receipt. Brickwood Contractors, Inc., B-290444, 2002 CPD ¶ 121 (Comp. Gen. 2002)

The rules regarding the acceptance of facsimile bid modifications are well settled: a facsimile bid modification must be rejected where the solicitation does not expressly authorize its submission. The government cannot orally modify an IFB to allow for receipt of facsimile bid modifications where the IFB prohibits their submission, because to do so may be prejudicial to the other bidders. PBM Construction, Inc., B-271344, 96-1 CPD ¶ 216 (Comp.

Gen. 1996)

§ 14.202-8 Electronic bids.

In accordance with Subpart 4.5, contracting officers may authorize use of electronic commerce for submission of bids. If electronic bids are authorized, the solicitation shall specify the electronic commerce method(s) that bidders may use.

United States Code Annotated

Contract requirements, see 41 USCA § 254.

Contracts, planning, solicitation, evaluation, and award procedures, see 10 USCA § 2305.

Definitions, see 10 USCA § 2302, 41 USCA §§ 259, 403.

Evaluation and award, see 41 USCA § 253b.

Kinds of contracts, see 10 USCA § 2306.

Planning and solicitation requirements, see 41 USCA § 253a.

Notes of Decisions

In general 1

1 In general

Where record shows that agency misread electronic version of awardee's bid as incomplete at the time of bid opening, and that, in fact, complete bid was received prior to bid opening time, there is no basis for questioning agency's award decision. Mitchell Roofing & Contracting, B-290462, 2002 CPD ¶ 108 (Comp. Gen. 2002)

§ 14.203 Methods of soliciting bids.

§ 14.203-1 Transmittal to prospective bidders.

Invitations for bids or presolicitation notices must be provided in accordance with 5.102. When a contracting office is located in the United States, any solicitation sent to a prospective bidder located outside the United States shall be sent by electronic data interchange or air mail if security classification permits.

United States Code Annotated

Contract requirements, see 41 USCA § 254.

Contracts, planning, solicitation, evaluation, and award procedures, see 10 USCA § 2305.

Definitions, see 10 USCA § 2302, 41 USCA §§ 259, 403.

Evaluation and award, see 41 USCA § 253b.

Kinds of contracts, see 10 USCA § 2306.

Planning and solicitation requirements, see 41 USCA § 253a.

§ 14.203-2 Dissemination of information concerning invitations for bids.

Procedures concerning display of invitations for bids in a public place, information releases to newspapers and trade journals, paid advertisements, and synopsizing through the Governmentwide point of entry (GPE) are set forth in 5.101 and Subpart 5.2.

United States Code Annotated

Contract requirements, see 41 USCA § 254.

Contracts, planning, solicitation, evaluation, and award procedures, see 10 USCA § 2305.

Definitions, see 10 USCA § 2302, 41 USCA §§ 259, 403.

Evaluation and award, see 41 USCA § 253b.

Kinds of contracts, see 10 USCA § 2306.

Planning and solicitation requirements, see 41 USCA § 253a.

§ 14.203-3 Master solicitation.

The master solicitation is provided to potential sources who are requested to retain it for continued and repetitive use. Individual solicitations must reference the date of the current master solicitation and identify any changes. The contracting officer must—

(a) Make available copies of the master solicitation on request; and

(b) Provide the cognizant contract administration activity a current copy of the master solicitation.

United States Code Annotated

Contract requirements, see 41 USCA § 254.

Contracts, planning, solicitation, evaluation, and award procedures, see 10 USCA § 2305.

Definitions, see 10 USCA § 2302, 41 USCA §§ 259, 403.

Evaluation and award, see 41 USCA § 253b.

Kinds of contracts, see 10 USCA § 2306.

Planning and solicitation requirements, see 41 USCA § 253a.

§ 14.204 Records of invitations for bids and records of bids.

(a) Each contracting office shall retain a record of each invitation that it issues and each abstract or record of bids. Contracting officers shall review and utilize the information available in connection with subsequent acquisitions of the same or similar items.

(b) The file for each invitation shall show the distribution that was made and the date the invitation was issued. The names and addresses of prospective bidders who requested the invitation and were not included on the original solicitation list shall be added to the list and made a part of the record.

United States Code Annotated

Contract requirements, see 41 USCA § 254.

Contracts, planning, solicitation, evaluation, and award procedures, see 10 USCA § 2305.

Definitions, see 10 USCA § 2302, 41 USCA §§ 259, 403.

Evaluation and award, see 41 USCA § 253b.

Kinds of contracts, see 10 USCA § 2306.

Planning and solicitation requirements, see 41 USCA § 253a.

§ 14.205 Presolicitation notices.

In lieu of initially forwarding complete bid sets, the contracting officer may send presolicitation notices to concerns. The notice shall—

(a) Specify the final date for receipt of requests for a complete bid set;

(b) Briefly describe the requirement and furnish other essential information to enable concerns to determine whether they have an interest in the invitation; and

(c) Normally not include drawings, plans, and specifications. The return date of the notice must be sufficiently in advance of the mailing date of the invitation for bids to permit an accurate estimate of the number of bid sets required. Bid sets shall be sent to concerns that request them in response to the notice.

United States Code Annotated

Contract requirements, see 41 USCA § 254.

Contracts, planning, solicitation, evaluation, and award procedures, see 10 USCA § 2305.

Definitions, see 10 USCA § 2302, 41 USCA §§ 259, 403.

Evaluation and award, see 41 USCA § 253b.

Kinds of contracts, see 10 USCA § 2306.

Planning and solicitation requirements, see 41 USCA § 253a.

Notes of Decisions

In general 1

1 In general

Government was under no obligation to solicit incumbent contractor on a delivery order from a Federal Supply Services (FSS) schedule contract, as sealed bidding regulation is not applicable to placement of a delivery order from an FSS schedule. Cybertech Group, Inc. v. U.S., 48 Fed. Cl. 638 (2001).

§ 14.206 [Reserved]

§ 14.207 Pre-bid conference.

A pre-bid conference may be used, generally in a complex acquisition, as a means of briefing prospective bidders and explaining complicated specifications and requirements to them as early as possible after the invitation has been issued and before the bids are opened. It shall never be used as a substitute for amending a defective or ambiguous invitation. The conference shall be conducted in accordance with the procedure prescribed in 15.201.

United States Code Annotated

Contract requirements, see 41 USCA § 254.

Contracts, planning, solicitation, evaluation, and award procedures, see 10 USCA § 2305.

Definitions, see 10 USCA § 2302, 41 USCA §§ 259, 403.

Evaluation and award, see 41 USCA § 253b.

Kinds of contracts, see 10 USCA § 2306.

Planning and solicitation requirements, see 41 USCA § 253a.

§ 14.208 Amendment of invitation for bids.

(a) If it becomes necessary to make changes in quantity, specifications, delivery schedules, opening dates, etc., or to correct a defective or ambiguous invitation, such changes shall be accomplished by amendment of the invitation for bids using Standard Form 30, Amendment of Solicitation/ Modification of Contract. The fact that a change was mentioned at a pre-bid conference does not relieve the necessity for issuing an amendment. Amendments shall be sent, before the time for bid opening, to everyone to whom invitations have been furnished and shall be displayed in the bid room.

(b) Before amending an invitation for bids, the period of time remaining until bid opening and the need to extend this period shall be considered. When only a short time remains before the time set for bid opening, consideration should be given to notifying bidders of an extension of time by telegrams or telephone. Such extension must be confirmed in the amendment.

(c) Any information given to a prospective bidder concerning an invitation for bids shall be furnished promptly to all other prospective bidders as an amendment to the invitation (1) if such information is necessary for bidders to submit bids or (2) if the lack of such information would be prejudicial to uninformed bidders. The information shall be furnished even though a pre-bid conference is held. No award shall be made on the invitation unless such amendment has been issued in sufficient time to permit all prospective bidders to consider such information in submitting or modifying their bids.

United States Code Annotated

Contract requirements, see 41 USCA § 254.

Contracts, planning, solicitation, evaluation, and award procedures, see 10 USCA § 2305.

Definitions, see 10 USCA § 2302, 41 USCA §§ 259, 403.

Evaluation and award, see 41 USCA § 253b.

Kinds of contracts, see 10 USCA § 2306.

Planning and solicitation requirements, see 41 USCA § 253a.

Notes of Decisions

In general 1

1 In general

Contracting agency's issuance of amendment to solicitation after bid submission did not violate the Federal Acquisition Regulation (FAR) on ground it altered a material term of the solicitation after the bid submission date; although amendment did affect technical and pricing aspects of bid proposals, and thus was material, there was no prejudice where final proposal revisions were not due until twenty-eight days after the issuance of amendment. 48 C.F.R. § 14.208. ABF Freight System, Inc. v. U.S., 55 Fed. Cl. 392 (2003). United States ☞64.25

Agency properly rejected low offer for failure to acknowledge a solicitation amendment where the amendment changed the legal relationship of the parties with regard to the contractor's obligations and the government's rights pertaining to the submission and approval of a first article test plan; there is no evidence that agency did not comply with applicable regulations regarding the distribution of amendments. Navistar Marine Instrument Corporation, B-277143, B-277143.2, 98-1 CPD ¶ 53 (Comp. Gen. 1998)

§ 14.209 Cancellation of invitations before opening.

(a) The cancellation of an invitation for bids usually involves a loss of time, effort, and money spent by the Government and bidders. Invitations should not be cancelled unless cancellation is clearly in the public interest; *e.g.*,

(1) Where there is no longer a requirement for the supplies or services; or

(2) Where amendments to the invitation would be of such magnitude that a new invitation is desirable.

(b) When an invitation issued other than electronically is cancelled, bids that have been received shall be returned unopened to the bidders and notice of cancellation shall be sent to all prospective bidders to whom invitations were issued. When an invitation issued electronically is cancelled, a general notice of cancellation shall be posted electronically, the bids received shall not be viewed, and the bids shall be purged from primary and backup data storage systems.

(c) The notice of cancellation shall—(1) identify the invitation for bids by number and short title or subject matter, (2) briefly explain the reason the invitation is being cancelled, and (3) where appropriate, assure prospective bidders that they will be given an opportunity to bid on any resolicitation of bids or any future requirements for the type of supplies or services involved. Cancellations shall be recorded in accordance with 14.403(d).

United States Code Annotated

Contract requirements, see 41 USCA § 254.

Contracts, planning, solicitation, evaluation, and award procedures, see 10 USCA § 2305.

Definitions, see 10 USCA § 2302, 41 USCA §§ 259, 403.

Evaluation and award, see 41 USCA § 253b.

Kinds of contracts, see 10 USCA § 2306.

Planning and solicitation requirements, see 41 USCA § 253a.

Notes of Decisions

Attorneys fees 9
Bad faith 5
Cancellation of invitations, generally 1
Costs of bid preparation 3
Discretion and authority of agency 2
Injunctions 6
Judicial review 10
Jurisdiction 7
Presumptions and burden of proof 8
Reason for cancellation of invitations 4

1 Cancellation of invitations, generally

Army was not required to cancel invitation for bids where invitation overstated Army's minimum needs. Delta Chemical Corp. v. West, 33 F.3d 380, 39 Cont. Cas. Fed. (CCH) P 76693 (4th Cir. 1994). United States ☞64.50

Army did not act arbitrarily and capriciously when it refused to cancel invitation for bids after determining that invitation overstated its minimum needs, where unsuccessful bidder was not prejudiced because its bid was nonresponsive for reason unrelated to overstatement.

Delta Chemical Corp. v. West, 33 F.3d 380, 39 Cont. Cas. Fed. (CCH) P 76693 (4th Cir. 1994). United States ☞64.50; United States ☞64.60(4)

Omission, from invitation for bid for manufacture of propeller shaft assembly approximately 56 feet long, of Defense Department restriction mandating against procurement of certain foreign forging products, including ship propulsion shafts greater than 50 feet in length, rendered invitation for bid defective under Federal Acquisition Regulations System and, thus, supported cancellation of invitation for bid. 10 U.S.C.A. § 2304(a)(16); Executive Order No. 11490, Oct. 28, 1969. National Forge Co. v. U.S., 779 F.2d 665, 33 Cont. Cas. Fed. (CCH) P 74149 (Fed. Cir. 1985). United States ☞64.25

Solicitation concerning past performance evaluation was overstated and overly restrictive of competition to the prejudice of other potential offerors in violation of the Competition in Contracting Act (CICA), warranting cancellation of solicitation. 10 U.S.C.A. § 2305(a)(1)(B)(ii); Federal Property and Administrative Services Act of 1949, § 303(a)(2)(B), 41 U.S.C.A. § 253(a)(2)(B); 48 C.F.R. § 14.101(a). Charles H. Tompkins Co. v. U.S., 43 Fed. Cl. 716 (1999). United States ☞64.50

When it becomes evident that solicitation fails to adequately reflect government's needs, it is proper to cancel solicitation; rule applies to sealed bidding and other competitive negotiation procedures. Shields Enterprises, Inc. v. U.S., 28 Fed. Cl. 615, 38 Cont. Cas. Fed. (CCH) P 76526 (1993). United States ☞64.50

For purpose of determining whether Government reasonably cancelled solicitation for bids for providing unarmed guard services, Government's need for two supervisors per eight-hour shift could not be inferred from provision of solicitation requiring that Government and contractor immediately after contract award coordinate to review performance requirements for guard post assignments. Vanguard Sec. Inc. v. U.S., 20 Cl. Ct. 90, 1990 WL 38036 (1990). United States ☞64.50

Regulatory admonitions that agency should not cancel solicitations just because their needs are for greater quantities than those listed in solicitation are meaningful only in context of supply contracts, as opposed to service contracts. Vanguard Sec. Inc. v. U.S., 20 Cl. Ct. 90, 1990 WL 38036 (1990). United States ☞64.50

For purpose of determining whether Government reasonably cancelled solicitation for bids for providing unarmed guard services, Government's need for two supervisors per eight-hour shift could not be inferred from solicitation's requirement that contractor furnish supervision on 24-houra-day basis. Vanguard Sec. Inc. v. U.S., 20 Cl. Ct. 90, 1990 WL 38036 (1990). United States ☞64.50

There was no basis for measuring decision to cancel solicitation of bids relating to coin production against standards or procedures contained in Office of Management Budget circular A-76, which stated that it is government policy to use private sources for government commercial activities in appropriate circumstances, since cancellation decision was based upon issue that is "jurisdictional" prerequisites of circular, that is, nongovernmental functions. Arrowhead Metals, Ltd. v. U.S., 8 Cl. Ct. 703, 33 Cont. Cas. Fed. (CCH) P 74026 (1985). United States ☞64.50

Office of Management Budget Circular A-76, which stated that it was government policy to use private sources for government commercial activities in appropriate circumstances, did not support claim that Government, in its cost analysis regarding coin production, as it related to decision to cancel solicitation of bids for production of coinage blanks, had to utilize historical costs for "strip" and could not utilize latest "strip" cost data. Arrowhead Metals, Ltd. v. U.S., 8 Cl. Ct. 703, 33 Cont. Cas. Fed. (CCH) P 74026 (1985). United States ☞64.50

It was not improper for United States Mint to consider actions taken or concerns raised by members of Congress in determining whether or not to cancel solicitation for bids in connection with contract for coin production; rather, issue was whether those factors affected contractor's right to full and fair consideration of its proposal. Arrowhead Metals, Ltd. v. U.S., 8 Cl. Ct. 703, 33 Cont. Cas. Fed. (CCH) P 74026 (1985). United States ☞64.50

Cancellation of solicitation bids in connection with contract for production of coins served interest of Government by allowing for further study of important policy issue of whether contracting out such work involved inherently governmental functions. Arrowhead Metals, Ltd. v. U.S., 8 Cl. Ct. 703, 33 Cont. Cas. Fed. (CCH) P 74026 (1985). United States ☞64.50

Foreign contractor's claim that United States Mint officials were prejudiced against it, thus leading to cancellation of solicitation for bids in connection with production of coins, could not be premised on language of Trade Agreement Act [Trade Agreements Act of 1979, §§ 1(a)-1112, 19 U.S.C.A. §§ 2501–2582] inasmuch as Act expressly denies private remedies not specifically provided for therein. Trade Agreements Act of 1979, §§ 3(f), 421, 19 U.S.C.A. § 2504(d), 2551. Arrowhead Metals, Ltd. v. U.S., 8 Cl. Ct. 703, 33 Cont. Cas. Fed. (CCH) P 74026 (1985). United States ☞64.60(1)

Offeror failed to establish that United States Air Force cancelled solicitation for lease of four aircraft in order to avoid bidder's protest or that air force air staff orchestrated plan to cancel solicitation and then rewrite specification to allow for use of C-12 aircraft at air field, either of which may have rendered cancellation of solicitation unreasonable. Aviation Enterprises, Inc. v. U.S., 8 Cl. Ct. 1, 32 Cont. Cas. Fed. (CCH) P 73403 (1985). United States ☞64.50

Cancellation of invitation for bids (IFB) prior to bid opening was in the public interest where agency failed to investigate whether procurement should be set aside for acquisition from National Institute for the Severely Handicapped or small business prior to issuing the IFB on an unrestricted basis. Diversified Management Group, A Joint Venture, B-288443.2, 2001 CPD ¶ 175 (Comp. Gen. 2001)

Agency properly canceled invitation for bids after bid opening where the solicitation specifications did not adequately set forth the agency's requirements, and prior to bid opening, the agency had provided only one of several offerors with informal clarifications regarding the actual requirements. Grot, Inc., B-276979, B-276979.2, B-277463, 97-2 CPD ¶ 50 (Comp. Gen. 1997)

2 Discretion and authority of agency

In the context of pre-award negotiations, a contracting officer is given latitude in deciding whether to cancel a solicitation and request new bids after price offers have been disclosed. Griffy's Landscape Maintenance LLC v. U.S., 51 Fed. Cl. 667 (2001). United States ☞64.50

Procurement official's decision to cancel solicitation in negotiated procurement is inherently discretionary. Shields Enterprises, Inc. v. U.S., 28 Fed. Cl. 615, 38 Cont. Cas. Fed. (CCH) P 76526 (1993). United States ☞64.50

Contracting officer did not act arbitrarily or capriciously by cancelling solicitation because supplies being contracted for were no longer required; solicitation granted to officer gave substantial discretion to reject bid or to cancel or amend solicitation. Durable Metals Products, Inc. v. U.S., 27 Fed. Cl. 472, 38 Cont. Cas. Fed. (CCH) P 76471 (1993), judgment aff'd, 11 F.3d 1071 (Fed. Cir. 1993). United States ☞64.50

Government reasonably and within its discretion determined that specifications in solicitation for bids for providing armed-guard services were ambiguous or inadequate with respect to Government's need for two supervisors per eighthour shift, and thus Government properly cancelled solicitation. Vanguard Sec. Inc. v. U.S., 20 Cl. Ct. 90, 1990 WL 38036 (1990). United States ☞64.50

Generally, government has discretion to reject all bids for a variety of reasons; that is to say, sealed bid solicitation does not per se limit agency's discretion. Arrowhead Metals, Ltd. v. U.S., 8 Cl. Ct. 703, 33 Cont. Cas. Fed. (CCH) P 74026 (1985). United States ☞64.50

United States Mint did not abandon its discretion to Congress in determining whether to cancel solicitation for bids in connection with contract for production of coins, but rather considered, in exercise of its own discretion, that public and congressional outcry raised issues worthy of investigation. Arrowhead Metals, Ltd. v. U.S., 8 Cl. Ct. 703, 33 Cont. Cas. Fed. (CCH) P 74026 (1985). United States ☞64.50

3 Costs of bid preparation

Claim for bid preparation costs depended on propriety of government cancellation of solicitation. Durable Metals Products, Inc. v. U.S., 27 Fed. Cl. 472, 38 Cont. Cas. Fed. (CCH) P 76471 (1993), judgment aff'd, 11 F.3d 1071 (Fed. Cir. 1993). United States ☞64.60(6)

Government's conduct in cancelling solicitation for bids is pertinent to bidder's claim for bid preparation costs. Vanguard Sec. Inc. v. U.S., 20 Cl. Ct. 90, 1990 WL 38036 (1990). United States ☜64.60(6)

Foreign contractor was not entitled to bid preparation costs after United States Mint had cancelled solicitation of bids, where cancellation decision had rational basis and where, at time solicitation was made, Mint had no knowledge, or reason to anticipate, that there would be any problems with solicitation. Arrowhead Metals, Ltd. v. U.S., 8 Cl. Ct. 703, 33 Cont. Cas. Fed. (CCH) P 74026 (1985). United States ☜64.60(6)

4 Reason for cancellation of invitations

Federal Energy Regulatory Commission (FERC) contracting officer did not have compelling reason for cancelling bid solicitation for stenographic services contract, making cancellation of contract abuse of discretion; reasons given for cancelling solicitation, including omission of clause requiring bid and performance bond, omission of organizational conflict of interest clause and omission of clause referring to potential loss of exhibits by stenographer, were inconsistent with reasons stated by FERC when initially cancelling the solicitation. Ace-Federal Reporters, Inc. v. F.E.R.C., 734 F. Supp. 20, 36 Cont. Cas. Fed. (CCH) P 75868 (D.D.C. 1990). United States ☜64.50

Social Security Administration's (SSA's) need to reassess whether some of work on computer contracts should be done in-house as well as its conclusion that it needed to revise scope of work, as articulated at time of cancellation, formed reasonable basis for cancelling request for proposals and was not arbitrary and capricious. Shields Enterprises, Inc. v. U.S., 28 Fed. Cl. 615, 38 Cont. Cas. Fed. (CCH) P 76526 (1993). United States ☜64.50

Government's principal motivation for cancellation of solicitation for bids for providing unarmed guard services, that solicitation did not allow Immigration and Naturalization Service to obtain additional services on immediate basis, lacked rational basis both in law and fact and could not be upheld as permissible exercise of agency's discretion. Vanguard Sec. Inc. v. U.S., 20 Cl. Ct. 90, 1990 WL 38036 (1990). United States ☜64.50

Government's decision to cancel solicitation for bids for providing unarmed guard services, based on perceived prejudice to bidders from ambiguity in contract as to whether bidders had to resubmit pricing information for additional hours, was without factual predicate, where no pricing sheet called for such information, and pricing sheet, which took precedence over instructions, specified that additional hours were to be compensated at unit price bid per hour. Vanguard Sec. Inc. v. U.S., 20 Cl. Ct. 90, 1990 WL 38036 (1990). United States ☜64.50

In determining whether Government reasonably cancelled solicitation for bids, Government would be allowed to advance post hoc justifications for cancellation. Vanguard Sec. Inc. v. U.S., 20 Cl. Ct. 90, 1990 WL 38036 (1990). United States ☜64.50

It is not the case that only decisions to cancel solicitation for bids based on changed requirements will be overridden due to agency's failure to make every effort timely to identify such changes. Vanguard Sec. Inc. v. U.S., 20 Cl. Ct. 90, 1990 WL 38036 (1990). United States ☜64.50

Procurement regulation, which required Government to make every effort to both anticipate changes in a requirement before bid opening and to notify bidders of resulting modification or cancellation so that bidders may change bids and so that Government may prevent unnecessary exposure of bid prices, was merely hortatory, and thus Government did not violate regulation when it cancelled solicitation for bids for providing unnamed guard services on basis that solicitation did not contain adequate personnel requirements, even though there was no evidence that procurement personnel made any effort to confirm that solicitation reflected actual, present, and prospective requirements for production guards. Vanguard Sec. Inc. v. U.S., 20 Cl. Ct. 90, 1990 WL 38036 (1990). United States ☜64.50

Government's failure to state needs adequately in solicitation for bids, such that significant modification to contract would be required if agency's needs were to be met during performance, is compelling reason to cancel solicitation. Vanguard Sec. Inc. v. U.S., 20 Cl. Ct. 90, 1990 WL 38036 (1990). United States ☜64.50

Government's understatement of guard post assignments in solicitation for bids for providing unarmed guard services was error which rendered solicitation defective, and thus Government reasonably and within its discretion deemed specifications inadequate and cancelled solicitation. Vanguard Sec. Inc. v. U.S., 20 Cl. Ct. 90, 1990 WL 38036 (1990). United States ☞64.50

Decision of Department of Treasury to cancel solicitation of bids for contract in connection with coin production was "compelling" as well as reasonable and rational, where critical reason was desire to review and weigh implications of contracting out coin blanking operations to private sector. Arrowhead Metals, Ltd. v. U.S., 8 Cl. Ct. 703, 33 Cont. Cas. Fed. (CCH) P 74026 (1985). United States ☞64.50

Decision of Department of Treasury to cancel solicitation of bids for contract relating to coin production was not without rational basis, given concern as to propriety and/or national interest factor of contracting out work that overseeing House subcommittee and others considered governmental function. Arrowhead Metals, Ltd. v. U.S., 8 Cl. Ct. 703, 33 Cont. Cas. Fed. (CCH) P 74026 (1985). United States ☞64.50

If party challenging cancellation of solicitation is unable to show that government officials involved in procurement process lacked rational or reasonable basis for their cancellation decision, party must present evidence of clear and prejudicial violation of applicable statute or regulations. Aviation Enterprises, Inc. v. U.S., 8 Cl. Ct. 1, 32 Cont. Cas. Fed. (CCH) P 73403 (1985). Public Contracts ☞5.1

Alleged violations of regulations requiring contracting officers to give reason for cancellation of solicitation and to assure prospective bidders of their opportunity to bid on any resolicitation of bids was insufficient to warrant any equitable or legal relief, where neither alleged violation denied dissatisfied bidder fair and full consideration of its proposal. Aviation Enterprises, Inc. v. U.S., 8 Cl. Ct. 1, 32 Cont. Cas. Fed. (CCH) P 73403 (1985). United States ☞64.50

Violation of regulation requiring that bidders be given reason for cancellation of solicitation was at most harmless error, where bidders were informed of reason for cancellation within reasonable time after first notification of cancellation. Aviation Enterprises, Inc. v. U.S., 8 Cl. Ct. 1, 32 Cont. Cas. Fed. (CCH) P 73403 (1985). United States ☞64.50

Contracting officer had both compelling reason to cancel solicitation, and cancellation was in public interest, thereby satisfying regulations governing cancellation of bids both before and after opening of bids, where it was necessary to rework specifications in order to include turbo-prop aircraft, and tenor and intent behind reasons justifying cancellation after opening encompassed overstated specifications in solicitation. Aviation Enterprises, Inc. v. U.S., 8 Cl. Ct. 1, 32 Cont. Cas. Fed. (CCH) P 73403 (1985). United States ☞64.50

In procurement terms "requirement" was synonymous with request for proposal and did not indicate that using facility need no longer existed at air force base; thus, notification of cancellation of solicitation in which it was noted there was no longer any requirement for aircraft was not inconsistent with official reason for cancellation that specifications were overstated. Aviation Enterprises, Inc. v. U.S., 8 Cl. Ct. 1, 32 Cont. Cas. Fed. (CCH) P 73403 (1985). United States ☞64.50

Defective specifications, mistaken contractual provisions and erroneous specifications, in appropriate cases, may be compelling reasons within discretion of contracting officer for rejection of all bids. Caddell Const. Co. v. U.S., 7 Cl. Ct. 236, 32 Cont. Cas. Fed. (CCH) P 73206 (1985). United States ☞64.50

In the circumstances, conclusion that unacceptably high prices were present because plaintiff's bid was 13.87 percent and only other bid was 16.7 percent over Government's estimate for construction of a submarine headquarters administration building was not unreasonable, and cancellation of the invitation for bids was appropriate. Caddell Const. Co. v. U.S., 7 Cl. Ct. 236, 32 Cont. Cas. Fed. (CCH) P 73206 (1985). United States ☞64.50

Protest challenging the agency's cancellation of an invitation for bids (IFB) is denied where the agency concerns regarding an ambiguity in the IFB regarding the price to be paid for mobilization and demobilization provided a compelling basis for cancellation. Great Lakes Dredge & Dock Co., LLC, B-407502.2, 2013 CPD ¶ 48 (Comp. Gen. 2013)

Cancellation of invitation for bids (IFB) prior to bid opening was in the public interest where agency failed to investigate whether procurement should be set aside for acquisition from National Institute for the Severely Handicapped or small business prior to issuing the IFB on an unrestricted basis. Diversified Management Group, A Joint Venture, B-288443.2, 2001 CPD ¶ 175 (Comp. Gen. 2001)

Agency properly canceled invitation for bids after bid opening where the solicitation specifications did not adequately set forth the agency's requirements, and prior to bid opening, the agency had provided only one of several offerors with informal clarifications regarding the actual requirements. Grot, Inc., B-276979, B-276979.2, B-277463, 97-2 CPD ¶ 50 (Comp. Gen. 1997)

5 Bad faith

Inference of bad faith of personnel of United States Mint in cancelling solicitation for bids to perform "blanking," annealing and upsetting processes could not be drawn from Mint's postbid opening cost analysis efforts. Arrowhead Metals, Ltd. v. U.S., 8 Cl. Ct. 703, 33 Cont. Cas. Fed. (CCH) P 74026 (1985). United States ☞64.50

Speculation that if foreign contractor were not low bidder on United States Treasury Department contract and American firm was low bidder, solicitation would not have been cancelled, did not support assertion of bad faith on part of Mint personnel in cancelling solicitation of bids. Arrowhead Metals, Ltd. v. U.S., 8 Cl. Ct. 703, 33 Cont. Cas. Fed. (CCH) P 74026 (1985). United States ☞64.50

Criteria for determining whether bid cancellation decisions lack rational basis include determination of existence of bad faith on part of defendant that deprive bidder of fair and honest consideration of its proposal; determination of whether reasonable basis for administrative decision exists; degree of proof needed for recovery is related to amount of discretion entrusted to procurement officials; and/or in some instances, proven violation of statute or regulation can be grounds for recovery. Arrowhead Metals, Ltd. v. U.S., 8 Cl. Ct. 703, 33 Cont. Cas. Fed. (CCH) P 74026 (1985). United States ☞64.50

Criteria used to evaluate whether Government lacked rational or reasonable basis for its decision or acted in arbitrary and capricious manner in cancelling solicitation of bids include: determination of existence of bad faith on part of Government which deprived bidder of fair and honest consideration of its proposal, and determination of whether reasonable basis for administrative decision exists; furthermore, degree of proof needed for recovery is related to amount of discretion entrusted to procurement officials, and in some instances, proven violation of statute or regulation can be grounds for recovery. Aviation Enterprises, Inc. v. U.S., 8 Cl. Ct. 1, 32 Cont. Cas. Fed. (CCH) P 73403 (1985). Public Contracts ☞5.1

6 Injunctions

For purpose of determining whether low bidder was entitled to enjoin Government's cancellation of solicitation for bids for providing unarmed guard services, language of schedule, which stated that prices bid for base hours carried over for additional requirements, prevailed over amended note on evaluation of bids and award criteria, which required that bidders must enter price for additional guard hours, where clause in solicitation stated that any inconsistency in solicitation shall be resolved by giving precedence to schedule. Vanguard Sec. Inc. v. U.S., 20 Cl. Ct. 90, 1990 WL 38036 (1990). United States ☞64.60(5.1)

For purpose of determining whether low bidder was entitled to enjoin Government's cancellation of solicitation for bids for providing unarmed guard services, amendment to solicitation providing that additional hours must be separately priced did not show that solicitation called for provision of additional services through options, as opposed to indefinite quantity requirement, where amendment did not also amend pricing sheet or otherwise advise bidders on how or in what manner they were to furnish additional information. Vanguard Sec. Inc. v. U.S., 20 Cl. Ct. 90, 1990 WL 38036 (1990). United States ☞64.60(5.1)

Low bidder showed irreparable damage if Government was not enjoined from cancelling solicitation for bids for providing unarmed guard services, where contractor could only recoup its bid preparation costs, and not its loss of anticipated profits, in suit for damages against Government. Vanguard Sec. Inc. v. U.S., 20 Cl. Ct. 90, 1990 WL 38036 (1990). United States ☞64.60(5.1)

Injunctive relief with respect to Government's cancellation of contract can be granted if contractor can establish clear and prejudicial violation of applicable procurement statute or regulation. 28 U.S.C.A. § 1491(a)(3). Vanguard Sec. Inc. v. U.S., 20 Cl. Ct. 90, 1990 WL 38036 (1990). United States ☞64.60(5.1)

For purpose of determining whether low bidder was entitled to enjoin Government's cancellation of solicitation for bids for providing unarmed guard services, insofar as amendment to solicitation attempted to convert indefinite quantity contract into fixed-price contract subject to options, amendment failed to displace contract provisions inherent in an indefinite contract. Vanguard Sec. Inc. v. U.S., 20 Cl. Ct. 90, 1990 WL 38036 (1990). United States ☞64.60(5.1)

For purpose of determining whether low bidder was entitled to enjoin Government's cancellation of solicitation for bids for providing unarmed guard services, solicitation's designation of contract as firm fixed-price contract was consistent with reaffirmation in same section that it was indefinite quantity contract, as meaning of contract was that prices for additional services, as well as for base and optional years, were firm fixed hourly rates. Vanguard Sec. Inc. v. U.S., 20 Cl. Ct. 90, 1990 WL 38036 (1990). United States ☞64.60(5.1)

For purpose of determining whether low bidder was entitled to enjoin Government's cancellation of solicitation for bids for providing unarmed guard services, even if solicitation could be characterized as unclear as to whether it was indefinite quantity contract or fixed-price contract subject to options, no bidder was confused about requirements of solicitation, as amended, that contract would be indefinite quantity contract. Vanguard Sec. Inc. v. U.S., 20 Cl. Ct. 90, 1990 WL 38036 (1990). United States ☞64.60(5.1)

Contractor which sought permanent injunction ordering United States to reinstate cancelled solicitation and to award contract to offerer with lowest price, that is, contractor, had very high burden of proof to surmount in establishing its entitlement to such relief; it had to establish by clear and convincing evidence that there was no rational basis for Treasury Department's cancellation of the solicitation. Arrowhead Metals, Ltd. v. U.S., 8 Cl. Ct. 703, 33 Cont. Cas. Fed. (CCH) P 74026 (1985). Injunction ☞128(7)

Air Force's decision to cancel solicitation based on specification, which overstated minimum needs of Air Force and restricted competition, was entirely reasonable, and therefore, dissatisfied bidder was not entitled to injunctive relief and bid preparation costs, where dissatisfied bidder failed to show that any of procuring officers had specific intent to injure bidder, bidder knew what reason for cancellation was and was able to challenge, air force procurement officials had high degree of discretion to cancel solicitations, and there were no regulatory violations which would render cancellation decision improper. Aviation Enterprises, Inc. v. U.S., 8 Cl. Ct. 1, 32 Cont. Cas. Fed. (CCH) P 73403 (1985). United States ☞64.50

Apparent low bidder of contract to construct submarine headquarters administration building was not entitled to a preliminary injunction prohibiting Government from proceeding with an award of a contract on a revised invitation for bids, in that there was a compelling reason for Government to cancel invitation for bids and revise project for resolicitation and, in instant procurement, preliminary injunction could only set aside invitation for bids and direct a new solicitation, which would not be in the public interest. Caddell Const. Co. v. U.S., 7 Cl. Ct. 236, 32 Cont. Cas. Fed. (CCH) P 73206 (1985). Injunction ☞138.63

7 Jurisdiction

Claims Court had jurisdiction to determine whether cancellation of invitation for bid for manufacture of propeller shaft assembly was proper, where plaintiff was seeking reinstatement of the cancelled solicitation, and no contract had been awarded. 28 U.S.C.A. § 1491(a)(3). National Forge Co. v. U.S., 779 F.2d 665, 33 Cont. Cas. Fed. (CCH) P 74149 (Fed. Cir. 1985). Federal Courts ☞1080

Allegation that contracting officer had orally promised to award contract to bidder, even though bidder was not lowest or next lowest bidder in sealed bidding procurement, was insufficient to establish implied in fact contract with United States, as required to establish Court of Federal Claims' jurisdiction over bidder's claim that this promise was breached, in that officer lacked authority to bind government in manner alleged. Domagala v. U.S., 30 Fed. Cl. 149, 39 Cont. Cas. Fed. (CCH) P 76600 (1993), aff'd, 39 F.3d 1196 (Fed. Cir. 1994). Federal Courts ☞1077; United States ☞69(2)

For purpose of determining whether low bidder would be granted injunctive relief with respect to Government's cancellation of solicitation for bids for providing unarmed guard services, injunction would not be in public interest, where immediate modification of contract would be necessary with respect to the number of guards to be provided by contractor, and other bidders had been denied opportunity to show whether they could provide lowest overall price to Government for larger quantity of guards. Vanguard Sec. Inc. v. U.S., 20 Cl. Ct. 90, 1990 WL 38036 (1990). United States ☞64.60(5.1)

For purpose of determining whether low bidder would be granted injunctive relief with respect to Government's cancellation of solicitation for bids for providing unarmed guard services, permanent injunction would have greater harm on Government and other bidders, where immediate modification to contract would be necessary to provide for further guards. Vanguard Sec. Inc. v. U.S., 20 Cl. Ct. 90, 1990 WL 38036 (1990). United States ☞64.60(5.1)

Jurisdiction of United States Claims Court to grant equitable relief in cases involving government contracts prior to award of the contracts includes claims questioning propriety of bid cancellations. 28 U.S.C.A. § 1491(a)(3). Arrowhead Metals, Ltd. v. U.S., 8 Cl. Ct. 703, 33 Cont. Cas. Fed. (CCH) P 74026 (1985). Federal Courts ☞1080

Where bidder contended that cancellation of solicitation of proposal from small businesses to supply the four aircraft, on lease basis, for use by United States Air Force, to which bidder and others had submitted bids, deprived bidder, and perhaps others, of fair and full consideration of their bids, Claims Court had equitable jurisdiction to review propriety of cancellation, despite fact that claim was filed with court after solicitation was cancelled. Aviation Enterprises, Inc. v. U.S., 8 Cl. Ct. 1, 32 Cont. Cas. Fed. (CCH) P 73403 (1985). Federal Courts ☞1076

Following proper cancellation of request for proposal there was no existing solicitation or bids responsive thereto which could form basis for implied-in-fact contract necessary to confer injunctive authority jurisdiction on Claims Court; thus, Claims Court lacked equitable jurisdiction to order resolicitation. Aviation Enterprises, Inc. v. U.S., 8 Cl. Ct. 1, 32 Cont. Cas. Fed. (CCH) P 73403 (1985). Federal Courts ☞1077

By complying with terms of agency solicitation bidder is entitled to have its bid fully and fairly considered by the agency and a claim that the agency improperly canceled the solicitation after bid was submitted falls squarely within jurisdiction of the Claims Court. National Forge Co. v. U.S., 7 Cl. Ct. 530, 32 Cont. Cas. Fed. (CCH) P 73355 (1985). Federal Courts ☞1076; United States ☞64.60(1)

Claims court has jurisdiction to entertain preaward actions initiated after cancellation of bid solicitation. 28 U.S.C.A. § 1491(a), (a)(3). Caddell Const. Co. v. U.S., 7 Cl. Ct. 236, 32 Cont. Cas. Fed. (CCH) P 73206 (1985). Federal Courts ☞1076

8 Presumptions and burden of proof

Foreign contractor failed to meet heavy burden required to overcome presumption of good faith on part of personnel of United States Mint in performing their official duties in cancelling bid solicitation; cancellation occurred due to concern over whether it was consistent with Mint's responsibilities for it to contract out "blanking" to private sector, director of Mint stated that Mint was fully prepared at time to award contract to lowest responsible bidder, whether foreign or domestic, and contractor remained eligible to bid on Mint procurements for "strip." Arrowhead Metals, Ltd. v. U.S., 8 Cl. Ct. 703, 33 Cont. Cas. Fed. (CCH) P 74026 (1985). United States ☞64.50

In establishing that cancellation of solicitation for bids was improper, party challenging cancellation has burden of showing that government officials involved in procurement process lacked rational or reasonable basis for their cancellation decision. Aviation Enterprises, Inc. v. U.S., 8 Cl. Ct. 1, 32 Cont. Cas. Fed. (CCH) P 73403 (1985). Public Contracts ☞5.1

To overcome presumption that government officials acted properly in procuring bids or cancelling solicitations law requires well-nigh irrefragable proof. Aviation Enterprises, Inc. v. U.S., 8 Cl. Ct. 1, 32 Cont. Cas. Fed. (CCH) P 73403 (1985). United States ☞64.25; United States ☞64.50

9 Attorneys fees

Agency's decision to cancel solicitation was not substantially justified, so as to preclude an award of attorney fees under the Equal Access to Justice Act (EAJA), where agency canceled solicitation in reliance on determination of the General Accounting Office (GAO) that one bid was untimely, as untimeliness of one bid did not provide a rational basis for canceling the solicitation. 28 U.S.C.A. § 2412(d). California Marine Cleaning, Inc. v. U.S.,

43 Fed. Cl. 724 (1999). United States ⊶147(12)

10 Judicial review

Claims Court correctly restricted its legal review to whether contracting officer's interpretation of, and later decision to cancel, solicitation of bids for manufacture of propeller shaft assembly was unreasonable or an abuse of discretion under requirements for cancellation set forth in Federal Acquisition Regulations System. National Forge Co. v. U.S., 779 F.2d 665, 33 Cont. Cas. Fed. (CCH) P 74149 (Fed. Cir. 1985). Federal Courts ⊶1118

After it was determined that Federal Energy Regulatory Commission (FERC) did not have rational basis to cancel bid solicitation for stenographic services contract, remand to FERC was required to determine which contractor provided most advantageous bid, although one contractor had submitted bonus bid that was responsive to solicitation. Ace-Federal Reporters, Inc. v. F.E.R.C., 734 F. Supp. 20, 36 Cont. Cas. Fed. (CCH) P 75868 (D.D.C. 1990). United States ⊶64.60(5.1)

Restrictions in Federal Acquisition Regulations regarding cancellation of solicitation limited only General Services Administration's power, so that while General Services Administration must have compelling reason to take such action, federal court's scope of review was governed by Administrative Procedure Act and under Act federal court had much broader authority to direct General Services Administration to resolicit bids for contracts. Federal Property and Administrative Services Act of 1949, § 301 et seq., as amended, 41 U.S.C.A. § 251 et seq.; 5 U.S.C.A. § 706(2). Abel Converting, Inc. v. U.S., 679 F. Supp. 1133, 34 Cont. Cas. Fed. (CCH) P 75449 (D.D.C. 1988). Administrative Law And Procedure ⊶751; United States ⊶64.60(3.1)

Upon contractor's complaint that regulation was violated by Government when cancelling solicitation for bids, Claims Court is to examine both whether agency determination to cancel is reasonable or abuse of discretion under applicable procurement regulation, and whether Government's conduct violated procedure set forth by cancellation regulation. 28 U.S.C.A. § 1491(a)(3). Vanguard Sec. Inc. v. U.S., 20 Cl. Ct. 90, 1990 WL 38036 (1990). United States ⊶64.50

In determining whether Government's motivation for cancellation of solicitation for bids lacked rational basis, whether officials may have considered incomplete documentation or no documentation at all when recommending cancellation was irrelevant if cancellation determination by commissioner and contracting officer accreted a reasonable basis. Vanguard Sec. Inc. v. U.S., 20 Cl. Ct. 90, 1990 WL 38036 (1990). United States ⊶64.50

Court asked to determine whether Government acted in bad faith in cancelling request for proposals cannot base finding of bad faith solely on speculation and innuendo. Aviation Enterprises, Inc. v. U.S., 8 Cl. Ct. 1, 32 Cont. Cas. Fed. (CCH) P 73403 (1985). United States ⊶64.50

§ 14.210 Qualified products.

(See Subpart 9.2.)

United States Code Annotated

Contract requirements, see 41 USCA § 254.

Contracts, planning, solicitation, evaluation, and award procedures, see 10 USCA § 2305.

Definitions, see 10 USCA § 2302, 41 USCA §§ 259, 403.

Evaluation and award, see 41 USCA § 253b.

Kinds of contracts, see 10 USCA § 2306.

Planning and solicitation requirements, see 41 USCA § 253a.

§ 14.211 Release of acquisition information.

(a) *Before solicitation.* Information concerning proposed acquisitions shall not be released outside the Government before solicitation except for presolicitation notices in accordance with 14.205 or 36.213-2, or long-range acquisition estimates in accordance with 5.404, or synopses in accordance with 5.201. Within the Government, such information shall be restricted to those having a legitimate interest. Releases of information shall be made (1) to all prospective bidders, and as nearly as possible at the same time, so that one prospective bidder shall not be given unfair advantage over another. See 3.104 regarding requirements for proprietary and source selection information including access to and disclosure thereof.

(b) *After solicitation.* Discussions with prospective bidders regarding a solicitation shall be conducted and technical or other information shall be transmitted only by the contracting officer or superiors having contractual authority or by others specifically authorized. Such personnel shall not furnish any information to a prospective bidder that alone or together with other information may afford an advantage over others. However, general information that would not be prejudicial to other prospective bidders may be furnished upon request; *e.g.,* explanation of a particular contract clause or a particular condition of the schedule in the invitation for bids, and more specific information or clarifications may be furnished by amending the solicitation (see 14.208).

United States Code Annotated
Contract requirements, see 41 USCA § 254.

Contracts, planning, solicitation, evaluation, and award procedures, see 10 USCA § 2305.

Definitions, see 10 USCA § 2302, 41 USCA §§ 259, 403.

Evaluation and award, see 41 USCA § 253b.

Kinds of contracts, see 10 USCA § 2306.

Planning and solicitation requirements, see 41 USCA § 253a.

§ 14.212 Economic purchase quantities (supplies).
Contracting officers shall comply with the economic purchase quantity planning requirements for supplies in Subpart 7.2. See 7.203 for instructions regarding use of the provision at 52.207-4, Economic Purchase Quantity—Supplies, and 7.204 for guidance on handling responses to that provision.

United States Code Annotated
Contract requirements, see 41 USCA § 254.

Contracts, planning, solicitation, evaluation, and award procedures, see 10 USCA § 2305.

Definitions, see 10 USCA § 2302, 41 USCA §§ 259, 403.

Evaluation and award, see 41 USCA § 253b.

Kinds of contracts, see 10 USCA § 2306.

Planning and solicitation requirements, see 41 USCA § 253a.

Subpart 14.3 Submission of Bids

§ 14.301 Responsiveness of bids.
(a) To be considered for award, a bid must comply in all material respects with the invitation for bids. Such compliance enables bidders to stand on an equal footing and maintain the integrity of the sealed bidding system.

(b) Telegraphic bids shall not be considered unless permitted by the invitation. The term "telegraphic bids" means bids submitted by telegram or by mailgram.

(c) Facsimile bids shall not be considered unless permitted by the solicitation (see 14.202-7).

(d) Bids should be filled out, executed, and submitted in accordance with the instructions in the invitation. If a bidder uses its own bid form or a letter to submit a bid, the bid may be considered only if—

(1) The bidder accepts all the terms and conditions of the invitation; and

(2) Award on the bid would result in a binding contract with terms and conditions that do not vary from the terms and conditions of the invitation.

(e) Bids submitted by electronic commerce shall be considered only if the electronic commerce method was specifically stipulated or permitted by the solicitation.

United States Code Annotated
Contract requirements, see 41 USCA § 254.

Contracts, planning, solicitation, evaluation, and award procedures, see 10 USCA § 2305.

Definitions, see 10 USCA § 2302, 41 USCA §§ 259, 403.

Evaluation and award, see 41 USCA § 253b.

Kinds of contracts, see 10 USCA § 2306.

Planning and solicitation requirements, see 41 USCA § 253a.

Notes of Decisions

Amendment of bid 4
Construction and application 8
Discretion of agency 2
Jurisdiction 7
Minor informalities or irregularities 5
Powers of attorney 6
Requirements of invitation 3
Responsibility distinguished 9
Responsiveness of bids, generally 1

1 Responsiveness of bids, generally

Contractor who was awarded contract despite fact that its bid was nonconforming could not subsequently assert claim that government violated procurement regulation by accepting its nonconforming bid, as regulation was designed to protect losing bidders in a bid contest, not the contractor that won the bid. Armour of America v. U.S., 69 Fed. Cl. 587 (2006)

FAR 14.404-2(d) states that a bid "shall be rejected when the bidder imposes conditions that would modify requirements of the invitation." Where an IFB requires that bidders use products on the Qualified Products List (QPL) and a bidder listed products not listed on the QPL, the agency was correct in finding the bid to be non-responsive. The Court finds that the bidder did not comply in all material respects with the IFB and modified the requirements by not bidding a qualified product. Therefore, the contracting officer correctly rejected the bid. Fire-Trol Holdings, LLC. v. U.S., 68 Fed. Cl. 281 (2005), aff'd, 205 Fed. Appx. 834 (Fed. Cir. 2006)

Offer in response to solicitation by the Department of Veterans Affairs (VA) for distribution of pharmaceutical products in 14 VA regions was an "all or none offer" within meaning of the Federal Acquisition Regulation (FAR), notwithstanding that offer recognized that the VA maintained the right to set aside three regions for small business concerns, where proposal limited acceptance to "all regions" contained in the offer. 48 C.F.R. § 14.404-5. AmerisourceBergen Drug Corp. v. U.S., 60 Fed. Cl. 30 (2004). United States ☞64.30

It was rational for contracting officer (CO) to reject bid bond as non-responsive because it was accompanied by a photocopied rather than original power of attorney, and absence of original power of attorney failed to provide sufficient authority to bind surety. 48 C.F.R. § 14.404-2(j). All Seasons Const., Inc. v. U.S., 55 Fed. Cl. 175 (2003). United States ☞64.35

Government's determination as to whether a bid is responsive must be based solely upon the bid documents as they appear at the time of the opening. 48 C.F.R. § 14.301(a). Interstate Rock Products, Inc. v. U.S., 50 Fed. Cl. 349 (2001), aff'd, 48 Fed. Appx. 331 (Fed. Cir. 2002). United States ☞64.30

Bid package was nonresponsive to invitation for bids; bond commitment and period of bid validity were entirely omitted from package, and such missing terms could not be incorporated by reference through amendment to invitation since bidder submitted only first page of that amendment, which did not contain omitted material terms. Firth Const. Co., Inc. v. U.S., 36 Fed. Cl. 268, 41 Cont. Cas. Fed. (CCH) P 76970 (1996). United States ☞64.30

In typical government contract case, solicitation and related regulations require contracting officer to make separate determinations on issue of bid's "responsiveness" to terms of solicitation and "responsibility" of bidder to perform contract work covered in solicitation prior to awarding contract to apparent low bidder. VMS Hotel Partners v. U.S., 30 Fed. Cl. 512, 39 Cont. Cas. Fed. (CCH) P 76631 (1994). United States ☞64.30; United States ☞64.45(2)

Unlike determining "responsiveness" of bid, in assessing contractor's "responsibility," contracting officer is not limited to information contained in bid when opened; rather, contracting officer may solicit and contractor may supply additional information to demonstrate that contractor is capable of performing contract work. VMS Hotel Partners v. U.S., 30 Fed. Cl. 512, 39 Cont. Cas. Fed. (CCH) P 76631 (1994). United States ☞64.45(2)

Apparent low bidder's designation of place of performance in bid to provide meals, lodging, and transportation for members of armed services raised exclusively issue of whether bidder was responsible to perform contract work covered in solicitation, rather than responsiveness of bid, and therefore contracting officer properly allowed bidder to change its place of performance after opening bids but before awarding contract. VMS Hotel Partners v. U.S., 30 Fed. Cl. 512, 39 Cont. Cas. Fed. (CCH) P 76631 (1994). United States ☞64.40(4)

"Responsive bid" to solicitation issued by Government is one that, if accepted by Government as submitted, will obligate contractor to perform exact thing called for in solicitation. Bean Dredging Corp. v. U.S., 22 Cl. Ct. 519, 36 Cont. Cas. Fed. (CCH) P 76017, 1991 WL 15601 (1991). United States ☞64.30

A bid that limits the bidder's liability to obtain permits and pay fees, which are responsibilities assigned the bidder under an invitation for bids (IFB) for a construction project, materially modifies the terms of the IFB and must be rejected as nonresponsive. Bishop Contractors, Inc., B-246526, 91-2 CPD ¶ 555 (Comp. Gen. 1991)

Bidder's failure to submit properly and completely executed certification regarding debarment, suspension, proposed debarment and other responsibility matters with bid at bid opening does not affect firm's material obligations under solicitation and therefore does not render bid nonresponsive. Intermountain Electric, Inc., B-236953, B-236953.2, 90-1 CPD ¶ 143 (Comp. Gen. 1990)

Protest alleging that bid was nonresponsive because it did not contain required information concerning whether bidder entered into a third party indemnification agreement in order to obtain bonds required by solicitation is denied. The information does not relate to the bidder's obligation to perform in accordance with the material terms and conditions of the solicitation, and therefore can be furnished any time before award. EDT Construction, Inc., and Northwest Paving & Construction Company, Inc., a joint venture, B-240343, 90-2 CPD ¶ 374 (Comp. Gen. 1990)

Failure of bidder to complete representation in its bid regarding its corporate status for taxpayer identification purposes has no bearing on the material aspects of the bid and thus does not render the bid nonresponsive. Watson Agency, Inc., B-241072, 90-2 CPD ¶ 506 (Comp. Gen. 1990)

Bid which attempts to limit government's rights and supplement bidder's rights under the termination for convenience clause in an invitation for bids (IFB) is nonresponsive since it contains a material deviation from the terms of the IFB. Gelco Payment Systems, Inc., B-234957, 89-2 CPD ¶ 27 (Comp. Gen. 1989)

2 Discretion of agency

Determination of whether a defect in a bid is material is committed to agency discretion. 48 C.F.R. §§ 14.301, 14.405. Tel-Instrument Electronics Corp. v. U.S., 56 Fed. Cl. 174 (2003), aff'd, 87 Fed. Appx. 752 (Fed. Cir. 2004). United States ☞64.30

A bid in which line item prices were omitted was properly rejected by the agency as nonresponsive where the line item prices were essential requirements of the IFB on which payments would be calculated. Matter of: Allbrite Office Cleaning, Inc., B-257188, 94-1 CPD ¶ 363 (Comp. Gen. 1994)

A bidder may not be afforded an opportunity after bid opening to explain or clarify its bid so as to make it responsive, since the bidder's intention must be determined from the bid and material available at bid opening. H.M. Kern Corporation, B-239821, 90-1 CPD ¶ 586 (Comp. Gen. 1990)

A nonresponsive bid must be rejected and may not be changed or corrected based on explanations offered by the bidder after bid opening; the importance of maintaining the integrity of the competitive bidding system outweighs the possibility that the government might realize monetary savings if a material deficiency in a bid is corrected or waived. AAA

Roofing Company Inc., B-240852, 90-2 CPD ¶ 485 (Comp. Gen. 1990)

3 Requirements of invitation

Bidder's failure to complete Buy American Certificate or check foreign source certificate in connection with its bid for contract from Washington Metropolitan Area Transit Authority (WMATA) rendered bid unresponsive; had bidder checked second option of foreign source certificate, either before or after opening of bids, WMATA would have been required by regulations to increase plaintiff's bid price by 10%, and allowing contractor to make choice after bids were submitted would thus have permitted material alteration of bid by allowing postbidding manipulation based on bids of other competitors. Buy American Act, §§ 1–3, 41 U.S.C.A. §§ 10c, 10a, 10b. Seal and Co., Inc. v. Washington Metropolitan Area Transit Authority, 768 F. Supp. 1150 (E.D. Va. 1991). Urban Railroads ⟶8

Bidder's failure to submit a properly executed bid guarantee by omitting penal sum on bid bond rendered its bid nonresponsive, and contracting agency was not permitted to consider bidder's explanation that omission of penal sum was a clerical error; moreover, bidder was not entitled to alter its bid with additional documents to correct the error following bid opening. 48 C.F.R. §§ 14.301(a), 14.404-2. Interstate Rock Products, Inc. v. U.S., 50 Fed. Cl. 349 (2001), aff'd, 48 Fed. Appx. 331 (Fed. Cir. 2002). United States ⟶64.30

Rationale for bid responsiveness requirement is to avoid unfairness to other contractors who submitted a sealed bid on the understanding that they must comply with all of the specifications and conditions in the invitation for bids, and who could have made a better proposal if they imposed conditions upon or variances from the contractual terms the government had specified. 10 U.S.C.A. § 2305(b)(3); Federal Property and Administrative Services Act of 1949, § 303B(c), 41 U.S.C.A. § 253b(c); 48 C.F.R. § 14.301. Ryan Co. v. U.S., 43 Fed. Cl. 646 (1999). United States ⟶64.30

In determining bid responsiveness, the contracting officer juxtaposes the bid against the invitation for bids to determine whether the former conforms in all material respects to the latter. 10 U.S.C.A. § 2305(b)(3); Federal Property and Administrative Services Act of 1949, § 303B(c), 41 U.S.C.A. § 253b(c); 48 C.F.R. § 14.301. Ryan Co. v. U.S., 43 Fed. Cl. 646 (1999). United States ⟶64.30

Request in invitation for bids (IFB) for submission of "catalog cuts" on major equipment for high voltage electrical power system was a matter of bid responsiveness, rather than bid responsibility, and bidder's failure to submit such descriptive information rendered its bid nonresponsive, where IFB informed bidders that such information would be used for bid evaluation, and that failure to furnish it would require rejection of the bid. 48 C.F.R. § 52.214-21. Ryan Co. v. U.S., 43 Fed. Cl. 646 (1999). United States ⟶64.30

To be deemed responsive, bid as submitted must obligate bidder to perform exactly what is being called for in solicitation. 48 C.F.R. §§ 14.301(a), 14.404-2(a). ECDC Environmental, L.C. v. U.S., 40 Fed. Cl. 236, 42 Cont. Cas. Fed. (CCH) P 77250 (1998). United States ⟶64.30

Regulation requiring that contract with joint venture be signed by each participant in joint venture did not become part of bid by implication under regulation requiring bid to be considered only if award on bid would result in binding contract with terms and conditions that did not vary from terms and conditions of invitation; bidders could not be held subject to unpublicized requirement. 48 C.F.R. §§ 4.102(d), 14.301(d). PCI/RCI v. U. S., 36 Fed. Cl. 761, 41 Cont. Cas. Fed. (CCH) P 77015 (1996). United States ⟶64.30

Bidder's exception to bid in business questionnaire rendered bid nonresponsive to invitation for bid, notwithstanding claim that questionnaire was not contract document but merely informative in nature; material submitted with bid which takes exception to IFB requirement renders bid nonresponsive. Blount, Inc. v. U.S., 22 Cl. Ct. 221, 36 Cont. Cas. Fed. (CCH) P 75981, 1990 WL 210734 (1990). United States ⟶64.30

4 Amendment of bid

Contracting officer's interpretation of solicitation to enable apparent low bidder to change place of performance would not have enabled apparent low bidder to terminate its bid, penalty free, by not finding suitable facility for performance and, therefore, did not impermissibly give apparent low bidder "two bites at the apple," whereby it could have waited to determine whether it would affirm or withdraw its bid after it became award of its competitor's bids. VMS Hotel Partners v. U.S., 30 Fed. Cl. 512, 39 Cont. Cas. Fed. (CCH) P 76631 (1994). United States ☞64.40(4)

Were contracting officer to award contract to bidder who had submitted nonresponsive bid after permitting bidder to change its response, award would be void ab initio. Blount, Inc. v. U.S., 22 Cl. Ct. 221, 36 Cont. Cas. Fed. (CCH) P 75981, 1990 WL 210734 (1990). United States ☞64.30

5 Minor informalities or irregularities

Bidder's submission of noncertified corporate check, rather than certified check as required by invitation of bids on public housing project, constituted material noncompliance with bidding process that warranted bidder's rejection. Professional Bldg. Concepts, Inc. v. City of Cent. Falls, 974 F.2d 1, 38 Cont. Cas. Fed. (CCH) P 76395 (1st Cir. 1992). United States ☞64.30; United States ☞82(3.3)

Determination of whether a defect in a bid is material is committed to agency discretion. 48 C.F.R. §§ 14.301, 14.405. Tel-Instrument Electronics Corp. v. U.S., 56 Fed. Cl. 174 (2003), aff'd, 87 Fed. Appx. 752 (Fed. Cir. 2004). United States ☞64.30

If a bidder on a government contract attempts to impose conditions that would modify material requirements of the solicitation, the bid is not responsive and must be rejected; "material requirements" include those affecting price, quantity, quality, or delivery of the solicited products, and thus are not minor informalities or irregularities. 48 C.F.R. § 14.405. Tel-Instrument Electronics Corp. v. U.S., 56 Fed. Cl. 174 (2003), aff'd, 87 Fed. Appx. 752 (Fed. Cir. 2004). United States ☞64.30

When a bid fails to conform with the invitation for bids, it will be rejected if it is nonconforming in a material respect; it follows that when a bid's only defect is an immaterial nonconformity, it is responsive. 48 C.F.R. § 14.301(a). Interstate Rock Products, Inc. v. U.S., 50 Fed. Cl. 349 (2001), aff'd, 48 Fed. Appx. 331 (Fed. Cir. 2002). United States ☞64.30

To be deemed responsive, bid as submitted must obligate bidder to perform exactly what is being called for in solicitation. 48 C.F.R. §§ 14.301(a), 14.404-2(a). ECDC Environmental, L.C. v. U.S., 40 Fed. Cl. 236, 42 Cont. Cas. Fed. (CCH) P 77250 (1998). United States ☞64.30

While a contract is to be awarded only to a bidder who fully responds to the federal government invitation for bids, where defect or omission in nonresponsive bid is trivial or a matter of a mere formality, law does not require that entire bid be rejected; rather, bidder may be given an opportunity to cure defect or government may waive those terms to which bid does not respond. Grade-Way Const. v. U.S., 7 Cl. Ct. 263, 32 Cont. Cas. Fed. (CCH) P 73209 (1985). United States ☞64.30

Protester's bid was responsive despite a discrepancy in the names of the bidder and the bid bond principal, where the record shows that the bidder and bid bond principal are the same entity so that it is certain that the surety would be liable to the government in the event that the bidder withdrew its bid or failed to execute a written contract or to furnish required performance and payment bonds. Matter of: Hostetter, Keach & Cassada Construction, LLC, B-403329, 2010 CPD ¶ 246 (Comp. Gen. 2010)

6 Powers of attorney

Contracting officer (CO) was not reasonable in rejecting computer-generated powers of attorney appointing officer to execute bid bonds and accompanying certificates on ground that mechanical signatures were applied after powers of attorney were generated. 48 C.F.R. § 52.228-1. Hawaiian Dredging Const. Co., Inc. v. U.S., 59 Fed. Cl. 305 (2004). United States ☞64.35

Powers of attorney appointing officer to execute bid bonds which contained mechanically applied signatures, as opposed to original, or wet, signatures, were adequate to establish unequivocally that surety intended to be bound, where powers of attorney were submitted with certificates restating board resolutions by which surety bound itself to facsimile signatures on a power of attorney or any certificate relating to the power of attorney, appointment was facially valid, and original corporate seal was affixed to the documents. 48 C.F.R. § 52.228-1. Hawaiian Dredging Const. Co., Inc. v. U.S., 59 Fed. Cl. 305 (2004). United States ☞64.35

7 Jurisdiction

Claims Court had jurisdiction over rejected bidder's challenge to validity of "responsive regulation" stating that failure of bidder to submit signed certificate with bid rendered it nonresponsive. 28 U.S.C.A. § 1491(a). McMaster Const., Inc. v. U.S., 23 Cl. Ct. 679, 37 Cont. Cas. Fed. (CCH) P 76150, 1991 WL 149281 (1991). United States ⊸64.60(1)

8 Construction and application

Contractor who was awarded contract despite fact that its bid was nonconforming could not subsequently assert claim that government violated procurement regulation by accepting its nonconforming bid, as regulation was designed to protect losing bidders in a bid contest, not the contractor that won the bid. Armour of America v. U.S., 69 Fed. Cl. 587 (2006). United States ⊸64.60(2)

9 Responsibility distinguished

In typical government contract case, solicitation and related regulations require contracting officer to make separate determinations on issue of bid's "responsiveness" to terms of solicitation and "responsibility" of bidder to perform contract work covered in solicitation prior to awarding contract to apparent low bidder. VMS Hotel Partners v. U.S., 30 Fed. Cl. 512, 39 Cont. Cas. Fed. (CCH) P 76631 (1994). United States ⊸64.30; United States ⊸64.45(2)

In identifying whether particular requirement is related to responsiveness or to responsibility, responsibility concerns question of bidder's performance capability and responsiveness concerns promise to perform contract. Bean Dredging Corp. v. U.S., 22 Cl. Ct. 519, 36 Cont. Cas. Fed. (CCH) P 76017, 1991 WL 15601 (1991). Public Contracts ⊸8; Public Contracts ⊸11

Government contractor was not entitled to injunction preventing award of contract to competing bidder, despite claim that competitor's bid was nonresponsive as result of failure to include schedule listing equipment to be used on project; listing of equipment on plant and equipment schedule related to responsibility and not to responsiveness. Bean Dredging Corp. v. U.S., 22 Cl. Ct. 519, 36 Cont. Cas. Fed. (CCH) P 76017, 1991 WL 15601 (1991). Injunction ⊸86

In government contract bid matter, preaward injunctive relief is extreme remedy which must be exercised with caution. Blount, Inc. v. U.S., 22 Cl. Ct. 221, 36 Cont. Cas. Fed. (CCH) P 75981, 1990 WL 210734 (1990). Injunction ⊸86

Fact that contracting officer requested clarification of bidder's response to business management questionnaire question in which bidder indicated that it intended to self-perform only 10% of contract work, while invitation for bid required self-performance of 20%, could not convert issue of nonresponsiveness of bid into issue of responsibility; procuring agency's authority to permit correction of bid mistakes is limited to bids that are responsive to solicitation. Blount, Inc. v. U.S., 22 Cl. Ct. 221, 36 Cont. Cas. Fed. (CCH) P 75981, 1990 WL 210734 (1990). United States ⊸64.30

Protest that awardee in fixed-price sealed bid acquisition submitted unrealistically low prices is dismissed, since question of whether a firm's pricing is too low does not involve the responsiveness of the firm's bid, but rather the firm's responsibility; agency, in making award, made an affirmative determination of responsibility, which is not for consideration under our Bid Protest Regulations except in circumstances not alleged by protester. AllWorld Language Consultants, Inc., B-298831, 2006 CPD ¶ 198 (Comp. Gen. 2006)

§ **14.302 Bid submission.**

(a) Bids shall be submitted so that they will be received in the office designated in the invitation for bids (referred to in paragraphs (b) and (c) of this section as the "designated office") not later than the exact time set for opening of bids.

(b) Except as specified in paragraph (c) of this section, if telegraphic bids are authorized, a telegraphic bid that is communicated by means of a telephone call to the designated office shall be considered if—

(1) Agency regulations authorize such consideration;

(2) The telephone call is made by the telegraph office that received the telegraphic bid;

(3) The telephone call is received by the designated office not later than the time set for the bid opening;

(4) The telegraph office that received the telegraphic bid sends the designated office the telegram that formed the basis for the telephone call;

(5) The telegram indicates on its face that it was received in the telegraph office before the telephone call was received by the designated office; and

(6) The bid in the telegram is identical in all essential respects to the bid received in the telephone call from the telegraph office.

(c) If the conditions in paragraph (b) of this section apply and the bid received by telephone is the apparent low bid, award may not be made until the telegram is received by the designated office; however, if the telegram is not received by the designated office within 5 days after the bid opening date, the bid shall be rejected.

United States Code Annotated

Contract requirements, see 41 USCA § 254.

Contracts, planning, solicitation, evaluation, and award procedures, see 10 USCA § 2305.

Definitions, see 10 USCA § 2302, 41 USCA §§ 259, 403.

Evaluation and award, see 41 USCA § 253b.

Kinds of contracts, see 10 USCA § 2306.

Planning and solicitation requirements, see 41 USCA § 253a.

Notes of Decisions

Timeliness 1

1 Timeliness

Term "local time" in solicitation provision setting forth deadline for electronic transmission of offer referred to the time in Naples, Italy, which was the location of government office designated in the solicitation, and not to United States Eastern Standard Time as contended by bid protestor based on language on contracting agency's web site. Conscoop-Consorzia Fra Coop. Di Prod. E Lavoro v. U.S., 62 Fed. Cl. 219 (2004), aff'd, 159 Fed. Appx. 184 (Fed. Cir. 2005)

Generally, only bids that are timely received by the procuring agency may be considered for award; to be considered timely, a bid must be delivered to the place specified in an invitation for bids (IFB) on or before the time and date specified in the IFB. 48 C.F.R. §§ 14. 301(a), 14.302(a). California Marine Cleaning, Inc. v. U.S., 42 Fed. Cl. 281, 42 Cont. Cas. Fed. (CCH) P 77398 (1998). United States ☞64.30

Bid protester bears the burden of proving by a preponderance of the evidence that its bid was timely submitted. California Marine Cleaning, Inc. v. U.S., 42 Fed. Cl. 281, 42 Cont. Cas. Fed. (CCH) P 77398 (1998). United States ☞64.55(2)

Fact that agency placed bid box in reception area and allowed bidders to date stamp their own bids did not afford a compelling reason for canceling and resoliciting the procurement; although agency's practice created difficulties in resolving timeliness of one bid, it did not call into question the entire solicitation or breach the integrity of the bidding system. 48 C.F.R. § 14.404-1(a)(1). California Marine Cleaning, Inc. v. U.S., 42 Fed. Cl. 281, 42 Cont. Cas. Fed. (CCH) P 77398 (1998). United States ☞64.50

Statement of requirements for second phase of concessions contract clearly required that applicants submit its best presentation of requested information at time application was sent to National Park Service (NPS) and, thus, applicant was not entitled to more time to submit information confirming commitments to satisfy $12 million capital equity requirement. YRT Services Corp. v. U.S., 28 Fed. Cl. 366, 38 Cont. Cas. Fed. (CCH) P 76512 (1993). United States ☞64.30

General Accounting Office's (GAO's) determination in bid protest case, that contractor's bid was submitted simultaneously with bid opening officer's announcement that time for receipt of bids had passed, had rational basis, precluding unsuccessful bidder from enjoining award of Navy construction contract to successful bidder. 28 U.S.C.A. § 1491(a)(3); 31 U.S.C.A. §§ 3551–3556. Carothers Const. Inc. v. U.S., 18 Cl. Ct. 745, 35 Cont. Cas. Fed. (CCH) P 75758, 1989 WL 143515 (1989). United States ☞64.30

Agency reasonably accepted late bid where the paramount cause of the late receipt was affirmative misdirection by the agency and where consideration of the late bid did not compromise the integrity of the competitive procurement system. In this case, the IFB listed the wrong room for delivery of bids. This error, which was attributable solely to the government, directly resulted in contractor submitting its bid 1 minute late. Weeks Marine, Inc., B-292758, 2003 CPD ¶ 183 (Comp. Gen. 2003)

Under request for proposals that designated closing time for submission of proposals as 14:00 hours, agency reasonably declined to reject as late a proposal received after 14:00 but before the time 14:01 was displayed on the time/date stamp clock used by the agency for determining timeliness of proposal submissions. The Haskell Company, B-292756, 2003 CPD ¶ 202 (Comp. Gen. 2003)

Bid in an envelope marked "BID ENCLOSED," which was hand-carried by commercial carrier to the contracting agency's mailroom several hours before bid opening but was not received by the contracting office where the bid depository was located until after bid opening, was late and not properly accepted for award; rather than government mishandling being the primary or paramount cause of the lateness, the mailroom's routing of the bid to another office in the same building that also handles bids was attributable to the bidder's failure to mark its commercial carrier-provided envelope as required by FAR 52.214-5 when using a commercial carrier to deliver a bid. Boines Construction & Equipment Co., Inc., B-279575, 98-1 CPD ¶ 175 (Comp. Gen. 1998)

Protest of rejection of late bid is denied where, while the agency changed the bid opening room less than 1 hour before bid opening, the agency reasonably determined that the bidder's actions significantly contributed to the late receipt of the bid. Adirondack Construction Corporation, B-280015, B-280015.2, 98-2 CPD ¶ 55 (Comp. Gen. 1998)

Agency improperly considered a late bid under the government mishandling exception where the evidence of record does not establish that the bid was timely received and remained under the government's control until it was first discovered 6 days after bid opening. Pacific Tank Cleaning Services, Inc., B-279111, B-279111.2, 98-2 CPD ¶ 2 (Comp. Gen. 1998)

Protest that agency improperly rejected protester's bid as late is sustained where: (1) agency amended solicitation so close to the deadline for submitting bids that bid submission by facsimile was the only practicable alternative available to bidders; (2) facsimile machine designated in solicitation became inoperable for some indefinite period of time during the morning of the bid submission deadline; (3) protester transmitted its bid to an alternate facsimile machine based on advice from an agency employee other than the designated point of contact only after unsuccessfully attempting to telephone the designated contact; and (4) the protester's bid package arrived at the installation and was in the hands of agency officials by the deadline for submitting bids. Brazos Roofing, Inc., B-275113, 97-1 CPD ¶ 43 (Comp. Gen. 1997)

Where the protester submitted its bid seconds after the bid opening officer reasonably declared that the time for bid opening stated in the solicitation had arrived, the agency properly rejected the bid as late, even though the bid opening clock continued to display the same minute in time. Matter of: Nueva Construction Company, Inc., B-270009, 96-1 CPD ¶ 84 (Comp. Gen. 1996)

Solicitation provided that bids were due at Savanna, Illinois by 2 p.m. local time, but low bidder sent its bid to Letterkenny Army Depot in Pennsylvania— which had issued the solicitation—at the direction of the Letterkenny contract specialist (identified in the solicitation as the person to contact for further information), where the bid was opened at 2 p.m. Letterkenny time (1 hour ahead of Savanna time). Acceptance of the bid was proper, since government misdirection of the bid to Letterkenny was the sole cause of the bid's nonreceipt at Savanna, and acceptance would not compromise the integrity of the competitive system. AABLE Tank Services, Inc., B-273010, 96-2 CPD ¶ 180 (Comp. Gen. 1996)

Protest challenging agency's rejection of facsimile bid modification as late is sustained on grounds that government mishandling was paramount cause of modification's late receipt where: (1) facsimile bid modification was received at least 7 minutes prior to bid opening time; (2) the facsimile machine was located a short distance from both the room designated in the solicitation for receipt of bids and the bid opening room; (3) the protester properly identified the bid modification as directed by the solicitation and provided timely telephone notice to the agency of its facsimile transmission; and (4) record establishes that mail room clerks unreasonably delayed promptly delivering the modification. Matter of: Butt Construction Co., Inc., B-258507, 95-1 CPD ¶ 45 (Comp. Gen. 1995)

The burden is on the claimant to present evidence of receipt of a claim in the proper office within the statutory period of limitations. The government activity's time/date stamp is not dispositive of the time of a claim's receipt, but in the absence of a clear proof of earlier actual receipt, we will assume receipt at the time and date indicated on the stamp. Matter of: Tri-State Motor Transit Company, B-253916, 1994 WL 86006 (Comp. Gen. 1994)

Hand-carried bid which was brought to the designated place for hand-carried bids and placed in the Navy's control at the exact time, 2 p.m., called for in the solicitation and prior to any declaration that the time for receipt of bids had passed is not late as the Federal Acquisition Regulation does not require that a bid be submitted prior to the time called for in the solicitation but rather not later than the exact time set for opening bids. Amfel Construction, Inc., B-233493, B-233493.2, 89-1 CPD ¶ 477 (Comp. Gen. 1989), on reconsideration, B-233493, B-233493.4, 89-2 CPD ¶ 292 (Comp. Gen. 1989)

§ 14.303 Modification or withdrawal of bids.

(a) Bids may be modified or withdrawn by any method authorized by the solicitation, if notice is received in the office designated in the solicitation not later than the exact time set for opening of bids. Unless proscribed by agency regulations, a telegraphic modification or withdrawal of a bid received in such office by telephone from the receiving telegraph office shall be considered. However, the message shall be confirmed by the telegraph company by sending a copy of the written telegram that formed the basis for the telephone call. If the solicitation authorizes facsimile bids, bids may be modified or withdrawn via facsimile received at any time before the exact time set for receipt of bids, subject to the conditions specified in the provision prescribed in 14.201-6(v). Modifications received by telegram (including a record of those telephoned by the telegraph company) or facsimile shall be sealed in an envelope by a proper official. The official shall write on the envelope (1) the date and time of receipt and by whom, and (2) the number of the invitation for bids, and shall sign the envelope. No information contained in the envelope shall be disclosed before the time set for bid opening.

(b) A bid may be withdrawn in person by a bidder or its authorized representative if, before the exact time set for opening of bids, the identity of the persons requesting withdrawal is established and that person signs a receipt for the bid.

(c) Upon withdrawal of an electronically transmitted bid, the data received shall not be viewed and shall be purged from primary and backup data storage systems.

United States Code Annotated

Contract requirements, see 41 USCA § 254.

Contracts, planning, solicitation, evaluation, and award procedures, see 10 USCA § 2305.

Definitions, see 10 USCA § 2302, 41 USCA §§ 259, 403.

Evaluation and award, see 41 USCA § 253b.

Kinds of contracts, see 10 USCA § 2306.

Planning and solicitation requirements, see 41 USCA § 253a.

Notes of Decisions

In general 1
Format of modification 2

1 In general

Officer in charge of bid opening violated federal acquisition regulation by giving apparently late bid back to bidder's bonding agent, but mistake was cured by testing envelope to determine if someone had opened and resealed it. Washington Mechanical Contractors, Inc. v. U.S. Dept. of Navy, 612 F. Supp. 1243 (N.D. Cal. 1984). United States ⟶64.30

Process of sealed bidding does not afford the opportunity for each bidder that might submit a defective bid bond to manifest its intent post-bid opening. 48 C.F.R. §§ 14.101(d), 14.208. Interstate Rock Products, Inc. v. U.S., 50 Fed. Cl. 349 (2001), aff'd, 48 Fed. Appx. 331 (Fed. Cir. 2002). United States ⟶64.30

Defense National Stockpile Center's (DNSC) domestic preference in solicitations for surplus material through formal advertising violated Federal Acquisition Regulations (FAR) to extent preference allowed bids to be modified after being opened. Federal Property and Administrative Services Act of 1949, § 303A(a)(2), as amended, 41 U.S.C.A. § 253a(a)(2); Strategic and Critical Materials Stock Piling Act, § 6(b), as amended, 50 U.S.C.A. § 98e(b); 48 C.F.R. § 14.408-6. Minor Metals, Inc. v. U.S., 38 Fed. Cl. 16, 41 Cont. Cas. Fed. (CCH) P 77145 (1997). United States ⊂▭64.15

A procuring agency properly considered a misplaced bid modification that resulted in the low bid, where the record establishes that the modification arrived at the proper office of the procuring agency 2 days before bid opening and remained in the agency's possession until it was discovered before award. Matter of, B-256827, 94-2 CPD ¶ 46 (Comp. Gen. 1994)

Contracting agency properly refused to allow modification that would have made protester's bid low where modification initially conveyed before bid opening by telephone would not have made bid low and confirming telegram containing different modification that would make bid low was not received until after bid opening; a pre-opening telephonic bid modification may be considered if subsequently confirmed by telegram, but there is no basis for accepting modification conveyed in the confirming telegram where that modification is different from the telephonic modification received before bid opening. Ibex, Ltd., B-240770, 90-2 CPD ¶ 483 (Comp. Gen. 1990)

2 Format of modification

Unsigned or uninitialed inscription on the outside envelope of the protester's bid purportedly modifying the bid price reflected on the protester's bid form is not an effective bid modification where the bid or modification is not otherwise accompanied by evidence of the bidder's intent to be bound by the modification. R.F. Lusa & Sons Sheetmetal, Inc., B-281180.2, 98-2 CPD ¶ 157 (Comp. Gen. 1998)

§ 14.304 Submission, modification, and withdrawal of bids.

(a) Bidders are responsible for submitting bids, and any modifications or withdrawals, so as to reach the Government office designated in the invitation for bid (IFB) by the time specified in the IFB. They may use any transmission method authorized by the IFB (i.e., regular mail, electronic commerce, or facsimile). If no time is specified in the IFB, the time for receipt is 4:30 p.m., local time, for the designated Government office on the date that bids are due.

(b) (1) Any bid, modification, or withdrawal of a bid received at the Government office designated in the IFB after the exact time specified for receipt of bids is "late" and will not be considered unless it is received before award is made, the contracting officer determines that accepting the late bid would not unduly delay the acquisition; and—

(i) If it was transmitted through an electronic commerce method authorized by the IFB, it was received at the initial point of entry to the Government infrastructure not later than 5:00 p.m. one working day prior to the date specified for receipt of bids; or

(ii) There is acceptable evidence to establish that it was received at the Government installation designated for receipt of bids and was under the Government's control prior to the time set for receipt of bids.

(2) However, a late modification of an otherwise successful bid, that makes its terms more favorable to the Government, will be considered at any time it is received and may be accepted.

(c) Acceptable evidence to establish the time of receipt at the Government installation includes the time/date stamp of that installation on the bid wrapper, other documentary evidence of receipt maintained by the installation, or oral testimony or statements of Government personnel.

(d) If an emergency or unanticipated event interrupts normal Government processes so that bids cannot be received at the Government office designated for receipt of bids by the exact time specified in the IFB, and urgent Government requirements preclude amendment of the bid opening date, the time specified for receipt of bids will be deemed to be extended to the same time of day specified in the IFB on the first work day on which normal Government processes resume.

(e) Bids may be withdrawn by written notice received at any time before the exact time set for receipt of bids. If the IFB authorizes facsimile bids, bids may be withdrawn via facsimile received at any time before the exact time set for receipt of bids, subject to the conditions specified in the provision at 52.214-31, Facsimile Bids. A bid may be withdrawn in person by a bidder or its authorized representative if, before the exact time set for receipt of bids, the identity of the person requesting withdrawal is established and the person signs a receipt for the bid. Upon withdrawal of an electronically transmitted bid, the data received must not be viewed and, where practicable, must be purged from primary and backup data storage systems.

(f) The contracting officer must promptly notify any bidder if its bid, modification, or withdrawal was received late, and must inform the bidder whether its bid will be considered, unless contract award is imminent and the notices prescribed in 14.409 would suffice.

(g) Late bids and modifications that are not considered must be held unopened, unless opened for identification, until after award and then retained with other unsuccessful bids. However, any bid bond or guarantee must be returned.

(h) If available, the following must be included in the contract files for each late bid, modification, or withdrawal:

(1) The date and hour of receipt.

(2) A statement, with supporting rationale, regarding whether the bid was considered for award.

(3) The envelope, wrapper, or other evidence of the date of receipt.

United States Code Annotated

Contract requirements, see 41 USCA § 254.

Contracts, planning, solicitation, evaluation, and award procedures, see 10 USCA § 2305.

Definitions, see 10 USCA § 2302, 41 USCA §§ 259, 403.

Evaluation and award, see 41 USCA § 253b.

Kinds of contracts, see 10 USCA § 2306.

Planning and solicitation requirements, see 41 USCA § 253a.

Notes of Decisions

Modification of bid 1
Time/date stamp 2
Timeliness 3

1 Modification of bid

Contracting agency properly refused to allow modification that would have made protester's bid low where modification initially conveyed before bid opening by telephone would not have made bid low and confirming telegram containing different modification that would make bid low was not received until after bid opening; a pre-opening telephonic bid modification may be considered if subsequently confirmed by telegram, but there is no basis for accepting modification conveyed in the confirming telegram where that modification is different from the telephonic modification received before bid opening. Ibex, Ltd., B-240770, 90-2 CPD ¶ 483 (Comp. Gen. 1990)

2 Time/date stamp

The language of FAR 14.304 regarding acceptable evidence to establish the time of receipt of a bid requires only that the agency maintain the time/date stamp device within the agency installation. This interpretation of the sentence merely precludes the acceptance of time/date stamps not made by the official device maintained by the agency, thus ensuring that all bids are time/date stamped using the same, official device. California Marine Cleaning, Inc. v. U.S., 42 Fed. Cl. 281, 42 Cont. Cas. Fed. (CCH) P 77398 (1998)

The burden is on the claimant to present evidence of receipt of a claim in the proper office within the statutory period of limitations. The government activity's time/date stamp is not dispositive of the time of a claim's receipt, but in the absence of a clear proof of earlier actual receipt, we will assume receipt at the time and date indicated on the stamp. Matter of: Tri-State Motor Transit Company, B-253916, 1994 WL 86006 (Comp. Gen. 1994)

3 Timeliness

Term "local time" in solicitation provision setting forth deadline for electronic transmission of offer referred to the time in Naples, Italy, which was the location of government office designated in the solicitation, and not to United States Eastern Standard Time as contended by bid protestor based on language on contracting agency's web site. Conscoop-Consorzia Fra Coop. Di Prod. E Lavoro v. U.S., 62 Fed. Cl. 219 (2004), aff'd, 159 Fed. Appx. 184 (Fed. Cir. 2005)

Generally, only bids that are timely received by the procuring agency may be considered for award; to be considered timely, a bid must be delivered to the place specified in an invitation for bids (IFB) on or before the time and date specified in the IFB. 48 C.F.R. §§ 14.301(a), 14.302(a). California Marine Cleaning, Inc. v. U.S., 42 Fed. Cl. 281, 42 Cont. Cas. Fed. (CCH) P 77398 (1998). United States ☞64.30

Bid protester bears the burden of proving by a preponderance of the evidence that its bid was timely submitted. California Marine Cleaning, Inc. v. U.S., 42 Fed. Cl. 281, 42 Cont. Cas. Fed. (CCH) P 77398 (1998). United States ☞64.55(2)

Fact that agency placed bid box in reception area and allowed bidders to date stamp their own bids did not afford a compelling reason for canceling and resoliciting the procurement; although agency's practice created difficulties in resolving timeliness of one bid, it did not call into question the entire solicitation or breach the integrity of the bidding system. 48 C.F.R. § 14.404-1(a)(1). California Marine Cleaning, Inc. v. U.S., 42 Fed. Cl. 281, 42 Cont. Cas. Fed. (CCH) P 77398 (1998). United States ☞64.50

Statement of requirements for second phase of concessions contract clearly required that applicants submit its best presentation of requested information at time application was sent to National Park Service (NPS) and, thus, applicant was not entitled to more time to submit information confirming commitments to satisfy $12 million capital equity requirement. YRT Services Corp. v. U.S., 28 Fed. Cl. 366, 38 Cont. Cas. Fed. (CCH) P 76512 (1993). United States ☞64.30

General Accounting Office's (GAO's) determination in bid protest case, that contractor's bid was submitted simultaneously with bid opening officer's announcement that time for receipt of bids had passed, had rational basis, precluding unsuccessful bidder from enjoining award of Navy construction contract to successful bidder. 28 U.S.C.A. § 1491(a)(3); 31 U.S.C.A. §§ 3551–3556. Carothers Const. Inc. v. U.S., 18 Cl. Ct. 745, 35 Cont. Cas. Fed. (CCH) P 75758, 1989 WL 143515 (1989). United States ☞64.30

Under request for proposals that designated closing time for submission of proposals as 14:00 hours, agency reasonably declined to reject as late a proposal received after 14:00 but before the time 14:01 was displayed on the time/date stamp clock used by the agency for determining timeliness of proposal submissions. The Haskell Company, B-292756, 2003 CPD ¶ 202 (Comp. Gen. 2003)

Bid in an envelope marked "BID ENCLOSED," which was hand-carried by commercial carrier to the contracting agency's mailroom several hours before bid opening but was not received by the contracting office where the bid depository was located until after bid opening, was late and not properly accepted for award; rather than government mishandling being the primary or paramount cause of the lateness, the mailroom's routing of the bid to another office in the same building that also handles bids was attributable to the bidder's failure to mark its commercial carrier-provided envelope as required by FAR 52.214-5 when using a commercial carrier to deliver a bid. Boines Construction & Equipment Co., Inc., B-279575, 98-1 CPD ¶ 175 (Comp. Gen. 1998)

Protest of rejection of late bid is denied where, while the agency changed the bid opening room less than 1 hour before bid opening, the agency reasonably determined that the bidder's actions significantly contributed to the late receipt of the bid. Adirondack Construction Corporation, B-280015, B-280015.2, 98-2 CPD ¶ 55 (Comp. Gen. 1998)

Agency improperly considered a late bid under the government mishandling exception where the evidence of record does not establish that the bid was timely received and remained under the government's control until it was first discovered 6 days after bid opening. Pacific Tank Cleaning Services, Inc., B-279111, B-279111.2, 98-2 CPD ¶ 2 (Comp. Gen. 1998)

Protest that agency improperly rejected protester's bid as late is sustained where: (1) agency amended solicitation so close to the deadline for submitting bids that bid submission by facsimile was the only practicable alternative available to bidders; (2) facsimile machine designated in solicitation became inoperable for some indefinite period of time during the morning of the bid submission deadline; (3) protester transmitted its bid to an alternate facsimile machine based on advice from an agency employee other than the designated point of contact only after unsuccessfully attempting to telephone the designated contact; and (4) the protester's bid package arrived at the installation and was in the hands of agency officials by the deadline for submitting bids. Brazos Roofing, Inc., B-275113, 97-1 CPD ¶ 43 (Comp. Gen. 1997)

Where the protester submitted its bid seconds after the bid opening officer reasonably declared that the time for bid opening stated in the solicitation had arrived, the agency properly rejected the bid as late, even though the bid opening clock continued to display the same minute in time. Matter of: Nueva Construction Company, Inc., B-270009, 96-1 CPD ¶ 84 (Comp. Gen. 1996)

Solicitation provided that bids were due at Savanna, Illinois by 2 p.m. local time, but low bidder sent its bid to Letterkenny Army Depot in Pennsylvania— which had issued the solicitation—at the direction of the Letterkenny contract specialist (identified in the solicitation as the person to contact for further information), where the bid was opened at 2 p.m. Letterkenny time (1 hour ahead of Savanna time). Acceptance of the bid was proper, since government misdirection of the bid to Letterkenny was the sole cause of the bid's nonreceipt at Savanna, and acceptance would not compromise the integrity of the competitive system. AABLE Tank Services, Inc., B-273010, 96-2 CPD ¶ 180 (Comp. Gen. 1996)

Where the bid opening officer receives a mailed bid from the agency mail clerk while he was walking en route from the building's foyer (where he declared that no more hand-carried bids would be accepted) to the bid opening room, bid was properly considered as timely received by the agency where solicitation did not designate particular office for receipt of bids and bid was received in the mailroom prior to the declared bid opening time. C.R. Hipp Construction Co., Inc., B-274328, 96-2 CPD ¶ 195 (Comp. Gen. 1996)

Protest challenging agency's rejection of facsimile bid modification as late is sustained on grounds that government mishandling was paramount cause of modification's late receipt where: (1) facsimile bid modification was received at least 7 minutes prior to bid opening time; (2) the facsimile machine was located a short distance from both the room designated in the solicitation for receipt of bids and the bid opening room; (3) the protester properly identified the bid modification as directed by the solicitation and provided timely telephone notice to the agency of its facsimile transmission; and (4) record establishes that mail room clerks unreasonably delayed promptly delivering the modification. Matter of: Butt Construction Co., Inc., B-258507, 95-1 CPD ¶ 45 (Comp. Gen. 1995)

Agency's acceptance of a late bid was proper where the failure of agency personnel to follow established procedures for receipt of express mail on weekends was the paramount cause of the late receipt. Watson Agency, Inc., B-241072, 90-2 CPD ¶ 506 (Comp. Gen. 1990)

Subpart 14.4 Opening of Bids and Award of Contract

§ 14.400 Scope of subpart.

This subpart contains procedures for the receipt, handling, opening, and disposition of bids including mistakes in bids, and subsequent award of contracts.

United States Code Annotated

Administrative determinations, see 41 USCA § 257.

Contract requirements, see 41 USCA § 254.

Contracts, planning, solicitation, evaluation, and award procedures, see 10 USCA § 2305.

Definitions, see 10 USCA § 2302, 41 USCA §§ 259, 403.

Determinations and decisions, see 10 USCA § 2310, 41 USCA § 262.

Evaluation and award, see 41 USCA § 253b.

Kinds of contracts, see 10 USCA § 2306.

Planning and solicitation requirements, see 41 USCA § 253a.

§ 14.401 Receipt and safeguarding of bids.

(a) All bids (including modifications) received before the time set for the opening of bids shall be kept secure. Except as provided in paragraph (b) of this section, the bids shall not be opened or viewed, and shall remain in a locked bid box, a safe, or in a secured, restricted-access electronic bid box. If an invitation for bids is cancelled, bids shall be returned to the bidders. Necessary precautions shall be taken to ensure the security of the bid box or safe. Before bid opening, information concerning the identity and number of bids received shall be made available only to Government employees. Such disclosure shall be only on a "need to know" basis. When bid samples are submitted, they shall be handled with sufficient care to prevent disclosure of characteristics before bid opening.

(b) Envelopes marked as bids but not identifying the bidder or the solicitation may be opened solely for the purpose of identification, and then only by an official designated for this purpose. If a sealed bid is opened by mistake (*e.g.*, because it is not marked as being a bid), the envelope shall be signed by the opener, whose position shall also be written thereon, and delivered to the designated official. This official shall immediately write on the envelope (1) an explanation of the opening, (2) the date and time opened, and (3) the invitation for bids number, and shall sign the envelope. The official shall then immediately reseal the envelope.

United States Code Annotated

Administrative determinations, see 41 USCA § 257.

Contract requirements, see 41 USCA § 254.

Contracts, planning, solicitation, evaluation, and award procedures, see 10 USCA § 2305.

Definitions, see 10 USCA § 2302, 41 USCA §§ 259, 403.

Determinations and decisions, see 10 USCA § 2310, 41 USCA § 262.

Evaluation and award, see 41 USCA § 253b.

Kinds of contracts, see 10 USCA § 2306.

Planning and solicitation requirements, see 41 USCA § 253a.

§ 14.402 Opening of bids.

§ 14.402-1 Unclassified bids.

(a) The bid opening officer shall decide when the time set for opening bids has arrived and shall inform those present of that decision. The officer shall then (1) personally and publicly open all bids received before that time, (2) if practical, read the bids aloud to the persons present, and (3) have the bids recorded. The original of each bid shall be carefully safeguarded, particularly until the abstract of bids required by 14.403 has been made and its accuracy verified.

(b) Performance of the procedure in paragraph (a) of this section may be delegated to an assistant, but the bid opening officer remains fully responsible for the actions of the assistant.

(c) Examination of bids by interested persons shall be permitted if it does not interfere unduly with the conduct of Government business. Original bids shall not be allowed to pass out of the hands of a Government official unless a duplicate bid is not available for public inspection. The original bid may be examined by the public only under the immediate supervision of a Government official and under conditions that preclude possibility of a substitution, addition, deletion, or alteration in the bid.

United States Code Annotated

Administrative determinations, see 41 USCA § 257.

Contract requirements, see 41 USCA § 254.

Contracts, planning, solicitation, evaluation, and award procedures, see 10 USCA § 2305.

Definitions, see 10 USCA § 2302, 41 USCA §§ 259, 403.

Determinations and decisions, see 10 USCA § 2310, 41 USCA § 262.

Evaluation and award, see 41 USCA § 253b.

Kinds of contracts, see 10 USCA § 2306.

Planning and solicitation requirements, see 41 USCA § 253a.

§ 14.402-2 Classified bids.

The general public may not attend bid openings for classified acquisitions. A bidder or its representative may attend and record the results if the individual has the appropriate security clearance. The contracting officer also may make the bids available at a later time to properly cleared individuals who represent bidders. No public record shall be made of bids or bid prices received in response to classified invitations for bids.

United States Code Annotated

Administrative determinations, see 41 USCA § 257.

Contract requirements, see 41 USCA § 254.

Contracts, planning, solicitation, evaluation, and award procedures, see 10 USCA § 2305.

Definitions, see 10 USCA § 2302, 41 USCA §§ 259, 403.

Determinations and decisions, see 10 USCA § 2310, 41 USCA § 262.

Evaluation and award, see 41 USCA § 253b.

Kinds of contracts, see 10 USCA § 2306.

Planning and solicitation requirements, see 41 USCA § 253a.

§ 14.402-3 Postponement of openings.

(a) A bid opening may be postponed even after the time scheduled for bid opening (but otherwise in accordance with 14.208) when—

(1) The contracting officer has reason to believe that the bids of an important segment of bidders have been delayed in the mails, or in the communications system specified for transmission of bids, for causes beyond their control and without their fault or negligence (*e.g.*, flood, fire, accident, weather conditions, strikes, or Government equipment blackout or malfunction when bids are due); or

(2) Emergency or unanticipated events interrupt normal governmental processes so that the conduct of bid opening as scheduled is impractical.

(b) At the time of a determination to postpone a bid opening under paragraph (a)(1) of this section, an announcement of the determination shall be publicly posted. If practical before issuance of a formal amendment of the invitation, the determination shall be otherwise communicated to prospective bidders who are likely to attend the scheduled bid opening.

(c) In the case of paragraph (a)(2) of this section, and when urgent Government requirements preclude amendment of the solicitation as prescribed in 14.208, the time specified for opening of bids will be deemed to be extended to the same time of day specified in the solicitation on the first work day on which normal Government processes resume. In such cases, the time of actual bid opening shall be deemed to be the time set for bid opening for the purpose of determining "late bids" under 14.304. A note should be made on the abstract of bids or otherwise added to the file explaining the circumstances of the postponement.

United States Code Annotated

Administrative determinations, see 41 USCA § 257.

Contract requirements, see 41 USCA § 254.

Contracts, planning, solicitation, evaluation, and award procedures, see 10 USCA § 2305.

Definitions, see 10 USCA § 2302, 41 USCA §§ 259, 403.

Determinations and decisions, see 10 USCA § 2310, 41 USCA § 262.

Evaluation and award, see 41 USCA § 253b.

Kinds of contracts, see 10 USCA § 2306.

Planning and solicitation requirements, see 41 USCA § 253a.

§ 14.403 Recording of bids.

(a) Standard Form 1409, Abstract of Offers, or Optional Form 1419, Abstract of Offers—Construction (or automated equivalent), shall be completed and certified as to its accuracy by the bid opening officer as soon after bid opening as practicable. Where bid items are too numerous to warrant complete recording of all bids, abstract entries for individual bids may be limited to item numbers and bid prices. In preparing these forms, the extra columns and SF 1410, Abstract of Offers—Continuation, and OF 1419A, Abstract of Offer—Construction, Continuation Sheet, may be used to label and record such information as the contracting activity deems necessary.

(b) Abstracts of offers for unclassified acquisitions shall be available for public inspection. Such abstracts shall not contain information regarding failure to meet minimum standards of responsibility, apparent collusion of bidders, or other notations properly exempt from disclosure to the public in accordance with agency regulations implementing Subpart 24.2.

(c) The forms identified in paragraph (a) of this section need not be used by the Defense Energy Support Center for acquisitions of coal or petroleum products or by the Defense Supply Center Philadelphia for perishable subsistence items.

(d) If an invitation for bids is cancelled before the time set for bid opening, this fact shall be recorded together with a statement of the number of bids invited and the number of bids received.

United States Code Annotated

Administrative determinations, see 41 USCA § 257.

Contract requirements, see 41 USCA § 254.

Contracts, planning, solicitation, evaluation, and award procedures, see 10 USCA § 2305.

Definitions, see 10 USCA § 2302, 41 USCA §§ 259, 403.

Determinations and decisions, see 10 USCA § 2310, 41 USCA § 262.

Evaluation and award, see 41 USCA § 253b.

Kinds of contracts, see 10 USCA § 2306.

Planning and solicitation requirements, see 41 USCA § 253a.

§ 14.404 Rejection of bids.

§ 14.404-1 Cancellation of invitations after opening.

(a) (1) Preservation of the integrity of the competitive bid system dictates that, after bids have been opened, award must be made to that responsible bidder who submitted the lowest responsive bid, unless there is a compelling reason to reject all bids and cancel the invitation.

(2) Every effort shall be made to anticipate changes in a requirement before the date of opening and to notify all prospective bidders of any resulting modification or cancellation. This will permit bidders to change their bids and prevent unnecessary exposure of bid prices.

(3) As a general rule, after the opening of bids, an invitation should not be cancelled and resolicited due solely to increased requirements for the items being acquired. Award should be made on the initial invitation for bids and the additional quantity should be treated as a new acquisition.

(b) When it is determined before award but after opening that the requirements of 11.201 (relating to the availability and identification of specifications) have not been met, the invitation shall be cancelled.

(c) Invitations may be cancelled and all bids rejected before award but after opening when, consistent with subparagraph (a)(1) of this section, the agency head determines in writing that—

(1) Inadequate or ambiguous specifications were cited in the invitation;

(2) Specifications have been revised;

(3) The supplies or services being contracted for are no longer required;

(4) The invitation did not provide for consideration of all factors of cost to the Government, such as cost of transporting Government-furnished property to bidders' plants;

(5) Bids received indicate that the needs of the Government can be satisfied by a less expensive article differing from that for which the bids were invited;

(6) All otherwise acceptable bids received are at unreasonable prices, or only one bid is received and the contracting officer cannot determine the reasonableness of the bid price;

(7) The bids were not independently arrived at in open competition, were collusive, or were submitted in bad faith (see Subpart 3.3 for reports to be made to the Department of

Justice);

(8) No responsive bid has been received from a responsible bidder;

(9) A cost comparison as prescribed in OMB Circular A-76 and Subpart 7.3 shows that performance by the Government is more economical; or

(10) For other reasons, cancellation is clearly in the public's interest.

(d) Should administrative difficulties be encountered after bid opening that may delay award beyond bidders' acceptance periods, the several lowest bidders whose bids have not expired (irrespective of the acceptance period specified in the bid) should be requested, before expiration of their bids, to extend in writing the bid acceptance period (with consent of sureties, if any) in order to avoid the need for resoliciting.

(e) Under some circumstances, completion of the acquisition after cancellation of the invitation for bids may be appropriate.

(1) If the invitation for bids has been cancelled for the reasons specified in subparagraphs (c)(6), (7), or (8) of this subsection, and the agency head has authorized, in the determination in paragraph (c) of this subsection, the completion of the acquisition through negotiation, the contracting officer shall proceed in accordance with paragraph (f) of this subsection.

(2) If the invitation for bids has been cancelled for the reasons specified in subparagraphs (c)(1), (2), (4), (5), or (10) of this subsection, or for the reasons in subparagraphs (c)(6), (7), or (8) of this subsection and completion through negotiation is not authorized under subparagraph (e)(1) of this subsection, the contracting officer shall proceed with a new acquisition.

(f) When the agency head has determined, in accordance with paragraph (e)(1) of this subsection, that an invitation for bids should be canceled and that use of negotiation is in the Government's interest, the contracting officer may negotiate (in accordance with Part 15, as appropriate) and make award without issuing a new solicitation provided—

(1) Each responsible bidder in the sealed bid acquisition has been given notice that negotiations will be conducted and has been given an opportunity to participate in negotiations; and

(2) The award is made to the responsible bidder offering the lowest negotiated price.

United States Code Annotated

Administrative determinations, see 41 USCA § 257.

Contract requirements, see 41 USCA § 254.

Contracts, planning, solicitation, evaluation, and award procedures, see 10 USCA § 2305.

Definitions, see 10 USCA § 2302, 41 USCA §§ 259, 403.

Determinations and decisions, see 10 USCA § 2310, 41 USCA § 262.

Evaluation and award, see 41 USCA § 253b.

Kinds of contracts, see 10 USCA § 2306.

Planning and solicitation requirements, see 41 USCA § 253a.

Notes of Decisions

Attorneys fees 9
Bad faith 4
Cancellation of invitations, generally 1
Discretion and authority of agency 2
Injunctions 5
Judicial review 10
Jurisdiction 6
Parties 7
Presumptions and burden of proof 8
Reason for cancellation of invitations 3

1 Cancellation of invitations, generally

Army was not required to cancel invitation for bids where invitation overstated Army's minimum needs. Delta Chemical Corp. v. West, 33 F.3d 380, 39 Cont. Cas. Fed. (CCH) P

76693 (4th Cir. 1994). United States ☞64.50

Army did not act arbitrarily and capriciously when it refused to cancel invitation for bids after determining that invitation overstated its minimum needs, where unsuccessful bidder was not prejudiced because its bid was nonresponsive for reason unrelated to overstatement. Delta Chemical Corp. v. West, 33 F.3d 380, 39 Cont. Cas. Fed. (CCH) P 76693 (4th Cir. 1994). United States ☞64.50; United States ☞64.60(4)

Omission, from invitation for bid for manufacture of propeller shaft assembly approximately 56 feet long, of Defense Department restriction mandating against procurement of certain foreign forging products, including ship propulsion shafts greater than 50 feet in length, rendered invitation for bid defective under Federal Acquisition Regulations System and, thus, supported cancellation of invitation for bid. 10 U.S.C.A. § 2304(a)(16); Executive Order No. 11490, Oct. 28, 1969. National Forge Co. v. U.S., 779 F.2d 665, 33 Cont. Cas. Fed. (CCH) P 74149 (Fed. Cir. 1985). United States ☞64.25

Contracting officer (CO) did not act arbitrarily or capriciously in canceling invitation for bids (IFB) after lowest bidder withdrew, where all remaining bids were in excess of amount available for construction, and all the remaining bids when added to design costs exceeded $4,000,000 cap for minor construction projects. 48 C.F.R. § 14.404-1(c)(6). First Enterprise v. U.S., 61 Fed. Cl. 109 (2004). United States ☞64.50

Solicitation concerning past performance evaluation was overstated and overly restrictive of competition to the prejudice of other potential offerors in violation of the Competition in Contracting Act (CICA), warranting cancellation of solicitation. 10 U.S.C.A. § 2305(a)(1)(B) (ii); Federal Property and Administrative Services Act of 1949, § 303(a)(2)(B), 41 U.S.C.A. § 253(a)(2)(B); 48 C.F.R. § 14.101(a). Charles H. Tompkins Co. v. U.S., 43 Fed. Cl. 716 (1999). United States ☞64.50

Agency's decision to cancel solicitation after bid opening could not be justified as an effort to avoid litigation in the Court of Federal Claims; agency's cancellation decision must be supported by evidence in the administrative record at the time of decision, not based upon post hoc rationalization, and the rationale could not be considering "compelling." 48 C.F.R. § 14.404-1(a)(1). California Marine Cleaning, Inc. v. U.S., 42 Fed. Cl. 281, 42 Cont. Cas. Fed. (CCH) P 77398 (1998). United States ☞64.50

Cancellation of an invitation for bids (IFB) is disfavored after bid opening and is generally inappropriate when other bidders would not be prejudiced by an award under an ostensibly deficient solicitation and when such an award would serve the actual needs of the government. 48 C.F.R. § 14.404-1. California Marine Cleaning, Inc. v. U.S., 42 Fed. Cl. 281, 42 Cont. Cas. Fed. (CCH) P 77398 (1998). United States ☞64.50

When it becomes evident that solicitation fails to adequately reflect government's needs, it is proper to cancel solicitation; rule applies to sealed bidding and other competitive negotiation procedures. Shields Enterprises, Inc. v. U.S., 28 Fed. Cl. 615, 38 Cont. Cas. Fed. (CCH) P 76526 (1993). United States ☞64.50

For purpose of determining whether Government reasonably cancelled solicitation for bids for providing unarmed guard services, Government's need for two supervisors per eight-hour shift could not be inferred from provision of solicitation requiring that Government and contractor immediately after contract award coordinate to review performance requirements for guard post assignments. Vanguard Sec. Inc. v. U.S., 20 Cl. Ct. 90, 1990 WL 38036 (1990). United States ☞64.50

Regulatory admonitions that agency should not cancel solicitations just because their needs are for greater quantities than those listed in solicitation are meaningful only in context of supply contracts, as opposed to service contracts. Vanguard Sec. Inc. v. U.S., 20 Cl. Ct. 90, 1990 WL 38036 (1990). United States ☞64.50

For purpose of determining whether Government reasonably cancelled solicitation for bids for providing unarmed guard services, Government's need for two supervisors per eight-hour shift could not be inferred from solicitation's requirement that contractor furnish supervision on 24-houra-day basis. Vanguard Sec. Inc. v. U.S., 20 Cl. Ct. 90, 1990 WL 38036 (1990). United States ☞64.50

There was no basis for measuring decision to cancel solicitation of bids relating to coin production against standards or procedures contained in Office of Management Budget circular A-76, which stated that it is government policy to use private sources for government commercial activities in appropriate circumstances, since cancellation decision was based upon issue that is "jurisdictional" prerequisites of circular, that is, nongovernmental functions. Arrowhead Metals, Ltd. v. U.S., 8 Cl. Ct. 703, 33 Cont. Cas. Fed. (CCH) P 74026 (1985). United States ☞64.50

Office of Management Budget Circular A-76, which stated that it was government policy to use private sources for government commercial activities in appropriate circumstances, did not support claim that Government, in its cost analysis regarding coin production, as it related to decision to cancel solicitation of bids for production of coinage blanks, had to utilize historical costs for "strip" and could not utilize latest "strip" cost data. Arrowhead Metals, Ltd. v. U.S., 8 Cl. Ct. 703, 33 Cont. Cas. Fed. (CCH) P 74026 (1985). United States ☞64.50

It was not improper for United States Mint to consider actions taken or concerns raised by members of Congress in determining whether or not to cancel solicitation for bids in connection with contract for coin production; rather, issue was whether those factors affected contractor's right to full and fair consideration of its proposal. Arrowhead Metals, Ltd. v. U.S., 8 Cl. Ct. 703, 33 Cont. Cas. Fed. (CCH) P 74026 (1985). United States ☞64.50

Cancellation of solicitation bids in connection with contract for production of coins served interest of Government by allowing for further study of important policy issue of whether contracting out such work involved inherently governmental functions. Arrowhead Metals, Ltd. v. U.S., 8 Cl. Ct. 703, 33 Cont. Cas. Fed. (CCH) P 74026 (1985). United States ☞64.50

Foreign contractor's claim that United States Mint officials were prejudiced against it, thus leading to cancellation of solicitation for bids in connection with production of coins, could not be premised on language of Trade Agreement Act [Trade Agreements Act of 1979, §§ 1(a)-1112, 19 U.S.C.A. §§ 2501–2582] inasmuch as Act expressly denies private remedies not specifically provided for therein. Trade Agreements Act of 1979, §§ 3(f), 421, 19 U.S.C.A. § 2504(d), 2551. Arrowhead Metals, Ltd. v. U.S., 8 Cl. Ct. 703, 33 Cont. Cas. Fed. (CCH) P 74026 (1985). United States ☞64.60(1)

Offeror failed to establish that United States Air Force cancelled solicitation for lease of four aircraft in order to avoid bidder's protest or that air force air staff orchestrated plan to cancel solicitation and then rewrite specification to allow for use of C-12 aircraft at air field, either of which may have rendered cancellation of solicitation unreasonable. Aviation Enterprises, Inc. v. U.S., 8 Cl. Ct. 1, 32 Cont. Cas. Fed. (CCH) P 73403 (1985). United States ☞64.50

2 Discretion and authority of agency

The authority vested in a contracting officer (CO) to decide whether to cancel an invitation for bids (IFB) and readvertise is extremely broad; CO's determination concerning the unreasonableness of the prices bid is a matter of administrative discretion which should not be questioned unless the determination is shown to be unreasonable or that there is a showing of fraud or bad faith. Contracting officer (CO) did not act arbitrarily or capriciously in canceling invitation for bids (IFB) after lowest bidder withdrew, where all remaining bids were in excess of amount available for construction, and all the remaining bids when added to design costs exceeded $4,000,000 cap for minor construction projects. First Enterprise v. U.S., 61 Fed. Cl. 109 (2004)

The authority vested in a contracting officer (CO) to decide whether to cancel an invitation for bids (IFB) and readvertise is extremely broad; CO's determination concerning the unreasonableness of the prices bid is a matter of administrative discretion which should not be questioned unless the determination is shown to be unreasonable or that there is a showing of fraud or bad faith. 48 C.F.R. § 14.404-1(c)(6). First Enterprise v. U.S., 61 Fed. Cl. 109 (2004). United States ☞64.50

In the context of pre-award negotiations, a contracting officer is given latitude in deciding whether to cancel a solicitation and request new bids after price offers have been disclosed. Griffy's Landscape Maintenance LLC v. U.S., 51 Fed. Cl. 667 (2001). United States ☞64.50

Authority vested in the contracting officer to decide whether to cancel an invitation for bids (IFB) and readvertise is extremely broad. 48 C.F.R. § 14.404-1(a)(1). Overstreet Elec. Co., Inc. v. U.S., 47 Fed. Cl. 728 (2000). United States ☞64.50

Agency's decision to cancel solicitation after bid opening could not be justified as an effort to avoid litigation in the Court of Federal Claims; agency's cancellation decision must be supported by evidence in the administrative record at the time of decision, not based upon post hoc rationalization, and the rationale could not be considering "compelling." California Marine Cleaning, Inc. v. U.S., 42 Fed. Cl. 281, 42 Cont. Cas. Fed. (CCH) P 77398 (1998)

Contracting officer's generally broad discretion to cancel a solicitation is substantially narrowed after bid opening to prevent harm to the integrity of the bidding system. 48 C.F.R. § 14.404-1. California Marine Cleaning, Inc. v. U.S., 42 Fed. Cl. 281, 42 Cont. Cas. Fed. (CCH) P 77398 (1998). United States ☞64.50

Procurement official's decision to cancel solicitation in negotiated procurement is inherently discretionary. Shields Enterprises, Inc. v. U.S., 28 Fed. Cl. 615, 38 Cont. Cas. Fed. (CCH) P 76526 (1993). United States ☞64.50

Contracting officer did not act arbitrarily or capriciously by cancelling solicitation because supplies being contracted for were no longer required; solicitation granted to officer gave substantial discretion to reject bid or to cancel or amend solicitation. Durable Metals Products, Inc. v. U.S., 27 Fed. Cl. 472, 38 Cont. Cas. Fed. (CCH) P 76471 (1993), judgment aff'd, 11 F.3d 1071 (Fed. Cir. 1993). United States ☞64.50

Government reasonably and within its discretion determined that specifications in solicitation for bids for providing armed-guard services were ambiguous or inadequate with respect to Government's need for two supervisors per eighthour shift, and thus Government properly cancelled solicitation. Vanguard Sec. Inc. v. U.S., 20 Cl. Ct. 90, 1990 WL 38036 (1990). United States ☞64.50

United States Mint did not abandon its discretion to Congress in determining whether to cancel solicitation for bids in connection with contract for production of coins, but rather considered, in exercise of its own discretion, that public and congressional outcry raised issues worthy of investigation. Arrowhead Metals, Ltd. v. U.S., 8 Cl. Ct. 703, 33 Cont. Cas. Fed. (CCH) P 74026 (1985). United States ☞64.50

Compelling reason to cancel invitation for bids (IFB) exists where IFB contained pricing specifications that were ambiguous and that led to total prices from bidders that lacked a common basis for comparison. Dynamic Corporation, B-296366, 2005 CPD ¶ 125 (Comp. Gen. 2005)

Agency lacked a reasonable basis to cancel a request for proposals (RFP) after disclosure of the offerors' proposed prices where the RFP provided only for a price competition and did not contain technical evaluation factors, the agency intends to issue an invitation for bids for this same requirement, and there is no basis to find the government or the integrity of the procurement system would be prejudiced if the RFP were not cancelled. Rand & Jones Enterprises Company, Inc., B-296483, 2005 CPD ¶ 142 (Comp. Gen. 2005)

Agency reasonably concluded it had a compelling reason to cancel invitation for bids after bid opening where the solicitation's language was ambiguous concerning certain certification requirements associated with the application and removal of paint from the steel structures of a bridge, creating a competition conducted on an unequal basis, and where one of the reasonable interpretations of the certification requirements would not meet the agency's actual needs. Brickwood Contractors, Inc., B-292171, 2003 CPD ¶ 120 (Comp. Gen. 2003)

Contracting agency had a reasonable basis to cancel request for quotations and recompete requirement for third party billing support services where the only quote that was received in response to the initial solicitation was evaluated as unacceptable and the record shows that during the course of evaluation the agency reasonably concluded that initial solicitation no longer meets the agency's needs. DataTrak Consulting, Inc., B-292502, B-292502.2, B-292503, B-292503.2, 2003 CPD ¶ 169 (Comp. Gen. 2003)

Agency had compelling reason to cancel an invitation for bids containing inconsistent provisions regarding the performance period and outdated Service Contract Act wage determinations. Paragon Van Lines, Inc., B-291820.2, B-291913, 2003 CPD ¶ 79 (Comp. Gen. 2003)

Compelling reason existed to cancel invitation for bids (IFB) after bid opening where IFB required performance of services that would be impossible to perform within the required time period. Chenega Management, LLC, B-290598, 2002 CPD ¶ 143 (Comp. Gen. 2002)

Agency properly converted the procurement from sealed bid to negotiated procedures, after bid opening, where the only acceptable bid received was at an unreasonable price. Agency's corrective action of canceling converted negotiated procurement was permissible where agency determined that a potentially ambiguous solicitation requirement may have resulted in unduly restricted competition. Matter of: FCS Construction Services, Inc., B-283726, B-283726.2, 2000 WL 2535 (Comp. Gen. 2000)

Cancellation of an invitation for bids after bid opening is proper where solicitation does not reflect changed requirements in work and award under the solicitation would not serve the government's actual needs. Eastern Technical Enterprises, Inc., B-281319, B-281320, 99-1 CPD ¶ 17 (Comp. Gen. 1999)

Agency did not have a compelling reason to cancel solicitation after bid opening based upon allegedly ambiguous pricing requirements, where the solicitation, when read as a whole, is susceptible to only one reasonable interpretation regarding how bidders were to structure their bids. Massaro Company; Poerio Inc., B-280772.2, B-280772.3, 98-2 CPD ¶ 123 (Comp. Gen. 1998)

3 Reason for cancellation of invitations

Government Printing Office can cancel bids only for compelling reasons once bids have been opened and made public. U.S. v. International Business Machines Corp., 892 F.2d 1006, 36 Cont. Cas. Fed. (CCH) P 75772 (Fed. Cir. 1989). United States ☞64.50

Federal Energy Regulatory Commission (FERC) contracting officer did not have compelling reason for cancelling bid solicitation for stenographic services contract, making cancellation of contract abuse of discretion; reasons given for cancelling solicitation, including omission of clause requiring bid and performance bond, omission of organizational conflict of interest clause and omission of clause referring to potential loss of exhibits by stenographer, were inconsistent with reasons stated by FERC when initially cancelling the solicitation. Ace-Federal Reporters, Inc. v. F.E.R.C., 734 F. Supp. 20, 36 Cont. Cas. Fed. (CCH) P 75868 (D.D.C. 1990). United States ☞64.50

Decision of contracting officer (CO) to cancel solicitation for harbor dredging because its specifications were inadequate was arbitrary and capricious; administrative record did not support government's contentions that solicitation was defective because it did not contain sufficient information regarding the hardness of the rock to be dredged, it prohibited blasting or other pre-treatment of the rock, and it did not provide for an open-water disposal site, resulting in decreased competition and inflated bids from those companies that did compete. 48 C.F.R. § 14.404-1(c)(1). Great Lakes Dredge & Dock Co. v. U.S., 60 Fed. Cl. 350 (2004). United States ☞64.50

Absent a compromise to the competitive bidding process, agency lacks a compelling reason for cancellation of a solicitation after bid opening. 48 C.F.R. § 14.404-1(a)(1). California Marine Cleaning, Inc. v. U.S., 42 Fed. Cl. 281, 42 Cont. Cas. Fed. (CCH) P 77398 (1998). United States ☞64.50

Social Security Administration's (SSA's) need to reassess whether some of work on computer contracts should be done in-house as well as its conclusion that it needed to revise scope of work, as articulated at time of cancellation, formed reasonable basis for cancelling request for proposals and was not arbitrary and capricious. Shields Enterprises, Inc. v. U.S., 28 Fed. Cl. 615, 38 Cont. Cas. Fed. (CCH) P 76526 (1993). United States ☞64.50

Government's principal motivation for cancellation of solicitation for bids for providing unarmed guard services, that solicitation did not allow Immigration and Naturalization Service to obtain additional services on immediate basis, lacked rational basis both in law and fact and could not be upheld as permissible exercise of agency's discretion. Vanguard Sec. Inc. v. U.S., 20 Cl. Ct. 90, 1990 WL 38036 (1990). United States ☞64.50

Government's decision to cancel solicitation for bids for providing unarmed guard services, based on perceived prejudice to bidders from ambiguity in contract as to whether bidders had to resubmit pricing information for additional hours, was without factual predicate, where no pricing sheet called for such information, and pricing sheet, which took precedence over instructions, specified that additional hours were to be compensated at unit price bid per hour. Vanguard Sec. Inc. v. U.S., 20 Cl. Ct. 90, 1990 WL 38036 (1990). United States ☞64.50

In determining whether Government reasonably cancelled solicitation for bids, Government would be allowed to advance post hoc justifications for cancellation. Vanguard Sec. Inc. v. U.S., 20 Cl. Ct. 90, 1990 WL 38036 (1990). United States ☞64.50

It is not the case that only decisions to cancel solicitation for bids based on changed requirements will be overridden due to agency's failure to make every effort timely to identify such changes. Vanguard Sec. Inc. v. U.S., 20 Cl. Ct. 90, 1990 WL 38036 (1990). United States ☞64.50

Procurement regulation, which required Government to make every effort to both anticipate changes in a requirement before bid opening and to notify bidders of resulting modification or cancellation so that bidders may change bids and so that Government may prevent unnecessary exposure of bid prices, was merely hortatory, and thus Government did not violate regulation when it cancelled solicitation for bids for providing unnamed guard services on basis that solicitation did not contain adequate personnel requirements, even though there was no evidence that procurement personnel made any effort to confirm that solicitation reflected actual, present, and prospective requirements for production guards. Vanguard Sec. Inc. v. U.S., 20 Cl. Ct. 90, 1990 WL 38036 (1990). United States ☞64.50

Government's failure to state needs adequately in solicitation for bids, such that significant modification to contract would be required if agency's needs were to be met during performance, is compelling reason to cancel solicitation. Vanguard Sec. Inc. v. U.S., 20 Cl. Ct. 90, 1990 WL 38036 (1990). United States ☞64.50

Government's understatement of guard post assignments in solicitation for bids for providing unarmed guard services was error which rendered solicitation defective, and thus Government reasonably and within its discretion deemed specifications inadequate and cancelled solicitation. Vanguard Sec. Inc. v. U.S., 20 Cl. Ct. 90, 1990 WL 38036 (1990). United States ☞64.50

Decision of Department of Treasury to cancel solicitation of bids for contract in connection with coin production was "compelling" as well as reasonable and rational, where critical reason was desire to review and weigh implications of contracting out coin blanking operations to private sector. Arrowhead Metals, Ltd. v. U.S., 8 Cl. Ct. 703, 33 Cont. Cas. Fed. (CCH) P 74026 (1985). United States ☞64.50

Decision of Department of Treasury to cancel solicitation of bids for contract relating to coin production was not without rational basis, given concern as to propriety and/or national interest factor of contracting out work that overseeing House subcommittee and others considered governmental function. Arrowhead Metals, Ltd. v. U.S., 8 Cl. Ct. 703, 33 Cont. Cas. Fed. (CCH) P 74026 (1985). United States ☞64.50

If party challenging cancellation of solicitation is unable to show that government officials involved in procurement process lacked rational or reasonable basis for their cancellation decision, party must present evidence of clear and prejudicial violation of applicable statute or regulations. Aviation Enterprises, Inc. v. U.S., 8 Cl. Ct. 1, 32 Cont. Cas. Fed. (CCH) P 73403 (1985). Public Contracts ☞5.1

Alleged violations of regulations requiring contracting officers to give reason for cancellation of solicitation and to assure prospective bidders of their opportunity to bid on any resolicitation of bids was insufficient to warrant any equitable or legal relief, where neither alleged violation denied dissatisfied bidder fair and full consideration of its proposal. Aviation Enterprises, Inc. v. U.S., 8 Cl. Ct. 1, 32 Cont. Cas. Fed. (CCH) P 73403 (1985). United States ☞64.50

Violation of regulation requiring that bidders be given reason for cancellation of solicitation was at most harmless error, where bidders were informed of reason for cancellation within reasonable time after first notification of cancellation. Aviation Enterprises, Inc. v. U.S., 8 Cl. Ct. 1, 32 Cont. Cas. Fed. (CCH) P 73403 (1985). United States ☞64.50

Contracting officer had both compelling reason to cancel solicitation, and cancellation was in public interest, thereby satisfying regulations governing cancellation of bids both before and after opening of bids, where it was necessary to rework specifications in order to include turbo-prop aircraft, and tenor and intent behind reasons justifying cancellation after opening encompassed overstated specifications in solicitation. Aviation Enterprises, Inc. v. U.S., 8 Cl. Ct. 1, 32 Cont. Cas. Fed. (CCH) P 73403 (1985). United States ☞64.50

In procurement terms "requirement" was synonymous with request for proposal and did not indicate that using facility need no longer existed at air force base; thus, notification of cancellation of solicitation in which it was noted there was no longer any requirement for aircraft was not inconsistent with official reason for cancellation that specifications were overstated. Aviation Enterprises, Inc. v. U.S., 8 Cl. Ct. 1, 32 Cont. Cas. Fed. (CCH) P 73403 (1985). United States ☜64.50

Defective specifications, mistaken contractual provisions and erroneous specifications, in appropriate cases, may be compelling reasons within discretion of contracting officer for rejection of all bids. Caddell Const. Co. v. U.S., 7 Cl. Ct. 236, 32 Cont. Cas. Fed. (CCH) P 73206 (1985). United States ☜64.50

In the circumstances, conclusion that unacceptably high prices were present because plaintiff's bid was 13.87 percent and only other bid was 16.7 percent over Government's estimate for construction of a submarine headquarters administration building was not unreasonable, and cancellation of the invitation for bids was appropriate. Caddell Const. Co. v. U.S., 7 Cl. Ct. 236, 32 Cont. Cas. Fed. (CCH) P 73206 (1985). United States ☜64.50

4 Bad faith

Inference of bad faith of personnel of United States Mint in cancelling solicitation for bids to perform "blanking," annealing and upsetting processes could not be drawn from Mint's postbid opening cost analysis efforts. Arrowhead Metals, Ltd. v. U.S., 8 Cl. Ct. 703, 33 Cont. Cas. Fed. (CCH) P 74026 (1985). United States ☜64.50

Speculation that if foreign contractor were not low bidder on United States Treasury Department contract and American firm was low bidder, solicitation would not have been cancelled, did not support assertion of bad faith on part of Mint personnel in cancelling solicitation of bids. Arrowhead Metals, Ltd. v. U.S., 8 Cl. Ct. 703, 33 Cont. Cas. Fed. (CCH) P 74026 (1985). United States ☜64.50

Criteria for determining whether bid cancellation decisions lack rational basis include determination of existence of bad faith on part of defendant that deprive bidder of fair and honest consideration of its proposal; determination of whether reasonable basis for administrative decision exists; degree of proof needed for recovery is related to amount of discretion entrusted to procurement officials; and/or in some instances, proven violation of statute or regulation can be grounds for recovery. Arrowhead Metals, Ltd. v. U.S., 8 Cl. Ct. 703, 33 Cont. Cas. Fed. (CCH) P 74026 (1985). United States ☜64.50

Criteria used to evaluate whether Government lacked rational or reasonable basis for its decision or acted in arbitrary and capricious manner in cancelling solicitation of bids include: determination of existence of bad faith on part of Government which deprived bidder of fair and honest consideration of its proposal, and determination of whether reasonable basis for administrative decision exists; furthermore, degree of proof needed for recovery is related to amount of discretion entrusted to procurement officials, and in some instances, proven violation of statute or regulation can be grounds for recovery. Aviation Enterprises, Inc. v. U.S., 8 Cl. Ct. 1, 32 Cont. Cas. Fed. (CCH) P 73403 (1985). Public Contracts ☜5.1

5 Injunctions

For purpose of determining whether low bidder was entitled to enjoin Government's cancellation of solicitation for bids for providing unarmed guard services, language of schedule, which stated that prices bid for base hours carried over for additional requirements, prevailed over amended note on evaluation of bids and award criteria, which required that bidders must enter price for additional guard hours, where clause in solicitation stated that any inconsistency in solicitation shall be resolved by giving precedence to schedule. Vanguard Sec. Inc. v. U.S., 20 Cl. Ct. 90, 1990 WL 38036 (1990). United States ☜64.60(5.1)

For purpose of determining whether low bidder was entitled to enjoin Government's cancellation of solicitation for bids for providing unarmed guard services, amendment to solicitation providing that additional hours must be separately priced did not show that solicitation called for provision of additional services through options, as opposed to indefinite quantity requirement, where amendment did not also amend pricing sheet or otherwise advise bidders on how or in what manner they were to furnish additional information. Vanguard Sec. Inc. v. U.S., 20 Cl. Ct. 90, 1990 WL 38036 (1990). United States ☜64.60(5.1)

Low bidder showed irreparable damage if Government was not enjoined from cancelling solicitation for bids for providing unarmed guard services, where contractor could only recoup its bid preparation costs, and not its loss of anticipated profits, in suit for damages against Government. Vanguard Sec. Inc. v. U.S., 20 Cl. Ct. 90, 1990 WL 38036 (1990). United States ☞64.60(5.1)

Injunctive relief with respect to Government's cancellation of contract can be granted if contractor can establish clear and prejudicial violation of applicable procurement statute or regulation. 28 U.S.C.A. § 1491(a)(3). Vanguard Sec. Inc. v. U.S., 20 Cl. Ct. 90, 1990 WL 38036 (1990). United States ☞64.60(5.1)

For purpose of determining whether low bidder was entitled to enjoin Government's cancellation of solicitation for bids for providing unarmed guard services, insofar as amendment to solicitation attempted to convert indefinite quantity contract into fixed-price contract subject to options, amendment failed to displace contract provisions inherent in an indefinite contract. Vanguard Sec. Inc. v. U.S., 20 Cl. Ct. 90, 1990 WL 38036 (1990). United States ☞64.60(5.1)

For purpose of determining whether low bidder was entitled to enjoin Government's cancellation of solicitation for bids for providing unarmed guard services, solicitation's designation of contract as firm fixed-price contract was consistent with reaffirmation in same section that it was indefinite quantity contract, as meaning of contract was that prices for additional services, as well as for base and optional years, were firm fixed hourly rates. Vanguard Sec. Inc. v. U.S., 20 Cl. Ct. 90, 1990 WL 38036 (1990). United States ☞64.60(5.1)

For purpose of determining whether low bidder was entitled to enjoin Government's cancellation of solicitation for bids for providing unarmed guard services, even if solicitation could be characterized as unclear as to whether it was indefinite quantity contract or fixed-price contract subject to options, no bidder was confused about requirements of solicitation, as amended, that contract would be indefinite quantity contract. Vanguard Sec. Inc. v. U.S., 20 Cl. Ct. 90, 1990 WL 38036 (1990). United States ☞64.60(5.1)

Contractor which sought permanent injunction ordering United States to reinstate cancelled solicitation and to award contract to offerer with lowest price, that is, contractor, had very high burden of proof to surmount in establishing its entitlement to such relief; it had to establish by clear and convincing evidence that there was no rational basis for Treasury Department's cancellation of the solicitation. Arrowhead Metals, Ltd. v. U.S., 8 Cl. Ct. 703, 33 Cont. Cas. Fed. (CCH) P 74026 (1985). Injunction ☞128(7)

Air Force's decision to cancel solicitation based on specification, which overstated minimum needs of Air Force and restricted competition, was entirely reasonable, and therefore, dissatisfied bidder was not entitled to injunctive relief and bid preparation costs, where dissatisfied bidder failed to show that any of procuring officers had specific intent to injure bidder, bidder knew what reason for cancellation was and was able to challenge, air force procurement officials had high degree of discretion to cancel solicitations, and there were no regulatory violations which would render cancellation decision improper. Aviation Enterprises, Inc. v. U.S., 8 Cl. Ct. 1, 32 Cont. Cas. Fed. (CCH) P 73403 (1985). United States ☞64.50

Where record established that plaintiff had submitted a bid on project, and that no contract had been awarded on that project when complaint was filed, and complaint asserted that, in solicitation of bids for construction project, requirements of regulation governing cancellation of invitations after opening had not been followed, plaintiff's application for a preliminary injunction was a contract claim within scope of statute governing Claims Court jurisdiction. 28 U.S.C.A. § 1491(a)(3). Caddell Const. Co. v. U.S., 7 Cl. Ct. 236, 32 Cont. Cas. Fed. (CCH) P 73206 (1985). Federal Courts ☞1076

Apparent low bidder of contract to construct submarine headquarters administration building was not entitled to a preliminary injunction prohibiting Government from proceeding with an award of a contract on a revised invitation for bids, in that there was a compelling reason for Government to cancel invitation for bids and revise project for resolicitation and, in instant procurement, preliminary injunction could only set aside invitation for bids and direct a new solicitation, which would not be in the public interest. Caddell Const. Co. v. U.S., 7 Cl. Ct. 236, 32 Cont. Cas. Fed. (CCH) P 73206 (1985). Injunction ☞138.63

Under invitation for bids for dredging, agency reasonably rejected bid as unbalanced where bidder failed to include cost of preparing a site for disposal of dredged sediment in its unit price for dredging sediment, for which payment would be made over the term of the project, and instead included disposal site costs in its lump sum price for grubbing and clearing, a minor work item, such that the disposal site costs comprised 99 percent of the price for grubbing and clearing; rejection of the bid was proper based on the agency's reasonable determination that the unbalancing posed an unreasonable risk that bidder would receive substantial up-front payment upon completing the grubbing and clearing work, whether or not it had completed the site preparation work. L.W. Matteson, Inc., B-290224, 2002 CPD ¶ 89 (Comp. Gen. 2002)

Where invitation for bids (IFB) expressly required option period prices to be determined solely by application of IFB's economic price adjustment clause, bid was properly rejected as nonresponsive for offering different option year prices, since the economic price adjustment clause is a material term of the IFB and any bid taking exception to it materially affects the legal rights of the bidder and the government. First American Engineered Solutions, B-289051, 2001 CPD ¶ 207 (Comp. Gen. 2001)

Agency properly rejected as nonresponsive a bid that included statements by the bidder that the government would provide various utilities, which materially altered the rights and obligations of the bidder and contracting agency. Walashek Industrial & Marine, B-281577, 99-1 CPD ¶ 30 (Comp. Gen. 1999)

Under invitation for bids (IFB) for construction of water control structure, agency reasonably rejected bid as unbalanced where bidder failed to allocate the cost of a cofferdam (a dewatering measure) among related work items requiring dewatering measures, as provided in the IFB, and instead included the cost of a cofferdam in its lump-sum line item price for a relatively minor work requirement for clearing, grubbing, and snagging of debris on the site, rendering the bidder's price for that line item many multiples higher than the government's estimate for the item and the other bids received; rejection of the bid was proper based upon agency's reasonable determination that the unbalancing posed an unacceptable risk that the government would make a substantial payment to the bidder upon completion of the required clearing, grubbing, and snagging work, without any assurance that the bidder would have constructed the cofferdam which was included in its price for that line item. Matter of: Industrial Builders, Inc., B-283749, 99-2 CPD ¶ 114 (Comp. Gen. 1999)

Agency properly reinstated a bid, previously rejected as nonresponsive, which failed to include a completed supplemental schedule of individual hourly rates where the schedule was not used in the evaluation of bid prices, and its omission did not affect the bidder's promise to perform as specified. Booth & Associates, Inc.—Advisory Opinion, B-277477, B-277477.2, 98-1 CPD ¶ 104 (Comp. Gen. 1998)

In a solicitation for a requirements contract, the agency reasonably rejected the apparent low bid as materially unbalanced where the bid included nominal prices for numerous line items and enhanced prices for other line items, and where uncertainty concerning the reliability of the solicitation's estimated quantities gave rise to a reasonable doubt that the unbalanced bid would actually represent the lowest price to the government. Alice Roofing & Sheet Metal Works, Inc., B-275477, 97-1 CPD ¶ 86 (Comp. Gen. 1997)

A bid that limits the bidder's liability to obtain permits and pay fees, which are responsibilities assigned the bidder under an invitation for bids (IFB) for a construction project, materially modifies the terms of the IFB and must be rejected as nonresponsive. Bishop Contractors, Inc., B-246526, 91-2 CPD ¶ 555 (Comp. Gen. 1991)

Bidder's failure to submit properly and completely executed certification regarding debarment, suspension, proposed debarment and other responsibility matters with bid at bid opening does not affect firm's material obligations under solicitation and therefore does not render bid nonresponsive. Intermountain Electric, Inc., B-236953, B-236953.2, 90-1 CPD ¶ 143 (Comp. Gen. 1990)

Protest alleging that bid was nonresponsive because it did not contain required information concerning whether bidder entered into a third party indemnification agreement in order to obtain bonds required by solicitation is denied. The information does not relate to the bidder's obligation to perform in accordance with the material terms and conditions of the solicitation, and therefore can be furnished any time before award. EDT Construction, Inc., and Northwest Paving & Construction Company, Inc., a joint venture, B-240343, 90-2 CPD ¶ 374 (Comp. Gen. 1990)

Failure of bidder to complete representation in its bid regarding its corporate status for taxpayer identification purposes has no bearing on the material aspects of the bid and thus does not render the bid nonresponsive. Watson Agency, Inc., B-241072, 90-2 CPD ¶ 506 (Comp. Gen. 1990)

Bid which attempts to limit government's rights and supplement bidder's rights under the termination for convenience clause in an invitation for bids (IFB) is nonresponsive since it contains a material deviation from the terms of the IFB. Gelco Payment Systems, Inc., B-234957, 89-2 CPD ¶ 27 (Comp. Gen. 1989)

6 Jurisdiction

Claims Court had jurisdiction to determine whether cancellation of invitation for bid for manufacture of propeller shaft assembly was proper, where plaintiff was seeking reinstatement of the cancelled solicitation, and no contract had been awarded. 28 U.S.C.A. § 1491(a)(3). National Forge Co. v. U.S., 779 F.2d 665, 33 Cont. Cas. Fed. (CCH) P 74149 (Fed. Cir. 1985). Federal Courts ☞1080

Allegation that contracting officer had orally promised to award contract to bidder, even though bidder was not lowest or next lowest bidder in sealed bidding procurement, was insufficient to establish implied in fact contract with United States, as required to establish Court of Federal Claims' jurisdiction over bidder's claim that this promise was breached, in that officer lacked authority to bind government in manner alleged. Domagala v. U.S., 30 Fed. Cl. 149, 39 Cont. Cas. Fed. (CCH) P 76600 (1993), aff'd, 39 F.3d 1196 (Fed. Cir. 1994). Federal Courts ☞1077; United States ☞69(2)

For purpose of determining whether low bidder would be granted injunctive relief with respect to Government's cancellation of solicitation for bids for providing unarmed guard services, injunction would not be in public interest, where immediate modification of contract would be necessary with respect to the number of guards to be provided by contractor, and other bidders had been denied opportunity to show whether they could provide lowest overall price to Government for larger quantity of guards. Vanguard Sec. Inc. v. U.S., 20 Cl. Ct. 90, 1990 WL 38036 (1990). United States ☞64.60(5.1)

For purpose of determining whether low bidder would be granted injunctive relief with respect to Government's cancellation of solicitation for bids for providing unarmed guard services, permanent injunction would have greater harm on Government and other bidders, where immediate modification to contract would be necessary to provide for further guards. Vanguard Sec. Inc. v. U.S., 20 Cl. Ct. 90, 1990 WL 38036 (1990). United States ☞64.60(5.1)

Jurisdiction of United States Claims Court to grant equitable relief in cases involving government contracts prior to award of the contracts includes claims questioning propriety of bid cancellations. 28 U.S.C.A. § 1491(a)(3). Arrowhead Metals, Ltd. v. U.S., 8 Cl. Ct. 703, 33 Cont. Cas. Fed. (CCH) P 74026 (1985). Federal Courts ☞1080

Where bidder contended that cancellation of solicitation of proposal from small businesses to supply the four aircraft, on lease basis, for use by United States Air Force, to which bidder and others had submitted bids, deprived bidder, and perhaps others, of fair and full consideration of their bids, Claims Court had equitable jurisdiction to review propriety of cancellation, despite fact that claim was filed with court after solicitation was cancelled. Aviation Enterprises, Inc. v. U.S., 8 Cl. Ct. 1, 32 Cont. Cas. Fed. (CCH) P 73403 (1985). Federal Courts ☞1076

Following proper cancellation of request for proposal there was no existing solicitation or bids responsive thereto which could form basis for implied-in-fact contract necessary to confer injunctive authority jurisdiction on Claims Court; thus, Claims Court lacked equitable jurisdiction to order resolicitation. Aviation Enterprises, Inc. v. U.S., 8 Cl. Ct. 1, 32 Cont. Cas. Fed. (CCH) P 73403 (1985). Federal Courts ☞1077

By complying with terms of agency solicitation bidder is entitled to have its bid fully and fairly considered by the agency and a claim that the agency improperly canceled the solicitation after bid was submitted falls squarely within jurisdiction of the Claims Court. National Forge Co. v. U.S., 7 Cl. Ct. 530, 32 Cont. Cas. Fed. (CCH) P 73355 (1985). Federal Courts ☞1076; United States ☞64.60(1)

That plaintiff claims improper cancellation of solicitation based upon a regulation has no bearing on Claims Court's jurisdiction; regulation limits agency's authority to cancel the solicitation after bidding is open governing one aspect of evaluation process and, as such, the regulation constitutes one of the terms of the implied contract of fair dealing that forms the court's jurisdiction. 28 U.S.C.A. § 1491(a)(3). National Forge Co. v. U.S., 7 Cl. Ct. 530, 32 Cont. Cas. Fed. (CCH) P 73355 (1985). Federal Courts ⚯1076

Claims court has jurisdiction to entertain preaward actions initiated after cancellation of bid solicitation. 28 U.S.C.A. § 1491(a), (a)(3). Caddell Const. Co. v. U.S., 7 Cl. Ct. 236, 32 Cont. Cas. Fed. (CCH) P 73206 (1985). Federal Courts ⚯1076

7 Parties

Second-lowest bidder is the only "interested party" entitled to protest award of government contract to General Services Board of Contract Appeals, where every disappointed bidder on formally advertised sealed-bid procurement offers essentially the same package of products and services, bids materially differ only as to price, solicitation itself is not challenged, and there is no reason to believe that secondlowest bid is not responsive. Federal Property and Administrative Services Act of 1949, § 111(f)(1), (f)(9)(B), as amended, 40 U.S.C.A. § 759(f)(1), (f)(9)(B). U.S. v. International Business Machines Corp., 892 F.2d 1006, 36 Cont. Cas. Fed. (CCH) P 75772 (Fed. Cir. 1989). United States ⚯64.55(2)

In order to establish standing, a bid protestor must show that it was an interested party prejudiced by the award by demonstrating that there was a substantial chance it would have received the contract award but for the error. First Enterprise v. U.S., 61 Fed. Cl. 109 (2004). United States ⚯64.60(2)

Prospective bidder had standing to file post-award bid protest claiming that its inability to bid was due to agency's failure to send it a copy of the amended solicitation. 31 U.S.C.A. § 3551(2). Razorcom Teleph & Net, LLC v. U.S., 56 Fed. Cl. 140 (2003). United States ⚯64.60(2)

Incumbent contractor was not an "interested party" with standing under the Administrative Dispute Resolution Act to contest government's alleged failure to perform a best value analysis and to award to the lowest cost alternative in solicitation for information technology services performed by contractor; although incumbent, who was not informed of the solicitation, suffered an injury in fact in loss of the contract, the injury was not fairly traceable to the government's evaluation of the awardee's price or value. 28 U.S.C.A. § 1491(b)(1). Cybertech Group, Inc. v. U.S., 48 Fed. Cl. 638 (2001). Federal Courts ⚯1110

Bidder whose bid was determined to be unresponsive, and whose only chance of winning the contract was in a resolicitation, was not an "interested party" within meaning of Tucker Act amendment giving Court of Federal Claims jurisdiction of postaward bid protest actions, and thus bidder lacked standing to assert deficiencies in agency's evaluation of the responsiveness of successful bid. Ryan Co. v. U.S., 43 Fed. Cl. 646 (1999). United States ⚯64.60(2)

In order to secure reinstatement of cancelled solicitation, party must first demonstrate standing to request such relief, that is, party must show that it was within zone of active consideration at time that solicitation was cancelled, and it must then show by clear and convincing evidence either that government officials involved in procurement process lacked rational or reasonable basis for decision to cancel solicitation or that procurement procedure involved clear and prejudicial violation of applicable statutes and regulations. Durable Metals Products, Inc. v. U.S., 27 Fed. Cl. 472, 38 Cont. Cas. Fed. (CCH) P 76471 (1993), judgment aff'd, 11 F.3d 1071 (Fed. Cir. 1993). United States ⚯64.50; United States ⚯64.60(2)

8 Presumptions and burden of proof

Foreign contractor failed to meet heavy burden required to overcome presumption of good faith on part of personnel of United States Mint in performing their official duties in cancelling bid solicitation; cancellation occurred due to concern over whether it was consistent with Mint's responsibilities for it to contract out "blanking" to private sector, director of Mint stated that Mint was fully prepared at time to award contract to lowest responsible bidder, whether foreign or domestic, and contractor remained eligible to bid on Mint procurements for "strip." Arrowhead Metals, Ltd. v. U.S., 8 Cl. Ct. 703, 33 Cont. Cas. Fed. (CCH) P 74026 (1985). United States ⚯64.50

In establishing that cancellation of solicitation for bids was improper, party challenging cancellation has burden of showing that government officials involved in procurement process lacked rational or reasonable basis for their cancellation decision. Aviation Enterprises, Inc. v. U.S., 8 Cl. Ct. 1, 32 Cont. Cas. Fed. (CCH) P 73403 (1985). Public Contracts ☞5.1

To overcome presumption that government officials acted properly in procuring bids or cancelling solicitations law requires well-nigh irrefragable proof. Aviation Enterprises, Inc. v. U.S., 8 Cl. Ct. 1, 32 Cont. Cas. Fed. (CCH) P 73403 (1985). United States ☞64.25; United States ☞64.50

9 Attorneys fees

Contracting agency was not substantially justified, so as to preclude an award of attorney fees to a bid protestor under the Equal Access to Justice Act (EAJA), when it attempted to convert solicitation from a sealed bid to negotiated procurement and when it failed to follow the procedures required by the Federal Acquisition Regulation for cancellation of an invitation for bids (IFB). 28 U.S.C.A. § 2412(d)(1)(A); 48 C.F.R. § 14.404-1. Brickwood Contractors, Inc. v. U.S., 49 Fed. Cl. 148 (2001). United States ☞147(12)

Agency's decision to cancel solicitation was not substantially justified, so as to preclude an award of attorney fees under the Equal Access to Justice Act (EAJA), where agency canceled solicitation in reliance on determination of the General Accounting Office (GAO) that one bid was untimely, as untimeliness of one bid did not provide a rational basis for canceling the solicitation. 28 U.S.C.A. § 2412(d). California Marine Cleaning, Inc. v. U.S., 43 Fed. Cl. 724 (1999). United States ☞147(12)

10 Judicial review

Claims Court correctly restricted its legal review to whether contracting officer's interpretation of, and later decision to cancel, solicitation of bids for manufacture of propeller shaft assembly was unreasonable or an abuse of discretion under requirements for cancellation set forth in Federal Acquisition Regulations System. National Forge Co. v. U.S., 779 F.2d 665, 33 Cont. Cas. Fed. (CCH) P 74149 (Fed. Cir. 1985). Federal Courts ☞1118

After it was determined that Federal Energy Regulatory Commission (FERC) did not have rational basis to cancel bid solicitation for stenographic services contract, remand to FERC was required to determine which contractor provided most advantageous bid, although one contractor had submitted bonus bid that was responsive to solicitation. Ace-Federal Reporters, Inc. v. F.E.R.C., 734 F. Supp. 20, 36 Cont. Cas. Fed. (CCH) P 75868 (D.D.C. 1990). United States ☞64.60(5.1)

Restrictions in Federal Acquisition Regulations regarding cancellation of solicitation limited only General Services Administration's power, so that while General Services Administration must have compelling reason to take such action, federal court's scope of review was governed by Administrative Procedure Act and under Act federal court had much broader authority to direct General Services Administration to resolicit bids for contracts. Federal Property and Administrative Services Act of 1949, § 301 et seq., as amended, 41 U.S.C.A. § 251 et seq.; 5 U.S.C.A. § 706(2). Abel Converting, Inc. v. U.S., 679 F. Supp. 1133, 34 Cont. Cas. Fed. (CCH) P 75449 (D.D.C. 1988). Administrative Law And Procedure ☞751; United States ☞64.60(3.1)

Upon contractor's complaint that regulation was violated by Government when cancelling solicitation for bids, Claims Court is to examine both whether agency determination to cancel is reasonable or abuse of discretion under applicable procurement regulation, and whether Government's conduct violated procedure set forth by cancellation regulation. 28 U.S.C.A. § 1491(a)(3). Vanguard Sec. Inc. v. U.S., 20 Cl. Ct. 90, 1990 WL 38036 (1990). United States ☞64.50

In determining whether Government's motivation for cancellation of solicitation for bids lacked rational basis, whether officials may have considered incomplete documentation or no documentation at all when recommending cancellation was irrelevant if cancellation determination by commissioner and contracting officer accreted a reasonable basis. Vanguard Sec. Inc. v. U.S., 20 Cl. Ct. 90, 1990 WL 38036 (1990). United States ☞64.50

Court asked to determine whether Government acted in bad faith in cancelling request for proposals cannot base finding of bad faith solely on speculation and innuendo. Aviation Enterprises, Inc. v. U.S., 8 Cl. Ct. 1, 32 Cont. Cas. Fed. (CCH) P 73403 (1985). United States ☞64.50

§ 14.404-2 Rejection of individual bids.

(a) Any bid that fails to conform to the essential requirements of the invitation for bids shall be rejected.

(b) Any bid that does not conform to the applicable specifications shall be rejected unless the invitation authorized the submission of alternate bids and the supplies offered as alternates meet the requirements specified in the invitation.

(c) Any bid that fails to conform to the delivery schedule or permissible alternates stated in the invitation shall be rejected.

(d) A bid shall be rejected when the bidder imposes conditions that would modify requirements of the invitation or limit the bidder's liability to the Government, since to allow the bidder to impose such conditions would be prejudicial to other bidders. For example, bids shall be rejected in which the bidder—

(1) Protects against future changes in conditions, such as increased costs, if total possible costs to the Government cannot be determined;

(2) Fails to state a price and indicates that price shall be "price in effect at time of delivery;"

(3) States a price but qualifies it as being subject to "price in effect at time of delivery;"

(4) When not authorized by the invitation, conditions or qualifies a bid by stipulating that it is to be considered only if, before date of award, the bidder receives (or does not receive) award under a separate solicitation;

(5) Requires that the Government is to determine that the bidder's product meets applicable Government specifications; or

(6) Limits rights of the Government under any contract clause.

(e) A low bidder may be requested to delete objectionable conditions from a bid provided the conditions do not go to the substance, as distinguished from the form, of the bid, or work an injustice on other bidders. A condition goes to the substance of a bid where it affects price, quantity, quality, or delivery of the items offered.

(f) Any bid may be rejected if the contracting officer determines in writing that it is unreasonable as to price. Unreasonableness of price includes not only the total price of the bid, but the prices for individual line items as well.

(g) Any bid may be rejected if the prices for any line items or subline items are materially unbalanced (see 15.404-1(g)).

(h) Bids received from any person or concern that is suspended, debarred, proposed for debarment or declared ineligible as of the bid opening date shall be rejected unless a compelling reason determination is made (see Subpart 9.4).

(i) Low bids received from concerns determined to be not responsible pursuant to subpart 9.1 shall be rejected (but if a bidder is a small business concern, see 19.6 with respect to certificates of competency).

(j) When a bid guarantee is required and a bidder fails to furnish the guarantee in accordance with the requirements of the invitation for bids, the bid shall be rejected, except as otherwise provided in 28.101-4.

(k) The originals of all rejected bids, and any written findings with respect to such rejections, shall be preserved with the papers relating to the acquisition.

(l) After submitting a bid, if all of a bidder's assets or that part related to the bid are transferred during the period between the bid opening and the award, the transferee may not be able to take over the bid. Accordingly, the contracting officer shall reject the bid unless the transfer is effected by merger, operation of law, or other means not barred by 41 U.S.C. 6305 or 31 U.S.C. 3727.

United States Code Annotated

Administrative determinations, see 41 USCA § 257.

Contract requirements, see 41 USCA § 254.

Contracts, planning, solicitation, evaluation, and award procedures, see 10 USCA § 2305.

Definitions, see 10 USCA § 2302, 41 USCA §§ 259, 403.

Determinations and decisions, see 10 USCA § 2310, 41 USCA § 262.

Evaluation and award, see 41 USCA § 253b.

Kinds of contracts, see 10 USCA § 2306.

Planning and solicitation requirements, see 41 USCA § 253a.

Notes of Decisions

1 Rejection of bid, generally

Public housing authority's vote to award contract to bidder did not preclude authority from later rejecting bid, where authority indicated that, before executing contract, its legal counsel would review issues. Professional Bldg. Concepts, Inc. v. City of Cent. Falls, 974 F.2d 1, 38 Cont. Cas. Fed. (CCH) P 76395 (1st Cir. 1992). United States ☞82(3.3)

Government's rejection of bid for purchase of textile fabrics and clothing articles was arbitrary and capricious; Government failed to establish that it based its rejection of bid on finding that it was unreasonable and there were no cogent and compelling reasons for its decision to reject bid. Arthur Forman Enterprises, Inc. v. U.S., 960 F.2d 154 (Fed. Cir. 1991). United States ☞64.40(2)

2 Discretion of agency

It was rational for contracting officer (CO) to reject bid bond as non-responsive because it was accompanied by a photocopied rather than original power of attorney, and absence of original power of attorney failed to provide sufficient authority to bind surety.

Determination of what is "so far out of line" on particular contract as to allow contracting agency to reject bid is a matter particularly committed to agency and contracting officer's discretion. 48 C.F.R. § 14.406-3(g)(5)(i, ii). Orbas & Associates v. Secretary of Navy, 863 F. Supp. 1186, 40 Cont. Cas. Fed. (CCH) P 76740 (E.D. Cal. 1994). United States ☞64.30

FAR 14.404-2(d) states that a bid "shall be rejected when the bidder imposes conditions that would modify requirements of the invitation." Where an IFB requires that bidders use products on the Qualified Products List (QPL) and a bidder listed products not listed on the QPL, the agency was correct in finding the bid to be non-responsive. The Court finds that the bidder did not comply in all material respects with the IFB and modified the requirements by not bidding a qualified product. Therefore, the contracting officer correctly rejected the bid. Fire-Trol Holdings, LLC. v. U.S., 68 Fed. Cl. 281 (2005), aff'd, 205 Fed. Appx. 834 (Fed. Cir. 2006)

Contracting agency was not reasonable in rejecting bid on ground that bidder's facially valid bid bond was nonresponsive based on post bid-opening communications from surety that contractor was not authorized to submit bid bond in the amount submitted, and from bidder that it would not have a payment or performance bond; regulation governing responsiveness of bid and performance bonds requires only that bid guarantee be proper on its face, and mandates post-award procedure to protect government if case of contractor's failure to furnish bonds. Aeroplate Corp. v. U.S., 67 Fed. Cl. 4 (2005)

Contracting officer (CO) was not reasonable in rejecting computer-generated powers of attorney appointing officer to execute bid bonds and accompanying certificates on ground that mechanical signatures were applied after powers of attorney were generated. Hawaiian Dredging Const. Co., Inc. v. U.S., 59 Fed. Cl. 305 (2004)

Protest alleging that agency improperly rejected protester's bid in violation of a solicitation clause is sustained where the clause contained a latent ambiguity regarding eligibility for an expedited verification review of the apparently successful offeror's status as a service-disabled veteran-owned small business concern, and the protester had no basis to be aware of the agency's contrary interpretation of the clause. Commandeer Construction Company LLC, B-405771, 2011 CPD ¶ 287, 2011 WL 6880720 (Comp. Gen. 2011)

Agency improperly rejected low bid as nonresponsive where the bid failed to acknowledge a solicitation amendment that merely clarified requirements already contained in the solicitation and otherwise had a negligible effect on the quality and price of the construction project bid upon. Matter of: Fort Mojave/Hummel, a Joint Venture, B-296961, 2005 CPD ¶ 181 (Comp. Gen. 2005)

A nonresponsive bid must be rejected and may not be changed or corrected based on explanations offered by the bidder after bid opening; the importance of maintaining the integrity of the competitive bidding system outweighs the possibility that the government might realize monetary savings if a material deficiency in a bid is corrected or waived. AAA Roofing Company Inc., B-240852, 90-2 CPD ¶ 485 (Comp. Gen. 1990)

3 Responsiveness of bid

Bid for public contract is mathematically unbalanced, such that bid is nonresponsive and must be rejected, when each line item in the bid does not reflect actual costs to bidder. 48 C.F.R. §§ 14.404-2(g), 15.814. McKnight Const. Co., Inc. v. Department of Defense, 85 F.3d 565, 40 Cont. Cas. Fed. (CCH) P 76942 (11th Cir. 1996). Public Contracts ⊙=8

Although Government has discretion to reject responsive bids as unreasonable, after bid opening, discretion is limited by requirement that contracting officer have cogent and compelling reasons to reject bids. Arthur Forman Enterprises, Inc. v. U.S., 960 F.2d 154 (Fed. Cir. 1991). United States ⊙=64.40(2)

Government's obligation to treat fairly responsive bids it receives is independent of Government's good-faith obligation and limits contracting officer's discretion to the extent officer may not act arbitrarily and capriciously in rejecting responsive bids. Arthur Forman Enterprises, Inc. v. U.S., 960 F.2d 154 (Fed. Cir. 1991). United States ⊙=64.40(2)

Contracting officer's decision to deny award of contract to low bidder was fully rational and reasonable; contracting officer was faced with very low bid, with significant disparities in two of three options, bidder's failure to respond to numerous requests for verification, nonresponsive representative at specially set bid verification meeting, unexplained discrepancies between portions of bid and subcontractor bids submitted to bidder, and lack of original bid worksheets. 48 C.F.R. § 14.406-3(g)(5)(i). Orbas & Associates v. Secretary of Navy, 863 F. Supp. 1186, 40 Cont. Cas. Fed. (CCH) P 76740 (E.D. Cal. 1994). United States ⊙=64.40(1); United States ⊙=64.40(3)

It was rational for contracting officer (CO) to reject bid bond as non-responsive because it was accompanied by a photocopied rather than original power of attorney, and absence of original power of attorney failed to provide sufficient authority to bind surety. 48 C.F.R. § 14.404-2(j). All Seasons Const., Inc. v. U.S., 55 Fed. Cl. 175 (2003). United States ⊙=64.35

Bids that fail to conform to essential requirements of invitation for bids must be rejected. 48 C.F.R. § 14.404-2(a). Firth Const. Co., Inc. v. U.S., 36 Fed. Cl. 268, 41 Cont. Cas. Fed. (CCH) P 76970 (1996). United States ⊙=64.40(1)

Bid on public contract which contains material nonconformity must be rejected; material nonconformity goes to substance of bid which affects price, quality, quantity, or delivery of article or service offered. Bean Dredging Corp. v. U.S., 22 Cl. Ct. 519, 36 Cont. Cas. Fed. (CCH) P 76017, 1991 WL 15601 (1991). Public Contracts ⊙=8

Rejection of a bid as nonresponsive for failing to provide the price for one of many line items included in the bid schedule was improper, where the item for which the price was omitted is divisible from the solicitation's overall requirements, *de minimis* as to total cost, and would not affect the competitive standing of the bidders; the omission should be waived as a minor informality under such circumstances. W.B. Construction and Sons, Inc., B-405818, B-405818.2, 2012 CPD ¶ 17, 2012 WL 32162 (Comp. Gen. 2012)

4 Timeliness

Bidder's failure to submit a properly executed bid guarantee by omitting penal sum on bid bond rendered its bid nonresponsive, and contracting agency was not permitted to consider bidder's explanation that omission of penal sum was a clerical error; moreover, bidder was not entitled to alter its bid with additional documents to correct the error following bid opening. 48 C.F.R. §§ 14.301(a), 14.404-2. Interstate Rock Products, Inc. v. U.S., 50 Fed. Cl. 349 (2001), aff'd, 48 Fed. Appx. 331 (Fed. Cir. 2002). United States ⊙=64.30

To be deemed responsive, bid as submitted must obligate bidder to perform exactly what is being called for in solicitation. 48 C.F.R. §§ 14.301(a), 14.404-2(a). ECDC Environmental, L.C. v. U.S., 40 Fed. Cl. 236, 42 Cont. Cas. Fed. (CCH) P 77250 (1998). United States ☞64.30

5 Reason for rejection of bid

Contracting officer has discretion to reject bid based upon unreasonable price alone. Arthur Forman Enterprises, Inc. v. U.S., 960 F.2d 154 (Fed. Cir. 1991). United States ☞64.60(1)

Sale of low bidder to another company did not provide grounds for Government Accounting Office's (GAO) recommendation of termination of contract between low bidder and Immigration and Naturalization Service (INS) to provide security guard services; bidder was an ongoing business with substantial tangible and intangible assets, bidder retained its pre-sale assets and employees after sale, and bidder continued to perform its contracts and to conduct business as it had for 14 years. Federal Property and Administrative Services Act of 1949, § 303B(c), as amended, 41 U.S.C.A. § 253B(c); 48 C.F.R. § 14.404-2. Lyons Sec. Services, Inc. v. U.S., 38 Fed. Cl. 783 (1997). United States ☞72.1(2)

If agency relies upon improper basis to cancel procurement, cancellation may be upheld if another proper basis for cancellation exists which is reasonable and not abuse of discretion. Shields Enterprises, Inc. v. U.S., 28 Fed. Cl. 615, 38 Cont. Cas. Fed. (CCH) P 76526 (1993). United States ☞64.60(3.1)

Under invitation for bids for dredging, agency reasonably rejected bid as unbalanced where bidder failed to include cost of preparing a site for disposal of dredged sediment in its unit price for dredging sediment, for which payment would be made over the term of the project, and instead included disposal site costs in its lump sum price for grubbing and clearing, a minor work item, such that the disposal site costs comprised 99 percent of the price for grubbing and clearing; rejection of the bid was proper based on the agency's reasonable determination that the unbalancing posed an unreasonable risk that bidder would receive substantial up-front payment upon completing the grubbing and clearing work, whether or not it had completed the site preparation work. L.W. Matteson, Inc., B-290224, 2002 CPD ¶ 89 (Comp. Gen. 2002)

Where invitation for bids (IFB) expressly required option period prices to be determined solely by application of IFB's economic price adjustment clause, bid was properly rejected as nonresponsive for offering different option year prices, since the economic price adjustment clause is a material term of the IFB and any bid taking exception to it materially affects the legal rights of the bidder and the government. First American Engineered Solutions, B-289051, 2001 CPD ¶ 207 (Comp. Gen. 2001)

Agency properly rejected as nonresponsive a bid that included statements by the bidder that the government would provide various utilities, which materially altered the rights and obligations of the bidder and contracting agency. Walashek Industrial & Marine, B-281577, 99-1 CPD ¶ 30 (Comp. Gen. 1999)

Under invitation for bids (IFB) for construction of water control structure, agency reasonably rejected bid as unbalanced where bidder failed to allocate the cost of a cofferdam (a dewatering measure) among related work items requiring dewatering measures, as provided in the IFB, and instead included the cost of a cofferdam in its lump-sum line item price for a relatively minor work requirement for clearing, grubbing, and snagging of debris on the site, rendering the bidder's price for that line item many multiples higher than the government's estimate for the item and the other bids received; rejection of the bid was proper based upon agency's reasonable determination that the unbalancing posed an unacceptable risk that the government would make a substantial payment to the bidder upon completion of the required clearing, grubbing, and snagging work, without any assurance that the bidder would have constructed the cofferdam which was included in its price for that line item. Matter of: Industrial Builders, Inc., B-283749, 99-2 CPD ¶ 114 (Comp. Gen. 1999)

Agency properly reinstated a bid, previously rejected as nonresponsive, which failed to include a completed supplemental schedule of individual hourly rates where the schedule was not used in the evaluation of bid prices, and its omission did not affect the bidder's promise to perform as specified. Booth & Associates, Inc.—Advisory Opinion, B-277477, B-277477.2, 98-1 CPD ¶ 104 (Comp. Gen. 1998)

In a solicitation for a requirements contract, the agency reasonably rejected the apparent low bid as materially unbalanced where the bid included nominal prices for numerous line items and enhanced prices for other line items, and where uncertainty concerning the reliability of the solicitation's estimated quantities gave rise to a reasonable doubt that the unbalanced bid would actually represent the lowest price to the government. Alice Roofing & Sheet Metal Works, Inc., B-275477, 97-1 CPD ¶ 86 (Comp. Gen. 1997)

A bid that limits the bidder's liability to obtain permits and pay fees, which are responsibilities assigned the bidder under an invitation for bids (IFB) for a construction project, materially modifies the terms of the IFB and must be rejected as nonresponsive. Bishop Contractors, Inc., B-246526, 91-2 CPD ¶ 555 (Comp. Gen. 1991)

Bidder's failure to submit properly and completely executed certification regarding debarment, suspension, proposed debarment and other responsibility matters with bid at bid opening does not affect firm's material obligations under solicitation and therefore does not render bid nonresponsive. Intermountain Electric, Inc., B-236953, B-236953.2, 90-1 CPD ¶ 143 (Comp. Gen. 1990)

Protest alleging that bid was nonresponsive because it did not contain required information concerning whether bidder entered into a third party indemnification agreement in order to obtain bonds required by solicitation is denied. The information does not relate to the bidder's obligation to perform in accordance with the material terms and conditions of the solicitation, and therefore can be furnished any time before award. EDT Construction, Inc., and Northwest Paving & Construction Company, Inc., a joint venture, B-240343, 90-2 CPD ¶ 374 (Comp. Gen. 1990)

Failure of bidder to complete representation in its bid regarding its corporate status for taxpayer identification purposes has no bearing on the material aspects of the bid and thus does not render the bid nonresponsive. Watson Agency, Inc., B-241072, 90-2 CPD ¶ 506 (Comp. Gen. 1990)

Bid which attempts to limit government's rights and supplement bidder's rights under the termination for convenience clause in an invitation for bids (IFB) is nonresponsive since it contains a material deviation from the terms of the IFB. Gelco Payment Systems, Inc., B-234957, 89-2 CPD ¶ 27 (Comp. Gen. 1989)

6 Minor informalities or irregularities

"Substantial deviation" that will require rejection of bid due to failure to conform with essential requirements of invitation for bids is defined as one which affects either price, quantity, or quality of article offered. 48 C.F.R. § 14.404-2(a). Firth Const. Co., Inc. v. U.S., 36 Fed. Cl. 268, 41 Cont. Cas. Fed. (CCH) P 76970 (1996). United States ☞64.40(1)

7 Mistakes

Not every error requires rejection of an agency's procurement action, and the court will not overturn a contract award based on de minimis errors made during the procurement process. Anderson Columbia Environmental, Inc. v. U.S., 43 Fed. Cl. 693 (1999). United States ☞64.55(1)

Absent other considerations, an obvious clerical error that deceives no one does not require rejection of bid. Sciaba Const. Corp. v. City of Boston, 35 Mass. App. Ct. 181, 617 N.E.2d 1023 (1993). Public Contracts ☞8

8 Bid preparation costs

Where considerable authority is granted to contracting officer to reject bids, high degree of proof is needed to establish right to recover bid preparation costs. Durable Metals Products, Inc. v. U.S., 27 Fed. Cl. 472, 38 Cont. Cas. Fed. (CCH) P 76471 (1993), judgment aff'd, 11 F.3d 1071 (Fed. Cir. 1993). United States ☞64.60(6)

9 Judicial review

Rejection of a bid based on the determination of ineligibility should not be overturned unless no rational basis exists for the contracting officer's determination. Walsh-Healey Act, § 1 et seq., 41 U.S.C.A. § 35 et seq.Mil-Tech Systems, Inc. v. U.S., 6 Cl. Ct. 26, 32 Cont. Cas. Fed. (CCH) P 72719 (1984). United States ☞64.60(4)

§ 14.404-3 Notice to bidders of rejection of all bids.

When it is determined necessary to reject all bids, the contracting officer shall notify each bidder that all bids have been rejected and shall state the reason for such action.

United States Code Annotated

Administrative determinations, see 41 USCA § 257.

Contract requirements, see 41 USCA § 254.

Contracts, planning, solicitation, evaluation, and award procedures, see 10 USCA § 2305.

Definitions, see 10 USCA § 2302, 41 USCA §§ 259, 403.

Determinations and decisions, see 10 USCA § 2310, 41 USCA § 262.

Evaluation and award, see 41 USCA § 253b.

Kinds of contracts, see 10 USCA § 2306.

Planning and solicitation requirements, see 41 USCA § 253a.

§ 14.404-4 Restrictions on disclosure of descriptive literature.

When a bid is accompanied by descriptive literature (as defined in 2.101), and the bidder imposes a restriction that prevents the public disclosure of such literature, the restriction may render the bid nonresponsive. The restriction renders the bid nonresponsive if it prohibits the disclosure of sufficient information to permit competing bidders to know the essential nature and type of the products offered or those elements of the bid that relate to quantity, price, and delivery terms. The provisions of this paragraph do not apply to unsolicited descriptive literature submitted by a bidder if such literature does not qualify the bid (see 14.202-5(e)).

United States Code Annotated

Administrative determinations, see 41 USCA § 257.

Contract requirements, see 41 USCA § 254.

Contracts, planning, solicitation, evaluation, and award procedures, see 10 USCA § 2305.

Definitions, see 10 USCA § 2302, 41 USCA §§ 259, 403.

Determinations and decisions, see 10 USCA § 2310, 41 USCA § 262.

Evaluation and award, see 41 USCA § 253b.

Kinds of contracts, see 10 USCA § 2306.

Planning and solicitation requirements, see 41 USCA § 253a.

Notes of Decisions

In general 1

1 In general

Where bidder restricted disclosure of required test data submitted to establish responsiveness of the bid, the agency properly rejected the bid as nonresponsive. Matter of: Industrial Acoustics Co., Inc.; Acoustic Systems, B-255123, B-255123.2, B-255123.3, B-255203, B-255203.2, B-255203.3, 94-1 CPD ¶ 220 (Comp. Gen. 1994)

Bid should not be rejected as nonresponsive merely because a drawing accompanying the bid contained a restriction on its disclosure where the drawing is not necessary to evaluate the bid. Cancellation of invitation for bids (IFB) because agency determined all bidders were nonresponsive to drawing requirement is not justified where the drawing is not necessary for evaluation of bids. Therefore, the agency should reinstate IFB and make award to the low, responsive bidder eligible for award. Colt Industries, B-225483, 87-1 CPD ¶ 288 (Comp. Gen. 1987)

§ 14.404-5 All or none qualifications.

Unless the solicitation provides otherwise, a bid may be responsive notwithstanding that the bidder specifies that award will be accepted only on all, or a specified group, of the items. Bidders shall not be permitted to withdraw or modify "all or none" qualifications after bid opening since such qualifications are substantive and affect the rights of other bidders.

United States Code Annotated

Administrative determinations, see 41 USCA § 257.

Contract requirements, see 41 USCA § 254.

Contracts, planning, solicitation, evaluation, and award procedures, see 10 USCA § 2305.

Definitions, see 10 USCA § 2302, 41 USCA §§ 259, 403.

Determinations and decisions, see 10 USCA § 2310, 41 USCA § 262.

Evaluation and award, see 41 USCA § 253b.

Kinds of contracts, see 10 USCA § 2306.

Planning and solicitation requirements, see 41 USCA § 253a.

Notes of Decisions

In general 1

1 In general

Offer in response to solicitation by the Department of Veterans Affairs (VA) for distribution of pharmaceutical products in 14 VA regions was an "all or none offer" within meaning of the Federal Acquisition Regulation (FAR), notwithstanding that offer recognized that the VA maintained the right to set aside three regions for small business concerns, where proposal limited acceptance to "all regions" contained in the offer. 48 C.F.R. § 14.404-5. AmerisourceBergen Drug Corp. v. U.S., 60 Fed. Cl. 30 (2004). United States ⬡64.30

Clause in solicitation which stated that contracting agency would "not accept any offers which are submitted only as an 'ALL OR NONE' offer" did not prohibit bidders from submitting any "all or none" offers; rather, clause unambiguously prohibited offerors from submitting only an "all or none" offer. 48 C.F.R. § 14.404-5. AmerisourceBergen Drug Corp. v. U.S., 60 Fed. Cl. 30 (2004). United States ⬡64.30

§ 14.405 Minor informalities or irregularities in bids.

A minor informality or irregularity is one that is merely a matter of form and not of substance. It also pertains to some immaterial defect in a bid or variation of a bid from the exact requirements of the invitation that can be corrected or waived without being prejudicial to other bidders. The defect or variation is immaterial when the effect on price, quantity, quality, or delivery is negligible when contrasted with the total cost or scope of the supplies or services being acquired. The contracting officer either shall give the bidder an opportunity to cure any deficiency resulting from a minor informality or irregularity in a bid or waive the deficiency, whichever is to the advantage of the Government. Examples of minor informalities or irregularities include failure of a bidder to—

(a) Return the number of copies of signed bids required by the invitation;

(b) Furnish required information concerning the number of its employees;

(c) Sign its bid, but only if—

(1) The unsigned bid is accompanied by other material indicating the bidder's intention to be bound by the unsigned bid (such as the submission of a bid guarantee or a letter signed by the bidder, with the bid, referring to and clearly identifying the bid itself); or

(2) The firm submitting a bid has formally adopted or authorized, before the date set for opening of bids, the execution of documents by typewritten, printed, or stamped signature and submits evidence of such authorization and the bid carries such a signature;

(d) Acknowledge receipt of an amendment to an invitation for bids, but only if—

(1) The bid received clearly indicates that the bidder received the amendment, such as where the amendment added another item to the invitation and the bidder submitted a bid on the item; or

(2) The amendment involves only a matter of form or has either no effect or merely a negligible effect on price, quantity, quality, or delivery of the item bid upon; and

(e) Execute the representations with respect to Equal Opportunity and Affirmative Action Programs, as set forth in the clauses at 52.222-22, Previous Contracts and Compliance Reports, and 52.222-25, Affirmative Action Compliance.

United States Code Annotated

Administrative determinations, see 41 USCA § 257.

Contract requirements, see 41 USCA § 254.

Contracts, planning, solicitation, evaluation, and award procedures, see 10 USCA § 2305.

Definitions, see 10 USCA § 2302, 41 USCA §§ 259, 403.

Determinations and decisions, see 10 USCA § 2310, 41 USCA § 262.

Evaluation and award, see 41 USCA § 253b.

Kinds of contracts, see 10 USCA § 2306.

Planning and solicitation requirements, see 41 USCA § 253a.

Notes of Decisions

In general 1
Discretion of agency 2
Rejection of bids 4
Responsiveness of bids 3

1 In general

Bidder's submission of noncertified corporate check, rather than certified check as required by invitation of bids on public housing project, constituted material noncompliance with bidding process that warranted bidder's rejection. Professional Bldg. Concepts, Inc. v. City of Cent. Falls, 974 F.2d 1, 38 Cont. Cas. Fed. (CCH) P 76395 (1st Cir. 1992). United States ⫟64.30; United States ⫟82(3.3)

While a contract is to be awarded only to a bidder who fully responds to the federal government invitation for bids, where defect or omission in nonresponsive bid is trivial or a matter of a mere formality, law does not require that entire bid be rejected; rather, bidder may be given an opportunity to cure defect or government may waive those terms to which bid does not respond. Grade-Way Const. v. U.S., 7 Cl. Ct. 263, 32 Cont. Cas. Fed. (CCH) P 73209 (1985). United States ⫟64.30

2 Discretion of agency

Determination of whether a defect in a bid is material is committed to agency discretion. 48 C.F.R. §§ 14.301, 14.405. Tel-Instrument Electronics Corp. v. U.S., 56 Fed. Cl. 174 (2003), aff'd, 87 Fed. Appx. 752 (Fed. Cir. 2004). United States ⫟64.30

By failing to acknowledge this amendment, the bidder obligated itself only to provide the agency a restroom built with red shingles and gray concrete, when the agency required amber shingles and brown concrete. In other words, absent acknowledgment of the amendment, the bidder has not bound itself to furnish the specified shingles. Even if an amendment's impact on price is trivial, the amendment is material if it affects the quality of performance in more than a negligible way. The color of an item can be a material requirement, as can compliance with a pre-existing color scheme or other aesthetic considerations. Matter of: Northern Sealcoating & Paving, Inc., B-299393, 2007 CPD ¶ 67 (Comp. Gen. 2007)

where a discrepancy between what is required in the IFB and what is offered is *de minimus,* and acceptance of the deviating bid will result in a contract that will meet the government's actual requirements and will not be prejudicial to any other bidder, the discrepancy may be waived as a minor informality. AllWorld Language Consultants, Inc., B-298831, 2006 CPD ¶ 198 (Comp. Gen. 2006)

Awardee's bid for dredging a boat basin and channel was responsive, even though it failed to acknowledge an amendment, which provided the precise location of disposal area for the dredging material, an area that was identified in the initial invitation for bids, because the amendment did not impose any additional legal obligations and therefore was not material. Singelton Enterprises, B-295562, 2005 CPD ¶ 42 (Comp. Gen. 2005)

Protest of award on basis that awardee failed to acknowledge solicitation amendment is denied where amendment provisions cited by protester merely clarified existing solicitation terms, and where any price difference attributable to those provisions is negligible; failure to acknowledge an amendment that is not material may be waived as a minor informality. Lumus Construction, Inc., B-287480, 2001 CPD ¶ 108 (Comp. Gen. 2001)

Bidder's failure to acknowledge a material amendment to an invitation for bids, which resolved an ambiguity between the product description and the bid schedule, and which imposed an additional requirement on the contractor, renders the bid nonresponsive since absent such an acknowledgment the government's acceptance of the bid would not legally obligate the bidder to meet the government's needs as identified in the amendment. John D. Lucas Printing Company, B-285730, 2000 CPD ¶ 154 (Comp. Gen. 2000)

The low bidder, a corporate entity, submitted a signed bid but did not place the word 'by' before the signature, as required by FAR 4.102. The protester, while not challenging the authority of the person who signed for the low bidder, contended that the bid should have been rejected as nonresponsive because the low bidder did not comply with the literal wording of FAR 4.102. The GAO denied the protest because FAR 4.102 deals with a contractor's signature on a *contract*, rather than on a bid, and there is no indication that FAR 4.102 was intended to apply to offers in response to a solicitation. Further, FAR 14.405 permits waiver of minor informalities or irregularities when their effect on price, quantity, quality, or delivery is negligible. As an example of a minor informality or irregularity, FAR, § 14.405(c) (1), lists an unsigned bid which is accompanied by other material indicating the bidder's intention to be bound by the unsigned bid. IBI Security Service, Inc., B-215732, 84-2 CPD ¶ 118 (Comp. Gen. 1984).

3 Responsiveness of bids

If a bidder on a government contract attempts to impose conditions that would modify material requirements of the solicitation, the bid is not responsive and must be rejected; "material requirements" include those affecting price, quantity, quality, or delivery of the solicited products, and thus are not minor informalities or irregularities. 48 C.F.R. § 14.405. Tel-Instrument Electronics Corp. v. U.S., 56 Fed. Cl. 174 (2003), aff'd, 87 Fed. Appx. 752 (Fed. Cir. 2004). United States ☞64.30

When a bid fails to conform with the invitation for bids, it will be rejected if it is nonconforming in a material respect; it follows that when a bid's only defect is an immaterial nonconformity, it is responsive. 48 C.F.R. § 14.301(a). Interstate Rock Products, Inc. v. U.S., 50 Fed. Cl. 349 (2001), aff'd, 48 Fed. Appx. 331 (Fed. Cir. 2002). United States ☞64.30

To be deemed responsive, bid as submitted must obligate bidder to perform exactly what is being called for in solicitation. 48 C.F.R. §§ 14.301(a), 14.404-2(a). ECDC Environmental, L.C. v. U.S., 40 Fed. Cl. 236, 42 Cont. Cas. Fed. (CCH) P 77250 (1998). United States ☞64.30

Where an invitation for bids required the submission of a bid guarantee, the awardee's failure to submit an original bid guarantee at bid opening could not be waived as a minor informality and rendered the bid nonresponsive. Hamilton Pac. Chamberlain, LLC, B-409795, 2014 CPD ¶ 227 (Comp. Gen. 2014)

4 Rejection of bids

"Substantial deviation" that will require rejection of bid due to failure to conform with essential requirements of invitation for bids is defined as one which affects either price, quantity, or quality of article offered. 48 C.F.R. § 14.404-2(a). Firth Const. Co., Inc. v. U.S., 36 Fed. Cl. 268, 41 Cont. Cas. Fed. (CCH) P 76970 (1996). United States ☞64.40(1)

§ 14.406 Receipt of an unreadable electronic bid.

If a bid received at the Government facility by electronic data interchange is unreadable to the degree that conformance to the essential requirements of the invitation for bids cannot be ascertained, the contracting officer immediately shall notify the bidder that the bid will be rejected unless the bidder provides clear and convincing evidence—

(a) Of the content of the bid as originally submitted; and

(b) That the unreadable condition of the bid was caused by Government software or hardware error, malfunction, or other Government mishandling.

United States Code Annotated

Administrative determinations, see 41 USCA § 257.

Contract requirements, see 41 USCA § 254.

Contracts, planning, solicitation, evaluation, and award procedures, see 10 USCA § 2305.

Definitions, see 10 USCA § 2302, 41 USCA §§ 259, 403.

Determinations and decisions, see 10 USCA § 2310, 41 USCA § 262.

Evaluation and award, see 41 USCA § 253b.

Kinds of contracts, see 10 USCA § 2306.

Planning and solicitation requirements, see 41 USCA § 253a.

§ 14.407 Mistakes in bids.

§ 14.407-1 General.

After the opening of bids, contracting officers shall examine all bids for mistakes. In cases of apparent mistakes and in cases where the contracting officer has reason to believe that a mistake may have been made, the contracting officer shall request from the bidder a verification of the bid, calling attention to the suspected mistake. If the bidder alleges a mistake, the matter shall be processed in accordance with this section 14.407. Such actions shall be taken before award.

United States Code Annotated

Administrative determinations, see 41 USCA § 257.

Contract requirements, see 41 USCA § 254.

Contracts, planning, solicitation, evaluation, and award procedures, see 10 USCA § 2305.

Definitions, see 10 USCA § 2302, 41 USCA §§ 259, 403.

Determinations and decisions, see 10 USCA § 2310, 41 USCA § 262.

Evaluation and award, see 41 USCA § 253b.

Kinds of contracts, see 10 USCA § 2306.

Planning and solicitation requirements, see 41 USCA § 253a.

Notes of Decisions

In general 1
Constructive notice of mistake 6
Duty to examine documents 4
Evidence 5
Mutual mistake 2
Unilateral mistake 3

1 In general

In limited circumstances, if the government has knowledge, or constructive knowledge, that a contractor's bid is based on a mistake, and the government accepts the bid and awards the contract despite knowledge of this mistake, then a trial court may reform or rescind the contract, but, generally, a contractor may obtain reformation or rescission of the contract only if the contractor establishes that its bid error resulted from a clear-cut clerical or arithmetical error, or a misreading of the specifications. Giesler v. U.S., 232 F.3d 864 (Fed. Cir. 2000). United States ☞72(1.1); United States ☞74(4)

Contracting officer reasonably suspected mistake and took appropriate steps where low bidder's aggregate bid on government procurement contract was 11% lower than government's estimate and 17% lower than next qualified bidder, and low bidder's base bid was 16% lower than government's estimate, while its option three bid was 957% higher than government's estimate. 48 C.F.R. § 14.406-3(g)(1)(i). Orbas & Associates v. Secretary of Navy, 863 F. Supp. 1186, 40 Cont. Cas. Fed. (CCH) P 76740 (E.D. Cal. 1994). United States ☞64.40(3)

Contractor's mistake in bid was not so gross that enforcement of contract without allowing for reformation was unconscionable, where contractor alleged that its mistake had affected its total bid of $17.2 million by $438,000, or about 2.5 percent; moreover, without correction of its bid mistake, contractor, at the time of award, still anticipated a profit of approximately 1.6%. Will H. Hall and Son, Inc. v. U.S., 54 Fed. Cl. 436 (2002). Reformation Of Instruments ☞17(1); United States ☞74(4)

A government contract may be reformed or rescinded if the contracting officer accepts a bid with actual or constructive knowledge that the bid contains a compensable mistake. Will H. Hall and Son, Inc. v. U.S., 54 Fed. Cl. 436 (2002). Reformation Of Instruments ☞17(1); United States ☞72(1.1)

Contracting officer's alleged failure to advise bidder of its option to withdraw after bidder discovered mistake in bid did not constitute a violation of the Federal Acquisition Regulation (FAR), as bidder was deemed to have constructive knowledge of applicable regulations allowing withdrawal, and FAR places an affirmative obligation on the bidder to request withdrawal. 48 C.F.R. § 14.407-3(a, b). Will H. Hall and Son, Inc. v. U.S., 54 Fed. Cl. 436 (2002). United States ☞64.40(4)

Bidder's alleged mistake in relying on quote from subcontractor which did not include work on a specification section was not an error in business judgment for which equitable relief was not available; although bidder's handling of quote was careless, it did not rise to the level of gross negligence, and bidder discovered the error six days after submitting its bid, and immediately notified the contracting officer. Will H. Hall and Son, Inc. v. U.S., 54 Fed. Cl. 436 (2002). United States ☞64.40(4)

An error in business judgment by a bidder is not a mistake for which equitable relief is available; such an error occurs where the bidder has the facts necessary to make the proper conclusion but, because of improper assumptions or faulty assessments of those facts, makes a bad business decision. Will H. Hall and Son, Inc. v. U.S., 54 Fed. Cl. 436 (2002). United States ☞74(4)

Since bid was responsive, bidder should have been allowed to correct mistake in its bid, omission of front-side of standard step-two form through clerical error, pursuant to mistake-in-bid procedures set out in regulation. 48 C.F.R. § 14.407. ECDC Environmental, L.C. v. U.S., 40 Fed. Cl. 236, 42 Cont. Cas. Fed. (CCH) P 77250 (1998). United States ☞64.30

Fact that contracting officer requested clarification of bidder's response to business management questionnaire question in which bidder indicated that it intended to self-perform only 10% of contract work, while invitation for bid required self-performance of 20%, could not convert issue of nonresponsiveness of bid into issue of responsibility; procuring agency's authority to permit correction of bid mistakes is limited to bids that are responsive to solicitation. Blount, Inc. v. U.S., 22 Cl. Ct. 221, 36 Cont. Cas. Fed. (CCH) P 75981, 1990 WL 210734 (1990). United States ☞64.30

Agency improperly failed to allow correction of claimed mistake in bid, where the bidder established its mistake and its intended bid (which was still low) by clear and convincing evidence and the agency denied the requested correction because of other suspected mistakes which were unrelated to the one claimed and which the agency did not bring to the bidder's attention, as required by FAR 14.407-1 and 14.407-3(g), and where the evidence in the record, including hearing testimony and worksheets, does not evidence that the bidder made additional mistakes (as suspected by the agency) or that the worksheets were not in good order. Matter of: Odyssey International, Inc., B-296855.2, 2006 CPD ¶ 49 (Comp. Gen. 2005)

Contracting agency properly allowed correction of firm's bid, which resulted in displacement of other competitors as the low bidder, where the firm's intended bid price is clearly evidenced in the firm's entire bid, including documents furnished with descriptive literature. George E. Failing Company, B-233207, 89-1 CPD ¶ 203 (Comp. Gen. 1989)

2 Mutual mistake

Government contractor could not invoke doctrine of mutual mistake to reform contract to include state sales tax in contract price, although both parties were mistaken concerning treatment of states sales tax in the contract, where contractor's mistake concerned the tax exemption status of materials used in the project, and government's mistake concerned the inclusion of state sales tax in unit prices contained in agency's Unit Price Book (UPB), and thus errors were separate and not mutual. C.W. Over & Sons, Inc. v. U.S., 54 Fed. Cl. 514 (2002). Reformation Of Instruments ☞19(2)

3 Unilateral mistake

Where reformation of contract is sought due to contractor's unilateral bid mistake, contractor must show by clear and convincing evidence that: (1) mistake in fact occurred prior to contract award; (2) mistake was clear-cut, clerical or mathematical error or misreading of specifications and not judgmental error; (3) prior to award Government knew, or should have known, that mistake had been made and, therefore, should have requested bid verification; (4) Government did not request bid verification or its request for bid verification was inadequate; and (5) proof of intended bid is established. 48 C.F.R. §§ 14.406-1, 14.406-3(g) (1992). McClure Elec. Constructors, Inc. v. Dalton, 132 F.3d 709, 42 Cont. Cas. Fed. (CCH) P 77246 (Fed. Cir. 1997). United States ☞72(1.1)

Bid verification request sent out by contracting officer was adequate to put contractor on notice of suspected bid mistake, and thus, contractor was not entitled to contract reformation to correct its unilateral bid mistake; although contracting officer did not expressly state that she suspected error, she did reveal amounts of all bids, and with this information in hand, contractor could see that next lowest bid was almost 20% higher than its bid, and that government estimate was almost twice contractor's bid. 48 C.F.R. §§ 14.406-1, 14.406-3(g) (1992). McClure Elec. Constructors, Inc. v. Dalton, 132 F.3d 709, 42 Cont. Cas. Fed. (CCH) P 77246 (Fed. Cir. 1997). United States ☞72(1.1)

Contract awardee established existence of a unilateral mistake in omission of salary of employee in its final price proposal, and thus was entitled to reformation of contract, where mistake occurred prior to award of contract, it was clerical in nature, contracting officer (CO) had constructive notice of error from disparity between awardee's bid and next lowest bid, government did not request verification, and awardee established by clear and convincing evidence the correct amount of its bid. Information Intern. Associates, Inc. v. U.S., 74 Fed. Cl. 192 (2006)

To be entitled to reformation under unilateral mistake, government contractor must show that the contracting officer knew or should have known of the contractor's unilateral mistake at the time its bid was accepted; moreover, the mistaken proposal must contain a clear cut clerical or arithmetical error, or misreading of the specifications. C.W. Over & Sons, Inc. v. U.S., 54 Fed. Cl. 514 (2002). Reformation Of Instruments ☞17(1)

In order to attain rescission on ground of unilateral mistake, government contractor must show: (1) the mistake in fact occurred prior to contract award; (2) the mistake was clerical, mathematical, or misreading of specification, not an error in judgment; (3) prior to award the government knew, or should have known, that a mistake had been made; and (4) the government did not request bid verification or the request was inadequate. Giesler v. U.S., 44 Fed. Cl. 737 (1999), rev'd in part on other grounds, 232 F.3d 864 (Fed. Cir. 2000). United States ☞72(1.1); United States ☞74(4)

Policy underlying doctrine of unilateral mistake is designed to prevent the government from overreaching by awarding a contract where it knows the contractor has made a significant mistake. Giesler v. U.S., 44 Fed. Cl. 737 (1999), rev'd in part on other grounds, 232 F.3d 864 (Fed. Cir. 2000). United States ☞74(4)

Doctrine of "unilateral mistake" holds that a government contract may be reformed or rescinded if the contracting officer accepts a bid with actual or constructive knowledge that it contains an error. Giesler v. U.S., 44 Fed. Cl. 737 (1999), rev'd in part on other grounds, 232 F.3d 864 (Fed. Cir. 2000). United States ☞74(4)

Despite protester's general assertion that it intends to perform in accordance with specifications, agency may reasonably reject low bid as mistaken where bid was significantly lower than the other responsive bids and the government estimate, and it appears that bid omitted costs of welding pipe, based on bidder's erroneous interpretation of specifications as not requiring welding. Matter of: Nova-CPF, Inc., B-261677, 95-2 CPD ¶ 181 (Comp. Gen. 1995)

4 Duty to examine documents

When the government has notice of a mistake in a particular bid, the government may have a duty to verify that bid by calling attention to the specific error suspected; however, this duty arises only where the contractor's mistake is a clear-cut clerical or arithmetical error, or a misreading of the specifications. Hunt Const. Group, Inc. v. U.S., 281 F.3d 1369 (Fed. Cir. 2002). United States ☞64.40(3)

In limited circumstances, if the government has breached its explicit regulatory duty to examine the contractor's bid for mistakes, then court may rescind a contract, despite an otherwise inexcusable error by the contractor. 48 C.F.R. § 14.407-1. Giesler v. U.S., 232 F.3d 864 (Fed. Cir. 2000). United States ☞74(4)

Though the government has a general duty to examine bids for mistakes, this duty does not extend to errors that may be contained in a contractor's subsequent filings. 48 C.F.R. §§ 14.407-1 to 14.407-3. Giesler v. U.S., 232 F.3d 864 (Fed. Cir. 2000). United States ☞64.40(1)

The government has no legal duty to examine for mistakes any paperwork submitted by contractors and subcontractors subsequent to the opening and acceptance of their bids, and after the completion of the pre-award survey report. 48 C.F.R. §§ 9.106, 14.407. Giesler v. U.S., 232 F.3d 864 (Fed. Cir. 2000). United States ☞64.40(1)

Rescission of contract to supply mixed nuts was not warranted due to the government's failure to examine subcontractor's facsimile which would have disclosed discrepancy between the requested nut mix and the nut mix subcontractor intended to produce; where the fax arrived after contractor's bid was opened and verified, and after the government had completed its pre-award survey of subcontractor, the government had no duty to examine the fax for errors. 48 C.F.R. §§ 14.407-1 to 14.407-3. Giesler v. U.S., 232 F.3d 864 (Fed. Cir. 2000). United States ☞74(4)

With respect to doctrine of unilateral mistake, the reasonableness of contractor's mistake is not relevant to the creation or discharge of the government's verification duty. Giesler v. U.S., 44 Fed. Cl. 737 (1999), rev'd in part on other grounds, 232 F.3d 864 (Fed. Cir. 2000). United States ☞74(4)

Contracting officer has duty to verify bid if all facts and circumstances suggest that it was reasonable to believe mistake had been made. 48 C.F.R. § 14.406-1. Dakota Tribal Industries v. U.S., 34 Fed. Cl. 593, 40 Cont. Cas. Fed. (CCH) P 76867 (1995). United States ☞64.40(3)

5 Evidence

Army Corps of Engineers' rule stating that uncorroborated statement is insufficient to satisfy the clear and convincing evidence standard required to show that the submitted bid was mistaken and what was the actual intended bid, such that bid is subject to correction, is not arbitrary and fact that some honest contractors may lose contracts because of minor errors on their part does not render Army's rule arbitrary. 48 C.F.R. § 14.406-3(a) (Repealed). McKnight Const. Co., Inc. v. Department of Defense, 85 F.3d 565, 40 Cont. Cas. Fed. (CCH) P 76942 (11th Cir. 1996). United States ☞64.30

Mistake, if any, in bidder's failure to include mark up in its bid price for beef patties to be supplied for federal child nutrition programs was noncompensable error in judgment; evidence showed that prevailing market prices for beef at time of bid solicitation were lower than those subsequently claimed by bidder, warranting inference that bidder knowingly decided to mark up its bids by lesser amount. Goldberger Foods, Inc. v. U.S., 960 F.2d 155 (Fed. Cir. 1992). United States ☞70(29)

Bidder on contract to furnish beef patties for federal child nutrition programs failed to establish that its omission of mark up from bid price was type of mistake that would have warranted allowing bidder to withdraw or correct its bid; bidder offered no evidence of raw beef prices quoted by its suppliers, prevailing market prices at time of solicitation were substantially lower than those claimed by bidder, and it was likely that bidder included substantial portion of mark up in preparing its bid. Goldberger Foods, Inc. v. U.S., 960 F.2d 155 (Fed. Cir. 1992). United States ☞70(29)

For purposes of correcting mistakes in government contract bids under Federal Acquisitions Regulations, there is no requirement that contractor's work papers be related in any way to specific line items of the bid. 48 C.F.R. § 14.406-3. McKnight Const. Co., Inc. v. Perry, 888 F. Supp. 1178 (S.D. Ga. 1994). United States ☞64.5

Under Federal Acquisition Regulations, bid work papers can be relied upon as best objective evidence of intended bid on government contract, but intended bid need not be established only from bid working papers in all cases of mistake. 48 C.F.R. § 14.406-3(g)(2). McKnight Const. Co., Inc. v. Perry, 888 F. Supp. 1178 (S.D. Ga. 1994). United States ☞64.60(1)

Bidder on federal government contract to renovate Army barracks presented sufficient evidence to clearly and convincingly establish its intended bid, even though bidder had made mistake in bid by transposing some of the line items in bid, where casual inspection of bid abstract revealed transpositional character of mistake, and bidder's company president submitted sworn affidavit in conjunction with bid itself that clarified the mistake. 48 C.F.R. § 14.406-3. McKnight Const. Co., Inc. v. Perry, 888 F. Supp. 1178 (S.D. Ga. 1994). United States ☞64.60(1)

Government contractor could not invoke doctrine of unilateral mistake to reform contract to include state sales tax in contract price, absent evidence that contracting officers knew of alleged mistake which was contractor's erroneous interpretation of contract clause as indicating that entire project was exempt from state tax; moreover, even if contracting officers should have known of contractor's mistake, it was a mistake in judgment and not a misreading of specifications, and thus was not compensable under the doctrine. C.W. Over & Sons, Inc. v. U.S., 54 Fed. Cl. 514 (2002). Reformation Of Instruments ☞17(1)

Under the Federal Acquisition Regulation (FAR), a bidder's request for an upward correction of its bid before award of the contract may be granted where the request is supported by clear and convincing evidence of both the existence of a mistake and the intended bid; the intended bid does not need to be an exact figure, as long as the bidder provides clear and convincing evidence to establish that the bid would fall within a narrow range of uncertainty and would remain the low bid if corrected. 48 C.F.R. § 14.407-3(a). Will H. Hall and Son, Inc. v. U.S., 54 Fed. Cl. 436 (2002). United States ☞64.40(4)

Bidder who alleged that its bid amount was based on mistake in subcontractor's quote failed to present clear and convincing evidence of its intended bid within a relatively narrow range, as required for correction of bid, where bidder would have had at least six options for its intended bid, and there was a range of 27 to 38.6 percent in possible intended bids. 48 C.F.R. § 14.407-3(a). Will H. Hall and Son, Inc. v. U.S., 54 Fed. Cl. 436 (2002). United States ☞64.40(4)

Pursuant to the Federal Acquisition Regulation (FAR), if the evidence is clear and convincing as to the existence of a bid mistake, but not the amount of the intended bid, or if the evidence only reasonably supports the existence of a mistake but is not clear and convincing, an agency official above the contracting officer may permit withdrawal of the bid. 48 C.F.R. § 14.407-3(c). Will H. Hall and Son, Inc. v. U.S., 54 Fed. Cl. 436 (2002). United States ☞64.40(4)

Affidavit of bidder's secretary and treasurer, who prepared and submitted its bid, which stated that he was unaware that subcontractor's quote was incomplete, did not rise to level of clear and convincing evidence of bid mistake, where bidder's worksheets did not corroborate that bidder was unaware that subcontractor's quote excluded certain work called for in contract. 48 C.F.R. § 14.407-3(a). Will H. Hall and Son, Inc. v. U.S., 54 Fed. Cl. 436 (2002). United States ☞74(11)

6 Constructive notice of mistake

A price disparity between a government contractor's bids is not enough by itself to impute constructive notice by the contracting officer (CO) of a possible error in the contractor's bid, if there are other factors that reasonably could explain the difference. Information Intern. Associates, Inc. v. U.S., 74 Fed. Cl. 192 (2006)

In limited circumstances, if the government has actual or constructive knowledge that a contractor's bid is based upon a mistake, and the government accepts the bid and awards the contract despite knowledge of this mistake, then the court may reform or rescind the contract. Contractor who performed ductwork for hospital renovation did not establish that it was entitled to reform contract based on unilateral mistake as to the degree of effort required in removing and replacing the air system diffusers and grilles, absent evidence that government knew or should have known of the mistake. Conner Brothers Const. Co., Inc. v. U.S., 65 Fed. Cl. 657 (2005)

§ 14.407-2 Apparent clerical mistakes.

(a) Any clerical mistake, apparent on its face in the bid, may be corrected by the contracting officer before award. The contracting officer first shall obtain from the bidder a verification of the bid intended. Examples of apparent mistakes are—

(1) Obvious misplacement of a decimal point;

(2) Obviously incorrect discounts (for example, 1 percent 10 days, 2 percent 20 days, 5 percent 30 days);

(3) Obvious reversal of the price f.o.b. destination and price f.o.b. origin; and

(4) Obvious mistake in designation of unit.

(b) Correction of the bid shall be effected by attaching the verification to the original bid and a copy of the verification to the duplicate bid. Correction shall not be made on the face of the bid; however, it shall be reflected in the award document.

(c) Correction of bids submitted by electronic data interchange shall be effected by including in the electronic solicitation file the original bid, the verification request, and the bid verification.

United States Code Annotated

Administrative determinations, see 41 USCA § 257.

Contract requirements, see 41 USCA § 254.

Contracts, planning, solicitation, evaluation, and award procedures, see 10 USCA § 2305.

Definitions, see 10 USCA § 2302, 41 USCA §§ 259, 403.

Determinations and decisions, see 10 USCA § 2310, 41 USCA § 262.

Evaluation and award, see 41 USCA § 253b.

Kinds of contracts, see 10 USCA § 2306.

Planning and solicitation requirements, see 41 USCA § 253a.

Notes of Decisions

In general 1

1 In general

Misunderstanding of the requirements of base bid and option three of government procurement contract did not fall within definition of "clerical mistake" for which bidder could be permitted to correct bid. 48 C.F.R. § 14.406-2. Orbas & Associates v. Secretary of Navy, 863 F. Supp. 1186, 40 Cont. Cas. Fed. (CCH) P 76740 (E.D. Cal. 1994). United States ☞64.40(3)

There was ample evidence before contracting officer that low bid on procurement contract could contain significant nonclerical errors; low bidder's aggregate bid was 11% lower than government's estimate and 17% lower than next lowest bidder, its base bid was 16% lower than government's estimate while its option three bid was 957% higher than government's estimate, bidder never verified original bid or error, and never specified in writing true amount of error, and there were other suspected errors in the bid. 48 C.F.R. § 14.406-3(g) (1). Orbas & Associates v. Secretary of Navy, 863 F. Supp. 1186, 40 Cont. Cas. Fed. (CCH) P 76740 (E.D. Cal. 1994). United States ☞64.40(3)

Contracting officer could not correct bidder's "clerical mistake" where bidder never verified original bid or error and never specified in writing true amount of the error. 48 C.F.R. § 14.406-2(a). Orbas & Associates v. Secretary of Navy, 863 F. Supp. 1186, 40 Cont. Cas. Fed. (CCH) P 76740 (E.D. Cal. 1994). United States ☞64.40(3)

The FAR required an examination by the CO of the bid for mistakes. Where the CO had reason to believe that a mistake in bid might have been made, verification of the bid was to be obtained from the bidder, calling attention to the suspected mistake. In the event of a clerical mistake, apparent on the face of the bid, the mistake could be corrected by the CO before award after first obtaining verification of the bid intended. Any such correction of a clerical mistake was to be reflected in the award document but not made on the face of the bid. In re Appeal of Walsh Const. Co. of Illinois, A.S.B.C.A. No. 52952, 02-2 B.C.A. (CCH) ¶ 32004, 2002 WL 31303013 (Armed Serv. B.C.A. 2002),

Contract awardee established existence of a unilateral mistake in omission of salary of employee in its final price proposal, and thus was entitled to reformation of contract, where mistake occurred prior to award of contract, it was clerical in nature, contracting officer (CO) had constructive notice of error from disparity between awardee's bid and next lowest bid, government did not request verification, and awardee established by clear and convincing evidence the correct amount of its bid. Information Intern. Associates, Inc. v. U.S., 74 Fed. Cl. 192 (2006)

Bidder's failure to submit a properly executed bid guarantee by omitting penal sum on bid bond rendered its bid nonresponsive, and contracting agency was not permitted to consider bidder's explanation that omission of penal sum was a clerical error; moreover, bidder was not entitled to alter its bid with additional documents to correct the error following bid opening. 48 C.F.R. §§ 14.301(a), 14.404-2. Interstate Rock Products, Inc. v. U.S., 50 Fed. Cl. 349 (2001), aff'd, 48 Fed. Appx. 331 (Fed. Cir. 2002). United States ∞64.30

Contracting agency's failure to inquire concerning absence of insurance information in bid was arbitrary and capricious, where absence of the information clearly indicated a clerical mistake, and bidder had performed two previous contracts for agency. 48 C.F.R. § 14.406-1 (1994). Griffy's Landscape Maintenance LLC v. U.S., 46 Fed. Cl. 257 (2000). United States ∞64.40(3)

Where the bidder correctly added contract line item amounts together to arrive at a total base year price but then used another figure on the next page of its bid schedule as its total base year price when calculating its option year prices, agency reasonably permitted correction of the obvious transcription error as a clerical mistake. Brazos Roofing, Inc., B-275319, B-275319.2, 97-1 CPD ¶ 66 (Comp. Gen. 1997)

§ 14.407-3 Other mistakes disclosed before award.

In order to minimize delays in contract awards, administrative determinations may be made as described in this 14.407-3 in connection with mistakes in bids alleged after opening of bids and before award. The authority to permit correction of bids is limited to bids that, as submitted, are responsive to the invitation and may not be used to permit correction of bids to make them responsive. This authority is in addition to that in 14.407-2 or that may be otherwise available.

(a) If a bidder requests permission to correct a mistake and clear and convincing evidence establishes both the existence of the mistake and the bid actually intended, the agency head may make a determination permitting the bidder to correct the mistake; provided, that if this correction would result in displacing one or more lower bids, such a determination shall not be made unless the existence of the mistake and the bid actually intended are ascertainable substantially from the invitation and the bid itself.

(b) If—

(1) A bidder requests permission to withdraw a bid rather than correct it;

(2) The evidence is clear and convincing both as to the existence of a mistake and as to the bid actually intended; and

(3) The bid, both as uncorrected and as corrected, is the lowest received, the agency head may make a determination to correct the bid and not permit its withdrawal.

(c) If, under paragraph (a) or (b) of this subsection, (1) the evidence of a mistake is clear and convincing only as to the mistake but not as to the intended bid, or (2) the evidence reasonably supports the existence of a mistake but is not clear and convincing, an official above the contracting officer, unless otherwise provided by agency procedures, may make a determination permitting the bidder to withdraw the bid.

(d) If the evidence does not warrant a determination under paragraph (a), (b), or (c) of this section, the agency head may make a determination that the bid be neither withdrawn nor corrected.

(e) Heads of agencies may delegate their authority to make the determinations under paragraphs (a), (b), (c), and (d) of this 14.407-3 to a central authority, or a limited number of authorities as necessary, in their agencies, without power of redelegation.

(f) Each proposed determination shall have the concurrence of legal counsel within the agency concerned before issuance.

(g) Suspected or alleged mistakes in bids shall be processed as follows. A mere statement by the administrative officials that they are satisfied that an error was made is insufficient.

(1) The contracting officer shall immediately request the bidder to verify the bid. Action taken to verify bids must be sufficient to reasonably assure the contracting officer that the bid as confirmed is without error, or to elicit the allegation of a mistake by the bidder. To assure that the bidder will be put on notice of a mistake suspected by the contracting officer, the bidder should be advised as appropriate—

(i) That its bid is so much lower than the other bids or the Government's estimate as to indicate a possibility of error;

(ii) Of important or unusual characteristics of the specifications;

(iii) Of changes in requirements from previous purchases of a similar item; or

(iv) Of any other information, proper for disclosure, that leads the contracting officer to believe that there is a mistake in bid.

(2) If the bid is verified, the contracting officer shall consider the bid as originally submitted. If the time for acceptance of bids is likely to expire before a decision can be made, the contracting officer shall request all bidders whose bids may become eligible for award to extend the time for acceptance of their bids in accordance with 14.404-1(d). If the bidder whose bid is believed erroneous does not (or cannot) grant an extension of time, the bid shall be considered as originally submitted (but see paragraph (g)(5) of this section). If the bidder alleges a mistake, the contracting officer shall advise the bidder to make a written request to withdraw or modify the bid. The request must be supported by statements (sworn statements, if possible) and shall include all pertinent evidence such as the bidder's file copy of the bid, the original worksheets and other data used in preparing the bid, subcontractors' quotations, if any, published price lists, and any other evidence that establishes the existence of the error, the manner in which it occurred, and the bid actually intended.

(3) When the bidder furnishes evidence supporting an alleged mistake, the contracting officer shall refer the case to the appropriate authority (see paragraph (e) of this section) together with the following data:

(i) A signed copy of the bid involved.

(ii) A copy of the invitation for bids and any specifications or drawings relevant to the alleged mistake.

(iii) An abstract or record of the bids received.

(iv) The written request by the bidder to withdraw or modify the bid, together with the bidder's written statement and supporting evidence.

(v) A written statement by the contracting officer setting forth—

(A) A description of the supplies or services involved;

(B) The expiration date of the bid in question and of the other bids submitted;

(C) Specific information as to how and when the mistake was alleged;

(D) A summary of the evidence submitted by the bidder;

(E) In the event only one bid was received, a quotation of the most recent contract price for the supplies or services involved or, in the absence of a recent comparable contract, the contracting officer's estimate of a fair price for the supplies or services;

(F) Any additional pertinent evidence; and

(G) A recommendation that either the bid be considered for award in the form submitted, or the bidder be authorized to withdraw or modify the bid.

(4) When time is of the essence because of the expiration of bids or otherwise, the contracting officer may refer the case by telegraph or telephone to the appropriate authority. Ordinarily, the contracting officer will not refer mistake in bid cases by telegraph or telephone to the appropriate authority when the determination set forth in paragraphs (a) or (b) of this section is applicable, since actual examination is generally necessary to determine whether the evidence presented is clear and convincing.

(5) Where the bidder fails or refuses to furnish evidence in support of a suspected or alleged mistake, the contracting officer shall consider the bid as submitted unless (i) the amount of the bid is so far out of line with the amounts of other bids received, or with the amount estimated by the agency or determined by the contracting officer to be reasonable, or (ii) there are other indications of error so clear, as to reasonably justify the conclusion that acceptance of the bid would be unfair to the bidder or to other bona fide bidders. Attempts made to obtain the information required and the action taken with respect to the bid shall be fully documented.

(h) Each agency shall maintain records of all determinations made in accordance with this subsection 14.407-3, the facts involved, and the action taken in each case. Copies of all such determinations shall be included in the file.

(i) Nothing contained in this subsection 14.407-3 prevents an agency from submitting doubtful cases to the Comptroller General for advance decision.

United States Code Annotated

Administrative determinations, see 41 USCA § 257.

Contract requirements, see 41 USCA § 254.

Contracts, planning, solicitation, evaluation, and award procedures, see 10 USCA § 2305.

Definitions, see 10 USCA § 2302, 41 USCA §§ 259, 403.

Determinations and decisions, see 10 USCA § 2310, 41 USCA § 262.

Evaluation and award, see 41 USCA § 253b.

Kinds of contracts, see 10 USCA § 2306.

Planning and solicitation requirements, see 41 USCA § 253a.

Notes of Decisions

In general 1
Correction of mistakes 6
Duty to examine documents 4
Evidence 5
Mutual mistake 2
Unilateral mistake 3

1 In general

In limited circumstances, if the government has knowledge, or constructive knowledge, that a contractor's bid is based on a mistake, and the government accepts the bid and awards the contract despite knowledge of this mistake, then a trial court may reform or rescind the contract, but, generally, a contractor may obtain reformation or rescission of the contract only if the contractor establishes that its bid error resulted from a clear-cut clerical or arithmetical error, or a misreading of the specifications. Giesler v. U.S., 232 F.3d 864 (Fed. Cir. 2000). United States ☞72(1.1); United States ☞74(4)

Contracting officer reasonably suspected mistake and took appropriate steps where low bidder's aggregate bid on government procurement contract was 11% lower than government's estimate and 17% lower than next qualified bidder, and low bidder's base bid was 16% lower than government's estimate, while its option three bid was 957% higher than government's estimate. 48 C.F.R. § 14.406-3(g)(1)(i). Orbas & Associates v. Secretary of Navy, 863 F. Supp. 1186, 40 Cont. Cas. Fed. (CCH) P 76740 (E.D. Cal. 1994). United States ☞64.40(3)

Contractor's mistake in bid was not so gross that enforcement of contract without allowing for reformation was unconscionable, where contractor alleged that its mistake had affected its total bid of $17.2 million by $438,000, or about 2.5 percent; moreover, without correction of its bid mistake, contractor, at the time of award, still anticipated a profit of approximately 1.6%. Will H. Hall and Son, Inc. v. U.S., 54 Fed. Cl. 436 (2002). Reformation Of Instruments ☞17(1); United States ☞74(4)

A government contract may be reformed or rescinded if the contracting officer accepts a bid with actual or constructive knowledge that the bid contains a compensable mistake. Will H. Hall and Son, Inc. v. U.S., 54 Fed. Cl. 436 (2002). Reformation Of Instruments ☞17(1); United States ☞72(1.1)

Contracting officer's alleged failure to advise bidder of its option to withdraw after bidder discovered mistake in bid did not constitute a violation of the Federal Acquisition Regulation (FAR), as bidder was deemed to have constructive knowledge of applicable regulations allowing withdrawal, and FAR places an affirmative obligation on the bidder to request withdrawal. 48 C.F.R. § 14.407-3(a, b). Will H. Hall and Son, Inc. v. U.S., 54 Fed. Cl. 436 (2002). United States ☞64.40(4)

Bidder's alleged mistake in relying on quote from subcontractor which did not include work on a specification section was not an error in business judgment for which equitable relief was not available; although bidder's handling of quote was careless, it did not rise to the level of gross negligence, and bidder discovered the error six days after submitting its bid, and immediately notified the contracting officer. Will H. Hall and Son, Inc. v. U.S., 54 Fed. Cl. 436 (2002). United States ☞64.40(4)

An error in business judgment by a bidder is not a mistake for which equitable relief is available; such an error occurs where the bidder has the facts necessary to make the proper conclusion but, because of improper assumptions or faulty assessments of those facts, makes a bad business decision. Will H. Hall and Son, Inc. v. U.S., 54 Fed. Cl. 436 (2002). United States ☞74(4)

Since bid was responsive, bidder should have been allowed to correct mistake in its bid, omission of front-side of standard step-two form through clerical error, pursuant to mistake-in-bid procedures set out in regulation. 48 C.F.R. § 14.407. ECDC Environmental, L.C. v. U.S., 40 Fed. Cl. 236, 42 Cont. Cas. Fed. (CCH) P 77250 (1998). United States ☞64.30

2 Mutual mistake

Government contractor could not invoke doctrine of mutual mistake to reform contract to include state sales tax in contract price, although both parties were mistaken concerning treatment of states sales tax in the contract, where contractor's mistake concerned the tax exemption status of materials used in the project, and government's mistake concerned the inclusion of state sales tax in unit prices contained in agency's Unit Price Book (UPB), and thus errors were separate and not mutual. C.W. Over & Sons, Inc. v. U.S., 54 Fed. Cl. 514 (2002). Reformation Of Instruments ☞19(2)

3 Unilateral mistake

Where reformation of contract is sought due to contractor's unilateral bid mistake, contractor must show by clear and convincing evidence that: (1) mistake in fact occurred prior to contract award; (2) mistake was clear-cut, clerical or mathematical error or misreading of specifications and not judgmental error; (3) prior to award Government knew, or should have known, that mistake had been made and, therefore, should have requested bid verification; (4) Government did not request bid verification or its request for bid verification was inadequate; and (5) proof of intended bid is established. 48 C.F.R. §§ 14.406-1, 14.406-3(g) (1992). McClure Elec. Constructors, Inc. v. Dalton, 132 F.3d 709, 42 Cont. Cas. Fed. (CCH) P 77246 (Fed. Cir. 1997). United States ☞72(1.1)

Bid verification request sent out by contracting officer was adequate to put contractor on notice of suspected bid mistake, and thus, contractor was not entitled to contract reformation to correct its unilateral bid mistake; although contracting officer did not expressly state that she suspected error, she did reveal amounts of all bids, and with this information in hand, contractor could see that next lowest bid was almost 20% higher than its bid, and that government estimate was almost twice contractor's bid. 48 C.F.R. §§ 14.406-1, 14.406-3(g) (1992). McClure Elec. Constructors, Inc. v. Dalton, 132 F.3d 709, 42 Cont. Cas. Fed. (CCH) P 77246 (Fed. Cir. 1997). United States ☞72(1.1)

To be entitled to reformation under unilateral mistake, government contractor must show that the contracting officer knew or should have known of the contractor's unilateral mistake at the time its bid was accepted; moreover, the mistaken proposal must contain a clear cut clerical or arithmetical error, or misreading of the specifications. C.W. Over & Sons, Inc. v. U.S., 54 Fed. Cl. 514 (2002). Reformation Of Instruments ☞17(1)

In order to attain rescission on ground of unilateral mistake, government contractor must show: (1) the mistake in fact occurred prior to contract award; (2) the mistake was clerical, mathematical, or misreading of specification, not an error in judgment; (3) prior to award the government knew, or should have known, that a mistake had been made; and (4) the government did not request bid verification or the request was inadequate. Giesler v. U.S., 44 Fed. Cl. 737 (1999), rev'd in part on other grounds, 232 F.3d 864 (Fed. Cir. 2000). United States ☞72(1.1); United States ☞74(4)

Policy underlying doctrine of unilateral mistake is designed to prevent the government from overreaching by awarding a contract where it knows the contractor has made a significant mistake. Giesler v. U.S., 44 Fed. Cl. 737 (1999), rev'd in part on other grounds, 232 F.3d 864 (Fed. Cir. 2000). United States ☞74(4)

Doctrine of "unilateral mistake" holds that a government contract may be reformed or rescinded if the contracting officer accepts a bid with actual or constructive knowledge that it contains an error. Giesler v. U.S., 44 Fed. Cl. 737 (1999), rev'd in part on other grounds, 232 F.3d 864 (Fed. Cir. 2000). United States ☞74(4)

4 Duty to examine documents

When the government has notice of a mistake in a particular bid, the government may have a duty to verify that bid by calling attention to the specific error suspected; however, this duty arises only where the contractor's mistake is a clear-cut clerical or arithmetical error, or a misreading of the specifications. Hunt Const. Group, Inc. v. U.S., 281 F.3d 1369 (Fed. Cir. 2002). United States ⊂⇒64.40(3)

In limited circumstances, if the government has breached its explicit regulatory duty to examine the contractor's bid for mistakes, then court may rescind a contract, despite an otherwise inexcusable error by the contractor. 48 C.F.R. § 14.407-1. Giesler v. U.S., 232 F.3d 864 (Fed. Cir. 2000). United States ⊂⇒74(4)

Though the government has a general duty to examine bids for mistakes, this duty does not extend to errors that may be contained in a contractor's subsequent filings. 48 C.F.R. §§ 14.407-1 to 14.407-3. Giesler v. U.S., 232 F.3d 864 (Fed. Cir. 2000). United States ⊂⇒64.40(1)

The government has no legal duty to examine for mistakes any paperwork submitted by contractors and subcontractors subsequent to the opening and acceptance of their bids, and after the completion of the pre-award survey report. 48 C.F.R. §§ 9.106, 14.407. Giesler v. U.S., 232 F.3d 864 (Fed. Cir. 2000). United States ⊂⇒64.40(1)

Rescission of contract to supply mixed nuts was not warranted due to the government's failure to examine subcontractor's facsimile which would have disclosed discrepancy between the requested nut mix and the nut mix subcontractor intended to produce; where the fax arrived after contractor's bid was opened and verified, and after the government had completed its pre-award survey of subcontractor, the government had no duty to examine the fax for errors. 48 C.F.R. §§ 14.407-1 to 14.407-3. Giesler v. U.S., 232 F.3d 864 (Fed. Cir. 2000). United States ⊂⇒74(4)

With respect to doctrine of unilateral mistake, the reasonableness of contractor's mistake is not relevant to the creation or discharge of the government's verification duty. Giesler v. U.S., 44 Fed. Cl. 737 (1999), rev'd in part on other grounds, 232 F.3d 864 (Fed. Cir. 2000). United States ⊂⇒74(4)

Contracting officer has duty to verify bid if all facts and circumstances suggest that it was reasonable to believe mistake had been made. 48 C.F.R. § 14.406-1. Dakota Tribal Industries v. U.S., 34 Fed. Cl. 593, 40 Cont. Cas. Fed. (CCH) P 76867 (1995). United States ⊂⇒64.40(3)

5 Evidence

Army Corps of Engineers' rule stating that uncorroborated statement is insufficient to satisfy the clear and convincing evidence standard required to show that the submitted bid was mistaken and what was the actual intended bid, such that bid is subject to correction, is not arbitrary and fact that some honest contractors may lose contracts because of minor errors on their part does not render Army's rule arbitrary. 48 C.F.R. § 14.406-3(a) (Repealed). McKnight Const. Co., Inc. v. Department of Defense, 85 F.3d 565, 40 Cont. Cas. Fed. (CCH) P 76942 (11th Cir. 1996). United States ⊂⇒64.30

Mistake, if any, in bidder's failure to include mark up in its bid price for beef patties to be supplied for federal child nutrition programs was noncompensable error in judgment; evidence showed that prevailing market prices for beef at time of bid solicitation were lower than those subsequently claimed by bidder, warranting inference that bidder knowingly decided to mark up its bids by lesser amount. Goldberger Foods, Inc. v. U.S., 960 F.2d 155 (Fed. Cir. 1992). United States ⊂⇒70(29)

Bidder on contract to furnish beef patties for federal child nutrition programs failed to establish that its omission of mark up from bid price was type of mistake that would have warranted allowing bidder to withdraw or correct its bid; bidder offered no evidence of raw beef prices quoted by its suppliers, prevailing market prices at time of solicitation were substantially lower than those claimed by bidder, and it was likely that bidder included substantial portion of mark up in preparing its bid. Goldberger Foods, Inc. v. U.S., 960 F.2d 155 (Fed. Cir. 1992). United States ⊂⇒70(29)

For purposes of correcting mistakes in government contract bids under Federal Acquisitions Regulations, there is no requirement that contractor's work papers be related in any way to specific line items of the bid. 48 C.F.R. § 14.406-3. McKnight Const. Co., Inc. v. Perry, 888 F. Supp. 1178 (S.D. Ga. 1994). United States ⊂⇒64.5

Under Federal Acquisition Regulations, bid work papers can be relied upon as best objective evidence of intended bid on government contract, but intended bid need not be established only from bid working papers in all cases of mistake. 48 C.F.R. § 14.406-3(g)(2). McKnight Const. Co., Inc. v. Perry, 888 F. Supp. 1178 (S.D. Ga. 1994). United States ☞64.60(1)

Bidder on federal government contract to renovate Army barracks presented sufficient evidence to clearly and convincingly establish its intended bid, even though bidder had made mistake in bid by transposing some of the line items in bid, where casual inspection of bid abstract revealed transpositional character of mistake, and bidder's company president submitted sworn affidavit in conjunction with bid itself that clarified the mistake. 48 C.F.R. § 14.406-3. McKnight Const. Co., Inc. v. Perry, 888 F. Supp. 1178 (S.D. Ga. 1994). United States ☞64.60(1)

Government contractor could not invoke doctrine of unilateral mistake to reform contract to include state sales tax in contract price, absent evidence that contracting officers knew of alleged mistake which was contractor's erroneous interpretation of contract clause as indicating that entire project was exempt from state tax; moreover, even if contracting officers should have known of contractor's mistake, it was a mistake in judgment and not a misreading of specifications, and thus was not compensable under the doctrine. C.W. Over & Sons, Inc. v. U.S., 54 Fed. Cl. 514 (2002). Reformation Of Instruments ☞17(1)

Under the Federal Acquisition Regulation (FAR), a bidder's request for an upward correction of its bid before award of the contract may be granted where the request is supported by clear and convincing evidence of both the existence of a mistake and the intended bid; the intended bid does not need to be an exact figure, as long as the bidder provides clear and convincing evidence to establish that the bid would fall within a narrow range of uncertainty and would remain the low bid if corrected. 48 C.F.R. § 14.407-3(a). Will H. Hall and Son, Inc. v. U.S., 54 Fed. Cl. 436 (2002). United States ☞64.40(4)

Bidder who alleged that its bid amount was based on mistake in subcontractor's quote failed to present clear and convincing evidence of its intended bid within a relatively narrow range, as required for correction of bid, where bidder would have had at least six options for its intended bid, and there was a range of 27 to 38.6 percent in possible intended bids. 48 C.F.R. § 14.407-3(a). Will H. Hall and Son, Inc. v. U.S., 54 Fed. Cl. 436 (2002). United States ☞64.40(4)

Pursuant to the Federal Acquisition Regulation (FAR), if the evidence is clear and convincing as to the existence of a bid mistake, but not the amount of the intended bid, or if the evidence only reasonably supports the existence of a mistake but is not clear and convincing, an agency official above the contracting officer may permit withdrawal of the bid. 48 C.F.R. § 14.407-3(c). Will H. Hall and Son, Inc. v. U.S., 54 Fed. Cl. 436 (2002). United States ☞64.40(4)

Affidavit of bidder's secretary and treasurer, who prepared and submitted its bid, which stated that he was unaware that subcontractor's quote was incomplete, did not rise to level of clear and convincing evidence of bid mistake, where bidder's worksheets did not corroborate that bidder was unaware that subcontractor's quote excluded certain work called for in contract. 48 C.F.R. § 14.407-3(a). Will H. Hall and Son, Inc. v. U.S., 54 Fed. Cl. 436 (2002). United States ☞74(11)

Protest that agency improperly refused to allow protester to correct alleged mistake in its price is denied where alleged mistake related to use of one set of indirect rates versus another, and protester provided no documentation to support its claimed mistake. Aeronautical Instrument & Radio Company, B-298582.2, B-298582.3, 2007 CPD ¶ 10 (Comp. Gen. 2007)

6 Correction of mistakes

Protest that agency improperly refused to allow protester to correct alleged mistake in its price is denied where alleged mistake related to use of one set of indirect rates versus another, and protester provided no documentation to support its claimed mistake. Aeronautical Instrument & Radio Company, B-298582.2, B-298582.3, 2007 CPD ¶ 10 (Comp. Gen. 2007)

Contracting agency's determination to permit bidder to upwardly correct its apparent low bid lacks a reasonable basis where bidder's explanation for alleged mistake is illogical and raises questions as to whether a mistake occurred, and where agency's determination fails to address these questions and relies on mischaracterizations of the bidder's explanation. Miramar Construction, Inc., B-298609, 2006 CPD ¶ 169 (Comp. Gen. 2006)

Agency improperly failed to allow correction of claimed mistake in bid, where the bidder established its mistake and its intended bid (which was still low) by clear and convincing evidence and the agency denied the requested correction because of other suspected mistakes which were unrelated to the one claimed and which the agency did not bring to the bidder's attention, as required by FAR 14.407-1 and 14.407-3(g), and where the evidence in the record, including hearing testimony and worksheets, does not evidence that the bidder made additional mistakes (as suspected by the agency) or that the worksheets were not in good order. Matter of: Odyssey International, Inc., B-296855.2, 2006 CPD ¶ 49 (Comp. Gen. 2005)

Where workpapers contain clear and convincing evidence that the low bidder mistakenly omitted an element of cost from its bid, the contracting agency properly permitted upward correction of the bid; even where the exact amount of the intended bid is not certain, determination to allow correction is reasonable where intended bid falls within a narrow range of uncertainty and would remain low after correction. Roy Anderson Corporation, B-292555, B-292555.2, 2003 CPD ¶ 179 (Comp. Gen. 2003)

Protest challenging agency's decision to allow awardee to upwardly correct its low bid is denied where it was not unreasonable for the agency to conclude that the awardee had presented clear and convincing evidence of the claimed mistake and the intended bid. Gulf-Atlantic Constructors, Inc., B-289032, 2002 CPD ¶ 2 (Comp. Gen. 2002)

Agency reasonably denied firm's request for upward correction of bid where the protester's claim of mistake was based on workpapers that the agency reasonably found not to be in good order and that did not establish the intended bid. Si-Nor, Inc., B-288990, 2001 CPD ¶ 204 (Comp. Gen. 2001)

Protest that contracting agency improperly denied request for bid correction is sustained where the worksheets submitted by the low bidder to support the claimed mistake in bid establish the existence of the mistake and the intended bid by clear and convincing evidence, and where the affidavit submitted along with the claim is entirely consistent with the worksheets. Cooper Construction, Inc., B-285880, 2000 CPD ¶ 153 (Comp. Gen. 2000)

Agency properly allowed correction of a mistake in bid by the low bidder where the existence of the mistake and the intended bid price were clear from the bidder's original bid preparation papers and the corrected bid remains significantly below the next low bid. Matter of: Merrick Construction Company, Inc., B-270661, 96-1 CPD ¶ 181 (Comp. Gen. 1996)

Contracting agency properly allowed correction of firm's bid, which resulted in displacement of other competitors as the low bidder, where the firm's intended bid price is clearly evidenced in the firm's entire bid, including documents furnished with descriptive literature. George E. Failing Company, B-233207, 89-1 CPD ¶ 203 (Comp. Gen. 1989)

§ 14.407-4 Mistakes after award.

If a contractor's discovery and request for correction of a mistake in bid is not made until after the award, it shall be processed under the procedures of Subpart 33.2 and the following:

(a) When a mistake in a contractor's bid is not discovered until after award, the mistake may be corrected by contract modification if correcting the mistake would be favorable to the Government without changing the essential requirements of the specifications.

(b) In addition to the cases contemplated in paragraph (a) of this section or as otherwise authorized by law, agencies are authorized to make a determination—

(1) To rescind a contract;

(2) To reform a contract—

(i) To delete the items involved in the mistake; or

(ii) To increase the price if the contract price, as corrected, does not exceed that of the next lowest acceptable bid under the original invitation for bids; or

(3) That no change shall be made in the contract as awarded, if the evidence does not warrant a determination under subparagraph (b)(1) or (2) of this section.

(c) Determinations under paragraph (b)(1) and (2) of this section may be made only on the basis of clear and convincing evidence that a mistake in bid was made. In addition, it must be clear that the mistake was—

(1) Mutual; or

(2) If unilaterally made by the contractor, so apparent as to have charged the contracting officer with notice of the probability of the mistake.

(d) Each proposed determination shall be coordinated with legal counsel in accordance with agency procedures.

(e) Mistakes alleged or disclosed after award shall be processed as follows:

(1) The contracting officer shall request the contractor to support the alleged mistake by submission of written statements and pertinent evidence, such as—

(i) The contractor's file copy of the bid,

(ii) The contractor's original worksheets and other data used in preparing the bid,

(iii) Subcontractors' and suppliers' quotations, if any,

(iv) Published price lists, and

(v) Any other evidence that will serve to establish the mistake, the manner in which the mistake occurred, and the bid actually intended.

(2) The case file concerning an alleged mistake shall contain the following:

(i) All evidence furnished by the contractor in support of the alleged mistake.

(ii) A signed statement by the contracting officer—

(A) Describing the supplies or services involved;

(B) Specifying how and when the mistake was alleged or disclosed;

(C) Summarizing the evidence submitted by the contractor and any additional evidence considered pertinent;

(D) Quoting, in cases where only one bid was received, the most recent contract price for the supplies or services involved, or in the absence of a recent comparable contract, the contracting officer's estimate of a fair price for the supplies or services and the basis for the estimate;

(E) Setting forth the contracting officer's opinion whether a bona fide mistake was made and whether the contracting officer was, or should have been, on constructive notice of the mistake before the award, together with the reasons for, or data in support of, such opinion;

(F) Setting forth the course of action with respect to the alleged mistake that the contracting officer considers proper on the basis of the evidence, and if other than a change in contract price is recommended, the manner by which the supplies or services will otherwise be acquired; and

(G) Disclosing the status of performance and payments under the contract, including contemplated performance and payments.

(iii) A signed copy of the bid involved.

(iv) A copy of the invitation for bids and any specifications or drawings relevant to the alleged mistake.

(v) An abstract of written record of the bids received.

(vi) A written request by the contractor to reform or rescind the contract, and copies of all other relevant correspondence between the contracting officer and the contractor concerning the alleged mistake.

(vii) A copy of the contract and any related change orders or supplemental agreements.

(f) Each agency shall include in the contract file a record of—

(1) All determinations made in accordance with this 14.407-4;

(2) The facts involved; and

(3) The action taken in each case.

United States Code Annotated

Administrative determinations, see 41 USCA § 257.

Contract requirements, see 41 USCA § 254.

Contracts, planning, solicitation, evaluation, and award procedures, see 10 USCA § 2305.

Definitions, see 10 USCA § 2302, 41 USCA §§ 259, 403.

Determinations and decisions, see 10 USCA § 2310, 41 USCA § 262.
Evaluation and award, see 41 USCA § 253b.
Kinds of contracts, see 10 USCA § 2306.
Planning and solicitation requirements, see 41 USCA § 253a.

Notes of Decisions

In general 1
Duty to examine documents 4
Evidence 5
Mutual mistake 2
Unilateral mistake 3

1 In general

Bidder's alleged mistake in relying on quote from subcontractor which did not include work on a specification section was not an error in business judgment for which equitable relief was not available; although bidder's handling of quote was careless, it did not rise to the level of gross negligence, and bidder discovered the error six days after submitting its bid, and immediately notified the contracting officer. Will H. Hall and Son, Inc.

In limited circumstances, if the government has knowledge, or constructive knowledge, that a contractor's bid is based on a mistake, and the government accepts the bid and awards the contract despite knowledge of this mistake, then a trial court may reform or rescind the contract, but, generally, a contractor may obtain reformation or rescission of the contract only if the contractor establishes that its bid error resulted from a clear-cut clerical or arithmetical error, or a misreading of the specifications. Giesler v. U.S., 232 F.3d 864 (Fed. Cir. 2000). United States ☞72(1.1); United States ☞74(4)

Contractor's mistake in bid was not so gross that enforcement of contract without allowing for reformation was unconscionable, where contractor alleged that its mistake had affected its total bid of $17.2 million by $438,000, or about 2.5 percent; moreover, without correction of its bid mistake, contractor, at the time of award, still anticipated a profit of approximately 1.6%. Will H. Hall and Son, Inc. v. U.S., 54 Fed. Cl. 436 (2002). Reformation Of Instruments ☞17(1); United States ☞74(4)

A government contract may be reformed or rescinded if the contracting officer accepts a bid with actual or constructive knowledge that the bid contains a compensable mistake. Will H. Hall and Son, Inc. v. U.S., 54 Fed. Cl. 436 (2002). Reformation Of Instruments ☞17(1); United States ☞72(1.1)

2 Mutual mistake

Government contractor could not invoke doctrine of mutual mistake to reform contract to include state sales tax in contract price, although both parties were mistaken concerning treatment of states sales tax in the contract, where contractor's mistake concerned the tax exemption status of materials used in the project, and government's mistake concerned the inclusion of state sales tax in unit prices contained in agency's Unit Price Book (UPB), and thus errors were separate and not mutual. C.W. Over & Sons, Inc. v. U.S., 54 Fed. Cl. 514 (2002). Reformation Of Instruments ☞19(2)

3 Unilateral mistake

Where reformation of contract is sought due to contractor's unilateral bid mistake, contractor must show by clear and convincing evidence that: (1) mistake in fact occurred prior to contract award; (2) mistake was clear-cut, clerical or mathematical error or misreading of specifications and not judgmental error; (3) prior to award Government knew, or should have known, that mistake had been made and, therefore, should have requested bid verification; (4) Government did not request bid verification or its request for bid verification was inadequate; and (5) proof of intended bid is established. 48 C.F.R. §§ 14.406-1, 14.406-3(g) (1992). McClure Elec. Constructors, Inc. v. Dalton, 132 F.3d 709, 42 Cont. Cas. Fed. (CCH) P 77246 (Fed. Cir. 1997). United States ☞72(1.1)

Bid verification request sent out by contracting officer was adequate to put contractor on notice of suspected bid mistake, and thus, contractor was not entitled to contract reformation to correct its unilateral bid mistake; although contracting officer did not expressly state that she suspected error, she did reveal amounts of all bids, and with this information in hand, contractor could see that next lowest bid was almost 20% higher than its bid, and that government estimate was almost twice contractor's bid. 48 C.F.R. §§ 14.406-1, 14.406-3(g) (1992). McClure Elec. Constructors, Inc. v. Dalton, 132 F.3d 709, 42 Cont. Cas. Fed. (CCH) P 77246 (Fed. Cir. 1997). United States ☞72(1.1)

To be entitled to reformation under unilateral mistake, government contractor must show that the contracting officer knew or should have known of the contractor's unilateral mistake at the time its bid was accepted; moreover, the mistaken proposal must contain a clear cut clerical or arithmetical error, or misreading of the specifications. C.W. Over & Sons, Inc. v. U.S., 54 Fed. Cl. 514 (2002). Reformation Of Instruments ☞17(1)

In order to attain rescission on ground of unilateral mistake, government contractor must show: (1) the mistake in fact occurred prior to contract award; (2) the mistake was clerical, mathematical, or misreading of specification, not an error in judgment; (3) prior to award the government knew, or should have known, that a mistake had been made; and (4) the government did not request bid verification or the request was inadequate. Giesler v. U.S., 44 Fed. Cl. 737 (1999), rev'd in part on other grounds, 232 F.3d 864 (Fed. Cir. 2000). United States ☞72(1.1); United States ☞74(4)

Policy underlying doctrine of unilateral mistake is designed to prevent the government from overreaching by awarding a contract where it knows the contractor has made a significant mistake. Giesler v. U.S., 44 Fed. Cl. 737 (1999), rev'd in part on other grounds, 232 F.3d 864 (Fed. Cir. 2000). United States ☞74(4)

Doctrine of "unilateral mistake" holds that a government contract may be reformed or rescinded if the contracting officer accepts a bid with actual or constructive knowledge that it contains an error. Giesler v. U.S., 44 Fed. Cl. 737 (1999), rev'd in part on other grounds, 232 F.3d 864 (Fed. Cir. 2000). United States ☞74(4)

4 Duty to examine documents

In limited circumstances, if the government has breached its explicit regulatory duty to examine the contractor's bid for mistakes, then court may rescind a contract, despite an otherwise inexcusable error by the contractor. 48 C.F.R. § 14.407-1. Giesler v. U.S., 232 F.3d 864 (Fed. Cir. 2000). United States ☞74(4)

Though the government has a general duty to examine bids for mistakes, this duty does not extend to errors that may be contained in a contractor's subsequent filings. 48 C.F.R. §§ 14.407-1 to 14.407-3. Giesler v. U.S., 232 F.3d 864 (Fed. Cir. 2000). United States ☞64.40(1)

The government has no legal duty to examine for mistakes any paperwork submitted by contractors and subcontractors subsequent to the opening and acceptance of their bids, and after the completion of the pre-award survey report. 48 C.F.R. §§ 9.106, 14.407. Giesler v. U.S., 232 F.3d 864 (Fed. Cir. 2000). United States ☞64.40(1)

Rescission of contract to supply mixed nuts was not warranted due to the government's failure to examine subcontractor's facsimile which would have disclosed discrepancy between the requested nut mix and the nut mix subcontractor intended to produce; where the fax arrived after contractor's bid was opened and verified, and after the government had completed its pre-award survey of subcontractor, the government had no duty to examine the fax for errors. 48 C.F.R. §§ 14.407-1 to 14.407-3. Giesler v. U.S., 232 F.3d 864 (Fed. Cir. 2000). United States ☞74(4)

With respect to doctrine of unilateral mistake, the reasonableness of contractor's mistake is not relevant to the creation or discharge of the government's verification duty. Giesler v. U.S., 44 Fed. Cl. 737 (1999), rev'd in part on other grounds, 232 F.3d 864 (Fed. Cir. 2000). United States ☞74(4)

5 Evidence

Army Corps of Engineers' rule stating that uncorroborated statement is insufficient to satisfy the clear and convincing evidence standard required to show that the submitted bid was mistaken and what was the actual intended bid, such that bid is subject to correction, is not arbitrary and fact that some honest contractors may lose contracts because of minor errors on their part does not render Army's rule arbitrary. 48 C.F.R. § 14.406-3(a)

(Repealed). McKnight Const. Co., Inc. v. Department of Defense, 85 F.3d 565, 40 Cont. Cas. Fed. (CCH) P 76942 (11th Cir. 1996). United States ☞64.30

Mistake, if any, in bidder's failure to include mark up in its bid price for beef patties to be supplied for federal child nutrition programs was noncompensable error in judgment; evidence showed that prevailing market prices for beef at time of bid solicitation were lower than those subsequently claimed by bidder, warranting inference that bidder knowingly decided to mark up its bids by lesser amount. Goldberger Foods, Inc. v. U.S., 960 F.2d 155 (Fed. Cir. 1992). United States ☞70(29)

Bidder on contract to furnish beef patties for federal child nutrition programs failed to establish that its omission of mark up from bid price was type of mistake that would have warranted allowing bidder to withdraw or correct its bid; bidder offered no evidence of raw beef prices quoted by its suppliers, prevailing market prices at time of solicitation were substantially lower than those claimed by bidder, and it was likely that bidder included substantial portion of mark up in preparing its bid. Goldberger Foods, Inc. v. U.S., 960 F.2d 155 (Fed. Cir. 1992). United States ☞70(29)

Bidder on federal government contract to renovate Army barracks presented sufficient evidence to clearly and convincingly establish its intended bid, even though bidder had made mistake in bid by transposing some of the line items in bid, where casual inspection of bid abstract revealed transpositional character of mistake, and bidder's company president submitted sworn affidavit in conjunction with bid itself that clarified the mistake. 48 C.F.R. § 14.406-3. McKnight Const. Co., Inc. v. Perry, 888 F. Supp. 1178 (S.D. Ga. 1994). United States ☞64.60(1)

A government contract may be reformed where the relevant contracting officer had actual or constructive knowledge that the bid was based on a clear, clerical or mathematical error or a misreading of the specifications. Information Intern. Associates, Inc. v. U.S., 74 Fed. Cl. 192 (2006)

Contract awardee established existence of a unilateral mistake in omission of salary of employee in its final price proposal, and thus was entitled to reformation of contract, where mistake occurred prior to award of contract, it was clerical in nature, contracting officer (CO) had constructive notice of error from disparity between awardee's bid and next lowest bid, government did not request verification, and awardee established by clear and convincing evidence the correct amount of its bid. Information Intern. Associates, Inc. v. U.S., 74 Fed. Cl. 192 (2006)

Government contractor could not invoke doctrine of unilateral mistake to reform contract to include state sales tax in contract price, absent evidence that contracting officers knew of alleged mistake which was contractor's erroneous interpretation of contract clause as indicating that entire project was exempt from state tax; moreover, even if contracting officers should have known of contractor's mistake, it was a mistake in judgment and not a misreading of specifications, and thus was not compensable under the doctrine. C.W. Over & Sons, Inc. v. U.S., 54 Fed. Cl. 514 (2002). Reformation Of Instruments ☞17(1)

Under the Federal Acquisition Regulation (FAR), a bidder's request for an upward correction of its bid before award of the contract may be granted where the request is supported by clear and convincing evidence of both the existence of a mistake and the intended bid; the intended bid does not need to be an exact figure, as long as the bidder provides clear and convincing evidence to establish that the bid would fall within a narrow range of uncertainty and would remain the low bid if corrected. 48 C.F.R. § 14.407-3(a). Will H. Hall and Son, Inc. v. U.S., 54 Fed. Cl. 436 (2002). United States ☞64.40(4)

Bidder who alleged that its bid amount was based on mistake in subcontractor's quote failed to present clear and convincing evidence of its intended bid within a relatively narrow range, as required for correction of bid, where bidder would have had at least six options for its intended bid, and there was a range of 27 to 38.6 percent in possible intended bids. 48 C.F.R. § 14.407-3(a). Will H. Hall and Son, Inc. v. U.S., 54 Fed. Cl. 436 (2002). United States ☞64.40(4)

Pursuant to the Federal Acquisition Regulation (FAR), if the evidence is clear and convincing as to the existence of a bid mistake, but not the amount of the intended bid, or if the evidence only reasonably supports the existence of a mistake but is not clear and convincing, an agency official above the contracting officer may permit withdrawal of the bid. 48 C.F.R. § 14.407-3(c). Will H. Hall and Son, Inc. v. U.S., 54 Fed. Cl. 436 (2002).

United States ⊙64.40(4)

Affidavit of bidder's secretary and treasurer, who prepared and submitted its bid, which stated that he was unaware that subcontractor's quote was incomplete, did not rise to level of clear and convincing evidence of bid mistake, where bidder's worksheets did not corroborate that bidder was unaware that subcontractor's quote excluded certain work called for in contract. 48 C.F.R. § 14.407-3(a). Will H. Hall and Son, Inc. v. U.S., 54 Fed. Cl. 436 (2002). United States ⊙74(11)

§ 14.408 Award.

§ 14.408-1 General.

(a) The contracting officer shall make a contract award (1) by written or electronic notice, (2) within the time for acceptance specified in the bid or an extension (see 14.404-1(d)), and (3) to that responsible bidder whose bid, conforming to the invitation, will be most advantageous to the Government, considering only price and the price-related factors (see 14.201-8) included in the invitation. Award shall not be made until all required approvals have been obtained and the award otherwise conforms with 14.103-2.

(b) If less than three bids have been received, the contracting officer shall examine the situation to ascertain the reasons for the small number of responses. Award shall be made notwithstanding the limited number of bids. However, the contracting officer shall initiate, if appropriate, corrective action to increase competition in future solicitations for the same or similar items, and include a notation of such action in the records of the invitation for bids (see 14.204).

(c) (1) Award shall be made by mailing or otherwise furnishing a properly executed award document to the successful bidder.

(2) When a notice of award is issued, it shall be followed as soon as possible by the formal award.

(3) When more than one award results from any single invitation for bids, separate award documents shall be suitably numbered and executed.

(4) When an award is made to a bidder for less than all of the items that may be awarded to that bidder and additional items are being withheld for subsequent award, the award shall state that the Government may make subsequent awards on those additional items within the bid acceptance period.

(5) All provisions of the invitation for bids, including any acceptable additions or changes made by a bidder in the bid, shall be clearly and accurately set forth (either expressly or by reference) in the award document. The award is an acceptance of the bid, and the bid and the award constitute the contract.

(d) (1) Award is generally made by using the Award portion of Standard Form (SF) 33, Solicitation, Offer, and Award, or SF 1447, Solicitation/Contract (see 53.214). If an offer from a SF 33 leads to further changes, the resulting contract shall be prepared as a bilateral document on SF 26, Award/Contract.

(2) Use of the Award portion of SF 33, SF 26, or SF 1447, does not preclude the additional use of informal documents, including telegrams or electronic transmissions, as notices of awards.

United States Code Annotated

Administrative determinations, see 41 USCA § 257.

Contract requirements, see 41 USCA § 254.

Contracts, planning, solicitation, evaluation, and award procedures, see 10 USCA § 2305.

Definitions, see 10 USCA § 2302, 41 USCA §§ 259, 403.

Determinations and decisions, see 10 USCA § 2310, 41 USCA § 262.

Evaluation and award, see 41 USCA § 253b.

Kinds of contracts, see 10 USCA § 2306.

Planning and solicitation requirements, see 41 USCA § 253a.

Notes of Decisions

Award of contract, generally 1

Delay in award of contract 2
Effect of pre-award submissions 4
Evaluation of bids 3

1 Award of contract, generally

Decision of contracting officer (CO) to select contract awardee's bid on alternate bid item 6, instead of bid protestor's offer on alternate bid item 5, was not arbitrary and capricious, where awardee's bid on alternate bid item 6 was lower than the independent government estimate for item 6, and awarding the contract to protestor for its bid on alternate bid item 5 would have exceeded the allocated funding. First Enterprise v. U.S., 61 Fed. Cl. 109 (2004). United States ☞64.45(1)

Under the arbitrary and capricious standard applicable to bid protests, a bid award may be set aside if either: (1) the procurement official's decision lacked a rational basis; or (2) the procurement procedure involved a violation of a regulation or procedure. 5 U.S.C.A. § 706(2)(A); 28 U.S.C.A. § 1491(b)(4). First Enterprise v. U.S., 61 Fed. Cl. 109 (2004). United States ☞64.60(3.1); United States ☞64.60(4)

The decision to award a government contract can only be set aside if the Court of Federal Claims determines that the contracting officer's decision lacked a rational basis or violated a regulation or procedure; it is not the role of the Court to substitute its own judgment for that of the contracting officer. Davis/HRGM Joint Venture v. U.S., 50 Fed. Cl. 539 (2001)

2 Delay in award of contract

Regulation concerning governmental delay in awarding bid is aimed at administrative efficiency and no substantive right is created on which contractor can erect damage claim. 48 C.F.R. § 14.404-1(d). Smith v. U.S., 34 Fed. Cl. 313, 40 Cont. Cas. Fed. (CCH) P 76854 (1995). United States ☞73(20)

3 Evaluation of bids

After lowest bidder withdrew, contracting officer (CO) acted properly in not awarding contract to the next lowest bidder, and instead concluding that remaining bids were unreasonable, where all the remaining bids were over the maximum amount the agency could spend on the construction portion of the contract. First Enterprise v. U.S., 61 Fed. Cl. 109 (2004). United States ☞64.50

An agency improperly made award to other than the lowest-priced bidder in a sealed bid procurement where the agency included pricing for options, even though the agency knew with a reasonable certainty that it lacked sufficient funding to exercise the options. Glen Mar Constr., Inc., B-410603, 2015 CPD ¶ 40 (Comp. Gen. 2015)

4 Effect of pre-award submissions

Pre-award submissions, such as a work plan, are not part of a government contract unless the contract specifically provides that they are to be incorporated. Teg-Paradigm Environmental, Inc. v. U.S., 465 F.3d 1329 (Fed. Cir. 2006). United States ☞70(12.1)

§ 14.408-2 Responsible bidder—reasonableness of price.

(a) The contracting officer shall determine that a prospective contractor is responsible (see Subpart 9.1) and that the prices offered are reasonable before awarding the contract. The price analysis techniques in 15.404-1(b) may be used as guidelines. In each case the determination shall be made in the light of all prevailing circumstances. Particular care must be taken in cases where only a single bid is received.

(b) The price analysis shall consider whether bids are materially unbalanced (see 15.404-1(g)).

United States Code Annotated

Administrative determinations, see 41 USCA § 257.

Contract requirements, see 41 USCA § 254.

Contracts, planning, solicitation, evaluation, and award procedures, see 10 USCA § 2305.

Definitions, see 10 USCA § 2302, 41 USCA §§ 259, 403.

Determinations and decisions, see 10 USCA § 2310, 41 USCA § 262.

Evaluation and award, see 41 USCA § 253b.

Kinds of contracts, see 10 USCA § 2306.

Planning and solicitation requirements, see 41 USCA § 253a.

Notes of Decisions

In general 1
Responsiveness distinguished 2

1 In general

Under the Federal Acquisition Regulation (FAR), a contracting officer (CO) is required to make a responsibility determination only for the one bidder selected for award; FAR does not require procuring agencies to evaluate conclusively the responsibility of other bidders. Greenleaf Const. Co., Inc. v. U.S., 67 Fed. Cl. 350 (2005). United States ☞64.45(2)

Failure of contracting agency to perform a cost realism analysis on contract awardee's offer was not error, as there was no requirement for such an analysis, where solicitation contemplated award of firm fixed price contract and contracting officer (CO) deemed awardee responsible to perform the project at the offered price. 48 C.F.R. § 15.404-1(d)(1). First Enterprise v. U.S., 61 Fed. Cl. 109 (2004). United States ☞64.40(1)

In assessing contractor's responsibility, the contracting officer is not limited to the information contained in the bid when opened, but instead is expected to solicit additional information demonstrating that the contractor is capable of performing the contract work. 48 C.F.R. § 9.105-1. Ryan Co. v. U.S., 43 Fed. Cl. 646 (1999). United States ☞64.40(1)

In typical government contract case, solicitation and related regulations require contracting officer to make separate determinations on issue of bid's "responsiveness" to terms of solicitation and "responsibility" of bidder to perform contract work covered in solicitation prior to awarding contract to apparent low bidder. VMS Hotel Partners v. U.S., 30 Fed. Cl. 512, 39 Cont. Cas. Fed. (CCH) P 76631 (1994). United States ☞64.30; United States ☞64.45(2)

"Responsibility" for purposes of public contract addresses performance capability of bidder including financial resources, experience, management, past performance, place of performance, and integrity, and evidence may be presented after bid opening until time of award. Bean Dredging Corp. v. U.S., 22 Cl. Ct. 519, 36 Cont. Cas. Fed. (CCH) P 76017, 1991 WL 15601 (1991). Public Contracts ☞11

2 Responsiveness distinguished

In identifying whether particular requirement is related to responsiveness or to responsibility, responsibility concerns question of bidder's performance capability and responsiveness concerns promise to perform contract. Bean Dredging Corp. v. U.S., 22 Cl. Ct. 519, 36 Cont. Cas. Fed. (CCH) P 76017, 1991 WL 15601 (1991). Public Contracts ☞8; Public Contracts ☞11

Fact that contracting officer requested clarification of bidder's response to business management questionnaire question in which bidder indicated that it intended to self-perform only 10% of contract work, while invitation for bid required self-performance of 20%, could not convert issue of nonresponsiveness of bid into issue of responsibility; procuring agency's authority to permit correction of bid mistakes is limited to bids that are responsive to solicitation. Blount, Inc. v. U.S., 22 Cl. Ct. 221, 36 Cont. Cas. Fed. (CCH) P 75981, 1990 WL 210734 (1990). United States ☞64.30

§ 14.408-3 Prompt payment discounts.

(a) Prompt payment discounts shall not be considered in the evaluation of bids. However, any discount offered will form a part of the award, and will be taken by the payment center if payment is made within the discount period specified by the bidder. As an alternative to indicating a discount in conjunction with the offer, bidders may prefer to offer discounts on individual invoices.

(b) See 32.111(b)(1), which prescribes the contract clause at 52.232-8, Discounts for Prompt Payment.

United States Code Annotated

Administrative determinations, see 41 USCA § 257.

Contract requirements, see 41 USCA § 254.

Contracts, planning, solicitation, evaluation, and award procedures, see 10 USCA § 2305.

Definitions, see 10 USCA § 2302, 41 USCA §§ 259, 403.

Determinations and decisions, see 10 USCA § 2310, 41 USCA § 262.

Evaluation and award, see 41 USCA § 253b.

Kinds of contracts, see 10 USCA § 2306.

Planning and solicitation requirements, see 41 USCA § 253a.

§ 14.408-4 Economic price adjustment.

(a) *Bidder proposes economic price adjustment.* (1) When a solicitation does not contain an economic price adjustment clause but a bidder proposes one with a ceiling that the price will not exceed, the bid shall be evaluated on the basis of the maximum possible economic price adjustment of the quoted base price.

(2) If the bid is eligible for award, the contracting officer shall request the bidder to agree to the inclusion in the award of an approved economic price adjustment clause (see 16.203) that is subject to the same ceiling. If the bidder will not agree to an approved clause, the award may be made on the basis of the bid as originally submitted.

(3) Bids that contain economic price adjustments with no ceiling shall be rejected unless a clear basis for evaluation exists.

(b) *Government proposes economic price adjustment.* (1) When an invitation contains an economic price adjustment clause and no bidder takes exception to the provisions, bids shall be evaluated on the basis of the quoted prices without the allowable economic price adjustment being added.

(2) When a bidder increases the maximum percentage of economic price adjustment stipulated in the invitation or limits the downward economic price adjustment provisions of the invitation, the bid shall be rejected as nonresponsive.

(3) When a bid indicates deletion of the economic price adjustment clause, the bid shall be rejected as nonresponsive since the downward economic price adjustment provisions are thereby limited.

(4) When a bidder decreases the maximum percentage of economic price adjustment stipulated in the invitation, the bid shall be evaluated at the base price on an equal basis with bids that do not reduce the stipulated ceiling. However, after evaluation, if the bidder offering the lower ceiling is in a position to receive the award, the award shall reflect the lower ceiling.

United States Code Annotated

Administrative determinations, see 41 USCA § 257.

Contract requirements, see 41 USCA § 254.

Contracts, planning, solicitation, evaluation, and award procedures, see 10 USCA § 2305.

Definitions, see 10 USCA § 2302, 41 USCA §§ 259, 403.

Determinations and decisions, see 10 USCA § 2310, 41 USCA § 262.

Evaluation and award, see 41 USCA § 253b.

Kinds of contracts, see 10 USCA § 2306.

Planning and solicitation requirements, see 41 USCA § 253a.

§ 14.408-5 [Reserved]

§ 14.408-6 Equal low bids.

(a) Contracts shall be awarded in the following order of priority when two or more low bids are equal in all respects:

(1) Small business concerns that are also labor surplus area concerns.

(2) Other small business concerns.

(3) Other business concerns.

(b) If two or more bidders still remain equally eligible after application of paragraph (a) of this section, award shall be made by a drawing by lot limited to those bidders. If time permits, the bidders involved shall be given an opportunity to attend the drawing. The drawing shall be witnessed by at least three persons, and the contract file shall contain the names and addresses of the witnesses and the person supervising the drawing.

(c) When an award is to be made by using the priorities under this 14.408-6, the contracting officer shall include a written agreement in the contract that the contractor will perform, or cause to be performed, the contract in accordance with the circumstances justifying the priority used to break the tie or select bids for a drawing by lot.

United States Code Annotated

Administrative determinations, see 41 USCA § 257.

Contract requirements, see 41 USCA § 254.

Contracts, planning, solicitation, evaluation, and award procedures, see 10 USCA § 2305.

Definitions, see 10 USCA § 2302, 41 USCA §§ 259, 403.

Determinations and decisions, see 10 USCA § 2310, 41 USCA § 262.

Evaluation and award, see 41 USCA § 253b.

Kinds of contracts, see 10 USCA § 2306.

Planning and solicitation requirements, see 41 USCA § 253a.

§ 14.408-7 Documentation of award.

(a) The contracting officer shall document compliance with 14.103-2 in the contract file.

(b) The documentation shall either state that the accepted bid was the lowest bid received, or list all lower bids with reasons for their rejection in sufficient detail to justify the award.

(c) When an award is made after receipt of equal low bids, the documentation shall describe how the tie was broken.

United States Code Annotated

Administrative determinations, see 41 USCA § 257.

Contract requirements, see 41 USCA § 254.

Contracts, planning, solicitation, evaluation, and award procedures, see 10 USCA § 2305.

Definitions, see 10 USCA § 2302, 41 USCA §§ 259, 403.

Determinations and decisions, see 10 USCA § 2310, 41 USCA § 262.

Evaluation and award, see 41 USCA § 253b.

Kinds of contracts, see 10 USCA § 2306.

Planning and solicitation requirements, see 41 USCA § 253a.

§ 14.408-8 Protests against award.

(See Subpart 33.1, Protests.)

United States Code Annotated

Administrative determinations, see 41 USCA § 257.

Contract requirements, see 41 USCA § 254.

Contracts, planning, solicitation, evaluation, and award procedures, see 10 USCA § 2305.

Definitions, see 10 USCA § 2302, 41 USCA §§ 259, 403.

Determinations and decisions, see 10 USCA § 2310, 41 USCA § 262.

Evaluation and award, see 41 USCA § 253b.

Kinds of contracts, see 10 USCA § 2306.

Planning and solicitation requirements, see 41 USCA § 253a.

§ 14.409 Information to bidders.

§ 14.409-1 Award of unclassified contracts.

(a) (1) The contracting officer shall as a minimum (subject to any restrictions in Subpart 9.4)—

(i) Notify each unsuccessful bidder in writing or electronically within three days after contract award, that its bid was not accepted. "Day," for purposes of the notification process, means calendar day, except that the period will run until a day which is not a Saturday, Sunday, or legal holiday;

(ii) Extend appreciation for the interest the unsuccessful bidder has shown in submitting a bid; and

(iii) When award is made to other than a low bidder, state the reason for rejection in the notice to each of the unsuccessful low bidders.

(2) For acquisitions covered by the World Trade Organization Government Procurement Agreement or a Free Trade Agreement (see 25.408(a)(5)), agencies must include in notices given unsuccessful bidders from World Trade Organization Government Procurement Agreement or Free Trade Agreement countries—

(i) The dollar amount of the successful bid; and

(ii) The name and address of the successful bidder.

(b) Information included in paragraph (a)(2) of this subsection shall be provided to any unsuccessful bidder upon request except when multiple awards have been made and furnishing information on the successful bids would require so much work as to interfere with normal operations of the contracting office. In such circumstances, only information concerning location of the abstract of offers need be given.

(c) When a request is received concerning an unclassified invitation from an inquirer who is neither a bidder nor a representative of a bidder, the contracting officer should make every effort to furnish the names of successful bidders and, if requested, the prices at which awards were made. However, when such requests require so much work as to interfere with the normal operations of the contracting office, the inquirer will be advised where a copy of the abstract of offers may be seen.

(d) Requests for records shall be governed by agency regulations implementing Subpart 24.2.

United States Code Annotated

Administrative determinations, see 41 USCA § 257.

Contract requirements, see 41 USCA § 254.

Contracts, planning, solicitation, evaluation, and award procedures, see 10 USCA § 2305.

Definitions, see 10 USCA § 2302, 41 USCA §§ 259, 403.

Determinations and decisions, see 10 USCA § 2310, 41 USCA § 262.

Evaluation and award, see 41 USCA § 253b.

Kinds of contracts, see 10 USCA § 2306.

Planning and solicitation requirements, see 41 USCA § 253a.

§ 14.409-2 Award of classified contracts.

In addition to 14.409-1, if classified information was furnished or created in connection with the solicitation, the contracting officer shall advise the unsuccessful bidders, including any who did not bid, to take disposition action in accordance with agency procedures. The name of the successful bidder and the contract price will be furnished to unsuccessful bidders only upon request. Information regarding a classified award shall not be furnished by telephone.

United States Code Annotated

Administrative determinations, see 41 USCA § 257.

Contract requirements, see 41 USCA § 254.

Contracts, planning, solicitation, evaluation, and award procedures, see 10 USCA § 2305.

Definitions, see 10 USCA § 2302, 41 USCA §§ 259, 403.

Determinations and decisions, see 10 USCA § 2310, 41 USCA § 262.

Evaluation and award, see 41 USCA § 253b.

Kinds of contracts, see 10 USCA § 2306.

Planning and solicitation requirements, see 41 USCA § 253a.

Subpart 14.5 Two-Step Sealed Bidding

§ 14.501 General.

Two-step sealed bidding is a combination of competitive procedures designed to obtain the benefits of sealed bidding when adequate specifications are not available. An objective is to permit the development of a sufficiently descriptive and not unduly restrictive statement of the Government's requirements, including an adequate technical data package, so that subsequent acquisitions may be made by conventional sealed bidding. This method is especially useful in acquisitions requiring technical proposals, particularly those for complex items. It is conducted in two steps:

(a) Step one consists of the request for, submission, evaluation, and (if necessary) discussion of a technical proposal. No pricing is involved. The objective is to determine the acceptability of the supplies or services offered. As used in this context, the word "technical" has a broad connotation and includes, among other things, the engineering approach, special manufacturing processes, and special testing techniques. It is the proper step for clarification of questions relating to technical requirements. Conformity to the technical requirements is resolved in this step, but not responsibility as defined in 9.1.

(b) Step two involves the submission of sealed priced bids by those who submitted acceptable technical proposals in step one. Bids submitted in step two are evaluated and the awards made in accordance with Subparts 14.3 and 14.4.

United States Code Annotated

Contract requirements, see 41 USCA § 254.

Contracts, planning, solicitation, evaluation, and award procedures, see 10 USCA § 2305.

Definitions, see 10 USCA § 2302, 41 USCA §§ 259, 403.

Evaluation and award, see 41 USCA § 253b.

Kinds of contracts, see 10 USCA § 2306.

Planning and solicitation requirements, see 41 USCA § 253a.

§ 14.502 Conditions for use.

(a) Unless other factors require the use of sealed bidding, two-step sealed bidding may be used in preference to negotiation when all of the following conditions are present:

(1) Available specifications or purchase descriptions are not definite or complete or may be too restrictive without technical evaluation, and any necessary discussion, of the technical aspects of the requirement to ensure mutual understanding between each source and the Government.

(2) Definite criteria exist for evaluating technical proposals.

(3) More than one technically qualified source is expected to be available.

(4) Sufficient time will be available for use of the two-step method.

(5) A firm-fixed-price contract or a fixed-price contract with economic price adjustment will be used.

(b) None of the following precludes the use of two-step sealed bidding:

(1) Multi-year contracting.

(2) Government property to be made available to the successful bidder.

(3) A total small business set-aside (see 19.502-2).

(4) The use of a set-aside or price evaluation preference for HUBZone small business concerns (see Subpart 19.13).

(5) The use of a set-aside for service-disabled veteran-owned small business concerns (see Subpart 19.14).

(6) The use of a set-aside for economically disadvantaged women-owned small business concerns and women-owned small business concerns eligible under the Women-Owned Small Business Program (see subpart 19.15).

(7) A first or subsequent production quantity is being acquired under a performance specification.

United States Code Annotated

Contract requirements, see 41 USCA § 254.

Contracts, planning, solicitation, evaluation, and award procedures, see 10 USCA § 2305.
Definitions, see 10 USCA § 2302, 41 USCA §§ 259, 403.
Evaluation and award, see 41 USCA § 253b.
Kinds of contracts, see 10 USCA § 2306.
Planning and solicitation requirements, see 41 USCA § 253a.

Notes of Decisions

In general 1

1 In general

Failure of agency to make determination that government contract should be negotiated, rather than made the subject of two-step formal advertising, constitutes an action committed to agency discretion by law, within the Administrative Procedure Act. 5 U.S.C.A. § 701(a) (2); 10 U.S.C.A. § 2304(a) (14). Wheelabrator Corp. v. Chafee, 455 F.2d 1306, 147 (D.C. Cir. 1971). Administrative Law And Procedure ⊕756; United States ⊕64.10

No abuse of discretion was shown in initiating two-step formal advertising procedure with respect to procurement of portable ship hull cleaning device for Navy, rather than negotiating contract with company which had allegedly developed new and unique device and acquired body of technology, special equipment and tooling, in absence of showing that formal advertising would be likely to result either in additional cost to the government by reason of duplication of investment or in duplication of necessary preparation which would unduly delay the procurement. Wheelabrator Corp. v. Chafee, 455 F.2d 1306, 1312 (D.C. Cir. 1971). United States ⊕64.10

FAR subpart 14.5, two-step sealed bidding, identifies two-step sealed bidding as "a combination of competitive procedures designed to obtain the benefits of sealed bidding . . .." FAR 14.501. While step one "consists of the request for, submission, evaluation, and (if necessary) discussion of a technical proposal," pricing is not involved. Conformity to the technical requirements is resolved in this step. FAR 14.501 (a). Step two involves submission of sealed bids priced by firms which submitted acceptable technical proposals in step one; award is based on the bids. FAR 14.501 (b). BMAR & Associates, Inc., B-281664, 99-1 CPD ¶ 62 (Comp. Gen. 1999)

§ 14.503 Procedures.

§ 14.503-1 Step one.

(a) Requests for technical proposals shall be synopsized in accordance with Part 5. The request must include, as a minimum, the following:

(1) A description of the supplies or services required.

(2) A statement of intent to use the two-step method.

(3) The requirements of the technical proposal.

(4) The evaluation criteria, to include all factors and any significant subfactors.

(5) A statement that the technical proposals shall not include prices or pricing information.

(6) The date, or date and hour, by which the proposal must be received (see 14.201-6(r)).

(7) A statement that—

(i) In the second step, only bids based upon technical proposals determined to be acceptable, either initially or as a result of discussions, will be considered for awards, and

(ii) Each bid in the second step must be based on the bidder's own technical proposals.

(8) A statement that—

(i) Offerors should submit proposals that are acceptable without additional explanation or information,

(ii) The Government may make a final determination regarding a proposal's acceptability solely on the basis of the proposal as submitted; and

(iii) The Government may proceed with the second step without requesting further information from any offeror; however, the Government may request additional information from offerors of proposals that it considers reasonably susceptible of being made acceptable, and may discuss proposals with their offerors.

(9) A statement that a notice of unacceptability will be forwarded to the offeror upon completion of the proposal evaluation and final determination of unacceptability.

(10) A statement either that only one technical proposal may be submitted by each offeror or that multiple technical proposals may be submitted. When specifications permit different technical approaches, it is generally in the Government's interest to authorize multiple proposals. If multiple proposals are authorized, see 14.201-6(s).

(b) Information on delivery or performance requirements may be of assistance to bidders in determining whether or not to submit a proposal and may be included in the request. The request shall also indicate that the information is not binding on the Government and that the actual delivery or performance requirements will be contained in the invitation issued under step two.

(c) Upon receipt, the contracting officer shall—

(1) Safeguard proposals against disclosure to unauthorized persons;

(2) Accept and handle data marked in accordance with 15.609 as provided in that section; and

(3) Remove any reference to price or cost.

(d) The contracting officer shall establish a time period for evaluating technical proposals. The period may vary with the complexity and number of proposals involved. However, the evaluation should be completed quickly.

(e) (1) Evaluations shall be based on the criteria in the request for proposals but not consideration of responsibility as defined in 9.1, Proposals, shall be categorized as—

(i) Acceptable;

(ii) Reasonably susceptible of being made acceptable; or

(iii) Unacceptable.

(2) Any proposal which modifies, or fails to conform to the essential requirements or specifications of, the request for technical proposals shall be considered nonresponsive and categorized as unacceptable.

(f) (1) The contracting officer may proceed directly with step two if there are sufficient acceptable proposals to ensure adequate price competition under step two, and if further time, effort and delay to make additional proposals acceptable and thereby increase competition would not be in the Government's interest. If this is not the case, the contracting officer shall request bidders whose proposals may be made acceptable to submit additional clarifying or supplementing information. The contracting office shall identify the nature of the deficiencies in the proposal or the nature of the additional information required. The contracting officer may also arrange discussions for this purpose. No proposal shall be discussed with any offeror other than the submitter.

(2) In initiating requests for additional information, the contracting officer shall fix an appropriate time for bidders to conclude discussions, if any, submit all additional information, and incorporate such additional information as part of their proposals submitted. Such time may be extended in the discretion of the contracting officer. If the additional information incorporated as part of a proposal within the final time fixed by the contracting officer establishes that the proposal is acceptable, it shall be so categorized. Otherwise, it shall be categorized as unacceptable.

(g) When a technical proposal is found unacceptable (either initially or after clarification), the contracting officer shall promptly notify the offeror of the basis of the determination and that a revision of the proposal will not be considered. Upon written request, the contracting officer shall debrief unsuccessful offerors (see 15.505 and 15.506).

(h) Late technical proposals are governed by 15.208(b), (c), and (f).

(i) If it is necessary to discontinue two-step sealed bidding, the contracting officer shall include a statement of the facts and circumstances in the contract file. Each offeror shall be notified in writing. When step one results in no acceptable technical proposal or only one acceptable technical proposal, the acquisition may be continued by negotiation.

United States Code Annotated

Contract requirements, see 41 USCA § 254.

Contracts, planning, solicitation, evaluation, and award procedures, see 10 USCA § 2305.

Definitions, see 10 USCA § 2302, 41 USCA §§ 259, 403.

Evaluation and award, see 41 USCA § 253b.

Kinds of contracts, see 10 USCA § 2306.

Planning and solicitation requirements, see 41 USCA § 253a.

§ 14.503-2 Step two.

(a) Sealed bidding procedures shall be followed except that invitations for bids shall—

(1) Be issued only to those offerors submitting acceptable technical proposals in step one;

(2) Include the provision prescribed in 14.201-6(t);

(3) Prominently state that the bidder shall comply with the specifications and the bidder's technical proposal; and

(4) Not be synopsized through the Governmentwide point of entry (GPE) as an acquisition opportunity nor publicly posted (see 5.101(a)).

(b) The names of firms that submitted acceptable proposals in step one will be listed through the GPE for the benefit of prospective subcontractors (see 5.207).

United States Code Annotated

Contract requirements, see 41 USCA § 254.

Contracts, planning, solicitation, evaluation, and award procedures, see 10 USCA § 2305.

Definitions, see 10 USCA § 2302, 41 USCA §§ 259, 403.

Evaluation and award, see 41 USCA § 253b.

Kinds of contracts, see 10 USCA § 2306.

Planning and solicitation requirements, see 41 USCA § 253a.

759

PART 15 CONTRACTING BY NEGOTIATION

Subpart 15.5 Preaward, Award, and Postaward Notifications, Protests, and Mistakes

Subpart 15.6 Unsolicited Proposals

§ 15.000 Scope of part.

This part prescribes policies and procedures governing competitive and noncompetitive negotiated acquisitions. A contract awarded using other than sealed bidding procedures is a negotiated contract (see 14.101).

United States Code Annotated

Contract requirements, see 41 USCA § 254.

Contracts, planning, solicitation, evaluation, and award procedures, see 10 USCA § 2305.

Definitions, see 10 USCA § 2302, 41 USCA §§ 259, 403.

Evaluation and award, see 41 USCA § 253b.

Kinds of contracts, see 10 USCA § 2306.

Planning and solicitation requirements, see 41 USCA § 253a.

§ 15.001 Definitions.

As used in this part—

"Deficiency" is a material failure of a proposal to meet a Government requirement or a combination of significant weaknesses in a proposal that increases the risk of unsuccessful contract performance to an unacceptable level.

"Proposal modification" is a change made to a proposal before the solicitation closing date and time, or made in response to an amendment, or made to correct a mistake at any time before award.

"Proposal revision" is a change to a proposal made after the solicitation closing date, at the request of or as allowed by a contracting officer, as the result of negotiations.

"Weakness" means a flaw in the proposal that increases the risk of unsuccessful contract performance. A "significant weakness" in the proposal is a flaw that appreciably increases the risk of unsuccessful contract performance.

United States Code Annotated

Contract requirements, see 41 USCA § 254.

Contracts, planning, solicitation, evaluation, and award procedures, see 10 USCA § 2305.

Definitions, see 10 USCA § 2302, 41 USCA §§ 259, 403.

Evaluation and award, see 41 USCA § 253b.

Kinds of contracts, see 10 USCA § 2306.

Planning and solicitation requirements, see 41 USCA § 253a.

Notes of Decisions

In general 1

1 In general

When the proposal of a contract program manager is a material solicitation requirement and an offeror cannot meet this requirement, this failure constitutes a "deficiency", rather than a "weakness." A weakness generally reflects a proposal flaw that increases the risk of unsuccessful performance, while a deficiency reflects the failure of a proposal to meet a material requirement. Paradigm Techs., Inc., B-409221.2, 2014 CPD ¶ 257 (Comp. Gen. 2014)

§ 15.002 Types of negotiated acquisition.

(a) *Sole source acquisitions.* When contracting in a sole source environment, the request for proposals (RFP) should be tailored to remove unnecessary information and requirements; *e.g.,* evaluation criteria and voluminous proposal preparation instructions.

(b) *Competitive acquisitions.* When contracting in a competitive environment, the procedures of this part are intended to minimize the complexity of the solicitation, the evaluation, and the source selection decision, while maintaining a process designed to foster an impartial and comprehensive evaluation of offerors' proposals, leading to selection of the proposal representing the best value to the Government (see 2.101).

United States Code Annotated

Contract requirements, see 41 USCA § 254.

Contracts, planning, solicitation, evaluation, and award procedures, see 10 USCA § 2305.

Definitions, see 10 USCA § 2302, 41 USCA §§ 259, 403.
Evaluation and award, see 41 USCA § 253b.
Kinds of contracts, see 10 USCA § 2306.
Planning and solicitation requirements, see 41 USCA § 253a.

Subpart 15.1 Source Selection Processes and Techniques

§ 15.100 Scope of subpart.

This subpart describes some of the acquisition processes and techniques that may be used to design competitive acquisition strategies suitable for the specific circumstances of the acquisition.

United States Code Annotated

Contract requirements, see 41 USCA § 254.
Contracts, planning, solicitation, evaluation, and award procedures, see 10 USCA § 2305.
Definitions, see 10 USCA § 2302, 41 USCA §§ 259, 403.
Evaluation and award, see 41 USCA § 253b.
Kinds of contracts, see 10 USCA § 2306.
Planning and solicitation requirements, see 41 USCA § 253a.

§ 15.101 Best value continuum.

An agency can obtain best value in negotiated acquisitions by using any one or a combination of source selection approaches. In different types of acquisitions, the relative importance of cost or price may vary. For example, in acquisitions where the requirement is clearly definable and the risk of unsuccessful contract performance is minimal, cost or price may play a dominant role in source selection. The less definitive the requirement, the more development work required, or the greater the performance risk, the more technical or past performance considerations may play a dominant role in source selection.

United States Code Annotated

Contract requirements, see 41 USCA § 254.
Contracts, planning, solicitation, evaluation, and award procedures, see 10 USCA § 2305.
Definitions, see 10 USCA § 2302, 41 USCA §§ 259, 403.
Evaluation and award, see 41 USCA § 253b.
Kinds of contracts, see 10 USCA § 2306.
Planning and solicitation requirements, see 41 USCA § 253a.

Notes of Decisions

In general 1

1 In general

GSA awarded 60 IDIQ contracts to offerors that were the "highest technically rated with a fair and reasonable price" without conducting a tradeoff of price and non-price factors. The protester alleged that this evaluation method violated the requirement to evaluate price, since the proposed prices of offerors not technically rated in the top 60 were not considered. GAO denied the protest and noted that the "Guiding Principles" in FAR 1.102 authorize agencies to use any acquisition procedure unless prohibited by law or regulation. Although FAR Part 15 describes only two procedures (the tradeoff process and the low price/technically acceptable process), it does not prohibit the approach used by the GSA. Sevatec, Inc., et al., B-413559.3, et al., 2017 CPD ¶ 3 (Comp. Gen. 2017)

§ 15.101-1 Tradeoff process.

(a) A tradeoff process is appropriate when it may be in the best interest of the Government to consider award to other than the lowest priced offeror or other than the highest technically rated offeror.

(b) When using a tradeoff process, the following apply:

(1) All evaluation factors and significant subfactors that will affect contract award and their relative importance shall be clearly stated in the solicitation; and

(2) The solicitation shall state whether all evaluation factors other than cost or price, when combined, are significantly more important than, approximately equal to, or significantly less important than cost or price.

(c) This process permits tradeoffs among cost or price and non-cost factors and allows the Government to accept other than the lowest priced proposal. The perceived benefits of the higher priced proposal shall merit the additional cost, and the rationale for tradeoffs must be documented in the file in accordance with 15.406.

United States Code Annotated

Contract requirements, see 41 USCA § 254.

Contracts, planning, solicitation, evaluation, and award procedures, see 10 USCA § 2305.

Definitions, see 10 USCA § 2302, 41 USCA §§ 259, 403.

Evaluation and award, see 41 USCA § 253b.

Kinds of contracts, see 10 USCA § 2306.

Planning and solicitation requirements, see 41 USCA § 253a.

Notes of Decisions

In general 1
Factor weights 3
Tradeoff process 2

1 In general

When an RFP contemplates that the relative merits of the proposals will be qualitatively compared, the evaluation may not properly be limited to determining whether proposals are merely technically acceptable. Rather, proposals must be further differentiated to distinguish their relative quality under each stated evaluation factor. Protest was sustained because there was no evidence in the source selection record showing that the agency performed a qualitative assessment of the merits of the offerors' differing approaches. M7 Aerospace LLC, Comp. Gen. Dec. B-411986, et al., 2016 CPD ¶ 100 (Comp. Gen. 2016)

Where solicitations provide for award on a "best value" or "most advantageous to the government" basis, it is the function of the source selection authority to perform a price/technical tradeoff, that is, to determine whether one proposal's technical superiority is worth the higher price, and the extent to which one is sacrificed for the other is governed only by the test of rationality and consistency with the stated evaluation criteria. Matter of: Remington Arms Company, Inc., B-297374, B-297374.2, 2006 CPD ¶ 32 (Comp. Gen. 2006).

2 Tradeoff process

"Best value" contract awards allow the government to accept other than the lowest priced proposal where the perceived benefits of the higher priced proposal merit the additional costs. B & S Transport, Inc. v. U.S., 68 Fed. Cl. 103 (2005). United States ☞64.45(1)

The government is only required to make a cost/technical tradeoff in considering proposals where one proposal is rated higher technically than another, but the other is lower in cost. Industrial Property Management, Inc. v. U.S., 59 Fed. Cl. 318 (2004). United States ☞64.45(1)

3 Factor weights

Both federal statutes and regulations require evaluation factors and significant subfactors to be listed in government's request for contract proposals; however, precise numerical weight to be used in evaluating each proposal submitted need not be disclosed. 10 U.S.C.A. § 2305(a)(2); Federal Property and Administrative Services Act of 1949, § 303A(b)(1), as amended, 41 U.S.C.A. § 253a(b)(1); 48 C.F.R. § 15.605(d)(1). Analytical & Research Technology, Inc. v. U.S., 39 Fed. Cl. 34, 442 Cont. Cas. Fed. (CCH) P 77228 (1997). United States ☞64.25

§ 15.101-2 Lowest price technically acceptable source selection process.

(a) The lowest price technically acceptable source selection process is appropriate when best value is expected to result from selection of the technically acceptable proposal with the lowest evaluated price.

(b) When using the lowest price technically acceptable process, the following apply:

(1) The evaluation factors and significant subfactors that establish the requirements of acceptability shall be set forth in the solicitation. Solicitations shall specify that award will be made on the basis of the lowest evaluated price of proposals meeting or exceeding the acceptability standards for non-cost factors. If the contracting officer documents the file pursuant to 15.304(c)(3)(iii), past performance need not be an evaluation factor in lowest price technically acceptable source selections. If the contracting officer elects to consider past performance as an evaluation factor, it shall be evaluated in accordance with 15.305. However, the comparative assessment in 15.305(a)(2)(i) does not apply. If the contracting officer determines that a small business' past performance is not acceptable, the matter shall be referred to the Small Business Administration for a Certificate of Competency determination, in accordance with the procedures contained in Subpart 19.6 and 15 U.S.C. 637(b)(7)).

(2) Tradeoffs are not permitted.

(3) Proposals are evaluated for acceptability but not ranked using the non-cost/price factors.

(4) Exchanges may occur (see 15.306).

United States Code Annotated

Contract requirements, see 41 USCA § 254.

Contracts, planning, solicitation, evaluation, and award procedures, see 10 USCA § 2305.

Definitions, see 10 USCA § 2302, 41 USCA §§ 259, 403.

Evaluation and award, see 41 USCA § 253b.

Kinds of contracts, see 10 USCA § 2306.

Planning and solicitation requirements, see 41 USCA § 253a.

Notes of Decisions

Lowest price technically acceptable 1
Minimum or material requirements 2

1 Lowest price technically acceptable

Protestor did not establish that contracting agency's rescoring of technical and management factors in solicitation had the effect of changing the solicitation from a "best value" procurement to "lowest price technically acceptable" procurement. 48 C.F.R. §§ 15.101-1(a), 15.101-2(a), (b)(2). Dismas Charities, Inc. v. U.S., 61 Fed. Cl. 191 (2004). United States ☞64.45(1)

2 Minimum or material requirements

A mandatory minimum requirement must be clearly identified as such within a solicitation so as to put offerors on notice of the serious consequences of failing to meet the requirement; such notice typically emphasizes that a proposal must meet the requirement in order to be eligible for evaluation or, conversely, that failure to comply with the requirement will lead to outright rejection of the proposal. ManTech Telecommunications and Information Systems Corp. v. U.S., 49 Fed. Cl. 57 (2001), decision aff'd, 30 Fed. Appx. 995 (Fed. Cir. 2002). United States ☞64.25

Solicitation's minimum education and experience provisions could not reasonably be read as imposing a minimum mandatory requirement; far from providing the requisite notice that failure to comply with the minimum experience and resume requirements would result in disqualification, the solicitation, as a whole, signaled that relatively minor deficiencies, rating something better than an exceptionally low score on a specific element or factor, would not result in a proposal being eliminated. ManTech Telecommunications and Information Systems Corp. v. U.S., 49 Fed. Cl. 57 (2001), decision aff'd, 30 Fed. Appx. 995 (Fed. Cir. 2002). United States ☞64.25

A mandatory minimum requirement (MMR) must be specified as such within a solicitation. 48 C.F.R. § 15.206(a). Cubic Defense Systems, Inc. v. U.S., 45 Fed. Cl. 450

(1999). United States ☞64.25

Government violated procurement statutes and regulations in awarding software contract, by relaxing minimum solicitation requirement without notifying all offerors that the evaluation criterion had changed. 10 U.S.C.A. § 2305(b)(1); 48 C.F.R. §§ 12.602(b, c), 15.305(a). Candle Corp. v. U.S., 40 Fed. Cl. 658, 42 Cont. Cas. Fed. (CCH) P 77276 (1998). United States ☞64.25

Requirement in Army's solicitation of proposals on contract for computer and data processing support, that proposed personnel have three years minimum experience within preceding five years, was not latently ambiguous as alleged by disappointed offeror; solicitation stated that proposed personnel must have requisite years of experience, defined the minimum years of experience required for proposed personnel, stated that proposed personnel would receive score of "unacceptable" if they did not meet minimum experience requirements, and further defined "unacceptable" as numerical score of zero. Analytical & Research Technology, Inc. v. U.S., 39 Fed. Cl. 34, 442 Cont. Cas. Fed. (CCH) P 77228 (1997). United States ☞64.25

In soliciting proposals on contract for computer and automated data processing support, Army could evaluate the requirement that proposed personnel have three years minimum experience within preceding five years as a "go/no-go" requirement which if not met would render that portion of offeror's proposal technically unacceptable, regardless of whether solicitation used term "go/no-go." 10 U.S.C.A. § 2305(a)(2); Federal Property and Administrative Services Act of 1949, § 303A(b)(1), as amended, 41 U.S.C.A. § 253a(b)(1); 48 C.F.R. § 15.605(d)(1). Analytical & Research Technology, Inc. v. U.S., 39 Fed. Cl. 34, 442 Cont. Cas. Fed. (CCH) P 77228 (1997). United States ☞64.40(1)

Statement of requirements for second phase of application process for concessions contract required that applicant not condition capital improvement fund contribution following change of operations on further negotiation. YRT Services Corp. v. U.S., 28 Fed. Cl. 366, 38 Cont. Cas. Fed. (CCH) P 76512 (1993). United States ☞64.30

§ 15.102 Oral presentations.

(a) Oral presentations by offerors as requested by the Government may substitute for, or augment, written information. Use of oral presentations as a substitute for portions of a proposal can be effective in streamlining the source selection process. Oral presentations may occur at any time in the acquisition process, and are subject to the same restrictions as written information, regarding timing (see 15.208) and content (see 15.306). Oral presentations provide an opportunity for dialogue among the parties. Pre-recorded videotaped presentations that lack real-time interactive dialogue are not considered oral presentations for the purposes of this section, although they may be included in offeror submissions, when appropriate.

(b) The solicitation may require each offeror to submit part of its proposal through oral presentations. However, representations and certifications shall be submitted as required in the FAR provisions at 52.204-8(d) or 52.212-3(b), and a signed offer sheet (including any exceptions to the Government's terms and conditions) shall be submitted in writing.

(c) Information pertaining to areas such as an offeror's capability, past performance, work plans or approaches, staffing resources, transition plans, or sample tasks (or other types of tests) may be suitable for oral presentations. In deciding what information to obtain through an oral presentation, consider the following:

    (1) The Government's ability to adequately evaluate the information;

    (2) The need to incorporate any information into the resultant contract;

    (3) The impact on the efficiency of the acquisition; and

    (4) The impact (including cost) on small businesses. In considering the costs of oral presentations, contracting officers should also consider alternatives to on-site oral presentations (e.g., teleconferencing, video teleconferencing).

(d) When oral presentations are required, the solicitation shall provide offerors with sufficient information to prepare them. Accordingly, the solicitation may describe—

    (1) The types of information to be presented orally and the associated evaluation factors that will be used;

    (2) The qualifications for personnel that will be required to provide the oral presentation(s);

(3) The requirements for, and any limitations and/or prohibitions on, the use of written material or other media to supplement the oral presentations;

(4) The location, date, and time for the oral presentations;

(5) The restrictions governing the time permitted for each oral presentation; and

(6) The scope and content of exchanges that may occur between the Government's participants and the offeror's representatives as part of the oral presentations, including whether or not discussions (see 15.306(d)) will be permitted during oral presentations.

(e) The contracting officer shall maintain a record of oral presentations to document what the Government relied upon in making the source selection decision. The method and level of detail of the record (*e.g.*, videotaping, audio tape recording, written record, Government notes, copies of offeror briefing slides or presentation notes) shall be at the discretion of the source selection authority. A copy of the record placed in the file may be provided to the offeror.

(f) When an oral presentation includes information that the parties intend to include in the contract as material terms or conditions, the information shall be put in writing. Incorporation by reference of oral statements is not permitted.

(g) If, during an oral presentation, the Government conducts discussions (see 15.306(d)), the Government must comply with 15.306 and 15.307.

United States Code Annotated

Contract requirements, see 41 USCA § 254.

Contracts, planning, solicitation, evaluation, and award procedures, see 10 USCA § 2305.

Definitions, see 10 USCA § 2302, 41 USCA §§ 259, 403.

Evaluation and award, see 41 USCA § 253b.

Kinds of contracts, see 10 USCA § 2306.

Planning and solicitation requirements, see 41 USCA § 253a.

Notes of Decisions

Oral presentation 1

1 Oral presentation

Decision of technical evaluation board to deduct 20 points from offeror's score on proposal because offeror's oral presentation was not given by its proposed project manager as required by solicitation but by his supervisor was not arbitrary or capricious; it is not unreasonable that agency would require that the project manager give the presentation, particularly when it is the project manager, not the supervisor who would be on-site at the project. Bean Stuyvesant, L.L.C. v. U.S., 48 Fed. Cl. 303 (2000). United States ⊙64.40(1)

Consensus scores of agency evaluators for offeror's proposal for beach renourishment and shore protection project reasonably reflected the merits of offeror's oral presentation on technical factors relating to transference of material from dredge to area inside the pipeline corridor, transference of material from dredge to area outside the pipeline corridor, and description of breakwater construction. Bean Stuyvesant, L.L.C. v. U.S., 48 Fed. Cl. 303 (2000). United States ⊙64.40(1)

Disappointed offeror did not establish that procuring agency engaged in technical leveling by suggesting, during successful offeror's first oral presentation, that it should replace one of its proposed candidates for project position with a candidate who was rated very highly by the technical evaluation committee (TEC). 48 C.F.R. § 15.610(d) (1995). Labat-Anderson, Inc. v. U.S., 42 Fed. Cl. 806 (1999). United States ⊙64.40(1)

Protest was sustained because the agency could not support its determination that the protester's proposal was unacceptable, which was based largely on the vendor's responses to questions following their oral presentation. Although the oral presentation was videotaped, the questions and answers following the presentation were not, and the documentation of the questions and answers was inadequate to support the agency's determination. Matter of: Resource Dimensions, LLC, B-404536, 2011 CPD ¶ 50 (Comp. Gen. 2011)

Agency's communications with awardee during oral presentation did not constitute discussions, and agency thus was not required to conduct discussions with and request revised proposals from all offerors in the competitive range, where information furnished by awardee (with respect to staffing of effort to develop health care network) in response to agency questions after oral presentation was merely a clarification of information previously furnished by awardee in the presentation slides and accompanying oral presentation of slides. Sierra Military Health Services, Inc.; Aetna Government Health Plans, B-292780, B-292780.2, B-292780.3, B-292780.4, B-292780.5, B-292780.6, 2004 CPD ¶ 55 (Comp. Gen. 2003)

Where agency personnel comment on, or raise substantive questions or concerns about, vendors' quotations or proposals in the course of an oral presentation, and either simultaneously or subsequently afford the vendors an opportunity to make revisions in light of the agency personnel's comments, questions, and concerns, discussions have occurred. TDS, Inc., B-292674, 2003 CPD ¶ 204 (Comp. Gen. 2003)

General Accounting Office cannot find that the agency reasonably evaluated the protester's oral presentation where the agency and protester disagree as to the content of the oral presentation, the contemporaneous record of the oral discussions and presentations—which consists only of the protester's presentation materials and the evaluators' scoresheets—does not support the evaluators' conclusions regarding the protester's approach, and the agency did not act in accordance with the terms of the solicitation where it disregarded the protester's previously submitted written proposal in evaluating the oral presentation. Checchi and Company Consulting, Inc., B-285777, 2001 CPD ¶ 132 (Comp. Gen. 2000).

In not allowing technically acceptable offerors to make oral presentations as part of their technical proposals, agency acted inconsistently with the solicitation provision that all offerors would be afforded the opportunity to make oral presentations. Kathpal Technologies, Inc.; Computer & Hi-Tech Management, Inc., B-283137.3, B-283137.4, B-283137.5, B-283137.6, 2000 CPD ¶ 6 (Comp. Gen. 1999)

Subpart 15.2 Solicitation and Receipt of Proposals and Information

§ 15.200 Scope of subpart.

This subpart prescribes policies and procedures for—

(a) Exchanging information with industry prior to receipt of proposals;

(b) Preparing and issuing requests for proposals (RFPs) and requests for information (RFIs); and

(c) Receiving proposals and information.

United States Code Annotated

Contract requirements, see 41 USCA § 254.

Contracts, planning, solicitation, evaluation, and award procedures, see 10 USCA § 2305.

Definitions, see 10 USCA § 2302, 41 USCA §§ 259, 403.

Evaluation and award, see 41 USCA § 253b.

Kinds of contracts, see 10 USCA § 2306.

Planning and solicitation requirements, see 41 USCA § 253a.

§ 15.201 Exchanges with industry before receipt of proposals.

(a) Exchanges of information among all interested parties, from the earliest identification of a requirement through receipt of proposals, are encouraged. Any exchange of information must be consistent with procurement integrity requirements (see 3.104). Interested parties include potential offerors, end users, Government acquisition and supporting personnel, and others involved in the conduct or outcome of the acquisition.

(b) The purpose of exchanging information is to improve the understanding of Government requirements and industry capabilities, thereby allowing potential offerors to judge whether or how they can satisfy the Government's requirements, and enhancing the Government's ability to obtain quality supplies and services, including construction, at reasonable prices, and increase efficiency in proposal preparation, proposal evaluation, negotiation, and contract award.

(c) Agencies are encouraged to promote early exchanges of information about future acquisitions. An early exchange of information among industry and the program manager, contracting officer, and other participants in the acquisition process can identify and resolve concerns regarding the acquisition strategy, including proposed contract type, terms and conditions, and acquisition planning schedules; the feasibility of the requirement, including performance requirements, statements of work, and data requirements; the suitability of the proposal instructions and evaluation criteria, including the approach for assessing past performance information; the availability of reference documents; and any other industry concerns or questions. Some techniques to promote early exchanges of information are—

    (1) Industry or small business conferences;

    (2) Public hearings;

    (3) Market research, as described in Part 10;

    (4) One-on-one meetings with potential offerors (any that are substantially involved with potential contract terms and conditions should include the contracting officer; also see paragraph (f) of this section regarding restrictions on disclosure of information);

    (5) Presolicitation notices;

    (6) Draft RFPs;

    (7) RFIs;

    (8) Presolicitation or preproposal conferences; and

    (9) Site visits.

(d) The special notices of procurement matters at 5.205(c), or electronic notices, may be used to publicize the Government's requirement or solicit information from industry.

(e) RFIs may be used when the Government does not presently intend to award a contract, but wants to obtain price, delivery, other market information, or capabilities for planning purposes. Responses to these notices are not offers and cannot be accepted by the Government to form a binding contract. There is no required format for RFIs.

(f) General information about agency mission needs and future requirements may be disclosed at any time. After release of the solicitation, the contracting officer must be the focal point of any exchange with potential offerors. When specific information about a proposed acquisition that would be necessary for the preparation of proposals is disclosed to one or more potential offerors, that information must be made available to the public as soon as practicable, but no later than the next general release of information, in order to avoid creating an unfair competitive advantage. Information provided to a potential offeror in response to its request must not be disclosed if doing so would reveal the potential offeror's confidential business strategy, and is protected under 3.104 or Subpart 24.2. When conducting a presolicitation or preproposal conference, materials distributed at the conference should be made available to all potential offerors, upon request.

United States Code Annotated

Contract requirements, see 41 USCA § 254.

Contracts, planning, solicitation, evaluation, and award procedures, see 10 USCA § 2305.

Definitions, see 10 USCA § 2302, 41 USCA §§ 259, 403.

Evaluation and award, see 41 USCA § 253b.

Kinds of contracts, see 10 USCA § 2306.

Planning and solicitation requirements, see 41 USCA § 253a.

§ 15.202 Advisory multi-step process.

    (a) The agency may publish a presolicitation notice (see 5.204) that provides a general description of the scope or purpose of the acquisition and invites potential offerors to submit information that allows the Government to advise the offerors about their potential to be viable competitors. The presolicitation notice should identify the information that must be submitted and the criteria that will be used in making the initial evaluation. Information sought may be limited to a statement of qualifications and other appropriate information (*e.g.*, proposed technical concept, past performance, and limited pricing information). At a minimum, the notice shall contain sufficient information to permit a potential offeror to make an informed decision about whether to participate in the acquisition. This process should not be used for multi-step acquisitions where it would result in offerors being required to submit identical information in response to the notice and in response to the initial step of the acquisition.

(b) The agency shall evaluate all responses in accordance with the criteria stated in the notice, and shall advise each respondent in writing either that it will be invited to participate in the resultant acquisition or, based on the information submitted, that it is unlikely to be a viable competitor. The agency shall advise respondents considered not to be viable competitors of the general basis for that opinion. The agency shall inform all respondents that, notwithstanding the advice provided by the Government in response to their submissions, they may participate in the resultant acquisition.

United States Code Annotated

Contract requirements, see 41 USCA § 254.

Contracts, planning, solicitation, evaluation, and award procedures, see 10 USCA § 2305.

Definitions, see 10 USCA § 2302, 41 USCA §§ 259, 403.

Evaluation and award, see 41 USCA § 253b.

Kinds of contracts, see 10 USCA § 2306.

Planning and solicitation requirements, see 41 USCA § 253a.

§ 15.203 Requests for proposals.

(a) Requests for proposals (RFPs) are used in negotiated acquisitions to communicate Government requirements to prospective contractors and to solicit proposals. RFPs for competitive acquisitions shall, at a minimum, describe the—

(1) Government's requirement;

(2) Anticipated terms and conditions that will apply to the contract:

(i) The solicitation may authorize offerors to propose alternative terms and conditions, including the contract line item number (CLIN) structure; and

(ii) When alternative CLIN structures are permitted, the evaluation approach should consider the potential impact on other terms and conditions or the requirement (e.g., place of performance or payment and funding requirements) (see 15.206);

(3) Information required to be in the offeror's proposal; and

(4) Factors and significant subfactors that will be used to evaluate the proposal and their relative importance.

(b) An RFP may be issued for OMB Circular A-76 studies. See Subpart 7.3 for additional information regarding cost comparisons between Government and contractor performance.

(c) Electronic commerce may be used to issue RFPs and to receive proposals, modifications, and revisions. In this case, the RFP shall specify the electronic commerce method(s) that offerors may use (see Subpart 4.5).

(d) Contracting officers may issue RFPs and/or authorize receipt of proposals, modifications, or revisions by facsimile.

(1) In deciding whether or not to use facsimiles, the contracting officer should consider factors such as—

(i) Anticipated proposal size and volume;

(ii) Urgency of the requirement;

(iii) Availability and suitability of electronic commerce methods; and

(iv) Adequacy of administrative procedures and controls for receiving, identifying, recording, and safeguarding facsimile proposals, and ensuring their timely delivery to the designated proposal delivery location.

(2) If facsimile proposals are authorized, contracting officers may request offeror(s) to provide the complete, original signed proposal at a later date.

(e) Letter RFPs may be used in sole source acquisitions and other appropriate circumstances. Use of a letter RFP does not relieve the contracting officer from complying with other FAR requirements. Letter RFPs should be as complete as possible and, at a minimum, should contain the following:

(1) RFP number and date;

(2) Name, address (including electronic address and facsimile address, if appropriate),

and telephone number of the contracting officer;

(3) Type of contract contemplated;

(4) Quantity, description, and required delivery dates for the item;

(5) Applicable certifications and representations;

(6) Anticipated contract terms and conditions;

(7) Instructions to offerors and evaluation criteria for other than sole source actions;

(8) Proposal due date and time; and

(9) Other relevant information; *e.g.,* incentives, variations in delivery schedule, cost proposal support, and data requirements.

(f) Oral RFPs are authorized when processing a written solicitation would delay the acquisition of supplies or services to the detriment of the Government and a notice is not required under 5.202 (*e.g.,* perishable items and support of contingency operations or other emergency situations). Use of an oral RFP does not relieve the contracting officer from complying with other FAR requirements.

(1) The contract files supporting oral solicitations should include—

(i) A description of the requirement;

(ii) Rationale for use of an oral solicitation;

(iii) Sources solicited, including the date, time, name of individuals contacted, and prices offered; and

(iv) The solicitation number provided to the prospective offerors.

(2) The information furnished to potential offerors under oral solicitations should include appropriate items from paragraph (e) of this section.

United States Code Annotated

Contract requirements, see 41 USCA § 254.

Contracts, planning, solicitation, evaluation, and award procedures, see 10 USCA § 2305.

Definitions, see 10 USCA § 2302, 41 USCA §§ 259, 403.

Evaluation and award, see 41 USCA § 253b.

Kinds of contracts, see 10 USCA § 2306.

Planning and solicitation requirements, see 41 USCA § 253a.

Notes of Decisions

Content of RFP 3
Disclosure of procedures 1
Latent ambiguity 5
Minimum or material requirements 2
Release of incumbent information 4

1 Disclosure of procedures

All factors and significant subfactors that will affect contract award and their relative importance shall be stated clearly in the solicitation (10 U.S.C. 2305(a)(2)(A)(i) and 41 U.S.C. 253a(b)(1)(A)). The rating method need not be disclosed in the solicitation. Beta Analytics Intern., Inc. v. U.S., 67 Fed. Cl. 384 (2005), subsequent determination, 69 Fed. Cl. 431 (2005), order clarified, 2006 WL 5628556 (Ct. Fed. Cl. 2006)

Failure to tell offerors the exact numerical weight of each factor and sub-factor in bid evaluation process was not arbitrary or capricious, where relative importance of factors and, within a factor, of the sub-factors, was specified in the solicitation, and was followed in the source selection plan and by evaluators. Beta Analytics Intern., Inc. v. U.S., 67 Fed. Cl. 384 (2005), subsequent determination, 69 Fed. Cl. 431 (2005), order clarified, 2006 WL 5628556 (Ct. Fed. Cl. 2006)

Assuming that simplified acquisition procedures found in Part 13 of the Federal Acquisition Regulation (FAR) were employed by agency in procurement, agency failed to provide adequate notice of that fact to offerors, and thus Court of Federal Claims would analyze agency's conduct in the procurement under the standard negotiated procurement regulations found in FAR Part 15. Dubinsky v. U.S., 43 Fed. Cl. 243 (1999). United States ⊂⇒64.40(1)

Notwithstanding statement in solicitation that simplified acquisition procedures were being used and authority at FAR 12.602(a) not to disclose the relative weight of evaluation factors when using simplified procedures, an agency's failure to disclose the relative weight of evaluation factors was unreasonable because basic fairness dictated disclosure of the relative weights where the agency required offerors to prepare detailed written proposals addressing unique government requirements. Finlen Complex, Inc., B-288280, 2001 CPD ¶ 167 (Comp. Gen. 2001) [Editorial Note: This case is aberrational because the agency's process was found to be unreasonable, although it complied with express guidance in the FAR.]

2 Minimum or material requirements

Even in negotiated procurement, procuring agency does not have discretion to disregard offeror's failure to satisfy material requirement in request for proposal. Howard Cooper Corp. v. U.S., 763 F. Supp. 829, 37 Cont. Cas. Fed. (CCH) P 76169 (E.D. Va. 1991). United States ☞64.5

A solicitation for a government contract must seek proposals that meet an agency's minimum needs, or else the solicitation represents an undue, improper restriction on competition. ABF Freight System, Inc. v. U.S., 55 Fed. Cl. 392 (2003). United States ☞64.25

A mandatory minimum requirement must be clearly identified as such within a solicitation so as to put offerors on notice of the serious consequences of failing to meet the requirement; such notice typically emphasizes that a proposal must meet the requirement in order to be eligible for evaluation or, conversely, that failure to comply with the requirement will lead to outright rejection of the proposal. ManTech Telecommunications and Information Systems Corp. v. U.S., 49 Fed. Cl. 57 (2001), decision aff'd, 30 Fed. Appx. 995 (Fed. Cir. 2002). United States ☞64.25

Solicitation's minimum education and experience provisions could not reasonably be read as imposing a minimum mandatory requirement; far from providing the requisite notice that failure to comply with the minimum experience and resume requirements would result in disqualification, the solicitation, as a whole, signaled that relatively minor deficiencies, rating something better than an exceptionally low score on a specific element or factor, would not result in a proposal being eliminated. ManTech Telecommunications and Information Systems Corp. v. U.S., 49 Fed. Cl. 57 (2001), decision aff'd, 30 Fed. Appx. 995 (Fed. Cir. 2002). United States ☞64.25

A mandatory minimum requirement (MMR) must be specified as such within a solicitation. 48 C.F.R. § 15.206(a). Cubic Defense Systems, Inc. v. U.S., 45 Fed. Cl. 450 (1999). United States ☞64.25

Government violated procurement statutes and regulations in awarding software contract, by relaxing minimum solicitation requirement without notifying all offerors that the evaluation criterion had changed. 10 U.S.C.A. § 2305(b)(1); 48 C.F.R. §§ 12.602(b, c), 15. 305(a). Candle Corp. v. U.S., 40 Fed. Cl. 658, 42 Cont. Cas. Fed. (CCH) P 77276 (1998). United States ☞64.25

Requirement in Army's solicitation of proposals on contract for computer and data processing support, that proposed personnel have three years minimum experience within preceding five years, was not latently ambiguous as alleged by disappointed offeror; solicitation stated that proposed personnel must have requisite years of experience, defined the minimum years of experience required for proposed personnel, stated that proposed personnel would receive score of "unacceptable" if they did not meet minimum experience requirements, and further defined "unacceptable" as numerical score of zero. Analytical & Research Technology, Inc. v. U.S., 39 Fed. Cl. 34, 442 Cont. Cas. Fed. (CCH) P 77228 (1997). United States ☞64.25

In soliciting proposals on contract for computer and automated data processing support, Army could evaluate the requirement that proposed personnel have three years minimum experience within preceding five years as a "go/no-go" requirement which if not met would render that portion of offeror's proposal technically unacceptable, regardless of whether solicitation used term "go/no-go." 10 U.S.C.A. § 2305(a)(2); Federal Property and Administrative Services Act of 1949, § 303A(b)(1), as amended, 41 U.S.C.A. § 253a(b)(1); 48 C.F.R. § 15. 605(d)(1). Analytical & Research Technology, Inc. v. U.S., 39 Fed. Cl. 34, 442 Cont. Cas. Fed. (CCH) P 77228 (1997). United States ☞64.40(1)

Statement of requirements for second phase of application process for concessions contract required that applicant not condition capital improvement fund contribution following change of operations on further negotiation. YRT Services Corp. v. U.S., 28 Fed. Cl. 366, 38 Cont. Cas. Fed. (CCH) P 76512 (1993). United States ☞64.30

Required purchase of concessioner, at price set by National Park Service (NPS), by successful applicant for concessions contract did not prejudice unsuccessful applicant or prevent that unsuccessful applicant from being fully and fairly considered in exactly same way as all other applicants; it was not clear that purchase price was necessarily higher than that which unsuccessful applicant could have negotiated, statement of requirements for second phase of application process called for package offer that took into account many other factors, and terms of purchase were same for all applicants. YRT Services Corp. v. U.S., 28 Fed. Cl. 366, 38 Cont. Cas. Fed. (CCH) P 76512 (1993). United States ☞64.40(2)

3 Content of RFP

GAO denied a protest challenging an agency's non-acceptance of a bid submitted during a reverse auction. Even though the offeror submitted its bid prior to the closing time for the reverse auction (by one second), the agency did not receive the bid prior to the closing time. It is an offeror's responsibility to ensure that an electronically submitted proposal is received by—not just submitted to—an agency prior to the time set for closing. C2G Ltd. Co., B-411131, 2015 CPD ¶ 157 (Comp.Gen. 2015)

Solicitations must describe the factors and significant subfactors that will be used to evaluate the proposals and their relative importance, and the evaluation of proposals must be based solely on the factors and subfactors contained in the solicitation. FAR 15.203(a)(4), 15.303(b)(4). In performing the evaluation, however, the agency may take into account specific, albeit not expressly identified, matters that are logically encompassed by the stated evaluation criteria. Colmek Systems Engineering, B-291931.2, 2003 CPD ¶ 123 (Comp. Gen. 2003)

4 Release of incumbent information

Agency is not required to release the names of the incumbent's subcontractors, service call log information and more detailed repair history information where the agency found the requested information to be proprietary and not subject to release. Knowledge as to the nature of the incumbent contractor's work force is strictly an advantage of incumbency, and the government thus has no obligation to disseminate that information to other offerors. Richen Management, LLC, B-406750 (July 31, 2012).

Decision by Air Force to not include historical cost information that offerors could use to project "other direct costs" (ODCs), which included real property costs, materials, tools, and other supplies required to perform a firm fixed price contract, was neither arbitrary nor capricious, since solicitations provided sufficient detail to allow offerors to compete intelligently and on relatively equal basis. Phoenix Mgmt., Inc. v. U.S., 127 Fed.Cl. 358 (2016)

5 Latent ambiguity

GAO sustained a protest where a latent ambiguity prevented the offerors from competing intelligently on a relatively equal basis. Past performance instructions contained a latent ambiguity because they could be interpreted as requiring that at least two past performance references pertain to the prime contractor *or* that at least two past performance references pertain to performance as a prime contractor, regardless of whether that past performance pertained to the prime contractor or a firm being proposed as a subcontractor. RELI Group, Inc., B-412380, 2016 CPD ¶ 51 (Comp. Gen. 2016)

§ 15.204 Contract format.

The use of a uniform contract format facilitates preparation of the solicitation and contract as well as reference to, and use of, those documents by offerors, contractors, and contract administrators. The uniform contract format need not be used for the following:

(a) Construction and architect-engineer contracts (see Part 36).

(b) Subsistence contracts.

(c) Supplies or services contracts requiring special contract formats prescribed elsewhere in this regulation that are inconsistent with the uniform format.

(d) Letter requests for proposals (see 15.203(e)).

(e) Contracts exempted by the agency head or designee.

United States Code Annotated

Contract requirements, see 41 USCA § 254.

Contracts, planning, solicitation, evaluation, and award procedures, see 10 USCA § 2305.

Definitions, see 10 USCA § 2302, 41 USCA §§ 259, 403.

Evaluation and award, see 41 USCA § 253b.

Kinds of contracts, see 10 USCA § 2306.

Planning and solicitation requirements, see 41 USCA § 253a.

§ 15.204-1 Uniform contract format.

(a) Contracting officers shall prepare solicitations and resulting contracts using the uniform contract format outlined in Table 15-1 of this subsection.

(b) Solicitations using the uniform contract format shall include Parts I, II, III, and IV (see 15.204-2 through 15.204-5). Upon award, contracting officers shall not physically include Part IV in the resulting contract, but shall retain it in the contract file. (See 4.1201(c).) The representations and certifications are incorporated by reference in the contract by using 52.204-19 (see 4.1202(b)) or for acquisitions of commercial items see 52.212-4(v).

TABLE 15-1—UNIFORM CONTRACT FORMAT

SECTION	TITLE
	Part I—The Schedule
A	Solicitation/contract form
B	Supplies or services and prices/costs
C	Description/specifications/statement of work
D	Packaging and marking
E	Inspection and acceptance
F	Deliveries or performance
G	Contract administration data
H	Special contract requirements
	Part II—Contract Clauses
I	Contract clauses
	Part III—List of Documents, Exhibits, and Other Attachments
J	List of attachments
	Part IV—Representations and Instructions
K	Representations, certifications, and other statements of offerors or respondents
L	Instructions, conditions, and notices to offerors or respondents
M	Evaluation factors for award

United States Code Annotated

Contract requirements, see 41 USCA § 254.

Contracts, planning, solicitation, evaluation, and award procedures, see 10 USCA § 2305.

Definitions, see 10 USCA § 2302, 41 USCA §§ 259, 403.

Evaluation and award, see 41 USCA § 253b.

Kinds of contracts, see 10 USCA § 2306.

Planning and solicitation requirements, see 41 USCA § 253a.

§ 15.204-2 Part I—The Schedule.

The contracting officer shall prepare the contract Schedule as follows:

(a) *Section A, Solicitation/contract form.* (1) Optional Form (OF) 308, Solicitation and Offer—Negotiated Acquisition, or Standard Form (SF) 33, Solicitation, Offer and Award, may be used to prepare RFPs.

(2) When other than OF 308 or SF 33 is used, include the following information on the first page of the solicitation:

(i) Name, address, and location of issuing activity, including room and building where proposals or information must be submitted.

(ii) Solicitation number.

(iii) Date of issuance.

(iv) Closing date and time.

(v) Number of pages.

(vi) Requisition or other purchase authority.

(vii) Brief description of item or service.

(viii) Requirement for the offeror to provide its name and complete address, including street, city, county, state, and ZIP code, and electronic address (including facsimile address), if appropriate.

(ix) Offer expiration date.

(b) *Section B, Supplies or services and prices / costs.* Include a brief description of the supplies or services; *e.g.,* item number, national stock number/part number if applicable, nouns, nomenclature, and quantities. (This includes incidental deliverables such as manuals and reports.)

(c) *Section C, Description / specifications / statement of work.* Include any description or specifications needed in addition to Section B (see Part 11, Describing Agency Needs).

(d) *Section D, Packaging and marking.* Provide packaging, packing, preservation, and marking requirements, if any.

(e) *Section E, Inspection and acceptance.* Include inspection, acceptance, quality assurance, and reliability requirements (see Part 46, Quality Assurance).

(f) *Section F, Deliveries or performance.* Specify the requirements for time, place, and method of delivery or performance (see Subpart 11.4, Delivery or Performance Schedules, and 47.301-1).

(g) *Section G, Contract administration data.* Include any required accounting and appropriation data and any required contract administration information or instructions other than those on the solicitation form. Include a statement that the offeror should include the payment address in the proposal, if it is different from that shown for the offeror.

(h) *Section H, Special contract requirements.* Include a clear statement of any special contract requirements that are not included in Section I, Contract clauses, or in other sections of the uniform contract format.

United States Code Annotated

Contract requirements, see 41 USCA § 254.

Contracts, planning, solicitation, evaluation, and award procedures, see 10 USCA § 2305.

Definitions, see 10 USCA § 2302, 41 USCA §§ 259, 403.

Evaluation and award, see 41 USCA § 253b.

Kinds of contracts, see 10 USCA § 2306.

Planning and solicitation requirements, see 41 USCA § 253a.

Notes of Decisions

Minimum or material requirements 1

1 Minimum or material requirements

In general, concept of responsiveness is not applicable to negotiation procurements where contracting officer is permitted to conduct oral or written discussions with offerors whose proposals vary from request for proposals; however, while concept of responsiveness is not technically applicable to negotiated procurements, even in negotiated procurement procuring agency does not have discretion to disregard offeror's failure to satisfy material requirement in request for proposal. Howard Cooper Corp. v. U.S., 763 F. Supp. 829, 37 Cont. Cas.

Fed. (CCH) P 76169 (E.D. Va. 1991). United States ☜64.5

A solicitation for a government contract must seek proposals that meet an agency's minimum needs, or else the solicitation represents an undue, improper restriction on competition. ABF Freight System, Inc. v. U.S., 55 Fed. Cl. 392 (2003). United States ☜64.25

A mandatory minimum requirement must be clearly identified as such within a solicitation so as to put offerors on notice of the serious consequences of failing to meet the requirement; such notice typically emphasizes that a proposal must meet the requirement in order to be eligible for evaluation or, conversely, that failure to comply with the requirement will lead to outright rejection of the proposal. ManTech Telecommunications and Information Systems Corp. v. U.S., 49 Fed. Cl. 57 (2001), decision aff'd, 30 Fed. Appx. 995 (Fed. Cir. 2002). United States ☜64.25

Solicitation's minimum education and experience provisions could not reasonably be read as imposing a minimum mandatory requirement; far from providing the requisite notice that failure to comply with the minimum experience and resume requirements would result in disqualification, the solicitation, as a whole, signaled that relatively minor deficiencies, rating something better than an exceptionally low score on a specific element or factor, would not result in a proposal being eliminated. ManTech Telecommunications and Information Systems Corp. v. U.S., 49 Fed. Cl. 57 (2001), decision aff'd, 30 Fed. Appx. 995 (Fed. Cir. 2002). United States ☜64.25

A mandatory minimum requirement (MMR) must be specified as such within a solicitation. 48 C.F.R. § 15.206(a). Cubic Defense Systems, Inc. v. U.S., 45 Fed. Cl. 450 (1999). United States ☜64.25

Government violated procurement statutes and regulations in awarding software contract, by relaxing minimum solicitation requirement without notifying all offerors that the evaluation criterion had changed. 10 U.S.C.A. § 2305(b)(1); 48 C.F.R. §§ 12.602(b, c), 15. 305(a). Candle Corp. v. U.S., 40 Fed. Cl. 658, 42 Cont. Cas. Fed. (CCH) P 77276 (1998). United States ☜64.25

Requirement in Army's solicitation of proposals on contract for computer and data processing support, that proposed personnel have three years minimum experience within preceding five years, was not latently ambiguous as alleged by disappointed bidder; solicitation stated that proposed personnel must have requisite years of experience, defined the minimum years of experience required for proposed personnel, stated that proposed personnel would receive score of "unacceptable" if they did not meet minimum experience requirements, and further defined "unacceptable" as numerical score of zero. Analytical & Research Technology, Inc. v. U.S., 39 Fed. Cl. 34, 442 Cont. Cas. Fed. (CCH) P 77228 (1997). United States ☜64.25

In soliciting proposals on contract for computer and automated data processing support, Army could evaluate the requirement that proposed personnel have three years minimum experience within preceding five years as a "go/no-go" requirement which if not met would render that portion of offeror's bid technically unacceptable, regardless of whether solicitation used term "go/no-go." 10 U.S.C.A. § 2305(a)(2); Federal Property and Administrative Services Act of 1949, § 303A(b)(1), as amended, 41 U.S.C.A. § 253a(b)(1); 48 C.F.R. § 15. 605(d)(1). Analytical & Research Technology, Inc. v. U.S., 39 Fed. Cl. 34, 442 Cont. Cas. Fed. (CCH) P 77228 (1997). United States ☜64.40(1)

Statement of requirements for second phase of application process for concessions contract required that applicant not condition capital improvement fund contribution following change of operations on further negotiation. YRT Services Corp. v. U.S., 28 Fed. Cl. 366, 38 Cont. Cas. Fed. (CCH) P 76512 (1993). United States ☜64.30

Required purchase of concessioner, at price set by National Park Service (NPS), by successful applicant for concessions contract did not prejudice unsuccessful applicant or prevent that unsuccessful applicant from being fully and fairly considered in exactly same way as all other applicants; it was not clear that purchase price was necessarily higher than that which unsuccessful applicant could have negotiated, statement of requirements for second phase of application process called for package offer that took into account many other factors, and terms of purchase were same for all applicants. YRT Services Corp. v. U.S., 28 Fed. Cl. 366, 38 Cont. Cas. Fed. (CCH) P 76512 (1993). United States ☜64.40(2)

§ 15.204-3 Part II—Contract Clauses.

Section I, Contract clauses. The contracting officer shall include in this section the clauses required by law or by this regulation and any additional clauses expected to be included in any resulting contract, if these clauses are not required in any other section of the uniform contract format. An index may be inserted if this section's format is particularly complex.

United States Code Annotated

Contract requirements, see 41 USCA § 254.

Contracts, planning, solicitation, evaluation, and award procedures, see 10 USCA § 2305.

Definitions, see 10 USCA § 2302, 41 USCA §§ 259, 403.

Evaluation and award, see 41 USCA § 253b.

Kinds of contracts, see 10 USCA § 2306.

Planning and solicitation requirements, see 41 USCA § 253a.

§ 15.204-4 Part III—List of Documents, Exhibits, and Other Attachments.

Section J, List of attachments. The contracting officer shall list the title, date, and number of pages for each attached document, exhibit, and other attachment. Cross-references to material in other sections may be inserted, as appropriate.

United States Code Annotated

Contract requirements, see 41 USCA § 254.

Contracts, planning, solicitation, evaluation, and award procedures, see 10 USCA § 2305.

Definitions, see 10 USCA § 2302, 41 USCA §§ 259, 403.

Evaluation and award, see 41 USCA § 253b.

Kinds of contracts, see 10 USCA § 2306.

Planning and solicitation requirements, see 41 USCA § 253a.

§ 15.204-5 Part IV—Representations and Instructions.

The contracting officer shall prepare the representations and instructions as follows:

(a) *Section K, Representations, certifications, and other statements of offerors.* Include in this section those solicitation provisions that require representations, certifications, or the submission of other information by offerors.

(b) *Section L, Instructions, conditions, and notices to offerors or respondents.* Insert in this section solicitation provisions and other information and instructions not required elsewhere to guide offerors or respondents in preparing proposals or responses to requests for information. Prospective offerors or respondents may be instructed to submit proposals or information in a specific format or severable parts to facilitate evaluation. The instructions may specify further organization of proposal or response parts, such as—

(1) Administrative;

(2) Management;

(3) Technical;

(4) Past performance; and

(5) Certified cost or pricing data (see Table 15-2 of 15.408) or data other than certified cost or pricing data.

(c) *Section M, Evaluation factors for award.* Identify all significant factors and any significant subfactors that will be considered in awarding the contract and their relative importance (see 15.304(d)). The contracting officer shall insert one of the phrases in 15.304(e).

United States Code Annotated

Contract requirements, see 41 USCA § 254.

Contracts, planning, solicitation, evaluation, and award procedures, see 10 USCA § 2305.

Definitions, see 10 USCA § 2302, 41 USCA §§ 259, 403.

Evaluation and award, see 41 USCA § 253b.

Kinds of contracts, see 10 USCA § 2306.

Planning and solicitation requirements, see 41 USCA § 253a.

Notes of Decisions
In general 1

1 In general

Protest that solicitation's instructions prohibiting the use of consultants to assist with proposal preparation is unduly restrictive is denied where the provision is reasonably related to the agency's desire to reduce performance risk by assessing the understanding and capabilities of the actual offeror and its proposed team, as opposed to those of a consultant, which has not been proposed to perform the contract. Advanced Commc'n Cabling, Inc., B-410898.2, 2015 CPD ¶ 113 (Comp. Gen. 2015)

§ 15.205 Issuing solicitations.

(a) The contracting officer shall issue solicitations to potential sources in accordance with the policies and procedures in 5.102, 19.202-4, and Part 6.

(b) A master solicitation, as described in 14.203-3, may also be used for negotiated acquisitions.

United States Code Annotated

Contract requirements, see 41 USCA § 254.

Contracts, planning, solicitation, evaluation, and award procedures, see 10 USCA § 2305.

Definitions, see 10 USCA § 2302, 41 USCA §§ 259, 403.

Evaluation and award, see 41 USCA § 253b.

Kinds of contracts, see 10 USCA § 2306.

Planning and solicitation requirements, see 41 USCA § 253a.

§ 15.206 Amending the solicitation.

(a) When, either before or after receipt of proposals, the Government changes its requirements or terms and conditions, the contracting officer shall amend the solicitation.

(b) Amendments issued before the established time and date for receipt of proposals shall be issued to all parties receiving the solicitation.

(c) Amendments issued after the established time and date for receipt of proposals shall be issued to all offerors that have not been eliminated from the competition.

(d) If a proposal of interest to the Government involves a departure from the stated requirements, the contracting officer shall amend the solicitation, provided this can be done without revealing to the other offerors the alternate solution proposed or any other information that is entitled to protection (see 15.207(b) and 15.306(e)).

(e) If, in the judgment of the contracting officer, based on market research or otherwise, an amendment proposed for issuance after offers have been received is so substantial as to exceed what prospective offerors reasonably could have anticipated, so that additional sources likely would have submitted offers had the substance of the amendment been known to them, the contracting officer shall cancel the original solicitation and issue a new one, regardless of the stage of the acquisition.

(f) Oral notices may be used when time is of the essence. The contracting officer shall document the contract file and formalize the notice with an amendment (see Subpart 4.5, Electronic Commerce in Contracting).

(g) At a minimum, the following information should be included in each amendment:

(1) Name and address of issuing activity.

(2) Solicitation number and date.

(3) Amendment number and date.

(4) Number of pages.

(5) Description of the change being made.

(6) Government point of contact and phone number (and electronic or facsimile address, if appropriate).

(7) Revision to solicitation closing date, if applicable.

United States Code Annotated

Contract requirements, see 41 USCA § 254.

Contracts, planning, solicitation, evaluation, and award procedures, see 10 USCA § 2305.
Definitions, see 10 USCA § 2302, 41 USCA §§ 259, 403.
Evaluation and award, see 41 USCA § 253b.
Kinds of contracts, see 10 USCA § 2306.
Planning and solicitation requirements, see 41 USCA § 253a.

Notes of Decisions

Amendment of solicitation 1
Canceling the RFP 2
Discretion of agency 3
Good faith 5
Notification 4

1 Amendment of solicitation

As long as a decision to amend a solicitation and request revised offers is made in good
faith, without the intent to change a particular offeror's ranking or to avoid an award to a
particular offeror, that decision will not be disturbed. Seaborn Health Care, Inc. v. U.S., 55
Fed. Cl. 520 (2003). United States ⊶64.25

Contracting agency's issuance of amendment to solicitation after proposal submission did
not violate the FAR on ground it altered a material term of the solicitation after the proposal submission date; although amendment did affect technical and pricing aspects of
proposals, and thus was material, there was no prejudice where final proposal revisions
were not due until twenty-eight days after the issuance of amendment. 48 C.F.R. § 14.208.
ABF Freight System, Inc. v. U.S., 55 Fed. Cl. 392 (2003). United States ⊶64.25

Generally, in a negotiated procurement, the contracting agency has broad discretion to
amend the solicitation when it determines that such action is necessary to ensure fair and
impartial competition and to permit the government to obtain its minimum requirements
at the most favorable price. ManTech Telecommunications and Information Systems Corp.
v. U.S., 49 Fed. Cl. 57 (2001), decision aff'd, 30 Fed. Appx. 995 (Fed. Cir. 2002). United
States ⊶64.25

Nothing in the section of the Federal Acquisition Regulation (FAR) authorizing the
proposed amendment of a solicitation precludes such an amendment from taking the form
of a clarification and reaffirmation of the prior solicitation's requirements. 48 C.F.R. § 15.
206(d). ManTech Telecommunications and Information Systems Corp. v. U.S., 49 Fed. Cl. 57
(2001), decision aff'd, 30 Fed. Appx. 995 (Fed. Cir. 2002). United States ⊶64.25

In a negotiated procurement, where an error has been alleged or detected, the government is not precluded from amending the solicitation, or even cancelling and resoliciting,
simply because the receipt of new proposals could cause the comparative adjectival ratings
of two competitors to shift. ManTech Telecommunications and Information Systems Corp. v.
U.S., 49 Fed. Cl. 57 (2001), decision aff'd, 30 Fed. Appx. 995 (Fed. Cir. 2002). United States
⊶64.25; United States ⊶64.50

Section of the Federal Acquisition Regulation specifying situations in which an agency
must amend a solicitation, by its terms, neither defines the only situations in which such
an amendment may be appropriate nor, conversely, precludes the agency from amending a
solicitation in other circumstances. 48 C.F.R. § 15.306(d). ManTech Telecommunications
and Information Systems Corp. v. U.S., 49 Fed. Cl. 57 (2001), decision aff'd, 30 Fed. Appx.
995 (Fed. Cir. 2002). United States ⊶64.25

Contracting agency's proposal to amend solicitation to clarify price requirements was not
arbitrary, capricious or contrary to law, where there was no evidence that agency was acting in bad faith, actuated by animus, with a specific intent to harm an offeror. ManTech
Telecommunications and Information Systems Corp. v. U.S., 49 Fed. Cl. 57 (2001), decision
aff'd, 30 Fed. Appx. 995 (Fed. Cir. 2002). United States ⊶64.25

An agency may amend a solicitation, and request and evaluate another round of best and
final offers (BAFOs) where the record shows that the agency made the decision to take this
action in good faith, without the specific intent of changing a particular offeror's technical
ranking or avoiding an award to a particular offeror. ManTech Telecommunications and

Information Systems Corp. v. U.S., 49 Fed. Cl. 57 (2001), decision aff'd, 30 Fed. Appx. 995 (Fed. Cir. 2002). United States ☞64.25

Elimination of an entire district from a solicitation requiring the contractor to provide courthouse security to nine districts in the Eleventh Circuit constituted a change necessitating an amendment to the solicitation under section of the Federal Acquisition Regulation. 48 C.F.R. § 15.206(a). MVM, Inc. v. U.S., 46 Fed. Cl. 126 (2000). United States ☞64.25

Protest is sustained where an agency made material modifications to the indemnification clause of the model contract in a commercial item solicitation without amending the solicitation or requesting revised proposals so that the other offerors could respond to the changed terms. Matter of: Diebold, Inc., B-404823, 2011 CPD ¶ 117 (Comp. Gen. 2011)

Where an agency's requirements change materially after a solicitation has been issued, it must issue an amendment notifying offerors of the change and affording them an opportunity to respond. FAR 15.206(a). This rule applies even after the submission of final proposal revisions, up until the time of award. Amending the solicitation provides offerors an opportunity to submit revised proposals on a common basis that reflects the agency's actual needs. Matter of: Global Solutions Network, Inc., B-298682.2, 2007 CPD ¶ 223 (Comp. Gen. 2007).

2 Canceling the RFP

Although an agency violated FAR 15.206 by changing a price evaluation factor without amending the RFP, the COFC granted the Government's motion for judgment on the administrative record because the error did not prejudice the protester because of the $49 million difference between the awardee's and protester's prices. Electronic Data Systems, LLC v. U.S., 93 Fed. Cl. 416 (2010)

Amendment of solicitation for contract to supply tie rods for Army helicopters which authorized an alternate material which met the Army's testing requirements was not so substantial that it required cancellation of contract and resolicitation; permitted deviation did not alter the nature, function, dimensions, or testing requirements of the part, and it could have been reasonably anticipated by offerors. Argencord Mach. & Equip., Inc. v. U.S., 68 Fed. Cl. 167 (2005). United States ☞64.25

In the context of pre-award negotiations, a contracting officer is given latitude in deciding whether to cancel a solicitation and request new proposals after price offers have been disclosed. Griffy's Landscape Maintenance LLC v. U.S., 51 Fed. Cl. 667 (2001). United States ☞64.50

Government contractor is never assured that it will receive award and government retains discretion to reject all proposals without liability. 48 C.F.R. § 15.608(b). Aero Corp., S.A. v. U.S., 38 Fed. Cl. 739, 42 Cont. Cas. Fed. (CCH) P 77213 (1997). United States ☞64.50

When it becomes evident that solicitation fails to adequately reflect government's needs, it is proper to cancel solicitation; rule applies to sealed bidding and other competitive negotiation procedures. Shields Enterprises, Inc. v. U.S., 28 Fed. Cl. 615, 38 Cont. Cas. Fed. (CCH) P 76526 (1993). United States ☞64.50

Procurement official's decision to cancel solicitation in negotiated procurement is inherently discretionary. Shields Enterprises, Inc. v. U.S., 28 Fed. Cl. 615, 38 Cont. Cas. Fed. (CCH) P 76526 (1993). United States ☞64.50

Where Government had reopened negotiations for technical support services contract due to failure to meet personnel qualification requirements, after Government had initially decided to award contract to one offeror and had disclosed that offeror's proposed costs, procuring agency could properly limit the scope of reopened negotiations to address only the information deficiencies noted in the contracting officer's letters, in order to preserve the integrity of the procurement process. Logicon, Inc. v. U.S., 22 Cl. Ct. 776, 37 Cont. Cas. Fed. (CCH) P 76066, 1991 WL 52823 (1991). United States ☞64.50

Contracting officer's refusal to resume negotiations after successful offeror on public contract obtained corporate surety did not lack rational basis; by time it was brought to officer's attention that offeror had obtained corporate surety, resolicitation had already been issued and officer determined proceeding under resolicitation would be more advantageous to Government. RADVA Corp. v. U.S., 17 Cl. Ct. 812, 35 Cont. Cas. Fed. (CCH) P 75706, 1989 WL 91318 (1989), judgment aff'd, 914 F.2d 271 (Fed. Cir. 1990). United States ☞64.50

GAO sustained a protest where an agency cancelled the RFP because the awardee refused to sign the contract and the Source Selection Authority (SSA) determined that that the other two offerors "did not meet critical parts of the agency's requirements." One of the offerors protested, and GAO sustained the protest because the SSA's decision lacked a reasonable basis inthat the source selection record did not indicate that the protester's proposal was considered unacceptable. Matter of: JER 370 Third Street, LLC, B-402025.2, B-402541, 2010 CPD ¶ 120 (Comp. Gen. 2010)

Protest challenging cancellation of solicitation is denied where the record supports the agency's assertion that by canceling the solicitation the agency could save money, enhance competition, and increase its purchasing flexibility. SEI Group, Inc., B-299108, 2007 CPD ¶ 35 (Comp. Gen. 2007)

A contracting agency need only establish a reasonable basis to support a decision to cancel an RFP. In this regard, so long as there is a reasonable basis for doing so, an agency may cancel a solicitation no matter when the information precipitating the cancellation first arises, even if it is not until proposals have been submitted and evaluated. Agencies must purchase supplies manufactured by FPI where, after conducting market research, the agency determines that supplies produced by FPI are comparable to those of the private sector in terms of price, quality, and time of delivery. FAR 8.602(a)(1), (3). Given that the agency was required to purchase the items from FPI, the agency acted reasonably in canceling the RFP. Management Solutions, L.C. d/b/a EssTech Engineering, B-298883, B-298883.2, 2006 CPD ¶ 197 (Comp. Gen. 2006)

Agency properly canceled solicitation and recompeted requirement for shuttle bus services where: (1) only one offer was received in response to original solicitation and that offeror failed to demonstrate that its price was fair and reasonable; and (2) during course of price discussions with sole offeror, agency discovered its minimum needs could be satisfied with alternative approach which presented reasonable possibility of increased competition and cost savings to the government. Matter of: JRW Management Company, Inc., B-260396, B-260396.2, 95-1 CPD ¶ 276 (Comp. Gen. 1995).

3 Discretion of agency

Amendment of solicitation to alter the threshold facility acceptability requirement after determining that only one of four offers met the requirement was not arbitrary, capricious, or otherwise contrary to law, where there was no evidence contracting officer (CO) who proposed amendment was acting in bad faith, actuated by animus and with a specific intent to harm sole offeror who met threshold requirement. EP Productions, Inc. v. U.S., 63 Fed. Cl. 220 (2005), aff'd, 163 Fed. Appx. 892 (Fed. Cir. 2006). United States ☞64.25

Standard for reviewing solicitation amendment for abuse of discretion is whether the action is taken in good faith, without the specific intent of changing a particular offeror's technical ranking or avoiding an award to a particular offer or. EP Productions, Inc. v. U.S., 63 Fed. Cl. 220 (2005), aff'd, 163 Fed. Appx. 892 (Fed. Cir. 2006). United States ☞64.25

Generally, in a negotiated procurement, the contracting agency has broad discretion to amend the solicitation when it determines that such action is necessary to ensure fair and impartial competition and to permit the government to obtain its minimum requirements at the most favorable price. ManTech Telecommunications and Information Systems Corp. v. U.S., 49 Fed. Cl. 57 (2001), decision aff'd, 30 Fed. Appx. 995 (Fed. Cir. 2002). United States ☞64.25

4 Notification

An agency violated FAR 15.206 by not giving an offeror timely notice of a solicitation amendment extending the deadline for submitting proposals. Allied Materials & Equipment Co., Inc. v. U.S., 81 Fed. Cl. 448 (2008)

Offerors must be notified of government's changed or relaxed requirements. 48 C.F.R. § 15.206(a, d). Candle Corp. v. U.S., 40 Fed. Cl. 658, 42 Cont. Cas. Fed. (CCH) P 77276 (1998). United States ☞64.25

5 Good faith

As long as a decision to amend a solicitation and request revised offers is made in good faith, without the intent to change a particular offeror's ranking or to avoid an award to a particular offeror, that decision will not be disturbed. Seaborn Health Care, Inc. v. U.S., 55 Fed. Cl. 520 (2003). United States ☞64.25

Contracting agency's proposal to amend solicitation to clarify price requirements was not arbitrary, capricious or contrary to law, where there was no evidence that agency was acting in bad faith, actuated by animus, with a specific intent to harm an offeror. ManTech Telecommunications and Information Systems Corp. v. U.S., 49 Fed. Cl. 57 (2001), decision aff'd, 30 Fed. Appx. 995 (Fed. Cir. 2002). United States ☞64.25

An agency may amend a solicitation, and request and evaluate another round of best and final offers (BAFOs) where the record shows that the agency made the decision to take this action in good faith, without the specific intent of changing a particular offeror's technical ranking or avoiding an award to a particular offeror. ManTech Telecommunications and Information Systems Corp. v. U.S., 49 Fed. Cl. 57 (2001), decision aff'd, 30 Fed. Appx. 995 (Fed. Cir. 2002). United States ☞64.25

§ 15.207 Handling proposals and information.

(a) Upon receipt at the location specified in the solicitation, proposals and information received in response to a request for information (RFI) shall be marked with the date and time of receipt and shall be transmitted to the designated officials.

(b) Proposals shall be safeguarded from unauthorized disclosure throughout the source selection process. (See 3.104 regarding the disclosure of source selection information (41 U.S.C. chapter 21, Restrictions on Obtaining and Disclosing Certain Information). Information received in response to an RFI shall be safeguarded adequately from unauthorized disclosure.

(c) If any portion of a proposal received by the contracting officer electronically or by facsimile is unreadable, the contracting officer immediately shall notify the offeror and permit the offeror to resubmit the unreadable portion of the proposal. The method and time for resubmission shall be prescribed by the contracting officer after consultation with the offeror, and documented in the file. The resubmission shall be considered as if it were received at the date and time of the original unreadable submission for the purpose of determining timeliness under 15.208(a), provided the offeror complies with the time and format requirements for resubmission prescribed by the contracting officer.

United States Code Annotated

Contract requirements, see 41 USCA § 254.

Contracts, planning, solicitation, evaluation, and award procedures, see 10 USCA § 2305.

Definitions, see 10 USCA § 2302, 41 USCA §§ 259, 403.

Evaluation and award, see 41 USCA § 253b.

Kinds of contracts, see 10 USCA § 2306.

Planning and solicitation requirements, see 41 USCA § 253a.

§ 15.208 Submission, modification, revision, and withdrawal of proposals.

(a) Offerors are responsible for submitting proposals, and any revisions, and modifications, so as to reach the Government office designated in the solicitation by the time specified in the solicitation. Offerors may use any transmission method authorized by the solicitation (*i.e.*, regular mail, electronic commerce, or facsimile). If no time is specified in the solicitation, the time for receipt is 4:30 p.m., local time, for the designated Government office on the date that proposals are due.

(b) (1) Any proposal, modification, or revision, that is received at the designated Government office after the exact time specified for receipt of proposals is "late" and will not be considered unless it is received before award is made, the contracting officer determines that accepting the late proposal would not unduly delay the acquisition; and—

    (i) If it was transmitted through an electronic commerce method authorized by the solicitation, it was received at the initial point of entry to the Government infrastructure not later than 5:00 p.m. one working day prior to the date specified for receipt of proposals; or

    (ii) There is acceptable evidence to establish that it was received at the Government installation designated for receipt of proposals and was under the Government's control prior to the time set for receipt of proposals; or

(iii) It was the only proposal received.

(2) However, a late modification of an otherwise successful proposal, that makes its terms more favorable to the Government, will be considered at any time it is received and may be accepted.

(c) Acceptable evidence to establish the time of receipt at the Government installation includes the time/date stamp of that installation on the proposal wrapper, other documentary evidence of receipt maintained by the installation, or oral testimony or statements of Government personnel.

(d) If an emergency or unanticipated event interrupts normal Government processes so that proposals cannot be received at the Government office designated for receipt of proposals by the exact time specified in the solicitation, and urgent Government requirements preclude amendment of the solicitation closing date, the time specified for receipt of proposals will be deemed to be extended to the same time of day specified in the solicitation on the first work day on which normal Government processes resume.

(e) Proposals may be withdrawn by written notice at any time before award. Oral proposals in response to oral solicitations may be withdrawn orally. The contracting officer must document the contract file when oral withdrawals are made. One copy of withdrawn proposals should be retained in the contract file (see 4.803(a)(10)). Extra copies of the withdrawn proposals may be destroyed or returned to the offeror at the offeror's request. Where practicable, electronically transmitted proposals that are withdrawn must be purged from primary and backup data storage systems after a copy is made for the file. Extremely bulky proposals must only be returned at the offeror's request and expense.

(f) The contracting officer must promptly notify any offeror if its proposal, modification, or revision was received late, and must inform the offeror whether its proposal will be considered, unless contract award is imminent and the notice prescribed in 15.503(b) would suffice.

(g) Late proposals and modifications that are not considered must be held unopened, unless opened for identification, until after award and then retained with other unsuccessful proposals.

(h) If available, the following must be included in the contracting office files for each late proposal, modification, revision, or withdrawal:

(1) The date and hour of receipt.

(2) A statement regarding whether the proposal was considered for award, with supporting rationale.

(3) The envelope, wrapper, or other evidence of date of receipt.

United States Code Annotated

Contract requirements, see 41 USCA § 254.

Contracts, planning, solicitation, evaluation, and award procedures, see 10 USCA § 2305.

Definitions, see 10 USCA § 2302, 41 USCA §§ 259, 403.

Evaluation and award, see 41 USCA § 253b.

Kinds of contracts, see 10 USCA § 2306.

Planning and solicitation requirements, see 41 USCA § 253a.

Notes of Decisions

In general 1
Amendment of proposals 2
Incomplete proposals 4
Time of submission 3

1 In general

Protest that contracting agency improperly refused to allow the protester to revive its expired proposal is sustained where the revival would not prejudice other offerors or the competitive system, given that the protester's proposal, the acceptance period for which expired on a Saturday, was revived by its extension of the acceptance period on the following Monday morning. Matter of: Ocean Services, LLC, B-404690, 2011 CPD ¶ 73 (Comp. Gen. 2011)

2 Amendment of proposals

Where, in a negotiated government procurement, an offeror's proposal does not comply with the solicitation's requirements, an agency is not required to eliminate the awardee from the competition, but may permit it to correct its proposal. Halter Marine, Inc. v. U.S., 56 Fed. Cl. 144 (2003). United States ☞64.30

Where, in a negotiated procurement, an offeror's proposal does not comply with the solicitation's requirements, an agency is not required to eliminate the awardee from the competition, but may permit it to correct its proposal. ManTech Telecommunications and Information Systems Corp. v. U.S., 49 Fed. Cl. 57 (2001), decision aff'd, 30 Fed. Appx. 995 (Fed. Cir. 2002). United States ☞64.30

Assuming that offeror's cost proposal did not conform to solicitation's requirements, it did not warrant offeror's total exclusion from the competition, but instead the defect could be remedied by steps designed to assist offeror in bringing its cost proposal into conformity with the agency's requirements. ManTech Telecommunications and Information Systems Corp. v. U.S., 49 Fed. Cl. 57 (2001), decision aff'd, 30 Fed. Appx. 995 (Fed. Cir. 2002). United States ☞64.30

3 Time of submission

Protest of agency's refusal to extend date for receipt of proposals because of problems experienced by the protester in accessing the solicitation is denied where the protester waited almost 3 weeks after solicitation was posted on FedBizOpps before first attempting to obtain a copy of the solicitation. Coyol International Group, B-408982.2, 2014 WL 279636 (Comp.Gen. 2014)

Offeror's late submission of proposal on Defense Commissary Agency's solicitation for supply of fresh pork products was not excused under FAR exception for disruption of normal government processes, since the disruption causing the delay had occurred at the offeror's, rather than the receiving agency's, location; although offeror claimed the one-day delay in delivery was caused by Federal Aviation Administration's restriction of aircraft ground operations in Alabama and Florida due to a flood emergency in extreme weather, the government office designated for receipt of offers was in Virginia, and normal government operations were not interrupted at that location. Global Military Marketing, Inc. v. U.S., 118 Fed.Cl. 624 (2014)

Contracting officer (CO) violated the "late is late" rule of the FAR, which precludes consideration of late submissions, by issuing post-hoc amendments to deadlines for acceptance of proposals to extend the deadlines and by accepting bidder's first and second revised proposals which were untimely under original deadlines. Geo-Seis Helicopters, Inc. v. U.S., 77 Fed. Cl. 633 (2007).

Section of the FAR excusing late receipt of a bid proposal was not applicable, where bidder did not deliver the proposal to "the government installation designated for receipt of proposals." The "designated office" refers to the particular location designated for the receipt of bids" and "government installation" refers to the entire government facility in which the "designated office" is located." Shirlington Limousine & Transp., Inc. v. U.S., 77 Fed. Cl. 157 (2007)

Offeror whose initial proposal for supply of helicopter tie rods was submitted late did not establish that it fell within exception permitting acceptance of late proposal when the proposal is the only proposal received, based on its contention that although agency received three other offers which were timely, the other offers should have been deemed nonresponsive because two of the offers lacked source approval and the third offer suggested an alternate material. Argencord Mach. & Equip., Inc. v. U.S., 68 Fed. Cl. 167 (2005). United States ☞64.30

Offeror's initial proposal could not be considered after its final proposal revision (FPR) was properly rejected as late, where solicitation was amended after the initial proposal to shift the period of contract performance, with result that initial proposal no longer conformed to material solicitation requirement of period of performance. Integrated Business Solutions, Inc. v. U.S., 58 Fed. Cl. 420 (2003). United States ☞64.40(1)

Contracting agency's refusal to consider offeror's initial proposal after its final proposal revision (FPR) was properly rejected as late was rational and in accordance with law; because offeror evidenced a clear intent to submit an FPR, albeit untimely, agency reasonably concluded that its right to accept offeror's initial proposal was extinguished. Integrated Business Solutions, Inc. v. U.S., 58 Fed. Cl. 420 (2003). United States ☞64.40(1)

Failure of offeror to confirm its initial proposal by an authorized representative precluded contracting agency's consideration of its initial proposal after its final proposal revision (FPR) was properly rejected as late. Integrated Business Solutions, Inc. v. U.S., 58 Fed. Cl. 420 (2003). United States ☞64.40(3)

Decision of contracting officer for government lease to allow late submission of proposal after deadline for initial proposals was contrary to Competition in Contracting Act of 1984 (CICA) requirement for provision of notice of due date for initial proposals in solicitation for offers (SFO) and Federal Acquisition Regulation (FAR) requiring that offerors submit initial offers by deadline for initial proposals as established in SFO, and thus Court of Federal Claims would enjoin award of instant contract to late offeror. Federal Property and Administrative Services Act of 1949, § 303A(b), (b)(2)(B)(ii), as amended, 41 U.S.C.A. § 253a(b), (b)(2)(B)(ii). Aerolease Long Beach v. U.S., 31 Fed. Cl. 342, 39 Cont. Cas. Fed. (CCH) P 76654, 39 Cont. Cas. Fed. (CCH) P 76655, 39 Cont. Cas. Fed. (CCH) P 76656 (1994), aff'd, 39 F.3d 1198 (Fed. Cir. 1994). Injunction ☞86; United States ☞64.40(1)

Late e-mail proposals may be considered under either the e-commerce exception (FAR 52. 215-1(c)(3)(ii)(A)(1)) or the "government mishandling" exception (FAR 52.215-1(c)(3)(ii)(A)(2)). If contractor's e-mail proposal was late, for failing to arrive in contracting officer's (CO) e-mail inbox until four minutes after deadline due to "mail storm" at the agency's e-mail servers, proposal's lateness was excused by government control exception to late proposal rule, where e-mail proposal was received at government installation designated for receipt of offers and was under government's control prior to deadline. Watterson Const. Co. v. U.S., 98 Fed.Cl. 84 (Fed.Cl.,2011)

Late e-mail proposals may be considered under either the e-commerce exception (FAR 52. 215-1(c)(3)(ii)(A)(1)) or the "emergency or unanticipated event" exception (FAR 52.215-1(c)(3)(iv)). If contractor's e-mail proposal was late, an unexplained "mail storm" disruption at that agency's e-mail servers that caused proposal to be delivered four minutes after deadline was an "emergency or unanticipated event" that interrupted normal government processes, thus warranting a one-day extension for contractor to submit e-mail proposal. Watterson Const. Co. v. U.S., 98 Fed. Cl. 84 (Fed.Cl.,2011)

Protest was sustained where an agency requested quotations for fuel, requiring next-day delivery, via the FedBid reverse auction website, and the protester (the lowest-priced technically acceptable vendor), responded timely and affirmatively to a FedBid "Bid Validation" request, but did not timely respond to the Contracting Officer's voicemail requesting confirmation of award within 45 minutes, causing the Contracting Officer to award to another vendor. AeroSage LLC, B-409627, 2014 CPD ¶ 192 (Comp. Gen. 2014)

Agency properly declined to accept Architect-Engineer Qualifications Statements submitted after closing date for such submissions where there is no evidence that improper government action caused the United States Postal Service's failure to make timely delivery of the submissions to the agency. Northwest Heritage Consultants, B-299547, 2007 CPD ¶ 93 (Comp. Gen. 2007)

Electronic proposal due by 3:00 p.m. and received at the agency's server at 2:57:41 p.m. was considered late because the proposal was not delivered to the contracting officer's e-mail box until 3:01:00 p.m. GAO held that receipt by the server did not trigger the "government control" exception applicable to hardcopy proposals. An electronic proposal received in the contracting officer's e-mail box after the time specified in the RFP is late unless it was received at the initial point of entry to the Government infrastructure not later than 5 p.m. 1 working day prior to the date specified for receipt of proposals. FAR 52.215-1(c)(3)(ii)(A)(1). Symetrics Industries, LLC, B-298759, 2006 CPD ¶ 154 (Comp. Gen. 2006).

Agency properly considered late proposal revision because agency action was paramount cause of late delivery of the revision and acceptance would not compromise the integrity of the competitive process, where agency extended the closing date for receipt of proposals to Saturday (not a business day of agency) from Friday after issuing a material amendment on Thursday; a commercial carrier unsuccessfully attempted delivery of the proposal revision on Saturday, but the agency's doors were locked and the agency had not posted delivery instructions for that day to advise that agency personnel were on-site to accept deliveries; and the proposal revision was delivered to agency by commercial carrier on Monday, the next business day. Matter of: Hospital Klean of Texas, Inc., B-295836, B-295836.2, 2005 CPD ¶ 185 (Comp. Gen. 2005)

A hand-carried proposal that arrives late may be considered if improper government action was the paramount cause for the late submission, and where consideration of the proposal would not compromise the integrity of the competitive procurement process. Agency properly rejected protester's hand-carried proposal as late where the delivery driver significantly contributed to the late receipt of the proposal by failing to allow sufficient time for timely delivery. O.S. Systems, Inc., B-292827, 2003 CPD ¶ 211 (Comp. Gen. 2003)

In a negotiated procurement that required offerors to submit both paper and electronic versions of proposals, rejection of the protester's proposal as late because the paper version of the proposal was not delivered by the time set for receipt of proposals was not reasonable, where a complete copy of protester's proposal was timely received in accordance with the solicitation instructions; the late delivery of the paper version was a minor informality that should have been waived. Tishman Construction Corporation, B-292097, 2003 CPD ¶ 94 (Comp. Gen. 2003)

Protest challenging the agency's rejection of the protester's proposal as late under a negotiated procurement that required the electronic submission of proposals is denied, where the protester waited until 13 minutes before the time set for receipt of proposals to transmit its proposal electronically to the agency's web-site and only the cover sheet of the electronic proposal was received by the agency by the time specified. PMTech, Inc., B-291082, 2002 CPD ¶ 172 (Comp. Gen. 2002)

Editor's Note: The holdings in COFC's *Watterson* decision, that the "government mishandling" and the "emergency or unanticipated event" exceptions apply *in addition to* the e-commerce exception, are directly contrary to GAO decisions holding that late e-mail bids/proposals may be considered under *only* the e-commerce exception. *See, e.g.,* Sea Box, Inc., B-291056, 2002 CPD ¶ 181 (Comp. Gen. 2002) and Symetrics Indus., LLC, B-298759, 2006 CPD ¶ 154, 2006 WL 2946848 (Comp. Gen. Oct. 16, 2006). The *Watterson* decision is also contrary to a prior COFC decision, Conscoop-Consorzia Fra Cooperative Di Prod. E Lavoro v. United States, 62 Fed. Cl. 219 (2004), which cited GAO's *Sea Box* decision in support of its holding that the "government mishandling" exception is inapplicable to electronic proposals. However, *Conscoop* was not expressly overruled by the *Watterson* decision.

Electronic proposal transmitted 11 minutes before the 1:00 deadline and received at the agency's initial point of entry (a Unix mail relay host server) between 8 and 10 minutes before the deadline, was late because it took approximately 17 to 33 minutes for the proposal to complete the agency's virus scanning process and did not arrive at the e-mail address designated in the RFP until over 7 minutes after the deadline. Sea Box, Inc., B-291056, 2002 CPD ¶ 181 (Comp. Gen. 2002).

In a procurement conducted by electronic commerce, where the solicitation materials were available only on the Internet, protest that it was improper for the agency to post an amendment with a short response time without specifically advising the protester was denied where the record shows that the protester failed to avail itself of every reasonable opportunity to obtain the amendment by either registering for e-mail notification or checking the Internet site, and that this failure was the reason the protester allegedly had insufficient time to protest the solicitation's terms. USA Information Systems, Inc., B-291488, 2002 CPD ¶ 205 (Comp. Gen. 2002).

In a procurement conducted by electronic commerce, where the solicitation materials were available only on the Internet, protest that the late delivery of the protester's proposal was caused by the unavailability of the agency's website on the date set for receipt of proposals and by the agency's refusal to delay the proposal closing date was denied, where the protester's failure to make reasonable efforts to promptly obtain the solicitation materials was the paramount cause of the late delivery and the reason that the protester allegedly had insufficient time to prepare its proposal. The protester did not avail itself of the opportunity to register for notification of amendments via the Navy's website and accordingly did not receive e-mail notice of the amendment. Performance Construction, Inc., B-286192, 2000 CPD ¶ 180 (Comp. Gen. 2000).

4 Incomplete proposals

Army acted rationally when it excluded bid protestor's contract proposal from consideration and returned unopened the protestor's late submission of data missing from the proposal; the solicitation clearly stated that an incomplete proposal "may" be disqualified, and the protestor failed to submit a complete proposal by the required deadline, as the protestor's proposal lacked information material to the Army's cost realism analysis, and the Army was under no obligation to accept or open late-submitted proposal materials or to open discussions to obtain the missing data. Orion Technology, Inc. v. U.S., 704 F.3d 1344 (Fed. Cir. 2013)

Agency properly rejected protester's proposal as late where the protester submitted its proposal via e-mail but failed to include its price proposal as an attachment, and the agency did not receive the protester's price proposal until after the designated closing time for receipt of proposals. JV Derichebourg-BMAR & Associates, LLC, B-408777, 2013 CPD ¶ 269 (Comp. Gen. 2013)

§ 15.209 Solicitation provisions and contract clauses.

When contracting by negotiation—

(a) The contracting officer shall insert the provision at 52.215-1, Instructions to Offerors—Competitive Acquisition, in all competitive solicitations where the Government intends to award a contract without discussions.

(1) If the Government intends to make award after discussions with offerors within the competitive range, the contracting officer shall use the basic provision with its Alternate I.

(2) If the Government would be willing to accept alternate proposals, the contracting officer shall alter the basic clause to add a new paragraph (c)(9) substantially the same as Alternate II.

(b) (1) Except as provided in paragraph (b)(2) of this section, the contracting officer shall insert the clause at 52.215-2, Audit and Records—Negotiation (10 U.S.C. 2313, 41 U.S.C. 4706, and Audit Requirements in the OMB Uniform Guidance at 2 CFR part 200, subpart F), in solicitations and contracts except those for—

(i) Acquisitions not exceeding the simplified acquisition threshold;

(ii) The acquisition of utility services at rates not exceeding those established to apply uniformly to the general public, plus any applicable reasonable connection charge; or

(iii) The acquisition of commercial items exempted under 15.403-1.

(2) (i) When using funds appropriated or otherwise made available by the American Recovery and Reinvestment Act of 2009 (Pub. L. 111-5)—

(A) The exceptions in paragraphs (b)(1)(i) through (b)(1)(iii) are not applicable; and

(B) Use the clause with its Alternate I.

(ii) (A) In the case of a bilateral contract modification that will use funds appropriated or otherwise made available by the American Recovery and Reinvestment Act of 2009, the contracting officer shall specify applicability of Alternate I to that modification.

(B) In the case of a task- or delivery-order contract in which not all orders will use funds appropriated or otherwise made available by the American Recovery and Reinvestment Act of 2009, the contracting officer shall specify the task or delivery orders to which Alternate I applies.

(3) For cost-reimbursement contracts with State and local Governments, educational institutions, and other nonprofit organizations, the contracting officer shall use the clause with its Alternate II.

(4) When the head of the agency has waived the examination of records by the Comptroller General in accordance with 25.1001, use the clause with its Alternate III.

(c) When issuing a solicitation for information or planning purposes, the contracting officer shall insert the provision at 52.215-3, Request for Information or Solicitation for Planning Purposes, and clearly mark on the face of the solicitation that it is for information or planning purposes.

(d) [Reserved]

(e) The contracting officer shall insert the provision at 52.215-5, Facsimile Proposals, in solicitations if facsimile proposals are authorized (see 15.203(d)).

(f) The contracting officer shall insert the provision at 52.215-6, Place of Performance, in solicitations unless the place of performance is specified by the Government.

(g) [Reserved]

(h) The contracting officer shall insert the clause at 52.215-8, Order of Precedence—Uniform Contract Format, in solicitations and contracts using the format at 15.204.

United States Code Annotated

Contract requirements, see 41 USCA § 254.

Contracts, planning, solicitation, evaluation, and award procedures, see 10 USCA § 2305.

Definitions, see 10 USCA § 2302, 41 USCA §§ 259, 403.

Evaluation and award, see 41 USCA § 253b.

Kinds of contracts, see 10 USCA § 2306.

Planning and solicitation requirements, see 41 USCA § 253a.

§ 15.210 Forms.

Prescribed forms are not required to prepare solicitations described in this part. The following forms may be used at the discretion of the contracting officer:

(a) Standard Form 33, Solicitation, Offer and Award, and Optional Form 308, Solicitation and Offer—Negotiated Acquisition, may be used to issue RFPs and RFIs.

(b) Standard Form 30, Amendment of Solicitation/ Modification of Contract, and Optional Form 309, Amendment of Solicitation, may be used to amend solicitations of negotiated contracts.

(c) Optional Form 17, Offer Label, may be furnished with each request for proposal.

United States Code Annotated

Contract requirements, see 41 USCA § 254.

Contracts, planning, solicitation, evaluation, and award procedures, see 10 USCA § 2305.

Definitions, see 10 USCA § 2302, 41 USCA §§ 259, 403.

Evaluation and award, see 41 USCA § 253b.

Kinds of contracts, see 10 USCA § 2306.

Planning and solicitation requirements, see 41 USCA § 253a.

Subpart 15.3 Source Selection

§ 15.300 Scope of subpart.

This subpart prescribes policies and procedures for selection of a source or sources in competitive negotiated acquisitions.

United States Code Annotated

Administrative determinations, see 41 USCA § 257.

Contract requirements, see 41 USCA § 254.

Contracts, planning, solicitation, evaluation, and award procedures, see 10 USCA § 2305.

Definitions, see 10 USCA § 2302, 41 USCA §§ 259, 403.

Determinations and decisions, see 10 USCA § 2310, 41 USCA § 262.

Evaluation and award, see 41 USCA § 253b.

Kinds of contracts, see 10 USCA § 2306.

Planning and solicitation requirements, see 41 USCA § 253a.

§ 15.301 [Reserved]

§ 15.302 Source selection objective.

The objective of source selection is to select the proposal that represents the best value.

United States Code Annotated

Administrative determinations, see 41 USCA § 257.

Contract requirements, see 41 USCA § 254.

Contracts, planning, solicitation, evaluation, and award procedures, see 10 USCA § 2305.

Definitions, see 10 USCA § 2302, 41 USCA §§ 259, 403.

Determinations and decisions, see 10 USCA § 2310, 41 USCA § 262.

Evaluation and award, see 41 USCA § 253b.

Kinds of contracts, see 10 USCA § 2306.

Planning and solicitation requirements, see 41 USCA § 253a.

§ 15.303 Responsibilities.

(a) Agency heads are responsible for source selection. The contracting officer is designated as the source selection authority, unless the agency head appoints another individual for a particular acquisition or group of acquisitions.

(b) The source selection authority shall—

(1) Establish an evaluation team, tailored for the particular acquisition, that includes appropriate contracting, legal, logistics, technical, and other expertise to ensure a comprehensive evaluation of offers;

(2) Approve the source selection strategy or acquisition plan, if applicable, before solicitation release;

(3) Ensure consistency among the solicitation requirements, notices to offerors, proposal preparation instructions, evaluation factors and subfactors, solicitation provisions or contract clauses, and data requirements;

(4) Ensure that proposals are evaluated based solely on the factors and subfactors contained in the solicitation (10 U.S.C. 2305(b)(4)(C) and 41 U.S.C. 3703(c));

(5) Consider the recommendations of advisory boards or panels (if any); and

(6) Select the source or sources whose proposal is the best value to the Government (10 U.S.C. 2305(b)(4)(C) and 41 U.S.C. 3703(c)).

(c) The contracting officer shall—

(1) After release of a solicitation, serve as the focal point for inquiries from actual or prospective offerors;

(2) After receipt of proposals, control exchanges with offerors in accordance with 15.306; and

(3) Award the contract(s).

United States Code Annotated

Administrative determinations, see 41 USCA § 257.

Contract requirements, see 41 USCA § 254.

Contracts, planning, solicitation, evaluation, and award procedures, see 10 USCA § 2305.

Definitions, see 10 USCA § 2302, 41 USCA §§ 259, 403.

Determinations and decisions, see 10 USCA § 2310, 41 USCA § 262.

Evaluation and award, see 41 USCA § 253b.

Kinds of contracts, see 10 USCA § 2306.

Planning and solicitation requirements, see 41 USCA § 253a.

Notes of Decisions

In general 1
Best value, generally 4
Cost evaluation, generally 4.5
Discretion of agency—In general 2
Discretion of agency—Best value, discretion of agency 3
Discussions with offerors 4.7
Timeliness 5

1 In general

Source selection authority (SSA) rationally concluded that offeror had no escalation policy for non-exempt personnel wage rates, where final proposal contained no such policy, despite offeror's contention that source selection evaluation team had asked it not to maintain an escalation policy. Computer Sciences Corp. v. U.S., 51 Fed. Cl. 297 (2002). United States ☞64.45(1)

Federal Acquisition Regulation (FAR) did not require source selection authority (SSA) to conduct his own contract-by-contract comparative assessment of past contract performance; as long as agency evaluators conducted a contract-by-contract assessment, the SSA could rely on such evaluation without performing the same detailed analysis. 48 C.F.R. §§ 15. 303(b)(5), 15.308. Computer Sciences Corp. v. U.S., 51 Fed. Cl. 297 (2002). United States ☞64.45(2)

2 Discretion of agency—In general

In formally advertised bidding the pertinent statutes and regulations are far more strict about the conduct of the procurement than in a negotiated one, and consequently in negotiated procurement the contracting officer is entrusted with a relatively high degree of discretion. Galen Medical Associates, Inc. v. U.S., 369 F.3d 1324 (Fed. Cir. 2004). United States ☞64.40(1)

Contracting officers enjoy substantially greater discretion when conducting negotiated procurements than when soliciting sealed bids. Howard Cooper Corp. v. U.S., 763 F. Supp. 829, 37 Cont. Cas. Fed. (CCH) P 76169 (E.D. Va. 1991). United States ☞59

In a negotiated procurement, contracting officers are generally afforded even greater decision-making discretion, in comparison to their role in sealed bid procurements. Maintenance Engineers v. U.S., 50 Fed. Cl. 399 (2001). United States ☞64.45(1)

Contracting officials in negotiated procurements have broad discretion to take corrective action where the agency determines that such action is necessary to ensure fair and impartial competition. ManTech Telecommunications and Information Systems Corp. v. U.S., 49 Fed. Cl. 57 (2001), decision aff'd, 30 Fed. Appx. 995 (Fed. Cir. 2002). United States ☞64.40(1)

Contracting officials are accorded broad discretion in conducting a negotiated procurement. Cube Corp. v. U.S., 46 Fed. Cl. 368 (2000). United States ☞64.40(1)

Contracting officials may properly exercise wide discretion in their evaluation of bids and the application of procurement regulations, and such discretion is especially broad in negotiated procurements. Impresa Construzioni Geom. Domenico Garufi v. U.S., 44 Fed. Cl. 540 (1999), aff'd in part, rev'd in part on other grounds, 238 F.3d 1324 (Fed. Cir. 2001). United States ☞64.40(1)

Courts allow agencies broad discretion in conducting negotiated procurements and determining which proposal is most advantageous to the government. Advanced Data Concepts, Inc. v. U.S., 43 Fed. Cl. 410 (1999), aff'd, 216 F.3d 1054 (Fed. Cir. 2000). United States ☞64.40(1)

Contracting officials in negotiated procurements have broad discretion to take corrective action where the agency determines that such action is necessary to ensure fair and impartial competition. 48 C.F.R. § 1.602-2. DGS Contract Service, Inc. v. U.S., 43 Fed. Cl. 227 (1999). United States ☞64.40(1)

Contracting officials may properly exercise wide discretion in their evaluation of bids and the application of procurement regulations, and such discretion is especially broad in negotiated procurements. DGS Contract Service, Inc. v. U.S., 43 Fed. Cl. 227 (1999). United States ☞64.40(1)

A contracting officer has broad discretion in conducting negotiations with an offeror. 48 C.F.R. § 15.610(b) (1995). Labat-Anderson, Inc. v. U.S., 42 Fed. Cl. 806 (1999). United States ☞64.40(1)

Discretion of contracting officials is especially broad where the contract was awarded through negotiated procurement. United Intern. Investigative Services, Inc. v. U.S., 41 Fed. Cl. 312, 42 Cont. Cas. Fed. (CCH) P 77336 (1998). United States ☞64.5

Contracting official's discretion in evaluating bids and applying procurement regulations is especially broad where contract was awarded through negotiated procurement. Delbert

Wheeler Const., Inc. v. U.S., 39 Fed. Cl. 239, 42 Cont. Cas. Fed. (CCH) P 77192, 42 Cont. Cas. Fed. (CCH) P 77257 (1997), aff'd, 155 F.3d 566 (Fed. Cir. 1998). United States ⊕64.40(1)

Under negotiated procurements, contracting officers are generally afforded greater discretion than they have in sealed bid procurements. Allied Technology Group, Inc. v. U.S., 39 Fed. Cl. 125, 41 Cont. Cas. Fed. (CCH) P 77179 (1997), aff'd, 173 F.3d 435 (Fed. Cir. 1998). United States ⊕64.40(1)

Contracting officials' discretion is especially broad in negotiated procurements. Aero Corp., S.A. v. U.S., 38 Fed. Cl. 739, 42 Cont. Cas. Fed. (CCH) P 77213 (1997). United States ⊕64.40(1)

In negotiated procurements, procurement officials possess high degree of discretion in their efforts to obtain contract most beneficial to government. E.W. Bliss Co. v. U.S., 33 Fed. Cl. 123, 40 Cont. Cas. Fed. (CCH) P 76769 (1995), judgment aff'd, 77 F.3d 445, 40 Cont. Cas. Fed. (CCH) P 76893 (Fed. Cir. 1996). United States ⊕64.40(2)

Government contracting officer has broad discretion in dealing with negotiation between government and offerors, including discretion to resolve any uncertainties concerning terms and conditions of proposal. Action Mfg. Co. v. U.S., 10 Cl. Ct. 474, 33 Cont. Cas. Fed. (CCH) P 74505 (1986). United States ⊕64.5

Deference accorded all procurement official's discretionary determinations must be given even greater weight where award of negotiated procurement is at stake. 28 U.S.C.A. § 1491(a)(3). Action Mfg. Co. v. U.S., 10 Cl. Ct. 474, 33 Cont. Cas. Fed. (CCH) P 74505 (1986). United States ⊕64.60(3.1)

Protest that solicitation gives undue weight to past performance because, in addition to past performance evaluation factor, certain non-price subfactors included under technical excellence and management factors concern past performance-related considerations, is denied; there is no limitation on weight agency can assign particular factors in evaluation. American Medical Information Services, B-288627, 2001 CPD ¶ 188 (Comp. Gen. 2001)

3 Discretion of agency—Best value, discretion of agency

Procurement officials have substantial discretion to determine which proposal represents the best value for the government. Dismas Charities, Inc. v. U.S., 61 Fed. Cl. 191 (2004). United States ⊕64.40(1)

Court of Federal Claims must accord broad deference to a contracting officer's decision as to which proposal in a negotiated procurement represents the best value. First Enterprise v. U.S., 61 Fed. Cl. 109 (2004). United States ⊕64.45(1)

Agency is entitled to broad discretion in evaluating proposals in a "best value" procurement. Information Technology & Applications Corp. v. U.S., 51 Fed. Cl. 340 (2001), decision aff'd, 316 F.3d 1312 (Fed. Cir. 2003). United States ⊕64.40(1)

Deference to agency procurement decision is particularly great when a negotiated procurement is involved and is greater still when the procurement is a "best value" procurement. Bean Stuyvesant, L.L.C. v. U.S., 48 Fed. Cl. 303 (2000). United States ⊕64.60(3.1)

Federal Acquisition Regulation (FAR) affords a procuring agency broad discretion in conducting discussions to obtain the best value for the government, and in the exercise of such discretion, a contracting officer need not discuss with offeror all areas in which its proposal could be improved. 48 C.F.R. § 15.306(d)(3). Dynacs Engineering Co., Inc. v. U.S., 48 Fed. Cl. 124 (2000). United States ⊕64.40(1)

Procurement officials have substantial discretion to determine which proposal represents the best value for the government. 48 C.F.R. § 15.101-1(c). Unified Architecture & Engineering, Inc. v. U.S., 46 Fed. Cl. 56 (2000), aff'd, 251 F.3d 170 (Fed. Cir. 2000). United States ⊕64.40(1)

Procuring agency's best value decision was made in accordance with the evaluation scheme outlined in the proposal, grounded in reason, and completely within the agency's discretion, despite protester's claim that agency disregarded the relative importance of the evaluation factors identified in the solicitation under the guise of a best value selection. Unified Architecture & Engineering, Inc. v. U.S., 46 Fed. Cl. 56 (2000), aff'd, 251 F.3d 170

(Fed. Cir. 2000). United States ☞64.40(1)

Procurement officials have substantial discretion to determine which proposal represents the best value for the government. ITT Federal Services Corp. v. U.S., 45 Fed. Cl. 174 (1999). United States ☞64.40(1)

Contracting officials have broad discretion in negotiated procurements to determine which technical proposal best meets its needs. Acra, Inc. v. U.S., 44 Fed. Cl. 288 (1999). United States ☞64.40(1)

4 Best value, generally

Award of contract in "best value" procurement to American firm which submitted lowest proposal was motivated by bias against French firm; even though source selection advisory council had recommended that contract be awarded to French firm, Assistant Director of Contract and Business Review refused to sign off on the decision and, after his senior procurement analyst raised "Buy American" considerations and political ramifications, demanded that negotiations be conducted with all the companies no matter how "unacceptable" their offers were. Latecoere Intern., Inc. v. U.S. Dept. of Navy, 19 F.3d 1342, 39 Cont. Cas. Fed. (CCH) P 76661 (11th Cir. 1994), as amended, (May 27, 1994). United States ☞64.40(2)

Source Selection Authority (SSA) gave reasoned explanation as to why he chose higher cost proposals as the best value to government, and General Services Administration Board of Contract Appeals (GSBCA) should have deferred to his reasonable decision. Federal Property and Administrative Services Act of 1949, § 111(f)(5)(B), as amended, 40 U.S.C.A. § 759(f)(5)(B); 48 C.F.R. § 15.605(c). Widnall v. B3H Corp., 75 F.3d 1577, 40 Cont. Cas. Fed. (CCH) P 76891 (Fed. Cir. 1996). United States ☞73(9)

Protestor did not establish that contracting agency's rescoring of technical and management factors in solicitation had the effect of changing the solicitation from a "best value" procurement to "lowest price technically acceptable" procurement. 48 C.F.R. §§ 15.101-1(a), 15.101-2(a), (b)(2). Dismas Charities, Inc. v. U.S., 61 Fed. Cl. 191 (2004). United States ☞64.45(1)

Protester did not establish that government's "best value" determination was arbitrary and capricious; although protester argued that the government essentially eliminated cost as a factor in the procurement, cost realism analysis conducted by the government placed the cost proposals of the protester and awardee relatively close, and the agency determined the technical advantage possessed by awardee was worth the relatively slightly higher evaluated cost of awardee's proposal. Cube Corp. v. U.S., 46 Fed. Cl. 368 (2000). United States ☞64.45(2)

Solicitation which indicated that the greater the equality of the proposals, the more important price would become in selecting "best value," provided a measure of latitude in the best value determination, permitting some price consideration with technically unequal proposals. ITT Federal Services Corp. v. U.S., 45 Fed. Cl. 174 (1999). United States ☞64.40(1)

4.5 Cost evaluation, generally

Protestor did not establish that source selection authority violated procurement statute and regulations by not accurately considering the most probable costs of two "weaknesses" noted by source evaluation board (SEB) in contract awardee's proposal, and thus could not properly have decided which of the competitive proposal was most advantageous to the government, as neither of the weaknesses had probable cost impacts that the SSA failed to address. Comprehensive Health Services, Inc. v. U.S., 70 Fed. Cl. 700 (2006). United States ☞64.45(1)

4.7 Discussions with offerors

Contracting agency's decision to award contract only on initial competitive proposals without discussions with offerors did not violate procurement statute requiring agency to award contract to offeror "whose proposal is most advantageous to the United States," or regulation mandating that agency select the "proposal [that] is the best value to the Government," notwithstanding protestor's contention that agency could not have determined which proposal was "most advantageous to" or "the best value to" government without engaging in discussions with all interested offerors. Rig Masters, Inc. v. U.S., 70 Fed. Cl. 413 (2006). United States ⬤64.45(1)

5 Timeliness

Procuring agency violated procurement statute and provisions of the Federal Acquisition Regulation by improperly crediting proposal with meeting technical requirements of the solicitation, even though offeror failed to identify a volunteer coordinator, as required by solicitation. 10 U.S.C.A. § 2305(b)(1); 48 C.F.R. §§ 15.303(b), 15.305(a), 15.308. Mangi Environmental Group, Inc. v. U.S., 47 Fed. Cl. 10 (2000). United States ⬤64.30

§ 15.304 Evaluation factors and significant subfactors.

(a) The award decision is based on evaluation factors and significant subfactors that are tailored to the acquisition.

(b) Evaluation factors and significant subfactors must—

(1) Represent the key areas of importance and emphasis to be considered in the source selection decision; and

(2) Support meaningful comparison and discrimination between and among competing proposals.

(c) The evaluation factors and significant subfactors that apply to an acquisition and their relative importance, are within the broad discretion of agency acquisition officials, subject to the following requirements:

(1) Price or cost to the Government shall be evaluated in every source selection (10 U.S.C. 2305(a)(3)(A)(ii) and 41 U.S.C. 3306(c)(1)(B)) (also see Part 36 for architect-engineer contracts);

(2) The quality of the product or service shall be addressed in every source selection through consideration of one or more non-cost evaluation factors such as past performance, compliance with solicitation requirements, technical excellence, management capability, personnel qualifications, and prior experience (10 U.S.C. 2305(a)(3)(A)(i) and 41 U.S.C. 3306(c)(1)(A)); and

(3) (i) Except as set forth in paragraph (c)(3)(iii) of this section, past performance shall be evaluated in all source selections for negotiated competitive acquisitions expected to exceed the simplified acquisition threshold.

(ii) For solicitations involving bundling that offer a significant opportunity for subcontracting, the contracting officer must include a factor to evaluate past performance indicating the extent to which the offeror attained applicable goals for small business participation under contracts that required subcontracting plans (15 U.S.C. 637(d)(4)(G)(ii)).

(iii) Past performance need not be evaluated if the contracting officer documents the reason past performance is not an appropriate evaluation factor for the acquisition.

(4) For solicitations involving bundling that offer a significant opportunity for subcontracting, the contracting officer must include proposed small business subcontracting participation in the subcontracting plan as an evaluation factor (15 U.S.C. 637(d)(4) (G)(i)).

(5) If telecommuting is not prohibited, agencies shall not unfavorably evaluate an offer that includes telecommuting unless the contracting officer executes a written determination in accordance with FAR 7.108(b).

(d) All factors and significant subfactors that will affect contract award and their relative importance shall be stated clearly in the solicitation (10 U.S.C. 2305(a)(2)(A)(i) and 41 U.S.C. 3306(b)(1)(A)) (see 15.204-5(c)). The rating method need not be disclosed in the solicitation. The general approach for evaluating past performance information shall be described.

(e) The solicitation shall also state, at a minimum, whether all evaluation factors other than cost or price, when combined, are—

(1) Significantly more important than cost or price;

(2) Approximately equal to cost or price; or

(3) Significantly less important than cost or price (10 U.S.C. 2305(a)(3)(A)(iii) and 41 U.S.C. 3306(c)(1)(C)).

United States Code Annotated

Administrative determinations, see 41 USCA § 257.

Contract requirements, see 41 USCA § 254.

Contracts, planning, solicitation, evaluation, and award procedures, see 10 USCA § 2305.

Definitions, see 10 USCA § 2302, 41 USCA §§ 259, 403.

Determinations and decisions, see 10 USCA § 2310, 41 USCA § 262.

Evaluation and award, see 41 USCA § 253b.

Kinds of contracts, see 10 USCA § 2306.

Planning and solicitation requirements, see 41 USCA § 253a.

Notes of Decisions

Discretion of agency—In general 1
Discretion of agency—Past performance, discretion of agency 2
Discretion of agency—Evaluation of proposals, discretion of agency 3
Evaluation factors—In general 5
Evaluation factors—Price, evaluation factors 6
Evaluation factors—Past performance, evaluation factors 7
Evaluation factors—HUBZones, evaluation factors 9
Evaluation factors—Disclosure of information, evaluation factors 10
Evaluation Factors—Risk 8
Evaluation factors—staffing 11
Minimum or material requirements 4

1 Discretion of agency—In general

In formally advertised bidding the pertinent statutes and regulations are far more strict about the conduct of the procurement than in a negotiated one, and consequently in negotiated procurement the contracting officer is entrusted with a relatively high degree of discretion. Galen Medical Associates, Inc. v. U.S., 369 F.3d 1324 (Fed. Cir. 2004). United States ☞64.40(1)

Contracting officers enjoy substantially greater discretion when conducting negotiated procurements than when soliciting sealed bids. Howard Cooper Corp. v. U.S., 763 F. Supp. 829, 37 Cont. Cas. Fed. (CCH) P 76169 (E.D. Va. 1991). United States ☞59

In a negotiated procurement, contracting officers are generally afforded even greater decision-making discretion, in comparison to their role in sealed bid procurements. Maintenance Engineers v. U.S., 50 Fed. Cl. 399 (2001). United States ☞64.45(1)

Contracting officials are accorded broad discretion in conducting a negotiated procurement. Cube Corp. v. U.S., 46 Fed. Cl. 368 (2000). United States ☞64.40(1)

2 Discretion of agency—Past performance, discretion of agency

Generally, a contracting agency is accorded broad discretion when conducting its past performance evaluations. Vantage Associates, Inc. v. U.S., 59 Fed. Cl. 1 (2003). United States ☞64.45(2)

An agency has discretion to determine the scope of an offeror's performance history to be considered provided all proposals are evaluated consistently. Seattle Sec. Services, Inc. v. U.S., 45 Fed. Cl. 560 (2000). United States ☞64.45(2)

Agency personnel engaged in procurement are generally given great discretion in determining what references to review in evaluating past performance of offerors; thus, there is no requirement that all references listed in a proposal be checked. Seattle Sec. Services, Inc. v. U.S., 45 Fed. Cl. 560 (2000). United States ☞64.45(2)

An agency's past performance evaluation was unreasonable because the agency did not consider relevant adverse past performance information that the protester had provided to the agency regarding the awardee. Protester had provided adverse information regarding the awardee's performance contained in an IG Report and a news article Matter of: Contrack International, Inc., B-401871.5, B-401871.6, B-401871.7, 2010 CPD ¶ 126 (Comp. Gen. 2010)

Protest that solicitation gives undue weight to past performance because, in addition to past performance evaluation factor, certain non-price subfactors included under technical excellence and management factors concern past performance-related considerations, is denied; there is no limitation on weight agency can assign particular factors in evaluation. American Medical Information Services, B-288627, 2001 CPD ¶ 188 (Comp. Gen. 2001)

3 Discretion of agency—Evaluation of proposals, discretion of agency

Contracting agency has great discretion in determining the scope of an evaluation factor. Maintenance Engineers v. U.S., 50 Fed. Cl. 399 (2001). United States ☞64.40(1)

4 Minimum or material requirements

In general, concept of responsiveness is not applicable to negotiation procurements where contracting officer is permitted to conduct oral or written discussions with offerors whose proposals vary from request for proposals; however, while concept of responsiveness is not technically applicable to negotiated procurements, even in negotiated procurement procuring agency does not have discretion to disregard offeror's failure to satisfy material requirement in request for proposal. Howard Cooper Corp. v. U.S., 763 F. Supp. 829, 37 Cont. Cas. Fed. (CCH) P 76169 (E.D. Va. 1991). United States ☞64.5

A solicitation for a government contract must seek proposals that meet an agency's minimum needs, or else the solicitation represents an undue, improper restriction on competition. ABF Freight System, Inc. v. U.S., 55 Fed. Cl. 392 (2003). United States ☞64.25

A mandatory minimum requirement must be clearly identified as such within a solicitation so as to put offerors on notice of the serious consequences of failing to meet the requirement; such notice typically emphasizes that a proposal must meet the requirement in order to be eligible for evaluation or, conversely, that failure to comply with the requirement will lead to outright rejection of the proposal. ManTech Telecommunications and Information Systems Corp. v. U.S., 49 Fed. Cl. 57 (2001), decision aff'd, 30 Fed. Appx. 995 (Fed. Cir. 2002). United States ☞64.25

Solicitation's minimum education and experience provisions could not reasonably be read as imposing a minimum mandatory requirement; far from providing the requisite notice that failure to comply with the minimum experience and resume requirements would result in disqualification, the solicitation, as a whole, signaled that relatively minor deficiencies, rating something better than an exceptionally low score on a specific element or factor, would not result in a proposal being eliminated. ManTech Telecommunications and Information Systems Corp. v. U.S., 49 Fed. Cl. 57 (2001), decision aff'd, 30 Fed. Appx. 995 (Fed. Cir. 2002). United States ☞64.25

A mandatory minimum requirement (MMR) must be specified as such within a solicitation. 48 C.F.R. § 15.206(a). Cubic Defense Systems, Inc. v. U.S., 45 Fed. Cl. 450 (1999). United States ☞64.25

Requirement in Army's solicitation of proposals on contract for computer and data processing support, that proposed personnel have three years minimum experience within preceding five years, was not latently ambiguous as alleged by disappointed offeror; solicitation stated that proposed personnel must have requisite years of experience, defined the minimum years of experience required for proposed personnel, stated that proposed personnel would receive score of "unacceptable" if they did not meet minimum experience requirements, and further defined "unacceptable" as numerical score of zero. Analytical & Research Technology, Inc. v. U.S., 39 Fed. Cl. 34, 442 Cont. Cas. Fed. (CCH) P 77228 (1997). United States ☞64.25

In soliciting proposals on contract for computer and automated data processing support, Army could evaluate the requirement that proposed personnel have three years minimum experience within preceding five years as a "go/no-go" requirement which if not met would render that portion of offeror's proposal technically unacceptable, regardless of whether solicitation used term "go/no-go." 10 U.S.C.A. § 2305(a)(2); Federal Property and Administrative Services Act of 1949, § 303A(b)(1), as amended, 41 U.S.C.A. § 253a(b)(1); 48 C.F.R. § 15. 605(d)(1). Analytical & Research Technology, Inc. v. U.S., 39 Fed. Cl. 34, 442 Cont. Cas. Fed. (CCH) P 77228 (1997). United States ☞64.40(1)

Clearly stated solicitation requirements are considered material to the needs of the government, and a quotation that fails to conform to material terms and conditions of the solicitation is unacceptable and cannot form the basis for award. Therefore, agency properly rejected a proposal that provided a lesser level of data rights than that required by the solicitation. Deloitte Consulting, LLP, B-411884, et al., 2016 CPD ¶ 2 (Comp. Gen. 2016)

Solicitation requirement that an offeror possess a secret facility clearance prior to the due date for proposals does not unduly restrict competition where the record shows that the requirement is reasonably related to the agency's needs. Contract Services, Inc., B-411153, 2015 CPD ¶ 161 (Comp.Gen. 2015)

5 Evaluation factors—In general

Solicitation for educational support services at Army installations violated the Federal Acquisition Regulation (FAR) by not clearly stating requirement that offerors bid on at lease 75 percent of services and requirement that offerors enter a loaded unit price in each blank of attachment. Heritage of America, LLC v. U.S., 77 Fed. Cl. 66 (2007)

Every solicitation of a government contract must identify the evaluation factors and significant subfactors which will be used to evaluate proposals, as well as the relative importance of each factor and subfactor. PHT Supply Corp. v. U.S., 71 Fed. Cl. 1 (2006). United States ☞64.25

A solicitation is not required to identify each element an agency is to consider during the course of evaluations when said element is intrinsic to the stated factors. Computer Sciences Corp. v. U.S., 51 Fed. Cl. 297 (2002). United States ☞64.25

Evaluation factors and significant subfactors must be clearly stated within a request for proposals (RFP), with a statement of the relative importance of such factors and subfactors. 10 U.S.C.A. § 2305a(2)(A); 48 C.F.R. § 15.304(d). Information Technology & Applications Corp. v. U.S., 51 Fed. Cl. 340 (2001), decision aff'd, 316 F.3d 1312 (Fed. Cir. 2003). United States ☞64.25

A solicitation need not identify each element to be considered by the agency during the course of the evaluation where such element is intrinsic to the stated factors. Maintenance Engineers v. U.S., 50 Fed. Cl. 399 (2001). United States ☞64.25

A solicitation must clearly state all significant factors and subfactors as well as their relative importance; in the absence of a statement of the relative importance of the factors or subfactors, each factor or subfactor must be weighed equally. 10 U.S.C.A. § 2305(a)(2)(A)(i, ii); 48 C.F.R. § 15.304(d). Bean Stuyvesant, L.L.C. v. U.S., 48 Fed. Cl. 303 (2000). United States ☞64.25; United States ☞64.40(1)

A solicitation need not identify each element to be considered by the agency during the course of proposal evaluation where such element is intrinsic to the stated factors. Bean Stuyvesant, L.L.C. v. U.S., 48 Fed. Cl. 303 (2000). United States ☞64.25

Offeror which submitted proposal on beach renourishment and shore protection project was on notice that "hardbottom" or reef protection would be singled out by evaluators as a significant subfactor, where solicitation stated that protection of existing reef system was "of paramount importance," and solicitation was replete with references to the hardbottom/reef resources and instructions to the potential contractor on how to protect and monitor such resources. Bean Stuyvesant, L.L.C. v. U.S., 48 Fed. Cl. 303 (2000). United States ☞64.25

Protesters did not establish that award of contract for Antarctic support services represented a clear departure from announced evaluation scheme, on ground that information technology/communications played an extremely important role in the evaluation process and consequently, should have been listed as an evaluation factor in the solicitation and assigned an evaluation weight. 48 C.F.R. § 15.304(d). Antarctic Support Associates v. U.S., 46 Fed. Cl. 145 (2000), aff'd, 251 F.3d 171 (Fed. Cir. 2000). United States ☞64.40(1)

A contract award may not be upheld when the source selection authority (SSA) improperly departs from stated evaluation criteria in a solicitation. ITT Federal Services Corp. v. U.S., 45 Fed. Cl. 174 (1999). United States ☞64.45(1)

6 Evaluation factors—Price, evaluation factors

Price must always be a factor in procuring agency's decision to award a contract. 10 U.S.C.A. § 2305(a)(3)(A); Federal Property and Administrative Services Act of 1949, § 303A(c)(1)(B), as amended, 41 U.S.C.A. § 253a(c)(1)(B); 48 C.F.R. § 15.304(c)(1). Bean Stuyvesant, L.L.C. v. U.S., 48 Fed. Cl. 303 (2000). United States ☞64.45(1)

The GAO sustained a protest of an agency's technical evaluation, source selection and conduct of discussions because the agency could not demonstrate the technical advantage offered by the awardee that would justify the payment of a price premium. "Even in a competition where price is of less importance than the non-price factors, an agency must meaningfully consider cost or price in making its selection decision." Matter of: ACCESS Systems, Inc., B-400623.3, 2009 CPD ¶ 56 (Comp. Gen. 2009)

7 Evaluation factors—Past performance, evaluation factors

In litigation challenging a default termination, the U.S. Court of Federal Claims denied the U.S. Postal Service's request to admit evidence of the contractor's past performance on other contracts. The COFC concluded that evidence of plaintiff's poor past performance on previous contracts did "not appear to be of a type that make the allegation of breach here— the failure to deliver the mail—more or less credible." Pinckney v. U.S., 85 Fed. Cl. 392 (2009)

Where solicitation was explicit that each of the three technical criteria of past performance, experience, and management capability, would be assessed on a pass/fail basis, Court of Federal Claims could not impose additional documentary requirements such as narrative justifications when neither the applicable regulations nor the evaluation criteria required anything more than what the agency performed. 48 C.F.R. §§ 15.101-1, 15.305. Al Ghanim Combined Group Co. Gen. Trad. & Cont. W.L.L. v. U.S., 56 Fed. Cl. 502 (2003). United States ⊕64.45(2)

Offeror waived alleged discrepancies between evaluation factors for past performance as stated in solicitation and the same factors as stated in questionnaires directed at offerors' past or current customers, where offeror failed to raise them prior to submission of proposal. Halter Marine, Inc. v. U.S., 56 Fed. Cl. 144 (2003). United States ⊕64.25

It was not error for contracting agency to distribute past performance questionnaires to offerors which contained a rating scale different from the scale used in the technical evaluation. Maintenance Engineers v. U.S., 50 Fed. Cl. 399 (2001). United States ⊕64.45(2)

Generally, an agency's evaluation under an experience factor is distinct from its evaluation of an offeror's past performance. Specifically, experience focuses on the degree to which an offeror has actually performed similar work, whereas past performance focuses on the quality of the work. The evaluation of experience and past performance, by its very nature, is subjective, and a vendor's disagreement with an agency's evaluation judgments does not demonstrate that those judgments are unreasonable. Amyx, Inc., B-410623, 2015 CPD ¶ 45 (Comp.Gen. 2015)

Protest was sustained where the Source Selection Authority used the awardee's good past performance to offset the relative technical weaknesses of the awardee's quotation, even though the awardee and the protester had the same past performance score. PricewaterhouseCoopers LLP, B-409537, 2014 CPD ¶ 255 (Comp. Gen. 2014)

Agency is not required to evaluate the past performance of key personnel or subcontractors. GAO held that an agency has a legitimate interest in assessing performance risk by considering only the experience and past performance of entities with which it will have contractual privity. HK Consulting, Inc., B- 408443, 2013 CPD ¶ 224 (Comp. Gen. 2013)

Protester's contention that agency past performance evaluation was unreasonable because the agency did not distinguish between degrees of relevance in evaluating each vendor's past performance is denied where the evaluation was reasonable, and consistent with the stated evaluation criteria; there is no *per se* requirement that an agency weight differently the ratings given each vendor based on an assessment of the relative relevance of the vendor's prior contracts. Matter of: Paragon Systems, Inc., B-299548.2, 2007 CPD ¶ 178 (Comp. Gen. 2007)

8 Evaluation Factors—Risk

GAO sustained a protest because an agency did not reasonably apply a solicitation criterion stating that offerors with existing production capabilities would be considered less risky than offerors that do not have currently existing facilities. The evaluation was unreasonable because the agency rated the awardee and the protester equally on the facility factor even though the protester currently had a suitable facility and the awardee had to make arrangements to acquire the necessary facilities. Matter of: Navistar Defense, LLC;

BAE Systems, Tactical Vehicle Systems LP, B-401865, B-401865.2, B-401865.3, B-401865.4, B-401865.5, B-401865.6, B-401865.7, 2009 CPD ¶ 258 (Comp. Gen. 2009).

9 Evaluation factors—HUBZones, evaluation factors

Contracting agency properly applied Historically Underutilized Business Zone (HUBZone) evaluation preference when it added a 10% margin to proposal prices offered by non-HUBZone offerors to determine whether price of HUBZone offeror could be deemed lower than that of the other offerors, but not for purpose of determining whether non-HUBZone offerors should be eliminated from competition because their proposal prices exceeded budget ceilings for line-items. Small Business Act, § 2[2](b)(3)(A), as amended, 15 U.S.C.A. § 657a(b)(3)(A). Metcalf Const. Co., Inc. v. U.S., 53 Fed. Cl. 617 (2002). United States ☞64.15

10 Evaluation factors—Disclosure of information, evaluation factors

Federal Government's undisclosed use of Army Materiel Systems Analysis Activity Technical Report No. 357, which projected reliability growth on basis of observed failures, raw test data, types of failures, and number of failures, was logically and reasonably related to identified reliability factor in request for proposal and did not need to be disclosed in request for proposal for variable reach, rough terrain forklift trucks for BMY, A Div. of HARSCO Corp. v. U.S., 693 F. Supp. 1232, 35 Cont. Cas. Fed. (CCH) P 75552 (D.D.C. 1988). United States ☞64.40(1)

Protest was sustained where agency did not inform offerors as to the weight of price and non-price evaluation factors. The sample task order RFP included in the master contract indicated that if both types of factors were to be considered in a task order RFP, they would receive approximately equal weight. The agency, instead, gave non-price factors three times the weight of the price factor. Thus, the guiding competition principles and procedures set forth in 41 U.S.C. § 253j(b), FAR 15.209(a) and FAR 15.304(e), were ignored in competing this task order. A & D Fire Protection, Inc. v. U.S., 72 Fed. Cl. 126 (2006)

Failure to tell offerors the exact numerical weight of each factor and sub-factor in bid evaluation process was not arbitrary or capricious, where relative importance of factors and, within a factor, of the sub-factors, was specified in the solicitation, and was followed in the source selection plan and by evaluators. Beta Analytics Intern., Inc. v. U.S., 67 Fed. Cl. 384 (2005), subsequent determination, 69 Fed. Cl. 431 (2005), order clarified, 2006 WL 5628556 (Ct. Fed. Cl. 2006)

Government may not rely upon undisclosed evaluation criteria when evaluating proposals, and must even disclose the factors' relative importance. 10 U.S.C.A. § 2305(a)(2)(A), (a) (3)(A); 48 C.F.R. § 15.305(a). Gulf Group, Inc. v. U.S., 56 Fed. Cl. 391 (2003). United States ☞64.40(1)

Although test and training/operational doctrine/data quality discriminator was a significant aspect of offerors' proposals relied upon by source selection authority (SSA) when making final decision in Air Force procurement for engineering and technical support services, SSA's actions did not result in elevating its requirements to the level of an undisclosed evaluation factor; rather, SSA acted within his discretion to consider it as an important discriminator when making his final decision. Computer Sciences Corp. v. U.S., 51 Fed. Cl. 297 (2002). United States ☞64.45(3)

In order to show entitlement to relief on a claim that government agency used undisclosed evaluation factors in reviewing proposals on government contract, plaintiff must prove that government evaluated the proposals received on a significantly different basis from that announced in solicitation and that plaintiff has been prejudiced as result. 10 U.S.C.A. § 2305(a)(2); Federal Property and Administrative Services Act of 1949, § 303A(b) (1), as amended, 41 U.S.C.A. § 253a(b)(1); 48 C.F.R. § 15.605(d)(1). Analytical & Research Technology, Inc. v. U.S., 39 Fed. Cl. 34, 442 Cont. Cas. Fed. (CCH) P 77228 (1997). United States ☞64.40(1)

Where a solicitation failed to disclose the relative weight of the listed subfactors of the primary technical factor, the subfactors should have been considered approximately equal in weight, even though the procurement was intended to be conducted using Federal Acquisition Regulation (FAR) Part 13 simplified acquisition procedures and FAR sect. 13.106-1(a)(2) states that the relative importance of evaluation factors and subfactors need

Part 15 Contracting by Negotiation   § 15.305

not be disclosed in a solicitation, because the solicitation did not indicate that the acquisition was being conducted under FAR Part 13 and the acquisition was conducted in a manner that was not distinguishable from a negotiated acquisition conducted under FAR Part 15, which requires that the relative weights of the evaluation factors and subfactors be stated in the solicitation. Bio-Rad Laboratories, Inc., B-297553, 2007 CPD ¶ 58 (Comp. Gen. 2006)

Agency's selection of a proposal for award was unreasonable where the solicitation was silent as to the relative weights of the subfactors of the primary technical evaluation factor, and the agency, rather than treating the subfactors as equal in weight in evaluating the relative merits of the competing proposals, considered the subfactors as listed in descending order of importance. Bio-Rad Laboratories, Inc., B-297553, 2007 CPD ¶ 58 (Comp. Gen. 2006)

Agency's determination to eliminate a proposal for a custody officer services contract from the competitive range, based solely on a minimum requirement for direct corporate experience that was neither stated in the solicitation nor disclosed to offerors prior to proposal submission, was improper. Omniplex World Services Corporation, B-290996.2, 2003 CPD ¶ 7 (Comp. Gen. 2003)

11 Evaluation factors—staffing

Protest challenging the evaluation of offerors' proposed staffing is sustained where the agency did not reasonably evaluate the offerors' proposals in accordance with solicitation's staffing plan subfactor. Specifically, the protester contended that the agency did not consider the effects of the awardee's proposed use of local nationals on their ability to perform the task order requirements. Exelis Sys. Corp., B-407111, 2012 CPD ¶ 340 (Comp. Gen. 2012)

§ 15.305 Proposal evaluation.

(a) Proposal evaluation is an assessment of the proposal and the offeror's ability to perform the prospective contract successfully. An agency shall evaluate competitive proposals and then assess their relative qualities solely on the factors and subfactors specified in the solicitation. Evaluations may be conducted using any rating method or combination of methods, including color or adjectival ratings, numerical weights, and ordinal rankings. The relative strengths, deficiencies, significant weaknesses, and risks supporting proposal evaluation shall be documented in the contract file.

(1) *Cost or price evaluation.* Normally, competition establishes price reasonableness. Therefore, when contracting on a firm-fixed-price or fixed-price with economic price adjustment basis, comparison of the proposed prices will usually satisfy the requirement to perform a price analysis, and a cost analysis need not be performed. In limited situations, a cost analysis (see 15.403-1(c)(1)(i)(B)) may be appropriate to establish reasonableness of the otherwise successful offeror's price. When contracting on a cost-reimbursement basis, evaluations shall include a cost realism analysis to determine what the Government should realistically expect to pay for the proposed effort, the offeror's understanding of the work, and the offeror's ability to perform the contract. (See 37.115 for uncompensated overtime evaluation.) The contracting officer shall document the cost or price evaluation.

(2) Past performance evaluation.

(i) Past performance information is one indicator of an offeror's ability to perform the contract successfully. The currency and relevance of the information, source of the information, context of the data, and general trends in contractor's performance shall be considered. This comparative assessment of past performance information is separate from the responsibility determination required under Subpart 9.1.

(ii) The solicitation shall describe the approach for evaluating past performance, including evaluating offerors with no relevant performance history, and shall provide offerors an opportunity to identify past or current contracts (including Federal, State, and local government and private) for efforts similar to the Government requirement. The solicitation shall also authorize offerors to provide information on problems encountered on the identified contracts and the offeror's corrective actions. The Government shall consider this information, as well as information obtained from any other sources, when evaluating the offeror's past performance. The source selection authority shall determine the relevance of similar past performance information.

799

(iii) The evaluation should take into account past performance information regarding predecessor companies, key personnel who have relevant experience, or subcontractors that will perform major or critical aspects of the requirement when such information is relevant to the instant acquisition.

(iv) In the case of an offeror without a record of relevant past performance or for whom information on past performance is not available, the offeror may not be evaluated favorably or unfavorably on past performance.

(v) The evaluation should include the past performance of offerors in complying with subcontracting plan goals for small disadvantaged business (SDB) concerns (see Subpart 19.7).

(3) *Technical evaluation.* When tradeoffs are performed (see 15.101-1), the source selection records shall include—

(i) An assessment of each offeror's ability to accomplish the technical requirements; and

(ii) A summary, matrix, or quantitative ranking, along with appropriate supporting narrative, of each technical proposal using the evaluation factors.

(4) *Cost information.* Cost information may be provided to members of the technical evaluation team in accordance with agency procedures.

(5) *Small business subcontracting evaluation.* Solicitations must be structured to give offers from small business concerns the highest rating for the evaluation factors in 15.304(c)(3)(ii) and (c)(4).

(b) The source selection authority may reject all proposals received in response to a solicitation, if doing so is in the best interest of the Government.

(c) For restrictions on the use of support contractor personnel in proposal evaluation, see 37.203(d).

United States Code Annotated

Administrative determinations, see 41 USCA § 257.

Contract requirements, see 41 USCA § 254.

Contracts, planning, solicitation, evaluation, and award procedures, see 10 USCA § 2305.

Definitions, see 10 USCA § 2302, 41 USCA §§ 259, 403.

Determinations and decisions, see 10 USCA § 2310, 41 USCA § 262.

Evaluation and award, see 41 USCA § 253b.

Kinds of contracts, see 10 USCA § 2306.

Planning and solicitation requirements, see 41 USCA § 253a.

Notes of Decisions

Protest against award 14
Ranking 10
Subcontractors 17.5
Tradeoff process 3

1 Discretion of agency—In general

If a company certifies that it meets the requirements of Section 508 in its proposal, the contracting officer may rely on the certification in awarding a contract. The company's potential failure to comply with the requirements is ordinarily a matter of contract administration, which does not affect the propriety of awarding a contract. Allied Technology Group, Inc. v. U.S., 649 F.3d 1320 (Fed. Cir. 2011)

Air Force solicitation for aircraft maintenance services specified a requirement for a process of maintenance information system (MIS) training so that a process of MIS training deficiency could be assigned to disappointed offeror. DynCorp Intern. LLC v. U.S., 76 Fed. Cl. 528 (2007).

The government may not rely upon undisclosed evaluation criteria in evaluating proposals; however, a solicitation need not identify each element to be considered by the agency during the course of the evaluation where such element is intrinsic to the stated factors. OTI America, Inc. v. U.S., 73 Fed. Cl. 758 (2006), aff'd, 227 Fed. Appx. 926 (Fed. Cir. 2007).

Contracting agency has great discretion in determining the scope of an evaluation factor. Maintenance Engineers v. U.S., 50 Fed. Cl. 399 (2001). United States ☞64.40(1)

In the context of a protest of a negotiated procurement, an agency is entitled to wide discretion in its evaluation of proposals. Tech Systems, Inc. v. U.S., 50 Fed. Cl. 216 (2001). United States ☞64.40(1)

Contracting officials may properly exercise wide discretion in their evaluation of proposals and the application of procurement regulations; discretion is especially broad in negotiated procurements. Hawpe Const., Inc. v. U.S., 46 Fed. Cl. 571 (2000), aff'd, 10 Fed. Appx. 957 (Fed. Cir. 2001). United States ☞64.40(1)

Procurement officials are entitled to broad discretion in evaluation of bids for government contracts and in the application of procurement regulations, particularly in those instances where negotiated procurement is at issue. Day & Zimmermann Services, a Div. of Day & Zimmermann, Inc. v. U.S., 38 Fed. Cl. 591, 42 Cont. Cas. Fed. (CCH) P 77186 (1997), dismissed, 132 F.3d 49 (Fed. Cir. 1997). United States ☞64.40(1)

Protest was sustained because agency gave undue emphasis to one of the evaluation subfactors, and treated offerors unequally by reading some offerors' proposals expansively and giving offerors the benefit of the doubt, while applying a much stricter standard when evaluating other offerors' proposals. Arctic Slope Mission Services, LLC, B-410992.5, B-410992.6, 2016 CPD ¶ 39 (Comp.Gen. 2016)

Protest challenging the award of an indefinite-delivery/indefinite-quantity contract was sustained because the agency knew, prior to award, that the agency's anticipated schedule for issuance of task orders was materially different from the assumptions set forth in the solicitation, upon which offerors were required to base their proposals. Matter of: Global Computer Enterprises, Inc.; Savantage Financial Services, Inc., B-404597, B-404597.2, B-404597.3, 2011 CPD ¶ 69 (Comp. Gen. 2011)

Agency unreasonably evaluated the protester's quotation for ambulance services as unacceptable under the solicitation's geographic coverage evaluation factor where, as described in its quotation, the protester offered to provide the same services within the required geographic coverage as it had performed under the incumbent contract and its quotation provided similar information to that provided by the awardee, which received an acceptable rating under this factor. Matter of: Douglas County Fire District %7b2, B-403228, 2010 CPD ¶ 239 (Comp. Gen. 2010)

Where solicitation established specific evaluation benchmarks for evaluation of offerors' experience, and provided for comparative assessments against those benchmarks, an agency may not substitute a previously unidentified "threshold of sufficiency" as an evaluation benchmark against which proposals are evaluated on a pass/fail basis. L-3 Communications Titan Corporation, B-299317, B-299317.2, B-299317.3, 2007 CPD ¶ 66 (Comp. Gen. 2007)

Protest against award for deactivation and decommissioning of nuclear reactor is sustained where, although solicitation provided that agency was committed to achieving an accelerated closure of the site, agency accorded little or no weight in the evaluation to the degree to which offerors proposed to accelerate completion ahead of required site closure date. Matter of: EPW Closure Services, LLC; FFTF Restoration Co., LLC, B-294910, B-294910.2, B-294910.3, B-294910.4, B-294910.5, B-294910.6, B-294910.7, 2006 CPD ¶ 3 (Comp. Gen. 2005)

Protest is sustained where Department of Treasury negotiated during procurement for network services a memorandum of understanding (with the Office of Management and Budget and General Services Administration's Federal Technology Service) that significantly changed the approach set forth in solicitation and Federal Acquisition Regulation to determining whether to exercise the options, making it significantly less likely that the options would be exercised, and thus materially altering the basis upon which offerors prepared their proposals. Northrup Grumman Information Technology, Inc.; Broadwing Communications LLC; Level 3 Communications, Inc.; QWest Government Services, Inc.; MCIWORLDCOM Communications, Inc., B-295526, B-295526.2, B-295526.3, B-295526.4, B-295526.5, B-295526.6, B-295526.7, 2005 CPD ¶ 45 (Comp. Gen. 2005)

General Accounting Office cannot find that the agency reasonably evaluated the protester's oral presentation where the agency and protester disagree as to the content of the oral presentation, the contemporaneous record of the oral discussions and presentations—which consists only of the protester's presentation materials and the evaluators' scoresheets—does not support the evaluators' conclusions regarding the protester's approach, and the agency did not act in accordance with the terms of the solicitation where it disregarded the protester's previously submitted written proposal in evaluating the oral presentation. Checchi and Company Consulting, Inc., B-285777, 2001 CPD ¶ 132 (Comp. Gen. 2000).

2 Discretion of agency—Past performance, discretion of agency

Protest that agency's evaluation of protester's past performance was unreasonable was sustained where the agency's evaluation was based on a numerical scoring system which had the effect of penalizing protester for submitting additional less relevant contracts, even though the contracts had "Superior" ratings. B-401679.8, 2010 CPD ¶ 211

Generally, a contracting agency is accorded broad discretion when conducting its past performance evaluations. Vantage Associates, Inc. v. U.S., 59 Fed. Cl. 1 (2003). United States ☞64.45(2)

An agency is accorded broad discretion when conducting its past performance evaluations during a procurement. Computer Sciences Corp. v. U.S., 51 Fed. Cl. 297 (2002). United States ☞64.45(2)

Evaluating an offeror's past performance based solely on the size of past contracts, without considering other indicators of complexity, may indicate an unreasonable emphasis on the factor; however, the consideration of the size of past contracts as one factor among a number of factors related to the relevance and quality of past performance is a proper and reasonable exercise of the agency's discretion. Maintenance Engineers v. U.S., 50 Fed. Cl. 399 (2001). United States ☞64.45(2)

An agency has discretion to determine the scope of an offeror's performance history to be considered provided all proposals are evaluated consistently. Seattle Sec. Services, Inc. v. U.S., 45 Fed. Cl. 560 (2000). United States ☞64.45(2)

Agency personnel engaged in procurement are generally given great discretion in determining what references to review in evaluating past performance of offerors; thus, there is no requirement that all references listed in a proposal be checked. Seattle Sec. Services, Inc. v. U.S., 45 Fed. Cl. 560 (2000). United States ☞64.45(2)

An agency's past performance evaluation was unreasonable because the agency did not consider relevant adverse past performance information that the protester had provided to the agency regarding the awardee. Protester had provided adverse information regarding the awardee's performance contained in an IG Report and a news article Matter of: Contrack International, Inc., B-401871.5, B-401871.6, B-401871.7, 2010 CPD ¶ 126 (Comp. Gen. 2010)

Past performance evaluation was unreasonable because the findings in the agency's evaluation report were not consistent with the information upon which the findings were based. The agency could not determine whether proper consideration was given to adverse past performance and the relevance of an offeror's prior contracts was not assessed. Matter of: DRSC3 Systems, LLC, B-310825, B-310825.2, 2008 CPD ¶ 103 (Comp. Gen. 2008)

An agency improperly evaluated proposals because it considered one of four factors on a pass/fail basis instead of the designated qualitative basis, and because it evaluated past performance with no contemporaneous documentation of oral discussion for the basis of the evaluation. Decision Matter of: Helicopter Transport Services LLC, B-400295, B-400295.2, 2008 CPD ¶ 180 (Comp. Gen. 2008)

Agency's past performance evaluation held unreasonable because it did not evaluate whether awardee's past performance projects contracts were similar in size to the protester's projects. GAO found that five out of six of the awardee's projects were between $2 million and $3.5 million, and used no more than a dozen employees. The sixth had a dollar value of about $30 million and 67 employees. By contrast, protester's projects included contracts with values of $600 million, $250 million, at least $100 million and $43.6 million, most involving more than 200 employees. The agency's contract was estimated to be nearly $200 million and was expected to involve more than 270 personnel. GAO considered the evaluation unreasonable because the agency essentially used a pass/fail criterion for the relative size of offerors' past performance references, contrary to the method described in the RFP. Matter of: ASRC Research & Technology Solutions, LLC, B-400217, B-400217.2, 2008 CPD ¶ 202 (Comp. Gen. 2008)

Agency's evaluation of vendor's past performance was reasonable where agency contacted an individual who was familiar with the vendor's performance, even though the individual was not the point of contact designated by the vendor in its past performance reference. Matter of: Paragon Systems, Inc., B-299548.2, 2007 CPD ¶ 178 (Comp. Gen. 2007)

Agency improperly attributed past performance of parent company or its other subsidiaries to awardee where record does not establish that parent company or subsidiaries will be involved in the performance of the protested contract. Universal Building Maintenance, Inc., B-282456, 99-2 CPD ¶ 32 (Comp. Gen. 1999)

3 Tradeoff process

Contracting agency's decision to exclude offeror from final cost/technical tradeoff between two other offerors was not arbitrary, capricious, or contrary to law, where offeror's proposal was more costly than that of the other offerors, and its technical rating was not superior to that of the offeror who had the highest technical rating in the tradeoff. Industrial Property Management, Inc. v. U.S., 59 Fed. Cl. 318 (2004). United States ☞64.45(1)

The government is only required to make a cost/technical tradeoff in considering proposals where one proposal is rated higher technically than another, but the other is lower in cost. Industrial Property Management, Inc. v. U.S., 59 Fed. Cl. 318 (2004). United States ☞64.45(1)

Where solicitation identified price as a factor in the bid process, and provided that "the significance of price as an evaluation factor will increase with the degree of equality of proposals in relationship to the technical scores," contracting agency reasonably relied upon price as the determining factor in awarding the contract when offerors both received overall Technical scores of "Outstanding," and contract awardee had the lower priced proposal. Vantage Associates, Inc. v. U.S., 59 Fed. Cl. 1 (2003).

Air Force committed procurement error by evaluating contract awardee's technically noncompliant proposal as an advantage under "cost as an independent variable" (CAIV) principles, allowing awardee to "trade off"its technical noncompliance for lowered cost, but only other offeror was not informed that CAIV tradeoffs would be considered in making the award decision. Gentex Corp. v. U.S., 58 Fed.Cl. 634 (2003).

Mere fact that protestor's proposal was lower than that of contract awardee did not establish that contracting officer's cost and technical tradeoff analysis was arbitrary, capricious, or irrational. Tech Systems, Inc. v. U.S., 50 Fed. Cl. 216 (2001). United States ☞64.40(1)

Agency reasonably determined that cost savings of $4.5 million dollars, or 8.4%, in selecting low bidder was not offset by the superior characteristics of higher bidder's management/

technical proposal. ITT Federal Services Corp. v. U.S., 45 Fed.Cl. 174 (1999).

Before an agency can select a higher-cost proposal that has been rated technically superior to a lower-cost, but acceptable one, the award decision must be supported by a rational explanation of why the higher-rated proposal is, in fact, superior, and explain why its technical superiority warrants paying a cost premium. DKW Commc'ns, Inc., B-411182, 2015 CPD ¶ 178 (Comp. Gen. 2015)

Protest was sustained because the RFP provided for a comparative best value evaluation of the technical factors and the agency failed to document that it qualitatively assessed the relative merits of the offerors' technical approaches. GAO found that the evaluation of the offerors' proposals under the staffing and implementation factors considered only whether the proposals were technically unacceptable or acceptable, and did not, as contemplated by the RFP, consider their relative qualitative merit. When an agency conducts a cost/technical tradeoff, adequate documentation requires more than just generalized statements of proposal equivalency. Trailboss Enters., Inc., B-407093, 2013 CPD ¶ 232 (Comp. Gen. 2013)

Protest is sustained where the agency's evaluation of protester's proposal was unreasonable because the agency conducted a tradeoff only between the three proposals with the highest point scores but did not consider the lower prices offered by other apparently technically acceptable lower-rated offerors. J.R. Conkey & Assocs., Inc. dba Solar Power Integrators, B-406024.4, 2012 CPD ¶ 241 (Comp. Gen. 2012)

In a best value procurement for maintenance services, protest is sustained where the record shows that the agency performed a tradeoff between two higher-rated, higher-priced quotations, but did not consider, in its tradeoff decision, the lower prices submitted by other lower-rated vendors, whose quotations were nonetheless found to be technically acceptable. Matter of: System Engineering International, Inc., B-402754, 2010 CPD ¶ 167 (Comp. Gen. 2010)

Protest is sustained where there is no evidence in the contemporaneous record that the contracting officer performed a proper price/technical trade-off-or, for that matter, even considered offerors' prices-prior to selecting the awardee. There is no evaluation of offerors' prices-on either an individual or comparative basis-in any of the source selection documentation. This is contrary to the requirement that price be considered in every source selection decision, 41 U.S.C. § 253a(c)(1)(B) (2002); FAR 15.304(c)(1), and the requirement that a source selection decision be based on a comparative assessment of proposals against all source selection criteria in the solicitation and that it be documented. Locus Technology, Inc., B-293012, 2004 CPD ¶ 16 (Comp. Gen. 2004)

4 Minimum or material requirements

Government's error in awarding contract to offeror whose proposal was technically noncompliant, due to failure to comply with specified test requirement, was prejudicial to unsuccessful offeror, which was only other offeror for contract, notwithstanding large price disparity between successful andunsuccessful proposals. Alfa Laval Separation, Inc. v. U.S., 175 F.3d 1365 (Fed. Cir. 1999).

In general, concept of responsiveness is not applicable to negotiation procurements where contracting officer is permitted to conduct oral or written discussions with offerors whose proposals vary from request for proposals; however, while concept of responsiveness is not technically applicable to negotiated procurements, even in negotiated procurement procuring agency does not have discretion to disregard offeror's failure to satisfy material requirement in request for proposal. Howard Cooper Corp. v. U.S., 763 F. Supp. 829, 37 Cont. Cas. Fed. (CCH) P 76169 (E.D. Va. 1991). United States ☞64.5

A mandatory minimum requirement must be clearly identified as such within a solicitation so as to put offerors on notice of the serious consequences of failing to meet the requirement; such notice typically emphasizes that a proposal must meet the requirement in order to be eligible for evaluation or, conversely, that failure to comply with the requirement will lead to outright rejection of the proposal. ManTech Telecommunications and Information Systems Corp. v. U.S., 49 Fed. Cl. 57 (2001), decision aff'd, 30 Fed. Appx. 995 (Fed. Cir. 2002). United States ☞64.25

Solicitation's minimum education and experience provisions could not reasonably be read as imposing a minimum mandatory requirement; far from providing the requisite notice that failure to comply with the minimum experience and resume requirements would result in disqualification, the solicitation, as a whole, signaled that relatively minor deficiencies, rating something better than an exceptionally low score on a specific element or factor, would not result in a proposal being eliminated. ManTech Telecommunications and Information Systems Corp. v. U.S., 49 Fed. Cl. 57 (2001), decision aff'd, 30 Fed. Appx. 995 (Fed. Cir. 2002). United States ☞64.25

Government violated procurement statutes and regulations in awarding software contract, by relaxing minimum solicitation requirement without notifying all offerors that the evaluation criterion had changed. 10 U.S.C.A. § 2305(b)(1); 48 C.F.R. §§ 12.602(b, c), 15. 305(a). Candle Corp. v. U.S., 40 Fed. Cl. 658, 42 Cont. Cas. Fed. (CCH) P 77276 (1998). United States ☞64.25

Requirement in Army's solicitation of proposals on contract for computer and data processing support, that proposed personnel have three years minimum experience within preceding five years, was not latently ambiguous as alleged by disappointed offeror; solicitation stated that proposed personnel must have requisite years of experience, defined the minimum years of experience required for proposed personnel, stated that proposed personnel would receive score of "unacceptable" if they did not meet minimum experience requirements, and further defined "unacceptable" as numerical score of zero. Analytical & Research Technology, Inc. v. U.S., 39 Fed. Cl. 34, 442 Cont. Cas. Fed. (CCH) P 77228 (1997). United States ☞64.25

In soliciting proposals on contract for computer and automated data processing support, Army could evaluate the requirement that proposed personnel have three years minimum experience within preceding five years as a "go/no-go" requirement which if not met would render that portion of offeror's proposal technically unacceptable, regardless of whether solicitation used term "go/no-go." 10 U.S.C.A. § 2305(a)(2); Federal Property and Administrative Services Act of 1949, § 303A(b)(1), as amended, 41 U.S.C.A. § 253a(b)(1); 48 C.F.R. § 15. 605(d)(1). Analytical & Research Technology, Inc. v. U.S., 39 Fed. Cl. 34, 442 Cont. Cas. Fed. (CCH) P 77228 (1997). United States ☞64.40(1)

Statement of requirements for second phase of application process for concessions contract required that applicant not condition capital improvement fund contribution following change of operations on further negotiation. YRT Services Corp. v. U.S., 28 Fed. Cl. 366, 38 Cont. Cas. Fed. (CCH) P 76512 (1993). United States ☞64.30

Required purchase of concessioner, at price set by National Park Service (NPS), by successful applicant for concessions contract did not prejudice unsuccessful applicant or prevent that unsuccessful applicant from being fully and fairly considered in exactly same way as all other applicants; it was not clear that purchase price was necessarily higher than that which unsuccessful applicant could have negotiated, statement of requirements for second phase of application process called for package offer that took into account many other factors, and terms of purchase were same for all applicants. YRT Services Corp. v. U.S., 28 Fed. Cl. 366, 38 Cont. Cas. Fed. (CCH) P 76512 (1993). United States ☞64.40(2)

If an agency is going to use internal staffing estimates to establish minimum requirements that all proposals must satisfy, it must disclose the internal staffing estimates to potential offerors. Protest was sustained because that agency mechanically and unequally applied undisclosed staffing estimates in evaluating the offerors' proposed staffing plans to determine whether proposals were acceptable or unacceptable. Orion Tech., Inc., et al., B-406769, 2012 CPD ¶ 268 (Comp. Gen. 2012)

Protest was sustained where solicitation required proposal of loaded labor rates to be used as ceiling rates in future task order competitions and awardee failed to propose rates for 20 labor categories. This omission in awardee's proposal constitutes material omission rendering proposal unacceptable. Raytheon Tech. Servs. Co. LLC, B-404655.4, 2011 CPD ¶ 236 (Comp. Gen. 2011)

Protest was sustained because agency waived a mandatory solicitation requirement to support staffing levels for one offeror, but did not disclose its willingness to waive the requirement to all offerors or provide them an opportunity to submit revised proposals. North Wind, Inc.; Earth Resources Technology, Inc., B-404880.4, B-404880.5, B-404880.6, 2011 CPD ¶ 246 (Comp. Gen. 2011)

An agency's award to a technically unacceptable offeror was inappropriate, the GAO determined, because the awardee did not have the five years of experience that the solicitation required. Although the protester had teamed with companies that did have over five years of experience, the solicitation specifically stated that the prime contractor must satisfy the experience requirement. Matter of: J2A2 JV, LLC, B-401663.4, 2010 CPD ¶ 102 (Comp. Gen. 2010)

An agency improperly rejected as unacceptable an offer that included data that provided a better understanding of the offeror's capabilities, the GAO determined. The agency requested a percentage of staff holding third-party certification, and the offeror submitted the actual number of staff members holding such certification. Although solicitation requirements are to be enforced as stated, the GAO noted, "the [protester's] table provided the evaluators with more, and more meaningful, information regarding its available staffing resources" and found that the agency's rejection of the proposal on this basis was unreasonable. Matter of: Engineering Management & Integration, Inc., B-400356.4, B-400356.5, 2009 CPD ¶ 114 (Comp. Gen. 2009)

Protest was sustained because the awardee did not affirmatively agree to meet a technical specification, even though the awardee's quotation and answers to questions demonstrated an apparent capacity to meet it. GAO held that, although the awardee may have had the capacity to meet the requirement, nowhere in its quote did it agree to do so within the time frame specified, as required by the RFQ. The awardee's quote discussed implementation of the capability, but did not address when the capability would be fully ready. GAO stated: "A vendor is responsible for affirmatively demonstrating the merits of its quotation and risks the rejection of its quotation if it fails to do so." Matter of: Carahsoft Technology Corporation, B-401169, B-401169.2, 2009 CPD ¶ 134 (Comp. Gen. 2009)

5 Evaluation factors—In general

In negotiated procurement, contracting officials have broad discretion to determine manner in which they will make use of technical and cost evaluation results; however, it is improper to induce offeror representing highest quality and then reject it in favor of materially inferior offer on basis of relatively insignificant price difference. Latecoere Intern., Inc. v. U.S. Dept. of Navy, 19 F.3d 1342 (11th Cir. 1994), as amended, (May 27, 1994).

The request for proposals clearly stated that offerors must address whether they had the capability to perform in nine designated metropolitan areas and that metropolitan presence would be considered in evaluating proposals. Therefore, the protester's assertion that the agency used an unstated evaluation criteria lacked merit and the COFC denied the protest. NEQ, LLC v. U.S., 88 Fed. Cl. 38 (2009)

Determination of source selection authority (SSA) that cost accounting discriminator under program management subfactor of mission capability factor slightly favored contract awardee in Air Force solicitation for engineering and technical support services was rationally based, despite protestor's challenge based on prior cost accounting analysis performed by the Defense Contract Audit Agency (DCAA). Computer Sciences Corp. v. U.S., 51 Fed. Cl. 297 (2002). United States ☞64.45(2)

A solicitation need not identify each element to be considered by the agency during the course of the evaluation where such element is intrinsic to the stated factors. Maintenance Engineers v. U.S., 50 Fed. Cl. 399 (2001). United States ☞64.25

Protesters did not establish that award of contract for Antarctic support services represented a clear departure from announced evaluation scheme, on ground that information technology/communications played an extremely important role in the evaluation process and consequently, should have been listed as an evaluation factor in the solicitation and assigned an evaluation weight. 48 C.F.R. § 15.304(d). Antarctic Support Associates v. U.S., 46 Fed. Cl. 145 (2000), aff'd, 251 F.3d 171 (Fed. Cir. 2000). United States ☞64.40(1)

A contract award may not be upheld when the source selection authority (SSA) improperly departs from stated evaluation criteria in a solicitation. ITT Federal Services Corp. v. U.S., 45 Fed. Cl. 174 (1999). United States ☞64.45(1)

Contracting agencies are required to evaluate proposals based on the content of the proposal itself; an offeror in a negotiated procurement must demonstrate within the four corners of its proposal that it is capable of performing the work upon the terms most advantageous to the government. Dubinsky v. U.S., 43 Fed. Cl. 243 (1999)

In making a best value source selection decision, an agency may properly rely on a single evaluation factor—even a lower-weighted factor—if it is determined to be a key discriminator. TriWest Healthcare Alliance Corp., B-401652.12; B-401652.13, 2012 CPD ¶ 191 (Comp. Gen. 2012)

5.5 Evaluation factors—Mission suitability, evaluation factors

Protestor did not establish that contracting agency violated procurement regulation by not explaining reason for re-evaluation of safety and health plan subfactor of mission suitability evaluation factor, or adequately justifying changes made in ratings of contract awardee and protestor following the re-evaluation; after the re-evaluation, the source evaluation board (SEB) presented detailed findings to support rescoring and re-rating the proposals, identifying the particular strengths of each and describing anticipated effects. Comprehensive Health Services, Inc. v. U.S., 70 Fed. Cl. 700 (2006). United States ☞64.45(1)

6 Evaluation factors—Past performance, evaluation factors

Although agencies have discretion to determine the scope of the past performance history it will consider, all quotations must be evaluated on the same basis. Protest was sustained because the agency engaged in disparate treatment of the awardee and protester by evaluating only the most recent CPARs for the projects identified by the protester, but when evaluating the awardee's past performance, the agency considered CPARs for other than the specific projects identified by the awardee. CSR, Inc., B-413973 2017 CPD ¶ 64 (Comp. Gen. 2017)

Army's use of a performance evaluation form in evaluating unsuccessful offeror's technical proposal was not unlawful, arbitrary, capricious, or an abuse of discretion; there was no prohibition in the RFP against use of form or against use of any other past performance evaluation to determining offeror's technical score, form was made specifically to evaluate a potential contractor's performance, and there was no evidence that Army was aware, before using form in procurement, of any problems with form. Kellie W. Tipton Const. Co. v. U.S., 4 Fed. Appx. 846 (Fed. Cir. 2001). United States ☞64.45(2)

Agency's "less than satisfactory" past performance rating of protester had a rational basis, and thus was entitled to deference. Although each reference rated protester's performance as "satisfactory" or "better" overall, negative comments in narrative portion of questionnaires detracted from positive ratings. There were several less than satisfactory subfactor ratings, protester had submitted late and incorrect estimates, its responses to questions were routinely delayed, and its corrective actions lacked sufficient detail. Glenn Def. Marine (ASIA), Pte. Ltd. v. U.S., 720 F.3d 901 (Fed. Cir. June 25, 2013)

Contracting officer was entitled to rely on offeror's past performance problems under a prior contract at Air Force base to which current contract pertained, in determining that offeror was not responsible, and fact that offeror may have been fulfilling a more recent contract at another base without problems did not make contracting officer's decision irrational or capricious. Tele-Sentry Sec., Inc. v. U.S. Dept. of Defense (Air Force), 705 F. Supp. 629 (D.D.C. 1989), judgment aff'd in part, vacated in part, 889 F.2d 1101 (Fed. Cir. 1989). United States ☞64.45(2)

Agency's past performance evaluation did not violate requirement that contractors receive impartial, fair, and equitable treatment, by evaluating ten task orders as one contract rather than as separate contracts, because the agency reasonably explained that "[h]earing from one COR on ten different task orders does not provide the same insight into a contractor's past performance as hearing from ten CORs on ten different contracts." Great S. Eng'g, Inc. v. U.S., 128 Fed. Cl. 739 (2016)

Protestor did not establish that contracting agency violated statute and regulations requiring it to evaluate proposals solely on basis of criteria stated in solicitation when it considered past contracts that were not technically "relevant" in evaluating past performance; based on solicitation's unambiguous language, source selection authority (SSA) acted within his discretion when he included non-relevant contracts as a part of his examination of general trends in the offerors' past performance. PHT Supply Corp. v. U.S., 71 Fed. Cl. 1 (2006). United States ☞64.45(2)

Source selection authority (SSA) did not violate procurement statute and regulation limiting evaluation of proposals to factors and subfactors specified in solicitation by considering offeror's past performances on 'large dollar value contracts" even though solicitation did not announce such a subfactor, as solicitation did not have to identify each element intrinsic to announced past performance evaluation factor. Comprehensive Health Services, Inc. v. U.S., 70 Fed. Cl. 700 (2006). United States ☞64.45(2)

Contracting agency did not abuse its discretion in solicitation for construction project by not seeking clarification from offeror concerning its past performance information after technical evaluation team (TET) determined that the information was inadequate to determine the scope of past projects, despite fact that the TET concluded that clarifications should be required, where source selection authority (SSA) subsequently explained that no clarification were sought because no discussions were conducted with any offeror. 48 C.F.R. § 15.306(a)(1, 2). Gulf Group Inc. v. U.S., 61 Fed. Cl. 338 (2004). United States ☞64.45(2)

Protestor did not establish that contracting agency failed to properly evaluate past performance factor in conducting price/technical tradeoff determination, notwithstanding protestor's contention that the three pages devoted to past performance in the source selection decision document (SSDD) were insufficient because the SSDD did not contain a "head-to-head" comparison of the various strengths and weakness of the offerors and did not list any weaknesses for protestor or contract awardee. Dismas Charities, Inc. v. U.S., 61 Fed. Cl. 191 (2004). United States ☞64.45(2)

Protestor did not establish that contracting agency violated procurement regulation requiring it to discuss "deficiencies, significant weaknesses, and adverse past performance information to which the offeror has not yet had an opportunity to respond" by not allowing protestor to address negative contractor evaluation forms (CEFs) regarding its performance of prior contracts; protestor cited no CEFs that were deemed "poor" or otherwise deficient, and protestor had the opportunity to respond to any CEFs that it considered adverse by submitting rebuttal comments with its proposals, but failed to do so. 48 C.F.R. § 15.306(d). Bannum, Inc. v. U.S., 60 Fed. Cl. 718 (2004). United States ☞64.45(2)

Contracting agency's downgrading of offeror for lack of past-performance data from the Construction Contractor Appraisal Support System (CCASS) database maintained by the Army Corps of Engineers amounted to error that operated to offeror's detriment, where direct cause of the lack of CCASS data for offeror appeared to be a failure on the part of governmental officials to complete evaluations regarding offeror's work under prior government contracts, as they were required to do by applicable regulations. 48 C.F.R. § 36.201. J.C.N. Const. Co., Inc. v. U.S., 60 Fed. Cl. 400 (2004), aff'd, 122 Fed. Appx. 514 (Fed. Cir. 2005). United States ☞64.45(2)

Divergence between past performance ratings assigned by offeror's references and those assigned by contracting agency's technical evaluation team did not constitute significant procurement error; offeror's focus on projects costing more than $500,000 could legitimately taken into account by agency's technical evaluation team (TET) as a negative element in making its evaluation for project costing less than $500,000. J.C.N. Const. Co., Inc. v. U.S., 60 Fed. Cl. 400 (2004), aff'd, 122 Fed. Appx. 514 (Fed. Cir. 2005). United States ☞64.45(2)

Although failure of government officials to complete evaluations for contractor's prior work under government contracts and to submit those evaluations to the Construction Contractor Appraisal Support System (CCASS) database was not in accord with regulations, it did not constitute significant error in subsequent procurement in which contractor was an unsuccessful offeror; although the absence of CCASS data for contract operated to its detriment in the subsequent procurement, that lack was attributable to a dereliction of duty by officials concerned with other construction contracts, and contractor had means available to it to confirm whether evaluations that should have been submitted in connection with earlier construction projects were in fact contained in the CCASS database. J.C.N. Const. Co., Inc. v. U.S., 60 Fed. Cl. 400 (2004), aff'd, 122 Fed. Appx. 514 (Fed. Cir. 2005). United States ☞64.45(2)

A contracting agency, in evaluating past performance, can give more weight to one contract over another if it is more relevant to an offeror's future performance on the solicited contract. Vantage Associates, Inc. v. U.S., 59 Fed. Cl. 1 (2003). United States ☞64.45(2)

Protestor did not establish that the Navy arbitrarily and capriciously awarded contract for gray radomes, based on its allegations that Navy failed to evaluate the quality and nature of awardee's past production of gray, rather than white, radomes, that the Navy failed to give proper weight to its experience with gray radomes, and unfairly downgraded its gray search radome based on awardee's critique. Vantage Associates, Inc. v. U.S., 59 Fed. Cl. 1 (2003). United States ☞64.45(2)

Where solicitation was explicit that each of the three technical criteria of past performance, experience, and management capability, would be assessed on a pass/fail basis, Court of Federal Claims could not impose additional documentary requirements such as narrative justifications when neither the applicable regulations nor the evaluation criteria required anything more than what the agency performed. 48 C.F.R. §§ 15.101-1, 15.305. Al Ghanim Combined Group Co. Gen. Trad. & Cont. W.L.L. v. U.S., 56 Fed. Cl. 502 (2003). United States ☞64.45(2)

Agency did not act arbitrarily, capriciously, or otherwise not in accordance with law, when it evaluated offeror's past performance as "satisfactory," despite offeror's contention that its lack of dredge disposal area experience instead should have led it to receive a "neutral" rating; agency did not assign offeror a "neutral" rating because it found that agency had relevant experience, including directly correlative experience with respect to several ☞tasks identified in the solicitation. Gulf Group, Inc. v. U.S., 56 Fed. Cl. 391 (2003). United States ☞64.45(2)

Protestor who alleged that its technical proposal should not have been downgraded due to its lack of experience as a prime contractor, did not establish that prime contracting experience was an undisclosed evaluation factor; solicitation clearly provided that in reviewing an offeror's past performance, contracting agency would look to contracts and subcontracts "similar in nature," and even if the contract had not so provided, the agency still would have been entitled to consider generically an offeror's experience in performing the specific tasks that were the subject of the procurement. Banknote Corp. of America, Inc. v. U.S., 56 Fed. Cl. 377 (2003), aff'd, 365 F.3d 1345 (Fed. Cir. 2004). United States ☞64.45(2)

Coast Guard did not act arbitrarily or capriciously in rating both disappointed and successful offerors on solicitation to construct Coast Guard icebreaker as "excellent" in past performance evaluation, despite fact that disappointed offeror was rated "excellent" on all four factors of past performance, while successful offeror received only a "good" rating on quality of product factor; solicitation's emphasis on overall customer satisfaction factor, on which successful offeror received a rating of "excellent," and which was equal in weight to the other three factors, cost control, timeliness of performance, and quality of product, combined, supported Coast Guard's evaluation. Halter Marine, Inc. v. U.S., 56 Fed. Cl. 144 (2003). United States ☞64.45(2)

Offeror waived alleged discrepancies between evaluation factors for past performance as stated in solicitation and the same factors as stated in questionnaires directed at offerors' past or current customers, where offeror failed to raise them prior to submission of proposal. Halter Marine, Inc. v. U.S., 56 Fed. Cl. 144 (2003). United States ☞64.25

With regard to procurement statute providing that offeror may not be evaluated favorably or unfavorably on factor of past performance when there is no information on past contract performance or such information is not available, proper approach to a "neutral rating" assigned a past performance factor pursuant to the statute is to exclude or completely eliminate that factor from the affected offeror's evaluation, rather than attempting to assign a quantitative value to the factor. Office of Federal Procurement Policy Act, § 6(j)(2), 41 U.S.C.A. § 405(j)(2). Metcalf Const. Co., Inc. v. U.S., 53 Fed. Cl. 617 (2002). United States ☞64.45(2)

Contracting agency violated statute providing that offeror may not be evaluated favorably or unfavorably on factor of past performance when there is no information on past contract performance by assigning a quantitative value to "neutral rating" given offeror on past performance subfactor of small business utilization factor pursuant to statute; rather, subfactor should have been completely eliminated from factor's evaluation, since subfactor was, in effect, "not applicable" to offeror. Office of Federal Procurement Policy Act, § 6(j)(2), 41 U.S.C.A. § 405(j)(2). Metcalf Const. Co., Inc. v. U.S., 53 Fed. Cl. 617 (2002). United States ☞64.45(2)

FAR did not require source selection authority (SSA) to conduct his own contract-by-contract comparative assessment of past contract performance; as long as agency evaluators conducted a contract-by-contract assessment, the SSA could rely on such evaluation without performing the same detailed analysis. 48 C.F.R. §§ 15.303(b)(5), 15.308. Computer Sciences Corp. v. U.S., 51 Fed. Cl. 297 (2002). United States ☞64.45(2)

Proposal assessment report (PAR) contained a sufficient analysis of past contract work, where approximately 19 pages were devoted to explaining the evaluations of each offeror's past performance. 48 C.F.R. § 15.308. Computer Sciences Corp. v. U.S., 51 Fed. Cl. 297 (2002). United States ☞64.45(2)

Even when past and present government contracts are similar, two sets of proposal evaluators can reasonably reach different conclusions concerning past performance evaluation factor. Computer Sciences Corp. v. U.S., 51 Fed. Cl. 297 (2002). United States ☞64.45(2)

Contracting agency did not act improperly in considering the past performance evaluations of successful offeror's subcontractors when evaluating its proposal and assigning a high confidence past performance rating to offeror. Information Technology & Applications Corp. v. U.S., 51 Fed. Cl. 340 (2001), decision aff'd, 316 F.3d 1312 (Fed. Cir. 2003). United States ☞64.45(2)

Contracting agency did not act improperly in considering the past performance evaluations of successful offeror's subcontractors when evaluating its proposal and assigning a high confidence past performance rating to offeror. Information Technology & Applications Corp. v. U.S., 51 Fed. Cl. 340 (2001), decision aff'd, 316 F.3d 1312 (Fed. Cir. 2003). United States ☞64.45(2)

It was not error for contracting agency to distribute past performance questionnaires to offerors which contained a rating scale different from the scale used in the technical evaluation. Maintenance Engineers v. U.S., 50 Fed. Cl. 399 (2001). United States ☞64.45(2)

A contracting agency's consideration of whether a contractor's past performance included work on contracts of a similar size and complexity is a proper consideration in determining the degree to which the past contracts are relevant to its current evaluation. Maintenance Engineers v. U.S., 50 Fed. Cl. 399 (2001). United States ☞64.45(2)

Contracting agency can give more weight to one past contract over another if it is more relevant to an offeror's future performance on the solicited contract, and provided the agency does not act arbitrarily or capriciously. Maintenance Engineers v. U.S., 50 Fed. Cl. 399 (2001). United States ☞64.45(2)

Evaluating an offeror's past performance based solely on the size of past contracts, without considering other indicators of complexity, may indicate an unreasonable emphasis on the factor; however, the consideration of the size of past contracts as one factor among a number of factors related to the relevance and quality of past performance is a proper and reasonable exercise of the agency's discretion. Maintenance Engineers v. U.S., 50 Fed. Cl. 399 (2001). United States ☞64.45(2)

Contracting agency's failure to combine the prices of two prior contracts on which offeror served as the incumbent contractor was not unreasonable, notwithstanding offeror's contention that since the contracts were run concurrently they showed an ability to manage a contract of the combined size, where there was no evidence that contracting agency automatically downgraded the offerors based on a threshold requirement of contract price. Maintenance Engineers v. U.S., 50 Fed. Cl. 399 (2001). United States ☞64.45(2)

Source selection authority's evaluations of both offerors' past performance as "Very Good" reflected a reasonable comparative evaluation of a highly relevant but not entirely positive performance history and a less relevant but very strong performance history, and the Court of Federal Claims would not disturb the evaluations absent a showing that they were without a rational basis. SDS Intern. v. U.S., 48 Fed. Cl. 759 (2001). United States ☞64.45(2)

Contracting agency may consider both relevance and quality of work in evaluating past performance and may give unequal weight to different contracts when the agency views one as more relevant than another. SDS Intern. v. U.S., 48 Fed. Cl. 759 (2001). United States ☞64.45(2)

Agency's decision to consider the manager with final authority for contract performance to be a "key person" for purpose of evaluating past performance of offeror was neither arbitrary nor capricious, notwithstanding fact that manager was not assigned to location of contract performance. 48 C.F.R. § 15.305(a)(2)(iii). SDS Intern. v. U.S., 48 Fed. Cl. 742 (2001). United States ☞64.45(2)

It was not improper for contacting agency to consider the positive corporate performance of manager's former employer when weighing the past performance of offerer on the basis of manager's past performance. SDS Intern. v. U.S., 48 Fed. Cl. 742 (2001). United States ☞64.45(2)

Even assuming that the Air Force did not know the precise extent of offeror's responsibility for problems in its performance of prior contract concerning Weapons School, it was not unreasonable for the Air Force to conclude that those problems raised "some doubt" that plaintiff would perform the proposed contract successfully. SDS Intern. v. U.S., 48 Fed. Cl. 742 (2001). United States ☞64.45(2)

Even if procuring agency violated statute and regulation by assigning protester a minor weakness for lack of past performance instead of a neutral rating, the error was not significant or prejudicial; even if agency had given protester a neutral rating, its overall rating for the experience and past performance factor would not have been affected. Office of Federal Procurement Policy Act, § 6(j)(2), as amended, 41 U.S.C.A. § 405(j)(2); 48 C.F.R. § 15.305(a)(2)(iv). Unified Architecture & Engineering, Inc. v. U.S., 46 Fed. Cl. 56 (2000), aff'd, 251 F.3d 170 (Fed. Cir. 2000). United States ☞64.45(2)

An agency, in evaluating past performance of offeror, can give more weight to one contract over another if it is more relevant to an offeror's future performance on the solicited contract. Seattle Sec. Services, Inc. v. U.S., 45 Fed. Cl. 560 (2000). United States ☞64.45(2)

Agency personnel engaged in procurement are generally given great discretion in determining what references to review in evaluating past performance of offerors; thus, there is no requirement that all references listed in a proposal be checked. Seattle Sec. Services, Inc. v. U.S., 45 Fed. Cl. 560 (2000). United States ☞64.45(2)

Contracting officer (CO) acted unreasonably in solicitation for armed guard services at federal buildings in Washington and Oregon, which combined previously separate contracts, in failing to evaluate incumbent contractor's past performance on the Oregon contract in combination with the Washington contract, as the information was simply too relevant and close at hand to ignore. Seattle Sec. Services, Inc. v. U.S., 45 Fed. Cl. 560 (2000). United States ☞64.45(2)

It is proper for evaluators of past performance of offerors to use their personal knowledge of an offeror's performance of a contract with an agency. Seattle Sec. Services, Inc. v. U.S., 45 Fed. Cl. 560 (2000). United States ☞64.45(2)

Contracting officer (CO) who made decision to award contract for repair of naval vessel did not violate section of the FAR requiring decision to set forth the rationale for any tradeoffs, including benefits associated with additional costs, where CO stated that award was based on difference between past performance ratings, and that the additional cost of award to highest proposal was justified by its higher performance rating. Marine Hydraulics Intern., Inc. v. U.S., 43 Fed. Cl. 664 (1999). United States ☞64.45(1)

Agency did not wrongfully fail to take into account offerer's past performance, where past evaluations proffered by offerer were not "interim evaluations," and they did not comply with agency's guidelines; moreover, agency sent requests for ad hoc performance evaluations to offerer's references, but none returned the questionnaire. Office of Federal Procurement Policy Act, § 6(j), 41 U.S.C.A. § 405(j); 48 C.F.R. § 42.1503(c); 48 C.F.R. § 15.608(a)(2)(ii). Advanced Data Concepts, Inc. v. U.S., 43 Fed. Cl. 410 (1999), aff'd, 216 F.3d 1054 (Fed. Cir. 2000). United States ☞64.45(2)

Contracting officer's ruling that offeror for contract to replace windows at Air Force Base was a "nonresponsible contractor" was rational and reasonable, where contractor's ratings, based on information by seven other contracting officers involved with contractor's other contracts with the military, were decidedly negative as to workmanship and timeliness. PNM Const., Inc. v. U.S., 13 Cl. Ct. 745, 34 Cont. Cas. Fed. (CCH) P 75409, 1987 WL 20987 (1987). United States ☞64.45(2)

Protest challenging agency's relevancy determinations for the awardee's past performance efforts was sustained where the solicitation required an assessment of the magnitude of the offerors' past efforts relative to the solicited requirement and where the record fails to show how the awardee's comparatively low-value past efforts reasonably could have been assessed as somewhat relevant. XPO Logistics Worldwide Gov't Servs., LLC, B-412628.6 et al., 2017 CPD ¶ 88 (Comp. Gen. 2017)

Agency's past performance evaluation was unreasonable because it downgraded the protester's past performance score despite additional, highly rated, past performance references. Specifically, the awardee and the protester both had two very relevant past performance contracts rated "exceptional" but the protester also had two additional references that were "relevant" and rated "exceptional" and another that was "very relevant" and rated "very good." The agency's evaluation was unreasonable because these additional past performance references resulted in a downgraded past performance rating. Patricio Enters., B-412740, 2016 CPD ¶ 145 (Comp. Gen. 2016)

Protest challenging the agency's past performance evaluation is sustained where the agency mechanically determined that, because the awardee and the protester both received "Satisfactory" past performance ratings, that past performance could be eliminated as a basis for award. The GAO held that this approach failed to "fulfill the requirement for a documented decision based on a comparative assessment of proposals against all source selection criteria in the solicitation." EFW Inc., B-412608, et al., 2016 CPD ¶ 304 (Comp. Gen. 2016)

Generally, an agency's evaluation under an experience factor is distinct from its evaluation of an offeror's past performance. Specifically, experience focuses on the degree to which an offeror has actually performed similar work, whereas past performance focuses on the quality of the work. The evaluation of experience and past performance, by its very nature, is subjective, and a vendor's disagreement with an agency's evaluation judgments does not demonstrate that those judgments are unreasonable. Amyx, Inc., B-410623, 2015 CPD ¶ 45 (Comp.Gen. 2015)

Protest that agency misevaluated proposals was sustained because agency improperly credited awardee with experience of two team members, even though the proposal did not clearly detail or explain how the team members would contribute meaningfully to contract performance, as required by solicitation. Alutiiq Pacific, LLC, B-409584, 2014 CPD ¶ 196 (Comp. Gen. 2014)

Protest was sustained where the Source Selection Authority used the awardee's good past performance to offset the relative technical weaknesses of the awardee's quotation, even though the awardee and the protester had the same past performance score. PricewaterhouseCoopers LLP, B-409537, 2014 CPD ¶ 255 (Comp. Gen. 2014)

A solicitation that provides that the experience and past performance of an offeror's affiliates will not be considered, even for proposals that demonstrate that affiliates will participate meaningfully in contract performance, is unduly restrictive of competition where the agency fails to provide an explanation—even during or after a hearing on the question—that sets forth a reasonable basis for the restriction. Iyabak Constr., LLC, B-409196, 2014 CPD ¶ 62 (Comp. Gen. 2014)

Protest was sustained because the source selection record was "devoid of any substantive consideration or comparative assessment as to the evaluated differences of the offerors' past performance." Although the agency identified clear differences between the protester's rating of "Substantial Confidence" and the awardee's rating of "Satisfactory Confidence", the source selection authority did not document her basis for concluding that the differences were insignificant. NOVA Corp., B-408046, 2013 CPD ¶ 127 (Comp. Gen. 2013)

An agency unreasonably credited a joint venture with past performance and corporate experience from one partner's separate affiliates, where the affiliates would not be relied upon during contract performance. IAP World Servs, Inc.; EMCOR Govt. Servs., B-407917.2, 2013 CPD ¶ 171 (Comp. Gen. 2013)

An agency properly may attribute the experience or past performance of a parent or affiliated company to an offeror where the firm's proposal or quotation demonstrates that the resources of the parent or affiliate will affect the performance of the offeror. The relevant consideration is whether the resources of the parent or affiliated company-e.g., its workforce, management, facilities or other resources-will be provided or relied upon for contract performance such that the parent or affiliate will have meaningful involvement in contract performance. IAP World Servs., Inc.; EMCOR Gov't Servs., B-407917.2 et al., 2013 CPD ¶ 171 (Comp. Gen. 2013)

Under a small business 8(a) set-aside in which the small business prime contractor was required to perform 51% of the work, GAO determined that it was reasonable for the agency to give greater weight to the past performance of the prime contractor than to that of the subcontractors. Miracle Sys. LLC, B-407324.7, 2013 CPD ¶ 78 (Comp. Gen. 2013)

Protest was sustained because the agency's evaluation of past performance was unreasonable and inconsistent with the solicitation, in that the agency did not meaningfully assess the relevance of the offerors' prior contracts. The past performance evaluations assumed that the past performance references were relevant and focused primarily on the quality of the offeror's past performance records. The Emergence Group, B-404844.5, 2012 CPD ¶ 132 (Comp. Gen. 2012)

GAO sustained protest challenging agency's assignment of highest possible experience/ past performance rating to awardee's proposal under size and complexity evaluation element where solicitation required prior contracts to meet a defined dollar threshold and none of awardee's contracts met the threshold. Supreme Foodservice GmbH, B-405400.3, 2012 CPD ¶ 292 (Comp. Gen. 2012)

Protest of an agency evaluation of the awardee's past performance is sustained, where the solicitation provided for the evaluation of projects that were similar in scope and complexity, and there is no explanation in the record or in response to the protest explaining why the awardee's smaller-value past performance projects were similar in scope and complexity. Matter of: U S Information Technologies Corporation, B-404357, B-404357.2, 2011 CPD ¶ 74 (Comp. Gen. 2011)

An agency's "exceptional" past performance rating for the awardee's proposal was not reasonable because the agency did not consider adverse past performance information received from prior customers of the awardee. Matter of: Northeast Military Sales, Inc., B-404153, 2011 CPD ¶ 2 (Comp. Gen. 2011)

An agency's past performance evaluation was unreasonable because the agency did not consider relevant adverse past performance information that the protester had provided to the agency regarding the awardee. Protester had provided adverse information regarding the awardee's performance contained in an IG Report and a news article Matter of: Contrack International, Inc., B-401871.5, B-401871.6, B-401871.7, 2010 CPD ¶ 126 (Comp. Gen. 2010)

Agency's solicitation requirement that prime contractor have two years of family advocacy program (FAP) experience was unduly restrictive because the agency did not show why the prime could not satisfy the experience requirement by teaming with a subcontractor with the requisite experience. Matter of: Total Health Resources, B-403209, 2010 CPD ¶ 226 (Comp. Gen. 2010)

An agency improperly failed to consider questionnaire responses it received regarding the protester's past performance. GAO held that, although agencies are not required to consider all past performance information, some information is so "close at hand" that it is unreasonable for an agency not to consider it. GAO stated that completed past performance questionnaires "in an agency's possession [is] information too close at hand to ignore." Matter of: Shaw-Parsons Infrastructure Recovery Consultants, LLC; Vanguard Recovery Assistance, Joint Venture, B-401679.4, B-401679.5, B-401679.6, B-401679.7, 2010 CPD ¶ 77 (Comp. Gen. 2010)

An agency improperly evaluated an awardee and protester unequally by crediting the awardee with its subcontractor's experience, but not crediting the protester with its subcontractor's experience, even though the agency viewed both subcontractors as having relevant experience. Matter of: Ahtna Support and Training Services, LLC, B-400947.2, 2009 CPD ¶ 119 (Comp. Gen. 2009)

Past performance evaluation was unreasonable because the findings in the agency's evaluation report were not consistent with the information upon which the findings were based. The agency could not determine whether proper consideration was given to adverse past performance and the relevance of an offeror's prior contracts was not assessed. Matter of: DRSC3 Systems, LLC, B-310825, B-310825.2, 2008 CPD ¶ 103 (Comp. Gen. 2008)

It is improper for an agency to consider the past experience of an offeror's parent or affiliated company as an indication of qualification for a project if a solicitation precludes such consideration The solicitation instructed that projects submitted should demonstrate the capabilities of the offeror and, more specifically, should only be ones for which the offeror or a primary teaming partner was the prime contractor. In contrast, the awardees in this case submitted projects performed by parent or affiliate corporations, and the agency ultimately relied on those projects. Matter of: Doyon-American Mechanical, JV; NAJV, LLC, B-310003, B-310003.2, 2008 CPD ¶ 50 (Comp. Gen. 2007)

The past performance of proposed subcontractors may properly be considered in evaluating the past performance of an offeror where the solicitation does not expressly prohibit its consideration. Indtai Inc., B-298432.3, 2007 CPD ¶ 13 (Comp. Gen. 2007)

Protester's contention that agency past performance evaluation was unreasonable because the agency did not distinguish between degrees of relevance in evaluating each vendor's past performance is denied where the evaluation was reasonable, and consistent with the stated evaluation criteria; there is no *per se* requirement that an agency weight differently the ratings given each vendor based on an assessment of the relative relevance of the vendor's prior contracts. Matter of: Paragon Systems, Inc., B-299548.2, 2007 CPD ¶ 178 (Comp. Gen. 2007)

Protest that the agency's evaluation of the protester's past performance was unreasonable is sustained where the record evidences that the protester and awardee were not treated equally with regard to the agency's efforts to contact past performance references, and the record does not provide a reasonable explanation for the agency's conclusions regarding the protester's past performance, including what if any impact the agency's receipt of contract performance assessment reports had on its evaluation. Family Entertainment Services, Inc., B-298047.3, 2007 CPD ¶ 59 (Comp. Gen. 2006)

Protest that past performance evaluation was unreasonable is sustained where agency used methodology to determine performance confidence ratings that improperly penalized offerors with relevant experience for their non-relevant experience and that effectively gave equal weight to highly relevant and non-relevant performance. United Paradyne Corporation, B-297758, 2006 CPD ¶ 47 (Comp. Gen. 2006)

Agency properly considered past performance record of predecessor company of awardee in evaluation where solicitation specifically provided that such information would be considered. Trailboss Enterprises, Inc., B-297742, 2006 CPD ¶ 64 (Comp. Gen. 2006)

Evaluators may consider and rely upon their personal knowledge in the course of evaluating an offeror's past performance. It is not necessarily improper for an agency evaluator to also serve as an offeror's past performance reference where there has been no showing of improper influence on the evaluation or award determination. Del-Jen International Corporation, B-297960, 2006 CPD ¶ 81 (Comp. Gen. 2006).

An agency may consider an offeror's lack of relevant past performance in conjunction with the "Exceptional" past performance of a proposed subcontractor and assign an overall past performance rating of "Very Good." There is nothing improper in an agency's giving weight to an offeror's own lack of relevant past performance-and the neutral weighting that goes with it-along with giving weight to, for example, a proposed subcontractor's past performance, when developing an overall rating for that offeror. Triad Logistics Services Corporation, B-296511.3, 2005 CPD ¶ 189 (Comp. Gen. 2005)

Under FAR 15.305(a)(2)(iv), an RFP may provide that firms lacking relevant past performance will receive a neutral/unknown confidence rating. An agency RFP provided that a neutral/unknown rating would have no positive or negative evaluation significance. The awardee lacked relevant experience and the agency assigned it a neutral rating for the past performance factor. Since the RFP stated that a neutral rating would have no negative effect on the evaluation, the agency properly determined that the awardee's neutral rating did not render the firm ineligible for award. Matter of: M & M Ret. Enterprises, LLC, B-297282, 2005 CPD ¶ 224 (Comp. Gen. 2005)

Agency's unfavorable evaluation of protester's proposal under a past performance subfactor was improper where the effect of the low rating was to penalize the protester for a lack of past performance information that the agency deemed relevant to this subfactor. The MIL Corporation, B-294836, 2005 CPD ¶ 29 (Comp. Gen. 2004)

Protesters contention that an agency's evaluation of its past performance was unreasonable because the agency overlooked the protesters most recent performance report related to the predecessor contract for the services being procured is denied where the agency's error was mitigated by its supplemental use of questionnaires and interviews related to the protesters performance on the earlier contract, resulting in the protesters receipt of the highest possible past performance rating. AIROD Sdn. Bhd., B-294127, 2004 CPD ¶ 156 (Comp. Gen. 2004).

In evaluating past performance, agency's assignment of neutral rating for past performance to the protester was reasonable where the protester's referenced past performance was either of far less magnitude than, or different from, the work being solicited. CMC & Maintenance, Inc., B-292081, 2003 CPD ¶ 107 (Comp. Gen. 2003)

Protest challenging agency's evaluation of the protester's and awardee's past performance, which found the two firms had essentially equal past performance, is sustained, where the agency did not consider awardee's record of integrity and business ethics, as required by the solicitation, and the record raises serious concerns that awardee may have problems in this area, and where agency did not document its assessment of protester's past performance, despite the fact that solicitation provided for qualitative assessment of offerors' past performance. Southwestern Bell Telephone Company, B-292476, 2003 CPD ¶ 177 (Comp. Gen. 2003)

Agency reasonably assigned the protester's past performance a neutral rating where the reference listed by the protester for the only contract considered relevant to the solicited work declined to respond to the past performance questionnaire, despite repeated requests by the agency. MCS of Tampa, Inc., B-288271.5, 2002 CPD ¶ 52 (Comp. Gen. 2002)

Agency reasonably found protester's proposal technically unacceptable under experience and past performance evaluation criterion, where record shows that protester failed to submit required detailed information showing that its proposed key subcontractors had previously performed contracts similar to the solicited effort; offerors have an affirmative duty to prepare an adequately written proposal. Menendez-Donnel & Associates, B-286599, 2001 CPD ¶ 15 (Comp. Gen. 2001)

Where the protester's proposal included negative performance information from an accrediting organization, and the protester failed to dispel the legitimate concerns raised by this information during discussions, the agency had no obligation to disregard the negative performance information simply because it did not suffice to deny the protester accreditation, nor was the agency required to contact the accrediting organization to investigate the information. Rotech Medical Corporation, B-283295.2, 99-2 CPD ¶ 86 (Comp. Gen. 1999).

Agency unequally evaluated the experience of the protester and the awardee, where both firms were newly formed corporations, yet the agency did not downgrade the awardee's proposal, as it did the protester's, for not evidencing significant corporate experience, but considered the experience of the awardee's proposed key personnel to determine the awardee's proposal to be superior in experience, but did not do so with regard to the protester's proposed personnel. U.S. Property Management Service Corporation, B-278727, 98-1 CPD ¶ 88 (Comp. Gen. 1998).

Protest that contracting agency improperly evaluated offerors' past performance is sustained where the record shows that, with respect to both offerors, the agency ignored relevant information that was personally known to one of the agency evaluators, and where the agency failed to comply with the solicitation's evaluation criteria with respect to the past performance evaluation. While there is no legal requirement that all past performance references be included in a valid review of past performance, some information is simply too close at hand to ignore. GTS Duratek, Inc., B-280511.2, B-280511.3, 98-2 CPD ¶ 130 (Comp. Gen. 1998).

Evaluators are prohibited from ignoring past performance information of which they are personally aware. Such information is simply too close at hand to be reasonably ignored in the agency's evaluation of proposals, even if omitted from the offeror's proposal. GTS Duratek, Inc., B-280511.2, B-280511.3, 98-2 CPD ¶ 130 (Comp. Gen. 1998).

The contracting officer properly considered the performance record of a proposed subcontractor in making a determination that an offeror was nonresponsible. A contracting officer must make an affirmative determination that a prospective prime contractor is responsible before awarding a contract. FAR 9.104(b). The quality of the subcontractors that a prospective prime contractor designates may influence the contracting officer's determination. FAR 9.104-4(a). While a prospective prime contractor generally determines the responsibility of its subcontractors, federal regulations authorize a contracting officer directly to determine a subcontractor's responsibility when a contract involves substantial subcontracting. Matter of: L & M Mercadeo Internacional, S.A., B-250637, 93-1 CPD ¶ 124 (Comp. Gen. 1993)

Where an offeror was involved as a subcontractor or joint venturer in performing work under a prior contract similar to work to be included under the instant contract, such experience may properly be considered in assessing that offeror's past performance. Matter of: Phillips National, Inc., B-253875, 93-2 CPD ¶ 252 (Comp. Gen. 1993).

6.5 Evaluation Factors—Risk

Agency unreasonably assigned performance risk to the protester's proposal because of the date of a Dun & Bradstreet (D&B) report, not because of the report's content. Matter of: Velos, Inc., B-400500.8, B-400500.9, 2010 CPD ¶ 13 (Comp. Gen. 2009)

GAO sustained a protest because an agency did not reasonably apply a solicitation criterion stating that offerors with existing production capabilities would be considered less risky than offerors that do not have currently existing facilities. The evaluation was unreasonable because the agency rated the awardee and the protester equally on the facility factor even though the protester currently had a suitable facility and the awardee had to make arrangements to acquire the necessary facilities. Matter of: Navistar Defense, LLC; BAE Systems, Tactical Vehicle Systems LP, B-401865, B-401865.2, B-401865.3, B-401865.4, B-401865.5, B-401865.6, B-401865.7, 2009 CPD ¶ 258 (Comp. Gen. 2009).

7 Evaluation factors—Personnel, evaluation factors

Protest challenging agency's determination that it's proposed key personnel were unacceptable was denied, even though the proposed key personnel met the minimum education and experience requirements. However, the resumes for the proposed key personnel did not address the specific skills referenced in the attachment to the position description, as required by the solicitation instructions. URS Fed. Servs., Inc., B-413333, 2016 CPD ¶ 286 (Comp. Gen. 2016)

Source selection authority's consideration of the experience of offeror's "key personnel" was not improper in evaluation of past performance on ground that the request for proposals (RFP) did not call for such consideration, as term "references" in the RFP did not specifically call for corporate experience as distinguished from experience of key personnel; moreover, the Federal Acquisition Regulation (FAR) provides that evaluators "should take into account" the experience of key personnel. 48 C.F.R. § 15.305(a)(2)(iii). SDS Intern. v. U.S., 48 Fed. Cl. 759 (2001). United States ☞64.45(2)

Apparent successful offeror on a Navy technical support services contract failed to prove that the harm it would realize due to the Government's reopening of negotiations after disclosure of the apparent successful offeror's proposed cost, would exceed the harm to the procurement process if negotiations were not reopened, in light of the damage that the procuring agency certainly would suffer if forced to accept personnel who did not satisfy minimum personnel qualification sheet requirements for experience in electronic warfare. Logicon, Inc. v. U.S., 22 Cl. Ct. 776, 37 Cont. Cas. Fed. (CCH) P 76066, 1991 WL 52823 (1991). United States ☞64.50

Protest challenging the agency's evaluation of the awardee's program manager, a key personnel position, was sustained because the proposed individual did not have managerial experience, as required by the solicitation. Prof'l Serv. Indus., Inc., B-412721.2, et al., 2016 CPD ¶ 234 (Comp. Gen. 2016)

To demonstrate an improper bait and switch of proposed key personnel, a protester must show that (1) the offeror knowingly or negligently misrepresented the personnel that it planned to use, (2) the agency relied on the misrepresentation and (3) the misrepresentation materially affected the evaluation results. An awardee's replacement of key personnel, hiring of incumbent personnel and recruitment efforts did not establish a bait and switch. Invertix Corp., B-411329.2, 2015 CPD ¶ 197 (Comp. Gen. 2015)

Protest that the issuance of a task order was inconsistent with the terms of a solicitation is sustained because the agency awarded the contract based on a proposal in which key personnel failed to satisfy several mandatory qualification requirements. Trandes Corp., B-411742, et al., 2015 CPD ¶ 317 (Comp. Gen. 2015)

GAO found that the agency applied unstated evaluation factors when it assessed a weakness under the key personnel factor because the Program Manager (PM) was not certified as a "program management professional" (PMP) and would also be serving as a corporate officer. Even though the RFP did advise offerors that the key personnel factor would be evaluated based on "the information contained in the resumes for potential staff members submitted with the proposals and their qualifications", the GAO found that PMP status and the PM's dual status were unstated evaluation factors and sustained the protest. Matter of: Powersolv, Inc., B-402534, B-402534.2, 2010 CPD ¶ 206 (Comp. Gen. 2010)

Protest that awardee misrepresented that three proposed key personnel had agreed to work for the firm is sustained where the record shows that the three individuals had not so agreed, and where the misrepresentation materially affected the evaluation of the awardee's proposal. ACS Government Services, Inc., B-293014, 2004 CPD ¶ 18 (Comp. Gen. 2004)

Agency properly eliminated protester's proposal from consideration on the basis of its inadequate proposed staffing where solicitation specifically directed offerors to address the staffing of the various contract requirements, advised offerors that their proposed staffing approach would be a subject for evaluation, stated that a proposal which failed to provide a proposed approach that would successfully meet the contract requirements would be rated as "unacceptable," and provided that any such proposal would be eliminated from the competition. TDF Corporation, B-288392, B-288392.2, 2001 CPD ¶ 178 (Comp. Gen. 2001)

Where an offeror proposes a particular individual for a key position with the intention of removing that individual from the position after an unspecified transition period under the contract, and the agency relies on the offeror's representation that the individual will be performing the work in evaluating its proposal, the agency reasonably rejected the proposal once the agency learned of the offeror's actual intent. S. C. Myers & Associates, Inc., B-286297, 2001 CPD ¶ 16 (Comp. Gen. 2000)

Proposal delivered by U.S. Postal Service Express Mail to agency mail room approximately 1 hour and 20 minutes before time established for receipt of proposals but not routed to the contracting office specified in solicitation until after the time set for receipt of proposals was properly rejected as late where: (1) offeror failed to identify the package as containing a proposal and otherwise failed to mark it with an identifying solicitation number or closing date deadline and time; and (2) offeror allowed only 1 day for delivery. Russo & Sons, Inc., B-280948, 98-2 CPD ¶ 141 (Comp. Gen. 1998)

8 Evaluation factors—HUBZones, evaluation factors

Contracting agency properly applied Historically Underutilized Business Zone (HUBZone) evaluation preference when it added a 10% margin to proposal prices offered by non-HUBZone offerors to determine whether price of HUBZone offeror could be deemed lower than that of the other offerors, but not for purpose of determining whether non-HUBZone offerors should be eliminated from competition because their proposal prices exceeded budget ceilings for line-items. Small Business Act, § 2[2](b)(3)(A), as amended, 15 U.S.C.A. § 657a(b)(3)(A). Metcalf Const. Co., Inc. v. U.S., 53 Fed. Cl. 617 (2002). United States ☞64.15

9 Evaluation of proposals, generally

Contracting officer's rejection of procurement of services proposal for private operation of Government wholesale distribution center, pursuant to federal acquisition regulations, was not irrational when based in part upon officer's finding that offeror did not understand complexity of center and would have understaffed it, where offeror was not able to demonstrate how it would assign and utilize personnel upon assuming operation, and where offeror's time and motion studies, used to support its staffing calculations, did not contain empirical data or factual bases for their conclusions. CACI Field Services, Inc. v. U.S., 854 F.2d 464, 34 Cont. Cas. Fed. (CCH) P 75537 (Fed. Cir. 1988). United States ☞64.45(3)

The COFC rejected protester's argument that NASA applied an unstated evaluation criterion. The protester relied on a statement in the Source Selection Authority's (SSA) decision document stating: "I was concerned that the proposal did not contain a backup plan in the event one of the major subcontractors was unable to perform," because the solicitation did not expressly require submission of a "backup plan." The COFC stated that a solicitation need not identify criteria intrinsic to the stated evaluation factors because agencies have great discretion in determining the scope of an evaluation factor. The court denied the protest based on its determination that the absence of a backup plan was fairly encompassed by the "management plan" subfactor, which the RFP stated would include an assessment of risk and soundness of the management approach. PlanetSpace, Inc. v. U.S., 92 Fed. Cl. 520 (2010), subsequent determination, 96 Fed. Cl. 119 (2010).

Protest was denied where the request for proposals indicated that metropolitan presence would be considered in evaluating proposals, and therefore the protester's assertion that the agency used an unstated evaluation criteria lacked merit. "Metropolitan presence" was considered to be within the scope of the stated evaluation factor of "response time." NEQ, LLC v. U.S., 88 Fed. Cl. 38 (2009)

Disappointed offerors who were included in competitive range were prejudiced by contracting officer's error in failing to consider price evaluation factor in establishing competitive range, where contract awardee's proposal would likely have been excluded from competitive range if price had been considered a factor, and thus disappointed offerors would have had a substantial chance of being awarded the contract. Information Sciences Corp. v. U.S., 73 Fed. Cl. 70 (2006), on reconsideration in part, 75 Fed. Cl. 406 (2007). United States ☞64.55(1)

Government is not permitted to rely upon undisclosed evaluation criteria when evaluating proposals during a procurement. Computer Sciences Corp. v. U.S., 51 Fed. Cl. 297 (2002). United States ☞64.40(2)

An agency's source selection decision is invalid when the underlying evaluation record does not support it. Computer Sciences Corp. v. U.S., 51 Fed. Cl. 297 (2002). United States ☞64.45(1)

A procuring agency may evaluate proposals only on the basis of the factors identified and their stated relative importance. Information Technology & Applications Corp. v. U.S., 51 Fed. Cl. 340 (2001), decision aff'd, 316 F.3d 1312 (Fed. Cir. 2003). United States ☞64.40(1)

Mere fact that a consensus score in a proposal evaluation may deviate from the agency's individual evaluators' scores, does not, per se, render the final consensus rating questionable. Bean Stuyvesant, L.L.C. v. U.S., 48 Fed. Cl. 303 (2000). United States ☞64.40(1)

Agency evaluators may meet to discuss the relative strengths and weaknesses of proposals, in order to reach a consensus rating, which often differs from the ratings given by individual evaluators, since such discussions generally operate to correct mistakes or misperceptions that may have occurred in the initial evaluation; overriding concern in the evaluation process is that the final scores assigned reasonably reflect the actual merits of the proposals, and not that they be mechanically traceable back to the scores initially given by the individual evaluators. Bean Stuyvesant, L.L.C. v. U.S., 48 Fed. Cl. 303 (2000). United States ☞64.40(1)

Procuring agency violated procurement statute and provisions of the Federal Acquisition Regulation by improperly crediting proposal with meeting technical requirements of the solicitation, even though offeror failed to identify a volunteer coordinator, as required by solicitation. 10 U.S.C.A. § 2305(b)(1); 48 C.F.R. §§ 15.303(b), 15.305(a), 15.308. Mangi Environmental Group, Inc. v. U.S., 47 Fed. Cl. 10 (2000). United States ☞64.30

Duty of verification of offer exists regardless of whether a solicitation is characterized as negotiated or sealed. 48 C.F.R. § 14.406-1 (1994). Griffy's Landscape Maintenance LLC v. U.S., 46 Fed. Cl. 257 (2000). United States ☞64.40(3)

Contract award was not required to be set aside, based upon noncompliance with proposal solicitation provision calling for members of evaluation board to score technical proposals individually, discuss proposals collectively and arrive at consensus for summary report to contracting officer, even though one member only rescored technical proposal, after initial scoring by board members, and recommendation went forward based on single member's scoring; board chairperson indicated that report represented "consensus" of board when transmitting it to contracting officer, rescoring reduced points of others besides disappointed offeror, and board report was merely advisory. Federal Property and Administrative Services Act of 1949, § 303b(a), as amended, 41 U.S.C.A. § 253b(a); 48 C.F.R. § 15.608(a). United Intern. Investigative Services v. U.S., 42 Fed. Cl. 73, 42 Cont. Cas. Fed. (CCH) P 77394 (1998), aff'd, 194 F.3d 1335 (Fed. Cir. 1999). United States ☞64.40(1)

Determination of evaluation panel, during second phase of application process for awarding concessions contract, that applicant did not satisfy financing criteria did not preclude applicant from further consideration, in view of use of negotiation procedure rather than sealed bidding procedure in awarding contract; applicant was considered at each stage of review, but was not awarded contract when competitor was found to have submitted best overall offer. YRT Services Corp. v. U.S., 28 Fed. Cl. 366, 38 Cont. Cas. Fed. (CCH) P 76512

(1993). United States ☞64.15

Protest was sustained where the agency unreasonably failed to consider the cost and performance impacts of the anticipated split of the awardee into two entities shortly after the performance start date of the contract. Wyle Labs. Inc., Comp. Gen. Dec. B-408112.2, 2014 CPD ¶ 16 (Comp. Gen. 2013)

Protest challenging the award decision under a GSA competition for federal office space was sustained because the Head of Contracting Activity (HCA) did not meaningfully consider the evaluated differences in the offerors' proposals in her selection decision. The solicitation required GSA to evaluate both the overall number of facility amenities offered as well as the variety. GSA's simple counting of categories, such as hair salons or automotive service stations, ignored the type of amenity being offered. Matter of: One Largo Metro LLC; Metroview Development Holdings, LLC; King Farm Associates, LLC, B-404896, B-404896.2, B-404896.3, B-404896.4, B-404896.5, B-404896.6, B-404896.7, 2011 CPD ¶ 128 (Comp. Gen. 2011).

Protest of agency evaluation is sustained where record reflects that agency failed to consider one of evaluation factors established by terms of solicitation. Agency's pass/fail evaluation of resumes was inconsistent with the qualitative approach described in the RFP. Mission Essential Personnel, LLC, B-404218.2, 2011 CPD ¶ 120 (Comp. Gen. 2011)

An agency's proposal evaluation was unreasonable because the agency favorably evaluated the awardee's proposal based on an enhancement, even though the proposal required the agency to accept the enhancement by a specific date and the date had passed without agency action. Med. Dev. Int'l, Inc., B-402198.2, 2011 CPD ¶ 185 (Comp. Gen. 2011)

Protest challenging agency's selection of firms with which to negotiate contracts for architect/engineering services is sustained where agency's final selections were based solely on results of oral interviews and did not consider specific evaluation factors listed in the solicitation. EBA Ernest Bland Assocs., P.C., B-404825.5, et al., 2011 CPD ¶ 212 (Comp. Gen. 2011)

Agency was not required to evaluate information relevant to one evaluation factor because the information was contained in a proposal section pertaining to another evaluation factor, even though the offeror cross-referenced the other proposal section. Although the RFP did not specifically prohibit cross-referencing, the solicitation specified page limitations for responses under each evaluation factor and considering information in another section would negate the intended effect of the page limitation. Outreach Process Partners, LLC, B-405529, 2011 CPD ¶ 255, 2011 WL 5866256 (Comp. Gen. 2011)

An agency's evaluation was unreasonable because it evaluated two proposals unequally by crediting the awardee for a subcontractor's experience and past performance, but not similarly crediting the protester, which proposed the same subcontractor. Matter of: Brican Inc., B-402602, 2010 CPD ¶ 141 (Comp. Gen. 2010)

An agency's evaluation of an awardee's proposal was unreasonable because the record did not demonstrate a reasonable basis for the evaluators' conclusion that the awardee complied with the solicitation's requirement to submit a transition plan and project milestones. Although the protester did submit these documents as attachments, the Contracting Officer removed them because the proposal exceeded the solicitation's page limitation, and the pertinent information was in the excess pages. Matter of: Irving Burton Associates, Inc., B-401983.3, 2010 CPD ¶ 92 (Comp. Gen. 2010)

An agency improperly rejected as unacceptable an offer that included data that provided a better understanding of the offeror's capabilities. The agency requested a percentage of staff holding third-party certification, and the offeror submitted the actual number of staff members holding such certification. Matter of: Engineering Management & Integration, Inc., B-400356.4, B-400356.5, 2009 CPD ¶ 114 (Comp. Gen. 2009)

An agency improperly evaluated proposals because it considered one of four factors on a pass/fail basis instead of the designated qualitative basis, and because it evaluated past performance with no contemporaneous documentation of oral discussion for the basis of the evaluation. Decision Matter of: Helicopter Transport Services LLC, B-400295, B-400295.2, 2008 CPD ¶ 180 (Comp. Gen. 2008)

A source selection decision that discusses strengths but not weaknesses of the awardee's proposal and relies on incorrectly calculated costs is not reasonably based, and justified sustaining the protest. Matter of: Fedcar Company, Ltd., B-310980, B-310980.2, B-310980.3, 2008 CPD ¶ 70 (Comp. Gen. 2008)

An agency's decision to award a contract was flawed because the agency did not hold meaningful discussions with an offeror on the significant weakness of its proposed staffing plan, materially affecting the final selection, the U.S. Comptroller General recently determined. The agency also lacked a reasonable basis for its vendor selection because it unreasonably did not consider the winning proposal's identified weakness. Matter of: AT & T Corp., B-299542.3, B-299542.4, 2008 CPD ¶ 65 (Comp. Gen. 2007)

An agency must follow the stated terms of its request for quotations in awarding a contract. When an RFQ states that technical factors will be given greater weight than price, an agency cannot then make an award determination based on price among technically acceptable quotations. Matter of: GlassLock, Inc., B-299931, B-299931.2, 2007 CPD ¶ 216 (Comp. Gen. 2007)

In not allowing technically acceptable offerors to make oral presentations as part of their technical proposals, agency acted inconsistently with the solicitation provision that all offerors would be afforded the opportunity to make oral presentations. Kathpal Technologies, Inc.; Computer & Hi-Tech Management, Inc., B-283137.3, B-283137.4, B-283137.5, B-283137.6, 2000 CPD ¶ 6 (Comp. Gen. 1999)

10 Ranking

Protestor did not establish that contracting agency disparately and unequally downgraded its technical and management scores when it rescored technical and management factors because chair of evaluation panel was concerned that panel members were incorrectly scoring the proposals; there was no indication that the panel applied different standards when re-scoring the proposals, and mere fact that the rescoring resulted in protestor's score going down, a disparate result, does not mean that protestor was treated unfairly or differently. Dismas Charities, Inc. v. U.S., 61 Fed. Cl. 191 (2004). United States ☞64.45(1)

Point scoring system used by contracting agency to evaluate technical proposals was proper and consistent with the solicitation, notwithstanding protestor's contention that method for converting the scores from raw points to weighted points was improper; it was acceptable and rational for agency to translate raw scores from evaluation checklists into a weighted score that reflected equal weight for each technical subfactor. Dismas Charities, Inc. v. U.S., 61 Fed. Cl. 191 (2004). United States ☞64.45(1)

Generally, the details of technical rating decisions in a procurement involve discretionary determinations that a court will not second guess. Dismas Charities, Inc. v. U.S., 61 Fed. Cl. 191 (2004). United States ☞64.45(1)

Protestor did not establish that contracting agency violated procurement regulation governing source selection decision by employing a "purely mathematical methodology" for calculating point totals and awarding contracts; rather, source selection authority (SSA) utilized points as a tool for weighing the strengths and weaknesses of each contractor in each different category, not as an impermissible purely mathematical calculation. 48 C.F.R. § 15.308. Bannum, Inc. v. U.S., 60 Fed. Cl. 718 (2004). United States ☞64.45(2)

Coast Guard did not act arbitrarily or capriciously in rating both disappointed and successful offerors on solicitation to construct Coast Guard icebreaker as "excellent" in past performance evaluation, despite fact that disappointed offeror was rated "excellent" on all four factors of past performance, while successful offeror received only a "good" rating on quality of product factor; solicitation's emphasis on overall customer satisfaction factor, on which successful offeror received a rating of "excellent," and which was equal in weight to the other three factors, cost control, timeliness of performance, and quality of product, combined, supported Coast Guard's evaluation. Halter Marine, Inc. v. U.S., 56 Fed. Cl. 144 (2003). United States ☞64.45(2)

Contracting agency acted arbitrarily when it ranked offeror third technically without providing support in the record for such ranking; agency ranked all three offerors "acceptable" on technical evaluation and failed to articulate the specific advantages that made one proposal of higher quality than another, and although it recorded the strengths and weakness of all of the offerors, it placed no particular emphasis on those areas, positively or negatively. Metcalf Const. Co., Inc. v. U.S., 53 Fed. Cl. 617 (2002). United States ☞64.40(1)

Error in rating offeror "acceptable (A)," rather than "highly acceptable (HA)," on small business utilization factor of technical evaluation was not prejudicial where, although offerer's elimination from competition might not have occurred if had a higher technical ranking, offeror's overall technical ranking was not the direct result of the number of HA's given, since the technical evaluation board (TEB) had previously ranked offeror third despite the fact that all offerors, as of that date, had two HA's and three A's. Metcalf Const. Co., Inc. v. U.S., 53 Fed. Cl. 617 (2002). United States ☞64.45(2)

Disappointed offeror did not establish that technical evaluation board (TEB) was arbitrary or capricious in giving its proposal a "poor" rating, where it offered little more than disagreements with the boards' overall assessment of the adequacy of its proposal, and did not show that the TEB's findings were unsupported by the administrative record or inconsistent with the evaluation criteria. JWK Intern. Corp. v. U.S., 52 Fed. Cl. 650 (2002), aff'd, 56 Fed. Appx. 474 (Fed. Cir. 2003). United States ☞64.45(2)

Protestor did not establish that contracting agency improperly weighed elements of cross-utilization, integration, and innovation which were present in mission capability subfactors; record reflected that agency evaluated the mission capability subfactors giving consideration, in accordance with the terms of the request for proposals (RFP), to those proposed innovations and enhancements that it deemed to be strengths. Information Technology & Applications Corp. v. U.S., 51 Fed. Cl. 340 (2001), decision aff'd, 316 F.3d 1312 (Fed. Cir. 2003). United States ☞64.45(2)

Protestor did not establish that high risk rating it received for subfactor of its technical proposal was based on an inaccurate independent cost estimate performed by the government which ignored its use of off-the-shelf solutions; protestor failed to explain in its proposal how the incorporation of the off-the-shelf technology would support the significant reduction in it proposed labor hours. Information Technology & Applications Corp. v. U.S., 51 Fed. Cl. 340 (2001), decision aff'd, 316 F.3d 1312 (Fed. Cir. 2003). United States ☞64.45(2)

A contracting officer (CO) does not have the discretion to employ a rigid point system for evaluating one offeror's references and not use the same system to evaluate another offeror's references. Seattle Sec. Services, Inc. v. U.S., 45 Fed. Cl. 560 (2000). United States ☞64.45(2)

Contracting officer (CO) acted unreasonably in employing evaluation forms which utilized a rigid point system to evaluate one offeror's references, but not employing the same forms in evaluating another offeror's references. Seattle Sec. Services, Inc. v. U.S., 45 Fed. Cl. 560 (2000). United States ☞64.45(2)

Protestor did not show that agency acted in a manner that was arbitrary, capricious, an abuse of discretion, and in bad faith when the source selection authority (SSA) rejected the recommendation of technical evaluation board to lower contract awardee's rating from highly satisfactory to acceptable. J & D Maintenance and Services v. U.S., 45 Fed. Cl. 532 (1999). United States ☞64.45(2)

Agency's award of contract for electronic scoreboards was arbitrary and capricious; agency's determination that awardee's proposal was technically acceptable was unreasonable, and protestor's proposals should have received higher evaluation ratings. Dubinsky v. U.S., 43 Fed. Cl. 243 (1999). United States ☞64.45(1)

Government's addition of one point to point total of offeror on proposals to furnish security services to federal courthouses, raising offeror from third place overall to first place, did not constitute rescoring to support predetermined procurement decision, in violation of procurement processes set forth in request for proposals; there was basis for increase, recognizing screening of prospective employees and in-house training programs not provided by other offerors. Federal Property and Administrative Services Act of 1949, § 303b(a), as amended, 41 U.S.C.A. § 253b(a); 48 C.F.R. § 15.608(a). United Intern. Investigative Services v. U.S., 42 Fed. Cl. 73, 42 Cont. Cas. Fed. (CCH) P 77394 (1998), aff'd, 194 F.3d 1335 (Fed. Cir. 1999). United States ☞64.40(2)

11 Cost and price analysis

Challenge to solicitation contemplating issuance of cost-reimbursable task orders was sustained because solicitation did not require offerors to propose cost-reimbursable labor rates for the services being procured, thereby precluding the agency from meaningfully evaluating the proposals' cost. The solicitation also did not request any information regarding the break-out of cost components such as direct labor, indirect labor, overhead, and/or general and administrative expenses to be evaluated. CACI, Inc.-Federal; Booz Allen Hamilton, Inc., B-413028, et al, 2016 WL 4582380(Comp.Gen. 2016)

Incumbent contractor failed to show, in its protest, prejudice from decision of the contracting officer not to enter into cost discussions with it, where even with a cost realism adjustment, incumbent contractor's proposal was still lower than that of the awardee, and it was more important that the incumbent contractor received lower ratings in the technical and management areas, because the contracting officer decided that the awardee's superiority in those areas outweighed the marginal cost difference between the two, which was a permissible judgment under the source selection regulation. 48 C.F.R. § 15.308. JWK Intern. Corp. v. U.S., 279 F.3d 985 (Fed. Cir. 2002). United States ⊕64.55(1)

Agency may use labor rate information from the awardee's prior contracts to assess the reasonableness of an awardee's proposed price. Agency's determination that the awardee's price was not unbalanced was reasonable. Survival Sys., USA, Inc. v. U.S., 102 Fed. Cl. 255 (2011)

Cost realism analysis performed by National Nuclear Security Administration (NNSA), with respect to bid solicitation for providing security system services for nuclear test site, was rationally based; NNSA established probable cost of each offeror's proposal, for purposes of evaluating best value, by adjusting proposed costs to reflect any additions or reductions in cost elements to realistic levels. Westech Intern., Inc. v. U.S., 79 Fed. Cl. 272 (2007)

Although the FAR requires that a procuring agency evaluate the reasonableness of an offeror's proposed price and, where cost data is required, the reasonableness of an offeror's proposed costs, the FAR does not mandate that either a "cost realism analysis" or "price realism analysis" be performed, unless the procurement is for a cost-reimbursement contract or the solicitation so requires. Information Sciences Corp. v. U.S., 73 Fed. Cl. 70 (2006), on reconsideration in part, 75 Fed. Cl. 406 (2007)

Failure of contracting agency to perform a cost realism analysis on contract awardee's offer was not error, as there was no requirement for such an analysis, where solicitation contemplated award of firm fixed price contract and contracting officer (CO) deemed awardee responsible to perform the project at the offered price. 48 C.F.R. § 15.404-1(d)(1). First Enterprise v. U.S., 61 Fed. Cl. 109 (2004). United States ⊕64.40(1)

Contracting agency violated procurement regulation when it reviewed only the total prices submitted in proposals and did not compare offerors' contract line item (CLIN) prices with the government's price estimates for the same CLINs to determine whether unit prices were unbalanced. Al Ghanim Combined Group Co. Gen.Trad. & Cont. W.L.L. v. U.S., 56 Fed. Cl. 502 (2003).

Contracting agency failed to perform a proper cost realism analysis of successful proposal on solicitation to provide health care services to immigration detainees in violation of the Federal Acquisition Regulation (FAR), where agency failed to adjust contract awardee's proposed costs for its unrealistically low assumed claims processing volume; moreover, protestor would have had a substantial chance of receiving the award, given the magnitude of the total contract value, as compared with the relatively narrow margin by which awardee purportedly underbid protestor. 48 C.F.R. § 15.404-1(d)(2)(i). United Payors & United Providers Health Services, Inc. v. U.S., 55 Fed. Cl. 323 (2003). United States ⊕64.45(1)

Provision of the FAR providing that agencies should not award cost-reimbursement contracts to the lowest-cost offeror without regard to other evaluation factors does not mandate cost-realism analysis in all cost-reimbursement procurements. 48 C.F.R. § 15.605(d) (1995). Labat-Anderson, Inc. v. U.S., 42 Fed. Cl. 806 (1999). United States ⊕64.40(1)

Provision of the FAR providing that "when cost or pricing data are required, the contracting officer shall make a cost analysis to evaluate the reasonableness of individual cost elements" does not create a mandatory requirement for a cost-realism analysis. 48 C.F.R. § 15.805-1(b) (1995). Labat-Anderson, Inc. v. U.S., 42 Fed. Cl. 806 (1999). United States ⊕64.40(1)

Protest was sustained where agency unreasonably evaluated the protester's pricing as unbalanced and conducted a technical-price tradeoff without meaningfully considering the lower prices set forth in the protester's BPA quotation. Unbalanced pricing may increase risk to the government, but agencies cannot reject an offer solely because it is unbalanced. Low prices (even below-cost prices), are not improper and do not establish unbalanced pricing. When establishing a BPA based on fixed unit prices, the agency had no reasonable basis to conclude that any unbalanced pricing would result in higher prices to the government. Triumvirate Envtl., Inc., B-406809, 2012 CPD ¶ 244 (Comp. Gen. 2012)

Protest that agency improperly rejected protester's proposal as unreasonably low priced is sustained where the agency based its conclusion on a comparison of the protester's price to the median price proposed by other offerors, including offerors whose proposals were determined to be unacceptable, ineligible for award, or priced unreasonably high. Lifecycle Constr. Servs., LLC, B-406907, 2012 CPD ¶ 269 (Comp. Gen. 2012).

GAO sustained protest challenging the evaluation of offerors' prices where the solicitation stated that a 5% royalty would be added to the total proposed prices of offerors without licenses to use certain technology, but evaluated proposals by applying the royalty adjustment only to specific components. Colt Defense, LLC, B-406696, 2012 CPD ¶ 302 (Comp. Gen. 2012)

Agency's decision to exclude the protester from a competition because the protester's submission of "other than cost or pricing data," as was contemplated by the solicitation, was considered to be inconsistent with the instructions in FAR 15.408, Table 15-2, was unreasonable where: (1) the instructions were only applicable to cost proposals when cost or pricing data is required, (2) the instructions were neither referenced nor incorporated into the RFP, (3) there was no evidence in the record that offerors were ever notified that their cost information had to be presented in accordance with Table 15-2, and (4) none of the audits of the other offerors' cost proposals were evaluated against this standard. Decision Matter of: PMO Partnership Joint Venture, B-403214, B-403214.2, 2010 CPD ¶ 256 (Comp. Gen. 2010)

Protest challenging agency's cost realism evaluation was sustained, where protester unequivocally proposed charging costs as overhead, instead of directly to the contract, to reduce costs and the agency ignored this aspect of the proposal and increased the protester's proposed cost to account for the labor costs that the agency believed would be charged as direct costs. Matter of: Marine Hydraulics International, Inc., B-403386, B-403386.2, 2010 CPD ¶ 255 (Comp. Gen. 2010)

Agency's cost-realism evaluation was unreasonable because the it failed to consider whether the material and supply costs in the Agency Tender Offer (ATO) were realistic under an Office of Management and Budget Circular A-76 competition. GAO found that the agency "simply assumed that the ATO's assertions were accurate, notwithstanding the fact that they were entirely unsupported." Matter of: New Dynamics Corporation, B-401272, 2009 CPD ¶ 150 (Comp. Gen. 2009)

Protest is sustained in a negotiated procurement for the award of a cost-reimbursement contract, where the agency in its cost realism assessment accepted the awardee's work allocation in its cost proposal, but that allocation was inconsistent with the firm's allocation of work in its technical proposal. Matter of: Earl Industries, LLC, B-309996, B-309996.4, 2007 CPD ¶ 203 (Comp. Gen. 2007)

When an agency evaluates a proposal for the award of a cost-reimbursement contract, as in this case, an offeror's proposed estimated costs are not dispositive because, regardless of the costs proposed, the government is bound to pay the contractor its actual and allowable costs. FAR 15.305(a)(1); 15.404-1(d). Consequently, the agency must perform a cost realism analysis to determine the extent to which an offeror's proposed costs are realistic for the work to be performed. An agency is not required to conduct an in-depth cost analysis or to verify each and every item in assessing cost realism; rather, the evaluation requires the exercise of informed judgment by the contracting agency. Matter of: ITT Industries Space Systems, LLC, B-309964, 2007 CPD ¶ 217 (Comp. Gen. 2007)

Agency's cost realism evaluation of awardee's proposal was unreasonable where agency failed to take into account cost adjustments made by its own cost analyst to awardee's proposal, and instead utilized awardee's proposed costs as the basis for its source selection decision. Matter of Magellan Health Services, B-298912, 2007 CPD ¶ 81 (Comp. Gen. 2007)

Agency did not perform a reasonable cost realism evaluation when it deleted a certain element of cost from awardee's proposed indirect costs because other offerors accounted for this element as a direct cost; this evaluation did not result in a reasonable assessment of the probable cost of performing the contract associated with the awardee's proposal, given that the adjustment was inconsistent with Cost Accounting Standards 401 and 402 and the firm's cost accounting practices, to which the firm was obligated to adhere in performing the contract. Kellogg Brown & Root Services, Inc., B-298694, B-298694.2, B-298694.3, 2006 CPD ¶ 160 (Comp. Gen. 2006)

Protest is sustained where agency failed to reconcile contradictory cost and technical evaluations regarding offerors' proposed staffing levels and unreasonably normalized offerors' proposed labor hours under its cost realism analysis. Matter of: Information Ventures, Inc., B-297276.2, B-297276.3, B-297276.4, 2006 CPD ¶ 45 (Comp. Gen. 2006)

Agency's cost realism evaluation of awardee's proposal was unreasonable where the awardee proposed to perform the solicitation requirements under a teaming arrangement whereby its proposed team members would perform almost [deleted] of the production work under the contract, but the agency failed to consider the impact of the team members' higher rates in determining the awardee's probable cost of performance under the contract. Metro Machine Corporation, B-297879.2, 2006 CPD ¶ 80 (Comp. Gen. 2006)

In a cost realism evaluation where the agency evaluated numerous areas under which the protester's proposed approach was inadequate and understaffed, the agency properly used its independent government estimate and prior experience on similar projects as tools to assess the amount of additional staffing that would be required under the protester's proposed approach. Pueblo Environmental Solution, LLC, B-291487, B-291487.2, 2003 CPD ¶ 14 (Comp. Gen. 2002)

Agency failed to perform a proper cost realism evaluation in awarding a cost reimbursement contract where the agency made no probable cost adjustments even where it identified costs that it believed were unrealistic and did not consider the proposed costs in light of the offeror's proposed technical proposals. Priority One Services, Inc., B-288836, B-288836.2, 2002 CPD ¶ 79 (Comp. Gen. 2001)

11.5 Price realism analysis

Contracting agency performed a price realism analysis in accordance with solicitation by providing a cogent analysis as to why successful offeror's price was lower than that of other offerors; agency explained that successful offeror proposed a totally automated approach that offered the government a substantial reduction of operating costs, and that it utilized a "managed" model that accounted for the price savings associated with its offer. Information Sciences Corp. v. U.S., 73 Fed. Cl. 70 (2006), on reconsideration in part, 75 Fed. Cl. 406 (2007). United States ☞64.45(1)

Protest challenging agency evaluation of protester's price as unrealistically low is sustained where the record shows that the agency's price analysis simply compared the protester's price to the government estimate and other offerors' prices without considering the protester's staffing approach. A price realism evaluation must consider each offeror's unique technical approach and an agency may not mechanically apply its own estimate to an offeror's proposal without considering the offeror's unique approach. Alcazar Trades, Inc., et al., B-410001.4, 2015 CPD ¶ 123 (Comp. Gen. 2015)

Protest alleging that the agency either failed to conduct a price realism analysis, or conducted an unreasonable analysis, is sustained where (1) the solicitation advised that proposals unrealistically high or low in price could be rejected; (2) the awardee's price was significantly lower than the other prices received and the government estimate; and (3) there is no evidence in the contemporaneous record that the agency conducted such an analysis. B&B Med. Servs., Inc.; Ed Med., Inc., B-409705.4 et al., 2015 CPD ¶ 198 (Comp. Gen. 2015)

Protest challenging the agency's evaluation of the protester's fixed-price quotation as *technically* unacceptable was sustained where the agency concluded that the protester's low price created a risk of unsuccessful performance, but the solicitation did not inform vendors that the agency would evaluate the realism of vendors' prices. Agencies therefore may not conduct a price realism analysis without first advising vendors that the agency intends to do so. W.P. Tax & Accounting Grp., B-411899, 2015 CPD ¶ 331 (Comp. Gen. 2015)

Price realism and price reasonableness are distinct concepts. Price realism measures whether a proposed price is so low that it poses a performance risk, whereas price reasonableness measures whether a proposed price is too high. An agency may not conduct a price realism analysis unless it advises offerors in the RFP that it intends to do so. Triad Int'l Maint. Corp., B-408374, 2013 CPD ¶ 208 (Comp. Gen. 2013)

Protest is sustained where solicitation for the issuance of a fixed-price time-and-materials task order did not place offerors on notice that the agency would conduct a price realism evaluation, yet the agency discounted the protester's lower price in its best value tradeoff decision based on its conclusion that the protester's low pricing posed performance risk and reflected a lack of understanding of the agency's requirements. Emergint Techs., Inc., B-407006, 2012 CPD ¶ 295 (Comp. Gen. 2012)

Protest challenging agency's price realism evaluation was sustained because the agency's price realism evaluation did not follow the solicitation terms. The agency compared prices from the awardee, the protester and the independent Government estimate (IGE), but not from all offerors, as the solicitation required. Digital Techs. Inc., B-406085, 2012 CPD ¶ 94 (Comp. Gen. 2012)

Allegation that agency failed to conduct price reasonableness analysis based on claim that awardee's price was unrealistically low fails to state valid basis for protest where solicitation provided for award of fixed-price contract and did not provide for price realism analysis. GAO distinguished between a price *reasonableness* analysis and a price *realism* analysis. Applied Business Management Solutions Incorporated, LLC, B-405724, 2012 CPD ¶ 14, 2011 WL 6960014 (Comp. Gen. 2011)

In a negotiated procurement for a fixed-price contract, a protest challenging the rejection of the protester's proposal on the basis that the price was too low was sustained because the evaluation record did not indicate the basis for the agency's determination. Rather, the record contained only the agency's conclusory judgment that the protester's fixed price was too low. Matter of: A1 Procurement, JVG, B-404618, 2011 CPD ¶ 53 (Comp. Gen. 2011)

Under a solicitation calling for award of fixed-price contract, GAO sustained a protest challenging the agency's determination that the protester's proposed price was unrealistically low because the solicitation lacked any evaluation criteria that reasonably would have put offerors on notice that agency intended to consider the realism of offerors' prices as reflecting lack of understanding or risk associated with the proposal. Matter of: Milani Construction, LLC, B-401942, 2010 CPD ¶ 87 (Comp. Gen. 2009)

Protester's contention that the agency failed to evaluate price proposals for completeness is sustained where the record shows that: (1) the solicitation expressly advised that price proposals would be assessed for completeness, including an assessment of the traceability of price estimates, and required that offerors submit detailed pricing data showing the traceability of those estimates in a work breakdown structure; (2) the agency never performed the completeness review; and (3) it is reasonable to conclude that, had it not been compelled to structure its proposal to comply with this solicitation requirement, the protester could have employed a different approach to structuring its proposal which could have resulted in a lower price. Advanced Systems Development, Inc., B-298411, B-298411.2, 2006 CPD ¶ 137 (Comp. Gen. 2006)

The elimination of the protester's proposal from the competition for the award of a fixed-price contract is unobjectionable where the agency reasonably determined under the solicitation's price realism evaluation factor that the protester's proposed price was unrealistically low and the agency was reasonably concerned that the protester's contract performance may therefore be adversely affected. Matter of: International Outsourcing Services, LLC, B-295959, 2006 CPD ¶ 6 (Comp. Gen. 2005)

An agency may eliminate a proposal from the competition based on price alone, without considering the high quality of the offeror's technical submission if the proposed price is unreasonable in an absolute (as opposed to relative) sense. Although the RFQ provided for a best value evaluation based on comparative technical and price considerations, an agency also must consider whether the quoted prices are too high in an absolute sense. The contracting officer rejected the protester's quotation because price was so high that award to the firm would not be in the public interest, no matter the quality of its technical submission. The protester's price was approximately 20 times the awardee's price, 8 times the third vendor's price, and 10 times the Government Estimate. Given this great disparity in pricing, there was nothing improper in the contracting officer's determination that the protester's price was unreasonable. Gold Cross Safety Corporation, B-296099, 2005 CPD ¶ 118 (Comp. Gen. 2005)

Below-cost pricing is not prohibited and the government cannot withhold an award from a responsible offeror merely because its low offer is or may be below cost. Nor can an agency, in evaluating an offeror's fixed-price proposal, make upward price adjustments for cost elements that agency contracting officials think may be priced too low. Where there is no relevant evaluation criterion pertaining to realism or understanding, a determination that an offeror's price on a fixed-price contract is too low generally concerns the offeror's responsibility, i.e., the offeror's ability and capacity to successfully perform the contract at its offered price. All Phase Environmental, Inc., B-292919.2, B-292919.3, B-292919.4, B-292919.5, B-292919.6, B-292919.7, 2004 CPD ¶ 62 (Comp. Gen. 2004)

Agency properly cancelled solicitation, issued as a small business set-aside, where the agency could not determine that the protester's proposed price, which exceeded the government estimate by more than 50 percent and was almost double the offer of a large business, was fair and reasonable. Nutech Laundry & Textiles, Inc., B-291739, 2003 CPD ¶ 34 (Comp. Gen. 2003)

Protest against award of primarily fixed-price incentive contracts for regional garrison food service at U.S. Marine Corps installations is sustained where agency did not properly assess realism of awardee's low proposed target price, which was the principal basis for determination that awardee's evaluated price was low. Eurest Support Services, B-285813.3, B-285813.4, B-285813.5, B-285882.4, B-285882.5, B-285882.7, 2003 CPD ¶ 139 (Comp. Gen. 2001)

12 Documentation

Contracting agency adequately articulated basis for its contract award in its source selection decision document when it explained that contract awardee's substantially better past performance and experience more that offset losing bidder's slightly better management subfactor proposal, and that $11 million dollar difference between proposed costs of awardee and losing bidder was mostly attributable to losing bidder's understaffing, which it considered detrimental; moreover, agency articulated the benefits it received in return for a higher price. Fort Carson Support Services v. U.S., 71 Fed. Cl. 571 (2006)

Where solicitation was explicit that each of the three technical criteria of past performance, experience, and management capability, would be assessed on a pass/fail basis, Court of Federal Claims could not impose additional documentary requirements such as narrative justifications when neither the applicable regulations nor the evaluation criteria required anything more than what the agency performed. 48 C.F.R. §§ 15.101-1, 15.305. Al Ghanim Combined Group Co. Gen. Trad. & Cont. W.L.L. v. U.S., 56 Fed. Cl. 502 (2003). United States ☞64.45(2)

Descriptions of offerors' proposals that Air Force evaluators provided when analyzing test and training/operational doctrine/data quality discriminator under technical performance subfactor did not prove that decision of source selection authority (SSA) did not comport with the underlying record of procurement for engineering and technical support services. Computer Sciences Corp. v. U.S., 51 Fed. Cl. 297 (2002). United States ☞64.45(3)

It is a fundamental principle of government accountability that an agency be able to produce a sufficient record to allow for a meaningful review when its procurement actions are challenged. An agency which fails to adequately document the rationale for its source selection, bears the risk that GAO will consider its determinations to be unsupported, and that absent such support, GAO may lack a basis to find that the agency had a reasonable basis for its determinations. Swets Info. Servs., B-410078, 2014 CPD ¶ 311 (Comp. Gen. 2014)

An agency is required to have adequate documentation to support its evaluation of proposals and its award decision. An award decision is not reasonable where there is no documentation or explanation to support the price/technical tradeoff and where the agency makes its award decision based strictly on a mechanical comparison of the offerors' total point scores. Documentation was considered inadequate where the evaluation record consists of one-paragraph summaries of the proposals, and charts showing for each evaluation factor the agency's assignment of raw scores, the calculation of weighted scores, and the total point score for each proposal. Such a record lacks any documentation reflecting a meaningful comparative analysis of proposals or any explanation of why the awardee's lower technically rated, lower-priced proposal was selected for award over protester's higher technically rated, higher-priced proposal. Midland Supply, Inc., B-298720, B-298720.2, 2007 CPD ¶ 2 (Comp. Gen. 2006)

Protest is sustained where source selection official failed to document rationale for source selection consistent with differential weighting of technical evaluation factors and emphasis on technical superiority as required by solicitation. YORK Building Services, Inc., B-296948.2, B-296948.3, B-296948.4, 2005 CPD ¶ 202 (Comp. Gen. 2005).

Protest is sustained where there is no evidence in the contemporaneous record that the contracting officer performed a proper price/technical trade-off—or, for that matter, even considered offerors' prices—prior to selecting the awardee. There is no evaluation of offerors' prices—on either an individual or comparative basis—in any of the source selection documentation. This is contrary to the requirement that price be considered in every source selection decision, 41 U.S.C. § 253a(c)(1)(B) (2002); FAR 15.304(c)(1), and the requirement that a source selection decision be based on a comparative assessment of proposals against all source selection criteria in the solicitation and that it be documented. Locus Technology, Inc., B-293012, 2004 CPD ¶ 16 (Comp. Gen. 2004)

Protest alleging that, because agency destroyed individual evaluator sheets, record does not include adequate documentation supporting the agency's evaluation and source selection decision, is denied where consensus evaluation materials and source selection decision contain a detailed explanation of the agency's evaluation conclusions and source selection decision. Joint Management and Technology Services, B-294229, B-294229.2, 2004 CPD ¶ 208 (Comp. Gen. 2004)

Where an agency makes award to a higher-priced offeror that has been ranked technically superior to a lower-priced offer, the award decision must be supported by a rational explanation demonstrating that the higher-rated proposal is in fact superior, and explaining why the technical superiority of the higher-priced proposal warrants the additional cost. Where neither the source selection decision nor the evaluation record supports the agency's conclusions, we will sustain a protest challenging the agency's award decision. Lockheed Martin Information Systems, B-292836, B-292836.2, B-292836.3, B-292836.4, 2003 CPD ¶ 230 (Comp. Gen. 2003)

Protest challenging the agency's best value source selection is sustained where the record shows that the agency failed to consider whether the awardee's higher-rated proposal was worth its higher price. Beacon Auto Parts, B-287483, 2001 CPD ¶ 116 (Comp. Gen. 2001)

13 Disclosure of information

Federal Government's undisclosed use of Army Materiel Systems Analysis Activity Technical Report No. 357, which projected reliability growth on basis of observed failures, raw test data, types of failures, and number of failures, was logically and reasonably related to identified reliability factor in request for proposal and did not need to be disclosed in request for proposal for variable reach, rough terrain forklift trucks for BMY, A Div. of HARSCO Corp. v. U.S., 693 F. Supp. 1232, 35 Cont. Cas. Fed. (CCH) P 75552 (D.D.C. 1988). United States ⟊64.40(1)

Government may not rely upon undisclosed evaluation criteria when evaluating proposals, and must even disclose the factors' relative importance. 10 U.S.C.A. § 2305(a)(2)(A), (a) (3)(A); 48 C.F.R. § 15.305(a). Gulf Group, Inc. v. U.S., 56 Fed. Cl. 391 (2003). United States ⟊64.40(1)

Although test and training/operational doctrine/data quality discriminator was a significant aspect of offerors' proposals relied upon by source selection authority (SSA) when making final decision in Air Force procurement for engineering and technical support services, SSA's actions did not result in elevating its requirements to the level of an undisclosed evaluation factor; rather, SSA acted within his discretion to consider it as an important discriminator when making his final decision. Computer Sciences Corp. v. U.S., 51 Fed. Cl. 297 (2002). United States ⟊64.45(3)

To obtain relief on a claim that government agency used undisclosed evaluation factors in reviewing proposals on government contract, plaintiff must prove that government evaluated the proposals received on a significantly different basis from that announced in solicitation and that plaintiff has been prejudiced as result. 10 U.S.C.A. § 2305(a)(2); Federal Property and Administrative Services Act of 1949, § 303A(b)(1), as amended, 41 U.S.C.A.

§ 253a(b)(1); 48 C.F.R. § 15.605(d)(1). Analytical & Research Technology, Inc. v. U.S., 39 Fed. Cl. 34, 442 Cont. Cas. Fed. (CCH) P 77228 (1997). United States ☞64.40(1)

14 Protest against award

Protestor did not establish that contracting agency failed to properly evaluate past performance factor in conducting price/technical tradeoff determination, notwithstanding protestor's contention that the three pages devoted to past performance in the source selection decision document (SSDD) were insufficient because the SSDD did not contain a "head-to-head" comparison of the various strengths and weakness of the offerors and did not list any weaknesses for protestor or contract awardee. Dismas Charities, Inc. v. U.S., 61 Fed. Cl. 191 (2004). United States ☞64.45(2)

While challenges to the terms of a solicitation are appropriate only prior to submission of final proposals, challenges to the evaluation may be raised after final proposal submission. Bannum, Inc. v. U.S., 60 Fed. Cl. 718 (2004). United States ☞64.25; United States ☞64.40(1)

Protest contesting contracting agency's formation and maintenance of protestor's files containing contractor evaluation forms (CEFs) upon completion of protestor's prior contracts was more properly characterized as a challenge of solicitation term than a challenge of the evaluation process, and since protestor failed to assert challenge before submitting its proposal, it waived its right to contest the evaluation process. Bannum, Inc. v. U.S., 60 Fed. Cl. 718 (2004). United States ☞64.25

Protester did not establish that contracting officer (CO) failed to evaluate all offers fairly, based on allegation that despite the fact that it and contract awardee were given the same scores for two subfactors within the overall performance risk category, when the subfactor scores were combined, awardee was unfairly given a more favorable score; CO permissibly chose to afford more weight to the financial risk and overall performance risk components of her analysis, and she identified specific "disadvantages" in protester's risk assessment not present in awardee's assessment. 48 C.F.R. § 1.102-2(c)(3). Ryder Move Management, Inc. v. U.S., 48 Fed. Cl. 380 (2001). United States ☞64.40(2)

Court of Federal Claims may grant an offeror relief if the offeror establishes that the agency evaluated its proposal on a basis different than that announced in the solicitation and that the offeror was prejudiced as a result. Bean Stuyvesant, L.L.C. v. U.S., 48 Fed. Cl. 303 (2000). United States ☞64.40(1); United States ☞64.55(1)

To obtain relief on its claim that the agency used undisclosed evaluation factors, protestor had to show that the government evaluated the submitted proposals on a significantly different basis than announced in the solicitation and that it was prejudiced as a result. ITT Federal Services Corp. v. U.S., 45 Fed. Cl. 174 (1999). United States ☞64.40(1)

Court of Federal Claims may grant relief in a protest case if the protester proves that the government evaluated proposals on a basis different from that announced in the solicitation and that it was prejudiced as a result. Dubinsky v. U.S., 43 Fed. Cl. 243 (1999). United States ☞64.60(5.1)

15 Incumbent advantage

Contracting officer (CO) acted unreasonably in solicitation for armed guard services at federal buildings in Washington and Oregon, which combined previously separate contracts, in failing to evaluate incumbent contractor's past performance on the Oregon contract in combination with the Washington contract, as the information was simply too relevant and close at hand to ignore. Seattle Sec. Services, Inc. v. U.S., 45 Fed. Cl. 560 (2000). United States ☞64.45(2)

It is proper for evaluators of past performance of offerors to use their personal knowledge of an offeror's performance of a contract with an agency. Seattle Sec. Services, Inc. v. U.S., 45 Fed. Cl. 560 (2000). United States ☞64.45(2)

Protest that awardee received improper competitive advantage due to status as incumbent contractor is denied; agency is not required to discount competitive advantage gained by virtue of performance as incumbent contractor. Matter of: Navarro Research and Engineering, Inc., B-299981, B-299981.3, 2007 CPD ¶ 195 (Comp. Gen. 2007)

16 Evaluation Factors—Technical

The Court deferred to the expertise of the agency and denied the protest where, the analysis of test results relating to protester's proposed equipment required a high level of technical expertise and, where the resolution of an issue "requires a high level of technical expertise," it is "properly left to the informed discretion of the responsible federal agencies." Terex Corp. v. U.S., 2012 WL 1574113 (Fed. Cl. 2012)

Solicitation provisions requiring the "contractor" to comply with FISMA IT security standards did not require offerors to demonstrate compliance before the source selection decision; such compliance is a performance requirement to be satisfied after award during contract performance. Discover Techs. LLC, B-412773, 2016 CPD ¶ 142 (Comp. Gen. 2016)

Protest was denied where the solicitation required that offerors' technical proposals include "a complete and detailed" description of the offeror's approach to accomplishing the PWS tasks. Although the protester's technical proposal described the firm's general capabilities, it did not provide the detailed explanation required by the solicitation. GeoSystems Analysis, Inc., B-413016, 2016 CPD ¶ 190 (Comp. Gen. 2016)

Agency's evaluation was unreasonable because it assigned a "Significant Strength" for a specific evaluation factor ("contingency plans for equipment downtime") based only on general experience in the field. Sterling Med. Corp., B-412407, 2016 CPD ¶ 73 (Comp. Gen. 2016)

A proposal or quotation that contains an ambiguity as to whether the offeror will comply with a material requirement of the solicitation renders the proposal unacceptable. Award decision was unreasonable because awardee's assertion that it would respond "promptly" failed to demonstrate compliance with the 1-hour response time specified in the solicitation. Bahrain Telecomms. Co., B.S.C., B-407682.2, 2013 CPD ¶ 71 (Comp. Gen. 2013)

Agency's assessment of a weaknesses under the technical evaluation factor, based on protester's proposed use of USB ports, lacked a reasonable basis because the solicitation prohibited only certain types of USB ports and the protester proposed a type of USB port that was not prohibited. Matter of: DRS ICAS, LLC, B-401852.4, B-401852.5, 2010 CPD ¶ 261 (Comp. Gen. 2010)

An agency's decision that the awardee's software proposal was technically superior to the protester's was unreasonable because the agency relied on a consultant evaluation that considered only the protester's discussion responses and not the full proposal, the GAO determined. The agency also unreasonably assigned performance risk to the protester's proposal because of the date of a Dun & Bradstreet (D&B) report, not because of the report's content. Matter of: Velos, Inc., B-400500.8, B-400500.9, 2010 CPD ¶ 13 (Comp. Gen. 2009)

17 Evaluation factors—staffing

Protest that agency unreasonably credited awardee for proposing to hire a large proportion of incumbent staff was sustained because the agency failed consider the fact that the awardee was proposing compensation that was substantially below what the incumbent proposed to pay the same staff, which created a potential risk that awardee would not be able to hire the proposed staff. Alutiiq Pacific, LLC, B-409584, 2014 CPD ¶ 196 (Comp. Gen. 2014)

Protest was sustained because agency found protester's proposed level of staffing to be a weakness based on mechanical application of an undisclosed government estimate, and this finding was of critical significance in agency's best value tradeoff decision. Native Res. Dev. Co., B-409617.3, 2014 CPD ¶ 217 (Comp. Gen. 2014)

Protest that agency misevaluated awardee's staffing plan was sustained because, although awardee proposed adequate staffing for the base year of the contract, its proposed staffing for the option years was significantly lower than that proposed in the base year, and the agency's evaluation failed to take this fact into consideration. Exelis Sys. Corp., B-407111.5, 2013 CPD ¶ 123 (Comp. Gen. 2013)

Protest challenging the evaluation of offerors' proposed staffing is sustained where the agency did not reasonably evaluate the offerors' proposals in accordance with solicitation's staffing plan subfactor. Specifically, the protester contended that the agency did not consider the effects of the awardee's proposed use of local nationals on their ability to perform the task order requirements. Exelis Sys. Corp., B-407111, 2012 CPD ¶ 340 (Comp. Gen. 2012)

17.5 Subcontractors

GAO sustained a protest that agency used unstated evaluation criteria in assessing a weakness in protester's proposal for failure to submit a list of subcontractors because the RFP did not require offerors to identify proposed subcontractors. The RFP in this IDIQ procurement stated that "[t]he *contractor* shall submit a list of subcontractors to be used on each individual task order," and did not require "offerors" to identify subcontracts at the time of the IDIQ competition. Coburn Contractors, LLC, B-408279.2, 2013 CPD ¶ 230 (Comp. Gen. 2013)

18 Ability to provide materials

Protest that agency improperly accepted awardee's proposal was sustained where record shows that the proposal offered to furnish certain equipment that was material to the acceptability of the awardee's proposal, but did not provide evidence of the awardee's ability to obtain the equipment, as required by the solicitation. Motorola Solutions, Inc., B-409148, 2014 CPD ¶ 59 (Comp. Gen. 2014)

19 Gender bias

GAO denied a protest alleging gender bias in the award of a contract for architect-engineering services. Although the protester submitted a number of reports and academic papers supporting the protester's arguments that women are discriminated in fields such as architecture and engineering, the record demonstrated that the agency reasonably evaluated the protester's experience and technical competence and found that the protester was not as capable as the awardee. AMEL Techs., Inc., B-412611, 2016 CPD ¶ 103 (Comp. Gen. 2016)

§ 15.306 Exchanges with offerors after receipt of proposals.

(a) Clarifications and award without discussions.

(1) Clarifications are limited exchanges, between the Government and offerors, that may occur when award without discussions is contemplated.

(2) If award will be made without conducting discussions, offerors may be given the opportunity to clarify certain aspects of proposals (*e.g.,* the relevance of an offeror's past performance information and adverse past performance information to which the offeror has not previously had an opportunity to respond) or to resolve minor or clerical errors.

(3) Award may be made without discussions if the solicitation states that the Government intends to evaluate proposals and make award without discussions. If the solicitation contains such a notice and the Government determines it is necessary to conduct discussions, the rationale for doing so shall be documented in the contract file (see the provision at 52.215-1) (10 U.S.C. 2305(b)(4)(A)(ii) and 41 U.S.C. 3703(a)(2)).

(b) *Communications with offerors before establishment of the competitive range.* Communications are exchanges, between the Government and offerors, after receipt of proposals, leading to establishment of the competitive range. If a competitive range is to be established, these communications—

(1) Shall be limited to the offerors described in paragraphs (b)(1)(i) and (b)(1)(ii) of this section and—

(i) Shall be held with offerors whose past performance information is the determining factor preventing them from being placed within the competitive range. Such communications shall address adverse past performance information to which an offeror has not had a prior opportunity to respond; and

(ii) May only be held with those offerors (other than offerors under paragraph (b)(1)(i) of this section) whose exclusion from, or inclusion in, the competitive range is uncertain;

(2) May be conducted to enhance Government understanding of proposals; allow reasonable interpretation of the proposal; or facilitate the Government's evaluation process. Such communications shall not be used to cure proposal deficiencies or material omissions, materially alter the technical or cost elements of the proposal, and/or otherwise revise the proposal. Such communications may be considered in rating proposals for the purpose of establishing the competitive range;

(3) Are for the purpose of addressing issues that must be explored to determine whether a proposal should be placed in the competitive range. Such communications shall not provide an opportunity for the offeror to revise its proposal, but may address—

(i) Ambiguities in the proposal or other concerns (*e.g.*, perceived deficiencies, weaknesses, errors, omissions, or mistakes (see 14.407)); and

(ii) Information relating to relevant past performance; and

(4) Shall address adverse past performance information to which the offeror has not previously had an opportunity to comment.

(c) Competitive range.

(1) Agencies shall evaluate all proposals in accordance with 15.305(a), and, if discussions are to be conducted, establish the competitive range. Based on the ratings of each proposal against all evaluation criteria, the contracting officer shall establish a competitive range comprised of all of the most highly rated proposals, unless the range is further reduced for purposes of efficiency pursuant to paragraph (c)(2) of this section.

(2) After evaluating all proposals in accordance with 15.305(a) and paragraph (c)(1) of this section, the contracting officer may determine that the number of most highly rated proposals that might otherwise be included in the competitive range exceeds the number at which an efficient competition can be conducted. Provided the solicitation notifies offerors that the competitive range can be limited for purposes of efficiency (see 52.215-1(f)(4)), the contracting officer may limit the number of proposals in the competitive range to the greatest number that will permit an efficient competition among the most highly rated proposals (10 U.S.C. 2305(b)(4) and 41 U.S.C. 3703).

(3) If the contracting officer, after complying with paragraph (d)(3) of this section, decides that an offeror's proposal should no longer be included in the competitive range, the proposal shall be eliminated from consideration for award. Written notice of this decision shall be provided to unsuccessful offerors in accordance with 15.503.

(4) Offerors excluded or otherwise eliminated from the competitive range may request a debriefing (see 15.505 and 15.506).

(d) *Exchanges with offerors after establishment of the competitive range.* Negotiations are exchanges, in either a competitive or sole source environment, between the Government and offerors, that are undertaken with the intent of allowing the offeror to revise its proposal. These negotiations may include bargaining. Bargaining includes persuasion, alteration of assumptions and positions, give-and-take, and may apply to price, schedule, technical requirements, type of contract, or other terms of a proposed contract. When negotiations are conducted in a competitive acquisition, they take place after establishment of the competitive range and are called discussions.

(1) Discussions are tailored to each offeror's proposal, and must be conducted by the contracting officer with each offeror within the competitive range.

(2) The primary objective of discussions is to maximize the Government's ability to obtain best value, based on the requirement and the evaluation factors set forth in the solicitation.

(3) At a minimum, the contracting officer must, subject to paragraphs (d)(5) and (e) of this section and 15.307(a), indicate to, or discuss with, each offeror still being considered for award, deficiencies, significant weaknesses, and adverse past performance information to which the offeror has not yet had an opportunity to respond. The contracting officer also is encouraged to discuss other aspects of the offeror's proposal that could, in the opinion of the contracting officer, be altered or explained to enhance materially the proposal's potential for award. However, the contracting officer is not required to discuss every area where the proposal could be improved. The scope and extent of discussions are a matter of contracting officer judgment.

(4) In discussing other aspects of the proposal, the Government may, in situations where the solicitation stated that evaluation credit would be given for technical solutions exceeding any mandatory minimums, negotiate with offerors for increased performance beyond any mandatory minimums, and the Government may suggest to offerors that have exceeded any mandatory minimums (in ways that are not integral to the design), that their proposals would be more competitive if the excesses were removed and the offered price decreased.

(5) If, after discussions have begun, an offeror originally in the competitive range is no longer considered to be among the most highly rated offerors being considered for award, that offeror may be eliminated from the competitive range whether or not all material aspects of the proposal have been discussed, or whether or not the offeror has been afforded an opportunity to submit a proposal revision (see 15.307(a) and 15.503(a)(1)).

(e) *Limits on exchanges.* Government personnel involved in the acquisition shall not engage in conduct that—

(1) Favors one offeror over another;

(2) Reveals an offeror's technical solution, including unique technology, innovative and unique uses of commercial items, or any information that would compromise an offeror's intellectual property to another offeror;

(3) Reveals an offeror's price without that offeror's permission. However, the contracting officer may inform an offeror that its price is considered by the Government to be too high, or too low, and reveal the results of the analysis supporting that conclusion. It is also permissible, at the Government's discretion, to indicate to all offerors the cost or price that the Government's price analysis, market research, and other reviews have identified as reasonable (41 U.S.C. 2102 and 2107);

(4) Reveals the names of individuals providing reference information about an offeror's past performance; or

(5) Knowingly furnishes source selection information in violation of 3.104 and 41 U.S.C. 2102 and 2107).

United States Code Annotated

Administrative determinations, see 41 USCA § 257.

Contract requirements, see 41 USCA § 254.

Contracts, planning, solicitation, evaluation, and award procedures, see 10 USCA § 2305.

Definitions, see 10 USCA § 2302, 41 USCA §§ 259, 403.

Determinations and decisions, see 10 USCA § 2310, 41 USCA § 262.

Evaluation and award, see 41 USCA § 253b.

Kinds of contracts, see 10 USCA § 2306.

Planning and solicitation requirements, see 41 USCA § 253a.

Notes of Decisions

Auctions 10
Award without discussions 12
Best value 2
Clarification 3
Competitive range 5
Definition of discussions 13
Disclosure of information 9
Discretion of agency 7
Exchanges with offerors, generally 1
Improper discussions 11
Meaningful discussions 4
Minimum or material requirements 8
Misleading discussions 14
Past performance 6

1 Exchanges with offerors, generally

In the context of a government contract proposal, the term "discussions" has a specific legal definition: discussions involve negotiations and are undertaken with the intent of allowing the offeror to revise its proposal. 48 C.F.R. § 15.306(d). Galen Medical Associates, Inc. v. U.S., 369 F.3d 1324 (Fed. Cir. 2004). United States ⊕64.40(1)

Disappointed offeror did not show that agency engaged in improper, or any, discussions with contract awardee, as required to prevail on argument that agency waived "without discussions" requirement for award of government contract; agency was allowed to receive clarifying information from offerors during bidding process. 48 C.F.R. § 15.306(a)(3). Galen Medical Associates, Inc. v. U.S., 369 F.3d 1324 (Fed. Cir. 2004). United States ⊕64.40(1)

Discussions with responsible offerors are intended to maximize the government's ability to obtain the "best value" in a contract award based on the requirements and the evaluation factors set forth in the solicitation; to that end, contracting agency has broad discretion in conducting discussions. 48 C.F.R. § 15.306(d)(3). JWK Intern. Corp. v. U.S., 49 Fed. Cl. 364 (2001), judgment aff'd, 279 F.3d 985 (Fed. Cir. 2002). United States ☞64.40(1)

Protestor did not establish that it was treated unequally by contracting agency when agency communicated to awardee a suggestion that it amend its proposal to enhance one of its features, where protestor also was informed of an area of its proposal that agency viewed as one for potential improvement or explanation. 48 C.F.R. § 15.306(d)(2, 3). Synetics, Inc. v. U.S., 45 Fed. Cl. 1 (1999). United States ☞64.40(2)

2 Best value

Where a contract has been awarded, but a bid protest has been sustained and the recommended corrective action is to make a new best value determination, the standard competition rules of the Competition in Contracting Act (CICA) and the Federal Acquisition Regulation (FAR) apply, and under such circumstances, if an agency conducts discussions, it must do so with all offerors in the competitive range. Chapman Law Firm Co. v. U.S., 71 Fed. Cl. 124 (2006), aff'd in part, rev'd in part and remanded on other grounds, 490 F.3d 934 (Fed. Cir. 2007). United States ☞64.40(1)

3 Clarification

Exchanges by which federal agency obtained additional information about subcontractors listed in offeror's proposal for professional services contract were "clarifications," rather than "discussions," under regulation that implemented statutes barring government from holding discussions with only one offeror for government contract; communications, through which offeror provided requested explanation as to which parts of project each subcontractor would support and detailed subcontractors' relevant experience regarding those tasks, did not qualify as "discussions," which were intended to occur in the context of negotiations during which offerors would have opportunity to revise their proposals, and agency's requests merely sought clarification of subcontractors' relevant experience, as authorized by regulation, even though additional, new information was sought. 10 U.S.C.A. § 2305(b)(4)(A); Federal Property and Administrative Services Act of 1949, § 303B(d)(1), as amended, 41 U.S.C.A. § 253b(d)(1); 48 C.F.R. § 15.306(a, d). Information Technology & Applications Corp. v. U.S., 316 F.3d 1312 (Fed. Cir. 2003). United States ☞64.40(1)

Amended regulations' definitions of terms "discussions" and "clarifications," which broadened scope of permitted "clarifications" to allow offerors to clarify certain aspects of their proposals, such as the relevance of offeror's past performance information and adverse past performance information to which offeror previously had no opportunity to respond, were reasonable interpretations of statutes barring government from holding discussions with only one offeror for government contract and thus were entitled to deference by court. 10 U.S.C.A. § 2305(b)(4)(A); Federal Property and Administrative Services Act of 1949, § 303B(d)(1), as amended, 41 U.S.C.A. § 253b(d)(1); 48 C.F.R. § 15.306(a, d). Information Technology & Applications Corp. v. U.S., 316 F.3d 1312 (Fed. Cir. 2003). United States ☞64.40(1)

To the extent that acquisition regulations were ambiguous, federal agency's interpretation of regulations as allowing it to treat as "clarifications" its requests for additional information about subcontractors listed in offeror's proposal for professional services contract was reasonable, and thus entitled to deference on judicial review. 10 U.S.C.A. § 2305(b)(4)(A); Federal Property and Administrative Services Act of 1949, § 303B(d)(1), as amended, 41 U.S.C.A. § 253b(d)(1); 48 C.F.R. § 15.306(a, d). Information Technology & Applications Corp. v. U.S., 316 F.3d 1312 (Fed. Cir. 2003). United States ☞64.40(1)

Although contracting officers generally have discretion to decide whether to seek clarifications, the COFC found that an agency abused its discretion by failing to inquire about a clerical error in an offeror's proposal. Where the same subcontractor was included in two offerors' proposals and the agency rated the subcontractor's experience acceptable under one proposal and unacceptable under the protester' proposal, it should have sought clarification of the apparent clerical error that resulted in the inconsistent ratings. The COFC granted the protester's request for an injunction barring the award and directing the agency to reevaluate proposals. BCPeabody Constr. Servs., Inc. v. U.S., 112 Fed.Cl. 502 (2013)

The general duty of contracting officers to act fairly with offerors does not create an affirmative duty to communicate with an offeror that failed to include required price and brand/model information for two line items. The Contracting Officer's decision to disqualify the offeror and not seek clarifications was, therefore, not arbitrary, capricious or an abuse of discretion. ST Net, Inc. v. U.S., 112 Fed.Cl. 99 (Fed. Cl. 2013)

Plaintiff argues that it is unfair to hold clarifications with one offeror and not the other. In support of this contention, plaintiff cites numerous FAR provisions which demand impartiality, fairness, equitable treatment, consistency and lack of favoritism in procurement processes. FAR 15.303(b). However, FAR 1.102-2(c)(3) states that: "All contractors and prospective contractors shall be treated fairly and impartially but need not be treated the same." Therefore, a procuring agency has the discretion to decline to enter into clarifications with an offeror, even if the agency has engaged in clarifications with another offeror. DynCorp Intern. LLC v. U.S., 76 Fed. Cl. 528 (2007).

Contracting agency did not abuse its discretion in solicitation for construction project by not seeking clarification from offeror concerning its past performance information after technical evaluation team (TET) determined that the information was inadequate to determine the scope of past projects, despite fact that the TET concluded that clarifications should be required, where source selection authority (SSA) subsequently explained that no clarification were sought because no discussions were conducted with any offerors. 48 C.F.R. § 15.306(a)(1, 2). Gulf Group Inc. v. U.S., 61 Fed. Cl. 338 (2004). United States ☞64.45(2)

Where dozens of fundamental deficiencies had been identified in offeror's proposals, source selection board (SSB) did not abuse its discretion in concluding that limited exchanges with offeror envisioned by regulation allowing clarifications when award will be made without conducting discussions would serve no purpose. 48 C.F.R. § 15.306(a)(2). JWK Intern. Corp. v. U.S., 52 Fed. Cl. 650 (2002), aff'd, 56 Fed. Appx. 474 (Fed. Cir. 2003). United States ☞64.45(1)

"Clarifications" are limited exchanges between the government and offerors that may occur when award without discussions is contemplated. Griffy's Landscape Maintenance LLC v. U.S., 46 Fed. Cl. 257 (2000). United States ☞64.40(3)

Awardee's submission of promised additional test data with its final proposal revisions did not constitute a "discussion" with contracting agency, obligating agency to reopen discussions with bid protestor; awardee's submission of data that had been previously addressed and anticipated by the agency, without requests for further clarification by the agency, lacked the element of exchange that is explicit in the regulatory treatment of "discussions." 48 C.F.R. § 15.306(d). Cubic Defense Systems, Inc. v. U.S., 45 Fed. Cl. 450 (1999). United States ☞64.40(5)

Contracting officer was not arbitrary and capricious in not engaging in another round of discussions with offeror after officer conducted one round of discussions of offeror's revised proposals, where revised proposal was repeatedly non-responsive to requests of the technical evaluation board (TEB) and the price evaluation board (PEB) for clarification, requests plainly stated in numerous questions. 48 C.F.R. § 15.306(d)(3). Impresa Construzioni Geom. Domenico Garufi v. U.S., 44 Fed. Cl. 540 (1999), aff'd in part, rev'd in part on other grounds, 238 F.3d 1324 (Fed. Cir. 2001). United States ☞64.40(5)

Clarifications are not to be used to cure proposal deficiencies or material omissions, or materially alter the technical or cost elements of the proposal, or otherwise revise the proposal. Protest was sustained because offeror's response to a "clarification" question was used to determine whether the proposal complied with minimum RFP requirements and GAO held that "this is quintessentially the nature of discussions, not clarifications." Cascadian Am. Enters., B-412208.3, et al., 2016 CPD ¶ 29 (Comp. Gen. 2016)

Protest that an agency was required to obtain clarifications from the protesters with respect to errors in their proposals is denied, because an agency may, but is not required to, engage in clarifications; clarifications may not be used to cure proposal deficiencies, such as those presented by the protesters' proposals. ADNET Systems, Inc., B-408685.3, 2014 CPD ¶ 173 (Comp.Gen. 2014)

Agency may request clarification from one offeror but not from another. The mere fact that an agency requests clarification from one offeror and not another, does not constitute unfair treatment under FAR 1.102-2(c)(3), which states that all contractors and prospective contractors must be treated fairly and impartially but need not be treated the same. Matter of Indus Technology, Inc., B-297800.13, 2007 CPD ¶ 116 (Comp. Gen. 2007).

Agency is not required to engage in clarifications to give offerors an opportunity to clarify an unacceptable subcontracting plan and may make award on initial proposals to another offeror submitting an acceptable proposal. Central Texas College, B-309947, 2007 CPD ¶ 187 (Comp.Gen. 2007)

Agency's post-proposal submission exchanges with awardee regarding price proposal were clarifications rather than discussions where the errors corrected were obvious on the face of the awardee's proposal. Other exchanges with awardee that may have resulted in discussions were not prejudicial to protester. IPlus, Inc., B-298020, B-298020.2, 2006 CPD ¶ 90 (Comp. Gen. 2006)

4 Meaningful discussions

Discussions were not "meaningful" because the agency did not submit any discussion questions on the protester's failure to describe how it would proactively detect problems, even though this perceived failure was specifically cited in the source selection decision document. Crowley Logistics, Inc., B-412628.2, 2016 CPD ¶ 120(Comp. Gen. 2016)

FAR does not require a contracting officer to enter into cost discussions with offerors whose cost proposals are deemed adequate. 48 C.F.R. §§ 15.304(c)(1, 2), 15.306(d)(3). JWK Intern. Corp. v. U.S., 279 F.3d 985 (Fed. Cir. 2002). United States ⊕64.40(1)

Federal contracting officer's notice of deficiency asking unsuccessful offeror to provide information about delivery performance on prior government contracts adequately notified offeror of importance of information, gave him opportunity to supplement submission as it saw fit, and complied with requirement to conduct meaningful negotiations. 10 U.S.C.A. § 2301 et seq.BMY, A Div. of HARSCO Corp. v. U.S., 693 F. Supp. 1232, 35 Cont. Cas. Fed. (CCH) P 75552 (D.D.C. 1988). United States ⊕64.40(1)

Agency-offeror discussions must be meaningful; to initiate meaningful discussions, an agency is required to point out weaknesses or deficiencies in a proposal as specifically as practical considerations permit so that the agency leads the offeror into areas of its proposal which require amplification or correction. Orca Northwest Real Estate Services v. U.S., 65 Fed. Cl. 1 (2005), on reconsideration, 65 Fed. Cl. 419 (2005). United States ⊕64.40(1)

Contracting officer's request, following delay in procurement process, for updated information about key personnel and subcontractors constituted limited "discussions" within purview of section of FAR, as updated information was used to evaluate technical subfactor, and thus offeror should have been informed of any deficiencies therein in order for such discussions to be meaningful. Consolidated Engineering Services, Inc. v. U.S., 64 Fed. Cl. 617 (2005). United States ⊕64.40(1)

Protestor failed to establish that contracting agency failed to conduct proper discussions on subject of its prior experience and past performance; record indicated that, consistent with its obligations under the FAR, technical evaluation panel (TEP) discussed aspects of offeror's proposal relating to past experience that weakened its proposal. Chapman Law Firm v. U.S., 63 Fed. Cl. 519 (2005), aff'd, 163 Fed. Appx. 889 (Fed. Cir. 2006). United States ⊕64.40(1)

Protestor did not establish that contracting agency violated procurement regulation requiring it to discuss "deficiencies, significant weaknesses, and adverse past performance information to which the offeror has not yet had an opportunity to respond" by not allowing protestor to address negative contractor evaluation forms (CEFs) regarding its performance of prior contracts; protestor cited no CEFs that were deemed "poor" or otherwise deficient, and protestor had the opportunity to respond to any CEFs that it considered adverse by submitting rebuttal comments with its proposals, but failed to do so. 48 C.F.R. § 15.306(d). Bannum, Inc. v. U.S., 60 Fed. Cl. 718 (2004). United States ⊕64.45(2)

Meaningful contract discussions must generally lead offerors into the areas of their proposals requiring amplification or correction, which means that discussions should be as specific as practical considerations permit; areas which require amplification or correction are those which either fail to meet the solicitation requirements or are in error. 48 C.F.R. § 15.306. Omega World Travel, Inc. v. U.S., 54 Fed. Cl. 570 (2002). United States ⊕64.40(1)

Government's failure to effectively notify other offerors of its interpretation of ambiguous term "budget ceiling" in request for proposals (RFP), using the same clear and unequivocal language in which another offeror was notified pursuant to a pre-proposal question, constituted unfair and unequal treatment in violation of the FAR; government clearly was required to notify other offerors regarding budget ceiling clarification when one offeror made an inquiry, particularly when inquiring offeror, itself, misunderstood government's answer. 48 C.F.R. § 15.306(d)(1). Metcalf Const. Co., Inc. v. U.S., 53 Fed. Cl. 617 (2002). United States ☞64.40(2)

Government's discussions with offeror regarding its price were adequate, where government told offeror that its prices were extremely high in comparison to the government estimate and instructed it to review its costs, repeatedly identified deficiencies in offeror's cost data, and gave offeror numerous opportunities to review its proposal. Process Control Technologies, a Div. of GMC Enterprises, Inc., 53 Fed. Cl. 71 (2002). United States ☞64.40(1)

Discussions between the government and offerors are meaningful if they include sufficient information to advise an offeror of the weaknesses in its proposal and enable it to address those weaknesses. 48 C.F.R. § 15.306(d). OAO Corp. v. U.S., 49 Fed. Cl. 478 (2001). United States ☞64.40(1)

Meaningful discussion requirement implies that contracting agency will consider an offeror's responses to the agency's questions and clarification requests. 48 C.F.R. § 15.306(d). OAO Corp. v. U.S., 49 Fed. Cl. 478 (2001). United States ☞64.40(1)

Contracting agencies need not discuss every aspect of a proposal that receives less than the maximum score or identify relative weaknesses in a proposal that is technically acceptable but presents a less desirable approach than others; rather, the agency should tailor its discussions to each offer, since the need for clarifications or revisions will vary with the proposals. 48 C.F.R. § 15.306. WorldTravelService v. U.S., 49 Fed. Cl. 431 (2001). United States ☞64.40(1)

While offerors must be given an equal opportunity to revise their proposals, and the FAR prohibits favoring one offeror over another, discussions need not be identical; rather, discussions are to be tailored to each offeror's proposal. 48 C.F.R. § 15.306. WorldTravelService v. U.S., 49 Fed. Cl. 431 (2001). United States ☞64.40(2)

In discussions with offerors, the procuring agency does not have to identify every item that might improve an offeror's proposal; rather, discussions need only address areas of weakness. 48 C.F.R. § 15.306(d)(3). JWK Intern. Corp. v. U.S., 49 Fed. Cl. 364 (2001), judgment aff'd, 279 F.3d 985 (Fed. Cir. 2002). United States ☞64.40(1)

Discussions with offerors whose proposals are found to be in the competitive range must be "meaningful," and requirement is not met if an offeror is not advised, in some way, of defects in its proposal that do not meet the requirements of the solicitation. 48 C.F.R. § 15.306(d). ManTech Telecommunications and Information Systems Corp. v. U.S., 49 Fed. Cl. 57 (2001), decision aff'd, 30 Fed. Appx. 995 (Fed. Cir. 2002). United States ☞64.40(1)

Discussions with an offeror are not required under the Federal Acquisition Regulation regarding opinions of a contracting agency drawn from data. 48 C.F.R. § 15.306(d)(3). Ryder Move Management, Inc. v. U.S., 48 Fed. Cl. 380 (2001). United States ☞64.40(1)

Contracting officer (CO) did not err in failing to conduct additional discussions with offeror regarding its financial condition, where the financial data was submitted by the offeror, accompanied by the offeror's explanation, and the data were not themselves in dispute, only the interpretation of the data. 48 C.F.R. § 15.306(d)(3). Ryder Move Management, Inc. v. U.S., 48 Fed. Cl. 380 (2001). United States ☞64.45(2)

An agency's failure to advise an offeror, in some way, of material proposal deficiencies vitiates the meaningfulness of contract discussions. 48 C.F.R. § 15.306(d). Dynacs Engineering Co., Inc. v. U.S., 48 Fed. Cl. 124 (2000). United States ☞64.40(1)

Agency's failure to identify two prior contracts that were considered in evaluating offeror's past performance did not violate agency's duty to conduct "meaningful discussions" with offeror, where performance problems associated with both contracts were identical to those found on other contracts that were cited, and thus offeror was not denied the opportunity to engage in meaningful discussions with evaluators on perceived management weaknesses. 48 C.F.R. § 15.306(d)(3). Cubic Defense Systems, Inc. v. U.S., 45 Fed. Cl. 450 (1999). United States ☞64.40(1)

Contracting officers are not required to engage in subsequent rounds of discussions and revised proposals simply because a disappointed offeror believes that additional rounds of discussions could somehow help it to construct an acceptable proposal. 48 C.F.R. § 15.306(d) (3). Impresa Construzioni Geom. Domenico Garufi v. U.S., 44 Fed. Cl. 540 (1999), aff'd in part, rev'd in part on other grounds, 238 F.3d 1324 (Fed. Cir. 2001). United States ☞64.40(5)

Offeror who protested Forest Service's award of contract to conduct tree stand exam did not establish that the Forest Service conducted any unfair discussions with awardee regarding past performance problems; rather, record showed that the Forest Service sought clarifications evenhandedly from offerors when it lacked information to fully evaluate the offers, as it was allowed to do under the FAR. 48 C.F.R. § 15.306(a)(1-2). Forestry Surveys and Data v. U.S., 44 Fed. Cl. 493 (1999). United States ☞64.40(2)

Discussions with offerors in course of negotiated procurements are "meaningful" as required under the FAR if they generally lead offerors into the areas of their proposals requiring amplification or correction, which means that discussions should be as specific as practical considerations permit. 48 C.F.R. § 15.610(c)(3)Advanced Data Concepts, Inc. v. U.S., 43 Fed. Cl. 410 (1999), aff'd, 216 F.3d 1054 (Fed. Cir. 2000). United States ☞64.40(1)

Contracting agency was not required, as part of "meaningful discussions" of negotiated procurement, to explain to offerer that it fundamentally misunderstood concepts used in agency; rather, agency was only required to give offerer a reasonable opportunity to correct its errors, and fact that its response did not satisfy the evaluators does not mean that the discussions were inadequate. 48 C.F.R. § 15.610(c)(3). Advanced Data Concepts, Inc. v. U.S., 43 Fed. Cl. 410 (1999), aff'd, 216 F.3d 1054 (Fed. Cir. 2000). United States ☞64.40(1)

Once contracting agency's request for final proposal revisions has been issued at the conclusion of discussions with offerors, agency generally may not engage in further discussions with any offerors. 48 C.F.R. § 15.307(b). Dubinsky v. U.S., 43 Fed. Cl. 243 (1999). United States ☞64.40(1)

Disappointed offeror did not establish that the contracting agency treated it unfairly by conducting multiple rounds of price discussions with, and receiving multiple revised price proposals from successful offeror on contract; agency did not violate the Federal Acquisition Regulation by conducting two rounds of price negotiations with successful offeror, while conducting only one with disappointed offeror. 48 C.F.R. § 15.306(e)(1). Miller-Holzwarth, Inc. v. U.S., 42 Fed. Cl. 643 (1999), aff'd, 232 F.3d 905 (Fed. Cir. 2000). United States ☞64.40(2)

Protest was sustained where discussions were conducted, but the protester was not provided with an opportunity to address the significant weaknesses identified in its proposal, even though one of the awardees had been provided the opportunity to revise its technical proposal in a significant way. Raytheon Company, B-404998, 2011 CPD ¶ 232 (Comp. Gen. 2011)

When an agency takes corrective action following a protest and reevaluates proposals, the agency must reopen discussions to address concerns identified in the reevaluations if the agency would have been required to raise those concerns if they were identified during the initial evaluation, the GAO concluded in sustaining a protest. The agency's concerns about the protester's proposal changed during the reevaluation such that the protester had to address the concerns to remain eligible for award. The agency's failure to reopen discussions rendered the discussions not meaningful. Matter of: Ewing Construction Co., Inc., B-401887.3, B-401887.4, 2010 CPD ¶ 108 (Comp. Gen. 2010)

Agencies are not required to afford offerors all-encompassing discussions or to discuss every aspect of a proposal that receives less than the maximum score, and are not required to advise an offeror of a minor weakness that is not considered significant, even where the weakness subsequently becomes a determinative factor in choosing between two closely ranked proposals. Apptis, Inc., B-403249, B-403249.3, 2010 CPD ¶ 237 (Comp. Gen. 2010)

The GAO determined that an agency failed to conduct meaningful discussions because it did not advise the protester that it considered the protester's schedule to be overly aggressive. Discussions must be sufficiently detailed to lead the vendor into the areas of its quotation requiring amplification or revision. Although the agency asked all offerors to provide a new project schedule, the GAO determined that the new schedule request did not inform the protester that the agency considered its schedule to be overly aggressive. Matter of: AINS, Inc., B-400760.4, B-400760.5, 2010 CPD ¶ 32 (Comp. Gen. 2010).

An agency failed to conduct meaningful discussions because it misled the protester by not conveying the true nature of its concerns about the choice of software proposed. GAO found that, by asking the protester to address only specific features of the proposed software, rather than the choice of the software, the agency misled the protester, thereby depriving the protester of an opportunity to address the agency's concern. Matter of: AMEC Earth & Environmental, Inc., B-401961, B-401961.2, 2010 CPD ¶ 151 (Comp. Gen. 2009)

Even though the agency complied with the FAR's minimum requirement to discuss "significant" weaknesses, GAO sustained a protest based on the agency's failure to discuss a non-significant weakness. GAO held: "Given the agency's decision to hold broad discussions with all firms, which went well beyond the FAR's minimum requirements, it was incumbent on the agency to do so with all offerors equally, and it may not now defend its failure to have apprised [the protester] of a perceived weakness in [its] proposal based on the FAR's minimum discussion requirements. Matter of: AMEC Earth & Environmental, Inc., B-401961, B-401961.2, 2010 CPD ¶ 151 (Comp. Gen. 2009)

Agency failed to conduct meaningful discussions where, after discussions had concluded, it determined that certain of the protester's proposed costs, which were set forth in the protester's initial and final revised proposals, were understated in comparison with those proposed by other offerors, and the agency adjusted the most probable cost estimate associated with the protester's costs upwards rather than reopening discussions to allow the protester an opportunity to address the issue. Matter of: CIGNA Government Services, LLC, B-401062.2, B-401062.3, 2010 CPD ¶ 283 (Comp. Gen. 2009)

In taking corrective action after a prior protest, an agency improperly limited discussions by not providing the protester with an opportunity to address significant weaknesses or deficiencies in its proposal because the agency limited it's discussions with the protester to a request for information showing that a proposed key position complied with the solicitation requirements. The agency provided the awardee with more extensive discussions and allowed it to revise its proposal. The protester, however, was not provided an opportunity to revise its proposal because the agency had previously revealed the awardee's price in the debriefing that preceded the earlier protest and believed that giving protester the opportunity to revise its proposal would confer an unfair competitive advantage. The GAO concluded that this was an insufficient justification. Matter of: American K-9 Detection Services, Inc., B-400464.6, 2009 CPD ¶ 107 (Comp. Gen. 2009)

Although not required by the RFQ, the agency conducted discussions. In such cases, the discussions, if held, must be meaningful, and must include a discussion of any deficiencies and significant weaknesses. FAR 15.306(d)(3). Because GSA based Tiger's ineligibility solely on price but did not raise the issue in discussions, the discussions were not meaningful, the Comp. Gen. found. It was possible that this prejudiced Tiger because it might otherwise have explained or reduced its price such that GSA would have found it fair and reasonable. Thus, the Comp. Gen. sustained Tiger's protest. Matter of: Tiger Truck, LLC, B-400685, 2009 CPD ¶ 19 (Comp. Gen. 2009)

An agency's decision to award a contract was flawed because the agency did not hold meaningful discussions with an offeror on the significant weakness of its proposed staffing plan, materially affecting the final selection, the U.S. Comptroller General recently determined. The agency also lacked a reasonable basis for its vendor selection because it unreasonably did not consider the winning proposal's identified weakness. Matter of: AT & T Corp., B-299542.3, B-299542.4, 2008 CPD ¶ 65 (Comp. Gen. 2007)

Protest that agency failed to provide meaningful discussions is denied where protester cannot establish prejudice because the record shows that protester's ordering systems for office supplies did not comply with a mandatory solicitation requirement, and shows that the protester did not plan to become compliant. Matter of OfficeMax, Inc., B-299340.2, 2007 CPD ¶ 158 (Comp. Gen. 2007)

In order for discussions in a negotiated procurement to be meaningful, an agency must advise the offeror of the deficiencies in its proposal, so that the offeror may have an opportunity to revise its proposal to satisfy the government's requirements. However, the content and extent of discussions is a matter of the contracting officer's judgment based on the particular facts of the procurement. In reviewing whether there has been sufficient disclosure of deficiencies, the focus is not on whether the agency described the deficiencies in such detail that there could be no doubt as to their identity and nature, but whether the information was sufficient in the context of the procurement to afford the offeror a fair and reasonable opportunity to identify and correct deficiencies in its proposal. Matter of: Alpha

Genesis, Inc., B-299859, 2007 CPD ¶ 167 (Comp. Gen. 2007)

Agency was not required to hold discussions regarding area of protester's proposal that was weak, but acceptable, and that did not prevent the protester from having a reasonable opportunity for award. Planning And Development Collaborative International, B-299041, 2007 CPD ¶ 28 (Comp. Gen. 2007)

Protester's contention that the agency conducted flawed discussions regarding price is sustained where (1) the agency corrected an error in the awardee's pricing; (2) the agency concluded that the awardee's price, as corrected, violated the solicitation's price target; (3) the agency advised the awardee in discussions that its price violated the solicitation's price target, though it did not, but never disclosed the upward adjustment it had made to correct the pricing error; (4) the awardee lowered its price in its final proposal, but repeated the pricing error it had made before; and (5) the agency selected that offeror for award after concluding that its significant price advantage offered the best value to the government. Thus, the record, as a whole, shows that the flawed discussions led the awardee to significantly lower its price, and the selection decision turned on the price differential between awardee and the protester. Advanced Systems Development, Inc., B-298411, B-298411.2, 2006 CPD ¶ 137 (Comp. Gen. 2006)

Agency was not required to discuss relative weaknesses in the protester's highly rated proposal that materialized as a result of oral presentations based on a comparative evaluation of the proposals by the agency, finding that the awardee's proposal had a superior technical approach. ManTech Security Technologies Corporation, B-297133.3, 2006 CPD ¶ 77 (Comp. Gen. 2006)

There generally is no obligation for an agency to set a competitive range and conduct discussions so that a deficient proposal may be made acceptable where the RFP specifically instructs offerors that award may be made on the basis of initial proposals. Matter of: Shaw Environmental, Inc., B-297294, 2005 CPD ¶ 218 (Comp. Gen. 2005)

Discussions are not inadequate simply because a weakness, which was not addressed during discussions, subsequently becomes a determinative factor in choosing between two closely ranked proposals, as was the case here. Gracon Corporation, B-293009, B-293009.2, B-293009.3, 2004 CPD ¶ 58 (Comp. Gen. 2004).

Where agency knew or should have known that the protester interpreted the solicitation as limiting technical proposals to 100 pages, discussions with the protester were not meaningful when the agency did not advise protester that the solicitation permitted 200 page proposals, declined to advise the protester of the agency's repeatedly expressed concerns that the protester's proposal lacked detail, and advised the protester there were no technical weaknesses in its proposal. Bank of America, B-287608, B-287608.2, 2001 CPD ¶ 137 (Comp. Gen. 2001)

Agency was not required to conduct discussions regarding two weaknesses identified in the protester's proposal regarding its past performance since the two weaknesses (which pertained to only 2 out of 20 performance questionnaire items) were not considered significant, and protester's performance record was rated acceptable overall. Agencies are not required to point out every element of acceptable proposals that receive less than the maximum evaluation rating. Digital Systems Group, Inc., B-286931, B-286931.2, 2001 CPD ¶ 50 (Comp. Gen. 2001)

Agency conducted meaningful discussions with the protester concerning its low evaluated staffing levels in certain functional areas where the agency informed the protester of the agency's concerns and of the amount by which the agency found the protester's proposed staffing low in these areas. IT Facility Services-Joint Venture, B-285841, 2000 CPD ¶ 177 (Comp. Gen. 2000)

Allegation that discussions with protester were not meaningful is sustained where the record shows that the evaluators were concerned over the protester's pricing methodology and the source selection official shared that concern, but the protester was not afforded an opportunity during discussions to explain its pricing strategy. ACS Government Solutions Group, Inc., B-282098, B-282098.2, B-282098.3, 99-1 CPD ¶ 106 (Comp. Gen. 1999).

Agency's determination, based on information acquired during preaward survey, that offeror lacked the understanding and capability to implement its proposed approach to meeting the specification requirements, constituted a nonresponsibility determination, not a revised technical evaluation. Agency therefore was not required to reopen discussions and request revised proposals. Matter of: TAAS-Israel Industries, Inc., B-251789, B-251789.3, 94-1 CPD ¶ 197 (Comp. Gen. 1994)

5 Competitive range

Disappointed offerors who were included in competitive range were prejudiced by contracting officer's error in failing to consider price evaluation factor in establishing competitive range, where contract awardee's bid would likely have been excluded from competitive range if price had been considered a factor, and thus disappointed offerors would have had a substantial chance of being awarded the contract. Information Sciences Corp. v. U.S., 73 Fed. Cl. 70 (2006), on reconsideration in part, 75 Fed. Cl. 406 (2007). United States ☜64.55(1)

Randolph-Sheppard Act and its implementing regulations do not contemplate or require a definition of competitive range different from that set forth in the Federal Acquisition Regulation. Randolph-Sheppard Vending Stand Act, § 1 et seq., as amended, 20 U.S.C.A. § 107 et seq.; 34 C.F.R. § 395.33(b); 48 C.F.R. § 15.306. North Carolina Div. of Services For Blind v. U.S., 53 Fed. Cl. 147 (2002), aff'd, 60 Fed. Appx. 826 (Fed. Cir. 2003). United States ☜57

Source selection board (SSB) did not violate section of the Federal Acquisition Regulation (FAR) governing communications with offerors before establishment of the competitive range, in not conducting discussions with offeror to allow it to explain the relevance of its prior contracts, where no competitive range was to be established. 48 C.F.R. § 15.306(b)(1). JWK Intern. Corp. v. U.S., 52 Fed. Cl. 650 (2002), aff'd, 56 Fed. Appx. 474 (Fed. Cir. 2003). United States ☜64.45(1)

It goes against principles of government contracting to exclude prematurely from competition an offeror whose proposal has a reasonable chance of being selected; federal acquisition policy favors inclusion of such an offeror within the competitive range in the early stages of a procurement. 48 C.F.R. §§ 15.306(c)(1), 15.609(a). Cubic Defense Systems, Inc. v. U.S., 45 Fed. Cl. 450 (1999). United States ☜64.40(1)

Government's elimination of offeror from the competitive range was not improper, where contracting officer established an initial competitive range of three offerors, and offeror was eliminated after its revised proposal was evaluated and discussions were held. FAR 15. 306(d)(4). Impresa Construzioni Geom. Domenico Garufi v. U.S., 44 Fed. Cl. 540 (1999), aff'd in part, rev'd in part, 238 F.3d 1324 (Fed. Cir. 2001) (The court ordered a limited deposition of the contracting officer, emphasizing "that such discovery of the contracting officer's reasoning is not lightly to be ordered and should not be ordered unless record evidence raises serious questions as to the rationality of the contracting officer's responsibility determination.") United States ☜64.40(1)

Contracting officer's disclosure to all offerors of their respective standing in the competitive price range, after agency disclosed such information during debriefing of one offeror and decided to reopen negotiations, did not violate the Procurement Integrity Act; informing all the offerors that they were in the high or low end of the competitive range was a reasonable means of serving to reduce the competitive advantage held by offeror who had received debriefing. Office of Federal Procurement Policy Act, § 27, as amended, 41 U.S.C.A. § 423. DGS Contract Service, Inc. v. U.S., 43 Fed. Cl. 227 (1999). United States ☜64.40(5)

Agency bulletin and attached instructions concerning when a proposal is in the competitive range was not a regulation entitled to the force and effect of law; bulletin was never promulgated, as it was distributed only to contracting personnel within the agency, and there was evidence that it was not intended to be a regulation, but merely an explication of requirement of the Federal Acquisition Regulation (FAR) that a contracting officer should err on the side of establishing a broad competitive range. 48 C.F.R. § 15.609(a). Labat-Anderson, Inc. v. U.S., 42 Fed. Cl. 806 (1999). Administrative Law And Procedure ☜417

Technically unacceptable proposals must generally be considered to be within the competitive range if capable of being made technically acceptable and if the proposal's cost or price term is competitive. Labat-Anderson, Inc. v. U.S., 42 Fed. Cl. 806 (1999). United States ☜64.30

Contracting agency acted within its discretion under federal acquisition regulation governing exchanges with offerors after receipt of proposals, when, in rejecting offeror's proposal, agency determined that it had not made a competitive range determination and was not obligated to engage in discussions with offeror concerning any weaknesses in its proposal. FAR 15.306. Firearms Training Systems, Inc. v. U.S., 41 Fed. Cl. 743, 42 Cont. Cas. Fed. (CCH) P 77369 (1998). United States ☞64.40(1)

Proposals need not be included within competitive range if they are so technically inferior or out of line as to price as to render discussions meaningless. 48 C.F.R. § 15.609(a). W & D Ships Deck Works, Inc. v. U.S., 39 Fed. Cl. 638, 42 Cont. Cas. Fed. (CCH) P 77222 (1997). United States ☞64.40(1)

Military Sealift Command, Atlantic (MSCLANT) acted reasonably in excluding offeror's proposal from competitive range of proposals for contract to perform work on ships; offeror's proposal failed to demonstrate how offeror would perform work required under contract, informational deficiencies in proposal tended to show that offeror did not understand scope of contract, and offeror would have had to rewrite most of its proposal in order to provide missing information. 48 C.F.R. § 15.609(a). W & D Ships Deck Works, Inc. v. U.S., 39 Fed. Cl. 638, 42 Cont. Cas. Fed. (CCH) P 77222 (1997). United States ☞64.40(1)

If a proposal fails to provide information sufficient to determine if offeror is technically acceptable, it is reasonable for agency to exclude it from competitive range. 48 C.F.R. § 15.609(a). W & D Ships Deck Works, Inc. v. U.S., 39 Fed. Cl. 638, 42 Cont. Cas. Fed. (CCH) P 77222 (1997). United States ☞64.40(1)

If offeror fails to demonstrate in its proposal how it will perform work required by contract, as required by solicitation, it is within agency's discretion to exclude proposal from competitive range. 48 C.F.R. § 15.609(a). W & D Ships Deck Works, Inc. v. U.S., 39 Fed. Cl. 638, 42 Cont. Cas. Fed. (CCH) P 77222 (1997). United States ☞64.40(1)

It is within agency's discretion to exclude technically unacceptable proposal from competitive range even if it is from the low price offeror. 48 C.F.R. § 15.609(a). W & D Ships Deck Works, Inc. v. U.S., 39 Fed. Cl. 638, 42 Cont. Cas. Fed. (CCH) P 77222 (1997). United States ☞64.40(1)

Relevant factors in reviewing agency decision to exclude proposal from competitive range include: (1) did solicitation specifically call for information that agency found lacking; (2) do informational deficiencies tend to show offeror did not understand contract's requirements; (3) does offeror essentially have to rewrite proposal to correct deficiencies; (4) was only one offeror left in competitive range; and (5) whether proposal, if reasonably correctable, would provide a cost savings. 48 C.F.R. § 15.609(a). W & D Ships Deck Works, Inc. v. U.S., 39 Fed. Cl. 638, 42 Cont. Cas. Fed. (CCH) P 77222 (1997). United States ☞64.40(1)

Close scrutiny of competitive range decisions is given by court only to decisions that result in competitive range of only one offeror. 48 C.F.R. § 15.609(a). W & D Ships Deck Works, Inc. v. U.S., 39 Fed. Cl. 638, 42 Cont. Cas. Fed. (CCH) P 77222 (1997). United States ☞64.60(3.1)

Agency decisions establishing competitive bidding range are primarily a matter of administrative discretion that will not be disturbed absent clear showing that determination lacked reasonable basis. 48 C.F.R. § 15.609(a). W & D Ships Deck Works, Inc. v. U.S., 39 Fed. Cl. 638, 42 Cont. Cas. Fed. (CCH) P 77222 (1997). United States ☞64.60(4)

Courts may not overrule agency competitive range decisions except where contracting officer's (CO) actions are clearly unreasonable. 48 C.F.R. § 15.609(a). W & D Ships Deck Works, Inc. v. U.S., 39 Fed. Cl. 638, 42 Cont. Cas. Fed. (CCH) P 77222 (1997). United States ☞64.60(4)

Offeror's proposal on public contract was not accorded disparate treatment during competitive range evaluation process in violation of regulation; offeror failed to show that deficiencies in other proposals, which allegedly were not treated as harshly as deficiencies in offeror's proposal, were of same magnitude as deficiencies in offeror's proposal, and offeror failed to show its proposal was considered under different standards. 48 C.F.R. § 15.603. Aero Corp., S.A. v. U.S., 38 Fed. Cl. 739, 42 Cont. Cas. Fed. (CCH) P 77213 (1997). United States ☞64.40(1)

Government's rejection of software process proposal did not violate regulation stating that competitive range shall be determined on basis of cost or price and other factors that were stated in solicitation; solicitation clearly indicated that costs would be considered in light of technical merits of each proposal, so that there would be no extensive cost analysis if evaluator determined that proposal's technical merit were comparatively weak, and evaluation sheets represented only portion of overall consideration of proposal. 48 C.F.R. § 15.609(a). Compubahn, Inc. v. U.S., 33 Fed. Cl. 677, 40 Cont. Cas. Fed. (CCH) P 76804 (1995). United States ☞64.40(1)

Agency reasonably excluded the protester's proposal from the competitive range because the protester failed to provide company experience information for one of its subcontractors and did not address the main experience areas described in the experience evaluation factor. As a result of these shortcomings, the protester's offer was not among the most highly rated proposals. Solstice Advertising, B-405529.2, 2011 CPD ¶ 256 (Comp. Gen. 2011)

An agency's exclusion of a proposal from the competitive range was improper because the agency relied solely on a technical-score cutoff to establish the competitive range and did not consider the proposal's cost to the Government. An agency may not exclude a technically acceptable proposal from the competitive range without considering the relative cost of that proposal. The agency's evaluation in this case was unreasonable because "there is no evidence that price was considered in deciding whether a proposal should be included or excluded," Matter of: Arc-Tech, Inc., B-400325.3, 2009 CPD ¶ 53 (Comp. Gen. 2009)

The determination of whether a proposal belongs in the competitive range is principally a matter within the discretion of the procuring agency. GAO will review an agency's evaluation of proposals and determination to exclude a proposal from the competitive range for reasonableness and consistency with the criteria and language of the solicitation, as well as applicable statues and regulations. Contracting agencies are not required to retain in the competitive range proposals that are not among the most highly rated or that the agency otherwise reasonably concludes have no realistic prospect of award. FAR 15.306(c)(1). Matter of: TELESIS Corporation, B-299804, 2007 CPD ¶ 150 (Comp. Gen. 2007)

Agency's decision to exclude protester's proposal from competition for failing to include option year pricing was reasonable, where the solicitation required that proposals contain this pricing and provided for award without discussions; agency was not required to allow protester to correct mistake because, although the omission was evident on the face of the proposal, the protester's intended pricing for the option years was not apparent. Battelle Memorial Institute, B-299533, 2007 CPD ¶ 94 (Comp. Gen. 2007)

Protest is denied where the protester's proposal was properly eliminated from competitive range because, among other reasons, the proposal requested addition of an advance payment term to the contract, and acknowledged that without the advance payment the protester could not perform, and the protester's objections to contracting officer's affirmative responsibility determination did not show a failure to consider available relevant information. Brian X. Scott, B-298568, 2006 CPD ¶ 156 (Comp. Gen. 2006)

Contracting agencies are not required to retain a proposal in a competitive range where the proposal is not among the most highly rated or where the agency otherwise reasonably concludes that the proposal has no realistic prospect of award. Where a proposal is technically unacceptable as submitted and would require major revisions to become acceptable, exclusion from the competitive range is generally permissible. Proposals with significant informational deficiencies may be excluded, whether the deficiencies are attributable to omitted or merely inadequate information. Hamilton Sundstrand Power Systems, B-298757, 2006 CPD ¶ 194 (Comp. Gen. 2006)

In procurement that placed greater importance on technical factors, agency's establishment of a competitive range of one, which consisted of the awardee's technically unacceptable initial proposal and which excluded protester's "highly acceptable" technical proposal, on the basis that protester's evaluated cost/price was 15 percent higher than the awardee's, was not reasonable where the agency's cost/price evaluation reflected various flaws and erroneous assumptions. Matter of: Global, A 1st Flagship Company, B-297235, B-297235.2, 2006 CPD ¶ 14 (Comp. Gen. 2005)

Agency's determination to eliminate a proposal for a custody officer services contract from the competitive range, based solely on a minimum requirement for direct corporate experience that was neither stated in the solicitation nor disclosed to offerors prior to proposal submission, was improper. Omniplex World Services Corporation, B-290996.2, 2003 CPD ¶ 7 (Comp. Gen. 2003)

Agency reasonably excluded protester's proposal from the competitive range where proposal was deficient in all three technical evaluation factors and, to become acceptable, would have required major revisions tantamount to submission of a new proposal. CMC & Maintenance, Inc., B-290152, 2002 CPD ¶ 107 (Comp. Gen. 2002)

In a procurement under simplified acquisition procedures where the agency elected to establish a competitive range and conduct discussions, the agency improperly excluded the protester's low-priced quote from the competitive range and conducted discussions with only the awardee, where the protester's and awardee's quotes failed to satisfy the same solicitation requirements and the record did not support the agency's determination that the protester would not have had a realistic chance of receiving award if it had been afforded discussions. Kathryn Huddleston and Associates, Ltd., B-289453, 2002 CPD ¶ 57 (Comp. Gen. 2002)

6 Past performance

Contracting agency did not abuse its discretion in solicitation for construction project by not seeking clarification from offeror concerning its past performance information after technical evaluation team (TET) determined that the information was inadequate to determine the scope of past projects, despite fact that the TET concluded that clarifications should be required, where source selection authority (SSA) subsequently explained that no clarification were sought because no discussions were conducted with any offerors. 48 C.F.R. § 15.306(a)(1, 2). Gulf Group Inc. v. U.S., 61 Fed. Cl. 338 (2004). United States ☞64.45(2)

Agency representative has broad discretion to decide whether to communicate with a contractor concerning its performance history, under section of the Federal Acquisition Regulation (FAR) providing that offerors "may" be given the opportunity to clarify certain aspects of proposals, including past performance information, where award will be made without conducting discussions. 48 C.F.R. § 15.306(a)(2). JWK Intern. Corp. v. U.S., 52 Fed. Cl. 650 (2002), aff'd, 56 Fed. Appx. 474 (Fed. Cir. 2003). United States ☞64.45(2)

Finding that a particular contract is not relevant or is not recent are not a findings of deficiency or significant weakness, nor does it constitute adverse past performance information. Therefore, an agency is not required to inform an offeror of such a finding during discussions for the discussions to be meaningful. Maywood Closure Company, LLC, B-408343, 2013 CPD ¶ 199 (Comp. Gen. 2013)

Agency is not required to evaluate the past performance of key personnel or subcontractors. GAO held that an agency has a legitimate interest in assessing performance risk by considering only the experience and past performance of entities with which it will have contractual privity. HK Consulting, Inc., B- 408443, 2013 CPD ¶ 224 (Comp. Gen. 2013)

Protest was sustained because the agency's evaluation of past performance was unreasonable and inconsistent with the solicitation, in that the agency did not meaningfully assess the relevance of the offerors' prior contracts. The past performance evaluations assumed that the past performance references were relevant and focused primarily on the quality of the offeror's past performance records. The Emergence Group, B-404844.5, 2012 CPD ¶ 132 (Comp. Gen. 2012)

Contracting agencies must provide an offeror with an opportunity to address adverse past performance information to which the offeror has not previously had an opportunity to respond. FAR 15.306(a)(2). There exists no requirement, however, that the agency find an offeror's rebuttals conclusive. TPL, Inc., B-297136.10, B-297136.11, 2006 CPD ¶ 104 (Comp. Gen. 2006).

While a competitive range of one means that the competition is at an end, we will not question a determination to establish a competitive range of one where the contracting officer had a reasonable basis to find that the excluded proposals lacked a reasonable chance of being selected for award. Information Systems Technology Corporation, B-291747, 2003 CPD ¶ 72, 2005 CPD ¶ 76 (Comp. Gen. 2003).

Agency was not required to conduct discussions regarding two weaknesses identified in the protester's proposal regarding its past performance since the two weaknesses (which pertained to only 2 out of 20 performance questionnaire items) were not considered significant, and protester's performance record was rated acceptable overall. Agencies are not required to point out every element of acceptable proposals that receive less than the maximum evaluation rating. Digital Systems Group, Inc., B-286931, B-286931.2, 2001 CPD ¶ 50 (Comp. Gen. 2001)

7 Discretion of agency

Decision of the contracting officer not to engage in cost discussions with the incumbent contractor because the Navy had determined that the cost proposal was acceptable was neither in bad faith nor an abuse of discretion, based on the contracting officer's judgment that a 1.79% difference in cost was not a weakness or deficiency. 48 C.F.R. §§ 15.301, 15.306(d) (3). JWK Intern. Corp. v. U.S., 279 F.3d 985 (Fed. Cir. 2002). United States ☞64.40(2)

Whether discussions should be conducted with offerors lies within the discretion of the contracting officer, as do all aspects of the discussions, their subject, breadth, and extent, and under the Federal Acquisition Regulation, aside from areas of significant weakness or deficiency, the contracting officer need not discuss areas in which a proposal may merely be improved. 48 C.F.R. § 15.306(d)(3). JWK Intern. Corp. v. U.S., 279 F.3d 985 (Fed. Cir. 2002). United States ☞64.40(1)

A contracting officer (CO) does not have discretion under the Federal Acquisition Regulation (FAR) to ignore an evaluation factor that is set forth in the solicitation when making the competitive range determination. Information Sciences Corp. v. U.S., 73 Fed. Cl. 70 (2006), on reconsideration in part, 75 Fed. Cl. 406 (2007). United States ☞64.40(1)

The decision to conduct discussions with an offeror and the scope of any discussions are left to the judgment of the contracting officer. 48 C.F.R. § 15.306. WorldTravelService v. U.S., 49 Fed. Cl. 431 (2001). United States ☞64.40(1)

In accordance with discretion provided under the Federal Acquisition Regulation, contracting agencies need not discuss every aspect of a proposal that receives less than the maximum score or identify relative weaknesses in a proposal that is technically acceptable but presents a less desirable approach than others. 48 C.F.R. § 15.306(d)(3). Ryder Move Management, Inc. v. U.S., 48 Fed. Cl. 380 (2001). United States ☞64.40(1)

FAR affords a procuring agency broad discretion in conducting discussions to obtain the best value for the government, and in the exercise of such discretion, a contracting officer need not discuss with offeror all areas in which its proposal could be improved. 48 C.F.R. § 15.306(d)(3). Dynacs Engineering Co., Inc. v. U.S., 48 Fed. Cl. 124 (2000). United States ☞64.40(1)

Both the decision to conduct discussions with offerors and the scope of any discussions are left to the judgment of the contracting officer. 48 C.F.R. § 15.306(d). Biospherics, Inc. v. U.S., 48 Fed. Cl. 1 (2000). United States ☞64.40(1)

An offeror in a lowest-priced, technically acceptable solicitation is not required to take part in discussions if the offeror's proposal was already deemed "technically acceptable." GAO reasoned that "because it was not possible for [the protester] to improve its technical proposal after the initial evaluation, the [agency's] subsequent discussions with offerors whose proposals were not technically acceptable did not deprive [the protester] of any opportunity afforded to other offerors." Matter of: Commercial Design Group, Inc., B-400923.4, 2009 CPD ¶ 157 (Comp. Gen. 2009)

8 Minimum or material requirements

In general, concept of responsiveness is not applicable to negotiation procurements where contracting officer is permitted to conduct oral or written discussions with offerors whose proposals vary from request for proposals; however, while concept of responsiveness is not technically applicable to negotiated procurements, even in negotiated procurement procuring agency does not have discretion to disregard offeror's failure to satisfy material requirement in request for proposal. Howard Cooper Corp. v. U.S., 763 F. Supp. 829, 37 Cont. Cas. Fed. (CCH) P 76169 (E.D. Va. 1991). United States ☞64.5

A solicitation for a government contract must seek proposals that meet an agency's minimum needs, or else the solicitation represents an undue, improper restriction on competition. ABF Freight System, Inc. v. U.S., 55 Fed. Cl. 392 (2003). United States ☞64.25

A mandatory minimum requirement must be clearly identified as such within a solicitation so as to put offerors on notice of the serious consequences of failing to meet the requirement; such notice typically emphasizes that a proposal must meet the requirement in order to be eligible for evaluation or, conversely, that failure to comply with the requirement will lead to outright rejection of the proposal. ManTech Telecommunications and Information Systems Corp. v. U.S., 49 Fed. Cl. 57 (2001), decision aff'd, 30 Fed. Appx. 995 (Fed. Cir. 2002). United States ☞64.25

Solicitation's minimum education and experience provisions could not reasonably be read as imposing a minimum mandatory requirement; far from providing the requisite notice that failure to comply with the minimum experience and resume requirements would result in disqualification, the solicitation, as a whole, signaled that relatively minor deficiencies, rating something better than an exceptionally low score on a specific element or factor, would not result in a proposal being eliminated. ManTech Telecommunications and Information Systems Corp. v. U.S., 49 Fed. Cl. 57 (2001), decision aff'd, 30 Fed. Appx. 995 (Fed. Cir. 2002). United States ☞64.25

A mandatory minimum requirement (MMR) must be specified as such within a solicitation. 48 C.F.R. § 15.206(a). Cubic Defense Systems, Inc. v. U.S., 45 Fed. Cl. 450 (1999). United States ☞64.25

Government violated procurement statutes and regulations in awarding software contract, by relaxing minimum solicitation requirement without notifying all offerors that the evaluation criterion had changed. 10 U.S.C.A. § 2305(b)(1); 48 C.F.R. §§ 12.602(b, c), 15. 305(a). Candle Corp. v. U.S., 40 Fed. Cl. 658, 42 Cont. Cas. Fed. (CCH) P 77276 (1998). United States ☞64.25

Requirement in Army's solicitation of proposals on contract for computer and data processing support, that proposed personnel have three years minimum experience within preceding five years, was not latently ambiguous as alleged by disappointed offeror; solicitation stated that proposed personnel must have requisite years of experience, defined the minimum years of experience required for proposed personnel, stated that proposed personnel would receive score of "unacceptable" if they did not meet minimum experience requirements, and further defined "unacceptable" as numerical score of zero. Analytical & Research Technology, Inc. v. U.S., 39 Fed. Cl. 34, 442 Cont. Cas. Fed. (CCH) P 77228 (1997). United States ☞64.25

In soliciting proposals on contract for computer and automated data processing support, Army could evaluate the requirement that proposed personnel have three years minimum experience within preceding five years as a "go/no-go" requirement which if not met would render that portion of offeror's proposal technically unacceptable, regardless of whether solicitation used term "go/no-go." 10 U.S.C.A. § 2305(a)(2); Federal Property and Administrative Services Act of 1949, § 303A(b)(1), as amended, 41 U.S.C.A. § 253a(b)(1); 48 C.F.R. § 15. 605(d)(1). Analytical & Research Technology, Inc. v. U.S., 39 Fed. Cl. 34, 442 Cont. Cas. Fed. (CCH) P 77228 (1997). United States ☞64.40(1)

Statement of requirements for second phase of application process for concessions contract required that applicant not condition capital improvement fund contribution following change of operations on further negotiation. YRT Services Corp. v. U.S., 28 Fed. Cl. 366, 38 Cont. Cas. Fed. (CCH) P 76512 (1993). United States ☞64.30

Required purchase of concessioner, at price set by National Park Service (NPS), by successful applicant for concessions contract did not prejudice unsuccessful applicant or prevent that unsuccessful applicant from being fully and fairly considered in exactly same way as all other applicants; it was not clear that purchase price was necessarily higher than that which unsuccessful applicant could have negotiated, statement of requirements for second phase of application process called for package offer that took into account many other factors, and terms of purchase were same for all applicants. YRT Services Corp. v. U.S., 28 Fed. Cl. 366, 38 Cont. Cas. Fed. (CCH) P 76512 (1993). United States ☞64.40(2)

9 Disclosure of information

Government did not improperly reveal incumbent contractor's proprietary information by advising another offeror of approximate amount by which its proposed salary rates were below "current average annual salaries"; government did not reveal incumbent's actual salary rates, and incumbent provided average salary rates to government without any claim that information was proprietary and should be protected. 48 C.F.R. § 15.306(e)(3). OMV Medical, Inc. v. U.S., 219 F.3d 1337 (Fed. Cir. 2000). United States ☞64.40(2)

Government may request further proposals after violation of regulation prohibiting disclosure of potential contractor's proposal, but only if government has rational or reasonable basis for doing so unrelated to violation; disclosure of one offeror's proposal does not make later negotiations per se illegal. 48 C.F.R. § 15.610(d) (1989). LaBarge Products, Inc. v. West, 46 F.3d 1547, 40 Cont. Cas. Fed. (CCH) P 76733 (Fed. Cir. 1995). United States ⚮64.25

Government did not abuse its discretion prior to award of contract for computer management and support services at naval air development center by denying disappointed offeror opportunity to inspect center's files inasmuch as review of competitor's proposal and negotiated procurements is not permitted. Applications Research Corp. v. Naval Air Development Center, 752 F. Supp. 660, 37 Cont. Cas. Fed. (CCH) P 76045 (E.D. Pa. 1990). United States ⚮64.40(1)

10 Auctions

An "auction" is the direct bidding of price between two competing offerors and not the negotiation of a price between an offeror and the government. FAR Part 15.306(e), provides that the government cannot favor one offeror over another, reveal an offeror's technical solution or reveal an offeror's price without that offeror's permission. No violation of these provisions occurred where there was no disclosure of proposals, including price, to other offerors; there was no cancelling of a contract award; no offeror was favored over another; and there was no "direct bidding of price" between the offerors. Accordingly, there was no auction. Southern Foods, Inc. v. U.S., 76 Fed. Cl. 769 (2007)

Contracting agency did not conduct an illegal "auction" when, after reopening contract negotiations, it disclosed to all offerors their respective placement in the price range and gave them the opportunity to revise their price proposals; there was no direct price bidding, and even if the contracting officer had disclosed prices, such action would not have constituted an auction. 48 C.F.R. § 15.306(e). DGS Contract Service, Inc. v. U.S., 43 Fed. Cl. 227 (1999). United States ⚮64.25

The conduct of an auction in a negotiated procurement is not per se improper. Logicon, Inc. v. U.S., 22 Cl. Ct. 776, 37 Cont. Cas. Fed. (CCH) P 76066, 1991 WL 52823 (1991). Public Contracts ⚮5.1

An improper auction would occur if the procuring agency, after initially determining the contractor to be the successful offeror, disclose the amount of contractor's offer and then express its desire to reopen negotiations, absent a reasonable or rational basis for deeming that the offerors fell short of meeting the Government's needs in the procurement, as all offerors would not possess equal knowledge of the same information as required to have a valid procurement. Logicon, Inc. v. U.S., 22 Cl. Ct. 776, 37 Cont. Cas. Fed. (CCH) P 76066, 1991 WL 52823 (1991). Public Contracts ⚮12

11 Improper discussions

If an agency identifies concerns during a reevaluation of proposals that should have been raised had they been identified before discussions were held, the agency must reopen discussions to permit the offeror to address those concerns. The agency's failure to do so deprived the protester of the opportunity to address and resolve the weaknesses in its Final Proposal Revision. Delfasco, LLC, B-409514.3, 2016CPD ¶ 192 (Comp. Gen. 2016)

Contracting agency did not hold improper discussions with successful offeror on solicitation for trash pick-up services when it inquired about offeror's proposed annual tonnage capacity for trash disposal; in reviewing offeror's proposal, agency noticed that it appeared offeror had inserted its monthly tonnage capacity, not the annual capacity required by the solicitation, and agency contacted offeror only to clarify whether it had submitted the monthly figure by mistake, and not to conduct negotiations. International Resource Recovery, Inc. v. U.S., 64 Fed. Cl. 150 (2005). United States ⚮64.40(1)

Contracting agency violated procurement regulation by engaging in improper discussions with offeror after the submission of amended proposals. 48 C.F.R. § 15.307(b). Dubinsky v. U.S., 43 Fed. Cl. 243 (1999). United States ⚮64.40(1)

Protest was sustained in a simplified acquisition procurement where agency engaged in discussions with the awardee and permitted the awardee to change the pricing terms in its quotation, but did not conduct discussions with the protester. Although an agency is not required to conduct discussions under simplified acquisition procedures, where an agency avails itself of negotiated procurement procedures, the agency should treat offerors fairly and reasonably in the conduct of those procedures. Int'l Waste Indus., B-411338, 2015 CPD ¶ 196 (Comp. Gen. 2015)

Protest that agency improperly evaluated the awardee's proposal and improperly conducted discussions with the awardee is sustained where the record reflects that the agency's reevaluation depended on a post-evaluation exchange with the firm that constituted discussions, not clarifications. The awardee was permitted to materially revise its technical proposal, to the protester's prejudice, because the agency improperly failed to request final proposal revisions from all competitive range offerors. Piquette & Howard Elec. Serv., Inc., B-408435.3, 2014 CPD ¶ 8 (Comp. Gen. 2014)

In taking corrective action after a prior protest, an agency improperly limited discussions by not providing the protester with an opportunity to address significant weaknesses or deficiencies in its proposal because the agency limited it's discussions with the protester to a request for information showing that a proposed key position complied with the solicitation requirements. The agency provided the awardee with more extensive discussions and allowed it to revise its proposal. The protester, however, was not provided an opportunity to revise its proposal because the agency had previously revealed the awardee's price in the debriefing that preceded the earlier protest and believed that giving protester the opportunity to revise its proposal would confer an unfair competitive advantage. The GAO concluded that this was an insufficient justification. Matter of: American K-9 Detection Services, Inc., B-400464.6, 2009 CPD ¶ 107 (Comp. Gen. 2009)

12 Award without discussions

Air Force's decision not to hold discussions in solicitation for aircraft maintenance services, even where only two proposals were received, was within discretion afforded a procuring agency; and it was reasonable for Air Force to seek information only from contract awardee to clarify aspects of its proposal or to correct minor errors where it planned to award contract without seeking revisions of either of the two proposals. DynCorp Intern. LLC v. U.S., 76 Fed. Cl. 528 (2007).

Contracting agency's decision in best value procurement to award contract without discussions, despite a price premium, was a reasonable exercise of agency's discretion, in light of the higher technical evaluation of awardee's proposal; higher price of awardee's proposal did not make agency's decision to award without discussions arbitrary or capricious, or contrary to statute or regulation. DynCorp Intern. LLC v. U.S., 76 Fed. Cl. 528 (2007).

Decision of contracting officer (CO) not to hold discussions with offerors did not render contract award arbitrary and capricious, despite offeror's claim that discussions would have provided it the opportunity to explain some of the purported deficiencies in its proposal, and it would have explained cost-saving mechanisms it used. Rig Masters, Inc. v. U.S., 70 Fed. Cl. 413 (2006). United States ☞64.40(1)

Agency's decision to exclude protester's proposal from competition for failing to include option year pricing was reasonable, where the solicitation required that proposals contain this pricing and provided for award without discussions; agency was not required to allow protester to correct mistake because, although the omission was evident on the face of the proposal, the protester's intended pricing for the option years was not apparent. Battelle Memorial Institute, B-299533, 2007 CPD ¶ 94 (Comp. Gen. 2007)

Protester's challenge that it should have been afforded the opportunity to comment on negative past performance information, which the protester had not previously had the opportunity to address, is denied where the solicitation indicated that award could be made without the benefit of discussions and there was no basis for the agency to have questioned the validity of the information since it was based on the agency's first-hand experience with the protester's performance. General Dynamics- Ordinance & Tactical Systems, B-295987, B-295987.2, 2005 CPD ¶ 114 (Comp. Gen. 2005)

13 Definition of discussions

In the context of a government contract proposal, the term "discussions" has a specific legal definition: discussions involve negotiations and are undertaken with the intent of allowing the offeror to revise its proposal. FAR 15.306(d). Galen Medical Associates, Inc. v. U.S., 369 F.3d 1324 (Fed. Cir. 2004). United States ☞64.40(1)

Exchanges by which federal agency obtained additional information about subcontractors listed in bidder's proposal for professional services contract were "clarifications," rather than "discussions," under regulation that implemented statutes barring government from holding discussions with only one bidder for government contract; communications, through which bidder provided requested explanation as to which parts of project each subcontractor would support and detailed subcontractors' relevant experience regarding those tasks, did not qualify as "discussions," which were intended to occur in the context of negotiations during which bidders would have opportunity to revise their proposals, and agency's requests merely sought clarification of subcontractors' relevant experience, as authorized by regulation, even though additional, new information was sought. Information Technology & Applications Corp. v. U.S., 316 F.3d 1312 (Fed. Cir. 2003)

In the context of evaluation notices (ENs) sent by contracting agency to offerors, when the agency does not give the offeror the opportunity to revise its proposal and the offeror does not change the terms of its proposal to make it more appealing to the agency, the ENs and an offeror's responses to the ENs are not "discussions" under the Federal Acquisition Regulation (FAR). DynCorp Intern. LLC v. U.S., 76 Fed. Cl. 528 (2007).

Exchanges between offeror and contracting agency regarding offeror's purchasing system, even if they produced changes in offeror's proposal, did not constitute "discussions" under the FAR, because they concerned only offeror's financial and fiscal responsibility. DynCorp Intern. LLC v. U.S., 76 Fed. Cl. 528 (2007).

No improper "discussions" were held where DCAA sought clarification of the eventual awardee's proposed labor rates while conducting its audit. These were not improper discussions under FAR 15.306(d) because they were not intended and did not lead toward any type of proposal revision. DCAA sought this information in order to verify the reasonableness of the offeror's price and its compliance with applicable labor law regarding fringe benefit rates. DCAA did not negotiate with the offeror and the contracting agency did not indicate that it would allow the offeror to revise its proposal. The information obtained by DCAA did not change a technically unacceptable proposal into an acceptable one. DCAA did not seek anything omitted from the proposal that was required to meet the technical acceptability standards. Therefore, the exchange did not constitute "discussions." SecureNet Co. Ltd. v. U.S., 72 Fed. Cl. 800 (2006)

Contracting agency's request for a subcontracting plan from successful offeror did not constitute "discussions" or require that revised proposals be solicited from all offerors; agency's action of requesting offeror's subcontracting plan, and negotiating with it to ensure that the subcontracting plan was acceptable, was required by FAR 19.705-4, and such negotiations were patently not of the type that would permit other offerors to revise their proposals. It is clear that *only* the "apparently successful offeror" need be engaged in subcontracting negotiations, and such negotiations are patently not of the type that permit offerors to revise their proposals. Consolidated Engineering Services, Inc. v. U.S., 64 Fed.Cl. 617 (2005)

Where the quality and completeness of the subcontracting plan was not to be evaluated as part of the comparative evaluation of proposals, the subcontracting plan requirement concerns a matter of responsibility. In this situation, an agency request for an updated subcontracting plan does not constitute discussions or require that revised proposals be solicited from all offerors. A P Logistics, LLC, B-401600, 2010 CPD ¶ 179 (Comp.Gen. 2010)

In a negotiated procurement, an agency's exchanges with offerors with respect to their proposed subcontracting plans were discussions, where the solicitation provided for the comparative assessment of the merits of the plans as part of the agency's technical evaluation, a number of the offerors' subcontracting plans were assessed as being unacceptable, and the offerors made material revisions in their plans in response to the exchanges with the agency that made them acceptable. Computer Sciences Corporation; Unisys Corporation; Northrop Grumman Information Technology, Inc., IBM Business Consulting Services-Federal, B-298494.2, B-298494.3, B-298494.4, B-298494.5, B-298494.6, B-298494.7, B-298494.8, B-298494.9, B-298494.10, B-298494.11, B-298494.12, B-298494.13, B-298494. 14, 2007 CPD ¶ 103 (Comp. Gen. 2007)

Discussions occur when an agency indicates to an offeror significant weaknesses, deficiencies, and other aspects of its proposal that could be altered or explained to materially enhance the proposal's potential for award. FAR 15.306(d)(3). When an agency conducts discussions with one offeror, it must conduct discussions with all other offerors in the competitive range. FAR 15.305(d)(1). Joint Venture Penauillie Italia S.p.A.; Cofathec S.p.A. ; SEB.CO S.a.s.; CO.PEL.S.a.s., B-298865, B-298865.2, 2007 CPD ¶ 7 (Comp. Gen. 2007)

The "acid test" for deciding whether discussions have been held is whether it can be said that an offeror was provided the opportunity to modify its proposal. Joint Venture Penauillie Italia S.p.A.; Cofathec S.p.A. ; SEB.CO S.a.s.; CO.PEL.S.a.s., B-298865, B-298865.2, 2007 CPD ¶ 7 (Comp. Gen. 2007)

Agency's communications with awardees following submission of initial proposals, during which awardees made multiple changes to the evaluated rates on which the agency's source selection decision was based, constituted discussions and required that the agency establish a competitive range and conduct discussions with all competitive range offerors. University of Dayton Research Institute, B-296946.6, 2006 CPD ¶ 102 (Comp. Gen. 2006)

Agency did not trigger requirement to hold discussions with all competitive range offerors by communicating with awardee regarding its subcontracting plan prior to award since these communications did not pertain to evaluation of the awardee's proposal and therefore did not constitute discussions. Rather, the negotiation and ultimate approval of a subcontracting plan involved a question of the awardee's responsibility. General Dynamics-Ordinance & Tactical Systems, B-295987; B-295987.2, 2005 CPD ¶ 114 (Comp. Gen. 2005)

It is the actions of the parties that determine whether discussions have been held and not merely the characterization of the exchanges by the agency. Gulf Copper Ship Repair, Inc., B-293706.5, 2005 CPD ¶ 108 (Comp. Gen. 2004)

Agency's communications with awardee during oral presentation did not constitute discussions, and agency thus was not required to conduct discussions with and request revised proposals from all offerors in the competitive range, where information furnished by awardee (with respect to staffing of effort to develop health care network) in response to agency questions after oral presentation was merely a clarification of information previously furnished by awardee in the presentation slides and accompanying oral presentation of slides. Sierra Military Health Services, Inc.; Aetna Government Health Plans, B-292780, B-292780.2, B-292780.3, B-292780.4, B-292780.5, B-292780.6, 2004 CPD ¶ 55 (Comp. Gen. 2003)

Where agency personnel comment on, or raise substantive questions or concerns about, vendors' quotations or proposals in the course of an oral presentation, and either simultaneously or subsequently afford the vendors an opportunity to make revisions in light of the agency personnel's comments, questions, and concerns, discussions have occurred. TDS, Inc., B-292674, 2003 CPD ¶ 204 (Comp. Gen. 2003)

Agency official's request for cost and pricing data from awardee and conversations with awardee's references to determine whether awardee could perform contract at the low price offered relate to responsibility—the firm's capability to perform the contract—and do not constitute discussions since the information solicited was not necessary to determine the acceptability of the awardee's proposal and did not provide the awardee an opportunity to modify its proposal. WECO Cleaning Specialists, Inc, B-279305, 98-1 CPD ¶ 154 (Comp. Gen. 1998).

14 Misleading discussions

Agency's discussions were misleading because the agency mistakenly informed the eventual awardee that its proposed price was greater than the independent government estimate, when, in fact, it was lower. The agency's misleading discussions caused the eventual awardee to lower its proposed price based on the false information provided by the agency and caused the ensuing price evaluation to be a sham. Caddell Constr. Co. v. U.S., 2016 WL 537314 (2016)

Disappointed offeror failed to establish the contracting officer (CO) conducted prejudicially misleading discussions during reopened negotiations in violation of regulation, absent evidence that agency treated disappointed offeror any differently than awardee when it asked certain questions during discussions. 48 C.F.R. § 15.306(e)(1). DGS Contract Service, Inc. v. U.S., 43 Fed. Cl. 227 (1999). United States ⇔64.40(1)

USTRANSCOM engaged in misleading discussions by requesting that an offeror delete several staffing assumptions from its proposal, even though the source selection record indicates that the agency did not have any concerns regarding the staffing assumptions.

Prejudice was established based on the protester's "reasonable assertion that it could have improved its competitive position" had the discussions not been misleading. Paragon Tech. Grp., Inc., B-412636, 2016 CPD ¶ 113 (Comp. Gen. 2016)

Protest alleging that agency engaged in misleading discussions was sustained because the agency's discussion questions addressed the level effort proposed for only one aspect of performance even though the agency had concerns with the level of effort proposed on the entire line item. EFW Inc., B-412608, et al., 2016 CPD ¶ 304 (Comp. Gen. 2016)

Protest was sustained where the agency engaged in misleading discussions. The agency relied on a significantly inflated Independent Government Cost Estimate (IGCE) to advise the protester that its labor rates were too low and indicated significant risk. This caused the protester to increase its rates. Thereafter, the agency revised its IGCE downward by over 50% but did not reopen discussions. Vencore Servs. & Solutions, Inc., B-412949, et al., 2016 CPD ¶ 346 (Comp. Gen. 2016)

Agency conducted misleading discussions where it advised protester during discussions that it should provide resumes for all proposed personnel for the lifespan of the contract, but in its protest response asserted that the RFP did not require such submission of resumes. KPMG LLP, B-406409, 2012 CPD ¶ 175 (Comp. Gen. 2012)

Protest is sustained where an agency misled the protester in discussions to increase its proposed staffing for the performance of a cost-plus-fixed-fee task order in order to obligate additional funds, without consideration of the protester's technical approach for performing the work. SeKON Enters., Inc.; Signature Consulting Group, B-405921, 2012 CPD ¶ 26 (Comp. Gen. 2012)

An agency conducted misleading discussions by accepting software license terms, but later rejecting the protester's revised proposal based on the accepted terms. An agency may not lead an offeror to respond in a way that fails to address the agency's concerns, misinform the offeror about a problem with its proposal or misinform the offeror about Government requirements. Matter of: Velos, Inc.; OmniComm Systems, Inc.; PercipEnz Technologies, Inc., B-400500, B-400500.2, B-400500.3, B-400500.4, B-400500.5, B-400500.6, B-400500.7, 2010 CPD ¶ 3 (Comp. Gen. 2008)

Discussions with protester were not meaningful, and protest therefore is sustained, where agency (1) failed to advise protester of significant weaknesses in its proposal, and (2) conducted misleading discussions concerning other weaknesses or deficiencies by advising protester prior to submission of final proposal revisions that agreement had been achieved as to all technical and cost issues raised during negotiations when in fact the agency's concerns had not been resolved. Cygnus Corporation, Inc., B-292649.3, B-292649.4, 2004 CPD ¶ 162 (Comp. Gen. 2003)

§ 15.307 Proposal revisions.

(a) If an offeror's proposal is eliminated or otherwise removed from the competitive range, no further revisions to that offeror's proposal shall be accepted or considered.

(b) The contracting officer may request or allow proposal revisions to clarify and document understandings reached during negotiations. At the conclusion of discussions, each offeror still in the competitive range shall be given an opportunity to submit a final proposal revision. The contracting officer is required to establish a common cut-off date only for receipt of final proposal revisions. Requests for final proposal revisions shall advise offerors that the final proposal revisions shall be in writing and that the Government intends to make award without obtaining further revisions.

United States Code Annotated

Administrative determinations, see 41 USCA § 257.

Contract requirements, see 41 USCA § 254.

Contracts, planning, solicitation, evaluation, and award procedures, see 10 USCA § 2305.

Definitions, see 10 USCA § 2302, 41 USCA §§ 259, 403.

Determinations and decisions, see 10 USCA § 2310, 41 USCA § 262.

Evaluation and award, see 41 USCA § 253b.

Kinds of contracts, see 10 USCA § 2306.

Planning and solicitation requirements, see 41 USCA § 253a.

Notes of Decisions

Exchanges with offerors 1
Final revised proposals 2

1 Exchanges with offerors

Once contracting agency's request for final proposal revisions has been issued at the conclusion of discussions with offerors, agency generally may not engage in further discussions with any offerors. 48 C.F.R. § 15.307(b). Dubinsky v. U.S., 43 Fed. Cl. 243 (1999). United States ⬤64.40(1)

Contracting agency violated procurement regulation by engaging in improper discussions with offeror after the submission of amended proposals. 48 C.F.R. § 15.307(b). Dubinsky v. U.S., 43 Fed. Cl. 243 (1999). United States ⬤64.40(1)

Contracting agency's failure to continue discussions with other offerors after submission of amended proposals and an additional round of discussions with successful offeror or to request final proposal revisions from all offerors remaining in the competitive range violated procurement regulations. 48 C.F.R. §§ 15.306(e), 15.307(b). Dubinsky v. U.S., 43 Fed. Cl. 243 (1999). United States ⬤64.40(2)

Contracting agency's discussions with one offeror after the issuance of a request for final proposal revisions that enable it to make its proposal technically acceptable are prohibited under the Federal Acquisition Regulations (FAR). 48 C.F.R. § 15.307(b). Dubinsky v. U.S., 43 Fed. Cl. 243 (1999). United States ⬤64.40(2)

2 Final revised proposals

Government's request for best and final offers on government contract was justified by legitimate need to add requirement on compatibility of components rather than sham designed to direct procurement to particular offeror and, thus, government's improper disclosure of low bid to competing offeror before requesting final offers did not entitle contractor to reform contract to higher price term in its original bid; disclosure did not impact final contract price in light of failure of government official who requested final offers and contractor who received contract to learn of disclosure, or of other officials' intent to influence negotiations, until after contract was awarded. 48 C.F.R. § 15.610(d) (1989). LaBarge Products, Inc. v. West, 46 F.3d 1547, 40 Cont. Cas. Fed. (CCH) P 76733 (Fed. Cir. 1995). United States ⬤64.40(1)

General Services Administration Board of Contract Appeals properly determined that contractor's errors in preparing best and final offer software inventory list were merely clerical, and thus could be corrected without reopening negotiations. Contract Disputes Act of 1978, § 10, 41 U.S.C.A. § 609; Federal Property and Administrative Services Act of 1949, § 111(f)(5)(B), as amended, 40 U.S.C.(1988 Ed.) § 759(f)(5)(B). Andersen Consulting v. U.S., 959 F.2d 929, 37 Cont. Cas. Fed. (CCH) P 76284 (Fed. Cir. 1992). United States ⬤64.40(1)

Department of the Navy conducted "discussions" with company that ultimately was awarded contract, and was therefore required to have discussions with the other offeror and to request best and final offers from both offerors, where Navy sent letters requesting explanations of the employment status of two of first company's key personnel who would be carrying out contract and of the capacity of that company's conference room; both issues involved information essential for determining acceptability of company's proposal. 48 C.F.R. §§ 15.601, 15.607, 15.610, 15.611(a). Strategic Analysis, Inc. v. U.S. Dept. of Navy, 939 F. Supp. 18, 41 Cont. Cas. Fed. (CCH) P 76992 (D.D.C. 1996). United States ⬤64.40(1)

Contracting agency committed procedural error during reevaluation of proposals following stipulated dismissal of bid protest by considering new information relevant to technical evaluation of offeror, as consideration of the information was to allowing only one of the two offerors to revise its technical proposal. Orca Northwest Real Estate Services v. U.S., 65 Fed. Cl. 1 (2005), on reconsideration, 65 Fed. Cl. 419 (2005). United States ⬤64.40(5)

Once an agency properly determines that a best and final proposal is technically unacceptable, the agency need not conduct further cost analysis or consider the cost of the unacceptable proposal since the proposal cannot be considered for award. Labat-Anderson, Inc. v. U.S., 42 Fed. Cl. 806 (1999). United States ⬤64.30

Because an agency generally may not reopen discussions after the submission of best and final offers (BAFOs), and because a technically unacceptable proposal cannot be considered for award, agencies must generally exclude a technically unacceptable BAFO from the competitive range, regardless of cost or price. 48 C.F.R. § 15.611(c) (1995). Labat-Anderson, Inc. v. U.S., 42 Fed. Cl. 806 (1999). United States ☞64.30

Contracting officer was not required to review offeror's cost proposal once he had determined, consistent with the recommendation of the technical evaluation committee (TEC), that offeror's second best and final technical proposal was technically unacceptable. 48 C.F.R. § 15.609. Labat-Anderson, Inc. v. U.S., 42 Fed. Cl. 806 (1999). United States ☞64.40(1)

Government was not required to consider technical proposal change contained in fourth "best and final offer" (BAFO) submitted by offeror seeking to provide security services for federal court, by virtue of sending letter to offerors complaining of bad experience on another contract arising from labor unrest and asking for review of price or technical proposals for areas not in best interest of program; before BAFO was submitted government issued clarification that earlier letter was informational only, and there was no solicitation of technical proposal changes. Federal Property and Administrative Services Act of 1949, § 303b(a), as amended, 41 U.S.C.A. § 253b(a); 48 C.F.R. § 15.608(a). United Intern. Investigative Services v. U.S., 42 Fed. Cl. 73, 42 Cont. Cas. Fed. (CCH) P 77394 (1998), aff'd, 194 F.3d 1335 (Fed. Cir. 1999). United States ☞64.25

In light of fact that Navy expressly reserved the right to reject any or all offers, initially successful offeror in negotiated procurement case was not prejudiced where Navy, in response to change in circumstances of initially unsuccessful offeror, requested new best and final offers from both offerors. Hayes Intern. Corp. v. U.S., 7 Cl. Ct. 681, 32 Cont. Cas. Fed. (CCH) P 73392 (1985). United States ☞64.40(5)

Contracting officials are accorded broad discretion in conducting a negotiated procurement including decision to request additional best and final offers. Hayes Intern. Corp. v. U.S., 7 Cl. Ct. 681, 32 Cont. Cas. Fed. (CCH) P 73392 (1985). United States ☞64.40(5)

In negotiated procurement case, Navy acted rationally and in the best interests of the government in withdrawing notice of a offeror's nonresponsibility after offeror, which was found nonresponsible on basis that it lacked capability to satisfactorily perform the contract on a particular site, received a certificate of competency from SBA on basis that a offeror could responsibly perform the contract at an alternate facility; furthermore in light of the changed circumstances, Navy was within its authority in requesting additional information through best and final offers from both offerors. Hayes Intern. Corp. v. U.S., 7 Cl. Ct. 681, 32 Cont. Cas. Fed. (CCH) P 73392 (1985). United States ☞64.45(2)

In a negotiated procurement which provided for a reverse auction, an agency reasonably determined to request revised price proposals after the end of the auction, in response to a protest which raised reasonable concerns that there were errors in the conduct of the reverse auction. Pacific Island Movers, B-287643.2, 2001 CPD ¶ 126 (Comp. Gen. 2001)

§ 15.308 Source selection decision.

The source selection authority's (SSA) decision shall be based on a comparative assessment of proposals against all source selection criteria in the solicitation. While the SSA may use reports and analyses prepared by others, the source selection decision shall represent the SSA's independent judgment. The source selection decision shall be documented, and the documentation shall include the rationale for any business judgments and tradeoffs made or relied on by the SSA, including benefits associated with additional costs. Although the rationale for the selection decision must be documented, that documentation need not quantify the tradeoffs that led to the decision.

United States Code Annotated

Administrative determinations, see 41 USCA § 257.

Contract requirements, see 41 USCA § 254.

Contracts, planning, solicitation, evaluation, and award procedures, see 10 USCA § 2305.

Definitions, see 10 USCA § 2302, 41 USCA §§ 259, 403.

Determinations and decisions, see 10 USCA § 2310, 41 USCA § 262.

Evaluation and award, see 41 USCA § 253b.

Kinds of contracts, see 10 USCA § 2306.

Planning and solicitation requirements, see 41 USCA § 253a.

Notes of Decisions

In general 1
Cost evaluation, generally 4.5
Discretion of agency 4
Documentation requirements 8
Necessity of independent rationale 6
Past performance 2
Ranking 3
Reasonableness of decision 7
Tradeoff process 5

1 In general

The FAR 15.308 requirement that independent judgment be exercised for source selection decisions does not apply to the contracting officer's decision to cancel a solicitation. Therefore, the contracting officer's decision to cancel a solicitation for medical services in support of its drug testing program was not arbitrary and capricious, or in violation of law, as would violate the Administrative Procedure Act (APA), even though a senior ranking official who lacked authority to make the cancellation decision attempted to influence the decision. RN Expertise, Inc. v. U.S., 97 Fed. Cl. 460 (2011)

Procuring agency violated procurement statute and provisions of the FAR by improperly crediting bid proposal with meeting technical requirements of the solicitation, even though offeror failed to identify a volunteer coordinator, as required by solicitation. 10 U.S.C.A. § 2305(b)(1); 48 C.F.R. §§ 15.303(b), 15.305(a), 15.308. Mangi Environmental Group, Inc. v. U.S., 47 Fed. Cl. 10 (2000). United States ☞64.30

2 Past performance

FAR did not require source selection authority (SSA) to conduct his own contract-by-contract comparative assessment of past contract performance; as long as agency evaluators conducted a contract-by-contract assessment, the SSA could rely on such evaluation without performing the same detailed analysis. 48 C.F.R. §§ 15.303(b)(5), 15.308. Computer Sciences Corp. v. U.S., 51 Fed. Cl. 297 (2002). United States ☞64.45(2)

Proposal assessment report (PAR) contained a sufficient analysis of past contract work, where approximately 19 pages were devoted to explaining the evaluations of each offeror's past performance. 48 C.F.R. § 15.308. Computer Sciences Corp. v. U.S., 51 Fed. Cl. 297 (2002). United States ☞64.45(2)

Protest challenging the agency's past performance evaluation is sustained where the agency mechanically determined that, because the awardee and the protester both received "Satisfactory" past performance ratings, that past performance could be eliminated as a basis for award. The GAO held that this approach failed to "fulfill the requirement for a documented decision based on a comparative assessment of proposals against all source selection criteria in the solicitation." EFW Inc., B-412608, et al., 2016 CPD ¶ 304 (Comp. Gen. 2016)

An agency improperly evaluated an awardee and protester unequally by crediting the awardee with its subcontractor's experience, but not crediting the protester with its subcontractor's experience, even though the agency viewed both subcontractors as having relevant experience. Matter of: Ahtna Support and Training Services, LLC, B-400947.2, 2009 CPD ¶ 119 (Comp. Gen. 2009)

3 Ranking

Incumbent contractor failed to show, in its protest, prejudice from decision of the contracting officer not to enter into cost discussions with it, where even with a cost realism adjustment, incumbent contractor's bid was still lower than that of the awardee, and it was more important that the incumbent contractor received lower ratings in the technical and management areas, because the contracting officer decided that the awardee's superiority in those areas outweighed the marginal cost difference between the two, which was a permissible judgment under the source selection regulation. 48 C.F.R. § 15.308. JWK Intern. Corp. v. U.S., 279 F.3d 985 (Fed. Cir. 2002). United States ☞64.55(1)

Disappointed offeror was prejudiced by error of source selection authority (SSA) in failing to exercise independent judgment when it decided to raise technical rating of contract awardee, where, prior to the decision, offeror was rated three steps above awardee, but after flawed determination, offeror's proposal was rated only one level higher than awardee's proposal, thus decreasing offeror's chances of receiving the award. Information Sciences Corp. v. U.S., 73 Fed. Cl. 70 (2006), on reconsideration in part, 75 Fed. Cl. 406 (2007). United States ☞64.55(1)

Protestor did not establish that contracting agency violated procurement regulation governing source selection decision by employing a "purely mathematical methodology" for calculating point totals and awarding contracts; rather, source selection authority (SSA) utilized points as a tool for weighing the strengths and weaknesses of each contractor in each different category, not as an impermissible purely mathematical calculation. 48 C.F.R. § 15.308. Bannum, Inc. v. U.S., 60 Fed. Cl. 718 (2004). United States ☞64.45(2)

4 Discretion of agency

If a company certifies that it meets the requirements of Section 508 in its proposal, the contracting officer may rely on the certification in awarding a contract. The company's potential failure to comply with the requirements is ordinarily a matter of contract administration, which does not affect the propriety of awarding a contract. Allied Technology Group, Inc. v. U.S., 649 F.3d 1320 (Fed. Cir. 2011)

In formally advertised bidding the pertinent statutes and regulations are far more strict about the conduct of the procurement than in a negotiated one, and consequently in negotiated procurement the contracting officer is entrusted with a relatively high degree of discretion. Galen Medical Associates, Inc. v. U.S., 369 F.3d 1324 (Fed. Cir. 2004). United States ☞64.40(1)

The Court deferred to the expertise of the agency and denied the protest where, the analysis of test results relating to protester's proposed equipment required a high level of technical expertise and, where the resolution of an issue "requires a high level of technical expertise," it is "properly left to the informed discretion of the responsible federal agencies." Terex Corp. v. U.S., 2012 WL 1574113 (Fed. Cl. 2012)

The government may not rely upon undisclosed evaluation criteria in evaluating proposals; however, a solicitation need not identify each element to be considered by the agency during the course of the evaluation where such element is intrinsic to the stated factors. OTI America, Inc. v. U.S., 73 Fed. Cl. 758 (2006), aff'd, 227 Fed. Appx. 926 (Fed. Cir. 2007).

In a negotiated procurement, contracting officers are generally afforded even greater decision-making discretion, in comparison to their role in sealed bid procurements. Maintenance Engineers v. U.S., 50 Fed. Cl. 399 (2001). United States ☞64.45(1)

Contracting officials in negotiated procurements have broad discretion to take corrective action where the agency determines that such action is necessary to ensure fair and impartial competition. ManTech Telecommunications and Information Systems Corp. v. U.S., 49 Fed. Cl. 57 (2001), decision aff'd, 30 Fed. Appx. 995 (Fed. Cir. 2002). United States ☞64.40(1)

Contracting officials are accorded broad discretion in conducting a negotiated procurement. Cube Corp. v. U.S., 46 Fed. Cl. 368 (2000). United States ☞64.40(1)

Contracting officials may properly exercise wide discretion in their evaluation of bids and the application of procurement regulations, and such discretion is especially broad in negotiated procurements. Impresa Construzioni Geom. Domenico Garufi v. U.S., 44 Fed. Cl. 540 (1999), aff'd in part, rev'd in part on other grounds, 238 F.3d 1324 (Fed. Cir. 2001). United States ☞64.40(1)

Courts allow agencies broad discretion in conducting negotiated procurements and determining which bid is most advantageous to the government. Advanced Data Concepts, Inc. v. U.S., 43 Fed. Cl. 410 (1999), aff'd, 216 F.3d 1054 (Fed. Cir. 2000). United States ☞64.40(1)

Contracting officials in negotiated procurements have broad discretion to take corrective action where the agency determines that such action is necessary to ensure fair and impartial competition. 48 C.F.R. § 1.602-2. DGS Contract Service, Inc. v. U.S., 43 Fed. Cl. 227 (1999). United States ☞64.40(1)

Contracting officials may properly exercise wide discretion in their evaluation of bids and the application of procurement regulations, and such discretion is especially broad in negotiated procurements. DGS Contract Service, Inc. v. U.S., 43 Fed. Cl. 227 (1999). United States ☞64.40(1)

A contracting officer has broad discretion in conducting negotiations with an offeror. 48 C.F.R. § 15.610(b) (1995). Labat-Anderson, Inc. v. U.S., 42 Fed. Cl. 806 (1999). United States ☞64.40(1)

Discretion of contracting officials is especially broad where the contract was awarded through negotiated procurement. United Intern. Investigative Services, Inc. v. U.S., 41 Fed. Cl. 312, 42 Cont. Cas. Fed. (CCH) P 77336 (1998). United States ☞64.5

Contracting official's discretion in evaluating bids and applying procurement regulations is especially broad where contract was awarded through negotiated procurement. Delbert Wheeler Const., Inc. v. U.S., 39 Fed. Cl. 239, 42 Cont. Cas. Fed. (CCH) P 77192, 42 Cont. Cas. Fed. (CCH) P 77257 (1997), aff'd, 155 F.3d 566 (Fed. Cir. 1998). United States ☞64.40(1)

Government contracting officer has broad discretion in dealing with negotiation between government and offerors, including discretion to resolve any uncertainties concerning terms and conditions of proposal. Action Mfg. Co. v. U.S., 10 Cl. Ct. 474, 33 Cont. Cas. Fed. (CCH) P 74505 (1986). United States ☞64.5

Deference accorded all procurement official's discretionary determinations must be given even greater weight where award of negotiated procurement is at stake. 28 U.S.C.A. § 1491(a)(3). Action Mfg. Co. v. U.S., 10 Cl. Ct. 474, 33 Cont. Cas. Fed. (CCH) P 74505 (1986). United States ☞64.60(3.1)

4.5 Cost evaluation, generally

Cost realism analysis performed by National Nuclear Security Administration (NNSA), with respect to bid solicitation for providing security system services for nuclear test site, was rationally based; NNSA established probable cost of each offeror's proposal, for purposes of evaluating best value, by adjusting proposed costs to reflect any additions or reductions in cost elements to realistic levels. Westech Intern., Inc. v. U.S., 79 Fed. Cl. 272 (2007)

Protestor did not establish that source selection authority violated procurement statute and regulations by not accurately considering the most probable costs of two "weaknesses" noted by source evaluation board (SEB) in contract awardee's proposal, and thus could not properly have decided which of the competitive proposal was most advantageous to the government, as neither of the weaknesses had probable cost impacts that the SSA failed to address. Comprehensive Health Services, Inc. v. U.S., 70 Fed. Cl. 700 (2006). United States ☞64.45(1)

Challenge to the evaluation of the realism of the awardee's proposed price and cost is sustained where the record does not demonstrate that the agency's evaluation was reasonable. Although the agency evaluated the realism of the offerors' labor rates; it did not evaluate the realism of the offerors' proposed labor mix or level of effort. Solers Inc., B-409079, 2014 CPD ¶ 74 (Comp. Gen. 2014)

An agency misevaluated proposals for a cost-reimbursement contract because the record did not show a logical connection between the agency's technical evaluation conclusions and its most probable cost evaluation conclusions, and provided no information to explain the apparent discrepancies. ITT Sys. Corp., B-405865, 2012 CPD ¶ 44 (Comp. Gen. 2012)

Protest is sustained in a negotiated procurement for the award of a cost-reimbursement contract, where the agency in its cost realism assessment accepted the awardee's work allocation in its cost proposal, but that allocation was inconsistent with the firm's allocation of work in its technical proposal. Matter of: Earl Industries, LLC, B-309996, B-309996.4, 2007 CPD ¶ 203 (Comp. Gen. 2007)

Agency's failure to address Defense Contract Audit Agency qualification of audit results regarding awardee's cost proposal due to awardee's noncompliance with cost accounting standards was not prejudicial where agency demonstrated that awardee's noncompliance would not result in any increased costs to the government. Matter of: ITT Industries Space Systems, LLC, B-309964, 2007 CPD ¶ 217 (Comp. Gen. 2007)

When an agency evaluates a proposal for the award of a cost-reimbursement contract, as in this case, an offeror's proposed estimated costs are not dispositive because, regardless of the costs proposed, the government is bound to pay the contractor its actual and allowable costs. FAR 15.305(a)(1); 15.404-1(d). Consequently, the agency must perform a cost realism analysis to determine the extent to which an offeror's proposed costs are realistic for the work to be performed. An agency is not required to conduct an in-depth cost analysis or to verify each and every item in assessing cost realism; rather, the evaluation requires the exercise of informed judgment by the contracting agency. Matter of: ITT Industries Space Systems, LLC, B-309964, 2007 CPD ¶ 217 (Comp. Gen. 2007)

Agency's cost realism evaluation of awardee's proposal was unreasonable where agency failed to take into account cost adjustments made by its own cost analyst to awardee's proposal, and instead utilized awardee's proposed costs as the basis for its source selection decision. Matter of Magellan Health Services, B-298912, 2007 CPD ¶ 81 (Comp. Gen. 2007)

5 Tradeoff process

Contracting agency's decision to exclude offeror from final cost/technical tradeoff between two other offerors was not arbitrary, capricious, or contrary to law, where offeror's proposal was more costly than that of the other offerors, and its technical rating was not superior to that of the offeror who had the highest technical rating in the tradeoff. Industrial Property Management, Inc. v. U.S., 59 Fed. Cl. 318 (2004). United States ☞64.45(1)

The government is only required to make a cost/technical tradeoff in considering proposals where one proposal is rated higher technically than another, but the other is lower in cost. Industrial Property Management, Inc. v. U.S., 59 Fed. Cl. 318 (2004). United States ☞64.45(1)

Mere fact that bid protestor's bid was lower than that of contract awardee did not establish that contracting officer's cost and technical tradeoff analysis was arbitrary, capricious, or irrational. Tech Systems, Inc. v. U.S., 50 Fed. Cl. 216 (2001). United States ☞64.40(1)

Protest was sustained because the RFP provided for a comparative best value evaluation of the technical factors and the agency failed to document that it qualitatively assessed the relative merits of the offerors' technical approaches. GAO found that the evaluation of the offerors' proposals under the staffing and implementation factors considered only whether the proposals were technically unacceptable or acceptable, and did not, as contemplated by the RFP, consider their relative qualitative merit. When an agency conducts a cost/technical tradeoff, adequate documentation requires more than just generalized statements of proposal equivalency. Trailboss Enters., Inc., B-407093, 2013 CPD ¶ 232 (Comp. Gen. 2013)

In a best value procurement for maintenance services, protest is sustained where the record shows that the agency performed a tradeoff between two higher-rated, higher-priced quotations, but did not consider, in its tradeoff decision, the lower prices submitted by other lower-rated vendors, whose quotations were nonetheless found to be technically acceptable. Matter of: System Engineering International, Inc., B-402754, 2010 CPD ¶ 167 (Comp. Gen. 2010)

The GAO sustained a protest of an agency's technical evaluation, source selection and conduct of discussions because the agency could not demonstrate the technical advantage offered by the awardee that would justify the payment of a price premium. "Even in a competition where price is of less importance than the non-price factors, an agency must meaningfully consider cost or price in making its selection decision." Matter of: ACCESS Systems, Inc., B-400623.3, 2009 CPD ¶ 56 (Comp. Gen. 2009)

Under solicitation providing for award to offeror whose proposal is found to be the most advantageous to the government based on past performance, delivery, and price, selection of lower technically rated, lower-priced proposal is improper where the record shows that selection decision was based on a mechanical comparison of offerors' total point scores and lacks any documentation indicating that a price/technical tradeoff was made. Midland Supply, Inc., B-298720, B-298720.2, 2007 CPD ¶ 2 (Comp. Gen. 2006)

An agency is required to have adequate documentation to support its evaluation of proposals and its award decision. An award decision is not reasonable where there is no documentation or explanation to support the price/technical tradeoff and where the agency makes its award decision based strictly on a mechanical comparison of the offerors' total point scores. Documentation was considered inadequate where the evaluation record consists of one-paragraph summaries of the proposals, and charts showing for each evaluation factor the agency's assignment of raw scores, the calculation of weighted scores, and the total point score for each proposal. Such a record lacks any documentation reflecting a meaningful comparative analysis of proposals or any explanation of why the awardee's lower technically rated, lower-priced proposal was selected for award over protester's higher technically rated, higher-priced proposal. Midland Supply, Inc., B-298720, B-298720.2, 2007 CPD ¶ 2 (Comp. Gen. 2006)

Where solicitations provide for award on a "best value" or "most advantageous to the government" basis, it is the function of the source selection authority to perform a price/technical tradeoff, that is, to determine whether one proposal's technical superiority is worth the higher price, and the extent to which one is sacrificed for the other is governed only by the test of rationality and consistency with the stated evaluation criteria. Matter of: Remington Arms Company, Inc., B-297374, B-297374.2, 2006 CPD ¶ 32 (Comp. Gen. 2006).

The propriety of such a price/past performance tradeoff decision turns not on the difference in scores or ratings *per se,* but on whether the selection official's judgment concerning the significance of the difference was reasonable and adequately justified in light of the RFP's evaluation scheme. Chenega Technical Products, LLC, B-295451.5, 2005 CPD ¶ 123 (Comp. Gen. 2005)

Protest is sustained where there is no evidence in the contemporaneous record that the contracting officer performed a proper price/technical trade-off—or, for that matter, even considered offerors' prices—prior to selecting the awardee. There is no evaluation of offerors' prices—on either an individual or comparative basis—in any of the source selection documentation. This is contrary to the requirement that price be considered in every source selection decision, 41 U.S.C. § 253a(c)(1)(B) (2002); FAR 15.304(c)(1), and the requirement that a source selection decision be based on a comparative assessment of proposals against all source selection criteria in the solicitation and that it be documented. Locus Technology, Inc., B-293012, 2004 CPD ¶ 16 (Comp. Gen. 2004)

Protest of the award to a firm with a higher past performance rating and a higher price is sustained where the source selection authority ignored the protester's significantly lower price and, as a result, failed to justify the payment of a substantial price premium. Beautify Professional Services Corporation, B-291954.3, 2003 CPD ¶ 178 (Comp. Gen. 2003).

Protest challenging the agency's best value source selection is sustained where the record shows that the agency failed to consider whether the awardee's higher-rated proposal was worth its higher price. Beacon Auto Parts, B-287483, 2001 CPD ¶ 116 (Comp. Gen. 2001)

6 Necessity of independent rationale

Source selection authority (SSA) violated requirement of the Federal Acquisition Regulation (FAR) that it exercise independent judgment when it raised two offerors' technical ratings based exclusively on its agreement with minority report of source selection evaluation board (SSEB) without providing an independent rationale for its agreement. Information Sciences Corp. v. U.S., 73 Fed. Cl. 70 (2006), on reconsideration in part, 75 Fed. Cl. 406 (2007). United States ☞64.45(1)

Protest challenging the evaluation of technical proposals is denied where the record establishes that the agency's evaluation was reasonable and consistent with the evaluation criteria; a source selection official's decision not to accept the findings and ratings of agency evaluators is unobjectionable if otherwise supported by the record. TPL, Inc., B-297136.10, B-297136.11, 2006 CPD ¶ 104 (Comp. Gen. 2006)

Where the RFP allows for a price/technical tradeoff, the source selection authority retains discretion to select a higher-priced, higher technically rated proposal if doing so is reasonably found to be in the government's best interest and is consistent with the solicitation's stated evaluation scheme. Although agencies must document the rationale for a source selection decision, including any tradeoffs, there is no requirement to quantify the specific cost or price value difference when selecting a higher-priced, higher technically rated offeror. Advanced Federal Services Corp., B-298662, 2006 CPD ¶ 174 (Comp. Gen. 2006)

Where a price/ technical tradeoff is made, the source selection decision must be documented, and the documentation must include the rationale for any tradeoffs made, including the benefits associated with additional costs. Matter of: Remington Arms Company, Inc., B-297374, B-297374.2, 2006 CPD ¶ 32 (Comp. Gen. 2006)

The SSA's analysis was unreasonable in that it failed to take into account the difference in the ratings of the two proposals with regard to performance risk. Where a price/technical tradeoff is made, the source selection decision must be documented, and the documentation must include the rationale for any tradeoffs made. A tradeoff determination in favor of a lower-rated, lower-priced proposal that fails to acknowledge significant strengths of the higher-rated proposal and furnish an explanation as to why they are not worth a price premium is not a sufficiently documented tradeoff determination. Matter of: Coastal Maritime Stevedoring, LLC, B-296627, 2005 CPD ¶ 186 (Comp. Gen. 2005)

A source selection official's adoption of an evaluation panel's findings and recommendation for award does not, without more, provide evidence that the selection official abdicated his responsibility to make independent judgments; protester's assertion that he did so is denied where the record shows that the selection official was clearly involved in the procurement from its outset to its conclusion. U.S. Facilities, Inc., B-293029, B-293029.2, 2004 CPD ¶ 17 (Comp. Gen. 2004)

7 Reasonableness of decision

The COFC rejected protester's argument that NASA applied an unstated evaluation criterion. The protester relied on a statement in the Source Selection Authority's (SSA) decision document stating: "I was concerned that the proposal did not contain a backup plan in the event one of the major subcontractors was unable to perform," because the solicitation did not expressly require submission of a "backup plan." The COFC stated that a solicitation need not identify criteria intrinsic to the stated evaluation factors because agencies have great discretion in determining the scope of an evaluation factor. The court denied the protest based on its determination that the absence of a backup plan was fairly encompassed by the "management plan" subfactor, which the RFP stated would include an assessment of risk and soundness of the management approach. PlanetSpace, Inc. v. U.S., 92 Fed.Cl. 250 (2010)

Protest was denied where the request for proposals indicated that metropolitan presence would be considered in evaluating proposals, and therefore the protester's assertion that the agency used an unstated evaluation criteria lacked merit. "Metropolitan presence" was considered to be within the scope of the stated evaluation factor of "response time." NEQ, LLC v. U.S., 88 Fed. Cl. 38 (2009)

Contracting agency was rational in its performance/price trade-off analysis whereby it awarded contract for repair or possible replacement of medium voltage switching station at Air Force base to higher-rated, higher-priced offeror based on determination that superior past/present performance of higher-priced offeror outweighed the difference in price; decision was reasonable given the Air Force's stated concerns about power failures occurring at base which was a major pilot training center. Overstreet Elec. Co., Inc. v. U.S., 59 Fed. Cl. 99 (2003). United States ☞64.45(2)

Protest was sustained where record shows that agency's source selection authority essentially disagreed with all of the negative findings of the agency's evaluators concerning awardee's proposal, but the record does not support a conclusion that his disagreement was reasonable. Prism Maritime, LLC, B-409267.2, 2014 CPD ¶ 124 (Comp. Gen. 2014)

Where an agency makes award to a higher-rated, higher-cost proposal in a best value acquisition, the award decision must be supported by a rational and adequately-documented explanation of why the higher-rated proposal is, in fact, superior, and why its technical superiority warrants paying a price premium. Nexant, Inc., Comp. Gen. Dec. B-407708, 2013 CPD ¶ 59 (Comp. Gen. 2013)

Protest challenging the award decision under a GSA competition for federal office space was sustained because the Head of Contracting Activity (HCA) did not meaningfully consider the evaluated differences in the offerors' proposals in her selection decision. The solicitation required GSA to evaluate both the overall number of amenities offered as well as the variety. GSA's simple counting of categories, such as hair salons or automotive service stations, ignored the type of amenity being offered. Matter of: One Largo Metro LLC; Metroview Development Holdings, LLC; King Farm Associates, LLC, B-404896, B-404896.2,

B-404896.3, B-404896.4, B-404896.5, B-404896.6, B-404896.7, 2011 CPD ¶ 128 (Comp. Gen. 2011)

An agency improperly made award to a vendor whose proposal took exception to a solicitation requirement to propose a fixed price by conditioning its offered price on a greater use of government facilities than contemplated or authorized by the solicitation, such that its offered price was conditional not firm. Matter of: Solers, Inc., B-404032.3, B-404032.4, 2011 CPD ¶ 83 (Comp. Gen. 2011)

An agency's evaluation of an awardee's proposal was unreasonable because the record did not demonstrate a reasonable basis for the evaluators' conclusion that the awardee complied with the solicitation's requirement to submit a transition plan and project milestones. Although the protester did submit these documents as attachments, the Contracting Officer removed them because the proposal exceeded the solicitation's page limitation, and the pertinent information was in the excess pages. Matter of: Irving Burton Associates, Inc., B-401983.3, 2010 CPD ¶ 92 (Comp. Gen. 2010)

An agency improperly rejected as unacceptable an offer that included data that provided a better understanding of the offeror's capabilities. The agency requested a percentage of staff holding third-party certification, and the offeror submitted the actual number of staff members holding such certification. Matter of: Engineering Management & Integration, Inc., B-400356.4, B-400356.5, 2009 CPD ¶ 114 (Comp. Gen. 2009)

An agency improperly evaluated an awardee and protester unequally by crediting the awardee with its subcontractor's experience, but not crediting the protester with its subcontractor's experience, even though the agency viewed both subcontractors as having relevant experience. Matter of: Ahtna Support and Training Services, LLC, B-400947.2, 2009 CPD ¶ 119 (Comp. Gen. 2009)

Protest was sustained because the awardee did not affirmatively agree to meet a technical specification, even though the awardee's quotation and answers to questions demonstrated an apparent capacity to meet it. GAO held that, although the awardee may have had the capacity to meet the requirement, nowhere in its quote did it agree to do so within the time frame specified, as required by the RFQ. The awardee's quote discussed implementation of the capability, but did not address when the capability would be fully ready. GAO stated: "A vendor is responsible for affirmatively demonstrating the merits of its quotation and risks the rejection of its quotation if it fails to do so." Matter of: Carahsoft Technology Corporation, B-401169, B-401169.2, 2009 CPD ¶ 134 (Comp. Gen. 2009)

An agency misevaluated protester's proposal and made an unreasonable source selection decision where the evaluation record was internally inconsistent, the agency relied on an overall adjectival rating and prices that failed to capture relative ratings, and the agency did not consider the protester in trade-off decisions where the protester's proposal was rated higher than the awardee's. Decision Matter of: T-C Transcription, Inc., B-401470, 2009 CPD ¶ 172 (Comp. Gen. 2009)

An agency improperly awarded a healthcare support services contract because its evaluation did not account for the network provider discounts associated with the protester's existing healthcare support services network. Under technical approach, the RFP stated that the "Government will consider offers that commit to higher performance standard(s) or requirements, if the offeror clearly describes the added benefit to the Government." GAO found that cost savings were a form of "benefit to the Government" and, therefore, had to be considered. Matter of: Humana Military Healthcare Services, B-401652.2, B-401652.4, B-401652.6, 2009 CPD ¶ 219 (Comp. Gen. 2009)

Agency's evaluation was unreasonable because the RFP set forth very clear and specific groundrules about how the agency would evaluate risk if an offeror did not have necessary tooling and equipment on hand and the selection decision was inconsistent with those groundrules. Second, because the agency was unable to produce critical relevant documents supporting its evaluation of the protester's past performance, GAO had no basis to conclude that the evaluation was reasonable. Matter of: Navistar Defense, LLC; BAE Systems, Tactical Vehicle Systems LP, B-401865, B-401865.2, B-401865.3, B-401865.4, B-401865.5, B-401865.6, B-401865.7, 2009 CPD ¶ 258 (Comp. Gen. 2009).

Agency's technical evaluation was unreasonable because it: 1) assigned a deficiency to protester's proposal based on an unstated evaluation factor; 2) rated similar aspects of competing proposals inconsistently; and 3) assigned the awardee an "excellent" rating without adequate support. Matter of: Public Communications Services, Inc., B-400058, B-400058.3, 2009 CPD ¶ 154 (Comp. Gen. 2008)

A source selection decision that discusses strengths but not weaknesses of the awardee's proposal and relies on incorrectly calculated costs is not reasonably based, and justified sustaining the protest. Matter of: Fedcar Company, Ltd., B-310980, B-310980.2, B-310980.3, 2008 CPD ¶ 70 (Comp. Gen. 2008)

An agency's decision to award a contract was flawed because the agency did not hold meaningful discussions with an offeror on the significant weakness of its proposed staffing plan, materially affecting the final selection, the U.S. Comptroller General recently determined. The agency also lacked a reasonable basis for its vendor selection because it unreasonably did not consider the winning proposal's identified weakness. Matter of: AT & T Corp., B-299542.3, B-299542.4, 2008 CPD ¶ 65 (Comp. Gen. 2007)

An agency must follow the stated terms of its request for quotations in awarding a contract. When an RFQ states that technical factors will be given greater weight than price, an agency cannot then make an award determination based on price among technically acceptable quotations. Matter of: GlassLock, Inc., B-299931, B-299931.2, 2007 CPD ¶ 216 (Comp. Gen. 2007)

Protest challenging agency's selection decision is sustained where the record shows that the awardee's proposal failed to address material solicitation requirements and that the agency failed to treat offerors equally by making award to the awardee despite the deficiencies in its proposal, while finding the protester's proposal unacceptable for similar deficiencies. Matter of: Wiltex Inc., B-297234.2, B-297234.3, 2006 CPD ¶ 13 (Comp. Gen. 2005)

Protest against award for deactivation and decommissioning of nuclear reactor is sustained where, although solicitation provided that agency was committed to achieving an accelerated closure of the site, agency accorded little or no weight in the evaluation to the degree to which offerors proposed to accelerate completion ahead of required site closure date. Matter of: EPW Closure Services, LLC; FFTF Restoration Co., LLC, B-294910, B-294910.2, B-294910.3, B-294910.4, B-294910.5, B-294910.6, B-294910.7, 2006 CPD ¶ 3 (Comp. Gen. 2005)

Protest is sustained where source selection official failed to document rationale for source selection consistent with differential weighting of technical evaluation factors and emphasis on technical superiority as required by solicitation. YORK Building Services, Inc., B-296948.2, B-296948.3, B-296948.4, 2005 CPD ¶ 202 (Comp. Gen. 2005).

In a negotiated procurement, which provided for award on the basis of a cost/technical tradeoff and under which past performance was stated to be the most important evaluation factor, the selection of the awardee's significantly higher-priced offer based upon that firm's technical superiority and better past performance was unreasonable, where the information provided to the source selection authority to support the awardee's and protester's past performance evaluation did not accurately reflect the firms' evaluation but instead erroneously conveyed the impression that the awardee had no evaluated past performance weaknesses and that the protester's past performance had nearly only weaknesses. Keeton Corrections, Inc., B-293348, 2005 CPD ¶ 44 (Comp. Gen. 2005)

Source selection decision selecting lower-priced proposal as the best-value under a solicitation containing an evaluation scheme that attached greater weight to technical merit was not reasonably based, where the lower-level evaluators found and documented that the protester's higher-priced proposal was technically superior, and the source selection authority determined the proposals were technically equal and made award based on the low-priced proposal, without considering the areas where the protester's proposal was found technically superior. SOS Interpreting, LTD., B-293026, B-293026.2, B-293026.3, 2005 CPD ¶ 26 (Comp. Gen. 2004)

Protest challenging an agency's evaluation and source selection decision that found the awardee's staffing and proposed marketing approach to be significant proposal strengths and discriminators in the selection decision is sustained, where the protester and awardee both addressed staffing and marketing approach, though not specifically requested by the solicitation, and the agency did not fairly consider the protester's similar proposed staffing and marketing approach. Spherix, Inc., B-294572, B-294572.2, 2005 CPD ¶ 3 (Comp. Gen. 2004)

Protest challenging proposal evaluation is sustained where record reveals that agency failed to consider significant portions of protester's revised proposal in its evaluation and failed to consider offerors' prices in source selection decision. Locus Technology, Inc., B-293012, 2004 CPD ¶ 16 (Comp. Gen. 2004)

Protest challenging the adequacy of a source selection decision is sustained where the selection official ultimately conceded that she knowingly mischaracterized in the source selection document the award recommendation of agency project officers, whose participation in the evaluation of proposals is anticipated by the agency's acquisition regulation— *i.e.*, she wrote that the project officers recommended award to the awardee, when, in fact, they recommended award to the protester—and, as a result, she fails to state any basis for rejecting their award recommendation. Without documentation in the record explaining the basis for rejecting the input of the project officers, the Government Accountability Office has no basis for determining whether those actions were reasonable. University Research Company, LLC, B-294358, B-294358.2, B-294358.3, B-294358.4, B-294358.5, 2004 CPD ¶ 217 (Comp. Gen. 2004)

Under request for proposals providing for award of multiple contracts, source selection authority's (SSA) decision to select lower technically rated, lower-priced proposals instead of protester's higher technically rated, higher-priced one was inadequately documented and thus could not be determined reasonable where SSA failed to furnish any explanation as to why he did not consider protester's higher-priced proposal to offer technical advantages or why he did not consider these advantages to be worth a price premium. Blue Rock Structures, Inc., B-293134, 2004 CPD ¶ 63 (Comp. Gen. 2004)

Protest that agency misevaluated proposals is sustained where record shows that agency's evaluation conclusions with respect to protester's proposal were either unrelated to the evaluation criteria or without a factual basis, and agency failed to note two deficiencies in awardee's proposal. Computer Information Specialist, Inc., B-293049, B-293049.2, 2004 CPD ¶ 1 (Comp. Gen. 2004)

Agency's determination that the awardee's proposal was acceptable cannot be considered reasonable where the contemporaneous record does not evidence that the agency meaningfully evaluated a relevant and apparently significant section of the awardee's technical proposal, and the agency, in defending the protest, states that its intent is to enter into post-award negotiations with the awardee regarding the protested aspects of the awardee's technical approach that should have been evaluated during the procurement process. Sabreliner Corporation, B-290515, B-290515.2, B-290515.3, 2003 CPD ¶ 4 (Comp. Gen. 2002)

In a negotiated procurement for a fixed-price construction contract, based upon a price/technical tradeoff, the selection of the higher-rated, higher-priced proposal was unreasonable where the source selection authority did not credit the protester for its substantially lower proposed price, but improperly viewed the protester's low price as too low and demonstrating the protester's lack of understanding of contract requirements, where the solicitation did not provide for an evaluation of offerors' understanding. CSE Construction, B-291268.2, 2002 CPD ¶ 207 (Comp. Gen. 2002)

Protest challenging the agency's "best value" source selection decision is sustained where the record shows that there is insufficient information and analysis in the record, which includes both a contemporaneous source selection statement and a post-protest addendum to that statement, to determine that the award selection was reasonable. Johnson Controls World Services, Inc., B-289942, B-289942.2, 2002 CPD ¶ 88 (Comp. Gen. 2002)

Agency reasonably found protester's proposal technically unacceptable under experience and past performance evaluation criterion, where record shows that protester failed to submit required detailed information showing that its proposed key subcontractors had previously performed contracts similar to the solicited effort; offerors have an affirmative duty to prepare an adequately written proposal. Menendez-Donnel & Associates, B-286599, 2001 CPD ¶ 15 (Comp. Gen. 2001)

A failure to maintain required contract file documentation in accordance with FAR 4.801 may be considered as evidence that an agency procurement decision was arbitrary. Matter of: Southwest Marine, Inc.; American Systems Engineering Corporation, B-265865, B-265865.3, B-265865.4, 96-1 CPD ¶ 56 (Comp. Gen. 1996).

8 Documentation requirements

Agency failure to retain evaluators' handwritten evaluation sheets does not furnish a basis for sustaining protest against determination that protesters' samples were noncompliant with specifications where comprehensive contemporaneous summary documents provided an adequate supporting rationale in the record from which to conclude that the agency had a reasonable basis for the evaluation. Custom Pak, Inc., et al., Comp. Gen. Dec. B-409308 et al., 2014 CPD ¶ 73 (Comp. Gen. 2014)

Subpart 15.4 Contract Pricing

§ 15.400 Scope of subpart.

This subpart prescribes the cost and price negotiation policies and procedures for pricing negotiated prime contracts (including subcontracts) and contract modifications, including modifications to contracts awarded by sealed bidding.

United States Code Annotated

Contract requirements, see 41 USCA § 254.

Contracts, planning, solicitation, evaluation, and award procedures, see 10 USCA § 2305.

Cost or pricing data, truth in negotiations, see 10 USCA § 2306a, 41 USCA § 254b.

Definitions, see 10 USCA § 2302, 41 USCA §§ 259, 403.

Evaluation and award, see 41 USCA § 253b.

Kinds of contracts, see 10 USCA § 2306.

Planning and solicitation requirements, see 41 USCA § 253a.

§ 15.401 Definitions.

As used in this subpart—

"Price" means cost plus any fee or profit applicable to the contract type.

"Subcontract" (except as used in 15.407-2) also includes a transfer of commercial items between divisions, subsidiaries, or affiliates of a contractor or a subcontractor (10 U.S.C. 2306a(h)(2) and 41 U.S.C. 3501(a)(3)).

United States Code Annotated

Contract requirements, see 41 USCA § 254.

Contracts, planning, solicitation, evaluation, and award procedures, see 10 USCA § 2305.

Cost or pricing data, truth in negotiations, see 10 USCA § 2306a, 41 USCA § 254b.

Definitions, see 10 USCA § 2302, 41 USCA §§ 259, 403.

Evaluation and award, see 41 USCA § 253b.

Kinds of contracts, see 10 USCA § 2306.

Planning and solicitation requirements, see 41 USCA § 253a.

§ 15.402 Pricing policy.

Contracting officers shall—

(a) Purchase supplies and services from responsible sources at fair and reasonable prices. In establishing the reasonableness of the offered prices, the contracting officer—

(1) Shall obtain certified cost or pricing data when required by 15.403-4, along with data other than certified cost or pricing data as necessary to establish a fair and reasonable price; or

(2) When certified cost or pricing data are not required by 15.403-4, shall obtain data other than certified cost or pricing data as necessary to establish a fair and reasonable price, generally using the following order of preference in determining the type of data required:

(i) No additional data from the offeror, if the price is based on adequate price competition, except as provided by 15.403-3(b).

(ii) Data other than certified cost or pricing data such as—

(A) Data related to prices (e.g., established catalog or market prices, sales to non-governmental and governmental entities), relying first on data available within the Government; second, on data obtained from sources other than the offeror; and, if necessary, on data obtained from the offeror. When obtaining data from the offeror is necessary, unless an exception under 15.403-1(b)(1) or (2) applies, such data submitted by the offeror shall include, at a minimum, appropriate data on the prices at which the same or similar items have been sold previously, adequate for evaluating the reasonableness of the price.

(B) Cost data to the extent necessary for the contracting officer to determine a fair and reasonable price.

(3) Obtain the type and quantity of data necessary to establish a fair and reasonable price, but not more data than is necessary. Requesting unnecessary data can lead to increased proposal preparation costs, generally extend acquisition lead time, and consume additional contractor and Government resources. Use techniques such as, but not limited to, price analysis, cost analysis, and/or cost realism analysis to establish a fair and reasonable price. If a fair and reasonable price cannot be established by the contracting officer from the analyses of the data obtained or submitted to date, the contracting officer shall require the submission of additional data sufficient for the contracting officer to support the determination of the fair and reasonable price.

(b) Price each contract separately and independently and not—

(1) Use proposed price reductions under other contracts as an evaluation factor; or

(2) Consider losses or profits realized or anticipated under other contracts.

(c) Not include in a contract price any amount for a specified contingency to the extent that the contract provides for a price adjustment based upon the occurrence of that contingency.

United States Code Annotated

Contract requirements, see 41 USCA § 254.

Contracts, planning, solicitation, evaluation, and award procedures, see 10 USCA § 2305.

Cost or pricing data, truth in negotiations, see 10 USCA § 2306a, 41 USCA § 254b.

Definitions, see 10 USCA § 2302, 41 USCA §§ 259, 403.

Evaluation and award, see 41 USCA § 253b.

Kinds of contracts, see 10 USCA § 2306.

Planning and solicitation requirements, see 41 USCA § 253a.

Notes of Decisions

Cost or pricing data 1
Evaluation factors 2
Price realism 3
Price reasonableness 4

1 Cost or pricing data

TINA requires the contractor to disclose all cost or pricing data "which *may* or will make up part of the total cost of a contract. Contractor's judgmental decision not to use three quotations from ball bearing suppliers in its bid/proposal was not cost or pricing data. However, the quotations themselves were clearly cost or pricing data because they might, and in this case did, become part of the cost of the contract. In re Appeal of GKS, Inc., A.S.B.C.A. No. 47692, A.S.B.C.A. No. 49296, 00-1 B.C.A. (CCH) ¶ 30914, 2000 WL 558100 (Armed Serv. B.C.A. 2000)

The definition of cost or pricing data includes purchase orders in the possession of the contractor for certain material parts and labor hours for manufacturing contract deliverables which became available prior to the execution of the pricing certification. Because the direct material costs and the direct labor hours involved are factual and verifiable, they are cost or pricing data within the meaning of TINA. In re McDonnell Douglas Helicopter Systems, A.S.B.C.A. No. 50341, 99-2 B.C.A. (CCH) ¶ 30546, 1999 WL 669549 (Armed Serv. B.C.A. 1999)

Regulation governing public contracts did not require contracting officer to obtain audit of successful bidder's cost and pricing data prior to award. RADVA Corp. v. U.S., 17 Cl. Ct.

812, 35 Cont. Cas. Fed. (CCH) P 75706, 1989 WL 91318 (1989), judgment aff'd, 914 F.2d 271 (Fed. Cir. 1990). Public Contracts ⊙⇒5.1

2 Evaluation factors

Where the Government is contractually obligated to pay an incumbent "plant shutdown costs," the Government may consider such costs as part of the total cost to be paid by the Government is a non-incumbent were to be selected for award. Such an approach would not violate FAR 15.402(b)(1), which prohibits the use of *"proposed* price reductions under other contracts as an evaluation factor." The plant shutdown costs that the Government would have to pay the incumbent if another offeror received the award are not *"proposed* price reductions"; rather, they are required under the incumbent's contract with the Government. Therefore, the shutdown costs may lawfully be added to the total evaluated price for offerors other than the incumbent. Arch Chemicals, Inc. v. U.S., 64 Fed. Cl. 380 (2005)

Contracting agency's failure to use the actual prices proposed by contract awardee in evaluating the reasonableness of awardee's prices was harmless error; although agency used incorrect numbers, it had no effect on the validity of the price analysis. Dismas Charities, Inc. v. U.S., 61 Fed. Cl. 191 (2004). United States ⊙⇒64.45(1)

Contracting agency violated procurement regulation when it reviewed only the total prices submitted in proposals and did not compare offerors' contract line item (CLIN) prices with the government's price estimates for the same CLINs to determine whether unit prices were unbalanced. 48 C.F.R. § 15.404-1(g)(1). Al Ghanim Combined Group Co. Gen. Trad. & Cont. W.L.L. v. U.S., 56 Fed. Cl. 502 (2003). United States ⊙⇒64.40(1)

Bidders on contract to provide grounds maintenance and landscaping at Navy facilities were on notice that the prices of past contracts would be evaluated as part of the past performance evaluation, considering that former contract prices were specifically requested, and that the information was reasonably related to a determination of the relevance of past contracts. Maintenance Engineers v. U.S., 50 Fed. Cl. 399 (2001). United States ⊙⇒64.45(2)

Price must always be a factor in procuring agency's decision to award a contract. 10 U.S.C.A. § 2305(a)(3)(A); Federal Property and Administrative Services Act of 1949, § 303A(c)(1)(B), as amended, 41 U.S.C.A. § 253a(c)(1)(B); 48 C.F.R. § 15.304(c)(1). Bean Stuyvesant, L.L.C. v. U.S., 48 Fed. Cl. 303 (2000). United States ⊙⇒64.45(1)

Pursuant to solicitation for offers (SFO) for government lease, contracting officer properly considered reasonableness of proposed cancellation and service costs in making award; with exception of service costs, officer was not required to perform any additional appraisals other than strict reasonableness determination, and determination of actual cancellation costs after award constituted clarification of costs dependent on amount of square footage, not separate, post-award price negotiation. Aerolease Long Beach v. U.S., 31 Fed. Cl. 342, 39 Cont. Cas. Fed. (CCH) P 76654, 39 Cont. Cas. Fed. (CCH) P 76655, 39 Cont. Cas. Fed. (CCH) P 76656 (1994), aff'd, 39 F.3d 1198 (Fed. Cir. 1994). United States ⊙⇒64.40(1)

3 Price realism

The Air Force's price-realism analysis was arbitrary and capricious because it did not account for the projected increasing costs of dealing with an aging fleet of tankers, the U.S. Court of Federal Claims recently held. The COFC nullified the agency's contract award because of the flawed price-realism analysis. Alabama Aircraft Industries, Inc.-Birmingham v. U.S., 83 Fed. Cl. 666 (2008), judgment rev'd, 586 F.3d 1372 (Fed. Cir. 2009)

Price reasonableness and price realism are distinct concepts. The purpose of a price reasonableness review is to determine whether the prices offered are too high, as opposed to too low. Conversely, a price realism review is to determine whether prices are too low, such that there may be a risk of poor performance. EFW Inc., B-412608, et al., 2016 CPD ¶ 304 (Comp. Gen. 2016)

Protest challenging agency's price realism evaluation was denied because the agency reasonably concluded that the awardee's price was not unrealistic based on a comparison with the total average price for the offerors. Kilda Group, LLC, B-409144, 2014 CPD ¶ 80 (Comp.Gen. 2014)

Protest is sustained where solicitation for the issuance of a fixed-price time-and-materials task order did not place offerors on notice that the agency would conduct a price realism evaluation, yet the agency discounted the protester's lower price in its best value tradeoff decision based on its conclusion that the protester's low pricing posed performance risk and reflected a lack of understanding of the agency's requirements. Emergint Techs., Inc., B-407006, 2012 CPD ¶ 295 (Comp. Gen. 2012)

In a negotiated procurement for a fixed-price contract, a protest challenging the rejection of the protester's proposal on the basis that the price was too low was sustained because the evaluation record did not indicate the basis for the agency's determination. Rather, the record contained only the agency's conclusory judgment that the protester's fixed price was too low. Matter of: A1 Procurement, JVG, B-404618, 2011 CPD ¶ 53 (Comp. Gen. 2011)

An agency improperly rejected a low-priced proposal as unrealistic because it did not reasonably consider the realism of the protester's labor rates, as the solicitation required. The agency's price evaluation consisted of a mechanical comparison to the government's cost estimate and the prices proposed for the sample tasks, without any consideration of the realism of the rates used in the sample task pricing. Matter of: I.M. Systems Group, B-404583, B-404583.2, B-404583.3, 2011 CPD ¶ 64 (Comp. Gen. 2011)

An agency's price realism evaluation was improper because the agency did not reconcile the staffing inconsistencies in the awardee's technical and price proposals. The awardee's technical proposal stated that it was "proactively engaged to achieve this staffing at contract startup and throughout the life of the contract." In contrast, the awardee's price proposal stated that staff levels would decrease steadily through the option years, to a level "significantly below" that identified in its technical proposal. Matter of: General Dynamics One Source, LLC; Unisys Corporation, B-400340.5, B-400340.6, 2010 CPD ¶ 45 (Comp. Gen. 2010).

Under a solicitation calling for award of fixed-price contract, GAO sustained a protest challenging the agency's determination that the protester's proposed price was unrealistically low because the solicitation lacked any evaluation criteria that reasonably would have put offerors on notice that agency intended to consider the realism of offerors' prices as reflecting lack of understanding or risk associated with the proposal. Matter of: Milani Construction, LLC, B-401942, 2010 CPD ¶ 87 (Comp. Gen. 2009)

An award was inappropriate because the agency could not provide documentation reflecting the price realism analysis and risk assessment required by the solicitation. Awardee's proposed price changed in Final Revised Proposal (FPR) by more than the difference between awardee's and protester's final total evaluated prices and the awardee's proposal did not explain the change. GAO sustained the protest because it could not determine whether the agency reasonably performed a price realism analysis or properly considered the potential risk flowing from the awardee's drastically changed FPR. Matter of: Pemco Aeroplex, Inc., B-310372, 2008 CPD ¶ 2 (Comp. Gen. 2007)

Agency performed a sufficient price analysis, which determined the awardees' prices were fair and reasonable based on adequate price competition, as required by FAR 15.402. However, FAR 15.402 does not require an agency to perform a price realism analysis to ascertain whether there were performance risks associated with awardees' low prices and the solicitation did not provide for such an analysis. Indtai Inc., B-298432.3, 2007 CPD ¶ 13 (Comp. Gen. 2007)

4 Price reasonableness

Reliance by contracting officer (CO) on other offerors' proposals to determine price reasonableness of bid by state licensing agency (SLA) for blind vendors was appropriate; although agency email indicated that a five percent calculation could be a valid benchmark for a CO to use in determining reasonableness of bid by an SLA, the email also stated that "the [CO]'s fair and reasonable price analysis may use 5% or some reasonable % as a benchmark in comparing the SLA's price to other vendors." Moore's Cafeteria Services v. U.S., 77 Fed. Cl. 180 (2007), aff'd, 314 Fed. Appx. 277 (Fed. Cir. 2008)

Even if independent government estimate (IGE) in solicitation for food services at Army installation was inaccurate, as contended by bid protestor, it did not prejudice protestor, where the IGE was not the sole basis for the price reasonableness determination of the contracting officer (CO); instead, the CO primarily relied upon a comparison of the contract awardee's offer to two other technically acceptable offers, and determined that the awardee's offer was reasonable. Moore's Cafeteria Services v. U.S., 77 Fed. Cl. 180 (2007), aff'd, 314 Fed. Appx. 277 (Fed. Cir. 2008)

Price reasonableness generally addresses whether a price is too high, whereas cost realism generally addresses whether a cost estimate is too low. While there is a requirement for the contracting officer to do a price reasonableness analysis, there is no similar requirement to do a cost realism analysis. The contracting officer is responsible for evaluating the reasonableness of proposed prices to ensure that the price to the government is fair and reasonable. First Enterprise v. U.S., 61 Fed. Cl. 109 (2004)

An agency may eliminate a proposal from the competition based on price alone, without considering the high quality of the offeror's technical submission if the proposed price is unreasonable in an absolute (as opposed to relative) sense. Although the RFQ provided for a best value evaluation based on comparative technical and price considerations, an agency also must consider whether the quoted prices are too high in an absolute sense. The contracting officer rejected the protester's quotation because price was so high that award to the firm would not be in the public interest, no matter the quality of its technical submission. The protester's price was approximately 20 times the awardee's price, 8 times the third vendor's price, and 10 times the Government Estimate. Given this great disparity in pricing, there was nothing improper in the contracting officer's determination that the protester's price was unreasonable. Gold Cross Safety Corporation, B-296099, 2005 CPD ¶ 118 (Comp. Gen. 2005)

Price reasonableness evaluation leading to award an indefinite-quantity contract was unreasonable where the agency evaluated only unit prices without also considering the estimated quantities of each line item. Such an approach does not satisfy the legal requirement to consider total cost to the government. Without using the estimated, the agency's evaluation failed to account for the difference in the relative proportions of the cost for each item in the total cost to the government, and, as a result, there was no direct relationship between the evaluated prices of a particular offeror and the actual price of performance by that offeror. R & G Food Service, Inc., d/b/a Port×A×Pit Catering, B-296435.4, B-296435.9, 2005 WL 3144073 (Comp. Gen. 2005).

A determination concerning price reasonableness is a matter of administrative discretion involving the exercise of business judgment, which our Office will not question unless that determination is unreasonable or there is a showing of bad faith or fraud. In this connection, a determination concerning price reasonableness may be based upon a comparison with such factors as government estimates, past procurement history, current market conditions, or any other relevant factors, including those which have been revealed by the competition received. Bristol Machining & Fabrication, Inc., B-244490, 91-2 CPD ¶ 315 (Comp. Gen. 1991)

§ 15.403 Obtaining cost or pricing data.

§ 15.403-1 Prohibition on obtaining certified cost or pricing data (10 U.S.C. 2306a and 41 U.S.C. chapter 35).

(a) Certified cost or pricing data shall not be obtained for acquisitions at or below the simplified acquisition threshold.

(b) Exceptions to certified cost or pricing data requirements. The contracting officer shall not require certified cost or pricing data to support any action (contracts, subcontracts, or modifications) (but may require data other than certified cost or pricing data as defined in FAR 2.101 to support a determination of a fair and reasonable price or cost realism)-

(1) When the contracting officer determines that prices agreed upon are based on adequate price competition (see standards in paragraph (c)(1) of this subsection);

(2) When the contracting officer determines that prices agreed upon are based on prices set by law or regulation (see standards in paragraph (c)(2) of this subsection);

(3) When a commercial item is being acquired (see standards in paragraph (c)(3) of this subsection);

(4) When a waiver has been granted (see standards in paragraph (c)(4) of this subsection); or

(5) When modifying a contract or subcontract for commercial items (see standards in paragraph (c)(3) of this sub section).

(c) Standards for exceptions from certified cost or pricing data requirements—

(1) Adequate price competition. A price is based on adequate price competition if—

(i) Two or more responsible offerors, competing independently, submit priced offers that satisfy the Government's expressed requirement and if—

(A) Award will be made to the offeror whose proposal represents the best value (see 2.101) where price is a substantial factor in source selection; and

(B) There is no finding that the price of the otherwise successful offeror is unreasonable. Any finding that the price is unreasonable must be supported by a statement of the facts and approved at a level above the contracting officer;

(ii) There was a reasonable expectation, based on market research or other assessment, that two or more responsible offerors, competing independently, would submit priced offers in response to the solicitation's expressed requirement, even though only one offer is received from a responsible offeror and if—

(A) Based on the offer received, the contracting officer can reasonably conclude that the offer was submitted with the expectation of competition, e.g., circumstances indicate that-

(1) The offeror believed that at least one other offeror was capable of submitting a meaningful offer; and

(2) The offeror had no reason to believe that other potential offerors did not intend to submit an offer; and

(B) The determination that the proposed price is based on adequate price competition and is reasonable has been approved at a level above the contracting officer; or

(iii) Price analysis clearly demonstrates that the proposed price is reasonable in comparison with current or recent prices for the same or similar items, adjusted to reflect changes in market conditions, economic conditions, quantities, or terms and conditions under contracts that resulted from adequate price competition.

(2) Prices set by law or regulation. Pronouncements in the form of periodic rulings, reviews, or similar actions of a governmental body, or embodied in the laws, are sufficient to set a price.

(3) Commercial items.

(i) Any acquisition of an item that the contracting officer determines meets the commercial item definition in 2.101, or any modification, as defined in paragraph (3)(i) of that definition, that does not change the item from a commercial item to a noncommercial item, is exempt from the requirement for certified cost or pricing data. If the contracting officer determines that an item claimed to be commercial is, in fact, not commercial and that no other exception or waiver applies, (e.g. the acquisition is not based on adequate price competition; the acquisition is not based on prices set by law or regulation; and the acquisition exceeds the threshold for the submission of certified cost or pricing data at 15.403-4(a)(1)) the contracting officer shall require submission of certified cost or pricing data.

(ii) In accordance with 41 U.S.C. 3501:

(A) When purchasing services that are not offered and sold competitively in substantial quantities in the commercial marketplace, but are of a type offered and sold competitively in substantial quantities in the commercial marketplace, they may be considered commercial items (thus meeting the purpose of 41 U.S.C. chapter 35 and 10 U.S.C. 2306a for truth in negotiations) only if the contracting officer determines in writing that the offeror has submitted sufficient information to evaluate, through price analysis, the reasonableness of the price of such services.

(B) In order to make this determination, the contracting officer may request the offeror to submit prices paid for the same or similar commercial items under comparable terms and conditions by both Government and commercial customers; and

(C) If the contracting officer determines that the information described in paragraph (c)(3)(ii)(B) of this section is not sufficient to determine the reasonableness of price, other relevant information regarding the basis for price or cost, including information on labor costs, material costs and overhead rates may be requested.

(iii) The following requirements apply to minor modifications defined in paragraph (3)(ii) of the definition of a commercial item at 2.101 that do not change the item from a commercial item to a noncommercial item;

(A) For acquisitions funded by any agency other than DoD, NASA, or Coast Guard, such modifications of a commercial item are exempt from the requirement for submission of certified cost or pricing data.

(B) For acquisitions funded by DoD, NASA, or Coast Guard, such modifications of a commercial item are exempt from the requirement for submission of certified cost or pricing data provided the total price of all such modifications under a particular contract action does not exceed the greater of the threshold for obtaining certified cost or pricing data in 15.403-4 or 5 percent of the total price of the contract at the time of contract award.

(C) For acquisitions funded by DoD, NASA, or Coast Guard such modifications of a commercial item are not exempt from the requirement for submission of certified cost or pricing data on the basis of the exemption provided for at 15.403-1(c)(3) if the total price of all such modifications under a particular contract action exceeds the greater of the threshold for obtaining certified cost or pricing data in 15.403-4 or 5 percent of the total price of the contract at the time of contract award.

(iv) Any acquisition for noncommercial supplies or services treated as commercial items at 12.102(f)(1), except sole source contracts greater than $19 million, is exempt from the requirements for certified cost or pricing data (41 U.S.C. 1903).

(4) Waivers. The head of the contracting activity (HCA) may, without power of delegation, waive the requirement for submission of certified cost or pricing data in exceptional cases. The authorization for the waiver and the supporting rationale shall be in writing. The HCA may consider waiving the requirement if the price can be determined to be fair and reasonable without submission of certified cost or pricing data. For example, if certified cost or pricing data were furnished on previous production buys and the contracting officer determines such data are sufficient, when combined with updated data, a waiver may be granted. If the HCA has waived the requirement for submission of certified cost or pricing data, the contractor or higher-tier subcontractor to whom the waiver relates shall be considered as having been required to provide certified cost or pricing data. Consequently, award of any lower-tier subcontract expected to exceed the certified cost or pricing data threshold requires the submission of certified cost or pricing data unless—

(i) An exception otherwise applies to the subcontract; or

(ii) The waiver specifically includes the subcontract and the rationale supporting the waiver for that subcontract.

United States Code Annotated

Contract requirements, see 41 USCA § 254.

Contracts, planning, solicitation, evaluation, and award procedures, see 10 USCA § 2305.

Cost or pricing data, truth in negotiations, see 10 USCA § 2306a, 41 USCA § 254b.

Definitions, see 10 USCA § 2302, 41 USCA §§ 259, 403.

Evaluation and award, see 41 USCA § 253b.

Kinds of contracts, see 10 USCA § 2306.

Planning and solicitation requirements, see 41 USCA § 253a.

Notes of Decisions

In general 1

1 In general

Regulation governing public contracts did not require contracting officer to obtain audit of successful bidder's cost and pricing data prior to award. RADVA Corp. v. U.S., 17 Cl. Ct. 812, 35 Cont. Cas. Fed. (CCH) P 75706, 1989 WL 91318 (1989), judgment aff'd, 914 F.2d 271 (Fed. Cir. 1990). Public Contracts ⊙5.1

§ 15.403-2 Other circumstances where certified cost or pricing data are not required.

(a) The exercise of an option at the price established at contract award or initial negotiation does not require submission of certified cost or pricing data.

(b) Certified cost or pricing data are not required for proposals used solely for overrun funding or interim billing price adjustments.

United States Code Annotated

Contract requirements, see 41 USCA § 254.

Contracts, planning, solicitation, evaluation, and award procedures, see 10 USCA § 2305.

Cost or pricing data, truth in negotiations, see 10 USCA § 2306a, 41 USCA § 254b.

Definitions, see 10 USCA § 2302, 41 USCA §§ 259, 403.

Evaluation and award, see 41 USCA § 253b.

Kinds of contracts, see 10 USCA § 2306.

Planning and solicitation requirements, see 41 USCA § 253a.

Notes of Decisions

Cost or pricing data 1
Format of submission 2
Incomplete or inaccurate data 3
Non-submission of data 4
Subcontractor data 5

1 Cost or pricing data

The government's claims for contract price reduction based upon misstatements or inaccuracies in an offeror's final revised proposal are not cognizable under the Truth in Negotiations Act (TINA) since a final revised proposal a is not cost or pricing data. United Technologies Corp., Appeals of, A.S.B.C.A. No. 51410, 04-1 B.C.A. (CCH) ¶ 32556, 2004 WL 483216 (Armed Serv. B.C.A. 2004), on reconsideration, A.S.B.C.A. No. 51410, A.S.B.C.A. No. 53089, A.S.B.C.A. No. 53349, 05-1 B.C.A. (CCH) ¶ 32860, 2005 WL 147601 (Armed Serv. B.C.A. 2005), decision aff'd, 463 F.3d 1261 (Fed. Cir. 2006)

A previously designed and built engineering advance applicable to the contract work being negotiated constituted factual data that was significant to the price negotiationsand must be disclosed in accordance with 10 U.S.C. § 2306(h)(1), which defines such facts as cost and pricing data which must be disclosed. In re Appeals of Lockheed Martin Corp., A.S.B.C.A. No. 50566, 02-2 B.C.A. (CCH) ¶ 31907, 2002 WL 1453988 (Armed Serv. B.C.A. 2002)

TINA requires the contractor to disclose all cost or pricing data "which *may* or will make up part of the total cost of a contract. Contractor's judgmental decision not to use three quotations from ball bearing suppliers in its bid/proposal was not cost or pricing data. However, the quotations themselves were clearly cost or pricing data because they might, and in this case did, become part of the cost of the contract. In re Appeal of GKS, Inc., A.S.B.C.A. No. 47692, A.S.B.C.A. No. 49296, 00-1 B.C.A. (CCH) ¶ 30914, 2000 WL 558100 (Armed Serv. B.C.A. 2000)

The definition of cost or pricing data includes purchase orders in the possession of the contractor for certain material parts and labor hours for manufacturing contract deliverables which became available prior to the execution of the pricing certification. Because the direct material costs and the direct labor hours involved are factual and verifiable, they are cost or pricing data within the meaning of TINA. In re McDonnell Douglas Helicopter Systems, A.S.B.C.A. No. 50341, 99-2 B.C.A. (CCH) ¶ 30546, 1999 WL 669549 (Armed Serv. B.C.A. 1999)

2 Format of submission

A prospective contractor must make the significance of the data known to the contracting officer if it does not physically deliver that data to the contracting officer but instead makes all of its records available. Thus, TINA requires the equalizing of cost or pricing data knowledge and does not require the creation of new cost or pricing data, a new analysis of furnished data, or the re-organization of furnished data. In re Appeals of Lockheed Martin Corp., A.S.B.C.A. No. 50566, 02-2 B.C.A. (CCH) ¶ 31907, 2002 WL 1453988 (Armed Serv. B.C.A. 2002)

Contractor satisfied its disclosure obligation by providing a copy of its final revised proposal to the resident DCAA auditor who evaluated the contractor's proposal. The cost and pricing information in the final revised proposal was in a usable, understandable format and was used by the auditor to advise the contracting officer of the specific pricing issue that is the subject of the government's defective pricing claim. Thus, both the auditor who reviewed the proposal and the contracting officer who negotiated the contract had actual knowledge of the pricing issue. Disclosure is not confined to a formal, written submission. Instead the contractor's disclosure obligation is fulfilled if the Government obtains the data in question in some other manner or had knowledge. Appeal of Alliant Techsystems, Inc., A.S.B.C.A. No. 47626, A.S.B.C.A. No. 51280, 00-2 B.C.A. (CCH) ¶ 31042, 2000 WL 1049163 (Armed Serv. B.C.A. 2000)

Contractor made adequate disclosure even though delivery was limited to granting of access to the data contained in the contractor's internal procurement management software program. Access was granted to audit personnel from the Defense Contract Audit Agency (DCAA) and Defense Plant Representative Office (DPRO) who were working in support of the contracting officer. The DCAA and DPRO personnel knew how to use the contractor's software program. In re McDonnell Douglas Helicopter Systems, A.S.B.C.A. No. 50447, A.S.B.C.A. No. 50448, A.S.B.C.A. No. 50449, 2000 WL 1286267 (Armed Serv. B.C.A. 2000)

It is not enough for the prospective contractor to make available or physically hand over to the Government for its inspection, files, which if examined, would disclose differences between proposal costs and lower historical costs. It is also necessary, in order to make a disclosure, to advise the Government representatives involved in the proposed procurement, of the kind and content of the cost or pricing data and their bearing on the prospective contractor's proposal which examination of the files would disclose. This disclosure obligation is satisfied if the Government personnel who participated in the proposal evaluation or contract negotiations were clearly advised of the relevant cost or pricing data or, if they were not so advised, nevertheless had actual knowledge thereof. Appeal of Texas Instruments, Inc., A.S.B.C.A. No. 23678, 87-3 B.C.A. (CCH) ¶ 20195, 1987 WL 41361 (Armed Serv. B.C.A. 1987)

3 Incomplete or inaccurate data

Contractor's failure to convert labor hours accumulated by work order number into hours per unit was excused because the contractor's accounting system did not accumulate labor hours by unit, the conversion had to be done manually and it would have required an "inordinate" amount of time to perform. Therefore, the data was not "reasonably available" at the time of certification so that its non-submission does not support the government's defective pricing claim. Appeal of Litton Systems, inc., Amecon Div., A.S.B.C.A. No. 34435, A.S.B.C.A. No. 37615, A.S.B.C.A. No. 37616, 93-2 B.C.A. (CCH) ¶ 25707, 1992 WL 379288 (Armed Serv. B.C.A. 1992)

Although cost and pricing data were apparently were in the contractor's possession and were relatively uncomplicated, they were not reasonably available for preparation of the proposal and the negotiations because the contractor was allowed less than two days on a weekend to verify and update the cost data in an area in which a war was going on. Appeal of Central Nav. and Trading Co., S.A., A.S.B.C.A. No. 23946, 82-2 B.C.A. (CCH) ¶ 16074, 1982 WL 7818 (Armed Serv. B.C.A. 1982)

In a defective pricing claim, the government must show, by a preponderance of the evidence, that more accurate, complete and current cost or pricing data were reasonably available to appellant on the date of certification under the prevailing circumstances. Because the procurement was negotiated under an exception to the Competition in Contract Act rules because it was determined to be necessary as a matter of public exigency, the contractor has convincingly demonstrated that its failure to produce more complete and more current cost or pricing data was not the result of a failure to make the necessary administrative effort to obtain them, but rather, that such data were simply not reasonably available within the time allowed. Appeal of LTV Electrosystems, Inc., Memcor Div., A.S.B.C.A. No. 16802, 73-1 B.C.A. (CCH) ¶ 9957, 1973 WL 1865 (Armed Serv. B.C.A. 1973), on reconsideration, A.S.B.C.A. No. 16802, 74-1 B.C.A. (CCH) ¶ 10380, 1973 WL 1901 (Armed Serv. B.C.A. 1973).

4 Non-submission of data

First-tier subcontractor responsible for electrical generator sets for Navy destroyers did not withhold cost or pricing data from prime contractor during contract renegotiations on redesigned units in violation of Truth in Negotiations Act, notwithstanding that first-tier subcontractor had anticipated by time of negotiations that cost of second-tier subcontractor's assembling redesigned units was likely to be less than original units, where subcontractors had not actually reached an agreement to lower assembly price at time of negotiations and first-tier subcontractor had no duty to disclose eventual agreement that did lower price because it was made 13 months after contract negotiations with shipyard. Truth in Negotiations, § 952(a)(1)(D)(i), 10 U.S.C.A. § 2306a(a)(1)(D)(i). U.S. ex rel. Sanders v. Allison Engine Co., Inc., 471 F.3d 610, 2006 FED App. 0463P (6th Cir. 2006), vacated and remanded, 553 U.S. 662, 128 S. Ct. 2123, 170 L. Ed. 2d 1030, 37 A.L.R. Fed. 2d 773 (2008). (The Supreme Court addressed only the issue of "whether subcontractors' invoices for allegedly defective construction of units violated FCA", finding that the circuit court incorrectly interpreted 31 U.S.C.A. § § 3729(a)(2) and (3).)

5 Subcontractor data

TINA requires submission of subcontractor cost or pricing data and certification that the cost or pricing data submitted is accurate, complete and current upon two occasions: (1) as of the date of final price agreement between the prime contractor and the Government, 10 U.S.C. § 2306a(a)(1), (2), and (2) when a subcontractor and prime contractor agree upon a negotiated subcontract price, which can occur months after agreement upon the Government's and prime contractor's contract price. In re Appeal of McDonnell Aircraft Co., A.S.B.C.A. No. 44504, 03-1 B.C.A. (CCH) ¶ 32154, 2003 WL 221003 (Armed Serv. B.C.A. 2003).

§ 15.403-3 Requiring data other than certified cost or pricing data.

(a)

(1) In those acquisitions that do not require certified cost or pricing data, the contracting officer shall—

(i) Obtain whatever data are available from Government or other secondary sources and use that data in determining a fair and reasonable price;

(ii) Require submission of data other than certified cost or pricing data, as defined in 2.101, from the offeror to the extent necessary to determine a fair and reasonable price (10 U.S.C. 2306a(d)(1) and 41 U.S.C. 3505(a)) if the contracting officer determines that adequate data from sources other than the offeror are not available. This includes requiring data from an offeror to support a cost realism analysis;

(iii) Consider whether cost data are necessary to determine a fair and reasonable price when there is not adequate price competition;

(iv) Require that the data submitted by the offeror include, at a minimum, appropriate data on the prices at which the same item or similar items have previously been sold, adequate for determining the reasonableness of the price unless an exception under 15.403-1(b)(1) or (2) applies; and

(v) Consider the guidance in section 3.3, chapter 3, volume I, of the Contract Pricing Reference Guide cited at 15.404-1(a)(7) to determine the data an offeror shall be required to submit.

(2) The contractor's format for submitting the data should be used (see 15.403-5(b)(2)).

(3) The contracting officer shall ensure that data used to support price negotiations are sufficiently current to permit negotiation of a fair and reasonable price. Requests for updated offeror data should be limited to data that affect the adequacy of the proposal for negotiations, such as changes in price lists.

(4) As specified in section 808 of the Strom Thurmond National Defense Authorization Act for Fiscal Year 1999 (Pub. L. 105-261), an offeror who does not comply with a requirement to submit data for a contract or subcontract in accordance with paragraph (a)(1) of this subsection is ineligible for award unless the HCA determines that it is in the best interest of the Government to make the award to that offeror, based on consideration of the following:

(i) The effort made to obtain the data.

(ii) The need for the item or service.

(iii) Increased cost or significant harm to the Government if award is not made.

(b) Adequate price competition. When adequate price competition exists (see 15.403-1(c)(1)), generally no additional data are necessary to determine the reasonableness of price. However, if there are unusual circumstances where it is concluded that additional data are necessary to determine the reasonableness of price, the contracting officer shall, to the maximum extent practicable, obtain the additional data from sources other than the offeror. In addition, the contracting officer should request data to determine the cost realism of competing offers or to evaluate competing approaches.

(c) Commercial items.

(1) At a minimum, the contracting officer must use price analysis to determine whether the price is fair and reasonable whenever the contracting officer acquires a commercial item (see 15.404-1(b)). The fact that a price is included in a catalog does not, in and of itself, make it fair and reasonable. If the contracting officer cannot determine whether an offered price is fair and reasonable, even after obtaining additional data from sources other than the offeror, then the contracting officer shall require the offeror to submit data other than certified cost or pricing data to support further analysis (see 15.404-1). This data may include history of sales to non-governmental and governmental entities, cost data, or any other information the contracting officer requires to determine the price is fair and reasonable. Unless an exception under 15.403-1(b)(1) or (2) applies, the contracting officer shall require that the data submitted by the offeror include, at a minimum, appropriate data on the prices at which the same item or similar items have previously been sold, adequate for determining the reasonableness of the price.

(2) *Limitations relating to commercial items (10 U.S.C. 2306a(d)(2) and 41 U.S.C. 3505(b)).*

(i) The contracting officer shall limit requests for sales data relating to commercial items to data for the same or similar items during a relevant time period.

(ii) The contracting officer shall, to the maximum extent practicable, limit the scope of the request for data relating to commercial items to include only data that are in the form regularly maintained by the offeror as part of its commercial operations.

(iii) The Government shall not disclose outside the Government data obtained relating to commercial items that is exempt from disclosure under 24.202(a) or the Freedom of Information Act (5 U.S.C. 552(b)).

(3) For services that are not offered and sold competitively in substantial quantities in the commercial marketplace, but are of a type offered and sold competitively in substantial quantities in the commercial marketplace, see 15.403-1(c)(3)(ii).

United States Code Annotated

Contract requirements, see 41 USCA § 254.

Contracts, planning, solicitation, evaluation, and award procedures, see 10 USCA § 2305.

Cost or pricing data, truth in negotiations, see 10 USCA § 2306a, 41 USCA § 254b.

Definitions, see 10 USCA § 2302, 41 USCA §§ 259, 403.

Evaluation and award, see 41 USCA § 253b.

Kinds of contracts, see 10 USCA § 2306.

Planning and solicitation requirements, see 41 USCA § 253a.

Notes of Decisions

In general 1

1 In general

Agency's decision to exclude the protester from a competition because the protester's submission of "other than cost or pricing data," as was contemplated by the solicitation, was determined to be inconsistent with the instructions in FAR 15.408, Table 15-2, was unreasonable where: (1) the instructions were only applicable to cost proposals when cost or pricing data is required, (2) the instructions were neither referenced nor incorporated into the RFP, (3) there was no evidence in the record that offerors were ever notified that their cost information had to be presented in accordance with Table 15-2, and (4) none of the audits of the other offerors' cost proposals were evaluated against this standard. Decision Matter of: PMO Partnership Joint Venture, B-403214, B-403214.2, 2010 CPD ¶ 256 (Comp. Gen. 2010)

§ 15.403-4 Requiring certified cost or pricing data (10 U.S.C. 2306a and 41 U.S.C. chapter 35).

(a) (1) The contracting officer shall obtain certified cost or pricing data only if the contracting officer concludes that none of the exceptions in 15.403-1(b) applies. However, if the contracting officer has reason to believe exceptional circumstances exist and has sufficient data available to determine a fair and reasonable price, then the contracting officer should consider requesting a waiver under the exception at 15.403-1(b)(4). The threshold for obtaining certified cost or pricing data is $750,000. Unless an exception applies, certified cost or pricing data are required before accomplishing any of the following actions expected to exceed the current threshold or, in the case of existing contracts, the threshold specified in the contract:

(i) The award of any negotiated contract (except for undefinitized actions such as letter contracts).

(ii) The award of a subcontract at any tier, if the contractor and each higher-tier subcontractor were required to furnish certified cost or pricing data (but see waivers at 15.403-1(c)(4)).

(iii) The modification of any sealed bid or negotiated contract (whether or not certified cost or pricing data were initially required) or any subcontract covered by paragraph (a)(1)(ii) of this subsection. Price adjustment amounts must consider both increases and decreases (e.g., a $200,000 modification resulting from a reduction of $500,000 and an increase of $300,000 is a pricing adjustment exceeding $750,000). This requirement does not apply when a unrelated and separately priced changes for which certified cost or pricing data would not otherwise be required are included for administrative convenience in the same modification. Negotiated final pricing actions (such as termination settlements and total final price agreements for fixed-price incentive and redeterminable contracts) are contract modifications requiring certified cost or pricing data if—

(A) The total final price agreement for such settlements or agreements exceeds the pertinent threshold set forth at paragraph (a)(1) of this subsection; or

(B) The partial termination settlement plus the estimate to complete the continued portion of the contract exceeds the pertinent threshold set forth at paragraph (a)(1) of this subsection (see 49.105(c)(15)).

(2) Unless prohibited because an exception at 15.403-1(b) applies, the head of the contracting activity, without power of delegation, may authorize the contracting officer to obtain certified cost or pricing data for pricing actions below the pertinent threshold in paragraph (a)(1) of this subsection, provided the action exceeds the simplified acquisition threshold. The head of the contracting activity shall justify the requirement for certified cost or pricing data. The documentation shall include a written finding that certified cost or pricing data are necessary to determine whether the price is fair and reasonable and the facts supporting that finding.

(b) When certified cost or pricing data are required, the contracting officer shall require the contractor or prospective contractor to submit to the contracting officer (and to have any subcontractor or prospective subcontractor submit to the prime contractor or appropriate subcontractor tier) the following in support of any proposal:

(1) The certified cost or pricing data and data other than certified cost or pricing data required by the contracting officer to determine that the price is fair and reasonable.

(2) A Certificate of Current Cost or Pricing Data, in the format specified in 15.406-2, certifying that to the best of its knowledge and belief, the cost or pricing data were accurate, complete, and current as of the date of agreement on price or, if applicable, an earlier date agreed upon between the parties that is as close as practicable to the date of agreement on price.

(c) If certified cost or pricing data are requested and submitted by an offeror, but an exception is later found to apply, the data must not be considered certified cost or pricing data as defined in 2.101 and must not be certified in accordance with 15.406-2

(d) The requirements of this subsection also apply to contracts entered into by an agency on behalf of a foreign government.

United States Code Annotated

Contract requirements, see 41 USCA § 254.

Contracts, planning, solicitation, evaluation, and award procedures, see 10 USCA § 2305.

Cost or pricing data, truth in negotiations, see 10 USCA § 2306a, 41 USCA § 254b.

Definitions, see 10 USCA § 2302, 41 USCA §§ 259, 403.

Evaluation and award, see 41 USCA § 253b.

Kinds of contracts, see 10 USCA § 2306.

Planning and solicitation requirements, see 41 USCA § 253a.

Notes of Decisions

In general 1
Disclosure of information 2

1 In general

Regulation governing public contracts did not require contracting officer to obtain audit of successful bidder's cost and pricing data prior to award. RADVA Corp. v. U.S., 17 Cl. Ct. 812, 35 Cont. Cas. Fed. (CCH) P 75706, 1989 WL 91318 (1989), judgment aff'd, 914 F.2d 271 (Fed. Cir. 1990). Public Contracts ☞5.1

2 Disclosure of information

"B-table" matrices of factors going into pricing of long distance telephone services in contract with General Services Administration (GSA) consisted of confidential information, which GSA was required to withhold from competitor making request under Freedom of Information Act (FOIA), and were consequently exempt from Federal Acquisition Regulation (FAR) requirement that unit pricing of contracts be disclosed. 5 U.S.C.A. § 552(b)(4); 48 C.F.R. § 15.503(b)(1). MCI Worldcom, Inc. v. General Services Admin., 163 F. Supp. 2d 28 (D.D.C. 2001). Records ☞59; United States ☞64.55(1)

Contractor that successfully bid on contract with Navy failed to show that Navy's disclosure of costs and pricing data and proprietary management strategies it included in its bid would cause substantial harm to its competitive position, as required for Freedom of Information Act's (FOIA) trade secret exemption to apply. 5 U.S.C.A. § 552(b)(4). Martin Marietta Corp. v. Dalton, 974 F. Supp. 37, 41 Cont. Cas. Fed. (CCH) P 77164 (D.D.C. 1997). Records ☞59

Cost and pricing information disclosed by contractor when it bid on contract with Navy was not disclosed voluntarily, in determining whether such information was exempt from disclosure under Freedom of Information Act (FOIA); contractor was required to submit information requested by Navy if it hoped to win contract. 5 U.S.C.A. § 552(b)(4); 48 C.F.R. § 15.804-6(b)(1). Martin Marietta Corp. v. Dalton, 974 F. Supp. 37, 41 Cont. Cas. Fed. (CCH) P 77164 (D.D.C. 1997). Records ☞59

In determining whether Freedom of Information Act's (FOIA) trade secret exemption applied to cost and pricing data and proprietary management strategies disclosed by contractor when it successfully bid on Navy contract, Navy's prior release of such information to limited number of requesters did not necessarily make information matter of public knowledge, or lessen likelihood contractor would suffer competitive harm if it was disclosed again to its competitors. 5 U.S.C.A. § 552(b)(4). Martin Marietta Corp. v. Dalton, 974 F. Supp. 37, 41 Cont. Cas. Fed. (CCH) P 77164 (D.D.C. 1997). Records ☞59

When an unsuccessful offeror lawfully obtains source selection information, such as a competitor's prices and technical scores, and the agency subsequently properly reopens negotiations, the agency may disclose similar information to all the competitors to eliminate any competitive advantage. 48 C.F.R. § 15.507. ManTech Telecommunications and Information Systems Corp. v. U.S., 49 Fed. Cl. 57 (2001), decision aff'd, 30 Fed. Appx. 995 (Fed. Cir. 2002). United States ☞64.40(5)

Agency would not be permitted to disclose to contract awardee price information contained in proposal of bid protestor, as part of proposed corrective action, even though agency disclosed to protestor the price of awardee's proposal during debriefing, where the pricing information contained in protestor's proposal was fundamentally different from what it received during debriefing, so that disclosure would not equalize the competition, but provide awardee with an unwarranted advantage. 48 C.F.R. § 15.507. ManTech Telecommunications and Information Systems Corp. v. U.S., 49 Fed. Cl. 57 (2001), decision aff'd, 30 Fed. Appx. 995 (Fed. Cir. 2002). United States ☞64.40(5)

Army did not violate provision of the Federal Acquisition Regulation (FAR) in solicitation for the manufacture of optically improved periscopes for the Army's Bradley fighting vehicle by providing successful bidder historical pricing data relating to prior contracts awarded to competitor for the manufacture and production of periscopes; provision would only have been violated if government personnel provided bidder with competitor's current offering prices. 48 C.F.R. § 15.306(e)(3). Miller-Holzwarth, Inc. v. U.S., 42 Fed. Cl. 643 (1999), aff'd, 232 F.3d 905 (Fed. Cir. 2000). United States ☞64.40(2)

Federal Acquisition Regulations (FAR) did not authorize agency's disclosure of offeror's unit pricing to other offerors on resolicitation of bid, where there was no contract award in original solicitation. 48 C.F.R. §§ 15.507, 15.1003(b), 15.1006. Fore Systems Federal, Inc. v. U.S., 40 Fed. Cl. 490 (1998). United States ☞64.40(2)

Government had a rational basis for reopening negotiations for a Navy technical support services contract after deciding initially to award the contract to one contractor and disclosing that contractor's proposed cost, based on contracting officer's determination that contractor's proposal did not affirmatively meet the personal qualification sheet requirements for specialized submarine experience in electronic warfare or specialized electronic warfare experience; Government could not be forced to accept service contracts that understated the Government's minimum personnel requirements. Logicon, Inc. v. U.S., 22 Cl. Ct. 776, 37 Cont. Cas. Fed. (CCH) P 76066, 1991 WL 52823 (1991). United States ☞64.50

In order for Government to substantiate its decision to reopen negotiation after disclosure of contractor's bid price, Government must show that contracting officer's decision to reopen negotiations was clearly in the agency's interest, in response to which contractor must prove by preponderance of the evidence that the justification was irrational or unreasonable or otherwise failed to satisfy applicable regulations. Logicon, Inc. v. U.S., 22 Cl. Ct. 776, 37 Cont. Cas. Fed. (CCH) P 76066, 1991 WL 52823 (1991). United States ☞64.50

§ 15.403-5 Instructions for submission of certified cost or pricing data and data other than certified cost or pricing data.

(a) Taking into consideration the policy at 15.402, the contracting officer shall specify in the solicitation (see 15.408 (l) and (m))—

(1) Whether certified cost or pricing data are required;

(2) That, in lieu of submitting certified cost or pricing data, the offeror may submit a request for exception from the requirement to submit certified cost or pricing data;

(3) Any requirement for data other than certified cost or pricing data; and

(4) The requirement for necessary preaward or postaward access to offeror's records.

(b) (1) *Format for submission of certified cost or pricing data.* When certification is required, the contracting officer may require submission of certified cost or pricing data in the format indicated in Table 15-2 of 15.408, specify an alternative format, or permit submission in the contractor's format (See 15.408(l)(1)), unless the data are required to be submitted on one of the termination forms specified in Subpart 49.6.

(2) *Format for submission of data other than certified cost or pricing data.* When required by the contracting officer, data other than certified cost or pricing data may be submitted in the offeror's own format unless the contracting officer decides that use of a specific format is essential for evaluating and determining that the price is fair and reasonable and the format has been described in the solicitation.

(3) *Format for submission of data supporting forward pricing rate agreements.* Data supporting forward pricing rate agreements or final indirect cost proposals shall be submitted in a form acceptable to the contracting officer.

United States Code Annotated

Contract requirements, see 41 USCA § 254.

Contracts, planning, solicitation, evaluation, and award procedures, see 10 USCA § 2305.

Cost or pricing data, truth in negotiations, see 10 USCA § 2306a, 41 USCA § 254b.

Definitions, see 10 USCA § 2302, 41 USCA §§ 259, 403.

Evaluation and award, see 41 USCA § 253b.

Kinds of contracts, see 10 USCA § 2306.

Planning and solicitation requirements, see 41 USCA § 253a.

§ 15.404 Proposal analysis.

§ 15.404-1 Proposal analysis techniques.

(a) *General.* The objective of proposal analysis is to ensure that the final agreed-to price is fair and reasonable.

(1) The contracting officer is responsible for evaluating the reasonableness of the offered prices. The analytical techniques and procedures described in this subsection may be used, singly or in combination with others, to ensure that the final price is fair and reasonable. The complexity and circumstances of each acquisition should determine the level of detail of the analysis required.

(2) Price analysis shall be used when certified cost or pricing data are not required (see paragraph (b) of this subsection and 15.404-3).

(3) Cost analysis shall be used to evaluate the reasonableness of individual cost elements when certified cost or pricing data are required. Price analysis should be used to verify that the overall price offered is fair and reasonable.

(4) Cost analysis may also be used to evaluate data other than certified cost or pricing data to determine cost reasonableness or cost realism when a fair and reasonable price cannot be determined through price analysis alone for commercial or non-commercial items.

(5) The contracting officer may request the advice and assistance of other experts to ensure that an appropriate analysis is performed.

(6) Recommendations or conclusions regarding the Government's review or analysis of an offeror's or contractor's proposal shall not be disclosed to the offeror or contractor without the concurrence of the contracting officer. Any discrepancy or mistake of fact (such as duplications, omissions, and errors in computation) contained in the certified cost or pricing data or data other than certified cost or pricing data submitted in support of a proposal shall be brought to the contracting officer's attention for appropriate action.

(7) The Air Force Institute of Technology (AFIT) and the Federal Acquisition Institute (FAI) jointly prepared a five-volume set of Contract Pricing Reference Guides to guide pricing and negotiation personnel. The five guides are: I Price Analysis, II Quantitative Techniques for Contract Pricing, III Cost Analysis, IV Advanced Issues in Contract Pricing, and V Federal Contract Negotiation Techniques. These references provide detailed discussion and examples applying pricing policies to pricing problems. They are to be used for instruction and professional guidance. However, they are not directive and should be considered informational only. They are available via the internet at http://www.acq.osd.mil/dpap/cpic/cp/contract_pricing_reference_guides.html.

(b) Price analysis for commercial and non-commercial items.

(1) Price analysis is the process of examining and evaluating a proposed price without evaluating its separate cost elements and proposed profit. Unless an exception from the requirement to obtain certified cost or pricing data applies under 15.403-1(b)(1) or (b)(2), at a minimum, the contracting officer shall obtain appropriate data, without certification, on the prices at which the same or similar items have previously been sold and determine if the data is adequate for evaluating the reasonableness of the price. Price analysis may include evaluating data other than certified cost or pricing data obtained from the offeror or contractor when there is no other means for determining a fair and reasonable price. Contracting officers shall obtain data other than certified cost or pricing data from the offeror or contractor for all acquisitions (including commercial item acquisitions), if that is the contracting officer's only means to determine the price to be fair and reasonable.

(2) The Government may use various price analysis techniques and procedures to ensure a fair and reasonable price. Examples of such techniques include, but are not limited to, the following:

(i) Comparison of proposed prices received in response to the solicitation. Normally, adequate price competition establishes a fair and reasonable price (see 15.403-1(c)(1)(i)).

(ii) Comparison of the proposed prices to historical prices paid, whether by the Government or other than the Government, for the same or similar items. This method may be used for commercial items including those "of a type" or requiring minor modifications.

(A) The prior price must be a valid basis for comparison. If there has been a significant time lapse between the last acquisition and the present one, if the terms and conditions of the acquisition are significantly different, or if the reasonableness of the prior price is uncertain, then the prior price may not be a valid basis for comparison.

(B) The prior price must be adjusted to account for materially differing terms and conditions, quantities and market and economic factors. For similar items, the contracting officer must also adjust the prior price to account for material differences between the similar item and the item being procured.

(C) Expert technical advice should be obtained when analyzing similar items, or commercial items that are "of a type" or requiring minor modifications, to ascertain the magnitude of changes required and to assist in pricing the required changes

(iii) Use of parametric estimating methods/application of rough yardsticks (such as dollars per pound or per horsepower, or other units) to highlight significant inconsistencies that warrant additional pricing inquiry.

(iv) Comparison with competitive published price lists, published market prices of commodities, similar indexes, and discount or rebate arrangements.

(v) Comparison of proposed prices with independent Government cost estimates.

(vi) Comparison of proposed prices with prices obtained through market research for the same or similar items.

(vii) Analysis of data other than certified cost or pricing data (as defined at 2.101) provided by the offeror.

(3) The first two techniques at 15.404-1(b)(2) are the preferred techniques. However, if the contracting officer determines that information on competitive proposed prices or previous contract prices is not available or is insufficient to determine that the price is fair and reasonable, the contracting officer may use any of the remaining techniques as appropriate to the circumstances applicable to the acquisition.

(4) Value analysis can give insight into the relative worth of a product and the Government may use it in conjunction with the price analysis techniques listed in paragraph (b)(2) of this section.

(c) Cost analysis.

(1) Cost analysis is the review and evaluation of any separate cost elements and profit or fee in an offeror's or contractor's proposal, as needed to determine a fair and reasonable price or to determine cost realism, and the application of judgment to determine how well the proposed costs represent what the cost of the contract should be, assuming reasonable economy and efficiency.

(2) The Government may use various cost analysis techniques and procedures to ensure a fair and reasonable price, given the circumstances of the acquisition. Such techniques and procedures include the following:

(i) Verification of cost data or pricing data and evaluation of cost elements, including—

(A) The necessity for, and reasonableness of, proposed costs, including allowances for contingencies;

(B) Projection of the offeror's cost trends, on the basis of current and historical cost or pricing data;

(C) Reasonableness of estimates generated by appropriately calibrated and validated parametric models or cost-estimating relationships; and

(D) The application of audited or negotiated indirect cost rates, labor rates, and cost of money or other factors.

(ii) Evaluating the effect of the offeror's current practices on future costs. In conducting this evaluation, the contracting officer shall ensure that the effects of inefficient or uneconomical past practices are not projected into the future. In pricing production of recently developed complex equipment, the contracting officer should perform a trend analysis of basic labor and materials, even in periods of relative price stability.

(iii) Comparison of costs proposed by the offeror for individual cost elements with—

(A) Actual costs previously incurred by the same offeror;

(B) Previous cost estimates from the offeror or from other offerors for the same or similar items;

(C) Other cost estimates received in response to the Government's request;

(D) Independent Government cost estimates by technical personnel; and

(E) Forecasts of planned expenditures.

(iv) Verification that the offeror's cost submissions are in accordance with the contract cost principles and procedures in Part 31 and, when applicable, the requirements and procedures in 48 CFR Chapter 99 (Appendix to the FAR looseleaf edition), Cost Accounting Standards.

(v) Review to determine whether any cost data or pricing data, necessary to make the offeror's proposal suitable for negotiation, have not been either submitted or identified in writing by the offeror. If there are such data, the contracting officer shall attempt to obtain and use them in the negotiations or make satisfactory allowance for the incomplete data.

(vi) Analysis of the results of any make-or-buy program reviews, in evaluating subcontract costs (see 15.407-2).

(d) Cost realism analysis.

(1) Cost realism analysis is the process of independently reviewing and evaluating specific elements of each offeror's proposed cost estimate to determine whether the estimated proposed cost elements are realistic for the work to be performed; reflect a clear understanding of the requirements; and are consistent with the unique methods of performance and materials described in the offeror's technical proposal.

(2) Cost realism analyses shall be performed on cost-reimbursement contracts to determine the probable cost of performance for each offeror.

(i) The probable cost may differ from the proposed cost and should reflect the Government's best estimate of the cost of any contract that is most likely to result from the offeror's proposal. The probable cost shall be used for purposes of evaluation to determine the best value.

(ii) The probable cost is determined by adjusting each offeror's proposed cost, and fee when appropriate, to reflect any additions or reductions in cost elements to realistic levels based on the results of the cost realism analysis.

(3) Cost realism analyses may also be used on competitive fixed-price incentive contracts or, in exceptional cases, on other competitive fixed-price-type contracts when new requirements may not be fully understood by competing offerors, there are quality concerns, or past experience indicates that contractors' proposed costs have resulted in quality or service shortfalls. Results of the analysis may be used in performance risk assessments and responsibility determinations. However, proposals shall be evaluated using the criteria in the solicitation, and the offered prices shall not be adjusted as a result of the analysis.

(e) Technical analysis.

(1) The contracting officer should request that personnel having specialized knowledge, skills, experience, or capability in engineering, science, or management perform a technical analysis of the proposed types and quantities of materials, labor, processes, special tooling, equipment or real property, the reasonableness of scrap and spoilage, and other associated factors set forth in the proposal(s) in order to determine the need for and reasonableness of the proposed resources, assuming reasonable economy and efficiency.

(2) At a minimum, the technical analysis should examine the types and quantities of material proposed and the need for the types and quantities of labor hours and the labor mix. Any other data that may be pertinent to an assessment of the offeror's ability to accomplish the technical requirements or to the cost or price analysis of the service or product being proposed should also be included in the analysis.

(3) The contracting officer should request technical assistance in evaluating pricing related to items that are "similar to" items being purchased, or commercial items that are "of a type" or requiring minor modifications, to ascertain the magnitude of changes required and to assist in pricing the required changes.

(f) Unit prices.

(1) Except when pricing an item on the basis of adequate price competition or catalog or market price, unit prices shall reflect the intrinsic value of an item or service and shall be in proportion to an item's base cost (e.g., manufacturing or acquisition costs). Any method of distributing costs to line items that distorts the unit prices shall not be used. For example, distributing costs equally among line items is not acceptable except when

there is little or no variation in base cost.

(2) Except for the acquisition of commercial items, contracting officers shall require that offerors identify in their proposals those items of supply that they will not manufacture or to which they will not contribute significant value, unless adequate price competition is expected (10 U.S.C. 2306a(b)(1)(A)(i) and 41 U.S.C. 3503(a)(1)(A)). Such information shall be used to determine whether the intrinsic value of an item has been distorted through application of overhead and whether such items should be considered for breakout. The contracting officer should require such information in all other negotiated contracts when appropriate.

(g) Unbalanced pricing.

(1) Unbalanced pricing may increase performance risk and could result in payment of unreasonably high prices. Unbalanced pricing exists when, despite an acceptable total evaluated price, the price of one or more contract line items is significantly over or understated as indicated by the application of cost or price analysis techniques. The greatest risks associated with unbalanced pricing occur when—

(i) Startup work, mobilization, first articles, or first article testing are separate line items;

(ii) Base quantities and option quantities are separate line items; or

(iii) The evaluated price is the aggregate of estimated quantities to be ordered under separate line items of an indefinite-delivery contract.

(2) All offers with separately priced line items or subline items shall be analyzed to determine if the prices are unbalanced. If cost or price analysis techniques indicate that an offer is unbalanced, the contracting officer shall—

(i) Consider the risks to the Government associated with the unbalanced pricing in determining the competitive range and in making the source selection decision; and

(ii) Consider whether award of the contract will result in paying unreasonably high prices for contract performance.

(3) An offer may be rejected if the contracting officer determines that the lack of balance poses an unacceptable risk to the Government.

United States Code Annotated

Contract requirements, see 41 USCA § 254.

Contracts, planning, solicitation, evaluation, and award procedures, see 10 USCA § 2305.

Cost or pricing data, truth in negotiations, see 10 USCA § 2306a, 41 USCA § 254b.

Definitions, see 10 USCA § 2302, 41 USCA §§ 259, 403.

Evaluation and award, see 41 USCA § 253b.

Kinds of contracts, see 10 USCA § 2306.

Planning and solicitation requirements, see 41 USCA § 253a.

Notes of Decisions

In general 1
Cost estimates 2
Cost realism 3
Cost reasonableness determination 7
Price realism analysis 4
Price reasonableness determination 6
Unbalanced pricing 5

1 In general

GAO sustained protest challenging the evaluation of offerors' prices where the solicitation stated that a 5% royalty would be added to the total proposed prices of offerors without licenses to use certain technology, but evaluated proposals by applying the royalty adjustment only to specific components. Colt Defense, LLC, B-406696, 2012 CPD ¶ 302 (Comp. Gen. 2012)

When an agency evaluates proposals for the award of a cost reimbursement contact, an offeror's proposed estimated costs are not dispositive, because regardless of the costs proposed, the government is bound to pay the contractor its actual and allowable costs. Consequently, a cost realism analysis must be performed by the agency to determine the extent to which an offeror's proposed costs represent what the contract should cost, assuming reasonable economy and efficiency. Battelle Memorial Institute, B-278673, 98-1 CPD ¶ 107 (Comp. Gen. 1998).

2 Cost estimates

Bid protestor did not establish that agency acted arbitrarily and capriciously when it issued solicitation, based on its assertions that agency was required to base its funding request on an independent government estimate of $3,596,111, not the agency's own construction estimate of $3,218,781, and that agency issued the solicitation without intent to award a contract because it should have known that using its own estimate would result in insufficient funding for the project. First Enterprise v. U.S., 61 Fed. Cl. 109 (2004). United States ☞64.25

Bid protestor did not establish that contracting agency was biased against it as reflected in agency's failure to conduct discussions with it regarding a cost estimate deemed unrealistic, absent evidence that agency had a specific intent to injure it; moreover, agency adhered to terms of request for proposals (RFP) in declining to seek further information regarding cost estimate. Information Technology & Applications Corp. v. U.S., 51 Fed. Cl. 340 (2001), decision aff'd, 316 F.3d 1312 (Fed. Cir. 2003). United States ☞64.40(3)

3 Cost realism

While the FAR precludes agencies from *adjusting* firm-fixed prices as a result of a cost realism analysis, it contemplates that such an analysis may be appropriate even in the context of firm-fixed price proposals and that the results may be used in performance risk assessments and responsibility determinations. Masai Technologies Corp. v. U.S., 79 Fed. Cl. 433 (2007)

For the court to overturn an agency's cost realism determination, the plaintiff must establish that the agency's decision lacked a rational basis. Decisions on cost realism are within the agency's sound discretion and expertise, and the judgment will not be overturned absent any rational basis. While an agency's cost realism analysis need not have been performed with "impeccable rigor" to be rational, the analysis must reflect that the agency considered the information available and did not make "irrational assumptions or critical miscalculations. Westech Intern., Inc. v. U.S., 79 Fed. Cl. 272 (2007)

Although the FAR requires that a procuring agency evaluate the reasonableness of an offeror's proposed price and, where cost data is required, the reasonableness of an offeror's proposed costs, the FAR does not mandate that either a "cost realism analysis" or "price realism analysis" be performed, unless the procurement is for a cost-reimbursement contract or the solicitation so requires. Information Sciences Corp. v. U.S., 73 Fed. Cl. 70 (2006), on reconsideration in part, 75 Fed. Cl. 406 (2007)

Failure of contracting agency to perform a cost realism analysis on contract awardee's offer was not error, as there was no requirement for such an analysis, where solicitation contemplated award of firm fixed price contract and contracting officer (CO) deemed awardee responsible to perform the project at the offered price. 48 C.F.R. § 15.404-1(d)(1). First Enterprise v. U.S., 61 Fed. Cl. 109 (2004). United States ☞64.40(1)

Contracting agency failed to perform a proper cost realism analysis of successful bid on solicitation to provide health care services to immigration detainees in violation of the Federal Acquisition Regulation (FAR), where agency failed to adjust contract awardee's proposed costs for its unrealistically low assumed claims processing volume; moreover, bid protestor would have had a substantial chance of receiving the award, given the magnitude of the total contract value, as compared with the relatively narrow margin by which awardee purportedly underbid protestor. 48 C.F.R. § 15.404-1(d)(2)(i). United Payors & United Providers Health Services, Inc. v. U.S., 55 Fed. Cl. 323 (2003). United States ☞64.45(1)

Provision of the Federal Acquisition Regulation (FAR) providing that agencies should not award cost-reimbursement contracts to the lowest-cost offeror without regard to other evaluation factors does not mandate cost-realism analysis in all cost-reimbursement procurements. 48 C.F.R. § 15.605(d) (1995). Labat-Anderson, Inc. v. U.S., 42 Fed. Cl. 806

(1999). United States ☞64.40(1)

Protest challenging agency's cost realism evaluation of proposals was sustained where record showed that agency's evaluation was based on a mechanical application of the government's internal cost estimate that did not take into account each offeror's unique technical approach, and therefore was not consistent with the terms of the solicitation and applicable procurement statutes and regulations. CFS-KBR Marianas Supp. Servs., LLC; Fluor Fed. Solutions LLC, B-410486, 2015 CPD ¶ 22 (Comp. Gen. 2015)

Protest challenging agency's cost realism analysis was sustained because the government misinterpreted the contractor's proposal regarding use of uncompensated overtime and unreasonably assumed that it would increase the most probably cost. Gen. Dynamics Advanced Info. Sys., Inc., B-411771, et al., 2015 CPD ¶ 322 (Comp. Gen. 2015)

Protest challenging agency's cost realism evaluation is sustained where evaluation failed adequately to consider the realism of the offerors' proposed costs, and record further shows that, in any event, agency improperly used the offerors' proposed—as opposed to evaluated—costs in making its source selection decision. Prism Maritime, LLC, B-409267.2, 2014 CPD ¶ 124 (Comp. Gen. 2014)

An agency misevaluated proposals for a cost-reimbursement contract because the record did not show a logical connection between the agency's technical evaluation conclusions and its most probable cost evaluation conclusions, and provided no information to explain the apparent discrepancies. ITT Sys. Corp., B-405865, 2012 CPD ¶ 44 (Comp. Gen. 2012)

Protest challenging agency's cost realism evaluation was sustained, where protester unequivocally proposed charging costs as overhead, instead of directly to the contract, to reduce costs and the agency ignored this aspect of the proposal and increased the protester's proposed cost to account for the labor costs that the agency believed would be charged as direct costs. Matter of: Marine Hydraulics International, Inc., B-403386, B-403386.2, 2010 CPD ¶ 255 (Comp. Gen. 2010)

An agency's cost-realism evaluation was found unreasonable because the agency failed to consider whether the agency tender's material and supply costs were realistic under an Office of Management and Budget Circular A-76 competition. Although the agency also prepared an analysis report on cost realism and reasonableness, it did not address the elements of the awardee's material and supply costs, or their reduction in the final revised proposal. Matter of: New Dynamics Corporation, B-401272, 2009 CPD ¶ 150 (Comp. Gen. 2009)

Protest is sustained in a negotiated procurement for the award of a cost-reimbursement contract, where the agency in its cost realism assessment accepted the awardee's work allocation in its cost proposal, but that allocation was inconsistent with the firm's allocation of work in its technical proposal. Matter of: Earl Industries, LLC, B-309996, B-309996.4, 2007 CPD ¶ 203 (Comp. Gen. 2007)

When an agency evaluates a proposal for the award of a cost-reimbursement contract, as in this case, an offeror's proposed estimated costs are not dispositive because, regardless of the costs proposed, the government is bound to pay the contractor its actual and allowable costs. FAR 15.305(a)(1); 15.404-1(d). Consequently, the agency must perform a cost realism analysis to determine the extent to which an offeror's proposed costs are realistic for the work to be performed. An agency is not required to conduct an in-depth cost analysis or to verify each and every item in assessing cost realism; rather, the evaluation requires the exercise of informed judgment by the contracting agency. Matter of: ITT Industries Space Systems, LLC, B-309964, 2007 CPD ¶ 217 (Comp. Gen. 2007)

Agency's cost realism evaluation of awardee's proposal was unreasonable where agency failed to take into account cost adjustments made by its own cost analyst to awardee's proposal, and instead utilized awardee's proposed costs as the basis for its source selection decision. Matter of Magellan Health Services, B-298912, 2007 CPD ¶ 81 (Comp. Gen. 2007)

Agency did not perform a reasonable cost realism evaluation when it deleted a certain element of cost from awardee's proposed indirect costs because other offerors accounted for this element as a direct cost; this evaluation did not result in a reasonable assessment of the probable cost of performing the contract associated with the awardee's proposal, given that the adjustment was inconsistent with Cost Accounting Standards 401 and 402 and the firm's cost accounting practices, to which the firm was obligated to adhere in performing the contract. Kellogg Brown & Root Services, Inc., B-298694, B-298694.2, B-298694.3, 2006 CPD ¶ 160 (Comp. Gen. 2006)

Agency's cost realism evaluation of awardee's proposal was unreasonable where the awardee proposed to perform the solicitation requirements under a teaming arrangement whereby its proposed team members would perform almost [deleted] of the production work under the contract, but the agency failed to consider the impact of the team members' higher rates in determining the awardee's probable cost of performance under the contract. Metro Machine Corporation, B-297879.2, 2006 CPD ¶ 80 (Comp. Gen. 2006)

In a cost realism evaluation where the agency evaluated numerous areas under which the protester's proposed approach was inadequate and understaffed, the agency properly used its independent government estimate and prior experience on similar projects as tools to assess the amount of additional staffing that would be required under the protester's proposed approach. Pueblo Environmental Solution, LLC, B-291487, B-291487.2, 2003 CPD ¶ 14 (Comp. Gen. 2002)

Agency failed to perform a proper cost realism evaluation in awarding a cost reimbursement contract where the agency made no probable cost adjustments even where it identified costs that it believed were unrealistic and did not consider the proposed costs in light of the offeror's proposed technical proposals. Priority One Services, Inc., B-288836, B-288836.2, 2002 CPD ¶ 79 (Comp. Gen. 2001)

4 Price realism analysis

The Air Force's price-realism analysis was arbitrary and capricious because it did not account for the projected increasing costs of dealing with an aging fleet of tankers, the U.S. Court of Federal Claims recently held. The COFC nullified the agency's contract award because of the flawed price-realism analysis. Alabama Aircraft Industries, Inc.-Birmingham v. U.S., 83 Fed. Cl. 666 (2008), judgment rev'd, 586 F.3d 1372 (Fed. Cir. 2009)

Bid protestor did not establish that contracting agency failed to follow evaluation criteria by improperly comparing its prices to national, rather than local salary levels, as statements favorably comparing contract awardee's price proposal to national rates were the only documented instance in evaluation where national rates were used; moreover, while request for quotations (RFQ) stated that prices were to be based on local levels, and encouraged offerors to extend discounts to the government on that basis, the RFQ did not expressly preclude the use of national standards in conducting a price reasonableness evaluation. Masai Technologies Corp. v. U.S., 79 Fed. Cl. 433 (2007)

The FAR does not require agencies to use its independent government estimate (IGE) to determine price realism. It does not direct agencies to use any particular tool in a price realism analysis. Instead, the FAR suggests that "independent government cost estimates" may be used in a price analysis comparison to determine price reasonableness, not price realism. FAR 15.404-1(b)(2)(v). Erinys Iraq Ltd. v. U.S., 78 Fed. Cl. 518 (2007)

Although the FAR requires that a procuring agency evaluate the reasonableness of an offeror's proposed price and, where cost data is required, the reasonableness of an offeror's proposed costs, the FAR does not mandate that either a "cost realism analysis" or "price realism analysis" be performed, unless the procurement is for a cost-reimbursement contract or the solicitation so requires. Information Sciences Corp. v. U.S., 73 Fed. Cl. 70 (2006), on reconsideration in part, 75 Fed. Cl. 406 (2007)

Price reasonableness generally addresses whether a price is too high, whereas cost realism generally addresses whether a cost estimate is too low. While there is a requirement for the contracting officer to do a price reasonableness analysis, there is no similar requirement to do a cost realism analysis. The contracting officer is responsible for evaluating the reasonableness of proposed prices to ensure that the price to the government is fair and reasonable. First Enterprise v. U.S., 61 Fed. Cl. 109 (2004)

Protest alleging that the agency either failed to conduct a price realism analysis, or conducted an unreasonable analysis, is sustained where (1) the solicitation advised that proposals unrealistically high or low in price could be rejected; (2) the awardee's price was significantly lower than the other prices received and the government estimate; and (3) there is no evidence in the contemporaneous record that the agency conducted such an analysis. B&B Med. Servs., Inc.; Ed Med., Inc., B-409705.4 et al., 2015 CPD ¶ 198 (Comp. Gen. 2015)

Protest challenging agency's price realism evaluation was denied because the agency reasonably concluded that the awardee's price was not unrealistic based on a comparison with the total average price for the offerors. Kilda Group, LLC, B-409144, 2014 CPD ¶ 80 (Comp.Gen. 2014)

Allegation that agency failed to conduct price reasonableness analysis based on claim that awardee's price was unrealistically low fails to state valid basis for protest where solicitation provided for award of fixed-price contract and did not provide for price realism analysis. GAO distinguished between a price *reasonableness* analysis and a price *realism* analysis. Applied Business Management Solutions Incorporated, LLC, B-405724, 2012 CPD ¶ 14, 2011 WL 6960014 (Comp. Gen. 2011)

In a negotiated procurement for a fixed-price contract, a protest challenging the rejection of the protester's proposal on the basis that the price was too low was sustained because the evaluation record did not indicate the basis for the agency's determination. Rather, the record contained only the agency's conclusory judgment that the protester's fixed price was too low. Matter of: A1 Procurement, JVG, B-404618, 2011 CPD ¶ 53 (Comp. Gen. 2011)

An agency improperly rejected a low-priced proposal as unrealistic because it did not reasonably consider the realism of the protester's labor rates, as the solicitation required. The agency's price evaluation consisted of a mechanical comparison to the government's cost estimate and the prices proposed for the sample tasks, without any consideration of the realism of the rates used in the sample task pricing. Matter of: I.M. Systems Group, B-404583, B-404583.2, B-404583.3, 2011 CPD ¶ 64 (Comp. Gen. 2011)

An agency's price realism evaluation was improper because the agency did not reconcile the staffing inconsistencies in the awardee's technical and price proposals. The awardee's technical proposal stated that it was "proactively engaged to achieve this staffing at contract startup and throughout the life of the contract." In contrast, the awardee's price proposal stated that staff levels would decrease steadily through the option years, to a level "significantly below" that identified in its technical proposal. Matter of: General Dynamics One Source, LLC; Unisys Corporation, B-400340.5, B-400340.6, 2010 CPD ¶ 45 (Comp. Gen. 2010).

Under a solicitation calling for award of fixed-price contract, GAO sustained a protest challenging the agency's determination that the protester's proposed price was unrealistically low because the solicitation lacked any evaluation criteria that reasonably would have put offerors on notice that agency intended to consider the realism of offerors' prices as reflecting lack of understanding or risk associated with the proposal. Matter of: Milani Construction, LLC, B-401942, 2010 CPD ¶ 87 (Comp. Gen. 2009)

Protest sustained by agency's price analysis of a telephone services contract was unreasonable because it: 1) evaluated proposals using a call rate that was different from the rate specified in the solicitation; 2) applied inconsistent workload levels to the proposals; and 3) evaluated call rates for only one country, even though the solicitation required proposal of call rates for six countries. Matter of: Public Communications Services, Inc., B-400058, B-400058.3, 2009 CPD ¶ 154 (Comp. Gen. 2008)

An award was inappropriate because the agency could not provide documentation reflecting the price realism analysis and risk assessment required by the solicitation. Awardee's proposed price changed in Final Revised Proposal (FPR) by more than the difference between awardee's and protester's final total evaluated prices and the awardee's proposal did not explain the change. GAO sustained the protest because it could not determine whether the agency reasonably performed a price realism analysis or properly considered the potential risk flowing from the awardee's drastically changed FPR. Matter of: Pemco Aeroplex, Inc., B-310372, 2008 CPD ¶ 2 (Comp. Gen. 2007)

Agency performed a sufficient price analysis, which determined the awardees' prices were fair and reasonable based on adequate price competition, as required by FAR 15.402. However, FAR 15.402 does not require an agency to perform a price realism analysis to ascertain whether there were performance risks associated with awardees' low prices and the solicitation did not provide for such an analysis. Indtai Inc., B-298432.3, 2007 CPD ¶ 13 (Comp. Gen. 2007)

Where solicitation contemplated award of fixed-price contract, agency's comparing proposed prices to government estimate and other proposed prices and ensuring that prices reflected labor categories and hours specified in solicitation constituted reasonable price realism analysis. Legacy Management Solutions, LLC, B-299981.2, B-299981.4, 2007 CPD ¶ 197 (Comp. Gen. 2007)

The elimination of the protester's proposal from the competition for the award of a fixed-price contract is unobjectionable where the agency reasonably determined under the solicitation's price realism evaluation factor that the protester's proposed price was unrealistically low and the agency was reasonably concerned that the protester's contract performance may therefore be adversely affected. Matter of: International Outsourcing Services, LLC, B-295959, 2006 CPD ¶ 6 (Comp. Gen. 2005)

Agency's rejection of fixed-price proposal submitted by HUBZone small business because the price was determined unrealistically low was improper, where the solicitation contains no evaluation criterion pertaining to price realism or understanding; such a determination concerns the offeror's responsibility, i.e., the offeror's ability and capacity to successfully perform the contract at its offered price, and must be submitted to the Small Business Administration for a possible certificate of competency. Matter of: J.A. Farrington Janitorial Services, B-296875, 2005 CPD ¶ 187 (Comp. Gen. 2005)

Where the award of a fixed-price contract is contemplated, a proposal's price realism is not ordinarily considered, since a fixed-price contract places the risk and responsibility for contract costs and resulting profit or loss on the contractor. An agency may, but is not required to, provide in the solicitation for a price realism analysis for such purposes as measuring an offeror's understanding of the solicitation requirements, or to avoid the risk of poor performance from a contractor who is forced to provide goods or services at little or no profit. Matter of: J.A. Farrington Janitorial Services, B-296875, 2005 CPD ¶ 187 (Comp. Gen. 2005)

Below-cost pricing is not prohibited and the government cannot withhold an award from a responsible offeror merely because its low offer is or may be below cost. Nor can an agency, in evaluating an offeror's fixed-price proposal, make upward price adjustments for cost elements that agency contracting officials think may be priced too low. Where there is no relevant evaluation criterion pertaining to realism or understanding, a determination that an offeror's price on a fixed-price contract is too low generally concerns the offeror's responsibility, i.e., the offeror's ability and capacity to successfully perform the contract at its offered price. All Phase Environmental, Inc., B-292919.2, B-292919.3, B-292919.4, B-292919.5, B-292919.6, B-292919.7, 2004 CPD ¶ 62 (Comp. Gen. 2004)

Protest against award of primarily fixed-price incentive contracts for regional garrison food service at U.S. Marine Corps installations is sustained where agency did not properly assess realism of awardee's low proposed target price, which was the principal basis for determination that awardee's evaluated price was low. Eurest Support Services, B-285813.3, B-285813.4, B-285813.5, B-285882.4, B-285882.5, B-285882.7, 2003 CPD ¶ 139 (Comp. Gen. 2001)

5 Unbalanced pricing

Bid protestor did not establish that contract awardee's proposal for aircraft maintenance contract contained materially unbalanced pricing merely by showing that they were lower than protestor's prices and lower than the prices for maintenance on another aircraft. Avtel Services, Inc. v. U.S., 70 Fed. Cl. 173 (2006). United States ⌑64.45(1)

Contracting agency violated procurement regulation when it reviewed only the total prices submitted in proposals and did not compare offerors' contract line item (CLIN) prices with the government's price estimates for the same CLINs to determine whether unit prices were unbalanced. 48 C.F.R. § 15.404-1(g)(1). Al Ghanim Combined Group Co. Gen. Trad. & Cont. W.L.L. v. U.S., 56 Fed. Cl. 502 (2003). United States ⌑64.40(1)

Agency's cost realism analysis was flawed because the agency limited its analysis to internal cost data provided by the offerors and did not assess the realism of the proposed rates through such methods as comparison of the rates to the prevailing market rates, the rates paid to incumbent employees, or the rates proposed by other offerors. GAO considered the cost realism evaluation to be unreasonable and sustained the protest. Target Media Mid Atlantic, Inc., B-412468.6, 2016 CPD ¶ 358 (Comp. Gen. 2017)

Protest was sustained where agency unreasonably evaluated the protester's pricing as unbalanced and conducted a technical-price tradeoff without meaningfully considering the lower prices set forth in the protester's BPA quotation. Unbalanced pricing may increase risk to the government, but agencies cannot reject an offer solely because it is unbalanced. Low prices (even below-cost prices), are not improper and do not establish unbalanced pricing. When establishing a BPA based on fixed unit prices, the agency had no reasonable basis to conclude that any unbalanced pricing would result in higher prices to the government. Triumvirate Envtl., Inc., B-406809, 2012 CPD ¶ 244 (Comp. Gen. 2012)

6 Price reasonableness determination

Agency may use labor rate information from the awardee's prior contracts to assess the reasonableness of an awardee's proposed price. Agency's determination that the awardee's price was not unbalanced was reasonable. Survival Sys., USA, Inc. v. U.S., 102 Fed. Cl. 255 (2011)

Contracting agency's failure to use the actual prices proposed by contract awardee in evaluating the reasonableness of awardee's prices was harmless error; although agency used incorrect numbers, it had no effect on the validity of the price analysis. Dismas Charities, Inc. v. U.S., 61 Fed. Cl. 191 (2004).

7 Cost reasonableness determination

Challenge to solicitation contemplating issuance of cost-reimbursable task orders was sustained because solicitation did not require offerors to propose cost-reimbursable labor rates for the services being procured, thereby precluding the agency from meaningfully evaluating the proposals' cost. The solicitation also did not request any information regarding the break-out of cost components such as direct labor, indirect labor, overhead, and/or general and administrative expenses to be evaluated. CACI, Inc.-Federal; Booz Allen Hamilton, Inc., B-413028, et al, 2016 WL 4582380(Comp.Gen. 2016)

§ 15.404-2 Data to support proposal analysis.

(a) Field pricing assistance.

(1) The contracting officer should request field pricing assistance when the information available at the buying activity is inadequate to determine a fair and reasonable price. The contracting officer shall tailor requests to reflect the minimum essential supplementary information needed to conduct a technical or cost or pricing analysis.

(2) The contracting officer shall tailor the type of information and level of detail requested in accordance with the specialized resources available at the buying activity and the magnitude and complexity of the required analysis. Field pricing assistance is generally available to provide—

(i) Technical, audit, and special reports associated with the cost elements of a proposal, including subcontracts;

(ii) Information on related pricing practices and history;

(iii) Information to help contracting officers determine commerciality and a fair and reasonable price, including—

(A) Verifying sales history to source documents;

(B) Identifying special terms and conditions;

(C) Identifying customarily granted or offered discounts for the item;

(D) Verifying the item to an existing catalog or price list;

(E) Verifying historical data for an item previously not determined commercial that the offeror is now trying to qualify as a commercial item; and

(F) Identifying general market conditions affecting determinations of commerciality and a fair and reasonable price.

(iv) Information relative to the business, technical, production, or other capabilities and practices of an offeror.

(3) When field pricing assistance is requested, contracting officers are encouraged to team with appropriate field experts throughout the acquisition process, including negotiations. Early communication with these experts will assist in determining the extent of assistance required, the specific areas for which assistance is needed, a realistic review schedule, and the information necessary to perform the review.

(4) When requesting field pricing assistance on a contractor's request for equitable adjustment, the contracting officer shall provide the information listed in 43.204(b)(5).

(5) Field pricing information and other reports may include proprietary or source selection information (see 2.101). This information must be appropriately identified and protected accordingly.

(b) *Reporting field pricing information.*

(1) Depending upon the extent and complexity of the field pricing review, results, including supporting rationale, may be reported directly to the contracting officer orally, in writing, or by any other method acceptable to the contracting officer.

(i) Whenever circumstances permit, the contracting officer and field pricing experts are encouraged to use telephonic and/or electronic means to request and transmit pricing information.

(ii) When it is necessary to have written technical and audit reports, the contracting officer shall request that the audit agency concurrently forward the audit report to the requesting contracting officer and the administrative contracting officer (ACO). The completed field pricing assistance results may reference audit information, but need not reconcile the audit recommendations and technical recommendations. A copy of the information submitted to the contracting officer by field pricing personnel shall be provided to the audit agency.

(2) Audit and field pricing information, whether written or reported telephonically or electronically, shall be made a part of the official contract file (see 4.807(f)).

(c) *Audit assistance for prime contracts or subcontracts.*

(1) The contracting officer should contact the cognizant audit office directly, particularly when an audit is the only field pricing support required. The audit office shall send the audit report, or otherwise transmit the audit recommendations, directly to the contracting officer.

(i) The auditor shall not reveal the audit conclusions or recommendations to the offeror/contractor without obtaining the concurrence of the contracting officer. However, the auditor may discuss statements of facts with the contractor.

(ii) The contracting officer should be notified immediately of any information disclosed to the auditor after submission of a report that may significantly affect the audit findings and, if necessary, a supplemental audit report shall be issued.

(2) The contracting officer shall not request a separate preaward audit of indirect costs unless the information already available from an existing audit, completed within the preceding 12 months, is considered inadequate for determining the reasonableness of the proposed indirect costs (41 U.S.C. 4706 and 10 U.S.C. 2313).

(3) The auditor is responsible for the scope and depth of the audit. Copies of updated information that will significantly affect the audit should be provided to the auditor by the contracting officer.

(4) General access to the offeror's books and financial records is limited to the auditor. This limitation does not preclude the contracting officer or the ACO, or their representatives, from requesting that the offeror provide or make available any data or records necessary to analyze the offeror's proposal.

(d) *Deficient proposals.* The ACO or the auditor, as appropriate, shall notify the contracting officer immediately if the data provided for review is so deficient as to preclude review or audit, or if the contractor or offeror has denied access to any records considered essential to conduct a satisfactory review or audit. Oral notifications shall be confirmed promptly in writing, including a description of deficient or denied data or records. The contracting officer immediately shall take appropriate action to obtain the required data. Should the offeror/contractor again refuse to provide adequate data, or provide access to necessary data, the contracting officer shall withhold the award or price adjustment and refer the contract action to a higher authority, providing details of the attempts made to resolve the matter and a statement of the practicability of obtaining the supplies or services from another source.

United States Code Annotated

Contract requirements, see 41 USCA § 254.

Contracts, planning, solicitation, evaluation, and award procedures, see 10 USCA § 2305.

Cost or pricing data, truth in negotiations, see 10 USCA § 2306a, 41 USCA § 254b.

Definitions, see 10 USCA § 2302, 41 USCA §§ 259, 403.

Evaluation and award, see 41 USCA § 253b.

Kinds of contracts, see 10 USCA § 2306.

Planning and solicitation requirements, see 41 USCA § 253a.

Notes of Decisions

In general 1

1 In general

Regulation governing public contracts did not require contracting officer to obtain audit of successful bidder's cost and pricing data prior to award. RADVA Corp. v. U.S., 17 Cl. Ct. 812, 35 Cont. Cas. Fed. (CCH) P 75706, 1989 WL 91318 (1989), judgment aff'd, 914 F.2d 271 (Fed. Cir. 1990). Public Contracts ◎5.1

§ 15.404-3 Subcontract pricing considerations.

(a) The contracting officer is responsible for the determination of a fair and reasonable price for the prime contract, including subcontracting costs. The contracting officer should consider whether a contractor or subcontractor has an approved purchasing system, has performed cost or price analysis of proposed subcontractor prices, or has negotiated the subcontract prices before negotiation of the prime contract, in determining the reasonableness of the prime contract price. This does not relieve the contracting officer from the responsibility to analyze the contractor's submission, including subcontractor's certified cost or pricing data.

(b) The prime contractor or subcontractor shall—

(1) Conduct appropriate cost or price analyses to establish the reasonableness of proposed subcontract prices;

(2) Include the results of these analyses in the price proposal; and

(3) When required by paragraph (c) of this subsection, submit subcontractor certified cost or pricing data to the Government as part of its own certified cost or pricing data.

(c) Any contractor or subcontractor that is required to submit certified cost or pricing data also shall obtain and analyze certified cost or pricing data before awarding any subcontract, purchase order, or modification expected to exceed the certified cost or pricing data threshold, unless an exception in 15.403-1(b) applies to that action.

(1) The contractor shall submit, or cause to be submitted by the subcontractor(s), certified cost or pricing data to the Government for subcontracts that are the lower of either—

(i) $13.5 million or more; or

(ii) Both more than the pertinent certified cost or pricing data threshold and more than 10 percent of the prime contractor's proposed price, unless the contracting officer believes such submission is unnecessary.

(2) The contracting officer should require the contractor or subcontractor to submit to the Government (or cause submission of) subcontractor certified cost or pricing data below the thresholds in paragraph (c)(1) of this subsection and data other than certified cost or pricing data that the contracting officer considers necessary for adequately pricing the prime contract.

(3) Subcontractor certified cost or pricing data shall be submitted in the format provided in Table 15-2 of 15.408 or the alternate format specified in the solicitation.

(4) Subcontractor certified cost or pricing data shall be current, accurate, and complete as of the date of price agreement, or, if applicable, an earlier date agreed upon by the parties and specified on the contractor's Certificate of Current Cost or Pricing Data. The contractor shall update subcontractor's data, as appropriate, during source selection and negotiations.

(5) If there is more than one prospective subcontractor for any given work, the contractor need only submit to the Government certified cost or pricing data for the prospective subcontractor most likely to receive the award.

United States Code Annotated

Contract requirements, see 41 USCA § 254.

Contracts, planning, solicitation, evaluation, and award procedures, see 10 USCA § 2305.

Cost or pricing data, truth in negotiations, see 10 USCA § 2306a, 41 USCA § 254b.

Definitions, see 10 USCA § 2302, 41 USCA §§ 259, 403.

Evaluation and award, see 41 USCA § 253b.

Kinds of contracts, see 10 USCA § 2306.

Planning and solicitation requirements, see 41 USCA § 253a.

Notes of Decisions

In general 1

1 In general

First-tier subcontractor responsible for electrical generator sets for Navy destroyers did not withhold cost or pricing data from prime contractor during contract renegotiations on redesigned units in violation of Truth in Negotiations Act, notwithstanding that first-tier subcontractor had anticipated by time of negotiations that cost of second-tier subcontractor's assembling redesigned units was likely to be less than original units, where subcontractors had not actually reached an agreement to lower assembly price at time of negotiations and first-tier subcontractor had no duty to disclose eventual agreement that did lower price because it was made 13 months after contract negotiations with shipyard. Truth in Negotiations, § 952(a)(1)(D)(i), 10 U.S.C.A. § 2306a(a)(1)(D)(i). U.S. ex rel. Sanders v. Allison Engine Co., Inc., 471 F.3d 610, 2006 FED App. 0463P (6th Cir. 2006), vacated and remanded, 553 U.S. 662, 128 S. Ct. 2123, 170 L. Ed. 2d 1030, 37 A.L.R. Fed. 2d 773 (2008)(The Supreme Court addressed only the issue of "whether subcontractors' invoices for allegedly defective construction of units violated FCA", finding that the circuit court incorrectly interpreted 31 U.S.C.A. § § 3729(a)(2) and (3).)

Contractor failed to show that it employed sound business practices and acted as a reasonably prudent business person in accepting subcontractor's proposed prices for change order concerning services for the Army, and thus, costs incurred by contractor were not reasonable. The fact that change order tripled the price for roughly double the troops being supported should have alerted contractor to at least request an explanation of how subcontractor arrived at its proposal, and in view of the disproportionate increase in costs, a prudent business person would have attempted to engage in arm's-length negotiations with subcontractor and would not have accepted subcontractor's proposal at face value. Kellogg Brown & Root Servs. v. U.S., 2014 WL 350072 (Fed. Cir. 2014)

§ 15.404-4 Profit.

(a) *General*. This subsection prescribes policies for establishing the profit or fee portion of the Government prenegotiation objective in price negotiations based on cost analysis.

(1) Profit or fee prenegotiation objectives do not necessarily represent net income to contractors. Rather, they represent that element of the potential total remuneration that contractors may receive for contract performance over and above allowable costs. This potential remuneration element and the Government's estimate of allowable costs to be incurred in contract performance together equal the Government's total prenegotiation objective. Just as actual costs may vary from estimated costs, the contractor's actual realized profit or fee may vary from negotiated profit or fee, because of such factors as efficiency of performance, incurrence of costs the Government does not recognize as allowable, and the contract type.

(2) It is in the Government's interest to offer contractors opportunities for financial rewards sufficient to stimulate efficient contract performance, attract the best capabilities of qualified large and small business concerns to Government contracts, and maintain a viable industrial base.

(3) Both the Government and contractors should be concerned with profit as a motivator of efficient and effective contract performance. Negotiations aimed merely at reducing prices by reducing profit, without proper recognition of the function of profit, are not in the Government's interest. Negotiation of extremely low profits, use of historical averages, or automatic application of predetermined percentages to total estimated costs do not provide proper motivation for optimum contract performance.

(b) Policy.

(1) Structured approaches (see paragraph (d) of this subsection) for determining profit or fee prenegotiation objectives provide a discipline for ensuring that all relevant factors

are considered. Subject to the authorities in 1.301(c), agencies making noncompetitive contract awards over $100,000 totaling $50 million or more a year—

(i) Shall use a structured approach for determining the profit or fee objective in those acquisitions that require cost analysis; and

(ii) May prescribe specific exemptions for situations in which mandatory use of a structured approach would be clearly inappropriate.

(2) Agencies may use another agency's structured approach.

(c) Contracting officer responsibilities.

(1) When the price negotiation is not based on cost analysis, contracting officers are not required to analyze profit.

(2) When the price negotiation is based on cost analysis, contracting officers in agencies that have a structured approach shall use it to analyze profit. When not using a structured approach, contracting officers shall comply with paragraph (d)(1) of this subsection in developing profit or fee prenegotiation objectives.

(3) Contracting officers shall use the Government prenegotiation cost objective amounts as the basis for calculating the profit or fee prenegotiation objective. Before applying profit or fee factors, the contracting officer shall exclude from the pre-negotiation cost objective amounts the purchase cost of contractor-acquired property that is categorized as equipment, as defined in FAR 45.101, and where such equipment is to be charged directly to the contract. Before applying profit or fee factors, the contracting officer shall exclude any facilities capital cost of money included in the cost objective amounts. If the prospective contractor fails to identify or propose facilities capital cost of money in a proposal for a contract that will be subject to the cost principles for contracts with commercial organizations (see Subpart 31.2), facilities capital cost of money will not be an allowable cost in any resulting contract (see 15.408(i)).

(4) (i) The contracting officer shall not negotiate a price or fee that exceeds the following statutory limitations, imposed by 10 U.S.C. 2306(d) and 41 U.S.C. 3905:

(A) For experimental, developmental, or research work performed under a cost-plus-fixed-fee contract, the fee shall not exceed 15 percent of the contract's estimated cost, excluding fee.

(B) For architect-engineer services for public works or utilities, the contract price or the estimated cost and fee for production and delivery of designs, plans, drawings, and specifications shall not exceed 6 percent of the estimated cost of construction of the public work or utility, excluding fees.

(C) For other cost-plus-fixed-fee contracts, the fee shall not exceed 10 percent of the contract's estimated cost, excluding fee.

(ii) The contracting officer's signature on the price negotiation memorandum or other documentation supporting determination of fair and reasonable price documents the contracting officer's determination that the statutory price or fee limitations have not been exceeded.

(5) The contracting officer shall not require any prospective contractor to submit breakouts or supporting rationale for its profit or fee objective but may consider it, if it is submitted voluntarily.

(6) If a change or modification calls for essentially the same type and mix of work as the basic contract and is of relatively small dollar value compared to the total contract value, the contracting officer may use the basic contract's profit or fee rate as the prenegotiation objective for that change or modification.

(d) Profit-analysis factors—

(1) *Common factors.* Unless it is clearly inappropriate or not applicable, each factor outlined in paragraphs (d)(1)(i) through (vi) of this subsection shall be considered by agencies in developing their structured approaches and by contracting officers in analyzing profit, whether or not using a structured approach.

(i) *Contractor effort.* This factor measures the complexity of the work and the resources required of the prospective contractor for contract performance. Greater profit opportunity should be provided under contracts requiring a high degree of professional and managerial skill and to prospective contractors whose skills, facilities, and technical assets can be expected to lead to efficient and economical contract performance. The subfactors in paragraphs (d)(1)(i)(A) through (D) of this subsection shall be considered in determining contractor effort, but they may be modified in specific situations to accommodate differences in the categories used by prospective contractors for listing costs—

(A) *Material acquisition.* This subfactor measures the managerial and technical effort needed to obtain the required purchased parts and material, subcontracted items, and special tooling. Considerations include the complexity of the items required, the number of purchase orders and subcontracts to be awarded and administered, whether established sources are available or new or second sources must be developed, and whether material will be obtained through routine purchase orders or through complex subcontracts requiring detailed specifications. Profit consideration should correspond to the managerial and technical effort involved.

(B) *Conversion direct labor.* This subfactor measures the contribution of direct engineering, manufacturing, and other labor to converting the raw materials, data, and subcontracted items into the contract items. Considerations include the diversity of engineering, scientific, and manufacturing labor skills required and the amount and quality of supervision and coordination needed to perform the contract task.

(C) *Conversion-related indirect costs.* This subfactor measures how much the indirect costs contribute to contract performance. The labor elements in the allocable indirect costs should be given the profit consideration they would receive if treated as direct labor. The other elements of indirect costs should be evaluated to determine whether they merit only limited profit consideration because of their routine nature, or are elements that contribute significantly to the proposed contract.

(D) *General management.* This subfactor measures the prospective contractor's other indirect costs and general and administrative (G&A) expense, their composition, and how much they contribute to contract performance. Considerations include how labor in the overhead pools would be treated if it were direct labor, whether elements within the pools are routine expenses or instead are elements that contribute significantly to the proposed contract, and whether the elements require routine as opposed to unusual managerial effort and attention.

(ii) Contract cost risk.

(A) This factor measures the degree of cost responsibility and associated risk that the prospective contractor will assume as a result of the contract type contemplated and considering the reliability of the cost estimate in relation to the complexity and duration of the contract task. Determination of contract type should be closely related to the risks involved in timely, cost-effective, and efficient performance. This factor should compensate contractors proportionally for assuming greater cost risks.

(B) The contractor assumes the greatest cost risk in a closely priced firm-fixed-price contract under which it agrees to perform a complex undertaking on time and at a predetermined price. Some firm-fixed-price contracts may entail substantially less cost risk than others because, for example, the contract task is less complex or many of the contractor's costs are known at the time of price agreement, in which case the risk factor should be reduced accordingly. The contractor assumes the least cost risk in a cost-plus-fixed-fee level-of-effort contract, under which it is reimbursed those costs determined to be allocable and allowable, plus the fixed fee.

(C) In evaluating assumption of cost risk, contracting officers shall, except in unusual circumstances, treat time-and-materials, labor-hour, and firm-fixed-price, level-of-effort term contracts as cost-plus-fixed-fee contracts.

(iii) *Federal socioeconomic programs.* This factor measures the degree of support given by the prospective contractor to Federal socioeconomic programs, such as those involving small business concerns, small business concerns owned and controlled by socially and economically disadvantaged individuals, women-owned small business concerns, veteran-owned, HUBZone, service-disabled veteran-owned small business concerns, sheltered workshops for workers with disabilities, and energy conservation. Greater profit opportunity should be provided contractors that have displayed unusual initiative in these programs.

(iv) *Capital investments*. This factor takes into account the contribution of contractor investments to efficient and economical contract performance.

(v) *Cost-control and other past accomplishments*. This factor allows additional profit opportunities to a prospective contractor that has previously demonstrated its ability to perform similar tasks effectively and economically. In addition, consideration should be given to measures taken by the prospective contractor that result in productivity improvements, and other cost-reduction accomplishments that will benefit the Government in follow-on contracts.

(vi) *Independent development*. Under this factor, the contractor may be provided additional profit opportunities in recognition of independent development efforts relevant to the contract end item without Government assistance. The contracting officer should consider whether the development cost was recovered directly or indirectly from Government sources.

(2) *Additional factors*. In order to foster achievement of program objectives, each agency may include additional factors in its structured approach or take them into account in the profit analysis of individual contract actions.

United States Code Annotated

Contract requirements, see 41 USCA § 254.

Contracts, planning, solicitation, evaluation, and award procedures, see 10 USCA § 2305.

Cost or pricing data, truth in negotiations, see 10 USCA § 2306a, 41 USCA § 254b.

Definitions, see 10 USCA § 2302, 41 USCA §§ 259, 403.

Evaluation and award, see 41 USCA § 253b.

Kinds of contracts, see 10 USCA § 2306.

Planning and solicitation requirements, see 41 USCA § 253a.

Notes of Decisions

In general 1
Incentive fee 3
Limitations 2

1 In general

FAR 15.404-4 provides a number of profit factors that should be considered when contracts are being *negotiated*. These factors include: (1) Common factors, (i) Contractor effort; (ii) Contract cost risk; (iii) Federal socioeconomic programs; (iv) Capital investments; (v) Cost-control and other past accomplishments; (vi) Independent development, and (2) Additional factors. The Contract Appeals Board looks to these factors for assistance in determining profit on an equitable adjustment. NVT Technologies, Inc., E.B.C.A. No. C-401372, 05-1 B.C.A. (CCH) ¶ 32969, 2005 WL 1077487 (Dep't Energy B.C.A. 2005)

2 Limitations

Portion of cost-plus-fixed-fee contract for project planning and construction management services which involved the provision of architectural and engineering (A&E) services for modernization of weather forecasting offices was void as a matter of law, where contracting officer failed to make a precontract estimate of the cost of the project, and thus failed to comply with section of the Brooks Act limiting fee for architectural and engineering (A&E) services in a government contract to 6% of the estimated cost of the contract as determined by the agency at the time of entering into the contract. Fluor Enterprises, Inc. v. U.S., 64 Fed. Cl. 461 (2005). United States ☞68

Section of the Brooks Act providing that a fee not in excess of 6% of the estimated cost is "authorized in contracts for architectural or engineering services related to any public works" was applicable to architectural and engineering (A&E) services rendered by contractor on project, notwithstanding that A&E services were only a minor part of cost-plus-fixed-fee contract; language of statute does not suggest that it applied only to contracts primarily or substantially for A & E services, and Federal Acquisition Regulation (FAR) implementing statute does not limit its applicability to such contracts. Fluor Enterprises, Inc. v. U.S., 64 Fed. Cl. 461 (2005). United States ☞70(18)

3 Incentive fee

GAO held that it was unreasonable for an agency to accept an offeror's proposed incentive fee percentage that was lower than what the agency stated was available. Because the solicitation stated that the "amount of incentive dollars potentially available to award to the Contractor in each quarter is five percent of the funds expended on core services," GAO sustained the protest because this language "did not reasonably put offerors on notice that they could propose a lower fee." Matter of: General Dynamics One Source, LLC; Unisys Corporation, B-400340.5, B-400340.6, 2010 CPD ¶ 45 (Comp. Gen. 2010).

§ 15.405 Price negotiation.

(a) The purpose of performing cost or price analysis is to develop a negotiation position that permits the contracting officer and the offeror an opportunity to reach agreement on a fair and reasonable price. A fair and reasonable price does not require that agreement be reached on every element of cost, nor is it mandatory that the agreed price be within the contracting officer's initial negotiation position. Taking into consideration the advisory recommendations, reports of contributing specialists, and the current status of the contractor's purchasing system, the contracting officer is responsible for exercising the requisite judgment needed to reach a negotiated settlement with the offeror and is solely responsible for the final price agreement. However, when significant audit or other specialist recommendations are not adopted, the contracting officer should provide rationale that supports the negotiation result in the price negotiation documentation.

(b) The contracting officer's primary concern is the overall price the Government will actually pay. The contracting officer's objective is to negotiate a contract of a type and with a price providing the contractor the greatest incentive for efficient and economical performance. The negotiation of a contract type and a price are related and should be considered together with the issues of risk and uncertainty to the contractor and the Government. Therefore, the contracting officer should not become preoccupied with any single element and should balance the contract type, cost, and profit or fee negotiated to achieve a total result—a price that is fair and reasonable to both the Government and the contractor.

(c) The Government's cost objective and proposed pricing arrangement directly affect the profit or fee objective. Because profit or fee is only one of several interrelated variables, the contracting officer shall not agree on profit or fee without concurrent agreement on cost and type of contract.

(d) If, however, the contractor insists on a price or demands a profit or fee that the contracting officer considers unreasonable, and the contracting officer has taken all authorized actions (including determining the feasibility of developing an alternative source) without success, the contracting officer shall refer the contract action to a level above the contracting officer. Disposition of the action should be documented.

United States Code Annotated

Contract requirements, see 41 USCA § 254.

Contracts, planning, solicitation, evaluation, and award procedures, see 10 USCA § 2305.

Cost or pricing data, truth in negotiations, see 10 USCA § 2306a, 41 USCA § 254b.

Definitions, see 10 USCA § 2302, 41 USCA §§ 259, 403.

Evaluation and award, see 41 USCA § 253b.

Kinds of contracts, see 10 USCA § 2306.

Planning and solicitation requirements, see 41 USCA § 253a.

Notes of Decisions

In general 1

1 In general

Agencies must consider cost to the government in evaluating proposals, 41 U.S.C. sect. 253a(b)(1)(A), (c)(1)(B), and while it is up to the agency to decide upon some appropriate and reasonable method for the evaluation of offerors' prices, an agency may not use an evaluation method that produces a misleading result. The method chosen must also include some reasonable basis for evaluating or comparing the relative costs of proposals, so as to establish whether one offeror's proposal would be more or less costly than another's. R & G Food Service, Inc., d/b/a Port×A×Pit Catering, B-296435.4, B-296435.9, 2005 WL 3144073

(Comp. Gen. 2005)

§ 15.406 Documentation.

§ 15.406-1 Prenegotiation objectives.

(a) The prenegotiation objectives establish the Government's initial negotiation position. They assist in the contracting officer's determination of fair and reasonable price. They should be based on the results of the contracting officer's analysis of the offeror's proposal, taking into consideration all pertinent information including field pricing assistance, audit reports and technical analysis, fact-finding results, independent Government cost estimates and price histories.

(b) The contracting officer shall establish prenegotiation objectives before the negotiation of any pricing action. The scope and depth of the analysis supporting the objectives should be directly related to the dollar value, importance, and complexity of the pricing action. When cost analysis is required, the contracting officer shall document the pertinent issues to be negotiated, the cost objectives, and a profit or fee objective.

United States Code Annotated

Contract requirements, see 41 USCA § 254.

Contracts, planning, solicitation, evaluation, and award procedures, see 10 USCA § 2305.

Cost or pricing data, truth in negotiations, see 10 USCA § 2306a, 41 USCA § 254b.

Definitions, see 10 USCA § 2302, 41 USCA §§ 259, 403.

Evaluation and award, see 41 USCA § 253b.

Kinds of contracts, see 10 USCA § 2306.

Planning and solicitation requirements, see 41 USCA § 253a.

§ 15.406-2 Certificate of Current Cost or Pricing Data.

(a) When certified cost or pricing data are required, the contracting officer shall require the contractor to execute a Certificate of Current Cost or Pricing Data, using the format in this paragraph, and must include the executed certificate in the contract file.

CERTIFICATE OF CURRENT COST OR PRICING DATA

This is to certify that, to the best of my knowledge and belief, the cost or pricing data (as defined in section 2.101 of the Federal Acquisition Regulation (FAR) and required under FAR subsection 15.403-4) submitted, either actually or by specific identification in writing, to the Contracting Officer or to the Contracting Officer's representative in support of _____* are accurate, complete, and current as of _____**. This certification includes the cost or pricing data supporting any advance agreements and forward pricing rate agreements between the offeror and the Government that are part of the proposal.

Firm _____
Signature _____
Name _____
Title _____
Date of execution*** _____

---

* Identify the proposal, request for price adjustment, or other submission involved, giving the appropriate identifying number (e.g., RFP No.).

** Insert the day, month, and year when price negotiations were concluded and price agreement was reached or, if applicable, an earlier date agreed upon between the parties that is as close as practicable to the date of agreement on price.

*** Insert the day, month, and year of signing, which should be as close as practicable to the date when the price negotiations were concluded and the contract price was agreed to.

(END OF CERTIFICATE)

(b) The certificate does not constitute a representation as to the accuracy of the contractor's judgment on the estimate of future costs or projections. It applies to the data upon which the judgment or estimate was based. This distinction between fact and judgment should be clearly understood. If the contractor had information reasonably available at the time of agreement showing that the negotiated price was not based on accurate, complete, and current data, the contractor's responsibility is not limited by any lack of personal knowledge of the information on the part of its negotiators.

(c) The contracting officer and contractor are encouraged to reach a prior agreement on criteria for establishing closing or cutoff dates when appropriate in order to minimize delays associated with proposal updates. Closing or cutoff dates should be included as part of the data submitted with the proposal and, before agreement on price, data should be updated by the contractor to the latest closing or cutoff dates for which the data are available. Use of cutoff dates coinciding with reports is acceptable, as certain data may not be reasonably available before normal periodic closing dates (e.g., actual indirect costs). Data within the contractor's or a subcontractor's organization on matters significant to contractor management and to the Government will be treated as reasonably available. What is significant depends upon the circumstances of each acquisition.

(d) Possession of a Certificate of Current Cost or Pricing Data is not a substitute for examining and analyzing the contractor's proposal.

(e) If certified cost or pricing data are requested by the Government and submitted by an offeror, but an exception is later found to apply, the data shall not be considered certified cost or pricing data and shall not be certified in accordance with this subsection.

United States Code Annotated

Contract requirements, see 41 USCA § 254.

Contracts, planning, solicitation, evaluation, and award procedures, see 10 USCA § 2305.

Cost or pricing data, truth in negotiations, see 10 USCA § 2306a, 41 USCA § 254b.

Definitions, see 10 USCA § 2302, 41 USCA §§ 259, 403.

Evaluation and award, see 41 USCA § 253b.

Kinds of contracts, see 10 USCA § 2306.

Planning and solicitation requirements, see 41 USCA § 253a.

§ 15.406-3 Documenting the negotiation.

(a) The contracting officer shall document in the contract file the principal elements of the negotiated agreement. The documentation (e.g., price negotiation memorandum (PNM)) shall include the following:

(1) The purpose of the negotiation.

(2) A description of the acquisition, including appropriate identifying numbers (e.g., RFP No.).

(3) The name, position, and organization of each person representing the contractor and the Government in the negotiation.

(4) The current status of any contractor systems (e.g., purchasing, estimating, accounting, and compensation) to the extent they affected and were considered in the negotiation.

(5) If certified cost or pricing data were not required in the case of any price negotiation exceeding the certified cost or pricing data threshold, the exception used and the basis for it.

(6) If certified cost or pricing data were required, the extent to which the contracting officer—

(i) Relied on the certified cost or pricing data submitted and used them in negotiating the price;

(ii) Recognized as inaccurate, incomplete, or noncurrent any certified cost or pricing data submitted; the action taken by the contracting officer and the contractor as a result; and the effect of the defective data on the price negotiated; or

(iii) Determined that an exception applied after the data were submitted and, therefore, considered not to be certified cost or pricing data.

(7) A summary of the contractor's proposal, any field pricing assistance recommendations, including the reasons for any pertinent variances from them, the Government's negotiation objective, and the negotiated position. Where the determination of a fair and reasonable price is based on cost analysis, the summary shall address each major cost

element. When determination of a fair and reasonable price is based on price analysis, the summary shall include the source and type of data used to support the determination.

(8) The most significant facts or considerations controlling the establishment of the prenegotiation objectives and the negotiated agreement including an explanation of any significant differences between the two positions.

(9) To the extent such direction has a significant effect on the action, a discussion and quantification of the impact of direction given by Congress, other agencies, and higher-level officials (*i.e.*, officials who would not normally exercise authority during the award and review process for the instant contract action).

(10) The basis for the profit or fee prenegotiation objective and the profit or fee negotiated.

(11) Documentation of fair and reasonable pricing.

(b) Whenever field pricing assistance has been obtained, the contracting officer shall forward a copy of the negotiation documentation to the office(s) providing assistance. When appropriate, information on how advisory field support can be made more effective should be provided separately.

United States Code Annotated

Contract requirements, see 41 USCA § 254.

Contracts, planning, solicitation, evaluation, and award procedures, see 10 USCA § 2305.

Cost or pricing data, truth in negotiations, see 10 USCA § 2306a, 41 USCA § 254b.

Definitions, see 10 USCA § 2302, 41 USCA §§ 259, 403.

Evaluation and award, see 41 USCA § 253b.

Kinds of contracts, see 10 USCA § 2306.

Planning and solicitation requirements, see 41 USCA § 253a.

§ 15.407 Special cost or pricing areas.

§ 15.407-1 Defective certified cost or pricing data.

(a) If, before agreement on price, the contracting officer learns that any certified cost or pricing data submitted are inaccurate, incomplete, or noncurrent, the contracting officer shall immediately bring the matter to the attention of the prospective contractor, whether the defective data increase or decrease the contract price. The contracting officer shall consider any new data submitted to correct the deficiency, or consider the inaccuracy, incompleteness, or noncurrency of the data when negotiating the contract price. The price negotiation memorandum shall reflect the adjustments made to the data or the corrected data used to negotiate the contract price.

(b) (1) If, after award, certified cost or pricing data are found to be inaccurate, incomplete, or noncurrent as of the date of final agreement on price or an earlier date agreed upon by the parties given on the contractor's or subcontractor's Certificate of Current Cost or Pricing Data, the Government is entitled to a price adjustment, including profit or fee, of any significant amount by which the price was increased because of the defective data. This entitlement is ensured by including in the contract one of the clauses prescribed in 15.408(b) and (c) and is set forth in the clauses at 52.215-10, Price Reduction for Defective Certified Cost or Pricing Data, and 52.215-11, Price Reduction for Defective Certified Cost or Pricing Data-Modifications. The clauses give the Government the right to a price adjustment for defects in certified cost or pricing data submitted by the contractor, a prospective subcontractor, or an actual subcontractor.

(2) In arriving at a price adjustment, the contracting officer shall consider the time by which the certified cost or pricing data became reasonably available to the contractor, and the extent to which the Government relied upon the defective data.

(3) The clauses referred to in paragraph (b)(1) of this subsection recognize that the Government's right to a price adjustment is not affected by any of the following circumstances:

(i) The contractor or subcontractor was a sole source supplier or otherwise was in a superior bargaining position;

(ii) The contracting officer should have known that the certified cost or pricing data in issue were defective even though the contractor or subcontractor took no affirmative action to bring the character of the data to the attention of the contracting officer;

(iii) The contract was based on an agreement about the total cost of the contract and there was no agreement about the cost of each item procured under such contract; or

(iv) Certified cost or pricing data were required; however, the contractor or subcontractor did not submit a Certificate of Current Cost or Pricing Data relating to the contract.

(4) Subject to paragraphs (b)(5) and (6) of this subsection, the contracting officer shall allow an offset for any understated certified cost or pricing data submitted in support of price negotiations, up to the amount of the Government's claim for overstated pricing data arising out of the same pricing action (e.g., the initial pricing of the same contract or the pricing of the same change order).

(5) An offset shall be allowed only in an amount supported by the facts and if the contractor—

(i) Certifies to the contracting officer that, to the best of the contractor's knowledge and belief, the contractor is entitled to the offset in the amount requested; and

(ii) Proves that the certified cost or pricing data were available before the "as of" date specified on the Certificate of Current Cost or Pricing Data but were not submitted. Such offsets need not be in the same cost groupings (e.g., material, direct labor, or indirect costs).

(6) An offset shall not be allowed if—

(i) The understated data were known by the contractor to be understated before the "as of" date specified on the Certificate of Current Cost or Pricing Data; or

(ii) The Government proves that the facts demonstrate that the price would not have increased in the amount to be offset even if the available data had been submitted before the "as of" date specified on the Certificate of Current Cost or Pricing Data.

(7) (i) In addition to the price adjustment, the Government is entitled to recovery of any overpayment plus interest on the overpayments. The Government is also entitled to penalty amounts on certain of these overpayments. Overpayment occurs only when payment is made for supplies or services accepted by the Government. Overpayments do not result from amounts paid for contract financing, as defined in 32.001.

(ii) In calculating the interest amount due, the contracting officer shall—

(A) Determine the defective pricing amounts that have been overpaid to the contractor;

(B) Consider the date of each overpayment (the date of overpayment for this interest calculation shall be the date payment was made for the related completed and accepted contract items; or for subcontract defective pricing, the date payment was made to the prime contractor, based on prime contract progress billings or deliveries, which included payments for a completed and accepted subcontract item); and

(C) Apply the underpayment interest rate(s) in effect for each quarter from the time of overpayment to the time of repayment, utilizing rate(s) prescribed by the Secretary of the Treasury under 26 U.S.C. 6621(a)(2).

(iii) In arriving at the amount due for penalties on contracts where the submission of defective certified cost or pricing data was a knowing submission, the contracting officer shall obtain an amount equal to the amount of overpayment made. Before taking any contractual actions concerning penalties, the contracting officer shall obtain the advice of counsel.

(iv) In the demand letter, the contracting officer shall separately include—

(A) The repayment amount;

(B) The penalty amount (if any);

(C) The interest amount through a specified date; and

(D) A statement that interest will continue to accrue until repayment is made.

(c) If, after award, the contracting officer learns or suspects that the data furnished were not accurate, complete, and current, or were not adequately verified by the contractor as of the time of negotiation, the contracting officer shall request an audit to evaluate the accuracy, completeness, and currency of the data. The Government may evaluate the profit-cost relationships only if the audit reveals that the data certified by the contractor were defective. The contracting officer shall not reprice the contract solely because the profit was greater than forecast or because a contingency specified in the submission failed to materialize.

(d) For each advisory audit received based on a postaward review that indicates defective pricing, the contracting officer shall make a determination as to whether or not the data submitted were defective and relied upon. Before making such a determination, the contracting officer should give the contractor an opportunity to support the accuracy, completeness, and currency of the data in question. The contracting officer shall prepare a memorandum documenting both the determination and any corrective action taken as a result. The contracting officer shall send one copy of this memorandum to the auditor and, if the contract has been assigned for administration, one copy to the administrative contracting officer (ACO). A copy of the memorandum or other notice of the contracting officer's determination shall be provided to the contractor. When the contracting officer determines that the contractor submitted defective cost or pricing data, the contracting officer, in accordance with agency procedures, shall ensure that information relating to the contracting officer's final determination is reported in accordance with 42.1503(h). Agencies shall ensure updated information that changes a contracting officer's prior final determination is reported into the FAPIIS module of PPIRS in the event of a—

(1) Contracting officer's decision in accordance with the Contract Disputes statute;

(2) Board of Contract Appeals decision; or

(3) Court decision.

(e) If both the contractor and subcontractor submitted, and the contractor certified, or should have certified, cost or pricing data, the Government has the right, under the clauses at 52.215-10, Price Reduction for Defective Certified Cost or Pricing Data, and 52.215-11, Price Reduction for Defective Certified Cost or Pricing Data—Modifications, to reduce the prime contract price if it was significantly increased because a subcontractor submitted defective data. This right applies whether these data supported subcontract cost estimates or supported firm agreements between subcontractor and contractor.

(f) If Government audit discloses defective subcontractor certified cost or pricing data, the information necessary to support a reduction in prime contract and subcontract prices may be available only from the Government. To the extent necessary to secure a prime contract price reduction, the contracting officer should make this information available to the prime contractor or appropriate subcontractors, upon request. If release of the information would compromise Government security or disclose trade secrets or confidential business information, the contracting officer shall release it only under conditions that will protect it from improper disclosure. Information made available under this paragraph shall be limited to that used as the basis for the prime contract price reduction. In order to afford an opportunity for corrective action, the contracting officer should give the prime contractor reasonable advance notice before determining to reduce the prime contract price.

(1) When a prime contractor includes defective subcontract data in arriving at the price but later awards the subcontract to a lower priced subcontractor (or does not subcontract for the work), any adjustment in the prime contract price due to defective subcontract data is limited to the difference (plus applicable indirect cost and profit markups) between the subcontract price used for pricing the prime contract, and either the actual subcontract price or the actual cost to the contractor, if not subcontracted, provided the data on which the actual subcontract price is based are not themselves defective.

(2) Under cost-reimbursement contracts and under all fixed-price contracts except firm-fixed-price contracts and fixed-price contracts with economic price adjustment, payments to subcontractors that are higher than they would be had there been no defective subcontractor certified cost or pricing data shall be the basis for disallowance or nonrecognition of costs under the clauses prescribed in 15.408(b) and (c). The Government has a continuing and direct financial interest in such payments that is unaffected by the initial agreement on prime contract price.

§ **15.407-2 Make-or-buy programs.**

(a) General. The prime contractor is responsible for managing contract performance, including planning, placing, and administering subcontracts as necessary to ensure the lowest overall cost and technical risk to the Government. When make-or-buy programs are required, the Government may reserve the right to review and agree on the contractor's make-or-buy program when necessary to ensure negotiation of reasonable contract prices, satisfactory performance, or implementation of socioeconomic policies. Consent to subcontracts and review of contractors' purchasing systems are separate actions covered in part 44.

(b) Definition. "Make item," as used in this subsection, means an item or work effort to be produced or performed by the prime contractor or its affiliates, subsidiaries, or divisions.

(c) Acquisitions requiring make-or-buy programs.

(1) Contracting officers may require prospective contractors to submit make-or-buy program plans for negotiated acquisitions requiring certified cost or pricing data whose estimated value is $13.5 million or more, except when the proposed contract is for research or development and, if prototypes or hardware are involved, no significant follow-on production is anticipated.

(2) Contracting officers may require prospective contractors to submit make-or-buy programs for negotiated acquisitions whose estimated value is under $13.5 million only if the contracting officer—

(i) Determines that the information is necessary; and

(ii) Documents the reasons in the contract file.

(d) Solicitation requirements. When prospective contractors are required to submit proposed make-or-buy programs, the solicitation shall include—

(1) A statement that the program and required supporting information must accompany the offer; and

(2) A description of factors to be used in evaluating the proposed program, such as capability, capacity, availability of small, small disadvantaged, women-owned, veteran-owned, HUBZone, and service-disabled veteran-owned small business concerns for subcontracting, establishment of new facilities in or near labor surplus areas, delivery or performance schedules, control of technical and schedule interfaces, proprietary processes, technical superiority or exclusiveness, and technical risks involved.

(e) Program requirements. To support a make-or-buy program, the following information shall be supplied by the contractor in its proposal:

(1) Items and work included. The information required from a contractor in a make-or-buy program shall be confined to those major items or work efforts that normally would require company management review of the make-or-buy decision because they are complex, costly, needed in large quantities, or require additional equipment or real property to produce. Raw materials, commercial items (see 2.101), and off-the-shelf items (see 46.101) shall not be included, unless their potential impact on contract cost or schedule is critical. Normally, make-or-buy programs should not include items or work efforts estimated to cost less than 1 percent of the total estimated contract price or any minimum dollar amount set by the agency.

(2) The offeror's program should include or be supported by the following information:

(i) A description of each major item or work effort.

(ii) Categorization of each major item or work effort as "must make," "must buy," or "can either make or buy."

(iii) For each item or work effort categorized as "can either make or buy," a proposal either to "make" or to "buy."

(iv) Reasons for categorizing items and work efforts as "must make" or "must buy," and proposing to "make" or to "buy" those categorized as "can either make or buy." The reasons must include the consideration given to the evaluation factors described in the solicitation and must be in sufficient detail to permit the contracting officer to evaluate the categorization or proposal.

(v) Designation of the plant or division proposed to make each item or perform each work effort, and a statement as to whether the existing or proposed new facility is in or near a labor surplus area.

(vi) Identification of proposed subcontractors, if known, and their location and size status (also see Subpart 19.7 for subcontracting plan requirements).

(vii) Any recommendations to defer make-or-buy decisions when categorization of some items or work efforts is impracticable at the time of submission.

(viii) Any other information the contracting officer requires in order to evaluate the program.

(f) Evaluation, negotiation, and agreement. Contracting officers shall evaluate and negotiate proposed make-or-buy programs as soon as practicable after their receipt and before contract award.

(1) When the program is to be incorporated in the contract and the design status of the product being acquired does not permit accurate precontract identification of major items or work efforts, the contracting officer shall notify the prospective contractor in writing that these items or efforts, when identifiable, shall be added under the clause at 52.215-9, Changes or Additions to Make-or-Buy Program.

(2) Contracting officers normally shall not agree to proposed "make items" when the products or services are not regularly manufactured or provided by the contractor and are available-quality, quantity, delivery, and other essential factors considered-from another firm at equal or lower prices, or when they are regularly manufactured or provided by the contractor, but are available-quality, quantity, delivery, and other essential factors considered-from another firm at lower prices. However, the contracting officer may agree to these as "make items" if an overall lower Governmentwide cost would result or it is otherwise in the best interest of the Government. If this situation occurs in any fixed-price incentive or cost-plus-incentive-fee contract, the contracting officer shall specify these items in the contract and state that they are subject to paragraph (d) of the clause at 52.215-9, Changes or Additions to Make-or-Buy Program (see 15.408(a)). If the contractor proposes to reverse the categorization of such items during contract performance, the contract price shall be subject to equitable reduction.

(g) Incorporating make-or-buy programs in contracts. The contracting officer may incorporate the make-or-buy program in negotiated contracts for—

(1) Major systems (see part 34) or their subsystems or components, regardless of contract type; or

(2) Other supplies and services if—

(i) The contract is a cost-reimbursable contract, or a cost-sharing contract in which the contractor's share of the cost is less than 25 percent; and

(ii) The contracting officer determines that technical or cost risks justify Government review and approval of changes or additions to the make-or-buy program.

United States Code Annotated

Contract requirements, see 41 USCA § 254.

Contracts, planning, solicitation, evaluation, and award procedures, see 10 USCA § 2305.

Cost or pricing data, truth in negotiations, see 10 USCA § 2306a, 41 USCA § 254b.

Definitions, see 10 USCA § 2302, 41 USCA §§ 259, 403.

Evaluation and award, see 41 USCA § 253b.

Kinds of contracts, see 10 USCA § 2306.

Planning and solicitation requirements, see 41 USCA § 253a.

§ 15.407-3 Forward pricing rate agreements.

(a) When certified cost or pricing data are required, offerors are required to describe any forward pricing rate agreements (FPRAs) in each specific pricing proposal to which the rates apply and to identify the latest cost or pricing data already submitted in accordance with the FPRA. All data submitted in connection with the FPRA, updated as necessary, form a part of the total data that the offeror certifies to be accurate, complete, and current at the time of agreement on price for an initial contract or for a contract modification. (See the Certificate of Current Cost or Pricing Data at 15.406-2.)

(b) Contracting officers will use FPRA rates as bases for pricing all contracts, modifications, and other contractual actions to be performed during the period covered by the agreement. Conditions that may affect the agreement's validity shall be reported promptly to the ACO. If the ACO determines that a changed condition invalidates the agreement, the ACO shall notify all interested parties of the extent of its effect and status of efforts to establish a revised FPRA.

(c) Contracting officers shall not require certification at the time of agreement for data supplied in support of FPRA's or other advance agreements. When a forward pricing rate agreement or other advance agreement is used to price a contract action that requires a certificate, the certificate supporting that contract action shall cover the data supplied to support the FPRA or other advance agreement, and all other data supporting the action.

United States Code Annotated

Contract requirements, see 41 USCA § 254.

Contracts, planning, solicitation, evaluation, and award procedures, see 10 USCA § 2305.

Cost or pricing data, truth in negotiations, see 10 USCA § 2306a, 41 USCA § 254b.

Definitions, see 10 USCA § 2302, 41 USCA §§ 259, 403.

Evaluation and award, see 41 USCA § 253b.

Kinds of contracts, see 10 USCA § 2306.

Planning and solicitation requirements, see 41 USCA § 253a.

§ 15.407-4 Should-cost review.

(a) *General.* (1) Should-cost reviews are a specialized form of cost analysis. Should-cost reviews differ from traditional evaluation methods because they do not assume that a contractor's historical costs reflect efficient and economical operation. Instead, these reviews evaluate the economy and efficiency of the contractor's existing work force, methods, materials, equipment, real property, operating systems, and management. These reviews are accomplished by a multifunctional team of Government contracting, contract administration, pricing, audit, and engineering representatives. The objective of should-cost reviews is to promote both short and long-range improvements in the contractor's economy and efficiency in order to reduce the cost of performance of Government contracts. In addition, by providing rationale for any recommendations and quantifying their impact on cost, the Government will be better able to develop realistic objectives for negotiation.

(2) There are two types of should-cost reviews—program should-cost review (see paragraph (b) of this subsection) and overhead should-cost review (see paragraph (c) of this subsection). These should-cost reviews may be performed together or independently. The scope of a should-cost review can range from a large-scale review examining the contractor's entire operation (including plant-wide overhead and selected major subcontractors) to a small-scale tailored review examining specific portions of a contractor's operation.

(b) *Program should-cost review.* (1) A program shouldcost review is used to evaluate significant elements of direct costs, such as material and labor, and associated indirect costs, usually associated with the production of major systems. When a program should-cost review is conducted relative to a contractor proposal, a separate audit report on the proposal is required.

(2) A program should-cost review should be considered, particularly in the case of a major system acquisition (see Part 34), when—

(i) Some initial production has already taken place;

(ii) The contract will be awarded on a sole source basis;

(iii) There are future year production requirements for substantial quantities of like items;

(iv) The items being acquired have a history of increasing costs;

(v) The work is sufficiently defined to permit an effective analysis and major changes are unlikely;

(vi) Sufficient time is available to plan and adequately conduct the should-cost review; and

(vii) Personnel with the required skills are available or can be assigned for the duration of the should-cost review.

(3) The contracting officer should decide which elements of the contractor's operation have the greatest potential for cost savings and assign the available personnel resources accordingly. The expertise of on-site Government personnel should be used, when appropriate. While the particular elements to be analyzed are a function of the contract work task, elements such as manufacturing, pricing and accounting, management and organization, and subcontract and vendor management are normally reviewed in a

should-cost review.

(4) In acquisitions for which a program should-cost review is conducted, a separate program should-cost review team report, prepared in accordance with agency procedures, is required. The contracting officer shall consider the findings and recommendations contained in the program should-cost review team report when negotiating the contract price. After completing the negotiation, the contracting officer shall provide the ACO a report of any identified uneconomical or inefficient practices, together with a report of correction or disposition agreements reached with the contractor. The contracting officer shall establish a follow-up plan to monitor the correction of the uneconomical or inefficient practices.

(5) When a program should-cost review is planned, the contracting officer should state this fact in the acquisition plan or acquisition plan updates (see Subpart 7.1) and in the solicitation.

(c) *Overhead should-cost review.* (1) An overhead shouldcost review is used to evaluate indirect costs, such as fringe benefits, shipping and receiving, real property, and equipment, depreciation, plant maintenance and security, taxes, and general and administrative activities. It is normally used to evaluate and negotiate an FPRA with the contractor. When an overhead should-cost review is conducted, a separate audit report is required.

(2) The following factors should be considered when selecting contractor sites for overhead should-cost reviews:

(i) Dollar amount of Government business.

(ii) Level of Government participation.

(iii) Level of noncompetitive Government contracts.

(iv) Volume of proposal activity.

(v) Major system or program.

(vi) Corporate reorganizations, mergers, acquisitions, or takeovers.

(vii) Other conditions (*e.g.,* changes in accounting systems, management, or business activity).

(3) The objective of the overhead should-cost review is to evaluate significant indirect cost elements in-depth, and identify and recommend corrective actions regarding inefficient and uneconomical practices. If it is conducted in conjunction with a program should-cost review, a separate overhead should-cost review report is not required. However, the findings and recommendations of the overhead shouldcost team, or any separate overhead should-cost review report, shall be provided to the ACO. The ACO should use this information to form the basis for the Government position in negotiating an FPRA with the contractor. The ACO shall establish a follow-up plan to monitor the correction of the uneconomical or inefficient practices.

United States Code Annotated

Contract requirements, see 41 USCA § 254.

Contracts, planning, solicitation, evaluation, and award procedures, see 10 USCA § 2305.

Cost or pricing data, truth in negotiations, see 10 USCA § 2306a, 41 USCA § 254b.

Definitions, see 10 USCA § 2302, 41 USCA §§ 259, 403.

Evaluation and award, see 41 USCA § 253b.

Kinds of contracts, see 10 USCA § 2306.

Planning and solicitation requirements, see 41 USCA § 253a.

§ 15.407-5 Estimating systems.

(a) Using an acceptable estimating system for proposal preparation benefits both the Government and the contractor by increasing the accuracy and reliability of individual proposals. Cognizant audit activities, when it is appropriate to do so, shall establish and manage regular programs for reviewing selected contractors' estimating systems or methods, in order to reduce the scope of reviews to be performed on individual proposals, expedite the negotiation process, and increase the reliability of proposals. The results of estimating system reviews shall be documented in survey reports.

(b) The auditor shall send a copy of the estimating system survey report and a copy of the official notice of corrective action required to each contracting office and contract administration office having substantial business with that contractor. Significant deficiencies not corrected by the contractor shall be a consideration in subsequent proposal analyses and negotiations.

§ 15.408 Solicitation provisions and contract clauses.

(a) Changes or Additions to Make-or-Buy Program. The contracting officer shall insert the clause at 52.215-9, Changes or Additions to Make-or-Buy Program, in solicitations and contracts when it is contemplated that a make-or-buy program will be incorporated in the contract. If a less economical "make" or "buy" categorization is selected for one or more items of significant value, the contracting officer shall use the clause with—

(1) Its Alternate I, if a fixed-price incentive contract is contemplated; or

(2) Its Alternate II, if a cost-plus-incentive-fee contract is contemplated.

(b) Price Reduction for Defective Certified Cost or Pricing Data. The contracting officer shall, when contracting by negotiation, insert the clause at 52.215-10, Price Reduction for Defective Certified Cost or Pricing Data, in solicitations and contracts when it is contemplated that certified cost or pricing data will be required from the contractor or any subcontractor (see 15.403-4).

(c) Price Reduction for Defective Certified Cost or Pricing Data-Modifications. The contracting officer shall, when contracting by negotiation, insert the clause at 52.215-11, Price Reduction for Defective Certified Cost or Pricing Data-Modifications, in solicitations and contracts when it is contemplated that certified cost or pricing data will be required from the contractor or any subcontractor (see 15.403-4) for the pricing of contract modifications, and the clause prescribed in paragraph (b) of this section has not been included.

(d) Subcontractor Certified Cost or Pricing Data. The contracting officer shall insert the clause at 52.215-12, Subcontractor Certified Cost or Pricing Data, in solicitations and contracts when the clause prescribed in paragraph (b) of this section is included.

(e) Subcontractor Certified Cost or Pricing Data-Modifications. The contracting officer shall insert the clause at 52.215-13, Subcontractor Certified Cost or Pricing Data-Modifications, in solicitations and contracts when the clause prescribed in paragraph (c) of this section is included.

(f) Integrity of Unit Prices.

(1) The contracting officer shall insert the clause at 52.215-14, Integrity of Unit Prices, in solicitations and contracts except for—

(i) Acquisitions at or below the simplified acquisition threshold;

(ii) Construction or architect-engineer services under part 36;

(iii) Utility services under part 41;

(iv) Service contracts where supplies are not required;

(v) Acquisitions of commercial items; and

(vi) Contracts for petroleum products.

(2) The contracting officer shall insert the clause with its Alternate I when contracting without adequate price competition or when prescribed by agency regulations. 52.215-15 part 31

(g) Pension Adjustments and Asset Reversions. The contracting officer shall insert the clause at 52.215-15, Pension Adjustments and Asset Reversions, in solicitations and contracts for which it is anticipated that certified cost or pricing data will be required or for which any preaward or postaward cost determinations will be subject to part 31.

(h) Facilities Capital Cost of Money. The contracting officer shall insert the provision at 52.215-16, Facilities Capital Cost of Money, in solicitations expected to result in contracts that are subject to the cost principles for contracts with commercial organizations (see Subpart 31.2).

(i) Waiver of Facilities Capital Cost of Money. If the prospective contractor does not propose facilities capital cost of money in its offer, the contracting officer shall insert the clause at 52.215-17, Waiver of Facilities Capital Cost of Money, in the resulting contract.

(j) Reversion or Adjustment of Plans for Postretirement Benefits (PRB) Other Than Pensions. The contracting officer shall insert the clause at 52.215-18, Reversion or Adjustment of Plans for Postretirement Benefits (PRB) Other Than Pensions, in solicitations and contracts for which it is anticipated that certified cost or pricing data will be required or for which any preaward or postaward cost determinations will be subject to part 31.

(k) Notification of Ownership Changes. The contracting officer shall insert the clause at 52.215-19, Notification of Ownership Changes, in solicitations and contracts for which it is contemplated that certified cost or pricing data will be required or for which any preaward or postaward cost determination will be subject to Subpart 31.2.

(l) Requirements for Certified Cost or Pricing Data and Data Other Than Certified Cost or Pricing Data. Considering the hierarchy at 15.402, the contracting officer shall insert the provision at 52.215-20, Requirements for Certified Cost or Pricing Data and Data Other Than Certified Cost or Pricing Data, in solicitations if it is reasonably certain that certified cost or pricing data or data other than certified cost or pricing data will be required. This provision also provides instructions to offerors on how to request an exception from the requirement to submit certified cost or pricing data. The contracting officer shall—

(1) Use the provision with its Alternate I to specify a format for certified cost or pricing data other than the format required by Table 15-2 of this section;

(2) Use the provision with its Alternate II if copies of the proposal are to be sent to the ACO and contract auditor;

(3) Use the provision with its Alternate III if submission via electronic media is required; and

(4) Replace the basic provision with its Alternate IV if certified cost or pricing data are not expected to be required because an exception may apply, but data other than certified cost or pricing data will be required as described in 15.403-3.

(m) Requirements for Certified Cost or Pricing Data and Data Other Than Certified Cost or Pricing Data-Modifications. Considering the hierarchy at 15.402, the contracting officer shall insert the clause at 52.215-21, Requirements for Certified Cost or Pricing Data and Data Other Than Certified Cost or Pricing Data-Modifications, in solicitations and contracts if it is reasonably certain that certified cost or pricing data or data other than certified cost or pricing data will be required for modifications. This clause also provides instructions to contractors on how to request an exception from the requirement to submit certified cost or pricing data. The contracting officer shall—

(1) Use the clause with its Alternate I to specify a format for certified cost or pricing data other than the format required by Table 15-2 of this section;

(2) Use the clause with its Alternate II if copies of the proposal are to be sent to the ACO and contract auditor;

(3) Use the clause with its Alternate III if submission via electronic media is required; and

(4) Replace the basic clause with its Alternate IV if certified cost or pricing data are not expected to be required because an exception may apply, but data other than certified cost or pricing data will be required as described in 15.403-3.

(n) Limitations on Pass-Through Charges.

(1) The contracting officer shall insert the provision at 52.215-22, Limitations on Pass-Through Charges-Identification of Subcontract Effort, in solicitations containing the clause at 52.215-23.

(2) (i) Except as provided in paragraph (n)(2)(ii), the contracting officer shall insert the clause 52.215-23, Limitations on Pass-Through Charges, in solicitations and contracts including task or delivery orders as follows:

(A) For civilian agencies, insert the clause when—

(1) The total estimated contract or order value exceeds the simplified acquisition threshold as defined in section 2.101 and

(2) The contemplated contract type is expected to be a cost-reimbursement type contract as defined in Subpart 16.3; or

(B) For DoD, insert the clause when—

(1) The total estimated contract or order value exceeds the threshold for obtaining cost or pricing data in 15.403-4; and

(2) The contemplated contract type is expected to be any contract type except—

(i) A firm-fixed-price contract awarded on the basis of adequate price competition;

(ii) A fixed-price contract with economic price adjustment awarded on the basis of adequate price competition;

    (iii) A firm-fixed-price contract for the acquisition of a commercial item;

    (iv) A fixed-price contract with economic price adjustment, for the acquisition of a commercial item;

    (v) A fixed-price incentive contract awarded on the basis of adequate price competition; or

    (vi) A fixed-price incentive contract for the acquisition of a commercial item.

    (ii) The clause may be used when the total estimated contract or order value is below the thresholds identified in 15.408(n)(2)(i) and for any contract type, when the contracting officer determines that inclusion of the clause is appropriate.

    (iii) Use the clause 52.215-23 with its Alternate I when the contracting officer determines that the prospective contractor has demonstrated that its functions provide added value to the contracting effort and there are no excessive pass-through charges.

Table 15-2—Instructions for Submitting Cost/Price Proposals When Certified Cost or Pricing Data Are Required

This document provides instructions for preparing a contract pricing proposal when certified cost or pricing data are required.

Note 1. There is a clear distinction between submitting certified cost or pricing data and merely making available books, records, and other documents without identification. The requirement for submission of certified cost or pricing data is met when all accurate certified cost or pricing data reasonably available to the offeror have been submitted, either actually or by specific identification, to the Contracting Officer or an authorized representative. As later data come into your possession, it should be submitted promptly to the Contracting Officer in a manner that clearly shows how the data relate to the offeror's price proposal. The requirement for submission of certified cost or pricing data continues up to the time of agreement on price, or an earlier date agreed upon between the parties if applicable.

Note 2. By submitting your proposal, you grant the Contracting Officer or an authorized representative the right to examine records that formed the basis for the pricing proposal. That examination can take place at any time before award. It may include those books, records, documents, and other types of factual data (regardless of form or whether the data are specifically referenced or included in the proposal as the basis for pricing) that will permit an adequate evaluation of the proposed price.

I. General Instructions

A. You must provide the following information on the first page of your pricing proposal:

    (1) Solicitation, contract, and/or modification number;

    (2) Name and address of offeror;

    (3) Name and telephone number of point of contact;

    (4) Name of contract administration office (if available);

    (5) Type of contract action (that is, new contract, change order, price revision/redetermination, letter contract, unpriced order, or other);

    (6) Proposed cost; profit or fee; and total;

    (7) Whether you will require the use of Government property in the performance of the contract, and, if so, what property;

    (8) Whether your organization is subject to cost accounting standards; whether your organization has submitted a CASB Disclosure Statement, and if it has been determined adequate; whether you have been notified that you are or may be in noncompliance with your Disclosure Statement or CAS (other than a noncompliance that the cognizant Federal agency official has determined to have an immaterial cost impact), and, if yes, an explanation; whether any aspect of this proposal is inconsistent with your disclosed practices or applicable CAS, and, if so, an explanation; and whether the proposal is consistent with your established estimating and accounting principles and procedures and FAR part 31, Cost Principles, and, if not, an explanation;

    (9) The following statement:

This proposal reflects our estimates and/or actual costs as of this date and conforms with the instructions in FAR 15.403-5(b)(1) and Table 15-2. By submitting this proposal, we grant the Contracting Officer and authorized representative(s) the right to examine, at any time before award, those records, which include books, documents, accounting procedures and practices, and other data, regardless of type and form or whether such supporting information is specifically referenced or included in the proposal as the basis for pricing, that will permit an adequate evaluation of the proposed price.

(10) Date of submission; and

(11) Name, title, and signature of authorized representative.

B. In submitting your proposal, you must include an index, appropriately referenced, of all the certified cost or pricing data and information accompanying or identified in the proposal. In addition, you must annotate any future additions and/or revisions, up to the date of agreement on price, or an earlier date agreed upon by the parties, on a supplemental index.

C. As part of the specific information required, you must submit, with your proposal—

(1) Certified cost or pricing data (as defined at FAR 2.101). You must clearly identify on your cover sheet that certified cost or pricing data are included as part of the proposal.

(2) Information reasonably required to explain your estimating process, including—

(i) The judgmental factors applied and the mathematical or other methods used in the estimate, including those used in projecting from known data; and

(ii) The nature and amount of any contingencies included in the proposed price.

D. You must show the relationship between contract line item prices and the total contract price. You must attach cost-element breakdowns for each proposed line item, using the appropriate format prescribed in the "Formats for Submission of Line Item Summaries" section of this table. You must furnish supporting breakdowns for each cost element, consistent with your cost accounting system.

E. When more than one contract line item is proposed, you must also provide summary total amounts covering all line items for each element of cost.

F. Whenever you have incurred costs for work performed before submission of a proposal, you must identify those costs in your cost/price proposal.

G. If you have reached an agreement with Government representatives on use of forward pricing rates/factors, identify the agreement, include a copy, and describe its nature.

H. As soon as practicable after final agreement on price or an earlier date agreed to by the parties, but before the award resulting from the proposal, you must, under the conditions stated in FAR 15.406-2, submit a Certificate of Current Cost or Pricing Data.

II. Cost Elements

Depending on your system, you must provide breakdowns for the following basic cost elements, as applicable:

A. Materials and services. Provide a consolidated priced summary of individual material quantities included in the various tasks, orders, or contract line items being proposed and the basis for pricing (vendor quotes, invoice prices, etc.). Include raw materials, parts, components, assemblies, and services to be produced or performed by others. For all items proposed, identify the item and show the source, quantity, and price. Conduct price analyses of all subcontractor proposals. Conduct cost analyses for all subcontracts when certified cost or pricing data are submitted by the subcontractor. Include these analyses as part of your own certified cost or pricing data submissions for subcontracts expected to exceed the appropriate threshold in FAR 15.403-4. Submit the subcontractor certified cost or pricing data and data other than certified cost or pricing data as part of your own certified cost or pricing data as required in paragraph IIA(2) of this table. These requirements also apply to all subcontractors if required to submit certified cost or pricing data.

(1) Adequate Price Competition. Provide data showing the degree of competition and the basis for establishing the source and reasonableness of price for those acquisitions (such as subcontracts, purchase orders, material order, etc.) exceeding, or expected to exceed, the appropriate threshold set forth at FAR 15.403-4 priced on the basis of adequate price competition. For interorganizational transfers priced at other than the cost of comparable competitive commercial work of the division, subsidiary, or affiliate of the contractor, explain the pricing method (see FAR 31.205-26(e)).

(2) All Other. Obtain certified cost or pricing data from prospective sources for those acquisitions (such as subcontracts, purchase orders, material order, etc.) exceeding the threshold set forth in FAR 15.403-4 and not otherwise exempt, in accordance with FAR 15.403-1(b) (i.e., adequate price competition, commercial items, prices set by law or regulation or waiver). Also provide data showing the basis for establishing source and reasonableness of price. In addition, provide a summary of your cost analysis and a copy of certified cost or pricing data submitted by the prospective source in support of each subcontract, or purchase order that is the lower of either $13.5 million or more, or both more than the pertinent certified cost or pricing data threshold and more than 10 percent of the prime contractor's proposed price. Also submit any information reasonably required to explain your estimating process (including the judgmental factors applied and the mathematical or other methods used in the estimate, including those used in projecting from known data, and the nature and amount of any contingencies included in the price). The Contracting Officer may require you to submit cost or pricing data in support of proposals in lower amounts. Subcontractor certified cost or pricing data must be accurate, complete and current as of the date of final price agreement, or an earlier date agreed upon by the parties, given on the prime contractor's Certificate of Current Cost or Pricing Data. The prime contractor is responsible for updating a prospective subcontractor's data. For standard commercial items fabricated by the offeror that are generally stocked in inventory, provide a separate cost breakdown, if priced based on cost. For interorganizational transfers priced at cost, provide a separate breakdown of cost elements. Analyze the certified cost or pricing data and submit the results of your analysis of the prospective source's proposal.When submission of a prospective source's certified cost or pricing data is required as described in this paragraph, it must be included as part of your own certified cost or pricing data. You must also submit any data other than certified cost or pricing data obtained from a subcontractor, either actually or by specific identification, along with the results of any analysis performed on that data.

B. Direct Labor. Provide a time-phased (e.g., monthly, quarterly, etc.) breakdown of labor hours, rates, and cost by appropriate category, and furnish bases for estimates.

C. Indirect Costs. Indicate how you have computed and applied your indirect costs, including cost breakdowns. Show trends and budgetary data to provide a basis for evaluating the reasonableness of proposed rates. Indicate the rates used and provide an appropriate explanation.

D. Other Costs. List all other costs not otherwise included in the categories described above (e.g., special tooling, travel, computer and consultant services, preservation, packaging and packing, spoilage and rework, and Federal excise tax on finished articles) and provide bases for pricing.

E. Royalties. If royalties exceed $1,500, you must provide the following information on a separate page for each separate royalty or license fee:

(1) Name and address of licensor.

(2) Date of license agreement.

(3) Patent numbers.

(4) Patent application serial numbers, or other basis on which the royalty is payable.

(5) Brief description (including any part or model numbers of each contract item or component on which the royalty is payable)

(6) Percentage or dollar rate of royalty per unit.

(7) Unit price of contract item.

(8) Number of units.

(9) Total dollar amount of royalties.

(10) If specifically requested by the Contracting Officer, a copy of the current license agreement and identification of applicable claims of specific patents (see FAR 27.202 and 31.205-37).

F. Facilities Capital Cost of Money. When you elect to claim facilities capital cost of money as an allowable cost, you must submit Form CASB-CMF and show the calculation of the proposed amount (see FAR 31.205-10).

III. Formats for Submission of Line Item Summaries

A. New Contracts (Including Letter Contracts)

Cost elements (1)	Proposed contract estimate—total cost (2)	Proposed contract estimate—unit cost (3)	Reference (4)

Column and Instruction

(1) Enter appropriate cost elements.

(2) Enter those necessary and reasonable costs that, in your judgment, will properly be incurred in efficient contract performance. When any of the costs in this column have already been incurred (e.g., under a letter contract), describe them on an attached supporting page. When preproduction or startup costs are significant, or when specifically requested to do so by the Contracting Officer, provide a full identification and explanation of them.

(3) Optional, unless required by the Contracting Officer.

(4) Identify the attachment in which the information supporting the specific cost element may be found. (Attach separate pages as necessary.)

B. Change Orders, Modifications, and Claims

Cost elements (1)	Estimated cost of all work deleted (2)	Cost of deleted work already performed (3)	Net cost to be deleted (4)	Cost of work added (5)	Net cost of change (6)	Reference (7)

Column and Instruction

(1) Enter appropriate cost elements.

(2) Include the current estimates of what the cost would have been to complete the deleted work not yet performed (not the original proposal estimates), and the cost of deleted work already performed.

(3) Include the incurred cost of deleted work already performed, using actuals incurred if possible, or, if actuals are not available, estimates from your accounting records. Attach a detailed inventory of work, materials, parts, components, and hardware already purchased, manufactured, or performed and deleted by the change, indicating the cost and proposed disposition of each line item. Also, if you desire to retain these items or any portion of them, indicate the amount offered for them.

(4) Enter the net cost to be deleted, which is the estimated cost of all deleted work less the cost of deleted work already performed. Column (2) minus Column (3) equals Column (4).

(5) Enter your estimate for cost of work added by the change. When nonrecurring costs are significant, or when specifically requested to do so by the Contracting Officer, provide a full identification and explanation of them. When any of the costs in this column have already been incurred, describe them on an attached supporting schedule.

(6) Enter the net cost of change, which is the cost of work added, less the net cost to be deleted. Column (5) minus Column (4) equals Column (6). When this result is negative, place the amount in parentheses.

(7) Identify the attachment in which the information supporting the specific cost element may be found. (Attach separate pages as necessary.)

C. Price Revision/Redetermination

Cut-off date (1)	Number of units completed (2)	Number of units to be completed (3)	Contract amount (4)	Redetermination proposal amount (5)	Difference (6)	Cost elements (7)	
Incurred cost—preproduction (8)	Incurred cost—completed units (9)	Incurred cost—work in process (10)	Total incurred cost (11)	Estimated cost to complete (12)	Estimated total cost (13)	Reference (14)	

(Use as applicable).

Column and Instruction

(1) Enter the cutoff date required by the contract, if applicable.

(2) Enter the number of units completed during the period for which experienced costs of production are being submitted.

(3) Enter the number of units remaining to be completed under the contract.

(4) Enter the cumulative contract amount.

(5) Enter your redetermination proposal amount.

(6) Enter the difference between the contract amount and the redetermination proposal amount. When this result is negative, place the amount in parentheses. Column (4) minus Column (5) equals Column (6).

(7) Enter appropriate cost elements. When residual inventory exists, the final costs established under fixed-price-incentive and fixed-price-redeterminable arrangements should be net of the fair market value of such inventory. In support of subcontract costs, submit a listing of all subcontracts subject to repricing action, annotated as to their status.

(8) Enter all costs incurred under the contract before starting production and other nonrecurring costs (usually referred to as startup costs) from your books and records as of the cutoff date. These include such costs as preproduction engineering, special plant rearrangement, training program, and any identifiable nonrecurring costs such as initial rework, spoilage, pilot runs, etc. In the event the amounts are not segregated in or otherwise available from your records, enter in this column your best estimates. Explain the basis for each estimate and how the costs are charged on your accounting records (e.g., included in production costs as direct engineering labor, charged to manufacturing overhead). Also show how the costs would be allocated to the units at their various stages of contract completion.

(9) Enter in Column (9) the production costs from your books and records (exclusive of preproduction costs reported in Column (8)) of the units completed as of the cutoff date.

(10) Enter in Column (10) the costs of work in process as determined from your records or inventories at the cutoff date. When the amounts for work in process are not available in your records but reliable estimates for them can be made, enter the estimated amounts in Column (10) and enter in Column (9) the differences between the total incurred costs (exclusive of preproduction costs) as of the cutoff date and these estimates. Explain the basis for the estimates, including identification of any provision for experienced or anticipated allowances, such as shrinkage, rework, design changes, etc. Furnish experienced unit or lot costs (or labor hours) from inception of contract to the cutoff date, improvement curves, and any other available production cost history pertaining to the item(s) to which your proposal relates.

(11) Enter total incurred costs (Total of Columns (8), (9), and (10)).

(12) Enter those necessary and reasonable costs that in your judgment will properly be incurred in completing the remaining work to be performed under the contract with respect to the item(s) to which your proposal relates.

(13) Enter total estimated cost (Total of Columns (11) and (12)).

(14) Identify the attachment in which the information supporting the specific cost element may be found. (Attach separate pages as necessary.)

Subpart 15.5 Preaward, Award, and Postaward Notifications, Protests, and Mistakes

§ 15.501 Definition.

"Day," as used in this subpart, has the meaning set forth at 33.101.

United States Code Annotated

Contract requirements, see 41 USCA § 254.

Contracts, planning, solicitation, evaluation, and award procedures, see 10 USCA § 2305.

Definitions, see 10 USCA § 2302, 41 USCA §§ 259, 403.

Evaluation and award, see 41 USCA § 253b.

Kinds of contracts, see 10 USCA § 2306.

Planning and solicitation requirements, see 41 USCA § 253a.

§ 15.502 Applicability.

This subpart applies to competitive proposals, as described in 6.102(b), and a combination of competitive procedures, as described in 6.102(c). The procedures in 15.504, 15.506, 15.507, 15.508, and 15.509, with reasonable modification, should be followed for sole source acquisitions and acquisitions described in 6.102(d)(1) and (2).

United States Code Annotated

Contract requirements, see 41 USCA § 254.

Contracts, planning, solicitation, evaluation, and award procedures, see 10 USCA § 2305.

Definitions, see 10 USCA § 2302, 41 USCA §§ 259, 403.

Evaluation and award, see 41 USCA § 253b.

Kinds of contracts, see 10 USCA § 2306.

Planning and solicitation requirements, see 41 USCA § 253a.

§ 15.503 Notifications to unsuccessful offerors.

(a) Preaward notices—

(1) *Preaward notices of exclusion from competitive range.* The contracting officer shall notify offerors promptly in writing when their proposals are excluded from the competitive range or otherwise eliminated from the competition. The notice shall state the basis for the determination and that a proposal revision will not be considered.

(2) Preaward notices for small business programs.

(i) In addition to the notice in paragraph (a)(1) of this section, the contracting officer shall notify each offeror in writing prior to award and upon completion of negotiations and determinations of responsibility—

(A) When using a small business set-aside (see Subpart 19.5);

(B) When using the HUBZone procedures in 19.1305 or 19.1307;

(C) When using the service-disabled veteran-owned small business procedures in 19.1405; or

(D) When using the Women-Owned Small Business Program procedures in 19.1505.

(ii) The notice shall state—

(A) The name and address of the apparently successful offeror;

(B) That the Government will not consider subsequent revisions of the offeror's proposal; and

(C) That no response is required unless a basis exists to challenge the size status or small business status of the apparently successful offeror (e.g., small business concern, small disadvantaged business concern, HUBZone small business concern, service-disabled veteran-owned small business concern, economically disadvantaged women-owned small business concern, or women-owned small business concern eligible under the Women-Owned Small Business Program).

(iii) The notice is not required when the contracting officer determines in writing that the urgency of the requirement necessitates award without delay or when the contract is entered into under the 8(a) program (see 19.805-2).

(b) Postaward notices.

(1) Within 3 days after the date of contract award, the contracting officer shall provide written notification to each offeror whose proposal was in the competitive range but was not selected for award (10 U.S.C. 2305(b)(5) and 41 U.S.C. 3704) or had not been previously notified under paragraph (a) of this section. The notice shall include—

(i) The number of offerors solicited;

(ii) The number of proposals received;

(iii) The name and address of each offeror receiving an award;

(iv) The items, quantities, and any stated unit prices of each award. If the number of items or other factors makes listing any stated unit prices impracticable at that time, only the total contract price need be furnished in the notice. However, the items, quantities, and any stated unit prices of each award shall be made publicly available, upon request; and

(v) In general terms, the reason(s) the offeror's proposal was not accepted, unless the price information in paragraph (b)(1)(iv) of this section readily reveals the reason. In no event shall an offeror's cost breakdown, profit, overhead rates, trade secrets, manufacturing processes and techniques, or other confidential business information be disclosed to any other offeror.

(2) Upon request, the contracting officer shall furnish the information described in paragraph (b)(1) of this section to unsuccessful offerors in solicitations using simplified acquisition procedures in Part 13.

(3) Upon request, the contracting officer shall provide the information in paragraph (b)(1) of this section to unsuccessful offerors that received a preaward notice of exclusion from the competitive range.

United States Code Annotated

Contract requirements, see 41 USCA § 254.

Contracts, planning, solicitation, evaluation, and award procedures, see 10 USCA § 2305.

Definitions, see 10 USCA § 2302, 41 USCA §§ 259, 403.

Evaluation and award, see 41 USCA § 253b.

Kinds of contracts, see 10 USCA § 2306.

Planning and solicitation requirements, see 41 USCA § 253a.

Notes of Decisions

Content of notice 1

Effect of improper notification 2

1 Content of notice

In the pre-award context, after receipt of proposals, FAR 15.306(e)(3) prevents government officials from, among other things, revealing one offeror's price to another offeror without the initial offeror's permission. In the post-award context, FAR 15.503(b)(2) requires a contracting officer, upon request, to furnish certain information to an unsuccessful offeror, including the number of offerors solicited, the number of proposals received, the name and address of each offeror receiving an award, the items, quantities, and stated unit prices of each award, and the general reasons the offeror's proposal was not accepted. Notably, FAR 15.503(b)(1)(v) prevents an offeror's cost breakdown, profit, overhead rates, trade secrets, manufacturing processes and techniques, or other confidential business information from being disclosed to another offeror. MTB Group, Inc. v. U.S., 65 Fed. Cl. 516 (2005)

2 Effect of improper notification

Bid protestor was not prejudiced by contracting officer's post-award notification which did not contain either the correct name or the awardee, or the awardee's bid price, notwithstanding protestor's claim that faulty notification caused it to delay filing a size protest with the Small Business Administration (SBA), as neither piece of information was critical to protestor's decision to file a size protest with the SBA. Tech Systems, Inc. v. U.S., 50 Fed. Cl. 216 (2001)

Where an agency fails to provide pre-award notification of the identity of the prospective awardee on a small business set-aside and the awardee is ultimately found by the Small Business Administration to be other than small based upon a timely size protest filed after award, the agency should terminate the contract and obtain the services from a small business offeror. Matter of: Spectrum Security Services, Inc., B-297320.2, B-297320.3, 2005 CPD ¶ 227 (Comp. Gen. 2005)

§ 15.504 Award to successful offeror.

The contracting officer shall award a contract to the successful offeror by furnishing the executed contract or other notice of the award to that offeror.

(a) If the award document includes information that is different than the latest signed proposal, as amended by the offeror's written correspondence, both the offeror and the contracting officer shall sign the contract award.

(b) When an award is made to an offeror for less than all of the items that may be awarded and additional items are being withheld for subsequent award, each notice shall state that the Government may make subsequent awards on those additional items within the proposal acceptance period.

(c) If the Optional Form (OF) 307, Contract Award, Standard Form (SF) 26, Award/Contract, or SF 33, Solicitation, Offer and Award, is not used to award the contract, the first page of the award document shall contain the Government's acceptance statement from Block 15 of that form, exclusive of the Item 3 reference language, and shall contain the contracting officer's name, signature, and date. In addition, if the award document includes information that is different than the signed proposal, as amended by the offeror's written correspondence, the first page shall include the contractor's agreement statement from Block 14 of the OF 307 and the signature of the contractor's authorized representative.

United States Code Annotated

Contract requirements, see 41 USCA § 254.

Contracts, planning, solicitation, evaluation, and award procedures, see 10 USCA § 2305.

Definitions, see 10 USCA § 2302, 41 USCA §§ 259, 403.

Evaluation and award, see 41 USCA § 253b.

Kinds of contracts, see 10 USCA § 2306.

Planning and solicitation requirements, see 41 USCA § 253a.

Notes of Decisions

Pre-award submissions 1

1 Pre-award submissions

Pre-award submissions, such as a work plan, are not part of a government contract unless the contract specifically provides that they are to be incorporated. Teg-Paradigm Environmental, Inc. v. U.S., 465 F.3d 1329 (Fed. Cir. 2006). United States ☞70(12.1)

§ 15.505 Preaward debriefing of offerors.

Offerors excluded from the competitive range or otherwise excluded from the competition before award may request a debriefing before award (10 U.S.C. 2305(b)(6)(A) and 41 U.S.C. 3705).

(a) (1) The offeror may request a preaward debriefing by submitting a written request for debriefing to the contracting officer within 3 days after receipt of the notice of exclusion from the competition.

(2) At the offeror's request, this debriefing may be delayed until after award. If the debriefing is delayed until after award, it shall include all information normally provided in a postaward debriefing (see 15.506(d)). Debriefings delayed pursuant to this paragraph could affect the timeliness of any protest filed subsequent to the debriefing.

(3) If the offeror does not submit a timely request, the offeror need not be given either a preaward or a postaward debriefing. Offerors are entitled to no more than one debriefing for each proposal.

(b) The contracting officer shall make every effort to debrief the unsuccessful offeror as soon as practicable, but may refuse the request for a debriefing if, for compelling reasons, it is not in the best interests of the Government to conduct a debriefing at that time. The rationale for delaying the debriefing shall be documented in the contract file. If the contracting officer delays the debriefing, it shall be provided no later than the time postaward debriefings are provided under 15.506. In that event, the contracting officer shall include the information at 15.506(d) in the debriefing.

(c) Debriefings may be done orally, in writing, or by any other method acceptable to the contracting officer.

(d) The contracting officer should normally chair any debriefing session held. Individuals who conducted the evaluations shall provide support.

(e) At a minimum, preaward debriefings shall include—

(1) The agency's evaluation of significant elements in the offeror's proposal;

(2) A summary of the rationale for eliminating the offeror from the competition; and

(3) Reasonable responses to relevant questions about whether source selection procedures contained in the solicitation, applicable regulations, and other applicable authorities were followed in the process of eliminating the offeror from the competition.

(f) Preaward debriefings shall not disclose—

(1) The number of offerors;

(2) The identity of other offerors;

(3) The content of other offerors' proposals;

(4) The ranking of other offerors;

(5) The evaluation of other offerors; or

(6) Any of the information prohibited in 15.506(e).

(g) An official summary of the debriefing shall be included in the contract file.

United States Code Annotated

Contract requirements, see 41 USCA § 254.

Contracts, planning, solicitation, evaluation, and award procedures, see 10 USCA § 2305.

Definitions, see 10 USCA § 2302, 41 USCA §§ 259, 403.

Evaluation and award, see 41 USCA § 253b.

Kinds of contracts, see 10 USCA § 2306.

Planning and solicitation requirements, see 41 USCA § 253a.

Notes of Decisions

Federal Supply Schedule procurements 1
Simplified acquisitions 2
Time to request debriefing 3

1 Federal Supply Schedule procurements

Although offeror requested a debriefing, GSA informed the offeror that because the procurement was conducted under the Federal Supply Schedule procedures established by FAR Subpart 8.4, as opposed to those under FAR Part 15, it was not required to provide the offeror with a formal debriefing as described under FAR sections 15.505 and 15.506. Rather, GSA was only required to provide the offeror with "a brief explanation of the basis for the award decision." FAR 8.405-2(d). Matter of: Computer Literacy World, Inc., B-299744, B-299744.4, 2007 CPD ¶ 154 (Comp. Gen. 2007)

2 Simplified acquisitions

Plaintiff's request for a debriefing also was based on the misunderstanding that this was a Part 15, rather than a Part 13, acquisition. Pre- and post-award debriefings are required (upon request) by FAR 15.505 and 15.506, respectively, and are not required by Part 13. FAR Part 13, see FAR § 13.106-3(d), merely provides that, upon request, contracting officers shall provide "information," "a brief explanation of the basis for the contract award decision." Seaborn Health Care, Inc. v. U.S., 55 Fed. Cl. 520 (2003)

3 Time to request debriefing

For purposes of FAR 15.505(a)(1), which provides that an offeror may request a preaward debriefing by submitting a written request for debriefing to the contracting officer within 3 days after receipt of the notice of exclusion from the competition, where e-mail notification of an offeror's exclusion from the competitive range enters the offeror's computer system after close of business or on a weekend or holiday and is not opened before the following business day, receipt of the notice is considered to have occurred on that business day. International Resources Group, B-286663, 2001 CPD ¶ 35 (Comp. Gen. 2001)

§ 15.506 Postaward debriefing of offerors.

(a) (1) An offeror, upon its written request received by the agency within 3 days after the date on which that offeror has received notification of contract award in accordance with 15.503(b), shall be debriefed and furnished the basis for the selection decision and contract award.

(2) To the maximum extent practicable, the debriefing should occur within 5 days after receipt of the written request. Offerors that requested a postaward debriefing in lieu of a preaward debriefing, or whose debriefing was delayed for compelling reasons beyond contract award, also should be debriefed within this time period.

(3) An offeror that was notified of exclusion from the competition (see 15.505(a)), but failed to submit a timely request, is not entitled to a debriefing.

(4) (i) Untimely debriefing requests may be accommodated.

(ii) Government accommodation of a request for delayed debriefing pursuant to 15.505(a)(2), or any untimely debriefing request, does not automatically extend the deadlines for filing protests. Debriefings delayed pursuant to 15.505(a)(2) could affect the timeliness of any protest filed subsequent to the debriefing.

(b) Debriefings of successful and unsuccessful offerors may be done orally, in writing, or by any other method acceptable to the contracting officer.

(c) The contracting officer should normally chair any debriefing session held. Individuals who conducted the evaluations shall provide support.

(d) At a minimum, the debriefing information shall include—

(1) The Government's evaluation of the significant weaknesses or deficiencies in the offeror's proposal, if applicable;

(2) The overall evaluated cost or price (including unit prices) and technical rating, if applicable, of the successful offeror and the debriefed offeror, and past performance information on the debriefed offeror;

(3) The overall ranking of all offerors, when any ranking was developed by the agency during the source selection;

(4) A summary of the rationale for award;

(5) For acquisitions of commercial items, the make and model of the item to be delivered by the successful offeror; and

(6) Reasonable responses to relevant questions about whether source selection

procedures contained in the solicitation, applicable regulations, and other applicable authorities were followed.

(e) The debriefing shall not include point-by-point comparisons of the debriefed offeror's proposal with those of other offerors. Moreover, the debriefing shall not reveal any information prohibited from disclosure by 24.202 or exempt from release under the Freedom of Information Act (5 U.S.C. 552) including—

(1) Trade secrets;

(2) Privileged or confidential manufacturing processes and techniques;

(3) Commercial and financial information that is privileged or confidential, including cost breakdowns, profit, indirect cost rates, and similar information; and

(4) The names of individuals providing reference information about an offeror's past performance.

(f) An official summary of the debriefing shall be included in the contract file.

United States Code Annotated

Contract requirements, see 41 USCA § 254.

Contracts, planning, solicitation, evaluation, and award procedures, see 10 USCA § 2305.

Definitions, see 10 USCA § 2302, 41 USCA §§ 259, 403.

Evaluation and award, see 41 USCA § 253b.

Kinds of contracts, see 10 USCA § 2306.

Planning and solicitation requirements, see 41 USCA § 253a.

Notes of Decisions

In general 1
Construction and application 2
Federal Supply Schedule procurements 3
Simplified acquisitions 4
Time to conduct debriefing 5
What cannot be released 7
What must be released 6

1 In general

Federal Acquisition Regulation (FAR) requiring disclosure to unsuccessful bidders of unit pricing information for government contracts, did not mandate disclosure of "B-tables" provided to General Services Administration (GSA) by providers of long distance telephone services; information in question consisted of pricing elements and components not required to be disclosed, rather than unit pricing. 48 C.F.R. §§ 15.503(b)(1), 15.506(d)(2). MCI Worldcom, Inc. v. General Services Admin., 163 F. Supp. 2d 28 (D.D.C. 2001). United States ☞64.55(1)

Contracting officer's disclosure to all offerors of their respective standing in the competitive price range, after agency disclosed such information during debriefing of one offeror and decided to reopen negotiations, did not violate the Procurement Integrity Act; informing all the offerors that they were in the high or low end of the competitive range was a reasonable means of serving to reduce the competitive advantage held by offeror who had received debriefing. Office of Federal Procurement Policy Act, § 27, as amended, 41 U.S.C.A. § 423. DGS Contract Service, Inc. v. U.S., 43 Fed. Cl. 227 (1999). United States ☞64.40(5)

2 Construction and application

Usual court deference to administrative agency, interpreting its own regulations, did not apply to case in which General Services Administration (GSA) was interpreting Federal Acquisition Regulation (FAR) as requiring disclosure to unsuccessful bidders of future years' pricing terms of long distance telephone services contract; FAR was joint product of several agencies. 48 C.F.R. §§ 15.503(b)(1), 15.506(d)(2). MCI Worldcom, Inc. v. General Services Admin., 163 F. Supp. 2d 28 (D.D.C. 2001). United States ☞64.55(1)

3 Federal Supply Schedule procurements

The whole of Part 15 is not applied to a solicitation under the Federal Supply Schedule

(FSS) merely because it employs some Part 15 procedures. Rather, only those portions that are particularly implicated by the procedures used will be applied to the solicitation. Where the solicitation did not specifically provide for a post-award debriefing, the post-award debriefing requirements found in subpart 15.506 are not applicable. Systems Plus, Inc. v. U.S., 68 Fed. Cl. 206 (2005)

Although offeror requested a debriefing, GSA informed the offeror that because the procurement was conducted under the Federal Supply Schedule procedures established by FAR Subpart 8.4, as opposed to those under FAR Part 15, it was not required to provide the offeror with a formal debriefing as described under FAR sections 15.505 and 15.506. Rather, GSA was only required to provide the offeror with "a brief explanation of the basis for the award decision." FAR 8.405-2(d). Matter of: Computer Literacy World, Inc., B-299744, B-299744.4, 2007 CPD ¶ 154 (Comp. Gen. 2007)

4 Simplified acquisitions

Plaintiff's request for a debriefing also was based on the misunderstanding that this was a Part 15, rather than a Part 13, acquisition. Pre- and post-award debriefings are required (upon request) by FAR 15.505 and 15.506, respectively, and are not required by Part 13. FAR Part 13, see FAR § 13.106-3(d), merely provides that, upon request, contracting officers shall provide "information," "a brief explanation of the basis for the contract award decision." Seaborn Health Care, Inc. v. U.S., 55 Fed. Cl. 520 (2003)

5 Time to conduct debriefing

Although the FAR states, "[t]o the extent practicable, the debriefing should occur within 5 days after the receipt of the written request," FAR 15.506(a)(2), it does not require that debriefings occur within five days. Plaintiff has not explained how, in light of the qualification provided by the first clause, the Government's delay in providing the debriefing slides violated FAR 15.506(a)(2). Heritage of America, LLC v. U.S., 77 Fed. Cl. 66 (2007)

Protest based on information obtained during post-award debriefing is not timely filed where protester who was excluded from competitive range requested that the debriefing be delayed until after award. United International Investigative Services, Inc., B-286327, 2000 CPD ¶ 173 (Comp. Gen. 2000)

6 What must be released

FAR 15.506(d)(2), which requires the contracting agency to release "the overall evaluated cost or price (including unit prices)," in a post-award debriefing, is qualfied by FAR 15.506(e), which prohibits release of "information . . . exempt from release under the Freedom of Information Act including . . . commercial and financial information that is privileged and confidential, including . . . profit, indirect cost rates, and similar information." Whether the overall cost or price or unit prices qualify as privileged or confidential turns on the particular facts of each case. Canadian Commercial Corp. v. Department of Air Force, 442 F. Supp. 2d 15 (D.D.C. 2006), judgment aff'd, 514 F.3d 37, 85 U.S.P.Q.2d 1693 (D.C. Cir. 2008).

7 What cannot be released

Information that is not releasable under the Freedom of Information Act (FOIA) cannot be released in a debriefing. Exemption 4 of FOIA protects from disclosure trade secrets and commercial or financial information obtained from a person that is privileged or confidential. 5 USCA § 552(b)(4). Commercial and financial information obtained involuntarily is confidential for purposes of the exemption if disclosure impairs the Government's ability to obtain necessary information in the future or causes substantial harm to the competitive position of the person from whom the information was obtained. The DC Circuit determined that line-item pricing in a Government contract is a confidential trade secret that may not be disclosed pursuant to a FOIA request if disclosure causes substantial harm to the competitive position of the contractor. Canadian Commercial Corp. v. Department of Air Force, 514 F.3d 37, 85 U.S.P.Q.2d 1693 (D.C. Cir. 2008)

Navy correctly refused to provide information to competitor of contractor that provided prototype of cylindrical orthogonal cylindrical arrangement air compressor that was new technology; if Government were forced to divulge every detail of new idea to competitor, then no company would be willing to go to government with novel or innovative concept. 10 U.S.C.A. § 2304(c)(1). Single Screw Compressor, Inc. v. U.S. Dept. of Navy, 791 F. Supp. 7,

38 Cont. Cas. Fed. (CCH) P 76403 (D.D.C. 1992). United States ☞64.10

§ 15.507 Protests against award.

(a) Protests against award in negotiated acquisitions shall be handled in accordance with Part 33. Use of agency protest procedures that incorporate the alternative dispute resolution provisions of Executive Order 12979 is encouraged for both preaward and postaward protests.

(b) If a protest causes the agency, within 1 year of contract award, to—

(1) Issue a new solicitation on the protested contract award, the contracting officer shall provide the information in paragraph (c) of this section to all prospective offerors for the new solicitation; or

(2) Issue a new request for revised proposals on the protested contract award, the contracting officer shall provide the information in paragraph (c) of this section to offerors that were in the competitive range and are requested to submit revised proposals.

(c) The following information will be provided to appropriate parties:

(1) Information provided to unsuccessful offerors in any debriefings conducted on the original award regarding the successful offeror's proposal; and

(2) Other nonproprietary information that would have been provided to the original offerors.

United States Code Annotated

Contract requirements, see 41 USCA § 254.

Contracts, planning, solicitation, evaluation, and award procedures, see 10 USCA § 2305.

Definitions, see 10 USCA § 2302, 41 USCA §§ 259, 403.

Evaluation and award, see 41 USCA § 253b.

Kinds of contracts, see 10 USCA § 2306.

Planning and solicitation requirements, see 41 USCA § 253a.

Notes of Decisions

Disclosure of information 1

1 Disclosure of information

When an unsuccessful offeror lawfully obtains source selection information, such as a competitor's prices and technical scores, and the agency subsequently properly reopens negotiations, the agency may disclose similar information to all the competitors to eliminate any competitive advantage. ManTech Telecommunications and Information Systems Corp. v. U.S., 49 Fed. Cl. 57 (2001), decision aff'd, 30 Fed. Appx. 995 (Fed. Cir. 2002)

Agency would not be permitted to disclose to contract awardee price information contained in proposal of bid protestor, as part of proposed corrective action, even though agency disclosed to protestor the price of awardee's proposal during debriefing, where the pricing information contained in protestor's proposal was fundamentally different from what it received during debriefing, so that disclosure would not equalize the competition, but provide awardee with an unwarranted advantage. ManTech Telecommunications and Information Systems Corp. v. U.S., 49 Fed. Cl. 57 (2001), decision aff'd, 30 Fed. Appx. 995 (Fed. Cir. 2002)

FAR 15.507 does not authorize agency's disclosure of offeror's unit pricing to other offerers on resolicitation of bid, where there was no contract award in original solicitation. Fore Systems Federal, Inc. v. U.S., 40 Fed. Cl. 490 (1998)

Protest that agency was required under FAR 15.507 to provide original awardee with information relating to unsuccessful offeror proposal prior to obtaining revised proposals is denied. When an agency reopens an acquisition as a consequence of a protest, FAR 15.507 requires only that the agency provide to all prospective offerors the information pertaining to the awardee's proposal that would have been provided to the other offerors in the course of a debriefing. Alatech Healthcare, LLC—Protest; Custom Services International, Inc.—Costs, B-289134.3, B-289134.4, 2002 CPD ¶ 73 (Comp. Gen. 2002)

Protest alleging that the agency violated the guidelines set forth at FAR 15.507, regarding competitions reopened in response to a protest, is denied where the agency concedes that it failed to advise the protester of the information regarding its proposal provided to unsuccessful offerors during their post-award debriefings, but the protester is unable to demonstrate how it was prejudiced by not receiving this information given the significant revisions to the solicitation between the initial and reopened competitions. Norvar Health Services—Protest and Reconsideration, B-286253.2, B-286253.3, B-286253.4, 2000 CPD ¶ 204 (Comp. Gen. 2000)

§ 15.508 Discovery of mistakes.

Mistakes in a contractor's proposal that are disclosed after award shall be processed substantially in accordance with the procedures for mistakes in bids at 14.407-4.

United States Code Annotated

Contract requirements, see 41 USCA § 254.

Contracts, planning, solicitation, evaluation, and award procedures, see 10 USCA § 2305.

Definitions, see 10 USCA § 2302, 41 USCA §§ 259, 403.

Evaluation and award, see 41 USCA § 253b.

Kinds of contracts, see 10 USCA § 2306.

Planning and solicitation requirements, see 41 USCA § 253a.

Notes of Decisions

In general 1

1 In general

A contractor seeking post-award reformation of its contract on grounds of unilateral mistake has the burden of proving by clear and convincing evidence the following five elements: (1) a mistake in fact occurred prior to contract award; (2) the mistake was a clear-cut, clerical or mathematical error or a misreading of the specifications and not a judgmental error; (3) prior to award the Government knew, or should have known, that a mistake had been made and, therefore, should have requested bid verification; (4) the Government did not request bid verification or its request for bid verification was inadequate; and (5) proof of the intended bid is established. A contractor is not precluded from recovery for unilateral mistake even though the contractor itself may have been negligent in preparing its bid or proposal. In re Holmes & Narver Constructions, Inc., A.S.B.C.A. No. 52429, 02-1, 02-1 B.C.A. (CCH) ¶ 31849, 2002 WL 1056380 (Armed Serv. B.C.A. 2002)

Contract awardee established existence of a unilateral mistake in omission of salary of employee in its final price proposal, and thus was entitled to reformation of contract, where mistake occurred prior to award of contract, it was clerical in nature, contracting officer (CO) had constructive notice of error from disparity between awardee's bid and next lowest bid, government did not request verification, and awardee established by clear and convincing evidence the correct amount of its bid. Information Intern. Associates, Inc. v. U.S., 74 Fed. Cl. 192 (2006)

Government contractor could not invoke doctrine of mutual mistake to reform contract to include state sales tax in contract price, although both parties were mistaken concerning treatment of states sales tax in the contract, where contractor's mistake concerned the tax exemption status of materials used in the project, and government's mistake concerned the inclusion of state sales tax in unit prices contained in agency's Unit Price Book (UPB), and thus errors were separate and not mutual. C.W. Over & Sons, Inc. v. U.S., 54 Fed. Cl. 514 (2002). Reformation Of Instruments ⟜19(2)

Government contractor could not invoke doctrine of unilateral mistake to reform contract to include state sales tax in contract price, absent evidence that contracting officers knew of alleged mistake which was contractor's erroneous interpretation of contract clause as indicating that entire project was exempt from state tax; moreover, even if contracting officers should have known of contractor's mistake, it was a mistake in judgment and not a misreading of specifications, and thus was not compensable under the doctrine. C.W. Over & Sons, Inc. v. U.S., 54 Fed. Cl. 514 (2002). Reformation Of Instruments ⟜17(1)

To be entitled to reformation under unilateral mistake, government contractor must show that the contracting officer knew or should have known of the contractor's unilateral mistake at the time its bid was accepted; moreover, the mistaken proposal must contain a clear cut clerical or arithmetical error, or misreading of the specifications. C.W. Over & Sons, Inc. v. U.S., 54 Fed. Cl. 514 (2002). Reformation Of Instruments ☞17(1)

Government contractor could not invoke doctrine of unilateral mistake to reform contract to include state sales tax in contract price, absent evidence that contracting agency knew of alleged mistake, or that the error was compensable. C.W. Over & Sons, Inc. v. U.S., 44 Fed. Cl. 18 (1999). United States ☞72(1.1); United States ☞74(4)

Government contractor could not invoke doctrine of mutual mistake to reform contract to include state sales tax in contract price, absent evidence that contacting agency mistakenly believed that the it was exempt from state sales tax, or that the agency was mistaken in its belief that the unit price book (UPB) already included sales tax. C.W. Over & Sons, Inc. v. U.S., 44 Fed. Cl. 18 (1999). United States ☞72(1.1)

In addition to establishing knowledge on the part of the contracting officer, contractor seeking to obtain relief from the government for a mistaken bid must demonstrate that the error is compensable, i.e., a clear cut clerical or arithmetical error, or misreading of the specification. C.W. Over & Sons, Inc. v. U.S., 44 Fed. Cl. 18 (1999). United States ☞74(4)

Under the doctrine of unilateral mistake, a contractor may obtain a remedy from the government for a mistaken bid only if the contracting officer knew or should have known of the contractor's unilateral mistake at the time the bid was accepted. C.W. Over & Sons, Inc. v. U.S., 44 Fed. Cl. 18 (1999). United States ☞74(4)

§ 15.509 Forms.

Optional Form 307, Contract Award, Standard Form (SF) 26, Award/Contract, or SF 33, Solicitation, Offer and Award, may be used to award negotiated contracts in which the signature of both parties on a single document is appropriate. If these forms are not used, the award document shall incorporate the agreement and award language from the OF 307.

United States Code Annotated

Contract requirements, see 41 USCA § 254.

Contracts, planning, solicitation, evaluation, and award procedures, see 10 USCA § 2305.

Definitions, see 10 USCA § 2302, 41 USCA §§ 259, 403.

Evaluation and award, see 41 USCA § 253b.

Kinds of contracts, see 10 USCA § 2306.

Planning and solicitation requirements, see 41 USCA § 253a.

Subpart 15.6 Unsolicited Proposals

§ 15.600 Scope of subpart.

This subpart sets forth policies and procedures concerning the submission, receipt, evaluation, and acceptance or rejection of unsolicited proposals.

United States Code Annotated

Contract requirements, see 41 USCA § 254.

Contracts, planning, solicitation, evaluation, and award procedures, see 10 USCA § 2305.

Definitions, see 10 USCA § 2302, 41 USCA §§ 259, 403.

Evaluation and award, see 41 USCA § 253b.

Kinds of contracts, see 10 USCA § 2306.

Planning and solicitation requirements, see 41 USCA § 253a.

§ 15.601 Definitions.

As used in this subpart—

"Advertising material" means material designed to acquaint the Government with a prospective contractor's present products, services, or potential capabilities, or designed to stimulate the Government's interest in buying such products or services.

"Commercial item offer" means an offer of a commercial item that the vendor wishes to see introduced in the Government's supply system as an alternate or a replacement for an existing supply item. This term does not include innovative or unique configurations or uses of commercial items that are being offered for further development and that may be submitted as an unsolicited proposal.

"Contribution" means a concept, suggestion, or idea presented to the Government for its use with no indication that the source intends to devote any further effort to it on the Government's behalf.

United States Code Annotated

Contract requirements, see 41 USCA § 254.

Contracts, planning, solicitation, evaluation, and award procedures, see 10 USCA § 2305.

Definitions, see 10 USCA § 2302, 41 USCA §§ 259, 403.

Evaluation and award, see 41 USCA § 253b.

Kinds of contracts, see 10 USCA § 2306.

Planning and solicitation requirements, see 41 USCA § 253a.

Notes of Decisions
Unsolicited proposals 1

1 Unsolicited proposals

Contracting officer for government lease did not improperly accept unsolicited proposal by bidder, where bidder submitted proposal for lease in view of outstanding solicitation for offers (SFO) for office space, and thus bidder's proposal was not "unsolicited proposal." Aerolease Long Beach v. U.S., 31 Fed. Cl. 342, 39 Cont. Cas. Fed. (CCH) P 76654, 39 Cont. Cas. Fed. (CCH) P 76655, 39 Cont. Cas. Fed. (CCH) P 76656 (1994), aff'd, 39 F.3d 1198 (Fed. Cir. 1994). United States ⬌64.40(1)

§ 15.602 Policy.

It is the policy of the Government to encourage the submission of new and innovative ideas in response to Broad Agency Announcements, Small Business Innovation Research topics, Small Business Technology Transfer Research topics, Program Research and Development Announcements, or any other Government-initiated solicitation or program. When the new and innovative ideas do not fall under topic areas publicized under those programs or techniques, the ideas may be submitted as unsolicited proposals.

United States Code Annotated

Contract requirements, see 41 USCA § 254.

Contracts, planning, solicitation, evaluation, and award procedures, see 10 USCA § 2305.

Definitions, see 10 USCA § 2302, 41 USCA §§ 259, 403.

Evaluation and award, see 41 USCA § 253b.

Kinds of contracts, see 10 USCA § 2306.

Planning and solicitation requirements, see 41 USCA § 253a.

§ 15.603 General.

(a) Unsolicited proposals allow unique and innovative ideas or approaches that have been developed outside the Government to be made available to Government agencies for use in accomplishment of their missions. Unsolicited proposals are offered with the intent that the Government will enter into a contract with the offeror for research and development or other efforts supporting the Government mission, and often represent a substantial investment of time and effort by the offeror.

(b) Advertising material, commercial item offers, or contributions, as defined in 15.601, or routine correspondence on technical issues, are not unsolicited proposals.

(c) A valid unsolicited proposal must—

(1) Be innovative and unique;

(2) Be independently originated and developed by the offeror;

(3) Be prepared without Government supervision, endorsement, direction, or direct Government involvement;

(4) Include sufficient detail to permit a determination that Government support could be worthwhile and the proposed work could benefit the agency's research and development or other mission responsibilities;

(5) Not be an advance proposal for a known agency requirement that can be acquired by competitive methods; and

(6) Not address a previously published agency requirement.

(d) Unsolicited proposals in response to a publicized general statement of agency needs are considered to be independently originated.

(e) Agencies must evaluate unsolicited proposals for energy-savings performance contracts in accordance with the procedures in 10 CFR 436.33(b).

United States Code Annotated

Contract requirements, see 41 USCA § 254.

Contracts, planning, solicitation, evaluation, and award procedures, see 10 USCA § 2305.

Definitions, see 10 USCA § 2302, 41 USCA §§ 259, 403.

Evaluation and award, see 41 USCA § 253b.

Kinds of contracts, see 10 USCA § 2306.

Planning and solicitation requirements, see 41 USCA § 253a.

Notes of Decisions

In general 1

1 In general

Protester, whose unsolicited proposal was rejected by the Navy, failed to meet burden to establish that the proposal had substantial chance of receiving a contract award, as required to have standing to bring action against United States asserting that he was prejudiced by alleged error in procurement process. The Contracting Officer reasonably determined that protester's unsolicited proposal failed to meet the requirement of FAR 15.603 that an unsolicited proposal be innovative and unique, which was a preliminary determination that necessarily preceded more comprehensive evaluation. Navy undertook serious review of proposal and carefully explained reasons for not initiating more comprehensive evaluation, and thus, even if proposal had been forwarded for comprehensive evaluation, there was not a substantial chance of receiving funding and contract award. Diaz v. U.S., 127 Fed.Cl. 664(2016)

§ 15.604 Agency points of contact.

(a) Preliminary contact with agency technical or other appropriate personnel before preparing a detailed unsolicited proposal or submitting proprietary information to the Government may save considerable time and effort for both parties (see 15.201). Agencies must make available to potential offerors of unsolicited proposals at least the following information:

(1) Definition (see 2.101) and content (see 15.605) of an unsolicited proposal acceptable for formal evaluation.

(2) Requirements concerning responsible prospective contractors (see Subpart 9.1), and organizational conflicts of interest (see Subpart 9.5).

(3) Guidance on preferred methods for submitting ideas/concepts to the Government, such as any agency: upcoming solicitations; Broad Agency Announcements; Small Business Innovation Research programs; Small Business Technology Transfer Research programs; Program Research and Development Announcements; or grant programs.

(4) Agency points of contact for information regarding advertising, contributions, and other types of transactions similar to unsolicited proposals.

(5) Information sources on agency objectives and areas of potential interest.

(6) Procedures for submission and evaluation of unsolicited proposals.

(7) Instructions for identifying and marking proprietary information so that it is protected and restrictive legends conform to 15.609.

(b) Only the cognizant contracting officer has the authority to bind the Government regarding unsolicited proposals.

United States Code Annotated

Contract requirements, see 41 USCA § 254.

Contracts, planning, solicitation, evaluation, and award procedures, see 10 USCA § 2305.

Definitions, see 10 USCA § 2302, 41 USCA §§ 259, 403.

Evaluation and award, see 41 USCA § 253b.

Kinds of contracts, see 10 USCA § 2306.

Planning and solicitation requirements, see 41 USCA § 253a.

§ 15.605 Content of unsolicited proposals.

Unsolicited proposals should contain the following information to permit consideration in an objective and timely manner:

(a) Basic information including—

(1) Offeror's name and address and type of organization; *e.g.,* profit, nonprofit, educational, small business;

(2) Names and telephone numbers of technical and business personnel to be contacted for evaluation or negotiation purposes;

(3) Identification of proprietary data to be used only for evaluation purposes;

(4) Names of other Federal, State, or local agencies or parties receiving the proposal or funding the proposed effort;

(5) Date of submission; and

(6) Signature of a person authorized to represent and contractually obligate the offeror.

(b) Technical information including—

(1) Concise title and abstract (approximately 200 words) of the proposed effort;

(2) A reasonably complete discussion stating the objectives of the effort or activity, the method of approach and extent of effort to be employed, the nature and extent of the anticipated results, and the manner in which the work will help to support accomplishment of the agency's mission;

(3) Names and biographical information on the offeror's key personnel who would be involved, including alternates; and

(4) Type of support needed from the agency; *e.g.,* Government property or personnel resources.

(c) Supporting information including—

(1) Proposed price or total estimated cost for the effort in sufficient detail for meaningful evaluation;

(2) Period of time for which the proposal is valid (a 6-month minimum is suggested);

(3) Type of contract preferred;

(4) Proposed duration of effort;

(5) Brief description of the organization, previous experience, relevant past performance, and facilities to be used;

(6) Other statements, if applicable, about organizational conflicts of interest, security clearances, and environmental impacts; and

(7) The names and telephone numbers of agency technical or other agency points of contact already contacted regarding the proposal.

United States Code Annotated

Contract requirements, see 41 USCA § 254.

Contracts, planning, solicitation, evaluation, and award procedures, see 10 USCA § 2305.

Definitions, see 10 USCA § 2302, 41 USCA §§ 259, 403.

Evaluation and award, see 41 USCA § 253b.

Kinds of contracts, see 10 USCA § 2306.

Planning and solicitation requirements, see 41 USCA § 253a.

§ 15.606 Agency procedures.

(a) Agencies shall establish procedures for controlling the receipt, evaluation, and timely disposition of unsolicited proposals consistent with the requirements of this subpart. The procedures shall include controls on the reproduction and disposition of proposal material, particularly data identified by the offeror as subject to duplication, use, or disclosure restrictions.

(b) Agencies shall establish agency points of contact (see 15.604) to coordinate the receipt and handling of unsolicited proposals.

United States Code Annotated

Contract requirements, see 41 USCA § 254.

Contracts, planning, solicitation, evaluation, and award procedures, see 10 USCA § 2305.

Definitions, see 10 USCA § 2302, 41 USCA §§ 259, 403.

Evaluation and award, see 41 USCA § 253b.

Kinds of contracts, see 10 USCA § 2306.

Planning and solicitation requirements, see 41 USCA § 253a.

§ 15.606-1 Receipt and initial review.

(a) Before initiating a comprehensive evaluation, the agency contact point shall determine if the proposal—

(1) Is a valid unsolicited proposal, meeting the requirements of 15.603(c);

(2) Is suitable for submission in response to an existing agency requirement (see 15.602);

(3) Is related to the agency mission;

(4) Contains sufficient technical information and costrelated or price-related information for evaluation;

(5) Has overall scientific, technical, or socioeconomic merit;

(6) Has been approved by a responsible official or other representative authorized to obligate the offeror contractually; and

(7) Complies with the marking requirements of 15.609.

(b) If the proposal meets these requirements, the contact point shall promptly acknowledge receipt and process the proposal.

(c) If a proposal is rejected because the proposal does not meet the requirements of paragraph (a) of this subsection, the agency contact point shall promptly inform the offeror of the reasons for rejection in writing and of the proposed disposition of the unsolicited proposal.

United States Code Annotated

Contract requirements, see 41 USCA § 254.

Contracts, planning, solicitation, evaluation, and award procedures, see 10 USCA § 2305.

Definitions, see 10 USCA § 2302, 41 USCA §§ 259, 403.

Evaluation and award, see 41 USCA § 253b.

Kinds of contracts, see 10 USCA § 2306.

Planning and solicitation requirements, see 41 USCA § 253a.

§ 15.606-2 Evaluation.

(a) Comprehensive evaluations shall be coordinated by the agency contact point, who shall attach or imprint on each unsolicited proposal, circulated for evaluation, the legend required by 15.609(d). When performing a comprehensive evaluation of an unsolicited proposal, evaluators shall consider the following factors, in addition to any others appropriate for the particular proposal:

(1) Unique, innovative, and meritorious methods, approaches, or concepts demonstrated by the proposal;

(2) Overall scientific, technical, or socioeconomic merits of the proposal;

(3) Potential contribution of the effort to the agency's specific mission;

(4) The offeror's capabilities, related experience, facilities, techniques, or unique combinations of these that are integral factors for achieving the proposal objectives;

(5) The qualifications, capabilities, and experience of the proposed principal investigator, team leader, or key personnel critical to achieving the proposal objectives; and

(6) The realism of the proposed cost.

(b) The evaluators shall notify the agency point of contact of their recommendations when the evaluation is completed.

United States Code Annotated

Contract requirements, see 41 USCA § 254.

Contracts, planning, solicitation, evaluation, and award procedures, see 10 USCA § 2305.

Definitions, see 10 USCA § 2302, 41 USCA §§ 259, 403.

Evaluation and award, see 41 USCA § 253b.

Kinds of contracts, see 10 USCA § 2306.

Planning and solicitation requirements, see 41 USCA § 253a.

§ 15.607 Criteria for acceptance and negotiation of an unsolicited proposal.

(a) A favorable comprehensive evaluation of an unsolicited proposal does not, in itself, justify awarding a contract without providing for full and open competition. The agency point of contact shall return an unsolicited proposal to the offeror, citing reasons, when its substance—

(1) Is available to the Government without restriction from another source;

(2) Closely resembles a pending competitive acquisition requirement;

(3) Does not relate to the activity's mission; or

(4) Does not demonstrate an innovative and unique method, approach, or concept, or is otherwise not deemed a meritorious proposal.

(b) The contracting officer may commence negotiations on a sole source basis only when—

(1) An unsolicited proposal has received a favorable comprehensive evaluation;

(2) A justification and approval has been obtained (see 6.302-1(a)(2)(i) for research proposals or other appropriate provisions of Subpart 6.3, and 6.303-2(c));

(3) The agency technical office sponsoring the contract furnishes the necessary funds; and

(4) The contracting officer has complied with the synopsis requirements of Subpart 5.2.

United States Code Annotated

Contract requirements, see 41 USCA § 254.

Contracts, planning, solicitation, evaluation, and award procedures, see 10 USCA § 2305.

Definitions, see 10 USCA § 2302, 41 USCA §§ 259, 403.

Evaluation and award, see 41 USCA § 253b.

Kinds of contracts, see 10 USCA § 2306.

Planning and solicitation requirements, see 41 USCA § 253a.

§ 15.608 Prohibitions.

(a) Government personnel shall not use any data, concept, idea, or other part of an unsolicited proposal as the basis, or part of the basis, for a solicitation or in negotiations with any other firm unless the offeror is notified of and agrees to the intended use. However, this prohibition does not preclude using any data, concept, or idea in the proposal that also is available from another source without restriction.

(b) Government personnel shall not disclose restrictively marked information (see 3.104 and 15.609) included in an unsolicited proposal. The disclosure of such information concerning trade secrets, processes, operations, style of work, apparatus, and other matters, except as authorized by law, may result in criminal penalties under 18 U.S.C. 1905.

United States Code Annotated

Contract requirements, see 41 USCA § 254.

Contracts, planning, solicitation, evaluation, and award procedures, see 10 USCA § 2305.

Definitions, see 10 USCA § 2302, 41 USCA §§ 259, 403.

Evaluation and award, see 41 USCA § 253b.

Kinds of contracts, see 10 USCA § 2306.

Planning and solicitation requirements, see 41 USCA § 253a.

Notes of Decisions

Constitutional issue 3
Non-proprietary information 1
Restrictively marked information 2

1 Non-proprietary information

Allegation that agency misappropriated information contained in protester's unsolicited proposal and developed specifications based on that information is denied where protester has not met its burden of showing proprietary nature of information allegedly misappropriated. Information that contractor was alleging was proprietary had been posted by the contractor on its website and once proprietary information becomes public knowledge, it is no longer considered proprietary. Digital Healthcare, Inc., B-296489, 2005 CPD ¶ 166 (Comp. Gen. 2005)

Solicitation did not improperly disclose protester's design information where information was contained in a brochure the protester previously had provided to the agency without restrictions on its use or disclosure, or any indication that the protester considered the information confidential or proprietary; restriction on the use of ideas in unsolicited proposal does not apply where information was furnished to agency in advertising material, not an unsolicited proposal. Metrick Systems Corporation, B-271578, 96-2 CPD ¶ 8 (Comp. Gen. 1996)

2 Restrictively marked information

Information included in unsolicited proposal by contractor to Patrick Air Force Base was not subject to proprietary data protections of federal acquisition regulations (FAR); although contractor marked title page of its unsolicited proposal, it failed to include restrictive legend on each sheet of data it wanted restricted. 48 C.F.R. §§ 15.608, 15.609. Xerxe Group, Inc. v. U.S., 278 F.3d 1357 (Fed. Cir. 2002). United States ⊶64.30

When United States Geological Survey received "unsolicited proposal" submitted by company which disclosed trade secrets but included restrictive legend which forbade use or disclosure for any purpose other than evaluation of proposal, there was meeting of the minds that Survey could use data but was scrupulously to safeguard confidentiality of data in accordance with terms of restrictive legend and not to use it unless permitted to do so by terms of legend itself. Airborne Data, Inc. v. U.S., 702 F.2d 1350, 217 U.S.P.Q. 297, 30 Cont. Cas. Fed. (CCH) ¶ 70905 (Fed. Cir. 1983)

No implied-in-fact contract was formed between the government and contractor who submitted unsolicited contract proposal whereby the government agreed to protect proprietary data in proposal, where contractor did not identify any proprietary information in his proposal that he wished to keep confidential in compliance with agency regulation governing unsolicited proposals, and thus government could not manifest its intent to protect the information. Block v. U.S., 66 Fed. Cl. 68 (2005)

Paragraph in Federal Aviation Administration (FAA) regulation admonishing FAA personnel against using information in unsolicited contract proposals did not create an implied-in-fact contract to maintain the confidentiality of proprietary information in such a proposal, where the FAA stated in its procurement regulations that even though the regulation required protection of unsolicited proposals, the FAA did not agree to be liable for disclosing or using data contained in such proposals. Block v. U.S., 66 Fed. Cl. 68 (2005)

3 Constitutional issue

When United States Geological Survey disclosed information contained in "unsolicited proposal" submitted by company which contained trade secrets but included restrictive legend which forbade use or disclosure for any purpose other than evaluation of proposal,

Survey's actions with respect to the technology did not amount to taking of private property for public purpose within meaning of Fifth Amendment. U.S.C.A. Const.Amend. 5. Airborne Data, Inc. v. U.S., 702 F.2d 1350, 217 U.S.P.Q. 297, 30 Cont. Cas. Fed. (CCH) ¶ 70905 (Fed. Cir. 1983)

Contractor who submitted unsolicited proposal for government contract to the Federal Aviation Administration (FAA) lost any property interest he had in alleged proprietary information in proposal which could be subject of a taking claim under the Fifth Amendment when he failed to mark his proposal "confidential" or "trade secret," or to place any restrictive markings on his proposal before submitting it to agency personnel. U.S.C.A. Const. Amend. 5. Block v. U.S., 66 Fed. Cl. 68 (2005)

§ 15.609 Limited use of data.

(a) An unsolicited proposal may include data that the offeror does not want disclosed to the public for any purpose or used by the Government except for evaluation purposes. If the offeror wishes to restrict the data, the title page must be marked with the following legend:

USE AND DISCLOSURE OF DATA

This proposal includes data that shall not be disclosed outside the Government and shall not be duplicated, used, or disclosed— in whole or in part—for any purpose other than to evaluate this proposal. However, if a contract is awarded to this offeror as a result of—or in connection with—the submission of these data, the Government shall have the right to duplicate, use, or disclose the data to the extent provided in the resulting contract. This restriction does not limit the Government's right to use information contained in these data if they are obtained from another source without restriction. The data subject to this restriction are contained in Sheets [insert numbers or other identification of sheets].

(b) The offeror shall also mark each sheet of data it wishes to restrict with the following legend: Use or disclosure of data contained on this sheet is subject to the restriction on the title page of this proposal.

(c) The agency point of contact shall return to the offeror any unsolicited proposal marked with a legend different from that provided in paragraph (a) of this section. The return letter will state that the proposal cannot be considered because it is impracticable for the Government to comply with the legend and that the agency will consider the proposal if it is resubmitted with the proper legend.

(d) The agency point of contact shall place a cover sheet on the proposal or clearly mark it as follows, unless the offeror clearly states in writing that no restrictions are imposed on the disclosure or use of the data contained in the proposal:

Unsolicited Proposal—Use of Data Limited

All Government personnel must exercise extreme care to ensure that the information in this proposal is not disclosed to an individual who has not been authorized access to such data in accordance with FAR 3.104, and is not duplicated, used, or disclosed in whole or in part for any purpose other than evaluation of the proposal, without the written permission of the offeror. If a contract is awarded on the basis of this proposal, the terms of the contract shall control disclosure and use. This notice does not limit the Government's right to use information contained in the proposal if it is obtainable from another source without restriction. This is a Government notice, and shall not by itself be construed to impose any liability upon the Government or Government personnel for disclosure or use of data contained in this proposal.

(e) Use the notice in paragraph (d) of this section solely as a manner of handling unsolicited proposals that will be compatible with this subpart. However, do not use this notice to justify withholding of a record, or to improperly deny the public access to a record, where an obligation is imposed by the Freedom of Information Act (5 U.S.C. 552). An offeror should identify trade secrets, commercial or financial information, and privileged or confidential information to the Government (see paragraph (a) of this section).

(f) When an agency receives an unsolicited proposal without any restrictive legend from an educational or nonprofit organization or institution, and an evaluation outside the Government is necessary, the agency point of contact shall—

(1) Attach a cover sheet clearly marked with the legend in paragraph (d) of this section;

(2) Change the beginning of this legend to read "All Government and non-Government personnel . . . ."; and

(3) Require any non-Government evaluator to agree in writing that data in the pro-

posal will not be disclosed to others outside the Government.

(g) If the proposal is received with the restrictive legend (see paragraph (a) of this section), the modified cover sheet shall also be used and permission shall be obtained from the offeror before release of the proposal for evaluation by non-Government personnel.

(h) When an agency receives an unsolicited proposal with or without a restrictive legend from other than an educational or nonprofit organization or institution, and evaluation by Government personnel outside the agency or by experts outside of the Government is necessary, written permission must be obtained from the offeror before release of the proposal for evaluation. The agency point of contact shall—

(1) Clearly mark the cover sheet with the legend in paragraph (d) or as modified in paragraph (f) of this section; and

(2) Obtain a written agreement from any non-Government evaluator stating that data in the proposal will not be disclosed to persons outside the Government.

United States Code Annotated

Contract requirements, see 41 USCA § 254.

Contracts, planning, solicitation, evaluation, and award procedures, see 10 USCA § 2305.

Definitions, see 10 USCA § 2302, 41 USCA §§ 259, 403.

Evaluation and award, see 41 USCA § 253b.

Kinds of contracts, see 10 USCA § 2306.

Planning and solicitation requirements, see 41 USCA § 253a.

Notes of Decisions

Damages for improper disclosure of data 3
Non-proprietary information 1
Restrictively marked information 2

1 Non-proprietary information

Allegation that agency misappropriated information contained in protester's unsolicited proposal and developed specifications based on that information is denied where protester has not met its burden of showing proprietary nature of information allegedly misappropriated. Information that contractor was alleging was proprietary had been posted by the contractor on its website and once proprietary information becomes public knowledge, it is no longer considered proprietary. Digital Healthcare, Inc., B-296489, 2005 CPD ¶ 166 (Comp. Gen. 2005)

Solicitation did not improperly disclose protester's design information where information was contained in a brochure the protester previously had provided to the agency without restrictions on its use or disclosure, or any indication that the protester considered the information confidential or proprietary; restriction on the use of ideas in unsolicited proposal does not apply where information was furnished to agency in advertising material, not an unsolicited proposal. Metrick Systems Corporation, B-271578, 96-2 CPD ¶ 8 (Comp. Gen. 1996)

2 Restrictively marked information

Information included in unsolicited proposal by contractor to Patrick Air Force Base was not subject to proprietary data protections of federal acquisition regulations (FAR); although contractor marked title page of its unsolicited proposal, it failed to include restrictive legend on each sheet of data it wanted restricted. 48 C.F.R. §§ 15.608, 15.609. Xerxe Group, Inc. v. U.S., 278 F.3d 1357 (Fed. Cir. 2002). United States ☞64.30

When United States Geological Survey received "unsolicited proposal" submitted by company which disclosed trade secrets but included restrictive legend which forbade use or disclosure for any purpose other than evaluation of proposal, there was meeting of the minds that Survey could use data but was scrupulously to safeguard confidentiality of data in accordance with terms of restrictive legend and not to use it unless permitted to do so by terms of legend itself. Airborne Data, Inc. v. U.S., 702 F.2d 1350, 217 U.S.P.Q. 297, 30 Cont. Cas. Fed. (CCH) ¶ 70905 (Fed. Cir. 1983)

No implied-in-fact contract was formed between the government and contractor who submitted unsolicited contract proposal whereby the government agreed to protect proprietary data in proposal, where contractor did not identify any proprietary information in his proposal that he wished to keep confidential in compliance with agency regulation governing unsolicited proposals, and thus government could not manifest its intent to protect the information. Block v. U.S., 66 Fed. Cl. 68 (2005)

Paragraph in Federal Aviation Administration (FAA) regulation admonishing FAA personnel against using information in unsolicited contract proposals did not create an implied-in-fact contract to maintain the confidentiality of proprietary information in such a proposal, where the FAA stated in its procurement regulations that even though the regulation required protection of unsolicited proposals, the FAA did not agree to be liable for disclosing or using data contained in such proposals. Block v. U.S., 66 Fed. Cl. 68 (2005)

3 Damages for improper disclosure of data

Where United States Geological Survey extended a valid and authorized invitation to submit unsolicited proposal containing ideas originated, conceived or developed by company and prescribed how, on submitting proposal, company might indicate that it did not want its ideas disclosed to public, Survey stated that all Government personnel would comply with terms of restrictive legend, and company accepted that invitation and submitted unsolicited proposal which disclosed trade secrets and contained restrictive legend, Government had obligation to maintain trade secrets and, upon breach of that obligation, right to monetary damages resulting from that breach was enforceable. Airborne Data, Inc. v. U.S., 702 F.2d 1350, 217 U.S.P.Q. 297, 30 Cont. Cas. Fed. (CCH) ¶ 70905 (Fed. Cir. 1983)

PART 16 TYPES OF CONTRACTS

Subpart 16.4 Incentive Contracts

Subpart 16.5 Indefinite-Delivery Contracts

Subpart 16.6 Time-and-Materials, Labor-Hour, and Letter Contracts

Subpart 16.7 Agreements

§ 16.000 Scope of part.

This part describes types of contracts that may be used in acquisitions. It prescribes policies and procedures and provides guidance for selecting a contract type appropriate to the circumstances of the acquisition.

§ 16.001 Definitions.

As used in this part—

Award-Fee Board means the team of individuals identified in the award-fee plan who have been designated to assist the Fee-Determining Official in making award-fee determinations.

Fee-Determining Official (FDO) means the designated Agency official(s) who reviews the recommendations of the Award-Fee Board in determining the amount of award fee to be earned by the contractor for each evaluation period.

Rollover of unearned award fee means the process of transferring unearned award fee, which the contractor had an opportunity to earn, from one evaluation period to a subsequent evaluation period, thus allowing the contractor an additional opportunity to earn that previously unearned award fee.

Subpart 16.1 Selecting Contract Types

§ 16.101 General.

(a) A wide selection of contract types is available to the Government and contractors in order to provide needed flexibility in acquiring the large variety and volume of supplies and services required by agencies. Contract types vary according to—

(1) The degree and timing of the responsibility assumed by the contractor for the costs of performance; and

(2) The amount and nature of the profit incentive offered to the contractor for achieving or exceeding specified standards or goals.

(b) The contract types are grouped into two broad categories: fixed-price contracts (see Subpart 16.2) and cost-reimbursement contracts (see Subpart 16.3). The specific contract types range from firm-fixed-price, in which the contractor has full responsibility for the performance costs and resulting profit (or loss), to cost-plus-fixed-fee, in which the contractor has minimal responsibility for the performance costs and the negotiated fee (profit) is fixed. In between are the various incentive contracts (see Subpart 16.4), in which the contractor's responsibility for the performance costs and the profit or fee incentives offered are tailored to the uncertainties involved in contract performance.

United States Code Annotated

Contract requirements, see 41 USCA § 254.

Contracts, planning, solicitation, evaluation, and award procedures, see 10 USCA § 2305.

Cost-type research and development contracts with educational institutions, see 41 USCA § 254a.

Definitions, see 10 USCA § 2302, 41 USCA §§ 259, 403.

Kinds of contracts, see 10 USCA § 2306.

Planning and solicitation requirements, see 41 USCA § 253a.

Task and delivery order contracts, definitions, see 10 USCA § 2304d, 41 USCA § 253k.

Task and delivery order contracts, general authority, see 10 USCA § 2304a, 41 USCA § 253h.

Task and delivery order contracts, orders, see 10 USCA § 2304c, 41 USCA § 253j.

Task order contracts, advisory and assistance services, see 10 USCA § 2304b, 41 USCA § 253i.

Notes of Decisions

Authority of officers to contract 18
Basic agreements, generally 16
Basic ordering agreements 17
Cost-plus-award-fee contracts 10
Cost-plus-fixed-fee contracts 8
Cost-plus-incentive-fee contracts 7
Cost-reimbursement contracts, generally 6
Court of Federal Claims jurisdiction 20
Economic price adjustment 4
Firm-fixed-price contracts 3
Fixed-price contracts, generally 2
Fixed-price incentive contracts 9
Indefinite-delivery contracts, generally 11

1 Negotiating contract type

Even if contracting officer abused his discretion under procurement regulations and directives by negotiating contract on a fixed-price basis, contractor that incurred costs in excess of price fixed in contract for research and development of technology for tracking ultra-quiet submarines had no remedy that could be provided in judicial forum, since cautionary and informative regulations and directives provided only internal governmental direction, and discipline to be administered was a responsibility of cognizant agency procurement officials. 48 C.F.R. §§ 16.103(a), 16.104, 35.006(b, c), 216.104. American Tel. and Tel. Co. v. U.S., 307 F.3d 1374 (Fed. Cir. 2002). United States ☞74(1)

2 Fixed-price contracts, generally

While Cost Accounting Standard (CAS) providing for adjustment of pension costs under government contracts in response to contractor's segment closings applies to both fixed- and flexibly-priced government contracts, determination of whether any adjustment was recoverable depended on terms of particular contract. 4 C.F.R. § 413-50(c)(12) (1986). Allegheny Teledyne Inc. v. U.S., 316 F.3d 1366, 30 Employee Benefits Cas. (BNA) 1753 (Fed. Cir. 2003). United States ☞70(18)

Amended version of Cost Accounting Standard (CAS), which provided for adjustment of pension costs under government contracts in response to contractor's segment closings, did not apply retroactively, where pension surplus that was attributable to CAS-covered government contracts arose under contracts that contained only the original "segment closing" provision, pursuant to which contractor was not liable for any pension surplus attributable to its fixed-price contracts; applying the CAS retroactively to such contracts would amount to a change in accounting practices and entitle contractor to equitable adjustment under another federal regulation. 48 C.F.R. § 52.230-2(a)(4)(i). Allegheny Teledyne Inc. v. U.S., 316 F.3d 1366, 30 Employee Benefits Cas. (BNA) 1753 (Fed. Cir. 2003). United States ☞70(18)

Procurement regulations and directives that guide a contracting officer's selection of contract type and grant the officer discretion to select type of contract did not prohibit contracting officer from negotiating contract for research and development of technology for tracking ultra-quiet submarines on a fixed-price basis, since those provisions merely cautioned against a fixed-price contract where substantial developmental risk rendered cost estimation merely hypothetical. 48 C.F.R. §§ 16.103(a), 16.104, 35.006(b, c), 216.104. American Tel. and Tel. Co. v. U.S., 307 F.3d 1374 (Fed. Cir. 2002). United States ☞70(15.1)

Navy contract for development of ship-towed, undersea surveillance system was for "major system or subsystem," for purposes of statute prohibiting Department of Defense from entering into fixed price contracts for development of major system or subsystem exceeding $10 million unless certain conditions were met, notwithstanding either agency's reliance on separate statute to define major system as having $75 million floor or fact that contract was funded over multiple years. 10 U.S.C.A. § 2302(5); Act December 22, 1987, § 101(b), Sec. 8118, 101 Stat. 1329. American Tel. & Tel. Co. v. U.S., 177 F.3d 1368 (Fed. Cir. 1999). United States ☞70(15.1)

Failure of Department of Defense to comply with statute setting forth internal review and reporting requirements for fixed price contract for development of major system or subsystem exceeding $10 million did not render such contract void ab initio, as statute itself did not announce sanction of contract invalidity, and contract had been fully performed. Act December 22, 1987, § 101(b), Sec. 8118, 101 Stat. 1329. American Tel. & Tel. Co. v. U.S., 177 F.3d 1368 (Fed. Cir. 1999). United States ☞70(15.1)

Fixed-price contracts assign risk to contractor that actual cost of performance will be higher than price of contract. 48 C.F.R. § 16.202-1. Dalton v. Cessna Aircraft Co., 98 F.3d 1298, 41 Cont. Cas. Fed. (CCH) P 76998 (Fed. Cir. 1996). United States ☞70(15.1)

Government did not breach fixed-price dredging contract that required the dredging, transporting, and depositing of material from two stockpile areas along the Mississippi River by refusing to pay contractor an additional $1,111,227.51 to contractor to compensate it for cost overrun caused by county's opposition to contractor's proposed disposal site on private property; as a party to a fixed-price contract, contractor assumed the risk of any cost overruns during the term of performance. 48 C.F.R. § 16.202-1. L.W. Matteson, Inc. v. U.S., 61 Fed. Cl. 296 (2004). United States ☞70(22.1)

Focus of fixed-price public contract is contractor output. 48 C.F.R. §§ 16.401, 16.403. McDonnell Douglas Corp. v. U.S., 37 Fed. Cl. 295, 41 Cont. Cas. Fed. (CCH) P 77046 (1997), order modified, 39 Fed. Cl. 665, 42 Cont. Cas. Fed. (CCH) P 77230 (1997). United States ☞70(15.1)

3 Firm-fixed-price contracts

Utility company's proposal for government contract relating to electrical services, which proposed that government would reimburse none of company's costs for replacing electrical system at issue and that government would pay company up to certain amount if specified contingencies arose, was cost-share type contract, not firm-fixed-price contract, and thus satisfied requirement in request for proposal (RFP) that bidders submit cost-reimbursement contract proposal. 48 C.F.R. §§ 16.202, 16.303. City & County of San Francisco v. U.S., 130 F.3d 873, 42 Cont. Cas. Fed. (CCH) P 77215 (9th Cir. 1997). United States ☞64.30

Costs of contractor's severance payments to six employees, following expiration of firm, fixed-price contract with United States Air Force, were not recoverable as "abnormal or mass severance costs" for which government would be liable for its "fair share" under Federal Acquisition Regulations (FAR) incorporated into contract; severance payments were normal severance when viewed in context of contract's expiration, which was foreseeable event when contract was entered into. 48 C.F.R. § 31.205-6(g)(2)(iii). ITT Federal Services Corp. v. Widnall, 132 F.3d 1448, 42 Cont. Cas. Fed. (CCH) P 77242 (Fed. Cir. 1997). United States ☞70(21)

Contractor was not entitled to recover cost of severance payments made to six employees who could not be placed with contractor or successor contractor following termination of firm, fixed-price contract with United States Air Force under continuity of services provision of Federal Acquisition Regulations (FAR) incorporated into contract; severance payments were not transition services costs provided for in provision, in that they did not result from activities to assist new contractor or government in taking over operations, nor were they designed to assure continuity of services during transition period. 48 C.F.R. § 52. 237-3. ITT Federal Services Corp. v. Widnall, 132 F.3d 1448, 42 Cont. Cas. Fed. (CCH) P 77242 (Fed. Cir. 1997). United States ☞70(21)

Flight training services contractor's interpretation of "17,000 airborne training service hours" provision of firm fixed-price contract with Navy as qualified by parenthetical reference to 58 hours per graduated student gave rise to patent ambiguity and corresponding duty to seek clarification before submitting proposal. Dalton v. Cessna Aircraft Co., 98 F.3d 1298, 41 Cont. Cas. Fed. (CCH) P 76998 (Fed. Cir. 1996). United States ☞64.5

Flight training services contractor that failed to seek clarification of its patently ambiguous interpretation of service hours required by firm fixed-price contract with Navy before it submitted winning proposal was barred from seeking equitable adjustment for subsequent change in Navy's training syllabus. Dalton v. Cessna Aircraft Co., 98 F.3d 1298, 41 Cont. Cas. Fed. (CCH) P 76998 (Fed. Cir. 1996). United States ☞70(24)

When viewing firm fixed-price contract for flight training services as whole, Navy reasonably interpreted parenthetical reference to 58 hours per graduated student in general provisions of contract as estimate, rather than binding provision; specific provisions of contract contained in attached training syllabus called for 17,000 hours of flight services for third, fourth, and fifth program years and for option years, without qualification as to the number of hours per student. Dalton v. Cessna Aircraft Co., 98 F.3d 1298, 41 Cont. Cas. Fed. (CCH)

P 76998 (Fed. Cir. 1996). United States ☞70(6.1)

In absence of language clearly and unambiguously placing qualification on manner in which Navy could consume services it was procuring through firm fixed-price contract for flight training services, it was reasonable for Navy to interpret contractual reference to 58 hours per graduated student as estimate. Dalton v. Cessna Aircraft Co., 98 F.3d 1298, 41 Cont. Cas. Fed. (CCH) P 76998 (Fed. Cir. 1996). United States ☞70(6.1)

Failure of contracting agency to perform a cost realism analysis on contract awardee's offer was not error, as there was no requirement for such an analysis, where solicitation contemplated award of firm fixed price contract and contracting officer (CO) deemed awardee responsible to perform the project at the offered price. 48 C.F.R. § 15.404-1(d)(1). First Enterprise v. U.S., 61 Fed. Cl. 109 (2004). United States ☞64.40(1)

Original version of Cost Accounting Standard (CAS) governing segment closing adjustment of pension costs under government contracts required contractor to examine both firm-fixed-price and flexibly-priced contracts to determine the pension surplus or deficit attributable to government contributions. 4 C.F.R. § 413-50(c)(12) (1986). Teledyne, Inc. v. U.S., 50 Fed. Cl. 155 (2001), aff'd, 316 F.3d 1366, 30 Employee Benefits Cas. (BNA) 1753 (Fed. Cir. 2003). United States ☞70(18)

Original version of Cost Accounting Standard (CAS) governing segment closing adjustment of pension costs under government contracts did not allow for the recovery of any pension surplus or the payment of any pension plan deficit attributable to government-reimbursed pension costs under firm-fixed-price contracts; thus, such adjustment would only be recoverable pursuant to an express contract provision. 4 C.F.R. § 413-50(c)(12) (1986). Teledyne, Inc. v. U.S., 50 Fed. Cl. 155 (2001), aff'd, 316 F.3d 1366, 30 Employee Benefits Cas. (BNA) 1753 (Fed. Cir. 2003). United States ☞70(18)

Original version of Cost Accounting Standard (CAS) governing segment closing adjustment of pension costs under government contracts required contractor to allocate the segment closing adjustment between firm-fixed-price contracts and flexibly-priced contracts that gave rise to the surplus or deficit attributable to government contributions; portion of surplus or deficit attributable to firm-fixed-price contracts must be identified in order to determine the recoverable portion of the segment closing adjustment. 4 C.F.R. § 413-50(c)(12) (1986). Teledyne, Inc. v. U.S., 50 Fed. Cl. 155 (2001), aff'd, 316 F.3d 1366, 30 Employee Benefits Cas. (BNA) 1753 (Fed. Cir. 2003). United States ☞70(18)

Applying amended version of Cost Accounting Standard (CAS) governing segment closing adjustment of pension costs to government contractor's sale of division amounted to a change in accounting practice that triggered equitable adjustment, where pension surplus that was attributable to CAS-covered government contracts arose under contracts that contained only the original segment closing provision pursuant to which contractor was not liable for pension surplus attributable to firm-fixed-price contracts. 4 C.F.R. § 413-50(c)(12) (1986); 48 C.F.R. §§ 52.230-2(a)(4)(i), 9904.413-50(c)(12). Teledyne, Inc. v. U.S., 50 Fed. Cl. 155 (2001), aff'd, 316 F.3d 1366, 30 Employee Benefits Cas. (BNA) 1753 (Fed. Cir. 2003). United States ☞70(21)

Amended version of Cost Accounting Standard (CAS) governing segment closing adjustment of pension costs under government contracts was not invalid on ground the Cost Accounting Standards Board (CASB) did not have authority under the Office of Federal Procurement Policy Act (OFPPA) to require price adjustments under firm-fixed-price contracts, as amended version did not clearly contradict the OFPPA which requires the measurement, assignment, and allocation of pension costs. Contract Disputes Act of 1978, § 26(f, h), as amended, 41 U.S.C.A. § 422(f, h). Teledyne, Inc. v. U.S., 50 Fed. Cl. 155 (2001), aff'd, 316 F.3d 1366, 30 Employee Benefits Cas. (BNA) 1753 (Fed. Cir. 2003). United States ☞70(18)

Cost Accounting Standards Board (CASB) complied with procedural requirements of the Office of Federal Procurement Policy Act (OFPPA) when it issued amended Cost Accounting Standard (CAS) making government contractor liable for pension surplus attributable to firm-fixed-price contracts in a segment closing adjustment; CASB gave adequate notice of the inclusion of firm-fixed-price contracts in the new segment closing adjustment provision in proposed illustrations, and received comments that addressed issue. Contract Disputes Act of 1978, § 26(g), as amended, 41 U.S.C.A. § 422(g); 48 C.F.R. § 9904.413-50(c)(12). Teledyne, Inc. v. U.S., 50 Fed. Cl. 155 (2001), aff'd, 316 F.3d 1366, 30 Employee Benefits

Cas. (BNA) 1753 (Fed. Cir. 2003). United States ☞70(18)

Contractor which willingly bid on a firm fixed price (FFP) contract, and willingly signed an FFP contract, thereby assuming the risks attendant to an FFP contract, could not raise claim that FFP provisions violated the Federal Acquisition Regulation. 48 C.F.R. §§ 16. 103(a), 16.202-2. PCL Const. Services, Inc. v. U.S., 47 Fed. Cl. 745 (2000). United States ☞70(15.1)

Firm-fixed-price contract for the operation and maintenance of two government-owned locks and dams did not require that contractor staff each lock and dam with a fulltime equipment mechanic, and thus it was improper for the government to reduce the contract price and withhold monies from contractor for periods during which equipment mechanic positions were vacant; term 'capability," as used in the solicitation and contract documents, did not mandate any specific "manpower" or "staffing levels." Omni Corp. v. U.S., 41 Fed. Cl. 585 (1998). United States ☞70(15.1)

In firm fixed-price contract between federal agency and corporation, corporation bore risk that it would be required to pay unforeseen premium wages to its employees for federal government furlough period after arbitrator ordered such wages, where agency did not take position that employees should be paid premium wages for holiday pay or require any changes in services as to scope, time or personnel during furlough period. Cleveland Telecommunications Corp. v. U.S., 39 Fed. Cl. 649, 42 Cont. Cas. Fed. (CCH) P 77199 (1997). United States ☞70(23)

For purpose of determining whether low bidder was entitled to enjoin Government's cancellation of solicitation for bids for providing unarmed guard services, solicitation's designation of contract as firm fixed-price contract was consistent with reaffirmation in same section that it was indefinite quantity contract, as meaning of contract was that prices for additional services, as well as for base and optional years, were firm fixed hourly rates. Vanguard Sec. Inc. v. U.S., 20 Cl. Ct. 90, 1990 WL 38036 (1990). United States ☞64.60(5.1)

Fact that solicitation for bids for providing unarmed guard services denominated contract as "firm fixed-price" did not show that solicitation called for provision of additional services through options, as opposed to indefinite quantity requirement. Vanguard Sec. Inc. v. U.S., 20 Cl. Ct. 90, 1990 WL 38036 (1990). United States ☞70(6.1)

4 Economic price adjustment

Under Federal Acquisition Regulation (FAR) governing economic price adjustments to fixed-price contracts, "contractor's established price" may be established by reference to either a catalog or market sources independent of the manufacturer or vendor. 48 C.F.R. § 16. 203. Tesoro Hawaii Corp. v. U.S., 405 F.3d 1339, 15 A.L.R. Fed. 2d 755 (Fed. Cir. 2005) United States ☞70(18)

Use of market-based references to determine adjustments to established prices in contracts for sale of jet fuel to military was authorized under Federal Acquisition Regulation (FAR) governing economic price adjustments to fixed price contracts. 48 C.F.R. § 16. 203. Tesoro Hawaii Corp. v. U.S., 405 F.3d 1339, 15 A.L.R. Fed. 2d 755 (Fed. Cir. 2005). United States ☞70(18)

Federal Acquisition Regulation (FAR) governing economic price adjustments to fixed price contracts permit use of contracts that include adjustments based on established prices, but do not limit those adjustments to changes only in the specific prices offered by an individual contractor. Tesoro Hawaii Corp. v. U.S., 405 F.3d 1339, 15 A.L.R. Fed. 2d 755 (Fed. Cir. 2005). United States ☞70(23)

Use of an economic price adjustment (EPA) clause tied particularly to a reference price in a market publication to determine price adjustments in fuel contracts did not violate Federal Acquisition Regulation (FAR) governing economic price adjustments to fixed price contracts; regulation did not require that adjustments be tied solely to changes in the prices charged by a particular contractor. 48 C.F.R. § 16.203-3. Tesoro Hawaii Corp. v. U.S., 405 F.3d 1339, 15 A.L.R. Fed. 2d 755 (Fed. Cir. 2005). United States ☞70(18)

To be authorized under the Federal Acquisition Regulation (FAR), economic price adjustment (EPA) clause in military fuel supply contracts had to fall within one of the three general types set forth in section of the FAR authorizing use of EPA clauses. 48 C.F.R. § 16.

203-1. Sunoco, Inc. v. U.S., 59 Fed. Cl. 390 (2004) (abrogated on other grounds by, Tesoro Hawaii Corp. v. U.S., 405 F.3d 1339, 15 A.L.R. Fed. 2d 755 (Fed. Cir. 2005)). United States ☞70(18)

Individual deviation or exemption from section of the Federal Acquisition Regulation (FAR) governing economic price adjustment clauses was invalid and illegal under the FAR, where deviation was applied not to a single contract but to multiple contracts issued under single solicitation, and was used to accommodate the government as a temporary measure until a permanent class deviation was obtained. 48 C.F.R. §§ 1.403, 1.404, 16.203-1. Calcasieu Refining Co. v. U.S., 2003 WL 22049528 (Ct. Fed. Cl. 2003). United States ☞70(18)

Section of the Federal Acquisition Regulation (FAR) which authorizes the government's use of "[f]ixed-price contracts with economic price adjustment" authorized the use of economic price adjustment (EPA) clauses that adopt market based price indexes to provide adjustments in a contractor's established prices. 48 C.F.R. § 16.203-1. Williams Alaska Petroleum, Inc. v. U.S., 57 Fed. Cl. 789 (2003). United States ☞70(18)

Defense Energy Support Center (DESC) had the authority to adopt market-based economic price adjustment (EPA) clauses in petroleum contracts awarded to military fuel suppliers during the years 1993 through 1999, pursuant to provisions of the Federal Acquisition Regulation (FAR) and individual and class deviations granted DESC during those years. 48 C.F.R. § 16.203-1. Williams Alaska Petroleum, Inc. v. U.S., 57 Fed. Cl. 789 (2003). United States ☞70(18)

If a fixed price government contract containing an economic price adjustment clause is in violation of the procurement regulations and does not meet the requirement that the selected index approximately tracks the economic changes affecting the contract, reformation is appropriate. Gold Line Refining, Ltd. v. U.S., 43 Fed. Cl. 291 (1999). United States ☞72(1.1)

Fixed price contract with economic price adjustment was required to comply with Federal Acquisition Regulations (FAR) on economic price adjustments, even if parties also intended indefinite-delivery indefinite-quantity contract. MAPCO Alaska Petroleum, Inc. v. U.S., 27 Fed. Cl. 405, 38 Cont. Cas. Fed. (CCH) P 76451 (1992) (abrogated on other grounds by, Tesoro Hawaii Corp. v. U.S., 405 F.3d 1339, 15 A.L.R. Fed. 2d 755 (Fed. Cir. 2005)). United States ☞70(23)

5 Level-of-effort

Government was not entitled to reimbursement of added costs paid to fiscal intermediary to providers of health care services operating under Medicare program in connection with intermediary's performance of authorized changes to its subcontract, notwithstanding that size of intermediary's work force declined during period for which added costs were paid; subcontract was not "level-of-effort" undertaking, nor did it obligate intermediary to dedicate fixed number of personnel to various tasks it had agreed to perform. Empire Blue Cross and Blue Shield v. U.S., 5 F.3d 1506 (Fed. Cir. 1993). United States ☞75(1); United States ☞88

6 Cost-reimbursement contracts, generally

State income taxes paid by sole shareholder of contractor, a Subchapter S corporation, were not reimbursable, allowable costs in cost-reimbursement contract between contractor and United States under the Federal Acquisition Regulation (FAR), since taxes were paid based on dividends paid to sole shareholder, and were not paid by the contracting entity. 48 C.F.R. § 31.205-41. Information Systems & Networks Corp. v. U.S., 549 U.S. 1179, 127 S. Ct. 1146, 166 L. Ed. 2d 993 (2007). United States ☞70(18)

Cost-share contract may be deemed cost-reimbursement contract, for purpose of request for proposal (RFP) relating to government contract, if RFP does not specify type of costreimbursement contract sought. 48 C.F.R. §§ 16.101(b), 16.303. City & County of San Francisco v. U.S., 130 F.3d 873, 42 Cont. Cas. Fed. (CCH) P 77215 (9th Cir. 1997). United States ☞64.25

Government would not be permitted to supplement the administrative record on final day of post-award bid protest hearing with 36 page document that explained the basis for government's most probable cost estimate (MPCE), which adjusted contractor's bid on a cost reimbursement contract, where government had intentionally failed to produce the document earlier, even though government was required by law to produce the document. 48 C.F.R. § 15.608(a). Day & Zimmermann Services, a Div. of Day & Zimmermann, Inc. v. U.S., 38 Fed. Cl. 591, 42 Cont. Cas. Fed. (CCH) P 77186 (1997), dismissed, 132 F.3d 49 (Fed. Cir. 1997). United States ☞64.60(1)

Government's unexplained failure to produce critically relevant document that explained basis for its most probable cost estimate (MPCE) for adjusting contractor's bid on cost reimbursement contract warranted an adverse inference; thus, court was constrained to infer that had government properly produced the document, it would have supported contractor's contention that the Army arbitrarily and capriciously determined the MPCE for its proposal, and court would not sustain Army's determination of MPCE for contractor's proposal as being a reasonable adjustment based on documented and creditable facts. Day & Zimmermann Services, a Div. of Day & Zimmermann, Inc. v. U.S., 38 Fed. Cl. 591, 42 Cont. Cas. Fed. (CCH) P 77186 (1997), dismissed, 132 F.3d 49 (Fed. Cir. 1997). Evidence ☞75; Evidence ☞87

7 Cost-plus-incentive-fee contracts

Incentive fee clause of cost-plus-incentive-fee (CPIF) contract for development of battlefield management aircraft was applied properly to reduce contractor's fee after contracting officer deleted or relaxed certain specifications to keep the project on track; clause permitted equitable adjustment of target cost and target fee and minimum and maximum fees when contractor's work was decreased by a modification to the contract. Northrop Grumman Corp. v. U.S., 41 Fed. Cl. 645, 42 Cont. Cas. Fed. (CCH) P 77361 (1998). United States ☞70(18)

"Best efforts" language in cost-plus-incentive-fee (CPIF) contract referred to government contractor's duty in a CPIF contract to use its "best efforts" to complete the project within the funding limit allocated to the contract; it did not address a dispute that involved the propriety of a fee reduction based on the deletion or relaxation of contract specifications. Northrop Grumman Corp. v. U.S., 41 Fed. Cl. 645, 42 Cont. Cas. Fed. (CCH) P 77361 (1998). United States ☞70(18)

8 Cost-plus-fixed-fee contracts

The "warranty of government specifications", also sometimes referred to as the "Spearin doctrine", provides that if the government furnishes specifications for the production or construction of an end product and proper application of those specifications does not result in a satisfactory end product, the contractor will be compensated for its efforts to produce the end product, notwithstanding the unsatisfactory results. PCL Const. Services, Inc. v. U.S., 47 Fed. Cl. 745 (2000). United States ☞73(17)

In architect and engineering cost-plus-fixed-fee contracts, government contractor receives fixed fee to design project and costs for construction effort, with fixed fee usually based on percentage of estimated cost of construction project, but increase in cost of construction does not per se justify increase in contractor's fixed fee; change in fee is proper only for work not contemplated at time fee was negotiated, not merely because greater than expected costs were being encountered doing work as originally contemplated. 48 C.F.R. § 16.306(a). Ralph L. Jones Co., Inc. v. U.S., 33 Fed. Cl. 327 (1995). United States ☞70(24)

9 Fixed-price incentive contracts

Despite fact that Department of Defense (DoD) violated DoD appropriation acts by incrementally funding fixed-price incentive contract without performing risk determinations in fiscal years 1990 to 1992, rendering the contract illegal, the Court of Federal Claims would enforce the contract as written, as such enforcement was not an unjust result where contractor was a sophisticated defense contractor, which had available to it all the information necessary to bid on the contract. Northrop Grumman Corp. v. U.S., 47 Fed. Cl. 20 (2000). United States ☞68

Department of Defense (DoD) violated DoD appropriation acts by incrementally funding fixed-price incentive contract without performing risk determinations in fiscal years 1990 to 1992. Department of Defense Appropriations Act, 1992, § 8037, 105 Stat. 1150; Department of Defense Appropriations Act, 1991, § 8038, 104 Stat. 1856; Department of Defense Appropriations Act, 1990, § 9048, 103 Stat. 1112. Northrop Grumman Corp. v. U.S., 47 Fed. Cl. 20 (2000). United States ☞70(15.1)

Contractor who contended that award of contract as a fixed-price incentive contract violated applicable regulatory requirements failed to prove that at the time of contracting the parties did not possess adequate cost and pricing information or that the risk was not reasonably apportioned. 48 C.F.R. § 16.403-1. Northrop Grumman Corp. v. U.S., 47 Fed. Cl. 20 (2000). United States ☞70(15.1)

Contractor did not satisfy its burden on claim that selection of award of contract as a fixed-price incentive contract violated provision of the Federal Acquisition Regulation concerning research and development acquisitions; even assuming that provision was applicable, provision was not mandatory in precluding use of fixed-price incentive contract. 48 C.F.R. § 35.006. Northrop Grumman Corp. v. U.S., 47 Fed. Cl. 20 (2000). United States ☞70(15.1)

Contractor did not satisfy its burden with regard to allegation that award of contract as a fixed-price incentive contract, rather than as a cost-reimbursement contract, violated Department of Defense (DoD) directive concerning appropriate contract type for research and development phases; obligation under the directive was to consider certain factors, not necessarily to adopt them as part of the procurement strategy. Northrop Grumman Corp. v. U.S., 47 Fed. Cl. 20 (2000). United States ☞70(15.1)

Contractor failed to establish that the government possessed superior knowledge, and did not disclose, that contract for a tactical air command and control system for the Marine Corps would require significant development and was unsuited for award as a fixed-price incentive contract; contractor did not undertake performance without vital knowledge, and the government did not fail to provide relevant information about the degree of development that the contract would require. Northrop Grumman Corp. v. U.S., 47 Fed. Cl. 20 (2000). United States ☞70(30)

Reformation to a cost-type contract was not the appropriate remedy for contract illegality which consisted of government's failure to perform risk assessment during each year of incremental funding by the Department of Defense (DoD) of fixed-price incentive contract; since Secretary of Defense did not make any determination that no lower cost alternatives were available, reformation to a cost-type contract would bring about another illegality. Northrop Grumman Corp. v. U.S., 47 Fed. Cl. 20 (2000). United States ☞72(1.1)

Contractor could not recover cost overruns on defense contract on ground of mutual mistake, as risk of mistake was allocated to contractor through the selection of fixed-price incentive contract. Northrop Grumman Corp. v. U.S., 47 Fed. Cl. 20 (2000). United States ☞74(4)

10 Cost-plus-award-fee contracts

Contract provision which purportedly divested jurisdiction of Armed Services Board of Contract Appeals to hear dispute concerning calculation of award fee under cost-plus-award-fee (CPAF) contract between Navy and contractor was void; provision otherwise depriving board of jurisdiction was not a matter of statute primacy, and thus parties could not on their own alter board's review under Contract Disputes Act (CDA). Contract Disputes Act of 1978, §§ 6(a), 10(a)(3), as amended, 41 U.S.C.A. §§ 605(a), 609(a)(3); 48 C.F.R. § 16. 404-2(a). Burnside-Ott Aviation Training Center v. Dalton, 107 F.3d 854, 41 Cont. Cas. Fed. (CCH) P 77043 (Fed. Cir. 1997). United States ☞68

11 Indefinite-delivery contracts, generally

Federal court had jurisdiction under Tucker Act over computer software manufacturer's action alleging that United States Department of Labor's (DOL) decision to standardize its software applications exclusively to software manufactured by competitor violated Competition in Contracting Act (CICA), where standardization decision was allegedly made in connection with its ultimate procurement of competitor's software licenses. 10 U.S.C.A. § 2304; 28 U.S.C.A. § 1491(b)(1); Federal Property and Administrative Services Act of 1949, § 303, as amended, 41 U.S.C.A. § 253; 48 C.F.R. §§ 16.501-1, 16.501-2. Corel Corp. v. U.S., 165 F. Supp. 2d 12 (D.D.C. 2001). United States ☞64.60(1)

12 Task or delivery order contracts

Federal Acquisition Streamlining Act (FASA) which prohibits protests "in connection with the issuance or proposed issuance of a task or delivery order" except under certain circumstances did not bar protest of award of blanket purchase agreement (BPA), as task order restriction does not apply to Federal Supply Schedule (FSS) procurements. Federal Property and Administrative Services Act of 1949, § 303j(d), as amended, 41 U.S.C.A. § 253j(d); 48 C.F.R. § 8.404(b)(4). Labat-Anderson Inc. v. U.S., 50 Fed. Cl. 99 (2001). United States ☞64.60(1)

Where an agency engages in a more comprehensive selection process than contemplated by the Federal Supply Schedule (FSS) scheme, a frustrated bidder may still challenge the agency award under the arbitrary and capricious standard, notwithstanding section of the Federal Acquisition Streamlining Act (FASA) which prohibits protests "in connection with the issuance or proposed issuance of a task or delivery order." 5 U.S.C.A. § 706(2)(A); Federal Property and Administrative Services Act of 1949, § 303j(d), as amended, 41 U.S.C.A. § 253j(d). Labat-Anderson Inc. v. U.S., 50 Fed. Cl. 99 (2001). United States ☞64.60(4)

13 Requirements contracts

Where company's contract to provide pest control services for Department of Housing and Urban Development (HUD) was neither requirements contract nor enforceable indefinite quantity contract, company was entitled to payment only for services actually ordered by HUD and provided by company. Coyle's Pest Control, Inc. v. Cuomo, 154 F.3d 1302, 42 Cont. Cas. Fed. (CCH) P 77373 (Fed. Cir. 1998). United States ☞70(19)

Essential element of requirements contract is promise by buyer to purchase subject matter of contract exclusively from seller. Modern Systems Technology Corp. v. U.S., 979 F.2d 200, 38 Cont. Cas. Fed. (CCH) P 76397 (Fed. Cir. 1992). Sales ☞71(4)

Requirements contract is formed when seller has exclusive right and legal obligation to fill all of buyer's needs for goods or services described in contract. Modern Systems Technology Corp. v. U.S., 979 F.2d 200, 38 Cont. Cas. Fed. (CCH) P 76397 (Fed. Cir. 1992). Sales ☞71(4)

Requirements contract calls for government to fill all its actual requirements for specified supplies or services during contract period by purchasing from awardee, who agrees to provide them at agreed price. Medart, Inc. v. Austin, 967 F.2d 579, 38 Cont. Cas. Fed. (CCH) P 76349 (Fed. Cir. 1992). United States ☞70(9)

Federal Acquisition Regulations require contracting officer to furnish estimated quantities in solicitation contemplating requirements contract; risks associated with variance between actual purchases and estimated quantities are allocated to contractor. Medart, Inc. v. Austin, 967 F.2d 579, 38 Cont. Cas. Fed. (CCH) P 76349 (Fed. Cir. 1992). United States ☞70(9)

Because actual purchases under requirements contracts vary significantly from government estimates does not ordinarily give rise to liability on part of government. Medart, Inc. v. Austin, 967 F.2d 579, 38 Cont. Cas. Fed. (CCH) P 76349 (Fed. Cir. 1992). United States ☞70(30)

Government may be liable in damages where contractor can show by preponderant evidence that government estimates made during solicitation for requirements contract were inadequately or negligently prepared, not in good faith, or grossly or unreasonably inadequate at time estimate was made. Medart, Inc. v. Austin, 967 F.2d 579, 38 Cont. Cas. Fed. (CCH) P 76349 (Fed. Cir. 1992). United States ☞70(30)

Estimating needs when soliciting for bids for requirements contract to supply metal storage cabinets based on last year's orders was reasonable and complied with Federal Acquisition Regulations, even though estimates exceeded actual orders. Medart, Inc. v. Austin, 967 F.2d 579, 38 Cont. Cas. Fed. (CCH) P 76349 (Fed. Cir. 1992). United States ☞70(30)

Requirements contract for computer repair services which required the Army to order all services and supplies from contractor that were "required to be purchased" did not entitle contractor to receive warranty work for machines purchased before contract performance which were still within their initial warranty period. Datalect Computer Services, Inc. v. U.S., 56 Fed. Cl. 178 (2003), aff'd, 97 Fed. Appx. 333 (Fed. Cir. 2004). United States ☞70(6.1)

Contractor under requirements contract for computer repair services could not recover under reformation theory damages for government's negligent estimates of repair needs for last two option years of contract, where it failed to prove that its damages were the result of government's breach. Datalect Computer Services, Inc. v. U.S., 56 Fed. Cl. 178 (2003), aff'd, 97 Fed. Appx. 333 (Fed. Cir. 2004). United States ☞74(13)

Jury verdict method of awarding damages could not be employed to formulate award for damages suffered by contractor under requirements contract for computer repair services due to government's negligent estimates of repair needs for last two option years of contract, under total loss theory measuring damages by the difference between the actual cost of performing the contract and the costs estimated in the contractor's proposal, where contractor provided insufficient evidence upon which to calculate award that was both fair and reasonable. Datalect Computer Services, Inc. v. U.S., 56 Fed. Cl. 178 (2003), aff'd, 97 Fed. Appx. 333 (Fed. Cir. 2004). United States ☞74(12.1)

Evidence supported conclusion that the Army violated requirements clause of contract for computer repair services which required the Army to order all services and supplies from contractor that were "required to be purchased" during the contract period by "purchasing" extensions to warranties on covered machinery from another contractor which supplied computer hardware, thereby depriving repair contractor of warranty work. Datalect Computer Services, Inc. v. U.S., 56 Fed. Cl. 178 (2003), aff'd, 97 Fed. Appx. 333 (Fed. Cir. 2004). United States ☞74(11)

Estimated government contract requirements do not represent a guarantee or warranty and, normally, significant variances between estimated requirements and actual orders will not result in liability on the part of the government in the absence of bad faith, negligence, or a showing of a grossly unreasonable estimate. 48 C.F.R. § 16.503(a)(1). Hi-Shear Technology Corp. v. U.S., 53 Fed. Cl. 420 (2002), decision aff'd, 356 F.3d 1372 (Fed. Cir. 2004). United States ☞70(30)

Consideration is satisfied in requirements contracts by the government purchaser's agreement to contractually limit its range of future options and to turn to the contractor for all such requirements as do develop. J. Cooper & Associates, Inc. v. U.S., 53 Fed. Cl. 8 (2002), aff'd, 65 Fed. Appx. 731 (Fed. Cir. 2003). United States ☞66

A "requirements contract" requires the contracting government entity to fill all of its actual requirements for supplies or services that are specified in the contract, during the contract period, by purchases from the contract awardee. 48 C.F.R. § 16.503(a). J. Cooper & Associates, Inc. v. U.S., 53 Fed. Cl. 8 (2002), aff'd, 65 Fed. Appx. 731 (Fed. Cir. 2003). United States ☞70(9)

A government purchaser who has entered into a requirements contract with a contractor for a specific item may not purchase that item from any other source for the duration of the contract. J. Cooper & Associates, Inc. v. U.S., 53 Fed. Cl. 8 (2002), aff'd, 65 Fed. Appx. 731 (Fed. Cir. 2003). United States ☞70(9)

Government has a duty of good faith and use of reasonable care in computing its estimated needs in a solicitation for a requirements contract. 48 C.F.R. § 16.503(a)(1). Educators Associates, Inc. v. U.S., 41 Fed. Cl. 811, 42 Cont. Cas. Fed. (CCH) P 77376 (1998). United States ☞70(9)

In a solicitation for a requirements contract, the contracting officer must provide a realistic estimate of the quantity of goods or services to be procured under the contract; however, the estimate is not a warranty as to quantity, but instead serves as a guideline as to the contract's magnitude and scope. 48 C.F.R. § 16.503(a)(1). Educators Associates, Inc. v. U.S., 41 Fed. Cl. 811, 42 Cont. Cas. Fed. (CCH) P 77376 (1998). United States ☞70(9); United States ☞70(30)

Contractor's contract reformation theory did not provide a reasonable basis for computing its damages under requirements contract for computer repair services; theory was based on the difference between what it actually received under the contract and what it would have bid if government had properly disclosed its estimated requirements, but contractor provided no credible evidence to demonstrate how the original bid prices were formulated, and thus its hypothetical bid was speculative. Datalect Computer Services, Ltd. v. U.S., 41 Fed. Cl. 720, 42 Cont. Cas. Fed. (CCH) P 77379 (1998), aff'd, 215 F.3d 1344 (Fed. Cir. 1999). United States ☞74(11)

Government contractor's "increased costs" theory did not provide a reasonable basis for computing its damages under requirements contract for computer repair services; pursuant to the theory, contractor calculated equitable adjustments to the fixed costs, spare parts costs, and the profit margin on those costs; although increased cost calculation purported to demonstrate contractor's projected costs and revenues at the time the bids were submitted as well as its actual costs in performing the contract, the figures were not supported by the record. Datalect Computer Services, Ltd. v. U.S., 41 Fed. Cl. 720, 42 Cont. Cas. Fed. (CCH) P 77379 (1998), aff'd, 215 F.3d 1344 (Fed. Cir. 1999). United States ☞74(11)

Although government contractor under requirements contract for computer repair services incurred monetary injury as a result of government's faulty estimate, "jury verdict" method of awarding damages could not be applied where contractor did not provide the court with sufficient evidence to make a reasonable approximation of the damages incurred. Datalect Computer Services, Ltd. v. U.S., 41 Fed. Cl. 720, 42 Cont. Cas. Fed. (CCH) P 77379 (1998), aff'd, 215 F.3d 1344 (Fed. Cir. 1999). United States ☞74(12.1)

Requirements contracts lack promise from buyer to order specific amount, but consideration is furnished, and contract is rendered enforceable, by buyer's promise to turn to seller for all such requirements as they develop. Datalect Computer Services, Ltd. v. U.S., 40 Fed. Cl. 28, 42 Cont. Cas. Fed. (CCH) P 77243 (1997), aff'd in part, vacated in part on other grounds, 215 F.3d 1344 (Fed. Cir. 1999). Sales ☞71(4)

Offeror on government contract is entitled to rely on government estimate set forth in contract as representing an honest and informed conclusion; government must act in good faith and use reasonable care in computing its estimated needs, and it must either reformulate its estimate when warranted by the information available, or notify offerors of situations or factors likely to affect the estimate. 48 C.F.R. § 16.503(a)(1). Datalect Computer Services, Ltd. v. U.S., 40 Fed. Cl. 28, 42 Cont. Cas. Fed. (CCH) P 77243 (1997), aff'd in part, vacated in part on other grounds, 215 F.3d 1344 (Fed. Cir. 1999). United States ☞70(30)

Principle that patent ambiguities place on contractor duty to inquire did not apply to dispute as to whether parties had entered a requirements contract or a contract for indefinite quantities. Crown Laundry and Dry Cleaners, Inc. v. U.S., 29 Fed. Cl. 506, 39 Cont. Cas. Fed. (CCH) P 76575 (1993). United States ☞70(30)

Contract for laundry and dry cleaning services was a requirements contract, even though it was labeled an indefinite quantities contract, where government intended to have all of its dry cleaning and laundry needs for arsenal serviced by the contract, contract provided that the government could arrange for services to be performed by another contractor if the contractor failed to perform any services covered by the contract, and the contract terms, read together were more consistent if taken as expression of requirements contract than as indefinite quantities contract. Crown Laundry and Dry Cleaners, Inc. v. U.S., 29 Fed. Cl. 506, 39 Cont. Cas. Fed. (CCH) P 76575 (1993). United States ☞70(6.1)

Variance of 5% to 15% between government's estimates of its need under requirements contract and the actual amount of its needs might be viewed as reasonable, but 45% variance is unreasonable. Crown Laundry and Dry Cleaners, Inc. v. U.S., 29 Fed. Cl. 506, 39 Cont. Cas. Fed. (CCH) P 76575 (1993). United States ☞70(6.1); United States ☞70(30)

Government was negligent in preparation of estimates of work to be performed under the requirements contract for laundry and dry cleaning at arsenal where it requested the using activities at the arsenal to estimate their needs for laundry and dry cleaning services, resulting estimates were submitted in monthly form and for variety of laundry and dry cleaning services, a contract specialist multiplied the monthly estimates by 12, estimates were not otherwise verified or checked for reasonableness or accuracy, historical data concerning use was not considered, and contracting officer was aware that using activities probably exaggerated their needs in order to insure that any increase in needs would be met by future procurement. Crown Laundry and Dry Cleaners, Inc. v. U.S., 29 Fed. Cl. 506, 39 Cont. Cas. Fed. (CCH) P 76575 (1993). United States ☞70(30)

Fact that actual work performed pursuant to requirements contract varies significantly from inaccurate estimates set forth in contract does not shift burden of persuasion to government to prove reasonableness of the estimating procedures; contractor has burden of persuasion to prove by preponderance of the evidence that inaccurate estimates were the result of negligent action by government personnel or lack of due care by personnel in preparation of the estimates. Crown Laundry and Dry Cleaners, Inc. v. U.S., 29 Fed. Cl. 506, 39 Cont. Cas. Fed. (CCH) P 76575 (1993). United States ☞74(10)

14 Indefinite-quantity contracts

An "indefinite delivery, indefinite quantity contract" (ID/IQ contract) differs from a "requirements contract" in that the former does not oblige the buyer to purchase more from the seller than a stated minimum quantity, whereas the latter obliges the buyer to buy from the seller all of its requirements of the relevant goods or services. Varilease Technology Group, Inc. v. U.S., 289 F.3d 795 (Fed. Cir. 2002). Sales ☞71(3); Sales ☞71(4)

Contract under which computer maintenance firm was to provide maintenance for certain computers owned by federal agency was an "indefinite delivery, indefinite quantity contract," or ID/IQ contract, rather than a "requirements contract," regardless of expectations of firm, where plain language of contract clearly, repeatedly, and unequivocally identified it as an ID/IQ contract, rather than a requirements contract, and contract had no language, express or implied, obligating the government to purchase its entire requirements for computer maintenance from firm, but did set forth the essentials of an ID/IQ contract. Varilease Technology Group, Inc. v. U.S., 289 F.3d 795 (Fed. Cir. 2002). United States ☞70(6.1)

Contract under which computer maintenance firm was to provide maintenance for certain computers owned by federal agency, which expressly indicated that it was an indefinite delivery, indefinite quantity contract, or ID/IQ contract, and established an initial six-month base period, followed by four 12-month options periods and one six-month option period, did not result in formation of a series of separate and distinct requirements contracts, even though option periods did not have a separate minimum quantity of services that would be required. 48 C.F.R. § 16.504(b). Varilease Technology Group, Inc. v. U.S., 289 F.3d 795 (Fed. Cir. 2002). United States ☞70(6.1)

General Services Administration (GSA) did not breach contract for provision of travel management services, although GSA did not inform contractor before it submitted its final bid that two agencies which comprised over half of the expected business in one of the states covered under the solicitation would not longer be utilizing GSA-contracted services; contract explicitly stated that it was a indefinitedelivery, indefinite-quantity (IDIQ) contract and that contractor was "a preferred source" of travel agency services, and GSA purchased minimum quantity stated in the contract. 48 C.F.R. § 16.504(a). Travel Centre v. Barram, 236 F.3d 1316 (Fed. Cir. 2001). United States ☞73(22)

Under an indefinite-delivery, indefinite-quantity (IDIQ) contract, the government is required to purchase the minimum quantity stated in the contract, but when the government makes that purchase its legal obligation under the contract is satisfied. 48 C.F.R. § 16.504(a). Travel Centre v. Barram, 236 F.3d 1316 (Fed. Cir. 2001). United States ☞70(6.1)

Once the government has purchased the minimum quantity stated in an indefinite-delivery, indefinite-quantity (IDIQ) contract from the contractor, it is free to purchase additional supplies or services from any other source it chooses. 48 C.F.R. § 16.504(a). Travel Centre v. Barram, 236 F.3d 1316 (Fed. Cir. 2001). United States ☞70(6.1)

Indefinite-delivery, Indefinite-quantity (IDIQ) contract does not provide any exclusivity to the contractor; government may, at its discretion and for its benefit, make its purchases for similar supplies and/or services from other sources. 48 C.F.R. § 16.504(a). Travel Centre v. Barram, 236 F.3d 1316 (Fed. Cir. 2001). United States ☞70(6.1)

When an indefinite-delivery, indefinite-quantity (IDIQ) contract between a contracting party and the government clearly indicates that the contracting party is guaranteed no more than a non-nominal minimum amount of sales, purchases exceeding that minimum amount satisfy the government's legal obligation under the contract. 48 C.F.R. § 16.504(a). Travel Centre v. Barram, 236 F.3d 1316 (Fed. Cir. 2001). United States ☞70(6.1)

Federal question subject matter jurisdiction existed over computer software manufacturer's action alleging that United States Department of Labor's (DOL) decision to standardize its software applications exclusively to software manufactured by competitor violated Administrative Procedure Act (APA) and Competition in Contracting Act (CICA), even if Federal Acquisition Streamlining Act (FASA) precluded review of DOL's issuance of delivery order issued under indefinite-delivery, indefinite-quantity contract pursuant to decision, where manufacturer's protest challenged DOL's overarching administrative decision to standardize to competitor's product, not issuance of individual delivery order. 5 U.S.C.A. § 701 et seq.; 10 U.S.C.A. § 2304; 28 U.S.C.A. § 1331; Federal Property and Administrative

Services Act of 1949, §§ 303, 303J(a)(2), as amended, 41 U.S.C.A. §§ 253, 253j(a)(2); 48 C.F.R. §§ 16.501-1, 16.501-2. Corel Corp. v. U.S., 165 F. Supp. 2d 12 (D.D.C. 2001). Federal Courts ☞232

Government did not breach indefinite delivery, indefinite quantity (ID/IQ) contract for asbestos removal when it renegotiated with contractor the price per square foot for encapsulation service to reduce it from $5.00 per square foot to $0.23 per square foot, after it purchased the contract minimum of $50,000; after satisfying the contract minimum, government had no further obligation to pay contractor $5.00 per square foot for encapsulation service. Abatement Contracting Corp. v. U.S., 58 Fed. Cl. 594 (2003). United States ☞73(22)

"Indefinite delivery, indefinite quantity contracts" obligate the government to purchase only a stated minimum quantity of supplies or services from the contractor, with deliveries to be scheduled as ordered by the government. 48 C.F.R. § 16.504. Abatement Contracting Corp. v. U.S., 58 Fed. Cl. 594 (2003). United States ☞70(6.1)

When the government enters into an indefinite delivery, indefinite quantity (ID/IQ) contract, it does not promise to fill all of its needs by purchasing from the contractor; it commits only to purchase the minimum quantity stated in the contract. 48 C.F.R. § 16.504. Abatement Contracting Corp. v. U.S., 58 Fed. Cl. 594 (2003). United States ☞70(6.1)

Economic duress did not void otherwise valid accord and satisfaction which settled dispute between contractor and government over price of asbestos encapsulation services, based on contractor's allegations that government withheld payments due, and threatened to hire other contractors for future work; contractor offered no evidence of withheld payments, and after ordering the contract minimum, the government had no further obligations to issue any more delivery orders to contractor under indefinite delivery, indefinite quantity (ID/IQ) contract. Abatement Contracting Corp. v. U.S., 58 Fed. Cl. 594 (2003). Accord And Satisfaction ☞20

Contractor did not establish that government breached indefinite delivery, indefinite quantity (ID/IQ) contract for asbestos removal by failing to accurately estimate the amount of asbestos encapsulation work that would be required, absent evidence of egregious conduct, beyond mere negligence, and rising to the level of bad faith. Abatement Contracting Corp. v. U.S., 58 Fed. Cl. 594 (2003). United States ☞74(11)

Contracting agency did not exercise its discretion irrationally, arbitrarily, or in bad faith in establishing the stated minimums for the procurement which involved multiple indefinite delivery/indefinite quantity (ID/IQ) contracts for freight transportation. 48 C.F.R. § 16. 504. ABF Freight System, Inc. v. U.S., 55 Fed. Cl. 392 (2003). United States ☞70(6.1)

Contracting agency's discretion in setting minimum quantities in an indefinite delivery/ indefinite quantity (ID/IQ) government contract is not unlimited; thus, a minimum is not acceptable in a situation where the agency has simply declined to try to establish a more exact level. 48 C.F.R. § 16.504. ABF Freight System, Inc. v. U.S., 55 Fed. Cl. 392 (2003). United States ☞70(6.1)

A contracting agency may exercise its discretion in setting stated minimums in an indefinite delivery/indefinite quantity (ID/IQ) government contract provided that the estimates are established in good faith or are based upon the best information available and accurately represent the agency's anticipated needs. 48 C.F.R. § 16.504. ABF Freight System, Inc. v. U.S., 55 Fed. Cl. 392 (2003). United States ☞70(6.1)

Contracting agency was under no obligation to terminate letter contract for convenience rather than allow it to lapse, where contract was for an indefinite delivery and indefinite quantity (IDIQ) contract, no task orders were interrupted or terminated by agency by its decision to allow the letter contract to lapse, and agency had paid contractor in excess of the minimum guarantee in the letter contract. J. Cooper & Associates, Inc. v. U.S., 53 Fed. Cl. 8 (2002), aff'd, 65 Fed. Appx. 731 (Fed. Cir. 2003). United States ☞72.1(1)

Contractor did not establish that contracting agency acted in bad faith in not awarding more work to contractor under indefinite delivery and indefinite quantity (IDIQ) contract, after assuring it of additional work, where agency became dissatisfied with contractor's accounting practices, pricing, and work quality, and gave contractor another chance by soliciting additional work proposals. J. Cooper & Associates, Inc. v. U.S., 53 Fed. Cl. 8 (2002), aff'd, 65 Fed. Appx. 731 (Fed. Cir. 2003). United States ☞72.1(2)

Government's failure to notify contractor that it was using other contractors to fulfill needs described in contract's statement of work was not evidence of bad faith, where contract was an indefinite delivery and indefinite quantity (IDIQ) contract, and government was under no obligation to notify contractor that it was using other contractors after the minimum guaranteed by the IDOQ contract was satisfied. J. Cooper & Associates, Inc. v. U.S., 53 Fed. Cl. 8 (2002), aff'd, 65 Fed. Appx. 731 (Fed. Cir. 2003). United States ⊶72.1(2)

Because letter contract to provide support services for agency recruitment campaign was an indefinite delivery and indefinite quantity (IDIQ) contract, government did not breach contract by failing to provide contractor with work in excess of the minimum quantity in the letter contract or by failing to award to contractor all of the work in the government's pre-contract estimate. J. Cooper & Associates, Inc. v. U.S., 53 Fed. Cl. 8 (2002), aff'd, 65 Fed. Appx. 731 (Fed. Cir. 2003). United States ⊶73(22)

An "indefinite delivery and indefinite quantity (IDIQ) contract" provides that the government will purchase an indefinite quantity of supplies or services from a contractor during a fixed period of time, and requires the government to order only a stated minimum quantity of supplies or services. J. Cooper & Associates, Inc. v. U.S., 53 Fed. Cl. 8 (2002), aff'd, 65 Fed. Appx. 731 (Fed. Cir. 2003). United States ⊶70(6.1)

An indefinite delivery and indefinite quantity (IDIQ) contract requires the government to order only a stated minimum quantity of supplies or services, and once the government has purchased the minimum quantity stated in an IDIQ contract from the contractor, it is free to purchase additional supplies or services from any other source it chooses. J. Cooper & Associates, Inc. v. U.S., 53 Fed. Cl. 8 (2002), aff'd, 65 Fed. Appx. 731 (Fed. Cir. 2003). United States ⊶70(6.1)

Government contractor stated a claim for inaccurate estimates in an indefinite-quantity (IDQ) contract, notwithstanding that it did not specifically incorporate the term "bad faith" into its complaint, where it alleged that contracting agency issued solicitation specifications which were knowingly and intentionally false, non-representative of the actual requirements, or in the alternative, issued with a reckless disregard of their truth or reliability, with the intent to induce contractor to rely on the flawed specifications to its detriment. Schweiger Const. Co., Inc. v. U.S., 49 Fed. Cl. 188 (2001). United States ⊶70(26)

Government contractor must present well-nigh irrefragable proof that the government acted in bad faith to recover for inaccurate quantity estimates in an indefinite-quantity contract (IDQ). Schweiger Const. Co., Inc. v. U.S., 49 Fed. Cl. 188 (2001). United States ⊶70(26)

Courts will not review the accuracy of quantity estimates in indefinite-quantity (IDQ) government contracts where mere negligence has been alleged; however, they will, permit recovery for inaccurate estimates in the event of more egregious governmental conduct, most usually defined as "bad faith." Schweiger Const. Co., Inc. v. U.S., 49 Fed. Cl. 188 (2001). United States ⊶70(26)

Fact that government has the obligation under an indefinite-quantity (IDQ) contract to order the contractual minimum does not preclude a contractor from recovering for inaccurate quantity estimates in an IDQ contract. Schweiger Const. Co., Inc. v. U.S., 49 Fed. Cl. 188 (2001). United States ⊶70(26)

With regard to whether a government contract is an indefinite quantity contract or a requirements contract, an indefinite quantity contract differs from a requirements contract in that under a requirements contract the government agrees to purchase all his requirements from the contractor; under an indefinite quantities contract, even if the government has requirements, it is not obligated to purchase from the contractor. Myers Investigative and Security Services, Inc. v. U.S., 47 Fed. Cl. 605 (2000), aff'd, 275 F.3d 1366 (Fed. Cir. 2002). United States ⊶70(9)

Section of Federal Acquisition Regulation giving preference to multiple awards of indefinite-quantity contracts under a single solicitation contemplates that contracting officer's contrary determination that a single award is appropriate will precede and form the basis of an agency decision to override the preference for multiple awards. Federal Property and Administrative Services Act of 1949, § 303h(d)(3), as amended, 41 U.S.C.A. § 253h(d)(3); 48 C.F.R. § 16.504(c)(1). WinStar Communications, Inc. v. U.S., 41 Fed. Cl. 748, 42 Cont. Cas. Fed. (CCH) P 77371 (1998). United States ⊶64.15

Decision of contracting officer (CO) to award a single indefinite delivery/indefinite quantity contract under a single solicitation, rather than multiple contracts, was arbitrary, capricious, and not in accordance with the legal preference for multiple awards, where the CO's analysis failed to address and weigh the benefits of awarding multiple contracts as required by the Federal Acquisition Regulation. 48 C.F.R. § 16.504(c)(1). WinStar Communications, Inc. v. U.S., 41 Fed. Cl. 748, 42 Cont. Cas. Fed. (CCH) P 77371 (1998). United States ☜64.15

Although agency's decision to award a single indefinite delivery/indefinite quantity contract under a single solicitation, rather than multiple contracts, was procedurally invalid because it was made before the contracting officer (CO) prepared the written determination required by section of the Federal Acquisition Regulation, violation was not prejudicial; if the matter were remanded solely on the basis of procedural error, agency would be free to adopt the substance of the CO's analysis and again conclude that a single award was appropriate. Federal Property and Administrative Services Act of 1949, § 303h(d)(3), as amended, 41 U.S.C.A. § 253h(d)(3); 48 C.F.R. § 16.504(c)(1). WinStar Communications, Inc. v. U.S., 41 Fed. Cl. 748, 42 Cont. Cas. Fed. (CCH) P 77371 (1998). United States ☜64.60(5.1)

Estimated quantities are not guarantees or warranties of quantity under requirements contract, and significant variance between estimated quantities and actual purchases under government contract does not, in itself, give rise to liability on part of government. 48 C.F.R. § 16.503(a)(1). Datalect Computer Services, Ltd. v. U.S., 40 Fed. Cl. 28, 42 Cont. Cas. Fed. (CCH) P 77243 (1997), aff'd in part, vacated in part on other grounds, 215 F.3d 1344 (Fed. Cir. 1999). United States ☜70(30)

Determination that justifies single award of contract for advisory and assistance services exceeding three years and $10 million must be made prior to issuance of solicitation. 10 U.S.C.A. § 2304b(e)(3); 48 C.F.R. § 16.504(c)(2)(i)(A). Cubic Applications, Inc. v. U.S., 37 Fed. Cl. 345, 41 Cont. Cas. Fed. (CCH) P 77075 (1997). United States ☜64.5

Service contract to maintain hardwood floors and paint interior walls of military family housing was an indefinite quantity contract, rather than a requirements contract, and thus, government fulfilled its obligations under contract when it exceeded the minimum quantity by 11 times the stated minimum, where contract clause stated it was an indefinite quantity contract for supplies or services specified and that government was required to order at least the quantity of supplies or services designated in schedule minimum, and an amendment to the contract specifically deleted requirements contracts clause from the agreement. 48 C.F.R. § 52.216-22. Rice Lake Contracting, Inc. v. U.S., 33 Fed. Cl. 144, 40 Cont. Cas. Fed. (CCH) P 76773 (1995). United States ☜70(6.1)

Under contract with Navy for manufacture of various types of hydrophone sensors, Navy's right to purchase "all or part" of items enabled it to limit purchase to portion of sensors under subline item numbers listed in contract, and did not require it to accept or reject entire quantity listed under subline item numbers included under each contract line item number; thus, contractor could not recover for increased unit price attributable to purchase of only part of quantities listed under some subline item numbers. International Transducer Corp. v. U.S., 30 Fed. Cl. 522, 39 Cont. Cas. Fed. (CCH) P 76630 (1994), aff'd, 48 F.3d 1235 (Fed. Cir. 1995). United States ☜70(9)

Because contract language could be interpreted to support finding that it was an indefinite quantity contract or finding that it was a requirements contract, intentions of the parties would be examined to determine what the parties really meant. Crown Laundry and Dry Cleaners, Inc. v. U.S., 29 Fed. Cl. 506, 39 Cont. Cas. Fed. (CCH) P 76575 (1993). Sales ☜71(4)

In determining whether contract with United States is for a definite quantity, for an indefinite quantity, or for requirements, court is not bound by the name or label given to the contract, interpretation which gives meaning to all parts of the contract is preferable to one which renders provisions of the contract meaningless or superfluous, and it will be assumed that the parties intended to form a binding contract, so the court will favor interpretation which saves the contract instead of voiding it. Crown Laundry and Dry Cleaners, Inc. v. U.S., 29 Fed. Cl. 506, 39 Cont. Cas. Fed. (CCH) P 76575 (1993). United States ☜70(6.1); United States ☜70(9)

Presence of requirements clause in contract does not preclude court from determining that contract is an indefinite quantities contract, and absence of requirements clause does not inhibit the court from deeming the contract to be a requirements contract. Crown Laundry and Dry Cleaners, Inc. v. U.S., 29 Fed. Cl. 506, 39 Cont. Cas. Fed. (CCH) P 76575 (1993). Contracts ☞71(4)

For purpose of determining whether low bidder was entitled to enjoin Government's cancellation of solicitation for bids for providing unarmed guard services, even if solicitation could be characterized as unclear as to whether it was indefinite quantity contract or fixed-price contract subject to options, no bidder was confused about requirements of solicitation, as amended, that contract would be indefinite quantity contract. Vanguard Sec. Inc. v. U.S., 20 Cl. Ct. 90, 1990 WL 38036 (1990). United States ☞64.60(5.1)

For purpose of determining whether low bidder was entitled to enjoin Government's cancellation of solicitation for bids for providing unarmed guard services, insofar as amendment to solicitation attempted to convert indefinite quantity contract into fixed-price contract subject to options, amendment failed to displace contract provisions inherent in an indefinite contract. Vanguard Sec. Inc. v. U.S., 20 Cl. Ct. 90, 1990 WL 38036 (1990). United States ☞64.60(5.1)

15 Letter contracts

A "letter contract" is an interim agreement that allows a government contractor to begin performance prior to issuance of a definitized contract. 48 C.F.R. § 16.603-1. Integrated Logistics Support Systems Intern., Inc. v. U.S., 47 Fed. Cl. 248 (2000), aff'd, 36 Fed. Appx. 650 (Fed. Cir. 2002). United States ☞63

Contracting agency's unilateral definitization of contract modification at the $2 million advanced to the contractor was in error, where modification indicated that the money advanced was projected to be less than half of the total amount needed for the contract modification. 48 C.F.R. § 16.603-2. Northrop Grumman Corp. v. U.S., 47 Fed. Cl. 20 (2000). United States ☞72(5)

16 Basic agreements, generally

Basic Purchasing Agreement with provider of telephone services involving "moves, adds and changes" to telephone configuration in Postal Service building did not create contractual obligation on part of Postal Service to utilize any telephone services; agreement contemplated that parties would enter into binding contracts in future through issuance of individual authorized orders, and merely provided price and other terms and conditions for such future contracts. Modern Systems Technology Corp. v. U.S., 979 F.2d 200, 38 Cont. Cas. Fed. (CCH) P 76397 (Fed. Cir. 1992). United States ☞70(6.1)

Basic Purchasing Agreement between provider of telephone services and Postal Service, providing for "moves, adds and changes" of telephone equipment, was not a requirements contract obligating Postal Service to have all such activities carried on through provider; there was no express contractual commitment to have all of the Postal Service's requirements so satisfied, nor were there any minimum purchase requirements. Modern Systems Technology Corp. v. U.S., 979 F.2d 200, 38 Cont. Cas. Fed. (CCH) P 76397 (Fed. Cir. 1992). United States ☞70(6.1)

Basic pricing agreement entered into by government agency and contractor was not binding contract but merely a framework for future contracts; there was no language in agreement indicating any present intent that either party be bound and terms were not sufficiently definite. Modern Systems Technology Corp. v. U.S., 979 F.2d 200, 38 Cont. Cas. Fed. (CCH) P 76397 (Fed. Cir. 1992). United States ☞70(15.1)

Facts and circumstances independent of basic agreement itself may form enforceable contract or transform basic agreement into binding obligation. Almar Industries, Inc. v. U.S., 16 Cl. Ct. 243, 35 Cont. Cas. Fed. (CCH) P 75621, 1989 WL 6470 (1989). Contracts ☞1

17 Basic ordering agreements

Basic ordering agreement between translator and State Department was not itself a contract, but rather contract arose only when translator accepted work order issued by State Department's Office of Language Services authorizing translator to perform various services and providing that payment would be made in accordance with schedule of rates in basic ordering agreement. Zoubi v. U.S., 25 Cl. Ct. 581, 37 Cont. Cas. Fed. (CCH) P 76287,

1992 WL 58983 (1992). United States ☞63

Memorandum of understanding executed each year for resupply of Air Force base was not a basic ordering agreement in that it contained sufficient contractual overtones to qualify as "contract" within ambit of statute governing jurisdiction over pre-award contract claims; however, even though sufficient request was made by Army transportation officer such as to form implied contract to fairly and honestly consider plaintiff's responding proposal, claims court lacked jurisdiction to consider plaintiff's request for equitable relief stemming from cancellation of certain resupply transportation requirements, where fuel contract was amended prior to suit to encompass transportation requirement previously solicited, thus making any contract claim filed as to this transportation requirement a postaward claim. 28 U.S.C.A. § 1491(a)(3). Western Pioneer, Inc. v. U.S., 8 Cl. Ct. 291, 32 Cont. Cas. Fed. (CCH) P 73617 (1985). Federal Courts ☞1076; Federal Courts ☞1077; Federal Courts ☞1080

18 Authority of officers to contract

Statement by Postal Service employee, that firm which had entered into Basic Purchasing Agreement with Postal Service covering "moves, adds and changes" to telephones within building would be getting all of Postal Service's business except that which was done in-house, did not contractually commit Postal Service to place orders with firm; employee was not a contracting officer entitled to bind Postal Service. Modern Systems Technology Corp. v. U.S., 979 F.2d 200, 38 Cont. Cas. Fed. (CCH) P 76397 (Fed. Cir. 1992). United States ☞60

19 Waiver

Contractor waived its claim for reformation of fixed-price contract for research and development of technology for tracking ultra-quiet submarines, although it incurred costs in excess of fixed price, where contractor, a sophisticated federal contractor, failed to seek a cost reimbursement contract during contract negotiations, and it successfully underbid technically superior competitors and retained contract with a vigorous defense against competitor's protest action. American Tel. and Tel. Co. v. U.S., 307 F.3d 1374 (Fed. Cir. 2002). Reformation Of Instruments ☞23

20 Court of Federal Claims jurisdiction

Court of Federal Claims lacked jurisdiction in government contractor's breach of contract suit to enter declaratory judgment holding indefinite-quantity (IDQ) specifications deficient as a matter of law where they bore no rational relationship to actual requirements within the contracting agency's superior knowledge at the time of solicitation, where such a ruling was not necessary to resolve contractor's claim for money damages. Schweiger Const. Co., Inc. v. U.S., 49 Fed. Cl. 188 (2001). Federal Courts ☞1078

Court of Federal Claims had jurisdiction over government contractor's claim that construction contract was illegal and that government violated provisions of the Federal Acquisition Regulation which address the type of contract to be used for procurement, in that procurement should have led to the award of a cost-reimbursement contract, rather than a firmfixed-price contract. 48 C.F.R. § 16.000. PCL Const. Services, Inc. v. U.S., 41 Fed. Cl. 242, 42 Cont. Cas. Fed. (CCH) P 77325 (1998), aff'd, 96 Fed. Appx. 672 (Fed. Cir. 2004). Federal Courts ☞1076

Court lacked jurisdiction to consider merits of government contractor's claim arising out of defense industrial supply center's removal of contractor's name from its automated procurement system; contractor failed to establish that it received sufficient benefit from participating in program to provide consideration to transform basic agreement with center into enforceable contract. Almar Industries, Inc. v. U.S., 16 Cl. Ct. 243, 35 Cont. Cas. Fed. (CCH) P 75621, 1989 WL 6470 (1989). Federal Courts ☞1076

21 Parties

Manufacturer of office automation systems was "interested party," for purposes of Tucker Act, and thus had standing to challenge Department of Labor's (DOL) decision to standardize its software applications exclusively to software manufactured by competitor as violative of Competition in Contracting Act (CICA), where DOL refused to engage in competitive procurement for its office automation systems, and manufacturer submitted bid nonetheless. 10 U.S.C.A. § 2304; 28 U.S.C.A. § 1491(b)(1); Federal Property and Administrative Services Act of 1949, § 303, as amended, 41 U.S.C.A. § 253; 48 C.F.R. §§ 16.501-1, 16.501-2. Corel Corp. v. U.S., 165 F. Supp. 2d 12 (D.D.C. 2001). United States ☞64.60(2)

22 Questions of law or fact

Whether a government contract is an indefinite quantity or a requirements contract is a matter of law for the Court of Federal Claims to decide. Myers Investigative and Security Services, Inc. v. U.S., 47 Fed. Cl. 605 (2000), aff'd, 275 F.3d 1366 (Fed. Cir. 2002). United States ☞70(9)

23 Summary judgment

Where question of whether contract was for requirements or indefinite quantities did not involve any factual disputes material to interpretation of the contract, summary judgment could be used to resolve the question. RCFC, Rule 56(c, d), 28 U.S.C.A.Crown Laundry and Dry Cleaners, Inc. v. U.S., 29 Fed. Cl. 506, 39 Cont. Cas. Fed. (CCH) P 76575 (1993). Federal Courts ☞1120

24 Selection of contract type

Sections of the FAR providing internal government direction and guidance for contracting officer's selection of contract type did not provide judicial remedy for contractor who alleged improper use of firm fixed-price contract. Short Bros., PLC v. U.S., 65 Fed. Cl. 695 (2005)

Contracting officer's determination to solicit proposals for the awards of cost-reimbursement, as opposed to fixed-price, contracts for the performance of shipboard preservation services was reasonable where, given the unpredictable nature of the variables associated with this type of work, cost-reimbursement contracts will allow the agency to work with contractors to achieve the solicitation's preservation requirements with maximum flexibility and minimal delays. Surface Technologies Corporation, B-288317, 2001 CPD ¶ 147 (Comp. Gen. 2001)

§ 16.102 Policies.

(a) Contracts resulting from sealed bidding shall be firm-fixed-price contracts or fixed-price contracts with economic price adjustment.

(b) Contracts negotiated under Part 15 may be of any type or combination of types that will promote the Government's interest, except as restricted in this part (see 10 U.S.C. 2306(a) and 41 U.S.C. 3901). Contract types not described in this regulation shall not be used, except as a deviation under Subpart 1.4.

(c) The cost-plus-a-percentage-of-cost system of contracting shall not be used (see 10 U.S.C. 2306(a) and 41 U.S.C. 3905(a)). Prime contracts (including letter contracts) other than firm-fixed-price contracts shall, by an appropriate clause, prohibit cost-plus-a-percentage-of-cost subcontracts (see clauses prescribed in Subpart 44.2 for cost-reimbursement contracts and Subparts 16.2 and 16.4 for fixed-price contracts).

(d) No contract may be awarded before the execution of any determination and findings (D&F's) required by this part. Minimum requirements for the content of D&F's required by this part are specified in 1.704.

United States Code Annotated

Contract requirements, see 41 USCA § 254.

Contracts, planning, solicitation, evaluation, and award procedures, see 10 USCA § 2305.

Cost-type research and development contracts with educational institutions, see 41 USCA § 254a.

Definitions, see 10 USCA § 2302, 41 USCA §§ 259, 403.

Kinds of contracts, see 10 USCA § 2306.

Planning and solicitation requirements, see 41 USCA § 253a.

Task and delivery order contracts, definitions, see 10 USCA § 2304d, 41 USCA § 253k.

Task and delivery order contracts, general authority, see 10 USCA § 2304a, 41 USCA § 253h.

Task and delivery order contracts, orders, see 10 USCA § 2304c, 41 USCA § 253j.

Task order contracts, advisory and assistance services, see 10 USCA § 2304b, 41 USCA

§ 253i.

Economic price adjustment 3
Firm-fixed-price contracts 2
Fixed-price contracts, generally 1

1 Fixed-price contracts, generally

Amended version of Cost Accounting Standard (CAS), which provided for adjustment of pension costs under government contracts in response to contractor's segment closings, did not apply retroactively, where pension surplus that was attributable to CAS-covered government contracts arose under contracts that contained only the original "segment closing" provision, pursuant to which contractor was not liable for any pension surplus attributable to its fixed-price contracts; applying the CAS retroactively to such contracts would amount to a change in accounting practices and entitle contractor to equitable adjustment under another federal regulation. 48 C.F.R. § 52.230-2(a)(4)(i). Allegheny Teledyne Inc. v. U.S., 316 F.3d 1366, 30 Employee Benefits Cas. (BNA) 1753 (Fed. Cir. 2003). United States ⊗═70(18)

While Cost Accounting Standard (CAS) providing for adjustment of pension costs under government contracts in response to contractor's segment closings applies to both fixed- and flexibly-priced government contracts, determination of whether any adjustment was recoverable depended on terms of particular contract. 4 C.F.R. § 413-50(c)(12) (1986). Allegheny Teledyne Inc. v. U.S., 316 F.3d 1366, 30 Employee Benefits Cas. (BNA) 1753 (Fed. Cir. 2003). United States ⊗═70(18)

Procurement regulations and directives that guide a contracting officer's selection of contract type and grant the officer discretion to select type of contract did not prohibit contracting officer from negotiating contract for research and development of technology for tracking ultra-quiet submarines on a fixed-price basis, since those provisions merely cautioned against a fixed-price contract where substantial developmental risk rendered cost estimation merely hypothetical. 48 C.F.R. §§ 16.103(a), 16.104, 35.006(b, c), 216.104. American Tel. and Tel. Co. v. U.S., 307 F.3d 1374 (Fed. Cir. 2002). United States ⊗═70(15.1)

Navy contract for development of ship-towed, undersea surveillance system was for "major system or subsystem," for purposes of statute prohibiting Department of Defense from entering into fixed price contracts for development of major system or subsystem exceeding $10 million unless certain conditions were met, notwithstanding either agency's reliance on separate statute to define major system as having $75 million floor or fact that contract was funded over multiple years. 10 U.S.C.A. § 2302(5); Act December 22, 1987, § 101(b), Sec. 8118, 101 Stat. 1329. American Tel. & Tel. Co. v. U.S., 177 F.3d 1368 (Fed. Cir. 1999). United States ⊗═70(15.1)

Failure of Department of Defense to comply with statute setting forth internal review and reporting requirements for fixed price contract for development of major system or subsystem exceeding $10 million did not render such contract void ab initio, as statute itself did not announce sanction of contract invalidity, and contract had been fully performed. Act December 22, 1987, § 101(b), Sec. 8118, 101 Stat. 1329. American Tel. & Tel. Co. v. U.S., 177 F.3d 1368 (Fed. Cir. 1999). United States ⊗═70(15.1)

Fixed-price contracts assign risk to contractor that actual cost of performance will be higher than price of contract. 48 C.F.R. § 16.202-1. Dalton v. Cessna Aircraft Co., 98 F.3d 1298, 41 Cont. Cas. Fed. (CCH) P 76998 (Fed. Cir. 1996). United States ⊗═70(15.1)

Government did not breach fixed-price dredging contract that required the dredging, transporting, and depositing of material from two stockpile areas along the Mississippi River by refusing to pay contractor an additional $1,111,227.51 to contractor to compensate it for cost overrun caused by county's opposition to contractor's proposed disposal site on private property; as a party to a fixed-price contract, contractor assumed the risk of any cost overruns during the term of performance. 48 C.F.R. § 16.202-1. L.W. Matteson, Inc. v. U.S., 61 Fed. Cl. 296 (2004). United States ⊗═70(22.1)

Focus of fixed-price public contract is contractor output. 48 C.F.R. §§ 16.401, 16.403. McDonnell Douglas Corp. v. U.S., 37 Fed. Cl. 295, 41 Cont. Cas. Fed. (CCH) P 77046 (1997), order modified, 39 Fed. Cl. 665, 42 Cont. Cas. Fed. (CCH) P 77230 (1997). United States ☞70(15.1)

2 Firm-fixed-price contracts

Utility company's proposal for government contract relating to electrical services, which proposed that government would reimburse none of company's costs for replacing electrical system at issue and that government would pay company up to certain amount if specified contingencies arose, was cost-share type contract, not firm-fixed-price contract, and thus satisfied requirement in request for proposal (RFP) that bidders submit cost-reimbursement contract proposal. 48 C.F.R. §§ 16.202, 16.303. City & County of San Francisco v. U.S., 130 F.3d 873, 42 Cont. Cas. Fed. (CCH) P 77215 (9th Cir. 1997). United States ☞64.30

Costs of contractor's severance payments to six employees, following expiration of firm, fixed-price contract with United States Air Force, were not recoverable as "abnormal or mass severance costs" for which government would be liable for its "fair share" under Federal Acquisition Regulations (FAR) incorporated into contract; severance payments were normal severance when viewed in context of contract's expiration, which was foreseeable event when contract was entered into. 48 C.F.R. § 31.205-6(g)(2)(iii). ITT Federal Services Corp. v. Widnall, 132 F.3d 1448, 42 Cont. Cas. Fed. (CCH) P 77242 (Fed. Cir. 1997). United States ☞70(21)

Contractor was not entitled to recover cost of severance payments made to six employees who could not be placed with contractor or successor contractor following termination of firm, fixed-price contract with United States Air Force under continuity of services provision of Federal Acquisition Regulations (FAR) incorporated into contract; severance payments were not transition services costs provided for in provision, in that they did not result from activities to assist new contractor or government in taking over operations, nor were they designed to assure continuity of services during transition period. 48 C.F.R. § 52. 237-3. ITT Federal Services Corp. v. Widnall, 132 F.3d 1448, 42 Cont. Cas. Fed. (CCH) P 77242 (Fed. Cir. 1997). United States ☞70(21)

Flight training services contractor's interpretation of "17,000 airborne training service hours" provision of firm fixed-price contract with Navy as qualified by parenthetical reference to 58 hours per graduated student gave rise to patent ambiguity and corresponding duty to seek clarification before submitting proposal. Dalton v. Cessna Aircraft Co., 98 F.3d 1298, 41 Cont. Cas. Fed. (CCH) P 76998 (Fed. Cir. 1996). United States ☞64.5

In absence of language clearly and unambiguously placing qualification on manner in which Navy could consume services it was procuring through firm fixed-price contract for flight training services, it was reasonable for Navy to interpret contractual reference to 58 hours per graduated student as estimate. Dalton v. Cessna Aircraft Co., 98 F.3d 1298, 41 Cont. Cas. Fed. (CCH) P 76998 (Fed. Cir. 1996). United States ☞70(6.1)

When viewing firm fixed-price contract for flight training services as whole, Navy reasonably interpreted parenthetical reference to 58 hours per graduated student in general provisions of contract as estimate, rather than binding provision; specific provisions of contract contained in attached training syllabus called for 17,000 hours of flight services for third, fourth, and fifth program years and for option years, without qualification as to the number of hours per student. Dalton v. Cessna Aircraft Co., 98 F.3d 1298, 41 Cont. Cas. Fed. (CCH) P 76998 (Fed. Cir. 1996). United States ☞70(6.1)

Flight training services contractor that failed to seek clarification of its patently ambiguous interpretation of service hours required by firm fixed-price contract with Navy before it submitted winning proposal was barred from seeking equitable adjustment for subsequent change in Navy's training syllabus. Dalton v. Cessna Aircraft Co., 98 F.3d 1298, 41 Cont. Cas. Fed. (CCH) P 76998 (Fed. Cir. 1996). United States ☞70(24)

Failure of contracting agency to perform a cost realism analysis on contract awardee's offer was not error, as there was no requirement for such an analysis, where solicitation contemplated award of firm fixed price contract and contracting officer (CO) deemed awardee responsible to perform the project at the offered price. 48 C.F.R. § 15.404-1(d)(1). First Enterprise v. U.S., 61 Fed. Cl. 109 (2004). United States ☞64.40(1)

Original version of Cost Accounting Standard (CAS) governing segment closing adjustment of pension costs under government contracts required contractor to examine both firm-fixed-price and flexibly-priced contracts to determine the pension surplus or deficit attributable to government contributions. 4 C.F.R. § 413-50(c)(12) (1986). Teledyne, Inc. v. U.S., 50 Fed. Cl. 155 (2001), aff'd, 316 F.3d 1366, 30 Employee Benefits Cas. (BNA) 1753 (Fed. Cir. 2003). United States ☞70(18)

Original version of Cost Accounting Standard (CAS) governing segment closing adjustment of pension costs under government contracts did not allow for the recovery of any pension surplus or the payment of any pension plan deficit attributable to government-reimbursed pension costs under firm-fixed-price contracts; thus, such adjustment would only be recoverable pursuant to an express contract provision. 4 C.F.R. § 413-50(c)(12) (1986). Teledyne, Inc. v. U.S., 50 Fed. Cl. 155 (2001), aff'd, 316 F.3d 1366, 30 Employee Benefits Cas. (BNA) 1753 (Fed. Cir. 2003). United States ☞70(18)

Original version of Cost Accounting Standard (CAS) governing segment closing adjustment of pension costs under government contracts required contractor to allocate the segment closing adjustment between firm-fixed-price contracts and flexibly-priced contracts that gave rise to the surplus or deficit attributable to government contributions; portion of surplus or deficit attributable to firm-fixed-price contracts must be identified in order to determine the recoverable portion of the segment closing adjustment. 4 C.F.R. § 413-50(c)(12) (1986). Teledyne, Inc. v. U.S., 50 Fed. Cl. 155 (2001), aff'd, 316 F.3d 1366, 30 Employee Benefits Cas. (BNA) 1753 (Fed. Cir. 2003). United States ☞70(18)

Applying amended version of Cost Accounting Standard (CAS) governing segment closing adjustment of pension costs to government contractor's sale of division amounted to a change in accounting practice that triggered equitable adjustment, where pension surplus that was attributable to CAS-covered government contracts arose under contracts that contained only the original segment closing provision pursuant to which contractor was not liable for pension surplus attributable to firm-fixed-price contracts. 4 C.F.R. § 413-50(c)(12) (1986); 48 C.F.R. §§ 52.230-2(a)(4)(i), 9904.413-50(c)(12). Teledyne, Inc. v. U.S., 50 Fed. Cl. 155 (2001), aff'd, 316 F.3d 1366, 30 Employee Benefits Cas. (BNA) 1753 (Fed. Cir. 2003). United States ☞70(21)

Cost Accounting Standards Board (CASB) complied with procedural requirements of the Office of Federal Procurement Policy Act (OFPPA) when it issued amended Cost Accounting Standard (CAS) making government contractor liable for pension surplus attributable to firm-fixed-price contracts in a segment closing adjustment; CASB gave adequate notice of the inclusion of firm-fixed-price contracts in the new segment closing adjustment provision in proposed illustrations, and received comments that addressed issue. Contract Disputes Act of 1978, § 26(g), as amended, 41 U.S.C.A. § 422(g); 48 C.F.R. § 9904.413-50(c)(12). Teledyne, Inc. v. U.S., 50 Fed. Cl. 155 (2001), aff'd, 316 F.3d 1366, 30 Employee Benefits Cas. (BNA) 1753 (Fed. Cir. 2003). United States ☞70(18)

Amended version of Cost Accounting Standard (CAS) governing segment closing adjustment of pension costs under government contracts was not invalid on ground the Cost Accounting Standards Board (CASB) did not have authority under the Office of Federal Procurement Policy Act (OFPPA) to require price adjustments under firm-fixed-price contracts, as amended version did not clearly contradict the OFPPA which requires the measurement, assignment, and allocation of pension costs. Contract Disputes Act of 1978, § 26(f, h), as amended, 41 U.S.C.A. § 422(f, h). Teledyne, Inc. v. U.S., 50 Fed. Cl. 155 (2001), aff'd, 316 F.3d 1366, 30 Employee Benefits Cas. (BNA) 1753 (Fed. Cir. 2003). United States ☞70(18)

Contractor which willingly bid on a firm fixed price (FFP) contract, and willingly signed an FFP contract, thereby assuming the risks attendant to an FFP contract, could not raise claim that FFP provisions violated the Federal Acquisition Regulation. 48 C.F.R. §§ 16.103(a), 16.202-2. PCL Const. Services, Inc. v. U.S., 47 Fed. Cl. 745 (2000). United States ☞70(15.1)

Firm-fixed-price contract for the operation and maintenance of two government-owned locks and dams did not require that contractor staff each lock and dam with a fulltime equipment mechanic, and thus it was improper for the government to reduce the contract price and withhold monies from contractor for periods during which equipment mechanic positions were vacant; term 'capability,' as used in the solicitation and contract documents, did not mandate any specific "manpower" or "staffing levels." Omni Corp. v. U.S., 41 Fed. Cl. 585 (1998). United States ☞70(15.1)

In firm fixed-price contract between federal agency and corporation, corporation bore risk that it would be required to pay unforeseen premium wages to its employees for federal government furlough period after arbitrator ordered such wages, where agency did not take position that employees should be paid premium wages for holiday pay or require any changes in services as to scope, time or personnel during furlough period. Cleveland Telecommunications Corp. v. U.S., 39 Fed. Cl. 649, 42 Cont. Cas. Fed. (CCH) P 77199 (1997). United States ☞70(23)

For purpose of determining whether low bidder was entitled to enjoin Government's cancellation of solicitation for bids for providing unarmed guard services, solicitation's designation of contract as firm fixed-price contract was consistent with reaffirmation in same section that it was indefinite quantity contract, as meaning of contract was that prices for additional services, as well as for base and optional years, were firm fixed hourly rates. Vanguard Sec. Inc. v. U.S., 20 Cl. Ct. 90, 1990 WL 38036 (1990). United States ☞64.60(5.1)

Fact that solicitation for bids for providing unarmed guard services denominated contract as "firm fixed-price" did not show that solicitation called for provision of additional services through options, as opposed to indefinite quantity requirement. Vanguard Sec. Inc. v. U.S., 20 Cl. Ct. 90, 1990 WL 38036 (1990). United States ☞70(6.1)

3 Economic price adjustment

Under Federal Acquisition Regulation (FAR) governing economic price adjustments to fixed-price contracts, "contractor's established price" may be established by reference to either a catalog or market sources independent of the manufacturer or vendor. 48 C.F.R. § 16. 203. Tesoro Hawaii Corp. v. U.S., 405 F.3d 1339, 15 A.L.R. Fed. 2d 755 (Fed. Cir. 2005) United States ☞70(18)

Use of market-based references to determine adjustments to established prices in contracts for sale of jet fuel to military was authorized under Federal Acquisition Regulation (FAR) governing economic price adjustments to fixed price contracts. 48 C.F.R. § 16. 203. Tesoro Hawaii Corp. v. U.S., 405 F.3d 1339, 15 A.L.R. Fed. 2d 755 (Fed. Cir. 2005). United States ☞70(18)

Federal Acquisition Regulation (FAR) governing economic price adjustments to fixed price contracts permit use of contracts that include adjustments based on established prices, but do not limit those adjustments to changes only in the specific prices offered by an individual contractor. Tesoro Hawaii Corp. v. U.S., 405 F.3d 1339, 15 A.L.R. Fed. 2d 755 (Fed. Cir. 2005). United States ☞70(23)

Use of an economic price adjustment (EPA) clause tied particularly to a reference price in a market publication to determine price adjustments in fuel contracts did not violate Federal Acquisition Regulation (FAR) governing economic price adjustments to fixed price contracts; regulation did not require that adjustments be tied solely to changes in the prices charged by a particular contractor. 48 C.F.R. § 16.203-3. Tesoro Hawaii Corp. v. U.S., 405 F.3d 1339, 15 A.L.R. Fed. 2d 755 (Fed. Cir. 2005). United States ☞70(18)

To be authorized under the Federal Acquisition Regulation (FAR), economic price adjustment (EPA) clause in military fuel supply contracts had to fall within one of the three general types set forth in section of the FAR authorizing use of EPA clauses. 48 C.F.R. § 16. 203-1. Sunoco, Inc. v. U.S., 59 Fed. Cl. 390 (2004) (abrogated on other grounds by, Tesoro Hawaii Corp. v. U.S., 405 F.3d 1339, 15 A.L.R. Fed. 2d 755 (Fed. Cir. 2005)). United States ☞70(18)

Individual deviation or exemption from section of the Federal Acquisition Regulation (FAR) governing economic price adjustment clauses was invalid and illegal under the FAR, where deviation was applied not to a single contract but to multiple contracts issued under single solicitation, and was used to accommodate the government as a temporary measure until a permanent class deviation was obtained. 48 C.F.R. §§ 1.403, 1.404, 16.203-1. Calcasieu Refining Co. v. U.S., 2003 WL 22049528 (Ct. Fed. Cl. 2003). United States ☞70(18)

Section of the Federal Acquisition Regulation (FAR) which authorizes the government's use of "[f]ixed-price contracts with economic price adjustment" authorized the use of economic price adjustment (EPA) clauses that adopt market based price indexes to provide adjustments in a contractor's established prices. 48 C.F.R. § 16.203-1. Williams Alaska Petroleum, Inc. v. U.S., 57 Fed. Cl. 789 (2003). United States ☞70(18)

Defense Energy Support Center (DESC) had the authority to adopt market-based economic price adjustment (EPA) clauses in petroleum contracts awarded to military fuel suppliers during the years 1993 through 1999, pursuant to provisions of the Federal Acquisition Regulation (FAR) and individual and class deviations granted DESC during those years. 48 C.F.R. § 16.203-1. Williams Alaska Petroleum, Inc. v. U.S., 57 Fed. Cl. 789 (2003). United States ☞70(18)

If a fixed price government contract containing an economic price adjustment clause is in violation of the procurement regulations and does not meet the requirement that the selected index approximately tracks the economic changes affecting the contract, reformation is appropriate. Gold Line Refining, Ltd. v. U.S., 43 Fed. Cl. 291 (1999). United States ☞72(1.1)

Fixed price contract with economic price adjustment was required to comply with Federal Acquisition Regulations (FAR) on economic price adjustments, even if parties also intended indefinite-delivery indefinite-quantity contract. MAPCO Alaska Petroleum, Inc. v. U.S., 27 Fed. Cl. 405, 38 Cont. Cas. Fed. (CCH) P 76451 (1992) (abrogated on other grounds by, Tesoro Hawaii Corp. v. U.S., 405 F.3d 1339, 15 A.L.R. Fed. 2d 755 (Fed. Cir. 2005)). United States ☞70(23)

§ 16.103 Negotiating contract type.

(a) Selecting the contract type is generally a matter for negotiation and requires the exercise of sound judgment. Negotiating the contract type and negotiating prices are closely related and should be considered together. The objective is to negotiate a contract type and price (or estimated cost and fee) that will result in reasonable contractor risk and provide the contractor with the greatest incentive for efficient and economical performance.

(b) A firm-fixed-price contract, which best utilizes the basic profit motive of business enterprise, shall be used when the risk involved is minimal or can be predicted with an acceptable degree of certainty. However, when a reasonable basis for firm pricing does not exist, other contract types should be considered, and negotiations should be directed toward selecting a contract type (or combination of types) that will appropriately tie profit to contractor performance.

(c) In the course of an acquisition program, a series of contracts, or a single long-term contract, changing circumstances may make a different contract type appropriate in later periods than that used at the outset. In particular, contracting officers should avoid protracted use of a cost-reimbursement or time-and-materials contract after experience provides a basis for firmer pricing.

(d) (1) Each contract file shall include documentation to show why the particular contract type was selected. This shall be documented in the acquisition plan, or in the contract file if a written acquisition plan is not required by agency procedures.

(i) Explain why the contract type selected must be used to meet the agency need.

(ii) Discuss the Government's additional risks and the burden to manage the contract type selected (e.g., when a cost-reimbursement contract is selected, the Government incurs additional cost risks, and the Government has the additional burden of managing the contractor's costs). For such instances, acquisition personnel shall discuss?

(A) How the Government identified the additional risks (e.g., pre-award survey, or past performance information);

(B) The nature of the additional risks (e.g., inadequate contractor's accounting system, weaknesses in contractor's internal control, non-compliance with Cost Accounting Standards, or lack of or inadequate earned value management system); and

(C) How the Government will manage and mitigate the risks.

(iii) Discuss the Government resources necessary to properly plan for, award, and administer the contract type selected (e.g., resources needed and the additional risks to the Government if adequate resources are not provided).

(iv) For other than a firm-fixed price contract, at a minimum the documentation should include?

(A) An analysis of why the use of other than a firm-fixed-price contract (e.g., cost reimbursement, time and materials, labor hour) is appropriate;

(B) Rationale that detail the particular facts and circumstances (e.g., complexity of the requirements, uncertain duration of the work, contractor's technical capability and financial responsibility, or adequacy of the contractor's accounting system), and associated reasoning essential to support the contract type selection;

(C) An assessment regarding the adequacy of Government resources that are necessary to properly plan for, award, and administer other than firm-fixed-price contracts; and

(D) A discussion of the actions planned to minimize the use of other than firm-fixed-price contracts on future acquisitions for the same requirement and to transition to firm-fixed-price contracts to the maximum extent practicable.

(v) A discussion of why a level-of-effort, price redetermination, or fee provision was included.

(2) Exceptions to the requirements at (d)(1) of this section are?

(i) Fixed-price acquisitions made under simplified acquisition procedures;

(ii) Contracts on a firm-fixed-price basis other than those for major systems or research and development; and

(iii) Awards on the set-aside portion of sealed bid partial set-asides for small business.

United States Code Annotated

Contract requirements, see 41 USCA § 254.

Contracts, planning, solicitation, evaluation, and award procedures, see 10 USCA § 2305.

Cost-type research and development contracts with educational institutions, see 41 USCA § 254a.

Definitions, see 10 USCA § 2302, 41 USCA §§ 259, 403.

Kinds of contracts, see 10 USCA § 2306.

Planning and solicitation requirements, see 41 USCA § 253a.

Task and delivery order contracts, definitions, see 10 USCA § 2304d, 41 USCA § 253k.

Task and delivery order contracts, general authority, see 10 USCA § 2304a, 41 USCA § 253h.

Task and delivery order contracts, orders, see 10 USCA § 2304c, 41 USCA § 253j.

Task order contracts, advisory and assistance services, see 10 USCA § 2304b, 41 USCA § 253i.

Notes of Decisions

In general 1
Remedies of contractors 2

1 In general

Procurement regulations and directives that guide a contracting officer's selection of contract type and grant the officer discretion to select type of contract did not prohibit contracting officer from negotiating contract for research and development of technology for tracking ultra-quiet submarines on a fixed-price basis, since those provisions merely cautioned against a fixed-price contract where substantial developmental risk rendered cost estimation merely hypothetical. 48 C.F.R. §§ 16.103(a), 16.104, 35.006(b, c), 216.104. American Tel. and Tel. Co. v. U.S., 307 F.3d 1374 (Fed. Cir. 2002). United States ☞70(15.1)

Even if contracting officer abused his discretion under procurement regulations and directives by negotiating contract on a fixed-price basis, contractor that incurred costs in excess of price fixed in contract for research and development of technology for tracking ultra-quiet submarines had no remedy that could be provided in judicial forum, since cautionary and informative regulations and directives provided only internal governmental direction, and discipline to be administered was a responsibility of cognizant agency procurement officials. 48 C.F.R. §§ 16.103(a), 16.104, 35.006(b, c), 216.104. American Tel. and Tel. Co. v. U.S., 307 F.3d 1374 (Fed. Cir. 2002). United States ☞74(1)

Defense procurement regulations and directives cautioning against use of a fixed-price contract where developmental risk makes cost estimation difficult did not prohibit use of fixed-price form of contract for development of cruise missile, as contracting officer (CO) was granted discretion to select contract type; moreover, even if CO abused his discretion by using a fixed-price contract, provisions supplied no remedy to contractor. Northrop

Grumman Corp. v. U.S., 63 Fed. Cl. 38 (2004). United States ☞70(15.1)

Contractor which willingly bid on a firm fixed price (FFP) contract, and willingly signed an FFP contract, thereby assuming the risks attendant to an FFP contract, could not raise claim that FFP provisions violated the Federal Acquisition Regulation. 48 C.F.R. §§ 16. 103(a), 16.202-2. PCL Const. Services, Inc. v. U.S., 47 Fed. Cl. 745 (2000). United States ☞70(15.1)

2 Remedies of contractors

Sections of the Federal Acquisition Regulation (FAR) providing internal government direction and guidance for contracting officer's selection of contract type did not provide judicial remedy for contractor who alleged improper use of firm fixed-price contract. Short Bros., PLC v. U.S., 65 Fed. Cl. 695 (2005). United States ☞74(1)

§ 16.104 Factors in selecting contract types.

There are many factors that the contracting officer should consider in selecting and negotiating the contract type. They include the following:

(a) *Price competition.* Normally, effective price competition results in realistic pricing, and a fixed-price contract is ordinarily in the Government's interest.

(b) *Price analysis.* Price analysis, with or without competition, may provide a basis for selecting the contract type. The degree to which price analysis can provide a realistic pricing standard should be carefully considered. (See 15.404-1(b).)

(c) *Cost analysis.* In the absence of effective price competition and if price analysis is not sufficient, the cost estimates of the offeror and the Government provide the bases for negotiating contract pricing arrangements. It is essential that the uncertainties involved in performance and their possible impact upon costs be identified and evaluated, so that a contract type that places a reasonable degree of cost responsibility upon the contractor can be negotiated.

(d) *Type and complexity of the requirement.* Complex requirements, particularly those unique to the Government, usually result in greater risk assumption by the Government. This is especially true for complex research and development contracts, when performance uncertainties or the likelihood of changes makes it difficult to estimate performance costs in advance. As a requirement recurs or as quantity production begins, the cost risk should shift to the contractor, and a fixed-price contract should be considered.

(e) *Combining contract types.* If the entire contract cannot be firm-fixed-price, the contracting officer shall consider whether or not a portion of the contract can be established on a firm-fixed-price basis.

(f) *Urgency of the requirement.* If urgency is a primary factor, the Government may choose to assume a greater proportion of risk or it may offer incentives tailored to performance outcomes to ensure timely contract performance.

(g) *Period of performance or length of production run.* In times of economic uncertainty, contracts extending over a relatively long period may require economic price adjustment or price redetermination clauses.

(h) *Contractor's technical capability and financial responsibility.*

(i) *Adequacy of the contractor's accounting system.* Before agreeing on a contract type other than firm-fixed-price, the contracting officer shall ensure that the contractor's accounting system will permit timely development of all necessary cost data in the form required by the proposed contract type. This factor may be critical?

(1) When the contract type requires price revision while performance is in progress; or

(2) When a cost-reimbursement contract is being considered and all current or past experience with the contractor has been on a fixed-price basis. See 42.302(a)(12).

(j) *Concurrent contracts.* If performance under the proposed contract involves concurrent operations under other contracts, the impact of those contracts, including their pricing arrangements, should be considered.

(k) *Extent and nature of proposed subcontracting.* If the contractor proposes extensive subcontracting, a contract type reflecting the actual risks to the prime contractor should be selected.

(l) *Acquisition history.* Contractor risk usually decreases as the requirement is repetitively acquired. Also, product descriptions or descriptions of services to be performed can be defined more clearly.

United States Code Annotated

Contract requirements, see 41 USCA § 254.

Contracts, planning, solicitation, evaluation, and award procedures, see 10 USCA § 2305.

Cost-type research and development contracts with educational institutions, see 41 USCA § 254a.

Definitions, see 10 USCA § 2302, 41 USCA §§ 259, 403.

Kinds of contracts, see 10 USCA § 2306.

Planning and solicitation requirements, see 41 USCA § 253a.

Task and delivery order contracts, definitions, see 10 USCA § 2304d, 41 USCA § 253k.

Task and delivery order contracts, general authority, see 10 USCA § 2304a, 41 USCA § 253h.

Task and delivery order contracts, orders, see 10 USCA § 2304c, 41 USCA § 253j.

Task order contracts, advisory and assistance services, see 10 USCA § 2304b, 41 USCA § 253i.

Notes of Decisions

Construction and application 1
Economic price adjustment 2
Rights and remedies of contractors 3

1 Construction and application

Procurement regulations and directives that guide a contracting officer's selection of contract type and grant the officer discretion to select type of contract did not prohibit contracting officer from negotiating contract for research and development of technology for tracking ultra-quiet submarines on a fixed-price basis, since those provisions merely cautioned against a fixed-price contract where substantial developmental risk rendered cost estimation merely hypothetical. 48 C.F.R. §§ 16.103(a), 16.104, 35.006(b, c), 216.104. American Tel. and Tel. Co. v. U.S., 307 F.3d 1374 (Fed. Cir. 2002). United States ☞70(15.1)

Defense procurement regulations and directives cautioning against use of a fixed-price contract where developmental risk makes cost estimation difficult did not prohibit use of fixed-price form of contract for development of cruise missile, as contracting officer (CO) was granted discretion to select contract type; moreover, even if CO abused his discretion by using a fixed-price contract, provisions supplied no remedy to contractor. Northrop Grumman Corp. v. U.S., 63 Fed. Cl. 38 (2004). United States ☞70(15.1)

2 Economic price adjustment

Under Federal Acquisition Regulation (FAR) governing economic price adjustments to fixed-price contracts, "contractor's established price" may be established by reference to either a catalog or market sources independent of the manufacturer or vendor. 48 C.F.R. § 16. 203. Tesoro Hawaii Corp. v. U.S., 405 F.3d 1339, 15 A.L.R. Fed. 2d 755 (Fed. Cir. 2005) United States ☞70(18)

Use of market-based references to determine adjustments to established prices in contracts for sale of jet fuel to military was authorized under Federal Acquisition Regulation (FAR) governing economic price adjustments to fixed price contracts. 48 C.F.R. § 16. 203. Tesoro Hawaii Corp. v. U.S., 405 F.3d 1339, 15 A.L.R. Fed. 2d 755 (Fed. Cir. 2005). United States ☞70(18)

Federal Acquisition Regulation (FAR) governing economic price adjustments to fixed price contracts permit use of contracts that include adjustments based on established prices, but do not limit those adjustments to changes only in the specific prices offered by an individual contractor. Tesoro Hawaii Corp. v. U.S., 405 F.3d 1339, 15 A.L.R. Fed. 2d 755 (Fed. Cir. 2005). United States ☞70(23)

Use of an economic price adjustment (EPA) clause tied particularly to a reference price in a market publication to determine price adjustments in fuel contracts did not violate Federal Acquisition Regulation (FAR) governing economic price adjustments to fixed price contracts; regulation did not require that adjustments be tied solely to changes in the prices charged by a particular contractor. 48 C.F.R. § 16.203-3. Tesoro Hawaii Corp. v. U.S., 405 F.3d 1339, 15 A.L.R. Fed. 2d 755 (Fed. Cir. 2005). United States ☞70(18)

To be authorized under the Federal Acquisition Regulation (FAR), economic price adjustment (EPA) clause in military fuel supply contracts had to fall within one of the three general types set forth in section of the FAR authorizing use of EPA clauses. 48 C.F.R. § 16.203-1. Sunoco, Inc. v. U.S., 59 Fed. Cl. 390 (2004) (abrogated on other grounds by, Tesoro Hawaii Corp. v. U.S., 405 F.3d 1339, 15 A.L.R. Fed. 2d 755 (Fed. Cir. 2005)). United States ☞70(18)

Individual deviation or exemption from section of the Federal Acquisition Regulation (FAR) governing economic price adjustment clauses was invalid and illegal under the FAR, where deviation was applied not to a single contract but to multiple contracts issued under single solicitation, and was used to accommodate the government as a temporary measure until a permanent class deviation was obtained. 48 C.F.R. §§ 1.403, 1.404, 16.203-1. Calcasieu Refining Co. v. U.S., 2003 WL 22049528 (Ct. Fed. Cl. 2003). United States ☞70(18)

Section of the Federal Acquisition Regulation (FAR) which authorizes the government's use of "[f]ixed-price contracts with economic price adjustment" authorized the use of economic price adjustment (EPA) clauses that adopt market based price indexes to provide adjustments in a contractor's established prices. 48 C.F.R. § 16.203-1. Williams Alaska Petroleum, Inc. v. U.S., 57 Fed. Cl. 789 (2003). United States ☞70(18)

Defense Energy Support Center (DESC) had the authority to adopt market-based economic price adjustment (EPA) clauses in petroleum contracts awarded to military fuel suppliers during the years 1993 through 1999, pursuant to provisions of the Federal Acquisition Regulation (FAR) and individual and class deviations granted DESC during those years. 48 C.F.R. § 16.203-1. Williams Alaska Petroleum, Inc. v. U.S., 57 Fed. Cl. 789 (2003). United States ☞70(18)

If a fixed price government contract containing an economic price adjustment clause is in violation of the procurement regulations and does not meet the requirement that the selected index approximately tracks the economic changes affecting the contract, reformation is appropriate. Gold Line Refining, Ltd. v. U.S., 43 Fed. Cl. 291 (1999). United States ☞72(1.1)

Fixed price contract with economic price adjustment was required to comply with Federal Acquisition Regulations (FAR) on economic price adjustments, even if parties also intended indefinite-delivery indefinite-quantity contract. MAPCO Alaska Petroleum, Inc. v. U.S., 27 Fed. Cl. 405, 38 Cont. Cas. Fed. (CCH) P 76451 (1992) (abrogated on other grounds by, Tesoro Hawaii Corp. v. U.S., 405 F.3d 1339, 15 A.L.R. Fed. 2d 755 (Fed. Cir. 2005)). United States ☞70(23)

3 Rights and remedies of contractors

Even if contracting officer abused his discretion under procurement regulations and directives by negotiating contract on a fixed-price basis, contractor that incurred costs in excess of price fixed in contract for research and development of technology for tracking ultra-quiet submarines had no remedy that could be provided in judicial forum, since cautionary and informative regulations and directives provided only internal governmental direction, and discipline to be administered was a responsibility of cognizant agency procurement officials. 48 C.F.R. §§ 16.103(a), 16.104, 35.006(b, c), 216.104. American Tel. and Tel. Co. v. U.S., 307 F.3d 1374 (Fed. Cir. 2002). United States ☞74(1)

Sections of the Federal Acquisition Regulation (FAR) providing internal government direction and guidance for contracting officer's selection of contract type did not provide judicial remedy for contractor who alleged improper use of firm fixed-price contract. Short Bros., PLC v. U.S., 65 Fed. Cl. 695 (2005). United States ☞74(1)

Procurement regulations providing guidance on the use of fixed-price contracts are instructional rather than mandatory, and, as such, grant no enforceable rights to contractors. 48 C.F.R. §§ 16.104, 35.006, 216.101, 216.104. American Tel. & Tel. Co. v. U.S., 48 Fed. Cl. 156 (2000), aff'd, 307 F.3d 1374 (Fed. Cir. 2002). United States ☞74(1)

§ 16.105 Solicitation provision.

The contracting officer shall complete and insert the provision at 52.216-1, Type of Contract, in a solicitation unless it is for—

(a) A fixed-price acquisition made under simplified acquisition procedures; or

(b) Information or planning purposes.

United States Code Annotated

Contract requirements, see 41 USCA § 254.

Contracts, planning, solicitation, evaluation, and award procedures, see 10 USCA § 2305.

Cost-type research and development contracts with educational institutions, see 41 USCA § 254a.

Definitions, see 10 USCA § 2302, 41 USCA §§ 259, 403.

Kinds of contracts, see 10 USCA § 2306.

Planning and solicitation requirements, see 41 USCA § 253a.

Task and delivery order contracts, definitions, see 10 USCA § 2304d, 41 USCA § 253k.

Task and delivery order contracts, general authority, see 10 USCA § 2304a, 41 USCA § 253h.

Task and delivery order contracts, orders, see 10 USCA § 2304c, 41 USCA § 253j.

Task order contracts, advisory and assistance services, see 10 USCA § 2304b, 41 USCA § 253i.

Subpart 16.2 Fixed-Price Contracts

§ 16.201 General.

(a) Fixed-price types of contracts provide for a firm price or, in appropriate cases, an adjustable price. Fixed-price contracts providing for an adjustable price may include a ceiling price, a target price (including target cost), or both. Unless otherwise specified in the contract, the ceiling price or target price is subject to adjustment only by operation of contract clauses providing for equitable adjustment or other revision of the contract price under stated circumstances. The contracting officer shall use firm-fixed-price or fixed-price with economic price adjustment contracts when acquiring commercial items, except as provided in 12.207(b).

(b) Time-and-materials contracts and labor-hour contracts are not fixed-price contracts.

United States Code Annotated

Contract requirements, see 41 USCA § 254.

Contracts, planning, solicitation, evaluation, and award procedures, see 10 USCA § 2305.

Cost-type research and development contracts with educational institutions, see 41 USCA § 254a.

Definitions, see 10 USCA § 2302, 41 USCA §§ 259, 403.

Kinds of contracts, see 10 USCA § 2306.

Planning and solicitation requirements, see 41 USCA § 253a.

Task and delivery order contracts, definitions, see 10 USCA § 2304d, 41 USCA § 253k.

Task and delivery order contracts, general authority, see 10 USCA § 2304a, 41 USCA § 253h.

Task and delivery order contracts, orders, see 10 USCA § 2304c, 41 USCA § 253j.

Task order contracts, advisory and assistance services, see 10 USCA § 2304b, 41 USCA § 253i.

Notes of Decisions

Economic price adjustment 2
Fixed-price contracts, generally 1
Waiver 3

1 Fixed-price contracts, generally

Amended version of Cost Accounting Standard (CAS), which provided for adjustment of pension costs under government contracts in response to contractor's segment closings, did not apply retroactively, where pension surplus that was attributable to CAS-covered government contracts arose under contracts that contained only the original "segment closing" provision, pursuant to which contractor was not liable for any pension surplus attributable to its fixed-price contracts; applying the CAS retroactively to such contracts would amount to a change in accounting practices and entitle contractor to equitable adjustment under another federal regulation. 48 C.F.R. § 52.230-2(a)(4)(i). Allegheny Teledyne Inc. v. U.S., 316 F.3d 1366, 30 Employee Benefits Cas. (BNA) 1753 (Fed. Cir. 2003). United States ☞70(18)

While Cost Accounting Standard (CAS) providing for adjustment of pension costs under government contracts in response to contractor's segment closings applies to both fixed- and flexibly-priced government contracts, determination of whether any adjustment was recoverable depended on terms of particular contract. 4 C.F.R. § 413-50(c)(12) (1986). Allegheny Teledyne Inc. v. U.S., 316 F.3d 1366, 30 Employee Benefits Cas. (BNA) 1753 (Fed. Cir. 2003). United States ☞70(18)

Procurement regulations and directives that guide a contracting officer's selection of contract type and grant the officer discretion to select type of contract did not prohibit contracting officer from negotiating contract for research and development of technology for tracking ultra-quiet submarines on a fixed-price basis, since those provisions merely cautioned against a fixed-price contract where substantial developmental risk rendered cost estimation merely hypothetical. 48 C.F.R. §§ 16.103(a), 16.104, 35.006(b, c), 216.104. American Tel. and Tel. Co. v. U.S., 307 F.3d 1374 (Fed. Cir. 2002). United States ☞70(15.1)

Navy contract for development of ship-towed, undersea surveillance system was for "major system or subsystem," for purposes of statute prohibiting Department of Defense from entering into fixed price contracts for development of major system or subsystem exceeding $10 million unless certain conditions were met, notwithstanding either agency's reliance on separate statute to define major system as having $75 million floor or fact that contract was funded over multiple years. 10 U.S.C.A. § 2302(5); Act December 22, 1987, § 101(b), Sec. 8118, 101 Stat. 1329. American Tel. & Tel. Co. v. U.S., 177 F.3d 1368 (Fed. Cir. 1999). United States ☞70(15.1)

Failure of Department of Defense to comply with statute setting forth internal review and reporting requirements for fixed price contract for development of major system or subsystem exceeding $10 million did not render such contract void ab initio, as statute itself did not announce sanction of contract invalidity, and contract had been fully performed. Act December 22, 1987, § 101(b), Sec. 8118, 101 Stat. 1329. American Tel. & Tel. Co. v. U.S., 177 F.3d 1368 (Fed. Cir. 1999). United States ☞70(15.1)

Fixed-price contracts assign risk to contractor that actual cost of performance will be higher than price of contract. 48 C.F.R. § 16.202-1. Dalton v. Cessna Aircraft Co., 98 F.3d 1298, 41 Cont. Cas. Fed. (CCH) P 76998 (Fed. Cir. 1996). United States ☞70(15.1)

Government did not breach fixed-price dredging contract that required the dredging, transporting, and depositing of material from two stockpile areas along the Mississippi River by refusing to pay contractor an additional $1,111,227.51 to contractor to compensate it for cost overrun caused by county's opposition to contractor's proposed disposal site on private property; as a party to a fixed-price contract, contractor assumed the risk of any cost overruns during the term of performance. 48 C.F.R. § 16.202-1. L.W. Matteson, Inc. v. U.S., 61 Fed. Cl. 296 (2004). United States ☞70(22.1)

Focus of fixed-price public contract is contractor output. 48 C.F.R. §§ 16.401, 16.403. McDonnell Douglas Corp. v. U.S., 37 Fed. Cl. 295, 41 Cont. Cas. Fed. (CCH) P 77046 (1997), order modified, 39 Fed. Cl. 665, 42 Cont. Cas. Fed. (CCH) P 77230 (1997). United States ☞70(15.1)

2 Economic price adjustment

Under Federal Acquisition Regulation (FAR) governing economic price adjustments to fixed-price contracts, "contractor's established price" may be established by reference to either a catalog or market sources independent of the manufacturer or vendor. 48 C.F.R. § 16.203. Tesoro Hawaii Corp. v. U.S., 405 F.3d 1339, 15 A.L.R. Fed. 2d 755 (Fed. Cir. 2005) United States ☞70(18)

Use of market-based references to determine adjustments to established prices in contracts for sale of jet fuel to military was authorized under Federal Acquisition Regulation (FAR) governing economic price adjustments to fixed price contracts. 48 C.F.R. § 16.

203. Tesoro Hawaii Corp. v. U.S., 405 F.3d 1339, 15 A.L.R. Fed. 2d 755 (Fed. Cir. 2005). United States ⊂⊃70(18)

Federal Acquisition Regulation (FAR) governing economic price adjustments to fixed price contracts permit use of contracts that include adjustments based on established prices, but do not limit those adjustments to changes only in the specific prices offered by an individual contractor. Tesoro Hawaii Corp. v. U.S., 405 F.3d 1339, 15 A.L.R. Fed. 2d 755 (Fed. Cir. 2005). United States ⊂⊃70(23)

Use of an economic price adjustment (EPA) clause tied particularly to a reference price in a market publication to determine price adjustments in fuel contracts did not violate Federal Acquisition Regulation (FAR) governing economic price adjustments to fixed price contracts; regulation did not require that adjustments be tied solely to changes in the prices charged by a particular contractor. 48 C.F.R. § 16.203-3. Tesoro Hawaii Corp. v. U.S., 405 F.3d 1339, 15 A.L.R. Fed. 2d 755 (Fed. Cir. 2005). United States ⊂⊃70(18)

To be authorized under the Federal Acquisition Regulation (FAR), economic price adjustment (EPA) clause in military fuel supply contracts had to fall within one of the three general types set forth in section of the FAR authorizing use of EPA clauses. 48 C.F.R. § 16.203-1. Sunoco, Inc. v. U.S., 59 Fed. Cl. 390 (2004) (abrogated on other grounds by, Tesoro Hawaii Corp. v. U.S., 405 F.3d 1339, 15 A.L.R. Fed. 2d 755 (Fed. Cir. 2005)). United States ⊂⊃70(18)

Individual deviation or exemption from section of the Federal Acquisition Regulation (FAR) governing economic price adjustment clauses was invalid and illegal under the FAR, where deviation was applied not to a single contract but to multiple contracts issued under single solicitation, and was used to accommodate the government as a temporary measure until a permanent class deviation was obtained. 48 C.F.R. §§ 1.403, 1.404, 16.203-1. Calcasieu Refining Co. v. U.S., 2003 WL 22049528 (Ct. Fed. Cl. 2003). United States ⊂⊃70(18)

Section of the Federal Acquisition Regulation (FAR) which authorizes the government's use of "[f]ixed-price contracts with economic price adjustment" authorized the use of economic price adjustment (EPA) clauses that adopt market based price indexes to provide adjustments in a contractor's established prices. 48 C.F.R. § 16.203-1. Williams Alaska Petroleum, Inc. v. U.S., 57 Fed. Cl. 789 (2003). United States ⊂⊃70(18)

Defense Energy Support Center (DESC) had the authority to adopt market-based economic price adjustment (EPA) clauses in petroleum contracts awarded to military fuel suppliers during the years 1993 through 1999, pursuant to provisions of the Federal Acquisition Regulation (FAR) and individual and class deviations granted DESC during those years. 48 C.F.R. § 16.203-1. Williams Alaska Petroleum, Inc. v. U.S., 57 Fed. Cl. 789 (2003). United States ⊂⊃70(18)

If a fixed price government contract containing an economic price adjustment clause is in violation of the procurement regulations and does not meet the requirement that the selected index approximately tracks the economic changes affecting the contract, reformation is appropriate. Gold Line Refining, Ltd. v. U.S., 43 Fed. Cl. 291 (1999). United States ⊂⊃72(1.1)

Fixed price contract with economic price adjustment was required to comply with Federal Acquisition Regulations (FAR) on economic price adjustments, even if parties also intended indefinite-delivery indefinite-quantity contract. MAPCO Alaska Petroleum, Inc. v. U.S., 27 Fed. Cl. 405, 38 Cont. Cas. Fed. (CCH) P 76451 (1992) (abrogated on other grounds by, Tesoro Hawaii Corp. v. U.S., 405 F.3d 1339, 15 A.L.R. Fed. 2d 755 (Fed. Cir. 2005)). United States ⊂⊃70(23)

3 Waiver

Contractor waived its claim for reformation of fixed-price contract for research and development of technology for tracking ultra-quiet submarines, although it incurred costs in excess of fixed price, where contractor, a sophisticated federal contractor, failed to seek a cost reimbursement contract during contract negotiations, and it successfully underbid technically superior competitors and retained contract with a vigorous defense against competitor's protest action. American Tel. and Tel. Co. v. U.S., 307 F.3d 1374 (Fed. Cir. 2002). Reformation Of Instruments ⊂⊃23

§ 16.202 Firm-fixed-price contracts.

§ 16.202-1 Description.

A firm-fixed-price contract provides for a price that is not subject to any adjustment on the basis of the contractor's cost experience in performing the contract. This contract type places upon the contractor maximum risk and full responsibility for all costs and resulting profit or loss. It provides maximum incentive for the contractor to control costs and perform effectively and imposes a minimum administrative burden upon the contracting parties. The contracting officer may use a firm-fixed-price contract in conjunction with an award-fee incentive (see 16.404) and performance or delivery incentives (see 16.402-2 and 16.402-3) when the award fee or incentive is based solely on factors other than cost. The contract type remains firm-fixed-price when used with these incentives.

United States Code Annotated

Contract requirements, see 41 USCA § 254.

Contracts, planning, solicitation, evaluation, and award procedures, see 10 USCA § 2305.

Cost-type research and development contracts with educational institutions, see 41 USCA § 254a.

Definitions, see 10 USCA § 2302, 41 USCA §§ 259, 403.

Kinds of contracts, see 10 USCA § 2306.

Planning and solicitation requirements, see 41 USCA § 253a.

Task and delivery order contracts, definitions, see 10 USCA § 2304d, 41 USCA § 253k.

Task and delivery order contracts, general authority, see 10 USCA § 2304a, 41 USCA § 253h.

Task and delivery order contracts, orders, see 10 USCA § 2304c, 41 USCA § 253j.

Task order contracts, advisory and assistance services, see 10 USCA § 2304b, 41 USCA § 253i.

Notes of Decisions

In general 1
Armed services contracts 3
Cost accounting standards 2
Injunctions 4
Reimbursements 5

1 In general

Utility company's proposal for government contract relating to electrical services, which proposed that government would reimburse none of company's costs for replacing electrical system at issue and that government would pay company up to certain amount if specified contingencies arose, was cost-share type contract, not firm-fixed-price contract, and thus satisfied requirement in request for proposal (RFP) that bidders submit cost-reimbursement contract proposal. 48 C.F.R. §§ 16.202, 16.303. City & County of San Francisco v. U.S., 130 F.3d 873, 42 Cont. Cas. Fed. (CCH) P 77215 (9th Cir. 1997). United States ☞64.30

Costs of contractor's severance payments to six employees, following expiration of firm, fixed-price contract with United States Air Force, were not recoverable as "abnormal or mass severance costs" for which government would be liable for its "fair share" under Federal Acquisition Regulations (FAR) incorporated into contract; severance payments were normal severance when viewed in context of contract's expiration, which was foreseeable event when contract was entered into. 48 C.F.R. § 31.205-6(g)(2)(iii). ITT Federal Services Corp. v. Widnall, 132 F.3d 1448, 42 Cont. Cas. Fed. (CCH) P 77242 (Fed. Cir. 1997). United States ☞70(21)

Contractor was not entitled to recover cost of severance payments made to six employees who could not be placed with contractor or successor contractor following termination of firm, fixed-price contract with United States Air Force under continuity of services provision of Federal Acquisition Regulations (FAR) incorporated into contract; severance payments were not transition services costs provided for in provision, in that they did not result from activities to assist new contractor or government in taking over operations, nor were they designed to assure continuity of services during transition period. 48 C.F.R. § 52. 237-3. ITT Federal Services Corp. v. Widnall, 132 F.3d 1448, 42 Cont. Cas. Fed. (CCH) P 77242 (Fed. Cir. 1997). United States ☞70(21)

Fixed-price contracts assign risk to contractor that actual cost of performance will be higher than price of contract. 48 C.F.R. § 16.202-1. Dalton v. Cessna Aircraft Co., 98 F.3d 1298, 41 Cont. Cas. Fed. (CCH) P 76998 (Fed. Cir. 1996). United States ☞70(15.1)

Government did not breach fixed-price dredging contract that required the dredging, transporting, and depositing of material from two stockpile areas along the Mississippi River by refusing to pay contractor an additional $1,111,227.51 to contractor to compensate it for cost overrun caused by county's opposition to contractor's proposed disposal site on private property; as a party to a fixed-price contract, contractor assumed the risk of any cost overruns during the term of performance. 48 C.F.R. § 16.202-1. L.W. Matteson, Inc. v. U.S., 61 Fed. Cl. 296 (2004). United States ☞70(22.1)

Failure of contracting agency to perform a cost realism analysis on contract awardee's offer was not error, as there was no requirement for such an analysis, where solicitation contemplated award of firm fixed price contract and contracting officer (CO) deemed awardee responsible to perform the project at the offered price. 48 C.F.R. § 15.404-1(d)(1). First Enterprise v. U.S., 61 Fed. Cl. 109 (2004). United States ☞64.40(1)

Contractor which willingly bid on a firm fixed price (FFP) contract, and willingly signed an FFP contract, thereby assuming the risks attendant to an FFP contract, could not raise claim that FFP provisions violated the Federal Acquisition Regulation. 48 C.F.R. §§ 16. 103(a), 16.202-2. PCL Const. Services, Inc. v. U.S., 47 Fed. Cl. 745 (2000). United States ☞70(15.1)

Firm-fixed-price contract for the operation and maintenance of two government-owned locks and dams did not require that contractor staff each lock and dam with a fulltime equipment mechanic, and thus it was improper for the government to reduce the contract price and withhold monies from contractor for periods during which equipment mechanic positions were vacant; term 'capability," as used in the solicitation and contract documents, did not mandate any specific "manpower" or "staffing levels." Omni Corp. v. U.S., 41 Fed. Cl. 585 (1998). United States ☞70(15.1)

In firm fixed-price contract between federal agency and corporation, corporation bore risk that it would be required to pay unforeseen premium wages to its employees for federal government furlough period after arbitrator ordered such wages, where agency did not take position that employees should be paid premium wages for holiday pay or require any changes in services as to scope, time or personnel during furlough period. Cleveland Telecommunications Corp. v. U.S., 39 Fed. Cl. 649, 42 Cont. Cas. Fed. (CCH) P 77199 (1997). United States ☞70(23)

Fact that solicitation for bids for providing unarmed guard services denominated contract as "firm fixed-price" did not show that solicitation called for provision of additional services through options, as opposed to indefinite quantity requirement. Vanguard Sec. Inc. v. U.S., 20 Cl. Ct. 90, 1990 WL 38036 (1990). United States ☞70(6.1)

2 Cost accounting standards

Original version of Cost Accounting Standard (CAS) governing segment closing adjustment of pension costs under government contracts required contractor to examine both firm-fixed-price and flexibly-priced contracts to determine the pension surplus or deficit attributable to government contributions. 4 C.F.R. § 413-50(c)(12) (1986). Teledyne, Inc. v. U.S., 50 Fed. Cl. 155 (2001), aff'd, 316 F.3d 1366, 30 Employee Benefits Cas. (BNA) 1753 (Fed. Cir. 2003). United States ☞70(18)

Original version of Cost Accounting Standard (CAS) governing segment closing adjustment of pension costs under government contracts did not allow for the recovery of any pension surplus or the payment of any pension plan deficit attributable to government-reimbursed pension costs under firm-fixed-price contracts; thus, such adjustment would only be recoverable pursuant to an express contract provision. 4 C.F.R. § 413-50(c)(12) (1986). Teledyne, Inc. v. U.S., 50 Fed. Cl. 155 (2001), aff'd, 316 F.3d 1366, 30 Employee Benefits Cas. (BNA) 1753 (Fed. Cir. 2003). United States ☞70(18)

Original version of Cost Accounting Standard (CAS) governing segment closing adjustment of pension costs under government contracts required contractor to allocate the segment closing adjustment between firm-fixed-price contracts and flexibly-priced contracts that gave rise to the surplus or deficit attributable to government contributions; portion of surplus or deficit attributable to firm-fixed-price contracts must be identified in order to determine the recoverable portion of the segment closing adjustment. 4 C.F.R. § 413-50(c)(12) (1986). Teledyne, Inc. v. U.S., 50 Fed. Cl. 155 (2001), aff'd, 316 F.3d 1366, 30 Employee Benefits Cas. (BNA) 1753 (Fed. Cir. 2003). United States ⏀70(18)

Applying amended version of Cost Accounting Standard (CAS) governing segment closing adjustment of pension costs to government contractor's sale of division amounted to a change in accounting practice that triggered equitable adjustment, where pension surplus that was attributable to CAS-covered government contracts arose under contracts that contained only the original segment closing provision pursuant to which contractor was not liable for pension surplus attributable to firm-fixed-price contracts. 4 C.F.R. § 413-50(c)(12) (1986); 48 C.F.R. §§ 52.230-2(a)(4)(i), 9904.413-50(c)(12). Teledyne, Inc. v. U.S., 50 Fed. Cl. 155 (2001), aff'd, 316 F.3d 1366, 30 Employee Benefits Cas. (BNA) 1753 (Fed. Cir. 2003). United States ⏀70(21)

Cost Accounting Standards Board (CASB) complied with procedural requirements of the Office of Federal Procurement Policy Act (OFPPA) when it issued amended Cost Accounting Standard (CAS) making government contractor liable for pension surplus attributable to firm-fixed-price contracts in a segment closing adjustment; CASB gave adequate notice of the inclusion of firm-fixed-price contracts in the new segment closing adjustment provision in proposed illustrations, and received comments that addressed issue. Contract Disputes Act of 1978, § 26(g), as amended, 41 U.S.C.A. § 422(g); 48 C.F.R. § 9904.413-50(c)(12). Teledyne, Inc. v. U.S., 50 Fed. Cl. 155 (2001), aff'd, 316 F.3d 1366, 30 Employee Benefits Cas. (BNA) 1753 (Fed. Cir. 2003). United States ⏀70(18)

Amended version of Cost Accounting Standard (CAS) governing segment closing adjustment of pension costs under government contracts was not invalid on ground the Cost Accounting Standards Board (CASB) did not have authority under the Office of Federal Procurement Policy Act (OFPPA) to require price adjustments under firm-fixed-price contracts, as amended version did not clearly contradict the OFPPA which requires the measurement, assignment, and allocation of pension costs. Contract Disputes Act of 1978, § 26(f, h), as amended, 41 U.S.C.A. § 422(f, h). Teledyne, Inc. v. U.S., 50 Fed. Cl. 155 (2001), aff'd, 316 F.3d 1366, 30 Employee Benefits Cas. (BNA) 1753 (Fed. Cir. 2003). United States ⏀70(18)

3 Armed services contracts

Flight training services contractor's interpretation of "17,000 airborne training service hours" provision of firm fixed-price contract with Navy as qualified by parenthetical reference to 58 hours per graduated student gave rise to patent ambiguity and corresponding duty to seek clarification before submitting proposal. Dalton v. Cessna Aircraft Co., 98 F.3d 1298, 41 Cont. Cas. Fed. (CCH) P 76998 (Fed. Cir. 1996). United States ⏀64.5

In absence of language clearly and unambiguously placing qualification on manner in which Navy could consume services it was procuring through firm fixed-price contract for flight training services, it was reasonable for Navy to interpret contractual reference to 58 hours per graduated student as estimate. Dalton v. Cessna Aircraft Co., 98 F.3d 1298, 41 Cont. Cas. Fed. (CCH) P 76998 (Fed. Cir. 1996). United States ⏀70(6.1)

Flight training services contractor that failed to seek clarification of its patently ambiguous interpretation of service hours required by firm fixed-price contract with Navy before it submitted winning proposal was barred from seeking equitable adjustment for subsequent change in Navy's training syllabus. Dalton v. Cessna Aircraft Co., 98 F.3d 1298, 41 Cont. Cas. Fed. (CCH) P 76998 (Fed. Cir. 1996). United States ⏀70(24)

When viewing firm fixed-price contract for flight training services as whole, Navy reasonably interpreted parenthetical reference to 58 hours per graduated student in general provisions of contract as estimate, rather than binding provision; specific provisions of contract contained in attached training syllabus called for 17,000 hours of flight services for third, fourth, and fifth program years and for option years, without qualification as to the number of hours per student. Dalton v. Cessna Aircraft Co., 98 F.3d 1298, 41 Cont. Cas. Fed. (CCH) P 76998 (Fed. Cir. 1996). United States ⏀70(6.1)

4 Injunctions

For purpose of determining whether low bidder was entitled to enjoin Government's cancellation of solicitation for bids for providing unarmed guard services, solicitation's designation of contract as firm fixed-price contract was consistent with reaffirmation in same section that it was indefinite quantity contract, as meaning of contract was that prices for additional services, as well as for base and optional years, were firm fixed hourly rates. Vanguard Sec. Inc. v. U.S., 20 Cl. Ct. 90, 1990 WL 38036 (1990). United States ⊕64.60(5.1)

5 Reimbursements

Under a fixed price contract, an increase in fuel costs was not a change to the contract that would trigger an equitable adjustment to the contract price. The contractor's requested adjustment was based on historical data that the agency provided for informational purposes only, and contractor failed to protect itself during contract negotiation, despite specifically recognizing the volatility of fuel prices. DG21, LLC v. Mabus, 819 F.3d 1358(Fed. Cir. 2016)

Government contractor was not entitled to "reimbursement" for state income tax payments incurred under its negotiated fixed-price contracts, because in the normal course there is no such thing as "reimbursement" of any costs in a fixed-price undertaking. Information Systems & Networks Corp. v. U.S., 64 Fed. Cl. 599 (2005). United States ⊕70(18)

§ 16.202-2 Application.

A firm-fixed-price contract is suitable for acquiring commercial items (see Parts 2 and 12) or for acquiring other supplies or services on the basis of reasonably definite functional or detailed specifications (see Part 11) when the contracting officer can establish fair and reasonable prices at the outset, such as when—

(a) There is adequate price competition;

(b) There are reasonable price comparisons with prior purchases of the same or similar supplies or services made on a competitive basis or supported by valid certified cost or pricing data;

(c) Available cost or pricing information permits realistic estimates of the probable costs of performance; or

(d) Performance uncertainties can be identified and reasonable estimates of their cost impact can be made, and the contractor is willing to accept a firm fixed price representing assumption of the risks involved.

United States Code Annotated

Contract requirements, see 41 USCA § 254.

Contracts, planning, solicitation, evaluation, and award procedures, see 10 USCA § 2305.

Cost-type research and development contracts with educational institutions, see 41 USCA § 254a.

Definitions, see 10 USCA § 2302, 41 USCA §§ 259, 403.

Kinds of contracts, see 10 USCA § 2306.

Planning and solicitation requirements, see 41 USCA § 253a.

Task and delivery order contracts, definitions, see 10 USCA § 2304d, 41 USCA § 253k.

Task and delivery order contracts, general authority, see 10 USCA § 2304a, 41 USCA § 253h.

Task and delivery order contracts, orders, see 10 USCA § 2304c, 41 USCA § 253j.

Task order contracts, advisory and assistance services, see 10 USCA § 2304b, 41 USCA § 253i.

Notes of Decisions

In general 1
Armed services contracts 3
Cost accounting standards 2
Injunctions 5
Waiver 4

1 In general

Utility company's proposal for government contract relating to electrical services, which proposed that government would reimburse none of company's costs for replacing electrical system at issue and that government would pay company up to certain amount if specified contingencies arose, was cost-share type contract, not firm-fixed-price contract, and thus satisfied requirement in request for proposal (RFP) that bidders submit cost-reimbursement contract proposal. 48 C.F.R. §§ 16.202, 16.303. City & County of San Francisco v. U.S., 130 F.3d 873, 42 Cont. Cas. Fed. (CCH) P 77215 (9th Cir. 1997). United States ☞64.30

Costs of contractor's severance payments to six employees, following expiration of firm, fixed-price contract with United States Air Force, were not recoverable as "abnormal or mass severance costs" for which government would be liable for its "fair share" under Federal Acquisition Regulations (FAR) incorporated into contract; severance payments were normal severance when viewed in context of contract's expiration, which was foreseeable event when contract was entered into. 48 C.F.R. § 31.205-6(g)(2)(iii). ITT Federal Services Corp. v. Widnall, 132 F.3d 1448, 42 Cont. Cas. Fed. (CCH) P 77242 (Fed. Cir. 1997). United States ☞70(21)

Contractor was not entitled to recover cost of severance payments made to six employees who could not be placed with contractor or successor contractor following termination of firm, fixed-price contract with United States Air Force under continuity of services provision of Federal Acquisition Regulations (FAR) incorporated into contract; severance payments were not transition services costs provided for in provision, in that they did not result from activities to assist new contractor or government in taking over operations, nor were they designed to assure continuity of services during transition period. 48 C.F.R. § 52. 237-3. ITT Federal Services Corp. v. Widnall, 132 F.3d 1448, 42 Cont. Cas. Fed. (CCH) P 77242 (Fed. Cir. 1997). United States ☞70(21)

Fixed-price contracts assign risk to contractor that actual cost of performance will be higher than price of contract. 48 C.F.R. § 16.202-1. Dalton v. Cessna Aircraft Co., 98 F.3d 1298, 41 Cont. Cas. Fed. (CCH) P 76998 (Fed. Cir. 1996). United States ☞70(15.1)

Government did not breach fixed-price dredging contract that required the dredging, transporting, and depositing of material from two stockpile areas along the Mississippi River by refusing to pay contractor an additional $1,111,227.51 to contractor to compensate it for cost overrun caused by county's opposition to contractor's proposed disposal site on private property; as a party to a fixed-price contract, contractor assumed the risk of any cost overruns during the term of performance. 48 C.F.R. § 16.202-1. L.W. Matteson, Inc. v. U.S., 61 Fed. Cl. 296 (2004). United States ☞70(22.1)

Failure of contracting agency to perform a cost realism analysis on contract awardee's offer was not error, as there was no requirement for such an analysis, where solicitation contemplated award of firm fixed price contract and contracting officer (CO) deemed awardee responsible to perform the project at the offered price. 48 C.F.R. § 15.404-1(d)(1). First Enterprise v. U.S., 61 Fed. Cl. 109 (2004). United States ☞64.40(1)

Contractor which willingly bid on a firm fixed price (FFP) contract, and willingly signed an FFP contract, thereby assuming the risks attendant to an FFP contract, could not raise claim that FFP provisions violated the Federal Acquisition Regulation. 48 C.F.R. §§ 16. 103(a), 16.202-2. PCL Const. Services, Inc. v. U.S., 47 Fed. Cl. 745 (2000). United States ☞70(15.1)

Firm-fixed-price contract for the operation and maintenance of two government-owned locks and dams did not require that contractor staff each lock and dam with a fulltime equipment mechanic, and thus it was improper for the government to reduce the contract price and withhold monies from contractor for periods during which equipment mechanic positions were vacant; term 'capability," as used in the solicitation and contract documents, did not mandate any specific "manpower" or "staffing levels." Omni Corp. v. U.S., 41 Fed. Cl. 585 (1998). United States ☞70(15.1)

In firm fixed-price contract between federal agency and corporation, corporation bore risk that it would be required to pay unforeseen premium wages to its employees for federal government furlough period after arbitrator ordered such wages, where agency did not take position that employees should be paid premium wages for holiday pay or require any changes in services as to scope, time or personnel during furlough period. Cleveland Telecommunications Corp. v. U.S., 39 Fed. Cl. 649, 42 Cont. Cas. Fed. (CCH) P 77199 (1997). United States ☞70(23)

Fact that solicitation for bids for providing unarmed guard services denominated contract as "firm fixed-price" did not show that solicitation called for provision of additional services through options, as opposed to indefinite quantity requirement. Vanguard Sec. Inc. v. U.S., 20 Cl. Ct. 90, 1990 WL 38036 (1990). United States ☞70(6.1)

2 Cost accounting standards

Original version of Cost Accounting Standard (CAS) governing segment closing adjustment of pension costs under government contracts required contractor to allocate the segment closing adjustment between firm-fixed-price contracts and flexibly-priced contracts that gave rise to the surplus or deficit attributable to government contributions; portion of surplus or deficit attributable to firm-fixed-price contracts must be identified in order to determine the recoverable portion of the segment closing adjustment. 4 C.F.R. § 413-50(c)(12) (1986). Teledyne, Inc. v. U.S., 50 Fed. Cl. 155 (2001), aff'd, 316 F.3d 1366, 30 Employee Benefits Cas. (BNA) 1753 (Fed. Cir. 2003). United States ☞70(18)

Applying amended version of Cost Accounting Standard (CAS) governing segment closing adjustment of pension costs to government contractor's sale of division amounted to a change in accounting practice that triggered equitable adjustment, where pension surplus that was attributable to CAS-covered government contracts arose under contracts that contained only the original segment closing provision pursuant to which contractor was not liable for pension surplus attributable to firm-fixed-price contracts. 4 C.F.R. § 413-50(c)(12) (1986); 48 C.F.R. §§ 52.230-2(a)(4)(i), 9904.413-50(c)(12). Teledyne, Inc. v. U.S., 50 Fed. Cl. 155 (2001), aff'd, 316 F.3d 1366, 30 Employee Benefits Cas. (BNA) 1753 (Fed. Cir. 2003). United States ☞70(21)

Amended version of Cost Accounting Standard (CAS) governing segment closing adjustment of pension costs under government contracts was not invalid on ground the Cost Accounting Standards Board (CASB) did not have authority under the Office of Federal Procurement Policy Act (OFPPA) to require price adjustments under firm-fixed-price contracts, as amended version did not clearly contradict the OFPPA which requires the measurement, assignment, and allocation of pension costs. Contract Disputes Act of 1978, § 26(f, h), as amended, 41 U.S.C.A. § 422(f, h). Teledyne, Inc. v. U.S., 50 Fed. Cl. 155 (2001), aff'd, 316 F.3d 1366, 30 Employee Benefits Cas. (BNA) 1753 (Fed. Cir. 2003). United States ☞70(18)

Cost Accounting Standards Board (CASB) complied with procedural requirements of the Office of Federal Procurement Policy Act (OFPPA) when it issued amended Cost Accounting Standard (CAS) making government contractor liable for pension surplus attributable to firm-fixed-price contracts in a segment closing adjustment; CASB gave adequate notice of the inclusion of firm-fixed-price contracts in the new segment closing adjustment provision in proposed illustrations, and received comments that addressed issue. Contract Disputes Act of 1978, § 26(g), as amended, 41 U.S.C.A. § 422(g); 48 C.F.R. § 9904.413-50(c)(12). Teledyne, Inc. v. U.S., 50 Fed. Cl. 155 (2001), aff'd, 316 F.3d 1366, 30 Employee Benefits Cas. (BNA) 1753 (Fed. Cir. 2003). United States ☞70(18)

Original version of Cost Accounting Standard (CAS) governing segment closing adjustment of pension costs under government contracts did not allow for the recovery of any pension surplus or the payment of any pension plan deficit attributable to government-reimbursed pension costs under firm-fixed-price contracts; thus, such adjustment would only be recoverable pursuant to an express contract provision. 4 C.F.R. § 413-50(c)(12) (1986). Teledyne, Inc. v. U.S., 50 Fed. Cl. 155 (2001), aff'd, 316 F.3d 1366, 30 Employee Benefits Cas. (BNA) 1753 (Fed. Cir. 2003). United States ☞70(18)

Original version of Cost Accounting Standard (CAS) governing segment closing adjustment of pension costs under government contracts required contractor to examine both firm-fixed-price and flexibly-priced contracts to determine the pension surplus or deficit attributable to government contributions. 4 C.F.R. § 413-50(c)(12) (1986). Teledyne, Inc. v. U.S., 50 Fed. Cl. 155 (2001), aff'd, 316 F.3d 1366, 30 Employee Benefits Cas. (BNA) 1753 (Fed. Cir. 2003). United States ☞70(18)

3 Armed services contracts

Flight training services contractor's interpretation of "17,000 airborne training service hours" provision of firm fixed-price contract with Navy as qualified by parenthetical reference to 58 hours per graduated student gave rise to patent ambiguity and corresponding duty to seek clarification before submitting proposal. Dalton v. Cessna Aircraft Co., 98 F.3d 1298, 41 Cont. Cas. Fed. (CCH) P 76998 (Fed. Cir. 1996). United States ☞64.5

In absence of language clearly and unambiguously placing qualification on manner in which Navy could consume services it was procuring through firm fixed-price contract for flight training services, it was reasonable for Navy to interpret contractual reference to 58 hours per graduated student as estimate. Dalton v. Cessna Aircraft Co., 98 F.3d 1298, 41 Cont. Cas. Fed. (CCH) P 76998 (Fed. Cir. 1996). United States ☞70(6.1)

Flight training services contractor that failed to seek clarification of its patently ambiguous interpretation of service hours required by firm fixed-price contract with Navy before it submitted winning proposal was barred from seeking equitable adjustment for subsequent change in Navy's training syllabus. Dalton v. Cessna Aircraft Co., 98 F.3d 1298, 41 Cont. Cas. Fed. (CCH) P 76998 (Fed. Cir. 1996). United States ☞70(24)

When viewing firm fixed-price contract for flight training services as whole, Navy reasonably interpreted parenthetical reference to 58 hours per graduated student in general provisions of contract as estimate, rather than binding provision; specific provisions of contract contained in attached training syllabus called for 17,000 hours of flight services for third, fourth, and fifth program years and for option years, without qualification as to the number of hours per student. Dalton v. Cessna Aircraft Co., 98 F.3d 1298, 41 Cont. Cas. Fed. (CCH) P 76998 (Fed. Cir. 1996). United States ☞70(6.1)

4 Waiver

Contractor waived its claim for reformation of fixed-price contract for research and development of technology for tracking ultra-quiet submarines, although it incurred costs in excess of fixed price, where contractor, a sophisticated federal contractor, failed to seek a cost reimbursement contract during contract negotiations, and it successfully underbid technically superior competitors and retained contract with a vigorous defense against competitor's protest action. American Tel. and Tel. Co. v. U.S., 307 F.3d 1374 (Fed. Cir. 2002). Reformation Of Instruments ☞23

5 Injunctions

For purpose of determining whether low bidder was entitled to enjoin Government's cancellation of solicitation for bids for providing unarmed guard services, solicitation's designation of contract as firm fixed-price contract was consistent with reaffirmation in same section that it was indefinite quantity contract, as meaning of contract was that prices for additional services, as well as for base and optional years, were firm fixed hourly rates. Vanguard Sec. Inc. v. U.S., 20 Cl. Ct. 90, 1990 WL 38036 (1990). United States ☞64.60(5.1)

§ 16.203 Fixed-price contracts with economic price adjustment.

§ 16.203-1 Description.

(a) A fixed-price contract with economic price adjustment provides for upward and downward revision of the stated contract price upon the occurrence of specified contingencies. Economic price adjustments are of three general types:

(1) *Adjustments based on established prices.* These price adjustments are based on increases or decreases from an agreed-upon level in published or otherwise established prices of specific items or the contract end items.

(2) *Adjustments based on actual costs of labor or material.* These price adjustments are based on increases or decreases in specified costs of labor or material that the contractor actually experiences during contract performance.

(3) *Adjustments based on cost indexes of labor or material.* These price adjustments are based on increases or decreases in labor or material cost standards or indexes that are specifically identified in the contract.

(b) The contracting officer may use a fixed-price contract with economic price adjustment in conjunction with an award-fee incentive (see 16.404) and performance or delivery incentives (see 16.402-2 and 16.402-3) when the award fee or incentive is based solely on factors other than cost. The contract type remains fixed-price with economic price adjustment when used with these incentives.

United States Code Annotated

Contract requirements, see 41 USCA § 254.

Contracts, planning, solicitation, evaluation, and award procedures, see 10 USCA § 2305.

Cost-type research and development contracts with educational institutions, see 41 USCA § 254a.

Definitions, see 10 USCA § 2302, 41 USCA §§ 259, 403.

Kinds of contracts, see 10 USCA § 2306.

Planning and solicitation requirements, see 41 USCA § 253a.

Task and delivery order contracts, definitions, see 10 USCA § 2304d, 41 USCA § 253k.

Task and delivery order contracts, general authority, see 10 USCA § 2304a, 41 USCA § 253h.

Task and delivery order contracts, orders, see 10 USCA § 2304c, 41 USCA § 253j.

Task order contracts, advisory and assistance services, see 10 USCA § 2304b, 41 USCA § 253i.

Notes of Decisions

Contractor's established price 1.5
Economic price adjustment, generally 1
Indexes 3
Modification 2

1 Economic price adjustment, generally

Federal Acquisition Regulation (FAR) governing economic price adjustments to fixed price contracts permit use of contracts that include adjustments based on established prices, but do not limit those adjustments to changes only in the specific prices offered by any individual contractor. Tesoro Hawaii Corp. v. U.S., 405 F.3d 1339, 15 A.L.R. Fed. 2d 755 (Fed. Cir. 2005). United States ☞70(18)

Economic price adjustment (EPA) clause in military fuel supply contracts which was based on average sale prices of refined petroleum products by region as reported by the Department of Energy in the Petroleum Marketing Monthly (PMM) was not defective on theory that Federal Acquisition Regulation (FAR) required that price adjustments be based only on changes in individual contractor's prices and not on changes in overall market prices. ConocoPhillips v. U.S., 73 Fed. Cl. 46 (2006), aff'd, 501 F.3d 1374 (Fed. Cir. 2007). United States ☞70(18)

To be authorized under the Federal Acquisition Regulation (FAR), economic price adjustment (EPA) clause in military fuel supply contracts had to fall within one of the three general types set forth in section of the FAR authorizing use of EPA clauses. 48 C.F.R. § 16.203-1. Sunoco, Inc. v. U.S., 59 Fed. Cl. 390 (2004) (abrogated on other grounds by, Tesoro Hawaii Corp. v. U.S., 405 F.3d 1339, 15 A.L.R. Fed. 2d 755 (Fed. Cir. 2005)). United States ☞70(18)

Individual deviation or exemption from section of the Federal Acquisition Regulation (FAR) governing economic price adjustment clauses was invalid and illegal under the FAR, where deviation was applied not to a single contract but to multiple contracts issued under single solicitation, and was used to accommodate the government as a temporary measure until a permanent class deviation was obtained. 48 C.F.R. §§ 1.403, 1.404, 16.203-1. Calcasieu Refining Co. v. U.S., 2003 WL 22049528 (Ct. Fed. Cl. 2003). United States ☞70(18)

Even assuming that class deviation from section of the Federal Acquisition Regulation (FAR) governing economic price adjustment (EPA) clauses was valid, it expired after three years pursuant to section of the Defense Logistics Acquisition Regulation (DLAR) imposing a normal three year time limitation on the validity of a class deviation. 48 C.F.R. § 16.203-1 et seq.Navajo Refining Co., L.P. v. U.S., 58 Fed. Cl. 200 (2003). United States ☞70(18)

Defense Energy Support Center (DESC) had the authority to adopt market-based economic price adjustment (EPA) clauses in petroleum contracts awarded to military fuel suppliers during the years 1993 through 1999, pursuant to provisions of the Federal Acquisition Regulation (FAR) and individual and class deviations granted DESC during those years. 48 C.F.R. § 16.203-1. Williams Alaska Petroleum, Inc. v. U.S., 57 Fed. Cl. 789 (2003). United States ☞70(18)

Fixed price contract with economic price adjustment was required to comply with Federal

Acquisition Regulations (FAR) on economic price adjustments, even if parties also intended indefinite-delivery indefinite-quantity contract. MAPCO Alaska Petroleum, Inc. v. U.S., 27 Fed. Cl. 405, 38 Cont. Cas. Fed. (CCH) P 76451 (1992) (abrogated on other grounds by, Tesoro Hawaii Corp. v. U.S., 405 F.3d 1339, 15 A.L.R. Fed. 2d 755 (Fed. Cir. 2005)). United States ☞70(23)

1.5 Contractor's established price

Under Federal Acquisition Regulation (FAR) governing economic price adjustments to fixed-price contracts, "contractor's established price" may be established by reference to either a catalog or market sources independent of the manufacturer or vendor. Tesoro Hawaii Corp. v. U.S., 405 F.3d 1339, 15 A.L.R. Fed. 2d 755 (Fed. Cir. 2005). United States ☞70(18)

2 Modification

If a fixed price government contract containing an economic price adjustment clause is in violation of the procurement regulations and does not meet the requirement that the selected index approximately tracks the economic changes affecting the contract, reformation is appropriate. Gold Line Refining, Ltd. v. U.S., 43 Fed. Cl. 291 (1999). United States ☞72(1.1)

3 Indexes

Petroleum Marketing Monthly (PMM), as basis for economic price adjustment (EPA) clause in contracts for fuel supplied to Defense Energy Support Center (DESC) for military uses, was sufficiently accurate measure of established prices to be permissible price adjustment mechanism, under regulatory requirement that price adjustments be based on published or otherwise established prices, where price was established from PMM's market-based compilation of actual fuel sales, independent of contract manufacturer or vendor, calculated by weighted average of market price for related fuel groups in different regions, PMM permissibly compiled sales figures as particular vendors' prices were not required and products were sufficiently closely related to constitute single market, and contractors agreed to PMM as market-based index when entering contract which did not guarantee that neither party could benefit from difference between PMM value and fair market value. ConocoPhillips v. U.S., 501 F.3d 1374 (Fed. Cir. 2007). United States ☞70(18)

Government's use of Petroleum Marketing Monthly (PMM) published by Department of Energy (DOE) as basis for economic price adjustments pursuant to economic price adjustment (EPA) clause of military fuel contracts satisfied requirement of Federal Acquisition Regulation (FAR) that EPA clauses be market based, as PPM compiled monthly average sale figures as reported by refiners. ConocoPhillips v. U.S., 73 Fed. Cl. 46 (2006), aff'd, 501 F.3d 1374 (Fed. Cir. 2007). United States ☞70(18)

Economic price adjustment (EPA) clause in contracts for supply of jet fuel was not valid under the Federal Acquisition Regulation (FAR) as an "adjustment based on established prices," where clause used as escalator the PPI Index derived from the Petroleum Marketing Monthly (PPM), a monthly government publication of petroleum sales data setting forth average prices for petroleum products, as term "established prices" refers to established market prices. 48 C.F.R. § 16.203-1(a). Calcasieu Refining Co. v. U.S., 2003 WL 22049528 (Ct. Fed. Cl. 2003). United States ☞70(18)

Economic price adjustment (EPA) clauses in contracts for supply of military jet fuel which based price of fuel on price indexes were not authorized by section of the Federal Acquisition Regulation (FAR) sanctioning EPA clauses based either on fluctuations in labor or material costs or on changes in the contractor's established prices that are reflective of industry-wide contingencies 48 C.F.R. § 16.203-1 et seq.Navajo Refining Co., L.P. v. U.S., 58 Fed. Cl. 200 (2003). United States ☞70(18)

Section of the Federal Acquisition Regulation (FAR) which authorizes the government's use of "[f]ixed-price contracts with economic price adjustment" authorized the use of economic price adjustment (EPA) clauses that adopt marketbased price indexes to provide adjustments in a contractor's established prices. 48 C.F.R. § 16.203-1. Williams Alaska Petroleum, Inc. v. U.S., 57 Fed. Cl. 789 (2003). United States ☞70(18)

§ 16.203-2 Application.

A fixed-price contract with economic price adjustment may be used when (i) there is serious doubt concerning the stability of market or labor conditions that will exist during an extended period of contract performance, and (ii) contingencies that would otherwise be included in the contract price can be identified and covered separately in the contract. Price adjustments based on established prices should normally be restricted to industry-wide contingencies. Price adjustments based on labor and material costs should be limited to contingencies beyond the contractor's control. For use of economic price adjustment in sealed bid contracts, see 14.408-4.

(a) In establishing the base level from which adjustment will be made, the contracting officer shall ensure that contingency allowances are not duplicated by inclusion in both the base price and the adjustment requested by the contractor under economic price adjustment clause.

(b) In contracts that do not require submission of certified cost or pricing data, the contracting officer shall obtain adequate data to establish the base level from which adjustment will be made and may require verification of data submitted.

United States Code Annotated

Contract requirements, see 41 USCA § 254.

Contracts, planning, solicitation, evaluation, and award procedures, see 10 USCA § 2305.

Cost-type research and development contracts with educational institutions, see 41 USCA § 254a.

Definitions, see 10 USCA § 2302, 41 USCA §§ 259, 403.

Kinds of contracts, see 10 USCA § 2306.

Planning and solicitation requirements, see 41 USCA § 253a.

Task and delivery order contracts, definitions, see 10 USCA § 2304d, 41 USCA § 253k.

Task and delivery order contracts, general authority, see 10 USCA § 2304a, 41 USCA § 253h.

Task and delivery order contracts, orders, see 10 USCA § 2304c, 41 USCA § 253j.

Task order contracts, advisory and assistance services, see 10 USCA § 2304b, 41 USCA § 253i.

Notes of Decisions

Economic price adjustment, generally 1
Indexes 3
Modification 2

1 Economic price adjustment, generally

Defense Energy Support Center's (DESC) use of marketbased references to determine adjustments to established prices in contracts for sale of jet fuel to military was authorized under Federal Acquisition Regulation (FAR) governing economic price adjustments to fixed-price contracts. Tesoro Hawaii Corp. v. U.S., 405 F.3d 1339, 15 A.L.R. Fed. 2d 755 (Fed. Cir. 2005). United States ☞70(18)

Federal Acquisition Regulations (FAR) governing economic price adjustments to fixed-price contracts permit use of contracts that include adjustments based on established prices, but do not limit those adjustments to changes only in the specific prices offered by an individual contractor. Tesoro Hawaii Corp. v. U.S., 405 F.3d 1339, 15 A.L.R. Fed. 2d 755 (Fed. Cir. 2005). United States ☞70(18)

To be authorized under the Federal Acquisition Regulation (FAR), economic price adjustment (EPA) clause in military fuel supply contracts had to fall within one of the three general types set forth in section of the FAR authorizing use of EPA clauses. 48 C.F.R. § 16.203-1. Sunoco, Inc. v. U.S., 59 Fed. Cl. 390 (2004) (abrogated on other grounds by, Tesoro Hawaii Corp. v. U.S., 405 F.3d 1339, 15 A.L.R. Fed. 2d 755 (Fed. Cir. 2005)). United States ☞70(18)

Individual deviation or exemption from section of the Federal Acquisition Regulation (FAR) governing economic price adjustment clauses was invalid and illegal under the FAR, where deviation was applied not to a single contract but to multiple contracts issued under single solicitation, and was used to accommodate the government as a temporary measure until a permanent class deviation was obtained. 48 C.F.R. §§ 1.403, 1.404, 16.203-1. Calcasieu Refining Co. v. U.S., 2003 WL 22049528 (Ct. Fed. Cl. 2003). United States ☞70(18)

Even assuming that class deviation from section of the Federal Acquisition Regulation (FAR) governing economic price adjustment (EPA) clauses was valid; it expired after three years pursuant to section of the Defense Logistics Acquisition Regulation (DLAR) imposing a normal threeyear time limitation on the validity of a class deviation. 48 C.F.R. § 16.203-1 et seq.Navajo Refining Co., L.P. v. U.S., 58 Fed. Cl. 200 (2003). United States ☞70(18)

Defense Energy Support Center (DESC) had the authority to adopt market-based economic price adjustment (EPA) clauses in petroleum contracts awarded to military fuel suppliers during the years 1993 through 1999, pursuant to provisions of the Federal Acquisition Regulation (FAR) and individual and class deviations granted DESC during those years. 48 C.F.R. § 16.203-1. Williams Alaska Petroleum, Inc. v. U.S., 57 Fed. Cl. 789 (2003). United States ☞70(18)

Fixed price contract with economic price adjustment was required to comply with Federal Acquisition Regulations (FAR) on economic price adjustments, even if parties also intended indefinite-delivery indefinite-quantity contract. MAPCO Alaska Petroleum, Inc. v. U.S., 27 Fed. Cl. 405, 38 Cont. Cas. Fed. (CCH) P 76451 (1992) (abrogated on other grounds by, Tesoro Hawaii Corp. v. U.S., 405 F.3d 1339, 15 A.L.R. Fed. 2d 755 (Fed. Cir. 2005)). United States ☞70(23)

2 Modification

If a fixed price government contract containing an economic price adjustment clause is in violation of the procurement regulations and does not meet the requirement that the selected index approximately tracks the economic changes affecting the contract, reformation is appropriate. Gold Line Refining, Ltd. v. U.S., 43 Fed. Cl. 291 (1999). United States ☞72(1.1)

3 Indexes

Use of market-based references to determine adjustments to established prices in contracts for sale of jet fuel to military was authorized under Federal Acquisition Regulation (FAR) governing economic price adjustments to fixed price contracts. 48 C.F.R. § 16.203. Tesoro Hawaii Corp. v. U.S., 405 F.3d 1339, 15 A.L.R. Fed. 2d 755 (Fed. Cir. 2005). United States ☞70(18)

Use of an economic price adjustment (EPA) clause tied particularly to a reference price in a market publication to determine price adjustments in fuel contracts did not violate Federal Acquisition Regulation (FAR) governing economic price adjustments to fixed price contracts; regulation did not require that adjustments be tied solely to changes in the prices charged by a particular contractor. 48 C.F.R. § 16.203-3. Tesoro Hawaii Corp. v. U.S., 405 F.3d 1339, 15 A.L.R. Fed. 2d 755 (Fed. Cir. 2005). United States ☞70(18)

Economic price adjustment (EPA) clause in contracts for supply of jet fuel was not valid under the Federal Acquisition Regulation (FAR) as an "adjustment based on established prices," where clause used as escalator the PPI Index derived from the Petroleum Marketing Monthly (PPM), a monthly government publication of petroleum sales data setting forth average prices for petroleum products, as term "established prices" refers to established market prices. 48 C.F.R. § 16.203-1(a). . Calcasieu Refining Co. v. U.S., 2003 WL 22049528 (Ct. Fed. Cl. 2003). United States ☞70(18)

Economic price adjustment (EPA) clauses in contracts for supply of military jet fuel which based price of fuel on price indexes were not authorized by section of the Federal Acquisition Regulation (FAR) sanctioning EPA clauses based either on fluctuations in labor or material costs or on changes in the contractor's established prices that are reflective of industry-wide contingencies 48 C.F.R. § 16.203-1 et seq.Navajo Refining Co., L.P. v. U.S., 58 Fed. Cl. 200 (2003). United States ☞70(18)

Section of the Federal Acquisition Regulation (FAR) which authorizes the government's use of "[f]ixed-price contracts with economic price adjustment" authorized the use of economic price adjustment (EPA) clauses that adopt marketbased price indexes to provide adjustments in a contractor's established prices. 48 C.F.R. § 16.203-1. Williams Alaska Petroleum, Inc. v. U.S., 57 Fed. Cl. 789 (2003). United States ☞70(18)

§ 16.203-3 Limitations.

A fixed-price contract with economic price adjustment shall not be used unless the contracting officer determines that it is necessary either to protect the contractor and the Government against significant fluctuations in labor or material costs or to provide for contract price adjustment in the event of changes in the contractor's established prices.

United States Code Annotated

Contract requirements, see 41 USCA § 254.

Contracts, planning, solicitation, evaluation, and award procedures, see 10 USCA § 2305.

Cost-type research and development contracts with educational institutions, see 41 USCA § 254a.

Definitions, see 10 USCA § 2302, 41 USCA §§ 259, 403.

Kinds of contracts, see 10 USCA § 2306.

Planning and solicitation requirements, see 41 USCA § 253a.

Task and delivery order contracts, definitions, see 10 USCA § 2304d, 41 USCA § 253k.

Task and delivery order contracts, general authority, see 10 USCA § 2304a, 41 USCA § 253h.

Task and delivery order contracts, orders, see 10 USCA § 2304c, 41 USCA § 253j.

Task order contracts, advisory and assistance services, see 10 USCA § 2304b, 41 USCA § 253i.

Notes of Decisions

In general 1

1 In general

Defense Energy Support Center's (DESC) use of an economic price adjustment (EPA) clause tied particularly to a reference price in a market publication to determine price adjustments in fuel contracts did not violate Federal Acquisition Regulation (FAR) governing economic price adjustments to fixed-price contracts; regulation did not require that adjustments be tied solely to changes in the prices charged by a particular contractor. Tesoro Hawaii Corp. v. U.S., 405 F.3d 1339, 15 A.L.R. Fed. 2d 755 (Fed. Cir. 2005). United States ☞70(18)

Government's use of Petroleum Marketing Monthly (PMM) published by Department of Energy (DOE) as basis for economic price adjustments pursuant to economic price adjustment (EPA) clause of military fuel contracts satisfied requirement of Federal Acquisition Regulation (FAR) that EPA clauses be market based, as PPM compiled monthly average sale figures as reported by refiners. ConocoPhillips v. U.S., 73 Fed. Cl. 46 (2006), aff'd, 501 F.3d 1374 (Fed. Cir. 2007). United States ☞70(18)

Economic price adjustment (EPA) clause in military fuel supply contracts which was based on average sale prices of refined petroleum products by region as reported by the Department of Energy in the Petroleum Marketing Monthly (PMM) was not defective on theory that Federal Acquisition Regulation (FAR) required that price adjustments be based only on changes in individual contractor's prices and not on changes in overall market prices. ConocoPhillips v. U.S., 73 Fed. Cl. 46 (2006), aff'd, 501 F.3d 1374 (Fed. Cir. 2007). United States ☞70(18)

§ 16.203-4 Contract clauses.

(a) *Adjustment based on established prices—standard supplies.* (1) The contracting officer shall, when contracting by negotiation, insert the clause at 52.216-2, Economic Price Adjustment—Standard Supplies, or an agency-prescribed clause as authorized in paragraph (a)(2) of this subsection, in solicitations and contracts when all of the following conditions apply:

(i) A fixed-price contract is contemplated.

(ii) The requirement is for standard supplies that have an established catalog or market price.

(iii) The contracting officer has made the determination specified in 16.203-3.

(2) If all the conditions in paragraph (a)(1) of this subsection apply and the contracting officer determines that the use of the clause at 52.216-2 is inappropriate, the contracting officer may use an agency-prescribed clause instead of the clause at 52.216-2.

(3) If the negotiated unit price reflects a net price after applying a trade discount from a catalog or list price, the contracting officer shall document in the contract file both the catalog or list price and the discount. (This does not apply to prompt payment or cash discounts.)

(b) *Adjustment based on established prices—semistandard supplies.* (1) The contracting officer shall, when contracting by negotiation, insert the clause at 52.216-3, Economic Price Adjustment—Semistandard Supplies, or an agency-prescribed clause as authorized in paragraph (b)(2) of this section, in solicitations and contracts when all of the following conditions apply:

(i) A fixed-price contract is contemplated.

(ii) The requirement is for semistandard supplies for which the prices can be reasonably related to the prices of nearly equivalent standard supplies that have an established catalog or market price.

(iii) The contracting officer has made the determination specified in 16.203-3.

(2) If all conditions in paragraph (b)(1) of this subsection apply and the contracting officer determines that the use of the clause at 52.216-3 is inappropriate, the contracting officer may use an agency-prescribed clause instead of the clause at 52.216-3.

(3) If the negotiated unit price reflects a net price after applying a trade discount from a catalog or list price, the contracting officer shall document in the contract file both the catalog or list price and the discount. (This does not apply to prompt payment or cash discounts.)

(4) Before entering into the contract, the contracting officer and contractor must agree in writing on the identity of the standard supplies and the corresponding contract line items to which the clause applies.

(5) If the supplies are standard, except for preservation, packaging, and packing requirements, the clause prescribed in 16.203-4(a) shall be used rather than this clause.

(c) *Adjustments based on actual cost of labor or material.* (1) The contracting officer shall, when contracting by negotiation, insert a clause that is substantially the same as the clause at 52.216-4, Economic Price Adjustment—Labor and Material, or an agency-prescribed clause as authorized in subparagraph (c)(2) of this section, in solicitations and contracts when all of the following conditions apply:

(i) A fixed-price contract is contemplated.

(ii) There is no major element of design engineering or development work involved.

(iii) One or more identifiable labor or material cost factors are subject to change.

(iv) The contracting officer has made the determination specified in 16.203-3.

(2) If all conditions in paragraph (c)(1) of this section apply and the contracting officer determines that the use of the clause at 52.216-4 is inappropriate, the contracting officer may use an agency-prescribed clause instead of the clause at 52.216-4.

(3) The contracting officer shall describe in detail in the contract Schedule—

(i) The types of labor and materials subject to adjustment under the clause;

(ii) The labor rates, including fringe benefits (if any) and unit prices of materials that may be increased or decreased; and

(iii) The quantities of the specified labor and materials allocable to each unit to be delivered under the contract.

(4) In negotiating adjustments under the clause, the contracting officer shall—

(i) Consider work in process and materials on hand at the time of changes in labor rates, including fringe benefits (if any) or material prices;

(ii) Not include in adjustments any indirect cost (except fringe benefits as defined in 31.205-6(m)) or profit; and

(iii) Consider only those fringe benefits specified in the contract Schedule.

(d) *Adjustments based on cost indexes of labor or material.* The contracting officer should consider using an economic price adjustment clause based on cost indexes of labor or material under the circumstances and subject to approval as described in paragraphs (d)(1) and (d)(2) of this section.

(1) A clause providing adjustment based on cost indexes of labor or materials may be appropriate when—

(i) The contract involves an extended period of performance with significant costs to be incurred beyond 1 year after performance begins;

(ii) The contract amount subject to adjustment is substantial; and

(iii) The economic variables for labor and materials are too unstable to permit a reasonable division of risk between the Government and the contractor, without this type of clause.

(2) Any clause using this method shall be prepared and approved under agency procedures. Because of the variations in circumstances and clause wording that may arise, no standard clause is prescribed.

United States Code Annotated

Contract requirements, see 41 USCA § 254.

Contracts, planning, solicitation, evaluation, and award procedures, see 10 USCA § 2305.

Cost-type research and development contracts with educational institutions, see 41 USCA § 254a.

Definitions, see 10 USCA § 2302, 41 USCA §§ 259, 403.

Kinds of contracts, see 10 USCA § 2306.

Planning and solicitation requirements, see 41 USCA § 253a.

Task and delivery order contracts, definitions, see 10 USCA § 2304d, 41 USCA § 253k.

Task and delivery order contracts, general authority, see 10 USCA § 2304a, 41 USCA § 253h.

Task and delivery order contracts, orders, see 10 USCA § 2304c, 41 USCA § 253j.

Task order contracts, advisory and assistance services, see 10 USCA § 2304b, 41 USCA § 253i.

§ 16.204 Fixed-price incentive contracts.

A fixed-price incentive contract is a fixed-price contract that provides for adjusting profit and establishing the final contract price by a formula based on the relationship of final negotiated total cost to total target cost. Fixed-price incentive contracts are covered in Subpart 16.4, Incentive Contracts. See 16.403 for more complete descriptions, application, and limitations for these contracts. Prescribed clauses are found at 16.406.

United States Code Annotated

Contract requirements, see 41 USCA § 254.

Contracts, planning, solicitation, evaluation, and award procedures, see 10 USCA § 2305.

Cost-type research and development contracts with educational institutions, see 41 USCA § 254a.

Definitions, see 10 USCA § 2302, 41 USCA §§ 259, 403.

Kinds of contracts, see 10 USCA § 2306.

Planning and solicitation requirements, see 41 USCA § 253a.

Task and delivery order contracts, definitions, see 10 USCA § 2304d, 41 USCA § 253k.

Task and delivery order contracts, general authority, see 10 USCA § 2304a, 41 USCA § 253h.

Task and delivery order contracts, orders, see 10 USCA § 2304c, 41 USCA § 253j.

Task order contracts, advisory and assistance services, see 10 USCA § 2304b, 41 USCA § 253i.

Notes of Decisions

In general 1

1 In general

Despite fact that Department of Defense (DoD) violated DoD appropriation acts by incrementally funding fixed-price incentive contract without performing risk determinations in fiscal years 1990 to 1992, rendering the contract illegal, the Court of Federal Claims would enforce the contract as written, as such enforcement was not an unjust result where contractor was a sophisticated defense contractor, which had available to it all the information necessary to bid on the contract. Northrop Grumman Corp. v. U.S., 47 Fed. Cl. 20 (2000). United States ☞68

Department of Defense (DoD) violated DoD appropriation acts by incrementally funding fixed-price incentive contract without performing risk determinations in fiscal years 1990 to 1992. Department of Defense Appropriations Act, 1992, § 8037, 105 Stat. 1150; Department of Defense Appropriations Act, 1991, § 8038, 104 Stat. 1856; Department of Defense Appropriations Act, 1990, § 9048, 103 Stat. 1112. Northrop Grumman Corp. v. U.S., 47 Fed. Cl. 20 (2000). United States ☞70(15.1)

Contractor who contended that award of contract as a fixed-price incentive contract violated applicable regulatory requirements failed to prove that at the time of contracting the parties did not possess adequate cost and pricing information or that the risk was not reasonably apportioned. 48 C.F.R. § 16.403-1. Northrop Grumman Corp. v. U.S., 47 Fed. Cl. 20 (2000). United States ☞70(15.1)

Contractor did not satisfy its burden on claim that selection of award of contract as a fixed-price incentive contract violated provision of the Federal Acquisition Regulation concerning research and development acquisitions; even assuming that provision was applicable, provision was not mandatory in precluding use of fixed-price incentive contract. 48 C.F.R. § 35.006. Northrop Grumman Corp. v. U.S., 47 Fed. Cl. 20 (2000). United States ☞70(15.1)

Contractor did not satisfy its burden with regard to allegation that award of contract as a fixed-price incentive contract, rather than as a cost-reimbursement contract, violated Department of Defense (DoD) directive concerning appropriate contract type for research and development phases; obligation under the directive was to consider certain factors, not necessarily to adopt them as part of the procurement strategy. Northrop Grumman Corp. v. U.S., 47 Fed. Cl. 20 (2000). United States ☞70(15.1)

Contractor failed to establish that the government possessed superior knowledge, and did not disclose, that contract for a tactical air command and control system for the Marine Corps would require significant development and was unsuited for award as a fixed-price incentive contract; contractor did not undertake performance without vital knowledge, and the government did not fail to provide relevant information about the degree of development that the contract would require. Northrop Grumman Corp. v. U.S., 47 Fed. Cl. 20 (2000). United States ☞70(30)

Reformation to a cost-type contract was not the appropriate remedy for contract illegality which consisted of government's failure to perform risk assessment during each year of incremental funding by the Department of Defense (DoD) of fixed-price incentive contract; since Secretary of Defense did not make any determination that no lower cost alternatives were available, reformation to a cost-type contract would bring about another illegality. Northrop Grumman Corp. v. U.S., 47 Fed. Cl. 20 (2000). United States ☞72(1.1)

Contractor could not recover cost overruns on defense contract on ground of mutual mistake, as risk of mistake was allocated to contractor through the selection of fixed-price incentive contract. Northrop Grumman Corp. v. U.S., 47 Fed. Cl. 20 (2000). United States ☞74(4)

§ 16.205 Fixed-price contracts with prospective price redetermination.

§ 16.205-1 Description.

A fixed-price contract with prospective price redetermination provides for—

(a) A firm fixed price for an initial period of contract deliveries or performance; and

(b) Prospective redetermination, at a stated time or times during performance, of the price for subsequent periods of performance.

United States Code Annotated

Contract requirements, see 41 USCA § 254.

Contracts, planning, solicitation, evaluation, and award procedures, see 10 USCA § 2305.

Cost-type research and development contracts with educational institutions, see 41 USCA § 254a.

Definitions, see 10 USCA § 2302, 41 USCA §§ 259, 403.

Kinds of contracts, see 10 USCA § 2306.

Planning and solicitation requirements, see 41 USCA § 253a.

Task and delivery order contracts, definitions, see 10 USCA § 2304d, 41 USCA § 253k.

Task and delivery order contracts, general authority, see 10 USCA § 2304a, 41 USCA § 253h.

Task and delivery order contracts, orders, see 10 USCA § 2304c, 41 USCA § 253j.

Task order contracts, advisory and assistance services, see 10 USCA § 2304b, 41 USCA § 253i.

§ 16.205-2 Application.

A fixed-price contract with prospective price redetermination may be used in acquisitions of quantity production or services for which it is possible to negotiate a fair and reasonable firm fixed price for an initial period, but not for subsequent periods of contract performance.

(a) The initial period should be the longest period for which it is possible to negotiate a fair and reasonable firm fixed price. Each subsequent pricing period should be at least 12 months.

(b) The contract may provide for a ceiling price based on evaluation of the uncertainties involved in performance and their possible cost impact. This ceiling price should provide for assumption of a reasonable proportion of the risk by the contractor and, once established, may be adjusted only by operation of contract clauses providing for equitable adjustment or other revision of the contract price under stated circumstances.

United States Code Annotated

Contract requirements, see 41 USCA § 254.

Contracts, planning, solicitation, evaluation, and award procedures, see 10 USCA § 2305.

Cost-type research and development contracts with educational institutions, see 41 USCA § 254a.

Definitions, see 10 USCA § 2302, 41 USCA §§ 259, 403.

Kinds of contracts, see 10 USCA § 2306.

Planning and solicitation requirements, see 41 USCA § 253a.

Task and delivery order contracts, definitions, see 10 USCA § 2304d, 41 USCA § 253k.

Task and delivery order contracts, general authority, see 10 USCA § 2304a, 41 USCA § 253h.

Task and delivery order contracts, orders, see 10 USCA § 2304c, 41 USCA § 253j.

Task order contracts, advisory and assistance services, see 10 USCA § 2304b, 41 USCA § 253i.

§ 16.205-3 Limitations.

This contract type shall not be used unless—

(a) Negotiations have established that—

(1) The conditions for use of a firm-fixed-price contract are not present (see 16.202-2); and

(2) A fixed-price incentive contract would not be more appropriate;

(b) The contractor's accounting system is adequate for price redetermination;

(c) The prospective pricing periods can be made to conform with operation of the contractor's accounting system; and

(d) There is reasonable assurance that price redetermination actions will take place promptly at the specified times.

United States Code Annotated

Contract requirements, see 41 USCA § 254.

Contracts, planning, solicitation, evaluation, and award procedures, see 10 USCA § 2305.

Cost-type research and development contracts with educational institutions, see 41 USCA § 254a.

Definitions, see 10 USCA § 2302, 41 USCA §§ 259, 403.

Kinds of contracts, see 10 USCA § 2306.

Planning and solicitation requirements, see 41 USCA § 253a.

Task and delivery order contracts, definitions, see 10 USCA § 2304d, 41 USCA § 253k.

Task and delivery order contracts, general authority, see 10 USCA § 2304a, 41 USCA § 253h.

Task and delivery order contracts, orders, see 10 USCA § 2304c, 41 USCA § 253j.

Task order contracts, advisory and assistance services, see 10 USCA § 2304b, 41 USCA § 253i.

§ 16.205-4 Contract clause.

The contracting officer shall, when contracting by negotiation, insert the clause at 52. 216-5, Price Redetermination— Prospective, in solicitations and contracts when a fixed-price contract is contemplated and the conditions specified in 16.205-2 and 16.205-3(a) through (d) apply.

United States Code Annotated

Contract requirements, see 41 USCA § 254.

Contracts, planning, solicitation, evaluation, and award procedures, see 10 USCA § 2305.

Cost-type research and development contracts with educational institutions, see 41 USCA § 254a.

Definitions, see 10 USCA § 2302, 41 USCA §§ 259, 403.

Kinds of contracts, see 10 USCA § 2306.

Planning and solicitation requirements, see 41 USCA § 253a.

Task and delivery order contracts, definitions, see 10 USCA § 2304d, 41 USCA § 253k.

Task and delivery order contracts, general authority, see 10 USCA § 2304a, 41 USCA § 253h.

Task and delivery order contracts, orders, see 10 USCA § 2304c, 41 USCA § 253j.

Task order contracts, advisory and assistance services, see 10 USCA § 2304b, 41 USCA § 253i.

§ 16.206 Fixed-ceiling-price contracts with retroactive price redetermination.

§ 16.206-1 Description.

A fixed-ceiling-price contract with retroactive price redetermination provides for—

(a) A fixed ceiling price; and

(b) Retroactive price redetermination within the ceiling after completion of the contract.

United States Code Annotated

Contract requirements, see 41 USCA § 254.

Contracts, planning, solicitation, evaluation, and award procedures, see 10 USCA § 2305.

Cost-type research and development contracts with educational institutions, see 41 USCA § 254a.

Definitions, see 10 USCA § 2302, 41 USCA §§ 259, 403.

Kinds of contracts, see 10 USCA § 2306.

Planning and solicitation requirements, see 41 USCA § 253a.

Task and delivery order contracts, definitions, see 10 USCA § 2304d, 41 USCA § 253k.

Task and delivery order contracts, general authority, see 10 USCA § 2304a, 41 USCA § 253h.

Task and delivery order contracts, orders, see 10 USCA § 2304c, 41 USCA § 253j.

Task order contracts, advisory and assistance services, see 10 USCA § 2304b, 41 USCA § 253i.

§ 16.206-2 Application.

A fixed-ceiling-price contract with retroactive price redetermination is appropriate for research and development contracts estimated at $150,000 or less when it is established at the outset that a fair and reasonable firm fixed price cannot be negotiated and that the amount involved and short performance period make the use of any other fixed-price contract type impracticable.

(a) A ceiling price shall be negotiated for the contract at a level that reflects a reasonable sharing of risk by the contractor. The established ceiling price may be adjusted only if required by the operation of contract clauses providing for equitable adjustment or other revision of the contract price under stated circumstances.

(b) The contract should be awarded only after negotiation of a billing price that is as fair and reasonable as the circumstances permit.

(c) Since this contract type provides the contractor no cost control incentive except the ceiling price, the contracting officer should make clear to the contractor during discussion before award that the contractor's management effectiveness and ingenuity will be considered in retroactively redetermining the price.

United States Code Annotated

Contract requirements, see 41 USCA § 254.

Contracts, planning, solicitation, evaluation, and award procedures, see 10 USCA § 2305.

Cost-type research and development contracts with educational institutions, see 41 USCA § 254a.

Definitions, see 10 USCA § 2302, 41 USCA §§ 259, 403.

Kinds of contracts, see 10 USCA § 2306.

Planning and solicitation requirements, see 41 USCA § 253a.

Task and delivery order contracts, definitions, see 10 USCA § 2304d, 41 USCA § 253k.

Task and delivery order contracts, general authority, see 10 USCA § 2304a, 41 USCA § 253h.

Task and delivery order contracts, orders, see 10 USCA § 2304c, 41 USCA § 253j.

Task order contracts, advisory and assistance services, see 10 USCA § 2304b, 41 USCA § 253i.

§ 16.206-3 Limitations.

This contract type shall not be used unless—

(a) The contract is for research and development and the estimated cost is $150,000 or less;

(b) The contractor's accounting system is adequate for price redetermination;

(c) There is reasonable assurance that the price redetermination will take place promptly at the specified time; and

(d) The head of the contracting activity (or a higher-level official, if required by agency procedures) approves its use in writing.

United States Code Annotated

Contract requirements, see 41 USCA § 254.

Contracts, planning, solicitation, evaluation, and award procedures, see 10 USCA § 2305.

Cost-type research and development contracts with educational institutions, see 41 USCA § 254a.

Definitions, see 10 USCA § 2302, 41 USCA §§ 259, 403.

Kinds of contracts, see 10 USCA § 2306.

Planning and solicitation requirements, see 41 USCA § 253a.

Task and delivery order contracts, definitions, see 10 USCA § 2304d, 41 USCA § 253k.

Task and delivery order contracts, general authority, see 10 USCA § 2304a, 41 USCA § 253h.

Task and delivery order contracts, orders, see 10 USCA § 2304c, 41 USCA § 253j.

Task order contracts, advisory and assistance services, see 10 USCA § 2304b, 41 USCA § 253i.

§ 16.206-4 Contract clause.

The contracting officer shall, when contracting by negotiation, insert the clause at 52.216-6, Price Redetermination— Retroactive, in solicitations and contracts when a fixed-price contract is contemplated and the conditions in 16.206-2 and 16.206-3(a) through (d) apply.

United States Code Annotated

Contract requirements, see 41 USCA § 254.

Contracts, planning, solicitation, evaluation, and award procedures, see 10 USCA § 2305.

Cost-type research and development contracts with educational institutions, see 41 USCA § 254a.

Definitions, see 10 USCA § 2302, 41 USCA §§ 259, 403.

Kinds of contracts, see 10 USCA § 2306.

Planning and solicitation requirements, see 41 USCA § 253a.

Task and delivery order contracts, definitions, see 10 USCA § 2304d, 41 USCA § 253k.

Task and delivery order contracts, general authority, see 10 USCA § 2304a, 41 USCA § 253h.

Task and delivery order contracts, orders, see 10 USCA § 2304c, 41 USCA § 253j.

Task order contracts, advisory and assistance services, see 10 USCA § 2304b, 41 USCA § 253i.

§ 16.207 Firm-fixed-price, level-of-effort term contracts.

§ 16.207-1 Description.

A firm-fixed-price, level-of-effort term contract requires—

(a) The contractor to provide a specified level of effort, over a stated period of time, on work that can be stated only in general terms; and

(b) The Government to pay the contractor a fixed dollar amount.

United States Code Annotated

Contract requirements, see 41 USCA § 254.

Contracts, planning, solicitation, evaluation, and award procedures, see 10 USCA § 2305.

Cost-type research and development contracts with educational institutions, see 41 USCA § 254a.

Definitions, see 10 USCA § 2302, 41 USCA §§ 259, 403.

Kinds of contracts, see 10 USCA § 2306.

Planning and solicitation requirements, see 41 USCA § 253a.

Task and delivery order contracts, definitions, see 10 USCA § 2304d, 41 USCA § 253k.

Task and delivery order contracts, general authority, see 10 USCA § 2304a, 41 USCA § 253h.

Task and delivery order contracts, orders, see 10 USCA § 2304c, 41 USCA § 253j.

Task order contracts, advisory and assistance services, see 10 USCA § 2304b, 41 USCA § 253i.

Notes of Decisions

Level-of-effort 1

1 Level-of-effort

Government was not entitled to reimbursement of added costs paid to fiscal intermediary to providers of health care services operating under Medicare program in connection with intermediary's performance of authorized changes to its subcontract, notwithstanding that size of intermediary's work force declined during period for which added costs were paid; subcontract was not "level-of-effort" undertaking, nor did it obligate intermediary to dedicate fixed number of personnel to various tasks it had agreed to perform. Empire Blue Cross and Blue Shield v. U.S., 5 F.3d 1506 (Fed. Cir. 1993). United States ☞75(1); United

States ☞88

§ 16.207-2 Application.

A firm-fixed-price, level-of-effort term contract is suitable for investigation or study in a specific research and development area. The product of the contract is usually a report showing the results achieved through application of the required level of effort. However, payment is based on the effort expended rather than on the results achieved.

United States Code Annotated

Contract requirements, see 41 USCA § 254.

Contracts, planning, solicitation, evaluation, and award procedures, see 10 USCA § 2305.

Cost-type research and development contracts with educational institutions, see 41 USCA § 254a.

Definitions, see 10 USCA § 2302, 41 USCA §§ 259, 403.

Kinds of contracts, see 10 USCA § 2306.

Planning and solicitation requirements, see 41 USCA § 253a.

Task and delivery order contracts, definitions, see 10 USCA § 2304d, 41 USCA § 253k.

Task and delivery order contracts, general authority, see 10 USCA § 2304a, 41 USCA § 253h.

Task and delivery order contracts, orders, see 10 USCA § 2304c, 41 USCA § 253j.

Task order contracts, advisory and assistance services, see 10 USCA § 2304b, 41 USCA § 253i.

Notes of Decisions

Level-of-effort 1

1 Level-of-effort

Government was not entitled to reimbursement of added costs paid to fiscal intermediary to providers of health care services operating under Medicare program in connection with intermediary's performance of authorized changes to its subcontract, notwithstanding that size of intermediary's work force declined during period for which added costs were paid; subcontract was not "level-of-effort" undertaking, nor did it obligate intermediary to dedicate fixed number of personnel to various tasks it had agreed to perform. Empire Blue Cross and Blue Shield v. U.S., 5 F.3d 1506 (Fed. Cir. 1993). United States ☞75(1); United States ☞88

§ 16.207-3 Limitations.

This contract type may be used only when—

(a) The work required cannot otherwise be clearly defined;

(b) The required level of effort is identified and agreed upon in advance;

(c) There is reasonable assurance that the intended result cannot be achieved by expending less than the stipulated effort; and

(d) The contract price is $150,000 or less, unless approved by the chief of the contracting office.

United States Code Annotated

Contract requirements, see 41 USCA § 254.

Contracts, planning, solicitation, evaluation, and award procedures, see 10 USCA § 2305.

Cost-type research and development contracts with educational institutions, see 41 USCA § 254a.

Definitions, see 10 USCA § 2302, 41 USCA §§ 259, 403.

Kinds of contracts, see 10 USCA § 2306.

Planning and solicitation requirements, see 41 USCA § 253a.

Task and delivery order contracts, definitions, see 10 USCA § 2304d, 41 USCA § 253k.

Task and delivery order contracts, general authority, see 10 USCA § 2304a, 41 USCA § 253h.

Task and delivery order contracts, orders, see 10 USCA § 2304c, 41 USCA § 253j.

Task order contracts, advisory and assistance services, see 10 USCA § 2304b, 41 USCA § 253i.

Notes of Decisions

Level-of-effort 1

1 Level-of-effort

Government was not entitled to reimbursement of added costs paid to fiscal intermediary to providers of health care services operating under Medicare program in connection with intermediary's performance of authorized changes to its subcontract, notwithstanding that size of intermediary's work force declined during period for which added costs were paid; subcontract was not "level-of-effort" undertaking, nor did it obligate intermediary to dedicate fixed number of personnel to various tasks it had agreed to perform. Empire Blue Cross and Blue Shield v. U.S., 5 F.3d 1506 (Fed. Cir. 1993). United States ☞75(1); United States ☞88

Subpart 16.3 Cost-Reimbursement Contracts

§ 16.301 General.

§ 16.301-1 Description.

Cost-reimbursement types of contracts provide for payment of allowable incurred costs, to the extent prescribed in the contract. These contracts establish an estimate of total cost for the purpose of obligating funds and establishing a ceiling that the contractor may not exceed (except at its own risk) without the approval of the contracting officer.

Notes of Decisions
Cost-reimbursement contracts, generally 1
Court of Federal Claims jurisdiction 2

1 Cost-reimbursement contracts, generally

Cost-share contract may be deemed cost-reimbursement contract, for purpose of request for proposal (RFP) relating to government contract, if RFP does not specify type of costreimbursement contract sought. 48 C.F.R. §§ 16.101(b), 16.303. City & County of San Francisco v. U.S., 130 F.3d 873, 42 Cont. Cas. Fed. (CCH) P 77215 (9th Cir. 1997). United States ☞64.25

State income taxes paid by sole shareholder of contractor, a Subchapter S corporation, were not reimbursable, allowable costs in cost-reimbursement contract between contractor and United States under the Federal Acquisition Regulation (FAR), since taxes were paid based on dividends paid to sole shareholder, and were not paid by the contracting entity. 48 C.F.R. § 31.205-41. Information Systems & Networks Corp. v. U.S., 437 F.3d 1173 (Fed. Cir. 2006). United States ☞70(33)

Government would not be permitted to supplement the administrative record on final day of post-award bid protest hearing with 36 page document that explained the basis for government's most probable cost estimate (MPCE), which adjusted contractor's bid on a cost reimbursement contract, where government had intentionally failed to produce the document earlier, even though government was required by law to produce the document. 48 C.F.R. § 15.608(a). Day & Zimmermann Services, a Div. of Day & Zimmermann, Inc. v. U.S., 38 Fed. Cl. 591, 42 Cont. Cas. Fed. (CCH) P 77186 (1997), dismissed, 132 F.3d 49 (Fed. Cir. 1997). United States ☞64.60(1)

Government's unexplained failure to produce critically relevant document that explained basis for its most probable cost estimate (MPCE) for adjusting contractor's bid on cost reimbursement contract warranted an adverse inference; thus, court was constrained to infer that had government properly produced the document, it would have supported contractor's contention that the Army arbitrarily and capriciously determined the MPCE for its proposal, and court would not sustain Army's determination of MPCE for contractor's proposal as being a reasonable adjustment based on documented and creditable facts. Day

& Zimmermann Services, a Div. of Day & Zimmermann, Inc. v. U.S., 38 Fed. Cl. 591, 42 Cont. Cas. Fed. (CCH) P 77186 (1997), dismissed, 132 F.3d 49 (Fed. Cir. 1997). Evidence ☞75; Evidence ☞87

2 Court of Federal Claims jurisdiction

Court of Federal Claims lacked jurisdiction in government contractor's breach of contract suit to enter declaratory judgment holding indefinite-quantity (IDQ) specifications deficient as a matter of law where they bore no rational relationship to actual requirements within the contracting agency's superior knowledge at the time of solicitation, where such a ruling was not necessary to resolve contractor's claim for money damages. Schweiger Const. Co., Inc. v. U.S., 49 Fed. Cl. 188 (2001). Federal Courts ☞1078

Court of Federal Claims had jurisdiction over government contractor's claim that construction contract was illegal and that government violated provisions of the Federal Acquisition Regulation which address the type of contract to be used for procurement, in that procurement should have led to the award of a cost-reimbursement contract, rather than a firmfixed-price contract. 48 C.F.R. § 16.000. PCL Const. Services, Inc. v. U.S., 41 Fed. Cl. 242, 42 Cont. Cas. Fed. (CCH) P 77325 (1998), aff'd, 96 Fed. Appx. 672 (Fed. Cir. 2004). Federal Courts ☞1076

Court lacked jurisdiction to consider merits of government contractor's claim arising out of defense industrial supply center's removal of contractor's name from its automated procurement system; contractor failed to establish that it received sufficient benefit from participating in program to provide consideration to transform basic agreement with center into enforceable contract. Almar Industries, Inc. v. U.S., 16 Cl. Ct. 243, 35 Cont. Cas. Fed. (CCH) P 75621, 1989 WL 6470 (1989). Federal Courts ☞1076

§ 16.301-2 Application.

(a) The contracting officer shall use cost-reimbursement contracts only when—

(1) Circumstances do not allow the agency to define its requirements sufficiently to allow for a fixed-price type contract (see 7.105); or

(2) Uncertainties involved in contract performance do not permit costs to be estimated with sufficient accuracy to use any type of fixed-price contract.

(b) The contracting officer shall document the rationale for selecting the contract type in the written acquisition plan and ensure that the plan is approved and signed at least one level above the contracting officer (see 7.103(j) and 7.105). If a written acquisition plan is not required, the contracting officer shall document the rationale in the contract file. See also 16.103(d).

Notes of Decisions

Cost-reimbursement contracts, generally 1
Court of Federal Claims jurisdiction 2

1 Cost-reimbursement contracts, generally

Cost-share contract may be deemed cost-reimbursement contract, for purpose of request for proposal (RFP) relating to government contract, if RFP does not specify type of costreimbursement contract sought. 48 C.F.R. §§ 16.101(b), 16.303. City & County of San Francisco v. U.S., 130 F.3d 873, 42 Cont. Cas. Fed. (CCH) P 77215 (9th Cir. 1997). United States ☞64.25

State income taxes paid by sole shareholder of contractor, a Subchapter S corporation, were not reimbursable, allowable costs in cost-reimbursement contract between contractor and United States under the Federal Acquisition Regulation (FAR), since taxes were paid based on dividends paid to sole shareholder, and were not paid by the contracting entity. 48 C.F.R. § 31.205-41. Information Systems & Networks Corp. v. U.S., 437 F.3d 1173 (Fed. Cir. 2006). United States ☞70(33)

Government would not be permitted to supplement the administrative record on final day of post-award bid protest hearing with 36 page document that explained the basis for government's most probable cost estimate (MPCE), which adjusted contractor's bid on a cost reimbursement contract, where government had intentionally failed to produce the document earlier, even though government was required by law to produce the document.

48 C.F.R. § 15.608(a). Day & Zimmermann Services, a Div. of Day & Zimmermann, Inc. v. U.S., 38 Fed. Cl. 591, 42 Cont. Cas. Fed. (CCH) P 77186 (1997), dismissed, 132 F.3d 49 (Fed. Cir. 1997). United States ⊕64.60(1)

Government's unexplained failure to produce critically relevant document that explained basis for its most probable cost estimate (MPCE) for adjusting contractor's bid on cost reimbursement contract warranted an adverse inference; thus, court was constrained to infer that had government properly produced the document, it would have supported contractor's contention that the Army arbitrarily and capriciously determined the MPCE for its proposal, and court would not sustain Army's determination of MPCE for contractor's proposal as being a reasonable adjustment based on documented and creditable facts. Day & Zimmermann Services, a Div. of Day & Zimmermann, Inc. v. U.S., 38 Fed. Cl. 591, 42 Cont. Cas. Fed. (CCH) P 77186 (1997), dismissed, 132 F.3d 49 (Fed. Cir. 1997). Evidence ⊕75; Evidence ⊕87

2 Court of Federal Claims jurisdiction

Court of Federal Claims lacked jurisdiction in government contractor's breach of contract suit to enter declaratory judgment holding indefinite-quantity (IDQ) specifications deficient as a matter of law where they bore no rational relationship to actual requirements within the contracting agency's superior knowledge at the time of solicitation, where such a ruling was not necessary to resolve contractor's claim for money damages. Schweiger Const. Co., Inc. v. U.S., 49 Fed. Cl. 188 (2001). Federal Courts ⊕1078

Court of Federal Claims had jurisdiction over government contractor's claim that construction contract was illegal and that government violated provisions of the Federal Acquisition Regulation which address the type of contract to be used for procurement, in that procurement should have led to the award of a cost-reimbursement contract, rather than a firmfixed-price contract. 48 C.F.R. § 16.000. PCL Const. Services, Inc. v. U.S., 41 Fed. Cl. 242, 42 Cont. Cas. Fed. (CCH) P 77325 (1998), aff'd, 96 Fed. Appx. 672 (Fed. Cir. 2004). Federal Courts ⊕1076

Court lacked jurisdiction to consider merits of government contractor's claim arising out of defense industrial supply center's removal of contractor's name from its automated procurement system; contractor failed to establish that it received sufficient benefit from participating in program to provide consideration to transform basic agreement with center into enforceable contract. Almar Industries, Inc. v. U.S., 16 Cl. Ct. 243, 35 Cont. Cas. Fed. (CCH) P 75621, 1989 WL 6470 (1989). Federal Courts ⊕1076

§ 16.301-3 Limitations.

(a) A cost-reimbursement contract may be used only when?

(1) The factors in 16.104 have been considered;

(2) A written acquisition plan has been approved and signed at least one level above the contracting officer;

(3) The contractor's accounting system is adequate for determining costs applicable to the contract or order; and

(4) Prior to award of the contract or order, adequate Government resources are available to award and manage a contract other than firm-fixed-priced (see 7.104(e)). This includes appropriate Government surveillance during performance in accordance with 1.602-2, to provide reasonable assurance that efficient methods and effective cost controls are used.

(i) Designation of at least one contracting officer's representative (COR) qualified in accordance with 1.602-2 has been made prior to award of the contract or order; and

(ii) Appropriate Government surveillance during performance to provide reasonable assurance that efficient methods and effective cost controls are used.

(b) The use of cost-reimbursement contracts is prohibited for the acquisition of commercial items (see Parts 2 and 12).

Notes of Decisions
Cost-reimbursement contracts, generally 1
Court of Federal Claims jurisdiction 3
Waiver 2

1 Cost-reimbursement contracts, generally

Cost-share contract may be deemed cost-reimbursement contract, for purpose of request for proposal (RFP) relating to government contract, if RFP does not specify type of costreimbursement contract sought. 48 C.F.R. §§ 16.101(b), 16.303. City & County of San Francisco v. U.S., 130 F.3d 873, 42 Cont. Cas. Fed. (CCH) P 77215 (9th Cir. 1997). United States ⚭64.25

State income taxes paid by sole shareholder of contractor, a Subchapter S corporation, were not reimbursable, allowable costs in cost-reimbursement contract between contractor and United States under the Federal Acquisition Regulation (FAR), since taxes were paid based on dividends paid to sole shareholder, and were not paid by the contracting entity. 48 C.F.R. § 31.205-41. Information Systems & Networks Corp. v. U.S., 437 F.3d 1173 (Fed. Cir. 2006). United States ⚭70(33)

Contractor did not satisfy its burden with regard to allegation that award of contract as a fixed-price incentive contract, rather than as a cost-reimbursement contract, violated Department of Defense (DoD) directive concerning appropriate contract type for research and development phases; obligation under the directive was to consider certain factors, not necessarily to adopt them as part of the procurement strategy. Northrop Grumman Corp. v. U.S., 47 Fed. Cl. 20 (2000). United States ⚭70(15.1)

Government's unexplained failure to produce critically relevant document that explained basis for its most probable cost estimate (MPCE) for adjusting contractor's bid on cost reimbursement contract warranted an adverse inference; thus, court was constrained to infer that had government properly produced the document, it would have supported contractor's contention that the Army arbitrarily and capriciously determined the MPCE for its proposal, and court would not sustain Army's determination of MPCE for contractor's proposal as being a reasonable adjustment based on documented and creditable facts. Day & Zimmermann Services, a Div. of Day & Zimmermann, Inc. v. U.S., 38 Fed. Cl. 591, 42 Cont. Cas. Fed. (CCH) P 77186 (1997), dismissed, 132 F.3d 49 (Fed. Cir. 1997). Evidence ⚭75; Evidence ⚭87

Government would not be permitted to supplement the administrative record on final day of post-award bid protest hearing with 36 page document that explained the basis for government's most probable cost estimate (MPCE), which adjusted contractor's bid on a cost reimbursement contract, where government had intentionally failed to produce the document earlier, even though government was required by law to produce the document. 48 C.F.R. § 15.608(a). Day & Zimmermann Services, a Div. of Day & Zimmermann, Inc. v. U.S., 38 Fed. Cl. 591, 42 Cont. Cas. Fed. (CCH) P 77186 (1997), dismissed, 132 F.3d 49 (Fed. Cir. 1997). United States ⚭64.60(1)

2 Waiver

Contractor waived its claim for reformation of fixed-price contract for research and development of technology for tracking ultra-quiet submarines, although it incurred costs in excess of fixed price, where contractor, a sophisticated federal contractor, failed to seek a cost reimbursement contract during contract negotiations, and it successfully underbid technically superior competitors and retained contract with a vigorous defense against competitor's protest action. American Tel. and Tel. Co. v. U.S., 307 F.3d 1374 (Fed. Cir. 2002). Reformation Of Instruments ⚭23

3 Court of Federal Claims jurisdiction

Court of Federal Claims lacked jurisdiction in government contractor's breach of contract suit to enter declaratory judgment holding indefinite-quantity (IDQ) specifications deficient as a matter of law where they bore no rational relationship to actual requirements within the contracting agency's superior knowledge at the time of solicitation, where such a ruling was not necessary to resolve contractor's claim for money damages. Schweiger Const. Co., Inc. v. U.S., 49 Fed. Cl. 188 (2001). Federal Courts ⚭1078

Court of Federal Claims had jurisdiction over government contractor's claim that construction contract was illegal and that government violated provisions of the Federal Acquisition Regulation which address the type of contract to be used for procurement, in that procurement should have led to the award of a cost-reimbursement contract, rather than a firmfixed-price contract. 48 C.F.R. § 16.000. PCL Const. Services, Inc. v. U.S., 41

Fed. Cl. 242, 42 Cont. Cas. Fed. (CCH) P 77325 (1998), aff'd, 96 Fed. Appx. 672 (Fed. Cir. 2004). Federal Courts ⬬1076

Court lacked jurisdiction to consider merits of government contractor's claim arising out of defense industrial supply center's removal of contractor's name from its automated procurement system; contractor failed to establish that it received sufficient benefit from participating in program to provide consideration to transform basic agreement with center into enforceable contract. Almar Industries, Inc. v. U.S., 16 Cl. Ct. 243, 35 Cont. Cas. Fed. (CCH) P 75621, 1989 WL 6470 (1989). Federal Courts ⬬1076

§ 16.302 Cost contracts.

(a) *Description.* A cost contract is a cost-reimbursement contract in which the contractor receives no fee.

(b) *Application.* A cost contract may be appropriate for research and development work, particularly with nonprofit educational institutions or other nonprofit organizations.

(c) *Limitations.* See 16.301-3.

United States Code Annotated

Contract requirements, see 41 USCA § 254.

Contracts, planning, solicitation, evaluation, and award procedures, see 10 USCA § 2305.

Cost-type research and development contracts with educational institutions, see 41 USCA § 254a.

Definitions, see 10 USCA § 2302, 41 USCA §§ 259, 403.

Kinds of contracts, see 10 USCA § 2306.

Planning and solicitation requirements, see 41 USCA § 253a.

Task and delivery order contracts, definitions, see 10 USCA § 2304d, 41 USCA § 253k.

Task and delivery order contracts, general authority, see 10 USCA § 2304a, 41 USCA § 253h.

Task and delivery order contracts, orders, see 10 USCA § 2304c, 41 USCA § 253j.

Task order contracts, advisory and assistance services, see 10 USCA § 2304b, 41 USCA § 253i.

§ 16.303 Cost-sharing contracts.

(a) *Description.* A cost-sharing contract is a cost-reimbursement contract in which the contractor receives no fee and is reimbursed only for an agreed-upon portion of its allowable costs.

(b) *Application.* A cost-sharing contract may be used when the contractor agrees to absorb a portion of the costs, in the expectation of substantial compensating benefits.

(c) *Limitations.* See 16.301-3.

United States Code Annotated

Contract requirements, see 41 USCA § 254.

Contracts, planning, solicitation, evaluation, and award procedures, see 10 USCA § 2305.

Cost-type research and development contracts with educational institutions, see 41 USCA § 254a.

Definitions, see 10 USCA § 2302, 41 USCA §§ 259, 403.

Kinds of contracts, see 10 USCA § 2306.

Planning and solicitation requirements, see 41 USCA § 253a.

Task and delivery order contracts, definitions, see 10 USCA § 2304d, 41 USCA § 253k.

Task and delivery order contracts, general authority, see 10 USCA § 2304a, 41 USCA § 253h.

Task and delivery order contracts, orders, see 10 USCA § 2304c, 41 USCA § 253j.

Task order contracts, advisory and assistance services, see 10 USCA § 2304b, 41 USCA § 253i.

Notes of Decisions

In general 1

1 In general

Utility company's proposal for government contract relating to electrical services, which proposed that government would reimburse none of company's costs for replacing electrical system at issue and that government would pay company up to certain amount if specified contingencies arose, was cost-share type contract, not firm-fixed-price contract, and thus satisfied requirement in request for proposal (RFP) that bidders submit cost-reimbursement contract proposal. 48 C.F.R. §§ 16.202, 16.303. City & County of San Francisco v. U.S., 130 F.3d 873, 42 Cont. Cas. Fed. (CCH) P 77215 (9th Cir. 1997). United States ☞64.30

Cost-share contract may be deemed cost-reimbursement contract, for purpose of request for proposal (RFP) relating to government contract, if RFP does not specify type of costreimbursement contract sought. 48 C.F.R. §§ 16.101(b), 16.303. City & County of San Francisco v. U.S., 130 F.3d 873, 42 Cont. Cas. Fed. (CCH) P 77215 (9th Cir. 1997). United States ☞64.25

§ 16.304 Cost-plus-incentive-fee contracts.

A cost-plus-incentive-fee contract is a cost-reimbursement contract that provides for an initially negotiated fee to be adjusted later by a formula based on the relationship of total allowable costs to total target costs. Cost-plus-incentive-fee contracts are covered in Subpart 16.4, Incentive Contracts. See 16.405-1 for a more complete description and discussion of application of these contracts. See 16.301-3 for limitations.

United States Code Annotated

Contract requirements, see 41 USCA § 254.

Contracts, planning, solicitation, evaluation, and award procedures, see 10 USCA § 2305.

Cost-type research and development contracts with educational institutions, see 41 USCA § 254a.

Definitions, see 10 USCA § 2302, 41 USCA §§ 259, 403.

Kinds of contracts, see 10 USCA § 2306.

Planning and solicitation requirements, see 41 USCA § 253a.

Task and delivery order contracts, definitions, see 10 USCA § 2304d, 41 USCA § 253k.

Task and delivery order contracts, general authority, see 10 USCA § 2304a, 41 USCA § 253h.

Task and delivery order contracts, orders, see 10 USCA § 2304c, 41 USCA § 253j.

Task order contracts, advisory and assistance services, see 10 USCA § 2304b, 41 USCA § 253i.

Notes of Decisions

In general 1

1 In general

Incentive fee clause of cost-plus-incentive-fee (CPIF) contract for development of battlefield management aircraft was applied properly to reduce contractor's fee after contracting officer deleted or relaxed certain specifications to keep the project on track; clause permitted equitable adjustment of target cost and target fee and minimum and maximum fees when contractor's work was decreased by a modification to the contract. Northrop Grumman Corp. v. U.S., 41 Fed. Cl. 645, 42 Cont. Cas. Fed. (CCH) P 77361 (1998). United States ☞70(18)

"Best efforts" language in cost-plus-incentive-fee (CPIF) contract referred to government contractor's duty in a CPIF contract to use its "best efforts" to complete the project within the funding limit allocated to the contract; it did not address a dispute that involved the propriety of a fee reduction based on the deletion or relaxation of contract specifications. Northrop Grumman Corp. v. U.S., 41 Fed. Cl. 645, 42 Cont. Cas. Fed. (CCH) P 77361 (1998). United States ☞70(18)

§ 16.305 Cost-plus-award-fee contracts.

A cost-plus-award-fee contract is a cost-reimbursement contract that provides for a fee consisting of (a) a base amount (which may be zero) fixed at inception of the contract and

(b) an award amount, based upon a judgmental evaluation by the Government, sufficient to provide motivation for excellence in contract performance. Cost-plus-award-fee contracts are covered in Subpart 16.4, Incentive Contracts. See 16.401(e) for a more complete description and discussion of the application of these contracts. See 16.301-3 and 16.401(e)(5) for limitations.

United States Code Annotated

Contract requirements, see 41 USCA § 254.

Contracts, planning, solicitation, evaluation, and award procedures, see 10 USCA § 2305.

Cost-type research and development contracts with educational institutions, see 41 USCA § 254a.

Definitions, see 10 USCA § 2302, 41 USCA §§ 259, 403.

Kinds of contracts, see 10 USCA § 2306.

Planning and solicitation requirements, see 41 USCA § 253a.

Task and delivery order contracts, definitions, see 10 USCA § 2304d, 41 USCA § 253k.

Task and delivery order contracts, general authority, see 10 USCA § 2304a, 41 USCA § 253h.

Task and delivery order contracts, orders, see 10 USCA § 2304c, 41 USCA § 253j.

Task order contracts, advisory and assistance services, see 10 USCA § 2304b, 41 USCA § 253i.

Notes of Decisions
In general 1

1 In general

Contract provision which purportedly divested jurisdiction of Armed Services Board of Contract Appeals to hear dispute concerning calculation of award fee under cost-plus-award-fee (CPAF) contract between Navy and contractor was void; provision otherwise depriving board of jurisdiction was not a matter of statute primacy, and thus parties could not on their own alter board's review under Contract Disputes Act (CDA). Contract Disputes Act of 1978, §§ 6(a), 10(a)(3), as amended, 41 U.S.C.A. §§ 605(a), 609(a)(3); 48 C.F.R. § 16.404-2(a). Burnside-Ott Aviation Training Center v. Dalton, 107 F.3d 854, 41 Cont. Cas. Fed. (CCH) P 77043 (Fed. Cir. 1997). United States ⚭68

§ 16.306 Cost-plus-fixed-fee contracts.

(a) *Description.* A cost-plus-fixed-fee contract is a costreimbursement contract that provides for payment to the contractor of a negotiated fee that is fixed at the inception of the contract. The fixed fee does not vary with actual cost, but may be adjusted as a result of changes in the work to be performed under the contract. This contract type permits contracting for efforts that might otherwise present too great a risk to contractors, but it provides the contractor only a minimum incentive to control costs.

(b) *Application.* (1) A cost-plus-fixed-fee contract is suitable for use when the conditions of 16.301-2 are present and, for example—

(i) The contract is for the performance of research or preliminary exploration or study, and the level of effort required is unknown; or

(ii) The contract is for development and test, and using a cost-plus-incentive-fee contract is not practical.

(2) A cost-plus-fixed-fee contract normally should not be used in development of major systems (see Part 34) once preliminary exploration, studies, and risk reduction have indicated a high degree of probability that the development is achievable and the Government has established reasonably firm performance objectives and schedules.

(c) *Limitations.* No cost-plus-fixed-fee contract shall be awarded unless the contracting officer complies with all limitations in 15.404-4(c)(4)(i) and 16.301-3.

(d) *Completion and term forms.* A cost-plus-fixed-fee contract may take one of two basic forms—completion or term.

(1) The completion form describes the scope of work by stating a definite goal or target and specifying an end product. This form of contract normally requires the contractor to

complete and deliver the specified end product (*e.g.*, a final report of research accomplishing the goal or target) within the estimated cost, if possible, as a condition for payment of the entire fixed fee. However, in the event the work cannot be completed within the estimated cost, the Government may require more effort without increase in fee, provided the Government increases the estimated cost.

(2) The term form describes the scope of work in general terms and obligates the contractor to devote a specified level of effort for a stated time period. Under this form, if the performance is considered satisfactory by the Government, the fixed fee is payable at the expiration of the agreed-upon period, upon contractor statement that the level of effort specified in the contract has been expended in performing the contract work. Renewal for further periods of performance is a new acquisition that involves new cost and fee arrangements.

(3) Because of the differences in obligation assumed by the contractor, the completion form is preferred over the term form whenever the work, or specific milestones for the work, can be defined well enough to permit development of estimates within which the contractor can be expected to complete the work.

(4) The term form shall not be used unless the contractor is obligated by the contract to provide a specific level of effort within a definite time period.

United States Code Annotated

Contract requirements, see 41 USCA § 254.

Contracts, planning, solicitation, evaluation, and award procedures, see 10 USCA § 2305.

Cost-type research and development contracts with educational institutions, see 41 USCA § 254a.

Definitions, see 10 USCA § 2302, 41 USCA §§ 259, 403.

Kinds of contracts, see 10 USCA § 2306.

Planning and solicitation requirements, see 41 USCA § 253a.

Task and delivery order contracts, definitions, see 10 USCA § 2304d, 41 USCA § 253k.

Task and delivery order contracts, general authority, see 10 USCA § 2304a, 41 USCA § 253h.

Task and delivery order contracts, orders, see 10 USCA § 2304c, 41 USCA § 253j.

Task order contracts, advisory and assistance services, see 10 USCA § 2304b, 41 USCA § 253i.

Notes of Decisions

In general 1
Level-of-effort 2

1 In general

The "warranty of government specifications", also sometimes referred to as the "Spearin doctrine", provides that if the government furnishes specifications for the production or construction of an end product and proper application of those specifications does not result in a satisfactory end product, the contractor will be compensated for its efforts to produce the end product, notwithstanding the unsatisfactory results. PCL Const. Services, Inc. v. U.S., 47 Fed. Cl. 745 (2000). United States ⚬═73(17)

In architect and engineering cost-plus-fixed-fee contracts, government contractor receives fixed fee to design project and costs for construction effort, with fixed fee usually based on percentage of estimated cost of construction project, but increase in cost of construction does not per se justify increase in contractor's fixed fee; change in fee is proper only for work not contemplated at time fee was negotiated, not merely because greater than expected costs were being encountered doing work as originally contemplated. 48 C.F.R. § 16.306(a). Ralph L. Jones Co., Inc. v. U.S., 33 Fed. Cl. 327 (1995). United States ⚬═70(24)

2 Level-of-effort

Government was not entitled to reimbursement of added costs paid to fiscal intermediary to providers of health care services operating under Medicare program in connection with intermediary's performance of authorized changes to its subcontract, notwithstanding that size of intermediary's work force declined during period for which added costs were paid; subcontract was not "level-of-effort" undertaking, nor did it obligate intermediary to dedicate fixed number of personnel to various tasks it had agreed to perform. Empire Blue Cross and Blue Shield v. U.S., 5 F.3d 1506 (Fed. Cir. 1993). United States ⊙⇒75(1); United States ⊙⇒88

§ 16.307 Contract clauses.

(a) (1) The contracting officer shall insert the clause at 52.216-7, Allowable Cost and Payment, in solicitations and contracts when a cost-reimbursement contract or a time-and-materials contract (other than a contract for a commercial item) is contemplated. If the contract is a time-and-materials contract, the clause at 52.216-7 applies in conjunction with the clause at 52.232-7), but only to the portion of the contract that provides for reimbursement of materials (as defined in the clause at 52.232-7) at actual cost. Further, the clause at 52.216-7 does not apply to labor-hour contracts.

(2) If the contract is a construction contract and contains the clause at 52.232-27, Prompt Payment for Construction Contracts, the contracting officer shall use the clause at 52.216-7 with its Alternate I.

(3) If the contract is with an educational institution, the contracting officer shall use the clause at 52.216-7 with its Alternate II.

(4) If the contract is with a State or local government, the contracting officer shall use the clause at 52.216-7 with its Alternate III.

(5) If the contract is with a nonprofit organization other than an educational institution, a State or local government, or a nonprofit organization exempted under the OMB Uniform Guidance at 2 CFR part 200, appendix VIII, the contracting officer shall use the clause at 52.216-7 with its Alternate IV.

(b) The contracting officer shall insert the clause at 52.216-8, Fixed Fee, in solicitations and contracts when a cost-plus-fixed-fee contract (other than a construction contract) is contemplated.

(c) The contracting officer shall insert the clause at 52.216-9, Fixed-Fee—Construction, in solicitations and contracts when a cost-plus-fixed-fee construction contract is contemplated.

(d) The contracting officer shall insert the clause at 52.216-10, Incentive Fee, in solicitations and contracts when a cost-plus-incentive-fee contract is contemplated.

(e) (1) The contracting officer shall insert the clause at 52.216-11, Cost Contract—No Fee, in solicitations and contracts when a cost-reimbursement contract is contemplated that provides no fee and is not a cost-sharing contract.

(2) If a cost-reimbursement research and development contract with an educational institution or a nonprofit organization that provides no fee or other payment above cost and is not a cost-sharing contract is contemplated, and if the contracting officer determines that withholding of a portion of allowable costs is not required, the contracting officer shall use the clause with its Alternate I.

(f) (1) The contracting officer shall insert the clause at 52.216-12, Cost-Sharing Contract—No Fee, in solicitations and contracts when a cost-sharing contract is contemplated.

(2) If a cost-sharing research and development contract with an educational institution or a nonprofit organization is contemplated, and if the contracting officer determines that withholding of a portion of allowable costs is not required, the contracting officer shall use the clause with its Alternate I.

(g) The contracting officer shall insert the clause at 52.216-15, Predetermined Indirect Cost Rates, in solicitations and contracts when a cost-reimbursement research and development contract with an educational institution (see 42.705-3(b)) is contemplated and predetermined indirect cost rates are to be used.

United States Code Annotated

Contract requirements, see 41 USCA § 254.

Contracts, planning, solicitation, evaluation, and award procedures, see 10 USCA § 2305.

Cost-type research and development contracts with educational institutions, see 41 USCA § 254a.

Definitions, see 10 USCA § 2302, 41 USCA §§ 259, 403.

Kinds of contracts, see 10 USCA § 2306.

Planning and solicitation requirements, see 41 USCA § 253a.

Task and delivery order contracts, definitions, see 10 USCA § 2304d, 41 USCA § 253k.

Task and delivery order contracts, general authority, see 10 USCA § 2304a, 41 USCA § 253h.

Task and delivery order contracts, orders, see 10 USCA § 2304c, 41 USCA § 253j.

Task order contracts, advisory and assistance services, see 10 USCA § 2304b, 41 USCA § 253i.

Subpart 16.4 Incentive Contracts

§ 16.401 General.

(a) Incentive contracts as described in this subpart are appropriate when a firm-fixed-price contract is not appropriate and the required supplies or services can be acquired at lower costs and, in certain instances, with improved delivery or technical performance, by relating the amount of profit or fee payable under the contract to the contractor's performance. Incentive contracts are designed to obtain specific acquisition objectives by—

(1) Establishing reasonable and attainable targets that are clearly communicated to the contractor; and

(2) Including appropriate incentive arrangements designed to—

(i) motivate contractor efforts that might not otherwise be emphasized; and

(ii) discourage contractor inefficiency and waste.

(b) When predetermined, formula-type incentives on technical performance or delivery are included, increases in profit or fee are provided only for achievement that sur-passes the targets, and decreases are provided for to the extent that such targets are not met. The incentive increases or decreases are applied to performance targets rather than minimum performance requirements.

(c) The two basic categories of incentive contracts are fixed-price incentive contracts (see 16.403 and 16.404) and cost-reimbursement incentive contracts (see 16.405). Since it is usually to the Government's advantage for the contractor to assume substantial cost responsibility and an appropriate share of the cost risk, fixed-price incentive contracts are preferred when contract costs and performance requirements are reasonably certain. Cost-reimbursement incentive contracts are subject to the overall limitations in 16.301 that apply to all cost-reimbursement contracts.

(d) A determination and finding, signed by the head of the contracting activity, shall be completed for all incentive- and award-fee contracts justifying that the use of this type of contract is in the best interest of the Government. This determination shall be documented in the contract file and, for award-fee contracts, shall address all of the suitability items in 16.401(e)(1).

(e) Award-fee contracts are a type of incentive contract.

(1) *Application.* An award-fee contract is suitable for use when—

(i) The work to be performed is such that it is neither feasible nor effective to devise predetermined objective incentive targets applicable to cost, schedule, and technical performance;

(ii) The likelihood of meeting acquisition objectives will be enhanced by using a contract that effectively motivates the contractor toward exceptional performance and provides the Government with the flexibility to evaluate both actual performance and the conditions under which it was achieved; and

(iii) Any additional administrative effort and cost required to monitor and evaluate performance are justified by the expected benefits as documented by a risk and cost benefit analysis to be included in the Determination and Findings referenced in 16. 401(e)(5)(iii).

(2) *Award-fee amount.* The amount of award fee earned shall be commensurate with the contractor's overall cost, schedule, and technical performance as measured against contract requirements in accordance with the criteria stated in the award-fee plan. Award fee shall not be earned if the contractor's overall cost, schedule, and technical performance in the aggregate is below satisfactory. The basis for all award-fee determina-

tions shall be documented in the contract file to include, at a minimum, a determination that overall cost, schedule and technical performance in the aggregate is or is not at a satisfactory level. This determination and the methodology for determining the award fee are unilateral decisions made solely at the discretion of the Government.

(3) *Award-fee plan.* All contracts providing for award fees shall be supported by an award-fee plan that establishes the procedures for evaluating award fee and an Award-Fee Board for conducting the award-fee evaluation. Award-fee plans shall—

(i) Be approved by the FDO unless otherwise authorized by agency procedures;

(ii) Identify the award-fee evaluation criteria and how they are linked to acquisition objectives which shall be defined in terms of contract cost, schedule, and technical performance. Criteria should motivate the contractor to enhance performance in the areas rated, but not at the expense of at least minimum acceptable performance in all other areas;

(iii) Describe how the contractor's performance will be measured against the award-fee evaluation criteria;

(iv) Utilize the adjectival rating and associated description as well as the award-fee pool earned percentages shown below in Table 16-1. Contracting officers may supplement the adjectival rating description. The method used to determine the adjectival rating must be documented in the award-fee plan;

Table 16-1

Award-Fee Adjectival Rating	Award-Fee Pool Available To Be Earned	Description
Excellent	91%–100%	Contractor has exceeded almost all of the significant award-fee criteria and has met overall cost, schedule, and technical performance requirements of the contract in the aggregate as defined and measured against the criteria in the award-fee plan for the award-fee evaluation period.
Very Good	76%–90%	Contractor has exceeded many of the significant award-fee criteria and has met overall cost, schedule, and technical performance requirements of the contract in the aggregate as defined and measured against the criteria in the award-fee plan for the award-fee evaluation period.
Good	51%–75%	Contractor has exceeded some of the significant award-fee criteria and has met overall cost, schedule, and technical performance requirements of the contract in the aggregate as defined and measured against the criteria in the award-fee plan for the award-fee evaluation period.
Satisfactory	No Greater Than 50%	Contractor has met overall cost, schedule, and technical performance requirements of the contract in the aggregate as defined and measured against the criteria in the award-fee plan for the award-fee evaluation period.
Unsatisfactory	0%	Contractor has failed to meet overall cost, schedule, and technical performance requirements of the contract in the aggregate as defined and measured against the criteria in the award-fee plan for the award-fee evaluation period.

(v) Prohibit earning any award fee when a contractor's overall cost, schedule, and technical performance in the aggregate is below satisfactory;

(vi) Provide for evaluation period(s) to be conducted at stated intervals during the contract period of performance so that the contractor will periodically be informed of the quality of its performance and the areas in which improvement is expected (*e.g.* six months, nine months, twelve months, or at specific milestones); and

(vii) Define the total award-fee pool amount and how this amount is allocated across each evaluation period.

(4) *Rollover of unearned award fee.* The use of rollover of unearned award fee is prohibited.

(5) *Limitations*. No award-fee contract shall be awarded unless—

(i) All of the limitations in 16.301-3, that are applicable to cost-reimbursement contracts only, are complied with;

(ii) An award-fee plan is completed in accordance with the requirements in 16.401(e)(3); and

(iii) A determination and finding is completed in accordance with 16.401(d) addressing all of the suitability items in 16.401(e)(1).

(f) *Incentive- and Award-Fee Data Collection and Analysis*. Each agency shall collect relevant data on award fee and incentive fees paid to contractors and include performance measures to evaluate such data on a regular basis to determine effectiveness of award and incentive fees as a tool for improving contractor performance and achieving desired program outcomes. This information should be considered as part of the acquisition planning process (see 7.105) in determining the appropriate type of contract to be utilized for future acquisitions.

(g) *Incentive- and Award-Fee Best Practices*. Each agency head shall provide mechanisms for sharing proven incentive strategies for the acquisition of different types of products and services among contracting and program management officials.

United States Code Annotated

Contract requirements, see 41 USCA § 254.

Contracts, planning, solicitation, evaluation, and award procedures, see 10 USCA § 2305.

Cost-type research and development contracts with educational institutions, see 41 USCA § 254a.

Definitions, see 10 USCA § 2302, 41 USCA §§ 259, 403.

Kinds of contracts, see 10 USCA § 2306.

Planning and solicitation requirements, see 41 USCA § 253a.

Task and delivery order contracts, definitions, see 10 USCA § 2304d, 41 USCA § 253k.

Task and delivery order contracts, general authority, see 10 USCA § 2304a, 41 USCA § 253h.

Task and delivery order contracts, orders, see 10 USCA § 2304c, 41 USCA § 253j.

Task order contracts, advisory and assistance services, see 10 USCA § 2304b, 41 USCA § 253i.

§ 16.402 Application of predetermined, formula-type incentives.

§ 16.402-1 Cost incentives.

(a) Most incentive contracts include only cost incentives, which take the form of a profit or fee adjustment formula and are intended to motivate the contractor to effectively manage costs. No incentive contract may provide for other incentives without also providing a cost incentive (or constraint).

(b) Except for award-fee contracts (see 16.404 and 16.405-2), incentive contracts include a target cost, a target profit or fee, and a profit or fee adjustment formula that (within the constraints of a price ceiling or minimum and maximum fee) provides that—

(1) Actual cost that meets the target will result in the target profit or fee;

(2) Actual cost that exceeds the target will result in downward adjustment of target profit or fee; and

(3) Actual cost that is below the target will result in upward adjustment of target profit or fee.

United States Code Annotated

Contract requirements, see 41 USCA § 254.

Contracts, planning, solicitation, evaluation, and award procedures, see 10 USCA § 2305.

Cost-type research and development contracts with educational institutions, see 41 USCA § 254a.

Definitions, see 10 USCA § 2302, 41 USCA §§ 259, 403.

Kinds of contracts, see 10 USCA § 2306.

Planning and solicitation requirements, see 41 USCA § 253a.

Task and delivery order contracts, definitions, see 10 USCA § 2304d, 41 USCA § 253k.

Task and delivery order contracts, general authority, see 10 USCA § 2304a, 41 USCA § 253h.

Task and delivery order contracts, orders, see 10 USCA § 2304c, 41 USCA § 253j.

Task order contracts, advisory and assistance services, see 10 USCA § 2304b, 41 USCA § 253i.

§ 16.402-2 Performance incentives.

(a) Performance incentives may be considered in connection with specific product characteristics (*e.g.*, a missile range, an aircraft speed, an engine thrust, or a vehicle maneuverability) or other specific elements of the contractor's performance. These incentives should be designed to relate profit or fee to results achieved by the contractor, compared with specified targets.

(b) To the maximum extent practicable, positive and negative performance incentives shall be considered in connection with service contracts for performance of objectively measurable tasks when quality of performance is critical and incentives are likely to motivate the contractor.

(c) Technical performance incentives may be particularly appropriate in major systems contracts, both in development (when performance objectives are known and the fabrication of prototypes for test and evaluation is required) and in production (if improved performance is attainable and highly desirable to the Government).

(d) Technical performance incentives may involve a variety of specific characteristics that contribute to the overall performance of the end item. Accordingly, the incentives on individual technical characteristics must be balanced so that no one of them is exaggerated to the detriment of the overall performance of the end item.

(e) Performance tests and/or assessments of work performance are generally essential in order to determine the degree of attainment of performance targets. Therefore, the contract must be as specific as possible in establishing test criteria (such as testing conditions, instrumentation precision, and data interpretation) and performance standards (such as the quality levels of services to be provided).

(f) Because performance incentives present complex problems in contract administration, the contracting officer should negotiate them in full coordination with Government engineering and pricing specialists.

(g) It is essential that the Government and contractor agree explicitly on the effect that contract changes (*e.g.*, pursuant to the Changes clause) will have on performance incentives.

(h) The contracting officer must exercise care, in establishing performance criteria, to recognize that the contractor should not be rewarded or penalized for attainments of Government-furnished components.

United States Code Annotated

Contract requirements, see 41 USCA § 254.

Contracts, planning, solicitation, evaluation, and award procedures, see 10 USCA § 2305.

Cost-type research and development contracts with educational institutions, see 41 USCA § 254a.

Definitions, see 10 USCA § 2302, 41 USCA §§ 259, 403.

Kinds of contracts, see 10 USCA § 2306.

Planning and solicitation requirements, see 41 USCA § 253a.

Task and delivery order contracts, definitions, see 10 USCA § 2304d, 41 USCA § 253k.

Task and delivery order contracts, general authority, see 10 USCA § 2304a, 41 USCA § 253h.

Task and delivery order contracts, orders, see 10 USCA § 2304c, 41 USCA § 253j.

Task order contracts, advisory and assistance services, see 10 USCA § 2304b, 41 USCA § 253i.

§ 16.402-3 Delivery incentives.

(a) Delivery incentives should be considered when improvement from a required delivery schedule is a significant Government objective. It is important to determine the Government's primary objectives in a given contract (*e.g.,* earliest possible delivery or earliest quantity production).

(b) Incentive arrangements on delivery should specify the application of the reward-penalty structure in the event of Government-caused delays or other delays beyond the control, and without the fault or negligence, of the contractor or subcontractor.

United States Code Annotated

Contract requirements, see 41 USCA § 254.

Contracts, planning, solicitation, evaluation, and award procedures, see 10 USCA § 2305.

Cost-type research and development contracts with educational institutions, see 41 USCA § 254a.

Definitions, see 10 USCA § 2302, 41 USCA §§ 259, 403.

Kinds of contracts, see 10 USCA § 2306.

Planning and solicitation requirements, see 41 USCA § 253a.

Task and delivery order contracts, definitions, see 10 USCA § 2304d, 41 USCA § 253k.

Task and delivery order contracts, general authority, see 10 USCA § 2304a, 41 USCA § 253h.

Task and delivery order contracts, orders, see 10 USCA § 2304c, 41 USCA § 253j.

Task order contracts, advisory and assistance services, see 10 USCA § 2304b, 41 USCA § 253i.

§ 16.402-4 Structuring multiple-incentive contracts.

A properly structured multiple-incentive arrangement should—

(a) Motivate the contractor to strive for outstanding results in all incentive areas; and

(b) Compel trade-off decisions among the incentive areas, consistent with the Government's overall objectives for the acquisition. Because of the interdependency of the Government's cost, the technical performance, and the delivery goals, a contract that emphasizes only one of the goals may jeopardize control over the others. Because outstanding results may not be attainable for each of the incentive areas, all multipleincentive contracts must include a cost incentive (or constraint) that operates to preclude rewarding a contractor for superior technical performance or delivery results when the cost of those results outweighs their value to the Government.

United States Code Annotated

Contract requirements, see 41 USCA § 254.

Contracts, planning, solicitation, evaluation, and award procedures, see 10 USCA § 2305.

Cost-type research and development contracts with educational institutions, see 41 USCA § 254a.

Definitions, see 10 USCA § 2302, 41 USCA §§ 259, 403.

Kinds of contracts, see 10 USCA § 2306.

Planning and solicitation requirements, see 41 USCA § 253a.

Task and delivery order contracts, definitions, see 10 USCA § 2304d, 41 USCA § 253k.

Task and delivery order contracts, general authority, see 10 USCA § 2304a, 41 USCA § 253h.

Task and delivery order contracts, orders, see 10 USCA § 2304c, 41 USCA § 253j.

Task order contracts, advisory and assistance services, see 10 USCA § 2304b, 41 USCA § 253i.

§ 16.403 Fixed-price incentive contracts.

(a) *Description.* A fixed-price incentive contract is a fixedprice contract that provides for adjusting profit and establishing the final contract price by application of a formula based on the relationship of total final negotiated cost to total target cost. The final price is subject to a price ceiling, negotiated at the outset. The two forms of fixed-price incentive contracts, firm target and successive targets, are further described in 16.403-1 and 16.403-2 below.

(b) *Application.* A fixed-price incentive contract is appropriate when—

(1) A firm-fixed-price contract is not suitable;

(2) The nature of the supplies or services being acquired and other circumstances of the acquisition are such that the contractor's assumption of a degree of cost responsibility will provide a positive profit incentive for effective cost control and performance; and

(3) If the contract also includes incentives on technical performance and/or delivery, the performance requirements provide a reasonable opportunity for the incentives to have a meaningful impact on the contractor's management of the work.

(c) *Billing prices.* In fixed-price incentive contracts, billing prices are established as an interim basis for payment. These billing prices may be adjusted, within the ceiling limits, upon request of either party to the contract, when it becomes apparent that final negotiated cost will be substantially different from the target cost.

United States Code Annotated

Contract requirements, see 41 USCA § 254.

Contracts, planning, solicitation, evaluation, and award procedures, see 10 USCA § 2305.

Cost-type research and development contracts with educational institutions, see 41 USCA § 254a.

Definitions, see 10 USCA § 2302, 41 USCA §§ 259, 403.

Kinds of contracts, see 10 USCA § 2306.

Planning and solicitation requirements, see 41 USCA § 253a.

Task and delivery order contracts, definitions, see 10 USCA § 2304d, 41 USCA § 253k.

Task and delivery order contracts, general authority, see 10 USCA § 2304a, 41 USCA § 253h.

Task and delivery order contracts, orders, see 10 USCA § 2304c, 41 USCA § 253j.

Task order contracts, advisory and assistance services, see 10 USCA § 2304b, 41 USCA § 253i.

Notes of Decisions

Construction and operation of contracts 1
Modification 3
Rights and remedies of contractors 4
Unauthorized or illegal contracts 2

1 Construction and operation of contracts

Department of Defense (DoD) violated DoD appropriation acts by incrementally funding fixed-price incentive contract without performing risk determinations in fiscal years 1990 to 1992. Department of Defense Appropriations Act, 1992, § 8037, 105 Stat. 1150; Department of Defense Appropriations Act, 1991, § 8038, 104 Stat. 1856; Department of Defense Appropriations Act, 1990, § 9048, 103 Stat. 1112. Northrop Grumman Corp. v. U.S., 47 Fed. Cl. 20 (2000). United States ☞70(15.1)

Contractor who contended that award of contract as a fixed-price incentive contract violated applicable regulatory requirements failed to prove that at the time of contracting the parties did not possess adequate cost and pricing information or that the risk was not reasonably apportioned. 48 C.F.R. § 16.403-1. Northrop Grumman Corp. v. U.S., 47 Fed. Cl. 20 (2000). United States ☞70(15.1)

Contractor did not satisfy its burden on claim that selection of award of contract as a fixed-price incentive contract violated provision of the Federal Acquisition Regulation concerning research and development acquisitions; even assuming that provision was applicable, provision was not mandatory in precluding use of fixed-price incentive contract. 48 C.F.R. § 35.006. Northrop Grumman Corp. v. U.S., 47 Fed. Cl. 20 (2000). United States ☞70(15.1)

Contractor failed to establish that the government possessed superior knowledge, and did not disclose, that contract for a tactical air command and control system for the Marine Corps would require significant development and was unsuited for award as a fixed-price incentive contract; contractor did not undertake performance without vital knowledge, and the government did not fail to provide relevant information about the degree of development that the contract would require. Northrop Grumman Corp. v. U.S., 47 Fed. Cl. 20 (2000). United States ☞70(30)

Contractor did not satisfy its burden with regard to allegation that award of contract as a fixed-price incentive contract, rather than as a cost-reimbursement contract, violated Department of Defense (DoD) directive concerning appropriate contract type for research and development phases; obligation under the directive was to consider certain factors, not necessarily to adopt them as part of the procurement strategy. Northrop Grumman Corp. v. U.S., 47 Fed. Cl. 20 (2000). United States ☞70(15.1)

Focus of fixed-price public contract is contractor output. 48 C.F.R. §§ 16.401, 16.403. McDonnell Douglas Corp. v. U.S., 37 Fed. Cl. 295, 41 Cont. Cas. Fed. (CCH) P 77046 (1997), order modified, 39 Fed. Cl. 665, 42 Cont. Cas. Fed. (CCH) P 77230 (1997). United States ☞70(15.1)

2 Unauthorized or illegal contracts

Despite fact that Department of Defense (DoD) violated DoD appropriation acts by incrementally funding fixed-price incentive contract without performing risk determinations in fiscal years 1990 to 1992, rendering the contract illegal, the Court of Federal Claims would enforce the contract as written, as such enforcement was not an unjust result where contractor was a sophisticated defense contractor, which had available to it all the information necessary to bid on the contract. Northrop Grumman Corp. v. U.S., 47 Fed. Cl. 20 (2000). United States ☞68

3 Modification

Reformation to a cost-type contract was not the appropriate remedy for contract illegality which consisted of government's failure to perform risk assessment during each year of incremental funding by the Department of Defense (DoD) of fixed-price incentive contract; since Secretary of Defense did not make any determination that no lower cost alternatives were available, reformation to a cost-type contract would bring about another illegality. Northrop Grumman Corp. v. U.S., 47 Fed. Cl. 20 (2000). United States ☞72(1.1)

4 Rights and remedies of contractors

Contractor could not recover cost overruns on defense contract on ground of mutual mistake, as risk of mistake was allocated to contractor through the selection of fixed-price incentive contract. Northrop Grumman Corp. v. U.S., 47 Fed. Cl. 20 (2000). United States ☞74(4)

§ 16.403-1 Fixed-price incentive (firm target) contracts.

(a) *Description*. A fixed-price incentive (firm target) contract specifies a target cost, a target profit, a price ceiling (but not a profit ceiling or floor), and a profit adjustment formula. These elements are all negotiated at the outset. The price ceiling is the maximum that may be paid to the contractor, except for any adjustment under other contract clauses. When the contractor completes performance, the parties negotiate the final cost, and the final price is established by applying the formula. When the final cost is less than the target cost, application of the formula results in a final profit greater than the target profit; conversely, when final cost is more than target cost, application of the formula results in a final profit less than the target profit, or even a net loss. If the final negotiated cost exceeds the price ceiling, the contractor absorbs the difference as a loss. Because the profit varies inversely with the cost, this contract type provides a positive, calculable profit incentive for the contractor to control costs.

(b) *Application*. A fixed-price incentive (firm target) contract is appropriate when the parties can negotiate at the outset a firm target cost, target profit, and profit adjustment formula that will provide a fair and reasonable incentive and a ceiling that provides for the contractor to assume an appropriate share of the risk. When the contractor assumes a considerable or major share of the cost responsibility under the adjustment formula, the target profit should reflect this responsibility.

(c) *Limitations*. This contract type may be used only when—

(1) The contractor's accounting system is adequate for providing data to support

negotiation of final cost and incentive price revision; and

(2) Adequate cost or pricing information for establishing reasonable firm targets is available at the time of initial contract negotiation.

(d) *Contract schedule.* The contracting officer shall specify in the contract schedule the target cost, target profit, and target price for each item subject to incentive price revision.

United States Code Annotated

Contract requirements, see 41 USCA § 254.

Contracts, planning, solicitation, evaluation, and award procedures, see 10 USCA § 2305.

Cost-type research and development contracts with educational institutions, see 41 USCA § 254a.

Definitions, see 10 USCA § 2302, 41 USCA §§ 259, 403.

Kinds of contracts, see 10 USCA § 2306.

Planning and solicitation requirements, see 41 USCA § 253a.

Task and delivery order contracts, definitions, see 10 USCA § 2304d, 41 USCA § 253k.

Task and delivery order contracts, general authority, see 10 USCA § 2304a, 41 USCA § 253h.

Task and delivery order contracts, orders, see 10 USCA § 2304c, 41 USCA § 253j.

Task order contracts, advisory and assistance services, see 10 USCA § 2304b, 41 USCA § 253i.

Notes of Decisions

In general 1

1 In general

Contractor who contended that award of contract as a fixed-price incentive contract violated applicable regulatory requirements failed to prove that at the time of contracting the parties did not possess adequate cost and pricing information or that the risk was not reasonably apportioned. 48 C.F.R. § 16.403-1. Northrop Grumman Corp. v. U.S., 47 Fed. Cl. 20 (2000). United States ⇐70(15.1)

§ 16.403-2 Fixed-price incentive (successive targets) contracts.

(a) *Description.* (1) A fixed-price incentive (successive targets) contract specifies the following elements, all of which are negotiated at the outset:

(i) An initial target cost.

(ii) An initial target profit.

(iii) An initial profit adjustment formula to be used for establishing the firm target profit, including a ceiling and floor for the firm target profit. (This formula normally provides for a lesser degree of contractor cost responsibility than would a formula for establishing final profit and price.)

(iv) The production point at which the firm target cost and firm target profit will be negotiated (usually before delivery or shop completion of the first item).

(v) A ceiling price that is the maximum that may be paid to the contractor, except for any adjustment under other contract clauses providing for equitable adjustment or other revision of the contract price under stated circumstances.

(2) When the production point specified in the contract is reached, the parties negotiate the firm target cost, giving consideration to cost experience under the contract and other pertinent factors. The firm target profit is established by the formula. At this point, the parties have two alternatives, as follows:

(i) They may negotiate a firm fixed price, using the firm target cost plus the firm target profit as a guide.

(ii) If negotiation of a firm fixed price is inappropriate, they may negotiate a formula for establishing the final price using the firm target cost and firm target profit. The final cost is then negotiated at completion, and the final profit is established by formula, as under the fixed-price incentive (firm target) contract (see 16.403-1 above).

(b) *Application.* A fixed-price incentive (successive targets) contract is appropriate when—

(1) Available cost or pricing information is not sufficient to permit the negotiation of a realistic firm target cost and profit before award;

(2) Sufficient information is available to permit negotiation of initial targets; and

(3) There is reasonable assurance that additional reliable information will be available at an early point in the contract performance so as to permit negotiation of either (i) a firm fixed price or (ii) firm targets and a formula for establishing final profit and price that will provide a fair and reasonable incentive. This additional information is not limited to experience under the contract, itself, but may be drawn from other contracts for the same or similar items.

(c) *Limitations.* This contract type may be used only when—

(1) The contractor's accounting system is adequate for providing data for negotiating firm targets and a realistic profit adjustment formula, as well as later negotiation of final costs; and

(2) Cost or pricing information adequate for establishing a reasonable firm target cost is reasonably expected to be available at an early point in contract performance.

(d) *Contract schedule.* The contracting officer shall specify in the contract schedule the initial target cost, initial target profit, and initial target price for each item subject to incentive price revision.

United States Code Annotated

Contract requirements, see 41 USCA § 254.

Contracts, planning, solicitation, evaluation, and award procedures, see 10 USCA § 2305.

Cost-type research and development contracts with educational institutions, see 41 USCA § 254a.

Definitions, see 10 USCA § 2302, 41 USCA §§ 259, 403.

Kinds of contracts, see 10 USCA § 2306.

Planning and solicitation requirements, see 41 USCA § 253a.

Task and delivery order contracts, definitions, see 10 USCA § 2304d, 41 USCA § 253k.

Task and delivery order contracts, general authority, see 10 USCA § 2304a, 41 USCA § 253h.

Task and delivery order contracts, orders, see 10 USCA § 2304c, 41 USCA § 253j.

Task order contracts, advisory and assistance services, see 10 USCA § 2304b, 41 USCA § 253i.

§ 16.404 Fixed-price contracts with award fees.

Award-fee provisions may be used in fixed-price contracts when the Government wishes to motivate a contractor and other incentives cannot be used because contractor performance cannot be measured objectively. Such contracts shall establish a fixed price (including normal profit) for the effort. This price will be paid for satisfactory contract performance. Award fee earned (if any) will be paid in addition to that fixed price. See 16.401(e) for the requirements relative to utilizing this contract type.

United States Code Annotated

Contract requirements, see 41 USCA § 254.

Contracts, planning, solicitation, evaluation, and award procedures, see 10 USCA § 2305.

Cost-type research and development contracts with educational institutions, see 41 USCA § 254a.

Definitions, see 10 USCA § 2302, 41 USCA §§ 259, 403.

Kinds of contracts, see 10 USCA § 2306.

Planning and solicitation requirements, see 41 USCA § 253a.

Task and delivery order contracts, definitions, see 10 USCA § 2304d, 41 USCA § 253k.

Task and delivery order contracts, general authority, see 10 USCA § 2304a, 41 USCA § 253h.

Task and delivery order contracts, orders, see 10 USCA § 2304c, 41 USCA § 253j.

Task order contracts, advisory and assistance services, see 10 USCA § 2304b, 41 USCA § 253i.

Notes of Decisions
Unauthorized or illegal contracts 1

1 Unauthorized or illegal contracts

Contract provision which purportedly divested jurisdiction of Armed Services Board of Contract Appeals to hear dispute concerning calculation of award fee under cost-plus-award-fee (CPAF) contract between Navy and contractor was void; provision otherwise depriving board of jurisdiction was not a matter of statute primacy, and thus parties could not on their own alter board's review under Contract Disputes Act (CDA). Contract Disputes Act of 1978, §§ 6(a), 10(a)(3), as amended, 41 U.S.C.A. §§ 605(a), 609(a)(3); 48 C.F.R. § 16.404-2(a). Burnside-Ott Aviation Training Center v. Dalton, 107 F.3d 854, 41 Cont. Cas. Fed. (CCH) P 77043 (Fed. Cir. 1997). United States ⊸68

§ 16.405 Cost-reimbursement incentive contracts.

See 16.301 for requirements applicable to all cost-reimbursement contracts, for use in conjunction with the following subsections.

United States Code Annotated

Contract requirements, see 41 USCA § 254.

Contracts, planning, solicitation, evaluation, and award procedures, see 10 USCA § 2305.

Cost-type research and development contracts with educational institutions, see 41 USCA § 254a.

Definitions, see 10 USCA § 2302, 41 USCA §§ 259, 403.

Kinds of contracts, see 10 USCA § 2306.

Planning and solicitation requirements, see 41 USCA § 253a.

Task and delivery order contracts, definitions, see 10 USCA § 2304d, 41 USCA § 253k.

Task and delivery order contracts, general authority, see 10 USCA § 2304a, 41 USCA § 253h.

Task and delivery order contracts, orders, see 10 USCA § 2304c, 41 USCA § 253j.

Task order contracts, advisory and assistance services, see 10 USCA § 2304b, 41 USCA § 253i.

§ 16.405-1 Cost-plus-incentive-fee contracts.

(a) *Description.* The cost-plus-incentive-fee contract is a cost-reimbursement contract that provides for the initially negotiated fee to be adjusted later by a formula based on the relationship of total allowable costs to total target costs. This contract type specifies a target cost, a target fee, minimum and maximum fees, and a fee adjustment formula. After contract performance, the fee payable to the contractor is determined in accordance with the formula. The formula provides, within limits, for increases in fee above target fee when total allowable costs are less than target costs, and decreases in fee below target fee when total allowable costs exceed target costs. This increase or decrease is intended to provide an incentive for the contractor to manage the contract effectively. When total allowable cost is greater than or less than the range of costs within which the fee-adjustment formula operates, the contractor is paid total allowable costs, plus the minimum or maximum fee.

(b) *Application.* (1) A cost-plus-incentive-fee contract is appropriate for services or development and test programs when—

(i) A cost-reimbursement contract is necessary (see 16.301-2); and

(ii) A target cost and a fee adjustment formula can be negotiated that are likely to motivate the contractor to manage effectively.

(2) The contract may include technical performance incentives when it is highly probable that the required development of a major system is feasible and the Government has established its performance objectives, at least in general terms. This approach also may apply to other acquisitions, if the use of both cost and technical performance incentives is desirable and administratively practical.

(3) The fee adjustment formula should provide an incentive that will be effective over the full range of reasonably foreseeable variations from target cost. If a high maximum fee is negotiated, the contract shall also provide for a low minimum fee that may be a

zero fee or, in rare cases, a negative fee.

(c) *Limitations.* No cost-plus-incentive-fee contract shall be awarded unless all limitations in 16.301-3 are complied with.

United States Code Annotated

Contract requirements, see 41 USCA § 254.

Contracts, planning, solicitation, evaluation, and award procedures, see 10 USCA § 2305.

Cost-type research and development contracts with educational institutions, see 41 USCA § 254a.

Definitions, see 10 USCA § 2302, 41 USCA §§ 259, 403.

Kinds of contracts, see 10 USCA § 2306.

Planning and solicitation requirements, see 41 USCA § 253a.

Task and delivery order contracts, definitions, see 10 USCA § 2304d, 41 USCA § 253k.

Task and delivery order contracts, general authority, see 10 USCA § 2304a, 41 USCA § 253h.

Task and delivery order contracts, orders, see 10 USCA § 2304c, 41 USCA § 253j.

Task order contracts, advisory and assistance services, see 10 USCA § 2304b, 41 USCA § 253i.

§ 16.405-2 Cost-plus-award-fee contracts.

A cost-plus-award-fee contract is a cost-reimbursement contract that provides for a fee consisting of (1) a base amount fixed at inception of the contract, if applicable and at the discretion of the contracting officer, and (2) an award amount that the contractor may earn in whole or in part during performance and that is sufficient to provide motivation for excellence in the areas of cost, schedule, and technical performance. See 16.401(e) for the requirements relative to utilizing this contract type.

United States Code Annotated

Contract requirements, see 41 USCA § 254.

Contracts, planning, solicitation, evaluation, and award procedures, see 10 USCA § 2305.

Cost-type research and development contracts with educational institutions, see 41 USCA § 254a.

Definitions, see 10 USCA § 2302, 41 USCA §§ 259, 403.

Kinds of contracts, see 10 USCA § 2306.

Planning and solicitation requirements, see 41 USCA § 253a.

Task and delivery order contracts, definitions, see 10 USCA § 2304d, 41 USCA § 253k.

Task and delivery order contracts, general authority, see 10 USCA § 2304a, 41 USCA § 253h.

Task and delivery order contracts, orders, see 10 USCA § 2304c, 41 USCA § 253j.

Task order contracts, advisory and assistance services, see 10 USCA § 2304b, 41 USCA § 253i.

§ 16.406 Contract clauses.

(a) Insert the clause at 52.216-16, Incentive Price Revision— Firm Target, in solicitations and contracts when a fixed-price incentive (firm target) contract is contemplated. If the contract calls for supplies or services to be ordered under a provisioning document or Government option and the prices are to be subject to the incentive price revision under the clause, the contracting officer shall use the clause with its Alternate I.

(b) Insert the clause at 52.216-17, Incentive Price Revision— Successive Targets, in solicitations and contracts when a fixed-price incentive (successive targets) contract is contemplated. If the contract calls for supplies or services to be ordered under a provisioning document or Government option and the prices are to be subject to incentive price revision under the clause, the contracting officer shall use the clause with its Alternate I.

(c) The clause at 52.216-7, Allowable Cost and Payment, is prescribed in 16.307(a) for insertion in solicitations and contracts when a cost-plus-incentive-fee contract or a cost-plus-award-fee contract is contemplated.

(d) The clause at 52.216-10, Incentive Fee, is prescribed in 16.307(d) for insertion in solicitations and contracts when a cost-plus-incentive-fee contract is contemplated.

(e) Insert an appropriate award-fee clause in solicitations and contracts when an award-fee contract is contemplated, provided that the clause—

(1) Is prescribed by or approved under agency acquisition regulations;

(2) Is compatible with the clause at 52.216-7, Allowable Cost and Payment; and

(3) Expressly provides that the award amount and the award-fee determination methodology are unilateral decisions made solely at the discretion of the Government.

United States Code Annotated

Contract requirements, see 41 USCA § 254.

Contracts, planning, solicitation, evaluation, and award procedures, see 10 USCA § 2305.

Cost-type research and development contracts with educational institutions, see 41 USCA § 254a.

Definitions, see 10 USCA § 2302, 41 USCA §§ 259, 403.

Kinds of contracts, see 10 USCA § 2306.

Planning and solicitation requirements, see 41 USCA § 253a.

Task and delivery order contracts, definitions, see 10 USCA § 2304d, 41 USCA § 253k.

Task and delivery order contracts, general authority, see 10 USCA § 2304a, 41 USCA § 253h.

Task and delivery order contracts, orders, see 10 USCA § 2304c, 41 USCA § 253j.

Task order contracts, advisory and assistance services, see 10 USCA § 2304b, 41 USCA § 253i.

Subpart 16.5 Indefinite-Delivery Contracts

§ 16.500 Scope of subpart.

(a) This subpart prescribes policies and procedures for making awards of indefinite-delivery contracts and establishes a preference for making multiple awards of indefinite-quantity contracts.

(b) This subpart does not limit the use of other than competitive procedures authorized by Part 6.

(c) Nothing in this subpart restricts the authority of the General Services Administration (GSA) to enter into schedule, multiple award, or task or delivery order contracts under any other provision of law. Therefore, GSA regulations and the coverage for the Federal Supply Schedule program in Subpart 8.4 and Part 38 take precedence over this subpart.

(d) The statutory multiple award preference implemented by this subpart does not apply to architect-engineer contracts subject to the procedures in Subpart 36.6. However, agencies are not precluded from making multiple awards for architectengineer services using the procedures in this subpart, provided the selection of contractors and placement of orders are consistent with Subpart 36.6.

United States Code Annotated

Contract requirements, see 41 USCA § 254.

Contracts, planning, solicitation, evaluation, and award procedures, see 10 USCA § 2305.

Cost-type research and development contracts with educational institutions, see 41 USCA § 254a.

Definitions, see 10 USCA § 2302, 41 USCA §§ 259, 403.

Kinds of contracts, see 10 USCA § 2306.

Planning and solicitation requirements, see 41 USCA § 253a.

Task and delivery order contracts, definitions, see 10 USCA § 2304d, 41 USCA § 253k.

Task and delivery order contracts, general authority, see 10 USCA § 2304a, 41 USCA § 253h.

Task and delivery order contracts, orders, see 10 USCA § 2304c, 41 USCA § 253j.

Task order contracts, advisory and assistance services, see 10 USCA § 2304b, 41 USCA § 253i.

Notes of Decisions
In general 1

1 In general

The Army Corps of Engineers properly used indefinite-delivery, indefinite-quantity contracts to procure design and construction of new facilities for soldiers and their families, the U.S. Court of Appeals for the Federal Circuit has held. The Corps acted lawfully and did not abuse its broad discretion by concluding that IDIQ contracts best served Government interests for the $40 billion military construction procurement. Tyler Const. Group v. U.S., 570 F.3d 1329 (Fed. Cir. 2009)

§ 16.501-1 Definitions.

As used in this subpart—

"Delivery order contract" means a contract for supplies that does not procure or specify a firm quantity of supplies (other than a minimum or maximum quantity) and that provides for the issuance of orders for the delivery of supplies during the period of the contract.

"Task order contract" means a contract for services that does not procure or specify a firm quantity of services (other than a minimum or maximum quantity) and that provides for the issuance of orders for the performance of tasks during the period of the contract.

United States Code Annotated

Contract requirements, see 41 USCA § 254.

Contracts, planning, solicitation, evaluation, and award procedures, see 10 USCA § 2305.

Cost-type research and development contracts with educational institutions, see 41 USCA § 254a.

Definitions, see 10 USCA § 2302, 41 USCA §§ 259, 403.

Kinds of contracts, see 10 USCA § 2306.

Planning and solicitation requirements, see 41 USCA § 253a.

Task and delivery order contracts, definitions, see 10 USCA § 2304d, 41 USCA § 253k.

Task and delivery order contracts, general authority, see 10 USCA § 2304a, 41 USCA § 253h.

Task and delivery order contracts, orders, see 10 USCA § 2304c, 41 USCA § 253j.

Task order contracts, advisory and assistance services, see 10 USCA § 2304b, 41 USCA § 253i.

Notes of Decisions
Jurisdiction 1
Parties 2

1 Jurisdiction

Federal question subject matter jurisdiction existed over computer software manufacturer's action alleging that United States Department of Labor's (DOL) decision to standardize its software applications exclusively to software manufactured by competitor violated Administrative Procedure Act (APA) and Competition in Contracting Act (CICA), even if Federal Acquisition Streamlining Act (FASA) precluded review of DOL's issuance of delivery order issued under indefinite-delivery, indefinite-quantity contract pursuant to decision, where manufacturer's protest challenged DOL's overarching administrative decision to standardize to competitor's product, not issuance of individual delivery order. 5 U.S.C.A. § 701 et seq.; 10 U.S.C.A. § 2304; 28 U.S.C.A. § 1331; Federal Property and Administrative Services Act of 1949, §§ 303, 303J(a)(2), as amended, 41 U.S.C.A. §§ 253, 253j(a)(2); 48 C.F.R. §§ 16.501-1, 16.501-2. Corel Corp. v. U.S., 165 F. Supp. 2d 12 (D.D.C. 2001). Federal Courts ⚖232

Federal court had jurisdiction under Tucker Act over computer software manufacturer's action alleging that United States Department of Labor's (DOL) decision to standardize its software applications exclusively to software manufactured by competitor violated Competition in Contracting Act (CICA), where standardization decision was allegedly made in connection with its ultimate procurement of competitor's software licenses. 10 U.S.C.A. § 2304; 28 U.S.C.A. § 1491(b)(1); Federal Property and Administrative Services Act of 1949, § 303, as amended, 41 U.S.C.A. § 253; 48 C.F.R. §§ 16.501-1, 16.501-2. Corel Corp. v. U.S., 165 F. Supp. 2d 12 (D.D.C. 2001). United States ☞64.60(1)

2 Parties

Manufacturer of office automation systems was "interested party," for purposes of Tucker Act, and thus had standing to challenge Department of Labor's (DOL) decision to standardize its software applications exclusively to software manufactured by competitor as violative of Competition in Contracting Act (CICA), where DOL refused to engage in competitive procurement for its office automation systems, and manufacturer submitted bid nonetheless. 10 U.S.C.A. § 2304; 28 U.S.C.A. § 1491(b)(1); Federal Property and Administrative Services Act of 1949, § 303, as amended, 41 U.S.C.A. § 253; 48 C.F.R. §§ 16.501-1, 16.501-2. Corel Corp. v. U.S., 165 F. Supp. 2d 12 (D.D.C. 2001). United States ☞64.60(2)

§ 16.501-2 General.

(a) There are three types of indefinite-delivery contracts: definite-quantity contracts, requirements contracts, and indefinite-quantity contracts. The appropriate type of indefinite-delivery contract may be used to acquire supplies and/or services when the exact times and/or exact quantities of future deliveries are not known at the time of contract award. Pursuant to 10 U.S.C. 2304d and 41 U.S.C. 4101, requirements contracts and indefinite-quantity contracts are also known as delivery-order contracts or task-order contracts.

(b) The various types of indefinite-delivery contracts offer the following advantages:

(1) All three types permit—

(i) Government stocks to be maintained at minimum levels; and

(ii) Direct shipment to users.

(2) Indefinite-quantity contracts and requirements contracts also permit—

(i) Flexibility in both quantities and delivery scheduling; and

(ii) Ordering of supplies or services after requirements materialize.

(3) Indefinite-quantity contracts limit the Government's obligation to the minimum quantity specified in the contract.

(4) Requirements contracts may permit faster deliveries when production lead time is involved, because contractors are usually willing to maintain limited stocks when the Government will obtain all of its actual purchase requirements from the contractor.

(c) Indefinite-delivery contracts may provide for any appropriate cost or pricing arrangement under Part 16. Cost or pricing arrangements that provide for an estimated quantity of supplies or services (*e.g.*, estimated number of labor hours) must comply with the appropriate procedures of this subpart.

United States Code Annotated

Contract requirements, see 41 USCA § 254.

Contracts, planning, solicitation, evaluation, and award procedures, see 10 USCA § 2305.

Cost-type research and development contracts with educational institutions, see 41 USCA § 254a.

Definitions, see 10 USCA § 2302, 41 USCA §§ 259, 403.

Kinds of contracts, see 10 USCA § 2306.

Planning and solicitation requirements, see 41 USCA § 253a.

Task and delivery order contracts, definitions, see 10 USCA § 2304d, 41 USCA § 253k.

Task and delivery order contracts, general authority, see 10 USCA § 2304a, 41 USCA § 253h.

Task and delivery order contracts, orders, see 10 USCA § 2304c, 41 USCA § 253j.

Task order contracts, advisory and assistance services, see 10 USCA § 2304b, 41 USCA § 253i.

Notes of Decisions

In general 1
Jurisdiction 2

1 In general

Manufacturer of office automation systems was "interested party," for purposes of Tucker Act, and thus had standing to challenge Department of Labor's (DOL) decision to standardize its software applications exclusively to software manufactured by competitor as violative of Competition in Contracting Act (CICA), where DOL refused to engage in competitive procurement for its office automation systems, and manufacturer submitted bid nonetheless. 10 U.S.C.A. § 2304; 28 U.S.C.A. § 1491(b)(1); Federal Property and Administrative Services Act of 1949, § 303, as amended, 41 U.S.C.A. § 253; 48 C.F.R. §§ 16.501-1, 16.501-2. Corel Corp. v. U.S., 165 F. Supp. 2d 12 (D.D.C. 2001). United States ☞64.60(2)

Federal court had jurisdiction under Tucker Act over computer software manufacturer's action alleging that United States Department of Labor's (DOL) decision to standardize its software applications exclusively to software manufactured by competitor violated Competition in Contracting Act (CICA), where standardization decision was allegedly made in connection with its ultimate procurement of competitor's software licenses. 10 U.S.C.A. § 2304; 28 U.S.C.A. § 1491(b)(1); Federal Property and Administrative Services Act of 1949, § 303, as amended, 41 U.S.C.A. § 253; 48 C.F.R. §§ 16.501-1, 16.501-2. Corel Corp. v. U.S., 165 F. Supp. 2d 12 (D.D.C. 2001). United States ☞64.60(1)

2 Jurisdiction

Federal question subject matter jurisdiction existed over computer software manufacturer's action alleging that United States Department of Labor's (DOL) decision to standardize its software applications exclusively to software manufactured by competitor violated Administrative Procedure Act (APA) and Competition in Contracting Act (CICA), even if Federal Acquisition Streamlining Act (FASA) precluded review of DOL's issuance of delivery order issued under indefinite-delivery, indefinite-quantity contract pursuant to decision, where manufacturer's protest challenged DOL's overarching administrative decision to standardize to competitor's product, not issuance of individual delivery order. 5 U.S.C.A. § 701 et seq.; 10 U.S.C.A. § 2304; 28 U.S.C.A. § 1331; Federal Property and Administrative Services Act of 1949, §§ 303, 303J(a)(2), as amended, 41 U.S.C.A. §§ 253, 253j(a)(2); 48 C.F.R. §§ 16.501-1, 16.501-2. Corel Corp. v. U.S., 165 F. Supp. 2d 12 (D.D.C. 2001). Federal Courts ☞232

§ 16.502 Definite-quantity contracts.

(a) *Description.* A definite-quantity contract provides for delivery of a definite quantity of specific supplies or services for a fixed period, with deliveries or performance to be scheduled at designated locations upon order.

(b) *Application.* A definite-quantity contract may be used when it can be determined in advance that—

(1) A definite quantity of supplies or services will be required during the contract period; and

(2) The supplies or services are regularly available or will be available after a short lead time.

United States Code Annotated

Contract requirements, see 41 USCA § 254.

Contracts, planning, solicitation, evaluation, and award procedures, see 10 USCA § 2305.

Cost-type research and development contracts with educational institutions, see 41 USCA § 254a.

Definitions, see 10 USCA § 2302, 41 USCA §§ 259, 403.

Kinds of contracts, see 10 USCA § 2306.

Planning and solicitation requirements, see 41 USCA § 253a.

Task and delivery order contracts, definitions, see 10 USCA § 2304d, 41 USCA § 253k.

Task and delivery order contracts, general authority, see 10 USCA § 2304a, 41 USCA § 253h.

Task and delivery order contracts, orders, see 10 USCA § 2304c, 41 USCA § 253j.

Task order contracts, advisory and assistance services, see 10 USCA § 2304b, 41 USCA § 253i.

§ 16.503 Requirements contracts.

(a) Description. A requirements contract provides for filling all actual purchase requirements of designated Government activities for supplies or services during a specified contract period (from one contractor), with deliveries or performance to be scheduled by placing orders with the contractor.

(1) For the information of offerors and contractors, the contracting officer shall state a realistic estimated total quantity in the solicitation and resulting contract. This estimate is not a representation to an offeror or contractor that the estimated quantity will be required or ordered, or that conditions affecting requirements will be stable or normal. The contracting officer may obtain the estimate from records of previous requirements and consumption, or by other means, and should base the estimate on the most current information available.

(2) The contract shall state, if feasible, the maximum limit of the contractor's obligation to deliver and the Government's obligation to order. The contract may also specify maximum or minimum quantities that the Government may order under each individual order and the maximum that it may order during a specified period of time.

(b) Application.

(1) A requirements contract may be appropriate for acquiring any supplies or services when the Government anticipates recurring requirements but cannot predetermine the precise quantities of supplies or services that designated Government activities will need during a definite period.

(2) No requirements contract in an amount estimated to exceed $112 million (including all options) may be awarded to a single source unless a determination is executed in accordance with 16.504(c)(1)(ii)(D).

(c) Government property furnished for repair. When a requirements contract is used to acquire work (e.g., repair, modification, or overhaul) on existing items of Government property, the contracting officer shall specify in the Schedule that failure of the Government to furnish such items in the amounts or quantities described in the Schedule as "estimated" or "maximum" will not entitle the contractor to any equitable adjustment in price under the Government Property clause of the contract.

(d) Limitations on use of requirements contracts for advisory and assistance services.

(1) Except as provided in paragraph (d)(2) of this section, no solicitation for a requirements contract for advisory and assistance services in excess of three years and $13.5 million (including all options) may be issued unless the contracting officer or other official designated by the head of the agency determines in writing that the services required are so unique or highly specialized that it is not practicable to make multiple awards using the procedures in 16.504.

(2) The limitation in paragraph (d)(1) of this section is not applicable to an acquisition of supplies or services that includes the acquisition of advisory and assistance services, if the contracting officer or other official designated by the head of the agency determines that the advisory and assistance services are necessarily incident to, and not a significant component of, the contract.

United States Code Annotated

Contract requirements, see 41 USCA § 254.

Contracts, planning, solicitation, evaluation, and award procedures, see 10 USCA § 2305.

Cost-type research and development contracts with educational institutions, see 41 USCA § 254a.

Definitions, see 10 USCA § 2302, 41 USCA §§ 259, 403.

Kinds of contracts, see 10 USCA § 2306.

Planning and solicitation requirements, see 41 USCA § 253a.

Task and delivery order contracts, definitions, see 10 USCA § 2304d, 41 USCA § 253k.

Task and delivery order contracts, general authority, see 10 USCA § 2304a, 41 USCA

§ 253h.

Task and delivery order contracts, orders, see 10 USCA § 2304c, 41 USCA § 253j.

Task order contracts, advisory and assistance services, see 10 USCA § 2304b, 41 USCA § 253i.

Notes of Decisions

In general 1
Breach of contract 9
Consideration 2
Estimates 3
Good faith 4
Indefinite quantity contracts distinguished 5
Questions of law or fact 6
Summary judgment 7
Termination 8

1 In general

Agency may award a multiple award requirements contract without guaranteeing any work to any awardee. A contract is not unenforceable merely because it does not fit neatly into a recognized category. As consideration for the contractors' promises regarding price, availability, delivery, and quantity, the government promised that it would purchase only from the contractors on the schedule, with few exceptions. The government's promise has substantial business value because there were only between two and five authorized sources in each of the designated geographic regions. Rather than vying with 18,000 other transcription services for the government's business, the contractors had to compete with only one to four other contractors. Ace-Federal Reporters, Inc. v. Barram, 226 F.3d 1329 (Fed. Cir. 2000)

Essential element of requirements contract is promise by buyer to purchase subject matter of contract exclusively from seller. Modern Systems Technology Corp. v. U.S., 979 F.2d 200, 38 Cont. Cas. Fed. (CCH) P 76397 (Fed. Cir. 1992). Sales ☞71(4)

Requirements contract is formed when seller has exclusive right and legal obligation to fill all of buyer's needs for goods or services described in contract. Modern Systems Technology Corp. v. U.S., 979 F.2d 200, 38 Cont. Cas. Fed. (CCH) P 76397 (Fed. Cir. 1992). Sales ☞71(4)

Requirements contract calls for government to fill all its actual requirements for specified supplies or services during contract period by purchasing from awardee, who agrees to provide them at agreed price. Medart, Inc. v. Austin, 967 F.2d 579, 38 Cont. Cas. Fed. (CCH) P 76349 (Fed. Cir. 1992). United States ☞70(9)

Under a fixed price requirements contract, the ASBCA determined that the Government was not negligent in estimating its requirements for a laundry services contract, although requirements decreased during contract performance after the Army deployed a division to Iraq. The Board also held that the sovereign acts doctrine precluded plaintiff from recovering lost revenue under the contract's changes clause. Appeal of Robertson & Penn, Inc., A.S.B.C.A. No. 55625, 08-2 B.C.A. (CCH) ¶ 33951, 2008 WL 4218367 (Armed Serv. B.C.A. 2008)

Contract Disputes Act (CDA) was applicable to multifaceted contract which called for lease by Office of Personnel Management (OPM) of a facility to be built by contractor for OPM management training center both for office space for its staff, conference space for all its training programs, and food, lodging and appurtenant facilities for program attendees; contract did not fall within CDA exception for "real property in being," as exception does not apply to contracts that create a new property interest, such as a leasehold at time of contracting. Contract Disputes Act of 1978, §§ 3(a)(1), 41 U.S.C.A. §§ 602(a)(1); Federal Group, Inc. v. U.S., 67 Fed. Cl. 87 (2005). United States ☞73(9)

Requirements contract for computer repair services which required the Army to order all services and supplies from contractor that were "required to be purchased" did not entitle contractor to receive warranty work for machines purchased before contract performance which were still within their initial warranty period. Datalect Computer Services, Inc. v.

U.S., 56 Fed. Cl. 178 (2003), aff'd, 97 Fed. Appx. 333 (Fed. Cir. 2004). United States ☞70(6.1)

Evidence supported conclusion that the Army violated requirements clause of contract for computer repair services which required the Army to order all services and supplies from contractor that were "required to be purchased" during the contract period by "purchasing" extensions to warranties on covered machinery from another contractor which supplied computer hardware, thereby depriving repair contractor of warranty work. Datalect Computer Services, Inc. v. U.S., 56 Fed. Cl. 178 (2003), aff'd, 97 Fed. Appx. 333 (Fed. Cir. 2004). United States ☞74(11)

A "requirements contract" requires the contracting government entity to fill all of its actual requirements for supplies or services that are specified in the contract, during the contract period, by purchases from the contract awardee. 48 C.F.R. § 16.503(a). J. Cooper & Associates, Inc. v. U.S., 53 Fed. Cl. 8 (2002), aff'd, 65 Fed. Appx. 731 (Fed. Cir. 2003). United States ☞70(9)

A government purchaser who has entered into a requirements contract with a contractor for a specific item may not purchase that item from any other source for the duration of the contract. J. Cooper & Associates, Inc. v. U.S., 53 Fed. Cl. 8 (2002), aff'd, 65 Fed. Appx. 731 (Fed. Cir. 2003). United States ☞70(9)

A "requirements contract" requires the contracting government entity to fill all of its actual requirements for supplies or services that are specified in the contract, during the contract period, by purchases from the contract awardee. To be valid and enforceable, a government contract must have both consideration to ensure mutuality of obligation, and sufficient definiteness so as to provide a basis for determining the existence of a breach and for giving an appropriate remedy. Consideration is satisfied in requirements contracts by the government purchaser's agreement to contractually limit its range of future options and to turn to the contractor for all such requirements as do develop. J. Cooper & Associates, Inc. v. U.S., 53 Fed. Cl. 8 (2002), aff'd, 65 Fed. Appx. 731 (Fed. Cir. 2003)

Government contractor's "increased costs" theory did not provide a reasonable basis for computing its damages under requirements contract for computer repair services; pursuant to the theory, contractor calculated equitable adjustments to the fixed costs, spare parts costs, and the profit margin on those costs; although increased cost calculation purported to demonstrate contractor's projected costs and revenues at the time the bids were submitted as well as its actual costs in performing the contract, the figures were not supported by the record. Datalect Computer Services, Ltd. v. U.S., 41 Fed. Cl. 720, 42 Cont. Cas. Fed. (CCH) P 77379 (1998), aff'd, 215 F.3d 1344 (Fed. Cir. 1999). United States ☞74(11)

Principle that patent ambiguities place on contractor duty to inquire did not apply to dispute as to whether parties had entered a requirements contract or a contract for indefinite quantities. Crown Laundry and Dry Cleaners, Inc. v. U.S., 29 Fed. Cl. 506, 39 Cont. Cas. Fed. (CCH) P 76575 (1993). United States ☞70(30)

Contract for laundry and dry cleaning services was a requirements contract, even though it was labeled an indefinite quantities contract, where government intended to have all of its dry cleaning and laundry needs for arsenal serviced by the contract, contract provided that the government could arrange for services to be performed by another contractor if the contractor failed to perform any services covered by the contract, and the contract terms, read together were more consistent if taken as expression of requirements contract than as indefinite quantities contract. Crown Laundry and Dry Cleaners, Inc. v. U.S., 29 Fed. Cl. 506, 39 Cont. Cas. Fed. (CCH) P 76575 (1993). United States ☞70(6.1)

2 Consideration

Consideration is satisfied in requirements contracts by the government purchaser's agreement to contractually limit its range of future options and to turn to the contractor for all such requirements as do develop. J. Cooper & Associates, Inc. v. U.S., 53 Fed. Cl. 8 (2002), aff'd, 65 Fed. Appx. 731 (Fed. Cir. 2003). United States ☞66

Requirements contracts lack promise from buyer to order specific amount, but consideration is furnished, and contract is rendered enforceable, by buyer's promise to turn to seller for all such requirements as they develop. Datalect Computer Services, Ltd. v. U.S., 40 Fed. Cl. 28, 42 Cont. Cas. Fed. (CCH) P 77243 (1997), aff'd in part, vacated in part on other grounds, 215 F.3d 1344 (Fed. Cir. 1999). Sales ☞71(4)

3 Estimates

A contractor can recover damages from the federal government for increased costs caused by a defective estimate of workload if it can show by preponderant evidence that the government's estimate was inadequately or negligently prepared, not in good faith, or grossly or unreasonably inadequate at the time the estimate was made. The Federal Circuit held although the government provided contractor with historical data, government possessed information indicating that its anticipated requirements were significantly greater than its historical requirements. Therefore, simply providing offerors with historical workload data was not sufficient. Agility Def. & Gov't Servs., Inc. v. U.S., 847 F.3d 1345 (Fed. Cir. 2017)

Federal Acquisition Regulations require contracting officer to furnish estimated quantities in solicitation contemplating requirements contract; risks associated with variance between actual purchases and estimated quantities are allocated to contractor. Medart, Inc. v. Austin, 967 F.2d 579, 38 Cont. Cas. Fed. (CCH) P 76349 (Fed. Cir. 1992). United States ☞70(9)

Because actual purchases under requirements contracts vary significantly from government estimates does not ordinarily give rise to liability on part of government. Medart, Inc. v. Austin, 967 F.2d 579, 38 Cont. Cas. Fed. (CCH) P 76349 (Fed. Cir. 1992). United States ☞70(30)

Estimating needs when soliciting for bids for requirements contract to supply metal storage cabinets based on last year's orders was reasonable and complied with Federal Acquisition Regulations, even though estimates exceeded actual orders. Medart, Inc. v. Austin, 967 F.2d 579, 38 Cont. Cas. Fed. (CCH) P 76349 (Fed. Cir. 1992). United States ☞70(30)

Jury verdict method of awarding damages could not be employed to formulate award for damages suffered by contractor under requirements contract for computer repair services due to government's negligent estimates of repair needs for last two option years of contract, under total loss theory measuring damages by the difference between the actual cost of performing the contract and the costs estimated in the contractor's proposal, where contractor provided insufficient evidence upon which to calculate award that was both fair and reasonable. Datalect Computer Services, Inc. v. U.S., 56 Fed. Cl. 178 (2003), aff'd, 97 Fed. Appx. 333 (Fed. Cir. 2004). United States ☞74(12.1)

Contractor under requirements contract for computer repair services could not recover under reformation theory damages for government's negligent estimates of repair needs for last two option years of contract, where it failed to prove that its damages were the result of government's breach. Datalect Computer Services, Inc. v. U.S., 56 Fed. Cl. 178 (2003), aff'd, 97 Fed. Appx. 333 (Fed. Cir. 2004). United States ☞74(13)

Estimated government contract requirements do not represent a guarantee or warranty and, normally, significant variances between estimated requirements and actual orders will not result in liability on the part of the government in the absence of bad faith, negligence, or a showing of a grossly unreasonable estimate. 48 C.F.R. § 16.503(a)(1). Hi-Shear Technology Corp. v. U.S., 53 Fed. Cl. 420 (2002), decision aff'd, 356 F.3d 1372 (Fed. Cir. 2004). United States ☞70(30)

In a solicitation for a requirements contract, the contracting officer must provide a realistic estimate of the quantity of goods or services to be procured under the contract; however, the estimate is not a warranty as to quantity, but instead serves as a guideline as to the contract's magnitude and scope. 48 C.F.R. § 16.503(a)(1). Educators Associates, Inc. v. U.S., 41 Fed. Cl. 811, 42 Cont. Cas. Fed. (CCH) P 77376 (1998). United States ☞70(9); United States ☞70(30)

Contractor's contract reformation theory did not provide a reasonable basis for computing its damages under requirements contract for computer repair services; theory was based on the difference between what it actually received under the contract and what it would have bid if government had properly disclosed its estimated requirements, but contractor provided no credible evidence to demonstrate how the original bid prices were formulated, and thus its hypothetical bid was speculative. Datalect Computer Services, Ltd. v. U.S., 41 Fed. Cl. 720, 42 Cont. Cas. Fed. (CCH) P 77379 (1998), aff'd, 215 F.3d 1344 (Fed. Cir. 1999). United States ☞74(11)

Although government contractor under requirements contract for computer repair services incurred monetary injury as a result of government's faulty estimate, "jury verdict" method of awarding damages could not be applied where contractor did not provide the court with sufficient evidence to make a reasonable approximation of the damages incurred. Datalect Computer Services, Ltd. v. U.S., 41 Fed. Cl. 720, 42 Cont. Cas. Fed. (CCH) P 77379 (1998), aff'd, 215 F.3d 1344 (Fed. Cir. 1999). United States ☞74(12.1)

Fact that actual work performed pursuant to requirements contract varies significantly from inaccurate estimates set forth in contract does not shift burden of persuasion to government to prove reasonableness of the estimating procedures; contractor has burden of persuasion to prove by preponderance of the evidence that inaccurate estimates were the result of negligent action by government personnel or lack of due care by personnel in preparation of the estimates. Crown Laundry and Dry Cleaners, Inc. v. U.S., 29 Fed. Cl. 506, 39 Cont. Cas. Fed. (CCH) P 76575 (1993). United States ☞74(10)

Variance of 5% to 15% between government's estimates of its need under requirements contract and the actual amount of its needs might be viewed as reasonable, but 45% variance is unreasonable. Crown Laundry and Dry Cleaners, Inc. v. U.S., 29 Fed. Cl. 506, 39 Cont. Cas. Fed. (CCH) P 76575 (1993). United States ☞70(6.1); United States ☞70(30)

Government was negligent in preparation of estimates of work to be performed under the requirements contract for laundry and dry cleaning at arsenal where it requested the using activities at the arsenal to estimate their needs for laundry and dry cleaning services, resulting estimates were submitted in monthly form and for variety of laundry and dry cleaning services, a contract specialist multiplied the monthly estimates by 12, estimates were not otherwise verified or checked for reasonableness or accuracy, historical data concerning use was not considered, and contracting officer was aware that using activities probably exaggerated their needs in order to insure that any increase in needs would be met by future procurement. Crown Laundry and Dry Cleaners, Inc. v. U.S., 29 Fed. Cl. 506, 39 Cont. Cas. Fed. (CCH) P 76575 (1993). United States ☞70(30)

4 Good faith

Government may be liable in damages where contractor can show by preponderant evidence that government estimates made during solicitation for requirements contract were inadequately or negligently prepared, not in good faith, or grossly or unreasonably inadequate at time estimate was made. Medart, Inc. v. Austin, 967 F.2d 579, 38 Cont. Cas. Fed. (CCH) P 76349 (Fed. Cir. 1992). United States ☞70(30)

If a government contractor under a requirements contract can show by a preponderance of the evidence that the government prepared estimates inadequately or negligently, not in good faith, or grossly or unreasonably inadequate at the time, the government could be liable for damages. Federal Group, Inc. v. U.S., 67 Fed. Cl. 87 (2005). United States ☞70(30)

Government has a duty of good faith and use of reasonable care in computing its estimated needs in a solicitation for a requirements contract. 48 C.F.R. § 16.503(a)(1). Educators Associates, Inc. v. U.S., 41 Fed. Cl. 811, 42 Cont. Cas. Fed. (CCH) P 77376 (1998). United States ☞70(9)

Offeror on government contract is entitled to rely on government estimate set forth in contract as representing an honest and informed conclusion; government must act in good faith and use reasonable care in computing its estimated needs, and it must either reformulate its estimate when warranted by the information available, or notify offerors of situations or factors likely to affect the estimate. 48 C.F.R. § 16.503(a)(1). Datalect Computer Services, Ltd. v. U.S., 40 Fed. Cl. 28, 42 Cont. Cas. Fed. (CCH) P 77243 (1997), aff'd in part, vacated in part on other grounds, 215 F.3d 1344 (Fed. Cir. 1999). United States ☞70(30)

5 Indefinite quantity contracts distinguished

Where company's contract to provide pest control services for Department of Housing and Urban Development (HUD) was neither requirements contract nor enforceable indefinite quantity contract, company was entitled to payment only for services actually ordered by HUD and provided by company. Coyle's Pest Control, Inc. v. Cuomo, 154 F.3d 1302, 42 Cont. Cas. Fed. (CCH) P 77373 (Fed. Cir. 1998). United States ☞70(19)

6 Questions of law or fact

Whether a government contract is an indefinite quantity or a requirements contract is a matter of law for the Court of Federal Claims to decide. Myers Investigative and Security Services, Inc. v. U.S., 47 Fed. Cl. 605 (2000), aff'd, 275 F.3d 1366 (Fed. Cir. 2002). United States ☞70(9)

7 Summary judgment

Where question of whether contract was for requirements or indefinite quantities did not involve any factual disputes material to interpretation of the contract, summary judgment could be used to resolve the question. RCFC, Rule 56(c, d), 28 U.S.C.A.Crown Laundry and Dry Cleaners, Inc. v. U.S., 29 Fed. Cl. 506, 39 Cont. Cas. Fed. (CCH) P 76575 (1993). Federal Courts ☞1120

8 Termination

Contractor was entitled to an equitable adjustment because Government's partial termination of a requirements contract eliminated work that would have permitted recovery of part of the fixed costs associated with the contract and thus increased the contractor's costs to perform the unterminated part of the contract. Mo. Dep't of Soc. Servs., ASBCA 59191, 16-1 BCA ¶ 36,563 (Armed Serv. B.C.A. 2016)

9 Breach of contract

Government breaches requirements contract when it has requirements for contract items or services but diverts business from contractor and does not use contractor to satisfy those requirements; contractor may be entitled to recover damages in form of lost profits for such breach. Rumsfeld v. Applied Cos., Inc., 325 F.3d 1328 (Fed. Cir. 2003)

To extent that government estimate for requirements contract is inadequately or negligently prepared, its inclusion in the contract constitutes misrepresentation that, whether deliberate or unintentional, amounts to breach of contract. Where an agency knew several months before award of requirements contract that the likely quantity to be purchased was only 10% of the estimate included in the RFP, but negligently failed to inform the contractor of that fact until after award, contractor was entitled to an equitable adjustment in price of units delivered to the agency to account for contractor's increased costs resulting the lower quantity, plus profit on that cost. Rumsfeld v. Applied Cos., Inc., 325 F.3d 1328 (Fed. Cir. 2003)

§ 16.504 Indefinite-quantity contracts.

(a) Description. An indefinite-quantity contract provides for an indefinite quantity, within stated limits, of supplies or services during a fixed period. The Government places orders for individual requirements. Quantity limits may be stated as number of units or as dollar values.

(1) The contract must require the Government to order and the contractor to furnish at least a stated minimum quantity of supplies or services. In addition, if ordered, the contractor must furnish any additional quantities, not to exceed the stated maximum. The contracting officer should establish a reasonable maximum quantity based on market research, trends on recent contracts for similar supplies or services, survey of potential users, or any other rational basis.

(2) To ensure that the contract is binding, the minimum quantity must be more than a nominal quantity, but it should not exceed the amount that the Government is fairly certain to order.

(3) The contract may also specify maximum or minimum quantities that the Government may order under each task or delivery order and the maximum that it may order during a specific period of time.

(4) A solicitation and contract for an indefinite quantity must—

(i) Specify the period of the contract, including the number of options and the period for which the Government may extend the contract under each option;

(ii) Specify the total minimum and maximum quantity of supplies or services the Government will acquire under the contract;

(iii) Include a statement of work, specifications, or other description, that reasonably describes the general scope, nature, complexity, and purpose of the supplies or services the Government will acquire under the contract in a manner that will enable a prospective offeror to decide whether to submit an offer;

(iv) State the procedures that the Government will use in issuing orders, including the ordering media, and, if multiple awards may be made, state the procedures and selection criteria that the Government will use to provide awardees a fair opportunity to be considered for each order (see 16.505(b)(1));

(v) Include the name, address, telephone number, facsimile number, and e-mail address of the agency task and delivery order ombudsman (see 16.505(b)(8)) if multiple awards may be made;

(vi) Include a description of the activities authorized to issue orders; and

(vii) Include authorization for placing oral orders, if appropriate, provided that the Government has established procedures for obligating funds and that oral orders are confirmed in writing.

(b) Application. Contracting officers may use an indefinite-quantity contract when the Government cannot predetermine, above a specified minimum, the precise quantities of supplies or services that the Government will require during the contract period, and it is inadvisable for the Government to commit itself for more than a minimum quantity. The contracting officer should use an indefinite-quantity contract only when a recurring need is anticipated.

(c) Multiple award preference—

(1) Planning the acquisition.

(i) Except for indefinite-quantity contracts for advisory and assistance services as provided in paragraph (c)(2) of this section, the contracting officer must, to the maximum extent practicable, give preference to making multiple awards of indefinite-quantity contracts under a single solicitation for the same or similar supplies or services to two or more sources.

(ii) (A) The contracting officer must determine whether multiple awards are appropriate as part of acquisition planning. The contracting officer must avoid situations in which awardees specialize exclusively in one or a few areas within the statement of work, thus creating the likelihood that orders in those areas will be awarded on a sole-source basis; however, each awardee need not be capable of performing every requirement as well as any other awardee under the contracts. The contracting officer should consider the following when determining the number of contracts to be awarded:

(1) The scope and complexity of the contract requirement.

(2) The expected duration and frequency of task or delivery orders.

(3) The mix of resources a contractor must have to perform expected task or delivery order requirements.

(4) The ability to maintain competition among the awardees throughout the contracts' period of performance.

(B) The contracting officer must not use the multiple award approach if—

(1) Only one contractor is capable of providing performance at the level of quality required because the supplies or services are unique or highly specialized;

(2) Based on the contracting officer's knowledge of the market, more favorable terms and conditions, including pricing, will be provided if a single award is made;

(3) The expected cost of administration of multiple contracts outweighs the expected benefits of making multiple awards;

(4) The projected task orders are so integrally related that only a single contractor can reasonably perform the work;

(5) The total estimated value of the contract is less than the simplified acquisition threshold; or

(6) Multiple awards would not be in the best interests of the Government.

(C) The contracting officer must document the decision whether or not to use multiple awards in the acquisition plan or contract file. The contracting officer may determine that a class of acquisitions is not appropriate for multiple awards (see Subpart 1.7).

(D)

(1) No task or delivery order contract in an amount estimated to exceed $112 million (including all options) may be awarded to a single source unless the head of the agency determines in writing that—

(i) The task or delivery orders expected under the contract are so integrally related that only a single source can reasonably perform the work;

(ii) The contract provides only for firm-fixed price (see 16.202) task or delivery orders for—

(A) Products for which unit prices are established in the contract; or

(B) Services for which prices are established in the contract for the specific tasks to be performed;

(iii) Only one source is qualified and capable of performing the work at a reasonable price to the Government; or

(iv) It is necessary in the public interest to award the contract to a single source due to exceptional circumstances.

(2) The head of the agency must notify Congress within 30 days after any determination under paragraph (c)(1)(ii)(D)(1)(iv) of this section.

(3) The requirement for a determination for a single-award contract greater than $112 million—

(i) Is in addition to any applicable requirements of Subpart 6.3; and

(ii) Is not applicable for architect-engineer services awarded pursuant to Subpart 36.6.

(2) Contracts for advisory and assistance services.

(i) Except as provided in paragraph (c)(2)(ii) of this section, if an indefinite-quantity contract for advisory and assistance services exceeds 3 years and $13.5 million, including all options, the contracting officer must make multiple awards unless—

(A) The contracting officer or other official designated by the head of the agency determines in writing, as part of acquisition planning, that multiple awards are not practicable. The contracting officer or other official must determine that only one contractor can reasonably perform the work because either the scope of work is unique or highly specialized or the tasks so integrally related;

(B) The contracting officer or other official designated by the head of the agency determines in writing, after the evaluation of offers, that only one offeror is capable of providing the services required at the level of quality required; or

(C) Only one offer is received.

(ii) The requirements of paragraph (c)(2)(i) of this section do not apply if the contracting officer or other official designated by the head of the agency determines that the advisory and assistance services are incidental and not a significant component of the contract.

United States Code Annotated

Contract requirements, see 41 USCA § 254.

Contracts, planning, solicitation, evaluation, and award procedures, see 10 USCA § 2305.

Cost-type research and development contracts with educational institutions, see 41 USCA § 254a.

Definitions, see 10 USCA § 2302, 41 USCA §§ 259, 403.

Kinds of contracts, see 10 USCA § 2306.

Planning and solicitation requirements, see 41 USCA § 253a.

Task and delivery order contracts, definitions, see 10 USCA § 2304d, 41 USCA § 253k.

Task and delivery order contracts, general authority, see 10 USCA § 2304a, 41 USCA § 253h.

Task and delivery order contracts, orders, see 10 USCA § 2304c, 41 USCA § 253j.

Task order contracts, advisory and assistance services, see 10 USCA § 2304b, 41 USCA § 253i.

Notes of Decisions

In general 1

Accord and satisfaction 7
Cost or Price Evaluation 15
Court of Federal Claims jurisdiction 10
Discretion of agency 2
Estimates 3
Good faith 4
Injunctions 9
Letter contracts 5
Minimum quantity 14
Multiple award preference 13
Questions of law or fact 11
Requirements contracts 6
Summary judgment 12
Task or delivery order contracts 8

1 In general

Under an indefinite-delivery, indefinite-quantity (IDIQ) contract, the government is required to purchase the minimum quantity stated in the contract, but when the government makes that purchase its legal obligation under the contract is satisfied. 48 C.F.R. § 16.504(a). Travel Centre v. Barram, 236 F.3d 1316 (Fed. Cir. 2001). United States ⚖70(6.1)

Once the government has purchased the minimum quantity stated in an indefinite-delivery, indefinite-quantity (IDIQ) contract from the contractor, it is free to purchase additional supplies or services from any other source it chooses. 48 C.F.R. § 16.504(a). Travel Centre v. Barram, 236 F.3d 1316 (Fed. Cir. 2001). United States ⚖70(6.1)

When an indefinite-delivery, indefinite-quantity (IDIQ) contract between a contracting party and the government clearly indicates that the contracting party is guaranteed no more than a non-nominal minimum amount of sales, purchases exceeding that minimum amount satisfy the government's legal obligation under the contract. 48 C.F.R. § 16.504(a). Travel Centre v. Barram, 236 F.3d 1316 (Fed. Cir. 2001). United States ⚖70(6.1)

General Services Administration (GSA) did not breach contract for provision of travel management services, although GSA did not inform contractor before it submitted its final bid that two agencies which comprised over half of the expected business in one of the states covered under the solicitation would not longer be utilizing GSA-contracted services; contract explicitly stated that it was a indefinitedelivery, indefinite-quantity (IDIQ) contract and that contractor was "a preferred source" of travel agency services, and GSA purchased minimum quantity stated in the contract. 48 C.F.R. § 16.504(a). Travel Centre v. Barram, 236 F.3d 1316 (Fed. Cir. 2001). United States ⚖73(22)

Government did not breach indefinite delivery, indefinite quantity (ID/IQ) contract for asbestos removal when it renegotiated with contractor the price per square foot for encapsulation service to reduce it from $5.00 per square foot to $0.23 per square foot, after it purchased the contract minimum of $50,000; after satisfying the contract minimum, government had no further obligation to pay contractor $5.00 per square foot for encapsulation service. Abatement Contracting Corp. v. U.S., 58 Fed. Cl. 594 (2003). United States ⚖73(22)

"Indefinite delivery, indefinite quantity contracts" obligate the government to purchase only a stated minimum quantity of supplies or services from the contractor, with deliveries to be scheduled as ordered by the government. 48 C.F.R. § 16.504. Abatement Contracting Corp. v. U.S., 58 Fed. Cl. 594 (2003). United States ⚖70(6.1)

When the government enters into an indefinite delivery, indefinite quantity (ID/IQ) contract, it does not promise to fill all of its needs by purchasing from the contractor; it commits only to purchase the minimum quantity stated in the contract. 48 C.F.R. § 16.504. Abatement Contracting Corp. v. U.S., 58 Fed. Cl. 594 (2003). United States ⚖70(6.1)

An "indefinite delivery and indefinite quantity (IDIQ) contract" provides that the government will purchase an indefinite quantity of supplies or services from a contractor during a fixed period of time, and requires the government to order only a stated minimum quantity of supplies or services. J. Cooper & Associates, Inc. v. U.S., 53 Fed. Cl. 8 (2002), aff'd, 65

Fed. Appx. 731 (Fed. Cir. 2003). United States ☞70(6.1)

An indefinite delivery and indefinite quantity (IDIQ) contract requires the government to order only a stated minimum quantity of supplies or services, and once the government has purchased the minimum quantity stated in an IDIQ contract from the contractor, it is free to purchase additional supplies or services from any other source it chooses. J. Cooper & Associates, Inc. v. U.S., 53 Fed. Cl. 8 (2002), aff'd, 65 Fed. Appx. 731 (Fed. Cir. 2003). United States ☞70(6.1)

Although agency's decision to award a single indefinite delivery/indefinite quantity contract under a single solicitation, rather than multiple contracts, was procedurally invalid because it was made before the contracting officer (CO) prepared the written determination required by section of the Federal Acquisition Regulation, violation was not prejudicial; if the matter were remanded solely on the basis of procedural error, agency would be free to adopt the substance of the CO's analysis and again conclude that a single award was appropriate. Federal Property and Administrative Services Act of 1949, § 303h(d)(3), as amended, 41 U.S.C.A. § 253h(d)(3); 48 C.F.R. § 16.504(c)(1). WinStar Communications, Inc. v. U.S., 41 Fed. Cl. 748, 42 Cont. Cas. Fed. (CCH) P 77371 (1998). United States ☞64.60(5.1)

Section of Federal Acquisition Regulation giving preference to multiple awards of indefinite-quantity contracts under a single solicitation contemplates that contracting officer's contrary determination that a single award is appropriate will precede and form the basis of an agency decision to override the preference for multiple awards. Federal Property and Administrative Services Act of 1949, § 303h(d)(3), as amended, 41 U.S.C.A. § 253h(d)(3); 48 C.F.R. § 16.504(c)(1). WinStar Communications, Inc. v. U.S., 41 Fed. Cl. 748, 42 Cont. Cas. Fed. (CCH) P 77371 (1998). United States ☞64.15

Decision of contracting officer (CO) to award a single indefinite delivery/indefinite quantity contract under a single solicitation, rather than multiple contracts, was arbitrary, capricious, and not in accordance with the legal preference for multiple awards, where the CO's analysis failed to address and weigh the benefits of awarding multiple contracts as required by the Federal Acquisition Regulation. 48 C.F.R. § 16.504(c)(1). WinStar Communications, Inc. v. U.S., 41 Fed. Cl. 748, 42 Cont. Cas. Fed. (CCH) P 77371 (1998). United States ☞64.15

Determination that justifies single award of contract for advisory and assistance services exceeding three years and $10 million must be made prior to issuance of solicitation. 10 U.S.C.A. § 2304b(e)(3); 48 C.F.R. § 16.504(c)(2)(i)(A). Cubic Applications, Inc. v. U.S., 37 Fed. Cl. 345, 41 Cont. Cas. Fed. (CCH) P 77075 (1997). United States ☞64.5

Under contract with Navy for manufacture of various types of hydrophone sensors, Navy's right to purchase "all or part" of items enabled it to limit purchase to portion of sensors under subline item numbers listed in contract, and did not require it to accept or reject entire quantity listed under subline item numbers included under each contract line item number; thus, contractor could not recover for increased unit price attributable to purchase of only part of quantities listed under some subline item numbers. International Transducer Corp. v. U.S., 30 Fed. Cl. 522, 39 Cont. Cas. Fed. (CCH) P 76630 (1994), aff'd, 48 F.3d 1235 (Fed. Cir. 1995). United States ☞70(9)

2 Discretion of agency

Although not specifically addressed in the FAR, the Federal Circuit held that the Army Corps of Engineers was authorized to award a $301 million IDIQ contract for design and construction work. The Court explained that the proper inquiry is not whether the FAR authorizes IDIQ contracts for construction, but whether any statutory or regulatory provisions preclude such use. Under FAR 1.102(d), agencies have authority to use any "strategy, practice, policy or procedure" that is not prohibited and "is in the best interests of the Government." The Army's use of IDIQ contracts for this procurement represents the type of innovation envisioned by FAR 1.102(d). Tyler Const. Group v. U.S., 570 F.3d 1329 (Fed. Cir. 2009)

Indefinite-delivery, Indefinite-quantity (IDIQ) contract does not provide any exclusivity to the contractor; government may, at its discretion and for its benefit, make its purchases for similar supplies and/or services from other sources. 48 C.F.R. § 16.504(a). Travel Centre v. Barram, 236 F.3d 1316 (Fed. Cir. 2001). United States ☞70(6.1)

Procurement process used by Defense Logistics Agency (DLA) for multiple indefinite-delivery, indefinite-quantity contracts, whereby all offerors submitting a compliant proposal would receive a contract, complied with Competition in Contracting Act, even though it did not provide for competition at the initial phase, but instead postponed true competition until the delivery order stage. Agency's efforts to create an online catalog of tents, which would be purchased later through delivery orders, was a permissible exercise of its discretion. SEK Solutions, Inc. v. U.S., 117 Fed. Cl. 43 (2014)

The Government's use of an indefinite-delivery, indefinite-quantity contract to acquire construction services is a permissible exercise of procurement authority because it is not specifically prohibited by law. Tyler Constr. Group v. U.S., 83 Fed. Cl. 94 (2008), aff'd, 570 F.3d 1329 (Fed. Cir. 2009)

Solicitation of the Army Corps of Engineers for maintenance dredging and shore protection projects using negotiated indefinite delivery indefinite quantity (IDIQ) multiple-award task order contracts rather than competitive sealed bidding procedures violated statute and related procurement regulations mandating use of sealed bidding procedures when time permits, awards are made solely based on price, discussions are not necessary, and the agency reasonably expects to receive more than one bid. Weeks Marine, Inc. v. U.S., 79 Fed. Cl. 22 (2007), aff'd in part, rev'd in part, 575 F.3d 1352 (Fed. Cir. 2009)

Contracting agency's discretion in setting minimum quantities in an indefinite delivery/indefinite quantity (ID/IQ) government contract is not unlimited; thus, a minimum is not acceptable in a situation where the agency has simply declined to try to establish a more exact level. 48 C.F.R. § 16.504. ABF Freight System, Inc. v. U.S., 55 Fed. Cl. 392 (2003). United States ☞70(6.1)

3 Estimates

Fact that government has the obligation under an indefinite quantity/indefinite delivery (IDIQ) contract to order the contractual minimum does not preclude a contractor from recovering for inaccurate quantity estimates in an IDIQ contract. Schweiger Const. Co., Inc. v. U.S., 49 Fed. Cl. 188 (2001). United States ☞70(26)

Price reasonableness evaluation leading to award of an indefinite-quantity contract was unreasonable where the agency evaluated only unit prices without also considering the estimated quantities of each line item. Such an approach does not satisfy the legal requirement to consider total cost to the government. By not considering the estimated cost, the agency's evaluation failed to account for the difference in the relative proportions of the cost for each item in the total cost to the government, and, as a result, there was no direct relationship between the evaluated prices of a particular offeror and the actual price of performance by that offeror. R & G Food Service, Inc., d/b/a Port×A×Pit Catering, B-296435.4, B-296435.9, 2005 WL 3144073 (Comp. Gen. 2005)

4 Good faith

Contractor did not establish that government breached indefinite delivery, indefinite quantity (ID/IQ) contract for asbestos removal by failing to accurately estimate the amount of asbestos encapsulation work that would be required, absent evidence of egregious conduct, beyond mere negligence, and rising to the level of bad faith. Abatement Contracting Corp. v. U.S., 58 Fed. Cl. 594 (2003). United States ☞74(11)

A contracting agency may exercise its discretion in setting stated minimums in an indefinite delivery/indefinite quantity (ID/IQ) government contract provided that the estimates are established in good faith or are based upon the best information available and accurately represent the agency's anticipated needs. 48 C.F.R. § 16.504. ABF Freight System, Inc. v. U.S., 55 Fed. Cl. 392 (2003). United States ☞70(6.1)

Contracting agency did not exercise its discretion irrationally, arbitrarily, or in bad faith in establishing the stated minimums for the procurement which involved multiple indefinite delivery/indefinite quantity (ID/IQ) contracts for freight transportation. 48 C.F.R. § 16.504. ABF Freight System, Inc. v. U.S., 55 Fed. Cl. 392 (2003). United States ☞70(6.1)

Contractor did not establish that contracting agency acted in bad faith in not awarding more work to contractor under indefinite delivery and indefinite quantity (IDIQ) contract, after assuring it of additional work, where agency became dissatisfied with contractor's accounting practices, pricing, and work quality, and gave contractor another chance by soliciting additional work proposals. J. Cooper & Associates, Inc. v. U.S., 53 Fed. Cl. 8 (2002), aff'd, 65 Fed. Appx. 731 (Fed. Cir. 2003). United States ☞72.1(2)

Government's failure to notify contractor that it was using other contractors to fulfill needs described in contract's statement of work was not evidence of bad faith, where contract was an indefinite delivery and indefinite quantity (IDIQ) contract, and government was under no obligation to notify contractor that it was using other contractors after the minimum guaranteed by the IDOQ contract was satisfied. J. Cooper & Associates, Inc. v. U.S., 53 Fed. Cl. 8 (2002), aff'd, 65 Fed. Appx. 731 (Fed. Cir. 2003). United States ☞72.1(2)

Government contractor must present well-nigh irrefragable proof that the government acted in bad faith to recover for inaccurate quantity estimates in an indefinite-quantity contract (IDQ). Schweiger Const. Co., Inc. v. U.S., 49 Fed. Cl. 188 (2001). United States ☞70(26)

Courts will not review the accuracy of quantity estimates in indefinite-quantity (IDQ) government contracts where mere negligence has been alleged; however, they will, permit recovery for inaccurate estimates in the event of more egregious governmental conduct, most usually defined as "bad faith." Schweiger Const. Co., Inc. v. U.S., 49 Fed. Cl. 188 (2001). United States ☞70(26)

Government contractor stated a claim for inaccurate estimates in an indefinite-quantity (IDQ) contract, notwithstanding that it did not specifically incorporate the term "bad faith" into its complaint, where it alleged that contracting agency issued solicitation specifications which were knowingly and intentionally false, non-representative of the actual requirements, or in the alternative, issued with a reckless disregard of their truth or reliability, with the intent to induce contractor to rely on the flawed specifications to its detriment. Schweiger Const. Co., Inc. v. U.S., 49 Fed. Cl. 188 (2001). United States ☞70(26)

5 Letter contracts

Because letter contract to provide support services for agency recruitment campaign was an indefinite delivery and indefinite quantity (IDIQ) contract, government did not breach contract by failing to provide contractor with work in excess of the minimum quantity in the letter contract or by failing to award to contractor all of the work in the government's pre-contract estimate. J. Cooper & Associates, Inc. v. U.S., 53 Fed. Cl. 8 (2002), aff'd, 65 Fed. Appx. 731 (Fed. Cir. 2003). United States ☞73(22)

Contracting agency was under no obligation to terminate letter contract for convenience rather than allow it to lapse, where contract was for an indefinite delivery and indefinite quantity (IDIQ) contract, no task orders were interrupted or terminated by agency by its decision to allow the letter contract to lapse, and agency had paid contractor in excess of the minimum guarantee in the letter contract. J. Cooper & Associates, Inc. v. U.S., 53 Fed. Cl. 8 (2002), aff'd, 65 Fed. Appx. 731 (Fed. Cir. 2003). United States ☞72.1(1)

6 Requirements contracts

An "indefinite delivery, indefinite quantity contract" (ID/IQ contract) differs from a "requirements contract" in that the former does not oblige the buyer to purchase more from the seller than a stated minimum quantity, whereas the latter obliges the buyer to buy from the seller all of its requirements of the relevant goods or services. Varilease Technology Group, Inc. v. U.S., 289 F.3d 795 (Fed. Cir. 2002). Sales ☞71(3); Sales ☞71(4)

Contract under which computer maintenance firm was to provide maintenance for certain computers owned by federal agency was an "indefinite delivery, indefinite quantity contract," or ID/IQ contract, rather than a "requirements contract," regardless of expectations of firm, where plain language of contract clearly, repeatedly, and unequivocally identified it as an ID/IQ contract, rather than a requirements contract, and contract had no language, express or implied, obligating the government to purchase its entire requirements for computer maintenance from firm, but did set forth the essentials of an ID/IQ contract. Varilease Technology Group, Inc. v. U.S., 289 F.3d 795 (Fed. Cir. 2002). United States ☞70(6.1)

Contract under which computer maintenance firm was to provide maintenance for certain computers owned by federal agency, which expressly indicated that it was an indefinite delivery, indefinite quantity contract, or ID/IQ contract, and established an initial six-month base period, followed by four 12-month options periods and one six-month option period, did not result in formation of a series of separate and distinct requirements contracts, even though option periods did not have a separate minimum quantity of services that would be required. 48 C.F.R. § 16.504(b). Varilease Technology Group, Inc. v. U.S., 289 F.3d 795 (Fed. Cir. 2002). United States ☞70(6.1)

Where company's contract to provide pest control services for Department of Housing and Urban Development (HUD) was neither requirements contract nor enforceable indefinite quantity contract, company was entitled to payment only for services actually ordered by HUD and provided by company. Coyle's Pest Control, Inc. v. Cuomo, 154 F.3d 1302, 42 Cont. Cas. Fed. (CCH) P 77373 (Fed. Cir. 1998). United States ☞70(19)

Government contract satisfied requirements for enforceable indefinite delivery, indefinite quantity (ID/IQ) contract, including that contract require order of stated minimum quantity of supplies or services and that such minimum quantity be more than nominal amount, when contract set minimum amount for award of $100,000 in base year of contract and provided that exercise of option would not reestablish contract minimum. International Data Products Corp. v. U.S., 64 Fed. Cl. 642 (2005). United States ☞70(6.1)

With regard to whether a government contract is an indefinite quantity contract or a requirements contract, an indefinite quantity contract differs from a requirements contract in that under a requirements contract the government agrees to purchase all his requirements from the contractor; under an indefinite quantities contract, even if the government has requirements, it is not obligated to purchase from the contractor. Myers Investigative and Security Services, Inc. v. U.S., 47 Fed. Cl. 605 (2000), aff'd, 275 F.3d 1366 (Fed. Cir. 2002). United States ☞70(9)

Estimated quantities are not guarantees or warranties of quantity under requirements contract, and significant variance between estimated quantities and actual purchases under government contract does not, in itself, give rise to liability on part of government. 48 C.F.R. § 16.503(a)(1). Datalect Computer Services, Ltd. v. U.S., 40 Fed. Cl. 28, 42 Cont. Cas. Fed. (CCH) P 77243 (1997), aff'd in part, vacated in part on other grounds, 215 F.3d 1344 (Fed. Cir. 1999). United States ☞70(30)

Service contract to maintain hardwood floors and paint interior walls of military family housing was an indefinite quantity contract, rather than a requirements contract, and thus, government fulfilled its obligations under contract when it exceeded the minimum quantity by 11 times the stated minimum, where contract clause stated it was an indefinite quantity contract for supplies or services specified and that government was required to order at least the quantity of supplies or services designated in schedule minimum, and an amendment to the contract specifically deleted requirements contracts clause from the agreement. 48 C.F.R. § 52.216-22. Rice Lake Contracting, Inc. v. U.S., 33 Fed. Cl. 144, 40 Cont. Cas. Fed. (CCH) P 76773 (1995). United States ☞70(6.1)

Principle that patent ambiguities place on contractor duty to inquire did not apply to dispute as to whether parties had entered a requirements contract or a contract for indefinite quantities. Crown Laundry and Dry Cleaners, Inc. v. U.S., 29 Fed. Cl. 506, 39 Cont. Cas. Fed. (CCH) P 76575 (1993). United States ☞70(30)

Contract for laundry and dry cleaning services was a requirements contract, even though it was labeled an indefinite quantities contract, where government intended to have all of its dry cleaning and laundry needs for arsenal serviced by the contract, contract provided that the government could arrange for services to be performed by another contractor if the contractor failed to perform any services covered by the contract, and the contract terms, read together were more consistent if taken as expression of requirements contract than as indefinite quantities contract. Crown Laundry and Dry Cleaners, Inc. v. U.S., 29 Fed. Cl. 506, 39 Cont. Cas. Fed. (CCH) P 76575 (1993). United States ☞70(6.1)

Presence of requirements clause in contract does not preclude court from determining that contract is an indefinite quantities contract, and absence of requirements clause does not inhibit the court from deeming the contract to be a requirements contract. Crown Laundry and Dry Cleaners, Inc. v. U.S., 29 Fed. Cl. 506, 39 Cont. Cas. Fed. (CCH) P 76575 (1993). Contracts ☞71(4)

In determining whether contract with United States is for a definite quantity, for an indefinite quantity, or for requirements, court is not bound by the name or label given to the contract, interpretation which gives meaning to all parts of the contract is preferable to one which renders provisions of the contract meaningless or superfluous, and it will be assumed that the parties intended to form a binding contract, so the court will favor interpretation which saves the contract instead of voiding it. Crown Laundry and Dry Cleaners, Inc. v. U.S., 29 Fed. Cl. 506, 39 Cont. Cas. Fed. (CCH) P 76575 (1993). United States ⚭70(6.1); United States ⚭70(9)

Because contract language could be interpreted to support finding that it was an indefinite quantity contract or finding that it was a requirements contract, intentions of the parties would be examined to determine what the parties really meant. Crown Laundry and Dry Cleaners, Inc. v. U.S., 29 Fed. Cl. 506, 39 Cont. Cas. Fed. (CCH) P 76575 (1993). Sales ⚭71(4)

For purpose of determining whether low bidder was entitled to enjoin Government's cancellation of solicitation for bids for providing unarmed guard services, even if solicitation could be characterized as unclear as to whether it was indefinite quantity contract or fixed-price contract subject to options, no bidder was confused about requirements of solicitation, as amended, that contract would be indefinite quantity contract. Vanguard Sec. Inc. v. U.S., 20 Cl. Ct. 90, 1990 WL 38036 (1990). United States ⚭64.60(5.1)

7 Accord and satisfaction

Economic duress did not void otherwise valid accord and satisfaction which settled dispute between contractor and government over price of asbestos encapsulation services, based on contractor's allegations that government withheld payments due, and threatened to hire other contractors for future work; contractor offered no evidence of withheld payments, and after ordering the contract minimum, the government had no further obligations to issue any more delivery orders to contractor under indefinite delivery, indefinite quantity (ID/IQ) contract. Abatement Contracting Corp. v. U.S., 58 Fed. Cl. 594 (2003). Accord And Satisfaction ⚭20

8 Task or delivery order contracts

Federal Acquisition Streamlining Act (FASA) which prohibits protests "in connection with the issuance or proposed issuance of a task or delivery order" except under certain circumstances did not bar protest of award of blanket purchase agreement (BPA), as task order restriction does not apply to Federal Supply Schedule (FSS) procurements. Federal Property and Administrative Services Act of 1949, § 303j(d), as amended, 41 U.S.C.A. § 253j(d); 48 C.F.R. § 8.404(b)(4). Labat-Anderson Inc. v. U.S., 50 Fed. Cl. 99 (2001). United States ⚭64.60(1)

Where an agency engages in a more comprehensive selection process than contemplated by the Federal Supply Schedule (FSS) scheme, a frustrated bidder may still challenge the agency award under the arbitrary and capricious standard, notwithstanding section of the Federal Acquisition Streamlining Act (FASA) which prohibits protests "in connection with the issuance or proposed issuance of a task or delivery order." 5 U.S.C.A. § 706(2)(A); Federal Property and Administrative Services Act of 1949, § 303j(d), as amended, 41 U.S.C.A. § 253j(d). Labat-Anderson Inc. v. U.S., 50 Fed. Cl. 99 (2001). United States ⚭64.60(4)

9 Injunctions

For purpose of determining whether low bidder was entitled to enjoin Government's cancellation of solicitation for bids for providing unarmed guard services, insofar as amendment to solicitation attempted to convert indefinite quantity contract into fixed-price contract subject to options, amendment failed to displace contract provisions inherent in an indefinite contract. Vanguard Sec. Inc. v. U.S., 20 Cl. Ct. 90, 1990 WL 38036 (1990). United States ⚭64.60(5.1)

10 Court of Federal Claims jurisdiction

Federal question subject matter jurisdiction existed over computer software manufacturer's action alleging that United States Department of Labor's (DOL) decision to standardize its software applications exclusively to software manufactured by competitor violated Administrative Procedure Act (APA) and Competition in Contracting Act (CICA), even if Federal Acquisition Streamlining Act (FASA) precluded review of DOL's issuance of delivery order issued under indefinite-delivery, indefinite-quantity contract pursuant to decision, where manufacturer's protest challenged DOL's overarching administrative decision to standardize to competitor's product, not issuance of individual delivery order. 5 U.S.C.A. § 701 et seq.; 10 U.S.C.A. § 2304; 28 U.S.C.A. § 1331; Federal Property and Administrative Services Act of 1949, §§ 303, 303J(a)(2), as amended, 41 U.S.C.A. §§ 253, 253j(a)(2); 48 C.F.R. §§ 16.501-1, 16.501-2. Corel Corp. v. U.S., 165 F. Supp. 2d 12 (D.D.C. 2001). Federal Courts ⟜232

Court of Federal Claims lacked jurisdiction in government contractor's breach of contract suit to enter declaratory judgment holding indefinite-quantity (IDQ) specifications deficient as a matter of law where they bore no rational relationship to actual requirements within the contracting agency's superior knowledge at the time of solicitation, where such a ruling was not necessary to resolve contractor's claim for money damages. Schweiger Const. Co., Inc. v. U.S., 49 Fed. Cl. 188 (2001). Federal Courts ⟜1078

Court of Federal Claims had jurisdiction over government contractor's claim that construction contract was illegal and that government violated provisions of the Federal Acquisition Regulation which address the type of contract to be used for procurement, in that procurement should have led to the award of a cost-reimbursement contract, rather than a firmfixed-price contract. 48 C.F.R. § 16.000. PCL Const. Services, Inc. v. U.S., 41 Fed. Cl. 242, 42 Cont. Cas. Fed. (CCH) P 77325 (1998), aff'd, 96 Fed. Appx. 672 (Fed. Cir. 2004). Federal Courts ⟜1076

Court lacked jurisdiction to consider merits of government contractor's claim arising out of defense industrial supply center's removal of contractor's name from its automated procurement system; contractor failed to establish that it received sufficient benefit from participating in program to provide consideration to transform basic agreement with center into enforceable contract. Almar Industries, Inc. v. U.S., 16 Cl. Ct. 243, 35 Cont. Cas. Fed. (CCH) P 75621, 1989 WL 6470 (1989). Federal Courts ⟜1076

11 Questions of law or fact

Whether a government contract is an indefinite quantity or a requirements contract is a matter of law for the Court of Federal Claims to decide. Myers Investigative and Security Services, Inc. v. U.S., 47 Fed. Cl. 605 (2000), aff'd, 275 F.3d 1366 (Fed. Cir. 2002). United States ⟜70(9)

12 Summary judgment

Where question of whether contract was for requirements or indefinite quantities did not involve any factual disputes material to interpretation of the contract, summary judgment could be used to resolve the question. RCFC, Rule 56(c, d), 28 U.S.C.A.Crown Laundry and Dry Cleaners, Inc. v. U.S., 29 Fed. Cl. 506, 39 Cont. Cas. Fed. (CCH) P 76575 (1993). Federal Courts ⟜1120

13 Multiple award preference

General Services Administration's (GSA) award of only one indefinite-delivery, indefinite-quantity (IDIQ) contract to provide travel management services for federal civilian agencies did not satisfy procurement law, permitting award of single IDIQ contract exceeding $103M if only one source was qualified and capable of performing work at reasonable price, where GSA failed to determine that disappointed bidder was not qualified and capable of performing work or had unreasonable price, and instead impermissibly relied on best value tradeoff to award contract to single offeror determined to be technically superior and priced lower than disappointed bidder that was assigned only marginal rating for proposal that did not meet government requirements necessary for acceptable contract performance, even though issues were correctable. CW Gov't Travel, Inc. v. U.S., 110 Fed.Cl. 462 (Fed. Cl. 2013)

When an agency does not implement the FAR's preference for making multiple awards under an Indefinite Delivery/Indefinite Quantity (ID/IQ) contract, the FAR plainly contemplates that the CO's determination to make a single award, whether set forth in the acquisition plan, in a class determination made under FAR subpart 1.7, or in a separate document, will precede and form the basis of an agency decision to override the preference for multiple awards. WinStar Communications, Inc. v. U.S., 41 Fed. Cl. 748, 42 Cont. Cas. Fed. (CCH) ¶ 77371 (1998)

Decision of contracting officer (CO) to award a single indefinite delivery/indefinite quantity contract under a single solicitation, rather than multiple contracts, was arbitrary, capricious, and not in accordance with the legal preference for multiple awards, where the CO's analysis failed to address and weigh the benefits of awarding multiple contracts as required by the Federal Acquisition Regulation. WinStar Communications, Inc. v. U.S., 41 Fed. Cl. 748, 42 Cont. Cas. Fed. (CCH) ¶ 77371 (1998)

14 Minimum quantity

Although a contract contained FAR clauses appropriate for an indefinite quantity contract, it was not a valid indefinite quantity contract because it lacked the stated minimum and maximum quantities that the agency promised to order, the Civilian Board of Contract Appeals has held. The CBCA said that the contract was binding only to the extent performed, and rejected the contractor's assertion that it was entitled to compensation for the entire quantity of services listed in the schedule, including services the contractor had not provided. Carrington Group v. Dep't of Veterans Affairs, CBCA 2091, 12-1 BCA ¶ 34993 (U.S. Civilian BCA 2012)

The Federal Circuit held that the general rule regarding recovery when the Government fails to order the minimum quantity under an IDIQ contract is that the amount of damages shall place the contractor in as good a position as it would have been in, had the Government fully performed its obligation. The contractor is generally entitled only to lost profits on the unordered minimum quantity (or the amount of lost profits on the entire minimum quantity if no orders were placed). White v. Delta Contr. Int'l., Inc., 285 F.3d 1040, 43 (Fed. Cir. 2002)

A contracting agency may exercise its discretion in setting stated minimums in an indefinite delivery/indefinite quantity (ID/IQ) government contract provided that the estimates are established in good faith or are based upon the best information available and accurately represent the agency's anticipated needs. Contracting agency's discretion in setting minimum quantities in an indefinite delivery/indefinite quantity (ID/IQ) government contract is not unlimited; thus, a minimum is not acceptable in a situation where the agency has simply declined to try to establish a more exact level. ABF Freight System, Inc. v. U.S., 55 Fed. Cl. 392 (2003). United States ⚯64.30

Under a solicitation that provides for the award of multiple indefinite-delivery, indefinite-quantity contracts for freight transportation services, protest that the minimum order quantity is inadequate is denied, where the guaranteed minimum amount is sufficient to support a binding contract and reflects the minimum amount the agency is fairly certain to order from each contractor. ABF Freight System, Inc.; Old Dominion Freight Line, Inc.; Overnite Transportation Co.; Roadway Express, Inc.; and Yellow Freight System, Inc., B-291185, 2002 CPD ¶ 201 (Comp. Gen. 2002)

15 Cost or Price Evaluation

Cost or price to the government must be included in every RFP as an evaluation factor, and agencies must consider cost or price to the government in evaluating competitive proposals. This requirement applies when awarding IDIQ contracts, even though the evaluation of cost or price often is difficult because of uncertainty regarding what ultimately will be procured. Protest to solicitation was sustained because the solicitation did not require offerors to propose cost-reimbursable labor rates for each labor category or contemplate the evaluation of any such rates for purposes of award. Further, the statutory requirement for considering cost to the government when evaluating and selecting proposals for award cannot be not satisfied by the promise to later consider cost or price when awarding individual task orders. CACI, Inc.-Federal; Booz Allen Hamilton, Inc., B-413028, et al, 2016 WL 4582380 (Comp.Gen. 2016)

GSA awarded 60 IDIQ contracts to offerors that were the "highest technically rated with a fair and reasonable price" without conducting a tradeoff of price and non-price factors. The protester alleged that this evaluation method violated the requirement to evaluate price, since the proposed prices of offerors not technically rated in the top 60 were not considered. GAO denied the protest and noted that the "Guiding Principles" in FAR 1.102 authorize agencies to use any acquisition procedure unless prohibited by law or regulation. Although FAR Part 15 describes only two procedures (the tradeoff process and the low price/technically acceptable process), it does not prohibit the approach used by the GSA. Sevatec, Inc., et al., B-413559.3, et al., 2017 CPD ¶ 3 (Comp. Gen. 2017)

§ 16.505 Ordering.

(a) General.

(1) In general, the contracting officer does not synopsize orders under indefinite-delivery contracts; except see 16.505(a)(4) and (11), and 16.505(b)(2)(ii)(D).

(2) Individual orders shall clearly describe all services to be performed or supplies to be delivered so the full cost or price for the performance of the work can be established when the order is placed. Orders shall be within the scope, issued within the period of performance, and be within the maximum value of the contract.

(3) Performance-based acquisition methods must be used to the maximum extent practicable, if the contract or order is for services (see 37.102(a) and Subpart 37.6).

(4) The following requirements apply when procuring items peculiar to one manufacturer:

(i) The contracting officer must justify restricting consideration to an item peculiar to one manufacturer (e.g., a particular brand-name, product, or a feature of a product that is peculiar to one manufacturer). A brand-name item, even if available on more than one contract, is an item peculiar to one manufacturer. Brand-name specifications shall not be used unless the particular brand-name, product, or feature is essential to the Government's requirements and market research indicates other companies' similar products, or products lacking the particular feature, do not meet, or cannot be modified to meet, the agency's needs.

(ii) Requirements for use of items peculiar to one manufacturer shall be justified and approved using the format(s) and requirements from paragraphs (b)(2)(ii)(A), (B), and (C) of this section, modified to show the brand-name justification. A justification is required unless a justification covering the requirements in the order was previously approved for the contract in accordance with 6.302-1(c) or unless the base contract is a single-award contract awarded under full and open competition. Justifications for the use of brand-name specifications must be completed and approved at the time the requirement for a brand-name is determined.

(iii) (A) For an order in excess of $30,000, the contracting officer shall—

(1) Post the justification and supporting documentation on the agency website used (if any) to solicit offers for orders under the contract; or

(2) Provide the justification and supporting documentation along with the solicitation to all contract awardees.

(B) The justifications for brand-name acquisitions may apply to the portion of the acquisition requiring the brand-name item. If the justification is to cover only the portion of the acquisition which is brand-name, then it should so state; the approval level requirements will then only apply to that portion.

(C) The requirements in paragraph (a)(4)(iii)(A) of this section do not apply when disclosure would compromise the national security (e.g., would result in disclosure of classified information) or create other security risks.

(D) The justification is subject to the screening requirement in paragraph (b)(2)(ii)(D)(4) of this section.

(5) When acquiring information technology and related services, consider the use of modular contracting to reduce program risk (see 39.103(a)).

(6) Orders may be placed by using any medium specified in the contract.

(7) Orders placed under indefinite-delivery contracts must contain the following information:

(i) Date of order.

(ii) Contract number and order number.

(iii) For supplies and services, contract item number and description, quantity, and unit price or estimated cost or fee.

(iv) Delivery or performance schedule.

(v) Place of delivery or performance (including consignee).

(vi) Any packaging, packing, and shipping instructions.

(vii) Accounting and appropriation data.

(viii) Method of payment and payment office, if not specified in the contract (see 32.1110(e)).

(8) Orders placed under a task-order contract or delivery-order contract awarded by another agency (i.e., a Governmentwide acquisition contract, or multi-agency contract)—

(i) Are not exempt from the development of acquisition plans (see Subpart 7.1), and an information technology acquisition strategy (see Part 39);

(ii) May not be used to circumvent conditions and limitations imposed on the use of funds (e.g., 31 U.S.C. 1501(a)(1)); and

(iii) Must comply with all FAR requirements for a bundled contract when the order meets the definition of "bundled contract" (see 2.101(b)).

(9) In accordance with section 1427(b) of Public Law 108-136 (40 U.S.C. 1103 note), orders placed under multi-agency contracts for services that substantially or to a dominant extent specify performance of architect-engineer services, as defined in 2.101, shall—

(i) Be awarded using the procedures at Subpart 36.6; and

(ii) Require the direct supervision of a professional architect or engineer licensed, registered or certified in the State, Federal District, or outlying area, in which the services are to be performed.

(10)

(i) No protest under Subpart 33.1 is authorized in connection with the issuance or proposed issuance of an order under a task-order contract or delivery-order contract, except for—

(A) A protest on the grounds that the order increases the scope, period, or maximum value of the contract; or

(B) A protest of an order valued in excess of $10 million. Protests of orders in excess of $10 million may only be filed with the Government Accountability Office, in accordance with the procedures at 33.104.

(ii) The authority to protest the placement of an order under (a)(10)(i)(B) of this section expires on September 30, 2016, for agencies other than DoD, NASA, and the Coast Guard (41 U.S.C. 4103(d) and 41 U.S.C. 4106(f)). The authority to protest the placement of an order under (a)(10)(i)(B) of this section does not expire for DoD, NASA, and the Coast Guard.

(11) Publicize orders funded in whole or in part by the American Recovery and Reinvestment Act of 2009 (Pub. L. 111-5) as follows:

(i) Notices of proposed orders shall follow the procedures in 5.704 for posting orders.

(ii) Award notices for orders shall follow the procedures in 5.705.

(12) When using the Governmentwide commercial purchase card as a method of payment, orders at or below the micro-purchase threshold are exempt from verification in the System for Award Management database as to whether the contractor has a delinquent debt subject to collection under the Treasury Offset Program (TOP).

(b) Orders under multiple-award contracts—

(1) Fair opportunity.

(i) The contracting officer must provide each awardee a fair opportunity to be considered for each order exceeding $3,500 issued under multiple delivery-order contracts or multiple task-order contracts, except as provided for in paragraph (b)(2) of this section.

(ii) The contracting officer may exercise broad discretion in developing appropriate order placement procedures. The contracting officer should keep submission requirements to a minimum. Contracting officers may use streamlined procedures, including oral presentations. If the order does not exceed the simplified acquisition threshold, the contracting officer need not contact each of the multiple awardees under the contract before selecting an order awardee if the contracting officer has information available to ensure that each awardee is provided a fair opportunity to be considered for each order. The competition requirements in Part 6 and the policies in Subpart 15.3 do not apply to the ordering process. However, the contracting officer must—

(A) Develop placement procedures that will provide each awardee a fair opportunity to be considered for each order and that reflect the requirement and other aspects of the contracting environment;

(B) Not use any method (such as allocation or designation of any preferred awardee) that would not result in fair consideration being given to all awardees prior to placing each order;

(C) Tailor the procedures to each acquisition;

(D) Include the procedures in the solicitation and the contract; and

(E) Consider price or cost under each order as one of the factors in the selection decision.

(iii) *Orders exceeding the simplified acquisition threshold.*

(A) Each order exceeding the simplified acquisition threshold shall be placed on a competitive basis in accordance with paragraph (b)(1)(iii)(B) of this section, unless supported by a written determination that one of the circumstances described at 16.505(b)(2)(i) applies to the order and the requirement is waived on the basis of a justification that is prepared in accordance with 16.505(b)(2)(ii)(B);

(B) The contracting officer shall—

(1) Provide a fair notice of the intent to make a purchase, including a clear description of the supplies to be delivered or the services to be performed and the basis upon which the selection will be made to all contractors offering the required supplies or services under the multiple-award contract; and

(2) Afford all contractors responding to the notice a fair opportunity to submit an offer and have that offer fairly considered.

(iv) *Orders exceeding $5.5 million.* For task or delivery orders in excess of $5.5 million, the requirement to provide all awardees a fair opportunity to be considered for each order shall include, at a minimum—

(A) A notice of the task or delivery order that includes a clear statement of the agency's requirements;

(B) A reasonable response period;

(C) Disclosure of the significant factors and subfactors, including cost or price, that the agency expects to consider in evaluating proposals, and their relative importance;

(D) Where award is made on a best value basis, a written statement documenting the basis for award and the relative importance of quality and price or cost factors; and

(E) An opportunity for a postaward debriefing in accordance with paragraph (b)(6) of this section.

(v) The contracting officer should consider the following when developing the procedures:

(A)

(1) Past performance on earlier orders under the contract, including quality, timeliness and cost control.

(2) Potential impact on other orders placed with the contractor.

(3) Minimum order requirements.

(4) The amount of time contractors need to make informed business decisions on whether to respond to potential orders.

(5) Whether contractors could be encouraged to respond to potential orders by outreach efforts to promote exchanges of information, such as—

(i) Seeking comments from two or more contractors on draft statements of work;

(ii) Using a multiphased approach when effort required to respond to a potential order may be resource intensive (e.g., requirements are complex or need continued development), where all contractors are initially considered on price considerations (e.g., rough estimates), and other considerations as appropriate (e.g., proposed conceptual approach, past performance). The contractors most likely to submit the highest value solutions are then selected for one-on-one sessions with the Government to increase their understanding of the requirements, provide suggestions for refining requirements, and discuss risk reduction measures.

(B) Formal evaluation plans or scoring of quotes or offers are not required.

(2) *Exceptions to the fair opportunity process.*

(i) The contracting officer shall give every awardee a fair opportunity to be considered for a delivery-order or task-order exceeding $3,500 unless one of the following statutory exceptions applies:

(A) The agency need for the supplies or services is so urgent that providing a fair opportunity would result in unacceptable delays.

(B) Only one awardee is capable of providing the supplies or services required at the level of quality required because the supplies or services ordered are unique or highly specialized.

(C) The order must be issued on a sole-source basis in the interest of economy and efficiency because it is a logical follow-on to an order already issued under the contract, provided that all awardees were given a fair opportunity to be considered for the original order.

(D) It is necessary to place an order to satisfy a minimum guarantee.

(E) For orders exceeding the simplified acquisition threshold, a statute expressly authorizes or requires that the purchase be made from a specified source.

(F) In accordance with section 1331 of Public Law 111-240 (15 U.S.C. 644(r)), contracting officers may, at their discretion, set aside orders for any of the small business concerns identified in 19.000(a)(3). When setting aside orders for small business concerns, the specific small business program eligibility requirements identified in part 19 apply.

(ii) The justification for an exception to fair opportunity shall be in writing as specified in paragraphs (b)(2)(ii)(A) or (B) of this section. No justification is needed for the exception described in paragraph (b)(2)(i)(F) of this section.

(A) Orders exceeding $3,500, but not exceeding the simplified acquisition threshold. The contracting officer shall document the basis for using an exception to the fair opportunity process. If the contracting officer uses the logical follow-on exception, the rationale shall describe why the relationship between the initial order and the follow-on is logical (e.g., in terms of scope, period of performance, or value).

(B) Orders exceeding the simplified acquisition threshold. As a minimum, each justification shall include the following information and be approved in accordance with paragraph (b)(2)(ii)(C) of this section:

(1) Identification of the agency and the contracting activity, and specific identification of the document as a "Justification for an Exception to Fair Opportunity."

(2) Nature and/or description of the action being approved.

(3) A description of the supplies or services required to meet the agency's needs (including the estimated value).

(4) Identification of the exception to fair opportunity (see 16.505(b)(2)) and the supporting rationale, including a demonstration that the proposed contractor's unique qualifications or the nature of the acquisition requires use of the exception cited. If the contracting officer uses the logical follow-on exception, the rationale shall describe why the relationship between the initial order and the follow-on is logical (e.g., in terms of scope, period of performance, or value).

(5) A determination by the contracting officer that the anticipated cost to the Government will be fair and reasonable.

(6) Any other facts supporting the justification.

(7) A statement of the actions, if any, the agency may take to remove or overcome any barriers that led to the exception to fair opportunity before any subsequent acquisition for the supplies or services is made.

(8) The contracting officer's certification that the justification is accurate and complete to the best of the contracting officer's knowledge and belief.

(9) Evidence that any supporting data that is the responsibility of technical or requirements personnel (e.g., verifying the Government's minimum needs or requirements or other rationale for an exception to fair opportunity) and which form a basis for the justification have been certified as complete and accurate by the technical or requirements personnel.

(10) A written determination by the approving official that one of the circum-

stances in (b)(2)(i)(A) through (E) of this section applies to the order.

(C) Approval.

(1) For proposed orders exceeding the simplified acquisition threshold, but not exceeding $700,000, the ordering activity contracting officer's certification that the justification is accurate and complete to the best of the ordering activity contracting officer's knowledge and belief will serve as approval, unless a higher approval level is established in accordance with agency procedures.

(2) For a proposed order exceeding $700,000, but not exceeding $13.5 million, the justification must be approved by the advocate for competition of the activity placing the order, or by an official named in paragraph (b)(2)(ii)(C)(3) or (4) of this section. This authority is not delegable.

(3) For a proposed order exceeding $13.5 million, but not exceeding $68 million (or, for DoD, NASA, and the Coast Guard, not exceeding $93 million), the justification must be approved by—

(i) The head of the procuring activity placing the order;

(ii) A designee who—

(A) If a member of the armed forces, is a general or flag officer;

(B) If a civilian, is serving in a position in a grade above GS-15 under the General Schedule (or in a comparable or higher position under another schedule); or

(iii) An official named in paragraph (b)(2)(ii)(C)(4) of this section.

(4) For a proposed order exceeding $68 million (or, for DoD, NASA, and the Coast Guard, over $93 million), the justification must be approved by the senior procurement executive of the agency placing the order. This authority is not delegable, except in the case of the Under Secretary of Defense for Acquisition, Technology, and Logistics, acting as the senior procurement executive for the Department of Defense.

(D) Posting.

(1) Except as provided in paragraph (b)(2)(ii)(D)(5) of this section, within 14 days after placing an order exceeding the simplified acquisition threshold that does not provide for fair opportunity in accordance with 16.505(b), the contract officer shall—

(i) Publish a notice in accordance with 5.301; and

(ii) Make publicly available the justification required at (b)(2)(ii)(B) of this section.

(2) The justification shall be made publicly available—

(i) At the GPE www.fedbizopps.gov;

(ii) On the Web site of the agency, which may provide access to the justifications by linking to the GPE; and

(iii) Must remain posted for a minimum of 30 days.

(3) In the case of an order permitted under paragraph (b)(2)(i)(A) of this subsection, the justification shall be posted within 30 days after award of the order.

(4) Contracting officers shall carefully screen all justifications for contractor proprietary data and remove all such data, and such references and citations as are necessary to protect the proprietary data, before making the justifications available for public inspection. Contracting officers shall also be guided by the exemptions to disclosure of information contained in the Freedom of Information Act (5 U.S.C. 552) and the prohibitions against disclosure in 24.202 in determining whether other data should be removed. Although the submitter notice process set out in Executive Order 12600 "Predisclosure Notification Procedures for Confidential Commercial Information" does not apply, if the justification appears to contain proprietary data, the contracting officer should provide the contractor that submitted the information an opportunity to review the justification for proprietary data before making the justification available for public inspection, redacted as necessary. This process must not prevent or delay the posting of the justification in accordance with the timeframes required in paragraphs (1) and

(3).

(5) The posting requirement of this section does not apply—

(i) When disclosure would compromise the national security (e.g., would result in disclosure of classified information) or create other security risks; or

(ii) To a small business set-aside under paragraph (b)(2)(i)(F).

(3) Pricing orders. If the contract did not establish the price for the supply or service, the contracting officer must establish prices for each order using the policies and methods in Subpart 15.4.

(4) For additional requirements for cost reimbursement orders see 16.301-3.

(5) For additional requirements for time-and-materials or labor-hour orders, see 16.601(e).

(6) Postaward Notices and Debriefing of Awardees for Orders Exceeding $5.5 million. The contracting officer shall notify unsuccessful awardees when the total price of a task or delivery order exceeds $5.5 million.

(i) The procedures at 15.503(b)(1) shall be followed when providing postaward notification to unsuccessful awardees.

(ii) The procedures at 15.506 shall be followed when providing postaward debriefing to unsuccessful awardees.

(iii) A summary of the debriefing shall be included in the task or delivery order file.

(7) Decision documentation for orders.

(i) The contracting officer shall document in the contract file the rationale for placement and price of each order, including the basis for award and the rationale for any tradeoffs among cost or price and non-cost considerations in making the award decision. This documentation need not quantify the tradeoffs that led to the decision.

(ii) The contract file shall also identify the basis for using an exception to the fair opportunity process (see paragraph (b)(2))

(8) Task-order and delivery-order ombudsman. The head of the agency shall designate a task-order and delivery-order ombudsman. The ombudsman must review complaints from contractors and ensure they are afforded a fair opportunity to be considered, consistent with the procedures in the contract. The ombudsman must be a senior agency official who is independent of the contracting officer and may be the agency's advocate for competition.

(c) Limitation on ordering period for task-order contracts for advisory and assistance services.

(1) Except as provided for in paragraphs (c)(2) and (c)(3), the ordering period of a task-order contract for advisory and assistance services, including all options or modifications, normally may not exceed 5 years.

(2) The 5-year limitation does not apply when—

(i) A longer ordering period is specifically authorized by a statute; or

(ii) The contract is for an acquisition of supplies or services that includes the acquisition of advisory and assistance services and the contracting officer, or other official designated by the head of the agency, determines that the advisory and assistance services are incidental and not a significant component of the contract.

(3) The contracting officer may extend the contract on a sole-source basis only once for a period not to exceed 6 months if the contracting officer, or other official designated by the head of the agency, determines that—

(i) The award of a follow-on contract is delayed by circumstances that were not reasonably foreseeable at the time the initial contract was entered into; and

(ii) The extension is necessary to ensure continuity of services, pending the award of the follow-on contract.

United States Code Annotated

Contract requirements, see 41 USCA § 254.

Contracts, planning, solicitation, evaluation, and award procedures, see 10 USCA § 2305.

Cost-type research and development contracts with educational institutions, see 41 USCA § 254a.

Definitions, see 10 USCA § 2302, 41 USCA §§ 259, 403.

Kinds of contracts, see 10 USCA § 2306.

Planning and solicitation requirements, see 41 USCA § 253a.

Task and delivery order contracts, definitions, see 10 USCA § 2304d, 41 USCA § 253k.

Task and delivery order contracts, general authority, see 10 USCA § 2304a, 41 USCA § 253h.

Task and delivery order contracts, orders, see 10 USCA § 2304c, 41 USCA § 253j.

Task order contracts, advisory and assistance services, see 10 USCA § 2304b, 41 USCA § 253i.

Notes of Decisions

Competition requirements 1
Fair opportunity 2
Protests 3
Terms and conditions 4

1 Competition requirements

Federal Acquisition Streamlining Act (FASA) permitted Department of Labor (DOL) to issue orders under an indefinite delivery/indefinite quantity (ID/IQ) contract with retailer for purchase of single manufacturer's software products without conducting full and open competition among manufacturers pursuant to Competition in Contracting Act (CICA), as long as DOL conducted full and open competition among retailers when making the ID/IQ awards. Federal Property and Administrative Services Act of 1949, §§ 303, 303J, as amended, 41 U.S.C.A. §§ 253, 253j. Corel Corp. v. U.S., 165 F. Supp. 2d 12 (D.D.C. 2001). United States ☞64.10

Bid protestor did not establish that agency's focus on experience with dredge disposal area maintenance in the context of an indefinite delivery/indefinite quantity (ID/IQ) contract effectively converted the contract into an illegal sole source contract because incumbent contractor was the only qualified small-business contractor in the Small Business Administration geographic region that had experience with dredge disposal area maintenance; actual results of competition in which five eligible offerors submitted proposals that were found to be within the competitive range belied any notion that the solicitation was a disguised sole source procurement. Gulf Group, Inc. v. U.S., 56 Fed. Cl. 391 (2003). United States ☞64.10

2 Fair opportunity

The Government's use of a cost realism analysis of an offeror's estimated costs breached the "fair opportunity to be considered" provision of an indefinite-delivery, indefinite-quantity contract. Use of the cost realism analysis was found to be fundamentally unfair because it was based on Government estimates and not on offerors' estimated hours and costs, and because the request for order proposals (RFOP) gave no notice that such an analysis would be performed. The claimant could recover bid and proposal (B&P) costs, but not lost or anticipatory profits because it did not show that, but for the Government's improper cost realism analysis, it would have received the delivery order. Appeal of L-3 Communications Corp., A.S.B.C.A. No. 54920, 08-1 B.C.A. (CCH) ¶ 33857, 2008 WL 2154902 (Armed Serv. B.C.A. 2008), appeal dismissed, 345 Fed. Appx. 535 (Fed. Cir. 2009)

Protests challenging the agency's issuance of two solicitations, under a multiple-award, indefinite-delivery, indefinite-quantity (IDIQ) contract for the issuance of a single delivery order under each solicitation were sustained because the solicitations contemplated the issuance of what amounted to a single, second-tier IDIQ instrument, under which the agency would place subsequent delivery orders, without providing the other multiple-award IDIQ contract holders a subsequent, fair opportunity to compete for those delivery orders. Harris IT Servs. Corp., B-411699; B-411796, 2015 CPD ¶ 293 (Comp. Gen. 2015)

When conducting a task order competition under FAR 16.505, agencies must provide contract holders with a "fair opportunity" to be considered for task orders. While FAR 16.505 does not establish specific requirements regarding the conduct of discussions under a task order competition, exchanges occurring with contract holders of multiple award contracts in a FAR 16.505 procurement, like other aspects of such a procurement, must be fair. In this regard, discussions, when conducted, must be meaningful, that is, they may not be misleading. CGI Federal Inc., B-403570, 2011 CPD ¶ 32 (Comp. Gen. 2011)

FAR 16.505 requires agencies to provide all awardees a "fair opportunity" to be considered for each order exceeding $3,000 issued under multiple delivery-order contracts or multiple task-order contracts. Where an agency conducts a competition that essentially abandons the multiple-award, fair-consideration scheme envisioned under the Federal Acquisition Streamlining Act in favor of selecting a single contractor for future orders under the ID/IQ contract, GAO has determined that such action constitutes an unauthorized downselection. Doug Boyd Enterprises, LLC, B-298237.2, 2007 CPD ¶ 147 (Comp. Gen. 2007)

3 Protests

Unsuccessful bidder's post-award bid protest alleging that GSA violated various laws by waiving organizational conflict of interest (OCI) after awarding task order fell within scope of Federal Acquisition Streamlining Act's bar on jurisdiction over protests in connection with issuance or proposed issuance of task or delivery order, and thus Court of Federal Claims lacked jurisdiction under Tucker Act over protest, even though unsuccessful bidder alleged violation of agency regulations, where OCI waiver was directly and causally connected to task order's issuance, and unsuccessful bidder sought rescission of task order's issuance. SRA Intern., Inc. v. U.S., 766 F.3d 1409 (Fed. Cir. 2014)

Even in cases in which an IDIQ contract holder is not statutorily authorized to protest an agency's task or delivery order award decision, the contractor could file a CDA claim. The same actions of the Government in awarding a delivery order under a multiple award indefinite quantity contract may be grounds for both a 'protest' seeking to cancel or modify the award and a 'claim' for damages for breach of the Awarding Orders clause of the contract. Appeal of L-3 Communications Corp., A.S.B.C.A. No. 54920, 08-1 B.C.A. (CCH) ¶ 33857, 2008 WL 2154902 (Armed Serv. B.C.A. 2008), appeal dismissed, 345 Fed. Appx. 535 (Fed. Cir. 2009)

The COFC determined that a protester's challenge to an agency's issuance of a non-competitive delivery order was barred by the protest restrictions applicable to Indefinite Delivery/Indefinite Quantity (ID/IQ) contracts, because the protester did not allege that the delivery order exceeded the scope, period or maximum value of the contract on which it was issued, as required by FAR 16.505(a)(9). DataMill, Inc. v. U.S., 91 Fed. Cl. 740 (2010)

A vendor under a multiple award ID/IQ contract may challenge the agency's failure to provide a "fair opportunity" to be considered via the claims process under the Contract Disputes Act, rather than as a protest. The Court of Federal Claims determined that a contractor's complaint asserting that the agency breached its duty to provide a fair opportunity in a task order competition, was in the nature of a breach of contract claim because it was not challenging the issuance or proposed issuance of a task order, but sought monetary damages based on an alleged breach of specific contractual language on ordering provisions in its ID/IQ contract with the government. Digital Technologies, Inc. v. U.S., 89 Fed. Cl. 711 (Fed. Cl. 2009)

The Government's award of a task order did not exceed the scope of the master IDIQ con¬tract. Protester alleged that a task order awarded to another IDIQ contract awardee required work that was beyond the scope of the awardee's original IDIQ contract. The COFC disagreed, finding the master IDIQ contract broad enough in scope to encompass the tasks envisioned in the task orders. Omega World Travel, Inc. v. U.S., 82 Fed. Cl. 452 (2008)

Provision of the Federal Acquisition Streamlining Act (FASA) prohibiting bid protests in connection with issuance of a task order or delivery order does not apply to protests relating to the placement of orders under GSA Federal Supply Schedule (FSS) contracts. 10 U.S.C.A. §§ 2304a, 2304b, 2304c(d). Idea Intern., Inc. v. U.S., 74 Fed. Cl. 129 (2006)

Federal Acquisition Streamlining Act (FASA) which prohibits protests "in connection with the issuance or proposed issuance of a task or delivery order" except under certain circumstances did not bar protest of award of blanket purchase agreement (BPA), as task order restriction does not apply to Federal Supply Schedule (FSS) procurements. Federal Property and Administrative Services Act of 1949, § 303j(d), as amended, 41 U.S.C.A. § 253j(d); 48 C.F.R. § 8.404(b)(4). Labat-Anderson Inc. v. U.S., 50 Fed. Cl. 99 (2001)

Because agency's decision to waive an organizational conflict of interest occurred after the award of a task order, the waiver decision was distinct from the issuance of the task order, and, therefore, the statutory bar on U.S. Court of Federal Claims jurisdiction over task order protests did not apply, and the COFC had jurisdiction over the challenge to the waiver. SRA Int'l, Inc. v. U.S., 2014 WL 171012 (Fed. Cl. Jan. 14, 2014)

GAO did not have jurisdiction to consider protest even though the protester's proposed price was over the $10M jurisdictional threshold, because the task order awarded to the awardee was below $10M. Goldbelt Glacier Health Servs., LLC, B-410378, 2014 CPD ¶ 281 (Comp.Gen. 2014)

GAO lacked jurisdiction to hear protest of task order solicitation where independent government estimate of task order's value, exclusive of the value of option to extend services, is below $10M and solicitation does not provide for evaluation of option to extend services. Edmond Scientific Co., B-410187.2, 2014 CPD ¶ 358 (Comp.Gen. 2014)

To determine whether a task order is beyond a contract's scope, the GAO considers whether there is a material difference between the task order and the contract. Two task order requests for proposals (TORPs) seeking mentoring, training, facilities and logistics support services for Afghanistan's Ministry of the Interior and the Afghan National Police were outside the scope of the counter-narcoterrorism indefinite-delivery, indefinite-quantity contracts, the U.S. Comptroller General recently determined. Decision Matter of: DynCorp International LLC, B-402349, 2010 CPD ¶ 59 (Comp. Gen. 2010).

GAO rejected an agency's argument that GAO's jurisdiction did not extend to a substantive review of the agency's task order award decision under an IDIQ contract. Section 843 of the National Defense Authorization Act for Fiscal Year 2008, P.L. 110-181, granted GAO jurisdiction over "a protest of an order valued in excess of $10,000,000," and requires agencies to provide IDIQ contract holders with specific information to meet the "fair opportunity to be considered" requirement if an order value exceeds $5 million. GAO rejected the agency's argument that contractors could protest an agency's failure to supply information on the bases for task and delivery order competition but could not challenge the merits of the award decision. Matter of: Triple Canopy, Inc., B-310566.4, 2008 CPD ¶ 207 (Comp. Gen. 2008)

The statutory limitation on General Accounting Office bid protest jurisdiction over challenges to the award of a task order under an indefinite-delivery/indefinite-quantity (ID/IQ) contract does not apply where the protester's challenge, although triggered by the issuance of a task order, in essence, raises the question of whether the solicitation for the underlying ID/IQ contract properly could be used to procure services which, the protester argues, must be set aside for small businesses. N&N Travel & Tours, Inc.; BCM Travel & Tours; Manassas Travel, Inc.; Alamo Travel, Inc.; Ravenel Bros., Inc.; and Bay Area Travel, Inc., B-285164.2, B-285164.3, 2000 CPD ¶ 146 (Comp. Gen. 2000)

4 Terms and conditions

Because the contractor previously accepted a series of delivery orders (DOs) issued by e-mail, equitable estoppel precluded the contractor from rejecting later DOs issued by e-mail in contravention of the contract's ordering clause, the U.S. Court of Appeals for the Federal Circuit has held, reversing a decision of the ASBCA. Mabus v. General Dynamics C4 Systems, Inc., 633 F.3d 1356 (Fed. Cir. 2011)

Contractor was not entitled to payment for performing work under an unsigned delivery order because the parties' correspondence showed that the contractor knew that delivery orders were not valid until the contracting officer signed them. The contractor's pre-performance request for a signed delivery order precluded the contractor from claiming that the requirement had been waived and that it detrimentally relied on the waiver, the ASBCA held. Appeal of MACH II, A.S.B.C.A. No. 56630, 10-1 B.C.A. (CCH) ¶ 34357, 2010 WL 292734 (Armed Serv. B.C.A. 2010)

An Indefinite Delivery/Indefinite Quantity (ID/IQ) contract for services contemplates the issuance of orders for the performance of tasks during the period of the contract. Such orders are contracts within the overall ID/IQ contract and are subject to the terms and conditions of that contract. 48 C.F.R. § 52.216-18(b). Sea-Land Service, Inc., B-278404, B-278404.2, 98-1 CPD ¶ 47 (Comp. Gen. 1998)

§ 16.506 Solicitation provisions and contract clauses.
(a) Insert the clause at 52.216-18, Ordering, in solicitations and contracts when a definite-

quantity contract, a requirements contract, or an indefinite-quantity contract is contemplated.

(b) Insert a clause substantially the same as the clause at 52.216-19, Order Limitations, in solicitations and contracts when a definite-quantity contract, a requirements contract, or an indefinite-quantity contract is contemplated.

(c) Insert the clause at 52.216-20, Definite Quantity, in solicitations and contracts when a definite-quantity contract is contemplated.

(d) (1) Insert the clause at 52.216-21, Requirements, in solicitations and contracts when a requirements contract is contemplated.

(2) If the contract is for nonpersonal services and related supplies and covers estimated requirements that exceed a specific Government activity's internal capability to produce or perform, use the clause with its Alternate I.

(3) If the contract includes subsistence for both Government use and resale in the same Schedule, and similar products may be acquired on a brand-name basis, use the clause with its Alternate II (but see paragraph (d)(5) of this section).

(4) If the contract involves a partial small business set-aside, use the clause with its Alternate III (but see paragraph (d)(5) of this section).

(5) If the contract—

(i) Includes subsistence for Government use and resale in the same schedule and similar products may be acquired on a brand-name basis; and

(ii) Involves a partial small business set-aside, use the clause with its Alternate IV.

(e) Insert the clause at 52.216-22, Indefinite Quantity, in solicitations and contracts when an indefinite-quantity contract is contemplated.

(f) Insert the provision at 52.216-27, Single or Multiple Awards, in solicitations for indefinite-quantity contracts that may result in multiple contract awards. Modify the provision to specify the estimated number of awards. Do not use this provision for advisory and assistance services contracts that exceed 3 years and $13.5 million (including all options).

(g) Insert the provision at 52.216-28, Multiple Awards for Advisory and Assistance Services, in solicitations for task-order contracts for advisory and assistance services that exceed 3 years and $13.5 million (including all options), unless a determination has been made under 16.504(c)(2)(i)(A). Modify the provision to specify the estimated number of awards.

(h) See 10.001(d) for insertion of the clause at 52.210-1, Market Research, when the contract is over $5.5 million for the procurement of items other than commercial items.

United States Code Annotated

Contract requirements, see 41 USCA § 254.

Contracts, planning, solicitation, evaluation, and award procedures, see 10 USCA § 2305.

Cost-type research and development contracts with educational institutions, see 41 USCA § 254a.

Definitions, see 10 USCA § 2302, 41 USCA §§ 259, 403.

Kinds of contracts, see 10 USCA § 2306.

Planning and solicitation requirements, see 41 USCA § 253a.

Task and delivery order contracts, definitions, see 10 USCA § 2304d, 41 USCA § 253k.

Task and delivery order contracts, general authority, see 10 USCA § 2304a, 41 USCA § 253h.

Task and delivery order contracts, orders, see 10 USCA § 2304c, 41 USCA § 253j.

Task order contracts, advisory and assistance services, see 10 USCA § 2304b, 41 USCA § 253i.

Subpart 16.6 Time-and-Materials, Labor-Hour, and Letter Contracts

§ 16.600 Scope.

Time-and-materials contracts and labor-hour contracts are not fixed-price contracts.

§ 16.601 Time-and-materials contracts.

(a) Definitions for the purposes of Time-and-Materials Contracts.

"Direct materials" means those materials that enter directly into the end product, or that are used or consumed directly in connection with the furnishing of the end product or service.

"Hourly rate" means the rate(s) prescribed in the contract for payment for labor that meets the labor category qualifications of a labor category specified in the contract that are—

(1) Performed by the contractor;

(2) Performed by the subcontractors; or

(3) Transferred between divisions, subsidiaries, or affiliates of the contractor under a common control.

"Materials" means—

(1) Direct materials, including supplies transferred between divisions, subsidiaries, or affiliates of the contractor under a common control;

(2) Subcontracts for supplies and incidental services for which there is not a labor category specified in the contract;

(3) Other direct costs (*e.g.*, incidental services for which there is not a labor category specified in the contract, travel, computer usage charges, etc.); and

(4) Applicable indirect costs.

(b) *Description*. A time-and-materials contract provides for acquiring supplies or services on the basis of—

(1) Direct labor hours at specified fixed hourly rates that include wages, overhead, general and administrative expenses, and profit; and

(2) Actual cost for materials (except as provided for in 31.205-26(e) and (f)).

(c) *Application*. A time-and-materials contract may be used only when it is not possible at the time of placing the contract to estimate accurately the extent or duration of the work or to anticipate costs with any reasonable degree of confidence. See 12.207(b) for the use of time-and-material contracts for certain commercial services.

(1) *Government surveillance*. A time-and-materials contract provides no positive profit incentive to the contractor for cost control or labor efficiency. Therefore, appropriate Government surveillance of contractor performance is required to give reasonable assurance that efficient methods and effective cost controls are being used.

(2) *Fixed hourly rates*.

(i) The contract shall specify separate fixed hourly rates that include wages, overhead, general and administrative expenses, and profit for each category of labor (see 16.601(f)(1)).

(ii) For acquisitions of noncommercial items awarded without adequate price competition (see 15.403-1(c)(1)), the contract shall specify separate fixed hourly rates that include wages, overhead, general and administrative expenses, and profit for each category of labor to be performed by—

(A) The contractor;

(B) Each subcontractor; and

(C) Each division, subsidiary, or affiliate of the contractor under a common control.

(iii) For contract actions that are not awarded using competitive procedures, unless exempt under paragraph (c)(2)(iv) of this section, the fixed hourly rates for services transferred between divisions, subsidiaries, or affiliates of the contractor under a common control—

(A) Shall not include profit for the transferring organization; but

(B) May include profit for the prime contractor.

(iv) For contract actions that are not awarded using competitive procedures, the fixed hourly rates for services that meet the definition of commercial item at 2.101 that are transferred between divisions, subsidiaries, or affiliates of the contractor under a common control may be the established catalog or market rate when—

(A) It is the established practice of the transferring organization to price interorganizational transfers at other than cost for commercial work of the contractor or any division, subsidiary or affiliate of the contractor under a common control; and

(B) The contracting officer has not determined the price to be unreasonable.

(3) *Material handling costs.* When included as part of material costs, material handling costs shall include only costs clearly excluded from the labor-hour rate. Material handling costs may include all appropriate indirect costs allocated to direct materials in accordance with the contractor's usual accounting procedures consistent with Part 31.

(d) *Limitations.* A time-and-materials contract or order may be used only if—

(1) The contracting officer prepares a determination and findings that no other contract type is suitable. The determination and finding shall be—

(i) Signed by the contracting officer prior to the execution of the base period or any option periods of the contracts; and

(ii) Approved by the head of the contracting activity prior to the execution of the base period when the base period plus any option periods exceeds three years; and

(2) The contract or order includes a ceiling price that the contractor exceeds at its own risk. Also see 12.207(b) for further limitations on use of time-and-materials or labor-hour contracts for acquisition of commercial items.

(e) *Post award requirements.* Prior to an increase in the ceiling price of a time-and-materials or labor-hour contract or order, the contracting officer shall—

(1) Conduct an analysis of pricing and other relevant factors to determine if the action is in the best interest of the Government;

(2) Document the decision in the contract or order file; and

(3) When making a change that modifies the general scope of—

(i) A contract, follow the procedures at 6.303;

(ii) An order issued under the Federal Supply Schedules, follow the procedures at 8.405-6; or

(iii) An order issued under multiple award task and delivery order contracts, follow the procedures at 16.505(b)(2).

(f) *Solicitation provisions.*

(1) The contracting officer shall insert the provision at 52.216-29, Time-and-Materials/Labor-Hour Proposal Requirements—Non-Commercial Item Acquisitions With Adequate Price Competition, in solicitations contemplating use of a Time-and-Materials or Labor-Hour type of contract for noncommercial items, if the price is expected to be based on adequate price competition. If authorized by agency procedures, the contracting officer may amend the provision to make mandatory one of the three approaches in paragraph (c) of the provision, and/or to require the identification of all subcontractors, divisions, subsidiaries, or affiliates included in a blended labor rate.

(2) The contracting officer shall insert the provision at 52.216-30, Time-and-Materials/Labor-Hour Proposal Requirements—Non-Commercial Item Acquisitions without Adequate Price Competition, in solicitations for noncommercial items contemplating use of a Time-and-Materials or Labor-Hour type of contract if the price is not expected to be based on adequate price competition.

(3) The contracting officer shall insert the provision at 52.216-31, Time-and-Materials/Labor-Hour Proposal Requirements—Commercial Item Acquisitions, in solicitations contemplating use of a Commercial Time-and-Materials or Labor-Hour contract.

United States Code Annotated

Contract requirements, see 41 USCA § 254.

Contracts, planning, solicitation, evaluation, and award procedures, see 10 USCA § 2305.

Cost-type research and development contracts with educational institutions, see 41 USCA § 254a.

Definitions, see 10 USCA § 2302, 41 USCA §§ 259, 403.

Kinds of contracts, see 10 USCA § 2306.

Planning and solicitation requirements, see 41 USCA § 253a.

Task and delivery order contracts, definitions, see 10 USCA § 2304d, 41 USCA § 253k.

Task and delivery order contracts, general authority, see 10 USCA § 2304a, 41 USCA

§ 253h.

Task and delivery order contracts, orders, see 10 USCA § 2304c, 41 USCA § 253j.

Task order contracts, advisory and assistance services, see 10 USCA § 2304b, 41 USCA § 253i.

Notes of Decisions

In general 1

1 In general

Under a T&M contract or a labor-hour contract, the government must pay the contractor for hours actually worked by the contractor's employees, regardless of whether the contractor paid the salaried employees for those hours. The ASBCA rejected the government's contention that reference to "actual payment" in the Payments clause (52.232-7) required actual payment of the employees by the contractor. GaN Corp., ASBCA 57834, 2012 WL 2997037 (July 13, 2012)

§ 16.602 Labor-hour contracts.

Description. A labor-hour contract is a variation of the time-and-materials contract, differing only in that materials are not supplied by the contractor. See 12.207(b), 16.601(c), and 16.601(d) for application and limitations, for time-andmaterials contracts that also apply to labor-hour contracts. See 12.207(b) for the use of labor-hour contracts for certain commercial services.

§ 16.603 Letter contracts.

§ 16.603-1 Description.

A letter contract is a written preliminary contractual instrument that authorizes the contractor to begin immediately manufacturing supplies or performing services.

United States Code Annotated

Contract requirements, see 41 USCA § 254.

Contracts, planning, solicitation, evaluation, and award procedures, see 10 USCA § 2305.

Cost-type research and development contracts with educational institutions, see 41 USCA § 254a.

Definitions, see 10 USCA § 2302, 41 USCA §§ 259, 403.

Kinds of contracts, see 10 USCA § 2306.

Planning and solicitation requirements, see 41 USCA § 253a.

Task and delivery order contracts, definitions, see 10 USCA § 2304d, 41 USCA § 253k.

Task and delivery order contracts, general authority, see 10 USCA § 2304a, 41 USCA § 253h.

Task and delivery order contracts, orders, see 10 USCA § 2304c, 41 USCA § 253j.

Task order contracts, advisory and assistance services, see 10 USCA § 2304b, 41 USCA § 253i.

Notes of Decisions

In general 1

1 In general

Contracting agency was under no obligation to terminate letter contract for convenience rather than allow it to lapse, where contract was for an indefinite delivery and indefinite quantity (IDIQ) contract, no task orders were interrupted or terminated by agency by its decision to allow the letter contract to lapse, and agency had paid contractor in excess of the minimum guarantee in the letter contract. J. Cooper & Associates, Inc. v. U.S., 53 Fed. Cl. 8 (2002), aff'd, 65 Fed. Appx. 731 (Fed. Cir. 2003). United States ⬦72.1(1)

Because letter contract to provide support services for agency recruitment campaign was an indefinite delivery and indefinite quantity (IDIQ) contract, government did not breach contract by failing to provide contractor with work in excess of the minimum quantity in the letter contract or by failing to award to contractor all of the work in the government's pre-contract estimate. J. Cooper & Associates, Inc. v. U.S., 53 Fed. Cl. 8 (2002), aff'd, 65 Fed. Appx. 731 (Fed. Cir. 2003). United States ☞73(22)

A "letter contract" is an interim agreement that allows a government contractor to begin performance prior to issuance of a definitized contract. 48 C.F.R. § 16.603-1. Integrated Logistics Support Systems Intern., Inc. v. U.S., 47 Fed. Cl. 248 (2000), aff'd, 36 Fed. Appx. 650 (Fed. Cir. 2002). United States ☞63

Contracting agency's unilateral definitization of contract modification at the $2 million advanced to the contractor was in error, where modification indicated that the money advanced was projected to be less than half of the total amount needed for the contract modification. 48 C.F.R. § 16.603-2. Northrop Grumman Corp. v. U.S., 47 Fed. Cl. 20 (2000). United States ☞72(5)

§ **16.603-2 Application.**

(a) A letter contract may be used when (1) the Government's interests demand that the contractor be given a binding commitment so that work can start immediately and (2) negotiating a definitive contract is not possible in sufficient time to meet the requirement. However, a letter contract should be as complete and definite as feasible under the circumstances.

(b) When a letter contract award is based on price competition, the contracting officer shall include an overall price ceiling in the letter contract.

(c) Each letter contract shall, as required by the clause at 52.216-25, Contract Definitization, contain a negotiated definitization schedule including (1) dates for submission of the contractor's price proposal, required certified cost or pricing data and data other than certified cost or pricing data; and, if required, make-or-buy and subcontracting plans, (2) a date for the start of negotiations, and (3) a target date for definitization, which shall be the earliest practicable date for definitization. The schedule will provide for definitization of the contract within 180 days after the date of the letter contract or before completion of 40 percent of the work to be performed, whichever occurs first. However, the contracting officer may, in extreme cases and according to agency procedures, authorize an additional period. If, after exhausting all reasonable efforts, the contracting officer and the contractor cannot negotiate a definitive contract because of failure to reach agreement as to price or fee, the clause at 52.216-25 requires the contractor to proceed with the work and provides that the contracting officer may, with the approval of the head of the contracting activity, determine a reasonable price or fee in accordance with Subpart 15.4 and Part 31, subject to appeal as provided in the Disputes clause.

(d) The maximum liability of the Government inserted in the clause at 52.216-24, Limitation of Government Liability, shall be the estimated amount necessary to cover the contractor's requirements for funds before definitization. However, it shall not exceed 50 percent of the estimated cost of the definitive contract unless approved in advance by the official that authorized the letter contract.

(e) The contracting officer shall assign a priority rating to the letter contract if it is appropriate under 11.604.

United States Code Annotated

Contract requirements, see 41 USCA § 254.

Contracts, planning, solicitation, evaluation, and award procedures, see 10 USCA § 2305.

Cost-type research and development contracts with educational institutions, see 41 USCA § 254a.

Definitions, see 10 USCA § 2302, 41 USCA §§ 259, 403.

Kinds of contracts, see 10 USCA § 2306.

Planning and solicitation requirements, see 41 USCA § 253a.

Task and delivery order contracts, definitions, see 10 USCA § 2304d, 41 USCA § 253k.

Task and delivery order contracts, general authority, see 10 USCA § 2304a, 41 USCA § 253h.

Task and delivery order contracts, orders, see 10 USCA § 2304c, 41 USCA § 253j.

Task order contracts, advisory and assistance services, see 10 USCA § 2304b, 41 USCA

§ 253i.

Notes of Decisions

In general 1

1 In general

Statement in Air Force's undefinitized contract award for electronic monitors, that failure to meet delivery schedule would result in work stoppage by aircraft manufacturer and additional charges, complied with statute which permits use of undefinitized contracts only when request for authorization includes description of "anticipated effect on requirements of the military department concerned if a delay is incurred." 10 U.S.C.A. § 2326. Mil-Com Electronics Corp. v. Aldridge, 712 F. Supp. 232, 35 Cont. Cas. Fed. (CCH) P 75658 (D.D.C. 1989). United States ☞64.10

A "letter contract" is an interim agreement that allows a government contractor to begin performance prior to issuance of a definitized contract. 48 C.F.R. § 16.603-1. Integrated Logistics Support Systems Intern., Inc. v. U.S., 47 Fed. Cl. 248 (2000), aff'd, 36 Fed. Appx. 650 (Fed. Cir. 2002). United States ☞63

Contracting agency's unilateral definitization of contract modification at the $2 million advanced to the contractor was in error, where modification indicated that the money advanced was projected to be less than half of the total amount needed for the contract modification. 48 C.F.R. § 16.603-2. Northrop Grumman Corp. v. U.S., 47 Fed. Cl. 20 (2000). United States ☞72(5)

§ 16.603-3 Limitations.

A letter contract may be used only after the head of the contracting activity or a designee determines in writing that no other contract is suitable. Letter contracts shall not—

(a) Commit the Government to a definitive contract in excess of the funds available at the time the letter contract is executed;

(b) Be entered into without competition when competition is required by Part 6; or

(c) Be amended to satisfy a new requirement unless that requirement is inseparable from the existing letter contract. Any such amendment is subject to the same requirements and limitations as a new letter contract.

United States Code Annotated

Contract requirements, see 41 USCA § 254.

Contracts, planning, solicitation, evaluation, and award procedures, see 10 USCA § 2305.

Cost-type research and development contracts with educational institutions, see 41 USCA § 254a.

Definitions, see 10 USCA § 2302, 41 USCA §§ 259, 403.

Kinds of contracts, see 10 USCA § 2306.

Planning and solicitation requirements, see 41 USCA § 253a.

Task and delivery order contracts, definitions, see 10 USCA § 2304d, 41 USCA § 253k.

Task and delivery order contracts, general authority, see 10 USCA § 2304a, 41 USCA § 253h.

Task and delivery order contracts, orders, see 10 USCA § 2304c, 41 USCA § 253j.

Task order contracts, advisory and assistance services, see 10 USCA § 2304b, 41 USCA § 253i.

§ 16.603-4 Contract clauses.

(a) The contracting officer shall include in each letter contract the clauses required by this regulation for the type of definitive contract contemplated and any additional clauses known to be appropriate for it.

(b) In addition, the contracting officer shall insert the following clauses in solicitations and contracts when a letter contract is contemplated:

(1) The clause at 52.216-23, Execution and Commencement of Work, except that this

clause may be omitted from letter contracts awarded on SF 26;

(2) The clause at 52.216-24, Limitation of Government Liability, with dollar amounts completed in a manner consistent with 16.603-2(d); and

(3) The clause at 52.216-25, Contract Definitization, with its paragraph (b) completed in a manner consistent with 16.603-2(c). If at the time of entering into the letter contract, the contracting officer knows that the definitive contract will be based on adequate price competition or will otherwise meet the criteria of 15.403-1 for not requiring submission of certified cost or pricing data, the words "and certified cost or pricing data in accordance with FAR 15.408, Table 15-2 supporting its proposal" may be deleted from paragraph (a) of the clause. If the letter contract is being awarded on the basis of price competition, the contracting officer shall use the clause with its Alternate I.

(c) The contracting officer shall also insert the clause at 52.216-26, Payments of Allowable Costs Before Definitization, in solicitations and contracts if a cost-reimbursement definitive contract is contemplated, unless the acquisition involves conversion, alteration, or repair of ships.

United States Code Annotated

Contract requirements, see 41 USCA § 254.

Contracts, planning, solicitation, evaluation, and award procedures, see 10 USCA § 2305.

Cost-type research and development contracts with educational institutions, see 41 USCA § 254a.

Definitions, see 10 USCA § 2302, 41 USCA §§ 259, 403.

Kinds of contracts, see 10 USCA § 2306.

Planning and solicitation requirements, see 41 USCA § 253a.

Task and delivery order contracts, definitions, see 10 USCA § 2304d, 41 USCA § 253k.

Task and delivery order contracts, general authority, see 10 USCA § 2304a, 41 USCA § 253h.

Task and delivery order contracts, orders, see 10 USCA § 2304c, 41 USCA § 253j.

Task order contracts, advisory and assistance services, see 10 USCA § 2304b, 41 USCA § 253i.

Subpart 16.7 Agreements

§ 16.701 Scope.

This subpart prescribes policies and procedures for establishing and using basic agreements and basic ordering agreements. (See 13.303 for blanket purchase agreements (BPA's) and see 35.015(b) for additional coverage of basic agreements with educational institutions and nonprofit organizations.)

United States Code Annotated

Contract requirements, see 41 USCA § 254.

Contracts, planning, solicitation, evaluation, and award procedures, see 10 USCA § 2305.

Cost-type research and development contracts with educational institutions, see 41 USCA § 254a.

Definitions, see 10 USCA § 2302, 41 USCA §§ 259, 403.

Kinds of contracts, see 10 USCA § 2306.

Planning and solicitation requirements, see 41 USCA § 253a.

Task and delivery order contracts, definitions, see 10 USCA § 2304d, 41 USCA § 253k.

Task and delivery order contracts, general authority, see 10 USCA § 2304a, 41 USCA § 253h.

Task and delivery order contracts, orders, see 10 USCA § 2304c, 41 USCA § 253j.

Task order contracts, advisory and assistance services, see 10 USCA § 2304b, 41 USCA § 253i.

Notes of Decisions

In general 1

1 In general

Statement by Postal Service employee, that firm which had entered into Basic Purchasing Agreement with Postal Service covering "moves, adds and changes" to telephones within building would be getting all of Postal Service's business except that which was done in-house, did not contractually commit Postal Service to place orders with firm; employee was not a contracting officer entitled to bind Postal Service. Modern Systems Technology Corp. v. U.S., 979 F.2d 200, 38 Cont. Cas. Fed. (CCH) P 76397 (Fed. Cir. 1992). United States ☞60

Basic Purchasing Agreement between provider of telephone services and Postal Service, providing for "moves, adds and changes" of telephone equipment, was not a requirements contract obligating Postal Service to have all such activities carried on through provider; there was no express contractual commitment to have all of the Postal Service's requirements so satisfied, nor were there any minimum purchase requirements. Modern Systems Technology Corp. v. U.S., 979 F.2d 200, 38 Cont. Cas. Fed. (CCH) P 76397 (Fed. Cir. 1992). United States ☞70(6.1)

Basic Purchasing Agreement with provider of telephone services involving "moves, adds and changes" to telephone configuration in Postal Service building did not create contractual obligation on part of Postal Service to utilize any telephone services; agreement contemplated that parties would enter into binding contracts in future through issuance of individual authorized orders, and merely provided price and other terms and conditions for such future contracts. Modern Systems Technology Corp. v. U.S., 979 F.2d 200, 38 Cont. Cas. Fed. (CCH) P 76397 (Fed. Cir. 1992). United States ☞70(6.1)

Basic pricing agreement entered into by government agency and contractor was not binding contract but merely a framework for future contracts; there was no language in agreement indicating any present intent that either party be bound and terms were not sufficiently definite. Modern Systems Technology Corp. v. U.S., 979 F.2d 200, 38 Cont. Cas. Fed. (CCH) P 76397 (Fed. Cir. 1992). United States ☞70(15.1)

§ 16.702 Basic agreements.

(a) *Description.* A basic agreement is a written instrument of understanding, negotiated between an agency or contracting activity and a contractor, that (1) contains contract clauses applying to future contracts between the parties during its term and (2) contemplates separate future contracts that will incorporate by reference or attachment the required and applicable clauses agreed upon in the basic agreement. A basic agreement is not a contract.

(b) *Application.* A basic agreement should be used when a substantial number of separate contracts may be awarded to a contractor during a particular period and significant recurring negotiating problems have been experienced with the contractor. Basic agreements may be used with negotiated fixed-price or cost-reimbursement contracts.

(1) Basic agreements shall contain—

(i) Clauses required for negotiated contracts by statute, executive order, and this regulation; and

(ii) Other clauses prescribed in this regulation or agency acquisition regulations that the parties agree to include in each contract as applicable.

(2) Each basic agreement shall provide for discontinuing its future applicability upon 30 days' written notice by either party.

(3) Each basic agreement shall be reviewed annually before the anniversary of its effective date and revised as necessary to conform to the requirements of this regulation. Basic agreements may need to be revised before the annual review due to mandatory statutory requirements. A basic agreement may be changed only by modifying the agree-ment itself and not by a contract incorporating the agreement.

(4) Discontinuing or modifying a basic agreement shall not affect any prior contract incorporating the basic agreement.

(5) Contracting officers of one agency should obtain and use existing basic agreements of another agency to the maximum practical extent.

(c) *Limitations.* A basic agreement shall not—

(1) Cite appropriations or obligate funds;

(2) State or imply any agreement by the Government to place future contracts or

orders with the contractor; or

(3) Be used in any manner to restrict competition.

(d) *Contracts incorporating basic agreements.* (1) Each contract incorporating a basic agreement shall include a scope of work and price, delivery, and other appropriate terms that apply to the particular contract. The basic agreement shall be incorporated into the contract by specific reference (including reference to each amendment) or by attachment.

(2) The contracting officer shall include clauses pertaining to subjects not covered by the basic agreement, but applicable to the contract being negotiated, in the same manner as if there were no basic agreement.

(3) If an existing contract is modified to effect new acquisition, the modification shall incorporate the most recent basic agreement, which shall apply only to work added by the modification, except that this action is not mandatory if the contract or modification includes all clauses required by statute, executive order, and this regulation as of the date of the modification. However, if it is in the Government's interest and the contractor agrees, the modification may incorporate the most recent basic agreement for application to the entire contract as of the date of the modification.

United States Code Annotated

Contract requirements, see 41 USCA § 254.

Contracts, planning, solicitation, evaluation, and award procedures, see 10 USCA § 2305.

Cost-type research and development contracts with educational institutions, see 41 USCA § 254a.

Definitions, see 10 USCA § 2302, 41 USCA §§ 259, 403.

Kinds of contracts, see 10 USCA § 2306.

Planning and solicitation requirements, see 41 USCA § 253a.

Task and delivery order contracts, definitions, see 10 USCA § 2304d, 41 USCA § 253k.

Task and delivery order contracts, general authority, see 10 USCA § 2304a, 41 USCA § 253h.

Task and delivery order contracts, orders, see 10 USCA § 2304c, 41 USCA § 253j.

Task order contracts, advisory and assistance services, see 10 USCA § 2304b, 41 USCA § 253i.

Notes of Decisions

In general 1
Authority officers to contract 2
Court of Federal Claims jurisdiction 3

1 In general

Basic Purchasing Agreement with provider of telephone services involving "moves, adds and changes" to telephone configuration in Postal Service building did not create contractual obligation on part of Postal Service to utilize any telephone services; agreement contemplated that parties would enter into binding contracts in future through issuance of individual authorized orders, and merely provided price and other terms and conditions for such future contracts. Modern Systems Technology Corp. v. U.S., 979 F.2d 200, 38 Cont. Cas. Fed. (CCH) P 76397 (Fed. Cir. 1992). United States ⊕70(6.1)

Basic Purchasing Agreement between provider of telephone services and Postal Service, providing for "moves, adds and changes" of telephone equipment, was not a requirements contract obligating Postal Service to have all such activities carried on through provider; there was no express contractual commitment to have all of the Postal Service's requirements so satisfied, nor were there any minimum purchase requirements. Modern Systems Technology Corp. v. U.S., 979 F.2d 200, 38 Cont. Cas. Fed. (CCH) P 76397 (Fed. Cir. 1992). United States ⊕70(6.1)

Basic pricing agreement entered into by government agency and contractor was not binding contract but merely a framework for future contracts; there was no language in agreement indicating any present intent that either party be bound and terms were not sufficiently definite. Modern Systems Technology Corp. v. U.S., 979 F.2d 200, 38 Cont. Cas. Fed. (CCH) P 76397 (Fed. Cir. 1992). United States ⊕70(15.1)

Facts and circumstances independent of basic agreement itself may form enforceable contract or transform basic agreement into binding obligation. Almar Industries, Inc. v. U.S., 16 Cl. Ct. 243, 35 Cont. Cas. Fed. (CCH) P 75621, 1989 WL 6470 (1989). Contracts ⚯1

2 Authority officers to contract

Statement by Postal Service employee, that firm which had entered into Basic Purchasing Agreement with Postal Service covering "moves, adds and changes" to telephones within building would be getting all of Postal Service's business except that which was done in-house, did not contractually commit Postal Service to place orders with firm; employee was not a contracting officer entitled to bind Postal Service. Modern Systems Technology Corp. v. U.S., 979 F.2d 200, 38 Cont. Cas. Fed. (CCH) P 76397 (Fed. Cir. 1992). United States ⚯60

3 Court of Federal Claims jurisdiction

Court of Federal Claims lacked jurisdiction in government contractor's breach of contract suit to enter declaratory judgment holding indefinite-quantity (IDQ) specifications deficient as a matter of law where they bore no rational relationship to actual requirements within the contracting agency's superior knowledge at the time of solicitation, where such a ruling was not necessary to resolve contractor's claim for money damages. Schweiger Const. Co., Inc. v. U.S., 49 Fed. Cl. 188 (2001). Federal Courts ⚯1078

Court of Federal Claims had jurisdiction over government contractor's claim that construction contract was illegal and that government violated provisions of the Federal Acquisition Regulation which address the type of contract to be used for procurement, in that procurement should have led to the award of a cost-reimbursement contract, rather than a firmfixed-price contract. 48 C.F.R. § 16.000. PCL Const. Services, Inc. v. U.S., 41 Fed. Cl. 242, 42 Cont. Cas. Fed. (CCH) P 77325 (1998), aff'd, 96 Fed. Appx. 672 (Fed. Cir. 2004). Federal Courts ⚯1076

Court lacked jurisdiction to consider merits of government contractor's claim arising out of defense industrial supply center's removal of contractor's name from its automated procurement system; contractor failed to establish that it received sufficient benefit from participating in program to provide consideration to transform basic agreement with center into enforceable contract. Almar Industries, Inc. v. U.S., 16 Cl. Ct. 243, 35 Cont. Cas. Fed. (CCH) P 75621, 1989 WL 6470 (1989). Federal Courts ⚯1076

§ 16.703 Basic ordering agreements.

(a) *Description.* A basic ordering agreement is a written instrument of understanding, negotiated between an agency, contracting activity, or contracting office and a contractor, that contains (1) terms and clauses applying to future contracts (orders) between the parties during its term, (2) a description, as specific as practicable, of supplies or services to be provided, and (3) methods for pricing, issuing, and delivering future orders under the basic ordering agreement. A basic ordering agreement is not a contract.

(b) *Application.* A basic ordering agreement may be used to expedite contracting for uncertain requirements for supplies or services when specific items, quantities, and prices are not known at the time the agreement is executed, but a substantial number of requirements for the type of supplies or services covered by the agreement are anticipated to be purchased from the contractor. Under proper circumstances, the use of these procedures can result in economies in ordering parts for equipment support by reducing administrative leadtime, inventory investment, and inventory obsolescence due to design changes.

(c) *Limitations.* A basic ordering agreement shall not state or imply any agreement by the Government to place future contracts or orders with the contractor or be used in any manner to restrict competition.

(1) Each basic ordering agreement shall—

(i) Describe the method for determining prices to be paid to the contractor for the supplies or services;

(ii) Include delivery terms and conditions or specify how they will be determined;

(iii) List one or more Government activities authorized to issue orders under the agreement;

(iv) Specify the point at which each order becomes a binding contract (*e.g.,* issuance of the order, acceptance of the order in a specified manner, or failure to reject the order within a specified number of days);

(v) Provide that failure to reach agreement on price for any order issued before its price is established (see paragraph (d)(3) of this section) is a dispute under the Disputes clause included in the basic ordering agreement; and

(vi) If fast payment procedures will apply to orders, include the special data required by 13.403.

(2) Each basic ordering agreement shall be reviewed annually before the anniversary of its effective date and revised as necessary to conform to the requirements of this regulation. Basic ordering agreements may need to be revised before the annual review due to mandatory statutory requirements. A basic ordering agreement shall be changed only by modifying the agreement itself and not by individual orders issued under it. Modifying a basic ordering agreement shall not retroactively affect orders previously issued under it.

(d) *Orders.* A contracting officer representing any Government activity listed in a basic ordering agreement may issue orders for required supplies or services covered by that agreement.

(1) Before issuing an order under a basic ordering agreement, the contracting officer shall—

(i) Obtain competition in accordance with Part 6;

(ii) If the order is being placed after competition, ensure that use of the basic ordering agreement is not prejudicial to other offerors; and

(iii) Sign or obtain any applicable justifications and approvals, and any determination and findings, and comply with other requirements in accordance with 1.602-1(b), as if the order were a contract awarded independently of a basic ordering agreement.

(2) Contracting officers shall—

(i) Issue orders under basic ordering agreements on Optional Form (OF) 347, Order for Supplies or Services, or on any other appropriate contractual instrument;

(ii) Incorporate by reference the provisions of the basic ordering agreement;

(iii) If applicable, cite the authority under 6.302 in each order; and

(iv) Comply with 5.203 when synopsis is required by 5.201.

(3) The contracting officer shall neither make any final commitment nor authorize the contractor to begin work on an order under a basic ordering agreement until prices have been established, unless the order establishes a ceiling price limiting the Government's obligation and either—

(i) The basic ordering agreement provides adequate procedures for timely pricing of the order early in its performance period; or

(ii) The need for the supplies or services is compelling and unusually urgent (*i.e.,* when the Government would be seriously injured, financially or otherwise, if the requirement is not met sooner than would be possible if prices were established before the work began). The contracting officer shall proceed with pricing as soon as practical. In no event shall an entire order be priced retroactively.

United States Code Annotated

Contract requirements, see 41 USCA § 254.

Contracts, planning, solicitation, evaluation, and award procedures, see 10 USCA § 2305.

Cost-type research and development contracts with educational institutions, see 41 USCA § 254a.

Definitions, see 10 USCA § 2302, 41 USCA §§ 259, 403.

Kinds of contracts, see 10 USCA § 2306.

Planning and solicitation requirements, see 41 USCA § 253a.

Task and delivery order contracts, definitions, see 10 USCA § 2304d, 41 USCA § 253k.

Task and delivery order contracts, general authority, see 10 USCA § 2304a, 41 USCA § 253h.

Task and delivery order contracts, orders, see 10 USCA § 2304c, 41 USCA § 253j.

Task order contracts, advisory and assistance services, see 10 USCA § 2304b, 41 USCA § 253i.

Notes of Decisions

In general 1

1 In general

Basic ordering agreement between translator and State Department was not itself a contract, but rather contract arose only when translator accepted work order issued by State Department's Office of Language Services authorizing translator to perform various services and providing that payment would be made in accordance with schedule of rates in basic ordering agreement. Zoubi v. U.S., 25 Cl. Ct. 581, 37 Cont. Cas. Fed. (CCH) P 76287, 1992 WL 58983 (1992). United States ⚖63

Memorandum of understanding executed each year for resupply of Air Force base was not a basic ordering agreement in that it contained sufficient contractual overtones to qualify as "contract" within ambit of statute governing jurisdiction over preaward contract claims; however, even though sufficient request was made by Army transportation officer such as to form implied contract to fairly and honestly consider plaintiff's responding proposal, claims court lacked jurisdiction to consider plaintiff's request for equitable relief stemming from cancellation of certain resupply transportation requirements, where fuel contract was amended prior to suit to encompass transportation requirement previously solicited, thus making any contract claim filed as to this transportation requirement a postaward claim. 28 U.S.C.A. § 1491(a)(3). Western Pioneer, Inc. v. U.S., 8 Cl. Ct. 291, 32 Cont. Cas. Fed. (CCH) P 73617 (1985). Federal Courts ⚖1076; Federal Courts ⚖1077; Federal Courts ⚖1080

PART 17 SPECIAL CONTRACTING METHODS

§ 17.000 Scope of part.

Subpart 17.1 Multi-year Contracting

Subpart 17.2 Options

Subpart 17.3 [Reserved]

Subpart 17.4 Leader Company Contracting

Subpart 17.5 Interagency Acquisitions Under the Economy Act

Subpart 17.6 Management and Operating Contracts

§ 17.600 Scope of subpart.
§ 17.601 Definition.
§ 17.602 Policy.
§ 17.603 Limitations.
§ 17.604 Identifying management and operating contracts.
§ 17.605 Award, renewal, and extension.

Subpart 17.7 Interagency Acquisitions: Acquisitions by Nondefense Agencies on Behalf of the Department of Defense

§ 17.700 Scope of subpart.
§ 17.701 Definitions.
§ 17.702 Applicability.
§ 17.703 Policy.

§ 17.000 Scope of part.

This part prescribes policies and procedures for the acquisition of supplies and services through special contracting methods, including—

(a) Multi-year contracting;

(b) Options; and

(c) Leader company contracting.

United States Code Annotated

Contract requirements, see 41 USCA § 254.

Contracts, planning, solicitation, evaluation, and award procedures, see 10 USCA § 2305.

Definitions, see 10 USCA § 2302, 41 USCA §§ 259, 403.

Kinds of contracts, see 10 USCA § 2306.

Planning and solicitation requirements, see 41 USCA § 253a.

Subpart 17.1 Multi-year Contracting

§ 17.101 Authority.

This subpart implements 41 U.S.C. 3903 and 10 U.S.C. 2306b and provides policy and procedures for the use of multi-year contracting.

United States Code Annotated

Contract requirements, see 41 USCA § 254.

Contracts, planning, solicitation, evaluation, and award procedures, see 10 USCA § 2305.

Definitions, see 10 USCA § 2302, 41 USCA §§ 259, 403.

Kinds of contracts, see 10 USCA § 2306.

Multiyear contracts, acquisition of property, see 10 USCA § 2306b.

Multiyear contracts, acquisition of services, see 10 USCA § 2306c.

Multiyear contracts, see 41 USCA § 254c.

Planning and solicitation requirements, see 41 USCA § 253a.

Severable services contracts for periods crossing fiscal years, see 41 USCA § 2531.

§ 17.102 Applicability.

For DoD, NASA, and the Coast Guard, the authorities cited in 17.101 do not apply to contracts for the purchase of supplies to which 40 U.S.C. 759 applies (information resource management supply contracts).

United States Code Annotated

Contract requirements, see 41 USCA § 254.

Contracts, planning, solicitation, evaluation, and award procedures, see 10 USCA § 2305.

Definitions, see 10 USCA § 2302, 41 USCA §§ 259, 403.

Kinds of contracts, see 10 USCA § 2306.

Multiyear contracts, acquisition of property, see 10 USCA § 2306b.

Multiyear contracts, acquisition of services, see 10 USCA § 2306c.

Multiyear contracts, see 41 USCA § 254c.

Planning and solicitation requirements, see 41 USCA § 253a.

Severable services contracts for periods crossing fiscal years, see 41 USCA § 253l.

§ 17.103 Definitions.

As used in this subpart—

"Cancellation" means the cancellation (within a contractually specified time) of the total requirements of all remaining program years. Cancellation results when the contracting officer—

(1) Notifies the contractor of nonavailability of funds for contract performance for any subsequent program year; or

(2) Fails to notify the contractor that funds are available for performance of the succeeding program year requirement.

"Cancellation ceiling" means the maximum cancellation charge that the contractor can receive in the event of cancellation.

"Cancellation charge" means the amount of unrecovered costs which would have been recouped through amortization over the full term of the contract, including the term canceled.

"Multi-year contract" means a contract for the purchase of supplies or services for more than 1, but not more than 5, program years. A multi-year contract may provide that performance under the contract during the second and subsequent years of the contract is contingent upon the appropriation of funds, and (if it does so provide) may provide for a cancellation payment to be made to the contractor if appropriations are not made. The key distinguishing difference between multiyear contracts and multiple year contracts is that multi-year contracts, defined in the statutes cited at 17.101, buy more than 1 year's requirement (of a product or service) without establishing and having to exercise an option for each program year after the first.

"Nonrecurring costs" means those costs which are generally incurred on a one-time basis and include such costs as plant or equipment relocation, plant rearrangement, special tooling and special test equipment, preproduction engineering, initial spoilage and rework, and specialized work force training.

"Recurring costs" means costs that vary with the quantity being produced, such as labor and materials.

United States Code Annotated

Contract requirements, see 41 USCA § 254.

Contracts, planning, solicitation, evaluation, and award procedures, see 10 USCA § 2305.

Definitions, see 10 USCA § 2302, 41 USCA §§ 259, 403.

Kinds of contracts, see 10 USCA § 2306.

Multiyear contracts, acquisition of property, see 10 USCA § 2306b.

Multiyear contracts, acquisition of services, see 10 USCA § 2306c.

Multiyear contracts, see 41 USCA § 254c.

Planning and solicitation requirements, see 41 USCA § 253a.

Notes of Decisions

Multiyear contracts 1

1 Multiyear contracts

"Multi-year contract" binds parties to public contract for more than one year, but funds need not be appropriated beyond current year. McDonnell Douglas Corp. v. U.S., 37 Fed. Cl.

295, 41 Cont. Cas. Fed. (CCH) P 77046 (1997), order modified, 39 Fed. Cl. 665, 42 Cont. Cas. Fed. (CCH) P 77230 (1997). United States ⟐70(1)

"Incremental funding" of public contract is one-year appropriation to multi-year contract. McDonnell Douglas Corp. v. U.S., 37 Fed. Cl. 295, 41 Cont. Cas. Fed. (CCH) P 77046 (1997), order modified, 39 Fed. Cl. 665, 42 Cont. Cas. Fed. (CCH) P 77230 (1997). United States ⟐70(15.1)

§ 17.104 General.

(a) Multi-year contracting is a special contracting method to acquire known requirements in quantities and total cost not over planned requirements for up to 5 years unless otherwise authorized by statute, even though the total funds ultimately to be obligated may not be available at the time of contract award. This method may be used in sealed bidding or contracting by negotiation.

(b) Multi-year contracting is a flexible contracting method applicable to a wide range of acquisitions. The extent to which cancellation terms are used in multi-year contracts will depend on the unique circumstances of each contract. Accordingly, for multi-year contracts, the agency head may authorize modification of the requirements of this subpart and the clause at 52.217-2, Cancellation Under Multi-year Contracts.

(c) Agency funding of multi-year contracts shall conform to the policies in OMB Circulars A-11 (Preparation and Submission of Budget Estimates) and A-34 (Instructions on Budget Execution) and other applicable guidance regarding the funding of multi-year contracts. As provided by that guidance, the funds obligated for multi-year contracts must be sufficient to cover any potential cancellation and/or termination costs; and multi-year contracts for the acquisition of fixed assets should be fully funded or funded in stages that are economically or programmatically viable.

(d) The termination for convenience procedure may apply to any Government contract, including multiyear contracts. As contrasted with cancellation, termination can be effected at any time during the life of the contract (cancellation is effected between fiscal years) and can be for the total quantity or partial quantity (where as cancellation must be for all subsequent fiscal years' quantities).

United States Code Annotated

Contract requirements, see 41 USCA § 254.

Contracts, planning, solicitation, evaluation, and award procedures, see 10 USCA § 2305.

Definitions, see 10 USCA § 2302, 41 USCA §§ 259, 403.

Kinds of contracts, see 10 USCA § 2306.

Multiyear contracts, acquisition of property, see 10 USCA § 2306b.

Multiyear contracts, acquisition of services, see 10 USCA § 2306c.

Multiyear contracts, see 41 USCA § 254c.

Planning and solicitation requirements, see 41 USCA § 253a.

Severable services contracts for periods crossing fiscal years, see 41 USCA § 2531.

Notes of Decisions

In general 1

1 In general

Agencies may use multiyear contracting procedures and use annual appropriations for the needs of future fiscal years, regardless of whether the contract procures nonseverable or severable services. GAO found that the plain language of 41 USC § 3903 establishes that this multiyear contracting authority applies to the acquisition of *all* services. Department of Health and Human Services—Multiyear Contracting and the *Bona Fide* Needs Rule, B-322455, 2013 WL 4398954 (Comp.Gen 2013)

"Multi-year contract" binds parties to public contract for more than one year, but funds need not be appropriated beyond current year. McDonnell Douglas Corp. v. U.S., 37 Fed. Cl. 295, 41 Cont. Cas. Fed. (CCH) P 77046 (1997), order modified, 39 Fed. Cl. 665, 42 Cont. Cas. Fed. (CCH) P 77230 (1997). United States ⟐70(1)

"Incremental funding" of public contract is one-year appropriation to multi-year contract.

McDonnell Douglas Corp. v. U.S., 37 Fed. Cl. 295, 41 Cont. Cas. Fed. (CCH) P 77046 (1997), order modified, 39 Fed. Cl. 665, 42 Cont. Cas. Fed. (CCH) P 77230 (1997). United States ☞70(15.1)

§ 17.105 Policy.

§ 17.105-1 Uses.

(a) Except for DoD, NASA, and the Coast Guard, the contracting officer may enter into a multi-year contract if the head of the contracting activity determines that—

(1) The need for the supplies or services is reasonably firm and continuing over the period of the contract; and

(2) A multi-year contract will serve the best interests of the United States by encouraging full and open competition or promoting economy in administration, performance, and operation of the agency's programs.

(b) For DoD, NASA, and the Coast Guard, the head of the agency may enter into a multi-year contract for supplies if—

(1) The use of such a contract will result in substantial savings of the total estimated costs of carrying out the program through annual contracts;

(2) The minimum need to be purchased is expected to remain substantially unchanged during the contemplated contract period in terms of production rate, procurement rate, and total quantities;

(3) There is a stable design for the supplies to be acquired, and the technical risks associated with such supplies are not excessive;

(4) There is a reasonable expectation that, throughout the contemplated contract period, the head of the agency will request funding for the contract at a level to avoid contract cancellation; and

(5) The estimates of both the cost of the contract and the cost avoidance through the use of a multi-year contract are realistic.

(c) The multi-year contracting method may be used for the acquisition of supplies or services.

(d) If funds are not appropriated to support the succeeding years' requirements, the agency must cancel the contract.

United States Code Annotated

Contract requirements, see 41 USCA § 254.

Contracts, planning, solicitation, evaluation, and award procedures, see 10 USCA § 2305.

Definitions, see 10 USCA § 2302, 41 USCA §§ 259, 403.

Kinds of contracts, see 10 USCA § 2306.

Multiyear contracts, acquisition of property, see 10 USCA § 2306b.

Multiyear contracts, acquisition of services, see 10 USCA § 2306c.

Multiyear contracts, see 41 USCA § 254c.

Planning and solicitation requirements, see 41 USCA § 253a.

Severable services contracts for periods crossing fiscal years, see 41 USCA § 253l.

Notes of Decisions

In general 1

1 In general

"Multi-year contract" binds parties to public contract for more than one year, but funds need not be appropriated beyond current year. McDonnell Douglas Corp. v. U.S., 37 Fed. Cl. 295, 41 Cont. Cas. Fed. (CCH) P 77046 (1997), order modified, 39 Fed. Cl. 665, 42 Cont. Cas. Fed. (CCH) P 77230 (1997). United States ☞70(1)

"Incremental funding" of public contract is one-year appropriation to multi-year contract. McDonnell Douglas Corp. v. U.S., 37 Fed. Cl. 295, 41 Cont. Cas. Fed. (CCH) P 77046 (1997), order modified, 39 Fed. Cl. 665, 42 Cont. Cas. Fed. (CCH) P 77230 (1997). United States ☞70(15.1)

§ 17.105-2 Objectives.

Use of multi-year contracting is encouraged to take advantage of one or more of the following:

(a) Lower costs.

(b) Enhancement of standardization.

(c) Reduction of administrative burden in the placement and administration of contracts.

(d) Substantial continuity of production or performance, thus avoiding annual startup costs, preproduction testing costs, make-ready expenses, and phaseout costs.

(e) Stabilization of contractor work forces.

(f) Avoidance of the need for establishing quality control techniques and procedures for a new contractor each year.

(g) Broadening the competitive base with opportunity for participation by firms not otherwise willing or able to compete for lesser quantities, particularly in cases involving high startup costs.

(h) Providing incentives to contractors to improve productivity through investment in capital facilities, equipment, and advanced technology.

United States Code Annotated

Contract requirements, see 41 USCA § 254.

Contracts, planning, solicitation, evaluation, and award procedures, see 10 USCA § 2305.

Definitions, see 10 USCA § 2302, 41 USCA §§ 259, 403.

Kinds of contracts, see 10 USCA § 2306.

Multiyear contracts, acquisition of property, see 10 USCA § 2306b.

Multiyear contracts, acquisition of services, see 10 USCA § 2306c.

Multiyear contracts, see 41 USCA § 254c.

Planning and solicitation requirements, see 41 USCA § 253a.

Severable services contracts for periods crossing fiscal years, see 41 USCA § 2531.

Notes of Decisions

In general 1

1 In general

"Multi-year contract" binds parties to public contract for more than one year, but funds need not be appropriated beyond current year. McDonnell Douglas Corp. v. U.S., 37 Fed. Cl. 295, 41 Cont. Cas. Fed. (CCH) P 77046 (1997), order modified, 39 Fed. Cl. 665, 42 Cont. Cas. Fed. (CCH) P 77230 (1997). United States ⟜70(1)

"Incremental funding" of public contract is one-year appropriation to multi-year contract. McDonnell Douglas Corp. v. U.S., 37 Fed. Cl. 295, 41 Cont. Cas. Fed. (CCH) P 77046 (1997), order modified, 39 Fed. Cl. 665, 42 Cont. Cas. Fed. (CCH) P 77230 (1997). United States ⟜70(15.1)

§ 17.106 Procedures.

§ 17.106-1 General.

(a) *Method of contracting.* The nature of the requirement should govern the selection of the method of contracting, since the multi-year procedure is compatible with sealed bidding, including two-step sealed bidding, and negotiation.

(b) *Type of contract.* Given the longer performance period associated with multi-year acquisition, consideration in pricing fixed-priced contracts should be given to the use of economic price adjustment terms and profit objectives commensurate with contractor risk and financing arrangements.

(c) *Cancellation procedures.* (1) All program years except the first are subject to cancellation. For each program year subject to cancellation, the contracting officer shall establish a cancellation ceiling. Ceilings must exclude amounts for requirements included in prior program years. The contracting officer shall reduce the cancellation ceiling for each program year in direct proportion to the remaining requirements subject to cancellation. For example, consider that the total nonrecurring costs (see 15.408, Table 15-2, Formats for Submission of Line Items Summaries C(8)) are estimated at 10 percent of the total multi-year price, and the percentages for each of the program year requirements for 5 years are (i) 30 in the first year, (ii) 30 in the second, (iii) 20 in the third, (iv) 10 in the fourth, and (v) 10 in the fifth. The cancellation percentages, after deducting 3 percent for the first program year, would be 7, 4, 2, and 1 percent of the total price applicable to the second, third, fourth, and fifth program years, respectively.

(2) In determining cancellation ceilings, the contracting officer must estimate reasonable preproduction or startup, labor learning, and other nonrecurring costs to be incurred by an "average" prime contractor or subcontractor, which would be applicable to, and which normally would be amortized over, the items or services to be furnished under the multi-year requirements. Nonrecurring costs include such costs, where applicable, as plant or equipment relocation or rearrangement, special tooling and special test equipment, preproduction engineering, initial rework, initial spoilage, pilot runs, allocable portions of the costs of facilities to be acquired or established for the conduct of the work, costs incurred for the assembly, training, and transportation to and from the job site of a specialized work force, and unrealized labor learning. They shall not include any costs of labor or materials, or other expenses (except as indicated above), which might be incurred for performance of subsequent program year requirements. The total estimate of the above costs must then be compared with the best estimate of the contract cost to arrive at a reasonable percentage or dollar figure. To perform this calculation, the contracting officer should obtain in-house engineering cost estimates identifying the detailed recurring and nonrecurring costs, and the effect of labor learning.

(3) The contracting officer shall establish cancellation dates for each program year's requirements regarding production lead time and the date by which funding for these requirements can reasonably be established. The contracting officer shall include these dates in the schedule, as appropriate.

(d) *Cancellation ceilings.* Cancellation ceilings and dates may be revised after issuing the solicitation if necessary. In sealed bidding, the contracting officer shall change the ceiling by amending the solicitation before bid opening. In two-step sealed bidding, discussions conducted during the first step may indicate the need for revised ceilings and dates which may be incorporated in step two. In a negotiated acquisition, negotiations with offerors may provide information requiring a change in cancellation ceilings and dates before final negotiation and contract award.

(e) *Payment of cancellation charges.* If cancellation occurs, the Government's liability will be determined by the terms of the applicable contract.

(f) *Presolicitation or pre-bid conferences.* To ensure that all interested sources of supply are thoroughly aware of how multi-year contracting is accomplished, use of presolicitation or pre-bid conferences may be advisable.

(g) *Payment limit.* The contracting officer shall limit the Government's payment obligation to an amount available for contract performance. The contracting officer shall insert the amount for the first program year in the contract upon award and modify it for successive program years upon availability of funds.

(h) *Termination payment.* If the contract is terminated for the convenience of the Government in whole, including requirements subject to cancellation, the Government's obligation shall not exceed the amount specified in the Schedule as available for contract performance, plus the cancellation ceiling.

United States Code Annotated

Contract requirements, see 41 USCA § 254.

Contracts, planning, solicitation, evaluation, and award procedures, see 10 USCA § 2305.

Definitions, see 10 USCA § 2302, 41 USCA §§ 259, 403.

Kinds of contracts, see 10 USCA § 2306.

Multiyear contracts, acquisition of property, see 10 USCA § 2306b.

Multiyear contracts, acquisition of services, see 10 USCA § 2306c.

Multiyear contracts, see 41 USCA § 254c.

Planning and solicitation requirements, see 41 USCA § 253a.

Severable services contracts for periods crossing fiscal years, see 41 USCA § 2531.

Notes of Decisions

In general 1

1 In general

"Multi-year contract" binds parties to public contract for more than one year, but funds need not be appropriated beyond current year. McDonnell Douglas Corp. v. U.S., 37 Fed. Cl. 295, 41 Cont. Cas. Fed. (CCH) P 77046 (1997), order modified, 39 Fed. Cl. 665, 42 Cont. Cas. Fed. (CCH) P 77230 (1997). United States ⊕70(1)

"Incremental funding" of public contract is one-year appropriation to multi-year contract. McDonnell Douglas Corp. v. U.S., 37 Fed. Cl. 295, 41 Cont. Cas. Fed. (CCH) P 77046 (1997), order modified, 39 Fed. Cl. 665, 42 Cont. Cas. Fed. (CCH) P 77230 (1997). United States ⊕70(15.1)

§ 17.106-2 Solicitations.

Solicitations for multi-year contracts shall reflect all the factors to be considered for evaluation, specifically including the following:

(a) The requirements, by item of supply or service, for the—

(1) First program year; and

(2) Multi-year contract including the requirements for each program year.

(b) Criteria for comparing the lowest evaluated submission on the first program year requirements to the lowest evaluated submission on the multi-year requirements.

(c) A provision that, if the Government determines before award that only the first program year requirements are needed, the Government's evaluation of the price or estimated cost and fee shall consider only the first year.

(d) A provision specifying a separate cancellation ceiling (on a percentage or dollar basis) and dates applicable to each program year subject to a cancellation (see 17.106-1(c) and (d)).

(e) A statement that award will not be made on less than the first program year requirements.

(f) The Government's administrative costs of annual contracting may be used as a factor in the evaluation only if they can be reasonably established and are stated in the solicitation.

(g) The cancellation ceiling shall not be an evaluation factor.

United States Code Annotated

Contract requirements, see 41 USCA § 254.

Contracts, planning, solicitation, evaluation, and award procedures, see 10 USCA § 2305.

Definitions, see 10 USCA § 2302, 41 USCA §§ 259, 403.

Kinds of contracts, see 10 USCA § 2306.

Multiyear contracts, acquisition of property, see 10 USCA § 2306b.

Multiyear contracts, acquisition of services, see 10 USCA § 2306c.

Multiyear contracts, see 41 USCA § 254c.

Planning and solicitation requirements, see 41 USCA § 253a.

Severable services contracts for periods crossing fiscal years, see 41 USCA § 2531.

§ 17.106-3 Special procedures applicable to DoD, NASA, and the Coast Guard.

(a) *Participation by subcontractors, suppliers, and vendors.* In order to broaden the defense industrial base, to the maximum extent practicable—

(1) Multi-year contracting shall be used in such a manner as to seek, retain, and promote the use under such contracts of companies that are subcontractors, suppliers, and vendors; and

(2) Upon accrual of any payment or other benefit under such a multi-year contract to any subcontractor, supplier, or vendor company participating in such contract, such payment or benefit shall be delivered to such company in the most expeditious manner practicable.

(b) *Protection of existing authority.* To the extent practicable, multi-year contracting shall not be carried out in a manner to preclude or curtail the existing ability of the Department or agency to provide for termination of a prime contract, the performance of which is deficient with respect to cost, quality, or schedule.

(c) *Cancellation or termination for insufficient funding.* In the event funds are not made available for the continuation of a multi-year contract awarded using the procedures in this section, the contract shall be canceled or terminated.

(d) Contracts awarded under the multi-year procedure shall be firm-fixed-price, fixed-price with economic price adjustment, or fixed-price incentive.

(e) *Recurring costs in cancellation ceiling.* The inclusion of recurring costs in cancellation ceilings is an exception to normal contract financing arrangements and requires approval by the agency head.

(f) *Annual and multi-year proposals.* Obtaining both annual and multi-year offers provides reduced lead time for making an annual award in the event that the multi-year award is not in the Government's interest. Obtaining both also provides a basis for the computation of savings and other benefits. However, the preparation and evaluation of dual offers may increase administrative costs and workload for both offerors and the Government, especially for large or complex acquisitions. The head of a contracting activity may authorize the use of a solicitation requesting only multi-year prices, provided it is found that such a solicitation is in the Government's interest, and that dual proposals are not necessary to meet the objectives in 17.105-2.

(g) *Level unit prices.* Multi-year contract procedures provide for the amortization of certain costs over the entire contract quantity resulting in identical (level) unit prices (except when the economic price adjustment terms apply) for all items or services under the multi-year contract. If level unit pricing is not in the Government's interest, the head of a contracting activity may approve the use of variable unit prices, provided that for competitive proposals there is a valid method of evaluation.

United States Code Annotated

Contract requirements, see 41 USCA § 254.

Contracts, planning, solicitation, evaluation, and award procedures, see 10 USCA § 2305.

Definitions, see 10 USCA § 2302, 41 USCA §§ 259, 403.

Kinds of contracts, see 10 USCA § 2306.

Multiyear contracts, acquisition of property, see 10 USCA § 2306b.

Multiyear contracts, acquisition of services, see 10 USCA § 2306c.

Multiyear contracts, see 41 USCA § 254c.

Planning and solicitation requirements, see 41 USCA § 253a.

Severable services contracts for periods crossing fiscal years, see 41 USCA § 2531.

§ 17.107 Options.

Benefits may accrue by including options in a multi-year contract. In that event, contracting officers must follow the requirements of Subpart 17.2. Options should not include charges for plant and equipment already amortized, or other nonrecurring charges which were included in the basic contract.

United States Code Annotated

Contract requirements, see 41 USCA § 254.

Contracts, planning, solicitation, evaluation, and award procedures, see 10 USCA § 2305.

Definitions, see 10 USCA § 2302, 41 USCA §§ 259, 403.

Kinds of contracts, see 10 USCA § 2306.

Multiyear contracts, acquisition of property, see 10 USCA § 2306b.

Multiyear contracts, acquisition of services, see 10 USCA § 2306c.

Multiyear contracts, see 41 USCA § 254c.

Planning and solicitation requirements, see 41 USCA § 253a.

Severable services contracts for periods crossing fiscal years, see 41 USCA § 2531.

Notes of Decisions

In general 1

1 In general

Disclosure of option year prices set forth in contract between Department of Air Force and aircraft maintenance and repair service provider, which provided for base year and eight option years, was likely to cause provider substantial competitive harm, and thus was exempt from disclosure under the Freedom of Information Act (FOIA) to provider's competitor; competitors could use such information to underbid the present contract if Air Force should choose to rebid it. 5 U.S.C.A. § 552(b)(4). McDonnell Douglas Corp. v. U.S. Dept. of the Air Force, 375 F.3d 1182, 1188 (D.C. Cir. 2004). Records ⊸⇒59

Contract under which computer maintenance firm was to provide maintenance for certain computers owned by federal agency, which expressly indicated that it was an indefinite delivery, indefinite quantity contract, or ID/IQ contract, and established an initial six-month base period, followed by four 12-month options periods and one six-month option period, did not result in formation of a series of separate and distinct requirements contracts, even though option periods did not have a separate minimum quantity of services that would be required. 48 C.F.R. § 16.504(b). Varilease Technology Group, Inc. v. U.S., 289 F.3d 795 (Fed. Cir. 2002). United States ⊸⇒70(6.1)

In construing ambiguity in government contract to supply audio cassette players, base unit price figure to which Consumer Price Index (CPI) adjustments were to be applied in future annual purchases pursuant to option provisions was the original base unit price, rather than subsequent CPI adjusted prices; applying CPI adjustment to already adjusted price would have compounded CPI adjustment well beyond inflation. Telex Communications, Inc. v. U.S., 40 Fed. Cl. 703, 42 Cont. Cas. Fed. (CCH) P 77281 (1998), dismissed, 168 F.3d 1317 (Fed. Cir. 1998). United States ⊸⇒70(30)

Option extensions to original agreement between Navy and government contractor were mere continuation of original agreement, which competitor was barred from challenging under Tucker Act after original contract had been awarded. 28 U.S.C.A. § 1491(a)(3). Unified Industries, Inc. v. U.S., 24 Cl. Ct. 570, 37 Cont. Cas. Fed. (CCH) P 76226, 1991 WL 255867 (1991). United States ⊸⇒64.55(1)

Federal government's use of option clauses is authorized in recognition of government's need in certain service contracts for continuity of operation where there is anticipated need for similar services beyond first contract period. 28 U.S.C.A. § 1491(a)(3). C.M.P., Inc. v. U.S., 8 Cl. Ct. 743, 33 Cont. Cas. Fed. (CCH) P 74027 (1985). United States ⊸⇒63

2 Solicitations

Purpose of option clause in solicitation of bid for government contract is to provide tool by which government may gain financial advantage in event that government later requires larger quantity than originally anticipated. Noa Airscrew Howden, Inc. v. Department of Army, 622 F. Supp. 984 (E.D. Mich. 1985). United States ⊸⇒64.25

Fact that solicitation for bids for providing unarmed guard services denominated contract as "firm fixed-price" did not show that solicitation called for provision of additional services through options, as opposed to indefinite quantity requirement. Vanguard Sec. Inc. v. U.S., 20 Cl. Ct. 90, 1990 WL 38036 (1990). United States ⊸⇒70(6.1)

3 Evaluations

Federal acquisition regulation requiring contracting officers to follow noncompetitive procedures before exercising option, when option price was not evaluated in original competitive solicitation, existed for benefit of government, not benefit of contractor, so regulation did not create cause of action on part of contractor that supplied small emplacement excavator (SEE) vehicles to government, and government's alleged failure to comply with regulation in exercising option to increase quantity of vehicles under supply contract would not render its exercise of option ineffective. 48 C.F.R. § 17.207(f). Freightliner Corp. v.

Caldera, 225 F.3d 1361 (Fed. Cir. 2000). United States ☞70(26); United States ☞74(3)

4 Exercise of options

Although government contractor had no obligation to perform under option clause of contract for demilitarization of bombs, because government did not validly exercise option, contractor was obligated to continue performance under contract's disputes clause, because option was not new contract but extension of obligations in original contract, and delivery rate set by contracting officer for option was not such drastic change as to constitute breach of contract; performance would be governed by terms set by Court of Federal Claims, which issued declaratory judgment prior to first delivery of option quantities required by contracting officer's decision. 48 C.F.R. § 17.201. Alliant Techsystems, Inc. v. U.S., 178 F.3d 1260 (Fed. Cir. 1999). United States ☞73(6)

Fixed price contract for missile fuses required government to exercise options in sequential order; contract permitted government to exercise options in accordance with schedule setting forth successive time periods for exercising each option, and price structure showed that options were priced according to learning curve to take into account savings anticipated through additional "learning" gained during earlier phases of production. Lockheed Martin Corp. v. Walker, 149 F.3d 1377, 42 Cont. Cas. Fed. (CCH) P 77341 (Fed. Cir. 1998). United States ☞70(26)

Factors that an agency must consider prior to exercising an option only restrict the agency from *exercising* the option. Non-exercise is unrestricted. Conditions are inherently negative concepts which limit exercise but make no sense in terms on non-exercise. This is not surprising as the concern of Congress was giving contracts to contractors who were unqualified performers. There are a large number of potential reasons why the option does not have to be exercised that are inherent in the concept of the option itself. There is no indication that Congress sought to limit the Government's discretion to not exercise an option in this situation. Thus, the option clause in the contract did not require the agency to consider certain factors in deciding not to exercise the option, as the factors applied only if the government decided to exercise the option. TMI Management Systems, Inc. v. U.S., 78 Fed. Cl. 445 (2007).

Oral communication or conduct were insufficient to exercise an option under the government contract providing that option had to be specifically exercised in writing. Green Management Corp. v. U.S., 42 Fed. Cl. 411 (1998). United States ☞72(2)

Government's failure to exercise an option in a contract does not ordinarily give rise to a breach of contract action; standard option provision in a government contract obliges the contractor to perform the additional contract work if the government chooses to exercise the option, but it does not create a legal obligation on the part of the government to exercise the option and require the work. Green Management Corp. v. U.S., 42 Fed. Cl. 411 (1998). United States ☞73(22)

Purchase orders whereby government exercised options to extend contract to supply audio cassette players beyond its first year were not binding and enforceable modifications and did not supersede the underlying contract, even though quantity and unit price were left open by the underlying contract, to be filled by subsequent purchase orders; purchase orders depended for their existence on the underlying contract, and were not freestanding contracts. Telex Communications, Inc. v. U.S., 40 Fed. Cl. 703, 42 Cont. Cas. Fed. (CCH) P 77281 (1998), dismissed, 168 F.3d 1317 (Fed. Cir. 1998). United States ☞72(2)

5 Parties

Current supplier under sole source contract for specialized parachutes used in bombs furnished to the armed services was not, at the pleading stage, shown to be a necessary party to prospective contractors' action seeking injunctive and declaratory relief arising from early exercise of option and order enjoining any activity under the option. Irvin Industries, Inc. v. U.S., 608 F. Supp. 907, 32 Cont. Cas. Fed. (CCH) P 73427 (D.D.C. 1985), order vacated, 612 F. Supp. 1105 (D.D.C. 1985). Federal Civil Procedure ☞214

Prospective government contractor had standing to challenge government's actions relating to early exercise of option in negotiated contract for procurement of specialized parachute used in a type of bomb supplied to the armed services, in that the contractor submitted persuasive affidavits indicating that it had and would suffer injury due to exercise of the option and contentions concerning exercise of option were within the "zone of interest" protected by government regulations designed to encourage competition in the procurement process and government did not provide a clear indication of legislative intent to preclude judicial review of exercise of an option. Irvin Industries, Inc. v. U.S., 608 F. Supp. 907, 32 Cont. Cas. Fed. (CCH) P 73427 (D.D.C. 1985), order vacated, 612 F. Supp. 1105 (D.D.C. 1985). Federal Civil Procedure ⟨key⟩103.2; United States ⟨key⟩64.60(2)

6 Injunctions

Four factors which plaintiff would have been required to establish for entitlement to injunctive relief restraining United States from exercising renewal option of public contract with competitor were that it would suffer specific irreparable injury if procurement was not enjoined, there was likelihood of success on merits of claim, harm to be suffered by it outweighed harm of Government and third parties if procurement was enjoined, and granting of injunctive relief would serve public interest. 28 U.S.C.A. § 1491(a)(3). C.M.P., Inc. v. U.S., 8 Cl. Ct. 743, 33 Cont. Cas. Fed. (CCH) P 74027 (1985). United States ⟨key⟩125(18)

7 Federal Court of Claims jurisdiction

Supplier's claim that federal agency wrongfully terminated supply contract by failing to exercise renewal option due to cronyism of contracting officer's technical representative (COTR) was federal contract claim lying within exclusive jurisdiction of Court of Federal Claims, and would be transferred there, despite contention that action was founded on agency's failure to follow procurement regulations making contracting officers (COs) solely responsible for option decisions, and notwithstanding that supplier sought specific performance. 28 U.S.C.A. §§ 1341(a)(2), 1491(b)(1, 2); Federal Property and Administrative Services Act of 1949, § 303(b)(1), 41 U.S.C.A. § 253(b)(1); Contract Disputes Act of 1978, §§ 2, 4, 41 U.S.C.A. §§ 601–613; 48 C.F.R. §§ 17.207, 43.102, 52.217-9. Information Systems & Networks Corp. v. U.S. Dept. of Health and Human Services, 970 F. Supp. 1, 41 Cont. Cas. Fed. (CCH) P 77149 (D.D.C. 1997). Federal Courts ⟨key⟩1139

For purposes of 28 U.S.C.A. § 1491(a)(3), governing Claims Court's jurisdiction to grant relief on contract claims brought before contract is awarded, "exercise of option" in existing contract is not equivalent of award of new contract, but, rather, element in continuation of unitary contract package. C.M.P., Inc. v. U.S., 8 Cl. Ct. 743, 33 Cont. Cas. Fed. (CCH) P 74027 (1985). Federal Courts ⟨key⟩1076

Renewal options of federal contract for computer maintenance services were essential part of total contractual relationship and were not severable from initial term as far as obligations of parties were concerned and, thus, Claims Court did not have jurisdiction pursuant to 28 U.S.C.A. § 1491(a)(3), governing jurisdiction of Claims Court to grant relief on contract claims brought before contract is awarded, to grant equitable relief in competitor's action seeking to restrain United States' from exercising renewal option, which action was brought prior to Government's exercise of renewal option, but after initial contract award. C.M.P., Inc. v. U.S., 8 Cl. Ct. 743, 33 Cont. Cas. Fed. (CCH) P 74027 (1985). Federal Courts ⟨key⟩1080

§ 17.108 Congressional notification.

(a) Except for DoD, NASA, and the Coast Guard, a multi-year contract which includes a cancellation ceiling in excess of $13.5 million may not be awarded until the head of the agency gives written notification of the proposed contract and of the proposed cancellation ceiling for that contract to the committees on appropriations of the House of Representatives and Senate and the appropriate oversight committees of the House and Senate for the agency in question. Information on such committees may not be readily available to contracting officers. Accordingly, agencies should provide such information through its internal regulations. The contract may not be awarded until the thirty-first day after the date of notification.

(b) For DoD, NASA, and the Coast Guard, a multi-year contract which includes a cancellation ceiling in excess of $135 million may not be awarded until the head of the agency gives written notification of the proposed contract and of the proposed cancellation ceiling for that contract to the committees on armed services and appropriations of the House of Representatives and Senate. The contract may not be awarded until the thirty-first day after the date of notification.

United States Code Annotated

Contract requirements, see 41 USCA § 254.

Contracts, planning, solicitation, evaluation, and award procedures, see 10 USCA § 2305.
Definitions, see 10 USCA § 2302, 41 USCA §§ 259, 403.
Kinds of contracts, see 10 USCA § 2306.
Multiyear contracts, acquisition of property, see 10 USCA § 2306b.
Multiyear contracts, acquisition of services, see 10 USCA § 2306c.
Multiyear contracts, see 41 USCA § 254c.
Planning and solicitation requirements, see 41 USCA § 253a.
Severable services contracts for periods crossing fiscal years, see 41 USCA § 253l.

§ 17.109 Contract clauses.

(a) The contracting officer shall insert the clause at 52.217-2, Cancellation Under Multi-year Contracts, in solicitations and contracts when a multi-year contract is contemplated.

(b) *Economic price adjustment clauses.* Economic price adjustment clauses are adaptable to multi-year contracting needs. When the period of production is likely to warrant a labor and material costs contingency in the contract price, the contracting officer should normally use an economic price adjustment clause (see 16.203). When contracting for services, the contracting officer—

(1) Shall add the clause at 52.222-43, Fair Labor Standards Act and Service Contract Labor Standards- Price Adjustment (Multiple Year and Option Contracts), when the contract includes the clause at 52.222-41, Service Contract Labor Standards;

(2) May modify the clause at 52.222-43 in overseas contracts when laws, regulations, or international agreements require contractors to pay higher wage rates; or

(3) May use an economic price adjustment clause authorized by 16.203, when potential fluctuations require coverage and are not included in cost contingencies provided for by the clause at 52.222-43.

United States Code Annotated

Contract requirements, see 41 USCA § 254.
Contracts, planning, solicitation, evaluation, and award procedures, see 10 USCA § 2305.
Definitions, see 10 USCA § 2302, 41 USCA §§ 259, 403.
Kinds of contracts, see 10 USCA § 2306.
Multiyear contracts, acquisition of property, see 10 USCA § 2306b.
Multiyear contracts, acquisition of services, see 10 USCA § 2306c.
Multiyear contracts, see 41 USCA § 254c.
Planning and solicitation requirements, see 41 USCA § 253a.
Severable services contracts for periods crossing fiscal years, see 41 USCA § 253l.

Notes of Decisions

In general 1

1 In general

Although Navy deviated from Cancellation of Items clause in drafting contract schedule that gave Navy until day after contract expired to exercise option to renew, without first obtaining proper authority to do so, contractor could not rely on deviation in arguing that Navy's exercise of options running for two fiscal years were ineffective, since Cancellation of Items clause was primarily for benefit of government. 48 C.F.R. § 17.109(a). Cessna Aircraft Co. v. Dalton, 126 F.3d 1442, 41 Cont. Cas. Fed. (CCH) P 77176 (Fed. Cir. 1997). United States ☞70(35)

Subpart 17.2 Options

§ 17.200 Scope of subpart.

This subpart prescribes policies and procedures for the use of option solicitation provi-sions and contract clauses. Except as provided in agency regulations, this subpart does not apply to contracts for (a) services involving the construction, alteration, or repair (including dredging, excavating, and painting) of buildings, bridges, roads, or other kinds of real property; (b) architect-engineer services; and (c) research and development services. However, it does not preclude the use of options in those contracts.

United States Code Annotated

Contract requirements, see 41 USCA § 254.

Contracts, planning, solicitation, evaluation, and award procedures, see 10 USCA § 2305.

Definitions, see 10 USCA § 2302, 41 USCA §§ 259, 403.

Kinds of contracts, see 10 USCA § 2306.

Planning and solicitation requirements, see 41 USCA § 253a.

§ 17.201 [Reserved]

§ 17.202 Use of options.

(a) Subject to the limitations of paragraphs (b) and (c) of this section, for both sealed bidding and contracting by negotiation, the contracting officer may include options in contracts when it is in the Government's interest. When using sealed bidding, the contracting officer shall make a written determination that there is a reasonable likelihood that the options will be exercised before including the provision at 52.217-5, Evaluation of Options, in the solicitation. (See 17.207(f) with regard to the exercise of options.)

(b) Inclusion of an option is normally not in the Government's interest when, in the judgment of the contracting officer—

(1) The foreseeable requirements involve—

(i) Minimum economic quantities (*i.e.*, quantities large enough to permit the recovery of startup costs and the production of the required supplies at a reasonable price); and

(ii) Delivery requirements far enough into the future to permit competitive acquisition, production, and delivery.

(2) An indefinite quantity or requirements contract would be more appropriate than a contract with options. However, this does not preclude the use of an indefinite quantity contract or requirements contract with options.

(c) The contracting officer shall not employ options if—

(1) The contractor will incur undue risks; *e.g.*, the price or availability of necessary materials or labor is not reasonably foreseeable;

(2) Market prices for the supplies or services involved are likely to change substantially; or

(3) The option represents known firm requirements for which funds are available unless—

(i) The basic quantity is a learning or testing quantity; and

(ii) Competition for the option is impracticable once the initial contract is awarded.

(d) In recognition of—

(1) The Government's need in certain service contracts for continuity of operations; and

(2) The potential cost of disrupted support, options may be included in service contracts if there is an anticipated need for a similar service beyond the first contract period.

United States Code Annotated

Contract requirements, see 41 USCA § 254.

Contracts, planning, solicitation, evaluation, and award procedures, see 10 USCA § 2305.

Definitions, see 10 USCA § 2302, 41 USCA §§ 259, 403.

Kinds of contracts, see 10 USCA § 2306.

Planning and solicitation requirements, see 41 USCA § 253a.

Notes of Decisions

In general 1
Cancellation 2
Federal Court of Claims jurisdiction 5

Injunctions 4
Parties 3

1 In general

Disclosure of option year prices set forth in contract between Department of Air Force and aircraft maintenance and repair service provider, which provided for base year and eight option years, was likely to cause provider substantial competitive harm, and thus was exempt from disclosure under the Freedom of Information Act (FOIA) to provider's competitor; competitors could use such information to underbid the present contract if Air Force should choose to rebid it. 5 U.S.C.A. § 552(b)(4). McDonnell Douglas Corp. v. U.S. Dept. of the Air Force, 375 F.3d 1182, 1188 (D.C. Cir. 2004). Records ☞59

Contract under which computer maintenance firm was to provide maintenance for certain computers owned by federal agency, which expressly indicated that it was an indefinite delivery, indefinite quantity contract, or ID/IQ contract, and established an initial six-month base period, followed by four 12-month options periods and one six-month option period, did not result in formation of a series of separate and distinct requirements contracts, even though option periods did not have a separate minimum quantity of services that would be required. 48 C.F.R. § 16.504(b). Varilease Technology Group, Inc. v. U.S., 289 F.3d 795 (Fed. Cir. 2002). United States ☞70(6.1)

In construing ambiguity in government contract to supply audio cassette players, base unit price figure to which Consumer Price Index (CPI) adjustments were to be applied in future annual purchases pursuant to option provisions was the original base unit price, rather than subsequent CPI adjusted prices; applying CPI adjustment to already adjusted price would have compounded CPI adjustment well beyond inflation. Telex Communications, Inc. v. U.S., 40 Fed. Cl. 703, 42 Cont. Cas. Fed. (CCH) P 77281 (1998), dismissed, 168 F.3d 1317 (Fed. Cir. 1998). United States ☞70(30)

Option extensions to original agreement between Navy and government contractor were mere continuation of original agreement, which competitor was barred from challenging under Tucker Act after original contract had been awarded. 28 U.S.C.A. § 1491(a)(3). Unified Industries, Inc. v. U.S., 24 Cl. Ct. 570, 37 Cont. Cas. Fed. (CCH) P 76226, 1991 WL 255867 (1991). United States ☞64.55(1)

Federal government's use of option clauses is authorized in recognition of government's need in certain service contracts for continuity of operation where there is anticipated need for similar services beyond first contract period. 28 U.S.C.A. § 1491(a)(3). C.M.P., Inc. v. U.S., 8 Cl. Ct. 743, 33 Cont. Cas. Fed. (CCH) P 74027 (1985). United States ☞63

2 Cancellation

Although Navy deviated from Cancellation of Items clause in drafting contract schedule that gave Navy until day after contract expired to exercise option to renew, without first obtaining proper authority to do so, contractor could not rely on deviation in arguing that Navy's exercise of options running for two fiscal years were ineffective, since Cancellation of Items clause was primarily for benefit of government. 48 C.F.R. § 17.109(a). Cessna Aircraft Co. v. Dalton, 126 F.3d 1442, 41 Cont. Cas. Fed. (CCH) P 77176 (Fed. Cir. 1997). United States ☞70(35)

For purpose of determining whether low bidder was entitled to enjoin Government's cancellation of solicitation for bids for providing unarmed guard services, insofar as amendment to solicitation attempted to convert indefinite quantity contract into fixed-price contract subject to options, amendment failed to displace contract provisions inherent in an indefinite contract. Vanguard Sec. Inc. v. U.S., 20 Cl. Ct. 90, 1990 WL 38036 (1990). United States ☞64.60(5.1)

For purpose of determining whether low bidder was entitled to enjoin Government's cancellation of solicitation for bids for providing unarmed guard services, even if solicitation could be characterized as unclear as to whether it was indefinite quantity contract or fixed-price contract subject to options, no bidder was confused about requirements of solicitation, as amended, that contract would be indefinite quantity contract. Vanguard Sec. Inc. v. U.S., 20 Cl. Ct. 90, 1990 WL 38036 (1990). United States ☞64.60(5.1)

For purpose of determining whether low bidder was entitled to enjoin Government's cancellation of solicitation for bids for providing unarmed guard services, solicitation's designation of contract as firm fixed-price contract was consistent with reaffirmation in same section that it was indefinite quantity contract, as meaning of contract was that prices for additional services, as well as for base and optional years, were firm fixed hourly rates. Vanguard Sec. Inc. v. U.S., 20 Cl. Ct. 90, 1990 WL 38036 (1990). United States ☞64.60(5.1)

For purpose of determining whether low bidder was entitled to enjoin Government's cancellation of solicitation for bids for providing unarmed guard services, amendment to solicitation providing that additional hours must be separately priced did not show that solicitation called for provision of additional services through options, as opposed to indefinite quantity requirement, where amendment did not also amend pricing sheet or otherwise advise bidders on how or in what manner they were to furnish additional information. Vanguard Sec. Inc. v. U.S., 20 Cl. Ct. 90, 1990 WL 38036 (1990). United States ☞64.60(5.1)

3 Parties

Current supplier under sole source contract for specialized parachutes used in bombs furnished to the armed services was not, at the pleading stage, shown to be a necessary party to prospective contractors' action seeking injunctive and declaratory relief arising from early exercise of option and order enjoining any activity under the option. Irvin Industries, Inc. v. U.S., 608 F. Supp. 907, 32 Cont. Cas. Fed. (CCH) P 73427 (D.D.C. 1985), order vacated, 612 F. Supp. 1105 (D.D.C. 1985). Federal Civil Procedure ☞214

Prospective government contractor had standing to challenge government's actions relating to early exercise of option in negotiated contract for procurement of specialized parachute used in a type of bomb supplied to the armed services, in that the contractor submitted persuasive affidavits indicating that it had and would suffer injury due to exercise of the option and contentions concerning exercise of option were within the "zone of interest" protected by government regulations designed to encourage competition in the procurement process and government did not provide a clear indication of legislative intent to preclude judicial review of exercise of an option. Irvin Industries, Inc. v. U.S., 608 F. Supp. 907, 32 Cont. Cas. Fed. (CCH) P 73427 (D.D.C. 1985), order vacated, 612 F. Supp. 1105 (D.D.C. 1985). Federal Civil Procedure ☞103.2; United States ☞64.60(2)

4 Injunctions

Four factors which plaintiff would have been required to establish for entitlement to injunctive relief restraining United States from exercising renewal option of public contract with competitor were that it would suffer specific irreparable injury if procurement was not enjoined, there was likelihood of success on merits of claim, harm to be suffered by it outweighed harm of Government and third parties if procurement was enjoined, and granting of injunctive relief would serve public interest. 28 U.S.C.A. § 1491(a)(3). C.M.P., Inc. v. U.S., 8 Cl. Ct. 743, 33 Cont. Cas. Fed. (CCH) P 74027 (1985). United States ☞125(18)

5 Federal Court of Claims jurisdiction

Supplier's claim that federal agency wrongfully terminated supply contract by failing to exercise renewal option due to cronyism of contracting officer's technical representative (COTR) was federal contract claim lying within exclusive jurisdiction of Court of Federal Claims, and would be transferred there, despite contention that action was founded on agency's failure to follow procurement regulations making contracting officers (COs) solely responsible for option decisions, and notwithstanding that supplier sought specific performance. 28 U.S.C.A. §§ 1341(a)(2), 1491(b)(1, 2); Federal Property and Administrative Services Act of 1949, § 303(b)(1), 41 U.S.C.A. § 253(b)(1); Contract Disputes Act of 1978, §§ 2, 4, 41 U.S.C.A. §§ 601–613; 48 C.F.R. §§ 17.207, 43.102, 52.217-9. Information Systems & Networks Corp. v. U.S. Dept. of Health and Human Services, 970 F. Supp. 1, 41 Cont. Cas. Fed. (CCH) P 77149 (D.D.C. 1997). Federal Courts ☞1139

For purposes of 28 U.S.C.A. § 1491(a)(3), governing Claims Court's jurisdiction to grant relief on contract claims brought before contract is awarded, "exercise of option" in existing contract is not equivalent of award of new contract, but, rather, element in continuation of unitary contract package. C.M.P., Inc. v. U.S., 8 Cl. Ct. 743, 33 Cont. Cas. Fed. (CCH) P 74027 (1985). Federal Courts ☞1076

Renewal options of federal contract for computer maintenance services were essential part of total contractual relationship and were not severable from initial term as far as obligations of parties were concerned and, thus, Claims Court did not have jurisdiction pursuant to 28 U.S.C.A. § 1491(a)(3), governing jurisdiction of Claims Court to grant relief on contract claims brought before contract is awarded, to grant equitable relief in competitor's action seeking to restrain United States' from exercising renewal option, which action was brought prior to Government's exercise of renewal option, but after initial contract award. C.M.P., Inc. v. U.S., 8 Cl. Ct. 743, 33 Cont. Cas. Fed. (CCH) P 74027 (1985). Federal Courts ⟨⤳⟩1080

§ 17.203 Solicitations.

(a) Solicitations shall include appropriate option provisions and clauses when resulting contracts will provide for the exercise of options (see 17.208).

(b) Solicitations containing option provisions shall state the basis of evaluation, either exclusive or inclusive of the option and, when appropriate, shall inform offerors that it is anticipated that the Government may exercise the option at time of award.

(c) Solicitations normally should allow option quantities to be offered without limitation as to price, and there shall be no limitation as to price if the option quantity is to be considered in the evaluation for award (see 17.206).

(d) Solicitations that allow the offer of options at unit prices which differ from the unit prices for the basic requirement shall state that offerors may offer varying prices for options, depending on the quantities actually ordered and the dates when ordered.

(e) If it is anticipated that the Government may exercise an option at the time of award and if the condition specified in paragraph (d) of this section applies, solicitations shall specify the price at which the Government will evaluate the option (highest option price offered or option price for specified requirements).

(f) Solicitations may, in unusual circumstances, require that options be offered at prices no higher than those for the initial requirement; *e.g.,* when—

(1) The option cannot be evaluated under 17.206; or;

(2) Future competition for the option is impracticable.

(g) Solicitations that require the offering of an option at prices no higher than those for the initial requirement shall—

(1) Specify that the Government will accept an offer containing an option price higher than the base price only if the acceptance does not prejudice any other offeror; and

(2) Limit option quantities for additional supplies to not more than 50 percent of the initial quantity of the same contract line item. In unusual circumstances, an authorized person at a level above the contracting officer may approve a greater percentage of quantity.

(h) Include the value of options in determining if the acquisition will exceed the World Trade Organization Government Procurement Agreement or Free Trade Agreement thresholds.

United States Code Annotated

Contract requirements, see 41 USCA § 254.

Contracts, planning, solicitation, evaluation, and award procedures, see 10 USCA § 2305.

Definitions, see 10 USCA § 2302, 41 USCA §§ 259, 403.

Kinds of contracts, see 10 USCA § 2306.

Planning and solicitation requirements, see 41 USCA § 253a.

Notes of Decisions

In general 1

1 In general

Purpose of option clause in solicitation of bid for government contract is to provide tool by which government may gain financial advantage in event that government later requires larger quantity than originally anticipated. Noa Airscrew Howden, Inc. v. Department of Army, 622 F. Supp. 984 (E.D. Mich. 1985). United States ⟨⤳⟩64.25

Fact that solicitation for bids for providing unarmed guard services denominated contract as "firm fixed-price" did not show that solicitation called for provision of additional services through options, as opposed to indefinite quantity requirement. Vanguard Sec. Inc. v. U.S., 20 Cl. Ct. 90, 1990 WL 38036 (1990). United States ⊂⇒70(6.1)

§ 17.204 Contracts.

(a) The contract shall specify limits on the purchase of additional supplies or services, or the overall duration of the term of the contract, including any extension.

(b) The contract shall state the period within which the option may be exercised.

(c) The period shall be set so as to provide the contractor adequate lead time to ensure continuous production.

(d) The period may extend beyond the contract completion date for service contracts. This is necessary for situations when exercise of the option would result in the obligation of funds that are not available in the fiscal year in which the contract would otherwise be completed.

(e) Unless otherwise approved in accordance with agency procedures, the total of the basic and option periods shall not exceed 5 years in the case of services, and the total of the basic and option quantities shall not exceed the requirement for 5 years in the case of supplies. These limitations do not apply to information technology contracts. However, statutes applicable to various classes of contracts, for example, the Service Contract Labor Standards statute (see 22.1002-1), may place additional restrictions on the length of contracts.

(f) Contracts may express options for increased quantities of supplies or services in terms of—

(1) Percentage of specific line items,

(2) Increase in specific line items; or

(3) Additional numbered line items identified as the option.

(g) Contracts may express extensions of the term of the contract as an amended completion date or as additional time for performance; e.g., days, weeks, or months.

United States Code Annotated

Contract requirements, see 41 USCA § 254.

Contracts, planning, solicitation, evaluation, and award procedures, see 10 USCA § 2305.

Definitions, see 10 USCA § 2302, 41 USCA §§ 259, 403.

Kinds of contracts, see 10 USCA § 2306.

Planning and solicitation requirements, see 41 USCA § 253a.

Notes of Decisions

Authority to extend contract 1

1 Authority to extend contract

The clause at FAR 52.217-9, Option to Extend the Term of the Contract, limiting performance to five years, did not bar a contract extension beyond five years under FAR 52.217-8, Option to Extend Services, the U.S. Court of Appeals for the Federal Circuit has held. FAR 52.217-8 allows the Government to extend contracts to avoid negotiating short extensions if there is a delay in awarding a new contract. The FAR 52.217-9 limit applies to the contract base year and options, the Federal Circuit held. Arko Executive Services, Inc. v. U.S., 553 F.3d 1375 (Fed. Cir. 2009)

§ 17.205 Documentation.

(a) The contracting officer shall justify in writing the quantities or the term under option, the notification period for exercising the option, and any limitation on option price under 17.203(g); and shall include the justification document in the contract file.

(b) Any justifications and approvals and any determination and findings required by Part 6 shall specify both the basic requirement and the increase permitted by the option.

United States Code Annotated

Contract requirements, see 41 USCA § 254.

Contracts, planning, solicitation, evaluation, and award procedures, see 10 USCA § 2305.

Definitions, see 10 USCA § 2302, 41 USCA §§ 259, 403.

Kinds of contracts, see 10 USCA § 2306.

Planning and solicitation requirements, see 41 USCA § 253a.

§ 17.206 Evaluation.

(a) In awarding the basic contract, the contracting officer shall, except as provided in paragraph (b) of this section, evaluate offers for any option quantities or periods contained in a solicitation when it has been determined prior to soliciting offers that the Government is likely to exercise the options. (See 17.208.)

(b) The contracting officer need not evaluate offers for any option quantities when it is determined that evaluation would not be in the best interests of the Government and this determination is approved at a level above the contracting officer. An example of a circumstance that may support a determination not to evaluate offers for option quantities is when there is a reasonable certainty that funds will be unavailable to permit exercise of the option.

United States Code Annotated

Contract requirements, see 41 USCA § 254.

Contracts, planning, solicitation, evaluation, and award procedures, see 10 USCA § 2305.

Definitions, see 10 USCA § 2302, 41 USCA §§ 259, 403.

Kinds of contracts, see 10 USCA § 2306.

Planning and solicitation requirements, see 41 USCA § 253a.

Notes of Decisions

In general 1

1 In general

Federal acquisition regulation requiring contracting officers to follow noncompetitive procedures before exercising option, when option price was not evaluated in original competitive solicitation, existed for benefit of government, not benefit of contractor, so regulation did not create cause of action on part of contractor that supplied small emplacement excavator (SEE) vehicles to government, and government's alleged failure to comply with regulation in exercising option to increase quantity of vehicles under supply contract would not render its exercise of option ineffective. 48 C.F.R. § 17.207(f). Freightliner Corp. v. Caldera, 225 F.3d 1361 (Fed. Cir. 2000). United States ⟜70(26); United States ⟜74(3)

§ 17.207 Exercise of options.

(a) When exercising an option, the contracting officer shall provide written notice to the contractor within the time period specified in the contract.

(b) When the contract provides for economic price adjustment and the contractor requests a revision of the price, the contracting officer shall determine the effect of the adjustment on prices under the option before the option is exercised.

(c) The contracting officer may exercise options only after determining that—

(1) Funds are available;

(2) The requirement covered by the option fulfills an existing Government need;

(3) The exercise of the option is the most advantageous method of fulfilling the Government's need, price and other factors (see paragraphs (d) and (e) of this section) considered;

(4) The option was synopsized in accordance with Part 5 unless exempted by 5.202(a)(11) or other appropriate exemptions in 5.202;

(5) The contractor is not listed in the System for Award Management Exclusions (see FAR 9.405-1);

(6) The contractor's past performance evaluations on other contract actions have been considered; and

(7) The contractor's performance on this contract has been acceptable, e.g., received satisfactory ratings.

(d) The contracting officer, after considering price and other factors, shall make the determination on the basis of one of the following:

(1) A new solicitation fails to produce a better price or a more advantageous offer than that offered by the option. If it is anticipated that the best price available is the option price or that this is the more advantageous offer, the contracting officer should not use this method of testing the market.

(2) An informal analysis of prices or an examination of the market indicates that the option price is better than prices available in the market or that the option is the more advantageous offer.

(3) The time between the award of the contract containing the option and the exercise of the option is so short that it indicates the option price is the lowest price obtainable or the more advantageous offer. The contracting officer shall take into consideration such factors as market stability and comparison of the time since award with the usual duration of contracts for such supplies or services.

(e) The determination of other factors under paragraph (c)(3) of this section—

(1) Should take into account the Government's need for continuity of operations and potential costs of disrupting operations; and

(2) May consider the effect on small business.

(f) Before exercising an option, the contracting officer shall make a written determination for the contract file that exercise is in accordance with the terms of the option, the requirements of this section, and Part 6. To satisfy requirements of Part 6 regarding full and open competition, the option must have been evaluated as part of the initial competition and be exercisable at an amount specified in or reasonably determinable from the terms of the basic contract, e.g.—

(1) A specific dollar amount;

(2) An amount to be determined by applying provisions (or a formula) provided in the basic contract, but not including renegotiation of the price for work in a fixed-price type contract;

(3) In the case of a cost-type contract, if—

(i) The option contains a fixed or maximum fee; or

(ii) The fixed or maximum fee amount is determinable by applying a formula contained in the basic contract (but see 16.102(c));

(4) A specific price that is subject to an economic price adjustment provision; or

(5) A specific price that is subject to change as the result of changes to prevailing labor rates provided by the Secretary of Labor.

(g) The contract modification or other written document which notifies the contractor of the exercise of the option shall cite the option clause as authority.

Notes of Decisions

In general 1

1 In general

Agency appropriately considered pricing and other information, and reasonably determined that exercising an option under a sole-source contract was the most advantageous way to meet its needs. In Genesis, Inc., Comp. Gen. Dec. B-412101.2, 2016 CPD ¶ 102(Comp. Gen. 2016)

Agency's exercise of an option with eight additional contract clauses not included in the original cotnract,invalidated the option). VARO, Inc., ASBCA No. 47945, 47946, 96-1 BCA ¶ 28,161 (Armed Serv. B.C.A. 1996)

§ 17.208 Solicitation provisions and contract clauses.

(a) Insert a provision substantially the same as the provision at 52.217-3, Evaluation Exclusive of Options, in solicitations when the solicitation includes an option clause and does not include one of the provisions prescribed in paragraph (b) or (c) of this section.

(b) Insert a provision substantially the same as the provision at 52.217-4, Evaluation of Options Exercised at Time of Contract Award, in solicitations when the solicitation includes an option clause, the contracting officer has determined that there is a reasonable likelihood that the option will be exercised, and the option may be exercised at the time of contract award.

(c) Insert a provision substantially the same as the provision at 52.217-5, Evaluation of Options, in solicitations when—

(1) The solicitation contains an option clause;

(2) An option is not to be exercised at the time of contract award;

(3) A firm-fixed-price contract, a fixed-price contract with economic price adjustment, or other type of contract approved under agency procedures is contemplated; and

(4) The contracting officer has determined that there is a reasonable likelihood that the option will be exercised. For sealed bids, the determination shall be in writing.

(d) Insert a clause substantially the same as the clause at 52.217-6, Option for Increased Quantity, in solicitations and contracts, other than those for services, when the inclusion of an option is appropriate (see 17.200 and 17.202) and the option quantity is expressed as a percentage of the basic contract quantity or as an additional quantity of a specific line item.

(e) Insert a clause substantially the same as the clause at 52.217-7, Option for Increased Quantity—Separately Priced Line Item, in solicitations and contracts, other than those for services, when the inclusion of an option is appropriate (see 17.200 and 17.202) and the option quantity is identified as a separately priced line item having the same nomenclature as a corresponding basic contract line item.

(f) Insert a clause substantially the same as the clause at 52.217-8, Option to Extend Services, in solicitations and contracts for services when the inclusion of an option is appropriate. (See 17.200, 17.202, and 37.111.)

(g) Insert a clause substantially the same as the clause at 52.217-9, Option to Extend the Term of the Contract, in solicitations and contracts when the inclusion of an option is appropriate (see 17.200 and 17.202) and it is necessary to include in the contract any or all of the following:

(1) A requirement that the Government must give the contractor a preliminary written notice of its intent to extend the contract.

(2) A statement that an extension of the contract includes an extension of the option.

(3) A specified limitation on the total duration of the contract.

United States Code Annotated

Contract requirements, see 41 USCA § 254.

Contracts, planning, solicitation, evaluation, and award procedures, see 10 USCA § 2305.

Definitions, see 10 USCA § 2302, 41 USCA §§ 259, 403.

Kinds of contracts, see 10 USCA § 2306.

Planning and solicitation requirements, see 41 USCA § 253a.

Notes of Decisions

In general 1

1 In general

Purpose of option clause in solicitation of bid for government contract is to provide tool by which government may gain financial advantage in event that government later requires larger quantity than originally anticipated. Noa Airscrew Howden, Inc. v. Department of Army, 622 F. Supp. 984 (E.D. Mich. 1985). United States ☞64.25

Bilateral modifications extending the periods of performance of the base period and options did not "count" against the 6-month limitation imposed by FAR 52.217-8, Option to Extend Services, because that clause authorizes unilateral modifications only. Glasgow Investigative Solutions, Inc., ASBCA 58111, 13-1 BCA ¶ 35286 (Armed Serv. B.C.A. 2013)

FAR 52.217-8, Option to Extend Services does not limit the Contracting Officer to extensions occurring after the exercise of all options. FAR 52.217-8 also authorizes the CO to extend the period of performance of the base period prior to the exercise of any options. Glasgow Investigative Solutions, Inc., ASBCA 58111, 13-1 BCA ¶ 35286 (Armed Serv. B.C.A. 2013)

Fact that solicitation for bids for providing unarmed guard services denominated contract as "firm fixed-price" did not show that solicitation called for provision of additional services through options, as opposed to indefinite quantity requirement. Vanguard Sec. Inc. v. U.S., 20 Cl. Ct. 90, 1990 WL 38036 (1990). United States ☞70(6.1)

Subpart 17.3 [Reserved]

Subpart 17.4 Leader Company Contracting

§ 17.401 General.

Leader company contracting is an extraordinary acquisition technique that is limited to special circumstances and utilized only when its use is in accordance with agency procedures. A developer or sole producer of a product or system is designated under this acquisition technique to be the leader company, and to furnish assistance and know-how under an approved contract to one or more designated follower companies, so they can become a source of supply. The objectives of this technique are one or more of the following:

(a) Reduce delivery time.

(b) Achieve geographic dispersion of suppliers.

(c) Maximize the use of scarce tooling or special equipment.

(d) Achieve economies in production.

(e) Ensure uniformity and reliability in equipment, compatibility or standardization of components, and interchangeability of parts.

(f) Eliminate problems in the use of proprietary data that cannot be resolved by more satisfactory solutions.

(g) Facilitate the transition from development to production and to subsequent competitive acquisition of end items or major components.

United States Code Annotated

Contract requirements, see 41 USCA § 254.

Contracts, planning, solicitation, evaluation, and award procedures, see 10 USCA § 2305.

Definitions, see 10 USCA § 2302, 41 USCA §§ 259, 403.

Kinds of contracts, see 10 USCA § 2306.

Planning and solicitation requirements, see 41 USCA § 253a.

§ 17.402 Limitations.

(a) Leader company contracting is to be used only when—

(1) The leader company has the necessary production know-how and is able to furnish required assistance to the follower(s);

(2) No other source can meet the Government's requirements without the assistance of a leader company;

(3) The assistance required of the leader company is limited to that which is essential to enable the follower(s) to produce the items; and

(4) Its use is authorized in accordance with agency procedures.

(b) When leader company contracting is used, the Government shall reserve the right to approve subcontracts between the leader company and the follower(s).

United States Code Annotated

Contract requirements, see 41 USCA § 254.

Contracts, planning, solicitation, evaluation, and award procedures, see 10 USCA § 2305.

Definitions, see 10 USCA § 2302, 41 USCA §§ 259, 403.

Kinds of contracts, see 10 USCA § 2306.

Planning and solicitation requirements, see 41 USCA § 253a.

§ 17.403 Procedures.

(a) The contracting officer may award a prime contract to a—

(1) Leader company, obligating it to subcontract a designated portion of the required

end items to a specified follower company and to assist it to produce the required end items;

(2) Leader company, for the required assistance to a follower company, and a prime contract to the follower for production of the items; or

(3) Follower company, obligating it to subcontract with a designated leader company for the required assistance.

(b) The contracting officer shall ensure that any contract awarded under this arrangement contains a firm agreement regarding disclosure, if any, of contractor trade secrets, technical designs or concepts, and specific data, or software, of a proprietary nature.

United States Code Annotated

Contract requirements, see 41 USCA § 254.

Contracts, planning, solicitation, evaluation, and award procedures, see 10 USCA § 2305.

Definitions, see 10 USCA § 2302, 41 USCA §§ 259, 403.

Kinds of contracts, see 10 USCA § 2306.

Planning and solicitation requirements, see 41 USCA § 253a.

Subpart 17.5 Interagency Acquisitions Under the Economy Act

§ 17.500 Scope of subpart.

(a) This subpart prescribes policies and procedures applicable to all interagency acquisitions under any authority, except as provided for in paragraph (c) of this section. In addition to complying with the interagency acquisition policy and procedures in this subpart, nondefense agencies acquiring supplies and services on behalf of the Department of Defense shall also comply with the policy and procedures at subpart 17.7.

(b) This subpart applies to interagency acquisitions, see 2.101 for definition, when—

(1) An agency needing supplies or services obtains them using another agency's contract; or

(2) An agency uses another agency to provide acquisition assistance, such as awarding and administering a contract, a task order, or delivery order.

(c) This subpart does not apply to—

(1) Interagency reimbursable work performed by Federal employees (other than acquisition assistance), or interagency activities where contracting is incidental to the purpose of the transaction; or

(2) Orders of $550,000 or less issued against Federal Supply Schedules.

United States Code Annotated

Agency agreements, see 31 USCA § 1535.

Contract requirements, see 41 USCA § 254.

Contracts, planning, solicitation, evaluation, and award procedures, see 10 USCA § 2305.

Definitions, see 10 USCA § 2302, 41 USCA §§ 259, 403.

Kinds of contracts, see 10 USCA § 2306.

Planning and solicitation requirements, see 41 USCA § 253a.

Notes of Decisions

In general 1

1 In general

United States Information Agency (USIA) could produce television news broadcasts for transmission to Cuba in-house, rather than through use of independent contractors procured by contract, without comparing costs of each alternative as required by Economy Act and Office of Management and Budget Circular; TV Marti Act called for "maximum utilization" of agency resources, and its specific requirements controlled over those of Economy Act, a statute having general applicability. Television Broadcasting to Cuba Act,

§ 244(b), 22 U.S.C.A. § 1465cc(b); 31 U.S.C.A. § 1535(a). Techniarts Engineering v. U.S., 51 F.3d 301, 311, 40 Cont. Cas. Fed. (CCH) P 76774 (D.C. Cir. 1995). United States ☞64.10

Air Force's Electronics Security Command was not prohibited by Competition in Contracting Act, in procuring automated data processing equipment, from changing from full and open competition procurement under that Act to procurement from another agency through existing contract under the Economy Act. 10 U.S.C.A. § 2304(a)(1), (c); 31 U.S.C.A. § 1535. National Gateway Telecom, Inc. v. Aldridge, 701 F. Supp. 1104 (D.N.J. 1988), judgment aff'd, 879 F.2d 858 (3d Cir. 1989). United States ☞64.10

§ 17.501 General.

(a) Interagency acquisitions are commonly conducted through indefinite-delivery contracts, such as task- and delivery-order contracts. The indefinite-delivery contracts used most frequently to support interagency acquisitions are Federal Supply Schedules (FSS), Governmentwide acquisition contracts (GWACs), and multi-agency contracts (MACs).

(b) An agency shall not use an interagency acquisition to circumvent conditions and limitations imposed on the use of funds.

(c) An interagency acquisition is not exempt from the requirements of subpart 7.3, Contractor Versus Government Performance.

(d) An agency shall not use an interagency acquisition to make acquisitions conflicting with any other agency's authority or responsibility (for example, that of the Administrator of General Services under title 40, United States Code, "Public Buildings, Property and Works" and 41 U.S.C. division C of subtitle I, Procurement.)

United States Code Annotated

Agency agreements, see 31 USCA § 1535.

Contract requirements, see 41 USCA § 254.

Contracts, planning, solicitation, evaluation, and award procedures, see 10 USCA § 2305.

Definitions, see 10 USCA § 2302, 41 USCA §§ 259, 403.

Kinds of contracts, see 10 USCA § 2306.

Planning and solicitation requirements, see 41 USCA § 253a.

§ 17.502 Procedures.

§ 17.502-1 General.

(a) Determination of best procurement approach.

(1) *Assisted acquisitions.* Prior to requesting that another agency conduct an acquisition on its behalf, the requesting agency shall make a determination that the use of an interagency acquisition represents the best procurement approach. As part of the best procurement approach determination, the requesting agency shall obtain the concurrence of the requesting agency's responsible contracting office in accordance with internal agency procedures. At a minimum, the determination shall include an analysis of procurement approaches, including an evaluation by the requesting agency that using the acquisition services of another agency—

(i) Satisfies the requesting agency's schedule, performance, and delivery requirements (taking into account factors such as the servicing agency's authority, experience, and expertise as well as customer satisfaction with the servicing agency's past performance);

(ii) Is cost effective (taking into account the reasonableness of the servicing agency's fees); and

(iii) Will result in the use of funds in accordance with appropriation limitations and compliance with the requesting agency's laws and policies.

(2) *Direct acquisitions.* Prior to placing an order against another agency's indefinite-delivery vehicle, the requesting agency shall make a determination that use of another agency's contract vehicle is the best procurement approach and shall obtain the concurrence of the requesting agency's responsible contracting office. At a minimum, the determination shall include an analysis, including factors such as:

(i) The suitability of the contract vehicle;

    (ii) The value of using the contract vehicle, including—

        (A) The administrative cost savings from using an existing contract;

        (B) Lower prices, greater number of vendors, and reasonable vehicle access fees; and

    (iii) The expertise of the requesting agency to place orders and administer them against the selected contract vehicle throughout the acquisition lifecycle.

  (b) Written agreement on responsibility for management and administration.

    (1) Assisted acquisitions.

    (i) Prior to the issuance of a solicitation, the servicing agency and the requesting agency shall both sign a written interagency agreement that establishes the general terms and conditions governing the relationship between the parties, including roles and responsibilities for acquisition planning, contract execution, and administration and management of the contract(s) or order(s). The requesting agency shall provide to the servicing agency any unique terms, conditions, and applicable agency-specific statutes, regulations, directives, and other applicable requirements for incorporation into the order or contract. In the event there are no agency unique requirements beyond the FAR, the requesting agency shall so inform the servicing agency contracting officer in writing. For acquisitions on behalf of the Department of Defense, also see Subpart 17.7. for patent rights, see 27.304-2. In preparing interagency agreements to support assisted acquisitions, agencies should review the Office of Federal Procurement Policy guidance, Interagency Acquisitions, available at http://www.whitehouse.go v/omb/assets/procurement/iac_revised.pdf.

    (ii) Each agency's file shall include the interagency agreement between the requesting and servicing agency, and shall include sufficient documentation to ensure an adequate audit consistent with 4.801(b).

    (2) *Direct acquisitions.* The requesting agency administers the order; therefore, no written agreement with the servicing agency is required.

  (c) *Business-case analysis requirements for multi-agency contracts and governmentwide acquisition contracts.* In order to establish a multi-agency or governmentwide acquisition contract, a business-case analysis must be prepared by the servicing agency and approved in accordance with the Office of Federal Procurement Policy (OFPP) business case guidance, available at http://www.whitehouse.gov/sites/default/files/omb/procurement/memo/dev elopment-review-and-approval-of-business-cases-for-certain-interagency-and-agency-specifi c-acquisitions-memo.pdf. The business-case analysis shall—

    (1) Consider strategies for the effective participation of small businesses during acquisition planning (see 7.103(u));

    (2) Detail the administration of such contract, including an analysis of all direct and indirect costs to the Government of awarding and administering such contract;

    (3) Describe the impact such contract will have on the ability of the Government to leverage its purchasing power, *e.g.*, will it have a negative effect because it dilutes other existing contracts;

    (4) Include an analysis concluding that there is a need for establishing the multi-agency contract; and

    (5) Document roles and responsibilities in the administration of the contract.

§ 17.502-2 The Economy Act.

  (a) The Economy Act (31 U.S.C. 1535) authorizes agencies to enter into agreements to obtain supplies or services from another agency. The FAR applies when one agency uses another agency's contract to obtain supplies or services. If the interagency business transaction does not result in a contract or an order, then the FAR does not apply. The Economy Act also provides authority for placement of orders between major organizational units within an agency; procedures for such intra-agency transactions are addressed in agency regulations.

  (b) The Economy Act applies when more specific statutory authority does not exist. Examples of more specific authority are 40 U.S.C. 501 for the Federal Supply Schedules (subpart 8.4), and 40 U.S.C. 11302(e) for Governmentwide acquisition contracts (GWACs).

  (c) Requirements for determinations and findings.

    (1) Each Economy Act order to obtain supplies or services by interagency acquisition

shall be supported by a determination and findings (D&F). The D&F shall—

(i) State that use of an interagency acquisition is in the best interest of the Government;

(ii) State that the supplies or services cannot be obtained as conveniently or economically by contracting directly with a private source; and

(iii) Include a statement that at least one of the following circumstances applies:

(A) The acquisition will appropriately be made under an existing contract of the servicing agency, entered into before placement of the order, to meet the requirements of the servicing agency for the same or similar supplies or services.

(B) The servicing agency has the capability or expertise to enter into a contract for such supplies or services that is not available within the requesting agency.

(C) The servicing agency is specifically authorized by law or regulation to purchase such supplies or services on behalf of other agencies.

(2) The D&F shall be approved by a contracting officer of the requesting agency with authority to contract for the supplies or services to be ordered, or by another official designated by the agency head, except that, if the servicing agency is not covered by the FAR, approval of the D&F may not be delegated below the senior procurement executive of the requesting agency.

(3) The requesting agency shall furnish a copy of the D&F to the servicing agency with the request for order.

(d) Payment.

(1) *The servicing agency may ask the* requesting agency, in writing, for advance payment for all or part of the estimated cost of furnishing the supplies or services. Adjustment on the basis of actual costs shall be made as agreed to by the agencies.

(2) If approved by the servicing agency, payment for actual costs may be made by the requesting agency after the supplies or services have been furnished.

(3) Bills rendered or requests for advance payment shall not be subject to audit or certification in advance of payment.

(4) In no event shall the servicing agency require, or the requesting agency pay, any fee or charge in excess of the actual cost (or estimated cost if the actual cost is not known) of entering into and administering the contract or other agreement under which the order is filled.

United States Code Annotated

Agency agreements, see 31 USCA § 1535.

Contract requirements, see 41 USCA § 254.

Contracts, planning, solicitation, evaluation, and award procedures, see 10 USCA § 2305.

Definitions, see 10 USCA § 2302, 41 USCA §§ 259, 403.

Kinds of contracts, see 10 USCA § 2306.

Planning and solicitation requirements, see 41 USCA § 253a.

Notes of Decisions

In general 1

1 In general

United States Information Agency (USIA) could produce television news broadcasts for transmission to Cuba in-house, rather than through use of independent contractors procured by contract, without comparing costs of each alternative as required by Economy Act and Office of Management and Budget Circular; TV Marti Act called for "maximum utilization" of agency resources, and its specific requirements controlled over those of Economy Act, a statute having general applicability. Television Broadcasting to Cuba Act, § 244(b), 22 U.S.C.A. § 1465cc(b); 31 U.S.C.A. § 1535(a). Techniarts Engineering v. U.S., 51 F.3d 301, 311, 40 Cont. Cas. Fed. (CCH) P 76774 (D.C. Cir. 1995). United States ⊕64.10

Air Force's Electronics Security Command was not prohibited by Competition in Contracting Act, in procuring automated data processing equipment, from changing from full and open competition procurement under that Act to procurement from another agency through existing contract under the Economy Act. 10 U.S.C.A. § 2304(a)(1), (c); 31 U.S.C.A. § 1535.

National Gateway Telecom, Inc. v. Aldridge, 701 F. Supp. 1104 (D.N.J. 1988), judgment aff'd, 879 F.2d 858 (3d Cir. 1989). United States ⊙64.10

§ 17.503 Ordering procedures.

(a) Before placing an order for supplies or services with another Government agency, the requesting agency shall follow the procedures in 17.502-1 and, if under the Economy Act, also 17.502-2.

(b) The order may be placed on any form or document that is acceptable to both agencies. The order should include—

(1) A description of the supplies or services required;

(2) Delivery requirements;

(3) A funds citation;

(4) A payment provision (see 17.502-2(d) for Economy Act orders); and

(5) Acquisition authority as may be appropriate (see 17.503(d)).

(c) The requesting and servicing agencies should agree to procedures for the resolution of disagreements that may arise under interagency acquisitions, including, in appropriate circumstances, the use of a third-party forum. If a third party is proposed, consent of the third party should be obtained in writing.

(d) When an interagency acquisition requires the servicing agency to award a contract, the following procedures also apply:

(1) If a justification and approval or a D&F (other than the requesting agency's D&F required in 17.502-2(c)) is required by law or regulation, the servicing agency shall execute and issue the justification and approval or D&F. The requesting agency shall furnish the servicing agency any information needed to make the justification and approval or D&F.

(2) The requesting agency shall also be responsible for furnishing other assistance that may be necessary, such as providing information or special contract terms needed to comply with any condition or limitation applicable to the funds of the requesting agency.

(3) The servicing agency is responsible for compliance with all other legal or regulatory requirements applicable to the contract, including—

(i) Having adequate statutory authority for the contractual action; and

(ii) Complying fully with the competition requirements of part 6 (see 6.002). However, if the servicing agency is not subject to the Federal Acquisition Regulation, the requesting agency shall verify that contracts utilized to meet its requirements contain provisions protecting the Government from inappropriate charges (for example, provisions mandated for FAR agencies by part 31), and that adequate contract administration will be provided.

(e) Nonsponsoring Federal agencies may use a Federally Funded Research and Development Center (FFRDC) only if the terms of the FFRDC's sponsoring agreement permit work from other than a sponsoring agency. Work placed with the FFRDC is subject to the acceptance by the sponsor and must fall within the purpose, mission, general scope of effort, or special competency of the FFRDC. (See 35.017; see also 6.302 for procedures to follow where using other than full and open competition.) The nonsponsoring agency shall provide to the sponsoring agency necessary documentation that the requested work would not place the FFRDC in direct competition with domestic private industry.

United States Code Annotated

Agency agreements, see 31 USCA § 1535.

Contract requirements, see 41 USCA § 254.

Contracts, planning, solicitation, evaluation, and award procedures, see 10 USCA § 2305.

Definitions, see 10 USCA § 2302, 41 USCA §§ 259, 403.

Kinds of contracts, see 10 USCA § 2306.

Planning and solicitation requirements, see 41 USCA § 253a.

Notes of Decisions

In general 1

1 In general

United States Information Agency (USIA) could produce television news broadcasts for transmission to Cuba in-house, rather than through use of independent contractors procured by contract, without comparing costs of each alternative as required by Economy Act and Office of Management and Budget Circular; TV Marti Act called for "maximum utilization" of agency resources, and its specific requirements controlled over those of Economy Act, a statute having general applicability. Television Broadcasting to Cuba Act, § 244(b), 22 U.S.C.A. § 1465cc(b); 31 U.S.C.A. § 1535(a). Techniarts Engineering v. U.S., 51 F.3d 301, 311, 40 Cont. Cas. Fed. (CCH) P 76774 (D.C. Cir. 1995). United States ⊕64.10

Air Force's Electronics Security Command was not prohibited by Competition in Contracting Act, in procuring automated data processing equipment, from changing from full and open competition procurement under that Act to procurement from another agency through existing contract under the Economy Act. 10 U.S.C.A. § 2304(a)(1), (c); 31 U.S.C.A. § 1535. National Gateway Telecom, Inc. v. Aldridge, 701 F. Supp. 1104 (D.N.J. 1988), judgment aff'd, 879 F.2d 858 (3d Cir. 1989). United States ⊕64.10

The COFC denied a protest challenging an agency's decision to cancel a solicitation and order the services from another agency under the Economy Act. Although the agency failed to prepare a properly signed Determination and Findings (D&F), as required by the Economy Act, the protester did not show that it was prejudiced by the violation and the agency had other adequate documentation indicating that purchase via the Economy Act would result in cost-savings. RN Expertise, Inc. v. U.S., 97 Fed. Cl. 460 (2011)

§ 17.504 Reporting requirements.

The senior procurement executive for each executive agency shall submit to the Director of OMB an annual report on interagency acquisitions, as directed by OMB.

United States Code Annotated
Agency agreements, see 31 USCA § 1535.

Contract requirements, see 41 USCA § 254.

Contracts, planning, solicitation, evaluation, and award procedures, see 10 USCA § 2305.

Definitions, see 10 USCA § 2302, 41 USCA §§ 259, 403.

Kinds of contracts, see 10 USCA § 2306.

Planning and solicitation requirements, see 41 USCA § 253a.

Notes of Decisions
In general 1

1 In general

United States Information Agency (USIA) could produce television news broadcasts for transmission to Cuba in-house, rather than through use of independent contractors procured by contract, without comparing costs of each alternative as required by Economy Act and Office of Management and Budget Circular; TV Marti Act called for "maximum utilization" of agency resources, and its specific requirements controlled over those of Economy Act, a statute having general applicability. Television Broadcasting to Cuba Act, § 244(b), 22 U.S.C.A. § 1465cc(b); 31 U.S.C.A. § 1535(a). Techniarts Engineering v. U.S., 51 F.3d 301, 311, 40 Cont. Cas. Fed. (CCH) P 76774 (D.C. Cir. 1995). United States ⊕64.10

Air Force's Electronics Security Command was not prohibited by Competition in Contracting Act, in procuring automated data processing equipment, from changing from full and open competition procurement under that Act to procurement from another agency through existing contract under the Economy Act. 10 U.S.C.A. § 2304(a)(1), (c); 31 U.S.C.A. § 1535. National Gateway Telecom, Inc. v. Aldridge, 701 F. Supp. 1104 (D.N.J. 1988), judgment aff'd, 879 F.2d 858 (3d Cir. 1989). United States ⊕64.10

Subpart 17.6 Management and Operating Contracts

§ 17.600 Scope of subpart.
This subpart prescribes policies and procedures for management and operating contracts for the Department of Energy and any other agency having requisite statutory authority.

United States Code Annotated

Contract requirements, see 41 USCA § 254.

Contracts, planning, solicitation, evaluation, and award procedures, see 10 USCA § 2305.

Definitions, see 10 USCA § 2302, 41 USCA §§ 259, 403.

Kinds of contracts, see 10 USCA § 2306.

Planning and solicitation requirements, see 41 USCA § 253a.

§ 17.601 Definition.

"Management and operating contract" means an agreement under which the Government contracts for the operation, maintenance, or support, on its behalf, of a Government-owned or -controlled research, development, special production, or testing establishment wholly or principally devoted to one or more major programs of the contracting Federal agency.

United States Code Annotated

Contract requirements, see 41 USCA § 254.

Contracts, planning, solicitation, evaluation, and award procedures, see 10 USCA § 2305.

Definitions, see 10 USCA § 2302, 41 USCA §§ 259, 403.

Kinds of contracts, see 10 USCA § 2306.

Planning and solicitation requirements, see 41 USCA § 253a.

Notes of Decisions

Management and operating contracts 1

1 Management and operating contracts

Government did not share a special relationship with employees of contractor which was party to a management and operating (M & O) contract such that government had obligation to ensure that employees received severance from contractor; government's only obligation was to reimburse contractor for severance pay that arose as result of the contract. Christos v. U.S., 48 Fed. Cl. 469 (2000), aff'd, 300 F.3d 1381 (Fed. Cir. 2002). United States ⊛70(5)

§ 17.602 Policy.

(a) Heads of agencies, with requisite statutory authority, may determine in writing to authorize contracting officers to enter into or renew any management and operating contract in accordance with the agency's statutory authority, or 41 U.S.C. chapter 33, and the agency's regulations governing such contracts. This authority shall not be delegated. Every contract so authorized shall show its authorization upon its face.

(b) Agencies may authorize management and operating contracts only in a manner consistent with the guidance of this subpart and only if they are consistent with the situations described in 17.604.

(c) Within 2 years of the effective date of this regulation, agencies shall review their current contractual arrangements in the light of the guidance of this subpart, in order to—

(1) Identify, modify as necessary, and authorize management and operating contracts; and

(2) Modify as necessary or terminate contracts not so identified and authorized, except that any contract with less than 4 years remaining as of the effective date of this regulation need not be terminated, nor need it be identified, modified, or authorized unless it is renewed or its terms are substantially renegotiated.

United States Code Annotated

Contract requirements, see 41 USCA § 254.

Contracts, planning, solicitation, evaluation, and award procedures, see 10 USCA § 2305.

Definitions, see 10 USCA § 2302, 41 USCA §§ 259, 403.

Kinds of contracts, see 10 USCA § 2306.

Planning and solicitation requirements, see 41 USCA § 253a.

Notes of Decisions

In general 1

1 In general

Government did not share a special relationship with employees of contractor which was party to a management and operating (M & O) contract such that government had obligation to ensure that employees received severance from contractor; government's only obligation was to reimburse contractor for severance pay that arose as result of the contract. Christos v. U.S., 48 Fed. Cl. 469 (2000), aff'd, 300 F.3d 1381 (Fed. Cir. 2002). United States ⊕70(5)

§ 17.603 Limitations.

(a) Management and operating contracts shall not be authorized for—

(1) Functions involving the direction, supervision, or control of Government personnel, except for supervision incidental to training;

(2) Functions involving the exercise of police or regulatory powers in the name of the Government, other than guard or plant protection services;

(3) Functions of determining basic Government policies;

(4) Day-to-day staff or management functions of the agency or of any of its elements; or

(5) Functions that can more properly be accomplished in accordance with Subpart 45.3, Authorizing the Use and Rental of Government Property.

(b) Since issuance of an authorization under 17.602(a) is deemed sufficient proof of compliance with paragraph (a) immediately above, nothing in paragraph (a) immediately above shall affect the validity or legality of such an authorization.

United States Code Annotated

Contract requirements, see 41 USCA § 254.

Contracts, planning, solicitation, evaluation, and award procedures, see 10 USCA § 2305.

Definitions, see 10 USCA § 2302, 41 USCA §§ 259, 403.

Kinds of contracts, see 10 USCA § 2306.

Planning and solicitation requirements, see 41 USCA § 253a.

Notes of Decisions

In general 1

1 In general

Government did not share a special relationship with employees of contractor which was party to a management and operating (M & O) contract such that government had obligation to ensure that employees received severance from contractor; government's only obligation was to reimburse contractor for severance pay that arose as result of the contract. Christos v. U.S., 48 Fed. Cl. 469 (2000), aff'd, 300 F.3d 1381 (Fed. Cir. 2002). United States ⊕70(5)

§ 17.604 Identifying management and operating contracts.

A management and operating contract is characterized both by its purpose (see 17.601) and by the special relationship it creates between Government and contractor. The following criteria can generally be applied in identifying management and operating contracts:

(a) Government-owned or -controlled facilities must be utilized; for instance—

(1) In the interest of national defense or mobilization readiness;

(2) To perform the agency's mission adequately; or

(3) Because private enterprise is unable or unwilling to use its own facilities for the work.

(b) Because of the nature of the work, or because it is to be performed in Government facilities, the Government must maintain a special, close relationship with the contractor and the contractor's personnel in various important areas (e.g., safety, security, cost control, site conditions).

(c) The conduct of the work is wholly or at least substantially separate from the contractor's other business, if any.

(d) The work is closely related to the agency's mission and is of a long-term or continuing nature, and there is a need—

(1) To ensure its continuity; and

(2) For special protection covering the orderly transition of personnel and work in the event of a change in contractors.

United States Code Annotated

Contract requirements, see 41 USCA § 254.

Contracts, planning, solicitation, evaluation, and award procedures, see 10 USCA § 2305.

Definitions, see 10 USCA § 2302, 41 USCA §§ 259, 403.

Kinds of contracts, see 10 USCA § 2306.

Planning and solicitation requirements, see 41 USCA § 253a.

§ 17.605 Award, renewal, and extension.

(a) Effective work performance under management and operating contracts usually involves high levels of expertise and continuity of operations and personnel. Because of program requirements and the unusual (sometimes unique) nature of the work performed under management and operating contracts, the Government is often limited in its ability to effect competition or to replace a contractor. Therefore contracting officers should take extraordinary steps before award to assure themselves that the prospective contractor's technical and managerial capacity are sufficient, that organizational conflicts of interest are adequately covered, and that the contract will grant the Government broad and continuing rights to involve itself, if necessary, in technical and managerial decisionmaking concerning performance.

(b) The contracting officer shall review each management and operating contract, following agency procedures, at appropriate intervals and at least once every 5 years. The review should determine whether meaningful improvement in performance or cost might reasonably be achieved. Any extension or renewal of an operating and management contract must be authorized at a level within the agency no lower than the level at which the original contract was authorized in accordance with 17.602(a).

(c) Replacement of an incumbent contractor is usually based largely upon expectation of meaningful improvement in performance or cost. Therefore, when reviewing contractor performance, contracting officers should consider—

(1) The incumbent contractor's overall performance, including, specifically, technical, administrative, and cost performance;

(2) The potential impact of a change in contractors on program needs, including safety, national defense, and mobilization considerations; and

(3) Whether it is likely that qualified offerors will compete for the contract.

United States Code Annotated

Contract requirements, see 41 USCA § 254.

Contracts, planning, solicitation, evaluation, and award procedures, see 10 USCA § 2305.

Definitions, see 10 USCA § 2302, 41 USCA §§ 259, 403.

Kinds of contracts, see 10 USCA § 2306.

Planning and solicitation requirements, see 41 USCA § 253a.

Subpart 17.7 Interagency Acquisitions: Acquisitions by Nondefense Agencies on Behalf of the Department of Defense

§ 17.700 Scope of subpart.

(a) Compliance with this subpart is in addition to the policies and procedures for interagency acquisitions set forth in Subpart 17.5. This subpart prescribes policies and procedures specific to acquisitions of supplies and services by nondefense agencies on behalf of the Department of Defense (DoD).

(b) This subpart implements Pub. L. 110-181, section 801, as amended (10 USC 2304 Note).

§ 17.701 Definitions.

As used in this subpart—

"Department of Defense (DoD) acquisition official" means—

(1) A DoD contracting officer; or

(2) Any other DoD official authorized to approve a direct acquisition or an assisted acquisition on behalf of DoD.

"Nondefense agency" means any department or agency of the Federal Government other than the Department of Defense.

"Nondefense agency that is an element of the intelligence community" means the agencies identified in 50 U.S.C. 401a(4) which include the—

(1) Office of the Director of National Intelligence;

(2) Central Intelligence Agency;

(3) Intelligence elements of the Federal Bureau of Investigation, Department of Energy, and Drug Enforcement Agency;

(4) Bureau of Intelligence and Research of the Department of State;

(5) Office of Intelligence and Analysis of the Department of the Treasury;

(6) The Office of Intelligence and Analysis of the Department of Homeland Security and the Office of Intelligence of the Coast Guard; and

(7) Such other elements of any department or agency as have been designated by the President, or designated jointly by the Director of National Intelligence and the head of the department or agency concerned, as an element of the intelligence community.

§ 17.702 Applicability.

This subpart applies to all acquisitions made by nondefense agencies on behalf of DoD. It does not apply to contracts entered into by a nondefense agency that is an element of the intelligence community for the performance of a joint program conducted to meet the needs of DoD and the nondefense agency.

§ 17.703 Policy.

(a) A DoD acquisition official may request a nondefense agency to conduct an acquisition on behalf of DoD in excess of the simplified acquisition threshold only if the head of the nondefense agency conducting the acquisition on DoD's behalf has certified that the agency will comply with applicable procurement requirements for that fiscal year except when waived in accordance with paragraph (e) of this section.

(b) A nondefense agency is compliant with applicable procurement requirements if the procurement policies, procedures, and internal controls of the nondefense agency applicable to the procurement of supplies and services on behalf of DoD, and the manner in which they are administered, are adequate to ensure the compliance of the nondefense department or agency with—

(1) The Federal Acquisition Regulation and other laws and regulations that apply to procurements of supplies and services by Federal agencies; and

(2) Laws and regulations that apply to procurements of supplies and services made by DoD through other Federal agencies, including DoD financial management regulations, the Defense Federal Acquisition Regulation Supplement (DFARS), DoD class deviations, and the DFARS Procedures, Guidance, and Information (PGI). (The DFARS, DoD class deviations, and PGI are accessible at: http://www.acq.osd.mil/dpap/dars).

(c) Within 30 days of the beginning of each fiscal year, submit nondefense agency certifications of compliance to the Director, Defense Procurement and Acquisition Policy, Department of Defense, 3060 Defense Pentagon, Washington D.C. 20301-3060.

(d) The DoD acquisition official, as defined at 17.701, shall provide to the servicing nondefense agency contracting officer any DoD-unique terms, conditions, other related statutes, regulations, directives, and other applicable requirements for incorporation into the order or contract. In the event there are no DoD-unique requirements beyond the FAR, the DoD acquisition official shall so inform the servicing nondefense agency contracting officer in writing. Nondefense agency contracting officers are responsible for ensuring support provided in response to DoD's request complies with paragraph (b) of this section.

(e) "Waiver". The limitation in paragraph (a) of this section shall not apply to the acquisition of supplies and services on behalf of DoD by a nondefense agency during any fiscal year for which the Under Secretary of Defense for Acquisition, Technology, and Logistics has determined in writing that it is necessary in the interest of DoD to acquire supplies and services through the nondefense agency during the fiscal year. The written determination shall identify the acquisition categories to which the waiver applies.

(f) Nondefense agency certifications, waivers, and additional information are available at http://www.acq.osd.mil/dpap/cpic/cp/interagency_acquisition.html.

ficer in writing. Nondefense agency contracting officers are responsible for ensuring support
provided in response to DoD's request complies with paragraph (b) of this section.

(c) "Waiver." The limitation in paragraph (a) of this section shall not apply to the acquisition of supplies or services for which the Secretary of Defense, after consulting any fiscal
year for which the DoD appropriation Act includes identical limitations, and Logistics
has determined in writing that it is necessary in the interest of ...
and services through the nondefense agency during the fiscal year. ...
tion shall identify the acquisition categories to which the waiver appli...

(d) Nondefense agency utilization waivers and additional information are available at
http:/...

PART 18 EMERGENCY ACQUISITIONS

§ 18.000 Scope of part.
§ 18.001 Definition.

Subpart 18.1 Available Acquisition Flexibilities

§ 18.101 General.
§ 18.102 System for Award Management.
§ 18.103 Synopses of proposed contract actions.
§ 18.104 Unusual and compelling urgency.
§ 18.105 Federal Supply Schedules (FSSs), multi-agency blanket purchase
agreements (BPAs), and multi-agency indefinite delivery contracts.
§ 18.106 Acquisitions from Federal Prison Industries, Inc. (FPI).
§ 18.107 AbilityOne specification changes.
§ 18.108 Qualifications requirements.
§ 18.109 Priorities and allocations.
§ 18.110 Soliciting from a single source.
§ 18.111 Oral requests for proposals.
§ 18.112 Letter contracts.
§ 18.113 Interagency acquisitions.
§ 18.114 Contracting with the Small Business Administration (The 8(a)
Program).
§ 18.115 HUBZone sole source awards.
§ 18.116 Service-disabled Veteran-owned Small Business (SDVOSB) sole source
awards.
§ 18.117 Awards to economically disadvantaged women-owned small business
concerns and women-owned small business concerns eligible under the
Women-Owned Small Business Program.
§ 18.118 Overtime approvals.
§ 18.119 Trade agreements.
§ 18.120 Use of patented technology under the North American Free Trade
Agreement.
§ 18.121 Bid guarantees.
§ 18.122 Advance payments.
§ 18.123 Assignment of claims.
§ 18.124 Electronic funds transfer.
§ 18.125 Protest to GAO.
§ 18.126 Contractor rent-free use of Government property.
§ 18.127 Extraordinary contractual actions.

Subpart 18.2 Emergency Acquisition Flexibilities

§ 18.201 Contingency operation.
§ 18.202 Defense or recovery from certain attacks.
§ 18.203 Emergency declaration or major disaster declaration.
§ 18.204 Humanitarian or peacekeeping operation.
§ 18.205 Resources.

§ **18.000 Scope of part.**
(a) This part identifies acquisition flexibilities that are available for emergency

acquisitions. These flexibilities are specific techniques or procedures that may be used to streamline the standard acquisition process. This part includes—

(1) Generally available flexibilities; and

(2) Emergency acquisition flexibilities that are available only under prescribed circumstances.

(b) The acquisition flexibilities in this part are not exempt from the requirements and limitations set forth in FAR Part 3, Improper Business Practices and Personal Conflicts of Interest.

(c) Additional flexibilities may be authorized in an executive agency supplement to the FAR.

§ 18.001 Definition.

"Emergency acquisition flexibilities", as used in this part, means flexibilities provided with respect to any acquisition of supplies or services by or for an executive agency that, as determined by the head of an executive agency, may be used—

(a) In support of a contingency operation as defined in 2.101;

(b) To facilitate the defense against or recovery from nuclear, biological, chemical, or radiological attack against the United States; or

(c) When the President declares an emergency declaration, or a major disaster declaration.

Subpart 18.1 Available Acquisition Flexibilities

§ 18.101 General.

The FAR includes many acquisition flexibilities that are available to the contracting officer when certain conditions are met. These acquisition flexibilities do not require an emergency declaration or designation of contingency operation.

§ 18.102 System for Award Management.

Contractors are not required to be registered in the System for Award Management (SAM) database for contracts awarded to support unusual and compelling needs or emergency acquisitions. (See 4.1102). However, contractors are required to register with SAM in order to gain access to the Disaster Response Registry. Contracting officers shall consult the Disaster Response Registry via https://www.acquisition.gov to determine the availability of contractors for debris removal, distribution of supplies, reconstruction, and other disaster or emergency relief activities inside the United States and outlying areas. (See 26.205).

§ 18.103 Synopses of proposed contract actions.

Contracting officers need not submit a synopsis notice when there is an unusual and compelling urgency and the Government would be seriously injured if the agency complied with the notice time periods. (See 5.202(a)(2).)

§ 18.104 Unusual and compelling urgency.

Agencies may limit the number of sources and full and open competition need not be provided for contracting actions involving urgent requirements. (See 6.302-2.)

§ 18.105 Federal Supply Schedules (FSSs), multi-agency blanket purchase agreements (BPAs), and multi-agency indefinite delivery contracts.

Streamlined procedures and a broad range of goods and services may be available under Federal Supply Schedule contracts (see Subpart 8.4), multi-agency BPAs (see 8.405-3(a)(6)), or multi-agency, indefinite-delivery contracts (see 16.505(a)(8)). These contracting methods may offer agency advance planning, pre-negotiated line items, and special terms and conditions that permit rapid response.

§ 18.106 Acquisitions from Federal Prison Industries, Inc. (FPI).

Purchase from FPI is not mandatory and a waiver is not required if public exigency requires immediate delivery or performance (see 8.605(b)).

§ 18.107 AbilityOne specification changes.

Contracting officers are not held to the notification required when changes in AbilityOne specifications or descriptions are required to meet emergency needs. (See 8.712(d).)

§ 18.108 Qualifications requirements.

Agencies may determine not to enforce qualification requirements when an emergency exists. (See 9.206-1.)

§ 18.109 Priorities and allocations.

The Defense Priorities and Allocations System (DPAS) supports approved national defense, emergency preparedness, and energy programs and was established to facilitate rapid industrial mobilization in case of a national emergency. (See Subpart 11.6.)

§ 18.110 Soliciting from a single source.

For purchases not exceeding the simplified acquisition threshold, contracting officers may solicit from one source under certain circumstances. (See 13.106-1(b).)

§ 18.111 Oral requests for proposals.

Oral requests for proposals are authorized under certain conditions. (See 15.203(f).)

§ 18.112 Letter contracts.

Letter contracts may be used when contract performance must begin immediately. (See 16.603.)

§ 18.113 Interagency acquisitions.

Interagency acquisitions are authorized under certain conditions. (See Subpart 17.5.)

§ 18.114 Contracting with the Small Business Administration (The 8(a) Program).

Contracts may be awarded to the Small Business Administration (SBA) for performance by eligible 8(a) firms on either a sole source or competitive basis. (See Subpart 19.8.)

§ 18.115 HUBZone sole source awards.

Contracts may be awarded to Historically Underutilized Business Zone (HUBZone) small business concerns on a sole source basis. (See 19.1306.)

§ 18.116 Service-disabled Veteran-owned Small Business (SDVOSB) sole source awards.

Contracts may be awarded to Service-disabled Veteranowned Small Business (SDVOSB) concerns on a sole source basis. (See 19.1406.)

§ 18.117 Awards to economically disadvantaged women-owned small business concerns and women-owned small business concerns eligible under the Women-Owned Small Business Program.

Contracts may be awarded to economically disadvantaged women-owned small business (EDWOSB) concerns and women-owned small business (WOSB) concerns eligible under the WOSB Program on a competitive or sole source basis. (See subpart 19.15.)

§ 18.118 Overtime approvals.

Overtime approvals may be retroactive if justified by emergency circumstances. (See 22.103-4(i).)

§ 18.119 Trade agreements.

The policies and procedures of FAR 25.4 may not apply to acquisitions not awarded under full and open competition (see 25.401(a)(5)).

§ 18.120 Use of patented technology under the North American Free Trade Agreement.

Requirement to obtain authorization prior to use of patented technology may be waived in circumstances of extreme urgency or national emergency. (See 27.204-1.)

§ 18.121 Bid guarantees.

The chief of the contracting office may waive the requirement to obtain a bid guarantee for emergency acquisitions when a performance bond or a performance bond and payment bond is required. (See 28.101-1(c).)

§ 18.122 Advance payments.

Agencies may authorize advance payments to facilitate the national defense for actions taken under Public Law 85-804 (see Subpart 50.1, Extraordinary Contractual Actions). These advance payments may be made at or after award of sealed bid contracts, as well as negotiated contracts. (See 32.405.)

§ 18.123 Assignment of claims.

The use of the no-setoff provision may be appropriate to facilitate the national defense in the event of a national emergency or natural disaster. (See 32.803(d).)

§ 18.124 Electronic funds transfer.

Electronic funds transfer payments may be waived for acquisitions to support unusual and compelling needs or emergency acquisitions. (See 32.1103(e).)

§ 18.125 Protest to GAO.

When urgent and compelling circumstances exist, agency protest override procedures allow the head of the contracting activity to determine that the contracting process may continue after GAO has received a protest. (See 33.104(b) and (c).)

§ 18.126 Contractor rent-free use of Government property.

Rental requirements do not apply to items of Government production and research property that are part of a general program approved by the Federal Emergency Management Agency and meet certain criteria. (See 45.301.)

§ 18.127 Extraordinary contractual actions.

Subpart 50.1 prescribes policies and procedures for entering into, amending, or modifying contracts in order to facilitate the national defense under the extraordinary emergency authority granted by Public Law 85-804 (50 U.S.C. 1431–1434). This includes—

(a) Amending contracts without consideration (see 50.103-2(a));

(b) Correcting or mitigating mistakes in a contract (see 50.103-2(b)); and

(c) Formalizing informal commitments (See 50.103-2(c)).

Subpart 18.2 Emergency Acquisition Flexibilities

§ 18.201 Contingency operation.

(a) Contingency operation is defined in 2.101.

(b) Micro-purchase threshold. The threshold increases when the head of the agency determines the supplies or services are to be used to support a contingency operation. (See 2.101 and 13.201(g).)

(c) Simplified acquisition threshold. The threshold increases when the head of the agency determines the supplies or services are to be used to support a contingency operation. (See 2.101.)

(d) SF 44, Purchase Order-Invoice-Voucher. The normal threshold for the use of the SF 44 is at or below the micro-purchase threshold. Agencies may, however, establish higher dollar limitations for purchases made to support a contingency operation. (See 13.306.)

(e) Simplified procedures for certain commercial items. The threshold limits authorized for use of this authority may be increased for acquisitions to support a contingency operation. (See 13.500(c).)

§ 18.202 Defense or recovery from certain attacks.

(a) Micro-purchase threshold. The threshold increases when the head of the agency determines the supplies or services are to be used to facilitate defense against or recovery from nuclear, biological, chemical, or radiological attack. (See 2.101.)

(b) Simplified acquisition threshold. The threshold increases when the head of the agency determines the supplies or services are to be used to facilitate defense against or recovery from nuclear, biological, chemical, or radiological attack. (See 2.101.)

(c) Commercial items to facilitate defense and recovery. Contracting officers may treat any acquisition of supplies or services as an acquisition of commercial items if the head of the agency determines the acquisition is to be used to facilitate the defense against or recovery from nuclear, biological, chemical, or radiological attack. (See 12.102(f)(1) and 13.500(c).)

(d) Simplified procedures for certain commercial items. The threshold limits authorized for use of this authority may be increased when it is determined the acquisition is to facilitate defense against or recovery from nuclear, biological, chemical, or radiological attack. (See 13.500(c).)

§ 18.203 Emergency declaration or major disaster declaration.

(a) Disaster or emergency assistance activities. Preference will be given to local organizations, firms, and individuals when contracting for major disaster or emergency assistance activities when the President has made a declaration under the Robert T. Stafford Disaster Relief and Emergency Assistance Act. Preference may take the form of local area set-asides or an evaluation preference. (See 6.208 and Subpart 26.2.)

(b) Ocean transportation by U.S. flag vessels. The provisions of the Cargo Preference Act of 1954 may be waived in emergency situations. (See 47.502(c).)

§ 18.204 Humanitarian or peacekeeping operation.

(a) A humanitarian or peacekeeping operation is defined in 2.101.

(b) Simplified acquisition threshold. The threshold increases when the head of the agency determines the supplies or services are to be used to support a humanitarian or peacekeeping operation. (See 2.101.)

§ 18.205 Resources.

(a) National Response Framework. The National Response Framework (NRF) is a guide to how the Nation conducts all-hazards response. This key document establishes a comprehensive, national, all-hazards approach to domestic incident response. The Framework identifies the key response principles, roles and structures that organize national response. It describes how communities, States, the Federal Government, the private-sector, and nongovernmental partners apply these principles for a coordinated, effective national response. It also describes special circumstances where the Federal Government exercises a larger role, including incidents where Federal interests are involved and catastrophic incidents where a State would require significant support. The NRF is available at http://www.fema.gov/emergency/nrf/.

(b) OFPP Guidelines. The Office of Federal Procurement Policy (OFPP) "Emergency Acquisitions Guide" is available at http://www.whitehouse.gov/sites/default/files/omb/assets/procurement_guides/emergency_acquisitions_guide.pdf.

Subchapter D Socioeconomic Programs

PART 19 SMALL BUSINESS PROGRAMS

Subpart 19.9 [Reserved]

Subpart 19.10 [Reserved]

Subpart 19.11 —[Reserved]

Subpart 19.12 —[Reserved]

Subpart 19.13 Historically Underutilized Business Zone (HUBZone) Program

Subpart 19.14 Service-Disabled Veteran-Owned Small Business Procurement Program

§ 19.1407 Contract clauses.

Subpart 19.15 —Women-Owned Small Business Program.

§ 19.1500 General.
§ 19.1501 Definition.
§ 19.1502 Applicability.
§ 19.1503 Status.
§ 19.1504 Exclusions.
§ 19.1505 Set-aside procedures.
§ 19.1506 Women-Owned Small Business Program sole source awards.
§ 19.1507 Contract clauses.

§ 19.000 Scope of part.

(a) This part implements the acquisition-related sections of the Small Business Act (15 U.S.C. 631, et seq.), applicable sections of the Armed Services Procurement Act (10 U.S.C. 2302, et seq.), 41 U.S.C. 3104, and Executive Order 12138, May 18, 1979. It covers—

(1) The determination that a concern is eligible for participation in the programs identified in this part;

(2) The respective roles of executive agencies and the Small Business Administration (SBA) in implementing the programs;

(3) Setting acquisitions aside for exclusive competitive participation by small business, 8(a) business development participants, HUBZone small business concerns, service-disabled veteran-owned small business concerns, and economically disadvantaged women-owned small business (EDWOSB) concerns and women-owned small business (WOSB) concerns eligible under the WOSB Program;

(4) The certificate of competency program;

(5) The subcontracting assistance program;

(6) The "8(a)" business development program (hereafter referred to as 8(a) program), under which agencies contract with the SBA for goods or services to be furnished under a subcontract by a small disadvantaged business concern;

(7) The use of a price evaluation preference for HUBZone small business concerns;

(8) The use of veteran-owned small business concerns; and

(9) Sole source awards to HUBZone small business concerns, service-disabled veteran-owned small business concerns, and EDWOSB concerns and WOSB concerns eligible under the WOSB Program.

(b) This part, except for Subpart 19.6, applies only in the United States or its outlying areas. Subpart 19.6 applies worldwide.

United States Code Annotated

Additional powers, see 15 USCA § 637.

Administrative determinations, see 41 USCA § 257.

Awards or contracts, see 15 USCA § 644.

Contract goal for small disadvantaged businesses and certain institutions of higher education, see 10 USCA § 2323.

Contract requirements, see 41 USCA § 254.

Contracts, planning, solicitation, evaluation, and award procedures, see 10 USCA § 2305.

Credit for Indian contracting in meeting certain subcontracting goals for small disadvantaged businesses and certain institutions of higher education, see 10 USCA § 2323a.

Definitions, see 10 USCA § 2302, 41 USCA §§ 259, 403.

Determinations and decisions, see 10 USCA § 2310, 41 USCA § 262.

HUBZone program, see 15 USCA § 657a.

Kinds of contracts, see 10 USCA § 2306.

Planning and solicitation requirements, see 41 USCA § 253a.

Procurement data, see 41 USCA § 417a.

Procurement program for small business concerns owned and controlled by service-disabled veterans, see 15 USCA § 657f.

Notes of Decisions
In general 1

1 In general

Agencies are not required to set-aside procurements outside the United States or its outlying areas. Protester's contention that the (Small Business Act, 15 U.S.C. § 644(j)(1)), requires agencies to set aside procurements under the simplified acquisition threshold for small businesses located outside the United States, unless the agency cannot obtain offers from two or more small businesses, is denied where the Act is silent on its application outside the U.S., and where FAR 19.000(b) expressly states that the set-aside requirement of the Act applies only in the U.S. or its outlying areas. Given the silence of the Act on its applicability outside the U.S. (and the silence of the SBA's regulations on the issue) the GAO held that the long-standing exclusion specified in FAR § 19.000(b) is consistent with the Small Business Act. Latvian Connection Gen. Trading & Constr. LLC, B-408633, 2013 CPD ¶ 225 (Comp. Gen. 2013).

§ 19.001 Definitions.

As used in this part—

"Concern" means any business entity organized for profit (even if its ownership is in the hands of a nonprofit entity) with a place of business located in the United States or its outlying areas and that makes a significant contribution to the U.S. economy through payment of taxes and/or use of American products, material and/or labor, etc. "Concern" includes but is not limited to an individual, partnership, corporation, joint venture, association, or cooperative. For the purpose of making affiliation findings (see 19.101), include any business entity, whether organized for profit or not, and any foreign business entity, i.e., any entity located outside the United States and its outlying areas.

"Fair market price" means a price based on reasonable costs under normal competitive conditions and not on lowest possible cost (see 19.202-6).

"Industry" means all concerns primarily engaged in similar lines of activity, as listed and described in the North American Industry Classification System (NAICS) manual.

"Nonmanufacturer rule" means that a contractor under a small business set-aside or 8(a) contract shall be a small business under the applicable size standard and shall provide either its own product or that of another domestic small business manufacturing or processing concern (see 13 CFR 121.406).

United States Code Annotated

Additional powers, see 15 USCA § 637.

Administrative determinations, see 41 USCA § 257.

Awards or contracts, see 15 USCA § 644.

Contract goal for small disadvantaged businesses and certain institutions of higher education, see 10 USCA § 2323.

Contract requirements, see 41 USCA § 254.

Contracts, planning, solicitation, evaluation, and award procedures, see 10 USCA § 2305.

Credit for Indian contracting in meeting certain subcontracting goals for small disadvantaged businesses and certain institutions of higher education, see 10 USCA § 2323a.

Definitions, see 10 USCA § 2302, 41 USCA §§ 259, 403.

Determinations and decisions, see 10 USCA § 2310, 41 USCA § 262.

HUBZone program, see 15 USCA § 657a.

Kinds of contracts, see 10 USCA § 2306.

Planning and solicitation requirements, see 41 USCA § 253a.

Procurement data, see 41 USCA § 417a.

Procurement program for small business concerns owned and controlled by service-disabled veterans, see 15 USCA § 657f.

Notes of Decisions
Economic disadvantage 3

Equal protection of laws 1
Small business concern 2

1 Equal protection of laws

Method of certification of disadvantaged business enterprises (DBEs) presuming economic disadvantage based on membership in certain racial groups, applied to federal highway subcontracting in 1996, was not narrowly tailored, so as to satisfy equal protection, but current regulations providing for an individualized determination of economic disadvantage are narrowly tailored. U.S.C.A. Const.Amend. 5; Small Business Act, § 2[8](a, d), as amended, 15 U.S.C.A. § 637(a, d); 13 C.F.R. §§ 124.104(b)(1), 124.1001 et seq., 124. 1002(a); 48 C.F.R. §§ 19.001, 19.703, 52.219-8; 49 C.F.R. § 26.67(b)(1). Adarand Constructors, Inc. v. Slater, 228 F.3d 1147 (10th Cir. 2000). Constitutional Law ☞215.2; Highways ☞113(1)

Current disadvantaged business enterprise (DBE) certification programs for federal highway subcontracting meet the requirements of narrow tailoring, and thus do not violate equal protection. U.S.C.A. Const.Amend. 5; Small Business Act, §§ 2[8](a, d), 2[15](g), as amended, 15 U.S.C.A. §§ 637(a, d), 644(g); Surface Transportation and Uniform Relocation Assistance Act of 1987, §§ 1 et seq., 23 U.S.C.A. § 101 note; Intermodal Surface Transportation Efficiency Act of 1991, §§ 1 et seq., 49 U.S.C.A. § 101 note; Transportation Equity Act for the 21st Century, §§ 1 et seq., 23 U.S.C.A. § 101 note; 13 C.F.R. §§ 124.104(c)(2), 124. 1014; 48 C.F.R. § 19.001; 49 C.F.R. §§ 26.65, 26.67(b). Adarand Constructors, Inc. v. Slater, 228 F.3d 1147 (10th Cir. 2000). Constitutional Law ☞234; Highways ☞113(1)

Insofar as Federal Lands Highway Program's (FLHP's) 1996 Subcontractor Compensation Clause (SCC) relied on Small Business Act's (SBA's) § 8(a) criteria, limiting duration of disadvantaged business enterprise (DBE) status, those criteria increased the narrow tailoring of the SCC raceconscious program, and current SBA § 8(d) program, incorporating regulations which provide for a certification of a business as socially and economically disadvantaged for three years after either the initial certification or other administrative determination, was narrowly tailored with regard to appropriate limitations on duration, for purposes of equal protection compliance, especially in light of extensive congressional debate prior to renewing the DBE program. Small Business Act, §§ 2[5](b)(6), 2[7](j)(10)(C) (i), (j)(10)(G), 2[8](a), (a)(6)(B, C), (d), as amended, 15 U.S.C.A. §§ 634(b)(6), 636(j)(10)(C)(i), (j)(10)(G), 637(a), (a)(6)(B, C), (d); 13 C.F.R. §§ 124.2, 124.110, 124.1002(a), 124.1014, 124. 1014(c); 48 C.F.R. § 19.001. Adarand Constructors, Inc. v. Slater, 228 F.3d 1147 (10th Cir. 2000). Constitutional Law ☞215.2; Highways ☞113(1)

The United States Court of Appeals for the Federal Circuit (CAFC) held that Department of Defense (DoD) preferences for small disadvantaged business concerns (SDBs) in 10 U.S.C. § 2323 violate the United States Constitution, specifically the equal protection component of the Fifth Amendment right to due process. The CAFC found that, in authorizing DoD to accord preferential treatment to SDBs on the basis of race, Congress did not have a "strong basis in evidence" upon which to conclude that DoD was a passive participant in pervasive, nationwide racial discrimination. As a result, the Court found that 10 U.S.C. § 2323 fails the "strict scrutiny" test that is applied to constitutional challenges of such race-based preferences. Rothe Development Corp. v. Department of Defense, 545 F.3d 1023, 91 Empl. Prac. Dec. (CCH) P 43388 (Fed. Cir. 2008)

2 Small business concern

Small disadvantaged business concern is "small business concern" for purposes of the Small Business Act and implementing regulations, as disadvantaged business participant qualifies as "small disadvantaged business concern" and "small business concern." Small Business Act, § 2[8](a), as amended, 15 U.S.C.A. § 637(a). Celtech, Inc. v. U.S., 24 Cl. Ct. 269, 37 Cont. Cas. Fed. (CCH) P 76181, 1991 WL 193295 (1991), vacated pursuant to settlement, 25 Cl. Ct. 368, 1992 WL 46122 (1992). United States ☞53(8)

Even if exception to mandatory requirement for referral to the Small Business Administration (SBA) if small business concern's offer is to be rejected because of determination of nonresponsibility applied to rejection of small disadvantaged business based on accounting system deficiencies identified in audit, Government violated referral requirement, as decision not to refer matter to SBA must be approved by chief of contracting office and no evidence was presented that chief of contracting office approved nonreferral decision.

Celtech, Inc. v. U.S., 24 Cl. Ct. 269, 37 Cont. Cas. Fed. (CCH) P 76181, 1991 WL 193295 (1991), vacated pursuant to settlement, 25 Cl. Ct. 368, 1992 WL 46122 (1992). United States ☞64.15

Small Business Administration's Office of Hearings and Appeals could relate back to original notice of appeal certification submission by second low bidder challenging low bidder's satisfaction of solicitation's "small business concern" requirement, and thus notice of appeal came within five-day rule for pending procurement, as certification was treated by OH&A as in nature of an amendment to previous notice of appeal, and original filing provided adequate notice. U.S.Cl. Ct.Rule 15(c), 28 U.S.C.A.Three S Constructors, Inc. v. U.S., 13 Cl. Ct. 41, 34 Cont. Cas. Fed. (CCH) P 75348 (1987). Administrative Law And Procedure ☞513; United States ☞64.55(2)

Process by which Small Business Administration's Office of Hearings and Appeals obtained second low bidder's certification on notice of appeal letter challenging low bidder's satisfaction of "small business concern" requirement was not prohibited ex parte contact, even though it would have been better practice to call attention to omission in manner which notified all parties. Three S Constructors, Inc. v. U.S., 13 Cl. Ct. 41, 34 Cont. Cas. Fed. (CCH) P 75348 (1987). United States ☞64.55(2)

Low bidder on government contract was not "small business concern" as required by solicitation and could not be awarded contract; "newly organized concern" rule applied and compelled aggregation of receipts of both low bidder and affiliated large businesses, as three sons involved in low bidder had been key officers of dissolving, but still existing, large businesses owned by their father and uncle, and assistance was being provided by large businesses to low bidder, which occupied facilities and performed remaining contracts of those businesses. Small Business Act, § 2[8](b)(6), 15 U.S.C.A. § 637(b)(6). Three S Constructors, Inc. v. U.S., 13 Cl. Ct. 41, 34 Cont. Cas. Fed. (CCH) P 75348 (1987). United States ☞64.15

3 Economic disadvantage

There was no constitutional relevance of the two slightly different definitions of economic disadvantage under different subsections of the Small Business Act (SBA), which has in any event disappeared in the current version of the regulations, and the two slightly different definitions did not create uncertainty as to who is a disadvantaged business enterprise (DBE), so as to preclude any finding of narrow tailoring, satisfying equal protection. U.S.C.A. Const. Amend. 5; Small Business Act, § 2[8](a, d), as amended, 15 U.S.C.A. § 637(a, d); 13 C.F.R. §§ 124.104(a), 124.106(b), 124.1001 et seq., 124.1002(a); 48 C.F.R. § 19.001. Adarand Constructors, Inc. v. Slater, 228 F.3d 1147 (10th Cir. 2000). Constitutional Law ☞225.4; United States ☞64.15

Subpart 19.1 Size Standards

§ 19.101 Explanation of terms.

As used in this subpart—

"Affiliates." Business concerns are affiliates of each other if, directly or indirectly, either one controls or has the power to control the other, or another concern controls or has the power to control both. In determining whether affiliation exists, consideration is given to all appropriate factors including common ownership, common management, and contractual relationships; provided, that restraints imposed by a franchise agreement are not considered in determining whether the franchisor controls or has the power to control the franchisee, if the franchisee has the right to profit from its effort, commensurate with ownership, and bears the risk of loss or failure. Any business entity may be found to be an affiliate, whether or not it is organized for profit or located in the United States or its outlying areas.

(1) *Nature of control.* Every business concern is considered as having one or more parties who directly or indirectly control or have the power to control it. Control may be affirmative or negative and it is immaterial whether it is exercised so long as the power to control exists.

(2) *Meaning of "party or parties."* The term "party" or "parties" includes, but is not limited to, two or more persons with an identity of interest such as members of the same family or persons with common investments in more than one concern. In determining who controls or has the power to control a concern, persons with an identity of interest

may be treated as though they were one person.

(3) Control through stock ownership.

(i) A party is considered to control or have the power to control a concern, if the party controls or has the power to control 50 percent or more of the concern's voting stock.

(ii) A party is considered to control or have the power to control a concern, even though the party owns, controls, or has the power to control less than 50 percent of the concern's voting stock, if the block of stock the party owns, controls, or has the power to control is large, as compared with any other outstanding block of stock. If two or more parties each owns, controls, or has the power to control, less than 50 percent of the voting stock of a concern, and such minority block is equal or substantially equal in size, and large as compared with any other block outstanding, there is a presumption that each such party controls or has the power to control such concern; however, such presumption may be rebutted by a showing that such control or power to control, in fact, does not exist.

(iii) If a concern's voting stock is distributed other than as described above, its management (officers and directors) is deemed to be in control of such concern.

(4) *Stock options and convertible debentures.* Stock options and convertible debentures exercisable at the time or within a relatively short time after a size determination and agreements to merge in the future, are considered as having a present effect on the power to control the concern. Therefore, in making a size determination, such options, debentures, and agreements are treated as though the rights held thereunder had been exercised.

(5) *Voting trusts.* If the purpose of a voting trust, or similar agreement, is to separate voting power from beneficial ownership of voting stock for the purpose of shifting control of or the power to control a concern in order that such concern or another concern may qualify as a small business within the size regulations, such voting trust shall not be considered valid for this purpose regardless of whether it is or is not valid within the appropriate jurisdiction. However, if a voting trust is entered into for a legitimate purpose other than that described above, and it is valid within the appropriate jurisdiction, it may be considered valid for the purpose of a size determination, provided such consideration is determined to be in the best interest of the small business program.

(6) *Control through common management.* A concern may be found as controlling or having the power to control another concern when one or more of the following circumstances are found to exist, and it is reasonable to conclude that under the circumstances, such concern is directing or influencing, or has the power to direct or influence, the operation of such other concern.

(i) *Interlocking management.* Officers, directors, employees, or principal stockholders of one concern serve as a working majority of the board of directors or officers of another concern.

(ii) *Common facilities.* One concern shares common office space and/or employees and/or other facilities with another concern, particularly where such concerns are in the same or related industry or field of operation, or where such concerns were formerly affiliated.

(iii) *Newly organized concern.* Former officers, directors, principal stockholders, and/or key employees of one concern organize a new concern in the same or a related industry or field operation, and serve as its officers, directors, principal stockholders, and/or key employees, and one concern is furnishing or will furnish the other concern with subcontracts, financial or technical assistance, and/or facilities, whether for a fee or otherwise.

(7) Control through contractual relationships—

(i) *Definition of a joint venture for size determination purposes.* A joint venture for size determination purposes is an association of persons or concerns with interests in any degree or proportion by way of contract, express or implied, consorting to engage in and carry out a single specific business venture for joint profit, for which purpose they combine their efforts, property, money, skill, or knowledge, but not on a continuing or permanent basis for conducting business generally. A joint venture is viewed as a business entity in determining power to control its management.

(A) For bundled requirements, apply size standards for the requirement to individual persons or concerns, not to the combined assets, of the joint venture.

(B) For other than bundled requirements, apply size standards for the requirement to individual persons or concerns, not to the combined assets, of the joint venture, if—

(1) A revenue-based size standard applies to the requirement and the estimated contract value, including options, exceeds one-half the applicable size standard; or

(2) An employee-based size standard applies to the requirement and the estimated contract value, including options, exceeds $10 million.

(ii) *HUBZone joint venture.* A HUBZone joint venture of two or more HUBZone small business concerns may submit an offer for a HUBZone contract as long as each concern is small under the size standard corresponding to the NAICS code assigned to the contract, provided one of the following conditions apply:

(A) The aggregate total of the joint venture is small under the size standard corresponding to the NAICS code assigned to the contract.

(B) The aggregate total of the joint venture is not small under the size standard corresponding to the NAICS code assigned to the contract and either—

(1) For a revenue-based size standard, the estimated contract value exceeds half the size standard corresponding to the NAICS code assigned to the contract; or

(2) For an employee-based size standard, the estimated contract value exceeds $10 million.

(iii) *Joint venture.* Concerns submitting offers on a particular acquisition as joint ventures are considered as affiliated and controlling or having the power to control each other with regard to performance of the contract. Moreover, an ostensible subcontractor which is to perform primary or vital requirements of a contract may have a controlling role such to be considered a joint venturer affiliated on the contract with the prime contractor. A joint venture affiliation finding is limited to particular contracts unless the SBA size determination finds general affiliation between the parties. The rules governing 8(a) Program joint ventures are described in 13 CFR 124.513.

(iv) Where a concern is not considered as being an affiliate of a concern with which it is participating in a joint venture, it is necessary, nevertheless, in computing annual receipts, etc., for the purpose of applying size standards, to include such concern's share of the joint venture receipts (as distinguished from its share of the profits of such venture).

(v) *Franchise and license agreements.* If a concern operates or is to operate under a franchise (or a license) agreement, the following policy is applicable: In determining whether the franchisor controls or has the power to control and, therefore, is affiliated with the franchisee, the restraints imposed on a franchisee by its franchise agreement shall not be considered, provided that the franchisee has the right to profit from its effort and the risk of loss or failure, commensurate with ownership. Even though a franchisee may not be controlled by the franchisor by virtue of the contractual relationship between them, the franchisee may be controlled by the franchisor or others through common ownership or common management, in which case they would be considered as affiliated.

(vi) *Size determination for teaming arrangements.* For size determination purposes, apply the size standard tests in paragraphs (7)(i)(A) and (B) of this section when a teaming arrangement of two or more business concerns submits an offer, as appropriate.

"Annual receipts."

(1) Annual receipts of a concern which has been in business for 3 or more complete fiscal years means the annual average gross revenue of the concern taken for the last 3 fiscal years. For the purpose of this definition, gross revenue of the concern includes revenues from sales of products and services, interest, rents, fees, commissions and/or whatever other sources derived, but less returns and allowances, sales of fixed assets, interaffiliate transactions between a concern and its domestic and foreign affiliates, and taxes collected for remittance (and if due, remitted) to a third party. Such revenues shall be measured as entered on the regular books of account of the concern whether on a cash, accrual, or other basis of accounting acceptable to the U.S. Treasury Department for the

purpose of supporting Federal income tax returns, except when a change in accounting method from cash to accrual or accrual to cash has taken place during such 3-year period, or when the completed contract method has been used.

(i) In any case of change in accounting method from cash to accrual or accrual to cash, revenues for such 3-year period shall, prior to the calculation of the annual average, be restated to the accrual method. In any case, where the completed contract method has been used to account for revenues in such 3-year period, revenues must be restated on an accrual basis using the percentage of completion method.

(ii) In the case of a concern which does not keep regular books of accounts, but which is subject to U.S. Federal income taxation, "annual receipts" shall be measured as reported, or to be reported to the U.S. Treasury Department, Internal Revenue Service, for Federal income tax purposes, except that any return based on a change in accounting method or on the completed contract method of accounting must be restated as provided for in the preceding paragraphs.

(2) Annual receipts of a concern that has been in business for less than 3 complete fiscal years means its total receipts for the period it has been in business, divided by the number of weeks including fractions of a week that it has been in business, and multiplied by 52. In calculating total receipts, the definitions and adjustments related to a change of accounting method and the completed contract method of paragraph (1) of this definition, are applicable.

"Number of employees" is a measure of the average employment of a business concern and means its average employment, including the employees of its domestic and foreign affiliates, based on the number of persons employed on a full-time, part-time, temporary, or other basis during each of the pay periods of the preceding 12 months. If a business has not been in existence for 12 months, "number of employees" means the average employment of such concern and its affiliates during the period that such concern has been in existence based on the number of persons employed during each of the pay periods of the period that such concern has been in business. If a business has acquired an affiliate during the applicable 12-month period, it is necessary, in computing the applicant's number of employees, to include the affiliate's number of employees during the entire period, rather than only its employees during the period in which it has been an affiliate. The employees of a former affiliate are not included, even if such concern had been an affiliate during a portion of the period.

United States Code Annotated

Additional powers, see 15 USCA § 637.

Administrative determinations, see 41 USCA § 257.

Awards or contracts, see 15 USCA § 644.

Contract goal for small disadvantaged businesses and certain institutions of higher education, see 10 USCA § 2323.

Contract requirements, see 41 USCA § 254.

Contracts, planning, solicitation, evaluation, and award procedures, see 10 USCA § 2305.

Credit for Indian contracting in meeting certain subcontracting goals for small disadvantaged businesses and certain institutions of higher education, see 10 USCA § 2323a.

Definitions, see 10 USCA § 2302, 41 USCA §§ 259, 403.

Determinations and decisions, see 10 USCA § 2310, 41 USCA § 262.

HUBZone program, see 15 USCA § 657a.

Kinds of contracts, see 10 USCA § 2306.

Planning and solicitation requirements, see 41 USCA § 253a.

Procurement data, see 41 USCA § 417a.

Procurement program for small business concerns owned and controlled by service-disabled veterans, see 15 USCA § 657f.

Notes of Decisions

Affiliation 4
Control through common management 2
Economic dependence 3

Size standards 1

1 Size standards

Bid protestor was not prejudiced by contracting officer's post-award notification which did not contain either the correct name or the awardee, or the awardee's bid price, notwithstanding protestor's claim that faulty notification caused it to delay filing a size protest with the Small Business Administration (SBA), as neither piece of information was critical to protestor's decision to file a size protest with the SBA. Tech Systems, Inc. v. U.S., 50 Fed. Cl. 216 (2001). United States ☞64.55(1)

Post-award bid protester who asserted that awardee's bid was nonresponsive for failure to meet requirement in solicitation for a Small Business Administration (SBA) size certification was not required to exhaust administrative remedies before the SBA, as protest was not concerned with size determination of awardee, but with whether the government breached implied-in-fact contract by not enforcing solicitation requirement. Hawpe Const., Inc. v. U.S., 46 Fed. Cl. 571 (2000), aff'd, 10 Fed. Appx. 957 (Fed. Cir. 2001). United States ☞64.55(2)

2 Control through common management

Common control did not exist between defense contractor and temporary staffing company for purposes of regulation limiting profits on sales between "divisions, subdivisions, subsidiaries or affiliates" under contractor's common control, given that company's sole shareholders held no direct shareholder interest in contractor and did not hold any positions of management, employment, or influence with contractor, shareholders ceded management and daily operational decision- making for company to its president-chief executive officer (CEO), president-CEO did not hold ownership interest in, or occupy any official or management position with, contractor, two businesses did not share common space or engage in business in same industry, and relationship between two businesses was fully disclosed to government entity that was responsible for ensuring that contractor's contract billings complied with federal regulations in all respects, which did not object in any of its audit reports. 48 C.F.R. §§ 2.101, 19.101, 31.205-26(e). U.S. ex rel. Kholi v. General Atomics, 2003 WL 21536816 (S.D. Cal. 2003). United States ☞70(12.1)

3 Economic dependence

A contractor that was alternately prime and subcontractor on several contracts with another firm was not an "affiliate" of that firm for purposes of a small business size determination, the Small Business Administration Office of Hearings and Appeals (OHA) determined. Subcontracts from the alleged affiliate accounted for less than 10 percent of the small business's receipts, and those subcontracts along with two subcontracts to the alleged affiliate were not enough to show economic dependence. Size Appeal of Diverse Constr. Group LLC, SBA No. SIZ-5112 (Feb. 2, 2010).

4 Affiliation

There is a rebuttable presumption that close family members have identical interests and must be treated as one person for purposes of determining if two firms are affiliated. A challenged firm may rebut the presumption of identity of interest if it is able to show "a clear line of fracture among the family members." Relevant factors include whether the firms share officers, employees, facilities, or equipment; whether the firms have different customers and lines of business; whether there is financial assistance, loans, or significant subcontracting between the firms; and whether the family members participate in multiple businesses together. Gregory Landscape Servs., SBA No. SIZ-5817, 2017 (S.B.A.), 2017 WL 1049487

SBA regulations provide for affiliation between "firms that are economically dependent through contractual or other relationships." 13 C.F.R. § 121.103(f). In interpreting this provision, OHA has long held, as a matter of law, that a firm that derives 70% or more of its revenue from another firm is economically dependent upon that firm. Further, SBA regulations state that "SBA may presume an identity of interest based upon economic dependence if the concern in question derived 70% or more of its receipts from another concern over the previous three fiscal years." Veterans Technology, LLC, SBA No. SIZ-5763, 2016 (S.B.A.), 2016 WL 5719600

Under the newly organized concern rule, firms are affiliated when former officers, directors, principal stockholders, or key employees of one firm organize a new firm in the same or a related industry or field of operation, and serve as its officers, directors, principal stockholders or key employees, and the one concern is furnishing or will furnish the other concern with subcontracts, financial or technical assistance, bid or performance bond indemnification, or other facilities, whether for a fee or otherwise. Affiliation under the newly organized concern rule is rebutted if the challenged firm can demonstrate a clear line of fracture between itself and the other firm. The purpose of the newly organized concern rule is to prevent circumvention of the size regulations by the creation of spin-off firms which appear to be small, independent firms, but are really affiliates or extensions of large firms, even absent evidence the new firm was formed to circumvent the size regulations. B,L. Harbert Int'l, LLC, SBA No. SIZ-4525 (S.B.A.), 2002 WL 31844946

§ 19.102 Size standards.

(a) (1) The SBA establishes small business size standards on an industry-by-industry basis. (See 13 CFR Part 121). Small business size standards matched to industry NAICS codes are published by the Small Business Administration and are available at http://www.sba.gov/content/table-small-business-size-standards.

(2) NAICS codes are updated by the Office of Management and Budget through its Economic Classification Policy Committee every five years. New NAICS codes are not available for use in Federal contracting until the Small Business Administration publishes corresponding industry size standards (see 19.102(a)(1)).

(b) Small business size standards are applied by—

(1) Classifying the product or service being acquired in the industry whose definition, as found in the North American Industry Classification System (NAICS) Manual (available at http://www.census.gov/eos/www/naics/), best describes the principal nature of the product or service being acquired;

(2) Identifying the size standard SBA established for that industry; and

(3) Specifying the size standard in the solicitation so that offerors can appropriately represent themselves as small or large.

(c) For size standard purposes, a product or service shall be classified in only one industry, whose definition best describes the principal nature of the product or service being acquired even though for other purposes it could be classified in more than one.

(d) When acquiring a product or service that could be classified in two or more industries with different size standards, contracting officers shall apply the size standard for the industry accounting for the greatest percentage of the contract price.

(e) If a solicitation calls for more than one item and allows offers to be submitted on any or all of the items, an offeror must meet the size standard for each item it offers to furnish. If a solicitation calling for more than one item requires offers on all or none of the items, an offeror may qualify as a small business by meeting the size standard for the item accounting for the greatest percentage of the total contract price.

(f) Any concern submitting a bid or offer in its own name, other than on a construction or service contract, that proposes to furnish an end product it did not manufacture (a "nonmanufacturer"), is a small business if it has no more than 500 employees, and—

(1) Except as provided in paragraphs (f)(4) through (f)(7) of this section, in the case of Government acquisitions set-aside for small businesses, furnishes in the performance of the contract, the product of a small business manufacturer or producer. The end product furnished must be manufactured or produced in the United States or its outlying areas. The term "nonmanufacturer" includes a concern that can, but elects not to, manufacture or produce the end product for the specific acquisition. For size determination purposes, there can be only one manufacturer of the end product being acquired. The manufacturer of the end product being acquired is the concern that, with its own forces, transforms inorganic or organic substances including raw materials and/or miscellaneous parts or components into the end product. However, see the limitations on subcontracting at 52.219-14 that apply to any small business offeror other than a nonmanufacturer for purposes of set-asides and 8(a) awards, 52.219-3 for HUBZone set-asides and HUBZone sole source awards, 52.219-27 for SDVOSB set-asides and SDVOSB sole source awards, 52.219-29 for economically disadvantaged women-owned small business (EDWOSB) set-asides and EDWOSB sole source awards, and 52.219-30 for set-asides and sole source

awards to women-owned small business (WOSB) concerns eligible under the WOSB Program.

(2) A concern which purchases items and packages them into a kit is considered to be a nonmanufacturer small business and can qualify as such for a given acquisition if it meets the size qualifications of a small nonmanufacturer for the acquisition, and if more than 50 percent of the total value of the kit and its contents are accounted for by items manufactured by small business.

(3) For the purpose of receiving a Certificate of Competency on an unrestricted acquisition, a small business nonmanufacturer may furnish any domestically produced or manufactured product.

(4) In the case of acquisitions set aside for small business or awarded under section 8(a) of the Small Business Act, when the acquisition is for a specific product (or a product in a class of products) for which the SBA has determined that there are no small business manufacturers or processors in the Federal market, then the SBA may grant a class waiver so that a nonmanufacturer does not have to furnish the product of a small business. For the most current listing of classes for which SBA has granted a waiver, contact an SBA Office of Government Contracting. A listing is also available on SBA's Internet Homepage at http://www.sba.gov/content/class-waivers. Contracting officers may request that the SBA waive the nonmanufacturer rule for a particular class of products. For procedures in requesting a waiver see 13 CFR 121.1204.

(5) For a specific solicitation, a contracting officer may request a waiver of that part of the nonmanufacturer rule which requires that the actual manufacturer or processor be a small business concern if no known domestic small business manufacturers or processors can reasonably be expected to offer a product meeting the requirements of the solicitation.

(6) Requests for waivers shall be sent to the—

Associate Administrator for Government Contracting
United States Small Business Administration
Mail Code 6250
409 Third Street, SW
Washington, DC 20416.

(7) The SBA provides for an exception to the nonmanufacturer rule if—

(i) The procurement of a manufactured end product processed under the procedures set forth in Part 13—

(A) Is set aside for small business; and

(B) Is not anticipated to exceed $25,000; and

(ii) The offeror supplies an end product that is manufactured or produced in the United States or its outlying areas.

(8) For non-manufacturer rules pertaining to HUBZone contracts, see 19.1303(e).

United States Code Annotated

Additional powers, see 15 USCA § 637.

Administrative determinations, see 41 USCA § 257.

Awards or contracts, see 15 USCA § 644.

Contract goal for small disadvantaged businesses and certain institutions of higher education, see 10 USCA § 2323.

Contract requirements, see 41 USCA § 254.

Contracts, planning, solicitation, evaluation, and award procedures, see 10 USCA § 2305.

Credit for Indian contracting in meeting certain subcontracting goals for small disadvantaged businesses and certain institutions of higher education, see 10 USCA § 2323a.

Definitions, see 10 USCA § 2302, 41 USCA §§ 259, 403.

Determinations and decisions, see 10 USCA § 2310, 41 USCA § 262.

HUBZone program, see 15 USCA § 657a.

Kinds of contracts, see 10 USCA § 2306.

Planning and solicitation requirements, see 41 USCA § 253a.

Procurement data, see 41 USCA § 417a.

Procurement program for small business concerns owned and controlled by service-disabled veterans, see 15 USCA § 657f.

Notes of Decisions

Non-manufacturer rule 4
North American Industry Classification System 3
Size standards 1
Small business concern 2

1 Size standards

Bid protestor was not prejudiced by contracting officer's post-award notification which did not contain either the correct name or the awardee, or the awardee's bid price, notwithstanding protestor's claim that faulty notification caused it to delay filing a size protest with the Small Business Administration (SBA), as neither piece of information was critical to protestor's decision to file a size protest with the SBA. Tech Systems, Inc. v. U.S., 50 Fed. Cl. 216 (2001). United States ☞64.55(1)

Post-award bid protester who asserted that awardee's bid was nonresponsive for failure to meet requirement in solicitation for a Small Business Administration (SBA) size certification was not required to exhaust administrative remedies before the SBA, as protest was not concerned with size determination of awardee, but with whether the government breached implied-in-fact contract by not enforcing solicitation requirement. Hawpe Const., Inc. v. U.S., 46 Fed. Cl. 571 (2000), aff'd, 10 Fed. Appx. 957 (Fed. Cir. 2001). United States ☞64.55(2)

2 Small business concern

Small disadvantaged business concern is "small business concern" for purposes of the Small Business Act and implementing regulations, as disadvantaged business participant qualifies as "small disadvantaged business concern" and "small business concern." Small Business Act, § 2[8](a), as amended, 15 U.S.C.A. § 637(a). Celtech, Inc. v. U.S., 24 Cl. Ct. 269, 37 Cont. Cas. Fed. (CCH) P 76181, 1991 WL 193295 (1991), vacated pursuant to settlement, 25 Cl. Ct. 368, 1992 WL 46122 (1992). United States ☞53(8)

Even if exception to mandatory requirement for referral to the Small Business Administration (SBA) if small business concern's offer is to be rejected because of determination of nonresponsibility applied to rejection of small disadvantaged business based on accounting system deficiencies identified in audit, Government violated referral requirement, as decision not to refer matter to SBA must be approved by chief of contracting office and no evidence was presented that chief of contracting office approved nonreferral decision. Celtech, Inc. v. U.S., 24 Cl. Ct. 269, 37 Cont. Cas. Fed. (CCH) P 76181, 1991 WL 193295 (1991), vacated pursuant to settlement, 25 Cl. Ct. 368, 1992 WL 46122 (1992). United States ☞64.15

Small Business Administration's Office of Hearings and Appeals could relate back to original notice of appeal certification submission by second low bidder challenging low bidder's satisfaction of solicitation's "small business concern" requirement, and thus notice of appeal came within five-day rule for pending procurement, as certification was treated by OH&A as in nature of an amendment to previous notice of appeal, and original filing provided adequate notice. U.S.Cl. Ct.Rule 15(c), 28 U.S.C.A.Three S Constructors, Inc. v. U.S., 13 Cl. Ct. 41, 34 Cont. Cas. Fed. (CCH) P 75348 (1987). Administrative Law And Procedure ☞513; United States ☞64.55(2)

Process by which Small Business Administration's Office of Hearings and Appeals obtained second low bidder's certification on notice of appeal letter challenging low bidder's satisfaction of "small business concern" requirement was not prohibited ex parte contact, even though it would have been better practice to call attention to omission in manner which notified all parties. Three S Constructors, Inc. v. U.S., 13 Cl. Ct. 41, 34 Cont. Cas. Fed. (CCH) P 75348 (1987). United States ☞64.55(2)

Low bidder on government contract was not "small business concern" as required by solicitation and could not be awarded contract; "newly organized concern" rule applied and compelled aggregation of receipts of both low bidder and affiliated large businesses, as three sons involved in low bidder had been key officers of dissolving, but still existing, large businesses owned by their father and uncle, and assistance was being provided by large businesses to low bidder, which occupied facilities and performed remaining contracts of those businesses. Small Business Act, § 2[8](b)(6), 15 U.S.C.A. § 637(b)(6). Three S Constructors, Inc. v. U.S., 13 Cl. Ct. 41, 34 Cont. Cas. Fed. (CCH) P 75348 (1987). United States ☞64.15

3 North American Industry Classification System

Air Force contracting officer (CO) violated procurement regulation when he selected North American Industry Classification System (NAICS) Code 811212, "Computer and Office Machine Repair and Maintenance" for solicitation to procure operations and maintenance services in support of base telephone system (BTS), as Code 811212 did not "best describ[e] the principal nature of the service being acquired" as required by regulation; decision was based on flawed premise that because computers are used to perform maintenance on a telephone switch, the BTS is therefore a computer. 13 C.F.R. § 121.402(b); 48 C.F.R. § 19.102(b)(1). Red River Service Corp. v. U.S., 60 Fed. Cl. 532 (2004), dismissed, 110 Fed. Appx. 887 (Fed. Cir. 2004). United States ☞64.25

Air Force contracting officer (CO) violated procurement regulation when he selected North American Industry Classification System (NAICS) Code 811212, "Computer and Office Machine Repair and Maintenance" for solicitation to procure operations and maintenance services in support of base telephone system (BTS); since 63% to 73% of the procurement was related more closely to the maintenance of a telecommunications system than a computer, "primary consideration" was not given to the "relative value and importance of the components of the procurement," as required by regulation. 13 C.F.R. § 121.402; 48 C.F.R. § 19.102(d). Red River Service Corp. v. U.S., 60 Fed. Cl. 532 (2004), dismissed, 110 Fed. Appx. 887 (Fed. Cir. 2004). United States ☞64.25

Pre-award bid protestor who prevailed on claim that Air Force contracting officer (CO) violated procurement regulations in selecting North American Industry Classification System (NAICS) Code for small business procurement was entitled to permanent injunction requiring Air Force to set aside solicitation until Code was changed; protestor would suffer irreparable harm of loss of opportunity to compete if Code was not changed, balance of hardships was in favor of protestor since the Air Force would suffer no financial harm, and public interest would be served by preserving integrity of procurement process. Red River Service Corp. v. U.S., 60 Fed. Cl. 532 (2004), dismissed, 110 Fed. Appx. 887 (Fed. Cir. 2004). Injunction ☞86

Prospective bidder whose pre-award bid protest resulted in declaratory judgment invalidating determination of the Small Business Administration (SBA) as to the proper North American Industry Classification System (NAICS) code for the solicitation, was not entitled to an injunction staying the procurement pending appeal after judicial review, considering that prospective bidder did not deconcentrate a likelihood of success on the merits, or that it would suffer irreparable harm. Ceres Environmental Services, Inc. v. U.S., 52 Fed. Cl. 23 (2002). Declaratory Judgment ☞387

Bid protestor challenging determination of the Small Business Administration (SBA) as to the proper North American Industry Classification System (NAICS) code for a solicitation must establish that the code determination had no rational basis or that in making the decision, the SBA violated an applicable procurement statute or regulation in a manner which was prejudicial to the potential offeror. 13 C.F.R. §§ 121.102, 121.402. Ceres Environmental Services, Inc. v. U.S., 52 Fed. Cl. 23 (2002). United States ☞64.55(1); United States ☞64.60(4)

Prospective bidder on solicitation for ice storm debris removal was prejudiced by irrational decision of the Small Business Administration (SBA) upholding contracting officer's decision to change the North American Industry Classification System (NAICS) code for the contract from a "construction" code to a "service" code, since code change rendered prospective bidder ineligible to compete for award. 13 C.F.R. §§ 121.102, 121.402. Ceres Environmental Services, Inc. v. U.S., 52 Fed. Cl. 23 (2002). United States ☞64.55(1)

Decision of the Small Business Administration (SBA), upholding contracting officer's change of the North American Industry Classification System (NAICS) classification code for a contract for ice storm debris removal from a "construction" code to a "service" code, lacked a rational basis, where the SBA failed to explain its departure from its own previous decisions. Ceres Environmental Services, Inc. v. U.S., 52 Fed. Cl. 23 (2002). United States

⚬64.25

4 Non-manufacturer rule

When determining whether a small business qualifies as the "manufacturer" of an end item for purposes of the non-manufacturer rule, the SBA considers the following factors: 1) The proportion of total value in the end item added by the efforts of the concern, excluding costs of overhead, testing, quality control, and profit; 2) the importance of the elements added by the concern to the function of the end item, regardless of their relative value; and 3) the concern's technical capabilities; plant, facilities and equipment; production or assembly line processes; packaging and boxing operations; labeling of products; and product warranties. Coulson Aviation USA, SBA No. SIZ-5815, 2017 (S.B.A.), 2017 WL 953491

The clear purpose of the non-manufacturer rule is "to prevent brokerage-type arrangements whereby small 'front' organizations are set up to bid on government contracts, but furnish the supplies of a large concern."Because the SBA fund that the awardee failed to comply with the non-manufacturer rule and because compliance was a requirement of the contract, the agency's decision to terminate for cause was proper. Third Coast Fresh Distribution, L.L.C., ASBCA 59696, 16-1 BCA ¶ 36,340 (Armed Serv. B.C.A. 2016)

Veterans Administration's solicitation for home oxygen supplies and services to be provided to veterans and beneficiaries was for contract that included supplies, thus requiring inclusion of Small Business Act's non-manufacturer rule in solicitation, even though solicitation was assigned North American Industry Classification System (NAICS) code designating services contract, where majority of solicitation's line items were for manufactured products to be provided to VA patients and only handful related to provision of services. Small Business Act § 2[8], 15 U.S.C.A. § 637(a)(17)(A). Rotech Healthcare Inc. v. U.S., 118 Fed.Cl. 408 (2014)

Protest that an agency failed to apply a HUBZone 10% price evaluation preference was denied because the agency reasonably found that the protester, a certified HUBZone small business, had not agreed to perform certain conditions required by FAR 52.219-4, Notice of Price Evaluation Preference for HUBZone Small Business Concerns, that was incorporated into the solicitation. Specifically, the protester did not demonstrate that it would comply with the HUBZone non-manufacturer rule. Wakan, LLC, B-408535, 2014 CPD ¶ 198 (Comp.Gen. 2014)

An agency's decision not to apply a statutory non-manufacturer rule to a Historically Underutilized Business Zone (HUBZone) set-aside was appropriate. The statutory non-manufacturer rule's plain language indicates that the rule applies only to 8(a) competitive procurement set-asides and general small business set-asides, which do not include HUBZone set-asides. SBA submitted comments arguing that the statutory non-manufacturer rule does not apply to HUBZone set-asides. Matter of: B & B Medical Services, Inc.; Rotech Healthcare, Inc., B-404241, B-404241.2, 2011 CPD ¶ 24 (Comp. Gen. 2011)

Subpart 19.2 Policies

§ 19.201 General policy.

(a) It is the policy of the Government to provide maximum practicable opportunities in its acquisitions to small business, veteran-owned small business, service-disabled veteran-owned small business, HUBZone small business, small disadvantaged business, and women-owned small business concerns. Such concerns must also have the maximum practicable opportunity to participate as subcontractors in the contracts awarded by any executive agency, consistent with efficient contract performance. The Small Business Administration (SBA) counsels and assists small business concerns and assists contracting personnel to ensure that a fair proportion of contracts for supplies and services is placed with small business.

(b) Heads of contracting activities are responsible for effectively implementing the small business programs within their activities, including achieving program goals. They are to ensure that contracting and technical personnel maintain knowledge of small business program requirements and take all reasonable action to increase participation in their activities' contracting processes by these businesses.

(c) The Small Business Act requires each agency with contracting authority to establish an Office of Small and Disadvantaged Business Utilization (see section (k) of the Small Business Act). For the Department of Defense, in accordance with section 904 of the National Defense Authorization Act for Fiscal Year 2006 (Public Law 109-163) (10 U.S.C. 144 note), the Office of Small and Disadvantaged Business Utilization has been redesignated as the Office of Small Business Programs. Management of the office shall be the responsibility of an officer or employee of the agency who shall, in carrying out the purposes of the Act—

(1) Be known as the Director of Small and Disadvantaged Business Utilization, or for the Department of Defense, the Director of Small Business Programs;

(2) Be appointed by the agency head;

(3) Be responsible to and report directly to the agency head or the deputy to the agency head;

(4) Be responsible for the agency carrying out the functions and duties in sections 8, 15, and 31 of the Small Business Act.

(5) Work with the SBA procurement center representative (or, if a procurement center representative is not assigned, see 19.402(a)) to—

(i) Identify proposed solicitations that involve bundling;

(ii) Facilitate small business participation as contractors including small business contract teams, where appropriate; and

(iii) Facilitate small business participation as subcontractors and suppliers where participation by small business concerns as contractors is unlikely;

(6) Assist small business concerns in obtaining payments under their contracts, late payment, interest penalties, or information on contractual payment provisions;

(7) Have supervisory authority over agency personnel to the extent that their functions and duties relate to sections 8, 15, and 31 of the Small Business Act.

(8) Assign a small business technical advisor to each contracting activity within the agency to which the SBA has assigned a representative (see 19.402)—

(i) Who shall be a full-time employee of the contracting activity, well qualified, technically trained, and familiar with the supplies or services contracted for by the activity; and

(ii) Whose principal duty is to assist the SBA's assigned representative in performing functions and duties relating to sections 8, 15, and 31 of the Small Business Act;

(9) Cooperate and consult on a regular basis with the SBA in carrying out the agency's functions and duties in sections 8, 15, and 31 of the Small Business Act;

(10) Make recommendations in accordance with agency procedures as to whether a particular acquisition should be awarded under subpart 19.5 as a small business set-aside, under subpart 19.8 as a Section 8(a) award, under subpart 19.13 as a HUBZone set-aside, under subpart 19.14 as a service-disabled veteran-owned small business set-aside, or under subpart 19.15 as a set-aside for economically disadvantaged women-owned small business (EDWOSB) concerns or women-owned small business (WOSB) concerns eligible under the WOSB Program.

(11) Conduct annual reviews to assess the—

(i) Extent to which small businesses are receiving a fair share of Federal procurements, including contract opportunities under the programs administered under the Small Business Act;

(ii) Adequacy of contract bundling documentation and justifications; and

(iii) Actions taken to mitigate the effects of necessary and justified contract bundling on small businesses.

(12) Provide a copy of the assessment made under paragraph (c)(11) of this section to the Agency Head and SBA Administrator.

(d) Small Business Specialists must be appointed and act in accordance with agency regulations.

United States Code Annotated

Additional powers, see 15 USCA § 637.

Administrative determinations, see 41 USCA § 257.

Awards or contracts, see 15 USCA § 644.

Contract goal for small disadvantaged businesses and certain institutions of higher education, see 10 USCA § 2323.

Contract requirements, see 41 USCA § 254.

Contracts, planning, solicitation, evaluation, and award procedures, see 10 USCA § 2305.

Credit for Indian contracting in meeting certain subcontracting goals for small disadvantaged businesses and certain institutions of higher education, see 10 USCA § 2323a.

Definitions, see 10 USCA § 2302, 41 USCA §§ 259, 403.

Determinations and decisions, see 10 USCA § 2310, 41 USCA § 262.

HUBZone program, see 15 USCA § 657a.

Kinds of contracts, see 10 USCA § 2306.

Planning and solicitation requirements, see 41 USCA § 253a.

Procurement data, see 41 USCA § 417a.

Procurement program for small business concerns owned and controlled by service-disabled veterans, see 15 USCA § 657f.

§ 19.202 Specific policies.

In order to further the policy in 19.201(a), contracting officers shall comply with the specific policies listed in this section and shall consider recommendations of the agency Director of Small and Disadvantaged Business Utilization, or the Director's designee, as to whether a particular acquisition should be awarded under subpart 19.5, 19.8, 19.13, 19.14, or 19.15. Agencies shall establish procedures including dollar thresholds for review of acquisitions by the Director or the Director's designee for the purpose of making these recommendations. The contracting officer shall document the contract file whenever the Director's recommendations are not accepted.

§ 19.202-1 Encouraging small business participation in acquisitions.

Small business concerns shall be afforded an equitable opportunity to compete for all contracts that they can perform to the extent consistent with the Government's interest. When applicable, the contracting officer shall take the following actions:

(a) Divide proposed acquisitions of supplies and services (except construction) into reasonably small lots (not less than economic production runs) to permit offers on quantities less than the total requirement.

(b) Plan acquisitions such that, if practicable, more than one small business concern may perform the work, if the work exceeds the amount for which a surety may be guaranteed by SBA against loss under 15 U.S.C. 694b.

(c) Ensure that delivery schedules are established on a realistic basis that will encourage small business participation to the extent consistent with the actual requirements of the Government.

(d) Encourage prime contractors to subcontract with small business concerns (see Subpart 19.7).

(e) (1) Provide a copy of the proposed acquisition package to the SBA procurement center representative (or, if a procurement center representative is not assigned, see 19.402(a)) at least 30 days prior to the issuance of the solicitation if—

(i) The proposed acquisition is for supplies or services currently being provided by a small business and the proposed acquisition is of a quantity or estimated dollar value, the magnitude of which makes it unlikely that small businesses can compete for the prime contract;

(ii) The proposed acquisition is for construction and seeks to package or consolidate discrete construction projects and the magnitude of this consolidation makes it unlikely that small businesses can compete for the prime contract; or

(iii) The proposed acquisition is for a bundled requirement. (See 10.001(c)(2)(i) for mandatory 30-day notice requirement to incumbent small business concerns.) The contracting officer shall provide all information relative to the justification of contract bundling, including the acquisition plan or strategy, and if the acquisition involves substantial bundling, the information identified in 7.107(e). When the acquisition involves substantial bundling, the contracting officer shall also provide the same information to the agency Office of Small and Disadvantaged Business Utilization.

(2) The contracting officer also must provide a statement explaining why the—

(i) Proposed acquisition cannot be divided into reasonably small lots (not less than economic production runs) to permit offers on quantities less than the total requirement;

(ii) Delivery schedules cannot be established on a realistic basis that will encourage small business participation to the extent consistent with the actual requirements of the Government;

(iii) Proposed acquisition cannot be structured so as to make it likely that small businesses can compete for the prime contract;

(iv) Consolidated construction project cannot be acquired as separate discrete projects; or

(v) Bundling is necessary and justified.

(3) The 30-day notification process shall occur concurrently with other processing steps required prior to the issuance of the solicitation.

(4) If the contracting officer rejects the SBA representative's recommendation made in accordance with 19.402(c)(2), the contracting officer shall document the basis for the rejection and notify the SBA representative in accordance with 19.505.

United States Code Annotated

Additional powers, see 15 USCA § 637.

Administrative determinations, see 41 USCA § 257.

Awards or contracts, see 15 USCA § 644.

Contract goal for small disadvantaged businesses and certain institutions of higher education, see 10 USCA § 2323.

Contract requirements, see 41 USCA § 254.

Contracts, planning, solicitation, evaluation, and award procedures, see 10 USCA § 2305.

Credit for Indian contracting in meeting certain subcontracting goals for small disadvantaged businesses and certain institutions of higher education, see 10 USCA § 2323a.

Definitions, see 10 USCA § 2302, 41 USCA §§ 259, 403.

Determinations and decisions, see 10 USCA § 2310, 41 USCA § 262.

HUBZone program, see 15 USCA § 657a.

Kinds of contracts, see 10 USCA § 2306.

Planning and solicitation requirements, see 41 USCA § 253a.

Procurement data, see 41 USCA § 417a.

Procurement program for small business concerns owned and controlled by service-disabled veterans, see 15 USCA § 657f.

Notes of Decisions

Contract bundling 1

1 Contract bundling

Protest that agency's bundling of requirements for spare parts for aircraft engine violated the Small Business Act and Competition in Contracting Act of 1984 is denied where agency has established measurably substantial benefit to government from consolidating spare part purchases under a single contract, and established that the single contract otherwise is necessary to meet agency needs. B.H. Aircraft Company, Inc., B-295399.2, 2005 CPD ¶ 138 (Comp. Gen. 2005)

Protest challenging bundling of system engineering and support services with other requirements under a single-award BPA issued under awardee's Federal Supply Schedule contract is sustained, where agency failed to perform bundling analysis or satisfy the requirements of FAR 7.107, 10.001(c)(2) and 19.202-1. The requirements that agencies perform a bundling analysis and notify the SBA when requirements are bundled are applicable to BPAs and orders placed against FSS contracts. Sigmatech, Inc., B-296401, 2005 CPD ¶ 156 (Comp. Gen. 2005)

Bundling, for purposes of the Small Business Act means consolidating 2 or more requirements for goods or services previously provided or performed under separate smaller contracts into a solicitation of offers for a single contract that is likely to be unsuitable for award to a small-business concern. Bundling does not occur when the procurement does not consolidate services previously performed under separate smaller contracts. Thus, there is no bundling if all of the services covered by a solicitation were previously performed under one predecessor contract. USA Information Systems, Inc., B-291417, 2002 CPD ¶ 224 (Comp. Gen. 2002)

Protester's contention that an agency's solicitation is an improperly bundled procurement, in violation of the bundling restrictions in the Small Business Act, 15 U.S.C. § 631(j) (3) (Supp. IV 1998), is denied where the solicitation, while clearly comprised of consolidated requirements, does not fall within the reach of the Act because the solicitation anticipates awards to six vendors, two of which will be small businesses. The contract will not, therefore, result in contracts that are "unsuitable for award to a small-business concern," within the meaning of 15 U.S.C. § 632(o)(2). Phoenix Scientific Corporation, B-286817, 2001 CPD ¶ 24 (Comp. Gen. 2001)

§ 19.202-2 Locating small business sources.

The contracting officer must, to the extent practicable, encourage maximum participation by small business, veteran-owned small business, service-disabled veteran-owned small business, HUBZone small business, small disadvantaged business, and women-owned small business concerns in acquisitions by taking the following actions:

(a) Before issuing solicitations, make every reasonable effort to find additional small business concerns, unless lists are already excessively long and only some of the concerns on the list will be solicited. This effort should include contacting the SBA procurement center representative (or, if a procurement center representative is not assigned, see 19.402(a)).

(b) Publicize solicitations and contract awards through the Governmentwide point of entry (see Subparts 5.2 and 5.3).

United States Code Annotated

Additional powers, see 15 USCA § 637.

Administrative determinations, see 41 USCA § 257.

Awards or contracts, see 15 USCA § 644.

Contract goal for small disadvantaged businesses and certain institutions of higher education, see 10 USCA § 2323.

Contract requirements, see 41 USCA § 254.

Contracts, planning, solicitation, evaluation, and award procedures, see 10 USCA § 2305.

Credit for Indian contracting in meeting certain subcontracting goals for small disadvantaged businesses and certain institutions of higher education, see 10 USCA § 2323a.

Definitions, see 10 USCA § 2302, 41 USCA §§ 259, 403.

Determinations and decisions, see 10 USCA § 2310, 41 USCA § 262.

HUBZone program, see 15 USCA § 657a.

Kinds of contracts, see 10 USCA § 2306.

Planning and solicitation requirements, see 41 USCA § 253a.

Procurement data, see 41 USCA § 417a.

Procurement program for small business concerns owned and controlled by service-disabled veterans, see 15 USCA § 657f.

§ 19.202-3 Equal low bids.

In the event of equal low bids (see 14.408-6), awards shall be made first to small business concerns which are also labor surplus area concerns, and second to small business concerns which are not also labor surplus area concerns.

United States Code Annotated

Additional powers, see 15 USCA § 637.

Administrative determinations, see 41 USCA § 257.

Awards or contracts, see 15 USCA § 644.

Contract goal for small disadvantaged businesses and certain institutions of higher education, see 10 USCA § 2323.

Contract requirements, see 41 USCA § 254.

Contracts, planning, solicitation, evaluation, and award procedures, see 10 USCA § 2305.

Credit for Indian contracting in meeting certain subcontracting goals for small disadvantaged businesses and certain institutions of higher education, see 10 USCA § 2323a.

Definitions, see 10 USCA § 2302, 41 USCA §§ 259, 403.

Determinations and decisions, see 10 USCA § 2310, 41 USCA § 262.

HUBZone program, see 15 USCA § 657a.

Kinds of contracts, see 10 USCA § 2306.

Planning and solicitation requirements, see 41 USCA § 253a.

Procurement data, see 41 USCA § 417a.

Procurement program for small business concerns owned and controlled by service-disabled veterans, see 15 USCA § 657f.

§ 19.202-4 Solicitation.

The contracting officer must encourage maximum response to solicitations by small business, veteran-owned small business, service-disabled veteran-owned small business, HUBZone small business, small disadvantaged business, and women-owned small business concerns by taking the following actions:

(a) Allow the maximum amount of time practicable for the submission of offers.

(b) Furnish specifications, plans, and drawings with solicitations, or furnish information as to where they may be obtained or examined.

(c) Provide to any small business concern, upon its request, a copy of bid sets and specifications with respect to any contract to be let, the name and telephone number of an agency contact to answer questions related to such prospective contract and adequate citations to each major Federal law or agency rule with which such business concern must comply in performing such contract other than laws or agency rules with which the small business must comply when doing business with other than the Government.

United States Code Annotated

Additional powers, see 15 USCA § 637.

Administrative determinations, see 41 USCA § 257.

Awards or contracts, see 15 USCA § 644.

Contract goal for small disadvantaged businesses and certain institutions of higher education, see 10 USCA § 2323.

Contract requirements, see 41 USCA § 254.

Contracts, planning, solicitation, evaluation, and award procedures, see 10 USCA § 2305.

Credit for Indian contracting in meeting certain subcontracting goals for small disadvantaged businesses and certain institutions of higher education, see 10 USCA § 2323a.

Definitions, see 10 USCA § 2302, 41 USCA §§ 259, 403.

Determinations and decisions, see 10 USCA § 2310, 41 USCA § 262.

HUBZone program, see 15 USCA § 657a.

Kinds of contracts, see 10 USCA § 2306.

Planning and solicitation requirements, see 41 USCA § 253a.

Procurement data, see 41 USCA § 417a.

Procurement program for small business concerns owned and controlled by service-disabled veterans, see 15 USCA § 657f.

§ 19.202-5 Data collection and reporting requirements.

Agencies must measure the extent of small business participation in their acquisition programs by taking the following actions:

(a) Require each prospective contractor to represent whether it is a small business, veteran-owned small business, service-disabled veteran-owned small business, HUBZone small business, small disadvantaged business, women-owned small business, EDWOSB concern, or WOSB concern eligible under the WOSB Program (see the provision at 52.219-1, Small Business Program Representations).

(b) Accurately measure the extent of participation by small business, veteran-owned small business, service-disabled veteran-owned small business, HUBZone small business, small disadvantaged business, and women-owned small business concerns in Government acquisitions in terms of the total value of contracts placed during each fiscal year, and report data to the SBA at the end of each fiscal year (see Subpart 4.6).

(c) When the contract includes the clause at 52.219-28, Post Award Small Business Program Rerepresentation, and the conditions in the clause for rerepresenting are met—

(1) Require a contractor that represented itself as a small business concern prior to award of the contract to rerepresent its size status; and

(2) Permit a contractor that represented itself as other than a small business concern prior to award to rerepresent its size status.

United States Code Annotated

Additional powers, see 15 USCA § 637.

Administrative determinations, see 41 USCA § 257.

Awards or contracts, see 15 USCA § 644.

Contract goal for small disadvantaged businesses and certain institutions of higher education, see 10 USCA § 2323.

Contract requirements, see 41 USCA § 254.

Contracts, planning, solicitation, evaluation, and award procedures, see 10 USCA § 2305.

Credit for Indian contracting in meeting certain subcontracting goals for small disadvantaged businesses and certain institutions of higher education, see 10 USCA § 2323a.

Definitions, see 10 USCA § 2302, 41 USCA §§ 259, 403.

Determinations and decisions, see 10 USCA § 2310, 41 USCA § 262.

HUBZone program, see 15 USCA § 657a.

Kinds of contracts, see 10 USCA § 2306.

Planning and solicitation requirements, see 41 USCA § 253a.

Procurement data, see 41 USCA § 417a.

Procurement program for small business concerns owned and controlled by service-disabled veterans, see 15 USCA § 657f.

§ 19.202-6 Determination of fair market price.

(a) The fair market price shall be the price achieved in accordance with the reasonable price guidelines in 15.404-1(b) for—

(1) Total and partial small business set-asides (see Subpart 19.5);

(2) HUBZone set-asides (see Subpart 19.13);

(3) Contracts utilizing the price evaluation preference for HUBZone small business concerns (see Subpart 19.13);

(4) Service-disabled veteran-owned small business set-asides (see subpart 19.14);

(5) Set-asides for EDWOSB concerns and WOSB concerns eligible under the WOSB Program (see subpart 19.15).

(b) For 8(a) contracts, both with respect to meeting the requirement at 19.806(b) and in order to accurately estimate the current fair market price, contracting officers shall follow the procedures at 19.807.

United States Code Annotated

Additional powers, see 15 USCA § 637.

Administrative determinations, see 41 USCA § 257.

Awards or contracts, see 15 USCA § 644.

Contract goal for small disadvantaged businesses and certain institutions of higher education, see 10 USCA § 2323.

Contract requirements, see 41 USCA § 254.

Contracts, planning, solicitation, evaluation, and award procedures, see 10 USCA § 2305.

Credit for Indian contracting in meeting certain subcontracting goals for small disadvantaged businesses and certain institutions of higher education, see 10 USCA § 2323a.

Definitions, see 10 USCA § 2302, 41 USCA §§ 259, 403.

Determinations and decisions, see 10 USCA § 2310, 41 USCA § 262.

HUBZone program, see 15 USCA § 657a.

Kinds of contracts, see 10 USCA § 2306.

Planning and solicitation requirements, see 41 USCA § 253a.

Procurement data, see 41 USCA § 417a.

Procurement program for small business concerns owned and controlled by service-disabled veterans, see 15 USCA § 657f.

§ 19.203 Relationship among small business programs.

(a) There is no order of precedence among the 8(a) Program (subpart 19.8), HUBZone Program (subpart 19.13), Service-Disabled Veteran-Owned Small Business (SDVOSB) Procurement Program (subpart 19.14), or the Women-Owned Small Business (WOSB) Program (subpart 19.15).

(b) At or below the simplified acquisition threshold. For acquisitions of supplies or services that have an anticipated dollar value exceeding $3,500 ($20,000 for acquisitions as described in 13.201(g)(1)), but not exceeding $150,000 ($300,000 for acquisitions described in paragraph (1)(i) of the simplified acquisition threshold definition at 2.101), the requirement at 19.502-2(a) to exclusively reserve acquisitions for small business concerns does not preclude the contracting officer from awarding a contract to a small business under the 8(a) Program, HUBZone Program, SDVOSB Program, or WOSB Program.

(c) Above the simplified acquisition threshold. For acquisitions of supplies or services that have an anticipated dollar value exceeding the simplified acquisition threshold definition at 2.101, the contracting officer shall first consider an acquisition for the small business socioeconomic contracting programs (i.e., 8(a), HUBZone, SDVOSB, or WOSB programs) before considering a small business set-aside (see 19.502-2(b)). However, if a requirement has been accepted by the SBA under the 8(a) Program, it must remain in the 8(a) Program unless the SBA agrees to its release in accordance with 13 CFR parts 124, 125, and 126.

(d) In determining which socioeconomic program to use for an acquisition, the contracting officer should consider, at a minimum—

(1) Results of market research that was done to determine if there are socioeconomic firms capable of satisfying the agency's requirement; and

(2) Agency progress in fulfilling its small business goals.

(e) Small business set-asides have priority over acquisitions using full and open competition. See requirements for establishing a small business set-aside at subpart 19.5.

Subpart 19.3 —Determination of Small Business Status for Small Business Programs

§ 19.301 Representations and rerepresentations.

§ 19.301-1 Representation by the offeror.

(a) To be eligible for award as a small business, an offeror must represent in good faith that it is a small business at the time of its written representation. An offeror may represent that it is a small business concern in connection with a specific solicitation if it meets the definition of a small business concern applicable to the solicitation and has not been determined by the Small Business Administration (SBA) to be other than a small business.

(b) The contracting officer shall accept an offeror's representation in a specific bid or proposal that it is a small business unless (1) another offeror or interested party challenges the concern's small business representation or (2) the contracting officer has a reason to question the representation. Challenges of and questions concerning a specific representation shall be referred to the SBA in accordance with 19.302.

(c) An offeror's representation that it is a small business is not binding on the SBA. If an offeror's small business status is challenged, the SBA will evaluate the status of the concern and make a determination, which will be binding on the contracting officer, as to whether the offeror is a small business. A concern cannot become eligible for a specific award by taking action to meet the definition of a small business concern after the SBA has determined that it is not a small business.

(d) If the SBA determines that the status of a concern as a small business, veteran-owned small business, service-disabled veteran-owned small business, HUBZone small business, small disadvantaged business, or women-owned small business has been misrepresented in order to obtain a set-aside contract, an 8(a) subcontract, a subcontract that is to be included as part or all of a goal contained in a subcontracting plan, or a prime or subcontract to be awarded as a result, or in furtherance of any other provision of Federal law that specifically references Section 8(d) of the Small Business Act for a definition of program eligibility, the SBA may take action as specified in Sections 16(a) or 16(d) of the Act. If the SBA declines to take action, the agency may initiate the process. The SBA's regulations on penalties for misrepresentations and false statements are contained in 13 CFR 121.108 for small business, 13 CFR 124.501 for 8(a) small business, 13 CFR 124.1004 for small disadvantaged business, 13 CFR 125.29 for veteran or service-disabled veteran-owned small business, 13 CFR 126.900 for HUBZone small business, and 13 CFR 127.700 for economically disadvantaged women-owned small business concerns and women-owned small business (WOSB) concerns eligible under the WOSB Program.

Notes of Decisions
In general 1

1 In general

A concern that represents itself and qualifies as an SDVO SBC at the time of initial offer (or other formal response to a solicitation), which includes price, including a Multiple Award Contract, is considered an SDVO SBC throughout the life of that contract. This means that if an SDVO SBC is qualified at the time of initial offer for a Multiple Award Contract, then it will be considered an SDVO SBC for each order issued against the contract, unless a contracting officer requests a new SDVO SBC certification in connection with a specific order. Redhorse Corp., SBA No. VET-261, 2017 (S.B.A.), 2017 WL 1104611

SBA will determine a challenged firm's receipts using those tax returns filed in the three-year period before the date of self-certification. If a challenged firm has not filed a tax return for one of the applicable years, that year will still be used to determine a challenged firm's size, and SBA will use any other available information to determine the challenged firm's receipts. 13 C.F.R. § 121.104(a)(2). The SBA determined that, "[t]here is no merit in Appellant's argument that the [most recent] return should not be used. The regulation clearly requires the use of receipts for the three fiscal years preceding self-certification to determine size, whether or not the Federal tax returns are available. Here, even though the 2001 return was filed late, it was available for the size determination. Educational Servs., Inc., SBA No. SIZ-4782 (S.B.A.), 2006 WL 1484897

§ 19.301-2 Rerepresentation by a contractor that represented itself as a small business concern.

(a) *Definition.* As used in this subsection—

Long-term contract means a contract of more than five years in duration, including options. However, the term does not include contracts that exceed five years in duration because the period of performance has been extended for a cumulative period not to exceed six months under the clause at 52.217-8, Option to Extend Services, or other appropriate authority.

(b) A contractor that represented itself as a small business concern before contract award must rerepresent its size status for the North American Industry Classification System (NAICS) code in the contract upon the occurrence of any of the following:

(1) Within 30 days after execution of a novation agreement or within 30 days after modification of the contract to include the clause at 52.219-28, Post-Award Small Business Program Rerepresentation, if the novation agreement was executed prior to inclusion of this clause in the contract.

(2) Within 30 days after a merger or acquisition of the contractor that does not require

novation or within 30 days after modification of the contract to include the clause at 52.219-28, Post-Award Small Business Program Rerepresentation, if the merger or acquisition occurred prior to inclusion of this clause in the contract.

(3) For long-term contracts—

(i) Within 60 to 120 days prior to the end of the fifth year of the contract; and

(ii) Within 60 to 120 days prior to the date specified in the contract for exercising any option thereafter.

(c) A contractor must rerepresent its size status in accordance with the size standard in effect at the time of its rerepresentation that corresponds to the NAICS code that was initially assigned to the contract.

(d) After a contractor rerepresents it is other than small in accordance with 52.219-28, the agency may no longer include the value of options exercised, modifications issued, orders issued, or purchases made under blanket purchase agreements on that contract in its small business prime contracting goal achievements. Agencies should issue a modification to the contract capturing the rerepresentation and report it to FPDS within 30 days after notification of the rerepresentation.

(e) A change in size status does not change the terms and conditions of the contract.

Notes of Decisions

In general 1

1 In general

When a firm is awarded an ID/IQ contract (including a GSA Federal Supply Schedule contract) as a small business, the firm is generally considered a small business throughout the life of that contract, and is not required to recertify its size status for each order issued under the contract. However, agencies have the discretion to request that vendors recertify their business status at the time of submission of proposals or quotations for an order. If a solicitation expressly requires a vendor to recertify its size status in response to a solicitation for an order, than the size of the vendor is determined as of the date of the recertification. GAO held that agency properly rejected the protester's quotation because the protester was no longer small at the time of the recertification and was not, therefore, an interested party eligible to protest. Technica Corp., Comp. Gen. Dec. B-413339, 2016 CPD ¶ 264 (Comp. Gen. 2016)

§ 19.301-3 Rerepresentation by a contractor that represented itself as other than a small business concern.

A contractor that represented itself as other than small before contract award may, but is not required to, rerepresent its size status when—

(a) The conditions in 19.301-2(b) apply; and

(b) The contractor qualifies as a small business concern under the applicable size standard in effect at the time of its rerepresentation.

§ 19.302 Protesting a small business representation or rerepresentation.

(a) (1) The Small Business Administration (SBA) regulations on small business size and size protests are found at 13 CFR part 121.

(2) An offeror, the SBA, or another interested party may protest the small business representation of an offeror in a specific offer. However, for competitive 8(a) contracts, the filing of a protest is limited to an offeror, the contracting officer, or the SBA.

(b) Any time after offers are opened, the contracting officer may question the small business representation of any offeror in a specific offer by filing a contracting officer's protest (see paragraph (c) of this section).

(c) (1) Any contracting officer who receives a protest, whether timely or not, or who, as the contracting officer, wishes to protest the small business representation of an offeror, or rerepresentation of a contractor, shall promptly forward the protest to the SBA Government Contracting Area Director at the Government Contracting Area Office serving the area in which the headquarters of the offeror is located.

(2) The protest, or confirmation if the protest was initiated orally, shall be in writing and shall contain the basis for the protest with specific, detailed evidence to support the allegation that the offeror is not small. The SBA will dismiss any protest that does not

contain specific grounds for the protest.

(3) The protest shall include a referral letter written by the contracting officer with information pertaining to the solicitation. The referral letter must include the following information to allow SBA to determine timeliness and standing:

(i) The protest and any accompanying materials.

(ii) A copy of the size self-certification.

(iii) Identification of the applicable size standard.

(iv) A copy or an electronic link to the solicitation and any amendments.

(v) The name, address, telephone number, email address, and fax number of the contracting officer.

(vi) Identification of the bid opening date or the date of notification provided to unsuccessful offerors.

(vii) The date the contracting officer received the protest.

(viii) A complete address and point of contact for the protested concern.

(d) In order to affect a specific solicitation, a protest must be timely. SBA's regulations on timeliness are contained in 13 CFR 121.1004. SBA's regulations on timeliness related to protests of disadvantaged status are contained in 13 CFR 124, Subpart B.

(1) To be timely, a protest by any concern or other interested party must be received by the contracting officer (see paragraphs (d)(1)(i) and (ii) of this section) by the close of business of the fifth business day after bid opening (in sealed bid acquisitions) or receipt of the special notification from the contracting officer that identifies the apparently successful offeror (in negotiated acquisitions) (see 15.503(a)(2)).

(i) A protest may be made orally if it is confirmed in writing and received by the contracting officer within the 5-day period or by letter postmarked no later than 1 business day after the oral protest.

(ii) A protest may be made in writing if it is delivered to the contracting officer by hand, telegram, mail, facsimile, e-mail, express or overnight delivery service.

(2) Except as provided in paragraph (d)(4) of this section, a protest filed by the contracting officer or SBA is always considered timely whether filed before or after award.

(3) A protest under a Multiple Award Schedule will be timely if received by SBA at any time prior to the expiration of the contract period, including renewals.

(4) A protest filed before bid opening, or notification to offerors of the selection of the apparent successful offeror, will be dismissed as premature by SBA.

(e) Upon receipt of a protest from or forwarded by the Contracting Office, the SBA will—

(1) Notify the contracting officer and the protester of the date it was received, and that the size of the concern being challenged is under consideration by the SBA; and

(2) Furnish to the concern whose representation is being protested a copy of the protest and a blank SBA Form 355, Application for Small Business Determination, by certified mail, return receipt requested.

(f) (1) Within 15 business days after receipt of a protest or request for a formal size determination or within any extension of time granted by the contracting officer the SBA Area Office will determine the size status of the challenged concern. The SBA Area Office will notify the contracting officer, the protester, and the challenged concern of its decision by a verifiable means, which may include facsimile, electronic mail, or overnight delivery service.

(2) Award may be made to a protested concern after the SBA Area Office has determined that either the protested concern is an eligible small business or has dismissed all protests against it.

(3) If SBA's Office of Hearings and Appeals (OHA) subsequently overturns the Area Office's determination of eligibility or dismissal, and contract award has not been made, the contracting officer may apply the OHA decision to the procurement in question.

(g) (1) After receiving a protest involving an offeror being considered for award, the contracting officer shall not award the contract until the SBA has made a size determination or 15 business days have expired since SBA's receipt of a protest, whichever occurs first; however, award shall not be withheld when the contracting officer determines in writing that an award must be made to protect the public interest.

(2) If SBA has not made a determination within 15 business days, or within any exten-

sion of time granted by the contracting officer, the contracting officer may award the contract after determining in writing that there is an immediate need to award the contract and that waiting until SBA makes its determination will be disadvantageous to the Government.

(3) SBA may, at its sole discretion, reopen a formal size determination to correct an error or mistake, if it is within the appeal period and no appeal has been filed with OHA or, a final decision has not been rendered by the SBA Area Office or OHA.

(4) If a protest is received that challenges the small business status of an offeror not being considered for award, the contracting officer is not required to suspend contract action. The contracting officer shall forward the protest to the SBA (see paragraph (c)(1) of this section) with a notation that the concern is not being considered for award, and shall notify the protester of this action.

(h) An appeal from an SBA size determination may be filed by any concern or other interested party whose protest of the small business representation of another concern has been denied by an SBA Government Contracting Area Director, any concern or other interested party that has been adversely affected by an SBA Government Contracting Area Director's decision, or the SBA Associate Administrator for the SBA program involved. The appeal must be filed with the Office of Hearings and Appeals, Small Business Administration, Suite 5900, 409 3rd Street, SW., Washington, DC 20416, within the time limits and in strict accordance with the procedures contained in Subpart C of 13 CFR 134. It is within the discretion of the SBA Judge whether to accept an appeal from a size determination. If a post-award appeal is submitted to OHA within the time limits specified in Subpart C of 13 CFR 134, the contracting officer shall consider suspending contract performance until an SBA Judge decides the appeal. SBA will inform the contracting officer of its ruling on the appeal. SBA's decision, if received before award, will apply to the pending acquisition. If the contracting officer has made a written determination in accordance with (g)(1) or (2) of this section, the contract has been awarded, the SBA rulings is received after award, and OHA finds the protested concern to be ineligible for award, the contracting officer shall terminate the contract unless termination is not in the best interests of the Government, in keeping with the circumstances described in the written determination. However, the contracting officer shall not exercise any options or award further task or delivery orders.

(i) SBA will dismiss untimely protests. A protest that is not timely, even though received before award, shall be forwarded to the SBA Government Contracting Area Office (see paragraph (c)(1) of this section), with a notation on it that the protest is not timely. A protest received by a contracting officer after award of a contract shall be forwarded to the SBA Government Contracting Area Office with a notation that award has been made.

(j) When a concern is found to be other than small under a protest concerning a size status rerepresentation made in accordance with the clause at 52.219-28, Post-Award Small Business Program Rerepresentation, a contracting officer may permit contract performance to continue, issue orders, or exercise option(s), because the contract remains a valid contract.

United States Code Annotated

Additional powers, see 15 USCA § 637.

Administrative determinations, see 41 USCA § 257.

Awards or contracts, see 15 USCA § 644.

Contract goal for small disadvantaged businesses and certain institutions of higher education, see 10 USCA § 2323.

Contract requirements, see 41 USCA § 254.

Contracts, planning, solicitation, evaluation, and award procedures, see 10 USCA § 2305.

Credit for Indian contracting in meeting certain subcontracting goals for small disadvantaged businesses and certain institutions of higher education, see 10 USCA § 2323a.

Definitions, see 10 USCA § 2302, 41 USCA §§ 259, 403.

Determinations and decisions, see 10 USCA § 2310, 41 USCA § 262.

HUBZone program, see 15 USCA § 657a.

Kinds of contracts, see 10 USCA § 2306.

Planning and solicitation requirements, see 41 USCA § 253a.

Procurement data, see 41 USCA § 417a.

Procurement program for small business concerns owned and controlled by service-disabled veterans, see 15 USCA § 657f.

Notes of Decisions

In general 1
Certificates of competency 2
Historically underutilized business zones 3
Injunctions 4

1 In general

Small business, which was disappointed bidder with respect to public contract, was entitled to preliminary injunction prohibiting successful bidder on small business set aside contract from continuing contract performance until decision was made by General Accounting Office (GAO) on disappointed bidder's protest; disappointed bidder's claim was not frivolous, disappointed bidder would suffer irreparable harm if it lost contract, it was unlikely that the United States would suffer injury if injunctive relief was granted, and granting of short duration injunction was in the public interest. United Power Corp. v. U.S. Defense Mapping Agency, 736 F. Supp. 354, 36 Cont. Cas. Fed. (CCH) P 75862 (D.D.C. 1990). Injunction ⟶138.63

Carrier, which had been engaged in transportation of military cargos pursuant to shipping contract with United States Navy Military Sealift Command, was entitled to preliminary injunction prohibiting Command from performing contract for transportation services with a competing carrier pending decision on the merits; carrier was likely to prevail on its claim that Command's failure to consider availability of continuing carrier's service to allow Small Business Administration and Government Accounting Office sufficient time to address its protests to awarding contract to competing carrier was arbitrary, capricious and contrary to law. Small Business Act, §§ 2[2] et seq., 15 U.S.C.A. §§ 631 et seq.Samson Tug & Barge Co., Inc. v. U.S., 695 F. Supp. 25 (D.D.C. 1988). Injunction ⟶138.63

Award to successful bidder of government contract that had been set aside for small businesses could not be challenged by unsuccessful bidder based on determination of successful bidder's size issued by Small Business Administration (SBA), where unsuccessful bidder did not file its administrative appeal and SBA's Office of Hearings and Appeals (OHA) did not rule on that appeal until after contract was awarded, and regulation made bidder size determinations issued after contract award applicable to prospective government procurements only, and therefore Court of Federal Claims could not supply declaratory or injunctive relief requested by unsuccessful bidder in its motion for preliminary injunction, and claim was not justiciable. Chapman Law Firm v. U.S., 63 Fed. Cl. 25 (2004). Declaratory Judgment ⟶203; Declaratory Judgment ⟶258; Federal Courts ⟶1119.1; United States ⟶64.15

Contracting officer's failure to bring technical protest of another bidder to technical evaluation team's attention was proper, where evaluation team had completed its review of all proposed aircraft and found aircraft in question acceptable under request for proposals from small businesses to supply the four aircraft, on lease basis, for use by United States Air Force. Aviation Enterprises, Inc. v. U.S., 8 Cl. Ct. 1, 32 Cont. Cas. Fed. (CCH) P 73403 (1985). United States ⟶64.55(2)

2 Certificates of competency

Small Business Administration (SBA) is final arbiter on responsibility determinations in bid protest proceedings. Small Business Act, § 2[8](b)(7), (A, C), 15 U.S.C.A. § 637(b)(7)(A, C). C & G Excavating, Inc. v. U.S., 32 Fed. Cl. 231, 39 Cont. Cas. Fed. (CCH) P 76715 (1994). United States ⟶64.60(3.1)

3 Historically underutilized business zones

A HUBZone status protest does not have to identify itself as such to be valid. 13 C.F.R. § 126.801(b). Mark Dunning Industries, Inc. v. U.S., 58 Fed. Cl. 216 (2003). United States ⟶64.55(2)

Language in bidder's fax to contract specialist sufficiently conveyed an expression of dissatisfaction with another bidder's HUBZone status as to constitute a HUBZone status protest, where bidder complained that "it would be upset" if it were determined that rival bidder was eligible for the HUBZone advantage, and submitted evidence that rival bidder might not be eligible for HUBZone status because, "according to the SBA HUB Zone locator their address IS NOT in a HUB Zone." 13 C.F.R. § 126.801(b). Mark Dunning Industries, Inc. v. U.S., 58 Fed. Cl. 216 (2003). United States ☞64.55(2)

Bidder's request in fax that the contracting officer (CO) "verify all certifications before making any determinations and applying any bid advantages" was sufficient request for corrective action to qualify fax as a valid HUBZone status protest, as context made it clear that bidder was requesting that CO make sure that rival bidder was actually qualified for HUBZone status certification. 13 C.F.R. § 126.801. Mark Dunning Industries, Inc. v. U.S., 58 Fed. Cl. 216 (2003). United States ☞64.55(2)

Protesting bidder did not abandon HUBZone status protest by not taking some sort of action after contracting officer (CO) did not forward the protest to the Small Business Administration (SBA), notwithstanding contention that bidder knew, or should have known, that CO had not forwarded the protest because it did not receive notice of receipt of the protest from the SBA; protestor was under no duty to acknowledge the receipt, or lack thereof, of the SBA's notice. 13 C.F.R. § 126.803(a). Mark Dunning Industries, Inc. v. U.S., 58 Fed. Cl. 216 (2003). United States ☞64.55(2)

Fact that bidder's HUBZone status protest in fax to contracting officer (CO) did not state all the specific grounds for the protest did not relieve CO of his duty under regulation to forward protest to the Small Business Administration (SBA); regulation clearly required CO to forward the protest to the SBA "notwithstanding whether he or she believes it is sufficiently specific." 13 C.F.R. § 126.801(b, e). Mark Dunning Industries, Inc. v. U.S., 58 Fed. Cl. 216 (2003). United States ☞64.55(2)

Whether bidder intended that his fax to contracting officer questioning the HUBZone status of rival bidder be treated as a HUBZone status protest was irrelevant with regard to the question whether CO should have treated it as such and forwarded it to the Small Business Administration (SBA). 13 C.F.R. § 126.801(e). Mark Dunning Industries, Inc. v. U.S., 58 Fed. Cl. 216 (2003). United States ☞64.55(2)

4 Injunctions

In finding, on motion for preliminary injunction, that claim in which unsuccessful bidder for small business contract challenged size determination made by Small Business Administration (SBA) for successful bidder was not justiciable, in light of unsuccessful bidder's post-award appeal and regulation making post-award bidder size determinations applicable to prospective government procurements only, Court of Federal Claims made finding on the merits warranting dismissal of action, in that unsuccessful bidder could not show requisite clear and prejudicial violation of regulations governing its appeal from its SBA size status protest. Chapman Law Firm v. U.S., 63 Fed. Cl. 25 (2004). United States ☞64.55(1)

§ 19.303 Determining North American Industry Classification System codes and size standards.

(a) (1) The contracting officer shall determine the appropriate North American Industry Classification System (NAICS) code and related small business size standard and include them in solicitations above the micro-purchase threshold. For information on size standards matched to industry NAICS codes, including the use of new NAICS codes, see also 19.102(a).

(2) The contracting officer shall select the NAICS code which best describes the principal purpose of the product or service being acquired. Primary consideration is given to the industry descriptions in the U.S. NAICS Manual, the product or service description in the solicitation and any attachments to it, the relative value and importance of the components of the procurement making up the end item being procured, and the function of the goods or services being purchased. A procurement is usually classified according to the component which accounts for the greatest percentage of contract value. A concern that submits an offer or quote for a contract where the NAICS code assigned to the contract is one for supplies, and furnishes a product it did not itself manufacture or produce, is categorized as a nonmanufacturer and deemed small if it meets the requirements of 19.102(f).

(b) If different products or services are required in the same solicitation, the solicitation shall identify the appropriate small business size standard for each product or service.

(c) The contracting officer's determination is final unless appealed as follows:

(1) An appeal from a contracting officer's NAICS code designation and the applicable size standard must be served and filed within 10 calendar days after the issuance of the initial solicitation or any amendment affecting the NAICS code or size standard. However, SBA may file a NAICS code appeal at any time before offers are due.

(2) Appeals from a contracting officer's NAICS code designation or applicable size standard may be filed with SBA's Office of Hearings and Appeals by—

(i) Any person adversely affected by a NAICS code designation or applicable size standard. However, with respect to a particular sole source 8(a) contract, only the SBA Associate Administrator for Business Development may appeal a NAICS code designation; or

(ii) The Associate or Assistant Director for the SBA program involved, through SBA's Office of General Counsel.

(3) Contracting officers shall advise the public, by amendment to the solicitation, of the existence of a NAICS code appeal (see 5.102(a)(1)). Such notices shall include the procedures and the deadline for interested parties to file and serve arguments concerning the appeal.

(4) SBA's Office of Hearings and Appeals (OHA) will dismiss summarily an untimely NAICS code appeal.

(5) (i) The appeal petition must be in writing and must be addressed to the Office of Hearings and Appeals, Small Business Administration, Suite 5900, 409 3rd Street, SW., Washington, DC 20416.

(ii) There is no required format for the appeal; however, the appeal must include—

(A) The solicitation or contract number and the name, address, email address, and telephone number of the contracting officer;

(B) A full and specific statement as to why the NAICS code designation is allegedly erroneous and argument supporting the allegation; and

(C) The name, address, telephone number, and signature of the appellant or its attorney.

(6) The appellant must serve the appeal petition upon—

(i) The contracting officer who assigned the NAICS code to the acquisition; and

(ii) SBA's Office of General Counsel, Associate General Counsel for Procurement Law, 409 Third Street, SW., Washington, DC 20416, facsimile 202-205-6873, or email at OPLService@sba.gov.

(7) Upon receipt of a NAICS code appeal, OHA will notify the contracting officer by a notice and order of the date OHA received the appeal, the docket number, and Judge assigned to the case. The contracting officer's response to the appeal, if any, must include argument and evidence (see 13 CFR Part 134), and must be received by OHA within 15 calendar days from the date of the docketing notice and order, unless otherwise specified by the Administrative Judge. Upon receipt of OHA's docketing notice and order, the contracting officer must withhold award, unless withholding award is not in the best interests of the Government, and immediately send to OHA an electronic link to or a paper copy of both the original solicitation and all amendments relating to the NAICS code appeal. The contracting officer will inform OHA of any amendments, actions, or developments concerning the procurement in question.

(8) After close of record, OHA will issue a decision and inform the contracting officer. If OHA's decision is received by the contracting officer before the date the offers are due, the decision shall be final and the solicitation must be amended to reflect the decision, if appropriate. OHA's decision received after the due date of the initial offers shall not apply to the pending solicitation but shall apply to future solicitations of the same products or services.

(d) SBA's regulations concerning appeals of NAICS code designations are found at 13 CFR 121.1101 to 121.1103 and 13 CFR part 134.

United States Code Annotated

Additional powers, see 15 USCA § 637.

Administrative determinations, see 41 USCA § 257.

Awards or contracts, see 15 USCA § 644.

Contract goal for small disadvantaged businesses and certain institutions of higher education, see 10 USCA § 2323.

Contract requirements, see 41 USCA § 254.

Contracts, planning, solicitation, evaluation, and award procedures, see 10 USCA § 2305.

Credit for Indian contracting in meeting certain subcontracting goals for small disadvantaged businesses and certain institutions of higher education, see 10 USCA § 2323a.

Definitions, see 10 USCA § 2302, 41 USCA §§ 259, 403.

Determinations and decisions, see 10 USCA § 2310, 41 USCA § 262.

HUBZone program, see 15 USCA § 657a.

Kinds of contracts, see 10 USCA § 2306.

Planning and solicitation requirements, see 41 USCA § 253a.

Procurement data, see 41 USCA § 417a.

Procurement program for small business concerns owned and controlled by service-disabled veterans, see 15 USCA § 657f.

Notes of Decisions

In general 1
Changes to the size standard 3
Injunctions 2

1 In general

A North American Industry Classification System (NAICS) code appeal must be filed with the Small Business Administration's Office of Hearings and Appeals (OHA) within 10 calendar days, OHA recently determined. The appellant had filed its appeal 14 calendar days, but 10 business days after the request for proposals was issued. NAICS Appeal of Eagle Home Med. Corp., SBA No. NAICS-5378 (2012)

SBA granted the challenge to the agency's use of an engineering services NAICS code (541330) because services comprised only approximately 25% of the total procurement cost and equipment costs comprised approximately 75%. Even among the 25% portion that pertained to services, it is not evident that *engineering* work is a significant portion. The SBA concluded: "[A]lthough engineering services are not totally irrelevant to these acquisitions, such services appear to represent a minor aspect of the overall RFPs. [T]he mere fact that a procurement calls for incidental or ancillary services 'does not justify classifying the procurement based upon the ancillary services,' even if those ancillary services are 'necessary to the procurement.'" NAICS Appeal of the SBA, SBA No. NAICS-5526, 2014 (S.B.A.), 2014 WL 183785

Dispute in which incumbent contractor challenged decision of the Office of Hearings and Appeals (OHA) of the Small Business Administration (SBA) which changed small business code designations in solicitation, rendering it ineligible to bid, was justiciable, notwithstanding government's contention that any relief could only be prospective under procurement regulation since OHA decision was received after due date of initial offers, as Court of Federal Claims could set a new date for submission of initial offers. Advanced Systems Technology, Inc. v. U.S., 69 Fed. Cl. 474 (2006). Federal Courts ☞13

Air Force contracting officer (CO) violated procurement regulation when he selected North American Industry Classification System (NAICS) Code 811212, "Computer and Office Machine Repair and Maintenance" for solicitation to procure operations and maintenance services in support of base telephone system (BTS), as Code 811212 did not "best describ[e] the principal nature of the service being acquired" as required by regulation; decision was based on flawed premise that because computers are used to perform maintenance on a telephone switch, the BTS is therefore a computer. 13 C.F.R. § 121.402(b); 48 C.F.R. § 19.102(b)(1). Red River Service Corp. v. U.S., 60 Fed. Cl. 532 (2004), dismissed, 110 Fed. Appx. 887 (Fed. Cir. 2004). United States ☞64.25

Air Force contracting officer (CO) violated procurement regulation when he selected North American Industry Classification System (NAICS) Code 811212, "Computer and Of-

fice Machine Repair and Maintenance" for solicitation to procure operations and maintenance services in support of base telephone system (BTS); since 63% to 73% of the procurement was related more closely to the maintenance of a telecommunications system than a
computer, "primary consideration" was not given to the "relative value and importance of
the components of the procurement," as required by regulation. 13 C.F.R. § 121.402; 48
C.F.R. § 19.102(d). Red River Service Corp. v. U.S., 60 Fed. Cl. 532 (2004), dismissed, 110
Fed. Appx. 887 (Fed. Cir. 2004). United States ⚎64.25

Bid protestor challenging determination of the Small Business Administration (SBA) as
to the proper North American Industry Classification System (NAICS) code for a solicitation must establish that the code determination had no rational basis or that in making the
decision, the SBA violated an applicable procurement statute or regulation in a manner
which was prejudicial to the potential offeror. 13 C.F.R. §§ 121.102, 121.402. Ceres
Environmental Services, Inc. v. U.S., 52 Fed. Cl. 23 (2002). United States ⚎64.55(1);
United States ⚎64.60(4)

Prospective bidder on solicitation for ice storm debris removal was prejudiced by irrational decision of the Small Business Administration (SBA) upholding contracting officer's decision to change the North American Industry Classification System (NAICS) code
for the contract from a "construction" code to a "service" code, since code change rendered
prospective bidder ineligible to compete for award. 13 C.F.R. §§ 121.102, 121.402. Ceres
Environmental Services, Inc. v. U.S., 52 Fed. Cl. 23 (2002). United States ⚎64.55(1)

Decision of the Small Business Administration (SBA), upholding contracting officer's
change of the North American Industry Classification System (NAICS) classification code
for a contract for ice storm debris removal from a "construction" code to a "service" code,
lacked a rational basis, where the SBA failed to explain its departure from its own previous
decisions. Ceres Environmental Services, Inc. v. U.S., 52 Fed. Cl. 23 (2002). United States
⚎64.25

2 Injunctions

Pre-award bid protestor who prevailed on claim that Air Force contracting officer (CO)
violated procurement regulations in selecting North American Industry Classification
System (NAICS) Code for small business procurement was entitled to permanent injunction requiring Air Force to set aside solicitation until Code was changed; protestor would
suffer irreparable harm of loss of opportunity to compete if Code was not changed, balance
of hardships was in favor of protestor since the Air Force would suffer no financial harm,
and public interest would be served by preserving integrity of procurement process. Red
River Service Corp. v. U.S., 60 Fed. Cl. 532 (2004), dismissed, 110 Fed. Appx. 887 (Fed. Cir.
2004). Injunction ⚎86

Prospective bidder whose pre-award bid protest resulted in declaratory judgment
invalidating determination of the Small Business Administration (SBA) as to the proper
North American Industry Classification System (NAICS) code for the solicitation, was not
entitled to an injunction staying the procurement pending appeal after judicial review,
considering that prospective bidder did not deconcentrate a likelihood of success on the
merits, or that it would suffer irreparable harm. Ceres Environmental Services, Inc. v. U.S.,
52 Fed. Cl. 23 (2002). Declaratory Judgment ⚎387

3 Changes to the size standard

Agencies are not required to amend solicitations to incorporate new size standards issued
by the Small Business Administration (SBA). SBA regulations (13 C.F.R. § 121.402) state
that contracting officers "may" amend solicitations and use new size standards when they
become effective before date initial bids are due, but the regulations do not require such
action. Orion Constr. Corp., 125 Fed.Cl. 668 (2016).

§ 19.304 Disadvantaged business status.

(a) The contracting officer may accept an offeror's representation that it is a small
disadvantaged business concern (SDB) concern.

(b) The provision at 52.219-1, Small Business Program Representations, or 52.212-3(c)(4),
Offeror Representations and Certifications-Commercial Items, is used to collect SDB data.

(c) A representation of SDB status on a Federal prime contract will be deemed a misrepresentation of SDB status if the firm does not meet the requirements of 13 CFR 124.

1001(b).

(d) Any person or entity that misrepresents a firm's status as an SDB concern in order to obtain a contracting opportunity in accordance with section 8(d) of the Small Business Act, (15 U.S.C. 637(d)) will be subject to the penalties imposed by section 16(d) of the Small Business Act, (15 U.S.C. 645(d)), as well as any other penalty authorized by law.

United States Code Annotated

Additional powers, see 15 USCA § 637.

Administrative determinations, see 41 USCA § 257.

Awards or contracts, see 15 USCA § 644.

Contract goal for small disadvantaged businesses and certain institutions of higher education, see 10 USCA § 2323.

Contract requirements, see 41 USCA § 254.

Contracts, planning, solicitation, evaluation, and award procedures, see 10 USCA § 2305.

Credit for Indian contracting in meeting certain subcontracting goals for small disadvantaged businesses and certain institutions of higher education, see 10 USCA § 2323a.

Definitions, see 10 USCA § 2302, 41 USCA §§ 259, 403.

Determinations and decisions, see 10 USCA § 2310, 41 USCA § 262.

HUBZone program, see 15 USCA § 657a.

Kinds of contracts, see 10 USCA § 2306.

Planning and solicitation requirements, see 41 USCA § 253a.

Procurement data, see 41 USCA § 417a.

Procurement program for small business concerns owned and controlled by service-disabled veterans, see 15 USCA § 657f.

§ 19.305 Protesting a representation of disadvantaged business status.

This section applies to reviews and protests of a small business concern's SDB status as a prime contractor or subcontractor.

(a) SBA may initiate the review of SDB status on any firm that has represented itself to be an SDB on a prime contract or subcontract to a Federal prime contract whenever it receives credible information calling into question the SDB status of the firm.

(b) Requests for an SBA review of SDB status may be forwarded to the Small Business Administration, Assistant Administrator for SDBCE, 409 Third Street, SW, Washington, DC 20416.

(c) An SBA review of a subcontractor's SDB status differs from a formal protest. Protests of a small business concern's SDB status as a subcontractor are processed under 19.703(a)(2). Protests of a concern's size as a prime contractor are processed under 19.302. Protests of a concern's size as a subcontractor are processed under 19.703(b).

United States Code Annotated

Additional powers, see 15 USCA § 637.

Administrative determinations, see 41 USCA § 257.

Awards or contracts, see 15 USCA § 644.

Contract goal for small disadvantaged businesses and certain institutions of higher education, see 10 USCA § 2323.

Contract requirements, see 41 USCA § 254.

Contracts, planning, solicitation, evaluation, and award procedures, see 10 USCA § 2305.

Credit for Indian contracting in meeting certain subcontracting goals for small disadvantaged businesses and certain institutions of higher education, see 10 USCA § 2323a.

Definitions, see 10 USCA § 2302, 41 USCA §§ 259, 403.

Determinations and decisions, see 10 USCA § 2310, 41 USCA § 262.

HUBZone program, see 15 USCA § 657a.

Kinds of contracts, see 10 USCA § 2306.

Planning and solicitation requirements, see 41 USCA § 253a.

Procurement data, see 41 USCA § 417a.

Procurement program for small business concerns owned and controlled by service-disabled veterans, see 15 USCA § 657f.

Notes of Decisions

Appeal of SBA determinations 3
Parties 2
Small business concern 1

1 Small business concern

Even if exception to mandatory requirement for referral to the Small Business Administration (SBA) if small business concern's offer is to be rejected because of determination of nonresponsibility applied to rejection of small disadvantaged business based on accounting system deficiencies identified in audit, Government violated referral requirement, as decision not to refer matter to SBA must be approved by chief of contracting office and no evidence was presented that chief of contracting office approved nonreferral decision. Celtech, Inc. v. U.S., 24 Cl. Ct. 269, 37 Cont. Cas. Fed. (CCH) P 76181, 1991 WL 193295 (1991), vacated pursuant to settlement, 25 Cl. Ct. 368, 1992 WL 46122 (1992). United States ☞64.15

Small disadvantaged business concern is "small business concern" for purposes of the Small Business Act and implementing regulations, as disadvantaged business participant qualifies as "small disadvantaged business concern" and "small business concern." Small Business Act, § 2[8](a), as amended, 15 U.S.C.A. § 637(a). Celtech, Inc. v. U.S., 24 Cl. Ct. 269, 37 Cont. Cas. Fed. (CCH) P 76181, 1991 WL 193295 (1991), vacated pursuant to settlement, 25 Cl. Ct. 368, 1992 WL 46122 (1992). United States ☞53(8)

2 Parties

Disappointed bidder established that it was prejudiced by decisions of contracting agency, and thus had standing to assert bid protest, based on allegations that it should have had a higher risk rating than successful bidder, and that failure to receive proper notice of the suspension of the small disadvantaged businesses (SDB) price evaluation adjustment induced it to place a higher bid than it would have; bidder would have had a substantial chance to have been awarded the contract had it been in a better risk category than successful bidder or had it submitted a bid that was ten percent lower than the one it actually submitted. Gulf Group Inc. v. U.S., 61 Fed. Cl. 338 (2004). United States ☞64.60(2)

3 Appeal of SBA determinations

Determination by SBA that a firm was not a small business because it was affiliated with another firm based on economic dependence, was arbitrary and capricious in violation of the Administrative Procedure Act. The SBA made contrary assumptions among various financial worksheets to calculate the three-year average receipts specified by the applicable NAICS code, SBA did not contact anyone to verify information contained in worksheets, and attorney made mathematical error in calculating revenues. Larry Grant Constr. v. Mills, __ Fed.Cl. __, 2013 WL 3816092 (D.D.C. 2013)

§ 19.306 Protesting a firm's status as a HUBZone small business concern.

(a) *Definition.* As used in this section—

"Interested party" has the meaning given in 13 CFR 126.103.

(b) (1) An offeror that is an interested party, the contracting officer, or the SBA may protest the apparently successful offeror's status as a qualified historically underutilized business zone (HUBZone) small business concern (see 13 CFR 126.800).

(2) SBA's protest regulations are found in subpart H "Protests" at 13 CFR 126.800 through 126.805.

(c) Protests relating to small business size status are subject to the procedures of 19.302. An interested party seeking to protest both the small business size and HUBZone status of an apparent successful offeror shall file two separate protests. Protests relating to small business size status for the acquisition and the HUBZone qualifying requirements will be processed concurrently by SBA.

(d) All protests must be in writing and must state all specific grounds for the protest.

(1) SBA will consider protests challenging the status of a concern if the protest presents evidence that—

(i) The concern is not a qualified HUBZone small business concern as described at 13 CFR 126.103 and 13 CFR 126.200;

(ii) The principal office is not located in a HUBZone; or

(iii) At least 35 percent of the employees do not reside in a HUBZone.

(2) Assertions that a protested concern is not a qualified HUBZone small business concern, without setting forth specific facts or allegations, will not be considered by SBA (see 13 CFR 126.801(b)).

(e) Protest by an interested party.

(1) An interested party shall submit its protest to the contracting officer—

(i) For sealed bids—

(A) By the close of business on the fifth business day after bid opening; or

(B) By the close of business on the fifth business day from the date of identification of the apparent successful offeror, if the price evaluation preference was not applied at the time of bid opening; or

(ii) For negotiated acquisitions, by the close of business on the fifth business day after notification by the contracting officer of the apparently successful offeror.

(2) Any protest received after the designated time limits is untimely, unless it is from the contracting officer or SBA.

(f) (1) The contracting officer shall forward all protests to SBA. The protests are to be submitted to the Director, HUBZone Program, U.S. Small Business Administration, 409 Third Street, SW, Washington, DC 20416 or by fax to 202-205-7167, Attn: HUBZone Small Business Status Protest.

(2) The protest shall include a referral letter written by the contracting officer with information pertaining to the solicitation. The referral letter must include the following information to allow SBA to determine timeliness and standing:

(i) The solicitation number (or an electronic link to or a paper copy of the solicitation).

(ii) The name, address, telephone number, fax number, and email address, of the contracting officer.

(iii) The type of HUBZone contract.

(iv) Whether the procurement was conducted using full and open competition with a HUBZone price evaluation preference, and whether the protester's opportunity for award was affected by the preference.

(v) If a HUBZone set-aside, whether the protester submitted an offer.

(vi) Whether the protested concern was the apparent successful offeror.

(vii) Whether the procurement was conducted using sealed bid or negotiated procedures.

(viii) The bid opening date, if applicable. If a price evaluation preference was applied after the bid opening date, also provide the date of identification of the apparent successful offeror.

(ix) The date the contracting officer received the protest.

(x) Whether a contract has been awarded.

(g) SBA will notify the protester and the contracting officer of the date SBA received the protest.

(h) Before SBA decision.

(1) After receiving a protest involving the apparent successful offeror's status as a HUBZone small business concern, the contracting officer shall either—

(i) Withhold award of the contract until SBA determines the status of the protested concern; or

(ii) Award the contract after receipt of the protest but before SBA issues its decision if the contracting officer determines in writing that an award must be made to protect the public interest.

(2) SBA will determine the merits of the status protest within 15 business days after receipt of a protest, or within any extension of time granted by the contracting officer.

(3) If SBA does not issue its determination within 15 business days, or within any

extension of time granted, the contracting officer may award the contract after determining in writing that there is an immediate need to award the contract and that waiting until SBA makes its determination will be disadvantageous to the Government. This determination shall be provided to the SBA's HUBZone Program Director.

(i) *After SBA decision.* The HUBZone Program Director will notify the contracting officer, the protester, and the protested concern of the SBA determination. The determination is effective immediately and is final unless overturned on appeal by SBA's Associate Administrator, Office of Government Contracting and Business Development (AA/GCBD).

(1) If the contracting officer has withheld contract award and SBA has determined that the protested concern is an eligible HUBZone or dismissed all protests against the protested concern, the contracting officer may award the contract to the protested concern. If AA/GCBD subsequently overturns the decision of the HUBZone Program Director, the contracting officer may apply the AA/GCBD decision to the procurement in question.

(2) If the contracting officer has withheld award and the HUBZone Program Director has determined that the protested concern is ineligible, and a timely AA/GCBD appeal has not been filed, then the contracting officer shall not award the contract to the protested concern.

(3) If the contracting officer has made a written determination in accordance with (h)(1)(ii) or (h)(3) of this section, awarded the contract, and the HUBZone Program Director's ruling sustaining the protest is received after award—

(i) The contracting officer shall terminate the contract, unless the contracting officer has made a written determination that termination is not in the best interests of the Government. However, the contracting officer shall not exercise any options or award further task or delivery orders under the contract;

(ii) The contracting officer shall update the Federal Procurement Data System to reflect the final decision of the HUBZone Program Director if no appeal is filed; and

(iii) The concern's designation as a certified HUBZone small business concern will be removed by SBA from the Dynamic Small Business Database. The concern shall not submit an offer as a HUBZone small business concern, until SBA issues a decision that the ineligibility is resolved.

(4) If the contracting officer has made a written determination in accordance with (h)(1)(ii) or (h)(3) of this section, awarded the contract, SBA has sustained the protest and determined that the concern is not a HUBZone small business, and a timely AA/GCBD appeal has been filed, then the contracting officer shall consider whether performance can be suspended until an AA/GCBD decision is rendered.

(5) If AA/GCBD affirms the decision of the HUBZone Program Director, finding the protested concern is ineligible, and contract award has occurred—

(i) The contracting officer shall terminate the contract, unless the contracting officer has made a written determination that termination is not in the best interest of the Government. However, the contracting officer shall not exercise any options or award further task or delivery orders.

(ii) The contracting officer shall update the FPDS to reflect the AA/GCBD decision; and

(iii) The SBA will remove the concern's designation as a certified HUBZone small business concern. The concern shall not submit an offer as a HUBZone small business concern until SBA issues a decision that the ineligibility is resolved or AA/GCBD finds the concern is eligible on appeal.

(6) A concern found to be ineligible during a HUBZone status protest is precluded from applying for HUBZone certification for 90 calendar days from the date of the SBA final decision.

(j) *Appeals of HUBZone status determinations.* The protested HUBZone small business concern, the protester, or the contracting officer may file appeals of protest determinations with SBA's AA/GC&BD. The AA/GC&BD must receive the appeal no later than 5 business days after the date of receipt of the protest determination. SBA will dismiss any untimely appeal.

(k) *The appeal must be in writing.* The appeal must identify the protest determination being appealed and must set forth a full and specific statement as to why the decision is erroneous or what significant fact the HUBZone Program Director failed to consider.

(l) (1) The party appealing the decision must provide notice of the appeal to—

(i) The contracting officer;

(ii) HUBZone Program Director, U.S. Small Business Administration, 409 Third Street, SW., Washington, DC 20416 or by fax to 202-205-7167; and

(iii) The protested HUBZone small business concern or the original protester, as appropriate.

(2) SBA will not consider additional information or changed circumstances that were not disclosed at the time of the Director/HUB's decision or that are based on disagreement with the findings and conclusions contained in the determination.

(m) The AA/GCBD will make its decision within 5 business days of the receipt of the appeal, if practicable, and will base its decision only on the information and documentation in the protest record as supplemented by the appeal. SBA will provide a copy of the decision to the contracting officer, the protester, and the protested HUBZone small business concern. The SBA decision, if received before award, will apply to the pending acquisition. The AA/GCBD's decision is the final decision.

(n) The AA/GC&BD will make its decision within 5 business days of the receipt of the appeal, if practicable, and will base its decision only on the information and documentation in the protest record as supplemented by the appeal. SBA will provide a copy of the decision to the contracting officer, the protester, and the protested HUBZone small business concern. The SBA decision, if received before award, will apply to the pending acquisition. SBA rulings received after award will not apply to that acquisition. The AA/GC&BD's decision is the final decision.

United States Code Annotated

Additional powers, see 15 USCA § 637.

Administrative determinations, see 41 USCA § 257.

Awards or contracts, see 15 USCA § 644.

Contract goal for small disadvantaged businesses and certain institutions of higher education, see 10 USCA § 2323.

Contract requirements, see 41 USCA § 254.

Contracts, planning, solicitation, evaluation, and award procedures, see 10 USCA § 2305.

Credit for Indian contracting in meeting certain subcontracting goals for small disadvantaged businesses and certain institutions of higher education, see 10 USCA § 2323a.

Definitions, see 10 USCA § 2302, 41 USCA §§ 259, 403.

Determinations and decisions, see 10 USCA § 2310, 41 USCA § 262.

HUBZone program, see 15 USCA § 657a.

Kinds of contracts, see 10 USCA § 2306.

Planning and solicitation requirements, see 41 USCA § 253a.

Procurement data, see 41 USCA § 417a.

Procurement program for small business concerns owned and controlled by service-disabled veterans, see 15 USCA § 657f.

Notes of Decisions

In general 1
Pleadings 2

1 In general

A HUBZone status protest does not have to identify itself as such to be valid. 13 C.F.R. § 126.801(b), Mark Dunning Industries, Inc. v. U.S., 58 Fed. Cl. 216 (2003). United States ⚖64.55(2)

Language in bidder's fax to contract specialist sufficiently conveyed an expression of dissatisfaction with another bidder's HUBZone status as to constitute a HUBZone status protest, where bidder complained that "it would be upset" if it were determined that rival bidder was eligible for the HUBZone advantage, and submitted evidence that rival bidder might not be eligible for HUBZone status because, "according to the SBA HUB Zone locator their address IS NOT in a HUB Zone." 13 C.F.R. § 126.801(b). Mark Dunning Industries,

Inc. v. U.S., 58 Fed. Cl. 216 (2003). United States ☞64.55(2)

Bidder's request in fax that the contracting officer (CO) "verify all certifications before making any determinations and applying any bid advantages" was sufficient request for corrective action to qualify fax as a valid HUBZone status protest, as context made it clear that bidder was requesting that CO make sure that rival bidder was actually qualified for HUBZone status certification. 13 C.F.R. § 126.801. Mark Dunning Industries, Inc. v. U.S., 58 Fed. Cl. 216 (2003). United States ☞64.55(2)

Protesting bidder did not abandon HUBZone status protest by not taking some sort of action after contracting officer (CO) did not forward the protest to the Small Business Administration (SBA), notwithstanding contention that bidder knew, or should have known, that CO had not forwarded the protest because it did not receive notice of receipt of the protest from the SBA; protestor was under no duty to acknowledge the receipt, or lack thereof, of the SBA's notice. 13 C.F.R. § 126.803(a). Mark Dunning Industries, Inc. v. U.S., 58 Fed. Cl. 216 (2003). United States ☞64.55(2)

Fact that bidder's HUBZone status protest in fax to contracting officer (CO) did not state all the specific grounds for the protest did not relieve CO of his duty under regulation to forward protest to the Small Business Administration (SBA); regulation clearly required CO to forward the protest to the SBA "notwithstanding whether he or she believes it is sufficiently specific." 13 C.F.R. § 126.801(b, e). Mark Dunning Industries, Inc. v. U.S., 58 Fed. Cl. 216 (2003). United States ☞64.55(2)

Whether bidder intended that his fax to contracting officer questioning the HUBZone status of rival bidder be treated as a HUBZone status protest was irrelevant with regard to the question whether CO should have treated it as such and forwarded it to the Small Business Administration (SBA). 13 C.F.R. § 126.801(e). Mark Dunning Industries, Inc. v. U.S., 58 Fed. Cl. 216 (2003). United States ☞64.55(2)

2 Pleadings

Bid protestor's statement in its verified complaint that it had not filed a valid HUBZone status protest did not preclude it from changing its position on the issue, where it corrected the assertion early in the case, and thus defendant was not prejudiced. Mark Dunning Industries, Inc. v. U.S., 58 Fed. Cl. 216 (2003). Federal Courts ☞1111

§ 19.307 Protesting a firm's status as a service-disabled veteran-owned small business concern.

(a) *Definition. Interested party*, as used in this section, has the meaning given in 13 CFR 125.8(b).

(b) (1) An offeror that is an interested party, the contracting officer, or the SBA may protest the apparently successful offeror's status as a service-disabled veteran-owned small business (SDVOSB) concern (see 13 CFR 125.24).

(2) SBA's protest regulations are found in subpart D "Protests" at 13 CFR 125.24 through 125.28.

(c) Protests relating to small business size status are subject to the procedures of 19.302. An interested party seeking to protest both the small business size and service-disabled veteran-owned small business status of an apparent successful offeror shall file two separate protests.

(d) All protests must be in writing and must state all specific grounds for the protest.

(1) SBA will consider protests challenging the service disabled veteran-owned status or the ownership and control of a concern if—

(i) For status protests, the protester presents evidence supporting the contention that the owner(s) cannot provide documentation from the Department of Veterans Affairs, Department of Defense determinations, or the U.S. National Archives and Records Administration to show that they meet the definition of "service-disabled veteran" or "service disabled veteran with a permanent and severe disability" as set forth in 13 CFR 125.8; or

(ii) For ownership and control protests, the protester presents evidence that the concern is not 51 percent owned and controlled by one or more service-disabled veterans. In the case of a veteran with a permanent and severe disability, the protester presents evidence that the concern is not controlled by the veteran, spouse, or permanent caregiver of such veteran.

(2) Assertions that a protested concern is not a service-disabled veteran-owned small business concern, without setting forth specific facts or allegations, will not be considered by SBA (see 13 CFR 125.25(b)).

(e) Protest by an interested party.

(1) An offeror shall submit its protest to the contracting officer

(i) To be received by close of business on the fifth business day after bid opening (in sealed bid acquisitions); or

(ii) To be received by close of business on the fifth business day after notification by the contracting officer of the apparently successful offeror for negotiated acquisitions).

(2) Any protest received after the designated time limits is untimely, unless it is from the contracting officer or SBA.

(f) (1) The contracting officer shall forward all protests to SBA. The protests are to be submitted to SBA's Director, Office of Government Contracting, U.S. Small Business Administration, 409 Third Street, SW, Washington, DC 20416 or by fax to 202-205-6390, Attn: Service-Disabled Veteran Status Protest.

(2) The protest shall include a referral letter written by the contracting officer with information pertaining to the solicitation. The referral letter must include the following information to allow SBA to determine timeliness and standing:

(i) The solicitation number (or an electronic link to or a paper copy of the solicitation).

(ii) The name, address, telephone number, fax number, and email address of the contracting officer.

(iii) Whether the contract was sole-source or set-aside.

(iv) Whether the protestor submitted an offer.

(v) Whether the protested concern was the apparent successful offeror.

(vi) When the protested concern submitted its offer.

(vii) Whether the acquisition was conducted using sealed bid or negotiated procedures.

(viii) The bid opening date, if applicable.

(ix) The date the contracting officer received the protest.

(x) The date the protestor received notification about the apparent successful offeror, if applicable.

(xi) Whether a contract has been awarded.

(g) SBA will notify the protester and the contracting officer of the date SBA received the protest.

(h) Before SBA decision.

(1) After receiving a protest involving the apparent successful offeror's status as a service-disabled veteran-owned small business concern, the contracting officer shall either—

(i) Withhold award of the contract until SBA determines the status of the protested concern; or

(ii) Award the contract after receipt of the protest but before SBA issues its decision if the contracting officer determines in writing that an award must be made to protect the public interest.

(2) SBA will determine the merits of the status protest within 15 business days after receipt of a protest, or within any extension of time granted by the contracting officer.

(3) If SBA does not issue its determination within 15 business days, or within any extension of time that is granted, the contracting officer may award the contract after determining in writing that there is an immediate need to award the contract and that waiting until SBA makes its determination will be disadvantageous to the government. This determination shall be provided to the SBA's Director, Office of Government Contracting and a copy shall be included in the contract file.

(i) *After SBA decision.* SBA will notify the contracting officer, the protester, and the protested concern of its determination. The determination is effective immediately and is final unless overturned on appeal by SBA's Office of Hearings and Appeals (OHA) pursuant to 13 CFR part 134.

(1) If the contracting officer has withheld contract award and SBA has determined that the protested concern is an eligible SDVOSB or dismissed all protests against the protested concern, the contracting officer may award the contract to the protested concern. If OHA subsequently overturns the SBA Director for Government Contracting's determination or dismissal, the contracting officer may apply the OHA decision to the procurement in question.

(2) If the contracting officer has withheld contract award, SBA has sustained the protest and determined that the concern is not an SDVOSB, and no OHA appeal has been filed, then the contracting officer shall not award the contract to the protested concern.

(3) If the contracting officer has made a written determination in accordance with (h)(1)(ii) or (h)(3) of this section, the contract has been awarded, and SBA's ruling sustaining the protest is received after award—

(i) The contracting officer shall terminate the contract, unless the contracting officer has made a written determination that termination is not in the best interests of the Government. However, the contracting officer shall not exercise any options or award further task or delivery orders;

(ii) The contracting officer shall update the FPDS to reflect the final SBA decision; and

(iii) The concern must remove its designation in the System for Award Management (SAM) as a SDVOSB concern, and shall not submit an offer as a SDVOSB concern, until SBA issues a decision that the ineligibility is resolved.

(4) If the contracting officer has made a written determination in accordance with (h)(1)(ii) or (h)(3) of this section and awarded the contract to the protested firm, SBA has sustained the protest and determined that the concern is not a SDVOSB, and a timely OHA appeal has been filed, then the contracting officer shall consider whether performance can be suspended until an OHA decision is rendered.

(5) If OHA affirms the SBA Director for Government Contracting's determination finding the protested concern is ineligible—

(i) The contracting officer shall terminate the contract unless the contracting officer has made a written determination that it is not in the best interest of the Government. However, the contracting officer shall not exercise any options or award further task or delivery orders;

(ii) The contracting officer shall update the FPDS to reflect OHA's decision; and

(iii) The concern shall remove its designation in SAM as a SDVOSB concern, until SBA issues a decision that the ineligibility is resolved or OHA finds the concern is eligible on appeal.

(6) A concern found to be ineligible may not submit future offers as an SDVOSB concern until the concern demonstrates to SBA's satisfaction that it has overcome the reason for the protest and SBA issues a decision to this effect.

(j) *Appeals of SDVOSB status determinations.* The protested SDVOSB small business concern, the protester, or the contracting officer may file appeals of protest determinations to OHA. OHA must receive the appeal no later than 10 business days after the date of receipt of the protest determination. SBA will dismiss an untimely appeal. See Subpart E "Rules of Practice for Appeals From Service-Disabled Veteran Owned Small Business Concerns Protests" at 13 CFR 134.501 through 134.515 for SBA's appeals regulations.

(k) *The appeal must be in writing.* The appeal must identify the protest determination being appealed and must set forth a full and specific statement as to why the SDVOSB protest determination is alleged to be based on a clear error of fact or law, together with an argument supporting such allegation.

(l) The party appealing the decision must provide notice of the appeal to—

(1) The contracting officer;

(2) Director, Office of Government Contracting, U.S. Small Business Administration, 409 Third Street, SW., Washington, DC 20416, facsimile 202-205-6390;

(3) The protested SDVOSB concern or the original protester, as appropriate; and

(4) Associate General Counsel for Procurement Law, U.S. Small Business Administration, 409 Third Street, SW., Washington, DC 20416, facsimile 202-205-6873, or e-mail at OPLService@sba.gov.

(m) OHA will make its decision within 15 business days of the receipt of the appeal, if practicable. SBA will provide a copy of the decision to the contracting officer, the protester, and the protested SDVOSB small business concern. The OHA decision regarding the status of the concern is final and is binding on the parties.

United States Code Annotated

Additional powers, see 15 USCA § 637.

Administrative determinations, see 41 USCA § 257.

Awards or contracts, see 15 USCA § 644.

Contract goal for small disadvantaged businesses and certain institutions of higher education, see 10 USCA § 2323.

Contract requirements, see 41 USCA § 254.

Contracts, planning, solicitation, evaluation, and award procedures, see 10 USCA § 2305.

Credit for Indian contracting in meeting certain subcontracting goals for small disadvantaged businesses and certain institutions of higher education, see 10 USCA § 2323a.

Definitions, see 10 USCA § 2302, 41 USCA §§ 259, 403.

Determinations and decisions, see 10 USCA § 2310, 41 USCA § 262.

HUBZone program, see 15 USCA § 657a.

Kinds of contracts, see 10 USCA § 2306.

Planning and solicitation requirements, see 41 USCA § 253a.

Procurement data, see 41 USCA § 417a.

Procurement program for small business concerns owned and controlled by service-disabled veterans, see 15 USCA § 657f.

Notes of Decisions

In general 1

1 In general

The SBA Office of Hearings and Appeals (OHA) rejected the contractor's contention that the agency unreasonably assumed that the awardees' self-certifications were valid, and that the agency unreasonably failed to verify whether the awardees were registered in the VetBiz database. OHA held that, "[t]hese arguments reflect misunderstanding of the SDVO SBC program. SBA's SDVO SBC program is a self-certification program, so Government officials are expected to rely upon offerors' representations absent some reason to question them. Here Appellant did not advance any basis to question the self-certifications . . . and the agency, therefore, properly accepted those representations. MJL Enterprises., LLC, SBA No. VET-240, 2013 (S.B.A.), 2013 WL 6056668

§ 19.308 Protesting a firm's status as an economically disadvantaged women-owned small business concern or women-owned small business concern eligible under the Women-Owned Small Business Program.

(a) Definition. Interested party, as used in this section, has the meaning given in 13 CFR 127.102.

(b) (1) For sole source acquisitions, the contracting officer or SBA may protest the offeror's status as an economically disadvantaged women-owned small business (EDWOSB) concern or as a WOSB concern eligible under the WOSB Program. For all other acquisitions, an interested party (see 13 CFR 127.102) may protest the apparent successful offeror's EDWOSB or WOSB status.

(2) SBA's protest regulations are found in subpart F "Protests" at 13 CFR 127.600 through 127.605.

(c) Protests relating to small business size status are subject to the procedures of 19.302. An interested party seeking to protest both the small business size and WOSB or EDWOSB status of an apparent successful offeror shall file two separate protests.

(d) All protests shall be in writing and must state all specific grounds for the protest.

(1) SBA will consider protests challenging the status of a concern if—

(i) The protest presents evidence that the concern is not at least 51 percent owned and controlled by one or more women who are United States citizens; or

(ii) The protest presents evidence that the concern is not at least 51 percent owned and controlled by one or more economically disadvantaged women, when it is in connection with an EDWOSB contract.

(2) SBA shall consider protests by a contracting officer when the apparent successful offeror has failed to provide all of the required documents, as set forth in 19.1503(c).

(3) Assertions that a protested concern is not a EDWOSB or WOSB concern eligible under the WOSB Program, without setting forth specific facts or allegations, will not be considered by SBA (see 13 CFR 127.603(a)).

(e) Protest by an interested party.

(1) An offeror shall submit its protest to the contracting officer—

(i) To be received by the close of business by the fifth business day after bid opening (in sealed bid acquisitions); or

(ii) To be received by the close of business by the fifth business day after notification by the contracting officer of the apparent successful offeror (in negotiated acquisitions).

(2) Any protest received after the designated time limit is untimely, unless it is from the contracting officer or SBA.

(f) (1) The contracting officer shall forward all protests to SBA. The protests are to be submitted to SBA's Director for Government Contracting, U.S. Small Business Administration, 409 Third Street, SW., Washington, DC 20416 or by fax to 202-205-6390, Attn: Women-owned Small Business Status Protest.

(2) The protest shall include a referral letter written by the contracting officer with information pertaining to the solicitation. The referral letter must include the following information to allow SBA to determine timeliness and standing:

(i) The solicitation number or electronic link to or a paper copy of the solicitation.

(ii) The name, address, telephone number, email address, and facsimile number of the contracting officer.

(iii) Whether the protestor submitted an offer.

(iv) Whether the protested concern was the apparent successful offeror.

(v) When the protested concern submitted its offer.

(vi) Whether the acquisition was conducted using sealed bid or negotiated procedures.

(vii) The bid opening date, if applicable.

(viii) The date the contracting officer received the protest.

(ix) The date the protestor received notification about the apparent successful offeror, if applicable.

(x) Whether a contract has been awarded.

(g) SBA will notify the protester and the contracting officer of the date SBA received the protest.

(h) Before SBA decision.

(1) After receiving a protest involving the apparent successful offeror's status as an EDWOSB or WOSB concern eligible under the WOSB Program, the contracting officer shall either—

(i) Withhold award of the contract until SBA determines the status of the protested concern; or

(ii) Award the contract after receipt of the protest but before SBA issues its decision if the contracting officer determines in writing that an award must be made to protect the public interest.

(2) SBA will determine the merits of the status protest within 15 business days after receipt of a protest, or within any extension of that time granted by the contracting officer.

(3) If SBA does not issue its determination within 15 business days, or within any extension of time granted, the contracting officer may award the contract after determining in writing that there is an immediate need to award the contract and that waiting until SBA makes its determination will be disadvantageous to the Government. This determination shall be provided to the SBA Director for Government Contracting and a copy shall be included in the contract file.

(i) After SBA decision. SBA will notify the contracting officer, the protester, and the protested concern of its determination. The determination is effective immediately and is final unless overturned on appeal by SBA's Office of Hearings and Appeals (OHA) pursuant to 13 CFR part 134.

(1) If the contracting officer has withheld contract award and SBA has denied or dismissed the protest, the contracting officer may award the contract to the protested concern. If OHA subsequently overturns the SBA Director for Government Contracting's determination or dismissal, the contracting officer may apply the OHA decision to the procurement in question.

(2) If the contracting officer has withheld contract award, SBA has sustained the protest and determined that the concern is not eligible under the WOSB Program, and no OHA appeal has been filed, then the contracting officer shall not award the contract to the protested concern.

(3) If the contracting officer has made a written determination in accordance with (h)(1)(ii) or (h)(3) of this section, awarded the contract, and SBA's ruling is received after award, and no OHA appeal has been filed, then—

(i) The contracting officer shall terminate the contract, unless the contracting officer has made a written determination that termination is not in the best interests of the Government. However, the contracting officer shall not exercise any options or award further task or delivery orders;

(ii) The contracting officer shall update the FPDS to reflect the final SBA decision; and

(iii) The concern must remove its designation in the System for Award Management (SAM) as an EDWOSB or WOSB concern eligible under the WOSB Program, and shall not submit an offer as an EDWOSB concern or WOSB concern eligible under the WOSB Program, until SBA issues a decision that the ineligibility is resolved.

(4) If the contracting officer has made a written determination in accordance with (h)(1)(ii) or (h)(3) of this section, contract award has occurred, SBA has sustained the protest and determined that the concern is not eligible under the WOSB Program, and a timely OHA appeal has been filed, then the contracting officer shall consider whether performance can be suspended until an OHA decision is rendered.

(5) If OHA affirms the SBA Director for Government Contracting's determination finding the protested concern is ineligible, then—

(i) The contracting officer shall terminate the contract, unless the contracting officer has made a written determination that termination is not in the best interests of the Government. However, the contracting officer shall not exercise any options or award further task or delivery orders;

(ii) The contracting officer shall update the FPDS to reflect OHA's decision; and

(iii) The concern must remove its designation in SAM as an EDWOSB or WOSB concern eligible under the WOSB Program, and shall not submit an offer as an EDWOSB concern or WOSB concern eligible under the WOSB Program, until SBA issues a decision that the ineligibility is resolved or OHA finds the concern is eligible on appeal.

(j) *Appeals of EDWOSB or WOSB concerns eligible under the WOSB Program status determinations.*

(1) The protested EDWOSB concern or WOSB concern eligible under the WOSB program, the protester, or the contracting officer may file an appeal of a WOSB or EDWOSB status protest determination with OHA.

(2) OHA must receive the appeal no later than 10 business days after the date of receipt of the protest determination. SBA will dismiss an untimely appeal.

(3) See subpart G "Rules of Practice for Appeals From Women-Owned Small Business Concerns (WOSB) and Economically Disadvantaged WOSB Concern (EDWOSB) Protests" at 13 CFR 134.701 through 134.715 for SBA's appeals regulations.

(k) The appeal must be in writing. The appeal must identify the protest determination being appealed and must set forth a full and specific statement as to why the EDWOSB concern or WOSB concern eligible under the WOSB program protest determination is alleged to be based on a clear error of fact or law, together with an argument supporting such allegation.

(l) The party appealing the decision must provide notice of the appeal to—

(1) The contracting officer;

(2) Director, Office of Government Contracting, U.S. Small Business Administration, 409 Third Street, SW., Washington, DC 20416, facsimile 202-205-6390;

(3) The protested EDWOSB concern or WOSB concern eligible under the WOSB program, or the original protester, as appropriate; and

(4) SBA's Office of General Counsel, Associate General Counsel for Procurement Law, U.S. Small Business Administration, 409 Third Street, SW., Washington, DC 20416, facsimile 202-205-6873, or e-mail at mailto:OPLService@sba.gov.

(m) OHA will make its decision within 15 business days of the receipt of the appeal, if practicable. SBA will provide a copy of the decision to the contracting officer, the protester, and the protested EDWOSB concern or WOSB concern eligible under the WOSB program. The OHA decision is the final agency decision and is binding on the parties.

§ 19.309 Solicitation provisions and contract clauses.

(a) (1) Insert the provision at 52.219-1, Small Business Program Representations, in solicitations exceeding the micro-purchase threshold when the contract will be performed in the United States or its outlying areas.

(2) Use the provision with its Alternate I in solicitations issued by DoD, NASA, or the Coast Guard.

(b) When contracting by sealed bidding, insert the provision at 52.219-2, Equal Low Bids, in solicitations when the contract will be performed in the United States or its outlying areas.

(c) Insert the clause at 52.219-28, Post-Award Small Business Program Rerepresentation, in solicitations and contracts exceeding the micro-purchase threshold when the contract will be performed in the United States or its outlying areas.

Subpart 19.4 Cooperation with the Small Business Administration

§ 19.401 General.

(a) The Small Business Act is the authority under which the Small Business Administration (SBA) and agencies consult and cooperate with each other in formulating policies to ensure that small business interests will be recognized and protected.

(b) The Director of Small and Disadvantaged Business Utilization serves as the agency focal point for interfacing with SBA.

United States Code Annotated

Additional powers, see 15 USCA § 637.

Administrative determinations, see 41 USCA § 257.

Awards or contracts, see 15 USCA § 644.

Contract goal for small disadvantaged businesses and certain institutions of higher education, see 10 USCA § 2323.

Contract requirements, see 41 USCA § 254.

Contracts, planning, solicitation, evaluation, and award procedures, see 10 USCA § 2305.

Credit for Indian contracting in meeting certain subcontracting goals for small disadvantaged businesses and certain institutions of higher education, see 10 USCA § 2323a.

Definitions, see 10 USCA § 2302, 41 USCA §§ 259, 403.

Determinations and decisions, see 10 USCA § 2310, 41 USCA § 262.

HUBZone program, see 15 USCA § 657a.

Kinds of contracts, see 10 USCA § 2306.

Planning and solicitation requirements, see 41 USCA § 253a.

Procurement data, see 41 USCA § 417a.

Procurement program for small business concerns owned and controlled by service-disabled veterans, see 15 USCA § 657f.

§ 19.402 Small Business Administration procurement center representatives.

(a) (1) The SBA may assign one or more procurement center representatives to any contracting activity or contract administration office to carry out SBA policies and programs. Assigned SBA procurement center representatives are required to comply with the contracting agency's directives governing the conduct of contracting personnel and the release of contract information. The SBA must obtain for its procurement center representatives security clearances required by the contracting agency.

(2) If a SBA procurement center representative is not assigned to the procuring activity or contract administration office, contact the SBA Office of Government Contracting Area Office serving the area in which the procuring activity is located for assistance in carrying out SBA policies and programs. See http://www.sba.gov/content/procurement-center-r epresentatives for the location of the SBA office servicing the activity.

(b) Upon their request and subject to applicable acquisition and security regulations, contracting officers shall give SBA procurement center representatives (or, if a procurement center representative is not assigned, see paragraph (a) of this section) access to all reasonably obtainable contract information that is directly pertinent to their official duties.

(c) The duties assigned by SBA to its procurement center representatives include the following:

(1) Reviewing proposed acquisitions to recommend—

(i) The setting aside of selected acquisitions not unilaterally set aside by the contracting officer;

(ii) New qualified small business sources, including veteran-owned small, service-disabled veteran-owned small, HUBZone small, small disadvantaged, economically disadvantaged women-owned small, and women-owned small eligible under the Women-Owned Small Business Program; and

(iii) Breakout of components for competitive acquisitions.

(2) Reviewing proposed acquisition packages provided in accordance with 19.202-1(e). If the SBA procurement center representative (or, if a procurement center representative is not assigned, see paragraph (a) of this section) believes that the acquisition, as proposed, makes it unlikely that small businesses can compete for the prime contract, the representative shall recommend any alternate contracting method that the representative reasonably believes will increase small business prime contracting opportunities. The recommendation shall be made to the contracting officer within 15 days after receipt of the package.

(3) Recommending concerns for inclusion on a list of concerns to be solicited in a specific acquisition.

(4) Appealing to the chief of the contracting office any contracting officer's determination not to solicit a concern recommended by the SBA for a particular acquisition, when not doing so results in no small business being solicited.

(5) Conducting periodic reviews of the contracting activity to which assigned to ascertain whether it is complying with the small business policies in this regulation.

(6) Sponsoring and participating in conferences and training designed to increase small business participation in the contracting activities of the office.

United States Code Annotated

Additional powers, see 15 USCA § 637.

Administrative determinations, see 41 USCA § 257.

Awards or contracts, see 15 USCA § 644.

Contract goal for small disadvantaged businesses and certain institutions of higher education, see 10 USCA § 2323.

Contract requirements, see 41 USCA § 254.

Contracts, planning, solicitation, evaluation, and award procedures, see 10 USCA § 2305.

Credit for Indian contracting in meeting certain subcontracting goals for small disadvantaged businesses and certain institutions of higher education, see 10 USCA § 2323a.

Definitions, see 10 USCA § 2302, 41 USCA §§ 259, 403.

Determinations and decisions, see 10 USCA § 2310, 41 USCA § 262.

HUBZone program, see 15 USCA § 657a.

Kinds of contracts, see 10 USCA § 2306.

Planning and solicitation requirements, see 41 USCA § 253a.

Procurement data, see 41 USCA § 417a.

Procurement program for small business concerns owned and controlled by service-disabled veterans, see 15 USCA § 657f.

§ 19.403 Small Business Administration breakout procurement center representative.

(a) The SBA is required by section 403 of Pub. L. 98-577 to assign a breakout procurement center representative to each major procurement center. A major procurement center means a procurement center that, in the opinion of the administrator, purchases substantial dollar amounts of other than commercial items, and which has the potential to incur significant savings as a result of the placement of a breakout procurement representative. The SBA breakout procurement center representative is an advocate for (1) the appropriate use of full and open competition, and (2) the breakout of items, when appropriate and while maintaining the integrity of the system in which such items are used. The SBA breakout procurement center representative is in addition to the SBA procurement center representative (see 19.402). When an SBA breakout procurement center representative is assigned, the SBA is required to assign at least two collocated small business technical advisors. Assigned SBA breakout procurement center representatives and technical advisors are required to comply with the contracting agency's directives governing the conduct of contracting personnel and the release of contract information. The SBA must obtain for its breakout procurement center representatives and technical advisors security clearances required by the contracting agency.

(b) Contracting officers shall comply with 19.402(b) in their relationships with SBA breakout procurement center representatives and SBA small business technical advisors.

(c) The SBA breakout procurement center representative is authorized to—

(1) Attend any provisioning conference or similar evaluation session during which determinations are made as to whether requirements are to be acquired using other than full and open competition and make recommendations with respect to such requirements to the members of such conference or session;

(2) Review, at any time, restrictions on competition previously imposed on items through acquisition method coding or similar procedures and recommend to personnel of the appropriate activity the prompt reevaluation of such limitations;

(3) Review restrictions on competition arising out of restrictions on the rights of the United States in technical data and, when appropriate, recommend that personnel of the appropriate activity initiate a review of the validity of such an asserted restriction;

(4) Obtain from any governmental source, and make available to personnel of the appropriate center, technical data necessary for the preparation of a competitive solicitation package for any item of supply or service previously acquired noncompetitively due to the unavailability of such technical data;

(5) Have access to procurement records and other data of the procurement center commensurate with the level of such representative's approved security clearance classification;

(6) Receive unsolicited engineering proposals and, when appropriate—

(i) Conduct a value analysis of such proposal to determine whether it, if adopted, will result in lower costs to the United States without substantially impeding legitimate acquisition objectives and forward to personnel of the appropriate center recommendations with respect to such proposal; or

(ii) Forward such proposals without analysis to personnel of the center responsible for reviewing them who shall furnish the breakout procurement center representative with information regarding the proposal's disposition;

(7) Review the systems that account for the acquisition and management of technical data within the procurement center to ensure that such systems provide the maximum availability and access to data needed for the preparation of offers to sell to the United States those supplies to which such data pertain which potential offerors are entitled to receive;

(8) Appeal the failure by the procurement center to act favorably on any recommendation made pursuant to paragraphs (c)(1) through (7) of this section. Such appeal must be in writing and shall be filed and processed in accordance with the appeal procedures set

out at 19.505;

(9) Conduct familiarization sessions for contracting officers and other appropriate personnel of the procurement center to which assigned. Such sessions shall acquaint the participants with the duties and objectives of the representative and shall instruct them in the methods designed to further the breakout of items for procurement through full and open competition; and

(10) Prepare and personally deliver an annual briefing and report to the head of the procurement center to which assigned. Such briefing and report shall detail the past and planned activities of the representative and shall contain recommendations for improvement in the operation of the center as may be appropriate. The head of such center shall personally receive the briefing and report and shall, within 60 calendar days after receipt, respond, in writing, to each recommendation made by the representative.

(d) The duties of the SBA small business technical advisors are to assist the SBA breakout procurement center representative in carrying out the activities described in paragraphs (c)(1) through (7) of this section to assist the SBA procurement center representatives (see FAR 19.402).

United States Code Annotated

Additional powers, see 15 USCA § 637.

Administrative determinations, see 41 USCA § 257.

Awards or contracts, see 15 USCA § 644.

Contract goal for small disadvantaged businesses and certain institutions of higher education, see 10 USCA § 2323.

Contract requirements, see 41 USCA § 254.

Contracts, planning, solicitation, evaluation, and award procedures, see 10 USCA § 2305.

Credit for Indian contracting in meeting certain subcontracting goals for small disadvantaged businesses and certain institutions of higher education, see 10 USCA § 2323a.

Definitions, see 10 USCA § 2302, 41 USCA §§ 259, 403.

Determinations and decisions, see 10 USCA § 2310, 41 USCA § 262.

HUBZone program, see 15 USCA § 657a.

Kinds of contracts, see 10 USCA § 2306.

Planning and solicitation requirements, see 41 USCA § 253a.

Procurement data, see 41 USCA § 417a.

Procurement program for small business concerns owned and controlled by service-disabled veterans, see 15 USCA § 657f.

Subpart 19.5 Set-Asides for Small Business

§ 19.501 General.

(a) The purpose of small business set-asides is to award certain acquisitions exclusively to small business concerns. A "set-aside for small business" is the reserving of an acquisition exclusively for participation by small business concerns. A small business set-aside may be open to all small businesses. A small business set-aside of a single acquisition or a class of acquisitions may be total or partial.

(b) The determination to make a small business set-aside may be unilateral or joint. A unilateral determination is one that is made by the contracting officer. A joint determination is one that is recommended by the Small Business Administration (SBA) procurement center representative (or, if a procurement center representative is not assigned, see 19.402(a)) and concurred in by the contracting officer.

(c) The contracting officer shall review acquisitions to determine if they can be set aside for small business, giving consideration to the recommendations of agency personnel having cognizance of the agency's small business programs. The contracting officer shall perform market research and document why a small business set-aside is inappropriate when an acquisition is not set aside for small business, unless an award is anticipated to a small business under the 8(a), HUBZone, SDVOSB, or WOSB Programs. If the acquisition is set aside for small business based on this review, it is a unilateral set-aside by the contracting officer. Agencies may establish threshold levels for this review depending upon their needs.

(d) At the request of an SBA procurement center representative, (or, if a procurement center representative is not assigned, see 19.402(a)) the contracting officer shall make available for review at the contracting office (to the extent of the SBA representative's security clearance) all proposed acquisitions in excess of the micro-purchase threshold that have not been unilaterally set aside for small business.

(e) To the extent practicable, unilateral determinations initiated by a contracting officer shall be used as the basis for small business set-asides rather than joint determinations by an SBA procurement center representative and a contracting officer.

(f) All solicitations involving set-asides must specify the applicable small business size standard and NAICS code (see 19.303).

(g) Except as authorized by law, a contract may not be awarded as a result of a small business set-aside if the cost to the awarding agency exceeds the fair market price.

United States Code Annotated

Additional powers, see 15 USCA § 637.

Administrative determinations, see 41 USCA § 257.

Awards or contracts, see 15 USCA § 644.

Contract goal for small disadvantaged businesses and certain institutions of higher education, see 10 USCA § 2323.

Contract requirements, see 41 USCA § 254.

Contracts, planning, solicitation, evaluation, and award procedures, see 10 USCA § 2305.

Credit for Indian contracting in meeting certain subcontracting goals for small disadvantaged businesses and certain institutions of higher education, see 10 USCA § 2323a.

Definitions, see 10 USCA § 2302, 41 USCA §§ 259, 403.

Determinations and decisions, see 10 USCA § 2310, 41 USCA § 262.

HUBZone program, see 15 USCA § 657a.

Kinds of contracts, see 10 USCA § 2306.

Planning and solicitation requirements, see 41 USCA § 253a.

Procurement data, see 41 USCA § 417a.

Procurement program for small business concerns owned and controlled by service-disabled veterans, see 15 USCA § 657f.

Notes of Decisions

In general 1
Market research 6
North American Industry Classification System 5
Set-aside challenges 3
Small business concern 4
Total set-asides 2

1 In general

Contractors, who brought suit against Army Corps of Engineers challenging suspension of minority set-aside program, failed to allege any facts showing that defense position was not substantially justified, and thus, award of attorney fees under Equal Access to Justice Act was not warranted; suspension of program was based on adverse decision by federal district court. Small Business Act, § 8(a), 15 U.S.C.A. § 637(a); 28 U.S.C.A. § 2412(d)(1)(A). Enplanar, Inc. v. Marsh, 11 F.3d 1284, 39 Cont. Cas. Fed. (CCH) P 76613, 27 Fed. R. Serv. 3d 1469 (5th Cir. 1994). United States ⚬147(12)

Contractors were barred from receiving injunctive relief against the Army Corps of Engineers concerning its administration of minority set-aside program, as Small Business Act precludes injunctive relief against Small Business Administration (SBA), and contractors could not obtain indirectly against Army what they could not obtain directly against SBA. Small Business Act, §§ 2[5](b)(1), 8(a), as amended, 15 U.S.C.A. §§ 634(b)(1), 637(a). Enplanar, Inc. v. Marsh, 11 F.3d 1284, 39 Cont. Cas. Fed. (CCH) P 76613, 27 Fed. R. Serv.

3d 1469 (5th Cir. 1994). United States ☞53(8)

Army Corps of Engineers' three-month suspension of decisions regarding submission of new minority set-aside projects was supported by articulated nondiscriminatory reason that Corps' practice of awarding large number of small business projects to minority set-aside program was improper, and contractors failed to show that articulated reason was pretext for discrimination. 42 U.S.C.A. §§ 1981, 1985(2); Civil Rights Act of 1964, § 601, 42 U.S.C.A. § 2000d; Small Business Act, § 8(a), 15 U.S.C.A. § 637(a). Enplanar, Inc. v. Marsh, 11 F.3d 1284, 39 Cont. Cas. Fed. (CCH) P 76613, 27 Fed. R. Serv. 3d 1469 (5th Cir. 1994). United States ☞64.15

There is no constitutional duty to offer government procurement contracts for competitive bidding. Small Business Act, § 2[8](a), 15 U.S.C.A. § 637(a). Ray Baillie Trash Hauling, Inc. v. Kleppe, 477 F.2d 696 (5th Cir. 1973). United States ☞64.10

Small Business Act did not preempt state law claims of unjust enrichment, intentional interference with economic advantage in securing contract rights, and fraud and misrepresentation asserted by unsuccessful bidder against low bidder on food service contract under small business set-aside program. Small Business Act, §§ 2[2]–2[23], as amended, 15 U.S.C.A. §§ 631–650. Integrity Management Intern., Inc. v. Tombs & Sons, Inc., 836 F.2d 485, 34 Cont. Cas. Fed. (CCH) P 75419 (10th Cir. 1987). States ☞18.15; States ☞98

Army's decision not to bid procurement for specialized computer equipment under small business set-aside program was reasonable, in light of Army's previous quality problems with computer hardware purchased from manufacturer challenging instant procurement decision, as well as legitimate concerns as to manufacturer's financial condition. 10 U.S.C.A. § 2301; 5 U.S.C.A. § 702; Small Business Act, § 2[2], 15 U.S.C.A. § 631. Genisco Technology Corp. v. Stone, 793 F. Supp. 357 (D.D.C. 1992). United States ☞64.15

Any error by Air Force in failing to include appropriate code for moving services in soliciting bids for warehousing services through small business set-aside was harmless, where any business small enough to qualify in warehouse trade was small enough to qualify in local business (moving services) trade. Small Business Act, § 2[8](a), (a)(4–6), as amended, 15 U.S.C.A. § 637(a), (a)(4–6). Young-Robinson Associates, Inc. v. U.S., 760 F. Supp. 212, 37 Cont. Cas. Fed. (CCH) P 76054 (D.D.C. 1991). United States ☞64.60(1)

Record did not support bidder's contention that contracting officer acted arbitrarily and capriciously by not even considering possibility of minority set-aside for interim solicitation for warehousing services by Air Force, where bidder's own complaint detailed Air Force's consideration or rejection of procurement through minority set-aside. Small Business Act, § 2[8](a), (a)(4–6), as amended, 15 U.S.C.A. § 637(a), (a)(4–6). Young-Robinson Associates, Inc. v. U.S., 760 F. Supp. 212, 37 Cont. Cas. Fed. (CCH) P 76054 (D.D.C. 1991). United States ☞64.15

Defense Department acquisition regulations precluded setting aside of interim contract for warehouse services at Air Force base for small socially and economically disadvantaged business, where warehousing services sought in solicitation had been previously acquired successfully on basis of small business set-aside. Small Business Act, § 2[8](a), (a)(4–6), as amended, 15 U.S.C.A. § 637(a), (a)(4–6). Young-Robinson Associates, Inc. v. U.S., 760 F. Supp. 212, 37 Cont. Cas. Fed. (CCH) P 76054 (D.D.C. 1991). United States ☞64.15

Where contracting officer (CO) based his decision to withdraw request for proposals (RFP) from the small business set aside program on comparison of independent government estimate (IGE) to remaining bidder's price, but there was no supporting documentation or discussion in the record regarding how the IGE was prepared, the Court of Federal Claims had no choice but to remand the matter to the CO for a new IGE. Nutech Laundry & Textile, Inc. v. U.S., 56 Fed. Cl. 588 (2003). United States ☞64.50

Contracting officer (CO) in contract procurement set-aside for small businesses did not abuse her discretion in determining that contract awardee qualified as a small business, notwithstanding that CO did not consult a listing of small businesses officially maintained by the Small Business Administration (SBA), where CO pursued other avenues of information about the bidders via a reputable financial service. Tech Systems, Inc. v. U.S., 50 Fed. Cl. 216 (2001). United States ☞64.15

Even assuming regulation that requires that Small Business Administration personnel be notified if small business set-aside is withdrawn was violated when solicitation itself is cancelled, dissatisfied bidder was neither entitled to injunctive relief nor bid preparation costs based upon that violation, where failure of Air Force to give notice to Small Business Administration did not deny dissatisfied bidder impartial consideration of its bid. Aviation Enterprises, Inc. v. U.S., 8 Cl. Ct. 1, 32 Cont. Cas. Fed. (CCH) P 73403 (1985). Injunction ⊕86; United States ⊕53(8).

2 Total set-asides

Contracting officer (CO) may consider and base its decision to set aside acquisition for small business participation on such factors as prior procurement history, the nature of the contract, market surveys, or advice of the agency's small business specialist. 48 C.F.R. § 19.502-2(b). MCS Management, Inc. v. U.S., 48 Fed. Cl. 506 (2001), aff'd, 25 Fed. Appx. 957 (Fed. Cir. 2001). United States ⊕64.15

Although section of the Federal Acquisition Regulation pertaining to small business set-aside does not require the use of any particular method for assessing the availability of small business offers, the contracting officer must undertake reasonable efforts to determine whether it is likely that offers will be received from at least two responsible small businesses at fair market prices. 48 C.F.R. § 19.502-2(b). MCS Management, Inc. v. U.S., 48 Fed. Cl. 506 (2001), aff'd, 25 Fed. Appx. 957 (Fed. Cir. 2001). United States ⊕64.15

3 Set-aside challenges

Where agency initially set Federal Supply Schedule (FSS) procurement aside for small businesses, but subsequently decided to conduct purchase on non-set-aside basis, agency's elimination of set-aside was unobjectionable; small business set-aside requirements do not apply to FSS purchases. Global Analytic Information Technology Services, Inc., B-297200.3, 2006 CPD ¶ 53 (Comp. Gen. 2006)

Protest challenging agency determination not to set aside procurement for small business concerns is sustained where the decision was based on an unreasonably limited search of the potential small business market, and the contracting officer did not consider the responses of several small businesses to the presolicitation notice in making her determination. Information Ventures, Inc., B-294267, 2004 CPD ¶ 205 (Comp. Gen. 2004)

Protest that procurement should have been set aside for small businesses is denied, where the agency reasonably determined that the items to be procured were available under the Federal Supply Schedule (FSS); agencies need not consider small business programs when purchasing from the FSS. Future Solutions, Inc., B-293194, 2004 CPD ¶ 39 (Comp. Gen. 2004)

Procurement under simplified acquisition threshold for a laboratory electronic sensor instrument was properly set aside for exclusive small business participation where contracting officer reasonably determined that there was a reasonable expectation of obtaining offers from at least two responsible small business concerns at a competitive market price. Nordic Sensor Technologies, Inc., B-282942, 99-2 CPD ¶ 22 (Comp. Gen. 1999)

4 Small business concern

Contracting officer's determination not to set aside solicitations for food service for the Marine Corps exclusively for small business concerns was not arbitrary or capricious or in violation of procurement law, where decision was based on a rational assessment of the scope and complexities of the solicitations, prior procurement history, input obtained from industry and consultations with the Small Business Administration (SBA) and the Marine Corps small business specialist. 48 C.F.R. § 19.502-2(b). MCS Management, Inc. v. U.S., 48 Fed. Cl. 506 (2001), aff'd, 25 Fed. Appx. 957 (Fed. Cir. 2001). United States ⊕64.15

Even if exception to mandatory requirement for referral to the Small Business Administration (SBA) if small business concern's offer is to be rejected because of determination of nonresponsibility applied to rejection of small disadvantaged business based on accounting system deficiencies identified in audit, Government violated referral requirement, as decision not to refer matter to SBA must be approved by chief of contracting office and no evidence was presented that chief of contracting office approved nonreferral decision. Celtech, Inc. v. U.S., 24 Cl. Ct. 269, 37 Cont. Cas. Fed. (CCH) P 76181, 1991 WL 193295 (1991), vacated pursuant to settlement, 25 Cl. Ct. 368, 1992 WL 46122 (1992). United States ⊕64.15

5 North American Industry Classification System

Pre-award bid protestor who prevailed on claim that Air Force contracting officer (CO) violated procurement regulations in selecting North American Industry Classification System (NAICS) Code for small business procurement was entitled to permanent injunction requiring Air Force to set aside solicitation until Code was changed; protestor would suffer irreparable harm of loss of opportunity to compete if Code was not changed, balance of hardships was in favor of protestor since the Air Force would suffer no financial harm, and public interest would be served by preserving integrity of procurement process. Red River Service Corp. v. U.S., 60 Fed. Cl. 532 (2004), dismissed, 110 Fed. Appx. 887 (Fed. Cir. 2004). Injunction ☞86

6 Market research

Protest is sustained where the agency's market research was insufficient to conclude that the agency would likely receive quotations from at least two responsible small business concerns that could meet the requirements in the RFQ. Agency's market research must address not only the existence of small businesses within the selected NAICS code, but also their capability to perform the particular contract. Triad Isotopes, Inc., B-411360, 2015 CPD ¶ 220 (Comp. Gen. 2015)

§ 19.502 Setting aside acquisitions.

§ 19.502-1 Requirements for setting aside acquisitions.

(a) The contracting officer shall set aside an individual acquisition or class of acquisitions for competition among small businesses when—

(1) It is determined to be in the interest of maintaining or mobilizing the Nation's full productive capacity, war or national defense programs; or

(2) Assuring that a fair proportion of Government contracts in each industry category is placed with small business concerns; and the circumstances described in 19.502-2 or 19.502-3(a) exist.

(b) This requirement does not apply to purchases of $3,500 or less ($20,000 or less for acquisitions as described in 13.201(g)(1)), or purchases from required sources of supply under Part 8 (e.g., Committee for Purchase From People Who are Blind or Severely Disabled, and Federal Supply Schedule contracts).

United States Code Annotated

Additional powers, see 15 USCA § 637.

Administrative determinations, see 41 USCA § 257.

Awards or contracts, see 15 USCA § 644.

Contract goal for small disadvantaged businesses and certain institutions of higher education, see 10 USCA § 2323.

Contract requirements, see 41 USCA § 254.

Contracts, planning, solicitation, evaluation, and award procedures, see 10 USCA § 2305.

Credit for Indian contracting in meeting certain subcontracting goals for small disadvantaged businesses and certain institutions of higher education, see 10 USCA § 2323a.

Definitions, see 10 USCA § 2302, 41 USCA §§ 259, 403.

Determinations and decisions, see 10 USCA § 2310, 41 USCA § 262.

HUBZone program, see 15 USCA § 657a.

Kinds of contracts, see 10 USCA § 2306.

Planning and solicitation requirements, see 41 USCA § 253a.

Procurement data, see 41 USCA § 417a.

Procurement program for small business concerns owned and controlled by service-disabled veterans, see 15 USCA § 657f.

Notes of Decisions

In general 1
Set-aside challenges 3
Total set-asides 2

1 In general

Contractors, who brought suit against Army Corps of Engineers challenging suspension of minority set-aside program, failed to allege any facts showing that defense position was not substantially justified, and thus, award of attorney fees under Equal Access to Justice Act was not warranted; suspension of program was based on adverse decision by federal district court. Small Business Act, § 8(a), 15 U.S.C.A. § 637(a); 28 U.S.C.A. § 2412(d)(1)(A). Enplanar, Inc. v. Marsh, 11 F.3d 1284, 39 Cont. Cas. Fed. (CCH) P 76613, 27 Fed. R. Serv. 3d 1469 (5th Cir. 1994). United States ☞147(12)

Contractors were barred from receiving injunctive relief against the Army Corps of Engineers concerning its administration of minority set-aside program, as Small Business Act precludes injunctive relief against Small Business Administration (SBA), and contractors could not obtain indirectly against Army what they could not obtain directly against SBA. Small Business Act, §§ 2[5](b)(1), 8(a), as amended, 15 U.S.C.A. §§ 634(b)(1), 637(a). Enplanar, Inc. v. Marsh, 11 F.3d 1284, 39 Cont. Cas. Fed. (CCH) P 76613, 27 Fed. R. Serv. 3d 1469 (5th Cir. 1994). United States ☞53(8)

Army Corps of Engineers' three-month suspension of decisions regarding submission of new minority set-aside projects was supported by articulated nondiscriminatory reason that Corps' practice of awarding large number of small business projects to minority set-aside program was improper, and contractors failed to show that articulated reason was pretext for discrimination. 42 U.S.C.A. §§ 1981, 1985(2); Civil Rights Act of 1964, § 601, 42 U.S.C.A. § 2000d; Small Business Act, § 8(a), 15 U.S.C.A. § 637(a). Enplanar, Inc. v. Marsh, 11 F.3d 1284, 39 Cont. Cas. Fed. (CCH) P 76613, 27 Fed. R. Serv. 3d 1469 (5th Cir. 1994). United States ☞64.15

Small Business Act did not preempt state law claims of unjust enrichment, intentional interference with economic advantage in securing contract rights, and fraud and misrepresentation asserted by unsuccessful bidder against low bidder on food service contract under small business set-aside program. Small Business Act, §§ 2[2]–2[23], as amended, 15 U.S.C.A. §§ 631–650. Integrity Management Intern., Inc. v. Tombs & Sons, Inc., 836 F.2d 485, 34 Cont. Cas. Fed. (CCH) P 75419 (10th Cir. 1987). States ☞18.15; States ☞98

Army's decision not to bid procurement for specialized computer equipment under small business set-aside program was reasonable, in light of Army's previous quality problems with computer hardware purchased from manufacturer challenging instant procurement decision, as well as legitimate concerns as to manufacturer's financial condition. 10 U.S.C.A. § 2301; 5 U.S.C.A. § 702; Small Business Act, § 2[2], 15 U.S.C.A. § 631. Genisco Technology Corp. v. Stone, 793 F. Supp. 357 (D.D.C. 1992). United States ☞64.15

Any error by Air Force in failing to include appropriate code for moving services in soliciting bids for warehousing services through small business set-aside was harmless, where any business small enough to qualify in warehouse trade was small enough to qualify in local business (moving services) trade. Small Business Act, § 2[8](a), (a)(4–6), as amended, 15 U.S.C.A. § 637(a), (a)(4–6). Young-Robinson Associates, Inc. v. U.S., 760 F. Supp. 212, 37 Cont. Cas. Fed. (CCH) P 76054 (D.D.C. 1991). United States ☞64.60(1)

Record did not support bidder's contention that contracting officer acted arbitrarily and capriciously by not even considering possibility of minority set-aside for interim solicitation for warehousing services by Air Force, where bidder's own complaint detailed Air Force's consideration or rejection of procurement through minority set-aside. Small Business Act, § 2[8](a), (a)(4–6), as amended, 15 U.S.C.A. § 637(a), (a)(4–6). Young-Robinson Associates, Inc. v. U.S., 760 F. Supp. 212, 37 Cont. Cas. Fed. (CCH) P 76054 (D.D.C. 1991). United States ☞64.15

Defense Department acquisition regulations precluded setting aside of interim contract for warehouse services at Air Force base for small socially and economically disadvantaged business, where warehousing services sought in solicitation had been previously acquired successfully on basis of small business set-aside. Small Business Act, § 2[8](a), (a)(4–6), as amended, 15 U.S.C.A. § 637(a), (a)(4–6). Young-Robinson Associates, Inc. v. U.S., 760 F. Supp. 212, 37 Cont. Cas. Fed. (CCH) P 76054 (D.D.C. 1991). United States ☞64.15

Where contracting officer (CO) based his decision to withdraw request for proposals (RFP) from the small business set aside program on comparison of independent government estimate (IGE) to remaining bidder's price, but there was no supporting documentation or discussion in the record regarding how the IGE was prepared, the Court of Federal

Claims had no choice but to remand the matter to the CO for a new IGE. Nutech Laundry & Textile, Inc. v. U.S., 56 Fed. Cl. 588 (2003). United States ⬥64.50

Contracting officer (CO) in contract procurement set-aside for small businesses did not abuse her discretion in determining that contract awardee qualified as a small business, notwithstanding that CO did not consult a listing of small businesses officially maintained by the Small Business Administration (SBA), where CO pursued other avenues of information about the bidders via a reputable financial service. Tech Systems, Inc. v. U.S., 50 Fed. Cl. 216 (2001). United States ⬥64.15

Contracting officer's determination not to set aside solicitations for food service for the Marine Corps exclusively for small business concerns was not arbitrary or capricious or in violation of procurement law, where decision was based on a rational assessment of the scope and complexities of the solicitations, prior procurement history, input obtained from industry and consultations with the Small Business Administration (SBA) and the Marine Corps small business specialist. 48 C.F.R. § 19.502-2(b). MCS Management, Inc. v. U.S., 48 Fed. Cl. 506 (2001), aff'd, 25 Fed. Appx. 957 (Fed. Cir. 2001). United States ⬥64.15

Even assuming regulation that requires that Small Business Administration personnel be notified if small business set-aside is withdrawn was violated when solicitation itself is cancelled, dissatisfied bidder was neither entitled to injunctive relief nor bid preparation costs based upon that violation, where failure of Air Force to give notice to Small Business Administration did not deny dissatisfied bidder impartial consideration of its bid. Aviation Enterprises, Inc. v. U.S., 8 Cl. Ct. 1, 32 Cont. Cas. Fed. (CCH) P 73403 (1985). Injunction ⬥86; United States ⬥53(8)

Agencies are not required to set-aside procurements outside the United States or its outlying areas. Protester's contention that the (Small Business Act, 15 U.S.C. § 644(j)(1)), requires agencies to set aside procurements under the simplified acquisition threshold for small businesses located outside the United States, unless the agency cannot obtain offers from two or more small businesses, is denied where the Act is silent on its application outside the U.S., and where FAR 19.000(b) expressly states that the set-aside requirement of the Act applies only in the U.S. or its outlying areas. Given the silence of the Act on its applicability outside the U.S. (and the silence of the SBA's regulations on the issue) the GAO held that the long-standing exclusion specified in FAR § 19.000(b) is consistent with the Small Business Act. Latvian Connection Gen. Trading & Constr. LLC, B-408633, 2013 CPD ¶ 225 (Comp. Gen. 2013).

2 Total set-asides

Contracting officer (CO) may consider and base its decision to set aside acquisition for small business participation on such factors as prior procurement history, the nature of the contract, market surveys, or advice of the agency's small business specialist. 48 C.F.R. § 19.502-2(b). MCS Management, Inc. v. U.S., 48 Fed. Cl. 506 (2001), aff'd, 25 Fed. Appx. 957 (Fed. Cir. 2001). United States ⬥64.15

Although section of the Federal Acquisition Regulation pertaining to small business set-aside does not require the use of any particular method for assessing the availability of small business offers, the contracting officer must undertake reasonable efforts to determine whether it is likely that offers will be received from at least two responsible small businesses at fair market prices. 48 C.F.R. § 19.502-2(b). MCS Management, Inc. v. U.S., 48 Fed. Cl. 506 (2001), aff'd, 25 Fed. Appx. 957 (Fed. Cir. 2001). United States ⬥64.15

3 Set-aside challenges

Contracting officer's determination not to set aside solicitations for commercial soft shelter tent systems for Defense Logistics Agency (DLA) exclusively for small business concerns was not arbitrary or capricious, or in violation of procurement law, where officer had called eleven companies to gauge their interest, compared the most popular tents under current system to those offered by small businesses that had submitted proposals, sought equivalent products amongst small businesses, and ultimately determined that although small businesses offered some of the products that would likely be obtained, soft shelter systems provided by both large and small businesses were necessary to achieve the full range of products required by the government. SEK Solutions, Inc. v. U.S., 117 Fed. Cl. 43 (2014)

Agency has discretion to procure via GSA's Federal Supply Schedules (FSS), rather than set-aside the procurement for small businesses, even though requirement had been previously performed by an 8(a) small business. Neither the Small Business Act, 15 USCA §§ 631–657, nor applicable regulations require the Government to obtain a service from a small business, including 8(a) firms, if it can meet its needs through the FSS. K-Lak Corp. v. U.S., 98 Fed. Cl. 1 (2011)

Where agency initially set Federal Supply Schedule (FSS) procurement aside for small businesses, but subsequently decided to conduct purchase on non-set-aside basis, agency's elimination of set-aside was unobjectionable; small business set-aside requirements do not apply to FSS purchases. Global Analytic Information Technology Services, Inc., B-297200.3, 2006 CPD ¶ 53 (Comp. Gen. 2006)

Protest challenging agency determination not to set aside procurement for small business concerns is sustained where the decision was based on an unreasonably limited search of the potential small business market, and the contracting officer did not consider the responses of several small businesses to the presolicitation notice in making her determination. Information Ventures, Inc., B-294267, 2004 CPD ¶ 205 (Comp. Gen. 2004)

Protest that procurement should have been set aside for small businesses is denied, where the agency reasonably determined that the items to be procured were available under the Federal Supply Schedule (FSS); agencies need not consider small business programs when purchasing from the FSS. Future Solutions, Inc., B-293194, 2004 CPD ¶ 39 (Comp. Gen. 2004)

Procurement under simplified acquisition threshold for a laboratory electronic sensor instrument was properly set aside for exclusive small business participation where contracting officer reasonably determined that there was a reasonable expectation of obtaining offers from at least two responsible small business concerns at a competitive market price. Nordic Sensor Technologies, Inc., B-282942, 99-2 CPD ¶ 22 (Comp. Gen. 1999)

§ 19.502-2 Total small business set-asides.

(a) Before setting aside an acquisition under this paragraph, refer to 19.203(b). Each acquisition of supplies or services that has an anticipated dollar value exceeding $3,500 ($20,000 for acquisitions as described in 13.201(g)(1)), but not over $150,000 ($300,000 for acquisitions described in paragraph (1) (i) of the simplified acquisition threshold definition at 2.101), is automatically reserved exclusively for small business concerns and shall be set aside for small business unless the contracting officer determines there is not a reasonable expectation of obtaining offers from two or more responsible small business concerns that are competitive in terms of market prices, quality, and delivery. If the contracting officer does not proceed with the small business set-aside and purchases on an unrestricted basis, the contracting officer shall include in the contract file the reason for this unrestricted purchase. If the contracting officer receives only one acceptable offer from a responsible small business concern in response to a set-aside, the contracting officer should make an award to that firm. If the contracting officer receives no acceptable offers from responsible small business concerns, the set-aside shall be withdrawn and the requirement, if still valid, shall be resolicited on an unrestricted basis. The small business reservation does not preclude the award of a contract as described in 19.203.

(b) Before setting aside an acquisition under this paragraph, refer to 19.203(c). The contracting officer shall set aside any acquisition over $150,000 for small business participation when there is a reasonable expectation that—

(1) Offers will be obtained from at least two responsible small business concerns offering the products of different small business concerns (see paragraph (c) of this section); and

(2) Award will be made at fair market prices. Total small business set-asides shall not be made unless such a reasonable expectation exists (see 19.502-3 as to partial set-asides). Although past acquisition history of an item or similar items is always important, it is not the only factor to be considered in determining whether a reasonable expectation exists. In making R&D small business set-asides, there must also be a reasonable expectation of obtaining from small businesses the best scientific and technological sources consistent with the demands of the proposed acquisition for the best mix of cost, performances, and schedules.

(c) For small business set-asides other than for construction or services, any concern proposing to furnish a product that it did not itself manufacture must furnish the product of a small business manufacturer unless the SBA has granted either a waiver or exception to the nonmanufacturer rule (see 19.102(f)). In industries where the SBA finds that there are no small business manufacturers, it may issue a waiver to the nonmanufacturer rule (see 19.102(f)(4) and (5)). In addition, SBA has excepted procurements processed under simplified acquisition procedures (see Part 13), where the anticipated cost of the procurement will not exceed $25,000, from the nonmanufacturer rule. Waivers permit small businesses to provide any firm's product. The exception permits small businesses to provide any domestic firm's product. In both of these cases, the contracting officer's determination in paragraph (b)(1) of this subsection or the decision not to set aside a procurement reserved for small business under paragraph (a) of this subsection will be based on the expectation of receiving offers from at least two responsible small businesses, including nonmanufacturers, offering the products of different concerns.

United States Code Annotated

Additional powers, see 15 USCA § 637.

Administrative determinations, see 41 USCA § 257.

Awards or contracts, see 15 USCA § 644.

Contract goal for small disadvantaged businesses and certain institutions of higher education, see 10 USCA § 2323.

Contract requirements, see 41 USCA § 254.

Contracts, planning, solicitation, evaluation, and award procedures, see 10 USCA § 2305.

Credit for Indian contracting in meeting certain subcontracting goals for small disadvantaged businesses and certain institutions of higher education, see 10 USCA § 2323a.

Definitions, see 10 USCA § 2302, 41 USCA §§ 259, 403.

Determinations and decisions, see 10 USCA § 2310, 41 USCA § 262.

HUBZone program, see 15 USCA § 657a.

Kinds of contracts, see 10 USCA § 2306.

Planning and solicitation requirements, see 41 USCA § 253a.

Procurement data, see 41 USCA § 417a.

Procurement program for small business concerns owned and controlled by service-disabled veterans, see 15 USCA § 657f.

Notes of Decisions

In general 1
Decision to set-aside procurement 4
Limitation on Subcontracting 2
The "Rule of Two" 3

1 In general

The Small Business Act imposes a number of requirements which businesses must satisfy if they wish to claim a small business preference in government procurements. The Act requires that nonmanufacturer recipients of small business set-aside contracts for manufactured products provide the product of domestic small manufacturers or processors on small business set-asides, the so-called 'nonmanufacturer rule. The clear purpose of the non-manufacturer rule is to prevent brokerage-type arrangements whereby small 'front' organizations are set up to bid [on] government contracts, but furnish the supplies of a large concern. Rotech Healthcare Inc. v. U.S., 71 Fed. Cl. 393 (2006)

A contracting officer's decision not to set a solicitation aside for small business concerns is a matter of business judgment within the contracting officer's discretion. 48 C.F.R. § 19.502-2(b). MCS Management, Inc. v. U.S., 48 Fed. Cl. 506 (2001), aff'd, 25 Fed. Appx. 957 (Fed. Cir. 2001). United States ⊗64.15

Contracting officer's determination not to set aside solicitations for food service for the Marine Corps exclusively for small business concerns was not arbitrary or capricious or in violation of procurement law, where decision was based on a rational assessment of the scope and complexities of the solicitations, prior procurement history, input obtained from industry and consultations with the Small Business Administration (SBA) and the Marine Corps small business specialist. 48 C.F.R. § 19.502-2(b). MCS Management, Inc. v. U.S., 48

Fed. Cl. 506 (2001), aff'd, 25 Fed. Appx. 957 (Fed. Cir. 2001). United States ☞64.15

Contracting officer (CO) may consider and base its decision to set aside acquisition for small business participation on such factors as prior procurement history, the nature of the contract, market surveys, or advice of the agency's small business specialist. 48 C.F.R. § 19.502-2(b). MCS Management, Inc. v. U.S., 48 Fed. Cl. 506 (2001), aff'd, 25 Fed. Appx. 957 (Fed. Cir. 2001). United States ☞64.15

Although section of the Federal Acquisition Regulation pertaining to small business set-aside does not require the use of any particular method for assessing the availability of small business offers, the contracting officer must undertake reasonable efforts to determine whether it is likely that offers will be received from at least two responsible small businesses at fair market prices. 48 C.F.R. § 19.502-2(b). MCS Management, Inc. v. U.S., 48 Fed. Cl. 506 (2001), aff'd, 25 Fed. Appx. 957 (Fed. Cir. 2001). United States ☞64.15

Protester's contention that the use of a government-wide unrestricted ID/IQ contract to procure travel management services at Travis Air Force Base, California, violates the requirement in FAR 19.502-2 to set aside procurements for small businesses where there is a reasonable expectation of receiving fair market price offers from at least two responsible small business concerns is sustained where the record shows that there is a significant pool of small business offerors who have responded to a recent solicitation for precisely these services, and where there is no evidence in the record of any reason why the agency could not set aside the procurement. N&N Travel & Tours, Inc.; BCM Travel & Tours; Manassas Travel, Inc.; Alamo Travel, Inc.; Ravenel Bros., Inc.; and Bay Area Travel, Inc., B-285164.2, B-285164.3, 2000 CPD ¶ 146 (Comp. Gen. 2000)

2 Limitation on Subcontracting

When reviewing compliance with the limitation on subcontracting clause at the time of contract award, the court considers whether a proposal, on its face, should lead an agency to the conclusion that an offeror could not and would not comply with the subcontracting limitation. Precision Standard, Inc. v. U.S., 69 Fed. Cl. 738 (2006), judgment aff'd, 228 Fed. Appx. 980 (Fed. Cir. 2007)

GAO denied protest where it determined that the protester's proposal took exception to the rule requiring small businesses in a set-aside procurement to perform 50% of the work with their own employees. The protester's price proposal lists a systems administrator as a "1099 Consultant," and not as a contractor employee. Protester's proposal represented that it would perform 53.3% of the work, but without the contribution of the 1099 consultant, the proposal committed the protester to perform only 45% of the personnel costs of performance with its own employees. MindPoint Group, LLC, B-409562, 2014 CPD ¶ 145 (Comp. Gen. 2014)

The Small Business Administration's (SBA) certificate of competency (COC) denial was inappropriate because the SBA applied the wrong standard in concluding that a Service Disabled Veteran Owned Small Business (SDVOSB) did not satisfy the requirement generally applicable to contracts for general construction that the small business concern perform at least 15% of the cost of the contract with its own employees. This requirement does not, however, apply to SDVOSBs, which are subject to a less stringent subcontracting threshold (13 C.F.R. § 125.6(b)), which the contractor satisfied. Construct Solutions, Inc., B-405288, 2011 CPD ¶ 214 (Comp. Gen. 2011)

Agency's award of a contract under a solicitation set aside for small businesses was improper where the awardee's proposal as submitted clearly did not meet the material solicitation requirement that at least 50 percent of the cost of contract performance incurred for personnel be expended for employees of the small business awardee, notwithstanding the United States Small Business Administration's (SBA) issuance of a Certificate of Competency to the small business awardee because SBA found that the awardee would be able to comply with the subcontracting limitation during the performance of the contract. TYBRIN Corporation, B-298364.6, B-298364.7, 2007 CPD ¶ 51 (Comp. Gen. 2007)

3 The "Rule of Two"

Department of Veterans Affairs (VA) is not excused from compliance with statutory Rule of Two for set asides, which states that the VA generally "shall award" a contract to a veteran-owned small business (VOSB) when there is a reasonable expectation that two or more such businesses will bid for the contract at a fair and reasonable price that offers the best value to the United States, even if the VA has already met its annual goals for awarding contracts to VOSBs, and even if the order is placed through the Federal Supply Schedule (FSS). Kingdomware Techs., Inc. v. U.S., 136 S.Ct. 1969 (U.S. June 16, 2016)

Protest challenging agency decision not to set aside for small business concerns is sustained where agency's decision was based on insufficient efforts to ascertain, and inaccurate assumptions of, small business capability to perform the contract. For example, the agency did not search available small business databases, including SBA's Dynamic Small Business Search database, despite the ease of doing so. DNO Inc., B-406256, 2012 CPD ¶ 136 (Comp. Gen. 2012)

The "Rule of Two" and the set-aside requirements of the Small Business Act, 15 U.S.C. § 644(a)), do not apply to procurements conducted under GSA's Federal Supply Schedule (FSS) contracts. GAO held: "Nothing in the Small Business Act suggests or requires that the Rule of Two. . . takes precedence over the FSS program. To the contrary. . . the implementing regulations for the small business set-aside program and the FSS program expressly provide that set-aside requirements for the program do not apply to FSS buys. Edmond Computer Company; Edmond Scientific Co., B-402863, 2010 CPD ¶ 200 (Comp. Gen. 2010)

Agency's decision to set aside delivery order under a multiple award indefinite-delivery/indefinite-quantity (ID/IQ) contract for the small business ID/IQ contract holders was reasonable where both small business contract holders represented to the agency that they could meet the delivery order requirements. In making set-aside decisions, agencies need not make actual determinations of responsibility; rather, they need only make an informed business judgment that there is a reasonable expectation of receiving acceptably priced offers from small business concerns that are capable of performing the contract. Ceradyne, Inc., B-402281, 2010 CPD ¶ 70 (Comp. Gen. 2010)

4 Decision to set-aside procurement

Department of Veterans Affairs' (VA) decision not to set aside a contract for an emergency notification service for VA medical centers and associated outpatient clinics the procurement for veteran-owned small businesses or service-disabled veteran-owned small businesses and instead procure the services from the Federal Supply Service was not arbitrary, capricious, or contrary to law; Veterans Benefits, Health Care, and Information Technology Act did not require the VA to comply with the Act's set-aside procedures. Kingdomware Techs., Inc. v. U.S., 107 Fed. Cl. 226 (Fed. Cl. 2012)

Protest that solicitation for the award of a cost reimbursement contract for a data coordination center should be set aside for small business concerns was denied, where agency reasonably found, based upon market research, past procurements and the publication of a sources sought notice, that the agency was not likely to receive proposals from at least two small businesses with sufficient experience to perform the overall requirement. EMMES Corp., B-402245, 2010 CPD ¶ 53 (Comp. Gen. 2010)

§ 19.502-3 Partial set-asides.

(a) The contracting officer shall set aside a portion of an acquisition, except for construction, for exclusive small business participation when—

(1) A total set-aside is not appropriate (see 19.502-2);

(2) The requirement is severable into two or more economic production runs or reasonable lots;

(3) One or more small business concerns are expected to have the technical competence and productive capacity to satisfy the set-aside portion of the requirement at a fair market price;

(4) The acquisition is not subject to simplified acquisition procedures; and

(5) A partial set-aside shall not be made if there is a reasonable expectation that only two concerns (one large and one small) with capability will respond with offers unless authorized by the head of a contracting activity on a case-by-case basis. Similarly, a class of acquisitions, not including construction, may be partially set aside. Under certain specified conditions, partial set-asides may be used in conjunction with multiyear contracting procedures.

(b) When the contracting officer determines that a portion of an acquisition is to be set aside, the requirement shall be divided into a set-aside portion and a non-set-aside portion, each of which shall (1) be an economic production run or reasonable lot and (2) have terms and a delivery schedule comparable to the other. When practicable, the set-aside portion should make maximum use of small business capacity.

(c) (1) The contracting officer shall award the non-set-aside portion using normal contracting procedures.

(2) (i) After all awards have been made on the non-setaside portion, the contracting officer shall negotiate with eligible concerns on the set-aside portion, as provided in the solicitation, and make award. Negotiations shall be conducted only with those offerors who have submitted responsive offers on the non-set-aside portion. Negotiations shall be conducted with small business concerns in the order of priority as indicated in the solicitation (but see paragraph (c)(2)(ii) of this section). The set-aside portion shall be awarded as provided in the solicitation. An offeror entitled to receive the award for quantities of an item under the non-set-aside portion and who accepts the award of additional quantities under the set-aside portion shall not be requested to accept a lower price because of the increased quantities of the award, nor shall negotiation be conducted with a view to obtaining such a lower price based solely upon receipt of award of both portions of the acquisition. This does not prevent acceptance by the contracting officer of voluntary reductions in the price from the low eligible offeror before award, acceptance of voluntary refunds, or the change of prices after award by negotiation of a contract modification.

(ii) If equal low offers are received on the non-setaside portion from concerns eligible for the set-aside portion, the concern that is awarded the non-set-aside part of the acquisition shall have first priority with respect to negotiations for the set-aside.

United States Code Annotated

Additional powers, see 15 USCA § 637.

Administrative determinations, see 41 USCA § 257.

Awards or contracts, see 15 USCA § 644.

Contract goal for small disadvantaged businesses and certain institutions of higher education, see 10 USCA § 2323.

Contract requirements, see 41 USCA § 254.

Contracts, planning, solicitation, evaluation, and award procedures, see 10 USCA § 2305.

Credit for Indian contracting in meeting certain subcontracting goals for small disadvantaged businesses and certain institutions of higher education, see 10 USCA § 2323a.

Definitions, see 10 USCA § 2302, 41 USCA §§ 259, 403.

Determinations and decisions, see 10 USCA § 2310, 41 USCA § 262.

HUBZone program, see 15 USCA § 657a.

Kinds of contracts, see 10 USCA § 2306.

Planning and solicitation requirements, see 41 USCA § 253a.

Procurement data, see 41 USCA § 417a.

Procurement program for small business concerns owned and controlled by service-disabled veterans, see 15 USCA § 657f.

§ 19.502-4 Methods of conducting set-asides.

In accordance with section 1331 of Public Law 111-240 (15 U.S.C. 644(r)) contracting officers may, at their discretion—

(a) When conducting multiple-award procurements using full and open competition, reserve one or more contract awards for any of the small business concerns identified in 19.000(a)(3). The specific program eligibility requirements identified in this part apply;

(b) Set aside part or parts of a multiple-award contract for any of the small business concerns identified in 19.000(a)(3). The specific program eligibility requirements identified in this part apply; or

(c) Set aside orders placed under multiple-award contracts for any of the small business concerns identified in 19.000(a)(3). For orders placed under the Federal Supply Schedules Program see 8.405-5. For all other multiple-award contracts see 16.505.

United States Code Annotated

Additional powers, see 15 USCA § 637.

Administrative determinations, see 41 USCA § 257.

Awards or contracts, see 15 USCA § 644.

Contract goal for small disadvantaged businesses and certain institutions of higher education, see 10 USCA § 2323.

Contract requirements, see 41 USCA § 254.

Contracts, planning, solicitation, evaluation, and award procedures, see 10 USCA § 2305.

Credit for Indian contracting in meeting certain subcontracting goals for small disadvantaged businesses and certain institutions of higher education, see 10 USCA § 2323a.

Definitions, see 10 USCA § 2302, 41 USCA §§ 259, 403.

Determinations and decisions, see 10 USCA § 2310, 41 USCA § 262.

HUBZone program, see 15 USCA § 657a.

Kinds of contracts, see 10 USCA § 2306.

Planning and solicitation requirements, see 41 USCA § 253a.

Procurement data, see 41 USCA § 417a.

Procurement program for small business concerns owned and controlled by service-disabled veterans, see 15 USCA § 657f.

§ 19.502-5 Insufficient causes for not setting aside an acquisition.

(a) Total small business set-asides may be conducted by using simplified acquisition procedures (see Part 13), sealed bids (see Part 14), or competitive proposals (see Part 15). Partial small business set-asides may be conducted using sealed bids (see Part 14), or competitive proposals (see Part 15).

(b) Except for offers on the non-set-aside portion of partial set-asides, offers received from concerns that do not qualify as small business concerns shall be considered nonresponsive and shall be rejected. However, before rejecting an offer otherwise eligible for award because of questions concerning the size representation, an SBA determination must be obtained (see Subpart 19.3).

United States Code Annotated

Additional powers, see 15 USCA § 637.

Administrative determinations, see 41 USCA § 257.

Awards or contracts, see 15 USCA § 644.

Contract goal for small disadvantaged businesses and certain institutions of higher education, see 10 USCA § 2323.

Contract requirements, see 41 USCA § 254.

Contracts, planning, solicitation, evaluation, and award procedures, see 10 USCA § 2305.

Credit for Indian contracting in meeting certain subcontracting goals for small disadvantaged businesses and certain institutions of higher education, see 10 USCA § 2323a.

Definitions, see 10 USCA § 2302, 41 USCA §§ 259, 403.

Determinations and decisions, see 10 USCA § 2310, 41 USCA § 262.

HUBZone program, see 15 USCA § 657a.

Kinds of contracts, see 10 USCA § 2306.

Planning and solicitation requirements, see 41 USCA § 253a.

Procurement data, see 41 USCA § 417a.

Procurement program for small business concerns owned and controlled by service-disabled veterans, see 15 USCA § 657f.

§ 19.502-6 Insufficient causes for not setting aside an acquisition.

None of the following is, in itself, sufficient cause for not setting aside an acquisition:

(a) A large percentage of previous contracts for the required item(s) has been placed with small business concerns.

(b) The item is on an established planning list under the Industrial Readiness Planning Program. However, a total small business set-aside shall not be made when the list contains a large business Planned Emergency Producer of the item(s) who has conveyed a desire to supply some or all of the required items.

(c) The item is on a Qualified Products List. However, a total small business set-aside shall not be made if the list contains the products of large businesses unless none of the large businesses desire to participate in the acquisition.

(d) A period of less than 30 days is available for receipt of offers.

(e) The acquisition is classified.

(f) Small business concerns are already receiving a fair proportion of the agency's contracts for supplies and services.

(g) A class small business set-aside of the item or service has been made by another contracting activity.

(h) A "brand name or equal" product description will be used in the solicitation.

§ 19.503 Setting aside a class of acquisitions for small business.

(a) A class of acquisitions of selected products or services, or a portion of the acquisitions, may be set aside for exclusive participation by small business concerns if individual acquisitions in the class will meet the criteria in 19.502-1, 19.502-2, or 19.502-3(a). The determination to make a class small business set-aside shall not depend on the existence of a current acquisition if future acquisitions can be clearly foreseen.

(b) The determination to set aside a class of acquisitions for small business may be either unilateral or joint.

(c) Each class small business set-aside determination shall be in writing and must—

(1) Specifically identify the product(s) and service(s) it covers;

(2) Provide that the set-aside does not apply to any acquisition automatically reserved for small business concerns under 19.502-2(a).

(3) Provide that the set-aside applies only to the (named) contracting office(s) making the determination; and

(4) Provide that the set-aside does not apply to any individual acquisition if the requirement is not severable into two or more economic production runs or reasonable lots, in the case of a partial class set-aside.

(d) The contracting officer shall review each individual acquisition arising under a class small business set-aside to identify any changes in the magnitude of requirements, specifications, delivery requirements, or competitive market conditions that have occurred since the initial approval of the class set-aside. If there are any changes of such a material nature as to result in probable payment of more than a fair market price by the Government or in a change in the capability of small business concerns to satisfy the requirements, the contracting officer may withdraw or modify (see 19.506(a)) the unilateral or joint set-aside by giving written notice to the SBA procurement center representative (or, if a procurement center representative is not assigned, see 19.402(a)) stating the reasons.

United States Code Annotated

Additional powers, see 15 USCA § 637.

Administrative determinations, see 41 USCA § 257.

Awards or contracts, see 15 USCA § 644.

Contract goal for small disadvantaged businesses and certain institutions of higher education, see 10 USCA § 2323.

Contract requirements, see 41 USCA § 254.

Contracts, planning, solicitation, evaluation, and award procedures, see 10 USCA § 2305.

Credit for Indian contracting in meeting certain subcontracting goals for small disadvantaged businesses and certain institutions of higher education, see 10 USCA § 2323a.

Definitions, see 10 USCA § 2302, 41 USCA §§ 259, 403.

Determinations and decisions, see 10 USCA § 2310, 41 USCA § 262.

HUBZone program, see 15 USCA § 657a.

Kinds of contracts, see 10 USCA § 2306.

Planning and solicitation requirements, see 41 USCA § 253a.

Procurement data, see 41 USCA § 417a.

Procurement program for small business concerns owned and controlled by service-disabled veterans, see 15 USCA § 657f.

§ 19.504 Inclusion of Federal Prison Industries, Inc.

When using competitive procedures in accordance with 8.602(a)(4), agencies shall include Federal Prison Industries, Inc. (FPI), in the solicitation process and consider a timely offer from FPI.

United States Code Annotated

Additional powers, see 15 USCA § 637.

Administrative determinations, see 41 USCA § 257.

Awards or contracts, see 15 USCA § 644.

Contract goal for small disadvantaged businesses and certain institutions of higher education, see 10 USCA § 2323.

Contract requirements, see 41 USCA § 254.

Contracts, planning, solicitation, evaluation, and award procedures, see 10 USCA § 2305.

Credit for Indian contracting in meeting certain subcontracting goals for small disadvantaged businesses and certain institutions of higher education, see 10 USCA § 2323a.

Definitions, see 10 USCA § 2302, 41 USCA §§ 259, 403.

Determinations and decisions, see 10 USCA § 2310, 41 USCA § 262.

HUBZone program, see 15 USCA § 657a.

Kinds of contracts, see 10 USCA § 2306.

Planning and solicitation requirements, see 41 USCA § 253a.

Procurement data, see 41 USCA § 417a.

Procurement program for small business concerns owned and controlled by service-disabled veterans, see 15 USCA § 657f.

§ 19.505 Rejecting Small Business Administration recommendations.

(a) If the contracting officer rejects a recommendation of the SBA procurement center representative (or, if a procurement center representative is not assigned, see 19.402(a)) or breakout procurement center representative, written notice shall be furnished to the appropriate SBA representative within 5 working days of the contracting officer's receipt of the recommendation.

(b) The SBA procurement center representative (or, if a procurement center representative is not assigned, see 19.402(a)) may appeal the contracting officer's rejection to the head of the contracting activity (or designee) within 2 working days after receiving the notice. The head of the contracting activity (or designee) shall render a decision in writing, and provide it to the SBA representative within 7 working days. Pending issuance of a decision to the SBA representative, the contracting officer shall suspend action on the acquisition.

(c) If the head of the contracting activity agrees that the contracting officer's rejection was appropriate—

(1) Within 2 working days, the SBA procurement center representative (or, if a procurement center representative is not assigned, see 19.402(a)) may request the contracting officer to suspend action on the acquisition until the SBA Administrator appeals to the agency head (see paragraph (f) of this section); and

(2) The SBA must be allowed 15 working days after making such a written request, within which the Administrator of SBA—

(i) May appeal to the Secretary of the Department concerned; and

(ii) Must notify the contracting officer whether the further appeal has, in fact, been taken. If notification is not received by the contracting officer within the 15-day period, it is deemed that the SBA request to suspend the contract action has been withdrawn and that an appeal to the Secretary was not taken.

(d) When the contracting officer has been notified within the 15-day period that the SBA has appealed to the agency head, the head of the contracting activity (or designee) shall forward justification for its decision to the agency head. The contracting officer shall suspend contract action until notification is received that the SBA appeal has been settled.

(e) The agency head shall reply to the SBA within 30 working days after receiving the appeal. The decision of the agency head shall be final.

(f) A request to suspend action on an acquisition need not be honored if the contracting officer determines that proceeding to contract award and performance is in the public interest. The contracting officer shall include in the contract file a statement of the facts justifying the determination, and shall promptly notify the SBA representative of the determination and provide a copy of the justification.

United States Code Annotated

Additional powers, see 15 USCA § 637.

Administrative determinations, see 41 USCA § 257.

Awards or contracts, see 15 USCA § 644.

Contract goal for small disadvantaged businesses and certain institutions of higher education, see 10 USCA § 2323.

Contract requirements, see 41 USCA § 254.

Contracts, planning, solicitation, evaluation, and award procedures, see 10 USCA § 2305.

Credit for Indian contracting in meeting certain subcontracting goals for small disadvantaged businesses and certain institutions of higher education, see 10 USCA § 2323a.

Definitions, see 10 USCA § 2302, 41 USCA §§ 259, 403.

Determinations and decisions, see 10 USCA § 2310, 41 USCA § 262.

HUBZone program, see 15 USCA § 657a.

Kinds of contracts, see 10 USCA § 2306.

Planning and solicitation requirements, see 41 USCA § 253a.

Procurement data, see 41 USCA § 417a.

Procurement program for small business concerns owned and controlled by service-disabled veterans, see 15 USCA § 657f.

§ 19.506 Withdrawing or modifying small business setasides.

(a) If, before award of a contract involving a small business set-aside, the contracting officer considers that award would be detrimental to the public interest (*e.g.*, payment of more than a fair market price), the contracting officer may withdraw the small business set-aside determination whether it was unilateral or joint. The contracting officer shall initiate a withdrawal of an individual small business set-aside by giving written notice to the agency small business specialist and the SBA procurement center representative (or, if a procurement center representative is not assigned, see 19.402(a)) stating the reasons. In a similar manner, the contracting officer may modify a unilateral or joint class small business set-aside to withdraw one or more individual acquisitions.

(b) If the agency small business specialist does not agree to a withdrawal or modification, the case shall be promptly referred to the SBA representative (or, if a procurement center representative is not assigned, see 19.402(a)) for review.

(c) The contracting officer shall prepare a written statement supporting any withdrawal or modification of a small business set-aside and include it in the contract file.

United States Code Annotated

Additional powers, see 15 USCA § 637.

Administrative determinations, see 41 USCA § 257.

Awards or contracts, see 15 USCA § 644.

Contract goal for small disadvantaged businesses and certain institutions of higher education, see 10 USCA § 2323.

Contract requirements, see 41 USCA § 254.

Contracts, planning, solicitation, evaluation, and award procedures, see 10 USCA § 2305.

Credit for Indian contracting in meeting certain subcontracting goals for small disadvantaged businesses and certain institutions of higher education, see 10 USCA § 2323a.

Definitions, see 10 USCA § 2302, 41 USCA §§ 259, 403.

Determinations and decisions, see 10 USCA § 2310, 41 USCA § 262.

HUBZone program, see 15 USCA § 657a.

Kinds of contracts, see 10 USCA § 2306.

Planning and solicitation requirements, see 41 USCA § 253a.

Procurement data, see 41 USCA § 417a.

Procurement program for small business concerns owned and controlled by service-disabled veterans, see 15 USCA § 657f.

§ 19.507 Automatic dissolution of a small business setaside.

(a) If a small business set-aside acquisition or portion of an acquisition is not awarded, the unilateral or joint determination to set the acquisition aside is automatically dissolved for the unawarded portion of the set-aside. The required supplies and/or services for which no award was made may be acquired by sealed bidding or negotiation, as appropriate.

(b) Before issuing a solicitation for the items called for in a small business set-aside that was dissolved, the contracting officer shall ensure that the delivery schedule is realistic in the light of all relevant factors, including the capabilities of small business concerns.

United States Code Annotated

Additional powers, see 15 USCA § 637.

Administrative determinations, see 41 USCA § 257.

Awards or contracts, see 15 USCA § 644.

Contract goal for small disadvantaged businesses and certain institutions of higher education, see 10 USCA § 2323.

Contract requirements, see 41 USCA § 254.

Contracts, planning, solicitation, evaluation, and award procedures, see 10 USCA § 2305.

Credit for Indian contracting in meeting certain subcontracting goals for small disadvantaged businesses and certain institutions of higher education, see 10 USCA § 2323a.

Definitions, see 10 USCA § 2302, 41 USCA §§ 259, 403.

Determinations and decisions, see 10 USCA § 2310, 41 USCA § 262.

HUBZone program, see 15 USCA § 657a.

Kinds of contracts, see 10 USCA § 2306.

Planning and solicitation requirements, see 41 USCA § 253a.

Procurement data, see 41 USCA § 417a.

Procurement program for small business concerns owned and controlled by service-disabled veterans, see 15 USCA § 657f.

§ 19.508 Solicitation provisions and contract clauses.

(a) [Reserved]

(b) [Reserved]

(c) The contracting officer shall insert the clause at 52.219-6, Notice of Total Small Business Set-Aside, in solicitations and contracts involving total small business set-asides or reserves. This includes multiple-award contracts when orders may be set aside for any of the small business concerns identified in 19.000(a)(3), as described in 8.405-5 and 16.505(b)(2)(i)(F). The clause at 52.219-6 with its Alternate I will be used when the acquisition is for a product in a class for which the Small Business Administration has waived the nonmanufacturer rule (see 19.102(f)(4) and (5)). Use the clause at 52.219-6 with its Alternate II when including FPI in the competition in accordance with 19.504.

(d) The contracting officer shall insert the clause at 52.219-7, Notice of Partial Small Business Set-Aside, in solicitations and contracts involving partial small business set-asides. This includes part or parts of multiple-award contracts, including those described in 38.101. The clause at 52.219-7 with its Alternate I will be used when the acquisition is for a product in a class for which the Small Business Administration has waived the nonmanufacturer rule (see 19.102(f)(4) and (5)). Use the clause at 52.219-7 with its Alternate II when including FPI in the competition in accordance with 19.504.

(e) The contracting officer shall insert the clause at 52.219-14, Limitations on

Subcontracting, in solicitations and contracts for supplies, services, and construction, if any portion of the requirement is to be set aside or reserved for small business and the contract amount is expected to exceed $150,000. This includes multiple-award contracts when orders may be set aside for small business concerns, as described in 8.405-5 and 16.505(b)(2)(i)(F).

(f) The contracting officer shall insert the clause at 52.219-13, Notice of Set-Aside of Orders, in solicitations and contracts to notify offerors if an order or orders are to be set aside for any of the small business concerns identified in 19.000(a)(3).

United States Code Annotated

Additional powers, see 15 USCA § 637.

Administrative determinations, see 41 USCA § 257.

Awards or contracts, see 15 USCA § 644.

Contract goal for small disadvantaged businesses and certain institutions of higher education, see 10 USCA § 2323.

Contract requirements, see 41 USCA § 254.

Contracts, planning, solicitation, evaluation, and award procedures, see 10 USCA § 2305.

Credit for Indian contracting in meeting certain subcontracting goals for small disadvantaged businesses and certain institutions of higher education, see 10 USCA § 2323a.

Definitions, see 10 USCA § 2302, 41 USCA §§ 259, 403.

Determinations and decisions, see 10 USCA § 2310, 41 USCA § 262.

HUBZone program, see 15 USCA § 657a.

Kinds of contracts, see 10 USCA § 2306.

Planning and solicitation requirements, see 41 USCA § 253a.

Procurement data, see 41 USCA § 417a.

Procurement program for small business concerns owned and controlled by service-disabled veterans, see 15 USCA § 657f.

Notes of Decisions

Payments to employees 1

1 Payments to employees

Contracting officer (CO) violated section of the Federal Acquisition Regulation (FAR) by not ensuring that contract awardee was in compliance with Small Business Administration (SBA) regulation requiring a small business concern awarded a set-aside contract to pay at least fifty percent of its labor costs on the contract to its own employees. Transatlantic Lines LLC v. U.S., 68 Fed. Cl. 48 (2005). United States ☞64.15

Subpart 19.6 Certificates of Competency and Determinations of Responsibility

§ 19.601 General.

(a) A Certificate of Competency (COC) is the certificate issued by the Small Business Administration (SBA) stating that the holder is responsible (with respect to all elements of responsibility, including, but not limited to, capability, competency, capacity, credit, integrity, perseverance, tenacity, and limitations on subcontracting) for the purpose of receiving and performing a specific Government contract.

(b) The COC program empowers the Small Business Administration (SBA) to certify to Government contracting officers as to all elements of responsibility of any small business concern to receive and perform a specific Government contract. The COC program does not extend to questions concerning regulatory requirements imposed and enforced by other Federal agencies.

(c) The COC program is applicable to all Government acquisitions. A contracting officer shall, upon determining an apparent successful small business offeror to be nonresponsible, refer that small business to the SBA for a possible COC, even if the next acceptable offer is also from a small business.

(d) When a solicitation requires a small business to adhere to the limitations on subcontracting, a contracting officer's finding that a small business cannot comply with the limitation shall be treated as an element of responsibility and shall be subject to the COC process. When a solicitation requires a small business to adhere to the definition of a nonmanufacturer, a contracting officer's determination that the small business does not comply shall be processed in accordance with Subpart 19.3.

(e) Contracting officers, including those located overseas, are required to comply with this subpart for U.S. small business concerns.

United States Code Annotated

Additional powers, see 15 USCA § 637.

Administrative determinations, see 41 USCA § 257.

Awards or contracts, see 15 USCA § 644.

Contract goal for small disadvantaged businesses and certain institutions of higher education, see 10 USCA § 2323.

Contract requirements, see 41 USCA § 254.

Contracts, planning, solicitation, evaluation, and award procedures, see 10 USCA § 2305.

Credit for Indian contracting in meeting certain subcontracting goals for small disadvantaged businesses and certain institutions of higher education, see 10 USCA § 2323a.

Definitions, see 10 USCA § 2302, 41 USCA §§ 259, 403.

Determinations and decisions, see 10 USCA § 2310, 41 USCA § 262.

HUBZone program, see 15 USCA § 657a.

Kinds of contracts, see 10 USCA § 2306.

Planning and solicitation requirements, see 41 USCA § 253a.

Procurement data, see 41 USCA § 417a.

Procurement program for small business concerns owned and controlled by service-disabled veterans, see 15 USCA § 657f.

Notes of Decisions

In general 1
Agency disagreement 9
Agency referral to SBA 10
Bid preparation and proposal costs 5
Court of Federal Claims jurisdiction 7
Disadvantaged businesses 3
Judicial review 8
Past performance 6
Responsibility determination 2
Suspension or debarment 4

1 In general

Certificate of competency issued by Small Business Administration to successful low bidder on navy contract for procurement of six marine thruster units would be set aside for failure to review compliance with "standard commercial product" clause in invitation for bids; Navy made no assessment of compliance despite fact that clause was part of product specification; SBA made only an after-the-fact, offhanded assessment of whether bidder met the specifications, accepting without question as evidence of "current offering for sale" a one-page flyer which described bidder's ability to produce all manner of thrust or propulsion systems. Small Business Act, § 2[8](b)(7), 15 U.S.C.A. § 637(b)(7). Ulstein Maritime, Ltd. v. U.S., 646 F. Supp. 720, 27 Wage & Hour Cas. (BNA) 1641 (D.R.I. 1986), judgment aff'd, 833 F.2d 1052, 34 Cont. Cas. Fed. (CCH) P 75405 (1st Cir. 1987). United States ⊚64.60(5.1)

Bidder on navy contract for procurement of six marine thruster units had not entered into "binding arrangements and commitments" to acquire for itself plant, equipment and personnel if awarded the contract, as required to qualify as a "newly entering" manufacturer under the Walsh-Healey Act, and thus the Small Business Administration acted contrary to law in issuing certificate of competency as to bidder's compliance with the Act. Walsh-

Healey Act, §§ 1–12, as amended, 41 U.S.C.A. §§ 35–45; Small Business Act, § 2[8](b)(7)(B), 15 U.S.C.A. § 637(b)(7)(B). Ulstein Maritime, Ltd. v. U.S., 646 F. Supp. 720, 27 Wage & Hour Cas. (BNA) 1641 (D.R.I. 1986), judgment aff'd, 833 F.2d 1052, 34 Cont. Cas. Fed. (CCH) P 75405 (1st Cir. 1987). United States ☞64.15

Government contractor did not establish that its prior debarment was a significant factor in determination of the Small Business Administration (SBA) to deny contractor a certificate of competency (COC); although report of SBA official referred to history of debarment, official was not a member of committee who made decision, and committee's minutes did not mention debarment. CRC Marine Services, Inc. v. U.S., 41 Fed. Cl. 66, 42 Cont. Cas. Fed. (CCH) P 77310 (1998). United States ☞64.45(2)

Government contractor failed to establish that Small Business Administration (SBA) was arbitrary or capricious in denying its application for a certificate of competency (COC) with respect to its bid on solicitation for transportation by barge of reactor vessels and steam generators. CRC Marine Services, Inc. v. U.S., 41 Fed. Cl. 66, 42 Cont. Cas. Fed. (CCH) P 77310 (1998). United States ☞64.45(2)

While Small Business Administration (SBA) or Navy may have had statutory duty to properly apply certificate of competency (CoC) requirements, it was not duty owed to incumbent contractor challenging proposed award of followon contract to another or to bidder responding to request for proposals (RFP), nor was it duty enforceable by Court of Federal Claims. Small Business Act, § 2[8](b)(7)(A), 15 U.S.C.A. § 637(b)(7)(A). Control Data Systems, Inc. v. U.S., 32 Fed. Cl. 520, 40 Cont. Cas. Fed. (CCH) P 76743 (1994). United States ☞64.40(1)

Small Business Administration (SBA) may not be required to request additional information when applicant for certificate of competency (COC) did not put forth required effort to complete COC application, especially since SBA must issue COC decision within 15 days of receiving contracting officer's referral. 13 C.F.R. § 125.5(d). C & G Excavating, Inc. v. U.S., 32 Fed. Cl. 231, 39 Cont. Cas. Fed. (CCH) P 76715 (1994). United States ☞64.15; United States ☞64.45(2)

2 Responsibility determination

While Small Business Administration's issuance of certificate of competency is binding on contracting officer, refusal to issue that certificate does not prevent contracting officer from later reversing denial of contract for nonresponsibility on basis of new evidence. Small Business Act, § 2[8], as amended, 15 U.S.C.A. § 637. Cavalier Clothes, Inc. v. U.S., 810 F.2d 1108, 33 Cont. Cas. Fed. (CCH) P 74983 (Fed. Cir. 1987). United States ☞64.45(2)

There was insufficient evidence that government acted "clearly illegally" or abused its discretion by concluding that successful bidder for contract for computer management and support services at naval air development center was a responsible small business concern that was capable of competently performing contract; evidence did not support disappointed bidder's contention that request for proposal required successful bidder to certify whether it was a womenowned small business concern. Applications Research Corp. v. Naval Air Development Center, 752 F. Supp. 660, 37 Cont. Cas. Fed. (CCH) P 76045 (E.D. Pa. 1990). United States ☞64.40(2)

Government agency which had failed to conduct proper responsibility determination for awarding contract could be ordered to reverse its award and to award contract to next lowest responsive and responsible bidder where evidence of awardee's looseness in reporting its finances and of potential violations of federal and local law associated with those actions would not permit finding of responsibility. Small Business Act, § 2[8](a), 15 U.S.C.A. § 637(a). Action Service Corp. v. Garrett, 790 F. Supp. 1188, 38 Cont. Cas. Fed. (CCH) P 76347 (D.P.R. 1992). United States ☞64.60(5.1)

Agency's failure to perform responsibility analysis of awardee prior to award of government contract constituted clear error prejudicial to disappointed bidder; contracting agency was required under applicable regulations to independently evaluate awardee's responsibility, and had awardee been found nonresponsible by agency and failed to receive certificate of competency from Small Business Administration, disappointed bidder would have had chance to win contract. Small Business Act, § 2[8](a), 15 U.S.C.A. § 637(a). Action Service Corp. v. Garrett, 790 F. Supp. 1188, 38 Cont. Cas. Fed. (CCH) P 76347 (D.P.R. 1992). United States ☞64.45(2); United States ☞64.60(5.1)

Government agency's failure to conduct responsibility determination prior to awarding procurement contract was material and not subject to correction by another agency's review; procurement regulations specifically require two separate evaluations of contracting firm's responsibility, one by contracting agency and one by Small Business Administration, and contracting agency can neither abdicate nor delegate its obligation to conduct responsibility determination. Small Business Act, § 2[8](a), 15 U.S.C.A. § 637(a). Action Service Corp. v. Garrett, 790 F. Supp. 1188, 38 Cont. Cas. Fed. (CCH) P 76347 (D.P.R. 1992). United States ⚞64.45(2)

Section of the Small Business Act requiring contracting agency to accept certification of responsibility of a bidder by the Small Business Administration, and section of the Act prohibiting courts from issuing injunctions against the SBA administrator, did not preclude declaratory and injunctive relief requested by disappointed bidders on navy contract, notwithstanding claim that any injunction which would issue against contracting agency was in actuality against the SBA which certified successful bidder. Small Business Act, §§ 2[5](b)(1), 2[8](b)(7), 15 U.S.C.A. §§ 634(b)(1), 637(b)(7). Ulstein Maritime, Ltd. v. U.S., 646 F. Supp. 720, 27 Wage & Hour Cas. (BNA) 1641 (D.R.I. 1986), judgment aff'd, 833 F.2d 1052, 34 Cont. Cas. Fed. (CCH) P 75405 (1st Cir. 1987). Injunction ⚞86

In reviewing a contractor's certificate of competency (COC) application, the Small Business Administration (SBA) is bound by the responsibility criteria set forth in the Federal Acquisition Regulation (FAR), and the criteria set out in the solicitation itself. Small Business Act, § 2[8](b)(7)(A), as amended, 15 U.S.C.A. § 637(b)(7)(A). CSE Const. Co., Inc. v. U.S., 58 Fed. Cl. 230 (2003). United States ⚞64.45(2)

Decision by Small Business Administration's certificate of competency (COC) review committee, that contractor seeking to haul government fuel was nonresponsible, and thus not entitled to COC, was not arbitrary and capricious; committee noted its concern that contractor had not completed installation of fuel gauges and alarms on equipment it proposed to use, that contractor had not fully implemented safety program, and that contractor had unacceptable number of oil spills. Stapp Towing Inc. v. U.S., 34 Fed. Cl. 300, 40 Cont. Cas. Fed. (CCH) P 76839 (1995). United States ⚞64.45(2)

When Small Business Administration (SBA) makes responsibility determination, for purposes of deciding whether to issue Certificate of Competency (COC) to government contractor, it is not limited to deficiencies cited in referring agency's non-responsibility decision, but may consider all aspects of responsibility it considers germane. 13 C.F.R. § 125. 5(a)(1). Stapp Towing Inc. v. U.S., 34 Fed. Cl. 300, 40 Cont. Cas. Fed. (CCH) P 76839 (1995). United States ⚞64.45(2)

Decision by Small Business Administration's certificate of competency (COC) review committee, that contractor seeking to haul government fuel was nonresponsible, and thus not entitled to COC, was not arbitrary and capricious; committee noted its concern that contractor had not completed installation of fuel gauges and alarms on equipment it proposed to use, that contractor had not fully implemented safety program, and that contractor had unacceptable number of oil spills. Stapp Towing Inc. v. U.S., 34 Fed. Cl. 300, 40 Cont. Cas. Fed. (CCH) P 76839 (1995). United States ⚞64.45(2)

When Small Business Administration (SBA) makes responsibility determination, for purposes of deciding whether to issue Certificate of Competency (COC) to government contractor, it is not limited to deficiencies cited in referring agency's non-responsibility decision, but may consider all aspects of responsibility it considers germane. 13 C.F.R. § 125. 5(a)(1). Stapp Towing Inc. v. U.S., 34 Fed. Cl. 300, 40 Cont. Cas. Fed. (CCH) P 76839 (1995). United States ⚞64.45(2)

Small Business Administration (SBA) may perform financial analysis in Miller Act cases, which require posting of performance and payment bonds for public contract award, but SBA must consider bonding requirement in assessing responsibility. Miller Act, §§ 1 et seq., 40 U.S.C.A. §§ 270a et seq.C & G Excavating, Inc. v. U.S., 32 Fed. Cl. 231, 39 Cont. Cas. Fed. (CCH) P 76715 (1994). United States ⚞64.15; United States ⚞64.45(2)

Evidence that contractor had outstanding Internal Revenue Service (IRS) deficiency and that it omitted 1993 financial statement demonstrated that Small Business Administration (SBA) did not act arbitrarily and capriciously in failing to pursue additional information or seek clarification before making finding of nonresponsibility in certification of competency review. C & G Excavating, Inc. v. U.S., 32 Fed. Cl. 231, 39 Cont. Cas. Fed. (CCH) P 76715

(1994). United States ☞64.40(3); United States ☞64.45(2)

Small Business Administration (SBA) was under no obligation to perform site visit to evaluate contractor's financial condition, given that subject of referral was another aspect of contractor responsibility. Small Business Act, § 2[8](b)(7), 15 U.S.C.A. § 637(b)(7). C & G Excavating, Inc. v. U.S., 32 Fed. Cl. 231, 39 Cont. Cas. Fed. (CCH) P 76715 (1994). United States ☞64.45(2)

Small Business Administration (SBA) properly considered contractor's financial status in making responsibility determination, though contracting officer cited capacity as only basis for her nonresponsibility decision; SBA may consider all aspects of responsibility in making certificate of competency determination. Small Business Act, § 2[8](a)(16)(A), (b)(7), 15 U.S.C.A. § 637(a)(16)(A), (b)(7); 13 C.F.R. § 125.5(e). C & G Excavating, Inc. v. U.S., 32 Fed. Cl. 231, 39 Cont. Cas. Fed. (CCH) P 76715 (1994). United States ☞64.45(2)

Burden rests with prospective contractor to demonstrate that it satisfies criteria underlying responsibility determination in certificate of competency proceeding with Small Business Administration (SBA). C & G Excavating, Inc. v. U.S., 32 Fed. Cl. 231, 39 Cont. Cas. Fed. (CCH) P 76715 (1994). United States ☞64.15

Small Business Administration's (SBA's) review of prospective contractor's competency to perform is not limited to situation in which contract negotiations are successful and result in procuring agency proposing to SBA that program participant be awarded contract; certificate of competency program requires procuring agency negotiating with small business to refer to SBA any determination that business is not responsible to perform particular contract. Small Business Act, § 2[8](a), (b)(7)(A), as amended, 15 U.S.C.A. § 637(a), (b)(7)(A). Celtech, Inc. v. U.S., 24 Cl. Ct. 269, 37 Cont. Cas. Fed. (CCH) P 76181, 1991 WL 193295 (1991), vacated pursuant to settlement, 25 Cl. Ct. 368, 1992 WL 46122 (1992). United States ☞53(8)

Certificate of competency program, which requires procuring agency negotiating with a small business to refer to the Small Business Administration (SBA) any determination that business is not responsible to perform particular contract was not limited in applicability only to competitive procurements, and contractors could seek certificates of competency when negotiating with government agencies on noncompetitive procurements. Celtech, Inc. v. U.S., 24 Cl. Ct. 269, 37 Cont. Cas. Fed. (CCH) P 76181, 1991 WL 193295 (1991), vacated pursuant to settlement, 25 Cl. Ct. 368, 1992 WL 46122 (1992). United States ☞64.15

Small Business Administration (SBA) is responsible for determining the responsibility of small businesses. SBA's investigation of government contract bidder, resulting in denial of certificate of competency, was thorough and unbiased, and did not violate bidder's due process rights, absent any evidence that SBA deviated from its standard operating procedure or in any manner deprived bidder of its right to submit pertinent information and to explain its case for a certificate of competency. U.S.C.A. Const.Amend. 5. PNM Const., Inc. v. U.S., 13 Cl. Ct. 745, 34 Cont. Cas. Fed. (CCH) P 75409, 1987 WL 20987 (1987). Constitutional Law ☞276(2); United States ☞64.20

Small Business Administration did not exceed its statutory authority, in ruling on bidder's certificate of competence application, by considering the contract specifications and conformity of the bid thereto; that aspect of review was a proper exercise of SBA's investigative responsibilities, particularly in view of bidder's track record of marginal and unsatisfactory performance on other government contracts. PNM Const., Inc. v. U.S., 13 Cl. Ct. 745, 34 Cont. Cas. Fed. (CCH) P 75409, 1987 WL 20987 (1987). United States ☞64.45(2)

Protest was sustained where FedBid, acting as the agent for the contracting agency, excluded the small business protester from the competition based on a perceived lack of business integrity, in effect making a negative responsibility determination, without referring the matter to the Small Business Administration under the Certificate of Competency procedures. Latvian Connection, LLC, B-410947, 2015 CPD ¶ 117 (Comp. Gen. 2015)

Protest was sustained where the agency found the small business protester to be nonresponsible based solely on what amounted to a pass/fail evaluation of the protester's past performance, without referring the matter to the Small Business Administration under the agency's Certificate of Competency procedures. FitNet Purchasing Alliance, B-410263, 2014 CPD ¶ 344 (Comp.Gen. 2015)

The Small Business Administration's (SBA) certificate of competency (COC) denial was inappropriate because the SBA applied the wrong standard in concluding that a Service Disabled Veteran Owned Small Business (SDVOSB) did not satisfy the requirement generally applicable to contracts for general construction that the small business concern perform at least 15% of the cost of the contract with its own employees. This requirement does not, however, apply to SDVOSBs, which are subject to a less stringent subcontracting threshold (13 C.F.R. § 125.6(b)), which the contractor satisfied. Construct Solutions, Inc., B-405288, 2011 CPD ¶ 214 (Comp. Gen. 2011)

3 Disadvantaged businesses

Current disadvantaged business enterprise (DBE) certification programs for federal highway subcontracting meet the requirements of narrow tailoring, and thus do not violate equal protection. U.S.C.A. Const.Amend. 5; Small Business Act, §§ 2[8](a, d), 2[15](g), as amended, 15 U.S.C.A. §§ 637(a, d), 644(g); Surface Transportation and Uniform Relocation Assistance Act of 1987, §§ 1 et seq., 23 U.S.C.A. § 101 note; Intermodal Surface Transportation Efficiency Act of 1991, §§ 1 et seq., 49 U.S.C.A. § 101 note; Transportation Equity Act for the 21st Century, §§ 1 et seq., 23 U.S.C.A. § 101 note; 13 C.F.R. §§ 124.104(c)(2), 124. 1014; 48 C.F.R. § 19.001; 49 C.F.R. §§ 26.65, 26.67(b). Adarand Constructors, Inc. v. Slater, 228 F.3d 1147 (10th Cir. 2000). Constitutional Law ☞234; Highways ☞113(1)

Method of certification of disadvantaged business enterprises (DBEs) presuming economic disadvantage based on membership in certain racial groups, applied to federal highway subcontracting in 1996, was not narrowly tailored, so as to satisfy equal protection, but current regulations providing for an individualized determination of economic disadvantage are narrowly tailored. U.S.C.A. Const.Amend. 5; Small Business Act, § 2[8](a, d), as amended, 15 U.S.C.A. § 637(a, d); 13 C.F.R. §§ 124.104(b)(1), 124.1001 et seq., 124. 1002(a); 48 C.F.R. §§ 19.001, 19.703, 52.219-8; 49 C.F.R. § 26.67(b)(1). Adarand Constructors, Inc. v. Slater, 228 F.3d 1147 (10th Cir. 2000). Constitutional Law ☞215.2; Highways ☞113(1)

Navy as contracting agency, rather than Small Business Administration (SBA), had duty to make responsibility determination with respect to best bidder and competitive bid. Small Business Act, § 2[8](a), as amended, 15 U.S.C.A. § 637(a). Action Service Corp. v. Garrett, 797 F. Supp. 82 (D.P.R. 1992). United States ☞64.45(2)

Regulations requiring procuring agency to refer contractor responsibility determinations to the Small Business Administration (SBA) apply to small disadvantaged business concerns, in accordance with the certificate of competency program, which requires procuring agency negotiating with small business to refer to SBA any determination that business is not responsible to perform particular contract. Small Business Act, § 2[8](a), (b)(7)(A), as amended, 15 U.S.C.A. § 637(a), (b)(7)(A). Celtech, Inc. v. U.S., 24 Cl. Ct. 269, 37 Cont. Cas. Fed. (CCH) P 76181, 1991 WL 193295 (1991), vacated pursuant to settlement, 25 Cl. Ct. 368, 1992 WL 46122 (1992). United States ☞53(8)

Department of State's violation of regulation by failing to notify the Small Business Administration (SBA) of determination that disadvantaged small business was not responsible to perform typewriter repair contract prejudiced business by depriving business of opportunity to apply for certificate of competency and possibly be awarded contract, thus breaching implied contract to fairly and honestly consider business' proposal and entitling business to recovery. Small Business Act, § 2[8](a), as amended, 15 U.S.C.A. § 637(a). Celtech, Inc. v. U.S., 24 Cl. Ct. 269, 37 Cont. Cas. Fed. (CCH) P 76181, 1991 WL 193295 (1991), vacated pursuant to settlement, 25 Cl. Ct. 368, 1992 WL 46122 (1992). United States ☞64.15

Exception to mandatory requirement that if small business concern's offer is to be rejected because of determination of nonresponsibility, contracting officers shall refer the matter to the Small Business Administration (SBA), which will decide whether to issue certificate of competency, did not apply to Department of State's rejection of disadvantaged small business for contract based on accounting system deficiencies identified in audit; exception applies if contracting officer determines business is unqualified because it does not meet standard of being "otherwise qualified and eligible to receive award," but different subsection lists as specific responsibility requirement that prospective contractor have necessary accounting and operational controls, so exception did not apply. Celtech, Inc. v. U.S., 24 Cl. Ct. 269, 37 Cont. Cas. Fed. (CCH) P 76181, 1991 WL 193295 (1991), vacated pursuant to settlement, 25 Cl. Ct. 368, 1992 WL 46122 (1992). United States ☞64.15

Small business eligible for the certificate of competency program was entitled to have the Department of State notify the Small Business Administration (SBA) prior to terminating negotiations on noncompetitive procurement with business which qualified as disadvantaged small business based on accounting system deficiencies in business identified in audit; business would then have had opportunity to apply for SBA assistance in curing perceived deficiencies and might ultimately have qualified for contract award. Small Business Act, § 2[8](a), (b)(7)(A), as amended, 15 U.S.C.A. § 637(a), (b)(7)(A). Celtech, Inc. v. U.S., 24 Cl. Ct. 269, 37 Cont. Cas. Fed. (CCH) P 76181, 1991 WL 193295 (1991), vacated pursuant to settlement, 25 Cl. Ct. 368, 1992 WL 46122 (1992). United States ☞64.15

4 Suspension or debarment

Small Business Act and Competition in Contracting Act provisions applicable when company is being considered for contract award are inapplicable to General Services Administration (GSA) action suspending or terminating government contract. Small Business Act, § 2[8](b)(7), as amended, 15 U.S.C.A. § 637(b)(7); Federal Property and Administrative Services Act of 1949, § 303B(c), (d)(2), as amended, 41 U.S.C.A. § 253b(c), (d)(2); 48 C.F.R. § 19.602-1(a)(2)(ii). Commercial Drapery Contractors, Inc. v. U.S., 967 F. Supp. 1, 41 Cont. Cas. Fed. (CCH) P 77172 (D.D.C. 1997), judgment aff'd, 133 F.3d 1, 39 Fed. R. Serv. 3d 825 (D.C. Cir. 1998). United States ☞72.1(1)

Government contractor did not establish that its prior debarment was a significant factor in determination of the Small Business Administration (SBA) to deny contractor a certificate of competency (COC); although report of SBA official referred to history of debarment, official was not a member of committee who made decision, and committee's minutes did not mention debarment. CRC Marine Services, Inc. v. U.S., 41 Fed. Cl. 66, 42 Cont. Cas. Fed. (CCH) P 77310 (1998). United States ☞64.45(2)

5 Bid preparation and proposal costs

Bid protestor was entitled to award of bid preparation costs, where contracting agency and the Small Business Administration (SBA) violated applicable statutes and regulations with respect to the protestor's application for a certificate of competency (COC), to the prejudice of protestor, and where the decision to deny it a COC lacked a rational basis. 28 U.S.C.A. § 1491(b)(3). CSE Const. Co., Inc. v. U.S., 58 Fed. Cl. 230 (2003). United States ☞64.60(6)

Costs incurred by bidder in responding to a Small Business Administration (SBA) size protest and investigation for purposes of an SBA certificate of competency (COC) were not recoverable as "bid preparation and proposal costs" within meaning of the Tucker Act, where eligibility to bid was not predicated on size, and compliance with COC investigation was not a term of the bid. 28 U.S.C.A. § 1491(b)(2). Lion Raisins, Inc. v. U.S., 52 Fed. Cl. 629 (2002), subsequent determination, 57 Fed. Cl. 505 (2003). United States ☞64.60(6)

Bidder who prevailed in bid protest was not entitled to award of 5,625.00 in attorney fees incurred in the course of responding to a Small Business Administration (SBA) size protest and investigation for purposes of an SBA certificate of competency (COC), as such fees were not allowable bid preparation costs. 28 U.S.C.A. § 1491(b)(2). Lion Raisins, Inc. v. U.S., 52 Fed. Cl. 629 (2002), subsequent determination, 57 Fed. Cl. 505 (2003). United States ☞64.60(6)

Unsuccessful bidder could not recover barge clean-up costs incurred in preparation for contract to haul fuel, absent showing that Small Business Administration's (SBA) denial of certificate of competency, necessary to be awarded contract, was arbitrary and capricious. Stapp Towing Inc. v. U.S., 34 Fed. Cl. 300, 40 Cont. Cas. Fed. (CCH) P 76839 (1995). United States ☞64.60(6)

6 Past performance

Bidder who was denied a certificate of competency (COC) by the Small Business Administration (SBA) was prejudiced by SBA's violation of regulatory requirements which occurred when it failed to consider unfavorable past performance references within the context of bidder's overall work record, and when it failed to consider whether the problems bidder encountered in past performance were beyond bidder's control and whether it took appropriate corrective action; in light of SBA's statement that the unfavorable references were a "major concern," there was a substantial chance that but for the violations the SBA would have issued the COC. 48 C.F.R. § 9.104-3(b). CSE Const. Co., Inc. v. U.S., 58 Fed. Cl. 230 (2003). United States ☞64.55(1)

On review of bidder's application for a certificate of competency, the Small Business Administration (SBA) was not required to give bidder the opportunity to clarify unfavorable past performance references the SBA had collected. CSE Const. Co., Inc. v. U.S., 58 Fed. Cl. 230 (2003). United States ☞64.45(2)

Failure of the Small Business Administration (SBA), on review of bidder's application for certificate of competency (COC), to consider whether bidder's past performance problems arose from circumstances beyond its control and whether bidder took appropriate corrective action to remedy the problems constituted a violation of SBA's obligations under both the solicitation and section of the Federal Acquisition Regulation (FAR). 48 C.F.R. § 9.104-3(b). CSE Const. Co., Inc. v. U.S., 58 Fed. Cl. 230 (2003). United States ☞64.45(2)

Upon bidder's application for certificate of competency (COC) from the Small Business Administration (SBA), contracting agency was required by regulation to supply the SBA with the results of its investigation into bidder's past performance, and the SBA was required to give consideration to the information collected by the agency concerning bidder's past performance. 13 C.F.R. § 125.5(c)(1); 48 C.F.R. § 19.602-1(c). CSE Const. Co., Inc. v. U.S., 58 Fed. Cl. 230 (2003). United States ☞64.45(2)

Decision of the Small Business Administration (SBA) to deny bidder a certificate of competency (COC) on the basis of poor past performance lacked a rational basis, where the SBA checked only three past references from extensive list of 105 submitted by bidder, and ignored contracting agency's conclusion that bidder's past performance was "very good"; moreover, SBA did not consider whether negative comments concerning past performance stemmed from circumstances beyond bidder's control, or even whether bidder had taken appropriate corrective action in the three instances. CSE Const. Co., Inc. v. U.S., 58 Fed. Cl. 230 (2003). United States ☞64.45(2)

In reviewing contractor's application for certificate of competency (COC), the Small Business Administration (SBA) violated section of the Federal Acquisition Regulation (FAR) charging agency evaluators to "consider the number of contracts involved and the extent of deficient performance in each contract" when making responsibility determinations, where SBA contacted only 3 of 35 project references submitted by contractor for the period since 2000 to the present. 48 C.F.R. § 9.104-3(b). CSE Const. Co., Inc. v. U.S., 58 Fed. Cl. 230 (2003). United States ☞64.45(2)

7 Court of Federal Claims jurisdiction

Court of Federal Claims had jurisdiction to review Small Business Administration's denial of bid protestor's application for a certificate of competency (COC) pursuant to the Court's jurisdiction over bid protests. Small Business Act, § 2[8](b)(7)(A), as amended, 15 U.S.C.A. § 637(b)(7)(A); 28 U.S.C.A. § 1491(b). CSE Const. Co., Inc. v. U.S., 58 Fed. Cl. 230 (2003). Federal Courts ☞1076

Court of Federal Claims has jurisdiction to review Small Business Administration's (SBA) Certificate of Competency (COC) determinations. Stapp Towing Inc. v. U.S., 34 Fed. Cl. 300, 40 Cont. Cas. Fed. (CCH) P 76839 (1995). Federal Courts ☞1073.1

8 Judicial review

Statute giving final disposition of competency certification of small business concern to Small Business Administration did not preclude small business contractor from obtaining judicial review of propriety of rejection of its low bid on ground of nonresponsibility; rejecting Speco Corp. v. U.S., 2 Cl. Ct. 335, 31 Cont. Cas. Fed. (CCH) P 71137 (1983) (rejected by, Cavalier Clothes, Inc. v. U.S., 810 F.2d 1108, 33 Cont. Cas. Fed. (CCH) P 74983 (Fed. Cir. 1987)). Small Business Act, § 2[8](b)(7)(A), as amended, 15 U.S.C.A. § 637(b)(7)(A). Cavalier Clothes, Inc. v. U.S., 810 F.2d 1108, 33 Cont. Cas. Fed. (CCH) P 74983 (Fed. Cir. 1987). United States ☞64.60(1)

9 Agency disagreement

An agency is authorized to determine that the offer of a small business is unacceptable even if the Small Business Administration has issued a Certificate of Competency (COC) certifying that the awardee is responsible. GAO sustained a protest against the award because it found the awardee's offer facially unacceptable in that it proposed to perform only 43% of the work, notwithstanding the requirements of the Limitations on Subcontracting clause (52.219-14), which requires the small business prime contractor to perform at least 50% of the services in a set-aside procurement. Centech Group, Inc. v. U.S., 554 F.3d 1029 (Fed. Cir. 2009)

Protest that contracting agency improperly rejected section 8(a) firm as nonresponsible despite determination of competency made by Small Business Administration's (SBA) Regional Office is denied where the contracting officer reasonably concluded that the Regional Office's determination did not adequately address contracting agency concerns regarding the technical capability of the firm to perform the contract, and subsequently appealed the Regional Office's decision to the SBA's Central Office, which declined to confirm the Regional Office's assessment that the protester was competent, and instead advised the contracting agency to make award to another 8(a) firm. Matter of: Joa Quin Manufacturing Corporation, B-255298, 94-1 CPD ¶ 140 (Comp. Gen. 1994)

10 Agency referral to SBA

Protest challenging rejection of small business protester's offer on the ground that the agency's decision constituted a nonresponsibility determination that should have been referred to the Small Business Administration is sustained where the basis of the agency's determination-that protester would be unable to obtain the required parts-relates directly to the firm's capability to perform the contract. Fabritech, Inc., B-298247, B-298247.2, 2006 CPD ¶ 112 (Comp. Gen. 2006)

Under the Small Business Act, agencies may not find a small business nonresponsible without referring the matter to the SBA, which has the ultimate authority to determine the responsibility of small businesses under its COC procedures. Capitol CREAG LLC, B-294958.4, 2005 CPD ¶ 31 (Comp. Gen. 2005)

Where a solicitation uses traditional responsibility factors as technical evaluation criteria and where the proposal of a small business concern which otherwise would be in line for award is found ineligible for award based on an agency's evaluation under those criteria, the agency has effectively made a determination that the small business offeror is not a responsible contractor capable of performing the solicitation requirements; accordingly, the agency must refer the matter of the firm's responsibility to the Small Business Administration (SBA) for the possible issuance of a certificate of competency (COC). Capitol CREAG LLC, B-294958.4, 2005 CPD ¶ 31 (Comp. Gen. 2005)

Agency is not required to refer a neutral past performance evaluation to the Small Business Administration for a possible certificate of competency. CMC & Maintenance, Inc., B-292081, 2003 CPD ¶ 107 (Comp. Gen. 2003)

Protest sustained where agency effectively determined small business, which submitted sole proposal on section 8(a) set-aside, to be nonresponsible based solely on what amounted to pass/fail evaluation of the protester's past performance, without referring the matter to the Small Business Administration under certificate of competency procedures. Phil Howry Company, B-291402.3, B-291402.4, 2003 CPD ¶ 33 (Comp. Gen. 2003)

§ 19.602 Procedures.

§ 19.602-1 Referral.

(a) Upon determining and documenting that an apparent successful small business offeror lacks certain elements of responsibility (including, but not limited to, capability, competency, capacity, credit, integrity, perseverance, tenacity, and limitations on subcontracting, but for sureties see 28.101-3(f) and 28.203(c)), the contracting officer shall—

    (1) Withhold contract award (see 19.602-3); and

    (2) Refer the matter to the cognizant SBA Government Contracting Area Office (Area Office) serving the area in which the headquarters of the offeror is located, in accordance with agency procedures, except that referral is not necessary if the small business concern—

       (i) Is determined to be unqualified and ineligible because it does not meet the standard in 9.104-1(g), provided, that the determination is approved by the chief of the contracting office; or

(ii) Is suspended or debarred under Executive Order 11246 or Subpart 9.4.

(b) If a partial set-aside is involved, the contracting officer shall refer to the SBA the entire quantity to which the concern may be entitled, if responsible.

(c) The referral shall include—

(1) A notice that a small business concern has been determined to be nonresponsible, specifying the elements of responsibility the contracting officer found lacking; and

(2) If applicable, a copy of the following:

(i) Solicitation.

(ii) Final offer submitted by the concern whose responsibility is at issue for the procurement.

(iii) Abstract of bids or the contracting officer's price negotiation memorandum.

(iv) Preaward survey.

(v) Technical data package (including drawings, specifications and statement of work).

(vi) Any other justification and documentation used to arrive at the nonresponsibility determination.

(d) For any single acquisition, the contracting officer shall make only one referral at a time regarding a determination of nonresponsibility.

(e) Contract award shall be withheld by the contracting officer for a period of 15 business days (or longer if agreed to by the SBA and the contracting officer) following receipt by the appropriate SBA Area Office of a referral that includes all required documentation.

United States Code Annotated

Additional powers, see 15 USCA § 637.

Administrative determinations, see 41 USCA § 257.

Awards or contracts, see 15 USCA § 644.

Contract goal for small disadvantaged businesses and certain institutions of higher education, see 10 USCA § 2323.

Contract requirements, see 41 USCA § 254.

Contracts, planning, solicitation, evaluation, and award procedures, see 10 USCA § 2305.

Credit for Indian contracting in meeting certain subcontracting goals for small disadvantaged businesses and certain institutions of higher education, see 10 USCA § 2323a.

Definitions, see 10 USCA § 2302, 41 USCA §§ 259, 403.

Determinations and decisions, see 10 USCA § 2310, 41 USCA § 262.

HUBZone program, see 15 USCA § 657a.

Kinds of contracts, see 10 USCA § 2306.

Planning and solicitation requirements, see 41 USCA § 253a.

Procurement data, see 41 USCA § 417a.

Procurement program for small business concerns owned and controlled by service-disabled veterans, see 15 USCA § 657f.

Notes of Decisions

Past performance 2
Suspension or debarment 1

1 Suspension or debarment

Small Business Act and Competition in Contracting Act provisions applicable when company is being considered for contract award are inapplicable to General Services Administration (GSA) action suspending or terminating government contract. Small Business Act, § 2[8](b)(7), as amended, 15 U.S.C.A. § 637(b)(7); Federal Property and Administrative Services Act of 1949, § 303B(c), (d)(2), as amended, 41 U.S.C.A. § 253b(c), (d)(2); 48 C.F.R. § 19.602-1(a)(2)(ii). Commercial Drapery Contractors, Inc. v. U.S., 967 F. Supp. 1, 41 Cont. Cas. Fed. (CCH) P 77172 (D.D.C. 1997), judgment aff'd, 133 F.3d 1, 39 Fed. R. Serv. 3d 825 (D.C. Cir. 1998). United States ☞72.1(1)

2 Past performance

Despite language in first paragraph of letter from contracting officer to authorized representative of bidder, that "your firm has been determined non-responsible," suggesting letter was finding that bidder was non-responsible in Small Business Act sense of that term, as would allegedly have required referral of finding to Small Business Administration, evidence established that letter was finding that bidder's proposal bond, rather than bidder, was nonresponsible; letter explained "[t]he basis of this determination is your inability to submit acceptable proposal bond within the allotted time frame." Small Business Act, § 2[8](b)(7)(A), as amended, 15 U.S.C.A. § 637(b)(7)(A). Radva Corp. v. U.S., 914 F.2d 271 (Fed. Cir. 1990). United States ☞64.45(2)

Although contracting agency determined that small business bidder was nonresponsibile, it was not obligated to refer the bidder to the Small Business Administration (SBA) for a determination of the bidder's responsibility under the SBA's certificate of competency program, where agency concurrently rejected bid on other ground of nonresponsiveness. Aeroplate Corp. v. U.S., 67 Fed. Cl. 4 (2005). United States ☞64.45(2)

Bidder who was denied a certificate of competency (COC) by the Small Business Administration (SBA) was prejudiced by SBA's violation of regulatory requirements which occurred when it failed to consider unfavorable past performance references within the context of bidder's overall work record, and when it failed to consider whether the problems bidder encountered in past performance were beyond bidder's control and whether it took appropriate corrective action; in light of SBA's statement that the unfavorable references were a "major concern," there was a substantial chance that but for the violations the SBA would have issued the COC. 48 C.F.R. § 9.104-3(b). CSE Const. Co., Inc. v. U.S., 58 Fed. Cl. 230 (2003). United States ☞64.55(1)

On review of bidder's application for a certificate of competency, the Small Business Administration (SBA) was not required to give bidder the opportunity to clarify unfavorable past performance references the SBA had collected. CSE Const. Co., Inc. v. U.S., 58 Fed. Cl. 230 (2003). United States ☞64.45(2)

Failure of the Small Business Administration (SBA), on review of bidder's application for certificate of competency (COC), to consider whether bidder's past performance problems arose from circumstances beyond its control and whether bidder took appropriate corrective action to remedy the problems constituted a violation of SBA's obligations under both the solicitation and section of the Federal Acquisition Regulation (FAR). 48 C.F.R. § 9.104-3(b). CSE Const. Co., Inc. v. U.S., 58 Fed. Cl. 230 (2003). United States ☞64.45(2)

Upon bidder's application for certificate of competency (COC) from the Small Business Administration (SBA), contracting agency was required by regulation to supply the SBA with the results of its investigation into bidder's past performance, and the SBA was required to give consideration to the information collected by the agency concerning bidder's past performance. 13 C.F.R. § 125.5(c)(1); 48 C.F.R. § 19.602-1(c). CSE Const. Co., Inc. v. U.S., 58 Fed. Cl. 230 (2003). United States ☞64.45(2)

Decision of the Small Business Administration (SBA) to deny bidder a certificate of competency (COC) on the basis of poor past performance lacked a rational basis, where the SBA checked only three past references from extensive list of 105 submitted by bidder, and ignored contracting agency's conclusion that bidder's past performance was "very good"; moreover, SBA did not consider whether negative comments concerning past performance stemmed from circumstances beyond bidder's control, or even whether bidder had taken appropriate corrective action in the three instances. CSE Const. Co., Inc. v. U.S., 58 Fed. Cl. 230 (2003). United States ☞64.45(2)

In reviewing contractor's application for certificate of competency (COC), the Small Business Administration (SBA) violated section of the Federal Acquisition Regulation (FAR) charging agency evaluators to "consider the number of contracts involved and the extent of deficient performance in each contract" when making responsibility determinations, where SBA contacted only 3 of 35 project references submitted by contractor for the period since 2000 to the present. 48 C.F.R. § 9.104-3(b). CSE Const. Co., Inc. v. U.S., 58 Fed. Cl. 230 (2003). United States ☞64.45(2)

Exception to mandatory requirement that if small business concern's offer is to be rejected because of determination of nonresponsibility, contracting officers shall refer the matter to the Small Business Administration (SBA), which will decide whether to issue certificate of competency, did not apply to Department of State's rejection of disadvantaged small business for contract based on accounting system deficiencies identified in audit; exception applies if contracting officer determines business is unqualified because it does not meet standard of being "otherwise qualified and eligible to receive award," but different subsection lists as specific responsibility requirement that prospective contractor have necessary accounting and operational controls, so exception did not apply. Celtech, Inc. v. U.S., 24 Cl. Ct. 269, 37 Cont. Cas. Fed. (CCH) P 76181, 1991 WL 193295 (1991), vacated pursuant to settlement, 25 Cl. Ct. 368, 1992 WL 46122 (1992). United States ☞64.15

§ 19.602-2 Issuing or denying a Certificate of Competency (COC).

Within 15 business days (or a longer period agreed to by the SBA and the contracting agency) after receiving a notice that a small business concern lacks certain elements of responsibility, the SBA Area Office will take the following actions:

(a) Inform the small business concern of the contracting officer's determination and offer it an opportunity to apply to the SBA for a COC. (A concern wishing to apply for a COC should notify the SBA Area Office serving the geographical area in which the headquarters of the offeror is located.)

(b) Upon timely receipt of a complete and acceptable application, elect to visit the applicant's facility to review its responsibility.

(1) The COC review process is not limited to the areas of nonresponsibility cited by the contracting officer.

(2) The SBA may, at its discretion, independently evaluate the COC applicant for all elements of responsibility, but may presume responsibility exists as to elements other than those cited as deficient.

(c) Consider denying a COC for reasons of nonresponsibility not originally cited by the contracting officer.

(d) When the Area Director determines that a COC is warranted (for contracts valued at $25,000,000 or less), notify the contracting officer and provide the following options:

(1) Accept the Area Director's decision to issue a COC and award the contract to the concern. The COC issuance letter will then be sent, including as an attachment a detailed rationale for the decision; or

(2) Ask the Area Director to suspend the case for one or more of the following purposes:

(i) To permit the SBA to forward a detailed rationale for the decision to the contracting officer for review within a specified period of time.

(ii) To afford the contracting officer the opportunity to meet with the Area Office to review all documentation contained in the case file and to attempt to resolve any issues.

(iii) To submit any information to the SBA Area Office that the contracting officer believes the SBA did not consider (at which time, the SBA Area Office will establish a new suspense date mutually agreeable to the contracting officer and the SBA).

(iv) To permit resolution of an appeal by the contracting agency to SBA Headquarters under 19.602-3. However, there is no contracting officer's appeal when the Area Office proposes to issue a COC valued at $100,000 or less.

(e) At the completion of the process, notify the concern and the contracting officer that the COC is denied or is being issued.

(f) Refer recommendations for issuing a COC on contracts greater than $25,000,000 to SBA Headquarters.

United States Code Annotated

Additional powers, see 15 USCA § 637.

Administrative determinations, see 41 USCA § 257.

Awards or contracts, see 15 USCA § 644.

Contract goal for small disadvantaged businesses and certain institutions of higher education, see 10 USCA § 2323.

Contract requirements, see 41 USCA § 254.

Contracts, planning, solicitation, evaluation, and award procedures, see 10 USCA § 2305.

Credit for Indian contracting in meeting certain subcontracting goals for small disadvantaged businesses and certain institutions of higher education, see 10 USCA § 2323a.

Definitions, see 10 USCA § 2302, 41 USCA §§ 259, 403.

Determinations and decisions, see 10 USCA § 2310, 41 USCA § 262.

HUBZone program, see 15 USCA § 657a.

Kinds of contracts, see 10 USCA § 2306.

Planning and solicitation requirements, see 41 USCA § 253a.

Procurement data, see 41 USCA § 417a.

Procurement program for small business concerns owned and controlled by service-disabled veterans, see 15 USCA § 657f.

Notes of Decisions

In general 1
Bid preparation and proposal costs 5
Determination of responsibility 2
Disadvantaged businesses 3
Past performance 6
Suspension or debarment 4

1 In general

Certificate of competency issued by Small Business Administration to successful low bidder on navy contract for procurement of six marine thruster units would be set aside for failure to review compliance with "standard commercial product" clause in invitation for bids; Navy made no assessment of compliance despite fact that clause was part of product specification; SBA made only an after-the-fact, offhanded assessment of whether bidder met the specifications, accepting without question as evidence of "current offering for sale" a one-page flyer which described bidder's ability to produce all manner of thrust or propulsion systems. Small Business Act, § 2[8](b)(7), 15 U.S.C.A. § 637(b)(7). Ulstein Maritime, Ltd. v. U.S., 646 F. Supp. 720, 27 Wage & Hour Cas. (BNA) 1641 (D.R.I. 1986), judgment aff'd, 833 F.2d 1052, 34 Cont. Cas. Fed. (CCH) P 75405 (1st Cir. 1987). United States ⚮64.60(5.1)

Bidder on navy contract for procurement of six marine thruster units had not entered into "binding arrangements and commitments" to acquire for itself plant, equipment and personnel if awarded the contract, as required to qualify as a "newly entering" manufacturer under the Walsh-Healey Act, and thus the Small Business Administration acted contrary to law in issuing certificate of competency as to bidder's compliance with the Act. Walsh-Healey Act, §§ 1–12, as amended, 41 U.S.C.A. §§ 35–45; Small Business Act, § 2[8](b)(7)(B), 15 U.S.C.A. § 637(b)(7)(B). Ulstein Maritime, Ltd. v. U.S., 646 F. Supp. 720, 27 Wage & Hour Cas. (BNA) 1641 (D.R.I. 1986), judgment aff'd, 833 F.2d 1052, 34 Cont. Cas. Fed. (CCH) P 75405 (1st Cir. 1987). United States ⚮64.15

Government contractor did not establish that its prior debarment was a significant factor in determination of the Small Business Administration (SBA) to deny contractor a certificate of competency (COC); although report of SBA official referred to history of debarment, official was not a member of committee who made decision, and committee's minutes did not mention debarment. CRC Marine Services, Inc. v. U.S., 41 Fed. Cl. 66, 42 Cont. Cas. Fed. (CCH) P 77310 (1998). United States ⚮64.45(2)

Government contractor failed to establish that Small Business Administration (SBA) was arbitrary or capricious in denying its application for a certificate of competency (COC) with respect to its bid on solicitation for transportation by barge of reactor vessels and steam generators. CRC Marine Services, Inc. v. U.S., 41 Fed. Cl. 66, 42 Cont. Cas. Fed. (CCH) P 77310 (1998). United States ⚮64.45(2)

Court of Federal Claims has jurisdiction to review Small Business Administration's (SBA) Certificate of Competency (COC) determinations. Stapp Towing Inc. v. U.S., 34 Fed. Cl. 300, 40 Cont. Cas. Fed. (CCH) P 76839 (1995). Federal Courts ⚮1073.1

While Small Business Administration (SBA) or Navy may have had statutory duty to properly apply certificate of competency (CoC) requirements, it was not duty owed to incumbent contractor challenging proposed award of followon contract to another or to bidder responding to request for proposals (RFP), nor was it duty enforceable by Court of

Federal Claims. Small Business Act, § 2[8](b)(7)(A), 15 U.S.C.A. § 637(b)(7)(A). Control Data Systems, Inc. v. U.S., 32 Fed. Cl. 520, 40 Cont. Cas. Fed. (CCH) P 76743 (1994). United States ☞64.40(1)

Small Business Administration (SBA) may not be required to request additional information when applicant for certificate of competency (COC) did not put forth required effort to complete COC application, especially since SBA must issue COC decision within 15 days of receiving contracting officer's referral. 13 C.F.R. § 125.5(d). C & G Excavating, Inc. v. U.S., 32 Fed. Cl. 231, 39 Cont. Cas. Fed. (CCH) P 76715 (1994). United States ☞64.15; United States ☞64.45(2)

2 Determination of responsibility

While Small Business Administration's issuance of certificate of competency is binding on contracting officer, refusal to issue that certificate does not prevent contracting officer from later reversing denial of contract for nonresponsibility on basis of new evidence. Small Business Act, § 2[8], as amended, 15 U.S.C.A. § 637. Cavalier Clothes, Inc. v. U.S., 810 F.2d 1108, 33 Cont. Cas. Fed. (CCH) P 74983 (Fed. Cir. 1987). United States ☞64.45(2)

There was insufficient evidence that government acted "clearly illegally" or abused its discretion by concluding that successful bidder for contract for computer management and support services at naval air development center was a responsible small business concern that was capable of competently performing contract; evidence did not support disappointed bidder's contention that request for proposal required successful bidder to certify whether it was a womenowned small business concern. Applications Research Corp. v. Naval Air Development Center, 752 F. Supp. 660, 37 Cont. Cas. Fed. (CCH) P 76045 (E.D. Pa. 1990). United States ☞64.40(2)

Government agency which had failed to conduct proper responsibility determination for awarding contract could be ordered to reverse its award and to award contract to next lowest responsive and responsible bidder where evidence of awardee's looseness in reporting its finances and of potential violations of federal and local law associated with those actions would not permit finding of responsibility. Small Business Act, § 2[8](a), 15 U.S.C.A. § 637(a). Action Service Corp. v. Garrett, 790 F. Supp. 1188, 38 Cont. Cas. Fed. (CCH) P 76347 (D.P.R. 1992). United States ☞64.60(5.1)

Agency's failure to perform responsibility analysis of awardee prior to award of government contract constituted clear error prejudicial to disappointed bidder; contracting agency was required under applicable regulations to independently evaluate awardee's responsibility, and had awardee been found nonresponsible by agency and failed to receive certificate of competency from Small Business Administration, disappointed bidder would have had chance to win contract. Small Business Act, § 2[8](a), 15 U.S.C.A. § 637(a). Action Service Corp. v. Garrett, 790 F. Supp. 1188, 38 Cont. Cas. Fed. (CCH) P 76347 (D.P.R. 1992). United States ☞64.45(2); United States ☞64.60(5.1)

Government agency's failure to conduct responsibility determination prior to awarding procurement contract was material and not subject to correction by another agency's review; procurement regulations specifically require two separate evaluations of contracting firm's responsibility, one by contracting agency and one by Small Business Administration, and contracting agency can neither abdicate nor delegate its obligation to conduct responsibility determination. Small Business Act, § 2[8](a), 15 U.S.C.A. § 637(a). Action Service Corp. v. Garrett, 790 F. Supp. 1188, 38 Cont. Cas. Fed. (CCH) P 76347 (D.P.R. 1992). United States ☞64.45(2)

Section of the Small Business Act requiring contracting agency to accept certification of responsibility of a bidder by the Small Business Administration, and section of the Act prohibiting courts from issuing injunctions against the SBA administrator, did not preclude declaratory and injunctive relief requested by disappointed bidders on navy contract, notwithstanding claim that any injunction which would issue against contracting agency was in actuality against the SBA which certified successful bidder. Small Business Act, §§ 2[5](b)(1), 2[8](b)(7), 15 U.S.C.A. §§ 634(b)(1), 637(b)(7). Ulstein Maritime, Ltd. v. U.S., 646 F. Supp. 720, 27 Wage & Hour Cas. (BNA) 1641 (D.R.I. 1986), judgment aff'd, 833 F.2d 1052, 34 Cont. Cas. Fed. (CCH) P 75405 (1st Cir. 1987). Injunction ☞86

In reviewing a contractor's certificate of competency (COC) application, the Small Business Administration (SBA) is bound by the responsibility criteria set forth in the Federal

Acquisition Regulation (FAR), and the criteria set out in the solicitation itself. Small Business Act, § 2[8](b)(7)(A), as amended, 15 U.S.C.A. § 637(b)(7)(A). CSE Const. Co., Inc. v. U.S., 58 Fed. Cl. 230 (2003). United States ☞64.45(2)

Decision by Small Business Administration's certificate of competency (COC) review committee, that contractor seeking to haul government fuel was nonresponsible, and thus not entitled to COC, was not arbitrary and capricious; committee noted its concern that contractor had not completed installation of fuel gauges and alarms on equipment it proposed to use, that contractor had not fully implemented safety program, and that contractor had unacceptable number of oil spills. Stapp Towing Inc. v. U.S., 34 Fed. Cl. 300, 40 Cont. Cas. Fed. (CCH) P 76839 (1995). United States ☞64.45(2)

When Small Business Administration (SBA) makes responsibility determination, for purposes of deciding whether to issue Certificate of Competency (COC) to government contractor, it is not limited to deficiencies cited in referring agency's non-responsibility decision, but may consider all aspects of responsibility it considers germane. 13 C.F.R. § 125. 5(a)(1). Stapp Towing Inc. v. U.S., 34 Fed. Cl. 300, 40 Cont. Cas. Fed. (CCH) P 76839 (1995). United States ☞64.45(2)

Evidence that contractor had outstanding Internal Revenue Service (IRS) deficiency and that it omitted 1993 financial statement demonstrated that Small Business Administration (SBA) did not act arbitrarily and capriciously in failing to pursue additional information or seek clarification before making finding of nonresponsibility in certification of competency review. C & G Excavating, Inc. v. U.S., 32 Fed. Cl. 231, 39 Cont. Cas. Fed. (CCH) P 76715 (1994). United States ☞64.40(3); United States ☞64.45(2)

Small Business Administration (SBA) was under no obligation to perform site visit to evaluate contractor's financial condition, given that subject of referral was another aspect of contractor responsibility. Small Business Act, § 2[8](b)(7), 15 U.S.C.A. § 637(b)(7). C & G Excavating, Inc. v. U.S., 32 Fed. Cl. 231, 39 Cont. Cas. Fed. (CCH) P 76715 (1994). United States ☞64.45(2)

Small Business Administration (SBA) properly considered contractor's financial status in making responsibility determination, though contracting officer cited capacity as only basis for her nonresponsibility decision; SBA may consider all aspects of responsibility in making certificate of competency determination. Small Business Act, § 2[8](a)(16)(A), (b)(7), 15 U.S.C.A. § 637(a)(16)(A), (b)(7); 13 C.F.R. § 125.5(e). C & G Excavating, Inc. v. U.S., 32 Fed. Cl. 231, 39 Cont. Cas. Fed. (CCH) P 76715 (1994). United States ☞64.45(2)

Burden rests with prospective contractor to demonstrate that it satisfies criteria underlying responsibility determination in certificate of competency proceeding with Small Business Administration (SBA). C & G Excavating, Inc. v. U.S., 32 Fed. Cl. 231, 39 Cont. Cas. Fed. (CCH) P 76715 (1994). United States ☞64.15

Small Business Administration's (SBA's) review of prospective contractor's competency to perform is not limited to situation in which contract negotiations are successful and result in procuring agency proposing to SBA that program participant be awarded contract; certificate of competency program requires procuring agency negotiating with small business to refer to SBA any determination that business is not responsible to perform particular contract. Small Business Act, § 2[8](a), (b)(7)(A), as amended, 15 U.S.C.A. § 637(a), (b)(7)(A). Celtech, Inc. v. U.S., 24 Cl. Ct. 269, 37 Cont. Cas. Fed. (CCH) P 76181, 1991 WL 193295 (1991), vacated pursuant to settlement, 25 Cl. Ct. 368, 1992 WL 46122 (1992). United States ☞53(8)

Certificate of competency program, which requires procuring agency negotiating with a small business to refer to the Small Business Administration (SBA) any determination that business is not responsible to perform particular contract was not limited in applicability only to competitive procurements, and contractors could seek certificates of competency when negotiating with government agencies on noncompetitive procurements. Celtech, Inc. v. U.S., 24 Cl. Ct. 269, 37 Cont. Cas. Fed. (CCH) P 76181, 1991 WL 193295 (1991), vacated pursuant to settlement, 25 Cl. Ct. 368, 1992 WL 46122 (1992). United States ☞64.15

3 Disadvantaged businesses

Current disadvantaged business enterprise (DBE) certification programs for federal highway subcontracting meet the requirements of narrow tailoring, and thus do not violate equal protection. U.S.C.A. Const.Amend. 5; Small Business Act, §§ 2[8](a, d), 2[15](g), as amended, 15 U.S.C.A. §§ 637(a, d), 644(g); Surface Transportation and Uniform Relocation Assistance Act of 1987, §§ 1 et seq., 23 U.S.C.A. § 101 note; Intermodal Surface Transportation Efficiency Act of 1991, §§ 1 et seq., 49 U.S.C.A. § 101 note; Transportation Equity Act for the 21st Century, §§ 1 et seq., 23 U.S.C.A. § 101 note; 13 C.F.R. §§ 124.104(c)(2), 124.1014; 48 C.F.R. § 19.001; 49 C.F.R. §§ 26.65, 26.67(b). Adarand Constructors, Inc. v. Slater, 228 F.3d 1147 (10th Cir. 2000). Constitutional Law ⟨≈⟩234; Highways ⟨≈⟩113(1)

Method of certification of disadvantaged business enterprises (DBEs) presuming economic disadvantage based on membership in certain racial groups, applied to federal highway subcontracting in 1996, was not narrowly tailored, so as to satisfy equal protection, but current regulations providing for an individualized determination of economic disadvantage are narrowly tailored. U.S.C.A. Const.Amend. 5; Small Business Act, § 2[8](a, d), as amended, 15 U.S.C.A. § 637(a, d); 13 C.F.R. §§ 124.104(b)(1), 124.1001 et seq., 124.1002(a); 48 C.F.R. §§ 19.001, 19.703, 52.219-8; 49 C.F.R. § 26.67(b)(1). Adarand Constructors, Inc. v. Slater, 228 F.3d 1147 (10th Cir. 2000). Constitutional Law ⟨≈⟩215.2; Highways ⟨≈⟩113(1)

Navy as contracting agency, rather than Small Business Administration (SBA), had duty to make responsibility determination with respect to best bidder and competitive bid. Small Business Act, § 2[8](a), as amended, 15 U.S.C.A. § 637(a). Action Service Corp. v. Garrett, 797 F. Supp. 82 (D.P.R. 1992). United States ⟨≈⟩64.45(2)

Regulations requiring procuring agency to refer contractor responsibility determinations to the Small Business Administration (SBA) apply to small disadvantaged business concerns, in accordance with the certificate of competency program, which requires procuring agency negotiating with small business to refer to SBA any determination that business is not responsible to perform particular contract. Small Business Act, § 2[8](a), (b)(7)(A), as amended, 15 U.S.C.A. § 637(a), (b)(7)(A). Celtech, Inc. v. U.S., 24 Cl. Ct. 269, 37 Cont. Cas. Fed. (CCH) P 76181, 1991 WL 193295 (1991), vacated pursuant to settlement, 25 Cl. Ct. 368, 1992 WL 46122 (1992). United States ⟨≈⟩53(8)

Department of State's violation of regulation by failing to notify the Small Business Administration (SBA) of determination that disadvantaged small business was not responsible to perform typewriter repair contract prejudiced business by depriving business of opportunity to apply for certificate of competency and possibly be awarded contract, thus breaching implied contract to fairly and honestly consider business' proposal and entitling business to recovery. Small Business Act, § 2[8](a), as amended, 15 U.S.C.A. § 637(a). Celtech, Inc. v. U.S., 24 Cl. Ct. 269, 37 Cont. Cas. Fed. (CCH) P 76181, 1991 WL 193295 (1991), vacated pursuant to settlement, 25 Cl. Ct. 368, 1992 WL 46122 (1992). United States ⟨≈⟩64.15

Exception to mandatory requirement that if small business concern's offer is to be rejected because of determination of nonresponsibility, contracting officers shall refer the matter to the Small Business Administration (SBA), which will decide whether to issue certificate of competency, did not apply to Department of State's rejection of disadvantaged small business for contract based on accounting system deficiencies identified in audit; exception applies if contracting officer determines business is unqualified because it does not meet standard of being "otherwise qualified and eligible to receive award," but different subsection lists as specific responsibility requirement that prospective contractor have necessary accounting and operational controls, so exception did not apply. Celtech, Inc. v. U.S., 24 Cl. Ct. 269, 37 Cont. Cas. Fed. (CCH) P 76181, 1991 WL 193295 (1991), vacated pursuant to settlement, 25 Cl. Ct. 368, 1992 WL 46122 (1992). United States ⟨≈⟩64.15

Small business eligible for the certificate of competency program was entitled to have the Department of State notify the Small Business Administration (SBA) prior to terminating negotiations on noncompetitive procurement with business which qualified as disadvantaged small business based on accounting system deficiencies in business identified in audit; business would then have had opportunity to apply for SBA assistance in curing perceived deficiencies and might ultimately have qualified for contract award. Small Business Act, § 2[8](a), (b)(7)(A), as amended, 15 U.S.C.A. § 637(a), (b)(7)(A). Celtech, Inc. v. U.S., 24 Cl. Ct. 269, 37 Cont. Cas. Fed. (CCH) P 76181, 1991 WL 193295 (1991), vacated pursuant to settlement, 25 Cl. Ct. 368, 1992 WL 46122 (1992). United States ⟨≈⟩64.15

4 Suspension or debarment

Small Business Act and Competition in Contracting Act provisions applicable when company is being considered for contract award are inapplicable to General Services Administration (GSA) action suspending or terminating government contract. Small Business Act, § 2[8](b)(7), as amended, 15 U.S.C.A. § 637(b)(7); Federal Property and Administrative Services Act of 1949, § 303B(c), (d)(2), as amended, 41 U.S.C.A. § 253b(c), (d)(2); 48 C.F.R. § 19.602-1(a)(2)(ii). Commercial Drapery Contractors, Inc. v. U.S., 967 F. Supp. 1, 41 Cont. Cas. Fed. (CCH) P 77172 (D.D.C. 1997), judgment aff'd, 133 F.3d 1, 39 Fed. R. Serv. 3d 825 (D.C. Cir. 1998). United States ☞72.1(1)

5 Bid preparation and proposal costs

Bid protestor was entitled to award of bid preparation costs, where contracting agency and the Small Business Administration (SBA) violated applicable statutes and regulations with respect to the protestor's application for a certificate of competency (COC), to the prejudice of protestor, and where the decision to deny it a COC lacked a rational basis. 28 U.S.C.A. § 1491(b)(3). CSE Const. Co., Inc. v. U.S., 58 Fed. Cl. 230 (2003). United States ☞64.60(6)

Costs incurred by bidder in responding to a Small Business Administration (SBA) size protest and investigation for purposes of an SBA certificate of competency (COC) were not recoverable as "bid preparation and proposal costs" within meaning of the Tucker Act, where eligibility to bid was not predicated on size, and compliance with COC investigation was not a term of the bid. 28 U.S.C.A. § 1491(b)(2). Lion Raisins, Inc. v. U.S., 52 Fed. Cl. 629 (2002), subsequent determination, 57 Fed. Cl. 505 (2003). United States ☞64.60(6)

Bidder who prevailed in bid protest was not entitled to award of 5,625.00 in attorney fees incurred in the course of responding to a Small Business Administration (SBA) size protest and investigation for purposes of an SBA certificate of competency (COC), as such fees were not allowable bid preparation costs. 28 U.S.C.A. § 1491(b)(2). Lion Raisins, Inc. v. U.S., 52 Fed. Cl. 629 (2002), subsequent determination, 57 Fed. Cl. 505 (2003). United States ☞64.60(6)

Unsuccessful bidder could not recover barge clean-up costs incurred in preparation for contract to haul fuel, absent showing that Small Business Administration's (SBA) denial of certificate of competency, necessary to be awarded contract, was arbitrary and capricious. Stapp Towing Inc. v. U.S., 34 Fed. Cl. 300, 40 Cont. Cas. Fed. (CCH) P 76839 (1995). United States ☞64.60(6)

6 Past performance

Bidder who was denied a certificate of competency (COC) by the Small Business Administration (SBA) was prejudiced by SBA's violation of regulatory requirements which occurred when it failed to consider unfavorable past performance references within the context of bidder's overall work record, and when it failed to consider whether the problems bidder encountered in past performance were beyond bidder's control and whether it took appropriate corrective action; in light of SBA's statement that the unfavorable references were a "major concern," there was a substantial chance that but for the violations the SBA would have issued the COC. 48 C.F.R. § 9.104-3(b). CSE Const. Co., Inc. v. U.S., 58 Fed. Cl. 230 (2003). United States ☞64.55(1)

On review of bidder's application for a certificate of competency, the Small Business Administration (SBA) was not required to give bidder the opportunity to clarify unfavorable past performance references the SBA had collected. CSE Const. Co., Inc. v. U.S., 58 Fed. Cl. 230 (2003). United States ☞64.45(2)

Failure of the Small Business Administration (SBA), on review of bidder's application for certificate of competency (COC), to consider whether bidder's past performance problems arose from circumstances beyond its control and whether bidder took appropriate corrective action to remedy the problems constituted a violation of SBA's obligations under both the solicitation and section of the Federal Acquisition Regulation (FAR). 48 C.F.R. § 9.104-3(b). CSE Const. Co., Inc. v. U.S., 58 Fed. Cl. 230 (2003). United States ☞64.45(2)

Upon bidder's application for certificate of competency (COC) from the Small Business Administration (SBA), contracting agency was required by regulation to supply the SBA with the results of its investigation into bidder's past performance, and the SBA was required to give consideration to the information collected by the agency concerning bidder's past performance. 13 C.F.R. § 125.5(c)(1); 48 C.F.R. § 19.602-1(c). CSE Const. Co., Inc.

v. U.S., 58 Fed. Cl. 230 (2003). United States ⊕64.45(2)

Decision of the Small Business Administration (SBA) to deny bidder a certificate of competency (COC) on the basis of poor past performance lacked a rational basis, where the SBA checked only three past references from extensive list of 105 submitted by bidder, and ignored contracting agency's conclusion that bidder's past performance was "very good"; moreover, SBA did not consider whether negative comments concerning past performance stemmed from circumstances beyond bidder's control, or even whether bidder had taken appropriate corrective action in the three instances. CSE Const. Co., Inc. v. U.S., 58 Fed. Cl. 230 (2003). United States ⊕64.45(2)

In reviewing contractor's application for certificate of competency (COC), the Small Business Administration (SBA) violated section of the Federal Acquisition Regulation (FAR) charging agency evaluators to "consider the number of contracts involved and the extent of deficient performance in each contract" when making responsibility determinations, where SBA contacted only 3 of 35 project references submitted by contractor for the period since 2000 to the present. 48 C.F.R. § 9.104-3(b). CSE Const. Co., Inc. v. U.S., 58 Fed. Cl. 230 (2003). United States ⊕64.45(2)

§ 19.602-3 Resolving differences between the agency and the Small Business Administration.

(a) *COCs valued between $100,000 and $25,000,000.* (1) When disagreements arise about a concern's ability to perform, the contracting officer and the SBA shall make every effort to reach a resolution before the SBA takes final action on a COC. This shall be done through the complete exchange of information and in accordance with agency procedures. If agreement cannot be reached between the contracting officer and the SBA Area Office, the contracting officer shall request that the Area Office suspend action and refer the matter to SBA Headquarters for review. The SBA Area Office shall honor the request for a review if the contracting officer agrees to withhold award until the review process is concluded. Without an agreement to withhold award, the SBA Area Office will issue the COC in accordance with applicable SBA regulations.

(2) SBA Headquarters will furnish written notice to the procuring agency's Director, Office of Small and Disadvantaged Business Utilization (OSDBU) or other designated official (with a copy to the contracting officer) that the case file has been received and that an appeal decision may be requested by an authorized official.

(3) If the contracting agency decides to file an appeal, it must notify SBA Headquarters through its procuring agency's Director, OSDBU, or other designated official, within 10 business days (or a time period agreed upon by both agencies) that it intends to appeal the issuance of the COC.

(4) The appeal and any supporting documentation shall be filed by the procuring agency's Director, OSDBU, or other designated official, within 10 business days (or a period agreed upon by both agencies) after SBA Headquarters receives the agency's notification in accordance with paragraph (a)(3) of this subsection.

(5) The SBA Associate Administrator for Government Contracting will make a final determination, in writing, to issue or to deny the COC.

(b) *SBA Headquarters' decisions on COCs valued over $25,000,000.* (1) Prior to taking final action, SBA Headquarters will contact the contracting agency and offer it the following options:

(i) To request that the SBA suspend case processing to allow the agency to meet with SBA Headquarters personnel and review all documentation contained in the case file; or

(ii) To submit to SBA Headquarters for evaluation any information that the contracting agency believes has not been considered.

(2) After reviewing all available information, the SBA will make a final decision to either issue or deny the COC.

(c) *Reconsideration of a COC after issuance.* (1) The SBA reserves the right to reconsider its issuance of a COC, prior to contract award, if—

(i) The COC applicant submitted false information or omitted materially adverse information; or

(ii) The COC has been issued for more than 60 days (in which case the SBA may investigate the firm's current circumstances).

(2) When the SBA reconsiders and reaffirms the COC, the procedures in subsection 19.602-2 do not apply.

(3) Denial of a COC by the SBA does not preclude a contracting officer from awarding a contract to the referred concern, nor does it prevent the concern from making an offer on any other procurement.

United States Code Annotated

Additional powers, see 15 USCA § 637.

Administrative determinations, see 41 USCA § 257.

Awards or contracts, see 15 USCA § 644.

Contract goal for small disadvantaged businesses and certain institutions of higher education, see 10 USCA § 2323.

Contract requirements, see 41 USCA § 254.

Contracts, planning, solicitation, evaluation, and award procedures, see 10 USCA § 2305.

Credit for Indian contracting in meeting certain subcontracting goals for small disadvantaged businesses and certain institutions of higher education, see 10 USCA § 2323a.

Definitions, see 10 USCA § 2302, 41 USCA §§ 259, 403.

Determinations and decisions, see 10 USCA § 2310, 41 USCA § 262.

HUBZone program, see 15 USCA § 657a.

Kinds of contracts, see 10 USCA § 2306.

Planning and solicitation requirements, see 41 USCA § 253a.

Procurement data, see 41 USCA § 417a.

Procurement program for small business concerns owned and controlled by service-disabled veterans, see 15 USCA § 657f.

Notes of Decisions

In general 1

1 In general

Certificate of competency issued by Small Business Administration to successful low bidder on Navy contract for procurement of six marine thruster units would be set aside for failure to review compliance with "standard commercial product" clause in invitation for bids; Navy made no assessment of compliance despite fact that clause was part of product specification; SBA made only an after-the-fact, offhanded assessment of whether bidder met the specifications, accepting without question as evidence of "current offering for sale" a one-page flyer which described bidder's ability to produce all manner of thrust or propulsion systems. Small Business Act, § 2[8](b)(7), 15 U.S.C.A. § 637(b)(7). Ulstein Maritime, Ltd. v. U.S., 646 F. Supp. 720, 27 Wage & Hour Cas. (BNA) 1641 (D.R.I. 1986), judgment aff'd, 833 F.2d 1052, 34 Cont. Cas. Fed. (CCH) P 75405 (1st Cir. 1987). United States ☞64.60(5.1)

Decision of the Small Business Administration (SBA) to deny bidder a certificate of competency (COC) on the basis of poor past performance lacked a rational basis, where the SBA checked only three past references from extensive list of 105 submitted by bidder, and ignored contracting agency's conclusion that bidder's past performance was "very good"; moreover, SBA did not consider whether negative comments concerning past performance stemmed from circumstances beyond bidder's control, or even whether bidder had taken appropriate corrective action in the three instances. CSE Const. Co., Inc. v. U.S., 58 Fed. Cl. 230 (2003). United States ☞64.45(2)

Government contractor failed to establish that Small Business Administration (SBA) was arbitrary or capricious in denying its application for a certificate of competency (COC) with respect to its bid on solicitation for transportation by barge of reactor vessels and steam generators. CRC Marine Services, Inc. v. U.S., 41 Fed. Cl. 66, 42 Cont. Cas. Fed. (CCH) P 77310 (1998). United States ☞64.45(2)

Government contractor did not establish that its prior debarment was a significant factor in determination of the Small Business Administration (SBA) to deny contractor a certificate of competency (COC); although report of SBA official referred to history of debarment, official was not a member of committee who made decision, and committee's minutes did not mention debarment. CRC Marine Services, Inc. v. U.S., 41 Fed. Cl. 66, 42 Cont. Cas. Fed. (CCH) P 77310 (1998). United States ☞64.45(2)

When Small Business Administration (SBA) makes responsibility determination, for purposes of deciding whether to issue Certificate of Competency (COC) to government contractor, it is not limited to deficiencies cited in referring agency's non-responsibility decision, but may consider all aspects of responsibility it considers germane. 13 C.F.R. § 125. 5(a)(1). Stapp Towing Inc. v. U.S., 34 Fed. Cl. 300, 40 Cont. Cas. Fed. (CCH) P 76839 (1995). United States ☞64.45(2)

Decision by Small Business Administration's certificate of competency (COC) review committee, that contractor seeking to haul government fuel was nonresponsible, and thus not entitled to COC, was not arbitrary and capricious; committee noted its concern that contractor had not completed installation of fuel gauges and alarms on equipment it proposed to use, that contractor had not fully implemented safety program, and that contractor had unacceptable number of oil spills. Stapp Towing Inc. v. U.S., 34 Fed. Cl. 300, 40 Cont. Cas. Fed. (CCH) P 76839 (1995). United States ☞64.45(2)

§ **19.602-4 Awarding the contract.**

(a) If new information causes the contracting officer to determine that the concern referred to the SBA is actually responsible to perform the contract, and award has not already been made under paragraph (c) of this subsection, the contracting officer shall reverse the determination of nonresponsibility, notify the SBA of this action, withdraw the referral, and proceed to award the contract.

(b) The contracting officer shall award the contract to the concern in question if the SBA issues a COC after receiving the referral. An SBA-certified concern shall not be required to meet any other requirements of responsibility. SBA COC's are conclusive with respect to all elements of responsibility of prospective small business contractors.

(c) The contracting officer shall proceed with the acquisition and award the contract to another appropriately selected and responsible offeror if the SBA has not issued a COC within 15 business days (or a longer period of time agreed to with the SBA) after receiving the referral.

United States Code Annotated

Additional powers, see 15 USCA § 637.

Administrative determinations, see 41 USCA § 257.

Awards or contracts, see 15 USCA § 644.

Contract goal for small disadvantaged businesses and certain institutions of higher education, see 10 USCA § 2323.

Contract requirements, see 41 USCA § 254.

Contracts, planning, solicitation, evaluation, and award procedures, see 10 USCA § 2305.

Credit for Indian contracting in meeting certain subcontracting goals for small disadvantaged businesses and certain institutions of higher education, see 10 USCA § 2323a.

Definitions, see 10 USCA § 2302, 41 USCA §§ 259, 403.

Determinations and decisions, see 10 USCA § 2310, 41 USCA § 262.

HUBZone program, see 15 USCA § 657a.

Kinds of contracts, see 10 USCA § 2306.

Planning and solicitation requirements, see 41 USCA § 253a.

Procurement data, see 41 USCA § 417a.

Procurement program for small business concerns owned and controlled by service-disabled veterans, see 15 USCA § 657f.

Notes of Decisions

In general 1

1 In general

Government agency is not required to award contract to contractor certified with respect to capacity and credit, and it was not improper for government agency to reject defaulting contractor's bid on replacement contract, even though his bid was lowest received and he had received Small Defense Plants Administration certification. Defense Production Act of 1950, § 714(f) (1), as added in 1951, 50 U.S.C.A.Appendix, § 2163a(f) (1). U.S. v. Thompson, 168 F. Supp. 281 (N.D. W. Va. 1958), judgment aff'd, 268 F.2d 426 (4th Cir. 1959). United States ☞64.45(2).

Subpart 19.7 The Small Business Subcontracting Program

§ 19.701 Definitions.

As used in this subpart—

"Alaska Native Corporation (ANC)" means any Regional Corporation, Village Corporation, Urban Corporation, or Group Corporation organized under the laws of the State of Alaska in accordance with the Alaska Native Claims Settlement Act, as amended (43 U.S.C. 1601, et seq.) and which is considered a minority and economically disadvantaged concern under the criteria at 43 U.S.C. 1626(e)(1). This definition also includes ANC direct and indirect subsidiary corporations, joint ventures, and partnerships that meet the requirements of 43 U.S.C. 1626(e)(2).

"Commercial plan" means a subcontracting plan (including goals) that covers the offeror's fiscal year and that applies to the entire production of commercial items sold by either the entire company or a portion thereof (e.g., division, plant, or product line).

"Electronic Subcontracting Reporting System (eSRS)" means the Governmentwide, electronic, web-based system for small business subcontracting program reporting.

"Failure to make a good faith effort to comply with the subcontracting plan" means willful or intentional failure to perform in accordance with the requirements of the subcontracting plan, or willful or intentional action to frustrate the plan.

"Indian tribe" means any Indian tribe, band, group, pueblo, or community, including native villages and native groups (including corporations organized by Kenai, Juneau, Sitka, and Kodiak) as defined in the Alaska Native Claims Settlement Act (43 U.S.C.A. 1601 et seq.), that is recognized by the Federal Government as eligible for services from the Bureau of Indian Affairs in accordance with 25 U.S.C. 1452(c). This definition also includes Indian-owned economic enterprises that meet the requirements of 25 U.S.C. 1452(e).

"Individual contract plan" means a subcontracting plan that covers the entire contract period (including option periods), applies to a specific contract, and has goals that are based on the offeror's planned subcontracting in support of the specific contract, except that indirect costs incurred for common or joint purposes may be allocated on a prorated basis to the contract.

"Master plan" means a subcontracting plan that contains all the required elements of an individual contract plan, except goals, and may be incorporated into individual contract plans, provided the master plan has been approved.

"Subcontract" means any agreement (other than one involving an employer-employee relationship) entered into by a Government prime contractor or subcontractor calling for supplies and/or services required for performance of the contract, contract modification, or subcontract.

United States Code Annotated

Additional powers, see 15 USCA § 637.

Administrative determinations, see 41 USCA § 257.

Awards or contracts, see 15 USCA § 644.

Contract goal for small disadvantaged businesses and certain institutions of higher education, see 10 USCA § 2323.

Contract requirements, see 41 USCA § 254.

Contracts, planning, solicitation, evaluation, and award procedures, see 10 USCA § 2305.

Credit for Indian contracting in meeting certain subcontracting goals for small disadvantaged businesses and certain institutions of higher education, see 10 USCA § 2323a.

Definitions, see 10 USCA § 2302, 41 USCA §§ 259, 403.

Determinations and decisions, see 10 USCA § 2310, 41 USCA § 262.

HUBZone program, see 15 USCA § 657a.

Kinds of contracts, see 10 USCA § 2306.

Planning and solicitation requirements, see 41 USCA § 253a.

Procurement data, see 41 USCA § 417a.

Procurement program for small business concerns owned and controlled by service-disabled veterans, see 15 USCA § 657f.

§ 19.702 Statutory requirements.

Any contractor receiving a contract for more than the simplified acquisition threshold must agree in the contract that small business, veteran-owned small business, service-disabled veteran-owned small business, HUBZone small business, small disadvantaged business, and women-owned small business concerns will have the maximum practicable opportunity to participate in contract performance consistent with its efficient performance. It is further the policy of the United States that its prime contractors establish procedures to ensure the timely payment of amounts due pursuant to the terms of their subcontracts with small business, veteran-owned small business, service-disabled veteran-owned small business, HUBZone small business, small disadvantaged business, and women-owned small business concerns.

(a) Except as stated in paragraph (b) of this section, Section 8(d) of the Small Business Act (15 U.S.C. 637(d)) imposes the following requirements regarding subcontracting with small businesses and small business subcontracting plans:

(1) In negotiated acquisitions, each solicitation of offers to perform a contract or contract modification, that individually is expected to exceed $700,000 ($1.5 million for construction) and that has subcontracting possibilities, shall require the apparently successful offeror to submit an acceptable subcontracting plan. If the apparently successful offeror fails to negotiate a subcontracting plan acceptable to the contracting officer within the time limit prescribed by the contracting officer, the offeror will be ineligible for award.

(2) In sealed bidding acquisitions, each invitation for bids to perform a contract or contract modification, that individually is expected to exceed $700,000 ($1.5 million for construction) and that has subcontracting possibilities, shall require the bidder selected for award to submit a subcontracting plan. If the selected bidder fails to submit a plan within the time limit prescribed by the contracting officer, the bidder will be ineligible for award.

(b) Subcontracting plans (see paragraphs (a)(1) and (2) of this section) are not required—

(1) From small business concerns;

(2) For personal services contracts;

(3) For contracts or contract modifications that will be performed entirely outside of the United States and its outlying areas; or

(4) For modifications to contracts within the general scope of the contract that do not contain the clause at 52.219-8, Utilization of Small Business Concerns (or equivalent prior clauses; e.g., contracts awarded before the enactment of Public Law 95-507).

(c) As stated in 15 U.S.C. 637(d)(8), any contractor or subcontractor failing to comply in good faith with the requirements of the subcontracting plan is in material breach of its contract. Further, 15 U.S.C. 637(d)(4)(F) directs that a contractor's failure to make a good faith effort to comply with the requirements of the subcontracting plan shall result in the imposition of liquidated damages.

(d) As authorized by 15 U.S.C. 637(d)(11), certain costs incurred by a mentor firm in providing developmental assistance to a protégé firm under the Department of Defense Pilot Mentor-Protégé Program, may be credited as if they were subcontract awards to a protégé firm for the purpose of determining whether the mentor firm attains the applicable goals under any subcontracting plan entered into with any executive agency. However, the mentor-protégé agreement must have been approved by the Director, Small Business Programs of the cognizant DoD military department or defense agency, before developmental assistance costs may be credited against subcontract goals. A list of approved agreements may be obtained at http://www.acq.osd.mil/osbp/mentor_protege/.

United States Code Annotated

Additional powers, see 15 USCA § 637.

Administrative determinations, see 41 USCA § 257.

Awards or contracts, see 15 USCA § 644.

Contract goal for small disadvantaged businesses and certain institutions of higher education, see 10 USCA § 2323.

Contract requirements, see 41 USCA § 254.

Contracts, planning, solicitation, evaluation, and award procedures, see 10 USCA § 2305.

Credit for Indian contracting in meeting certain subcontracting goals for small disadvantaged businesses and certain institutions of higher education, see 10 USCA § 2323a.

Definitions, see 10 USCA § 2302, 41 USCA §§ 259, 403.

Determinations and decisions, see 10 USCA § 2310, 41 USCA § 262.

HUBZone program, see 15 USCA § 657a.

Kinds of contracts, see 10 USCA § 2306.

Planning and solicitation requirements, see 41 USCA § 253a.

Procurement data, see 41 USCA § 417a.

Procurement program for small business concerns owned and controlled by service-disabled veterans, see 15 USCA § 657f.

Notes of Decisions

In general 1
Disadvantaged businesses 2
Revised proposals 3

1 In general

District court lacked jurisdiction over subsubcontractors' action alleging that Small Business Administration had breached its statutory, regulatory, and fiduciary duties of care and fair dealing by awarding subcontract to minority contractor without determining acceptability of proposed sureties and without determining that subcontractor was capable of successfully performing and completing contract, where subsubcontractors alleged duty sounding in tort, but subsubcontractors had not complied with Federal Tort Claims Act. 28 U.S.C.A. § 2671 et seq.J.C. Driskill, Inc. v. Abdnor, 901 F.2d 383, 36 Cont. Cas. Fed. (CCH) P 75843 (4th Cir. 1990). United States ⟋127(2)

Even if a showing of "deliberate indifference" was sufficient to prove intentional discrimination in the context of civil rights statute addressing racial discrimination in contractual relationships, defendant's alleged violation of federal regulations regarding minority business participation in federal contracts by, for example, failing to file certain reports, by failing to achieve its 5% minority participation goal, or by setting a 5% minority participation goal while knowing that such a goal would be impossible to achieve, would not support an inference of racial animus or intentional discrimination against African-Americans contractors in general or plaintiffs in particular. 42 U.S.C.A. § 1981; 48 C.F.R. § 19.701PAS Communications, Inc. v. Sprint Corp., 139 F. Supp. 2d 1149 (D. Kan. 2001). Civil Rights ⟋1406

Bidder's failure to include a subcontracting plan in its proposal did not render it nonresponsive, where solicitation was ambiguous with respect to whether subcontracting plan had to be submitted with proposal as indicated in attachment or whether subcontracting plan was due "upon request by the Contracting Officer," as provided in addenda to solicitation; ambiguity had to be resolved in favor of addenda under clause setting forth order of preference in event of inconsistencies within solicitation. Consolidated Engineering Services, Inc. v. U.S., 64 Fed. Cl. 617 (2005). United States ⟋64.30

Case challenging public utility's alleged noncompliance with minority subcontracting requirements of Small Business Act was not mooted when minority subcontracting plan was adopted by utility after plaintiff had filed complaint; question remained whether there were any consequences flowing to third parties due to utility's past failure to comply. Small Business Act, §§ 2[2], 2[8](c), as amended, 15 U.S.C.A. §§ 631, 637(c). Jordan v. Public Service Com'n, 622 A.2d 1106, 148 Pub. Util. Rep. 4th (PUR) 112 (D.C. 1993). Electricity ⟋1

Remand was required for Public Service Commission (PSC) to determine, in light of its own precedents, whether it had authority to entertain complaint challenging utility's alleged noncompliance with minority subcontractor provisions of Small Business Act. Small Business Act, § 2[8](c), (c)(4)(B), as amended, 15 U.S.C.A. § 637(c), (c)(4)(B); D.C.Code 1981, § 43-503. Jordan v. Public Service Com'n, 622 A.2d 1106, 148 Pub. Util. Rep. 4th (PUR) 112 (D.C. 1993). Electricity ⬤1

Fact that public utility may have in good faith believed that it was not subject to minority subcontracting requirements of Small Business Act did not mean that those requirements could not be enforced against public utility. Small Business Act, §§ 2[2], 2[8](c), as amended, 15 U.S.C.A. §§ 631, 637(c). Jordan v. Public Service Com'n, 622 A.2d 1106, 148 Pub. Util. Rep. 4th (PUR) 112 (D.C. 1993). Electricity ⬤1

2 Disadvantaged businesses

Subcontractor that challenged subcontractor compensation clause of government highway contract, offering financial incentives to prime contractor for hiring disadvantaged subcontractors was not required to demonstrate that it had been, or would be, low bidder on government contract to have standing to challenge clause on equal protection grounds. (Per opinion of Justice O'Connor, with three Justices concurring and one Justice concurring in part and concurring in judgment.) U.S.C.A. Const.Amend. 5; Small Business Act, § 2[8](d) (2, 3), 15 U.S.C.A. § 637(d)(2, 3). Adarand Constructors, Inc. v. Pena, 515 U.S. 200, 115 S. Ct. 2097, 132 L. Ed. 2d 158, 67 Fair Empl. Prac. Cas. (BNA) 1828, 40 Cont. Cas. Fed. (CCH) P 76756, 66 Empl. Prac. Dec. (CCH) P 43556 (1995). Constitutional Law ⬤42.2(2)

Subcontractor that was not awarded guardrail portion of federal highway contract as result of contract's subcontractor compensation clause, offering financial incentives to prime contractor for hiring disadvantaged subcontractor, had standing to seek forward-looking declaratory and injunctive relief against future use of such compensation clauses on equal protection grounds; evidence indicated that government let contracts involving guardrail work that contained such clauses at least once per year in state, that subcontractor was likely to bid on each such contracts, and was required to compete for such contracts against small disadvantaged businesses. (Per opinion of Justice O'Connor, with three Justices concurring and one Justice concurring in part and concurring in judgment.) U.S.C.A. Const.Amend. 5; Small Business Act, § 2[8](d)(2, 3), 15 U.S.C.A. § 637(d)(2, 3). Adarand Constructors, Inc. v. Pena, 515 U.S. 200, 115 S. Ct. 2097, 132 L. Ed. 2d 158, 67 Fair Empl. Prac. Cas. (BNA) 1828, 40 Cont. Cas. Fed. (CCH) P 76756, 66 Empl. Prac. Dec. (CCH) P 43556 (1995). Constitutional Law ⬤42.2(2)

Remand was required to determine whether subcontractor compensation clauses in federal highway contracts, offering financial incentives to prime contractor for hiring disadvantaged subcontractors, with presumption that minority-owned subcontractors were disadvantaged, served compelling governmental interest, as required by strict scrutiny equal protection test. (Per opinion of Justice O'Connor, with three Justices concurring and one Justice concurring in part and concurring in judgment.) Small Business Act, § 2[8](d)(2, 3), 15 U.S.C.A. § 637(d)(2, 3); Surface Transportation and Uniform Relocation Assistance Act of 1987, § 106(c)(1), 23 U.S.C.A. § 101 note; 13 C.F.R. § 124.106(a), (b)(1); 48 C.F.R. § 19. 703(a)(2); 49 C.F.R. § 23.62; 49 C.F.R. Part 23, Subpart D, App. C. Adarand Constructors, Inc. v. Pena, 515 U.S. 200, 115 S. Ct. 2097, 132 L. Ed. 2d 158, 67 Fair Empl. Prac. Cas. (BNA) 1828, 40 Cont. Cas. Fed. (CCH) P 76756, 66 Empl. Prac. Dec. (CCH) P 43556 (1995). Federal Courts ⬤462

To extent subcontractor compensation program, offering financial incentives to prime contractors on government projects for hiring disadvantaged subcontractors, was based on disadvantage, not race, it was subject to relaxed equal protection scrutiny. (Per opinion of Justice O'Connor, with three Justices concurring and one Justice concurring in part and concurring in judgment.) U.S.C.A. Const.Amend. 5; Small Business Act, § 2[8](d)(2, 3), 15 U.S.C.A. § 637(d)(2, 3). Adarand Constructors, Inc. v. Pena, 515 U.S. 200, 115 S. Ct. 2097, 132 L. Ed. 2d 158, 67 Fair Empl. Prac. Cas. (BNA) 1828, 40 Cont. Cas. Fed. (CCH) P 76756, 66 Empl. Prac. Dec. (CCH) P 43556 (1995). Constitutional Law ⬤219.1

Defense Logistics Agency did not show that information compiled by government contractors regarding their compliance with Small Business Act's goals for subcontracting with small disadvantaged business (SDB) was privileged or confidential commercial information within Exemption 4 to Freedom of Information Act (FOIA) where data would have provided little, if any, help to competitors attempting to estimate and undercut contractor's bids. 5

U.S.C.A. § 552(b)(4). GC Micro Corp. v. Defense Logistics Agency, 33 F.3d 1109, 39 Cont. Cas. Fed. (CCH) P 76701 (9th Cir. 1994). Records ☞59

For purposes of strict scrutiny equal protection test, Congress had compelling governmental interest in federal program allowing subcontractor compensation clauses in federal highway contracts which offered financial incentives to prime contractor for hiring disadvantaged subcontractors with presumption that minority-owned subcontractors were disadvantaged, and findings of discriminatory barriers in federal construction industry nationwide were sufficient to show compelling interest, despite fact that Congress had not made particularized findings of discrimination in highway industry of particular city or state. U.S.C.A. Const.Amend. 5; Small Business Act, § 2[8](d)(2, 3), 15 U.S.C.A. § 637(d)(2, 3); Surface Transportation and Uniform Relocation Assistance Act of 1987, § 106(c)(1), 23 U.S.C.A. § 101 note; 13 C.F.R. § 124.106(a), (b)(1); 48 C.F.R. § 19.703(a)(2); 49 C.F.R. § 23.62; 49 C.F.R. Part 23, Subpart D, App. C. Adarand Constructors, Inc. v. Pena, 965 F. Supp. 1556, 41 Cont. Cas. Fed. (CCH) P 77118 (D. Colo. 1997), vacated, 169 F.3d 1292 (10th Cir. 1999), cert. granted, judgment rev'd, 528 U.S. 216, 120 S. Ct. 722, 145 L. Ed. 2d 650, 81 Fair Empl. Prac. Cas. (BNA) 1016, 77 Empl. Prac. Dec. (CCH) P 46195 (2000) and rev'd, 228 F.3d 1147 (10th Cir. 2000) (On final reversal, the circuit court said that "[t]he purpose of strict scrutiny of race-based measures, in determining whether such measures violate equal protection principles, is to 'smoke out' illegitimate uses of race by assuring that the legislative body is pursuing a goal important enough to warrant the use of a highly suspect tool.") Constitutional Law ☞215.2; Highways ☞97.5

Statutes and regulations implementing federal program allowing subcontractor compensation clauses in federal highway contracts which offered financial incentives to prime contractor for hiring disadvantaged subcontractors, with presumption that minority-owned subcontractors were disadvantaged, created racial classification that was not narrowly tailored to goal of overcoming discriminatory barriers in federal construction industry nationwide, and, thus, program as well as statutes and regulations implementing program violated equal protection clause under strict scrutiny test; statutes and regulations governing program were both over inclusive, in that they presumed that all those in named minority groups were economically or socially challenged, and under inclusive as they excluded certain groups whose members are economically and socially disadvantaged. U.S.C.A. Const.Amend. 5; Small Business Act, §§ 2[8](d)(2, 3), 2[15](g), 15 U.S.C.A. §§ 637(d) (2, 3), 644(g); Surface Transportation and Uniform Relocation Assistance Act of 1987, § 106(c)(1), 23 U.S.C.A. § 101 note; 13 C.F.R. § 124.106(a), (b)(1); 48 C.F.R. § 19.703(a)(2); 49 C.F.R. § 23.62; 49 C.F.R. Part 23, Subpart D, App. C.Adarand Constructors, Inc. v. Pena, 965 F. Supp. 1556, 41 Cont. Cas. Fed. (CCH) P 77118 (D. Colo. 1997), vacated, 169 F.3d 1292 (10th Cir. 1999), cert. granted, judgment rev'd, 528 U.S. 216, 120 S. Ct. 722, 145 L. Ed. 2d 650, 81 Fair Empl. Prac. Cas. (BNA) 1016, 77 Empl. Prac. Dec. (CCH) P 46195 (2000) and rev'd, 228 F.3d 1147 (10th Cir. 2000) (The 10th Circuit finally found that the programs originally at issue were "insufficiently narrowly tailored" but that the defects were remedied after the fact and were narrowly tailored.) Constitutional Law ☞215.2; Highways ☞97.5; Highways ☞113(1)

3 Revised proposals

Contracting agency's request for a subcontracting plan from successful offeror did not constitute "discussions" or require that revised proposals be solicited from all offerors; agency's action of requesting offeror's subcontracting plan, and negotiating with it to ensure that the subcontracting plan was acceptable, was required by section of the Federal Acquisition Regulation (FAR), and such negotiations were patently not of the type that would permit other offerors to revise their proposals. Consolidated Engineering Services, Inc. v. U.S., 64 Fed. Cl. 617 (2005). United States ☞64.40(1)

§ 19.703 Eligibility requirements for participating in the program.

(a) Except as provided in paragraph (c) of this section, to be eligible as a subcontractor under the program, a concern must represent itself as a small business, veteran-owned small business, service-disabled veteran-owned small business, HUBZone small business, small disadvantaged business, or women-owned small business concern.

(1) To represent itself as a small business, veteran-owned small business, service-disabled veteran-owned small business, HUBZone small business, small disadvantaged business, or women-owned small business concern, a concern must meet the appropriate

definition (see 2.101 and 19.001).

(2) In connection with a subcontract, the contracting officer or the SBA may protest the disadvantaged status of a proposed subcontractor. Such protests will be processed in accordance with 13 CFR 124.1007 through 124.1014. Other interested parties may submit information to the contracting officer or the SBA in an effort to persuade the contracting officer or the SBA to initiate a protest. Such protests, in order to be considered timely, must be submitted to the SBA prior to completion of performance by the intended subcontractor.

(b) A contractor acting in good faith may rely on the written representation of its subcontractor regarding the subcontractor's status as a small business, small disadvantaged business, veteran-owned small business, service-disabled veteran-owned small business, or a women-owned small business concern. The contractor, the contracting officer, or any other interested party can challenge a subcontractor's size status representation by filing a protest, in accordance with 13 CFR 121.1001 through 121.1008. Protests challenging a subcontractor's small disadvantaged business representation must be filed in accordance with 13 CFR 124.1007 through 124.1014.

(c) (1) In accordance with 43 U.S.C. 1626, the following procedures apply:

(i) Subcontracts awarded to an ANC or Indian tribe shall be counted towards the subcontracting goals for small business and small disadvantaged business (SDB) concerns, regardless of the size or Small Business Administration certification status of the ANC or Indian tribe.

(ii) Where one or more subcontractors are in the subcontract tier between the prime contractor and the ANC or Indian tribe, the ANC or Indian tribe shall designate the appropriate contractor(s) to count the subcontract towards its small business and small disadvantaged business subcontracting goals.

(A) In most cases, the appropriate contractor is the contractor that awarded the subcontract to the ANC or Indian tribe.

(B) If the ANC or Indian tribe designates more than one contractor to count the subcontract toward its goals, the ANC or Indian tribe shall designate only a portion of the total subcontract award to each contractor. The sum of the amounts designated to various contractors cannot exceed the total value of the subcontract.

(C) The ANC or Indian tribe shall give a copy of the written designation to the contracting officer, the prime contractor, and the subcontractors in between the prime contractor and the ANC or Indian tribe within 30 days of the date of the subcontract award.

(D) If the contracting officer does not receive a copy of the ANC's or the Indian tribe's written designation within 30 days of the subcontract award, the contractor that awarded the subcontract to the ANC or Indian tribe will be considered the designated contractor.

(2) A contractor acting in good faith may rely on the written representation of an ANC or an Indian tribe as to the status of the ANC or Indian tribe unless an interested party challenges its status or the contracting officer has independent reason to question its status. In the event of a challenge of a representation of an ANC or Indian tribe, the interested parties shall follow the procedures at 26.103(b) through (e).

(d) (1) The contractor shall confirm that a subcontractor representing itself as a HUBZone small business concern is certified by SBA as a HUBZone small business concern by accessing the System for Award Management database or by contacting the SBA. Options for contacting the SBA include—

(i) HUBZone small business database search application web page at http://dsbs.sba. gov/dsbs/dsp_searchhubzone.cfm or www.sba.gov/hubzone;

(ii) In writing to the—

Director/HUB,
U.S. Small Business Administration,
409 3rd Street, SW.,
Washington DC 20416; or

(iii) E-mail at mailto:hubzone@sba.gov.

(2) Protests challenging HUBZone small business concern size status must be filed in

accordance with 13 CFR 121.411.

§ 19.704 Subcontracting plan requirements.

(a) Each subcontracting plan required under 19.702(a)(1) and (2) must include—

(1) Separate percentage goals for using small business (including ANCs and Indian tribes), veteran-owned small business, service-disabled veteran-owned small business, HUBZone small business, small disadvantaged business (including ANCs and Indian tribes) and women-owned small business concerns as subcontractors;

(2) A statement of the total dollars planned to be subcontracted and a statement of the total dollars planned to be subcontracted to small business (including ANCs and Indian tribes), veteran-owned small business, service-disabled veteran-owned small business, HUBZone small business, small disadvantaged business (including ANCs and Indian tribes) and women-owned small business concerns;

(3) A description of the principal types of supplies and services to be subcontracted and an identification of types planned for subcontracting to small business (including ANCs and Indian tribes), veteran-owned small business, service-disabled veteran-owned small business, HUBZone small business, small disadvantaged business (including ANCs and Indian tribes), and women-owned small business concerns;

(4) A description of the method used to develop the subcontracting goals;

(5) A description of the method used to identify potential sources for solicitation purposes;

(6) A statement as to whether or not the offeror included indirect costs in establishing subcontracting goals, and a description of the method used to determine the proportionate share of indirect costs to be incurred with small business (including ANCs and Indian tribes), veteran-owned small business, service-disabled veteran-owned small business, HUBZone small business, small disadvantaged business (including ANCs and Indian tribes), and women-owned small business concerns;

(7) The name of an individual employed by the offeror who will administer the offeror's subcontracting program, and a description of the duties of the individual;

(8) A description of the efforts the offeror will make to ensure that small business, veteran-owned small business, service-disabled veteran-owned small business, HUBZone small business, small disadvantaged business, and women-owned small business concerns have an equitable opportunity to compete for subcontracts;

(9) Assurances that the offeror will include the clause at 52.219-8, Utilization of Small Business Concerns (see 19.708(a)), in all subcontracts that offer further subcon- tracting opportunities, and that the offeror will require all subcontractors (except small business concerns) that receive subcontracts in excess of $700,000 ($1.5 million for construction) to adopt a plan that complies with the requirements of the clause at 52.219-9, Small Business Subcontracting Plan (see 19.708(b));

(10) Assurances that the offeror will—

(i) Cooperate in any studies or surveys as may be required;

(ii) Submit periodic reports so that the Government can determine the extent of compliance by the offeror with the subcontracting plan;

(iii) Submit the Individual Subcontract Report (ISR), and the Summary Subcontract Report (SSR) using the Electronic Subcontracting Reporting System (eSRS) (http://www.esrs.gov), following the instructions in the eSRS;

(A) The ISR shall be submitted semi-annually during contract performance for the periods ending March 31 and September 30. A report is also required for each contract within 30 days of contract completion. Reports are due 30 days after the close of each reporting period, unless otherwise directed by the contracting officer. Reports are required when due, regardless of whether there has been any subcontracting activity since the inception of the contract or the previous reporting period.

(B) The SSR shall be submitted as follows: For DoD and NASA, the report shall be submitted semi-annually for the six months ending March 31 and the twelve months ending September 30. For civilian agencies, except NASA, it shall be submitted annually for the twelve-month period ending September 30. Reports are due 30 days after the close of each reporting period.

(iv) Ensure that its subcontractors with subcontracting plans agree to submit the ISR and/or the SSR using the eSRS;

(v) Provide its prime contract number, its DUNS number, and the e-mail address of the offeror's official responsible for acknowledging receipt of or rejecting the ISRs to all first-tier subcontractors with subcontracting plans so they can enter this information into the eSRS when submitting their ISRs; and

(vi) Require that each subcontractor with a subcontracting plan provide the prime contract number, its own DUNS number, and the e-mail address of the subcontractor's official responsible for acknowledging receipt of or rejecting the ISRs, to its subcontractors with subcontracting plans.

(11) A description of the types of records that will be maintained concerning procedures adopted to comply with the requirements and goals in the plan, including establishing source lists; and a description of the offeror's efforts to locate small business, veteran-owned small business, service-disabled veteran-owned small business, HUBZone small business, small disadvantaged business, and women-owned small business concerns and to award subcontracts to them.

(b) Contractors may establish, on a plant or division-wide basis, a master plan (see 19.701) that contains all the elements required by the clause at 52.219-9, Small Business Subcontracting Plan, except goals. Master plans shall be effective for a 3-year period after approval by the contracting officer; however, it is incumbent upon contractors to maintain and update master plans. Changes required to update master plans are not effective until approved by the contracting officer. A master plan, when incorporated in an individual plan, shall apply to that contract throughout the life of the contract.

(c) For multiyear contracts or contracts containing options, the cumulative value of the basic contract and all options is considered in determining whether a subcontracting plan is necessary (see 19.705-2(a)). If a plan is necessary and the offeror is submitting an individual contract plan, the plan shall contain all the elements required by paragraph (a) of this section and shall contain separate statements and goals for the basic contract and for each option.

(d) A commercial plan (as defined in 19.701) is the preferred type of subcontracting plan for contractors furnishing commercial items. Once a contractor's commercial plan has been approved, the Government shall not require another subcontracting plan from the same contractor while the plan remains in effect, as long as the product or service being provided by the contractor continues to meet the definition of a commercial item. The contractor shall—

(1) Submit the commercial plan to either the first contracting officer awarding a contract subject to the plan during the contractor's fiscal year, or, if the contractor has ongoing contracts with commercial plans, to the contracting officer responsible for the contract with the latest completion date. The contracting officer shall negotiate the commercial plan for the Government. The approved commercial plan shall remain in effect during the contractor's fiscal year for all Government contracts in effect during that period;

(2) Submit a new commercial plan, 30 working days before the end of the Contractor's fiscal year, to the contracting officer responsible for the uncompleted Government contract with the latest completion date. The contractor must provide to each contracting officer responsible for an ongoing contract subject to the plan, the identity of the contracting officer that will be negotiating the new plan;

(3) When the new commercial plan is approved, provide a copy of the approved plan to each contracting officer responsible for an ongoing contract that is subject to the plan; and

(4) Comply with the reporting requirements stated in paragraph (a)(10) of this section by submitting one SSR in eSRS, for all contracts covered by its commercial plan. This report will be acknowledged or rejected in eSRS by the contracting officer who approved the plan. The report shall be submitted within 30 days after the end of the Government's fiscal year.

United States Code Annotated

Additional powers, see 15 USCA § 637.

Administrative determinations, see 41 USCA § 257.

Awards or contracts, see 15 USCA § 644.

Contract goal for small disadvantaged businesses and certain institutions of higher education, see 10 USCA § 2323.

Contract requirements, see 41 USCA § 254.

Contracts, planning, solicitation, evaluation, and award procedures, see 10 USCA § 2305.

Credit for Indian contracting in meeting certain subcontracting goals for small disadvantaged businesses and certain institutions of higher education, see 10 USCA § 2323a.

Definitions, see 10 USCA § 2302, 41 USCA §§ 259, 403.

Determinations and decisions, see 10 USCA § 2310, 41 USCA § 262.

HUBZone program, see 15 USCA § 657a.

Kinds of contracts, see 10 USCA § 2306.

Planning and solicitation requirements, see 41 USCA § 253a.

Procurement data, see 41 USCA § 417a.

Procurement program for small business concerns owned and controlled by service-disabled veterans, see 15 USCA § 657f.

Notes of Decisions

Subcontracting, generally 1
Subcontracting plans 2

1 Subcontracting, generally

District court lacked jurisdiction over subsubcontractors' action alleging that Small Business Administration had breached its statutory, regulatory, and fiduciary duties of care and fair dealing by awarding subcontract to minority contractor without determining acceptability of proposed sureties and without determining that subcontractor was capable of successfully performing and completing contract, where subsubcontractors alleged duty sounding in tort, but subsubcontractors had not complied with Federal Tort Claims Act. 28 U.S.C.A. § 2671 et seq. J.C. Driskill, Inc. v. Abdnor, 901 F.2d 383, 36 Cont. Cas. Fed. (CCH) P 75843 (4th Cir. 1990). United States ⚖127(2)

Even if a showing of "deliberate indifference" was sufficient to prove intentional discrimination in the context of civil rights statute addressing racial discrimination in contractual relationships, defendant's alleged violation of federal regulations regarding minority business participation in federal contracts by, for example, failing to file certain reports, by failing to achieve its 5% minority participation goal, or by setting a 5% minority participation goal while knowing that such a goal would be impossible to achieve, would not support an inference of racial animus or intentional discrimination against African-Americans contractors in general or plaintiffs in particular. 42 U.S.C.A. § 1981; 48 C.F.R. § 19.701PAS Communications, Inc. v. Sprint Corp., 139 F. Supp. 2d 1149 (D. Kan. 2001). Civil Rights ⚖1406

Case challenging public utility's alleged noncompliance with minority subcontracting requirements of Small Business Act was not mooted when minority subcontracting plan was adopted by utility after plaintiff had filed complaint; question remained whether there were any consequences flowing to third parties due to utility's past failure to comply. Small Business Act, §§ 2[2], 2[8](c), as amended, 15 U.S.C.A. §§ 631, 637(c). Jordan v. Public Service Com'n, 622 A.2d 1106, 148 Pub. Util. Rep. 4th (PUR) 112 (D.C. 1993). Electricity ⚖1

Remand was required for Public Service Commission (PSC) to determine, in light of its own precedents, whether it had authority to entertain complaint challenging utility's alleged noncompliance with minority subcontractor provisions of Small Business Act. Small Business Act, § 2[8](c), (c)(4)(B), as amended, 15 U.S.C.A. § 637(c), (c)(4)(B); D.C.Code 1981, § 43-503. Jordan v. Public Service Com'n, 622 A.2d 1106, 148 Pub. Util. Rep. 4th (PUR) 112 (D.C. 1993). Electricity ⚖1

Fact that public utility may have in good faith believed that it was not subject to minority subcontracting requirements of Small Business Act did not mean that those requirements could not be enforced against public utility. Small Business Act, §§ 2[2], 2[8](c), as amended, 15 U.S.C.A. §§ 631, 637(c). Jordan v. Public Service Com'n, 622 A.2d 1106, 148 Pub. Util. Rep. 4th (PUR) 112 (D.C. 1993). Electricity ⚖1

2 Subcontracting plans

Where a solicitation states a small business participation goal of 40%, such a goal is not an unachievable mandatory condition, notwithstanding the provision stating that, "[i]f the apparently successful offeror fails to negotiate a subcontracting plan acceptable to the contracting officer before contract award, the offeror will be ineligible for award." This provision did not speak in terms of failing to meet any bright-line threshold and fell far short of indicating that any proposal falling short of this 40% goal could be rejected as nonresponsive. FirstLine Transp. Sec., Inc. v. U.S., 107 Fed.Cl. 189 (2012)

Where a solicitation states a small business participation goal of 40%, compliance may be measured as a percentage of total contract price, even though Federal Acquisition Regulation (FAR) applies the percentage against the total subcontracting dollars. Nothing in the FAR prohibits a procuring agency from setting a small business goal expressed as percentage of total contract price, and because offerors knew total contract dollars that they intended to subcontract, their small business goals could be readily expressed in terms of both total contracting dollars and subcontracting dollars. FirstLine Transp. Sec., Inc. v. U.S., 107 Fed.Cl. 189 (2012)

Bidder's failure to include a subcontracting plan in its proposal did not render it nonresponsive, where solicitation was ambiguous with respect to whether subcontracting plan had to be submitted with proposal as indicated in attachment or whether subcontracting plan was due "upon request by the Contracting Officer," as provided in addenda to solicitation; ambiguity had to be resolved in favor of addenda under clause setting forth order of preference in event of inconsistencies within solicitation. Consolidated Engineering Services, Inc. v. U.S., 64 Fed.Cl. 617 (2005)

In a negotiated procurement that provided for the evaluation of small business subcontracting plans on a pass/fail basis, the rejection of the protester's proposal as technically unacceptable on the basis of the acceptability of its small business subcontracting plan was unreasonable. MANCON, B-405663, 2012 CPD ¶ 68 (Comp.Gen. 2012)

GAO denied protest that agency's evaluation of protester's subcontracting plan was unreasonable. The protester did not explain what work would be performed by its proposed small business subcontractors and the evaluators could not, therefore, assess the feasibility of the subcontracting plan. GAO found that, without any information as to the types of services to be subcontracted, the agency reasonably concluded that it could not determine whether the protester's small business goals were realistic. L-3 STRATIS, B-404865, 2011 CPD ¶ 119 (Comp.Gen. 2011)

Protest of agency's determination that the protester failed to comply with the solicitation's subcontracting plan requirement was denied because the protester failed to include a small business subcontracting plan with its proposal. The protester's assertion that the relevant information was scattered throughout the proposal was rejected by GAO. It is an offeror's responsibility to submit a well-written proposal, with adequately detailed information which clearly demonstrates compliance with the solicitation requirements and allows a meaningful review by the procuring agency. Having failed to submit the small business subcontracting plan, the protester cannot reasonably require the agency to assemble the plan itself from various disparate portions of the proposal. eTouch Federal Systems, LLC B-404894.3, 2011 CPD ¶ 160, 2011 WL 3609466 (Comp.Gen. 2011)

The agency reasonably determined that the protester's subcontracting plan was unacceptable because the plan did not meet the total small business subcontracting percentages listed as "goals" in the solicitation. The agency further determined that the protester did not provide an adequate supporting rationale for its proposed total small business percentage and for the lower HUBZone, WOSB, SDB, VOSB, and SDVOSB percentages. As a result, the agency's conclusion that the protester's proposal was technically unacceptable was reasonable. Granite Construction Co., B-400706, 2009 CPD ¶ 20 (Comp.Gen. 2009)

§ 19.705 Responsibilities of the contracting officer under the subcontracting assistance program.

§ 19.705-1 General support of the program.
The contracting officer may encourage the development of increased subcontracting opportunities in negotiated acquisition by providing monetary incentives such as payments based on actual subcontracting achievement or award-fee contracting (see the clause at 52.219-10, Incentive Subcontracting Program, and 19.708(c)). When using any contractual

incentive provision based upon rewarding the contractor monetarily for exceeding goals in the subcontracting plan, the contracting officer must ensure that (a) the goals are realistic and (b) any rewards for exceeding the goals are commensurate with the efforts the contractor would not have otherwise expended. Incentive provisions should normally be negotiated after reaching final agreement with the contractor on the subcontracting plan.

United States Code Annotated

Additional powers, see 15 USCA § 637.

Administrative determinations, see 41 USCA § 257.

Awards or contracts, see 15 USCA § 644.

Contract goal for small disadvantaged businesses and certain institutions of higher education, see 10 USCA § 2323.

Contract requirements, see 41 USCA § 254.

Contracts, planning, solicitation, evaluation, and award procedures, see 10 USCA § 2305.

Credit for Indian contracting in meeting certain subcontracting goals for small disadvantaged businesses and certain institutions of higher education, see 10 USCA § 2323a.

Definitions, see 10 USCA § 2302, 41 USCA §§ 259, 403.

Determinations and decisions, see 10 USCA § 2310, 41 USCA § 262.

HUBZone program, see 15 USCA § 657a.

Kinds of contracts, see 10 USCA § 2306.

Planning and solicitation requirements, see 41 USCA § 253a.

Procurement data, see 41 USCA § 417a.

Procurement program for small business concerns owned and controlled by service-disabled veterans, see 15 USCA § 657f.

§ 19.705-2 Determining the need for a subcontracting plan.

The contracting officer must take the following actions to determine whether a proposed contractual action requires a subcontracting plan:

(a) Determine whether the proposed contractual action will meet the dollar threshold in 19.702(a)(1) or (2). If the action includes options or similar provisions, include their value in determining whether the threshold is met.

(b) Determine whether subcontracting possibilities exist by considering relevant factors such as—

(1) Whether firms engaged in the business of furnishing the types of items to be acquired customarily contract for performance of part of the work or maintain sufficient in-house capability to perform the work; and

(2) Whether there are likely to be product prequalification requirements.

(c) If it is determined that there are no subcontracting possibilities, the determination must be approved at a level above the contracting officer and placed in the contract file.

(d) In solicitations for negotiated acquisitions, the contracting officer may require the submission of subcontracting plans with initial offers, or at any other time prior to award. In determining when subcontracting plans should be required, as well as when and with whom plans should be negotiated, the contracting officer must consider the integrity of the competitive process, the goal of affording maximum practicable opportunity for small business, veteran-owned small business, service-disabled veteran-owned small business, HUBZone small business, small disadvantaged business, and women-owned small business concerns to participate, and the burden placed on offerors.

(e) A contract may have no more than one plan. When a modification meets the criteria in 19.702 for a plan, or an option is exercised, the goals associated with the modification or option shall be added to those in the existing subcontract plan.

United States Code Annotated

Additional powers, see 15 USCA § 637.

Administrative determinations, see 41 USCA § 257.

Awards or contracts, see 15 USCA § 644.

Contract goal for small disadvantaged businesses and certain institutions of higher

education, see 10 USCA § 2323.

Contract requirements, see 41 USCA § 254.

Contracts, planning, solicitation, evaluation, and award procedures, see 10 USCA § 2305.

Credit for Indian contracting in meeting certain subcontracting goals for small disadvantaged businesses and certain institutions of higher education, see 10 USCA § 2323a.

Definitions, see 10 USCA § 2302, 41 USCA §§ 259, 403.

Determinations and decisions, see 10 USCA § 2310, 41 USCA § 262.

HUBZone program, see 15 USCA § 657a.

Kinds of contracts, see 10 USCA § 2306.

Planning and solicitation requirements, see 41 USCA § 253a.

Procurement data, see 41 USCA § 417a.

Procurement program for small business concerns owned and controlled by service-disabled veterans, see 15 USCA § 657f.

§ 19.705-3 Preparing the solicitation.

The contracting officer shall provide the Small Business Administration's (SBA's) procurement center representative (or, if a procurement center representative is not assigned, see 19.402(a)) a reasonable period of time to review any solicitation requiring submission of a subcontracting plan and to submit advisory findings before the solicitation is issued.

United States Code Annotated

Additional powers, see 15 USCA § 637.

Administrative determinations, see 41 USCA § 257.

Awards or contracts, see 15 USCA § 644.

Contract goal for small disadvantaged businesses and certain institutions of higher education, see 10 USCA § 2323.

Contract requirements, see 41 USCA § 254.

Contracts, planning, solicitation, evaluation, and award procedures, see 10 USCA § 2305.

Credit for Indian contracting in meeting certain subcontracting goals for small disadvantaged businesses and certain institutions of higher education, see 10 USCA § 2323a.

Definitions, see 10 USCA § 2302, 41 USCA §§ 259, 403.

Determinations and decisions, see 10 USCA § 2310, 41 USCA § 262.

HUBZone program, see 15 USCA § 657a.

Kinds of contracts, see 10 USCA § 2306.

Planning and solicitation requirements, see 41 USCA § 253a.

Procurement data, see 41 USCA § 417a.

Procurement program for small business concerns owned and controlled by service-disabled veterans, see 15 USCA § 657f.

§ 19.705-4 Reviewing the subcontracting plan.

The contracting officer shall review the subcontracting plan for adequacy, ensuring that the required information, goals, and assurances are included (see 19.704).

(a) No detailed standards apply to every subcontracting plan. Instead, the contracting officer shall consider each plan in terms of the circumstances of the particular acquisition, including—

(1) Previous involvement of small business concerns as prime contractors or subcontractors in similar acquisitions;

(2) Proven methods of involving small business concerns as subcontractors in similar acquisitions; and

(3) The relative success of methods the contractor intends to use to meet the goals and requirements of the plan, as evidenced by records maintained by contractors.

(b) If, under a sealed bid solicitation, a bidder submits a plan that does not cover each of the 11 required elements (see 19.704), the contracting officer shall advise the bidder of the deficiency and request submission of a revised plan by a specific date. If the bidder does not submit a plan that incorporates the required elements within the time allotted, the bidder shall be ineligible for award. If the plan, although responsive, evidences the bidder's intention not to comply with its obligations under the clause at 52.219-8, Utilization of Small Business Concerns, the contracting officer may find the bidder nonresponsible.

(c) In negotiated acquisitions, the contracting officer shall determine whether the plan is acceptable based on the negotiation of each of the 11 elements of the plan (see 19.704). Subcontracting goals should be set at a level that the parties reasonably expect can result from the offeror expending good faith efforts to use small business, veteran-owned small business, service-disabled veteran-owned small business, HUBZone small business, small disadvantaged business, and women-owned small business subcontractors to the maximum practicable extent. The contracting officer shall take particular care to ensure that the offeror has not submitted unreasonably low goals to minimize exposure to liquidated damages and to avoid the administrative burden of substantiating good faith efforts. Additionally, particular attention should be paid to the identification of steps that, if taken, would be considered a good faith effort. No goal should be negotiated upward if it is apparent that a higher goal will significantly increase the Government's cost or seriously impede the attainment of acquisition objectives. An incentive subcontracting clause (see 52.219-10, Incentive Subcontracting Program), may be used when additional and unique contract effort, such as providing technical assistance, could significantly increase subcontract awards to small business, small disadvantaged business, veteran-owned small business, service-disabled veteran-owned small business, HUBZone small business, or women-owned small business concerns.

(d) In determining the acceptability of a proposed subcontracting plan, the contracting officer should take the following actions:

(1) Obtain information available from the cognizant contract administration office, as provided for in 19.706(a), and evaluate the offeror's past performance in awarding subcontracts for the same or similar products or services to small business, veteran-owned small business, service-disabled veteran-owned small business, HUBZone small business, small disadvantaged business, and women-owned small business concerns. If information is not available on a specific type of product or service, evaluate the offeror's overall past performance and consider the performance of other contractors on similar efforts.

(2) In accordance with 15 U.S.C. 637(d)(4)(F)(iii), ensure that the goals offered are attainable in relation to—

(i) The subcontracting opportunities available to the contractor, commensurate with the efficient and economical performance of the contract;

(ii) The pool of eligible subcontractors available to fulfill the subcontracting opportunities; and

(iii) The actual performance of such contractor in fulfilling the subcontracting goals specified in prior plans.

(3) Ensure that the subcontracting goals are consistent with the offeror's certified cost or pricing data or data other than certified cost or pricing data.

(4) Evaluate the offeror's make-or-buy policy or program to ensure that it does not conflict with the offeror's proposed subcontracting plan and is in the Government's interest. If the contract involves products or services that are particularly specialized or not generally available in the commercial market, consider the offeror's current capacity to perform the work and the possibility of reduced subcontracting opportunities.

(5) Evaluate subcontracting potential, considering the offeror's make-or-buy policies or programs, the nature of the supplies or services to be subcontracted, the known availability of small business, veteran-owned small business, service-disabled veteran-owned small business, HUBZone small business, small disadvantaged business, and women-owned small business concerns in the geographical area where the work will be performed, and the potential contractor's long-standing contractual relationship with its suppliers.

(6) Advise the offeror of available sources of information on potential small business, veteran-owned small business, service-disabled veteran-owned small business, HUBZone small business, small disadvantaged business, and women-owned small business subcontractors, as well as any specific concerns known to be potential subcontractors. If

the offeror's proposed goals are questionable, the contracting officer must emphasize that the information should be used to develop realistic and acceptable goals.

(7) Obtain advice and recommendations from the SBA procurement center representative (or, if a procurement center representative is not assigned, see 19.402(a)) and the agency small business specialist.

United States Code Annotated

Additional powers, see 15 USCA § 637.

Administrative determinations, see 41 USCA § 257.

Awards or contracts, see 15 USCA § 644.

Contract goal for small disadvantaged businesses and certain institutions of higher education, see 10 USCA § 2323.

Contract requirements, see 41 USCA § 254.

Contracts, planning, solicitation, evaluation, and award procedures, see 10 USCA § 2305.

Credit for Indian contracting in meeting certain subcontracting goals for small disadvantaged businesses and certain institutions of higher education, see 10 USCA § 2323a.

Definitions, see 10 USCA § 2302, 41 USCA §§ 259, 403.

Determinations and decisions, see 10 USCA § 2310, 41 USCA § 262.

HUBZone program, see 15 USCA § 657a.

Kinds of contracts, see 10 USCA § 2306.

Planning and solicitation requirements, see 41 USCA § 253a.

Procurement data, see 41 USCA § 417a.

Procurement program for small business concerns owned and controlled by service-disabled veterans, see 15 USCA § 657f.

Notes of Decisions

In general 1

1 In general

Contracting agency's request for a subcontracting plan from successful offeror did not constitute "discussions" or require that revised proposals be solicited from all offerors; agency's action of requesting offeror's subcontracting plan, and negotiating with it to ensure that the subcontracting plan was acceptable, was required by FAR 19.705-4, and such negotiations were patently not of the type that would permit other offerors to revise their proposals. It is clear that *only* the "apparently successful offeror" need be engaged in subcontracting negotiations, and such negotiations are patently not of the type that permit offerors to revise their proposals. Consolidated Engineering Services, Inc. v. U.S., 64 Fed.Cl. 617 (2005)

In a negotiated procurement that provided for the evaluation of small business subcontracting plans on a pass/fail basis, the rejection of the protester's proposal as technically unacceptable on the basis of the acceptability of its small business subcontracting plan was unreasonable. Because the plans were evaluated on a pass/fail basis, the agency's evaluation of those plans concern an offeror's responsibility and not the technical merit of the offeror's proposal. Since there was no indication that the offeror would not be able to comply with the terms of the subcontracting plan, rejection of the proposal was unreasonable. MANCON, B-405663, 2012 CPD ¶ 68 (Comp. Gen 2012)

§ 19.705-5 Awards involving subcontracting plans.

(a) In making an award that requires a subcontracting plan, the contracting officer shall be responsible for the following:

(1) Consider the contractor's compliance with the subcontracting plans submitted on previous contracts as a factor in determining contractor responsibility.

(2) Assure that a subcontracting plan was submitted when required.

(3) Notify the SBA procurement center representative (or, if a procurement center representative is not assigned, see 19.402(a)) of the opportunity to review the proposed contract (including the plan and supporting documentation). The notice shall be issued in sufficient time to provide the representative a reasonable time to review the material and

submit advisory recommendations to the contracting officer. Failure of the representative to respond in a reasonable period of time shall not delay contract award.

(4) Determine any fee that may be payable if an incentive is used in conjunction with the subcontracting plan.

(5) Ensure that an acceptable plan is incorporated into and made a material part of the contract.

(b) Letter contracts and similar undefinitized instruments, which would otherwise meet the requirements of 19.702(a)(1) and (2), shall contain at least a preliminary basic plan addressing the requirements of 19.704 and in such cases require the negotiation of the final plan within 90 days after award or before definitization, whichever occurs first.

United States Code Annotated

Additional powers, see 15 USCA § 637.

Administrative determinations, see 41 USCA § 257.

Awards or contracts, see 15 USCA § 644.

Contract goal for small disadvantaged businesses and certain institutions of higher education, see 10 USCA § 2323.

Contract requirements, see 41 USCA § 254.

Contracts, planning, solicitation, evaluation, and award procedures, see 10 USCA § 2305.

Credit for Indian contracting in meeting certain subcontracting goals for small disadvantaged businesses and certain institutions of higher education, see 10 USCA § 2323a.

Definitions, see 10 USCA § 2302, 41 USCA §§ 259, 403.

Determinations and decisions, see 10 USCA § 2310, 41 USCA § 262.

HUBZone program, see 15 USCA § 657a.

Kinds of contracts, see 10 USCA § 2306.

Planning and solicitation requirements, see 41 USCA § 253a.

Procurement data, see 41 USCA § 417a.

Procurement program for small business concerns owned and controlled by service-disabled veterans, see 15 USCA § 657f.

Notes of Decisions

In general 1

1 In general

An offeror's proposal need not affirmatively demonstrate compliance with FAR 52.219-14 (Limitation on Subcontracting). The plain language of FAR 52.219-14 provides that the act of proposal submission itself is sufficient to demonstrate agreement to be bound by the limitation and, in the absence of any contradictory language, the agency may presume that the offeror will comply with the clause. Mare Solutions, Inc., B-413238, 2016 WL 5110438(Comp.Gen. 2016)

In a negotiated procurement that provided for the evaluation of small business subcontracting plans on a pass/fail basis, the rejection of the protester's proposal as technically unacceptable on the basis of the acceptability of its small business subcontracting plan was unreasonable. Because the plans were evaluated on a pass/fail basis, the agency's evaluation of those plans concern an offeror's responsibility and not the technical merit of the offeror's proposal. Since there was no indication that the offeror would not be able to comply with the terms of the subcontracting plan, rejection of the proposal was unreasonable. MANCON, B-405663, 2012 CPD ¶ 68 (Comp. Gen 2012)

§ 19.705-6 Postaward responsibilities of the contracting officer.

After a contract or contract modification containing a subcontracting plan is awarded, the contracting officer who approved the plan is responsible for the following:

(a) Notifying the SBA of the award by sending a copy of the award document to the Area Director, Office of Government Contracting, in the SBA area office where the contract will be performed.

(b) Forwarding a copy of each commercial plan and any associated approvals to the Area

Director, Office of Government Contracting, in the SBA area office where the contractor's headquarters is located.

(c) Giving to the SBA procurement center representative (or, if a procurement center representative is not assigned, see 19.402(a)) a copy of—

(1) Any subcontracting plan submitted in response to a sealed bid solicitation; and

(2) The final negotiated subcontracting plan that was incorporated into a negotiated contract or contract modification.

(d) Notifying the SBA procurement center representative (or, if a procurement center representative is not assigned, see 19.402(a)) of the opportunity to review subcontracting plans in connection with contract modifications.

(e) Forwarding a copy of each plan, or a determination that there is no requirement for a subcontracting plan, to the cognizant contract administration office.

(f) Initiating action to assess liquidated damages in accordance with 19.705-7 upon a recommendation by the administrative contracting officer or receipt of other reliable evidence to indicate that such action is warranted.

(g) Taking action to enforce the terms of the contract upon receipt of a notice under 19.706(f).

(h) Acknowledging receipt of or rejecting the ISR and the SSR in the eSRS. Acknowledging receipt does not mean acceptance or approval of the report. The report shall be rejected if it is not adequately completed, for instance, if there are errors, omissions, or incomplete data. Failure to meet the goals of the subcontracting plan is not a valid reason for rejecting the report.

United States Code Annotated

Additional powers, see 15 USCA § 637.

Administrative determinations, see 41 USCA § 257.

Awards or contracts, see 15 USCA § 644.

Contract goal for small disadvantaged businesses and certain institutions of higher education, see 10 USCA § 2323.

Contract requirements, see 41 USCA § 254.

Contracts, planning, solicitation, evaluation, and award procedures, see 10 USCA § 2305.

Credit for Indian contracting in meeting certain subcontracting goals for small disadvantaged businesses and certain institutions of higher education, see 10 USCA § 2323a.

Definitions, see 10 USCA § 2302, 41 USCA §§ 259, 403.

Determinations and decisions, see 10 USCA § 2310, 41 USCA § 262.

HUBZone program, see 15 USCA § 657a.

Kinds of contracts, see 10 USCA § 2306.

Planning and solicitation requirements, see 41 USCA § 253a.

Procurement data, see 41 USCA § 417a.

Procurement program for small business concerns owned and controlled by service-disabled veterans, see 15 USCA § 657f.

§ 19.705-7 Liquidated damages.

(a) Maximum practicable utilization of small business, veteran-owned small business, service-disabled veteran-owned small business, HUBZone small business, small disadvantaged business, and women-owned small business concerns as subcontractors in Government contracts is a matter of national interest with both social and economic benefits. When a contractor fails to make a good faith effort to comply with a subcontracting plan, these objectives are not achieved, and 15 U.S.C. 637(d)(4)(F) directs that liquidated damages shall be paid by the contractor.

(b) The amount of damages attributable to the contractor's failure to comply shall be an amount equal to the actual dollar amount by which the contractor failed to achieve each subcontracting goal.

(c) If, at completion of the basic contract or any option, or in the case of a commercial plan, at the close of the fiscal year for which the plan is applicable, a contractor has failed to meet its subcontracting goals, the contracting officer shall review all available information for an indication that the contractor has not made a good faith effort to comply with the plan. If no such indication is found, the contracting officer shall document the file accordingly. If the contracting officer decides in accordance with paragraph (d) of this subsection that the contractor failed to make a good faith effort to comply with its subcontracting plan, the contracting officer shall give the contractor written notice specifying the failure, advising the contractor of the possibility that the contractor may have to pay to the Government liquidated damages, and providing a period of 15 working days (or longer period as necessary) within which to respond. The notice shall give the contractor an opportunity to demonstrate what good faith efforts have been made before the contracting officer issues the final decision, and shall further state that failure of the contractor to respond may be taken as an admission that no valid explanation exists.

(d) In determining whether a contractor failed to make a good faith effort to comply with its subcontracting plan, a contracting officer must look to the totality of the contractor's actions, consistent with the information and assurances provided in its plan. The fact that the contractor failed to meet its subcontracting goals does not, in and of itself, constitute a failure to make a good faith effort. For example, notwithstanding a contractor's diligent effort to identify and solicit offers from small business, veteran-owned small business, service-disabled veteran-owned small business, HUBZone small business, small disadvantaged business, and women-owned small business concerns, factors such as unavailability of anticipated sources or unreasonable prices may frustrate achievement of the contractor's goals. However, when considered in the context of the contractor's total effort in accordance with its plan, the following, though not all inclusive, may be considered as indicators of a failure to make a good faith effort: a failure to attempt to identify, contact, solicit, or consider for contract award small business, veteran-owned small business, service-disabled veteran-owned small business, HUBZone small business, small disadvantaged business, or womenowned small business concerns; a failure to designate and maintain a company official to administer the subcontracting program and monitor and enforce compliance with the plan; a failure to submit the ISR, or the SSR, using the eSRS, or as provided in agency regulations; a failure to maintain records or otherwise demonstrate procedures adopted to comply with the plan; or the adoption of company policies or procedures that have as their objectives the frustration of the objectives of the plan.

(e) If, after consideration of all the pertinent data, the contracting officer finds that the contractor failed to make a good faith effort to comply with its subcontracting plan, the contracting officer shall issue a final decision to the contractor to that effect and require the payment of liquidated damages in an amount stated. The contracting officer's final decision shall state that the contractor has the right to appeal under the clause in the contract entitled Disputes.

(f) With respect to commercial plans approved under the clause at 52.219-9, Small Business Subcontracting Plan, the contracting officer that approved the plan shall—

(1) Perform the functions of the contracting officer under this subsection on behalf of all agencies with contracts covered by the commercial plan;

(2) Determine whether or not the goals in the commercial plan were achieved and, if they were not achieved, review all available information for an indication that the contractor has not made a good faith effort to comply with the plan, and document the results of the review;

(3) If a determination is made to assess liquidated damages, in order to calculate and assess the amount of damages, the contracting officer shall ask the contractor to provide—

(i) Contract numbers for the Government contracts subject to the plan;

(ii) The total Government sales during the contractor's fiscal year; and

(iii) The amount of payments made under the Government contracts subject to that plan that contributed to the contractor's total sales during the contractor's fiscal year; and

(4) When appropriate, assess liquidated damages on the Government's behalf, based on the pro rata share of subcontracting attributable to the Government contracts. For example: The contractor's total actual sales were $50 million and its actual subcontracting was $20 million. The Government's total payments under contracts subject to the plan contributing to the contractor's total sales were $5 million, which accounted for 10 percent of the contractor's total sales. Therefore, the pro rata share of subcontracting attributable to the Government contracts would be 10 percent of $20 million, or $2 million.

To continue the example, if the contractor failed to achieve its small business goal by 1 percent, the liquidated damages would be calculated as 1 percent of $2 million, or $20,000. The contracting officer shall make similar calculations for each category of small business where the contractor failed to achieve its goal and the sum of the dollars for all of the categories equals the amount of the liquidated damages to be assessed. A copy of the contracting officer's final decision assessing liquidated damages shall be provided to other contracting officers with contracts subject to the commercial plan.

(g) Liquidated damages shall be in addition to any other remedies that Government may have.

(h) Every contracting officer with a contract that is subject to a commercial plan shall include in the contract file a copy of the approved plan and a copy of the final decision assessing liquidating damages, if applicable.

United States Code Annotated

Additional powers, see 15 USCA § 637.

Administrative determinations, see 41 USCA § 257.

Awards or contracts, see 15 USCA § 644.

Contract goal for small disadvantaged businesses and certain institutions of higher education, see 10 USCA § 2323.

Contract requirements, see 41 USCA § 254.

Contracts, planning, solicitation, evaluation, and award procedures, see 10 USCA § 2305.

Credit for Indian contracting in meeting certain subcontracting goals for small disadvantaged businesses and certain institutions of higher education, see 10 USCA § 2323a.

Definitions, see 10 USCA § 2302, 41 USCA §§ 259, 403.

Determinations and decisions, see 10 USCA § 2310, 41 USCA § 262.

HUBZone program, see 15 USCA § 657a.

Kinds of contracts, see 10 USCA § 2306.

Planning and solicitation requirements, see 41 USCA § 253a.

Procurement data, see 41 USCA § 417a.

Procurement program for small business concerns owned and controlled by service-disabled veterans, see 15 USCA § 657f.

§ 19.706 Responsibilities of the cognizant administrative contracting officer.

The administrative contracting officer is responsible for assisting in evaluating subcontracting plans, and for monitoring, evaluating, and documenting contractor performance under the clause prescribed in 19.708(b) and any subcontracting plan included in the contract. The contract administration office shall provide the necessary information and advice to support the contracting officer, as appropriate, by furnishing—

(a) Documentation on the contractor's performance and compliance with subcontracting plans under previous contracts;

(b) Information on the extent to which the contractor is meeting the plan's goals for subcontracting with eligible small business, veteran-owned small business, service-disabled veteran-owned small business, HUBZone small business, small disadvantaged business, and women-owned small business concerns;

(c) Information on whether the contractor's efforts to ensure the participation of small business, veteran-owned small business, service-disabled veteran-owned small business, HUBZone small business, small disadvantaged business, and women-owned small business concerns are in accordance with its subcontracting plan;

(d) Information on whether the contractor is requiring its subcontractors to adopt similar subcontracting plans;

(e) Immediate notice if, during performance, the contractor is failing to meet its commitments under the clause prescribed in 19.708(b) or the subcontracting plan;

(f) Immediate notice and rationale if, during performance, the contractor is failing to comply in good faith with the subcontracting plan; and

(g) Immediate notice that performance under a contract is complete, that the goals were or were not met, and, if not met, whether there is any indication of a lack of a good faith effort to comply with the subcontracting plan.

United States Code Annotated

Additional powers, see 15 USCA § 637.

Administrative determinations, see 41 USCA § 257.

Awards or contracts, see 15 USCA § 644.

Contract goal for small disadvantaged businesses and certain institutions of higher education, see 10 USCA § 2323.

Contract requirements, see 41 USCA § 254.

Contracts, planning, solicitation, evaluation, and award procedures, see 10 USCA § 2305.

Credit for Indian contracting in meeting certain subcontracting goals for small disadvantaged businesses and certain institutions of higher education, see 10 USCA § 2323a.

Definitions, see 10 USCA § 2302, 41 USCA §§ 259, 403.

Determinations and decisions, see 10 USCA § 2310, 41 USCA § 262.

HUBZone program, see 15 USCA § 657a.

Kinds of contracts, see 10 USCA § 2306.

Planning and solicitation requirements, see 41 USCA § 253a.

Procurement data, see 41 USCA § 417a.

Procurement program for small business concerns owned and controlled by service-disabled veterans, see 15 USCA § 657f.

§ 19.707 The Small Business Administration's role in carrying out the program.

(a) Under the program, the SBA may—

(1) Assist both Government agencies and contractors in carrying out their responsibilities with regard to subcontracting plans;

(2) Review (within 5 working days) any solicitation that meets the dollar threshold in 19.702(a)(1) or (2) before the solicitation is issued;

(3) Review (within 5 working days) before execution any negotiated contractual document requiring a subcontracting plan, including the plan itself, and submit recommendations to the contracting officer, which shall be advisory in nature; and

(4) Evaluate compliance with subcontracting plans, either on a contract-by-contract basis, or, in the case of contractors having multiple contracts, on an aggregate basis.

(b) The SBA is not authorized to—

(1) Prescribe the extent to which any contractor or subcontractor shall subcontract,

(2) Specify concerns to which subcontracts will be awarded, or

(3) Exercise any authority regarding the administration of individual prime contracts or subcontracts.

United States Code Annotated

Additional powers, see 15 USCA § 637.

Administrative determinations, see 41 USCA § 257.

Awards or contracts, see 15 USCA § 644.

Contract goal for small disadvantaged businesses and certain institutions of higher education, see 10 USCA § 2323.

Contract requirements, see 41 USCA § 254.

Contracts, planning, solicitation, evaluation, and award procedures, see 10 USCA § 2305.

Credit for Indian contracting in meeting certain subcontracting goals for small disadvantaged businesses and certain institutions of higher education, see 10 USCA § 2323a.

Definitions, see 10 USCA § 2302, 41 USCA §§ 259, 403.

Determinations and decisions, see 10 USCA § 2310, 41 USCA § 262.

HUBZone program, see 15 USCA § 657a.

Kinds of contracts, see 10 USCA § 2306.

Planning and solicitation requirements, see 41 USCA § 253a.

Procurement data, see 41 USCA § 417a.

Procurement program for small business concerns owned and controlled by service-disabled veterans, see 15 USCA § 657f.

§ 19.708 Contract clauses.

(a) Insert the clause at 52.219-8, Utilization of Small Business Concerns, in solicitations and contracts when the contract amount is expected to exceed the simplified acquisition threshold unless—

(1) A personal services contract is contemplated (see 37.104); or

(2) The contract, together with all of its subcontracts, will be performed entirely outside of the United States and its outlying areas.

(b) (1) Insert the clause at 52.219-9, Small Business Subcontracting Plan, in solicitations and contracts that offer subcontracting possibilities, are expected to exceed $700,000 ($1.5 million for construction of any public facility), and are required to include the clause at 52.219-8, Utilization of Small Business Concerns, unless the acquisition is set aside or is to be accomplished under the 8(a) program. When—

(i) Contracting by sealed bidding rather than by negotiation, the contracting officer shall use the clause with its Alternate I.

(ii) Contracting by negotiation, and subcontracting plans are required with initial proposals as provided for in 19.705-2(d), the contracting officer shall use the clause with its Alternate II.

(iii) The contract action will not be reported in the Federal Procurement Data System pursuant to 4.606(c)(5), or (c)(6), the contracting officer shall use the clause with its Alternate III.

(2) Insert the clause at 52.219-16, Liquidated Damages-Subcontracting Plan, in all solicitations and contracts containing the clause at 52.219-9, Small Business Subcontracting Plan, or the clause with its Alternate I, II, or III.

(c) (1) The contracting officer may, when contracting by negotiation, insert in solicitations and contracts a clause substantially the same as the clause at 52.219-10, Incentive Subcontracting Program, when a subcontracting plan is required (see 19.702), and inclusion of a monetary incentive is, in the judgment of the contracting officer, necessary to increase subcontracting opportunities for small business, veteran-owned small business, service-disabled veteran-owned small business, HUBZone small business, small disadvantaged business, and women-owned small business concerns, and is commensurate with the efficient and economical performance of the contract; unless the conditions in paragraph (c)(3) of this section are applicable. The contracting officer may vary the terms of the clause as specified in paragraph (c)(2) of this section.

(2) Various approaches may be used in the development of small business, veteran-owned small business, service-disabled veteran-owned small business, HUBZone small business, small disadvantaged business, and women-owned small business concerns' subcontracting incentives. They can take many forms, from a fully quantified schedule of payments based on actual subcontract achievement to an award-fee approach employing subjective evaluation criteria (see paragraph (c)(3) of this section). The incentive should not reward the contractor for results other than those that are attributable to the contractor's efforts under the incentive subcontracting program.

(3) As specified in paragraph (c)(2) of this section, the contracting officer may include small business, veteran-owned small business, service-disabled veteran-owned small business, HUBZone small business, small disadvantaged business, and women-owned small business subcontracting as one of the factors to be considered in determining the award fee in a cost-plus-award-fee contract; in such cases, however, the contracting officer shall not use the clause at 52.219-10, Incentive Subcontracting Program.

United States Code Annotated

Additional powers, see 15 USCA § 637.

Administrative determinations, see 41 USCA § 257.

Awards or contracts, see 15 USCA § 644.

Contract goal for small disadvantaged businesses and certain institutions of higher education, see 10 USCA § 2323.

Contract requirements, see 41 USCA § 254.

Contracts, planning, solicitation, evaluation, and award procedures, see 10 USCA § 2305.

Credit for Indian contracting in meeting certain subcontracting goals for small disadvantaged businesses and certain institutions of higher education, see 10 USCA § 2323a.

Definitions, see 10 USCA § 2302, 41 USCA §§ 259, 403.

Determinations and decisions, see 10 USCA § 2310, 41 USCA § 262.

HUBZone program, see 15 USCA § 657a.

Kinds of contracts, see 10 USCA § 2306.

Planning and solicitation requirements, see 41 USCA § 253a.

Procurement data, see 41 USCA § 417a.

Procurement program for small business concerns owned and controlled by service-disabled veterans, see 15 USCA § 657f.

Subpart 19.8 Contracting with the Small Business Administration (The 8(a) Program)

§ 19.800 General.

(a) Section 8(a) of the Small Business Act (15 U.S.C. 637(a)) established a program that authorizes the Small Business Administration (SBA) to enter into all types of contracts with other agencies and award subcontracts for performing those contracts to firms eligible for program participation. The SBA's subcontractors are referred to as "8(a) contractors."

(b) Contracts may be awarded to the SBA for performance by eligible 8(a) firms on either a sole source or competitive basis.

(c) When, acting under the authority of the program, the SBA certifies to an agency that the SBA is competent and responsible to perform a specific contract, the contracting officer is authorized, in the contracting officer's discretion, to award the contract to the SBA based upon mutually agreeable terms and conditions.

(d) The SBA refers to this program as the 8(a) Business Development (BD) Program.

(e) The contracting officer shall comply with 19.203 before deciding to offer an acquisition to a small business concern under the 8(a) Program. For acquisitions above the simplified acquisition threshold, the contracting officer shall consider 8(a) set-asides or sole source awards before considering small business set-asides.

(f) When SBA has delegated its 8(a) Program contract execution authority to an agency, the contracting officer must refer to its agency supplement or other policy directives for appropriate guidance.

United States Code Annotated

Additional powers, see 15 USCA § 637.

Administrative determinations, see 41 USCA § 257.

Awards or contracts, see 15 USCA § 644.

Contract goal for small disadvantaged businesses and certain institutions of higher education, see 10 USCA § 2323.

Contract requirements, see 41 USCA § 254.

Contracts, planning, solicitation, evaluation, and award procedures, see 10 USCA § 2305.

Credit for Indian contracting in meeting certain subcontracting goals for small disadvantaged businesses and certain institutions of higher education, see 10 USCA § 2323a.

Definitions, see 10 USCA § 2302, 41 USCA §§ 259, 403.

Determinations and decisions, see 10 USCA § 2310, 41 USCA § 262.

HUBZone program, see 15 USCA § 657a.

Kinds of contracts, see 10 USCA § 2306.

Planning and solicitation requirements, see 41 USCA § 253a.

Procurement data, see 41 USCA § 417a.

Procurement program for small business concerns owned and controlled by service-disabled veterans, see 15 USCA § 657f.

Notes of Decisions

In general 1

Bid protest 2
Unconstitutionality 3

1 In general

United States Army Corps of Engineers was not required to conduct proportional impact analysis before offering contract to build recreation park in Mississippi into Small Business Administration (SBA) "8(a)" program for socially and economically disadvantaged small business concerns; Corps' interpretation of federal regulation to require impact analysis only when recurring contracts were redesignated as exclusively available to disadvantaged contractors was well-reasoned and consistent with regulation's plain meaning. Small Business Act, § 2[8](a), 15 U.S.C.A. § 637(a). Valley Const. Co. v. Marsh, 984 F.2d 133, 38 Cont. Cas. Fed. (CCH) P 76484 (5th Cir. 1993). United States ☞64.15

Small Business Act provides no private right of action to enforce goals of encouraging government contractors to subcontract to small disadvantaged businesses (SDBs). Small Business Act, §§ 2[8](a)(1)(B), 2[15](g), 15 U.S.C.A. §§ 637(a)(1)(B), 644(g). GC Micro Corp. v. Defense Logistics Agency, 33 F.3d 1109, 39 Cont. Cas. Fed. (CCH) P 76701 (9th Cir. 1994). Action ☞3

Insofar as Federal Lands Highway Program's (FLHP's) 1996 Subcontractor Compensation Clause (SCC) relied on Small Business Act's (SBA's) § 8(a) criteria, limiting duration of disadvantaged business enterprise (DBE) status, those criteria increased the narrow tailoring of the SCC raceconscious program, and current SBA § 8(d) program, incorporating regulations which provide for a certification of a business as socially and economically disadvantaged for three years after either the initial certification or other administrative determination, was narrowly tailored with regard to appropriate limitations on duration, for purposes of equal protection compliance, especially in light of extensive congressional debate prior to renewing the DBE program. Small Business Act, §§ 2[5](b)(6), 2[7](j)(10)(C) (i), (j)(10)(G), 2[8](a), (a)(6)(B, C), (d), as amended, 15 U.S.C.A. §§ 634(b)(6), 636(j)(10)(C)(i), (j)(10)(G), 637(a), (a)(6)(B, C), (d); 13 C.F.R. §§ 124.2, 124.110, 124.1002(a), 124.1014, 124. 1014(c); 48 C.F.R. § 19.001. Adarand Constructors, Inc. v. Slater, 228 F.3d 1147 (10th Cir. 2000). Constitutional Law ☞215.2; Highways ☞113(1)

Air Force's interpretation of Small Business Administration Section 8(a) program to mean that contract which had historically been set aside for small business participation could not be set aside under 8(a) program was reasonable interpretation not contradicted by plain meaning of regulations, and thus, interpretation was required to be accepted by district court. Small Business Act, § 2[8](a), as amended, 15 U.S.C.A. § 637(a). Young-Robinson Associates, Inc. v. U.S., 760 F. Supp. 212, 37 Cont. Cas. Fed. (CCH) P 76054 (D.D.C. 1991). United States ☞64.15

Government contractor could not maintain a cause of action based on statute and regulation governing the estimate of the government's fair market price in a Section 8(a) contract, as the provisions concerned internal operating procedures and existed primarily for the benefit of the government. Small Business Act, § 2[8](a)(3)(B)(ii), as amended, 15 U.S.C.A. § 637(a)(3)(B)(ii). D.V. Gonzalez Elec. & General Contractors, Inc. v. U.S., 55 Fed. Cl. 447 (2003). United States ☞74(1)

Government's duty to fairly and honestly consider proposal does not arise only in context of competitive bidding, and cause of action exists for breach of implied contract to fairly and honestly consider proposal submitted in small disadvantaged business environment. Small Business Act, § 2[8](a), as amended, 15 U.S.C.A. § 637(a). Celtech, Inc. v. U.S., 24 Cl. Ct. 269, 37 Cont. Cas. Fed. (CCH) P 76181, 1991 WL 193295 (1991), vacated pursuant to settlement, 25 Cl. Ct. 368, 1992 WL 46122 (1992). United States ☞64.40(2)

Evidence showed that there was rational basis for Air Force to request that Small Business Administration provide new contractor for performance of janitorial services at Air Force base under section 8(a) contract and that Air Force did not act in bad faith in making the request in view of complaints which had arisen over the performance of the contractor. Small Business Act, § 2[8](a), as amended, 15 U.S.C.A. § 637(a). Harris Systems Intern., Inc. v. U.S., 5 Cl. Ct. 253, 32 Cont. Cas. Fed. (CCH) P 72486 (1984). United States ☞53(8)

In essence, a "section 8(a) contract" is one in which the Small Business Administration contracts with a federal agency having procurement powers for the performance by the SBA of the work required under a so-called prime contract; in turn, the SBA subcontracts the actual performance of the work to a section 8(a) contractor which the SBA determines to be a socially and economically disadvantaged small business concern. Small Business Act, § 2[8](a), as amended, 15 U.S.C.A. § 637(a). Harris Systems Intern., Inc. v. U.S., 5 Cl. Ct. 253, 32 Cont. Cas. Fed. (CCH) P 72486 (1984). United States ☞53(8)

Air Force did not abuse its discretion with respect to participation in the section 8(a) program with the Small Business Administration by indicating that it would not accept, for the final option year of a contract, the contractor which had been performing the work. Small Business Act, § 2[8](a), as amended, 15 U.S.C.A. § 637(a). Harris Systems Intern., Inc. v. U.S., 5 Cl. Ct. 253, 32 Cont. Cas. Fed. (CCH) P 72486 (1984). United States ☞53(8)

2 Bid protest

Editor Note: On September 27, 2010, the "Small Business Jobs Act" (HR 5297) ended the long-running debate within the federal government regarding whether set-asides for HUBZone vendors had priority over awards to either an 8(a) vendor or a service disabled veteran-owned small business. Section 1347 of the Act amends the HUBZone statute (15 USC § 657a) by changing "shall" set-aside to "may" set-aside, when it is expected that offers will be received from two or more qualified HUBZone firms.

3 Unconstitutionality

Definition of "socially disadvantaged" in Small Business Act 8(a) program for government contracting with socially and economically disadvantaged individuals, which included "those who have been subjected to racial or ethnic prejudice or cultural bias because of their identity as a member of a group without regard to their individual qualities," did not contain a racial classification, and thus application of the "strict scrutiny" test to the 8(a) statute was not warranted, where definition envisioned an individual-based approach that focused on experience rather than a group characteristic, a person of any racial or ethnic background may have suffered such discrimination, causing them to fall within definition, and not all members of a minority group had necessarily been subjected to racial or ethnic prejudice or cultural bias. Rothe Dev., Inc. v. U.S. Dep't of Def., 2016 WL 4719049 (D.C. Cir. 2016)

Small Business Act's 8(a) program for government contracting with socially and economically disadvantaged individuals satisfied the less stringent "rational basis" test (rather than "strict scrutiny" test) to survive small business owner's equal protection challenge to statute, where Act sought to remedy effects of prejudice and bias that impeded business formation and development and suppressed fair competition for government contracts, and counteracting discrimination was a legitimate government interest. Rothe Dev., Inc. v. U.S. Dep't of Def., 2016 WL 4719049 (D.C. Cir. 2016)

District court prohibited DoD and SBA from awarding contracts for military simulators based on race of contractors under the 8(a) Program. The agencies failed to meet their burden of proving a history of discrimination in the military simulation and training industry sufficient to demonstrate a compelling interest, which is constitutionally necessary to discriminate based on race. DynaLantic Corp. v. U.S. Dept. of Defense, 885 F.Supp.2d 237 (D.D.C. 2012)

§ 19.801 [Reserved]

§ 19.802 Selecting concerns for the 8(a) Program.

Selecting concerns for the 8(a) Program is the responsibility of the SBA and is based on the criteria established in 13 CFR 124.101-112.

United States Code Annotated

Additional powers, see 15 USCA § 637.

Administrative determinations, see 41 USCA § 257.

Awards or contracts, see 15 USCA § 644.

Contract goal for small disadvantaged businesses and certain institutions of higher education, see 10 USCA § 2323.

Contract requirements, see 41 USCA § 254.

Contracts, planning, solicitation, evaluation, and award procedures, see 10 USCA § 2305.

Credit for Indian contracting in meeting certain subcontracting goals for small

disadvantaged businesses and certain institutions of higher education, see 10 USCA § 2323a.

Definitions, see 10 USCA § 2302, 41 USCA §§ 259, 403.

Determinations and decisions, see 10 USCA § 2310, 41 USCA § 262.

HUBZone program, see 15 USCA § 657a.

Kinds of contracts, see 10 USCA § 2306.

Planning and solicitation requirements, see 41 USCA § 253a.

Procurement data, see 41 USCA § 417a.

Procurement program for small business concerns owned and controlled by service-disabled veterans, see 15 USCA § 657f.

§ 19.803 Selecting acquisitions for the 8(a) Program.

Through their cooperative efforts, the SBA and an agency match the agency's requirements with the capabilities of 8(a) concerns to establish a basis for the agency to contract with the SBA under the program. Selection is initiated in one of three ways—

(a) The SBA advises an agency contracting activity through a search letter of an 8(a) firm's capabilities and asks the agency to identify acquisitions to support the firm's business plans. In these instances, the SBA will provide at least the following information in order to enable the agency to match an acquisition to the firm's capabilities:

(1) Identification of the concern and its owners.

(2) Background information on the concern, including any and all information pertaining to the concern's technical ability and capacity to perform.

(3) The firm's present production capacity and related facilities.

(4) The extent to which contracting assistance is needed in the present and the future, described in terms that will enable the agency to relate the concern's plans to present and future agency requirements.

(5) If construction is involved, the request shall also include the following:

(i) The concern's capabilities in and qualifications for accomplishing various categories of maintenance, repair, alteration, and construction work in specific categories such as mechanical, electrical, heating and air conditioning, demolition, building, painting, paving, earth work, waterfront work, and general construction work.

(ii) The concern's capacity in each construction category in terms of estimated dollar value (*e.g.*, electrical, up to $100,000).

(b) The SBA identifies a specific requirement for a particular 8(a) firm or firms and asks the agency contracting activity to offer the acquisition to the 8(a) Program for the firm(s). In these instances, in addition to the information in paragraph (a) of this section, the SBA will provide—

(1) A clear identification of the acquisition sought; *e.g.*, project name or number;

(2) A statement as to how any additional needed equipment and real property will be provided in order to ensure that the firm will be fully capable of satisfying the agency's requirements;

(3) If construction, information as to the bonding capability of the firm(s); and

(4) Either—

(i) If sole source request—

(A) The reasons why the firm is considered suitable for this particular acquisition; *e.g.*, previous contracts for the same or similar supply or service; and

(B) A statement that the firm is eligible in terms of NAICS code, business support levels, and business activity targets; or

(ii) If competitive, a statement that at least two 8(a) firms are considered capable of satisfying the agency's requirements and a statement that the firms are also eligible in terms of the NAICS code, business support levels, and business activity targets. If requested by the contracting activity, SBA will identify at least two such firms and provide information concerning the firms' capabilities.

(c) Agencies may also review other proposed acquisitions for the purpose of identifying requirements which may be offered to the SBA. Where agencies independently, or through the self marketing efforts of an 8(a) firm, identify a requirement for the 8(a) Program, they may offer on behalf of a specific 8(a) firm, for the 8(a) Program in general, or for 8(a) competition.

United States Code Annotated

Additional powers, see 15 USCA § 637.

Administrative determinations, see 41 USCA § 257.

Awards or contracts, see 15 USCA § 644.

Contract goal for small disadvantaged businesses and certain institutions of higher education, see 10 USCA § 2323.

Contract requirements, see 41 USCA § 254.

Contracts, planning, solicitation, evaluation, and award procedures, see 10 USCA § 2305.

Credit for Indian contracting in meeting certain subcontracting goals for small disadvantaged businesses and certain institutions of higher education, see 10 USCA § 2323a.

Definitions, see 10 USCA § 2302, 41 USCA §§ 259, 403.

Determinations and decisions, see 10 USCA § 2310, 41 USCA § 262.

HUBZone program, see 15 USCA § 657a.

Kinds of contracts, see 10 USCA § 2306.

Planning and solicitation requirements, see 41 USCA § 253a.

Procurement data, see 41 USCA § 417a.

Procurement program for small business concerns owned and controlled by service-disabled veterans, see 15 USCA § 657f.

Notes of Decisions

In general 1
Violations 2

1 In general

Agency has discretion to procure via GSA's Federal Supply Schedules (FSS), rather than set-aside the procurement for small businesses, even though requirement had been previously performed by an 8(a) small business. Neither the Small Business Act, 15 USCA §§ 631–657, nor applicable regulations require the Government to obtain a service from a small business, including 8(a) firms, if it can meet its needs through the FSS. K-Lak Corp. v. U.S., 98 Fed. Cl. 1 (2011)

2 Violations

Small Business Administration (SBA) did not violate sole source regulations by recommending two firms to procuring agency in sole source procurement conducted under sole source provisions of section 8(a) of the Small Business Act, and thereby convert sole source procurement to a competitive procurement; SBA and procuring agency acted within strictures of applicable regulations when two section 8(a) firms were nominated by the SBA, and procuring agency chose between the two eligible firms. Innovative Resources v. U.S., 63 Fed. Cl. 287 (2004). United States ⬦64.10

§ 19.804 Evaluation, offering, and acceptance.

§ 19.804-1 Agency evaluation.

In determining the extent to which a requirement should be offered in support of the 8(a) Program, the agency should evaluate—

(a) Its current and future plans to acquire the specific items or work that 8(a) contractors are seeking to provide, identified in terms of—

(1) Quantities required or the number of construction projects planned; and

(2) Performance or delivery requirements, including required monthly production rates, when applicable;

(b) Its current and future plans to acquire items or work similar in nature and complexity to that specified in the business plan;

(c) Problems encountered in previous acquisitions of the items or work from the 8(a) contractors and/or other contractors;

(d) The impact of any delay in delivery;

(e) Whether the items or work have previously been acquired using small business set-asides; and

(f) Any other pertinent information about known 8(a) contractors, the items, or the work. This includes any information concerning the firms' capabilities. When necessary, the contracting agency shall make an independent review of the factors in 19.803(a) and other aspects of the firms' capabilities which would ensure the satisfactory performance of the requirement being considered for commitment to the 8(a) Program.

United States Code Annotated

Additional powers, see 15 USCA § 637.

Administrative determinations, see 41 USCA § 257.

Awards or contracts, see 15 USCA § 644.

Contract goal for small disadvantaged businesses and certain institutions of higher education, see 10 USCA § 2323.

Contract requirements, see 41 USCA § 254.

Contracts, planning, solicitation, evaluation, and award procedures, see 10 USCA § 2305.

Credit for Indian contracting in meeting certain subcontracting goals for small disadvantaged businesses and certain institutions of higher education, see 10 USCA § 2323a.

Definitions, see 10 USCA § 2302, 41 USCA §§ 259, 403.

Determinations and decisions, see 10 USCA § 2310, 41 USCA § 262.

HUBZone program, see 15 USCA § 657a.

Kinds of contracts, see 10 USCA § 2306.

Planning and solicitation requirements, see 41 USCA § 253a.

Procurement data, see 41 USCA § 417a.

Procurement program for small business concerns owned and controlled by service-disabled veterans, see 15 USCA § 657f.

§ 19.804-2 Agency offering.

(a) After completing its evaluation, the agency must notify the SBA of the extent of its plans to place 8(a) contracts with the SBA for specific quantities of items or work. The notification must identify the time frames within which prime contract and subcontract actions must be completed in order for the agency to meet its responsibilities. The notification must also contain the following information applicable to each prospective contract:

(1) A description of the work to be performed or items to be delivered, and a copy of the statement of work, if available.

(2) The estimated period of performance.

(3) The NAICS code that applies to the principal nature of the acquisition.

(4) The anticipated dollar value of the requirement, including options, if any.

(5) Any special restrictions or geographical limitations on the requirement (for construction, include the location of the work to be performed).

(6) Any special capabilities or disciplines needed for contract performance.

(7) The type of contract anticipated.

(8) The acquisition history, if any, of the requirement, including the names and addresses of any small business contractors that have performed this requirement during the previous 24 months.

(9) A statement that prior to the offering no solicitation for the specific acquisition has been issued as a small business, HUBZone, service-disabled veteran-owned small business set-aside, or a set-aside under the Women-Owned Small Business (WOSB) Program, and that no other public communication (such as a notice through the Governmentwide point of entry (GPE)) has been made showing the contracting agency's clear intention to set-aside the acquisition for small business, HUBZone small business, service-disabled veteran-owned small business concerns, or a set-aside under the WOSB Program.

(10) Identification of any particular 8(a) concern designated for consideration, including

a brief justification, such as—

(i) The 8(a) concern, through its own efforts, marketed the requirement and caused it to be reserved for the 8(a) Program; or

(ii) The acquisition is a follow-on or renewal contract and the nominated concern is the incumbent.

(11) Bonding requirements, if applicable.

(12) Identification of all SBA field offices that have asked for the acquisition for the 8(a) Program.

(13) A request, if appropriate, that a requirement with an estimated contract value under the applicable competitive threshold be awarded as an 8(a) competitive contract (see 19.805-1(d)).

(14) A request, if appropriate, that a requirement with a contract value over the applicable competitive threshold be awarded as a sole source contract (see 19.805-1(b)).

(15) Any other pertinent and reasonably available data.

(b) (1) An agency offering a construction requirement for which no specific offeror is nominated should submit it to the SBA District Office for the geographical area where the work is to be performed.

(2) An agency offering a construction requirement on behalf of a specific offeror should submit it to the SBA District Office servicing that concern.

(3) Sole source requirements, other than construction, should be forwarded directly to the district office that services the nominated firm. If the contracting officer is not nominating a specific firm, the offering letter should be forwarded to the district office servicing the geographical area in which the contracting office is located.

(c) All requirements for 8(a) competition, other than construction, should be forwarded to the district office servicing the geographical area in which the contracting office is located. All requirements for 8(a) construction competition should be forwarded to the district office servicing the geographical area in which all or the major portion of the construction is to be performed. All requirements, including construction, must be synopsized through the GPE. For construction, the synopsis must include the geographical area of the competition set forth in the SBA's acceptance letter.

United States Code Annotated

Additional powers, see 15 USCA § 637.

Administrative determinations, see 41 USCA § 257.

Awards or contracts, see 15 USCA § 644.

Contract goal for small disadvantaged businesses and certain institutions of higher education, see 10 USCA § 2323.

Contract requirements, see 41 USCA § 254.

Contracts, planning, solicitation, evaluation, and award procedures, see 10 USCA § 2305.

Credit for Indian contracting in meeting certain subcontracting goals for small disadvantaged businesses and certain institutions of higher education, see 10 USCA § 2323a.

Definitions, see 10 USCA § 2302, 41 USCA §§ 259, 403.

Determinations and decisions, see 10 USCA § 2310, 41 USCA § 262.

HUBZone program, see 15 USCA § 657a.

Kinds of contracts, see 10 USCA § 2306.

Planning and solicitation requirements, see 41 USCA § 253a.

Procurement data, see 41 USCA § 417a.

Procurement program for small business concerns owned and controlled by service-disabled veterans, see 15 USCA § 657f.

§ 19.804-3 SBA acceptance.

(a) Upon receipt of the contracting agency's offer, the SBA will determine whether to accept the requirement for the 8(a) Program. The SBA's decision whether to accept the requirement will be transmitted to the contracting agency in writing within 10 working days of receipt of the offer if the contract is likely to exceed the simplified acquisition threshold and within 2 days of receipt if the contract is at or below the simplified acquisition threshold. The contracting agency may grant an extension of these time periods. If SBA does not respond to an offering letter within 10 days, the contracting activity may seek SBA's acceptance through the Associate Administrator.

(b) If the acquisition is accepted as a sole source, the SBA will advise the contracting activity of the 8(a) firm selected for negotiation. Generally, the SBA will accept a contracting activity's recommended source.

(c) For acquisitions not exceeding the simplified acquisition threshold, when the contracting activity makes an offer to the 8(a) Program on behalf of a specific 8(a) firm and does not receive a reply to its offer within 2 days, the contracting activity may assume the offer is accepted and proceed with award of an 8(a) contract.

(d) As part of the acceptance process, SBA will review the appropriateness of the NAICS code designation assigned to the requirement by the contracting activity.

(1) SBA will not challenge the NAICS code assigned to the requirement by the contracting activity if it is reasonable, even though other NAICS codes may also be reasonable.

(2) If SBA and the contracting activity are unable to agree on a NAICS code designation for the requirement, SBA may refuse to accept the requirement for the 8(a) Program, appeal the contracting officer's determination to the head of the agency pursuant to 19.810, or appeal the NAICS code designation to the SBA Office of Hearings and Appeals under Subpart C of 13 CFR Part 134.

United States Code Annotated

Additional powers, see 15 USCA § 637.

Administrative determinations, see 41 USCA § 257.

Awards or contracts, see 15 USCA § 644.

Contract goal for small disadvantaged businesses and certain institutions of higher education, see 10 USCA § 2323.

Contract requirements, see 41 USCA § 254.

Contracts, planning, solicitation, evaluation, and award procedures, see 10 USCA § 2305.

Credit for Indian contracting in meeting certain subcontracting goals for small disadvantaged businesses and certain institutions of higher education, see 10 USCA § 2323a.

Definitions, see 10 USCA § 2302, 41 USCA §§ 259, 403.

Determinations and decisions, see 10 USCA § 2310, 41 USCA § 262.

HUBZone program, see 15 USCA § 657a.

Kinds of contracts, see 10 USCA § 2306.

Planning and solicitation requirements, see 41 USCA § 253a.

Procurement data, see 41 USCA § 417a.

Procurement program for small business concerns owned and controlled by service-disabled veterans, see 15 USCA § 657f.

Notes of Decisions

Violations 1

1 Violations

Small Business Administration (SBA) did not violate sole source regulations by recommending two firms to procuring agency in sole source procurement conducted under sole source provisions of section 8(a) of the Small Business Act, and thereby convert sole source procurement to a competitive procurement; SBA and procuring agency acted within strictures of applicable regulations when two section 8(a) firms were nominated by the SBA, and procuring agency chose between the two eligible firms. Innovative Resources v. U.S., 63 Fed. Cl. 287 (2004). United States ☞64.10

§ 19.804-4 Repetitive acquisitions.

In order for repetitive acquisitions to be awarded through the 8(a) Program, there must be separate offers and acceptances. This allows the SBA to determine—

(a) Whether the requirement should be a competitive 8(a) award;

(b) A nominated firm's eligibility, whether or not it is the same firm that performed the previous contract;

(c) The effect that contract award would have on the equitable distribution of 8(a) contracts; and

(d) Whether the requirement should continue under the 8(a) Program.

United States Code Annotated

Additional powers, see 15 USCA § 637.

Administrative determinations, see 41 USCA § 257.

Awards or contracts, see 15 USCA § 644.

Contract goal for small disadvantaged businesses and certain institutions of higher education, see 10 USCA § 2323.

Contract requirements, see 41 USCA § 254.

Contracts, planning, solicitation, evaluation, and award procedures, see 10 USCA § 2305.

Credit for Indian contracting in meeting certain subcontracting goals for small disadvantaged businesses and certain institutions of higher education, see 10 USCA § 2323a.

Definitions, see 10 USCA § 2302, 41 USCA §§ 259, 403.

Determinations and decisions, see 10 USCA § 2310, 41 USCA § 262.

HUBZone program, see 15 USCA § 657a.

Kinds of contracts, see 10 USCA § 2306.

Planning and solicitation requirements, see 41 USCA § 253a.

Procurement data, see 41 USCA § 417a.

Procurement program for small business concerns owned and controlled by service-disabled veterans, see 15 USCA § 657f.

§ 19.804-5 Basic ordering agreements.

(a) The contracting activity must offer, and SBA must accept, each order under a basic ordering agreement (BOA) in addition to offering and accepting the BOA itself.

(b) SBA will not accept for award on a sole-source basis any order that would cause the total dollar amount of orders issued under a specific BOA to exceed the competitive threshold amount in 19.805-1.

(c) Once an 8(a) concern's program term expires, the concern otherwise exits the 8(a) Program, or becomes other than small for the NAICS code assigned under the BOA, SBA will not accept new orders for the concern.

United States Code Annotated

Additional powers, see 15 USCA § 637.

Administrative determinations, see 41 USCA § 257.

Awards or contracts, see 15 USCA § 644.

Contract goal for small disadvantaged businesses and certain institutions of higher education, see 10 USCA § 2323.

Contract requirements, see 41 USCA § 254.

Contracts, planning, solicitation, evaluation, and award procedures, see 10 USCA § 2305.

Credit for Indian contracting in meeting certain subcontracting goals for small disadvantaged businesses and certain institutions of higher education, see 10 USCA § 2323a.

Definitions, see 10 USCA § 2302, 41 USCA §§ 259, 403.

Determinations and decisions, see 10 USCA § 2310, 41 USCA § 262.

HUBZone program, see 15 USCA § 657a.

Kinds of contracts, see 10 USCA § 2306.

Planning and solicitation requirements, see 41 USCA § 253a.

Procurement data, see 41 USCA § 417a.

Procurement program for small business concerns owned and controlled by service-disabled veterans, see 15 USCA § 657f.

§ 19.804-6 Indefinite delivery contracts.

(a) Separate offers and acceptances must not be made for individual orders under multiple award, Federal Supply Schedule (FSS), multi-agency contracts or Governmentwide acquisition contracts. SBA's acceptance of the original contract is valid for the term of the contract.

(b) The requirements of 19.805-1 of this part do not apply to individual orders that exceed the competitive threshold as long as the original contract was competed.

(c) An 8(a) concern may continue to accept new orders under a multiple award, Federal Supply Schedule (FSS), multi-agency contract or Governmentwide acquisition contract even after a concern's program term expires, the concern otherwise exits the 8(a) Program, or the concern becomes other than small for the NAICS code assigned under the contract.

United States Code Annotated

Additional powers, see 15 USCA § 637.

Administrative determinations, see 41 USCA § 257.

Awards or contracts, see 15 USCA § 644.

Contract goal for small disadvantaged businesses and certain institutions of higher education, see 10 USCA § 2323.

Contract requirements, see 41 USCA § 254.

Contracts, planning, solicitation, evaluation, and award procedures, see 10 USCA § 2305.

Credit for Indian contracting in meeting certain subcontracting goals for small disadvantaged businesses and certain institutions of higher education, see 10 USCA § 2323a.

Definitions, see 10 USCA § 2302, 41 USCA §§ 259, 403.

Determinations and decisions, see 10 USCA § 2310, 41 USCA § 262.

HUBZone program, see 15 USCA § 657a.

Kinds of contracts, see 10 USCA § 2306.

Planning and solicitation requirements, see 41 USCA § 253a.

Procurement data, see 41 USCA § 417a.

Procurement program for small business concerns owned and controlled by service-disabled veterans, see 15 USCA § 657f.

§ 19.805 Competitive 8(a).

§ 19.805-1 General.

(a) Except as provided in paragraph (b) of this subsection, an acquisition offered to the SBA under the 8(a) Program shall be awarded on the basis of competition limited to eligible 8(a) firms if—

    (1) There is a reasonable expectation that at least two eligible and responsible 8(a) firms will submit offers and that award can be made at a fair market price; and

    (2) The anticipated total value of the contract, including options, will exceed $7 million for acquisitions assigned manufacturing North American Industry Classification System (NAICS) codes and $4 million for all other acquisitions.

(b) Where an acquisition exceeds the competitive threshold, the SBA may accept the requirement for a sole source 8(a) award if—

    (1) There is not a reasonable expectation that at least two eligible and responsible 8(a) firms will submit offers at a fair market price; or

    (2) SBA accepts the requirement on behalf of a concern owned by an Indian tribe or an Alaska Native Corporation.

(c) A proposed 8(a) requirement with an estimated value exceeding the applicable competitive threshold amount shall not be divided into several requirements for lesser amounts in order to use 8(a) sole source procedures for award to a single firm.

(d) The SBA Associate Administrator for 8(a) Business Development (AA/BD) may approve an agency request for a competitive 8(a) award below the competitive thresholds. Such requests will be approved only on a limited basis and will be primarily granted where technical competitions are appropriate or where a large number of responsible 8(a) firms are available for competition. In determining whether a request to compete below the threshold will be approved, the AA/BD will, in part, consider the extent to which the requesting agency is supporting the 8(a) Program on a noncompetitive basis. The agency may include recommendations for competition below the threshold in the offering letter or by separate correspondence to the AA/BD.

United States Code Annotated

Additional powers, see 15 USCA § 637.

Administrative determinations, see 41 USCA § 257.

Awards or contracts, see 15 USCA § 644.

Contract goal for small disadvantaged businesses and certain institutions of higher education, see 10 USCA § 2323.

Contract requirements, see 41 USCA § 254.

Contracts, planning, solicitation, evaluation, and award procedures, see 10 USCA § 2305.

Credit for Indian contracting in meeting certain subcontracting goals for small disadvantaged businesses and certain institutions of higher education, see 10 USCA § 2323a.

Definitions, see 10 USCA § 2302, 41 USCA §§ 259, 403.

Determinations and decisions, see 10 USCA § 2310, 41 USCA § 262.

HUBZone program, see 15 USCA § 657a.

Kinds of contracts, see 10 USCA § 2306.

Planning and solicitation requirements, see 41 USCA § 253a.

Procurement data, see 41 USCA § 417a.

Procurement program for small business concerns owned and controlled by service-disabled veterans, see 15 USCA § 657f.

Notes of Decisions

HUBZone set-aside priority 3
Splitting of procurements 1
Violations 2

1 Splitting of procurements

Substantial evidence supported arbitrator's finding that federal employee participated with contracting agent in improper splitting of procurements in order to avoid competitive threshold. Hursh v. General Services Admin., 136 Fed. Appx. 355 (Fed. Cir. 2005). Labor And Employment ☜1588

2 Violations

Small Business Administration (SBA) did not violate sole source regulations by recommending two firms to procuring agency in sole source procurement conducted under sole source provisions of section 8(a) of the Small Business Act, and thereby convert sole source procurement to a competitive procurement; SBA and procuring agency acted within strictures of applicable regulations when two section 8(a) firms were nominated by the SBA, and procuring agency chose between the two eligible firms. Innovative Resources v. U.S., 63 Fed. Cl. 287 (2004). United States ☜64.10

3 HUBZone set-aside priority

Editor Note: On September 27, 2010, the "Small Business Jobs Act" (HR 5297) ended the long-running debate within the federal government regarding whether set-asides for HUBZone vendors had priority over awards to either an 8(a) vendor or a service disabled veteran-owned small business. Section 1347 of the Act amends the HUBZone statute (15 USC § 657a) by changing "shall" set-aside to "may" set-aside, when it is expected that offers will be received from two or more qualified HUBZone firms.

§ 19.805-2 Procedures.

(a) Offers shall be solicited from those sources identified in accordance with 19.804-3.

(b) The SBA will determine the eligibility of the firms for award of the contract. Eligibility will be determined by the SBA as of the time of submission of initial offers which include price. Eligibility is based on Section 8(a) Program criteria.

(1) In sealed bid acquisitions, upon receipt of offers, the contracting officer will provide the SBA a copy of the solicitation, the estimated fair market price, and a list of offerors ranked in the order of their standing for award (*i.e.*, first low, second low, etc.) with the

total evaluated price for each offer, differentiating between basic requirements and any options. The SBA will consider the eligibility of the first low offeror. If the first low offeror is not determined to be eligible, the SBA will consider the eligibility of the next low offeror until an eligible offeror is identified. The SBA will determine the eligibility of the firms and advise the contracting officer within 5 working days after its receipt of the list of bidders. Once eligibility has been established by the SBA, the successful offeror will be determined by the contracting activity in accordance with normal contracting procedures.

(2) In negotiated acquisition, the SBA will determine eligibility when the successful offeror has been established by the agency and the contract transmitted for signature unless a referral has been made under 19.809, in which case the SBA will determine eligibility at that point.

(c) In any case in which a firm is determined to be ineligible, the SBA will notify the firm of that determination.

(d) The eligibility of an 8(a) firm for a competitive 8(a) award may not be challenged or protested by another 8(a) firm or any other party as part of a solicitation or proposed contract award. Any party with information concerning the eligibility of an 8(a) firm to continue participation in the 8(a) Program may submit such information to the SBA in accordance with 13 CFR 124.517.

United States Code Annotated

Additional powers, see 15 USCA § 637.

Administrative determinations, see 41 USCA § 257.

Awards or contracts, see 15 USCA § 644.

Contract goal for small disadvantaged businesses and certain institutions of higher education, see 10 USCA § 2323.

Contract requirements, see 41 USCA § 254.

Contracts, planning, solicitation, evaluation, and award procedures, see 10 USCA § 2305.

Credit for Indian contracting in meeting certain subcontracting goals for small disadvantaged businesses and certain institutions of higher education, see 10 USCA § 2323a.

Definitions, see 10 USCA § 2302, 41 USCA §§ 259, 403.

Determinations and decisions, see 10 USCA § 2310, 41 USCA § 262.

HUBZone program, see 15 USCA § 657a.

Kinds of contracts, see 10 USCA § 2306.

Planning and solicitation requirements, see 41 USCA § 253a.

Procurement data, see 41 USCA § 417a.

Procurement program for small business concerns owned and controlled by service-disabled veterans, see 15 USCA § 657f.

§ 19.806 Pricing the 8(a) contract.

(a) The contracting officer shall price the 8(a) contract in accordance with Subpart 15.4. If required by Subpart 15.4, the SBA shall obtain certified cost or pricing data from the 8(a) contractor. If the SBA requests audit assistance to determine the proposed price to be fair and reasonable in a sole source acquisition, the contracting activity shall furnish it to the extent it is available.

(b) An 8(a) contract, sole source or competitive, may not be awarded if the price of the contract results in a cost to the contracting agency which exceeds a fair market price.

(c) If requested by the SBA, the contracting officer shall make available the data used to estimate the fair market price within 10 working days.

(d) The negotiated contract price and the estimated fair market price are subject to the concurrence of the SBA. In the event of a disagreement between the contracting officer and the SBA, the SBA may appeal in accordance with 19.810.

United States Code Annotated

Additional powers, see 15 USCA § 637.

Administrative determinations, see 41 USCA § 257.

Awards or contracts, see 15 USCA § 644.

Contract goal for small disadvantaged businesses and certain institutions of higher

education, see 10 USCA § 2323.

Contract requirements, see 41 USCA § 254.

Contracts, planning, solicitation, evaluation, and award procedures, see 10 USCA § 2305.

Credit for Indian contracting in meeting certain subcontracting goals for small disadvantaged businesses and certain institutions of higher education, see 10 USCA § 2323a.

Definitions, see 10 USCA § 2302, 41 USCA §§ 259, 403.

Determinations and decisions, see 10 USCA § 2310, 41 USCA § 262.

HUBZone program, see 15 USCA § 657a.

Kinds of contracts, see 10 USCA § 2306.

Planning and solicitation requirements, see 41 USCA § 253a.

Procurement data, see 41 USCA § 417a.

Procurement program for small business concerns owned and controlled by service-disabled veterans, see 15 USCA § 657f.

§ 19.807 Estimating fair market price.

(a) The contracting officer shall estimate the fair market price of the work to be performed by the 8(a) contractor.

(b) In estimating the fair market price for an acquisition other than those covered in paragraph (c) of this section, the contracting officer shall use cost or price analysis and consider commercial prices for similar products and services, available in-house cost estimates, data (including certified cost or pricing data) submitted by the SBA or the 8(a) contractor, and data obtained from any other Government agency.

(c) In estimating a fair market price for a repeat purchase, the contracting officer shall consider recent award prices for the same items or work if there is comparability in quantities, conditions, terms, and performance times. The estimated price should be adjusted to reflect differences in specifications, plans, transportation costs, packaging and packing costs, and other circumstances. Price indices may be used as guides to determine the changes in labor and material costs. Comparison of commercial prices for similar items may also be used.

United States Code Annotated

Additional powers, see 15 USCA § 637.

Administrative determinations, see 41 USCA § 257.

Awards or contracts, see 15 USCA § 644.

Contract goal for small disadvantaged businesses and certain institutions of higher education, see 10 USCA § 2323.

Contract requirements, see 41 USCA § 254.

Contracts, planning, solicitation, evaluation, and award procedures, see 10 USCA § 2305.

Credit for Indian contracting in meeting certain subcontracting goals for small disadvantaged businesses and certain institutions of higher education, see 10 USCA § 2323a.

Definitions, see 10 USCA § 2302, 41 USCA §§ 259, 403.

Determinations and decisions, see 10 USCA § 2310, 41 USCA § 262.

HUBZone program, see 15 USCA § 657a.

Kinds of contracts, see 10 USCA § 2306.

Planning and solicitation requirements, see 41 USCA § 253a.

Procurement data, see 41 USCA § 417a.

Procurement program for small business concerns owned and controlled by service-disabled veterans, see 15 USCA § 657f.

§ 19.808 Contract negotiation.

§ 19.808-1 Sole source.

(a) The SBA may not accept for negotiation a sole-source 8(a) contract that exceeds $22 million unless the requesting agency has completed a justification in accordance with the requirements of 6.303.

(b) The SBA is responsible for initiating negotiations with the agency within the time established by the agency. If the SBA does not initiate negotiations within the agreed time and the agency cannot allow additional time, the agency may, after notifying the SBA, proceed with the acquisition from other sources.

(c) The SBA should participate, whenever practicable, in negotiating the contracting terms. When mutually agreeable, the SBA may authorize the contracting activity to negotiate directly with the 8(a) contractor. Whether or not direct negotiations take place, the SBA is responsible for approving the resulting contract before award.

United States Code Annotated

Additional powers, see 15 USCA § 637.

Administrative determinations, see 41 USCA § 257.

Awards or contracts, see 15 USCA § 644.

Contract goal for small disadvantaged businesses and certain institutions of higher education, see 10 USCA § 2323.

Contract requirements, see 41 USCA § 254.

Contracts, planning, solicitation, evaluation, and award procedures, see 10 USCA § 2305.

Credit for Indian contracting in meeting certain subcontracting goals for small disadvantaged businesses and certain institutions of higher education, see 10 USCA § 2323a.

Definitions, see 10 USCA § 2302, 41 USCA §§ 259, 403.

Determinations and decisions, see 10 USCA § 2310, 41 USCA § 262.

HUBZone program, see 15 USCA § 657a.

Kinds of contracts, see 10 USCA § 2306.

Planning and solicitation requirements, see 41 USCA § 253a.

Procurement data, see 41 USCA § 417a.

Procurement program for small business concerns owned and controlled by service-disabled veterans, see 15 USCA § 657f.

§ 19.808-2 Competitive.

In competitive 8(a) acquisitions subject to Part 15, the contracting officer conducts negotiations directly with the competing 8(a) firms. Conducting competitive negotiations among 8(a) firms prior to SBA's formal acceptance of the acquisition for the 8(a) Program may be grounds for SBA's not accepting the acquisition for the 8(a) Program.

United States Code Annotated

Additional powers, see 15 USCA § 637.

Administrative determinations, see 41 USCA § 257.

Awards or contracts, see 15 USCA § 644.

Contract goal for small disadvantaged businesses and certain institutions of higher education, see 10 USCA § 2323.

Contract requirements, see 41 USCA § 254.

Contracts, planning, solicitation, evaluation, and award procedures, see 10 USCA § 2305.

Credit for Indian contracting in meeting certain subcontracting goals for small disadvantaged businesses and certain institutions of higher education, see 10 USCA § 2323a.

Definitions, see 10 USCA § 2302, 41 USCA §§ 259, 403.

Determinations and decisions, see 10 USCA § 2310, 41 USCA § 262.

HUBZone program, see 15 USCA § 657a.

Kinds of contracts, see 10 USCA § 2306.

Planning and solicitation requirements, see 41 USCA § 253a.

Procurement data, see 41 USCA § 417a.

Procurement program for small business concerns owned and controlled by service-disabled veterans, see 15 USCA § 657f.

§ 19.809 Preaward considerations.

The contracting officer should request a preaward survey of the 8(a) contractor whenever considered useful. If the results of the preaward survey or other information available to the contracting officer raise substantial doubt as to the firm's ability to perform, the contracting officer must refer the matter to SBA for Certificate of Competency consideration under Subpart 19.6.

United States Code Annotated

Additional powers, see 15 USCA § 637.

Administrative determinations, see 41 USCA § 257.

Awards or contracts, see 15 USCA § 644.

Contract goal for small disadvantaged businesses and certain institutions of higher education, see 10 USCA § 2323.

Contract requirements, see 41 USCA § 254.

Contracts, planning, solicitation, evaluation, and award procedures, see 10 USCA § 2305.

Credit for Indian contracting in meeting certain subcontracting goals for small disadvantaged businesses and certain institutions of higher education, see 10 USCA § 2323a.

Definitions, see 10 USCA § 2302, 41 USCA §§ 259, 403.

Determinations and decisions, see 10 USCA § 2310, 41 USCA § 262.

HUBZone program, see 15 USCA § 657a.

Kinds of contracts, see 10 USCA § 2306.

Planning and solicitation requirements, see 41 USCA § 253a.

Procurement data, see 41 USCA § 417a.

Procurement program for small business concerns owned and controlled by service-disabled veterans, see 15 USCA § 657f.

§ 19.810 SBA appeals.

(a) The SBA Administrator may submit the following matters for determination to the agency head if the SBA and the contracting officer fail to agree on them:

(1) The decision not to make a particular acquisition available for award under the 8(a) Program.

(2) A contracting officer's decision to reject a specific 8(a) firm for award of an 8(a) contract after SBA's acceptance of the requirement for the 8(a) Program.

(3) The terms and conditions of a proposed 8(a) contract, including the contracting activity's NAICS code designation and estimate of the fair market price.

(b) Notification of a proposed appeal to the agency head by the SBA must be received by the contracting officer within 5 working days after the SBA is formally notified of the contracting officer's decision. The SBA will provide the agency Director for Small and Disadvantaged Business Utilization a copy of this notification of the intent to appeal. The SBA must send the written appeal to the head of the contracting activity within 15 working days of SBA's notification of intent to appeal or the contracting activity may consider the appeal withdrawn. Pending issuance of a decision by the agency head, the contracting officer must suspend action on the acquisition. The contracting officer need not suspend action on the acquisition if the contracting officer makes a written determination that urgent and compelling circumstances that significantly affect the interests of the United States will not permit waiting for a decision.

(c) If the SBA appeal is denied, the decision of the agency head shall specify the reasons for the denial, including the reasons why the selected firm was determined incapable of performance, if appropriate. The decision shall be made a part of the contract file.

United States Code Annotated

Additional powers, see 15 USCA § 637.

Administrative determinations, see 41 USCA § 257.

Awards or contracts, see 15 USCA § 644.

Contract goal for small disadvantaged businesses and certain institutions of higher education, see 10 USCA § 2323.

Contract requirements, see 41 USCA § 254.

Contracts, planning, solicitation, evaluation, and award procedures, see 10 USCA § 2305.

Credit for Indian contracting in meeting certain subcontracting goals for small disadvantaged businesses and certain institutions of higher education, see 10 USCA § 2323a.

Definitions, see 10 USCA § 2302, 41 USCA §§ 259, 403.

Determinations and decisions, see 10 USCA § 2310, 41 USCA § 262.

HUBZone program, see 15 USCA § 657a.

Kinds of contracts, see 10 USCA § 2306.

Planning and solicitation requirements, see 41 USCA § 253a.

Procurement data, see 41 USCA § 417a.

Procurement program for small business concerns owned and controlled by service-disabled veterans, see 15 USCA § 657f.

§ 19.811 Preparing the contracts.

§ 19.811-1 Sole source.

(a) The contract to be awarded by the agency to the SBA shall be prepared in accordance with agency procedures and in the same detail as would be required in a contract with a business concern. The contracting officer shall use the Standard Form 26 as the award form, except for construction contracts, in which case the Standard Form 1442 shall be used as required in 36.701(a).

(b) The agency shall prepare the contract that the SBA will award to the 8(a) contractor in accordance with agency procedures, as if the agency were awarding the contract directly to the 8(a) contractor, except for the following:

(1) The award form shall cite 41 U.S.C. 3304(a)(5) or 10 U.S.C. 2304(c)(5) (as appropriate) as the authority for use of other than full and open competition.

(2) Appropriate clauses shall be included, as necessary, to reflect that the contract is between the SBA and the 8(a) contractor.

(3) The following items shall be inserted by the SBA:

(i) The SBA contract number.

(ii) The effective date.

(iii) The typed name of the SBA's contracting officer.

(iv) The signature of the SBA's contracting officer.

(v) The date signed.

(4) The SBA will obtain the signature of the 8(a) contractor prior to signing and returning the prime contract to the contracting officer for signature. The SBA will make every effort to obtain signatures and return the contract, and any subsequent bilateral modification, to the contracting officer within a maximum of 10 working days.

(c) Except in procurements where the SBA will make advance payments to its 8(a) contractor, the agency contracting officer may, as an alternative to the procedures in paragraphs (a) and (b) of this subsection, use a single contract document for both the prime contract between the agency and the SBA and its 8(a) contractor. The single contract document shall contain the information in paragraphs (b) (1), (2), and (3) of this subsection. Appropriate blocks on the Standard Form (SF) 26 or 1442 will be asterisked and a continuation sheet appended as a tripartite agreement which includes the following:

(1) Agency acquisition office, prime contract number, name of agency contracting officer and lines for signature, date signed, and effective date.

(2) The SBA office, the SBA contract number, name of the SBA contracting officer, and lines for signature and date signed.

(3) Name and lines for the 8(a) subcontractor's signature and date signed.

(d) For acquisitions not exceeding the simplified acquisition threshold, the contracting officer may use the alternative procedures in paragraph (c) of this subsection with the appropriate simplified acquisition forms.

United States Code Annotated

Additional powers, see 15 USCA § 637.

Administrative determinations, see 41 USCA § 257.

Awards or contracts, see 15 USCA § 644.

Contract goal for small disadvantaged businesses and certain institutions of higher education, see 10 USCA § 2323.

Contract requirements, see 41 USCA § 254.

Contracts, planning, solicitation, evaluation, and award procedures, see 10 USCA § 2305.

Credit for Indian contracting in meeting certain subcontracting goals for small disadvantaged businesses and certain institutions of higher education, see 10 USCA § 2323a.

Definitions, see 10 USCA § 2302, 41 USCA §§ 259, 403.

Determinations and decisions, see 10 USCA § 2310, 41 USCA § 262.

HUBZone program, see 15 USCA § 657a.

Kinds of contracts, see 10 USCA § 2306.

Planning and solicitation requirements, see 41 USCA § 253a.

Procurement data, see 41 USCA § 417a.

Procurement program for small business concerns owned and controlled by service-disabled veterans, see 15 USCA § 657f.

§ 19.811-2 Competitive.

(a) The contract will be prepared in accordance with 14.408-1(d), except that appropriate blocks on the Standard Form 26 or 1442 will be asterisked and a continuation sheet appended as a tripartite agreement which includes the following:

(1) The agency contracting activity, prime contract number, name of agency contracting officer, and lines for signature, date signed, and effective date.

(2) The SBA office, the SBA subcontract number, name of the SBA contracting officer and lines for signature and date signed.

(b) The process for obtaining signatures shall be as specified in 19.811-1(b)(4).

United States Code Annotated

Additional powers, see 15 USCA § 637.

Administrative determinations, see 41 USCA § 257.

Awards or contracts, see 15 USCA § 644.

Contract goal for small disadvantaged businesses and certain institutions of higher education, see 10 USCA § 2323.

Contract requirements, see 41 USCA § 254.

Contracts, planning, solicitation, evaluation, and award procedures, see 10 USCA § 2305.

Credit for Indian contracting in meeting certain subcontracting goals for small disadvantaged businesses and certain institutions of higher education, see 10 USCA § 2323a.

Definitions, see 10 USCA § 2302, 41 USCA §§ 259, 403.

Determinations and decisions, see 10 USCA § 2310, 41 USCA § 262.

HUBZone program, see 15 USCA § 657a.

Kinds of contracts, see 10 USCA § 2306.

Planning and solicitation requirements, see 41 USCA § 253a.

Procurement data, see 41 USCA § 417a.

Procurement program for small business concerns owned and controlled by service-disabled veterans, see 15 USCA § 657f.

§ 19.811-3 Contract clauses.

(a) The contracting officer shall insert the clause at 52.219-11, Special 8(a) Contract Conditions, in contracts between the SBA and the agency when the acquisition is accomplished using the procedures of 19.811-1(a) and (b).

(b) The contracting officer shall insert the clause at 52.219-12, Special 8(a) Subcontract Conditions, in contracts between the SBA and its 8(a) contractor when the acquisition is accomplished using the procedures of 19.811-1(a) and (b).

(c) The contracting officer shall insert the clause at 52.219-17, Section 8(a) Award, in competitive solicitations and contracts when the acquisition is accomplished using the procedures of 19.805 and in sole source awards which utilize the alternative procedure in 19.811-1(c).

(d) The contracting officer shall insert the clause at 52.219-18, Notification of Competition Limited to Eligible 8(a) Concerns, in competitive solicitations and contracts when the acquisition is accomplished using the procedures of 19.805.

(1) The clause at 52.219-18 with its Alternate I will be used when competition is to be limited to 8(a) concerns within one or more specific SBA districts pursuant to 19.804-2.

(2) The clause at 52.219-18 with its Alternate II will be used when the acquisition is for a product in a class for which the Small Business Administration has waived the nonmanufacturer rule (see 19.102(f)(4) and (5)).

(e) The contracting officer shall insert the clause at 52.219-14, Limitations on Subcontracting, in any solicitation and contract resulting from this subpart. This includes multiple-award contracts when orders may be set aside for 8(a) concerns as described in 8.405-5 and 16.505(b)(2)(i)(F).

United States Code Annotated

Additional powers, see 15 USCA § 637.

Administrative determinations, see 41 USCA § 257.

Awards or contracts, see 15 USCA § 644.

Contract goal for small disadvantaged businesses and certain institutions of higher education, see 10 USCA § 2323.

Contract requirements, see 41 USCA § 254.

Contracts, planning, solicitation, evaluation, and award procedures, see 10 USCA § 2305.

Credit for Indian contracting in meeting certain subcontracting goals for small disadvantaged businesses and certain institutions of higher education, see 10 USCA § 2323a.

Definitions, see 10 USCA § 2302, 41 USCA §§ 259, 403.

Determinations and decisions, see 10 USCA § 2310, 41 USCA § 262.

HUBZone program, see 15 USCA § 657a.

Kinds of contracts, see 10 USCA § 2306.

Planning and solicitation requirements, see 41 USCA § 253a.

Procurement data, see 41 USCA § 417a.

Procurement program for small business concerns owned and controlled by service-disabled veterans, see 15 USCA § 657f.

§ **19.812 contract administration.**

(a) The contracting officer shall assign contract administration functions, as required, based on the location of the 8(a) contractor (see Federal Directory of Contract Administration Services Components (available via the Internet at https://pubapp.dcma.mil/CASD/main.jsp)).

(b) The agency shall distribute copies of the contract(s) in accordance with Part 4. All contracts and modifications, if any, shall be distributed to both the SBA and the firm in accordance with the timeframes set forth in 4.201.

(c) To the extent consistent with the contracting activity's capability and resources, 8(a) contractors furnishing requirements shall be afforded production and technical assistance, including, when appropriate, identification of causes of deficiencies in their products and suggested corrective action to make such products acceptable.

(d) An 8(a) contract, whether in the base or an option year, must be terminated for convenience if the 8(a) concern to which it was awarded transfers ownership or control of the firm or if the contract is transferred or novated for any reason to another firm, unless the Administrator of the SBA waives the requirement for contract termination (13 CFR 124. 515). The Administrator may waive the termination requirement only if certain conditions exist. Moreover, a waiver of the requirement for termination is permitted only if the 8(a) firm's request for waiver is made to the SBA prior to the actual relinquishment of ownership or control, except in the case of death or incapacity where the waiver must be submitted within 60 days after such an occurrence. The clauses in the contract entitled "Special 8(a) Contract Conditions" and "Special 8(a) Subcontract Conditions" require the SBA and the 8(a) subcontractor to notify the contracting officer when ownership of the firm is being transferred. When the contracting officer receives information that an 8(a) contractor is planning to transfer ownership or control to another firm, the contracting officer must take action immediately to preserve the option of waiving the termination requirement. The contracting officer should determine the timing of the proposed transfer and its effect on contract performance and mission support. If the contracting officer determines that the SBA does not intend to waive the termination requirement, and termination of the contract would severely impair attainment of the agency's program objectives or mission, the contracting officer should immediately notify the SBA in writing that the agency is requesting a waiver. Within 15 business days thereafter, or such longer period as agreed to by the agency and the SBA, the agency head must either confirm or withdraw the request for waiver. Unless a waiver is approved by the SBA, the contracting officer must terminate the contract for convenience upon receipt of a written request by the SBA. This requirement for a convenience termination does not affect the Government's right to terminate for default if the cause for termination of an 8(a) contract is other than the transfer of ownership or control.

United States Code Annotated

Additional powers, see 15 USCA § 637.

Administrative determinations, see 41 USCA § 257.

Awards or contracts, see 15 USCA § 644.

Contract goal for small disadvantaged businesses and certain institutions of higher education, see 10 USCA § 2323.

Contract requirements, see 41 USCA § 254.

Contracts, planning, solicitation, evaluation, and award procedures, see 10 USCA § 2305.

Credit for Indian contracting in meeting certain subcontracting goals for small disadvantaged businesses and certain institutions of higher education, see 10 USCA § 2323a.

Definitions, see 10 USCA § 2302, 41 USCA §§ 259, 403.

Determinations and decisions, see 10 USCA § 2310, 41 USCA § 262.

HUBZone program, see 15 USCA § 657a.

Kinds of contracts, see 10 USCA § 2306.

Planning and solicitation requirements, see 41 USCA § 253a.

Procurement data, see 41 USCA § 417a.

Procurement program for small business concerns owned and controlled by service-disabled veterans, see 15 USCA § 657f.

Subpart 19.9 [Reserved]

Subpart 19.10 [Reserved]

Subpart 19.11 —[Reserved]

Subpart 19.12 —[Reserved]

Subpart 19.13 Historically Underutilized Business Zone (HUBZone) Program

§ 19.1301 General.

(a) The Historically Underutilized Business Zone (HUBZone) Act of 1997 (15 U.S.C. 631 note) created the HUBZone Program.

(b) The purpose of the HUBZone Program is to provide Federal contracting assistance for qualified small business concerns located in historically underutilized business zones, in an effort to increase employment opportunities, investment, and economic development in those areas.

United States Code Annotated

Additional powers, see 15 USCA § 637.

Administrative determinations, see 41 USCA § 257.

Awards or contracts, see 15 USCA § 644.

Contract goal for small disadvantaged businesses and certain institutions of higher education, see 10 USCA § 2323.

Contract requirements, see 41 USCA § 254.

Contracts, planning, solicitation, evaluation, and award procedures, see 10 USCA § 2305.

Credit for Indian contracting in meeting certain subcontracting goals for small disadvantaged businesses and certain institutions of higher education, see 10 USCA § 2323a.

Definitions, see 10 USCA § 2302, 41 USCA §§ 259, 403.

Determinations and decisions, see 10 USCA § 2310, 41 USCA § 262.

HUBZone program, see 15 USCA § 657a.

Kinds of contracts, see 10 USCA § 2306.

Planning and solicitation requirements, see 41 USCA § 253a.

Procurement data, see 41 USCA § 417a.

Procurement program for small business concerns owned and controlled by service-disabled veterans, see 15 USCA § 657f.

Notes of Decisions

In general 1
Pleadings 4
Protest 3
Set-asides 2

1 In general

Administrative Procedure Act's arbitrary and capricious standard of review did not apply to Navy contracting officer's designation of certain contract bid solicitations as Historically Underutilized Business Zone ("HUBZone")-only, since officer was carrying out legal duty she believed to be required by Small Business Act implementing regulations. Small Business Act, § 2[31], as amended, 15 U.S.C.A. § 657a; 13 C.F.R. § 126.607; 48 C.F.R. § 19.1305. Contract Management, Inc. v. Rumsfeld, 291 F. Supp. 2d 1166 (D. Haw. 2003), aff'd, 434 F.3d 1145 (9th Cir. 2006). United States ☞64.15

Omission of clause in request for proposals (RFP) giving notice of price evaluation preference for HUBZone small business concerns was not prejudicial procurement error, where RFP required offerors to list their small business or HUBZone small business status, and bidders did so, indicating clear knowledge as to the existence of small business and HUBZone provisions. Small Business Act, § 2[31](b)(3)(A), as amended, 15 U.S.C.A. § 657a(b)(3)(A); 48 C.F.R. § 52.219-4. Delaney Const. Corp. v. U.S., 56 Fed. Cl. 470, 197 A.L.R. Fed. 719 (2003). United States ☞64.25

Where contract was awarded without a HUBZone price evaluation preference on the basis of a faulty small business certification of the contract awardee, it was appropriate to take corrective action by terminating the contract, and proceeding to make a new award based on the proposals previously received with application of the HUBZone price evaluation preference mandated by statute; however, it was not necessary to amend the request for proposals (RFP) to include the HUBZone notice clause and then obtain new price proposals, as there was no evidence that presence of clause would have any additional impact on price competition, and prices proposed by all offerors for the contract have been mistakenly disclosed by the contracting agency. Small Business Act, § 2[31](b)(3)(A), as amended, 15 U.S.C.A. § 657a(b)(3)(A); 48 C.F.R. §§ 19.1307(b)(2), 52.219-4. Delaney Const. Corp. v. U.S., 56 Fed. Cl. 470, 197 A.L.R. Fed. 719 (2003). United States ☞64.40(5)

Mandatory procurement preference for blind vendors provided by the Randolph—Sheppard Vending Stand Act, and Department of Defense procurement regulation implementing the preference, is not incompatible with disadvantaged business preference provided by the

Historically Underutilized Business Zone Act; fact that blind vendor preference carries more weight in military vending procurement does not, per se, create a conflict. Small Business Act, § 2[3](p), as amended, 15 U.S.C.A. § 632(p); Randolph—Sheppard Vending Stand Act, §§ 1–10, as amended, 20 U.S.C.A. §§ 107–107f. Automated Communication Systems, Inc. v. U.S., 49 Fed. Cl. 570 (2001). United States ☞57

2 Set-asides

Editor Note: On September 27, 2010, the "Small Business Jobs Act" (HR 5297) ended the long-running debate within the federal government regarding whether set-asides for HUBZone vendors had priority over awards to either an 8(a) vendor or a service disabled veteran-owned small business. Section 1347 of the Act amends the HUBZone statute (15 USC § 657a) by changing "shall" set-aside to "may" set-aside, when it is expected that offers will be received from two or more qualified HUBZone firms.

Federal regulations that implemented Small Business Act's Historically Underutilized Business Zone ("HUBZone") program by mandating HUBZone set-asides for government contracts in certain circumstances did not frustrate overarching goals of Act, even though they benefited narrow group of small businesses. Small Business Act, §§ 2[2](a), 2[15](g), 2[31](b)(2), as amended, 15 U.S.C.A. §§ 631(a), 644(g), 657a(b)(2); 13 C.F.R. § 126.607; 48 C.F.R. §§ 19.1301(b), 19.1305. Contract Management, Inc. v. Rumsfeld, 291 F. Supp. 2d 1166 (D. Haw. 2003), aff'd, 434 F.3d 1145 (9th Cir. 2006). United States ☞64.15

Small Business Act's Historically Underutilized Business Zone ("HUBZone") program was not limited to new contracts, nor did it require that contracts set aside for HUBZone businesses be performed within HUBZones. Small Business Act, § 2[31], as amended, 15 U.S.C.A. § 657a. Contract Management, Inc. v. Rumsfeld, 291 F. Supp. 2d 1166 (D. Haw. 2003), aff'd, 434 F.3d 1145 (9th Cir. 2006). United States ☞64.15

Fact that Small Business Act program for disadvantaged small businesses mandated competition of eligible government contractors, while leaving to agency discretion initial offer and acceptance of contracts into program, did not require that Act's Historically Underutilized Business Zone ("HUBZone") program extend same discretion; thus, HUBZone implementing regulations that mandated HUBZone set-asides in certain circumstances were valid. Small Business Act, §§ 2[8](a)(1)(D)(i), 2[31](b)(2)(B), as amended, 15 U.S.C.A. §§ 637(a)(1)(D)(i), 657a(b)(2)(B); 13 C.F.R. § 126.607; 48 C.F.R. § 19.1305. Contract Management, Inc. v. Rumsfeld, 291 F. Supp. 2d 1166 (D. Haw. 2003), aff'd, 434 F.3d 1145 (9th Cir. 2006). United States ☞64.15

Small Business Administration (SBA) reasonably resolved conflict between congressional objective of parity between Small Business Act program for disadvantaged small businesses and second program for Historically Underutilized Business Zone ("HUBZone") businesses, on one hand, and mandatory status of HUBZone set-asides, on other, by limiting scope of HUBZone preference so that it did not affect other program. Small Business Act, § 2[31](b)(2), as amended, 15 U.S.C.A. § 657a(b)(2); 13 C.F.R. § 126.605; 48 C.F.R. § 19.1304(d). Contract Management, Inc. v. Rumsfeld, 291 F. Supp. 2d 1166 (D. Haw. 2003), aff'd, 434 F.3d 1145 (9th Cir. 2006). United States ☞64.15

Bidder's interpretation of solicitation as incorporating HUBZone set-aside clause, by virtue of its incorporation of regulation listing that clause and other standard clauses, created a patent ambiguity regarding which of the clauses, if any, applied to the solicitation, since set-aside clause was mutually exclusive of another clause listed in regulation, and bidder's failure to inquire meant that solicitation had to be construed against it. 48 C.F.R. §§ 52.212-5(b), 52.219-3. J & H Reinforcing and Structural Erectors, Inc. v. U.S., 50 Fed. Cl. 570 (2001). United States ☞64.25

Bidder who contended it was misled in believing that solicitation was a special HUBZone set-aside could not rely on oral representations or misrepresentations by contracting personnel; rather, under regulation, bidder was required to inquire in writing. 48 C.F.R. § 52.214-6. J & H Reinforcing and Structural Erectors, Inc. v. U.S., 50 Fed. Cl. 570 (2001). United States ☞64.25

3 Protest

Language in bidder's fax to contract specialist sufficiently conveyed an expression of dissatisfaction with another bidder's HUBZone status as to constitute a HUBZone status protest, where bidder complained that "it would be upset" if it were determined that rival bidder was eligible for the HUBZone advantage, and submitted evidence that rival bidder might not be eligible for HUBZone status because, "according to the SBA HUB Zone locator their address IS NOT in a HUB Zone." 13 C.F.R. § 126.801(b). Mark Dunning Industries, Inc. v. U.S., 58 Fed. Cl. 216 (2003). United States ☞64.55(2)

Fact that bidder's HUBZone status protest in fax to contracting officer (CO) did not state all the specific grounds for the protest did not relieve CO of his duty under regulation to forward protest to the Small Business Administration (SBA); regulation clearly required CO to forward the protest to the SBA "notwithstanding whether he or she believes it is sufficiently specific." 13 C.F.R. § 126.801(b, e). Mark Dunning Industries, Inc. v. U.S., 58 Fed. Cl. 216 (2003). United States ☞64.55(2)

Bidder's request in fax that the contracting officer (CO) "verify all certifications before making any determinations and applying any bid advantages" was sufficient request for corrective action to qualify fax as a valid HUBZone status protest, as context made it clear that bidder was requesting that CO make sure that rival bidder was actually qualified for HUBZone status certification. 13 C.F.R. § 126.801. Mark Dunning Industries, Inc. v. U.S., 58 Fed. Cl. 216 (2003). United States ☞64.55(2)

4 Pleadings

Bid protestor's statement in its verified complaint that it had not filed a valid HUBZone status protest did not preclude it from changing its position on the issue, where it corrected the assertion early in the case, and thus defendant was not prejudiced. Mark Dunning Industries, Inc. v. U.S., 58 Fed. Cl. 216 (2003). Federal Courts ☞1111

§ 19.1302 Applicability.

The procedures in this subpart apply to all Federal agencies that employ one or more contracting officers.

United States Code Annotated

Additional powers, see 15 USCA § 637.

Administrative determinations, see 41 USCA § 257.

Awards or contracts, see 15 USCA § 644.

Contract goal for small disadvantaged businesses and certain institutions of higher education, see 10 USCA § 2323.

Contract requirements, see 41 USCA § 254.

Contracts, planning, solicitation, evaluation, and award procedures, see 10 USCA § 2305.

Credit for Indian contracting in meeting certain subcontracting goals for small disadvantaged businesses and certain institutions of higher education, see 10 USCA § 2323a.

Definitions, see 10 USCA § 2302, 41 USCA §§ 259, 403.

Determinations and decisions, see 10 USCA § 2310, 41 USCA § 262.

HUBZone program, see 15 USCA § 657a.

Kinds of contracts, see 10 USCA § 2306.

Planning and solicitation requirements, see 41 USCA § 253a.

Procurement data, see 41 USCA § 417a.

Procurement program for small business concerns owned and controlled by service-disabled veterans, see 15 USCA § 657f.

§ 19.1303 Status as a HUBZone small business concern.

(a) Status as a HUBZone small business concern is determined by the Small Business Administration (SBA) in accordance with 13 CFR Part 126.

(b) If the SBA determines that a concern is a HUBZone small business concern, it will issue a certification to that effect and will add the concern to the List of Qualified HUBZone Small Business Concerns at http://dsbs.sba.gov/dsbs/search/dsp_searchhubzone.cfm. Only firms on the list are HUBZone small business concerns, eligible for HUBZone preferences. HUBZone preferences apply without regard to the place of performance. Information on HUBZone small business concerns can also be obtained at www.sba.gov/hubzone or by writing to the Director for the HUBZone Program (Director/HUB) at U.S. Small Business Administration, 409 3rd Street, SW., Washington, DC 20416 or at mailto:hubzone@sba.gov.

(c) A joint venture may be considered a HUBZone small business concern if it meets the criteria in the explanation of affiliates (see 19.101).

(d) To be eligible for a HUBZone contract under this section, a HUBZone small business concern must be a HUBZone small business concern both at the time of its initial offer and at the time of contract award.

(e) A HUBZone small business concern may submit an offer for supplies as a nonmanufacturer if it meets the requirements of the nonmanufacturer rule set forth at 13 CFR 121.406(b)(1) and if the small business manufacturer providing the end item is also a HUBZone small business concern.

(1) There are no waivers to the nonmanufacturer rule for HUBZone contracts.

(2) For HUBZone contracts at or below $25,000 in total value, a HUBZone small business concern may supply the end item of any manufacturer, including a large business, so long as the product acquired is manufactured or produced in the United States.

United States Code Annotated

Additional powers, see 15 USCA § 637.

Administrative determinations, see 41 USCA § 257.

Awards or contracts, see 15 USCA § 644.

Contract goal for small disadvantaged businesses and certain institutions of higher education, see 10 USCA § 2323.

Contract requirements, see 41 USCA § 254.

Contracts, planning, solicitation, evaluation, and award procedures, see 10 USCA § 2305.

Credit for Indian contracting in meeting certain subcontracting goals for small disadvantaged businesses and certain institutions of higher education, see 10 USCA § 2323a.

Definitions, see 10 USCA § 2302, 41 USCA §§ 259, 403.

Determinations and decisions, see 10 USCA § 2310, 41 USCA § 262.

HUBZone program, see 15 USCA § 657a.

Kinds of contracts, see 10 USCA § 2306.

Planning and solicitation requirements, see 41 USCA § 253a.

Procurement data, see 41 USCA § 417a.

Procurement program for small business concerns owned and controlled by service-disabled veterans, see 15 USCA § 657f.

Notes of Decisions

In general 1
Non-manufacturer rule 4
Pleadings 3
Set-asides 2

1 In general

Editor Note: On September 27, 2010, the "Small Business Jobs Act" (HR 5297) ended the long-running debate within the federal government regarding whether set-asides for HUBZone vendors had priority over awards to either an 8(a) vendor or a service disabled veteran-owned small business. Section 1347 of the Act amends the HUBZone statute (15 USC § 657a) by changing "shall" set-aside to "may" set-aside, when it is expected that offers will be received from two or more qualified HUBZone firms.

Administrative Procedure Act's arbitrary and capricious standard of review did not apply to Navy contracting officer's designation of certain contract bid solicitations as Historically Underutilized Business Zone ("HUBZone")-only, since officer was carrying out legal duty she believed to be required by Small Business Act implementing regulations. Small Business Act, § 2[31], as amended, 15 U.S.C.A. § 657a; 13 C.F.R. § 126.607; 48 C.F.R. § 19. 1305. Contract Management, Inc. v. Rumsfeld, 291 F. Supp. 2d 1166 (D. Haw. 2003), aff'd, 434 F.3d 1145 (9th Cir. 2006). United States ☞64.15

A HUBZone contractor has "safe harbor" from the requirement that at least 35 percent of its employees reside in the HUBZone, if it "attempts to maintain" that percentage. However, the provision permits the firm to maintain HUBZone status only for an existing contract. A firm claiming HUBZone status for a new contract must actually satisfy the requirements for HUBZone status, rather than simply attempt to meet the requirements, both at the time it submits its proposal and at the time of award. Mission Critical Solutions v. U.S., 96 Fed. Cl. 657 (2011)

Omission of clause in request for proposals (RFP) giving notice of price evaluation preference for HUBZone small business concerns was not prejudicial procurement error, where RFP required offerors to list their small business or HUBZone small business status, and bidders did so, indicating clear knowledge as to the existence of small business and HUBZone provisions. Small Business Act, § 2[31](b)(3)(A), as amended, 15 U.S.C.A. § 657a(b)(3)(A); 48 C.F.R. § 52.219-4. Delaney Const. Corp. v. U.S., 56 Fed. Cl. 470, 197 A.L.R. Fed. 719 (2003). United States ☞64.25

Where contract was awarded without a HUBZone price evaluation preference on the basis of a faulty small business certification of the contract awardee, it was appropriate to take corrective action by terminating the contract, and proceeding to make a new award based on the proposals previously received with application of the HUBZone price evaluation preference mandated by statute; however, it was not necessary to amend the request for proposals (RFP) to include the HUBZone notice clause and then obtain new price proposals, as there was no evidence that presence of clause would have any additional impact on price competition, and prices proposed by all offerors for the contract have been mistakenly disclosed by the contracting agency. Small Business Act, § 2[31](b)(3)(A), as amended, 15 U.S.C.A. § 657a(b)(3)(A); 48 C.F.R. §§ 19.1307(b)(2), 52.219-4. Delaney Const. Corp. v. U.S., 56 Fed. Cl. 470, 197 A.L.R. Fed. 719 (2003). United States ☞64.40(5)

Mandatory procurement preference for blind vendors provided by the Randolph—Sheppard Vending Stand Act, and Department of Defense procurement regulation implementing the preference, is not incompatible with disadvantaged business preference provided by the Historically Underutilized Business Zone Act; fact that blind vendor preference carries more weight in military vending procurement does not, per se, create a conflict. Small Business Act, § 2[3](p), as amended, 15 U.S.C.A. § 632(p); Randolph—Sheppard Vending Stand Act, §§ 1–10, as amended, 20 U.S.C.A. §§ 107–107f. Automated Communication Systems, Inc. v. U.S., 49 Fed. Cl. 570 (2001). United States ☞57

2 Set-asides

Small Business Act's Historically Underutilized Business Zone ("HUBZone") program was not limited to new contracts, nor did it require that contracts set aside for HUBZone businesses be performed within HUBZones. Small Business Act, § 2[31], as amended, 15 U.S.C.A. § 657a. Contract Management, Inc. v. Rumsfeld, 291 F. Supp. 2d 1166 (D. Haw. 2003), aff'd, 434 F.3d 1145 (9th Cir. 2006). United States ☞64.15

Bidder's interpretation of solicitation as incorporating HUBZone set-aside clause, by virtue of its incorporation of regulation listing that clause and other standard clauses, created a patent ambiguity regarding which of the clauses, if any, applied to the solicitation, since set-aside clause was mutually exclusive of another clause listed in regulation, and bidder's failure to inquire meant that solicitation had to be construed against it. 48 C.F.R. §§ 52.212-5(b), 52.219-3. J & H Reinforcing and Structural Erectors, Inc. v. U.S., 50 Fed. Cl. 570 (2001). United States ☞64.25

Bidder who contended it was misled in believing that solicitation was a special HUBZone set-aside could not rely on oral representations or misrepresentations by contracting personnel; rather, under regulation, bidder was required to inquire in writing. 48 C.F.R. § 52.214-6. J & H Reinforcing and Structural Erectors, Inc. v. U.S., 50 Fed. Cl. 570 (2001). United States ☞64.25

3 Pleadings

Bid protestor's statement in its verified complaint that it had not filed a valid HUBZone status protest did not preclude it from changing its position on the issue, where it corrected the assertion early in the case, and thus defendant was not prejudiced. Mark Dunning Industries, Inc. v. U.S., 58 Fed. Cl. 216 (2003). Federal Courts ☞1111

4 Non-manufacturer rule

An agency's decision not to apply a statutory non-manufacturer rule to a Historically Underutilized Business Zone (HUBZone) set-aside was appropriate. The statutory non-manufacturer rule's plain language indicates that the rule applies only to 8(a) competitive procurement set-asides and general small business set-asides, which do not include HUBZone set-asides. SBA submitted comments arguing that the statutory non-manufacturer rule does not apply to HUBZone set-asides. Matter of: B & B Medical Services, Inc.; Rotech Healthcare, Inc., B-404241, B-404241.2, 2011 CPD ¶ 24 (Comp. Gen. 2011)

§ 19.1304 Exclusions.

This subpart does not apply to—

(a) Requirements that can be satisfied through award to—

(1) Federal Prison Industries, Inc. (see Subpart 8.6); or

(2) AbilityOne participating non-profit agencies for the blind or severely disabled (see Subpart 8.7);

(b) Orders under indefinite-delivery contracts (see subpart 16.5). (But see 16.505(b)(2)(i)(F) for discretionary set-asides of orders);

(c) Orders against Federal Supply Schedules (see subpart 8.4). (But see 8.405-5 for discretionary set-asides of orders);

(d) Requirements currently being performed by an 8(a) participant or requirements SBA has accepted for performance under the authority of the 8(a) Program, unless SBA has consented to release the requirements from the 8(a) Program;

(e) Requirements that do not exceed the micro-purchase threshold; or

(f) Requirements for commissary or exchange resale items.

United States Code Annotated

Additional powers, see 15 USCA § 637.

Administrative determinations, see 41 USCA § 257.

Awards or contracts, see 15 USCA § 644.

Contract goal for small disadvantaged businesses and certain institutions of higher education, see 10 USCA § 2323.

Contract requirements, see 41 USCA § 254.

Contracts, planning, solicitation, evaluation, and award procedures, see 10 USCA § 2305.

Credit for Indian contracting in meeting certain subcontracting goals for small disadvantaged businesses and certain institutions of higher education, see 10 USCA § 2323a.

Definitions, see 10 USCA § 2302, 41 USCA §§ 259, 403.

Determinations and decisions, see 10 USCA § 2310, 41 USCA § 262.

HUBZone program, see 15 USCA § 657a.

Kinds of contracts, see 10 USCA § 2306.

Planning and solicitation requirements, see 41 USCA § 253a.

Procurement data, see 41 USCA § 417a.

Procurement program for small business concerns owned and controlled by service-disabled veterans, see 15 USCA § 657f.

§ 19.1305 HUBZone set-aside procedures.

(a) The contracting officer—

(1) Shall comply with 19.203 before deciding to set aside an acquisition under the HUBZone Program;

(2) May set aside acquisitions exceeding the micro-purchase threshold for competition restricted to HUBZone small business concerns when the requirements of paragraph (b) of this section can be satisfied; and

(3) Shall consider HUBZone set-asides before considering HUBZone sole source awards (see 19.1306) or small business set-asides (see subpart 19.5).

(b) To set aside an acquisition for competition restricted to HUBZone small business concerns, the contracting officer must have a reasonable expectation that—

(1) Offers will be received from two or more HUBZone small business concerns; and

(2) Award will be made at a fair market price.

(c) If the contracting officer receives only one acceptable offer from a qualified HUBZone small business concern in response to a set aside, the contracting officer should make an award to that concern. If the contracting officer receives no acceptable offers from HUBZone small business concerns, the HUBZone set-aside shall be withdrawn and the requirement, if still valid, set aside for small business concerns, as appropriate (see 19.203).

(d) The procedures at 19.202-1 and, except for acquisitions not exceeding the simplified acquisition threshold, at 19.402 apply to this section.

(1) When the SBA intends to appeal a contracting officer's decision to reject a recommendation of the SBA procurement center representative (or, if a procurement center representative is not assigned, see 19.402(a)) to set aside an acquisition for competition restricted to HUBZone small business concerns, the SBA procurement center representative shall notify the contracting officer, in writing, of its intent within 5 business days of receiving the contracting officer's notice of rejection.

(2) Upon receipt of notice of SBA's intent to appeal, the contracting officer shall suspend action on the acquisition unless the head of the contracting activity makes a written determination that urgent and compelling circumstances, which significantly affect the interests of the Government, exist.

(3) Within 15 business days of SBA's notification to the contracting officer, SBA must file its formal appeal with the head of the agency, or the appeal will be deemed withdrawn. The head of the agency shall reply to SBA within 15 business days of receiving the appeal. The decision of the head of the agency shall be final.

United States Code Annotated

Additional powers, see 15 USCA § 637.

Administrative determinations, see 41 USCA § 257.

Awards or contracts, see 15 USCA § 644.

Contract goal for small disadvantaged businesses and certain institutions of higher education, see 10 USCA § 2323.

Contract requirements, see 41 USCA § 254.

Contracts, planning, solicitation, evaluation, and award procedures, see 10 USCA § 2305.

Credit for Indian contracting in meeting certain subcontracting goals for small disadvantaged businesses and certain institutions of higher education, see 10 USCA § 2323a.

Definitions, see 10 USCA § 2302, 41 USCA §§ 259, 403.

Determinations and decisions, see 10 USCA § 2310, 41 USCA § 262.

HUBZone program, see 15 USCA § 657a.

Kinds of contracts, see 10 USCA § 2306.

Planning and solicitation requirements, see 41 USCA § 253a.

Procurement data, see 41 USCA § 417a.

Procurement program for small business concerns owned and controlled by service-disabled veterans, see 15 USCA § 657f.

Notes of Decisions

In general 1

1 In general

Editor Note: On September 27, 2010, the "Small Business Jobs Act" (HR 5297) ended the long-running debate within the federal government regarding whether set-asides for HUBZone vendors had priority over awards to either an 8(a) vendor or a service disabled veteran-owned small business. Section 1347 of the Act amends the HUBZone statute (15 USC § 657a) by changing "shall" set-aside to "may" set-aside, when it is expected that offers will be received from two or more qualified HUBZone firms.

However, Air Force's decision to grant and award contract for recycling and solid waste management services at Air Force base via a sole source solicitation did not lack a rational basis, where contract awardee was only company that had requisite Washington State

Utilities and Transportation Commission (WUTC) solid waste disposal certificate; although other companies could apply for a temporary certificate, it was uncertain whether a temporary certificate would issue at all, and, even if it did, then that temporary certificate would last, at most, only 120 days. Blue Dot Energy Co., Inc. v. U.S., 179 Fed. Appx. 40 (Fed. Cir. 2006)

Administrative Procedure Act's arbitrary and capricious standard of review did not apply to Navy contracting officer's designation of certain contract bid solicitations as Historically Underutilized Business Zone ("HUBZone")-only, since officer was carrying out legal duty she believed to be required by Small Business Act implementing regulations. Small Business Act, § 2[31], as amended, 15 U.S.C.A. § 657a; 13 C.F.R. § 126.607; 48 C.F.R. § 19. 1305. Contract Management, Inc. v. Rumsfeld, 291 F. Supp. 2d 1166 (D. Haw. 2003), aff'd, 434 F.3d 1145 (9th Cir. 2006). United States ☞64.15

A contracting officer must make reasonable efforts to ascertain if it is likely that at least two small businesses capable of performing the work will submit offers, so as to satisfy requirement for a HUBZone program set aside. Small Business Act, § 2[31](b)(2)(B), 15 U.S.C.A. § 657a(b)(2)(B). Blue Dot Energy Co., Inc. v. U.S., 76 Fed. Cl. 783 (2004), rev'd on other grounds, 179 Fed. Appx. 40 (Fed. Cir. 2006)

Agency's decision to issue sole-source solicitation and contract for solid waste collection and disposal services, instead of conducting a competitive procurement in compliance with HUBZone small business set-aside requirements, lacked a rational basis insofar as it was based on its determination that offers would not be received from two or more Hubzone small business concerns; given prior procurement history and nature of contract, it was reasonable to assume that two or more HUBZone small business concerns would submit offers for any future solicitations. Small Business Act, § 2[31](b)(2)(B), 15 U.S.C.A. § 657a(b)(2)(B); 48 C.F.R. § 19.1305. Blue Dot Energy Co., Inc. v. U.S., 76 Fed. Cl. 783 (2004), rev'd, 179 Fed. Appx. 40 (Fed. Cir. 2006)

§ 19.1306 HUBZone sole source awards.

(a) A contracting officer shall consider a contract award to a HUBZone small business concern on a sole source basis (see 6.302-5(b)(5)) before considering a small business set-aside (see 19.203 and subpart 19.5), provided none of the exclusions at 19.1304 apply; and—

(1) The contracting officer does not have a reasonable expectation that offers would be received from two or more HUBZone small business concerns;

(2) The anticipated price of the contract, including options, will not exceed—

(i) $7 million for a requirement within the North American Industry Classification System (NAICS) codes for manufacturing; or

(ii) $4 million for a requirement within all other NAICS codes;

(3) The requirement is not currently being performed by an 8(a) participant under the provisions of Subpart 19.8 or has been accepted as a requirement by SBA under Subpart 19.8;

(4) The acquisition is greater than the simplified acquisition threshold (see Part 13);

(5) The HUBZone small business concern has been determined to be a responsible contractor with respect to performance; and

(6) Award can be made at a fair and reasonable price.

(b) The SBA has the right to appeal the contracting officer's decision not to make a HUBZone sole source award.

United States Code Annotated

Additional powers, see 15 USCA § 637.

Administrative determinations, see 41 USCA § 257.

Awards or contracts, see 15 USCA § 644.

Contract goal for small disadvantaged businesses and certain institutions of higher education, see 10 USCA § 2323.

Contract requirements, see 41 USCA § 254.

Contracts, planning, solicitation, evaluation, and award procedures, see 10 USCA § 2305.

Credit for Indian contracting in meeting certain subcontracting goals for small

disadvantaged businesses and certain institutions of higher education, see 10 USCA § 2323a.

Definitions, see 10 USCA § 2302, 41 USCA §§ 259, 403.

Determinations and decisions, see 10 USCA § 2310, 41 USCA § 262.

HUBZone program, see 15 USCA § 657a.

Kinds of contracts, see 10 USCA § 2306.

Planning and solicitation requirements, see 41 USCA § 253a.

Procurement data, see 41 USCA § 417a.

Procurement program for small business concerns owned and controlled by service-disabled veterans, see 15 USCA § 657f.

§ 19.1307 Price evaluation preference for HUBZone small business concerns.

(a) The price evaluation preference for HUBZone small business concerns shall be used in acquisitions conducted using full and open competition. The preference shall not be used—

(1) Where price is not a selection factor so that a price evaluation preference would not be considered (*e.g.,* Architect/Engineer acquisitions); or

(2) Where all fair and reasonable offers are accepted (*e.g.,* the award of multiple award schedule contracts).

(b) The contracting officer shall give offers from HUBZone small business concerns a price evaluation preference by adding a factor of 10 percent to all offers, except—

(1) Offers from HUBZone small business concerns that have not waived the evaluation preference; or

(2) Otherwise successful offers from small business concerns.

(c) The factor of 10 percent shall be applied on a line item basis or to any group of items on which award may be made. Other evaluation factors, such as transportation costs or rent-free use of Government property, shall be added to the offer to establish the base offer before adding the factor of 10 percent.

(d) When the two highest rated offerors are a HUBZone small business concern and a large business, and the evaluated offer of the HUBZone small business concern is equal to the evaluated offer of the large business after considering the price evaluation preference, the contracting officer shall award the contract to the HUBZone small business concern.

United States Code Annotated

Additional powers, see 15 USCA § 637.

Administrative determinations, see 41 USCA § 257.

Awards or contracts, see 15 USCA § 644.

Contract goal for small disadvantaged businesses and certain institutions of higher education, see 10 USCA § 2323.

Contract requirements, see 41 USCA § 254.

Contracts, planning, solicitation, evaluation, and award procedures, see 10 USCA § 2305.

Credit for Indian contracting in meeting certain subcontracting goals for small disadvantaged businesses and certain institutions of higher education, see 10 USCA § 2323a.

Definitions, see 10 USCA § 2302, 41 USCA §§ 259, 403.

Determinations and decisions, see 10 USCA § 2310, 41 USCA § 262.

HUBZone program, see 15 USCA § 657a.

Kinds of contracts, see 10 USCA § 2306.

Planning and solicitation requirements, see 41 USCA § 253a.

Procurement data, see 41 USCA § 417a.

Procurement program for small business concerns owned and controlled by service-disabled veterans, see 15 USCA § 657f.

Notes of Decisions

In general 1

1 In general

Where contract was awarded without a HUBZone price evaluation preference on the basis of a faulty small business certification of the contract awardee, it was appropriate to take corrective action by terminating the contract, and proceeding to make a new award based on the proposals previously received with application of the HUBZone price evaluation preference mandated by statute; however, it was not necessary to amend the request for proposals (RFP) to include the HUBZone notice clause and then obtain new price proposals, as there was no evidence that presence of clause would have any additional impact on price competition, and prices proposed by all offerors for the contract have been mistakenly disclosed by the contracting agency. Small Business Act, § 2[31](b)(3)(A), as amended, 15 U.S.C.A. § 657a(b)(3)(A); 48 C.F.R. §§ 19.1307(b)(2), 52.219-4. Delaney Const. Corp. v. U.S., 56 Fed. Cl. 470, 197 A.L.R. Fed. 719 (2003). United States ☞64.40(5)

The 10% price evaluation preference in favor of HUBZone firms applies to lease procurements. Although GAO determined that the FAR does not apply to the acquisition of real property leasehold interests, a real property lease is a contract and the HUBZone Act does not limit the type of contract to which it applies. As a result, GAO concluded that the 10$ price evaluation preference broadly applies to all federal contracts that involve full and open competition. Argos Group, LLC, B-406040, 2012 CPD ¶ 32, 2012 WL 235017 (Comp. Gen. 2012)

In a procurement that required a best value tradeoff, agency was required to apply Historically Underutilized Business Zone (HUBZone) price evaluation preference in evaluating proposals, even though HUBZone proposal was lower in price than the large business proposal, where the plain language of the solicitation, which incorporated Federal Acquisition Regulation clause 52.219-4, required that the price evaluation preference be applied. Explo Sys., Inc., B-404952, 2011 CPD ¶ 127 (Comp. Gen. 2011)

Protester, a non-HUBZone small business, alleged that the Government erred by not applying a 10% to the prices proposed by two large businesses with which it was competing. GAO denied the protest and held that the Government is not required to apply the HUBZone small business price-evaluation preference for an offeror that is not a HUBZone small business. Matter of: Martin Electronics, Inc.; AMTEC Corporation, B-404197, B-404197.2, B-404197.3, B-404197.4, B-404197.5, 2011 CPD ¶ 25 (Comp. Gen. 2011)

§ 19.1308 Performance of work requirements (limitations on subcontracting) for general construction or construction by special trade contractors.

(a) Before issuing a solicitation for general construction or construction by special trade contractors, the contracting officer shall determine if at least two HUBZone small business concerns can spend at least 50 percent of the cost of contract performance to be incurred for personnel on their own employees or subcontract employees of other HUBZone small business concerns.

(b) The clause at 52.219-3, Notice of HUBZone Set-Aside or Sole Source Award, or 52.219-4, Notice of Price Evaluation Preference for HUBZone Small Business Concerns, shall be used, as applicable, with its Alternate I to waive the 50 percent requirement (see 19.1309) if at least two HUBZone small business concerns cannot meet the conditions of paragraph (a); but, the HUBZone prime contractor can still meet the following—

(1) For general construction, at least 15 percent of the cost of the contract performance to be incurred for personnel using the concern's employees; or

(2) For construction by special trade contractors, at least 25 percent of the cost of contract performance to be incurred for personnel using the concern's employees.

(c) See 13 CFR 125.6 for definitions of terms used in paragraph (a) of this section.

United States Code Annotated

Additional powers, see 15 USCA § 637.

Administrative determinations, see 41 USCA § 257.

Awards or contracts, see 15 USCA § 644.

Contract goal for small disadvantaged businesses and certain institutions of higher education, see 10 USCA § 2323.

Contract requirements, see 41 USCA § 254.

Contracts, planning, solicitation, evaluation, and award procedures, see 10 USCA § 2305.

Credit for Indian contracting in meeting certain subcontracting goals for small

disadvantaged businesses and certain institutions of higher education, see 10 USCA § 2323a.

Definitions, see 10 USCA § 2302, 41 USCA §§ 259, 403.

Determinations and decisions, see 10 USCA § 2310, 41 USCA § 262.

HUBZone program, see 15 USCA § 657a.

Kinds of contracts, see 10 USCA § 2306.

Planning and solicitation requirements, see 41 USCA § 253a.

Procurement data, see 41 USCA § 417a.

Procurement program for small business concerns owned and controlled by service-disabled veterans, see 15 USCA § 657f.

§ 19.1309 Contract clauses.

(a) The contracting officer shall insert the clause 52.219-3, Notice of HUBZone Set-Aside or Sole Source Award, in solicitations and contracts for acquisitions that are set aside, or reserved for, or awarded on a sole source basis to, HUBZone small business concerns under 19.1305 or 19.1306. This includes multiple-award contracts when orders may be set aside for HUBZone small business concerns as described in 8.405-5 and 16.505(b)(2)(i)(F).

(1) The contracting officer shall use the clause with its Alternate I to waive the 50 percent requirement if the conditions at 19.1308(b) apply.

(2) If a waiver is granted, the HUBZone small business prime contractor must still meet the performance of work requirements set forth in 13 CFR 125.6(c).

(b) The contracting officer shall insert the clause at FAR 52.219-4, Notice of Price Evaluation Preference for HUBZone Small Business Concerns, in solicitations and contracts for acquisitions conducted using full and open competition.

(1) The contracting officer shall use the clause with its Alternate I to waive the 50 percent requirement if the conditions at 19.1308(b) apply.

(2) If a waiver is granted, the HUBZone small business prime contractor must still meet the performance of work requirements set forth in 13 CFR 125.6(c).

Subpart 19.14 Service-Disabled Veteran-Owned Small Business Procurement Program

§ 19.1401 General.

(a) The Veterans Benefit Act of 2003 (15 U.S.C. 657f) created the procurement program for small business concerns owned and controlled by service-disabled veterans (commonly referred to as the "Service-Disabled Veteran-owned Small Business (SDVOSB) Procurement Program").

(b) The purpose of the Service-Disabled Veteran-Owned Small Business Program is to provide Federal contracting assistance to service-disabled veteran-owned small business concerns.

United States Code Annotated

Additional powers, see 15 USCA § 637.

Administrative determinations, see 41 USCA § 257.

Awards or contracts, see 15 USCA § 644.

Contract goal for small disadvantaged businesses and certain institutions of higher education, see 10 USCA § 2323.

Contract requirements, see 41 USCA § 254.

Contracts, planning, solicitation, evaluation, and award procedures, see 10 USCA § 2305.

Credit for Indian contracting in meeting certain subcontracting goals for small disadvantaged businesses and certain institutions of higher education, see 10 USCA § 2323a.

Definitions, see 10 USCA § 2302, 41 USCA §§ 259, 403.

Determinations and decisions, see 10 USCA § 2310, 41 USCA § 262.

HUBZone program, see 15 USCA § 657a.

Kinds of contracts, see 10 USCA § 2306.

Planning and solicitation requirements, see 41 USCA § 253a.

Procurement data, see 41 USCA § 417a.

Procurement program for small business concerns owned and controlled by service-disabled veterans, see 15 USCA § 657f.

§ 19.1402 Applicability.

The procedures in this subpart apply to all Federal agencies that employ one or more contracting officers.

United States Code Annotated

Additional powers, see 15 USCA § 637.

Administrative determinations, see 41 USCA § 257.

Awards or contracts, see 15 USCA § 644.

Contract goal for small disadvantaged businesses and certain institutions of higher education, see 10 USCA § 2323.

Contract requirements, see 41 USCA § 254.

Contracts, planning, solicitation, evaluation, and award procedures, see 10 USCA § 2305.

Credit for Indian contracting in meeting certain subcontracting goals for small disadvantaged businesses and certain institutions of higher education, see 10 USCA § 2323a.

Definitions, see 10 USCA § 2302, 41 USCA §§ 259, 403.

Determinations and decisions, see 10 USCA § 2310, 41 USCA § 262.

HUBZone program, see 15 USCA § 657a.

Kinds of contracts, see 10 USCA § 2306.

Planning and solicitation requirements, see 41 USCA § 253a.

Procurement data, see 41 USCA § 417a.

Procurement program for small business concerns owned and controlled by service-disabled veterans, see 15 USCA § 657f.

§ 19.1403 Status as a service-disabled veteran-owned small business concern.

(a) Status as a service-disabled veteran-owned small business concern is determined in accordance with 13 CFR Parts 125.8 through 125.13; also see 19.307.

(b) At the time that a service-disabled veteran-owned small business concern submits its offer, it must represent to the contracting officer that it is a—

(1) Service-disabled veteran-owned small business concern; and

(2) Small business concern under the North American Industry Classification System (NAICS) code assigned to the procurement.

(c) A joint venture may be considered a service-disabled veteran owned small business concern if—

(1) At least one member of the joint venture is a servicedisabled veteran-owned small business concern, and makes the representations in paragraph (b) of this section;

(2) Each other concern is small under the size standard corresponding to the NAICS code assigned to the procurement;

(3) The joint venture meets the requirements of paragraph 7 of the explanation of Affiliates in 19.101; and

(4) The joint venture meets the requirements of 13 CFR 125.15(b).

(d) Any service-disabled veteran-owned small business concern (nonmanufacturer) must meet the requirements in 19.102(f) to receive a benefit under this program.

United States Code Annotated

Additional powers, see 15 USCA § 637.

Administrative determinations, see 41 USCA § 257.

Awards or contracts, see 15 USCA § 644.

Contract goal for small disadvantaged businesses and certain institutions of higher education, see 10 USCA § 2323.

Contract requirements, see 41 USCA § 254.

Contracts, planning, solicitation, evaluation, and award procedures, see 10 USCA § 2305.

Credit for Indian contracting in meeting certain subcontracting goals for small disadvantaged businesses and certain institutions of higher education, see 10 USCA § 2323a.

Definitions, see 10 USCA § 2302, 41 USCA §§ 259, 403.

Determinations and decisions, see 10 USCA § 2310, 41 USCA § 262.

HUBZone program, see 15 USCA § 657a.

Kinds of contracts, see 10 USCA § 2306.

Planning and solicitation requirements, see 41 USCA § 253a.

Procurement data, see 41 USCA § 417a.

Procurement program for small business concerns owned and controlled by service-disabled veterans, see 15 USCA § 657f.

Notes of Decisions
In general 1

1 In general

Cancellation of government contractor's certification for service-disabled veteran-owned small business (SDVOSB) eligibility by the Veterans Affairs (VA) contravened Administrative Procedure Act's (APA) provision setting forth the minimal procedural requirements for an informal adjudication. The agency did not notify the contractor that it was the subject of an agency-initiated status protest, and since contractor was entirely unaware of the investigation and cancellation of eligibility until it was disqualified for a contract, despite being the apparent responsible, responsive lowest-cost bidder, it had no opportunity to respond or submit documentation regarding its status. AmBuild Company, LLC v. U.S., 119 Fed.Cl. 10 (2014)

§ 19.1404 Exclusions.

This subpart does not apply to—

(a) Requirements that can be satisfied through award to—

(1) Federal Prison Industries, Inc. (see Subpart 8.6);

(2) AbilityOne participating non-profit agencies for the blind or severely disabled (see Subpart 8.7);

(b) Orders under indefinite-delivery contracts (see subpart 16.5). (But see 16.505(b)(2)(i)(F) for discretionary set-asides of orders);

(c) Orders against Federal Supply Schedules (see subpart 8.4). (But see 8.405-5 for discretionary set-asides of orders); or

(d) Requirements currently being performed by an 8(a) participant or requirements SBA has accepted for performance under the authority of the 8(a) Program, unless SBA has consented to release the requirements from the 8(a) Program.

United States Code Annotated

Additional powers, see 15 USCA § 637.

Administrative determinations, see 41 USCA § 257.

Awards or contracts, see 15 USCA § 644.

Contract goal for small disadvantaged businesses and certain institutions of higher education, see 10 USCA § 2323.

Contract requirements, see 41 USCA § 254.

Contracts, planning, solicitation, evaluation, and award procedures, see 10 USCA § 2305.

Credit for Indian contracting in meeting certain subcontracting goals for small disadvantaged businesses and certain institutions of higher education, see 10 USCA § 2323a.

Definitions, see 10 USCA § 2302, 41 USCA §§ 259, 403.

Determinations and decisions, see 10 USCA § 2310, 41 USCA § 262.

HUBZone program, see 15 USCA § 657a.

Kinds of contracts, see 10 USCA § 2306.

Planning and solicitation requirements, see 41 USCA § 253a.

Procurement data, see 41 USCA § 417a.

Procurement program for small business concerns owned and controlled by service-disabled veterans, see 15 USCA § 657f.

§ 19.1405 Service-disabled veteran-owned small business set-aside procedures.

(a) The contracting officer—

(1) Shall comply with 19.203 before deciding to set aside an acquisition under the SDVOSB Program;

(2) May set-aside acquisitions exceeding the micro-purchase threshold for competition restricted to SDVOSB concerns when the requirements of paragraph (b) of this section can be satisfied; and

(3) Shall consider SDVOSB set-asides before considering SDVOSB sole source awards (see 19.1406) or small business set-asides (see subpart 19.5).

(b) To set aside an acquisition for competition restricted to service-disabled veteran-owned small business concerns, the contracting officer must have a reasonable expectation. that—

(1) Offers will be received from two or more service-disabled veteran-owned small business concerns; and

(2) Award will be made at a fair market price.

(c) If the contracting officer receives only one acceptable offer from a service-disabled veteran-owned small business concern in response to a set-aside, the contracting officer should make an award to that concern. If the contracting officer receives no acceptable offers from service-disabled veteran-owned small business concerns, the service-disabled veteran-owned set-aside shall be withdrawn and the requirement, if still valid, set aside for small business concerns, as appropriate (see 19.203).

(d) The procedures at 19.202-1 and, except for acquisitions not exceeding the simplified acquisition threshold, at 19.402 apply to this section. When the SBA intends to appeal a contracting officer's decision to reject a recommendation of the SBA procurement center representative (or, if a procurement center representative is not assigned, see 19.402(a)) to set aside an acquisition for competition restricted to service-disabled veteran-owned small business concerns, the SBA procurement center representative shall notify the contracting officer, in writing, of its intent within 5 working days of receiving the contracting officer's notice of rejection. Upon receipt of notice of SBA's intent to appeal, the contracting officer shall suspend action on the acquisition unless the head of the contracting activity makes a written determination that urgent and compelling circumstances, which significantly affect the interests of the Government, exist. Within 15 working days of SBA's notification to the contracting officer, SBA shall file its formal appeal with the head of the contracting activity, or that agency may consider the appeal withdrawn. The head of the contracting activity shall reply to SBA within 15 working days of receiving the appeal. The decision of the head of the contracting activity shall be final.

United States Code Annotated

Additional powers, see 15 USCA § 637.

Administrative determinations, see 41 USCA § 257.

Awards or contracts, see 15 USCA § 644.

Contract goal for small disadvantaged businesses and certain institutions of higher education, see 10 USCA § 2323.

Contract requirements, see 41 USCA § 254.

Contracts, planning, solicitation, evaluation, and award procedures, see 10 USCA § 2305.

Credit for Indian contracting in meeting certain subcontracting goals for small disadvantaged businesses and certain institutions of higher education, see 10 USCA § 2323a.

Definitions, see 10 USCA § 2302, 41 USCA §§ 259, 403.

Determinations and decisions, see 10 USCA § 2310, 41 USCA § 262.

HUBZone program, see 15 USCA § 657a.

Kinds of contracts, see 10 USCA § 2306.

Planning and solicitation requirements, see 41 USCA § 253a.

Procurement data, see 41 USCA § 417a.

Procurement program for small business concerns owned and controlled by service-disabled veterans, see 15 USCA § 657f.

Notes of Decisions

In general 1

1 In general

Department of Veterans Affairs (VA) is not excused from compliance with statutory Rule of Two for set asides, which states that the VA generally "shall award" a contract to a veteran-owned small business (VOSB) when there is a reasonable expectation that two or more such businesses will bid for the contract at a fair and reasonable price that offers the best value to the United States, even if the VA has already met its annual goals for awarding contracts to VOSBs, and even if the order is placed through the Federal Supply Schedule (FSS). Kingdomware Techs., Inc. v. U.S., 136 S.Ct. 1969 (U.S. June 16, 2016)

Contracting officer lacked rational basis for failing to comply with Department of Veterans Affairs' (DVA) guidelines (which give first priority to service-disabled veteran-owned (SDVO) and veteran-owned (VO) small businesses) by awarding laundry services contract on a sole-source basis to JWOD contractor under AbilityOne program, since agency guidelines did not exempt placements on AbilityOne procurement list. Angelica Textile Services, Inc. v. U.S., 95 Fed. Cl. 208 (2010)

The U.S. Court of Federal Claims held that it lacked subject matter jurisdiction over a plaintiff's claims because plaintiff was not eligible for a contract and, thus, lacked standing to challenge the award. Plaintiff was the lowest bidder for a service-disabled veteran-owned small business set-aside, but was found ineligible because it was not listed in the Department of Veterans Affairs' vendor information pages (VIP) database, www.VetBiz.gov. CS-360, LLC v. U.S., 94 Fed. Cl. 488 (2010)

Protest is sustained where the agency's determination that there was not a reasonable expectation of receiving offers from two or more service-disabled veteran-owned small business (SDVOSB) concerns was not supported by the record in that the agency imposed a geographic restriction, even though most of the work would be performed at the contractor's site. Fire Risk Mgmt., Inc., B-411552, 2015 CPD ¶ 259 (Comp.Gen. 2015)

Protest from a woman-owned small business that agency unreasonably set aside an acquisition for service-disabled, veteran-owned small businesses was denied because the agency's market research demonstrated that at least two such firms would be likely to submit proposals and that award could be made at a fair and reasonable price. Starlight Corporation, Inc., B-410471.2, 2014 CPD ¶ 383 (Comp.Gen. 2014)

Protest that Department of Veterans Affairs (VA) improperly used non-mandatory Federal Supply Schedule procedures to procure items, rather than using a set-aside for service-disabled veteran-owned small businesses, is sustained, where the applicable statute-the Veterans Benefits, Health Care, and Information Technology Act of 2006-and implementing regulations require the VA to use such set-asides where the statutory prerequisites are met. Aldevra, B-405271, 2011 CPD ¶ 183 (Comp. Gen. 2011)

Protests that Department of Veterans Affairs improperly failed to set aside architect-engineering services procurements for service-disabled veteran-owned small businesses are sustained, where the applicable statute, the Veterans Benefits, Health Care, and Information Technology Act of 2006 (38 U.S.C. §§ 8127–8128), and implementing regulations require such set asides if the contracting officer has a reasonable expectation that two or more small business concerns owned and controlled by veterans will submit offers and that the award can be made at a fair and reasonable price. Matter of: Powerhouse Design Architects & Engineers, Ltd., B-403174, B-403175, B-403176, B-403177, B-403633, B-403647, B-403648, B-403649, 2010 CPD ¶ 240 (Comp. Gen. 2010)

An agency determined that the bid of a service-disabled veteran-owned small business (SDVOSB) concern was nonresponsive for not adhering to the IFB requirement that joint ventures designate the SDVOSB firm as the managing partner of the venture. GAO sustained the protest of the SDVOSB because the agency's determination was based on matters external to the bid and because only the Small Business Administration can make a status determination. Decision Matter of: Singleton Enterprises-GMT Mechanical, A Joint Venture, B-310552, 2008 CPD ¶ 16 (Comp. Gen. 2008)

Agencies are may, but are not required to, set aside procurements for service-disabled veteran-owned small business (SDVOSB) concerns. In contrast to the mandatory language in the HUBZone statute and implementing regulations, the statutory provisions establishing the SDVOSB program and the implementing regulations use the following permissive language, "a contracting officer may award contracts on the basis of competition restricted to small business concerns owned and controlled by service-disabled veterans." 15 USCA § 657f(b). Decision Matter of: International Program Group, Inc., B-400278, B-400308, 2008 CPD ¶ 172 (Comp. Gen. 2008)

§ 19.1406 Sole source awards to service-disabled veteran-owned small business concerns.

(a) A contracting officer shall consider a contract award to a SDVOSB concern on a sole source basis (see 6.302-5(b)(6)), before considering small business set-asides (see 19.203 and subpart 19.5) provided none of the exclusions of 19.1404 apply and—

(1) The contracting officer does not have a reasonable expectation that offers would be received from two or more service-disabled veteran-owned small business concerns;

(2) The anticipated award price of the contract, including options, will not exceed—

(i) $6.5 million for a requirement within the NAICS codes for manufacturing; or

(ii) $4 million for a requirement within any other NAICS code;

(3) The requirement is not currently being performed by an 8(a) participant under the provisions of Subpart 19.8 or has been accepted as a requirement by SBA under Subpart 19.8;

(4) The service-disabled veteran-owned small business concern has been determined to be a responsible contractor with respect to performance; and

(5) Award can be made at a fair and reasonable price.

(b) The SBA has the right to appeal the contracting officer's decision not to make a service-disabled veteran-owned small business sole source award.

United States Code Annotated

Additional powers, see 15 USCA § 637.

Administrative determinations, see 41 USCA § 257.

Awards or contracts, see 15 USCA § 644.

Contract goal for small disadvantaged businesses and certain institutions of higher education, see 10 USCA § 2323.

Contract requirements, see 41 USCA § 254.

Contracts, planning, solicitation, evaluation, and award procedures, see 10 USCA § 2305.

Credit for Indian contracting in meeting certain subcontracting goals for small disadvantaged businesses and certain institutions of higher education, see 10 USCA § 2323a.

Definitions, see 10 USCA § 2302, 41 USCA §§ 259, 403.

Determinations and decisions, see 10 USCA § 2310, 41 USCA § 262.

HUBZone program, see 15 USCA § 657a.

Kinds of contracts, see 10 USCA § 2306.

Planning and solicitation requirements, see 41 USCA § 253a.

Procurement data, see 41 USCA § 417a.

Procurement program for small business concerns owned and controlled by service-disabled veterans, see 15 USCA § 657f.

§ 19.1407 Contract clauses.

The contracting officer shall insert the clause 52.219-27, Notice of Service-Disabled Veteran-Owned Small Business Set-Aside, in solicitations and contracts for acquisitions that are set aside or reserved for, or awarded on a sole source basis to, service-disabled veteran-owned small business concerns under 19.1405 and 19.1406. This includes multiple-award contracts when orders may be set aside for service-disabled veteran-owned small business concerns as described in 8.405-5 and 16.505(b)(2)(i)(F).

United States Code Annotated

Additional powers, see 15 USCA § 637.

Administrative determinations, see 41 USCA § 257.

Awards or contracts, see 15 USCA § 644.

Contract goal for small disadvantaged businesses and certain institutions of higher education, see 10 USCA § 2323.

Contract requirements, see 41 USCA § 254.

Contracts, planning, solicitation, evaluation, and award procedures, see 10 USCA § 2305.

Credit for Indian contracting in meeting certain subcontracting goals for small disadvantaged businesses and certain institutions of higher education, see 10 USCA § 2323a.

Definitions, see 10 USCA § 2302, 41 USCA §§ 259, 403.

Determinations and decisions, see 10 USCA § 2310, 41 USCA § 262.

HUBZone program, see 15 USCA § 657a.

Kinds of contracts, see 10 USCA § 2306.

Planning and solicitation requirements, see 41 USCA § 253a.

Procurement data, see 41 USCA § 417a.

Procurement program for small business concerns owned and controlled by service-disabled veterans, see 15 USCA § 657f.

Subpart 19.15 —Women-Owned Small Business Program.

§ 19.1500 General.

(a) Section 8(m) of the Small Business Act (15 U.S.C. 637(m)) created the Women-Owned Small Business (WOSB) Program.

(b) The purpose of the WOSB Program is to ensure women-owned small business concerns have an equal opportunity to participate in Federal contracting and to assist agencies in achieving their women-owned small business participation goals (see 13 part CFR 127).

(c) An economically disadvantaged women-owned small business (EDWOSB) concern or WOSB concern eligible under the WOSB Program is a subcategory of "women-owned small business concern" as defined in 2.101.

§ 19.1501 Definition.

"WOSB Program Repository" means a secure, Web-based application that collects, stores, and disseminates documents to the contracting community and SBA, which verify the eligibility of a business concern for a contract to be awarded under the WOSB Program.

§ 19.1502 Applicability.

The procedures in this subpart apply to all Federal agencies that employ one or more contracting officers.

§ 19.1503 Status.

(a) Status as an EDWOSB concern or WOSB concern eligible under the WOSB Program is determined in accordance with 13 CFR part 127.

(b) The contracting officer shall verify that the offeror—

(1) Is registered in the System for Award Management (SAM);

(2) Is self-certified as an EDWOSB or WOSB concern in SAM; and

(3) Has submitted documents verifying its eligibility at the time of initial offer to the WOSB Program Repository. The contract shall not be awarded until all required documents are received.

(c) (1) An EDWOSB concern or WOSB concern eligible under the WOSB Program that has been certified by a SBA approved third party certifier, (which includes SBA certification under the 8(a) Program), must provide the following eligibility requirement documents—

(i) The third-party certification;

(ii) SBA's WOSB Program Certification form (SBA Form 2413 for WOSB concerns eligible under the WOSB Program and SBA Form 2414 for EDWOSB concerns); and

(iii) The joint venture agreement, if applicable.

(2) An EDWOSB concern or WOSB concern eligible under the WOSB Program that has not been certified by an SBA approved third party certifier or by SBA under the 8(a) Program, must provide the following documents:

(i) The U.S. birth certificate, naturalization documentation, or unexpired U.S. passport for each woman owner.

(ii) The joint venture agreement, if applicable.

(iii) For limited liability companies, articles of organization (also referred to as certificate of organization or articles of formation) and any amendments, and the operating agreement and any amendments.

(iv) For corporations, articles of incorporation and any amendments, by-laws and any amendments, all issued stock certificates, including the front and back copies, signed in accord with the by-laws, stock ledger, and voting agreements, if any.

(v) For partnerships, the partnership agreement and any amendments.

(vi) For sole proprietorships, corporations, limited liability companies and partnerships if applicable, the assumed/fictitious name certificate(s).

(vii) SBA's WOSB Program Certification form (SBA Form 2413 for WOSB concerns eligible under the WOSB Program and SBA Form 2414 for EDWOSB concerns).

(viii) For EDWOSB concerns, in addition to the above, the SBA Form 413, Personal Financial Statement, available to the public at http://www.sba.gov/tools/Forms/index.html, for each woman claiming economic disadvantage.

(d) (1) A contracting officer may accept a concern's self-certification as accurate for a specific procurement reserved for award under this subpart if—

(i) The apparent successful WOSB eligible under the WOSB Program or EDWOSB offeror provided the required documents;

(ii) There has been no protest or other credible information that calls into question the concern's eligibility as an EDWOSB concern or WOSB concern eligible under the WOSB Program; and

(iii) There has been no decision issued by SBA as a result of a current eligibility examination finding the concern did not qualify as an EDWOSB concern or WOSB concern eligible under the WOSB Program at the time it submitted its initial offer.

(2) The contracting officer shall file a status protest in accordance with 19.308 if—

(i) There is information that questions the eligibility of a concern; or

(ii) The concern fails to provide all of the required documents to verify its eligibility.

(e) If there is a decision issued by SBA as a result of a current eligibility examination finding that the concern did not qualify as an EDWOSB concern or WOSB concern eligible under the WOSB Program, the contracting officer may terminate the contract, and shall not exercise any option nor award further task or delivery orders. The contracting officer shall not count or include the award toward the small business accomplishments for an EDWOSB concern or WOSB concern eligible under the WOSB Program and must update FPDS from the date of award.

(f) A joint venture may be considered an EDWOSB concern or WOSB concern eligible under the WOSB Program if it meets the requirements of 13 CFR 127.506.

(g) An EDWOSB concern or WOSB concern eligible under the WOSB Program that is a non-manufacturer, as defined in 13 CFR 121.406(b), may submit an offer on a requirement set aside for an EDWOSB concern or a WOSB concern eligible under the WOSB Program with a NAICS code for supplies, if it meets the requirements under the non-manufacturer rule set forth in that regulation.

§ 19.1504 Exclusions.

This subpart does not apply to—

(a) Requirements that an 8(a) concern is currently performing under the 8(a) Program or that SBA has accepted for performance under the authority of the 8(a) Program, unless SBA has consented to release the requirements from the 8(a) Program;

(b) Requirements that can be satisfied through award to—

(1) Federal Prison Industries, Inc. (see subpart 8.6); or

(2) AbilityOne participating non-profit agencies for the blind or severely disabled (see subpart 8.7);

(c) Orders under indefinite-delivery contracts (see subpart 16.5). (But see 16.505(b)(2)(i)(F) for discretionary set-asides of orders); or

(d) Orders against Federal Supply Schedules (see subpart 8.4). (But see 8.405-5 for discretionary set-asides of orders.)

§ 19.1505 Set-aside procedures.

(a) The contracting officer—

(1) Shall comply with 19.203 before deciding to set aside an acquisition under the WOSB Program.

(2) May set aside acquisitions exceeding the micro-purchase threshold for competition restricted to EDWOSB concerns or WOSB concerns eligible under the WOSB Program when the acquisition—

(i) Is assigned a NAICS code in which SBA has determined that WOSB concerns are underrepresented in Federal procurement; or

(ii) Is assigned a NAICS code in which SBA has determined that WOSB concerns are substantially underrepresented in Federal procurement, as specified on SBA's Web site at http://www.sba.gov/WOSB.

(b) For requirements in NAICS codes designated by SBA as underrepresented, a contracting officer may restrict competition to EDWOSB concerns if the contracting officer has a reasonable expectation based on market research that—

(1) Two or more EDWOSB concerns will submit offers for the contract and;

(2) Contract award will be made at a fair and reasonable price.

(c) A contracting officer may restrict competition to WOSB concerns eligible under the WOSB Program (including EDWOSB concerns), for requirements in NAICS codes designated by SBA as substantially underrepresented if there is a reasonable expectation based on market research that—

(1) Two or more WOSB concerns eligible under the WOSB Program (including EDWOSB concerns), will submit offers and;

(2) Contract award may be made at a fair and reasonable price.

(d) The contracting officer may make an award, if only one acceptable offer is received from a qualified EDWOSB concern or WOSB concern eligible under the WOSB Program.

(e) The contracting officer must check whether the apparently successful offeror filed all the required eligibility documents, and file a status protest if any documents are missing. See 19.1503(d)(2).

(f) If no acceptable offers are received from an EDWOSB concern or WOSB concern eligible under the WOSB Program, the set-aside shall be withdrawn and the requirement, if still valid, must be considered for set aside in accordance with 19.203 and subpart 19.5.

(g) If the contracting officer rejects a recommendation by SBA's Procurement Center Representative—

(1) The contracting officer shall notify the procurement center representative as soon as practicable;

(2) SBA shall notify the contracting officer of its intent to appeal the contracting officer's decision no later than five business days after receiving notice of the contracting officer's decision;

(3) The contracting officer shall suspend further action regarding the procurement until the head of the agency issues a written decision on the appeal, unless the head of the agency makes a written determination that urgent and compelling circumstances which significantly affect the interests of the United States compel award of the contract;

(4) Within 15 business days of SBA's notification to the head of the contracting activity, SBA shall file a formal appeal to the head of the agency, or the appeal will be determined withdrawn; and

(5) The head of the agency, or designee, shall specify in writing the reasons for a denial of an appeal brought under this section.

§ 19.1506 Women-Owned Small Business Program sole source awards.

(a) A contracting officer shall consider a contract award to an EDWOSB concern on a sole source basis (see 6.302-5(b)(7)) before considering small business set-asides (see 19.203 and subpart 19.5) provided none of the exclusions at 19.1504 apply and—

(1) The acquisition is assigned a NAICS code in which SBA has determined that WOSB concerns are underrepresented in Federal procurement;

(2) The contracting officer does not have a reasonable expectation that offers would be received from two or more EDWOSB concerns; and

(3) The conditions in paragraph (c) of this section exist.

(b) A contracting officer shall consider a contract award to a WOSB concern (including EDWOSB concerns) eligible under the WOSB Program on a sole source basis (see 6.302-5(b)(7)) before considering small business set-asides (see 19.203 and subpart 19.5) provided none of the exclusions at 19.1504 apply and—

(1) The acquisition is assigned a NAICS code in which SBA has determined that WOSB concerns are substantially underrepresented in Federal procurement;

(2) The contracting officer does not have a reasonable expectation that offers would be received from two or more WOSB concerns (including EDWOSB concerns); and

(3) The conditions in paragraph (c) of this section exist.

(c) (1) The anticipated award price of the contract, including options, will not exceed—

(i) $6.5 million for a requirement within the NAICS codes for manufacturing; or

(ii) $4 million for a requirement within any other NAICS codes.

(2) The EDWOSB concern or WOSB concern has been determined to be a responsible contractor with respect to performance.

(3) The award can be made at a fair and reasonable price.

(d) The SBA has the right to appeal the contracting officer's decision not to make a sole source award to either an EDWOSB concern or WOSB concern eligible under the WOSB program.

§ 19.1507 Contract clauses.

(a) The contracting officer shall insert the clause 52.219-29, Notice of Set-Aside for, or Sole Source Award to, Economically Disadvantaged Women-owned Small Business Concerns, in solicitations and contracts for acquisitions that are set aside or reserved for, or awarded on a sole source basis to, EDWOSB concerns under 19.1505(b) or 19.1506(a). This includes multiple-award contracts when orders may be set aside for EDWOSB concerns as described in 8.405-5 and 16.505(b)(2)(i)(F).

(b) The contracting officer shall insert the clause 52.219-30, Notice of Set-Aside for, or Sole Source Award to, Women-Owned Small Business Concerns Eligible Under the Women-Owned Small Business Program, in solicitations and contracts for acquisitions that are set aside or reserved for, or awarded on a sole source basis to WOSB concerns under 19.1505(c) or 19.1506(b). This includes multiple-award contracts when orders may be set aside for WOSB concerns eligible under the WOSB Program as described in 8.405-5 and 16.505(b)(2)(i)(F).

PART 20 RESERVED

PART 21 RESERVED

PART 22 APPLICATION OF LABOR LAWS TO GOVERNMENT ACQUISITIONS

Subpart 22.5 [Reserved]

Subpart 22.6 Walsh-Healey Public Contracts Act

Subpart 22.7 [Reserved]

Subpart 22.8 Equal Employment Opportunity

Subpart 22.11 Professional Employee Compensation

Subpart 22.12 Nondisplacement of Qualified Workers Under Service Contracts

Subpart 22.13 —Equal Opportunity for Veterans

§ 22.1904 Annual Executive Order Minimum Wage Rate.
§ 22.1905 Enforcement of Executive Order Minimum Wage Requirements.
§ 22.1906 Contract clause.

§ 22.000 Scope of part.
This part—

(a) Deals with general policies regarding contractor labor relations as they pertain to the acquisition process;

(b) Prescribes contracting policy and procedures for implementing pertinent labor laws; and

(c) Prescribes contract clauses with respect to each pertinent labor law.

United States Code Annotated
Contract requirements, see 41 USCA § 254.

Contracts, planning, solicitation, evaluation, and award procedures, see 10 USCA § 2305.

Definitions, see 10 USCA § 2302, 41 USCA §§ 259, 403.

Kinds of contracts, see 10 USCA § 2306.

Planning and solicitation requirements, see 41 USCA § 253a.

§ 22.001 Definitions.
"Administrator" or "Administrator, Wage and Hour Division," as used in this part, means the—

Administrator
Wage and Hour Division
Employment Standards Administration
U.S. Department of Labor
Washington, DC 20210

or an authorized representative.

"Agency labor advisor" means an individual responsible for advising contracting agency officials on Federal contract labor matters.

"e98" means the Department of Labor's approved electronic application (http://www.wdol.gov), whereby a contracting officer submits pertinent information to the Department of Labor and requests a Service Contract Labor Standards statute wage determination directly from the Wage and Hour Division.

"Service contract" means any Government contract, or subcontract thereunder, the principal purpose of which is to furnish services in the United States through the use of service employees, except as exempted by 41 U.S.C. chapter 67, Service Contract Labor Standards; see 22.1003-3 and 22.1003-4). See 22.1003-5 and 29 CFR 4.130 for a partial list of services covered by the Service Contract Labor Standards statute.

"Service employee" means any person engaged in the performance of a service contract other than any person employed in a bona fide executive, administrative, or professional capacity, as those terms are defined in 29 CFR part 541. The term "service employee" includes all such persons regardless of any contractual relationship that may be alleged to exist between a contractor or subcontractor and such persons.

"Wage Determinations OnLine (WDOL)" means the Government Internet website for both Construction Wage Rate Requirements statute and Service Contract Labor Standards statute wage determinations available at http://www.wdol.gov.

Subpart 22.1 Basic Labor Policies

§ 22.101 Labor relations.

§ 22.101-1 General.
(a) Agencies shall maintain sound relations with industry and labor to ensure (1) prompt receipt of information involving labor relations that may adversely affect the Government

acquisition process and (2) that the Government obtains needed supplies and services without delay. All matters regarding labor relations shall be handled in accordance with agency procedures.

(b) Agencies shall remain impartial concerning any dispute between labor and contractor management and not undertake the conciliation, mediation, or arbitration of a labor dispute. To the extent practicable, agencies should ensure that the parties to the dispute use all available methods for resolving the dispute, including the services of the National Labor Relations Board, Federal Mediation and Conciliation Service, the National Mediation Board and other appropriate Federal, State, local, or private agencies.

(c) Agencies should, when practicable, exchange information concerning labor matters with other affected agencies to ensure a uniform Government approach concerning a particular plant or labor-management dispute.

(d) Agencies should take other actions concerning labor relations problems to the extent consistent with their acquisition responsibilities. For example, agencies should—

(1) Notify the agency responsible for conciliation, mediation, arbitration, or other related action of the existence of any labor dispute affecting or threatening to affect agency acquisition programs;

(2) Furnish to the parties to a dispute factual information pertinent to the dispute's potential or actual adverse impact on these programs, to the extent consistent with security regulations; and

(3) Seek a voluntary agreement between management and labor, notwithstanding the continuance of the dispute, to permit uninterrupted acquisition of supplies and services. This shall only be done, however, if the attempt to obtain voluntary agreement does not involve the agency in the merits of the dispute and only after consultation with the agency responsible for conciliation, mediation, arbitration, or other related action.

(e) The head of the contracting activity may designate programs or requirements for which it is necessary that contractors be required to notify the Government of actual or potential labor disputes that are delaying or threaten to delay the timely contract performance (see 22.103-5(a)).

United States Code Annotated

Contract requirements, see 41 USCA § 254.

Contracts, planning, solicitation, evaluation, and award procedures, see 10 USCA § 2305.

Definitions, see 10 USCA § 2302, 41 USCA §§ 259, 403.

Kinds of contracts, see 10 USCA § 2306.

Planning and solicitation requirements, see 41 USCA § 253a.

§ 22.101-2 Contract pricing and administration.

(a) Contractor labor policies and compensation practices, whether or not included in labor-management agreements, are not acceptable bases for allowing costs in cost-reimbursement contracts or for recognition of costs in pricing fixed-price contracts if they result in unreasonable costs to the Government. For a discussion of allowable costs resulting from labor-management agreements, see 31.205-6(b).

(b) Labor disputes may cause work stoppages that delay the performance of Government contracts. Contracting officers shall impress upon contractors that each contractor shall be held accountable for reasonably avoidable delays. Standard contract clauses dealing with default, excusable delays, etc., do not relieve contractors or subcontractors from the responsibility for delays that are within the contractors' or their subcontractors' control. A delay caused by a strike that the contractor or subcontractor could not reasonably prevent can be excused; however, it cannot be excused beyond the point at which a reasonably diligent contractor or subcontractor could have acted to end the strike by actions such as—

(1) Filing a charge with the National Labor Relations Board to permit the Board to seek injunctive relief in court;

(2) Using other available Government procedures; and

(3) Using private boards or organizations to settle disputes.

(c) Strikes normally result in changing patterns of cost incurrence and therefore may have an impact on the allowability of costs for cost-reimbursement contracts or for recognition of costs in pricing fixed-price contracts. Certain costs may increase because of strikes; *e.g.,* guard services and attorney's fees. Other costs incurred during a strike may not fluctuate (*e.g.,* "fixed costs" such as rent and depreciation), but because of reduced production, their proportion of the unit cost of items produced increases. All costs incurred during strikes shall be carefully examined to ensure recognition of only those costs necessary for performing the contract in accordance with the Government's essential interest.

(d) If, during a labor dispute, the inspectors' safety is not endangered, the normal functions of inspection at the plant of a Government contractor shall be continued without regard to the existence of a labor dispute, strike, or picket line.

United States Code Annotated

Contract requirements, see 41 USCA § 254.

Contracts, planning, solicitation, evaluation, and award procedures, see 10 USCA § 2305.

Definitions, see 10 USCA § 2302, 41 USCA §§ 259, 403.

Kinds of contracts, see 10 USCA § 2306.

Planning and solicitation requirements, see 41 USCA § 253a.

§ 22.101-3 Reporting labor disputes.

The office administering the contract shall report, in accordance with agency procedures, any potential or actual labor disputes that may interfere with performing any contracts under its cognizance. If a contract contains the clause at 52.222-1, Notice to the Government of Labor Disputes, the contractor also must report any actual or potential dispute that may delay contract performance.

United States Code Annotated

Contract requirements, see 41 USCA § 254.

Contracts, planning, solicitation, evaluation, and award procedures, see 10 USCA § 2305.

Definitions, see 10 USCA § 2302, 41 USCA §§ 259, 403.

Kinds of contracts, see 10 USCA § 2306.

Planning and solicitation requirements, see 41 USCA § 253a.

§ 22.101-4 Removal of items from contractors' facilities affected by work stoppages.

(a) Items shall be removed from contractors' facilities affected by work stoppages in accordance with agency procedures. Agency procedures should allow for the following:

(1) Determine whether removal of items is in the Government's interest. Normally the determining factor is the critical needs of an agency program.

(2) Attempt to arrange with the contractor and the union representative involved their approval of the shipment of urgently required items.

(3) Obtain appropriate approvals from within the agency.

(4) Determine who will remove the items from the plant(s) involved.

(b) Avoid the use or appearance of force and prevent incidents that might detrimentally affect labor-management relations.

(c) When two or more agencies' requirements are or may become involved in the removal of items, the contract administration office shall ensure that the necessary coordination is accomplished.

United States Code Annotated

Contract requirements, see 41 USCA § 254.

Contracts, planning, solicitation, evaluation, and award procedures, see 10 USCA § 2305.

Definitions, see 10 USCA § 2302, 41 USCA §§ 259, 403.

Kinds of contracts, see 10 USCA § 2306.

Planning and solicitation requirements, see 41 USCA § 253a.

§ 22.102 Federal and State labor requirements.

§ 22.102-1 Policy.

Agencies shall cooperate, and encourage contractors to cooperate with Federal and State agencies responsible for enforcing labor requirements such as—

(a) Safety;

(b) Health and sanitation;

(c) Maximum hours and minimum wages;

(d) Equal employment opportunity;

(e) Child and convict labor;

(f) Age discrimination;

(g) Disabled and Vietnam veteran employment;

(h) Employment of workers with disabilities; and

(i) Eligibility for employment under United States immigration laws.

United States Code Annotated

Contract requirements, see 41 USCA § 254.

Contracts, planning, solicitation, evaluation, and award procedures, see 10 USCA § 2305.

Definitions, see 10 USCA § 2302, 41 USCA §§ 259, 403.

Kinds of contracts, see 10 USCA § 2306.

Planning and solicitation requirements, see 41 USCA § 253a.

§ 22.102-2 Administration.

(a) Agencies shall cooperate with, and encourage contractors to use to the fullest extent practicable, the United States Employment Service (USES) and its affiliated local State Employment Service offices in meeting contractors' labor requirements. These requirements may be to staff new or expanding plant facilities, including requirements for workers in all occupations and skills from local labor market areas or through the Federal-State employment clearance system.

(b) Local State employment offices are operated throughout the United States, Puerto Rico, Guam, and the U.S. Virgin Islands. In addition to providing recruitment assistance to contractors, cooperation with the local State Employment Service offices will further the national program of maintaining continuous assessment of manpower requirements and resources on a national and local basis.

(c) (1) The U.S. Department of Labor is responsible for the administration and enforcement of the Occupational Safety and Health Act. The Department of Labor's Wage and Hour Division is responsible for administration and enforcement of numerous wage and hour statutes including—

(i) 40 U.S.C. chapter 31, subchapter IV, Wage Rate Requirements (Construction);

(ii) 40 U.S.C. chapter 37, Contract Work Hours and Safety Standards;

(iii) The Copeland Act (18 U.S.C. 874 and 40 U.S.C. 3145);

(iv) 41 U.S.C. chapter 65, Contracts for Materials, Supplies, Articles, and Equipment Exceeding $15,000;

(v) 41 U.S.C. chapter 67, Service Contract Labor Standards.

(2) Contracting officers should contact the Wage and Hour Division's regional offices when required by the subparts relating to these statutes unless otherwise specified. Addresses for these offices may be found at 29 CFR 1, Appendix B.

United States Code Annotated

Contract requirements, see 41 USCA § 254.

Contracts, planning, solicitation, evaluation, and award procedures, see 10 USCA § 2305.

Definitions, see 10 USCA § 2302, 41 USCA §§ 259, 403.

Kinds of contracts, see 10 USCA § 2306.

Planning and solicitation requirements, see 41 USCA § 253a.

§ 22.103 Overtime.

§ 22.103-1 Definition.

"Normal workweek," as used in this subpart, means, generally, a workweek of 40 hours. Outside the United States and its outlying areas, a workweek longer than 40 hours is considered normal if—

(1) The workweek does not exceed the norm for the area, as determined by local custom, tradition, or law; and

(2) The hours worked in excess of 40 in the workweek are not compensated at a premium rate of pay.

United States Code Annotated

Contract requirements, see 41 USCA § 254.

Contracts, planning, solicitation, evaluation, and award procedures, see 10 USCA § 2305.

Definitions, see 10 USCA § 2302, 41 USCA §§ 259, 403.

Kinds of contracts, see 10 USCA § 2306.

Planning and solicitation requirements, see 41 USCA § 253a.

§ 22.103-2 Policy.

Contractors shall perform all contracts, so far as practicable, without using overtime, particularly as a regular employment practice, except when lower overall costs to the Government will result or when it is necessary to meet urgent program needs. Any approved overtime, extra-pay shifts, and multishifts should be scheduled to achieve these objectives.

United States Code Annotated

Contract requirements, see 41 USCA § 254.

Contracts, planning, solicitation, evaluation, and award procedures, see 10 USCA § 2305.

Definitions, see 10 USCA § 2302, 41 USCA §§ 259, 403.

Kinds of contracts, see 10 USCA § 2306.

Planning and solicitation requirements, see 41 USCA § 253a.

Notes of Decisions

In general 1

1 In general

Department of Navy solicitation was ambiguous and, thus, had to be construed against Navy on whether it could use overtime rates to evaluate overtime hours where prospective bidders inquired during prebid phase of procurement, even though Navy did not act in bad faith; Navy developed and published ambiguous solicitation language, it initially evaluated offers received using overtime rates in accordance with its own interpretation of language in solicitation, and it refused to respond meaningfully to multiple inquiries on how to calculate overtime in evaluation process. Allied Technology Group, Inc. v. U.S., 39 Fed. Cl. 125, 41 Cont. Cas. Fed. (CCH) P 77179 (1997), aff'd, 173 F.3d 435 (Fed. Cir. 1998). United States ☞64.25

§ 22.103-3 Procedures.

(a) Solicitations normally shall not specify delivery or performance schedules that may require overtime at Government expense.

(b) In negotiating contracts, contracting officers should, consistent with the Government's needs, attempt to—

(1) Ascertain the extent that offers are based on the payment of overtime and shift premiums; and

(2) Negotiate contract prices or estimated costs without these premiums or obtain the requirement from other sources.

(c) When it becomes apparent during negotiations of applicable contracts (see 22.103-

5(b)) that overtime will be required in contract performance, the contracting officer shall secure from the contractor a request for all overtime to be used during the life of the contract, to the extent that the overtime can be estimated with reasonable certainty. The contractor's request shall contain the information required by paragraph (b) of the clause at 52.222-2, Payment for Overtime Premiums.

United States Code Annotated

Contract requirements, see 41 USCA § 254.

Contracts, planning, solicitation, evaluation, and award procedures, see 10 USCA § 2305.

Definitions, see 10 USCA § 2302, 41 USCA §§ 259, 403.

Kinds of contracts, see 10 USCA § 2306.

Planning and solicitation requirements, see 41 USCA § 253a.

§ 22.103-4 Approvals.

(a) The contracting officer shall review the contractor's request for overtime. Approval of the use of overtime may be granted by an agency approving official after determining in writing that overtime is necessary to—

(1) Meet essential delivery or performance schedules;

(2) Make up for delays beyond the control and without the fault or negligence of the contractor; or

(3) Eliminate foreseeable extended production bottlenecks that cannot be eliminated in any other way.

(b) Approval by the designated official of use and total dollar amount of overtime is required before inclusion of an amount in paragraph (a) of the clause at 52.222-2, Payment for Overtime Premiums.

(c) Contracting officer approval of payment of overtime premiums is required for time-and-materials and labor-hour contracts (see paragraph (a)(8) of the clause at 52.232-7, Payments Under Time-and-Materials and Labor-Hour Contracts).

(d) No approvals are required for paying overtime premiums under other types of contracts.

(e) Approvals by the agency approving official (see 22.103-4(a)) may be for an individual contract, project, program, plant, division, or company, as practical.

(f) During contract performance, contractor requests for overtime exceeding the amount authorized by paragraph (a) of the clause at 52.222-2, Payment for Overtime Premiums, shall be submitted as stated in paragraph (b) of the clause to the office administering the contract. That office will review the request and if it approves, send the request to the contracting officer. If the contracting officer determines that the requested overtime should be approved in whole or in part, the contracting officer shall request the approval of the agency's designated approving official and modify paragraph (a) of the clause to reflect any approval.

(g) Overtime premiums at Government expense should not be approved when the contractor is already obligated, without the right to additional compensation, to meet the required delivery date.

(h) When the use of overtime is authorized under a contract, the office administering the contract and the auditor should periodically review the use of overtime to ensure that it is allowable in accordance with the criteria in Part 31. Only overtime premiums for work in those departments, sections, etc., of the contractor's plant that have been individually evaluated and the necessity for overtime confirmed shall be considered for approval.

(i) Approvals for using overtime shall ordinarily be prospective, but, if justified by emergency circumstances, approvals may be retroactive.

United States Code Annotated

Contract requirements, see 41 USCA § 254.

Contracts, planning, solicitation, evaluation, and award procedures, see 10 USCA § 2305.

Definitions, see 10 USCA § 2302, 41 USCA §§ 259, 403.

Kinds of contracts, see 10 USCA § 2306.

Planning and solicitation requirements, see 41 USCA § 253a.

§ 22.103-5 Contract clauses.

(a) The contracting officer shall insert the clause at 52.222-1, Notice to the Government of Labor Disputes, in solicitations and contracts that involve programs or requirements that have been designated under 22.101-1(e).

(b) The contracting officer shall include the clause at 52.222-2, Payment for Overtime Premiums, in solicitations and contracts when a cost-reimbursement contract is contemplated and the contract amount is expected to exceed the simplified acquisition threshold; unless—

(1) A cost-reimbursement contract for operation of vessels is contemplated; or

(2) A cost-plus-incentive-fee contract that will provide a swing from the target fee of at least plus or minus 3 percent and a contractor's share of at least 10 percent is contemplated.

United States Code Annotated

Contract requirements, see 41 USCA § 254.

Contracts, planning, solicitation, evaluation, and award procedures, see 10 USCA § 2305.

Definitions, see 10 USCA § 2302, 41 USCA §§ 259, 403.

Kinds of contracts, see 10 USCA § 2306.

Planning and solicitation requirements, see 41 USCA § 253a.

Notes of Decisions

Overtime 1

1 Overtime

Department of Navy solicitation was ambiguous and, thus, had to be construed against Navy on whether it could use overtime rates to evaluate overtime hours where prospective bidders inquired during prebid phase of procurement, even though Navy did not act in bad faith; Navy developed and published ambiguous solicitation language, it initially evaluated offers received using overtime rates in accordance with its own interpretation of language in solicitation, and it refused to respond meaningfully to multiple inquiries on how to calculate overtime in evaluation process. Allied Technology Group, Inc. v. U.S., 39 Fed. Cl. 125, 41 Cont. Cas. Fed. (CCH) P 77179 (1997), aff'd, 173 F.3d 435 (Fed. Cir. 1998). United States ☞64.25

Subpart 22.2 Convict Labor

§ 22.201 General.

(a) Executive Order 11755, December 29, 1973, as amended by Executive Order 12608, September 9, 1987, and Executive Order 12943, December 13, 1994, states: "The development of the occupational and educational skills of prison inmates is essential to their rehabilitation and to their ability to make an effective return to free society. Meaningful employment serves to develop those skills. It is also true, however, that care must be exercised to avoid either the exploitation of convict labor or any unfair competition between convict labor and free labor in the production of goods and services." The Executive order does not prohibit the contractor, in performing the contract, from employing—

(1) Persons on parole or probation;

(2) Persons who have been pardoned or who have served their terms;

(3) Federal prisoners; or

(4) Nonfederal prisoners authorized to work at paid employment in the community under the laws of a jurisdiction listed in the Executive order if—

(i) The worker is paid or is in an approved work training program on a voluntary basis;

(ii) Representatives of local union central bodies or similar labor union organizations have been consulted;

(iii) Paid employment will not—

(A) Result in the displacement of employed workers;

(B) Be applied in skills, crafts, or trades in which there is a surplus of available gainful labor in the locality; or

(C) Impair existing contracts for services;

(iv) The rates of pay and other conditions of employment will not be less than those for work of a similar nature in the locality where the work is being performed; and

(v) The Attorney General of the United States has certified that the work-release laws or regulations of the jurisdiction involved are in conformity with the requirements of Executive Order 11755, as amended.

(b) Department of Justice regulations authorize the Director of the Bureau of Justice Assistance to exercise the power and authority vested in the Attorney General by the Executive order to certify and to revoke the certification of work-release laws or regulations (see 28 CFR 0.94-1(b)).

United States Code Annotated

Contract requirements, see 41 USCA § 254.

Contracts, planning, solicitation, evaluation, and award procedures, see 10 USCA § 2305.

Definitions, see 10 USCA § 2302, 41 USCA §§ 259, 403.

Kinds of contracts, see 10 USCA § 2306.

Planning and solicitation requirements, see 41 USCA § 253a.

§ 22.202 Contract clause.

Insert the clause at 52.222-3, Convict Labor, in solicitations and contracts above the micro-purchase threshold, when the contract will be performed in the United States, Puerto Rico, the Northern Mariana Islands, American Samoa, Guam, or the U.S. Virgin Islands; unless—

(a) The contract will be subject to 41 U.S.C. chapter 65, Contracts for Materials, Supplies, Articles, and Equipment Exceeding $15,000 (see Subpart 22.6), which contains a separate prohibition against the employment of convict labor;

(b) The supplies or services are to be purchased from Federal Prison Industries, Inc. (see Subpart 8.6); or

(c) The acquisition involves the purchase, from any State prison, of finished supplies that may be secured in the open market or from existing stocks, as distinguished from supplies requiring special fabrication.

United States Code Annotated

Contract requirements, see 41 USCA § 254.

Contracts, planning, solicitation, evaluation, and award procedures, see 10 USCA § 2305.

Definitions, see 10 USCA § 2302, 41 USCA §§ 259, 403.

Kinds of contracts, see 10 USCA § 2306.

Planning and solicitation requirements, see 41 USCA § 253a.

Subpart 22.3 Contract Work Hours and Safety Standards Act

§ 22.300 Scope of subpart.

This subpart prescribes policies and procedures for applying the requirements of 40 U.S.C. chapter 37, Contract Work Hours and Safety Standards (the statute) to contracts that may require or involve laborers or mechanics. In this subpart, the term "laborers or mechanics" includes apprentices, trainees, helpers, watchmen, guards, firefighters, fireguards, and workmen who perform services in connection with dredging or rock excavation in rivers or harbors, but does not include any employee employed as a seaman.

United States Code Annotated

Contract requirements, see 41 USCA § 254.

Contractor certification or contract clause in acquisition of commercial items not required, see 37 USCA § 3707.

Contracts, planning, solicitation, evaluation, and award procedures, see 10 USCA § 2305.

Criminal penalties, see 37 USCA § 3708.

Definition and application, see 37 USCA § 3701.

Definitions, see 10 USCA § 2302, 41 USCA §§ 259, 403.

Health and safety standards in building trades and construction industry, see 37 USCA § 3704.

Kinds of contracts, see 10 USCA § 2306.

Limitations, variations, tolerances, and exemptions, see 37 USCA § 3706.

Planning and solicitation requirements, see 41 USCA § 253a.

Report of violations and withholding of amounts for unpaid wages and liquidated damages, see 37 USCA § 3703.

Work hours, see 37 USCA § 3702.

§ 22.301 Statutory requirement.

The statute requires that certain contracts contain a clause specifying that no laborer or mechanic doing any part of the work contemplated by the contract shall be required or permitted to work more than 40 hours in any workweek unless paid for all such overtime hours at not less than 1 1/2 times the basic rate of pay.

United States Code Annotated

Contract requirements, see 41 USCA § 254.

Contractor certification or contract clause in acquisition of commercial items not required, see 37 USCA § 3707.

Contracts, planning, solicitation, evaluation, and award procedures, see 10 USCA § 2305.

Criminal penalties, see 37 USCA § 3708.

Definition and application, see 37 USCA § 3701.

Definitions, see 10 USCA § 2302, 41 USCA §§ 259, 403.

Health and safety standards in building trades and construction industry, see 37 USCA § 3704.

Kinds of contracts, see 10 USCA § 2306.

Limitations, variations, tolerances, and exemptions, see 37 USCA § 3706.

Planning and solicitation requirements, see 41 USCA § 253a.

Report of violations and withholding of amounts for unpaid wages and liquidated damages, see 37 USCA § 3703.

Work hours, see 37 USCA § 3702.

§ 22.302 Liquidated damages and overtime pay.

(a) When an overtime computation discloses under-payments, the responsible contractor or subcontractor must pay the affected employee any unpaid wages and pay liquidated damages to the Government. The contracting officer must assess liquidated damages at the rate of $10 per affected employee for each calendar day on which the employer required or permitted the employee to work in excess of the standard workweek of 40 hours without paying overtime wages required by the statute.

(b) If the contractor or subcontractor fails or refuses to comply with overtime pay requirements of the statute and the funds withheld by Federal agencies for labor standards violations do not cover the unpaid wages due laborers and mechanics and the liquidated damages due the Government, make payments in the following order—

(1) Pay laborers and mechanics the wages they are owed (or prorate available funds if they do not cover the entire amount owed); and

(2) Pay liquidated damages.

(c) If the head of an agency finds that the administratively determined liquidated damages due under paragraph (a) of this section are incorrect, or that the contractor or subcontractor inadvertently violated the statute despite the exercise of due care, the agency head may—

(1) Reduce the amount of liquidated damages assessed for liquidated damages of $500 or less;

(2) Release the contractor or subcontractor from the liability for liquidated damages of $500 or less; or

(3) Recommend that the Secretary of Labor reduce or waive liquidated damages over $500.

(d) After the contracting officer determines the liquidated damages and the contractor makes appropriate payments, disburse any remaining assessments in accordance with agency procedures.

United States Code Annotated

Contract requirements, see 41 USCA § 254.

Contractor certification or contract clause in acquisition of commercial items not required, see 37 USCA § 3707.

Contracts, planning, solicitation, evaluation, and award procedures, see 10 USCA § 2305.

Criminal penalties, see 37 USCA § 3708.

Definition and application, see 37 USCA § 3701.

Definitions, see 10 USCA § 2302, 41 USCA §§ 259, 403.

Health and safety standards in building trades and construction industry, see 37 USCA § 3704.

Kinds of contracts, see 10 USCA § 2306.

Limitations, variations, tolerances, and exemptions, see 37 USCA § 3706.

Planning and solicitation requirements, see 41 USCA § 253a.

Report of violations and withholding of amounts for unpaid wages and liquidated damages, see 37 USCA § 3703.

Work hours, see 37 USCA § 3702.

§ 22.303 Administration and enforcement.

The procedures and reports required for construction contracts in Subpart 22.4 also apply to investigations of alleged violations of the statute on other than construction contracts.

United States Code Annotated

Contract requirements, see 41 USCA § 254.

Contractor certification or contract clause in acquisition of commercial items not required, see 37 USCA § 3707.

Contracts, planning, solicitation, evaluation, and award procedures, see 10 USCA § 2305.

Criminal penalties, see 37 USCA § 3708.

Definition and application, see 37 USCA § 3701.

Definitions, see 10 USCA § 2302, 41 USCA §§ 259, 403.

Health and safety standards in building trades and construction industry, see 37 USCA § 3704.

Kinds of contracts, see 10 USCA § 2306.

Limitations, variations, tolerances, and exemptions, see 37 USCA § 3706.

Planning and solicitation requirements, see 41 USCA § 253a.

Report of violations and withholding of amounts for unpaid wages and liquidated damages, see 37 USCA § 3703.

Work hours, see 37 USCA § 3702.

§ 22.304 Variations, tolerances, and exemptions.

(a) The Secretary of Labor, under 40 U.S.C. 3706, upon the Secretary's initiative or at the request of any Federal agency, may provide reasonable limitations and allow variations, tolerances, and exemptions to and from any or all provisions of the statute (see 29 CFR 5.15).

(b) The Secretary of Labor may make variations, tolerances, and exemptions from the regulatory requirements of applicable parts of 29 CFR when the Secretary finds that such action is necessary and proper in the public interest or to prevent injustice and undue hardship (see 29 CFR 5.14).

United States Code Annotated

Contract requirements, see 41 USCA § 254.

Contractor certification or contract clause in acquisition of commercial items not required, see 37 USCA § 3707.

Contracts, planning, solicitation, evaluation, and award procedures, see 10 USCA § 2305.

Criminal penalties, see 37 USCA § 3708.

Definition and application, see 37 USCA § 3701.

Definitions, see 10 USCA § 2302, 41 USCA §§ 259, 403.

Health and safety standards in building trades and construction industry, see 37 USCA § 3704.

Kinds of contracts, see 10 USCA § 2306.

Limitations, variations, tolerances, and exemptions, see 37 USCA § 3706.

Planning and solicitation requirements, see 41 USCA § 253a.

Report of violations and withholding of amounts for unpaid wages and liquidated damages, see 37 USCA § 3703.

Work hours, see 37 USCA § 3702.

§ 22.305 Contract clause.

Insert the clause at 52.222-4, Contract Work Hours and Safety Standards—Overtime Compensation, in solicitations and contracts (including, for this purpose, basic ordering agreements) when the contract may require or involve the employment of laborers or mechanics. However, do not include the clause in solicitations and contracts—

(a) Valued at or below $150,000;

(b) For commercial items;

(c) For transportation or the transmission of intelligence;

(d) To be performed outside the United States, Puerto Rico, American Samoa, Guam, the U.S. Virgin Islands, Johnston Island, Wake Island, and the outer Continental Shelf as defined in the Outer Continental Shelf Lands Act (43 U.S.C. 1331) (29 CFR 5.15);

(e)) For work to be done solely in accordance with 41 U.S.C. chapter 65, Contracts for Materials, Supplies, Articles, and Equipment Exceeding $15,000 (see Subpart 22.6);

(f) For supplies that include incidental services that do not require substantial employment of laborers or mechanics; or

(g) Exempt under regulations of the Secretary of Labor (29 CFR 5.15).

United States Code Annotated

Contract requirements, see 41 USCA § 254.

Contractor certification or contract clause in acquisition of commercial items not required, see 37 USCA § 3707.

Contracts, planning, solicitation, evaluation, and award procedures, see 10 USCA § 2305.

Criminal penalties, see 37 USCA § 3708.

Definition and application, see 37 USCA § 3701.

Definitions, see 10 USCA § 2302, 41 USCA §§ 259, 403.

Health and safety standards in building trades and construction industry, see 37 USCA § 3704.

Kinds of contracts, see 10 USCA § 2306.

Limitations, variations, tolerances, and exemptions, see 37 USCA § 3706.

Planning and solicitation requirements, see 41 USCA § 253a.

Report of violations and withholding of amounts for unpaid wages and liquidated damages, see 37 USCA § 3703.

Work hours, see 37 USCA § 3702.

Subpart 22.4 Labor Standards for Contracts Involving Construction

§ 22.400 Scope of subpart.

This subpart implements the statutes which prescribe labor standards requirements for contracts in excess of $2,000 for construction, alteration, or repair, including painting and decorating, of public buildings and public works. (See definition of "Construction, alteration, or repair" in section 22.401.) Labor relations requirements prescribed in other subparts of Part 22 may also apply.

United States Code Annotated

Contract requirements, see 41 USCA § 254.

Contracts, planning, solicitation, evaluation, and award procedures, see 10 USCA § 2305.

Definitions, see 10 USCA § 2302, 41 USCA §§ 259, 403.

Kickbacks from public works employees, see 18 USCA § 874.

Kinds of contracts, see 10 USCA § 2306.

Planning and solicitation requirements, see 41 USCA § 253a.

Rate of wages for laborers and mechanics, see 40 USCA § 3142.

Work hours, see 40 USCA § 3702.

§ 22.401 Definitions.

As used in this subpart—

"Apprentice" means a person—

(1) Employed and individually registered in a bona fide apprenticeship program registered with the U.S. Department of Labor, Employment and Training Administration, Office of Apprenticeship Training, Employer, and Labor Services (OATELS), or with a State Apprenticeship Agency recognized by OATELS; or

(2) Who is in the first 90 days of probationary employment as an apprentice in an apprenticeship program, and is not individually registered in the program, but who has been certified by the OATELS or a State Apprenticeship Agency (where appropriate) to be eligible for probationary employment as an apprentice.

"Construction, alteration, or repair" means all types of work done by laborers and mechanics employed by the construction contractor or construction subcontractor on a particular building or work at the site thereof, including without limitations—

(1) Altering, remodeling, installation (if appropriate) on the site of the work of items fabricated off-site;

(2) Painting and decorating;

(3) Manufacturing or furnishing of materials, articles, supplies, or equipment on the site of the building or work;

(4) Transportation of materials and supplies between the site of the work within the meaning of paragraphs (1)(i) and (ii) of the "site of the work" definition of this section, and a facility which is dedicated to the construction of the building or work and is deemed part of the site of the work within the meaning of paragraph (2) of the "site of work" definition of this section; and

(5) Transportation of portions of the building or work between a secondary site where a significant portion of the building or work is constructed, which is part of the "site of the work" definition in paragraph (1)(ii) of this section, and the physical place or places where the building or work will remain (paragraph (1)(i) in the "site of the work" definition of this section).

"Laborers or mechanics."—

(1) Means—

(i) Workers, utilized by a contractor or subcontractor at any tier, whose duties are manual or physical in nature (including those workers who use tools or who are performing the work of a trade), as distinguished from mental or managerial;

(ii) Apprentices, trainees, helpers, and, in the case of contracts subject to the Contract Work Hours and Safety Standards statute, watchmen and guards;

(iii) Working foremen who devote more than 20 percent of their time during a workweek performing duties of a laborer or mechanic, and who do not meet the criteria of 29 CFR part 541, for the time so spent; and

(iv) Every person performing the duties of a laborer or mechanic, regardless of any contractual relationship alleged to exist between the contractor and those individuals; and

(2) Does not include workers whose duties are primarily executive, supervisory (except as provided in paragraph (1)(iii) of this definition), administrative, or clerical, rather than manual. Persons employed in a bona fide executive, administrative, or professional capacity as defined in 29 CFR part 541 are not deemed to be laborers or mechanics.

"Public building or public work" means building or work, the construction, prosecution, completion, or repair of which, as defined in this section, is carried on directly by authority of, or with funds of, a Federal agency to serve the interest of the general public regardless of whether title thereof is in a Federal agency.

"Site of the work."—

(1) Means—

(i) *The primary site of the work.* The physical place or places where the construction called for in the contract will remain when work on it is completed; and

(ii) *The secondary site of the work, if any.* Any other site where a significant portion of the building or work is constructed, provided that such site is—

(A) Located in the United States; and

(B) Established specifically for the performance of the contract or project;

(2) Except as provided in paragraph (3) of this definition, includes fabrication plants, mobile factories, batch plants, borrow pits, job headquarters, tool yards, etc., provided—

(i) They are dedicated exclusively, or nearly so, to performance of the contract or project; and

(ii) They are adjacent or virtually adjacent to the "primary site of the work" as defined in paragraphs (1)(i) of "the secondary site of the work" as defined in paragraph (1)(ii) of this definition;

(3) Does not include permanent home offices, branch plant establishments, fabrication plants, or tool yards of a contractor or subcontractor whose locations and continuance in operation are determined wholly without regard to a particular Federal contract or project. In addition, fabrication plants, batch plants, borrow pits, job headquarters, yards, etc., of a commercial or material supplier which are established by a supplier of materials for the project before opening of bids and not on the project site, are not included in the "site of the work." Such permanent, previously established facilities are not a part of the "site of the work", even if the operations for a period of time may be dedicated exclusively, or nearly so, to the performance of a contract.

"Trainee" means a person registered and receiving on-the-job training in a construction occupation under a program which has been approved in advance by the U.S. Department of Labor, Employment and Training Administration, Office of Apprenticeship Training, Employer, and Labor Services (OATELS), as meeting its standards for on-the-job training programs and which has been so certified by that Administration.

"Wages" means the basic hourly rate of pay; any contribution irrevocably made by a contractor or subcontractor to a trustee or to a third person pursuant to a bona fide fringe benefit fund, plan, or program; and the rate of costs to the contractor or subcontractor which may be reasonably anticipated in providing bonafide fringe benefits to laborers and mechanics pursuant to an enforceable commitment to carry out a financially responsible plan or program, which was communicated in writing to the laborers and mechanics affected. The fringe benefits enumerated in the Construction Wage Rate Requirements statute include medical or hospital care, pensions on retirement or death, compensation for injuries or illness resulting from occupational activity, or insurance to provide any of the foregoing; unemployment benefits; life insurance, disability insurance, sickness insurance, or accident insurance; vacation or holiday pay; defraying costs of apprenticeship or other similar programs; or other bona fide fringe benefits. Fringe benefits do not include benefits required by other Federal, State, or local law.

United States Code Annotated

Contract requirements, see 41 USCA § 254.

Contracts, planning, solicitation, evaluation, and award procedures, see 10 USCA § 2305.

Definitions, see 10 USCA § 2302, 41 USCA §§ 259, 403.

Kickbacks from public works employees, see 18 USCA § 874.

Kinds of contracts, see 10 USCA § 2306.

Planning and solicitation requirements, see 41 USCA § 253a.

Rate of wages for laborers and mechanics, see 40 USCA § 3142.

Work hours, see 40 USCA § 3702.

§ 22.402 Applicability.

(a) Contracts for construction work.

(1) The requirements of this subpart apply—

(i) Only if the construction work is, or reasonably can be foreseen to be, performed at a particular site so that wage rates can be determined for the locality, and only to construction work that is performed by laborers and mechanics at the site of the work;

(ii) To dismantling, demolition, or removal of improvements if a part of the construction contract, or if construction at that site is anticipated by another contract as provided in Subpart 37.3;

(iii) To the manufacture or fabrication of construction materials and components conducted in connection with the construction and on the site of the work by the contractor or a subcontractor under a contract otherwise subject to this subpart; and

(iv) To painting of public buildings or public works, whether performed in connection with the original construction or as alteration or repair of an existing structure.

(2) The requirements of this subpart do not apply to—

(i) The manufacturing of components or materials off the site of the work or their subsequent delivery to the site by the commercial supplier or materialman;

(ii) Contracts requiring construction work that is so closely related to research, experiment, and development that it cannot be performed separately, or that is itself the subject of research, experiment, or development (see paragraph (b) of this section for applicability of this subpart to research and development contracts or portions thereof involving construction, alteration, or repair of a public building or public work);

(iii) Employees of railroads operating under collective bargaining agreements that are subject to the Railway Labor Act; or

(iv) Employees who work at contractors' or subcontractors' permanent home offices, fabrication shops, or tool yards not located at the site of the work. However, if the employees go to the site of the work and perform construction activities there, the requirements of this subpart are applicable for the actual time so spent, not including travel unless the employees transport materials or supplies to or from the site of the work.

(b) Nonconstruction contracts involving some construction work.

(1) The requirements of this subpart apply to construction work to be performed as part of nonconstruction contracts (supply, service, research and development, etc.) if—

(i) The construction work is to be performed on a public building or public work;

(ii) The contract contains specific requirements for a substantial amount of construction work exceeding the monetary threshold for application of the Construction Wage Rate Requirements statute (the word "substantial" relates to the type and quantity of construction work to be performed and not merely to the total value of construction work as compared to the total value of the contract); and

(iii) The construction work is physically or functionally separate from, and is capable of being performed on a segregated basis from, the other work required by the contract.

(2) The requirements of this subpart do not apply if—

(i) The construction work is incidental to the furnishing of supplies, equipment, or services (for example, the requirements do not apply to simple installation or alteration at a public building or public work that is incidental to furnishing supplies or equipment under a supply contract; however, if a substantial and segregable amount of construction, alteration, or repair is required, such as for installation of heavy generators or large refrigerator systems or for plant modification or rearrangement, the requirements of this subpart apply); or

    (ii) The construction work is so merged with non- construction work or so fragmented in terms of the locations or time spans in which it is to be performed, that it is not capable of being segregated as a separate contractual requirement.

United States Code Annotated

Contract requirements, see 41 USCA § 254.

Contracts, planning, solicitation, evaluation, and award procedures, see 10 USCA § 2305.

Definitions, see 10 USCA § 2302, 41 USCA §§ 259, 403.

Kickbacks from public works employees, see 18 USCA § 874.

Kinds of contracts, see 10 USCA § 2306.

Planning and solicitation requirements, see 41 USCA § 253a.

Rate of wages for laborers and mechanics, see 40 USCA § 3142.

Work hours, see 40 USCA § 3702.

§ 22.403 Statutory and regulatory requirements.

§ 22.403-1 Construction Wage Rate Requirements statute.

40 U.S.C. chapter 31, subchapter IV, Wage Rate Requirements (Construction), formerly known as the Davis-Bacon Act, provides that contracts in excess of $2,000 to which the United States or the District of Columbia is a party for construction, alteration, or repair (including painting and decorating) of public buildings or public works within the United States, shall contain a clause (see 52.222-6) that no laborer or mechanic employed directly upon the site of the work shall receive less than the prevailing wage rates as determined by the Secretary of Labor.

United States Code Annotated

Contract requirements, see 41 USCA § 254.

Contracts, planning, solicitation, evaluation, and award procedures, see 10 USCA § 2305.

Definitions, see 10 USCA § 2302, 41 USCA §§ 259, 403.

Kickbacks from public works employees, see 18 USCA § 874.

Kinds of contracts, see 10 USCA § 2306.

Planning and solicitation requirements, see 41 USCA § 253a.

Rate of wages for laborers and mechanics, see 40 USCA § 3142.

Work hours, see 40 USCA § 3702.

Notes of Decisions

In general 1
Construction and application 3
Purpose 2

1 In general

Wage and Hour Administrator's determination that batch plant was part of "site of the work" for highway construction project, so that prevailing wage requirement of Davis-Bacon Act applied to truck drivers hauling asphalt from plant to project, was not arbitrary or capricious; plant was located approximately three miles from midpoint of project at facility of supplier of coarse aggregate required for bituminous mix to resurface highway, decision to establish plant was made at preconstruction meeting convened to discuss project, plant produced material exclusively or nearly exclusively for project, and plant was dismantled after completion of project.

Davis-Bacon Act essentially provides that all laborers and mechanics working on federally funded construction projects be paid not less than prevailing wage in locality in which work is performed. Davis-Bacon Act, § 1 et seq., 40 U.S.C.A. § 276a et seq.Sheet Metal Workers Intern. Ass'n, Local Union No. 19 v. U.S. Dept. of Veterans Affairs, 135 F.3d 891, 4 Wage & Hour Cas. 2d (BNA) 580 (3d Cir. 1998). Labor And Employment ☞2304

Davis-Bacon Act requires contractors on all federally assisted construction projects to pay their employees the prevailing wage, as specified by the United States Department of Labor, in cash, or in contributions to bona fide employee benefit plans. Davis-Bacon Act, § 1, as amended, 40 U.S.C.A. § 276a. In re Schimmels, 85 F.3d 416, 36 Collier Bankr. Cas. 2d (MB) 143, 34 Fed. R. Serv. 3d 1596 (9th Cir. 1996). Labor And Employment ⊙2304

Under the Davis-Bacon Act, contractors on federally assisted construction projects must pay employees in compliance with the Act and must certify compliance on weekly basis; payment of federal funds to contractors is expressly contingent upon receipt of contractors' weekly certifications of compliance. 40 U.S.C.A. § 276c; Davis-Bacon Act, § 2, as amended, 40 U.S.C.A. § 276a-1; 29 C.F.R. §§ 5.9–5.12. In re Schimmels, 85 F.3d 416, 36 Collier Bankr. Cas. 2d (MB) 143, 34 Fed. R. Serv. 3d 1596 (9th Cir. 1996). Labor And Employment ⊙2304

Department of Labor's definition, for purposes of the Davis-Bacon Act, of class of employees known as "helpers," pursuant to which agency would approve helper classification only if it is a separate and distinct class of worker that prevails in the area, the duties of which can be differentiated from the duties of journey-level workers, did not abuse its broad discretion under the Act to recognize and define various classes of workers for whom prevailing wage must be determined. Davis-Bacon Act, § 1, 40 U.S.C.A. § 276a. Associated Builders & Contractors, Inc. v. Herman, 976 F. Supp. 1 (D.D.C. 1997). Labor And Employment ⊙2304

Davis-Bacon Act, § 1 et seq., 40 U.S.C.A. § 276a et seq.; 29 C.F.R. § 5.2(l). L.P. Cavett Co. v. U.S. Dept. of Labor, 892 F. Supp. 973, 2 Wage & Hour Cas. 2d (BNA) 1458, 131 Lab. Cas. (CCH) P 33372 (S.D. Ohio 1995), judgment rev'd, 101 F.3d 1111, 3 Wage & Hour Cas. 2d (BNA) 993, 133 Lab. Cas. (CCH) P 33480, 1996 FED App. 0369P (6th Cir. 1996). Labor And Employment ⊙2243; Labor And Employment ⊙2304

On review of decision of Wage Appeals Board finding prevailing wage requirement applicable to truck drivers hauling asphalt from temporary batch plant to highway construction project, controlling statute for purposes of determining validity of regulation defining "site of the work" was Davis-Bacon Act, rather than Federal Aid Highways Act which contains no language limiting "site of the work"; Federal Aid Highways Act incorporates method of determining prevailing wage rates under Davis-Bacon Act, and legislative history of Federal Aid Highways Act indicated that workers on federally funded highway construction were to be given same wage protection as workers covered by Davis-Bacon Act. 23 U.S.C.A. § 113; Davis-Bacon Act, § 1 et seq., 40 U.S.C.A. § 276a et seq.; 29 C.F.R. §§ 5.1(a), 5.2(l). L.P. Cavett Co. v. U.S. Dept. of Labor, 892 F. Supp. 973, 2 Wage & Hour Cas. 2d (BNA) 1458, 131 Lab. Cas. (CCH) P 33372 (S.D. Ohio 1995), judgment rev'd, 101 F.3d 1111, 3 Wage & Hour Cas. 2d (BNA) 993, 133 Lab. Cas. (CCH) P 33480, 1996 FED App. 0369P (6th Cir. 1996). Labor And Employment ⊙2243; Labor And Employment ⊙2304

Agency unreasonably evaluated awardee's proposal as responsive to the terms of the solicitation where the awardee did not expressly commit to pay applicable Davis-Bacon wage rates, and, instead, expressly committed only to pay those rates for a subset of the work anticipated. Fed. Builders, LLC-The James R. Belk Trust, B-409952, 2014 CPD ¶ 285 (Comp. Gen. 2014)

2 Purpose

Dual purposes of Davis-Bacon Act are to give local laborers and contractors fair opportunity to participate in building programs when federal money is involved and to protect local wage standards by preventing contractors from basing their bids on wages lower than those prevailing in area. Davis-Bacon Act, § 1 et seq., 40 U.S.C.A. § 276a et seq. L.P. Cavett Co. v. U.S. Dept. of Labor, 892 F. Supp. 973, 2 Wage & Hour Cas. 2d (BNA) 1458, 131 Lab. Cas. (CCH) P 33372 (S.D. Ohio 1995), judgment rev'd, 101 F.3d 1111, 3 Wage & Hour Cas. 2d (BNA) 993, 133 Lab. Cas. (CCH) P 33480, 1996 FED App. 0369P (6th Cir. 1996). Labor And Employment ⊙2243; Labor And Employment ⊙2304

3 Construction and application

Davis-Bacon Act protects local contractors from being underbid on federally funded construction projects and applies to all government contracts for construction, alteration, and/or repair; Act mandates that government contractors and subcontractors pay covered employees wages at least as high as those prevailing in area in which public work is sited.

Contracting agency has initial responsibility for determining whether particular contract is subject to Davis-Bacon Act, and if agency determines such contract is subject to Act, it must determine appropriate prevailing wage rate and ensure that rate chosen is inserted in requests for bids on project, as well as in any resulting contract. Davis-Bacon Act, §§ 1 et seq., 1(a) as amended 40 U.S.C.A. §§ 276a et seq., 276a(a); 40 U.S.C.A. § 276c. Universities Research Ass'n, Inc. v. Coutu, 450 U.S. 754, 101 S. Ct. 1451, 67 L. Ed. 2d 662, 24 Wage & Hour Cas. (BNA) 1273, 28 Cont. Cas. Fed. (CCH) P 81199, 91 Lab. Cas. (CCH) P 33992 (1981). Labor And Employment ☞2298; Labor And Employment ☞2304

Davis-Bacon Act, § 1 et seq., 40 U.S.C.A. § 276a et seq.Building and Const. Trades Dept. AFL-CIO v. U.S. Dept. of Labor Wage Appeals Bd., 932 F.2d 985, 30 Wage & Hour Cas. (BNA) 497, 37 Cont. Cas. Fed. (CCH) P 76099, 118 Lab. Cas. (CCH) P 35491 (D.C. Cir. 1991). Labor And Employment ☞2304

Davis-Bacon Act minimum-wage, maximum-hours law applicable to workers under federal contract who are employed directly upon site of work is remedial act for benefit of construction workers and is liberally construed to effectuate its beneficent purpose. Davis-Bacon Act, § 1, 40 U.S.C.A. § 276a. Drivers, Salesmen, Warehousemen, Milk Processors, Cannery, Dairy Emp. and Helpers Local Union No. 695 v. N. L. R. B., 361 F.2d 547 (D.C. Cir. 1966). Labor And Employment ☞2304; Labor And Employment ☞2220(2)

§ 22.403-2 Copeland Act.

The Copeland (Anti-Kickback) Act (18 U.S.C. 874 and 40 U.S.C. 3145) makes it unlawful to induce, by force, intimidation, threat of procuring dismissal from employment, or otherwise, any person employed in the construction or repair of public buildings or public works, financed in whole or in part by the United States, to give up any part of the compensation to which that person is entitled under a contract of employment. The Copeland Act also requires each contractor and subcontractor to furnish weekly a statement of compliance with respect to the wages paid each employee during the preceding week. Contracts subject to the Copeland Act shall contain a clause (see 52.222-10) requiring contractors and subcontractors to comply with the regulations issued by the Secretary of Labor under the Copeland Act.

United States Code Annotated

Contract requirements, see 41 USCA § 254.

Contracts, planning, solicitation, evaluation, and award procedures, see 10 USCA § 2305.

Definitions, see 10 USCA § 2302, 41 USCA §§ 259, 403.

Kickbacks from public works employees, see 18 USCA § 874.

Kinds of contracts, see 10 USCA § 2306.

Planning and solicitation requirements, see 41 USCA § 253a.

Work hours, see 40 USCA § 3702.

Notes of Decisions

In general 1

1 In general

Davis-Bacon Act can properly reach conduct that is not also in violation of Copeland Act; accordingly, Davis-Bacon Act's command that contractor or subcontractor pay employees the full amount accrued without subsequent deduction or rebate does not apply only to kickbacks as described in Copeland Act. Davis-Bacon Act, § 1 et seq., as amended, 40 U.S.C.A. § 276a et seq.; 18 U.S.C.A. § 874. International Broth. of Elec. Workers, Local 357, AFL-CIO v. Brock, 68 F.3d 1194, 2 Wage & Hour Cas. 2d (BNA) 1633, 131 Lab. Cas. (CCH) P 33307 (9th Cir. 1995). Labor And Employment ☞2304

Davis-Bacon Act can properly reach conduct that is not also in violation of Copeland Act; accordingly, Davis-Bacon Act's command that contractor or subcontractor pay employees the full amount accrued without subsequent deduction or rebate does not apply only to kickbacks as described in Copeland Act. Davis-Bacon Act, § 1 et seq., as amended, 40 U.S.C.A. § 276a et seq.; 18 U.S.C.A. § 874. Building and Const. Trades Dept., AFL-CIO v. Reich, 40 F.3d 1275, 2 Wage & Hour Cas. 2d (BNA) 737, 129 Lab. Cas. (CCH) P 33183 (D.C. Cir. 1994). Labor And Employment ☞2304

§ 22.403-3 Contract Work Hours and Safety Standards.

40 U.S.C. chpater 37, Contract Work Hours and Safety Standards, requires that certain

contracts (see 22.305) contain a clause (see 52.222-4) specifying that no laborer or mechanic doing any part of the work contemplated by the contract shall be required or permitted to work more than 40 hours in any workweek unless paid for all additional hours at not less than 1 1/2 times the basic rate of pay (see 22.301).

United States Code Annotated

Contract requirements, see 41 USCA § 254.

Contracts, planning, solicitation, evaluation, and award procedures, see 10 USCA § 2305.

Definitions, see 10 USCA § 2302, 41 USCA §§ 259, 403.

Kickbacks from public works employees, see 18 USCA § 874.

Kinds of contracts, see 10 USCA § 2306.

Planning and solicitation requirements, see 41 USCA § 253a.

Rate of wages for laborers and mechanics, see 40 USCA § 3142.

Work hours, see 40 USCA § 3702.

§ 22.403-4 Department of Labor regulations.

(a) Under the statutes referred to in this 22.403 and Reorganization Plan No. 14 of 1950 (3 CFR 1949-53 Comp, p. 1007), the Secretary of Labor has issued regulations in Title 29, Subtitle A, *Code of Federal Regulations*, prescribing standards and procedures to be observed by the Department of Labor and the Federal contracting agencies. Those standards and procedures applicable to contracts involving construction are implemented in this subpart.

(b) The Department of Labor regulations include—

(1) Part 1, relating to Construction Wage Rate Requirements statute minimum wage rates;

(2) Part 3, relating to the Copeland (Anti-Kickback) Act and requirements for submission of weekly statements of compliance and the preservation and inspection of weekly payroll records;

(3) Part 5, relating to enforcement of the (i) Construction Wage Rate Requirements statute, (ii) Contract Work Hours and Safety Standards statute and (iii) Copeland (Anti-Kickback) Act;

(4) Part 6, relating to rules of practice for appealing the findings of the Administrator, Wage and Hour Division, in enforcement cases under the various labor statutes, and by which Administrative Law Judge hearings are held; and

(5) Part 7, relating to rules of practice by which contractors and other interested parties may appeal to the Department of Labor Administrative Review Board, decisions issued by the Administrator, Wage and Hour Division, or administrative law judges under the various labor statutes.

(c) Refer all questions relating to the application and interpretation of wage determinations (including the classifications therein) and the interpretation of the Department of Labor regulations in this subsection to the Administrator, Wage and Hour Division.

United States Code Annotated

Contract requirements, see 41 USCA § 254.

Contracts, planning, solicitation, evaluation, and award procedures, see 10 USCA § 2305.

Definitions, see 10 USCA § 2302, 41 USCA §§ 259, 403.

Kickbacks from public works employees, see 18 USCA § 874.

Kinds of contracts, see 10 USCA § 2306.

Planning and solicitation requirements, see 41 USCA § 253a.

Rate of wages for laborers and mechanics, see 40 USCA § 3142.

Work hours, see 40 USCA § 3702.

Notes of Decisions

Damages 4

Discretion of department 1

Helpers 3

Jurisdiction 5
Site of work 2

1 Discretion of department

After expiration of congressional rider prohibiting expenditure of funds to implement revised regulations governing class of employees known as "helpers" working on federal construction projects covered by the Davis-Bacon Act, it was within discretion of Department of Labor to seek an indefinite postponement of the effective date of such regulations, assuming a rational basis for agency's findings concerning changed circumstances. Davis-Bacon Act, § 1, 40 U.S.C.A. § 276a. Associated Builders & Contractors, Inc. v. Herman, 976 F. Supp. 1 (D.D.C. 1997). Labor And Employment ☞2304

2 Site of work

Regulation defining "site of the work" for purposes of Davis-Bacon Act, which requires payment of prevailing wage to workers employed directly upon "site of the work," to include off-site facility which is adjacent or nearby actual construction location, is dedicated exclusively, or nearly so, to performance of contract at issue, and is not permanent was reasonable interpretation of Act; regulation was consistent with Department of Labor's longstanding interpretation of Act, and regulation prohibited contractor from creating artificial off-site facility to evade payment of prevailing wages. Davis-Bacon Act, § 1 et seq., 40 U.S.C.A. § 276a et seq.; 29 C.F.R. § 5.2(l). L.P. Cavett Co. v. U.S. Dept. of Labor, 892 F. Supp. 973, 2 Wage & Hour Cas. 2d (BNA) 1458, 131 Lab. Cas. (CCH) P 33372 (S.D. Ohio 1995), judgment rev'd, 101 F.3d 1111, 3 Wage & Hour Cas. 2d (BNA) 993, 133 Lab. Cas. (CCH) P 33480, 1996 FED App. 0369P (6th Cir. 1996). Labor And Employment ☞2243; Labor And Employment ☞2304

For purposes of determining validity of regulation defining "site of the work," with regard to highway and other construction projects such as aqueducts, bridges, and dams, phrase "directly upon the site of the work" used in Davis-Bacon Act is ambiguous; in such projects, which by their nature are long and narrow and require large amounts of construction material, site of construction work must, by necessity, spill over onto nearby areas, although those areas are outside land occupied by final construction work. Davis-Bacon Act, § 1 et seq., 40 U.S.C.A. § 276a et seq.; 29 C.F.R. § 5.2(l). L.P. Cavett Co. v. U.S. Dept. of Labor, 892 F. Supp. 973, 2 Wage & Hour Cas. 2d (BNA) 1458, 131 Lab. Cas. (CCH) P 33372 (S.D. Ohio 1995), judgment rev'd, 101 F.3d 1111, 3 Wage & Hour Cas. 2d (BNA) 993, 133 Lab. Cas. (CCH) P 33480, 1996 FED App. 0369P (6th Cir. 1996). Labor And Employment ☞2243; Labor And Employment ☞2304

3 Helpers

Davis-Bacon Act regulation establishing formula of 2:3 for calculating cap on ratio of helpers to journeyman on federal construction projects is arbitrary and capricious; basis upon which 40% cap was selected as a numerical limit for use of helpers on Davis-Bacon Act projects was unexplained, and agency stated only that a 2:3 ratio better reflected industry use of helpers than a 1:5 ratio. Davis-Bacon Act, § 1 et seq., 40 U.S.C.A. § 276a et seq.Building & Const. Trades Dept., AFL-CIO v. Martin, 961 F.2d 269, 30 Wage & Hour Cas. (BNA) 1430, 38 Cont. Cas. Fed. (CCH) P 76313, 121 Lab. Cas. (CCH) P 35628 (D.C. Cir. 1992). Labor And Employment ☞2304

Secretary of Labor did not act arbitrarily in promulgating regulation under the Davis-Bacon Act setting forth alternative tests for determining whether the use of helpers "prevails" in a particular locality; under the test, any federal project employing helper category will reflect either practice of contractors employing a majority of journeymen in locality or majority of workers engaged in relevant employment in a weighted average locality; in neither instance would determination that a practice prevails be contrary to Act's purpose of aligning wages on federal projects with local rates. Davis-Bacon Act, § 1 et seq., 40 U.S.C.A. § 276a et seq.Building & Const. Trades Dept., AFL-CIO v. Martin, 961 F.2d 269, 30 Wage & Hour Cas. (BNA) 1430, 38 Cont. Cas. Fed. (CCH) P 76313, 121 Lab. Cas. (CCH) P 35628 (D.C. Cir. 1992). Labor And Employment ☞2304

Conformance regulations implementing Davis-Bacon Act which prescribe procedure for adding an employee classification to specifications of an existing government contract are not arbitrary and capricious, notwithstanding claim that regulations allow a lower-paid helper classification to replace higher-paid class of semi-skilled laborers already in the wage determination and working under supervision of a journeyman, as regulation specifically prohibits addition of a lowerpaid classification to replace existing classification of semiskilled workers. Davis-Bacon Act, § 1 et seq., 40 U.S.C.A. § 276a et seq.Building & Const. Trades Dept., AFL-CIO v. Martin, 961 F.2d 269, 30 Wage & Hour Cas. (BNA) 1430, 38 Cont. Cas. Fed. (CCH) P 76313, 121 Lab. Cas. (CCH) P 35628 (D.C. Cir. 1992). Labor And Employment ⚯2304

Definition of "helper" in regulation implementing the Davis-Bacon Act does not subvert Act's purpose by allowing members of lower paid and lower skilled class to be hired to perform tasks which a higher class normally performs in cases where tasks overlap. Davis-Bacon Act, § 1 et seq., 40 U.S.C.A. § 276a et seq.Building & Const. Trades Dept., AFL-CIO v. Martin, 961 F.2d 269, 30 Wage & Hour Cas. (BNA) 1430, 38 Cont. Cas. Fed. (CCH) P 76313, 121 Lab. Cas. (CCH) P 35628 (D.C. Cir. 1992). Labor And Employment ⚯2304

Revised regulations governing class of employees known as "helpers" working on federal construction projects covered by the Davis-Bacon Act were subject to implementation immediately upon expiration of congressional rider prohibiting expenditure of funds to implement them; thus, on April 26, 1996, Department of Labor was required to take necessary steps to implement revised helper regulations, absent "good cause" circumstances that would have justified continuation of their suspension without notice and an opportunity for comment. 5 U.S.C.A. § 553(b)(3)(B); Davis-Bacon Act, § 1, 40 U.S.C.A. § 276a. Associated Builders & Contractors, Inc. v. Herman, 976 F. Supp. 1 (D.D.C. 1997). Labor And Employment ⚯2304

4 Damages

Court of Federal Claims may award monetary relief based on the violation of regulation that tracks the Labor Department's authority to monitor compliance with the Davis-Bacon Act. Davis-Bacon Act, § 1 et seq., 40 U.S.C.A. § 276a et seq.; 48 C.F.R. 22.403-4. Reidell v. U.S., 43 Fed. Cl. 770, 6 Wage & Hour Cas. 2d (BNA) 444 (1999). Federal Courts ⚯1073.1

5 Jurisdiction

Court of Federal Claims had jurisdiction to enforce ruling of the Department of Labor that employees of subcontractor on government project were entitled to be paid prevailing wages pursuant to the Davis-Bacon Act, as employees were asking for enforcement of a determination by a government agency that the United States owed money to them. 28 U.S.C.A. § 1491; Davis-Bacon Act, § 1 et seq., 40 U.S.C.A. § 276a et seq.; 29 C.F.R. § 1.6(f). Reidell v. U.S., 43 Fed. Cl. 770, 6 Wage & Hour Cas. 2d (BNA) 444 (1999). Federal Courts ⚯1073.1

§ 22.403-5 Executive Order 13658.

Executive Order 13658 establishes minimum wages for certain workers. The wage rate is subject to annual increases by an amount determined by the Secretary of Labor. See Subpart 22.19. The clause at 52.222-55, Minimum Wages under Executive Order 13658, requires the Executive Order 13658 minimum wage rate to be paid if it is higher than other minimum wage rates, such as the Subpart 22.4 statutory wage determination amount.

§ 22.404 Construction Wage Rate Requirements statute wage determinations.

The Department of Labor is responsible for issuing wage determinations reflecting prevailing wages, including fringe benefits. The wage determinations apply only to those laborers and mechanics employed by a contractor upon the site of the work including drivers who transport to or from the site materials and equipment used in the course of contract operations. Determinations are issued for different types of construction, such as building, heavy, highway, and residential (referred to as rate schedules), and apply only to the types of construction designated in the determination.

§ 22.404-1 Types of wage determinations.

(a) General wage determinations.

(1) A general wage determination contains prevailing wage rates for the types of construction designated in the determination, and is used in contracts performed within a specified geographical area. General wage determinations contain no expiration date

and remain valid until modified, superseded, or canceled by the Department of Labor. Once incorporated in a contract, a general wage determination normally remains effective for the life of the contract, unless the contracting officer exercises an option to extend the term of the contract (see 22.404-12). These determinations shall be used whenever possible. They are issued at the discretion of the Department of Labor either upon receipt of an agency request or on the Department of Labor's own initiative.

(2) General wage determinations are published on the WDOL website. General wage determinations are effective on the publication date of the wage determination or upon receipt of the wage determination by the contracting agency, whichever occurs first. "Publication" within the meaning of this section shall occur on the first date the wage determination is published on the WDOL. Archived Davis-Bacon Act general wage determinations that are no longer current may be accessed in the "Archived DB WD" database on WDOL for information purposes only. Contracting officers may not use an archived wage determination in a contract action without obtaining prior approval of the Department of Labor. To obtain prior approval, contact the Department of Labor, Wage and Hour Division, using http://www.wdol.gov, or contact the procurement agency labor advisor listed on http://www.wdol.gov.

(b) *Project wage determinations.* A project wage determination is issued at the specific request of a contracting agency. It is used only when no general wage determination applies, and is effective for 180 calendar days from the date of the determination. However, if a determination expires before contract award, it may be possible to obtain an extension to the 180-day life of the determination (see 22.404-5(b)(2)). Once incorporated in a contract, a project wage determination normally remains effective for the life of the contract, unless the contracting officer exercises an option to extend the term of the contract (see 22.404-12).

United States Code Annotated

Contract requirements, see 41 USCA § 254.

Contracts, planning, solicitation, evaluation, and award procedures, see 10 USCA § 2305.

Definitions, see 10 USCA § 2302, 41 USCA §§ 259, 403.

Kinds of contracts, see 10 USCA § 2306.

Planning and solicitation requirements, see 41 USCA § 253a.

Rate of wages for laborers and mechanics, see 40 USCA § 3142.

Work hours, see 40 USCA § 3702.

§ 22.404-2 General requirements.

(a) The contracting officer must incorporate only the appropriate wage determinations in solicitations and contracts and must designate the work to which each determination or part thereof applies. The contracting officer must not include project wage determinations in contracts or options other than those for which they are issued. When exercising an option to extend the term of a contract, the contracting officer must select the most current wage determination(s) from the same schedule(s) as the wage determination(s) incorporated into the contract.

(b) If the wage determination is a general wage determination or a project wage determination containing more than one rate schedule, the contracting officer shall either include only the rate schedules that apply to the particular types of construction (building, heavy, highway, etc.) or include the entire wage determination and clearly indicate the parts of the work to which each rate schedule shall be applied. Inclusion by reference is not permitted.

(c) The Wage and Hour Division has issued the following general guidelines for use in selecting the proper schedule(s) of wage rates:

(1) *Building* construction is generally the construction of sheltered enclosures with walk-in access, for housing persons, machinery, equipment, or supplies. It typically includes all construction of such structures, installation of utilities and equipment (both above and below grade level), as well as incidental grading, utilities and paving, unless there is an established area practice to the contrary.

(2) *Residential* construction is generally the construction, alteration, or repair of single family houses or apartment buildings of no more than four (4) stories in height, and typically includes incidental items such as site work, parking areas, utilities, streets and

sidewalks, unless there is an established area practice to the contrary.

(3) *Highway* construction is generally the construction, alteration, or repair of roads, streets, highways, runways, taxiways, alleys, parking areas, and other similar projects that are not incidental to "building," "residential," or "heavy" construction.

(4) *Heavy* construction includes those projects that are not properly classified as either "building," "residential," or "highway," and is of a catch-all nature. Such heavy projects may sometimes be distinguished on the basis of their individual characteristics, and separate schedules issued (*e.g.,*"dredging," "water and sewer line," "dams," "flood control," etc.).

(5) When the nature of a project is not clear, it is necessary to look at additional factors, with primary consideration given to locally established area practices. If there is any doubt as to the proper application of wage rate schedules to the type or types of construction involved, guidance shall be sought before the opening of bids, or receipt of best and final offers, from the Administrator, Wage and Hour Division. Further examples are contained in Department of Labor All Agency Memoranda Numbers 130 and 131.

United States Code Annotated

Contract requirements, see 41 USCA § 254.

Contracts, planning, solicitation, evaluation, and award procedures, see 10 USCA § 2305.

Definitions, see 10 USCA § 2302, 41 USCA §§ 259, 403.

Kickbacks from public works employees, see 18 USCA § 874.

Kinds of contracts, see 10 USCA § 2306.

Planning and solicitation requirements, see 41 USCA § 253a.

Rate of wages for laborers and mechanics, see 40 USCA § 3142.

Work hours, see 40 USCA § 3702.

Notes of Decisions

In general 1
Construction and application 2
Helpers 4
Site of work 3

1 In general

Contracting agency has initial responsibility for determining whether particular contract is subject to Davis-Bacon Act, and if agency determines such contract is subject to Act, it must determine appropriate prevailing wage rate and ensure that rate chosen is inserted in requests for bids on project, as well as in any resulting contract. Davis-Bacon Act, §§ 1 et seq., 1(a) as amended 40 U.S.C.A. §§ 276a et seq., 276a(a); 40 U.S.C.A. § 276c. Universities Research Ass'n, Inc. v. Coutu, 450 U.S. 754, 101 S. Ct. 1451, 67 L. Ed. 2d 662, 24 Wage & Hour Cas. (BNA) 1273, 28 Cont. Cas. Fed. (CCH) P 81199, 91 Lab. Cas. (CCH) P 33992 (1981). Labor And Employment ⟨⟨⟩⟩2298; Labor And Employment ⟨⟨⟩⟩2304

An area practice survey conducted by the Department of Labor is not a prerequisite to the determination of prevailing wage rates or job classifications under Davis-Bacon Act and related federal laws. Davis-Bacon Act, § 1 et seq., 40 U.S.C.A. § 276a et seq.U.S. ex rel. Plumbers and Steamfitters Local Union No. 38 v. C.W. Roen Const. Co., 183 F.3d 1088, 5 Wage & Hour Cas. 2d (BNA) 808, 138 Lab. Cas. (CCH) P 33916 (9th Cir. 1999). Labor And Employment ⟨⟨⟩⟩2304

Although it is the Department of Labor's statutory responsibility under the Davis-Bacon Act to issue wage determinations for all classes of laborers and mechanics which prevail in every locality where they do prevail, Department has broad discretion to recognize and define the various classes of workers for whom the prevailing wage must be determined. Davis-Bacon Act, § 1, 40 U.S.C.A. § 276a. Associated Builders & Contractors, Inc. v. Herman, 976 F. Supp. 1 (D.D.C. 1997). Labor And Employment ⟨⟨⟩⟩2304

2 Construction and application

Davis-Bacon Act minimum-wage, maximum-hours law applicable to workers under federal contract who are employed directly upon site of work is remedial act for benefit of construction workers and is liberally construed to effectuate its beneficent purpose. Davis-Bacon Act, § 1, 40 U.S.C.A. § 276a. Drivers, Salesmen, Warehousemen, Milk Processors, Cannery, Dairy Emp. and Helpers Local Union No. 695 v. N. L. R. B., 361 F.2d 547, 553 (D.C. Cir. 1966). Labor And Employment ⚬2304; Labor And Employment ⚬2220(2)

3 Site of work

On review of decision of Wage Appeals Board finding prevailing wage requirement applicable to truck drivers hauling asphalt from temporary batch plant to highway construction project, controlling statute for purposes of determining validity of regulation defining "site of the work" was Davis-Bacon Act, rather than Federal Aid Highways Act which contains no language limiting "site of the work"; Federal Aid Highways Act incorporates method of determining prevailing wage rates under Davis-Bacon Act, and legislative history of Federal Aid Highways Act indicated that workers on federally funded highway construction were to be given same wage protection as workers covered by Davis-Bacon Act. 23 U.S.C.A. § 113; Davis-Bacon Act, § 1 et seq., 40 U.S.C.A. § 276a et seq.; 29 C.F.R. §§ 5.1(a), 5.2(l). L.P. Cavett Co. v. U.S. Dept. of Labor, 892 F. Supp. 973, 2 Wage & Hour Cas. 2d (BNA) 1458, 131 Lab. Cas. (CCH) P 33372 (S.D. Ohio 1995), judgment rev'd, 101 F.3d 1111, 3 Wage & Hour Cas. 2d (BNA) 993, 133 Lab. Cas. (CCH) P 33480, 1996 FED App. 0369P (6th Cir. 1996). Labor And Employment ⚬2243; Labor And Employment ⚬2304

Wage and Hour Administrator's determination that batch plant was part of "site of the work" for highway construction project, so that prevailing wage requirement of Davis-Bacon Act applied to truck drivers hauling asphalt from plant to project, was not arbitrary or capricious; plant was located approximately three miles from midpoint of project at facility of supplier of coarse aggregate required for bituminous mix to resurface highway, decision to establish plant was made at preconstruction meeting convened to discuss project, plant produced material exclusively or nearly exclusively for project, and plant was dismantled after completion of project. Davis-Bacon Act, § 1 et seq., 40 U.S.C.A. § 276a et seq.; 29 C.F.R. § 5.2(l). L.P. Cavett Co. v. U.S. Dept. of Labor, 892 F. Supp. 973, 2 Wage & Hour Cas. 2d (BNA) 1458, 131 Lab. Cas. (CCH) P 33372 (S.D. Ohio 1995), judgment rev'd, 101 F.3d 1111, 3 Wage & Hour Cas. 2d (BNA) 993, 133 Lab. Cas. (CCH) P 33480, 1996 FED App. 0369P (6th Cir. 1996). Labor And Employment ⚬2243; Labor And Employment ⚬2304

4 Helpers

Department of Labor's definition, for purposes of the Davis-Bacon Act, of class of employees known as "helpers," pursuant to which agency would approve helper classification only if it is a separate and distinct class of worker that prevails in the area, the duties of which can be differentiated from the duties of journey-level workers, did not abuse its broad discretion under the Act to recognize and define various classes of workers for whom prevailing wage must be determined. Davis-Bacon Act, § 1, 40 U.S.C.A. § 276a. Associated Builders & Contractors, Inc. v. Herman, 976 F. Supp. 1 (D.D.C. 1997). Labor And Employment ⚬2304

§ 22.404-3 Procedures for requesting wage determinations.

(a) *General wage determinations.* If there is a general wage determination on the WDOL website applicable to the project, the agency may use it without notifying the Department of Labor. When necessary, a request for a general wage determination may be made by submitting Standard Form (SF) 308, Request for Determination and Response to Request (see 53.301-308), to the Administrator, Wage and Hour Division, Attention: Branch of Construction Contract Wage Determinations, 200 Constitution Avenue, NW, Washington, DC 20210.

(b) *Project wage determinations.* If a general wage determination is not available on WDOL, a contracting agency shall submit requests for project wage determinations on SF 308 to the Department of Labor. The requests shall include the following information:

(1) The location, including the county (or other civil subdivision) and State in which the proposed project is located.

(2) The name of the project and a sufficiently detailed description of the work to indicate the types of construction involved (*e.g.,* building, heavy, highway, residential, or other type).

(3) Any available pertinent wage payment information, unless wage patterns in the area are clearly established.

(4) The estimated cost of each project.

(5) All the classifications of laborers and mechanics likely to be employed.

(c) *Time for submission of requests.* (1) The time required by the Department of Labor for processing requests for project wage determinations varies according to the facts and circumstances in each case. An agency should expect the processing to take at least 30 days. Accordingly, agencies should submit requests for project wage determinations for the primary site of the work to the Department of Labor at least 45 days (60 days if possible) before issuing the solicitation or exercising an option to extend the term of a contract.

(2) Agencies should promptly submit to the Department of Labor an offeror's request for a project wage determination for a secondary site of the work.

(d) *Review of wage determinations.* Immediately upon receipt, the contracting agency shall examine the wage determination and inform the Department of Labor of any changes necessary or appropriate to correct errors. Private parties requesting changes should be advised to submit their requests to the Department of Labor.

United States Code Annotated

Contract requirements, see 41 USCA § 254.

Contracts, planning, solicitation, evaluation, and award procedures, see 10 USCA § 2305.

Definitions, see 10 USCA § 2302, 41 USCA §§ 259, 403.

Kickbacks from public works employees, see 18 USCA § 874.

Kinds of contracts, see 10 USCA § 2306.

Planning and solicitation requirements, see 41 USCA § 253a.

Rate of wages for laborers and mechanics, see 40 USCA § 3142.

Work hours, see 40 USCA § 3702.

Notes of Decisions

In general 1
Helper 2
Site of work 3

1 In general

Contracting agency has initial responsibility for determining whether particular contract is subject to Davis-Bacon Act, and if agency determines such contract is subject to Act, it must determine appropriate prevailing wage rate and ensure that rate chosen is inserted in requests for bids on project, as well as in any resulting contract. Davis-Bacon Act, §§ 1 et seq., 1(a) as amended 40 U.S.C.A. §§ 276a et seq., 276a(a); 40 U.S.C.A. § 276c. Universities Research Ass'n, Inc. v. Coutu, 450 U.S. 754, 101 S. Ct. 1451, 67 L. Ed. 2d 662, 24 Wage & Hour Cas. (BNA) 1273, 28 Cont. Cas. Fed. (CCH) P 81199, 91 Lab. Cas. (CCH) P 33992 (1981). Labor And Employment ⟐2298; Labor And Employment ⟐2304

An area practice survey conducted by the Department of Labor is not a prerequisite to the determination of prevailing wage rates or job classifications under Davis-Bacon Act and related federal laws. Davis-Bacon Act, § 1 et seq., 40 U.S.C.A. § 276a et seq.U.S. ex rel. Plumbers and Steamfitters Local Union No. 38 v. C.W. Roen Const. Co., 183 F.3d 1088, 5 Wage & Hour Cas. 2d (BNA) 808, 138 Lab. Cas. (CCH) P 33916 (9th Cir. 1999). Labor And Employment ⟐2304

Although it is the Department of Labor's statutory responsibility under the Davis-Bacon Act to issue wage determinations for all classes of laborers and mechanics which prevail in every locality where they do prevail, Department has broad discretion to recognize and define the various classes of workers for whom the prevailing wage must be determined. Davis-Bacon Act, § 1, 40 U.S.C.A. § 276a. Associated Builders & Contractors, Inc. v. Herman, 976 F. Supp. 1 (D.D.C. 1997). Labor And Employment ⟐2304

2 Helper

Department of Labor's definition, for purposes of the Davis-Bacon Act, of class of employees known as "helpers," pursuant to which agency would approve helper classification only if it is a separate and distinct class of worker that prevails in the area, the duties of which can be differentiated from the duties of journey-level workers, did not abuse its broad discretion under the Act to recognize and define various classes of workers for whom prevailing wage must be determined. Davis-Bacon Act, § 1, 40 U.S.C.A. § 276a. Associated Builders & Contractors, Inc. v. Herman, 976 F. Supp. 1 (D.D.C. 1997). Labor And Employment ☞2304

3 Site of work

On review of decision of Wage Appeals Board finding prevailing wage requirement applicable to truck drivers hauling asphalt from temporary batch plant to highway construction project, controlling statute for purposes of determining validity of regulation defining "site of the work" was Davis-Bacon Act, rather than Federal Aid Highways Act which contains no language limiting "site of the work"; Federal Aid Highways Act incorporates method of determining prevailing wage rates under Davis-Bacon Act, and legislative history of Federal Aid Highways Act indicated that workers on federally funded highway construction were to be given same wage protection as workers covered by Davis-Bacon Act. 23 U.S.C.A. § 113; Davis-Bacon Act, § 1 et seq., 40 U.S.C.A. § 276a et seq.; 29 C.F.R. §§ 5.1(a), 5.2(l). L.P. Cavett Co. v. U.S. Dept. of Labor, 892 F. Supp. 973, 2 Wage & Hour Cas. 2d (BNA) 1458, 131 Lab. Cas. (CCH) P 33372 (S.D. Ohio 1995), judgment rev'd, 101 F.3d 1111, 3 Wage & Hour Cas. 2d (BNA) 993, 133 Lab. Cas. (CCH) P 33480, 1996 FED App. 0369P (6th Cir. 1996). Labor And Employment ☞2243; Labor And Employment ☞2304

Wage and Hour Administrator's determination that batch plant was part of "site of the work" for highway construction project, so that prevailing wage requirement of Davis-Bacon Act applied to truck drivers hauling asphalt from plant to project, was not arbitrary or capricious; plant was located approximately three miles from midpoint of project at facility of supplier of coarse aggregate required for bituminous mix to resurface highway, decision to establish plant was made at preconstruction meeting convened to discuss project, plant produced material exclusively or nearly exclusively for project, and plant was dismantled after completion of project. Davis-Bacon Act, § 1 et seq., 40 U.S.C.A. § 276a et seq.; 29 C.F.R. § 5.2(l). L.P. Cavett Co. v. U.S. Dept. of Labor, 892 F. Supp. 973, 2 Wage & Hour Cas. 2d (BNA) 1458, 131 Lab. Cas. (CCH) P 33372 (S.D. Ohio 1995), judgment rev'd, 101 F.3d 1111, 3 Wage & Hour Cas. 2d (BNA) 993, 133 Lab. Cas. (CCH) P 33480, 1996 FED App. 0369P (6th Cir. 1996). Labor And Employment ☞2243; Labor And Employment ☞2304

§ 22.404-4 Solicitations issued without wage determinations for the primary site of the work.

(a) If a solicitation is issued before the wage determination for the primary site of the work is obtained, a notice shall be included in the solicitation that the schedule of minimum wage rates to be paid under the contract will be issued as an amendment to the solicitation.

(b) In sealed bidding, bids may not be opened until a reasonable time after the wage determination for the primary site of the work has been furnished to all bidders.

(c) In negotiated acquisitions, the contracting officer may open proposals and conduct negotiations before obtaining the wage determination for the primary site of the work. However, the contracting officer shall incorporate the wage determination for the primary site of the work into the solicitation before submission of best and final offers.

United States Code Annotated

Contract requirements, see 41 USCA § 254.

Contracts, planning, solicitation, evaluation, and award procedures, see 10 USCA § 2305.

Definitions, see 10 USCA § 2302, 41 USCA §§ 259, 403.

Kickbacks from public works employees, see 18 USCA § 874.

Kinds of contracts, see 10 USCA § 2306.

Planning and solicitation requirements, see 41 USCA § 253a.

Rate of wages for laborers and mechanics, see 40 USCA § 3142.

Work hours, see 40 USCA § 3702.

§ 22.404-5 Expiration of project wage determinations.

(a) The contracting officer shall make every effort to ensure that contract award is made before expiration of the project wage determination included in the solicitation.

(b) The following procedure applies when contracting by sealed bidding:

(1) If a project wage determination for the primary site of the work expires before bid opening, or if it appears before bid opening that a project wage determination may expire before award, the contracting officer shall request a new determination early enough to ensure its receipt before bid opening. If necessary, the contracting officer shall postpone the bid opening date to allow a reasonable time to obtain the determination, amend the solicitation to incorporate the new determination, and permit bidders to amend their bids. If the new determination does not change the wage rates and would not warrant amended bids, the contracting officer shall amend the solicitation to include the number and date of the new determination.

(2) If a project wage determination for the primary site of the work expires after bid opening but before award, the contracting officer shall request an extension of the project wage determination expiration date from the Administrator, Wage and Hour Division. The request for extension shall be supported by a written finding, which shall include a brief statement of factual support, that the extension is necessary and proper in the public interest to prevent injustice or undue hardship or to avoid serious impairment of the conduct of Government business. If necessary, the contracting officer shall delay award to permit either receipt of the extension or receipt and processing of a new determination. If the request is granted, the contracting officer shall award the contract and modify it to apply the extended expiration date to the already incorporated project wage determination. (See 43.103(b)(1).) If the request is denied, the Administrator will proceed to issue a new project wage determination. Upon receipt, the contracting officer shall process the new determination as follows:

(i) If If the new determination for the primary site of the work changes any wage rates for classifications to be used in the contract, the contracting officer may cancel the solicitation only in accordance with 14.404-1. Otherwise the contracting officer shall award the contract and incorporate the new determination to be effective on the date of contract award. The contracting officer shall equitably adjust the contract price for any increased or decreased cost of performance resulting from any changed wage rates.

(ii) If the new determination for the primary site of the work does not change any wage rates, the contracting officer shall award the contract and modify it to include the number and date of the new determination. (See 43.103(b)(1).)

(c) The following procedure applies when contracting by negotiation:

(1) If a project wage determination will or does expire before contract award, the contracting officer shall request a new wage determination from the Department of Labor. If necessary, the contracting officer shall delay award while the new determination is obtained and processed.

(2) The contracting officer need not delay opening and reviewing proposals or discussing them with the offerors while a new determination for the primary site of the work is being obtained. The contracting officer shall request offerors to extend the period for acceptance of any proposal if that period expires or may expire before receipt and full processing of the new determination.

(3) If the new determination for the primary site of the work changes any wage rates, the contracting officer shall amend the solicitation to incorporate the new determination, and furnish the wage rate information to all prospective offerors that were sent a solicitation if the closing date for receipt of proposals has not yet occurred, or to all offerors that have not been eliminated from the competition if the closing date has passed. All offerors to whom wage rate information has been furnished shall be given reasonable opportunity to amend their proposals.

(4) If the new determination for the primary site of the work does not change any wage rates, the contracting officer shall amend the solicitation to include the number and date of the new determination and award the contract.

United States Code Annotated

Contract requirements, see 41 USCA § 254.

Contracts, planning, solicitation, evaluation, and award procedures, see 10 USCA § 2305.

Definitions, see 10 USCA § 2302, 41 USCA §§ 259, 403.

Kickbacks from public works employees, see 18 USCA § 874.

Kinds of contracts, see 10 USCA § 2306.

Planning and solicitation requirements, see 41 USCA § 253a.

Rate of wages for laborers and mechanics, see 40 USCA § 3142.

Work hours, see 40 USCA § 3702.

§ 22.404-6 Modifications of wage determinations.

(a) *General.* (1) The Department of Labor may modify a wage determination to make it current by specifying only the items being changed or by reissuing the entire determination with changes incorporated.

(2) All project wage determination modifications expire on the same day as the original determination. The need to include a modification of a project wage determination for the primary site of the work in a solicitation is determined by the time of receipt of the modification by the contracting agency. Therefore, the contracting agency must annotate the modification of the project wage determination with the date and time immediately upon receipt.

(3) The need for inclusion of the modification of a general wage determination for the primary site of the work in a solicitation is determined by the date the modified wage determination is published on the WDOL, or by the date the agency receives actual written notice of the modification from the Department of Labor, whichever occurs first. (Note the distinction between receipt by the agency (modification is effective) and receipt by the contracting officer, which may occur later.) During the course of the solicitation, the contracting officer shall monitor the WDOL website to determine whether the applicable wage determination has been revised. Revisions published on the WDOL website or otherwise communicated to the contracting officer within the timeframes prescribed at 22.404-6(b) and (c) are applicable and must be included in the resulting contract. Monitoring can be accomplished by use of the WDOL website's "Alert Service".

(b) The following applies when contracting by sealed bidding:

(1) A written action modifying a wage determination shall be effective if:

(i) It is received by the contracting agency, or is published on the WDOL, 10 or more calendar days before the date of bid opening; or

(ii) It is received by the contracting agency, or is published on the WDOL, less than 10 calendar days before the date of bid opening, unless the contracting officer finds that there is not reasonable time available before bid opening to notify the prospective bidders. (If the contracting officer finds that there is not reasonable time to notify bidders, a written report of the finding shall be placed in the contract file and shall be made available to the Department of Labor upon request.)

(2) All written actions modifying wage determinations received by the contracting agency after bid opening, or modifications to general wage determinations published on the WDOL after bid opening, shall not be effective and shall not be included in the solicitation (but see paragraph (b)(6) of this subsection).

(3) If an effective modification of the wage determination for the primary site of the work is received by the contracting officer before bid opening, the contracting officer shall postpone the bid opening, if necessary, to allow a reasonable time to amend the solicitation to incorporate the modification and permit bidders to amend their bids. If the modification does not change the wage rates and would not warrant amended bids, the contracting officer shall amend the solicitation to include the number and date of the modification.

(4) If an effective modification of the wage determination for the primary site of the work is received by the contracting officer after bid opening, but before award, the contracting officer shall follow the procedures in 22.404-5(b)(2)(i) or (ii).

(5) If an effective modification is received by the contracting officer after award, the contracting officer shall modify the contract to incorporate the wage modification retroactive to the date of award and equitably adjust the contract price for any increased or decreased cost of performance resulting from any changed wage rates. If the modification does not change any wage rates and would not warrant contract price adjustment, the

contracting officer shall modify the contract to include the number and date of the modification.

(6) If an award is not made within 90 days after bid opening, any modification to a general wage determination which is published on the WDOL before award, shall be effective for any resultant contract unless an extension of the 90-day period is obtained from the Administrator, Wage and Hour Division. An agency head may request such an extension from the Administrator. The request must be supported by a written finding, which shall include a brief statement of factual support, that the extension is necessary and proper in the public interest to prevent injustice, undue hardship, or to avoid serious impairment in the conduct of Government business. The contracting officer shall follow the procedures in 22.404-5(b)(2).

(c) The following applies when contracting by negotiation:

(1) All written actions modifying wage determinations received by the contracting agency before contract award, or modifications to general wage determinations published on the WDOL before award, shall be effective.

(2) If an effective wage modification is received by the contracting officer before award, the contracting officer shall follow the procedures in 22.404-5(c)(3) or (4).

(3) If an effective wage modification is received by the contracting officer after award, the contracting officer shall follow the procedures in 22.404-6(b)(5).

(d) The following applies when modifying a contract to exercise an option to extend the term of a contract:

(1) A modified wage determination is effective if—

(i) The contracting agency receives a written action from the Department of Labor prior to exercise of the option, or within 45 days after submission of a wage determination request (22.404-3(c)), whichever is later; or

(ii) The Department of Labor publishes the modification to a general wage determination on the WDOL before exercise of the option.

(2) If the contracting officer receives an effective modified wage determination either before or after execution of the contract modification to exercise the option, the contracting officer must modify the contract to incorporate the modified wage determination, and any changed wage rates, effective as of the date that the option to extend was effective.

United States Code Annotated

Contract requirements, see 41 USCA § 254.

Contracts, planning, solicitation, evaluation, and award procedures, see 10 USCA § 2305.

Definitions, see 10 USCA § 2302, 41 USCA §§ 259, 403.

Kickbacks from public works employees, see 18 USCA § 874.

Kinds of contracts, see 10 USCA § 2306.

Planning and solicitation requirements, see 41 USCA § 253a.

Rate of wages for laborers and mechanics, see 40 USCA § 3142.

Work hours, see 40 USCA § 3702.

§ 22.404-7 Correction of wage determinations containing clerical errors.

Upon the Department of Labor's own initiative or at the request of the contracting agency, the Administrator, Wage and Hour Division, may correct any wage determination found to contain clerical errors. Such corrections will be effective immediately, and will apply to any solicitation or active contract. Before contract award, the contracting officer must follow the procedures in 22.404-5(b)(1) or (2)(i) or (ii) in sealed bidding, and the procedures in 22.404-5(c)(3) or (4) in negotiations. After contract award, the contracting officer must follow the procedures at 22.404-6(b)(5), except that for contract modifications to exercise an option to extend the term of the contract, the contracting officer must follow the procedures at 22.404-6(d)(2).

United States Code Annotated

Contract requirements, see 41 USCA § 254.

Contracts, planning, solicitation, evaluation, and award procedures, see 10 USCA § 2305.

Definitions, see 10 USCA § 2302, 41 USCA §§ 259, 403.

Kickbacks from public works employees, see 18 USCA § 874.

Kinds of contracts, see 10 USCA § 2306.

Planning and solicitation requirements, see 41 USCA § 253a.

Rate of wages for laborers and mechanics, see 40 USCA § 3142.

Work hours, see 40 USCA § 3702.

§ 22.404-8 Notification of improper wage determination before award.

(a) The following written notifications by the Department of Labor shall be effective immediately without regard to 22.404-6 if received by the contracting officer prior to award:

(1) A solicitation includes the wrong wage determination or the wrong rate schedule; or

(2) A wage determination is withdrawn by the Administrative Review Board.

(b) In sealed bidding, the contracting officer shall proceed in accordance with the following:

(1) If the notification of an improper wage determination for the primary site of the work reaches the contracting officer before bid opening, the contracting officer shall postpone the bid opening date, if necessary, to allow a reasonable time to—

(i) Obtain the appropriate determination if a new wage determination is required;

(ii) Amend the solicitation to incorporate the determination (or rate schedule); and

(iii) Permit bidders to amend their bids. If the appropriate wage determination does not change any wage rates and would not warrant amended bids, the contracting officer shall amend the solicitation to include the number and date of the new determination.

(2) If the notification of an improper wage determination for the primary site of the work reaches the contracting officer after bid opening but before award, the contracting officer shall delay awarding the contract, if necessary, and if required, obtain the appropriate wage determination. The appropriate wage determination shall be processed in accordance with 22.404-5(b)(2)(i) or (ii).

(c) In negotiated acquisitions, the contracting officer shall delay award, if necessary, and process the notification of an improper wage determination for the primary site of the work in the manner prescribed for a new wage determination at 22.404-5(c)(3).

United States Code Annotated

Contract requirements, see 41 USCA § 254.

Contracts, planning, solicitation, evaluation, and award procedures, see 10 USCA § 2305.

Definitions, see 10 USCA § 2302, 41 USCA §§ 259, 403.

Kickbacks from public works employees, see 18 USCA § 874.

Kinds of contracts, see 10 USCA § 2306.

Planning and solicitation requirements, see 41 USCA § 253a.

Rate of wages for laborers and mechanics, see 40 USCA § 3142.

Work hours, see 40 USCA § 3702.

§ 22.404-9 Award of contract without required wage determination.

(a) If a contract is awarded without the required wage determination (*i.e.*, incorporating no determination, containing a clearly inapplicable general wage determination, or containing a project determination which is inapplicable because of an inaccurate description of the project or its location), the contracting officer shall initiate action to incorporate the required determination in the contract immediately upon discovery of the error. If a required wage determination (valid determination in effect on the date of award) is not available, the contracting officer shall expeditiously request a wage determination from the Department of Labor, including a statement explaining the circumstances and giving the date of the contract award.

(b) The contracting officer shall—

(1) Modify the contract to incorporate the required wage determination (retroactive to the date of award) and equitably adjust the contract price if appropriate; or

(2) Terminate the contract.

United States Code Annotated

Contract requirements, see 41 USCA § 254.

Contracts, planning, solicitation, evaluation, and award procedures, see 10 USCA § 2305.

Definitions, see 10 USCA § 2302, 41 USCA §§ 259, 403.

Kickbacks from public works employees, see 18 USCA § 874.

Kinds of contracts, see 10 USCA § 2306.

Planning and solicitation requirements, see 41 USCA § 253a.

Rate of wages for laborers and mechanics, see 40 USCA § 3142.

Work hours, see 40 USCA § 3702.

Notes of Decisions

In general 1

1 In general

A contractor was entitled to an equitable adjustment, including profit and overhead, to compensate for the additional costs attributable to a contract modification issued because the contract included a Davis-Bacon Act wage determination that was out of date when the contract was awarded. The contractor was entitled to an equitable adjustment for the increased wage rate for all affected hours reasonably worked, even if those hours were not in the contractor's bid estimate. Construction Company v. GSA, CBCA 1495, 11-1 BCA ¶ 34638, (U.S. Civilian BCA 2010)

§ 22.404-10 Posting wage determinations and notice.

The contractor must keep a copy of the applicable wage determination (and any approved additional classifications) posted at the site of the work in a prominent place where the workers can easily see it. The contracting officer shall furnish to the contractor, Department of Labor Form WH-1321, Notice to Employees Working on Federal and Federally Financed Construction Projects, for posting with the wage rates. The name, address, and telephone number of the Government officer responsible for the administration of the contract shall be indicated in the poster to inform workers to whom they may submit complaints or raise questions concerning labor standards.

United States Code Annotated

Contract requirements, see 41 USCA § 254.

Contracts, planning, solicitation, evaluation, and award procedures, see 10 USCA § 2305.

Definitions, see 10 USCA § 2302, 41 USCA §§ 259, 403.

Kickbacks from public works employees, see 18 USCA § 874.

Kinds of contracts, see 10 USCA § 2306.

Planning and solicitation requirements, see 41 USCA § 253a.

Rate of wages for laborers and mechanics, see 40 USCA § 3142.

Work hours, see 40 USCA § 3702.

§ 22.404-11 Wage determination appeals.

The Secretary of Labor has established an Administrative Review Board which decides appeals of final decisions made by the Department of Labor concerning Construction Wage Rate Requirements statute wage determinations. A contracting agency or other interested party may file a petition for review under the procedures in 29 CFR Part 7 if reconsideration by the Administrator has been sought pursuant to 29 CFR 1.8 and denied.

United States Code Annotated

Contract requirements, see 41 USCA § 254.

Contracts, planning, solicitation, evaluation, and award procedures, see 10 USCA § 2305.

Definitions, see 10 USCA § 2302, 41 USCA §§ 259, 403.

Kickbacks from public works employees, see 18 USCA § 874.

Kinds of contracts, see 10 USCA § 2306.

Planning and solicitation requirements, see 41 USCA § 253a.

Rate of wages for laborers and mechanics, see 40 USCA § 3142.

Work hours, see 40 USCA § 3702.

§ 22.404-12 Labor standards for contracts containing construction requirements and option provisions that extend the term of the contract.

(a) Each time the contracting officer exercises an option to extend the term of a contract for construction, or a contract that includes substantial and segregable construction work, the contracting officer must modify the contract to incorporate the most current wage determination.

(b) If a contract with an option to extend the term of the contract has indefinite-delivery or indefinite-quantity construction requirements, the contracting officer must incorporate the wage determination incorporated into the contract at the exercise of the option into task orders issued during that option period. The wage determination will be effective for the complete period of performance of those task orders without further revision.

(c) The contracting officer must include in fixed-price contracts a clause that specifies one of the following methods, suitable to the interest of the Government, to provide an allowance for any increases or decreases in labor costs that result from the inclusion of the current wage determination at the exercise of an option to extend the term of the contract:

(1) The contracting officer may provide the offerors the opportunity to bid or propose separate prices for each option period. The contracting officer must not further adjust the contract price as a result of the incorporation of a new or revised wage determination at the exercise of each option to extend the term of the contract. Generally, this method is used in construction-only contracts (with options to extend the term) that are not expected to exceed a total of 3 years.

(2) The contracting officer may include in the contract a separately specified pricing method that permits an adjustment to the contract price or contract labor unit price at the exercise of each option to extend the term of the contract. At the time of option exercise, the contracting officer must incorporate a new wage determination into the contract, and must apply the specific pricing method to calculate the contract price adjustment. An example of a contract pricing method that the contracting officer might separately specify is incorporation in the solicitation and resulting contract of the pricing data from an annually published unit pricing book (e.g., the U.S. Army Computer-Aided Cost Estimating System or similar commercial product), which is multiplied in the contract by a factor proposed by the contractor (e.g., .95 or 1.1). At option exercise, the contracting officer incorporates the pricing data from the latest annual edition of the unit pricing book, multiplied by the factor agreed to in the basic contract. The contracting officer must not further adjust the contract price as a result of the incorporation of the new or revised wage determination.

(3) The contracting officer may provide for a contract price adjustment based solely on a percentage rate determined by the contracting officer using a published economic indicator incorporated into the solicitation and resulting contract. At the exercise of each option to extend the term of the contract, the contracting officer will apply the percentage rate, based on the economic indicator, to the portion of the contract price or contract unit price designated in the contract clause as labor costs subject to the provisions of the Construction Wage Rate Requirements statute. The contracting officer must insert 50 percent as the estimated portion of the contract price that is labor unless the contracting officer determines, prior to issuance of the solicitation, that a different percentage is more appropriate for a particular contract or requirement. This percentage adjustment to the designated labor costs must be the only adjustment made to cover increases in wages and/or benefits resulting from the incorporation of a new or revised wage determination at the exercise of the option.

(4) The contracting officer may provide a computation method to adjust the contract price to reflect the contractor's actual increase or decrease in wages and fringe benefits (combined) to the extent that the increase is made to comply with, or the decrease is voluntarily made by the contractor as a result of incorporation of, a new or revised wage determination at the exercise of the option to extend the term of the contract. Generally, this method is appropriate for use only if contract requirements are predominately services subject to the Service Contract Labor Standards statute and the construction

requirements are substantial and segregable. The methods used to adjust the contract price for the service requirements and the construction requirements would be similar.

United States Code Annotated
Contract requirements, see 41 USCA § 254.

Contracts, planning, solicitation, evaluation, and award procedures, see 10 USCA § 2305.

Definitions, see 10 USCA § 2302, 41 USCA §§ 259, 403.

Kickbacks from public works employees, see 18 USCA § 874.

Kinds of contracts, see 10 USCA § 2306.

Planning and solicitation requirements, see 41 USCA § 253a.

Rate of wages for laborers and mechanics, see 40 USCA § 3142.

Work hours, see 40 USCA § 3702.

United States Code Annotated
Contract requirements, see 41 USCA § 254.

Contracts, planning, solicitation, evaluation, and award procedures, see 10 USCA § 2305.

Definitions, see 10 USCA § 2302, 41 USCA §§ 259, 403.

Kickbacks from public works employees, see 18 USCA § 874.

Kinds of contracts, see 10 USCA § 2306.

Planning and solicitation requirements, see 41 USCA § 253a.

Rate of wages for laborers and mechanics, see 40 USCA § 3142.

Work hours, see 40 USCA § 3702.

Notes of Decisions
Construction and application 1

1 Construction and application

Davis-Bacon Act minimum-wage, maximum-hours law applicable to workers under federal contract who are employed directly upon site of work is remedial act for benefit of construction workers and is liberally construed to effectuate its beneficent purpose. Davis-Bacon Act, § 1, 40 U.S.C.A. § 276a. Drivers, Salesmen, Warehousemen, Milk Processors, Cannery, Dairy Emp. and Helpers Local Union No. 695 v. N. L. R. B., 361 F.2d 547, 553 (D.C. Cir. 1966). Labor And Employment ☞2304; Labor And Employment ☞2220(2)

§ 22.405 [Reserved]

§ 22.406 Administration and enforcement.

§ 22.406-1 Policy.

(a) *General.* Contracting agencies are responsible for ensuring the full and impartial enforcement of labor standards in the administration of construction contracts. Contracting agencies shall maintain an effective program that shall include—

(1) Ensuring that contractors and subcontractors are informed, before commencement of work, of their obligations under the labor standards clauses of the contract;

(2) Adequate payroll reviews, on-site inspections, and employee interviews to determine compliance by the contractor and subcontractors, and prompt initiation of corrective action when required;

(3) Prompt investigation and disposition of complaints; and

(4) Prompt submission of all reports required by this subpart.

(b) *Preconstruction letters and conferences.* Before construction begins, the contracting officer shall inform the contractor of the labor standards clauses and wage determination requirements of the contract and of the contractor's and any subcontractor's responsibilities under the contract. Unless it is clear that the contractor is fully aware of the requirements, the contracting officer shall issue an explanatory letter and/or arrange a conference with the contractor promptly after award of the contract.

United States Code Annotated
Contract requirements, see 41 USCA § 254.

Contracts, planning, solicitation, evaluation, and award procedures, see 10 USCA § 2305.

Definitions, see 10 USCA § 2302, 41 USCA §§ 259, 403.

Kickbacks from public works employees, see 18 USCA § 874.

Kinds of contracts, see 10 USCA § 2306.

Planning and solicitation requirements, see 41 USCA § 253a.

Rate of wages for laborers and mechanics, see 40 USCA § 3142.

Work hours, see 40 USCA § 3702.

Notes of Decisions

In general 1

1 In general

Contractor violated False Claims Act (FCA) where its Davis-Bacon Act payroll certifications were expressly false because they stated that they were complete, when in fact no subcontractor employees who worked on the project were listed, and the certifications wrongly represented that the prevailing wages were paid to its subcontracted employees; contractor made false statements, acted in reckless disregard of the truth or falsity of the information, and the false statements were "material" to the government's decision to make the payment sought in contractor's claim. U.S. ex rel. Wall v. Circle C Constr., LLC, 697 F.3d 345 (6th Cir. Oct. 1, 2012)

The CBCA held that, because a contract for federal construction did not contain a clause excluding overhead and profit from the equitable adjustment, and therefore the contractor was entitled to these amounts. Construction Company v. General Services Administration, CBCA 1495, 11-1 B.C.A. (CCH) ¶ 34638, 2010 WL 5904458 (U.S. Civilian BCA 2010)

A contractor was entitled to an equitable adjustment to compensate for the additional costs attributable to a contract modification increasing a Davis-Bacon Act wage determination that was set too low in the original contract. The contractor was entitled to compensation for the increased wage rate for all affected hours reasonably worked, even if those hours were not in the contractor's bid estimate. Construction Company v. General Services Administration, CBCA 1495, 11-1 B.C.A. (CCH) ¶ 34638, 2010 WL 5904458 (U.S. Civilian BCA 2010)

§ 22.406-2 Wages, fringe benefits, and overtime.

(a) In computing wages paid to a laborer or mechanic, the contractor may include only the following items:

(1) Amounts paid in cash to the laborer or mechanic, or deducted from payments under the conditions set forth in 29 CFR 3.5.

(2) Contributions (except those required by Federal, State, or local law) the contractor makes irrevocably to a trustee or a third party under any bona fide plan or program to provide for medical or hospital care, pensions, compensation for injuries or illness resulting from occupational activity, unemployment benefits, life insurance, disability and sickness insurance, accident insurance, or any other bona fide fringe benefit.

(3) Other contributions or anticipated costs for bona fide fringe benefits to the extent expressly approved by the Secretary of Labor.

(b) (1) The contractor may satisfy the obligation under the clause at 52.222-6, Construction Wage Rate Requirements, by providing wages consisting of any combination of contributions or costs as specified in paragraph (a) of this subsection, if the total cost of the combination is not less than the total of the basic hourly rate and fringe benefits payments prescribed in the wage determination for the classification of laborer or mechanic concerned.

(2) Wages provided by the contractor and fringe benefits payments required by the wage determination may include items that are not stated as exact cash amounts. In these cases, the hourly cash equivalent of the cost of these items shall be determined by dividing the employer's contributions or costs by the employee's hours worked during the period covered by the costs or contributions. For example, if a contractor pays a monthly health insurance premium of $112 for a particular employee who worked 125 hours during the month, the hourly cash equivalent is determined by dividing $112 by 125 hours,

which equals $0.90 per hour. Similarly, the calculation of hourly cash equivalent for nine paid holidays per year for an employee with a hourly rate of pay of $5.00 is determined by multiplying $5.00 by 72 (9 days at 8 hours each), and dividing the result of $360 by the number of hours worked by the employee during the year. If the interested parties (contractor, contracting officer, and employees or their representative) cannot agree on the cash equivalent, the contracting officer shall submit the question for final determination to the Department of Labor as prescribed by agency procedures. The information submitted shall include—

(i) A comparison of the payments, contributions, or costs in the wage determination with those made or proposed as equivalents by the contractor; and

(ii) The comments and recommendations of the contracting officer.

(c) In computing required overtime payments, (*i.e.*, 1 1/2 times the basic hourly rate of pay) the contractor shall use the basic hourly rate of pay in the wage determination, or the basic hourly rate actually paid by the contractor, if higher. The basic rate of pay includes employee contributions to fringe benefits, but excludes the contractor's contributions, costs, or payment of cash equivalents for fringe benefits. Overtime shall not be computed on a rate lower than the basic hourly rate in the wage determination.

United States Code Annotated

Contract requirements, see 41 USCA § 254.

Contracts, planning, solicitation, evaluation, and award procedures, see 10 USCA § 2305.

Definitions, see 10 USCA § 2302, 41 USCA §§ 259, 403.

Kickbacks from public works employees, see 18 USCA § 874.

Kinds of contracts, see 10 USCA § 2306.

Planning and solicitation requirements, see 41 USCA § 253a.

Rate of wages for laborers and mechanics, see 40 USCA § 3142.

Work hours, see 40 USCA § 3702.

§ 22.406-3 Additional classifications.

(a) If any laborer or mechanic is to be employed in a classification that is not listed in the wage determination applicable to the contract, the contracting officer, pursuant to the clause at 52.222-6, Construction Wage Rate Requirements, shall require that the contractor submit to the contracting officer, Standard Form (SF) 1444, Request for Authorization of Additional Classification and Rate, which, along with other pertinent data, contains the proposed additional classification and minimum wage rate including any fringe benefits payments.

(b) Upon receipt of SF 1444 from the contractor, the contracting officer shall review the request to determine whether it meets the following criteria:

(1) The classification is appropriate and the work to be performed by the classification is not performed by any classification contained in the applicable wage determination.

(2) The classification is utilized in the area by the construction industry.

(3) The proposed wage rate, including any fringe benefits, bears a reasonable relationship to the wage rates in the wage determination in the contract.

(c) (1) If the criteria in paragraph (b) of this subsection are met and the contractor and the laborers or mechanics to be employed in the additional classification (if known) or their representatives agree to the proposed additional classification, and the contracting officer approves, the contracting officer shall submit a report (including a copy of SF 1444) of that action to the Administrator, Wage and Hour Division, for approval, modification, or disapproval of the additional classification and wage rate (including any amount designated for fringe benefits); or

(2) If the contractor, the laborers or mechanics to be employed in the classification or their representatives, and the contracting officer do not agree on the proposed additional classification, or if the criteria are not met, the contracting officer shall submit a report (including a copy of SF 1444) giving the views of all interested parties and the contracting officer's recommendation to the Administrator, Wage and Hour Division, for determination of appropriate classification and wage rate.

(d) (1) Within 30 days of receipt of the report, the Administrator, Wage and Hour Division, will complete action and so advise the contracting officer, or will notify the contracting officer that additional time is necessary.

(2) Upon receipt of the Department of Labor's action, the contracting officer shall forward a copy of the action to the contractor, directing that the classification and wage rate be posted in accordance with paragraph (a) of the clause at 52.222-6 and that workers in the affected classification receive no less than the minimum rate indicated from the first day on which work under the contract was performed in the classification.

(e) In each option to extend the term of the contract, if any laborer or mechanic is to be employed during the option in a classification that is not listed (or no longer listed) on the wage determination incorporated in that option, the contracting officer must require that the contractor submit a request for conformance using the procedures noted in paragraphs (a) through (d) of this section.

United States Code Annotated

Contract requirements, see 41 USCA § 254.

Contracts, planning, solicitation, evaluation, and award procedures, see 10 USCA § 2305.

Definitions, see 10 USCA § 2302, 41 USCA §§ 259, 403.

Kickbacks from public works employees, see 18 USCA § 874.

Kinds of contracts, see 10 USCA § 2306.

Planning and solicitation requirements, see 41 USCA § 253a.

Rate of wages for laborers and mechanics, see 40 USCA § 3142.

Work hours, see 40 USCA § 3702.

§ 22.406-4 Apprentices and trainees.

(a) The contracting officer shall review the contractor's employment and payment records of apprentices and trainees made available pursuant to the clause at 52.222-8, Payrolls and Basic Records, to ensure that the contractor has complied with the clause at 52.222-9, Apprentices and Trainees.

(b) If a contractor has classified employees as apprentices, trainees, or helpers without complying with the requirements of the clause at 52.222-9, the contracting officer shall reject the classification and require the contractor to pay the affected employees at the rates applicable to the classification of the work actually performed.

United States Code Annotated

Contract requirements, see 41 USCA § 254.

Contracts, planning, solicitation, evaluation, and award procedures, see 10 USCA § 2305.

Definitions, see 10 USCA § 2302, 41 USCA §§ 259, 403.

Kickbacks from public works employees, see 18 USCA § 874.

Kinds of contracts, see 10 USCA § 2306.

Planning and solicitation requirements, see 41 USCA § 253a.

Rate of wages for laborers and mechanics, see 40 USCA § 3142.

Work hours, see 40 USCA § 3702.

§ 22.406-5 Subcontracts.

In accordance with the requirements of the clause at 52.222-11, Subcontracts (Labor Standards), the contractor and subcontractors at any tier are required to submit a fully executed SF 1413, Statement and Acknowledgment, upon award of each subcontract.

United States Code Annotated

Contract requirements, see 41 USCA § 254.

Contracts, planning, solicitation, evaluation, and award procedures, see 10 USCA § 2305.

Definitions, see 10 USCA § 2302, 41 USCA §§ 259, 403.

Kickbacks from public works employees, see 18 USCA § 874.

Kinds of contracts, see 10 USCA § 2306.

Planning and solicitation requirements, see 41 USCA § 253a.

Rate of wages for laborers and mechanics, see 40 USCA § 3142.

Work hours, see 40 USCA § 3702.

§ 22.406-6 Payrolls and statements.

(a) *Submission*. In accordance with the clause at 52.222-8, Payrolls and Basic Records, the contractor must submit or cause to be submitted, within 7 calendar days after the regular payment date of the payroll week covered, for the contractor and each subcontractor, (1) copies of weekly payrolls applicable to the contract, and (2) weekly payroll statements of compliance. The contractor may use the Department of Labor Form WH-347, Payroll (For Contractor's Optional Use), or a similar form that provides the same data and identical representation.

(b) *Withholding for nonsubmission*. If the contractor fails to submit copies of its or its subcontractors' payrolls promptly, the contracting officer shall, from any payment due to the contractor, withhold approval of an amount that the contracting officer considers necessary to protect the interest of the Government and the employees of the contractor or any subcontractor.

(c) *Examination*. (1) The contracting officer shall examine the payrolls and payroll statements to ensure compliance with the contract and any statutory or regulatory requirements. Particular attention should be given to—

(i) The correctness of classifications and rates;

(ii) Fringe benefits payments;

(iii) Hours worked;

(iv) Deductions; and

(v) Disproportionate employment ratios of laborers, apprentices or trainees to journeymen.

(2) Fringe benefits payments, contributions made, or costs incurred on other than a weekly basis shall be considered as a part of weekly payments to the extent they are creditable to the particular weekly period involved and are otherwise acceptable.

(d) *Preservation*. The contracting agency shall retain payrolls and statements of compliance for 3 years after completion of the contract and make them available when requested by the Department of Labor at any time during that period. Submitted payrolls shall not be returned to a contractor or subcontractor for any reason, but copies thereof may be furnished to the contractor or subcontractor who submitted them, or to a higher tier contractor or subcontractor.

(e) *Disclosure of payroll records*. Contractor payroll records in the Government's possession must be carefully protected from any public disclosure which is not required by law, since payroll records may contain information in which the contractor's employees have a privacy interest, as well as information in which the contractor may have a proprietary interest that the Government may be obliged to protect. Questions concerning release of this information may involve the Freedom of Information Act (FOIA).

United States Code Annotated

Contract requirements, see 41 USCA § 254.

Contracts, planning, solicitation, evaluation, and award procedures, see 10 USCA § 2305.

Definitions, see 10 USCA § 2302, 41 USCA §§ 259, 403.

Kickbacks from public works employees, see 18 USCA § 874.

Kinds of contracts, see 10 USCA § 2306.

Planning and solicitation requirements, see 41 USCA § 253a.

Rate of wages for laborers and mechanics, see 40 USCA § 3142.

Work hours, see 40 USCA § 3702.

§ 22.406-7 Compliance checking.

(a) *General*. The contracting officer shall make checks and investigations on all contracts covered by this subpart as may be necessary to ensure compliance with the labor standards requirements of the contract.

(b) *Regular compliance checks*. Regular compliance checking includes the following activities:

(1) Employee interviews to determine correctness of classifications, rates of pay, fringe benefits payments, and hours worked. (See Standard Form 1445.)

(2) On-site inspections to check type of work performed, number and classification of workers, and fulfillment of posting requirements.

(3) Payroll reviews to ensure that payrolls of prime contractors and subcontractors have been submitted on time and are complete and in compliance with contract requirements.

(4) Comparison of the information in this paragraph (b) with available data, including daily inspector's report and daily logs of construction, to ensure consistency.

(c) *Special compliance checks.* Situations that may require special compliance checks include—

(1) Inconsistencies, errors, or omissions detected during regular compliance checks; or

(2) Receipt of a complaint alleging violations. If the complaint is not specific enough, the complainant shall be so advised and invited to submit additional information.

United States Code Annotated

Contract requirements, see 41 USCA § 254.

Contracts, planning, solicitation, evaluation, and award procedures, see 10 USCA § 2305.

Definitions, see 10 USCA § 2302, 41 USCA §§ 259, 403.

Kickbacks from public works employees, see 18 USCA § 874.

Kinds of contracts, see 10 USCA § 2306.

Planning and solicitation requirements, see 41 USCA § 253a.

Rate of wages for laborers and mechanics, see 40 USCA § 3142.

Work hours, see 40 USCA § 3702.

Notes of Decisions

In general 1

1 In general

Contractor violated False Claims Act (FCA) where its Davis-Bacon Act payroll certifications were expressly false because they stated that they were complete, when in fact no subcontractor employees who worked on the project were listed, and the certifications wrongly represented that the prevailing wages were paid to its subcontracted employees; contractor made false statements, acted in reckless disregard of the truth or falsity of the information, and the false statements were "material" to the government's decision to make the payment sought in contractor's claim. U.S. ex rel. Wall v. Circle C Constr., LLC, 697 F.3d 345 (6th Cir. Oct. 1, 2012)

§ 22.406-8 Investigations.

Conduct labor standards investigations when available information indicates such action is warranted. In addition, the Department of Labor may conduct an investigation on its own initiative or may request a contracting agency to do so.

(a) *Contracting agency responsibilities.* Conduct an investigation when a compliance check indicates that substantial or willful violations may have occurred or violations have not been corrected.

(1) The investigation must—

(i) Include all aspects of the contractor's compliance with contract labor standards requirements;

(ii) Not be limited to specific areas raised in a complaint or uncovered during compliance checks; and

(iii) Use personnel familiar with labor laws and their application to contracts.

(2) Do not disclose contractor employees' oral or written statements taken during an investigation or the employee's identity to anyone other than an authorized Government official without that employee's prior signed consent.

(3) Send a written request to the Administrator, Wage and Hour Division, to obtain—

(i) Investigation and enforcement instructions; or

(ii) Available pertinent Department of Labor files.

(4) Obtain permission from the Department of Labor before disclosing material obtained from Labor Department files, other than computations of back wages and liquidated damages and summaries of back wages due, to anyone other than Government contract administrators.

(b) *Investigation report.* The contracting officer must review the investigation report on receipt and make preliminary findings. The contracting officer normally must not base adverse findings solely on employee statements that the employee does not wish to have disclosed. However, if the investigation establishes a pattern of possible violations that are based on employees' statements that are not authorized for disclosure, the pattern itself may support a finding of noncompliance.

(c) *Contractor Notification.* After completing the review, the contracting officer must—

(1) Provide the contractor any written preliminary findings and proposed corrective actions, and notice that the contractor has the right to request that the basis for the findings be made available and to submit written rebuttal information.

(2) Upon request, provide the contractor with rationale for the findings. However, under no circumstances will the contracting officer permit the contractor to examine the investigation report. Also, the contracting officer must not disclose the identity of any employee who filed a complaint or who was interviewed, without the prior consent of the employee.

(3) (i) The contractor may rebut the findings in writing within 60 days after it receives a copy of the preliminary findings. The rebuttal becomes part of the official investigation record. If the contractor submits a rebuttal, evaluate the preliminary findings and notify the contractor of the final findings.

(ii) If the contracting officer does not receive a timely rebuttal, the contracting officer must consider the preliminary findings final.

(4) If appropriate, request the contractor to make restitution for underpaid wages and assess liquidated damages. If the request includes liquidated damages, the request must state that the contractor has 60 days to request relief from such assessment.

(d) *Contracting officer's report.* After taking the actions prescribed in paragraphs (b) and (c) of this subsection—

(1) The contracting officer must prepare and forward a report of any violations, including findings and supporting evidence, to the agency head. Standard Form 1446, Labor Standards Investigation Summary Sheet, is the first page of the report; and

(2) The agency head must process the report as follows:

(i) The contracting officer must send a detailed enforcement report to the Administrator, Wage and Hour Division, within 60 days after completion of the investigation, if—

(A) A contractor or subcontractor underpaid by $1,000 or more;

(B) The contracting officer believes that the violations are aggravated or willful (or there is reason to believe that the contractor has disregarded its obligations to employees and subcontractors under the Construction Wage Rate Requirements statute);

(C) The contractor or subcontractor has not made restitution; or

(D) Future compliance has not been assured.

(ii) If the Department of Labor expressly requested the investigation and none of the conditions in paragraph (d)(2)(i) of this subsection exist, submit a summary report to the Administrator, Wage and Hour Division. The report must include—

(A) A summary of any violations;

(B) The amount of restitution paid;

(C) The number of workers who received restitution;

(D) The amount of liquidated damages assessed under the Contract Work Hours and Safety Standards statute;

(E) Corrective measures taken; and

(F) Any information that may be necessary to review any recommendations for an appropriate adjustment in liquidated damages.

(iii) If none of the conditions in paragraphs (d)(2)(i) or (ii) of this subsection are present, close the case and retain the report in the appropriate contract file.

(iv) If substantial evidence is found that violations are willful and in violation of a criminal statute, (generally 18 U.S.C. 874 or 1001), forward the report (supplemented if necessary) to the Attorney General of the United States for prosecution if the facts warrant. Notify the Administrator, Wage and Hour Division, when the report is forwarded for the Attorney General's consideration.

(e) *Department of Labor investigations.* The Department of Labor will furnish the contracting officer an enforcement report detailing violations found and any corrective action taken by the contractor, in investigations that disclose—

(1) Underpayments totaling $1,000 or more;

(2) Aggravated or willful violations (or, when the contracting officer believes that the contractor has disregarded its obligations to employees and subcontractors under the Construction Wage Rate Requirements statute); or

(3) Potential assessment of liquidated damages under the Contract Work Hours and Safety Standards statute.

(f) *Other investigations.* The Department of Labor will provide a letter summarizing the findings of the investigation to the contracting officer for all investigations that are not described in paragraph (e) of this subsection.

United States Code Annotated

Contract requirements, see 41 USCA § 254.

Contracts, planning, solicitation, evaluation, and award procedures, see 10 USCA § 2305.

Definitions, see 10 USCA § 2302, 41 USCA §§ 259, 403.

Kickbacks from public works employees, see 18 USCA § 874.

Kinds of contracts, see 10 USCA § 2306.

Planning and solicitation requirements, see 41 USCA § 253a.

Rate of wages for laborers and mechanics, see 40 USCA § 3142.

Work hours, see 40 USCA § 3702.

§ 22.406-9 Withholding from or suspension of contract payments.

(a) *Withholding from contract payments.* If the contracting officer believes a violation exists (see 22.406-8), or upon request of the Department of Labor, the contracting officer must withhold from payments due the contractor an amount equal to the estimated wage underpayment and estimated liquidated damages due the United States under the Contract Work Hours and Safety Standards statute. (See 22.302.)

(1) If the contracting officer believes a violation exists or upon request of the Department of Labor, the contracting officer must withhold funds from any current Federal contract or Federally assisted contract with the same prime contractor that is subject to either Construction Wage Rate Requirements statute or Contract Work Hours and Safety Standards statute requirements.

(2) If a subsequent investigation confirms violations, the contracting officer must adjust the withholding as necessary. However, if the Department of Labor requested the withholding, the contracting officer must not reduce or release the withholding without written approval of the Department of Labor.

(3) Use withheld funds as provided in paragraph (c) of this subsection to satisfy assessed liquidated damages, and unless the contractor makes restitution, validated wage underpayments.

(b) *Suspension of contract payments.* If a contractor or subcontractor fails or refuses to comply with the labor standards clauses of the Construction Wage Rate Requirements statute and related statutes, the agency, upon its own action or upon the written request of the Department of Labor, must suspend any further payment, advance, or guarantee of funds until the violations cease or until the agency has withheld sufficient funds to compensate employees for back wages, and to cover any liquidated damages due.

(c) Disposition of contract payments withheld or suspended—

(1) *Forwarding wage underpayments to the Secretary of Labor.* Upon final administrative determination, if the contractor or subcontractor has not made restitution, the contracting officer must follow the Department of Labor guidance published in Wage and

Hour Division, All Agency Memorandum (AAM) No. 215, Streamlining Claims for Federal Contractor Employees Act. The AAM No. 215 can be obtained at http://www.dol.gov/whd/govcontracts/dbra.htm; under Guidance there is a link for All Agencies Memoranda (AAMs).

(2) *Returning of withheld funds to contractor.* When funds withheld exceed the amount required to satisfy validated wage underpayments and assessed liquidated damages, return the funds to the contractor.

(3) *Limitation on returning funds.* If the Department of Labor requested the withholding or if the findings are disputed (see 22.406-10(e)), the contracting officer must not return the funds to the contractor without approval by the Department of Labor.

(4) *Liquidated damages.* Upon final administrative determination, the contracting officer must dispose of funds withheld or collected for liquidated damages in accordance with agency procedures.

United States Code Annotated

Contract requirements, see 41 USCA § 254.

Contracts, planning, solicitation, evaluation, and award procedures, see 10 USCA § 2305.

Definitions, see 10 USCA § 2302, 41 USCA §§ 259, 403.

Kickbacks from public works employees, see 18 USCA § 874.

Kinds of contracts, see 10 USCA § 2306.

Planning and solicitation requirements, see 41 USCA § 253a.

Rate of wages for laborers and mechanics, see 40 USCA § 3142.

Work hours, see 40 USCA § 3702.

§ 22.406-10 Disposition of disputes concerning construction contract labor standards enforcement.

(a) The areas of possible differences of opinion between contracting officers and contractors in construction contract labor standards enforcement include—

(1) Misclassification of workers;

(2) Hours of work;

(3) Wage rates and payment;

(4) Payment of overtime;

(5) Withholding practices; and

(6) The applicability of the labor standards requirements under varying circumstances.

(b) Generally, these differences are settled administratively at the project level by the contracting agency. If necessary, these differences may be settled with assistance from the Department of Labor.

(c) When requesting the contractor to take corrective action in labor violation cases, the contracting officer shall inform the contractor of the following:

(1) Disputes concerning the labor standards requirements of the contract are handled under the contract clause at 52.222-14, Disputes Concerning Labor Standards, and not under the clause at 52.233-1, Disputes.

(2) The contractor may appeal the contracting officer's findings or part thereof by furnishing the contracting officer a complete statement of the reasons for the disagreement with the findings.

(d) The contracting officer shall promptly transmit the contracting officer's findings and the contractor's statement to the Administrator, Wage and Hour Division.

(e) The Administrator, Wage and Hour Division, will respond directly to the contractor or subcontractor, with a copy to the contracting agency. The contractor or subcontractor may appeal the Administrator's findings in accordance with the procedures outlined in Labor Department Regulations (29 CFR 5.11). Hearings before administrative law judges are conducted in accordance with 29 CFR Part 6, and hearings before the Labor Department Administrative Review Board are conducted in accordance with 29 CFR Part 7.

(f) The Administrator, Wage and Hour Division, may institute debarment proceedings against the contractor or subcontractor if the Administrator finds reasonable cause to believe that the contractor or subcontractor has committed willful or aggravated violations of the Contract Work Hours and Safety Standards statute or the Copeland (Anti-Kickback) Act, or any of the applicable statutes listed in 29 CFR 5.1 other than the Construction Wage Rate Requirements statute, or has committed violations of the Construction Wage Rate Requirements statute that constitute a disregard of its obligations to employees or subcontractors under 40 U.S.C. 3144.

United States Code Annotated

Contract requirements, see 41 USCA § 254.

Contracts, planning, solicitation, evaluation, and award procedures, see 10 USCA § 2305.

Definitions, see 10 USCA § 2302, 41 USCA §§ 259, 403.

Kickbacks from public works employees, see 18 USCA § 874.

Kinds of contracts, see 10 USCA § 2306.

Planning and solicitation requirements, see 41 USCA § 253a.

Rate of wages for laborers and mechanics, see 40 USCA § 3142.

Work hours, see 40 USCA § 3702.

§ 22.406-11 Contract terminations.

If a contract or subcontract is terminated for violation of the labor standards clauses, the contracting agency shall submit a report to the Administrator, Wage and Hour Division. The report shall include—

(a) The number of the terminated contract;

(b) The name and address of the terminated contractor or subcontractor;

(c) The name and address of the contractor or subcontractor, if any, who is to complete the work;

(d) The amount and number of the replacement contract, if any; and

(e) A description of the work.

United States Code Annotated

Contract requirements, see 41 USCA § 254.

Contracts, planning, solicitation, evaluation, and award procedures, see 10 USCA § 2305.

Definitions, see 10 USCA § 2302, 41 USCA §§ 259, 403.

Kickbacks from public works employees, see 18 USCA § 874.

Kinds of contracts, see 10 USCA § 2306.

Planning and solicitation requirements, see 41 USCA § 253a.

Rate of wages for laborers and mechanics, see 40 USCA § 3142.

Work hours, see 40 USCA § 3702.

§ 22.406-12 Cooperation with the Department of Labor.

(a) The contracting agency shall cooperate with representatives of the Department of Labor in the inspection of records, interviews with workers, and all other aspects of investigations undertaken by the Department of Labor. When requested, the contracting agency shall furnish to the Secretary of Labor any available information on contractors, subcontractors, current and previous contracts, and the nature of the contract work.

(b) If a Department of Labor representative undertakes an investigation at a construction project, the contracting officer shall inquire into the scope of the investigation, and request to be notified immediately of any violations discovered under the Construction Wage Rate Requirements statute, the Contract Work Hours and Safety Standards statute, or the Copeland (Anti-Kickback) Act.

United States Code Annotated

Contract requirements, see 41 USCA § 254.

Contracts, planning, solicitation, evaluation, and award procedures, see 10 USCA § 2305.

Definitions, see 10 USCA § 2302, 41 USCA §§ 259, 403.

Kickbacks from public works employees, see 18 USCA § 874.

Kinds of contracts, see 10 USCA § 2306.

Planning and solicitation requirements, see 41 USCA § 253a.

Rate of wages for laborers and mechanics, see 40 USCA § 3142.

Work hours, see 40 USCA § 3702.

§ 22.406-13 Semiannual enforcement reports.

A semiannual report on compliance with and enforcement of the construction labor standards requirements of the Construction Wage Rate Requirements statute and Contract Work Hours and Safety Standards statute is required from each contracting agency. The reporting periods are October 1 through March 31 and April 1 through September 30. The reports shall only contain information as to the enforcement actions of the contracting agency and shall be prepared as prescribed in Department of Labor memoranda and submitted to the Department of Labor within 30 days after the end of the reporting period. This report has been assigned interagency report control number 1482-DOL-SA.

United States Code Annotated

Contract requirements, see 41 USCA § 254.

Contracts, planning, solicitation, evaluation, and award procedures, see 10 USCA § 2305.

Definitions, see 10 USCA § 2302, 41 USCA §§ 259, 403.

Kickbacks from public works employees, see 18 USCA § 874.

Kinds of contracts, see 10 USCA § 2306.

Planning and solicitation requirements, see 41 USCA § 253a.

Rate of wages for laborers and mechanics, see 40 USCA § 3142.

Work hours, see 40 USCA § 3702.

§ 22.407 Solicitation provision and contract clauses.

(a) Insert the following clauses in solicitations and contracts in excess of $2,000 for construction within the United States:

(1) 52.222-6, Construction Wage Rate Requirements.

(2) 52.222-7, Withholding of Funds.

(3) 52.222-8, Payrolls and Basic Records.

(4) 52.222-9, Apprentices and Trainees.

(5) 52.222-10, Compliance with Copeland Act Requirements.

(6) 52.222-11, Subcontracts (Labor Standards).

(7) 52.222-12, Contract Termination-Debarment.

(8) 52.222-13, Compliance with Construction Wage Rate Requirements and Related Regulations.

(9) 52.222-14, Disputes Concerning Labor Standards.

(10) 52.222-15, Certification of Eligibility.

(b) Insert the clause at 52.222-16, Approval of Wage Rates, in solicitations and contracts in excess of $2,000 for cost-reimbursement construction to be performed within the United States, except for contracts with a State or political subdivision thereof.

(c) A contract that is not primarily for construction may contain a requirement for some construction work to be performed in the United States. If under 22.402(b) the requirements of this subpart apply to the construction work, insert in such solicitations and contracts the applicable construction labor standards clauses required in this section and identify the item or items of construction work to which the clauses apply.

(d) [Reserved]

(e) Insert the clause at 52.222-30, Construction Wage Rate Requirements—Price Adjustment (None or Separately Specified Pricing Method), in solicitations and contracts if the contract is expected to be—

(1) A fixed-price contract subject to the Construction Wage Rate Requirements statute that will contain option provisions by which the contracting officer may extend the term of the contract, and the contracting officer determines the most appropriate contract price adjustment method is the method at 22.404-12(c)(1) or (2); or

(2) A cost-reimbursable type contract subject to the Construction Wage Rate Requirements statute that will contain option provisions by which the contracting officer may extend the term of the contract.

(f) Insert the clause at 52.222-31, Construction Wage Rate Requirements-Price Adjustment (Percentage Method), in solicitations and contracts if the contract is expected to be a fixed-price contract subject to the Construction Wage Rate Requirements statute that will contain option provisions by which the contracting officer may extend the term of the contract, and the contracting officer determines the most appropriate contract price adjustment method is the method at 22.404-12(c)(3).

(g) Insert the clause at 52.222-32, Construction Wage Rate Requirements-Price Adjustment (Actual Method), in solicitations and contracts if the contract is expected to be a fixed-price contract subject to the Construction Wage Rate Requirements statute that will contain option provisions by which the contracting officer may extend the term of the contract, and the contracting officer determines the most appropriate method to establish contract price is the method at 22.404-12(c)(4).

(h) Insert the provision at 52.222-5, Construction Wage Rate Requirements—Secondary Site of the Work, in solicitations in excess of $2,000 for construction within the United States.

United States Code Annotated

Contract requirements, see 41 USCA § 254.

Contracts, planning, solicitation, evaluation, and award procedures, see 10 USCA § 2305.

Definitions, see 10 USCA § 2302, 41 USCA §§ 259, 403.

Kickbacks from public works employees, see 18 USCA § 874.

Kinds of contracts, see 10 USCA § 2306.

Planning and solicitation requirements, see 41 USCA § 253a.

Rate of wages for laborers and mechanics, see 40 USCA § 3142.

Work hours, see 40 USCA § 3702.

Subpart 22.5 [Reserved]

Subpart 22.6 Walsh-Healey Public Contracts Act

§ 22.601 [Reserved]

§ 22.602 Statutory requirements.

Except for the exemptions at 22.604, all contracts subject to 41 U.S.C. chapter 65, Contracts for Materials, Supplies, Articles, and Equipment Exceeding $15,000 (the statute), and entered into by any executive department, independent establishment, or other agency or instrumentality of the United States, or by the District of Columbia, or by any corporation (all the stock of which is beneficially owned by the United States) for the manufacture or furnishing of materials, supplies, articles, and equipment (referred to in this subpart as supplies) in any amount exceeding $15,000, shall include or incorporate by reference the stipulations required by the statute pertaining to such matters as minimum wages, maximum hours, child labor, convict labor, and safe and sanitary working conditions.

United States Code Annotated

Contract requirements, see 41 USCA § 254.

Contracts, planning, solicitation, evaluation, and award procedures, see 10 USCA § 2305.

Contracts for materials, etc., exceeding $10,000, representations
and stipulations, see 41 USCA § 35.

Definitions, see 10 USCA § 2302, 41 USCA §§ 259, 403.

Kinds of contracts, see 10 USCA § 2306.

Planning and solicitation requirements, see 41 USCA § 253a.

Notes of Decisions

In general 1

Locality 2

1 In general

Unsuccessful bidder for public contract suffered no prejudice by alleged failure of military agency and Small Business Administration (SBA) to explicitly consider bidder's preaward Walsh-Healey protest, as agency addressed in substance each element of protest. Walsh-Healey Act, § 1 et seq., as amended, 41 U.S.C.A. § 35 et seq.J.G.B. Enterprises, Inc. v. U.S., 921 F. Supp. 91, 40 Cont. Cas. Fed. (CCH) P 76941 (N.D. N.Y. 1996). United States ⊕64.55(2)

Military agency's alleged failure to follow regulations in processing unsuccessful bidder's preaward Walsh-Healey protest relating to public contract for supplying water storage systems did not warrant invalidation of contract, as regulations which agency failed to follow were not applicable where agency was required by regulation to forward chosen bid to Small Business Administration (SBA) and agency could thus not immediately act on protest. Walsh-Healey Act, § 1 et seq., as amended, 41 U.S.C.A. § 35 et seq.; 13 C.F.R. § 125.5(d); 48 C.F.R. § 219.602-1(a)(ii)(A) (1994). J.G.B. Enterprises, Inc. v. U.S., 921 F. Supp. 91, 40 Cont. Cas. Fed. (CCH) P 76941 (N.D. N.Y. 1996). United States ⊕64.55(2)

Unsuccessful bidder for public contract submitted proper preaward protest under Walsh-Healey Act, despite similarity of that protest to bidder's responsibility protest, in view of overlapping nature of responsibility and Walsh-Healey eligibility issues. Walsh-Healey Act, § 1 et seq., as amended, 41 U.S.C.A. § 35 et seq.J.G.B. Enterprises, Inc. v. U.S., 921 F. Supp. 91, 40 Cont. Cas. Fed. (CCH) P 76941 (N.D. N.Y. 1996). United States ⊕64.55(2)

2 Locality

"Locality" as used in Walsh-Healey Act is not synonymous with "locality" as used in Service Contract Act. Service Contract Act of 1965, § 2(a)(1), 41 U.S.C.A. § 351(a)(1); Walsh-Healey Act, § 1, 41 U.S.C.A. § 35. Southern Packaging and Storage Co., Inc. v. U.S., 618 F.2d 1088, 24 Wage & Hour Cas. (BNA) 701, 27 Cont. Cas. Fed. (CCH) P 80382, 89 Lab. Cas. (CCH) P 33930 (4th Cir. 1980). Labor And Employment ⊕2304

Under Walsh-Healey Act section directing Secretary of Labor to determine prevailing minimum wages for persons employed in similar work, or persons employed in particular or similar industries, or persons employed in groups of industries "currently operating in the locality" in which materials are to be furnished under government contract, considerable degree of discretion is vested in the Secretary to determine what shall constitute locality for particular purpose, but entire United States may not be regarded as a single "locality". Walsh-Healey Act, § 1 et seq., and § 10, as added in 1952, 41 U.S.C.A. §§ 35 et seq., Covington Mills v. Mitchell, 129 F. Supp. 740 (D. D.C. 1955). Labor And Employment ⊕2304

§ 22.603 Applicability.

The requirements in 22.602 apply to contracts (including for this purpose, indefinite-delivery contracts, basic ordering agreements, and blanket purchase agreements) and subcontracts under Section 8(a) of the Small Business Act, for the manufacture or furnishing of supplies that—

(a) Will be performed in the United States, Puerto Rico, or the U.S. Virgin Islands;

(b) Exceed or may exceed $15,000; and

(c) Are not exempt under 22.604.

United States Code Annotated

Contract requirements, see 41 USCA § 254.

Contracts, planning, solicitation, evaluation, and award procedures, see 10 USCA § 2305.

Contracts for materials, etc., exceeding $10,000, representations and stipulations, see 41 USCA § 35.

Definitions, see 10 USCA § 2302, 41 USCA §§ 259, 403.

Kinds of contracts, see 10 USCA § 2306.

Planning and solicitation requirements, see 41 USCA § 253a.

§ 22.604 Exemptions.

§ 22.604-1 Statutory exemptions.

Contracts for acquisition of the following supplies are exempt from the statute:

(a) Any item in those situations where the contracting officer is authorized by the express language of a statute to purchase "in the open market" generally (such as commercial items, see Part 12); or where a specific purchase is made under the conditions described in 6.302-2 in circumstances where immediate delivery is required by the public exigency.

(b) Perishables, including dairy, livestock, and nursery products.

(c) Agricultural or farm products processed for first sale by the original producers.

(d) Agricultural commodities or the products thereof purchased under contract by the Secretary of Agriculture.

United States Code Annotated

Contract requirements, see 41 USCA § 254.

Contracts, planning, solicitation, evaluation, and award procedures, see 10 USCA § 2305.

Contracts for materials, etc., exceeding $10,000, representations and stipulations, see 41 USCA § 35.

Definitions, see 10 USCA § 2302, 41 USCA §§ 259, 403.

Kinds of contracts, see 10 USCA § 2306.

Planning and solicitation requirements, see 41 USCA § 253a.

§ 22.604-2 Regulatory exemptions.

(a) Contracts for the following acquisitions are fully exempt from the statute (see 41 CFR 50-201.603):

(1) Public utility services.

(2) Supplies manufactured outside the United States, Puerto Rico, and the U.S. Virgin Islands.

(3) Purchases against the account of a defaulting contractor where the stipulations of the statute were not included in the defaulted contract.

(4) Newspapers, magazines, or periodicals, contracted for with sales agents or publisher representatives, which are to be delivered by the publishers thereof.

(b) (1) Upon the request of the agency head, the Secretary of Labor may exempt specific contracts or classes of contracts from the inclusion or application of one or more of the Act's stipulations; provided, that the request includes a finding by the agency head stating the reasons why the conduct of Government business will be seriously impaired unless the exemption is granted.

(2) Those requests for exemption that relate solely to safety and health standards shall be transmitted to the—

Assistant Secretary for Occupational Safety and Health
U.S. Department of Labor
Washington, DC 20210.

All other requests shall be transmitted to the—

Administrator of the Wage and Hour Division
U.S. Department of Labor
Washington, DC 20210.

United States Code Annotated

Contract requirements, see 41 USCA § 254.

Contracts, planning, solicitation, evaluation, and award procedures, see 10 USCA § 2305.

Contracts for materials, etc., exceeding $10,000, representations and stipulations, see 41 USCA § 35.

Definitions, see 10 USCA § 2302, 41 USCA §§ 259, 403.

Kinds of contracts, see 10 USCA § 2306.

Planning and solicitation requirements, see 41 USCA § 253a.

§ 22.605 Rulings and interpretations of the statute.

(a) As authorized by the Act, the Secretary of Labor has issued rulings and interpretations concerning the administration of the statute (see 41 CFR 50-206). The substance of certain rulings and interpretations is as follows:

(1) If a contract for $15,000 or less is subsequently modified to exceed $15,000, the contract becomes subject to the statute for work performed after the date of the modification.

(2) If a contract for more than $15,000 is subsequently modified by mutual agreement to $15,000 or less, the contract is not subject to the statute for work performed after the date of the modification.

(3) If a contract awarded to a prime contractor contains a provision whereby the prime contractor is made an agent of the Government, the prime contractor is required to include the stipulations of the statute in contracts in excess of $15,000 awarded for and on behalf of the Government for supplies that are to be used in the construction and equipment of Government facilities.

(4) If a contract subject to the statute is awarded to a contractor operating Government-owned facilities, the stipulations of the statute affect the employees of that contractor the same as employees of contractors operating privately owned facilities.

(5) Indefinite-delivery contracts, including basic ordering agreements and blanket purchase agreements, are subject to the statute unless it can be determined in advance that the aggregate amount of all orders estimated to be placed thereunder for 1 year after the effective date of the agreement will not exceed $15,000. A determination shall be made annually thereafter if the contract or agreement is extended, and the contract or agreement modified if necessary.

(b) [Reserved]

United States Code Annotated

Contract requirements, see 41 USCA § 254.

Contracts, planning, solicitation, evaluation, and award procedures, see 10 USCA § 2305.

Contracts for materials, etc., exceeding $10,000, representations and stipulations, see 41 USCA § 35.

Definitions, see 10 USCA § 2302, 41 USCA §§ 259, 403.

Kinds of contracts, see 10 USCA § 2306.

Planning and solicitation requirements, see 41 USCA § 253a.

§ 22.606 [Reserved]

§ 22.607 [Reserved]

§ 22.608 Procedures.

(a) *Award.* When a contract subject to the statute is awarded, the contracting officer, in accordance with regulations or instructions issued by the Secretary of Labor and individual agency procedures, shall furnish to the contractor DOL publication WH-1313, Notice to Employees Working on Government Contracts.

(b) *Breach of stipulation.* In the event of a violation of a stipulation required under the statute, the contracting officer shall, in accordance with agency procedures, notify the appropriate regional office of the DOL, Wage and Hour Division (see 29 CFR part 1, Appendix B), and furnish any information available.

United States Code Annotated

Contract requirements, see 41 USCA § 254.

Contracts, planning, solicitation, evaluation, and award procedures, see 10 USCA § 2305.

Contracts for materials, etc., exceeding $10,000, representations and stipulations, see 41 USCA § 35.

Definitions, see 10 USCA § 2302, 41 USCA §§ 259, 403.

Kinds of contracts, see 10 USCA § 2306.

Planning and solicitation requirements, see 41 USCA § 253a.

§ 22.609 [Reserved]

§ 22.610 Contract clause.

The contracting officer shall insert the clause at 52.222-20, Contracts for Materials, Supplies, Articles, and Equipment Exceeding $15,000, in solicitations and contracts covered by the statute (see 22.603, 22.604, and 22.605).

United States Code Annotated

Contract requirements, see 41 USCA § 254.

Contracts, planning, solicitation, evaluation, and award procedures, see 10 USCA § 2305.

Contracts for materials, etc., exceeding $10,000, representations and stipulations, see 41 USCA § 35.

Definitions, see 10 USCA § 2302, 41 USCA §§ 259, 403.

Kinds of contracts, see 10 USCA § 2306.

Planning and solicitation requirements, see 41 USCA § 253a.

Subpart 22.7 [Reserved]

Subpart 22.8 Equal Employment Opportunity

§ 22.800 Scope of subpart.

This subpart prescribes policies and procedures pertaining to nondiscrimination in employment by contractors and subcontractors.

United States Code Annotated

Contract requirements, see 41 USCA § 254.

Contracts, planning, solicitation, evaluation, and award procedures, see 10 USCA § 2305.

Definitions, see 10 USCA § 2302, 41 USCA §§ 259, 403.

Kinds of contracts, see 10 USCA § 2306.

Planning and solicitation requirements, see 41 USCA § 253a.

§ 22.801 Definitions.

As used in this subpart—

"Affirmative action program" means a contractor's program that complies with Department of Labor regulations to ensure equal opportunity in employment to minorities and women.

"Compliance evaluation" means any one or combination of actions that the Office of Federal Contract Compliance Programs (OFCCP) may take to examine a Federal contractor's compliance with one or more of the requirements of E.O. 11246.

"Contractor" includes the terms "prime contractor" and "subcontractor."

"Deputy Assistant Secretary" means the Deputy Assistant Secretary for Federal Contract Compliance, U.S. Department of Labor, or a designee.

"Equal Opportunity clause" means the clause at 52.222-26, Equal Opportunity, as prescribed in 22.810(e).

"E.O. 11246" means Parts II and IV of Executive Order 11246, September 24, 1965 (30 FR 12319), and any Executive order amending or superseding this order (see 22.802). This term specifically includes the Equal Opportunity clause at 52.222-26, and the rules, regulations, and orders issued pursuant to E.O. 11246 by the Secretary of Labor or a designee.

"Prime contractor" means any person who holds, or has held, a Government contract subject to E.O. 11246.

"Recruiting and training agency" means any person who refers workers to any contractor or provides or supervises apprenticeship or training for employment by any contractor.

"Site of construction" means the general physical location of any building, highway, or other change or improvement to real property that is undergoing construction, rehabilitation, alteration, conversion, extension, demolition, or repair; and any temporary location or facility at which a contractor or other participating party meets a demand or performs a function relating to a Government contract or subcontract.

"Subcontract" means any agreement or arrangement between a contractor and any person (in which the parties do not stand in the relationship of an employer and an employee)—

(1) For the purchase, sale, or use of personal property or nonpersonal services that, in whole or in part, are necessary to the performance of any one or more contracts; or

(2) Under which any portion of the contractor's obligation under any one or more contracts is performed, undertaken, or assumed.

"Subcontractor" means any person who holds, or has held, a subcontract subject to E.O. 11246. The term "first-tier subcontractor" means a subcontractor holding a subcontract with a prime contractor.

"United States" means the 50 States, the District of Columbia, Puerto Rico, the Northern Mariana Islands, American Samoa, Guam, the U.S. Virgin Islands, and Wake Island.

United States Code Annotated

Contract requirements, see 41 USCA § 254.

Contracts, planning, solicitation, evaluation, and award procedures, see 10 USCA § 2305.

Definitions, see 10 USCA § 2302, 41 USCA §§ 259, 403.

Kinds of contracts, see 10 USCA § 2306.

Planning and solicitation requirements, see 41 USCA § 253a.

§ 22.802 General.

(a) Executive Order 11246, as amended, sets forth the Equal Opportunity clause and requires that all agencies—

(1) Include this clause in all nonexempt contracts and subcontracts (see 22.807); and

(2) Act to ensure compliance with the clause and the regulations of the Secretary of Labor to promote the full realization of equal employment opportunity for all persons, regardless of race, color, religion, sex, or national origin.

(b) No contract or modification involving new acquisition shall be entered into, and no subcontract shall be approved by a contracting officer, with a person who has been found ineligible by the Deputy Assistant Secretary for reasons of noncompliance with the requirements of E.O. 11246.

(c) No contracting officer or contractor shall contract for supplies or services in a manner so as to avoid applicability of the requirements of E.O. 11246.

(d) Contractor disputes related to compliance with its obligation shall be handled according to the rules, regulations, and relevant orders of the Secretary of Labor (see 41 CFR 60-1.1).

United States Code Annotated

Contract requirements, see 41 USCA § 254.

Contracts, planning, solicitation, evaluation, and award procedures, see 10 USCA § 2305.

Definitions, see 10 USCA § 2302, 41 USCA §§ 259, 403.

Kinds of contracts, see 10 USCA § 2306.

Planning and solicitation requirements, see 41 USCA § 253a.

§ 22.803 Responsibilities.

(a) The Secretary of Labor is responsible for the—

(1) Administration and enforcement of prescribed parts of E.O. 11246; and

(2) Adoption of rules and regulations and the issuance of orders necessary to achieve the purposes of E.O. 11246.

(b) The Secretary of Labor has delegated authority and assigned responsibility to the Deputy Assistant Secretary for carrying out the responsibilities assigned to the Secretary by E.O. 11246, except for the issuance of rules and regulations of a general nature.

(c) The head of each agency is responsible for ensuring that the requirements of this subpart are carried out within the agency, and for cooperating with and assisting the OFCCP in fulfilling its responsibilities.

(d) In the event the applicability of E.O. 11246 and implementing regulations is questioned, the contracting officer shall forward the matter to the Deputy Assistant Secretary, through agency channels, for resolution.

United States Code Annotated

Contract requirements, see 41 USCA § 254.

Contracts, planning, solicitation, evaluation, and award procedures, see 10 USCA § 2305.

Definitions, see 10 USCA § 2302, 41 USCA §§ 259, 403.

Kinds of contracts, see 10 USCA § 2306.

Planning and solicitation requirements, see 41 USCA § 253a.

§ 22.804 Affirmative action programs.

§ 22.804-1 Nonconstruction.

Except as provided in 22.807, each nonconstruction prime contractor and each subcontractor with 50 or more employees and either a contract or subcontract of $50,000 or more, or Government bills of lading that in any 12-month period total, or can reasonably be expected to total, $50,000 or more, is required to develop a written affirmative action program for each of its establishments. Each contractor and subcontractor shall develop its written affirmative action programs within 120 days from the commencement of its first such Government contract, subcontract, or Government bill of lading.

United States Code Annotated

Contract requirements, see 41 USCA § 254.

Contracts, planning, solicitation, evaluation, and award procedures, see 10 USCA § 2305.

Definitions, see 10 USCA § 2302, 41 USCA §§ 259, 403.

Kinds of contracts, see 10 USCA § 2306.

Planning and solicitation requirements, see 41 USCA § 253a.

§ 22.804-2 Construction.

(a) Construction contractors that hold a nonexempt (see 22.807) Government construction contract are required to meet—

(1) The contract terms and conditions citing affirmative action requirements applicable to covered geographical areas or projects; and

(2) Applicable requirements of 41 CFR 60-1 and 60-4.

(b) Each agency shall maintain a listing of covered geographical areas that are subject to affirmative action requirements that specify goals for minorities and women in covered construction trades. Information concerning, and additions to, this listing will be provided to the principally affected contracting officers in accordance with agency procedures. Any contracting officer contemplating a construction project in excess of $10,000 within a geographic area not known to be covered by specific affirmative action goals shall request instructions on the most current information from the OFCCP regional office, or as otherwise specified in agency regulations, before issuing the solicitation.

(c) Contracting officers shall give written notice to the OFCCP regional office within 10 working days of award of a construction contract subject to these affirmative action requirements. The notification shall include the name, address, and telephone number of the contractor; employer identification number; dollar amount of the contract; estimated starting and completion dates of the contract; the contract number; and the geographical area in which the contract is to be performed. When requested by the OFCCP regional office, the contracting officer shall arrange a conference among contractor, contracting activity, and compliance personnel to discuss the contractor's compliance responsibilities.

United States Code Annotated

Contract requirements, see 41 USCA § 254.

Contracts, planning, solicitation, evaluation, and award procedures, see 10 USCA § 2305.

Definitions, see 10 USCA § 2302, 41 USCA §§ 259, 403.

Kinds of contracts, see 10 USCA § 2306.

Planning and solicitation requirements, see 41 USCA § 253a.

§ 22.805 Procedures.

(a) *Preaward clearances for contracts and subcontracts of $10 million or more (excluding construction).* (1) Except as provided in paragraphs (a)(4) and (a)(8) of this section, if the estimated amount of the contract or subcontract is $10 million or more, the contracting officer shall request clearance from the appropriate OFCCP regional office before—

(i) Award of any contract, including any indefinite delivery contract or letter contract; or

(ii) Modification of an existing contract for new effort that would constitute a contract award.

(2) Preaward clearance for each proposed contract and for each proposed first-tier subcontract of $10 million or more shall be requested by the contracting officer directly from the OFCCP regional office(s). Verbal requests shall be confirmed by letter or facsimile transmission.

(3) When the contract work is to be performed outside the United States with employees recruited within the United States, the contracting officer shall send the request for a preaward clearance to the OFCCP regional office serving the area where the proposed contractor's corporate home or branch office is located in the United States, or the corporate location where personnel recruiting is handled, if different from the contractor's corporate home or branch office. If the proposed contractor has no corporate office or location within the United States, the preaward clearance request action should be based on the location of the recruiting and training agency in the United States.

(4) The contracting officer does not need to request a preaward clearance if—

(i) The specific proposed contractor is listed in OFCCP's National Preaward Registry via the Internet at *http://www.dol-esa.gov/preaward/*;

(ii) The projected award date is within 24 months of the proposed contractor's Notice of Compliance completion date in the Registry; and

(iii) The contracting officer documents the Registry review in the contract file.

(5) The contracting officer shall include the following information in the preaward clearance request:

(i) Name, address, and telephone number of the prospective contractor and of any corporate affiliate at which work is to be performed.

(ii) Name, address, and telephone number of each proposed first-tier subcontractor with a proposed subcontract estimated at $10 million or more.

(iii) Anticipated date of award.

(iv) Information as to whether the contractor and first-tier subcontractors have previously held any Government contracts or subcontracts.

(v) Place or places of performance of the prime contract and first-tier subcontracts estimated at $10 million or more, if known.

(vi) The estimated dollar amount of the contract and each first-tier subcontract, if known.

(6) The contracting officer shall allow as much time as feasible before award for the conduct of necessary compliance evaluation by OFCCP. As soon as the apparently successful offeror can be determined, the contracting officer shall process a preaward clearance request in accordance with agency procedures, assuring, if possible, that the preaward clearance request is submitted to the OFCCP regional office at least 30 days

before the proposed award date.

(7) Within 15 days of the clearance request, OFCCP will inform the awarding agency of its intention to conduct a preaward compliance evaluation. If OFCCP does not inform the awarding agency within that period of its intention to conduct a preaward compliance evaluation, clearance shall be presumed and the awarding agency is authorized to proceed with the award. If OFCCP informs the awarding agency of its intention to conduct a preaward compliance evaluation, OFCCP shall be allowed an additional 20 days after the date that it so informs the awarding agency to provide its conclusions. If OFCCP does not provide the awarding agency with its conclusions within that period, clearance shall be presumed and the awarding agency is authorized to proceed with the award.

(8) If the procedures specified in paragraphs (a)(6) and (a)(7) of this section would delay award of an urgent and critical contract beyond the time necessary to make award or beyond the time specified in the offer or extension thereof, the contracting officer shall immediately inform the OFCCP regional office of the expiration date of the offer or the required date of award and request clearance be provided before that date. If the OFCCP regional office advises that a preaward evaluation cannot be completed by the required date, the contracting officer shall submit written justification for the award to the head of the contracting activity, who, after informing the OFCCP regional office, may then approve the award without the preaward clearance. If an award is made under this authority, the contracting officer shall immediately request a postaward evaluation from the OFCCP regional office.

(9) If, under the provisions of paragraph (a)(8) of this section, a postaward evaluation determines the contractor to be in noncompliance with E.O. 11246, the Deputy Assistant Secretary may authorize the use of the enforcement procedures at 22.809 against the noncomplying contractor.

(b) *Furnishing posters.* The contracting officer shall furnish to the contractor appropriate quantities of the poster entitled "Equal Employment Opportunity Is The Law." These shall be obtained in accordance with agency procedures.

United States Code Annotated

Contract requirements, see 41 USCA § 254.

Contracts, planning, solicitation, evaluation, and award procedures, see 10 USCA § 2305.

Definitions, see 10 USCA § 2302, 41 USCA §§ 259, 403.

Kinds of contracts, see 10 USCA § 2306.

Planning and solicitation requirements, see 41 USCA § 253a.

§ 22.806 Inquiries.

(a) An inquiry from a contractor regarding status of its compliance with E.O. 11246, or rights of appeal to any of the actions in 22.809, shall be referred to the OFCCP regional office.

(b) Labor union inquiries regarding the revision of a collective bargaining agreement in order to comply with E.O. 11246 shall be referred to the Deputy Assistant Secretary.

United States Code Annotated

Contract requirements, see 41 USCA § 254.

Contracts, planning, solicitation, evaluation, and award procedures, see 10 USCA § 2305.

Definitions, see 10 USCA § 2302, 41 USCA §§ 259, 403.

Kinds of contracts, see 10 USCA § 2306.

Planning and solicitation requirements, see 41 USCA § 253a.

§ 22.807 Exemptions.

(a) Under the following exemptions, all or part of the requirements of E.O. 11246 may be excluded from a contract subject to E.O. 11246:

(1) *National security.* The agency head may determine that a contract is essential to the national security and that the award of the contract without complying with one or more of the requirements of this subpart is necessary to the national security. Upon making such a determination, the agency shall notify the Deputy Assistant Secretary in writ-

ing within 30 days.

(2) *Specific contracts.* The Deputy Assistant Secretary may exempt an agency from requiring the inclusion of one or more of the requirements of E.O. 11246 in any contract if the Deputy Assistant Secretary deems that special circumstances in the national interest so require. Groups or categories of contracts of the same type may also be exempted if the Deputy Assistant Secretary finds it impracticable to act upon each request individually or if group exemptions will contribute to convenience in the administration of E.O. 11246.

(b) The following exemptions apply even though a contract or subcontract contains the Equal Opportunity clause:

(1) *Transactions of $10,000 or less.* The Equal Opportunity clause is required to be included in prime contracts and subcontracts by 22.802(a). Individual prime contracts or subcontracts of $10,000 or less are exempt from application of the Equal Opportunity clause, unless the aggregate value of all prime contracts or subcontracts awarded to a contractor in any 12-month period exceeds, or can reasonably be expected to exceed, $10,000. (Note: Government bills of lading, regardless of amount, are not exempt.)

(2) *Work outside the United States.* Contracts are exempt from the requirements of E.O. 11246 for work performed outside the United States by employees who were not recruited within the United States.

(3) *Contracts with State or local governments.* The requirements of E.O. 11246 in any contract with a State or local government (or any agency, instrumentality, or subdivision thereof) shall not be applicable to any agency, instrumentality, or subdivision of such government that does not participate in work on or under the contract.

(4) *Work on or near Indian reservations.* It shall not be a violation of E.O. 11246 for a contractor to extend a publicly announced preference in employment to Indians living on or near an Indian reservation in connection with employment opportunities on or near an Indian reservation. This applies to that area where a person seeking employment could reasonably be expected to commute to and from in the course of a work day. Contractors extending such a preference shall not, however, discriminate among Indians on the basis of religion, sex, or tribal affiliation, and the use of such preference shall not excuse a contractor from complying with E.O. 11246, rules and regulations of the Secretary of Labor, and applicable clauses in the contract.

(5) *Facilities not connected with contracts.* The Deputy Assistant Secretary may exempt from the requirements of E.O. 11246 any of a contractor's facilities that the Deputy Assistant Secretary finds to be in all respects separate and distinct from activities of the contractor related to performing the contract, provided, that the Deputy Assistant Secretary also finds that the exemption will not interfere with, or impede the effectiveness of, E.O. 11246.

(6) *Indefinite-quantity contracts.* With respect to indefinite-quantity contracts and subcontracts, the Equal Opportunity clause applies unless the contracting officer has reason to believe that the amount to be ordered in any year under the contract will not exceed $10,000. The applicability of the Equal Opportunity clause shall be determined by the contracting officer at the time of award for the first year, and annually thereafter for succeeding years, if any. Notwithstanding the above, the Equal Opportunity clause shall be applied to the contract whenever the amount of a single order exceeds $10,000. Once the Equal Opportunity clause is determined to be applicable, the contract shall continue to be subject to such clause for its duration regardless of the amounts ordered, or reasonably expected to be ordered, in any year.

(7) *Contracts with religious entities.* Pursuant to E.O. 13279, Section 202 of E.O. 11246, shall not apply to a Government contractor or subcontractor that is a religious corporation, association, educational institution, or society, with respect to the employment of individuals of a particular religion to perform work connected with the carrying on by such corporation, association, educational institution, or society of its activities. Such contractors and subcontractors are not exempted or excused from complying with the other requirements contained in the order.

(c) To request an exemption under paragraph (a)(2) or (b)(5) of this section, the contracting officer shall submit, under agency procedures, a detailed justification for omitting all, or part of, the requirements of E.O. 11246. Requests for exemptions under paragraph (a)(2) or (b)(5) of this section shall be submitted to the Deputy Assistant Secretary for approval.

(d) The Deputy Assistant Secretary may withdraw the exemption for a specific contract, or group of contracts, if the Deputy Assistant Secretary deems that such action is necessary and appropriate to achieve the purposes of E.O. 11246. Such withdrawal shall not apply—

(1) To contracts awarded before the withdrawal; or

(2) To any sealed bid contract (including restricted sealed bidding), unless the withdrawal is made more than 10 days before the bid opening date.

United States Code Annotated

Contract requirements, see 41 USCA § 254.

Contracts, planning, solicitation, evaluation, and award procedures, see 10 USCA § 2305.

Definitions, see 10 USCA § 2302, 41 USCA §§ 259, 403.

Kinds of contracts, see 10 USCA § 2306.

Planning and solicitation requirements, see 41 USCA § 253a.

§ 22.808 Complaints.

Complaints received by the contracting officer alleging violation of the requirements of E.O. 11246 shall be referred immediately to the OFCCP regional office. The complainant shall be advised in writing of the referral. The contractor that is the subject of a complaint shall not be advised in any manner or for any reason of the complainant's name, the nature of the complaint, or the fact that the complaint was received.

United States Code Annotated

Contract requirements, see 41 USCA § 254.

Contracts, planning, solicitation, evaluation, and award procedures, see 10 USCA § 2305.

Definitions, see 10 USCA § 2302, 41 USCA §§ 259, 403.

Kinds of contracts, see 10 USCA § 2306.

Planning and solicitation requirements, see 41 USCA § 253a.

§ 22.809 Enforcement.

Upon the written direction of the Deputy Assistant Secretary, one or more of the following actions, as well as administrative sanctions and penalties, may be exercised against contractors found to be in violation of E.O. 11246, the regulations of the Secretary of Labor, or the applicable contract clauses:

(a) Publication of the names of the contractor or its unions.

(b) Cancellation, termination, or suspension of the contractor's contracts or portion thereof.

(c) Debarment from future Government contracts, or extensions or modifications of existing contracts, until the contractor has established and carried out personnel and employment policies in compliance with E.O. 11246 and the regulations of the Secretary of Labor.

(d) Referral by the Deputy Assistant Secretary of any matter arising under E.O. 11246 to the Department of Justice or to the Equal Employment Opportunity Commission (EEOC) for the institution of appropriate civil or criminal proceedings.

United States Code Annotated

Contract requirements, see 41 USCA § 254.

Contracts, planning, solicitation, evaluation, and award procedures, see 10 USCA § 2305.

Definitions, see 10 USCA § 2302, 41 USCA §§ 259, 403.

Kinds of contracts, see 10 USCA § 2306.

Planning and solicitation requirements, see 41 USCA § 253a.

§ 22.810 Solicitation provisions and contract clauses.

(a) When a contract is contemplated that will include the clause at 52.222-26, Equal Opportunity, the contracting officer shall insert—

(1) The clause at 52.222-21, Prohibition of Segregated Facilities, in the solicitation and contract; and

(2) The provision at 52.222-22, Previous Contracts and Compliance Reports, in the solicitation.

(b) The contracting officer shall insert the provision at 52.222-23, Notice of Requirement for Affirmative Action to Ensure Equal Employment Opportunity for Construction, in solicitations for construction when a contract is contemplated that will include the clause at 52.222-26, Equal Opportunity, and the amount of the contract is expected to be in excess of $10,000.

(c) The contracting officer shall insert the provision at 52.222-24, Preaward On-Site Equal Opportunity Compliance Evaluation, in solicitations other than those for construction when a contract is contemplated that will include the clause at 52.222-26, Equal Opportunity, and the amount of the contract is expected be $10 million or more.

(d) The contracting officer shall insert the provision at 52.222-25, Affirmative Action Compliance, in solicitations, other than those for construction, when a contract is contemplated that will include the clause at 52.222-26, Equal Opportunity.

(e) The contracting officer shall insert the clause at 52.222-26, Equal Opportunity, in solicitations and contracts (see 22.802) unless the contract is exempt from all of the requirements of E.O. 11246 (see 22.807(a)). If the contract is exempt from one or more, but not all, of the requirements of E.O. 11246, the contracting officer shall use the clause with its Alternate I.

(f) The contracting officer shall insert the clause at 52.222-27, Affirmative Action Compliance Requirements for Construction, in solicitations and contracts for construction that will include the clause at 52.222-26, Equal Opportunity, when the amount of the contract is expected to be in excess of $10,000.

(g) The contracting officer shall insert the clause at 52.222-29, Notification of Visa Denial, in contracts that will include the clause at 52.222-26, Equal Opportunity, if the contractor is required to perform in or on behalf of a foreign country.

United States Code Annotated

Contract requirements, see 41 USCA § 254.

Contracts, planning, solicitation, evaluation, and award procedures, see 10 USCA § 2305.

Definitions, see 10 USCA § 2302, 41 USCA §§ 259, 403.

Kinds of contracts, see 10 USCA § 2306.

Planning and solicitation requirements, see 41 USCA § 253a.

Subpart 22.9 Nondiscrimination Because of Age

§ 22.901 Policy.

Executive Order 11141, February 12, 1964 (29 FR 2477), states that the Government policy is as follows:

(a) Contractors and subcontractors shall not, in connection with employment, advancement, or discharge of employees, or the terms, conditions, or privileges of their employment, discriminate against persons because of their age except upon the basis of a bona fide occupational qualification, retirement plan, or statutory requirement.

(b) Contractors and subcontractors, or persons acting on their behalf, shall not specify in solicitations or advertisements for employees to work on Government contracts, a maximum age limit for employment unless the specified maximum age limit is based upon a bona fide occupational qualification, retirement plan, or statutory requirement.

(c) Agencies will bring this policy to the attention of contractors. The use of contract clauses is not required.

§ 22.902 Handling complaints.

Agencies shall bring complaints regarding a contractor's compliance with this policy to that contractor's attention (in writing, if appropriate), stating the policy, indicating that the contractor's compliance has been questioned, and requesting that the contractor take any appropriate steps that may be necessary to comply.

Subpart 22.10 Service Contract Act of 1965, as Amended

§ 22.1000 Scope of subpart.

This subpart prescribes policies and procedures implementing the provisions of 41 U.S.C. chapter 67, Service Contract Labor Standards (formerly known as the Service Contract Act of 1965), the applicable provisions of the Fair Labor Standards Act of 1938, as amended (29 U.S.C. 201, *et seq.*), and related Secretary of Labor regulations and instructions (29 CFR parts 4, 6, 8, and 1925).

United States Code Annotated

Contract requirements, see 41 USCA § 254.

Contracts, planning, solicitation, evaluation, and award procedures, see 10 USCA § 2305.

Definitions, see 10 USCA § 2302, 41 USCA §§ 259, 403.

Kinds of contracts, see 10 USCA § 2306.

List of violators, prohibition of contract award to firms appearing on list, actions to recover underpayments, payment of sums recovered, see 41 USCA § 354.

Planning and solicitation requirements, see 41 USCA § 253a.

Required contract provisions, minimum wages, see 41 USCA § 351.

Violations, see 41 USCA § 352.

Notes of Decisions

In general 1
Construction and application 2

1 In general

Under Service Contract Act, which requires that successor contractor grant employees the same wages and fringe benefits as were provided under predecessor's collective bargaining agreement, successor contractor was not required to recognize successorship and seniority rights acquired by predecessor contractor's employees under collective bargaining agreement with predecessor. Service Contract Act of 1965, § 4(c), 41 U.S.C.A. § 353(c). Clark v. Unified Services, Inc., 659 F.2d 49, 25 Wage & Hour Cas. (BNA) 145, 29 Cont. Cas. Fed. (CCH) P 81955, 92 Lab. Cas. (CCH) P 34074, 63 A.L.R. Fed. 786 (5th Cir. 1981). Labor And Employment ⟜2304

Service Contract Act contemplates that a successor employer will provide benefits to its employees that the predecessor provided its own employees; there is nothing in the statute which requires the successor to extend benefits to the predecessor's employees absent formation of an employeremployee relationship between the successor and the predecessor's employees. Service Contract Act of 1965, § 2(a), (a)(1-5), (b)(1) as amended 41 U.S.C.A. § 351(a), (a)(1–5), (b)(1). Trinity Services, Inc. v. Marshall, 593 F.2d 1250, 24 Wage & Hour Cas. (BNA) 216, 25 Cont. Cas. Fed. (CCH) P 82955, 85 Lab. Cas. (CCH) P 33731 (D.C. Cir. 1978). Labor And Employment ⟜2304

Even if Service Contract Act applied to keypunch operators, applicable wage determination with respect to bidder on government keypunching contract would be those prevailing for keypunch operators in Wilmington, Delaware area, the locality of bidder's principal place of business, and not the Washington, D.C. area, the locality of government installation. Service Contract Act of 1965, §§ 2-10, 41 U.S.C.A. §§ 351–358. Descomp, Inc. v. Sampson, 377 F. Supp. 254, 21 Wage & Hour Cas. (BNA) 999, 74 Lab. Cas. (CCH) P 33111 (D. Del. 1974). Labor And Employment ⟜2304

2 Construction and application

The Service Contract Act is remedial labor legislation which must be liberally construed. Service Contract Act of 1965, § 2 et seq. as amended 41 U.S.C.A. § 351 et seq.Midwest Maintenance & Const. Co., Inc. v. Vela, 621 F.2d 1046, 24 Wage & Hour Cas. (BNA) 696, 27 Cont. Cas. Fed. (CCH) P 80391, 88 Lab. Cas. (CCH) P 33905 (10th Cir. 1980). Labor And Employment ⟜2304

Secretary of Labor's interpretation of Service Contract Act has controlling weight unless plainly erroneous or inconsistent with Act. Service Contract Act of 1965, § 2 et seq., 41

U.S.C.A. § 351 et seq.Service Employees Intern. Union, AFL-CIO v. General Services Admin., 830 F. Supp. 5, 1 Wage & Hour Cas. 2d (BNA) 974 (D.D.C. 1993). Statutes ⊸219(8)

§ 22.1001 Definitions.

As used in this subpart—

"Contractor" includes a subcontractor at any tier whose subcontract is subject to the provisions of the statute.

"Multiple year contracts" means contracts having a term of more than 1 year regardless of fiscal year funding. The term includes multiyear contracts (see 17.103).

"United States" means the 50 States, the District of Columbia, Puerto Rico, the Northern Mariana Islands, American Samoa, Guam, the U.S. Virgin Islands, Johnston Island, Wake Island, and the outer Continental Shelf as defined in the Outer Continental Shelf Lands Act (43 U.S.C. 1331, et seq.), but does not include any other place subject to U.S. jurisdiction or any U.S. base or possession within a foreign country (29 CFR 4.112).

"Wage and Hour Division" means the unit in the Employment Standards Administration of the Department of Labor to which is assigned functions of the Secretary of Labor under the Service Contract Labor Standards statute.

"Wage determination"means a determination of minimum wages or fringe benefits made under 41 U.S.C. 6703 or 6707(c) applicable to the employment in a given locality of one or more classes of service employees.

United States Code Annotated

Contract requirements, see 41 USCA § 254.

Contracts, planning, solicitation, evaluation, and award procedures, see 10 USCA § 2305.

Definitions, see 10 USCA § 2302, 41 USCA §§ 259, 403.

Kinds of contracts, see 10 USCA § 2306.

List of violators, prohibition of contract award to firms appearing on list, actions to recover underpayments, payment of sums recovered, see 41 USCA § 354.

Planning and solicitation requirements, see 41 USCA § 253a.

Required contract provisions, minimum wages, see 41 USCA § 351.

Violations, see 41 USCA § 352.

Notes of Decisions

Fringe benefit 3
Locality 2
Services 1

1 Services

Contract for sale of timber on Indian reservation was not principally for "services," within meaning of Service Contract Act, and thus that Act's requirement that contractor provide its employees with occupational compensation insurance and accident insurance was not applicable. Service Contract Act of 1965, § 2(a)(2), 41 U.S.C.A. § 351(a)(2). Bear Medicine v. U.S., 47 F. Supp. 2d 1172 (D. Mont. 1999), judgment rev'd, 241 F.3d 1208, 31 Envtl. L. Rep. 20501 (9th Cir. 2001). Indians ⊸17

2 Locality

"Locality" as used in Walsh-Healey Act is not synonymous with "locality" as used in Service Contract Act. Service Contract Act of 1965, § 2(a)(1), 41 U.S.C.A. § 351(a)(1); Walsh-Healey Act, § 1, 41 U.S.C.A. § 35. Southern Packaging and Storage Co., Inc. v. U.S., 618 F.2d 1088, 24 Wage & Hour Cas. (BNA) 701, 27 Cont. Cas. Fed. (CCH) P 80382, 89 Lab. Cas. (CCH) P 33930 (4th Cir. 1980). Labor And Employment ⊸2304

Appropriate "locality" for determining prevailing minimum wage under Service Contract Act was standard metropolitan statistical area in which contractor was located, not entire nation. Service Contract Act of 1965, § 2(a)(1), 41 U.S.C.A. § 351(a)(1). Southern Packaging and Storage Co., Inc. v. U.S., 618 F.2d 1088, 24 Wage & Hour Cas. (BNA) 701, 27 Cont. Cas. Fed. (CCH) P 80382, 89 Lab. Cas. (CCH) P 33930 (4th Cir. 1980). Labor And Employment ⊸2304

Determination of Secretary of Labor that word "locality" within prevailing wage rate period of Service Contract Act included entire continental United States exceeded boundaries set by Congress and, hence, would be rejected as not in accordance with law. Federal Property and Administrative Services Act of 1949, § 303(a), 41 U.S.C.A. § 253(a); 5 U.S.C.A. § 706(2)(A). Southern Packaging and Storage Co. v. U.S., 458 F. Supp. 726, 23 Wage & Hour Cas. (BNA) 1085, 25 Cont. Cas. Fed. (CCH) P 82844, 84 Lab. Cas. (CCH) P 33719 (D.S.C. 1978), judgment aff'd, 618 F.2d 1088, 24 Wage & Hour Cas. (BNA) 701, 27 Cont. Cas. Fed. (CCH) P 80382, 89 Lab. Cas. (CCH) P 33930 (4th Cir. 1980). Labor And Employment ☞2304

In enacting Service Contract Act, Congress required wage levels based on prevailing wage rates in locality and further required Secretary of Labor, in determining "locality," to take a realistic view of type of contract intended to be covered by determination. Federal Property and Administrative Services Act of 1949, § 303(a), 41 U.S.C.A. § 253(a); 5 U.S.C.A. § 706(2)(A). Southern Packaging and Storage Co. v. U.S., 458 F. Supp. 726, 23 Wage & Hour Cas. (BNA) 1085, 25 Cont. Cas. Fed. (CCH) P 82844, 84 Lab. Cas. (CCH) P 33719 (D.S.C. 1978), judgment aff'd, 618 F.2d 1088, 24 Wage & Hour Cas. (BNA) 701, 27 Cont. Cas. Fed. (CCH) P 80382, 89 Lab. Cas. (CCH) P 33930 (4th Cir. 1980). Labor And Employment ☞2304

Word "locality," within prevailing wage rate provision of Service Contract Act, did not include entire continental United States as contended by Secretary of Labor, but referred to standard metropolitan statistical area, if available, or specific county where bidding party's plant or facility was located. Federal Property and Administrative Services Act of 1949, § 303(a), 41 U.S.C.A. § 253(a); 5 U.S.C.A. § 706(2)(A). Southern Packaging and Storage Co. v. U.S., 458 F. Supp. 726, 23 Wage & Hour Cas. (BNA) 1085, 25 Cont. Cas. Fed. (CCH) P 82844, 84 Lab. Cas. (CCH) P 33719 (D.S.C. 1978), judgment aff'd, 618 F.2d 1088, 24 Wage & Hour Cas. (BNA) 701, 27 Cont. Cas. Fed. (CCH) P 80382, 89 Lab. Cas. (CCH) P 33930 (4th Cir. 1980). Labor And Employment ☞2304

3 Fringe benefit

For purpose of Service Contract Act, a bona fide "fringe benefit" is one which involves the present cost or the present risk of a future cost to the employer of the workers and is a benefit of the type of which its value to the recipient is capable of being ascertained in a different amount. Service Contract Act of 1965, § 2(a)(2) as amended 41 U.S.C.A. § 351(a)(2). Trinity Services, Inc. v. Marshall, 593 F.2d 1250, 24 Wage & Hour Cas. (BNA) 216, 25 Cont. Cas. Fed. (CCH) P 82955, 85 Lab. Cas. (CCH) P 33731 (D.C. Cir. 1978). Labor And Employment ☞2304

Seniority is not a "fringe benefit" within meaning of Service Contract Act but, rather, is a means of determining how wages and fringe benefits are to be allocated. Service Contract Act of 1965, §§ 2(a)(2), 4(c) as amended 41 U.S.C.A. §§ 351(a)(2), 353(c). Trinity Services, Inc. v. Marshall, 593 F.2d 1250, 24 Wage & Hour Cas. (BNA) 216, 25 Cont. Cas. Fed. (CCH) P 82955, 85 Lab. Cas. (CCH) P 33731 (D.C. Cir. 1978). Labor And Employment ☞2304

A pure severance payment obligation under which any employer might incur an obligation to make payments with its employees when it lays them off constitutes a bona fide "fringe benefit" for purpose of Service Contract Act. Service Contract Act of 1965, § 2(a)(2) as amended 41 U.S.C.A. § 351(a)(2). Trinity Services, Inc. v. Marshall, 593 F.2d 1250, 24 Wage & Hour Cas. (BNA) 216, 25 Cont. Cas. Fed. (CCH) P 82955, 85 Lab. Cas. (CCH) P 33731 (D.C. Cir. 1978). Labor And Employment ☞2304

§ 22.1002 Statutory requirements.

§ 22.1002-1 General.

Service contracts over $2,500 shall contain mandatory provisions regarding minimum wages and fringe benefits, safe and sanitary working conditions, notification to employees of the minimum allowable compensation, and equivalent Federal employee classifications and wage rates. Under 41 U.S.C. 6707(d), service contracts may not exceed 5 years.

United States Code Annotated

Contract requirements, see 41 USCA § 254.

Contracts, planning, solicitation, evaluation, and award procedures, see 10 USCA § 2305.

Definitions, see 10 USCA § 2302, 41 USCA §§ 259, 403.

Kinds of contracts, see 10 USCA § 2306.

List of violators, prohibition of contract award to firms appearing on list, actions to recover underpayments, payment of sums recovered, see 41 USCA § 354.

Planning and solicitation requirements, see 41 USCA § 253a.

Required contract provisions, minimum wages, see 41 USCA § 351.

Violations, see 41 USCA § 352.

Notes of Decisions

Fringe benefit 1

1 Fringe benefit

For purpose of Service Contract Act, a bona fide "fringe benefit" is one which involves the present cost or the present risk of a future cost to the employer of the workers and is a benefit of the type of which its value to the recipient is capable of being ascertained in a different amount. Service Contract Act of 1965, § 2(a)(2) as amended 41 U.S.C.A. § 351(a)(2). Trinity Services, Inc. v. Marshall, 593 F.2d 1250, 24 Wage & Hour Cas. (BNA) 216, 25 Cont. Cas. Fed. (CCH) P 82955, 85 Lab. Cas. (CCH) P 33731 (D.C. Cir. 1978). Labor And Employment ∞2304

Seniority is not a "fringe benefit" within meaning of Service Contract Act but, rather, is a means of determining how wages and fringe benefits are to be allocated. Service Contract Act of 1965, §§ 2(a)(2), 4(c) as amended 41 U.S.C.A. §§ 351(a)(2), 353(c). Trinity Services, Inc. v. Marshall, 593 F.2d 1250, 24 Wage & Hour Cas. (BNA) 216, 25 Cont. Cas. Fed. (CCH) P 82955, 85 Lab. Cas. (CCH) P 33731 (D.C. Cir. 1978). Labor And Employment ∞2304

A pure severance payment obligation under which any employer might incur an obligation to make payments with its employees when it lays them off constitutes a bona fide "fringe benefit" for purpose of Service Contract Act. Service Contract Act of 1965, § 2(a)(2) as amended 41 U.S.C.A. § 351(a)(2). Trinity Services, Inc. v. Marshall, 593 F.2d 1250, 24 Wage & Hour Cas. (BNA) 216, 25 Cont. Cas. Fed. (CCH) P 82955, 85 Lab. Cas. (CCH) P 33731 (D.C. Cir. 1978). Labor And Employment ∞2304

§ 22.1002-2 Wage determinations based on prevailing rates.

Contractors performing on service contracts in excess of $2,500 to which no predecessor contractor's collective bargaining agreement applies shall pay their employees at least the wages and fringe benefits found by the Department of Labor to prevail in the locality or, in the absence of a wage determination, the minimum wage set forth in the Fair Labor Standards Act.

United States Code Annotated

Contract requirements, see 41 USCA § 254.

Contracts, planning, solicitation, evaluation, and award procedures, see 10 USCA § 2305.

Definitions, see 10 USCA § 2302, 41 USCA §§ 259, 403.

Kinds of contracts, see 10 USCA § 2306.

List of violators, prohibition of contract award to firms appearing on list, actions to recover underpayments, payment of sums recovered, see 41 USCA § 354.

Planning and solicitation requirements, see 41 USCA § 253a.

Required contract provisions, minimum wages, see 41 USCA § 351.

Violations, see 41 USCA § 352.

Notes of Decisions

Fringe benefit 1

1 Fringe benefit

For purpose of Service Contract Act, a bona fide "fringe benefit" is one which involves the present cost or the present risk of a future cost to the employer of the workers and is a benefit of the type of which its value to the recipient is capable of being ascertained in a different amount. Service Contract Act of 1965, § 2(a)(2) as amended 41 U.S.C.A. § 351(a)(2). Trinity Services, Inc. v. Marshall, 593 F.2d 1250, 24 Wage & Hour Cas. (BNA) 216, 25 Cont. Cas. Fed. (CCH) P 82955, 85 Lab. Cas. (CCH) P 33731 (D.C. Cir. 1978). Labor And Employment ⊸2304

Seniority is not a "fringe benefit" within meaning of Service Contract Act but, rather, is a means of determining how wages and fringe benefits are to be allocated. Service Contract Act of 1965, §§ 2(a)(2), 4(c) as amended 41 U.S.C.A. §§ 351(a)(2), 353(c). Trinity Services, Inc. v. Marshall, 593 F.2d 1250, 24 Wage & Hour Cas. (BNA) 216, 25 Cont. Cas. Fed. (CCH) P 82955, 85 Lab. Cas. (CCH) P 33731 (D.C. Cir. 1978). Labor And Employment ⊸2304

A pure severance payment obligation under which any employer might incur an obligation to make payments with its employees when it lays them off constitutes a bona fide "fringe benefit" for purpose of Service Contract Act. Service Contract Act of 1965, § 2(a)(2) as amended 41 U.S.C.A. § 351(a)(2). Trinity Services, Inc. v. Marshall, 593 F.2d 1250, 24 Wage & Hour Cas. (BNA) 216, 25 Cont. Cas. Fed. (CCH) P 82955, 85 Lab. Cas. (CCH) P 33731 (D.C. Cir. 1978). Labor And Employment ⊸2304

§ 22.1002-3 Wage determinations based on collective bargaining agreements.

(a) Successor contractors performing on contracts in excess of $2,500 for substantially the same services performed in the same locality must pay wages and fringe benefits (including accrued wages and benefits and prospective increases) at least equal to those contained in any bona fide collective bargaining agreement entered into under the predecessor contract. This requirement is self-executing and is not contingent upon incorporating a wage determination or the wage and fringe benefit terms of the predecessor contractor's collective bargaining agreement in the successor contract. This requirement will not apply if the Secretary of Labor determines—

(1) After a hearing, that the wages and fringe benefits are substantially at variance with those which prevail for services of a similar character in the locality; or

(2) That the wages and fringe benefits are not the result of arm's length negotiations.

(b) Paragraphs in this Subpart 22.10 which deal with this statutory requirement and the Department of Labor's implementing regulations are 22.1010, concerning notification to contractors and bargaining representatives of procurement dates; 22.1012-2, explaining when a collective bargaining agreement will not apply due to late receipt by the contracting officer; and 22.1013 and 22.1021, explaining when the application of a collective bargaining agreement can be challenged due to a variance with prevailing rates or lack of arm's length bargaining.

United States Code Annotated

Contract requirements, see 41 USCA § 254.

Contracts, planning, solicitation, evaluation, and award procedures, see 10 USCA § 2305.

Definitions, see 10 USCA § 2302, 41 USCA §§ 259, 403.

Kinds of contracts, see 10 USCA § 2306.

List of violators, prohibition of contract award to firms appearing on list, actions to recover underpayments, payment of sums recovered, see 41 USCA § 354.

Planning and solicitation requirements, see 41 USCA § 253a.

Required contract provisions, minimum wages, see 41 USCA § 351.

Violations, see 41 USCA § 352.

Notes of Decisions

Fringe benefit 1

1 Fringe benefit

For purpose of Service Contract Act, a bona fide "fringe benefit" is one which involves the present cost or the present risk of a future cost to the employer of the workers and is a benefit of the type of which its value to the recipient is capable of being ascertained in a different amount. Service Contract Act of 1965, § 2(a)(2) as amended 41 U.S.C.A. § 351(a)(2). Trinity Services, Inc. v. Marshall, 593 F.2d 1250, 24 Wage & Hour Cas. (BNA) 216, 25 Cont. Cas. Fed. (CCH) P 82955, 85 Lab. Cas. (CCH) P 33731 (D.C. Cir. 1978). Labor And Employment ⊸2304

Seniority is not a "fringe benefit" within meaning of Service Contract Act but, rather, is a means of determining how wages and fringe benefits are to be allocated. Service Contract Act of 1965, §§ 2(a)(2), 4(c) as amended 41 U.S.C.A. §§ 351(a)(2), 353(c). Trinity Services, Inc. v. Marshall, 593 F.2d 1250, 24 Wage & Hour Cas. (BNA) 216, 25 Cont. Cas. Fed. (CCH) P 82955, 85 Lab. Cas. (CCH) P 33731 (D.C. Cir. 1978). Labor And Employment ⟳2304

A pure severance payment obligation under which any employer might incur an obligation to make payments with its employees when it lays them off constitutes a bona fide "fringe benefit" for purpose of Service Contract Act. Service Contract Act of 1965, § 2(a)(2) as amended 41 U.S.C.A. § 351(a)(2). Trinity Services, Inc. v. Marshall, 593 F.2d 1250, 24 Wage & Hour Cas. (BNA) 216, 25 Cont. Cas. Fed. (CCH) P 82955, 85 Lab. Cas. (CCH) P 33731 (D.C. Cir. 1978). Labor And Employment ⟳2304

§ 22.1002-4 Application of the Fair Labor Standards Act minimum wage.

No contractor or subcontractor holding a service contract for any dollar amount shall pay any of its employees working on the contract less than the minimum wage specified in section 6(a)(1) of the Fair Labor Standards Act (29 U.S.C. 206).

United States Code Annotated

Contract requirements, see 41 USCA § 254.

Contracts, planning, solicitation, evaluation, and award procedures, see 10 USCA § 2305.

Definitions, see 10 USCA § 2302, 41 USCA §§ 259, 403.

Kinds of contracts, see 10 USCA § 2306.

List of violators, prohibition of contract award to firms appearing on list, actions to recover underpayments, payment of sums recovered, see 41 USCA § 354.

Planning and solicitation requirements, see 41 USCA § 253a.

Required contract provisions, minimum wages, see 41 USCA § 351.

Violations, see 41 USCA § 352.

§ 22.1002-5 Executive Order 13658.

Executive Order 13658 establishes minimum wages for certain workers. The wage rate is subject to annual increases by an amount determined by the Secretary of Labor. See Subpart 22.19. The clause at 52.222-55, Minimum Wages under Executive Order 13658, requires the Executive Order 13658 minimum wage rate to be paid if it is higher than other minimum wage rates, such as the Subpart 22.10 statutory wage determination amount.

§ 22.1003 Applicability.

§ 22.1003-1 General.

This Subpart 22.10 applies to all Government contracts, the principal purpose of which is to furnish services in the United States through the use of service employees, except as exempted in 22.1003-3 and 22.1003-4 of this section, or any subcontract at any tier thereunder. This subpart does not apply to individual contract requirements for services in contracts not having as their principal purpose the furnishing of services. The nomenclature, type, or particular form of contract used by contracting agencies is not determinative of coverage.

United States Code Annotated

Contract requirements, see 41 USCA § 254.

Contracts, planning, solicitation, evaluation, and award procedures, see 10 USCA § 2305.

Definitions, see 10 USCA § 2302, 41 USCA §§ 259, 403.

Kinds of contracts, see 10 USCA § 2306.

List of violators, prohibition of contract award to firms appearing on list, actions to recover underpayments, payment of sums recovered, see 41 USCA § 354.

Planning and solicitation requirements, see 41 USCA § 253a.

Required contract provisions, minimum wages, see 41 USCA § 351.

Violations, see 41 USCA § 352.

§ 22.1003-2 Geographical coverage of the Act.

The Service Contract Labor Standards statute applies to service contracts performed in the United States (see 22.1001). The Service Contract Labor Standards statute does not apply to contracts performed outside the United States.

United States Code Annotated

Contract requirements, see 41 USCA § 254.

Contracts, planning, solicitation, evaluation, and award procedures, see 10 USCA § 2305.

Definitions, see 10 USCA § 2302, 41 USCA §§ 259, 403.

Kinds of contracts, see 10 USCA § 2306.

List of violators, prohibition of contract award to firms appearing on list, actions to recover underpayments, payment of sums recovered, see 41 USCA § 354.

Planning and solicitation requirements, see 41 USCA § 253a.

Required contract provisions, minimum wages, see 41 USCA § 351.

Violations, see 41 USCA § 352.

§ 22.1003-3 Statutory exemptions.

The Service Contract Labor Standards statute does not apply to—

(a) Any contract for construction, alteration, or repair of public buildings or public works, including painting and decorating;

(b) Any work required to be done in accordance with the provisions of 41 U.S.C. chapter 65, Contracts for Materials, Supplies, Articles, and Equipment Exceeding $15,000;

(c) Any contract for transporting freight or personnel by vessel, aircraft, bus, truck, express, railroad, or oil or gas pipeline where published tariff rates are in effect;

(d) Any contract for furnishing services by radio, telephone, telegraph, or cable companies subject to the Communications Act of 1934;

(e) Any contract for public utility services;

(f) Any employment contract providing for direct services to a Federal agency by an individual or individuals; or

(g) Any contract for operating postal contract stations for the U.S. Postal Service.

United States Code Annotated

Contract requirements, see 41 USCA § 254.

Contracts, planning, solicitation, evaluation, and award procedures, see 10 USCA § 2305.

Definitions, see 10 USCA § 2302, 41 USCA §§ 259, 403.

Kinds of contracts, see 10 USCA § 2306.

List of violators, prohibition of contract award to firms appearing on list, actions to recover underpayments, payment of sums recovered, see 41 USCA § 354.

Planning and solicitation requirements, see 41 USCA § 253a.

Required contract provisions, minimum wages, see 41 USCA § 351.

Violations, see 41 USCA § 352.

§ 22.1003-4 Administrative limitations, variations, tolerances, and exemptions.

(a) The Secretary of Labor may provide reasonable limitations and may make rules and regulations allowing reasonable variations, tolerances, and exemptions to and from any or all provisions of the Service Contract Labor Standards statute other than 41 U.S.C. 6707(f). These will be made only in special circumstances where it has been determined that the limitation, variation, tolerance, or exemption is necessary and proper in the public interest or to avoid the serious impairment of Government business, and is in accord with the remedial purpose of the Service Contract Labor Standards statute to protect prevailing labor standards (41 U.S.C. 6707(b)). See 29 CFR 4.123 for a listing of administrative exemptions, tolerances, and variations. Requests for limitations, variances, tolerances, and exemptions from the Service Contract Labor Standards statute shall be submitted in writing through contracting channels and the agency labor advisor to the Wage and Hour Administrator.

(b) In addition to the statutory exemptions cited in 22.1003-3 of this subsection, the Secretary of Labor has exempted the following types of contracts from all provisions of the Service Contract Labor Standards statute:

(1) Contracts entered into by the United States with common carriers for the carriage of mail by rail, air (except air star routes), bus, and ocean vessel, where such carriage is performed on regularly scheduled runs of the trains, airplanes, buses, and vessels over regularly established routes and accounts for an insubstantial portion of the revenue therefrom.

(2) Any contract entered into by the U.S. Postal Service with an individual owner-operator for mail service if it is not contemplated at the time the contract is made that the owner-operator will hire any service employee to perform the services under the contract except for short periods of vacation time or for unexpected contingencies or emergency situations such as illness, or accident.

(3) Contracts for the carriage of freight or personnel if such carriage is subject to rates covered by section 10721 of the Interstate Commerce Act.

(c) *Contracts for maintenance, calibration or repair of certain equipment.*—

(1) *Exemption.* The Secretary of Labor has exempted from the Service Contract Labor Standards statute contracts and subcontracts in which the primary purpose is to furnish maintenance, calibration, or repair of the following types of equipment, if the conditions at paragraph (c)(2) of this subsection are met:

(i) Automated data processing equipment and office information/word processing systems.

(ii) Scientific equipment and medical apparatus or equipment if the application of micro-electronic circuitry or other technology of at least similar sophistication is an essential element (for example, Federal Supply Classification (FSC) Group 65, Class 6515, "Medical Diagnostic Equipment;" Class 6525, "X-Ray Equipment;" FSC Group 66, Class 6630, "Chemical Analysis Instruments;" and Class 6665, "Geographical and Astronomical Instruments," are largely composed of the types of equipment exempted in this paragraph).

(iii) Office/business machines not otherwise exempt pursuant to paragraph (c)(1)(i) of this subsection, if such services are performed by the manufacturer or supplier of the equipment.

(2) *Conditions.* The exemption at paragraph (c)(1) of this subsection applies if all the following conditions are met for a contract (or a subcontract):

(i) The items of equipment to be serviced under the contract are used regularly for other than Government purposes and are sold or traded by the contractor in substantial quantities to the general public in the course of normal business operations.

(ii) The services will be furnished at prices which are, or are based on, established catalog or market prices for the maintenance, calibration, or repair of such equipment. As defined at 29 CFR 4.123(e)(1)(ii)(B)—

(A) An established catalog price is a price included in a catalog price list, schedule, or other form that is regularly maintained by the manufacturer or the contractor, is either published or otherwise available for inspection by customers, and states prices at which sales currently, or were last, made to a significant number of buyers constituting the general public.

(B) An established market price is a current price, established in the usual course of trade between buyers and sellers free to bargain, which can be substantiated from sources independent of the manufacturer or contractor.

(iii) The contractor will use the same compensation (wage and fringe benefits) plan for all service employees performing work under the contract as the contractor uses for these employees and equivalent employees servicing the same equipment of commercial customers.

(iv) The apparent successful offeror certifies to the conditions in paragraph (c)(2)(i) through (iii) of this subsection. (See 22.1006(e).)

(3) *Affirmative determination and contract award.*

(i) For source selections where the contracting officer has established a competitive range, if the contracting officer determines that one or more of the conditions in paragraphs 22.1003-4 (c)(2)(i) through (iii) of an offeror's certification will not be met, the contracting officer shall identify the deficiency to the offeror before receipt of the final proposal revisions. Unless the offeror provides a revised offer acknowledging applicability of the Service Contract Labor Standards statute or demonstrating to the satisfaction of the contracting officer an ability to meet all required conditions for exemption, the offer will not be further considered for award.

(ii) The contracting officer shall determine in writing the applicability of this exemption to the contract before contract award. If the apparent successful offeror will meet all conditions in paragraph (c)(2) of this subsection, the contracting officer shall make an affirmative determination and award the contract without the otherwise applicable Service Contract Labor Standards clause(s).

(iii) If the apparent successful offeror does not certify to the conditions in paragraph (c)(2)(i) through (iii) of this subsection, the contracting officer shall incorporate in the contract the Service Contract Act clause (see 22.1006(a)) and, if the contract will exceed $2,500, the appropriate Department of Labor wage determination (see 22.1007).

(4) *Department of Labor determination.*

(i) If the Department of Labor determines after award of the contract that any condition for exemption in paragraph (c)(2) of this subsection has not been met, the exemption shall be deemed inapplicable, and the contract shall become subject to the Service Contract Labor Standards statute, effective as of the date of the Department of Labor determination. In such case, the procedures at 29 CFR 4.123(e)(1)(iv) and 29 CFR 4.5(c) shall be followed.

(ii) If the Department of Labor determines that any conditions in paragraph (c)(2) of this subsection have not been met with respect to a subcontract, the exemption shall be deemed inapplicable. The contractor may be responsible for ensuring that the subcontractor complies with the Service Contract Labor Standards statute, effective as of the date of the subcontract award.

(d) *Contracts for certain services.*—

(1) *Exemption.* Except as provided in paragraph (d)(5) of this subsection, the Secretary of Labor has exempted from tthe Service Contract Labor Standards statute contracts and subcontracts in which the primary purpose is to provide the following services, if the conditions in paragraph (d)(2) of this subsection are met:

(i) Automobile or other vehicle (*e.g.*, aircraft) maintenance services (other than contracts or subcontracts to operate a Government motor pool or similar facility).

(ii) Financial services involving the issuance and servicing of cards (including credit cards, debit cards, purchase cards, smart cards, and similar card services).

(iii) Hotel/motel services for conferences, including lodging and/or meals, that are part of the contract or subcontract for the conference (which must not include ongoing contracts for lodging on an as needed or continuing basis).

(iv) Maintenance, calibration, repair, and/or installation (where the installation is not subject to the Construction Wage Rate Requirements statute, as provided in 29 CFR 4.116(c)(2)) services for all types of equipment where the services are obtained from the manufacturer or supplier of the equipment under a contract awarded on a sole source basis.

(v) Transportation by common carrier of persons by air, motor vehicle, rail, or marine vessel on regularly scheduled routes or via standard commercial services (not including charter services).

(vi) Real estate services, including real property appraisal services, related to housing Federal agencies or disposing of real property owned by the Government.

(vii) Relocation services, including services of real estate brokers and appraisers to assist Federal employees or military personnel in buying and selling homes (which shall not include actual moving or storage of household goods and related services).

(2) *Conditions.* The exemption for the services in paragraph (d)(1) of this subsection applies if all the following conditions are met for a contract (or for a subcontract):

(i) (A) Except for services identified in paragraph (d)(1)(iv) of this subsection, the contractor will be selected for award based on other factors in addition to price or cost, with the combination of other factors at least as important as price or cost; or

(B) The contract will be awarded on a sole source basis.

(ii) The services under the contract are offered and sold regularly to non-Governmental customers, and are provided by the contractor (or subcontractor in the case of an exempt subcontract) to the general public in substantial quantities in the course of normal business operations.

(iii) The contract services are furnished at prices that are, or are based on, established catalog or market prices. As defined at 29 CFR 4.123(e)(2)(ii)(C)—

(A) An established catalog price is a price included in a catalog, price list, schedule, or other form that is regularly maintained by the contractor, is either published or otherwise available for inspection by customers, and states prices at which sales are currently, or were last, made to a significant number of buyers constituting the general public; and

(B) An established market price is a current price, established in the usual course of trade between buyers and sellers free to bargain, which can be substantiated from sources independent of the manufacturer or contractor.

(iv) Each service employee who will perform the services under the contract will spend only a small portion of his or her time (a monthly average of less than 20 percent of the available hours on an annualized basis, or less than 20 percent of available hours during the contract period if the contract period is less than a month) servicing the Government contract.

(v) The contractor will use the same compensation (wage and fringe benefits) plan for all service employees performing work under the contract as the contractor uses for these employees and equivalent employees servicing commercial customers.

(vi) The contracting officer (or contractor with respect to a subcontract) determines in advance before issuing the solicitation, based on the nature of the contract requirements and knowledge of the practices of likely offerors, that all or nearly all offerors will meet the conditions in paragraph (d)(2)(ii) through (v) of this subsection. If the services are currently being performed under contract, the contracting officer (or contractor with respect to a subcontract) shall consider the practices of the existing contractor in making a determination regarding the conditions in paragraphs (d)(2)(ii) through (v) of this subsection.

(vii) (A) The apparent successful offeror certifies that the conditions in paragraphs (d)(2)(ii) through (v) will be met; and

(B) For other than sole source awards, the contracting officer determines that the same certification is obtained from substantially all other offerors that are—

(1) In the competitive range, if discussions are to be conducted (see FAR 15.306(c)); or

(2) Considered responsive, if award is to be made without discussions (see FAR 15.306(a)).

(3) *Contract award or resolicitation.*

(i) If the apparent successful offeror does not certify to the conditions, the contracting officer shall insert in the contract the applicable Service Contract Labor Standards clause(s) (see 22.1006) and, if the contract will exceed $2,500, the appropriate Department of Labor wage determination (see 22.1007).

(ii) The contracting officer shall award the contract without the otherwise applicable Service Contract Labor Standards clause(s) if—

(A) The apparent successful offeror certifies to the conditions in paragraphs (d)(2)(ii) through (v) of this subsection;

(B) The contracting officer determines that the same certification is obtained from substantially all other offerors that are—

(1) In the competitive range, if discussions are to be conducted (see FAR 15.306); or

(2) Considered responsive, if award is to be made without discussions (see FAR 15.306(a)); and

(C) The contracting officer has no reason to doubt the certification.

(iii) If the conditions in paragraph (d)(3)(ii) of this subsection are not met, then the contracting officer shall resolicit, amending the solicitation by removing the exemption provision from the solicitation as prescribed at 22.1006(e)(3). The contract will include the applicable Service Contract Labor Standards clause(s) as prescribed at 22.1006 and, if the contract will exceed $2,500, the appropriate Department of Labor wage determination (see 22.1007).

(4) *Department of Labor determination.*

(i) If the Department of Labor determines after award of the contract that any conditions for exemption at paragraph (d)(2) of this subsection have not been met, the exemption shall be deemed inapplicable, and the contract shall become subject to the Service Contract Labor Standards statute. In such case, the procedures at 29 CFR 4.123(e)(2)(iii) and 29 CFR 4.5(c) shall be followed.

(ii) If the Department of Labor determines that any conditions in paragraph (d)(2) of this subsection have not been met with respect to a subcontract, the exemption shall be deemed inapplicable. The contractor may be responsible for ensuring that the subcontractor complies with the Service Contract Labor Standards statute, effective as of the date of the subcontract award.

(5) *Exceptions.* The exemption at paragraph (d)(1) of this subsection does not apply to solicitations and contracts (subcontracts)—

(i) Awarded under, 41 U.S.C. chapter 85, Committee for Purchase from People Who Are Blind or Severely Disabled (see Subpart 8.7).

(ii) For the operation of a Government facility, or part of a Government facility (but may be applicable to subcontracts for services); or

(iii) Subject to 41 U.S.C. 6707(c) (see 22.1002-3).

United States Code Annotated

Contract requirements, see 41 USCA § 254.

Contracts, planning, solicitation, evaluation, and award procedures, see 10 USCA § 2305.

Definitions, see 10 USCA § 2302, 41 USCA §§ 259, 403.

Kinds of contracts, see 10 USCA § 2306.

List of violators, prohibition of contract award to firms appearing on list, actions to recover underpayments, payment of sums recovered, see 41 USCA § 354.

Planning and solicitation requirements, see 41 USCA § 253a.

Required contract provisions, minimum wages, see 41 USCA § 351.

Violations, see 41 USCA § 352.

Notes of Decisions

Fringe benefit 1

1 Fringe benefit

For purpose of Service Contract Act, a bona fide "fringe benefit" is one which involves the present cost or the present risk of a future cost to the employer of the workers and is a benefit of the type of which its value to the recipient is capable of being ascertained in a different amount. Service Contract Act of 1965, § 2(a)(2) as amended 41 U.S.C.A. § 351(a)(2). Trinity Services, Inc. v. Marshall, 593 F.2d 1250, 24 Wage & Hour Cas. (BNA) 216, 25 Cont. Cas. Fed. (CCH) P 82955, 85 Lab. Cas. (CCH) P 33731 (D.C. Cir. 1978). Labor And Employment ☞2304

Seniority is not a "fringe benefit" within meaning of Service Contract Act but, rather, is a means of determining how wages and fringe benefits are to be allocated. Service Contract Act of 1965, §§ 2(a)(2), 4(c) as amended 41 U.S.C.A. §§ 351(a)(2), 353(c). Trinity Services, Inc. v. Marshall, 593 F.2d 1250, 24 Wage & Hour Cas. (BNA) 216, 25 Cont. Cas. Fed. (CCH) P 82955, 85 Lab. Cas. (CCH) P 33731 (D.C. Cir. 1978). Labor And Employment ☞2304

A pure severance payment obligation under which any employer might incur an obligation to make payments with its employees when it lays them off constitutes a bona fide "fringe benefit" for purpose of Service Contract Act. Service Contract Act of 1965, § 2(a)(2) as amended 41 U.S.C.A. § 351(a)(2). Trinity Services, Inc. v. Marshall, 593 F.2d 1250, 24 Wage & Hour Cas. (BNA) 216, 25 Cont. Cas. Fed. (CCH) P 82955, 85 Lab. Cas. (CCH) P 33731 (D.C. Cir. 1978). Labor And Employment ☞2304

§ 22.1003-5 Some examples of contracts covered.

The following examples, while not definitive or exclusive, illustrate some of the types of services that have been found to be covered by the Service Contract Labor Standards statute (see 29 CFR 4.130 for additional examples):

PART 22 APPLICATION OF LABOR LAWS

(a) Motor pool operation, parking, taxicab, and ambulance services.

(b) Packing, crating, and storage.

(c) Custodial, janitorial, housekeeping, and guard services.

(d) Food service and lodging.

(e) Laundry, dry-cleaning, linen-supply, and clothing alteration and repair services.

(f) Snow, trash, and garbage removal.

(g) Aerial spraying and aerial reconnaissance for fire detection.

(h) Some support services at installations, including grounds maintenance and landscaping.

(i) Certain specialized services requiring specific skills, such as drafting, illustrating, graphic arts, stenographic reporting, or mortuary services.

(j) Electronic equipment maintenance and operation and engineering support services.

(k) Maintenance and repair of all types of equipment, for example, aircraft, engines, electrical motors, vehicles, and electronic, office and related business and construction equipment. (But see 22.1003-4(c)(1) and (d)(1)(iv).)

(l) Operation, maintenance, or logistics support of a Federal facility.

(m) Data collection, processing and analysis services.

United States Code Annotated

Contract requirements, see 41 USCA § 254.

Contracts, planning, solicitation, evaluation, and award procedures, see 10 USCA § 2305.

Definitions, see 10 USCA § 2302, 41 USCA §§ 259, 403.

Kinds of contracts, see 10 USCA § 2306.

List of violators, prohibition of contract award to firms appearing on list, actions to recover underpayments, payment of sums recovered, see 41 USCA § 354.

Planning and solicitation requirements, see 41 USCA § 253a.

Required contract provisions, minimum wages, see 41 USCA § 351.

Violations, see 41 USCA § 352.

§ 22.1003-6 Repair distinguished from remanufacturing of equipment.

(a) Contracts principally for remanufacturing of equipment which is so extensive as to be equivalent to manufacturing are subject to 41 U.S.C. chapter 65, Contracts for Materials, Supplies, Articles, and Equipment Exceeding $15,000, rather than to the Service Contract Labor Standards statute. Remanufacturing shall be deemed to be manufacturing when the criteria in either subparagraphs (a)(1) or (a)(2) of this subsection are met.

(1) Major overhaul of an item, piece of equipment, or material which is degraded or inoperable, and under which all of the following conditions exist:

(i) The item or equipment is required to be completely or substantially torn down into individual component parts.

(ii) Substantially all of the parts are reworked, rehabilitated, altered and/or replaced.

(iii) The parts are reassembled so as to furnish a totally rebuilt item or piece of equipment.

(iv) Manufacturing processes similar to those which were used in the manufacturing of the item or piece of equipment are utilized.

(v) The disassembled components, if usable (except for situations where the number of items or pieces of equipment involved are too few to make it practicable) are commingled with existing inventory and, as such, lose their identification with respect to a particular piece of equipment.

(vi) The items or equipment overhauled are restored to original life expectancy, or nearly so.

(vii) Such work is performed in a facility owned or operated by the contractor.

(2) Major modification of an item, piece of equipment, or material which is wholly or partially obsolete, and under which all of the following conditions exist:

(i) The item or equipment is required to be completely or substantially torn down.

(ii) Outmoded parts are replaced.

(iii) The item or equipment is rebuilt or reassembled.

(iv) The contract work results in the furnishing of a substantially modified item in a usable and serviceable condition.

(v) The work is performed in a facility owned or operated by the contractor.

(b) Remanufacturing does not include the repair of damaged or broken equipment which does not require a complete teardown, overhaul, and rebuild as described in subparagraphs (a)(1) and (a)(2) of this subsection, or the periodic and routine maintenance, preservation, care, adjustment, upkeep, or servicing of equipment to keep it in usable, serviceable, working order. Such contracts typically are billed on an hourly rate (labor plus materials and parts) basis. Any contract principally for this type of work is subject to the Service Contract Labor Standards statute. Examples of such work include the following:

(1) Repair of an automobile, truck, or other vehicle, construction equipment, tractor, crane, aerospace, air conditioning and refrigeration equipment, electric motors, and ground powered industrial or vehicular equipment.

(2) Repair of typewriters and other office equipment (but see 22.1003-4(c)(1) and (d)(1)(iv)).

(3) Repair of appliances, radios, television sets, calculators, and other electronic equipment.

(4) Inspecting, testing, calibration, painting, packaging, lubrication, tune-up, or replacement of internal parts of equipment listed in subparagraphs (b)(1), (b)(2), and (b)(3) of this subsection.

(5) Reupholstering, reconditioning, repair, and refinishing of furniture.

United States Code Annotated

Contract requirements, see 41 USCA § 254.

Contracts, planning, solicitation, evaluation, and award procedures, see 10 USCA § 2305.

Definitions, see 10 USCA § 2302, 41 USCA §§ 259, 403.

Kinds of contracts, see 10 USCA § 2306.

List of violators, prohibition of contract award to firms appearing on list, actions to recover underpayments, payment of sums recovered, see 41 USCA § 354.

Planning and solicitation requirements, see 41 USCA § 253a.

Required contract provisions, minimum wages, see 41 USCA § 351.

Violations, see 41 USCA § 352.

§ 22.1003-7 Questions concerning applicability of the Service Contract Labor Standards statute.

If the contracting officer questions the applicability of the Service Contract Labor Standards statute to an acquisition, the contracting officer shall request the advice of the agency labor advisor. Unresolved questions shall be submitted in a timely manner to the Administrator, Wage and Hour Division, for determination.

United States Code Annotated

Contract requirements, see 41 USCA § 254.

Contracts, planning, solicitation, evaluation, and award procedures, see 10 USCA § 2305.

Definitions, see 10 USCA § 2302, 41 USCA §§ 259, 403.

Kinds of contracts, see 10 USCA § 2306.

List of violators, prohibition of contract award to firms appearing on list, actions to recover underpayments, payment of sums recovered, see 41 USCA § 354.

Planning and solicitation requirements, see 41 USCA § 253a.

Required contract provisions, minimum wages, see 41 USCA § 351.

Violations, see 41 USCA § 352.

§ 22.1004 Department of Labor responsibilities and regulations.

Under the Service Contract Labor Standards statute, the Secretary of Labor is authorized and directed to enforce the provisions of the Service Contract Labor Standards statute, make rules and regulations, issue orders, hold hearings, make decisions, and take other appropriate action. The Department of Labor has issued implementing regulations on such matters as—

(a) Service contract labor standards provisions and procedures (29 CFR Part 4, Subpart A);

(b) Wage determination procedures (29 CFR part 4, subparts A and B);

(c) Application of the Service Contract Labor Standards statute (rulings and interpretations) (29 CFR Part 4, Subpart C);

(d) Compensation standards (29 CFR Part 4, Subpart D);

(e) Enforcement (29 CFR Part 4, Subpart E);

(f) Safe and sanitary working conditions (29 CFR Part 1925);

(g) Rules of practice for administrative proceedings enforcing service contract labor standards (29 CFR Part 6); and

(h) Practice before the Administrative Review Board (29 CFR part 8).

United States Code Annotated

Contract requirements, see 41 USCA § 254.

Contracts, planning, solicitation, evaluation, and award procedures, see 10 USCA § 2305.

Definitions, see 10 USCA § 2302, 41 USCA §§ 259, 403.

Kinds of contracts, see 10 USCA § 2306.

List of violators, prohibition of contract award to firms appearing on list, actions to recover underpayments, payment of sums recovered, see 41 USCA § 354.

Planning and solicitation requirements, see 41 USCA § 253a.

Required contract provisions, minimum wages, see 41 USCA § 351.

Violations, see 41 USCA § 352.

Notes of Decisions

Wage revisions 1

1 Wage revisions

Wage revisions made during base period of contracts to provide key entry operators of Postal Service, after discovery that original wage determinations were low, were governed by changes clause of contracts rather than price adjustment clause and, thus, contractor could recover indirect costs associated with revised wage determination, including general and administrative costs, overhead, and profit. 29 C.F.R. § 4.4(d); 48 C.F.R. §§ 22.1004(b), 22.1007. Lockheed Support Systems, Inc. v. U.S., 36 Fed. Cl. 424, 3 Wage & Hour Cas. 2d (BNA) 785 (1996). United States ☞74(12.1)

§ 22.1005 [Reserved]

§ 22.1006 Solicitation provisions and contract clauses.

(a) (1) The contracting officer shall insert the clause at 52.222-41, Service Contract Labor Standards, in solicitations and contracts (except as provided in paragraph (a)(2) of this section) if the contract is subject to the Service Contract Labor Standards statute and is—

    (i) Over $2,500; or

    (ii) For an indefinite dollar amount and the contracting officer does not know in advance that the contract amount will be $2,500 or less.

(2) The contracting officer shall not insert the clause at 52.222-41 (or any of the associated Service Contract Labor Standards statute clauses as prescribed in this section for possible use when 52.222-41 applies) in the resultant contract if—

    (i) The solicitation includes the provision at—

        (A) 52.222-48, Exemption from Application of the Service Contract Labor Standards statute to Contracts for Maintenance, Calibration, or Repair of Certain Equipment—Certification;

        (B) 52.222-52, Exemption from Application of the Service Contract Labor Standards statute to Contracts for Certain Services—Certification; or

(C) Either of the comparable certifications is checked as applicable in the provision at 52.204-8(c)(2) or 52.212-3(k); and

(ii) The contracting officer has made the determination, in accordance with paragraphs (c)(3) or (d)(3) of subsection 22.1003-4, that the Service Contract Labor Standards statute does not apply to the contract. (In such case, insert the clause at 52.222-51, Exemption from Application of the Service Contract Labor Standards to Contracts for Maintenance, Calibration, or Repair of Certain Equipment-Requirements, or 52.222-53, Exemption from Application of the Service Contract Labor Standards to Contracts for Certain Services-Requirements, in the contract, in accordance with the prescription at paragraph (e)(2)(ii) or (e)(4)(ii) of this subsection).

(b) The contracting officer shall insert the clause at 52.222-42, Statement of Equivalent Rates for Federal Hires, in solicitations and contracts if the contract amount is expected to be over $2,500 and the Service Contract Labor Standards statute is applicable. (See 22.1016.)

(c) (1) The contracting officer shall insert the clause at 52.222-43, Fair Labor Standards Act and Service Contract Labor Standards—Price Adjustment (Multiple Year and Option Contracts), or another clause which accomplishes the same purpose, in solicitations and contracts if the contract is expected to be a fixed-price, time-and-materials, or labor-hour service contract containing the clause at 52.222-41, Service Contract Labor Standards, and is a multiple year contract or is a contract with options to renew which exceeds the simplified acquisition threshold. The clause may be used in contracts that do not exceed the simplified acquisition threshold. The clause at 52.222-43, Fair Labor Standards Act and Service Contract Labor Standards—Price Adjustment (Multiple Year and Option Contracts), applies to both contracts subject to area prevailing wage determinations and contracts subject to the incumbent contractor's collective bargaining agreement in effect during this contract's preceding contract period (see 22.1002-2 and 22.1002-3). Contracting officers shall ensure that contract prices or contract unit price labor rates are adjusted only to the extent that a contractor's increases or decreases in applicable wages and fringe benefits are made to comply with the requirements set forth in the clauses at 52.222-43 (subparagraphs (d)(1), (2) and (3)), or 52.222-44 (subparagraphs (b)(1) and (2)). (For example, the prior year wage determination required a minimum wage rate of $4.00 per hour. The contractor actually paid $4.10. The new wage determination increases the minimum rate to $4.50. The contractor increases the rate actually paid to $4.75 per hour. The allowable price adjustment is $.40 per hour.)

(2) The contracting officer shall insert the clause at 52.222-44, Fair Labor Standards Act and Service Contract Labor Standards—Price Adjustment, in solicitations and contracts if the contract is expected to be a fixed-price, time-and-materials, or labor-hour service contract containing the clause at 52.222-41, Service Contract Labor Standards, exceeds the simplified acquisition threshold, and is not a multiple year contract or is not a contract with options to renew. The clause may be used in contracts that do not exceed the simplified acquisition threshold. The clause at 52.222-44, Fair Labor Standards Act and Service Contract Labor Standards—Price Adjustment, applies to both contracts subject to area prevailing wage determinations and contracts subject to contractor collective bargaining agreements (see 22.1002-2 and 22.1002-3).

(3) The clauses prescribed in paragraph 22.1006(c)(1) cover situations in which revised minimum wage rates are applied to contracts by operation of law, or by revision of a wage determination in connection with (i) exercise of a contract option or (ii) extension of a multiple year contract into a new program year. If a clause prescribed in 16.203-4(d) is used, it must not conflict with, or duplicate payment under, the clauses prescribed in this paragraph 22.1006(c).

(d) [Reserved]

(e) (1) The contracting officer shall insert the provision at 52.222-48, Exemption from Application of the Service Contract Labor Standards to Contracts for Maintenance, Calibration, or Repair of Certain Equipment-Certification, in solicitations that—

(i) Include the clause at 52.222-41, Service Contract Labor Standards; and

(ii) The contract may be exempt from the Service Contract Labor Standards statute in accordance with 22.1003-4(c).

(2) The contracting officer shall insert the clause at 52.222-51, Exemption from Ap-

plication of the Service Contract Labor Standards to Contracts for Maintenance, Calibration, or Repair of Certain Equipment-Requirements—

(i) In solicitations that include the provision at 52.222-48, or the comparable provision is checked as applicable in the clause at 52.204-8(c)(2) or 52.212-3(k)(1); and

(ii) In resulting contracts in which the contracting officer has determined, in accordance with 22.1003-4(c)(3), that the Service Contract Labor Standards statute does not apply.

(3) (i) Except as provided in paragraph (e)(3)(ii) of this section, the contracting officer shall insert the provision at 52.222-52, Exemption from Application of the Service Contract Labor Standards to Contracts for Certain Services—Certification, in solicitations that—

(A) Include the clause at 52.222-41, Service Contract Labor Standards, and

(B) The contract may be exempt from the Service Contract Labor Standards statute in accordance with 22.1003-4(d).

(ii) When resoliciting in accordance with 22.1003-4(d)(3)(iii), amend the solicitation by removing the provision at 52.222-52 from the solicitation.

(4) The contracting officer shall insert the clause at 52.222-53, Exemption from Application of the Service Contract Labor Standards to Contracts for Certain Services— Requirements—

(i) In solicitations that include the provision at 52.222-52, or the comparable provision is checked as applicable in 52.204-8(c)(2) or 52.212-3(k)(2); and

(ii) In resulting contracts in which the contracting officer has determined, in accordance with 22.1003-4(d)(3), that the Service Contract Labor Standards statute does not apply.

(f) The contracting officer shall insert the clause at 52.222-49, Service Contract Labor Standards-Place of Performance Unknown, if using the procedures prescribed in 22.1009-4.

United States Code Annotated

Contract requirements, see 41 USCA § 254.

Contracts, planning, solicitation, evaluation, and award procedures, see 10 USCA § 2305.

Definitions, see 10 USCA § 2302, 41 USCA §§ 259, 403.

Kinds of contracts, see 10 USCA § 2306.

List of violators, prohibition of contract award to firms appearing on list, actions to recover underpayments, payment of sums recovered, see 41 USCA § 354.

Planning and solicitation requirements, see 41 USCA § 253a.

Required contract provisions, minimum wages, see 41 USCA § 351.

Violations, see 41 USCA § 352.

Notes of Decisions

Fringe benefit 1

1 Fringe benefit

For purpose of Service Contract Act, a bona fide "fringe benefit" is one which involves the present cost or the present risk of a future cost to the employer of the workers and is a benefit of the type of which its value to the recipient is capable of being ascertained in a different amount. Service Contract Act of 1965, § 2(a)(2) as amended 41 U.S.C.A. § 351(a)(2). Trinity Services, Inc. v. Marshall, 593 F.2d 1250, 24 Wage & Hour Cas. (BNA) 216, 25 Cont. Cas. Fed. (CCH) P 82955, 85 Lab. Cas. (CCH) P 33731 (D.C. Cir. 1978). Labor And Employment ⬡2304

Seniority is not a "fringe benefit" within meaning of Service Contract Act but, rather, is a means of determining how wages and fringe benefits are to be allocated. Service Contract Act of 1965, §§ 2(a)(2), 4(c) as amended 41 U.S.C.A. §§ 351(a)(2), 353(c). Trinity Services, Inc. v. Marshall, 593 F.2d 1250, 24 Wage & Hour Cas. (BNA) 216, 25 Cont. Cas. Fed. (CCH) P 82955, 85 Lab. Cas. (CCH) P 33731 (D.C. Cir. 1978). Labor And Employment ⬡2304

A pure severance payment obligation under which any employer might incur an obligation to make payments with its employees when it lays them off constitutes a bona fide "fringe benefit" for purpose of Service Contract Act. Service Contract Act of 1965, § 2(a)(2) as amended 41 U.S.C.A. § 351(a)(2). Trinity Services, Inc. v. Marshall, 593 F.2d 1250, 24 Wage & Hour Cas. (BNA) 216, 25 Cont. Cas. Fed. (CCH) P 82955, 85 Lab. Cas. (CCH) P 33731 (D.C. Cir. 1978). Labor And Employment ⊙⊷2304

§ 22.1007 Requirement to obtain wage determinations.

The contracting officer shall obtain wage determinations for the following service contracts:

(a) Each new solicitation and contract in excess of $2,500.

(b) Each contract modification which brings the contract above $2,500 and—

(1) Extends the existing contract pursuant to an option clause or otherwise; or

(2) Changes the scope of the contract whereby labor requirements are affected significantly.

(c) Each multiple year contract in excess of $2,500 upon—

(1) Annual anniversary date if the contract is subject to annual appropriations; or

(2) Biennial anniversary date if the contract is not subject to annual appropriations and its proposed term exceeds 2 years—unless otherwise advised by the Wage and Hour Division.

United States Code Annotated

Contract requirements, see 41 USCA § 254.

Contracts, planning, solicitation, evaluation, and award procedures, see 10 USCA § 2305.

Definitions, see 10 USCA § 2302, 41 USCA §§ 259, 403.

Kinds of contracts, see 10 USCA § 2306.

List of violators, prohibition of contract award to firms appearing on list, actions to recover underpayments, payment of sums recovered, see 41 USCA § 354.

Planning and solicitation requirements, see 41 USCA § 253a.

Required contract provisions, minimum wages, see 41 USCA § 351.

Violations, see 41 USCA § 352.

Notes of Decisions

Wage revisions 1

1 Wage revisions

Wage revisions made during base period of contracts to provide key entry operators of Postal Service, after discovery that original wage determinations were low, were governed by changes clause of contracts rather than price adjustment clause and, thus, contractor could recover indirect costs associated with revised wage determination, including general and administrative costs, overhead, and profit. 29 C.F.R. § 4.4(d); 48 C.F.R. §§ 22.1004(b), 22.1007. Lockheed Support Systems, Inc. v. U.S., 36 Fed. Cl. 424, 3 Wage & Hour Cas. 2d (BNA) 785 (1996). United States ⊙⊷74(12.1)

§ 22.1008 Procedures for obtaining wage determinations.

§ 22.1008-1 Obtaining wage determinations.

(a) Contracting officers may obtain most prevailing wage determinations using the WDOL website. Contracting officers may also use the Department of Labor's e98 electronic process, located on the WDOL website, to request a wage determination directly from the Department of Labor. If the WDOL database does not contain the applicable prevailing wage determination for a contract action, the contracting officer must use the e98 process to request a wage determination from the Department of Labor.

(b) In using the e98 process to obtain prevailing wage determinations, contracting officers shall provide as complete and accurate information on the e98 as possible. Contracting officers shall ensure that the email address submitted on an e98 request is accurate.

(c) The contracting officer must anticipate the amount of time required to gather the information necessary to obtain a wage determination, including sufficient time, if necessary, to contact the Department of Labor to request wage determinations that are not available through use of the WDOL.

(d) Although the WDOL website provides assistance to the contracting agency to select the correct wage determination, the contracting agency remains responsible for the wage determination selected. If the contracting agency has used the e98 process, the Department of Labor will respond to the contracting agency based on the information provided on the e98. The contracting agency may rely upon the Department of Labor response as the correct wage determination for the contract.

(e) To obtain the applicable wage determination for each contract action, the contracting officer shall determine the following information concerning the service employees expected to be employed by the contractor and any subcontractors in performing the contract:

(1) Determine the classes of service employees to be utilized in performance of the contract using the Wage and Hour Division's *Service Contract Act Directory of Occupations* (Directory). The Directory can be found on WDOL's Library Page, and is for sale by the Superintendent of Documents, U.S. Government Printing Office.

(2) Determine the locality where the services will be performed (see 22.1009).

(3) Determine whether 41 U.S.C. 6707(c) applies (see 22.1008-2, 22.1010 and 22.1002-2).

(4) Determine the wage rate that would be paid each class if employed by the agency and subject to the wage provisions of 5 U.S.C. 5341 and/or 5332 (see 22.1016).

(f) If the contracting officer has questions regarding the procedures for obtaining a wage determination, or questions regarding the selection of a wage determination, the contracting officer should request assistance from the agency labor advisor.

United States Code Annotated

Contract requirements, see 41 USCA § 254.

Contracts, planning, solicitation, evaluation, and award procedures, see 10 USCA § 2305.

Definitions, see 10 USCA § 2302, 41 USCA §§ 259, 403.

Kinds of contracts, see 10 USCA § 2306.

List of violators, prohibition of contract award to firms appearing on list, actions to recover underpayments, payment of sums recovered, see 41 USCA § 354.

Planning and solicitation requirements, see 41 USCA § 253a.

Required contract provisions, minimum wages, see 41 USCA § 351.

Violations, see 41 USCA § 352.

§ 22.1008-2 Successorship with incumbent contractor collective bargaining agreement.

(a) Early in the acquisition cycle, the contracting officer shall determine whether 41 U.S.C. 6707(c) affects the new acquisition. The contracting officer shall determine whether there is a predecessor contract covered by the Service Contract Labor Standards statute and, if so, whether the incumbent prime contractor or its subcontractors and any of their employees have a collective bargaining agreement.

(b) 41 U.S.C. 6707(c) provides that a successor contractor must pay wages and fringe benefits (including accrued wages and benefits and prospective increases) to service employees at least equal to those agreed upon by a predecessor contractor under the following conditions:

(1) The services to be furnished under the proposed contract will be substantially the same as services being furnished by an incumbent contractor whose contract the proposed contract will succeed.

(2) The services will be performed in the same locality.

(3) The incumbent prime contractor or subcontractor is furnishing such services through the use of service employees whose wages and fringe benefits are the subject of one or more collective bargaining agreements.

(c) The application of 41 U.S.C. 6707(c) is subject to the following limitations:

(1) 41 U.S.C. 6707(c) will not apply if the incumbent contractor enters into a collective bargaining agreement for the first time and the agreement does not become effective until after the expiration of the incumbent's contract.

(2) If the incumbent contractor enters into a new or revised collective bargaining agree-

ment during the period of the incumbent's performance on the current contract, the terms of the new or revised agreement shall not be effective for the purposes of 41 U.S.C. 6707(c) under the following conditions:

   (i) (A) In sealed bidding, the contracting agency receives notice of the terms of the collective bargaining agreement less than 10 days before bid opening and finds that there is not reasonable time still available to notify bidders (see 22.1002-2(a)); or

      (B) For contractual actions other than sealed bidding, the contracting agency receives notice of the terms of the collective bargaining agreement after award, provided that the start of performance is within 30 days of award (see 22.1002-2(b)); and

   (ii) The contracting officer has given both the incumbent contractor and its employees' collective bargaining agent timely written notification of the applicable acquisition dates (see 22.1010).

(d) (1) If 41 U.S.C. 6707(c) applies, the contracting officer shall obtain a copy of any collective bargaining agreement between an incumbent contractor or subcontractor and its employees. Obtaining a copy of an incumbent contractor's collective bargaining agreement may involve coordination with the administrative contracting officer responsible for administering the predecessor contract. (Paragraph (m) of the clause at 52.222-41, Service Contract Labor Standards, requires the incumbent prime contractor to furnish the contracting officer a copy of each collective bargaining agreement.)

   (2) If the contracting officer has timely received the collective bargaining agreement, the contracting officer may use the WDOL website to prepare a wage determination referencing the agreement and incorporate that wage determination, attached to a complete copy of the collective bargaining agreement, into the successor contract action. In using the WDOL process, it is not necessary to submit a copy of the collective bargaining agreement to the Department of Labor unless requested to do so.

   (3) The contracting officer may also use the e98 process on WDOL to request that the Department of Labor prepare the cover wage determination. The Department of Labor's response to the e98 may include a request for the contracting officer to submit a complete copy of the collective bargaining agreement. Any questions regarding the applicability of the Service Contract Labor Standards statute to a collective bargaining agreement should be directed to the agency labor advisor.

(e) (1) 41 U.S.C. 6707(c) will not apply if the Secretary of Labor determines (i) after a hearing, that the wages and fringe benefits in the predecessor contractor's collective bargaining agreement are substantially at variance with those which prevail for services of a similar character in the locality, or (ii) that the wages and fringe benefits in the predecessor contractor's collective bargaining agreement are not the result of arm's length negotiations (see 22.1013 and 22.1021). The Department of Labor (DOL) has concluded that contingent collective bargaining agreement provisions that attempt to limit a contractor's obligations by means such as requiring issuance of a wage determination by the DOL, requiring inclusion of the wage determination in the contract, or requiring the Government to adequately reimburse the contractor, generally reflect a lack of arm's length negotiations.

   (2) If the contracting officer's review (see 22.1013) indicates that monetary provisions of the collective bargaining agreement may be substantially at variance or may not have been reached as a result of arm's length bargaining, the contracting officer shall immediately contact the agency labor advisor to consider if further action is warranted.

(f) If the services are being furnished at more than one location and the collectively bargained wage rates and fringe benefits are different at different locations or do not apply to one or more locations, the contracting officer shall identify the locations to which the agreements apply.

(g) If the collective bargaining agreement does not apply to all service employees under the contract, the contracting officer shall access WDOL to obtain the prevailing wage determination for those service employee classifications that are not covered by the collective bargaining agreement. The contracting officer shall separately list in the solicitation and contract the service employee classifications—

   (1) Subject to the collective bargaining agreement; and

   (2) Not subject to any collective bargaining agreement.

United States Code Annotated

Contract requirements, see 41 USCA § 254.

Contracts, planning, solicitation, evaluation, and award procedures, see 10 USCA § 2305.

Definitions, see 10 USCA § 2302, 41 USCA §§ 259, 403.

Kinds of contracts, see 10 USCA § 2306.

List of violators, prohibition of contract award to firms appearing on list, actions to recover underpayments, payment of sums recovered, see 41 USCA § 354.

Planning and solicitation requirements, see 41 USCA § 253a.

Required contract provisions, minimum wages, see 41 USCA § 351.

Violations, see 41 USCA § 352.

Notes of Decisions

Fringe benefit 1

1 Fringe benefit

For purpose of Service Contract Act, a bona fide "fringe benefit" is one which involves the present cost or the present risk of a future cost to the employer of the workers and is a benefit of the type of which its value to the recipient is capable of being ascertained in a different amount. Service Contract Act of 1965, § 2(a)(2) as amended 41 U.S.C.A. § 351(a)(2). Trinity Services, Inc. v. Marshall, 593 F.2d 1250, 24 Wage & Hour Cas. (BNA) 216, 25 Cont. Cas. Fed. (CCH) P 82955, 85 Lab. Cas. (CCH) P 33731 (D.C. Cir. 1978). Labor And Employment ☞2304

Seniority is not a "fringe benefit" within meaning of Service Contract Act but, rather, is a means of determining how wages and fringe benefits are to be allocated. Service Contract Act of 1965, §§ 2(a)(2), 4(c) as amended 41 U.S.C.A. §§ 351(a)(2), 353(c). Trinity Services, Inc. v. Marshall, 593 F.2d 1250, 24 Wage & Hour Cas. (BNA) 216, 25 Cont. Cas. Fed. (CCH) P 82955, 85 Lab. Cas. (CCH) P 33731 (D.C. Cir. 1978). Labor And Employment ☞2304

A pure severance payment obligation under which any employer might incur an obligation to make payments with its employees when it lays them off constitutes a bona fide "fringe benefit" for purpose of Service Contract Act. Service Contract Act of 1965, § 2(a)(2) as amended 41 U.S.C.A. § 351(a)(2). Trinity Services, Inc. v. Marshall, 593 F.2d 1250, 24 Wage & Hour Cas. (BNA) 216, 25 Cont. Cas. Fed. (CCH) P 82955, 85 Lab. Cas. (CCH) P 33731 (D.C. Cir. 1978). Labor And Employment ☞2304

§ 22.1009 Place of performance unknown.

§ 22.1009-1 General.

If the place of performance is unknown, the contracting officer may use the procedures in this section. The contracting officer should first attempt to identify the specific places or geographical areas where the services might be performed (see 22.1009-2) and then may follow the procedures either in 22.1009-3 or in 22.1009-4.

United States Code Annotated

Contract requirements, see 41 USCA § 254.

Contracts, planning, solicitation, evaluation, and award procedures, see 10 USCA § 2305.

Definitions, see 10 USCA § 2302, 41 USCA §§ 259, 403.

Kinds of contracts, see 10 USCA § 2306.

List of violators, prohibition of contract award to firms appearing on list, actions to recover underpayments, payment of sums recovered, see 41 USCA § 354.

Planning and solicitation requirements, see 41 USCA § 253a.

Required contract provisions, minimum wages, see 41 USCA § 351.

Violations, see 41 USCA § 352.

§ 22.1009-2 Attempt to identify possible places of performance.

The contracting officer should attempt to identify the specific places or geographical areas where the services might be performed. The following may indicate possible places of performance:

(a) Locations of previous contractors and their competitors.

(b) Databases available via the Internet for lists of prospective offerors and contractors.

(c) Responses to a presolicitation notice (see 5.204).

United States Code Annotated

Contract requirements, see 41 USCA § 254.

Contracts, planning, solicitation, evaluation, and award procedures, see 10 USCA § 2305.

Definitions, see 10 USCA § 2302, 41 USCA §§ 259, 403.

Kinds of contracts, see 10 USCA § 2306.

List of violators, prohibition of contract award to firms appearing on list, actions to recover underpayments, payment of sums recovered, see 41 USCA § 354.

Planning and solicitation requirements, see 41 USCA § 253a.

Required contract provisions, minimum wages, see 41 USCA § 351.

Violations, see 41 USCA § 352.

§ 22.1009-3 All possible places of performance identified.

(a) If the contracting officer can identify all the possible places or areas of performance (even though the actual place of performance will not be known until the successful offeror is chosen), the contracting officer shall obtain a wage determination for each locality where services may be performed (see 22.1008).

(b) If the contracting officer subsequently learns of any potential offerors in previously unidentified places before the closing date for submission of offers, the contracting officer shall—

(1) Obtain wage determinations for the additional places of performance and amend the solicitation to include all wage determinations. If necessary, the contracting officer shall extend the time for submission of final offers; and

(2) Follow the procedures in 22.1009-4.

United States Code Annotated

Contract requirements, see 41 USCA § 254.

Contracts, planning, solicitation, evaluation, and award procedures, see 10 USCA § 2305.

Definitions, see 10 USCA § 2302, 41 USCA §§ 259, 403.

Kinds of contracts, see 10 USCA § 2306.

List of violators, prohibition of contract award to firms appearing on list, actions to recover underpayments, payment of sums recovered, see 41 USCA § 354.

Planning and solicitation requirements, see 41 USCA § 253a.

Required contract provisions, minimum wages, see 41 USCA § 351.

Violations, see 41 USCA § 352.

§ 22.1009-4 All possible places of performance not identified.

If the contracting officer believes that there may be offerors interested in performing in unidentified places or areas, the contracting officer may use the following procedures:

(a) Include the following information in the synopsis and solicitation:

(1) That the place of performance is unknown.

(2) The possible places or areas of performance that the contracting officer has already identified.

(3) That the contracting officer will obtain wage determinations for additional possible places of performance if asked to do so in writing.

(4) The time and date by which offerors must notify the contracting officer of additional places of performance.

(b) Include the information required by paragraphs (a)(2) and (a)(4) of this section in the clause at 52.222-49, Service Contract Labor Standards–Place of Performance Unknown (see 22.1006(f)). The closing date for receipt of offerors' requests for wage determinations for additional possible places of performance should allow reasonable time for potential offerors to review the solicitation and determine their interest in competing. Generally, 10 to 15 days from the date of issuance of the solicitation may be considered a reasonable period of time.

(c) The procedures in 14.304 shall apply to late receipt of offerors' requests for wage determinations for additional places of performance. However, late receipt of an offeror's request for a wage determination for additional places of performance does not preclude the offeror's competing for the proposed acquisition.

(d) If the contracting officer receives any timely requests for wage determinations for additional places of performance the contracting officer shall—

(1) Obtain wage determinations for the additional places of performance; and

(2) Amend the solicitation to include all wage determinations and, if necessary, extend the time for submission of final offers.

(e) If the successful offeror did not make a timely request for a wage determination and will perform in a place of performance for which the contracting officer therefore did not request a wage determination, the contracting officer shall—

(1) Award the contract;

(2) Obtain a wage determination; and

(3) Incorporate the wage determination in the contract, retroactive to the date of contract award and with no adjustment in contract price, pursuant to the clause at 52.222-49, Service Contract Labor Standards–Place of Performance Unknown.

United States Code Annotated

Contract requirements, see 41 USCA § 254.

Contracts, planning, solicitation, evaluation, and award procedures, see 10 USCA § 2305.

Definitions, see 10 USCA § 2302, 41 USCA §§ 259, 403.

Kinds of contracts, see 10 USCA § 2306.

List of violators, prohibition of contract award to firms appearing on list, actions to recover underpayments, payment of sums recovered, see 41 USCA § 354.

Planning and solicitation requirements, see 41 USCA § 253a.

Required contract provisions, minimum wages, see 41 USCA § 351.

Violations, see 41 USCA § 352.

§ 22.1010 Notification to interested parties under collective bargaining agreements.

(a) The contracting officer should determine whether the incumbent prime contractor's or its subcontractors' service employees performing on the current contract are represented by a collective bargaining agent. If there is a collective bargaining agent, the contracting officer shall give both the incumbent contractor and its employees' collective bargaining agent written notification of—

(1) The forthcoming successor contract and the applicable acquisition dates (issuance of solicitation, opening of bids, commencement of negotiations, award of contract, or start of performance, as the case may be); or

(2) The forthcoming contract modification and applicable acquisition dates (exercise of option, extension of contract, change in scope, or start of performance, as the case may be); or

(3) The forthcoming multiple year contract anniversary date (annual anniversary date or biennial date, as the case may be).

(b) This written notification must be given at least 30 days in advance of the earliest applicable acquisition date or the applicable annual or biennial anniversary date in order for the time-of-receipt limitations in paragraphs 22.1012-2(a) and (b) to apply. The contracting officer shall retain a copy of the notification in the contract file.

United States Code Annotated

Contract requirements, see 41 USCA § 254.

Contracts, planning, solicitation, evaluation, and award procedures, see 10 USCA § 2305.

Definitions, see 10 USCA § 2302, 41 USCA §§ 259, 403.

Kinds of contracts, see 10 USCA § 2306.

List of violators, prohibition of contract award to firms appearing on list, actions to recover underpayments, payment of sums recovered, see 41 USCA § 354.

Planning and solicitation requirements, see 41 USCA § 253a.

Required contract provisions, minimum wages, see 41 USCA § 351.

Violations, see 41 USCA § 352.

§ 22.1011 [Reserved]

§ 22.1012 Applicability of revisions to wage determinations.

§ 22.1012-1 Prevailing wage determinations.

(a) (1) The Wage and Hour Administrator may issue revisions to prevailing wage determinations periodically. The need for inclusion of a revised prevailing wage determination in a solicitation, contract or contract modification (see 22.1007) is determined by the date of receipt of the revised prevailing wage determination by the contracting agency. (Note the distinction between receipt by the agency and receipt by the contracting officer which may occur later.)

(i) For purposes of using WDOL, the time of receipt by the contracting agency shall be the first day of publication of the revised prevailing wage determination on the website.

(ii) For purposes of using the e98 process, the time of receipt by the contracting agency shall be the date the agency receives actual notice of a new or revised prevailing wage determination from the Department of Labor as an e98 response.

(2) In selecting a prevailing wage determination from the WDOL website for use in a solicitation or other contract action, the contracting officer shall monitor the WDOL website to determine whether the applicable wage determination has been revised. Revisions published on the WDOL website or otherwise communicated to the contracting officer within the timeframes prescribed at 22.1012-1(b) and (c) are effective and must be included in the resulting contract. Monitoring can be accomplished by use of the WDOL website's "Alert Service".

(b) The following shall apply when contracting by sealed bidding: a revised prevailing wage determination shall not be effective if it is received by the contracting agency less than 10 days before the opening of bids, and the contracting officer finds that there is not reasonable time to incorporate the revision in the solicitation.

(c) For contractual actions other than sealed bidding, a revised prevailing wage determination received by the contracting agency after award of a new contract or a modification as specified in 22.1007(b) shall not be effective provided that the start of performance is within 30 days of the award or the specified modification. If the contract does not specify a start of performance date which is within 30 days of the award or the specified modification, and if contract performance does not commence within 30 days of the award or the specified modification, any revision received by the contracting agency not less than 10 days before commencement of the work shall be effective.

(d) If the contracting officer has submitted an e98 to the Department of Labor requesting a prevailing wage determination and has not received a response within 10 days, the contracting officer shall contact the Wage and Hour Division by telephone to determine when the wage determination can be expected. (The telephone number is provided on the e98 website.)

United States Code Annotated

Contract requirements, see 41 USCA § 254.

Contracts, planning, solicitation, evaluation, and award procedures, see 10 USCA § 2305.

Definitions, see 10 USCA § 2302, 41 USCA §§ 259, 403.

Kinds of contracts, see 10 USCA § 2306.

List of violators, prohibition of contract award to firms appearing on list, actions to recover underpayments, payment of sums recovered, see 41 USCA § 354.

Planning and solicitation requirements, see 41 USCA § 253a.

Required contract provisions, minimum wages, see 41 USCA § 351.

Violations, see 41 USCA § 352.

Notes of Decisions

Fringe benefit 1

1 Fringe benefit

For purpose of Service Contract Act, a bona fide "fringe benefit" is one which involves the present cost or the present risk of a future cost to the employer of the workers and is a benefit of the type of which its value to the recipient is capable of being ascertained in a different amount. Service Contract Act of 1965, § 2(a)(2) as amended 41 U.S.C.A. § 351(a)(2). Trinity Services, Inc. v. Marshall, 593 F.2d 1250, 24 Wage & Hour Cas. (BNA) 216, 25 Cont. Cas. Fed. (CCH) P 82955, 85 Lab. Cas. (CCH) P 33731 (D.C. Cir. 1978). Labor And Employment ⚮2304

Seniority is not a "fringe benefit" within meaning of Service Contract Act but, rather, is a means of determining how wages and fringe benefits are to be allocated. Service Contract Act of 1965, §§ 2(a)(2), 4(c) as amended 41 U.S.C.A. §§ 351(a)(2), 353(c). Trinity Services, Inc. v. Marshall, 593 F.2d 1250, 24 Wage & Hour Cas. (BNA) 216, 25 Cont. Cas. Fed. (CCH) P 82955, 85 Lab. Cas. (CCH) P 33731 (D.C. Cir. 1978). Labor And Employment ⚮2304

A pure severance payment obligation under which any employer might incur an obligation to make payments with its employees when it lays them off constitutes a bona fide "fringe benefit" for purpose of Service Contract Act. Service Contract Act of 1965, § 2(a)(2) as amended 41 U.S.C.A. § 351(a)(2). Trinity Services, Inc. v. Marshall, 593 F.2d 1250, 24 Wage & Hour Cas. (BNA) 216, 25 Cont. Cas. Fed. (CCH) P 82955, 85 Lab. Cas. (CCH) P 33731 (D.C. Cir. 1978). Labor And Employment ⚮2304

§ 22.1012-2 Wage determinations based on collective bargaining agreements.

(a) In sealed bidding, a new or changed collective bargaining agreement shall not be effective under 41 U.S.C. 6707(c) if the contracting agency has received notice of the terms of the new or changed collective bargaining agreement less than 10 days before bid opening and the contracting officer determines that there is not reasonable time to incorporate the new or changed terms of the collective bargaining agreement in the solicitation.

(b) For contractual actions other than sealed bidding, a new or changed collective bargaining agreement shall not be effective under 41 U.S.C. 6707(c) if notice of the terms of the new or changed collective bargaining agreement is received by the contracting agency after award of a successor contract or a modification as specified in 22.1007(b), provided that the contract start of performance is within 30 days of the award of the contract or of the specified modification. If the contract does not specify a start of performance date which is within 30 days of the award of the contract or of the specified modification, or if contract performance does not commence within 30 days of the award of the contract or of the specified modification, any notice of the terms of a new or changed collective bargaining agreement received by the agency not less than 10 days before commencement of the work shall be effective for purposes of the successor contract under 41 U.S.C. 6707(c).

(c) The limitations in paragraphs (a) and (b) of this subsection shall apply only if timely notification required in 22.1010 has been given.

(d) If the contracting officer has submitted an e98 to Department of Labor requesting a wage determination based on a collective bargaining agreement and has not received a response from the Department of Labor within 10 days, the contracting officer shall contact the Wage and Hour Division by telephone to determine when the wage determination can be expected. (The telephone number is provided on the e98 website.) If the Department of Labor is unable to provide the wage determination by the latest date needed to maintain the acquisition schedule, the contracting officer shall incorporate the collective bargaining agreement itself in a solicitation or other contract action (*e.g.*, exercise of option) and include a wage determination referencing that collective bargaining agreement created by use of the WDOL website (see 22.1008-1(d)(2)).

United States Code Annotated

Contract requirements, see 41 USCA § 254.

Contracts, planning, solicitation, evaluation, and award procedures, see 10 USCA § 2305.

Definitions, see 10 USCA § 2302, 41 USCA §§ 259, 403.

Kinds of contracts, see 10 USCA § 2306.

List of violators, prohibition of contract award to firms appearing on list, actions to recover underpayments, payment of sums recovered, see 41 USCA § 354.

Planning and solicitation requirements, see 41 USCA § 253a.

Required contract provisions, minimum wages, see 41 USCA § 351.

Violations, see 41 USCA § 352.

Notes of Decisions
Fringe benefit 1

1 Fringe benefit

For purpose of Service Contract Act, a bona fide "fringe benefit" is one which involves the present cost or the present risk of a future cost to the employer of the workers and is a benefit of the type of which its value to the recipient is capable of being ascertained in a different amount. Service Contract Act of 1965, § 2(a)(2) as amended 41 U.S.C.A. § 351(a)(2). Trinity Services, Inc. v. Marshall, 593 F.2d 1250, 24 Wage & Hour Cas. (BNA) 216, 25 Cont. Cas. Fed. (CCH) P 82955, 85 Lab. Cas. (CCH) P 33731 (D.C. Cir. 1978). Labor And Employment ⚖2304

Seniority is not a "fringe benefit" within meaning of Service Contract Act but, rather, is a means of determining how wages and fringe benefits are to be allocated. Service Contract Act of 1965, §§ 2(a)(2), 4(c) as amended 41 U.S.C.A. §§ 351(a)(2), 353(c). Trinity Services, Inc. v. Marshall, 593 F.2d 1250, 24 Wage & Hour Cas. (BNA) 216, 25 Cont. Cas. Fed. (CCH) P 82955, 85 Lab. Cas. (CCH) P 33731 (D.C. Cir. 1978). Labor And Employment ⚖2304

A pure severance payment obligation under which any employer might incur an obligation to make payments with its employees when it lays them off constitutes a bona fide "fringe benefit" for purpose of Service Contract Act. Service Contract Act of 1965, § 2(a)(2) as amended 41 U.S.C.A. § 351(a)(2). Trinity Services, Inc. v. Marshall, 593 F.2d 1250, 24 Wage & Hour Cas. (BNA) 216, 25 Cont. Cas. Fed. (CCH) P 82955, 85 Lab. Cas. (CCH) P 33731 (D.C. Cir. 1978). Labor And Employment ⚖2304

§ 22.1013 Review of wage determination.

(a) *Based on incumbent collective bargaining agreement.* (1) If wages, fringe benefits, or periodic increases provided for in a collective bargaining agreement vary substantially from those prevailing for similar services in the locality, the contracting officer shall immediately contact the agency labor advisor to consider instituting the procedures in 22.1021.

(1) If the contracting officer believes that an incumbent or predecessor contractor's agreement was not the result of arm's length negotiations, the contracting officer shall contact the agency labor advisor to determine appropriate action.

(b) *Based on other than incumbent collective bargaining agreement.* Upon receiving a wage determination not predicated upon a collective bargaining agreement, the contracting officer shall ascertain—

(1) If the wage determination does not conform with wages and fringe benefits prevailing for similar services in the locality; or

(2) If the wage determination contains significant errors or omissions. If either subparagraph (b)(1) or (b)(2) of this section is evident, the contracting officer shall contact the agency labor advisor to determine appropriate action.

United States Code Annotated

Contract requirements, see 41 USCA § 254.

Contracts, planning, solicitation, evaluation, and award procedures, see 10 USCA § 2305.

Definitions, see 10 USCA § 2302, 41 USCA §§ 259, 403.

Kinds of contracts, see 10 USCA § 2306.

List of violators, prohibition of contract award to firms appearing on list, actions to recover underpayments, payment of sums recovered, see 41 USCA § 354.

Planning and solicitation requirements, see 41 USCA § 253a.

Required contract provisions, minimum wages, see 41 USCA § 351.

Violations, see 41 USCA § 352.

Notes of Decisions
Fringe benefit 1

1 Fringe benefit

For purpose of Service Contract Act, a bona fide "fringe benefit" is one which involves the present cost or the present risk of a future cost to the employer of the workers and is a benefit of the type of which its value to the recipient is capable of being ascertained in a different amount. Service Contract Act of 1965, § 2(a)(2) as amended 41 U.S.C.A. § 351(a)(2). Trinity Services, Inc. v. Marshall, 593 F.2d 1250, 24 Wage & Hour Cas. (BNA) 216, 25 Cont. Cas. Fed. (CCH) P 82955, 85 Lab. Cas. (CCH) P 33731 (D.C. Cir. 1978). Labor And Employment ☞2304

Seniority is not a "fringe benefit" within meaning of Service Contract Act but, rather, is a means of determining how wages and fringe benefits are to be allocated. Service Contract Act of 1965, §§ 2(a)(2), 4(c) as amended 41 U.S.C.A. §§ 351(a)(2), 353(c). Trinity Services, Inc. v. Marshall, 593 F.2d 1250, 24 Wage & Hour Cas. (BNA) 216, 25 Cont. Cas. Fed. (CCH) P 82955, 85 Lab. Cas. (CCH) P 33731 (D.C. Cir. 1978). Labor And Employment ☞2304

A pure severance payment obligation under which any employer might incur an obligation to make payments with its employees when it lays them off constitutes a bona fide "fringe benefit" for purpose of Service Contract Act. Service Contract Act of 1965, § 2(a)(2) as amended 41 U.S.C.A. § 351(a)(2). Trinity Services, Inc. v. Marshall, 593 F.2d 1250, 24 Wage & Hour Cas. (BNA) 216, 25 Cont. Cas. Fed. (CCH) P 82955, 85 Lab. Cas. (CCH) P 33731 (D.C. Cir. 1978). Labor And Employment ☞2304

§ 22.1014 Delay over 60 days in bid opening or commencement of work.

If a wage determination was obtained through the e98 process, and bid opening, or commencement of work under a negotiated contract has been delayed, for whatever reason, more than 60 days from the date indicated on the previously submitted e98, the contracting officer shall submit a new e98. Any revision of a wage determination received by the contracting agency as a result of that communication shall supersede the earlier response as the wage determination applicable to the particular acquisition subject to the time frames in 22.1012-1(b) and (c).

United States Code Annotated

Contract requirements, see 41 USCA § 254.

Contracts, planning, solicitation, evaluation, and award procedures, see 10 USCA § 2305.

Definitions, see 10 USCA § 2302, 41 USCA §§ 259, 403.

Kinds of contracts, see 10 USCA § 2306.

List of violators, prohibition of contract award to firms appearing on list, actions to recover underpayments, payment of sums recovered, see 41 USCA § 354.

Planning and solicitation requirements, see 41 USCA § 253a.

Required contract provisions, minimum wages, see 41 USCA § 351.

Violations, see 41 USCA § 352.

§ 22.1015 Discovery of errors by the Department of Labor.

If the Department of Labor discovers and determines, whether before or after a contract award, that a contracting officer made an erroneous determination that the Service Contract Labor Standards statute did not apply to a particular acquisition or failed to include an appropriate wage determination in a covered contract, the contracting officer, within 30 days of notification by the Department of Labor, shall include in the contract the clause at 52.222-41 and any applicable wage determination issued by the Administrator. If the contract is subject to 41 U.S.C. 6707(c), the Administrator may require retroactive application of that wage determination. The contracting officer shall equitably adjust the contract price to reflect any changed cost of performance resulting from incorporating a wage determination or revision.

United States Code Annotated

Contract requirements, see 41 USCA § 254.

Contracts, planning, solicitation, evaluation, and award procedures, see 10 USCA § 2305.

Definitions, see 10 USCA § 2302, 41 USCA §§ 259, 403.

Kinds of contracts, see 10 USCA § 2306.

List of violators, prohibition of contract award to firms appearing on list, actions to recover underpayments, payment of sums recovered, see 41 USCA § 354.

Planning and solicitation requirements, see 41 USCA § 253a.

Required contract provisions, minimum wages, see 41 USCA § 351.

Violations, see 41 USCA § 352.

§ 22.1016 Statement of equivalent rates for Federal hires.

(a) The statement required under the clause at 52.222-42, Statement of Equivalent Rates for Federal Hires, (see 22.1006(b)) shall set forth those wage rates and fringe benefits that would be paid by the contracting activity to the various classes of service employees expected to be utilized under the contract if 5 U.S.C. 5332 (General Schedule—white collar) and/or 5 U.S.C. 5341 (Wage Board—blue collar) were applicable.

(b) Procedures for computation of these rates are as follows:

(1) Wages paid blue collar employees shall be the basic hourly rate for each class. The rate shall be Wage Board pay schedule step two for nonsupervisory service employees and step three for supervisory service employees.

(2) Wages paid white collar employees shall be an hourly rate for each class. The rate shall be obtained by dividing the general pay schedule step one biweekly rate by 80.

(3) Local civilian personnel offices can assist in determining and providing grade and salary data.

United States Code Annotated

Contract requirements, see 41 USCA § 254.

Contracts, planning, solicitation, evaluation, and award procedures, see 10 USCA § 2305.

Definitions, see 10 USCA § 2302; 41 USCA §§ 259, 403.

Kinds of contracts, see 10 USCA § 2306.

List of violators, prohibition of contract award to firms appearing on list, actions to recover underpayments, payment of sums recovered, see 41 USCA § 354.

Planning and solicitation requirements, see 41 USCA § 253a.

Required contract provisions, minimum wages, see 41 USCA § 351.

Violations, see 41 USCA § 352.

Notes of Decisions

Fringe benefit 1

1 Fringe benefit

For purpose of Service Contract Act, a bona fide "fringe benefit" is one which involves the present cost or the present risk of a future cost to the employer of the workers and is a benefit of the type of which its value to the recipient is capable of being ascertained in a different amount. Service Contract Act of 1965, § 2(a)(2) as amended 41 U.S.C.A. § 351(a)(2). Trinity Services, Inc. v. Marshall, 593 F.2d 1250, 24 Wage & Hour Cas. (BNA) 216, 25 Cont. Cas. Fed. (CCH) P 82955, 85 Lab. Cas. (CCH) P 33731 (D.C. Cir. 1978). Labor And Employment ☞2304

Seniority is not a "fringe benefit" within meaning of Service Contract Act but, rather, is a means of determining how wages and fringe benefits are to be allocated. Service Contract Act of 1965, §§ 2(a)(2), 4(c) as amended 41 U.S.C.A. §§ 351(a)(2), 353(c). Trinity Services, Inc. v. Marshall, 593 F.2d 1250, 24 Wage & Hour Cas. (BNA) 216, 25 Cont. Cas. Fed. (CCH) P 82955, 85 Lab. Cas. (CCH) P 33731 (D.C. Cir. 1978). Labor And Employment ☞2304

A pure severance payment obligation under which any employer might incur an obligation to make payments with its employees when it lays them off constitutes a bona fide "fringe benefit" for purpose of Service Contract Act. Service Contract Act of 1965, § 2(a)(2) as amended 41 U.S.C.A. § 351(a)(2). Trinity Services, Inc. v. Marshall, 593 F.2d 1250, 24 Wage & Hour Cas. (BNA) 216, 25 Cont. Cas. Fed. (CCH) P 82955, 85 Lab. Cas. (CCH) P 33731 (D.C. Cir. 1978). Labor And Employment ☞2304

§ 22.1017 [Reserved]

§ 22.1018 Notification to contractors and employees.

The contracting officer shall take the following steps to ensure that service employees are notified of minimum wages and fringe benefits.

(a) As soon as possible after contract award, inform the contractor of the labor standards requirements of the contract relating to the Service Contract Labor Standards statute and of the contractor's responsibilities under these requirements, unless it is clear that the contractor is fully informed.

(b) At the time of award, furnish the contractor Department of Labor Publication WH-1313, Notice to Employees Working on Government Contracts, for posting at a prominent and accessible place at the worksite before contract performance begins. The publication advises employees of the compensation (wages and fringe benefits) required to be paid or furnished under the Service Contract Labor Standards statute and satisfies the notice requirements in paragraph (g) of the clause at 52.222-41, Service Contract Labor Standards.

(c) Attach any applicable wage determination to Publication WH-1313.

United States Code Annotated

Contract requirements, see 41 USCA § 254.

Contracts, planning, solicitation, evaluation, and award procedures, see 10 USCA § 2305.

Definitions, see 10 USCA § 2302, 41 USCA §§ 259, 403.

Kinds of contracts, see 10 USCA § 2306.

List of violators, prohibition of contract award to firms appearing on list, actions to recover underpayments, payment of sums recovered, see 41 USCA § 354.

Planning and solicitation requirements, see 41 USCA § 253a.

Required contract provisions, minimum wages, see 41 USCA § 351.

Violations, see 41 USCA § 352.

Notes of Decisions

Fringe benefit 1

1 Fringe benefit

For purpose of Service Contract Act, a bona fide "fringe benefit" is one which involves the present cost or the present risk of a future cost to the employer of the workers and is a benefit of the type of which its value to the recipient is capable of being ascertained in a different amount. Service Contract Act of 1965, § 2(a)(2) as amended 41 U.S.C.A. § 351(a)(2). Trinity Services, Inc. v. Marshall, 593 F.2d 1250, 24 Wage & Hour Cas. (BNA) 216, 25 Cont. Cas. Fed. (CCH) P 82955, 85 Lab. Cas. (CCH) P 33731 (D.C. Cir. 1978). Labor And Employment ☞2304

Seniority is not a "fringe benefit" within meaning of Service Contract Act but, rather, is a means of determining how wages and fringe benefits are to be allocated. Service Contract Act of 1965, §§ 2(a)(2), 4(c) as amended 41 U.S.C.A. §§ 351(a)(2), 353(c). Trinity Services, Inc. v. Marshall, 593 F.2d 1250, 24 Wage & Hour Cas. (BNA) 216, 25 Cont. Cas. Fed. (CCH) P 82955, 85 Lab. Cas. (CCH) P 33731 (D.C. Cir. 1978). Labor And Employment ☞2304

A pure severance payment obligation under which any employer might incur an obligation to make payments with its employees when it lays them off constitutes a bona fide "fringe benefit" for purpose of Service Contract Act. Service Contract Act of 1965, § 2(a)(2) as amended 41 U.S.C.A. § 351(a)(2). Trinity Services, Inc. v. Marshall, 593 F.2d 1250, 24 Wage & Hour Cas. (BNA) 216, 25 Cont. Cas. Fed. (CCH) P 82955, 85 Lab. Cas. (CCH) P 33731 (D.C. Cir. 1978). Labor And Employment ☞2304

§ 22.1019 Additional classes of service employees.

(a) If the contracting officer is aware that contract performance involves classes of service employees not included in the wage determination, the contracting officer shall require the contractor to classify the unlisted classes so as to provide a reasonable relationship (*i.e.*, appropriate level of skill comparison) between the unlisted classifications and the classifications listed in the determination (see paragraph (c) of the clause at 52.222-41, Service

Contract Labor Standards). The contractor shall initiate the conforming procedure before unlisted classes of employees perform contract work. The contractor shall submit Standard Form (SF) 1444, Request For Authorization of Additional Classification and Rate. The contracting officer shall review the proposed classification and rate and promptly submit the completed SF 1444 (which must include information regarding the agreement or disagreement of the employees' representative or the employees themselves together with the agency recommendation) and all other pertinent information to the Wage and Hour Division. Within 30 days of receipt of the request, the Wage and Hour Division will (1) approve, modify, or disapprove the request when the parties are in agreement or (2) render a final determination in the event of disagreement among the parties. If the Wage and Hour Division will require more than 30 days to take action, it will notify the contracting officer within 30 days of receipt of the request that additional time is necessary.

(b) Some wage determinations will list a series of classes within a job classification family, for example, Computer Operators, level I, II, and III, or Electronic Technicians, level I, II, and III, or Clerk Typist, level I and II. Generally, level I is the lowest level. It is the entry level, and establishment of a lower level through conformance is not permissible. Further, trainee classifications may not be conformed. Helpers in skilled maintenance trades (for example, electricians, machinists, and automobile mechanics) whose duties constitute, in fact, separate and distinct jobs may also be used if listed on the wage determination, but may not be conformed. Conformance may not be used to artificially split or subdivide classifications listed in the wage determination. However, conforming procedures may be used if the work which an employee performs under the contract is not within the scope of any classification listed on the wage determination, regardless of job title. (See 29 CFR 4.152.)

(c) Subminimum rates for apprentices, student learners, and disabled workers are permissible in accordance with paragraph (q) of the clause at 52.222-41, Service Contract Labor Standards.

United States Code Annotated

Contract requirements, see 41 USCA § 254.

Contracts, planning, solicitation, evaluation, and award procedures, see 10 USCA § 2305.

Definitions, see 10 USCA § 2302, 41 USCA §§ 259, 403.

Kinds of contracts, see 10 USCA § 2306.

List of violators, prohibition of contract award to firms appearing on list, actions to recover underpayments, payment of sums recovered, see 41 USCA § 354.

Planning and solicitation requirements, see 41 USCA § 253a.

Required contract provisions, minimum wages, see 41 USCA § 351.

Violations, see 41 USCA § 352.

§ 22.1020 Seniority lists.

If a contract is performed at a Federal facility where employees may be hired/retained by a succeeding contractor, the incumbent prime contractor is required to furnish a certified list of all service employees on the contractor's or subcontractor's payroll during the last month of the contract, together with anniversary dates of employment, to the contracting officer no later than 10 days before contract completion. (See paragraph (n) of the clause at 52.222-41, Service Contract Labor Standards.) At the commencement of the succeeding contract, the contracting officer shall provide a copy of the list to the successor contractor for determining employee eligibility for vacation or other fringe benefits which are based upon length of service, including service with predecessor contractors if such benefit is required by an applicable wage determination.

United States Code Annotated

Contract requirements, see 41 USCA § 254.

Contracts, planning, solicitation, evaluation, and award procedures, see 10 USCA § 2305.

Definitions, see 10 USCA § 2302, 41 USCA §§ 259, 403.

Kinds of contracts, see 10 USCA § 2306.

List of violators, prohibition of contract award to firms appearing on list, actions to recover underpayments, payment of sums recovered, see 41 USCA § 354.

Planning and solicitation requirements, see 41 USCA § 253a.

Required contract provisions, minimum wages, see 41 USCA § 351.

Violations, see 41 USCA § 352.

Notes of Decisions

Fringe benefit 1

1 Fringe benefit

For purpose of Service Contract Act, a bona fide "fringe benefit" is one which involves the present cost or the present risk of a future cost to the employer of the workers and is a benefit of the type of which its value to the recipient is capable of being ascertained in a different amount. Service Contract Act of 1965, § 2(a)(2) as amended 41 U.S.C.A. § 351(a)(2). Trinity Services, Inc. v. Marshall, 593 F.2d 1250, 24 Wage & Hour Cas. (BNA) 216, 25 Cont. Cas. Fed. (CCH) P 82955, 85 Lab. Cas. (CCH) P 33731 (D.C. Cir. 1978). Labor And Employment ⌐2304

Seniority is not a "fringe benefit" within meaning of Service Contract Act but, rather, is a means of determining how wages and fringe benefits are to be allocated. Service Contract Act of 1965, §§ 2(a)(2), 4(c) as amended 41 U.S.C.A. §§ 351(a)(2), 353(c). Trinity Services, Inc. v. Marshall, 593 F.2d 1250, 24 Wage & Hour Cas. (BNA) 216, 25 Cont. Cas. Fed. (CCH) P 82955, 85 Lab. Cas. (CCH) P 33731 (D.C. Cir. 1978). Labor And Employment ⌐2304

A pure severance payment obligation under which any employer might incur an obligation to make payments with its employees when it lays them off constitutes a bona fide "fringe benefit" for purpose of Service Contract Act. Service Contract Act of 1965, § 2(a)(2) as amended 41 U.S.C.A. § 351(a)(2). Trinity Services, Inc. v. Marshall, 593 F.2d 1250, 24 Wage & Hour Cas. (BNA) 216, 25 Cont. Cas. Fed. (CCH) P 82955, 85 Lab. Cas. (CCH) P 33731 (D.C. Cir. 1978). Labor And Employment ⌐2304

§ 22.1021 Request for hearing.

(a) A contracting agency or other interested party may request a hearing on an issue presented in 22.1013(a). To obtain a hearing for the contracting agency, the contracting officer shall submit a written request through appropriate channels (ordinarily the agency labor advisor) to—

Administrator, Wage and Hour Division
Employment Standards Administration
U.S. Department of Labor
Washington, DC 20210

(b) A request for a substantial variance hearing shall include sufficient data to show that the rates at issue vary substantially from those prevailing for similar services in the locality. The request shall also include—

(1) The number of the wage determinations at issue;

(2) The name of the contracting agency whose contract is involved;

(3) A brief description of the services to be performed under the contract;

(4) The status of the procurement and any estimated procurement dates, such as bid opening, contract award, and commencement date of the contract or its follow-up option period;

(5) A statement of the applicant's case, setting forth in detail the reasons why the applicant believes that a substantial variance exists with respect to some or all of the wages and/or fringe benefits;

(6) Names and addresses (to the extent known) of interested parties; and

(7) Any other data required by the Administrator.

(c) A request for an arm's length hearing shall include—

(1) A statement of the applicant's case, setting forth in detail the reasons why the applicant believes that the wages and fringe benefits contained in the collective bargaining agreement were not reached as a result of arm's length negotiations;

(2) A statement regarding the status of the procurement and any estimated procurement dates, such as bid opening, contract award, and commencement date of the contract

or its follow-up option period; and

(3) Names and addresses (to the extent known) of interested parties.

(d) Unless the Administrator determines that extraordinary circumstances exist, the Administrator will not consider requests for a hearing unless received as follows:

(1) For sealed bid contracts, more than 10 days before the award of the contract; or

(2) For negotiated contracts and for contracts with provisions exceeding the initial term by option, before the commencement date of the contract or the follow-up option period.

United States Code Annotated

Contract requirements, see 41 USCA § 254.

Contracts, planning, solicitation, evaluation, and award procedures, see 10 USCA § 2305.

Definitions, see 10 USCA § 2302, 41 USCA §§ 259, 403.

Kinds of contracts, see 10 USCA § 2306.

List of violators, prohibition of contract award to firms appearing on list, actions to recover underpayments, payment of sums recovered, see 41 USCA § 354.

Planning and solicitation requirements, see 41 USCA § 253a.

Required contract provisions, minimum wages, see 41 USCA § 351.

Violations, see 41 USCA § 352.

Notes of Decisions

Fringe benefit 1

1 Fringe benefit

For purpose of Service Contract Act, a bona fide "fringe benefit" is one which involves the present cost or the present risk of a future cost to the employer of the workers and is a benefit of the type of which its value to the recipient is capable of being ascertained in a different amount. Service Contract Act of 1965, § 2(a)(2) as amended 41 U.S.C.A. § 351(a)(2). Trinity Services, Inc. v. Marshall, 593 F.2d 1250, 24 Wage & Hour Cas. (BNA) 216, 25 Cont. Cas. Fed. (CCH) P 82955, 85 Lab. Cas. (CCH) P 33731 (D.C. Cir. 1978). Labor And Employment ⊙2304

Seniority is not a "fringe benefit" within meaning of Service Contract Act but, rather, is a means of determining how wages and fringe benefits are to be allocated. Service Contract Act of 1965, §§ 2(a)(2), 4(c) as amended 41 U.S.C.A. §§ 351(a)(2), 353(c). Trinity Services, Inc. v. Marshall, 593 F.2d 1250, 24 Wage & Hour Cas. (BNA) 216, 25 Cont. Cas. Fed. (CCH) P 82955, 85 Lab. Cas. (CCH) P 33731 (D.C. Cir. 1978). Labor And Employment ⊙2304

A pure severance payment obligation under which any employer might incur an obligation to make payments with its employees when it lays them off constitutes a bona fide "fringe benefit" for purpose of Service Contract Act. Service Contract Act of 1965, § 2(a)(2) as amended 41 U.S.C.A. § 351(a)(2). Trinity Services, Inc. v. Marshall, 593 F.2d 1250, 24 Wage & Hour Cas. (BNA) 216, 25 Cont. Cas. Fed. (CCH) P 82955, 85 Lab. Cas. (CCH) P 33731 (D.C. Cir. 1978). Labor And Employment ⊙2304

§ 22.1022 Withholding of contract payments.

Any violations of the clause at 52.222-41, Service Contract Labor Standards, as amended, renders the responsible contractor liable for the amount of any deductions, rebates, refunds, or underpayments (which includes nonpayment) of compensation due employees performing the contract. The contracting officer may withhold—or, upon written request of the Department of Labor from a level no lower than that of Deputy Regional Administrator, Wage and Hour Division, Employment Standards Administration, Department of Labor, shall withhold—the amount needed to pay such underpaid employees from accrued payments due the contractor on the contract, or on any other prime contract (whether subject to the Service Contract Labor Standards statute or not) with the contractor. The agency shall place the amount withheld in a deposit fund. Such withheld funds shall be transferred to the Department of Labor for disbursement to the underpaid employees on order of the Secretary (or authorized representatives), and Administrative Law Judge, or the Administrative Review Board. In addition, the Department of Labor has given blanket approval to forward withheld funds pending completion of an investigation or other administrative proceeding when disposition of withheld funds remains the final action necessary to close out a contract.

United States Code Annotated

Contract requirements, see 41 USCA § 254.

Contracts, planning, solicitation, evaluation, and award procedures, see 10 USCA § 2305.

Definitions, see 10 USCA § 2302, 41 USCA §§ 259, 403.

Kinds of contracts, see 10 USCA § 2306.

List of violators, prohibition of contract award to firms appearing on list, actions to recover underpayments, payment of sums recovered, see 41 USCA § 354.

Planning and solicitation requirements, see 41 USCA § 253a.

Required contract provisions, minimum wages, see 41 USCA § 351.

Violations, see 41 USCA § 352.

§ 22.1023 Termination for default.

As provided by the Service Contract Labor Standards statute, any contractor failure to comply with the requirements of the contract clauses related to the Service Contract Labor Standards statute may be grounds for termination for default (see paragraph (k) of the clause at 52.222-41, Service Contract Labor Standards).

United States Code Annotated

Contract requirements, see 41 USCA § 254.

Contracts, planning, solicitation, evaluation, and award procedures, see 10 USCA § 2305.

Definitions, see 10 USCA § 2302, 41 USCA §§ 259, 403.

Kinds of contracts, see 10 USCA § 2306.

List of violators, prohibition of contract award to firms appearing on list, actions to recover underpayments, payment of sums recovered, see 41 USCA § 354.

Planning and solicitation requirements, see 41 USCA § 253a.

Required contract provisions, minimum wages, see 41 USCA § 351.

Violations, see 41 USCA § 352.

§ 22.1024 Cooperation with the Department of Labor.

The contracting officer shall cooperate with Department of Labor representatives in the examination of records, interviews with service employees, and all other aspects of investigations undertaken by the Department. When asked, agencies shall furnish the Wage and Hour Administrator or a designee, any available information on contractors, subcontractors, their contracts, and the nature of the contract services. The contracting officer shall promptly refer, in writing to the appropriate regional office of the Department, apparent violations and complaints received. Employee complaints shall not be disclosed to the employer.

United States Code Annotated

Contract requirements, see 41 USCA § 254.

Contracts, planning, solicitation, evaluation, and award procedures, see 10 USCA § 2305.

Definitions, see 10 USCA § 2302, 41 USCA §§ 259, 403.

Kinds of contracts, see 10 USCA § 2306.

List of violators, prohibition of contract award to firms appearing on list, actions to recover underpayments, payment of sums recovered, see 41 USCA § 354.

Planning and solicitation requirements, see 41 USCA § 253a.

Required contract provisions, minimum wages, see 41 USCA § 351.

Violations, see 41 USCA § 352.

§ 22.1025 Ineligibility of violators.

A list of persons or firms found to be in violation of the Service Contract Labor Standards statute is contained in the System for Award Management Exclusions (see 9.404). No Government contract may be awarded to any violator so listed because of a violation of the Service Contract Labor Standards statute, or to any firm, corporation, partnership, or association in which the violator has a substantial interest, without the approval of the Secretary of Labor. This prohibition against award to an ineligible contractor applies to both prime and subcontracts.

§ 22.1026 Disputes concerning labor standards.

Disputes concerning labor standards requirements of the contract are handled under paragraph (t) of the contract clause at 52.222-41, Service Contract Labor Standards, and not under the clause at 52.233-1, Disputes.

United States Code Annotated

Contract requirements, see 41 USCA § 254.

Contracts, planning, solicitation, evaluation, and award procedures, see 10 USCA § 2305.

Definitions, see 10 USCA § 2302, 41 USCA §§ 259, 403.

Kinds of contracts, see 10 USCA § 2306.

List of violators, prohibition of contract award to firms appearing on list, actions to recover underpayments, payment of sums recovered, see 41 USCA § 354.

Planning and solicitation requirements, see 41 USCA § 253a.

Required contract provisions, minimum wages, see 41 USCA § 351.

Violations, see 41 USCA § 352.

Subpart 22.11 Professional Employee Compensation

§ 22.1101 Applicability.

The Service Contract Act of 1965, now codified at 41 U.S.C. chapter 67, Service Contract Labor Standards, was enacted to ensure that Government contractors compensate their blue-collar service workers and some white-collar service workers fairly, but it does not cover bona fide executive, administrative, or professional employees.

United States Code Annotated

Contract requirements, see 41 USCA § 254.

Contracts, planning, solicitation, evaluation, and award procedures, see 10 USCA § 2305.

Definitions, see 10 USCA § 2302, 41 USCA §§ 259, 403.

Kinds of contracts, see 10 USCA § 2306.

List of violators, prohibition of contract award to firms appearing on list, actions to recover underpayments, payment of sums recovered, see 41 USCA § 354.

Planning and solicitation requirements, see 41 USCA § 253a.

Required contract provisions, minimum wages, see 41 USCA § 351.

Violations, see 41 USCA § 352.

§ 22.1102 Definition.

"Professional employee," as used in this subpart, means any person meeting the definition of "employee employed in a bona fide . . . professional capacity" given in 29 CFR 541. The term embraces members of those professions having a recognized status based upon acquiring professional knowledge through prolonged study. Examples of these professions include accountancy, actuarial computation, architecture, dentistry, engineering, law, medicine, nursing, pharmacy, the sciences (such as biology, chemistry, and physics, and teaching). To be a professional employee, a person must not only be a professional but must be involved essentially in discharging professional duties.

United States Code Annotated

Contract requirements, see 41 USCA § 254.

Contracts, planning, solicitation, evaluation, and award procedures, see 10 USCA § 2305.

Definitions, see 10 USCA § 2302, 41 USCA §§ 259, 403.

Kinds of contracts, see 10 USCA § 2306.

List of violators, prohibition of contract award to firms appearing on list, actions to recover underpayments, payment of sums recovered, see 41 USCA § 354.

Planning and solicitation requirements, see 41 USCA § 253a.

Required contract provisions, minimum wages, see 41 USCA § 351.

Violations, see 41 USCA § 352.

§ 22.1103 Policy, procedures, and solicitation provision.

All professional employees shall be compensated fairly and properly. Accordingly, the contracting officer shall insert the provision at 52.222-46, Evaluation of Compensation for Professional Employees, in solicitations for negotiated contracts when the contract amount is expected to exceed $700,000 and services are to be provided which will require meaningful numbers of professional employees. This provision requires that offerors submit for evaluation a total compensation plan setting forth proposed salaries and fringe benefits for professional employees working on the contract. Supporting information will include data, such as recognized national and regional compensation surveys and studies of professional, public and private organizations, used in establishing the total compensation structure. Plans indicating unrealistically low professional employee compensation may be assessed adversely as one of the factors considered in making an award.

United States Code Annotated

Contract requirements, see 41 USCA § 254.

Contracts, planning, solicitation, evaluation, and award procedures, see 10 USCA § 2305.

Definitions, see 10 USCA § 2302, 41 USCA §§ 259, 403.

Kinds of contracts, see 10 USCA § 2306.

List of violators, prohibition of contract award to firms appearing on list, actions to recover underpayments, payment of sums recovered, see 41 USCA § 354.

Planning and solicitation requirements, see 41 USCA § 253a.

Required contract provisions, minimum wages, see 41 USCA § 351.

Violations, see 41 USCA § 352.

Notes of Decisions

In general 1

1 In general

Even assuming that General Services Administration Board of Contract Appeals (GSBCA) erred in holding that soliciting agency's cost evaluation was proper, and that contracting officer did not abuse his discretion by not including "professional employee compensation clause" in solicitation, unsuccessful bidder on government services contract failed to demonstrate that such errors were prejudicial, where alleged errors only affected degree of price differential between its bid and less expensive bid of successful bidder, and there was no evidence that result would have been different if price differential was not as great. Statistica, Inc. v. Christopher, 102 F.3d 1577, 41 Cont. Cas. Fed. (CCH) P 77026 (Fed. Cir. 1996). United States ⊜64.55(1)

Subpart 22.12 Nondisplacement of Qualified Workers Under Service Contracts

§ 22.1200 Scope of subpart.

This subpart prescribes policies and procedures for implementing Executive Order 13495 of January 30, 2009, Nondisplacement of Qualified Workers Under Service Contracts, and related Secretary of Labor regulations and instructions (see 29 CFR part 9).

§ 22.1201 Definitions.

As used in this subpart—

"United States" means the 50 States, the District of Columbia, Puerto Rico, the Northern

Mariana Islands, American Samoa, Guam, the U.S. Virgin Islands, Johnston Island, Wake Island, and outer Continental Shelf as defined in the Outer Continental Shelf Lands Act (43 U.S.C. 1331, *et seq.*), but does not include any other place subject to United States jurisdiction or any United States base or possession in a foreign country (see 29 CFR 4.112).

§ 22.1202 Policy.

(a) When a service contract succeeds a contract for performance of the same or similar services, as defined at 29 CFR 9.2, at the same location, the successor contractor and its subcontractors are required to offer those service employees that are employed under the predecessor contract, and whose employment will be terminated as a result of the award of the successor contract, a right of first refusal of employment under the contract in positions for which they are qualified. Executive Order 13495 generally prohibits employment openings under the successor contract until such right of first refusal has been provided, when consistent with applicable law.

(b) Nothing in Executive Order 13495 shall be construed to permit a contractor or subcontractor to fail to comply with any provision of any other Executive order or law. For example, the requirements of the HUBZone Program (see subpart 19.13), Executive Order 11246 (Equal Employment Opportunity), and the Vietnam Era Veterans' Readjustment Assistance Act of 1974 may, in certain circumstances, conflict with the requirements of Executive Order 13495. All applicable laws and Executive orders must be satisfied in tandem with, and if necessary prior to, the requirements of Executive Order 13495 and this subpart.

§ 22.1203 Applicability.

§ 22.1203-1 General.

This subpart applies to service contracts that succeed contracts for the same or similar services (29 CFR 9.2) at the same location.

§ 22.1203-2 Exemptions.

(a) This subpart does not apply to—

(1) Contracts and subcontracts under the simplified acquisition threshold;

(2) Contracts or subcontracts awarded pursuant to 41 U.S.C. chapter 85, Committee for Purchase from People Who Are Blind or Severely Disabled;

(3) Guard, elevator operator, messenger, or custodial services provided to the Government under contracts or subcontracts with sheltered workshops employing the "severely handicapped" as described in 40 U.S.C. 593;

(4) Agreements for vending facilities entered into pursuant to the preference regulations issued under the Randolph Sheppard Act, 20 U.S.C. 107; or

(5) Service employees who were hired to work under a Federal service contract and one or more nonfederal service contracts as part of a single job, provided that the service employees were not deployed in a manner that was designed to avoid the purposes of this subpart.

(b) The exemptions in paragraphs (a)(2) through (a)(4) of this subsection apply when either the predecessor or successor contract has been awarded for services produced or provided by the "severely handicapped."

§ 22.1203-3 Waiver.

(a) The senior procurement executive of the procuring agency may waive some or all of the provisions of this subpart after determining in writing that the application of this subpart would not serve the purposes of Executive Order 13495 or would impair the ability of the Federal Government to procure services on an economical and efficient basis. Such waivers may be made for a contract, subcontract, or purchase order, or with respect to a class of contracts, subcontracts, or purchase orders. See 29 CFR 9.4(d)(4) for regulatory provisions addressing circumstances in which a waiver could or would not be appropriate. The waiver must be reflected in a written analysis as described in 29 CFR 9.4(d)(4)(i) and must be completed by the contract solicitation date, or the waiver is inoperative. The senior procurement executive shall not redelegate this waiver authority.

(b) (1) When an agency exercises its waiver authority with respect to any contract, subcontract, or purchase order, the contracting officer shall direct the contractor to notify affected workers and their collective bargaining representative in writing, no later than five business days after the solicitation issuance date, of the agency's determination. The notice shall include facts supporting the determination. The contracting officer's failure to direct that the contractor provide the notice as provided in this subparagraph shall render the waiver decision inoperative, and the contracting officer shall include the clause at 52.222-17 in the solicitation.

(2) Where a contracting agency waives application to a class of contracts, subcontracts, or purchase orders, the contracting officer shall, with respect to each individual solicitation, direct the contractor to notify incumbent workers and their collective bargaining representatives in writing, no later than five business days after each solicitation issuance date, of the agency's determination. The notice shall include facts supporting the determination. The contracting officer's failure to direct that the contractor provide the notice provided in this subparagraph shall render the waiver decision inoperative, and the contracting officer shall include the clause at 52.222-17 in the solicitation.

(3) In addition, the agency shall notify the Department of Labor of its waiver decision and provide the Department of Labor with a copy of its written analysis no later than five business days after the solicitation issuance date (see 29 CFR 9.4(d)(2)). Failure to comply with this notification requirement shall render the waiver decision inoperative, and the contracting officer shall include the clause at 52.222-17 in the solicitation. The waiver decision and related written analysis shall be sent to the following address: U.S. Department of Labor, Wage and Hour Division, Branch of Government Contracts Enforcement, 200 Constitution Avenue, Room S-3006, Washington, D.C. 20210, or email to: Displaced@dol.gov.

§ 22.1203-4 Method of job offer.

A job offer made by a successor contractor must be a bona fide express offer of employment on the contract. Each bona fide express offer made to a qualified service employee on the predecessor contract must have a stated time limit of not less than 10 days for an employee response. Prior to the expiration of the 10-day period, the contractor is prohibited from offering employment on the contract to any other person, subject to the exceptions at 22.1203-5. Any question concerning an employee's qualifications shall be decided based upon the individual's education and employment history, with particular emphasis on the employee's experience on the predecessor contract, and a contractor may utilize employment screening processes only when such processes are provided for by the contracting agency, are conditions of the service contract, and are consistent with the Executive Order. An offer of employment will be presumed to be bona fide even if it is not for a position similar to the one the employee previously held, but is one for which the employee is qualified, and even if it is subject to different employment terms and conditions, including changes to pay or benefits. (See 29 CFR 9.12(b) for regulatory provisions addressing circumstances in which a bona fide offer of employment can occur.)

§ 22.1203-5 Exceptions.

(a) A successor contractor or its subcontractors are not required to offer employment to any service employee of the predecessor contractor who—

(1) Will be retained by the predecessor contractor.

(2) The successor contractor or any of its subcontractors reasonably believes, based on the particular service employee's past performance, has failed to perform suitably on the job. (See 29 CFR 9.12(c)(4) for regulatory provisions addressing circumstances in which this exception would or would not be appropriate.)

(b) A successor contractor or its subcontractors may employ under the contract any of its current service employees who (1) have worked for the successor contractor or its subcontractors for at least three months immediately preceding the commencement of the successor contract, and (2) would otherwise face lay-off or discharge.

(c) The successor contractor bears the responsibility of demonstrating the appropriateness of claiming any of the preceding exceptions and the exemption listed at 22.1203-2(a)(5) involving nonfederal work.

§ 22.1203-6 Reduced staffing.

A successor contractor and its subcontractors may employ fewer service employees than the predecessor contractor employed in connection with performance of the work. Thus, the successor contractor need not offer employment on the contract to all service employees on the predecessor contract, but must offer employment only to the number of eligible service employees the successor contractor believes necessary to meet its anticipated staffing pattern. Where a successor contractor does not initially offer employment to all the predecessor contract service employees, the obligation to offer employment shall continue for 90 days after the successor contractor's first date of performance on the contract. (See 29 CFR 9.12(d) for regulatory provisions addressing circumstances in which reduced staffing can occur.)

§ 22.1204 Certified service employee lists.

(a) Not less than 30 days before completion of the contract, the predecessor contractor is required to furnish to the contracting officer a certified list of the names of all service employees working under the contract and its subcontracts at the time the list is submitted. The certified list must also contain anniversary dates of employment of each service employee under the contract and subcontracts for services. The information on this list is the same as that on the seniority list required by paragraph (n) of the clause at 52.222-41, Service Contract Labor Standards. If there are no changes to the workforce before the predecessor contract is completed, then the predecessor contractor is not required to submit a revised list 10 days prior to completion of performance and the requirements of 52.222-41(n) are met. When there are changes to the workforce after submission of the 30-day list, the predecessor contractor shall submit a revised certified list not less than 10 days prior to performance completion.

(b) Immediately upon receipt of the certified service employee list but not before contract award, the contracting officer shall provide the certified service employee list to the successor contractor, and, if requested, to employees of the predecessor contractor or subcontractors or their authorized representatives.

§ 22.1205 Notification to contractors and service employees.

(a) The contracting officer shall direct that the predecessor contractor provides written notice to service employees of their possible right to an offer of employment with the successor contractor. The written notice shall be—

(1) Posted in a conspicuous place at the worksite; or

(2) Delivered to the service employees individually. If such delivery is via e-mail, the notification must result in an electronic delivery receipt or some other reliable confirmation that the intended recipient received the notice.

(b) Contracting officers may advise contractors to provide the notice in Appendix B to 29 CFR chapter 9. Where a significant portion of the predecessor contractor's workforce is not fluent in English, the contractor shall provide the notice in English and the language(s) with which service employees are more familiar. English and Spanish versions of the notice are available on the Department of Labor website at http://www.dol.gov/whd/govcontracts.

§ 22.1206 Remedies and sanctions for violations of this subpart.

(a) The Secretary of Labor has the authority to issue orders prescribing appropriate remedies, including, but not limited to, requiring the successor contractor to offer employment, in positions for which the employees are qualified, to service employees from the predecessor contract and payment of wages lost. (See 29 CFR 9.24(a)).

(b) After an investigation (see 29 CFR 9.23) and a determination by the Administrator, Wage and Hour Division, Department of Labor, that lost wages or other monetary relief is due, the Administrator may direct that so much of the accrued payments due on either the contract or any other contract between the contractor and the Government shall be withheld as are necessary to pay the monies due. Upon the final order of the Secretary of Labor that such monies are due, the Administrator may direct that such withheld funds be transferred to the Department of Labor for disbursement. (See 29 CFR 9.24(c)).

(c) If the contracting officer or the Administrator, Wage and Hour Division, Department of Labor, finds that the predecessor contractor has failed to provide the list required by 22.1204, the contracting officer may, in his or her discretion, or on request by the Administrator, suspend contract payment until such time as the contractor provides the list to the contracting officer.

(d) The Secretary of Labor may also suspend or debar a contractor or subcontractor for a period of up to three years for violations of 29 CFR part 9.

§ **22.1207 Contract clause.**

The contracting officer shall insert the clause at 52.222-17, Nondisplacement of Qualified Workers, in solicitations and contracts for (1) service contracts, as defined at 22.001, (2) that succeed contracts for performance of the same or similar work at the same location and (3) that are not exempted by 22.1203-2 or waived in accordance with 22.1203-3.

Subpart 22.13 —Equal Opportunity for Veterans

§ **22.1300 Scope of subpart.**

This subpart prescribes policies and procedures for implementing the following:

(a) The Vietnam Era Veterans' Readjustment Assistance Act of 1972 (38 U.S.C. 4211 and 4212) (the Act).

(b) The Veterans Employment Opportunities Act of 1998, Public Law 105-339.

(c) The Jobs for Veterans Act, Public Law 107-288.

(d) Executive Order 11701, January 24, 1973 (3 CFR 1971 - 1975 Comp., p. 752).

(e) The regulations of the Secretary of Labor (41 CFR parts 60-300 and 61-300).

United States Code Annotated

Contract requirements, see 41 USCA § 254.

Contracts, planning, solicitation, evaluation, and award procedures, see 10 USCA § 2305.

Definitions, see 10 USCA § 2302, 41 USCA §§ 259, 403.

Kinds of contracts, see 10 USCA § 2306.

Planning and solicitation requirements, see 41 USCA § 253a.

Veterans' employment emphasis under Federal contracts, see 38 USCA § 4212.

§ **22.1301 Definitions.**

As used in this subpart—

"Active duty wartime or campaign badge veteran" means a veteran who served on active duty in the U.S. military, ground, naval, or air service, during a war or in a campaign or expedition for which a campaign badge has been authorized under the laws administered by the Department of Defense.

"Armed Forces service medal veteran" means any veteran who, while serving on active duty in the U.S. military, ground, naval, or air service, participated in a United States military operation for which an Armed Forces service medal was awarded pursuant to Executive Order 12985 (61 FR 1209).

"Disabled veteran" means—

(1) A veteran of the U.S. military, ground, naval, or air service, who is entitled to compensation (or who, but for the receipt of military retired pay, would be entitled to compensation) under laws administered by the Secretary of Veterans Affairs; or

(2) A person who was discharged or released from active duty because of a service-connected disability.

"Executive and senior management" means—

(1) Any employee—

(i) Compensated on a salary basis at a rate of not less than $455 per week (or $380 per week, if employed in American Samoa by employers other than the Federal Government), exclusive of board, lodging, or other facilities;

(ii) Whose primary duty consists of the management of the enterprise in which the individual is employed or of a customarily recognized department or subdivision thereof;

(iii) Who customarily and regularly directs the work of two or more other employees; and

(iv) Who has the authority to hire or fire other employees or whose suggestions and recommendations as to the hiring or firing and as to the advancement and promotion or any other change of status of other employees will be given particular weight; or

(2) Any employee who owns at least a bona fide 20-percent equity interest in the enterprise in which the employee is employed, regardless of whether the business is a corporate or other type of organization, and who is actively engaged in its management.

"Protected veteran" means a veteran who is protected under the non-discrimination and affirmative action provisions of 38 U.S.C. 4212; specifically, a veteran who may be classified as a "disabled veteran," "recently separated veteran," "active duty wartime or campaign badge veteran," or an "Armed Forces service medal veteran," as defined by this section.

"Qualified disabled veteran" means a disabled veteran who has the ability to perform the essential functions of the employment positions with or without reasonable accommodation.

"Recently separated veteran" means any veteran during the three-year period beginning on the date of such veteran's discharge or release from active duty in the U.S. military, ground, naval, or air service.

"United States", means the 50 States, the District of Columbia, Puerto Rico, the Northern Mariana Islands, American Samoa, Guam, the U.S. Virgin Islands, and Wake Island.

United States Code Annotated

Contract requirements, see 41 USCA § 254.

Contracts, planning, solicitation, evaluation, and award procedures, see 10 USCA § 2305.

Definitions, see 10 USCA § 2302, 41 USCA §§ 259, 403.

Kinds of contracts, see 10 USCA § 2306.

Planning and solicitation requirements, see 41 USCA § 253a.

Veterans' employment emphasis under Federal contracts, see 38 USCA § 4212.

§ 22.1302 Policy.

(a) Contractors and subcontractors, when entering into contracts and subcontracts subject to the Act, are required to—

(1) List all employment openings, with the appropriate employment service delivery system where the opening occurs, except for—

(i) Executive and senior management positions;

(ii) Positions to be filled from within the contractor's organization; and

(iii) Positions lasting three days or less.

(2) Take affirmative action to employ, advance in employment, and otherwise treat qualified individuals, including qualified disabled veterans, without discrimination based upon their status as a protected veteran, in all employment practices;

(3) Undertake appropriate outreach and positive recruitment activities that are reasonably designed to effectively recruit protected veterans; and

(4) Establish a hiring benchmark and apply it to hiring of protected veterans in each establishment, on an annual basis, in the manner prescribed in the regulations of the Secretary of Labor.

(b) Except for contracts for commercial items or contracts that do not exceed the simplified acquisition threshold, contracting officers must not obligate or expend funds appropriated for the agency for a fiscal year to enter into a contract for the procurement of personal property and nonpersonal services (including construction) with a contractor that has not submitted the required annual VETS-4212, Federal Contractor Veterans' Employment Report (VETS-4212 Report), with respect to the preceding fiscal year if the contractor was subject to the reporting requirements of 38 U.S.C. 4212(d) for that fiscal year.

United States Code Annotated

Contract requirements, see 41 USCA § 254.

Contracts, planning, solicitation, evaluation, and award procedures, see 10 USCA § 2305.

Definitions, see 10 USCA § 2302, 41 USCA §§ 259, 403.

Kinds of contracts, see 10 USCA § 2306.

Planning and solicitation requirements, see 41 USCA § 253a.

Veterans' employment emphasis under Federal contracts, see 38 USCA § 4212.

§ 22.1303 Applicability.

(a) The Act applies to all contracts and subcontracts for personal property and nonpersonal services (including construction) of $150,000 or more except as waived by the Secretary of Labor.

(b) The requirements of the clause at 52.222-35, Equal Opportunity for Veterans, in any contract with a State or local government (or any agency, instrumentality, or subdivision) do not apply to any agency, instrumentality, or subdivision of that government that does not participate in work on or under the contract.

(c) The Act requires submission of the VETS-4212 Report in all cases where the contractor or subcontractor has received an award of $150,000 or more, except for awards to State and local governments, and foreign organizations where the workers are recruited outside of the United States.

United States Code Annotated

Contract requirements, see 41 USCA § 254.

Contracts, planning, solicitation, evaluation, and award procedures, see 10 USCA § 2305.

Definitions, see 10 USCA § 2302, 41 USCA §§ 259, 403.

Kinds of contracts, see 10 USCA § 2306.

Planning and solicitation requirements, see 41 USCA § 253a.

Veterans' employment emphasis under Federal contracts, see 38 USCA § 4212.

§ 22.1304 Procedures.

To verify if a proposed contractor is current with its submission of the VETS-4212 Report, the contracting officer may—

(a) Query the Department of Labor's VETS-4212 Database via the Internet at http://www.dol.gov/vets/vets4212.htm under "Filing Verification"; and

(b) Contact the VETS-4212 customer support via e-mail at mailto:VETS-4212-customersupport@dol.gov for confirmation, if the proposed contractor represents that it has submitted the VETS-4212 Report and is not listed on the verification file.

United States Code Annotated

Contract requirements, see 41 USCA § 254.

Contracts, planning, solicitation, evaluation, and award procedures, see 10 USCA § 2305.

Definitions, see 10 USCA § 2302, 41 USCA §§ 259, 403.

Kinds of contracts, see 10 USCA § 2306.

Planning and solicitation requirements, see 41 USCA § 253a.

Veterans' employment emphasis under Federal contracts, see 38 USCA § 4212.

§ 22.1305 Waivers.

(a) The Director, Office of Federal Contract Compliance Programs, Department of Labor, may waive any or all of the terms of the clause at 52.222-35, Equal Opportunity for Veterans, for—

(1) Any contract if a waiver is in the national interest; or

(2) Groups or categories of contracts if a waiver is in the national interest and it is—

(i) Impracticable to act on each request individually; and

(ii) Determined that the waiver will substantially contribute to convenience in administering the Act.

(b) The head of the agency may waive any requirement in this subpart when it is determined that the contract is essential to the national security, and that its award without complying with such requirements is necessary to the national security. Upon making such a determination, the head of the agency must notify the Deputy Assistant Secretary of Labor in writing within 30 days.

(c) The contracting officer must submit requests for waivers in accordance with agency procedures.

(d) The Deputy Assistant Secretary of Labor may withdraw an approved waiver for a specific contract or group of contracts to be awarded, when in the Deputy's judgment such action is necessary to achieve the purposes of the Act. The withdrawal does not apply to awarded contracts. For procurements entered into by sealed bidding, such withdrawal does not apply unless the withdrawal is made more than 10 calendar days before the date set for the opening of bids.

United States Code Annotated

Contract requirements, see 41 USCA § 254.

Contracts, planning, solicitation, evaluation, and award procedures, see 10 USCA § 2305.

Definitions, see 10 USCA § 2302, 41 USCA §§ 259, 403.

Kinds of contracts, see 10 USCA § 2306.

Planning and solicitation requirements, see 41 USCA § 253a.

Veterans' employment emphasis under Federal contracts, see 38 USCA § 4212.

§ 22.1306 Department of Labor notices and reports.

(a) The contracting officer must furnish to the contractor appropriate notices for posting when they are prescribed by the Deputy Assistant Secretary of Labor (see http://www.dol.g ov/ofccp/regs/compliance/posters/ofccpost.htm).

(b) The Act requires contractors and subcontractors to submit a report at least annually to the Secretary of Labor regarding employment of protected veterans (i.e., active duty wartime or campaign badge veterans, Armed Forces service medal veterans, disabled veterans, and recently separated veterans, unless all of the terms of the clause at 52.222-35, Equal Opportunity for Veterans, have been waived see 22.1305). The contractor and subcontractor must file VETS-4212, Federal Contractor Veterans' Employment Report (see "VETS-4212 Federal Contractor Reporting" and "Filing Your VETS-4212 Report" at http://w ww.dol.gov/vets/vets4212.htm).

United States Code Annotated

Contract requirements, see 41 USCA § 254.

Contracts, planning, solicitation, evaluation, and award procedures, see 10 USCA § 2305.

Definitions, see 10 USCA § 2302, 41 USCA §§ 259, 403.

Kinds of contracts, see 10 USCA § 2306.

Planning and solicitation requirements, see 41 USCA § 253a.

Veterans' employment emphasis under Federal contracts, see 38 USCA § 4212.

§ 22.1307 Collective bargaining agreements.

. If performance under the clause at 52.222-35, Equal Opportunity for Veterans, may necessitate a revision of a collective bargaining agreement, the contracting officer must advise the affected labor unions that the Department of Labor will give them appropriate opportunity to present their views. However, neither the contracting officer nor any representative of the contracting officer may discuss with the contractor or any labor representative any aspect of the collective bargaining agreement.

United States Code Annotated

Contract requirements, see 41 USCA § 254.

Contracts, planning, solicitation, evaluation, and award procedures, see 10 USCA § 2305.

Definitions, see 10 USCA § 2302, 41 USCA §§ 259, 403.

Kinds of contracts, see 10 USCA § 2306.

Planning and solicitation requirements, see 41 USCA § 253a.

Veterans' employment emphasis under Federal contracts, see 38 USCA § 4212.

§ 22.1308 Complaint procedures.

Following agency procedures, the contracting office must forward any complaints received about the administration of the Act to the Veterans' Employment and Training Service of the Department of Labor, or to the Director, Office of Federal Contract Compliance

Programs, 200 Constitution Avenue, NW., Washington, DC 20210, or to any OFCCP regional, district, or area office or through the local Veterans' Employment Representative or designee, at the local State employment office. The Director, Office of Federal Contract Compliance Programs, is responsible for investigating complaints.

United States Code Annotated

Contract requirements, see 41 USCA § 254.

Contracts, planning, solicitation, evaluation, and award procedures, see 10 USCA § 2305.

Definitions, see 10 USCA § 2302, 41 USCA §§ 259, 403.

Kinds of contracts, see 10 USCA § 2306.

Planning and solicitation requirements, see 41 USCA § 253a.

Veterans' employment emphasis under Federal contracts, see 38 USCA § 4212.

§ 22.1309 Actions because of noncompliance.

The contracting officer must take necessary action as soon as possible upon notification by the appropriate agency official to implement any sanctions imposed on a contractor by the Department of Labor for violations of the clause at 52.222-35, Equal Opportunity for Veterans. These sanctions (see 41 CFR 60-300.66) may include—

(a) Withholding progress payments;

(b) Termination or suspension of the contract; or

(c) Debarment of the contractor.

United States Code Annotated

Contract requirements, see 41 USCA § 254.

Contracts, planning, solicitation, evaluation, and award procedures, see 10 USCA § 2305.

Definitions, see 10 USCA § 2302, 41 USCA §§ 259, 403.

Kinds of contracts, see 10 USCA § 2306.

Planning and solicitation requirements, see 41 USCA § 253a.

Veterans' employment emphasis under Federal contracts, see 38 USCA § 4212.

§ 22.1310 Solicitation provision and contract clauses.

(a) (1) Insert the clause at 52.222-35, Equal Opportunity for Veterans, in solicitations and contracts if the expected value is $150,000 or more, except when—

(i) Work is performed outside the United States by employees recruited outside the United States; or

(ii) The Director, Office of Federal Contract Compliance Programs of the U.S. Department of Labor, has waived, in accordance with 22.1305(a), or the head of the agency has waived, in accordance with 22.1305(b), all of the terms of the clause.

(2) If the Director, Office of Federal Contract Compliance Programs of the U.S. Department of Labor, or the head of the agency waives one or more (but not all) of the terms of the clause, use the basic clause with its Alternate I.

(b) Insert the clause at 52.222-37, Employment Reports on Veterans, in solicitations and contracts containing the clause at 52.222-35, Equal Opportunity for Veterans.

(c) Insert the provision at 52.222-38, Compliance with Veterans' Employment Reporting Requirements, in solicitations when it is anticipated the contract award will exceed the simplified acquisition threshold and the contract is not for acquisition of commercial items.

United States Code Annotated

Contract requirements, see 41 USCA § 254.

Contracts, planning, solicitation, evaluation, and award procedures, see 10 USCA § 2305.

Definitions, see 10 USCA § 2302, 41 USCA §§ 259, 403.

Kinds of contracts, see 10 USCA § 2306.

Planning and solicitation requirements, see 41 USCA § 253a.

Veterans' employment emphasis under Federal contracts, see 38 USCA § 4212.

Subpart 22.14 Employment of Workers with Disabilities

§ 22.1400 Scope of subpart.

This subpart prescribes policies and procedures for implementing section 503 of the Rehabilitation Act of 1973, as amended (29 U.S.C. 793) (the Act); Executive Order 11758, January 15, 1974; and the regulations of the Secretary of Labor (41 CFR Part 60-741). In this subpart, the terms "contract" and "contractor" include "subcontract" and "subcontractor."

United States Code Annotated

Contract requirements, see 41 USCA § 254.

Contracts, planning, solicitation, evaluation, and award procedures, see 10 USCA § 2305.

Definitions, see 10 USCA § 2302, 41 USCA §§ 259, 403.

Employment under Federal contracts, see 29 USCA § 793.

Kinds of contracts, see 10 USCA § 2306.

Planning and solicitation requirements, see 41 USCA § 253a.

§ 22.1401 Policy.

Contractors and subcontractors, when entering into contracts and subcontracts subject to the Act, are required to—

(a) Take affirmative action to employ, and advance in employment, qualified individuals with disabilities, and to otherwise treat qualified individuals without discrimination based on their physical or mental disability;

(b) Undertake appropriate outreach and positive recruitment activities that are reasonably designed to effectively recruit qualified individuals with disabilities; and

(c) Compare the utilization of individuals with disabilities in their workforces to the utilization goal, as prescribed in the regulations of the Secretary of Labor, on an annual basis.

United States Code Annotated

Contract requirements, see 41 USCA § 254.

Contracts, planning, solicitation, evaluation, and award procedures, see 10 USCA § 2305.

Definitions, see 10 USCA § 2302, 41 USCA §§ 259, 403.

Employment under Federal contracts, see 29 USCA § 793.

Kinds of contracts, see 10 USCA § 2306.

Planning and solicitation requirements, see 41 USCA § 253a.

§ 22.1402 Applicability.

(a) Section 503 of the Act applies to all Government contracts in excess of $15,000 for supplies and services (including construction) except as waived by the Secretary of Labor. The clause at 52.222-36, Equal Opportunity for Workers with Disabilities, implements the Act.

(b) The requirements of the clause at 52.222-36, Equal Opportunity for Workers with Disabilities, in any contract with a State or local government (or any agency, instrumentality, or subdivision) shall not apply to any agency, instrumentality, or subdivision of that government that does not participate in work on or under the contract.

United States Code Annotated

Contract requirements, see 41 USCA § 254.

Contracts, planning, solicitation, evaluation, and award procedures, see 10 USCA § 2305.

Definitions, see 10 USCA § 2302, 41 USCA §§ 259, 403.

Employment under Federal contracts, see 29 USCA § 793.

Kinds of contracts, see 10 USCA § 2306.

Planning and solicitation requirements, see 41 USCA § 253a.

§ 22.1403 Waivers.

(a) The Director of the Office of Federal Contract Compliance Programs of the U.S. Department of Labor (Director of OFCCP), may waive the application of any or all of the terms of the clause at 52.222-36, Equal Opportunity for Workers with Disabilities, for—

(1) Any contract if a waiver is deemed to be in the national interest; or

(2) Groups or categories of contracts if a waiver is in the national interest and it is—

(i) Impracticable to act on each request individually; and

(ii) Determined that the waiver will substantially contribute to convenience in administering the Act.

(b) The head of an agency may waive any requirement in this subpart when it is determined that the contract is essential to the national security, and that its award without complying with such requirements is necessary to the national security. Upon making such a determination, the head of the agency shall notify the Director of OFCCP in writing within 30 days.

(c) The contracting officer shall submit requests for waivers in accordance with agency procedures.

(d) A waiver granted for a particular class of contracts may be withdrawn for any contract within that class whenever considered necessary by the Director of OFCCP to achieve the purposes of the Act. The withdrawal shall not apply to contracts awarded before the withdrawal. The withdrawal shall not apply to solicitations under any means of sealed bidding unless it is made more than 10 days before the date set for bid opening.

United States Code Annotated

Contract requirements, see 41 USCA § 254.

Contracts, planning, solicitation, evaluation, and award procedures, see 10 USCA § 2305.

Definitions, see 10 USCA § 2302, 41 USCA §§ 259, 403.

Employment under Federal contracts, see 29 USCA § 793.

Kinds of contracts, see 10 USCA § 2306.

Planning and solicitation requirements, see 41 USCA § 253a.

§ 22.1404 Department of Labor notices.

The contracting officer shall furnish to the contractor appropriate notices that state the contractor's obligations and the rights of individuals with disabilities. The contracting officer may obtain these notices from the Office of Federal Contract Compliance Programs (OFCCP) regional office.

United States Code Annotated

Contract requirements, see 41 USCA § 254.

Contracts, planning, solicitation, evaluation, and award procedures, see 10 USCA § 2305.

Definitions, see 10 USCA § 2302, 41 USCA §§ 259, 403.

Employment under Federal contracts, see 29 USCA § 793.

Kinds of contracts, see 10 USCA § 2306.

Planning and solicitation requirements, see 41 USCA § 253a.

§ 22.1405 Collective bargaining agreements.

If performance under the clause at 52.222-36, Equal Opportunity for Workers with Disabilities, may necessitate a revision of a collective bargaining agreement, the contracting officer shall advise the affected labor unions that the Department of Labor will give them appropriate opportunity to present their views. However, neither the contracting officer nor any representative of the contracting officer shall discuss with the contractor or any labor representative any aspect of the collective bargaining agreement.

United States Code Annotated

Contract requirements, see 41 USCA § 254.

Contracts, planning, solicitation, evaluation, and award procedures, see 10 USCA § 2305.

Definitions, see 10 USCA § 2302, 41 USCA §§ 259, 403.

Employment under Federal contracts, see 29 USCA § 793.

Kinds of contracts, see 10 USCA § 2306.

Planning and solicitation requirements, see 41 USCA § 253a.

§ 22.1406 Complaint procedures.

(a) Following agency procedures, the contracting office shall forward any complaints received about the administration of the Act to—

(1) Director, Office of Federal Contract Compliance Programs, U.S. Department of Labor, 200 Constitution Avenue, NW, Washington, DC 20210; or

(2) Any OFCCP regional or area office.

(b) The OFCCP shall institute investigation of each complaint and shall be responsible for developing a complete case record.

United States Code Annotated

Contract requirements, see 41 USCA § 254.

Contracts, planning, solicitation, evaluation, and award procedures, see 10 USCA § 2305.

Definitions, see 10 USCA § 2302, 41 USCA §§ 259, 403.

Employment under Federal contracts, see 29 USCA § 793.

Kinds of contracts, see 10 USCA § 2306.

Planning and solicitation requirements, see 41 USCA § 253a.

§ 22.1407 Actions because of noncompliance.

The contracting officer shall take necessary action, as soon as possible upon notification by the appropriate agency official, to implement any sanctions imposed on a contractor by the Department of Labor for violations of the clause at 52.222-36, Equal Opportunity for Workers with Disabilities. These sanctions (see 41 CFR 60-741.66) may include—

(a) Withholding from payments otherwise due;

(b) Termination or suspension of the contract; or

(c) Debarment of the contractor.

United States Code Annotated

Contract requirements, see 41 USCA § 254.

Contracts, planning, solicitation, evaluation, and award procedures, see 10 USCA § 2305.

Definitions, see 10 USCA § 2302, 41 USCA §§ 259, 403.

Employment under Federal contracts, see 29 USCA § 793.

Kinds of contracts, see 10 USCA § 2306.

Planning and solicitation requirements, see 41 USCA § 253a.

§ 22.1408 Contract clause.

(a) Insert the clause at 52.222-36, Equal Opportunity for Workers with Disabilities, in solicitations and contracts that exceed or are expected to exceed $15,000, except when—

(1) Both the performance of the work and the recruitment of workers will occur outside the United States, Puerto Rico, the Northern Mariana Islands, American Samoa, Guam, the U.S. Virgin Islands, and Wake Island; or

(2) The Director of OFCCP or agency head has waived, in accordance with 22.1403(a) or 22.1403(b) all the terms of the clause.

(b) If the Director of OFCCP or agency head waives one or more (but not all) of the terms of the clause in accordance with 22.1403(a) or 22.1403(b), use the basic clause with its Alternate I.

United States Code Annotated

Contract requirements, see 41 USCA § 254.

Contracts, planning, solicitation, evaluation, and award procedures, see 10 USCA § 2305.

Definitions, see 10 USCA § 2302, 41 USCA §§ 259, 403.

Employment under Federal contracts, see 29 USCA § 793.
Kinds of contracts, see 10 USCA § 2306.
Planning and solicitation requirements, see 41 USCA § 253a.

Subpart 22.15 Prohibition of Acquisition of Products Produced by Forced or Indentured Child Labor

§ 22.1500 Scope.

This subpart applies to acquisitions of supplies that exceed the micro-purchase threshold.

United States Code Annotated

Contract requirements, see 41 USCA § 254.

Contracts, planning, solicitation, evaluation, and award procedures, see 10 USCA § 2305.

Contracts for materials, etc., exceeding $10,000, representations
and stipulations, see 41 USCA § 35.

Definitions, see 10 USCA § 2302, 41 USCA §§ 259, 403.

Kinds of contracts, see 10 USCA § 2306.

Planning and solicitation requirements, see 41 USCA § 253a.

§ 22.1501 Definitions.

As used in this subpart—

"Forced or indentured child labor" means all work or service—

(1) Exacted from any person under the age of 18 under the menace of any penalty for its nonperformance and for which the worker does not offer himself voluntarily; or

(2) Performed by any person under the age of 18 pursuant to a contract the enforcement of which can be accomplished by process or penalties.

"List of Products Requiring Contractor Certification as to Forced or Indentured Child Labor" means the list published by the Department of Labor in accordance with E.O. 13126 of June 12, 1999, Prohibition of Acquisition of Products Produced by Forced or Indentured Child Labor. The list identifies products, by their country of origin, that the Departments of Labor, Treasury, and State have a reasonable basis to believe might have been mined, produced, or manufactured by forced or indentured child labor.

United States Code Annotated

Contract requirements, see 41 USCA § 254.

Contracts, planning, solicitation, evaluation, and award procedures, see 10 USCA § 2305.

Contracts for materials, etc., exceeding $10,000, representations and stipulations, see 41 USCA § 35.

Definitions, see 10 USCA § 2302, 41 USCA §§ 259, 403.

Kinds of contracts, see 10 USCA § 2306.

Planning and solicitation requirements, see 41 USCA § 253a.

§ 22.1502 Policy.

Agencies must take appropriate action to enforce the laws prohibiting the manufacture or importation of products that have been mined, produced, or manufactured wholly or in part by forced or indentured child labor, consistent with 19 U.S.C. 1307, 29 U.S.C. 201, *et seq.*, and 41 U.S.C. chapter 65. Agencies should make every effort to avoid acquiring such products.

United States Code Annotated

Contract requirements, see 41 USCA § 254.

Contracts, planning, solicitation, evaluation, and award procedures, see 10 USCA § 2305.

Contracts for materials, etc., exceeding $10,000, representations and stipulations, see 41 USCA § 35.

Definitions, see 10 USCA § 2302, 41 USCA §§ 259, 403.

Kinds of contracts, see 10 USCA § 2306.

Planning and solicitation requirements, see 41 USCA § 253a.

§ 22.1503 Procedures for acquiring end products on the List of Products Requiring Contractor Certification as to Forced or Indentured Child Labor.

(a) When issuing a solicitation for supplies expected to exceed the micro-purchase threshold, the contracting officer must check the List of Products Requiring Contractor Certification as to Forced or Indentured Child Labor (the List) (www.dol.gov/ilab/) (see 22.1505(a)). Appearance of a product on the List is not a bar to purchase of any such product mined, produced, or manufactured in the identified country, but rather is an alert that there is a reasonable basis to believe that such product may have been mined, produced, or manufactured by forced or indentured child labor.

(b) The requirements of this subpart that result from the appearance of any end product on the List do not apply to a solicitation or contract if the identified country of origin on the List is—

(1) Canada, and the anticipated value of the acquisition is $25,000 or more (subpart 25.4);

(2) Israel, and the anticipated value of the acquisition is $50,000 or more (see 25.406);

(3) Mexico, and the anticipated value of the acquisition is $77,533 or more (see subpart 25.4); or

(4) Armenia, Aruba, Austria, Belgium, Bulgaria, Croatia, Cyprus, Czech Republic, Denmark, Estonia, Finland, France, Germany, Greece, Hong Kong, Hungary, Iceland, Ireland, Italy, Japan, Korea, Latvia, Liechtenstein, Lithuania, Luxembourg, Malta, Montenegro, Netherlands, New Zealand, Norway, Poland, Portugal, Romania, Singapore, Slovak Republic, Slovenia, Spain, Sweden, Switzerland, Taiwan, or the United Kingdom and the anticipated value of the acquisition is $191,000 or more (see 25.402(b)).

(c) Except as provided in paragraph (b) of this section, before the contracting officer may make an award for an end product (regardless of country of origin) of a type identified by country of origin on the List the offeror must certify that—

(1) It will not supply any end product on the List that was mined, produced, or manufactured in a country identified on the List for that product, as specified in the solicitation by the contracting officer in the Certification Regarding Knowledge of Child Labor for Listed End Products; or

(2) (i) It has made a good faith effort to determine whether forced or indentured child labor was used to mine, produce, or manufacture any end product to be furnished under the contract that is on the List and was mined, produced, or manufactured in a country identified on the List for that product; and

(ii) On the basis of those efforts, the offeror is unaware of any such use of child labor.

(d) Absent any actual knowledge that the certification is false, the contracting officer must rely on the offerors' certifications in making award decisions.

(e) Whenever a contracting officer has reason to believe that forced or indentured child labor was used to mine, produce, or manufacture an end product furnished pursuant to a contract awarded subject to the certification required in paragraph (c) of this section, the contracting officer must refer the matter for investigation by the agency's Inspector General, the Attorney General, or the Secretary of the Treasury, whichever is determined appropriate in accordance with agency procedures, except to the extent that the end product is from the country listed in paragraph (b) of this section, under a contract exceeding the applicable threshold.

(f) Proper certification will not prevent the head of an agency from imposing remedies in accordance with section 22.1504(a)(4) if it is later discovered that the contractor has furnished an end product or component that has in fact been mined, produced, or manufactured, wholly or in part, using forced or indentured child labor.

§ 22.1504 Violations and remedies.

(a) *Violations.* The Government may impose remedies set forth in paragraph (b) of this section for the following violations (note that the violations in paragraphs (a)(3) and (a)(4) of this section go beyond violations of the requirements relating to certification of end products) (see 22.1503):

(1) The contractor has submitted a false certification regarding knowledge of the use of forced or indentured child labor.

(2) The contractor has failed to cooperate as required in accordance with the clause at 52.222-19, Child Labor Cooperation with Authorities and Remedies, with an investigation of the use of forced or indentured child labor by an Inspector General, the Attorney General, or the Secretary of the Treasury.

(3) The contractor uses forced or indentured child labor in its mining, production, or manufacturing processes.

(4) The contractor has furnished an end product or component mined, produced, or manufactured, wholly or in part, by forced or indentured child labor. Remedies in paragraphs (b)(2) and (b)(3) of this section are inappropriate unless the contractor knew of the violation.

(b) *Remedies.* (1) The contracting officer may terminate the contract.

(2) The suspending official may suspend the contractor in accordance with the procedures in Subpart 9.4.

(3) The debarring official may debar the contractor for a period not to exceed 3 years in accordance with the procedures in Subpart 9.4.

United States Code Annotated

Contract requirements, see 41 USCA § 254.

Contracts, planning, solicitation, evaluation, and award procedures, see 10 USCA § 2305.

Contracts for materials, etc., exceeding $10,000, representations and stipulations, see 41 USCA § 35.

Definitions, see 10 USCA § 2302, 41 USCA §§ 259, 403.

Kinds of contracts, see 10 USCA § 2306.

Planning and solicitation requirements, see 41 USCA § 253a.

§ 22.1505 Solicitation provision and contract clause.

(a) Except as provided in paragraph (b) of 22.1503, insert the provision at 52.222-18, Certification Regarding Knowledge of Child Labor for Listed End Products, in all solicitations that are expected to exceed the micro-purchase threshold and are for the acquisition of end products (regardless of country of origin) of a type identified by country of origin on the List of Products Requiring Contractor Certification as to Forced or Indentured Child Labor, except solicitations for commercial items that include the provision at 52.212-3, Offeror Representations and Certifications—Commercial Items. The contracting officer must identify in paragraph (b) of the provision at 52.222-18, Certification Regarding Knowledge of Child Labor for Listed End Products, or paragraph (i)(1) of the provision at 52.212-3, any applicable end products and countries of origin from the List. For solicitations estimated to equal or exceed $25,000, the contracting officer must exclude from the List in the solicitation end products from any countries identified at 22.1503(b), in accordance with the specified thresholds.

(b) Insert the clause at 52.222-19, Child Labor—Cooperation with Authorities and Remedies, in all solicitations and contracts for the acquisition of supplies that are expected to exceed the micro-purchase thresholds.

United States Code Annotated

Contract requirements, see 41 USCA § 254.

Contracts, planning, solicitation, evaluation, and award procedures, see 10 USCA § 2305.

Contracts for materials, etc., exceeding $10,000, representations and stipulations, see 41 USCA § 35.

Definitions, see 10 USCA § 2302, 41 USCA §§ 259, 403.

Kinds of contracts, see 10 USCA § 2306.

Planning and solicitation requirements, see 41 USCA § 253a.

Subpart 22.16 Notification of Employee Rights Under the National Labor Relations Act

§ 22.1600 Scope of subpart.

This subpart prescribes policies and procedures to implement Executive Order 13496, dated January 30, 2009 (74 FR 6107, February 4, 2009).

§ 22.1601 Definitions.

As used in this subpart—

"Secretary" means the Secretary of Labor, U.S. Department of Labor.

"United States" means the 50 States, the District of Columbia, Puerto Rico, the Commonwealth of the Northern Mariana Islands, American Samoa, Guam, the U.S. Virgin Islands, and Wake Island.

§ 22.1602 Policy.

(a) Executive Order 13496 requires contractors to post a notice informing employees of their rights under Federal labor laws.

(b) The Secretary has determined that the notice must contain employee rights under the National Labor Relations Act (Act), 29 U.S.C. 151 et seq. The Act encourages collective bargaining, and protects the exercise by employees of their freedom to associate, to self-organize, and to designate representatives of their own choosing for the purpose of negotiating the terms and conditions of their employment or other mutual aid or protection.

§ 22.1603 Exceptions.

(a) The requirements of this subpart do not apply to—

(1) Contracts under the simplified acquisition threshold;

(2) Subcontracts of $10,000 or less; and

(3) Contracts or subcontracts for work performed exclusively outside the United States.

(b) Exemptions granted by the Secretary.

(1) If the Secretary finds that the requirements of the Executive Order impair the ability of the Government to procure goods and services on an economical and efficient basis or if special circumstances require an exemption in order to serve the national interest, the Secretary may exempt a contracting department or agency, or groups of departments or agencies, from the requirements of any or all of the provisions of this Executive Order with respect to a particular contract or subcontract, or any class of contracts or subcontracts, including the requirement to include the clause at 52.222-40, or parts of that clause, in contracts.

(2) Requests for exemptions may be submitted in accordance with Department of Labor regulations at 29 CFR 471.3.

§ 22.1604 Compliance evaluation and complaint investigations and sanctions for violations.

(a) The Secretary may conduct compliance evaluations or investigate complaints of any contractor or subcontractor to determine if any of the requirements of the clause at 52.222-40 have been violated.

(b) Contracting departments and agencies shall cooperate with the Secretary and provide such information and assistance as the Secretary may require in the performance of the Secretary's functions.

(c) If the Secretary determines that there has been a violation, the Secretary may take such actions as set forth in 29 CFR 471.14.

(d) The Secretary may not terminate or suspend a contract or suspend or debar a contractor if the agency head has provided written objections, which must include a statement of reasons for the objection and a finding that the contractor's performance is essential to the agency's mission, and continues to object to the imposition of such sanctions and penalties. Procedures for enforcement by the Secretary are set out in 29 CFR 471.10 through 29 CFR 471.16.

§ 22.1605 Contract clause.

(a) Insert the clause at 52.222-40, Notification of Employee Rights under the National Labor Relations Act, in all solicitations and contracts, including acquisitions for commercial items and commercially available off-the-shelf items, except acquisitions—

(1) *Under the simplified acquisition threshold.* For indefinite-quantity contracts, include the clause only if the value of orders in any calendar year of the contract is expected to exceed the simplified acquisition threshold;

(2) For work performed exclusively outside the United States; or

(3) Covered (in their entirety) by an exemption granted by the Secretary.

(b) A contracting agency may modify the clause at 52.222-40, if necessary, to reflect an exemption granted by the Secretary (see 22.1603(b)).

Subpart 22.17 Combating Trafficking in Persons

§ 22.1700 Scope of subpart.

This subpart prescribes policy for implementing 22 U.S.C. chapter 78 and Executive Order 13627, Strengthening Protections Against Trafficking in Persons in Federal Contracts, dated September 25, 2012.

§ 22.1701 Applicability.

(a) This subpart applies to all acquisitions.

(b) The requirement at 22.1703(c) for a certification and compliance plan applies only to any portion of a contract or subcontract that—

(1) Is for supplies, other than commercially available off-the-shelf (COTS) items, to be acquired outside the United States, or services to be performed outside the United States; and

(2) Has an estimated value that exceeds $500,000.

§ 22.1702 Definitions.

As used in this subpart—

"Agent" means any individual, including a director, an officer, an employee, or an independent contractor, authorized to act on behalf of the organization.

"Coercion" means—

(1) Threats of serious harm to or physical restraint against any person;

(2) Any scheme, plan, or pattern intended to cause a person to believe that failure to perform an act would result in serious harm to or physical restraint against any person; or

(3) The abuse or threatened abuse of the legal process.

"Commercial sex act" means any sex act on account of which anything of value is given to or received by any person.

"Debt bondage" means the status or condition of a debtor arising from a pledge by the debtor of his or her personal services or of those of a person under his or her control as a security for debt, if the value of those services as reasonably assessed is not applied toward the liquidation of the debt or the length and nature of those services are not respectively limited and defined.

"Employee" means an employee of the Contractor directly engaged in the performance of work under the contract who has other than a minimal impact or involvement in contract performance.

"Forced labor" means knowingly providing or obtaining the labor or services of a person—

(1) By threats of serious harm to, or physical restraint against, that person or another person;

(2) By means of any scheme, plan, or pattern intended to cause the person to believe that, if the person did not perform such labor or services, that person or another person would suffer serious harm or physical restraint; or

(3) By means of the abuse or threatened abuse of law or the legal process.

"Involuntary servitude" includes a condition of servitude induced by means of—

(1) Any scheme, plan, or pattern intended to cause a person to believe that, if the person did not enter into or continue in such conditions, that person or another person would suffer serious harm or physical restraint; or

(2) The abuse or threatened abuse of the legal process.

"Severe forms of trafficking in persons" means—

(1) Sex trafficking in which a commercial sex act is induced by force, fraud, or coercion, or in which the person induced to perform such act has not attained 18 years of age; or

(2) The recruitment, harboring, transportation, provision, or obtaining of a person for labor or services, through the use of force, fraud, or coercion for the purpose of subjection to involuntary servitude, peonage, debt bondage, or slavery.

"Sex trafficking" means the recruitment, harboring, transportation, provision, or obtaining of a person for the purpose of a commercial sex act.

"Subcontract" means any contract entered into by a subcontractor to furnish supplies or services for performance of a prime contract or a subcontract.

"Subcontractor" means any supplier, distributor, vendor, or firm that furnishes supplies or services to or for a prime contractor or another subcontractor.

"United States" means the 50 States, the District of Columbia, and outlying areas.

§ 22.1703 Policy.

The United States Government has adopted a policy prohibiting trafficking in persons, including the trafficking-related activities below. Additional information about trafficking in persons may be found at the website for the Department of State's Office to Monitor and Combat Trafficking in Persons at http://www.state.gov/g/tip. Government solicitations and contracts shall—

(a) Prohibit contractors, contractor employees, subcontractors, subcontractor employees, and their agents from—

(1) Engaging in severe forms of trafficking in persons during the period of performance of the contract;

(2) Procuring commercial sex acts during the period of performance of the contract;

(3) Using forced labor in the performance of the contract;

(4) Destroying, concealing, confiscating, or otherwise denying access by an employee to the employee's identity or immigration documents, such as passports or drivers' licenses, regardless of issuing authority;

(5) (i) Using misleading or fraudulent practices during the recruitment of employees or offering of employment, such as failing to disclose, in a format and language accessible to the worker, basic information or making material misrepresentations during the recruitment of employees regarding the key terms and conditions of employment, including wages and fringe benefits, the location of work, the living conditions, housing and associated costs (if employer or agent provided or arranged), any significant costs to be charged to the employee, and, if applicable, the hazardous nature of the work;

(ii) Using recruiters that do not comply with local labor laws of the country in which the recruiting takes place;

(6) Charging employees recruitment fees;

(7)

(i) (A) Failing to provide return transportation or pay for the cost of return transportation upon the end of employment, for an employee who is not a national of the country in which the work is taking place and who was brought into that country for the purpose of working on a U.S. Government contract or subcontract, for portions of contracts and subcontracts performed outside the United States; or

(B) Failing to provide return transportation or pay for the cost of return transportation upon the end of employment, for an employee who is not a United States national and who was brought into the United States for the purpose of working on a U.S. Government contract or subcontract, if the payment of such costs is required under existing temporary worker programs or pursuant to a written agreement with the employee for portions of contracts and subcontracts performed inside the United States; except that—

(ii) The requirements of paragraph (a)(7)(i) of this section do not apply to an employee who is—

(A) Legally permitted to remain in the country of employment and who chooses to do so; or

(B) Exempted by an authorized official of the contracting agency, designated by the agency head in accordance with agency procedures, from the requirement to provide return transportation or pay for the cost of return transportation;

(iii) The requirements of paragraph (a)(7)(i) of this section are modified for a victim of trafficking in persons who is seeking victim services or legal redress in the country of employment, or for a witness in an enforcement action related to trafficking in persons. The contractor shall provide the return transportation or pay the cost of return transportation in a way that does not obstruct the victim services, legal redress, or witness activity. For example, the contractor shall also offer return transportation to a witness at a time that supports the witness' need to testify. This paragraph does not apply when the exemptions at paragraph (a)(7)(ii) of this section apply.

(8) Providing or arranging housing that fails to meet the host country housing and safety standards; or

(9) If required by law or contract, failing to provide an employment contract, recruitment agreement, or other required work document in writing. Such written document shall be in a language the employee understands. If the employee must relocate to perform the work, the work document shall be provided to the employee at least five days prior to the employee relocating. The employee's work document shall include, but is not limited to, details about work description, wages, prohibition on charging recruitment fees, work location(s), living accommodations and associated costs, time off, roundtrip transportation arrangements, grievance process, and the content of applicable laws and regulations that prohibit trafficking in persons. The contracting officer shall consider the risk that the contract or subcontract will involve services or supplies susceptible to trafficking in persons, and the number of non-U.S. citizens expected to be employed, when deciding whether to require work documents in the contract;

(b) Require contractors and subcontractors to notify employees of the prohibited activities described in paragraph (a) of this section and the actions that may be taken against them for violations;

(c) With regard to certification and a compliance plan—

(1) (i) Require the apparent successful offeror to provide, before contract award, a certification (see 52.222-56) that the offeror has a compliance plan if any portion of the contract or subcontract—

(A) Is for supplies, other than COTS items (see 2.101), to be acquired outside the United States, or services to be performed outside the United States; and

(B) The estimated value exceeds $500,000.

(ii) The certification must state that—

(A) The offeror has implemented the plan and has implemented procedures to prevent any prohibited activities and to monitor, detect, and terminate the contract with a subcontractor or agent engaging in prohibited activities; and

(B) After having conducted due diligence, either—

(1) To the best of the offeror's knowledge and belief, neither it nor any of its agents, proposed subcontractors, or their agents, has engaged in any such activities; or

(2) If abuses relating to any of the prohibited activities identified in 52.222-50(b) have been found, the offeror or proposed subcontractor has taken the appropriate remedial and referral actions;

(2) Require annual certifications (see 52.222-50(h)(5)) during performance of the contract, when a compliance plan was required at award;

(3) (i) Require the contractor to obtain a certification from each subcontractor, prior to award of a subcontract, if any portion of the subcontract—

(A) Is for supplies, other than COTS items (see 2.101), to be acquired outside the United States, or services to be performed outside the United States; and

(B) The estimated value exceeds $500,000.

(ii) The certification must state that—

(A) The subcontractor has implemented a compliance plan; and

(B) After having conducted due diligence, either—

(1) To the best of the subcontractor's knowledge and belief, neither it nor any of its agents, subcontractors, or their agents, has engaged in any such activities; or

(2) If abuses relating to any of the prohibited activities identified in 52.222-50(b) have been found, the subcontractor has taken the appropriate remedial and referral actions;

(4) Require the contractor to obtain annual certifications from subcontractors during performance of the contract, when a compliance plan was required at the time of subcontract award; and

(5) Require that any compliance plan or procedures shall be appropriate to the size and complexity of the contract and the nature and scope of its activities, including the number of non-U.S. citizens expected to be employed and the risk that the contract or subcontract will involve services or supplies susceptible to trafficking in persons. The minimum elements of the plan are specified at 52.222-50(h);

(d) Require the contractor and subcontractors to—

(1) Disclose to the contracting officer and the agency Inspector General information sufficient to identify the nature and extent of an offense and the individuals responsible for the conduct;

(2) Provide timely and complete responses to Government auditors' and investigators' requests for documents;

(3) Cooperate fully in providing reasonable access to their facilities and staff (both inside and outside the U.S.) to allow contracting agencies and other responsible Federal agencies to conduct audits, investigations, or other actions to ascertain compliance with the Trafficking Victims Protection Act (22 U.S.C. chapter 78), Executive Order 13627, or any other applicable law or regulation establishing restrictions on trafficking in persons, the procurement of commercial sex acts, or the use of forced labor; and

(4) Protect all employees suspected of being victims of or witnesses to prohibited activities, prior to returning to the country from which the employee was recruited, and shall not prevent or hinder the ability of these employees from cooperating fully with Government authorities; and

(e) Provide suitable remedies, including termination, to be imposed on contractors that fail to comply with the requirements of paragraphs (a) through (d) of this section.

§ 22.1704 Violations and remedies.

(a) Violations. It is a violation of the Trafficking Victims Protection Act of 2000, as amended, (22 U.S.C. chapter 78), E.O. 13627, or the policies of this subpart if—

(1) The contractor, contractor employee, subcontractor, subcontractor employee, or agent engages in severe forms of trafficking in persons during the period of performance of the contract;

(2) The contractor, contractor employee, subcontractor, subcontractor employee, or agent procures a commercial sex act during the period of performance of the contract;

(3) The contractor, contractor employee, subcontractor, subcontractor employee, or agent uses forced labor in the performance of the contract; or

(4) The contractor fails to comply with the requirements of the clause at 52.222-50, Combating Trafficking in Persons.

(b) Credible information. Upon receipt of credible information regarding a violation listed in paragraph (a) of this section, the contracting officer—

(1) Shall promptly notify, in accordance with agency procedures, the agency Inspector General, the agency debarring and suspending official, and if appropriate, law enforcement officials with jurisdiction over the alleged offense; and

(2) May direct the contractor to take specific steps to abate the alleged violation or enforce the requirements of its compliance plan.

(c) Receipt of agency Inspector General report.

(1) The head of an executive agency shall ensure that the contracting officer is provided a copy of the agency Inspector General report of an investigation of a violation of the traf-

ficking in persons prohibitions in 22.1703(a) and 52.222-50(b).

(2) (i) Upon receipt of a report from the agency Inspector General that provides support for the allegations, the head of the executive agency, in accordance with agency procedures, shall delegate to an authorized agency official, such as the agency suspending or debarring official, the responsibility to—

(A) Expeditiously conduct an administrative proceeding, allowing the contractor the opportunity to respond to the report;

(B) Make a final determination as to whether the allegations are substantiated; and

(C) Notify the contracting officer of the determination.

(ii) Whether or not the official authorized to conduct the administrative proceeding is the suspending and debarring official, the suspending and debarring official has the authority, at any time before or after the final determination as to whether the allegations are substantiated, to use the suspension and debarment procedures in subpart 9.4 to suspend, propose for debarment, or debar the contractor, if appropriate, also considering the factors at 22.1704(d)(2).

(d) Remedies. After a final determination in accordance with paragraph (c)(2)(ii) of this section that the allegations of a trafficking in persons violation are substantiated, the contracting officer shall—

(1) Enter the violation in FAPIIS (see 42.1503(h)); and

(2) Consider taking any of the remedies specified in paragraph (e) of the clause at 52.222-50, Combating Trafficking in Persons. These remedies are in addition to any other remedies available to the United States Government. When determining the appropriate remedies, the contracting officer may consider the following factors:

(i) Mitigating factors. The contractor had a Trafficking in Persons compliance plan or awareness program at the time of the violation, was in compliance with the plan at the time of the violation, and has taken appropriate remedial actions for the violations, that may include reparation to victims for such violations.

(ii) Aggravating factors. The contractor failed to abate an alleged violation or enforce the requirements of a compliance plan, when directed by a contracting officer to do so.

§ 22.1705 Contract clause.

(a) (1) Insert the clause at 52.222-50, Combating Trafficking in Persons, in all solicitations and contracts.

(2) Use the clause with its Alternate I when the contract will be performed outside the United States (as defined at 22.1702) and the contracting officer has been notified of specific U.S. directives or notices regarding combating trafficking in persons (such as general orders or military listings of "off-limits" local establishments) that apply to contractor employees at the contract place of performance.

(b) Insert the provision at 52.222-56, Certification Regarding Trafficking in Persons Compliance Plan, in solicitations if

(1) It is possible that at least $500,000 of the value of the contract may be performed outside the United States; and

(2) The acquisition is not entirely for commercially available off-the-shelf items.

Subpart 22.18 Employment Eligibility Verification

§ 22.1800 Scope.

This subpart prescribes policies and procedures requiring contractors to utilize the Department of Homeland Security (DHS), United States Citizenship and Immigration Service's employment eligibility verification program (E-Verify) as the means for verifying employment eligibility of certain employees.

§ 22.1801 Definitions.

As used in this subpart—

"Commercially available off-the-shelf (COTS) item"—

(1) Means any item of supply that is—

(i) A commercial item (as defined in paragraph (1) of the definition at 2.101);

(ii) Sold in substantial quantities in the commercial marketplace; and

(iii) Offered to the Government, without modification, in the same form in which it is sold in the commercial marketplace; and

(2) Does not include bulk cargo, as defined in 46 U.S.C. 40102(4), such as agricultural products and petroleum products. Per 46 CFR 525.1 (c)(2), "bulk cargo" means cargo that is loaded and carried in bulk onboard ship without mark or count, in a loose unpackaged form, having homogenous characteristics. Bulk cargo loaded into intermodal equipment, except LASH or Seabee barges, is subject to mark and count and, therefore, ceases to be bulk cargo.

"Employee assigned to the contract" means an employee who was hired after November 6, 1986 (after November 27, 2009, in the Commonwealth of the Northern Mariana Islands), who is directly performing work, in the United States, under a contract that is required to include the clause prescribed at 22.1803. An employee is not considered to be directly performing work under a contract if the employee—

(1) Normally performs support work, such as indirect or overhead functions; and

(2) Does not perform any substantial duties applicable to the contract.

"Subcontract" means any contract, as defined in 2.101, entered into by a subcontractor to furnish supplies or services for performance of a prime contract or a subcontract. It includes but is not limited to purchase orders, and changes and modifications to purchase orders.

"Subcontractor" means any supplier, distributor, vendor, or firm that furnishes supplies or services to or for a prime contractor or another subcontractor.

"United States", as defined in 8 U.S.C. 1101(a)(38), means the 50 States, the District of Columbia, Puerto Rico, Guam, the Commonwealth of Northern Mariana Islands, and the U.S. Virgin Islands.

§ 22.1802 Policy.

(a) Statutes and Executive orders require employers to abide by the immigration laws of the United States and to employ in the United States only individuals who are eligible to work in the United States. The E-Verify program provides an Internet-based means of verifying employment eligibility of workers employed in the United States, but is not a substitute for any other employment eligibility verification requirements.

(b) Contracting officers shall include in solicitations and contracts, as prescribed at 22.1803, requirements that Federal contractors must—

(1) Enroll as Federal contractors in E-Verify;

(2) Use E-Verify to verify employment eligibility of all new hires working in the United States, except that the contractor may choose to verify only new hires assigned to the contract if the contractor is—

(i) An institution of higher education (as defined at 20 U.S.C. 1001(a));

(ii) A State or local government or the government of a Federally recognized Indian tribe; or

(iii) A surety performing under a takeover agreement entered into with a Federal agency pursuant to a performance bond;

(3) Use E-Verify to verify employment eligibility of all employees assigned to the contract; and

(4) Include these requirements, as required by the clause at 52.222-54, in subcontracts for—

(i) Commercial or noncommercial services, except for commercial services that are part of the purchase of a COTS item (or an item that would be a COTS item, but for minor modifications), performed by the COTS provider, and are normally provided for that COTS item; and

(ii) Construction.

(c) Contractors may elect to verify employment eligibility of all existing employees working in the United States who were hired after November 6, 1986 (after November 27, 2009, in the Commonwealth of the Northern Mariana Islands) instead of just those employees assigned to the contract. The contractor is not required to verify employment eligibility of—

(1) Employees who hold an active security clearance of confidential, secret, or top se-

cret; or

(2) Employees for whom background investigations have been completed and credentials issued pursuant to Homeland Security Presidential Directive (HSPD)-12.

(d) In exceptional cases, the head of the contracting activity may waive the E-Verify requirement for a contract or subcontract or a class of contracts or subcontracts, either temporarily or for the period of performance. This waiver authority may not be delegated.

(e) DHS and the Social Security Administration (SSA) may terminate a contractor's MOU and deny access to the E-Verify system in accordance with the terms of the MOU. If DHS or SSA terminates a contractor's MOU, the terminating agency must refer the contractor to a suspension or debarment official for possible suspension or debarment action. During the period between termination of the MOU and a decision by the suspension or debarment official whether to suspend or debar, the contractor is excused from its obligations under paragraph (b) of the clause at 52.222-54. If the contractor is suspended or debarred as a result of the MOU termination, the contractor is not eligible to participate in E-Verify during the period of its suspension or debarment. If the suspension or debarment official determines not to suspend or debar the contractor, then the contractor must reenroll in E-Verify.

§ 22.1803 Contract clause.

Insert the clause at 52.222-54, Employment Eligibility Verification, in all solicitations and contracts that exceed the simplified acquisition threshold, except those that—

(a) Are only for work that will be performed outside the United States;

(b) Are for a period of performance of less than 120 days; or

(c) Are only for—

(1) Commercially available off-the-shelf items;

(2) Items that would be COTS items, but for minor modifications (as defined at paragraph (3)(ii) of the definition of "commercial item" at 2.101);

(3) Items that would be COTS items if they were not bulk cargo; or

(4) Commercial services that are—

(i) Part of the purchase of a COTS item (or an item that would be a COTS item, but for minor modifications);

(ii) Performed by the COTS provider; and

(iii) Are normally provided for that COTS item.

Subpart 22.19 —Establishing a Minimum Wage for Contractors

§ 22.1900 Scope of subpart.

This subpart prescribes policies and procedures to implement Executive Order (E.O.) 13658, Establishing a Minimum Wage for Contractors, dated February 12, 2014, and Department of Labor (DOL) implementing regulations at 29 CFR part 10.

§ 22.1901 Definitions.

"Worker", as used in this subpart (in accordance with 29 CFR 10.2)—

(1) Means any person engaged in performing work on, or in connection with, a contract covered by Executive Order 13658, and

(i) Whose wages under such contract are governed by the Fair Labor Standards Act (29 U.S.C. chapter 8), the Service Contract Labor Standards statute (41 U.S.C. chapter 67), or the Wage Rate Requirements (Construction) statute (40 U.S.C. chapter 31, subchapter IV),

(ii) Other than individuals employed in a bona fide executive, administrative, or professional capacity, as those terms are defined in 29 CFR part 541,

(iii) Regardless of the contractual relationship alleged to exist between the individual and the employer.

(2) Includes workers performing on, or in connection with, the contract whose wages are calculated pursuant to special certificates issued under 29 U.S.C. 214(c).

(3) Also includes any person working on, or in connection with, the contract and

individually registered in a bona fide apprenticeship or training program registered with the Department of Labor's Employment and Training Administration, Office of Apprenticeship, or with a State Apprenticeship Agency recognized by the Office of Apprenticeship.

§ 22.1902 Policy.

(a) Pursuant to Executive Order 13658, the minimum hourly wage rate required to be paid to workers performing on, or in connection with, contracts and subcontracts subject to this subpart is at least $10.10 per hour beginning January 1, 2015, and beginning January 1, 2016, and annually thereafter, an amount determined by the Secretary of Labor. The Administrator of the Wage and Hour Division (the Administrator) will notify the public of the new E.O. minimum wage rate at least 90 days before it is to take effect. (See 22.1904.)

(b) Relationship with other wage rates.

(1) Nothing in this subpart shall excuse noncompliance with any applicable Federal or State prevailing wage law or any applicable law or municipal ordinance establishing a minimum wage higher than the E.O. minimum wage. However, wage increases under such other laws or municipal ordinances are not subject to price adjustment under this subpart.

(2) The E.O. minimum wage rate applies whenever it is higher than any applicable collective bargaining agreement(s) wage rate.

(c) Application to tipped workers. Policies and procedures in DOL regulations at 29 CFR 10.24(b) and 10.28 address the relationship between the E.O. minimum wage and wages of workers engaged in an occupation in which they customarily and regularly receive more than $30 a month in tips.

§ 22.1903 Applicability.

(a) This subpart applies to contracts covered by the Service Contract Labor Standards statute (41 U.S.C. chapter 67, formerly known as the Service Contract Act, Subpart 22.10), or the Wage Rate Requirements (Construction) statute (40 U.S.C. chapter 31, Subchapter IV, formerly known as the Davis Bacon Act, Subpart 22.4), that require performance in whole or in part within the United States. When performance is in part within and in part outside the United States, this subpart applies to the part of the contract that is performed within the United States.

(b) (1) This subpart applies to workers as defined at 22.1901. As provided in that definition—

(i) Workers are covered regardless of the contractual relationship alleged to exist between the contractor or subcontractor and the worker;

(ii) Workers with disabilities whose wages are calculated pursuant to special certificates issued under 29 U.S.C. 214(c) are covered; and

(iii) Workers who are registered in a bona fide apprenticeship program or training program registered with the Department of Labor's Employment and Training Administration, Office of Apprenticeship, or with a State Apprenticeship Agency recognized by the Office of Apprenticeship, are covered.

(2) This subpart does not apply to—

(i) Fair Labor Standards Act (FLSA)-covered individuals performing in connection with contracts covered by the E.O., i.e., those individuals who perform duties necessary to the performance of the contract, but who are not directly engaged in performing the specific work called for by the contract, and who spend less than 20 percent of their hours worked in a particular workweek performing in connection with such contracts;

(ii) Individuals exempted from the minimum wage requirements of the FLSA under 29 U.S.C. 213(a) and 214(a) and (b), unless otherwise covered by the Service Contract Labor Standards statute or the Wage Rate Requirements (Construction) statute. These individuals include but are not limited to—

(A) Learners, apprentices, or messengers whose wages are calculated pursuant to special certificates issued under 29 U.S.C. 214(a);

(B) Students whose wages are calculated pursuant to special certificates issued under 29 U.S.C. 214(b); and

(C) Those employed in a bona fide executive, administrative, or professional capacity (29 U.S.C. 213(a)(1) and 29 CFR part 541).

(c) Agency Labor Advisors, as defined at 22.001, are listed at http://wdol.gov, and are available to provide guidance and assistance with the application of this subpart.

§ 22.1904 Annual Executive Order Minimum Wage Rate.

(a) For the E.O. minimum wage rate that becomes effective on January 1, 2016, and annually thereafter, the Administrator will—

(1) Notify the public of the new E.O. minimum wage rate at least 90 days before it becomes effective by publishing a notice in the Federal Register;

(2) Publish and maintain on Wage Determinations OnLine (WDOL), http://www.wdol.gov, or any successor site, the E.O. minimum wage rate; and

(3) Include a general notice on wage determinations which are issued under the Service Contract Labor Standards statute or the Wage Rate Requirements (Construction) statute. The notice will provide information on the E.O. minimum wage and how to obtain annual updates.

(b) (1) The contractor may request a price adjustment only after the effective date of a new annual E.O. minimum wage determination published pursuant to paragraph (a). Prices will be adjusted only for increased labor costs (including subcontractor labor costs) as a result of the annual E.O. minimum wage, and for associated labor costs (including those for subcontractors). Associated labor costs shall include increases or decreases that result from changes in social security and unemployment taxes and workers' compensation insurance, but will not otherwise include any amount for general and administrative costs, overhead, or profit.

(2) The wage rate price adjustment under this clause is the lowest amount calculated by subtracting from the new E.O. wage rate the following: the current E.O. minimum wage rate; the current service or construction wage determination rate under the contract (if the wage rate is applicable to that worker); or the actual wage currently paid the worker. If the amount is zero or below, there will be no increase paid for this worker.

(i) Example 1 - New E.O. wage rate is $11.10.

Previous E.O. wage rate is $10.70.

The current service or construction wage determination rate applicable to this worker under the contract is $10.75.

The actual wage currently paid to the worker is $10.80.

Analysis: The calculation is $11.10 - $10.80 = $.30. The price adjustment for this worker is $.30.

(ii) Example 2 - New E.O. wage rate is $10.50.

Previous E.O. wage rate is $10.10.

The current service or construction wage determination rate applicable to this worker under the contract is $10.75.

The actual wage currently paid to the worker is $10.80.

Analysis: The calculation is $10.50 - $10.80 = -$.30. There is no price adjustment for this worker.

(3) The contracting officer shall not adjust the contract price for any costs other than those identified in paragraph (b)(1) of this section, and shall not provide duplicate price adjustments with any price adjustment under clauses implementing the Service Contract Labor Standards statute or the Wage Rate Requirements (Construction) statute.

§ 22.1905 Enforcement of Executive Order Minimum Wage Requirements.

(a) Authority.

(1) Section 5 of the E.O. grants the authority for investigating potential violations of, and obtaining compliance with, the E.O. to the Secretary of Labor. The Secretary of Labor, in promulgating the implementing regulations required by Section 4 of the E.O., has assigned this authority to the Administrator. Contracting agencies do not have authority to conduct compliance investigations under 29 CFR part 10 as implemented in this subpart. This does not limit the contracting officer's authority to otherwise enforce the terms and conditions of the contract.

(2) Contracting officers shall withhold payment at the direction of the Administrator.

(3) The contracting officer shall withhold payment, without a request from the Administrator, if the contractor fails to comply with the requirements in paragraph (e)(2) of 52.222-55, Minimum Wages Under Executive Order 13658 to furnish payroll records, until such time as the noncompliance is corrected.

(b) Complaints.

(1) Complaints may be filed with the contracting officer or the Administrator by any person, entity, or organization that believes a violation of this subpart has occurred.

(2) The identity of any individual who makes a written or oral statement as a complaint or in the course of an investigation, as well as portions of the statement which would reveal the individual's identity, shall not be disclosed in any manner to anyone other than Federal officials without the prior consent of the individual, unless otherwise authorized by law.

(3) Upon receipt of a complaint, or if notified that the Administrator has received a complaint, the contracting officer shall report the following information, within 14 days, if available without conducting an investigation, to the Department of Labor, Wage and Hour Division, Office of Government Contracts, 200 Constitution Avenue N.W., Room S3006, Washington, D.C. 20210.

(i) The complaint or description of the alleged violation;

(ii) Available statements by the worker, contractor, or any other person regarding the alleged violation;

(iii) Evidence that clause 52.222-55, Minimum Wages Under Executive Order 13658, was included in the contract;

(iv) Information concerning known settlement negotiations between the parties, if applicable; and

(v) Any other relevant facts known to the contracting officer or other information requested by the Wage and Hour Division.

(c) Investigations. Complaints will be investigated by the Administrator, if warranted, in accordance with the procedures in 29 CFR part 10.43.

(d) Remedies and sanctions–

(1) Unpaid wages. When the Administrator's investigation reveals that a contractor has failed to pay the applicable E.O. minimum wage, the Administrator will notify the contractor and the contracting agency of the unpaid wage violation, and request that the contractor remedy the violation. If the contractor does not remedy the violation, the Administrator may direct withholding of payments due on the contract or any other contract between the contractor and the Federal Government. Upon final decision and direction of the Administrator, the contracting agency shall transfer the withheld funds to the Department of Labor for disbursement in accordance with the procedures at 22.406-9(c).

(2) Antiretaliation. When a contractor has been found to have violated paragraph (i) of clause 52.222-55, Minimum Wages Under Executive Order 13658, the Administrator may provide for relief to the worker in accordance with 29 CFR 10.44.

(3) Debarment.

(i) The Department of Labor may initiate debarment proceedings under 29 CFR 10.52 whenever a contractor is found to have disregarded its obligations under 29 CFR part 10.

(ii) Contracting officers shall consider notifying the agency suspending and debarring official in accordance with agency procedures when a contractor commits significant violations of contract terms and conditions related to this subpart.

(4) Retroactive inclusion of contract clause. If a contracting agency fails to include the contract clause in a contract to which the E.O. applies, the contracting agency, on its own initiative or within 15 calendar days of notification by an authorized representative of the Department of Labor, shall incorporate the contract clause in the contract retroactive to commencement of performance under the contract through the exercise of any and all authority that may be needed (including, where necessary, its authority to negotiate or amend, its authority to pay any necessary additional costs, and its authority under any contract provision authorizing changes, cancellation and termination).

§ 22.1906 Contract clause.

Insert the clause at 52.222-55, Minimum Wages Under Executive Order 13658, in solicitations and contracts that include the clause at 52.222-6, Construction Wage Rate Requirements, or 52.222-41, Service Contract Labor Standards, where work is to be performed, in whole or in part, in the United States (the 50 States and the District of Columbia).

PART 23 ENVIRONMENT, ENERGY AND WATER EFFICIENCY, RENEWABLE ENERGY TECHNOLOGIES, OCCUPATIONAL SAFETY, AND DRUG-FREE WORKPLACE

§ 23.000 Scope.

This part prescribes acquisition policies and procedures supporting the Government's program for ensuring a drug-free workplace, for protecting and improving the quality of the environment, and to foster markets for sustainable technologies, materials, products, and services, and encouraging the safe operation of vehicles by—

(a) Reducing or preventing pollution;

(b) Managing efficiently and reducing energy and water use in Government facilities;

(c) Using renewable energy and renewable energy technologies;

(d) Acquiring energy-efficient and water-efficient products and services, environmentally preferable (including EPEAT®-registered, and non-toxic and less toxic) products, products containing recovered materials, biobased products, non-ozone-depleting products, and products and services that minimize or eliminate, when feasible, the use, release, or emission of high global warming potential hydrofluorocarbons, such as by using reclaimed instead of virgin hydrofluorocarbons;

(e) Requiring contractors to identify hazardous materials;

(f) Encouraging contractors to adopt and enforce policies that ban text messaging while driving; and

(g) Requiring contractors to comply with agency environmental management systems.

United States Code Annotated

Contract requirements, see 41 USCA § 254.

Contracts, planning, solicitation, evaluation, and award procedures, see 10 USCA § 2305.

Definitions, see 10 USCA § 2302, 41 USCA §§ 259, 403.

Kinds of contracts, see 10 USCA § 2306.

Planning and solicitation requirements, see 41 USCA § 253a.

§ 23.001 Definitions.

As used in this part—

"Environmental" means environmental aspects of internal agency operations and activities, including those aspects related to energy and transportation functions.

"Greenhouse gases" means carbon dioxide, methane, nitrous oxide, hydrofluorocarbons, perfluorocarbons, and sulfur hexafluoride.

"Toxic chemical" means a chemical or chemical category listed in 40 CFR 372.65.

"United States", except as used in subpart 23.10, means—

(1) The fifty States;

(2) The District of Columbia;

(3) The commonwealths of Puerto Rico and the Northern Mariana Islands;

(4) The territories of Guam, American Samoa, and the United States Virgin Islands; and

(5) Associated territorial waters and airspace.

United States Code Annotated

Contract requirements, see 41 USCA § 254.

Contracts, planning, solicitation, evaluation, and award procedures, see 10 USCA § 2305.

Definitions, see 10 USCA § 2302, 41 USCA §§ 259, 403.

Kinds of contracts, see 10 USCA § 2306.

Planning and solicitation requirements, see 41 USCA § 253a.

§ 23.002 Policy.

Executive Order 13423 sections 3(e) and (f) require that contracts for contractor operation of a Government-owned or -leased facility and contracts for support services at a Government-owned or -operated facility include provisions that obligate the contractor to comply with the requirements of the order to the same extent as the agency would be required to comply if the agency operated or supported the facility. Compliance includes developing programs to promote and implement cost-effective waste reduction.

Subpart 23.1 Sustainable Acquisition Policy

§ 23.101 Definition.

As used in this subpart—

"Contract action" means any oral or written action that results in the purchase, rent, or lease of supplies or equipment, services, or construction using appropriated dollars, including purchases below the micro-purchase threshold. Contract action does not include grants, cooperative agreements, other transactions, real property leases, requisitions from Federal stock, training authorizations, or other non-FAR based transactions.

§ 23.102 Authorities.

(a) Executive Order 13423 of January 24, 2007, Strengthening Federal Environmental, Energy, and Transportation Management.

(b) Executive Order 13514 of October 5, 2009, Federal Leadership in Environmental, Energy, and Economic Performance.

(c) All of the authorities specified in subparts 23.2, 23.4, 23.7, 23.8, 23.9, and 23.10.

§ 23.103 Sustainable acquisitions.

(a) Federal agencies shall advance sustainable acquisition by ensuring that 95 percent of new contract actions for the supply of products and for the acquisition of services (including construction) require that the products are—

(1) Energy-efficient (ENERGY STAR® or Federal Energy Management Program (FEMP)-designated);

(2) Water-efficient;

(3) Biobased;

(4) Environmentally preferable (e.g., EPEAT®-registered, or non-toxic or less toxic alternatives);

(5) Non-ozone depleting; or

(6) Made with recovered materials.

(b) The required products in the contract actions for services include products that are—

(1) Delivered to the Government during performance;

(2) Acquired by the contractor for use in performing services at a Federally-controlled facility; or

(3) Furnished by the contractor for use by the Government.

(c) The required products in the contract actions must meet agency performance requirements.

(d) For purposes of meeting the 95 percent sustainable acquisition requirement, the term "contract actions" includes new contracts (and task and delivery orders placed against them) and new task and delivery orders on existing contracts.

§ 23.104 Exceptions.

This subpart does not apply to the following acquisitions:

(a) Contracts performed outside of the United States, unless the agency head determines that such application is in the interest of the United States.

(b) Weapon systems.

§ 23.105 Exemption authority.

(a) The head of an agency may exempt—

(1) Intelligence activities of the United States, and related personnel, resources, and facilities, to the extent the Director of National Intelligence or agency head determines it necessary to protect intelligence sources and methods from unauthorized disclosure;

(2) Law enforcement activities of that agency and related personnel, resources, and facilities, to the extent the head of an agency determines it necessary to protect undercover operations from unauthorized disclosure;

(3) Law enforcement, protective, emergency response, or military tactical vehicle fleets of that agency; and

(4) Agency activities and facilities in the interest of national security.

(b) If the head of the agency issues an exemption under paragraph (a) of this section, the agency must notify the Chair of the Council on Environmental Quality in writing within 30 days of the issuance of the exemption.

(c) The agency head may submit through the Chair of the Council on Environmental Quality a request for exemption of an agency activity other than those activities listed in paragraph (a) of this section and related personnel, resources, and facilities.

Subpart 23.2 Energy and Water Efficiency and Renewable Energy

§ 23.200 Scope.

(a) This subpart prescribes policies and procedures for—

(1) Acquiring energy- and water-efficient products and services, and products that use renewable energy technology; and

(2) Using an energy-savings performance contract to obtain energy-efficient technologies at Government facilities without Government capital expense.

(b) This subpart applies to acquisitions in the United States and its outlying areas. Agencies conducting acquisitions outside of theses areas must use their best efforts to comply with this subpart.

United States Code Annotated

Authority to enter into contracts, see 42 USCA § 8287.

Contract requirements, see 41 USCA § 254.

Contracts, planning, solicitation, evaluation, and award procedures, see 10 USCA § 2305.

Definitions, see 10 USCA § 2302, 41 USCA §§ 259, 403.

Energy management requirements, see 42 USCA § 8253.

Kinds of contracts, see 10 USCA § 2306.

Planning and solicitation requirements, see 41 USCA § 253a.

Procurement and identification of energy efficient products, see 42 USCA § 8262g.

§ 23.201 Authorities.

(a) Energy Policy and Conservation Act (42 U.S.C. 6361(a)(1)) and Resource Conservation and Recovery Act of 1976 (42 U.S.C. 6901, *et seq.*).

(b) National Energy Conservation Policy Act (42 U.S.C. 8253, 8259b, 8262g, and 8287).

(c) Section 706 of Division D, Title VII of the Omnibus Appropriations Act, 2009 (Pub. L. 111-8).

(d) Title VI of the Clean Air Act, as amended (42 U.S.C. 7671, *et seq.*).

(e) Executive Order 11912 of April 13, 1976, Delegations of Authority under the Energy Policy and Conservation Act.

(f) Executive Order 13221 of July 31, 2001, Energy-Efficient Standby Power Devices.

(g) Executive Order 13423 of January 24, 2007, Strengthening Federal Environmental, Energy, and Transportation Management.

(h) Executive Order 13514 of October 5, 2009, Federal Leadership in Environmental, Energy, and Economic Performance.

United States Code Annotated

Authority to enter into contracts, see 42 USCA § 8287.

Contract requirements, see 41 USCA § 254.

Contracts, planning, solicitation, evaluation, and award procedures, see 10 USCA § 2305.

Definitions, see 10 USCA § 2302, 41 USCA §§ 259, 403.

Energy management requirements, see 42 USCA § 8253.

Kinds of contracts, see 10 USCA § 2306.

Planning and solicitation requirements, see 41 USCA § 253a.

Procurement and identification of energy efficient products, see 42 USCA § 8262g.

§ 23.202 Policy.

(a) *Introduction.* The Government's policy is to acquire supplies and services that promote a clean energy economy that increases our Nation's energy security, safeguards the health of our environment, and reduces greenhouse gas emissions from direct and indirect Federal activities. To implement this policy, Federal acquisitions will foster markets for sustainable technologies, products, and services. This policy extends to all acquisitions, including those below the simplified acquisition threshold and those at or below the micro-purchase threshold (including those made with a Government purchase card).

(b) *Water-efficient.* In accordance with Executive Order 13514, dated October 5, 2009, Federal Leadership in Environmental, Energy, and Economic Performance, it is the policy and objective of the Government to use and manage water through water-efficient means by—

(1) Reducing potable water consumption intensity to include low-flow fixtures and efficient cooling towers;

(2) Reducing agency, industry, landscaping, and agricultural water consumption; and

(3) Storm water management in accordance with section 438 of the Energy Independence and Security Act of 2007 (42 U.S.C. 17094) as implemented in http://www.epa.gov/nps/lid/section438.

United States Code Annotated

Authority to enter into contracts, see 42 USCA § 8287.

Contract requirements, see 41 USCA § 254.

Contracts, planning, solicitation, evaluation, and award procedures, see 10 USCA § 2305.

Definitions, see 10 USCA § 2302, 41 USCA §§ 259, 403.

Energy management requirements, see 42 USCA § 8253.

Kinds of contracts, see 10 USCA § 2306.

Planning and solicitation requirements, see 41 USCA § 253a.

Procurement and identification of energy efficient products, see 42 USCA § 8262g.

§ 23.203 Energy-efficient products.

(a) Unless exempt as provided at 23.204—

(1) When acquiring energy-consuming products listed in the ENERGY STAR® Program or Federal Energy Management Program (FEMP)—

(i) Agencies shall purchase ENERGY STAR® or FEMP-designated products; and

(ii) For products that consume power in a standby mode and are listed on FEMP's Low Standby Power Devices product listing, agencies shall—

(A) Purchase items which meet FEMP's standby power wattage recommendation or document the reason for not purchasing such items; or

(B) If FEMP has listed a product without a corresponding wattage recommendation, purchase items which use no more than one watt in their standby power consuming mode. When it is impracticable to meet the one watt requirement, agencies shall purchase items with the lowest standby wattage practicable; and

(2) When contracting for services or construction that will include the provision of energy-consuming products, agencies shall specify products that comply with the applicable requirements in paragraph (a)(1) of this section.

(b) Information is available via the Internet about—

(1) ENERGY STAR® at *http://www.energystar.gov/products*; and

(2) FEMP at *http://www1.eere.energy.gov/femp/procurement/eep_requirements.html*.

United States Code Annotated

Authority to enter into contracts, see 42 USCA § 8287.

Contract requirements, see 41 USCA § 254.

Contracts, planning, solicitation, evaluation, and award procedures, see 10 USCA § 2305.

Definitions, see 10 USCA § 2302, 41 USCA §§ 259, 403.

Energy management requirements, see 42 USCA § 8253.

Kinds of contracts, see 10 USCA § 2306.

Planning and solicitation requirements, see 41 USCA § 253a.

Procurement and identification of energy efficient products, see 42 USCA § 8262g.

§ 23.204 Procurement exemptions.

An agency is not required to procure an ENERGY STAR® or FEMP-designated product if the head of the agency determines in writing that—

(a) No ENERGY STAR® or FEMP-designated product is reasonably available that meets the functional requirements of the agency; or

(b) No ENERGY STAR® or FEMP-designated product is cost effective over the life of the product taking energy cost savings into account.

United States Code Annotated

Authority to enter into contracts, see 42 USCA § 8287.

Contract requirements, see 41 USCA § 254.

Contracts, planning, solicitation, evaluation, and award procedures, see 10 USCA § 2305.

Definitions, see 10 USCA § 2302, 41 USCA §§ 259, 403.

Energy management requirements, see 42 USCA § 8253.

Kinds of contracts, see 10 USCA § 2306.

Planning and solicitation requirements, see 41 USCA § 253a.

Procurement and identification of energy efficient products, see 42 USCA § 8262g.

§ 23.205 Energy-savings performance contracts.

(a) Agencies should make maximum use of the authority provided in the National Energy Conservation Policy Act (42 U.S.C. 8287) to use an energy-savings performance contract (ESPC), when life-cycle cost-effective, to reduce energy use and cost in the agency's facilities and operations.

(b) (1) Under an ESPC, an agency can contract with an energy service company for a period not to exceed 25 years to improve energy efficiency in one or more agency facilities at no direct capital cost to the United States Treasury. The energy service company finances the capital costs of implementing energy conservation measures and receives, in return, a contractually determined share of the cost savings that result.

(2) Except as provided in 10 CFR 436.34, ESPC's are subject to Subpart 17.1.

(c) To solicit and award an ESPC, the contracting officer—

(1) Must use the procedures, selection method, and terms and conditions provided in 10 CFR Part 436, Subpart B; at http://www1.eere.energy.gov/femp/financing/espcs_regulations.html; and

(2) May use the "Qualified List" of energy service companies established by the Department of Energy and other agencies.

Notes of Decisions

In general 1

1 In general

The ESPC statute does not permit the inclusion of sales of Solar Renewable Energy Certificates (SRECs) among the energy savings generated by an ESPC in order to calculate the payments due to the contractor. A SREC represents one megawatt-hour of solar energy produced from a facility connected to New Jersey's distribution system. The contract authorized the contractor to sell SRECs earned via energy savings and use the proceeds to procure more energy savings equipment under the contract. The ASBCA held that the proceeds from SREC sales are not themselves "energy savings" and, therefore, consideration of such sales is not authorized by the ESPC statute (42 USC § 8287c). The ASBCA further determined that the contracting officer was not authorized to permit the contractor to sell the SRECs because the SRECs were government property and must be disposed of in accordance with GSA's government property disposal regulations (41 CFR §§ 102-35 thru 102-42).

§ 23.206 Contract clause.

Unless exempt pursuant to 23.204, insert the clause at 52.223-15, Energy Efficiency in Energy-Consuming Products, in solicitations and contracts when energy-consuming products listed in the ENERGY STAR® Program or FEMP will be—

(a) Delivered;

(b) Acquired by the contractor for use in performing services at a Federally-controlled facility;

(c) Furnished by the contractor for use by the Government; or

(d) Specified in the design of a building or work, or incorporated during its construction, renovation, or maintenance.

Subpart 23.3 Hazardous Material Identification and Material Safety Data

§ 23.300 Scope of subpart.

This subpart prescribes policies and procedures for acquiring deliverable items, other than ammunition and explosives, that require the furnishing of data involving hazardous materials. Agencies may prescribe special procedures for ammunition and explosives.

United States Code Annotated

Contract requirements, see 41 USCA § 254.

Contracts, planning, solicitation, evaluation, and award procedures, see 10 USCA § 2305.

Definitions, see 10 USCA § 2302, 41 USCA §§ 259, 403.

Kinds of contracts, see 10 USCA § 2306.

Planning and solicitation requirements, see 41 USCA § 253a.

§ 23.301 Definition.

"Hazardous material" is defined in the latest version of Federal Standard No. 313 (Federal Standards are sold to the public and Federal agencies through—

General Services Administration
Specifications Unit (3FBP-W)
7th & D Sts. SW
Washington, DC 20407.

United States Code Annotated

Contract requirements, see 41 USCA § 254.

Contracts, planning, solicitation, evaluation, and award procedures, see 10 USCA § 2305.

Definitions, see 10 USCA § 2302, 41 USCA §§ 259, 403.

Kinds of contracts, see 10 USCA § 2306.

Planning and solicitation requirements, see 41 USCA § 253a.

§ 23.302 Policy.

(a) The Occupational Safety and Health Administration (OSHA) is responsible for issuing and administering regulations that require Government activities to apprise their employees of—

(1) All hazards to which they may be exposed;

(2) Relative symptoms and appropriate emergency treatment; and

(3) Proper conditions and precautions for safe use and exposure.

(b) To accomplish this objective, it is necessary to obtain certain information relative to the hazards which may be introduced into the workplace by the supplies being acquired. Accordingly, offerors and contractors are required to submit hazardous materials data whenever the supplies being acquired are identified as hazardous materials. The latest version of Federal Standard No. 313 (Material Safety Data Sheet, Preparation and Submission of) includes criteria for identification of hazardous materials.

(c) Hazardous material data (Material Safety Data Sheets (MSDS)) are required—

(1) As specified in the latest version of Federal Standard No. 313 (including revisions adopted during the term of the contract);

(2) For any other material designated by a Government technical representative as potentially hazardous and requiring safety controls.

(d) MSDS's must be submitted—

(1) By the apparent successful offeror prior to contract award if hazardous materials are expected to be used during contract performance.

(2) For agencies other than the Department of Defense, again by the contractor with the supplies at the time of delivery.

(e) The contracting officer shall provide a copy of all MSDS's received to the safety officer or other designated individual.

United States Code Annotated

Contract requirements, see 41 USCA § 254.

Contracts, planning, solicitation, evaluation, and award procedures, see 10 USCA § 2305.

Definitions, see 10 USCA § 2302, 41 USCA §§ 259, 403.

Kinds of contracts, see 10 USCA § 2306.

Planning and solicitation requirements, see 41 USCA § 253a.

§ 23.303 Contract clause.

(a) The contracting officer shall insert the clause at 52.223-3, Hazardous Material Identification and Material Safety Data, in solicitations and contracts if the contract will require the delivery of hazardous materials as defined in 23.301.

(b) If the contract is awarded by an agency other than the Department of Defense, the contracting officer shall use the clause at 52.223-3 with its Alternate I.

United States Code Annotated

Contract requirements, see 41 USCA § 254.

Contracts, planning, solicitation, evaluation, and award procedures, see 10 USCA § 2305.

Definitions, see 10 USCA § 2302, 41 USCA §§ 259, 403.

Kinds of contracts, see 10 USCA § 2306.

Planning and solicitation requirements, see 41 USCA § 253a.

Subpart 23.4 Use of Recovered Materials and Biobased Products

§ 23.400 Scope of subpart.

(a) The procedures in this subpart apply to all agency acquisitions of an Environmental Protection Agency (EPA) or United States Department of Agriculture (USDA)-designated item, if—

(1) The price of the designated item exceeds $10,000; or

(2) The aggregate amount paid for designated items, or for functionally equivalent designated items, in the preceding fiscal year was $10,000 or more.

(b) While micro-purchases are included in determining the aggregate amount paid under paragraph (a)(2) of this section, it is not recommended that an agency track micro-purchases when—

(1) The agency anticipates the aggregate amount paid will exceed $10,000; or

(2) The agency intends to establish or continue an affirmative procurement program in

the following fiscal year.

United States Code Annotated

Contract requirements, see 41 USCA § 254.

Contracts, planning, solicitation, evaluation, and award procedures, see 10 USCA § 2305.

Definitions, see 10 USCA § 2302, 41 USCA §§ 259, 403.

Federal procurement, see 42 USCA § 6962.

Kinds of contracts, see 10 USCA § 2306.

Planning and solicitation requirements, see 41 USCA § 253a.

§ 23.401 Definitions.

As used in this subpart—

(a) "EPA-designated item" means a product that is or can be made with recovered material—

(1) That is listed by EPA in a procurement guideline (40 CFR part 247); and

(2) For which EPA has provided purchasing recommendations in a related Recovered Materials Advisory Notice (RMAN) (available at http://www.epa.gov/epawaste/conserve/tools/cpg/index.htm).

(b) "USDA-designated item" means a generic grouping of products that are or can be made with biobased materials—

(1) That is listed by USDA in a procurement guideline (7 CFR part 3201, subpart B); and

(2) For which USDA has provided purchasing recommendations.

United States Code Annotated

Contract requirements, see 41 USCA § 254.

Contracts, planning, solicitation, evaluation, and award procedures, see 10 USCA § 2305.

Definitions, see 10 USCA § 2302, 41 USCA §§ 259, 403.

Federal procurement, see 42 USCA § 6962.

Kinds of contracts, see 10 USCA § 2306.

Planning and solicitation requirements, see 41 USCA § 253a.

§ 23.402 Authorities.

(a) The Resource Conservation and Recovery Act of 1976 (RCRA), 42 U.S.C. 6962.

(b) The Farm Security and Rural Investment Act of 2002 (FSRIA), 7 U.S.C. 8102.

(c) Executive Order 13423 of January 24, 2007, Strengthening Federal Environmental, Energy, and Transportation Management.

(d) The Energy Policy Act of 2005, Pub. L. 109-58.

(e) Executive Order 13514 of October 5, 2009, Federal Leadership in Environmental, Energy, and Economic Performance.

United States Code Annotated

Contract requirements, see 41 USCA § 254.

Contracts, planning, solicitation, evaluation, and award procedures, see 10 USCA § 2305.

Definitions, see 10 USCA § 2302, 41 USCA §§ 259, 403.

Federal procurement, see 42 USCA § 6962.

Kinds of contracts, see 10 USCA § 2306.

Planning and solicitation requirements, see 41 USCA § 253a.

§ 23.403 Policy.

Government policy on the use of products containing recovered materials and biobased products considers cost, availability of competition, and performance. Agencies shall purchase these products or require in the acquisition of services, the delivery, use, or furnishing (see 23.103(b)) of such products. Agency contracts should specify that these products are composed of the highest percent of recovered material or biobased content practicable, or at least meet, but may exceed, the minimum recovered materials or biobased content of an EPA- or USDA- designated product. Agencies shall purchase these products to the maximum extent practicable without jeopardizing the intended use of the product while maintaining a satisfactory level of competition at a reasonable price. Such products shall meet the reasonable performance standards of the agency and be acquired competitively, in a cost-effective manner. Except as provided at 23.404(b), virgin material shall not be required by the solicitation (see 11.302).

United States Code Annotated

Contract requirements, see 41 USCA § 254.

Contracts, planning, solicitation, evaluation, and award procedures, see 10 USCA § 2305.

Definitions, see 10 USCA § 2302, 41 USCA §§ 259, 403.

Federal procurement, see 42 USCA § 6962.

Kinds of contracts, see 10 USCA § 2306.

Planning and solicitation requirements, see 41 USCA § 253a.

§ 23.404 Agency affirmative procurement programs.

(a) An agency must establish an affirmative procurement program for EPA and USDA-designated items if the agency's purchases of designated items exceed the threshold set forth in 23.400.

(1) Agencies have a period of 1 year to revise their procurement program(s) after the designation of any new item by EPA or USDA.

(2) Technical or requirements personnel and procurement personnel are responsible for the preparation, implementation, and monitoring of affirmative procurement programs.

(3) Agency affirmative procurement programs must include—

(i) A recovered materials and biobased products preference program;

(ii) An agency promotion program;

(iii) For EPA-designated items only, a program for requiring reasonable estimates, certification, and verification of recovered material used in the performance of contracts. Both the recovered material content and biobased programs require preaward certification that the products meet EPA or USDA recommendations. A second certification is required at contract completion for recovered material content; and

(iv) Annual review and monitoring of the effectiveness of the program.

(b) "Exemptions".

(1) Agency affirmative procurement programs must require that 100 percent of purchases of EPA or USDA-designated items contain recovered material or biobased content, respectively, unless the item cannot be acquired—

(i) Competitively within a reasonable time frame;

(ii) Meeting reasonable performance standards; or

(iii) At a reasonable price.

(2) EPA and USDA may provide categorical exemptions for items that they designate, when procured for a specific purpose. For example, all USDA-designated items (see 7 CFR 3201.3 (e)) are exempt from the preferred procurement requirement for the following:

(i) Spacecraft system and launch support equipment.

(ii) Military equipment, i.e., a product or system designed or procured for combat or combat-related missions.

(c) Agency affirmative procurement programs must provide guidance for purchases of EPA-designated items at or below the micro-purchase threshold.

(d) Agencies may use their own specifications or commercial product descriptions when procuring products containing recovered materials or biobased products. When using either, the contract should specify—

(1) For products containing recovered materials, that the product is composed of the—

(i) Highest percent of recovered materials practicable; or

(ii) Minimum content standards in accordance with EPA's Recovered Materials Advisory Notices; and

(2) For biobased products, that the product is composed of—

(i) The highest percentage of biobased material practicable; or

(ii) USDA's recommended minimum contents standards.

(e) Agencies shall treat as eligible for the preference for biobased products, products from "designated countries," as defined in 25.003, provided that those products—

(1) Meet the criteria for the definition of biobased product, except that the products need not meet the requirement that renewable agricultural materials or forestry materials in such product must be domestic; and

(2) Otherwise meet all requirements for participation in the preference program.

United States Code Annotated

Contract requirements, see 41 USCA § 254.

Contracts, planning, solicitation, evaluation, and award procedures, see 10 USCA § 2305.

Definitions, see 10 USCA § 2302, 41 USCA §§ 259, 403.

Federal procurement, see 42 USCA § 6962.

Kinds of contracts, see 10 USCA § 2306.

Planning and solicitation requirements, see 41 USCA § 253a.

§ 23.405 Procedures.

(a) *Designated items and procurement guidelines.*

(1) *Recovered Materials.* Contracting officers should refer to EPA's list of EPA-designated items (available via the Internet at http://www.epa.gov/cpg/products.htm) and to their agencies' affirmative procurement program when purchasing products that contain recovered material, or services that could include the use of products that contain recovered material.

(2) *Biobased products.* Contracting officers should refer to USDA's list of USDA-designated items (available through the Internet at http://www.biopreferred.gov) and to their agencies affirmative procurement program when purchasing supplies that contain biobased material or when purchasing services that could include supplies that contain biobased material.

(3) When acquiring recovered material or biobased products, the contracting officer may request information or data on such products, including recycled or biobased content or related standards of the products (see 11.302(c)).

(b) *Procurement exemptions.*

(1) Once an item has been designated by either EPA or USDA, agencies shall purchase conforming products unless an exemption applies (see 23.404(b)).

(2) When an exemption is used for an EPA-designated item or the procurement of a product containing recovered material does not meet or exceed the EPA recovered material content guidelines, the contracting officer shall place a written justification in the contract file.

(c) *Program priorities.* When both the USDA-designated item and the EPA-designated item will be used for the same purposes, and both meet the agency's needs, the agency shall purchase the EPA-designated item.

United States Code Annotated

Contract requirements, see 41 USCA § 254.

Contracts, planning, solicitation, evaluation, and award procedures, see 10 USCA § 2305.

Definitions, see 10 USCA § 2302, 41 USCA §§ 259, 403.

Federal procurement, see 42 USCA § 6962.

Kinds of contracts, see 10 USCA § 2306.

Planning and solicitation requirements, see 41 USCA § 253a.

§ 23.406 Solicitation provisions and contract clauses.

(a) Insert the provision at 52.223-1, Biobased Product Certification, in solicitations that—

(1) Require the delivery or specify the use of USDA-designated items; or

(2) Include the clause at 52.223-2.

(b) Insert the clause at 52.223-2, Affirmative Procurement of Biobased Products Under Service and Construction Contracts, in service or construction solicitations and contracts, unless the contract will not involve the use of USDA-designated items at http://www.biopre ferred.gov or 7 CFR part 3201.

(c) Except for the acquisition of commercially available off-the-shelf items, insert the provision at 52.223-4, Recovered Material Certification, in solicitations that—

(1) Require the delivery or specify the use of EPA-designated items; or

(2) Include the clause at 52.223-17, Affirmative Procurement of EPA-designated Items in Service and Construction Contracts.

(d) Except for the acquisition of commercially available off-the-shelf items, insert the clause at 52.223-9, Estimate of Percentage of Recovered Material Content for EPA-designated Items, in solicitations and contracts exceeding $150,000 that are for, or specify the use of, EPA-designated items containing recovered materials. If technical personnel advise that estimates can be verified, use the clause with its Alternate I.

(e) Insert the clause at 52.223-17, Affirmative Procurement of EPA-designated Items in Service and Construction Contracts, in service or construction solicitations and contracts unless the contract will not involve the use of EPA-designated items.

United States Code Annotated

Contract requirements, see 41 USCA § 254.

Contracts, planning, solicitation, evaluation, and award procedures, see 10 USCA § 2305.

Definitions, see 10 USCA § 2302, 41 USCA §§ 259, 403.

Federal procurement, see 42 USCA § 6962.

Kinds of contracts, see 10 USCA § 2306.

Planning and solicitation requirements, see 41 USCA § 253a.

Subpart 23.5 Drug-Free Workplace

§ 23.500 Scope of subpart.

This subpart implements 41 U.S.C. chapter 81, Drug-Free Workplace.

United States Code Annotated

Contract requirements, see 41 USCA § 254.

Contracts, planning, solicitation, evaluation, and award procedures, see 10 USCA § 2305.

Definitions, Drug-free workplace, see 41 USCA § 706.

Definitions, see 10 USCA § 2302, 41 USCA §§ 259, 403.

Drug-free workplace requirements for Federal contractors, see 41 USCA § 701.

Employee sanctions and remedies, see 41 USCA § 703.

Kinds of contracts, see 10 USCA § 2306.

Planning and solicitation requirements, see 41 USCA § 253a.

§ 23.501 Applicability.

This subpart applies to contracts, including contracts with 8(a) contractors under FAR Subpart 19.8 and modifications that require a justification and approval (see Subpart 6.3), except contracts—

(a) At or below the simplified acquisition threshold; however, the requirements of this subpart apply to all contracts of any value awarded to an individual;

(b) For the acquisition of commercial items (see Part 12);

(c) Performed outside the United States and its outlying areas or any part of a contract performed outside the United States and its outlying areas;

(d) By law enforcement agencies, if the head of the law enforcement agency or designee involved determines that application of this subpart would be inappropriate in connection with the law enforcement agency's undercover operations; or

(e) Where application would be inconsistent with the international obligations of the United States or with the laws and regulations of a foreign country.

United States Code Annotated

Contract requirements, see 41 USCA § 254.

Contracts, planning, solicitation, evaluation, and award procedures, see 10 USCA § 2305.

Definitions, Drug-free workplace, see 41 USCA § 706.

Definitions, see 10 USCA § 2302, 41 USCA §§ 259, 403.

Drug-free workplace requirements for Federal contractors, see 41 USCA § 701.

Employee sanctions and remedies, see 41 USCA § 703.

Kinds of contracts, see 10 USCA § 2306.

Planning and solicitation requirements, see 41 USCA § 253a.

Waiver, see 41 USCA § 704.

§ 23.502 Authority.

41 U.S.C. chapter 81, Drug-Free Workplace.

United States Code Annotated

Contract requirements, see 41 USCA § 254.

Contracts, planning, solicitation, evaluation, and award procedures, see 10 USCA § 2305.

Definitions, Drug-free workplace, see 41 USCA § 706.

Definitions, see 10 USCA § 2302, 41 USCA §§ 259, 403.

Drug-free workplace requirements for Federal contractors, see 41 USCA § 701.

Employee sanctions and remedies, see 41 USCA § 703.

Kinds of contracts, see 10 USCA § 2306.

Planning and solicitation requirements, see 41 USCA § 253a.

Waiver, see 41 USCA § 704.

§ 23.503 Definitions.

As used in this subpart—

"Controlled substance" means a controlled substance in schedules I through V of section 202 of the Controlled Substances Act (21 U.S.C. 812), and as further defined in regulation at 21 CFR 1308.11–1308.15.

"Conviction" means a finding of guilt (including a plea of nolo contendere) or imposition of sentence, or both, by any judicial body charged with the responsibility to determine violations of the Federal or State criminal drug statutes.

"Criminal drug statute" means a Federal or non-Federal criminal statute involving the manufacture, distribution, dispensing, possession, or use of any controlled substance.

"Employee" means an employee of a contractor directly engaged in the performance of work under a Government contract. "Directly engaged" is defined to include all direct cost employees and any other contract employee who has other than a minimal impact or involvement in contract performance.

"Individual" means an offeror/contractor that has no more than one employee including the offeror/contractor.

United States Code Annotated

Contract requirements, see 41 USCA § 254.

Contracts, planning, solicitation, evaluation, and award procedures, see 10 USCA § 2305.

Definitions, Drug-free workplace, see 41 USCA § 706.

Definitions, see 10 USCA § 2302, 41 USCA §§ 259, 403.

Drug-free workplace requirements for Federal contractors, see 41 USCA § 701.

Employee sanctions and remedies, see 41 USCA § 703.

Kinds of contracts, see 10 USCA § 2306.

Planning and solicitation requirements, see 41 USCA § 253a.

Waiver, see 41 USCA § 704.

§ 23.504 Policy.

(a) No offeror other than an individual shall be considered a responsible source (see 9.104-1(g) and 19.602-1(a)(2)(i)) for a contract that exceeds the simplified acquisition threshold, unless it agrees that it will provide a drug-free workplace by—

(1) Publishing a statement notifying its employees that the unlawful manufacture, distribution, dispensing, possession, or use of a controlled substance is prohibited in the contractor's workplace, and specifying the actions that will be taken against employees for violations of such prohibition;

(2) Establishing an ongoing drug-free awareness program to inform its employees about—

(i) The dangers of drug abuse in the workplace;

(ii) The contractor's policy of maintaining a drugfree workplace;

(iii) Any available drug counseling, rehabilitation, and employee assistance programs; and

(iv) The penalties that may be imposed upon employees for drug abuse violations occurring in the workplace;

(3) Providing all employees engaged in performance of the contract with a copy of the statement required by paragraph (a)(1) of this section;

(4) Notifying all employees in writing in the statement required by paragraph (a)(1) of this section, that as a condition of employment on a covered contract, the employee will—

(i) Abide by the terms of the statement; and

(ii) Notify the employer in writing of the employee's conviction under a criminal drug statute for a violation occurring in the workplace no later than 5 days after such conviction;

(5) Notifying the contracting officer in writing within 10 days after receiving notice under subdivision (a)(4)(ii) of this section, from an employee or otherwise receiving actual notice of such conviction. The notice shall include the position title of the employee;

(6) Within 30 days after receiving notice under paragraph (a)(4) of this section of a conviction, taking one of the following actions with respect to any employee who is convicted of a drug abuse violation occurring in the workplace:

(i) Taking appropriate personnel action against such employee, up to and including termination; or

(ii) Requiring such employee to satisfactorily participate in a drug abuse assistance or rehabilitation program approved for such purposes by a Federal, State, or local health, law enforcement, or other appropriate agency.

(7) Making a good faith effort to maintain a drug-free workplace through implementation of paragraphs (a)(1) through (a)(6) of this section.

(b) No individual shall be awarded a contract of any dollar value unless that individual agrees not to engage in the unlawful manufacture, distribution, dispensing, possession, or use of a controlled substance while performing the contract.

(c) For a contract of 30 days or more performance duration, the contractor shall comply with the provisions of paragraph (a) of this section within 30 days after contract award, unless the contracting officer agrees in writing that circumstances warrant a longer period of time to comply. Before granting such an extension, the contracting officer shall consider such factors as the number of contractor employees at the worksite, whether the contractor has or must develop a drug-free workplace program, and the number of contractor worksites. For contracts of less than 30 days performance duration, the contractor shall comply with the provisions of paragraph (a) of this section as soon as possible, but in any case, by a date prior to when performance is expected to be completed.

United States Code Annotated

Contract requirements, see 41 USCA § 254.

Contracts, planning, solicitation, evaluation, and award procedures, see 10 USCA § 2305.

Definitions, Drug-free workplace, see 41 USCA § 706.

Definitions, see 10 USCA § 2302, 41 USCA §§ 259, 403.

Drug-free workplace requirements for Federal contractors, see 41 USCA § 701.

Employee sanctions and remedies, see 41 USCA § 703.

Kinds of contracts, see 10 USCA § 2306.

Planning and solicitation requirements, see 41 USCA § 253a.

Waiver, see 41 USCA § 704.

§ 23.505 Contract clause.

Except as provided in 23.501, insert the clause at 52.223-6, Drug-Free Workplace, in solicitations and contracts.

United States Code Annotated

Contract requirements, see 41 USCA § 254.

Contracts, planning, solicitation, evaluation, and award procedures, see 10 USCA § 2305.

Definitions, Drug-free workplace, see 41 USCA § 706.

Definitions, see 10 USCA § 2302, 41 USCA §§ 259, 403.

Drug-free workplace requirements for Federal contractors, see 41 USCA § 701.

Employee sanctions and remedies, see 41 USCA § 703.

Kinds of contracts, see 10 USCA § 2306.

Planning and solicitation requirements, see 41 USCA § 253a.

Waiver, see 41 USCA § 704.

§ 23.506 Suspension of payments, termination of contract, and debarment and suspension actions.

(a) After determining in writing that adequate evidence to suspect any of the causes at paragraph (d) of this section exists, the contracting officer may suspend contract payments in accordance with the procedures at 32.503-6(a)(1).

(b) After determining in writing that any of the causes at paragraph (d) of this section exist, the contracting officer may terminate the contract for default.

(c) Upon initiating action under paragraph (a) or (b) of this section, the contracting officer shall refer the case to the agency suspension and debarment official, in accordance with agency procedures, pursuant to Subpart 9.4.

(d) The specific causes for suspension of contract payments, termination of a contract for default, or suspension and debarment are—

(1) The contractor has failed to comply with the requirements of the clause at 52.223-6, Drug-Free Workplace; or

(2) The number of contractor employees convicted of violations of criminal drug statutes occurring in the workplace indicates that the contractor has failed to make a good faith effort to provide a drug-free workplace.

(e) A determination under this section to suspend contract payments, terminate a contract for default, or debar or suspend a contractor may be waived by the agency head for a particular contract, in accordance with agency procedures, only if such waiver is necessary to prevent a severe disruption of the agency operation to the detriment of the Federal Government or the general public (see Subpart 9.4). The waiver authority of the agency head cannot be delegated.

United States Code Annotated

Contract requirements, see 41 USCA § 254.

Contracts, planning, solicitation, evaluation, and award procedures, see 10 USCA § 2305.

Definitions, Drug-free workplace, see 41 USCA § 706.

Definitions, see 10 USCA § 2302, 41 USCA §§ 259, 403.

Drug-free workplace requirements for Federal contractors, see 41 USCA § 701.

Employee sanctions and remedies, see 41 USCA § 703.

Kinds of contracts, see 10 USCA § 2306.

Planning and solicitation requirements, see 41 USCA § 253a.

Waiver, see 41 USCA § 704.

Subpart 23.6 Notice of Radioactive Material

§ 23.601 Requirements.

(a) The clause at 52.223-7, Notice of Radioactive Materials, requires the contractor to notify the contracting officer prior to delivery of radioactive material.

(b) Upon receipt of the notice, the contracting officer shall notify receiving activities so that appropriate safeguards can be taken.

(c) The clause permits the contracting officer to waive the notification if the contractor states that the notification on prior deliveries is still current. The contracting officer may waive the notice only after consultation with cognizant technical representatives.

(d) The contracting officer is required to specify in the clause at 52.223-7, the number of days in advance of delivery that the contractor will provide notification. The determination of the number of days should be done in coordination with the installation/facility radiation protection officer (RPO). The RPO is responsible for insuring the proper license, authorization or permit is obtained prior to receipt of the radioactive material.

United States Code Annotated

Contract requirements, see 41 USCA § 254.

Contracts, planning, solicitation, evaluation, and award procedures, see 10 USCA § 2305.

Definitions, see 10 USCA § 2302, 41 USCA §§ 259, 403.

Kinds of contracts, see 10 USCA § 2306.

Planning and solicitation requirements, see 41 USCA § 253a.

§ 23.602 Contract clause.

The contracting officer shall insert the clause at 52.223-7, Notice of Radioactive Materials, in solicitations and contracts for supplies which are, or which contain—(a) radioactive material requiring specific licensing under regulations issued pursuant to the Atomic Energy Act of 1954; or (b) radioactive material not requiring specific licensing in which the specific activity is greater than 0.002 microcuries per gram or the activity per item equals or exceeds 0.01 microcuries. Such supplies include, but are not limited to, aircraft, ammunition, missiles, vehicles, electronic tubes, instrument panel gauges, compasses and identification markers.

United States Code Annotated

Contract requirements, see 41 USCA § 254.

Contracts, planning, solicitation, evaluation, and award procedures, see 10 USCA § 2305.

Definitions, see 10 USCA § 2302, 41 USCA §§ 259, 403.

Kinds of contracts, see 10 USCA § 2306.

Planning and solicitation requirements, see 41 USCA § 253a.

Subpart 23.7 Contracting for Environmentally Preferable Products and Services

§ 23.700 Scope.

This subpart prescribes policies for acquiring environmentally preferable products and services.

United States Code Annotated

Contract requirements, see 41 USCA § 254.

Contracts, planning, solicitation, evaluation, and award procedures, see 10 USCA § 2305.

Definitions, see 10 USCA § 2302, 41 USCA §§ 259, 403.

Kinds of contracts, see 10 USCA § 2306.

Planning and solicitation requirements, see 41 USCA § 253a.

Procurement and identification of energy efficient products, see 42 USCA § 8262g.

§ 23.701 Definitions.

As used in this subpart—

"Computer" means a device that performs logical operations and processes data. Computers are composed of, at a minimum:

(1) A central processing unit (CPU) to perform operations;

(2) User input devices such as a keyboard, mouse, digitizer, or game controller; and

(3) A computer display screen to output information. Computers include both stationary and portable units, including desktop computers, integrated desktop computers, notebook computers, thin clients, and workstations. Although computers must be capable of using input devices and computer displays, as noted in paragraphs (2) and (3) of this definition, computer systems do not need to include these devices on shipment to meet this definition. This definition does not include server computers, gaming consoles, mobile telephones, portable hand-held calculators, portable digital assistants (PDAs), MP3 players, or any other mobile computing device with displays less than 4 inches, measured diagonally.

"Computer display" means a display screen and its associated electronics encased in a single housing or within the computer housing (*e.g.*, notebook or integrated desktop computer) that is capable of displaying output information from a computer via one or more inputs such as a VGA, DVI, USB, DisplayPort, and/or IEEE 1394-2008™, Standard for High Performance Serial Bus. Examples of computer display technologies are the cathode-ray tube (CRT) and liquid crystal display (LCD).

"Desktop computer" means a computer where the main unit is intended to be located in a permanent location, often on a desk or on the floor. Desktops are not designed for portability and utilize an external computer display, keyboard, and mouse. Desktops are designed for a broad range of home and office applications.

"Electronic products" means products that are dependent on electric currents or electromagnetic fields in order to work properly.

"Imaging equipment" means the following products:

(1) *Copier*–A commercially available imaging product with a sole function of the production of hard copy duplicates from graphic hard-copy originals. The unit is capable of being powered from a wall outlet or from a data or network connection. This definition is intended to cover products that are marketed as copiers or upgradeable digital copiers (UDCs).

(2) *Digital duplicator*–A commercially available imaging product that is sold in the market as a fully automated duplicator system through the method of stencil duplicating with digital reproduction functionality. The unit is capable of being powered from a wall outlet or from a data or network connection. This definition is intended to cover products that are marketed as digital duplicators.

(3) *Facsimile machine (fax machine)*–A commercially available imaging product whose primary functions are scanning hard-copy originals for electronic transmission to remote units and receiving similar electronic transmissions to produce hard-copy output. Electronic transmission is primarily over a public telephone system but also may be via computer network or the Internet. The product also may be capable of producing hard copy duplicates. The unit is capable of being powered from a wall outlet or from a data or network connection. This definition is intended to cover products that are marketed as fax machines.

(4) *Mailing machine*–A commercially available imaging product that serves to print postage onto mail pieces. The unit is capable of being powered from a wall outlet or from a data or network connection. This definition is intended to cover products that are marketed as mailing machines.

(5) *Multifunction device (MFD)*–A commercially available imaging product, which is a physically integrated device or a combination of functionally integrated components, that

performs two or more of the core functions of copying, printing, scanning, or faxing. The copy functionality as addressed in this definition is considered to be distinct from single-sheet convenience copying offered by fax machines. The unit is capable of being powered from a wall outlet or from a data or network connection. This definition is intended to cover products that are marketed as MFDs or multifunction products.

(6) *Printer*–A commercially available imaging product that serves as a hard-copy output device and is capable of receiving information from single-user or networked computers, or other input devices (e.g., digital cameras). The unit is capable of being powered from a wall outlet or from a data or network connection. This definition is intended to cover products that are marketed as printers, including printers that can be upgraded into MFDs in the field.

(7) *Scanner*–A commercially available imaging product that functions as an electro-optical device for converting information into electronic images that can be stored, edited, converted, or transmitted, primarily in a personal computing environment. The unit is capable of being powered from a wall outlet or from a data or network connection. This definition is intended to cover products that are marketed as scanners.

"Integrated desktop computer" means a desktop system in which the computer and computer display function as a single unit that receives its AC power through a single cable. Integrated desktop computers come in one of two possible forms:

(1) A system where the computer display and computer are physically combined into a single unit; or

(2) A system packaged as a single system where the computer display is separate but is connected to the main chassis by a DC power cord and both the computer and computer display are powered from a single power supply. As a subset of desktop computers, integrated desktop computers are typically designed to provide similar functionality as desktop systems.

"Notebook computer" means a computer designed specifically for portability and to be operated for extended periods of time either with or without a direct connection to an AC power source. Notebooks must utilize an integrated computer display and be capable of operation off of an integrated battery or other portable power source. In addition, most notebooks use an external power supply and have an integrated keyboard and pointing device. Notebook computers are typically designed to provide similar functionality to desktops, including operation of software similar in functionality to that used in desktops. Docking stations are considered accessories for notebook computers, not notebook computers. Tablet PCs, which may use touch-sensitive screens along with, or instead of, other input devices, are considered notebook computers.

"Personal computer product" means a computer, computer display, desktop computer, integrated desktop computer, or notebook computer.

"Television", or "TV", means a commercially available electronic product designed primarily for the reception and display of audiovisual signals received from terrestrial, cable, satellite, Internet Protocol TV (IPTV), or other digital or analog sources. A TV consists of a tuner/receiver and a display encased in a single enclosure. The product usually relies upon a cathode-ray tube (CRT), liquid crystal display (LCD), plasma display, or other display technology. Televisions with computer capability (*e.g.*, computer input port) may be considered to be a TV as long as they are marketed and sold to consumers primarily as televisions.

United States Code Annotated

Contract requirements, see 41 USCA § 254.

Contracts, planning, solicitation, evaluation, and award procedures, see 10 USCA § 2305.

Definitions, see 10 USCA § 2302, 41 USCA §§ 259, 403.

Kinds of contracts, see 10 USCA § 2306.

Planning and solicitation requirements, see 41 USCA § 253a.

Procurement and identification of energy efficient products, see 42 USCA § 8262g.

§ 23.702 Authorities.

(a) Resource Conservation and Recovery Act (RCRA) (42 U.S.C. 6901, *et seq.*).

(b) National Energy Conservation Policy Act (42 U.S.C. 8262g).

(c) Pollution Prevention Act of 1990 (42 U.S.C. 13101, *et seq.*).

(d) Farm Security and Rural Investment Act of 2002 (FSRIA) (7 U.S.C. 8102).

(e) Executive Order 13221 of July 31, 2001, Energy Efficient Standby Power Devices.

(f) Executive Order 13423 of January 24, 2007, Strengthening Federal Environmental, Energy, and Transportation Management.

(g) Executive Order 13514 of October 5, 2009, Federal Leadership in Environmental, Energy, and Economic Performance.

United States Code Annotated

Contract requirements, see 41 USCA § 254.

Contracts, planning, solicitation, evaluation, and award procedures, see 10 USCA § 2305.

Definitions, see 10 USCA § 2302, 41 USCA §§ 259, 403.

Kinds of contracts, see 10 USCA § 2306.

Planning and solicitation requirements, see 41 USCA § 253a.

Procurement and identification of energy efficient products, see 42 USCA § 8262g.

§ 23.703 Policy.

Agencies must—

(a) Implement cost-effective contracting preference programs promoting energy-efficiency, water conservation, and the acquisition of environmentally preferable products and services; and

(b) Employ acquisition strategies that affirmatively implement the following environmental objectives:

(1) Maximize the utilization of environmentally preferable products and services (based on EPA-issued guidance).

(2) Promote energy-efficiency and water conservation.

(3) Eliminate or reduce the generation of hazardous waste and the need for special material processing (including special handling, storage, treatment, and disposal).

(4) Promote the use of nonhazardous and recovered materials.

(5) Realize life-cycle cost savings.

(6) Promote cost-effective waste reduction when creating plans, drawings, specifications, standards, and other product descriptions authorizing material substitutions, extensions of shelf-life, and process improvements.

(7) Promote the use of biobased products.

(8) Purchase only plastic ring carriers that are degradable (7 USC 8102(c)(1), 40 CFR part 238).

United States Code Annotated

Contract requirements, see 41 USCA § 254.

Contracts, planning, solicitation, evaluation, and award procedures, see 10 USCA § 2305.

Definitions, see 10 USCA § 2302, 41 USCA §§ 259, 403.

Kinds of contracts, see 10 USCA § 2306.

Planning and solicitation requirements, see 41 USCA § 253a.

Procurement and identification of energy efficient products, see 42 USCA § 8262g.

§ 23.704 Electronic products environmental assessment tool.

(a) (1) *General.* As required by E.O.s 13423 and 13514, agencies shall acquire Electronic Product Environmental Assessment Tool (EPEAT®)-registered electronic products, unless—

(i) There is no EPEAT® standard for such products; or

(ii) The agency head, in accordance with agency procedures, determines that—

(A) No EPEAT®-registered product meets agency requirements; or

(B) The EPEAT®-registered product will not be cost effective over the life of the product.

(2) This subpart applies to acquisitions of electronic products to be used in the United States, unless otherwise provided by agency procedures. When acquiring electronic products to be used outside the United States, agencies must use their best efforts to comply with this subpart.

(b) *Personal computer products, imaging equipment, and televisions.* These are categories of EPEAT®-registered electronic products.

(1) The IEEE 1680.1™-2009 Standard for the Environmental Assessment of Personal Computer Products, the IEEE 1680.2™-2012 Standard for the Environmental Assessment of Imaging Equipment, and the IEEE 1680.3™-2012 Standard for the Environmental Assessment of Televisions—

(i) Were as issued by the Institute of Electrical and Electronics Engineers, Inc., on March 5, 2010; October 19, 2012, and October 19, 2012, respectively;

(ii) Are voluntary consensus standards consistent with section 12(d) of Pub. L. 104-113, the "National Technology Transfer and Advancement Act of 1995", (see 11.102);

(iii) Meets EPA-issued guidance on environmentally preferable products and services; and

(iv) Are described in more detail at *www.epa.gov/epeat*.

(2) A list of EPEAT® product categories and EPEAT®-registered electronic products that are in conformance with these standards can be found at *www.epa.gov/epeat*.

(3) EPEAT® electronic products are designated "bronze-," "silver-," or "gold-" registered.

(4) Agencies shall, at a minimum, acquire EPEAT® bronze-registered products.

(5) Agencies are encouraged to acquire EPEAT® silver- or gold-registered products.

§ 23.705 Contract clauses.

(a) Insert the clause at 52.223-10, Waste Reduction Program, in all solicitations and contracts for contractor operation of Government-owned or -leased facilities and all solicitations and contracts for support services at Government-owned or -operated facilities.

(b) (1) Unless an exception applies in accordance with 23.704(a), insert the clause at 52.223-16, Acquisition of EPEAT®-Registered Personal Computer Products, in all solicitations and contracts when personal computer products will be—

(i) Delivered;

(ii) Acquired by the contractor for use in performing services at a Federally controlled facility; or

(iii) Furnished by the contractor for use by the Government.

(2) Agencies may use the clause with its Alternate I when there are sufficient EPEAT® silver- or gold-registered products available to meet agency needs.

(c) (1) Unless an exception applies in accordance with 23.704(a), insert the clause at 52.223-13, Acquisition of EPEAT®-Registered Imaging Equipment, in all solicitations and contracts when imaging equipment (copiers, digital duplicators, facsimile machines, mailing machines, multifunction devices, printers, and scanners) will be—

(i) Delivered;

(ii) Acquired by the contractor for use in performing services at a Federally controlled facility; or

(iii) Furnished by the contractor for use by the Government.

(2) Agencies may use the clause with its Alternate I when there are sufficient EPEAT® silver- or gold-registered products available to meet agency needs.

(d) (1) Unless an exception applies in accordance with 23.704(a), insert the clause at 52.223-14, Acquisition of EPEAT®-Registered Televisions, in all solicitations and contracts when televisions will be—

(i) Delivered;

(ii) Acquired by the contractor for use in performing services at a Federally controlled facility; or

(iii) Furnished by the contractor for use by the Government.

(2) Agencies may use the clause with its Alternate I when there are sufficient EPEAT® silver- or gold-registered products available to meet agency needs.

Subpart 23.8 —Ozone-Depleting Substances and Hydrofluorocarbons

§ 23.800 Scope of subpart.

This subpart sets forth policies and procedures for the acquisition of items that–

(a) Contain, use, or are manufactured with ozone-depleting substances; or

(b) Contain or use high global warming potential hydrofluorocarbons.

United States Code Annotated

Contract requirements, see 41 USCA § 254.

Contracts, planning, solicitation, evaluation, and award procedures, see 10 USCA § 2305.

Definitions, ozone protection terms, see 42 USCA § 7671.

Definitions, see 10 USCA § 2302, 41 USCA §§ 259, 403.

Federal procurement, see 42 USCA § 7671l.

Kinds of contracts, see 10 USCA § 2306.

Planning and solicitation requirements, see 41 USCA § 253a.

Safe alternatives policy, see 42 USCA § 7671k.

§ 23.801 Authorities.

(a) Title VI of the Clean Air Act (42 U.S.C. 7671, et seq.).

(b) Section 706 of Division D, Title VII of the Omnibus Appropriations Act, 2009 (Pub. L. 111-8).

(c) Executive Order 13693 of March 25, 2015, Planning for Federal Sustainability in the Next Decade.

(d) Environmental Protection Agency (EPA) regulations, Protection of Stratospheric Ozone (40 CFR part 82).

United States Code Annotated

Contract requirements, see 41 USCA § 254.

Contracts, planning, solicitation, evaluation, and award procedures, see 10 USCA § 2305.

Definitions, ozone protection terms, see 42 USCA § 7671.

Definitions, see 10 USCA § 2302, 41 USCA §§ 259, 403.

Federal procurement, see 42 USCA § 7671l.

Kinds of contracts, see 10 USCA § 2306.

Planning and solicitation requirements, see 41 USCA § 253a.

Safe alternatives policy, see 42 USCA § 7671k.

§ 23.802 Policy.

It is the policy of the Federal Government that Federal agencies–

(a) Implement cost-effective programs to minimize the procurement of materials and substances that contribute to the depletion of stratospheric ozone and/or result in the use, release or emission of high global warming potential hydrofluorocarbons; and

(b) Give preference to the procurement of acceptable alternative chemicals, products, and manufacturing processes that reduce overall risks to human health and the environment by minimizing-

(1) The depletion of ozone in the upper atmosphere; and

(2) The potential use, release, or emission of high global warming potential hydrofluorocarbons.

§ 23.803 Procedures.

In preparing specifications and purchase descriptions, and in the acquisition of products and services, agencies shall–

(a) Comply with the requirements of title VI of the Clean Air Act, section 706 of division D, title VII of Pub. L. 111-8, Executive Order 13693, and 40 CFR 82.84(a)(2), (3), (4), and

1363

(5);

(b) Substitute acceptable alternatives to ozone-depleting substances, as identified under 42 U.S.C. 7671k, to the maximum extent practicable, as provided in 40 CFR 82.84(a)(1), except in the case of Class I substances being used for specified essential uses, as identified under 40 CFR 82.4(n);

(c) Unless a particular contract requires otherwise, specify that, when feasible, contractors shall use another acceptable alternative in lieu of a high global warming potential hydrofluorocarbon in products and services in a particular end use for which EPA's Significant New Alternatives Policy (SNAP) program has identified other acceptable alternatives that have lower global warming potential; and

(d) Refer to EPA's SNAP program for the list of alternatives, found at 40 CFR part 82, subpart G as well as supplemental tables of alternatives (available at http://www.epa.gov/snap).

United States Code Annotated

Contract requirements, see 41 USCA § 254.

Contracts, planning, solicitation, evaluation, and award procedures, see 10 USCA § 2305.

Definitions, ozone protection terms, see 42 USCA § 7671.

Definitions, see 10 USCA § 2302, 41 USCA §§ 259, 403.

Federal procurement, see 42 USCA § 7671l.

Kinds of contracts, see 10 USCA § 2306.

Planning and solicitation requirements, see 41 USCA § 253a.

Safe alternatives policy, see 42 USCA § 7671k.

§ 23.804 Contract clauses.

Except for contracts for supplies that will be delivered outside the United States and its outlying areas, or contracts for services that will be performed outside the United States and its outlying areas, insert the following clauses:

(a) 52.223-11, Ozone-Depleting Substances and High Global Warming Potential Hydrofluorocarbons, in solicitations and contracts for—

(1) Refrigeration equipment (in product or service code (PSC) 4110);

(2) Air conditioning equipment (PSC 4120);

(3) Clean agent fire suppression systems/equipment (e.g., installed room flooding systems, portable fire extinguishers, aircraft/tactical vehicle fire/explosion suppression systems) (in PSC 4210);

(4) Bulk refrigerants and fire suppressants (in PSC 6830);

(5) Solvents, dusters, freezing compounds, mold release agents, and any other miscellaneous chemical specialty that may contain ozone-depleting substances or high global warming potential hydrofluorocarbons (in PSC 6850);

(6) Corrosion prevention compounds, foam sealants, aerosol mold release agents, and any other preservative or sealing compound that may contain ozone-depleting substances or high global warming potential hydrofluorocarbons (in PSC 8030);

(7) Fluorocarbon lubricants (primarily aerosols) (in PSC 9150); and

(8) Any other manufactured end products that may contain or be manufactured with ozone-depleting substances.

(b) 52.223-12, Maintenance, Service, Repair, or Disposal of Refrigeration Equipment and Air Conditioners, in solicitations and contracts that include the maintenance, service, repair, or disposal of—

(1) Refrigeration equipment, such as refrigerators, chillers, or freezers; or

(2) Air conditioners, including air conditioning systems in motor vehicles.

(c) 52.223-20, Aerosols, in solicitations and contracts—

(1) For products that may contain high global warming potential hydrofluorocarbons as a propellant, or as a solvent; or

(2) That involve maintenance or repair of electronic or mechanical devices.

(d) 52.223-21, Foams, in solicitations and contracts for—

(1) Products that may contain high global warming potential hydrofluorocarbons or refrigerant blends containing hydrofluorocarbons as a foam blowing agent, such as building foam insulation or appliance foam insulation; or

(2) Construction of buildings or facilities.

United States Code Annotated

Contract requirements, see 41 USCA § 254.

Contracts, planning, solicitation, evaluation, and award procedures, see 10 USCA § 2305.

Definitions, ozone protection terms, see 42 USCA § 7671.

Definitions, see 10 USCA § 2302, 41 USCA §§ 259, 403.

Federal procurement, see 42 USCA § 7671l.

Kinds of contracts, see 10 USCA § 2306.

Planning and solicitation requirements, see 41 USCA § 253a.

Safe alternatives policy, see 42 USCA § 7671k.

Subpart 23.9 Contractor Compliance with Environmental Management Systems

§ 23.900 Scope.

This subpart implements the environmental management systems requirements for contractors.

§ 23.901 Authority.

(a) Executive Order 13423 of January 24, 2007, Strengthening Federal Environmental, Energy, and Transportation Management.

(b) Executive Order 13514 of October 5, 2009, Federal Leadership in Environmental, Energy, and Economic Performance.

United States Code Annotated

Contract requirements, see 41 USCA § 254.

Contracts, planning, solicitation, evaluation, and award procedures, see 10 USCA § 2305.

Definitions, see 10 USCA § 2302, 41 USCA §§ 259, 403.

Kinds of contracts, see 10 USCA § 2306.

Planning and solicitation requirements, see 41 USCA § 253a.

Source reduction and recycling data collection, see 42 USCA § 13106.

Toxic chemical release forms, see 42 USCA § 11023.

§ 23.902 Policy.

(a) Agencies shall implement environmental management systems (EMS) at all appropriate organizational levels. Where contractor activities affect an agency's environmental management aspects, EMS requirements shall be included in contracts to ensure proper implementation and execution of EMS roles and responsibilities.

(b) The contracting officer shall—

(1) Specify the EMS directives with which the contractor must comply; and

(2) Ensure contractor compliance to the same extent as the agency would be required to comply, if the agency operated the facilities or vehicles.

United States Code Annotated

Contract requirements, see 41 USCA § 254.

Contracts, planning, solicitation, evaluation, and award procedures, see 10 USCA § 2305.

Definitions, see 10 USCA § 2302, 41 USCA §§ 259, 403.

Kinds of contracts, see 10 USCA § 2306.

Planning and solicitation requirements, see 41 USCA § 253a.

Source reduction and recycling data collection, see 42 USCA § 13106.

Toxic chemical release forms, see 42 USCA § 11023.

§ 23.903 Contract clause.

The contracting officer shall insert the clause at 52.223-19, Compliance With Environmental Management Systems, in all solicitations and contracts for contractor operation of Government-owned or -leased facilities or vehicles, located in the United States. For facilities located outside the United States, the agency head may determine that use of the clause is in the best interest of the Government.

United States Code Annotated

Contract requirements, see 41 USCA § 254.

Contracts, planning, solicitation, evaluation, and award procedures, see 10 USCA § 2305.

Definitions, see 10 USCA § 2302, 41 USCA §§ 259, 403.

Kinds of contracts, see 10 USCA § 2306.

Planning and solicitation requirements, see 41 USCA § 253a.

Source reduction and recycling data collection, see 42 USCA § 13106.

Toxic chemical release forms, see 42 USCA § 11023.

§ 23.904 Policy.

(a) It is the policy of the Government to purchase supplies and services that have been produced with a minimum adverse impact on community health and the environment.

(b) Federal agencies, to the greatest extent practicable, shall contract with companies that report in a public manner on toxic chemicals released to the environment.

United States Code Annotated

Contract requirements, see 41 USCA § 254.

Contracts, planning, solicitation, evaluation, and award procedures, see 10 USCA § 2305.

Definitions, see 10 USCA § 2302, 41 USCA §§ 259, 403.

Kinds of contracts, see 10 USCA § 2306.

Planning and solicitation requirements, see 41 USCA § 253a.

Source reduction and recycling data collection, see 42 USCA § 13106.

Toxic chemical release forms, see 42 USCA § 11023.

§ 23.905 Requirements.

(a) E.O. 13148 requires that solicitations for competitive contracts expected to exceed $100,000 include, to the maximum extent practicable, as an award eligibility criterion, a certification by an offeror that, if awarded a contract, either—

(1) As the owner or operator of facilities to be used in the performance of the contract that are subject to Form R filing and reporting requirements, the offeror will file, and will continue to file throughout the life of the contract, for such facilities, the Toxic Chemical Release Inventory Form (Form R) as described in EPCRA sections 313(a) and (g) and PPA section 6607; or

(2) Facilities to be used in the performance of the contract are exempt from Form R filing and reporting requirements because the facilities—

(i) Do not manufacture, process, or otherwise use any toxic chemicals listed under section 313(c) of EPCRA, 42 U.S.C. 11023(c);

(ii) Do not have 10 or more full-time employees as specified in section 313(b)(1)(A) of EPCRA, 42 U.S.C. 11023(b)(1)(A);

(iii) Do not meet the reporting thresholds of toxic chemicals established under section 313(f) of EPCRA, 42 U.S.C. 11023(f) (including the alternate thresholds at 40 CFR 372. 27, provided an appropriate certification form has been filed with EPA);

(iv) Do not fall within the following Standard Industrial Classification (SIC) codes or their corresponding North American Industry Classification System sectors:

(A) Major group code 10 (except 1011, 1081, and 1094.

(B) Major group code 12 (except 1241).

(C) Major group codes 20 through 39.

(D) Industry code 4911, 4931, or 4939 (limited to facilities that combust coal and/or oil for the purpose of generating power for distribution in commerce).

(E) Industry code 4953 (limited to facilities regulated under the Resource Conservation and Recovery Act, Subtitle C (42 U.S.C. 6921, *et seq.*), or 5169, or 5171, or 7389 (limited to facilities primarily engaged in solvent recovery services on a contract or fee basis); or

(v) Are not located in the United States and its outlying areas.

(b) A determination that it is not practicable to include the solicitation provision at 52. 223-13, Certification of Toxic Chemical Release Reporting, in a solicitation or class of solicitations shall be approved by a procurement official at a level no lower than the head of the contracting activity. Prior to making such a determination for a solicitation or class of solicitations with an estimated value in excess of $500,000 (including all options), the agency shall consult with the Environmental Protection Agency, Director, Environmental Assistance Division, Office of Pollution Prevention and Toxic Substances (Mail Code 7408), Washington, DC 20460.

(c) Award shall not be made to offerors who do not certify in accordance with paragraph (a) of this section when the provision at 52.223-13, Certification of Toxic Chemical Release Reporting, is included in the solicitation. If facilities to be used by the offeror in the performance of the contract are not subject to Form R filing and reporting requirements and the offeror fails to check the appropriate box(es) in 52.223-13, Certification of Toxic Chemical Release Reporting, such failure shall be considered a minor informality or irregularity.

(d) The contracting officer shall cooperate with EPA representatives and provide such advice and assistance as may be required to aid EPA in the performance of its responsibilities under E.O. 13148.

(e) EPA, upon determining that a contractor is not filing the necessary forms or is filing incomplete information, may recommend to the head of the contracting activity that the contract be terminated for convenience. The head of the contracting activity shall consider the EPA recommendation and determine if termination or some other action is appropriate.

United States Code Annotated

Contract requirements, see 41 USCA § 254.

Contracts, planning, solicitation, evaluation, and award procedures, see 10 USCA § 2305.

Definitions, see 10 USCA § 2302, 41 USCA §§ 259, 403.

Kinds of contracts, see 10 USCA § 2306.

Planning and solicitation requirements, see 41 USCA § 253a.

Source reduction and recycling data collection, see 42 USCA § 13106.

Toxic chemical release forms, see 42 USCA § 11023.

§ 23.906 Solicitation provision and contract clause.

Except for acquisitions of commercial items as defined in Part 2, the contracting officer shall—

(a) Insert the provision at 52.223-13, Certification of Toxic Chemical Release Reporting, in all solicitations for competitive contracts expected to exceed $100,000 and competitive 8(a) contracts, unless it has been determined in accordance with 23.905(b) that to do so is not practicable; and

(b) Insert the clause at 52.223-14, Toxic Chemical Release Reporting, in competitively awarded contracts exceeding $100,000 and competitively awarded 8(a) contracts, except when the determination at 23.905(b) has been made.

United States Code Annotated

Contract requirements, see 41 USCA § 254.

Contracts, planning, solicitation, evaluation, and award procedures, see 10 USCA § 2305.

Definitions, see 10 USCA § 2302, 41 USCA §§ 259, 403.

Kinds of contracts, see 10 USCA § 2306.

Planning and solicitation requirements, see 41 USCA § 253a.

Source reduction and recycling data collection, see 42 USCA § 13106.

Toxic chemical release forms, see 42 USCA § 11023.

Subpart 23.10 Federal Compliance with Right-to-Know Laws and Pollution Prevention Requirements

§ 23.1000 Scope.

This subpart prescribes policies and procedures for obtaining information needed for Government—

(a) Compliance with right-to-know laws and pollution prevention requirements;

(b) Implementation of an environmental management system (EMS) at a Federal facility; and

(c) Completion of facility compliance audits (FCAs) at a Federal facility.

United States Code Annotated

Contract requirements, see 41 USCA § 254.

Contracts, planning, solicitation, evaluation, and award procedures, see 10 USCA § 2305.

Definitions, see 10 USCA § 2302, 41 USCA §§ 259, 403.

Kinds of contracts, see 10 USCA § 2306.

Planning and solicitation requirements, see 41 USCA § 253a.

Source reduction and recycling data collection, see 42 USCA § 13106.

Toxic chemical release forms, see 42 USCA § 11023.

§ 23.1001 Authorities.

(a) Emergency Planning and Community Right-to-Know Act of 1986, 42 U.S.C. 11001–11050 (EPCRA).

(b) Pollution Prevention Act of 1990, 42 U.S.C. 13101–13109 (PPA).

(c) Executive Order 13423 of January 24, 2007, Strengthening Federal Environmental, Energy, and Transportation Management.

(d) Executive Order 13514 of October 5, 2009, Federal Leadership in Environmental, Energy, and Economic Performance.

United States Code Annotated

Contract requirements, see 41 USCA § 254.

Contracts, planning, solicitation, evaluation, and award procedures, see 10 USCA § 2305.

Definitions, see 10 USCA § 2302, 41 USCA §§ 259, 403.

Kinds of contracts, see 10 USCA § 2306.

Planning and solicitation requirements, see 41 USCA § 253a.

Source reduction and recycling data collection, see 42 USCA § 13106.

Toxic chemical release forms, see 42 USCA § 11023.

§ 23.1002 Applicability.

The requirements of this subpart apply to facilities owned or operated by an agency in the customs territory of the United States.

United States Code Annotated

Contract requirements, see 41 USCA § 254.

Contracts, planning, solicitation, evaluation, and award procedures, see 10 USCA § 2305.

Definitions, see 10 USCA § 2302, 41 USCA §§ 259, 403.

Kinds of contracts, see 10 USCA § 2306.

Planning and solicitation requirements, see 41 USCA § 253a.

Source reduction and recycling data collection, see 42 USCA § 13106.

Toxic chemical release forms, see 42 USCA § 11023.

§ 23.1003 Definitions.

As used in this subpart—

"Federal agency" means an executive agency (see 2.101).

United States Code Annotated

Contract requirements, see 41 USCA § 254.

Contracts, planning, solicitation, evaluation, and award procedures, see 10 USCA § 2305.

Definitions, see 10 USCA § 2302, 41 USCA §§ 259, 403.

Kinds of contracts, see 10 USCA § 2306.

Planning and solicitation requirements, see 41 USCA § 253a.

Source reduction and recycling data collection, see 42 USCA § 13106.

Toxic chemical release forms, see 42 USCA § 11023.

§ 23.1004 Requirements.

(a) Federal facilities are required to comply with—

(1) The emergency planning and toxic release reporting requirements in EPCRA and PPA; and

(2) The toxic chemical, and hazardous substance release and use reduction goals of sections 2(e) and 3(a)(vi) of Executive Order 13423.

(b) Pursuant to EPCRA, PPA, E.O. 13423, and any agency implementing procedures, every new contract that provides for performance on a Federal facility shall require the contractor to provide information necessary for the Federal agency to comply with the—

(1) Requirements in paragraph (a) of this section; and

(2) Requirements for EMSs and FCAs if the place of performance is at a Federal facility designated by the agency.

United States Code Annotated

Contract requirements, see 41 USCA § 254.

Contracts, planning, solicitation, evaluation, and award procedures, see 10 USCA § 2305.

Definitions, see 10 USCA § 2302, 41 USCA §§ 259, 403.

Kinds of contracts, see 10 USCA § 2306.

Planning and solicitation requirements, see 41 USCA § 253a.

Source reduction and recycling data collection, see 42 USCA § 13106.

Toxic chemical release forms, see 42 USCA § 11023.

§ 23.1005 Contract clause.

(a) Insert the clause at 52.223-5, Pollution Prevention and Right-to-Know Information, in solicitations and contracts that provide for performance, in whole or in part, on a Federal facility.

(b) Use the clause with its Alternate I if the contract provides for contractor—

(1) Operation or maintenance of a Federal facility at which the agency has implemented or plans to implement an EMS; or

(2) Activities and operations—

(i) To be performed at a Government-operated Federal facility that has implemented or plans to implement an EMS; and

(ii) That the agency has determined are covered within the EMS.

(c) Use the clause with its Alternate II if—

(1) The contract provides for contractor activities on a Federal facility; and

(2) The agency has determined that the contractor activities should be included within the FCA or an environmental management system audit.

United States Code Annotated

Contract requirements, see 41 USCA § 254.

Contracts, planning, solicitation, evaluation, and award procedures, see 10 USCA § 2305.

Definitions, see 10 USCA § 2302, 41 USCA §§ 259, 403.

Kinds of contracts, see 10 USCA § 2306.

Planning and solicitation requirements, see 41 USCA § 253a.

Source reduction and recycling data collection, see 42 USCA § 13106.

Toxic chemical release forms, see 42 USCA § 11023.

Subpart 23.11 Encouraging Contractor Policies to Ban Text Messaging While Driving

§ 23.1101 Purpose.

This subpart implements the requirements of the Executive Order (E.O.) 13513, dated October 1, 2009 (74 FR 51225, October 6, 2009), Federal Leadership on Reducing Text Messaging while Driving.

§ 23.1102 Applicability.

This subpart applies to all solicitations and contracts.

§ 23.1103 Definitions.

As used in this subpart—

"Driving"—

(1) Means operating a motor vehicle on an active roadway with the motor running, including while temporarily stationary because of traffic, a traffic light, stop sign, or otherwise.

(2) Does not include operating a motor vehicle with or without the motor running when one has pulled over to the side of, or off, an active roadway and has halted in a location where one can safely remain stationary.

"Text messaging" means reading from or entering data into any handheld or other electronic device, including for the purpose of short message service texting, e-mailing, instant messaging, obtaining navigational information, or engaging in any other form of electronic data retrieval or electronic data communication. The term does not include glancing at or listening to a navigational device that is secured in a commercially designed holder affixed to the vehicle, provided that the destination and route are programmed into the device either before driving or while stopped in a location off the roadway where it is safe and legal to park.

§ 23.1104 Policy.

Agencies shall encourage contractors and subcontractors to adopt and enforce policies that ban text messaging while driving—

(a) Company-owned or -rented vehicles or Government-owned vehicles; or

(b) Privately-owned vehicles when on official Government business or when performing any work for or on behalf of the Government.

§ 23.1105 Contract clause.

The contracting officer shall insert the clause at 52.223-18, Encouraging Contractor Policies to Ban Text Messaging While Driving, in all solicitations and contracts.

PART 24 PROTECTION OF PRIVACY AND FREEDOM OF INFORMATION

§ 24.000 Scope of part.

Subpart 24.1 Protection of Individual Privacy
§ 24.101 Definitions.
§ 24.102 General.
§ 24.103 Procedures.
§ 24.104 Contract clauses.

Subpart 24.2 Freedom of Information Act
§ 24.201 Authority.
§ 24.202 Prohibitions.
§ 24.203 Policy.

§ 24.000 Scope of part.

This part prescribes policies and procedures that apply requirements of the Privacy Act of 1974 (5 U.S.C. 552a) (the Act) and OMB Circular No. A-130, December 12, 1985, to Government contracts and cites the Freedom of Information Act (5 U.S.C. 552, as amended).

United States Code Annotated

Contract requirements, see 41 USCA § 254.

Contracts, planning, solicitation, evaluation, and award procedures, see 10 USCA § 2305.

Definitions, see 5 USCA § 554, 10 USCA § 2302, 41 USCA § 403.

Kinds of contracts, see 10 USCA § 2306.

Planning and solicitation requirements, see 41 USCA § 253a.

Public information, agency rules, opinions, orders, records, and proceedings, see 5 USCA § 552.

Records maintained on individuals, see 5 USCA § 552a.

Subpart 24.1 Protection of Individual Privacy

§ 24.101 Definitions.

As used in this subpart—

"Agency" means any executive department, military department, Government corporation, Government controlled corporation, or other establishment in the executive branch of the Government (including the Executive Office of the President), or any independent regulatory agency.

"Individual" means a citizen of the United States or an alien lawfully admitted for permanent residence.

"Maintain" means maintain, collect, use, or disseminate.

"Operation of a system of records" means performance of any of the activities associated with maintaining the system of records, including the collection, use, and dissemination of records.

"Record" means any item, collection, or grouping of information about an individual that is maintained by an agency, including, but not limited to, education, financial transactions, medical history, and criminal or employment history, and that contains the individual's name, or the identifying number, symbol, or other identifying particular assigned to the individual, such as a fingerprint or voiceprint or a photograph.

1371

"System of records on individuals" means a group of any records under the control of any agency from which information is retrieved by the name of the individual or by some identifying number, symbol, or other identifying particular assigned to the individual.

United States Code Annotated

Contract requirements, see 41 USCA § 254.

Contracts, planning, solicitation, evaluation, and award procedures, see 10 USCA § 2305.

Definitions, see 5 USCA § 554, 10 USCA § 2302, 41 USCA § 403.

Kinds of contracts, see 10 USCA § 2306.

Planning and solicitation requirements, see 41 USCA § 253a.

Public information, agency rules, opinions, orders, records, and proceedings, see 5 USCA § 552.

Records maintained on individuals, see 5 USCA § 552a.

§ 24.102 General.

(a) The Act requires that when an agency contracts for the design, development, or operation of a system of records on individuals on behalf of the agency to accomplish an agency function the agency must apply the requirements of the Act to the contractor and its employees working on the contract.

(b) An agency officer or employee may be criminally liable for violations of the Act. When the contract provides for operation of a system of records on individuals, contractors and their employees are considered employees of the agency for purposes of the criminal penalties of the Act.

(c) If a contract specifically provides for the design, development, or operation of a system of records on individuals on behalf of an agency to accomplish an agency function, the agency must apply the requirements of the Act to the contractor and its employees working on the contract. The system of records operated under the contract is deemed to be maintained by the agency and is subject to the Act.

(d) Agencies, which within the limits of their authorities, fail to require that systems of records on individuals operated on their behalf under contracts be operated in conformance with the Act may be civilly liable to individuals injured as a consequence of any subsequent failure to maintain records in conformance with the Act.

United States Code Annotated

Contract requirements, see 41 USCA § 254.

Contracts, planning, solicitation, evaluation, and award procedures, see 10 USCA § 2305.

Definitions, see 5 USCA § 554, 10 USCA § 2302, 41 USCA § 403.

Kinds of contracts, see 10 USCA § 2306.

Planning and solicitation requirements, see 41 USCA § 253a.

Public information, agency rules, opinions, orders, records, and proceedings, see 5 USCA § 552.

Records maintained on individuals, see 5 USCA § 552a.

§ 24.103 Procedures.

(a) The contracting officer shall review requirements to determine whether the contract will involve the design, development, or operation of a system of records on individuals to accomplish an agency function.

(b) If one or more of those tasks will be required, the contracting officer shall—

(1) Ensure that the contract work statement specifically identifies the system of records on individuals and the design, development, or operation work to be performed; and

(2) Make available, in accordance with agency procedures, agency rules and regulation implementing the Act.

United States Code Annotated

Contract requirements, see 41 USCA § 254.

Contracts, planning, solicitation, evaluation, and award procedures, see 10 USCA § 2305.

Definitions, see 5 USCA § 554, 10 USCA § 2302, 41 USCA § 403.

Kinds of contracts, see 10 USCA § 2306.

Planning and solicitation requirements, see 41 USCA § 253a.

Public information, agency rules, opinions, orders, records, and proceedings, see 5 USCA § 552.

Records maintained on individuals, see 5 USCA § 552a.

§ 24.104 Contract clauses.

When the design, development, or operation of a system of records on individuals is required to accomplish an agency function, the contracting officer shall insert the following clauses in solicitations and contracts:

(a) The clause at 52.224-1, Privacy Act Notification.

(b) The clause at 52.224-2, Privacy Act.

United States Code Annotated

Contract requirements, see 41 USCA § 254.

Contracts, planning, solicitation, evaluation, and award procedures, see 10 USCA § 2305.

Definitions, see 5 USCA § 554, 10 USCA § 2302, 41 USCA § 403.

Kinds of contracts, see 10 USCA § 2306.

Planning and solicitation requirements, see 41 USCA § 253a.

Public information, agency rules, opinions, orders, records, and proceedings, see 5 USCA § 552.

Records maintained on individuals, see 5 USCA § 552a.

Subpart 24.2 Freedom of Information Act

§ 24.201 Authority.

The Freedom of Information Act (5 U.S.C. 552, as amended) provides that information is to be made available to the public either by—

(a) Publication in the *Federal Register*;

(b) Providing an opportunity to read and copy records at convenient locations; or

(c) Upon request, providing a copy of a reasonably described record.

United States Code Annotated

Contract requirements, see 41 USCA § 254.

Contracts, planning, solicitation, evaluation, and award procedures, see 10 USCA § 2305.

Cost or pricing data, truth in negotiations, see 10 USCA § 2306a, 41 USCA § 254b.

Definitions, see 5 USCA § 554, 10 USCA § 2302, 41 USCA § 403.

Kinds of contracts, see 10 USCA § 2306.

Planning and solicitation requirements, see 41 USCA § 253a.

Public information, agency rules, opinions, orders, records, and proceedings, see 5 USCA § 552.

Records maintained on individuals, see 5 USCA § 552a.

§ 24.202 Prohibitions.

(a) A proposal in the possession or control of the Government, submitted in response to a competitive solicitation, shall not be made available to any person under the Freedom of Information Act. This prohibition does not apply to a proposal, or any part of a proposal, that is set forth or incorporated by reference in a contract between the Government and the contractor that submitted the proposal. (See 10 U.S.C. 2305(g) and 41 U.S.C. 4702.)

(b) No agency shall disclose any information obtained pursuant to 15.403-3(b) that is exempt from disclosure under the Freedom of Information Act. (See 10 U.S.C. 2306a(d)(2) (C) and 41 U.S.C. 3505(b)(3).)

(c) A dispute resolution communication that is between a neutral person and a party to alternative dispute resolution proceedings, and that may not be disclosed under 5 U.S.C. 574, is exempt from disclosure under the Freedom of Information Act (5 U.S.C. 552(b)(3)).

United States Code Annotated

Contract requirements, see 41 USCA § 254.

Contracts, planning, solicitation, evaluation, and award procedures, see 10 USCA § 2305.

Cost or pricing data, truth in negotiations, see 10 USCA § 2306a, 41 USCA § 254b.

Definitions, see 5 USCA § 554, 10 USCA § 2302, 41 USCA § 403.

Kinds of contracts, see 10 USCA § 2306.

Planning and solicitation requirements, see 41 USCA § 253a.

Public information, agency rules, opinions, orders, records, and proceedings, see 5 USCA § 552.

Records maintained on individuals, see 5 USCA § 552a.

Notes of Decisions

Disclosure of information 2
General 1

1 General

Contracting agency did not violate the Trade Secrets Act, which barred government officials from disclosing or making known "to any extent not authorized by law" confidential and trade secret information, when it released incumbent contractor's unit prices for current and future option years, pursuant to Freedom of Information Act (FOIA) request, to its competitor, before imminent re-solicitation of substantially similar contract; release of contractor's unit prices, which were in the public domain, was authorized by FOIA. R & W Flammann GmbH v. U.S., 339 F.3d 1320 (Fed. Cir. 2003)

2 Disclosure of information

After a contractor pinpoints technical information it believes its competitors could use in their own operations, an agency's summary conclusion that disclosing that information is not likely to cause substantial competitive harm is insufficient to justify release of the information under the Freedom of Information Act. The FOIA request sought a Defense Contract Management Agency (DCMA) audit report on the contractor's quality-control system and manufacturing techniques. United Technologies Corp. v. U.S. Dept. of Defense, 601 F.3d 557 (D.C. Cir. 2010)

Exemption 4 of FOIA protects from disclosure trade secrets and commercial or financial information obtained from a person that is privileged or confidential. 5 U.S.C.A. § 552(b)(4). Commercial and financial information obtained involuntarily is confidential for purposes of the exemption if disclosure impairs the Government's ability to obtain necessary information in the future or causes substantial harm to the competitive position of the person from whom the information was obtained. The DC Circuit determined that line-item pricing in a Government contract is a confidential trade secret that may not be disclosed pursuant to a FOIA request if disclosure causes substantial harm to the competitive position of the contractor. Canadian Commercial Corp. v. Department of Air Force, 514 F.3d 37, 85 U.S.P. Q.2d 1693 (D.C. Cir. 2008)

Because disclosing the unit prices contained in contracts for jet engine parts would likely cause substantial competitive harm to the spare-parts manufacturer, the unit prices are confidential and protected from disclosure by Freedom of Information Act Exemption 4. Although this particular contract was a sole source award, competitive harm was established based on future competitive opportunities. General Elec. Co. v. Department of Air Force, 648 F. Supp. 2d 95 (D.D.C. 2009)

The Air Force properly found that a contractor's labor-rate information, which was contained in the contract, was not protected from disclosure by Freedom of Information Act Exemption 4, 5 USCA § 552(b)(4), which applies to trade secrets and commercial or financial information, the U.S. District Court for the District of Columbia has held. The contractor did not refute the Air Force's finding that the labor rates varied from year to year, and thus the rates from prior years would not allow a competitor to predict future rates. Because the contractor did not show a clear link between the information and the possibility of competitive harm, the Air Force decision was not arbitrary and capricious, the Court held. Boeing Co. v. U.S. Dept. of Air Force, 616 F. Supp. 2d 40 (D.D.C. 2009)

"B-table" matrices of factors going into pricing of long distance telephone services in contract with General Services Administration (GSA) consisted of confidential information, which GSA was required to withhold from competitor making request under Freedom of Information Act (FOIA), and were consequently exempt from Federal Acquisition Regulation (FAR) requirement that unit pricing of contracts be disclosed. 5 U.S.C.A. § 552(b)(4); 48 C.F.R. § 15.503(b)(1). MCI Worldcom, Inc. v. General Services Admin., 163 F. Supp. 2d 28 (D.D.C. 2001). Records ☞59; United States ☞64.55(1)

Contractor that successfully bid on contract with Navy failed to show that Navy's disclosure of costs and pricing data and proprietary management strategies it included in its bid would cause substantial harm to its competitive position, as required for Freedom of Information Act's (FOIA) trade secret exemption to apply. 5 U.S.C.A. § 552(b)(4). Martin Marietta Corp. v. Dalton, 974 F. Supp. 37, 41 Cont. Cas. Fed. (CCH) P 77164 (D.D.C. 1997). Records ☞59

Cost and pricing information disclosed by contractor when it bid on contract with Navy was not disclosed voluntarily, in determining whether such information was exempt from disclosure under Freedom of Information Act (FOIA); contractor was required to submit information requested by Navy if it hoped to win contract. 5 U.S.C.A. § 552(b)(4); 48 C.F.R. § 15.804–6(b)(1). Martin Marietta Corp. v. Dalton, 974 F. Supp. 37, 41 Cont. Cas. Fed. (CCH) P 77164 (D.D.C. 1997). Records ☞59

In determining whether Freedom of Information Act's (FOIA) trade secret exemption applied to cost and pricing data and proprietary management strategies disclosed by contractor when it successfully bid on Navy contract, Navy's prior release of such information to limited number of requesters did not necessarily make information matter of public knowledge, or lessen likelihood contractor would suffer competitive harm if it was disclosed again to its competitors. 5 U.S.C.A. § 552(b)(4). Martin Marietta Corp. v. Dalton, 974 F. Supp. 37, 41 Cont. Cas. Fed. (CCH) P 77164 (D.D.C. 1997). Records ☞59

When an unsuccessful offeror lawfully obtains source selection information, such as a competitor's prices and technical scores, and the agency subsequently properly reopens negotiations, the agency may disclose similar information to all the competitors to eliminate any competitive advantage. 48 C.F.R. § 15.507. ManTech Telecommunications and Information Systems Corp. v. U.S., 49 Fed. Cl. 57 (2001), decision aff'd, 30 Fed. Appx. 995 (Fed. Cir. 2002). United States ☞64.40(5)

§ 24.203 Policy.

(a) The Act specifies, among other things, how agencies shall make their records available upon public request, imposes strict time standards for agency responses, and exempts certain records from public disclosure. Each agency's implementation of these requirements is located in its respective title of the *Code of Federal Regulations* and referenced in Subpart 24.2 of its implementing acquisition regulations.

(b) Contracting officers may receive requests for records that may be exempted from mandatory public disclosure. The exemptions most often applicable are those relating to classified information, to trade secrets and confidential commercial or financial information, to interagency or intra-agency memoranda, or to personal and medical information pertaining to an individual. Other exemptions include agency personnel practices, and law enforcement. Since these requests often involve complex issues requiring an in-depth knowledge of a large and increasing body of court rulings and policy guidance, contracting officers are cautioned to comply with the implementing regulations of their agency and to obtain necessary guidance from the agency officials having Freedom of Information Act responsibility. If additional assistance is needed, authorized agency officials may contact the Department of Justice, Office of Information and Privacy. A Freedom of Information Act guide and other resources are available at the Department of Justice website under FOIA reference materials: *http://www.usdoj.gov/oip*.

United States Code Annotated

Contract requirements, see 41 USCA § 254.

Contracts, planning, solicitation, evaluation, and award procedures, see 10 USCA § 2305.

Cost or pricing data, truth in negotiations, see 10 USCA § 2306a, 41 USCA § 254b.

Definitions, see 5 USCA § 554, 10 USCA § 2302, 41 USCA § 403.

Kinds of contracts, see 10 USCA § 2306.

Planning and solicitation requirements, see 41 USCA § 253a.

Public information, agency rules, opinions, orders, records, and proceedings, see 5 USCA § 552.

Records maintained on individuals, see 5 USCA § 552a.

PART 25 FOREIGN ACQUISITION

Subpart 25.9 Customs and Duties
§ 25.900 Scope of subpart.
§ 25.901 Policy.
§ 25.902 Procedures.
§ 25.903 Exempted supplies.

Subpart 25.10 Additional Foreign Acquisition Regulations
§ 25.1001 Waiver of right to examination of records.
§ 25.1002 Use of foreign currency.

Subpart 25.11 Solicitation Provisions and Contract Clauses
§ 25.1101 Acquisition of supplies.
§ 25.1102 Acquisition of construction.
§ 25.1103 Other provisions and clauses.

§ 25.000 Scope of part.
(a) This part provides policies and procedures for—

(1) Acquisition of foreign supplies, services, and construction materials; and

(2) Contracts performed outside the United States.

(b) It implements 41 U.S.C. chapter 83, Buy American; trade agreements; and other laws and regulations.

United States Code Annotated
Administrative determinations, see 41 USCA § 257.

American materials required for public use, see 41 USCA § 10a.

Clarification of Congressional intent regarding sections 10a and 10b(a), see 41 USCA § 10d.

Contract requirements, see 41 USCA § 254.

Contracts, planning, solicitation, evaluation, and award procedures, see 10 USCA § 2305.

Contracts for public works, specification for use of American materials, blacklisting contractors violating requirements, see 41 USCA § 10b.

Definition of terms used in sections 10a, 10b, and 10c, see 41 USCA § 10c.

Definitions, see 10 USCA § 2302, 41 USCA §§ 259, 403.

Determinations and decisions, see 10 USCA § 2310, 41 USCA § 262.

Kinds of contracts, see 10 USCA § 2306.

Limitation on authority to waive Buy American Act requirement, see 41 USCA § 10b-2.

Planning and solicitation requirements, see 41 USCA § 253a.

§ 25.001 General.
(a) 41 U.S.C. chapter 83, Buy American—

(1) Restricts the purchase of supplies, that are not domestic end products, for use within the United States. A foreign end product may be purchased if the contracting officer determines that the price of the lowest domestic offer is unreasonable or if another exception applies (see Subpart 25.1); and

(2) Requires, with some exceptions, the use of only domestic construction materials in contracts for construction in the United States (see Subpart 25.2).

(b) The restrictions in the Buy American statute are not applicable in acquisitions subject to certain trade agreements (see Subpart 25.4). In these acquisitions, end products and construction materials from certain countries receive nondiscriminatory treatment in evaluation with domestic offers. Generally, the dollar value of the acquisition determines which of the trade agreements applies. Exceptions to the applicability of the trade agreements are described in Subpart 25.4.

(c) The test to determine the country of origin for an end product under the Buy American statute (see the various country "end product" definitions in 25.003) is different from the test to determine the country of origin for an end product under the trade agreements, or the criteria for the representation on end products manufactured outside the United States (see 52.225-18).

(1) The Buy American statute uses a two-part test to define a "domestic end product"or "domestic construction material" (manufactured in the United States and a formula based on cost of domestic components). The component test has been waived for acquisition of commercially available off-the-shelf items.

(2) Under the trade agreements, the test to determine country of origin is "substantial transformation" (*i.e.*, transforming an article into a new and different article of commerce, with a name, character, or use distinct from the original article).

(3) For the representation at 52.225-18, the only criterion is whether the place of manufacture of an end product is in the United States or outside the United States, without regard to the origin of the components.

(4) When using funds appropriated under the American Recovery and Reinvestment Act of 2009 (Pub. L. 111-5), the definition of "domestic manufactured construction material" requires manufacture in the United States but does not include a requirement with regard to the origin of the components. If the construction material consists wholly or predominantly of iron or steel, the iron or steel must be produced in the United States.

Notes of Decisions

In general 1

1 In general

GAO denied protest alleging that an agency's determination of noncompliance with the Trade Agreements Act was unreasonable because agency reasonably determined that major components of the protester's end item would be sourced in China and the protester's assembly and manufacturing processes would not "substantially transform" the product in the U.S. or a designated country. Thus, the protester's item did not qualify as a U.S.-made end product. Sea Box, Inc., B-409963.3, 2015 CPD ¶ 72(Comp.Gen. 2015)

§ 25.002 Applicability of subparts.

The following table shows the applicability of the subparts. Subpart 25.5 provides comprehensive procedures for offer evaluation and examples.

SUBPART	SUPPLIES FOR USE		CONSTRUCTION		SERVICES PERFORMED	
	INSIDE U.S.	OUTSIDE U.S.	INSIDE U.S.	OUTSIDE U.S.	INSIDE U.S.	OUTSIDE U.S.
25.1 Buy American—Supplies	X	—	—	—	—	—
25.2 Buy American—Construction Materials	—	—	X	—	—	—
25.3 Contracts Performed Outside the United States	—	X	—	X	—	X
25.4 Trade Agreements	X	X	X	X	X	X
25.5 Evaluating Foreign Offers—Supply Contracts	X	X	—	—	—	—
25.6 American Recovery and Reinvestment Act—Buy American statute—Construction Materials			X			
25.7 Prohibited Sources	X	X	X	X	X	X

SUBPART	SUPPLIES FOR USE		CONSTRUCTION		SERVICES PERFORMED	
	INSIDE U.S.	OUTSIDE U.S.	INSIDE U.S.	OUTSIDE U.S.	INSIDE U.S.	OUTSIDE U.S.
25.8 Other International Agreements and Coordination	X	X	—	X	—	X
25.9 Customs and Duties	X	—	—	—	—	—
25.10 Additional Foreign Acquisition Regulations	X	X	X	X	X	X
25.11 Solicitation Provisions and Contract Clauses	X	X	X	X	X	X

United States Code Annotated

Administrative determinations, see 41 USCA § 257.

American materials required for public use, see 41 USCA § 10a.

Clarification of Congressional intent regarding sections 10a and 10b(a), see 41 USCA § 10d.

Contract requirements, see 41 USCA § 254.

Contracts, planning, solicitation, evaluation, and award procedures, see 10 USCA § 2305.

Contracts for public works, specification for use of American materials, blacklisting contractors violating requirements, see 41 USCA § 10b.

Definition of terms used in sections 10a, 10b, and 10c, see 41 USCA § 10c.

Definitions, see 10 USCA § 2302, 41 USCA §§ 259, 403.

Determinations and decisions, see 10 USCA § 2310, 41 USCA § 262.

Kinds of contracts, see 10 USCA § 2306.

Limitation on authority to waive Buy American Act requirement, see 41 USCA § 10b-2.

Planning and solicitation requirements, see 41 USCA § 253a.

§ 25.003 Definitions.

As used in this part—

"Caribbean Basin country" means any of the following countries: Antigua and Barbuda, Aruba, Bahamas, Barbados, Belize, Bonaire, British Virgin Islands, Curacao, Dominica, Grenada, Guyana, Haiti, Jamaica, Montserrat, Saba, St. Kitts and Nevis, St. Lucia, St. Vincent and the Grenadines, Sint Eustatius, Sint Maarten, or Trinidad and Tobago.

"Caribbean Basin country end product"—

(1) Means an article that—

(i) (A) Is wholly the growth, product, or manufacture of a Caribbean Basin country; or

(B) In the case of an article that consists in whole or in part of materials from another country, has been substantially transformed in a Caribbean Basin country into a new and different article of commerce with a name, character, or use distinct from that of the article or articles from which it was transformed; and

(ii) Is not excluded from duty-free treatment for Caribbean countries under 19 U.S.C. 2703(b).

(A) For this reason, the following articles are not Caribbean Basin country end products:

(1) Tuna, prepared or preserved in any manner in airtight containers.

(2) Petroleum, or any product derived from petroleum.

(3) Watches and watch parts (including cases, bracelets, and straps) of whatever type including, but not limited to, mechanical, quartz digital, or quartz analog, if such watches or watch parts contain any material that is the product

of any country to which the Harmonized Tariff Schedule of the United States (HTSUS) column 2 rates of duty apply (i.e., Afghanistan, Cuba, Laos, North Korea, and Vietnam).

(4) Certain of the following: textiles and apparel articles; footwear, handbags, luggage, flat goods, work gloves, and leather wearing apparel; or handloomed, handmade, and folklore articles.

(B) Access to the HTSUS to determine duty-free status of articles of the types listed in paragraph (1)(ii)(A)(4) of this definition is available via the Internet at ht tp://www.usitc.gov/tata/hts/. In particular, see the following:

(1) General Note 3(c), Products Eligible for Special Tariff treatment.

(2) General Note 17, Products of Countries Designated as Beneficiary Countries under the United States-Caribbean Basin Trade Partnership Act of 2000.

(3) Section XXII, Chapter 98, Subchapter II, Articles Exported and Returned, Advanced or Improved Abroad, U.S. Note 7(b).

(4) Section XXII, Chapter 98, Subchapter XX, Goods Eligible for Special Tariff Benefits under the United States-Caribbean Basin Trade Partnership Act; and

(2) Refers to a product offered for purchase under a supply contract, but for purposes of calculating the value of the acquisition, includes services (except transportation services) incidental to the article, provided that the value of those incidental services does not exceed that of the article itself.

"Civil aircraft and related articles" means—

(1) All aircraft other than aircraft to be purchased for use by the Department of Defense or the U.S. Coast Guard;

(2) The engines (and parts and components for incorporation into the engines) of these aircraft;

(3) Any other parts, components, and subassemblies for incorporation into the aircraft; and

(4) Any ground flight simulators, and parts and components of these simulators, for use with respect to the aircraft, whether to be used as original or replacement equipment in the manufacture, repair, maintenance, rebuilding, modification, or conversion of the aircraft and without regard to whether the aircraft or articles receive duty-free treatment under section 601(a)(2) of the Trade Agreements Act.

"Component" means an article, material, or supply incorporated directly into an end product or construction material.

"Construction material" means an article, material, or supply brought to the construction site by a contractor or subcontractor for incorporation into the building or work. The term also includes an item brought to the site preassembled from articles, materials, or supplies. However, emergency life safety systems, such as emergency lighting, fire alarm, and audio evacuation systems, that are discrete systems incorporated into a public building or work and that are produced as complete systems, are evaluated as a single and distinct construction material regardless of when or how the individual parts or components of those systems are delivered to the construction site. Materials purchased directly by the Government are supplies, not construction material.

"Cost of components" means—

(1) For components purchased by the contractor, the acquisition cost, including transportation costs to the place of incorporation into the end product or construction material (whether or not such costs are paid to a domestic firm), and any applicable duty (whether or not a duty-free entry certificate is issued); or

(2) For components manufactured by the contractor, all costs associated with the manufacture of the component, including transportation costs as described in paragraph (1) of this definition, plus allocable overhead costs, but excluding profit. Cost of components does not include any costs associated with the manufacture of the end product.

"Designated country" means any of the following countries:

(1) A World Trade Organization Government Procurement Agreement (WTO GPA) country (Armenia, Aruba, Austria, Belgium, Bulgaria, Canada, Croatia, Cyprus, Czech Republic, Denmark, Estonia, Finland, France, Germany, Greece, Hong Kong, Hungary,

Iceland, Ireland, Israel, Italy, Japan, Korea (Republic of), Latvia, Liechtenstein, Lithuania, Luxembourg, Malta, Montenegro, Netherlands, New Zealand, Norway, Poland, Portugal, Romania, Singapore, Slovak Republic, Slovenia, Spain, Sweden, Switzerland, Taiwan (known in the World Trade Organization as "the Separate Customs Territory of Taiwan, Penghu, Kinmen and Matsu" (Chinese Taipei)) or United Kingdom);

(2) A Free Trade Agreement (FTA) country (Australia, Bahrain, Canada, Chile, Colombia, Costa Rica, Dominican Republic, El Salvador, Guatemala, Honduras, Korea (Republic of), Mexico, Morocco, Nicaragua, Oman, Panama, Peru, or Singapore);

(3) A least developed country (Afghanistan, Angola, Bangladesh, Benin, Bhutan, Burkina Faso, Burundi, Cambodia, Central African Republic, Chad, Comoros, Democratic Republic of Congo, Djibouti, Equatorial Guinea, Eritrea, Ethiopia, Gambia, Guinea, Guinea-Bissau, Haiti, Kiribati, Laos, Lesotho, Liberia, Madagascar, Malawi, Mali, Mauritania, Mozambique, Nepal, Niger, Rwanda, Samoa, Sao Tome and Principe, Senegal, Sierra Leone, Solomon Islands, Somalia, South Sudan, Tanzania, Timor-Leste, Togo, Tuvalu, Uganda, Vanuatu, Yemen, or Zambia); or

(4) A Caribbean Basin country (Antigua and Barbuda, Aruba, Bahamas, Barbados, Belize, Bonaire, British Virgin Islands, Curacao, Dominica, Grenada, Guyana, Haiti, Jamaica, Montserrat, Saba, St. Kitts and Nevis, St. Lucia, St. Vincent and the Grenadines, Sint Eustatius, Sint Maarten, or Trinidad and Tobago).

"Designated country end product" means a WTO GPA country end product, an FTA country end product, a least developed country end product, or a Caribbean Basin country end product.

"Domestic construction material" means—

(1) (i) An unmanufactured construction material mined or produced in the United States;

(ii) A construction material manufactured in the United States, if—

(A) The cost of the components mined, produced, or manufactured in the United States exceeds 50 percent of the cost of all its components. Components of foreign origin of the same class or kind for which nonavailability determinations have been made are treated as domestic; or

(B) The construction material is a COTS item;

(2) Except that for use in subpart 25.6, see the definition in 25.601.

"Domestic end product" means—

(1) An unmanufactured end product mined or produced in the United States;

(2) An end product manufactured in the United States, if—

(i) The cost of its components mined, produced, or manufactured in the United States exceeds 50 percent of the cost of all its components. Components of foreign origin of the same class or kind as those that the agency determines are not mined, produced, or manufactured in sufficient and reasonably available commercial quantities of a satisfactory quality are treated as domestic. Scrap generated, collected, and prepared for processing in the United States is considered domestic; or

(ii) The end product is a COTS item.

"Domestic offer" means an offer of a domestic end product. When the solicitation specifies that award will be made on a group of line items, a domestic offer means an offer where the proposed price of the domestic end products exceeds 50 percent of the total proposed price of the group.

"Eligible offer" means an offer of an eligible product. When the solicitation specifies that award will be made on a group of line items, an eligible offer means a foreign offer where the combined proposed price of the eligible products and the domestic end products exceeds 50 percent of the total proposed price of the group.

"Eligible product" means a foreign end product, construction material, or service that, due to applicability of a trade agreement to a particular acquisition, is not subject to discriminatory treatment.

"End product" means those articles, materials, and supplies to be acquired for public use.

"Foreign construction material" means a construction material other than a domestic construction material.

"Foreign contractor" means a contractor or subcontractor organized or existing under the laws of a country other than the United States.

"Foreign end product" means an end product other than a domestic end product.

"Foreign offer" means any offer other than a domestic offer.

"Free Trade Agreement country" means Australia, Bahrain, Canada, Chile, Colombia, Costa Rica, Dominican Republic, El Salvador, Guatemala, Honduras, Korea (Republic of), Mexico, Morocco, Nicaragua, Oman, Panama, Peru, or Singapore.

"Free Trade Agreement country end product" means an article that—

(1) Is wholly the growth, product, or manufacture of a Free Trade Agreement (FTA) country; or

(2) In the case of an article that consists in whole or in part of materials from another country, has been substantially transformed in an FTA country into a new and different article of commerce with a name, character, or use distinct from that of the article or articles from which it was transformed. The term refers to a product offered for purchase under a supply contract, but for purposes of calculating the value of the end product, includes services (except transportation services) incidental to the article, provided that the value of those incidental services does not exceed that of the article itself.

"Israeli end product" means an article that—

(1) Is wholly the growth, product, or manufacture of Israel; or

(2) In the case of an article that consists in whole or in part of materials from another country, has been substantially transformed in Israel into a new and different article of commerce with a name, character, or use distinct from that of the article or articles from which it was transformed.

"Least developed country" means any of the following countries: Afghanistan, Angola, Bangladesh, Benin, Bhutan, Burkina Faso, Burundi, Cambodia, Central African Republic, Chad, Comoros, Democratic Republic of Congo, Djibouti, Equatorial Guinea, Eritrea, Ethiopia, Gambia, Guinea, Guinea-Bissau, Haiti, Kiribati, Laos, Lesotho, Liberia, Madagascar, Malawi, Mali, Mauritania, Mozambique, Nepal, Niger, Rwanda, Samoa, Sao Tome and Principe, Senegal, Sierra Leone, Solomon Islands, Somalia, South Sudan, Tanzania, Timor-Leste, Togo, Tuvalu, Uganda, Vanuatu, Yemen, or Zambia.

"Least developed country end product" means an article that—

(1) Is wholly the growth, product, or manufacture of a least developed country; or

(2) In the case of an article that consists in whole or in part of materials from another country, has been substantially transformed in a least developed country into a new and different article of commerce with a name, character, or use distinct from that of the article or articles from which it was transformed. The term refers to a product offered for purchase under a supply contract, but for purposes of calculating the value of the end product, includes services (except transportation services) incidental to the article, provided that the value of those incidental services does not exceed that of the article itself.

"Noneligible offer" means an offer of a noneligible product.

"Noneligible product" means a foreign end product that is not an eligible product.

"United States" means the 50 States, the District of Columbia, and outlying areas.

"U.S.-made end product" means an article that is mined, produced, or manufactured in the United States or that is substantially transformed in the United States into a new and different article of commerce with a name, character, or use distinct from that of the article or articles from which it was transformed.

"World Trade Organization Government Procurement Agreement (WTO GPA) country" means any of the following countries: Armenia, Aruba, Austria, Belgium, Bulgaria, Canada, Croatia, Cyprus, Czech Republic, Denmark, Estonia, Finland, France, Germany, Greece, Hong Kong, Hungary, Iceland, Ireland, Israel, Italy, Japan, Korea (Republic of), Latvia, Liechtenstein, Lithuania, Luxembourg, Malta, Montenegro, Netherlands, New Zealand, Norway, Poland, Portugal, Romania, Singapore, Slovak Republic, Slovenia, Spain, Sweden, Switzerland, Taiwan, or United Kingdom.

"WTO GPA country end product" means an article that—

(1) Is wholly the growth, product, or manufacture of a WTO GPA country; or

(2) In the case of an article that consists in whole or in part of materials from another country, has been substantially transformed in a WTO GPA country into a new and dif-

ferent article of commerce with a name, character, or use distinct from that of the article or articles from which it was transformed. The term refers to a product offered for purchase under a supply contract, but for purposes of calculating the value of the end product includes services (except transportation services) incidental to the article, provided that the value of those incidental services does not exceed that of the article itself.

Notes of Decisions

Definitions 1

1 Definitions

Because the definition of "domestic end product" focuses on where the product is manufactured and not the country affiliation of the manufacturer, foreign companies can produce "domestic end products" and U.S. based companies can produce "foreign end products." Military Optic, Inc., B-245010.3, 92-1 CPD ¶ 78 (Comp. Gen. 1992).

The BAA applies only at the end item level and the content restrictions do not flow down to subcontractors. The prime contractor is responsible for delivering a product that meets the domestic end product definition. A "component" under the BAA is either entirely foreign or entirely domestic. A component is domestic only if it is manufactured in the United States. Computer Hut Int'l, Inc., B-249421, 92-2 CPD ¶ 364 (Comp. Gen. 1992).

Subpart 25.1 Buy American Act—Supplies

§ 25.100 Scope of subpart.

(a) This subpart implements—

(1) 41 U.S.C. chapter 83, Buy American;

(2) Executive Order 10582, December 17, 1954; and

(3) Waiver of the component test of the Buy American statute for acquisition of commercially available off-the-shelf (COTS) items in accordance with 41 U.S.C 1907.

(b) It applies to supplies acquired for use in the United States, including supplies acquired under contracts set aside for small business concerns, if—

(1) The supply contract exceeds the micro-purchase threshold; or

(2) The supply portion of a contract for services that involves the furnishing of supplies (*e.g.*, lease) exceeds the micro-purchase threshold.

United States Code Annotated

Administrative determinations, see 41 USCA § 257.

American materials required for public use, see 41 USCA § 10a.

Clarification of Congressional intent regarding sections 10a and 10b(a), see 41 USCA § 10d.

Contract requirements, see 41 USCA § 254.

Contracts, planning, solicitation, evaluation, and award procedures, see 10 USCA § 2305.

Contracts for public works, specification for use of American materials, blacklisting contractors violating requirements, see 41 USCA § 10b.

Definition of terms used in sections 10a, 10b, and 10c, see 41 USCA § 10c.

Definitions, see 10 USCA § 2302, 41 USCA §§ 259, 403.

Determinations and decisions, see 10 USCA § 2310, 41 USCA § 262.

Kinds of contracts, see 10 USCA § 2306.

Limitation on authority to waive Buy American Act requirement, see 41 USCA § 10b-2.

Planning and solicitation requirements, see 41 USCA § 253a.

§ 25.101 General.

(a) The Buy American statute restricts the purchase of supplies that are not domestic end products. For manufactured end products, the Buy American statute uses a two-part test to define a domestic end product.

(1) The article must be manufactured in the United States; and

(2) The cost of domestic components must exceed 50 percent of the cost of all the components. In accordance with 41 U.S.C 1907, this component test of the Buy American statute has been waived for acquisitions of COTS items (see 12.505(a)).

(b) The Buy American statute applies to small business set-asides. A manufactured product of a small business concern is a U.S.-made end product, but is not a domestic end product unless it meets the component test in paragraph (a)(2) of this section.

(c) Exceptions that allow the purchase of a foreign end product are listed at 25.103. The unreasonable cost exception is implemented through the use of an evaluation factor applied to low foreign offers that are not eligible offers. The evaluation factor is not used to provide a preference for one foreign offer over another. Evaluation procedures and examples are provided in Subpart 25.5.

United States Code Annotated

Administrative determinations, see 41 USCA § 257.

American materials required for public use, see 41 USCA § 10a.

Clarification of Congressional intent regarding sections 10a and 10b(a), see 41 USCA § 10d.

Contract requirements, see 41 USCA § 254.

Contracts, planning, solicitation, evaluation, and award procedures, see 10 USCA § 2305.

Contracts for public works, specification for use of American materials, blacklisting contractors violating requirements, see 41 USCA § 10b.

Definition of terms used in sections 10a, 10b, and 10c, see 41 USCA § 10c.

Definitions, see 10 USCA § 2302, 41 USCA §§ 259, 403.

Determinations and decisions, see 10 USCA § 2310, 41 USCA § 262.

Kinds of contracts, see 10 USCA § 2306.

Limitation on authority to waive Buy American Act requirement, see 41 USCA § 10b-2.

Planning and solicitation requirements, see 41 USCA § 253a.

Notes of Decisions

In general 1

1 In general

Termination for of the contract for default is proper if the contractor's product does not contain over 50% (by cost) domestic or qualifying country components. H&R Machinists Co., ASBCA. No. 38440, 91-1 BCA ¶ 23,373 (Armed Serv. BCA 1991).

As a general rule, an agency should go beyond a firm's self-certification for Buy American Act purposes and should not rely upon the validity of that certification where the agency has reason to believe, prior to award, that a foreign end product will be furnished. On the other hand, where a contracting officer has no information prior to award that would lead to the conclusion that the product to be furnished is a foreign end product, the contracting officer may properly rely upon an offeror's self-certification without further investigation. Leisure-Lift, Inc., B-291878.3, 2003 CPD ¶ 189 (Comp.Gen. 2003)

The nationality of the company that manufactures an end item is irrelevant. What is relevant under the BAA is whether an item is manufactured, mined or produced in the U.S. Military Optic, Inc., B-245010.3, 92-1 CPD ¶ 78 (Comp. Gen. 1992)

To satisfy the requirements of the Buy American Act, an item must be "manufactured" in the United States. "Manufacture" means completion of the article in the form required for use by the government. General Kinetics, Inc, Cryptek Div., B-242052.2, 70 Comp. Gen. 473, 91-1 CPD ¶ 445 (Comp. Gen. 1991)

The Buy American Act does not provide a basis for challenging a sole-source procurement, since the act does not impose an absolute prohibition on the purchase of foreign-made products, but merely requires a price comparison between competing offers, domestic and foreign. Bartlett Technologies Corp., B-218786, 85-2 CPD ¶ 198 (Comp. Gen. 1983)

§ 25.102 Policy.

Except as provided in 25.103, acquire only domestic end products for public use inside the United States.

United States Code Annotated

Administrative determinations, see 41 USCA § 257.

American materials required for public use, see 41 USCA § 10a.

Clarification of Congressional intent regarding sections 10a and 10b(a), see 41 USCA § 10d.

Contract requirements, see 41 USCA § 254.

Contracts, planning, solicitation, evaluation, and award procedures, see 10 USCA § 2305.

Contracts for public works, specification for use of American materials, blacklisting contractors violating requirements, see 41 USCA § 10b.

Definition of terms used in sections 10a, 10b, and 10c, see 41 USCA § 10c.

Definitions, see 10 USCA § 2302, 41 USCA §§ 259, 403.

Determinations and decisions, see 10 USCA § 2310, 41 USCA § 262.

Kinds of contracts, see 10 USCA § 2306.

Limitation on authority to waive Buy American Act requirement, see 41 USCA § 10b-2.

Planning and solicitation requirements, see 41 USCA § 253a.

§ 25.103 Exceptions.

When one of the following exceptions applies, the contracting officer may acquire a foreign end product without regard to the restrictions of the Buy American statute:

(a) *Public interest.* The head of the agency may make a determination that domestic preference would be inconsistent with the public interest. This exception applies when an agency has an agreement with a foreign government that provides a blanket exception to the Buy American Act.

(b) *Nonavailability.* The Buy American statute does not apply with respect to articles, materials, or supplies if articles, materials, or supplies of the class or kind to be acquired, either as end items or components, are not mined, produced, or manufactured in the United States in sufficient and reasonably available commercial quantities and of a satisfactory quality.

(1) Class determinations.

(i) A nonavailability determination has been made for the articles listed in 25.104. This determination does not necessarily mean that there is no domestic source for the listed items, but that domestic sources can only meet 50 percent or less of total U.S. Government and nongovernment demand.

(ii) Before acquisition of an article on the list, the procuring agency is responsible to conduct market research appropriate to the circumstances, including seeking of domestic sources. This applies to acquisition of an article as—

(A) An end product; or

(B) A significant component (valued at more than 50 percent of the value of all the components).

(iii) The determination in paragraph (b)(1)(i) of this section does not apply if the contracting officer learns at any time before the time designated for receipt of bids in sealed bidding or final offers in negotiation that an article on the list is available domestically in sufficient and reasonably available commercial quantities of a satisfactory quality to meet the requirements of the solicitation. The contracting officer must—

(A) Ensure that the appropriate Buy American statute provision and clause are included in the solicitation (see 22.1101(a), 22.1101(b), or 25.1102);

(B) Specify in the solicitation that the article is available domestically and that offerors and contractors may not treat foreign components of the same class or kind as domestic components; and

(C) Submit a copy of supporting documentation to the appropriate council identified in 1.201-1, in accordance with agency procedures, for possible removal of the article from the list.

(2) Individual determinations.

(i) The head of the contracting activity may make a determination that an article, material, or supply is not mined, produced, or manufactured in the United States in sufficient and reasonably available commercial quantities of a satisfactory quality.

(ii) If the contracting officer considers that the nonavailability of an article is likely to affect future acquisitions, the contracting officer may submit a copy of the determination and supporting documentation to the appropriate council identified in 1.201-1, in accordance with agency procedures, for possible addition to the list in 25.104.

(3) A written determination is not required if all of the following conditions are present:

(i) The acquisition was conducted through use of full and open competition.

(ii) The acquisition was synopsized in accordance with 5.201.

(iii) No offer for a domestic end product was received.

(c) *Unreasonable cost.* The contracting officer may determine that the cost of a domestic end product would be unreasonable, in accordance with 25.105 and Subpart 25.5.

(d) *Resale.* The contracting officer may purchase foreign end products specifically for commissary resale.

(e) *Information technology that is a commercial item.* The restriction on purchasing foreign end products does not apply to the acquisition of information technology that is a commercial item, when using fiscal year 2004 or subsequent fiscal year funds (Section 535(a) of Division F, Title V, Consolidated Appropriations Act, 2004, and similar sections in subsequent appropriations acts).

United States Code Annotated

Administrative determinations, see 41 USCA § 257.

American materials required for public use, see 41 USCA § 10a.

Clarification of Congressional intent regarding sections 10a and 10b(a), see 41 USCA § 10d.

Contract requirements, see 41 USCA § 254.

Contracts, planning, solicitation, evaluation, and award procedures, see 10 USCA § 2305.

Contracts for public works, specification for use of American materials, blacklisting contractors violating requirements, see 41 USCA § 10b.

Definition of terms used in sections 10a, 10b, and 10c, see 41 USCA § 10c.

Definitions, see 10 USCA § 2302, 41 USCA §§ 259, 403.

Determinations and decisions, see 10 USCA § 2310, 41 USCA § 262.

Kinds of contracts, see 10 USCA § 2306.

Limitation on authority to waive Buy American Act requirement, see 41 USCA § 10b-2.

Planning and solicitation requirements, see 41 USCA § 253a.

§ 25.104 Nonavailable articles.

(a) The following articles have been determined to be nonavailable in accordance with 25.103(b)(1)(i):

Acetylene, black.

Agar, bulk.

Anise.

Antimony, as metal or oxide.

Asbestos, amosite, chrysotile, and crocidolite.

Bamboo shoots.

Bananas.

Bauxite.

Beef, corned, canned.

Beef extract.

Bephenium hydroxynapthoate.

Bismuth.

Books, trade, text, technical, or scientific; newspapers; pamphlets; magazines; periodicals; printed briefs and films; not printed in the United States and for which domestic editions are not available.

Brazil nuts, unroasted
Cadmium, ores and flue dust.
Calcium cyanamide.
Capers.
Cashew nuts.
Castor beans and castor oil.
Chalk, English.
Chestnuts.
Chicle.
Chrome ore or chromite.
Cinchona bark.
Cobalt, in cathodes, rondelles, or other primary ore and metal forms.
Cocoa beans.
Coconut and coconut meat, unsweetened, in shredded, desiccated, or similarly prepared form.
Coffee, raw or green bean.
Colchicine alkaloid, raw.
Copra.
Cork, wood or bark and waste.
Cover glass, microscope slide.
Crane rail (85-pound per foot).
Cryolite, natural.
Dammar gum.
Diamonds, industrial, stones and abrasives.
Emetine, bulk.
Ergot, crude.
Erythrityl tetranitrate.
Fair linen, altar.
Fibers of the following types: abaca, abace, agave, coir, flax, jute, jute burlaps, palmyra, and sisal.
Goat and kidskins.
Goat hair canvas.
Grapefruit sections, canned.
Graphite, natural, crystalline, crucible grade.
Hand file sets (Swiss pattern).
Handsewing needles.
Hemp yarn.
Hog bristles for brushes.
Hyoscine, bulk.
Ipecac, root.
Iodine, crude.
Kaurigum.
Lac.
Leather, sheepskin, hair type.
Lavender oil.
Manganese.
Menthol, natural bulk.
Mica.
Microprocessor chips (brought onto a Government construction site as separate units for incorporation into building systems during construction or repair and alteration of real property).
Modacrylic fiber.

Nickel, primary, in ingots, pigs, shots, cathodes, or similar forms; nickel oxide and nickel salts.

Nitroguanidine (also known as picrite).

Nux vomica, crude.

Oiticica oil.

Olive oil.

Olives (green), pitted or unpitted, or stuffed, in bulk.

Opium, crude.

Oranges, mandarin, canned.

Petroleum, crude oil, unfinished oils, and finished products.

Pine needle oil.

Pineapple, canned.

Platinum and related group metals, refined, as sponge, powder, ingots, or cast bars.

Pyrethrum flowers.

Quartz crystals.

Quebracho.

Quinidine.

Quinine.

Rabbit fur felt.

Radium salts, source and special nuclear materials.

Rosettes.

Rubber, crude and latex.

Rutile.

Santonin, crude.

Secretin.

Shellac.

Silk, raw and unmanufactured.

Spare and replacement parts for equipment of foreign manufacture, and for which domestic parts are not available.

Spices and herbs, in bulk.

Sugars, raw.

Swords and scabbards.

Talc, block, steatite.

Tantalum.

Tapioca flour and cassava.

Tartar, crude; tartaric acid and cream of tartar in bulk.

Tea in bulk.

Thread, metallic (gold).

Thyme oil.

Tin in bars, blocks, and pigs.

Triprolidine hydrochloride.

Tungsten.

Vanilla beans.

Venom, cobra.

Water chestnuts.

Wax, carnauba.

Wire glass.

Woods; logs, veneer, and lumber of the following species: Alaskan yellow cedar, angelique, balsa, ekki, greenheart, lignum vitae, mahogany, and teak.

Yarn, 50 Denier rayon.

Yeast, active dry and instant active dry.

(b) This list will be published in the *Federal Register* for public comment no less frequently than once every five years. Unsolicited recommendations for deletions from this list may be submitted at any time and should provide sufficient data and rationale to permit evaluation (see 1.502).

United States Code Annotated

Administrative determinations, see 41 USCA § 257.

American materials required for public use, see 41 USCA § 10a.

Clarification of Congressional intent regarding sections 10a and 10b(a), see 41 USCA § 10d.

Contract requirements, see 41 USCA § 254.

Contracts, planning, solicitation, evaluation, and award procedures, see 10 USCA § 2305.

Contracts for public works, specification for use of American materials, blacklisting contractors violating requirements, see 41 USCA § 10b.

Definition of terms used in sections 10a, 10b, and 10c, see 41 USCA § 10c.

Definitions, see 10 USCA § 2302, 41 USCA §§ 259, 403.

Determinations and decisions, see 10 USCA § 2310, 41 USCA § 262.

Kinds of contracts, see 10 USCA § 2306.

Limitation on authority to waive Buy American Act requirement, see 41 USCA § 10b-2.

Planning and solicitation requirements, see 41 USCA § 253a.

§ 25.105 Determining reasonableness of cost.

(a) The contracting officer—

(1) Must use the evaluation factors in paragraph (b) of this section unless the head of the agency makes a written determination that the use of higher factors is more appropriate. If the determination applies to all agency acquisitions, the agency evaluation factors must be published in agency regulations; and

(2) Must not apply evaluation factors to offers of eligible products if the acquisition is subject to a trade agreement under Subpart 25.4.

(b) If there is a domestic offer that is not the low offer, and the restrictions of the Buy American statute apply to the low offer, the contracting officer must determine the reasonableness of the cost of the domestic offer by adding to the price of the low offer, inclusive of duty—

(1) 6 percent, if the lowest domestic offer is from a large business concern; or

(2) 12 percent, if the lowest domestic offer is from a small business concern. The contracting officer must use this factor, or another factor established in agency regulations, in small business set-asides if the low offer is from a small business concern offering the product of a small business concern that is not a domestic end product (see Subpart 19.5).

(c) The price of the domestic offer is reasonable if it does not exceed the evaluated price of the low offer after addition of the appropriate evaluation factor in accordance with paragraph (a) or (b) of this section. (See evaluation procedures at Subpart 25.5.)

United States Code Annotated

Administrative determinations, see 41 USCA § 257.

American materials required for public use, see 41 USCA § 10a.

Clarification of Congressional intent regarding sections 10a and 10b(a), see 41 USCA § 10d.

Contract requirements, see 41 USCA § 254.

Contracts, planning, solicitation, evaluation, and award procedures, see 10 USCA § 2305.

Contracts for public works, specification for use of American materials, blacklisting contractors violating requirements, see 41 USCA § 10b.

Definition of terms used in sections 10a, 10b, and 10c, see 41 USCA § 10c.

Definitions, see 10 USCA § 2302, 41 USCA §§ 259, 403.

Determinations and decisions, see 10 USCA § 2310, 41 USCA § 262.

Kinds of contracts, see 10 USCA § 2306.

Limitation on authority to waive Buy American Act requirement, see 41 USCA § 10b-2.

Planning and solicitation requirements, see 41 USCA § 253a.

Subpart 25.2 Buy American Act—Construction Materials

§ 25.200 Scope of Subpart.
(a) This subpart implements—

(1) 41 U.S.C. chapter 83, Buy American;

(2) Executive Order 10582, December 17, 1954; and

(3) Waiver of the component test of the Buy American statute for acquisition of commercially available off-the-shelf (COTS) items in accordance with 41 U.S.C 1907.

(b) It applies to contracts for the construction, alteration, or repair of any public building or public work in the United States.

(c) When using funds appropriated or otherwise provided by the American Recovery and Reinvestment Act of 2009 (Pub. L. 111-5) (Recovery Act) for construction, see Subpart 25.6.

United States Code Annotated
Administrative determinations, see 41 USCA § 257.

American materials required for public use, see 41 USCA § 10a.

Clarification of Congressional intent regarding sections 10a and 10b(a), see 41 USCA § 10d.

Contract requirements, see 41 USCA § 254.

Contracts, planning, solicitation, evaluation, and award procedures, see 10 USCA § 2305.

Contracts for public works, specification for use of American materials, blacklisting contractors violating requirements, see 41 USCA § 10b.

Definition of terms used in sections 10a, 10b, and 10c, see 41 USCA § 10c.

Definitions, see 10 USCA § 2302, 41 USCA §§ 259, 403.

Determinations and decisions, see 10 USCA § 2310, 41 USCA § 262.

Kinds of contracts, see 10 USCA § 2306.

Limitation on authority to waive Buy American Act requirement, see 41 USCA § 10b-2.

Planning and solicitation requirements, see 41 USCA § 253a.

§ 25.201 Policy.
Except as provided in 25.202, use only domestic construction materials in construction contracts performed in the United States.

United States Code Annotated
Administrative determinations, see 41 USCA § 257.

American materials required for public use, see 41 USCA § 10a.

Clarification of Congressional intent regarding sections 10a and 10b(a), see 41 USCA § 10d.

Contract requirements, see 41 USCA § 254.

Contracts, planning, solicitation, evaluation, and award procedures, see 10 USCA § 2305.

Contracts for public works, specification for use of American materials, blacklisting contractors violating requirements, see 41 USCA § 10b.

Definition of terms used in sections 10a, 10b, and 10c, see 41 USCA § 10c.

Definitions, see 10 USCA § 2302, 41 USCA §§ 259, 403.

Determinations and decisions, see 10 USCA § 2310, 41 USCA § 262.

Kinds of contracts, see 10 USCA § 2306.

Limitation on authority to waive Buy American Act requirement, see 41 USCA § 10b-2.

Notes of Decisions
Contract construction, generally 1
Domestic construction material 2

False claims against the United States 4
Instructions 5
Waiver of act 3

1 Contract construction, generally

Buy American clause for construction contracts could be treated as requirement of federal construction contract, even though parties had stricken clause and erroneously inserted version of clause applicable to supply contracts. Buy American Act, § 3, 41 U.S.C.A. § 10b. S.J. Amoroso Const. Co., Inc. v. U.S., 12 F.3d 1072, 39 Cont. Cas. Fed. (CCH) P 76603 (Fed. Cir. 1993). United States ☞70(8); United States ☞70(29)

2 Domestic construction material

Under Buy American Act (BAA), only domestic construction materials are to be used in public construction contracts in the United States unless agency head, after timely application for waiver, determines that use of only domestic construction materials would be inconsistent with public interest or that cost of those materials is unreasonable. 41 U.S.C.A. § 10d; Executive Order No. 10582, § 1 et seq., 41 U.S.C.(1982 Ed.) § 10d note. S.J. Amoroso Const. Co., Inc. v. U.S., 12 F.3d 1072, 39 Cont. Cas. Fed. (CCH) P 76603 (Fed. Cir. 1993). United States ☞70(8)

Each steel beam brought to construction site for incorporation into building had to satisfy domestic content requirements of Buy American Act (BAA), even though beams were later combined with other materials. Buy American Act, § 3, 41 U.S.C.A. § 10b. S.J. Amoroso Const. Co., Inc. v. U.S., 12 F.3d 1072, 39 Cont. Cas. Fed. (CCH) P 76603 (Fed. Cir. 1993). United States ☞70(8)

Cost of labor and transportation of steel beams to construction site were not to be included in cost of each beam for purposes of domestic content requirements of Buy American Act (BAA). Buy American Act, § 3, 41 U.S.C.A. § 10b. S.J. Amoroso Const. Co., Inc. v. U.S., 12 F.3d 1072, 39 Cont. Cas. Fed. (CCH) P 76603 (Fed. Cir. 1993). United States ☞70(8)

Buy American Act (BAA) required construction contractor to calculate domestic portion of each piece of structural steel delivered to construction site, and did not permit determination of domestic percentage based upon aggregate of all structural steel. Buy American Act, § 2 et seq., as amended, 41 U.S.C.A. § 10a et seq. S.J. Amoroso Const. Co., Inc. v. U.S., 12 F.3d 1072, 39 Cont. Cas. Fed. (CCH) P 76603 (Fed. Cir. 1993). United States ☞70(9)

Contractor's labor and transportation costs could not be included in computations for purposes of determining whether domestic portion of each individual piece of structural steel delivered to construction site was at least 50% domestic, as required under Buy American Act (BAA). Buy American Act, § 2 et seq., as amended, 41 U.S.C.A. § 10a et seq. S.J. Amoroso Const. Co., Inc. v. U.S., 12 F.3d 1072, 39 Cont. Cas. Fed. (CCH) P 76603 (Fed. Cir. 1993). United States ☞70(9)

Buy American Act (BAA) provision mandating that each individual component delivered to construction site be at least 50% domestic material applied to contract, even though parties erroneously included clause that would have governed supply contract, rather than construction contract, whether error was advertent or inadvertent. Buy American Act, § 2 et seq., as amended, 41 U.S.C.A. § 10a et seq. S.J. Amoroso Const. Co., Inc. v. U.S., 12 F.3d 1072, 39 Cont. Cas. Fed. (CCH) P 76603 (Fed. Cir. 1993). United States ☞70(9)

Contractor did not make timely request for waiver of statute requiring government to give preference to domestic construction materials, though contractor requested postaward approval of foreign wire, where it did not make formal request for waiver; remark by contracting officer that nothing could be done about higher cost of domestic product could not reasonably be understood as formal denial of formal request for waiver. Buy American Act, § 2 et seq., 41 U.S.C.A. § 10a et seq.; 41 U.S.C.A. § 10d. C. Sanchez and Son, Inc. v. U.S., 6 F.3d 1539, 39 Cont. Cas. Fed. (CCH) P 76578 (Fed. Cir. 1993). United States ☞70(21); United States ☞70(36)

Labor costs of adapting Canadian steel angles and doors for use in contract to provide elevator at air base could not be included in determining whether 50 percent of their cost was incurred in United States, for purposes of qualifying items as "domestic construction material" under Buy America Act. Buy American Act, § 3(b), 41 U.S.C.A. § 10b(b); 48 C.F.R. § 25.202. Glazer Const. Co., Inc. v. U.S., 50 F. Supp. 2d 85, 185 A.L.R. Fed. 717 (D. Mass.

1999). United States ☞70(8)

3 Waiver of act

Contractor, which never formally requested waiver of Buy American Act with regard to subcontractor's use of wire in construction of artificial battlefield, until after construction had been completed and transferred to Government, did not satisfactorily request postaward waiver of the Act, either orally or by its actions; although subcontractor orally informed contracting officer's representative that use of domestic material would be much more expensive and that domestic material was not available in sufficient quantities, assertions were not submitted in writing and were not accompanied by any information concerning actual price differentials. Buy American Act, §§ 1–3, 41 U.S.C.A. §§ 10c, 10a, 10b; National Military Establishment Appropriation Act, 1950, § 633, 41 U.S.C.A. § 10d; Executive Order No. 10582, §§ 1 et seq., 2(b, c), 41 U.S.C.A. § 10d note. C. Sanchez and Son, Inc. v. U.S., 6 F.3d 1539, 39 Cont. Cas. Fed. (CCH) P 76578 (Fed. Cir. 1993). United States ☞70(8)

Appropriate time to request waiver of Buy American Act is in first instance before contract award, or at least before contract has been performed, so that grant of waiver, if warranted, will avoid increased construction costs. Buy American Act, § 2 et seq., 41 U.S.C.A. § 10a et seq. C. Sanchez and Son, Inc. v. U.S., 6 F.3d 1539, 39 Cont. Cas. Fed. (CCH) P 76578 (Fed. Cir. 1993). United States ☞70(36)

Regulations setting forth requirements for preaward request for waiver of the Buy American Act apply also for a contractor requesting postaward waiver; contractor must submit to agency a description of materials for which waiver is sought, including quantity, estimated costs, and detailed justification of impracticability of using domestic materials. Buy American Act, §§ 1–3, 41 U.S.C.A. §§ 10c, 10a, 10b; National Military Establishment Appropriation Act, 1950, § 633, 41 U.S.C.A. § 10d; Executive Order No. 10582, §§ 1 et seq., 2(b, c), 41 U.S.C.A. § 10d note. C. Sanchez and Son, Inc. v. U.S., 6 F.3d 1539, 39 Cont. Cas. Fed. (CCH) P 76578 (Fed. Cir. 1993). United States ☞70(6.1)

4 False claims against the United States

Issue of whether hacksaw blades sold to the General Services Administration were domestic end products as certified by supplier under the Buy American Act, so that Government could not recover penalties under the False Claims Act, was for the jury in view of dispute over whether component manufacture had taken place, even though underlying facts were not in dispute. 31 U.S.C.A. § 3729 et seq.; Buy American Act, §§ 1–3, 41 U.S.C.A. §§ 10c, 10a, 10b. U.S. v. Rule Industries, Inc., 878 F.2d 535, 11 Int'l Trade Rep. (BNA) 1634, 35 Cont. Cas. Fed. (CCH) P 75678 (1st Cir. 1989). United States ☞122

Finding that claims for payment from the Government for products delivered were knowingly made, if false, was supported by evidence that supplier thought that blanks were "components" of the hacksaw blades which he was selling to the Government and that the blades were not domestic end products for purposes of the Buy American Act, that one employee of the supplier falsely told a GSA official that supplier would be using domestic steel to make the blades, and that it destroyed packaging of foreign hacksaw blanks which contained the wording "Made in Sweden." 31 U.S.C.A. § 3729 et seq.; Buy American Act, §§ 1–3, 41 U.S.C.A. §§ 10c, 10a, 10b. U.S. v. Rule Industries, Inc., 878 F.2d 535, 11 Int'l Trade Rep. (BNA) 1634, 35 Cont. Cas. Fed. (CCH) P 75678 (1st Cir. 1989). United States ☞122

5 Instructions

Trial court's instructions regarding the Buy American Act and the False Claims Act as applied to dispute over whether goods supplied by supplier were domestic end products were adequate. 31 U.S.C.A. § 3729 et seq.; Buy American Act, §§ 1–3, 41 U.S.C.A. §§ 10c, 10a, 10b. U.S. v. Rule Industries, Inc., 878 F.2d 535, 11 Int'l Trade Rep. (BNA) 1634, 35 Cont. Cas. Fed. (CCH) P 75678 (1st Cir. 1989). Federal Civil Procedure ☞2173.1(3)

§ 25.202 Exceptions.

(a) When one of the following exceptions applies, the contracting officer may allow the contractor to acquire foreign construction materials without regard to the restrictions of the Buy American statute:

(1) Impracticable or inconsistent with public-interest. The head of the agency may determine that application of the restrictions of the Buy American statute to a particular construction material would be impracticable or would be inconsistent with the public interest. The public interest exception applies when an agency has an agreement with a foreign government that provides a blanket exception to the Buy American statute.

(2) Nonavailability. The head of the contracting activity may determine that a particular construction material is not mined, produced, or manufactured in the United States in sufficient and reasonably available commercial quantities of a satisfactory quality. The determinations of nonavailability of the articles listed at 25.104(a) and the procedures at 25.103(b)(1) also apply if any of those articles are acquired as construction materials.

(3) Unreasonable cost. The contracting officer concludes that the cost of domestic construction material is unreasonable in accordance with 25.204.

(4) Information technology that is a commercial item. The restriction on purchasing foreign construction material does not apply to the acquisition of information technology that is a commercial item, when using Fiscal Year 2004 or subsequent fiscal year funds (Section 535(a) of Division F, Title V, Consolidated Appropriations Act, 2004, and similar sections in subsequent appropriations acts).

(b) Determination and findings. When a determination is made for any of the reasons stated in this section that certain foreign construction materials may be used, the contracting officer must list the excepted materials in the contract. The agency must make the findings justifying the exception available for public inspection.

(c) Acquisitions under trade agreements. For construction contracts with an estimated acquisition value of $7,358,000 or more, see subpart 25.4.

§ 25.203 Preaward determinations.

(a) For any acquisition, an offeror may request from the contracting officer a determination concerning the inapplicability of the Buy American statute for specifically identified construction materials. The time for submitting the request is specified in the solicitation in paragraph (b) of either 52.225-10 or 52.225-12, whichever applies. The information and supporting data that must be included in the request are also specified in the solicitation in paragraphs (c) and (d) of either 52.225-9 or 52.225-11, whichever applies.

(b) Before award, the contracting officer must evaluate all requests based on the information provided and may supplement this information with other readily available information.

United States Code Annotated

Administrative determinations, see 41 USCA § 257.

American materials required for public use, see 41 USCA § 10a.

Clarification of Congressional intent regarding sections 10a and 10b(a), see 41 USCA § 10d.

Contract requirements, see 41 USCA § 254.

Contracts, planning, solicitation, evaluation, and award procedures, see 10 USCA § 2305.

Contracts for public works, specification for use of American materials, blacklisting contractors violating requirements, see 41 USCA § 10b.

Definition of terms used in sections 10a, 10b, and 10c, see 41 USCA § 10c.

Definitions, see 10 USCA § 2302, 41 USCA §§ 259, 403.

Determinations and decisions, see 10 USCA § 2310, 41 USCA § 262.

Kinds of contracts, see 10 USCA § 2306.

Limitation on authority to waive Buy American Act requirement, see 41 USCA § 10b-2.

Planning and solicitation requirements, see 41 USCA § 253a.

Notes of Decisions

In general 1
Waiver of act 2

1 In general

The contracting officer may rely on the offeror's certification that its product is domestic, unless, prior to award, the contracting officer has reason to question the certification. New York Elevator Co., B-250992, Mar. 3, 1993, 93-1 CPD ¶ 196

2 Waiver of act

Contractor, which never formally requested waiver of Buy American Act with regard to subcontractor's use of wire in construction of artificial battlefield, until after construction had been completed and transferred to Government, did not satisfactorily request postaward waiver of the Act, either orally or by its actions; although subcontractor orally informed contracting officer's representative that use of domestic material would be much more expensive and that domestic material was not available in sufficient quantities, assertions were not submitted in writing and were not accompanied by any information concerning actual price differentials.

Buy American Act, §§ 1–3, 41 U.S.C.A. §§ 10c, 10a, 10b; National Military Establishment Appropriation Act, 1950, § 633, 41 U.S.C.A. § 10d; Executive Order No. 10582, §§ 1 et seq., 2(b, c), 41 U.S.C.A. § 10d note. C. Sanchez and Son, Inc. v. U.S., 6 F.3d 1539, 39 Cont. Cas. Fed. (CCH) P 76578 (Fed. Cir. 1993). United States ☞70(8)

Appropriate time to request waiver of Buy American Act is in first instance before contract award, or at least before contract has been performed, so that grant of waiver, if warranted, will avoid increased construction costs. Buy American Act, § 2 et seq., 41 U.S.C.A. § 10a et seq. C. Sanchez and Son, Inc. v. U.S., 6 F.3d 1539, 39 Cont. Cas. Fed. (CCH) P 76578 (Fed. Cir. 1993). United States ☞70(36)

Regulations setting forth requirements for preaward request for waiver of the Buy American Act apply also for a contractor requesting postaward waiver; contractor must submit to agency a description of materials for which waiver is sought, including quantity, estimated costs, and detailed justification of impracticability of using domestic materials. Buy American Act, §§ 1–3, 41 U.S.C.A. §§ 10c, 10a, 10b; National Military Establishment Appropriation Act, 1950, § 633, 41 U.S.C.A. § 10d; Executive Order No. 10582, §§ 1 et seq., 2(b, c), 41 U.S.C.A. § 10d note. C. Sanchez and Son, Inc. v. U.S., 6 F.3d 1539, 39 Cont. Cas. Fed. (CCH) P 76578 (Fed. Cir. 1993). United States ☞70(6.1)

§ 25.204 Evaluating offers of foreign construction material.

(a) Offerors proposing to use foreign construction material other than that listed by the Government in the applicable clause at 52.225-9, paragraph (b)(2), or 52.225-11, paragraph (b)(3), or covered by the WTO GPA or a Free Trade Agreement (paragraph (b)(2) of 52.225-11), must provide the information required by paragraphs (c) and (d) of the respective clauses.

(b) Unless the head of the agency specifies a higher percentage, the contracting officer must add to the offered price 6 percent of the cost of any foreign construction material proposed for exception from the requirements of the Buy American statute based on the unreasonable cost of domestic construction materials. In the case of a tie, the contracting officer must give preference to an offer that does not include foreign construction material excepted at the request of the offeror on the basis of unreasonable cost.

(c) Offerors also may submit alternate offers based on use of equivalent domestic construction material to avoid possible rejection of the entire offer if the Government determines that an exception permitting use of a particular foreign construction material does not apply.

(d) If the contracting officer awards a contract to an offeror that proposed foreign construction material not listed in the applicable clause in the solicitation (paragraph (b)(2) of 52.225-9, or paragraph (b)(3) of 52.225-11), the contracting officer must add the excepted materials to the list in the contract clause.

United States Code Annotated

Administrative determinations, see 41 USCA § 257.

American materials required for public use, see 41 USCA § 10a.

Clarification of Congressional intent regarding sections 10a and 10b(a), see 41 USCA § 10d.

Contract requirements, see 41 USCA § 254.

Contracts, planning, solicitation, evaluation, and award procedures, see 10 USCA § 2305.

Contracts for public works, specification for use of American materials, blacklisting contractors violating requirements, see 41 USCA § 10b.

Definition of terms used in sections 10a, 10b, and 10c, see 41 USCA § 10c.

Definitions, see 10 USCA § 2302, 41 USCA §§ 259, 403.

Determinations and decisions, see 10 USCA § 2310, 41 USCA § 262.

Kinds of contracts, see 10 USCA § 2306.

Limitation on authority to waive Buy American Act requirement, see 41 USCA § 10b-2.

Planning and solicitation requirements, see 41 USCA § 253a.

§ 25.205 Postaward determinations.

(a) If a contractor requests a determination regarding the inapplicability of the Buy American statute after contract award, the contractor must explain why it could not request the determination before contract award or why the need for such determination otherwise was not reasonably foreseeable. If the contracting officer concludes that the contractor should have made the request before contract award, the contracting officer may deny the request.

(b) The contracting officer must base evaluation of any request for a determination regarding the inapplicability of the Buy American statute made after contract award on information required by paragraphs (c) and (d) of the applicable clause at 52.225-9 or 52.225-11 and/or other readily available information.

(c) If a determination, under 25.202(a), is made after contract award that an exception to the Buy American statute applies, the contracting officer must negotiate adequate consideration and modify the contract to allow use of the foreign construction material. When the basis for the exception is the unreasonable price of a domestic construction material, adequate consideration is at least the differential established in 25.202(a) or in accordance with agency procedures.

United States Code Annotated

Administrative determinations, see 41 USCA § 257.

American materials required for public use, see 41 USCA § 10a.

Clarification of Congressional intent regarding sections 10a and 10b(a), see 41 USCA § 10d.

Contract requirements, see 41 USCA § 254.

Contracts, planning, solicitation, evaluation, and award procedures, see 10 USCA § 2305.

Contracts for public works, specification for use of American materials, blacklisting contractors violating requirements, see 41 USCA § 10b.

Definition of terms used in sections 10a, 10b, and 10c, see 41 USCA § 10c.

Definitions, see 10 USCA § 2302, 41 USCA §§ 259, 403.

Determinations and decisions, see 10 USCA § 2310, 41 USCA § 262.

Kinds of contracts, see 10 USCA § 2306.

Limitation on authority to waive Buy American Act requirement, see 41 USCA § 10b-2.

Planning and solicitation requirements, see 41 USCA § 253a.

Notes of Decisions

Waiver of act 1

1 Waiver of act

Contractor, which never formally requested waiver of Buy American Act with regard to subcontractor's use of wire in construction of artificial battlefield, until after construction had been completed and transferred to Government, did not satisfactorily request postaward waiver of the Act, either orally or by its actions; although subcontractor orally informed contracting officer's representative that use of domestic material would be much more expensive and that domestic material was not available in sufficient quantities, assertions were not submitted in writing and were not accompanied by any information concerning actual price differentials. Buy American Act, §§ 1–3, 41 U.S.C.A. §§ 10c, 10a, 10b; National Military Establishment Appropriation Act, 1950, § 633, 41 U.S.C.A. § 10d; Executive Order No. 10582, §§ 1 et seq., 2(b, c), 41 U.S.C.A. § 10d note. C. Sanchez and Son, Inc. v. U.S., 6 F.3d 1539, 39 Cont. Cas. Fed. (CCH) P 76578 (Fed. Cir. 1993). United States ☞70(8)

Appropriate time to request waiver of Buy American Act is in first instance before contract award, or at least before contract has been performed, so that grant of waiver, if warranted, will avoid increased construction costs. Buy American Act, § 2 et seq., 41 U.S.C.A. § 10a et seq. C. Sanchez and Son, Inc. v. U.S., 6 F.3d 1539, 39 Cont. Cas. Fed. (CCH) P 76578 (Fed. Cir. 1993). United States ☞70(36)

Regulations setting forth requirements for preaward request for waiver of the Buy American Act apply also for a contractor requesting postaward waiver; contractor must submit to agency a description of materials for which waiver is sought, including quantity, estimated costs, and detailed justification of impracticability of using domestic materials. Buy American Act, §§ 1–3, 41 U.S.C.A. §§ 10c, 10a, 10b; National Military Establishment Appropriation Act, 1950, § 633, 41 U.S.C.A. § 10d; Executive Order No. 10582, §§ 1 et seq., 2(b, c), 41 U.S.C.A. § 10d note. C. Sanchez and Son, Inc. v. U.S., 6 F.3d 1539, 39 Cont. Cas. Fed. (CCH) P 76578 (Fed. Cir. 1993). United States ☞70(6.1)

§ 25.206 Noncompliance.

The contracting officer must—

(a) Review allegations of Buy American statute violations;

(b) Unless fraud is suspected, notify the contractor of the apparent unauthorized use of foreign construction material and request a reply, to include proposed corrective action; and

(c) If the review reveals that a contractor or subcontractor has used foreign construction material without authorization, take appropriate action, including one or more of the following:

(1) Process a determination concerning the inapplicability of the Buy American statute in accordance with 25.205.

(2) Consider requiring the removal and replacement of the unauthorized foreign construction material.

(3) If removal and replacement of foreign construction material incorporated in a building or work would be impracticable, cause undue delay, or otherwise be detrimental to the interests of the Government, the contracting officer may determine in writing that the foreign construction material need not be removed and replaced. A determination to retain foreign construction material does not constitute a determination that an exception to the Buy American statute applies, and this should be stated in the determination. Further, a determination to retain foreign construction material does not affect the Government's right to suspend or debar a contractor, subcontractor, or supplier for violation of the Buy American statute, or to exercise other contractual rights and remedies, such as reducing the contract price or terminating the contract for default.

(4) If the noncompliance is sufficiently serious, consider exercising appropriate contractual remedies, such as terminating the contract for default. Also consider preparing and forwarding a report to the agency suspending or debarring official in accordance with Subpart 9.4. If the noncompliance appears to be fraudulent, refer the matter to other appropriate agency officials, such as the officer responsible for criminal investigation.

United States Code Annotated

Administrative determinations, see 41 USCA § 257.

American materials required for public use, see 41 USCA § 10a.

Clarification of Congressional intent regarding sections 10a and 10b(a), see 41 USCA § 10d.

Contract requirements, see 41 USCA § 254.

Contracts, planning, solicitation, evaluation, and award procedures, see 10 USCA § 2305.

Contracts for public works, specification for use of American materials, blacklisting contractors violating requirements, see 41 USCA § 10b.

Definition of terms used in sections 10a, 10b, and 10c, see 41 USCA § 10c.

Definitions, see 10 USCA § 2302, 41 USCA §§ 259, 403.

Determinations and decisions, see 10 USCA § 2310, 41 USCA § 262.

Kinds of contracts, see 10 USCA § 2306.

Limitation on authority to waive Buy American Act requirement, see 41 USCA § 10b-2.

Planning and solicitation requirements, see 41 USCA § 253a.

Notes of Decisions

In general 1

1 In general

Contractor's replacement of items not conforming with Buy America Act (BAA) with conforming items, after contractor was informed of non-compliance with BAA, did not cure violations. Buy American Act, § 3, 41 U.S.C.A. § 10b; 48 C.F.R. § 25.206(c)(3). Glazer Const. Co., Inc. v. U.S., 50 F. Supp. 2d 85, 185 A.L.R. Fed. 717 (D. Mass. 1999). United States ☞70(8)

Subpart 25.3 Contracts Performed Outside the United States

§ 25.301 Contractor personnel in a designated operational area or supporting a diplomatic or consular mission outside the United States.

§ 25.301-1 Scope.

(a) This section applies to contracts requiring contractor personnel to perform outside the United States—

(1) In a designated operational area during—

(i) Contingency operations;

(ii) Humanitarian or peacekeeping operations; or

(iii) Other military operations or military exercises, when designated by the combatant commander; or

(2) When supporting a diplomatic or consular mission—

(i) That has been designated by the Department of State as a danger pay post (see *http://aoprals.state.gov/Web920/danger_pay_all.asp*); or

(ii) That the contracting officer determines is a post at which application of the clause at FAR 52.225-19, Contractor Personnel in a Designated Operational Area or Supporting a Diplomatic or Consular Mission outside the United States, is appropriate.

(b) Any of the types of operations listed in paragraph (a)(1) of this section may include stability operations such as—

(1) Establishment or maintenance of a safe and secure environment; or

(2) Provision of emergency infrastructure reconstruction, humanitarian relief, or essential governmental services (until feasible to transition to local government).

(c) This section does not apply to personal services contracts (see FAR 37.104), unless specified otherwise in agency procedures.

§ 25.301-2 Government support.

(a) Generally, contractors are responsible for providing their own logistical and security support, including logistical and security support for their employees. The agency shall provide logistical or security support only when the appropriate agency official, in accordance with agency guidance, determines that—

(1) Such Government support is available and is needed to ensure continuation of essential contractor services; and

(2) The contractor cannot obtain adequate support from other sources at a reasonable cost.

(b) The contracting officer shall specify in the contract, and in the solicitation if possible, the exact support to be provided, and whether this support is provided on a reimbursable basis, citing the authority for the reimbursement.

§ 25.301-3 Weapons.

The contracting officer shall follow agency procedures and the weapons policy established by the combatant commander or the chief of mission when authorizing contractor personnel to carry weapons (see paragraph (i) of the clause at 52.225-19, Contractor Personnel in a Designated Operational Area or Supporting a Diplomatic or Consular Mission outside the United States).

§ 25.301-4 Contract clause.

Insert the clause at 52.225-19, Contractor Personnel in a Designated Operational Area or Supporting a Diplomatic or Consular Mission outside the United States, in solicitations and contracts, other than personal service contracts with individuals, that will require contractor personnel to perform outside the United States—

(a) In a designated operational area during—

(1) Contingency operations;

(2) Humanitarian or peacekeeping operations; or

(3) Other military operations or military exercises, when designated by the combatant commander; or

(b) When supporting a diplomatic or consular mission—

(1) That has been designated by the Department of State as a danger pay post (see *htt p://aoprals.state.gov/Web920/danger_pay_all.asp*); or

(2) That the contracting officer determines is a post at which application of the clause FAR 52.225-19, Contractor Personnel in a Designated Operational Area or Supporting a Diplomatic or Consular Mission outside the United States, is appropriate.

§ 25.302 Contractors performing private security functions outside the United States.

§ 25.302-1 Scope.

This section prescribes policy for implementing section 862 of the National Defense Authorization Act (NDAA) for Fiscal Year (FY) 2008 (Pub. L. 110-181), as amended by section 853 of the NDAA for FY 2009 (Pub. L. 110-417), and sections 831 and 832 of the NDAA for FY 2011 (Pub. L. 111-383) (see 10 U.S.C. 2302 Note).

§ 25.302-2 Definitions.

As used in this section—

"Area of combat operations" means an area of operations designated as such by the Secretary of Defense when enhanced coordination of contractors performing private security functions working for Government agencies is required.

"Other significant military operations" means activities, other than combat operations, as part of a contingency operation outside the United States that is carried out by United States Armed Forces in an uncontrolled or unpredictable high-threat environment where personnel performing security functions may be called upon to use deadly force (see 25.302-3(b)(2)).

"Private security functions means" activities engaged in by a contractor, as follows—

(1) Guarding of personnel, facilities, designated sites, or property of a Federal agency, the contractor or subcontractor, or a third party; or

(2) Any other activity for which personnel are required to carry weapons in the performance of their duties in accordance with the terms of the contract.

§ 25.302-3 Applicability.

(a) *DoD*: This section applies to acquisitions by Department of Defense components under a contract that requires performance—

(1) During contingency operations outside the United States;

(2) In an area of combat operations as designated by the Secretary of Defense; or

(3) In an area of other significant military operations as designated by the Secretary of Defense, and only upon agreement of the Secretary of Defense and the Secretary of State.

(b) *Non-DoD agencies*: This section applies to acquisitions by non-DoD agencies under a contract that requires performance—

(1) In an area of combat operations as designated by the Secretary of Defense; or

(2) In an area of other significant military operations as designated by the Secretary of Defense, and only upon agreement of the Secretary of Defense and the Secretary of State.

(c) These designations can be found at http://www.acq.osd.mil/dpap/pacc/cc/designated_ar eas_of_other_significant_military_operations.html and http://www.acq.osd.mil/dpap/pacc/cc/ designated_areas_of_combat_operations.html.

(d) When the applicability requirements of this subsection are met, contractors and subcontractors must comply with 32 CFR part 159, whether the contract is for the performance of private security functions as a primary deliverable or the provision of private security functions is ancillary to the stated deliverables.

(e) The requirements of section 25.302 shall not apply to—

(1) Contracts entered into by elements of the intelligence community in support of intelligence activities; or

(2) Temporary arrangements entered into on a non-DoD contract for the performance of private security functions by individual indigenous personnel not affiliated with a local or expatriate security company. These temporary arrangements must still comply with local law.

§ 25.302-4 Policy.

(a) General.

(1) The policy, responsibilities, procedures, accountability, training, equipping, and conduct of personnel performing private security functions in designated areas are addressed at 32 CFR part 159, entitled "Private Security Contractors (PSCs) Operating in Contingency Operations, Combat Operations, or Other Significant Military Operations." Contractor responsibilities include ensuring that employees are aware of, and comply with, relevant orders, directives, and instructions; keeping appropriate personnel records; accounting for weapons; registering and identifying armored vehicles, helicopters, and other military vehicles; and reporting specified incidents in which personnel performing private security functions under a contract are involved.

(2) In addition, contractors are required to cooperate with any Government-authorized investigation into incidents reported pursuant to paragraph (c)(3) of the clause at 52.225-26, Contractors Performing Private Security Functions Outside the United States, by providing access to employees performing private security functions and relevant information in the possession of the contractor regarding the incident concerned.

(b) *Implementing guidance.* In accordance with 32 CFR part 159—

(1) Geographic combatant commanders will provide DoD contractors performing private security functions with guidance and procedures for the operational environment in their area of responsibility; and

(2) In a designated area of combat operations, or areas of other significant military operations, as designated by the Secretary of Defense and only upon agreement of the Secretary of Defense and the Secretary of State, the relevant Chief of Mission will provide implementing instructions for non-DoD contractors performing private security functions and their personnel consistent with the standards set forth by the geographic combatant commander. In accordance with 32 CFR 159.4(c), the Chief of Mission has the option of instructing non-DoD contractors performing private security functions and their personnel to follow the guidance and procedures of the geographic combatant commander and/or a sub-unified commander or joint force commander where specifically authorized by the combatant commander to do so and notice of that authorization is provided to non-DoD agencies.

§ 25.302-5 Remedies.

(a) In addition to other remedies available to the Government—

(1) The contracting officer may direct the contractor, at its own expense, to remove and replace any contractor or subcontractor personnel performing private security functions who fail to comply with or violate applicable requirements. Such action may be taken at the Government's discretion without prejudice to its rights under any other contract provision, *e.g.*, termination for default;

(2) The contracting officer shall include the contractor's failure to comply with the requirements of this section in appropriate databases of past performance and consider any such failure in any responsibility determination or evaluation of past performance;

and

(3) In the case of award-fee contracts, the contracting officer shall consider a contractor's failure to comply with the requirements of this subsection in the evaluation of the contractor's performance during the relevant evaluation period, and may treat such failure as a basis for reducing or denying award fees for such period or for recovering all or part of award fees previously paid for such period.

(b) If the performance failures are severe, prolonged, or repeated, the contracting officer shall refer the matter to the appropriate suspending and debarring official.

§ 25.302-6 Contract clause.

(a) Use the clause at 52.225-26, Contractors Performing Private Security Functions Outside the United States, in the following solicitations and contracts:

(1) A DoD contract for performance in an area of—

(i) Contingency operations outside the United States;

(ii) Combat operations, as designated by the Secretary of Defense; or

(iii) Other significant military operations, as designated by the Secretary of Defense only upon agreement of the Secretary of Defense and the Secretary of State.

(2) A contract of a non-DoD agency for performance in an area of—

(i) Combat operations, as designated by the Secretary of Defense; or

(ii) Other significant military operations, as designated by the Secretary of Defense and only upon agreement of the Secretary of Defense and the Secretary of State.

(b) The clause is not required to be used for—

(1) Contracts entered into by elements of the intelligence community in support of intelligence activities; or

(2) Temporary arrangements entered into by non-DoD contractors for the performance of private security functions by individual indigenous personnel not affiliated with a local or expatriate security company.

Subpart 25.4 Trade Agreements

§ 25.400 Scope of subpart.

(a) This subpart provides policies and procedures applicable to acquisitions that are covered by—

(1) The World Trade Organization Government Procurement Agreement (WTO GPA), as approved by Congress in the Uruguay Round Agreements Act (Public Law 103-465);

(2) Free Trade Agreements (FTA), consisting of—

(i) NAFTA (the North American Free Trade Agreement, as approved by Congress in the North American Free Trade Agreement Implementation Act of 1993 (Pub. L. 103-182) (19 U.S.C. 3301 note));

(ii) Chile FTA (the United States-Chile Free Trade Agreement, as approved by Congress in the United States-Chile Free Trade Agreement Implementation Act of 1993 (Pub. L. 108-77) (19 U.S.C. 3805 note));

(iii) Singapore FTA (the United States-Singapore Free Trade Agreement, as approved by Congress in the United States-Singapore Free Trade Agreement Implementation Act (Pub. L. 108-78) (19 U.S.C. 3805 note));

(iv) Australia FTA (the United States-Australia Free Trade Agreement, as approved by Congress in the United States-Australia Free Trade Agreement Implementation Act (Pub. L. 108-286) (19 U.S.C. 3805 note));

(v) Morocco FTA (The United States-Morocco Free Trade Agreement, as approved by Congress in the United States-Morocco Free Trade Agreement Implementation Act (Pub. L. 108-302) (19 U.S.C. 3805 note));

(vi) CAFTA-DR (The Dominican Republic-Central America-United States Free Trade Agreement, as approved by Congress in the Dominican Republic-Central America-United States Free Trade Agreement Implementation Act (Pub. L. 109-53) (19 U.S.C. 4001 note));

(vii) Bahrain FTA (the United States-Bahrain Free Trade Agreement, as approved by

Congress in the United States-Bahrain Free Trade Agreement Implementation Act (Pub. L. 109-169) (19 U.S.C. 3805 note));

(viii) Oman FTA (the United States-Oman Free Trade Agreement, as approved by Congress in the United States-Oman Free Trade Agreement Implementation Act (Pub. L. 109-283) (19 U.S.C. 3805 note));

(ix) Peru FTA (the United States-Peru Trade Promotion Agreement, as approved by Congress in the United States-Peru Trade Promotion Agreement Implementation Act (Pub. L. 110-138) (19 U.S.C. 3805 note));

(x) Korea FTA (the United States–Korea Free Trade Agreement Implementation Act (Pub. L. 112-41) (19 U.S.C. 3805));

(xi) Colombia FTA (the United States–Colombia Trade Promotion Agreement Implementation Act (Pub. L. 112-42) (19 U.S.C. 3805 note)); and

(xii) Panama FTA (the United States-Panama Trade Promotion Agreement Implementation Act (Pub. L. 112-43) (19 U.S.C. 3805 note));

(3) The least developed country designation made by the U.S. Trade Representative, pursuant to the Trade Agreements Act (19 U.S.C. 2511(b)(4)), in acquisitions covered by the WTO GPA;

(4) The Caribbean Basin Trade Initiative (CBTI) (determination of the U.S. Trade Representative that end products or construction material granted duty-free entry from countries designated as beneficiaries under the Caribbean Basin Economic Recovery Act (19 U.S.C. 2701, *et seq.*), with the exception of Panama, must be treated as eligible products in acquisitions covered by the WTO GPA);

(5) The Israeli Trade Act (the U.S.-Israel Free Trade Area Agreement, as approved by Congress in the United States-Israel Free Trade Area Implementation Act of 1985 (19 U.S.C. 2112 note)); or

(6) The Agreement on Trade in Civil Aircraft (U.S. Trade Representative waiver of the Buy American statute for signatories of the Agreement on Trade in Civil Aircraft, as implemented in the Trade Agreements Act of 1979 (19 U.S.C. 2513)).

(b) For application of the trade agreements that are unique to individual agencies, see agency regulations.

United States Code Annotated

Administrative determinations, see 41 USCA § 257.

American materials required for public use, see 41 USCA § 10a.

Clarification of Congressional intent regarding sections 10a and 10b(a), see 41 USCA § 10d.

Contract requirements, see 41 USCA § 254.

Contracts, planning, solicitation, evaluation, and award procedures, see 10 USCA § 2305.

Contracts for public works, specification for use of American materials, blacklisting contractors violating requirements, see 41 USCA § 10b.

Definition of terms used in sections 10a, 10b, and 10c, see 41 USCA § 10c.

Definitions, see 10 USCA § 2302, 41 USCA §§ 259, 403.

Determinations and decisions, see 10 USCA § 2310, 41 USCA § 262.

Kinds of contracts, see 10 USCA § 2306.

Limitation on authority to waive Buy American Act requirement, see 41 USCA § 10b-2.

Planning and solicitation requirements, see 41 USCA § 253a.

§ 25.401 Exceptions.

(a) This subpart does not apply to—

(1) Acquisitions set aside for small businesses;

(2) Acquisitions of arms, ammunition, or war materials, or purchases indispensable for national security or for national defense purposes;

(3) Acquisitions of end products for resale;

(4) Acquisitions from Federal Prison Industries, Inc., under Subpart 8.6, and acquisitions under Subpart 8.7, Acquisition from Nonprofit Agencies Employing People Who Are

Blind or Severely Disabled; and

(5) Other acquisitions not using full and open competition, if authorized by Subpart 6.2 or 6.3, when the limitation of competition would preclude use of the procedures of this subpart; or sole source acquisitions justified in accordance with 13.501(a).

(b) In the World Trade Organization Government Procurement Agreement (WTO GPA) and each FTA, there is a U.S. schedule that lists services that are excluded from that agreement in acquisitions by the United States. Acquisitions of the following services are excluded from coverage by the U.S. schedule of the WTO GPA or an FTA as indicated in this table:

	THE SERVICE (FEDERAL SERVICE CODES FROM THE FEDERAL PROCUREMENT DATA SYSTEM PRODUCT/SERVICE CODE MANUAL ARE INDICATED IN PARENTHESES FOR SOME SERVICES.)	WTO GPA AND KOREA FTA	BAHRAIN FTA, CAFTA–DR, CHILE FTA, COLOMBIA FTA, NAFTA, OMAN FTA, PANAMA FTA, AND PERU FTA	SINGAPORE FTA	AUSTRALIA AND MOROCCO FTA
(1)	All services purchased in support of military services overseas.	X	X	X	X
(2)	(i) Automatic data processing (ADP) telecommunications and transmission services (D304), except enhanced (i.e., value-added) telecommunications services.	X	X		
	(ii) ADP teleprocessing and timesharing services (D305), telecommunications network management services (D316), automated news services, data services or other information services (D317), and other ADP and telecommunications services (D399).	X	X		
	(iii) Basic telecommunications network services (i.e., voice telephone services, packet-switched data transmission services, circuit-switched data transmission services, telex services, telegraph services, facsimile services, and private leased circuit services, but not information services, as defined in 47 U.S.C. 153(20)).	*	*	X	X
(3)	Dredging.	X	X	X	X
(4)	(i) Operation and management contracts of certain Government or privately owned facilities used for Government purposes, including Federally Funded Research and Development Centers.	X		X	

THE SERVICE (FEDERAL SERVICE CODES FROM THE FEDERAL PROCUREMENT DATA SYSTEM PRODUCT/SERVICE CODE MANUAL ARE INDICATED IN PARENTHESES FOR SOME SERVICES.)		WTO GPA AND KO-REA FTA	BAHRAIN FTA, CAFTA–DR, CHILE FTA, COLOMBIA FTA, NAFTA, OMAN FTA, PANAMA FTA, AND PERU FTA	SINGA-PORE FTA	AUSTRALIA AND MO-ROCCO FTA
	(ii) Operation of all Department of Defense, Department of Energy, or the National Aeronautics and Space Administration facilities; and all Government-owned research and development facilities or Government-owned environmental laboratories.	**	X	**	X
(5)	Research and development.	X	X	X	X
(6)	Transportation services (including launching services, but not including travel agent services).	X	X	X	X
(7)	Utility services.	X	X	X	X
(8)	Maintenance, repair, modification, rebuilding and installation of equipment related to ships (J019).		X		X
(9)	Nonnuclear ship repair (J998).		X		X

* Note 1. Acquisitions of the services listed at (2)(iii) of this table are a subset of the excluded services at (2)(i) and (ii), and are therefore not covered under the WTO GPA.

** Note 2. Acquisitions of the services listed at (4)(ii) of this table are a subset of the excluded services at (4)(i), and are therefore not covered under the WTO GPA.

United States Code Annotated

Administrative determinations, see 41 USCA § 257.

American materials required for public use, see 41 USCA § 10a.

Clarification of Congressional intent regarding sections 10a and 10b(a), see 41 USCA § 10d.

Contract requirements, see 41 USCA § 254.

Contracts, planning, solicitation, evaluation, and award procedures, see 10 USCA § 2305.

Contracts for public works, specification for use of American materials, blacklisting contractors violating requirements, see 41 USCA § 10b.

Definition of terms used in sections 10a, 10b, and 10c, see 41 USCA § 10c.

Definitions, see 10 USCA § 2302, 41 USCA §§ 259, 403.

Determinations and decisions, see 10 USCA § 2310, 41 USCA § 262.

Kinds of contracts, see 10 USCA § 2306.

Limitation on authority to waive Buy American Act requirement, see 41 USCA § 10b-2.

Planning and solicitation requirements, see 41 USCA § 253a.

Notes of Decisions

In general 1
Evaluation 4
Injunctions 3
War materials 2

1 In general

Substantial transformation established for hardware components assembled into complete Ethernet switches in China, which are then shipped to the U.S., where they are programmed with software developed in the U.S. at significant cost to the manufacturer and over many years. For 5 years, over 140 software engineers have developed the software and more than 80% of the manufacturer's R&D spending has been on this software development. The U.S.-origin software enables the imported switches to interact with other network switches, and allows for the management of functions such as network performance monitoring and security and access control. Without this software, the imported devices could not function as Ethernet switches. As a result of the programming performed in the U.S., with software developed in the U.S., the imported switches are "substantially transformed" in the U.S. Arista Networks LAN Switches, CBP Decision HQ H175415 (October 4, 2011)

If the TAA applies to the purchase, only domestic products, products from designated foreign countries, qualifying country products, and products which, though comprised of over 50% foreign components, are "substantially transformed" in the United States or a designated country, are eligible for award. Compuadd Corp. v. Dep't of the Air Force, GSBCA No. 12021-P, 93-2 BCA ¶ 25,811 (Gen. Serv. BCA 1993)

Government contractor's reliance on distributor's certification as to country of origin (COO) of technology products, for Trade Agreements Act (TAA) purposes, was reasonable, and thus contractor's presentation of claims for payment did not violate False Claims Act (FCA), even though contractor had received email indicating that some products were produced in nondesignated country. U.S. ex rel. Folliard v. Gov't Acquisitions, Inc. et al., 2014 WL 4251150 (D.C. Cir. 2014)

Although RFP requirement that vendors identify country of origin of product is inconsistent with customary commercial practice (and therefore, inconsistent with the general policy of FAR 12.302 that commercial item contracts adopt commercial terms), the provision was reasonably related to ensuring compliance with the Trade Agreements Act. FAR clause 52.212-4(q) requires a contractor under a commercial items contract to "comply with all applicable Federal, State and local laws, executive orders, rules and regulations applicable to its performance under [the] contract." Bridges System Integration, LLC, B-411020, 2015 CPD ¶ 144 (Comp.Gen. 2015).

2 War materials

United States General Services Administration (GSA) acted arbitrarily and capriciously when, in determining that manufacturer's tactical products made in Vietnam did not meet "war materials" exemption to prohibition, under Trade Agreements Act (TAA), against federal agencies buying products from countries which had not signed Agreement on Government Procurement, GSA adopted interpretation of exemption that required products to be used exclusively by Department of Defense (DoD) for military purposes in war environment, reading out language in regulation that applied exemption to products "indispensable for national security or for national defense purposes," and applied exemption through ad hoc procedure under which manufacturer was required to supply supporting letters that higher DoD officials, due to advice of government counsel, could not provide. Blackhawk Industries Products Group Unlimited, LLc. v. U.S. General Services Admin., 348 F. Supp. 2d 649 (E.D. Va. 2004). War And National Emergency ⟲41

In opposing preliminary injunction requested by manufacturer of tactical products, which sought to prevent government from removing its products made in Vietnam from federal supply schedule pursuant to "war materials" exemption from Trade Agreements Act (TAA), government did not establish harm through its contention that other suppliers of similar products would seek same exemption of their products if preliminary injunction was granted, inasmuch as products proven to be within exemption were intended to be exempted under federal regulations. Blackhawk Industries Products Group Unlimited, LLc. v. U.S. General Services Admin., 348 F. Supp. 2d 649 (E.D. Va. 2004). Injunction ⟲138.63

3 Injunctions

Manufacturer of tactical products was entitled to preliminary injunction barring United States General Services Administration (GSA) from removing manufacturer's products made in Vietnam from federal supply schedule pursuant to Trade Agreements Act (TAA), given that injunction would maintain status quo, that manufacturer would suffer irreparable harm without injunctive relief but GSA would suffer no significant harm due to such relief, that manufacturer established likelihood of success on the merits that it qualified for exemption to TAA for "war materials," in light of showing that GSA's definition and application of exemption was arbitrary and capricious, and that public interest strongly supported preliminary injunction. Blackhawk Industries Products Group Unlimited, LLc. v. U.S. General Services Admin., 348 F. Supp. 2d 649 (E.D. Va. 2004). Injunction ☞138.63

4 Evaluation

GAO denied protest alleging that an agency's determination of noncompliance with the Trade Agreements Act was unreasonable because agency reasonably determined that major components of the protester's end item would be sourced in China and the protester's assembly and manufacturing processes would not "substantially transform" the product in the U.S. or a designated country. Thus, the protester's item did not qualify as a U.S.-made end product. Sea Box, Inc., B-409963.3, 2015 CPD ¶ 72(Comp.Gen. 2015)

Even though solicitation did not include provision (DFARS § 252.225-7020) advising offerors that the agency would evaluate compliance with the Trade Agreements Act (TAA), GAO upheld the agency's rejection of a proposal that did not comply with the TAA because the contracting officer's Final Proposal Revision letter advised offerors that, after award, deliverables must either comply with the TAA or be approved under a waiver. Refinery Assocs. of Texas, Inc., B-410911.2, 2015 CPD ¶ 116 (Comp. Gen. 2015)

Protest that agency improperly evaluated offers for compliance with the Trade Agreements Act (TAA) was denied because firms were advised that such an evaluation would occur and throughout the acquisition, protester offered a product that was not compliant with the TAA and continued to do so notwithstanding the associated risk-even after being advised during discussions that its proposal might be found unacceptable on that basis. Refinery Associates of Texas, Inc., B-410911.2, 2015 CPD ¶ 116 (Comp.Gen. 2015)

Agency improperly awarded contract based upon a proposal where the offeror expressly declined to certify that the product to be provided would comply with the Trade Agreements Act as was required by the terms of the solicitation. Wyse Technology, Inc., B- 297454, 2006 CPD ¶ 23 (Comp.Gen. 2006)

§ 25.402 General.

(a) (1) The Trade Agreements Act (19 U.S.C. 2501, et seq.) provides the authority for the President to waive the Buy American statute and other discriminatory provisions for eligible products from countries that have signed an international trade agreement with the United States, or that meet certain other criteria, such as being a least developed country. The President has delegated this waiver authority to the U.S. Trade Representative. In acquisitions covered by the WTO GPA, Free Trade Agreements, or the Israeli Trade Act, the U.S. Trade Representative has waived the Buy American statute and other discriminatory provisions for eligible products. Offers of eligible products receive equal consideration with domestic offers.

(2) The contracting officer shall determine the origin of services by the country in which the firm providing the services is established. See subpart 25.5 for evaluation procedures for supply contracts covered by trade agreements.

(b) The value of the acquisition is a determining factor in the applicability of trade agreements. Most of these dollar thresholds are subject to revision by the U.S. Trade Representative approximately every 2 years. The various thresholds are summarized as follows:

Trade Agreement	Supply Contract (equal to or exceeding)	Service Contract (equal to or exceeding)	Construction Contract (equal to or exceeding)
WTO GPA	$191,000	$191,000	$7,358,000
FTAs			
Australia FTA	77,533	77,533	7,358,000
Bahrain FTA	191,000	191,000	10,079,365
CAFTA-DR (Costa Rica, Dominican Republic, El Salvador, Guatemala, Honduras, and Nicaragua)	77,533	77,533	7,358,000

Trade Agreement	Supply Contract (equal to or exceeding)	Service Contract (equal to or exceeding)	Construction Contract (equal to or exceeding)
Chile FTA	77,533	77,533	7,358,000
Colombia FTA	77,533	77,533	7,358,000
Korea FTA	100,000	100,000	7,358,000
Morocco FTA	191,000	191,000	7,358,000
NAFTA			
—Canada	25,000	77,533	10,079,365
—Mexico	77,533	77,533	10,079,365
Oman FTA	191,000	191,000	10,079,365
Panama	191,000	191,000	7,358,000
Peru FTA	191,000	191,000	7,358,000
Singapore FTA	77,533	77,533	7,358,000
Israeli Trade Act	50,000	—	—

§ 25.403 World Trade Organization Government Procurement Agreement and Free Trade Agreements.

(a) Eligible products from WTO GPA and FTA countries are entitled to the nondiscriminatory treatment specified in 25.402(a)(1). The WTO GPA and FTAs specify procurement procedures designed to ensure fairness (see 25.408).

(b) Thresholds.

(1) To determine whether the acquisition of products by lease, rental, or lease-purchase contract (including lease-to-ownership, or lease-with-option-to purchase) is covered by the WTO GPA or an FTA, calculate the estimated acquisition value as follows:

(i) If a fixed-term contract of 12 months or less is contemplated, use the total estimated value of the acquisition.

(ii) If a fixed-term contract of more than 12 months is contemplated, use the total estimated value of the acquisition plus the estimated residual value of the leased equipment at the conclusion of the contemplated term of the contract.

(iii) If an indefinite-term contract is contemplated, use the estimated monthly payment multiplied by the total number of months that ordering would be possible under the proposed contract, *i.e.*, the initial ordering period plus any optional ordering periods.

(iv) If there is any doubt as to the contemplated term of the contract, use the estimated monthly payment multiplied by 48.

(2) The estimated value includes the value of all options.

(3) If, in any 12-month period, recurring or multiple awards for the same type of product or products are anticipated, use the total estimated value of these projected awards to determine whether the WTO GPA or an FTA applies. Do not divide any acquisition with the intent of reducing the estimated value of the acquisition below the dollar threshold of the WTO GPA or an FTA.

(c) Purchase restriction.

(1) Under the Trade Agreements Act (19 U.S.C. 2512), in acquisitions covered by the WTO GPA, acquire only U.S.-made or designated country end products or U.S. or designated country services, unless offers for such end products or services are either not received or are insufficient to fulfill the requirements. This purchase restriction does not apply below the WTO GPA threshold for supplies and services, even if the acquisition is covered by an FTA.

(2) This restriction does not apply to purchases of supplies by the Department of Defense from a country with which it has entered into a reciprocal agreement, as provided in departmental regulations.

United States Code Annotated

Administrative determinations, see 41 USCA § 257.

American materials required for public use, see 41 USCA § 10a.

Clarification of Congressional intent regarding sections 10a and 10b(a), see 41 USCA § 10d.

Contract requirements, see 41 USCA § 254.

Contracts, planning, solicitation, evaluation, and award procedures, see 10 USCA § 2305.

Contracts for public works, specification for use of American materials, blacklisting contractors violating requirements, see 41 USCA § 10b.

Definition of terms used in sections 10a, 10b, and 10c, see 41 USCA § 10c.

Definitions, see 10 USCA § 2302, 41 USCA §§ 259, 403.

Determinations and decisions, see 10 USCA § 2310, 41 USCA § 262.

Kinds of contracts, see 10 USCA § 2306.

Limitation on authority to waive Buy American Act requirement, see 41 USCA § 10b-2.

Planning and solicitation requirements, see 41 USCA § 253a.

§ 25.404 Least developed countries.

For acquisitions covered by the WTO GPA, least developed country end products, construction material, and services must be treated as eligible products.

United States Code Annotated

Administrative determinations, see 41 USCA § 257.

American materials required for public use, see 41 USCA § 10a.

Clarification of Congressional intent regarding sections 10a and 10b(a), see 41 USCA § 10d.

Contract requirements, see 41 USCA § 254.

Contracts, planning, solicitation, evaluation, and award procedures, see 10 USCA § 2305.

Contracts for public works, specification for use of American materials, blacklisting contractors violating requirements, see 41 USCA § 10b.

Definition of terms used in sections 10a, 10b, and 10c, see 41 USCA § 10c.

Definitions, see 10 USCA § 2302, 41 USCA §§ 259, 403.

Determinations and decisions, see 10 USCA § 2310, 41 USCA § 262.

Kinds of contracts, see 10 USCA § 2306.

Limitation on authority to waive Buy American Act requirement, see 41 USCA § 10b-2.

Planning and solicitation requirements, see 41 USCA § 253a.

§ 25.405 Caribbean Basin Trade Initiative.

Under the Caribbean Basin Trade Initiative, the United States Trade Representative has determined that, for acquisitions covered by the WTO GPA, Caribbean Basin country end products, construction material, and services must be treated as eligible products. In accordance with Section 201 (a)(3) of the Dominican Republic-Central America-United States Free Trade Implementation Act (Pub. L. 109-53) (19 U.S.C. 4031), when the CAFTA-DR agreement enters into force with respect to a country, that country is no longer designated as a beneficiary country for purposes of the Caribbean Basin Economic Recovery Act, and is therefore no longer included in the definition of "Caribbean Basin country" for purposes of the Caribbean Basin Trade Initiative.

United States Code Annotated

Administrative determinations, see 41 USCA § 257.

American materials required for public use, see 41 USCA § 10a.

Clarification of Congressional intent regarding sections 10a and 10b(a), see 41 USCA § 10d.

Contract requirements, see 41 USCA § 254.

Contracts, planning, solicitation, evaluation, and award procedures, see 10 USCA § 2305.

Contracts for public works, specification for use of American materials, blacklisting contractors violating requirements, see 41 USCA § 10b.

Definition of terms used in sections 10a, 10b, and 10c, see 41 USCA § 10c.

Definitions, see 10 USCA § 2302, 41 USCA §§ 259, 403.

Determinations and decisions, see 10 USCA § 2310, 41 USCA § 262.

Kinds of contracts, see 10 USCA § 2306.

Limitation on authority to waive Buy American Act requirement, see 41 USCA § 10b-2.

Planning and solicitation requirements, see 41 USCA § 253a.

§ 25.406 Israeli Trade Act.

Acquisitions of supplies by most agencies are covered by the Israeli Trade Act, if the estimated value of the acquisition is $50,000 or more but does not exceed the WTO GPA threshold for supplies (see 25.402(b)). Agencies other than the Department of Defense, the Department of Energy, the Department of Transportation, the Bureau of Reclamation of the Department of the Interior, the Federal Housing Finance Board, and the Office of Thrift Supervision must evaluate offers of Israeli end products without regard to the restrictions of the Buy American statute. The Israeli Trade Act does not prohibit the purchase of other foreign end products.

United States Code Annotated

Administrative determinations, see 41 USCA § 257.

American materials required for public use, see 41 USCA § 10a.

Clarification of Congressional intent regarding sections 10a and 10b(a), see 41 USCA § 10d.

Contract requirements, see 41 USCA § 254.

Contracts, planning, solicitation, evaluation, and award procedures, see 10 USCA § 2305.

Contracts for public works, specification for use of American materials, blacklisting contractors violating requirements, see 41 USCA § 10b.

Definition of terms used in sections 10a, 10b, and 10c, see 41 USCA § 10c.

Definitions, see 10 USCA § 2302, 41 USCA §§ 259, 403.

Determinations and decisions, see 10 USCA § 2310, 41 USCA § 262.

Kinds of contracts, see 10 USCA § 2306.

Limitation on authority to waive Buy American Act requirement, see 41 USCA § 10b-2.

Planning and solicitation requirements, see 41 USCA § 253a.

§ 25.407 Agreement on Trade in Civil Aircraft.

Under the authority of Section 303 of the Trade Agreements Act, the U.S. Trade Representative has waived the Buy American statute for civil aircraft and related articles that meet the substantial transformation test of the Trade Agreements Act, from countries that are parties to the Agreement on Trade in Civil Aircraft. Those countries are Albania, Austria, Belgium, Bulgaria, Canada, Croatia, Cyprus, Czech Republic, Denmark, Egypt, Estonia, Finland, France, Georgia, Germany, Greece, Hungary, Ireland, Italy, Japan, Latvia, Lithuania, Luxembourg, Macao China, Malta, Montenegro, the Netherlands, Norway, Poland, Portugal, Romania, Slovakia, Slovenia, Spain, Sweden, Switzerland, Taiwan (Chinese Taipei), and the United Kingdom.

§ 25.408 Procedures.

(a) If the WTO GPA or an FTA applies (see 25.401), the contracting officer must—

(1) Comply with the requirements of 5.203, Publicizing and response time;

(2) Comply with the requirements of 5.207, Preparation and transmittal of synopses;

(3) Not include technical requirements in solicitations solely to preclude the acquisition of eligible products;

(4) Specify in solicitations that offerors must submit offers in the English language and in U.S. dollars (see 52.214-34, Submission of Offers in the English Language, and 52.214-35, Submission of Offers in U.S. Currency, or paragraph (c)(5) of 52.215-1, Instruction to Offerors—Competitive Acquisitions); and

(5) Provide unsuccessful offerors from WTO GPA or FTA countries notice in accordance with 14.409-1 or 15.503.

(b) See Subpart 25.5 for evaluation procedures and examples.

United States Code Annotated

Administrative determinations, see 41 USCA § 257.

American materials required for public use, see 41 USCA § 10a.

Clarification of Congressional intent regarding sections 10a and 10b(a), see 41 USCA § 10d.

Contract requirements, see 41 USCA § 254.

Contracts, planning, solicitation, evaluation, and award procedures, see 10 USCA § 2305.

Contracts for public works, specification for use of American materials, blacklisting contractors violating requirements, see 41 USCA § 10b.

Definition of terms used in sections 10a, 10b, and 10c, see 41 USCA § 10c.

Definitions, see 10 USCA § 2302, 41 USCA §§ 259, 403.

Determinations and decisions, see 10 USCA § 2310, 41 USCA § 262.

Kinds of contracts, see 10 USCA § 2306.

Limitation on authority to waive Buy American Act requirement, see 41 USCA § 10b-2.

Planning and solicitation requirements, see 41 USCA § 253a.

Subpart 25.5 Evaluating Foreign Offers—Supply Contracts

§ 25.501 General.

The contracting officer—

(a) Must apply the evaluation procedures of this subpart to each line item of an offer unless either the offer or the solicitation specifies evaluation on a group basis (see 25.503);

(b) May rely on the offeror's certification of end product origin when evaluating a foreign offer;

(c) Must identify and reject offers of end products that are prohibited in accordance with Subpart 25.7; and

(d) Must not use the Buy American statute evaluation factors prescribed in this subpart to provide a preference for one foreign offer over another foreign offer.

United States Code Annotated

Administrative determinations, see 41 USCA § 257.

American materials required for public use, see 41 USCA § 10a.

Clarification of Congressional intent regarding sections 10a and 10b(a), see 41 USCA § 10d.

Contract requirements, see 41 USCA § 254.

Contracts, planning, solicitation, evaluation, and award procedures, see 10 USCA § 2305.

Contracts for public works, specification for use of American materials, blacklisting contractors violating requirements, see 41 USCA § 10b.

Definition of terms used in sections 10a, 10b, and 10c, see 41 USCA § 10c.

Definitions, see 10 USCA § 2302, 41 USCA §§ 259, 403.

Determinations and decisions, see 10 USCA § 2310, 41 USCA § 262.

Kinds of contracts, see 10 USCA § 2306.

Limitation on authority to waive Buy American Act requirement, see 41 USCA § 10b-2.

Planning and solicitation requirements, see 41 USCA § 253a.

§ 25.502 Application.

(a) Unless otherwise specified in agency regulations, perform the following steps in the order presented:

(1) Eliminate all offers or offerors that are unacceptable for reasons other than price; *e.g.,* nonresponsive, debarred or suspended, or a prohibited source (see Subpart 25.7).

(2) Rank the remaining offers by price.

(3) If the solicitation specifies award on the basis of factors in addition to cost or price,

apply the evaluation factors as specified in this section and use the evaluated cost or price in determining the offer that represents the best value to the Government.

(b) For acquisitions covered by the WTO GPA (see Subpart 25.4)—

(1) Consider only offers of U.S.-made or designated country end products, unless no offers of such end products were received;

(2) If the agency gives the same consideration given eligible offers to offers of U.S.-made end products that are not domestic end products, award on the low offer. Otherwise, evaluate in accordance with agency procedures; and

(3) If there were no offers of U.S.-made or designated country end products, make a nonavailability determination (see 25.103(b)(2)) and award on the low offer (see 25.403(c)).

(c) For acquisitions not covered by the WTO GPA, but subject to the Buy American statute (an FTA or the Israeli Trade Act also may apply), the following applies:

(1) If the low offer is a domestic offer or an eligible offer under an FTA or the Israeli Trade Act, award on that offer.

(2) If the low offer is a noneligible offer and there were no domestic offers (see 25.103(b)(3)), award on the low offer.

(3) If the low offer is a noneligible offer and there is an eligible offer that is lower than the lowest domestic offer, award on the low offer. The Buy American statute provides an evaluation preference only for domestic offers.

(4) Otherwise, apply the appropriate evaluation factor provided in 25.105 to the low offer.

(i) If the evaluated price of the low offer remains less than the lowest domestic offer, award on the low offer.

(ii) If the price of the lowest domestic offer is less than the evaluated price of the low offer, award on the lowest domestic offer.

(d) Ties.

(1) If application of an evaluation factor results in a tie between a domestic offer and a foreign offer, award on the domestic offer.

(2) If no evaluation preference was applied (*i.e.*, offers afforded nondiscriminatory treatment under the Buy American statute), resolve ties between domestic and foreign offers by a witnessed drawing of lots by an impartial individual.

(3) Resolve ties between foreign offers from small business concerns (under the Buy American statute, a small business offering a manufactured article that does not meet the definition of "domestic end product" is a foreign offer) or foreign offers from a small business concern and a large business concern in accordance with 14.408-6(a).

United States Code Annotated

Administrative determinations, see 41 USCA § 257.

American materials required for public use, see 41 USCA § 10a.

Clarification of Congressional intent regarding sections 10a and 10b(a), see 41 USCA § 10d.

Contract requirements, see 41 USCA § 254.

Contracts, planning, solicitation, evaluation, and award procedures, see 10 USCA § 2305.

Contracts for public works, specification for use of American materials, blacklisting contractors violating requirements, see 41 USCA § 10b.

Definition of terms used in sections 10a, 10b, and 10c, see 41 USCA § 10c.

Definitions, see 10 USCA § 2302, 41 USCA §§ 259, 403.

Determinations and decisions, see 10 USCA § 2310, 41 USCA § 262.

Kinds of contracts, see 10 USCA § 2306.

Limitation on authority to waive Buy American Act requirement, see 41 USCA § 10b-2.

Planning and solicitation requirements, see 41 USCA § 253a.

§ 25.503 Group offers.

(a) If the solicitation or an offer specifies that award can be made only on a group of line items or on all line items contained in the solicitation or offer, reject the offer—

(1) If any part of the award would consist of prohibited end products (see Subpart 25. 7); or

(2) If the acquisition is covered by the WTO GPA and any part of the offer consists of items restricted in accordance with 22.403(c).

(b) If an offer restricts award to a group of line items or to all line items contained in the offer, determine for each line item whether to apply an evaluation factor (see 25.504-4, Example 1).

(1) First, evaluate offers that do not specify an award restriction on a line item basis in accordance with 25.502, determining a tentative award pattern by selecting for each line item the offer with the lowest evaluated price.

(2) Evaluate an offer that specifies an award restriction against the offered prices of the tentative award pattern, applying the appropriate evaluation factor on a line item basis.

(3) Compute the total evaluated price for the tentative award pattern and the offer that specified an award restriction.

(4) Unless the total evaluated price of the offer that specified an award restriction is less than the total evaluated price of the tentative award pattern, award based on the tentative award pattern.

(c) If the solicitation specifies that award will be made only on a group of line items or all line items contained in the solicitation, determine the category of end products on the basis of each line item, but determine whether to apply an evaluation factor on the basis of the group of items (see 25.504-4, Example 2).

(1) If the proposed price of domestic end products exceeds 50 percent of the total proposed price of the group, evaluate the entire group as a domestic offer. Evaluate all other groups as foreign offers.

(2) For foreign offers, if the proposed price of domestic end products and eligible products exceeds 50 percent of the total proposed price of the group, evaluate the entire group as an eligible offer.

(3) Apply the evaluation factor to the entire group in accordance with 25.502.

United States Code Annotated

Administrative determinations, see 41 USCA § 257.

American materials required for public use, see 41 USCA § 10a.

Clarification of Congressional intent regarding sections 10a and 10b(a), see 41 USCA § 10d.

Contract requirements, see 41 USCA § 254.

Contracts, planning, solicitation, evaluation, and award procedures, see 10 USCA § 2305.

Contracts for public works, specification for use of American materials, blacklisting contractors violating requirements, see 41 USCA § 10b.

Definition of terms used in sections 10a, 10b, and 10c, see 41 USCA § 10c.

Definitions, see 10 USCA § 2302, 41 USCA §§ 259, 403.

Determinations and decisions, see 10 USCA § 2310, 41 USCA § 262.

Kinds of contracts, see 10 USCA § 2306.

Limitation on authority to waive Buy American Act requirement, see 41 USCA § 10b-2.

§ 25.504 Evaluation examples.

The following examples illustrate the application of the evaluation procedures in 25.502 and 25.503. The examples assume that the contracting officer has eliminated all offers that are unacceptable for reasons other than price or a trade agreement (see 25.502(a)(1)). The evaluation factor may change as provided in agency regulations.

§ 25.504-1 Buy American Act.

(a) (1) *Example 1.*

Offer A $12,000   Domestic end product, small business

| Offer B | $11,700 | Domestic end product, small business |
| Offer C | $10,000 | U.S.-made end product (not domestic), small business |

(2) *Analysis:* This acquisition is for end products for use in the United States and is set aside for small business concerns. The Buy American Act applies. Since the acquisition value is less than $25,000 and the acquisition is set aside, none of the trade agreements apply. Perform the steps in 25.502(a). Offer C is evaluated as a foreign end product because it is the product of a small business, but is not a domestic end product (see 25.502(c)(4)). Since Offer B is a domestic offer, apply the 12 percent factor to Offer C (see 25.105(b)(2)). The resulting evaluated price of $11,200 remains lower than Offer B. The cost of Offer B is therefore unreasonable (see 25.105(c)). Award on Offer C at $10,000 (see 25.502(c)(4)(i)).

(b) (1) *Example 2.*

Offer A	$11,000	Domestic end product, small business
Offer B	$10,700	Domestic end product, small business
Offer C	$10,200	U.S.-made end product (not domestic), small business

(2) *Analysis*: This acquisition is for end products for use in the United States and is set aside for small business concerns. The Buy American Act applies. Perform the steps in 25.502(a). Offer C is evaluated as a foreign end product because it is the product of a small business but is not a domestic end product (see 25.502(c)(4)). After applying the 12 percent factor, the evaluated price of Offer C is $11,424. Award on Offer B at $10,700 (see 25.502(c)(4)(ii)).

United States Code Annotated

Administrative determinations, see 41 USCA § 257.

American materials required for public use, see 41 USCA § 10a.

Clarification of Congressional intent regarding sections 10a and 10b(a), see 41 USCA § 10d.

Contract requirements, see 41 USCA § 254.

Contracts, planning, solicitation, evaluation, and award procedures, see 10 USCA § 2305.

Contracts for public works, specification for use of American materials, blacklisting contractors violating requirements, see 41 USCA § 10b.

Definition of terms used in sections 10a, 10b, and 10c, see 41 USCA § 10c.

Definitions, see 10 USCA § 2302, 41 USCA §§ 259, 403.

Determinations and decisions, see 10 USCA § 2310, 41 USCA § 262.

Kinds of contracts, see 10 USCA § 2306.

Limitation on authority to waive Buy American Act requirement, see 41 USCA § 10b-2.

Planning and solicitation requirements, see 41 USCA § 253a.

§ 25.504-2 WTO GPA/Caribbean Basin Trade Initiative/FTAs.

Example 1.

Offer A	$304,000	U.S.-made end product (not domestic)
Offer B	$303,000	U.S.-made end product (domestic), small business
Offer C	$300,000	Eligible product
Offer D	$295,000	Noneligible product (not U.S.-made)

Analysis: Eliminate Offer D because the acquisition is covered by the WTO GPA and there is an offer of a U.S.-made or an eligible product (see 25.502(b)(1)). If the agency gives the same consideration given eligible offers to offers of U.S.-made end products that are not domestic offers, it is unnecessary to determine if U.S.-made end products are domestic (large or small business). No further analysis is necessary. Award on the low remaining offer, Offer C (see 25.502(b)(2)).

United States Code Annotated

Administrative determinations, see 41 USCA § 257.

American materials required for public use, see 41 USCA § 10a.

Clarification of Congressional intent regarding sections 10a and 10b(a), see 41 USCA § 10d.

Contract requirements, see 41 USCA § 254.

Contracts, planning, solicitation, evaluation, and award procedures, see 10 USCA § 2305.

Contracts for public works, specification for use of American materials, blacklisting contractors violating requirements, see 41 USCA § 10b.

Definition of terms used in sections 10a, 10b, and 10c, see 41 USCA § 10c.

Definitions, see 10 USCA § 2302, 41 USCA §§ 259, 403.

Determinations and decisions, see 10 USCA § 2310, 41 USCA § 262.

Kinds of contracts, see 10 USCA § 2306.

Limitation on authority to waive Buy American Act requirement, see 41 USCA § 10b-2.

Planning and solicitation requirements, see 41 USCA § 253a.

§ 25.504-3 FTA/Israeli Trade Act.

(a) *Example 1.*

Offer A	$105,000	Domestic end product, small business
Offer B	$100,000	Eligible product

Analysis: Since the low offer is an eligible offer, award on the low offer (see 25.502(c)(1)).

(b) *Example 2.*

Offer A	$105,000	Eligible product
Offer B	$103,000	Noneligible product

Analysis: Since the acquisition is not covered by the WTO GPA, the contracting officer can consider the noneligible offer. Since no domestic offer was received, make a nonavailability determination and award on Offer B (see 25.502(c)(2)).

(c) *Example 3.*

Offer A	$105,000	Domestic end product, large business
Offer B	$103,000	Eligible product
Offer C	$100,000	Noneligible product

Analysis: Since the acquisition is not covered by the WTO GPA, the contracting officer can consider the noneligible offer. Because the eligible offer (Offer B) is lower than the domestic offer (Offer A), no evaluation factor applies to the low offer (Offer C). Award on the low offer (see 25.502(c)(3)).

United States Code Annotated

Administrative determinations, see 41 USCA § 257.

American materials required for public use, see 41 USCA § 10a.

Clarification of Congressional intent regarding sections 10a and 10b(a), see 41 USCA § 10d.

Contract requirements, see 41 USCA § 254.

Contracts, planning, solicitation, evaluation, and award procedures, see 10 USCA § 2305.

Contracts for public works, specification for use of American materials, blacklisting contractors violating requirements, see 41 USCA § 10b.

Definition of terms used in sections 10a, 10b, and 10c, see 41 USCA § 10c.

Definitions, see 10 USCA § 2302, 41 USCA §§ 259, 403.

Determinations and decisions, see 10 USCA § 2310, 41 USCA § 262.

Kinds of contracts, see 10 USCA § 2306.

Limitation on authority to waive Buy American Act requirement, see 41 USCA § 10b-2.

Planning and solicitation requirements, see 41 USCA § 253a.

§ 25.504-4 Group award basis.

Key:

DO	=	Domestic end product
EL	=	Eligible product
NEL	=	Noneligible product

(a) *Example 1*.

	OFFERS		
ITEM	A	B	C
1	DO = $55,000	EL = $56,000	NEL = $50,000
2	NEL = 13,000	EL = 10,000	EL = 13,000
3	NEL = 11,500	DO = 12,000	DO = 10,000
4	NEL = 24,000	EL = 28,000	NEL = 22,000
5	DO = 18,000	NEL = 10,000	DO = 14,000
	$121,500	$116,000	$109,000

Problem: Offeror C specifies all-or-none award. Assume all offerors are large businesses. The acquisition is not covered by the WTO GPA.

Analysis: (see 25.503)

STEP 1: Evaluate Offers A & B before considering Offer C and determine which offer has the lowest evaluated cost for each line item (the tentative award pattern):

Item 1: Low offer A is domestic; select A.

Item 2: Low offer B is eligible; do not apply factor; select B.

Item 3: Low offer A is noneligible and Offer B is a domestic offer. Apply a 6 percent factor to Offer A. The evaluated price of Offer A is higher than Offer B; select B.

Item 4: Low offer A is noneligible. Since neither offer is a domestic offer, no evaluation factor applies; select A.

Item 5: Low offer B is noneligible; apply a 6 percent factor to Offer B. Offer A is still higher than Offer B; select B.

STEP 2: Evaluate Offer C against the tentative award pattern for Offers A and B:

	OFFERS		
ITEM	LOW OF-FER	TENTATIVE AWARD PATTERN FROM A AND B	C
1	A	DO = $ 55,000	NEL = $53,000*
2	B	EL = 10,000	EL = 13,000
3	B	DO = 12,000	DO = 10,000
4	A	NEL = 24,000	NEL = 22,000
5	B	NEL = 10,600*	DO = 14,000
		$111,600	$112,000

* Offer + 6 percent.

On a line item basis, apply a factor to any noneligible offer if the other offer for that line item is domestic.

For Item 1, apply a factor to Offer C because Offer A is domestic and the acquisition was not covered by the WTO GPA. The evaluated price of Offer C, Item 1, becomes $53,000 ($50,000 plus 6 percent). Apply a factor to Offer B, Item 5, because it is a noneligible product and Offer C is domestic. The evaluated price of Offer B is $10,600 ($10,000 plus 6 percent). Evaluate the remaining items without applying a factor.

STEP 3: The tentative unrestricted award pattern from Offers A and B is lower than the evaluated price of Offer C. Award the combination of Offers A and B. Note that if Offer C had not specified all-or-none award, award would be made on Offer C for line items 1, 3, and 4, totaling an award of $82,000.

(b) *Example 2.*

OFFERS			
ITEM	A	B	C
1	DO = $50,000	EL = $50,500	NEL = $50,000
2	NEL = 10,300	NEL = 10,000	EL = 10,200
3	EL = 20,400	EL = 21,000	NEL = 20,200
4	DO = 10,500	DO = 10,300	DO = 10,400
	$91,200	$91,800	$90,800

Problem: The solicitation specifies award on a group basis. Assume the Buy American statute applies and the acquisition cannot be set aside for small business concerns. All offerors are large businesses.

Analysis: (see 25.503(c))

STEP 1: Determine which of the offers are domestic (see 25.503(c)(1)):

	DOMESTIC%	DETERMINATION
A	60,500/91,200 = 66.3%	Domestic
B	10,300/91,800 = 11.2%	Foreign
C	10,400/90,800 = 11.5%	Foreign

STEP 2: Determine whether foreign offers are eligible or noneligible offers (see 25.503(c)(2)):

	DOMESTIC + ELIGIBLE%	DETERMINATION
A	N/A	Domestic
B	81,800/91,800 = 89.1%	Eligible
C	20,600/90,800 = 22.7%	Noneligible

STEP 3: Determine whether to apply an evaluation factor (see 25.503(c)(3)). The low offer (Offer C) is a foreign offer. There is no eligible offer lower than the domestic offer. Therefore, apply the factor to the low offer. Addition of the 6 percent factor (use 12 percent if Offer A is a small business) to Offer C yields an evaluated price of $96,248 ($90,800 + 6 percent). Award on Offer A (see 25.502(c)(4)(ii)). Note that, if Offer A were greater than Offer B, an evaluation factor would not be applied and award would be on Offer C (see 25.502(c)(3)).

United States Code Annotated

Administrative determinations, see 41 USCA § 257.

American materials required for public use, see 41 USCA § 10a.

Clarification of Congressional intent regarding sections 10a and 10b(a), see 41 USCA § 10d.

Contract requirements, see 41 USCA § 254.

Contracts, planning, solicitation, evaluation, and award procedures, see 10 USCA § 2305.

Contracts for public works, specification for use of American materials, blacklisting contractors violating requirements, see 41 USCA § 10b.

Definition of terms used in sections 10a, 10b, and 10c, see 41 USCA § 10c.

Definitions, see 10 USCA § 2302, 41 USCA §§ 259, 403.

Determinations and decisions, see 10 USCA § 2310, 41 USCA § 262.

Kinds of contracts, see 10 USCA § 2306.

Limitation on authority to waive Buy American Act requirement, see 41 USCA § 10b-2.

Planning and solicitation requirements, see 41 USCA § 253a.

Subpart 25.6 American Recovery and Reinvestment Act— Buy American Act—Construction Materials

§ 25.600 Scope of subpart.

This subpart implements section 1605 in Division A of the American Recovery and Reinvestment Act of 2009 (Pub. L. 111-5) (Recovery Act) with regard to manufactured construction material and the 41 U.S.C. chapter 83, Buy American (referred to in this subpart as the Buy American statute) with regard to unmanufactured construction material. It applies to construction projects that use funds appropriated or otherwise provided by the Recovery Act.

§ 25.601 Definitions.

As used in this subpart—

"Domestic construction material" means the following:

(1) An unmanufactured construction material mined or produced in the United States. (The Buy American statute applies.)

(2) A manufactured construction material that is manufactured in the United States and, if the construction material consists wholly or predominantly of iron or steel, the iron or steel was produced in the United States. (Section 1605 of the Recovery Act applies.)

"Foreign construction material" means a construction material other than a domestic construction material.

"Manufactured construction material" means any construction material that is not unmanufactured construction material.

"Public building or public work" means a building or work, the construction, prosecution, completion, or repair of which is carried on directly or indirectly by authority of, or with funds of, a Federal agency to serve the interest of the general public regardless of whether title thereof is in a Federal agency (see 22.401). These buildings and works may include, without limitation, bridges, dams, plants, highways, parkways, streets, subways, tunnels, sewers, mains, power lines, pumping stations, heavy generators, railways, airports, terminals, docks, piers, wharves, ways, lighthouses, buoys, jetties, breakwaters, levees, and canals, and the construction, alteration, maintenance, or repair of such buildings and works.

"Recovery Act designated country" means a World Trade Organization Government Procurement Agreement country, a Free Trade Agreement country, or a least developed country.

"Steel" means an alloy that includes at least 50 percent iron, between.02 and 2 percent carbon, and may include other elements.

"Unmanufactured construction material" means raw material brought to the construction site for incorporation into the building or work that has not been—

(1) Processed into a specific form and shape; or

(2) Combined with other raw material to create a material that has different properties than the properties of the individual raw materials.

§ 25.602 Policy.

§ 25.602-1 Section 1605 of the Recovery Act.

Except as provided in 25.603—

(a) None of the funds appropriated or otherwise made available by the Recovery Act may be used for a project for the construction, alteration, maintenance, or repair of a public building or public work unless the public building or public work is located in the United States and—

(1) All of the iron, steel, and manufactured goods used as construction material in the project are produced or manufactured in the United States.

(i) All manufactured construction material must be manufactured in the United States.

(ii) *Iron or steel components.*

(A) Iron or steel components of construction material consisting wholly or predominantly of iron or steel must be produced in the United States. This does not restrict the origin of the elements of the iron or steel, but requires that all manufacturing processes of the iron or steel must take place in the United States, except metallurgical processes involving refinement of steel additives.

(B) The requirement in paragraph (a)(1)(ii)(A) of this section does not apply to iron or steel components or subcomponents in construction material that does not consist wholly or predominantly of iron or steel.

(iii) *All other components.* There is no restriction on the origin or place of production or manufacture of components or subcomponents that do not consist of iron or steel.

(iv) *Examples.*

(A) If a steel guardrail consists predominantly of steel, even though coated with aluminum, then the steel would be subject to the section 1605 restriction requiring that all stages of production of the steel occur in the United States, in addition to the requirement to manufacture the guardrail in the United States. There would be no restrictions on the other components of the guardrail.

(B) If a wooden window frame is delivered to the site as a single construction material, there is no restriction on any of the components, including the steel lock on the window frame; or

(2) If trade agreements apply, the manufactured construction material shall either comply with the requirements of paragraph (a)(1) of this subsection, or be wholly the product of or be substantially transformed in a Recovery Act designated country;

(b) Manufactured materials purchased directly by the Government and delivered to the site for incorporation into the project shall meet the same domestic source requirements as specified for manufactured construction material in paragraphs (a)(1) and (a)(2) of this section; and

(c) A project may include several contracts, a single contract, or one or more line items on a contract.

§ 25.602-2 Buy American statute

Except as provided in 25.603, use only unmanufactured construction material mined or produced in the United States, as required by the Buy American statute or, if trade agreements apply, unmanufactured construction material mined or produced in a designated country may also be used.

§ 25.603 Exceptions.

(a) (1) When one of the following exceptions applies, the contracting officer may allow the contractor to incorporate foreign manufactured construction materials without regard to the restrictions of section 1605 of the Recovery Act or foreign unmanufactured construction material without regard to the restrictions of the Buy American statute:

(i) Nonavailability. The head of the contracting activity may determine that a particular construction material is not mined, produced, or manufactured in the United States in sufficient and reasonably available commercial quantities of a satisfactory quality. The determinations of nonavailability of the articles listed at 25.104(a) and the procedures at 25.103(b)(1) also apply if any of those articles are acquired as construction materials.

(ii) Unreasonable cost. The contracting officer concludes that the cost of domestic construction material is unreasonable in accordance with 25.605.

(iii) Inconsistent with public interest. The head of the agency may determine that application of the restrictions of section 1605 of the Recovery Act to a particular manufactured construction material, or the restrictions of the Buy American statute to a particular unmanufactured construction material would be inconsistent with the public interest.

(2) In addition, the head of the agency may determine that application of the Buy American statute to a particular unmanufactured construction material would be impracticable.

(b) Determinations. When a determination is made, for any of the reasons stated in this section, that certain foreign construction materials may be used—

(1) The contracting officer shall list the excepted materials in the contract; and

(2) For determinations with regard to the inapplicability of section 1605 of the Recovery Act, unless the construction material has already been determined to be domestically nonavailable (see list at 25.104), the head of the agency shall provide a notice to the Federal Register within three business days after the determination is made, with a copy to the Administrator for Federal Procurement Policy and to the Recovery Accountability and Transparency Board. The notice shall include—

(i) The title "Buy American Exception under the American Recovery and Reinvestment Act of 2009";

(ii) The dollar value and brief description of the project; and

(iii) A detailed justification as to why the restriction is being waived.

(c) Acquisitions under trade agreements.

(1) For construction contracts with an estimated acquisition value of $7,358,000 or more, also see subpart 25.4. Offers proposing the use of construction material from a designated country shall receive equal consideration with offers proposing the use of domestic construction material.

(2) For purposes of applying section 1605 of the Recovery Act to evaluation of manufactured construction material, designated countries do not include the Caribbean Basin Countries.

§ 25.604 Preaward determination concerning the inapplicability of section 1605 of the Recovery Act or the Buy American statute.

(a) For any acquisition, an offeror may request from the contracting officer a determination concerning the inapplicability of section 1605 of the Recovery Act or the Buy American statute for specifically identified construction materials. The time for submitting the request is specified in the solicitation in paragraph (b) of either 52.225-22 or 52.225-24, whichever applies. The information and supporting data that must be included in the request are also specified in the solicitation in paragraphs (c) and (d) of either 52.225-21 or 52.225-23, whichever applies.

(b) Before award, the contracting officer must evaluate all requests based on the information provided and may supplement this information with other readily available information.

(c) Determination based on unreasonable cost of domestic construction material.

(1) *Manufactured construction material.* The contracting officer must compare the offered price of the contract using foreign manufactured construction material (*i.e.,* any construction material not manufactured in the United States, or construction material consisting predominantly of iron or steel and the iron or steel is not produced in the United States) to the estimated price if all domestic manufactured construction material were used. If use of domestic manufactured construction material would increase the overall offered price of the contract by more than 25 percent, then the contracting officer shall determine that the cost of the domestic manufactured construction material is unreasonable

(2) *Unmanufactured construction material.* The contracting officer must compare the cost of each foreign unmanufactured construction material to the cost of domestic unmanufactured construction material. If the cost of the domestic unmanufactured construction material exceeds the cost of the foreign unmanufactured construction material by more than 6 percent, then the contracting officer shall determine that the cost of the domestic unmanufactured construction material is unreasonable.

§ 25.605 Evaluating offers of foreign construction material.

(a) If the contracting officer has determined that an exception applies because the cost of certain domestic construction material is unreasonable, in accordance with section 25.604, then the contracting officer shall apply evaluation factors to the offer incorporating the use of such foreign construction material as follows:

(1) Use an evaluation factor of 25 percent, applied to the total offered price of the contract, if foreign manufactured construction material is incorporated in the offer based on an exception for unreasonable cost of comparable domestic construction material requested by the offeror.

(2) In addition, use an evaluation factor of 6 percent applied to the cost of foreign unmanufactured construction material incorporated in the offer based on an exception for unreasonable cost of comparable domestic unmanufactured construction material requested by the offeror.

(3) Total evaluated price = offered price + (.25 x offered price, if (a)(1) applies) + (.06 x cost of foreign unmanufactured construction material, if (a)(2) applies).

(b) If the solicitation specifies award on the basis of factors in addition to cost or price, apply the evaluation factors as specified in paragraph (a) of this section and use the evaluated price in determining the offer that represents the best value to the Government

(c) Unless paragraph (b) applies, if two or more offers are equal in price, the contracting officer must give preference to an offer that does not include foreign construction material excepted at the request of the offeror on the basis of unreasonable cost.

(d) Offerors also may submit alternate offers based on use of equivalent domestic construction material to avoid possible rejection of the entire offer if the Government determines that an exception permitting use of a particular foreign construction material does not apply.

(e) If the contracting officer awards a contract to an offeror that proposed foreign construction material not listed in the applicable clause in the solicitation (paragraph (b)(3) of 52.225-21, or paragraph (b)(3) of 52.225-23), the contracting officer must add the excepted materials to the list in the contract clause.

§ **25.606 Postaward determinations.**

(a) If a contractor requests a determination regarding the inapplicability of section 1605 of the Recovery Act or the Buy American statute after contract award, the contractor must explain why it could not request the determination before contract award or why the need for such determination otherwise was not reasonably foreseeable. If the contracting officer concludes that the contractor should have made the request before contract award, the contracting officer may deny the request.

(b) The contracting officer must base evaluation of any request for a determination regarding the inapplicability of section 1605 of the Recovery Act or the Buy American statute made after contract award on information required by paragraphs (c) and (d) of the applicable clause at 52.225-21 or 52.225-23 and/or other readily available information.

(c) If a determination, under 25.603(a), is made after contract award that an exception to section 1605 of the Recovery Act or to the Buy American statute applies, the contracting officer must negotiate adequate consideration and modify the contract to allow use of the foreign construction material. When the basis for the exception is the unreasonable cost of a domestic construction material, adequate consideration is at least the differential established in 25.605(a).

§ **25.607 Noncompliance.**

The contracting officer must—

(a) Review allegations of violations of section 1605 of the Recovery Act or Buy American statute;

(b) Unless fraud is suspected, notify the contractor of the apparent unauthorized use of foreign construction material and request a reply, to include proposed corrective action; and

(c) If the review reveals that a contractor or subcontractor has used foreign construction material without authorization, take appropriate action, including one or more of the following:

(1) Process a determination concerning the inapplicability of section 1605 of the Recovery Act or the Buy American statute in accordance with 25.606.

(2) Consider requiring the removal and replacement of the unauthorized foreign

construction material.

(3) If removal and replacement of foreign construction material incorporated in a building or work would be impracticable, cause undue delay, or otherwise be detrimental to the interests of the Government, the contracting officer may determine in writing that the foreign construction material need not be removed and replaced. A determination to retain foreign construction material does not constitute a determination that an exception to section 1605 of the Recovery Act or the Buy American statute applies, and this should be stated in the determination. Further, a determination to retain foreign construction material does not affect the Government's right to suspend or debar a contractor, subcontractor, or supplier for violation of section 1605 of the Recovery Act or the Buy American statute, or to exercise other contractual rights and remedies, such as reducing the contract price or terminating the contract for default.

(4) If the noncompliance is sufficiently serious, consider exercising appropriate contractual remedies, such as terminating the contract for default. Also consider preparing and forwarding a report to the agency suspending or debarring official in accordance with subpart 9.4. If the noncompliance appears to be fraudulent, refer the matter to other appropriate agency officials, such as the agency's inspector general or the officer responsible for criminal investigation.

Subpart 25.7 Prohibited Sources

§ 25.700 Scope of subpart.

This subpart implements—

(a) Economic sanctions administered by the Office of Foreign Assets Control (OFAC) in the Department of the Treasury prohibiting transactions involving certain countries, entities, and individuals;

(b) The Sudan Accountability and Divestment Act of 2007 (Pub. L. 110-174) (50 U.S.C. 1701 note);

(c) The Iran Sanctions Act of 1996 (Iran Sanctions Act) (Pub. L. 104-172; 50 U.S.C. 1701 note), including amendments by the Iran Freedom Support Act (Pub. L. 109-293), section 102 of the Comprehensive Iran Sanctions, Accountability, and Divestment Act of 2010 (Pub. L. 111-195), and Titles II and III of the Iran Threat Reduction and Syria Human Rights Act of 2012 (Pub. L. 112-158); and

(d) Prohibition against contracting with entities that export sensitive technologies to Iran (22 U.S.C. 8515).

§ 25.701 Restrictions administered by the Department of the Treasury on acquisitions of supplies or services from prohibited sources.

(a) Except as authorized by OFAC, agencies and their contractors and subcontractors must not acquire any supplies or services if any proclamation, Executive order, or statute administered by OFAC, or if OFAC's implementing regulations at 31 CFR Chapter V, would prohibit such a transaction by a person subject to the jurisdiction of the United States.

(b) Except as authorized by OFAC, most transactions involving Cuba, Iran, and Sudan are prohibited, as are most imports from Burma or North Korea into the United States or its outlying areas. In addition, lists of entities and individuals subject to economic sanctions are included in OFAC's List of Specially Designated Nationals and Blocked Persons at http://www.treas.gov/offices/enforcement/ofac/sdn. More information about these restrictions, as well as updates, is available in OFAC's regulations at 31 CFR Chapter V and/or on OFAC's website at http://www.treas.gov/offices/enforcement/ofac.

(c) Refer questions concerning the restrictions in paragraphs (a) or (b) of this section to the—

Department of the Treasury
Office of Foreign Assets Control
Washington, DC 20220
(Telephone (202) 622-2490).

Notes of Decisions

In general 1

1 In general

Illegal performance of government contract for air transportation of humanitarian relief supplies, which occurred when subcontractor employed an Iranian carrier to transport the supplies, did not render contract per se unenforceable by contractor seeking payment of full contract price; first, determination had to be made whether, under the circumstances, contractor was responsible for the illegal performance of its subcontractor and, then, applying the balancing test of the Restatement of Contracts, whether the nature of the illegality was such as to warrant the forfeiture of all compensation. Restatement (Second) of Contracts § 178. Transfair Intern., Inc. v. U.S., 54 Fed. Cl. 78 (2002). United States ☞70(15.1)

§ 25.702 Prohibition on contracting with entities that conduct restricted business operations in Sudan.

§ 25.702-1 Definitions.

As used in this section—

"Appropriate Congressional committees" means—

(1) The Committee on Banking, Housing, and Urban Affairs, The Committee on Foreign Relations, and the Select Committee on Intelligence of the Senate; and

(2) The Committee on Financial Services, the Committee on Foreign Relations, and the Permanent Select Committee on Intelligence of the House of Representatives.

"Business operations" means engaging in commerce in any form, including by acquiring, developing, maintaining, owning, selling, possessing, leasing, or operating equipment, facilities, personnel, products, services, personal property, real property, or any other apparatus of business or commerce.

"Marginalized populations of Sudan" means—

(1) Adversely affected groups in regions authorized to receive assistance under section 8(c) of the Darfur Peace and Accountability Act (Pub. L. 109-344) (50 U.S.C. 1701 note); and

(2) Marginalized areas in Northern Sudan described in section 4(9) of such Act.

"Restricted business operations"—

(1) Means, except as provided in paragraph (2) of this definition, business operations in Sudan that include power production activities, mineral extraction activities, oil-related activities, or the production of military equipment, as those terms are defined in the Sudan Accountability and Divestment Act of 2007 (Pub. L. 110-174).

(2) Does not include business operations that the person (as that term is defined in Section 2 of the Sudan Accountability and Divestment Act of 2007) conducting the business can demonstrate—

(i) Are conducted under contract directly and exclusively with the regional government of southern Sudan;

(ii) Are conducted pursuant to specific authorization from the Office of Foreign Assets Control in the Department of the Treasury, or are expressly exempted under Federal law from the requirement to be conducted under such authorization;

(iii) Consist of providing goods or services to marginalized populations of Sudan;

(iv) Consist of providing goods or services to an internationally recognized peacekeeping force or humanitarian organization;

(v) Consist of providing goods or services that are used only to promote health or education; or

(vi) Have been voluntarily suspended.

§ 25.702-2 Certification.

As required by the Sudan Accountability and Divestment Act of 2007 (Pub. L. 110-174), each offeror must certify that it does not conduct restricted business operations in Sudan.

§ 25.702-3 Remedies.

Upon the determination of a false certification under subsection 25.702-2—

(a) The contracting officer may terminate the contract;

(b) The suspending official may suspend the contractor in accordance with the procedures in Subpart 9.4; and

(c) The debarring official may debar the contractor for a period not to exceed 3 years in accordance with the procedures in Subpart 9.4.

§ 25.702-4 Waiver.

(a) The President may waive the requirement of subsection 25.702-2 on a case-by-case basis if the President determines and certifies in writing to the appropriate congressional committees that it is in the national interest to do so.

(b) An agency seeking waiver of the requirement shall submit the request to the Administrator of the Office of Federal Procurement Policy (OFPP), allowing sufficient time for review and approval. Upon receipt of the waiver request, OFPP shall consult with the President's National Security Council, Office of African Affairs, and the Department of State Sudan Office and Sanctions Office to assess foreign policy aspects of making a national interest recommendation.

(c) Agencies may request a waiver on an individual or class basis; however, waivers are not indefinite and can be cancelled if warranted.

(1) A class waiver may be requested only when the class of supplies is not available from any other source and it is in the national interest.

(2) Prior to submitting the waiver request, the request must be reviewed and cleared by the agency head.

(3) All waiver requests must include the following information:

(i) Agency name, complete mailing address, and point of contact name, telephone number, and email address;

(ii) Offeror's name, complete mailing address, and point of contact name, telephone number, and email address;

(iii) Description/nature of product or service;

(iv) The total cost and length of the contract;

(v) Justification, with market research demonstrating that no other offeror can provide the product or service and stating why the product or service must be procured from this offeror, as well as why it is in the national interest for the President to waive the prohibition on contracting with this offeror that conducts restricted business operations in Sudan, including consideration of foreign policy aspects identified in consultation(s) pursuant to 25.702-4(b);

(vi) Documentation regarding the offeror's past performance and integrity (see the Past Performance Information Retrieval System including the Federal Awardee Performance Information and Integrity System at www.ppirs.gov and any other relevant information);

(vii) Information regarding the offeror's relationship or connection with other firms that conduct prohibited business operations in Sudan; and

(viii) Any humanitarian efforts engaged in by the offeror, the human rights impact of doing business with the offeror for which the waiver is requested, and the extent of the offeror's business operations in Sudan.

(d) The consultation in 25.702-4(b) and the information in 25.702-4(c)(3) will be considered in determining whether to recommend that the President waive the requirement of subsection 25.702-2. In accordance with section 6(c) of the Sudan Accountability and Divestment Act of 2007, OFPP will semiannually submit a report to Congress, on April 15th and October 15th, on the waivers granted.

§ 25.703 Prohibition on contracting with entities that engage in certain activities or transactions relating to Iran.

§ 25.703-1 Definitions.

As used in this section—

"Person"—

(1) Means—

(i) A natural person;

(ii) A corporation, business association, partnership, society, trust, financial institution, insurer, underwriter, guarantor, and any other business organization, any other nongovernmental entity, organization, or group, and any governmental entity operating as a business enterprise; and

(iii) Any successor to any entity described in paragraph (1)(ii) of this definition; and

(2) Does not include a government or governmental entity that is not operating as a business enterprise.

"Sensitive technology"—

(1) Means hardware, software, telecommunications equipment, or any other technology that is to be used specifically—

(i) To restrict the free flow of unbiased information in Iran; or

(ii) To disrupt, monitor, or otherwise restrict speech of the people of Iran; and

(2) Does not include information or informational materials the export of which the President does not have the authority to regulate or prohibit pursuant to section 203(b)(3) of the International Emergency Economic Powers Act (50 U.S.C. 1702(b)(3)).

§ 25.703-2 Iran Sanctions Act.

(a) Certification.

(1) Certification relating to activities described in section 5 of the Iran Sanctions Act. As required by section 6(b)(1)(A) of the Iran Sanctions Act (50 U.S.C. 1701 note), unless an exception applies in accordance with paragraph (c) of this subsection, or a waiver is granted in accordance with 25.703-4, each offeror must certify that the offeror, and any person owned or controlled by the offeror, does not engage in any activity for which sanctions may be imposed under section 5 of the Iran Sanctions Act. Such activities, which are described in detail in section 5 of the Iran Sanctions Act, relate to the energy sector of Iran and development by Iran of weapons of mass destruction or other military capabilities.

(2) Certification relating to transactions with Iran's Revolutionary Guard Corps. As required by section 6(b)(1)(B) of the Iran Sanctions Act (50 U.S.C. 1701 note), unless an exception applies in accordance with paragraph (c) of this subsection, or a waiver is granted in accordance with 25.703-4, each offeror must certify that the offeror, and any person owned or controlled by the offeror, does not knowingly engage in any significant transaction (i.e., a transaction that exceeds $3,500) with Iran's Revolutionary Guard Corps or any of its officials, agents, or affiliates, the property and interests in property of which are blocked pursuant to the International Emergency Economic Powers Act (50 U.S.C. 1701 et seq.)(see OFAC's Specially Designated Nationals and Blocked Persons List at http://www.treasury.gov/ofac/downloads/t11sdn.pdf).

(b) Remedies. Upon the determination of a false certification under paragraph (a) of this subsection, the agency shall take one or more of the following actions:

(1) The contracting officer terminates the contract in accordance with procedures in part 49, or for commercial items, see 12.403.

(2) The suspending official suspends the contractor in accordance with the procedures in subpart 9.4.

(3) The debarring official debars the contractor for a period of at least two years in accordance with the procedures in subpart 9.4.

(c) Exception for trade agreements. The certification requirements of paragraph (a) of this subsection do not apply if the acquisition is subject to trade agreements and the offeror certifies that all the offered products are designated country end products or designated country construction material (see subpart 25.4).

§ 25.703-3 Prohibition on contracting with entities that export sensitive technology to Iran.

(a) The head of an executive agency may not enter into or extend a contract for the procurement of goods or services with a person that exports certain sensitive technology to Iran, as determined by the President and listed in the System for Award Management Exclusions via http://www.acquisition.gov (22 U.S.C. 8515).

(b) Each offeror must represent that it does not export any sensitive technology to the government of Iran or any entities or individuals owned or controlled by, or acting on behalf or at the direction of, the government of Iran.

(c) *Exception for trade agreements.* The representation requirement of paragraph (b) of this subsection does not apply if the acquisition is subject to trade agreements and the offeror certifies that all the offered products are designated country end products or designated country construction material (see subpart 25.4).

§ 25.703-4 Waiver.

(a) An agency or contractor seeking a waiver of the requirements of 25.703-2 or 25.703-3, consistent with section 6(b)(5) of the Iran Sanctions Act or 22 U.S.C. 8551(b), respectively, and the Presidential Memorandum of September 23, 2010 (75 FR 67025), shall submit the request to the Office of Federal Procurement Policy, allowing sufficient time for review and approval.

(b) Agencies may request a waiver on an individual or class basis; however, waivers are not indefinite and can be cancelled, if warranted.

(1) A class waiver may be requested only when the class of supplies or equipment is not available from any other source and it is in the national interest.

(2) Prior to submitting the waiver request, the request must be reviewed and cleared by the agency head.

(c) In general, all waiver requests should include the following information:

(1) Agency name, complete mailing address, and point of contact name, telephone number, and e-mail address.

(2) Offeror's name, complete mailing address, and point of contact name, telephone number, and e-mail address.

(3) Description/nature of product or service.

(4) The total cost and length of the contract.

(5) Justification, with market research demonstrating that no other offeror can provide the product or service and stating why the product or service must be procured from this offeror.

(i) If the offeror exports sensitive technology to the government of Iran or any entities or individuals owned or controlled by, or acting on behalf or at the direction of, the government of Iran, provide rationale why it is in the national interest for the President to waive the prohibition on contracting with this offeror, as required by 22 U.S.C. 8551(b).

(ii) If the offeror conducts activities for which sanctions may be imposed under section 5 of the Iran Sanctions Act or engages in any transaction that exceeds $3,500 with Iran's Revolutionary Guard Corps or any of its officials, agents, or affiliates, the property and interests in property of which are blocked pursuant to the International Emergency Economic Powers Act, provide rationale why it is essential to the national security interests of the United States for the President to waive the prohibition on contracting with this offeror, as required by section 6(b)(5) of the Iran Sanctions Act.

(6) Documentation regarding the offeror's past performance and integrity (see the Past Performance Information Retrieval System and the Federal Awardee Performance Information and Integrity System at www.ppirs.gov, and any other relevant information).

(7) Information regarding the offeror's relationship or connection with other firms that—

(i) Export sensitive technology to the government of Iran or any entities or individuals owned or controlled by, or acting on behalf or at the direction of, the government of Iran;

(ii) Conduct activities for which sanctions may be imposed under section 5 of the Iran Sanctions Act; or

(iii) Conduct any transaction that exceeds $3,500 with Iran's Revolutionary Guard Corps or any of its officials, agents, or affiliates, the property and interests in property of which are blocked pursuant to the International Emergency Economic Powers Act.

(8) Describe—

(i) The sensitive technology and the entity or individual to which it was exported (i.e., the government of Iran or an entity or individual owned or controlled by, or acting on behalf or at the direction of, the government of Iran);

(ii) The activities in which the offeror is engaged for which sanctions may be imposed under section 5 of the Iran Sanctions Act; or

(iii) The transactions that exceed $3,500 with Iran's Revolutionary Guard Corps or any of its officials, agents, or affiliates, the property and interests in property of which are blocked pursuant to the International Emergency Economic Powers Act.

Subpart 25.8 Other International Agreements and Coordination

§ 25.801 General.

Treaties and agreements between the United States and foreign governments affect the evaluation of offers from foreign entities and the performance of contracts in foreign countries.

United States Code Annotated

Contract requirements, see 41 USCA § 254.

Contracts, planning, solicitation, evaluation, and award procedures, see 10 USCA § 2305.

Definitions, see 10 USCA § 2302, 41 USCA §§ 259, 403.

Kinds of contracts, see 10 USCA § 2306.

Planning and solicitation requirements, see 41 USCA § 253a.

§ 25.802 Procedures.

(a) When placing contracts with contractors located outside the United States, for performance outside the United States, contracting officers must—

(1) Determine the existence and applicability of any international agreements and ensure compliance with these agreements; and

(2) Conduct the necessary advance acquisition planning and coordination between the appropriate U.S. executive agencies and foreign interests as required by these agreements.

(b) The Department of State publishes many international agreements in the "United States Treaties and Other International Agreements" series. Copies of this publication normally are available in overseas legal offices and U.S. diplomatic missions.

(c) Contracting officers must award all contracts with Taiwanese firms or organizations through the American Institute of Taiwan (AIT). AIT is under contract to the Department of State.

United States Code Annotated

Contract requirements, see 41 USCA § 254.

Contracts, planning, solicitation, evaluation, and award procedures, see 10 USCA § 2305.

Definitions, see 10 USCA § 2302, 41 USCA §§ 259, 403.

Kinds of contracts, see 10 USCA § 2306.

Planning and solicitation requirements, see 41 USCA § 253a.

Subpart 25.9 Customs and Duties

§ 25.900 Scope of subpart.

This subpart provides policies and procedures for exempting from import duties certain supplies purchased under Government contracts.

§ 25.901 Policy.

United States laws impose duties on foreign supplies imported into the customs territory of the United States. Certain exemptions from these duties are available to Government agencies. Agencies must use these exemptions when the anticipated savings to appropriated funds will outweigh the administrative costs associated with processing required documentation.

§ 25.902 Procedures.

For regulations governing importations and duties, see the Customs Regulations issued by the U.S. Customs Service, Department of the Treasury (19 CFR Chapter 1). Except as provided elsewhere in the Customs Regulations (see 19 CFR 10.100), all shipments of imported supplies purchased under Government contracts are subject to the usual Customs entry and examination requirements. Unless the agency obtains an exemption (see 25.903), those shipments are also subject to duty.

§ 25.903 Exempted supplies.

(a) Subchapters VIII and X of Chapter 98 of the Harmonized Tariff Schedule of the United States (19 U.S.C. 1202) list supplies for which exemptions from duty may be obtained when imported into the customs territory of the United States under a Government contract. For certain of these supplies, the contracting agency must certify to the Commissioner of Customs that they are for the purpose stated in the Harmonized Tariff Schedule (see 19 CFR 10.102–104, 10.114, and 10.121 and 15 CFR Part 301 for requirements and formats).

(b) Supplies (excluding equipment) for Government-operated vessels or aircraft may be withdrawn from any customsbonded warehouse, from continuous customs custody elsewhere than in a bonded warehouse, or from a foreign-trade zone, free of duty and internal revenue tax as provided in 19 U.S.C. 1309 and 1317. The contracting activity must cite this authority on the appropriate customs form when making purchases (see 19 CFR 10.59–10.65).

Subpart 25.10 Additional Foreign Acquisition Regulations

§ 25.1001 Waiver of right to examination of records.

(a) *Policy.* The clause at 52.215-2, Audit and Records—Negotiation, prescribed at 15.209(b), and paragraph (d) of the clause at 52.212-5, Contract Terms and Conditions Required to Implement Statutes or Executive Orders—Commercial Items, prescribed at 12.301(b)(4), implement 10 U.S.C. 2313 and 41 U.S.C. 4706. The basic clauses authorize examination of records by the Comptroller General.

(1) Insert the appropriate basic clause, whenever possible, in negotiated contracts with foreign contractors.

(2) The contracting officer may use 52.215-2 with its Alternate III or 52.212-5 with its Alternate I after—

(i) Exhausting all reasonable efforts to include the basic clause;

(ii) Considering factors such as alternate sources of supply, additional cost, and time of delivery; and

(iii) The head of the agency has executed a determination and findings in accordance with paragraph (b) of this section, with the concurrence of the Comptroller General. However, concurrence of the Comptroller General is not required if the contractor is a foreign government or agency thereof or is precluded by the laws of the country involved from making its records available for examination.

(b) *Determination and findings.* The determination and findings must—

(1) Identify the contract and its purpose, and identify if the contract is with a foreign contractor or with a foreign government or an agency of a foreign government;

(2) Describe the efforts to include the basic clause;

(3) State the reasons for the contractor's refusal to include the basic clause;

(4) Describe the price and availability of the supplies or services from the United States and other sources; and

(5) Determine that it will best serve the interest of the United States to use the appropriate alternate clause in paragraph (a)(2) of this section.

United States Code Annotated

Contract requirements, see 41 USCA § 254.

Definitions, see 10 USCA § 2302, 41 USCA §§ 259, 403.

Examination of records of contractor, see 10 USCA § 2313, 41 USCA § 254d.

Kinds of contracts, see 10 USCA § 2306.

§ 25.1002 Use of foreign currency.

(a) Unless an international agreement or the WTO GPA (see 25.408(a)(4)) requires a specific currency, contracting officers must determine whether solicitations for contracts to be entered into and performed outside the United States will require submission of offers in U.S. currency or a specified foreign currency. In unusual circumstances, the contracting officer may permit submission of offers in other than a specified currency.

(b) To ensure a fair evaluation of offers, solicitations generally should require all offers to be priced in the same currency. However, if the solicitation permits submission of offers in other than a specified currency, the contracting officer must convert the offered prices to U.S. currency for evaluation purposes. The contracting officer must use the current market exchange rate from a commonly used source in effect as follows:

(1) For acquisitions conducted using sealed bidding procedures, on the date of bid opening.

(2) For acquisitions conducted using negotiation procedures—

(i) On the date specified for receipt of offers, if award is based on initial offers; otherwise

(ii) On the date specified for receipt of final proposal revisions.

(c) If a contract is priced in foreign currency, the agency must ensure that adequate funds are available to cover currency fluctuations to avoid a violation of the Anti-Deficiency Act (31 U.S.C. 1341, 1342, 1511–1519).

United States Code Annotated

Contract requirements, see 41 USCA § 254.

Contracts, planning, solicitation, evaluation, and award procedures, see 10 USCA § 2305.

Definitions, see 10 USCA § 2302, 41 USCA §§ 259, 403.

Kinds of contracts, see 10 USCA § 2306.

Planning and solicitation requirements, see 41 USCA § 253a.

Subpart 25.11 Solicitation Provisions and Contract Clauses

§ 25.1101 Acquisition of supplies.

The following provisions and clauses apply to the acquisition of supplies and the acquisition of services involving the furnishing of supplies.

(a) (1) Insert the clause at 52.225-1, Buy American—Supplies, in solicitations and contracts with a value exceeding the micro-purchase threshold but not exceeding $25,000; and in solicitations and contracts with a value exceeding $25,000, if none of the clauses prescribed in paragraphs (b) and (c) of this section apply, except if—

(i) The solicitation is restricted to domestic end products in accordance with subpart 6.3;

(ii) The acquisition is for supplies for use within the United States and an exception to the Buy American statute applies (e.g., nonavailability, public interest, or information technology that is a commercial item); or

(iii) The acquisition is for supplies for use outside the United States.

(2) Insert the provision at 52.225-2, Buy American Certificate, in solicitations containing the clause at 52.225-1.

(b) (1)

(i) Insert the clause at 52.225-3, Buy American—Free Trade Agreements—Israeli Trade Act, in solicitations and contracts if—

(A) The acquisition is for supplies, or for services involving the furnishing of supplies, for use within the United States, and the acquisition value is $25,000 or more, but is less than $191,000;

(B) The acquisition is not for information technology that is a commercial item, using fiscal year 2004 or subsequent fiscal year funds; and

(C) No exception in 25.401 applies. For acquisitions of agencies not subject to the Israeli Trade Act (see 25.406), see agency regulations.

(ii) If the acquisition value is $25,000 or more but is less than $50,000, use the clause with its Alternate I.

(iii) If the acquisition value is $50,000 or more but is less than $77,533, use the clause with its Alternate II.

(iv) If the acquisition value is $77,533 or more but is less than $100,000, use the clause with its Alternate III.

(2) (i) Insert the provision at 52.225-4, Buy American—Free Trade Agreements—Israeli Trade Act Certificate, in solicitations containing the clause at 52.225-3.

(ii) If the acquisition value is $25,000 or more but is less than $50,000, use the provision with its Alternate I.

(iii) If the acquisition value is $50,000 or more but is less than $77,533, use the provision with its Alternate II.

(iv) If the acquisition value is $77,533 or more, but is less than $100,000, use the provision with its Alternate III.

(c) (1) Insert the clause at 52.225-5, Trade Agreements, in solicitations and contracts valued at $191,000 or more, if the acquisition is covered by the WTO GPA (see subpart 25.4) and the agency has determined that the restrictions of the Buy American statute are not applicable to U.S.-made end products. If the agency has not made such a determination, the contracting officer must follow agency procedures.

(2) Insert the provision at 52.225-6, Trade Agreements Certificate, in solicitations containing the clause at 52.225-5.

(d) Insert the provision at 52.225-7, Waiver of Buy American Statute for Civil Aircraft and Related Articles, in solicitations for civil aircraft and related articles (see 25.407), if the acquisition value is less than $191,000.

(e) Insert the clause at 52.225-8, Duty-Free Entry, in solicitations and contracts for supplies that may be imported into the United States and for which duty-free entry may be obtained in accordance with 25.903(a), if the value of the acquisition—

(1) Exceeds the simplified acquisition threshold; or

(2) Does not exceed the simplified acquisition threshold, but the savings from waiving the duty is anticipated to be more than the administrative cost of waiving the duty. When used for acquisitions that do not exceed the simplified acquisition threshold, the contracting officer may modify paragraphs (c)(1) and (j)(2) of the clause to reduce the dollar figure.

(f) Insert the provision at 52.225-18, Place of Manufacture, in solicitations that are predominantly for the acquisition of manufactured end products (i.e., the estimated value of the manufactured end products exceeds the estimated value of other items to be acquired as a result of the solicitation).

§ 25.1102 Acquisition of construction.

When using funds other than those appropriated under the American Recovery and Reinvestment Act of 2009 (Pub. L. 111-5) (Recovery Act), follow the prescriptions in paragraphs (a) through (d) of this section. Otherwise, follow the prescription in paragraph (e).

(a) Insert the clause at 52.225-9, Buy American—Construction Materials, in solicitations and contracts for construction that is performed in the United States valued at less than $7,358,000.

(1) List in paragraph (b)(2) of the clause all foreign construction material excepted from the requirements of the Buy American statute.

(2) If the head of the agency determines that a higher percentage is appropriate, substitute the higher evaluation percentage in paragraph (b)(3)(i) of the clause.

(b) (1) Insert the provision at 52.225-10, Notice of Buy American Requirement—Construction Materials, in solicitations containing the clause at 52.225-9.

(2) If insufficient time is available to process a determination regarding the inapplicability of the Buy American statute before receipt of offers, use the provision with its

Alternate I.

(c) Insert the clause at 52.225-11, Buy American—Construction Materials under Trade Agreements, in solicitations and contracts for construction that is performed in the United States valued at $7,358,000 or more.

(1) List in paragraph (b)(3) of the clause all foreign construction material excepted from the requirements of the Buy American statute, other than designated country construction material.

(2) If the head of the agency determines that a higher percentage is appropriate, substitute the higher evaluation percentage in paragraph (b)(4)(i) of the clause.

(3) For acquisitions valued at $7,358,000 or more, but less than $10,079,365, use the clause with its Alternate I. List in paragraph (b)(3) of the clause all foreign construction material excepted from the requirements of the Buy American statute, unless the excepted foreign construction material is from a designated country other than Bahrain, Mexico, and Oman.

(d) (1) Insert the provision at 52.225-12, Notice of Buy American Requirement—Construction Materials under Trade Agreements, in solicitations containing the clause at 52.225-11.

(2) If insufficient time is available to process a determination regarding the inapplicability of the Buy American statute before receipt of offers, use the provision with its Alternate I.

(3) For acquisitions valued at $7,358,000 or more, but less than $10,079,365, use the provision with its Alternate II.

(e) (1) When using funds appropriated under the Recovery Act for construction, use provisions and clauses 52.225-21, 52.225-22, 52.225-23, or 52.225-24 (with appropriate Alternates) in lieu of the provisions and clauses 52.225-9, 52.225-10, 52.225-11, or 52.225-12 (with appropriate Alternates), respectively, that would be applicable as prescribed in paragraphs (a) through (d) of this section if Recovery Act funds were not used.

(2) If these Recovery Act provisions and clauses are only applicable to a project consisting of certain line items in the contract, identify in the schedule the line items to which the provisions and clauses apply.

(3) When using clause 52.225-23, list foreign construction material in paragraph (b)(3) of the clause as follows:

(i) Basic clause. List all foreign construction materials excepted from the Buy American statute or section 1605 of the Recovery Act, other than manufactured construction material from a Recovery Act designated country or unmanufactured construction material from a designated country.

(ii) Alternate I. List in paragraph (b)(3) of the clause all foreign construction material excepted from the Buy American statute or section 1605 of the Recovery Act, other than—

(A) Manufactured construction material from a Recovery Act designated country other than Bahrain, Mexico, or Oman; or

(B) Unmanufactured construction material from a designated country other than Bahrain, Mexico, or Oman.

§ 25.1103 Other provisions and clauses.

(a) *Restrictions on certain foreign purchases.* Insert the clause at 52.225-13, Restrictions on Certain Foreign Purchases, in solicitations and contracts, unless an exception applies.

(b) *Translations.* Insert the clause at 52.225-14, Inconsistency Between English Version and Translation of Contract, in solicitations and contracts if anticipating translation into another language.

(c) *Foreign currency offers.* Insert the provision at 52.225-17, Evaluation of Foreign Currency Offers, in solicitations that permit the use of other than a specified currency. Insert in the provision the source of the rate to be used in the evaluation of offers.

(d) The contracting officer shall include in each solicitation for the acquisition of products or services (other than commercial items procured under Part 12) the provision at 52.225-20, Prohibition on Conducting Restricted Business Operations in Sudan—Certification.

(e) The contracting officer shall include in all solicitations the provision at 52.225-25, Prohibition on Contracting with Entities Engaging in Certain Activities or Transactions Relating to Iran-Representation and Certifications.

United States Code Annotated

American materials required for public use, see 41 USCA § 10a.

Clarification of Congressional intent regarding sections 10a and 10b(a), see 41 USCA § 10d.

Contract requirements, see 41 USCA § 254.

Contracts, planning, solicitation, evaluation, and award procedures, see 10 USCA § 2305.

Contracts for public works, specification for use of American materials, blacklisting contractors violating requirements, see 41 USCA § 10b.

Definition of terms used in sections 10a, 10b, and 10c, see 41 USCA § 10c.

Definitions, see 10 USCA § 2302, 41 USCA §§ 259, 403.

Kinds of contracts, see 10 USCA § 2306.

Limitation on authority to waive Buy American Act requirement, see 41 USCA § 10b-2.

Planning and solicitation requirements, see 41 USCA § 253a.

PART 26 OTHER SOCIOECONOMIC PROGRAMS

Subpart 26.1 Indian Incentive Program

Subpart 26.2 Disaster or Emergency Assistance Activities

Subpart 26.3 Historically Black Colleges and Universities and Minority Institutions

Subpart 26.4 Food Donations to Nonprofit Organizations

Subpart 26.1 Indian Incentive Program

NOTE: This part has been created to facilitate promulgation of additional FAR and agency level socioeconomic coverage which properly fall under FAR Subchapter D— Socioeconomic Programs, but neither implements nor supplements existing FAR Parts 19, 20, or 22 through 25.

§ 26.100 Scope of subpart.

This subpart implements 25 U.S.C. 1544, which provides an incentive to prime contractors that use Indian organizations and Indian-owned economic enterprises as subcontractors.

United States Code Annotated

Additional compensation to contractors of Federal agency, see 25 USCA § 1544.

Contract requirements, see 41 USCA § 254.

Contracts, planning, solicitation, evaluation, and award procedures, see 10 USCA § 2305.

Definitions, see 10 USCA § 2302, 41 USCA §§ 259, 403.

Kinds of contracts, see 10 USCA § 2306.

Planning and solicitation requirements, see 41 USCA § 253a.

§ 26.101 Definitions.

As used in this subpart—

"Indian" means any person who is a member of any Indian tribe, band, group, pueblo, or community that is recognized by the Federal Government as eligible for services from the Bureau of Indian Affairs (BIA) in accordance with 25 U.S.C. 1452(c) and any "Native" as defined in the Alaska Native Claims Settlement Act (43 U.S.C. 1601).

"Indian organization" means the governing body of any Indian tribe or entity established or recognized by the governing body of an Indian tribe for the purposes of 25 U.S.C., Chapter 17.

"Indian-owned economic enterprise" means any Indianowned (as determined by the Secretary of the Interior) commercial, industrial, or business activity established or organized for the purpose of profit, provided that Indian ownership constitutes not less than 51 percent of the enterprise.

"Indian tribe" means any Indian tribe, band, pueblo, or community, including native villages and native groups (including corporations organized by Kenai, Juneau, Sitka, and Kodiak) as defined in the Alaska Native Claims Settlement Act, that is recognized by the Federal Government as eligible for services from BIA in accordance with 25 U.S.C. 1452(c).

"Interested party" means a prime contractor or an actual or prospective offeror whose direct economic interest would be affected by the award of a subcontract or by the failure to award a subcontract.

United States Code Annotated

Additional compensation to contractors of Federal agency, see 25 USCA § 1544.

Contract requirements, see 41 USCA § 254.

Contracts, planning, solicitation, evaluation, and award procedures, see 10 USCA § 2305.

Definitions, see 10 USCA § 2302, 41 USCA §§ 259, 403.

Kinds of contracts, see 10 USCA § 2306.

Planning and solicitation requirements, see 41 USCA § 253a.

§ 26.102 Policy.

Indian organizations and Indian-owned economic enterprises shall have the maximum practicable opportunity to participate in performing contracts awarded by Federal agencies. In fulfilling this requirement, the Indian Incentive Program allows an incentive payment equal to 5 percent of the amount paid to a subcontractor in performing the contract, if the contract so authorizes and the subcontractor is an Indian organization or Indian-owned economic enterprise.

United States Code Annotated

Additional compensation to contractors of Federal agency, see 25 USCA § 1544.

Contract requirements, see 41 USCA § 254.

Contracts, planning, solicitation, evaluation, and award procedures, see 10 USCA § 2305.

Definitions, see 10 USCA § 2302, 41 USCA §§ 259, 403.

Kinds of contracts, see 10 USCA § 2306.

Planning and solicitation requirements, see 41 USCA § 253a.

Notes of Decisions

In general 1

1 In general

The award of a contract under a Buy Indian Act set-aside to a company that had no American Indians in management positions was proper because the request for proposals did not impose specific criteria for eligibility and awardee was a wholly owned subsidiary of a qualifying corporation. Matter of: Native American Industrial Distributors, Inc., B-310737.3, B-310737.4, B-310737.5, 2008 CPD ¶ 76 (Comp. Gen. 2008)

§ 26.103 Procedures.

(a) Contracting officers and prime contractors, acting in good faith, may rely on the representation of an Indian organization or Indian-owned economic enterprise as to its eligibility, unless an interested party challenges its status or the contracting officer has independent reason to question that status.

(b) In the event of a challenge to the representation of a subcontractor, the contracting officer shall refer the matter to the—

U.S. Department of the Interior
Bureau of Indian Affairs (BIA)
Attn: Chief, Division of Contracting and Grants
Administration
1849 C Street, NW
MS-2626-MIB
Washington, DC 20240-4000.

The BIA will determine the eligibility and notify the contracting officer.

(c) The BIA will acknowledge receipt of the request from the contracting officer within 5 working days. Within 45 additional working days, BIA will advise the contracting officer, in writing, of its determination.

(d) The contracting officer will notify the prime contractor upon receipt of a challenge.

(1) To be considered timely, a challenge shall—

(i) Be in writing;

(ii) Identify the basis for the challenge;

(iii) Provide detailed evidence supporting the claim; and

(iv) Be filed with and received by the contracting officer prior to award of the subcontract in question.

(2) If the notification of a challenge is received by the prime contractor prior to award, it shall withhold award of the subcontract pending the determination by BIA, unless the prime contractor determines, and the contracting officer agrees, that award must be made in order to permit timely performance of the prime contract.

(3) Challenges received after award of the subcontract shall be referred to BIA, but the BIA determination shall have prospective application only.

(e) If the BIA determination is not received within the prescribed time period, the contracting officer and the prime contractor may rely on the representation of the subcontractor.

(f) Subject to the terms and conditions of the contract and the availability of funds, contracting officers shall authorize an incentive payment of 5 percent of the amount paid to the subcontractor. Contracting officers shall seek funding in accordance with agency procedures.

United States Code Annotated

Additional compensation to contractors of Federal agency, see 25 USCA § 1544.

Contract requirements, see 41 USCA § 254.

Contracts, planning, solicitation, evaluation, and award procedures, see 10 USCA § 2305.

Definitions, see 10 USCA § 2302, 41 USCA §§ 259, 403.

Kinds of contracts, see 10 USCA § 2306.

Planning and solicitation requirements, see 41 USCA § 253a.

§ 26.104 Contract clause.

Contracting officers in civilian agencies may insert the clause at 52.226-1, Utilization of

Indian Organizations and Indian-Owned Economic Enterprises, in solicitations and contracts if—

(a) In the opinion of the contracting officer, subcontracting possibilities exist for Indian organizations or Indian-owned economic enterprises; and

(b) Funds are available for any increased costs as described in paragraph (b)(2) of the clause at 52.226-1.

United States Code Annotated

Additional compensation to contractors of Federal agency, see 25 USCA § 1544.

Contract requirements, see 41 USCA § 254.

Contracts, planning, solicitation, evaluation, and award procedures, see 10 USCA § 2305.

Definitions, see 10 USCA § 2302, 41 USCA §§ 259, 403.

Kinds of contracts, see 10 USCA § 2306.

Planning and solicitation requirements, see 41 USCA § 253a.

Subpart 26.2 Disaster or Emergency Assistance Activities

§ 26.200 Scope of subpart.

This subpart implements the Robert T. Stafford Disaster Relief and Emergency Assistance Act (42 U.S.C. 5150), which provides a preference for local organizations, firms, and individuals when contracting for major disaster or emergency assistance activities.

United States Code Annotated

Contract requirements, see 41 USCA § 254.

Contracts, planning, solicitation, evaluation, and award procedures, see 10 USCA § 2305.

Definitions, see 10 USCA § 2302, 41 USCA §§ 259, 403.

Kinds of contracts, see 10 USCA § 2306.

Planning and solicitation requirements, see 41 USCA § 253a.

Use of local firms and individuals, see 42 USCA § 5150.

§ 26.201 Definitions.

"Emergency response contract" means a contract with private entities that supports assistance activities in a major disaster or emergency area, such as debris clearance, distribution of supplies, or reconstruction.

"Local firm" means a private organization, firm, or individual residing or doing business primarily in a major disaster or emergency area.

"Major disaster or emergency area" means the area included in the official Presidential declaration(s) and any additional areas identified by the Department of Homeland Security. Major disaster declarations and emergency declarations are published in the Federal Register and are available at *http://www.fema.gov/news/disasters.fema*.

United States Code Annotated

Contract requirements, see 41 USCA § 254.

Contracts, planning, solicitation, evaluation, and award procedures, see 10 USCA § 2305.

Definitions, see 10 USCA § 2302, 41 USCA §§ 259, 403.

Kinds of contracts, see 10 USCA § 2306.

Planning and solicitation requirements, see 41 USCA § 253a.

Use of local firms and individuals, see 42 USCA § 5150.

§ 26.202 Local area preference.

When awarding emergency response contracts during the term of a major disaster or emergency declaration by the President of the United States under the authority of the Robert T. Stafford Disaster Relief and Emergency Assistance Act (42 U.S.C. 5121, *et seq.*), preference shall be given, to the extent feasible and practicable, to local firms. Preference may be given through a local area set-aside or an evaluation preference.

§ 26.202-1 Local area set-aside.

The contracting officer may set aside solicitations to allow only local firms within a specific geographic area to compete (see 6.208).

(a) The contracting officer, in consultation with the requirements office, shall define the specific geographic area for the local set-aside.

(b) A major disaster or emergency area may span counties in several contiguous States. The set-aside area need not include all the counties in the declared disaster/emergency area(s), but cannot go outside it.

(c) The contracting officer shall also determine whether a local area set-aside should be further restricted to small business concerns in the set-aside area (see Part 19).

§ 26.202-2 Evaluation preference.

The contracting officer may use an evaluation preference, when authorized in agency regulations or procedures.

§ 26.203 Transition of work.

(a) In anticipation of potential emergency response requirements, agencies involved in response planning should consider awarding emergency response contracts before a major disaster or emergency occurs to ensure immediate response and relief. These contracts should be structured to respond to immediate emergency response needs, and should not be structured in any way that may inhibit the transition of emergency response work to local firms (e.g., unnecessarily broad scopes of work or long periods of performance).

(b) 42 U.S.C. 5150(b)(2) requires that agencies performing response, relief, and reconstruction activities transition to local firms any work performed under contracts in effect on the date on which the President declares a major disaster or emergency, unless the head of such agency determines in writing that it is not feasible or practicable. This determination may be made on an individual contract or class basis. The written determination shall be prepared within a reasonable time given the circumstances of the emergency.

(c) In effecting the transition, agencies are not required to terminate or renegotiate existing contracts. Agencies should transition the work at the earliest practical opportunity after consideration of the following:

(1) The potential duration of the disaster or emergency.

(2) The severity of the disaster or emergency.

(3) The scope and structure of the existing contract, including its period of performance and the milestone(s) at which a transition is reasonable (e.g., before exercising an option).

(4) The potential impact of a transition, including safety, national defense, and mobilization.

(5) The expected availability of qualified local offerors who can provide the products or services at a reasonable price.

(d) The agency shall transition the work to local firms using the local area set-aside identified in 26.202-1.

§ 26.204 Justification for expenditures to other than local firms.

(a) 42 U.S.C. 5150(b)(1) requires that, subsequent to any Presidential declaration of a major disaster or emergency, any expenditure of Federal funds, under an emergency response contract not awarded to a local firm, must be justified in writing in the contract file. The justification should include consideration for the scope of the major disaster or emergency and the immediate requirements or needs of supplies and services to ensure life is protected, victims are cared for, and property is protected.

(b) The justification may be made on an individual or class basis. The contracting officer approves the justification.

§ 26.205 Disaster Response Registry.

(a) Contracting officers shall consult the Disaster Response Registry via https://www.acqu isition.gov to determine the availability of contractors for debris removal, distribution of supplies, reconstruction, and other disaster or emergency relief activities inside the United States and outlying areas.

(b) A list of prospective vendors voluntarily participating in the Disaster Response Registry can be retrieved using the System for Award Management (SAM) search tool, which can be accessed via https://www.acquisition.gov. These vendors may be identified by selecting the criteria for "Disaster Response Contractors". Contractors are required to register with SAM in order to gain access to the Disaster Response Registry.

§ 26.206 Solicitation provision and contract clauses.

(a) The contracting officer shall insert the provision at 52.226-3, Disaster or Emergency Area Representation, in solicitations involving the local area set-aside. For commercial items, see 12.301(e)(4).

(b) The contracting officer shall insert the clause at 52.226-4, Notice of Disaster or Emergency Area Set-aside in solicitations and contracts involving local area set-asides.

(c) The contracting officer shall insert the clause at 52.226-5, Restrictions on Subcontracting Outside Disaster or Emergency Area, in all solicitations and contracts that involve local area set-asides.

Subpart 26.3 Historically Black Colleges and Universities and Minority Institutions

§ 26.300 Scope of subpart.

(a) This subpart implements Executive Order 12928 of September 16, 1994, which promotes participation of Historically Black Colleges and Universities (HBCUs) and Minority Institutions (MIs) in Federal procurement.

(b) This subpart does not pertain to contracts performed entirely outside the United States and its outlying areas.

United States Code Annotated

Contract requirements, see 41 USCA § 254.

Contracts, planning, solicitation, evaluation, and award procedures, see 10 USCA § 2305.

Definitions, see 10 USCA § 2302, 41 USCA §§ 259, 403.

Kinds of contracts, see 10 USCA § 2306.

Planning and solicitation requirements, see 41 USCA § 253a.

§ 26.301 [Reserved]

§ 26.302 General policy.

It is the policy of the Government to promote participation of HBCUs and MIs in Federal procurement.

United States Code Annotated

Contract requirements, see 41 USCA § 254.

Contracts, planning, solicitation, evaluation, and award procedures, see 10 USCA § 2305.

Definitions, see 10 USCA § 2302, 41 USCA §§ 259, 403.

Kinds of contracts, see 10 USCA § 2306.

Planning and solicitation requirements, see 41 USCA § 253a.

§ 26.303 Data collection and reporting requirements.

Executive Order 12928 requires periodic reporting to the President on the progress of departments and agencies in complying with the laws and requirements mentioned in the Executive order.

United States Code Annotated

Contract requirements, see 41 USCA § 254.

Contracts, planning, solicitation, evaluation, and award procedures, see 10 USCA § 2305.

Definitions, see 10 USCA § 2302, 41 USCA §§ 259, 403.

Kinds of contracts, see 10 USCA § 2306.

Planning and solicitation requirements, see 41 USCA § 253a.

§ 26.304 Solicitation provision.

Insert the provision at 52.226-2, Historically Black College or University and Minority Institution Representation, in solicitations exceeding the micro-purchase threshold, for research, studies, supplies, or services of the type normally acquired from higher educational institutions.

United States Code Annotated

Contract requirements, see 41 USCA § 254.

Contracts, planning, solicitation, evaluation, and award procedures, see 10 USCA § 2305.

Definitions, see 10 USCA § 2302, 41 USCA §§ 259, 403.

Kinds of contracts, see 10 USCA § 2306.

Planning and solicitation requirements, see 41 USCA § 253a.

Subpart 26.4 Food Donations to Nonprofit Organizations

§ 26.400 Scope of subpart.

This section implements the Federal Food Donation Act of 2008 (42 U.S.C 1792).

§ 26.401 Definitions.

As used in this subpart—

"Apparently wholesome food" means food that meets all quality and labeling standards imposed by Federal, State, and local laws and regulations even though the food may not be readily marketable due to appearance, age, freshness, grade, size, surplus, or other conditions, in accordance with (b)(2) of the Bill Emerson Good Samaritan Food Donation Act (42 U.S.C. 1791(b)).

"Excess food" means food that—

(1) Is not required to meet the needs of the executive agencies; and

(2) Would otherwise be discarded.

"Food-insecure" means inconsistent access to sufficient, safe, and nutritious food.

"Nonprofit organization" means any organization that is—

(1) Described in section 501(c) of the Internal Revenue Code of 1986; and

(2) Exempt from tax under section 501(a) of that Code.

§ 26.402 Policy.

The Government encourages executive agencies and their contractors, to the maximum extent practicable and safe, to donate excess apparently wholesome food to nonprofit organizations that provide assistance to food-insecure people in the United States.

§ 26.403 Procedures.

(a) In accordance with the Federal Food Donation Act of 2008 an executive agency shall comply with the following:

(1) *Encourage donations.* In the applicable contracts stated at section 26.404, encourage contractors, to the maximum extent practicable and safe, to donate apparently wholesome excess food to nonprofit organizations that provide assistance to food-insecure people in the United States.

(2) *Costs.*

(i) In any case in which a contractor enters into a contract with an executive agency under which apparently wholesome food is donated to food-insecure people in the United States, the head of the executive agency shall not assume responsibility for the costs and logistics of collecting, transporting, maintaining the safety of, or distributing excess, apparently wholesome food to food-insecure people in the United States under this Act.

(ii) The Government will not reimburse any costs incurred by the contractor against this contract or any other contract for the donation of Federal excess foods. Any costs incurred for Federal excess food donations are not considered allowable public relations costs in accordance with 31.205-1(f)(8).

(3) *Liability.* An executive agency (including an executive agency that enters into a contract with a contractor) and any contractor making donations pursuant to this Act shall be exempt from civil and criminal liability to the extent provided under the Bill Emerson Good Samaritan Food Donation Act (42 U.S.C. 1791).

§ 26.404 Contract clause.

Insert the clause at 52.226-6, Promoting Excess Food Donation to Nonprofit Organizations, in solicitations and contracts greater than $25,000 for the provision, service, or sale of food in the United States.